LET'S GO

■ THE RESOURCE FOR THE INDEPENDENT TRAVELER

"The guides are aimed not only at young budget travelers but at the indepedent traveler; a sort of streetwise cookbook for traveling alone."

—The New York Times

"Unbeatable; good sight-seeing advice; up-to-date info on restaurants, hotels, and inns; a commitment to money-saving travel; and a wry style that brightens nearly every page."

—The Washington Post

"Lighthearted and sophisticated, informative and fun to read. [Let's Go] helps the novice traveler navigate like a knowledgeable old hand."

—Atlanta Journal-Constitution

"A world-wise traveling companion—always ready with friendly advice and helpful hints, all sprinkled with a bit of wit."

—The Philadelphia Inquirer

■ THE BEST TRAVEL BARGAINS IN YOUR PRICE RANGE

"All the dirt, dirt cheap."

—People

"Anything you need to know about budget traveling is detailed in this book."

—The Chicago Sun-Times

"Let's Go follows the creed that you don't have to toss your life's savings to the wind to travel—unless you want to."

—The Salt Lake Tribune

■ REAL ADVICE FOR REAL EXPERIENCES

"The writers seem to have experienced every rooster-packed bus and lunar-surfaced mattress about which they write."

—The New York Times

"Value-packed, unbeatable, accurate, and comprehensive."

—The Los Angeles Times

"[Let's Go's] devoted updaters really walk the walk (and thumb the ride, and trek the trail). Learn how to fish, haggle, find work—anywhere."

—Food & Wine

LET'S GO PUBLICATIONS

TRAVEL GUIDES

Australia 8th edition
Austria & Switzerland 12th edition
Brazil 1st edition
Britain & Ireland 2005
California 10th edition
Central America 9th edition
Chile 2nd edition
China 5th edition
Costa Rica 2nd edition
Eastern Europe 2005
Ecuador 1st edition **NEW TITLE**
Egypt 2nd edition
Europe 2005
France 2005
Germany 12th edition
Greece 2005
Hawaii 3rd edition
India & Nepal 8th edition
Ireland 2005
Israel 4th edition
Italy 2005
Japan 1st edition
Mexico 20th edition
Middle East 4th edition
Peru 1st edition **NEW TITLE**
Puerto Rico 1st edition
South Africa 5th edition
Southeast Asia 9th edition
Spain & Portugal 2005
Thailand 2nd edition
Turkey 5th edition
USA 2005
Vietnam 1st edition **NEW TITLE**
Western Europe 2005

ROADTRIP GUIDE

Roadtripping USA **NEW TITLE**

ADVENTURE GUIDES

Alaska 1st edition
New Zealand **NEW TITLE**
Pacific Northwest **NEW TITLE**
Southwest USA 3rd edition

CITY GUIDES

Amsterdam 3rd edition
Barcelona 3rd edition
Boston 4th edition
London 2005
New York City 15th edition
Paris 13th edition
Rome 12th edition
San Francisco 4th edition
Washington, D.C. 13th editi

POCKET CITY GUIDES

Amsterdam
Berlin
Boston
Chicago
London
New York City
Paris
San Francisco
Venice
Washington, D.C.

LET'S GO

SOUTHEAST ASIA

Deysia L. Dundas Editor
Megan Prado Associate Editor
Colin Shepherd Associate Editor

Researcher-Writers
Kelzie E Beebe
Leila Chirayath
Dennis Feehan
Adrian Foo
Greg Schmeller

Leila Strachan Map Editor
Ella M. Steim Managing Editor

St. Martin's Press New York

HELPING LET'S GO. If you want to share your discoveries, suggestions, or corrections, please drop us a line. We read every piece of correspondence, whether a postcard, a 10-page email, or a coconut. **Address mail to:**

Let's Go: Southeast Asia
67 Mount Auburn Street
Cambridge, MA 02138
USA

Visit Let's Go at **http://www.letsgo.com,** or send email to:

feedback@letsgo.com
Subject: "Let's Go: Southeast Asia"

In addition to the invaluable travel advice our readers share with us, many are kind enough to offer their services as researchers or editors. Unfortunately, our charter enables us to employ only currently enrolled Harvard students.

Distributed outside the USA and Canada by Macmillan, an imprint of Pan Macmillan Ltd.
20 New Wharf Road, London N1 9RR
Basingstoke and Oxford
Associated companies throughout the world
www.panmacmillan.com

ISBN: 0-312-33567-9
EAN: 978-0312-33567-0
First edition
10 9 8 7 6 5 4 3 2 1

Let's Go: Southeast Asia is written by Let's Go Publications, 67 Mount Auburn Street, Cambridge, MA 02138, USA.

CONTENTS

RESEARCHER-WRITERS

Kelzie E Beebe *Myanmar*

Having previously researched for *Let's Go* in India, Namibia, and Nepal, Kelzie was well equipped to tackle the highs and lows of Myanmar. This mistress of dead-tree awed us with her candid portrayal of locals. Surmounting every obstacle, Kelzie vanquished her unwieldy itinerary. Whether she was sleeping on a crate of onions, trekking barefoot through cow dung, or nursing the two baby mice that she rescued, this researcher-writer proved her mettle.

Leila Chirayath *Sarawak, Sabah, Luzon*

A veteran of the *Let's Go* Brazil and South Africa guides, Leila pulled out all the stops leaving a trail of dust and broken hearts in her wake. Her research was impeccable and demonstrated a knack for unique experiences. Leila cast her spell over typhoons, smog-filled cities, and random rock stars, making her our pick for the *Let's Go* Developing World Triple Crown.

Adrian Foo *Singapore, Peninsular Malaysia*

A native son of Singapore who likes his *laksa* extra spicy, Adrian emerged from the rainforests of Southeast Asia bearing, um, bundles of hot, fresh copy. After a return to his former stomping grounds, he set off for Malaysia to discover pristine beaches, frosty Tiger beer, and rare architectural gems. Although Adrian's whereabouts are currently unknown, he was supposedly last seen in the jungle muttering about a collection of rattan furniture and 1960s matchbook covers from the peninsula.

Greg Schmeller *The Visayas*

During his time with *Let's Go*, Greg has been charged by a moose in northern BC and escaped a sinking ship in the Philippines. We are fairly sure that, given only a modest length of rope and few kumquats, the skilled young Greg could make his way around the world in less than sixteen hours, and probably break a handful of young hearts along the way. A perfect researcher-writer in every respect, Greg sent us lengthy, sagacious copy that was always complete, always thorough, and always amusing.

Dennis Feehan *Cambodia, Laos*

The quiet yet observant Dennis felt right at home in Southeast Asia. He filled kilo-sized copy with anthropological observations, tales of fruitless romances, and allusions to Sheena Warrior Princess. Dennis found so much blissss in Cambodia that he never returned! If you should encounter the popular and eligible bachelor in your tracks, send him our regards.

CONTRIBUTING WRITERS

Anna Byrne *Bangkok, Central Thailand*

Despite her irrational fear of collapsing malls, Anna did an amazing job seeking out hidden gems in the frenetic labyrinth that is Bangkok. We have no doubt Thailand will miss her as she tackles her next challenge. We will too.

Stephen Fan *Northeast Thailand*

Making new friends at every turn, Steve wandered through the rustic villages of Thailand's northeastern plateau. We wish we could say that he enjoyed himself, but his mouth was always too full of food for us to understand him on the phone.

Dan Ramsey *Northern Thailand*

Hailing from the American South, Dan chose to switch it up on his second researching stint for *Let's Go*, trekking through the mountains of northern Thailand. Despite his Indiana Jones-style antics, Dan completed his copy in top form.

Nitin Shah *Northern Thailand, Southern Thailand*

After narrowly escaping death by coconut (the doctors say there won't be any permanent damage), Nitin did an amazing job finishing up his itinerary (although he had the cushiest route. Where else would sitting on the beach be called "work"?).

Sarah Selim *Editor,* Let's Go: Thailand

Anne Patrone *Associate Editor,* Let's Go: Thailand

Marianne Cook *Hồ Chí Minh City, Mekong Delta*

Mare: cool as iced tea.
Let's Go vet, globetrotter, and
karaoke buff.

Danny Koski-Karell *Southern Central Coast, Central Highlands*

"Fixed" monk's stereo.
Perceptive, bearded heartthrob
flaunts his Hội An threads.

Malgorzata Kurjanska *Northern Central Vietnam, Northern Coast*

One word: prolific.
Loves nature, biking, chè, Huế,
and not eating meat.

Hendrik Jan Rick Slettenhaar *Hà Nội, Northern Coast*

Stars in upcoming
"How Hà Nội Got Its Groove Back."
His next stop: Oxford.

J Zac Stein *Northwest Highlands, Northern Vietnam*

Floods and sketchy cops?
For our road warrior, it's
all in a day's work.

Jesse Reid Andrews *Editor,* Let's Go: Vietnam

Scottie Thompson *Associate Editor,* Let's Go: Vietnam

Joshua Levin is a graduate of Harvard University and a former researcher-writer for *Let's Go* China and Tibet. An avid traveler to Southeast Asia, Joshua most recently worked for Conservation International in Cambodia, where he tracked and monitored endangered species. Joshua is interested in education and human development: he designed an environmental education program for military personnel in Cambodia, volunteered for an education NGO in Indonesia, and currently runs an education company in the Boston area.

Raymond Lum is Asian Bibliographer for Widener Library, Librarian for Western Languages at the Harvard-Yenching Library, and Instructor in Chinese in the Harvard University Extension School. A former Peace Corps Volunteer in Malaysian Borneo, Mr. Lum holds an M.A. and Ph.D. from the Department of East Asian Languages and Civilizations. He regularly travels to Southeast Asia to acquire new publications for the Harvard College Library.

Sarah Rotman is a graduate of Harvard University and a former *Let's Go* researcher-writer, editor, and manager. An experienced traveler to Asia, she developed websites for local businesses in Hà Nội while living in Vietnam in 2003. Sarah is also an avid student of international business; she recently returned from Seoul, Korea, where she assisted in teaching a pre-MBA course at Korea University. She currently designs educational programs for businesses and schools in the US and Korea.

HOW TO USE THIS BOOK

Southeast Asia is a land of tradition and flux, so be prepared to experience and enjoy both. *Let's Go* lists thousand-year-old temples that will still be around when you get there and two-year-old guesthouses that may bite the proverbial dust before the year is up. Let these pages and your instinct be your guide and trust no other.

THE "MEAT". Each chapter covers a country, and all are in alphabetical order. The **Life and Times** sections of each chapter provide a general introduction to the art, culture, politics, and history of the region. In each city or town's section, we list places to stay, places to eat, and things to do. The **black tabs** in the margins help you navigate among chapters.

THE DOWN LOW. All the practical information involved in traveling can get downright pesky. **Discover Southeast Asia,** the first chapter, provides an overview of travel in Southeast Asia, including **Regional Highlights** that tell you what you shouldn't miss. Flip to the **Essentials** section to get the quick and easy guide to Southeast Asia, including getting there, getting around, finding a place to stay, and staying safe.

TRANSPORTATION INFO. Each city and town includes **transportation** info in as exact a form as we can put it; bear in mind that departure/arrival times can be imprecise and may have changed after we researched them. Prepare to be flexible. If you want to get to Town X, but can't find it in the transportation section of the city you're in, you'll probably need to find an intermediate hub. Parenthetical bus/train info is divided like so: "(duration, departure time, price)."

SCHOLARLY ARTICLES. We've included three articles written by experts to share information on Southeast Asia's ethnic Chinese (p. 646), environment (p. 81), and service abroad opportunities (p. 53). Read them; they're good for you.

FEATURES. When you hire witty, talented people, you get the best stories there are to offer. Interesting local lore, recent news items, hidden deals, big splurges, major celebrations, regional cuisine, and researchers' tales from the road abound throughout the book. Read these; they're good for you too.

PRICE DIVERSITY. With each accommodation and food listing, you'll find an icon listing a price range; ranges are listed on p. xiv. We rank establishments in order of quality, *not* price. Our favorites are indicated with a **thumbs-up.**

THE END. Our delightful **Appendix** (p. 990) introduces you to the various languages of Southeast Asia, with a **pronunciation guide,** a **phrasebook,** and a **glossary.** The reader is invited to partake of sundry **conversion charts** as well.

A NOTE TO OUR READERS. The information for this book was gathered by *Let's Go* researchers from January through August of 2004. Each listing is based on one researcher's opinion, formed during his or her visit at a particular time. Those traveling at other times may have different experiences since prices, dates, hours, and conditions are always subject to change. You are urged to check the facts presented in this book beforehand to avoid inconvenience and surprises.

ACKNOWLEDGMENTS

TEAM SEAS THANKS: Ella!!! Our wonderful researchers; Laura, for your dedication; Kirkie, for keeping the checks rolling; Ella!!!; Joshua Levin, Raymond Lum, Sarah Rotman, Proofers; Anne Chisholm; and our predecessors for keeping SEAS alive.

DEYS THANKS: Ella Bella, a supreme being and wonderful manager; Megan, for pushing through; Leila S., you held it down for SEAS; Laura, the other AE I wish I had; Colin, for the flava; my steadfast RWs; Joshua, my chi and better half; and my fam and friends for their unconditional love and unwavering support. Love always, me.

MEGAN THANKS: Ella, thanks for setting the standard. Deys, Leila S., and Laura for seeing things through. Colin for keeping it light. Kirkie and W/EUR for being such lovely podmates. Kelzie, Greg, Leila C.—thanks for the interesting mail. Mom, Dad, JBH.

COLIN THANKS: Jon Bardin's iPod; even though you are gone, I will always remember the way you made me feel. Marcel; for being vocal. RBK, for the summertime. Leanna; for covering first base with me and running from the law. Stevie Wonder; for making all that music. My brothers; for being the best. Emma Firestone, for trying. EMS, DD, MP & LS; *A+*.

LEILA THANKS: Elizabeth and all of Mapland; I really feel like we got to know each other through those team-building exercises we did every morning. Deys, Colin, and Megan: Thanks for taking a crazy chance on a rookie kid. You guys are my heart. To my RWs: You taught me to hope again. *Let's Go*: Never change!

Editor
Deysia L. Dundas
Associate Editors
Megan Prado, Colin Shepherd
Managing Editor
Ella M. Steim
Map Editor
Leila Strachan
Typesetter
Melissa Rudolph

Publishing Director
Emma Nothmann
Editor-in-Chief
Teresa Elsey
Production Manager
Adam R. Perlman
Cartography Manager
Elizabeth Halbert Peterson
Design Manager
Amelia Aos Showalter
Editorial Managers
Briana Cummings, Charlotte Douglas, Ella M. Steim, Joel August Steinhaus, Lauren Truesdell, Christina Zaroulis
Financial Manager
R. Kirkie Maswoswe
Marketing and Publicity Managers
Stef Levner, Leigh Pascavage
Personnel Manager
Jeremy Todd
Low-Season Manager
Clay H. Kaminsky
Production Associate
Victoria Esquivel-Korsiak
IT Director
Matthew DePetro
Web Manager
Rob Dubbin
Associate Web Manager
Patrick Swieskowski
Web Content Manager
Tor Krever
Research and Development Consultant
Jennifer O'Brien
Office Coordinators
Stephanie Brown, Elizabeth Peterson

Director of Advertising Sales
Elizabeth S. Sabin
Senior Advertising Associates
Jesse R. Loffler, Francisco A. Robles, Zoe M. Savitsky
Advertising Graphic Designer
Christa Lee-Chuvala

President
Ryan M. Geraghty
General Manager
Robert B. Rombauer
Assistant General Manager
Anne E. Chisholm

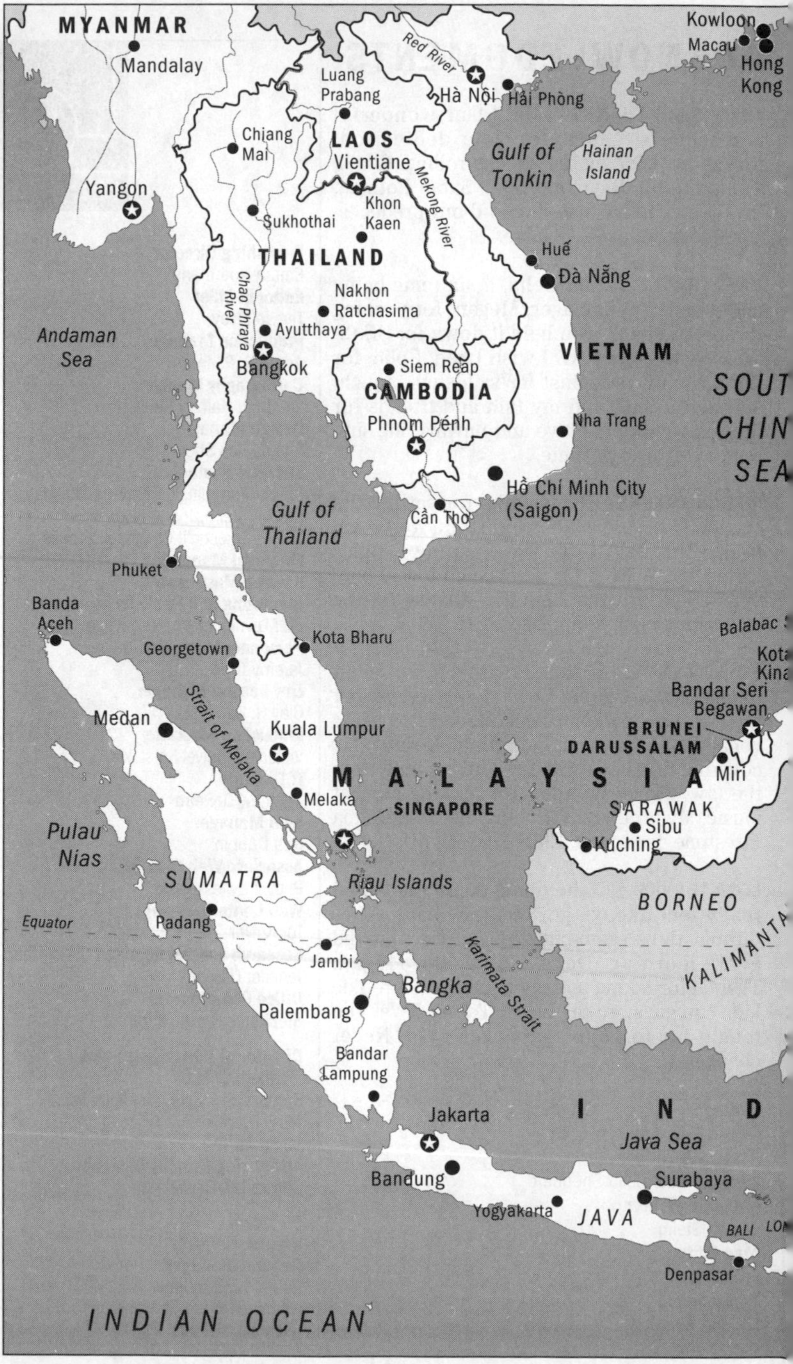
MYANMAR
Mandalay
Yangon
Andaman Sea
Chiang Mai
Sukhothai
THAILAND
Chao Phraya River
Nakhon Ratchasima
Ayutthaya
Bangkok
Luang Prabang
LAOS
Vientiane
Khon Kaen
Mekong River
Red River
Hà Nội
Hải Phòng
Gulf of Tonkin
Hainan Island
Kowloon
Macau
Hong Kong
Huế
Đà Nẵng
VIETNAM
Siem Reap
CAMBODIA
Phnom Pénh
Nha Trang
Hồ Chí Minh City (Saigon)
Cần Thơ
Gulf of Thailand
SOUT
CHIN
SEA
Phuket
Banda Aceh
Kota Bharu
Georgetown
Strait of Melaka
Medan
Kuala Lumpur
Melaka
MALAYSIA
SINGAPORE
Balabac
Kota Kina
Bandar Seri Begawan
BRUNEI DARUSSALAM
Miri
SARAWAK
Sibu
Kuching
Pulau Nias
SUMATRA
Riau Islands
BORNEO
Equator
Padang
Jambi
Karimata Strait
KALIMANTA
Bangka
Palembang
Bandar Lampung
Jakarta
I N D
Java Sea
Bandung
Surabaya
Yogyakarta
JAVA
BALI
LOM
Denpasar
INDIAN OCEAN

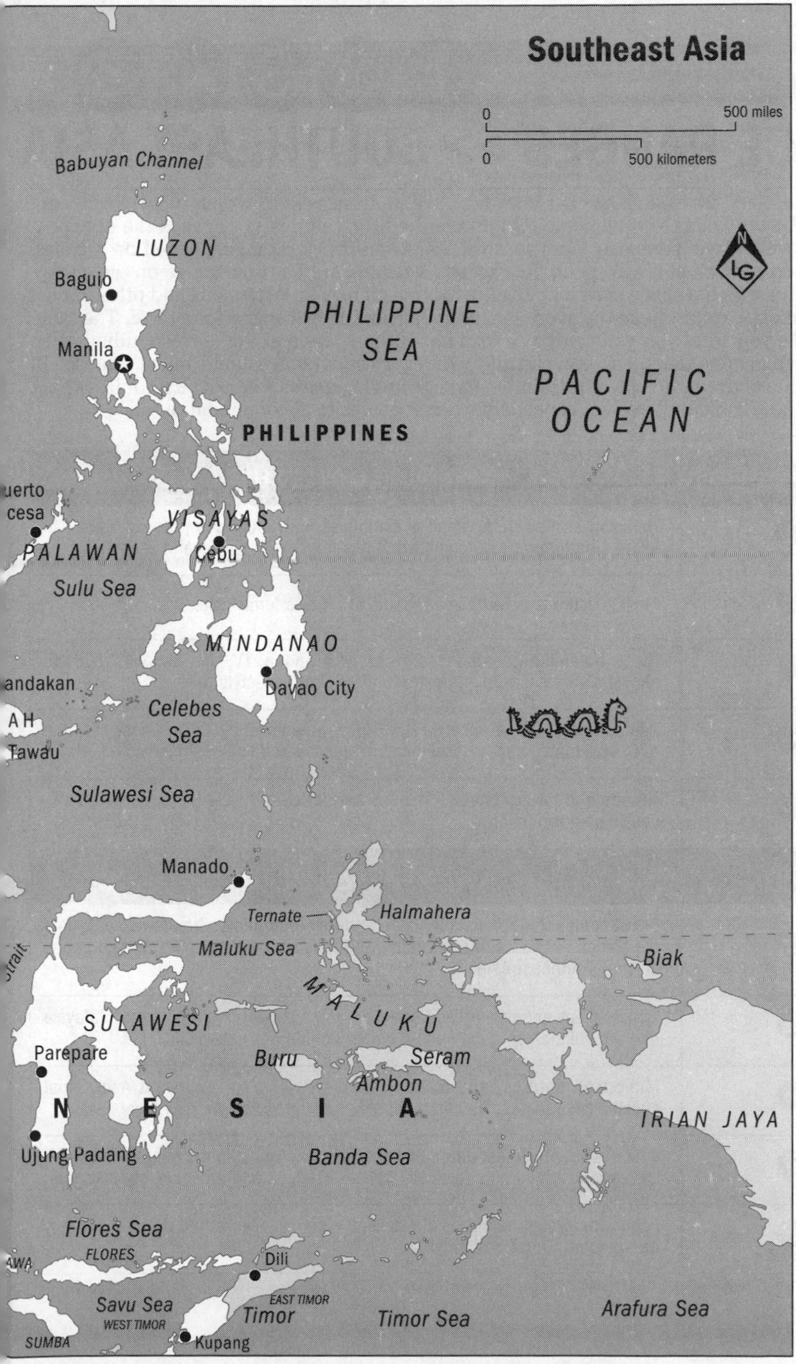
Southeast Asia
0
500 miles
0
500 kilometers
Babuyan Channel
LUZON
Baguio
Manila
PHILIPPINE SEA
PACIFIC OCEAN
PHILIPPINES
uerto
cesa
VISAYAS
PALAWAN
Cebu
Sulu Sea
MINDANAO
andakan
Davao City
AH
Celebes Sea
Tawau
Sulawesi Sea
Manado
Ternate
Halmahera
Maluku Sea
Biak
MALUKU
SULAWESI
Parepare
Buru
Seram
Ambon
N E S I A
IRIAN JAYA
Ujung Padang
Banda Sea
Flores Sea
FLORES
Dili
EAST TIMOR
Savu Sea
WEST TIMOR
Timor
Timor Sea
Arafura Sea
SUMBA
Kupang

PRICE RANGES >> SOUTHEAST ASIA

Our researchers list establishments in order of value from best to worst; our favorites are denoted by the Let's Go thumbs-up (👍). Since the best value is not always the cheapest price, however, we have also incorporated a system of price ranges, based on a rough expectation of what you will spend. For **accommodations,** we base our range on the cheapest price for which a single traveler can stay for one night. For **restaurants** and other dining establishments, we estimate the average amount a traveler will spend for a meal. The table below tells you what you will *typically* find in Southeast Asia at the corresponding price range; keep in mind that no system can allow for every individual establishment's quirks. In general, these are good rules of thumb—except in **Singapore**, where you should expect prices to be significantly higher, especially when it comes to accommodations.

ACCOMMODATIONS	WHAT YOU'RE *LIKELY* TO FIND
1	Hammocks, nipa huts, small guesthouses, and most dorm rooms. Expect to share a bathroom; you may have to provide or rent towels and sheets.
2	Most guesthouses, with small rooms and basic furnishings.
3	Nicer, hotel-like guesthouses, often with phone, TV, and usually A/C. You should also have a private bathroom with Western-style toilet.
4	A larger room, with a private bath. Expect amenities, including phone, TV, and A/C. Well-manicured, professional, or well-located establishments.
5	Resorts and luxury hotels. If it's a 5 and it doesn't have the perks you want, you've paid too much.

FOOD	WHAT YOU'RE *LIKELY* TO FIND
1	Street-corner stands, market stalls, and fast-food joints. Simple rice and noodle dishes in Laos and Cambodia. Small snacks in Singapore. Baked goods all over Southeast Asia.
2	Typical meat entrees in Laos and Cambodia. Lower-end entrees in Malaysia and the Philippines; *halo halo* in pricier Philippines eateries.
3	Mid-priced entrees, and most western-style fare in Southeast Asia. Most guesthouse eateries. Tip can bump you up slightly, as you may have a waiter.
4	A somewhat fancy restaurant or a steakhouse. Expect loads of ambience, and more exotic ingredients (typically Italian-, French-, and American-style dishes).
5	Food with foreign names and a decent wine list. Slacks and dress shirts may be expected. Don't order PB&J.

DISCOVER SOUTHEAST ASIA

From the vibrant floating markets of Vietnam and Thailand to the endangered komodo dragons of the Indonesian archipelago, Southeast Asia encompasses an overwhelming display of geographical, ecological, and cultural diversity. Shimmering crater lakes await the tranquil traveler, while the steamy streets of the bustling big cities challenge even the hardiest urban adventurer. Whether you prefer the vast array of eco- and adventure-tour opportunities—including trekking, mountain biking, scuba diving, and elephant riding, to name only a few—or would rather imbibe the local ambience of traditional hill-tribe villages, travel in Southeast Asia offers an educational experience that will continually awe, frighten, challenge, and spell-bind. The region's shared Chinese and Indian origins, rooted in thousands of years of sea trade, religious conflict, colonial influence, and political turmoil, have since spawned one of the most complex ethnic mixes in the world, a diversity made all the more remarkable by the persistence of traditional lifestyles alongside the products of rapid industrialization. Sugar-sand beaches, colorful reefs teeming with endangered species, still abundant rainforest, and seven-tiered waterfalls coexist with burgeoning metropolises, like Bangkok, Jakarta, and Manila, which are responsible for the increasing levels of pollution now threatening Southeast Asia's fragile ecosystems. More extended travel in the region takes many forms, from teaching English to novice monks, to helping preserve the wealth of natural resources by building more self-sustainable communities. Whatever path you choose to explore, you will leave impressed with the challenges and rewards of Southeast Asia's dynamic fusion between ancient traditions and the relatively recent pandemonium of modern development.

FACTS AND FIGURES

POPULATION: 555,019,898.

COUPS SINCE 1950: 42.

WATS, PAGODAS, OR TEMPLES: We stopped counting at 17,500,010.

AVG. # OF WHEELS PER VEHICLE: 2.79.

COUNTRIES: 10.

SEX CHANGE OPERATIONS: 21,473.

ISLANDS: 25,390.

AVG. LENGTH OF THAI ISLAND PARTIES: 31hr.

AVG. COST OF 31HR. THAI ISLAND PARTIES: US$6.

WHEN TO GO

Southeast Asia has dry and rainy seasons that roughly correspond to high and low tourism seasons. The rainy season results in rougher seas, causing some beaches, islands, and roads to shut down depending on the weather. Sights are often less crowded, and there are fewer services—however, guesthouses and airlines frequently offer reduced prices. Generally the best time to visit the region is between November and February, when most of the region experiences drier, cooler weather. Malaysia is the main exception to this rule, and the dry and rainy seasons vary between the east and west coasts; April to October is the best time to visit, when both Borneo and the east coast of peninsular Malaysia have the least rain. As you move closer to the equator, the weather becomes hotter and there is less variation among seasons. Singapore, for instance, is rainy the majority of the time, with June and July being the driest months. The weather in Southeast Asia is hot and humid; temperatures hover around 27°C (80°F) year-round everywhere except in the extreme uplands of the mainland, where nighttime temperatures can fall to near freezing. For a rough conversion from °C to °F, multiply by two and add 30. (See the conversion chart in the **Appendix,** p. 990.)

Also keep an eye on public holidays and festivals, as these generally contribute to the influx of tourists. Particularly between December and February, when most of the region celebrates a succession of holidays including the Chinese New Year, Thaipusam Festival, Hari Raya, and the Muslim New Year, it is a good idea to make travel plans early.

WHAT TO DO

With ten countries and countless destinations, planning an itinerary in Southeast Asia can be as difficult as getting Yaks to mate at low altitudes. Luckily for you, this section details routes, suggested itineraries, and must-dos to give you an idea of the country-hopping, beach-bumming, mountain-climbing, budget-living days that lie ahead of you. Whether you plan on trekking up mountainsides or plunging your toes into the crystal waters of island coves, lazing resort-side or roughing it in rural villages, we've got the goods right here.

SAND AND SURF

Southeast Asia has more than its fair share of gorgeous beaches. While some beachfront towns have been invaded by luxury resorts and bland hotels (like **Phuket,** Thailand and **Bali,** Indonesia), budget accommodations—bathed in the same sunlight—are still available pretty much everywhere. The islands of **Ko Samet, Ko Tao, Ko Phi Phi Don,** and **Khao Lak** in Thailand; **Pulau Tioman, the Perhentian Islands, Pangkor Laut,** and **Similajau National Park** in Malaysia; **Pulau Nias** off Sumatra, **Kuta Beach** off Bali, and the **Gilis** off Lombok in Indonesia; and **Borocay, Biliran,** and **Malapascua** in the Philippines should be on every self-respecting beach bunny's to-do list. In general, Thailand's beach scene is more raucous, especially compared to sleepy Laos and Cambodia. The **Full Moon**

TOP TEN PLACES TO GET WET

In a region where the sun blazes around the clock, every traveler needs to cool off. Below are some of the finest ways to immerse yourself in water and the best ways to survive the heat.

Serasa Beach (p. 72). This beach in Brunei is a magnet for watersports enthusiasts. Let the waves soak you while jet skiing, kayaking, windsurfing, water-skiing or power boat racing. Enough? Never! Get back on the water and play some more!

Bali (p. 168). Despite its past disturbances, Bali's beaches remain some of the most beautiful destinations in Southeast Asia. The sky's the limit when it comes to watersports and activities. Take your pick.

Yak Lom Lake (p. 103). Legend has it that this crater lake was formed 700,000 years ago by the footprint of a giant. He surely left an indelible mark; this small, secluded body of water is probably the most beautiful place to swim in Cambodia.

Wat Sokpaluang (p. 293). Set in the lush greenery of Sokpaluang Temple, this sauna provides the best R&R in Laos. Soothe away aches with a massage offered by the divine nuns. You should be fully dry by the end.

Poring Hot Springs (p. 443). Located near Kota Kinabalu, Malaysia, these sulfurous waters are believed to relieve muscle

Party—thrown every month in **Ko Phangan,** Thailand—is an all-night rave, not to be missed. It's not the only option either; in recent years, Bali's **Kuta Beach** and the Philippines **Boracay Island** have upped the ante with harder, longer, and even more infamous trances into partydom. If that's exactly what you want to avoid, head to **Lovina** or **Sanur** off **Bali** in Indonesia, or the quieter beaches on the coast of Vietnam. Those who find themselves in more touristy areas usually need only walk or bike a short while from the hubbub to see relatively untouched beauty. Avid divers swarm to sites around **Bali,** much of **Malaysia,** and the splendid **Visayas** in the Philippines. Offshore reefs and a smorgasbord of gorgeous fish await trained and amateur divers alike, making this some of Asia's best diving. There are also several good places to surf, particularly around Bali and in some parts of the **Philippines.** In general, the waves are unpredictable in Southeast Asia; several sites are hit or miss, or only suitable for the master surfer. Because of this, most travelers stick to snorkeling and scuba-diving.

OVER THE RIVER AND THRU THE WOODS

Since the mid-1980s, jungle trekking and its trendy 90s cousin, ecotourism, have drawn many tourists to Southeast Asia. The rage began 20 years ago in **Northern Thailand,** and quality trips are still affordable. Numerous national parks offer cool, peaceful respites from the summer heat. Backpackers trek, climb, and spelunk in the parks of **Sabah** and **Sarawak. Taman Negara,** a national park in the world's oldest rainforest, offers everything from canopy walking on rickety rope bridges to week-long camping stays. **Palawan** in the Philippines has the world's longest underground river. For hikers, Southeast Asia presents peaks of varying difficulty, including **Fansipan** in northern Vietnam, **Gunung Kinabalu** in Sabah, **Gunung Agung** in Bali, **Gunung Rinjani** in Lombok, and the **Mayon** volcano and **Mt. Apo** in the Philippines. The last has an annoying habit of erupting every once in a while.

WILL YOU BE MY FRIEND? OR NOT.

THE BACKPACKER SCENE...

Love it or hate it—in every major city, backpackers huddle in their ghettos, meeting other travelers, and exchanging tales, tips, and reading material. Some travelers relish the opportunity to spend weeks holed

aches. Bathe in hot or cold water, either alone or with that hot backpacker you met on the trail.

Thingyan Festival (p. 459). Every April, all of Myanmar goes into party mode to celebrate the New Year with this water festival. According to ancient tradition, sins are washed by the splashing or throwing of water on one another. If you're feeling particularly bad, hop on an open-jeep and cruise around.

Malapascua Island (p. 593). Swim in crystalline waters on this popular island at the northern tip of Cebu, Philippines. Besides its beautiful waters and white-sand beaches, Malapascua is one of the few places in the world where the big Thresher Shark comes close to the surface. Watch out.

Sentosa Beach (p. 648). This island theme park in Singapore is tourist-ridden, but a great place to get soaked on the beach or on the water rides of Fantasy Island. Dry off while viewing Singapore's history on display amid lights, colors, and water. Then get wet again.

Ko Phi Phi (p. 809). Once a secluded paradise, this island in Thailand is second only to Phuket in popularity. Shimmering turquoise waters invite you to cool off and relax. When the sun goes down, break a sweat at one of the many nightclubs.

Phú Quốc (p. 987). Saturate your body in the sparkling sea and dry off on the white sands of Vietnam's Sao Beach. For a more majestic scene, head to Suối Đá Bàn where you can bathe in waterfalls and natural springs.

up in cheap guesthouses, avoiding the outside world. Others strive to well, avoid each other. To these types, the "singular experience" is paramount—and apparently, the greatest decoration one can achieve is to be able to say, "I was hanging out in this village where they've never seen a white man before." Still, during the high season, grungy, scantily clad foreigners seem to outnumber the locals at haunts like: Bangkok's **Khaosan Road, Chang Mai, Nong Khai,** and the **islands** in Thailand; **Georgetown, the Perhantian Islands,** and **Pulau Tioman** in Malaysia; **Jogjakarta** on Java, **Ubud** and **Kuta** on Bali, the **Gilis** off Lombok, and **Bukit Tinggi** and **Lake Toba** on Sumatra, all in **Indonesia; Sabang, Baguio,** and **Boracay** in the Philippines; **Hồ Chí Minh City** and **Hội An** in Vietnam; and **Singapore.**

AND HOW TO AVOID IT

Those who would rather avoid the throngs of fellow *farang* can find respite in more isolated regions—most of which tend to see visitors more interested in exploring than in partying. Some of these include: **Northeast Thailand,** Cambodia's **Mekong River,** the **Mekong Delta** of Vietnam, **Sarawak** and Malaysia's east coast, **Naga Pulu, Flores** and northern **Sulawesi** in Indonesia, **Negros** and **Davao** in the Philippines, southern **Laos,** and all of **Myanmar.** Traveling during the low season is an excellent way to dodge crowds almost anywhere, though fewer services are available and many resorts may be closed altogether.

ROLLING WITH THE LOCALS

Many tourists come to the region seeking "traditional" Southeast Asian culture. At its worst, "ethnotourism" leads to human zoos such as the long-neck **Karen villages** of Northern Thailand or the so-called **"Chicken Village"** outside Đà Lạt, Vietnam; in most cases, however, travelers are welcome to observe and participate in local ceremonies and festivals. Chances to respectfully interact with indigenous cultures include: visiting **longhouses** in **Sarawak** and **Sabah;** participating in massive **funerals** in **Tana Toraja** in Sulawesi; traveling down the **Mekong** by **barge** with a Lao family; staying with a **hill-tribe village** in **Mai Chñu,** Vietnam; or living in a **Malay kampung,** a **Thai Muslim fishing community,** or an **Ifugao village** in the **Central Cordillera** of Luzon. Be sensitive and respectful of your surroundings.

LOTS AND LOTS OF WATS

Southeast Asia is overrun by awesome temples, palaces, and *wats*, and the assorted ruins thereof. The **three wonders** of classical Southeast Asia are **Angkor** in Cambodia, **Bagan** in Myanmar, and **Borobudur** on Java in Indonesia. The imperial city in **Huế,** Vietnam—a microcosm of Beijing's Forbidden City—serves as counterpoint to the Indic-influenced monuments everywhere else in the region. Though it suffered serious bombing in 1968, it remains exotic, striking, and immense. **Luang Prabang** in Laos, "the jewel of Indochina," may be the best-preserved ancient city in the region. Declared a UNESCO world heritage sight in 1995, the city sports a plethora of gorgeous temples, with breathtakingly steep wing-style roofs. In Thailand, the former capitals of **Sukhothai** and **Ayutthaya** shouldn't be missed. While not as well preserved as Luang Prabang, they sport thrilling silhouettes and fantastically grand stone statues, guaranteed to awaken marvel in even the most worldly traveler.

FOOD GLORIOUS FOOD

The unbelievable cuisine alone is worth the trip to Southeast Asia. Cuisines vary depending upon a country's religion, ethnicity, and history of colonial occupation. Savor the richness of seasonings fundamental to the region's palate, from the aromatic roots of the ginger family, to the spicy-hot chillies imported from 16th-century Portugal, to common ingredients like coconut milk, garlic, lemongrass, basil, turmeric, and lime. Among the culinary highlights are the **hawker stalls** of Singapore, the **nyonya** cuisine of Penang and Melaka in Malaysia, the spicy **padang** food of Sumatra, the Vietnamese delicacies found in Huế, the European-inspired hybrid dishes of **Ubud** in Bali, and just about anything in Thailand. Eating at the vibrant **night markets** of Thailand and Malaysia, where the locals dine, is one of the truly great pleasures of traveling there. Menu listings can range from pigeon and rat to squid, cobra, or giant fried spiders. There are abundant vegetarian options everywhere that will keep the less carnivorously inclined well fed and content. Food is generally safe to eat, but be wary when buying from street vendors in countries other than Singapore. Always try to avoid the consumption of uncooked or unpeeled fruits and vegetables.

THE HUSTLE AND BUSTLE

Southeast Asia's big cities are stories in themselves. Though Bangkok, Jakarta, and Manila are often portrayed as smog-ridden, choking ovens, these cities bustle with an unmatched energy, diversity, and chaos—the essence of modern-day Southeast Asia. The region's major cities gather architectural, cultural, and culinary attractions all in one place. **Singapore**'s ultra clean and regimented atmosphere is a respite from the disorder of other Southeast Asian cities; **Hà Nội, Luang Prabang, Yangon, Kuching, Davao,** and **Cebu** also deserve exploration. For nightlife, **Bangkok, Hồ Chí Minh City, Kuala Lumpur, Jakarta,** and **Manila** lead the pack.

LET'S GO PICKS: SOUTHEAST ASIA

BEST GENITALIA-SHAPED ROCK: The "grandmother and grandfather" rocks of **Ko Samui** (p. 824), Thailand win this prize.

BEST MEMORIALS: Phnom Penh's **Tuol Sleng Genocide Museum** demands reflection, as does the **War Remnants Museum** (p. 973) in Hồ Chí Minh City.

BEST REASON TO GET UP IN THE MORNING: The sunrise over **Angkor Wat** is one of the world's spectacular sights.

BEST LUNAR CYCLE: The **Full Moon Parties,** on the beaches of Southern Thailand, or for that matter the beaches themselves, are the party centers of Southeast Asia.

BEST WAY TO SWEAT WITH THE LOCALS: Catch an impromptu soccer game in the parks of Hà Nội, or indulge in the Philippines's favorite, basketball. If you fancy yourself a real athlete, try *sepak takraw* in Kuala Lumpur.

BEST PLACE TO GET SERVED IN BED: Recline on divans while staffers dressed like spaceship travelers excite your taste buds at the **Bed Supper Club.**

BEST PLACE TO SEE WILDLIFE: Catch the mini-dinosaurs on **Komodo Island** (p. 214) in Indonesia, on your way to **Gunung Leseur National Park.** Malaysia's **Taman Negara National Park** (p. 382) and the *babirusa* (pig-deer) of **Sulawesi** finish off the list (p. 222).

BEST PLACE TO EAT WILDLIFE: You choose: Cambodian crickets; Filipino duck embryos, ox balls, or blood soup; Vietnamese snakes and rats; Indonesian squids. What can we get you today?

BEST PLACE TO LOSE YOUR LOINS: **Bangkok**'s best hospitals have one special skill: they help Michael find the Michelle within.

BEST TRADITIONAL REMEDY: Sabang Beach (p. 575) in the Philippines, offers you the **"Feeling Shitty"** breakfast of coffee, 2 cigarettes, Coke, and ibuprofen for P70 (under US$2).

BEST PLACE FOR SOME BLING BLING: **Myanmar** boasts some of the most beautiful gems in Southeast Asia, but beware that proceeds go to the government.

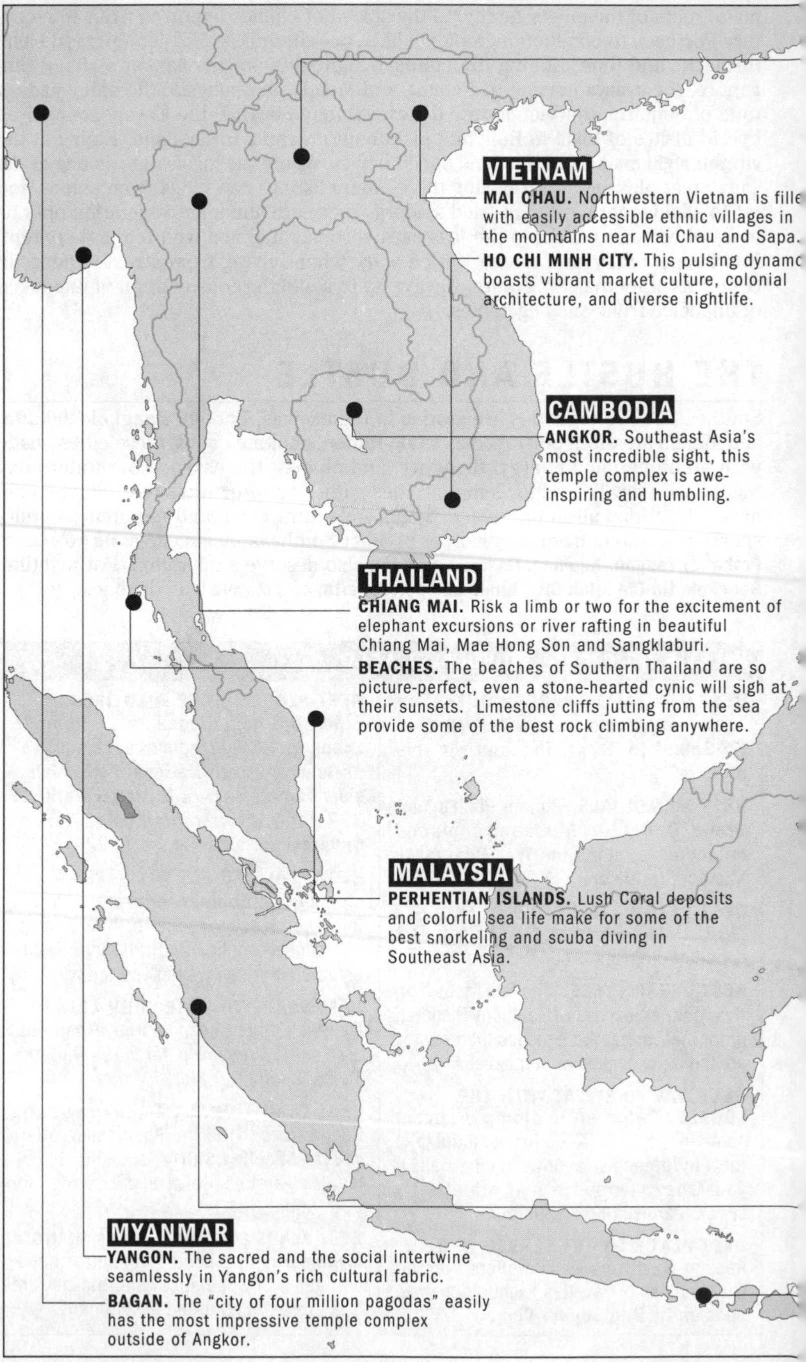
VIETNAM
MAI CHAU. Northwestern Vietnam is fille with easily accessible ethnic villages in the mountains near Mai Chau and Sapa.
HO CHI MINH CITY. This pulsing dynamo boasts vibrant market culture, colonial architecture, and diverse nightlife.
CAMBODIA
ANGKOR. Southeast Asia's most incredible sight, this temple complex is awe-inspiring and humbling.
THAILAND
CHIANG MAI. Risk a limb or two for the excitement of elephant excursions or river rafting in beautiful Chiang Mai, Mae Hong Son and Sangklaburi.
BEACHES. The beaches of Southern Thailand are so picture-perfect, even a stone-hearted cynic will sigh at their sunsets. Limestone cliffs jutting from the sea provide some of the best rock climbing anywhere.
MALAYSIA
PERHENTIAN ISLANDS. Lush Coral deposits and colorful sea life make for some of the best snorkeling and scuba diving in Southeast Asia.
MYANMAR
YANGON. The sacred and the social intertwine seamlessly in Yangon's rich cultural fabric.
BAGAN. The "city of four million pagodas" easily has the most impressive temple complex outside of Angkor.

Highlights of Southeast Asia

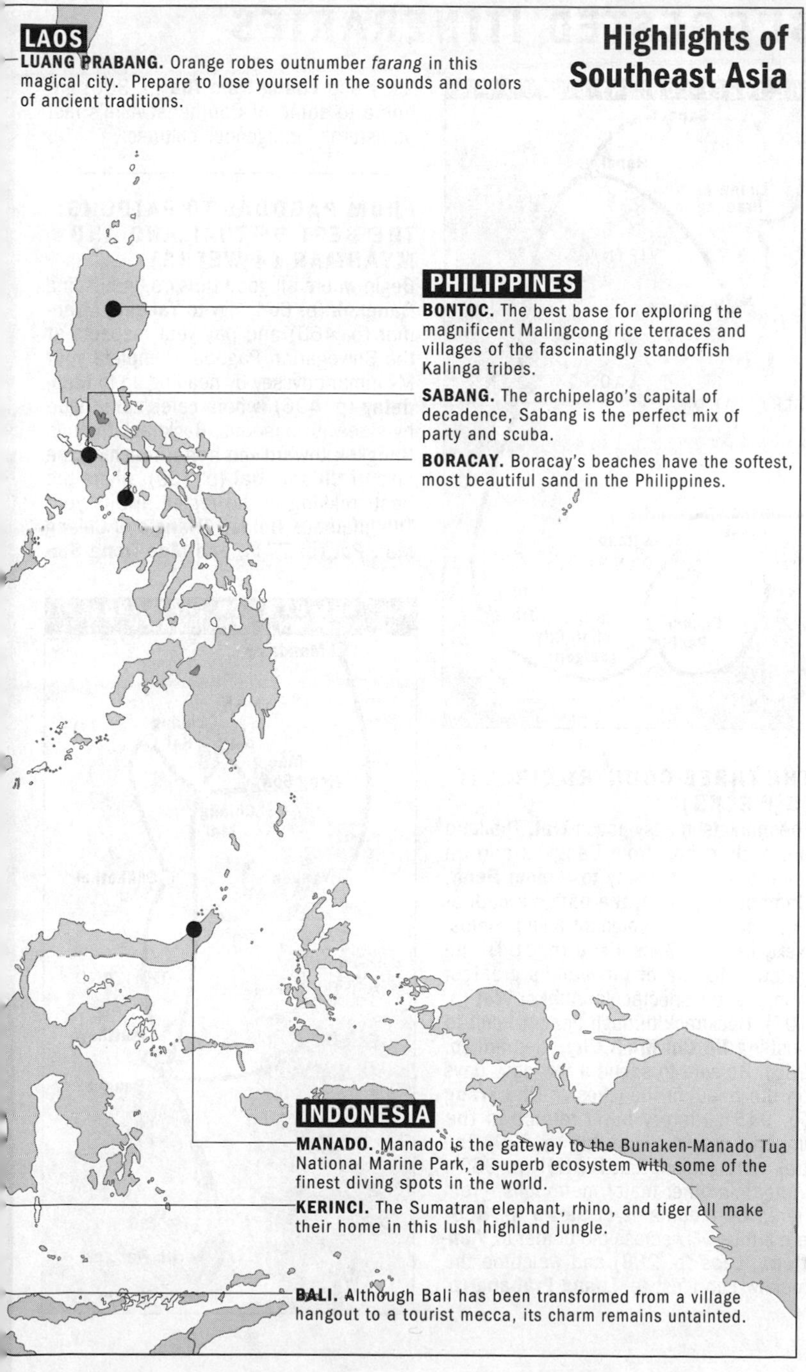

LAOS

LUANG PRABANG. Orange robes outnumber *farang* in this magical city. Prepare to lose yourself in the sounds and colors of ancient traditions.

PHILIPPINES

BONTOC. The best base for exploring the magnificent Malingcong rice terraces and villages of the fascinatingly standoffish Kalinga tribes.

SABANG. The archipelago's capital of decadence, Sabang is the perfect mix of party and scuba.

BORACAY. Boracay's beaches have the softest, most beautiful sand in the Philippines.

INDONESIA

MANADO. Manado is the gateway to the Bunaken-Manado Tua National Marine Park, a superb ecosystem with some of the finest diving spots in the world.

KERINCI. The Sumatran elephant, rhino, and tiger all make their home in this lush highland jungle.

BALI. Although Bali has been transformed from a village hangout to a tourist mecca, its charm remains untainted.

SUGGESTED ITINERARIES

THE THREE-COUNTRY CIRCUIT

THE THREE-COUNTRY CIRCUIT (5 WEEKS)

The markets in easy-paced **Trat,** Thailand are a short hop from Bangkok and an ideal stop on the way to **Phnom Penh,** Cambodia (p. 87), the nation's capital and home of the poignant Killing Fields. Next, head to **Siem Reap** (p. 104), the gateway to one of the world's greatest wonders, the spectacular **Angkor Wat** (p. 107). Backtrack through Phnom Penh to bustling **Hồ Chí Minh City,** Vietnam (p. 965). Be sure to spend a few easy days on the beautiful beaches of **Nha Trang** (p. 946). History buffs rejoice in the imperial capital city of **Huế** (p. 920). The trek north finishes at **Hà Nội** (p. 850), Vietnam's other major metropolis. From here, the mountains of **Sa Pa** (p. 868) are a must. Fly across the border to **Vientiane,** Laos (p. 288) and welcome the mellow Lao lifestyle. **Luang Prabang** (p. 297) and **Luang Nam Tha** (p. 306) are home to some of Southeast Asia's last undisturbed indigenous cultures.

FROM PAGODAS TO PATPONG: THE BEST OF THAILAND AND MYANMAR (4 WEEKS)

Begin where all good trips do, in bustling **Bangkok** (p. 664). Fly to **Yangon,** Myanmar (p. 466) and pay your respects at the Shwegadon Pagoda. Complete your Myanmar odyssey by heading up to **Mandalay** (p. 496), where cafes stand side by side with pagodas. Backtrack through Bangkok toward the north, reaching the hills of **Chiang Mai** (p. 759), where the best trekking in the region awaits you. The infamous **Golden Triangle** of Chiang Mai, **Pai** (p. 771), and **Mae Hong Son**

THE BEST OF THAILAND AND MYANMAR

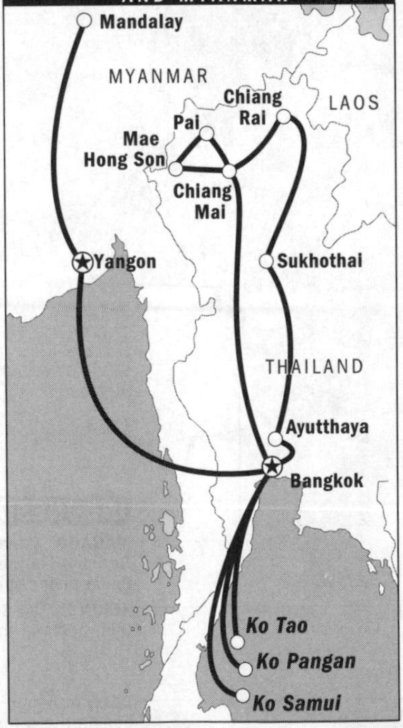

(p. 772) bring together the best of indigenous Thai culture, amazing mountain views, and respite from the sizzling Southeast Asian summer. Having conquered the triangle, move on to gentler **Chiang Rai** (p. 792). Head back to Bangkok via the ancient capital of **Sukhothai** (p. 780), whose ruins will remind you of the deep history of Thailand. Another former capital, **Ayutthaya** (p. 709) showcases the Indic influences on Thailand's past. Then shoot south to the **Kos** (any one will do; see **Southern Thailand,** p. 798) and reflect on your trip on the world's best beaches. Click your ruby heels, and you're back in **Bangkok,** where it all began.

SMORGASBORD: BEACHES, MOUNTAINS, AND THE ODD SKYSCRAPER (3 WEEKS)

Begin in **Bangkok** (p. 664) and soak up the urban chaos. Start the journey south at **Hua Hin** (p. 722) for an introduction to Thailand's pristine white sand. Now, island-hop from the diver's paradise to **Ko Tao** (p. 834) to the **Full Moon Party** on **Ko Phangan** (p. 829), and to tourist friendly **Ko Samui** (p. 824). Still craving beaches? Cut across to **Krabi** (p. 812) and **Phuket** (p. 804). On to **Penang,** Malaysia (p. 366) and its scrumptious street food. Then venture inland to the **Cameron Highlands** (p. 379) and challenge yourself with jungle hikes. **Kuala Lumpur** (p. 339) will serve as a fitting adventure for any urban guru. As a reward, plunge into Malaysian history in **Melaka** (p. 350). End your whirlwind tour of cities, beaches, mountains, and coast in **Singapore** (p. 625), the ultimate city-state.

BEACHES, MOUNTAINS, AND THE ODD SKYSCRAPER

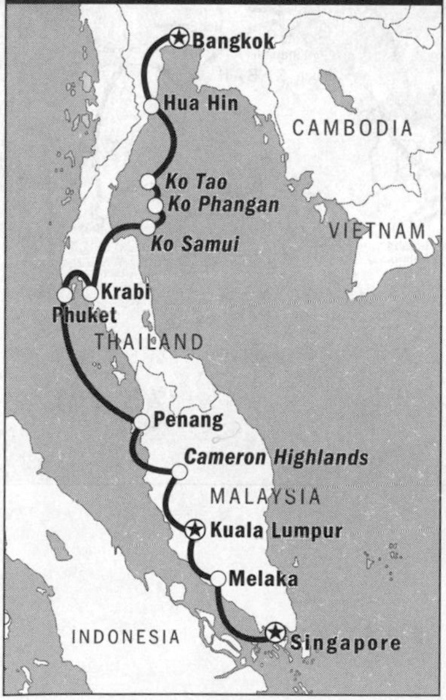

TALES OF AMPHIBIOUS TOURISTS: THE BEST OF THE PHILIPPINES (4 WEEKS)

Stay in **Manila** (p. 543) long enough to hit the pumping nightlife and check out Intramuros, then catch your breath amid the rice paddies in the northern hills of **Banaue** (p. 561). Linger in lazy **Sagada** (p. 563) for a while, then backtrack through Manila south to beautiful **Lake Taal** (p. 570). Next, hop over to **Mindoro Island** (p. 575) for an introduction to Filipino beach culture. After an overnight stay in **Panay** (p. 604), a brief sun-soak-

THE BEST OF THE PHILIPPINES

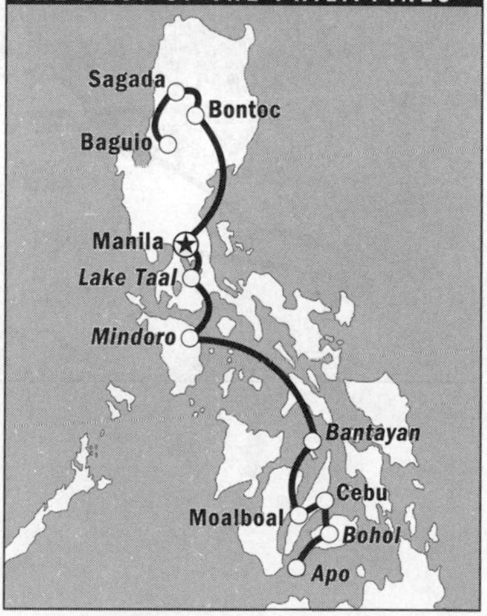

DISCOVER

ing session on **Bantayan Island** (p. 592) or undiscovered **Malapascua Island** (p. 593), and world-class diving on **Moalboal** (p. 591), steam into **Cebu City** (p. 585) to appease your Bacchanalian impulses. Catch a ferry to **Bohol** (p. 593), indulge in the Chocolate Hills, and bask on the isolated beaches of **Panglao Island** (p. 595). Continue island-hopping to your finale at **Apo Island** (p. 603), where you'll find the Philippines's best-preserved marine sanctuary.

THE BEST OF BORNEO—SARAWAK AND SABAH (3 WEEKS)

Begin your adventure with a flight into **Tawau,** Sabah (p. 434)—gateway to the luxurious **Sipadan Islands.** On return to Sabah, catch a bus to **Sandakan** (p. 443), a stone's throw from the Sepilok Orangutan Center and the lush wilds of the **Kinabatangan River** (p. 447). Make your way back to civilization in **Kota Kinabalu** (p. 434), stopping for some deserved R&R at the fantastic **Poring Hot Springs** (p. 443). After restocking, set your sights on the marvelous mosques and palaces of **Bandar Seri Begawan, Brunei,** reached from KK via boat connection in **Pulau Labuan.** When you're done enjoying the high life, take a bus to **Miri** (p. 428) and waste no time catching a flight to **Gunung Mulu**'s (p. 431) incredible Pinnacles, caves, and creatures. Be sure not to miss the exquisite beauty of **Lambir Hills National Park** (p. 427), also accessible via Miri. When you've had your fill of the park's world-famous forests, catch a bus to **Similajau** (p. 426), where you can bum around on the beach, and make connections to **Sibu** (p. 419) or **Kapit** (p. 421)—the best places to explore indigenous longhouse culture. End your journey in **Kuching,** a splendid city, where scores of cheap flights can take you back to **Kuala Lumpur** (p. 339) and beyond.

THE BEST OF BORNEO

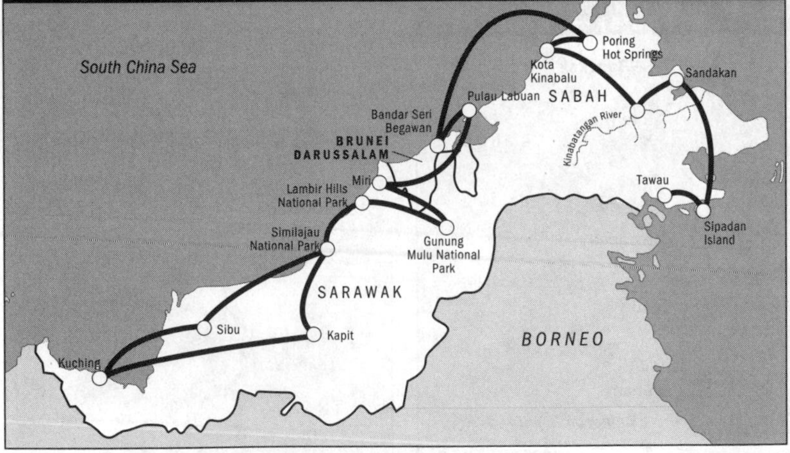

ESSENTIALS

PLANNING YOUR TRIP

BEFORE YOU GO

Passport (p. 11). Required for citizens of all countries. Most countries will require that your passport be valid for 6 months beyond your anticipated departure date. See individual country introductions for specifics.

Visa (p. 13). Many countries in Southeast Asia require an entry visa that must be obtained in advance from a consulate abroad. Some countries, namely the Philippines and Singapore, do not require a visa, but do require **proof of onward travel,** which can be demonstrated with a plane ticket. For multiple entries, applying for re-entry permits may be necessary. For specific visa requirements, see the **Essentials** section of each individual country. Check entrance requirements at the nearest embassy for up-to-date information before departure. US citizens can take advantage of the **Center for International Business and Travel** (☎800-925-2428), which secures visas for travel to almost all countries for a variable service charge.

Work Permit (p. 12). Required for foreigners planning to work in Southeast Asia.

Required Vaccinations (p. 25).

Recommended Vaccinations (p. 25).

Vaccination/Health Certificates (p. 25). Visitors who have been in Africa or South America must have a certificate of vaccination against yellow fever.

Other Health: Malaria pills are recommended for those traveling to malaria risk areas (p. 28). If your regular **medical insurance policy** (p. 26) does not cover travel abroad, you may wish to purchase additional coverage.

DOCUMENTS AND FORMALITIES

PASSPORTS

REQUIREMENTS

You need a valid passport to enter all Southeast Asian nations and to return to your home country. Most countries will require that your passport be valid for six months beyond your anticipated departure date. See individual country introductions for specifics.

NEW PASSPORTS

Citizens of Australia, Canada, Ireland, New Zealand, the UK, and the US can apply for a passport at passport offices, courts of law, and certain post offices. Any new passport or renewal applications must be filed well in advance of the departure date, although most passport offices offer rush services for a very steep fee. Even rush services, however, can take up to two weeks.

PASSPORT MAINTENANCE

Photocopy the page of your passport with your photo, as well as your visas, traveler's check serial numbers, and any other important documents. Carry one set of copies in a safe place, apart from the originals, and leave another set at home. Consulates also recommend that you carry an expired passport or an official copy of your birth certificate in a part of your baggage separate from other documents.

If you lose your passport, notify the local police and the nearest embassy or consulate of your home government. To expedite its replacement, you should know all information previously recorded, show ID and proof of citizenship. A replacement may take weeks to process, and may be valid only for a limited time. Any visas stamped in your old passport will be lost. In an emergency, ask for immediate temporary traveling papers that will permit you to re-enter your home country.

VISAS, INVITATIONS, AND WORK PERMITS

Many countries in Southeast Asia require an entry visa that must be obtained in advance from a consulate abroad. For specific visa requirements (as of Aug. 2004), see the **Essentials** section of each individual country. Double-check entrance requirements at the nearest embassy or consulate (also listed in the **Essentials** chapter of each country.) for up-to-date info before departure. US citizens can also consult the **Center for International Business and Travel** (☎800-925-2428), which secures visas for travel to almost all countries for a variable service charge, or try www.pueblo.gsa.gov/cic_text/travel/foreign/foreignentryreqs.

VISA REQUIREMENTS

	AUS	CAN	IRE	NZ	UK	US
BRUNEI	Y	N^3	Y^3	N^3	N^1	N^2
CAMBODIA	Y	Y	Y	Y	Y	Y
INDONESIA	N^5	N^5	N^5	N^5	N^5	N^5
LAOS	Y	Y	Y	Y	Y	Y
MALAYSIA	N	N^5	N	N	N	N^2
MYANMAR	Y	Y	Y	Y	Y	Y
PHILIPPINES	N^6	N^6	N^6	N^6	N^6	N^6
SINGAPORE	N^1	N^1	N^1	N^1	N^1	N^1
THAILAND	N^1	N^1	N^1	N^1	N^1	N^1
VIETNAM	Y	Y	Y	Y	Y	Y

KEY: Y tourists must obtain a visa; **N** tourists do not need a visa, or do not need a visa with the following stipulations: **1** tourists can stay up to 30 days without visa; **2** tourists can stay up to 90 days without a visa; **3** tourists can stay up to 14 days without a visa; **4** tourists can stay for 6 months without a visa; **5** tourists can stay up to 60 days without a visa; **6** tourists can stay 21 days without a visa. Extensions issued within country.

Admission as a visitor does not include the right to work, which is authorized only by a work permit. Entering Southeast Asian countries to study or work requires a special visa that can be obtained with letters of sponsorship or invitation from businesses, organizations, or universities in Southeast Asia. Teaching English is the easiest way to enter the workforce. Large cities like Bangkok, Kuala Lumpur, and Hồ Chí Minh City have a lot of opportunities.Contact the embassy for specific details. For more information, see **Alternatives to Tourism** (p. 51).

IDENTIFICATION

When you travel, always carry at least two forms of identification on your person, including at least one photo ID; a passport and a driver's license or birth certificate is usually adequate. Students should carry a school ID. Never carry all of your IDs together; split them up, and keep copies of them in your luggage and at home.

STUDENT, TEACHER, AND YOUTH IDENTIFICATION

The **International Student Identity Card (ISIC),** the most widely accepted form of student ID, provides discounts on some sights, accommodations, food, and transport, access to a 24hr. emergency helpline, and insurance benefits for US cardholders (see **Insurance,** p. 26). Applicants must be full-time secondary or post-secondary school students at least 12 years of age. Because of the proliferation of fake ISICs, some services (particularly airlines) require additional proof of student identity.

The **International Teacher Identity Card (ITIC)** offers teachers the same insurance coverage as the ISIC and similar but limited discounts. For travelers who are 25 years old or under but are not students, the **International Youth Travel Card (IYTC)** also offers many of the same benefits as the ISIC.

Each of these identity cards costs US$22 or the equivalent. ISIC and ITIC cards are valid for the rest of the calendar year if bought between January and September; if bought between October and December, they are valid through December of the following year. IYTC cards are valid for one year from the date of issue. Many student travel agencies (p. 32) issue the cards; for a list of issuing agencies, see the **International Student Travel Confederation (ISTC)** website (www.istc.org).

The **International Student Exchange Card (ISE)** is a similar identification card available to students, faculty, and youth aged 12 to 26. The card provides discounts, medical benefits, access to a 24hr. emergency helpline, and the ability to purchase student airfares. The card costs US$25; call US ☎800-255-8000 for more info, or visit www.isecard.com. There are only discounts in a few Southeast Asian countries, including Indonesia, Malaysia and Singapore; see http://68.14.208.174:591/world/index to check for updated information.

CUSTOMS

Customs requirements vary from country to country in Southeast Asia. Upon entering you must declare certain items from abroad and pay a duty on the value of those articles if they exceed the allowance established by that country's customs service. Southeast Asian governments have harsh penalties for **drug possession and trafficking,** often considered synonymous. Note that goods and gifts purchased at **duty-free** shops abroad are not exempt from duty or sales tax at your point of return and must be declared as well. Several countries in Southeast Asia require official certification before cultural goods or artifacts can be taken out of the countries. Such certification often takes three to five days to process; if you do not complete the process, your purchases cannot leave the country with you. The import of **weapons** and **pornography** is prohibited by all Southeast Asian countries.

Upon returning home, you must declare all articles acquired abroad and pay a duty on the value of articles in excess of your home country's allowance. In order to expedite your return, register any valuables brought from home with customs before traveling abroad, and be sure to keep receipts for all goods acquired abroad. Additional country-specific customs regulations are listed below.

Brunei: There are strict regulations regarding temporary importation into or export of items such as firearms, antiquities, medications, currency restrictions, religious materials, ivory, and alcohol. Non-Muslims are permitted a limited amount of alcohol for personal consumption.

Cambodia: The export of antiquities, drugs, firearms, and ivory is strictly forbidden. There is no restriction on the export of local currency, but foreign nationals are restricted to a US$10,000 (cash) import limit.

Indonesia: Enforcement of Indonesia's strict customs regulations is inconsistent. Travelers can bring 1L of distilled alcohol and 200 cigarettes or 50 cigars or 100g of tobacco products. Chinese medicines and printings, firearms and ammunition, narcotics, pornography, fresh fruit, and cordless telephones are not permitted. Consult the Indonesian embassy in your country for more information.

Laos: No antique cultural items or Buddha images may leave the country without government authorization. Silver or copper items are subject to customs duties. Adult travelers are allowed to bring in a maximum of 500 cigarettes and 1L of alcohol. Drugs, firearms and ammunition, and pornography are not allowed in the country.

Malaysia: The importation of illicit drugs carries the mandatory death penalty in Malaysia. There are no general restrictions on the import or export of currency, but it is illegal to leave with over RM10,000 in cash. Pornography, publications that could be offensive to the government, knives, and most broadcast receivers are prohibited. A permit is necessary to import precious stones or gold for business purposes (coins issued by the Central Bank of Malaysia and personal jewelry are permissible).

Myanmar: Non-residents can bring the equivalent of US$2000 without declaration. Jewelry, electronic items, and cameras must be declared but are exempt from duty. Antique or archaeological souvenirs cannot be exported. Gems, jewelry, and silverware accompanied by an export-guarantee voucher from authorized gift shops may be exported.

Philippines: Visitors bringing in over US$3000 must declare the total at the Central Bank counter at customs. Drugs, coral, certain orchid species, mussels, animal parts (e.g. turtle shells), and local currency over P1000 may not leave the country. A certificate from the National Museum must accompany all antiques purchased in the country.

Singapore: Prohibited from importation are tobacco, obscene material, "seditious and treasonable material," and toy currency. Drug possession is considered trafficking in Singapore. Also prohibited is bringing live dogs of certain breeds in Singapore.

Thailand: Travelers may bring one still camera with 10 rolls of film, or one video camera with three tapes; these restrictions are meant to ensure the film and equipment is for personal use only and are flexible. Firearms and pornography are prohibited. The total amount of currency taken out should not exceed the amount taken in (max. US$10,000). No authentic Buddha or Bodhisattva images, or fragments thereof, may be exported without permission from the Bangkok National Museum (☎02 224 1333) and the Department of Fine Arts; you must prove you are a practicing Buddhist or are using them for cultural or academic purposes. These rules do not apply to souvenirs. For art purchased in the country, keep receipts for customs.

Vietnam: Visitors to Vietnam are allowed to bring in 200 cigarettes or the equivalent (50 cigars or 150g of tobacco); 1.5L of liquor; and other items (not forbidden goods) of the total value beneath US$300. Items that you can't bring into Vietnam include weapons, munitions, explosives and other flammable items, firecrackers of all kinds, opium and drugs, toxic chemicals, harmful children's toys, and cultural materials deemed unsuitable to Vietnamese society (pornographic or other seditious publications, films, and photos). Videotapes will be confiscated and checked upon arrival, and returned several days later.

MONEY

CURRENCY AND EXCHANGE

Up-to-date **exchange rates** and information on local currencies are in each country's **Essentials** section. As a general rule, it's cheaper to convert money at your destination. Bring enough currency to last for the first 24 to 72 hours of your trip—banks might be closed when you arrive. Travelers from the US can get foreign currency from the comfort of home: **International Currency Express** (☎888-278-6628) delivers currency or traveler's checks overnight (US$25) or second-day (US$12) at competitive exchange rates. Store your money in several forms; ideally, at any given time you will be carrying some cash, traveler's checks, and an ATM and/or credit card. Travelers should carry US dollars (about US$50 worth) even if it isn't their national currency, as many establishments in Southeast Asia prefer transactions in US dollars. For small transactions, put your dollars away and use local currency. Throwing dollars around for preferential treatment is offensive and attracts thieves. If you use traveler's checks or bills, carry some in small denominations (the equivalent of US$50 or less) for times when you are forced to exchange money at disadvantageous rates, but bring a range of denominations since charges may be levied per check cashed.

Banks generally have the best rates outside the black market. A good rule of thumb is to go only to banks that have at most a 5% margin between their buy and sell prices. **Convert large sums** (unless the currency is depreciating rapidly), **but no more than you'll need.** Freelancers on the black market often offer excellent rates, but you run the risk of being swindled or arrested.

TRAVELER'S CHECKS

Traveler's checks are one of the safest and least troublesome means of carrying funds. American Express and Visa are the most recognized brands. Many banks and agencies sell them for a small commission. Check issuers provide refunds if the checks are lost or stolen, and many provide additional services, such as toll-free refund hotlines abroad and stolen credit card assistance. Most Southeast Asian countries accept traveler's checks in well-traveled areas, especially at banks and hotels. They are less widely accepted in smaller towns and rural areas. Traveler's checks may not be accepted in Myanmar. Check individual country listings for more information. Ask about toll-free refund hotlines and the location of refund centers when purchasing checks, and always carry emergency cash.

American Express: Checks available with commission at select banks, at all AmEx offices, and online (www.americanexpress.com; US residents only). AmEx cardholders can purchase checks by phone (☎800-721-9768). Checks available in Australian, Canadian, British, Euro, Japanese, and US currencies. For purchase locations or more information contact AmEx's service centers: Australia ☎800 68 80 22; New Zealand 0508 555 358; the UK 0800 587 6023; the US and Canada 800-221-7282; elsewhere, call the US collect at 801-964-6665.

Visa: Checks available (generally with commission) at banks worldwide. For the location of the nearest office, call Visa's service centers: in the UK ☎0800 59 50 78; in the US 800-227-6811; elsewhere, call the UK collect at 44 173 331 8949. Checks available in British, Canadian, Euro, Japanese, and US currencies. AAA (p. 37) offers commission-free checks to its members.

Travelex/Thomas Cook: In the UK call ☎0800 62 21 01; in the US and Canada call 800-287-7362; elsewhere call the UK collect at 44 1733 31 89 50. Issues V traveler's checks. Members of AAA and affiliated automobile associations receive a 25% commission discount on check purchases. Checks accepted only in Singapore.

CREDIT, DEBIT, AND ATM CARDS

Where they are accepted, credit cards often offer superior exchange rates—up to 5% better than the retail rate used by banks and other currency exchange establishments. Credit cards may also offer services such as insurance or emergency help, and are sometimes required to reserve hotel rooms or rental cars. **Mastercard** and **Visa** are the most welcomed; **American Express** cards work at some ATMs and at AmEx offices and major airports.

ATMs are common in Brunei, Indonesia, Hong Kong, Malaysia, the Philippines, Singapore, and Thailand. They are rare in Cambodia, Laos, and Vietnam, except in large, central cities. The two major international money networks are **Cirrus** (US ☎800-424-7787) and **Visa/PLUS** (US ☎800-843-7587). Call these numbers to locate ATMs anywhere in the world, or consult http://usa.visa.com/personal/atm_locator/plus_atm or www.mastercard.com/cardholderservices/atm. Depending on the system that your home bank uses, you can most likely access your personal bank account from abroad. ATMs get the same wholesale exchange rate as credit cards, but there is often a limit on the amount you can withdraw per day (around US$500), and computer networks sometimes fail. There is typically a surcharge of US$1-5 per withdrawal. Have your home bank issue you a four-digit PIN, the only variety accepted at some Southeast Asian ATMs. Be sure to memorize your PIN in numeric form, since machines abroad often don't have letters on their keys.

A debit card can be used wherever its associated credit card company (usually MC or V) is accepted, yet the money is withdrawn directly from the holder's checking account. Debit cards often also function as ATM cards and can be used to withdraw cash from associated banks and ATMs throughout Southeast Asia.

Visa TravelMoney is a system that allows you to access money from any Visa ATM for a small fee. Deposit money before you travel, and you can withdraw up to that sum. The cards give you the same favorable exchange rate for withdrawals as a regular Visa. Check with your local bank to see if it issues TravelMoney cards (☎877-394-2247; www.usa.visa.com/personal/cards/visa_travel_money).

GETTING MONEY FROM HOME

If you run out of money while traveling, the easiest and cheapest solution is to have someone back home make a deposit to your account. Failing that, consider the following options. The online **International Money Transfer Consumer Guide** (http://international-money-transfer-consumer-guide.info) may also be of help.

WIRING MONEY

It is possible to arrange a **bank money transfer,** which means asking a bank back home to wire money to a bank in most Southeast Asian countries. This is the cheapest way to transfer cash, but it's also the slowest, usually taking several days or more. Note that some banks may only release your funds in local currency, potentially sticking you with a poor exchange rate; inquire about this in advance. Money transfer services like **Western Union** are faster and more convenient than bank transfers—but also much pricier. Western Union has many locations worldwide. To find one, visit www.westernunion.com, or call in Australia ☎800 501 500; in Canada 800-235-0000; in the UK 0800 83 38 33; in the US 800-325-6000. See individual chapters for locations and phone numbers within Southeast Asia. Money transfer services are also available at **American Express** offices. However, American Express is not offered in Brunei, Cambodia, Laos, or Myanmar.

US STATE DEPARTMENT (US CITIZENS ONLY)

In serious emergencies only, the US State Department will forward money within hours to the nearest consular office, which will then disburse it according to instructions for a US$30 fee. If you wish to use this service, you must contact the Overseas Citizens Service division of the US State Department (☎317-472-2328; nights, Su, and holidays 202-647-4000).

COSTS

The cost of your trip will vary considerably, depending on where you go, how you travel, and where you stay. The single biggest cost of your trip will probably be your round-trip **airfare** (see **By Plane,** p. 32). Traveling in Southeast Asia can be done on a rather small budget, spending as little as US$5 per day in some parts of the region. Before you go, spend some time calculating a reasonable daily **budget** that will meet your needs. But always keep emergency reserve funds (at least US$200) when planning how much money you'll need.

STAYING ON A BUDGET

With the exception of Singapore, a traveler's cost of living is very low in Southeast Asia relative to most Western countries. The difference between the cheapest option and the mid-range option is often only a few dollars, giving the budget traveler the option of an occasional night of luxury. To give you a general idea, a bare-bones day in most of Southeast Asia (camping or sleeping in hostels or guesthouses, buying food at supermarkets) would cost about US$10; a slightly more comfortable day (sleeping in hostels or guesthouses and the occasional budget hotel, eating 1 meal per day at a restaurant, going out at night) would cost US$15; for a luxurious day, the sky's the limit.

MADE TO MEASURE
Ladies & Gents Custom Tailoring / BESPOKE SUITS & SHIRTS
To make an appointment with the Most Awarded Tailor
visit at: www.smartfashion.com/form.htm
On our next visit to Europe / UK we will introduce the latest and finest fabric collection from Super 120's wool and cashmere.
SPECIAL OFFER
2 Suits
2 Extra Pants
2 Shirts
2 Ties
from US$
159
Fax & Voicemail
UK No: 020 7681 1794
E-mail: somsak11@inet.co.th
Website: www.smartfashion.com
For free pick up in Bangkok
Call: 02 253 2993
Hong Kong Tailors
Address: 28-28/1 Sukhumvit Soi 19 (Soi wattana) Bangkok 10110, Thailand
Tel: 00 662 253 2993 Fax: 00 662 255 4518
SAM'S LODGE
BANGKOK
Special Opening Rates @US$15 and up
GUESTHOUSE WITH COMMON CLEAN HYGIENIC BATHROOM. ACCESS TO EVERY FLOOR WITH ELEVATOR AND A NICE GARDEN ROOF TOP WITH AN EXCELLENT VIEW.
E-mail: stay@samslodge.com
For more information please visit:
www.samslodge.com
CENTRALLY LOCATED IN SUKHUMVIT AREA (SOI 19)
EASY 1 MINUTE REACH BY SKY TRAIN (ASOKE STATION)
FOR FURTHER INFORMATION, PLEASE CALL 02 253 6069
28-28/1 Sukhumvit Soi 19 (Soi Wattana) Wattana, Bangkok, Thailand.
Booking: 02 253 2993 or 02 255 4516 Fax: +66 2 255 4518

TIPS FOR SAVING MONEY

Some simpler ways to save include searching out opportunities for free entertainment, splitting accommodation and food costs with trustworthy fellow travelers, and buying food in supermarkets rather than eating out. Bring a sleepsack (p. 19) to save on sheet charges, and do your laundry in the sink (unless you're explicitly prohibited from doing so). However, although staying within your budget is important, don't do so at the expense of your health or a great travel experience.

TIPPING AND BARGAINING

There are many unspoken rules for tipping and especially bargaining in the developing world. Bargaining is commonplace. Tipping is not customary in Southeast Asia. However, a general rule is: the more Western the establishment, the more likely a tip is expected. If an establishment includes a service charge in the bill tipping is not necessary. Still, most people will welcome the extra kip, riel, đồng, or baht, as the average yearly income for some in Southeast Asia is as low as US$150.

While corruption is rife in many Southeast Asian countries, as a general rule, officials are unwilling to accept bribes from foreigners, and it is unwise to initiate an under-the-table transaction. If an official demands a fee or fine that you feel may be illegal, proceed with caution. Paying the bribe might be preferable to the alternative, but keep in mind that it is also illegal. If you politely ask for a receipt, or to speak with the official's superior, you might be able to defuse the situation. As a last resort, threatening to contact your embassy may also be effective.

PACKING

Pack lightly: Lay out only what you absolutely need, then take half the clothes and twice the money. The Travelite FAQ (www.travelite.org) is a good resource for tips on traveling light. The online **Universal Packing List** (http://upl.codeq.info) will generate a list of suggested items based on your trip length, the climate, your activities, and other factors. If you plan to hike, consult **Camping,** p. 43.

Luggage: If you plan to cover most of your itinerary on foot, a sturdy **frame backpack** is unbeatable. (For the basics on buying a pack, see p. 44.) Toting a **suitcase** or **trunk** is fine if you plan to live in one or two cities and explore from there, but not a great idea if you plan to move around frequently. In addition to your main piece of luggage, a **daypack** (a small backpack or courier bag) is useful.

Clothing: Clothing is very inexpensive in Southeast Asia, so the best thing to do is pack very little and buy what you need on the road. Due to the region's hot climate, there's an urge to wear less. However, the general rule is to dress modestly. Women should be covered past the shoulders and at least to the knees. Men should avoid going around topless. The best way to stay cool is to wear loose cotton or linen. If you plan to visit religious or cultural sites, remember that you will need respectful dress.

Sleepsack: Some hostels require that you either provide your own linen or rent sheets from them. Save cash by making your own sleepsack: fold a full-size sheet in half the long way, then sew it closed along the long side and one of the short sides.

Converters and Adapters: In Southeast Asia, electricity ranges from 220 to 240 volts AC, enough to fry any 120V North American appliance. 220/240V electrical appliances won't work with a 120V current, either. Americans and Canadians should buy an adapter (which changes the shape of the plug; US$5) and a converter (which changes the voltage; US$20-30). Don't make the mistake of using only an adapter (unless appliance instructions explicitly state otherwise). New Zealand, UK, and Australian travelers (who use 230V at home) won't need a converter, but will need a set of adapters. For more on all things adaptable, check out http://kropla.com/electric.htm.

TIP **THE ART OF THE DEAL.** Bargaining in Southeast Asia is a given: no price is set in stone, and vendors and drivers will automatically quote you a price that is several times too high; it's up to you to get them down to a reasonable rate. With the following tips and some finesse, you might be able to impress even the most hardened hawkers:

1. **Bargaining needn't be a fierce struggle laced with barbs.** Quite the opposite: good-natured wrangling with a cheerful face may prove your best weapon.
2. **Use your poker face.** The less your face betrays your interest in the item the better. If you touch an item to inspect it, the vendor will be sure to "encourage" you to name a price or make a purchase. Coming back again and again to admire a trinket is a good way of ensuring that you pay a ridiculously high price. Never get too enthusiastic about the object in question; point out flaws in workmanship and design. Be cool.
3. **Know when to bargain.** In most cases, it's quite clear when it's appropriate to bargain. Most private transportation fares and things for sale in outdoor markets are all fair game. Don't bargain on prepared or pre-packaged foods on the street or in restaurants. In some stores, signs will indicate whether "fixed prices" prevail. When in doubt, ask tactfully, "Is that your lowest price?" or whether discounts are given.
4. **Never underestimate the power of peer pressure.** Bargaining with more than one person at a time always leads to higher prices. Alternately, try having a friend discourage you from your purchase—if you seem to be reluctant, the merchant will want to drop the price to interest you again.
5. **Know when to turn away.** Feel free to refuse any vendor or driver who bargains rudely, and don't hesitate to move on to another vendor if one will not be reasonable about the final price he offers. However, to start bargaining without an intention to buy is a major *faux pas*. Agreeing on a price and declining it is also poor form. Turn away slowly with a smile and a "thank you" upon hearing a ridiculous price—the price may plummet.
6. **Start low.** Never feel guilty offering a ridiculously low price. Your starting price should be no more than one-third to one-half the asking price.

ESSENTIALS

Toiletries: Toothbrushes, towels, cold-water soap, talcum powder (to keep feet dry), deodorant, razors, tampons, and condoms are often available, but may be difficult to find; bring extras. Contact lenses are likely to be expensive and difficult to find, so bring enough extra pairs and solution for your entire trip. Also bring your glasses and a copy of your prescription in case you need emergency replacements. If you use heat-disinfection, either switch temporarily to a chemical disinfection system (check first to make sure it's safe with your brand of lenses), or buy a converter to 220/240V.

First-Aid Kit: For a basic first-aid kit, pack bandages, a pain reliever, antibiotic cream, a thermometer, a Swiss Army knife, tweezers, moleskin, decongestant, motion-sickness remedy, diarrhea or upset-stomach medication (Pepto Bismol or Imodium), an antihistamine, sunscreen, insect repellent, burn ointment, and a syringe for emergencies (get an explanatory letter from your doctor).

Film: Film and developing in Southeast Asia range in price from US$4-10 for a roll of 24 color exposure, depending on the country. The quality also varies, so bring along enough film for your entire trip and develop it at home. Less serious photographers may want to bring a disposable camera. Despite disclaimers, airport security X-rays can fog film, so buy a lead-lined pouch at a camera store or ask security to hand-inspect it. Pack film in your carry-on, since higher-intensity X-rays are used on checked luggage.

Other Useful Items: For safety purposes, you should bring a **money belt** and small **padlock.** Basic **outdoors equipment** (plastic water bottle, compass, waterproof matches, pocketknife, sunglasses, sunscreen, hat) may also prove useful. Quick repairs of torn garments can be done on the road with a needle and thread; also consider bringing electrical tape for patching tears. If you want to do laundry by hand, bring detergent, a small rubber ball to stop up the sink, and string for a makeshift clothes line. Other things you're liable to forget are an umbrella, sealable **plastic bags** (for damp clothes, soap, food, shampoo, and other spillables), an **alarm clock,** safety pins, rubber bands; a flashlight, earplugs, garbage bags, and a small **calculator.** A **cell phone** can be a life-saver (literally) on the road; see p. 41 for information on acquiring one in Southeast Asia.

Important Documents: Don't forget your passport, traveler's checks, ATM or credit cards, adequate ID, and photocopies of all of these in case these documents are lost or stolen (p. 13). Check that you have the following: driver's license (p. 13); travel insurance forms; and ISIC card (p. 13).

HEALTH AND SAFETY

GENERAL ADVICE

In any type of crisis situation, the most important thing to do is **stay calm.** Your country's embassy abroad is usually your best resource when things go wrong; registering with that embassy upon arrival in the country is often a good idea. The government offices listed in the **Travel Advisories** box (p. 13) can provide information on the services they offer their citizens in case of emergencies abroad.

DRUGS AND ALCOHOL

Drugs are often easily accessible in Southeast Asia and, especially in some rural communities, drug use may seem to be common and public. All drug use, however, is illegal. Buying or selling *any* type of drug may lead to anything from a prison sentence to the death penalty, especially in Malaysia, Singapore, and Cambodia. Don't think you can talk or pay your way out of trouble. A meek "I didn't know it was illegal" will not suffice; if you break the law, your home embassies **cannot and will not do anything else** to help. Alcohol consumption varies from country to country, often reflecting the dominant religious values.

PROSTITUTION AND SEX TOURISM

Prostitution in Southeast Asia has developed into a lucrative business that affects employment and national income and contributes immensely to the region's economic growth. Every year, people travel to Southeast Asia to exploit women and children who have no alternative means to support themselves and their families. Many of these sex slaves are trafficked abroad for close to nothing.

Sexual exploitation and trafficking of women and children should be taken very seriously. Keep in mind the danger of contracting HIV/AIDS and STDs. Penalties in Southeast Asia for pedophiles are severe, and countries around the world prosecute and punish pedophilia offenses committed abroad. Several organizations are working to curb child prostitution and child pornography. For more information, visit the website of **End Child Prostitution and Trafficking** (Ecpat; www.ecpat.net).

NATURAL DISASTERS

TYPHOONS. Typhoons are severe tropical storms (equivalent to hurricanes in the Atlantic) with very high winds that occur from May to November, with most in August and September. During a typhoon, move inside, keep away from windows, and stay informed on the storm's movement. Most of Southeast Asia is not subject to typhoons, which form over the Pacific and track northwest toward the Asian mainland. However, typhoons occasionally strike the Philippines and Vietnam.

TERRORISM

Southeast Asia is emerging as one of the most important centers of Islamic terrorism outside of the Arab East. Political-religious violence, including armed activities against the governments, is well established in several Southeast Asian countries, especially Indonesia, the Philippines, and Thailand. Travelers to Southeast Asia should always check travel advisories and world news for the countries they will be visiting before departure. It is always helpful—and sometimes essential—to be aware of the political situation in the region; using current, proper titles for government officials and organizations is a must. Currently, one of the most prominent terrorist groups in Southeast Asia is the Jemaah Islamiya, an Islamic separatist organization operating primarily in Indonesia. It is suspected that the JI has ties with al Qaeda, and that a number of its leaders have undergone training in Pakistan and Afghanistan. The Philippines-based terrorist Abu Sayyaf Group poses an ongoing threat in areas near Malaysia and the Philippines. The box on travel advisories (p. 24) lists offices to contact and webpages to visit to get the most updated list of your home country's government's advisories about travel.

COUNTRY-SPECIFIC CONCERNS

BRUNEI. Violent crime is rare, but burglaries and theft are on the rise. Brunei has a mandatory death penalty for many narcotic offenses depending on the amount. Possession of small amounts will land you in jail for 20 years after a caning.

CAMBODIA. **Landmines** litter the country. Though de-mining operations have made significant progress, much of Cambodia remains mined, especially in rural areas. **Stay on well-traveled roads.** Bandits are still at large, and corrupt police forces are always looking for extra cash. Overland travel is the most dangerous mode of transport due to raids, unofficial police "checkpoints," and road conditions.

INDONESIA. A specific, credible terrorist threat in areas of Central, Southern and Southwestern Sulawesi in May 2004 led many Westerners to evacuate those areas. Anti-Western violence has been increasing over the past few years; the nightclub bombings in Bali were preceded by a failed attack on the US embassy, and it is not yet known what groups are currently the most active. Radical Islamic groups have gained momentum in the country, and both separatist movements and interreligious violence threaten political and social stability. The floundering economy of the past several years has aggravated tensions. Militant groups in Surakarta have threatened to push Americans off Indonesian soil, though government forces have prevented them from acting on such threats. Foreign travelers should exercise caution: keep a low profile and avoid demonstrations. Travel is currently considered unsafe in the **Aceh Province, Central and South Sulawesi, West Timor, Central and West Kalimantan, Irian Jaya,** and **Maluku and North Maluku.** Check with your embassy for up-to-date safety information.

LAOS. Laos has a low crime rate, but travelers shouldn't let their guard down, especially as incidents of theft, burglary, and assault have recently risen. In 2003, 12 people were killed and injured on Rte. 13, and two bombs detonated outside a market in Vientiane and in Savannakhet province. There have been sporadic attacks at selected points along the Lao-Thai border and in a number of northern provinces. Be especially careful in the **Golden Triangle** area near the Thai-Burmese-Lao border, which is known for its opium production. Provinces that require extreme caution are Xieng Khouang; Luang Prabang; Houaphan; Sayaboury, Saysomboun Special Zone and north of Van Vieng in Vientiane Province (not to be confused with the separate municipality of Vientiane). Although several non-governmental organizations have taken up de-mining, some bombs remain, killing or injuring about 10 people per month. Laos has strict rules regarding **public morality.** (Remember, this is the country that outlawed karaoke in its capital city.) Bringing a Laotian into your hotel room could land you in prison.

MALAYSIA. International trafficking of **illegal drugs** is punishable by death. Very little violent crime threatens travelers; criminals stop at theft and minor cons.

MYANMAR. Ethnic clashes have made eastern Myanmar and Thai border regions dangerous in recent months, so check the news and your embassy before going to the Shan state. **Do not talk about politics.** Stay away from demonstrations and do not engage in political conversations, no matter how harmless the topic may seem. **Political conversations put locals at risk of interrogation and arrest.** Do not photograph bridges, military installations, or anything else of economic or military importance. Officials carefully screen books and magazines at the airport. These officials may not understand English, but they are attentive to political articles, books, and pictures related to **Aung San Suu Kyi.**

THE PHILIPPINES. Personable Filipinos go to great lengths to give directions and point out proper jeepney routes. However, be wary of taking drinks from anyone you don't know—unsuspecting travelers have been given drinks spiked with **sedatives.** Manila seems to be a haven for such wayward pharmacists, but exercise caution everywhere. Another concern for travelers is the use of firearms by security guards protecting restaurants, banks, and clubs. Standing in front of banks and armored vehicles is unsafe, as these are often targets. Venturing unchaperoned into rarely frequented areas may make you a target for **radical separatist groups.**

SINGAPORE. Singaporean law can be quite strict by most Western standards. Jaywalking is prohibited and may result in a fine. The sale (and purchase) of chewing gum is no longer prohibited. Smoking in enclosed public spaces and eating or drinking on public transportation are prohibited. The penalty for importing illegal drugs can be as severe as execution and will almost definitely involve a long prison sentence. Singapore is one of the safest places in the world. Women are rarely catcalled, and often walk alone after dark. Nevertheless, petty crime happens, and travelers should not surrender their street smarts.

THAILAND. Recently, Northern Thailand and its border with Myanmar have been prone to violence due to the **Myanmar ethnic conflict.** Travelers considering heading to the deep south (specifically, Narathiwat, Pattani, Yala, and Songkhla provinces) should closely monitor the religious tensions which have been the source of violence during the spring of 2004. Check the news and at your embassy before going to those areas. Thailand has a good safety record. Nevertheless, scams abound: taxi and *tuk-tuk* drivers, guesthouse operators, and fellow travelers have all been known to attempt various con-games and thievery. On buses and trains and in the airport, be careful when accepting food or drink from strangers; travelers have been drugged and robbed. Most likely their friendliness is genuine, but exercise common sense. Crime committed against foreigners is usually petty thievery; violence is rare. Most Thai cities have separate tourist police forces. **All narcotic drugs in Thailand are illegal,** despite what your guesthouse owner may tell you. Penalties for drug-related crimes can be very stiff—up to life in prison.

VIETNAM. Never leave valuables unguarded (especially your passport); **thefts** are not uncommon within guesthouses, sometimes even under the management's orchestration. Keep an eye out for con artists, pickpockets, and purse or backpack snatchers, especially prevalent in Hồ Chí Minh City. Pedicab passengers are particularly vulnerable to thieves. Avoid photographing bridges, border crossings, power stations, and military and government structures. In the past few years, minority protests have caused certain areas to be closed to travelers; check with your embassy for detailed information.

TRAVEL ADVISORIES. The following government offices provide travel information and advisories by telephone or via the web:

Australian Department of Foreign Affairs and Trade: ☎13 00 555135; www.dfat.gov.au.

Canadian Department of Foreign Affairs and International Trade (DFAIT): In Canada and the US call ☎800-267-8376, elsewhere call ☎1 613-944-4000; www.dfait-maeci.gc.ca. Call for their free booklet, *Bon Voyage...But.*

New Zealand Ministry of Foreign Affairs: ☎04 439 8000; www.mft.govt.nz/travel/index.html.

United Kingdom Foreign and Commonwealth Office: ☎020 7008 0232; www.fco.gov.uk.

US Department of State: ☎202-647-5225; http://travel.state.gov. For *A Safe Trip Abroad,* call ☎202-512-1800.

ESSENTIALS

PERSONAL SAFETY

EXPLORING AND TRAVELING

To avoid unwanted attention, try to blend in as much as possible. Respecting local customs (in many cases, dressing more conservatively than you would at home) may placate would-be hecklers. Familiarize yourself with your surroundings before setting out, and carry yourself with confidence. Check maps in shops and restaurants rather than on the street. If you are traveling alone, be sure someone at home knows your itinerary, and never admit that you're by yourself. When walking at night, stick to busy, well-lit streets and avoid dark alleyways. If you ever feel uncomfortable, leave the area as quickly and directly as you can.

There is no sure-fire way to avoid all the threatening situations you might encounter while traveling, but a good **self-defense course** will give you concrete ways to react to unwanted advances. **Impact, Prepare, and Model Mugging** can refer you to local self-defense courses in the US (☎800-345-5425). Visit the website at www.impactsafety.org for a list of nearby chapters. Workshops (2-3hr.) start at US$50; full courses (20hr.) run US$350-500.

If you are using a **car,** learn local driving signals and wear a seatbelt. Children under 40 lbs. should ride only in specially designed carseats, available for a small fee from most car rental agencies. Study route maps before you hit the road, and if you plan on spending a lot of time driving, consider bringing spare parts. If your car breaks down, wait for the police to assist you. For long drives in desolate areas, invest in a cellular phone and a roadside assistance program (p. 37). Park your vehicle in a garage or well-traveled area, and use a steering wheel locking device in larger cities. **Sleeping in your car** is one of the most dangerous (and often illegal) ways to get your rest. For info on the perils of **hitchhiking,** see p. 38.

POSSESSIONS AND VALUABLES

Never leave your belongings unattended; crime occurs in even the most demure-looking hostel or hotel. Bring your own **padlock** for hostel lockers, and don't ever store valuables in a locker. Be particularly careful on **buses** and **trains;** horror stories abound about determined thieves who wait for travelers to fall asleep. Carry your pack in front of you where you can see it. When traveling with others, sleep in alternate shifts. When alone, use good judgment in selecting a train compartment: never stay in an empty one, and use a lock to secure your pack to the luggage rack. Try to sleep on top bunks with your luggage stored above you (if not in bed with you), and keep important documents and other valuables on your person.

There are a few steps you can take to minimize the financial risk associated with traveling. First, **bring as little with you as possible.** Second, buy a few combination **padlocks** to secure your belongings either in your pack or in a hostel or train station locker. Third, **carry as little cash as possible.** Keep your traveler's checks and ATM/credit cards in a **money belt**—not a "fanny pack"—along with your passport and ID cards. Fourth, **keep a small cash reserve separate from your primary stash.** This should be about US$50 sewn into or stored in the depths of your pack, along with your traveler's check numbers and important photocopies.

In large cities **con artists** often work in groups and may involve children. Beware of certain classics: sob stories that require money, rolls of bills "found" on the street, mustard spilled (or saliva spit) onto your shoulder to distract you while they snatch your bag. **Never let your passport and your bags out of your sight.** Beware of **pickpockets** in city crowds, especially on public transportation. Also, be alert in public telephone booths: if you must say your calling card number, do so very quietly; if you punch it in, make sure no one can look over your shoulder.

If traveling with electronic devices, such as a laptop or PDA, check if your homeowner's insurance covers loss, theft, or damage when you travel. If not, you might consider purchasing a low-cost separate insurance policy. **Safeware** (☎US 800-800-1492; www.safeware.com) specializes in covering computers and charges US$90 for 90-day comprehensive international travel coverage up to US$4000.

ESSENTIALS

PRE-DEPARTURE HEALTH

In your **passport,** write the names of any people you wish to be contacted in case of a medical emergency, and list any allergies or medical conditions. Matching a prescription to a foreign equivalent is not always easy, safe, or possible; if you take prescription drugs, consider carrying up-to-date, legible prescriptions or a statement from your doctor stating the medication's trade name, manufacturer, chemical name, and dosage. While traveling, keep all medication with you in your carry-on luggage. For tips on packing a **first-aid kit** and other health essentials, see p. 20.

IMMUNIZATIONS AND PRECAUTIONS

Travelers over two-years-old should make sure that the following vaccines are up to date: MMR (for measles, mumps, and rubella); DTaP or Td (for diphtheria, tetanus, and pertussis); IPV (for polio); Hib (for *haemophilus* influenza B); and HepB (for Hepatitis B). Adults traveling to the developing world on trips longer than four weeks should consider the following additional immunizations: Hepatitis A vaccine and/or immune globulin (IG), an additional dose of Polio vaccine, typhoid and cholera vaccines—particularly if traveling off the beaten path—as well as a meningitis vaccine, Japanese encephalitis vaccine, rabies vaccine, and yearly influenza vaccines. While yellow fever is only endemic to parts of South America and sub-Saharan Africa, many countries may deny entrance to travelers arriving from these zones without a certificate of vaccination. For recommendations on immunizations and prophylaxis, consult the CDC (p. 16) in the US or the equivalent in your home country, and check with a doctor for guidance.

INOCULATION REQUIREMENTS AND RECOMMENDATIONS. The inoculations needed for travel in Southeast Asia vary with the length of your trip and the activities you plan to pursue. Visit your doctor at least 4-6 weeks prior to your departure to allow time for the shots to take effect. Be sure to keep your inoculation records with you as you travel–you may be required to show them to border officials.

Diptheria, tetanus, measles, and **polio** booster doses recommended as needed.
Typhoid strongly recommended.
Hepatitis A or immune globulin (IG), recommended.
Hepatitis B if traveling for 6 months or more, or if exposure to blood, needle-sharing, or sexual contact is likely. Important for healthcare workers and those who might seek medical treatment abroad.
Japanese Encephalitis, only if you will be in rural areas for 4 weeks or more, or if there are known outbreaks in the regions you plan to visit; elevated risk usually from May-Oct.
Rabies, if you might be exposed to animals as you travel.
Yellow Fever, if traveling from South America or sub-Saharan Africa; certificate of vaccination may be required for entry into some countries. There is no risk in Southeast Asia.

INSURANCE

Travel insurance covers four basic areas: medical and health problems, property loss, trip cancellation or interruption, and emergency evacuation. Though regular insurance policies may well extend to travel-related accidents, you should consider purchasing separate travel insurance if the cost of potential trip cancellation, interruption, or emergency medical evacuation is greater than you can absorb. Prices for travel insurance purchased separately generally run about US$50 per week for full coverage, while trip cancellation or interruption may be purchased separately at a rate of US$3-5 per day depending on length of stay.

Medical insurance (especially university policies) often covers costs incurred abroad; check with your provider. **US Medicare** does not cover foreign travel. **Canadian** provincial health insurance plans increasingly do not cover foreign travel; check with the provincial Ministry of Health or Health Plan Headquarters for details. **Homeowners' insurance** (or your family's coverage) often covers theft during travel and loss of travel documents (passport, plane ticket, etc.) up to US$500.

ISIC and **ITIC** (p. 13) provide basic insurance benefits to US cardholders, including US$100 per day of in-hospital sickness for up to 60 days and US$5000 of accident-related medical reimbursement (see www.isicus.com for details). Cardholders have access to a toll-free 24hr. helpline for medical, legal, and financial emergencies overseas. **American Express** (US ☎ 800-528-4800) grants most cardholders automatic collision and theft car rental insurance and ground travel accident coverage of US$100,000 on flight purchases made with the card.

INSURANCE PROVIDERS

STA (p. 32) offers a range of plans that can supplement your basic coverage. Other private insurance providers in the US and Canada include: Access America (☎ 800-284-8300; www.accessamerica.com); Berkely Group (☎ 800-797-4514; www.berkely.com); Globalcare Travel Insurance (☎ 800-821-2488; www.globalcare-cocco.com); Travel Assistance International (☎ 800-821-2828; www.europ-assistance.com); and Travel Guard (☎800-826-4919; www.travelguard.com). Columbus Direct (☎020 7375 0011; www.columbusdirect.co.uk) operates in the UK and AFTA (☎02 9264 3299; www.afta.com.au) in Australia.

USEFUL ORGANIZATIONS AND PUBLICATIONS

The US **Centers for Disease Control and Prevention** (**CDC;** ☎877-FYI-TRIP; www.cdc.gov/travel) maintains an international travelers' hotline and an informative website. The CDC's comprehensive booklet *Health Information for International Travel* (The Yellow Book), an annual rundown of disease, immunization, and general health advice, is free online or for US$29-40 via the Public Health Foundation (☎877-252-1200; http://bookstore.phf.org). Consult the appropriate government agency of your home country for consular information sheets on health, entry requirements, and other issues for various countries (see the box on **Travel Advisories,** p. 24). For quick information on health and other travel warnings, call the **Overseas Citizens Services** (M-F 8am-8pm ☎888-407-4747, after-hours 202-647-4000, overseas 317-472-2328), or contact a passport agency, embassy, or consulate abroad. For information on medical evacuation services and travel insurance firms, see the US government's website at http://travel.state.gov/medical.html or the **British Foreign and Commonwealth Office** (www.fco.gov.uk). For general health info, contact the **American Red Cross** (☎800-564-1234; www.redcross.org)

STAYING HEALTHY

Common sense is the simplest prescription for good health while you travel. Drink lots of fluids to prevent dehydration and constipation, and wear sturdy, broken-in shoes and clean socks.

ONCE IN SOUTHEAST ASIA

ENVIRONMENTAL HAZARDS

Prickly heat: Prickly heat is a lasting heat rash that blocks the pores of the sweat glands, resulting in tiny bumps or even water blisters. It is common in Southeast Asia due to the heat and humidity. If you develop prickly heat, gently cleanse the skin with a soap containing salicylic acid, and apply hydrocortisone cream (not ointment) to alleviate itching. Antibiotics may be needed if the rash becomes infected. Once treated, prickly heat should disappear within 2-3 days.

Heat exhaustion and dehydration: Heat exhaustion leads to nausea, excessive thirst, headaches, and dizziness. Avoid it by drinking plenty of fluids, eating salty foods (e.g. crackers), abstaining from dehydrating beverages (e.g. alcohol and caffeinated beverages), and always wearing sunscreen. Continuous heat stress can eventually lead to heatstroke, characterized by a rising temperature, severe headache, delirium and cessation of sweating. Victims should be cooled off with wet towels and taken to a doctor.

Heatstroke: Heatstroke is an illness caused by prolonged exposure to very hot temperatures or dehydration. Symptoms include dizziness, fatigue, headache, rapid pulse, rapid breathing, hot, flushed skin, muscle cramps, no sweating, high body temperature, and loss of consciousness. To alleviate heat stroke, cool down the body with cold water and consult a doctor immediately. Failure to seek treatment could result in death.

Sunburn: To prevent sunburn, apply sunscreen (SPF 30 is good) at least every 2hr., and wear a wide-brimmed hat and sunglasses, especially if you're near water or sand. Wearing less will not keep you cooler and will not protect you from the sun. Wear loose cotton or linen pants and longsleeved shirts. Don't let a cloudy sky fool you; the sun's rays will find their way to your skin. Treat a sunburn with aloe, calamine lotion, or Vitamin E ointment. For mild sunburn, a hot shower increases peeling and alleviates discomfort sooner. Severe sunburns can lead to sun poisoning, a condition that affects the entire body with fever, chills, nausea, and vomiting. Sun poisoning should always be treated by a doctor.

High altitude: More than 50% of travelers have trouble adjusting to high altitudes. Symptoms include headache, vomiting, nausea, dizziness, fatigue, coughing and irritability. Mild symptoms can be treated with rest and descending if necessary. **Do not go higher if you experience any symptoms.** Several preventative drugs are recommended by doctors, namely acetazolamide and dexamethasin; however, because the full effect of these drugs is unclear, we do not recommend them for travelers. You need more fluids at higher altitudes so remain well hydrated. Those with heart or lung disease or high blood pressure should consult a doctor before traveling above 4000m. Be particularly cautious if you are travelling to Mt. Kinabalu in Malaysian Borneo, or the higher peaks of Indonesia and northern Myanmar. Allow your body a couple of days to adjust to less oxygen. Note that alcohol is more potent and UV rays are stronger at high elevations.

Air pollution: The quality of air in Southeast Asia is unpredictable. Vehicle pollution is on the rise and forest fires in Kalimantan and Sumatra, Indonesia have affected the air throughout the region. Health effects may range from difficulty in breathing, including coughing and wheezing, to aggravation of existing cardiac and respiratory conditions. Pollution can also cause dry throat, irritated eyes, and sinusitis. Fresh air will usually alleviate irritation due to pollution.

INSECT-BORNE DISEASES

Many diseases are transmitted by insects—mainly mosquitoes, fleas, ticks, and lice. Be aware of insects in wet or forested areas, especially while hiking and camping; wear long pants and long sleeves, tuck your pants into your socks, and use a mosquito net. Use insect repellents such as DEET and soak or spray your gear with permethrin (licensed in the US only for use on clothing). **Mosquitoes**—responsible for malaria, Dengue fever, yellow fever, and Japanese encephalitis, among others—can be particularly dangerous in wet, swampy, or wooded areas. **Ticks**—responsible for Lyme and other diseases—can be particularly dangerous in rural and forested regions throughout Southeast Asia.

Malaria: Transmitted by *Anopheles* mosquitoes that bite at night. The incubation period varies anywhere between 10 days and 4 weeks. Early symptoms include fever, chills, aches, and fatigue, followed by high fever and sweating, sometimes with vomiting and diarrhea. See a doctor for any flu-like sickness that occurs after travel in a risk area. To reduce the risk of contracting malaria, use mosquito repellent, particularly in the evenings and when visiting forested areas. Make sure you see a doctor at least 4-6 weeks before a trip to a high-risk area to get up-to-date malaria prescriptions and recommendations. A doctor may prescribe oral prophylactics, like **mefloquine** or **doxycycline.** Be aware that mefloquine can have very serious side effects, including paranoia and nightmares. Malaria is a risk in all Southeast Asian countries except Singapore and Brunei.

Dengue fever: An "urban viral infection" transmitted by *Aedes* mosquitoes, which bite during the day rather than at night. The incubation period is 3-14 days, usually 4-7 days. Early symptoms include a high fever, severe headaches, swollen lymph nodes, and muscle aches. Many patients also suffer from nausea, vomiting, and a pink rash. If you experience these symptoms, see a doctor immediately, drink plenty of liquids, and take fever-reducing medication such as acetaminophen (Tylenol). *Never take aspirin to treat Dengue fever.* There is no vaccine available for Dengue fever. There is a risk throughout Southeast Asia. Wear insect repellent throughout the day.

Tick-borne encephalitis: A viral infection of the central nervous system transmitted during the summer by tick bites (primarily in wooded areas) or by consumption of unpasteurized dairy products. The risk of contracting the disease is relatively low, especially if precautions are taken against tick bites.

Japanese encephalitis: Another mosquito-borne disease, most prevalent during the rainy season in rural, agricultural areas near rice fields and livestock pens. Aside from delirium, most symptoms are flu-like: chills, headache, fever, vomiting, muscle fatigue. Since the disease carries a high mortality rate, it's vital to go to a hospital as soon as any symptoms appear. While the JE-VAX vaccine, usually given in 3 shots over a 30-day period, is effective for a year, it has been associated with serious side effects. According to the CDC, there is little chance of being infected if proper precautions are taken, such as using mosquito repellents containing DEET and sleeping under mosquito nets. JE is a risk in all Southeast Asian countries, with the exception of Singapore.

Lyme disease: A bacterial infection carried by ticks and marked by a circular bull's-eye rash of 2 in. or more. Later symptoms include fever, headache, fatigue, and aches and pains. Antibiotics are effective if administered early. Left untreated, Lyme can cause problems in joints, the heart, and the nervous system. If you find a tick attached to your skin, grasp the head with tweezers as close to your skin as possible and apply slow, steady traction. Removing a tick within 24hr. greatly reduces the risk of infection. Do not try to remove ticks with petroleum jelly, nail polish remover, or a hot match. Tick bites usually occur in moist, shaded environments and heavily wooded areas. If you are going to be hiking in these areas, wear long clothes and DEET.

FOOD- AND WATER-BORNE DISEASES

The **tap water** in Southeast Asia (with the exception of Singapore) is not safe, even for brushing teeth. Prevention is the best cure: be sure that your food is properly cooked and the water you drink is clean. Peel fruits and vegetables and avoid tap water (including ice cubes and anything washed in tap water, like salad). Watch out for food from markets or street vendors that may have been cooked in unhygienic conditions. Other culprits are raw shellfish, unpasteurized milk, and sauces containing raw eggs. Buy bottled water, or purify your own water by bringing it to a rolling boil or treating it with **iodine tablets**; note, however, that some parasites such as *giardia* have exteriors that resist iodine treatment, so boiling is more reliable. Always wash your hands before eating or bring a quick-drying purifying liquid hand cleaner.

Traveler's diarrhea: Results from drinking fecally contaminated water or eating uncooked and contaminated foods. Symptoms include nausea, bloating, and urgency. Try quick-energy, non-sugary foods with protein and carbohydrates to keep your strength up. Over-the-counter anti-diarrheals (e.g. Imodium) may counteract the problems. The most dangerous side effect is dehydration; drink 8 oz. of water with ½ tsp. of sugar or honey and a pinch of salt, try uncaffeinated soft drinks, or eat salted crackers. If you develop a fever or your symptoms don't go away after 4-5 days, consult a doctor. Consult a doctor immediately for treatment of diarrhea in children.

Dysentery: Results from a serious intestinal infection caused by certain bacteria in contaminated food or water. The most common type is bacillary dysentery. Symptoms include bloody diarrhea (sometimes mixed with mucus), fever, and abdominal pain and tenderness. Bacillary dysentery generally only lasts a week, but it is highly contagious. Amoebic dysentery, which develops more slowly, is a more serious disease and may cause long-term damage if left untreated. A stool test can determine which kind you have; seek medical help immediately. Dysentery can be treated with the drugs norfloxacin or ciprofloxacin (commonly known as Cipro). If you are traveling in high-risk (especially rural) regions, consider obtaining a prescription before you leave home. Dehydration can be a problem; be sure to drink plenty of water or eat salted crackers.

Cholera: An intestinal disease caused by a bacteria found in contaminated food. Symptoms include severe diarrhea, dehydration, and vomiting. See a doctor immediately; if left untreated, it may be deadly, even within a few hours. Antibiotics are available, but the most important treatment is rehydration. There is no vaccine available.

Hepatitis A: A viral infection of the liver acquired primarily through contaminated water, including through shellfish in water. Symptoms include fatigue, fever, loss of appetite, nausea, dark urine, jaundice, vomiting, aches and pains, and light stools. The risk is highest in rural areas and the countryside, but it is also present in urban areas. Ask your doctor about the Hepatitis A vaccine (Havrix or Vaqta) or an injection of immune globulin (IG; formerly called gamma globulin).

Schistosomiasis: A parasitic disease caused when the larvae of a certain fresh-water snail species penetrate unbroken skin. Symptoms include an itchy localized rash, followed in 4-6 weeks by fever, fatigue, headaches, muscle and joint aches, painful urination, diarrhea, nausea, loss of appetite, and night sweats. To avoid it, try not to swim in fresh water in areas with poor sanitation; if exposed to untreated water, rub the area vigorously with a towel and apply rubbing alcohol. Only the Philippines, Vietnam, and Sulawesi, Indonesia pose a risk.

Typhoid fever: Caused by the salmonella bacteria; common in villages and rural areas in all Southeast Asia, except Singapore. While mostly transmitted through contaminated food and water, it may also be acquired by direct contact with another person. Early symptoms include a persistent, high fever, headaches, fatigue, loss of appetite, constipation, and sometimes a rash on the abdomen or chest. Antibiotics can treat typhoid, but a vaccination (70-90% effective) is recommended.

OTHER INFECTIOUS DISEASES

Rabies: Transmitted through the saliva of infected animals, often through dogs; fatal if untreated. By the time symptoms (thirst and muscle spasms) appear, the disease is in its terminal stage. If you are bitten, wash the wound thoroughly, seek immediate medical care, and try to have the animal located. A rabies vaccine, which consists of 3 shots given over a 21-day period, is available and recommended for developing world travel, but is only semi-effective. Rabies is found throughout Southeast Asia except in Singapore and Brunei.

Hepatitis B: A viral infection of the liver transmitted via blood or other bodily fluids. Symptoms, which may not surface until years after infection, include jaundice, loss of appetite, fever, and joint pain. It is transmitted through activities like unprotected sex, injections of illegal drugs, and unprotected health work. A 3-shot vaccination sequence is recommended for health-care workers, sexually-active travelers, and anyone planning to seek medical treatment abroad; it must begin 6 months before traveling.

Hepatitis C: Like Hepatitis B, but the mode of transmission differs. IV drug users, those with occupational exposure to blood, hemodialysis patients, and recipients of blood transfusions are at the highest risk, but the disease can also be spread through sexual contact or sharing items like razors and toothbrushes that may have traces of blood on them. No symptoms are usually exhibited, but if there are any, they can include loss of appetite, abdominal pain, fatigue, nausea, and jaundice. Go to a doctor immediately if you experience any of these symptoms; if untreated, Hepatitis C can lead to liver failure.

Severe Acute Respiratory Syndrome (SARS): A viral respiratory illness transmitted through droplets. Early symptoms include fever, chills, headache, and muscle ache. Steroids and antiviral agents such as oseltamivir and ribavirin have been used as therapy; in many cases, however, SARS is fatal.

Avian Influenza (Birdflu): A virulent strain of flu largely restricted to birds; cases of bird-to-human transmission in Vietnam and Thailand in early 2004 led to international fears that a SARS-like outbreak was imminent, which happily was not the case. Symptoms include fever, cough, sore throat, pneumonia, and severe respiratory problems. There have been no recorded cases of human-to-human transmission, and travelers who avoid large-scale contact with poultry and their feces shouldn't be at any risk. Travelers who do not avoid aforementioned contact should reconsider their travel priorities.

AIDS and HIV: For detailed information on Acquired Immune Deficiency Syndrome (AIDS) in Southeast Asia, call the US Centers for Disease Control's 24hr. hotline (☎800-342-2437), or contact the Joint United Nations Programme on HIV/AIDS (UNAIDS), 20 ave. Appia, CH-1211 Geneva 27, Switzerland (☎41 22 791 3666; fax 22 791 4187).

Sexually transmitted diseases (STDs): Gonorrhea, chlamydia, genital warts, syphilis, herpes, and other STDs are easier to catch than HIV and can be just as deadly. **Hepatitis** B and C can also be transmitted sexually. Though condoms may protect you from some STDs, oral or even tactile contact can lead to transmission. If you think you may have contracted an STD, see a doctor immediately.

OTHER HEALTH CONCERNS

MEDICAL CARE ON THE ROAD

Hospitals in Southeast Asia vary from region to region, but generally larger, centralized cities like Singapore, Bangkok, and Kuala Lumpur have high-quality facilities. Public hospitals tend be more crowded and less expensive than private hospitals, which are more likely to have English-speaking doctors, language interpreters, foreign insurance claim assistance, international emergency medical evacuation access, and embassy liaison services. For the most trusted medical care, go to Thailand or Singapore.

If you are concerned about obtaining medical assistance while traveling, you may wish to employ special support services. The *MedPass* from **GlobalCare, Inc.**, 6875 Shiloh Rd. East, Alpharetta, GA 30005, USA (☎800-860-1111; www.globalcare.net), provides 24hr. international medical assistance, support, and medical evacuation resources. The **International Association for Medical Assistance to Travelers** (**IAMAT;** US ☎716-754-4883, Canada 519-836-0102; www.cybermall.co.nz/NZ/IAMAT) has free membership, lists English-speaking doctors worldwide, and offers detailed info on immunization requirements and sanitation. If your regular **insurance** policy does not cover travel abroad, you may wish to purchase additional coverage (p. 26).

Those with medical conditions (including diabetes, allergies to antibiotics, epilepsy, and heart conditions) may want to obtain a **Medic Alert** membership (first year US$35, annually thereafter US$20), which includes a stainless steel ID tag, among other benefits, and a 24hr. collect-call number. Contact the Medic Alert Foundation, 2323 Colorado Ave, Turlock, CA 95382, USA (☎888-633-4298, outside the US 209-668-3333; www.medicalert.org).

WOMEN'S HEALTH

Women traveling in unsanitary conditions are vulnerable to urinary tract and bladder infections, common and severely uncomfortable bacterial conditions that cause a burning sensation and painful, frequent urination. Over-the-counter medicines can sometimes alleviate symptoms, but if they persist, see a doctor. The hot and humid climate of Southeast Asia also makes women especially susceptible to vaginal yeast infections. Wearing loose-fitting trousers or a skirt and cotton underwear will help, as will over-the-counter remedies like Monistat or Gynelotrimin. Bring supplies from home if you are prone to infection, as they may be difficult to find on the road. In a pinch, some travelers use a natural alternative such as a plain yogurt and lemon juice douche. Since tampons, pads, and reliable contraceptive devices are sometimes hard to find in Southeast Asia, bring supplies from home. Women using birth-control pills should bring enough to allow for possible loss or extended stays. Also bring a prescription, since forms of the pill vary considerably. Abortion is illegal or restricted in many countries in Southeast Asia. Even in countries where it is readily available (for as little as US$5 in some cases), it may not always be safe. Make sure you are informed about the country or countries you are visiting. Information about family planning centers can be obtained through the **International Planned Parenthood Federation,** European Regional Office, Regent's College Inner Circle, Regent's Park, London NW1 4NS, UK (☎020 7487 7900).

TOILETS

Squat toilets are the norm throughout Southeast Asia. Some squat toilets have an automatic flush; most do not. There should be a reservoir of water with an accompanying scoop to flush all bodily wastes and to cleanse yourself. Carry a wad of toilet paper with you at all times. Rural areas might only have some planks over a hole. Should you find a sit-down toilet, be aware that the plumbing may not be able to take heavy loads of toilet paper.

BATHING

Most guesthouses and hotels do not have hot-water showers. Some do offer hot water for some extra cash. Some hotels in rural towns provide basins with a scoop or have cement troughs filled with water for bathing. Outside the city, especially if you decide to stay over in a village or camp outdoors, you may have to bathe in rivers or streams. Nudity is unacceptable, so men and women should bring or purchase a sarong.

GETTING TO SOUTHEAST ASIA

BY PLANE

When it comes to airfare, a little effort can save you a bundle. If your plans are flexible enough to deal with the restrictions, courier fares are the cheapest. Tickets bought from consolidators and standby seating are also good deals, but last-minute specials, airfare wars, and charter flights often beat these fares. The key is to hunt around, to be flexible, and to ask persistently about discounts. Students, seniors, and those under 26 should never pay full price for a ticket.

BUDGET AND STUDENT TRAVEL AGENCIES

While knowledgeable agents specializing in flights to Southeast Asia can make your life easy and help you save, they may not spend the time to find you the lowest possible fare—they get paid on commission. Travelers holding **ISIC** and **IYTC** cards (p. 13) qualify for big discounts from student travel agencies. Most flights from budget agencies are on major airlines, but in peak season some may sell seats on less reliable chartered aircraft.

STA Travel, 5900 Wilshire Blvd., Ste. 900, Los Angeles, CA 90036 USA (24hr. reservations and info ☎800-781-4040; www.sta-travel.com). A student and youth travel organization with over 150 offices worldwide (check their website for a listing of all their offices), including US offices in Boston, Chicago, L.A., New York, San Francisco, Seattle, and Washington, D.C. Ticket booking, travel insurance, railpasses, and more. Walk-in offices are located throughout Australia (☎03 9349 4344), New Zealand (☎09 309 9723), and the UK (☎0870 1 600 599).

CTS Travel, 30 Rathbone Pl., London W1T 1GQ, UK (☎0207 209 0630; www.ctstravel.co.uk). A British student travel agency with offices in 39 countries including the US, Empire State Building, 350 Fifth Ave., Ste. 7813, New York, NY 10118 (☎877-287-6665; www.ctstravelusa.com).

Travel CUTS (Canadian Universities Travel Services Limited), 187 College St., Toronto, ON M5T 1P7 (☎416-979-2406; www.travelcuts.com). Offices across Canada and the US including Los Angeles, New York, San Francisco, and Seattle.

USIT, 19-21 Aston Quay, Dublin 2 (☎01 602 1777; www.usitworld.com), Ireland's leading student and budget travel agency has 22 offices throughout Northern Ireland and the Republic of Ireland. Offers programs to work in North America.

FLIGHT PLANNING ON THE INTERNET. The Internet may be the budget traveler's dream when it comes to finding and booking bargain fares, but the array of options can be overwhelming.

Many airline sites offer special last-minute deals on the Web. Check out Cheapflights (www.cheapflights.com), Onetravel (www.onetravel.com), Bridge The World (www.bridgetheworld.com), and Avia Travel (www.aviatravel.com).

STA (www.sta-travel.com) and **StudentUniverse** (www.studentuniverse.com) provide quotes on student tickets, while **Orbitz** (www.orbitz.com), **Expedia** (www.expedia.com), and **Travelocity** (www.travelocity.com) offer full travel services. **Zuji** (www.zuji.com) offers great deals on travel throughout Asia. **Priceline** (www.priceline.com) lets you specify a price, and obligates you to buy any ticket that meets or beats it; **Hotwire** (www.hotwire.com) offers bargain fares, but won't reveal the airline or flight times until you buy. Other sites that compile deals for you include: www.bestfares.com, www.flights.com, www.lowestfare.com, and www.travelzoo.com.

Increasingly, there are online tools available to help sift through multiple offers; **SideStep** (www.sidestep.com; download required) and **Booking Buddy** (www.bookingbuddy.com) let you enter your trip information once and search multiple sites.

An indispensable resource on the Internet is the **Air Traveler's Handbook** (www.faqs.org/faqs/travel/air/handbook), a comprehensive listing of links to everything you need to know before you board a plane.

COMMERCIAL AIRLINES

The commercial airlines' lowest regular offer is the **APEX** (Advance Purchase Excursion) fare, which provides confirmed reservations and allows "open-jaw" tickets. Generally, reservations must be made 7 to 21 days ahead of departure, with 7 to 14-day minimum-stay and up to 90-day maximum-stay restrictions. These fares carry hefty cancellation and change penalties (fees rise in summer). Book peak-season APEX fares early. Use **Microsoft Expedia** (www.expedia.com) or **Travelocity** (www.travelocity.com) to get an idea of the lowest published fares, then use the resources outlined here to try and beat those fares. Low-season fares should be appreciably cheaper than the high-season (mid-June to Aug.) ones listed here.

TRAVELING FROM NORTH AMERICA

Round-trip fares to Southeast Asia are pricey. It is cheaper to fly from the west coast than the east coast. Flights usually depart from San Francisco, Los Angeles, New York and other major cities. Standard commercial carriers like American and United will probably offer the most convenient flights, but they may not be the

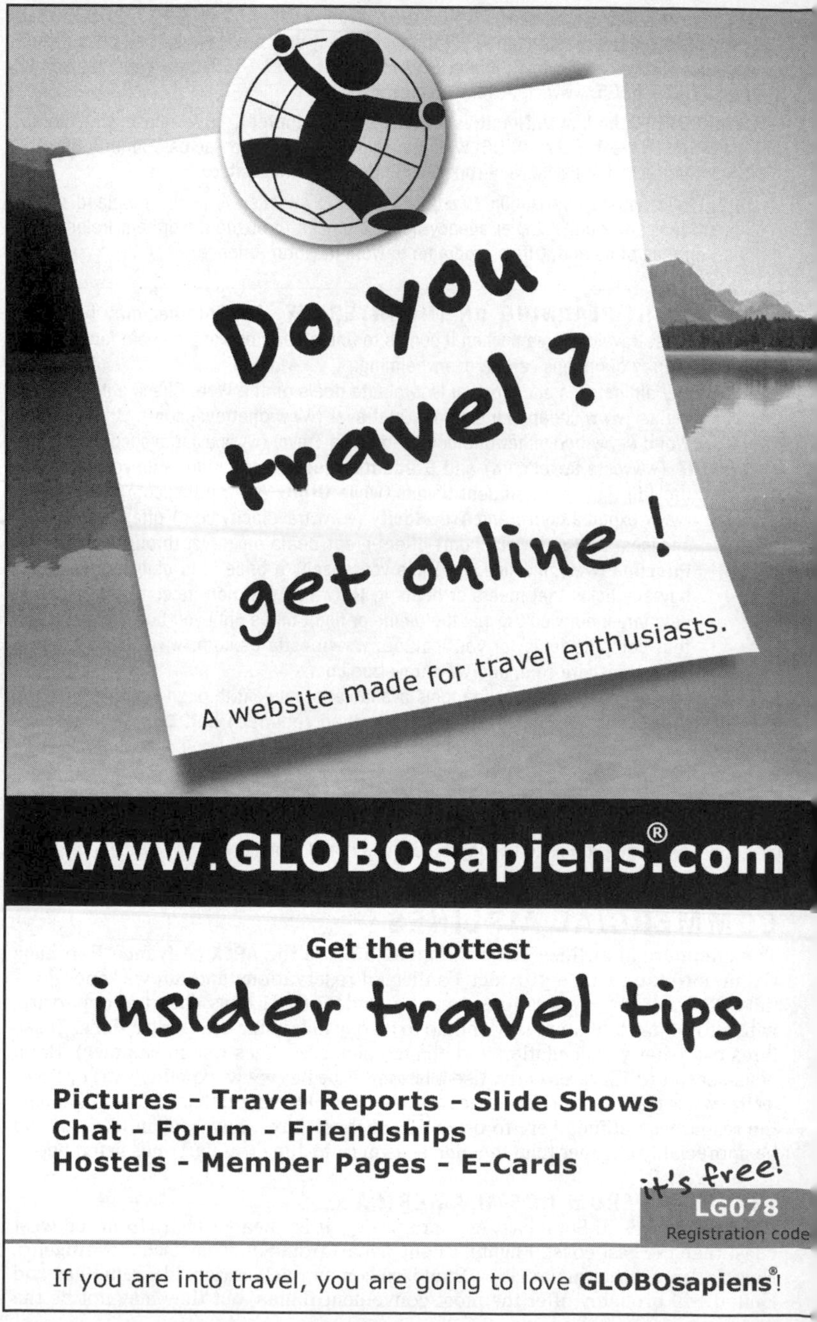
Do you travel? get online!
A website made for travel enthusiasts.
www.GLOBOsapiens®.com
Get the hottest
insider travel tips
Pictures - Travel Reports - Slide Shows
Chat - Forum - Friendships
Hostels - Member Pages - E-Cards
it's free!
LG078
Registration code
If you are into travel, you are going to love GLOBOsapiens®!

cheapest, unless you manage to grab a special promotion or airfare war ticket. You will probably find flying "discount" airlines a better deal, if any of their limited departure points is convenient for you.

TRAVELING FROM THE UK, AUSTRALIA, AND NEW ZEALAND

In London, the **Air Travel Advisory Bureau** (☎020 7636 5000; www.atab.co.uk) can provide names of reliable consolidators and discount flight specialists. In Australia and New Zealand, look for consolidator ads in the travel section of the *Sydney Morning Herald* and other papers.

TICKET CONSOLIDATORS

Ticket consolidators, or **"bucket shops,"** buy unsold tickets in bulk from commercial airlines and sell them at discounted rates. The best place to look is in the Sunday travel section of any major newspaper (such as the *New York Times*), where many bucket shops place tiny ads. Call quickly, as availability is typically extremely limited. Not all bucket shops are reliable, so insist on a receipt that gives full details of restrictions, refunds, and tickets, and pay by credit card (in spite of the 2-5% fee) so you can stop payment if you never receive your tickets. For more info, see www.travel-library.com/air-travel/consolidators.

Travel Avenue (☎800-333-3335; www.travelavenue.com) searches for best available published fares and then uses several consolidators to attempt to beat that fare. Other consolidators worth trying are **Travel Leaders** (☎800-468-3796 or 305-445-2999; www.traveleaders.com), **Cheap Tickets** (☎800-652-4327; www.cheaptickets.com), and **Flights.com** (www.flights.com). Yet more consolidators on the web include **Internet Travel Network** (www.itn.com), **Travel Information Services** (www.tiss.com), and **TravelHUB** (www.travelhub.com). Keep in mind that these are just suggestions to get you started in your research; *Let's Go* does not endorse any of these agencies. As always, be cautious, and research companies before you hand over your credit card number.

CHARTER FLIGHTS

Charters are flights a tour operator contracts with an airline to fly extra loads of passengers during peak season. Charter flights fly less frequently than major airlines, make refunds particularly difficult, and are almost always fully booked. Schedules and itineraries may also change or be cancelled at the last moment (as late as 48hr. before the trip, and without a full refund), and check-in, boarding, and baggage claim are often much slower. However, they can also be cheaper.

Discount clubs and fare brokers offer members savings on last-minute charter and tour deals. Study contracts closely; you don't want to end up with an unwanted overnight layover. **Travelers Advantage,** 7 Cambridge Dr., Trumbull, CT 06611, USA (☎877-259-2691; www.travelersadvantage.com; US$90 annual fee includes discounts and cheap flight directories) offers specials and travel packages to Southeast Asia.

BY BUS

Bus travel between countries can be arranged within the regions of Cambodia, Laos, and Vietnam; Myanmar, Thailand, and Malaysia. A/C buses can be very comfortable and reliable, but others offer sparse leg room and bumpy rides. Inquire about purchasing tickets; some buses require reservations in advance, whereas others sell tickets upon departure and don't leave the station until completely full. Check visa availability before taking a bus ride; visas may not always be available at the border and must be acquired in advance in other towns. Most tourist cafes can help you with information and reservations.

BORDER CROSSINGS

Overland border crossing points represent legal points of transit between Southeast Asian countries. For detailed information on possible crossing points and requirements, refer to the **Getting There** section of individual countries. Check local news agencies and embassies to confirm which border crossing points are open.

GETTING AROUND SOUTHEAST ASIA

BY PLANE

Flights between countries in Southeast Asia are inexpensive. Find the best deals on tickets in Bangkok, Singapore, Hong Kong, Kuala Lumpur, and Penang. Popular airlines include Malaysia Airlines, Singapore Airlines, Thai International, Cathay Pacific, and KLM Airlines. Booking tickets should be relatively worry-free, but travel agents can scam you. Be sure to make sure your deal is legitimate before you buy. *Let's Go* lists reliable tourist offices and travel offices in the **Practical Information** section of large cities. In general, use common sense—don't trust agents vending tickets in coffee bars. To be sure, always reconfirm with the airlines after receiving your ticket.

AIRCRAFT SAFETY. The airlines of developing world nations do not always meet safety standards. The *Official Airline Guide* (www.oag.com) and many travel agencies can tell you the type and age of aircraft on a particular route. This can be especially useful in Southeast Asia, where less reliable equipment is often used for internal or short flights. The **International Airline Passengers Association** (US ☎800-821-4272, UK 020 8681 6555) provides region-specific safety information. The **Federal Aviation Administration** (www.faa.gov) reviews the airline authorities for countries whose airlines enter the US. **US State Department** travel advisories (☎202-647-5225; http://travel.state.gov/travel_warnings) sometimes involve foreign carriers, especially when terrorist bombings or hijackings may be a threat.

BY CAR

Car rental is possible in Southeast Asia. However, it is not the safest means of travel throughout the region as many roads are tenuous and banditry is common. Should you choose to rent a car, Western car rental companies can be found in major cities.

ON THE ROAD

Small vehicles yield to buses and trucks, regardless of whose turn it is to go. If you wish to pass a vehicle, use the middle of the road and use your horn to notify other vehicles. **Petrol (gasoline)** prices vary, but average about 20฿ per liter in cities and from 19.5฿ per liter in outlying areas.

DRIVING PRECAUTIONS. When traveling during the dry season, bring substantial amounts of **water** (a suggested 5L of water per person per day) for drinking and for the radiator. For long drives to unpopulated areas, register with police before beginning the trek, and again upon arrival at the destination. Check with the local automobile club for details. When traveling for long distances, make sure tires are in good repair and have enough air, and get good maps. A **compass** and a **car manual** can also be very useful. You should always carry a **spare tire** and **jack, jumper cables, extra oil, flares, a flashlight (torch),** and **heavy blankets** (in case your car breaks down at night or in the winter). If you don't know how to **change a tire,** learn before heading out, especially if you are planning on traveling in deserted areas. Blowouts on dirt roads are exceedingly common. If you do have a breakdown, **stay with your car;** if you wander off, there's less likelihood trackers will find you. Before you get on the road, check the tires, look out for oil leaks, and check the brakes.

DANGERS

Roads in Cambodia and Laos are not well-paved and hijacking does occur. Many towns do not have streetlights and it is not always clear which streets are one-way. Deaths due to motorcycle and automobile accidents are very common throughout the region, particularly in Vietnam, Cambodia, and Laos.

DRIVING PERMITS AND CAR INSURANCE

INTERNATIONAL DRIVING PERMIT (IDP)

If you plan to drive a car while in Southeast Asia , you must be over 18 and have an International Driving Permit (IDP), though certain countries allow travelers to drive with your home driving license (e.g. Malaysia). It may be a good idea to get

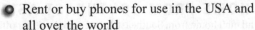

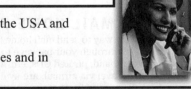

one anyway, in case you're in a situation (e.g. an accident or stranded in a small town) where the police do not know English; information on the IDP is printed in ten languages, including Chinese and French.

Your IDP, valid for one year, must be issued in your own country before you depart. An application for an IDP usually requires one or two photos, a current local license, an additional form of identification, and a fee. To apply, contact the national or local branch of your home country's automobile association. If you make a purchase anywhere other than your home automobile association, be aware that many vendors sell permits of questionable legitimacy for higher prices.

CAR INSURANCE

Most credit cards cover standard insurance. If you rent, lease, or borrow a car, you will need a **green card,** or **International Insurance Certificate,** to certify that you have liability insurance and that it applies abroad. Green cards can be obtained at car rental agencies, car dealers (for those leasing cars), some travel agents, and some border crossings. Rental agencies may require you to purchase theft insurance in countries that they consider to have a high risk of auto theft.

BY MOPED, BICYCLE, ETC.

Travel by moped, bicycles, and motorcycles is very common throughout Southeast Asia. However, it is also extremely dangerous. See individual country chapters for more information.

BY THUMB

> *Let's Go* never recommends hitchhiking as a safe means of transportation, and none of the information presented here is intended to do so.

Let's Go strongly urges you to consider the risks before you choose to hitchhike. In Southeast Asia, hitchhiking is particularly dangerous for Western travelers. Should you choose to hitchhike, do not do it alone.

KEEPING IN TOUCH

BY MAIL

SENDING MAIL HOME FROM SOUTHEAST ASIA

Airmail is the best way to send mail home from Southeast Asia. Be advised that officials may check through your package to make sure it doesn't have any offending items like contraband, pirated CDs, etc. **Aerogrammes,** printed sheets that fold into envelopes and travel via airmail, are available at post offices. Write "airmail" and "par avion" all over the front; if you want to send it express, choose a special **EMS** (Express Mail Service) envelope and refrain from writing "airmail" on it. Most post offices will charge exorbitant fees or simply refuse to send aerogrammes with enclosures. **Surface mail** is by far the cheapest and slowest way to send mail. It takes one to two months to cross the Atlantic and one to three months to cross the Pacific—good for heavy items you won't need for a while, such as souvenirs or other articles you've acquired along the way that are weighing down your pack. These are standard rates for mail from Southeast Asia to:

Australia: Allow 7-10 days for regular airmail home. Postcards/aerogrammes and letters up to 20g cost US$0.73; packages up to 0.5kg US$14.55.

Canada: Allow 10-14 days for regular airmail home. Postcards/aerogrammes and letters up to 20g cost US$0.73; packages up to 0.5kg US$19.09.

Ireland: Allow 7-10 days for regular airmail home. Postcards/aerogrammes and letters up to 20g cost US$0.73; packages up to 0.5kg US$20-22.

New Zealand: Allow 7-10 days for regular airmail home. Postcards/aerogrammes and letters up to 20g cost US$0.73; packages up to 0.5kg US$20.82.

UK: Allow 7-10 days for regular airmail home. Postcards/aerogrammes and letters up to 20g cost US$0.73; packages up to 0.5kg US$19.82.

US: Allow 10-14 days for regular airmail home. Postcards/aerogrammes and letters up to 20g cost US$0.73; packages up to 0.5kg US$21.36.

SENDING MAIL TO SOUTHEAST ASIA

To ensure timely delivery, mark envelopes "airmail" and "par avion." In addition to the standard postage system whose rates are listed below, **Federal Express** (www.fedex.com; Australia ☎ 13 26 10, Canada and US 800-463-3339, Ireland 1800 535 800, New Zealand 0800 733 339, UK 0800 123 800) handles express mail services from most countries to Southeast Asia. All major cities in Southeast Asia have a post office. Listed below are the average prices and transit times.

Australia: Allow 4-5 days for regular airmail. Postcards and letters up to 20g cost AUS$1; packages up to 0.5kg AUS$6.60, up to 2kg AUS$34.50. EMS can get a letter to most countries in Southeast Asia in 3-4 days for AUS$30. www.auspost.com.au/pac.

Canada: Allow 7 days for regular airmail. Postcards and letters up to 30g cost CDN$1.40; packages up to 0.5kg CDN$11.20, up to 2kg CDN$37.35. Purolator International can get a letter to most countries in Southeast Asia in 4-6 days for CDN$52. www.canadapost.ca/personal/rates/default-e.asp.

Ireland: Allow 7 days for regular airmail. Postcards and letters up to 20g cost €0.65; packages up to 0.5kg €5.00, up to 2kg €16.00. www.letterpost.ie.

New Zealand: Allow 4-10 days for regular airmail. Postcards and letters up to 20g cost NZ$6.83; packages up to 0.5kg NZ$15.82, up to 2kg NZ$49.56. International Express can get a letter to most countries in Southeast Asia in 2-4 days for NZ$49.44. www.nzpost.co.nz/nzpost/inrates.

UK: Allow 5 days for regular airmail. Letters up to 20g cost UK£0.68; packages up to 0.5kg UK£5, up to 2kg UK£18.52. www.royalmail.co.uk/calculator.

US: Allow 4-7 days for regular airmail. Letters up to 1 oz. cost US$0.80; packages up to 1 lb. US$14.50, up to 5 lb. US$32.75. US Express Mail takes 2-3 days and costs US$32. http://ircalc.usps.gov.

RECEIVING MAIL IN SOUTHEAST ASIA

There are several ways to arrange pick-up of letters sent to you by friends and relatives while you are abroad. Mail can be sent via **Poste Restante** (General Delivery) to almost any major city or town in Southeast Asia with a post office, and is reliable by developing-world standards; however, you may be required to provide extensive documentation to prove your identity. Address *Poste Restante* letters like so:

Firstname LASTNAME
Poste Restante
City, Việt Nam

The mail will go to a special desk in the central post office, unless you specify a post office by street address or postal code. It's best to use the largest post office, since mail may be sent there regardless. It is usually safer and quicker, though more expensive, to send mail express or registered. Bring your passport (or other photo ID) for pick-up; there may be a small fee. If the clerks insist that there is nothing for you, have them check under your first name as well. *Let's Go* lists post offices in the **Practical Information** section for each city and most towns.

BY TELEPHONE

CALLING HOME FROM SOUTHEAST ASIA

A **calling card** is probably your cheapest bet. Calls are billed collect or to your account. You can frequently call collect without even possessing a company's calling card just by calling their access number and following the instructions.

CALLING WITHIN SOUTHEAST ASIA

The simplest way to call within the country is to use a coin-operated phone. **Prepaid phone cards** (available at many guesthouses, shops, and restaurants), which carry a certain amount of phone time depending on the card's denomination, usually save time and money in the long run. The computerized phone will tell you how much time, in units, you have left on your card. Another kind of prepaid telephone card comes with a Personal Identification Number (PIN) and a toll-free access number. Instead of inserting the card into the phone, you call the access number and follow the directions on the card. These cards can be used to make international as well as domestic calls. Phone rates typically tend to be highest in the morning, lower in the evening, and lowest on Sunday and late at night. Before settling on a calling card plan, be sure to research your options in order to pick the one that best fits both your needs and your destination.

CELLULAR PHONES

Cellular phones are readily available throughout Southeast Asia, with the exception of Myanmar. The standard for cell phones is **GSM**, a system that began in Europe and has spread to much of the rest of the world. To make and receive calls in Southeast Asia you will need a GSM-compatible phone and a SIM (subscriber identity module) card—a country-specific, thumbnail-sized chip that gives you a local phone number and plugs you into the local network. Many SIM cards are prepaid, meaning that they come with calling time included and you don't need to sign up for a monthly service plan. Incoming calls are frequently free. When you use up the prepaid time, you can buy additional cards or vouchers (usually available at convenience stores) to get more. For more information on GSM phones, check out www.telestial.com, www.vodafone.com, www.orange.co.uk, www.roadpost.com, www.t-mobile.com, or www.planetomni.com. Companies like Cellular Abroad (www.cellularabroad.com) rent cell phones that work in a variety of destinations around the world, providing a simpler option than picking up a phone in-country.

TIP **GSM PHONES.** Just having a GSM phone doesn't mean you're necessarily good to go when you travel abroad. The majority of GSM phones sold in the United States operate on a different **frequency** (1900) than international phones (900/1800) and will not work abroad. Tri-band phones work on all three frequencies (900/1800/1900) and will operate through most of the world. As well, some GSM phones are **SIM-locked** and will only accept SIM cards from a single carrier. You'll need a **SIM-unlocked** phone to use a SIM card from a local carrier when you travel.

TIME DIFFERENCES

Most of Southeast Asia is either seven or eight hours ahead of Greenwich Mean Time (GMT). Brunei, Malaysia, the Philippines, and Singapore are eight hours ahead of GMT/UTC. Therefore, at midnight in Malaysia, it is 11am the previous day in New York, 8am the previous day in Vancouver and San Francisco, and 2am in Sydney and New Zealand. Cambodia, Laos, Thailand, and Vietnam are seven hours ahead of GMT. At midnight in Thailand, it is noon the previous day in New York, 9am in Vancouver and San Francisco, and 3am in Sydney and New Zealand. Myanmar is 6½ hours ahead of GMT. At midnight in Myanmar, it is 12:30pm the previous day in New York, 9:30am the previous day in Vancouver and San Francisco, and 3:30am in Sydney and New Zealand.

BY EMAIL AND INTERNET

Internet access is common in all Southeast Asian countries. In Myanmar, you can send and receive email, but cannot log on to the Internet.

Though in some places it's possible to forge a remote link with your home server, in most cases this is a much slower (and thus more expensive) option than taking advantage of free **web-based email accounts** (e.g., www.hotmail.com and www.yahoo.com). **Internet cafes** and the occasional free Internet terminal at a public library or university are listed in the **Practical Information** sections of major cities. Increasingly, travelers find that taking their **laptop computers** on the road with them can be a convenient option for staying connected. Laptop users can call an Internet service provider via a modem using long-distance phone cards specifically intended for such calls. They may also find Internet cafes that allow them to connect their laptops to the Internet. And most excitingly, travelers with wireless-enabled computers may be able to take advantage of an increasing number of Internet "hot spots," where they can get online for free or for a small fee. Newer computers can detect these hot spots automatically; otherwise, websites like www.jiwire.com, www.wi-fihotspotlist.com, and www.locfinder.net can help you find them. For information on insuring your laptop while traveling, see p. 25.

ACCOMMODATIONS

Choosing accommodations in Southeast Asia can sometimes be a gamble, as electricity, running water, and air conditioning have not yet reached many rural areas. Finding inexpensive accommodations, however, never proves to be a problem. Hotels and guesthouses line the streets of major cities and towns throughout Southeast Asia, many with Internet facilities and small cafes. For a few dollars, facilities can vary from a shared room with several beds to a single room with a private bath and fan. Modern and more expensive hotels can be found in highly touristed areas.

While you should make reservations at the more expensive lodgings, finding a hotel on a day's notice is not difficult. It is not uncommon, and most often is expected, to ask to see rooms before committing to a hotel; this also allows room for bargaining. In some parts of Southeast Asia, including in all of Vietnam, the law requires that you leave your passport with your hotel or guesthouse during your stay. If you feel uncomfortable about doing this, some places will allow you to leave your customs slip from immigration.

THE GREAT OUTDOORS

TREKKING

Trekking is a great way to get off the beaten path and see relatively "untouched" beauty. Southeast Asia's rainforests, undulating terrain, and extraordinary vistas offer a range of trekking styles. Nascent trekkers may want to start with a guided tour of one of the **national parks**. Experienced trekkers can venture up some of the highest peaks in the world. However, even the most adept of trekkers should seek a guide to smooth out cultural and linguistic barriers. UNESCO offers "ecologically and culturally responsible" treks into remote villages. Tourist offices also offer tours, both daily and overnight. Keep in mind that trekking doesn't come cheap at US$30-40 per person per day.

DIVING AND SNORKELING

Its tropical location and long-established professional operations make Southeast Asia one of the world's greatest dive and snorkel destinations. Make sure your instructor has PADI certification (or the equivalent). In the Philippines, Boracay has long been regarded as the holy grail of SEAS diving—with its lush beaches and abundance of colorful sea life. In Thailand, Similan Island is regarded as the place to go for divers, and Phuket's west coast has eco-diving options. Many sites offer diving lessons. Terengganu is regarded as the best diving on Peninsular Malaysia.

LEAVE NO TRACE. *Let's Go* encourages travelers to embrace the "Leave No Trace" ethic, minimizing their impact on natural environments and protecting them for future generations. Trekkers and wilderness enthusiasts should set up camp on durable surfaces, use cookstoves instead of campfires, bury human waste away from water supplies, bag trash and carry it out with them, and respect wildlife and natural objects. For more detailed information, contact the **Leave No Trace Center for Outdoor Ethics,** PO Box 997, Boulder, CO 80306, USA (☎800-332-4100 or 303-442-8222; www.lnt.org).

CAMPING

The Great Outdoor Recreation Pages (www.gorp.com) provides excellent general information for travelers planning on camping or spending time in the outdoors.

NATIONAL PARKS

Southeast Asia faces serious environmental hazards due to deforestation, mining, population growth, and poaching. Indonesia's rainforest is currently being deforested at the devastating rate of 10 acres per minute, or 2.4 million hectares per year. In order to combat these trends, countries like Thailand are aggressively setting aside land for preservation. Currently, 12.8% of Thailand's total land mass is set aside for 79 national parks, 89 wildlife and nonhunting sanctuaries, and 35 forest reserves. Most sites are open to tourism and function as single destinations for ecotourism like Khao Yai National Park, Thailand's first consecrated national park northeast of Bangkok. Indonesia, Malaysia, and Thailand have the most extensive systems of national parks in Southeast Asia, all of which present an excellent opportunity to experience the region's natural beauty. Although it is unlikely that you will witness any large mammalian species, you will most certainly encounter Southeast Asia's vast diversity of plant, marine, and bird wildlife. Most will agree that ecotourism is less invasive and consumeristic than other forms of travel, serving to increase awareness about threats to Southeast Asia's natural resources. It is important to book adventure and eco-tours well in advance, especially if planning to travel during the peak season.

WILDERNESS SAFETY

Staying **warm, dry, and well-hydrated** is key to a happy and safe wilderness experience. For any hike, prepare yourself for an emergency by packing a first-aid kit, a reflector, a whistle, high-energy food, extra water, raingear, a hat, and mittens. For warmth, wear wool or insulating synthetic materials designed for the outdoors. Cotton is a bad choice since it dries painfully slowly.

Check **weather forecasts** often and pay attention to the skies when hiking, as weather patterns can change suddenly. Always let someone, either a friend, your hostel, or a park ranger, know when and where you are going hiking. Know your physical limits and do not attempt a hike beyond your ability. See **Safety and Health**, p. 21, for information on outdoor ailments and medical concerns.

WILDLIFE

Illegal wildlife trade in the region totals billions of dollars a year globally. Many animals are facing extinction due to poaching and habitat loss. They include tigers, elephants, rhinoceroses, monkeys, fresh-water tortoises and turtles, snakes, cobra, rats, and monitor lizards. There is an impressive array of birds in Southeast Asia, particularly in Indonesia's Papua, the Borneo rainforests, and Thailand. If you look at a ceiling or wall and see nothing but geckos, do not be alarmed. They are literally everywhere in Southeast Asia, and they are harmless. The *tookay* lizard is louder than the gecko, but rarely seen. The Indonesian island of Komodo and a few neighboring islands are home to the world's largest lizard. The only great ape species is the orangutan.

CAMPING AND HIKING EQUIPMENT

WHAT TO BUY

Good camping equipment is both sturdy and light. North American suppliers tend to offer the most competitive prices.

Sleeping Bags: Most sleeping bags are rated by season; "summer" means 30-40°F (around 0°C) at night; "four-season" or "winter" often means below 0°F (-17°C). Bags are made of **down** (warm and light, but expensive, and miserable when wet) or of **synthetic** material (heavy, durable, and warm when wet). Prices range US$50-250 for a summer synthetic to US$200-300 for a good, down winter bag. **Sleeping bag pads** include foam pads (US$10-30), air mattresses (US$15-50), and self-inflating mats (US$30-120). Bring a **stuff sack** to store your bag and keep it dry.

Tents: The best tents are free-standing (with their own frames and suspension systems), set up quickly, and only require staking in high winds. Low-profile dome tents are the best all-around. Worthy 2-person tents start at US$100, 4-person at US$160. Make sure your tent has a rain fly and seal its seams with waterproofer. Other useful accessories include a **battery-operated lantern,** a plastic **groundcloth,** and a nylon **tarp.**

Backpacks: Internal-frame packs mold well to your back, keep a lower center of gravity, and flex adequately to allow you to hike difficult trails, while **external-frame packs** are more comfortable for long hikes over even terrain, as they carry weight higher and distribute it more evenly. Make sure your pack has a strong, padded hip-belt to transfer weight to your legs. There are models designed specifically for women. Any serious backpacking requires a pack of at least 4000 $in.^3$ (16,000cc), plus 500 in^3 for sleeping bags in internal-frame packs. Sturdy backpacks cost anywhere from US$125 to US$420—your pack is an area where it doesn't pay to economize. On your hunt for the perfect pack, fill up the prospective model with something heavy, strap it on correctly, and walk around to get a sense of how the model distributes weight. Either buy a **rain cover** (US$10-20) or store all of your belongings in plastic bags inside your pack.

Boots: Be sure to wear hiking boots with good **ankle support.** They should fit snugly and comfortably over 1-2 pairs of **wool socks** and a pair of thin **liner socks.** Break in boots over several weeks before you go to spare yourself blisters.

Other Necessities: Synthetic layers, like those made of polypropylene or polyester, and a pile jacket will keep you warm even when wet. Plastic **water bottles** are vital; look for shatter-and-leak resistant models. Carry **water-purification tablets** for when you can't boil water. Although most campgrounds provide campfire sites, you may want to bring a small **metal grate** or **grill.** For those places that forbid fires or the gathering of firewood, you'll need a **camp stove** (the classic Coleman starts at US$50) and a propane-filled **fuel bottle** to operate it. Also bring a **first-aid kit**, a **pocketknife**, **insect repellent**, and **waterproof matches** or a **lighter.**

ESSENTIALS

SPECIFIC CONCERNS

SUSTAINABLE TRAVEL

As the number of travelers on the road continues to rise, the detrimental effect they can have on natural environments becomes an increasing concern. With this in mind, *Let's Go* promotes the philosophy of **sustainable travel.** Through a sensitivity to issues of ecology and sustainability, today's travelers can be a powerful force in preserving and restoring the places they visit.

Ecotourism, a rising trend in sustainable travel, focuses on the conservation of natural habitats and using them to build up the economy without exploitation or overdevelopment. Travelers can make a difference by doing advance research and by supporting organizations and establishments that pay attention to their impact on their natural surroundings and strive to be environmentally-friendly.

RESPONSIBLE TRAVEL

The impact of tourist dollars on the destinations you visit should not be underestimated. The choices you make during your trip can have potent effects on local communities—for better or for worse. Travelers who care about the destinations and environments they explore should become aware of the social and cultural and political implications of the choices they make when they travel.

Community-based tourism aims to channel tourist dollars into the local economy by emphasizing tours and cultural programs that are run by members of the host community and that often benefit disadvantaged groups. This is particularly relevant in Myanmar. Throughout the Myanmar chapter, government-operated businesses are noted. An excellent resource for general information on community-based travel is *The Good Alternative Travel Guide* (UK£10), a project of **Tourism Concern** (☎ 020 7133 3330; www.tourismconcern.org.uk).

TRAVELING ALONE

There are many benefits to traveling alone—independence and a greater interaction with locals. On the other hand, a solo traveler is a more vulnerable target for harassment and street theft. As a lone traveler, try not to stand out as a tourist, look confident, and be careful in deserted or crowded areas. If questioned, never admit that you are traveling alone. Maintain regular contact with someone at home who knows your itinerary. For more tips, pick up *Traveling Solo* by Eleanor Berman (Globe Pequot Press, US$18), visit www.travelaloneandloveit.com, or subscribe to **Connecting: Solo Travel Network,** 689 Park Rd., Unit 6, Gibsons, BC V0N 1V7, Canada (☎604-886-9099; www.cstn.org; membership US$28-45).

WOMEN TRAVELERS

Women exploring on their own inevitably face some additional safety concerns, but it's easy to be adventurous without taking undue risks. If you are concerned, consider staying in hostels which offer single rooms that lock from the inside or in religious organizations with rooms for women only. Stick to centrally located accommodations and avoid solitary late-night treks or metro rides.

Always carry extra money for a phone call, bus, or taxi. **Hitchhiking** is never safe for lone women, or even for two women traveling together. Look as if you know where you're going and approach older women or couples for directions if you're lost or uncomfortable. The less you look like a tourist, the better off you'll be. Dress conservatively, especially in rural areas. Wearing a **wedding band** sometimes prevents unwanted overtures.

Your best answer to verbal harassment is no answer at all; feigning deafness, sitting motionless, and staring straight ahead at nothing in particular will do a world of good that reactions usually don't achieve. The extremely persistent can sometimes be dissuaded by a firm, loud, and very public "Go away!" in the appropriate language. Don't hesitate to seek out a police officer or a passerby if you are being harassed. Memorize the emergency numbers in places you visit, and consider carrying a whistle on your keychain. A self-defense course will prepare you for a potential attack and raise your level of awareness of your surroundings (see **Self Defense,** p. 25). Also be aware of health concerns that women face when traveling (p. 31).

GAY, LESBIAN, BISEXUAL, AND TRANSGENDERED TRAVELERS

The enormous range of sexualities in Southeast Asia defies easy categorization. From the *waria* communities of Indonesia to the *bakla* of the Philippines and the *kathoey* transgender communities of Thailand, the prospective gay traveler can find a trip to Southeast Asia an enlightening experience. Although active gay communities exist in **Bangkok, Hong Kong, Jakarta, Kuala Lumpur, Manila,** and **Singapore,** Southeast Asian governments still have an unfavorable outlook on homosexuality (even if laws banning homosexuality no longer exist) and rural communities may be much less accepting. Homosociality (camaraderie between members of the same sex, particularly men) is much more common than you may be accustomed to; hand-holding between two men cannot be interpreted according to typical "Western" norms. The stigma of the sex trade is such that many gay travelers find it difficult to integrate themselves into local communities. Lesbian life tends to be inaccessible to outsiders. Travelers should keep in mind that the people of Southeast Asia often disapprove of public displays of affection among anyone. *Let's Go* lists resources for gay and lesbian travelers in the **Life and Times** sections of specific countries. Listed below are contact organizations, mail-order bookstores, and publishers that offer materials addressing some specific concerns. **Out and About** (www.planetout.com) offers a bi-weekly newsletter addressing travel concerns and a comprehensive site addressing gay travel concerns. The online newspaper **365gay.com** also has a travel section (www.365gay.com/travel/travelchannel).

Gay's the Word, 66 Marchmont St., London WC1N 1AB, UK (☎44 20 7278 7654; www.gaystheword.co.uk). The largest gay and lesbian bookshop in the UK, with both fiction and non-fiction titles. Mail-order service available.

Giovanni's Room, 1145 Pine St., Philadelphia, PA 19107 USA (☎215-923-2960; www.queerbooks.com). An international lesbian, feminist, and gay bookstore with mail-order service (carries many of the publications listed below).

International Lesbian and Gay Association (ILGA), 81 rue Marché-au-Charbon, B-1000 Brussels, Belgium (☎32 2 502 2471; www.ilga.org). Provides political information, such as homosexuality laws of individual countries.

FURTHER READING: BISEXUAL, GAY, AND LESBIAN.

Spartacus 2003-2004: International Gay Guide. Bruno Gmunder Verlag (US$33).

Damron Men's Travel Guide, Damron Accommodations Guide, Damron City Guide, and *Damron Women's Traveller.* Damron Travel Guides (US$11-19). For info, call ☎800-462-6654 or visit www.damron.com.

Ferrari Guides' Gay Travel A to Z, Ferrari Guides' Men's Travel in Your Pocket, Ferrari Guides' Women's Travel in Your Pocket, and *Ferrari Guides' Inn Places.* Ferrari Publications (US$16-20).

The Gay Vacation Guide: The Best Trips and How to Plan Them, Mark Chesnut. Kensington Books (US$15).

TRAVELERS WITH DISABILITIES

Southeast Asia, excluding Singapore, is ill-equipped to accommodate disabled travelers. Those with disabilities should inform airlines and hotels of their disabilities when making arrangements for travel; some time may be needed to prepare special accommodations. Hospitals cannot be relied upon to replace broken braces or prostheses; orthopedic materials, even in Bangkok, Jakarta, and Manila, are faulty at best. All public transportation is completely inaccessible. Rural areas have no sidewalks, and larger cities are packed with curbs and steps.

Attitudes toward disabled people vary. In Laos and Cambodia, where an uncommonly large part of the population consists of amputees (from landmines and cluster-bombs), disabilities are common. Thai people with disabilities rarely come out in public. Despite this, bold travelers will find many people eager to aid them. Call ahead to restaurants, museums, and other facilities to find out if they are wheelchair-accessible. **Guide dog owners** should inquire as to the quarantine policies of each destination country.

USEFUL ORGANIZATIONS

Access Abroad, www.umabroad.umn.edu/access. A website devoted to making study abroad available to students with disabilities. The site is maintained by Disability Services Research and Training, University of Minnesota, University Gateway, Ste. 180, 200 Oak St. SE, Minneapolis, MN 55455 USA (☎612-624-6884).

Accessible Journeys, 35 West Sellers Ave., Ridley Park, PA 19078 USA (☎800-846-4537; www.disabilitytravel.com). Designs tours for wheelchair users and slow walkers. The site has tips and forums for all travelers.

Directions Unlimited, 123 Green Ln., Bedford Hills, NY 10507 USA (☎800-533-5343). Books individual vacations for the physically disabled; not an info service.

Flying Wheels, 143 W. Bridge St., P.O. Box 382, Owatonna, MN 55060 USA (☎507-451-5005; www.flyingheelstravel.com). Specializes in escorted trips to Europe for people with physical disabilities; plans custom accessible trips worldwide.

Mobility International USA (MIUSA), P.O. Box 10767, Eugene, OR 97440 USA (☎541-343-1284; www.miusa.org). Provides a variety of books and other publications containing information for travelers with disabilities.

Society for Accessible Travel & Hospitality (SATH), 347 Fifth Ave., #610, New York, NY 10016 USA (☎212-447-7284; www.sath.org). An advocacy group that publishes free online travel information and the travel magazine *OPEN WORLD* (annual subscription US$13, free for members). Annual membership US$45, students and seniors US$30.

MINORITY TRAVELERS

People in Southeast Asia are largely accepting of minority travelers. However, travelers of African descent have reported stray incidents of harassment, though there have been no reports of violence. To be safe, travelers of African descent are advised not to travel alone in rural areas. In addition, ethnic Chinese in Indonesia and Malaysia have been a target of discrimination. Though violence is rare, some travelers report inferior service and stray incidents of harassment.

DIETARY CONCERNS

Although Southeast Asian food often contains meat or uses meat bases, **vegetarian** dishes abound. For more information about traveling as a vegetarian, contact **North American Vegetarian Society,** P.O. Box 72, Dolgeville, NY 13329 USA (☎518-568-7970; www.navs-online.org), which publishes *Vegetarian Asia* (US$10). While **kosher** meals are practically nonexistent, the Muslim presence in Southeast Asia makes **halal** food a large part of the cuisine, especially in the Malay-speaking world. (For more information on kosher food, see www.shamash.org/kosher.) If you are strict in your observance, consider preparing your own food. For more information, visit your local bookstore, health food store, or library, and consult *The Vegetarian Traveler: Where to Stay if You're Vegetarian, Vegan, Environmentally Sensitive*, by Jed and Susan Civic (Larson Publications, US$16).

OTHER RESOURCES

Let's Go tries to cover all aspects of budget travel, but we can't put *everything* in our guides. Listed below are books and websites that can serve as jumping-off points for your own research.

USEFUL PUBLICATIONS

LITERATURE

Southeast Asia: An Introductory History, by Milton Osborne (1995). A basic survey of Southeast Asian history, revised and updated many times.

The Lands of Charm and Cruelty: Travels in Southeast Asia, by Stan Sesser (1994). A collection of essays originally published in the *New Yorker.*

Into the Heart of Borneo, by Redmond O'Hanlon (1987). Follows the real-life, humorous adventures of a *London Times* reviewer with poet friend, James Benton.

A Fortune-Teller Told Me: Earthbound Travels in the Far East, by Tiziano Terzani (2001). A journalist treks through Southeast Asia, focusing on myth, religion, and fortune-tellers.

TRAVEL PUBLISHERS AND BOOKSTORES

Hippocrene Books, Inc., 171 Madison Ave., New York, NY 10016 USA (☎212-685-4371, orders 718-454-2366; www.hippocrenebooks.com). Free catalog. Publishes foreign language dictionaries and language learning guides.

Hunter Publishing, 470 W. Broadway, 2nd fl., South Boston, MA 02127 USA (☎617-269-0700; www.hunterpublishing.com). Has an extensive catalog of travel guides and diving and adventure travel books.

Rand McNally, 8255 N. Central Park, Skokie, IL 60076 USA (☎847-329-8100; www.randmcnally.com). Publishes road atlases.

Adventurous Traveler Bookstore, P.O. Box 2221, Williston, VT 05495 USA (☎800-282-3963 or 802-860-6776; www.adventuroustraveler.com).

Travel Books & Language Center, Inc., 4437 Wisconsin Ave. NW, Washington, D.C. 20016 USA (☎800-220-2665 or 202-237-1322; www.bookweb.org/bookstore/travelbks). Over 60,000 titles from around the world.

WORLD WIDE WEB

Almost every aspect of budget travel is accessible via the web—in 10min. you can make a hostel reservation and get advice on travel hot spots from other travelers.

Listed here are some regional and travel-related sites to start off your surfing; other relevant websites are listed throughout the book. Because website turnover is high, use search engines (such as www.google.com) to strike out on your own.

WWW.LETSGO.COM. Our freshly redesigned website features extensive content from our guides; community forums where travelers can connect with each other and ask questions or advice–as well as share stories and tips; and expanded resources to help you plan your trip. Visit us soon to browse by destination, find information about ordering our titles, and sign up for our e-newsletter!

THE ART OF TRAVEL

How to See the World: www.artoftravel.com. A compendium of great travel tips, from cheap flights to self defense to interacting with local culture.

Travel Library: www.travel-library.com. A fantastic set of links for general information and personal travelogues.

Travel Intelligence: www.travelintelligence.net. A large collection of travel writing by distinguished travel writers.

World Hum: www.worldhum.com. An independently produced collection of "travel dispatches from a shrinking planet."

BootsnAll.com: www.bootsnall.com. Numerous resources for independent travelers, from planning your trip to reporting on it when you get back.

INFORMATION ON SOUTHEAST ASIA

CIA World Factbook: www.odci.gov/cia/publications/factbook/index.html. Tons of vital statistics on the geography, government, economy, and people of Southeast Asia.

MyTravelGuide: www.mytravelguide.com. Country overviews, with everything from history to transportation to live web cam coverage of Southeast Asia.

Geographia: www.geographia.com. Highlights, culture, and people of Southeast Asia.

Atevo Travel: www.atevo.com/guides/destinations. Detailed introductions, travel tips, and suggested itineraries.

Time-Asia Now: www.time.com/time/asia. The international version of *Time Magazine* covers current events, cultural information, and technology news throughout Asia.

ALTERNATIVES TO TOURISM

A PHILOSOPHY FOR TRAVELERS

Let's Go believes that the connection between travelers and their destinations is an important one. Over the years, we've watched the growth of the "ignorant tourist" stereotype with dismay, knowing that even conscientious tourists can inadvertently damage natural wonders and harm cultural environments. With this "Alternatives to Tourism" chapter, *Let's Go* hopes to promote a better understanding of Southeast Asia, and enhance your experiences there.

In the developing world, there are several different options for those who seek to participate in alternatives to tourism. Opportunities for **volunteering** abound, both with local and international organizations. **Studying** can also be instructive, either in the form of direct enrollment in a local university or in an independent research project. *Let's Go* discourages **working** in the developing world due to high unemployment rates and weak economies. With so few jobs as it is—especially in the tourism industry—these locales can better use your assistance elsewhere.

As a **volunteer** in Southeast Asia, you can participate in projects that range from disaster relief to plastic surgery, on a short-term basis or as the main component of your trip. Help bring decent healthcare to struggling rural areas, or make a child's day by teaching her skills she can use to support herself and her family. Below, we recommend organizations that can help you find the opportunities that best suit your interests, whether you're looking to pitch in for a day or a year.

Studying at a college or language program is another great option. While many colleges offer language instruction, there are several small-time operations worth considering. While smaller language centers usually cannot offer official course credit, small classes mean an intimate environment and more personal attention. Weigh your options carefully before setting out.

> Start your search at **www.beyondtourism.com,** Let's Go's brand-new searchable database of Alternatives to Tourism, where you can find exciting feature articles and helpful program listings divided by country, continent, and program type.

VOLUNTEERING

Volunteer opportunities in Southeast Asia center around projects that further peace, human rights, education, health, conservation, and community development. Many positions are available for professionals with valuable skills in business and management, industry, science and technology, agriculture, healthcare, and social services. Programs aid locals in building infrastructures that will promote self-sufficiency in these developing nations. There are also positions and internships available that do not require professional expertise, particularly in the areas of conservation, agriculture, human rights, and education. Participate in community agricultural and construction projects or provide language instruction to local healthcare professionals. There are many service projects in Southeast

Asia that need volunteers, with time commitments ranging from a few days or weeks to a year, and beyond. Some volunteer programs require participants to pay fees; most often this money is used to pay for housing, food, and sometimes airfare, and to purchase the resources needed to help enrich the local community.

HEALTH

Doctors Without Borders, 333 7th Ave., 2nd fl., New York, NY 10001-5004, USA (☎212-679-6800; www.doctorswithoutborders.org); 2525 Main St., Ste. 110, Santa Monica, CA 90405 (☎310-399-0049). Provides emergency aid to victims of armed conflict, epidemics, and natural and manmade disasters in Cambodia, Indonesia, Laos, Myanmar, the Philippines, and Thailand. Medical positions require 2 years' experience.

Health Volunteers Overseas, 1900 L St. N.W., Ste. 310, Washington, DC 20036, USA (☎202-296-0928; www.hvousa.org). Sends qualified health professionals overseas to train local healthcare providers. Placement is according to medical specialty, with sites in Cambodia, the Philippines, and Vietnam.

Interplast, 300-B Pioneer Way, Mountain View, CA 94041-1506, USA (☎888-467-5278 or 650-962-0123; www.interplast.org). Provides reconstructive plastic surgery for children and adults. Sends medical teams to perform operations and educate local professionals in Myanmar and Vietnam.

Operation Smile, 6435 Tidewater Dr., Norfolk, VA 23509, USA (☎757-321-7645; www.operationsmile.org). Provides reconstructive surgery to children and related healthcare and training to professionals in Cambodia, the Philippines, Thailand, and Vietnam.

DEVELOPMENT

Mango Treehouse, Rev. Craig Edwards, Executive Director, ASCF, 24 Pakinas St., Proj. 8, Quezon City, Manila (craig@ascf.ph). Volunteers teach English and other subjects at a home for abandoned children in Manila. University students welcome.

Aram Kindergarten, Jesus Christ Church of the Nations, Pastor Purisimo R. Ramirez (☎63 (0) 918 259 9414; john_cardel23@yahoo.com). Looking for university students and adults to volunteer teaching English and other subjects in Myanmar.

Involvement Volunteers Association Inc., P.O. Box 218, Port Melbourne, Victoria 3207, Australia (☎613 9646 9392; www.volunteering.org.au). Offers a variety of opportunities in Cambodia, Malaysia (Sabah), Thailand, and Vietnam. Teach science, business, or agriculture in Cambodia; help conserve the Malaysian jungle; teach orphaned children or work on an organic farm in northeast Thailand (teacher positions are female-only; farmer positions are male-only).

Relief for Oppressed People Everywhere (ROPE), 12 Church St., Rickmansworth, Hertfordshire, WD3 1BS, UK (☎44 019 2377 1821; www.rope.org.uk/default.html). A Christian volunteer charity that promotes educational, medical, agricultural, and other practical projects to increase self-sufficiency in 85 countries. Operates in Cambodia, Indonesia, Laos, Myanmar, the Philippines, Thailand, and Vietnam. Benefits widows, orphans, refugees, the unemployed, and the homeless.

Australian Aid for Cambodia Fund, P.O. Box 81, Bundoora, Victoria 3081, Australia (☎613-9489-6240; www.aacf.ws/default.html). Dedicated to bringing peace and prosperity to Cambodia through education, medical care, and human resource development. Teach business, science, agriculture, rural development, or languages for 9-12 months at Maharishi Vedic University.

COMMUNITY INVOLVEMENT

Hope for Cambodia's Youth

ıs a tourist in Cambodia, I often felt ıneasy as a witness to extreme poverty, uffering, and pain. Certainly the most difïcult experience was the "genocide tour" of the Killing Fields and the accompanying nuseum and former torture prison, Tuol Sleng. Riding to the outskirts of Phnom Penh to do this tour, my friend and I hared the back of a motorbike driven by former welder who found it more profitıble to earn a living by shuttling tourists round on his Honda. His mother had een killed by the Khmer Rouge. The bike agged under our triple weight, kicking up lust every time we hit a rut in the dirt oad. At a crossroads, our driver asked if ve would like to take the right fork to the hooting range—where you can detonate ust about anything—before we went out o the fields. We declined.

Tourists in Cambodia often face these hoices: the activities that have been idenified as things that tourists like to do are ften violent, like shooting rocket launchrs; they are often exploitative, like freuenting Phnom Penh's nightmare rothels; or they involve bearing witness o the violent and exploitative acts that ompose Cambodia's recent history. Even hopping becomes an odd ethical hoice—at the Russian Market the best uys are the second-hand goods from vell-known clothing store chains. While umping foreign currency into the econmy is undoubtedly a good thing, many ravelers visit Cambodia and feel the need o do more.

Volunteering without language skills or pecialized degrees can be a challenge (if ou are a Khmer-speaking surgeon you'll ave no problem), but it's not impossible. One area in which there exists great need s in educating and supporting street chilren. In Phnom Penh, 1200 children live lone on the streets, and another 500-1500 ive on the streets with their families. These children are at high risk for physical nd emotional exploitation—many are bused and drugged by adults to make hem look more pathetic as beggars. With 6% of the Cambodian population under 9, the future of the country depends on he strength of this young generation. Volınteering with a local NGO can be a ewarding way to fulfill this need in sociıty while connecting with Cambodian taff and the children you are helping.

In Phnom Penh, Mith Samlanh Friends (www.streetfriends.org) runs a residential center for homeless children, as well as several businesses where children develop practical work experience while generating income to support Friends' other outreach programs. At Friends Restaurant, just north of the National Museum, students are trained to prepare and serve food to guests; next door, street youth repair and resell electronics. At Condom Café, students serve Khmer food and offer education on reproductive health. The income generated by these businesses support outreach programs including AIDS/HIV awareness and care, substance abuse prevention and treatment, and a mobile library. Volunteers can propose new projects or work on existing jobs; for information on how to apply see the Friends website or email Sebastion Marot (friends@everyday.com.kh).

If you are seeking a more rugged volunteer experience, the Cambodian Association for Orphan Development (CAFOD), a smaller organization with a similar mission, runs a farm in Kandal Province, Saang District (about 25km southeast of Phnom Penh) where orphans learn skills for sustainable living in rural Cambodia. Twenty orphans, aged 9-14, live and work at the farm, learning English and environmentally responsible agriculture. Volunteers can work with the students at the farm or at an affiliated school in Siem Riep, the Australian Friendship Institute (AFI). Profits from AFI, where students learn languages, computer skills, and hospitality trades, help support the CAFOD farm initiatives. CAFOD and AFI are run by a husband-and-wife team, both dedicated to improving the lives of young Cambodians. For information on volunteering, contact Sophal (☎855 (0)12 755 913) or Kathy (☎855 (0)12 675 838), or email afi@everyday.com.kh.

These organizations and dozens of other NGOs operate innovative and successful programs that are transforming Cambodia's future. Whether you are seeking transformation yourself, or just a more fulfilling travel experience, volunteering to work with Cambodia's youth can be a worthwhile alternative to the typical tourist track.

Sarah Rotman is a former Let's Go *researcher-writer, editor, and manager. An avid traveler to Asia, she developed websites for local businesses while living in Vietnam in 2003. She currently designs educational programs for businesses and schools in the US and Korea.*

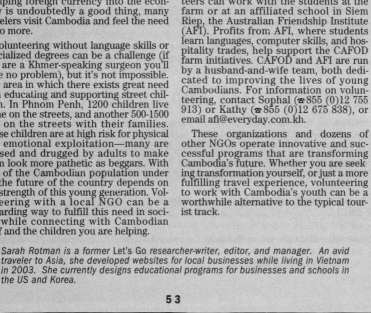

United Nations Volunteers, Postfach 260 111, D-53153 Bonn, Germany (☎49 228 815 2000; www.unv.org). The UN recruits professionals, humanitarian workers, executives, and IT specialists to work for up to 2 years in developing countries. Placement is at the discretion of the agency and is based on the applicant's skills.

Population and Community Development Association, 8 Sukhumvit, Soi 12, Bangkok 10110, Thailand (☎662 229 4611; www.sli.unimelb.edu.au/pda). Organizes volunteers to Thailand working on projects involving village mapping, journalism, teaching, agriculture, and the construction of affordable housing.

Cross Cultural Solutions, 2 Clinton Pl., New Rochelle, NY 10801, USA (☎800-380-4777 or 914-632-0022; www.crossculturalsolutions.org). 3-12 week programs in Thailand. Teach English to monks, work with HIV/AIDS patients, or alongside locals in rural and urban community projects. Some volunteers research with local development organizations. Thai lessons are available twice weekly. Tax-deductible US$2000-5000.

Global Service Corps, 300 Broadway, Ste. 28, San Francisco, CA 94133-3312, USA (☎415-788-3666; www.globalservicecorps.org). Programs and internships in Thailand, in education, healthcare, and Buddhist immersion. 2-10 weeks (US$2000-4000). Sites include local schools, colleges, monasteries, hospitals, and orphanages. Homestays and 1-on-1 training and language assistance with local volunteers.

Teaching and Projects Abroad, Gerrard House, Rustington, West Sussex BN16 1AW, UK (☎440 1903 859911; www.teaching-abroad.co.uk). Programs in Thailand, in teaching or in care-giving at orphanages and nurseries. 3 months or less US$2700.

CUSO, 500-2255 Carling Ave., Ottawa, Ontario K2B 1A6, Canada (Canada ☎888-434-2876, 613-829-7445; www.cuso.org). 2-year volunteer opportunities for Canadian citizens in Indonesia, Laos, the Philippines, Thailand, and Vietnam. Work to further human rights, legal advocacy, and development. Airfare, housing, and stipend provided.

PROFESSIONAL

ACDI/VOCA, 50 F St. NW, Ste. 1100, Washington, D.C. 20001, USA (☎800-929-8622 or 202-383-4961; www.acdivoca.org). Projects for professionals in Indonesia, the Philippines, Thailand, and Vietnam. Provide short-term assistance in banking, business, cooperative planning, and agricultural production. 2-4 weeks. All expenses paid.

International Executive Service Corps, 901 15th St. NW, Ste. 350, Washington D.C. 20005, USA (☎202-326-0280; www.iesc.org) sends professionals to Indonesia, Thailand, and Vietnam to serve as consultants to businesses, government organizations, and non-profits. 1 week to 2 months; long-term work available. Major travel expenses and spouses' expenses are covered if the project lasts for more than 1 month.

ENVIRONMENTAL AND AGRICULTURAL

World-Wide Opportunities on Organic Farms, P.O. Box 2675, Lewes BN7 1RB, UK (www.wwoof.org). Provides connections between volunteers and organic farms in the Philippines and Thailand. There is a minimal WWOOF membership fee.

Ecovolunteer, 1st fl., 577/579 Fishponds Rd., Bristol BS16 3AF, UK (☎0117 965 8333; www.ecovolunteer.org). Connects volunteers with wildlife conservation projects in Indonesia and Thailand.

Coral Cay Conservation Ltd., The Tower, 13th fl., 125 High St., Colliers Wood, London SW19 2JG, UK (☎44 0870 750 0668). Volunteer with conservation and sustainable development projects in Malaysia and the Philippines.

International Conservation Holidays, Conservation Centre, 163 Balby Rd., Doncaster, South Yorkshire DN4 0RH, UK (☎44 0130 257 2244; www.btcv.org/international). Runs conservation ecology trips.

HUMAN RIGHTS

Peace Brigades International, Box 9, 33 Boundary Trail, Clearwater, Manitoba ROK OMO, Canada (☎204-873-2563; www.peacebrigades.org). Work in Indonesia to promote a safe space for human rights defenders and provide nonviolent conflict resolution. All expenses in the field are covered.

Suaram, 383, 1st fl., Jl. 5/59, Petaling Gardens, 46000 Petaling Jaya, Selangor, Malaysia (☎603 7784 3525; www.suaram.org/home.htm). An activist organization working to further human rights progress in Malaysia. Runs educational campaigns.

Free Burma Coalition (FBC), 1101 Pennsylvania Ave., SE #204 Washington, DC 20003, USA (☎202-547-5985; www.freeburmacoalition.org). Modeled after the anti-apartheid movement in South Africa and working jointly with the National League for Democracy (NLD). Mobilizes groups around the world to promote freedom and democracy in Myanmar (Burma). Offers a wide range of volunteer opportunities for students and professionals alike, both in Myanmar and in other countries across the globe.

STUDYING ABROAD

Options for study abroad in Southeast Asia include language classes and English-language cultural and history courses. Some programs can be very pricey; most do not include international airfare in the tuition price. Students hoping to get degree credit for courses taken abroad should check with their college's academic offices. For information concerning student visas, see **Visas,** p. 12.

AMERICAN PROGRAMS

Council-International Study Programs: Vietnam, Cambodia, Laos, 633 Third Ave., 20th fl., New York, NY 10017, USA (☎800-407-8839; www.ciee.org). Introduces students to contemporary development in Indochina in a comparative framework. Based in Hà Nội, but there are also extended study components in Cambodia, Laos, and Thailand.

Pacific Challenge, P.O. Box 3151, Eugene, OR 97401, USA (☎541-343-4124; www.pacificchallenge.org). Adventure travel program in Cambodia, Laos, Thailand, and Vietnam. US$4700 includes airfare, activities, accommodations, and visas.

Where There Be Dragons (☎800-982-9203; www.wheretherebedragons.com/). Runs youth summer programs and short trips for adults to Cambodia, Laos, Thailand, and Vietnam. Youth programs cost US$5950-6150. Adult programs cost US$3550-4500. Fee includes food, accommodations, and internal travel.

International Association for the Exchange of Students for Technical Experience (IAESTE), 10400 Little Patuxent Pkwy. #250, Columbia, MD 21044, USA (☎410-997-3069; www.iaeste.org). 8- to 12-week programs in Indonesia and Thailand for college students who have done 2 years of technical study. US$25 application fee.

Naropa University, Office of International Education, 2130 Arapahoe Ave., Boulder, CO 80302, USA (www.naropa.edu/studyabroad). Offers semester programs in Bali, Indonesia focusing on arts and spirituality in contemporary Balinese culture. Room, board, and tuition cost US$8450 for undergrads; college credit available.

School for International Training: College Semester Abroad, Admissions, Kipling Rd., P.O. Box 676, Brattleboro, VT 05302, USA (toll-free ☎888-272-7881 or 802-258-3212; www.sit.edu). Semester-long programs in Bali, Indonesia, and Vietnam. US$12,000. Financial aid; US financial aid is transferable.

American University, 4400 Massachusetts Ave. NW, Washington, D.C. 20016, USA (☎202-865-6000; summer@american.edu). With a branch based in Kuala Lumpur, American University provides 3-week summer programs exploring "interstate relations."

Kolej Damansara Utama, School of American Programs, KDO Petaling Jaya Jalan SS 22141 Damansara Jaya, 4700 Petaling Jaya Selangar (☎603 718 8123, ext. 308; www.kdu.edu.my/). Focuses on practical skills in the tourism sector, including hotel and restaurant management, as well as more academic concerns.

International Partnership for Service Learning, 815 2nd Ave., Ste. 315, New York, NY 10017, USA (☎212-986-0989; info@ipsl.org). Pursue a full range of academic studies at Manila's Trinity College, and volunteer 15hr. a week for a nearby service agency or program. Summer-, semester-, and year-long programs. Summer US$4900; semester US$7200; year-long US$14,200. Applications are due 2 months prior to program.

Tagalog On Site, 161 Judge Juan Luna St., San Francisco Del Monte, Quezon City, Manila (☎2 371 6296; http://members.aol.com/tagalogusa). Specifically designed for Filipino-American students. TOS participants spend the summer or fall semesters studying the language, history, and contemporary culture of the Philippines. Online application. Program costs US$2552.

Experiment in International Living (toll-free ☎800-345-2929 or 802-27-7751; www.usexperiment.org). Founded in 1932, the program is run by the School for International Training: College Semester Abroad. Offers cross-cultural, educational homestays, and community work in Thailand. Programs are 5 weeks (US$2550-5000).

ITTA, 3600 S. 60th Ave., Shelby, MI 49455, USA (☎231-861-0481). Massage classes (175hr. CEU) and travel in Thailand. US$1800 includes airfare and accommodations.

Brockport Vietnam Program, Office of International Education, SUNY Brockport, 350 New Campus Dr., Brockport, NY 14420, USA (☎800-298-7869; www.brockport-abroad.com/thirdlvl/vietnam_3rd.html). Study for a semester in Đà Nẵng through the State University of New York College at Brockport program. Students take courses in history, language, culture, and politics and participate in community service projects. The US$8150 program fee covers airfare.

Center for Study Abroad, CSA International, 325 Washington Ave. South #93, Kent, Washington 98032, USA (☎206-583-8191; www.centerforstudyabroad.com). Offers programs at Vietnam National University in Hồ Chí Minh City. Vietnamese language instruction for all levels. 9-week summer programs US$1395; semester programs US$3295; airfare and housing not included.

CULINARY AND CULTURAL STUDY

Juwita Cafe, on Tuk Tuk Peninsula on Pulau Samosir. Cooking classes are offered daily 1-4pm. See **Pulau Samosir,** p. 250.

Lucy Batik Gallery and Losmen, Sosrowijayan Wetan GT 1/94, Jogjakarta (☎513 429). Offers *batik* courses starting at 9am. Rp30,000-75,000. See **Jogjakarta** (p. 152) for further information and directions.

Elderhostel, Inc., 11 Ave. de Lafayette, Boston, MA 02111-1746, USA (☎877-426-8056; www.elderhostel.org). Sends adults ages 55+ on "learning adventures" to Cambodia, Indonesia, Laos, Malaysia, Thailand, and Vietnam. Costs average US$100 per day plus airfare.

Semarang 2000 Indonesian Language Center, Ms. Augustina Prasetyo, Semarang 2000, Ruko Semarang Indah E1, 12A-14, Semarang 50144, Java (☎62 24 762 0009; info@semarang2000.com). Provides instruction in Bahasa Indonesia to students of all ages (US$10 per hour). Extra activities include lessons in *batik* and Indonesian cooking. Accommodations available (some meals included; US$15, with A/C US$20).

Viavia, Jl. Prawirotaman 24B, Jogjakarta (☎386 557; viavia@yogya.wasantara.net.id). Offers courses in language (Rp30,000), cooking (Rp35,000), and massage (Rp40,000). Open 8am-10pm. See **Jogjakarta** (p. 152) for more information.

Chiang Mai Thai Cookery, 1-3 Moon Muang Rd., Chiang Mai 50200 (☎66 53 206 388; www.thaicookeryschool.com). Offers courses for up to 5 days in Thai cooking and fruit tasting (5 days US$100).

Hai Cafe, 98 Nguyễn Thái Học, Hội An (p. 936). The cafe offers a nightly cooking class. During the 1hr. class, the chef instructs students on how to make grilled fish in banana leaves, spring rolls, and squid salad. Afterward, students chow down on their own creations in addition to Hội An specialties like white rose and fried wonton. US$5 covers enrollment and the meal.

Lexia International, 25 South Main St., Hanover, NH 03755, USA (☎800-775-3942 or 603-643-9898; www.lexiaintl.org). Lexia offers a progressive curriculum of language, cultural, and field study drawing on cultural study in the social sciences and humanities. Summer-, semester-, and year-long programs in Thailand (US$5000-20,000).

LANGUAGE SCHOOLS

The Royal University of Phnom Penh, M. V. Confédération de la Russie, Khan Tuol Kork, Phnom Penh (☎12 812 017; http://www.aun.chula.ac.th/cambodia.htm). Offers courses in Khmer language for foreigners.

Indonesia Australia Language Foundation (www.ialf.edu), offers courses in Bahasa Indonesia, organizes group study tours, and provides individualized tuition. Homestays available. IALF offers programs in: Denpasar (Jl. Kapten Agung 17, Denpasar 80232, Bali; ☎62 361 225 243; ialfbali@ialf.edu); Jakarta (Jl. Rasuna Said Kav C-6, Jakarta 12940; ☎62 21 521 3350; ialfjkt@ialf.edu); Surabaya (Jl. Sumatera No. 49, Surabaya 60281, East Java; ☎62 31 502 6400; ialfsby@ialf.edu).

Lembaga Bahasa Colorado, Jl. Demangan Baru 33, Jogjakarta 55281 (☎62 274 562 874; www.lbcolorado.or.id). Courses in Bahasa Indonesia for all levels (1 student US$8 per hour). Language training for business or pleasure. Homestays available.

Puri Bahasa Indonesia, Dr. Unang Liesanggoro, Academic Coordinator, Puri Bahasa Indonesia, Jl. Bausasran 59, Jogjakarta 55211 (☎62 274 588 192; http://indigo.ie/~noelrubt). Programs for beginning to advanced students. 1-on-1 or group instruction (US$5 per hr. for 1 student; US$10 per hr. for 4). Homestays or accommodation at local guesthouses. Organizes cultural activities including *batik,* yoga, and *wayang.*

Realia Indonesian Language Training, Jl. Pandga Marta V/6, Pogung Utara, Jogjakarta 55281 (☎62 274 583 229; http://realians.com/). Intensive and less intensive language training programs for up to 4 students (1 student US$10 per hr.; 4 students US$14 per hour). Professional or social focus. Complimentary homestay can be arranged for participants in the intensive program.

Wisma Bahasa, Jl. Rajawali, Gg. Nuri No. 6, Demangan Baru, Jogjakarta 55281 (☎62 274 588 409; www.wisma-bahasa.or.id). Courses for all proficiency levels in English, Indonesian, Javanese, and Tetun, the language of East Timor. Homestays, private tuition, and cultural activities. Class size varies from 1 student (about US$7.50 per hr.) to 4 students (about US$14 per hour). Student and volunteer discounts.

The University of the Philippines-Diliman, Kolehiyo ng Arte at Literatura, Unibersidad ng Pilipinas, Diliman, Lunsod Quezon 1101, Manila (☎2 920 5301; www.upd.org.ph). Offers courses and degree programs in Filipino language and Philippine studies.

Vietnam National University, 12 Đinh Tien Hoang, Hồ Chí Minh City (☎822 50 09). Regular and intensive Vietnamese language study available through the Department of Vietnamese Studies and Vietnamese Language for Foreigners, University of Social Sciences and Humanities. 6 levels of study. All foreigners with a Vietnamese visa are eligible to enroll. Dorm housing for those with student visa (US$160-220 per month).

WORKING

Unless you happen to land a job with an American company abroad, teaching English is the easiest way to gain entry into the workforce in Southeast Asia. Through some universities and employment websites, you can find opportunities in various fields. Most of these jobs, are located in the more developed countries of Malaysia and Singapore. If you have your eyes set on a particular field, your best bet is to get a work permit, and search away.

TEACHING

International Schools Services, Educational Staffing Program, P.O. Box 5910, Princeton, NJ 08543, USA (☎609-452-0990; www.iss.edu). Recruits teachers and administrators for schools in Cambodia, Indonesia, Laos, Malaysia, Myanmar, the Philippines, Singapore, Thailand, and Vietnam.

Panyathip Bilingual School and Thames Business School, 07/146, Singsavong Rd., Naxay Village, Vientiane, Vientiane Municipality 10000 (☎856 21 414 084). Frequently needs English teachers.

Sengsavanh, 190 Moot Banna, Vientiane, Vientiane Municipality (☎038 671 112). Local school kindergarten through grade 6 and continuing education; often needs English teachers.

The Vientiane International School (VIS), P.O. Box 3180, Vientiane (☎856 21 313 606; fax 856 21 313 008; vis@laonet.net). A private day school encompassing preschool through grade 9, mostly for the children of foreign nationals. Has occasional teaching opportunities. Contact Mr. John Ritter, Director.

ELS Language Centers in Malaysia, A-2-1 Wisma, H.B., Megan Phileo Ave., 12 Jl. Yap Kwan Seng, 50450 Kuala Lumpur (☎603 2166 5530; www.els.edu.my). Places teachers certified to instruct Malaysians in English. 5 centers, various placements.

Teaching Opportunities. Teach English or German to young children on the island of Moalboal to support your diving habit (p. 591). Contact Jochen Hanika (planet@han-grp.de).

International English Club Vietnam, 537 3 Thang 2 St., District 10, Hồ Chí Minh City. (☎848-853-3929; www.ilavietnam.com). Positions teaching English at all levels; payment varies. Serve as a preschool English teacher for room, board, and a stipend.

ILA Vietnam, 402 Nguyen Thi Minh Khai St., District 3, Hồ Chí Minh City (☎848-929-0100; www.ilavietnam.com) and 155 Nguyen Thai Hoc St., 4th Fl., Ward 7, Vung Tau City. (☎846-457-2347; www.ilavietnam.com). ILA Vietnam seeks experienced English teachers to provide instruction in social and business English. Salaries vary.

TEFL International, 367/11-12 Yaowarat Rd., Muang, Phuket Town, Phuket 83000, Thailand, offers a 4-week intensive training course in teaching English (6-12 MA credits through the University of Washington). Course fee US$1290, with housing US$1690. After completing the course, teachers are placed in schools throughout Vietnam.

University of Lethbridge Work-Study in Malaysia. Contact Andrea Amelinckx (E560), (☎403-329-2148; www.uleth.ca/man-int/students/countries/malaysia.shtml). Run jointly by the University of Lethbridge and the University of Victoria MBA Program. Offers students first-hand international business experience working for a Malaysian company in Kuala Lumpur. Students complete a "cross-cultural study in Malaysia," and study Malaysian culture, politics, and business. 5-week program usually in the spring.

Malaysia Employment Center (www.asiadragons.com/malaysia/employment/). This website serves as a employment information hub. Potential employees and employers alike can post and search for suitable matches.

BRUNEI DARUSSALAM

HIGHLIGHTS OF BRUNEI DARUSSALAM

JAW-DROPPING SITES. The **Omar Ali Saifuddien Mosque** (p. 71) inspires awe with its gaudy glory. From dazzling gold domes to diamond-studded entrance signs, not a detail has been overlooked. Enjoy the view from the bridge that leads to its entrance.

STOMACH-RENDING FUN. At the **Jerudong Park Playground** (p. 72), guests can savor the joy flying 100m skyward in a metal cage. Afterwards, they can collect their wits at the fabulous 20,000 gal. "Dancing Fountain"—a stunning laser show.

ROLLIN' ON THE RIVER. Visitors stroll along the **Brunei River,** viewing lovely **water villages** (p. 71), or barrel down it on **water taxis** (p. 68). Unrivaled views of parks, water-houses, and the palace make the river the place to be.

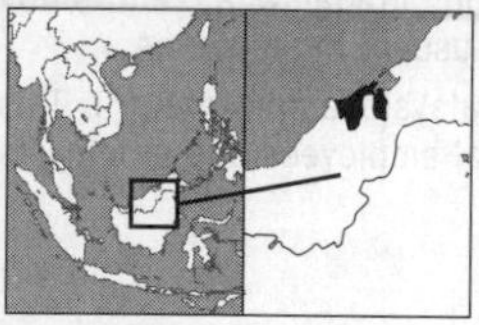

Citizens of Brunei describe their ruler—His Majesty Paduka Seri Baginda Sultan Haji Hassanal Bolkiah Mu'izzaddin Waddaulah—as a man with a heart of gold. One visit to this geographically tiny yet fabulously wealthy country, and you may start taking them literally. Over the past 20 years, oil has transformed this Islamic sultanate into an impressive "Shellfare state" that offers its citizens free education and healthcare, no income tax, and subsidized houses, cars, and pilgrimages to Mecca. Bandar Seri Begawan, the stunning capital, has a skyline pierced with some of Asia's most lavish mosques and, courtesy of Jerudong Park Playground, Asia's tallest roller coasters. Ostentatious buildings like the royal palace are balanced by the more humble water villages and relatively well-protected rainforest. Unfortunately, Brunei Darussalam—translated as "The Abode of Peace"—should be more appropriately translated as "The Abode of Boredom." Nightlife is nonexistent, and the sale and consumption of liquor by locals has been banned since 1991. Fortunately this doesn't apply to foreigners; the country's generous policy allows the import of two bottles of liquor and five cans of beer twice daily.

LIFE AND TIMES

AN OVERVIEW

About two thirds of Brunei's population are **Malay** (67%), but there are significant **Chinese** (15%) and **indigenous** (6%) minorities. The remaining 12% is made up of several immigrant and non-native populations. While not particularly well integrated, Brunei's ethnic groups manage to get along without much ado.

Malay is the official language of Brunei, spoken by almost all of the country's citizens. **English** is widely understood as well, and holds the distinction of being the de facto language of business. **Chinese** is spoken among the Chinese minority, and some indigenous groups speak their own dialects, like **Iban.**

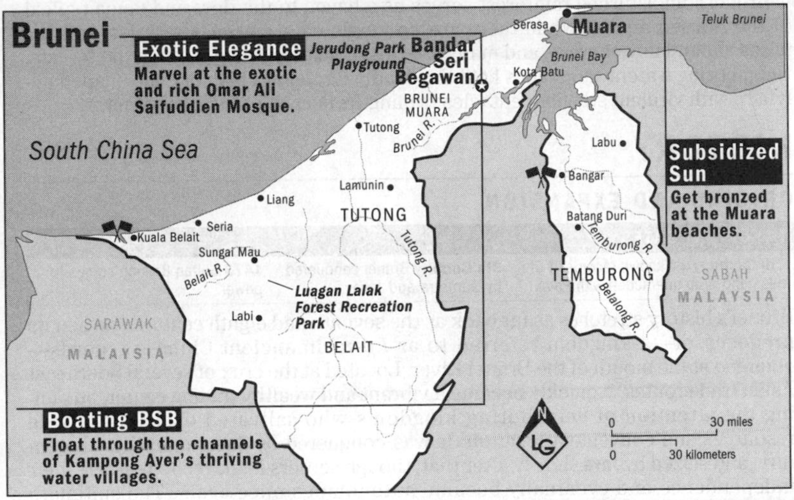

The Malay majority in Brunei adheres strictly to **Islam** (67%), thé country's official religion. Under its auspices, drinking is forbidden, as are immodest dress and sex outside of marriage. The 1984 constitution provides for universal religious freedom, and there are notable **Buddhist** (13%) and **Christian** (10%) demographics. The remaining 10% of the population practices other major world religions or subscribes to indigenous **tribal beliefs.**

Brunei borders **Malaysia** to the west, south, and east, and the **South China Sea** to the north. While **mountains** rise in the country's eastern regions, most of the country's land is low and hilly—part of a broad coastal plain. Lush **rainforest** covers 70% of Brunei's land area, and thanks to the sultanate's fabulous wealth, the forest remains largely untouched. Arable land is at a stark premium, so Brunei imports the vast majority of its foodstuffs, including beef, fruits, and vegetables, from other countries.

FACTS AND FIGURES

Official Name: Negara Brunei Darussalam.

Government: Constitutional Sultanate.

Capital: Bandar Seri Begawan.

Land Area: 5270km².

Geography: Borders Malaysia. Hills and lowlands in the west; coastal plains rising to mountains in the east.

Climate: Tropical; holding steady at 80°F year round; rainy season Sep.-Jan. Average humidity, 79%.

Phone Codes: Country code: 673. International dialing prefix: 00.

Major Cities: Kuala Belait, Muara, Seria.

Population: 365,251.

Life Expectancy: Women: 77.09 years. Men: 72.13 years.

Language: Malay (official), English, Chinese.

Religion: Muslim (67%), Buddhist (13%), Christian (10%), other (10%).

Literacy Rate: 91.8% overall; 94.8% of men, 88.5% of women.

Major Exports: Crude oil, natural gas, and refined products.

Random Fact: His Majesty's wife has 16 names!

Brunei's undisturbed rainforest serves as a haven to the flora and fauna typical of the Borneo region. While there are no jungle cats, **crocodiles, turtles,** and **tortoises** abound in wet areas, and many species of **monkey** swing through the forests. Neighboring waters sometimes host the deadly **Box Jelly**—a bell- or cube-shaped jellyfish, with virulent stinging tentacles trailing from each of its four corners.

HISTORY

ORIGINS AND EXPANSION

IMPORTANT DATES		
7th Century First known records of Chinese and Arab interaction with *Po-ni.*	**9th Century** Brunei conquered by Sumatra and Java.	**1473** Sultan Bolkiah comes to power.

Brunei's history stretches as far back as the seventh and eighth centuries, when its predecessor—a kingdom referred to as *Po-ni* in ancient Chinese records—emerged at the mouth of the Brunei River. Located at the crux of several Southeast Asian trade routes, it quickly became a vibrant and wealthy trading center, attracting the attention of neighboring kingdoms who salivated over its growing resources and convenient location. It was conquered by **Sumatra** in the 9th century, and seized by **Java** shortly after that, though settlers managed to reassert their independence and eventually became autonomous once again. The sultanate known today did not materialize until the 15th and 16th centuries, when a string of strong leaders, particularly the **Sultan Bolkiah** (1473-1521), helped expand Brunei's territory into parts of **Malaysia** and the **Philippines.**

BRUNEI DARUSSALAM

FORMING A NATIONAL IDENTITY

IMPORTANT DATES		
1605 Sultan Hassan comes to power.	**1619** Hassan's reign ends, marking descent into infighting.	**1838** James Brooke arrives in Brunei.

With Sultan Hassan (1605-19) came Brunei's famous courtly image, replete in palaces and stalwart imperial decrees. While not the most skilled ruler, Hassan made his mark by promoting a strong governmental hierarchy and setting numerous precedents. Following his death, however, no precedents could save the kingdom from petty infighting and multiple claims to the Brunei throne. The country was especially vulnerable to the growing forces of colonialism in Southeast Asia. Beginning with the arrival of English adventurer **James Brooke** in 1838—who won the sultan's support by helping put down a rebellion—the kingdom saw its power gradually usurped by the **British crown,** as Brooke pressured the sultan to accept caustic treaties and trade agreements.

PAYDIRT

IMPORTANT DATES		
1929 Oil is discovered in Brunei.	**1959** Brunei's constitution is written.	**1984** Brunei becomes fully independent from the British crown.

With the discovery of oil in 1929, however, Brunei's fate would change. The seemingly endless source of income, coupled with the decline of British colonialism in the first half of the 20th century, brought the tiny sultanate both property and independence. So began the days of government-subsidized housing, free education, and zero income tax. In 1959 Brunei made its first constitution, declaring its status as a semi-autonomous state, although Britain still maintained a say in many of its foreign and commercial affairs. In 1979, however, Brunei signed a friendship treaty with the UK—effectively limiting British involvement in Brunei's government—and on January 1, 1984, Brunei declared itself fully independent.

BRUNEI TODAY

The transition has not been entirely smooth, however. Recent years have had their blemishes, as **Prince Jefri**—the sultan **Hassanal Bolkiah**'s youngest brother and Finance Minister—led the family-owned **Amedeo Development Corporation** to bankruptcy at the nadir of the Asian financial crisis. Jefri was fired from the position of Finance Minister, but Brunei's holdings have dropped to just a third of their peak value; the sultan brought a lawsuit against his brother, but settled when Prince Jefri agreed to give back assets he had acquired while he was Finance Minister.

On the heels of the Amedeo crash, Jefri's actions were further questioned by a former Miss USA, who sued both him and the sultan for US$56 million, claiming that she was lured to Brunei and pressured to become a sex slave. The case was dismissed because of state immunity. Jefri has since faced a multi-million-dollar civil lawsuit brought by creditors. Thanks to these costly legal tangles, the prince was forced to auction off thousands of his personal possessions, including hundreds of gold-plated toilet brush holders, two fire engines, and a Comanche attack helicopter simulator. While his family has forgiven him, they have apparently also advised him to make himself scarce; his antics no longer make front page news, and when he does make public appearances, it is usually with his family.

CUSTOMS AND ETIQUETTE

Strongly rooted in the Muslim faith, Brunei is quite conservative when it comes to clothing and behavior. It's best to avoid outfits that reveal vast expanses of flesh—particularly the shoulders, stomach, and legs. Kissing and other public displays of affection are inadvisable, especially for single Muslims (who are subject to fines and even imprisonment if caught getting too close in public). As in other Southeast Asian countries, it is considered rude to use the left hand when passing things (dishes, documents), so always use the right. When entering a mosque, always remove your shoes.

BRUNEI COOKING. Brunei's location puts it at the crossroads of several gustatory cultures, including Chinese, Indonesian, Indian, and Malaysian, to name a few. Most foodstuffs are imported, so it's possible to find everything from Japanese beef to Irish potatoes. In general, Brunei's residents relish rich and spicy dishes, and rice and noodles play a central role. Be sure to try:

Malu Abulthiyal: Fish steamed or baked in a sauce of curry leaves, tumeric, garlic, and goraka–a small, sweet, purple fruit (not unlike tamarind). An example of Brunei's marvelous melting-pot cuisine.

Chicken Kurma: Pungently spicy and sweet; pieces of chicken are plunged into pan-fried garlic and onion, flavored with cardamom and anise, and then made sweet with coconut milk and cream. Served with rice.

Beriani: Chicken, cooked with garlic, onion, cashews, almonds, ginger, poppy seeds and cloves. Heaped with coconut rice, in traditional Malaysian fashion.

ARTS

Brunei possesses little in the way of artistic and literary traditions. Indulge your senses in the (somewhat gaudy) opulence of Bandar Seri Begawan's mosques and palace, which boast lavish amounts of 24k gold, Italian marble, and diamonds.

HOLIDAYS AND FESTIVALS (2005)

DATE	NAME	DESCRIPTION
Jan. 1	New Year's Day	National.
Jan. 21	Hari Raya Haji	Festival of sacrifice, usually four days long.
Feb. 9	Chinese New Year	Celebrated by the Chinese community over two full weeks.
Feb. 22	Islamic New Year	Muslim.
Feb. 23	National Day	National.
May 1	Labor Day	National.
May 15	Vesak Day	Commemorates the birth and enlightenment of Buddha.
Aug. 9	National Day	National.
Oct. 23	Deepavali (Diwali)	Indian—five-day festival of lights, celebrating the Ramayana.
Oct. 5	Start of Ramadan	Muslim—begins month of fasting.
Nov. 3	Hari Raya Puasa	Muslim feast that marks the end of Ramadan.
Dec. 25	Christmas Day	A colorful Christian celebration.

BRUNEI DARUSSALAM

ADDITIONAL RESOURCES

LITERATURE

History of Brunei, by Graham Saunders (2002). An impeccable and comprehensive volume, shedding light onto Brunei's history from its earliest days as a sultanate right up to the present day.

New World Hegemony In The Malay World, by Geoffrey C. Gunn (2000). Has a decent account of the rise of the Brunei sultanate.

ON THE WEB

The Sultan of Brunei Online (www.bruneisultan.com). Features charming opening animation, and a comprehensive background on the royal family, its residences, and politics.

Brunei News Online (http://bruneinews.net/). Regional news (occasionally of import), updated daily.

ESSENTIALS

BRUNEI PRICE ICONS					
SYMBOL:	❶	❷	❸	❹	❺
ACCOMM.	Under US$15 Under B$17	US$15-40 B$17-34	US$40-60 B$34-52	US$60-100 B$52-68	Over US$100 Over B$68
FOOD	Under US$5 Under B$5	US$5-10 B$5-11	US$10-20 B$11-22	US$20-35 B$22-34	Over US$35 Over B$34

EMBASSIES AND CONSULATES

BRUNEI CONSULAR SERVICES ABROAD

Australia: High Commission, 16 Bulwarra Close, Canberra, Australia (☎61-6 29018012).

Canada: High Comission, 395 Laurier Ave. East, Ottawa, Ontario K1N 6R4 (☎613-234-5656).

UK: High Commission, 19-20 Belgrave Square, London, SW1X 8PG (☎44 171 581 0521).

US: Embassy, 3520 International Court NW, Washington D.C. 20008 (☎202-237-1838; www.bruneiembassy.org).

CONSULAR SERVICES IN BRUNEI

For embassies and consulates of other countries in Brunei, please see **Practical information: Embassies,** p.481.

DOCUMENTS AND FORMALITIES

Most travelers will not need a visa to enter Brunei; only a valid passport is needed for short stays. Citizens of Canada, New Zealand, and most European countries are allowed to remain in Brunei for up to 14 days without a visa, New Zealanders and UK citizens for up to 30, and US citizens for up to 90 days. Citizens of Australia can obtain a single entry visa (B$20) for a stay of 10 days or a multiple entry visa (US$30) for a stay of a month upon arrival. Only BND cash and Singapore dollars are accepted, and there is no moneychanger inside the terminal behind the immigration barrier, so bring the necessary amount with you.

MONEY

CURRENCY AND EXCHANGE

The currency chart below is based on August 2004 exchange rates between local currency and Australian dollars (AUS$), Canadian dollars (CDN$), European Union euros (EUR€), New Zealand dollars (NZ$), British pounds (UK£), and US dollars (US$). Check the currency converter on websites like www.xe.com or www.bloomberg.com or a large newspaper for the latest exchange rates.

CURRENCY (B$)		
	AUS$1 = B$0.93 (BRUNEI DOLLAR)	B$1 = AUS$1.08
	CDN$1 = B$1.13	B$1 = CDN$0.88
	EUR€1 = B$1.59	B$1 = EUR€0.63
	NZ$1 = B$0.77	B$1 = NZ$1.30
	UK£1 = B$2.54	B$1 = UK£0.39
	US$1 = B$1.75	B$1 = US$0.57

The **Brunei Dollar (B$)** comes in denominations of B$1, 5, 10, 25, 50, 100, 500, 1000, and 10,000; coins come in 1, 5, 10, 20, and 50 cent amounts. Cash and traveler's checks can be exchanged at most banks; US$ and UK£ traveler's checks are preferred. The Singapore Dollar (S$) circulates widely, and is often used to pay for goods and services (the Singapore ringgit, however, is frowned upon). All major credit cards are accepted, and ATMs abound in all corners of Bandar Seri Begawan. Remember that there is a 10% service charge in hotels and air-conditioned restaurants; it is unnecessary to tip taxi drivers.

GETTING THERE AND GETTING AROUND

For comprehensive information concerning travel to and in Brunei, see **Intercity Transportation** for Bandar Seri Begawan, p. 66.

HEALTH AND SAFETY

EMERGENCY NUMBERS: Police: ☎ 993. Fire: ☎ 995. Ambulance: ☎ 991.

WOMEN TRAVELERS. Strict adherence to Muslim codes means that women should dress conservatively—taking care not to bare thighs, chest, upper arms, or shoulders. As long as women visitors respect these customs, there should be no problems; catcalls, leers, and other tomfoolery are virtually nonexistent in Brunei.

HEALTH RISKS. While there is no risk of contracting malaria in Brunei, Dengue fever does occur; take precautions to avoid insect bites. It is relatively easy to get proper medical attention in the hospital facilities of Bandar Seri Begawan.

GLBT TRAVELERS. By law, homosexuality is illegal in Brunei. Unlike other Southeast Asian countries where it is banned, there is no bustling gay scene to be found in Brunei. PDA for both gay and straight couples is inadvisable. Technically, if convicted, offending homosexuals could be sentenced to up to 10 years in prison or face a US$30 fine.

KEEPING IN TOUCH

The postal service is fairly reliable in Brunei. Offices are usually open M-Th and Sa 7:45am-4:30pm, F 8-11am and 2-4pm, and *Poste Restante* service is reasonably secure. For phone calls, purchase a HelloKad or JTB phone card, available in most stores and Telecom offices. Call ☎ 113 for directory assistance. For Home Country Direct (HCD) numbers from Brunei, refer to the table on the inside back cover.

BANDAR SERI BEGAWAN ☎ 02

Lavish royal monuments like Omar Ali Saifuddien Mosque and the new Yayasan Sultan Haji Hassanal Bolkiah Mall reflect Brunei's true faiths—Islam and opulence. Shiny SUVs and beaming BMWs crowd the compact city center where banks dot every corner. Reckless speedboats snake through the city's sole canal and across the Brunei River to Kampung Ayer, arguably BSB's most charming locale. There, an active water village—home to houses, restaurants, and a floating mosque—pulses with life at all hours.

INTERCITY TRANSPORTATION

BY PLANE. The international airport, **Lapangan Terbang Antarabangsa,** is accessible by buses #11, 23, 24, 36, 38, and 57 from downtown BSB (B$1). A Purple Pelangi (PPP) taxi costs B$25-35. Airport departure tax is B$5 for destinations in Malaysia or Singapore (B$12 for other destinations). Airlines serving BSB include: **Garuda Indonesia,** 49-50 Jl. Sultan, Wisma Raya Building, 3rd fl. (☎ 235 870; open M-F 8:30am-5pm, Sa 8:30am-12:30pm); **MAS,** 144 Jl. Pemancha (☎ 223 404); **Royal Brunei Airlines,** RBA Plaza, Jl. Sultan (☎ 242 222); **Singapore Airlines,** 49-50 Jl. Sultan, ground fl. Wisma Raya Building (☎ 227 253). Travel agents offer cheaper airfare than the airlines. Some tickets do not include the airport tax (B$5 to destinations Kota Kinabalu and Kuching; B$12 all other destinations); inquire in advance.

DESTINATION	FREQUENCY	PRICE	DESTINATION	FREQUENCY	PRICE
Bangkok	5 per week	B$550	**Kuala Lumpur**	19 per week	B$421
Denpasar	2 per week	B$471	**Kuching**	3 per week	B$240
Hong Kong	5 per week	B$695	**Manila**	5 per week	B$458
Jakarta	6 per week	B$471	**Singapore**	14 per week	B$360
Kota Kinabalu	7 per week	B$75	**Surabaya**	4 per week	B$471

BY BOAT. Boats to and from **Lawas** in Sarawak and **Pulau Labuan** in Sabah (4 per day, B$15) stop at **Muara Port,** 30km east of BSB. The port is accessible by the express bus to Muara from the bus station (every 20min. 6:50am-4:50pm, B$2) or by taxi (B$25-30). A B$1 service charge applies. If continuing on to **Kota Kinabalu,** purchase a ticket at **Pulau Labuan, Malaysia** (2½hr., RM30). **Ferry Raja Wali** (☎087 413 827) departs Muara Port for Labuan at 1pm daily. **Express Kinabalu** (☎088 236 834) offers a connecting ferry at 3pm. Boats to **Limbang** (12 passengers, leave when full 7am-4pm, B$10) depart from the **ferry terminal** on Jl. McArthur in BSB.

BY BUS. The **bus station** in BSB is on Jl. Cator between Jl. Sultan and Jl. Sungai Kianggeh. Buses leave in the morning for **Seria** (1½hr., B$5), with connections to **Kuala Belait** (20min., every hr., B$1). At Kuala Belait, take a bus (30min., free) to the border, where buses go to **Miri, Malaysia** (45min., RM10). Get an early start; buses depart infrequently but post departure times in the front windows. The trip will take at least 5hr.

BORDER CROSSINGS: MALAYSIA. The main overland crossing is by bus from Kuala Belait in Brunei to Kuala Baram (Miri) in Sarawak (**P. 428**). Ferries are the most convenient means to cross into Limbang or Liwas. Ferries connect Brunei to Pulau Labuan in the Malaysian province of Sabah.

BRUNEI DARUSSALAM

ORIENTATION

A sliver of Malaysia known as Limbang divides Brunei Darussalam into two areas. To the west are the **Belait, Tutong,** and **Brunei-Muara** regions. To the east is the **Temburong** region. BSB is in Brunei-Muara. Downtown BSB, often called "Bandar," extends south to the Brunei River. The **bus station** sits on **Jl. Cator** in the heart of Bandar. Jl. Cator meets **Jl. Sultan,** BSB's main street, to the west and **Jl. Sungai Kianggeh** to the east. The **canal** runs adjacent to Jl. Sungai Kianggeh. Across from the canal is the **market** and **Pusat Belia.** Both Jl. Sungai Kianggeh and Jl. Sultan end at **Jl. McArthur,** which runs west along the waterfront to the **water taxi stand** and to the Yayasan Sultan Haji Hassanal Bolkiah Mall. Behind the mall is the Omar Ali Saifuddien Mosque. Across the river is **Kampung Ayer,** the city's water village. The **Gadong** area houses the Yaohan Shopping Mall, Kiarong Complex, and the Jame'Asr Hassanal Bolkiah Mosque, and borders the Jerudong Park Playground.

LOCAL TRANSPORTATION

Buses: Purple buses with A/C run from the **bus station** on Jl. Cator 6:30am-6pm or earlier (B$1). Express bus #33 to **Muara** B$2. Bus #11 runs most frequently, making a circular route by the hospital, Center Point shopping district, government buildings, and the immigration office. Bus #55 goes to **Jerudong Park,** #39 to the **museum,** #21 to **Kiarong Complex,** and #22 to **Jame'Asr Hassanal Bolkiah Mosque.** Pick up a schedule at the tourist office.

THE ROYAL REGALIA MUSEUM

One visit to Brunei's Royal Regalia Museum will satiate any appetite for over-the-top luxury. The modern complex houses an extraordinary collection of solid gold coronation accessories, jeweled gifts to the sultan from various heads of state, and mannequins swathed in gold-embroidered formal wear. Best of all, to see this 24-karat opulence doesn't cost a single sen.

Start the tour on the first floor, where there's a small glass case with enough gold to put even the gaudiest baroque cathedrals to shame. The royal couple's exquisite 1968 coronation crowns alone, inlaid with hundreds of rubies, emeralds and diamonds, warrant a trip to Brunei. The second floor offers prime ogling of some of the sultan's many gifts, ranging from ostentatious filigreed daggers from the Emirates to a modest bronze eagle donated by Colin Powell.

In a gallery off the lobby, a giant Royal Chariot used for his majesty's 1992 silver jubilee procession stands behind an army of 100 life-sized soldiers, providing a glimpse of the grandeur for those who missed it. At this rate, the gold jubilee replica might well require its own museum.

(From the Tourist Information Center on Jl. Elizabeth Dua, turn right on Jl. Sultffdan and pass the Brunei History Center. The Museum is on the left. Open daily 10am-5pm.)

Taxis: PPP taxis (☎394 949) wait outside major hotels and the bus station. Most are metered. Taxis run 6am-10pm to: the **airport** (B$25-30); **Gadong** (B$10); **Jeradong Park** (B$25). Destinations within town, B$3. It's difficult to hail cabs, so call the office or head to a hotel instead. Booking fee B$1. **John Kwang** (☎08 731 818) is fast, reliable, and skillful.

Water taxis: Hail water taxis at the stand behind the Yayasan Sultan Haji Hassanal Bolkiah Mall or along the canal by the market on Jl. Sungai Kianggeh. B$0.50-3, tours B$10 per 30-60min. Fares are negotiable.

PRACTICAL INFORMATION

TOURIST, FINANCIAL, AND LOCAL SERVICES

Tourist Offices: Information counter at airport (☎330 142, ext. 364). **Tourist Information Center,** Jl. Elizabeth Dua, next door to the post office. Free maps and brochures. Useful *Explore Brunei* booklet at both locations. Both open daily 8am-4:30pm.

Tours: Freme Travel Service Sdn., Unit 403B, Wisma Jaya, Jl. Pemancha (☎234 280). Tours B$36-140 per person; inquire about min. number of people. Open M-F 8am-noon and 1:30-5pm, Sa 8am-noon. Tourism guru **Danny** (danny25174@hotmail.com) hangs out near the bus station.

Embassies and Consulates: Australian High Commission, 4th fl., Teck Guan Plaza, Jl. Sultan (☎229 435; ozcombrn@brunet.bn). Open M-Th 8am-4:30pm, F 8am-4pm. **British High Commission,** 2nd fl., Block D, Complex Yayasan Sultan Haji Hassanal Bolkiah (☎222 231; brithc@brunei.bn). Open M-Th 8:30am-5pm, F 8:30am-12:30pm. **Cambodia,** No. 8, Simpang 845, Kampong Tasek Meradun, Jl. Tutong BF 1520 (☎654 046). Open M-F 8:30am-5pm. **Canadian High Commission,** 5th fl., 1 Jl. McArthur (☎220 043). Open M-F 8:30am-5pm. **Laos,** No. 11, Simpang 480, Jl. Kebangsaan Lama (☎345 666; hicomcda@brunet.bn). **Malaysian High Commission,** No. 27 and 29, Simpang 396-39, Kampung Sungai Akar, Mukim Berakas B, Jl. Kebangsaan (☎345 652). Open M-Th and Sa 9am-noon and 3-4pm. **Myanmar,** No. 14, Simpang 212, Jl. Kampong Rimba, Gadong BE 3119 (☎450 506). Open M-F 8am-4:30pm. **Philippines,** Rooms 1 and 2, 6th fl., Badi'ah Building, Mile 1, Jl. Tutong (☎241 465). Open M-F 8:30am-12:30pm and 1:30-5:30pm, Sa 9am-noon. **Singapore High Commission,** No. 8, Simpang 74, Jl. Subok (☎262 741; singa@brunet.bn). Open M-F 8:30am-5pm. **Thailand,** No. 2, Simpang 52-86-16, Kampong Bunut, Jl. Tutong BF 1320 (☎653 108).

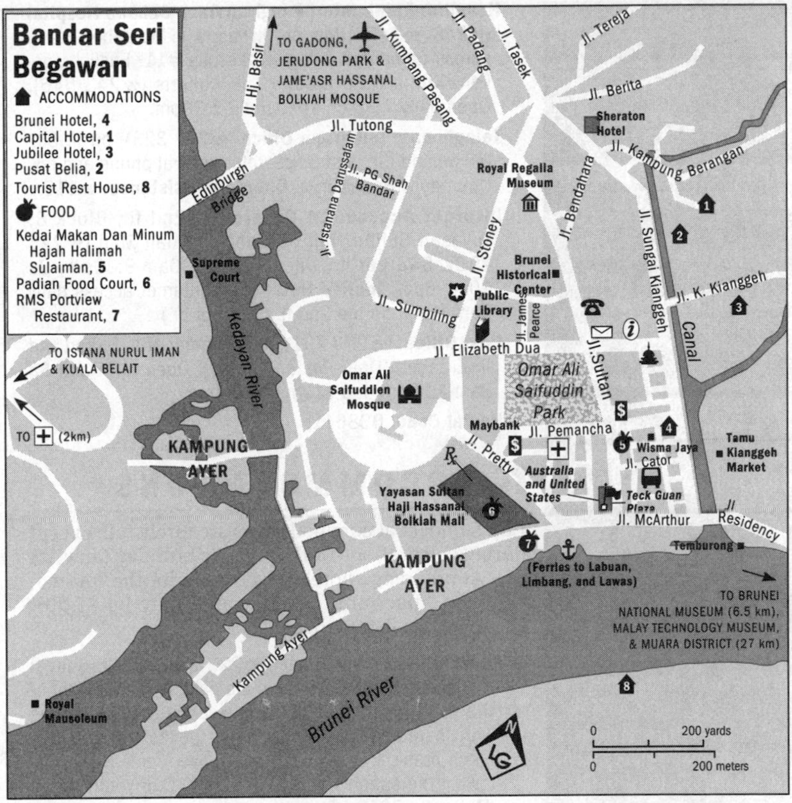

Open M-F 9am-5pm. **US,** 3rd fl., Teck Guan Plaza, Jl. Sultan (☎229 670). Open M-F 8am-4:30pm. **Vietnam,** House 16, Simpang 538-37-2. Jl. Kebangsaan Lama (☎343 167). Open M-Sa 8-10am and 2-4:30pm.

Currency Exchange: Hong Kong Bank (☎242 305), Jl. Sultan and Jl. Pemancha. Open M-F 9am-3pm, Sa 9-11am. Cirrus **ATM. Standard Chartered Bank,** 51-55 Jl. Sultan (☎242 386). Unlimited exchange B$15. Open M-F 9am-3pm, Sa 9-11am. Moneychangers can be found in every major shopping complex.

Markets: Tamu Kianggeh Market, on the opposite side of the canal from Jl. Sungai Kianggeh. Open daily 8am-6pm. **Pasar Malam** (night market), opposite the Sheraton Hotel on Jl. Tasek. Savory *satay* and good souvenirs. Small shops with basic provisions line the waterfront.

EMERGENCY AND COMMUNICATIONS

Emergency: ☎993. **Fire:** ☎995. **Ambulance:** ☎991.

Police: (☎242 334), on Jl. Stoney near the intersection with Jl. Elizabeth Dua.

Pharmacies: Guardian Pharmacy, Yayasan Sultan Haji Hassanal Bolkiah Mall, ground fl. Open daily 10am-9:45pm.

THE BIG SPLURGE

THE EMPIRE HOTEL AND COUNTRY CLUB

Billed as "the most distinctive and exclusive property in Asia today," the **Empire Hotel** ❺ lives up to its reputation. After eight years of construction and an estimated US$1.5 billion price tag, the hotel opened its doors in [redacted] to immense acclaim. [redacted] had it that the international hotel rating system would have to add a star.

The hotel's unmatched opulence is apparent as soon as the doormen do their job. The marble used in the intricate mosaic flooring was the last of its kind in the world; the Sultan bought out the reserve in Italy to finish the lobby.

On sunny days, light shines through the five-story atrium, refracts through chandeliers, and reflects off towers lined with genuine gold trim. Don't leave your sunglasses at home! As if the Empire needed more sumptuousness, a US$250,000 crystal camel graces the hotel lobby.

The 423 rooms, suites, and villas pamper guests at every corne[redacted]he deluxe rooms, the cheapest in the hotel, start at B$500 per night, offer a long list of luxurious amenities.

The executive suites start at B$1000 per night, and include myriad gold-plated touches, all necessary for a life of champagne kisses and caviar dreams.

(On the Muara-Tutong Highway, Kampong Jerudong. 418 888; www.empire.com.bn.)

Hospital: Rajah Isteri Pengiran Anak Saheha Hospital (RIPAS; ☎242 424), on Jl. Putera Al-Muhtadee Billah across Edinburgh Bridge. Take bus #11. English spoken. **Klinik Kuin Mee,** 72 Jl. Roberts (☎243 546). Open daily 7:30am-1pm and 2-5:30pm.

Telephones: Telegraph Office (☎222 323), on Jl. Sultan behind the post office. International phone and fax. Open daily 8am-10pm. **Directory Assistance:** ☎113.

internet Access: LA Cybercafe, 2nd fl., Block B, Yayasan Sultan Haji Hassanal Bolkiah Mall (☎225 298). B$3 per hr. Open M-Sa 9:30am-9:30pm, Su 10am-6pm. **Jubilee Hotel** offers Internet access daily 9am-10pm on the 2nd fl. (B$1 per hr.)

Post Office: (☎228 291), at the corner of Jl. Sultan and Jl. Elizabeth Dua. *Poste Restante.* Open M-Th and Sa 8am-4:30pm, F 8-11am and 2-4pm.

Postal Code: BS8611.

ACCOMMODATIONS

BSB's budget accommodations are rarely full, except during celebrations of the sultan's birthday (July 15-31). At mid-range hotels, always ask for the "promotion" or "discount" rates, which may be 25-30% cheaper than listed prices.

Pusat Belia (Youth Hostel; ☎222 900), on Jl. Sungai Kianggeh. With the canal on the right, it's to the right of the youth center. Clean, single-sex 4-bed A/C dorms with shared baths. Check in early; the staff takes a long lunch break. Curfew 10:30pm. Closed for 2 weeks following the sultan's birthday. Bring ISIC or youth hostel ID. Dorms B$13. ❶

Tourist Rest House, Ketua Kampong (☎202 140), across the river in Kampung Ayer. Take a boat from town (B$0.50) and head for the cream-colored building with a green roof. Clean rooms have A/C and breakfast. Check-out noon. B$22 per person. ❷

Jubilee Hotel, Jubilee Plaza, Jl. Kampung Kianggeh (☎228 070; jubilee@brunet.bn). Turn right past the temple; Jubilee is before Pusat Belia. Free breakfast, transport to and from the airport, Internet access, and cafe. Singles and doubles B$60. AmEx/MC/V. ❹

Capital Hotel, No. 7, Simpang 2, Jl. Kampung Berangan (☎223 561), behind Pusat Belia. Go down Jl. Sungai Kianggeh, right on Jl. Berangan, and right on Simpang 2. Laundry service. Weekly rates available. Singles B$55; doubles B$60. AmEx/MC/V. ❹

Brunei Hotel, 95 Jl. Pemancha (☎242 372), opposite the canal. Big rooms in the heart of the city for a relatively small price. Free breakfast, minibar, and satellite TV. Singles B$88; doubles B$99. AmEx/MC/V. ❺

FOOD

Near Pusat Belia, the **night market** behind the Chinese temple on Jl. Elizabeth Dua provides a selection of dishes and iced drinks (most items B$1). A similar night market sets up at the end of Jl. Sungai Kianggeh on the waterfront. (Both open daily sundown-midnight.) Pork-lovers and alcoholics be warned. As a strict Islamic state, Brunei follows a "no booze, no bacon" policy. Servers are often willing to oblige if you bring your own liquor; be prepared to pay a corkage fee at upscale establishments. **Kedai Makan Dan Minum Hajah Halimah Sulaiman ❶,** No. 34 Jl. Sultan, opposite the Hong Kong Bank on Jl. Pemancha, has generous servings of the best Indian and Malay fare around. (☎234 803. *Dosai* with chicken B$3.50. Open daily 6am-8pm.) In Block H, Yayasan Mall, **RMS Portview Restaurant ❸** serves up Brunei's best seafood. (☎231 465. Savory steamboats with fish, crab, vegetables, and noodles B$15 per person. Set menus include several courses B$26-30. Open daily 10am-2am. AmEx/MC/V.) On the first floor of the Yayasan Mall, **Padian Food Court ❶** offers Malay, Indian, Indonesian, and Chinese cuisine. (Most entrees B$3-5. Fresh squid soup B$12. Open daily 9am-9:30pm.) The Empire Hotel's poolside **Pantai Restaurant ❺** hosts sheikh-worthy barbecues for B$38 per person; choose from an array of succulent seafoods and meats for grilling and top off your meal with an elaborate dessert bar. Vegetarian and Western options available. (Open nightly 7-11pm. AmEx/MC/V.)

BRUNEI DARUSSALAM

SIGHTS

For those short on time, the best of Brunei can be seen via water taxi; ask for a 1hr. tour (negotiable; B$10-20).

OMAR ALI SAIFUDDIEN MOSQUE. Built in 1958 and costing US$500 million, this is the city's most visible landmark. Its golden dome—covered with 3.3 million pieces of Venetian glass mosaic—is only part of the grandeur. Italian marble and English stained glass dominate the interior. The replica 16th century royal barge in its manmade lagoon occasionally hosts Qur'an-reading competitions. Worshippers wash before entering at the fountain on the far side. Dress conservatively and remove shoes. *(On the west side of downtown; enter on Jl. Elizabeth Dua. Open M-W and Su 8am-noon, 1-3:30pm, and 4:30-5:30pm, F 4:30-5:30pm. Closed Th to non-Muslims.)*

KAMPUNG AYER AND ENVIRONS. Behind the mosque, **water villages** unfold along the Brunei River. This labyrinth of bright homes and restaurants sits on stilts above the water. Boardwalks link the neighborhoods of Kampung Ayer, but a less strenuous option is to explore the area by water taxi. Make sure the taxi driver goes to the newest residential development at the far end, where white cookie-cutter homes stand on concrete piles, in contrast to the rickety wooden structures closer to town. While barreling around the Brunei River, check out the **Persiaran Damuan,** a landscaped park across the river on Jl. Tutong; it offers the city's best view of the **Istana Nurul Iman,** the world's largest palace and residence of the sultan. Visitors are allowed inside the palace once a year—at the end of Ramadan. Surprise: more golden domes and marble await inside this grand building.

BRUNEI MUSEUM. His Majesty's Muslim art and artifacts, rescued from shipwrecks, exhibit the history of wealth in the sultanate. The collection has Qur'ans carved from sheets of gold and a shrine to the oil industry. *(6.5km east of BSB. Take bus #39 or an express bus to Muara. Open Su-Th 9:30am-5pm, F 9:30-11:30am and 2:30-5pm.)*

JAME'ASR HASSANAL BOLKIAH MOSQUE. This fancy mosque beckons worshippers, architecture enthusiasts, and tourists alike. Recently completed in commemoration of His Majesty's 25 years on the throne, Jame'Asr Hassanal Bolkiah Mosque, the largest in Brunei, trumps Omar Ali Saifuddien Mosque in every category. The sultan prays here on Fridays. Upon entry, remove your shoes and register at the security post. *(In Gadong. Take bus #21 or 22. Open M-W and Su 8am-noon, 1-1:30pm, and 4:30-5:30pm, F 4:30-5:30pm. Closed Th to non-Muslims.)*

ENTERTAINMENT

JERUDONG PARK PLAYGROUND. Even in alcohol-free Brunei nights don't have to be tame. **Jerudong Park Playground,** the greatest attraction in BSB and, perhaps, the country, delivers an adrenaline high to Bruneians and visitors alike. Rides like the **Giant Drop** and the exhilarating **Pusing Lagi** shoot passengers nearly 100m above the state-of-the-art amusement park. While airborne, guests are also privy to amazing views of the South China Sea. The less adventurous can enjoy the more mundane merry-go-round, bumper cars, and beautifully landscaped botanical gardens—all connected by a locomotive system. Each night, the spectacular "Dancing Fountain" laser show electrifies visitors with lurid lighting amidst 1216 nozzles spraying 20,000 gal. of water upward. A food court is next to the parking lot. Although the park was built in 1994 by the sultan as a gift to his people, the formerly free attraction began charging an admission fee during the 2001 season. (B$1, B$4 per ride.) Alternatively, visitors can purchase an unlimited pass, which includes admission and as many rides as you can stomach. (B$15, children B$5.) The cheapest option, which includes transportation, is to purchase an all-inclusive ticket (B$15) available from the Tourist Information Center one day in advance. Jerudong is beyond the Bandar city limits. *(Take bus #55 before 5pm and arrange for a PPP cab to take you back for B$25. The manager of Pusat Belia also takes groups of 4 for B$10. ☎ 261 2044; www.jerudong-park.com. Open W-F and Su 5pm-midnight, Sa 5pm-1am.)*

BRUNEI DARUSSALAM

OTHER ENTERTAINMENT. Outside BSB are a few scattered sights, all difficult to reach by public transportation. **Muara and Serasa beaches,** in Muara District, are considered Brunei's finest. Temburong District is home to **Ulu Temburong National Park, Peradayan Forest Recreational Park,** and the **Rainforest Field Studies Center (FSC)** at Kuala Belalong in Batu Apoi Forest Reserve. Travelers must go with a tour; **Freme Travel** (see **Tours,** p. 68) runs expeditions. (B$140, with rafting B$180; overnight tours start at B$220. 2-person min.)

CAMBODIA

HIGHLIGHTS OF CAMBODIA

CULTURAL HERITAGE. Amidst the vines and creatures of Cambodia's jungle, **Angkor**'s (p. 107) statues, temples and towers rise up, holding quiet dominion. These are arguably the most awe-inspiring sights in Southeast Asia—reason enough to visit Cambodia. The **Tuol Sleng Genocide Museum,** in Phnom Penh, attests to equally hair-raising human feats (p. 93), preserving the Khmer Rouge legacy of cruelty and horror.

HANGING OUT. The guesthouses and restaurants of **Phnom Penh** (p. 87) and **Siem Reap** (p. 104) attract a fun-loving bunch. Expats and locals fill the bars, sharing tips and experiences. Nature-lovers will enjoy quiet **Ban Lung** (p. 102), where tribespeople live in remote peace, tending to the rustic countryside.

BEACHES. The beaches of **Sihanoukville** (p. 96), with their fine white sand, affordable guesthouses, and delicious seafood, have only been discovered by the weekending Cambodian crowd. Deserted during the week, they're a great place to lounge in the sun, feel the sand in your toes, and experience the laid-back ease of today's Cambodia.

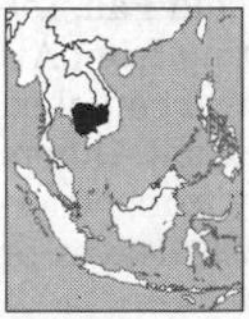

The story of modern Cambodia is a dark one, steeped in bloodshed and tragedy. It has been a thousand years since the god-kings of Angkor built their vast empire, and Cambodians still strive to recapture a sliver of their ancestors' glory. Nowadays, the classic five-column silhouette of Angkor Wat adorns countless products and logos, including a popular brand of beer ("Angkor: My Country, My Beer"). Still, such veneration of the past cannot hide the more gruesome realities of the present. North of Phnom Penh, a once graceful temple, lies in ruins—its central sanctuary pockmarked with bullet holes. Poverty dominates in Cambodian cities and villages, and implicitly in the country's faulty roads, schools, and public works. The relative stability of recent years is a welcome change from the constant civil war since the 1970s, but no one is celebrating just yet. The Khmer Rouge may be defunct, but political corruption, violence, massive unemployment, illiteracy, and landmines are its legacies. Perhaps one day Cambodia will leave this past behind, but for now it lingers, both a comfort and a curse.

FACTS AND FIGURES

Official Name: Kingdom of Cambodia.

Government: Multi-party democracy under a constitutional monarchy.

Capital: Phnom Penh.

Land Area: 176,520 km^2.

Geography: Borders Thailand, Laos, and Vietnam. River systems: Mekong, Bassac, Tonle Sap. Mountain ranges: Cardamom, Dangrek, Elephant.

Climate: Dry (high season) Dec.-Apr., rainy (low season) May-Nov.

Phone Codes: Country code: 855. International dialing prefix: 00.

Major Cities: Battambang, Siem Reap, Sihanoukville (Kompong Som).

Population: 13,124,754.

Language: Khmer (official), English, French.

Religion: Buddhism (95%), other (5%).

Literacy Rate: 69.9% overall; 80.5% of men, 60.3% of women.

Major Exports: Timber, coffee, tin, textiles, electricity, opium.

LIFE AND TIMES

DEMOGRAPHICS

Cambodia's pre-1975 population included **Khmer, Khmer Loeu** (upland Khmer hilltribes), and minority ethnic groups, including **Chinese, Vietnamese,** and **Cham** (Muslim Khmer). The Khmer Rouge genocide (see **Civil War and the Khmer Rouge,** p. 77), however, targeted minority populations, and Cambodia's population is now, consequently, almost 90 percent Khmer. The Chinese minority, which had been a large part of the merchant class in pre-Khmer Rouge Cambodia, is now rebounding. Hill-tribes such as the Pro, Krung, and Jarai eke out an existence through subsistence agriculture along the Lao and Vietnamese borders, but the growing logging industry threatens their lifestyle. The Vietnamese, known by the pejorative term *yuon*, remain subject to virulent racism.

LANGUAGE

Although the official language of Cambodia is **Khmer,** the country is functionally multilingual. Indigenous groups speak their own **tribal languages,** while **English** is spoken by young, educated, urban elites and people associated with the tourism industry. The older generation learned **French** under colonial rule, and **Chinese** is often the *de facto* language of business. Drawing on both Sanskrit and Pali, the Khmer language is ancient, with the earliest Khmer inscription dating from AD 612. Both Sanskrit and Khmer are used in inscriptions in the Angkor Wat complex. Aside from these, only three Khmer literary works are known to be extant. Others may have survived as folk legends that have been passed down orally from generation to generation, but since the ancient Khmer often wrote on *latina* leaves or animal skins, many documents and works of literature have been lost.

RELIGION

THERAVADA BUDDHISM. Introduced to Cambodia in the 12th century from Sri Lanka, Theravada Buddhism's anti-materialist teachings helped cause the decline of the ancient Angkor empire. Buddhist beliefs influence nearly all aspects of day-to-day life in Cambodia, and have become closely linked with the Khmer identity. Over 90% of the population identifies itself as Buddhist. Only about 500 monks managed to survive the Khmer Rouge's national purge, however, and today the link between Cambodian Buddhism and nationalism is weakening.

ISLAM. There are approximately 500,000 Muslims in Cambodia, mostly from the **Cham** and **Malay** minorities. The Cham combine Muslim beliefs with non-Islamic deities, and are staunch believers in the power of magic. Only 20 of the original 113 Cham clergy survived the Khmer Rouge, but today the community is growing—mostly due to the support of Wahabi (fundamentalist) Muslim countries like Saudi Arabia, and the aid of nearby Malaysia and Indonesia.

CHRISTIANITY. Since 1990, when Christianity was recognized as a legal religion in Cambodia, the Christian population has risen to approximately 60,000. Even Khieu Samphan, accused of the murders of 16,000 individuals under the Khmer Rouge, has become a born-again Christian. Some missionaries worry, however, that Cambodians are becoming only **"rice-bowl Christians,"** relying on the material benefits offered by the mission's aid programs rather than being true converts.

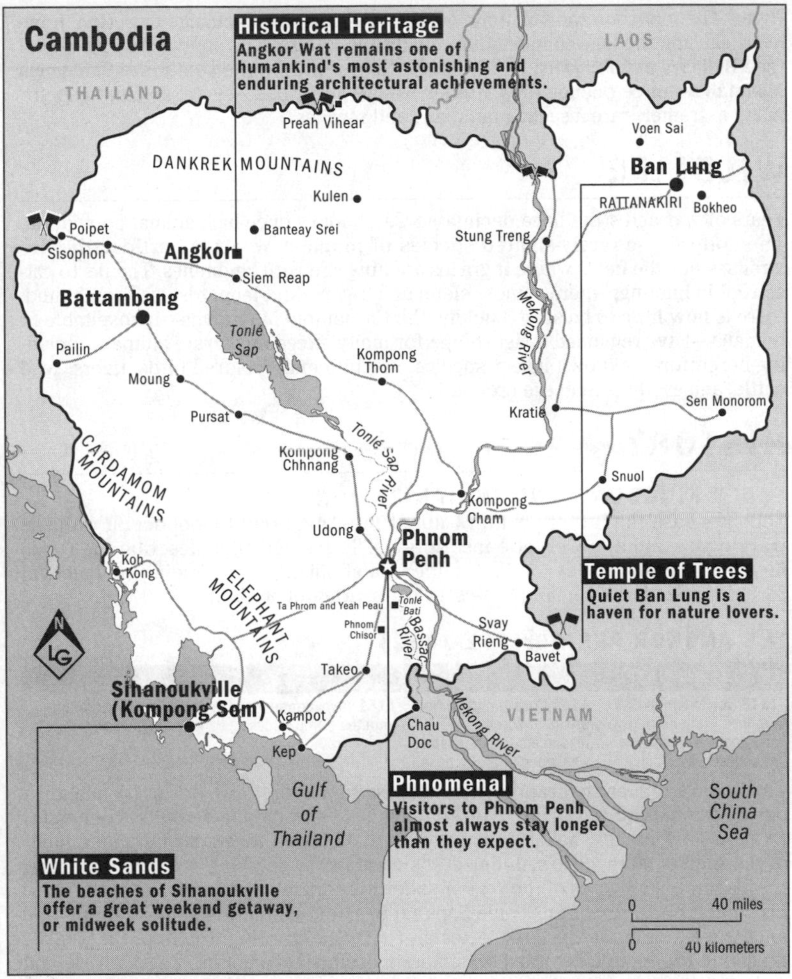

ANIMISM. Found predominantly in remote rural areas, these beliefs encompass **local deities** as well as **ancestral spirits,** and are passed down from generation to generation as part of an oral tradition. Charms and amulets (made by a *kru*, or sorcerer) are used to ward off evil spirits or to ensure good luck. Animism lies at the heart of many folk arts, including traditional Khmer medicine.

LAND

Cambodia's land is incredibly fertile. The **Tonle Sap,** the largest freshwater lake in Southeast Asia, provides an abundance of fish and natural irrigation for the area's rice growers. The Tonle Sap is also the only waterway in the world in which the current flows in different directions depending on the time of year. From November to May, the water from the Tonle Sap flows as expected, into the Mekong

River. The monsoon rains in June force the Tonle Sap to change direction, however, causing the lake to more than quadruple in size. The annual Water Festival (see **Holidays and Festivals,** p. 82) marks this event. To the south, the **Cardamom Mountains**—once occupied by Khmer Rouge guerrillas—serve as sanctuary for many extremely rare insects, mammals, and reptiles.

WILDLIFE

Years of war and strife have decimated Cambodia's once-lush animal population. The kouprey—a rarely-sighted species of jungle-cow—is in particularly dire straits, since the fields where it grazes are now rife with landmines. Thanks to catastrophic hunting, where rhinos, elephants, tigers, and leopards used to abound, there is now little to be seen. Luckily, the Cardamom Mountains—inhospitable to humans—have remained a last refuge for many exceedingly rare animals, including heretofore unknown insect species, magnificently colored birds, tigers, wild cattle, and even the Siamese crocodile.

HISTORY

EARLY KINGDOMS AND INDIANIZATION

Scholars base the little they know about pre-Angkorian Cambodia on Chinese travelogues and a few cryptic inscriptions. These accounts describe the **Funan Kingdom** (AD 100-500) as the first unified Cambodian polity. Trading contacts led to an **Indianization** of Khmer politics, religion, art, and literature.

THE ANGKOR PERIOD (802-1432)

IMPORTANT DATES			
1113 Suryavarman II expands Khmer territory and goes on a massive wat-construction binge.	**1177** Construction binge drains national resources; Cham invade weakened Kambujadesa.	**1181** Jayavarman VII reunites Kambujadesa.	**1200** Construction on Angkor Thom begins.

Cambodia's Khmer civilization (**Kambujadesa** in inscriptions) was at its mightiest during this period, towering over its neighbors and drawing tribute from as far away as present-day Thailand, Myanmar, and Malaysia. **Jayavarman II,** the founder of the Angkor state, declared himself its **devaraja,** or god-king, ruthlessly bringing the disparate kingdoms of the region under his control. Eventually, he established his capital northeast of the Tonle Sap and began constructing the mammoth temple complex of **Angkor** (p. 110). A testament to the dazzling wealth of the Angkor kingdom, the temple complex was made possible by a boom in agriculture and technological advancements. Later rulers struggled to maintain the glory achieved under Jayavarman II, and the kingdom's wealth waxed and waned. Under **Suryavarman II,** for example, Khmer territory expanded again, and construction of Angkor Wat increased, this time sapping the country of its strength and leaving it vulnerable to Cham invasions in 1177. In 1181, **Jayavarman VII** reunited the kingdom and instituted an ambitious public works program. Following his death, Kambujadesa suffered a slow decline, its territory steadily encroached upon by the Thai and Lao. In 1431, the Thai Ayutthaya Kingdom claimed the capital, Angkor Thom.

POST-ANGKOR COLONIALISM (1431-1945)

IMPORTANT DATES		
1594 Thais sack Angkor.	**1863** French establish a protectorate in Cambodia and kick off 90 years of colonial rule.	**1941** Playboy Prince Norodom Sihanouk comes to power as supposed "puppet king" but surprises everyone.

Referred to as "Cambodia's Dark Ages," the five centuries following the sack of Angkor were blighted by stagnation and decay. In the mid-15th century, the country's capital shifted from Angkor to **Phnom Penh,** a trade hub at the confluence of the Mekong, Tonle Sap, and Bassac Rivers, bringing Cambodia into greater contact with the outside world. By the 19th century Cambodia was caught between its ambitious and mutually antagonistic neighbors, Vietnam and Thailand. Each invaded Cambodian territory several times, and may well have swallowed the country up permanently were it not for French colonists who established a protectorate there in 1863. Colonialism, of course, took its toll: heavy taxes, onerous *corvée* labor, and paltry funding for education and social welfare weighed heavily on the long-beleaguered nation. By the 1930s, an emerging educated elite in Phnom Penh responded with the first stirrings of Cambodian nationalism, recalling the pride of Angkor and Cambodia's past. Co-opted by the French, Cambodian kings were content to collaborate with colonists. Thinking they had selected a pliant puppet, the French placed **Norodom Sihanouk** on the throne in 1941. Equal parts playboy and patriot, Sihanouk surprised them by agitating for independence.

INDEPENDENCE (1945-1970)

IMPORTANT DATES			
1945 US B-29s bomb Phnom Penh.	**1953** Pol Pot returns to Cambodia from France; Sihanouk declares Cambodian independence.	**1965** Sihanouk breaks off relations with US and allows North Vietnamese to set up bases in Cambodia.	**1970** Vietnam War leads to US invasion of Cambodia.

Cambodian independence came in stages, without the drama and bloodshed of the Vietnamese war against the French. French attempts to romanize the Khmer language—giving it western letters and standardized pronunciation—outraged nationalistically inclined Khmers, and spurred the formation of pro-independence groups like the **Khmer Issarak (Free Khmer)** party. In 1949, the French signed a treaty granting Cambodia limited sovereignty, and complete independence followed peacefully in 1953. The next decade belonged to Sihanouk, who rose to the challenge of leading an independent people, with strong domestic and foreign policies. In the end, however, Sihanouk's careful focus and neutrality were thwarted, as the war in South Vietnam sent shock waves throughout the region. Sihanouk gave the North Vietnamese tacit permission to use Cambodia as a sanctuary and staging ground for their operations in South Vietnam. Desperate to eliminate the Viet Cong sanctuaries, US military commanders requested permission from the Nixon White House (and, some say, from Sihanouk) to begin a series of secret, devastating bombing campaigns over Cambodia—eventually invading the country outright in 1970, planting mines that continue to haunt its inhabitants.

CIVIL WAR AND THE KHMER ROUGE (1970-1975)

IMPORTANT DATES	
1970 Khmer Rouge control most of the country.	**1975** Khmer Rouge occupy Phnom Penh; Pol Pot founds Democratic Kampuchea (DK) and declares the Year Zero.

The **Khmer People's Revolutionary Party (KPRP)** began picking up steam in the 1950s, drawing support from leftist Khmer Issarak members and Khmer students returning from study in France. Among these ambitious students, known as the **"Paris Circle,"** was Saloth Sar—better known as **Pol Pot,** mastermind of the Cambodian genocides. He had studied engineering in Paris but spent most of his time reading Rousseau and attending Stalinist discussion groups. Poor grades necessitated his return to Cambodia in the early 1950s, and set in motion his rapid rise to power. The Marxist revolutionary movement renamed itself the **Communist Party of Kampuchea (CPK),** known popularly as the **Khmer Rouge.** Led by Pol Pot, it steadily expanded its influence until it had almost a quarter of the country's votes; in March 1970, Cambodia's Prime Minister, the US-backed General **Lon Nol,** deposed Sihanouk in a bloodless coup. At this time, the Khmer Rouge only grew more rapidly, accruing territory with abandon until April 1975, when Pol Pot's forces marched into Phnom Penh and declared the founding of **Democratic Kampuchea (DK).** The Khmer Rouge leadership quickly set about to transform Cambodia into a self-sufficient agrarian utopia, and Pol Pot, a shadowy figure whose true identity few knew, declared that the present day **"Year Zero,"** would mark the beginning of a massive restructuring of Cambodian society.

DEMOCRATIC KAMPUCHEA (1975-1979)

IMPORTANT DATES			
1975 Khmer Rouge evacuate Cambodians from cities and put them to work in the countryside.	**1975-79** Cambodian genocide engineered by Khmer Rouge kills millions.	**1978** Vietnamese invasion finally ends Khmer Rouge power.	**1979** Pro-Hà Nội government installed with Hun Sen appointed prime minister.

In 1975 the Khmer Rouge ordered the evacuation of all the country's cities, as part of its effort to purify Cambodian society. Phnom Penh's transition was especially wrenching, as its two million residents fled into US bombing in the countryside, and were relocated to slave labor camps. The government abolished money and systematically eradicated all vestiges of pre-revolutionary society, including 5857 schools, 796 hospitals, conservatories and laboratories, 1968 Buddhist pagodas, and 104 mosques—not to mention the teachers, doctors, monks, and artists who worked there. Anyone suspected of being educated—as evidenced by wearing glasses or speaking a foreign language, for example—was shot or clubbed to death and then buried in a mass grave. Under the Khmer Rouge, an estimated 1.7 million people (approximately one-fifth of the 1975 population) were either murdered, or perished of malnutrition and disease. Consumed by ideals of ethnic purity, the Khmer Rouge turned their hatred on Cambodia's perennial enemy, the Vietnamese, whom they blamed for the post-Angkor decline of the Khmer nation. Raids on Vietnamese border villages provoked a Vietnamese invasion of Cambodia in December 1978. Two weeks later, Vietnamese forces seized Phnom Penh and instituted the **People's Republic of Kampuchea (PRK),** a pro-Hà Nội regime. Pol Pot and his followers carried on their struggle from jungle strongholds along the Thai-Cambodian border, supporting themselves through timber and gem smuggling.

FOREIGN INTERVENTION AND HUN SEN'S COUP (1979-1997)

IMPORTANT DATES				
1980 US places embargo and recognizes Khmer Rouge as Cambodian government.	**1991** Paris Peace Accords; UNTAC tries unsuccessfully to resolve internal conflict.	**1993** Elections result in shaky coalition government.	**1994** Thousands of Khmer Rouge guerrillas surrender in response to government amnesty.	**1997** Hun Sen seizes control of government in coup.

Led by **Heng Samrin** and **Hun Sen** (the prime minister), the PRK struggled to rebuild Cambodia's shattered nationhood, but countryside guerrilla warfare hampered their efforts. Making matters worse, the US, which recognized the Khmer Rouge as the legitimate government of Cambodia, engineered an embargo that further stifled recovery, and fermented economic strife. For a while, it seemed that things were beginning to look up for the troubled nation in September 1989. The Vietnamese announced a unilateral withdrawal of their forces from Cambodia, and cleared the way for the 1991 Paris Peace Accords. Furthermore, the UN oversaw the **United Nations Transitional Authority in Cambodia (UNTAC),** an ambitious mission to resolve the civil war and hold elections. In reality, however, UNTAC would prove an embarrassing fiasco; the UN failed to disarm the Khmer Rouge, which, rather than participating in the peace process, marred the elections with intimidation and violence. The May 1993 election resulted in a shaky coalition between Prince Norodom Ranariddh's **United Front for an Independent, Neutral, Peaceful, and Cooperative Cambodia (FUNCINPEC)** and Hun Sen's **Cambodia People's Party (CPP).** But the two factions were never more than uneasy partners, and the Khmer Rouge continued to wage war from border-area strongholds. Eventually, Hun Sen seized sole control of the government in a July 1997 coup, and Ranariddh went into exile.

CAMBODIA TODAY

CAMBODIA

KHMER ROUGE TRIALS. Pol Pot, held under house arrest from 1997 until his death in early 1998, defiantly declared, "My conscience is clear," to the fury (but not the surprise) of genocide survivors. While many former Khmer Rouge officials stuck amnesty deals with the Cambodian government in the 1990s, strides have been made to hold the regime's leaders accountable. Two senior leaders, **Ta Mok** (nicknamed "The Butcher") and **Kang Kek Ieu** (known better as **Duch**), were arrested in the spring of 1999. The latter had been Pol Pot's security chief and head of **Tuol Sleng** (codenamed **S-21**), one of Southeast Asia's largest genocidal prisons. Duch was discovered in remote western Cambodia, a born-again Christian relief worker living under the assumed name of **Hong Pin.** Former DK Head of State **Khieu Samphan** abandoned the Khmer Rouge just before its collapse and still lives freely in Pailin, where he supports his family by tending ducks; he denies involvement with any killings and has not been charged with war crimes or genocide. In 2001, after prodding from the UN, US, Australia, and UK, legislation was approved to establish a **war crimes tribunal** for those accused of genocide. Unfortunately, Sihanouk's legislation was unacceptable to the UN, and fearing that international standards of justice could not be guaranteed in the tribunal proposed by Cambodia, the UN withdrew its support altogether. In defense of Cambodia's proposal, Hun Sen asserted that, if mismanaged, these trials could incite further civil war; cynics, however, note that the prime minister has a vested interest in keeping important political allies out of jail. Hun Sen is just one of several government officials with a Khmer Rouge background, but he has not been charged with any crimes. While 2002 saw a revived interest in holding war crimes trials, a hotly contested July election—and subsequent government deadlock—put Khmer Rouge justice on hold yet again. Since June 2003, the government's two rival parties, Prime Minister Hun Sen's Cambodian People's Party and the royalist FUNCINPEC party, have bickered for controlling interest in the Cambodian governing bodies. Budget estimates for the trials also loom over the Cambodian people, already suffering from extensive poverty.

LANDMINES. Over 25 years of civil war have left Cambodia with many sad legacies, perhaps the most devastating being the six to ten million anti-personnel mines strewn about the countryside. If you stray far from Phnom Penh, you're bound to see warning signs. There are also 500,000 tons of unexploded ordnance (UXO) that the US dropped during the Vietnam War. In 1996, demining groups estimated that, at the current rate, it will take nearly 300 years to clear the fields. In December 1997, a Japanese company introduced Mine Eye, a new landmine sensor that is able to differentiate between mines and scrap metal. If contributions continue to increase, CMAC may clear the fields within 10 or 20 years. For now, however, never stray from appropriately marked paths when traveling outside touristed centers.

FROM KILLING FIELDS TO CHILLING FIELDS. The year 2004 saw robust growth in Cambodia's tourism industry, which had previously been stymied by the decrease in tourist travel after the September 11 attacks on the US. Especially in **Siem Reap** (the gateway city to **Angkor Wat**), hotel construction has risen to unprecedented rates. In a somewhat symbolic gesture, Cambodia is in the process of converting Pol Pot's jungle hideout at **Anlong Veng** as well as Ta Mok's opulent home into tourist resorts. These attractions come hot on the heels of other Khmer Rouge sites turned tourist destinations, including the **Killing Fields,** the main execution grounds for the Khmer Rouge, and S-21, a high school that the Khmer Rouge converted into a secret interrogation center. Due to its imminent decay, Cambodian tourism officials dismantled the legendary S-21 **"skull map,"** a wall-size map of Cambodia made of the skulls of 300 prisoners executed under the Khmer Rouge; in its place, the museum has erected a Buddhist shrine. For slightly different reasons, conservationists have also been hard at work on the Angkor temple complex, making replicas of the statues and replacing the originals, which are now housed in an obscure storage warehouse near Siem Reap. For centuries, the international stolen art market has been flooded with Khmer carvings; nowadays, **Angkor Conservancy** is trying to force art thieves to flood this market with fakes. In general, visitors will enjoy a laid-back attitude and a warm welcome in Cambodia today. Hospitality, curiosity, and friendliness emanate from its people, who have risen above this immense hardship to make Cambodia a better place.

CUSTOMS AND ETIQUETTE

TABOOS. Cambodia is often considered less fervent about Buddhist doctrine than its neighbors. However, the basics still hold: don't point your feet toward people or images of the Buddha, don't touch people on the head (the head is sacred), don't lose your calm in public. Unlike the rest of Southeast Asia, shorts and t-shirts are accepted at some Cambodian temples. Note that crossing one's fingers, considered a sign of good luck in many Western countries, is considered obscene in Cambodia. Similarly obscene is the use of one's left hand; always use both hands or the right one only when passing something.

DINING RULES. In Cambodia, as in the rest of Asia, natives always have tea on hand. Coffee, brought to Cambodia by the French, is quite sweet (it's customary to add sweetened condensed milk to it). Typically, it is most polite to use chopsticks, a spoon, or your fingers to eat. As always, take cues from the locals around you. If invited to dine with a Cambodian family, bring a token of your appreciation—a small gift, decoration, or hard-to-find food item.

Development and Deforestation

1945, 75% of Southeast Asia was covered by rest. By 1995, the number had dropped to 25%, d logging has continued to accelerate in the maining forests. Experts predict that the gion will shortly become characterized by nall islands of forest surrounded by vast seas developed land and agriculture. They expect at more than 40% of the plant and animal spe-es in the region will be extinct by the end of is century.

Colonial deforestation marked the beginning unsustainable land management in Southeast ia, but it was minor compared to post-colonial forestation. Following WWII and successful colonization, Southeast Asian countries were disarray, without social allegiances, and reatened by civil war. In warring countries, mil-ry logging and American defoliating agents curred major environmental damage. In "sta-e" nations (dictatorships), national and multi-tional corporations took the place of colonial terprises, selling the same natural resources to e same places.

These corporations were largely Asian-owned, eled with foreign investment, and operating in litically irresponsible environments. Southeast ian leaders rapidly privatized public resources d gave incentives for logging, mining, and low-nd monoculture. In many cases, they were quired or induced to do so by the IMF and orld Bank as part of structural adjustment poli-es and loan conditionalities. The ostensible al was to create foreign exchange earnings to pay loans and to create a climate conducive to reign investment.

By the early 1970s, Southeast Asia had come the main source of the tropical timber ade. Booming demand for wood from urban tes in East Asia and certain parts of Southeast ia added to existing demand in Europe and nerica, and the market took off. By around 90, countries including Thailand and Malaysia d cleared their forests for export, yet were aking in domestic demand. Southeast Asian-vned corporations became multi-national as ey moved into countries and took advantage of rrupt and impoverished governance to wipe t forests. In Cambodia, one of the last large vaths of lowland evergreen forest has come der attack from logging interests. Of particu-r concern has been the rapid depletion of resin ees, because local indigenous communities harvest the resin sustainably to be sold for commercial uses. Increased pressures on the ecosystem caused the Cambodian government to revoke the license of one logging company, the Malaysian GAT corporation, in 2002, signalling that they would begin to take forest management more seriously.

Everyone from the World Bank to local governments is now paying lip service to conservation, but a precedent for destruction has been set and is out of control. In Indonesia, the pulp and paper industries have grown by nearly 700 percent in the last 20 years, fueling a rapid rise in the demand for raw timber. Experts estimate that on the island of Sumatra, 60% of the total forestland has been destroyed over the century. The conspicuous lack of management policies and the demand of pulp mills, which have difficulty distinguishing between legal and illegal sources of timber, have contributed mightily to the problem. The World Bank predicted in a 2001 study that all of Sumatra's lowland forests will be gone by the end of 2005, and if significant countermeasures are not taken, all of Indonesia will be deforested by 2015. Still, there is some hope: deforestation has reportedly slowed a bit in recent years due to market forces, and the Indonesian government has begun to take a more conservationist stance. In August 2004, Tesso Nilo, one of the most fought-over tracts of Sumatran forest, was designated a national park.

Nevertheless, as each nation's post-colonial rulers strive to "develop," they sell what they have—forest resources. The hope is to grow rich enough to repay their debt to already wealthy nations. The beneficiaries of this giant harvest are only a small, urban elite. The majority of the population lives in nearly the exact same way it has been for hundreds of years, or worse. Once the "developing" country has generated a large enough class of educated urban elites who can produce other export products beyond trees, like household products and semi-conductors, they demand houses and furniture of their own, but the trees are gone. So the logging companies move elsewhere, paying a small, powerful group of, say, Cambodians, for their national forests. The result is that Cambodia, a 2000-year-old civilization that has always relied on the products of its forests, has lost half of its resources in less than 20 years.

Joshua Levin is a graduate of Harvard University and a former researcher-writer for Let's Go China. *Joshua most recently worked for Conservation International in Cambodia. He has designed an environmental education program for military personnel in Cambodia and has volunteered for an education NGO in Indonesia.*

PUBLIC BEHAVIOR. Always ask permission before taking someone's picture—especially before photographing monks and villagers in remote areas who may not have much exposure to Westerners and their cameras. Keep your social place in mind when interacting with Cambodians; it is not polite to make eye contact with those who are older than or socially superior to you.

CAMBODIAN COOKING. The staples of every Cambodian meal are rice and fish. You'll find that lemon grass, hot peppers, ginger, and mint flavor most dishes. Meat is a rare find in Cambodia for many reasons, and is usually used only as a an accent to vegetables. The French *baguette* is ubiquitous, as are vermin-based delicacies; don't be surprised to see plates heaped high with giant fried spiders.
Prohoc: a rite of passage for the Westerner: rotten fish is left to ferment further before it is added to rice as a paste; it has a strong flavor.
Amok: fish cooked in coconut milk.
Num ansom: cylinder cake, for special celebrations.
Non kaom: sweet coconut sticky-rice cake. Cambodian desserts are very sweet.
Samlaw misur: noodle soup.

ARTS AND RECREATION

Because of the destruction wrought on Cambodian cultural traditions under Pol Pot and the Khmer Rouge, there's a dearth of artistic professionals in Cambodia today; however, those who survived are catalyzing a cultural renaissance.

ARCHITECTURE. The **Angkor Wat** temple complex near Siem Reap is, without a doubt, one of the world's most marvelous architectural gems. Built in accordance with Hindu mythology—which states that the gods live on top of five mountains including central Mt. Meru, surrounded by the cosmic ocean—the structure consists of four smaller towers and one prominent one, as well as a surrounding moat. Buildings in today's towns are built on stilts to prevent flooding and infestation by insects during the monsoon season.

WEAVING. Handed down by women from generation to generation, Khmer weaving incorporates intricate patterns and mythological scenes into its cloth designs. During its cultural crackdown, the Khmer Rouge destroyed the mulberry trees that house the silk worms used in production, effectively destroying the trade. Today, however, thanks to the efforts of NGOs, the trees are being replanted, and Cambodians are being encouraged to again take up weaving as a source of income.

HOLIDAYS AND FESTIVALS (2005)

DATE	NAME	DESCRIPTION
Jan. 7	Victory Day	Commemorates the fall of the Khmer Rouge in 1979.
Mid-Apr. (lunar)	Bonn Chaul Chnam (Cambodian New Year's Festival)	Spans 3 days after the end of the harvest season during which Cambodians douse each other with water and clean their homes.
May 16	Visaka Buja Day	Commemorates the birth of the Buddha.
Late May (lunar)	Bonn Chroat Preah Nongkoal (Royal Ploughing Ceremony)	Commemorates the beginning of the planting season.
Jun. 18	Queen's Birthday	Parades and a festive atmosphere mark this day.
Late Oct. (lunar)	Bonn Dak Ben & Pchum Ben	Day to remember and honor ancestors; families bring offerings of food to the local wat and prepare for the afterlife.

CAMBODIA

DATE	NAME	DESCRIPTION
Oct. 30	King's Birthday	People from all over the country converge on Phnom Penh to enjoy the fireworks, parades, and festivals.
Nov. 9	Independence Day (from France)	Parade in front of Royal Palace in Phnom Penh.
Mid-Nov. (lunar)	Bonn Om Touk Water Festival	Marks the reversal of the current in the Tonle Sap. Celebration includes boat races and fireworks.
Dec. 10	UN Human Rights Day	Cambodia's recent past lends a particular poignancy to this international holiday.

ADDITIONAL RESOURCES

GENERAL HISTORY

Cambodia, Pol Pot, and the United States: A Faustian Pact, by Michael Haas (1991). An exhaustive examination of the disastrous US foreign policy in Cambodia.

The Civilization of Angkor, by Charles Higham (2001). A look at Khmer civilization at its high point.

FICTION AND NON-FICTION

Cambodia: Report from a Stricken Land, by Henry Kamm (1999). An explanation of modern Cambodia's political instability as a legacy of the Khmer Rouge genocide.

Children of Cambodia's Killing Fields: Memoirs by Survivors, by Kim Depaul, Ben Kiernan, and Dith Pran, eds. (1999). A series of moving eyewitness accounts of the Khmer Rouge atrocities.

The Stones Cry Out: A Cambodian Childhood 1975-1980, by Molyda Szymusiak. Trans. Linda Coverdale (1999). A fascinating first-person narrative highlighting the hypocrisy in Khmer Rouge rhetoric and Khmer Rouge action.

TRAVEL BOOKS

The Ends of the Earth: From Togo to Turkmenistan, from Iran to Cambodia, a Journey to the Frontiers of Anarchy, by Robert Kaplan (1997). A pessimistically realistic look at what the future might have in store for us.

Off the Rails in Phnom Penh: Into the Dark Heart of Guns, Girls, and Ganja, by Amit Gilboa (1998). A gripping travel narrative about the legacy of 3 decades of civil strife.

FILMS

The Killing Fields, dir. Roland Joffé (1984). A moving drama based on the real-life relationship between a *New York Times* reporter and his Khmer assistant, this film portrays the atrocities of the Khmer Rouge regime. One of the best war stories around.

ESSENTIALS

CAMBODIA PRICE ICONS					
SYMBOL:	❶	❷	❸	❹	❺
ACCOMM.	Under US$3 Under 12,000r	US$3-7 12,000-28,000r	US$7-12 28,000-48,000r	US$12-20 48,000-80,000r	Over US$20 Over 80,000r
FOOD	Under US$2 Under 8000r	US$2-4 8000-16,000r	US$4-8 16,000-32,000r	US$8-12 32,000-48,000r	Over US$12 Over 48,000r

EMBASSIES AND CONSULATES

CAMBODIAN CONSULAR SERVICES ABROAD

Australia: Embassy, 5 Canterbury Cres., Deakin, Canberra, ACT 2600 (☎02 6273 1259; embassyofcambodia.org.nz/au.htm). Also accredited to **New Zealand** (to which no Cambodian embassy is formally accredited).

France: Embassy, 4 Rue Adolphe Yvon, 75116 Paris (☎33 1 4503 4720; fax: 33 1 4503 4740). Also recommended for citizens of **Ireland** and the **UK** (to which no Cambodian embassy is formally accredited).

Thailand: No. 185 Rajddamri Rd., Lumpini Patumwan, Bangkok 10330 (☎662 2 546630; fax 662 2 539859; recbkk@cscoms.com)

US: Embassy, 4530 16th St. NW, Washington, DC 20011 (☎202-726-7742; www.embassy.org/cambodia). Also recommended for citizens of **Canada** (to which no Cambodian embassy is formally accredited).

CONSULAR SERVICES IN CAMBODIA

Australia: Embassy, Villa 11, St. 254, Daun Penh District, Phnom Penh (☎23 213 470; http://www.embassy.gov.au/kh.html). Also provides consular services to Canadians.

Canada: Embassy, St. 254, Sangkat Chaktamouk, Daun Penh District, Phnom Penh (☎23 426 000; www.dfait-maeci.gc.ca/cambodia/). For consular services, except if in need of an emergency passport, use the Australian Embassy in Phnom Penh (see above). In case of an after hours emergency, those in need of assistance should call the **Emergency Operations Center** in Ottawa (☎613-996-8885).

UK: Embassy, #27-29, St. 75, Phnom Penh (☎23 427 124; www.britishembassy.gov.uk/cambodia).

US: Embassy, 16, St. 228 (between Street 51 and 63), Phnom Penh (☎23 216 436; http://usembassy.state.gov/cambodia/).

CAMBODIA

TOURIST SERVICES

There are several tourism offices throughout Cambodia. For more information, visit www.visit-mekong.com/cambodia/mot/.

DOCUMENTS AND FORMALITIES

Foreigners entering Cambodia must have valid passports and visas, and passports should be valid for at least four months after date of entry. Note that a visa's validity period begins at date of issue, *not* after a traveler's date of entry. International consulates issue one-month visas for US$20, and two-month extensions cost US$45; allow three business days for processing. Thirty-day tourist visas are available at **Pochentong International Airport** in Phnom Penh (p. 87) or **Siem Reap Airport** in Siem Reap (p. 104) upon arrival for US$20. Those traveling overland from Vietnam can apply for same-day visas (US$30) in Hồ Chí Minh City at the Cambodian Consulate. The Cambodian Embassy in Bangkok issues 30-day visas (US$20, 2-day processing); many travel agencies can secure visas in one day. The Cambodian Embassy in Vientiane can also supply visas (US$20; 1-day processing), and **extensions** are available through the Immigration Office in Phnom Penh at No. 5, St. 200. Beware of scams when obtaining visas at border crossings; drivers may exhort you to obtain visas with their aid. It is easier and cheaper to do it yourself.

MONEY

CURRENCY AND EXCHANGE

The currency chart below is based on August 2004 exchange rates between local currency and Australian dollars (AUS$), Canadian dollars (CDN$), European Union euros (EUR€), New Zealand dollars (NZ$), British pounds (UK£), and US dollars (US$). Check the currency converter on websites like www.xe.com or www.bloomberg.com or a large newspaper for the latest exchange rates.

CURRENCY (R)

AUS$1 = 2088.21R	1000R = AUS$0.48
CDN$1 = 2446.62R	1000R = CDN$0.41
EUR€1 = 3746.86R	1000R = EUR0€0.27
NZ$1 = 1791.04R	1000R = NZ$0.56
UK£1 = 5948.75R	1000R = UK£0.17
US$1 = 3815.80R	1000R = US$0.26

The Cambodian **riel (R)** comes in denominations of 50, 100, 200, 500, 1000, and 10,000R notes. It's usually not necessary to exchange a lot of money because US dollars and Thai baht are widely accepted. If you pay in either currency, you'll be given change in Cambodian riel. Small denominations of riel are helpful for small expenses such as cab or motorcycle rides (note that coins are frowned upon, and almost never accepted by locals). **Tipping** is not necessary but appreciated. A tip of around 2500R is appropriate for moto and cyclo drivers, and at less expensive restaurants. Credit cards are not widely accepted, and there are no **ATMs** in Cambodia. Traveler's checks and US dollars can be exchanged, and most banks (in Phnom Penh and other cities) and local moneychangers often have decent rates.

GETTING THERE

BY PLANE. Cambodia has two **international airports:** Pochentong International Airport in Phnom Penh (p. 87) and Siem Reap Airport (p. 104). The country has no national airline, but several Southeast Asian airlines such as **Silk Air, Bangkok Airways, Thai Airways, Lao Airlines,** and **Vietnam Airlines** also fly into these airports. **Air France** also flies into Phnom Penh.

GETTING AROUND

Inexpensive daily **flights** connect all of Cambodia's major cities. **Boats** are a fairly safe, pleasant option for travel between Phnom Penh and Siem Reap and along the Mekong River. Roads in Cambodia, except for the road from Kompong Cham to Phnom Penh and the road from Phnom Penh to Sihanoukville, are lined with pot holes—take a boat wherever possible. When traveling overland and in remote regions, **4WD pick-ups** are the best bet, servicing every corner of the country. **Motorcycles** are ubiquitous, and although safety is suspect and helmets are rare, almost every visitor finds himself on the back of a motorcycle at some point. Foreigners should avoid public transportation whenever possible; **private bus lines** run between Phnom Penh and major cities. Hiring a **shared taxi** is a smart option for border crossings; it's cheaper than flying and more secure than taking a bus.

LAOS. The border crossing between **Stung Treng** (p. 101) in northern Cambodia and **Don Khong** in southern Laos is open to those willing to pay US$20 to cross, but is still unpredictable. Check with your embassy, and be sure to have a valid visa *before* you go, as they are not available upon arrival.

THAILAND. Boats run regularly from Sihanoukville (p. 96) to Trat. From Siem Reap, trucks take travelers through Sisophon to the border at Aranyaprathet/Poipet (p. 708). The 7hr. overland route is uncomfortable and bumpy, and during the rainy season muddy roads sometimes make the route impassable. Visas are available, but travelers should consider getting them in advance, in order to avoid potential hassles.

VIETNAM. Buses, minivans, and rickety share-taxis head from **Phnom Penh** through **Bavet (Svay Rieng)** to **Mộc Bài (Tây Ninh),** Vietnam. From here, travelers can continue to Saigon. The ferry that departs from **Chau Doc** crosses the border at **Vinh Xuong** and is well worth it for a trip through the Mekong Delta. The trip to the Vietnamese border takes 4-5hr. Boats also make the trip from Phnom Penh to the Vietnamese border; from there, another boat or bus will take you to HCMC. Visas available.The third crossing, which has recently opened, is 25km west of Chau Doc at **Tinh Bien.** You must have a Cambodian visa to cross here. You can reach the crossing by taxi or hire a motorbike and driver.

HEALTH AND SAFETY

EMERGENCY NUMBERS: Police/Fire/Ambulance: ☎ 119.

HEALTH RISKS. Malaria is omnipresent in Cambodia; take a trusted brand of antimalarial drugs, and beware of fake medications hawked by many merchants. Wearing a strong insect repellent helps, since Cambodia's insect army also spreads Dengue fever, tick-borne encephalitis, Japanese encephalitis, Lyme disease, and yellow fever. Water is also a major concern for travelers in the countryside. Dangerous parasites and bacteria abound in streams and rivers (especially in the Mekong Delta), so only drink purified and filtered water. Getting serious medical attention means heading to Phnom Penh or even Bangkok—the only places in the region where hospital facilities are halfway decent.

GLBT. There is little or no openly gay life in Cambodia. Rumors of underground communities abound, but finding them is entirely a matter of luck. Be careful and discreet; con men are known to run scams involving gay travelers. For helpful listings, and insider info, see **Utopia Asia Cambodia** (www.utopia-asia.com/tipscam).

KEEPING IN TOUCH

Cambodia's **postal service** is unreliable—**postal codes** are not used, and mail takes over two weeks to get to and from Cambodia. Phnom Penh and Siem Reap offer *Poste Restante* and **telephone** service. **Long distance calls** placed from Cambodia are costly. Incoming calls are accepted at most hotels and some communication centers. **IDD calls** can be placed from Telstra phone booths around Phnom Penh. For **Home Country Direct (HCD)** numbers from Cambodia, refer to the table on the inside back cover of this book. HCD calls can be made from phone booths with orange handsets instead of blue ones. **Internet** access is found often, but by no means everywhere.

SOUTHERN CAMBODIA

PHNOM PENH ☎23

Phnom Penh's citizens have spent the past 29 years improvising with the leftovers from disaster. Purged of its population in April 1975, Phnom Penh sat empty for the four-year Pol Pot regime, while nearby provinces faced hard labor, famine, fear, and death. Though the city has been more stable in recent years, the past is more than just a memory: many streets are still rutted and unpaved, blackouts are common, and bored policemen loiter on street corners. French colonial architecture mixes with modern kitsch, and there are still plenty of guns on the streets, making parts of the city dangerous at night. Still, Phnom Penh does present a brighter side, with a number of cafes and restaurants that feed hungry visitors high-quality Khmer and Western food. Travelers who make it to Phnom Penh may stay longer than they expect.

INTERCITY TRANSPORTATION

BY PLANE. Most guesthouses and hotels help arrange bus, boat, taxi, and air services to Siem Reap, Battambang, Hồ Chí Minh City in Vietnam, and Sihanoukville. Non-guests can also use these services.

DESTINATION	FREQUENCY	PRICE	DESTINATION	FREQUENCY	PRICE
Bangkok	daily	US$120	**Siem Reap**	daily	US$55
Hồ Chí Minh City	daily	US$179	**Singapore**	daily	US$214
Kuala Lumpur	5 per week	US$217	**Vientiane**	4 per week	US$133

Flights to Phnom Penh arrive at **Pochentong Airport,** 3km west of the city. Airport tax US$25 on international flights, US$6 on domestic flights. Taxis (US$5) go to the airport from town. Ticketing can be done at the airport or at these offices in and around the city: **Bangkok Airways,** 61A, St. 214 (☎722 544; open daily 8am-5pm); one-way to **Bangkok** US$102. **Lao Airlines,** 58B R.V. Samdech Preah Sihanouk (☎216 563; open M-F 8-11:30am and 1-4pm); flights to **Vientiane** (daily, one-way US$133) and **Pakse** (Sa, one-way US$73). **Malaysia Airlines,** 72-184 M.V. Preah Monivong, on the second floor of the Diamond Hotel (☎218 923; open M-F 8am-4:30pm and Sa 8am-12:30pm); flights to **Kuala Lumpur** (daily, one-way US$217) and **Singapore** (one-way US$214). **Phnom Penh Airways,** 209, St. 19 (☎990 964; open M-Sa 8am-5:30pm and Su 8am-3pm); flights to **Siem Ream** (Tu, Th, Sa; one-way US$55) and **Ban Lung** (M, W, F; one-way US$55). **Silk Air,** 313 M.V. Preah Sisowath Quay, in the Micasa Hotel (☎426 808; open M-F 1:15-5pm, Sa 8am-noon); flights to **Singapore. Thai Airways,** Regency Sq., 294 Mao Tsé Toung, in the Hotel Inter-Continental (☎214 359; open M-F 8am-4:30pm and Sa 8am-noon). **Vietnam Airlines,** 41 P. 214 (☎363 396; open M-F 8am-noon and 1:30-4:30pm, Sa 8am-noon); flights to **HCMC** (daily, one-way US$79), **Hà Nội** (daily, one-way $US189), and many other cities.

> **!** Train travel for foreigners was recently legalized, and although cheap, it remains somewhat dangerous and is not recommended, especially for those traveling alone. The train station is a yellow, Art Deco building set back from M.V. Preah Monivong, north of M.V. Conféderation de la Russie (Pochentong Blvd.).

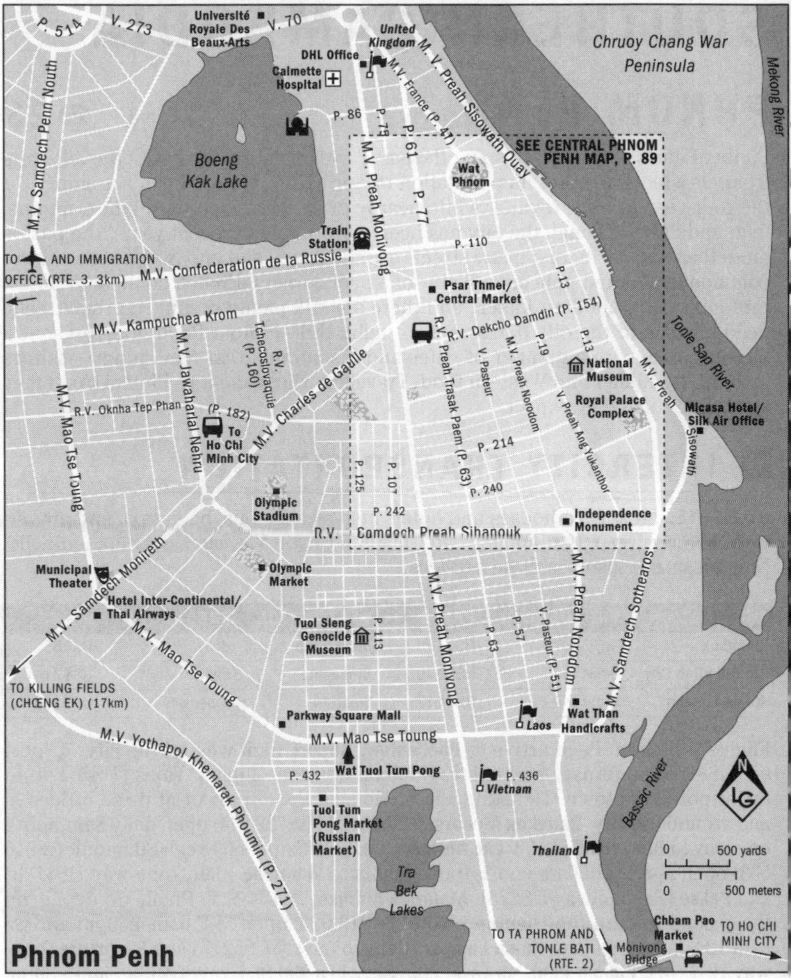

BY BUS. Most travelers arrange their tickets through guesthouses. Buses depart near the Central Market (New Market) and go to: **Battambang** (6-7hr.; 6 per day 6:30-7:45am; 15,000r); **Kompong Cham** (3hr; 7 per day 6:45am-1:45pm); **Hồ Chí Minh City** (Tu, Th, Sa, 6:30am; US$12); **Sihanoukville** (4hr.; 4 per day 7:15am-1:30pm; 12,000r); **Poipet** border (9-10hr.; 6:40am; 25,000r); **Siem Reap** (8hr.; 3 per day 6:30-7:30am; US$4). The roads to Battambang, Poipet, and Siem Reap are terrible.

BY BOAT. With Cambodia's abundance of bad roads and wide rivers, boats are the most expedient travel option. Beware that in the dry season trips can take longer and service may be suspended. Most boats leave from the Japanese Bridge (Rte. 5). Guesthouses can usually arrange **express boat** service to **Kratie**

(5hr., 7am; 30,000r) and **Siem Reap** (5hr., 7am, US$23). The ferries, many of which lack adequate safety equipment, can be overloaded, so it's best to travel on the roof. Boats leave 6-7am.

BY TAXI. Taxis can be hired on M.V. Charles de Gaulle between M.V. Preah Monivong and the New Market. Hire a taxi by the seat or by the car; a car to **Sihanoukville** costs around US$20. If you purchase just a seat (around US$3), expect to be crammed into a Toyota Corolla with six other people; buying two seats is a more comfortable option. Shared taxis to the Vietnamese border at **Bavet/Mộc Bài** (US$10 per person) and **Siem Reap** (25,000r per person). Most destinations between 2-4hr. from Phnom Penh cost US$15-20 per car. Before hiring a taxi by the New Market, check with guesthouses for cheaper options.

ORIENTATION

Three major north-south boulevards divide central Phnom Penh. In the east, **M.V. Preah Sisowath,** with its cafes and bars, runs alongside the **Tonle Sap River. M.V. Preah Norodom,** west of the river, is lined with embassies, government ministries, banks, and NGOs. One block to the east, toward the Tonle Sap, are the **National Museum, Royal Palace,** and **Silver Pagoda** complexes. The main thoroughfare, **M.V. Preah Monivong,** runs straight down the center of the city. Most accommodations and restaurants are between the Tonle Sap River and M.V. Preah Monivong. The **New Market (Psar Thmei)** sits between M.V. Preah Monivong and Norodom just south of **M.V. Conféderation de la Russie** (called **Pochentong Boulevard** everywhere but on maps). The east-west thoroughfares are M.V. Conféderation de la Russie (Pochentong Blvd.), **R.V. Samdech Preah Sihanouk,** and **M.V. Mao Tsé Toung.** Most named streets have a number as well; both are printed on street signs.

LOCAL TRANSPORTATION

Motos and pedicabs: Motorcycle taxis (motos) and **pedicabs** go anywhere in the city for low fares (1000-2000r). Moto drivers also take passengers to sites outside of town, including **Chœng Ek, Tonle Bati,** and **Udong.** Drivers outside expatriate and backpacker haunts speak some English. There's a lot of competition for customers, which is to your advantage; bargaining is recommended. If going out alone at night, use a motorcycle driver whom you know (like the one who took you to Chœng Ek during the day). Female travelers should note that while sitting side-saddle might be customary, it is also dangerous and extremely uncomfortable on longer and less-traveled routes.

Rentals: Lucky Motorcycles, 413 M.V. Preah Monivong (☎212 788), north of the Hong Kong Hotel near Wat Koh. Motos (US$5 per day), dirtbikes (US$7-10). Discounts available for extended rental. Insurance US$3.40 per day. A passport or cash deposit is required. English spoken. Open daily 7:30am-6:30pm.

PRACTICAL INFORMATION

TOURIST AND FINANCIAL SERVICES

Tourist Offices: The understaffed tourist offices in Phnom Penh are not very helpful. Speak to a guesthouse manager for good travel advice and bookings. Information regarding safety outside Phnom Penh should be verified at an embassy.

Tours: Diethelm Travel, 65 P. 240 (☎219 151). West of the American Embassy, it is better than most agencies. Arranges trips to Sihanoukville and Siem Reap. Open M-F 8am-6pm, Sa 8am-noon. Issues AmEx traveler's checks for a 1% commission. AmEx/MC/V. **K.K. International Travel and Tours,** 15 P. 13 (☎846 213) also arranges tours, car rentals, and airline tickets. Open M-F 8am-noon and 1:30-5pm, Sa 8am-noon.

Embassies: Australia and Canada, Villa 11, P. 254 (☎213 470). Consular services open M-Th 8am-noon and 1:30-5pm, F 8am-noon and 1:30-4:15pm. **Laos,** 15-17 M.V. Mao Tsé Toung (☎982 632). Visa office open M-F 8-11:30am and 2-5pm; 15-day and 1-month tourist visas US$45. 2 passport photos required. Same-day processing. **Thailand,** 196 M.V. Preah Norodom (☎300 857). Visa office open M-F 9am-noon and 2-5pm; consular services M-F 8:30am-11am. Transit visa US$20 per entry; tourist visa US$25 per entry. 2-day processing. **UK,** 27-29 P. 75 (☎427 124). Office open M-Th 8am-noon and 1:30-5pm, F 8am-1pm. Consular services available M-Th 8:30-11:30am and 1:30-3pm, F 8:30-11:30am. Also serves **New Zealand** citizens. **US,** 16-18 P. 228

(☎216 436 or 216 438). Open M-F 8am-noon and 1-5pm. Consular services open M-F 9am-noon and 1-3pm. In an after hours emergency, speak to the guard. **Vietnam,** 436 M.V. Preah Monivong (☎362 531). Visa office open M-F 8-11am and 2-4pm, Sa 8-11am. Visa applicants must specify point of entry. Visas US$40 for 2-day processing; US$35 for 3-day processing.

Currency Exchange: Moneychangers on the street who post their exchange rates may offer good rates, but banks are more trustworthy. **Cambodian Commercial Bank,** 26 M.V. Preah Monivong (☎213 602), on the corner of M.V. Conféderation de la Russie on the right. AmEx/MC/V cash advances (2% commission, min. US$5). Cashes traveler's checks (2% commission, min. US$1). Open M-F 8am-3pm; exchange booth open Sa-Su 9am-noon and 1-5pm. **Union Commercial Bank,** 61 P. 130 (☎214 159) issues cash advances. Cashes traveler's checks (2% commission, min US$2). Open M-F 8am-3:30pm and Sa 8am-noon. In the modern shopping mall next to the Cultural Market is a branch of **Canada Bank** that provides similar services and is open M-F 8am-3:30pm, Sa 8-11:30am. **There are no ATMs in Phnom Penh.**

American Express: At **Diethelm Travel** (see **Tours,** p. 91). No surcharge on AmEx purchases. Issues Traveler's Cheques (1% commission). Also accepts MC/V. Open M-F 8am-6pm, Sa 8am-noon.

English-Language Bookstore: Monument Books, 111 Preah Norodom (☎217 617). Good selection of English books on Cambodian politics and history. Open M 7:30am-5pm, Tu-Su 7:30am-7pm. MC/V. Monument also has a branch in the Foreign Correspondents Club, open daily 9am-7pm.

EMERGENCY AND COMMUNICATIONS

Emergency: Police ☎117. **Medical** ☎119. Free from any orange phone.

Police: Bureau des Etrangers (Office of Foreign Affairs), P. 154 (☎226 847), off V. Pasteur/P. 151. Some English spoken. Come here with complaints, but in emergencies go immediately to your embassy. Open daily M-F 7-11:30am and 2-5:30pm.

Pharmacies: A high percentage of drugs sold in Phnom Penh have expired or are fraudulent. **Pharmacie de la Gare,** 81 M.V. Preah Monivong (☎426 855), on the corner of Confedération de la Russie just before the train station, is the most reliable in Phnom Penh. Some English spoken. Open M-Sa 7am-7pm, Su 8:30am-noon.

Hospitals: Healthcare in Cambodia is well below international standards. **AEA International/SOS Assistance,** 161 P. 51 (24hr. ☎216 911), near P. 228, specializes in emergency care and will provide evacuation to Bangkok. Australian or Khmer-French doctor on-call 24hr. Open M-F 8:30am-5pm, Sa 8am-noon. **Tropical & Travelers Medical Clinic,** 88 P. 108 (☎015 912 1000 or 012 898 981), specializes in travelers' needs. British doctor. Open M-F 8:30am-noon and 2-5pm, Sa 8am-noon.

Telephones: IDD calls can be made from Telstra phone booths at the GPO, the Ministry of Tourism, and outside many hotels on M.V. Preah Monivong. Phone cards sold at GPO and many hotels. Internet cafes can often place international calls at reduced quality and price over the Internet.

Internet Access: Internet cafes are everywhere. Many are associated with the guesthouses on Bœng Kak Lake next to all the Western restaurants, or along the river. The going rate is 2000r per hr. Some cafes have a minimum charge of 500r.

Post Office: GPO, on P. 13, at the intersection with P. 102 south of Wat Phnom. A large, yellow colonial building. Overseas calls, fax, telegram service. EMS mail available. Sells phone cards for local phone booths. *Poste Restante.* Open daily 8am-5pm.

Express Mail: DHL, 28 M.V. Preah Monivong (☎427 726), north past the intersection with Conféderation de la Russie. Open M-Sa 8am-5:30pm.

ACCOMMODATIONS

Guesthouses (US$3-10) in Phnom Penh provide beds and a backpacker-friendly atmosphere. Hotels (US$10 and up) keep travelers cooler and cleaner, but many of them are nondescript. Hangouts line Bœng Kak (pronounced Bangkok) Lake, which feels a world away from the bustle of Phnom Penh. Many good hotels are along Preah Monivong. Most guesthouses listed arrange visas and transportation.

Sister (No. 9) Guest House, 9 P. 93. Head toward Bœng Kak Lake on M.V. Preah Monivong, then turn left on V. Moat Chrouk (P. 86). At the end of the street, just before the mosque, turn left and walk 500m. It's on the right. Loll in hammocks on the lakeside porch with fellow backpackers. Rooms have mosquito nets. Arranges transportation to Siem Reap, Sihanoukville, and HCMC. ❷

Royal Guest House, 91 P. 154 (☎854 806), near the intersection with M.V. Preah Norodom. Convenient location and wide range of room options make the few extra dollars worth it. Arranges moto driver for US$5 per day. Singles with shared bath US$3-4. All other rooms with bath, fridge, and cable TV. With fan US$5-7. ❷

Narin Guest House No. 50, 50 P. 125 (☎982 584; touchnarin@hotmail.com). Follow M.V. Preah Monivong from the city center, turn right at the Ministry of Tourism (P. 232), then left on P. 125. Good food (US$1-3) and clean rooms. Patio and balcony give guests a place to socialize. Organizes onward travel; taxis to Vietnam US$5. Singles US$2-3; doubles US$5, with bath US$0-9. ❷

Keov Mean Guest House, 1 V. Pasteur St. (☎723 067), near P. 51 between P. 118 and P. 126. Tidy rooms within 2 blocks of the New Market. Wrap-around balconies. Rooms have fan and bath. Rooms US$5-6, with A/C US$10. ❷

CAMBODIA

FOOD

Phnom Penh is full of opportunities to eat well, no matter what your budget is. Restaurants geared toward tourists and expats line **Sisowath Quay,** but **P. 240,** behind the Royal Palace Complex, is more peaceful and less crowded with tourists. The food on **P. 240** is also generally higher in quality. Dozens of cafes worthy of exploration line **M.V. Preah Monivong** and **M.V. Samdech Preah Sihanouk.** Cheap and adventurous eats are at the markets. **Lucky Market Group** has two stores, one at 160 Samdech Preah Sihanouk (open daily 8am-8pm), and a large one in the Parkway Square complex, on M.V. Mao Tsé Toung near the intersection with M.V. Preah Monivong (open M-F 9am-8:30pm, Sa-Su 9am-9pm). At 5:30pm, foodstalls materialize near **Wat Koh** at the **Independence Monument.** The restaurants over the **Chruoy Changvar** (Cambodian-Japanese Friendship Bridge), northeast of the city, are popular with locals. Of the restaurants in this area, **Bœng Meas** (on the left) has the best food and **Hang Neak** (farther down the strip on the right) has great decor and entertainment. These restaurants are open from 9am-10pm. On weekends, they start filling up after 8pm. The emerging backpackers' hangout by **Boeng Kak Lake** has brought with it a host of inexpensive eateries. A range of options, including (at last count) no fewer than four Indian restaurants all within a stone's throw of one another, makes it a good place to get a bite.

Athena Restaurant and Steve's Steakhouse, at the corner of St. 51 and 282. This place serves up excellent Greek and eastern Mediterranean food, as well as steaks. Delicious *meze* plate US$4; Greek food US$4-6; steaks US$6 and up. ❸

The Shop, 39 P.240 (☎986 964) is the sort of bakery-cafe you'd expect to find in Notting Hill or the Upper East Side. Western magazines available for reading. Good coffee US$1; focaccia pockets US$3. Open daily 7am-7pm. ❷

Garden Center Cafe, 23, St. 57. Set in a tropical garden, this restaurant serves a full range of Asian and Western food. Great breakfast options. Entrees US$5-10; burgers US$3; quiche US$2.50. Open Tu-Su 7am-10pm; last seating 9pm. ❷

The Sugar Palace, on P. 240, 15m from the intersection with P. 19 on the right, has well-prepared, upscale Khmer food, like mango salad and *amok*. Entrees US$4-6. ❸

SIGHTS

Phnom Penh is better for aimless exploration than scheduled sightseeing. There are few jaw-dropping attractions, but some are more profound, deserving plenty of time and attention. Chief among these are the **Tuol Sleng Genocide Museum** and the **Killing Fields** at **Chœng Ek.** Guesthouses arrange motorcycle drivers for the day (US$7, more for a trip to the Killing Fields; bargain for the best price). A moto driver to Tuol Sleng or Chœng Ek should cost you no more than US$3. Many government tourist attractions close on Mondays, but a gratuity may open the doors.

TUOL SLENG GENOCIDE MUSEUM. At this former high school in a residential neighborhood of Southern Phnom Penh, the Khmer Rouge imprisoned and killed over 14,000 people. Only seven survived; the rest were sent to the Killing Fields of Chœng Ek. When the Vietnamese arrived in 1979, they found at Tuol Sleng a morbidly well-documented hell. The most telling memorial of the Khmer Rouge years, Tuol Sleng has been left as it was found in 1979. There are no velvet museum barricades—visitors walk freely through closet-sized detention cells and torture chambers. Many documents of torture are now displayed on the walls, including hundreds of photographs taken of each victim upon arrival. Be sure to time your visit to catch the documentary movie, about 1 hr. long, shown at 10am and 3pm each day. *(On P. 103. Open Tu-Sa 7:30-11am and 2-5pm. US$2. Photography permitted.)*

CHŒNG EK KILLING FIELDS. The Killing Fields were the final destination for more than 40,000 victims of Pol Pot's reign of terror. Only one person survived the massacre here. He was shot but didn't die and was buried alive. When the Vietnamese found the Killing Fields, they unearthed him, barely alive. A *stupa* was erected in 1988; a glass case inside contains 17 levels of human skulls and bones from exhumed bodies. Bits of bone and cloth still come up from the earth. *(17km south of the city. Open Tu-Su 7am-5pm, though on M a donation might open the gates. Entry US$2.)*

WAT PHNOM. With its beautiful lawn and Buddhist statues, Wat Phnom is the most sacred sight in Phnom Penh. According to legend, an aristocrat named Lady Penh founded a monastery atop this hill to house Buddha statues that she had found inside a log. It's a great place for a picnic. *(On a hill north of the Old Market on M.V. Preah Norodom. US$1.)*

ROYAL PALACE AND SILVER PAGODA COMPLEX. The Royal Palace is closed when the royal family is home, but visitors can peek in the huge windows. English-speaking guides or English programs are available, as most of the buildings are unlabeled. Along the walls of the Silver Pagoda complex, in the southeastern corner complex, frescoes portray scenes from the *Ramayana* and of the palace in ancient times. A large *stupa* holds the ashes of King Ang Duong (r. 1845-59). The pavilion beyond shelters a statue of King Norodom on horseback and a footprint of the Buddha. At the center of the complex is the **Silver Pagoda,** which derives its name from the 5000 silver blocks covering the floor. **Wat Phra Kaew** (Temple of the Emerald Buddha) contains, not surprisingly, an emerald Buddha from the 1600s. A Buddha statue in the likeness of King Norodom, made of gold and inlaid with thousands of diamonds, is also on display. *(Along M.V. Sothearos, south of Wat Ounalom. Open daily 7:30-11am and 2-5pm. US$3, camera fee US$2, video camera fee US$3.)*

NATIONAL MUSEUM OF ARTS. The museum houses fine Angkorian wooden and stone figures as well as pre-Angkorian sculptures. *(North of the Royal Palace along P. 13. Open Tu-Su 8am-5pm. Admission US$3; video camera permit US$3.)*

OTHER SIGHTS. In the park at the intersection of Norodom and Sihanouk, the **Liberation Monument (Cambodia-Laos-Vietnam Monument)** features a giant statue of three figures that commemorates the 1979 Vietnamese liberation of Cambodia. Phnom Penh also has wats, though many were wrecked by the Khmer Rouge in the late 1970s. The remaining ones serve as schools and shelters for the poor and disabled; they are not designed for tourists. **Wat Ounalom,** on the corner of P. 154 and M.V. Preah Sisowath Quay, is the cornerstone of Cambodian Buddhism. **Wat Tuol Tum Pong,** on the corner of M.V. Mao Tsé Toung and P.155, just before the market, has budding linguists who greet visitors with enthusiastic "hellos." **Wat Koh,** on M.V. Preah Monivong, south of the New Market, has an English school.

ENTERTAINMENT

Check the calendar of *The Cambodia Daily*'s Friday edition for cultural events. The **Sovanna Phum Association,** 111 P. 360, near the Tuol Sleng Genocide Museum, performs dance and shadow-puppet shows. (☎012 846 020; shows every Friday; tickets US$3.) The **Mekong Island Park,** intended as an "authentic showcase" of traditional Cambodian culture, hosts Khmer music and theater. Trips leave daily from the **Mekong Island Park Office,** 13 P. 240, at the corner of P. 19, and return at 3pm. Tickets include lunch, a visit to the zoo, an elephant ride, and a dance show. (☎016 851 1361; 4-person min.; US$32.) The easiest and cheapest way to observe Khmer music and dance is to visit the **Université Royale des Beaux-Arts,** on P. 70, off M.V. Preah Monivong, north of the French Embassy. On the right is the university, where the faculty struggles to preserve Khmer art. Students learn the *apsara* dance, flute music, and scenes from the *Ramayana.* Unobtrusive foreigners are welcome. (Classes M-F 7-11am, Sa 8-11am.) At sundown, locals head to the decorated restaurants northeast of the city center, where cool river breezes accompany diverse menus and lively entertainment of the karaoke variety.

SHOPPING

Phnom Penh boasts more than seven markets, and most vendors set up at 6:30am and don't leave until 5pm. Markets are best visited in the early morning. **Cobblers** on P. 143, due west of the Tuol Sleng Genocide Museum, sell custom-fit, all-leather shoes and sandals (US$10-40). In addition to its traditional markets, Phnom Penh has a few Western-style shopping malls, complete with A/C and food courts. The tall glass tower next to the Central Market has one (open daily 8am-9pm). On M.V. Mao Tse Roung, near the Russian Market, is the Parkway Shopping Mall, which has a health club with a swimming pool and a bowling alley ("Super Bowl").

Russian Market (Tuol Tom Pong Market), between P. 163 and P. 155, south of the wat of the same name. This market wins high marks for its beautiful silk and cotton print sarongs, *krama* (used as either a scarf, headdress, or bathing suit), and a wide selection of cheap pirated CDs. There are many wood and stone sculptures here as well. It's probably the best place in Cambodia to buy souvenirs. Don't forget to bargain.

New Market (Psar Thmei). The hub of Phnom Penh, this large yellow structure is often referred to as "Central Market." Large Art Deco structure built in the 1930s. Generally has higher prices than the other markets. Purchase up-to-date maps, Angkor guides, and Khmer phrasebooks here.

Old Market (Psar Char), northeast of the New Market along P. 108 and P. 15. If you want to purchase silk by the yard, this is the place. The atmosphere is less touristy and the vendors are less aggressive than in the other markets.

Wat Tan Handicrafts, 206a M.V. Preah Norodom, next to the Royal Air Cambodge Office. Trains students in tailoring, weaving, and carpentry as part of an effort to aid those disabled by landmines and polio. The fruits of their labor are sold at the Wat Than showroom. Items include silk pillows, clothing, and pocketbooks. Tailor-made outfits specially-ordered. Open M-F 8am-5pm, Sa 8am-noon.

NIGHTLIFE

Going out at night in Phnom Penh invariably means seeing lots of beautiful Khmer girls paired up with suspiciously unattractive Western guys. Popular bars and cafes, including **The Globe** and **Rising Sun,** line **Preah Sisowath.** There are many other bars near Norodom Blvd. and toward Independence Monument, including **Walkabout,** at the corner of St. 174 and 51 (open 24hr.), and **Sharky Bar,** at 126 St. 130. **Be careful at night**—tourists have been mugged.

Foreign Correspondents Club of Cambodia (FCCC), 363 M.V. Preah Sisowath Quay (☎427 757), on the river north of the Royal Palace. Mission-style furniture on a terrace overlooking the river. Western menu, pool table. Imported beers, mixed drinks, and restaurant. The entryway is lined with photos taken during Phnom Penh's fall to the Khmer Rouge in 1975. The 2-level building also features rotating art exhibits. FCC also has a bookshop and, at street level, a deli. Happy hour 5-7pm. Open daily 7am-midnight.

Heart of Darkness Bar, 26 P. 51, near the corner of P. 174. Red-lit bamboo and Angkor-inspired decor, good music and ambience. An expat and backpacker bar par excellence. Inexpensive beer and mixed drinks US$1-3. Open daily 8pm-sunrise.

The Cambodia Club (☎556 677), at the intersection of Sisowath Quay and P. 178, is a pleasant cafe, restaurant, and bar all rolled into one. Its a great place to watch the Mekong River in the evening.

DAYTRIPS FROM PHNOM PENH

UDONG

The city bus from Phnom Penh has the cheapest rate to Udong. Buses leave from the bus station at the New Market (every 45min. 6:30am-6:30pm, 25000r) for the village of Udong. From there, it is a moto ride to the temples (4000r). Capitol Travel at the Capitol Guest House in Phnom Penh offers an A/C bus to Udong daily (9am, US$5, 4-person minimum). Alternatively, a moto can be chartered round-trip for about US$10. Get there early, as the hill tends to simmer even when the surrounding countryside basks in a picnic-friendly breeze.

Udong, Cambodia's capital from 1618 to 1866, sits 45km northwest of Phnom Penh. The site sees few tourists, though Phnom Penh natives pour in for weekend picnics. The **twin hills of Udong** are visible from miles away; one is sprinkled with temples and *stupas.* From the parking lot area at the hill's base, the road on the extreme left leads to a mosque and temple, both of which suffered greatly in the civil war. From there, paths lead to countless vistas and *stupas.*

PHNOM CHISOR

Phnom Chisor is 22km from Phnom Tamao. The turn-off is on the left beyond the school. From there, a dusty dirt track winds 6km through a small village and past lush rice fields to the foot of the hill. Hire a moto to go there (about US$5 round-trip), or inquire about buses to Takeo at the bus station.

Phnom Chisor temple rises high above the flat plains of Takeo Province. The kings rode elephants, but visitors must now walk up more than 500 steps to get there. Built in 1150 of laterite and sandstone, the temple was a regular stop on the pilgrimage circuit, though it was nearly destroyed by US bombers in 1973. The central sanctuary houses the original reclining Buddha statue. To protect it from thieves, the monks have concealed it behind newer images. The original can be viewed only by climbing back into the tiny sanctuary with a candle and a 500r tip. Facing east, in line with Phnom Chisor, stand two laterite gates, **Sen Thomol** and **Sen Ravang.** On their way to Phnom Chisor in earlier times, Brahmin priests would bathe in Tonle Oun, the lake in front of the first gate. The original steps leading down to the gates are still visible.

ALONG ROUTE 2

There are several worthwhile sights near the capital, each of which can be visited on a half-day excursion. The easiest way to reach them is by motorcycle or car. Most drivers charge tourists about US$10-15. Or inquire about the Taeko bus at the Ho Wah Genting station by the Central Market.

Ta Phrom temple is 32km south of Phnom Penh along Rte. 2. The turn-off is on the right; look for a gate with three large Angkor-inspired towers. The first Phrom temple was constructed in the 7th century. The current one, built of laterite and sandstone in the Bayon style, is believed to have been erected during the rule of Jayavarman VII (1191-1218). Originally constructed as a Brahmanic temple, it was later reconsecrated as a Buddhist temple. Nearby, **Yeah Peau** temple is also worth a peek. The nearby lake of **Tonle Bati** is a popular weekend retreat for urbanites. Vendors offer beer, fried chicken, cold drinks, fruit, and young coconut juice out of the shell. **Phnom Tamao** (US$1) is a wildlife center and zoological preserve near Tonle Bati. Monkeys, tigers, birds, and bears are caged in the setting of lush jungles, except during the dry season.

CAMBODIA

SIHANOUKVILLE ☎034

Sihanoukville, the country's only deep-water port, was rebuilt with Soviet aid after being ravaged under Pol Pot's regime. Tourism has been on the rise in recent years, but while the number of hotels in the town has grown, the beaches remain largely deserted. Somehow, the town still feels incomplete, with stretches of countryside between built up segments on the beaches and hills. It's a good place to hang up the rucksack and take it easy for a couple of days—as if you hadn't been doing that already.

TRANSPORTATION

Buses: Guesthouses and hotels can arrange bus tickets to **Phnom Penh.** Three bus companies, all along V. Ekareach, go to Phnom Penh: **Capitol Tours,** east of the city center (7:30am, 12:30pm; 12,000r); **GST Express** (☎012 820 559), next to Chaok Sakor Hotel (4hr., 4 per day 7:15am-1:30pm, 12,000r); **Ho Wah Genting Transport Co. Ltd.** (☎933 888), next to the Cambodian Commercial Bank (4hr., 5 per day 7:10am-2pm, 12,000r). Arrive 15min. early. **Capitol Tours** and **Ho Wah Genting** also have **minibuses** to the **Thai Border** (7:15am, US$13).

Ferries: Look for signs saying "Port of Passenger Ship" at the ferry dock north of Sihanoukville, off Hun Sen Beach Dr., or inquire at **Ho Wah Genting,** which also runs ferries. Take the boat to **Koh Kong** (3½-4hr., noon, US$15), where smaller boats run to the **Thai border** (10min.; 100฿).

Local Transportation: Motorcycle taxis cost 1000-2500r, depending on distance. Arrange early morning transport in advance. Hire a **taxi** at the **Central Market** (Psar Loer). To **Phnom Penh** US$25-30. Night travel not recommended.

Rentals: Uncrowded roads make Sihanoukville an ideal place to rent **motorbikes.** Check your guesthouse, the GST and D.H. bus stations, or look for tables set up along V. Ekareach. Most places charge US$4-5 per day.

BORDER CROSSING: SIHANOUKVILLE/TRAT. Thirty-day Thai visas are issued at the border. Take a speedboat from the ferry dock off Hun Sen Beach Dr. to **Koh Kong** (3½hr., noon, US$15). Cross the river (5000r) and take a short moto ride to the border (3000r). Alternatively, arrange for a minibus in town (US$13). Walk across the border, get your exit stamp, and enter Thailand at the border town of **Had Lek.** Take a minibus or taxi from Had Lek to **Trat,** where further transportation to Bangkok can be found. The border is open from 7am-5pm, but since you will probably arrive in Koh Kong in the late afternoon from Sihanoukville, do not waste time in crossing. If the border is closed when you arrive, there are accommodations in town.

ORIENTATION AND PRACTICAL INFORMATION

The town is spread thinly over hills, with long stretches of road between it and the beaches. The town's main thoroughfare is **V. Ekareach,** which runs east-west from **Victory Beach** to the city center (2km) and then elbows south to the **Golden Lion Traffic Circle** (1.5km). The main beach road, **2 Thnou Street,** follows the coast past **Independence** and **Sokha Beaches. Ochheuteal Beach** lies to the south of the Golden Lion Traffic Circle. The most popular guesthouses and the main **post office** are above Victory Beach. The *Sihanoukville Visitors Guide*, published yearly and available in restaurants and hotels, includes a map. **Canadia Bank** and **Union Commercial Bank** are next to one another in the center of town on V. Ekareadh. Canadia offers MC cash advances while UCC has Visa cash advances (both open M-F 8am-3:30pm, Sa 8-11:30am). The **Central Market (Psar Loer)** is a raucous night market near the Okinawa Thmey Hotel. (Open daily 5am-6pm.) Other services include the **police** (☎833 222), on V. Ekareach at the top of the hill 1km west of city center and the **Chuen Min Hospital** (☎933 111), on V. Ekareach near the city center. **International calls** and **Internet** access are available from several shops on V. Ekareach, including **Ana Internet,** 150m past the Ho Wah Geatry bus station on the left (US$1 per hour). Weather Station Hill, above Victory Beach, also has a couple of net cafes. The going rate there is around 4500r per hr. The **post office** is in the building across the street from the market on 7 Makara. (Open M-F 8am-noon and 1-5pm.) Next to the market is **Pharmacie Prachea Chun,** where some of the staff speak English (☎838 280; open daily 6:30am-9pm). **Casablanca Books,** above the Starfish Cafe (see **Accommodations and Food**, below), has a decent collection of used novels and books on Cambodia as well as a small selection of books in French.

ACCOMMODATIONS AND FOOD

On Weather Station Hill above Victory Beach, **MASH & Melting Pot ❶** is characterized by its idiosyncratic charm. There is an attached restaurant, a bar, and a library of books about Cambodia and Southeast Asia. (☎012 913 714. MASH section 1-2 person US$3-4; Melting Pot section US$4-6.) **Mealy Chenda Guest House ❶,** on the bluff above Victory Beach, is a new backpacker-friendly haven with an open-air balcony and rooftop restaurant. (☎933 472. Moto rental US$4 per day. Free pick-

CAMBODIA

up at bus station. 3-bed dorms with shared bath US$2; singles with shared bath US$3; doubles with bath US$5-6, with balcony US$7-8.) On Serendipity Beach west of Ochheuteal Beach, **Serendipity Guest House ❶** has basic accommodations in a great location from which to take advantage of local nightlife.

Sihanoukville has excellent seafood, especially shrimp and crab. Most guest-houses sport a wide selection of food, but one can feast at the **night market;** food-stalls line V. Ekareach. **Les Feuilles Restaurant ❹,** 400m east of the Golden Lion Traffic Circle on Kanda 1 St., serves excellent French, Western, and Khmer food. (Great *luk-lak* US$5. Open daily 7am-10pm.) In the middle of town, down a small alley on the right side of the road towards the market (look for the sign) is **Starfish Café ❷,** which has good breakfast options (US$1-1.75) and sandwiches served in a peaceful garden (US$2-2.50). **Chez Claude Restaurant ❺,** off 2 Thnou St. on a ridge high above Sokha Beach, has fantastic Asian and French cuisine and a beautiful view of the sunset over the Gulf of Thailand. (Entrees US$5-10.) **Hawaii Seaview ❸,** on South Victory Beach, has excellent seafood with a great view of the beach. (Entrees US$2-5. Open daily 9am-late.)

SIGHTS AND ENTERTAINMENT

Sihanoukville's major attractions are the many stretches of sugary sand that surround the town. However, there are a few other sights worth a look. Atop the 132m high **Sihanoukville Mountain,** the town's wat overlooks a stunning panorama of land and seascape. Head east on National Rte. 4 (toward Phnom Penh), turn right at the **Cambrew Brewery** (home of Angkor Beer), and follow the dirt road up the ridge. About an hour by moto outside of the town is a **waterfall** that is a popular bathing spot. Moto drivers will do the round-trip for US$4. **Angkor Arms Pub,** on V. Ekareach near the city center, is a self-proclaimed traditional British pub and a Sihanoukville institution offering beer, darts, and a restaurant. (Beer US$0.75. Happy hour 5-7pm. Open daily 4pm-midnight.) Next door, **Espresso Kampuchea** is a good place to sip some coffee before catching your bus out of town (espresso US$1).

BEACHES

At the southeastern end of the peninsula is **Ochheuteal Beach**—long, uncrowded, and backed by some of Sihanoukville's nicest hotels. Farther west is **Independence Beach,** which has clear water and few hawkers. There is great boulder-hopping on the rocky shorelines between beaches. **Sokha Beach,** back to the east a bit, is the most popular beach. Throngs of vendors sell snacks and fresh coconuts (1000r) here, and inner tubes can be rented. Rent a motorbike at **Victory Beach,** just south of the Port of Sihanoukville, for 3000-5000r.

UP THE MEKONG

KOMPONG CHAM ☎042

It may not feel like it, but Kompong Cham is Cambodia's third-largest city and the first major stop for travelers heading up the Mekong River. With the opening of the Lao border north of Stung Treng and the recent completion of a gargantuan bridge across the Mekong, Kompong Cham has also become a transit point to the north and east of the country. Despite the fact that there is not a whole lot to see or do, Kompong Cham is a pleasant provincial city, and there are certainly worse places to be stuck for a night.

TRANSPORTATION. The road between Phnom Penh and Kompong Cham is in excellent condition. **Buses** leave Kompong Cham from behind the market on the same street as the Canadia Bank for **Phnom Penh** (3hr., 6per day 7am-4:15pm, 8000r). The road to **Kratie** is horrible and there is no need to take it, since **boats** run to Kratie year-round. But if you're so inclined, pick-up trucks leave for Kratie from the market. Preferable are the boats that go to **Kratie** (fast boat 3hr.; 7:30, 9am, 2pm; $US7) and **Phnom Penh** (fast boat 3hr., 9:30am, 15,000r).

ORIENTATION AND PRACTICAL INFORMATION. Kompong Cham sits on the west bank of the Mekong River, 120km northeast of Phnom Penh. Fast boats from Phnom Penh and Kratie dock opposite the Mekong Hotel, on **Preah Bat Sihanouk,** the riverside road. Just south of the Mekong Hotel, Sihanouk supports a string of guesthouses and intersects **Rue Pasteur,** which runs inland past the police station. Heading north from the Mekong Hotel, Sihanouk bends inland to a six-way intersection, abutting the market, which is also a bus stop. One block north, **Kosamak Neary Rath** runs inland through a roundabout to the governor's mansion.

The **tourist office,** in front of the governor's mansion on Kosamak Neary Rath, is eager to help but low on resources. (Open M-F 8-11am and 2-4pm.) **Canadia Bank** will exchange currency and cash traveler's checks (US$2 commission) and disburse cash to MC holders. (Open M-F 8:30am-5:30pm, Sa 8am-noon.) A **provincial market** sits next to the six-way intersection of Preah Bat Sihanouk. Here you can buy fine *kramas* (traditional checkered scarves). The **police** are located on Rue Pasteur one block from the river. The **Kompong Cham Provincial Hospital** runs a bare-bones operation on Rue Pasteur, one block from the river. The **post office** is on Khemarak Pumin, one block north of Kosamak Neary Rath. (Open M-F 7-11am and 2-5pm.) Long distance calls can be made from shops around the city, including some on Rue Jayavarman VII, one block north of the police station, and from an international phone booth at the edge of the market. **Internet** cafes surround the market and nearby streets; a decent connection will cost about 2000r for 20min. Many also offer international calls at good rates.

ACCOMMODATIONS AND FOOD. Cheap guesthouses line Preah Bat Sihanouk south of the dock. **Bo Pear Guest House ❶,** two blocks away from the river of Rue Pasteur, has clean rooms and good prices (rooms US$2, with bath US$3). A glut of rooms in Kompong Cham means hotel-style accommodations come cheap; the **Mittapheap Hotel ❷,** across the roundabout from Canadia Bank, has flush toilets and fans. (☎941 565. Rooms US$5, with A/C US$10.) One block from the dock, on Preah Bat Sihanouk, the **Speanthmey Guest House ❶** provides the most room for your riel and the upstairs balcony offers a great view. (Singles US$3, with TV US$4; doubles with TV US$5, with A/C US$8.) The **Kim Srung Guest House ❶,** a few doors down from Speanthmey, has nice rooms and an attached restaurant. (Singles US$3; doubles US$5.) Along the river, many vendors sell pots of food for 2000r, including steamed rice. More formal restaurants are scarce, but many of the nicer hotels serve decent fare. One quality eatery is **Hoa An ❶,** four blocks inland on Rue Pasteur. This local institution serves up Chinese and Khmer food with lots of beer. The menu has pictures of every dish; check out the fish heads and pig intestines. (Fried rice with pork sausage and egg 6500r. Open daily 6am-8:30pm.)

SIGHTS AND NIGHTLIFE. Wat Nokor, an 11th-century Buddhist temple made from sandstone and laterite, claims top billing in Kompong Cham, which is not saying much. Many of the statues in the temple were defaced by the Khmer Rouge, and all the paintings on the walls of the scenes of the Buddha's life were painted over in black. Since then the temple has been reconstructed in its former image. Next to the temple is a cemetery; one of the *stupas* has hundreds of human skulls from the Khmer Rouge days inside. The ruins contain an active temple 2km west of town. From the road to Phnom Penh, take a left at the roundabout or hire a moto driver (US$2). **Phnom Pros** and **Phnom Sray** are 5km farther toward Phnom Penh. They feature nice (if not outright amazing) views of the countryside and a wat where you can buy bananas (1000r for a large bundle) with which to **feed the monkeys.** This is surprisingly entertaining—the animals have fascinating habits and mannerisms. A moto-trip costs US$2 round-trip.

Nightlife is not one of Kompong Cham's strong points. Only **Phnom Prosh Nightclub** in the Phnom Prosh Hotel can pass as a spot for nighttime entertainment. If karaoke is your thing, try the open-air places that have opened up on the other side of the new bridge and are quite popular with the locals.

KRATIE

A worthy stop on any journey heading north or south, Kratie (KRA-cheh) is a pleasant town along the Mekong; it's just the right size, and the best place in the world to see the rare Irrawaddy dolphin.

TRANSPORTATION. The road north to Stung Treng and south to Kompong Cham is in very poor condition. Luckily, boats go south to Kompong Cham year-round. During the dry season, however, low water levels make traveling north by boat nearly impossible. **Pick-up Trucks** leave from the market and go to **Ban Lung** (9-12hr., 7am; US$10); **Mondulkiri** (8hr.; 6, 7am; US$10); **Stung Treng** (6-8hr., 6am, US$6). Shared **taxis** follow the same routes to **Ban Lung** (US$13), **Mondulkiri** US$8.75), and **Stung Treng** (US$7.50) in the rainy season. **Boats** are a much friendlier option. Boats go south year-round to **Kompong Cham** (daily fast boat 3hr.; 6, 11am), where you can catch a bus to **Phnom Penh** (see **Kompong Cham,** p. 98), and north to **Stung Treng** (US$7.50).

ORIENTATION AND PRACTICAL INFORMATION. Kratie dozes on the east bank of the Mekong, northeast of Kompong Cham and Phnom Penh. Navigation couldn't be easier. Kratie's two main streets run parallel to the river, with **V. Preah Sura Marit** along the bank and **V. Samdech Preah Sihanouk** one block back. Streets numbered from north to south, with the town's center situated between Rue 7 and Rue 10, intersect these two roads. The **market** is on Sihanouk between Rue 8 and Rue 10, and the **post office** (open M-F 7-11am and 2-5pm) sits between the two main streets on Rue 12. The **police station** (☎971 499) is off Rue 15 near the radio tower. International phone calls can be made from the Kodak Express MiniLab on Preah Sihanouk past Hy Heng Guest House.

ACCOMMODATIONS AND FOOD. A profusion of cheap rooms graces Preah Sihanouk near the market. Sometimes bargaining is possible, so ask if there are discounts available. **U Hong Guest House ❶**, on Sihanouk and Rue 10, is right next to the market and has clean rooms, a nice atmosphere, and a great balcony. Don't listen to touts, who claim that the market makes the rooms too loud—they're not. (Singles US$2; doubles US$4; enormous double with balcony overlooking the market US$5.) **Heng Oudom Hotel ❶,** at 85 St. 10, is also very close to the market and has beautiful new rooms (☎12 276 030, US$3-4, some with TV). **Santepheap Hotel ❷** is on Preah Sura Marit across from the docks. This classy yellow hotel has large modern rooms and great management. (Doubles with fan and bath US$5, with A/C US$10.) **Prom Meas ❶** (☎924 826), on Sihanouk a block down from Star Guest House, has tiled rooms with desks. (Rooms 10,000r and up.)

Market ❶ food is exceptionally cheap in Kratie. The standard market meal costs 1500r; most of the town shows up to partake. For a more formal setting, try the **Mekong Restaurant ❶**, on Rue 9, which has attentive service, a host of local patrons, and quality fried chicken with pineapple (5000r). The **Star Guest House Restaurant ❶** is an excellent place to have breakfast and watch the market.

SIGHTS. The best place in Cambodia to see endangered **Irrawaddy dolphins** is 15km north of Kratie. Hundreds more survive in Laos. As soon as you arrive, your guesthouse proprietor will want to arrange your moto to the pavilion; bargaining should start at US$4, which is a ridiculous price. A local moto driver will take you for US$1-1.50. A boatman will pole you out on the river for a closer look (US$2-3, depending on the season). The nearby stretch of the river is also nice for swimming, and there are small rapids as well.

BORDER CROSSING: STUNG TRENG/VEUNKHAM. This border crossing is only unofficially open, and you **cannot** obtain a Cambodian or a Laos visa at the border. There are corrupt border officials, though, and you can charter a boat from Stung Treng to **Veunkham** (1hr., anytime during the day, US$6). You will be required to pay US$2-5 to leave Cambodia, and then your boat will take you across the river to Laos immigration. There you will be required to pay US$1-2 to enter Laos. Go back to your boat and continue on to **Don Khong** or **Don Det.** There is **no bank** in Veunkham, Don Det, or Don Khong. Bring dollars or baht, which are readily negotiable all over Laos.

STUNG TRENG

Just off the Mekong, Stung Treng is a tiny town on the San River that unfortunately constitutes a near-necessary overnight stop for those heading north to Laos or east to Ban Lung and Rattanakiri. Perhaps the opening of the Lao border will spur a growth in Stung Treng's tourist attractions and infrastructure. Right now, though, one night here is plenty for most travelers.

Boat travel is the best way to get north or south from Stung Treng, but during the dry season travel by boat is not always possible. Check for availability. Boats go to Kratie (6hr., US$15) and Kompong Cham (3hr., US$7-8). To go to Phnom Phenh, take the boat to Kompong Cham and then take a bus to the capital (3hr., US$2; see **Kampong Chang**). Boats can be chartered any time of the day to go north to the Lao border (US$6). The roads are extremely poor around Stung Treng, especially toward Kratie. Nevertheless, 4WD **pick-up trucks** leave from the lot between the dock to and Sunset Guest House (6-8hr. of pain, around 7am, US$5). Pick-ups also leave for (4hr., around 7am, US$5-6), and the road is halfway decent, although it is almost comically dusty. Don't wear clothing you don't want to get very dirty, or pay an extra dollar to sit inside the pick-up's cab. Be sure your bag is covered with a tarp, or it will soon become caked with grime. **Internet** access is available at an Internet cafe at the southwest corner of the market, but it's very expensive. (Open daily 7am-8pm. 300r per min.) From the roundabout at the dock, walk away from the river and pass the market on your left. The shop is on the left at the corner past the market. The best place to buy your boat ticket (and practice your French) is at **Dona Restaurant ❶**, next to Sunset Guest House. The proprietor, Mr. Taing, lived in Paris for many years and is helpful and kind. His tickets are often US$1-2 cheaper than those of other agents. There is **no bank** in Stung Treng; plan ahead and have a supply of dollars or baht, particularly if you are arriving from Laos. Sunset Guest

House will cash traveler's checks for a hefty 8% commission. If you're in a bind, the best place to change hard currency (including dollars, baht, and kip) is in the market at a **jewelry stall.** Look for glass cases with different currencies on display, and familiarize yourself with the exchange rates before you conduct any transactions. Budget accommodations are not plentiful in Stung Treng. **Sunset Guest House** ❶ has basic rooms for US$2-4 and is convenient to both the pier and the pick-up truck lot. **Sekong Hotel ❶,** opposite the docks, has basic rooms with mosquito nets and fans for US$3. The genial owner can help those headed to Laos. Nicer but pricier is the **Sok Sombat Hotel** ❷ on the north side of the market. (Rooms with flush toilet and fan US$5-7, with A/C US$15-25.) Eating options are limited in Stung Treng. The cheapest is the small **market ❶,** one block behind the Amatak Guest House (2000r). Of the touristy places surrounding Sunset Guest House, **Dara Restaurant** ❸ is the best pick (large range of entrees US$12). **Soup Gaot Restaurant ❶,** two blocks from the docks going away from the market and next to the Sekong Hotel, serves decent Khmer fare (entrees about 3000r).

BAN LUNG ☎075

Far removed from the bustle of Phnom Penh, Rattanakiri Province is defined by its countryside, dusty clay roads, and populations of fiercely independent minorities. Isolated in the mountainous northeast border between Laos and Vietnam, the people of the region have resisted lowland hegemony for centuries. Even the Khmer Rouge left the ethnic minorities largely to their own devices. Since 1986, when Ban Lung was made the provincial capital, increasing numbers of Khmer, Vietnamese, and Chinese have migrated here, but a vibrant mix of Jarai, Krung, and Tumpuon people continues to dwell in small, insular communities and farms. Itself small and sleepy, Ban Lung is an excellent place to explore the Cambodian countryside, with waterfalls, gem mines, and hill-tribes all within a 2hr. radius.

TRANSPORTATION. The dirt strip **airfield** is 400m south of town. **President's Airlines** (☎012 958 721; open daily 7:30-11:30am and 1-5pm) runs flights to Phnom Penh (3 per week, US$55). **Phnom Penh Airlines** (open M-Th and Sa 7:30-11:30am and 1-5pm) also runs flights to Phnom Penh (M, F; US$55). All flights must be confirmed, and departures can change without formal notice. **Pick-up trucks** run from the market in Ban Lung to Kratie (9-12hr., leave when full, around 7am, US$10) via Stung Treng (4hr., US$5). Inquire at the Mountain Guest House or Ratanak Hotel (see **Accommodations and Food,** below) the night before you want to leave to arrange a pick-up. The stretch of road from Stung Treng to Kratie is in horrible condition. If possible, take a **boat** from Stung Treng to Kratie (3-4hr., 7am, US$7-8).

ORIENTATION AND PRACTICAL INFORMATION. The town has only one main road, so finding your way around Ban Lung isn't difficult. Heading north on the airport road brings you to the intersection with **Route 19,** Ban Lung's wide artery, which runs east-west through town and on to the Vietnamese border only 70km away. A right turn leads to town. Another right at the *naga* pillars leads past a **police station** and Ban Lung's utilitarian **market.** The road also passes the **President Airlines office** (☎012 958 721; open daily 7:30-11:30am and 1-5pm). **Phnom Penh Airlines** is to the left of the market (open daily 7:30-11:30am and 1-5pm). **Rattanakiri Provincial Hospital,** 2km north of the airport road and Rte. 19 intersection, is not for the faint of heart. The **post office** (open daily 8-11am and 2-5pm) is 1km east of the *naga* pillar, next to the **telecommunications office** (☎974 006; open daily 7:30am-noon and 2-5pm), which offers international service (US$1.30 per minute).

ACCOMMODATIONS AND FOOD. Shrewd bargaining can greatly reduce prices from March to June. The pleasant **Mountain Guest House** ❷ is on the airport road 400m north of Rte. 19. Plates of fruit mysteriously appear as you lounge on the veranda. (☎974 047. Large rooms with double beds, fans, and shared baths US$3-4.) Towards town on the same road, just past the *naga* and on the right side (same side as the market) is **Hotel Cheng Lok** ❷ which has beautiful, brand-new rooms. (☎974 121. US$5 with fan and TV, with A/C US$10.) Across the street is **Rattanak Hotel** ❷, another excellent choice; all rooms are fully tiled with fan and private bath. (Doubles US$5.) Mrs. Kim at the Mountain and Mr. Leng at the Ratanak are both excellent sources of information about the surrounding area and can arrange for guides, bike rental, and transportation from Ban Lung. The **American Restaurant** ❶, diagonally across from Mountain Guest House, has savory fruit and is bound to be the highlight of any visit. (Beef *lok-lak* 4000r.) The **Rattanak Hotel** ❷ has a good restaurant as well. (Khmer barbecue 15,000r, but enough for 3.)

SIGHTS. There is little to see in Ban Lung proper, but there is a lot to see and do in the surrounding area. Get a map from Ratanak Hotel or Mountain Guest House. About 2km west of the airport road intersection on Rte. 19 is **Wat Phnom Suay.** At the top of Phnom Suay, 1km beyond the temple along the dirt path that runs through the temple grounds, is a large statue of the **Sleeping Buddha.** The Enlightened One's view from the top, with the jagged peaks of the Central Highlands in the distance, is magnificent. **Yak Lom Lake,** a magical little crater lake, is 4km east on Rte. 19. The water is quite clear and the swimming excellent. To get there, head east on Rte. 19 past several rubber plantations. After 2km, there's a roundabout topped with statues of hill-tribesmen. Take a right and the lake is 1.5km farther, past a hill-tribe village. It makes a nice walk if the weather cooperates. There is also a **museum** at Yak Lom Lake featuring exhibits on tribes in the Rattanakiri area and their handicrafts. (Entry to lake, including museum, US$1; for a trekking guide call ☎012 981 226 or check out www.geocities.com/yeak_laom.)

DAYTRIPS FROM BAN LUNG. Many travelers use Ban Lung merely as a base camp from which to see the province's attractions. The region is a patchwork of highland minorities, many of whom continue to live as they have for millennia in small, isolated communities. Indeed, during the rainy season, many villages may be largely, if not completely, deserted. At this time families head off into the forest to clear and cultivate mountain rice, their staple crop. The best way to see the countryside is to hire a motorcycle and driver in Ban Lung (US$10-15 per day; inquire at Mountain Guest House). The best places to see hill-tribes are at **Ta Vang,** at the eastern edge of Virachay Park (51km, 2-2½hr. by motorbike), and at **Vocun Sai** (38km, 1-2hr. by motorbike), at the western edge of the park. There are **Pro, Lao,** and **Krung villages** near both places. While you can explore on your own it is best to bring a guide, for very few people speak English in the villages. The road to Ta Vang is especially difficult for inexperienced moto drivers. There are active gem mines within a 2hr. moto ride from Ban Lung. East on the road to Vietnam is **Bokeo,** home to several **sapphire mines,** Jarai and Lao tribe villages, and a waterfall. There are also three **waterfalls** close to Ban Lung off the main road.

To experience the wonders of **Virachay National Park**, rent a motorbike or hire a guide to either Ta Vang, at the eastern edge of the park, or Vocun Sai, at the western edge. There you will need to hire a ranger to take you into the forest. Rangers are generally on duty Monday to Friday, and it is best to arrive in the morning to secure one. (Entrance fee US$5. Rangers charge US$10 per day.) It is best to go on at least a 2-night trek into the forest, for it takes more than a full day's hike to reach the jungle. Bring bug spray, iodine pills or water purifier, and a hammock with mosquito net (Mountain Guest House, see **Accommodations and Food,** p. 103, will rent one for US$3). Virachay National Park, bordering Laos and Vietnam, is still largely unexplored, and is home to dense jungle and many different kinds of birds and mammals, including elephants, tigers, gaur, and leopards. Many different hill-tribes also live on the outskirts of the forest. Another option is to see the jungle by boat on the river which skirts the park. Boats can be chartered from Ta Vang to Vocun Sai (6-8hr., US$40 per boat). Inquire at the ranger station. If stuck in Ta Vang or Vocun Sai, you can stay the night for very cheap, or even for free.

NORTHERN CAMBODIA

SIEM REAP ☎063

Spurred by improved safety in the region, tourism has taken off in the dusty little city of Siem Reap, which functions chiefly as a gateway to the nearby temples of Angkor. Five-star resorts and restaurants line the outskirts of town, and package tour buses are a regular sight on the way to the temples. Siem Reap may have the highest concentration of moto drivers in the whole country, but its secluded waterfalls and isolated temples remain a secret travelers can explore in peace.

TRANSPORTATION

The **airport** is 8km northwest of town off Rte. 6. International departure tax is US$20 and domestic is US$4. **Bangkok Airways,** 571 Rte. 6 (☎380 191; open daily 8am-4:30pm), flies to **Bangkok** (5 per day, reduced service in low season, US$158). **Siem Reap Airlines,** in the same office as Bangkok Airways, flies to **Phnom Penh** (3 per day, US$64). **Vietnam Airlines,** 108 Rte. 6 (☎063 964 488), flies to **Hà Nội** (daily, US$226) and **Hồ Chí Minh City** (4 per day,US$104). **Minibuses** and **pick-ups** go to **Bangkok** (13hr., 7am, US$10) via **Poi Pot** (5-6hr., US$4) and **Phnom Penh** (7-9hr., 7am, US$4). Inquire at your guesthouse the night before you leave, and the bus will pick you up. If you are tired of bad roads you can take a **speedboat** to **Battambang** (4hr., 7am, US$12) and **Phnom Penh** (7hr., 7am, US$23). Boat service may be restricted or may take longer in the dry season. It is advisable to leave Siem Reap at 5:45-6am to catch the boat because it is 18km from Siem Reap to the river and the road is bad. Any moto driver in town will take you to the temples (US$5-6 per day for the main temples, US$10-12 per day for Banteay Srei and the far temples; US$4-6 extra to see the waterfalls beyond Banteay Srei). A **car** and driver can be rented for the day at the tourist office (US$20).

ORIENTATION AND PRACTICAL INFORMATION

Siem Reap can be navigated by foot, but the heat and unlabeled streets make traveling by moto preferable. **Rte. 6** cuts through the north part of town, running east to the **New Market** and west to the **airport.** Those arriving by boat will follow a road heading north from Tonle Sap. The road forks into **V. Sivatha** on the left and the **West Bank River Road** on the right. V. Sivatha traces the west edge of town, intersecting Rte. 6 in a flurry of guesthouse signs. North of its intersection with Rte. 6, the West Bank River Rd. runs past the roundabout and the Grand Hotel, and on to Angkor, 7km away. Running north-south, the **Siem Reap River** traces the eastern edge of town. The dirt road parallel to the east bank road is **V. Wat Bo,** home to several popular guesthouses.

Tourist Office: Opposite the Grand Hotel on the road to Angkor (☎964 371). Maps of Angkor and Siem Reap. Motorcycle with driver US$8 per day. A/C car with driver US$20 per day. Licensed guides US$20 per day. Open M-F 8am-noon and 2-5pm. Next door is the **Tour Guides Association** (☎063 964 347; khmerang@camintel.com), which has guides in a variety of languages, including English, French, German, and Thai. Guides US$20 per day. Open daily 7-11am and 2-5pm.

Currency Exchange: US dollars and Thai baht are accepted everywhere. **Cambodian Commercial Bank** (☎964 392), at the intersection of Vithei Siratha and Achamean St., exchanges traveler's checks (2% commission, US$1 min.) and offers MC/V cash advances (2% commission, US$5 min.). Open M-F 8am-3pm.

Books: The Lazy Mango (☎963 875) next to the **Angkor What?** bar, has a decent selection of second-hand paperbacks, as well as an assortment of titles on Angkor and Cambodia in general. Open daily 9am-10pm.

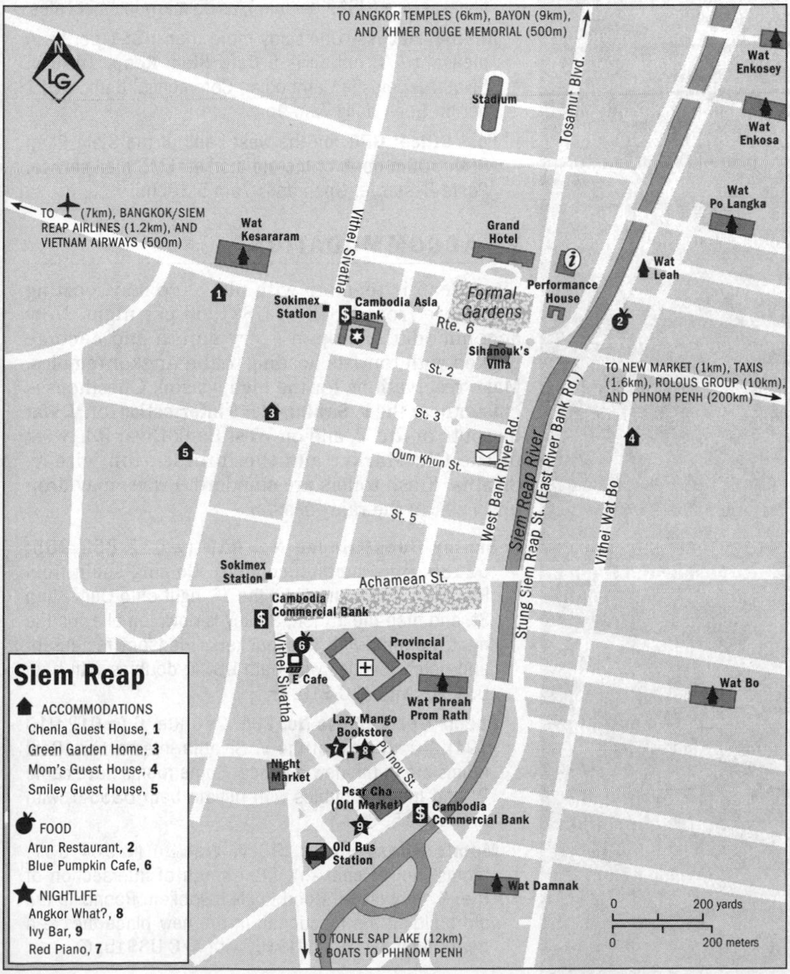

CAMBODIA

THE LOCAL STORY

MOST DANGEROUS COW IN THE EAST

Cambodia's national animal is the critically endangered kouprey *(Bos sauveli)*, a wild, forest-dwelling cow. Males have frayed horns and a huge dewlap. They stand 2m at the shoulder and can weigh up to 900kg. It is estimated that there are probably no more than 200 kouprey left in northern Cambodia, and only a few spill into northeastern Thailand, southern Laos, and central Vietnam.

Thanks to the folly of human warfare in the 20th century, it has become not only nearly impossible for the unlucky cow to survive, but also for specialists to study the bovine. During WWII, a captive kouprey calf starved to death in a Paris zoo during German occupation. Since then, a handful of 50s field notes, one grainy 1967 photograph, and a few unverified sightings have comprised the best research in the kouprey's war-torn home turf; the official UN Conservation Plan states that kouprey data is "of a very sketchy nature."

Beyond its mystery and rarity, the kouprey could be profitably interbred with domestic cattle to produce disease-resistant, tropics-adapted livestock. When hiking through Rattanakiri in search of this elusive bovine, be sure to bring the proper equipment: malaria pills, a flashlight, an armed escort, de-mining equipment, and for heaven's sake, a decent camera.

Markets: New Market (Psar Leu), 1km east of town on Rte. 6. The touristy **Old Market (Psar Cha)** is at the southern end of the West Bank River Rd.

Police: Foreigner Office (☎779 181), on the corner of Rte. 6 and V. Sivatha.

Pharmacies: Many located around the town center.

Medical Services: Rustic **Siem Reap Provincial Hospital** (☎761 119), down the side-street off V. Sivatha that veers east at Cambodian Commercial Bank, opposite the Apsara Tours branch office. Doctors on-call M-F 7-11am and 2-5pm, Sa 6am-noon.

Telephones: Many guesthouses offer international service (US$2-3 per min.). The post office also offers international service (US$2 per min.), as do many Internet cafes.

Internet Access: Don't pay more than US$1 per hr. A pleasant A/C option is **E Cafe Siem Reap,** 147B V. Sivatha, opposite Cambodian Commercial Bank. US$1 per hr. Open daily 7am-9pm.

Post Office: GPO, on the west bank of the Siem Reap River 500m north of the old market. EMS mail service. *Poste Restante.* Open daily 7am-5:30pm.

ACCOMMODATIONS

Siem Reap is teeming with places to stay, costing anywhere from US$2 to US$1900 per night. New accommodations open every month and become packed with tourists heading to the Angkor temples. Make reservations for the high season. Guesthouses cluster near the **V. Sivatha-Rte. 6 intersection,** on **V. Wat Bo** south of Rte. 6, and on West Bank River Rd., west of the Old Market and the intersection with V. Sivatha. Flush toilets are standard. Prices may drop up to 20% in the rainy season.

Smiley Guest House No. 019 (☎012 852 955; 021852955@mobitel.com.kh). Coming south from Rte. 6 on V. Sivatha, take the 1st right onto Oum Khun St. and then the 1st left; Smiley is down an alley on the right. Popular with backpackers. Pleasant restaurant and porch. Singles with bath US$4; doubles with bath US$5-6, with A/C $10. ❶

Chenla Guest House No. 260, 260 Rte. 6 (☎012 910 794), 200m west of the V. Sivatha intersection. Best rooms are in the new building. Some rooms have cable TV and fridge. Doubles with private bath US$5-6, with A/C US$15. ❷

Mom's Guest House, 99 V. Wat Bo (☎964 037; moms@online.com.kh), 30m south of intersection of Rte. 6. Very clean. Good English spoken. Rooms in the old building are functional; in the new place they're a treat. Rooms with fan US$6, with A/C US$15. ❷

Green Garden Home, 051 V. Sivatha (☎012 963 342), about 200m south of the Rte. 6 intersection, and down a street to the right; look for the blue sign on V. Sivatha. Lovely rooms with bamboo furniture and relaxing verandas all set in a flower garden. Rooms have A/C, bath with hot water, fridge, cable TV, and fan. Rooms $US15-25. ❸

FOOD

A small night market on V. Sivatha, north of Cambodian Commercial Bank, serves noodles for under US$1. Food vendors also line the road to Angkor and the east bank of the river parallel to the guesthouse strip. For a sit-down meal, **Arun Restaurant** ❸, off East Bank River Rd. 50m north of the Rte. 6 intersection, has generous portions of Cambodian and Chinese food. (☎964 227. Grilled beef with tofu sauce US$4. Open daily 10am-10pm.) On Pitnou St. across from the hospital, **The Blue Pumpkin** ❷ is a chic bakery/cafe with the best coffee in town (US$1). They also have some delicious baked goods (2000r and up) and lunch food. (☎946 277. US$1.50 and up. Open daily 6am-10pm.) Simple and cheap pan-Asia and Khmer food is available at **Lucky Restaurant** ❷ and next door at **Teck Wain Hainanese Chicken** ❷; both places offer a happy medium between sit-down restaurants and cheap market food. Both are located on V. Sivatha, south of the Cambodian Commercial Bank. (Entrees US$1-2.)

SIGHTS

A somber **memorial** to Khmer Rouge atrocities is on the road to Angkor. Take the dirt road turn-off at the "Welcome" sign, 500m past the Grand Hotel. Follow the road to a small wat, next to the ramshackle wooden pavilion that is filled waist-deep with human skulls and bones. For those who can't get enough of Angkor architecture, **Wat Leah,** along the east bank of the river north of Arun Restaurant, has two well-preserved Angkor-period brick sanctuaries behind the modern pagoda. For a chance to watch highly-skilled craftsmen create traditional Khmer wood carvings, head to the **Khmer Art of Carving Center.** Look for the sign on the left heading out of town on the road to the temples. (Open M-Sa 7:30am-4:30pm.) Across the road there is also a small **stone carving workshop.** Small pieces start at US$25; high rollers can spend hundreds of dollars.

NIGHTLIFE

Although nightlife in Siem Reap is picking up, it is hampered by the fact that many people get up at dawn to see the temples. The amusingly named **Angkor What?,** a block north of the Old Market on one of V. Sivatha's side-streets, and the **Ivy Bar,** at the south end of the Old Market, are both youthful late-night drinking spots. **Lotus Bar,** at the north end of the market, is open 24hr. For an expensive nightcap, try the **Elephant Bar** in the Grand Hotel d'Angkor, at the north end of the West Bank River Rd. (happy hour 4-8pm). You can see Khmer dancing at the **Bayon II Restaurant,** on Rd. 6 on the east side of the river (nightly performances US$4, with buffet dinner US$11; show starts at 7:30pm). The **Red Piano,** 50m northwest of the Old Market, is a chic restaurant/bar whose claim to fame is that it was the headquarters of the "Tomb Raider" cast and crew while they filmed at Angkor.

ANGKOR

With their unrivaled beauty and majesty, the temples of Angkor deserve their reputation as one of the great manmade wonders of the world. Begun in the 9th century, the building process lasted well into the 15th century. The temples are the remains of the mighty Khmer empire that, at its height, ruled over most of the Malay peninsula and modern-day Cambodia, Laos, and Vietnam. In the 15th century, the Khmer kings abandoned Angkor and moved their capital to the site of modern-day Phnom Penh. Angkor lay in relative obscurity until the diaries of French naturalist Henri Mouhot were published in 1864. Mouhot's description of the beautiful temples sparked international interest, drawing the numerous travelers who now come to see the rising sun break over the temple *stupas* in what the Khmer believe is the gateway between the mortal and celestial worlds.

TRANSPORTATION

Many travelers stay the night in Siem Reap and hire a **motorcycle** (US$5-6 per day for the main temples, US$10-12 per day for the far temples like Banteay Srei) or **bicycle** (US$1-2 per day) to see the temples. Those considering renting a bicycle should think it through and plan carefully: some temples aren't terribly far from town, but they are in the jungle, and the weather gets very hot from the late morning to the evening. Rentals can be arranged through guesthouses or at the Siem Reap Tourist Office (p. 104) and require a passport as deposit. **Cars** with drivers can be hired for US$20 per day from hotels or the tourist office.

PRACTICAL INFORMATION

Foreigners can buy one-day (US$20), three-day (US$40), or seven-day (US$60) temple passes from the onsite ticket checkpoint. Officials appreciate it if you bring your own passport-size photo for your ticket. However, if you don't have one they'll take one for free. Multi-day passes must be used on consecutive days. There is a steep US$80 fine for misusing tickets.

SIGHTS

The following descriptions are arranged in the order that most travelers see the monuments. Beginning at Angkor Wat, the route proceeds clockwise on a roughly rectangular track. Angkor's magnificent ruins hold enough secret nooks and crannies for a lifetime of exploration, but with a little planning and prioritizing you can see most of the temple complex in a few days. Try to get an early start; by 11am temperatures can rise to over 39°C (100°F). Bring a map of the temple complex, a flashlight, drinking water, and extra film, or buy all these things from vendors outside the temples at inflated prices. *A Guide to Angkor*, by Dawn Rooney, sold by child vendors at Angkor Wat (US$3-6), has temple plans and is especially useful while navigating the complexities of Ta Prohm, Bayon, and Angkor Wat. If locals come up to you in one of the temples and start to give you information, they will demand US$1 at the end. Don't listen if you don't want to pay.

SAFETY CONCERNS AND TEMPLE ETIQUETTE. Keep in mind the following concerns and customs while at Angkor:

Mines: The government claims that Angkor has been demined, but to be safe, stay on well-trodden paths, especially at more remote temples.

Wildlife: The jungles have poisonous snakes like small bright green *kraits.* King cobras, with enough venom to bring down a bull elephant, are rare but not unheard of—avoid dark, isolated chambers within the temples. Also, roadside monkeys are fascinating—and, yes, cute—but they are not tame; keep your distance.

Tickets: Guards check passes at the entrances to most of the temples; it's now virtually impossible to slip in without paying.

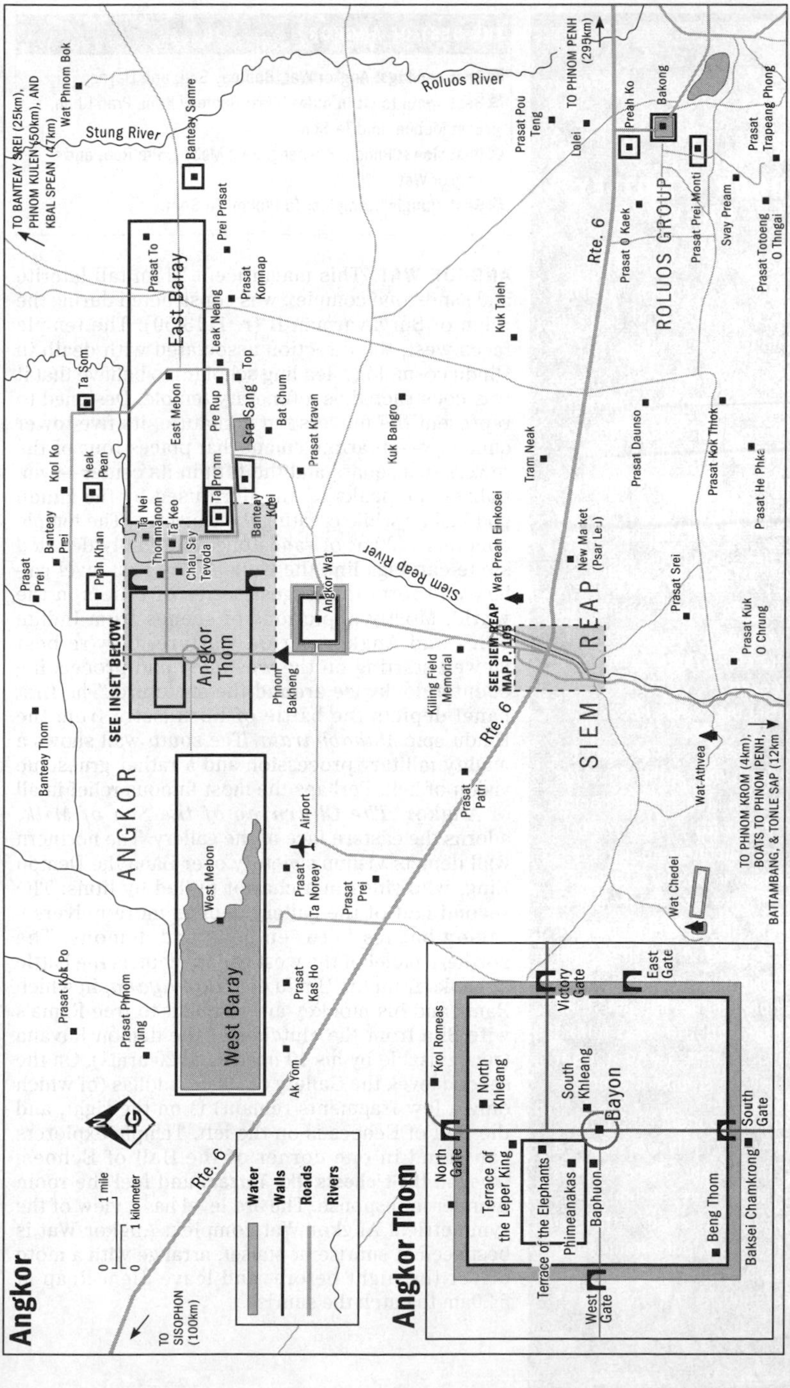
Angkor
0 1 mile
0 1 kilometer
LG
N
Water
Walls
Roads
Rivers
Rte. 6
TO SISOPHON (100km)
ANGKOR
SEE INSET BELOW
Angkor Thom
West Baray
West Mebon
East Baray
Siem Reap River
SIEM REAP
SEE SIEM REAP MAP P. 105
Rte. 6
Roluos River
Stung River
TO BANTEAY SREI (25km), PHNOM KULEN (50km), AND KBAL SPEAN (47km)
TO PHNOM PENH (295km)
TO PHNOM KROM (4km), BOATS TO PHNOM PENH, BATTAMBANG, & TONLE SAP (12km)
ROLUOS GROUP
Wat Phnom Bok
Banteay Samre
Prei Prasat
Prasat To
Prasat Komnap
Leak Neang
Ta Som
Top
East Mebon
Pre Rup
Sra Sang
Bat Chum
Krol Ko
Neak Pean
Ta Prohm
Banteay Kdei
Prasat Kravan
Kuk Bangro
Banteay Prei
Ta Nei
Thommanom
Ta Keo
Chau Say Tevoda
Prasat Prei
Preah Khan
Angkor Wat
Phnom Bakheng
Killing Field Memorial
Wat Preah Einkosei
New Market (Psar Leu)
Tram Neak
Kuk Talen
Prasat Pou Teng
Lolei
Preah Ko
Bakong
Prasat Trapeang Phong
Prasat Prei Monti
Svay Pream
Prasat Totoeng O Thngai
Prasat O Kaek
Prasat Daunso
Prasat Kok Thlok
Prasat He Phke
Prasat Srei
Prasat Kuk O Chrung
Wat Athvea
Wat Chedei
Banteay Thom
Airport
Prasat Ta Noreay
Prasat Prei
Prasat Patri
Prasat Kok Po
Prasat Phnom Rung
Prasat Kas Ho
Ak Yom
Angkor Thom
North Gate
Krol Romeas
North Khleang
Victory Gate
East Gate
South Khleang
Bayon
Terrace of the Leper King
Terrace of the Elephants
Phimeanakas
Baphuon
West Gate
Beng Thom
Baksei Chamkrong
South Gate

CAMBODIA

THE LOCAL STORY

ANGKOR'S MOTLEY CREW

There are several recurring figures in the carvings of Angkor Wat. This is *Let's Go*'s Who's Who guide to the world-famous temple.

Naga: Sanskrit for "snake." These multi-headed, half-human, half-serpentine creatures appear in both Buddhist and Hindu mythology, and are frequently depicted on the balustrades of Angkor's temples. It is said that the Khmer people descended from the union between a foreigner and a *naga*. According to Hindu myths, the *naga* swallowed the waters of life and were either ruptured by Indra or squeezed by Vishnu's entourage to set the waters free.

Apsara: These celestial beauties sprang forth during the Churning of the Sea of Milk and have since become virtually synonymous with Khmer architecture. Their perfect, sensuous beauty is believed to hold highly refined powers of seduction. Angkor Wat's apsaras, widely regarded as the most beautiful nymphs of all the temples, appear alone, flaunting their individual appearances, unlike the Bayon apsaras who appear collectively, in groups of three.

Vishnu: An important Hindu deity, Vishnu was widely worshipped during the height of the Angkor period. Married to Lakshmi, he is frequently portrayed with four arms and a sampot (ornamental waist sash). Whenever the earth is threatened by evil, he acts as

THE BEST OF ANGKOR

- **Best carvings:** Angkor Wat, Banteay Srei, and Bayon.
- **Best spots to sit in quiet bliss:** Banteay Kdei, Prah Khan, East Mebon, and Ta Som.
- **Best views:** Phnom Bakheng, East Mebon, Pre Rup, and Angkor Wat.
- **Best "jungle" temples:** Ta Prohm, Ta Som.

ANGKOR WAT. This magnificent 213m tall laterite and sandstone complex was constructed during the reign of Suryavarman II (r. 1113-50). The temple faces west, the direction associated with death in Hindu cosmology, leading scholars to believe that it was constructed as a funerary temple. Designed to represent the universe in miniature, its five-tower quincunx—an arrangement that places four of the towers in a square and the fifth in its center—symbolizes the peaks of Mt. Meru used by the Hindu god Vishnu while creating the Universe. The temple contains $1200m^3$ of sandstone. Incredibly detailed stone carvings line the walls of the first-level gallery and form the largest series of reliefs in the world. Mostly depictions of scenes from Indian epics and Angkor period warfare, they're best viewed starting on the west side and proceeding counterclockwise around the structure. The first panel depicts the battle of Kuruksetra from the Hindu epic *Mahabharata*. The south wall shows a mighty military procession and a rather gruesome vision of hell. Perhaps the most famous relief in all of Angkor, *The Churning of the Sea of Milk*, adorns the eastern face of the gallery. The northern wall depicts Vishnu's victory over Bana the Demon King, who rides in a chariot pulled by lions. The second half of the gallery depicts more universe-saving battles between gods and demons. The northern panel of the west gallery depicts the battle of Lanka from the Hindu epic *Ramayana*, in which Rama and his monkey army sought to free Rama's wife Sita from the clutches of the demon Ravana (recognizable by his 10 heads and 20 arms). On the second level, the Gallery of 1000 Buddhas (of which only a few fragments remain) is on the right, and the Hall of Echoes is on the left. Temple explorers can stand in one corner of the Hall of Echoes, **pound their chests like Tarzan,** and feel the room thunder in response. The 3rd level has a view of the symmetrical Angkor Wat complex. Angkor Wat is best seen at sunrise or sunset; arrange with a moto driver the night before, and leave Siem Reap at 5:30am to catch the sunrise.

ANGKOR THOM. The large temple complex of Angkor Thom (literally "Great City"), constructed by Jayavarman VII (1181-1219), lies 1.5km north of Angkor Wat. Angkor Thom shares Angkor Wat's cosmological layout: a moat symbolizes the oceans, the walls are the land, and the towers represent the peaks of Mt. Meru. The remaining ruins are mainly temples, though it's believed that this city once housed many administrative buildings that didn't survive the test of time. Angkor Thom's south entrance passes through a causeway lined with 54 guardian statues of gods and demons. The Angkor Conservancy has replaced many of the original heads to prevent theft. An all-seeing, four-faced, smiling head tops the tower gates.

THE BAYON. Rising in the exact center of Angkor Thom, the Bayon was erected by Jayavarman VII and is dedicated to Buddhism. Its reliefs depict, in addition to the usual epics, scenes of everyday life in Angkorian Cambodia. The Bayon contains two sets of bas-reliefs meant to be viewed clockwise. The southern gallery contains perhaps the finest of the Bayon's bas-reliefs depicting a battle between the Khmers and Chams, while the lower tier of reliefs presents a more peaceful view of Angkorian life. The northern gallery, only some of which was completed, contains a depiction of an Angkor circus. The upper gallery contains stories from Hindu epics dotted with faces believed to represent the Bodhisattva Avalokitesvara, who selflessly delayed attaining enlightenment to aid humanity.

BAPHUON. A few hundred meters northwest of the Bayon stands the Hindu temple of Baphuon, built by Udayadityavarman II in the late 11th century.

PHIMEANAKAS. Situated just north of Baphuon, this Hindu monument was erected by three successive kings: Rajendravarman, Jayavarman V, and Udayadityavarman I. If the monument is open, the steep climb to the top of the central sanctuary is worth the view that awaits. The steep laterite "stairs" are best attempted early in the day before the sun or rain set in. The west staircase has a metal rail that makes climbing slightly easier.

TERRACE OF THE ELEPHANTS. First laid out by Suryavarman I, the Terrace of the Elephants (the Royal Terrace) stretches 300m from Baphuon to the beginning of the Terrace of the Leper King, past Phimeanakas. The **bas-reliefs** of near life-sized elephants seem to emerge like ghosts from the stones. Along the wall near the Terrace of the Leper King is a carving of a five-headed horse.

its savior in the form of an *avatara* (earthly incarnation). He is seen in the bas-reliefs of Angkor Wat both in the form of a human and as a tortoise in the Churning of the Sea of Milk.

Ganesha: Parvati created Ganesha, the elephant-headed Hindu god of wisdom, to guard her bath. When Parvati's husband, the powerful god Shiva, tried to gain admittance to her chambers while she was bathing, Ganesha refused to let him pass. Shiva called upon Vishnu for help, and together they decapitated Ganesha. Rightly furious, Parvati began to wreak havoc, destroying the world. Since even the mighty Shiva could not handle a woman's scorn, he resurrected Ganesha. But instead of replacing Ganesha's head, Shiva instead placed upon Ganesha's body the head of the first being he saw—that of an elephant.

Garuda: A late addition to Angkor's characters, this half-man, half-bird is the enemy of the *naga*. He is also Vishnu's preferred means of transportation.

Makara: With a face like that of a Chinese dragon and the body of a crocodile, representations of this demonic sea monster are often found on lintel beams. Frequently he is pictured with other hideous creatures—like the *naga*—coming from his mouth. Lolei, one of the Roluos temples, has a fine representation of this creature.

TERRACE OF THE LEPER KING. Another legacy of Jayavarman VII, the monument lies north of the Terrace of the Elephants. Two galleries of bas-reliefs line the terrace, while mythological creatures and *apsaras* decorate the outer wall. The statue of the Leper King himself is a replica. The National Museum in Phnom Penh now houses the original. Some believe Jayavarman VII may have suffered from leprosy himself, though others believe that the statue portrays the Hindu god of death, Yama, or Kubera, the god of wealth.

PRAH KHAN. Located northeast of the Bayon outside Angkor Thom, Prah Khan is one of the largest temple complexes. It was built as a Buddhist temple by Jayavarman VII in memory of his father, and Prah Khan literally means "Sacred Sword." Some archaeologists believe that the two-story building in the northeastern corner of the compound, a location rarely used in Khmer architecture, might once have housed an Asian Excalibur, left by Jayavarman VII for his descendants.

NEAK PEAN. This Buddhist temple, east of Prah Khan along the Grand Circuit access road, was also built by Jayavarman VII. Unlike any other Angkor temple, this small and charming spot was once five ponds, that are now covered in grass. A temple stands in the exact center of what was the large, central pond. Neak Pean is said to represent Lake Anayatapa, a sacred body of water in the Himalayas. The four symmetrical ponds, one at each cardinal point, represent the earth's four rivers. A stone horse, believed to be the sacred steed *Balaha*, drags several marooned sailors toward the island sanctuary in the middle of Neak Pean.

TA SOM. Lying east of Neak Pean along the access road, Ta Som was also built by Jayavarman VII. A small, quiet temple with one sanctuary, it is unrestored and largely in ruins. A four-faced *bayon* (a monument distinguished by its many sculpted faces) casts its inscrutable smile over visitors as they enter from the west. Continuing to the east gate, the *bayon* is almost entirely in the clutches of fig tree roots, giving its smile an eerie feel.

EAST MEBON. Built in the 10th century by Rajendravarman II in memory of his parents, tranquil East Mebon stands southeast of Ta Som and is accessible only by boat. In the Angkor era, the temple stood in the middle of the large manmade lake *(baray)*. Impressive sculptures of elephants and lions guard each entrance.

PHNOM BAKHENG. Just north and slightly west of Angkor Wat, Phnom Bakheng was built by Yasovarman I in the late ninth century. Travelers struggle up the steep and rocky slope to enjoy a spectacular sunset and view of Angkor Wat. An elephant carriage is available to take the weary to the top (US$15). Originally, 109 towers, corresponding to the animal zodiac cycle, graced the *phnom*. In January and February, a sunrise directly over Angkor rewards early risers.

WEST BARAY. West of Angkor Thom, this half-filled lake is best seen from Phnom Bakheng. Believed to date from the 11th century, West Baray was built during the reign of Udayadityavarman II. A small, largely destroyed temple, **West Mebon,** stands in the center of the *baray* and is accessible by boat.

TA PROHM. West of Pre Rup and bordering Banteay Kdei, Ta Prohm was built as a Buddhist temple by Jayavarman VII in his mother's memory. This vast, crumbling temple competes with the Bayon and Angkor Wat as the most awe-inspiring of Angkor's treasures and is the most authentic "jungle" temple. Ancient trees have grown into and out of the buildings themselves, creating the visage of a "lost city." Inscriptions reveal that 79,365 people were employed in Ta Prohm's upkeep during its heyday. Early risers can witness its stunning beauty in the morning light.

PRE RUP. Five hundred meters due south of East Mebon lies Pre Rup, a Hindu temple built by Rajendravarman II in the second half of the 10th century to honor Shiva. More impressive than its contemporary East Mebon, this multi-tiered structure affords views of East Baray to the north. Two halls parallel to the laterite wall as you enter from the east are believed to have housed pilgrims who journeyed here to worship. The temple is thought to have funerary associations. The vat near the east staircase is thought to have been used at cremations.

BANTEAY KDEI. Banteay Kdei is a Buddhist temple built by Jayavarman VII, southeast of Pre Rup near the Sra Srang Reservoir. A *bayon* oversees the entrance to this unrestored temple. Lying largely in ruins, Banteay Kdei is more a spot for calm reflection than active exploration.

BANTEAY SREI. Detailed and beautiful Banteay Srei (Citadel of Women) stands 35km northeast of the main cluster of Angkor temples. Described as the "precious queen" by French archaeologists, Banteay Srei's construction spanned two kingships in the second half of the 10th century. Though smaller in scale than the temples at Angkor, this pinkish temple is home to many exquisite carvings that are based on Indian epics. The south library shows Ravana shaking Mt. Kailusa (east pediment). The north library depicts Indra casting down heavenly rain and Krishna killing his murderous uncle King Kamsa. Unfortunately, moto drivers will charge you US$12 for the day to get to Banteay Srei and the other far temples.

ROLUOS GROUP. About 30min. by moto on the incredibly dusty Rte. 6, this collection of three temples represents the very earliest of the Angkor period and is interesting only to die-hard Angkor enthusiasts. Jayavarman II made this capital of Hariharalaya in the 9th century. All three temples were originally consecrated to Hinduism. **Lolei** (north of the other two off Rte. 6), the site of a modern Buddhist wat, has not been preserved very well but boasts a few beautiful lintel beams on the four brick towers of the main sanctuary. **Preah Ko** (south of Rte. 6 and north of Bakong), or "Sacred Ox," consists of a central sanctuary with six brick towers. **Bakong,** the largest and most impressive of the Roluos Group is a temple mountain representing Mt. Meru and was once the ancient capital of Hariharalaya.

KBAL SPEAN. About 10km down the road from Banteay Srei, Kbal Spean, "The Head of the Bridge," offers a free and less crowded opportunity to see riverbed *linga.* A *linga* is a symbol of the creative power of nature and is shaped like a male phallus. About 15min. up the hill lies the secluded **River of the Thousand Linga.** The stretch of riverbed before the waterfall is carved with *linga* and images of deities. The carvings bless the river's waters as they flow to the temples and fields of Angkor. Its proximity to Banteay Srei makes it practical to combine a visit to the two sites. Moto drivers will try to charge you US$4-6 extra to see Kbal Spean; bargain hard. **Stay on the path marked by red tree-trunks, as mines remain a risk.**

PHNOM KULEN. Phnom Kulen looms 50km northeast of Angkor Thom. Due to its distance from Siem Reap, the US$20 entry fee, and the presence of more impressive riverbed carvings at Kbal Spean, the trek to Phnom Kulen is not for the temple-weary. The mountain is one of Cambodia's most sacred sites and on the weekend plays host to hordes of pilgrims. They come to see the **reclining Buddha,** perched on top of a huge boulder on one of the mountain's peaks. The temple sheltering the Buddha has magnificent views over the surrounding mountains, but remember to remove your shoes before climbing the staircase. Ten meters down the hill from the river on the right is a side road leading to a **waterfall,** a popular bathing spot. The quickest way to get to Phnom Kulen is by moto (1½hr. each way, US$20-25 for the whole day). **Be sure you have a reliable guide before venturing off the main road; keep to well-trodden paths, as mines remain a risk.**

INDONESIA

> **ALERT, ALERT.** The September 9, 2004 bombing of the Australian embassy in Jakarta, which killed 9 and injured more than 180, was only the latest in a string of terrorist incidents. Bombings of hotels and nightclubs in recent years suggest that foreigners are being specifically targeted. At press time, non-essential travel to certain parts of Indonesia was not recommended. See the **Travel Advisories** box (p. 24) to get the most recent information.
>
> As our researchers' safety is our number one priority, the coverage of Indonesia for our 2005 edition was not researched from the road. However, thanks to Alexander Graham Bell and Al Gore, we were able to update Indonesia as much as possible with phone and Internet research.

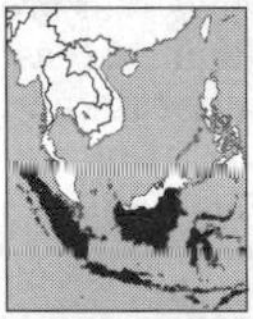

Indonesia's national motto, "*Bhinneka Tunggal Ika,*" translates to "Unity In Diversity." This simple idea has recently become the goal of political leaders, who have found that unity isn't as easy as diversity. The country is home to over 350 ethnic groups, adding cultural hodgepodge to the geographic mix of volcanoes, islands, and beaches. Achieving political unity has been most challenging: President Suharto's resignation signaled the end of the iron-fisted New Order era and the beginning of *Reformasi*, complete with student protests, strikes, and rioting. The recovering tourist industry and peaceful parliamentary elections of 1999 sparked renewed hope in divided Indonesia, although violence in East Timor, the Malukus, and Aceh Province signifies that unity remains tenuous in the wake of continuing political upheaval. Still, wary travelers can maneuver around points of instability and immerse themselves in the strongholds of Indonesia—its stunning landscapes, cultural diversity, historical legacies, and gracious people.

HIGHLIGHTS OF INDONESIA

BEACHES. Despite recent troubles, **Bali** and **Kuta** (p. 174)–is still home to some of the world's most beautiful beaches. Lombok's northwestern **Gili Islands** (p. 207) has smooth sands. **Manado** (p. 230), at Sulawesi's north tip, offers first-rate scuba diving. **Pulau Nias** (p. 254) off Sumatra draws a surfer crowd.

CULTURAL HERITAGE. **Yogjakarta** (p. 152) is easily Java's best city. Colorful **Tana Toraja** (p. 227) in Sulawesi throws killer funerals. **Pura Besakih** (p. 187) is the mother of Balinese temples. **Bukittinggi** (p. 256) and **Padang** (p. 260) showcase both the artistic and culinary culture of Sumatra's Minangkabau people.

HANGING OUT. Hip **Ubud** (p. 179) on Bali has the best cafes and meditation workshops. Lombok's **Tetebatu** (p. 205), and Sulawesi's **Rantepao** (p. 228) all offer cool respite from the lowland heat. **Lake Toba** (p. 247) on Sumatra is an ethereal detour.

LIFE AND TIMES

DEMOGRAPHICS

With over 200 million people, Indonesia is the fourth most populous nation in the world. Over 75% of Indonesians live on Java and Sumatra, which together represent only a fraction of the country's total land mass. The **Javanese** and **Sundanese,**

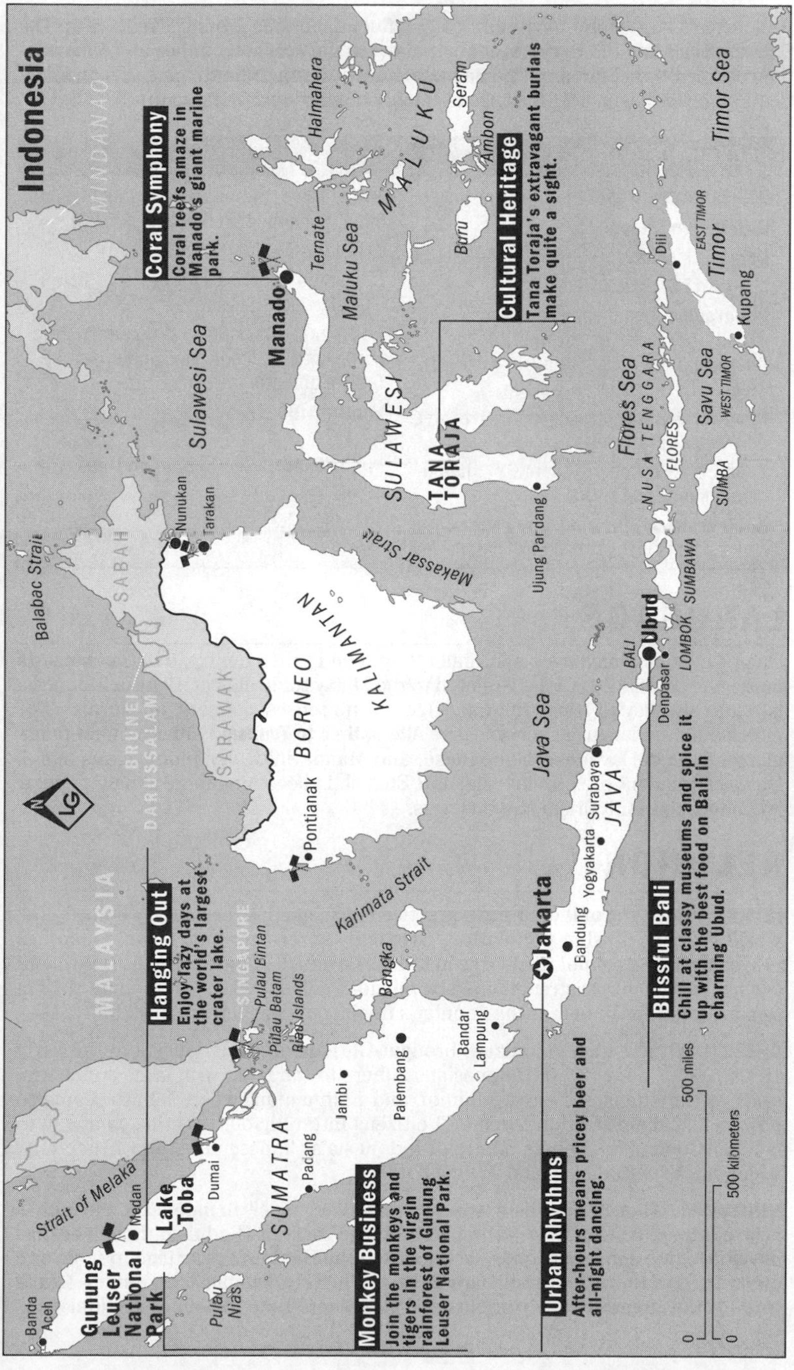
Indonesia
Gunung Leuser National Park
Lake Toba
Monkey Business
Join the monkeys and tigers in the virgin rainforest of Gunung Leuser National Park.
Hanging Out
Enjoy lazy days at the world's largest crater lake.
Urban Rhythms
After-hours means pricey beer and all-night dancing.
Blissful Bali
Chill at classy museums and spice it up with the best food on Bali in charming Ubud.
Coral Symphony
Coral reefs amaze in Manado's giant marine park.
Cultural Heritage
Tana Toraja's extravagant burials make quite a sight.
Jakarta
Ubud
Manado
TANA TORAJA
Banda Aceh
Medan
Strait of Melaka
Dumai
Pulau Nias
SUMATRA
Padang
Jambi
Palembang
Bandar Lampung
Pulau Batam
Pulau Bintan
Riau Islands
SINGAPORE
MALAYSIA
Bangka
Karimata Strait
Pontianak
BORNEO
KALIMANTAN
SARAWAK
BRUNEI DARUSSALAM
SABAH
Balabac Strait
Nunukan
Tarakan
Makassar Strait
Ujung Pandang
Bandung
Yogyakarta
Surabaya
JAVA
Java Sea
BALI
Denpasar
LOMBOK
SUMBAWA
NUSA TENGGARA
FLORES
SUMBA
Flores Sea
Savu Sea
WEST TIMOR
Kupang
Timor
EAST TIMOR
Dili
Timor Sea
SULAWESI
Sulawesi Sea
MINDANAO
Ternate
Maluku Sea
Halmahera
MALUKU
Buru
Seram
Ambon
500 miles
500 kilometers
0

Indonesia's largest and most politically influential ethnic groups, live in Java. The Islamic **Bugis** and the **Torajans** inhabit Sulawesi; the **Acehnese, Batak,** and **Minangkabau** people live in Sumatra. The **Balinese,** known for their flourishing arts and dedication to Hinduism, host Indonesia's most popular tourist destination.

FACTS AND FIGURES

Official Name: Republic of Indonesia.

Government: Republic.

Capital: Jakarta.

Land Area: 1,919,440km².

Geography: Archipelago of over 17,000 islands bordered by the Indian Ocean. Shares Borneo with Malaysia and New Guinea with Papua New Guinea.

Climate: Dry (high season) May-Oct., wet (low season) Nov.-Apr.

Phone Codes: Country code: 62. International dialing prefix: 001, 008.

Random Fact: The word "boogieman" is derived from the Bugis people of Indonesia.

Major Cities: Bandung, Medan, Palembang, Semarang, Surabaya.

Population: 238,452,952.

Language: Bahasa Indonesia (official), English, Dutch, Javanese.

Religions: Islam 88%, Christianity 8%, Hinduism 2%, Mahayana Buddhism 1%, Taoism and other religions 1%.

Literacy: 88.5% overall; 92.9% of men, 84.1% of women.

Major Exports: Petroleum and gas, plywood, textiles, rubber.

LANGUAGE

One of over 300 languages and dialects spoken in the country, **Bahasa Indonesia** unites the population. Closely related to the Malay trade dialect, Bahasa Indonesia is relatively easy to learn; the language has no tenses, genders, or plurals. (For information on language schools, see **Alternatives to Tourism.**) Other common languages include Javanese, Sundanese, and Mandarin. Older Indonesians speak Dutch, a remnant of colonial rule, and English is becoming increasingly popular and important for tourism and business.

RELIGION

ISLAM. About 88% of Indonesians practice Islam, making the country home to the world's largest Muslim population. Originally spread through trade, Islam has proved an important political force in Indonesia; much of the nationalist sentiment against the Dutch was strengthened by religious belief. Today, agitation by Muslim separatist groups threatens the country's fragile political and social stability.

CHRISTIANITY. Dutch colonizers brought Christianity to Indonesia in the early 1600s. Today, about 8% of Indonesians adhere to the faith, with large concentrations of Christians in Flores, Maluku, and Kalimantan. When Suharto came to power, his administration forced all citizens into religious practice as a way to combat Communist beliefs. Many of Indonesia's Chinese adopted Christianity, widening the cultural gap and fueling conflict.

HINDUISM. Though Hinduism was once practiced widely in Indonesia, the faith is now confined primarily to Bali. The Balinese form of Hinduism, however, has developed into something quite distinct from the Hinduism practiced in India and other areas of the world. Visit Pura Besakih, "Mother Temple," on Gunung Agung to study the largest temple complex and most sacred site of Balinese Hinduism.

BUDDHISM. Before the introduction of Islam, Sumatra was primarily Buddhist, while Hinduism dominated Java. Though few followers remain today, the strong influence of Buddhism is nonetheless still evident throughout the archipelago. For a glimpse of some of Southeast Asia's most stunning Buddhist architecture and a lesson in Buddhist philosophy, visit the Borobudur temple near Yogyakarta.

LAND

Indonesia's rich natural environment—which includes 10% of the world's forest cover and the third largest tropical rain forest—has suffered terrible environmental abuses due to industrialization and urbanization. In 2002, President Megawati Soekarnoputri dissolved the Environmental Impact Control Agency (Bapedal), which handled the cases of 23 environmental law violations—including forest fires and illegal logging. Illegal logging has started to take its toll in the southern lowland forests of Sumatra, where the depletion of their natural habitat has driven tigers and elephants into villages to look for food. Floods and landslides are also the result of massive deforestation, precipitating deterioration of the natural environment on all fronts.

More than 30,000 flowering plant species thrive on Indonesia's tropical islands. The rainforest hosts many different kinds of tree species, including pine, teak, bamboo, and meranti—a dark red wood that makes up over 50% of Indonesia's timber exports. River gorges are also home to the sacred Banyan and Pule trees. In addition to thousands of delicate orchid species, Indonesia is also home to the world's largest flower, *Rafflesia*, whose blossoms measure nearly a meter in diameter and smell like rotting flesh.

WILDLIFE

As an archipelago of over 17,000 islands, Indonesia boasts the largest diversity of marine life in the world and sustains 17% of the world's bird species. Ecologists classify the fauna of the islands according to the **Wallace Line,** which runs between Kalimantan and Sulawesi, extending down between Bali and Lombok. Named after British naturalist Alfred Russell Wallace, this invisible dividing line distinguishes the Australian fauna to the east from the Asian fauna to the west. Asian mammals west of the line include leopards, black panthers, the Sumatran tiger, orangutans (found only in Sumatra and Borneo), the Asian elephant, Sumatran rhinos, and the Javan one-horned rhino. On the Australian side live komodo dragons (the world's largest lizard), kangaroos, and other marsupials, which nurse their immature young in abdominal pouches. The eastern islands also support colorful birds, including many species from the parrot family, and small mammalian species like the *babirusa* (jungle-dwelling pig related to the hippopotamus, whose name translates to "pig-deer" because of its antler-like tusks) and the *monyet hitam* (a type of black monkey). Indonesia's coral reefs are home to the fast-disappearing giant sea turtle, and shoreline mangrove forests host a vast array of rare crab, shrimp, and fish species.

In the 19th century, British naturalist Alfred Russel Wallace asserted that wildlife in Borneo is Asian, while Sulawesi's animal friends are Austronesian. Indeed, Sulawesi's bizarre fauna often has more in common with the creatures of Australia than with those of much closer Indonesian islands. Sulawesi's isolation from larger landmasses has resulted in a proliferation of unique species; over 60% of Sulawesi's mammals and a third of its birds are endemic. Three species are particularly celebrated on the island. Lucky travelers might catch a glimpse of the famous *babirusa*, which has monstrous tusks that curve through the roof of its mouth. Another fearsome beast is the *anoa* (miniature buffalo), whose size belies its ferocity. Rounding out the trio is the *maleo* bird, a megapode that digs big holes in the ground with its enormous feet to bury its eggs. Unfortunately, development and poaching threaten these species with extinction.

HISTORY

HINDU-BUDDHIST KINGDOMS (AD 600-1478)

IMPORTANT DATES			
7th Century Indian traders introduce Buddhism, Hinduism.	**7th-12th Centuries** Shrivijaya Kingdom controls trade routes.	**8th-10th Centuries** Saliendra Kingdom expands into Indochina.	**1292-1478** Majapahit Empire leads Java's Golden Age.

Indonesian history begins with the **Shrivijaya Kingdom,** which gained power by controlling trade routes. Simultaneously, a succession of neighboring kingdoms in Central Java prospered through intensive agricultural development. At its height, the Mahayana Buddhist **Sailendra Kingdom** reconquered parts of Indochina. The **Sanjaya Kingdom** built impressive monuments during the 9th century; the temples of **Prambanan,** dedicated to the Hindu god Shiva, still exist today near Yogyakarta. Indonesia's last great Hindu-Buddhist kingdom, East Java's **Majapahit Empire,** unified the islands before the Dutch arrived. Its greatest rulers, **Hayam Wuruk** and **Gajah Mada,** fostered Java's Golden Age.

ISLAMIC SULTANATES (1200-1700)

IMPORTANT DATES		
13th Century First Sumatran Muslim kingdom. Islamization begins.	**14th-16th Century** Islam spreads throughout the archipelago.	**16th-17th Century** Zenith of Achinese sultanate.

Arab and Indian traders introduced Islam as early as the 7th century, but Muslim communities weren't prominent in Indonesia until 600 years later when the first sultanates were established in Northern Sumatra. These soon became centralized under the state of **Aceh.** Though Islam spread as far east as Maluku and the Southern Philippines, Bali remained staunchly Hindu. During the 15th and 16th centuries, a series of sultanates arose along the coast of Java, and Islam finally penetrated inland, mixing with preexisting Hindu-Buddhist tradition. Aceh remains a Muslim stronghold today.

DUTCH COLONIALISM (1700-1927)

IMPORTANT DATES			
1602 Dutch East India Company formed.	**1825-30** Locals lose Java to Dutch.	**1873-80** Achinese War. Aceh province rebels against Dutch armies.	**1900-30** Ethical Policy tries to spread European values.

The Portuguese left Indonesia with some ruins, a few street names, and about five serious Catholics. The Dutch, on the other hand, monitored by the **Dutch East India Company,** were more successful (and brutal) colonizers. Military force and exploitative diplomacy gave the Dutch a regional trade monopoly and funneled all profits away from locals. A "divide and subjugate" strategy created power imbalances among increasingly Dutch-dependent local rulers.

The Dutch East India Company went bankrupt in 1799, but the Dutch, intent on trade, stepped in to pursue what came to be known as the **Dutch East Indies.** Colonists set up an administration with compliant local rulers as middlemen. The early

20th century saw the creation of the **Ethical Policy** aimed at improving education and public health and bringing Indonesians closer to European ideals. Indonesians began organizing themselves by religious or ethnic identity and political ideology. Trade cooperatives became vehicles for political action, but internal conflicts prevented the formation of a united nationalist movement.

REVOLUTION AND INDEPENDENCE (1927-1950)

IMPORTANT DATES				
1924 Indonesian Communist Party (PKI) established.	**1927** Partai Nasional Indonesia (PNI) founded.	**1942** Brief, brutal Japanese rule.	**1945** Independence declared.	**1945-1950** Indonesian Revolution forces out the Dutch.

The stage was set for the rise of the **Partai Nasional Indonesia (PNI),** a nationalist party founded in 1927 that practiced civil disobedience and was led by charismatic **President Sukarno.** Bahasa Indonesia, the national language, was adopted in 1928 to further an ever-increasing sense of national unity.

During World War II, Japan defeated the Dutch and invaded Indonesia for its rich oil deposits. Indonesians welcomed the Japanese as they liberated them from European control, but soon discovered that incorporation into the **Greater East Asia Co-Prosperity Sphere** was a fate worse than Dutch rule. Power again changed hands as Japan's brutal 3½-year regime ended with their surrender to the Allies in 1945. Eager to take charge before the Dutch returned, Sukarno declared independence several days later. The Dutch had hoped to restore their former colonial empire, but, to their dismay, they found a mobilized and chaotic population willing to fight for the newly declared **Republik Indonesia.** The **Indonesian Revolution** (1945-50) further unified the nation against the Dutch, who, for once, quietly bowed out. The new government, however, faced raging internal disputes, especially among the **Indonesian Communist Party (PKI),** the Nationalists and their ragtag military, and an array of Islamic parties.

SUKARNO'S RULE (1950-1965)

IMPORTANT DATES		
1950-57 Sukarno's first years in power, relative politic freedom.	**1957** Sukarno introduces "Guided Democracy."	**1963** *Konfrontasi* campaign against Malaysia.

By 1950, the Dutch, embarrassed by international criticism, officially transferred sovereignty to Indonesia. Sukarno wrote the **Pancasila,** the ideological basis of the Indonesian constitution, which consisted of **Five Principles:** belief in one supreme God, humanitarianism, nationalism and national unity, social justice, and democracy. Sukarno's attempts to form a government based on representative democracy in the 1950s were the most politically free years in Indonesian history but they resulted in corruption and stagnation in a largely poor and illiterate nation.

By 1957, after economic failure and several regional rebellions, Sukarno announced his **Guided Democracy** concept, which abolished political parties and granted the president dictatorial powers. In the early 60s, matters came to a head when the masses called for "liberation" of western **New Guinea.** Under US pressure, the Dutch handed over the territory to the UN, which transferred the territory to Indonesia, with the agreement that a vote of self-determination would take place within five years. The vote never came, and the province was officially incorporated into the Indonesian Republic under the name **Irian Jaya.** To this day, conflict over the region's sovereignty persists (see **Indonesia Today,** p. 120).

THE NEW ORDER (1965-1998)

IMPORTANT DATES		
1965 Rise of Suharto's "New Order."	**1975** East Timor annexed.	**1997-1998** Anti Suharto student protests.

Sukarno's balancing act collapsed in 1965, when he was implicated in a failed coup, supposedly perpetrated by the PKI. The coup involved the murder of six high-ranking generals and resulted in a right-wing military backlash. During the following "Year of Living Dangerously," the military slaughtered between 500,000 and one million suspected Communists. Pragmatic and mild-mannered **Major General Suharto** emerged as supreme commander, dismantling Sukarno's powers and replacing the Guided Democracy with his **New Order** government. He promptly banned the PKI and encouraged investment from the West.

Under the New Order, the next 30 years brought political stability, impressive economic growth, and major improvements in infrastructure, public health, and education—at the expense of free speech and individual human rights under military control. The suppression of independence movements by Suharto's regime resulted in the deaths of 200,000 people in East Timor and 2000 in Northern Sumatra. Newly independent **East Timor** was on the verge of forming its own government when civil war broke out. Claiming that the Timorese posed a Communist threat to the region, the Indonesian army invaded in 1975.

INDONESIA TODAY

IMPORTANT DATES		
1998 Economic crisis, Suharto resigns presidency to VP Habibie.	**1999** Wahid is first democratically elected president.	**2001** Wahid impeached in July. VP Megawati Soekarnoputri assumes presidential responsibilities.

GOVERNMENT AND POLITICS. In March 1998, economic crisis caused by currency devaluation and stringent IMF regulations resulted in factory closings, bank liquidations, withdrawal of foreign investment, and spiraling inflation and unemployment rates. Popular opinion turned decisively against Suharto. Later that year, the military killed four student protesters in Jakarta, provoking serious outrage. Rioting, fires, and looting quickly swept cities throughout the archipelago. Meanwhile, thousands of students staged a sit-in at the House of Representatives, demanding Suharto's resignation. One by one, government ministers and high-ranking political figures stepped down, calling upon Suharto to do the same. Suharto finally resigned the presidency to Vice President **B.J. Habibie** in May 1998.

Protests subsided as Habibie, in a bid to regain confidence in the Indonesian presidency and government, released political prisoners, opened dialogue on the East Timor issue, distanced himself from Suharto, and addressed the concerns of ethnic Chinese, who had been the victims of many attacks during the riots. The most dramatic change during this so-called *reformasi* (reformation) era was an easing of censorship; political pundits now openly criticize the government. Fifty new political parties formed before the 1999 parliamentary elections, each espousing the aspirations of a different portion of Indonesian society. The **Indonesian Democratic Party (PDI),** headed by Sukarno's daughter **Megawati Soekarnoputri,** received the most votes, followed by Habibie's **GOLKAR** party.

In late 1999, **Abdurrahman Wahid** defeated front-runner Megawati in the presidential election; Megawati accepted the position of VP. Wahid's leadership over the next months, however, proved flawed. Accusations of financial scandal were leveled against the president, who responded by dismissing several top government officials. Amid confusion and intense political maneuvering, the parliament voted to impeach Wahid on July 23, 2001, and presidential responsibilities were handed over to Megawati. The 2004 elections will determine who will continue to face the immense task of holding Indonesia together amid political turmoil, ethnic and religious violence, and economic malaise.

SEPARATIST MOVEMENTS. In the months after Suharto stepped down, his enforced unity crumbled as various groups scrambled to fill the power vacuum. The most violent separatist movements erupted in **East Timor** and the **Aceh** province of Northern Sumatra. East Timor voted for independence in 1999; UN peacekeeping forces were sent in to control the resulting violence between pro-Indonesia and pro-independence factions. Under global pressure, Indonesia removed troops from East Timor and renounced claims to the territory. East Timor remained under UN administration until May 20, 2002, when the nation gained official independence and autonomy. Recently, the Indonesian government has come under criticism for its treatment of East Timorese refugees.

Wahid responded to separatist agitation in the Aceh province of Northern Sumatra by holding secret peace talks with the rebels, culminating in a truce in May of 2000. Jakarta continues to deny the region independence, but the government has granted Aceh more autonomy. There is a similar situation in **Irian Jaya,** where resentments flare over past military abuses and exploited natural resources. The province claimed independence in June 2000; the government offered autonomy and dialogue. Continuing tensions keep these areas dangerous. In August 2004, Acting Coordinating Minister for Political and Security Affairs Hari Sabarno cleared four senior military figures who were implicated for the violence surrounding East Timor's 1999 independence vote.

ETHNIC AND RELIGIOUS VIOLENCE. Ethnic and religious violence plagues Indonesia. In **Kalimantan,** Muslim settlers have come into conflict with indigenous Dayaks and Malays. In February of 2001, 400 Muslims were massacred on the island; over 500,000 Muslims have fled in the wake of this Dayak hostility. Years of Muslim-Christian tension in **Maluku** and **Ambon** prompted the government to declare a state of emergency in the region on June 26, 2000. Church bombings throughout the country on December 24, 2000 injured over a 100 people and left 16 dead. Sectarian and ethnic strife also wrack **Lombok** and **Central and South Sulawesi.** The fragile economic situation heightens tensions all over Indonesia. Religious tensions are still high in Indonesia. An Easter shooting in 2004 wounded seven and in July

PLIGHT OF THE CHINESE. In the aftermath of the 1997 financial crisis, Indonesia's 7 million Chinese bear a large burden; comprising only 3.5% of the population, they control 70% of the nation's wealth. This wealth, however, is their only security against institutionalized repression. Even though most Chinese are Indonesian-born, they are considered second-class citizens. Until recently, identity cards labeled them as Chinese. The government has lifted the ban on Chinese-language schools, publications bearing Chinese characters, and publicly spoken Chinese, but all Chinese must still adopt indigenous Indonesian surnames and can't serve in the military. In spring 1998, anti-Chinese riots rocked Indonesia. Many are convinced that the government, through its ambivalence, encourages anti-Chinese sentiment to provide a scapegoat for the frustration caused by economic conditions. The violence has led to an exodus of Chinese and their billions, which threatens to worsen the economy and heighten racial hatred. Chinese travelers to the region should be extremely careful.

2004, unidentified gunmen killed a reverend and four members of her congregation as she delivered a sermon. Religious leaders in Indonesia continue to insist that the violence is being provoked by individuals seeking to incite religous unrest in order to justify a new military crackdown.

CUSTOMS AND ETIQUETTE

Adat, or common law, explains many Indonesian customs. *Adat,* originally rooted in religion and adapted over many years, is one of the few things that diverse Indonesians have in common. Though unwritten and unspoken, *adat* still remains an important code of conduct.

Friendliness is valued in Indonesia. Just keep smiling—Indonesians are known to hide negative feelings and avoid confrontation, rarely raising their voices. Indonesians also place less emphasis on punctuality than Westerners; travelers sometimes become frustrated with the country's "rubber time." Be patient, as it is considered disrespectful to show signs of annoyance.

CLOTHING. As Indonesia is largely an Islamic country, revealing clothes are inappropriate, especially if you plan to visit a mosque. Women should take special care to dress conservatively.

TABOOS. Avoid eating, passing dishes, and giving or receiving objects with the left hand, which is considered unclean. Though shaking hands is normal with introductions, never shake with the left. Indonesians regard the feet as the least sacred part of the body, so avoid pointing your feet at anyone. Conversely, don't touch anyone on the head, even young children. Pointing with a forefinger is considered impolite. To beckon someone, extend your hand with the palm down and make a scratching motion with your fingers. Finally, remember that observant Muslims do not consume pork or alcohol, while Hindus avoid beef and leather.

TABLE MANNERS. Accept hosts' offers of food and drink. Most dishes are eaten with the right hand. Forks and spoons are the main utensils; knives are rarely used. Leave a portion of your meal on your plate to signal your satisfaction with the meal. When entering an Indonesian's house, remove your shoes if your hosts take off theirs.

ARTS AND RECREATION

BATIK AND OTHER CRAFTS. Batik, a world-renowned textile art of producing intricate patterns, often with animal motifs, is common throughout Southeast Asia. Originally done by hand, *batik tulis* is now made with a tool that holds a small amount of liquid wax and is used like a pencil to create designs on fabric. Various colored dyes are absorbed by the parts of the fabric not covered by wax. The cheaper *batik cap* is made with pre-patterned metal stamps dipped in wax and then pressed repeatedly onto fabric. *Batik* shirts are common formal dress for men; women often wear *batik* sarongs. Recently, *batik* **paintings** have become a popular art form. The best and cheapest *batik* paintings are around Yogyakarta; many galleries also give visitors a chance to make their own paintings. **Ikat** is a type of weaving in which already-dyed threads are woven into designs, while the rest of the fabric is dyed in a contrasting color. **Traditional wood-carvings,** from masks and life-size puppets to weapons and furniture, are uniquely reflective of Indonesia's many cultures. In places where Hindu culture was strongest, metalworking recreates the ancient artifacts of *moko,* bronze kettle drums, and the legendary *kris,* a ceremonial sword. For those with a hankering for gold, silver, and semi-precious stones, Indonesian artists offer inexpensive and intricate jewelry.

INDONESIAN COOKING. Two words describe Indonesian dishes: deep fried. Travelers will often encounter the term "*goreng*," which means "fried." *Warungs* (foodstalls) offer the tastiest and cheapest food. Take cues from locals. Some of Indonesia's most popular dishes (listed below) can be found at most *warungs.*

Bakso: Meatball soup.

Sambal: Indonesian hot sauce. Exported all over the island. Yogya does it best.

Bolang-baling: Fried doughnuts.

Nasi goreng: Fried rice, the national dish. Not too spicy. *Ayam* means that chicken is mixed in, *daging* includes beef, *kambing* is lamb, and *kampung* means egg.

Gado-gado: A vegetarian staple in Indonesia. This vegetable stir fry in a light peanut sauce provides a healthy alternative to heavier fare.

Soto: Indonesian soup. *Soto ayam madura* is a popular, tangy chicken soup.

Pisang goreng: Yes, even bananas can be fried. The result is not overly sweet, making for a lovely dessert or light meal.

Lalapan: Raw vegetables served with *samble* (chilli sauce) on the side.

Mie goreng: Fried noodles.

Nasi uduk: Rice cooked in coconut milk and *pandan* leaves topped with fried shallots. This is a native Jakartan dish but can be found throughout Indonesia.

Bakso: *Mie soto* (noodle soup) in a beef or ox broth with meat and deep fried tofu. This would be excellent on a chilly day–if such a thing existed on Java.

Bandrek: A cool and refreshing drink made with ginger, sugar, and coconut milk. *Bajigur* is the version without ginger.

Srabi: Even from *warung*, this specialty is still made the traditional way, in clay pots over low fires. Sweet coconut milk and rice flour are combined with *cokolat* (chocolate), *pisang* (bananas), coconut, or condensed milk for sweet *srabi,* with cheese and meats for the savory version.

DANCE AND DRAMA. Indonesian dance traditions are highly developed, especially in Java and Bali. Javanese dance is meditative, deliberate, involving limber movements and contemplative pauses. Balinese dancing also requires meticulous maneuvering but is distinguished by its fast, jerky movements accompanied by the explosive Balinese *gamelan.* The most popular dances are the *Barong*, which is a battle between good and evil, and *Kecak* (**Monkey Dance**), which reenacts a scene of the Hindu epic *Ramayana* around flame torches while 100 or more men sit in concentric circles shouting and chanting in rhythm. Most modern drama has developed in Java. *Ludruk* is an all-male performance in which roles of women are humorously, if somewhat derogatorily, depicted on stage. *Kethoprak* adds a contemporary twist on classic epic stories and myths of India and Java.

MUSIC AND WAYANG. The **gamelan** orchestra, a sophisticated ensemble of gongs, metallophones, drums, vocalists, and string and wind instruments, is unique to Java and Bali. Javanese *gamelan* is trance-like, while the Balinese version is fast-paced and dramatic. *Gamelan* accompanies many events, among them dance and *wayang* (shadow puppetry). Indonesia's diverse set of popular music traditions draws upon outside influences and traditions across the islands. Lilting *kroncong* music reflects the influence of the Portuguese, while *dangdut* music shares Indian and Arabic rhythms. The Batak of North Sumatra are famed for their beautiful voices and melancholy tunes, which frequently feature unabashed sobbing by the vocalists. The ancient Javanese art of **shadow puppetry** *(wayang)* probably has its roots in ancestor worship, with the *dalang* (puppeteer) considered a conduit of spirits. Today he's highly respected for his ability to manipulate several puppets at once, to conduct the *gamelan* orchestra behind him, and to keep it going nonstop for nine hours. The stories are drawn from the *Ramayana* and *Mahabharata* Indian epics as well as indigenous stories.

HOLIDAYS AND FESTIVALS (2005)

DATE	NAME	DESCRIPTION AND LOCATION
Jan. 1	New Year's Day	Mainly celebrated by expats.
Jan. 21	Idul Adha	Celebrates Abraham's willingness to sacrifice his son.
Feb. 9	Chinese New Year	Known locally as *Imlek* and now a national holiday.
Feb. 10	Islamic New Year	Celebrates the day Muhammad left Mecca to found a new community in Medina.
Mar. 20-27	Holy Week	Christian holiday week leading up to Easter.
Apr. 9	Nyepi	Hindu New Year.
Apr. 21	Maulid Nabi	Prophet Muhammad's birthday
May 22	Waisak	A central Buddhist festival, celebrating the enlightenment of the Buddha. Observant Buddhists gather at the Borobudur temple near Yogyakarta.
Aug. 17	Indonesian Independence Day	Celebrates Sukarno's declaration of independence in 1945.
Sept. 2	Isra Mi'raj	Muslim celebration of the ascension of Muhammad.
Oct. 3	Beginning of Ramadan	The Muslim month of fasting and religious contemplation.
Nov. 3-4	Idul Fitri	The most important Muslim festival of the year, celebrated at the end of Ramadan.
Dec. 25	Christmas Day	Christian holiday commemorating the birth of Jesus.

ADDITIONAL RESOURCES

GENERAL HISTORY

A History of Modern Indonesia Since c.1300, by MC Ricklefs (1993). A comprehensive and readable history of Indonesia, with a focus on the colonial period.

The Buru Tetralogy: This Earth of Mankind, Child of All Nations, Footsteps, and *House of Glass,* by Pramoedya Ananta Toer. Historical novels about the Indonesian national consciousness by Indonesia's most famous dissident writer. Pramoedya languished in the country's prison and has been under house arrest since 1965.

NON-FICTION

Nathaniel's Nutmeg: How One Man's Courage Changed the Course of History, by Giles Milton (1999). An in-depth study of the battle between European nations for control of the valuable spices of the eastern islands of present-day Indonesia.

The Religion of Java, by Clifford Geertz (1990). Released in 1960, this book is an overview of the Javanese cultural and religious landscape.

TRAVEL BOOKS

In Search of Conrad, by Gavin Young (1991). Retraces Joseph Conrad's travels around Java, Bali, Sumatra, Kalimantan, and Sulawesi.

The Malay Archipelago, by Alfred Russel Wallace (1990). An 1869 account of British biologist and naturalist's journeys throughout the Indonesian archipelago.

FILM

Short Films and Animation Work by Gotot Prakosa, dir. Gotot Prakosa. A collection of work done between 1974 and 1987 by Gotot Prakosa while he was a student at the Jakarta Institute of the Arts.

Tamu Agung (Exalted Guest), dir. Usmar Ismail (1955). A classic and satire of early Indonesian cinema on President Sukarno and political leadership in Indonesia.

ON THE WEB

Inside Indonesia (www.insideindonesia.org). The online version of this quarterly magazine offers information on current events.

The Jakarta Post (www.thejarkatapost.com). The largest English newspaper in Indonesia, *The Jakarta Post* features the latest news and information on Indonesia.

ESSENTIALS

INDONESIA PRICE ICONS

SYMBOL:	❶	❷	❸	❹	❺
ACCOMM.	Rp15,000 and under	Rp15,000-30,000	Rp30,000-50,000	Rp50,000-80,000	Rp80,000 and over
FOOD	Rp7000 and under	Rp7000-12,000	Rp12,000-20,000	Rp20,000-30,000	Rp30,000 and over

EMBASSIES AND CONSULATES

INDONESIAN CONSULAR SERVICES ABROAD

Australia: Embassy, 8 Darwin Ave., Yarralumla, Canberra, ACT 2600; P.O. Box 616, Kingston 2604 (☎02 6250 8600). **Consulates,** East Perth, WA (☎08 9221 5858); Darwin, NT (☎08 8941 0048); Melbourne, VIC (☎03 9525 2755); Maroubra, NSW (☎02 9344 9933); Wayville, SA (☎08 8357 8955); Brisbane, QLD (☎07 3309 0858).

Canada: Embassy, 55 Parkdale Ave., Ottawa, ON K1Y 1E5 (☎613-724-1100; www.indonesia-ottawa.org). **Consulates,** Vancouver, BC (☎604-682-8855; www.kjrivcr.org); Toronto, ON (☎416-360-4020).

New Zealand: Embassy, 70 Glen Rd., Kelburn; P.O. Box 3543, Wellington (☎04 475 8697 or 475 8698).

UK: Embassy, 38 Grosvenor Sq., London W1K 2HW (☎020 7499 7661).

US: Embassy, 2020 Massachusetts Ave. NW, Washington, D.C. 20036 (☎202-775-5200). **Consulates,** New York (☎212-879-0600); Chicago (☎312-595-1777); Los Angeles (☎213-383-5126); San Francisco (☎415-474-9571); Houston (☎713-785-1691).

CONSULAR SERVICES IN INDONESIA

Australia: Embassy, Jl. H.R. Rasuna Said Kav. C15-16, Kuningan, Jakarta Selatan 12940 (☎62 21 2550 5555). **Consulates,** in Denpasar (p. 171) and Medan (p. 237).

Canada: Embassy, World Trade Center, 6th fl., Jl. Jend. Sudirman Kav. 29-31, Jakarta 12920; P.O. Box 8324/JKS.MP, Jakarta 12920 (☎62 021 2550 7800). **Consulate,** in Surabaya (p. 164).

New Zealand: Embassy, BRI II Building, 23rd fl., Jl. Jend. Sudirman Kav. 44-46, Jakarta; P.O. Box 2439, Jakarta (☎62 21 573 5268).

UK: Embassy, Jl. M.H. Thamrin No. 75, Jakarta 10310 (☎62 21 315 6264). **Consulates,** Medan (p. 234) and Surabaya (p. 164).

US: Embassy, Jl. Medan Merdeka Selatan 5, Jakarta 10110 (☎62 21 3435 9000). **Consulates,** in Denpasar (p. 171) and Surabaya (p. 164)

DOCUMENTS AND FORMALITIES

Indonesia strictly enforces its entry requirements. Travelers need a passport valid for at least six months, proof of onward travel (return ticket, US$1000 or a valid credit card), and a visa. A three-day visa is available for US$10 or 30-day visa for US$25. Both visas are non-extendable, and travelers must leave for a minimum of two weeks before they can return. Travelers visiting for business purposes or social/cultural stays can extend their stay with a letter of intent/sponsorship from the employer and/or sponsor.

MONEY

CURRENCY AND EXCHANGE

The currency chart below is based on August 2004 exchange rates between local currency and Australian dollars (AUS$), Canadian dollars (CDN$), European Union euros (EUR€), New Zealand dollars (NZ$), British pounds (UK£), and US dollars (US$). Check the currency converter on websites like www.xe.com or www.bloomberg.com or a large newspaper for the latest exchange rates.

CURRENCY (Rp)		
	AUS$1 = RP6436.52	RP1000 = AUS$.155401
	CDN$1 = RP6758.24	RP1000 = CDN$.147909
	EUR€1 = RP11,059.71	RP1000 = EUR€.0904225
	NZ$1 = RP5858.19	RP1000 = NZ$.170671
	UK£1 = RP16,580.02	RP1000 = UK£.0603104
	US$1 = RP8910	RP1000 = US$.112233

The Indonesian **rupiah (Rp)** comes in denominations of Rp100, 500, 1000, 5000, 10,000, 20,000, 50,000, and 100,000, and coins come in Rp25, 50, 100, 500, and 1000. The US dollar is the most readily accepted foreign currency. Personal checks are basically unheard of. Traveler's checks can be exchanged at banks, moneychangers, and some hotels. Credit cards and traveler's checks are accepted in bigger towns and tourist destinations, but if you are traveling in rural or unfrequented areas, cash is your best (and sometimes only) bet. Most major cities have ATMs. Credit card fraud is common and merchants often charge customers a 3% service fee. Counterfeit money has become a serious problem as well—check all bills, even in banks. Exchanging bills at major hotels usually include a 10% service charge. Tipping is not expected, but a 5-10% tip is always appreciated. Tips for taxi and hired car drivers are not necessary, but for satisfactory taxi service a tip of Rp500-1000 is appropriate; give a bit more for a hired car. Airport porters should be given Rp2000 for small bags and Rp3000 for bags over 20kg.

GETTING THERE

BY PLANE. Indonesia has a number of **international airports**, including Soekarno-Hatta Airport in Jakarta (p. 130), Adi Sumarmo Airport in Surakarta (p. 159), Juanda Airport in Surabaya (p. 163), Ngurah Rai International Airport in Denpasar (p. 169), Polonia Airport in Medan (p. 234), Sam Ratulangi Airport in Manado (p. 230), and Selaparang Airport in Lombok (p. 195). **Garuda** (www.garuda-indonesia.com) runs the most flights to these airports.

BY LAND. Refer to the following table for overland border crossings in Indonesia.

BORDER CROSSINGS:

MALAYSIA. You can cross from Entikong in West Kalimantan (near Pontianak) to Tebedu in Sarawak (near Kuching, p. 411), or from Nunukan in East Kalimantan to Tawau in Sabah. Ferries connect Sumatra and Peninsular Malaysia via a number of routes: Medan (p. 234) to Penang (p. 366); Dumai to Melaka (p. 350); and Pulau Batam to Johor Bahru (near Singapore).

SINGAPORE. Ferries and speedboats connect Singapore (p. 625) to **Riau Islands** (p. 266).

GETTING AROUND

BY PLANE. Air travel is the easiest and most comfortable way to get around Indonesia, although the economic crisis has forced many airlines to bump up fares. National carriers **Garuda** and **Merpati** (www.merpati.co.id) run to all provincial district capitals, and **Bouraq** and **Mandala** fly to more domestic destinations. DAS Mandala, Jatayu, Lion Air, and Pelita also offer domestic services.

BY BOAT. Government-owned **Pelayaran Nasional Indonesia**'s (PELNI) air-conditioned ships serve all domestic main points biweekly with spartan accommodations, basic food, slow journeys, and mediocre prices. Reserve ahead. Go early to claim a mattress and floor space. Check out the useful website at www.pelni.co.id.

BY TRAIN OR BUS. Trains run in Java and parts of Sumatra; they're often slow and delayed but prove more comfortable than buses for long trips. Most locals take buses, which, like trains, are slow and unpredictable. Though buses get crowded, tickets are cheap. Overnight buses are usually faster, but more nerve-wracking and arrive at inconvenient hours. Combined bus/ferry tickets make island-hopping easy. Beware of pickpockets on any public transportation. Also note that buses often will not depart with fewer than five passengers, which can make travel unpredictable in rural areas.

BY CAR OR TAXI. Hired cars with driver cost 80,000-300,000Rp per day in major cities. Taxis are metered in large cities and carry five passengers on major routes—to avoid getting ripped off, make sure the driver runs the meter. If there's no meter, agree on a price before hopping in.

OTHER LOCAL TRANSPORTATION. Other forms of transport include the *andong* or *dokar* (horse-drawn cart), *angkot* or *colt* (minibus), *bajaj* (ba-JA-ee; orange motorized three-wheeler), *becak* (BAY-chuck; bicycle rickshaw), *bemo* (canopied pickup truck that runs on a regular route), *ojek* (motorcycle taxi), *oplet* or *microlet* (a larger form of *bemo*), and *sudako* (minivans that travel a set route). Some can be hired for private use. When navigating by foot or **bicycle,** keep in mind that Jl. is an abbreviation of *jalan* (street).

HEALTH AND SAFETY

EMERGENCY NUMBERS: Police: ☎110 Fire: ☎113 Ambulance: ☎118.

MEDICAL EMERGENCIES. The general level of sanitation and healthcare in Indonesia is far below Western standards. Routine medical care is available in major cities. However, serious medical problems should be handled in Singapore or Australia, the closest locations with extensive medical care.

HEALTH RISKS. In January 2004, there was an outbreak of Dengue fever affecting all 30 provinces. There were several human cases of avian influenza in January and June of 2004. Contracting malaria is always a risk. Although no laws deal specifically with AIDS or HIV, affected persons may be denied entry or even quarantined under other restrictions.

GLBT. Public displays of affection are not advisable for *any* couples, straight or gay. Men holding hands is usually a sign of friendship. All large Indonesian cities have a substantial gay nightlife scene, but it may take some time or the advice of locals to figure out what's currently *en vogue*. Defying categories assigned by the West, Indonesia has an alternate gender, known as *waria*, which is defined as a man *(pria)* with the soul of a woman *(wanita)*. While not wholly accepted by Indonesian society, *waria* participate in a subculture of their own. For more information on Indonesia's gay and lesbian scene, *waria* communities, and AIDS activism, pick up a copy of *GAYa Nusantara*, a magazine published in Surabaya. (☎593 4924. Offices at Jl. Mulyosari Timur 46, Surabaya, East Java, 60112.)

KEEPING IN TOUCH

MAIL. Indonesia's postal service is not terribly reliable—**register important mail.** Check **Practical Information** listings in each town for *Poste Restante* availability. *Kantor pos* means "post office."

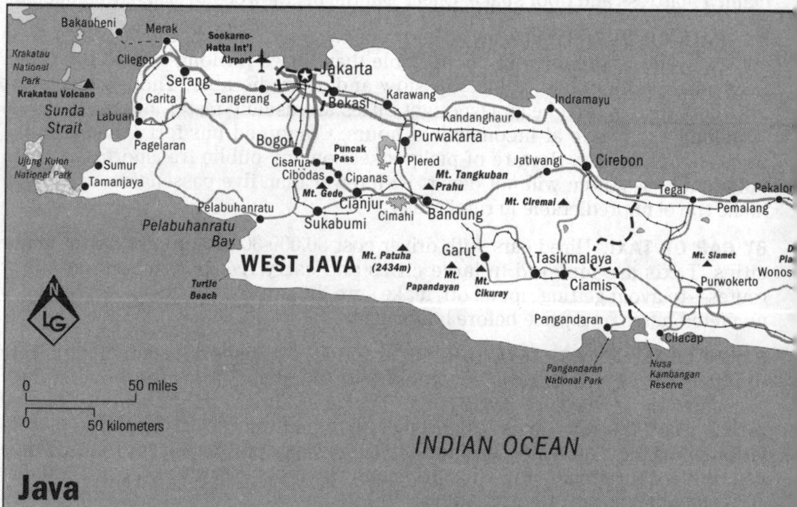

TELEPHONES. Most towns have Perumtel or *wartel* offices, which often also send **faxes.** Offices usually have private booths for callers; a digital display tells you how long you have been talking and how much the call costs. International calls are fairly simple, though you might have trouble using your phone card. IDD is widely available. For **Home Country Direct (HCD)** numbers from Indonesia, refer to the table on the inside back cover of this book. When calling home, remember that Indonesia falls into three separate **time zones:** west (Java and Sumatra) is seven hours ahead of GMT; central (Nusa Tenggara and Sulawesi) is eight hours ahead; and east (Maluku) is nine hours ahead. Calls to the USA cost roughly US$1 per minute.

INTERNET ACCESS. You'll have no problems checking your email in big cities and major tourist destinations. Rates average around Rp8000 per hour. In more rural areas, Internet access is harder to find and more expensive.

JAVA

Packing over 60% of Indonesia's population onto only 8% of its landmass, Java takes center stage both politically and culturally. The island's fertile volcanic soil has supported the development of sophisticated court cultures from the 7th century through the Republic's modern government. Although alone it presents an incomplete portrait of Indonesia, Java offers a wealth of ancient, colonial, and modern sites. Most travelers make a beeline from Yogyakarta to Gunung Bromo, but for those willing to step off the beaten path, Java's labyrinthine cities and mountainous landscapes are ripe for exploration.

JAKARTA ☎021

Plagued by overcrowding and political instability, Jakarta is caught in transition. While it is one of the world's most cosmopolitan cities, Jakarta is nonetheless steeped in the chaos and frenetic energy of the developing world. Shiny skyscrapers sidle up next to weathered metal shacks while sleek Mercedes cut off smog-

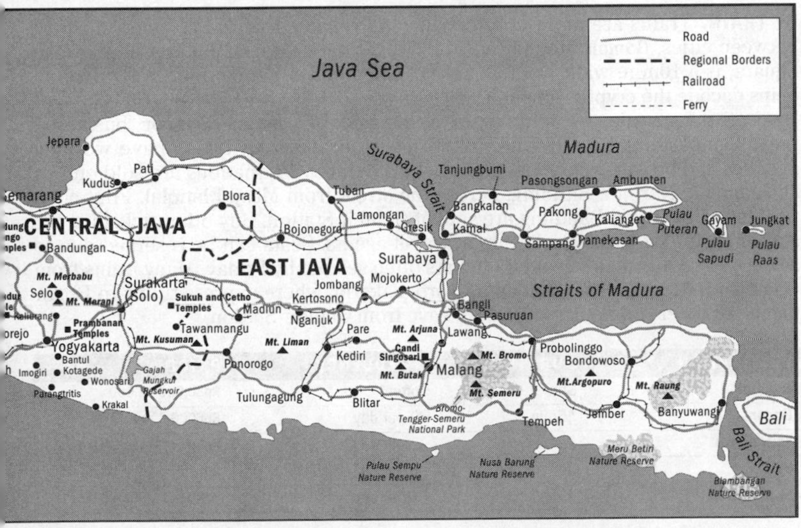

spewing *bajaj* on the streets. McDonald's meets 100% *Halal* and Dunkin' Donuts serves durian-flavored next to honey-glazed. Those willing to venture away from backpacker hangouts will witness the harsh reality of the city. Many tourists prefer other parts of the archipelago, though attractions such as the thriving harbor and exciting nightlife reward those who stick around. Travelers should be extra sensitive to potential crime. Pickpocketing is the main problem, but walking the streets late at night might be tempting fate.

INTERCITY TRANSPORTATION

BY PLANE. International and domestic flights arrive at **Soekarno-Hatta Airport** (departure/arrival info ☎550 5307), 35km northwest of the city. Departure tax is Rp75,000 for international and Rp11,000 for domestic travel. From the airport, **DAMRI** buses go to **Bogor** (Rp10,000), **Gambir Station** (every hr., A/C Rp8000), and other locations. A metered taxi to the city costs roughly Rp52,000 (including toll). The one-way plane fares below may be lower during the winter months.

DESTINATION	FREQUENCY	PRICE	DESTINATION	FREQUENCY	PRICE
Bangkok	1 per day	US$270	**Kuala Lumpur**	1 per day	US$70
Denpasar	4 per day	Rp700,000	**Medan**	3 per day	Rp600,000
Hong Kong	1 per day	US$265	**Singapore**	1 per day	US$90

Major airlines that serve Jakarta include: **Bouraq,** Jl. Angkasa 1 (☎628 8827); **Garuda,** Jl. Merdeka Selatan 13 (☎231 1801); **Malaysian Airlines,** World Trade Center, Jl. Sudirman (☎522 9682); **Mandala** (☎381 1107), Jl. Veteran near Mesjid Istiqlal; **Merpati,** Jl. Angasa, Kemayoran, in front of the PELNI office (☎654 6789); and **Singapore Airlines/Silk Air,** Jl. Rasuda Said (☎5790 3747). Other international airlines are in the BDN Building, Jl. Thamrin 5, next to the Sari Pan Pacific Hotel, including: **American Airlines** (☎230 0033; open M-F 8am-5pm, Sa 9am-1pm); **British Airways/Qantas** (☎230 0277; open M-F 8:30am-5pm, Sa 8:30am-12:30pm); **Continental** (☎334 417; open M-F 8:30am-4:30pm, Sa 8:30am-1pm); and **Thai Airlines** (☎230 2551; open M-F 8am-5pm, Sa 8am-noon).

BY TRAIN. Trains are more comfortable and reliable than other land transport between cities. **Gambir Station** (☎384 2777), at the center of Jakarta in Merdeka Square, is a 10min. walk from Jl. Jaksa. The information counter at the station helps decode the cryptic schedule. Tickets are sold for three classes: **first-class,** or "executive," provides reclining seats, meals, and A/C; **second-class,** or "business," means smokers galore and non-reclining seats; **economy** trains have wooden benches and broken fans. First-class tickets to most destinations are sold only at Jl. Juanda 1, Narinda Building, across the street from Mesjid Istiqlal. First-class tickets to Bogor and Bandung are sold at Gambir Station. Buy other tickets at the station or for a Rp15,000 markup at travel agents. Seats can be reserved one to seven days in advance. Weekend tickets often sell out by Friday. Many trains from Gambir run through **Kota Station** in North Jakarta, where express trains to Bogor begin. All other trains (listed below) leave from Gambir Station.

DESTINATION	DURATION	FREQUENCY	PRICE
Bandung	3hr.	often	Rp30,000-45,000
Bogor	45min.	9 per day	Rp6000-8000
Yogyakarta	7-9hr.	2 per day	Rp50,000-150,000
Solo	9hr.	2 per day	Rp18,500-185,000
Surabaya	10hr.	4 per day	Rp23,000-250,000

BUS SAVVY. The buses *Let's Go* lists are only suggestions; hundreds of buses are sure to go your way. Yelling out your destination or asking someone at the stop is a good way to make sure you're on the right bus. Overcharging foreigners for bus fares is common. Some bus operators will insist on high fares; others will laugh and accept the lower fare when they realize that you know their ploy. Ask another passenger to make sure you don't pay too much.

BY BUS. Travel agencies around Jl. Jaksa hire comfortable private buses (non-stop, usually with A/C, and far less crowded than public buses) that whisk travelers to Java's tourist destinations. Pay for public buses on board. Bus terminals are outside Jakarta and require a complicated 1-2hr. of travel by public transportation. To get to **Kali Deres Stasiun,** take bus #77 from in front of McDonald's in Sarinah (Jl. Wahid Hasyim and Jl. Thamrin). Bus #507 goes to **Pulo Gadung Terminal** from Jl. Kebon Sirih. Many buses, including #79 and 10, leave Sarinah for **Kp. Rambutan Terminal.** Travel agents do not advise economy class due to heat and risk of theft. Executive class means A/C, while Super Executive provides A/C, TV and food. All prices below include A/C.

DESTINATION	TIME	FREQUENCY	PRICE
FROM KALI DERES STASIUN			
Bengkulu	30hr.	1 per day	Rp160,000
Bukittinggi	36hr.	3 per day	Rp160,000; Super Executive Rp310,000
Medan	48hr.	many 2-3pm	Rp230,000; Super Executive Rp330,000
Padang	30hr.	2 per day 2-3pm	Rp160,000; Super Executive Rp310,000
FROM PULO GADUNG TERMINAL			
Denpasar	24hr.	often, 3-6pm	Rp170,500; Super Executive Rp230,000
Yogyakarta	12hr.	often, 3-5pm	Rp100,000
Surabaya	14hr.	often, 2-6pm	Rp138,500
FROM KP. RAMBUTAN TERMINAL			
Bandung	3-4hr.	every 20min. 6am-10pm	Rp25,000
Banjar	6hr.	hourly	Rp30,000
Bogor	1hr.	every 20min. 6am-10pm	Rp6500

BY BOAT. The state-run **PELNI Company** on Jl. Angkasa #18, Kemayoran (sales ☎421 1921, info 6385 7773) has a small fleet of A/C ships that wind their way between major harbors throughout Indonesia. Those with a supply of Dramamine and a tolerance for spartan accommodations and erratic schedules can travel on them at a reasonable cost. For tickets, head to the PELNI office or pay a surcharge and buy from a travel agency on Jl. Jaksa. PELNI offers four classes: the expensive 1st and 2nd classes have toilets and TVs; 3rd and 4th don't; *wisata* class provides a bed and a locker; economy is split into seat and non-seat (read: floor) areas.

ORIENTATION

Jakarta is divided into five regions: central Jakarta and four quadrants that run north, south, east, and west.

CENTRAL JAKARTA (JAKARTA DUSIT). The area revolves around **Medan Merdeka (Freedom Square),** home to **Monas,** the national monument, and **Gambir Station.** Bordering the square is the **National Museum** to the west, **Istana Merdeka** (the Presidential Palace) to the northwest, and the **Mesjid Istiqlal** to the northeast. A 10min. walk away is **Jl. Jaksa,** home to a myriad of budget *losmen* and eateries. Another 10min. away, **Jl. Thamrin** boasts skyscrapers, banks, shopping plazas, and international hotels. Jl. Thamrin runs north-south; at Medan Merdeka it becomes **Jl. Merdeka Barat** (Freedom Road West) and **Jl. Hayum Wuuk** farther north.

NORTH JAKARTA (TANJUNG PRIOK). The district includes **Sunda Kelapar** (the harbor), the museum-filled **old Dutch district** (Kota), the electronics-peddling **Chinatown** (Glodok), and enormous **Jaya Ancol** leisure park. To go north, hop on any bus bound for Kota Bus Terminal.

SOUTH JAKARTA. Jl. Kemang is expat-friendly, lined with expensive bars, jazz clubs, restaurants, and a disproportionate number of furniture galleries. Farther south is **Ragunan Zoo.** The heart of south Jakarta is **Block M** station, though much of the area is referred to as "Block M."

EAST AND WEST JAKARTA. East Jakarta is largely industrial. Closer to Block M is the huge **Taman Mini Indonesia Indah** complex. **West Jakarta** is the site of mass flower cultivation and distribution, offering little else to visitors.

LOCAL TRANSPORTATION

There's no easy way to get around in Jakarta. A combination of patience, a *Let's Go* guide, and a sense of adventure provides the quickest way to any destination.

Bajaj: Pronounced "BA-ja-ee." Rickety, smog-spewing orange three-wheelers zoom all over the city. Convenient for short trips; fix a price beforehand (Rp4000 per km).

Taxis: A/C comfort and less need for life insurance. Taxis are everywhere in Jakarta; calling for one can mean up to an hour wait. **Blue Bird Group** (☎798 9000) is by far the best, with consistent rates and safe driving. **Citra** (☎781 7233), **Silver Bird** (☎794 1234), and **Express** (☎576 1313) are decent. Get out of any taxi that does not run the meter. Rp3000 for the 1st km, Rp1300 per km after.

Buses: Run on all major roads; look for the destination on the windshield. Tickets are sold on board or at major stops. Ask locals to find the right route.

Microlet: Minibuses and **vans,** also known as *oplet,* run various routes. Look for the destination on the windshield or tell the driver your destination.

Rentals: Avis, Jl. Diponegoro 25 (☎314 2900). Rp395,000-585,000 per day.

PRACTICAL INFORMATION

TOURIST AND FINANCIAL SERVICES

Tourist Office: Visitor Information Center, Jl. M.H. Thamrin 9 (☎314 2067), opposite Sarinah Plaza. From Jl. Jaksa, walk south (away from Monas) to the end of the street and turn right on Jl. Wahid Hasyim. The entrance is in the Djakarta Theater building. Open unreliably M-F 9am-5pm, Sa 9am-1pm. Another booth is in the **airport** near baggage claim, before customs. Both have free maps, brochures, shopping guides, and English-speaking help. **Information:** ☎108.

Tours: Many Jl. Jaksa establishments book bus tours and transportation. Budget travel offices on Jl. Jaksa and K.H. Wahid Hasyim cover the travel spectrum, booking seats on chartered buses to **Denpasar, Yogyakarta,** and other destinations at a small markup. **Pacto Travel,** in the BDN building, Jl. Thamrin 5 (☎230 0336, httjky@cbn.net.id), has 3-day package tours to Southeast Asian cities. Open M-F 8:30am-5pm, Sa 8:30am-noon.

Embassies and Consulates: Australia, Jl. Rasuna Said Kav. C15-16 (☎2550 5555; www.austembjak.or.id). Take bus #P11 or #19 to Kuningan Plaza. Open M-F 7:45am-12:30pm and 1:30-4pm. **Brunei,** 8th fl. Wisma BCA, Jl. Sudirman Kav 22-23 (☎471 2180). Open M-Th 8am-4pm. **Canada,** World Trade Center, 6th fl., Jl. Sudirman Kav. 29 (☎525 0709). Take bus for Block M and stop at Karel in front of the Meridian Hotel. Open M-Th 7:30am-4pm, F 7:30am-1pm. Visas M-F 8:30am-noon. **Laos,** Jl. Kintamani Raya C15 #33 (☎520 2673). Open M-F 8am-4pm. **Malaysia,** Jl. H.R. Rasuna Said Kav. X/6 1-3 (☎522 4947). Take bus #P11 or #66 to Jl. Prof. Dr. Satriol. Open M-Th 9am-4pm. **New Zealand** (☎570 9460), 23rd fl. BRI building, Jl. Sudirman Kav. 44-46. Open M-Th 7:30am-4pm, F 7:30am-1pm. **Philippines,** Menteng Jakarta Pusat (☎315 5118). Open M-F 8am-5pm. **Singapore,** Jl. H.R. Rasuna Said Blok X4 Kav. 2 (www.mfa.gov.sg/jkt, ☎520 1489). Take bus #P11 to Mesjid. Open M-F 8:30am-5pm. Visas 8:30am-noon. **Thailand,** Jl. Imam Bonjol 74 (☎390 4052, thaijkt@indo.net.id). Head 500m southwest from the roundabout on Jl. Imam Bonjol. Open M-F 8:30am-4:30pm, consular services 8:30am-1:30pm. **UK,** Jl. M.H. Thamrin 75 (☎315 6264, www.britain-in-indonesia.or.id), near Jl. Jaksa. Open M-Th 7:45am-4pm, F 7:45am-12:45pm. **US,** Jl. Merdeka Selatan 5 (☎3435 9000; www.usembassyjakarta.org). Open M-F 7:30am-4pm. **Vietnam,** Jl. Teuku Umar 25 (☎310 0357), southeast of Jl. Jaksa. Open M-F 8:30-11:30am and 1:30-4:30pm. Best time for visa applications is 9am-noon.

Currency Exchange: Airport banks offer decent rates without commission. In the city, many banks and **ATMs,** which offer slightly better rates, cluster near the Jl. Jaksa area. Traveler's checks not in US dollars can be difficult to cash, except at international banks. **BCA Bank,** Jl. Wahid Hosyim 82 (☎390 3979), cashes traveler's checks. Open M-F 8:30am-3pm. **Citibank,** Landmark Bldg., Jl. Jend Suriman 1 (☎252 9999). Hordes of 24hr. **ATMs** can be found at most banks, Sarinah Plaza, and elsewhere. Some credit cards fail at certain establishments, so carry two.

American Express: Jl. Rasuna Said Blok X/1 (☎521 6111). Traveler's check services. Open M-F 8:30am-3pm.

LOCAL SERVICES

Luggage Storage: ☎550 5581. Airport Terminal D. Rp3300 per day. Open 24hr.

English-Language Bookstores and Publications: Times, on the lower level of Plaza Indonesia Shopping Center beneath the Grand Hyatt on Jl. M.H. Thamrin, has British tabloids and English books. Open daily 10am-9pm. Several small book-trading posts and book-peddlers cluster along Jl. Jaksa. **The Jakarta Post** is the daily English-language newspaper. The weekly **Djakarta** magazine is half in English, half in Bahasa Indonesia and has nightlife, film, and theater listings (Rp17,500).

Pharmacies: Apotik Cerme, Jl. Wahid Hasyim 64 (☎326 207). Walk north on Jl. Jaksa and turn left; it's 100m down on the left. Open daily 8am-11:30pm. **Apotek Melawai Cabang Selemba,** Jl. Salemba Raya 57-59 (☎315 0589). Open 24hr. Additional pharmacies on Kebon Sirih, in the basement of Plaza Indonesia, and in Plaza Senayan.

Medical Services: Best service by doctors between 8am and 8pm. All are open 24hr. for emergencies. General hospitals **MMC Kuningan,** Jl. Rasuna Said Kav. C21 (☎522 5201 or 520 3435), and **RS Jakarta,** Jl. Sudirman Kav. 49 (☎573 22 41). **Ufar Madica Clinic** (☎310 2870), next to Gambir Apotik on Jl. Kebon Sirih.

EMERGENCY AND COMMUNICATIONS

Emergency: Police: ☎110. **Fire:** ☎113. **Ambulance:** ☎118.

Tourist Police: ☎526 4347. Some English spoken.

Police: Jl. Sudirman 55 (☎525 0110). Another post at the corner of Jl. Wahid Hasyim and Jl. Agus Salim, near Jl. Jaksa.

Telephones: Coin (blue) and card (gray) phones on almost every street block are for local use only. For better connections, try phones in shopping centers and public buildings. **Indosat** offers **HCD** service from phones at the airport. There are several *wartel* on Jl. Jaksa. The one in the **Graha Inanta,** Jl. Jaksa 15A, offers HCD for Rp5000. **Click Internet,** Jl. Jaksa 29, has a free HCD phone. Open daily 9am-midnight.

Internet Access: Access can be found in travel agencies along Jl. Jaksa, public buildings like the Central Post Office, and, of all places, McDonald's. **Bloem Steen Hostel,** Jl. K.S. Timur I 174. Rp10,000 per hr. Open 24hr. **Click Internet** (see above) charges Rp3000 for 15min. or Rp8000 per hr. Open daily 9am-midnight. **Pinguin Internet,** 2nd fl. Sarinah Thamrin (beside Hard Rock Café). Rp8000 per hr. **Graha Inanta,** Jl. Jaksa 15A, upstairs from the travel agency. Rp10,000 per hr. Open daily 8:30am-10pm.

Express Mail: DHL (☎314 1708, ext. 2128), in the Djakarta Theater building, opposite Amigos bar. Open M-F 8am-4:30pm.

Post Offices: GPO, Jl. Pos 2, Pasar Baru (☎385 9889), opposite the West Indonesia Freedom Memorial, 3 buildings east of the Cathedral. Take bus #P12. *Poste Restante* at counter 43 (open M-Sa 8am-3pm). Open M-F 8am-8pm, Sa 8am-7pm, Su 8:30am-2pm. **Pt. Pos Indonesia,** on the 5th fl. of Sarinah Plaza on Jl. M.H. Thamrin (☎381 4427). Open M-Th 8am-3pm, F 8am-2pm, Sa 8am-noon.

Postal Code: 10000.

ACCOMMODATIONS

Jakarta's accommodations, known locally as *losmen,* vary dramatically in terms of prices and of comfort. **Jl. Jaksa** (1km south of Gambir Station, a 15min. walk or Rp3000-3500 by *bajaj*) hosts the backpacker district. Hostel doors often close at midnight. Mosquitoes are bad, so pick up some incense coils, buy a net, or get an A/C room. It's also a good idea to bring a padlock for your door. Almost all accommodations in Jakarta have Western toilets, but eventually you'll have to get used to using a *mandi,* which involves bathing with a bucket of cold water.

Bloem Steen Hostel, Jl. K.S. Timur I 175, 50m up the path by Le Margot Seafood. Clean, quiet rooms with fans. Best bargain in town. Shared baths, 24hr. Internet. Door padlocks provided. Singles Rp15,000; doubles Rp20,000-25,000. ❶

Wisma Delima, Jl. Jaksa 5 (☎392 3850). The closest accommodation to Gambir Station, this popular but weathered guesthouse offers basic rooms with fans. Cafe. Midnight lockout. Strict no drugs or alcohol policy. Books A/C buses. Rooms have shared bath downstairs. Rooms Rp30,000, with A/C Rp50,000. ❷

Yusran Hostel, Jl. Jaksa 9 (☎391 9958). Removed from the bustle of the street. Cheap, quiet rooms with fans. Shared *mandi*. Tiny singles Rp20,000; doubles Rp30,000. ❷

Djody Hotel, Jl. Jaksa 35 (☎315 1404). Large range of rooms with fan or A/C. No lockout. Small singles Rp30,000; A/C doubles with bath Rp60,000; upstairs doubles and triples with shared bath and Western toilets Rp40,000-50,000. ❸

Hotel Arcadia, Jl. K.H. Wahid Hasyim 114 (☎230 0050; arcadia@indosat.net.id). Western accommodation at an Indonesian price. Rooms include TV, phone, guest bar, and private Western baths. Stylish cafe in lobby. Rooms US$28-50 without tax. ❺

FOOD

In Jakarta, you're never more than a block away from **warung** (foodstalls), which specialize in delicious *satay,* fresh seafood, and spicy *padang* food. Ranging from little stalls to larger areas with chairs and tables, these are your best bet for good, cheap food all over the city. The homesick can rely on international chains at one of the many malls ("plazas") in town. Cheap backpacker restaurants cluster on **Jl. Jaksa** and one block over on **Jl. H.A. Salim.** Jl. Salim also hosts fancier restaurants, including some with A/C. Food chains pack **Jl. Wahid Hasyim** and the **Sarinah Plaza** on the corner of Jl. Hasyim and Jl. Thamrin. **Hero** and **Ramayana** supermarkets, at Sarinah and Jl. Salim 22A/B, provide the do-it-yourself option. A more upscale grocery store in the basement of Plaza Indonesia offers Western and specialty foods. Popular with expats and Indonesians alike, **Jl. Kemang Raya** hops with fancier Western bars and restaurants with higher prices. Take a cab from Jl. Jaksa (Rp20,000) or a bus from Block M.

Ya Udah, Jl. Jaksa near Jl. Wahid Hasyim, opposite Hotel Karya. Huge portions and cheap prices attract backpackers and locals alike. Good selection of German, Western, and local food. Espresso Rp4500 per pot. ❶

Memori Cafe, Jl. Jaksa 17, under the Carlsberg sign. Jam to contemporary music and rub elbows with locals and travelers while enjoying Indonesian and Western food. Often shows major sporting events on TV. Typical meal Rp8000-10,000. Open 24hr. ❷

Jimbani Cafe and Gallery, Jl. Kemang Raya 85 (☎719 8938). One of many "resto-galleries" in this trendy area, though this is more of a food-serving bar frequented by young Indonesians and expats. Pool table. Live music on weekends. Irish coffee Rp28,500. Cocktails Rp39,900. Happy hour 4-7pm, half-price drinks. Open daily 11am-2am. ❸

Hazara, Jl. Wahid Hasyim 112 (☎315 0424), next to Hotel Arcadia. Upstairs bar, pool table, the 2-for-1 happy hour before dinner, and excellent service make Hazara the expat restaurant of choice. Pricey, but the food is worth it. Entrees Rp30,000-65,000. Open daily noon-2:30pm lunch, 6-10:30pm dinner. ❺

CAFES

Jakarta's cafes serve as trendy business meeting spots, but can also be a nice way to escape backpacker hangouts and read or relax in air-conditioned comfort. Plaza Senayan is the best place for cafes, but Plaza Indonesia holds its own.

The Coffee Bean & Tea Leaf, Plaza Senayan 1st fl., Jl. Asia Afrika 8 (☎572 5303). This popular meeting spot offers Western coffee shop staples at Western prices. Iced drinks Rp30,140. Muffins Rp15,000. Open daily 10am-10pm. ❹

Tamani Cafe, Jl. Kemang Raya 3A (☎719 8077). This restaurant/cafe sells awesome frozen drinks, cocktails, and desserts. Try the brownies with fudge and ice cream. Drinks Rp15,000-37,000. ❸

Phoenam, Jl. Wahid Hasyim 106 (☎314 7813). The Indonesian take on the coffee shop. Replace muffins and scones with *roti bakar* and you have Phoenam. Cheap prices go well with the A/C and cozy decor. Open daily 6:30am-10:30pm. ❶

SIGHTS

MEDAN MERDEKA (FREEDOM SQUARE)

MESJID ISTIQLAL. Northeast of the square is the dome of Mesjid Istiqlal, the largest mosque in Southeast Asia, with a capacity of 100,000. Visitors are welcome if clothed appropriately (pants, long sleeves, and covered head). Noon prayer is crowded, but breathtaking. Listen for the five daily "calls to prayer" for the best times to visit. The entrance is on the north side, on Jl. Veteran. *(Free.)*

MONAS. In the center of the square is Monas, Indonesia's national monument. Also known as **Sukarno's Last Erection,** this 132m monument represents the strength, freedom, and fertility of the nation, and also makes a good reference point. The base of the monument contains a diorama of Indonesia's fight for independence. *(Monument and museum open daily 8:30am-5pm, closed last M of every month. Rp5100, students Rp3600, children Rp2600.)*

NATIONAL MUSEUM. Across the street 300m to the west, the museum is recognizable by a small elephant statue out front. It has a vast stockpile of artifacts from all over the archipelago, ranging from Ming Dynasty pottery to models of traditional houses from the islands. *(Open Tu-Th and Su 8:30am-2:30pm, F 8:30-11:30am, Sa 8:30am-1:30pm. Free tours Tu-Th 9:30am, second Sa and last Su of every month 10:30am. Rp750, students Rp250, children Rp150.)*

FATAHILLAH SQUARE

One kilometer northeast of Kota Station is Fatahillah Square, surrounded by Dutch period buildings where public executions were held.

JAKARTA HISTORY MUSEUM. This weathered building with teal shutters was formerly known as the Batavia Town Hall. Antique Dutch and traditional Indonesian furniture and a dozen ornate muskets are displayed. Some descriptions are in English. *(☎692 9101. Open Tu-Su 9am-3pm. Rp2000, students Rp1000, children Rp600.)*

WAYANG MUSEUM. The Dutch museum on the west side of the square houses an extensive collection of *wayang kulit* (leather) and *wayang golek* (wooden) puppets. There are puppets of modern-day bureaucrats and vignettes from revolutionary movements. Descriptions are somewhat lacking, making the displays hard to follow. *(☎629 2560. Open Tu-Su 9am-3pm. Rp2000, students Rp1000, children Rp600.)*

FINE ARTS AND CERAMICS MUSEUM. The large museum is set back on the east side of the square. Ceramics include modern *kreatif*, foreign pieces, and eerie carved tree-trunk totems. The tree in front of the building provides a welcome bit of shade. *(☎690 7062. Open Tu-Su 9am-3pm. Rp2000, students Rp1000, children Rp600.)*

OTHER SIGHTS

SUNDA KELAPA (OLD HARBOR). Northwest of Fatahillah Square, the Old Harbor features panoramic **Jl. Pasar Ikan,** which begins under a metal gate and continues past shops of all sorts to the water (see **Markets,** below). The **Museum Bahari (Maritime Museum),** on the beginning of Jl. Pasar Ilkan, is in the breezy storehouses of the Dutch East India Company, where the feel of old Batavia still lingers. The sight of old Makassar schooners sailing in the morning is truly one of the most impressive sights in Jakarta. *(☎669 3406. 20min. walk, or take a* bajaj *(Rp3000). Open Tu-Th and Su 9am-3pm, F 9am-2pm, Sa 9am-1pm. Rp2000, students 1000, children Rp600.)*

RAGUNAN ZOO. A large, green zoo where animals are kept in their natural habitats. All sorts of standard zoo animals roam here, but the most fabulous by far are the Komodo dragons, who bask like mini-dinosaurs. *(Take bus #19 from Jl. Thamrin. Open daily 8am-6pm. Rp2000, children under 12 Rp2000; Rp1500 extra for snake house.)*

TAMAN MINI INDONESIA INDAH. In this huge complex on the southeast corner of Jakarta, "you can see all of Indonesia in a day." The complex includes the **Museum Indonesia,** which displays traditional artwork, cultural dioramas, and flicks about Indonesia at the IMAX Theater. English-speaking guides lead tours of 27 full-size provincial houses. Other areas, from the aviary to the Islamic museum, appeal to specialized interests. On crowded Sunday mornings, there are traditional dance performances. *(☎840 9210. Take bus #P11 from Sarinah, or bus #P15 from Block M, and then take a* microlet *from the Kampung Rambutan Station. Open Tu-Su 8am-5pm. Rp4000, children Rp3000, Sa-Su Rp1000 extra. Museum of Indonesia open daily 9am-4pm. Rp3000. IMAX every hr. 11am-4pm. Rp6000. Rp25,000 for full-day all-access pass.)*

MARKETS

Huge malls and open-air markets are scattered throughout Jakarta and frequented by upperclass families. Other markets cater to the everyday man.

Pasar Ikan, in Sunda Kelapa. The fish market is a tile-roofed building on Jl. Pasar Ikan, 400m up from the Maritime Museum. Activity is almost endless, but when the catch comes in after 9pm, everything else shuts down. The fish on sale come in every shape, size, and color imaginable. Beyond the Maritime Museum, shops sell gear to prepare ships for sea—huge anchors, chains, and cables are carted from place to place.

Pasar Antik, running along Jl. Surabaya, a Rp5000 *bajaj* ride from Jl. Jaksa, is full of beautiful handicrafts from around the archipelago. Decorative items from ship wheels to ebony sculptures and ashtrays overflow from the stalls. Shopkeepers do their utmost to get you bargaining—once you've started it's expected you'll buy. Open daily 8am-6pm.

Pasar Burung, on Jl. Pramuka behind the big yellow and blue Pasar Pramuka, a Rp4000 *bajaj* ride from Jl. Jaksa. The twitter of birds slowly grows louder until millions are visible in their cages—from colorful budgies to magnificent (and outlawed) eagles. Pesky peddlers are known to hassle travelers. Open daily 6am-6pm.

Pasar Mangga Dua, on Jl. Mangga Dua, is full of electronics. Shops continue down from the top of Jl. Hayam Wuruk. **Jl. Pancuran** leads off Jl. Hayam Wuruk 300m down and through Glodok, boasting a huge **fruit market** running the length of the street. Although this market is full of deals, peddlers can be aggressive.

SHOPPING

Teenage mall culture is all the rage in Jakarta. Pricey and sterile foodstalls cater to hordes of school kids while the chic-chic head straight to the designer stores.

Sarinah Department Store, on the corner of Jl. Wahid Hasyim and Jl. Thamrin, a 10min. walk from Jl. Jaksa. Look for a frighteningly large inflatable Ronald McDonald. Less extravagant than some malls in town, Sarinah is the place for lesser designer clothes and Rp70,000 CDs. Supermarket downstairs. Several 24hr. **ATMS** outside.

Plaza Senayan, Jl. Asia Afrika 8. Senayan has a cinema, bowling alley, and pool as well as American food chains and European couturiers. A daytime hangout for rich kids, it's best used for its recreational facilities and cafes (see **Cafes,** p. 136). Open M-F 8am-9pm, Sa-Su 8am-midnight.

Plaza Indonesia, Grand Hyatt Hotel, Jl. Thamrin. 1km up from Sarinah on the right. Much of the Hyatt's grandeur has leaked down to this 5 fl. A/C mall. Piano music wafts through the air and Italian shoes sell for Rp3,000,000. A grocery store in the basement offers affordable foods and a lovely bakery. Open daily 10am-10pm.

ENTERTAINMENT

At the end of the day, Jakarta has the typical big city offerings: movies, bowling, and billiards abound. Many malls offer these distractions in one stop.

CENTRAL JAKARTA. Djakarta Theater, at the corner of Jl. Wahid Hasyim and Jl. Thamrin, 10min. from Jl. Jaksa, has three screens showing last year's English movies beginning at 2pm. A similar setup runs at **Plaza Senayan,** on Jl. Asia Afrika. Plaza Senayan also boasts 30 **bowling lanes** and a big pool hall. (Bowling Rp12,000 before 4pm, Rp15,000 after. Pool Rp18,000 per hr. before 4pm, Rp24,000 after. Open daily 10am-10pm.) English movies play on the 4th floor of the plaza (Rp40,000).

NORTHERN JAKARTA. Jaya Ancol is a massive entertainment complex of Disney-like proportions. A resort facility on the coast, it's next to the mercury-laden sea, but the nearby **waterpark** has decent slides. (Open M-F 9am-4pm, Sa-Su 7am-7pm. M-F Rp15,000, Sa-Su Rp17,500.) Near the main entrance to Jaya Ancol is **Jaya Ancol Bowl.** (Rp9000 per game before 4pm, Rp13,000 after. Shoes Rp3000. Open daily 10am-1am.) **Dunia Fantasi** has a roller coaster, a ferris wheel, and other rides and games for children. (Open M-Sa 9am-4pm, Su 10am-10pm. Full pass Rp40,000.) **Sea World** aquarium boasts over 6000 aquatic animals and daily sting ray and shark feedings in the main aquarium. To get there, take bus #P64 from Kota, *microlet* #15 from Sunda Kelapa, or bus #60 up Jl. Gunung Sahar. (☎641 0080. Open M-F 9am-6pm, Sa-Su 9am-7:30pm. Feedings M-F 11am, 3:30pm; Sa-Su 11am, 2:30, 5:30pm. Rp25,000.)

NIGHTLIFE

Cheap beer flows nightly along Jl. Jaksa as live music softens the murmur of backpacker chit-chat. The dancing queen in everyone is well served by Jakarta's many nightclubs. Some establishments are rather seedy, pushing the skin trade, while others are the height of glamor.

NEAR JL. JAKSA

Hard Rock Café, Sarinah Jl. Thamrin. Locals claim it is the best Hard Rock in Southeast Asia. Although that's questionable, this club is dependable and quite popular with locals and expats alike. Beer Rp23,500-36,000. Happy hour before 8pm. Open M-Th 8:30am-10:30pm, F-Sa 8:30am-11pm, Su 8:30am-10:30pm.

Vera's Pub, Jl. Wahid Hasyim 116 (☎391 3592), 5min. from Jl. Jaksa down a side street after Dyna Pub. A Jl. Jaksa crowd. Stake out your space on the small dance floor. Beer Rp19,500. Open daily 9pm-3am.

Dyna Pub, Jl. Wahid Hasyim 116A, down the side street after Bank BCA. Quiet and cozy—somewhere between an Irish pub and old gentlemen's club. Ideal for a drink away from the backpacker droves. Bintang or Guinness Rp19,000. Open daily 11am-2am.

Dejavu Club, Jl. Wahid Hasyim 88, upstairs from Parkit Restaurant. Boasting an "artist" clientele and gentle, jazz-like music nightly. Older Indonesian family crowd. Partner dancing. Beer Rp19,000. Open daily 9pm-2am.

ELSEWHERE IN JAKARTA

Jl. Hayam Wuruk in **Glodok** has a reputation for extremely large, overwhelming, and seedier clubs. The most happening places are in luxurious hotels. Cover charges and drinks aren't budget-friendly, but the clubs provide a chance to observe the top end of Jakarta's society. Taxis are the only way to get around.

Retro, on Jl. Gatoto Subroto Kav 2-3, in the Crown Plaza Hotel. Another hangout of the rich and beautiful (and some mere mortals). Reputedly some of the best music in town—Top 40 with good lights and enough space to enjoy it. Torn trousers won't do. Cover W and F-Sa Rp50,000. Open Su-Tu and Th 10pm-1am, W 10pm-3am, F-Sa 10pm-4am.

Musro, Hotel Borobudur, Jl. Lapangan Banteng near Station Juanda. For a taste of local swanky nightlife, go to Musro. Music is a mix of Top 40 and Indonesian dance. Rp100,000 cover includes all non-alcoholic drinks. Open M-F 9am-8pm, Sa 6pm-2am.

Tanamur, Jl. Abang Timur 14 (☎380 5233). Jostle with tourists, expats, and Indonesians in this club. Fast music. Beer Rp25,000. Go-go dancers M-Sa at midnight, 1, and 2am. Gay-friendly. Cover Rp30,000. Open daily 9pm-3am.

BOGOR ☎0251

Dubbed "*Sans-Souci*" or "without worries" by the Dutch, Bogor was originally the site (chosen for its temperate climate) of capitals built by ancient Hindu-Buddhist kings. Centuries later, colonists made the town a site for weekend retreats, and the city retains a similar role today. Virtually a suburb of Jakarta, Bogor is cosmopolitan enough to satisfy a traveler's longing for creature comforts, yet small enough to provide refuge from the madness of the city. Most find it preferable to stay in Bogor and explore Jakarta rather than vice-versa. Bogor's world-renowned botanical gardens, the city's heart and soul, flourish with the nourishment of the high rainfall of West Java. Don't miss the peaceful waterfalls at Air Terjun Cilember (see **Daytrips**, p. 143) or the hot springs of nearby Puncak.

TRANSPORTATION

Trains: The **train station** (☎324 529), on Jl. Permas, is northwest of the Botanical Gardens off Jl. Kapten Muslihat. To get from the hostels on Jl. Palendang to the train station, take *angkot* #02 northbound and get off at the end of the road. Walk down the road to the right, turn left into the alley with *warungs* and street vendors. The station will be on your left. To **Jakarta** (economy 1hr., every 30min. 4am-9:30pm, Rp6000; executive express 30min., 9 per day until 5pm, Rp8000). Major central and east Javanese city routes go through Jakarta; ask a travel agent for these destinations.

Buses: The **terminal** is 1km southeast of the Botanical Gardens on Jl. Raya Pajajaran. To **Bandung** (economy up to 7hr., express 4hr.; Rp12,000-20,000) and **Jakarta** (Kali Deres, Tanjung Priok, and Pulo Gadung: 1½hr.; every 15min., Rp3000-5000; Kp. Rambutan: 45min., every 15min., Rp3000-5000). Buses to **Yogyakarta** and **Surabaya** go through Jakarta.

Local Transportation: Short-distance **angkot** head to the Puncak and surrounding areas from the Sukasari minibus "terminal" in South Bogor–take *angkot* #2 to the "terminal." *Angkot* swarm local roads on fixed routes at fixed rates (Rp1000), and **becak** are everywhere. Prices vary with weight and distance but should generally be around Rp3000 and never exceed Rp5000. Slower **delman** (pony carts) linger by gardens, but the ride is not so romantic when stuck in traffic.

ORIENTATION AND PRACTICAL INFORMATION

Bogor is built around the rectangular **Botanical Gardens,** home to many plant species and one of five Indonesian Presidential Palaces, the **Istana Bogor.** The gardens are bounded by **Jl. Ir. H. Juanda** to the west, **Jl. Otista** to the south, and **Jl. Raya Pajajaran** to the east (which leads to the **bus station**). Extending away from the palace to the west is **Jl. Kapten Muslihat,** toward **Taman Topi (Hat Park)** and the **train station.** Most guesthouses lie on Jl. Raya Pajajaran and Jl. Palendang.

Tourist Office: Jl. Palendang 35 (☎332 775). Hidden behind two white buildings. Maps and palace tours available. Open M-F 8am-4pm. **Tourist Information Center,** in Taman Topi, on Jl. Permas side. Unreliably open M-F 8am-7pm.

Tours: Travel Bureau Mulia Rahayu, Jl. Mayor Oking 18-20 (☎324 150). Books airplane and PELNI boat tickets. Open daily 8am-5pm. **Larasati Tours and Travel** (☎338 361), on Jl. Kapten Muslihat, in a hat-shaped building at Taman Topi, southeast of the train station. Open M-F 8am-5pm, Sa 8am-4pm, Su 9am-1pm.

Currency Exchange: Bank Bali, Jl. Kapten Muslihat 17A (☎312 990), near the railway station. **ATM.** Open M-F 8am-3pm; exchange available M-F 10am-2pm. Numerous other banks with ATMs are along Jl. Raya Pajajaran and Jl. Juanda.

Markets: Pasar Anyar, on Jl. Dewi Sartika beside Taman Topi, offers everything from *anjaman* (weaving) to *zaitun minyac* (olive oil). **Pasar Bogor,** Jl. Suryakencana 3, is near the gate to the Botanical Gardens behind **Bogor Plaza Shopping Center.**

Emergency: Police: ☎110. **Fire:** ☎113. **Ambulance:** ☎118.

Police: Jl. Kapten Muslihat 16 (☎381 360), opposite the soldier statue at Taman Topi. Open 24hr.

Medical Services: RS Salak, Jl. Jend. Sudirman 8 (☎344 609), with **pharmacy** (☎320 496) next door. **RSU PMI,** on Jl. Rumah Sakit II. Both open 24hr.

Telephones: *Wartel,* Jl. Pengadilan 14, to the left of Telkom, offers **international calls** daily 4:30am-midnight. **Wartel Exotica,** Jl. Kapten Muslihat 51, at Taman Topi. Open daily 7am-midnight.

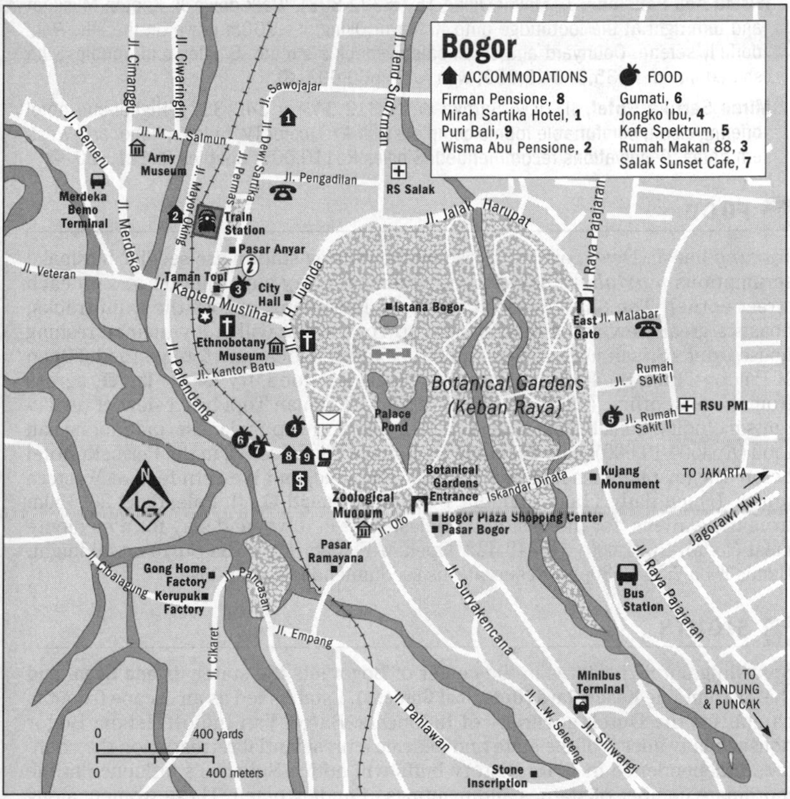

Internet Access: Internet cafes full of schoolchildren on "Lovemail" abound. Around Rp5000 per hr. **B@linet,** Jl. Palendang 50. Attached to Puri Bali Guest House. Open daily 9am-midnight. **Blue Corner Net,** at Taman Topi, is a popular hangout among local college students. Rp85 per min. Open daily 9am-9pm. **Infonet,** Jl. Pajajaran 34, next to Pangrango Hotel. Open 24hr.

Post Office: GPO, Jl. Ir. H. Juanda 5, 200m north of where Jl. Palendang intersects with the gardens. *Poste Restante.* Open M-Sa 8am-4pm.

Postal Code: 16124.

ACCOMMODATIONS

Bogor has numerous guesthouses. In addition to those listed, several more are on **Jl. Raya Pajajaran** east of the gardens. All of these listings offer free tea, need no reservations (except where noted), and accept cash only.

Firman Pensione, Jl. Palendang 48 (☎323 3246), past Puri Bali on the left. This social *wisma* has several sitting areas that look out over the valley to the peak. Breakfast included; cafe offers other meals as well. Hang out in the main floor sitting area—the owner often graces it with her delicious, free, homemade snacks. Doubles Rp25,000, with *mandi* Rp30,000-40,000. ❷

Wisma Abu Pensione, Jl. Mayor Oking 15 (☎322 893). Walk down Jl. Kapten Muslihat and turn right at the footbridge onto Jl. Mayor Oking; it's 300m down on the left. Wonderfully serene. Courtyard and small cafe overlook a stream. Singles and doubles with shared *mandi* Rp35,000-45,000, with A/C Rp60,000. ❸

Mirah Sartika Hotel, Jl. Dewi Sartika 6A (☎312 343 or 340 387). Higher-end hotel offering clean, comfortable rooms complete with A/C, color TV, fridge, phone, and Western baths. Reservations recommended. Singles Rp110,000; doubles Rp121,000. ❺

FOOD

Warung line Jl. Dewi Sartika. Those by the railway station are seedier but make scrumptious *martabak*. **Bakeries** are in almost every supermarket and on each street corner. The **Salak Sunset Cafe ❷,** Jl. Palendang, across the train tracks, boasts a great view and a relaxed setting. Your wallet will enjoy their refreshing house drink (Sirsak juice Rp5000) and the fantastic local and foreign food. (Open M-F noon-11pm, Su 4-11pm.) For great Sundanese food, try **Jongko Ibu ❸,** across from the post office. (Open daily 9am-10:30pm.) Taman Topi has a slew of restaurants including **Rumah Makan 88 ❶,** which serves cheap Sudanese and Indonesian food (Rp4000-10,000). **Kafe Spektrum ❺,** Jl. Raya Pajajaran 35, in the Permata Hotel before the hospital, has nightly live music, karaoke, and Western food at Western prices. (Open daily 11am-midnight.) Come to **Gumati ❺,** Jl. Palendang 26, 150m from the gardens, for the best and priciest view in town, and stay for a mediocre meal (oxtail Rp21,000). (☎313 422. Open M-F 10am-11pm, Sa-Su 10am-midnight. Bands F-Sa 7:30-10:30pm. Reservations recommended Sa-Su. Visa.)

SIGHTS

Sprawling out 87 hectares in the center of Bogor sits the stately **Istana Bogor** and the surrounding **Kebun Raya (Botanical Gardens).** Established as an escape from the capital for the Dutch governor of Indonesia, Baron Van Imhoff, Istana Bogor housed many guests of the state and became a presidential retreat upon the country's independence in 1945. History buffs will notice Sukarno's influence in the inordinate number of statues and paintings of nude women. These women, along with his four wives, surely brightened up Sukarno's house arrest here (1967-70). Gaining admission to the grounds is a bit tricky—a consequence of Indonesian politics. Children are not admitted to the palace, and only groups of 10 or more can visit if they request permission one week in advance, but all are welcome on national holidays.

Viewing **Kebun Raya** is simpler. The park's entrance is on the south side on Jl. Otista. Formerly part of Bogor Palace, these gardens were converted to a collection of indigenous, foreign, and exotic botanical species for educational and scientific purpose in the late 18th and early 19th centuries. Those in the mood for a soothing stroll can meander along the four recommended routes (about 1hr. each), and guides give naturalists the scoop on the thousands of unique species. (Open daily 8am-5pm. Last tickets sold at 3pm. Rp3000. Guides Rp25,000.)

Across the street from the Pasar Ramayana food market are the inanimate skeletons and stuffed animals of the **Zoological Museum,** 200m west of the entrance to the gardens. (Open daily 8am-4pm. Rp1000.)

Tourists can also visit the **Gong Home Factory,** Jl. Pancasan 17. A small donation of a couple thousand rupiahs is expected. Bring a pack of cigarettes to make a whole bunch of friends while enjoying the musical rhythms of metal-hammering. (Take blue *angkot* #3 from the Zoological Museum. Open Sa-Th 8am-noon and 1-4pm.) Head up the hill and turn right at the dentist sign to visit a **kerupuk factory.**

The dough is kneaded, spun into cakes, dried, and dropped into hot oil. (Open daily 6am-noon and 1-4pm.) An ancient **stone inscription** *batutulis*, dating from the mid-14th century and the Pajajaran Kingdom, can be seen on Jl. Batutulis. Take *angkot* #2 10min. south of the garden, or walk (30min.).

DAYTRIPS FROM BOGOR

Buses from the main bus terminal or the Sukusari bus terminal (via green *angkot* #2) reach countless destinations in the outlying areas near Bogor. Travelers can escape to **Pelabuhanratu,** a hill-bounded coastal town to the southwest. It takes four hours by share-taxi (total Rp250,000 can be split by up to 8 people) and an indeterminate amount of time by bus (economy Rp8000; A/C Rp15,000). Beaches around **Ujung Genteng** have great surfing and reasonable accommodations. Share the beaches at twilight with night-loving giant turtles. From Pelabuhanratu a bus will take you to Suradi and a *bemo* will get you to Genteng.

To reach the seven peaceful **Air Terjun Cilember** (Cilember Waterfalls), one of the few places near Jakarta where the air doesn't smell like exhaust, take *angkot* #2 to Terminal Sukasari and then a blue #2 minibus halfway to Cisarva (Rp2500). Look for the blue gates and then catch an *ojek* (Rp2000-4000) to the entrance. The tough hike is deserted on weekdays; solo travelers might consider visiting on weekends. (Entrance fee Rp2000. Guides for less traversed routes roughly Rp5000-10,000.)

Taman Safari, in Cisarva, is more like a drive-through zoo than a safari. A swimming pool and other entertainment make this a fun half-day trip from Puncak. (☎0251 253 222. Take an *angkot* 30min. from Cilember (Rp1000); tell the driver to stop at the Safari. An *ojek* (Rp1500) will take you to the gate. Open M-F 9am-5pm, Sa-Su 8:30am-5:30pm. Tour Rp30,000, children Rp25,000. Night tours on the Taman Safari bus Sa 7-9pm.)

THE PUNCAK ☎0263

Meaning "peak" in Bahasa Indonesia, "Puncak" understates the beauty of the mountain pass connecting Jakarta and Bogor to Bandung. Tea plantations stretch for miles on either side of Rte. 2 (Jl. Raya), which winds through the towns of Cisarua and Cipanas. Enjoy the refreshing sight of lush green fields stretching for kilometers with traditional thatched huts interspersed. From here the floral Jl. Raya Cobodas branches off and leads to the Gede Pangrango National Park and the Cibodas Botanical Gardens. Terraced rice paddies and the peaks of Gunung Gede and Gunung Pangrango are visible from any patio on the hill. Beyond the park's gates, avid trekkers will find exciting wildlife, impressive waterfalls, and seemingly bottomless volcano craters on the way to the top. The view of the mountain path alone is well worth the challenging hike.

TRANSPORTATION. On weekdays, **buses** run almost every 30min. from **Jakarta, Bogor,** and **Bandung.** On the weekend, public buses are forbidden from traveling on Rte. 2 (Jl. Raya) because traffic is so heavy, though white minibuses do still make the trip from Bogor (1hr., Rp3000-5000). From Bandung, travelers can reach **Cibodas** by taking a bus to **Cianjur** and then traveling by *angkot* to Cibodas via **Cipanas** (total Rp6000-7000).

PRACTICAL INFORMATION. The **medical clinic, post office,** *wartel*, and **bank** reside on **Jl. Raya Cipanas,** the stretch of the road connecting Bogor and Bandung. A couple of kilometers from the heart of Cipanas toward Bogor, **Jl. Raya Cibodas** branches off and stretches to the parks and gardens above, where most guesthouses are located.

INDONESIA

The Cipanas **angkot station** is next to the **post office,** Jl. Raya Cipanas 109. (Open M-Th 8am-3pm, F 8-11am, Sa 8am-1pm.) Painfully slow Internet and a *wartel* are next door. (Open daily 6am-midnight.) A few hundred meters back toward the pass is **BNI Cipanas,** Jl. Raya Cipanas 167, which has a 24hr. **ATM.** (☎512 022. Open M-F 8am-3pm.) BCA **ATM** (Cirrus/MC/V) is 100m toward Bandung and across the street. Next door is a general **pharmacy.** There is a 24hr. health clinic (☎512 465) at the Jl. Raya Cibodas and Jl. Raya Cipanas intersection. **Postal Code:** 43253.

ACCOMMODATIONS AND FOOD. A short *angkot* ride up Jl. Raya Cibodas leads to several well-situated accommodations, overlooking the beautiful terraced valley and a mere 10min. walk from the Botanical Gardens and Gunung Gede. **Freddy's ❷,** 500m from the Cibodas gate, is the lodging of choice. This relaxed, friendly home has the only knowledgeable English-speaking guides in the area. Breakfast and tea are complimentary. (☎515 473. Doubles Rp50,000. Shared *mandi.*) Past the Cibodas Gate to the right is the **Wisma Jamur ❸,** a good option for groups of three to six, offering clean rooms with great views of the Puncak from its veranda. (Around Rp50,000 with *mandi*, depending on size and degree of privacy.) Next door, the **Pondok Pemuda Hostel ❸,** intended for groups of four to 24, evokes memories of summer camp with its dorm-style rooms. (☎512 807. Quads Rp40,000.) Expect these hostels to be packed on weekends and holidays.

The best options for delicious, satiating eats are the guesthouses above, all of which offer hot, cheap, home-cooked meals. Dozens of fruit stands and countless *warung* offering fried noodles and rice line the road leading to the garden gates, providing a quick post-trek snack for a few thousand rupiah. Several cafes inside the gardens offer somewhat more extensive menus. **Jl. Raya Cipanas** houses fancy hotel-restaurants, sleepless *warung*, and cheap *padang* joints for spice fanatics.

SIGHTS. The walk or ride up **Jl. Raya Cibodas** is breathtaking (*angkot* Rp1000). Thanks to residents who participate in the nursery business, flowering plants and bonsai line the whole 4km stretch. The **Kebun Raya Cibodas,** an extension of the Bogor Botanical Gardens 1km beyond the Cibodas gates, is a hiking and bird-watching paradise. **Avoid crowded weekend and holiday explorations.** (Open daily 7am-6pm; last ticket sold at 4pm. Rp3000.) The gardens spread out on the lower fringe of **Gede Pangrango National Park,** a volcanic range that extends from Sumatra through Java. For Rp2500, visitors can hike roughly one hour to a mystical bat cave (guide required), three waterfalls, and a path alongside the fresh spewings of an active volcano. Another 1½hr. finds a hot spring, one of the least visited in all of Java—perfect for a secluded retreat. A round-trip day-hike to the summit of Gunung Gede (14km) is another option for those who start early enough. Those with a tent and sleeping bag can spend the night near the summit of **Gunung Pangrango,** a neighboring mountain. Quality maps with suggested trails and required visitor's permits are available at the Visitors Center. Though costly, guides are strongly recommended for night hikes.

The **Taman Bunga Nusantara** (National Flower Garden) has pleasant landscaping with colorful greenhouses (around Rp10,000). An *angkot* headed toward Mariwati from Cipanas will drop you at the gate. The tea-picking process can be seen at the fascinating **Gunung Mas Pabrik Teh** (Gunung Mas Tea Factory) between Bogor and Cipanas. From the gates, walk 10min. to get the factory—passing a teahouse, gift shop, and women tirelessly picking away. (Grounds open daily 8am-6pm. Rp1500. Factory open Sa-Th 8am-2pm. Rp2000, plus Rp5000 for required guide.)

BANDUNG ☎022

With less pollution, a cooler climate, and extensive factory outlet shopping, Bandung often beats out Indonesia's capital as the big city of choice. Although not evident from the unpleasant backpacker ghetto, the residual European glamor and sophistication earn Bandung the title of "Paris of the East Indies." The city, West Java's capital, is home to over 50 schools and universities. With the high concentration of young people, nightlife in Bandung is more comfortable and benign than in other Javanese cities and should not be passed over.

TRANSPORTATION

Flights: Husen Sastra Negara Airport, 5km west of the city. Take a taxi from the town center (15-30min. depending on traffic; Rp20,000-40,000). Contact **Merpati** at the airport (☎603 47 44) and in Hotel Papandayan on Jl. Gabot Sobroto (☎730 27 37) for flight times and arrangements. Open M-F 8am-4:30pm, Sa 9am-2pm, Su 9am-1pm. Flights Tu, Th, and Sa to **Denpasar** (Rp815,000); **Lombok** (Rp 912,000); **Surabaya** (Rp530,500); **Ujung Pandang** (Rp1,199,000).

Trains: Terminal Staslun (☎420 69 17), behind the *angkot* station on Jl. Stasiun Barat, off Jl. Kebonjati. To: **Jakarta** (3hr.; every hr. 5am-6pm; Express/Special M-F 6:30 and 9pm, F-Sa 4pm, Su and holidays 7, 8pm; Rp30,000-45,000); **Yogyakarta** (around 7hr.; 4 per day; Rp60,000-85,000); **Surabaya** (11hr.; 7am, 5, 7pm; Rp75,000-160,000). Prices depend on class (1st, 2nd) and type (standard, executive) of train.

Buses: Leuwi Panjang Terminal (☎522 07 68), on Jl. Sukarno-Hatta a few kilometers south of the train station. Take bus Ledeng-Leuwi Panjang or an *angkot* from *alun-alun.* To **Bogor** (3hr.; every hr. 24hr.; Rp8000-12,000) and **Jakarta** (4hr.; every hr. 24hr.; Rp25,000). **Terminal Cicaheum** (☎727 95 49), on Jl. A. Yani northeast of town center. Take bus Cicaheum-Kebon Kelapa or bus #9 Cicaheum-Leuwi Panjang from *alun-alun.* To: **Cirebon** (4hr.; every hr. 6am-6pm; Rp15,000-20,000); **Denpasar** (24hr.; 2pm; Rp132,000); **Yogyakarta** (10hr.; 6:30pm; Rp60,000); **Surabaya** (12hr.; 2pm; Rp82,000).

Local Transportation: City buses (Rp1000-1500) have north-south and east-west routes. A network of **angkot** run through city streets (Rp1000-1500) and the surrounding area. Navigation can be difficult, but locals can help. Terminals are **Station Hall** and **Kebon Kelapa** (old bus terminal). **Becak** are convenient and cheaper than elsewhere (Rp4000 gets you from Jl. Suniaraja to anyplace within 15min.). **Taxis** rarely use meters, so bargain. Share-taxi to **Pangandaran** (6hr.) Rp25,000.

ORIENTATION AND PRACTICAL INFORMATION

Busy **Jl. Asia-Afrika** runs east-west passing *alun-alun,* the town center. **Jl. Otto Iskandardinata** runs north-south and ends at the Governor's Mansion, where **Jl. Merdeka** takes over as the major north-south route two blocks east. **Jl. Kebonjati** becomes **Jl. Suniaraja** in front of the train station and then runs parallel to and north of Jl. Asia-Afrika. **Jl. Braga** runs north-south by the **Museum Asia-Afrika.** Keep in mind that street signs are placed perpendicular to the streets they name.

Tourist Office: Tourist Information Center (☎420 6644), at the northeast corner of *alun-alun;* it's the small office past the parked cars. Books tours in and around Bandung. Open M-Sa 9am-5pm. The **information counter** (☎421 6648), at the railway station, has locked luggage storage (Rp2000 per day). Open daily 8am-5:30pm.

Tours: Sari Holiday, Jl. Naicpan 45 (☎422 0716), 1 block northeast of the Museum Asia-Afrika. Open M-Sa 8am-4pm. **Pacto Tours and Travel,** Jl. Karapitan 87 (☎733 39 42) provides AmEx services. Open M-F 8:30am-4:30pm, Sa 8:30am-1pm.

Currency Exchange: Golden Moneychanger, Jl. Otto Iskandardinata 180 (☎423 84 38). Open M-F 9am-4:30pm, Sa 9am-1pm. Banks and ATMs are all over the city, including a **BCA ATM** at the corner of Jl. Suniaraja and Jl. Banceuy, and a full-service **Bank Bali,** Jl. Merdeka 66 (☎423 4366). Open M-F 8am-3pm.

Markets: Pasar Baru, along Jl. Otto Iskandardinata in Chinatown. Bandung's oldest market, dating back to 1812. Textiles, shoes, fish, fruit, and a disproportionate number of bedcovers. Open daily 7am-4pm. **Pasar Ciroyom,** west of town, sells second-hand goods, food, and household products. Catch a red westward *angkot* from the train station. **Night markets** along Jl. Sudirman and Jl. Belakang Pasar are a cheap cure for midnight munchies. 2 blocks north of the train station, a flashy shopping strip on **Jeans Street (Jl. Cihampelas)** sells cheap denim products. Swanky **Plaza Bandung Indah,** Jl. Merdeka 56, features big-name foreign stores and a seven-screen cinema. (Open daily 8am-6pm, Sa 9am-8pm). For *warung,* try **Pasar Malam,** off *alun-alun*'s northeast corner.

Emergency: Police: ☎110. **Ambulance:** ☎118. **Fire:** ☎113.

Police: Main Station (☎420 3500), on Jl. Merdeka.

Pharmacy: Kimia Farma 12, Jl. Ir. H. Juanda 1 (☎420 5421), at the intersection with Jl. Hasannudin. Open 24hr. Pharmacies in town are open daily 8am-8pm.

Medical Services: Hospital RS Kebonjati, Jl. Kebonjati 152 (☎601 4058). 24hr. **emergency** clinic.

Telephones: International phones at **GPO.** *Wartel* are abundant in town.

Internet Access: Ega Kineta, Jl. Braga 111 (☎420 6291). Rp5000 per hr. Open M-Sa 8am-7pm. **Cybernet,** Jl. Gardu Jati 33. Rp5000 per hr. Open daily 10am-10pm. Although far away, the fastest and most reliable Internet cafes line Jl. Dago.

Express Mail: DHL, Jl. Asia-Afrika 81 (☎423 1631), in the Grand Hotel Preanger. Open M-F 8am-5pm, Sa 8am-1pm.

Post Office: GPO, Jl. Asia-Afrika 49 (☎420 7081). Enter on the side past the stands. **International phones.** *Poste Restante.* Western Union service available. Open daily 8am-8pm.

Postal Code: 40111.

INDONESIA

ACCOMMODATIONS

Cheap accommodations line both streets near the railway station and Jl. Pangarang, two blocks south of the Museum Asia-Afrika.

By "Moritz," Luxor Permai 35 (☎420 5788), at intersection with Jl. Belakang Pasar. A sign on the south side of Jl. Kebonjati points out the way. Comfortable, colorful, and clean. Breakfast and virtuoso guitarists included. All rooms have shared, clean, Western *mandi*. Dorms Rp16,000; singles Rp22,000; doubles Rp32,000; triples Rp43,000. ❷

Hotel Patrudissa II, Jl. Pasirkaliki 12 (☎420 2645). Follow the "Hotel" sign down a well-lit alley. Private *mandi,* hot water, maps, and info about Bandung. Colored lights give the bland rooms character. Blue, green, or red singles and doubles Rp45,000. ❸

Hotel Surabaya, Jl. Kebonjati 71-75 (☎423 3679). Echoey, spacious rooms are clean and comfortable. Free tea. Singles Rp25,000; doubles Rp35,000; triples Rp45,000; quads Rp50,000; deluxe Rp55,000. ❷

Wisma Nusaindah, Jl. Lodaya 95 (☎730 05 05). Walk east down Jl. Asia-Afrika and turn right onto Jl. Palasari, then left onto Jl. Lodaya. Although quite Western in appearance, it's popular with Indonesians. Singles with shared *mandi* and fan Rp35,000-50,000; doubles Rp70,000, with TV and hot bath Rp80,000-100,000. ❸

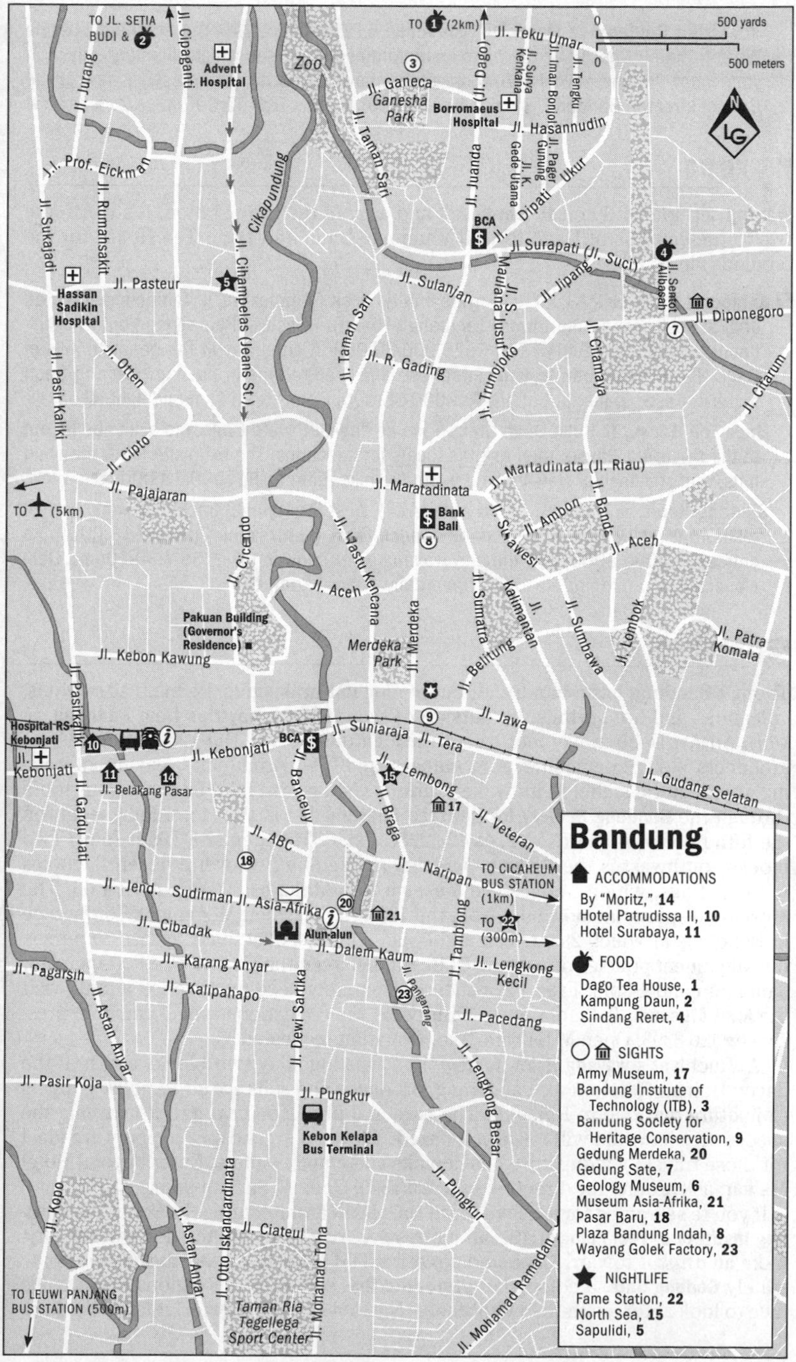
Bandung
ACCOMMODATIONS
By "Moritz," 14
Hotel Patrudissa II, 10
Hotel Surabaya, 11
FOOD
Dago Tea House, 1
Kampung Daun, 2
Sindang Reret, 4
SIGHTS
Army Museum, 17
Bandung Institute of Technology (ITB), 3
Bandung Society for Heritage Conservation, 9
Gedung Merdeka, 20
Gedung Sate, 7
Geology Museum, 6
Museum Asia-Afrika, 21
Pasar Baru, 18
Plaza Bandung Indah, 8
Wayang Golek Factory, 23
NIGHTLIFE
Fame Station, 22
North Sea, 15
Sapulidi, 5
0
500 yards
500 meters
TO JL. SETIA BUDI & 2
TO 1 (2km)
Jl. Teku Umar
Jl. Cipaganti
Advent Hospital
Zoo
Jl. Jurang
Jl. Ganeca
Ganesha Park
Borromaeus Hospital
Jl. Hasannudin
Jl. Taman Sari
Jl. Juanda (Jl. Dago)
Jl. Prof. Eickman
Jl. Rumahsakit
Jl. Sukajadi
Cikapundung
Jl. Dipati Ukur
BCA
Jl Surapati (Jl. Suci)
Jl. Pasteur
Hassan Sadikin Hospital
Jl. Cihampelas (Jeans St.)
Jl. Sulanjan
Jl. Jipang
Jl. Diponegoro
Jl. Otten
Jl. R. Gading
Jl. Trunojoko
Jl. Cilamaya
Jl. Citarum
Jl. Pasir Kaliki
Jl. Cipto
Jl. Pajajaran
TO (5km)
Jl. Maratadinata
Jl. Martadinata (Jl. Riau)
Bank Bali
Jl. Ambon
Jl. Banda
Jl. Aceh
Jl. Cicendo
Jl. Wastu Kencana
Jl. Sumatra
Jl. Kalimantan
Jl. Sumbawa
Jl. Lombok
Pakuan Building (Governor's Residence)
Merdeka Park
Jl. Merdeka
Jl. Belitung
Jl. Patra Komala
Jl. Kebon Kawung
Hospital RS Kebonjati
Jl. Pasirkaliki
Jl. Jawa
Jl. Suniaraja
Jl. Tera
Jl. Kebonjati
Jl. Gudang Selatan
Jl. Belakang Pasar
Jl. Banceuy
Jl. Lembong
Jl. Braga
Jl. Veteran
Jl. Gardu Jati
Jl. ABC
Jl. Naripan
TO CICAHEUM BUS STATION (1km)
Jl. Jend. Sudirman
Jl. Asia-Afrika
Jl. Cibadak
Alun-alun
TO 22 (300m)
Jl. Dalem Kaum
Jl. Tamblong
Jl. Lengkong Kecil
Jl. Karang Anyar
Jl. Pagarsih
Jl. Kalipahapo
Jl. Pangarang
Jl. Pacedang
Jl. Astan Anyar
Jl. Dewi Sartika
Jl. Lengkong Besar
Jl. Pasir Koja
Jl. Pungkur
Kebon Kelapa Bus Terminal
Jl. Kopo
Jl. Otto Iskandardinata
Jl. Ciateul
Jl. Mohamad Toha
Jl. Mohamad Ramadan
TO LEUWI PANJANG BUS STATION (500m)
Taman Ria Tegellega Sport Center

INDONESIA

Asia-Afrika Conference Hotel, Jl. Asia-Afrika 112 (☎423 22 44). A standard upscale Western hotel. Check out the historical information and see which dignitary stayed in your room. Rooms have TV, A/C, bathtub, shower, and an unimpressive view of the busiest street in Bandung. Singles Rp422,000; doubles Rp452,000, plus 21% tax. ❺

FOOD

Warung set up nightly on **Jl. Gardu Jati** and around the train station. It's worth the trip to the suburbs of Dago to visit Kampung Daun and Dago Tea House for the fabulous views.

Kampung Daun (☎278 7915), in the Trinity Villas Complex on Jl. Cihideung. Take an *angkot* up Jl. Setia Budi toward Lembang (15min). Transit in Parongpong onto Jl. Cihideung on the left (10min). Taxi Rp25,000-30,000. A hideaway in the beautiful hills of Dago, Bandung's suburb. Fine Sudanese and Mediterranean cuisine. *Jaipong* upon request. Reserve ahead. Entrees Rp9000-35,000. Open Tu-F 11am-midnight. ❹

Dago Tea House, Jl. Bukit Dago Utara. Take an *angkot* toward Dago and ask to be let out at the Dago Tea House, then ask the locals for directions. The exquisite food, thatched huts, and spectacular view make it worth the hike. Entrees Rp7000-18,000. ❸

Sindang Reret, Jl. Surapati 53 (☎250 1474), past the running track. Performance hall restaurant provides both a great Sudanese feast (fish dishes Rp9000-18,000; rice entrees Rp3000-8000) and the only *wayang golek* show in town (Sa 7:30-10pm). Delicious *sarikaya* pudding Rp1750. Open daily 10am-11pm. ❷

SIGHTS

Though Bandung has a handful of interesting cultural sights, its main attractions, volcanoes and hot springs, lie outside of the city (see **Daytrips from Bandung,** p. 149). An Art Deco movement swept through this area in the 1930s (courtesy of architects Wolf Shoemacher, A.F. Aalbers, and F.W. Brinkman), leaving interesting architectural sights in its wake. Curious visitors can take free one-hour tours through the **Bandung Society for Heritage Conservation** in the Hotel Panghegar, on the fifth floor of Jl. Merdeka 2. (☎423 2286, ext. 8554. Open M-F 10am-4pm.) Two blocks southwest is the **Gedung Merdeka,** marked by its several dozen flagpoles without flags, which houses the **Museum Asia-Afrika** at Jl. Asia-Afrika 65. The museum displays memorabilia from the 1955 Non-Aligned Movement Conference in Bandung, at which 29 African and Asian nations collectively agreed to pursue non-alignment policies during the Cold War between the US and USSR. (Open M-F 8am-noon and 1-3pm. Free.) For those desperately needing to touch a tank, visit the **Army Museum,** Jl. Lembong 38. Otherwise, the collection is small and unimpressive (☎420 3393. Open M-Sa 8am-1pm. Donation requested.)

A. Ruchiyat's **wayang golek factory,** in a twisting alley two blocks south of the Savoy Homan Hotel off Jl. Pangarang, produces and sells *wayang golek* puppets (miniature marionette Rp6000). The care and precision that go into carving the special albasia wood will leave you dazed. The smaller, cheaper puppets are ideal for those traveling with stuffed backpacks and empty wallets. Enter beyond Hotel Mawar; ask around for directions. (☎420 1335. Open M-Sa 8am-9pm.)

If you're searching for some modern European architecture, check out the **Bandung Institute of Technology (ITB),** an impressive Art Deco building north of the city. Take an *angkot* toward Dago and get off at ITB. Also in the north suburbs is the stately **Gedung Sate,** a colonial-era building that serves as the regional capital. It's nice to look at for a minute, but nothing to go out of your way for. It faces the **Geol-**

ogy Museum, Jl. Diponegoro 57 (☎720 3205), which is worth a visit if you're into rocks. The most impressive fossils include those of an enormous elephant, a Tyrannosaurus Rex, and a prehistoric **Java Man's skull.**

ENTERTAINMENT AND NIGHTLIFE

Wayang golek puppet performances are free with dinner at **Sindang Reret** on Jl. Surapati (Sa 7:30-10pm), while Jl. Tegalega offers traditional *jaipong* dance. Bandung's clubs all have cover bands and so much cigarette smoke that you will not make it through the night without eye drops. The centers of Bandung's nightlife are **Jl. Dago** and **Jl. Cihampelas (Jeans Street).** On Saturday nights, hordes of suburban youth congregate on Jl. Dago, where dance competitions have been known to break out. Live cover bands play *dangdut* music at most clubs on weekends. Saturday is the best night to go clubbing. Drinks, alcoholic and otherwise, are expensive.

Fame Station, on the 11th fl. of the Wisma Lippo tower on Jl. Asia-Afrika. Suburban youth and the occasional foreigner just having a good time. Don't come if you're not going to dance. Pool hall in back. Cover Rp40,000, includes one non-alcoholic drink. Try Tyson, a compound of 18 liquors, Rp165,000. Open M-Sa 9pm-2am.

Sapulidi, Jl. Cihampelas 107. Self-proclaimed "fancy bar" packed with local hipsters and serious cover bands. A favorite with the local college crowd and older men trying to hit on the college crowd. Cover Rp30,000 includes one drink. Open M-Sa 11pm-2am.

North Sea, Jl. Braga 82. Nautically-themed bar with international crowd. Drown your sorrows and have a maritime. Bir Bintang Rp12,000. Live music F-Sa. Free pool table, though it's usually occupied. Open M-F 5pm-1am, Sa-Su noon-3am.

DAYTRIPS FROM BANDUNG

Bandung hides a wealth of sights in its mountain ridges, best seen through guided tours (about Rp75,000 per daytrip) or by renting a car (Rp200,000-300,000 per day). You can brave the *angkot*/minibus system for a cheaper viewing; take *angkot* from the train station toward Lembang and get out before Subang. Travelers can trek to **Tangkuban Prahu,** the "capsized boat" crater, from the town of **Lembang,** a 90min. *angkot* ride from the railway station. Those with time should get off at Jl. Jayagiri after one hour and hike the remaining 10km up through pine and tropical forests. The forest trail emerges at the lower parking lot and gate. (Open daily 6am-5pm.) The big gray **Ratu** (1830m) spits sulfur and steam. A path leads to the smaller **Domas Caldera** from the lower lot; get a guide for this route (available at the tourist office, Rp20,000-30,000). Those who have had their fill of vistas can take an *angkot* toward Subang. Get off at the top of the road at the "Air Panas Crater," the **hot springs** at **Sari Ater Resort,** Jl. Taman Sari 72. To see some stars, it's best to settle in the therapeutic hot baths among natural waterfalls around 9pm. (☎250 31 88. Open 24hr.) Full-day car rentals available at the hot springs (Rp250,000) or five hour rentals at the tourist information center (Rp175,000).

Check out a **silk factory** in Garut at the **Candi Cangkuang Temple,** the oldest Hindu temple on West Java, dating from the 8th century. Take an *angkot* from Terminal Cicaheum, in the direction of Garut, and after one hour get out in Kadungora. It's a 4km walk or *delman* ride from there. Continue on to Garut, switch *angkots* and head to Cisurupan, a 9km hike from the crystal studded **Papandayan Volcano.** After the hike, take a soak in the **Tarogong Hot Springs** to help you relax (take *angkot* from Garut directly to Tarogong). The volcano and hot springs are worth splurging for a guided drive and hike. Tours are offered at most hostels (Rp110,000 per person from By "Moritz").

PANGANDARAN ☎0265

Though Pangandaran is known for its beach, the real attraction of this small coastal town is Green Canyon, a magnificent jade-colored river flowing between cliffs and over waterfalls. Travelers looking for black sands might be disappointed—the beach is a bit dirty and dangerous currents make it unsafe for swimming. However, nearby villages with welcoming locals and bustling industries, coupled with lush forest and a quiet unimaginable in other parts of Java, make Pangandaran ideal for a short visit.

TRANSPORTATION

Buses: The **terminal,** 50m from main gateshas buses to: **Bandung** (6hr.; every hr. 4-9am and noon, 3, 6, 9pm; Rp22,000. A/C chartered minibus Rp45,000); **Banjar** (1½hr.; every 10min. 4am-4pm; Rp10,000); **Bogor** (8hr.; 7am, 7pm; Rp23,000); **Jakarta** (9hr.; 5, 7, 9am and every hr. 5-9pm; Rp35,000); **Yogyakarta** (9hr.; Rp70,000); **Wonosobo** (Rp60,000). Charter minibuses available at Lotus Tours (see **Tours,** below).

Local Transportation: *Becak,* motorcycles, and bicycles rule the roads.

Rentals: Rent bicycles (Rp 20,000 per day) and mopeds (Rp 35,000 per day) from the *ojek* stand opposite the market, or from most hotels.

ORIENTATION AND PRACTICAL INFORMATION

From the bus terminal, turn left and enter the first red gates. Sign the guest book and pay a one-time cover charge of Rp3000 to enter the city. Inside the gates, a well-lit boulevard leads directly to the waves of the **west beach.** Perpendicular at the boulevard's end, **Jl. Pamugaran/Pantai Barat** stretches north-south along the shore. One kilometer south, busy **Jl. Bulak Laut** connects Jl. Pantai Barat with the town's former main road **Jl. Kidang Pananjung,** the town's former main road lined with cheap *losmen* and restaurants extending all the way back to the bus station.

Tours: Countless tourist information services, hotels, and restaurants sell similar package tours. One of the more popular is **Lotus Tours,** Jl. Bulak Laut 7 (☎639 635). Open daily 6am-10pm. Buses head to: **Bandung** (Rp35,000, with A/C Rp45,000); **Jakarta** (Rp35,000); **Wonosobo** (Rp50,000). A wonderful **river boat/bus trip** offers a stress-free ride to **Yogyakarta** (10hr.; Rp70,000 through an agent). Alternatively, take an early Banjar-bound bus to **Calipucang** (Rp3000), a *becak* to the harbor (Rp5000), a boat to **Cilacap** (4hr.; 6am, though known to launch late; Rp5000), a *becak* to the bus station (Rp4000), and a bus to **Yogyakarta** (6hr.; Rp25,000).

Currency Exchange: The town's greatest tourist attraction is its only 24hr. **ATM,** behind the market by **Bank Negara Indonesia,** Jl. Merdeka 312 (☎639 700). Often empty, the machine also frequently rejects cards at random—bring enough money to get to the next city. **Bank Rakyat Indonesia,** Jl. Kidang Pananjung 212 (☎639 288), by the intersection with Jl. E. Jaga Lautan. **Branch** on Jl. Merdeka behind the market. Cashes traveler's checks at reasonable rates. All banks open M-F 8am-2pm.

Markets: A narrow **main market** lies outside the entrance gates by the bus terminal. Supplier of all goods known to man. (Open daily 6am-4pm; crowded on M and Th.) The sadly deserted **fish market** and a mass of tourist shops are in the south, by the east beach and west beach respectively. Open daily 5am-4pm.

Emergency: Police: ☎110.

Police: Jl. Merdeka 177 (☎639 110), behind the main market and 400m to the left. Open M-Sa 7am-2pm. Police officers stationed at main gate 24hr.

Pharmacy: Apotik Pangandaran Farma (☎639 524), in back of the main market. A 2nd pharmacy resides on Jl. Kidang Pananjung (☎639 983), 100m west of the hospital.

Medical Services: Hospital, Jl. Parapat 1 (☎639 118). Small hospital with ambulance service. 24hr. **emergency** care.

Telephones: Telkom office, Jl. Kidang Pananjung 65 (☎639 333). **Open** 24hr. **HCD** and fax. **Adam's,** Jl. Pantai Barat 164, has **international phone** service 8am-10pm.

Post Office: Jl. Kidang Pananjung 129 (☎639 284). *Poste Restante.* Open M-Th 7:30am-3pm, F 7:30-11:30am, Sa 7:30am-1pm.

Postal Code: 49396.

ACCOMMODATIONS

The town has a surplus of exceptional budget lodgings. Sundry accommodations are cluttered on the west beach road. The farther inland you go, the cheaper they get. Most places have a two-night minimum and prices decrease with length of stay. Indonesia's tourism slump has hit Pangandaran particularly hard, as it is a vacation spot for Indonesians unable to afford Bali. Prices have been driven down and many establishments have been forced to close.

Laguna Beach Bungalows (☎639 761), off Jl. Pengadilan Kebon, 2km outside the city. Laguna offers pick-up service for a price (one-way Rp10,000; call reception or ☎081 223 68806). A raft-ride or 30min. walk from the city, the most popular stay in Pangandaran offers a lip-smacking welcome drink from the full-fledged restaurant. Rooms with porches, hammocks, and a beautiful view of coconut trees and the beach. Standard singles Rp35,000; doubles and triples Rp50,000-75,000. ❸

Bamboo House (☎639 419), on Jl. Baru. This popular stay offers quality bungalows far from traffic. Breakfast Rp5000. Private bath. Singles Rp20,000; doubles Rp30,000, with a lovely porch and jungle-themed *mandi* Rp40,000. ❷

Pondok Cocobana, Jl. Pamugaran 177, 200m north of the street to the west beach. 3-day minimum. Beautiful, spacious rooms with fan, shower, and porch. Free breakfast with stay. Singles Rp30,000; doubles Rp45,000; triples Rp60,000. ❷

FOOD

Pangandaran's food scene ranges from the usual *warung* to busy cafes and seafood spots. Eateries in the old center, the southern end of Jl. Kidang Pananjung, are cheap (Rp5000-10,000 per meal) and open daily 8am-11pm. Farther north on the east beach road, the **fish market** offers the freshest food in town at low prices.

Green Garden Cafe, Jl. Kidang Pananjung 116. Next to Pondok Ibu. Seafood with a Western twist and tasty Indonesian dinner served *al fresco* (Rp6000-10,000). Very relaxed atmosphere. Open daily 5-10pm. ❷

Bunga Laut Restaurant, Jl. Bulak Laut 8-11. Opposite Lotus Tours. Savory soups (Rp5000), delightful desserts (Rp2000-4000), and sizzling seafood entrees (Rp7000-15,000). The *pisang goreng* (fried banana) with chocolate is alone worth the trip. ❷

Bamboo Cafe, on Jl. Pantai Barat beside Adam's. A popular roadside joint with a fantastic view, known to grill a mean fish (around Rp25,000). Essential fried rice Rp5000. Chicken dishes around Rp10,000. ❸

SIGHTS

Pangandaran has two major sights, **Penanjung National Park** and **Green Canyon.** Travelers can enter Penanjung National Park (Rp2000; open daily 7am-4pm) and check out black-sand beaches that promise great snorkeling (Rp60,000) and hungry monkeys. Although much of the park is technically closed, hikers can see some areas on their own or hire a guide for eco-friendly tours (Rp30,000). Expect to see limestone caves, bats with 2m wingspans, lizards, monkeys, deer, porcupines, and enormous rafflesia flowers that bloom for only four days and reek from 30m away. The Green Canyon holds a jade-colored river of reputedly holy water, which winds past sharp cliffs and through waterfalls. Majestic rock formations surround clear pools separated from the main river. Bring a swimsuit, but ask hotels about safe bathing areas or book a tour for Rp40,000. Tours include stops at **Batu Keras Beach,** ideal for beginners looking to ride waves (plastic boards Rp10,000 per hour).

YOGYAKARTA ☎0274

There are at least three full days of quality things to see and do in Yogya (as it is often called)—a city full of commission-earning locals and *becak* drivers all clamoring to "help" you through it. The abundance of cheap and excellent food and accommodations is unfortunately balanced by steep US$ entry fees to many sights. If you are here for a short time, the overpriced tours may be necessary in order to see it all, but they can easily be avoided with the excellent public transportation system. However you do it, Yogya must be visited.

TRANSPORTATION

Flights: The **airport** (☎566 666) is on Jl. Adisucipto, 5km from the city center. Take a taxi–by public transportation, the trip is excessively complicated, requiring 2-3 bus transfers. **Garuda** (☎522 148), in Amparukmu Hotel on Jl. Laksda Adisucipto. (Open daily 5:30am-8pm.) Daily flights to **Denpasar, Jakarta,** and **Mataram. Merpati** (airport office ☎512 727) is open daily 8am-4:30pm. Flies daily to **Surabaya.** Flights to **Sulawesi** start at Rp793,600 plus tax. Purchase tickets through a travel agent. Rp9000 tax is added to the flight prices listed below.

DESTINATION	FREQUENCY	PRICE
Denpasar	3 per day	Rp426,000; 1st class Rp574,500
Jakarta	5 per day	Rp456,800; 1st class Rp616,300
Mataram	1 per day	Rp530,700; 1st class Rp714,400
Surabaya	2 per day	Rp241,200

Trains: Tugu Train Station, Jl. Mangkubumi 1 (☎589 685), on Jl. Pasar Kembang. Tourist staff at the station can help de-mystify the schedule. Arrive 30min. early to purchase tickets. **Lempuyangan Train Station** on Jl. Lempuyangan serves economy trains only.

DESTINATION	DURATION	FREQUENCY	PRICE
Bandung	7hr.	business 2 per day, executive 3 per day	business Rp60,000; executive Rp90,000-185,000
Jakarta	7-8hr.	business 5 per day, executive 8 per day	business Rp50,000-120,000; executive Rp150,000-235,000
Solo	1hr.	business 7 per day, executive 4 per day	business Rp5000-6000; executive Rp9000-23,500
Surabaya	5hr.	business 3 per day, executive 5 per day	business Rp35,000-60,000; executive Rp60,000-240,000

Buses: Umbulharjo Terminal, Jl. Veteran (☎376 013), southeast of the city. Take buses #4 and 2 from Malioboro and Prawirotaman areas, respectively. Buses (usually with evening departures) go all over Java, Sumatra, and Bali. Schedules, fares, express buses, and peace of mind available at ticket agencies on Jl. Mangkubumi, Sosrowijayan, and Prawirotaman. To: **Denpasar** (17hr.; 2:30pm; Rp125,000); **Jakarta** (9-14hr.; 4pm; Rp100,000).

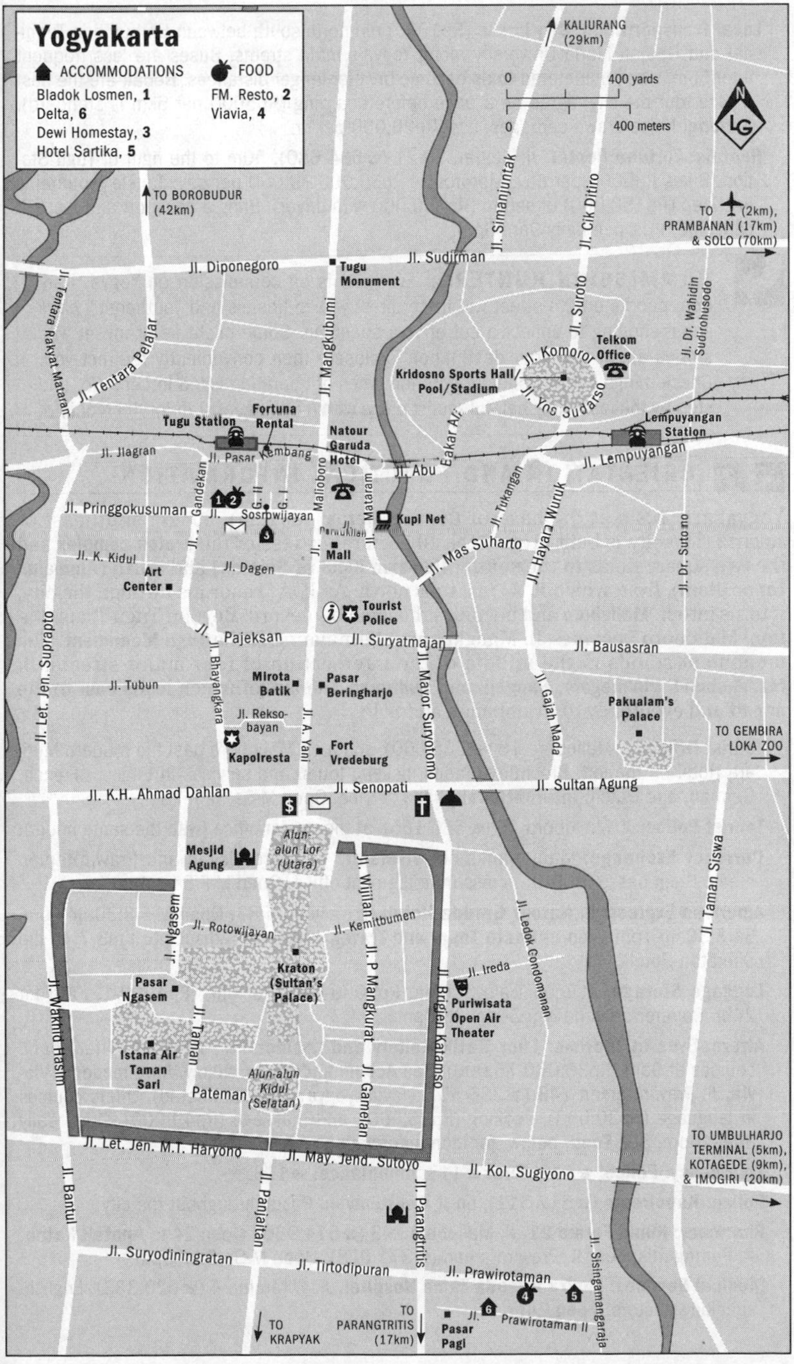
Yogyakarta
ACCOMMODATIONS
Bladok Losmen, 1
Delta, 6
Dewi Homestay, 3
Hotel Sartika, 5
FOOD
FM. Resto, 2
Viavia, 4
KALIURANG (29km)
0 400 yards
0 400 meters
TO BOROBUDUR (42km)
TO (2km), PRAMBANAN (17km) & SOLO (70km)
Jl. Diponegoro
Tugu Monument
Jl. Sudirman
Jl. Simanjuntak
Jl. Cik Ditiro
Jl. Suroto
Jl. Dr. Wahidin Sudirohusodo
Jl. Tentara Rakyat Mataram
Jl. Tentara Pelajar
Jl. Mangkubumi
Telkom Office
Jl. Komoro
Kridosno Sports Hall/ Pool/Stadium
Jl. Yos Sudarso
Tugu Station
Fortuna Rental
Natour Garuda Hotel
Lempuyangan Station
Jl. Jlagran
Jl. Pasar Kembang
Jl. Abu Bakar Ali
Jl. Lempuyangan
Jl. Gandekan
Jl. Pringgokusuman
Jl. Sosrowijayan
Jl. Malioboro
Jl. Mataram
Jl. Tukangan
Jl. Hayam Wuruk
Kupi Net
Jl. Perwakilan
Mall
Jl. Mas Suharto
Jl. Dr. Sutomo
Jl. K. Kidul
Art Center
Jl. Dagen
Tourist Police
Jl. Pajeksan
Jl. Suryatmajan
Jl. Bausasran
Jl. Let. Jen. Suprapto
Jl. Tubun
Jl. Bhayangkara
Mirota Batik
Pasar Beringharjo
Jl. Reksobayan
Jl. A. Yani
Jl. Mayor Suryotomo
Jl. Gajah Mada
Pakualam's Palace
TO GEMBIRA LOKA ZOO
Kapolresta
Fort Vredeburg
Jl. K.H. Ahmad Dahlan
Jl. Senopati
Jl. Sultan Agung
Mesjid Agung
Alun-alun Lor (Utara)
Jl. Wijilan
Jl. Taman Siswa
Jl. Ngasem
Jl. Rotowijayan
Jl. Kemitbumen
Jl. Ledok Condomanan
Kraton (Sultan's Palace)
Jl. P Mangkurat
Jl. Brigjen Katamso
Jl. Ireda
Jl. Wahid Hasim
Pasar Ngasem
Puriwisata Open Air Theater
Jl. Taman
Istana Air Taman Sari
Pateman
Alun-alun Kidul (Selatan)
Jl. Gamelan
Jl. Let. Jen. M.T. Haryono
Jl. May. Jend. Sutoyo
Jl. Kol. Sugiyono
TO UMBULHARJO TERMINAL (5km), KOTAGEDE (9km), & IMOGIRI (20km)
Jl. Bantul
Jl. Panjaitan
Jl. Parangtritis
Jl. Suryodiningratan
Jl. Tirtodipuran
Jl. Prawirotaman
Jl. Sisingamangaraja
Jl. Prawirotaman II
TO KRAPYAK
TO PARANGTRITIS (17km)
Pasar Pagi

INDONESIA

Local Transportation: City buses (Rp1000) run north-south between Umbulharjo Terminal and Gadjah Mada University along Yogya's main streets. Buses are less frequent after 5pm, when unmetered **taxis** become best for longer distances. **Becak** are the best way to tour the city; agree on a price before boarding (Rp5000 per 5km is standard). **Andong,** horse-drawn carriages, cost Rp20,000 per hr.

Rentals: Fortuna Rental, Jl. Jlagran 20-21 (☎564 680), 50m to the right of Tugu Station. Bikes Rp5000 per day. Motorbikes Rp50,000-75,000 per day. Tackle mountains in a jeep (Rp150,000) or sedan (Rp350,000 with driver). Bring a passport and a credit card (MC/V). Open daily 9am-6pm.

COMMISSION HUNTERS. Everyone is on commission on Yogya. Random people on the street will try to direct you to hostels and "authentic" *batik* shops—hoping to collect a cut of your spending. Some might lie or invent wild stories about why your destination is closed—then conveniently redirect you. Check things out for yourself, note the times of operation listed in *Let's Go,* and stop by the incredibly helpful tourist office with multilingual staff for the real info.

ORIENTATION AND PRACTICAL INFORMATION

Yogyakarta rests at the base of **Gunung Merapi** (2911m), 603km southeast of Jakarta. The city is built around the 10-hectare fortress of the **kraton complex** and the two square fields to the south (**Alun-alun Kidul** or **Selatan**) and north (**Alun-alun Lor** or **Utara**), from which **Jl. A. Yani** runs north. As Jl. A. Yani runs through the city, it turns into **Jl. Malioboro** and becomes the main boulevard. Beyond Tugu Train Station, Malioboro becomes Jl. Mangkubumi, terminating at the **Tugu Monument.** The monument stands in the middle of the intersection of four major streets: **Jl. Mangkubumi, Diponegoro, Sangaji,** and **Sudirman,** the last of which leads east to the **airport** and eventually to Prambanan and Solo.

Tourist Office: Jl. Malioboro 16 (☎566 000), south on Malioboro past the modern Mutiara Hotel on the left. Brochures, maps, tickets, tours, and services in English, French, German, and Dutch. **International phone** service. Open M-Sa 8am-7pm.

Tourist Police: Jl. Malioboro 16 (☎566 165), at the tourist office (with the same hours).

Currency Exchange: Many banks and **ATMs** are in Sosrowijayan and Prawirotaman areas. Bring passport. **BNI,** across from the post office. Open M-F 8am-4pm.

American Express: In **Natour Garuda Hotel,** Jl. Malioboro 89. Open M-F 8:30am-4pm, Sa 8:30am-1pm. Also at **Pacto Tours and Travel,** Jl. Laksda Adisucipto Km8.7, in the Sheraton Hotel.

Luggage Storage: At Tugu Train Station. Rp2000-6000 for 6hr.; Rp4000-12,000 for 24hr. Counter open daily 5:30am-9:30pm.

Alternatives to Tourism: Lucy Batik Gallery and Losmen (☎513 429). Offers *batik* courses at 9am (Rp30,000-75,000). See **Accommodations,** below, for directions. **Via-via,** Jl. Prawirotaman 24B (☎386 557; viavia@yogya.wasantara.net.id). Offers courses in language (Rp30,000), cooking (Rp35,000), and massage (Rp40,000). Open daily 8am-10pm. See **Food,** below, for more information.

Emergency: Police: ☎110. **Fire:** ☎113. **Ambulance:** ☎118.

Police: Kapolresta (☎512 511), on Jl. Reksobayan. Posts throughout the city.

Pharmacy: Kimia Farma 21, Jl. Malioboro 123 (☎514 980). Open 24hr. **Apotek Ratna,** Jl. Parangtritis, near Jl. Prawirotaman (☎371 028). Open M-Sa 8am-9pm.

Medical Services: Ludira Husada Tama Hospital, Jl. Wiratama 4 (☎620 333). English-speaking doctors. **Open** 24hr.

Telephones: Wartel all over town including the tourist office place **international** calls (no credit cards). **Telkom office,** next to Komodor Yos Sudarso Rotary, and at the **Natour Garuda Hotel,** Jl. Malioboro 89. Both are overpriced, as are the *wartel* on Jl. Sosrowijayan, and neither accepts phone cards.

Internet Access: Küpi Net, on Jl. Mataram, is cheap and fast, like many other 24hr. cybercafes along Prawirotaman and Jl. Jend. Sudirman. Rp3500 per hr. Cybercafes in the backpacker community are slower and overpriced.

Post Office: Express Mail: DHL, Jl. Dr. Wahidin 58 (☎511 950). **GPO,** Jl. Senopati 2 (☎384 237), on the corner with Jl. A. Yani. *Poste Restante.* Open M-Sa 8am-8:30pm. Get stamps at Jl. Sosrowijayan 53. Open M-Th and Sa 8am-2pm, F 8am-noon.

Postal Code: 55000.

ACCOMMODATIONS

Budget accommodations cluster in two main areas. In the *gangs* (alleys) that connect **Jl. Pasar Kembang** to **Jl. Sosrowijayan (Sosro),** accommodations and restaurants are plentiful and span a large cost range. This trendy, popular area is close to **Jl. Malioboro.** A 25min. walk south, **Jl. Prawirotaman** is farther from the action. Though still a tourist neighborhood, this area is nice if you're looking for more seclusion. Accommodations at the two areas are similar. Near both, commission-earning "friends" claim to know the best places; close your ears to them.

JL. SOSROWIJAYAN

Dewi Homestay, Jl. Sosrowijayan Wetan GT 1/115 (☎516 014; dewihomestay@hotmail.com). One of the best deals in Yogya. Authentically artistic and fantastically clean. Huge rooms with private *mandi.* Singles Rp25,000; doubles Rp40,000. ❷

Bladok Losmen, Jl. Sosrowijayan 76 (☎/fax 523 832). A hit with the families hopping over from Bali, this place comes with every Western amenity. Swimming pool and one of Sosro's most popular restaurants. Standard rooms with bath Rp50,000; with private balcony Rp75,000; executive rooms with hot water and refrigerator Rp95,000; with A/C and TV Rp145,000. ❹

JL. PRAWIROTAMAN

Delta, Jl. Prawirotaman II MG 111 597A (☎082 274 3177). Relaxed, with a nice courtyard and pool. Free safebox. Breakfast included. Singles Rp25,000, with *mandi* Rp45,000-70,000; doubles Rp32,500/Rp50,000-75,000. ❷

Hotel Sartika, Jl. Prawirotaman 44A (☎372 669). Need a bath? This quiet refuge has spacious rooms with fans and bathtubs! Free breakfast. Singles and doubles from Rp35,000, rooms with tubs Rp40,000 and up. ❸

INDONESIA

FOOD

On Sosrowijayan, pricey restaurants serve Western, Chinese, and—if you're lucky—even Indonesian food. For more authentic and cheaper eats, join the locals at the *warung* on the upper levels of **Pasar Beringharjo** (see **Markets,** p. 156) during the day, or on the sidewalks of **Jl. Malioboro** sitting on woven mats, playing cards, and eating *lesehan*-style at night.

FM. Resto, Jl. Sosrowijayan 54. You have a better chance of finding your long-lost Australian cousin here than anywhere else. Reason: good food, good music, incredibly friendly staff, and relaxed atmosphere. Come late to hang out with the locals. Lemon-honey juice Rp5000. Open daily 8am-3am. ❷

YOGYA YUMMIES. As a separate sultanate within Java, Yogya has developed some truly local specialties not available anywhere else. Indonesia isn't known for its desserts, but Jl. Mataram is lined with sweet shops. Try **Tape Mataram Baru,** Jl. Mataram 191. Don't miss these Yogyan eats and treats:
Gudeg (Nasi Gudeg): Rice served in a sweet sauce of coconut, spices, and jackfruit. Often comes with egg, *tempe,* or *kercek* (cow hide).
Geplak: These colored coconut-and-sugar bombs sit in sweet shop windows.
Wajik: Sticky-rice soaked in palm sugar and coconut milk.
Yangko: Chewy, rice flour candies in mango, chocolate, and durian flavors.
Bakpia: Gelatinous squares made of sweet red and green bean paste. The least sweet is the lightest of the bunch.

Viavia, Jl. Prawirotaman 24B (☎386 557; viavia@yogya.wasantara.net.id). Hippie hangout with good food and courses in language (Rp30,000), cooking (Rp35,000), and massage (Rp40,000). Walking tours from Rp275,000 for 2 people to Rp355,000 for 6 people. Entrees Rp9000-28,000. Open daily 8am-10pm. ❸

SIGHTS

Many of Yogya's historical and cultural sights are within the *kraton* walls. The **Sultan's Palace** and its pavilions sit at the center of the enclosure. The buildings, built at various times throughout the city's history, display the development of Javanese architecture since 1755. Multilingual guides lead visitors through the home of Yogya's past 10 sultans. Hamengku Buwono X, the beloved current Sultan, resides in the *kraton* with his family. (Open M-Th 8:30am-2pm, F 8:30am-1pm; avoid noon prayer. Rp7500. Camera Rp500 extra, video Rp1000. Respectful dress required—tank tops and short-shorts are not acceptable.)

The ruins of **Istana Air Taman Sari** (water castle and fragrant garden) can be seen a few blocks west behind **Pasar Ngasem** (a bird market). Animal lovers should avoid the market and head straight to the beautiful, wildly exotic ruins of the water castle. A mixture of Javanese and Portuguese architecture built shortly after the *kraton*, Taman Sari (meaning beautiful park) was used briefly as the royal family's pleasure garden. (Rp2000 at the pool complex.) Past the initially unimpressive view lie a network of tunnels, a deteriorated underground mosque, and ruins (best climbed early in the morning, when Gunung Merapi is visible). According to legend, the tunnels extend for 27km to Parangtritis (see p. 159). Parts of Taman Sari have been restored, including the now goopy green bathing pools of the 20 royal wives, where boys sit on the stone lily pads and fish the day away.

Mesjid Agung, the grand mosque of the *kraton*, stands at the southwest corner of Alun-alun Utara. For over two centuries, the yearly **Sekaten** festival has honored the Prophet Muhammad's birth. *Sekaten* is celebrated annually from June 7 to July 7, during which time the *alun-alun* is filled with amusement-park games.

INDONESIA

MARKETS

Ironically, the cheapest way to spend an afternoon in Yogya is to go shopping. Just a walk through the narrow passageways of **Pasar Beringharjo** can be very enriching. Head upstairs for more organized shops and cheap *warung* food. The early bird catches the discount (open until 4pm). For the barter-worn, **Mirota Batik,** opposite Pasar Beringharjo, sells quality *batik* clothes and other crafts at fixed prices. *Penjahit* (tailors) will convert *batik* cloth into an outfit of your liking. **Pasar Ngasem** is reliable but a bit more pricey. For a good deal, try the turquoise **Art Center,** 20m down an alley off Jl. Pajeksan. *Batiks* are labeled with a letter that corresponds to a price; sellers give you a price guide and leave you to browse without pressure. An informal bazaar on the west side of **Jl. Malioboro** sells Yogya's signature handcrafts. **Kotagede market,** to the southeast of Yogya, is renowned for its silver. Take bus #8 south to Basen. Jl. Kemasan is lined with shops that take orders for brass, copper, and silver pieces. Most tour packages include a stop at **Borobudur Silver** (just in case you're dying for a set of sterling silver toothpicks).

ENTERTAINMENT AND NIGHTLIFE

It would be criminal to come to Yogya and not see the *Ramayana* **ballet** at the Prambanan Temples (see below). The story of Prince Rama is played out with the view of the illuminated temples behind, bats flying overhead, and if you come at the right time, the full moon rising next to the temples. (Alternating days, 7:30-9:30pm. Rp25,000-100,000.) If you cannot get to Prambanan, the condensed version is danced indoors at **Trimurti Theater.** (Tu, Th 7:30-9:30pm.) **Purawisata Open Air Theater** on Jl. Brigjen Katamso has nightly performances as well. (8-9:30pm. Rp90,000 for the ballet, dinner combos available.) Once a religious ceremony, **wayang kulit** is now a Javanese art form. This unique theater form, in which leather shadow puppets depict the heroism of mythological ancestors, is performed at the **Sonobudoyo Archaeological Museum** on Jl. Trikora (daily 7:30-9:30pm) and in Alun-alun Selatan (every 2nd Sa of the month 9pm-5:30am). Free performances, such as classical Yogyan dance (at the Sultan's Palace, Jl. KHA Dahlan 71; Su 10:30am-noon) and *wayang golek* puppet shows with traditional *gamelan* music (M-Sa 11am-1pm). At night, **fire-eaters** perform at the south end of Jl. Malioboro/Jl. A. Yani. Participate in a **blindfold walk** between the banyan trees at **Alun-alun Kidul,** south of the *kraton.* If you like dancing alone, head over to **Papillon,** Jl. Mayor Suryotomo 26, which was once Yogya's hottest nightclub. (☎564 343. Cover Rp15,000. Ladies' night Su-Tu, Th; gay night F. Open Su-Tu, Th 10pm-2am; W, F-Sa 10pm-3am.) A little more popular but still not exactly hopping is **Yogya-Yogya Music House** in Borobudur Plaza on Jl. Magelang. (Open daily 9pm-2am.)

DAYTRIPS FROM YOGYAKARTA

BOROBUDUR. Few sights on the planet can compare to the misty sunrise over Borobudur, the world's largest Buddhist temple. Built between AD 750 and 850 during the Sailendra dynasty, Borobudur is one of the three wonders of classical Southeast Asia (along with Myanmar's Bagan and Cambodia's Angkor Wat). The temple, topped by a 40m *stupa*, consists of ten levels, symbolic of the ten stages of the Buddhist cosmic system. Along the walls, carvings depict scenes from the life of Buddha, the thousands of reincarnations and manifestations, and the final quest for truth. The three highest levels of Arupadhatu stand for the freedom from earthly bonds and represent "Karma," the highest stage of Buddhahood. Here, an exposed stone Buddha figure meditates among encapsulated neighbors. His expression of suffering communicates that life is pain because of desire, which can only be controlled by meditation. (Open daily 6am-5:15pm.)

Before facing the breathtaking climb and view, visitors often go to the **Audio Visual Center** to watch an enlightening 35min. video. (First showing 8am. Rp4000.) Many visitors try to improve their luck by reaching into any of the 432 stupas to touch the stone Buddhas' hands and navels. Use your right hand, as the left hand is considered unclean. If you're visiting in the summer, every schoolchild in Indonesia will be visiting as well, so for pictures of the temple free of the crowds, go early (6am). For an awesome view, climb the hills behind the monument. **Mendut** and

Pawon, two nearby historic temples, are sites of the actual religious ceremonies (included in tours). Devotees from as far away as China have walked across Java to attain enlightenment from Borobudur via Mendut and Pawon. *(42km northwest of Yogya, Borobudur can be reached by local buses from* ***Umbulharjo*** *(Jl. Veteran), which run to Borobudur (6am-6pm, Rp2000-6000) or Muntilan, a transfer point. Tourist offices along Jl. Sosrowijayan and Jl. Prawirotaman offer package tours. US$7/Rp63,000, students with valid ID US$4 or Rp34,000. Guide Rp30,000.)*

PRAMBANAN TEMPLES. Built in the 9th century during the Hindu Sanjaya dynasty, the complex consists of temples dedicated to the Hindu Trinity: Shiva the destroyer, Vishnu the protector, and Brahma the creator. The rubble littering the area is what remains of the temples destroyed by Gunung Merapi's eruption in 1006. Within the park, smaller temples, including **Candi Lumbung, Bubrah, Sewu,** and **Sojiwan,** are worth a look. Monuments to the north (**Candi Plaosan, Banyunibo, Sari, Kalasan,** and **Sambisari**) are best seen by bike or becak, but beware the gods of inflation. **Kraton Ratu Boko,** 2km south of Prambanam, offers a splendid view. Bike south along the road on the west side of the market and follow signs to the palace gate (Rp750). The Prambanan park holds Ramayana ballets in an outdoor theater during the summer; it's indoors the rest of the year (see **Entertainment,** above). (Camera pass Rp2000, video pass Rp15,000.) **Ny Muharti Guest House ❷** (☎496 103), Jl. Tampumas Ngankruk 2-3, opposite Prambanan's entrance, is an option for early-rising temple-goers. (Singles Rp25,000; doubles Rp35,000.) *(The Prambanan temples are 17km northeast of Yogya toward Solo. A direct bus runs from Umbulharjo Terminal (45min., Rp3500). On arrival, the peaks of Gunung Merapi and the main Prambanan temple should be visible. Maps are complimentary at the tourist office inside the entrance gate. Entry US$7 or Rp63,000, students US$4/Rp34,000. To avoid the tourist scene and see more than the main temple, rent a bike (Rp5000 per day).*

> **WARNING.** Gunung Merapi killed dozens when it erupted in November 1994. In July 1998, Merapi erupted for days in a row, spewing ash over the countryside. Hiking up to see live lava can be exciting, but it is extremely risky. *Let's Go* does not recommend falling into live lava.

INDONESIA

GUNUNG MERAPI AND KALIURANG. Gunung Merapi, 30km north of Yogya, rises high above sea level and can be seen from all surrounding areas. **Vogel's,** Jl. Astamulya 76, offers recommended and reasonably priced tours. Wear layers, as temperatures increase dramatically with daybreak. Spend the night at the **hostel ❷** to avoid risky night buses. (☎895 208. Rp25,000-30,000.) For a tamer adventure, stick around **Kaliurang,** 28km north of Yogya on the slopes of Merapi. From Yogya, take a 1hr. bus ride from Umbulharjo or an *angkot* from the Terban Terminal on Jl. Simanjuntak (both Rp2000). Kaliurang offers several cheap hotels, a campground, and a youth hostel, **Vogel's ❶.** (Dorms Rp6000, 10% discount for HI members; singles Rp12,500; doubles Rp17,500-25,000.) While in the **market,** look out for Kaliurang's specialties: sweet, brown-red *tempe* or *tahu bacem* and the mild *jadah,* made from glutinous rice. To explore the town's hiking trails and nature park, head to **Hutan Wisata Kaliurang,** 1km from the youth hostel. Cool off by clambering up the observatory for a stunning view of the valley and Mt. Merapi. *(From the Umbulharjo Terminal, take a bus to Kartosuro, then to Boyolali, then to Selo. Start at 1am to reach the summit in time for sunrise, as the hike will take around 4hr.)*

IMOGIRI ROYAL CEMETERY. Imogiri Royal Cemetery, 12km south of Yogya, is the resting place for the deceased members of the Royal Houses of Yogyakarta and Surakarta, including Yogya's first sultan, Hamengku Buwono I. Built in 1645 by Sultan Agung, three distinct courtyards constitute the cemetery. To the left rests the royalty of Solo, to the right, the sultans of Yogya, and at the center, the ancient Mataram kings. All visitors are expected to wear formal Javanese clothing in the tombs; after climbing the 345 steps, discard your sweaty garments and rent appropriate attire (Rp1500). Men should wear a sarong, a long-sleeved shirt, and a hat. Women can put on a sarong and *batik* halter top. The tombs are best visited with a guide, but maps are available at the dressing station. In each room, enter quietly, make a donation (Rp100 will do), and kneel by the cool marble. After paying your respects, visit the sacred burial chambers of Sultan Agung and Hamengku Buwono I. *(Buses to Imogiri leave from Umbulharjo Terminal (45min., Rp2000). Open M 10am-noon, F 1-4pm. Rp1500 for outfit.)*

PARANGTRITIS. While the harsh cliffs and clear water are inarguably beautiful, there is something a little unsatisfying about a "look, but don't touch" beach—there is no swimming or surfing allowed. However, the **meditation caves** are very well reputed. Try doing a Yogya-Imogiri-Siluk-Parangtritis route. The 35km connect Imogiri Cemetery, Kotagede silver market, and some beautiful scenery. *(27km south of Yogya. Take a public bus (Rp4500) from Umbulharjo Terminal, or a minibus from Jl. Parangtritis (Rp3000) at the southeast corner of the* kraton. *The last bus back leaves Parangtritis at 5pm. For those left stranded, dozens of guesthouses (Rp20,000-50,000 per night) line the beachfront.)*

SURAKARTA (SOLO) ☎0271

Few tourists stop in Solo, but that only adds to the charm of this old-world city. Solo is about food and *batik*. The local specialty, *nasi liwet* (rice served in a mildly spicy coconut milk curry) is consistently good, and the *batik* is exported all over the world (but cheapest here). The *kratons* (palaces) are not spectacular, and there is no nightlife to speak of, but Solo is truly lovely if you want to stop in an inexpensive place where you're not constantly on a mission to see and do all.

TRANSPORTATION

Flights: Adi Sumarmo Airport (☎780 400), 10km northwest of Solo. To get to town, take a blue minibus to Kartosuro Terminal (Rp700-1000) and a bus or a taxi (Rp20,000) to Jl. Slamet Riyadi. **Garuda,** Jl. Slamet Riyadi 201 (☎630 082), in Hotel Cakra. Open M-F 7:30am-5pm, Sa-Su 9am-noon. To **Jakarta** (2 per day; 9:20am, 5:30pm; Rp460,300). **Silk Air,** Jl. Slamet Riyadi 272 (☎724 606), at Hotel Novotel, flies to **Singapore** (Tu 3:40pm, Th and Su 10:20am; US$210). Domestic airport tax Rp8000; international tax Rp30,000.

Trains: Balapan Railway Station (☎644 122), Jl. Monginsidi 112. Trains to: **Bandung** (7hr.; 8am, 9pm; Rp30,000-120,000); **Jakarta** (8-12hr.; 8pm; Rp35,000-185,000); **Yogyakarta** (1hr., 7 per day 6am-7pm, Rp4000); **Surabaya** (3hr.; 2:45, 4:30pm; Rp40,000-130,000). Bandung and Jakarta trains stop in Yogyakarta.

Buses: The main intercity **bus terminal** is **Tirtonadi,** Jl. Ahmad Yani 262 (☎717 297), on the north side of town. Buses to: **Bandung** (11hr.; 4pm; Rp30,000-75,000); **Jakarta** (12hr.; 5, 7pm; Rp35,000-100,000); **Yogyakarta** (1½hr., every 30min., Rp3000); **Surabaya** (6hr.; every hr.; Rp15,000-25,000). **Gilingan Minibus Terminal,** connected to Tirtonadi, serves all major destinations. Special overnight buses must be pre-booked. Contact **Raya,** Jl. Sultan Syahir 13 (☎635 838), for buses to **Bogor** (Rp100,000) and **Jakarta** (Rp120,000); **Bandung Cepat,** Jl. Kapten Mulyadi 27 (☎653 836), for buses to **Bandung** (Rp97,500); and **Cakrawala,** Jl. Setia Budi (☎711 710), for buses to **Denpasar** (Rp120,000).

Local Transportation: The plentiful **becak** are most convenient. Metered **taxis** congregate at all major hotels. **Double-decker** and **regular buses,** the cheapest option, travel along Jl. Slamet Riyadi and Jl. Veteran (every 10min. 5am-9pm, Rp1000). Orange **minibuses** (Rp1000) run along many other routes.

ORIENTATION AND PRACTICAL INFORMATION

The city's main boulevard and bus artery, **Jl. Slamet Riyadi,** runs east-west through town. The **tourist office** is on its west side, and many restaurants and foodstalls cluster on connecting streets. The **Puro Mangkunegaran Kraton** is at the northern edge. The **post** and **telephone offices** are off **Jl. Sudirman** on Jl. Slamet Riyadi's east side. Homestays are off Jl. Slamet Riyadi: to the north by **Jl. A. Dahlan,** and in the alleys between **Jl. Gatot Subroto** and **Jl. Yos Sudarso** to the south. The **Kraton Surakarta** and the bustling **batik market** are southeast, while **Tirtonadi/Gilingan Terminal** and **Balapan Train Station** are north of the city center.

Tourist Offices: Dinas Pariwisata, Jl. Slamet Riyadi 275 (☎711 435), beside the Museum Radya Pustaka on the far west end of Solo's main boulevard. Brochures, calendar of events, and a super-useful booklet. Free city maps. Open M-Sa noon-4pm.

Tours: High-priced tours at agencies along Jl. Slamet Riyadi and at many *losmen.* Try **Warung Baru Restaurant** on Jl. A. Dahlan.

Currency Exchange: BNI, Jl. Arifin 2 (☎645 909). Open M-F 7am-noon and 1-3pm. Numerous others are on Jl. Slamet Riyadi and the south end of Jl. Sudirman.

Markets: Pasar Klewer, near Kraton Surakarta, is an endless indoor maze of inexpensive but quality *batiks.* **Pasar Gede,** on Jl. Slamet Riyadi near the *Alun-alun,* sells fruits, vegetables, and spices. **Pasar Burung** is an outdoor aviary on the outskirts of town near Tirtonadi/Gilingan Terminal. All are open daily 8am-4pm.

Emergency: Police: ☎110. **Fire:** ☎113. **Ambulance:** ☎118.

Police: Adisucipto Manahan (☎712 600) and other stations all over town.

Pharmacy: Pasar Pon, Jl. Slamet Riyadi 124 (☎645 802), and **Rapi,** Jl. Ronggowarsito 161 (☎713 067), are convenient and well stocked. The *apotik* at **Rumah Sakit Kasih Ibu Hospital** is open 24hr.

Medical Services: Rumah Sakit PKU Muhammadiyah, Jl. Ronggowarsito 130 (☎719 743). Open 24hr. **Klinik Prodia Laboratorium,** Jl. Ronggowarsito 143 (☎463 78), is a modern diagnostic clinic. Open M-F 7am-8pm, Sa 7am-5pm. MC/V.

Telephones: Telkom Office, Jl. Mayor Kusmanto 1 (☎644 606), opposite the GPO. Open 24hr.

Internet Access: Aloha Internet Cafe, at the Hotel Sahid Kusuma. Delightfully speedy. Rp3600 per hr. Open daily 8am-10:30pm. **NETPluzz,** Jl. Yos Sudarso 174, 500m off Jl. Slamet Riyadi. Rp4000 per hr. Open 9am-11pm.

Post Office: GPO, Jl. Sudirman 8, off the east end of Jl. Slamet Riyadi. *Poste Restante.* Open M-Sa 7am-8pm.

Postal Code: 57111.

ACCOMMODATIONS

Quality *losmen* abound near **Jl. A. Dahlan** and **Kemlayan Kidul,** connecting Jl. Gatot Subroto and Jl. Yos Sudarso. Most are in nondescript alleys, but locals are more than willing to give directions.

INDONESIA

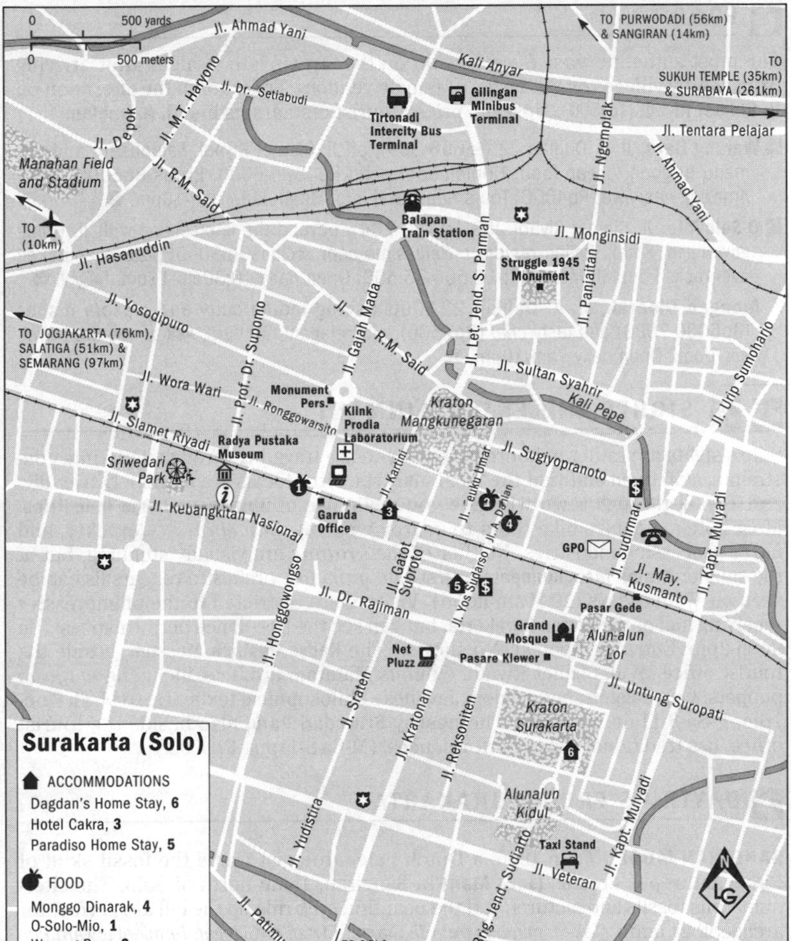

Dagdan's Home Stay, Baluwerti 02/7 42 (☎669 324), within the *kraton*, 400m past the museum entrance. Lush courtyard, meditation garden, and airy rooms. Special long-term rates. Singles Rp15,000; doubles Rp20,000. ❷

Paradiso Home Stay, Kemlayan Kidul 1/3 (☎652 960). Gorgeous Dutch building furnished with plants, pottery, and a cafe, though rooms are plain. Ring bell after 10pm. Singles Rp25,000, with *mandi* Rp30,000-50,000; doubles Rp35,000-50,000. ❷

Hotel Cakra, Jl. Slamet Riyadi 201 (☎458 47). Upscale hotel with a swimming pool, billiard room, and in-room satellite TV and sound system. All rooms have double beds. Standard Rp195,000; family cottage Rp712,500. AmEx/DC/MC/V. ❺

FOOD

The most authentic *nasi liwet* is sold on the streets late at night after arriving from nearby villages on the backs of female vendors. Try *srabi* in the afternoon on **Jl. Slamet Riyadi** (Rp500). Upscale, pricey tourist restaurants line **Jl. A. Dahlan.**

Warung Baru, Jl. A. Dahlan 23 (☎656 369), off Jl. Slamet Riyadi. Famous for a titanic menu of good, cheap food. Homemade bread Rp4500-6000. Pizzas Rp6000-7500. Amazing *nasi liwet* Rp4000. Tours and travel info. Open daily 7am-10pm. ❶

O-Solo-Mio, Jl. Slamet Riyadi 253 (☎727 264), beyond the intersection with Jl. Honggowongso. Small, Italian *restoran. Bellissimo* cappuccinos Rp8000; pizza oven-baked over rocks from Mt. Merapi Rp16,500-35,500. Open daily 10:30am-11pm. MC/V. ❹

Monggo Dinarak, Jl. A. Dahlan 22. Outstanding Indian curry and *masala* dishes (Rp6000-7000) and tasty *chai* (Rp2500), plus elegant furniture. Ask to see the travelers' book. Open daily 7am-10pm. ❶

SIGHTS AND ENTERTAINMENT

Solo's sights are rather unimpressive—if you are traveling through with time constraints, skip them and visit the local markets. Most locals are extremely friendly, and a walk through town will give you a glimpse of numerous **home industries.** Most hotels organize bike tours to nearby weaving, *gamelan*, rice cracker, and *batik* processing industries. Neither of the *kratons* are visually stunning, but at the smaller **Kraton Mangkunegaran,** first-rate *gamelan* orchestra rehearsals can be seen on Wednesdays (10:30am-noon). Visitors are restricted to the unimpressive receiving hall of the **Kraton Surakarta,** but can see the free dance performances. (Su noon-2pm. Entrance Rp5000. No shorts.) The **Radya Pustaka Museum,** beside the tourist office on Jl. Slamet Riyadi, exhibits Mataram artifacts, including *wayang* puppets, *kris* daggers, and ancient Javanese philosophical texts. (Open M-Th 8am-1pm, F-Sa 8-11am. Rp1000.) The nearby **Sriwedari Park,** also beside the tourist office, has traditional dance performances. (M-Sa 8-11pm. Rp3000.)

INDONESIA

DAYTRIPS FROM SURAKARTA

SANGIRAN MUSEUM. In 1936, a Dutch paleontologist found the fossil skull of Pithecanthropus erectus **(Java Man)** in Sangiran, 15km north of Solo. The site's numerous fossils and pictures and the beautiful *ojek* ride up the hill are perfect for archaeology buffs. *(Take a minibus from Jl. Slamet Riyadi or Gilingan Terminal toward Purwodadi or Kalijambe and ask to get off near Sangiran (1hr.), where* ojek *haul visitors up the hill to the museum. To return to Solo from the* ojek *stand, hop on a large bus with "Berseri" printed on the front. Open M-Sa 8am-5pm. Rp1500.)*

SUKUH TEMPLE. On the slopes of Gunung Lawu 34km northeast of Solo, the Sukuh Temple is difficult to reach, but its views make the journey worthwhile. Built in the 15th century, it was one of the last Hindu temples constructed before the rise of Islam. Due to some very suggestive and descriptive reliefs, many believe that a fertility cult built the temple as a "sex education" exhibit. Even more difficult to reach (*ojek* is the only reliable way), **Candi Cetho,** 8km away, offers more stunning views of the tobacco and tea plantations below in addition to a larger temple complex now used exclusively for meditation. *(Catch a double-decker bus from Jl. Slamet Riyadi to Palur and then a big bus to Karang Pandan (30min.). From here, take a minibus to Sukuh (20min.). Except on market days, the minibus will drop you off at the bottom of a hill. Take an* ojek *to the temple (Rp3500) or walk 45min. to the top.)*

DIENG PLATEAU

This quiet mountain village offers cool, clean air and a wealth of unspoiled natural and man-made sights. A 2-3hr. walk reveals the multicolored **Telaga Warna Lake** (fed from a sulfur hot spring), mushroom and potato terraces, smoldering craters, and ancient Hindu temples. The plateau of **Kawahsi Kidang** merits exploration.

The **tourist office** next to the bus terminal **stores luggage.** Minibuses go from the terminal into town. Travelers who wish to enjoy the mountain air for a little longer can stay at **Dieng Plateau ❶,** opposite the *ojek* stand. (☎92 823. Singles Rp15,000; doubles Rp20,000.) It serves food (Rp3000-7000), as do numerous *warung*. **Losmen Jawa Tengah ❷,** toward the department store on Jl. A. Yani, 150m north of the intersection with Jl. Pasman, has minimal but satisfactory rooms (Rp20,000).

With the freedom of a car, you'll have the chance to visit small hill villages. Alternatively, buses scurry from the town of **Wonosobo** to the highland (45min., 7am-3pm, Rp3000). Yogyakarta has direct buses to Wonosobo, but the trip from Surakarta requires transfer at Bawen Magelang. From the Wonosobo **bus terminal** (open daily 7am-3pm), connect to **Magelang** (1½hr.; every 15min., last bus 5pm; Rp3000). Head left from where the bus drops you off and walk 1km or ride an *ojek* to the gate, where maps are available (Rp2000).

SURABAYA ☎031

As the second-largest city in Indonesia, Surabaya has six-lane streets, a formidable skyline, and five indoor shopping complexes the size of small towns. Travelers seeking an "authentic Java" may be put off by the city's restless pace, but with connections to every island in the archipelago by ferry, plane, or bus, it's an important transit city with luxuries not found in other parts of east Java.

WARNING. Surabaya can be dangerous, especially for female and solo travelers. *Let's Go* includes this city because it is an important transportation hub, but recommends avoiding it when possible. If you must go, be on your guard.

TRANSPORTATION

Flights: Juanda Airport (☎866 7513, ext. 9), 18km south of Surabaya. Taxis (Rp20,000-30,000) and DAMRI buses (Rp2500) shuttle visitors into town, leaving when full. To: **Bandar Seri Bagawan** (M, W, F; US$237, US$351 round-trip); **Denpasar** (6am, 7:20pm; Rp295,000-310,000); **Jakarta** (every 2hr. 6am-8pm; Rp457,000-625,000); **Yogyakarta** (4:20pm; Rp230,000). **Garuda** (☎534 5886; open M and Sa 9am-1pm, Tu-Th 7:30am-4:30pm, F 7:30am-5pm) and **Royal Brunei Airlines** (☎532 6407; open M-F 9am-5pm, Sa 9am-noon) are both on Jl. Basuki Rakhmat 106-128, next door to the Hyatt Regency. **Merpati,** Jl. Raya Darmo 111 (☎568 8111).

Trains: Stations are **Gubeng,** on Jl. Gubeng Masjid (☎503 3115); **Kota/Semut,** on Jl. Stasiun Kota; and **Pasar Turi** (☎534 5014), on Jl. Semarang. Trains traveling through Gubeng stop at Kota/Semut. From Gubeng, trains go to: **Bandung** (10½hr.; 7am; Rp158,800) via **Solo** (4½hr.) and **Yogyakarta** (5hr.; Rp48,500-138,500); **Banyuwangi** (5hr.; 8am, 10pm; Rp27,000-40,000); **Jakarta** (12hr.; 6pm; Rp148,500). From Pasar Turi, executive trains go to **Jakarta** (12-13hr.; 6 per day 9am-9pm; Rp56,000-227,000) via **Semarang** (8hr.; Rp44,500-217,000) and **Cirebon** (10hr.; Rp44,500-217,000). Ticket offices open daily 8am-5pm.

Buses: Bungurasih/Purabaya Terminal (☎853 1701), 10km south of town. All southbound **DAMRI** and **Patas buses** finish their routes at Bungurasih/Purabaya. Executive/deluxe buses with A/C, video, reclining seat, toilet, and food go to: **Bandung** (10hr.; 3,

3:30, 4, 4:30pm; Rp87,500); **Banyuwangi** (6hr.; every 15min.; Rp30,000); **Denpasar** (7hr.; every hr. 4-9pm; Rp55,000); **Jakarta** (11hr.; every 30min. 2-4:30pm; Rp87,500); **Probolingo** (1½hr.; every 10min.; Rp10,000); and **Solo/Yogyakarta** (4½-5½hr.; every hr. 10am-midnight, 12:30am; Rp24,000-28,500). Pay on the bus. Economy buses are slower, more crowded, leave when full, and charge half the price.

Ferries: The **port** is 100m from Tanjung Perak Terminal (see **Local Transportation,** below). **PELNI office,** Jl. Pahlawan 112 (☎355 9950). Open M-Th 8am-4pm, F 8-11am and 1-4pm. Purchase tickets at least 3 days in advance; cash only. Boats go to: **Bali** (Rp90,000-127,000); **Jakarta** (Rp105,000-327,000); **Ujung Pandang** (Rp119,000-374,000). Ask at the PELNI office for departure times and other destinations.

Local Transportation: Joyoboyo Terminal, on Jl. Joyoboyo by Surabaya Zoo, is the main local bus terminal. From Bungurasih Terminal, DAMRI (Rp1000) and P-1 Patas (Rp2000) **buses** run by the zoo, Tunjungan Plaza, Pasar Turi Station, the PELNI office, the GPO, and the Madura Ferry Terminal, ending at **Tanjung Perak Terminal.** Buses run 6am-9pm. There are 30 **bemo** routes, labeled alphabetically; almost half use Joyoboyo Terminal as a base. **Becak** are useful for short distances (Rp2000-3000).

Taxis: The best way to get around. Make sure they turn on the meter. Rp2800 for 1st km, about Rp800 each additional km. **Taxi Citra,** Jl. Arif Rahmuin 147 (☎592 5555). **Zebra Taxi** (☎841 1111).

Rentals: Toyota Rent-A-Car, Jl. Raya Waru Km15 (☎853 0909), 2km from the airport, and Jl. Basuki Rakhmat 116 (☎546 2500). Rp275,000 per day. International Driver's Permit (see p. 37) or driver (Rp99,000 per day) required. Open daily 8am-4pm.

ORIENTATION AND PRACTICAL INFORMATION

Surabaya is a sprawling harbor city with a branching river that snakes around its more popular spots, making navigation difficult. The huge **Tunjungan Plaza** marks the intersection of **Jl. Tunjungan** and **Jl. Pemuda,** two main commercial streets. **Jl. Yos Sudarso** and Jl. Pemuda meet four blocks east around the center of town. **Gubeng Train Station** is a few blocks down at the end of Jl. Pemuda across the river, after the Surabaya Plaza. Following the river north brings you to **Jl. Peneleh,** which has some reasonably priced accommodations. Farther upriver are the **GPO, Kota Station,** the **Arab Quarter,** and **Chinatown. Jl. Tanjung Perak** and the river eventually head to the **Madura Ferry Terminal** and to Surabaya's harbor.

Tourist Office: Regional Office (☎853 1815), 7km south of the city toward the airport on Jl. Wisata Menanggal. More convenient **branch** at Jl. Basuki Rakhmat 121 (☎534 4710), opposite the Hyatt Regency. Both open M-F 7am-1pm.

Tours: Dozens of agencies around Tunjungan Plaza and the Hyatt Regency on Jl. Basuki Rakhmat. **P.T. Haryono Tours and Travel,** Jl. Sulawesi 27-29 (☎503 4000), books transport as well as tours. **Branch,** Jl. Sudirman 93 (☎532 5800).

Consulates: Canada, Jl. Kembang Jepun 38-40 (☎354 4330; fax 354 4331). **UK,** Jl. Basuki Rakhmat 106-128 3rd fl., Hyatt Regency (☎550 5500). Open M-F 9am-5pm. **US,** Jl. Dr. Sutomo 33 (☎567 6880). Open M-F 8am-4pm.

Currency Exchange: Banks with ATMs line Jl. Pemuda and Jl. Urip Sumoharjo. **Danamon** (☎534 8700), on Jl. Pemuda. AmEx Traveler's Cheques. MC/V cash advances. Open M-F 8:30am-3pm. **Bank Bali,** Jl. Tunjungan 52. 24hr. **ATM** (AmEx/Cirrus/V).

American Express: Pacto, Jl. Basuki Rakhmat (☎531 1234), in the Hyatt Regency. Open M-F 9am-5pm, Sa 9am-1pm.

Luggage Storage: At Gubeng Train Station. Rp2000 per day.

INDONESIA

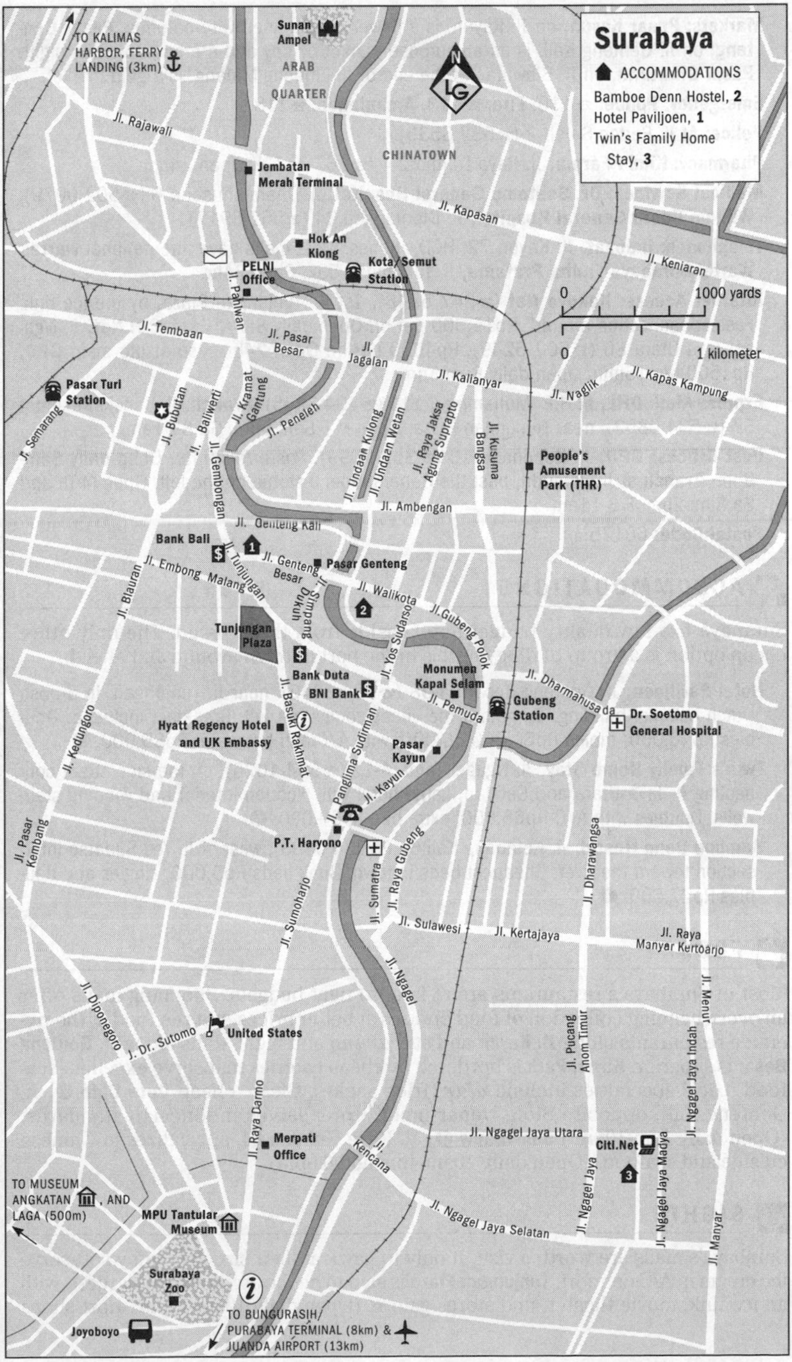
Surabaya
ACCOMMODATIONS
Bamboe Denn Hostel, 2
Hotel Paviljoen, 1
Twin's Family Home Stay, 3
0 1000 yards
0 1 kilometer
TO KALIMAS HARBOR, FERRY LANDING (3km)
Sunan Ampel
ARAB QUARTER
CHINATOWN
Jl. Rajawali
Jembatan Merah Terminal
Jl. Kapasan
Hok An Kiong
PELNI Office
Kota/Semut Station
Jl. Keniaran
Jl. Pahlwan
Jl. Tembaan
Jl. Pasar Besar
Jl. Jagalan
Jl. Kalianyar
Jl. Naglik
Jl. Kapas Kampung
Pasar Turi Station
Jl. Bubutan
Jl. Baliwerti
Jl. Kramat Gantung
Jl. Peneleh
Jl. Semarang
Jl. Gembongan
Jl. Undaan Kulong
Jl. Undaan Wetan
Jl. Raya Jaksa Agung Suprapto
Jl. Kusuma Bangsa
People's Amusement Park (THR)
Jl. Ambengan
Jl. Genteng Kali
Bank Bali
Jl. Tunjungan
Jl. Genteng Besar
Pasar Genteng
Jl. Embong Malang
Jl. Simpang Dukuh
Jl. Walikota
Jl. Gubeng Polok
Jl. Blauran
Tunjungan Plaza
Jl. Yos Sudarso
Bank Duta
BNI Bank
Monumen Kapal Selam
Jl. Dharmahusada
Gubeng Station
Jl. Pemuda
Dr. Soetomo General Hospital
Hyatt Regency Hotel and UK Embassy
Jl. Basuki Rakhmat
Jl. Panglima Sudirman
Pasar Kayun
Jl. Kayun
Jl. Kedungoro
Jl. Pasar Kembang
P.T. Haryono
Jl. Raya Gubeng
Jl. Sumatra
Jl. Sumoharjo
Jl. Dharawangsa
Jl. Sulawesi
Jl. Kertajaya
Jl. Raya Manyar Kertoarjo
Jl. Ngagel
Jl. Menur
Jl. Diponegoro
J. Dr. Sutomo
United States
Jl. Pucang Anom Timur
Jl. Ngagel Jaya Indah
Jl. Raya Darmo
Merpati Office
Jl. Ngagel Jaya Utara
Jl. Kencana
Citi.Net
Jl. Ngagel Jaya
Jl. Ngagel Jaya Madya
TO MUSEUM ANGKATAN, AND LAGA (500m)
MPU Tantular Museum
Jl. Ngagel Jaya Selatan
Jl. Manyar
Surabaya Zoo
Joyoboyo
TO BUNGURASIH/ PURABAYA TERMINAL (8km) & JUANDA AIRPORT (13km)
INDONESIA

Markets: Pasar Kayun, on Jl. Kayun, is a flower market lined with eateries. **Pasar Genteng,** on Jl. Genteng Kali, is an all-purpose market by day and a food market by night. **Pasar Blawuran,** on Jl. Blawuran at the end of Jl. Embong Malang, is a gold market.

Emergency: Police: ☎110. **Fire:** ☎113. **Ambulance:** ☎118.

Police: At Jl. Raden Saleh 2 (☎532 8535).

Pharmacy: Kimia Farma, Jl. Raya Darmo 2-4 (☎567 7777). Open 24hr.

Medical Services: Dr. Soetomo General Hospital, Jl. Dharmahusada 6 (☎502 0079). **William Booth General Hospital,** Jl. Diponegoro 34 (☎567 8917).

Telephones: Indosat, Jl. Kayun 72. HCD phones. Most malls have international **wartel. Wartel Surabaya Yudha Pratama,** Jl. Tunjungan 53k. Open 24hr.

Internet Access: Kokuyo Net (☎547 5848), 1st fl., Tunjungan Plaza, by the ice rink. Fastest connection around. Rp15,000 per hr. Open daily 8am-10pm. **Citi.Net,** Jl. Ngagel Jaya Utara 80 (☎502 5249). Rp4000 per hr. Open 24hr. Also at the main **GPO.** Rp1500 per 15min. Open daily 8am-5pm.

Express Mail: DHL, Jl. H.R. Muhammad 111 (☎734 3435). **Branch,** Jl. Basuki Rakhmat 57 (☎534 0852), near Tunjungan Plaza. Open M-F 8am-5pm, Sa 8-11am.

Post Offices: GPO, Jl. Kebonrojo 10 (☎352 2099). *Poste Restante.* Open daily 8am-9pm. **Branch** at Jl. Pemuda, past the General Soerjo statue on the left. Open M-Th and Sa 8am-2pm, F 8-11am.

Postal Code: 60175.

ACCOMMODATIONS

Surabaya has few quality budget hotels aside from those listed. The only other cheap option is a group of dingy hotels in the part of town around Jl. Peneleh.

Hotel Paviljoen, Jl. Genteng Besar 94-98 (☎534 3449), near Jl. Tunjungan. In a posh Dutch colonial building. Bargain if the cheap rooms are full. Breakfast included. Doubles Rp40,000; triples Rp60,000-65,000, with A/C and hot water Rp85,000. ❸

Twin's Family Home Stay, Jl. Ngagel Tama A-12 (☎504 1026), on the side street connecting Jl. Jaya Utara and Selatan. Large hotel with wooden interior and winding stairwells. Doubles with A/C Rp65,000; extra bed Rp30,000. ❹

Bamboe Denn Hostel, Jl. Ketabang Kali 6A (☎534 0333), west of Jl. Yos Sudarso intersection toward the river. Cheapest beds in town. Bunk beds Rp5,000; singles and doubles Rp27,500. ❶

INDONESIA

FOOD

Most of Surabaya's restaurants aren't kind to tight budgets. Shopping malls offer an overwhelming collection of food options at better prices, but the food at the riverside restaurants along **Jl. Kayun** and at *warung* and night stalls along **Jl. Genteng Besar** is superior. **Kayun Park** is bordered by cheap eateries that serve excellent seafood. Local specialties include *ular* (fried snake). Clean, cheap **Duta Cafe** ❷, Jl. Genteng Kali, opposite Siola Department Store, serves Indonesian standards. (Open daily 7am-10pm.) **San Thauw** ❸, Jl. Raya Gubeng 64, specializes in Chinese cuisine and seafood. (Open daily 10am-4pm and 6-9pm).

SIGHTS

Surabaya's malls are worth a visit, if only to gawk at their size and enjoy soft-serve ice cream in A/C comfort. **Tunjungan Plaza** is said to be the archipelago's largest, with an ice rink, movie theater, and stores galore. (Open daily 10am-11pm; most shops close by 9pm.) The **People's Amusement Park (THR),** behind the THR Mall, offers traditional dance and music performances. Schedules are available at the tourist office. (☎534 0956. Open Th and Sa 7pm-midnight. Rp350.) The real thrills, however, are at nearby **Taman Remaja**'s ferris wheel and mini roller coasters (Rp2000).

The **Surabaya Zoo** is Southeast Asia's largest, but animal lovers might be turned off by the unnatural, cramped living spaces and the crude spectators. From the Tunjungan area, catch a bus (15min.) south on Jl. Sudirman; ask to get off at "Kebun Binatang." (Komodo dragon feedings the 5th and 20th of every month. Open daily 7am-6pm. Rp3000. Elephant and camel rides Rp2000.)

The **Arab Quarter** and the monumental **Sunan Ampel Mosque,** the oldest mosque in East Java, can be visited in a few hours and are worth the trip for architecture buffs. The mosque was built by Sunan Ampel, one of the *wali songo*—nine Muslim holy men who initiated the spread of Islam in Java. To get there, take any *bemo* (#10 is ideal) to Jembatan Merah Terminal and then hop on a *becak* (Rp2000) or walk 15min. northeast to Sunan Ampel. Be warned that tensions are high in this area as a result of recent religious fighting.

NIGHTLIFE

Plenty of discotheques and karaoke bars scattered around **Tunjungan Plaza** are crowded on weekends. Surabaya's major hotels are known for their bars with nightly live music, Bintang beer at around Rp20,000, and decent vibes for a Rp40,000 cover charge. Low-key **Tavern Pub** in the Hyatt Regency, Chinese-filled **Desperado** in Sanggrila Hotel, tropical **Bongos** in the Sheraton, and the similar **Java Jimmies** in the Westin complete the hotel pub crawl. All close around 3am. You'll need to take cabs to get around, so just make sure they are metered. **Colors,** Jl. Sumatra 81, is a cozy bar/cafe crowded with hungry hip cats and kittens on the prowl. (Excellent pop bands after 9pm. Bintang Rp11,000; pitchers Rp36,000. Happy hour 7-9pm daily. Open daily 5pm-2am.) Cheap and popular on weekends, **Laga,** Jl. May Jen Sungkono 107, is one of the few "bars" that neither costs more than a hotel room nor blasts deafening dance music. (☎568 1826. Live music from 10:30pm. Cover F Rp3000, Sa Rp5000. Open M-F 6pm-1:20am, Sa 6pm-2:30am.)

INDONESIA

GUNUNG BROMO ☎0335

At 2923m, dramatic Gunung Bromo is one of the most magnificent sights in Indonesia. "Bromo" refers not only to the ash-gray, semi-active crater named after the Hindu god Brahma, but also to an entire cluster of volcanoes set in an enormous crater spanning 40km, the Bromo-Semeru Massif, known as Tengger. A breathtaking sunrise seen from the lookout point on Gunung Penanjaka, followed by a 5hr. hike, will give you a chance to take in the vistas. If you aren't in a hurry, the mountain air merits an extra night or two—if you don't mind the hordes of tourists.

TRANSPORTATION. Gunung Bromo is most commonly reached by tourist bus via the town of Probolinggo. From there, take a crowded public *bemo* to Cemorolawang (2½hr., last bus 5pm, Rp8000), the stop for the Gunung Bromo area. Most locals will get out at the market halfway to Gunung Bromo; refuse offers for express buses and wait for the *bemo* to refill (around 10min.). For late arrivals, direct **minibuses** can be chartered from the Probolinggo bus terminal (1hr.; Rp50,000-60,000). Alternatively, Gunung Bromo can also be approached from its northern edge via the coastal town of Pasuruan. From Pasuruan, minibuses run to Tosari, where visitors can hire a jeep to the crater or take a minibus to Penanjakan, the premier sunrise viewpoint.

To leave, purchase bus tickets at the **Probolinggo bus terminal** or take a bus from Cemorolawang. Avoid the travel agencies in Probolinggo. Minibuses constantly run downhill to Probolinggo. From there, buses continue to **Denpasar** (8hr.; 10:30am, 12:15, 7, 8, 9pm; Rp60,000) and Solo/Yogyakarta (economy: 11-12hr.; 7, 8, 9pm; Rp45,000; executive: 9-10hr.; 10:30am, 8pm; Rp60,000). Alternatively, take a bus to Panuangi (4hr., every 30min., Rp8000), a *bemo* to Ketapong (45min., Rp1750), and a final bus to Denpasar (3½hr.; Rp10,000). **Public buses** travel to Surabaya (2hr., every 30min., Rp8000).

ACCOMMODATIONS AND FOOD. The best deal in the Gunung Bromo area is **Yoschi ❷**, Jl. Wonokerto Km2, Ngadisari, 7km before Cemorolawang. Though it's a *bemo* ride or a steep 45min. walk from the crater, Yoschi's classy facilities, including a restaurant and morning jacket rentals, trump the competition. (☎541 018. Hot water. Doubles Rp25,000.) In Cemorolawang, on the lip of the crater, *losmen* are close together and travelers should shop around—note that *bemo* drivers often take commissions from *losmen* operators. **Hotel Lava's ❷**, beyond the entrance gate 50m up the left road, has a friendly and comfortable cafe (try the pancakes) and attracts the most tourists. (☎541 020. Doubles Rp30,000, with *mandi* and breakfast Rp85,000.) **Cemara Indah ❷** is 100m up the road to the right, where you're most likely to get dropped off. (☎541 019. Singles Rp20,000; doubles Rp25,000-30,000; deluxe rooms Rp85,000; superior deluxe Rp200,000.) Restaurants are limited to those attached to hotels. (Entrees Rp5000-15,000.) *Warung* are easy to come by on village roads (Rp1000-4000). Get your dinner early—the town shuts down after 8pm.

If you're stranded in Probolinggo, **Hotel Ratna ❸**, Jl. Sudirman 16, has pricey rooms. (☎421 597. Breakfast included. Rooms Rp35,000-75,000.) **Rumah Makan Sumber Hidup ❷**, next to Hotel Ratna at the corner at Jl. Moch Saleh 2, serves ice cream and Indonesian fare. (Dishes Rp8000-15,000. Open daily 7am-9pm).

TREKKING. Gunung Bromo and its surrounding peaks can be climbed at any time of day, but to hike by the light of the magnificent sunrise, set your alarm clock for 3:30am. Rub your eyes and make your way to the lookout point at **Gunung Penanjaka,** which provides a premium postcard panorama at daybreak. Follow the road from Cemara Indah. Bring warm clothes to wear in layers, water, a flashlight, and hiking buddies if you're going without a guide. If you stray from the path, locals will follow your flashlight and direct you to safety for a small fee (Rp10,000 per group). Alternatively, a convoy of jeeps leaves at 4am, hauling crowds of people to Gunung Penanjaka. Purchase tickets for Rp25,000 through any Cemorolawang accommodation. After the dawn breaks, jeeps rumble back down the mountain across *Laut Pasir*, the "sea of sand," and to Gunung Bromo, where a short 15min. jaunt up the trail will take you to the caldera's edge. Expect to be surrounded by desperate men trying to rent wheezing horses—remember that the ride may be more strenuous than walking.

INDONESIA

BALI

011 62 361 + tel

One million tourists flock to this little island (5700 km²) every year, looking for everything from enlightenment to drunken debauchery. Bali balances precariously between Eden and Eden after the Fall: though McDonald's has colonized Kuta, escapists can still find virgin expanse and a paradise not yet lost. You may have to share the shores and volcanoes with droves of travelers, but the white coral, black lava beaches, and gorgeous vistas are worth it. Though no part of Bali's main attractions remains untouched by tourism, the island's beauty cannot be denied.

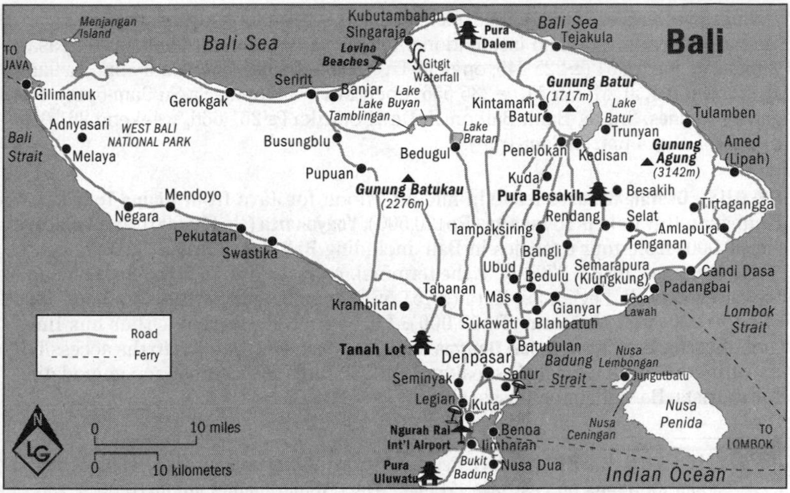

THE VIEW FROM ABOVE
Main Cities: Denpasar, Kuta, Singaraja, and Ubud.
Highlights: Enjoying dolphins in Lovina, partying in Kuta, absorbing culture in Ubud.
Something Fun: Climb Gunung Agung and Gunung Batur, surf in Legian, visit the Monkey Forest.

DENPASAR ☎0361

Chock full of art, markets, malls, karaoke, museums, and international cuisine, Denpasar is Bali's urban center of schmooze. Since most travelers skip over the city, it is more typically Indonesian than the rest of the island. Though the streets can be filthy, they offer a mosaic of treasures, from the literal to the metaphoric. With puppies and birds for sale and paintings and Dutch cannons to admire, the eclectic nature of Denpasar's streets should not be missed.

INDONESIA

TRANSPORTATION

BY PLANE. Ngurah Rai International Airport (☎751 011, 24hr. info ext. 164) is 30min. south of Kuta by taxi or direct shuttle. A moneychanger, luggage storage (Rp5500 per day), and **ATM** (Cirrus/MC/Plus/V) are available. The Rp75,000 international departure tax must be paid in cash; the domestic departure tax is Rp30,000. From the airport, fixed-rate taxis go to: **Denpasar** (Rp27,000-37,500); **Nusa Dua** (Rp30,000); **Sanur** (Rp30,000); and **Ubud** (Rp90,000). Cheaper public *bemo* and vehicles available for charter linger outside the airport on the main road. Beware of porters who carry your luggage without being asked and then demand large sums for their effort.

DESTINATION	FREQUENCY	PRICE	DESTINATION	FREQUENCY	PRICE
Bima	1 per day	Rp478,800	**Mataram**	5 per day	Rp233,500
Jakarta	8 per day	Rp802,200	**Singapore**	1 per day	US$255
Yogyakarta	3 per day	Rp426,000	**Ujung Pandang**	1 per day	Rp555,800
Kupang	1 per day	Rp803,300			

Singapore Airlines, Garuda, and **Merpati** have information desks at the airport, between the domestic and international terminals, and main offices in Denpasar: **Garuda,** Jl. Melati 61 (☎225 245; open M-Th 7:30am-4:30pm, F 7:30am-5pm, Sa 9am-1pm); **Merpati,** Jl. Melati 51 (☎235 556; open M-F 8am-5pm, Sa-Su 9am-5pm); **Singapore Airlines,** 3rd fl., Bank Bali on Jl. Dewi Sartika (☎261 666, weekend 261 669; open M-F 8am-5pm, Sa 8am-1pm).

BY BUS. Overnight buses leave in mid-afternoon for Java from **Ubung Terminal** in Denpasar. Buy tickets to **Jakarta** (Rp170,500), **Yogyakarta** (Rp110,000), and **Surabaya** (Rp50,000) from tour agencies in Bali, including **Bali Buana Artha,** Jl. Diponegoro 131A, Denpasar (☎227 370), or at the terminal. A/C buses go to **Bima/Sape** on Sumbawa. **Perama,** Jl. Legian 39, Kuta (☎751 551), has daily departures to **Bima/Sape** (Rp130,000) and **Mataram** (Rp50,000). Fares include ferries. Other bus lines include **Langsung Indah, Safari Dharma Raya,** and **Simpatik,** but due to the accessibility of its offices and English-speaking staff, Perama is the most accommodating for tourists. Be vigilant on buses, as theft is common.

ISLAND-HOPPING. Ferries run between **Gilimanuk** on the west tip of Bali and **Ketapang** on East Java (20min., every 30min. 5am-9pm, Rp10,000). Ferries to **Lombok** leave from **Padangbai** (see p. 193) on Bali's east coast (4-5hr., every 1½hr., Rp9500). **Mabua Express** leaves for **Lembar** on Lombok (2½hr., 8am, US$25-30) from **Benoa Harbor** (☎721 272) in South Bali. **PELNI** ships also serve Benoa Harbor. For schedules and tickets, contact their ticket office in Benoa (☎721 377). To get to Benoa, take a taxi from Denpasar (15minutes).

BY BEMO. Public *bemo*, identified by yellow license plates (government vehicles have red plates; private ones have black), are easiest to catch in the early morning and generally stop running after 9pm in Southern Bali and 6pm in the north. They can also be chartered privately. **Denpasar** is the hub of *bemo* activity for Southern Bali. Four terminals serve the island:

Batubulan, 6km northeast of Denpasar, runs *bemo* east to **Bangli, Padangbai, Candi Dasa, Amlapura,** and **Tirtagangga** and north to **Ubud** via **Kediri** and **Penelokan.**

Kereneng, on the east end of Denpasar off Jl. Hayam Wuruk, has connecting *bemo* to the other terminals.

Tegal, on the west end near the intersection of Jl. G. Willis and Jl. Imam Bonjol, runs *bemo* south to **Kuta, Legian, Ngurah Rai Airport, Nusa Dua, Sanur,** and **Uluwatu.**

Ubung, north of Denpasar on Jl. Cokroaminoto, handles trips to the north and west, including **Bedugul, Gilimanuk, Singaraja, Tanah Lot,** and points in **Java.**

LOCAL TRANSPORTATION

Metered taxis around town start at Rp3000; bargaining is usually more expensive. Taxis don't stop where *bemo* or local drivers are parked, so catch one elsewhere. The light-blue **Bali Taxi** (☎701 111) offers professional service. **Ojek** can be hired anywhere. **Dokar** (horse-drawn carts) are used in Denpasar.

TOURIST PRICE. Tourists are usually charged more than locals for transportation. If you're up to the challenge, ask locals how much they pay to determine a fair price. Good luck.

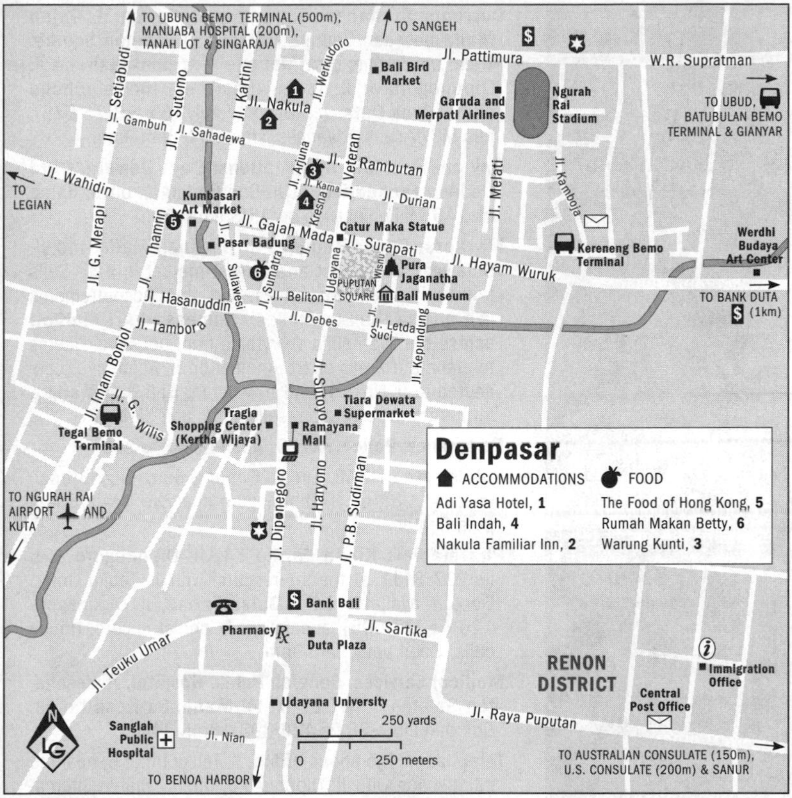

ORIENTATION AND PRACTICAL INFORMATION

North of Denpasar, dense **Pasar Badung** lies between the two parallel east-west streets, **Jl. Hasanuddin** and **Jl. Gajah Mada,** which are connected by **Jl. Sulawesl.** Jl. Gajah Mada becomes **Jl. Surapati** to the east, which later becomes **Jl. Hayam Wuruk. Puputan Square** is east of the market, between the same streets. At one corner of the square, where Jl. Gajah Mada, **Jl. Veteran, Jl. Surapadial,** and **Jl. Udayana** meet, sits **Catur Maka statue.** The **central post office** and **Bali Government Tourist Office** are both in the **Renon District** near **Jl. Raya Puputan. Udayan University** and the massive **Duta Plaza Shopping Center** border **Jl. Diponegoro,** which heads north to the market.

Tourist Office: Dinas Pariwisata, Jl. Surapati 7 (☎234 569), near the Bali Museum. Friendly and informative. Free maps, brochures, and schedule of events. Staff helps demystify *bemo* routes. Open M-Th 7am-2pm, F 7-11am, Sa 7am-12:30pm.

Tours: Miraz Tours, Jl. Diponegoro 81 (☎246 007), books tours around Bali. Open M-Sa 8am-8pm, Su 8am-4pm.

PELNI Office: Jl. Diponegoro 165 (☎234 680). Helps with transportation and other tourist-related questions. Open daily 8am-7pm.

Consulates: Australia, Jl. Prof. Yamin 4, Renon District (☎235 092). Open M-F 8am-4pm. **US,** Jl. Hayam Wuruk 188 (☎233 605), by Hotel Sanno. Open M-F 8am-4:30pm.

INDONESIA

THE LOCAL STORY

A WARIA WARRIOR

Fitra is anatomically male, but says that she and her boyfriend, a Javanese policeman, aren't gay.

"He doesn't like men," Fitra insists. Like most *waria*—members of Indonesia's alternate gender—she believes that God gave her a female soul inside a male body.

When Fitra was 13, she dressed in a woman's clothes and went to a mosque—a way of confronting her identity. She sat on the female side of the room, but the women near her began to shift away uneasily. As Fitra explains it, they felt she was polluting the purity of their prayer.

Fitra doesn't go to the mosque anymore. She prays alone in her room, a concrete cell in a compound filled with other Javanese immigrants hoping to strike it rich in Denpasar. The intricacies of Fitra's belief distinguish her from transvestites, hermaphrodites, homosexuals, and transsexuals. She is not a "cross-dresser." In a masculine body, she believes that her female soul distinguishes her from homosexual men.

Fitra has recently updated her National Identity Card. The card describes her status—once printed as male—as *waria*. While declaring this publicly is somewhat easy in urban areas, being *waria* is hard in the country. Fitra knows that where she came from her counterparts will continue to report hardships of alienation, abuse, and misunderstanding. It's a hard reality to deal with.

Currency Exchange: Big **banks** cluster on **Jl. Gajah Mada** between Badung Market and Puputan Square. There are dozens of **ATMs;** one is at **Bank Bali,** on Jl. Diponegoro at Jl. Teuku Umar near the telephone office. **Bank Duta,** Jl. Hayam Wuruk 165 (☎226 578), has MC/V cash advances. Open M-F 8am-3pm.

Gay and Lesbian Organizations: Gaya Dewata/Citra Usadua Foundation, at Jl. Sari Gading 1, off Jl. Ratna (☎246 757). Focuses on AIDS education.

Markets: Pasar Badung, at Jl. Gajah Mada and Jl. Sulawesi. The oldest and largest market in Bali. Sells fruit and spices, appliances, and ritual accoutrements like *pajong* (Bali umbrellas). **Kumbasari Art Market,** across the river, sells everything from household items to elaborate works of art. Another on Jl. Abimanyu (connected to Jl. Nokula) and Jl. Veteran. **Bali Bird Market,** farther down Jl. Veteran, sells fabric and birds.

Emergency: Police: ☎110. **Ambulance:** ☎118.

Police: ☎424 346. On Jl. Gunung Sangiong. Branch (☎234 928), on Jl. Diponegoro near the Tragia Shopping Contor.

Pharmacies: Kimia Farma 34, Jl. Diponegoro 125 (☎227 811), at the intersection with Jl. Teuku Umar. Doctors available 24hr. **Bulan Farma,** Jl. Diponegoro 126 (☎227 605), specializes in pediatric care. House calls. Open daily 5am-9pm.

Medical Services: Sanglah Public Hospital, Jl. Kesehatan Selatan 1 (☎227 911). **Manuaba Hospital,** Jl. Cokroaminoto 28 (☎426 393). Both 24hr.

Telephones: The **phone office,** Jl. Teuku Umar 6, near the intersection with Jl. Diponegoro, offers reliable international, collect, and calling card calls. **Wartel,** also offering international calls, are scattered about town.

Internet Access: 3rd fl. of Ramayana Mall. Rp50,000 per hr.

Express Mail: DHL, Jl. Hayam Wuruk 146 (☎262 713). Open M-F 8am-5pm, Sa 8am-1pm.

Post Offices: GPO (☎223 565), south on Jl. Raya Puputan in Renon District. *Poste Restante.* Branch, Jl. Kamboja 6 (☎222 004), outside Kereneng Terminal. Both open daily 8am-8pm.

Postal Code: 80235.

ACCOMMODATIONS

Nakula Familiar Inn, Jl. Nakula 4 (☎226 446). Run by a friendly local family, it's easily the top pick in the city. Huge, clean singles or doubles with porch, ceiling fan, and private bath. Breakfast Rp15,000. Laundry with ironing Rp2500 per article. Singles Rp40,000; doubles Rp60,000. ❸

Adi Yasa Hotel, Jl. Nakula 23B (☎222 679), 50m from Nakula Familiar Inn. *Losmen*-style accommodations. Inexpensive, worn rooms with private combination *mandi* and fan. Clean and relatively safe. Singles Rp25,000; doubles Rp40,000. ❷

Bali Indah, Jl. Kresna 11 (☎225 226). From the Catur Maka statue, the first right off Jl. Gajah Mada. A quiet hotel in noisy Denpasar, near all the sights. Fewer tourists make it ideal for mingling with locals. Doubles with private *mandi* and fan Rp50,000, with A/C, TV, bath, and hot water Rp120,000. ❸

FOOD

Denpasar's diverse ethnic population makes for exciting dining. You'll find *warung* and cheap eateries everywhere in town, especially along **Jl. Sumatra-Diponegoro** and at the Kereneng Terminal. A **night market** behind Pasar Badung offers *warung* dishes. (Open daily 6pm-midnight.) Another night market comes to life on Jl. Diponegoro near the **Kertha Wijaya Shopping Center. Tragia Market,** Jl. Diponegoro 98, part of the Kertha Wijaya Shopping Center, sells a large selection of fruits and vegetables. (Open daily until 10pm.) **Tiara Dewata Supermarket** is at the northern end of Jl. Sudirman. Western cuisine is easy to find.

Rumah Makan Betty, Jl. Sumatra 56. 1 block east of Jl. Sulawesi. A small, low-budget cafeteria. Clean, roomy, friendly. East Javanese food and vegetarian options. Betty also gives the best directions in town. Open M-Sa 8am-9pm, Su 8am-2pm. ❷

Warung Kunti, Jl. Arjuna 37. Take 2nd right down Jl. Gajah Mada from the Catur Maka statue. A tiny mom-and-pop operation, Kunti is far from traffic and serves spicy Balinese food. Meal with rice Rp5000. Open daily 7am-2pm. ❶

The Food of Hong Kong, Jl. Gajah Mada 99 (☎434 926), next to Pasar Badung, serves up delectable and diverse Southeast Asian meals. Dishes Rp10,000-50,000. ❹

SIGHTS

BALI MUSEUM. Rebuilt in 1932 after the original collapsed in a 1917 earthquake, this museum is Denpasar's primary attraction. The building itself, a blend of Balinese temple and palace architecture, is the finest exhibit. It houses artifacts that provide an introduction to Balinese society and culture from the prehistoric age to today. While the museum lacks detailed labels, the courtyards are well-maintained and the rooms are informative, especially for those interested in Balinese woodcarving, weaving, and painting. *(On Jl. Mayor Wisnu east of Puputan Sq. Open Tu-F 8am-2:45pm, Sa 8am-3:15pm, Su 8am-3:45pm. Rp750, children Rp250.)*

PURA JAGANATHA. This temple, dedicated to the supreme god Sanghyang Widi, is a symbolic representation of the cosmos. A gold statue of Sanghyang Widi sits atop a tall spire. The eight gods, each clad in a symbolic color, are beneath, and under them are two dragons that balance the earth. The spire, built of white coral, is surrounded by a moat with goldfish and sacred lilies. Guides, often religion or history students, will give you a crash course on Balinese Hinduism for a few dollars. At 7pm during *purnama* (full moon) and *tilem* (dark moon), the temple is crowded with Balinese bringing offerings and Hindu intellectuals meeting for religious readings. *Wayang kulit* (shadow puppet performances) begin around 10pm during *purnama*. *(Next to the Bali Museum. Open daily 7am-6pm.)*

WERDHI BUDAYA ART CENTER. Every June and July, the **Bali Arts Festival** kicks off in Denpasar at Werdhi Budaya Art Center. The large, outdoor amphitheater and exhibition halls are a perfect home for Balinese painting. The tourist office (see **Practical Information,** p. 171) provides a schedule of events. Call ahead to find out what's on display. English-speaking guides are available—bargain with them. *(On the corner of Jl. Hayam Wuruk and Jl. Nusa Indah. ☎227 176. Open daily 8am-2pm. Rp1000.)*

PUPUTAN SQUARE. This large park, with a fountain and monument depicting a family preparing for battle, commemorates the solemn, suicidal *puputan* (final flight) of 1906, when Badung's last king, followed by family and court, refused to surrender and marched into the bullets of Dutch soldiers. Locals eat lunch and lounge around the square throughout the week. *(Opposite the Bali Museum.)*

NUSA LEMBONGAN

With white sand, blue waters, and barreling waves, Nusa Lembongan is the domain of surfers who brave the three large breaks over its reef. Looking from the beach to the off-shore reefs, the major breaks (from right to left) are: **Shipwreck, Lacerations,** and **Playground.** The most reliable surf is at Shipwreck, a clean right-hand break. Almost as good as the surf is the snorkeling at **Mangrove Bay.** The cheapest way to get to Nusa Lembongan is by **public boat** from the end of Jl. Hang Tuah in Sanur. The boat leaves at 8am but requires a minimum number of people (Rp40,000). **Perama boats** leave at 10:30am. Tickets cost Rp50,000; show up at the Warung Pojok depot at 10:15am on the day of the trip. Returning boats, both public and Perama, leave around 8am from Nusa Lembongan. The strait between the islands is rough and the only way to navigate it is by chartering a boat. On the island, boats are readily available for rent, and guides will take you around the island for some of the best snorkeling on Bali. (Rp100,000; Rp20,000 when boat is full.) The best places for cheap food and accommodations are on the northwest corner of the island at Jungubatu Village, 500m from the boat drop-off (with the water to your back, walk left). There is little difference among the bungalows along the shore, and none of them include breakfast. **Ketut's Losmen ❹** has new, modern bungalows. (Singles Rp70,000; doubles Rp80,000.) **Ketut's Warung ❸,** past Agung's Lodge and 50m inland, has one of the cheapest options, with simple rooms with bath. (Singles Rp40,000; doubles Rp50,000.) **Agung's Lodge ❸** offers a carnival atmosphere and full amenities. (Singles Rp50,000; doubles Rp60,000.) The best place to eat is beachside at the **Mainski Inn and Restaurant ❸,** which offers fresh seafood and shows American movies at 7:30pm. (Tasty chips and bean dip Rp10,000.) The 2½hr. walk around the island is pleasant, especially at dusk. The nearby island of **Nusa Penida,** which serves primarily as a seaweed plantation, has a spectacular reef for snorkeling and is also out of the way of passing motorboats. However, it has no restaurants and a few shabby accommodations on the shore.

KUTA ☎0361

What has long been known as one of the most vibrant areas on Bali was shaken by the devastating bombings of two crowded nightspots along Jl. Legian on October 12, 2002. About 180 people were killed in the attacks, which seemed to be aimed specifically at Western tourists. Kuta's economy is largely driven by tourism and its lighthearted reputation, and the attacks had serious repercussions on local businesses and the livelihood of the area's residents. However, Kuta is recovering and on its way to becoming a full-fledged tourist destination once again.

ACCOMMODATIONS

Poppies Lane II, just meters from the surf shops and nightlife, attracts a young crowd, while **Poppies Lane I** is quieter. (Accommodations in these areas are the most likely to have been affected by the recent bombings.) Cheap beds are harder to come by in Legian; however, what does exist exudes an air of sophistication not found in Kuta proper.

Senen Beach Inn, Camplung Mas Ln. 25 (☎755 470), in an alley off Jl. Melasti. One of the cheapest options in Legian. Unusually friendly and laid-back staff help plan trips and book shuttles. Quiet garden. Restaurant. Tea fairy leaves you a fresh thermos every morning. Fan, private bath. Singles Rp30,000; doubles Rp35,000. ❷

Puri Agung (☎750 054), on Gang Bedugul. Turn onto Poppies Ln. I from Jl. Legian, turn right at T.J.'s; it's a short way down on the right. Central location and gated entrance. Singles with fan and private bath Rp30,000; doubles Rp40,000. ❷

Suka Beach Inn (☎752 793). Turn onto Poppies Ln. II from Jl. Legian and then turn right at the Adrenalin Park sign on Jl. Bene Sari and walk 100m. Popular among surfers. Free storage for boards and bags. Breakfast included. Bike (from Rp30,000 per day) and car (from Rp70,000 per day) rental. Singles with fan Rp40,000; doubles Rp50,000. ❸

FOOD

Kuta's tourist hordes eschew local food and instead eat at a variety of Western-style restaurants (anything from McDonald's fast food to fine European cuisine). The locals, however, will share their own cooking at the **night market** ❷. From Jl. Pantai Kuta, walk away from the beach and take the fifth right; it's 100m down on the left.) For cheap eats, a few **warung** ❶ dot the beach boardwalk.

Ryoshi Japanese Restaurant (☎761 852), 300m from the water on Jl. Melasti. Branch at Jl. Seminyak 17 (☎731 152). Fresh sashimi melts in your mouth. White mackerel roll Rp9500. Open daily noon-midnight. MC/V. ❷

Aromas Cafe, on Jl. Legian, 30m south of the intersection with Jl. Melasti. More Bombay than Bali, this venue for "exotic vegetarian cuisine" will tempt even the most carnivorous. Many vegan options as well—try the avocado salad (Rp18,000). MC/V. ❹

WHAT'S YOUR SIGN?

Upon visiting Bali for the first time, tourists are sometimes shocked by the use of a threatening, highly evocative symbol: the swastika. Reviled in the West as an emblem of Nazi terror, the symbol has another, more benevolent history that dates back over 3000 years to when the term first appeared in the Vedas, the holy texts of Hinduism.

Indeed—the swastika is a Sanskrit sun symbol, a common motif in both Hindu and Buddhist art, and a sort of "good luck" symbol in a range of other ancient cultures. The four "legs" represent dynamic cyclical change, like phases or seasons, circling endlessly. In Bali and other areas influenced by Hinduism, the swastika is a ubiquitous blessing that imbues statues and buildings with religious significance.

While some cultures have differentiated the clockwise and counter-clockwise symbols—often holding the latter to be evil or inauspicious—the idea of a fundamentally evil swastika is a relatively recent, 20th-century development. While it is imperative to remember the evil done under the sign of the Nazis, travelers should also remember the symbol's other story. More ancient than even the Egyptian Ankh life symbol, its good meaning reaches almost as far back as civilization itself.

T.J.'s (☎751 093), on Poppies Ln. I, 1 block from the beach. Classy, tropical atmosphere with indoor reflecting pool. The food isn't authentic Mexican but is still fresh and tasty. Enchiladas with crab meat and green chilli Rp35,000. Open daily 8am-11pm. Bar open until 11:30pm. MC/V. ❺

Warung '96, Jl. Bene Sari, off Poppies Ln. II. Branch at Jl. Abimanyu 200A (☎733 800). Serves burgers and way too much J. Lo and Green Day. Join the surfers for a King Sized Burger (with beef, bacon, ham, pineapple, egg, and cheese; Rp7500). Open daily 7am-midnight. ❸

NIGHTLIFE

The Sari Club, one of the most popular clubs in Kuta, was the primary target of the October 12, 2002 bombings. Other establishments were damaged as well, and the future of many businesses seems bleak. Travelers who remember Kuta's once-legendary night scene, however, are beginning to return, and the nightlife is slowly becoming revitalized.

Double Six (☎251 266), in north Legian, at the beach end of Jl. Arjuna. Trendy place is worth the hefty cover (Rp40,000; includes 1 drink) on weekends. Mixed crowd boogies to Euro-house/trance music. Open daily midnight-dawn.

Q Bar and Cafe, on Jl. Abimanyu off Jl. Raya Seminyak in Seminyak. Gay-friendly establishment with nightly dancing, a clothing boutique, and occasional fashion shows. Open daily 9pm-2am.

Blue Train, on Jl. Raya Seminyak No. 28, in Seminyak. Best jazz on Bali. Bands vary throughout the week. Open Tu-Su 11am-2am.

The Bounty Ship, one location at the intersection of Jl. Legian and Poppies Ln. I, another on Jl. Legian just north of Jl. Melasti. Built to look like ships, these 2 joints fill up with large weekend crowds. 2-for-1 drinks 5-7pm. Open 24hr.

Cafe Luna (☎730 805), in north Legian on Jl. Raya Seminyak, 100m north of Jl. Pura Bagus Teruna. Salsa with live bands (Tu and Th 10pm-midnight) or go-go dancers (Sa midnight). Mixed crowd. Drinks Rp20,000-30,000; pizza Rp18,000-32,000.

Peanuts (☎754 149), at the intersection of Jl. Legian and Jl. Melasti. Attracts a fast crowd looking to hook up. Hosts a pub crawl (May-Sept. Tu and Sa); Rp50,000 cover includes transport, entrance fees, and drop-off at the end.

OUTDOOR ACTIVITIES

If you're a surfer, welcome home. If you aren't, now is the time to become one. While the surf is safe, the rental selection is rather poor. **Motor boats** regularly go from **Kuta Beach** to the airport reefs (Rp10,000, but don't pay full price in advance to ensure a quick pickup). Many hotels will transport surfers to beaches in **Seminyak** or **Uluwatu.** Swing by **Tubes Surf Bar and Restaurant,** on Jl. Legian between Poppies Ln. I and II, to pick up a free tide chart. (☎753 510. Open daily 10am-midnight.) Even if getting crazy barrel is not your thing, Kuta still has plenty to get you excited, including four **bungee-jumping** towers, a **waterslide park,** several **billiard halls,** and a few **arcades. Waterbom Park,** on Jl. Kartika Plaza in Tuban, a 5min. walk south from the *bemo* corner, has waterslides, a wave pool, and masseurs. (☎755 676. US$15; massage extra. Open daily 9am-6pm.) Bungee-jumping packages are available at **A.J. Hackett** (☎730 666), next to Double Six Nightclub; **Bali Bungy Co.,** on Jl. Pura Puseh (☎752 658; open daily 9am-7pm); **Adrenalin Park,** Jl. Bene Sari 69 in Legian (☎757 841; open daily noon-7pm); and **Bungee in Bali** (☎941 102), 30min. away in Gianyar. Bungee in Bali drops jumpers over a waterfall; the others do it over a pool.

Budi Shady Gully Guest House (☎976 027), on Jl. Jembawan. A 5min. walk from the intersection with Jl. Raya Ubud. Serene jungle views overlooking a river. Family-run and impeccably well maintained. Pricey rooms with outside bath. Doubles US$10. ❺

FOOD

Ubud lives up to its reputation for having Bali's best food. The city's international cuisine may beat out local fare for ingenuity and flavor. Trendy cafes, health food stores, and vegetarian restaurants are popular among expats—their quality and selection leave no doubt as to why. **Tino Drug Store,** on Jl. Raya Ubud near the Tourist Information Office, has a supermarket. (☎975 020. Open daily 8am-10pm.)

Casa Luna (☎977 409; www.casalunabali.com), on Jl. Raya Ubud. Serves not only the best bread in Bali, but also incredible entrees and desserts. Outdoor patio overlooks dense tropical forest. "Killer Brownie" concoction Rp9000. MC/V. ❸

Bali Buddha, on Jl. Jembawan, opposite the post office. Bright hippie colors and trendy drinks. Awesome place to sit and relax. Organic grocery, bakery. 3-level sitting area and a sandbox for the kids. Banana-date soy milkshake Rp6500. Open daily 7am-10pm. ❷

Ary's Warung, on Jl. Raya Ubud by the Tourist Information Office. Classy atmosphere and walls covered with black and white photos from Ary's backpacker days. Expensive, though the *paella* sets you back only Rp35,000. Open daily 7:30am-1am. MC/V. ❺

Cafe Mekar, Jl. Sugriwa 33. Minimal atmosphere, but cheap and hearty Indonesian food. Entrees under Rp15,000. Open daily 10am-11pm. ❷

Rumah Makan Senak, Jl. Hanoman 7. Cheap, clean, and basic, with *padang*-style sauces. Rice with tofu Rp1500, with beef Rp3500. ❶

SIGHTS

Ubud, with its classy cafes, souvenir shops, scenic boulevards, and nearby villages, is one giant sight in itself. Even so, you won't want to miss the city's rich museums or a stroll through the renowned Monkey Forest.

MONKEY FOREST. Ubud's most popular site is a miniature jungle in the middle of the city. Giant trees loom on either side of the trail, providing a habitat for about 200 monkeys. The monkeys aren't shy, so the problem isn't spotting them but keeping them from stealing your hat and sunglasses. Don't carry food—it's sure to attract some monkey business. Inside the forest is Ubud's **Pura Dalem** ("Temple of the Dead"), flanked by statues of ogres devouring children. *(On the southern bend of Jl. Monkey Forest. Open daily 8am-5:30pm. Rp10,000.)* Paths lead from the forest to southern villages, including **Nyuhkuning,** where you will find a **woodcarving museum.**

NEKA ART MUSEUM. Set in idyllic grounds overlooking a river valley, this museum displays an extensive collection of Balinese and Bali-inspired art. One of the museum's annexes, the Arie Smit Pavilion, houses work by the Dutch expat and examples of the "Young Artist" style he established. The photography archive collection preserves photographs of Balinese ceremonies from colonial times, while the back room has a megalomaniacal tribute to the museum's founder, Suteja Neka. All paintings are labeled in English. *(Follow Jl. Raya Ubud west until it crosses the river and becomes Jl. Raya Campuhan, then walk 1km farther until it turns right. ☎975 074. Open daily 9am-5pm. Rp10,000.)*

ANTONIO BLANCO GALLERY. The former home of the "Dalí of Bali" now showcases his art. Antonio Blanco's style was eccentric, expressive, exotic, and highly erotic. The house itself is a great exhibit; the Balinese architecture is done with

BALINESE COCKFIGHT

Cockfighting is still a cultural keystone in Bali, and the rituals surrounding it can be fairly lavish. On the day of the fight, the cock-master usually prepares a concoction of meat and purified jackfruit, a potent mix intended to thicken the blood and make the cock stand strong, tall, and ready. While cockfights are common in Ubud, they accrue additional meaning on the day of *tabah rah* (literally "pouring of the blood"), a sacred event in which demons are fed sacrifices.

After the Demangku (lay priest) gives the initial offering of rice wine, it's down to business for the chickens. The masters pass their birds around to be prodded, pulled, and plucked so that spectators can evaluate the strength and ferocity of each one. The owners then attach a 10-15cm long *taji* (blade) to each cock's leg. From there, it's winner-take-all. Bets are placed in codes; for example, the cry of "cok, cok, cok" in quick succession indicates 4:3 odds that the underdog will win. When the gong sounds, the cocks fly at each other in a frenzy of feathers and feet until the fatal blow is struck. The *pemsang taji* (master of the winning cock) wins the leg of the losing cock with the *taji* still attached. Hoisted up high, the winning cock lives to fight another day. The losing cock becomes dinner.

over-the-top pastel colors and a giant archway. *(Facing the Tourist Information Office, turn right down Jl. Raya Ubud and take the 1st left before the suspension bridge. ☎975 502. Open daily 8am-5pm. Rp10,000.)*

AGUNG RAI MUSEUM OF ART. Opened in 1996, ARMA has examples of traditional styles of Balinese painting and Bali's only works of the Russian-German artist Walter Spies. An open-air stage hosts traditional dances every night at 6pm. *(On Jl. Hanoman 500m south of Jl. Monkey Forest. ☎976 659. Open daily 9am-6pm. Rp10,000.)*

MUSEUM PURI LUKISAN. Built to preserve Bali's artistic heritage, the museum focuses on traditional painting styles and woodcarvings. At the center of the museum compound is a garden and lotus pool, complete with elegant shrine islands. *(Opposite the Tourist Information Office. ☎975 136. Open daily 8am-4pm. Rp10,000.)*

ENTERTAINMENT

To catch all the performances you want to see, go to the Ubud Tourist Information Center (see **Tourist Offices,** p. 180) and pick up a schedule of events as soon as you arrive in Ubud. Dance and *gamelan* are performed nightly throughout the city. Ubud's shows are well-rehearsed and elaborately staged. More natural and traditional performances are held in the surrounding area. (Shows 7pm. Tickets sold at the Tourist Information Center, tour agencies, and on the street. For shows in neighboring villages, the Tourist Information Center provides free transport.) Particularly worthwhile are the *wayang kulit* (shadow puppet shows) and the powerful *kecak* (monkey) dance, in which men beat out rhythms on their bare chests.

Ganesha Bookstore, on Jl. Raya Ubud, offers **gamelan lessons;** no previous musical knowledge is required. (☎963 59. Rp45,000.) **Balinese dance courses** are available at **Dewi Sekar Ayu,** Jl. Hanoman 26. With your back to Jl. Dewi Sita, turn right at the intersection with Jl. Hanoman and walk 100m. Take away a lasting memento from the **batik course** offered at the **Crackpot Gallery** on Jl. Monkey Forest. With the football field on the left, the Crackpot is 100m down. Design your own shirt or cushion cover. (☎973 411. Open daily 9am-8pm.) The **Meditation Shop,** on Jl. Monkey Forest, 400m from the Monkey Forest, allows visitors to observe **meditation workshops** for free. Stop by for details or join the daily 6-7pm meditation. (☎976 206. Open daily 5-9:30pm.) **Casa Luna Restaurant** offers **Balinese cooking classes.** Sign up early for the Tuesday **market tour,** as spots are limited to eight. (M and W 10am-2pm, Tu 8am-noon.

Rp100,000, includes 1 meal.) **Massages** and **skin treatments** are available at competitive prices. De-stress and rejuvenate at **Ubud Sari Health Resort,** Jl. Kajeng 35, at the end of the road. (Massages US$12 per hr.) The health food restaurant and juice bar serve high-quality dishes and drinks. (☎974 393. Open daily 8am-8pm.)

Although most of Ubud's draws are cultural or artistic, rafting and other adventure sport options exist for thrill-seekers. Contact **Sobek** (☎287 059), **Unda Adventures,** Jl. Raya Ubud 33 (☎977 169), or **Bali Adventure Tours** (☎751 292). You can also arrange whitewater rafting tours in the area. Daytrips include transportation and a meal (about US$60).

NIGHTLIFE

An artsy town inhabited by bohemian tourists, Ubud has a calmer nightlife than Kuta that tends to revolve around cafes rather than bars. The coffee shops on Jl. Dewi Sata are popular—both **Tutmak Warung Kopi Espresso** (☎975 754; open daily 9am-11pm) and **Kafe Batan Waru** (☎977 528; open daily 8am-midnight) fill up after dance performances end. A few places on Jl. Monkey Forest pit American movies against Balinese dancing. For the bar-goer, the **Sai Sai Bar** plays Top 40 (M) and reggae (Th). At the **Funky Monkey,** known for its mysterious trance atmosphere, patrons sit under a black-lit, star-studded ceiling. (☎390 3729. Open daily 11am-1am.) The **Jazz Cafe** is packed nightly and plays pop, jazz, and blues. (Open daily 11am-midnight.) As the evening winds down and the night starts, crowds head to **Putra Bar.** (Open daily from 11am until the last person leaves.)

DAYTRIPS FROM UBUD

Villages and rice paddies lie within 1km of Ubud, and any road leading away from the main drag will reward the explorer with breathtaking scenery.

GOA GAJAH (ELEPHANT CAVE). There never were elephants on Bali—Goa Gajah gets its name from the floppy-eared demon carved at its entrance. One section contains idols of Ganesha, the other *hingham* (phallic representations), and the Hindu trinity: Brahma, Vishnu, and Shiva. A thousand years of existence have taken their toll on Goa Gajah's carvings—many are worn. Whether it's worth the hassle of pushy souvenir hawkers is up to you. *(1km outside of Ubud on the road to Gianyar. Take a red or green* bemo *Rp3100.)*

YEH PULU. For the time being, the bas-relief of Yeh Pulu is vendor-free. The walk there passes an ungentrified Balinese neighborhood and terraced rice fields. *(From Gao Gajah, walk 1km away from Ubud; the route is clearly marked by signs on the road.)*

GUNUNG KAWI. **Tampaksiring village's** Gunung Kawi is a mysterious complex of tombs surrounding a central temple. The river divides the two cliff faces, hewn from rock in the 11th century. The area left of the stone archway is thought to be the burial site of King Anak Wungsu's four concubines. Across the river are the tombs of the king and his four wives. Beside the **royal tombs** lie a courtyard and a series of caves and rock passages. Gunung Kawi is best seen in the early morning or late afternoon, when visitors can avoid hordes of tourists and share the grounds only with local villagers who bathe in the river. **Titra Empul,** at the north end of Tampaksiring village, is a temple near natural spring pools. The holy water is said to have therapeutic power. *(Take an orange or blue* bemo *for Gianyar and get off in Bedulu. From there, take a* bemo *or* ojek *north to Tampaksiring. If you bike, prepare for an arduous 15km ride uphill that lasts about 1hr. Each sight Rp3100. Where necessary, sarong and sash are free.)*

ANIMAL PARKS. Two animal parks were recently built in **Singapadu.** The **Bali Reptile Park (Rimba Reptil)** features reptiles from around the world, including cobras and Komodo dragons, as well as a petting zoo with huge pythons and iguanas. The conditions here are much better than those in other zoos around Indonesia. *(☎ 299 344. Open daily 8:30am-6pm. Rp57,000.)* Next door is the **Bali Bird Park (Taman Burung),** home to exquisite landscaping and fantastic birds, including the endangered Bali starling. *(Catch a bemo toward Batubulan from Jl. Raya Ubud and tell the driver "tempat burung, di Singapadu" (the bird place in Singapadu). The trip takes 30min., and the bemo will probably let you off at the turn-off to Celuk. From there it's a 20min. walk to the parks. Private vans may be easier, but bargain hard—don't pay more than 5 times what the bemo ride would cost. ☎ 299 352. Open daily 8am-7pm. Rp57,000. Combination ticket for both parks Rp103,000.)*

LOVINA ☎ 0362

Get it all in Lovina: multicolor sunsets, great snorkeling, superb dolphin-watching, a black lava beach, exquisite Balinese seafood, and cheap accommodations. It's a refuge for ocean-goers who want to trade in the crowded beach scene for calmer waters and relaxed Balinese hospitality. But as dollars roll in, loud nightlife and the ever-growing tourist infrastructure increasingly threaten Lovina's serenity.

TRANSPORTATION

Buses: *Bemo* run west to **Gilimanuk,** where a ferry goes to **East Java,** and east to **Singaraja,** where further connections are available to anywhere in Bali. **Perama** (☎ 411 04), on the main road next to B.U. Warung, goes to: **Candi Dasa** (3hr.; Rp50,000); **Denpasar/Kuta** (2hr.; Rp40,000); **Gunung Batur** (2hr.; Rp20,000); **Ubud** (2½hr.; Rp40,000). For the cheapest rates but rougher, longer travel, take a *bemo* to Singaraja's **Banyuasri Terminal** and catch **public bus** connections there.

Rentals: Motorcycles (Rp40,000), **cars** (Rp80,000), and **bicycles** available. **Su-kha Rentals** (☎ 411 56), on Jl. Bhina Ria, rents bikes for Rp10,000 per day. Open daily 8am-10pm.

INDONESIA

ORIENTATION AND PRACTICAL INFORMATION

"Lovina" describes an 8km stretch of beach along the Bali Sea. The main road, **Jl. Singaraja,** runs parallel to the beach and is lined with restaurants and hotels. The strip includes several villages. From east to west, they are **Pemaron, Tukadmungga Anturan** (Happy Beach), **Kalibukbuk,** and **Kaliasem** (Lovina). Tourist activity is heaviest on Kalibukbuk and Kaliasem, through which **Jl. Bhina Ria,** marked by a dolphin statue, is the main road to the beach. A smaller beach road, **Jl. Pantai Mawar,** branches from Jl. Singaraja 300m farther east. In addition, there are many smaller, unnamed beach roads lined with bungalows and restaurants. As Jl. Singaraja leaves town, it heads east to **Singaraja** (10min.) and west to the ferry point of **Gilimanuk** (2hr.) and the **Bali Barat National Park** (1¼ hours).

Tourist Office: ☎ 419 10. On Jl. Singaraja in Kalibukbuk between B.U. Warung and Malibu Restaurant. Diving information and directions to local sights. Open M-Sa 8am-8pm, but phones may not be answered after 2pm.

Currency Exchange: Several moneychangers along the main road offer slightly better rates than at Singaraja's banks. Most are open until 9pm. Bank BCA 24hr. **ATM** on Jl. Singaraja in Kalibukuk (Cirrus/MC/PLUS/V).

Emergency: Police: ☎ 110. **Ambulance:** ☎ 118.

Police: (☎ 419 10). On Jl. Singaraja between Jl. Bhina Ria and Seririt.

Medical Services: Darma Bakti (☎412 11), on Jl. Singaraja, 1km to the right (with your back to the tourist office). English-speaking doctor. Open M-Sa 9am-noon and 5-7pm.

Pharmacy: Lovina has no pharmacy, but **Angosaka Mini-Market** (☎411 30), in front of Pasar Kalibukbuk on the main road, sells some medicine. Open daily 8am-10pm.

Telephones: Several **wartel** along Jl. Bhina Ria charge a small fee for international calling cards and are typically open daily 8am-midnight.

Internet Access: Internet cafes line Jl. Bhina Ria. Rp400 per min.

Post Office: GPO (☎413 92), on Jl. Singaraja. With your back to the tourist office, turn right (to the west) and walk 20min.; it's on the left. Open M-Sa 8am-2pm.

ACCOMMODATIONS

Most of Lovina's accommodations are clean and well attended. The price range comes from added amenities such as swimming pools, mosquito nets, and proximity to the beach. The region is known for its mosquitoes and for gigolos. Pick up a mosquito coil from a corner store; you're on your own with the gigolos. Expect to pay more for rooms during peak season.

Susila 2 Backpackers Hostel (☎410 80), on Jl. Bhina Ria. Best value in town. Clean, with mosquito nets, table, fan, and private bath. Breakfast included. Free use of next-door Angsoka Beach Inn's swimming pool. Singles Rp40,000; doubles Rp50,000. ❸

Angsoka Beach Inn (☎410 80), on Jl. Bhina Ria. Well-kept bungalows have ceiling fans, spacious porches, and comfy beds. Swimming pool, mosquito nets, and laundry service. Singles from Rp65,000; doubles from Rp80,000. ❹

Pulesti Beach Hotel (☎410 35), 25m from the beach on the main beach road. Hard to miss; the bright facade opens onto a landscaped pool with man-made waterfalls. Singles with fans and mosquito nets Rp75,000; doubles with open-air bath Rp90,000. ❹

Billibo Beach Cottages (☎413 55), opposite the post office on Lovina's western edge. Owner helps plan itineraries. Removed from tourist noise despite being just a few meters from the beach. Rooms with fans and screened windows from Rp75,000. ❹

Hotel Dupa (☎413 84), on the main road opposite the beach, is cheap, clean, and close to the action. The view of rice fields from upper rooms is worth the extra rupiah. Laundry service. Low rooms from Rp30,000; higher floors Rp10,000 extra. ❷

Mas Bungalows (☎417 73). Facing the tourist information office, walk 1km to the right or catch a *bemo*. Take a left on Jl. Lasiana; it's on the right. Shelter from downtown means quiet evenings. Singles Rp40,000; doubles Rp50,000. ❸

FOOD

Although Western dishes are available, Lovina's premier tastebud sensations are Balinese seafood and roasted duck. Establishments offering these local specialties have signs posted on their windows; be sure to order a few hours in advance for dinner, as roasting duck takes a while.

Kakatu Bar & Restaurant (☎413 44), on Jl. Bhina Ria right before the beach, has an international menu. Mexican, Indian, Balinese, and Thai dishes go for Rp15,000-30,000. Watch your meal prepared in the open-air kitchen. Open daily 8am-11pm. ❹

Bali Bintang (☎413 59), on Jl. Bhina Ria, offers steamed duck (order 1 day in advance). Otherwise, its menu is typical Western/Indonesian (meals Rp15,000-35,000). Open daily 8am-11pm. ❹

Poco Evolution Bar (☎415 35), on Jl. Bhina Ria, has occasional live music, but otherwise plays movies or music videos while you eat. Extensive Mexican and Indonesian menu; tasty nachos Rp10,000. Open daily 8am-midnight. ❹

B.U. Warung, next door to the Perama office, is cheap and unpretentious, with scrumptious *pepes*, tuna, and lemon papaya juice. Recommendations from past visitors displayed outside in myriad languages. Open daily noon-9pm. ❷

Waru Bali (☎415 53), at the end of Jl. Mawar, is the place for breakfast after chasing dolphins. It lives up to the fresh-seafood potential of its location directly on the beach. Fresh filet of the day Rp15,000-30,000, depending on size. Open daily 7am-10pm. ❸

SIGHTS AND ENTERTAINMENT

Lovina's main attractions are pre-dawn boat rides to see **dolphins** and midday **snorkeling** excursions. Local fishermen offer early-morning rides past the reef for roughly Rp20,000 with hard bargaining. If the dolphins don't show (only a 20% chance), the sunrise is a glorious consolation. Lovina's snorkeling is some of Bali's best, and shallow waters make it safe for beginners and children. **Scuba diving** possibilities abound. **Spice Dive** (☎415 09), on Jl. Bhina Ria, is a professional, PADI-certified outfit. Facing the tourist information office, head left 500m; it's on the left, opposite Joni's Restaurant. Spice offers full certification courses (4 days US$250), dives for beginners (US$65), and night dives. Waterskiing (Rp120,000) and parasailing (Rp89,000) are also offered. (Open daily 8am-8pm.) Fishing enthusiasts can rent boats, motorboats, traditional *sanpan* (bamboo-stabilized canoes), and other equipment on the beach. (Fishing with guide Rp20,000.)

Tiga Wasa village, a pleasant 1½hr. walk from the west edge of Lovina, makes ornate bamboo handicrafts. Follow the main road west past the post office; the turn-off is clearly marked on the left—it is then a 5km climb uphill. There are no official stores, but bamboo items are visible from the road. At the first house, a pathway to the right leads you to the **Sing Sing Waterfalls,** perfect for a dip. There are no signs, but ask and someone will help you. Although no problems have been documented, the village and waterfall are remote, so it's best to visit with a friend.

In the evening, the best place to catch a film is on top of **Mailaku Bar and Restaurant.** Seats fill up, so get there early. (Shows 6 and 8pm.) The hot, friendly bar in town is **Zigiz,** on Jl. Bhina Ria, with a full bar and live music every night. (Open daily 11am-midnight.) If you're still going strong, it's on to the **Malibu Cafe,** on the main road, for more live music, dancing, and partying until dawn.

DAYTRIPS FROM LOVINA

Though *bemo* transport to Lovina's three main excursions is both easy and cheap, many tourists still charter a car and driver in order to see all three at once. A full six-person *bemo* should cost Rp30,000.

GITGIT WATERFALL. The only thing more spectacular than the 40m high waterfall is the kilometer-long line of souvenir stalls. Local legend says that couples who swim together in the pools beneath the falls will soon separate. If you've been looking for a way out, here's your chance. *(Take a* bemo *from Sukasada Terminal in Singaraja toward Ubung Station (15min., Rp2000). At the sign to Gitgit, walk 1km along the path to the falls. Open daily 8:30am-5pm. Rp3800.)*

BANJAR BUDDHIST MONASTERY. On a forested hilltop with stunning ocean views, the monastery was damaged in the 1976 earthquake that flattened Seririt. The monks have since repaired it, and it once again houses Buddha sculptures and a lotus pool. Proper dress is required and can be borrowed from the shop next door. Talking is frowned upon in monastery grounds, and a donation (albeit a small one) over and above the admission fee is expected. *(Catch a* bemo *from Lovina toward Seririt and get off at Dencarik Village (15min.). Grab an* ojek *or* bemo *3km to the monastery; ask the driver to go to* tempat buddha. *Open daily 8am-6pm. Rp3000.)*

BANJAR HOT SPRINGS. Perhaps more popular than the monastery itself are the nearby hot springs. The pools, located among manicured gardens and palm trees, are often filled with tourists. *(Near the Banjar Buddhist Monastery.)*

GUNUNG AGUNG

For Balinese Hindus, Gunung Agung is the religious focus of the universe—the vantage point from which the gods observe human life in Bali and beyond. Some 3142m high and thought to be the son of the larger Mt. Semuru on Java, Gunung Agung dominates eastern Bali. An active volcano, it erupted most recently in 1963, killing thousands. Many believed the eruption to be a punishment for neglecting religious duty, so high priests were sent to appease the gods at Mt. Semuru. The most sacred temple complex on Bali lies on the southern slope of Gunung Agung and was untouched by the eruption as lava flowed down the other side of the mountain. It is only 6km from the village of Besakih, and once a year, in March or April, representatives from every town in Bali come to this "Mother Temple" for the Betara Turun Kabeh ceremony. The mountain gives the visitor a gorgeous view of the countryside and is a welcome escape from the bustle of more touristed areas.

TRANSPORTATION AND PRACTICAL INFORMATION. Public **bemo** run to Besakih from Klungkung (50min., Rp3500) and Amlapura (1½hr., Rp4000). While the official schedule is every 30min. until the last *bemo* at 3pm, it may be necessary to flag down local *ojeks* or trucks. A common place to change *bemo* is at Redang between Besakih and Klungkung. Here, *bemo* can be caught to Selat (30min., Rp2000) and onward to Amlapura. Though most foreign visitors to the area come on package tours from Candi Dasa and Ubud, tourist facilities do exist. Below the main parking lot and beyond the ticket booth is a *dinas pariwisata*, or **tourist information bureau.** (Open daily 7am-1pm.) When this is closed, you can make do with the maps at the end of the road leading to the temples.

ACCOMMODATIONS AND FOOD. If you're climbing Gunung Agung from Besakih, it is more convenient to stay at one of the many unmarked **losmen** ❶ that line the street from the car park to the hotel. Ask any local; he or she will show you where they are. Usually the *mandi* is shared and rooms are noisy, so bargain for a cheap price. Rp15,000 is fair. **Food** ❷ can be found at the base of the temple, after the parking lot. Hit the *satay ayam* cart before dark for a cheap, filling meal. Fruit and souvenir **vendors** ❶ line the path up to the temple; try the "snakeskin" fruit, found only in Bali.

SIGHTS. Pura Besakih (The Mother Temple) is the most sacred Balinese sanctuary. The largest temple complex in Bali, consisting of nearly 30 temples, it sits 900m above sea level on the southwestern slope of Gunung Agung, affording fantastic views of southern Bali. A pantheon of Hindu gods and goddesses is worshipped at Besakih; Shiva, Brahma, and Vishnu are most important. The Shiva temple is the first and largest. A phalanx of statues protect Shiva; those on the left represent *fandwa* (good spirits), the ones on the right *krawa* (bad spirits). The three gods sit inside the temple, with Shiva in the center, Brahma on the right, and Vishnu on the left. The temple at the far right belongs to Brahma and the one at the far left belongs to Vishnu.

The temple complex is extensive, and the lack of brochures or other English-language tourist information makes hiring a local guide tempting. The same organization that supervises the Gunung Agung guides also manages guides at Pura Besakih. The base price is Rp25,000, the only required fee, although the guide may want more than this as a tip or commission or as an extra *ojek* charge if you took the ride up. Decide on a price before setting out, as guides can demand outrageous sums after 5min. "tours" or a 1min. *ojek* ride to the temple, which they claim is 1km. It is important to note that the organization has a monopoly on tours of Besakih; if you bring an outside guide, you are still expected to pay the organization Rp25,000. Additionally, the central temple at Besakih is off-limits to all save worshippers. The path around the temple's rather low outer walls gives good views of the inside, however. Another option is to pay one of the temple "caretakers" at its front gates Rp20,000 to be let in to "worship" (and take pictures). While Rp20,000 may seem like a bargain, during the requisite prayer at one of Besakih's shrines, tourists are pressured to make "offerings" of Rp50,000 or more. (Complex open daily 6am-6pm. Admission Rp7500, parking costs extra.) Besakih's great annual festival, **Bhatara Turun Kabeh** (Gods Descend Together), occurs on the full moon of the 10th lunar month *(purnama kadasa)*, in March or April. This month-long festival, during which the gods of all temples in Bali take up residence in Besakih's main shrine, attracts thousands of worshippers from all over Bali.

TREKKING. Gunung Agung is a rigorous climb, dangerous in its steeper portions, but it's an exhilarating experience for the physically fit who want a perch from which to view Bali—provided they arrive at the summit before the clouds do. Climbers should aim to reach the top near daybreak, and definitely no later than 8am, when the mist begins to roll in. The two most popular climbs from Besakih and Selat require climbers to spend a night in the region. The one from the **Besakih** temple is a 4- to 6-hr., 6km ascent to the highest point on Gunung Agung; one should leave around 2am. Another route starting in **Selat** enables hikers to take transportation up to within 2km of the summit, although the climb itself is steeper. For this route, one should leave around 4am. A guide is necessary as parts of the trail are hard to find; arrangements should be made at least a day in advance. The **tourist police stations** in Besakih (☎230 82) and Selat (☎241 87) have lists of **guides** in the area, or you can ask at the temple's **ticket booth.** In Selat it's possible to shop around among different guides. **Gung Bawa Trekking** (☎243 79) is one reputable outfit. (1 person Rp100,000; 4 people Rp200,000. Guide and breakfast included. A night in Selat, Rp50,000 per person is required.) The guides from Besakih have been cartelized, and the standard price from there is US$50 for one person, US$75 for two, and US$100 for three. You cannot choose your guide; the cartel's members take turns on a strict system. Wear sturdy shoes and warm clothing, and bring a flashlight and something to eat. Beware of loose topsoil and falling rocks.

GUNUNG BATUR

The serene beauty of Lake Batur, which rests inside an enormous volcanic crater, masks the volcano's volatility. Gunung Batur's 1917 eruption demolished the village of Batur, killing 1400 and destroying 65,000 homes, curiously sparing only the town's temple. Believing this to be a sign of good fortune, the villagers remained in Batur until the eruption of 1926, which devastated the village again and convinced Batur residents to relocate to the outer rim. The most recent eruption occurred in 1994. The Batur region offers lavish scenery, but aggressive merchants, pricey accommodations, and mediocre food have marred many a traveler's stay here.

TRANSPORTATION. Orange **bemo** travel between Bangli and Penulisan (30min., Rp2000). To see Gunung Batur from the rim, get off at Penelokan. *Bemo* arriving in Gunung Batur stop in Kintamani, where connections run to other villages. **Taxis** and **ojek** also pick up passengers at the *bemo* stop. **Public buses** depart from Penelokan to other island destinations. Morning departures (7-9am) are most frequent. Travelers can also arrange for shuttle connections through transport agents along the main road in Toya Bungkah (also known as Tirta). Perama goes to: Kuta (3hr.; Rp30,000); Lovina (2½hr.; Rp20,000); Ubud (1½hr.; Rp20,000).

ORIENTATION AND PRACTICAL INFORMATION. The Batur area occupies Bali's northeast corner. The villages of **Penulisan, Batur, Kintamani,** and **Penelokan,** on the crater's west edge, are at the highest elevations and offer spectacular views. Of the two most frequented, **Kedisan** (on the west corner) runs boat trips across the lake, while **Toya Bungkah** (at the southern base of Batur) provides easy access to the mountains. The village of **Trunyan,** famed for its aboriginal Balinese residents, the **Bali Aga,** lies across the lake.

The **tourist office** is opposite the fork in the road at Penelokan. (Open daily 9am-3pm.) **Made "Dizzy" Darsana** (☎517 54), a guide who has been climbing Gunung Batur since he was 12, is the best resource for tourists intent on exploring. His knowledge of the area is unsurpassed and his English is excellent. Find him at Hotel Putra Mulya. Visitors should change money elsewhere, as rates here are poor. The **post office** is on Jl. Bayung Gede in Kintamani. (Open M-Th 8am-2pm, F 8am-11pm, Sa 8am-12:30pm.)

ACCOMMODATIONS AND FOOD. If circumstances require a night on the rim, **Miranda ❷** (☎520 22), 5km from Penelokan in Kintamani, has basic singles with *mandi* (Rp20,000) and doubles (Rp40,000). Be sure to get a room away from the main road. Toya Bungkah is the place to stay if you are climbing Batur or soaking up the view from the lake. **Arlinas Bungalows ❸,** in Toya Bungkah, arranges treks up Gunung Batur. (☎511 65. Singles Rp30,000; doubles Rp40,000.) **Wisma Tirtha Yatra ❷,** on the lake's edge, is the cheapest in town. Follow the main road from Penelokan and take the first right after the hot springs. (Singles Rp20,000.)

Segara Cafe ❷, opposite the boat harbor in Kedisan, prepares small but delicious fish for Rp10,000. (☎511 35. Open daily 7am-10pm.) If you are only visiting the rim, **Ramana ❷** has simple fare and an unforgettable view. Facing the Penelokan police station at the fork in the road, turn left and walk 5min. around the corner. (Open daily 10am-5pm.) Make sure to visit a neighborhood *warung* to taste *bantal* (pillow cake): coconut, rice, and banana or peanuts wrapped in a coconut leaf.

SIGHTS. Close to Kintamani in the village of **Penulisan,** at an altitude of 1745m, stands **Pura Tegeh Kuripan,** Bali's highest temple. Built in the 9th century, the temple offers exquisite views of Gunung Batur and Bali's north coast, and houses *linga* statues, symbols of the god Shiva. (Open during daylight. Rp3000.)

Tours of **Lake Batur** can be arranged from the harbor in **Kedisan.** From Kedisan, the boat goes to the **Bali Aga** village of Trunyan, **Trunyan cemetery** (both are accessible only by boat), and the hot springs at **Toya Bungkah.** (US$5 to swim. Open daily 8am-8pm.) The boat waits as long as you like at each stop. Standard tours last 1½-2hr. Guides are assigned and prices are fixed. (Rp196,500 for 1 person, includes admission and donation at Trunyan and the cemetery; prices go down with more people.) Beware of locals aggressively asking you for "donations."

The base of Gunung Batur is encircled by a road; the scenic walk around the base takes 4-5hr. Among the highlights is **Lucky Temple** in the northwest corner, which has miraculously survived all lava flows.

INDONESIA

TREKKING. A spectacular sunrise and a view of the entire Gunung Batur area is the reward for a steep, challenging climb. On a clear day you can even see Lombok's Gunung Rinjani peak. During the day, a guide is unnecessary, however, locals claim it is "illegal" to climb before sunrise without a guide. This "law" is enforced by the Komesariat Gunung Bator, the union of local guides, who harass and threaten independent climbers. All guides must be hired through the Komesariat. (☎523 62. Rp150,000 for up to 4 people; additional Rp20,000 for breakfast and ground transportation.) Many *losmen* charge commissions that can double or triple this price. Wear warm clothes.

To climb on your own, find the yellow "Welcome to Toya Bungkah" sign at the Kedisan side of town. A dirt road next to the sign heads toward the mountain. Take this road and, when it bears right after the houses, continue following it 70m. It will then bear left; follow it. When the road reaches a temple on the right, take the narrow footpath just before the temple wall and follow it around the temple into the woods. Stick with the path for 45min. until the trees stop and the terrain turns to volcanic rock, sand, and ash. From here, there are no real "paths"—the only way to go is up. Most day-trekkers leave between 8 and 9am. If you depart much later you might be shrouded in mist before reaching the summit (2 hours).

TIRTAGANGGA

Bali's Karangasem *rajah* built Tirtagangga in 1947 as a holiday retreat and named it after Hinduism's holiest river, the Ganges. Lying 13km northwest of Amlapura, Tirtagangga is home to multi-level ornate pools fed by a spring on the slopes of Gunung Agung. The idyllic pools offer the perfect setting in which to swim, rest, and rejuvenate yourself. (Open daily 6am-6pm. Admission to springs Rp3000, children Rp1600; privilege of swimming Rp6000, Rp4000; still cameras Rp1500, video cameras Rp2500.) **Bemo** run between Amlapura (15min.) and Tirtagangga (every 20min. until 6pm); Tirtagangga is also served by Perama shuttles: at the entrance to the parking lot, the **Good Karma Restaurant ❷** (☎224 45) sells tickets to destinations all over the island. The main road from Tirtagangga, leading away from Amlapura to **Culik** (30min.), passes some of the most picture-perfect scenery in Bali, from dense tropical forests to rugged arid mountains.

For those staying here overnight, the best value is at **Pondok Lembeh-Dukuh ❷**, three secluded bungalows on a hill. Getting there is an adventure. From the parking lot, head toward Singaraja on the main road until you come across an irrigation canal. Follow the canal through rice paddies and past houses until you reach the forest. A path there leads to a long stairway to Pondok Lembeh-Dukuh. Gorgeous views of the area more than compensate for the trek. (Breakfast included. Singles Rp30,000; doubles Rp40,000.) Cheaper accommodations can be found at **Kusuma Taya Inn ❸.** On the main road, with your back to the pools, turn left and climb up the stairs 300m. (☎212 50. Breakfast included. Rooms from Rp45,000, but prices fluctuate depending on availability.)

AMED (LIPAH)

The sleepy fishing village of Amed conjures up the Bali of 30 years ago. The village's quiet seaside air is conducive to relaxing on the warm lava-black beaches or snorkeling in the clear calm waters. Along the main road north of Amlapura/Tirtagangga, **bemo** pass the village of Culik, from which point they run to Amed up until 11am (after that, hire an *ojek*). Change money before arriving, as there are no banks or currency exchanges. No longer inexpensive, many once-budget places in Amed have gone up-market or closed down. It is hard to find single-person accommodation for under Rp60,000. The best option is the newly merged **Amed Beach Cottages/Amed Cafe ❹.** On the main drag at the center of town, its cheaper rooms are clean and well maintained, with fan, private bath, and mosquito nets. (Doubles including breakfast Rp80,000.) Similarly priced rooms with similar amenities are 50m farther away from the center of town at **Bamboo Bali Bungalows** ❹. (Singles Rp70,000; doubles Rp90,000.) **Warung Congkang Three Brothers** ❷ will cook your catch and serve it with good humor. Most menu entrees are under Rp15,000. (Open daily 8am-9pm.) The wreck of the **USAT Liberty,** torpedoed by a Japanese submarine during WWII, is at nearby **Tulamben,** and it makes both Tulamben and Amed meccas for divers. All accommodations rent diving and snorkeling equipment and normally offer dive packages. **Amed Dive Shop** comes highly recommended. (1-day, 2-dive packages US$85; introductory courses US$55. MC/V.)

CANDI DASA ☎0363

Once upon a time, there was a beach at Candi Dasa. The beach attracted tourists. The tourists needed bungalows. To build the bungalows, the locals needed cement. To make cement, the coral along the coast was ripped out and ground up. Without the coral to break the tides, the beach washed away. There is no beach in Candi Dasa anymore, but there are still bungalows. Despite the lack of a beach, watersports still attract tourists to the area. In addition, Candi Dasa is the only designated resort area in eastern Bali; budget accommodations and decent restaurants abound and are scant elsewhere in the area. In turn, Candi Dasa is not as lonely for a traveler as, for example, Amlapura or Amed. The sights in Bangli, Klungkung, and Amlapura, along with the two villages of Tenganan and Trunyan, are easily accessible from Candi Dasa and make a few nights here worthwhile.

TRANSPORTATION

Local Transportation: Bemo run regularly on the main road until 6pm. With your back to the water, *bemo* going right are headed to **Amlapura** (20min., with connections to Tirtagangga and Singaraja). Those going left are headed to **Padangbai** (20min.) and **Klungkung** (40min., with connections to Gianyar, Besakih, Penelokan, Batubulan). **Perama,** next to the police office at the west end of town, has daily morning bus departures to: **Denpasar/Kuta/Sanur/Airport** (Rp20,000); **Lovina/Singaraja** (3hr.; Rp50,000); **Penelokan/Kintamani** (2½hr.; Rp30,000); **Tirtagangga** (30min.; Rp20,000); **Ubud** (1½hr.; Rp15,000).

Rentals and Diving: Many accommodations and tour agencies rent **bicycles** (Rp10,000), **motor bikes** (Rp30,000), and **snorkeling equipment** (Rp15,000) by the day. **Baruna Dive** (☎411 85), at the center of Candi Dasa's main road, offers diving and snorkeling expeditions to surrounding areas.

ORIENTATION AND PRACTICAL INFORMATION

Candi Dasa is a 1km strip on Bali's east coast along the Klungkung-Amlapura Rd. With your back to the water, Klungkung is to the left (west) and Amlapura is to the right (east). Murky **Candi Dasa Lagoon** is on the seaward side of the main road at its east end; the local temple is directly across the lagoon. The waters of **Amuk Bay** border Candi Dasa on the south and hilly rice terraces to the north. From the sand, the island straight ahead is Nusa Penida (see **Nusa Lembongan,** p. 174).

Tourist Offices: Besides the plethora of private tourist information centers offering tours, rentals and shuttle services, there is the official (but not very useful) **Candidasa Tourist Information Office** (☎412 04). As you're walking on the main road with the lagoon on the right, the office is 1 house past the end of the lagoon. Open daily 8am-noon.

Currency Exchange: Moneychangers all along the main road offer reasonable rates and take traveler's checks. Most close by 9pm. 24hr. BNI **ATM** about 100m south of the lagoon on the beachside.

Emergency: Police: ☎ 110. **Ambulance:** ☎ 118.

Police: (☎ 416 77.) At the west end of the main road, where the road runs along the bay.

Hospital: Candidasa Clinic Laboratory & Apotik (☎ 413 21). Traveling on the road to Padangbai, it's 100m past the turn-off to Tenganan on the left. Open M-Sa. On Su, the area is serviced by a doctor from Denpasar (☎ 0361 463 093).

Telephones: Wartel at the center of town on the main road. International cash calls only. Open daily 8am-11pm. **HCD** booth at Tourist Information.

Internet Access: Scattered along the main road. Rp300 per min.

Post Offices: There are several **postal agents** on the main street, including **Asri's Convenience Store.** These may take mail and sell stamps, but no more. Open until 10pm. The nearest **post office** is 20min. away in Amlapura.

Postal Code: 80851.

ACCOMMODATIONS

Budget beachside bungalows run the length of Candi Dasa, but the quieter ones cluster at either end. In the low season, it's possible to negotiate cheaper prices.

Barong Beach Inn (☎ 411 27). When the road bends sharply to Amlapura at the east end, go straight and take the 1st right. Best price in town. Breakfast included. Singles Rp20,000; doubles Rp25,000; beachfront rooms (nothing special) Rp40,000. ❷

Ida Home Stay (☎ 410 96), on the west side of the lagoon. 6 private 2-story bungalows with large rooms, modern baths, and deck chairs on private verandas. Guests include many families. Rooms available for 4 or more. Breakfast included. Doubles Rp90,000; additional persons Rp25,000. ❺

Dewi Bungalows (☎ 411 66; fax 411 77), bordering the eastern side of the lagoon. Private bungalows with fans around a nice garden. Breakfast included. Laundry and massages. Singles Rp50,000; doubles Rp70,000. ❸

Rama Bungalows (☎ 417 78). With the lagoon on the right, walk down the path toward the beach; it's on the left. Set among gardens. Quiet, well-screened rooms with fan and full bath. Breakfast included. Laundry. Singles Rp40,000; doubles Rp60,000. ❸

FOOD

For a small strip along the beach, Candi Dasa offers a surprisingly large selection of culinary delights. Cheap tourist-oriented restaurants face the street. *Warung*, only slightly cheaper, cluster at the west end of town. More expensive restaurants have superior service and atmosphere, and are worth the extra cost. Some restaurants also serve as the source of nighttime entertainment with movies, dance floors, or live bands on weekends.

TJ's (☎ 41 540), across the street (to the west) from the lagoon, is on the exquisite side of food consumption with fantastic and creatively prepared daily catches (Rp30,000). Vegetarian friendly. MC/V. ❹

Raja's Bar and Restaurant, opposite Tourist Information on the main road, offers a large Western menu with burgers, pasta, and barbecue (Rp12,000-28,000). English-language movies—mainly Hollywood flicks—shown from 7:30pm. MC/V. Open daily 10am-11pm. ❸

Ciao (☎411 74), set back off the main road near Candidasa Beach Bungalows, features great Italian spaghetti, pizzas, and gelato. Entrees Rp13,000-25,000. Movies M-F 7:30pm. A band plays Sa and a dance floor opens up below the dining area. Open daily 9am-10pm. ❸

Warung Astawa (☎413 63), on the main road at the east edge of Candi Dasa. Seafood sampler (Rp18,000) with shrimp cocktail, fish in banana leaves, and dessert. Tropical atmosphere, bamboo furniture. *Legong* dancing at 7:45pm. Open daily 7am-10pm. ❸

Warung Srijati, opposite the Ida Home Stay west of the mucky lagoon. Nicer than a real *warung,* cheaper than a real restaurant. Tasty Balinese food for under Rp10,000. Fresh fruit juice. Vegetarian-friendly. Open daily 7am-10pm. ❶

Koeno (☎420 11), 150m south of the lagoon. Tiki decor, extensive seafood menu as well as pasta and curry offerings. Entrees Rp15,500-26,000. Live band at night. Open daily 8am-10pm. ❹

PADANGBAI ☎0363

Set along a crescent of narrow beach, the village is a quiet pocket of colorful outriggers, ocean-view bungalows, and cheap seafood. For many, Padangbai is no more than a busy transit point on the way to Lombok. Yet, for a modest port village, Padangbai has much to offer, including diving, snorkeling, and convenient swimmable beaches, as well as the opportunity to fish for your dinner.

TRANSPORTATION. Buses whisk travelers to destinations on Bali, Lombok, and Java. Prices include ferry fees. Tickets can be purchased along the water or at many accommodations. Perama (☎414 19), at Dona cafe opposite the *bemo* on the entrance road, runs several shuttles to: Bangsal (5½hr.; Rp30,000); Gili Air (7hr.); Gili Meno (7hr.); Gili Trawangan (7hr.; Rp60,000); Kintamani (2hr.; Rp30,000); Kuta (2½hr.; Rp25,000); Mataram (5hr.; Rp30,000); Sanur (2hr.; Rp25,000); Senggigi (5½hr.; Rp30,000); Ubud (1hr.; Rp15,000). Various **commercial buses** run to: Jakarta; Yogyakarta/Surakarta; Probolinggo/Surabaya. **Ferries** run continuously to **Lombok** (5hr.; every 1½hr.; Rp8500, 1st class A/C Rp17,000). **Motorcycle** (Rp30,000) and **car rentals** (Rp80,000) are available through **Hotel Puri Rai** and **Kerti Beach Inn.** *Bemo* wait at the ferry terminal end of the entrance road.

WARNING. When waiting for a boat, keep your luggage with you at all times and do not let the porters take it. Some have been known to threaten to throw it overboard unless you pay a ridiculous amount (on the order of Rp100,000).

ORIENTATION AND PRACTICAL INFORMATION. Padangbai is 50km northeast of Denpasar, off the main road between Klungkung and Candi Dasa. At the end of the road entering Padangbai are the harbor gates and the overbearing ferry terminal. Facing the terminal, in the left corner closest to the water, is **Jl. Segaran.** This crosses a parking lot and runs into **Jl. SilIyutl,** which continues to head away from the port. Most accommodations lie off Jl. Segaran and Jl. Siliyuti. A helpful **tourist office** at the front of the ferry terminal can direct you toward the best snorkeling and beaches in the area, but has no printed information. **Snorkeling equipment** is available everywhere. **Moneychangers** abound on the beach boardwalk and market; most take traveler's checks. A *wartel* on the street leading from the harbor gates toward the main road to Candi Dasa offers cash-only **international calls** and faxes. (Open daily 6am-12:30pm.) **Ozone Cafe** has **Internet** access (Rp300 per min.). To get to the **post office,** walk to the harbor gates next to the ferry, walk straight ahead, and take the first left at the **police station** (open daily 7am-11pm). The post office will be 50m ahead on the right. (*Poste Restante.* Open M-Th 8am-2pm, F 8-11am, Sa 8am-12:30pm.) **Postal Code:** 80872.

ACCOMMODATIONS AND FOOD. Several cheap accommodations lie to the left of Jl. Siliyuti at the point where it meets Jl. Segara. **Parta ❸** is the most well maintained. Rooms are worth the extra rupiah for the space, privacy, fan, and private bath. (☎414 75. Singles with fan Rp40,000; doubles Rp50,000, with hot water Rp70,000.) The **Bagus Inn ❷** has basic rooms with ceiling fans and *mandi*-style baths. (☎41 398. Breakfast included. Singles Rp25,000; doubles Rp30,000.) For a bed closer to the water, continue away from the port along Jl. Siliyuti and the beach. At **Topi Inn ❷**, try for one of the three rooms that have private *mandi*. (Singles Rp30,000; doubles Rp40,000; bungalows Rp50,000.) **Kerti Beach Inn ❸**, next to Hotel Puri Rai, has clean rooms and well-designed bungalows with an open-air lounge room and mosquito nets. (Breakfast included. Singles Rp30,000; doubles Rp50,000; bungalows Rp60,000.) **Padangbai Beach Home Stay ❹** has rooms with private bath and fan, as well as bungalows with A/C. All have springy beds and mosquito nets. (☎479 46. Breakfast included. Basic singles Rp50,000, with A/C Rp90,000; doubles Rp80,000/Rp120,000.)

Padangbai's seafood is exceptional—prawns, shark, and barracuda are local specialties, served with generous amounts of garlic. The cheapest prices are found away from the water and at hotel-attached restaurants. **Kondedes Restaurant ❷** on Jl. Silayuti, has a sizable menu of cheap, tasty Indonesian food. The second-floor seating has a good view of the ocean or, if you prefer, a better one of the graveyard. Laid-back **Ozone Cafe ❸**, before Parta, has a backpacker-friendly atmosphere, loud music, and an owner who will beat you at Scrabble. (Scrumptious pizzas from Rp15,000.) **Puri Rai Restaurant ❹**, attached to Hotel Puri Rai, is a classy tiki bar. On the water, **Warung Pantai Ayu ❷** is cheap. (Garlic prawns Rp15,000.)

OOOOH—BARRACUDA! Welcome to Bali, land of fresh seafood. From shark to shellfish, amazing meals from the ocean are prepared everywhere around the island; off the east coast, one specialty is barracuda. Flooding the Lombok Strait in May, these fish feed locals and tourists alike until August. Local fishermen, mostly in traditional narrow boats, catch the 1-1.5m long, 10-15kg fish. On shore, the barracuda are cleaned and gutted. Their bodies are then sliced like a loaf of French bread, into thick round fillets. A 10kg fish provides approximately 40 fillets for serving. Chefs then fire up the grill. The flaky white barracuda is dipped in a sauce of garlic, salt, pepper, and melted butter. The fillet is served with three sauces: the first, a spicy chilli sauce, the second, only slightly milder, is *sambal matah,* an onion and chilli sauce served cold, the final sauce is similar to the grilling sauce: finely minced garlic with butter and spices. Each one brings out the fish's flavor. Whichever sauce you decide on, the thick barracuda fillets, often served with rice and vegetables, make a filling meal. Prepare your cutlery and appetite, and enjoy!

Before eating barracuda, it is advisable to check that it comes from waters at low risk of ciguatera poisoning. The Lombok Strait's barracuda are not currently considered especially dangerous, but get the latest information to be safe.

SIGHTS AND BEACHES. Padangbai offers a surprisingly large range of water-recreation options. **Equator,** the local PADI- and CAMS-certified dive shop, offers dives in nearby waters (full day US$50, cash only). PADI-certified **Geko Dive** in Pandan Restaurant offers similar packages. All-inclusive diving packages to

Nusa Penida cost US$70. If you can find a group of four or more divers, tagging along to snorkel is only US$10, including lunch. The best swimming option is the popular **Bias Tugel.** With your back to the ferry port, turn left at the police station. The turn-off to Bias Tugel is 50m ahead on the left before the road rises steeply. Another popular and more convenient recreation area is **Blue Lagoon,** at the opposite end of Jl. Siliyuti from the ferry-port bay. The turn-off to the Blue Lagoon is immediately after Topi Inn. The best place from which to explore the surrounding rocky coastline is **Pura Silayukti,** the temple commemorating the man who introduced the caste system to Bali. It's a 5min. walk along the sealed road from Topi Inn. When the road forks, head to the left; Pura Silayukti is the temple to the left. From high on the ridge, dirt paths lead to the shoreline, where several *pantai kecil* (little beaches) and interesting rock pools can be found. Immaculate and deserted, these beaches provide solitude and serenity.

NUSA TENGGARA

LOMBOK

Since the riots of January 2000, tourists have been wary of visiting this island; however, as its safety rating has improved, travelers seeking relief from Bali and its excessive tourism are beginning once again to flock to Lombok's serenity. The resort life of Senggigi is well known, the trek through Gunung Rinjani is more than just a touristy sleep-over, and a simple unhurried stroll through rice and tobacco paddies in Tetebatu is exquisitely calm. Meanwhile, the ever-accessible diving and snorkeling keep the adventuresome ferrying in

THE VIEW FROM ABOVE

The Lowdown: Bali's quieter, gentler sibling.

Major towns: Greater Mataram, Senggigi, Tetebatu

Highlights: Climbing Gunung Rinjani, walking through the rice paddies of Tetebatu, riding the surf in Kuta.

GETTING TO LOMBOK

BY PLANE. Lombok's **Selaparang Airport** (☎622 987, ext. 108) marks the northern edge of Mataram, the official capital. **Taxis** have set rates and are in front of the airport (Mataram Rp9500; Senggigi Rp15,000). **Bemo** go to Ampenan (Rp1000). **Merpati** flies to: **Bima** (1¼hr.; Th, Sa; Rp475,500); **Denpasar** (30min.; 3 per day; Rp240,000); **Jakarta** (1 per day; Rp.888,000) via **Yogyakarta** (1 per day; Rp530,000); **Surabaya** (M, W, Sa; Rp380,900). **Silk Air** flies to **Singapore** (Tu, F-Su; one-way US$225, round-trip US$350). International departure tax is Rp60,000; domestic departure tax is Rp8000.

BY BOAT. Ferries cross from **Lembar,** Lombok to **Padangbai,** Bali (4-5hr., every 1½hr., Rp8500), and a similar ferry system runs between **Labuhan,** Lombok and **Poto Tano,** Sumbawa (1½hr.; every hr.; Rp10,000). The **Mabua Express** (☎811 95) operates daily between Lembar and **Benoa,** Bali (2½hr., returns 5:30pm, US$25-30). Two **PELNI** ships dock at Lembar. The **KM Awu** departs once every two weeks to: **Berau; Denpasar** (Rp21,500); **Dili; Ende; Kaladahi; Kupang; Makassar; Maumere; Nunukan; Tarakan;** and **Waingapu.** The **KM Tilongkabilu** leaves every two weeks and travels to: **Bima** (Rp53,000); **Denpasar; Kumai; Labuanbajo** (Rp79,300); **Makassar; Sampit;** and **Surabaya.** Buy tickets and confirm ship arrival dates at the harbor in Lembar or at the PELNI office on Jl. Industri (☎637 212), opposite Hotel Nitour in Ampenan.

BY BUS. Buses to destinations on other islands depart Sweta Terminal, on the east side of greater Mataram (see below), around noon to: **Denpasar** (7hr., Rp50,000); **Jakarta** (Rp175,000); **Yogyakarta** (Rp135,000); and **Surabaya** (19hr., Rp85,000). **Langsung Indah** has the most comfortable buses, departing daily at noon and 2:30pm to: **Bima** (13hr., Rp44,400); **Dompu** (11hr., Rp40,500); **Sape** (15hr.; Rp47,500). There are also buses to: **Jereveh** (Rp20,000); **Lonyuk** (Rp28,000); **Plompang** (Rp30,000); and **Taliwerg** (Rp15,000-20,000). Confirm times a day in advance. Buy tickets for night buses 24hr. before departure. Long rides often include dinner.

GETTING AROUND LOMBOK

Buses departing from Sweta Terminal cost less than *bemo* and run to the same places. **Taxis** run in Greater Mataram, but aren't common outside the city. **Ojek** save time but not money. Combined, buses and **bemo** will run almost everywhere. Beware of empty *bemo*—drivers will assume that you are chartering the vehicle. **Cidomo**—horse-drawn carts with car tires and axles—ferry people around small locales. They're ubiquitous on Lombok, even in cosmopolitan Mataram. If you'd rather get yourself around, **motorcycle** rentals are everywhere, and you can rent a **car** from **Rinjani Rent Car,** on Jl. Panca Usaha in Mataram. (☎632 259. Suzuki Jimmys Rp75,000.) The following are Lombok's major terminals, in Greater Mataram:

Sweta, on the east side of Greater Mataram. Lombok's transportation hub. Serves: **Bangsal** (1½hr.); **Bayan** (20min.); **Labuhan** (2hr.); **Lembar** (1hr.); **Greater Mataram** (10min.); **Narmada** (20min.); **Praya** (1hour).

Ampenan, north of the city's main intersection. Serves as a stop for Mataram routes from Sweta Terminal, with *bemo* running north to **Senggigi** (15min.).

Praya, in the town center. Serves the south: **Kuta** (30min.); **Sengkol** (30min.).

Narmada, in the center of town. Serves central Lombok: **Masbagik** (2hr.); **Pomotong** (1hr.); **Suranadi** (15min.); **Tetebatu** (2hr.); and points east of Greater Mataram.

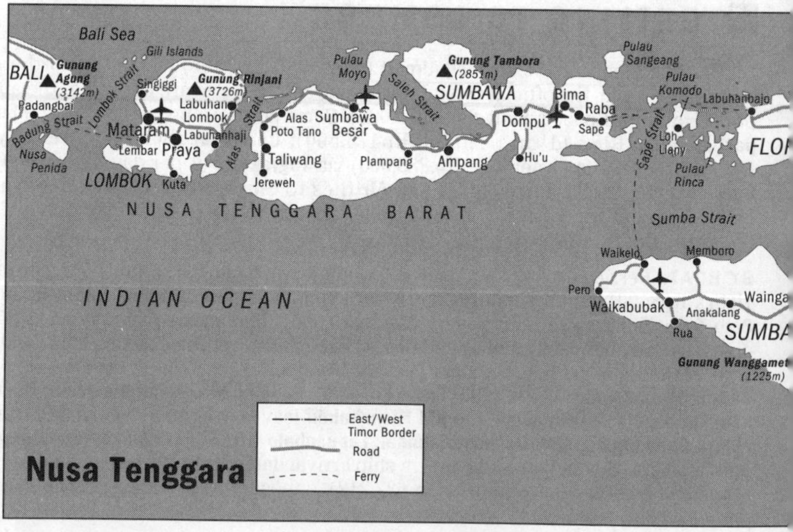

GREATER MATARAM ☎0370

Home to 10% of Lombok's 2.5 million people, Greater Mataram consists of three cities—Ampenan, Mataram, and Cakranegara (Cakra for short)—along 10km of one wide street. The worst rioting in January 2000 ravaged hot and dusty Ampenan. As you browse the art and jewelry stores, you won't be able to ignore the burnt ruins of churches that serve as a sobering backdrop. As the capital of Nusa Tenggara Barat, Mataram has seen some development and investment. In the mid-90s it was busy transforming itself from sleepy provincial headquarters to a modern city. The currency crisis and the riots of 2000 halted that process. Now Mataram is in the process of reintroducing tourism and enlivening shopping and nightlife—although outside night markets, nightlife is, so far, nonexistent.

ORIENTATION AND PRACTICAL INFORMATION

Traffic courses through Greater Mataram on two parallel roads. *Bemo* circle between terminals at both ends. **Jl. Yos Sudarso** goes from Ampenan to Cakra, then turns into **Jl. Langko, Jl. Pejanggik,** and finally **Jl. Selaparang. Jl. Tumpang Sari** runs east-west from Cakra to Ampenan, one block south, and becomes **Jl. Panca Usaha, Jl. Pancawarga,** and finally **Jl. Pendidikan.** Giant, official-looking buildings flank the tree-lined streets of **Mataram,** the administrative center. Outside Cakra are the transportation hubs of **Sweta** and **Bertals.**

Tourist Office: Provincial Tourist Service, Jl. Singosari 2 (☎634 800), off Jl. Majapahit near central post office. Friendly staff dispenses maps and a plethora of pamphlets. Open M-Th 7am-2pm, F 7-11am, Sa 7am-12:30pm.

Tours: Perama, Jl. Pejanggik 66 (☎635 928), east of the hospital. Runs buses and cruises to Flores, Java, and Sumbawa. Many accommodations also offer tour and shuttle services.

Currency Exchange: Moneychangers and **ATMs** abound at Ampenan's main intersection, on Jl. Pejanggik in Cakra, and opposite Sweta Terminal on Jl. Sandubaya. **BCA** (☎632 588), on Jl. Pejanggik, has a 24hr. **ATM** (Cirrus/MC/PLUS/V). Open M-F 8am-2:30pm.

Emergency: Police: ☎110. **Ambulance:** ☎118.

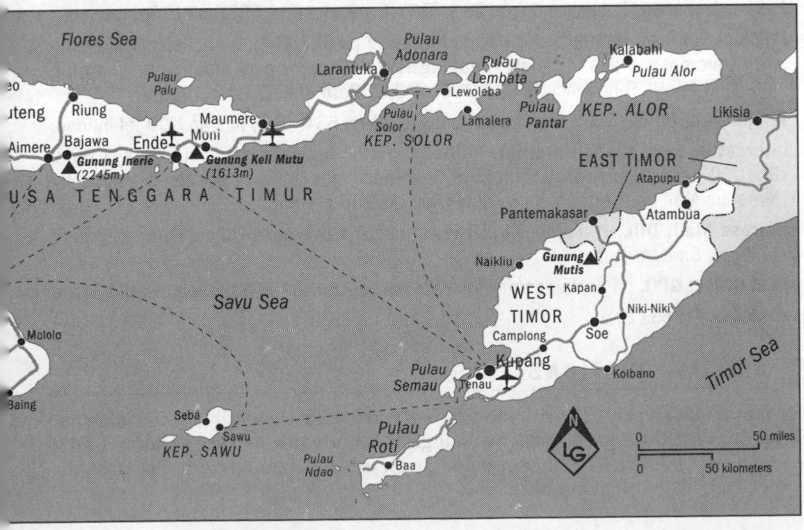

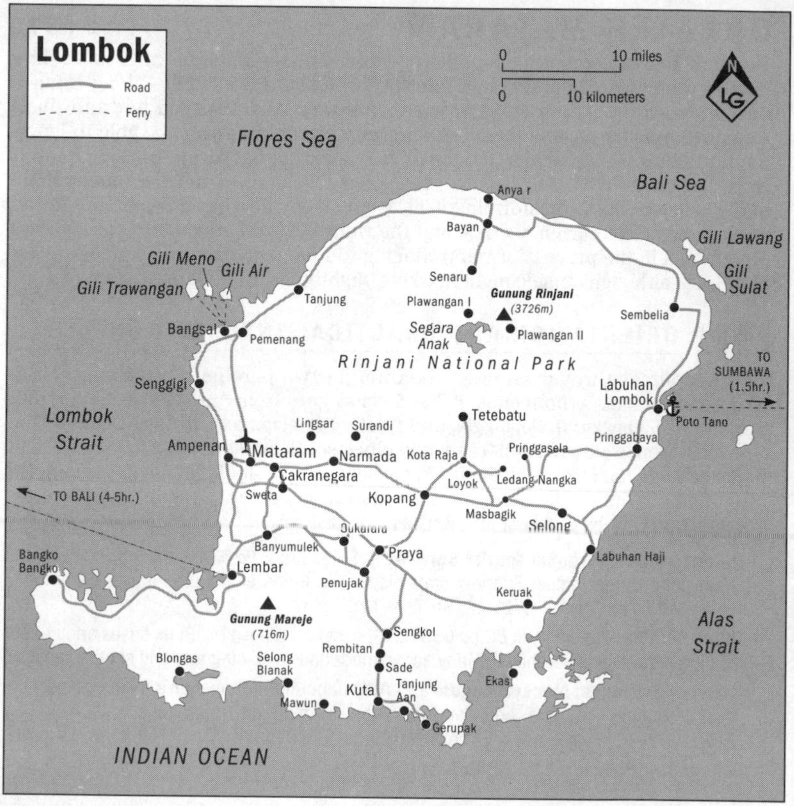

Police: Ampenan, Jl. Langko 17 (☎633 733). **Sweta** (☎632 682), on Jl. Selaparang.

Medical Services: Rumah Sakit Umum Mataram (☎622 254), on Jl. Pejanggik, east of the Governor's office. English-speaking female doctor available in the morning. Attached **Apotik** (pharmacy; ☎637 326). MC/V. Both open 24hr.

Telephones: The big **Telkom office,** Jl. Langko 23 (☎634 466), has an **HCD** telephone.

Internet Access: Global Internet, in the strip mall opposite the Lombok Raya Hotel. Rp1000 per hr. Open daily 8am-8pm. **Internet** cafes are also scattered around the Mataram Mall area, but are more expensive (Rp200 per min.).

Express Mail: DHL, Jl. Pejanggik 20, west of the Governor's Office. Open M-F 8am-4:30pm, Sa 8am-1pm.

Post Office: GPO, on Jl. Majapahit. *Poste Restante.* Open M-Th 8am-3pm, F-Sa 8-11am. **Postal Code:** 83114.

ACCOMMODATIONS

Accommodations pander equally to tourists and locals. Generally comfortable and cheap, they are far from the beach and nightlife, both of which are easier to find in **Senggigi** (see p. 202). The cheapest lodgings, in Ampenan along **Jl. Koperasi,** are noisier and dustier than in Cakra.

Shanti Puri Hotel and Restaurant, Jl. Maktal 15 (☎632 649), 100m south off Jl. Pejanggik in east Cakra. Comfort exceeds price. Friendly staff, cozy restaurant. Clean rooms with fan. Singles and doubles with *mandi* Rp30,000, with toilets Rp40,000. ❸

Inap Keluagra Oka (Oka), Jl. Repatmaja 5 (☎622 406), 200m south of Jl. Pejanggik at Bank Danamon in Cakra, on a side street. Shady courtyard and *losmen*-quality rooms. Friendly staff. Breakfast included. Singles Rp20,000; doubles Rp25,000. ❷

Karthika II Hotel, Jl. Subak 6 (☎641 776), north of Jl. Pejanggik. Rooms around a bright courtyard on a surprisingly quiet side street near the heart of Cakra. Breakfast included. Singles Rp32,500, with A/C and TV Rp60,000; basic doubles Rp37,500/Rp70,000. ❸

Losmen Ayu (☎621 761), on Jl. Nursiwan, 100m south of the BCA ATM in Cakra at the corner with Jl. Panca Usaha, has clean rooms. Free unlimited tea and coffee. Singles and doubles with *mandi* Rp25,000, with toilets Rp40,000, with A/C Rp75,000. ❷

Hotel Wisata, Jl. Koperasi 19 (☎269 71), in Ampenan. A variety of rooms just secluded enough to get away from street noise. Close to antique and art shops. Singles with bath Rp35,000; doubles Rp40,000. ❸

FOOD

In Cakra, there are a variety of *warung* and numerous scrumptious night stalls. The regional specialty is spicy *sasak taliwang*, food smothered in hot chili peppers. If you can't handle the heat, ask for it *"kurang pedes"* (less spicy) and ignore the snickers.

Restaurant Betawi, at the intersection of Jl. Koperasai, Jl. Saleh Sungkar, and Jl. Yos Sudarso, in a "Colonial Grand Style." Famous among expatriates, Betawi had us all worried when it closed briefly due to the 2000 riots. Thankfully, it quickly resumed offering up some lip-smacking dishes from its balcony overlooking the heart of Ampenan. Red snapper with Rico Rico (sweet tomato with chilli) sauce Rp22,000. ❹

Suharti Sate House, Jl. Maktal 9 (☎637 958), next to the Shanti Puri. Run by Romy Rahiem, a Mataram-renowned Indonesian master chef. Tasty *nasi goreng* (Rp5000). Open daily 9am-10pm. ❷

Kania Satu-Rumah Makan Taliwang, on Jl. Pejanggik, opposite Bank BCA in Cakra. Spicy Lombok-style food. *Ayam goreng taliwang* Rp15,000. Open daily 7am-11pm. ❸

Aroma, Jl. Palapa 12, in west Cakra, south of Jl. Pejanggik at Bank BTN. Clean, quiet, quick, and cool. Large portions of Chinese seafood. Young pigeon Rp18,000. ❸

INDONESIA

SHOPPING

If it's modernity—escalators, bright lights, A/C, and fixed prices—you seek, then the **Mataram Mall** (formerly Glinoya Shopping Center), on Jl. Pejonggik, is your place. Here you'll find clothes and electronics, and a bookstore with English, French, and German texts to boot. If you prefer a noisy rush and bargaining, then the **market** in Cakra is at the Mataram Complex farther up Jl. Pejanggik and condenses at the intersection of Jl. Pejanggik and Jl. Gede Ngurah. It offers similar items, minus the foreign books, for cheaper prices. For art, woodcraft, jewelry, and antiques, go to **Jl. Saleh Sungkar,** in Ampenan center. One art shop certainly worth the trip is the **Yufi Artshop,** Jl. Saleh Sungklar 22, which has brilliant and affordable pottery in all shapes and sizes. Much more art for sale can be found near the beginning of **the road to Senggigi** from Ampenan.

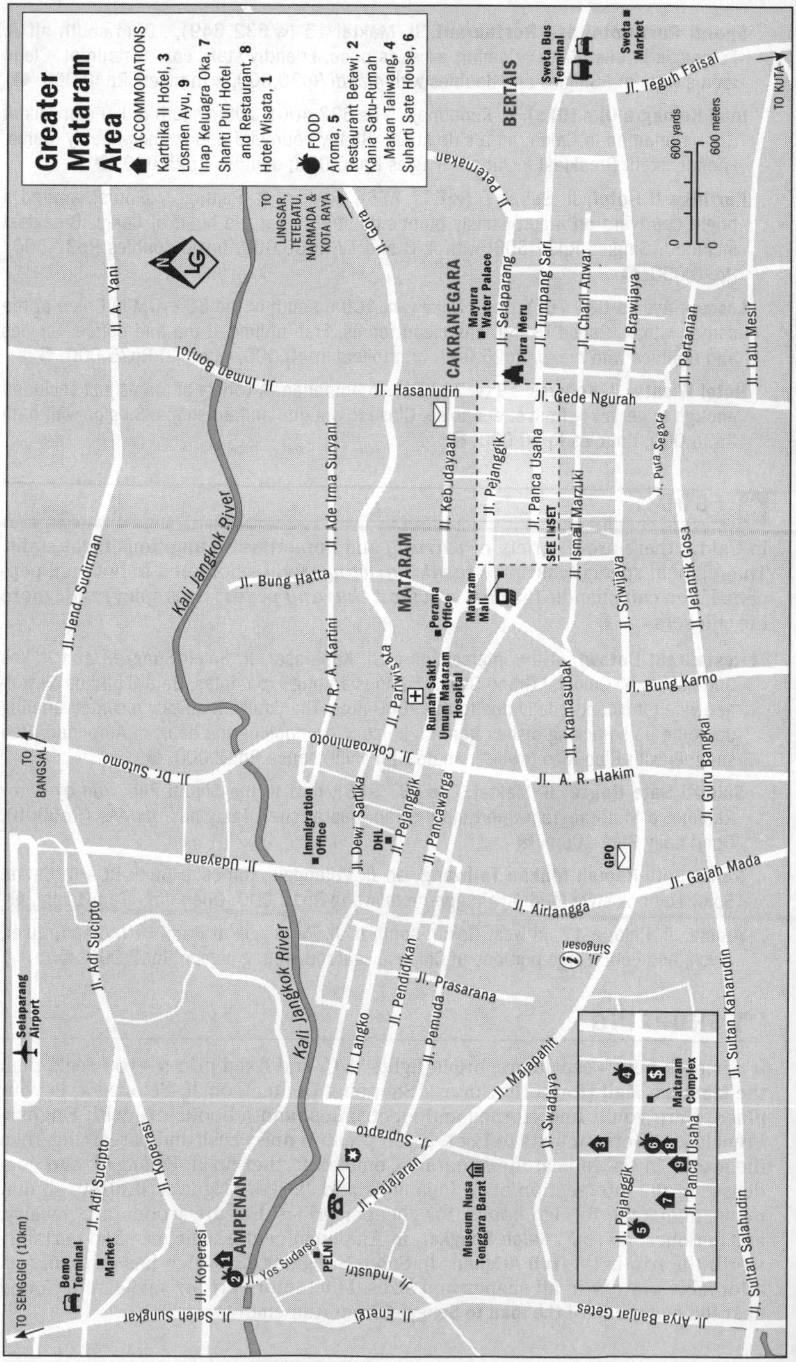

Greater Mataram Area
ACCOMMODATIONS
Karthika II Hotel, 3
Losmen Ayu, 9
Inap Keluagra Oka, 7
Shanti Puri Hotel and Restaurant, 8
Hotel Wisata, 1
FOOD
Aroma, 5
Restaurant Betawi, 2
Kania Satu-Rumah Makan Taliwang, 4
Suharti Sate House, 6
TO LINGSAR, TETEBATU, NARMADA & KOTA RAYA
TO SENGGIGI (10km)
TO BANGSAL
TO KUTA
600 yards
600 meters
Selaparang Airport
Bemo Terminal
Market
AMPENAN
PELNI
Museum Nusa Tenggara Barat
Immigration Office
DHL
GPO
Rumah Sakit Umum Mataram Hospital
Perama Office
Mataram Mall
MATARAM
CAKRANEGARA
Mayura Water Palace
Pura Meru
BERTAIS
Sweta Bus Terminal
Sweta Market
SEE INSET
Mataram Complex
Kali Jangkok River
Jl. Saleh Sungkar
Jl. Koperasi
Jl. Adi Sucipto
Jl. Yos Sudarso
Jl. Industri
Jl. Energi
Jl. Pajajaran
Jl. Suprapto
Jl. Langko
Jl. Pendidikan
Jl. Pemuda
Jl. Prasarana
Jl. Majapahit
Jl. Swadaya
Jl. Singosari
Jl. Airlangga
Jl. Gajah Mada
Jl. Udayana
Jl. Dewi Sartika
Jl. Pejanggik
Jl. Pancawarga
Jl. Dr. Sutomo
Jl. Cokroaminoto
Jl. Pariwisata
Jl. R. A. Kartini
Jl. A. R. Hakim
Jl. Kramasubak
Jl. Bung Karno
Jl. Guru Bangkal
Jl. Sultan Kaharudin
Jl. Sultan Salahudin
Jl. Arya Banjar Getes
Jl. Jend. Sudirman
Jl. Bung Hatta
Jl. Ade Irma Suryani
Jl. Kebudayaan
Jl. Panca Usaha
Jl. Ismail Marzuki
Jl. Sriwijaya
Jl. Jelantik Gosa
Jl. Pura Segara
Jl. Hasanudin
Jl. Gede Ngurah
Jl. Selaparang
Jl. Tumpang Sari
Jl. Charil Anwar
Jl. Brawijaya
Jl. Pertanian
Jl. Lalu Mesir
Jl. Iman Bonjol
Jl. A. Yani
Jl. Gora
Jl. Peternakan
Jl. Teguh Faisal

SIGHTS

In the small fishing village on the north side of Ampenan is **Pura Segara.** Off Jl. Yos Sudarso, the temple is still used for Hindu burial ceremonies. The front gates are locked; sometimes the gate around back is open, allowing a better look. Regardless, the surrounding fishing village warrants the trip. Pura Segara is best visited early, when the rugged foothills of Gunung Rinjani are visible. A **Chinese cemetery,** on the way to Pura Segara, is an exhibition of above-ground tombs enshrined in ornate tiles of Chinese characters and colors. Sections of the grounds have gone to seed, though, and it is not unusual for locals to graze cattle inside.

In 1894, Balinese and Western Sasaks crept to the walls of the **Mayura Water Palace,** fired on Dutch soldiers camped there, and drove them out of this former Balinese court. Deteriorating fountains, statues, and cannons are all that remain (entrance Rp5000). Across Jl. Pejanggik from the Water Palace is **Pura Meru,** Lombok's *grande dame* of Balinese temples, with 33 shrines and three big, plain, empty pagodas. Commissioned by Anak Agung Made Karang of the Singosari Kingdom in 1772, the three pagodas honor the Hindu trinity of Brahma, Vishnu, and Shiva, and the three volcanos, Agung, Bromo, and Rinjani. Sashes are lent out for free, but the entrance fee is Rp10,000.

Museum Nusa Tenggara Barat, on Jl. Panji Tilar Negara in southeast Ampenan, displays 1239 palm-leaf Indonesian manuscripts and exhibits in English on the history, geology, and cultures of Lombok and Sumbawa. One of the curators speaks English and leads tours. (Open Tu-Su 8am-4pm. Rp1000.)

DAYTRIPS FROM GREATER MATARAM

NARMADA. On the south side of the main road in Narmada is the **Pura Kalasa Water Palace,** a temple built into a hill and encircled by three pools. In 1805, King Ana Agun Gedengurah built the complex as a reproduction of Gunung Rinjani when he was too old to make his annual climb of the mountain. The central pool replicates Lake Segara Anak, the small pools represent the cascading hot springs near the lake, and the temple itself, built at the top of the hill, symbolizes Gunung Rinjani's peak. The water palace sated the king's lust; the Balinese monarch would watch his harems bathe in the pool from his small two-room house on the hill: one room for his wife and one for his concubine. Guides (fairly useless) will approach you near the entrance. The water palace is more popular with the locals than with tourists—it's packed on weekends. The main pool, originally for the king's use only, is now complete with starting blocks and lane markings and is used for regional and local swim meets. Locals use the lower pools for swimming and laundry, while it is believed that the higher pool's water gives eternal life if drunk. Tourists can join in the splashing for a small fee (Rp1000, Rp1000 extra to bathe). During the full moon of the 5th Balinese lunar month in December, townspeople give live ducks and other offerings to the lake in a ritual called *pujawali.* *(Bemo (15min., Rp1000) run from the Sweta Terminal eastward to Narmada.)*

LINGSAR. The **Pura Lingsar** temples, consisting of the Sasak **Kemaliq** and the Hindu **Pura Gaduh,** built in 1714, sit 7km northwest of Narmada (15min. from Sindu), near the village Lingsar. Both temples are simple and sparse. The complex celebrates the peaceful coexistence of Balinese and Sasaks. Annual weeklong ceremonies at the start of the wet season (late Nov. or early Dec.) known as **Perang Topat (Topat War)** mark these events. As a symbol of tolerance between the two religions, Hindus and Sasaks pelt each other with ketupat (rice wrapped in coconut leaves) after giving thanks for last year's rain and asking for it to return again. A spring-water **eel pool** lies within the Kemaliq section of Pura Lingsar. Eggs to feed the eels are sold at the gate. It is said that if an eel rises to eat your egg, you will have good luck. There is no fee to enter the complex, but a donation is expected for the two temples (sash provided). *(Bemo (10min., admission by donation) run to Lingsar from Narmada.)*

SENGGIGI ☎0370

With one main drag and paradise-like bungalow resorts, Senggigi is the small but hip height of nightlife and leisure on Lombok, offering everything from fine food to dancing to drag shows—and an amazing sunset over the Gilis.

ORIENTATION AND PRACTICAL INFORMATION. Only 15min. from Ampenan by *bemo* (Rp1000), Senggigi makes a nice base for exploration into north and west Lombok. Most hotels and restaurants are spread out along a 2km strip that incorporates two sandy bays.

Services, which cluster near **Pacific Supermarket,** on Jl. Raya Senggigi (☎693 005; open daily 8:30am-9:30pm), include: the **Perama Office** (☎693 007), opposite Lina's Cottages, which provides information on trips to the Gilis and Gunung Rinjani; **BNI,** next to the supermarket (☎693 546; 24hr. **ATM** accepts Cirrus/MC/PLUS/V); the **police** (☎693 267), at the north end of Jl. Raya Senggigi, a 24hr. **medical clinic** (☎693 210, ext. 1730), with an attached **pharmacy,** at the Senggigi Beach Hotel; a **Telekom Office,** opposite the Sheraton Hotel; a **wartel,** in Pacific Supermarket (offers international calls; open daily 8am-10pm); an **HCD** booth outside the supermarket; several **Internet cafes** along the main strip (all open daily around 8am-11pm; Rp250 per min.); and the **post office,** opposite the supermarket (*Poste Restante;* open M-Sa 8am-8pm, Su 8am-noon). **Postal Code:** 83355.

ACCOMMODATIONS AND FOOD. Although Senggigi is resort-oriented, the lack of tourists has depressed prices considerably. Don't be afraid to bargain down from quoted prices; outside of the high season (July-Aug.) actual prices are even lower. **Lombok Coconut ❸,** at the far north end of Jl. Raya Senggigi past the Sheraton, has ocean views from the swimming pool and free evening transport into town. (☎693 195. Singles Rp35,000; doubles Rp60,000.) **Batu Bolong Hotel ❹** offers daily cleaning services, towels, and free tea all day long. Opposite the beach, it's a 10min walk below the main strip (on the same street), or a 3min. *bemo* ride. (☎693 065. Doubles Rp70,000.) **Sonya ❷,** on the main road behind Kastika Restaurant, is the cheapest place in town with great hospitality and a delicious breakfast. (☎693 447. Singles Rp20,000; doubles Rp30,000.)

Fine international cuisine is on **Jl. Raya Senggigi ❹** (Rp20,000-30,000 per dish), but cheaper eats are scarce. Some establishments offer transportation to and from restaurants; call ahead. **Restoran Taman Senggigi ❸** (☎693 842) features a fountain with goldfish, multi-level seating, and Cajun tuna steak (Rp26,000). Its lunch sandwiches are also a good deal (Rp10,000-20,000). **Bumbu ❸,** 300m south of Pacific Supermarket, has the best curry dishes (Rp15,000-25,000) in Senggigi. The art market in the north end is cluttered with beachside dining. **Cafe Coco Loco ❸,** next to the Sheraton Hotel end of the market, prepares an excellent *olah olah,* a spicy Sasak dish with vegetables in coconut milk. (Entrees Rp8000-18,000.) For basic dining, four **warung ❷,** located before the bridge leading to the center of town, serve scrumptious *ikan laut* (ocean fish). The cheap **Senang Restaurant ❶,** in the supermarket complex, offers spicy *nasi pecal* for Rp6000. (Open daily 9am-9pm.)

SIGHTS AND ENTERTAINMENT. Pura Batu Bolong (Hole-in-Rock Temple), one of Lombok's most stunning Balinese temples, is within walking distance of the main strip to the south. The rocky promontory yields a gorgeous view of the ocean. It is thought that the Balinese once hurled virgins from Batu Bolong into the sea, though locals today are often not sure why. A donation is expected, and sashes can be borrowed for free at the gate. Despite the increasingly grand views, tourism wanes as you go farther north, perhaps because of the simultaneously increasing hills. Much of the desolate beach is accessible from the road. *Bemo* run often along the long road as far as **Mangsit** (15min., Rp1000) until 6pm, and most rented motorbikes can manage the hills. On the way to Mangsit, buy some coconut milk from a roadside vendor, sit atop a lookout hill on the coastal road, and watch the sun drop behind the Gilis. At 10pm the to-and-fro migration between two dance clubs begins: **Club Tropicana** and **The Blue Coral,** about a half-kilometer apart on the main drag. Both offer contemporary dance music with the occasional 70s or 80s song. Sometimes a band comes on; if you don't like it, just move on to the other club. (☎693 173. Cover Rp20,000-25,000.) **Pondok Senggigi** hosts an all-male cabaret (Sa 11pm) and **Warung Pojok,** next to Millennium Internet, titillates with an evening drag show (9pm).

KUTA ☎0370

Kuta, not to be confused with Kuta on Bali, is a rock-bottom-priced stop for surfers, beachcombers, and budget travelers in the center of Lombok's south coast. Pristine white sand clashes with a jagged, rocky shoreline in this fishing town once slated for massive tourist development. Kuta was hit hard by the economic crisis. While the villagers are friendly, the struggling populace has become desperate, and robberies are on the rise; watch your wallet and belongings carefully.

TRANSPORTATION AND PRACTICAL INFORMATION. A **Perama bus** to Kuta from Mataram costs five times more than a *bemo* but saves hours (2hr.; Rp45,000). Explore Sasak villages on the way to Kuta by taking a bus or *bemo* from Mataram via **Praya** (Rp2000) and Sengkol (Rp1500). *Bemo* from Sengkol continue on to Tanjung Aan Beach. Most tourist services, including the **police, Perama Office, moneychangers,** and the **Ocean Blue Surf Shop,** are on the beachfront road, **Jl. Raya Pantai Kuta.** The closest **hospital** is in Praya, but Kuta has a **public health clinic** 500m out of town on the road to Sengkol (doctor available M-Sa 4-6pm; attached **apotik (pharmacy)** open 24 hours). There is a *wartel* (open M-Sa 7:30am-10:30pm) and another Perama office across the intersection from Matahari Inn. **Collect** and **international calls** can be made from Wisma Segara Anak and Kuta Indah.

ACCOMMODATIONS AND FOOD. The bungalows along the beachfront all offer similar quality and price. **Anda Bungalows and Restaurant ❷** provides service worthy of a resort, although it's best to eat elsewhere. (Singles from Rp30,000; doubles Rp35,000.) **Ketapang Cafe and Bungalow ❷,** on the corner of the beachfront and road leading inland, has a relaxing restaurant. It is clean, although the *mandi* are somewhat old. Breakfast included. (Singles Rp20,000; doubles Rp25,000.) Farther toward Mandalika Tourist Resort, **Rinjani Agung ❸** has a range of rooms with safes and night security. (☎654 852. Singles from Rp30,000; rooms with A/C Rp100,000.) For its landscaped gardens and the luxury of a pool, **Matahari Inn ❹** wins the non-beach prize. (Rp60,000. MC/V.) Most accommodations in Kuta have their own restaurants, but the half-dozen waterfront **warung ❷** are cheaper and closer to the main street's activity. **Rinjani Agung ❸** features international dishes like Thai chicken salad (Rp10,500) and spinach and feta crepes (Rp14,000).

BEACHES AND NIGHTLIFE. Kuta's beach, **Putri Nyale,** is too rocky for swimming but great for exploring. It hosts the **Bau Nyale,** a celebration of the mating of *nyale* (seaworms), four to eight days after the second full moon of the year (in February or March). The origin of the festival stems from the story of the beautiful Princess Mandalika, who, instead of choosing one man, threw herself into the ocean where she was transformed into a *nyale* in order to be shared by everyone. The celebration marks the anniversary of her transformation. Thousands of people camp on the beach before the *nyale* make their appearance. The young eat the worms, which are supposedly powerful aphrodisiacs. The region also boasts great **surf,** and boats can be chartered to choice spots. Check the **Blue Ocean Surf Shop** for local excursions as well as trips to the breaks on Sumbawa. (☎653 911. Board rentals Rp25,000 per day.) A local favorite for surfing is **Maun Beach,** 30min. outside Kuta. (*Ojek* Rp25,000.) **Tanjungon Beach,** good for swimming and snorkeling, is 5km east of Kuta. (*Bemo* from Kuta Rp1500.) **Sartinng Beach,** completely isolated and visited most often by locals, is another swimmable white-sand beach with surrounding rock formations.

Jungle Bay, across from the Matahari Inn, sometimes has live music. If not, an eclectic selection of jazz blares through the speakers. The bar serves a parade of cocktails and Bintang draught beer (Rp10,000). Their pool is free of charge. (☎655 410. Open daily from 11am until the last person leaves.)

SOUTH COAST BEACHES. Due to threats against foreigners since 1998, coverage of the South Coast Beaches is not included in this edition of *Let's Go: Southeast Asia.* Check embassies for current safety information.

GUNUNG RINJANI

Magnificent Gunung Rinjani, which last erupted in 1994, rises 3726m in the center of the north coast and is Lombok's holiest site. Many local Balinese Hindus make an annual pilgrimage to the summit to toss goldfish and jewelry into Segara Anak, the crater lake, much to the delight of local fishers. Sasak Muslims believe that on the ninth day after death, spirits travel to Gunung Rinjani. By journeying to the volcano, Sasaks draw power from their ancestors. Members of both religions also believe that the waters of the lake and nearby hot springs have healing power.

TRANSPORTATION AND PRACTICAL INFORMATION. Senaru is the Rinjani's gateway town. Due to the popularity of treks, private tourist information centers in Senggigi and on the Gili Islands arrange transportation from there as part of package tours. Be sure your package includes return transport. Cars (Rp100,000) and *ojek* (Rp40,000) can be hired from Senggigi or Senaru. Self-fashioned expeditions cost less but require finding supplies and transportation—and you won't have a guide. *Bemo* to **Bayan** start in Mataram (3hr., Rp5000) or can be picked up on the northwest coastal road in Pemenang or Tanjung. Past Bayan, *bemo* run to Senaru (30min., Rp1500) via Anchak. Transportation is possible to Anchak from Labuhan Lombok (2½hr., Rp7000) or Pringgabaya. Before coming to Senaru, the base for the trek, be prepared: there is **no wartel, post office, bank, hospital,** or **police** in the small town. **Emy's Cafe** (see **Accommodations and Food,** below) changes **currency** and traveler's checks. Bayan has a **wartel** and **post office.**

ACCOMMODATIONS AND FOOD. All accommodations in Senaru rent equipment and provide advice for treks. **Pondok Indah ❷,** on the south end of Senaru, has fairly new rooms and a great view of the coastline and valley. The staff helps organize transport for travelers starting or completing the climb in Sembalan Lawang. (Singles Rp30,000; doubles Rp35,000.) **Segara Anak Bungalows and Restaurant ❷,** across the road from Pondok Indah, has an equally stunning view of the

INDONESIA

river valley. The rooms are plainer, though the food is tastier. (Singles Rp25,000; doubles Rp30,000.) The most convenient option is the **Bale Bayan ❸,** on the trailhead opposite the Rinjani Trek Center. (Singles Rp35,000; doubles Rp50,000.) **Emy's Cafe ❶** offers cheap food. Most trek outfitting happens here as well; they usually give hikers free tea or even lunch. (Most dishes Rp3000-8000.)

WATERFALLS. In Gunung Rinjani's picturesque foothills, Senaru itself contains the spectacular **Sindang Gile Waterfall.** The path leading to the falls appears off the main road in Senaru when the falls first come into view. A second waterfall upstream from Sindang Gile, **Tiu Kelep Waterfall,** is equally powerful and has a pool ideal for swimming. Although locals will tell you that a guide is needed to reach it, experienced trekkers can follow the path at the bottom of the steps as they descend to Sindang Gile. The path crosses an aqueduct and fades out 500m before the waterfall at the bend in the river. From there, follow the noise and the riverbed to reach the base of the falls. A third waterfall, **Betara Lenjang,** is past the Rinjani trailhead.

CLIMBING GUNUNG RINJANI. Climbing Gunung Rinjani, one of the most exhilarating experiences on Lombok, should be tried only by those prepared for a long trek. Climbers can reach the summit from nearly all sides—Tetebatu, Saesot, or Torean. The most popular route is via Batu Koq/Senaru and Sembalan Lawang in Gunung Rinjani's northern foothills.

In January 2002, the trekking system in Senaru was changed. The government built the **Rinjani Trek Center** at the base of the trail in Senaru and set up criteria for guides. All guides brief hikers here before hitting the trail. With this new system also came the organization of trek services in Senaru, which means two things: first, trek prices are now set and it is more difficult to bargain, especially if you begin planning your trip in Senaru rather than, say, in Senggigi or the Gili Islands; second, the quality of the hiking and the safety precautions have improved. Trek prices vary depending on duration and desired amenities. All-inclusive packages (with guide, porters, three meals per day and snacks, water, and necessary equipment) cost US$20 per day for one person. The per-person price drops rapidly for larger groups; the trek will also be cheaper if you carry your own gear and food. Additionally, paths are clearly marked and it is possible to do the trek totally on your own, though this isn't recommended for groups of fewer than four people. In this case, the only fee is the Rp25,000 park entrance fee. Bring a flashlight, warm clothing (the temperature drops at night), and a bathing suit for the hot springs.

The hike up Rinjani is not easy, and those who attempt it should be in moderate shape. The most popular route is the three-day, two-night trek to the crater rims and lakeside from **Senaru.** This hike does not actually reach the top of Rinjani—for that, an extra day should be budgeted, and because the views from the summit depend heavily on the weather, many hikers feels that this fourth day is not worth it. The first night ends on the crater rim at **Base Camp V,** a 6-8hr. hike from the Trek Center. The second day starts early with a 2hr. hike after sunrise down to Lake Segara and the hot springs (2hr.), leaving gear behind at the rim. After merriment there, and lunch, it's back up to the rim again (2½ hours). When going down into the caldera, watch your step; past hikers have slipped to their deaths. The final descent to **Sembalan Lawang** is a 4-5hr. hike on the third day.

TETEBATU ☎0370

Tetebatu sits on the cusp between foothills and farmland. *Pondok* and *losmen* stand between fields of rice and tobacco in picturesque contrast to Lombok's beach attractions. Wander through the fields toward the Monkey Forest to the north, the jungle waterfalls to the east, or the natural springs to the west. If placid Tetebatu loses its charm, visit the nearby local craft villages by motorbike.

TRANSPORTATION AND PRACTICAL INFORMATION. To get to Tetebatu, catch a *bemo* to Promotong. From there, *bemo* go as far as Kotaraja (Rp1000), where *ojek* and *cidomo* go the extra distance to Tetebatu (Rp2000). **Perama** also makes the trip (Rp80,000 from Mataram). Tetebatu's northern and southern central areas are 1km apart. Losmen are in two clusters, one between Tetebatu's two centers, the other on the eastbound side road, **Jl. Waterfall.** The Monkey Forest is to the north, past Soedjones Hotel. A **Perama office** is in the **Green Orry Inn** on the south side of Jl. Waterfall from lower Tetebatu. Soedjones Hotel offers **currency exchange.** Warung Salabusa rents **motorbikes** (Rp30,000) and **cars** (Rp100,000), and the wartel, next door, offers cash international and collect calls. The nearest **post office** and **police station** are in Masbagik.

ACCOMMODATIONS AND FOOD. Tetebatu has high-quality accommodations south of the town center and along the eastbound road. The lack of tourists means that all prices are negotiable. **Cendrawasih Cottages ❷,** along Jl. Waterfall, has colorful Sasak-style Lumbung bungalows with back balconies. Only one of the four has a Western bath, but all are spotless and cheap. (Doubles Rp30,000.) **Pondok Tetebatu ❷,** along the main road, has bright bungalows with private *mandi*. (Singles Rp20,000-25,000; doubles Rp30,000.) Directly behind, **Merkarsari ❷** has rooms of slightly lower quality, though slightly cheaper, farther from the road. (☎22 772. Rp20,000.) **Soedjones Hotel ❸,** at the far north end of Jl. Monkey Forest, has overpriced rooms and a swimming pool. (☎62 376 22522. Bungalows with *mandi* Rp45,000; cottages with Western bath Rp50,000.) Every hotel comes with a good-quality restaurant or cafe. **Green Orry Inn's cafe ❷** serves delicious *lassis* (Rp3000-3500) and chicken curry (Rp15,000). **Harmony Cafe ❷,** on the main road, is vegetarian-friendly (vegetables with coconut milk Rp7500). **Tetebatu Cafe ❸** has billiards and an occasional band (F-Sa), and serves a small menu of cheap food (fried chicken Rp12,500). **Warung Salabuse ❸,** the other nightspot down the main road from Harmony Cafe, is also open for lunch. Nightly movies, Saturday night bands, and karaoke round out this lively cafe. (☎836 62. Entrees Rp8000-18,000.)

SIGHTS. Local hospitality makes Tetebatu a peaceful retreat. The paths around the glorious tobacco fields and terraced rice paddies merit a day of exploring. To get to the **Monkey Forest,** follow the main road north until it veers right; a dirt road marked by a park sign continues north for 4km before reaching the *hutan*. Local boys gather here to offer their services as guides. **Otak Kokok Gading (Joben Waterfall),** west of Tetebatu, is frequented by locals who believe the natural springs have healing powers. Far more impressive are the **Jeruk Manis Waterfalls,** 7km to the east of Tetebatu. To reach these falls, follow the signs along the eastbound road out of Tetebatu's southern hub to a carpark. From there it's a 30min. walk to the falls. There's a new **police** post at the entrance. Guides are recommended, but choose a local guide, as there have been reports of non-local "guides" mugging their tourists. (Guides Rp20,000 for the falls, Rp50,000 to motorbike to all sights, including villages. Admission to Jeruk Manis Waterfalls Rp1500.)

DAYTRIPS FROM TETEBATU. Rural Lombok towns are full of textiles and craftwork. *Ojek* drivers and bungalow owners offer tourists various packages around the handicraft loop. *Bemo* and *cidomo* cover all destinations and, if you travel early, shouldn't be hard to catch. The frugal can walk to nearby villages.

The market town of **Kotaraja** is 3km south of Tetebatu. Its daily market, which carries mainly produce and petrol, is dwarfed by the massive turnouts on Wednesday and Friday. The next village, **Loyok,** is known for bamboo and rattan weaving. On its main street is a "handicraft center," but residential shops are more interesting. Visitors who ask to see weaving can get a lesson in bamboo-ring making. Five hundred meters east, in **Rungkang,** locals sell burnt-sienna pots that resemble over-baked Grecian urns. **Masbagik,** however, is the commercial center for terra-cotta pieces. East of Pomotong on the main drag, Masbagik has a market on Mondays. **Pringgasela** lies farther from Masbagik (go east toward Rempung, then veer north off the main road), but it's worth the trip to see *Sasak ikat* weaving at its finest.

The **Radiah** ❷ in **Lendang Nangka** is an unorthodox way to experience central Lombok. Radiah is a teacher who leads walks through fields and teaches guests how rice is planted and harvested. Meals consist of Sasak food: *urap-urap* (veggies with young coconut and garlic), *olah olah* (veggies with coconut milk), *sayurbening* (plain boiled veggies), and *pelecing kangkung* (very spicy boiled veggies). There are two walks a day—one (from sunrise until 7:30am) to witness how Sasak farmers start their day, and another (from 4pm to sunset) to see how their day ends. Walks are free for guests, but non-guests can also tag along for Rp25,000 (includes one meal). Buses stop at Masbagik from Labuhan Lombok and Sweta. Take a *cidomo* (Rp1500) to Lendang Nangka and ask for Radiah. (Meals included. Singles Rp25,000; doubles Rp35,000; plantation room Rp45,000. If business is slow, the plantation rooms close and guests are boarded with the family.)

THE GILI ISLANDS

Gili Trawangan, Gili Air, and Gili Meno are tourist magnets, popular for their glorious blue-green reefs, white sand, and fun-loving crowds. Each island has a niche of its own: Gili Trawangan hops with an eternal party, Gili Meno is the perfect romantic getaway, and Gili Air is the best place to hide from the drunks and mushy couples. Snorkeling and diving packages are everywhere—sea life and shark sightings attract tourists. However, in addition to the harm done by rapid development, environmental changes and rising water temperatures have endangered the coral along the shore and sparked conservation efforts.

THE VIEW FROM ABOVE

The Lowdown: Three islands—Gili Air, Gili Meno, and Gili Trawangan—off Lombok's northwestern coast.

Highlights: Partying at the bar shacks of Gili Trawangan, scuba diving in Gili Air's coral reefs, and finding peace and quiet on Gili Meno.

GETTING AROUND THE GILI ISLANDS

From **Mataram** (p. 197), take a **bemo** to **Pemenang** (1½hr., Rp4000), where **cidomo** go 1km to the port of **Bangsal.** Once at Bangsal, you can reach the Gilis by public, shuttle, or chartered boat. **Public boats,** the cheapest option, leave when full (at least 15 passengers and up to 2hr. wait) for Gili Air (Rp1500), Gili Meno (Rp1900), and Gili Trawangan (Rp2000). **Shuttle boats** run at 10am and 4:30pm to Gili Air (Rp3500), Gili Meno (Rp4000), and Gili Trawangan (Rp4500) and leave for the return at 8:15am from Gili Air and Gili Meno and 8:30am from Gili Trawangan. Boats can be chartered from the Bangsal port or the islands. Prices are never fixed, but trips under 5hr. should be Rp100,000 per boat or less. **Perama** is a reputable boat operator that runs boats to the Gilis from virtually anywhere on Bali and Lombok. Direct boats leave from **Senggigi** (Rp40,000). **Island-hopping shuttles** (Rp7000 one-way) allow daytrips to other islands and leave twice daily from Gili Air (8:30am and 3pm). Other information is available at the ticket office.

GILI TRAWANGAN

Gili Trawangan, the party center of the Gilis, bustles with backpackers who come for the bars and a hip beach resort with low prices. In 1992, President Suharto marked the northwest corner of the island for massive tourist development and ordered all establishments there to shut down. In July 1998, following Suharto's resignation, the people regained possession of their land. As they returned to their beachside plots, most set up stores and simple *warung* that contrast with the more upscale resorts near the landing. The island is a great place for snorkeling and scuba diving, and stretches of undeveloped beach await exploration.

The **boat landing** is at the midpoint of the eastern coast. The **Perama Office** is just south of the landing. A **medical clinic** is next door to Villa-Ombok on the south side of the main strip. There are **wartel** scattered along the strip that offer cash and collect calls. (Most open daily 8am-midnight.) **Moneychangers** line the strip and a few offer Visa advances at outrageous rates (8-10%). **Wiggis Internet,** next to the Perama Office, suffers the fewest chance disconnections. (Rp500 per min. Open daily 8:30am-11pm.) *Cidomo*, bicycles, and walking suffice for local transportation. There is **no post office.** Trawangan has more options for diving than the other Gilis. **Blue Marlin Dive Center,** with a PADI 5-star IDC rating, is one of the island's three professional dive centers (2 dives US$45.) Compare prices with **Reef Seekers** and **Dream Divers;** bargain for **snorkeling** prices around US$10.

Most accommodations line a narrow strip along the eastern coast; the northern and southern ends are more secluded. Most lodgings come with electricity, fan, mosquito nets, and breakfast. In the high season, the better hotels may be booked, forcing travelers to put down a deposit while staying elsewhere for the first night. **Creatif Bungalows II ❸,** a 10min. walk north from the boat landing and just a short stroll to the best swimming area, has private hammocks in a beautiful garden. (Singles Rp30,000; doubles Rp40,000.) The cheapest option is **Mawar I Bungalows ❶,** past the southern end of the strip, with bamboo bungalows. (Singles Rp10,000; doubles Rp12,000.) For peace and quiet, head to **Pondok Santi ❷,** south of Mawar I. (Singles Rp25,000; doubles Rp40,000.) **Pondok Jessica ❸,** 100m inland from the ferry port, has well-kept cottages and fresh-water showers. (Rp40,000-60,000.) In addition to the **warung ❶** that line the beach north of the landing, many fine restaurants line the southern end of the beach strip. **Brobudur ❸** has an extensive menu including large burgers (Rp18,000) and even larger fish (Rp15,000-25,000). **Dream Divers ❹** grills fresh fish every night. (☎634 496. Entrees Rp14,000-42,000.) **Blue-Marlin Dive Center ❹** serves tasty meals on beachside tables. (Sweet and sour prawns Rp25,000.) **Villa-Ombok ❹** has delicious food that's worth the price tag (entrees Rp30,000). Try the crepes *partisia* (apple or mango and custard in a crepe drizzled with orange sauce; Rp15,500). Most of the backpacker cafes and *warung* serve the local specialty—Indonesian magic mushrooms.

GILI AIR

Gili Air is just busy enough. It has the bustle of a tourist town yet retains a small-town air. Greener than the other Gilis, it supports coconut groves. It also has the largest permanent population of the three islands, and the local presence is felt beyond the hawkers and massage-ladies. Swimming is best in the southeastern corner of the island, but once-good snorkeling sites have deteriorated due to seaweed farming and dynamite fishing.

An obvious road traces the perimeter of the island, and a few unnamed paths cut through the village center. Most tourist services are on the beachfront. **Boats** land on the south side of the island. **Horsecarts** traverse the island constantly, but **bicycles** are the most efficient transport. The **Perama Office** (☎637 816), 100m inland from the jetty, arranges **glass-bottom boat trips** all over Lombok. Most hotels offer tickets to destinations in Bali, Lombok, and Sumbawa at similar prices. Gili Air has **no hospital, police, post office,** or **bank,** but there's a **health clinic** (*Puskesmas*) on the south side in the village, and **moneychangers** are everywhere. Hotel Gili Indah has a **wartel.** (☎636 341. Open daily 7am-10pm.) **Internet cafes** (around Rp500 per min.) are popping up all over, including at **Gili Air Santay** (see below). Several dive shops and guesthouses offer **scuba-diving** trips and courses, and most bungalows rent **snorkeling** equipment. Even if you don't dive with **Reefseekers** (☎641 008), stop by to ask the staff for a tour of the **Turtle Farm.** Endangered eggs are bought from markets and hatched. The turtles are then returned to the sea.

Night owls will be grateful for the island's 24hr. electricity. Most bungalows offer rooms with mosquito nets, *mandi*, and breakfast; the variables are showers, hammocks, and location. Outside of high season (June-Sept.), it is possible to bargain down from the prices listed here. Otherwise, arrive early, as rooms are usually booked before noon. **Safari Cottages ❸,** along the south coast, has respectable bungalows on a stretch of secluded, if scruffy, beach. (Singles Rp30,000; doubles Rp45,000.) **Gili Air Santay ❸,** halfway along the eastern shore, is more expensive than others, but the cleanliness and tiled baths make it worth the extra rupiah. (Singles Rp40,000; doubles Rp50,000.) Slightly farther north on the east coast, **Coconut Cottages ❸** has a range of accommodations. (Bamboo bungalows with veranda Rp40,000-50,000.) The restaurant in **Hotel Gili Air ❹,** with beachside seating along the northern coast, is a great place to watch the sunset and chow down on pan-fried tuna (Rp27,500). Order their homemade pastas a day in advance. Next door, the **Pondok Wisata Santi ❸** features pavilions and delicious sweet-and-sour chicken (Rp15,000). **Il Pirata ❹,** in a pirate ship 100m west and inland from the landing (follow the signs), serves Italian cuisine (most entrees Rp20,000-25,000).

GILI MENO

Gili Meno is the least visited of the Gilis, making it the preferred island for a real getaway. The northern part of the island is empty, but the livelier southeast shore is entrancing, and has the island's only decent beach. An inland **salt-water lake** can be reached by the road next to Royal Reef Hotel. There is also a **bird reserve** about 300m inland. During the low season (late Nov.-Apr.), Gili Meno operates at half speed; bungalows stay open, but restaurants usually close.

Boats arrive at the southeast shore. Most tourist facilities, including a **Perama** outpost and **moneychangers,** are near the landing. The **Blue Marlin Dive Center** offers Visa and Mastercard advances and has spotty **Internet** connections (Rp300 per min.). The **wartel,** south of the landing at the Gazebo Meno Hotel, has unreliable connections. **Royal Reef Hotel,** north of the landing, offers **phone service.** There is **no post office** or **hospital** on Meno. Generators produce the only electricity on Gili Meno; lights are switched off 10pm-midnight (or whenever the owners feel like it).

Kontiki Cottages ❹, south of the landing, has elegant, clean bungalows with Western baths. (☎632 824. Singles Rp60,000; doubles Rp80,000.) **Matahari Bungalows ❷,** 50m from the beach, is the cheapest option, with clean bungalows that have mosquito nets. The manager doesn't turn on the generator unless he has to. (Rooms Rp25,000-35,000.) **Mallia's Child Bungalows ❹,** next door to Kontiki, tempts travelers with its beachfront location. (Bungalows with *mandi* Rp50,000-75,000.) Saleswomen hawk *gado-gado* and *nasi campur* on the beach. Most accommodations have restaurants attached. The **restaurant at Kontiki Cottages ❷** has great beach views and cheap, tasty meals (entrees Rp10,000-15,000). The cheap **Good Heart Restaurant ❸** is on the northwest side of the island (entrees Rp6000-30,000). Time your visit with the setting sun—but bring a flashlight for the walk back.

SUMBAWA

Hot, dry, dusty Sumbawa is rarely visited by foreigners. Though a fairly good road system exists, Sumbawa is still primarily a residential island. The friendly residents are eager to practice their English with visitors, but otherwise keep to themselves. Surfers will appreciate Hu'u's waves—for others, however, Sumbawa is probably just dry scenery rolling by on the long bus trip from Poto Tano to Sape.

THE VIEW FROM ABOVE

The Lowdown: The island that Indonesia forgot lies between Lombok and Flores.

Gateway Cities: Poto Tano, Sape.

Major Towns: Bima, Sape, Sumbawa Besar.

Highlights: Surfing Lakey's Beach in Hu'u and Taliwang's waters, stopping by the Sultan's Palace in Bima.

GETTING TO SUMBAWA

BY PLANE. Bima's airport lies 19km from town along the main road to Bima. As a major regional hub for Merpati, Bima offers island-hopping flights to: Denpasar (Tu, Th, Sa-Su; Rp528,800); Kupang (Th, Su; Rp720,900) via Ruteng (Rp284,100); Labuhanbajo, Flores (M, Sa; Rp223,200); Mataram (Th, Sa; Rp352,300). **Sumbawa Besar's airport,** on Jl. Garuda at the western edge of town, is easily reached by yellow *bemo* (Rp1000), though flights from here are less frequent than from Bima. Flights go to: Yogyakarta and Surabaya.

BY FERRY. Ferries run between Labuhan Lombok on Lombok's east coast to Poto Tano on Sumbawa's west coast (2hr., every hr., Rp8000). Purchase tickets at the piers. Alternatively, buy a combined ferry and A/C bus ticket (Rp27,000), which will take you directly to Mataram (see p. 197) on Lombok. A ferry/bus combination going in the other direction, from Mataram to Sumbawa Besar, costs Rp20,000, but buses have no A/C. Ferries also leave Sape for Labuhanbajo, Flores (8-12hr.; 8am; Rp16,000) and Waikelo, Sumba (M 8pm; Rp21,000).

BY BOAT. PELNI ships dock at Bima and at Badas. The KM *Tata Mailau* departs from both harbors every two weeks for Denpasar, Dobo, Labuhanbajo, Larantuka, Saumlaki, and Tual. The KM *Tilongkabila* leaves sporadically from Bima for Denpasar, Kumai, Lembar, Sampit, and Surabaya. The KM *Pangrango* leaves from Badas about once a week to Ende, Labuhanbajo, Surabaya, Waingapu, and beyond. The Bima PELNI Office, Jl. Pelabuhan 103, is beside the harbor. Barito, on Jl. Hasanudin (☎437 37), runs express boats from Bima to **Denpasar** (6hr.; business Rp146,000, executive Rp176,000).

HU'U ☎0373

Surf-lovers and professionals come to roast, play, and be photographed in Hu'u's aquamarine Cempi Bay before rainy-season winds dampen surfing conditions. The surrounding reefs make for great snorkeling opportunities for non-surfers—though few without boards ever make their way down here. Surfers will appreciate the easy offshore access to the successive breaks from Lakey's Beach: **Lakey's Peak, Lakey's Pipe,** and **Nanges.** For intrepid surfers, two right-hand breaks off Lakey's Beach lie to the north (**Cobblestone,** a 15min. walk) and south (**Periscope,** a 30min. walk). If you're not a professional surfer and can't tell the difference, ask anyone with a board. But be careful with your belongings at the outer breaks and do not bring valuables, as thefts have been reported.

TIP **BAHASA INDONESIA, 101.** When traveling by bus on rural islands like Sumba, where few people speak English, knowledge of Bahasa Indonesia is essential. Useful phrases include "Apakah masih ada bis dari sini ke 'X' hari ini?" (Is there still a bus from here to 'X' today?), "Di mana bisa saya naik bis ke 'X'?" (Where can I catch a bus to 'X'?), and "Berapa ongkos dari sini ke 'X'?" (How much is the fare from here to 'X'?). If you hear responses like "Tidak ada lagi" (There are no more) or "Besok pagi" (Tomorrow morning), then ask about spending the night. "Di mana bisa saya menginap malam ini?" means "Where can I spend the night this evening?" Also ask about chartering private transport to the highway junction: "Apakah ada orang di sini yang bisa mengantar saya ke jalan raya?" means "Is there someone here who can take me to the highway?" Be prepared to shell out rupiah for an *ojek* or private *bemo* ride.

Accommodations on **Lakey's Beach** are kilometers away from the nearest villages, so most lodgings have restaurants and general stores. **Mona Lisa Bungalows ❸,** about the fourth hotel from the northern edge of Lakey's Beach, has straw and bamboo huts with private *mandi*. (Breakfast included. Singles Rp30,000, with A/C 60,000; doubles Rp40,000/Rp75,000.) **Puma Cottages ❸** is larger with Western-style baths and a helpful staff. (Breakfast included. Laundry service. Singles Rp35,000; doubles Rp60,000.) The rooms, service, and amenities at **Hotel Aman Gati ❺** are exquisite. (☎623 031. Breakfast included. Rooms Rp140,000-210,000, with A/C and hot water Rp240,000-320,000. Extra beds Rp70,000. MC/V.) Once the low tide kills the surf, the happening **Fatma's Hand Restaurant ❸** gets lively. Come for the quiche (from Rp22,000), fresh fish (from Rp15,000), a movie, or just to hear the word "gnarly" spoken without irony.

Exchange **currency** in Bima, Dompu, or Sumbawa—rates in Hu'u are terrible. **Intan Lestari** rents **bicycles** (Rp 15,000) and **snorkeling gear** (Rp10,000). Most hotels and bungalows provide **international call** service. Fatma's Hand Restaurant provides **fax** service, transportation **bookings,** and **surfboard rental** (Rp25,000 per day). To get to Hu'u, take a bus from Bima (2hr., Rp5000) to Dompu. In Dompu, take a *bemo* from the Northern Terminal to the city center (Rp500) and then a *cidomo* (Rp500) to the Southern Terminal. From here, pricey and sporadic transport heads to Hu'u. Accommodations such as the Hotel Aman Gati arrange transportation; call ahead and they may pick you up.

BIMA ☎0374

Whether in the night market's vendors or in the *dokar* careening down its streets, Bima's energy envelopes every visitor as hundreds of bright, colored lights illuminate up every awning, storefront, and mosque while teenagers blast music, turning downtown into a virtual discotheque. The **Sultan's Palace** (now a museum) contains an impressive display of ceremonial *kris* (swords). (At the western end of Jl. Sumbawa. Open M-F 9am-4pm. Free, but guide tip expected.)

La'mbitu Hotel ❸ is easily the best value on Sumbawa. (☎422 22. Breakfast included. Classy rooms with bath Rp45,000, with A/C, TV, and bath Rp70,000). Next door, **Hotel Liligraha ❷,** older and more worn, gives you less for the money. (Breakfast included. Rooms Rp15,000-20,000; doubles with bath Rp50,000, with bath and fan Rp60,000.) The numerous **food carts ❶** that line Bima's back streets and the **night market ❶** (just south of Jl. Hasanuddin) compensate for a paucity of restaurants. Both hotels listed above have cheap, tasty **eateries ❷** inside (most entrees Rp4000-12,000). In town, **Rumah Makan Anda ❷,** on Jl. Kaharnuddin before the bridge on the way to the terminal, delights with freshly baked goods and a large Chinese menu. (Limited vegetarian dishes. Entrees Rp4000-11,000. Open daily 8am-10pm.) **Ayam Goreng Pemuda ❸,** Jl. Sulawesi 12, by the night market, weighs a bit heavier on the vegetarian side. Try the vegetables in chilli sauce for Rp4000. (Large fish with tomato Rp20,000. Open daily 9am-3pm and 5-10pm.)

Buses go from **Kumbe Terminal** on Jl. Sukarno-Hatta and the **Town Bus Terminal,** across the river after Jl. Kaharnuddin, to: **Dompu** (2hr., Rp3500); Sape (1½hr., every 30min. 7am-4pm, Rp3000). Bima sits between two rivers. **Jl. Terminal Baru** stretches north from the airport (south of the southern river) and becomes **Jl. Kaharnuddin,** the main street. It first intersects **Jl. Karantina/Sukarno-Hatta,** the main eastbound road that leads to **Raba,** Bima's administrative center. **Jl. Sumbawa,** which collides with the Sultan's Palace complex, runs two blocks up and parallel to Jl. Sukarno-Hatta. Along Jl. Sukarno-Hatta, Raba has a 24hr. **Telkom Office** with collect calls and **Internet** (Rp12,000 per hr.); the **police** (☎430 26; **emergency** ☎110); and the **hospital,** Jl. Langsat 1 (24hr. **emergency** ☎431 42; **ambulance** ☎118). **BNI,** on Jl. Sultan Hasanuddin, has a 24hr. **ATM.** (Open M-F 8am-3pm. Cirrus/MC/PLUS/V.) The **GPO** is on the eastern extension of Jl. Hasanuddin/Diponegoro at Jl. Gajah Mada. (*Poste Restante.* Open M-Sa 8am-2:30pm, Su 9am-noon.) **Postal Code:** 84100.

FLORES

With its magnificent landscape, Flores ranks as one of Indonesia's most spectacular islands. Lush rainforests set Flores apart from barren Sumba and Sumbawa, nurtured and protected by volcanic mountains and ridges that break the passing clouds. Flores still bears the legacy of colonialism; Roman Catholicism is the faith of choice and names are often Portuguese. "Flores," in fact, is Portuguese for "flower," though the island wasn't named for its vegetation. Rather, it was so dubbed because the colonists who first circumnavigated the island believed it to be flower-shaped. Though colonialism left significant marks on Flores and its people, old habits die hard, and European influences have not supplanted traditional culture. In most remote areas, "Catholic" villages still practice traditional animistic rites and rituals along with the sacraments.

THE VIEW FROM ABOVE

The Lowdown: Bali's quieter neighbor preserves the wonders of nature.

Main Cities: Labuhanbajo, Ruteng, Bajawa, Ende, Maumere

Highlights: Tricolored crater lakes, sunrises over Golo Curu, the dragons of Komodo and Rinca.

GETTING THERE

BY PLANE. An **airport** is 2km southeast of Labuhanbajo; take the road heading inland at the south end of town and turn left at the sign. **Merpati** (☎411 77) has an office on the way, as well as in Ende (see **Transportation,** p. 217) and flies a few times per week to **Denpasar** (once a week via **Bima**), **Jakarta,** and **Kupang.** Maumere's airport is a busy hub to and from Bali, with flights to **Denpasar** (3 per week; Rp883,000) and **Jakarta** (Rp921,000). Be warned that flights are frequently cancelled and, in the high season, often booked well in advance (especially the Maumere-Denpasar route). **Bajawa Airport,** 25km north of Bajawa, has flights to **Kupang** (Rp220,000).

BY BOAT. A main **ferry landing** is at the north end of Labuhanbajo. Ferries go to **Sape** (8-12hr.; W, Sa; Rp16,000). Check at the harbor to confirm the erratic ferry schedule. To get to the **PELNI office** (☎411 06), walk away from the water at the har-

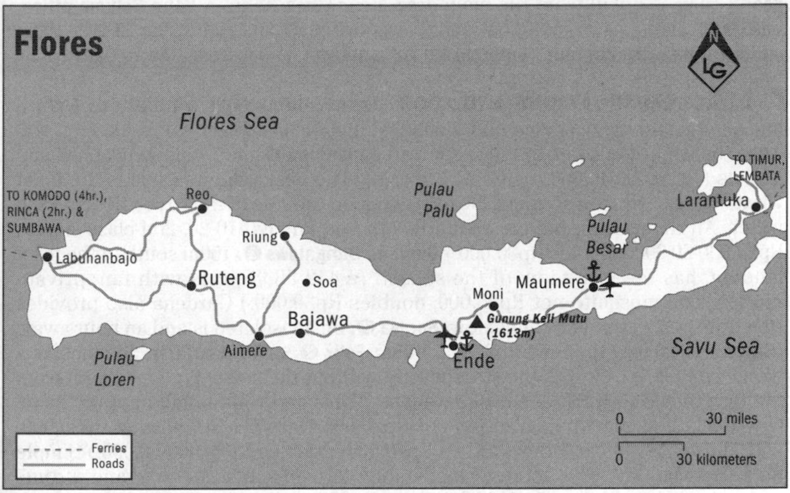

bor, take the main road to the right, and then take the first left. Go through the intersection up the dirt road; it's 50m up on the left, cleverly disguised as a house. Check on boats to **Bali, Lombok, Sumba, Surabaya,** and **Timor** here. PELNI also has a main port in Ende, where boats depart to similar destinations. Larantuka, in the east, has a regular ferry service to **Kupang** and **Lembata.** PELNI boats also occasionally sail from Maumere. The 14hr. fast ferry, also leaving from Maumere, goes directly to **Benoa** (M; Rp275,000) before continuing on to **Surabaya** (Rp330,000).

LABUHANBAJO ☎0385

While Labuhanbajo's excellent accommodations and relaxing seaside atmosphere should make it a destination in its own right, it is still mainly a point of departure to Rinca and Komodo. Since the cancellation of regular ferry service to Komodo, most tourists book tours out of the port here. A 15min. walk will bring you to a fine stretch of sand and beach hotels; more secluded resorts lie on islands or the mainland beaches north of town.

TRANSPORTATION. While Labuhanbajo has no bus terminal, **buses** leave in the morning bound for Ruteng (6hr.; Rp15,000) and Bajawa (10hr.; Rp20,000); flag one down on the main road. Check with hotels for times and to arrange a pickup.

ORIENTATION AND PRACTICAL INFORMATION. Labuhanbajo is a simple coastal crescent stretching 1.5km. The **national parks office,** on the inland road heading to the airport, has brochures, maps, and information about **Rinca** and **Komodo,** as well as a Komodo dragon skeleton that's worth a look. (☎410 04. Open M-Sa 7am-2pm.) Most hotels on **Jl. Sukarno/Yos Sudarso/Pelabuhan** arrange snorkeling trips and island treks. Many local tourist agencies take visitors diving (about US$75 per day). Hotels also rent out snorkeling equipment.

Bank Negara Indonesia, in the market across from Hotel Witasa, has good rates. (Open M-F 7:30am-2:30pm, Sa 7:30-11:30am.) The main **police station** (☎411 10) is inconveniently located south of the town center on the road to the **Pasar Baru** (new market), which is a 20min. walk from the center of town or a Rp1000 *bemo* ride. A

INDONESIA

health clinic is uphill from the main drag, near Chez Felix. A 24hr. **Telkom office,** with **HCD** phone, is past the national parks office on the right. The **GPO** is 400m south of the ferry landing. (Open M-Th 7:30am-3pm, F 7:30-11am, Sa 7:30am-1pm.)

ACCOMMODATIONS AND FOOD. Labuhanbajo has a number of good budget and mid-range accommodations that include breakfast. For seekers of solitude, beach hotels offer free transport to **bungalows ❷** on secluded beaches and islands (Rp20,000-40,000 including 3 meals). The best value in town is the **Hotel Wisata ❷,** about 1.2km south of the ferry dock on the side of the street closer to the water. All rooms have private Western bath and fan. (☎410 20. 2nd-class singles Rp25,000-30,000; doubles Rp30,000.) **Gardena Bungalows ❷,** 150m south of the ferry landing, has the best view of the sunset. (☎412 58. Singles with fan, private *mandi*, and mosquito net Rp25,000; doubles Rp30,000.) Gardena also provides free transport to its sister bungalow, **Seraya ❷,** on an isolated island an hour away. (Singles Rp20,000; doubles Rp25,000.) **Chez Felix ❷,** on Jl. Prof. Dr. Johanes, is a wonderful place to watch the street bustle without the noise. Walking south from the ferry dock, turn left at the sign (about 800m) and walk uphill another 200m. (☎410 32. Singles with shared *mandi* Rp20,000, with private *mandi* Rp25,000, with mosquito nets and flush toilets Rp40,000; doubles Rp20,000-50,000.) Simple **Hotel Matahari ❷,** 300m south of the landing, provides fans, shower and *mandi* and a view of the harbor. (☎410 83. Singles Rp25,000; doubles Rp30,000.)

The restaurants at Gardena Bungalows, Hotel Wisata, and Chez Felix have lively atmospheres and cheap prices. **Borobudur Restaurant ❸,** a couple of doors south of Gardena Bungalows, has a spectacular view and food to match. The chocolate milkshakes are an incredible treat (Rp6000), especially after a plate of sweet and sour prawns (Rp15,000). The steak, chicken, and prawn dishes at **Dewata Ayu Restaurant ❸,** also next door to Gardena, are all worth the wait (Rp20,000). Both restaurants are open until 10pm.

NEAR LABUHANBAJO: KOMODO AND RINCA ISLANDS

The beautiful blue water of the coast of Flores is dotted with multiple islands, known for their reptilian inhabitants with ravenous appetites. The **Komodo dragon,** over 3m long and a hefty 50kg, is the largest of the monitor lizard family. The dragons have long claws, sharp teeth, and powerful tails. Although they're sedentary in the heat of day, they can sprint short distances and hunt with considerable prowess. Much like a snake, a Komodo can expand its chest cavity enough to swallow a goat whole. Wandering the islands alone has been forbidden since 1974, when an elderly Swiss gentleman took a walk and never came back. Though Komodo Island is perhaps better known, Rinca is equally interesting (if not more so), with savannah-like scenery and diverse wildlife, including buffalo, monkeys, deer, and the occasional cobra. The national park offices on each island lead tours in the early morning and late afternoon. (Rp6000 each for 1-2 persons, Rp2000 each for 3 or more. Entrance fee at both Rp10,000.) On Komodo, guides lead an hour-long walk to **Banu Ngulung,** a dry riverbed where the lazy dragons sunbathe. For the motivated, a hike up **Gunung Gara** (7-8km) affords magnificent views of the rugged landscape. On Rinca, the tour heads uphill toward a vista of the surroundings and then back to the port (2 hours).

SAFETY WATCH. Before signing up for any overnight cruise, check the boat. Typically, boats do not have life vests or a radio, making stormy nights nerve-wracking. There have been reports of stolen money and women being molested in the middle of the night. **Women should not go alone.**

Getting to Komodo can be difficult. Since regular ferry service has been cancelled, travelers must now go through a tour agency in Labuhanbajo or charter a boat from Sape. In Labuhanbajo, the most popular tour is a two-day, one-night trip to Komodo and Rinca. Most tours include lunch both days, as well as dinner, breakfast, and a mattress on the deck. Trips block out extra time for snorkeling; make sure snorkeling gear is included or rent it before you leave. On a boat of at least 8 people, prices range Rp140,000-180,000. Alternatively, a daytrip to just one of the islands ranges Rp60,000-100,000 depending on group size, while a two-day tour is Rp100,000-130,000 (not including meals). It's also possible to visit both islands in one day, though this won't be any easier on your wallet (Rp140,000-150,000 including lunch and snacks). Extended boat trips are also available, usually including snorkeling or diving. Some leave from Labuhanbajo (diving packages start at US$50 per day), while others are booked in Lombok and make a four-day journey past Sumbawa to Komodo and Rinca, ending at Labuhanbajo (Rp350,000-500,000). Fishing boats can be chartered from Labuhanbajo or Sape (around Rp100,000; discounts for groups), though it is then necessary to spend a night at either Komodo or Rinca. Both have government-run **accommodations** ❷ near the park offices. (Singles Rp20,000; doubles Rp25,000.)

BAJAWA ☎0384

This market town of the Ngada people has weathered its transition into the modern world with grace. Although Bajawa's hotels are seldom empty, life goes on undisturbed, and nearby villages have maintained traditional homes.

TRANSPORTATION AND PRACTICAL INFORMATION. The road branching off the **Trans-Flores Highway** enters from the south, running into **Jl. Ahmed Yani (Jl. A. Yani),** which marks the town's southern border. **Watujaji Bus Terminal,** 3km south of town, is a Rp500 *bemo* ride away. Buses go to **Ende** (4hr.; Rp20,000) and Ruteng (4hr.; Rp10,000). **Bajawa Airport,** 25km north, is accessible by a Merpati shuttle (Rp5000) or chartered *bemo* (Rp20,000). **Merpati** has an office near the market. (☎210 50. Open daily 8am-1pm.)

The tiny town isn't tough to navigate. The tourist office, **Dinas Pariwisata,** is on the corner where Jl. Sukarno turns sharply to the right to become Jl. A. Yani. **Jl. Sukarno-Hatta** marks the east side of town; perpendicular to it, **Jl. Gajah Mada** runs through the center of town, past the **bemo stand.** The **market** is in the middle of town. For medical services, **Rumah Sakit Umum** (☎210 30) is on Jl. Diponegoro in the north of town. For an **ambulance,** call ☎118; in an **emergency,** call ☎110. Along Jl. Sukarno-Hatta are **Bank Rakyat Indonesia** (☎210 24; open M-F 7:30am-3:45pm, Sa 7:30-11:30am), the **Telkom office** (☎210 00; open 24hr.) with **Internet** access (Rp16,000 per hr.; available 7am-5pm), and the **post office** (open M-Th 7:30am-3pm, F 7:30-11:30am, Sa 7:30am-1pm). **Postal Code:** 86415.

ACCOMMODATIONS AND FOOD. There are few good values among Bajawa's many hotels. Bargaining is worthwhile, especially in the low season. Breakfast is always included. Highland nights get cold, so make sure your hotel provides blankets. Hotel Elizabeth ❹ is the nicest place around (but with a price to match), with bright, airy rooms and private baths. (☎212 23. Singles Rp50,000; doubles Rp60,000.) To get there, take a left from Jl. Sukarno-Hatta after the tourist office onto a gravel road; it's on the left. Hotel Korina ❸, on Jl. A. Yani at the southern end of town, has decent rooms with bath, blankets, and breakfast. (Book exchange. Singles Rp35,000; doubles Rp45,000.) One of the few budget places that still charges budget rates, Hotel Dam ❶, on a side street with the church, south of the market, has cozy rooms. (Rp12,000 per person with shared bath.)

The local specialty, **dog,** is only prepared for special occasions. Few tourists are interested in trying it, so it's left off the menu at the more touristy spots. Several *padang* joints cluster near the market. For more ambience, sample the extensive international menu at **Borobudur Garden ❶,** one block toward town from Jl. A. Yani. (Squid in chilli sauce Rp15,000.) **Restaurant Carmellia ❷,** Jl. A. Yani 82, across from Hotel Korina, is acclaimed for its spring rolls and guacamole. (Entrees Rp6000-15,000.) **Restaurant Kasih Bahagia ❷,** on Jl. Gajah Mada east of the town center, serves typical Chinese favorites. (Entrees Rp5000-12,000.)

DAYTRIP FROM BAJAWA: NGADA HIGHLANDS AND WAWOMUDHA RED LAKES. Traditional **Ngada villages** dot the mountainous region around Bajawa, characterized by windowless thatched-roof houses, intricate carvings, and clusters of monoliths. Two distinctive structures can be seen in this area, evidence of the ancestor worship still practiced here: the *bhaga*, a small carved thatched-roof house, commemorates female ancestors, while the *ngadhu*, a wooden pole topped by a conical thatched roof, honors male ancestors. **Bena,** 13km south of Bajawa, is the most interesting village (Rp2500). Although it's possible to visit Bena and other villages on your own, you'll get the most for your money on a guided tour. In town, ask for the extremely knowledgeable Lukas Dua (☎864 12), who still lives in a traditional village himself. Don't miss a relaxing soak at the superb **hot springs** near **Soa,** 25km north of Bajawa. The volcanic eruption on January 7, 2001, resulted in the formation of numerous crater lakes in this area. Most have since evaporated, but four blood-red ponds known as the **Wawomudha Red Lakes** still remain. The intense color of the waters contrasts starkly with the surrounding white-gray rock and the green scenery of the hike up.

ARRAK ATTACK. Grapes may give rise to the wine of some gods, but in Nusa Tenggara, the gods like their drink a little bit stronger. Arrak, also called palm wine *(tuak putih)*, is made from the fruit of palm trees. "Wine," however, is a misnomer–arrak is distilled, giving its taste a bit more kick and making its drinker a bit more wrecked. (The joke goes: "I had two blankets last night–one of cotton, one of arrak.") The fruit, which looks like a long bean, is cut from the trees and sliced open to collect the juice. The sweet liquid is then placed in a container with the bark *(denu)* of the tree, which serves to ferment the juice and give it a bitter flavor. What results is a slightly spicy beverage with an alcohol content of about 5%. But it is rare to see the palm wine in this form–the process is usually continued to make arrak. The fermented juice is placed in a large clay pot over an open fire. The pot has a narrow mouth connected to a long bamboo tube. The vapors rise through the shoot and drip out on the other side, distilling the wine to create arrak. A fast, hot fire creates Arrak #3, which is approximately 20% alcohol, but the best arrak is kept over a slow fire for three to four days, creating Arrak #1, of 60% alcohol content. Arrak #1, an elixir for immediate inebriation, is also touted for helping to keep cholesterol low and to strengthen muscles. It is served on special occasions with honey, citrus, and egg yolk.

Occasional *bemo* run from Bajawa to Bena in the Ngada Highlands. Trips to the nearby volcano, crater lakes, and villages are easily arranged with a guide. Using public transport, a guide is usually Rp40,000 per person for groups of 4 or more. Private transport is required to go to Soa, bumping the price to Rp60,000 per person. Tours include lunch. It's also possible to get to Wawomudha Lakes without a guide: take a *bemo* to Ngornale (Rp1500). It's a 1hr. walk to the rim from there.

ENDE ☎038

One of Flores's more developed cities, Ende stretches along a coastline of black-sand beaches, surrounded by rolling hills and islands. As one of the main ports for Sumba and a stop on the way to the much-visited Keli Mutu, with bustling markets, and many of the comforts you thought you could do without.

TRANSPORTATION

Flights: Merpati (☎213 55), on Jl. Nangka. Open M-Tu and Th-Sa 8am-1pm and 4-5pm, Su and holidays 10am-noon.

Buses: Ende has the best bus connections anywhere on Flores—at least 2 buses per day go to both ends of the Trans-Flores Hwy. **Ndao Bus Terminal** is on Jl. Mesjid, north of the city proper. Several buses per day go to: **Bajawa** (5hr.; Rp10,000); **Labuhanbajo** (10hr.; Rp27,000); **Ruteng** (8hr.; Rp20,000). **Wolowana Terminal,** east of town on Jl. A. Yani, has buses to: **Larantuka** (10hr.; Rp20,000); **Maumere** (6hr.; Rp20,000); **Moni** (2hr., Rp6000).

Ferries: PELNI, Jl. Katedral 2 (☎210 43), has info on the 2 PELNI ships that dock here, and for smaller, more frequent ferries to **Timor** (Rp31,000) and **Waingapu** (Rp22,000).

Local Transportation: *Bemo* buzz along the main streets (Rp1000). *Ojek* are quicker. Prices vary according to distance and bargaining skill.

Rentals: Hotel Ikhlas (See **Accommodations,** below) rents **cars** and **motorcycles.**

ORIENTATION AND PRACTICAL INFORMATION

Ende stretches across the neck of a peninsula, with **Ende Harbor** to the west and **Ipi Harbor** to the southeast. Most accommodations post a map on the wall. Otherwise, you can pick one up at the tourist office. In front of the Ende Harbor, the streets form rectangular blocks; **Jl. Sukarno, Jl. Kemakmuran, Jl. Pasar,** and **Jl. Yos Sudarso** run north-south, parallel to the harbor. The intersecting streets are small and mostly unnamed. Outside this grid, the city's blocks become larger and irregular. Leading directly out of the harbor is **Jl. Katedral,** which then becomes **Jl. A. Yani,** the southern border of the town. At the airport, this road turns into **Jl. Gatot** as it turns north toward the **bus station. Jl. Adi Sucipto** branches off Jl. Katedral to head to Ipi Harbor. **Jl. Sudirman** heads from its intersection with Jl. Yos Sudarso to become **Jl. Kelimutu.** Another main street, **Jl. Prof. WZ Johanes,** borders the south end of town and intersects with **Jl. Gatot Subroto.**

Tourist Office: Ende Regency Tourism Office, Jl. Sukarno 4 (☎213 03). Has maps and informative, colorful brochures about Ende and the surrounding sights. Free stickers.

Currency Exchange: Bank Rakyat Indonesia, Jl. Yos Sudarso 27 (☎216 15), in Dwi Putra Hotel. Exchanges currency and traveler's checks. Open M-F 8am-3pm. **BNI,** on Jl. Gatot Subroto, 200m east of the airport roundabout, has a 24hr. **ATM** (Cirrus/MC/PLUS/V).

Emergency: Police: ☎110. **Ambulance:** ☎118.

Police: ☎210 95. On Jl. Polisi, a few blocks up Jl. Pahlawan, on the right.

Pharmacy: Sumber Sehat, Jl. Sudirman 6 (☎216 15). Open daily 8am-1am.

Hospital: Rumah Sakit Umum (☎210 31), far from the town center on Jl. Prof. WZ Johanes.

Telephones: 24hr. **Telkom office,** Jl. Kelimutu 5.

Post Offices: GPO, Jl. Basuki Rahmat 15 (☎212 03), northeast of town, near the Pahjawan-El Tari intersection. (Jl. Basuki Rahmat is the continuation of Jl. El Tari.) *Poste Restante.* Open 24hr. **Branch** is at Jl. Yos Sudarso 4, opposite Dwi Putra Hotel. Open M-Th 7:30am-3pm, F 7:30-11am, Sa 7:30am-1pm.

Postal Code: 86318.

ACCOMMODATIONS

Ende's accommodations are cheaper and more tourist-friendly than most other places in Flores. The nicest places are east of the town center.

Dwi Putra, Jl. Yos Sudarso, next door to Bank Rakyat Indonesia. Lounge with cable TV and spacious rooms. The main attraction is the not-to-be-missed aerobics class. Laundry service and complimentary breakfast. Singles Rp40,000; doubles Rp45,000. ❸

Hotel Ikhlas (☎216 95), on Jl. A. Yani, 200m from the roundabout to the airport. Cheap rooms, lounge (with CNN and MTV), restaurant, and HCD phone. Basic singles Rp10,000, with bath Rp15,000-20,000; doubles Rp15,000/Rp20,000-25,000. ❶

Nurjaya Hotel, Jl. A. Yani 20 (☎212 52), closer to town center. Clean, simply furnished rooms with shared bath. Complimentary breakfast with excellent ginger coffee. Singles Rp15,000; doubles Rp25,000. ❶

FOOD

The capital's proximity to the ocean translates into good seafood. Downtown abounds with Indonesian restaurants, where window displays of delicious dishes will torture the indecisive. **Istana Bambu** ❸, Jl. Pasar 39, downtown, offers Chinese and Indonesian food. (☎214 80. Shrimp in butter sauce Rp15,000.) A rival restaurant, the other **Istana Bambu** ❷, Jl. Kemakmuran 30 (☎219 21), one block east, tempts customers with fresh sweet-and-sour squid (Rp12,500) and baked goods.

MONI

The village of Moni offers fabulous views, cool weather, hot springs, and waterfalls. Its proximity to the base of Keli Mutu's tricolored crater lakes make this town a convenient respite en route to the nearby peaks.

Moni is 50km from Ende and 100km from Maumere. Buses run regularly from both (from Ende: 2hr., Rp6000; from Maumere: 4hr.; Rp10,000). Queasy travelers should note that the route from both cities winds along the narrow sides of jagged ravines and over antiquated bridges. The road toward **Keli Mutu** is a 15min. walk uphill on the Ende side of town. There's a **wartel** at Restaurant Kelimutu, 100m from the **police office** near the turn-off to Keli Mutu.

Arwanti Bungalows ❶, near the town center, is the best bet for groups (Rp60,000), each has two separate rooms and a sitting area. Accommodations that were once very cheap now lean toward being overpriced and dirty. Be sure to bargain—don't pay more than Rp10,000 per person or Rp20,000 with private *mandi*, including breakfast. The staff at **Wisma Kelimutu Moni** ❶ is often praised for its helpfulness and honesty. **Nusa Bunga** ❶, near the east end of town, and **Daniel** ❶ (in the center of the village) are both adequate for a night's sleep. (All three singles Rp10,000; doubles Rp20,000.) There are some nicer options farther away, with quiet settings, impressive vistas, and bungalow-style housing. One of the most pleasant is **Watugana Bungalows** ❸, not far uphill from the market. (Singles Rp30,000; doubles Rp40,000.) The **Arwanti Restaurant** ❷, in the Arwanti Bungalows, serves real vermicelli. People usually go to **Restaurant Kelimutu** ❷, near the turn-off to Keli Mutu, to enjoy the view rather than the food, but it's a decent spot for a simple meal. Mary, of **Mary's ❷**, can cook up a traditional dinner banquet for Rp10,000 per person if you ask her by 2pm. Bring your own drinks, as beverages can be limited and pricey (Rp15,000).

While you're here, enjoy the nightly **traditional dance performance** at the *rumah adat*, 20m off the main road, opposite the market. The bamboo dance—traditionally performed only every few years to bless children—makes it almost worth the Rp15,000 admission, though the performance is short. (Show daily at 8pm.)

DAYTRIPS FROM MONI

KELI MUTU. Moni's tourist trappings are the result of the village's proximity to Flores's grandest natural wonder—the tricolored crater lakes. The water changes color over time due to a geological process not fully understood. As of July 2002, the three lakes were turquoise, black, and eggplant. Previously, the middle lake was milky white; for a long time before that the lakes were maroon, blue, and white. Locals consider the pools to be the resting place of spirits, where color indicates morality; the three pools are akin to Heaven, Hell, and Purgatory. *(A truck up Keli Mutu (Rp15,000) leaves daily at 4am and stops at the park office (entrance fee Rp1000). The ride down (Rp15,000) leaves at 7am. To avoid the crowds on the truck, charter a bemo (Rp50,000) or walk the 13km from Moni. A shortcut* (jalan potong) *begins opposite Rumah Makan Sarty on the road to Ende, 500m from the market, and ends near the park office—it's only recommended for the descent, however, as the way up can be steep and slippery. It's possible to ascend Keli Mutu later in the day, but those who wait to climb will miss the sunrise and risk having the views obscured by a cloud cover. By road, the ascent takes 3-4hr., while the shortcut takes 2hr.)*

WEAVING VILLAGES. Central Flores is renowned for its gorgeous *ikat* weaving. Sarongs, shawls, and blankets in rich rust and orange tones are woven with elaborate patterns featuring mountains, spiders, gongs, flowers, and other motifs. The entire process, from the dyeing of the cotton to the stitching of the cloth, is done by hand. Although it's easy to find affordable, decent cloth in Moni and Ende, the villages south of **Wolowaru,** 12km east of Moni on the Maumere road, display the best work. **Jopu,** the first village, lies 5km south of Wolowaru, followed by **Wolonjita** 6km farther south. At the end of the road, a full 17km from Wolowaru, is **Nggela,** on a promontory overlooking the Savu Sea. Nggela's weaving is the best in the area; the finest pieces can sell for millions of rupiah. At any of the villages, simply ask in any house and usually a few sarongs will be brought out for display. The asking price for a high-quality sarong is usually Rp100,000, though it's often possible to end up paying half that or less. In Moni, there is a large market on Saturdays and Mondays where weavers sell their work; this is the best bet for finding good quality at the best price. Keep in mind though that the aim of haggling is to reach an acceptable price for both parties—one that recognizes the work that goes into the *ikat* cloth. *(Buses run directly from Moni to Nggela a few times every morning (Rp1500). Alternatively, take a bus to Wolowaru (or get off a Maumere-bound bus there; Rp4000) and walk south to Nggela. A bemo usually heads to Wolowaru in the afternoon (Rp1000). From Wolowaru, catch a bus back to Moni.)*

MAUMERE ☎0382

Hit hard by the 1992 earthquake and a resulting tsunami that rocked East Flores, Maumere is slowly rebuilding itself. There's not much to occupy tourists here, and the town also sees its fair share of unrest—most travelers stay only to catch a flight out, head west to Keli Mutu, or venture east to Larantuka, a gateway to Timor and the islands off the east coast. Those who linger stay at one of several beachside resorts east of the city and wander through the markets and surrounding villages.

TRANSPORTATION. The **airport** is 3km east of the town center. *Bemo* and taxis ask Rp10,000 for the trip, but ignore them and walk 500m to the highway, where passing *bemo* can be hailed (Rp1000). **Merpati,** Jl. Don Tomas da Silva 19, is in the center of town. (☎213 42. Open daily 8am-8pm.) Frequent **buses** heading east to Larantuka (4hr.; Rp10,000) leave from **Terminal Waioti,** several kilometers east of town, but you can catch them on their way out of the city. **Terminal Madawat,** a few kilometers southwest of town, is the departure point for transport headed to western destinations, including Ende (6hr., Rp20,000) and Moni (use an Ende-bound bus, as direct *bemo* are infrequent; 4hr., Rp10,000). The **PELNI office** (☎210 13), on Jl. Slamet Riyadi, across the west bridge at the end of town, handles ship reservations for the KM *Awu* and can point you in the right direction for fast-ferry reservations to Bali (14hr., M, Rp275,000) and Surabaya (20hr., M, Rp325,000).

ORIENTATION AND PRACTICAL INFORMATION. Most of the town is concentrated in a wedge between the main east-west road (the **Trans-Flores Highway**) and the water. The downtown area centers around the **Old Market** on **Jl. A. Yani** in the west part of town. The market's west edge is formed by **Jl. Raja Centris,** which is home to most of the restaurants in Maumere. The **New Market,** on Jl. Anylik, is on the western border of the city. The **Sikka Regency tourist information office,** in the western reaches of town, has maps of Maumere. Turn left on Jl. Gajah Mada, follow Jl. A. Yani as it turns left across the river, and take the second right onto Jl. Wairklau at the sign; it's 250m up. (☎216 52. Open M-Th 7am-2pm, F 7-11am, Sa 7am-12:30pm.) The best place to change money and traveler's checks is **BNI,** Jl. Sukarno-Hatta 4, about a block south of the highway. (Open M-F 8am-3pm.) The 24hr. **ATM** accepts Cirrus/MC/PLUS/V. The **police** (☎211 10, **emergency** ☎110) are at the west end of Jl. A. Yani. The new **hospital,** Rumah Sakit Umum Daerah (☎216 17, ambulance ☎118), is on Jl. Wairklau, past the tourist information office. The **pharmacy** is on Jl. Moa Toda near the **Harapan Jaya Artshop,** which has a collection of weavings and Indonesian art (artshop open M-Sa 7:15am-8pm, Su 8am-noon and 4-8pm). The 24hr. **Telkom office** with **HCD** phone is opposite the police station. The **post office** is one block east of Jl. Sukarno-Hatta on the corner of the main road. *Poste Restante.* (Open M-F 8am-5pm, Sa 8am-4pm.) **Postal Code:** 86100.

INDONESIA

ACCOMMODATIONS AND FOOD. Despite a relative lack of tourists, Maumere has several decent budget spots that serve complimentary breakfasts. **Gardena Hotel ❶,** one block north of the soccer field on Jl. Patirangga, has very clean and inexpensive rooms. (Singles with bath and fan Rp15,000, with A/C Rp40,000; doubles Rp25,000-50,000.) The hotel can arrange an English-speaking guide. Call ahead for reservations. **Wini Rai Hotel ❷,** Jl. Gagah Mada 50, down the street from Terminal Madawat, 2km into the town center, is clean and welcoming with a garden and great location. (☎213 88. Singles with fan Rp25,000, with A/C Rp45,000; doubles Rp55,000-70,000.) Popular **Senja Wair Bubuk ❶,** Jl. Komodor Yos Sudarso 81, on the waterfront street in the east part of the town center, is a friendly place. (☎214 98. Singles Rp12,000-22,000, with A/C Rp27,500; doubles Rp17,800-30,500/Rp35,200.) Dining options are limited, though **Jl. Raja Centris** has a couple of decent places, the Chinese **Restaurant Sarinah ❷** being the best. The tourist favorite is the **Golden Fish Restaurant ❺,** on Jl. Hasanuddin as you walk toward the pier. It has fresh seafood, but at the highest prices in town (lobster Rp100,000).

In **Wairterang,** only 27km east of Maumere, travelers will find some of the best values in **beach resorts** in Indonesia. **Ankermi Bungalows ❷** sits on a secluded bay shared only with local fishermen. Guests can enjoy activities ranging from climbing the island volcano to snorkeling. Jump in one of the canoes (free at either resort) at night and observe the mesmerizing phosphorescent glow in the water. Their PADI-certified diving facility also offers **dive trips** (US$30 per dive). After working up an appetite in the sun, head to the restaurant to satisfy your cravings. The food is exceptional—try the Ankermi cake for Rp10,000. The bungalows at Ankermi are immaculate with spotless outdoor *mandi*. Electricity is only on from 6pm to 6am. (Singles Rp30,000; doubles Rp35,000; quad bungalows Rp45,000.) To get to Wairterang, take any *bemo* or bus east toward Lurantuka and ask for Ankermi (Rp2000).

NEAR MAUMERE: LARANTUKA AND BEYOND

Larantuka, a seaport 4hr. east of Maumere, is the last stop on the Trans-Flores Hwy. (almost 700km from its beginning in Labuhanbajo). The town's setting is its most attractive feature—it runs along the coast and up the slopes of volcanic **Mount Ile Mandiri.** Although the surrounding area has a few sweet spots of sand and sleepy villages, there's little of note in the town itself. Most people visit here on their way to the islands off Flores's east coast. The **Solor** and **Alor Archipelagos** offer scenic seclusion and the chance to join a whale-hunting expedition in Lamalera (on the island of **Lembata**), where hunters still use hand-thrown harpoons. Even if they don't catch a whale, the hunters will get in the water and act out the entire process. (Rp20,000-50,000 per person, depending on group and boat size.) Daily **boats** head from Larantuka to Lewoleba (1pm, Rp12,000), the largest city on Lembata (from where infrequent boats go to Lamalera). Less frequent boats voyage to other islands in the archipelagos and to **Kupang,** Timor. Several **buses** per day head west to **Maumere** (4hr., Rp10,000), and a few continue farther west to **Ende** (Rp20,000). The **bus terminal** is several kilometers southwest of Larantuka, though most buses drive through town in hopes of picking up extra passengers.

Everything you need is on the waterfront boulevard or the parallel street a block uphill. Money can be changed (at horrible rates) at **BNI** (open M-F 7:30am-1:30pm) or at the main **Bank Rakyat Indonesia** (open M-F 7:30am-2:30pm, Sa 7:30-11:30am), around the corner from its branch on the main road. The **PELNI office** is on the main road in the western part of town. (Open daily 7:30am-5pm.) A **hospital** is off the main road 2km west of the town (**emergency** ☎ 110, ambulance ☎ 118).

There are only a handful of places to stay in the area. **Hotel Rulies ❷,** on the main street a bit west of what might be called downtown Lewoleba, is the most popular spot with backpackers. (☎ 0383 211 98. Singles with shared *mandi* Rp25,000; doubles Rp40,000.) **Hotel Tresna ❷,** next door, caters more to locals. (☎ 0383 210 72. Singles Rp20,000, with *mandi* Rp25,000; doubles Rp25,000-30,000.) Dining options are similarly limited. A few *rumah makan* cluster in the center of town by the monument, but **Restaurant Nirwana's ❷** Chinese food, east on the waterfront, is a better bet. (Entrees Rp7000-18,000.)

INDONESIA

SULAWESI

Indonesia's third-largest island, Sulawesi has a population of 11 million, including the Muslim Makarese and Bugis in the south, the Minahasans in the north, and the animist-Christian Torajans in the central-south region. While major tourist spots are accessible by plane and are traveler-friendly, many of the twisty roads are

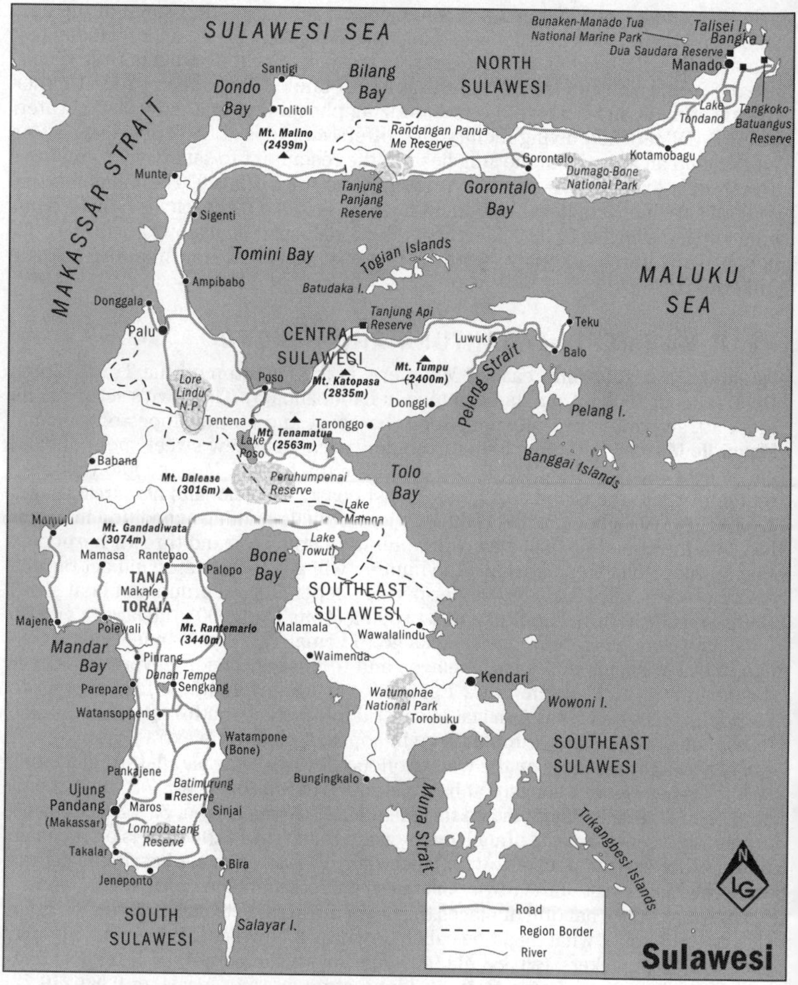

damaged and the rickety smoke-filled vehicles are overcrowded. Nonetheless, travelers tend to stay longer than intended, seeing more than any guidebook could cover. For those who are up to the challenge of traveling in Sulawesi, the rewards of exquisite natural beauty and unforgettable cultural exchanges are plentiful.

SOUTH SULAWESI (SULAWESI SELATAN)

Convoluted Sulawesi seems to have as much coastline as land. Nowhere is its wealth of beachfront life as rich or textured as in the ports of South Sulawesi. North of Makassar, the peninsula becomes increasingly lush, and mountains rise dramatically from coastal plains. Farther north, Tana Toraja gives way to the labyrinthine topography of mountain valleys, offering even more natural beauty.

MAKASSAR (UJUNG PANDANG) ☎0411

Centuries after the Gowa Kingdom established Makassar as a trading *entrepot*, the site retains all the characteristics of a lively port city. Cluttered markets clatter with buyers and sellers, and waterfront bars help sailors drown their sorrows. Equally fascinating is the ethnic diversity resulting from ages of fighting over the largest city in the spice islands. Violent anti-Chinese riots in 1998 and continued tensions reveal that the racial mix is not necessarily a stable one.

TRANSPORTATION

Flights: Hasanuddin Airport, 23km from downtown. Walk 500m to the "Halte bus" hut or to the main road and flag down a *bemo* (Rp2000) to Makassar Mall. Fixed-rate taxis are available from in front of the terminal building (Rp40,000 to most hotels). From Makassar, you can fly just about anywhere within Indonesia; **Silk Air** runs 3 flights per week to **Singapore.** The best place to make ticket reservations is **Limbunan Travel Service,** 40-42 Jl. Gunung Bawakaraeng (☎315 010). Prices often much cheaper than official airline rates. Open M-Sa 8am-5pm. **Merpati,** Jl. Gunung Bawakaraeng 109 (☎442 471). **Garuda,** Jl. A.P. Pettarani 18B-C (☎423 737). **Bouraq,** Jl. Veteran 1 (☎453 139). **Mandala,** Latanet Plaza and on Jl. Cokroaminoto (info ☎323 592, reservations ☎314 880). Ask offices for exact departure times.

Buses: Panaikan Station, a 20min. drive out of town on the airport road. Serves points north and east. Take a *bemo* from Makassar Mall. The **Trans-Sulawesi Highway (Transul)** connects Makassar in the south to Manado at the northernmost tip of the island. **Public buses** to: **Mamasa** (12hr., Rp45,000); **Parepare** (3hr., Rp15,000); **Rantepao** (8hr., Rp30,000-60,000); **Sengkang** (6hr., Rp20,000-25,000).

> **TRANS-SULAWESI TRAVEL WARNING.** Sectarian violence and frequent shoot-outs mean that parts of the Trans-Sulawesi HIghway are not considered safe for non-essential travel. Tourists should avoid traveling by land across Central Sulawesi (especially the areas around Poso). Check with your embassy for the latest information and advice.

Boats: PELNI office, Jl. Sudirman 38 (☎331 401; www. pelni.co.id). Buy tickets there or from a travel agent. Fares are cheaper than air tickets, but travel time is in the scale of days. Most boats run on 2-week loops. Ferries to: **Bima; Denpasar; Jakarta; Kupang; Labuhanbajo; Manado; Surabaya.** Check PELNI office or online for times, prices, current schedules, and ticket reservations.

ORIENTATION AND PRACTICAL INFORMATION

Although the clamor of Makassar seems to reach as far as the **airport** some 23km to the east, the heart of the city is relatively compact and easy to navigate. **Jl. A. Yani,** the main thoroughfare, starts at the waterfront in the western edge of town. **Jl. Martadinata** runs to the north, **Jl. Ujung Pandang** (which passes **Fort Rotterdam** and morphs into **Jl. Pasar Ikan, Jl. Penghibur,** and **Jl. Rajawali**) to the south. A block inland, a gentle right turn off Jl. A. Yani leads to **Jl. Slamet Riyadi,** which becomes **Jl. Hasanuddin** and then **Jl. Cendrawasih** as it heads south out of town. Two blocks farther east, Jl. A. Yani passes the **Lampangan Karebosi** football field in the city center, changes to **Jl. Bulusarung,** and then intersects **Jl. Cokroaminoto,** a major boulevard and home to **Makassar Mall** and the central **bemo station.** Jl. Bulusarung continues eastward to meet northbound **Jl. Andalas,** which heads to **Paotere Harbor** via **Jl. Yos Sudarso.**

Tourist Office: Government Tourist Office (☎443 355), off Jl. Sudirman by the Mandala Monument. Open M-Th 8am-3pm, F 8am-noon, Sa 8am-1pm. Staff at Legend Hostel and other hotels are more helpful.

Tours: Sena Tours, Jl. Jampea 1A (☎323 906), on the same lane as Legend Hostel.

Currency Exchange: Over a dozen **banks,** several with 24hr. **ATMs,** line Jl. A. Yani. Most open M-F 8am-2pm. **BNI,** Jl. Sudirman 1, at the Jl. A. Yani intersection at the top of Lampangan Karebosi, **changes cash** and traveler's checks. Open M-Th 8am-4pm, F 7:30am-4pm.

Markets: Renowned primarily for its jewelry, **Jl. Somba Opu** runs parallel to the waterfront a bit south of the fort. **Sutera Alam,** Jl. Onta Lama 47, is a silk-weaving center on a side street running east off Jl. Dr. Ratulangi.

Emergency: Police: ☎110. **Fire:** ☎113. **Ambulance:** ☎118.

Police: Jl. A. Yani 9 (☎319 277), opposite Jl. Balaikota.

Pharmacies: Apotik Kimia Farma are all over town, including 24hr. branches at Jl. Hasanuddin 36 (☎324 442), south of Galael supermarket, and Jl. A. Yani 17-19 (☎316 722).

Medical Services: Rumah Sakit Akademis Jaury (☎317 343), on Jl. Akademis off Jl. Bulusarung. 24hr. emergency care.

Telephones: Wartel are at Jl. Bali 71, Jl. Kajaolaliddo 2G-4, Jl. Balaikota 2, Jl. Veteran 28, and on Jl. Sulawesi and Jl. Nusantara. **HCD** phones in big hotels; try Hotel Makassar Golden.

Internet Access: Warnet Utama, Jl. A. Yani 17. Best price. Rp3600 per hr. **Surf@cybercafe,** Jl. A. Yani 2, 3rd fl., above Pizza Ria Kafe. Drinks, snacks, lightning-quick connections (Rp6000 per hour). Open M-Th, Su 8am-11pm and F-Sa 8am-midnight.

Post Office: Jl. Slamet Riyadi 10 (☎323 180), 1 block south of Jl. A. Yani. *Poste Restante*. Open M-Sa 8am-8pm, Su 9am-4pm.

Postal Code: 90111.

ACCOMMODATIONS

Budget accommodations are not easy to find. This scarcity has resulted in the virtual monopolization of the backpacker trade by the renowned "Legend."

Legend Hostel, Jl. Jampea 5G (☎328 203), next to Yasmin Hotel, on a small side street north of Jl. A. Yani. Travel agency, cafe, sitting room, bottomless teacups, and cheap rooms. Dorms Rp15,000; singles Rp29,000-36,000; doubles Rp35,000-39,000. ❶

Richardson's Homestay, Jl. Mochtar Lufti 21 (☎320 348), 2 blocks east of Jl. Penghibur near Bundt's Orchid Garden. Comfortable, clean rooms arranged around a central dining area. Shared *mandi*. Doubles with fan Rp40,000, with A/C Rp50,000. ❸

Hotel Makassar Golden, Jl. Pasar Ikan 52 (☎333 000; mghupg@indosat.net.id). Right on the bay, a few minutes from the fort and Jl. A. Yani. Peaceful luxury hotel; rooms have superb views out to sea and all the perks: A/C, satellite TV, attached Western baths with hot showers. Doubles Rp240,000-390,000. ❺

Losari Beach Hotel, Jl. Penghibur 10 (☎326 002; fax 313 978). Centrally located mid-range hotel with views of the bay. All rooms come with A/C, satellite TV, hot showers, and phones. Doubles Rp300,000-450,000. ❺

FOOD

Makassar is a seafood lover's heaven. **Food carts** ❶ and seafood **warung** ❶ set up early every evening along Jl. Penghibur to make up **Pantai Losari,** named after its beachside locale. Delicious fish, crab, and squid dishes are served until well into the night, and a full meal will normally cost less than Rp10,000. If you're in the mood for a drink, grab a beer at one of Jl. Penghibur's cafes.

Istana Laut, Jl. Datumuseng 1, around the corner from Richardson's Homestay and Bundt's Orchid Garden. *The* place for tasty, fresh seafood. Fish from Rp15,000. Fried prawns Rp16,000. Crab in butter sauce Rp40,000-60,000. Open daily 9am-11pm. ❹

New Shogun Japanese Restaurant, Jl. Penghibur 2. Near the fort, on the left as you walk down Jl. Penghibur with the sea on the right. Real soy sauce, real wasabi, and real Japanese pop music. Sublime sashimi (Rp78,500) and sushi (Rp76,500) are obvious choices, but if you're thinking in yen, try the imported *shabu-shabu* (Rp79,500) too. Open daily 11:30am-3pm and 6-11pm. ❺

Warung Pak Toba, on Jl. Penghibur, right next to the fort. A series of tarpaulin-covered stalls serving outstanding seafood at unbeatable prices. Often packed. Squid, crab, fish, and chicken—all around Rp8000. Open daily 3pm-4am. ❷

Pizza Ria Kafe, Jl. A. Yani 2, on the right, just before Lampangan Karebosi. Winner of the All-Indonesia Pizza Hut Look-Alike Competition, 2002. A/C American-food wonderland. Pizzas Rp20,000-30,000. Pasta and salad bar. Call ☎336 336 for delivery. Branches at Jl. G. Latimojong 152, on the corner with Jl. Saddang, and at Jl. Boulevard Rako Ruby 12. Open daily 6:30am-11pm. ❹

Rumah Makan Maxim II, Jl. Sulawesi 78. Large A/C dining room with a TV humming to itself quietly in the corner. Chinese-style seafood. Prawns Rp20,000-35,000. Crab Rp22,500-40,000. Beef, frog, fish, and chicken also available. Open daily 10am-2:30pm and 6-11pm. ❹

SIGHTS AND NIGHTLIFE

Once called Fort Jumpandang (from which Ujung Pandang derives its name), the structure near the waterfront on Jl. Penghibur was renamed **Fort Rotterdam** after the Dutch gained control of the area in 1669. There has been a fortification on this site since at least 1545, but most of what remains today is Dutch-built. It now houses government offices and the **La Galigo Museum.** One wing displays a collection of ethnographic exhibits from around Indonesia; a second features artifacts from various kingdoms of Southern Sulawesi. (Fort open daily 7am-6pm. Museum open Tu-Su 8am-1pm. Admission by donation.) Clustered north of the fort are several Chinese temples, including the **Temple of the Heavenly Queen,** whose front altar was reduced to rubble during anti-Chinese riots. The shrine, dedicated to the sailor-protecting goddess Tian Hou Gong, is located at the corner of Jl. Sulawesi and Jl. Serui, one block north of Jl. A. Yani. Farther up Jl. Sulawesi at Jl. Bali is the **Temple of the Dragon Apparition,** whose central altar celebrates Xian Mu, the mother of immortals. Farther north is the Javanese-style **Tomb of Diponegoro,** inside a rustic cemetery near the intersection of Jl. Diponegoro and Jl. Akademis. One of Indonesia's favorite national heroes (just count the roads named after him), Diponegoro was a beloved prince of Yogyakarta who led pro-independence forces against the Dutch during the Java War of 1825-30. For his troubles, he was exiled to Celebes (modern-day Sulawesi), where he lived in imprisonment until his death in Makassar. South of the fort off Jl. Penghibur is **Bundt's Orchid Garden (Taman Anggrek),** Jl. Mochtar Lufti 15, a pleasantly shaded yard with a stunning seashell shop. Ask multilingual Clara to show you the "Golden Cowrie" and "Glory of the Sea." (☎322 572. Open daily dawn to dusk.)

Shark Cafe ❸, Jl. Penghibur 33, on the left as you walk down the street from the fort with the sea on your right. Cold beers and loud music make this a good spot to sit and enjoy some Bintang (large Rp15,000) at an outdoor table—as long as you don't mind a healthy dose of traffic fumes with your beer. (Open daily 6pm-midnight.) **Kareba Music Café ❸,** Jl. Penghibur 12, next door to the Losari Beach Hotel, has a pleasant beer-garden atmosphere with (mostly atrocious) live music nightly. It's a popular foreigners' hangout. (Large beer Rp16,000. Open daily 4pm-1am.)

DAYTRIPS FROM MAKASSAR

MAKASSAR BAY. Home to a collection of white-sand islands and some of the finest coral reefs in the region, Makassar Bay is ideal for aquatic exploration. Unfortunately, careless snorkeling and explosives used in dynamite fishing have nearly destroyed reefs close to shore; decent dives sites are at least 10km out. **Samalona** is the jewel of the bay, with budget bamboo huts on the beach, while the secluded island of **Kodingareng Keke** provides a quiet retreat. The ocean floor near **Kapoposang** drops dramatically and teems with sea life. In Makassar, sporting goods stores on Jl. Somba Opu sell and rent snorkeling gear. **Makassar Diving Center,** Jl. Ujung Pandang 4, 50m north of the fort, rents masks, snorkels, and fins and offers 4hr. snorkeling and island sightseeing trips (US$25), 1-day diving trips (US$50-100), or multi-day package tours (US$25-200). *(Charter boats (up to 6 people; Rp100,000 each) leave from the Tumba Kayu Bangkoa Pier, south of the intersection of Jl. Pattimura and Jl. Penghibur, for the islands of Barang Caddi (1hr.), Barang Lompo (1hr.), and Samalona (30min.). Boats to Kodingareng Keke (1hr.) and Bone Tambung (1½hr.) cost Rp200,000.)*

MAROS CAVES. With over 55 caverns, the Maros Caves are a wonderland of bizarre rock formations, running streams, and prehistoric wall paintings. The most visited site is the "Prehistoric Park" at **Leang-Leang,** where two caves are decorated with paintings of babirusa (wild pig) believed to be 5000 years old. *(Take a bemo (Rp2000) or DAMRI bus (Rp3500) directly to Maros (1½hr.) and ask to be let off at the caves (gua). Bring a flashlight. Open daily 8am-6pm. Rp2500.)*

BANTIMURUNG WATERFALL. Bantimurung Falls, 1½hr. northeast of Makassar, is a park reserve surrounded by impressive cliffs that are worth the trip in themselves. The waterfalls are nothing special by Indonesian standards, but the butterfly-filled walk up the stairs to the left is delightful. A 15min. promenade up the riverbed leads to **Store Cave,** harboring a waterfall, a secluded pool, and smaller caves within. Before the main waterfall, there's a quieter walk up to **Gua Mimpi (Dream Cave),** a pitch-dark cave filled with stalactites and stalagmites and weirdly shaped rock formations. You'll have a rotten time without a flashlight. Guide hire is around Rp10,000 per person. *(Take a* bemo *(Rp2000) or DAMRI bus (Rp3500) from Ujung Pandang's Makassar Mall to Maros (1½hr.), then jump on a* bemo *(Rp1500) to Bantimurung.)*

GOWA. Along the Jeneberang River, 11km south of Ujung Padang, lie the scattered remains of the once great kingdom of Gowa, including the ruins of the fortress **Somba Opu,** the strongest of the forts that once protected Makassar. **Old Gowa,** where ancient mosques, royal tombs, and legendary coronation stones remain standing, is farther east. The sacred **Tomb of Syech Yusuf** stands in the northwest section. A religious-scholar-turned-resistance-fighter, Syech Yusuf (1626-94) purportedly brought Islam to Sri Lanka and South Africa during his Dutch-imposed exile. A road south of the tomb runs southeast to **Katangka Mosque,** Sulawesi's oldest mosque, supposedly built in 1605, shortly after Islam became Gowa's official religion. Walk 300m down the road from the mosque, make a right, and then make another to reach Gowa's kings' **Batu Pelantikan** (Coronation Stone). Beside it is the **Tomb of Hasanuddin,** the celebrated 12th king of Gowa, who waged war against the Dutch before his final defeat in 1660. *(Take a* bemo *from Makassar Mall and get off at Tangul Patompo (Rp1000). From there, boats (Rp1000) cross the river.)*

TANA TORAJA

Beautiful Tana Toraja (or "Tator") is the heart of Sulawesi's tourist trade. People from all over the world flock here by the thousands, drawn to the glorious scenery and fascinating culture of the Torajan people. Rantepao, the regional hub, is nothing to write home about, but within easy striking distance of town—often just an hour's walk away—are the countless attractions that have helped turn "Torajaland" into one of the most popular tourist destinations in the whole of Indonesia. If the English-menu restaurants and Euro-tourists around Rantepao start to get you down, consider making the trek to Mamasa, an unforgettable three-day adventure through some of the most beautiful, untouched areas in the country.

RANTEPAO ☎0423

Rantepao is geared toward the affluent outsider. Sleek tour buses buzz past rice farmers, and "traditional houses" are touched up annually with fresh paint. Restaurants cater to European tourists with fragile digestive systems, and guides think they know exactly what you want to see. But just beyond the town limits, stretching in all directions, lies a lush green mountain paradise that remains every bit as impressive as it must have been before the tour buses arrived. Most tourists follow the same well-trodden path between the best-known cultural and natural attractions; if you're prepared to head out on your own and do a bit of exploring, you'll probably find you have the place almost to yourself.

TRANSPORTATION

Buses: Bus companies line Jl. Mappanyuki. **Limon Express** and **Litha & Co.** run frequently to **Ujung Pandang** and **Parepare.** Daily service to **Palu** (26hr.; Rp50,000) and **Ujung Pandang** (9hr.; 7:30am, 1, 6:30, 9pm; Rp30,000-60,000). Regional instability has made routes through Central Sulawesi unpredictable and potentially dangerous; keep your ears open and ask agencies and hotels for up-to-date information.

Local Transportation: Bemo run regularly between Rantepao and **Makale,** 18km south, passing many of the popular tourist sights on the way. **Becak** are also hard to miss.

Rentals. Motorcycles (Rp00,000 per day) and **bicycles** (Rp30,000 per day) available at several establishments in town, including **Holiday Tourist Service,** Jl. Mangadil 25 (☎254 68), and **Bagus Tourist Service,** Jl. Dr. Ratulangi 62, close to Wisma Maria I.

ORIENTATION AND PRACTICAL INFORMATION

Rantepao, 18km north of Makale, centers around a mercantile north-south thoroughfare, which enters from the south as **Jl. Pongtiku,** becomes **Jl. A. Yani** in the center of town, and then changes names again to become **Jl. Mappanyuki** past the large intersection with Jl. Diponegoro. Farther north, the same road (now known as **Jl. Pahlawan**) continues across the north curve of the **Sa'dan River** and leads to **Jl. Suloara,** to the left beyond the bridge. A general **market** is in the center of town, but the real market life is 1km up Jl. Diponegoro.

Tourist Office: Pusat Informasi Wisata, Jl. A. Yani 62A (☎212 77). Free maps and a listing of ceremonies. Open M-Sa 8am-2pm.

Tours: Several agencies and guide services on Jl. A. Yani/Mappanyuki. **Holiday Tourist Service,** Jl. Mangadil 25 (☎254 68), and **Bagus Tourist Service,** Jl. Dr. Ratulangi 62, both arrange guides for trips to Torajan villages and ceremonies.

Currency Exchange: BNI, Jl. A. Yani 84 (☎243 16), exchanges cash and traveler's checks. Open M-F 8am-2pm.

Bookstore: Celebes Tourist Service, Jl. Mangadil 11, has a small selection of secondhand English books for sale.

Emergency: Police: ☎110. **Ambulance:** ☎118.

Police: At the corner of Jl. A. Yani and Jl. Landorundun, close to the central market.

Pharmacy: Rayndi Farma, Jl. A. Yani 99 (☎210 13). Open M-Sa 8am-8:30pm.

Medical Services: Rumah Sakit Elim, Jl. A. Yani 68 (☎212 58), 500m out of town on the left as you head toward Makale. Open 24hr.

Telephones: Telkom office (☎211 08), next to the post office. Allows collect and credit-card calls from a card phone. Open 24hr. **Wartel Citra,** next to the Wisma Pasadena Hotel on Jl. Mappanyuki, is also open 24hr.

Post Office: Jl. A. Yani 111, opposite the bigger of the 2 Bank Rakyats. *Poste Restante.* Open M-Th 8am-2pm, F 8-11am, Sa 8am-1pm.

Postal Code: 91831.

ACCOMMODATIONS

Rantepao's supply of rooms exceeds demand for much of the year. Most of the best places are on the outskirts of town, a short walk from the bustle and noise of the main road. Prices generally include a simple breakfast.

Wisma Malita, Jl. Suloara 110 (☎210 11). Go north on the main road through town and cross the Sa'dan river, then take the first left onto Jl. Suloara; it's on the right after about 700m. A quiet refuge from tourist chaos with newly renovated rooms and a small garden. Doubles with Western toilets and showers Rp35,000-40,000. ❸

Wisma Maria I, Jl. Ratulangi 23 (☎211 65). Backpacker favorite. Clean doubles with attached baths along open corridors overlooking a pleasant garden courtyard. Singles Rp25,000-50,000; doubles Rp40,000-80,000. ❷

Hotel Indra Toraja, Jl. Landorundun 63 (☎215 83; fax 215 47), at the bottom of the road, opposite the church. Mid-range hotel with A/C rooms around a courtyard and mini-jungle. Doubles with Western toilets and showers Rp100,000-150,000.❺

Wisma Monika, Jl. Ratulangi 36 (☎212 16), a few doors down from Maria I. Friendly family-run hostel with large, clean rooms. Christian iconography on the walls and Jesus look-alikes in most of the rooms. Doubles with Western bath Rp40,000. ❸

Wisma Surya, Jl. Monginsidi 36 (☎213 12), right by the river. Good bare-bones budget option. Singles and doubles Rp25,000. ❷

FOOD

Tourist restaurants in Rantepao turn local specialties, such as bamboo-tube-cooked meats *(pa' piong)*, black rice, and palm wine, into bland fare. Small restaurants and *warung* off the main road, however, serve *pa' piong* the old-fashioned way. To eat with locals, ask around for directions to **Warung Ni'Buri ❷,** on Jl. Emmy Saelan. *Tuak* (palm wine) is cheapest in markets, but taste before you buy—it goes bad quickly. To satisfy pancake cravings, try any of the backpacker hangouts in the center of town. **Riman ❸,** Jl. Mappanyuki 115, is a popular spot on the left of the main road toward the bridge. (Roast pork Rp18,500; large beer Rp12,500. Open daily 8am-10pm.) **Mambo ❹,** opposite the Wisma Maria I, is a good place for a few beers or a quick meal. (Hamburgers Rp25,000; fried chicken Rp25,000; large Bintang Rp12,500. Open daily 6:30am-10pm.) **Mart's Cafe ❸,** on Jl. Ratulangi by the football field, has decent food, including tourist-friendly versions of local specialties. (*Pa' piong* Rp20,000; chicken and cheese sandwich Rp11,500.)

SIGHTS

Tana Toraja is a walker's paradise. The best time to trek is March through October, when clouds at the end of the dry season protect hikers from the harsh sun. Avoid the wet season, when roads turn into leech-infested mudslides. Guides are recommended for longer trips. Tourist attractions charge Rp10,000 entrance fees.

Many of the area's most popular sights are just a few kilometers south of Rantepao, off the main road to Makale. **Londa,** 6km from Rantepao toward Makale, is famous for its collection of *tau-tau* effigies (carved as part of Torajan burial ceremonies) and two caves filled with decaying coffins and hundreds of human skulls. Guides can help you find your way with oil lamps (Rp10,000). Braving the death-dark, bone-strewn caves without a light is not a good idea. **Lemo,** 6km farther south, has one of the most spectacular cliff-graves in all of Tana Toraja, fronted by dozens of *tau-tau* effigies. Most figures have their right hand extended, symbolically accepting offerings, and their left protecting the graves from evil spirits. Many of the carvings here are replicas financed by the government after a heist in the late 1980s. For a relaxing daytrip, catch a Makale-bound *bemo* in Rantepao and get off at the road to Lemo (Rp1000). After studying the *tau-tau,* walk north along the small paths to **Tilanga** and its swimming hole. Continue to Londa and catch a *bemo* to Rantepao. **Ke'te Kesu',** whose well-preserved *tongkonan* houses and rice barns have made it one of the most visited villages in the area, is 4km southeast of Rantepao. A path leads back from the rows of houses to a cliff gravesite packed with coffins, skulls, and *tau-tau.* Any *bemo* from Rantepao to Makale can drop you at the turn-off for Ke'te Kesu'; from there, it's a 20min. walk uphill to the village itself. Excursions into the countryside north of Rantepao take you through some of the most spectacular scenery in Sulawesi. To follow a popular route, take a *bemo* from **Terminal Bolu** north of Rantepao to **Lempo** (45min., Rp2500) and to walk uphill from there to **Batutumonga** for some stunning views out over the whole region. From here, continue uphill to the turn-off for **Pana.** Pana has a modest cliff-grave with some nearby tree-graves used for infants. A pleasant downhill walk leads to **Tikala,** where you can catch *bemo* back to Rantepao.

NORTH SULAWESI (SULAWESI UTARA)

The smallest of the island's provinces, North Sulawesi is the most prosperous. Blessed with fertile soil fed by volcanic ash and seasonally heavy rains, the region has cashed in on coconuts and cloves. The most visible remnant of the Dutch colonial presence is the predominance of Christianity among the Minahasa people, who constitute the province's largest ethnic group. Today, most tourists come to North Sulawesi for the exquisite diving near Manado.

MANADO ☎0431

The prosperity of Manado, North Sulawesi's capital, is evident in its lively markets and Chinese and Minahasa traditions and cuisines. Thus far, the city has avoided direct ethnic conflict; during the 1998 riots, Chinese from across the archipelago come here seeking refuge from ethnic violence. For most tourists, Manado is the gateway to the world-class diving at Bunaken-Manado Tua National Marine Park.

TRANSPORTATION

Flights: Sam Ratulangi Airport, 15km out of town. Walk left downhill to catch a *microlet* to the Paal 2 Bus Terminal in the center of town, or take a cab (Rp40,000 to most hotels). Airport tax Rp15,000 domestic, Rp75,000 international. Manado is a major air hub; there are several flights per day to most major cities in Indonesia, as well as international flights to **Singapore** (Silk Air; M, W, Sa; US$180) and **Davao, Philippines** (Bouraq; M and F; US$150). For flight bookings, try **Limbunan,** 159 Jl. Sam Ratulangi (☎857 555), an official agent for most airlines. Often has cheaper fares than the airlines themselves. **Bouraq,** Jl. Sarapung 28 (☎841 470). **Garuda,** Jl. Diponegoro 15 (☎852 154). **Mandala,** Jl. Sam Ratulangi 175 (☎859 333); **Merpati,** Jl. Martadinata 43 (☎853 213), near the Paal 2 Terminal. **Silk Air,** Jl. Sarapung 5 (☎863 744).

Ferries: PELNI boats depart from **Bitung** (see p. 233). **PELNI office,** Jl. Sam Ratulangi 7 (☎855 115). Open M-F 8am-3pm. Destinations include: **Balikpapan** (Rp214,000-724,000); **Bima; Denpasar; Makassar** (Rp350,000-1,194,500); **Surabaya; Tanjung Priok** (for **Jakarta;** Rp525,000-1,798,500); **Ternate** (Rp93,500-305,500).

Buses: Buses leave from the **Paal 2 Terminal,** east of the city, to: **Airmadidi** (30min., Rp2000); **Bitung** (1hr., every 30min. 7am-9pm, Rp2500); **Tondano** (1hr., frequent, Rp2500). From **Karombasan Station,** south of town in Wanea, buses leave for **Tomohon** (1hr., Rp2500) and destinations farther into the Minahasan heartland. From the **Malalayang Terminal,** southwest of Manado, buses leave for: **Kotamobagu** (4hr.; Rp10,000); **Makassar** (3 days; 9am; Rp150,000); **Palu** (24-30hr.; Rp60,000).

ORIENTATION AND PRACTICAL INFORMATION

North-south **Jl. Sam Ratulangi,** parallel to **Jl. Piere Tendean (Waterfront Boulevard),** has all the goods and services a traveler needs. Another road, called **Jl. Lasut** at the top and **Jl. Sarapung** at the bottom, runs one block inland from the northern part of Jl. Sam Ratulangi. **Jl. Walanda Maramis** (sometimes called **Jl. Tendean**), is a shopping street that runs farther inland from Jl. Sam Ratulangi and Jl. Lasut. At the far northern end of **Pasar 45,** *microlets* head anywhere in the city for Rp1000 but are often full and sometimes unwilling to stop for travelers with large bags.

Tourist Office: Government Tourist Office, Jl. Diponegoro 111 (☎851 723). Open M-Th 8am-2pm, F 8-11am, Sa 8am-1pm.

Currency Exchange: BNI, at the north end of Jl. Lasut. Open M-F 8am-4pm.

Markets: Pasar Bersehati is north of the harbor, past the end of Jl. Sam Ratulangi. The **Matahari** supermarket and department store is on Jl. Sam Ratulangi, not far from the post office (on the right as you head south).

Bookstore: Gramedia, Jl. Sam Ratulangi, on the right as you head south from the post office. Open daily 9am-9pm.

Police: Central station, on southern Jl. Diponegoro. **Branch** at the Telkom office on Jl. Sam Ratulangi.

Emergency: ☎110. **Ambulance:** ☎118.

Pharmacy: Apotik Kimia Farma, Jl. Sam Ratulangi 31 (☎864 012), opposite Gramedia bookstore, on the left as you walk south from the post office. Open 24hr.

Medical Services: Rumah Sakit Gmim, Jl. Raya Talete 1 (☎352 712), in Tomohon, 30min. from Manado, at the end of the *microlet* line. The region's best hospital.

Telephones: Telkom office, Jl. Sam Ratulangi 4 (☎861 447), on the left as you head north, opposite the PELNI office. Open 24hr. **Wartel Virgo,** Jl. Sam Ratulangi 5, on the right as you head north from the post office. Open 24hr.

Internet Access: The News Cafe, Jl. Sam Ratulangi 50 (☎846 870), on the left south of the post office. Speedy connections, A/C, and a full menu. Probably the best Internet cafe in Indonesia. Rp150 per min. Open daily 7:30am-midnight. **Cybernet,** Jl. Sam Ratulangi 23, by the post office. Rp6000 per hr. Open daily 9am-10pm.

Post Offices: GPO, Jl. Sam Ratulangi 19 (☎852 301). *Poste Restante.* Open M-Th 8am-7pm, F 8-11am and 1-7pm, Sa 8am-6pm. **Express Mail: DHL** (☎852 778), on Jl. Sam Ratulangi between Jl. Sudirman and Jl. Walanda Maramis. Open M-F 8am-6pm.

Postal Code: 95111.

ACCOMMODATIONS

Hotel Minahasa, Jl. Sam Ratulangi 199 (☎862 559 or 862 059; fax 854 041), at the far southern end of Jl. Sam Ratulangi. Cottage-style rooms with fine views come with private Western toilets and showers. Breakfast included. Singles with fan Rp55,000, with A/C Rp115,000; doubles Rp75,000/Rp140,000. MC/V. ❹

Hotel Celebes, Jl. Rumambi 8A (☎870 425 or 859 069; fax 859 068), north of Jl. Sam Ratulangi, right on the port. Best location in town if you're going to Bunaken in the morning. Restaurant and travel agent. Economy rooms with shared *mandi* Rp40,000, with A/C and private bath Rp60,000, with hot water Rp100,000-120,000. ❸

Manado Bersehati Hotel, Jl. Jend. Sudirman 20 (☎855 022; fax 857 238), on a side street 1 block inland from the Jl. Sudirman and Jl. Sarapung intersection. Clean, bare rooms. Economy rooms with shared bath and fan Rp22,500; singles/doubles with private bath Rp45,000/Rp55,000; doubles with A/C Rp67,000; VIP rooms with shower, A/C, and "living room" Rp75,000-97,500. ❷

Rex Hotel, Jl. Sugiono 3 (☎851 136 or 856 650; fax 867 706). Head inland on Jl. Walanda Maramis from Jl. Sam Ratulangi and make the 4th left. Clean and affordable. Economy singles with shared *mandi* Rp22,500, with A/C and private Western bath; doubles Rp37,500/Rp75,000. ❷

FOOD

Minahasan cuisine features spicy specialties such as forest rat, bat, dog, and *tinutuan* (vegetable breakfast porridge). The best place to sample these delicacies is at the string of restaurants overlooking Manado near the town of **Tinoor** on the road to Tomohon. More conventional fare is available at the cheap *warung* that line the upper part of **Jl. Sam Ratulangi.**

Tinoor Jaya, Jl. Sam Ratulangi 167, close to Hotel Minahasa. Has all of Manado's specialties. There's no menu—ask for *rintek wuuk* (spicy dog), *kawaok* (fried forest rat), or *lawang pangang* (stewed bat). Most dishes around Rp6000. Open daily 1-5pm. ❶

Green Garden, on Jl. Sam Ratulangi, on the right as you head south, just past the post office. Pleasant, airy, Chinese-run place. Crab Rp7000; prawns Rp30,000; fried chicken Rp25,000-50,000. Open daily 10am-midnight; closed last Su of the month. ❹

Kawan Baru, Jl. Sam Ratulangi 212, just south of the Hotel Minahasa. Trendy youngsters' hangout. Simple Indonesian fast-food (*mie goreng* Rp10,000) and a wide range of fruit juices (*jus alpokat* Rp6000). Open daily 9am-9pm. **Branch** at Jl. Walanda Maramis 45, near the Jl. Sam Ratulangi intersection. ❷

Peony Restaurant, Jl. Sarapung 33, heading north up Jl. Sam Ratulangi, turn right just after Gramedia bookstore (opposite the Pusat Protestant Church), and take the first left; it's on the right, about 50m up. Good Chinese food in well-polished surroundings. Squid Rp23,000. Chicken in oyster sauce Rp18,000. Open daily 10am-10pm. ❸

Padang Raya, Jl. Sam Ratulangi 5, opposite the Telkom office. Good, spicy, *padang*-style food. Most dishes around Rp5000. Open daily 8:30am-10:30pm. ❶

SIGHTS AND ENTERTAINMENT

The **Provincial Museum of North Sulawesi,** at Jl. Supratman 72, contains a collection of traditional clothing, pottery, and handicrafts from North Sulawesi. (Open M-F 8am-2pm. Admission by donation.) The **Ban Hian Kiong Buddhist-Confucian Temple,** on Jl. Panjaitan in the city center, serves Manado's large Chinese population. In February, two weeks after the Chinese New Year, it is home to one of Southeast Asia's largest **Toa Pa Kong Festival** celebrations.

Amigo Billiards Hall, on Jl. Walanda Maramis, is as friendly as the name suggests. (Pool Rp10,000 per hr. Open daily 9am-1am.) Word travels quickly about **Hot Gossip,** a popular bar and nightclub on Jl. Sam Ratulangi, on the left as you head north, a 5min. walk from the post office. The club is packed nightly with dancers grinding to ear-splitting disco. (Cover Rp10,000. Open 10pm-3am.)

NEAR MANADO

BUNAKEN

The 753 sq. km **Bunaken-Manado Tua National Marine Park,** one of the best diving spots in the world, has turned Manado into a major stop on the backpacker circuit. There are dozens of world-class dive sites here, and many run excellent dive centers. Underwater novices can content themselves with snorkeling or take an introductory scuba course. All visitors to the park must pay an entrance fee, proceeds of which are funneled into the care of Bunaken's fragile ecosystem. Daily tickets cost Rp50,000; year-long passes are Rp150,000. From Manado, take a **boat** from behind Pasar Bersehati to **Bunaken** (1½hr.; departs roughly 2pm, returns about 7 or 8am; Rp15,000) or charter an **outrigger** (Rp50,000-100,000).

The best way to explore Bunaken is to stay at one of the dive resorts on the island itself. **Liang Beach,** 100m from the drop-off, is home to several posh dive centers and a good range of budget accommodation. Simple **cottages** ❸ with *mandi* run about Rp30,000-60,000 per person. **Papa Boa, Ibu Konda, Santika,** and **Panorama Cottages** are all good budget options. On the other side of the island, **Pangalisang Beach** has a similar range of places to stay, including **MC** ❸ (rooms Rp30,000), **Daniel's** ❸ (rooms Rp35,000), **Lorenso's Cottage** ❸ (rooms Rp30,000), and **Seabreeze** ❸ (rooms Rp40,000-60,000).

Bunaken's beaches may not be paradise, but the island's world-class dive sites more than make up for it. Turtles, tuna, and whitetip sharks frequent **Lekuan,** a superb wall dive. Schools of barracuda are often spotted in **Pangalisang,** and **Sachiko**'s spectacular density of fish and strong currents attract schools of pelagics. **Cela Cela** is an ideal site to observe reef life at night.

Sulawesi Dive Quest, on Liang Beach, is one of the island's best dive centers, with mint-condition gear and knowledgeable instructors. (☎863 023; info@sulawesi-dive-quest.com. 2 dives US$40; 5-day PADI open-water course US$340.) **Froggies** ❺ is an impressive, all-inclusive hotel and dive shop. (☎812 430; manado@divefroggies.com. 2 dives US$60; accommodations US$15-35 per person.) Other dive resorts include **Two Fishes Divers** ❹ (☎0811 432 805) and **Living Colours** ❺ (☎8124 306 063) both on Pangalisang Beach. (Two Fishes Divers: info@twofishdivers.com. US$25 per dive; PADI open-water course US$360; advanced course US$250; accommodations US$7-12 per person. Living Colours: info@livingcoloursdiving.com. US$30 per dive; PADI open-water course US$360; cottages US$20 per person).

The pricier dive centers on Manado offer better accommodations, more amenities, and easier access to shops and banks. The only downside is a 1hr. commute to the dive sites. **Nusantara Diving Center** ❺ (**NDC;** ☎863 988) is in Molas, north of Manado. (Take a *microlet* to Tuminting and then an *oplet* to Molas, or call NDC for pickup from Manado. 2 dives US$60, with accommodation US$80; PADI open-water course US$400.) Small and intimate **Murex Dive Resort** ❺, Jl. Sudirman 28 (☎866 280; fax 852 116; info@murexdive.com), has bungalows south of the city.

BITUNG AND TANGKOKO

By the 1960s, Manado's port was too silted for cargo boats, and most shipping traffic moved to **Bitung** on the other side of the peninsula. The only reason to come here is to catch **PELNI ferries.** From the Paal 2 Terminal in Manado, take a bus to Bitung (1hr., frequent departures, Rp2500). **Tangkoko**'s main attraction is the **Tangkoko-Batuangus Dua Saudara National Park.** Home to the endemic *maleo* bird and the Spectral Tarsier (the world's smallest species of primate), Tangkoko supports a wealth of diverse species. To get to Tangkoko, take the Bitung bus to **Girian** (45min., Rp2000), then catch a jeep north to **Batuputih** (30min., Rp2500).

SUMATRA

One of Indonesia's largest islands, Sumatra plays second fiddle only to Java in politics and economics. Notorious for its poor roads and fickle climate, Sumatra is no jetsetter's paradise. Many regions prove inaccessible for even the most determined, and women traveling alone may experience harassment. Still, the Medan-Padang route via Lake Toba, Nias, and Bukittinggi is well traveled and promises intrepid visitors a memorable experience. With hikeable jungle terrain, crystalline crater lakes, and rich cultural character, Sumatra should not be overlooked by those with the desire—and stomach—for adventure.

NORTH SUMATRA

MEDAN ☎061

With a population of nearly 2 million, Medan is Sumatra's largest city by far, and the third-largest in Indonesia. It is also a major port of entry for travelers, and first impressions tend to range from disappointment to dismay. Medan is characterized by an uncompromising atmosphere of mad honking chaos, and many travelers, confronted with the smoke and grime of the traffic-choked streets, scurry straight to the safety of their hotels—emerging only to catch the first bus out of town. Behind all the fumes and noise, however, lie neighborhoods full of character, with a richness of food and architecture that reflects the diverse local population. Mosques dot the city, from the handsome Mesjid Raya to decrepit constructions weathered by the past. Colorful Hindu and Buddhist temples find their place west and east of the town center in Little India and Chinatown, neighborhoods bursting with their own tales, tongues, and tastes. If you have a secret fondness for shopping malls, McDonald's, and movie theaters, Medan is a good place to get your last fix before setting off on the backpacker trail south to Lake Toba and beyond.

TRANSPORTATION

Flights: Polonia International Airport (☎456 5777), 3km south of town at the end of Jl. Imam Bonjol. Regular public transportation does not run to the airport; take a *becak* (Rp10,000) or taxi (Rp20,000) instead. Airlines accept MC/V.

Garuda, Jl. Balai Kota 2 (☎451 6400), across from the post office. Open M-F 8am-5pm, Sa 9am-1pm. Daily flights to: **Banda Aceh** (1hr.; Rp400,000); **Denpasar** (3hr.; Rp1,684,000); **Jakarta** (2hr.; Rp1,159,900).

Malaysian Airlines, Jl. Imam Bonjol 17 (☎451 9333), ground fl. of the Danau Toba Hotel. Open M-F 8:30am-4:30pm, Sa 8:30am-1:30pm. Daily flights to **Kuala Lumpur** (US$85) and **Penang** (US$85).

Merpati, Jl. Brigjen Katamso 219 (☎455 1888). Open M-F 8am-4:30 pm, Sa 9am-2pm. To: **Palembang** (Rp1,355,700); **Pekan Baru** (Rp 991,600); **Pontianak** (Rp1,170,900).

Silk Air/Singapore Airlines (☎453 7744), on the lower back side of the Tiara Convention Center off Jl. Imam Bonjol. Open M-F 8am-5pm, Sa 8am-noon. To **Singapore** (US$115).

Buses: There are 2 main terminals and a 3rd smaller one; *Sudako* #64 runs between them. *Sudako* can also take you from either terminal to travelers' hangouts on Jl. Sisingamangaraja. Ask around for transport to the **Mesjid Raya** (about Rp1000). Both terminals have dozens of different bus company offices–shop around for the best fares.

Amplas Terminal, 10km south of the city center at the end of Jl. Sisingamangaraja, serves most destinations south of Medan, as well as long-distance buses to Java. From the city center take any *sudako* (20min., Rp1000) marked "Amplas" running south along Jl. Sisingamangaraja; ask to get

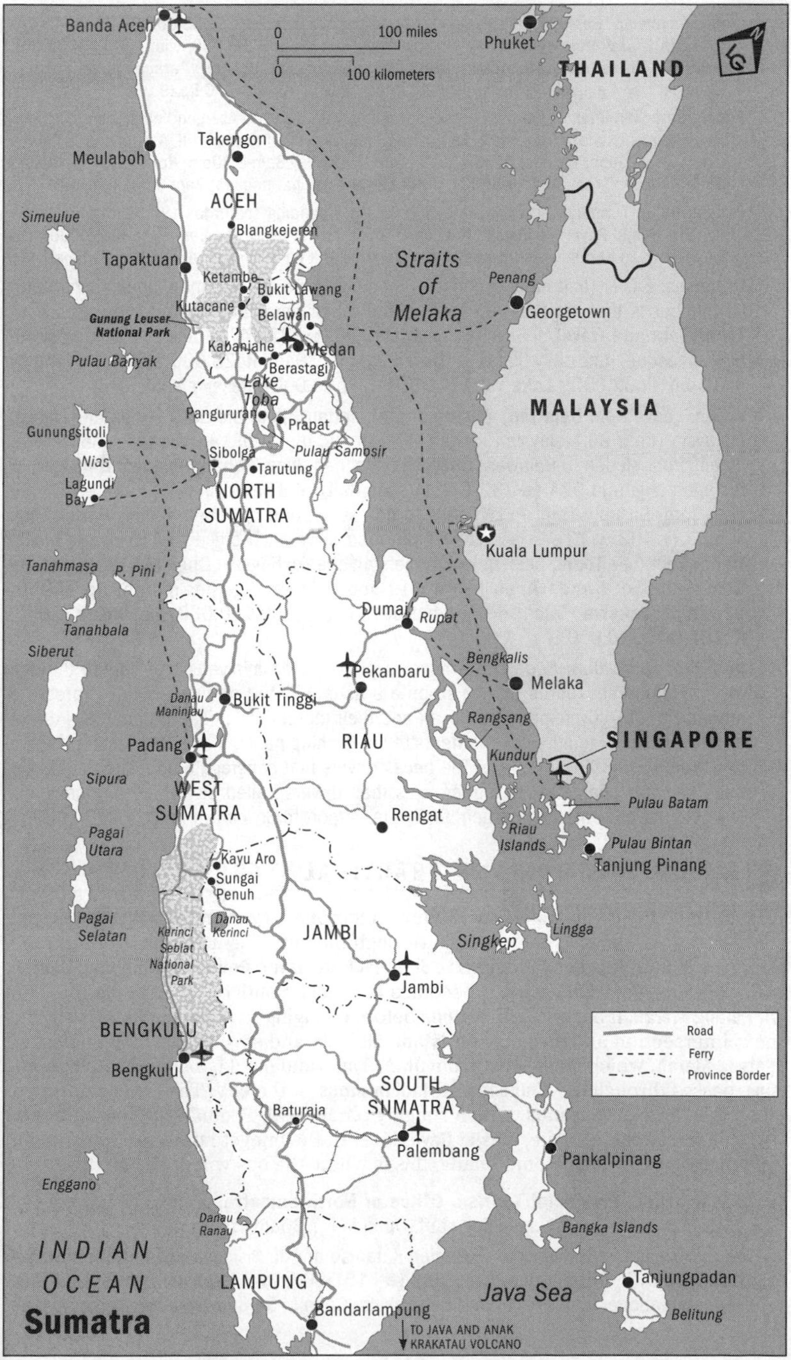
Banda Aceh
0 100 miles
0 100 kilometers
Phuket
THAILAND
Meulaboh
Takengon
ACEH
Simeulue
Blangkejeren
Tapaktuan
Ketambe
Bukit Lawang
Kutacane
Gunung Leuser National Park
Belawan
Straits of Melaka
Penang
Georgetown
Kabanjahe
Medan
Berastagi
Pulau Banyak
Lake Toba
Pangururan
Prapat
MALAYSIA
Gunungsitoli
Nias
Sibolga
Pulau Samosir
Tarutung
Lagundi Bay
NORTH SUMATRA
Kuala Lumpur
Tanahmasa
P. Pini
Tanahbala
Dumai
Rupat
Siberut
Pekanbaru
Bengkalis
Melaka
Danau Maninjau
Bukit Tinggi
Rangsang
Padang
RIAU
SINGAPORE
Kundur
Sipura
WEST SUMATRA
Pulau Batam
Riau Islands
Rengat
Pulau Bintan
Tanjung Pinang
Pagai Utara
Kayu Aro
Sungai Penuh
Danau Kerinci
Pagai Selatan
Kerinci Seblat National Park
JAMBI
Lingga
Singkep
Jambi
Road
Ferry
Province Border
BENGKULU
Bengkulu
SOUTH SUMATRA
Baturaja
Palembang
Pankalpinang
Enggano
Danau Ranau
Bangka Islands
INDIAN OCEAN
LAMPUNG
Java Sea
Tanjungpadan
Belitung
Sumatra
Bandarlampung
TO JAVA AND ANAK KRAKATAU VOLCANO

INDONESIA

off at *"terminal."* Buses to: **Bukittinggi** (24hr.; 6 per day 8am-2pm; Rp63,000-96,000, with A/C Rp112,000); **Jakarta** (48hr.; every hr. 8am-7pm; Rp175,000-265,000, with A/C Rp300,000); **Padang** (24hr.; 6 per day 8am-2pm; Rp63,000, with A/C Rp112,000); **Parapat** (4hr.; 5 regular buses per day, frequent minibuses 7am-midnight; Rp24,000, with A/C Rp29,000).

Pinang Baris Terminal, 12km west of the city center, with buses to Aceh and other closer destinations. Frequent *sudako* (marked *P. Baris*, 30-40min., Rp1000) run along Jl. A. Yani and Jl. Palang Merah. Destinations include: **Banda Aceh** (14hr.; 8 per day 8am-8:30pm; Rp60,000); **Berastagi** (2½hr., frequent 7am-5pm, Rp3500); **Bukit Lawang** (3½hr., frequent 7am-5pm, Rp4000).

Padang Bulan Terminal, accessible via *Sudako* #41, heading south down Jl. Sisingamangaraja past the **Mesjid Raya.** Travelers to **Kutacane** (6hr.; roughly every 2hr. 8am-5pm; Rp25,000) and connections to **Ketambe** and **Blangkejeren** might find it easier to use this smaller terminal.

Minibuses: Easier (and more expensive) than public buses are small, privately run tourist minibuses that run between Medan and major destinations throughout Sumatra. **Tobali Tour and Travel,** Jl Sisingamangaraja 79C (☎732 4471), across from and south of the mosque, runs daily buses to: **Berastagi** (11:30am; Rp28,000); **Bukit Lawang** (3 and 5pm; Rp32,000); **Lake Toba** (11:30am; Rp40,000). Reserve seats early.

Ferries: Leave from **Belawan,** 26km north of Medan. There are daily ferries to **Penang,** Malaysia (4hr.; 90 Malaysian Ringgit (RM), round-trip 160RM). Fares include transfer by bus from Medan to Belawan. Children travel half-price. **Penang Express Bahagia,** Jl. Sisingamangaraja 92A (☎732 0421) sails daily at 10am. Open M-F 8am-5pm, Sa 8am-3pm, Su 8am-1pm. **PELNI** sails to domestic ports. The main office, Jl. Kol. Sugiorno 5 (☎453 8772), is less convenient than the branch office (☎415 5777) inside Trophy Tour (see **Tours,** below), where the staff speaks English. Open M-F 8am-5pm, Sa 8am-noon. To: **Banda Aceh** (16hr.; 12 sporadic sailings per month; Rp75,000-230,000); **Jakarta** (58hr.; every other day; Rp190,000-600,000) via **Batan** (20hr.; Rp105,000-310,000).

Local Transportation: *Sudako* are rickety, multi-colored minivans that careen through the city along set routes; major stops are usually listed on windshields. Fares are around Rp1000. Cycle-powered *becak* and their motor-driven big brothers prowl downtown. If you don't mind a few moments of life-flashing panic, they're the fastest. Expect to pay Rp4000-8000 for a ride. The *becak* drivers that congregate opposite the Mesjid Raya typically charge much higher rates than drivers hailed elsewhere around town. **Taxis** do not have meters—bargain for a rate. Airport to downtown roughly Rp20,000.

ORIENTATION AND PRACTICAL INFORMATION

The heart of the city is made up of a few major one-way avenues with names that change several times as they ramble through the city. The main north-south road starts as **Jl. Putri Hijau** and changes to **Jl. Balai Kota** at the **Deli Plaza Shopping Center.** After passing **Merdeka Square,** it becomes **Jl. A. Yani.** South of the intersection with **Jl. Palang Merah,** it becomes **Jl. Pemuda** before changing to **Jl. Brigjen Katamso** at the next intersection and passing the **Istana Maimun** and several travel agencies. **Jl. Palang Merah,** which leads west from Jl. A. Yani (and quickly becomes **Jl. H. Z. Arifin**), passes through the **Chinese** and **Indian areas** of the city. The other important road is **Jl. Sisingamangaraja,** which roughly parallels Jl. Pemuda/Brigjen Katamso, passing the Grand Mosque, **Mesjid Raya.** Most of the budget hotels are here, and if you're arriving by boat from Penang, this is where the bus will drop you off.

Tourist Office: Provincial Tourism Office of North Sumatra, Jl. A. Yani 107 (☎453 8101). Friendly, English-speaking staff. Open M-F 7:30am-4:30pm.

Tours: Dozens of agencies line Jl. Brigjen Katamso and Jl. Sisingamangaraja. The best is **Trophy Tour,** Jl. Brigjen Katamso 33D-E (☎415 5666; www.trophytour.com). Domestic and international ferry, plane, and bus tickets. Open M-Sa 8am-5pm, Su 8am-noon.

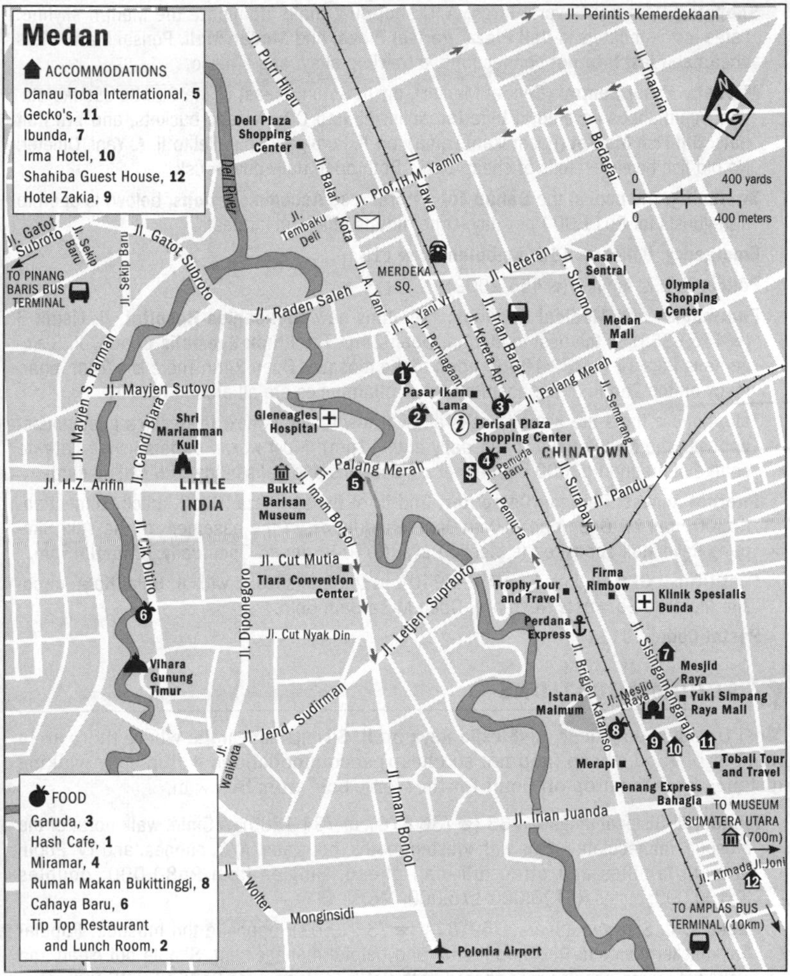

Consulates: Australia, Jl. Kartini 32 (☎415 7810). Open M-F 8am-4:30pm. **Malaysia,** Jl. Diponegoro 43 (☎453 1342). Open M-F 8am-1pm and 2-4pm. **Singapore,** Jl. Tengku Daud 3 (☎451 3366). Open M-F 8am-12:30pm and 1:30-4:30pm. **UK,** Jl. Kaptan Pattimura 459 (☎821 0559). Open M-F 8am-noon.

Currency Exchange: Change money here—rates are often worse outside Medan. Most banks are along Jl. Pemuda/Jl. A. Yani, including **BNI,** Jl. Pemuda 12 (☎453 8166). Open M-F 8am-3pm. Many guesthouses also change money. There are a number of **ATMs** around town, most are open 24hr. and accept international cards. Try BNI and other banks, shopping malls, and the Danau Toba Hotel on Jl. Palang Merah.

Bookstore: Gramedia, Jl. Gajah Mada 23, west of Jl. Palang Merah, has a decent selection of English books. Open M-F 9am-8:45pm, Sa-Su 9am-9:15pm. **Firma Rimbow,** Jl. Sisingamangaraja 14 (☎736 8538), also has a small number.

Shopping Centers: Several large, A/C shopping malls dominate the Medan skyline. Large movie theaters in **Deli Plaza, Perisai Plaza,** and **Medan Mall.** Perisai Plaza offers cheap and fast **Internet** connections, a bowling alley, and a disco.

Markets: Pasar Sentral (Central Market), off Jl. Sutomo, east of the Sambu *sudako* station. Amid shops covered in blue tarpaulin. Pirated CDs, plastic buckets, and live fruit bats. **Old Fish Market** (Pasar Ikam Lama), on Jl. Pernigaan, parallel to Jl. A. Yani. Quieter. No old fish here—just rolls of cheap *batik*. Both open daily dawn-dusk.

Swimming: The pool at the **Danau Toba Hotel** (see **Accommodations,** below) is open to non-guests for Rp11,000 per day. Other hotels offer similar deals.

Emergency: Police: ☎110. **Ambulance:** ☎118.

Police: Jl. H.Z. Arifin 7 (☎455 2000).

Pharmacies and Medical Services: The shiny new **Gleneagles Hospital,** Jl. Listrik 6 (☎456 6368), is the best in Medan. Open 24hr. The **Klinik Spesialis Bunda,** Jl. Sisingamangaraja 17 (☎732 1666), north of the mosque. Open 24hr. There is a 24hr. pharmacy on the 2nd fl. of the hospital. Other pharmacies are all around the city.

Telephones: There are *wartel* kiosks all over town. One is next to Gecko's guesthouse, opposite the Mesjid Raya (open daily until 11pm). Most *wartel* owners levy a flat-rate charge of around Rp3000 per call for collect calls and calls made with calling cards.

Internet Access: Paragon Computer, 2nd fl. of Perisai Plaza. Good, quick connection. Rp3000 per hr. Open daily 10am-9pm. **Hokkibear,** in the basement of the Yuki Simpang Raya Mall opposite the Mesjid Raya. Rp4000 per hr. Open daily 10am-9:45pm.

Post Office: GPO, Jl. Pos 1 (☎456 8940), at the intersection with Jl. Balai Kota, opposite Merdeka Sq. *Poste Restante.* Open M-Sa 8am-6pm.

Postal Code: 20111.

ACCOMMODATIONS

Most travelers stay near the **Mesjid Raya** on **Jl. Sisingamangaraja,** where there are a number of good, cheap (and not so cheap) accommodations within easy walking distance from the drop-off point for the "ferry bus" from Belawan.

Ibunda, Jl. Sisingamangaraja 33 (☎736 8787 or 734 1285). A 5min. walk north of the mosque. Immaculate rooms with Western baths, hot water, A/C, phones, and TV. Popular with families and often full—call ahead. Singles from Rp80,000; doubles Rp100,000; suites Rp120,000-175,000. MC/V. ❹

Gecko's, Jl. Sisingamangaraja 59/81A (☎734 3507), opposite the mosque. Popular backpacker hangout. Restaurant area and helpful management. Simple but clean and well-kept rooms. Singles with shared bath Rp25,000; doubles Rp30,000-35,000. ❷

Danau Toba International, Jl. Imam Bonjol 17 (☎415 7000; hdti@nusa.net.id). Large complex at the westernmost end of Jl. Palang Merah. Large, comfortable, A/C rooms. Swimming pool, billiard room, fitness center, restaurants, and a bar with live music. Doubles Rp169,000-214,500. ❺

Hotel Zakia (☎732 2413), on Jl. Sipiso Piso, the small lane immediately before the mosque as you head north up Jl. Sisingamangaraja (with the mosque on your left). Veteran favorite of the bare-bones backpacker crowd. 2nd fl. rooms are perfect to enjoy the *muezzin*'s 5am call to prayer. Most rooms come with Western toilet. Check-out noon. Dorms Rp8000; singles from Rp22,500; doubles Rp30,000-35,000. ❶

Irma Hotel, Jl. Tengah 1B. Just south of Mesjid Raya, around the corner from Hotel Zakia. Turn left after the cafe/restaurant on the corner. Basic but clean. Very friendly management. Doubles with shared bath Rp20,000, with private bath Rp30,000. ❷

Shahiba Guest House, Jl. Armada 1A (☎ 736 8528). Head south on Jl. Sisingamangaraja; at the end of Bukit Barisan Hero's Cemetery, turn right onto Jl. Armada. Simple rooms with *mandi.* Dorms Rp8000; singles Rp20,000; doubles Rp25,000-50,000. ❶

FOOD

Medan's chief culinary attraction is spicy *padang* food, the ethnic specialty of West Sumatra's Minang people. There are cheap stalls all over town. Waiters bring a number of dishes to your table—you eat and pay for what you want. In the evenings, stalls selling cheap and delicious Chinese food line **Jl. Semarang,** between Jl. Pandu and Jl. Bandung. (Open daily 6pm-midnight.) There's an excellent Chinese place north of Jl. Semarang, at the intersection of Jl. A. Yani V and Jl. Perniagaan, which serves superb stir-fry dishes for Rp15,000. (Open M-Sa 10am-9pm). A few bakeries and Indian foodstalls are in the Indian quarter, near the intersection of Jl. H. Z. Arifin and Jl. Cik Ditiro. *Satay* and juice stands on Jl. Sisingamangaraja toward the Bukit Barisan Hero's Cemetery stay open late.

Miramar, Jl. Pemuda, opposite BNI. A/C Indonesian restaurant with a Costa del Sol party atmosphere. Popular with locals. "Special" chicken Rp20,000. Cuttlefish Rp5000. *Cap chai* Rp15,000. Open daily 11am-10pm. AmEx/MC/V. ❸

Garuda, Palang Merah 26, just east of Jl. Pemuda. Heading north up Jl. Pemuda, turn right before the tourist information office. Shiny-clean *padang* place with uniformed waiters. Wide selection of excellent food; dishes Rp4000-5000. Open 24hr. ❶

Hash Cafe, Jl. Jend A. Yani 50. The huge red Bintang beer sign is hard to miss. Dark, smoky expatriate watering hole complete with bar stools. Good steaks from Rp32,000; fried chicken Rp20,000; fried calamari Rp18,000. Draft beer Rp11,500. Open daily 11am-11pm. Also **Entertainment.** ❹

Tip Top Restaurant and Lunch Room, Jl. A. Yani 92. North of the intersection with Jl. Palang Merah. An old Dutch-era restaurant that retains the flavor of slower-paced times. Mutton curry Rp5500. Frog legs Rp17,500. Open daily 8:30am-10:30pm. ❷

Rumah Makan Bukittinggi, Jl. Brigjen Katamso 456, opposite the Istana Maimun. Clean canteen-style place serving great pick-and-point *padang* food. Large number of chicken, mutton, and fish dishes (most around Rp5000). Open daily 7am-10pm. ❶

Cahaya Baru, Jl. Cik Ditiro 8L. Heading west along Jl. H. Z. Arifin, turn left onto Jl. Cik Ditiro. The restaurant is a 10-15min. walk south. 4-table A/C nook serves tasty curries and South Indian staples. The **Maharaja** restaurant, next door, is also good. *Alu gobi* Rp6000. Mutton curry Rp8000. *Dosas* Rp2500-17,500. Open daily 10am-10pm. ❷

SIGHTS

Medan is never going to win any prizes as a sight-seeing city. Many travelers stay here only as long as it takes to book a ticket out of town. If you aren't in a hurry to follow the crowds, however, there is enough to keep you occupied here for at least a day or two. Medan is relatively easy to navigate, and some visitors might be interested in exploring a large Indonesian city barely affected by foreign tourism—unlike most of the other stops along the backpacker trail through Sumatra and beyond. Apart from the real-life charm of Medan's residential neighborhoods, the city's main attraction is its **architecture.** Many of its most interesting buildings line Jl. Pemuda/Jl. A. Yani. The entire length of this street is littered with architectural relics of the colonial period, and if you can imagine away all the traffic fumes and KFC billboards, it's still possible to get a sense of what the place might have looked like back in the days when all the street signs were written in Dutch. Old-world remnants include the **Tip Top Restaurant** (see **Food,** above) and the **headquarters** of the London-Sumatera trading company (just south of Merdeka Sq.). Also worth a quick peek is the multi-colored, tumbledown **Tjong A Fie** mansion at Jl. A. Yani 105, built in a mixture of Chinese and European styles. The black domes, turquoise tiles, and soaring minarets of the **Mesjid Raya (Grand Mosque),** at Jl. Sisingamangaraja and Jl. Mesjid Raya, were built by a Dutch architect in 1908. The well-kept gardens around the mosque are a popular local hangout— people come here to chat, sleep, or play football, while the elderly pray beside the graveyard where the Sultan is buried. Non-Muslims may visit the interior of the mosque between prayer times. (Open daily dawn-dusk. Admission by donation.)

Near Mesjid Raya, where Jl. Brigjen Katamso meets Jl. Mesjid Raya, is the **Istana Maimun (Maimun Palace).** Built with tobacco money, the palace has housed the Deli Sultans since 1888. The 12th Sultan and his family still live here. The throne room is open to the public. (Open daily 8am-5pm. Admission by donation.) A Hindu temple, **Shri Mariamman Kuil,** is on Jl. H. Z. Arifin. Renovated and expanded in 1991, it turns heads with its brightly colored and ornate depictions of gods, heroes, and mythical creatures. (Open daily dawn to dusk. Free.) **Vihara Gunung Timur,** a Buddhist temple sacred to Medan's Chinese community, stands on Jl. Hang Tuah in a quiet residential suburb off Jl. Cik Ditiro. The temple is worth a visit for its impressive, cluttered interior, clouded by sweet incense and colored by flowers and fruit. (Open daily 8am-5pm. Free.) To get there, turn left onto Jl. Cik Ditiro shortly after the Hindu temple, and walk south for 20min. It's down a small lane, opposite the Methodist church. The **Museum Sumatera Utara,** Jl. H.M. Joni 51, documents the geological and cultural history of the province. An informative tour takes about 1hr. (Take any *sudako* heading south on Jl. Sisingamangaraja, or walk 1.5km from Mesjid Raya. From the south end of the Bukit Barisan Hero's Cemetery, the museum is 700m. Open Tu-Su 8am-3:30pm. Admission by donation.)

ENTERTAINMENT

Travelers in search of late-night parties featuring last year's Euro-hits and magic mushrooms will find slim pickings in Medan. But this doesn't mean that people stuck here need to spend their nights watching pro-wrestling on TV. The ancient and noble pastime of drinking large amounts of beer and talking large amounts of nonsense is all over town. For a dark, smoky atmosphere, the **Hash Café** on Jl. A. Yani (see **Food,** above) is your best bet. Mugs of draft beer go for Rp11,500. The cafe is the unofficial watering hole of the Medan branch of the **Hash House Harriers,** an Asia-wide expatriate obsession that involves weekly runs through the local countryside, followed by ritualistic boozing. Visitors are welcome to join in the fun for a small entrance free. (Runs most M and Th. Ask for details of upcoming events.) Three live bands play nightly at the **Danau Toba International Hotel.** (See **Accommodations,** above. Beatles night Su. Open daily 6pm-1am.) There is also a popular **"billiard centre,"** where a game of 8-ball pool costs Rp2000. (Open daily 10am-1am.) The Danau Toba's **disco** was closed down at press time, but may have opened again by the time you read this. There is a large new **bowling alley** on the top floor of the Perisai Plaza on Jl. A. Yani. (Rp5000 per game M-F; Rp6000 Sa-Su. Open daily 11am-midnight.) Also at the top of the Perisai Plaza are a cheap **video arcade** and the **Kristal Disco,** a fun place to look silly with the locals on a Saturday night. There are **cinemas** showing English-language movies (Rp12,000) at several of Medan's shopping malls, including Perisai Plaza, Deli Plaza, and Medan Mall.

BERASTAGI ☎0628

Set against the ethereal beauty of North Sumatra's mountainous hinterland, Berastagi is a slightly scruffy hill town within easy reach of a large number of natural and cultural attractions. A number of traditional Batak Karo villages are scattered among the surrounding Karo Highlands, within daytripping distance. Using Berastagi as a base, volcano climbers can tackle steaming Gunung Sibayak or jungle-covered Gunung Sinabung. Or, visitors can take a stroll in one of the town's parks or sit in a local coffeehouse with some of the friendliest people in Sumatra.

TRANSPORTATION

Most buses from Berastagi are **minibuses,** though buses from Medan occasionally pass through on their way south. The **main terminal** is in front of the market on Jl. Veteran. Buses go to: Kutacane (5-6hr.; every 20min. 9am-6pm; Rp18,000); Medan (2½hr., frequent trips 5am-8pm, Rp2500); Pangururan (5hr.; 3-4 per day 8am-1pm; Rp10,000). Buses to Tapaktuan (8hr.; 2 per day 7-9pm; Rp20,000) depart from a second terminal 5km out of town. (Take a *sudako* from the main terminal. Ask for Kutugadung or the PMTOH terminal. Rp500.) **Tourist buses** provide the only direct service from Berastagi to **Bukit Lawang** and **Parapat (Lake Toba).** Buy tickets at least a day ahead from **Raymond's Steak House** or **Losmen Sibayak Guest House.** Tourist buses usually only leave with 5 or more people. To Bukit Lawang (5hr.; 10am and 2pm; Rp45,000-50,000) and Parapat (6hr.; 10am and 2pm; Rp40,000-50,000).

ORIENTATION AND PRACTICAL INFORMATION

Berastagi is a small town, with a single, divided thoroughfare, **Jl. Veteran,** which forks at a 5m **war monument** at its north end. The left branch becomes **Jl. Gundaling,** which leads uphill past the **fruit market** toward **Mt. Sibayak;** the right branch leads downhill out of town, becoming the **Berastagi-Medan Hwy.** The tourist information center, post office, and *wartel* are near the monument. Most budget accommodations are on Jl. Veteran. Heading south, Jl. Veteran passes the **bus terminal** and **central market** before forking again at a large sculpture of a **cabbage** in the middle of the road. The left branch continues 11km to **Kabanjahe,** and the right branch, **Jl. Udara,** leads to **Gunung Sinabung** and the Karo village of **Lingga.**

Tourist Offices: Tourist Information Center, Jl. Gundaling 1 (☎910 84). Left of the war memorial. Offers little more than trekking maps of Gunung Sibayak and Gunung Sinabung. Arranges more arduous trekking and rafting expeditions and trips to nearby Karo villages, but at prices much higher than elsewhere. Open M-Sa 8am-6pm. The **information desk** at the Losmen Sibayak is useful, with up-to-date advice and boards advertising travelers looking to put together groups for climbing, trekking, and rafting.

Tours: Mr. Telah Bangun, an excellent **guide** who speaks English and organizes treks (US$30 per person per day, min. 4 people) in Gunung Leuser National Park.

Tour and Travel, Jl. Veteran 49 (☎921 60; fax 915 13), above Raymond's Steak House. Mr. Bangun's English students are available as guides **for free,** in exchange for a chance to practice their English. Generally available M-Sa 8am-8pm, varies Su. For plane and ferry tickets, try **P. T. Persiar Indah,** Jl. Veteran 55 (☎911 50), inside the *wartel* office as you head south from the monument. Open daily 7:30am-midnight.

Currency Exchange: BNI, Jl. Veteran 22, several blocks down from the monument, on the right as you head south. Open M-Th 8:30am-3:30pm, F 8:30am-noon and 2-3:30pm. 24hr. **ATM** takes international cards.

INDONESIA

Markets: Pasar Sentral winds along the narrow lanes around the main bus terminal on Jl. Veteran. Sells everything from live fish to rubber boots and pirated CDs. **Pasar Buah,** the fruit market, on the left of Jl. Gundaling, has Berastagi's trademark *marquisa* passion fruit among the piles. Tourist tack is also for sale. Both open daily 6am-9pm.

Pharmacy: Dharma Bakti, Jl. Veteran 49A, past the central market before the cabbage. Open daily 8:30am-8pm. A 24hr. pharmacy is in the Public Health Center (see below).

Medical Services: Public Health Center, Jl. Veteran 34. (☎910 28). English-speaking doctors normally available in the mornings. Open 24hr.

Telephones: Telkom office, Jl. Perwira 1, next to the post office. Open daily 7am-midnight. International calls also available at the *wartel* office at Jl. Veteran 55, on the left as you head south from the monument. Open daily 7:30am-midnight.

Internet Access: Sporadic service at **Mikie Holiday Hotel,** 2km out of town on the main road to Medan (*Sudako* Rp700). Rp5000 per hr. Open daily 9am-4pm.

Post Office: Jl. Veteran 4, next to the tourist office. Open M-Th and Sa 8am-2pm, F 8-11am.

Postal Code: 22156.

ACCOMMODATIONS

Berastagi has some of the finest guesthouses in North Sumatra. Many double as trek and rafting organizers and travel agents.

Elshaddai Hotel and Restaurant, Jl. Veteran 65/66 (☎910 23; fax 915 13). Just north of the monument. Well-run budget hotel. Rooftop patio with a nice view. Shared *mandi* with hot shower (Rp3000). Singles Rp10,000; doubles Rp15,000. ❶

Losmen Sibayak Guest House, Jl. Veteran 119 (☎910 95; fax 911 22). Head south from the war monument; it's 200m down on the left. Organizes trekking, rafting, and guides to local volcanoes. Hot showers Rp2000. Dorms Rp8000; simple singles with shared *mandi* Rp15,000, with bath Rp25,000; doubles Rp20,000. ❶

Sibayak Multinational Rest House, Jl. Pendidikan 93 (☎910 31). Beautiful, quiet, secluded hotel on the grounds of an old Dutch home 2km from the war monument, on the road that leads up to Sibayak volcano. Follow directions to Gunung Sibayak (see **Hiking,** below), or take a *sudako* from the monument (Rp1000). Faultlessly clean rooms with marble floors and balconies overlooking well-kept gardens. All rooms have Western baths and hot showers. Doubles Rp35,000-50,000. ❸

Sinabung Resort Hotel, Jl. Kolam Renang, (☎914 00; fax 913 00), about 1km out of town. From the monument, walk up Jl. Gundaling past the fruit market, turn right at the sign onto Jl. Kolam Renang by the football field. The best upscale hotel in town. Immaculate rooms with satellite TV, Western baths, and hot water. Heated swimming pool, mini-golf, beauty salon, tennis courts, and health center. Doubles Rp400,000; deluxe cottages Rp550,000 and up. Discounts often available mid-week. AmEx/MC/V. ❺

Wisma Sibayak Guest House, Jl. Udara 1 (☎911 04). Head south on Jl. Veteran from the bus terminal; it's set back from the road where Jl. Udara branches right just after the cabbage sculpture. Excursions into the surrounding area. Dorms Rp8000; singles Rp10,000-15,000; doubles 25,000-40,000. Higher-end rooms have Western bath. ❶

FOOD

For such a small town, Berastagi has a surprising number of good places to eat. Most *losmen* offer extensive menus of Indonesian and Western standbys, including hearty trekkers' breakfasts. Along **Jl. Veteran,** options range from fried banana stands and *satay* stalls to shiny restaurants with window displays of mouth-watering *padang* and *batak* dishes. Jl. Veteran, between the monument and **Losmen Sibayak,** comes alive each night with cheap *warung* selling everything from fried chicken to delicious shellfish *(kerang rebus)*, most for Rp5000 or less.

Bundok Andung, Jl. Veteran 20, on the right as you walk from the post office toward BNI. Sparkling clean with simmering piles of spicy chicken, fish, and shrimp dishes. Rp15,000-20,000 for a full meal. Open daily 7am-10pm. ❸

Muslimin, Jl. Veteran 128, close to the bus terminal. Good place to meet locals, who come here every night for tasty food in an unpretentious atmosphere. Most dishes Rp5000-7000. Open daily 7am-10pm. ❶

Eropah, Jl. Veteran 60, on the right as you head south from the monument. Good Chinese food and a range of Western and Indonesian staples. Fried chicken Rp15,000. Sweet and sour pork Rp15,000. Large beer Rp10,000. Open daily 7am-9am. ❸

Raymond's, Jl. Veteran 49, on the left as you walk south from the monument. Popular foreigner's hangout with a good selection of Western and Indonesian food. Steaks Rp4000-5000. Spaghetti Rp6000-14,000. Open daily 6:30am-10pm. ❷

SIGHTS AND ENTERTAINMENT

The **highland region** around Berastagi constitutes the heart of Karo Batak country, and several **Karo villages** are close enough to visit on daytrips. **Peceren,** 2km past the war monument on the road to Medan, is the closest. Traditional Karo longhouses, complete with buffalo horns and thatched roofs, stand alongside modern, concrete buildings with satellite dishes. Ask for directions to the *rumah adat* (traditional houses). Although guesthouse operators decry Perceren as "impure," it perhaps provides a more realistic look at contemporary Karo life than other more "traditional" settlements popular with tour groups and sightseers. It's also easy to get to the larger village of **Lingga,** where a dozen or so traditional houses are interspersed with more modern buildings (as well as the rusted shells of a number of abandoned vehicles). Thanks to its easy accessibility from Berastagi, Lingga sees more tourist traffic than other Karo Batak villages; as a result, it can feel somewhat commercialized. It may be better to visit later in the day, after most of the postcard vendors have gone home. Visitors are intercepted as they get off the bus and escorted to the "Tourist Information Center" to pay a donation (around Rp5000), after which they are free to roam and mingle as they please. To get to Lingga from Berastagi, take a *sudako* to Kabanjahe (Rp1000), then change to another minibus to Lingga (Rp1000). Other Karo villages, including **Cingkas** and **Dokan,** are slightly farther out of town. They remain slightly less "spoiled." There are hourly buses to Cingkas from Kabanjahe (Rp2500); for Dokan, take any bus from Kabanjahe bound for Siantar and ask to be let off at the turn-off for "Desa Dokan." From here, it's a 30min. walk to the village. Telah Bangun, of Tobali Tour and Travel (see **Tours,** p. 241), offers an overnight tour of **Serdang** during which you sleep and eat in a Batak longhouse. (3-person min. Rp60,000.) The Losmen Sibayak Guest House offers a afternoon's walking tour from Berastagi through several smaller villages to Lingga. Check its office for details.

Tahura National Park, 15min. by *sudako* (Rp700) from Berastagi on the road to Medan, is home to gibbons, hornbills, and hundreds of other kinds of (mostly elusive) wildlife. You'd be quite lucky to see more than the occasional monkey, but a stroll along one of the park's marked trails is nonetheless a good way to get away from the traffic and back into the fresh air. (Open daily 8am-6pm. Rp1100.)

Back in town, **Arihta,** Jl. Veteran 36, near the splendid cabbage sculpture, is the town pool hall, where dozens of locals can be found mis-spending their youth and practicing trick shots. (Rp1000. Open daily 7am-11pm.)

HIKING

Most visitors spend their time hiking up the two spectacular volcanoes close to town. Most popular is **Gunung Sibayak** (2100m), an active volcano with clouds of sulfurous steam billowing from its peak. A well-maintained trail with concrete steps winds up the west slope to the crater. A second "jungle" trail winds up from the Berastagi-Medan Hwy., but this unmarked route is hard to follow and should not be attempted without a guide.

To reach the west route, walk north on Jl. Veteran, bearing left onto Jl. Gundaling. Turn right onto Jl. Pendidikan and follow the road past the football field. The road meanders slowly uphill through a small village, before veering right after a stretch of fields. The small bamboo shack on the left is the *pondok masuk*, where you pay your Rp1000 entrance fee. The hiking trail begins just to the left of the *pondok masuk;* take the lower path to the left of the thatched gateway. Note the sign bearing the names of the half-dozen or so unlucky tourists who came this way before but never made it home. Although a guide is not necessary for climbing the volcano via the western route, some hikers may feel safer joining up with a group. The walk uphill from here, along a pot-holed logging road through the forest, takes 2-3hr. At the summit, several steep trails lead downhill. The one on the right by the crater lake, before the radio antenna, leads down a steep flight of worn steps to the **hot springs** (Rp1000) and the village of **Semargat Gunung.** From the hot springs, regular *suduko* run back to the terminal in Berastagi (Rp2000). Maps of the route are available from the Tourist Information Office and from several of the hotels.

Gunung Sinabung (2417m), 27km west of Berastagi, makes for a much more challenging climb, requiring a good level of fitness and some previous climbing experience. Trails are rudimentary and devoid of markings. Several people have died on Sinabung over the years. Guides are available from the Losmen Sibayak guest house for Rp150,000 for a group of three. Most hikers begin at the village of Sigaranggarang and end at Lake Kawar for a post-climb swim. Much of the hike is unspoiled jungle. The final few hundred meters cover loose rock. The ascent takes 3hr.; the earlier you begin, the better the view. On a clear day, it is possible to see the northern tip of shimmering Lake Toba, 30km to the south. Leave by 9am for the safest and most comfortable (cool on the way up, warm on top) climb.

BUKIT LAWANG ☎061

"Welcome to the jungle" is a common greeting in Bukit Lawang. But the "jungle" in this tiny town, beautifully set on the Bohorok River, is as apt a description of the tourist colony as it is of the nature that cradles it. Carved out of the rubber and cocoa plantations northwest of Medan, Bukit Lawang consists of a string of restaurants and guesthouses lining the riverbank. Most people come here to visit the Bohorok Orangutan Rehabilitation Center, where the world's gentlest primates are reintroduced to their natural habitat. This is also a popular point of entry to the Gunung Leuser National Park, and many people get caught up in the beauty of the place, whiling away their time trekking, rafting, or tubing down the lazy river. Visitors looking for peace and quiet should avoid the weekends, when the party bus rolls in from Medan, often leaving devastation in its wake.

TRANSPORTATION

The **"bus terminal"** is the large sandy lot near the Visitors Center. Buses go to Medan (2½hr., every 30min. 5am-5pm, Rp5000). Tourist buses leave daily for Berastagi (5hr.; 8:30am; Rp45,000) and Parapat (10hr.; 8:30am; Rp60,000). Book at least one day in advance. Purchase tickets pretty much anywhere in town.

INDONESIA

ORIENTATION AND PRACTICAL INFORMATION

The **Visitors Center, PHPA office,** and **tourist office** cluster near a dirt lot known as the **bus terminal.** The path leading upriver from the bus stop is **Jl. Orangutan,** lined with stalls selling blowpipes and mineral water, and (farther upriver) a dozen or so mellow bars and restaurants catering to the backpacker crowd. About 800m upriver, a gate marks the entrance to a **public campground;** the most popular guesthouses are beyond the campground along the river. The **Bohorok Orangutan Center** is about 1.5km upriver from the **Visitors Center,** on the opposite bank.

Tourist Offices: PHPA Ranger Station (☎542 574), on Jl. Orangutan, opposite the bus lot. Organizes treks and nature walks. Sells permits to see orangutan feedings. Rp20,500 per person, good for 2 feedings in a day. Open daily 7am-3pm. **Bukit Lawang Visitors Center,** next door, has interesting exhibits about local wildlife. Videos screened M, W, F at 8pm. Open daily 8am-3pm. The **Tourist Information Center,** down a small path opposite the PHPA office, recruits tourists for its trekking and rafting expeditions. Open daily 7am-4pm. Most guesthouses arrange these trips as well (roughly US$15 per person per day).

Currency Exchange: There are **no banks** in Bukit Lawang. Most guesthouses and travel agents will change money, but often at poor rates. The **wartel** kiosk also exchanges cash and traveler's checks and stays open until midnight.

Police: Opposite the bus terminal. Open 24hr.

Medical Services: There is a **polyclinic** opposite the PHPA office. Open daily 8am-8pm.

Telephones: Wartel kiosk off the path to Bukit Lawang Cottages; turn left off Jl. Orangutan at the sign. International collect calls Rp3000. Open daily 6am-midnight.

Internet Access: Natrabu Tours and Travel, on Jl. Orangutan, opposite the Visitors Center. Also available at the **Wisma Leuser Sibayak Guest House.** Both charge Rp10,000 per 30min. and are open daily roughly 8am-9pm.

Post Office: No post office, though several shops sell stamps. Most guesthouses will mail letters for you if you're planning to be away in the jungle for a while.

ACCOMMODATIONS

Excellent accommodations line both banks for 1.5km upstream from the bus terminal. For late-night music and reggae bars, stay at one of the places close to the bus terminal in the center of the village. Places farther upriver (past the campground) are much quieter. For the cheapest sleep in town, head to the campground about 10min. upriver from the main village, on the right-hand bank as you head upstream. (Rp1000 entrance fee. Basic facilities.)

Jungle Inn (☎08 681 210 5758; thejungleinn2000@yahoo.com), 400m beyond the campground entrance gate, across the river from the Rehabilitation Center. One of the most original guesthouses in the whole of Sumatra. Restaurant and a range of "jungle-themed" doubles featuring 4-poster beds, hand-carved furniture, and hammocks. Ask to see the waterfall room. Doubles with bath Rp30,000-75,000. ❷

Pongo Resort (☎454 2574; dirganet@indosat.net.id), next to the Orangutan Rehabilitation Center, a 30min. walk upstream from the bus terminal. Luxury thatched huts on the river banks, surrounded by waterfalls and rainforest. A peaceful piece of paradise. Attached restaurant. Prices include breakfast and orangutan feeding permits. Doubles (all with Western toilets and showers) Rp100,000-200,000. ❺

Bukit Lawang Cottages (☎414 5061; lawang@indosat.net.id), across the river from the bus terminal. Spacious grounds right on the river—close to town but away from the crowds. Smaller bungalows with bath and 2nd-floor patio Rp15,000; bungalows with veranda Rp30,000; orangutan bungalow with "jungle" bath Rp40,000. ❷

Wisma Leuser Sibayak (☎550 576), across the river from the main "village," over one of the first bridges you reach from the bus terminal. Popular restaurant with live music and sing-alongs. Internet. Basic rooms/bungalows with bath Rp20,000-30,000. ❷

Queen Resort, a 10min. walk upstream from the bus terminal, past the campground. Away from the crowds, but within easy walking distance of pizza and cold beer. Large bamboo rooms with comfy beds and private bath go for Rp15,000-45,000. ❶

Green Paradise Backpacker and Café, a 10min. walk upriver from the bus terminal on the right. Dorm beds (Rp6000) are the cheapest in town. Basic doubles Rp15,000. ❶

FOOD

Cheap *warung* and *padang* joints are all along the river near the bus terminal. Most guesthouses and hotels have their own restaurants. One of the best is the **Wisma Leuser Sibayak Resort** ❹ (see above), which serves Indonesian and Western food, often with live music. (Chicken *satay* Rp12,500. Shrimp with ginger sauce Rp13,500.) **Bamboo Pizzeria** ❸, opposite the Bukit Lawang Indah Guest House, serves excellent fresh-baked pizzas (Rp15,000-19,000) and pasta (spaghetti carbonara Rp15,000) in a classy, laid-back atmosphere. Also popular is **Lina's** ❸, a little farther upstream, with seating inside and out by the river, and a large menu of Western and Indonesian food. (Fried squid Rp13,000. Chicken with chilli Rp17,000.) Most restaurants generally stay open until at least 10pm and often much later.

SIGHTS AND ENTERTAINMENT

Most people come to Bukit Lawang in the hope of getting up close and personal with the local population of *Pongo pygmaeus abelli*, or orangutans. About 1.5km upstream from the bus terminals the world-famous **Orangutan Rehabilitation Center,** founded in 1973 with grants from the World Wildlife Fund and the Frankfurt Zoological Society to reintroduce illegally captured orangutans to their natural habitat. Since then, the rehabilitation project has successfully returned more than 120 animals to the rainforest. Two **daily feedings** (8-9am and 3-4pm) take place near the Rehabilitation Center, when wild and semi-wild orangutans can usually be seen feasting on bananas and swinging slowly from tree to tree. A small boat ferries visitors across the river before each feeding. Day-long **permits** (good for both feedings) can be obtained at the PHPA office (see p. 245) for Rp20,500. Visitors keen to share less orchestrated time with the primates can go on one of the **one-day treks** organized by most guesthouses, or the PHPA, where guides will normally guarantee at least one sighting of the animals in the wild.

The superb **Bat Cave** is 15min. from the village center. The trail starts behind Bukit Lawang Cottages and winds through a rubber plantation before turning right to the cave. The cavern is filled with bats and leads some 600m into the hillside. A flashlight is essential. You can normally rent one (Rp3000) at the entrance, where a Rp1000 fee is charged.

Bukit Lawang is a popular point of entry into the **Gunung Leuser National Park. Treks** and expeditions can be arranged through the PHPA office, or at most guesthouses. Prices are generally the same wherever you arrange your trip, and range from US$15 per person for a one-day "jungle trek" to three-day excursions to Berastagi (US$65), six-day hikes to Kutacane (US$250), and seven-day jungle expeditions (US$250). **Rafting** down the Bohorok River is another popular pastime here; one-day trekking and rafting combos cost US$25 per person.

Most guesthouses at Bukit Lawang have **inner tubes** for use on the Bohorok River (Rp3000 per day). During the dry season (Feb. to June), the water level may be too low to float safely. Check with the Visitors Center first. You can also float 6km down to Bohorok village (2-3 hours). Local buses ferry the drenched back to Bukit Lawang (Rp500).

NIGHTLIFE

For a tiny, nondescript settlement in the middle of nowhere, Bukit Lawang has an impressively active nightlife—especially on weekends, when bus loads of people buzz in from Medan to party primate-style through the night. The narrow pathway along the right-hand side of the river (heading upstream from the bus terminal) is home to a number of laid-back bars, cafes, and restaurants with tourist-oriented menus (and music collections). Among the most popular are **Tony's Restaurant** and **Lina's Coffee Shop,** both serving food and drink into the wee hours. Lina's organizes a late-night "dance party" every Saturday night. Next door is an incredibly mellow wooden **reggae shack** with dim lighting, floor cushions, and the best music collection in town.

DANAU TOBA (LAKE TOBA)

Southeast Asia's largest freshwater lake and the largest crater lake in the world, majestic Lake Toba is Sumatra's top tourist destination, and one of the most awe-inspiring natural sights in Southeast Asia. The steep slopes that ring Toba form the rim of an ancient volcano, whose cataclysmic eruption some 75,000 years ago created the lake, and may have even triggered the last ice age. Undiscovered by the outside world until the 1850s, the area around Lake Toba is the homeland of the Batak Toba, now a predominantly Christian people whose unique language and culture still thrive today. A remarkably relaxed and laid-back place, with an abundance of excellent guesthouses, bars, and restaurants sprinkled along the waterfront, Lake Toba offers breathtaking views, welcoming people, and rich cultural heritage. This is the perfect spot to kick back and take a break from traveling for a while. Be warned—Lake Toba can be a difficult place to leave behind.

TONGGING

Unspoiled and resplendent at the head of Lake Toba, Tongging is a secluded spot that not many tourists visit—a great place to get a feel for what this area must have looked like, in the days before pizza parlors and late-night bars set up shop.

There is plenty to do around Tongging aside from admiring your reflection in the lake. **Sipisopiso and Sidompah waterfalls** are both within a 2hr. hike, with breathtaking views of Lake Toba from the top of Gunung Sipisopiso. Several nearby villages afford spectacular views **(Sibaulangit),** longhouses **(Bage),** and a monument to the Batak ancestors **(Silalahi).** Wisma Sibayak rents canoes (Rp20,000) and fishing rods (Rp5000) and will help you cook your catch.

Easily reached from Berastagi, Tongging is a good alternative to Parapat as an access point to Samosir Island, the hub of Lake Toba's tourist activity. From Kabanjahe (a short *sudako* ride from Berastagi), there are frequent buses to Situngaling (30min., Rp2000). From there, take a bus to Tongging (20min., Rp1500), or walk down the steep, winding road that leads to the lake. There are also usually four direct buses a day from Kabanjahe (1½hr., Rp2000). Buses run regularly from nearby Merek to Pangururan, on the western shore of Samosir

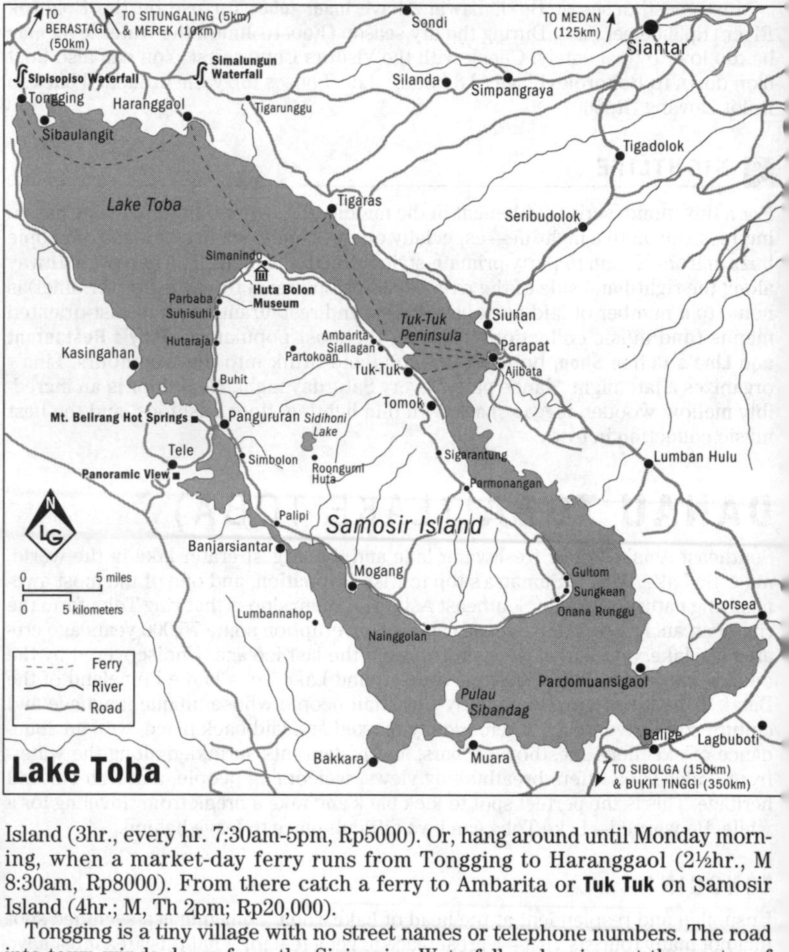

Lake Toba

Island (3hr., every hr. 7:30am-5pm, Rp5000). Or, hang around until Monday morning, when a market-day ferry runs from Tongging to Haranggaol (2½hr., M 8:30am, Rp8000). From there catch a ferry to Ambarita or **Tuk Tuk** on Samosir Island (4hr.; M, Th 2pm; Rp20,000).

Tongging is a tiny village with no street names or telephone numbers. The road into town winds down from the Sipisopiso Waterfall and arrives at the center of the village at the top of the lake. If you want to mail a letter, make a call, or chat it up with the police, head up the road to **Merek.** Your best source for **information** on the local area is also the town's only **guesthouse,** the **Wisma Sibayak ❷**, about 1.5km down the road from the bus drop-off point. (Decent sized doubles with shared *mandi* Rp20,000-25,000; bungalow-style rooms with Western bath Rp35,000.) There is also a **restaurant ❸** with a somewhat pricey, limited selection. (Fried chicken Rp15,000.) Otherwise, you'll have to catch dinner yourself, or go back to "town," where *warung* serve cheap chicken and fish meals by the harbor.

PARAPAT ☎0625

The rolling hills of Lake Toba's eastern shoreline have drawn tourists since the 1930s, when Parapat was a popular holiday retreat for the ruling Dutch. Crowds still flock here every weekend from Medan and elsewhere in Sumatra, filling the modern resorts that now dominate the skyline. The views across the lake to Samosir are hard to beat, with spectacular sunsets almost every night. For most foreign visitors, however, Parapat is little more than a transit point to Samosir, where the views are just as stunning and everything moves at a much calmer pace.

TRANSPORTATION

Buses: Public buses and private coaches depart from the terminal on Jl. Sisingamangaraja, 1km east of the police station. All buses originate in Medan and get to Parapat around midday; talk to travel agents about exact times. Minibuses booked ahead will often pick you up at your hotel. To: **Bukittinggi** (15hr.; 5 per day noon-8pm; Rp90,000-150,000); **Jakarta** (4-5hr.; 5 per day noon-5:30pm; Rp170,000-400,000); **Medan** (4hr.; 3 per day and frequent minibuses 10am-4pm; Rp25,000-40,000); **Padang** (17hr.; 5 per day noon-8pm; Rp100,000-160,000); **Sibolga** (6hr.; 11:30am and noon; Rp35,000-60,000). **Tourist buses** head to: **Berastagi** (4hr.; Rp40,000); **Bukit Lawang** (7hr.; Rp60,000-70,000); **Bukittinggi** (12hr.; Rp110,000).

Ferries: Passenger ferries to **Pulau Samosir** leave from Tiga Raja Pier, dropping passengers off at guesthouses in Tuk Tuk (30-45min., every hr. 8:30am-7:30pm, Rp3000).

Local Transportation: *Sudako* follow streets counter-clockwise (with your back to Samosir Island), from Tiga Raja Pier to the bus terminal, down Jl. Sisingamangaraja and then down Jl. Sinagara/Haranggaol back to Tiga Raja (Rp1000).

ORIENTATION AND PRACTICAL INFORMATION

Jl. Sisingamangaraja, the main road, swings northwest-southeast through town, passing the **police, wartel, post office,** and **bus terminal** before rejoining the Trans-Sumatra Highway and heading south to Bukittinggi. **Jl. Kol. TPR Sinaga** (a.k.a. **Jl. Pulau Samosir**) branches off Jl. Sisingamangaraja at a **Welcome Gate** along the lake and follows the shore before crossing a ridge, becoming **Jl. Haranggaol** at the Natour Parapat Hotel, and leading to the **Tiga Raja Pier.** Buses usually drop backpackers off at the ferry.

Tourist Information and Tours: Use travel agents. Try **PT Dolok Silau,** Jl. Haranggaol 118 (☎415 49), near the ferry. Open daily 8am-6pm. **Branch** at Jl. Sisingamangaraja 56 (☎414 67), close to Singgalang Hotel, up the road from the police. **Andilo Nancy Travel Service** (☎415 48) has an office at the bus terminal. Open daily 6am-10pm.

Currency Exchange: Moneychangers line Jl. Haranggaol. There is a BNI **ATM** on Jl. Sisingamangaraja, but no bank. From Jl. Pulau Samosir, turn right after the gate onto Jl. Sisingamangaraja—past the police station and the mosque—and head straight uphill. It's 700m or so. **Cash advances** on credit cards are available (for a 10% commission) at the Singgalang Hotel.

Police: ☎421 10. On Jl. Sisingamangaraja next to the Welcome Gate. Open 24hr.

Medical Services: Parapat Public Hospital (☎413 32), on Jl. Ompu Ranjo, 800m past the bus terminal, left off Jl. Sisingamangaraja at the sign, and set back 300m on a hill.

Telephones: There are plenty of **wartel** along Jl. Haranggaol, and one 24hr. *wartel* at Jl. Sisingamangaraja 177, across the road from the ATM, up past the gas station.

Internet Access: Sporadic service available at the *wartel,* Jl. Haranggaol 74. Rp300 per min. Open daily 7am-midnight.

Post Office: Jl. Sisingamangaraja 75 (☎414 88), by the Welcome Gate. *Poste Restante.* Open M-Th 7:30am-3pm, F 7:30-11:30am, Sa 7:30am-1pm.

Postal Code: 21174.

ACCOMMODATIONS

Most of the cheaper hotels are on **Jl. Haranggaol** and lower **Jl. Sisingamangaraja.**

Riris Inn, Jl. Haranggaol 43 (☎413 92), 250m up Jl. Haranggaol from the harbor. Beautiful views from a flowery porch. Clean doubles with Western bath Rp30,000. ❸

Singgalang Hotel, Jl. Sisingamangaraja 52 (☎412 60), 50m up from the police station on the right. Large, clean rooms with 3-4 beds off peaceful, wood-floored corridors. All with shared *mandi.* Chinese restaurant downstairs. Rp20,000 per person. ❷

Charlie Inn (☎412 77), overlooking the market in front of the ferry landing, to the right as you face the water. Restaurant downstairs. A perfect spot for the early-morning ferry. Decent, well-kept rooms with bath Rp15,000-30,000. ❷

FOOD

There are plenty of good *padang*-style restaurants along Jl. Sisingamangaraja and Jl. Haranggaol, several serving the local specialty: fresh goldfish from the lake.

Hidangan Khas Minang, Jl. Sisingamangaraja 108, 100m up from Singgalang Hotel on the right. Clean and friendly *padang* restaurant with an English menu. Fried goldfish Rp9000. Octopus chilli Rp8000. Mutton curry Rp15,000. Open daily 6am-11pm. ❷

Mitudo Cafe, Jl. Pulau Samosir, 400m past the Welcome Gate. Deck with the best views in town is perfect for a sundown drink. Guinness Rp14,000. Open daily 7am-2am. ❷

Hong Kong Restaurant, Jl. Haranggaol 9/11, near the crest of the hill. Sweet and sour pork Rp20,000. Fish hot plate Rp25,000. Open daily 7:30am-10pm. ❹

PULAU SAMOSIR

Samosir Island, larger in area than Singapore, is the focal point of North Sumatra's tourist industry—when foreign travelers wax lyrical about "Lake Toba," it's Samosir they're talking about. A bridge connects Samosir with the mainland to the west, but most travelers arrive by ferry from Parapat. Many never make it beyond the Tuk Tuk peninsula, a mellow tourist enclave of lakeside guesthouses, bars, and restaurants. Those who do venture farther afield will find ancient relics of Batak culture, lush green countryside, and spectacular scenery.

INDONESIA

TRANSPORTATION

Buses: Nearly all travelers to Samosir use the ferry to and from **Parapat,** but those who take the bus from Pangururan are rewarded with stunning views of Lake Toba's western shore. On Mondays, a market-day ferry connects **Tongging** (see p. 247) to **Haranggaol,** where another ferry runs to **Ambarita** and **Tuk Tuk** on Samosir. For regular public **buses** to elsewhere in Sumatra, you'll have to go via Parapat (or less conveniently, west across the bridge from Pangururan). Tourist agencies on the island (most in Tuk Tuk) can help arrange tickets in advance. Tourist buses go to: **Berastagi** (Rp40,000-50,000); **Bukit Lawang** (Rp60,000-70,000); **Bukittinggi** (Rp110,000); **Medan** (Rp40,000).

Ferries: Ferries chug along the shoreline every hr. throughout the day, stopping off to pick up passengers from their guesthouses. From **Tuk Tuk** to **Parapat** (7am-6pm, Rp3000). Wave from your pier to flag one down. Also from **Tomok** (8am-7pm, Rp3000), and on market days from **Ambarita** (Tu, Th, Sa; Rp3000).

Local Transportation: Buses shuttle between **Pangururan** and **Tomok** (every hr. 6am-5pm, Rp7000) tracing the north shore via **Simanindo** (Rp5000). From Tuk Tuk, you'll have to walk to the north or south of the peninsula to catch a bus on the main road.

Rentals: Guesthouses and cafes in Tuk Tuk rent **mountain bikes** (Rp20,000) and **motorcycles** (Rp40,000); usually for the day only. Bargain down later in the day.

ORIENTATION AND PRACTICAL INFORMATION

Pulau Samosir is 40km long and 20km wide. The largest town is **Pangururan,** the seat of local government, on the west shore. A single **perimeter road** circles the north half of the island, connecting Pangururan with **Tomok** on the east. At the north tip is the village of **Simanindo.** Most visitors stay on the mushroom-shaped **Tuk Tuk Peninsula,** 4km north of Tomok. The **Tuk Tuk Ring Rd.** branches off the main road to the right, 3km north of Tomok. After 2km, at the south neck of the peninsula, the shortcut to the small village of **Ambarita** branches left, and guesthouses appear on the right. The narrow pavement follows Tuk Tuk's gold coast of guesthouses and *warung* for 2km, joining the shortcut at the north neck and continuing to Ambarita, 3km up the coast. About 8km inland from Ambarita is the hamlet of **Partokoan,** a popular stopover point on the Ambarita-Pangururan traverse.

Tours: Agencies are everywhere in Tuk Tuk, selling airline tickets and tourist bus and ferry tickets from Medan to Penang. Guesthouses book tourist buses at slightly higher rates.

Currency Exchanges: Several places along the Tuk Tuk tourist trail change money, but rates are generally poor. Use the **ATM** in Parapat (see p. 249).

Bookstores: Gokhon Library, roughly halfway around the peninsular road, has a good selection of English books for rent or sale. There is another second-hand bookshop inside the Bagus Bay (see **Accommodations,** below).

Police: The **main station** (☎451 091) is in Ambarita, opposite a large football field, on the road from Tuk Tuk. There is a small **police post** in Tuk Tuk, near Carolina Cottages.

Medical Services: Health center (☎451 075), at the south end of the Tuk Tuk peninsula, round the corner from Carolina Cottages. Doctor speaks some English. Open 24hr. In an **emergency,** return to Parapat or Medan.

Telephones: There is a **wartel** (one of many) opposite Brando's Blues Bar at the north end of Tuk Tuk. Most guesthouses have **international** service and free call-backs.

Internet Access: Bagus Bay, at the south end of Tuk Tuk. Rp400 per min. Open daily 8:30am-10pm. **Samosir Cottages** (for both, see **Accommodations,** below) Rp25,000 per hr. Open daily 7am-midnight. **Sibayak,** just past Tony's at the northern end of the peninsula. Rp18,000 per hr. Open daily 8am-10pm.

Post Office: Ambarita, Jl. Raya 39. Open M-Th 7:30am-3pm, F 7:30-11:30am, Sa 7:30am-1pm.

Postal Code: 22395.

ACCOMMODATIONS

As North Sumatra's premier tourist destinations, Tuk Tuk and Ambarita are full of cheap guesthouses offering first-rate services. Almost all guesthouses will show movies upon request. All the places listed below have views of the lake.

Bagus Bay Homestay and Restaurant (☎451 287), at the southern end of the peninsula, past Tabo cottages. One of Tuk Tuk's most popular backpacker hangouts. Movies every night, free Batak dance performances W and Sa 8:15pm. Table tennis, spacious garden, **Internet,** second-hand bookshop, and a cafe that's never empty. Dorm beds Rp7500; rooms and bungalows with bath Rp25,000-90,000. ❶

Tony's Guest House (☎451 209), on the north end of the peninsula. Batak-style chalets with patios facing the lake. Cafe and TV/living room overlook the water. Sunbathing platform. Good value. Doubles with bath Rp15,000-25,000. ❷

INDONESIA

Tabo Cottages (☎451 318; tabores@indo.net.id), on the south neck, past the Ambarita shortcut road. A cut above average, with stylish rooms, table tennis, **Internet,** vegetarian restaurant, and "wellness program." Delicious fresh-baked bread. Rooms with Western bath Rp19,000-39,000; bungalows Rp49,000-99,000. ❷

Carolina Hotel (☎415 520; fax 415 21), toward the southern end of Tuk Tuk, on a side lane that juts off the main strip just before it leads uphill to Tabo Cottages. Spacious grounds overlooking the lake. Well-appointed rooms and Batak-style villas, most with hot showers and Western toilets. Attached restaurant. Attracts a slightly more well-heeled crowd. Rooms Rp27,500-90,000. ❸

FOOD

Most travelers eat at their guesthouses, which tend to offer uninspiring menus with typical Western and Indonesian staples, but there are alternatives along the main road through Tuk Tuk. If you've been craving fresh pizza (or magic mushroom omelettes), you've come to the right place. The following are all in Tuk Tuk.

Bamboo, at the north end of the peninsula, on the right. Lovely restaurant serving tasty food accompanied by superb views over the lake. Pillows, cushions, and lots of comfy bamboo chairs. *Gado-gado* Rp8000. Pasta Rp10,000-13,000. Curries Rp8000-12,000. Large beer Rp12,000. Open daily 7am-midnight. ❷

Pizzeria Rumba, with branches in the north (past Tony's) and south (past the health clinic) of Tuk Tuk Peninsula. Rumba was the first of Tuk Tuk's countless pizzerias, and still the best. Pizza Rp19,000, extra toppings Rp1000-4000 apiece. Cheaper in the north, better in the south. Both open daily 8am-10pm. ❸

Tabo Vegetarian Restaurant and Bakery, at the cottages. Excellent fish and vegetarian food on a beautiful wooden veranda. Best are the homemade German bread (Rp2500), cake (Rp3000), and ice cream (Rp3500). Salads Rp5000-12,000. ❷

Endy's Restaurant, next to Gokhon Library, roughly halfway around the peninsular road. An excellent place to relax with a book from the lending library next door. Excellent sandwiches made with fresh brown bread. Bread Rp3000 per slice. Avocado sandwich Rp8000. Chicken sandwich Rp10,000. Open daily 9am-8pm. ❷

Juwita Cafe, toward the southern end of the peninsula, on the road that leads uphill past the health clinic. Downstairs cafe is nondescript, but the views from the hillside terrace are unbeatable. Daily cooking classes advertised (1-4pm). Coconut curries with beef Rp17,500. Fresh goldfish from the lake also available. Open daily 7am-10pm. ❸

Mafir, up the road from Juwita (see above), 50m down from the Roy's Pub sign. Wide-ranging menu and tie-dyed surroundings. Chicken *satay* Rp13,000. Curry chicken Rp13,000. Large beer Rp12,000. Fruit juices Rp5000. Open daily 7am-10pm. ❸

Rumah Makan Islam Murni, close to Carolina's, after the police post. Escape from the banana pancake crowd and remind yourself that you're in Indonesia. Airy, *padang*-style restaurant. Chicken Rp7000. Fish Rp8000. Open daily 7:30am-9:30pm. ❷

Tempo Doeloe Ruman Makan Islam, next to Brando's Blues Bar toward the north of the peninsula. Garish murals depict local scenery—and Bob Marley. Good *padang* food (beef *rendang* Rp12,500). Open daily 8am-midnight. ❸

SIGHTS

Most travelers come to spend a few lazy days chilling out and splashing in the lake, but there are also cultural attractions along the eastern shore, within 20km of Tomok. Motorcycles and bicycles are the most convenient modes of transport, but be careful: the only roads safely navigable by motorcycle are the north coast road from Tomok to Pangururan (passing through Ambarita and Simanindo) and the Tuk Tuk Ring Rd. The whole island can be circled in about seven hours, but the roads in the south are treacherous and should only be tackled in good light.

TOMOK AND AMBARITA. There are several megalithic **tomb complexes** in Tomok, 10min. by motorbike south of Tuk Tuk. Featuring moss-covered stone statues of humans and animals, they were built to hold the remains of local Batak kings, the Sidobutars, whose descendants still live in Tomok today. Signs from the main road to Tuk Tuk lead uphill through a maze of souvenir stalls to a **carved stone coffin,** guarded by stone elephants, on the right about 500m up. The nearby **Museum of King Sidobutar** was closed indefinitely when we last visited (July 2002), but may have re-opened since. The **tomb of Rajah Ompu Soribuntu Sidobutar** is farther uphill, under a *hariam* tree. More interesting and slightly less commercialized, **Siallagan village** lies 8km up the road in Ambarita, behind the post office near the town harbor. As you drive along the main road from Tuk Tuk, look for the "Stone Chairs" sign on your left. Hidden behind a row of houses are several intricately **carved stone chairs,** about 300 years old—the site of village councils, where village chiefs arbitrated quarrels and gave out sentences. The second set of monoliths mark the site of the cannibalistic practices that made the Batak notorious following their first contact with Europeans. People found guilty of serious offenses (and enemies captured in battle) were brought here for execution. Once the poor victim's flesh had been tenderized with a stone mallet, he would be killed and cooked here—the main course at a banquet to which the whole village was invited. Cannibalism was never common practice among the Batak (it was reserved as punishment for serious offenses and as an economical way of dealing with prisoners of war), and by the early decades of the 20th century had died out completely.

SIMANINDO AND PANGURURAN. Some 20km north of Ambarita, the road reaches the village of **Simanindo,** on the north tip of the island. Here, a former chieftain's house has been converted into a **museum** full of dusty artifacts supposed to shed light on traditional Batak life. (Look for the sign on the right advertising the Huta Bolon Museum.) Daily performances of **traditional Batak dances** took place in the village until recently, but have been suspended. They may well have started up again by the time you read this; ask around in Tuk Tuk for the latest developments. Uninspiring **Pangururan** provides a base for forays into the hills on the mainland. The **Mt. Belirang Hot Springs** (Rp500) offer sulfurous comfort 4km west of town—look for signs on the main road. Although most visitors to Samosir seem to come here, the springs are unimpressive. Motorcycle enthusiasts can take a trip up **Mount Tele,** the steep ridge on the mainland. Beware of buses careening downhill. If for some reason you get stranded in Pangururan (or if you simply prefer urban grime to fresh air and fun), you can stay at **Hotel Wisata Samosir ❶,** 42 Dr. T.B. Simatupang, next to the Telkom office on Jl. Sisingamangaraja. (☎200 50. Doubles with bath Rp10,000-48,000.) A tour of all these villages can be organized at the **Bagus Bay Guest House** (Rp50,000).

ENTERTAINMENT

Many guesthouses show English movies nightly, in a cozy atmosphere with drinks. A few of the bars and restaurant along the main Tuk Tuk road stay open as long as there are customers, serving beer and tea until the wee hours to the strum of Batak folk songs. The discos go till dawn on Saturday nights.

Brando's Blues Bar, a popular pub on the northern end of the peninsula, is a 5min. walk south from Tony's. No blues in evidence here (think U2 and Tracy Chapman), but this is a mellow, popular nightspot nonetheless—with a free pool table outside and beer (Rp14,000) and food (chicken *satay* Rp12,000) served until late. (Dance floor. Open throughout the day till 2am.) **Elios Bar,** at the southern end of Tuk Tuk, packs in the locals on Saturday nights for frantic gyrating to the pulsating beat of Indonesian house "music." (Open Sa 9pm-5am.) The nearby **Tumba Disco** is a similar affair, and is also open late on Saturday nights (closed during the week). **Roy's Pub,** down the road, is open nightly, but is often deserted during the week.

HIKING ACROSS PULAU SAMOSIR

An invigorating hike across the island brings you through well-preserved Batak communities, much less impacted by tourism than those close to Tuk Tuk. The easiest and most pleasant route runs between Ambarita in the east and Pangururan in the west, and can be walked in either direction. Well-marked trails wind around coffee and tapioca plantations. It's possible to finish in one day if you start early. Alternatively, you can stay overnight in one of several villages with simple guesthouses. Hikers setting out from Ambarita pass tiny **Partokoan,** which has two guesthouses, **John's ❷** and **Jennie's ❷.** From Partokoan, a rocky cart path heads 9km up to the larger village of **Roongurni Huta,** where it meets the road left to Tomok (24km) and right to Pangururan (16km). The latter arrives after 6km at **Sidihoni Lake,** where **Weny Guest House ❶** puts up hikers for Rp5000 per night on the shore of the lake. The last 10km down to Pangururan offer stunning views of the steep crater walls and **Gunung Pusuk Buhit** on the western mainland.

PULAU NIAS

More than 100km west of mainland Sumatra, Pulau Nias is like nowhere else in Indonesia. Outside the two major towns, much of the interior of the island is thickly forested and remains relatively untouched by the outside world. The Niha people who inhabit the island are the proud inheritors of a unique language and culture, and Nias's rich tradition of monolithic stone sculptures and wood carving can still be seen today in dozens of villages around the island. Most visitors will pass through Gunung Sitoli, the not-so-interesting capital, on their way to the more popular southern part of the island. Many people come to Nias to surf—Sorake Beach, just a few kilometers outside Teluk Dalam, is renowned in zinc-nosed circles as home to some of the best waves in the world.

SIBOLGA ☎0631

Everything bad thing you've heard about Sibolga is true. Since this decidedly unpretty little town is the transit point to Pulau Nias, touts and aggressive hustlers swarm around the ferry and bus terminals. Happily, there is no reason why you should be stuck here for more than a couple of hours. **Scuba diving** and the **Internet** are two things you'll find in Sibolga and not on Nias.

The cheapest and safest way to buy **boat tickets** for Nias is to purchase them directly from the shipping offices. For **PT ASDP** boats to Gunung Sitoli, small branch offices at the port sell tickets right up to sailing time. If you're willing to fork out a bit of extra cash to forego the hassle of buying your own ticket, **Helen's Tourist Information Service,** Jl. Diponegoro 33 (☎2542), a shack across from Mesjid Agung mosque, offers ferry and bus tickets at a hefty commission as well as transport to the port and bus terminal and temporary bag storage. As always, rates can be negotiated and are better for groups. **Overnight ferries** shuttle from Sibolga to Gunung Sitoli and Teluk Dalam. **PT Simeulue,** Jl. Pelabuhan 9, close to the old harbor and a *becak* ride from the port, operates small wooden boats from Sibolga to **Teluk Dalam** (10-12hr.; Tu, Th, Sa 8pm; return W, F, and sometimes M 8pm; deck Rp32,500). A few cabins are normally available for at least double the regular fare.

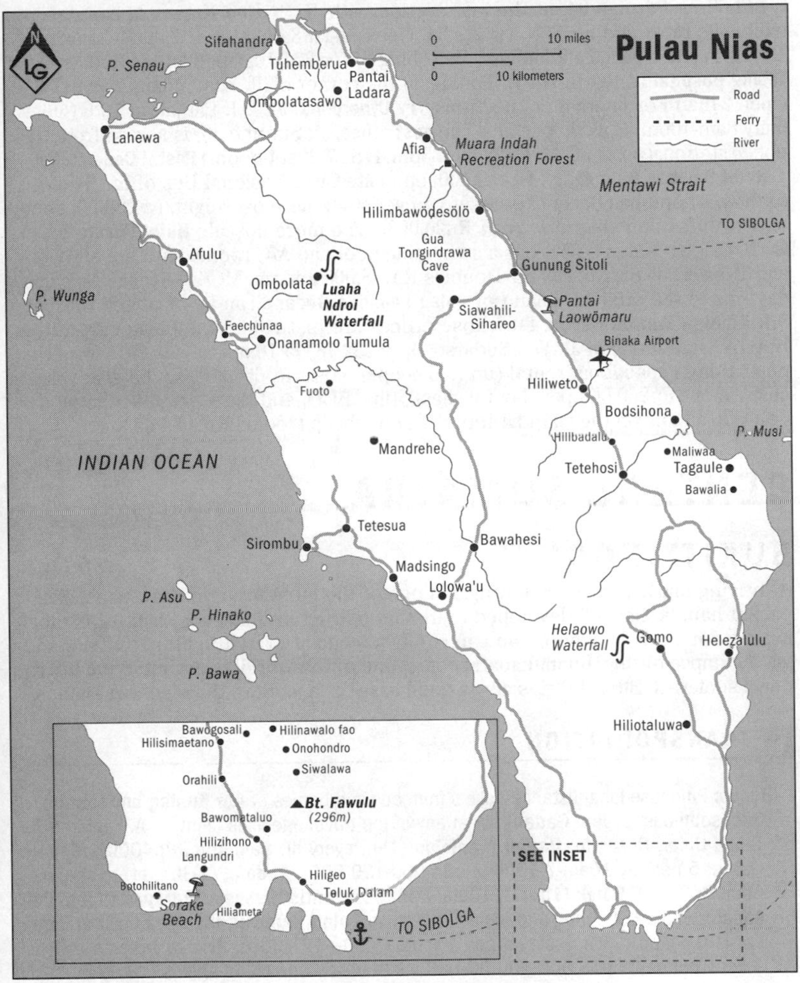

(☎214 97. Office open M-Sa 8:30am-6pm.) **PT ASDP,** Jl. Sisingamangaraja 161, runs regular boats from Sibolga to **Gunung Sitoli** (10hr.; M-Sa 8pm; economy Rp19,500, A/C lounge Rp26,000, non-A/C cabin Rp55,000-60,000) and back. (☎217 52. Open M-Sa 8am-5pm.) Alternating **PELNI** ships stop in Sibolga most Saturdays and provide direct links to **Padang** (Rp75,000-250,000) before sailing on to **Jakarta, Makassar, Surabaya,** and **Ternate.** The **PELNI office,** Jl. Horas 89 (☎222 91), is a 5min. walk from the port, on the right as you head away from the sea.

Buses leave from private company offices by the port and from the terminal on Jl. Sisingamangaraja in Sibolga (Rp1000 by *becak* from the pier) to: **Medan** (8hr.; several departures 7-9am and 7-9pm; Rp30,000-40,000); **Padang** (16hr.) via **Bukittinggi** (14hr.; 8, 9am, 3:30, 4, 8, 9pm; Rp30,000-50,000); **Parapat** (6hr.; 8, 10am, 2, 8pm; Rp30,000). Many of the bus companies have offices close to the port, along Jl. Horas and Jl. Diponegoro; buy tickets a few hours ahead if you can.

BNI, Jl. S. Parman 34, at the intersection with Jl. Brigjen Katamso, has decent exchange rates and an **ATM.** (☎227 24. Open M-Th 8am-4pm, F 7:30am-noon and 1:30-4pm.) The **police station** is at Jl. Tobing 35. (☎251 10. Open 24hr.) **RSU Dr. F.L. Tobing Hospital** is nearby on Jl. Tobing, at the corner of Jl. Yos Sudarso. (☎247 25. Open 24hr.) For **Internet** connections, try **Cyberpunk,** Jl. D.I. Panjaitan 100. (Open daily 8am-10pm. Rp6000 per hr.) The **post office,** Jl. Sutomo 40, is across from the police station. (☎221 62. M-Th 7:30am-3pm, F-Sa 7:30am-noon.) **Postal Code**: 22500.

Hotel Sambas Baru ❷, Jl. Horas 100, opposite Citra Nasional Bus office, is close to the port and has decent rooms if you get stuck here overnight. (☎228 57. Doubles with fan and shared *mandi* Rp20,000.) The more upscale **Hotel Wisata Indah ❺,** Jl. Brigjen Katamso 51, has a swimming pool and A/C rooms with hot showers and TVs. (☎236 88; fax 239 88. Doubles Rp178,000 and up. MC/V.) **Scuba diving** and daytrips to the offshore island of **Pulau Pooncan Gadang** can be arranged through **P.T. Sibolga Marina Resort ❺,** whose offices are just round the corner from the Hotel Wisata Indah at Jl. Yos Sudarso 29 (☎232 78), a 10min. *becak* ride from the port. A day's speedboat rental (up to 6 people) costs Rp650,000; scuba gear rental costs about Rp260,000 per day for mask, fins, BCD, and the works. Accommodation is available on the island, though it's not cheap (rooms Rp260,000 and up).

CENTRAL SUMATRA

BUKITTINGGI ☎0752

A thriving market town, Bukittinggi is one of the most urban of Sumatra's backpacker haunts. Its well-developed tourist infrastructure makes it ideal for exploring the countryside, where you can climb volcanoes, watch fighting buffalo, and get a glimpse of the Minangkabau people, one of the world's only surviving matrilineal societies. Bukittinggi is also a good base for a jaunt to the Mentawi Islands.

TRANSPORTATION

Buses: Purchase long-distance tickets from bus companies at **Aur Kuning bus terminal,** 3km southeast of Jam Gadang, or at any of the travel agencies lining Jl. A. Yani and Jl. Teuku Umar. Buses to: **Danau Maninjau** (1hr., every hr. 8am-4pm, Rp4000); **Medan** (18hr.; 5 per day 10am-7:30pm; Rp85,000-120,000); **Padang** (2-3hr., every hr. 6am-6pm, Rp8000); **Solok** (1hr.; 9, 10am; Rp6000). **Tourist buses** to **Parapat** stop at the equator and a hot spring and include a ferry to **Pulau Samosir,** though a night in Parapat is required (13hr.; several per day; Rp78,000-127,000). Also to **Jakarta** (40hr.; several per day; Rp75,000-260,000). Book at hotels and travel agents.

Ferries: To get to **Melaka,** first take a bus (12hr.; 7am, 2, 4pm; Rp35,000) or minibus (10hr.; 7:30pm; Rp55,000) to **Dumai.** From there, ferries run to **Melaka** (1¾hr.; every hr. 11am-3pm; Rp125,000). A bus to **Sibolga** (10hr.; 10am and 7pm; Rp55,000) will get you to the Nias ferries.

Local Transportation: Microlet minivans follow a roughly clockwise route up Jl. Sudirman, Jl. A. Yani, Pasar Bawah (lower market), and Aur Kuning bus terminal (Rp1000). **Dokar** (horse drawn carriages) clop around town for about Rp5000 a ride.

ORIENTATION AND PRACTICAL INFORMATION

Jam Gadang—the Dutch clocktower—and the surrounding square dominate the town center. **Pasar Atas** (upper market) is next to the square on the northeast. **Jl. A. Yani** heads roughly northwest from the square until it bends right at a four-way

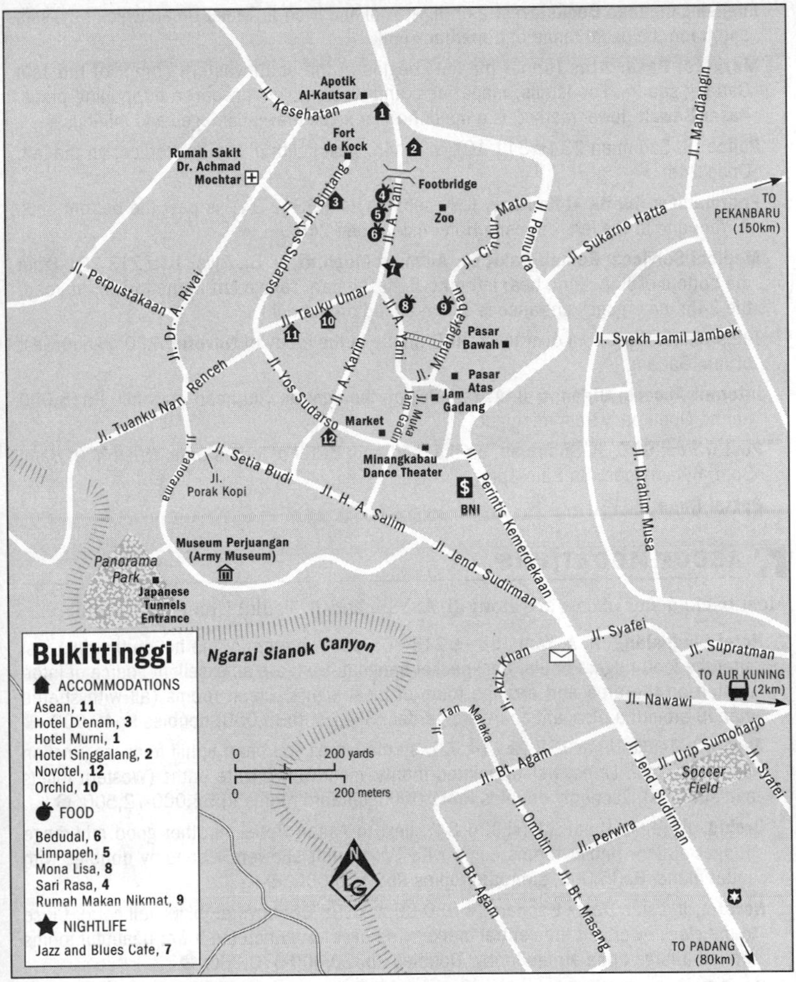

INDONESIA

intersection and continues downhill under the towering footbridge past the **zoo** and the old Dutch **Fort de Kock,** into **Kampong Cina (Chinatown).** Most of the budget hotels and cafes are on Jl. A. Yani and the adjoining **Jl. Teuku Umar.** Back from the four-way intersection, **Jl. A. Karim** climbs to the southwest (with **Novotel** at its summit), and Jl. Teuku Umar (which becomes **Jl. Tengku Nan Renceh**) climbs uphill to the west, intersecting **Jl. Yos Sudarso.**

Tours: Outfits on Jl. A. Yani arrange flights, buses, taxis, and tours. Hotels and cafes along Jl. A. Yani are great place to meet guides for the local area (Rp65,000 for a day's tour) and treks up Gunung Merapi (Rp150,000 per person for overnight climb).

Currency Exchange: BNI, Perintis Kemerdekaan 15 (☎225 78), has an **ATM.** Open M-F 8am-3pm. **Branch** by the Hotel Singgalang on Jl. A. Yani. 24hr. **ATM.**

English-Language Bookstores: 2 on Jl. A. Yani and 1 on Jl. Teuku Umar, which buy, sell, and trade the usual range of paperback junk.

Markets: Pasar Atas (upper market) begins in the southwestern corner of the Jam Gadang square. Foodstalls, magazines, and women's underwear–a happening place. **Pasar Bawah** (lower market) is a major hub for horse drawn carriages and minibuses.

Police: Jl. Sudirman 23 (☎311 10), a 10min. walk south of the post office, on the left. Open 24hr.

Pharmacies: Apotik Al-Kautsar, Jl. Kesehatan 17 (☎312 34), is past the bottom of Jl. A. Yani and to the left, opposite Hotel Asia. Open 24hr.

Medical Services: Rumah Sakit Dr. Achmad Mochtar, Jl. Dr. Rivai 1 (☎213 22). From the bottom of Jl. A. Yani, bear left onto Jl. Kesehatan. Take a left at the fork in the road; the 24hr. emergency entrance is 100m ahead on the right.

Telephones: Wartel all over town. HCD phone in the lobby of **Novotel,** 300m southwest of Jam Gadang.

Internet Access: Giganet, Jl. A. Yani 96, on the right as you head downhill. Rp15,000 per hr. Open daily 9am-midnight.

Post Office: GPO, Jl. Sudirman, up the road from BNI. *Poste Restante.* Open M-Th 8am-3pm, F 8am-noon, Sa 8am-1pm.

Postal Code: 26116.

ACCOMMODATIONS

Most backpacker places are along Jl. A. Yani and Jl. Teuku Umar, up the hill.

Hotel Singgalang, Jl. A. Yani 130 (☎215 76), at the bottom of the hill on the right just after the footbridge. Popular backpacker hangout. Staff are an excellent source of information on the area and arrange tours of local sights. Clean rooms (all with shared *mandi*) around a pleasant courtyard garden. Singles Rp35,000; doubles Rp40,000. ❷

Asean, Jl. Teuku Umar 13B (☎214 92), on the left as you head uphill from the junction with Jl. A. Yani. Large, well-appointed rooms, most with private baths (Western toilets and showers). Economy doubles Rp41,000; standard rooms Rp52,000-72,500. ❸

Orchid, Jl. Teuku Umar 11 (☎326 84), next to Asean Hotel. Another good mid-range budget option; pricier rooms come with TV and hot showers. Economy doubles with squat *mandi* Rp35,000; standard rooms Rp50-70,000. ❸

Novotel, Jl. Laras Datuk Bandaro (☎350 00; fax 238 00; novotel_bkt@mail.com). Close to the clocktower and the central market. The best luxury hotel in town; beautiful rooms around a large open atrium lobby. Doubles Rp320,000-370,000. ❺

Hotel D'enam, Jl. Yos Sudarso 4 (☎213 33), close to the back of the fort. Small, clean, family-run guesthouse on a secluded street away from the noise. Doubles with shared *mandi* Rp17,000, with private *mandi* and Western toilet Rp20,000. ❷

Hotel Murni, Jl. A. Yani 115 (☎355 69), at the bottom of the road, on the left. Helpful staff. Good, cheap option; simple twin-bedded rooms with shared *mandi* Rp15,000. ❶

FOOD

Tasty, atomic-hot Minangkabau cuisine (known across the archipelago as *padang* food) dominates the menus of most local restaurants and *warung.* The cheapest meals can be had at the foodstalls in **Pasar Atas** or on Jl. A. Yani itself. **Backpacker cafes** cluster at the bottom of **Jl. A. Yani** and up into **Jl. Teuku Umar,** all serving a range of Western and Indonesian favorites.

Sari Rasa, Jl. A. Yani 31, opposite BNI and next to Hotel Yany. Classy little wooden place serving excellent *padang* food as well as a range of other Indonesian, Chinese, and Western dishes. There's an English menu on display at the door, but locals eat here too. *Daging rending* Rp12,000. *Gulai ayam* Rp12,000. Open daily 8am-11pm. ❷

Bedudal, Jl. A. Yani 95/105, on the left as you head downhill. Probably the best of the backpacker restaurants/bars. Raised wooden tables and cushioned seating areas. Popular spot for an evening beer. Pizza Rp19,000; sandwiches Rp8500-14,500; steak Rp20,000-35,000; chocolate cake Rp5000. Open daily 9am-12:30am. ❹

Mona Lisa, Jl. A. Yani 58, up the hill from the bridge and left at the crossroads; it's on the left. Dark narrow corridor of a restaurant serving decent Chinese food. Sweet and sour pork Rp11,000; *cap cai* Rp8000. Open daily 7:30am-9:30pm. ❷

Rumah Makan Nikmat, Jl. Minangkabau 77, upstairs on the left as you turn onto Jl. Minangkabau from the clock square. Clean cafeteria serving good, cheap *padang*-style food. Most dishes around Rp4000. Open daily 6am-9pm. ❶

Limpapeh, Jl. A. Yani, next to the *wartel* opposite Hotel Singgalang. *Padang* restaurant serving tasty, spicy fare for around Rp10,000 a meal. Open daily 8am-9pm. ❷

SIGHTS

Towering above Bukittinggi's skyline, the Minangkabau-Dutch hybrid **Jam Gadang** clocktower oversees the frenetic market. Almost nothing remains of the Dutch **Fort de Kock** at the end of Jl. Bintang except a few rusty cannons, but it's a pleasant spot for a relaxing walk. (Open daily 8am-6pm. Rp1000.) The footbridge over Jl. A. Yani, with superb views across the city to Gunung Merapi, connects Fort de Kock to the **city zoo,** where a pair of overweight and shaggy-coated orangutans are the chief exhibits. (Open daily 8am-6pm; Rp2000.) Within the zoo grounds is a small **museum** of Minangkabau culture, worth a look if only for the freakish display of deformed animals hidden at the back (Rp900). **Panorama Park** looks out across the **Ngarai Sianok Canyon,** and its clusters of *warung* afford spectacular views. Also within the park is a complex of **Japanese Tunnels,** built with forced labor during World War II, but they're nothing to write home about. (Open daily 8am-6pm. Rp1500.) Not far past the park entrance on Jl. Panorama is the **Museum Perjuangan** (Army Museum) with an old fighter plane outside. The museum contains an impressive collection of weapons dating from the struggle for independence, and a grisly exhibition of photographs of the gloriously dead. (Open daily 8am-5pm. Admission by donation.)

Two volcanoes, **Gunung Singgalang** (2878m) and **Gunung Merapi** (2891m), dominate Bukittinggi's horizon. A guide is recommended for either 9hr. round-trip ascent; the trail may be hard to find alone. Travel companies in Bukittinggi leave at 11pm in order to catch the sunrise (around Rp150,000). Merapi, the more popular climb, is still active and erupted in 1974; the police will close it down if it starts smoking. The view from the summit can be spectacular.

Slightly farther afield, there are a number of traditional **Minangkabau villages,** native reserves, and a swimming lake. Public transportation can be unpredictable; either rent a motorbike or go with a tour. **Lake Singkarak** and surrounding villages can be visited in six hours on a motorbike (Rp65,000 per day). **Harau Canyon** is a pristine reserve northeast of Bukittinggi. Rental places can give you directions.

Pandai Sikat, a handicraft town specializing in carvings and *songket* weavings, is a popular stop on Minangkabau area tours; it's also accessible by *microlet* from the bus station (Rp1000). **Pariangan** is a village with *rumah gadang* homes; take a bus from **Aur Kuning** (1hr., every hr. 7am-6pm, Rp2000). Buses also run to **Batang Palupuh** (15min., Rp1000), a nature reserve for the rafflesia flower. Worthwhile day tours of the region can be arranged just about anywhere in town for Rp65,000 per person.

ENTERTAINMENT AND NIGHTLIFE

Nightly **Minangkabau dance performances** are held at a theater on Jl. Lenggogeni 1 (opposite BNI, on the lane that leads from the market and the clocktower toward Jl. Perintis Kemerdekaan). The show includes local martial arts, wedding celebrations with elaborate costumes, and the harvest celebration dance, where dancers jump and thrash around in a heap of shattered china. Purchase tickets at hotels or travel agencies, or at the door (Rp20,000). **Buffalo fighting** is also popular. Fights take place every Saturday evening, and on either Tuesday or Wednesday night (normally 5-7pm), but not always in the same place. Ask around at cafes and hotels for details and directions. (Most hotels and restaurants arrange special fight-day minibuses to ferry tourists to and from the fights. Rp25,000 per person.) Area daytrips on fight days finish with the match-up.

The **Jazz and Blues Cafe** is on Jl. A. Yani, up the road on the left from the Hotel Singgalang. With tables on the street and drawings of jazz and blues greats on the walls inside, this is a good place to have a beer or two with a mostly local crowd. (Large beer Rp14,000. Open daily 9:30am-10pm.)

DANAU MANINJAU

A smaller, less touristed version of Lake Toba, Lake Maninjau is a crater lake 36km west of Bukittinggi. Extreme weather patterns created by the crater's micro-climate cause eerie mists, freak downpours, and dazzling sunsets. For daytrips near the lake, **bicycles** (Rp20,000) and **motorbikes** (Rp70,000) can be rented in **Maninjau village.** Painfully slow **Internet** is available at **Jack's Place** in Maninjau village, on the right as you walk along the main road toward Bayur (Rp23,000 per hour).

A number of waterfront guesthouses have sprouted north of Maninjau Village and past **Bayur,** 3km north of Maninjau. Maninjau village is more developed, with a growing number of hotels and cafes catering to the tourist crowd. Homestays in Bayur are more peaceful, separated from the main road by rice paddies. **Lili's** ❷ is the most popular of a string of similar places by the lakeside, and has rooms and bungalows for Rp20,000-30,000, as well as a decent restaurant. The great views and the unhurried air make this a wonderful place to take it easy for a few days.

Travel to Maninjau is an ordeal: the last descent from Bukittinggi involves 44 hairpin turns. **Buses** from Bukittinggi will drop you at any lakeside guesthouse. Alternatively, you can get off at **Lawang,** climb 2hr. uphill to **Puncak Lawang** (the highest point around the lake), and then hike 4hr. down to Bayur village. Regular **buses** run to **Bukittinggi** (1½hr., Rp4000). To get to **Padang** (4hr., Rp8000) you have to first go to **Lubuk Basung,** 1hr. up the road from Bayur.

PADANG ☎0751

The offshore islands near Padang, the southernmost stop on Northern Sumatra's backpacker ant-trail, offer excellent opportunities for beach-side frolicking. Aside from roaming the Pasar Raya, there's not much to do in the city. Padang's weather complicates any travels: the scorching sun turns anything more than a 5min. stroll into a physical endurance test, and torrential rains often wash out the views. Padang's trademark hot and spicy cuisine is famous all over the archipelago, and excellent restaurants serving local specialties can be found all over town.

TRANSPORTATION

Flights: Bandara Tabing Airport, 9km north of town. Catch *bis kota* #14 up Jl. Sudirman (Rp1000) or an *oplet* (Rp1000) up Jl. Pemuda. Taxis Rp10,000. Departure tax Rp15,000 (domestic) or Rp60,000 (international). **Merpati,** Jl. Juanda 79 (☎444

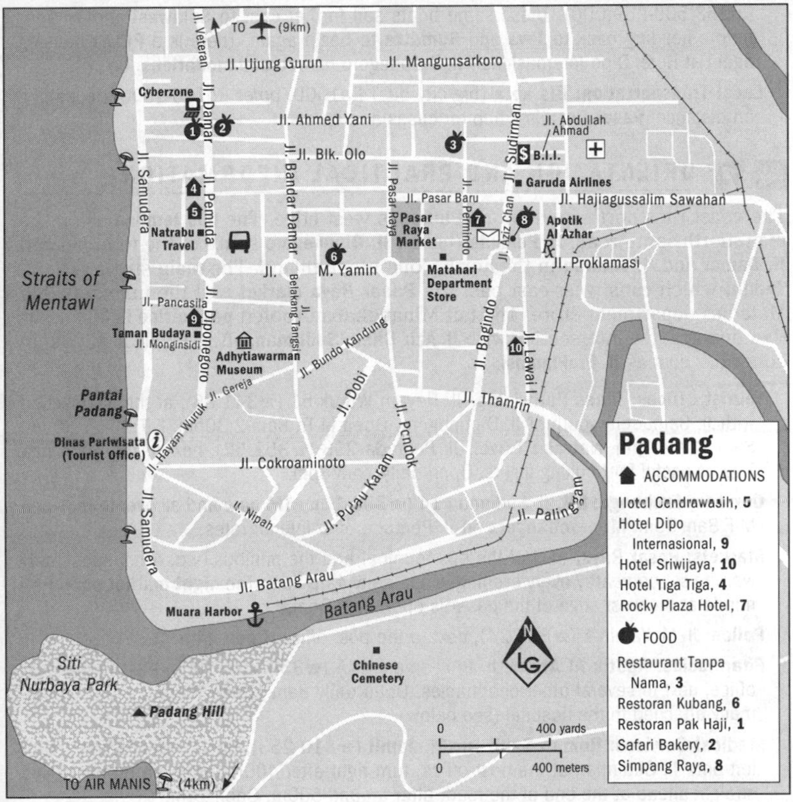

831), inside Hotel Pangerna, flies to: **Batam** (Tu, Th, Su; Rp586,000) and **Palembang** (Tu, Th, Su; Rp1,151,900). Open M-F 8am-4:30pm, Sa-Su 9am-1pm. **Garuda,** Jl. Sudirman 2 (☎301 73), in between Bank Mandisi and Bank Bukopin, flies to **Jakarta** (2 per day; Rp700,000). Open M-F 8am-4pm, Sa-Su 9am-1pm. **Mandala,** Jl. Veteran 20C (☎397 37), has the cheapest flights to **Jakarta** (daily; Rp604,000). **Silk Air** has flights to **Singapore** (3 per week).

Buses: The **terminal** is on Jl. Pemuda, west of Pasar Raya. Buy tickets from the many companies at the bus station. Each company handles 1 or 2 routes; ask around. To: **Bengkulu** (16hr.; 2pm; Rp40,000, with A/C Rp60,000); **Bukittinggi** (2½hr., every hr. 6am-6pm, Rp8000); **Jakarta** (30hr.; economy 1pm, Rp100,000; A/C 1pm, Rp170,000; A/C toilet 10am, Rp270,000); **Medan** (17hr.; economy 11am, Rp60,000; A/C 1pm, Rp135,000; A/C toilet 2pm, Rp135,000); **Pekanbaru** (10hr.; 8am, 7pm; Rp30,000); **Sungai Penuh** (10hr., 5pm, Rp35,000; minibuses 5hr., 9, 9:30am, 6, 6:30pm, Rp35,000; 1pm, Rp45,000).

Ferries: PELNI, Jl. Teluk Bayur 32 (☎616 24), in Teluk Bayur, near the port. The modern passenger ferries **Lambelu** and **Kambuna** dock at Padang as part of their bi-weekly travel around the archipelago. To: **Gunung Sitoli** (15hr.; Su 7am and 6pm; Rp79,500-263,000); **Jakarta** (36hr.; Tu 7am and 8pm; Rp160,500-543,500); **Sibolga** (10hr.; Su 7am and 6pm; Rp86,000-285,000); **Surabaya** (2 days; Tu 7am and 8pm;

Rp283,500-969,000). These same boats sail farther east to **Sulawesi** and **Ambon,** before heading back to **Java** and **Sumatra** to begin again. There is a **PELNI** booking agent at Hotel Dipo Internasional, Jl. Diponegoro (see **Accommodations,** below).

Local Transportation: Bis kota (big city bus) Rp1000, *oplet* Rp700-1500, depending on distance. **Pasar Raya** is a hub for buses and *oplets*.

ORIENTATION AND PRACTICAL INFORMATION

The coast runs north-south along Padang's west edge. The **bus terminal** is on the main north-south road, **Jl. Pemuda** (called **Jl. Diponegoro** south of the terminal and **Jl. Damar** and **Jl. Veteran** in the north), one block inland. The main street is **Jl. M. Yamin,** which runs west-east past the **Pasar Raya market** and the unmistakable Matahari department store. The tall Minangkabau-roofed **post office** is 300m farther down, at the intersection with **Jl. Aziz Chan/Sudirman,** after which Jl. M. Yamin continues east as **Jl. Proklamasi.**

Tourist Offices: Dinas Pariwisata, Jl. Hayam Wuruk 51 (☎341 86), at the intersection with Jl. Samudera south of Jl. Diponegoro. Open M-Th 8am-2:30pm, F 7:30-11:30am, Sa 7:30am-1pm. **Natrabu Travel,** Jl. Pemuda 29B (☎352 52), next to the Hotel Tiga Tiga, is useful for booking flights. Open daily 7am-8pm.

Currency Exchange: BII, Jl. Sudirman 14 (☎308 11). **ATM** here and all over town. Open M-F 8am-3pm. **Moneychangers** on Jl. Pemuda offer inferior rates.

Markets: Pasar Raya, east of the bus terminal and the minibus hub. A hot spot. Tasty *warung* set up nearby every evening. Open daily 4am-7pm. The **night market** on Jl. Permindo at the west edge of the *pasar* is open until 9pm.

Police: Jl. M. Yamin 1 (☎337 24), next to the post office. Open 24hr.

Pharmacies: Apotik Al Azhar, Jl. Proklamasi 44A (☎359 26), 100m east of the post office, next to several other pharmacies. Open daily 8am-10pm. There is a 24hr. pharmacy attached to the hospital (see below).

Medical Services: Rumah Sakit Dr. M. Jamil (☎810 253), on Jl. Kemerdekaan. Turn left onto Jl. Sudirman at the post office, turn right after 400m (after the BII bank). It's straight ahead at the end of the road, after around 500m. Open 24hr.

Telephones: Free HCD phone in the **Hotel Dipo International,** Jl. Diponegoro 13 (see **Accommodations,** below). Open 24hr. There is a 24hr. wartel about halfway up Jl. M. Yamin, on the right as you head toward the post office.

Internet Access: Cyberzone, Jl. Veteran 3, slightly north of the Safari Bakery, on the opposite side of the road. Rp4000 per hr. Open daily 9am-11pm.

Post Office: Pos Besar Padang, Jl. Aziz Chan 7 (☎343 58), on the corner with Jl. M. Yamin. *Poste Restante.* Open daily 7:45am-6pm (closed F 11:30am-1:30pm).

Postal Code: 25111.

ACCOMMODATIONS

Budget hotels are along **Jl. Pemuda** near the bus terminal; quieter places lie scattered about town. Stifling heat and bloodthirsty mosquitoes make this a good place to think about upgrading to an A/C room.

Rocky Plaza Hotel, Jl. Permindo 40 (☎840 888; fax 841 230), on the right as you head away from the market. Snazzy new international-standard hotel with all the perks. All rooms have A/C, satellite TV, IDD phone, and hot showers. Swimming pool, bar, and 24hr. coffee shop. If rates stay this low, this is the best mid-range deal in town. Doubles (including breakfast and tax) Rp205,000-230,000. AmEx/MC/V. ❺

Hotel Sriwijaya, Jl. Alang Lawas I 15 (☎235 77). Head right 100m east of the post office on Jl. M. Yamin/Proklamasi, down Jl. Alang Lawas I; it's on the right on a quiet back street within walking distance of the city center. Comfy lounge. Economy singles/doubles with fan and shared squat *mandi* Rp25,000/Rp35,000, with private squat *mandi* Rp40,000/Rp45,000, with A/C Rp45,000/Rp50,000. ❷

Hotel Cendrawasih, Jl. Pemuda 27 (☎228 94), next to Tiga Tiga. Simple budget rooms within spitting distance of the bus station. Economy singles/doubles with shared squat *mandi* Rp15,000/Rp25,000, with private squat *mandi* Rp25,000/Rp35,000; VIP rooms with fan, shower, and Western toilets Rp50,000. ❶

Hotel Dipo Internasional, Jl. Diponegoro 25 (☎342 61; fax 342 65), south of Jl. M. Yamin, on the right. Excellent mid-range option. All rooms have A/C with private Western toilets. In-house travel agency books buses and flights. 24hr. currency exchange and 24hr. restaurant. Singles Rp130,000-180,000; doubles 140,000-200,000, plus 21% tax. Credit cards accepted. ❺

Hotel Tiga Tiga, Jl. Pemuda 31 (☎226 23), opposite the bus terminal. Labyrinth of rooms set around a sitting area. Late-night cafe and TV. Popular with backpackers. Pricier rooms have private Western toilets. Singles Rp20,000-50,000; doubles 30,000-60,000. A newer and more upscale **branch** is farther north, at Jl. Veteran 33. ❷

FOOD

Padang is famous all over Indonesia for its delicious spicy food. In a *padang*-style restaurant, the waiter brings you many small dishes as soon as you sit down—you only pay for what you eat. Typical dishes include dry beef *rending* and *kao ayam*, a creamy chicken curry. Lunch *warung* cluster at the bus terminal and east toward Pasar Raya. At night, Jl. M. Yamin and Jl. Permindo on the west edge of the *pasar* come to life. *Warung* with a view set up along **Pantai Padang,** where Jl. M. Yamin ends on the west edge of town, until the evening.

Simpang Raya, Jl. Aziz Chan 24, left on Jl. M. Yamin at the post office; it's on the right. A/C non-smoking restaurant serving a superb range of *padang*-style food and fresh-squeezed fruit juices. Most dishes around Rp10,000. Open daily 7am-9pm. ❷

Restaurant Tanpa Nama, Jl. Rohana Kudus 87. Head 300m north on Jl. Permindo from Pasar Raya to Jl. Rohana Kudus. Great *padang* food and fruit juices in shiny A/C diner popular with young student types. Dishes Rp5000-15,000. Open Sa-Th 8am-9pm. ❷

Restoran Kubang, Jl. M. Yamin 138, east of the bus terminal. Late-night street stall complex with fan-cooled indoor cafeteria seating attached. *Martabak* pancakes with meat and vegetables are the speciality (Rp5000); simple dishes like *satay* and fried rice also available. Open daily 2pm-midnight. ❶

Safari Bakery, Jl. Damar 50C, 500m north of the bus station on the right. Good breakfast spot. Gaggles of teeny-boppers and students flock here for the best selection of pastries (Rp2500) and cakes (Rp1600-2500) in town. Fresh coffee and excellent range of fruit juices also available. Open daily 8am-9pm. ❶

Restoran Pak Haji, Jl. Damar 67C, opposite Safari Bakery, on the left as you head north from the bus terminal. Cafeteria style place serving cheap *martabak* (Rp5000) and *mie goreng* (Rp6000). Excellent avocado juice Rp4000. Open daily 10am-11pm. ❶

SIGHTS

The **Adhytiawarman Museum,** Jl. Diponegoro 10, presides over a fenced park with a playground, garden, and benches. The museum houses a marginally interesting exhibit of folk cultures from around West Sumatra. (Open Tu-Su 8am-3:30pm. Rp800.) Across the street at Jl. Diponegoro 19 is the **Taman Budaya (Cultural Center),** which stages outdoor dance and martial arts shows. A schedule is usually posted.

Pantai Padang extends along the western edge of town and is lined with *warung* that stay open late into the evening. The beach and water are dirty, but the view at sunset is spectacular. **Air Manis,** Padang's most famous beach, is a 2hr. hike away; from Air Manis there are great views of **Pulau Pisang Ketek** (Small Banana Island), to which you can wade during low tide. To get to Air Manis, walk south along Pantai Padang to the Arau River, where rickety canoes will ferry you across for Rp1000. On the other side, the scenic path leads past Japanese fortifications, through a Chinese cemetery, and eventually to the beach 4km down. Alternatively, *oplets* run from Pasar Raya for Rp1000. You'll have to change *oplets* at the turn-off to the beach (another Rp1000). In the opposite direction, **Pasir Jambak** (15km north of the city) is Padang's best beach for swimming. Straight out of an Indiana Jones flick, the **Jembatan Akar** (Root Bridge) in **Pulut-Pulut** spans 40m over raging rapids. The bridge is formed entirely from the interwoven roots of two giant Beringin trees on either side of the river. Usually, three buses travel daily to the village of Pulut-Pulut (2hr., Rp6000).

KERINCI SEBLAT NATIONAL PARK

Spanning four provinces and almost 15,000 sq. km, Kerinci Seblat National Park is Sumatra's hotspot for ecotourism. Designated a national park in 1982 and now an ASEAN heritage site, the park is dominated by 3805m Gunung Kerinci, Indonesia's second-highest volcano. Animal lovers come to the park in search of rare Sumatran tigers, rhinos, and elephants, as well as the mysterious *orang pendek* (short man) with the head of a man and the body of an ape, a "species" so elusive that scientists still aren't sure whether it really exists. The world's largest flower, the rafflesia, can be found here, as well as hundreds of species of birds, including the bronze-tailed peacock pheasant.

SUNGAI PENUH ☎0748

Sungai Penuh is the only town in Jambi Province that sees any kind of foreign tourism. Surrounded by beautiful scenery, this small-scale provincial capital is a convenient base for travelers wishing to explore the national park—a good place to organize climbing and trekking expeditions into the surrounding countryside.

INDONESIA

TRANSPORTATION AND PRACTICAL INFORMATION. It's not hard to get your bearings here; Sungai Penuh is a small town with a well-defined center. South of the square, an obelisk sits at the top of **Jl. Martadinata,** the town's main road. **Jl. Agus Salini,** on the left 100m from the obelisk (away from the grass square), leads past the main **market** to the **bus terminal.** The square is flanked on the northwest by Jl. Sudirman and on the southeast and northeast by Jl. Diponegoro, which becomes Jl. Muradi north past the square. **Buses** depart from **Terminal Sungai Penuh** to: **Bengkulu** (17hr.; noon; Rp30,000-35,000); **Jambi** (11hr.; 8am and 5-8pm; Rp30,000-50,000); **Padang** (10hr.; every 2hr. 9am-8pm; Rp25,000-35,000); as well as **Bedeng Dua, Kersik Tua,** and **Pelompek** (1½hr., every 15min., Rp4000).

To get to **Kerinci National Park Headquarters,** Jl. Basuki Rahmat 11, follow Jl. Muradi 300m from the square. After the second set of concrete gateposts on either side of the road, turn left onto Jl. Basuki Rahmat; the office is at the top of the hill on the right. The office issues permits to climb Kerinci or visit Danau Gunung Tujuh (Rp15,000 per person per day) and arranges guides (Rp150,000 per day) for trekking. (☎222 50. Open M-Th 9am-2pm, F 9-11am.) **BNI,** Jl. A. Yani opposite Hotel Matahari, has an **ATM.** The **police,** Jl. Diponegoro 2, are at the far right end of the square as you approach it from Jl. Martadinata and the center of town. (☎211 70. Open 24hr.) A pharmacy, **Apotik Usaha Baru,** Jl. Diponegoro 4-12, is on the southeast side of the square. (☎323 583. Open daily 8am-9pm.) The **hospital,** Rumah

Sakit Umum Daerah, is on Jl. Basuki Rahmat, on the left before the park office as you walk uphill. (☎118. Intensive care unit open 24hr.) The **Telkom office,** Jl. Imam Bonjol 2, is to the left of the obelisk as you emerge from Jl. Martadinata with the square in front of you. (Open daily 7am-1am.) The **post office** is in the far left corner of the square as you approach it from Jl. Martadinata. (Open M-Th 8am-3pm, F 8-11:30am, Sa 8am-1pm.) **Postal Code:** 37114.

ACCOMMODATIONS AND FOOD. A block beyond the post office and 150m uphill on the left is **Hotel Matahari ❸,** Jl. A. Yani 25, a friendly family-run place with comfortable rooms and helpful information on the area. (☎210 61. Economy doubles with shared *mandi* Rp30,000; VIP doubles with private Western bath Rp50,000-60,000.) At the bottom left corner of the square as you approach it from Jl. Martadinata, **Hotel Aroma ❷,** Jl. Imam Bonjol 14, has a wide range of rooms and a decent restaurant. (☎211 42. Economy doubles with shared *mandi* Rp20,000, with private bath Rp30,000, with TV, hot water, and fan Rp60,000.) Just off the square on the right, the **Yani Hotel ❷,** Jl. Muradi 1 (☎214 09), has economy doubles with shared *mandi* (Rp25,000-50,000) and huge VIP rooms with full-length mirrors and boat-sized beds. **Hotel Kayu Manis ❶,** Jl. Martadinata 34, has simple rooms and a central location on the town's main road. (☎212 26. Economy rooms with shared *mandi* Rp10,000-20,000, with private bath Rp20,000-35,000.)

Warung and hole-in-the-wall establishments flourish around the square's north-east edge and continue down along Jl. Muradi. Most of the busiest places are along **Jl. Martadinata,** which brims with *nasi goreng* joints, *satay* and *martabak* vendors, and syrupy-sweet *es* (iced) goodies. **Bofet Sate Kambing ❶,** Jl. Martadinata 45, is a friendly, relaxing place to enjoy a plate of *satay* (Rp5000) or *martabak* (Rp4000) and hang out with locals. (Open daily 9am-10pm.)

SIGHTS AND ENTERTAINMENT. **Mesjid Agung Pondok Tinggi,** 200m from the post office on Jl. Depati Payung, was built in 1874 without a single nail. Tourists may enter. (Rp10,000 donation goes to the mosque's charity box.) The unimpressive **Semurup Hot Springs,** 9km north of town, soothes bathers. Communal *mandi* disperse hot water in the long building directly before the springs. Catch a minivan from the bus terminal; ask for "Air Panas Semurup." Most buses will drop you off at the intersection of the main road (Rp1000). From the intersection, it's a 2km walk or Rp1000 *ojek* ride; bear right at the fork after 1km and then left after another 700m. (Open M-Sa 8am-6pm, Su 6am-6pm. Rp1500.)

Traditional Kerinci dances include *Asyiek*, which contacts the spirits of dead ancestors, and *Pencak Silat*, a martial art involving swords. Music unique to the area includes *Basikie*, a complex mix of drum beats, and *Seruling Bambu*, singing with bamboo flute accompaniment. Ask about local village festivals.

KAYU ARO REGION

Dominated by Gunung Sitoli and covered with tea plantations and cinnamon groves, the beautiful Kayu Aro Region is home to three towns each a short bus ride apart: Bedeng Dua, with a tea factory; Kersik Tua, 7km north and a base for mountain treks; and Pelompek, another 10km up, the starting point for hikes to Danau Gunung Tujuh. Visitors may be treated to *Kuda Kepang*, a frenetic fruit-throwing, bamboo-pounding ceremony that blends Kerinci and Javanese traditions.

TRANSPORTATION AND PRACTICAL INFORMATION. **Bedeng Dua, Kersik Tua,** and **Pelompek** are easily negotiated, one-street towns. Buses and minivans shuttle between **Kayu Aro** and **Sungai Penuh** (1-1½hr., every 15min. 6am-4pm, Rp4000), and can be flagged down for transit between the three Kayu Aro towns

INDONESIA

(Rp1000). Buses to **Padang** pass through at around 10am (5hr.; Rp25,000; reservation recommended) and 9pm (10hr.; Rp35,000). To climb Gunung Kerinci or visit Danau Gunung Tujuh, buy permits (Rp15,000 per day) at the **park headquarters** in Sungai Penuh or at the **Subandi guest house** in Kersik Tua. Each town has a **police post, health clinic,** and a local **wartel. Postal Code:** 37163.

ACCOMMODATIONS AND FOOD. There are several good guesthouses along the main road in Kersik Tua, all offering clean rooms, a cozy atmosphere, complimentary tea and coffee, and shared Western toilets. The most popular is **Subandi ❷,** whose owner is an excellent source of information on the local area. (Rp30,000 per person.) If you want to eat out, **Ojo Lali ❶,** across from the tiger statue, makes great *bakso* noodle soup with meatballs for Rp5000. (Open daily 7am-9pm.) Several *losmen* and restaurants dot Pelompek, but the best are found at the park, near **Sungai Jernih** village. **Losmen Mt. Solok ❷,** 150m from the PHPA hut, with bundles of sweet cinnamon downstairs, is a prime spot for hikers ready for that early climb up Danau Gunung Tujuh. (Rooms Rp15,000 per person.)

SIGHTS. The sprawling **PTP Nusantara-VI tea plantation** yields 18 tons of black tea daily, most of which is exported to Europe. (Tours 7am-5pm. Expect to be asked for a "donation" of Rp10,000-15,000.) Ensconced in dense jungle, **Danau Gunung Tujuh,** at 1996m, is the highest freshwater lake in Southeast Asia. From Pelompek, you can hike up to swim in its icy waters and marvel at the seven mountains from which the lake takes its name. A guide is helpful but not necessary for the 7km hike from Sungai Jernih village. From the end of the asphalt road at Sungai Jernih (2km east of Pelompek), a gate marks the park's entrance. Buy your permit at the **PHPA hut** (Rp15,000) and follow the path, making sure not to take the turn-off to the left at the bridge 1km up. Don't forget snacks, water, rain gear, insect repellent, and a sweater. **Telun Berasap Waterfall** cascades into a pool 50m below. From Pelompek, catch a northbound bus 4km to **Letter village** (Rp1000); the waterfall is 300m away. Guides for all activities usually charge Rp150,000 per day.

CLIMBING KERINCI. Take a guide for the two-day climb up Gunung Kerinci (about Rp150,000 per day)—as recently as 1999, an experienced Swiss climber disappeared on the mountain. The first day of hiking is not strenuous: about 6hr. through the tea plantation to the park boundary (permits Rp15,000 at the PPA hut here), then a climb up through the jungle to Camp 2, a shelter at 3000m. The final steep ascent to the summit should be done in the morning, when skies are clearest. The weather at high altitudes can be freezing and fickle (snow and hail are not unheard of), so take warm clothes and a sleeping bag (rent one in Kersik Tua for Rp10,000 per night). Also remember to bring a large supply of water, as there are no sources for replenishment along the trail.

PULAU BINTAN

Three times the size of Singapore with only a fraction of its population, the majority of Pulau Bintan remains largely undeveloped—rainforests and quiet beaches lined with palm trees dominate the landscape. The major industries are fishing and mining, while the construction of new malls and beach resorts also provides employment for island residents. The locals seem to coexist peacefully, despite the practice of Islam, Hinduism, Christianity, and Buddhism. Many travelers stay in Tanjung Pinang to access the Buddhist temples in Senggarang or Pulau Penyengat, a popular pilgrimage site for Malays. Others head to Trikora Beach to pretend they're on a deserted island. In fact, the sand on Trikora Beach is so highly desired that it's exported to Singapore's Sentosa Island. Hotel prices are steep in the posh Bintan resorts to the north, but Singaporeans come anyway, bringing their families for the weekend to fish and break some of the rules of their hometown.

THE VIEW FROM ABOVE

Main Cities: Tanjung Pinang, Senggarang, Kijang, Tanjung Uban.
Highlights: Trikora Beach, Snake River, Pulau Penyengat.
Something Fun: Snorkeling at Pulau Bralas, Tanjung Pinang's water village.

TANJUNG PINANG ☎0771

Home to many services on Pulau Bintan, Tanjung Pinang is primarily a gateway city, but also boasts an intriguing water village and nearby temples. Beware of pickpockets who loiter near the harbor and often harass unsuspecting tourists. You can always seek assistance from local tourist agents, who will show you the safest areas of town and might even accompany you on your excursions.

TRANSPORTATION

Ferries: Ferry schedule and prices vary with the season. Check with travel agents around the port exit on Jl. Merdeka. To **Singapore** (1½hr.; 10 per day 7am-6:30pm; Rp100,000-120,000, round-trip Rp200,000-240,000). Exit tax to Singapore is Rp15,000. Ferries to **Jakarta** leave from the pier to the right, as you are facing Tg. Pinang (**Pt. Pelni,** 20hr., M 9am, Rp140,000; **Samudra Jaya,** 2 days, Th 5pm, Rp175,000; **ASDD Fast Ferry,** 14hr., Rp237,000 with beds). To **Pekan Baru** (8hr., daily 6:30am, Rp160,000).

Buses: The **bus terminal** is best reached by minibus (20min., Rp3500). From here, buses travel northwest to **Tanjung Uban** (every 30min. until 3am, Rp12,000).

Taxis: Bargain for fares to **Kijang** (Rp50,000 per car); **Senggarang** (Rp35,000); **Trikora Beach** (Rp85,000).

Boat Rental: To get to **Pulau Penyengat,** face away from the docks and go to the jetty on the very left. Catch a motorboat (20min., Rp20,000) or charter one if there is no group waiting to go (Rp30,000). Pick up a **motorboat** to **Senggarang** from Jl. Pelantar I by the water (Rp150,000 per 2-3hr. trip). **Pulau Batam speedboats** leave from the main pier (every hour from 7am-5pm, Rp18,000-25,000). There are two harbors in Batam, **Telaga Punggun** and **Sekupang.**

Local Transportation: Honking **minibuses** abound. Within the city Rp1300 with A/C. **Motorcycle rental** Rp150,000 per day, includes helmet, required by law. Motorcycle "taxis" go for Rp2500 per km up to 10km, when the rate goes up to Rp10,000 per km.

ORIENTATION AND PRACTICAL INFORMATION

Ferries from Singapore dock at the port in **Tanjung Pinang** or north of the island at **Bintan Resort. Pulau Penyengat** is offshore to the west. **Trikora Beach** hugs the east coast, but is cut off from ferry ports by lack of transportation. Development will soon bring resorts to the entire northern coast of Pulau Bintan. Upon arrival at **Bandar Bintan Telani** (BBT) in Bintan Resort, take a **taxi** to the resort area (S$5-10). Getting to Tanjung Pinang is more difficult. From the drop-off point, take a minibus to the **bus terminal** and a bus onward to Tanjung Pinang (Rp12,000). In Tanjung Pinang, most travelers arrive at the main pier on the east end. Down the pier past the dock offices is **Jl. Merdeka,** which runs east-west from the arch near the pier to the fruit market. Walking through the Merdeka intersection leads to **Jl. Bintan.** Parallel and to the east is **Jl. Teuku Umar,** home to the night market. **Jl. Pos** begins opposite Jl. Bintan, close to the **post office,** and turns at the wharves. The **police station** and **bus terminal** outside of town are accessible by minibus.

Tourist Office: Riau Archipelago Tourist Office, Jl. Samudra No. 7 (☎/fax 253 73; www.indosat.id/bintan_tourist_promotions).

Currency Exchange: Bank Negara Indonesia, Jl. Teuku Umar 630 (☎214 32). Cashes traveler's checks. Open M-F 8am-6:15pm, Sa 8:30-11:30am. **Moneychangers** are near the Jl. Pos and Jl. Merdeka intersection. Open daily 8am-8pm. Many hotels will also accept Singapore dollars. **Bank Indonesia International** and **Lippo Bank,** both on Jl. Teuku Umar across from the post office, also cash traveler's checks.

Police: ☎110. At Km5 Jl. A. Yani. **Police box** at the corner of Jl. Merdeka and Jl. Ketapang. Police phone line is 24hr.

Medical Services: Along Jl. Sudirman, in the south of the city or in the General or Navy Hospitals near the Top View Hotel. Facilities at the Navy Hospital are superior.

Telephones: Telkom office (☎281 83), on Jl. Hang Tuah. Follow the road to your right from the main pier near the large waterfront seashell statue. Long distance **24hr.**

Internet Access: Bintan Internet Cafe, on the second floor of Bintan Mall on Jl. Pos across from fruit stands. Rp5000 per 30min., Rp8000 per hr. Open 9am-5pm daily.

Post Office: On Jl. Merdeka No. 7 (☎210 71). *Poste Restante.* Located at the corner of Jl. Pos and Jl. Merdeka, 100m through the western arch on the left. Open M-Sa 8am-8pm, Su 8am-1pm.

Postal Code: 29111.

PULAU BINTAN PRICES. Since many prices in Pulau Bintan are given in Singapore dollars, the price icons below will reflect Singapore's price levels—not Indonesia's. Please review the price ranges for Singapore (see p. 625).

ACCOMMODATIONS

While Tanjung Pinang is lacking in cheap stays (for Indonesia, that is), it does offer a great deal of comfort—mostly at Singapore prices. If you are determined to pinch pennies, you may want to consider the budget accommodations at Trikora Beach instead. The ones in Tanjung Pinang on Jl. Bintan are not in a terrific area.

Hotel Laut Jaya, Jl. Plantar II No. 98 (☎627 71), next to the night market. View of the water village. Breakfast included. All rooms with A/C. Standard S$20; deluxe S$25. ❷

Bintan Beach Resort, Jl. Pantai Impian No. 1 (☎236 64, fax 239 95), has a garden with starfruit groves leading to the sea. Enjoy the swimming pool, tennis court, or a drink at the 24hr. coffee house. English spoken. All rooms have A/C and TV. Reserve in advance. Breakfast included. Standard S$46.40; deluxe S$58; sea view S$69.60 including tax. ❹

Hotel Surya, Jl. Bintan 49 (☎218 11). A hotel atmosphere with hostel prices. Its proximity to the harbor and peaceful courtyard with goldfish pond explain its popularity. Call ahead. Double with fan Rp40,000, with A/C Rp55,000, newly renovated with A/C Rp60,000. ❶

FOOD

If you don't find the local chicken heart and beef lung curry appetizing, it's best to head to the **night markets** ❶, where you can choose from a variety of food vendors that cook up the fare as soon as you order. Try the one at **Bukit Cermin,** one of the highest points in the city, on top of a residential hill (Open 7pm to 1am). Another equally photogenic spot is the night market near the **water village** (open 6pm-1am). Opposite Bank Degong Negara on Jl. Teuka Umar, and on Jl. Ganbir, three blocks up Jl. Merdeka, plenty of options exist to appease taste-buds, such as Malay satay, *mie goreng* (Rp5000), and *chap chye* (cooked mixed vegetables; Rp4500). To escape the outdoor heat, try **Jawa Timur**, Jl. Raja Ali Haji No. 8, which serves Indonesian and Singaporean dishes. The staff doesn't speak English, but the whole menu is in photos so that you may point and choose from small, medium, or large servings of favorites like *ayam goreng* (fried chicken) for Rp60,000 and seafood *lumpia* (egg roll) for Rp28,000. (☎245 32. Open 10am-9pm.)

SIGHTS AND NIGHTLIFE

One of the truly amazing sights of Tanjung Pinang is the **water village** at the northern end of town, down Jl. Pasar Ikan. **Senggarang,** home of impressive 200-year-old Buddhist temples and colorful modern statues, can be reached by motorboat (20min., Rp21,000) from the fishing village on stilts at Jl. Pelantar I. Just north of Senggarang is **Snake River,** a picturesque boat ride (charter boat Rp60,000) through a curving waterway that leads to **Snake River Temple.** At night, hit the clubs on Jl. Gatot Subroto near Bintan Plaza. **Club 5** plays house music (cover Rp10,000; open Su-Th 9pm-late, F-Sa 9pm-6am), while **Singapore Discotheque** spins electronic and Indonesian hits (cover Rp5000; open Su-Th 9:30pm-2am, F-Sa 9:30pm-3am).

DAYTRIP FROM TANJUNG PINANG

PULAU PENYENGAT

Catch a motorboat (10min., Rp40,000) from the pier to the left of the middle pier when you are facing Tanjung Pinang. On Pulau Penyengat, the pier is off Jl. Pos, hidden opposite the bank. The boats drop anchor at Penyengat jetty.

Pulau Penyengat, the seat of the Riau *rajah*'s far-flung kingdom for hundreds of years, is Bintan's greatest treasure. **Mesjid Raya Sultan Riau,** a 178-year-old mosque, is just beyond the jetty. Jl. Ahmadi, to the left of this mosque, leads to the **Raja Ali Grave.** Directly past this grave is the **Tengku Bilik Building** and the **Raja Jakfar Grave,** the oldest building on the island. The **tomb of Rajah Abdurrachman** is 100m to the right, and the **island fort,** the highest point on the island, is directly behind the tomb. The path then winds through the quiet **Rajah Ali's palace,** abandoned this century. Go farther down the track to the road's end and take a right to get to the modern **Riau palace.** Pilgrims travel here to admire the royal internments of **Rajah Ali Jajai,** writer of the first Malay grammar, who received the isle as her dowry.

SOUTHERN SUMATRA

BANDAR LAMPUNG ☎0721

The capital of Lampung Province and a bustling transportation hub, Bandar Lampung is a convenient stop between Jakarta and the rest of Sumatra. Made up of the port city, Teluk Betung, and its hillside neighbor, Tanjung Karang, this urban region is known for its distinctive "ship cloth" tapestries and *tapis* sarongs. Its proximity to nearby attractions, including the Way Kambas Elephant Training Center and Krakatau, the infamous island-volcano whose eruption in 1883 demolished Teluk Betung, make it an ideal starting point for exploration. Every July, the people of Lampung attempt to appease the volcano gods with traditional dances and music, along with parades, races, car rallies, and a biathlon.

TRANSPORTATION

Flights: Radin Inten II Airport, 24km north of town. Take a public DAMRI bus from Rajabasa Bus Terminal (Rp1000), or a purple *angkot* bound for Teluk Betung (Rp2000). Taxis to the airport cost Rp30,000-40,000. **Merpati,** Jl. Diponegoro 189 (☎263 226), at the intersection with Jl. A. Yani, has daily flights to **Jakarta** (40min.; daily 3:30pm and M, Th, Sa 8:20am; Rp340,000). Open M-F 8am-5pm, Sa-Su 8am-1pm.

Trains: Stasium Tanjung Karang, Jl. Kotaraja 1 (☎262 854). Open prior to departures. Trains to **Palembang** (8hr.; 8:30, 9:30am, 8:30pm; Rp30,000-70,000) via **Baturaja.**

Buses: Rajabasa Bus Terminal, 25min. north via light blue *microlet.* Buses to and from just about anywhere in Sumatra and Java pass through Bandar Lampung at some point. To: **Bahanheri** (for boats to Java; 2hr.; every hr. throughout the day; Rp7000-10,000); **Baturaja** (7hr.; 7am, 7pm; Rp24,000); **Bengkulu** (18hr.; noon, 5pm; Rp55,000-140,000); **Jakarta** (7hr.; many per day; Rp54,000-70,000); **Medan** (48hr.; noon, 7pm, midnight; Rp150,000-375,000); **Padang** (20hr.; 3 per day; Rp125,000-225,000); **Palembang** (12hr.; 7am, 9pm; Rp50,000). Deluxe A/C DAMRI buses to **Jakarta** leave from the train station daily in the morning (8-9am) and at night (9pm); Rp65,000-85,000. Unlike most buses passing through, these all leave from Bandar Lampung—you have a better chance of finding a seat. Reserve in advance to be sure.

Ferries: Run to Java from **Bahanheri,** 90km southeast of Bandar Lampung (roughly every hr.; Rp20,000). If you're on one of the buses to Jakarta or other places on Java, the price of the crossing is included in your ticket.

Local Transportation: Small, color-coded *angkot* zip around the city: **purple** (Tanjung Karang to Teluk Betung); **green** (Tanjung Karang to Garuntang); **red** (Kemiling to Bambu Kuning); and **blue** (Tanjung Karang to Rajabasa Bus Terminal). All Rp1000. The main station is next to the train station at the corner of Jl. Kotaraja and Jl. Raden Intan.

Taxis: All over town. For door-to-door service, try **Herodiza Taksi** (☎270 139) or **Siger Taksi** (☎771 999).

INDONESIA

ORIENTATION AND PRACTICAL INFORMATION

The bus terminal and airport are north of the city. The train station is at the end of **Jl. Kotaraja,** which intersects with **Jl. Kartini,** one of the city's main roads, in the center of **Tanjung Karang.** Jl. Kartini runs north-south and changes into **Jl. Teuku Umar** farther north and to **Jl. Monginsidi** in the south. **Jl. Diponegoro** runs from Tanjung Karang toward Teluk Betung.

Tourist Office: Jl. J. Sudirman 29 (☎266 184), can be reached via green *angkot.* Maps, brochures, and English-speaking staff. Open M-Th 8:30am-2:30pm, F 8:30-11am, Sa 8:30am-1:30pm.

Tours: Elendra Tours and Travel, Jl. Sultan Agung 32 (☎704 737), runs daytrip tours to Way Kambas (Rp275,000 per person), Way Kanan (Rp275,000 per person), and Krakatau (Rp325,000 per person). Open M-Sa 8am-4:30pm, Su 10am-1:30pm.

Currency Exchange: Banks with **ATMs** are everywhere. For currency exchange, try **BNI,** Jl. Teuku Umar 17 (☎252 145). Open M-F 8:30am-2:30pm.

Markets: Bambu Kuning Plaza, on Jl. Imam Bonjol, offers fresh mangoes, American films, and everything in between. **Tanjung Karang Plaza,** a slightly glitzier version 1km down Jl. Kartini, offers McD's, cinemas, and general kitsch. **Pasar Seni,** Jl. Majapahit, features local artwork and *batik.* **Teluk Betung's Pasar Mambo** on Jl. Sultan Hasanudin is a popular spot for late-night seafood. Open daily 6pm-1am.

Police: ☎253 283. At the intersection of Jl. Kartini and Jl. Imam Bonjol. Open 24hr.

Medical Services: RS Dr. H. Abdul Moeloek, Jl. Dr. Rivai 6 (☎703 312), 2km down Jl. Teuku Umar in a blue *angkot*. **Open 24hr.,** as is the **pharmacy** in front.

Telephones: There are a number of **wartel** around town, including one by the **Telkom** building on Jl. Bukittinggi, close to the police station. Open daily 7:30am-10pm.

Internet Access: Dawiel Internet Station, Jl. Kartini 40 (☎257 893). 2min. walk down Jl. Kartini from the Tanjung Karang Plaza, with the plaza on your left. Dawiel's is on the right. A/C teeny-bopper paradise. Rp6000 per hr. Open daily 9am-10pm.

Post Office: GPO, Jl. A. Dahlan 21. Take a green *microlet.* Open M-Sa 8am-6pm. **Branch** at Jl. Kotaraja, off Jl. Kartini. Open M-Sa 8am-5pm.

Postal Code: 35111.

ACCOMMODATIONS

To get to the center of Tanjung Karang from the bus terminal, take a light blue *angkot* and ask to be dropped off at the intersection of Jl. Kartini and Jl. Kotaraja (by the roundabout with the gray marble obelisk). Hotels on **Jl. Kartini** and **Jl. Raden Intan** cater to local businessmen and are generally clean and comfortable. Call ahead to make a reservation, as many hotels fill up quickly.

Lampung Inn, Jl. W. Monginsidi 178 (☎471 674), 3km south of Bambu Kuning. Head up Jl. Kartini with the plaza on your right, and follow Jl. Monginsidi downhill. Large clean doubles in a rickety house, all with fans and private squat *mandi.* Rooms Rp45,000. ❸

Marcopolo Hotel, Jl. Dr. Susilo 4 (☎262 511). Posh mid-range hotel., a short taxi ride from town center. Well-appointed rooms (A/C, attached Western bath, showers, satellite TV) have views out over the bay. Restaurant, drugstore, swimming pool, and billiard room. Standard doubles Rp118,600; deluxe rooms Rp155,900-228,700; superior rooms Rp186,300-272,250, excluding tax. AmEx/MC/V. ❺

Hotel Ria, Jl. Kartini 79 (☎266 404). From the train station, walk up Jl. Kotaraja and turn left onto Jl. Kartini; it's on the right. The cheaper end of the traveling salesman bracket. Wide range of rooms, some with bath and A/C. Doubles Rp52,500-83,500. ❹

FOOD

Bakeries with names like "Roti French, London, and European" are everywhere along Jl. Kartini and Jl. Pemuda, along with standard-issue *padang* restaurants.

Garuda Restaurant, Jl. Kartini 31, before Tanjung Karang Plaza. Excellent *padang*-style restaurant serves beef *rendang* (Rp10,000) and creamy avocado juice (Rp6500). A/C dining room with gurgling waterfall. Attentive service. Open daily 7am-10pm. ❷

Rumah Makan Shinta, Jl. W. Monginsidi 44B, on the right as you head downhill. Clean, Chinese-run cafeteria serves *nasi goreng* (Rp6000), *gado-gado* (Rp5000), and fried chicken (Rp28,000). Fresh fruit juices Rp5000-10,000. Open daily 9am-9pm. ❷

Kamang, on Jl. Dwi Warna, near the mosque, down a small alley just past Hotel Ria, off Jl. Kartini. An open-air cafeteria constantly enveloped by clouds of sweet-smelling *kretek* smoke. *The* place to mingle with locals and gobble down a plate of *martabak* and a cup of coffee. Yummy *padang* dishes, most Rp5000. Open daily 7am-8pm. ❶

DAYTRIPS FROM BANDAR LAMPUNG

Getting out to the sights and beaches around Bandar Lampung by public transportation can be a frustrating and time-consuming business. If all you're interested in is a short daytrip, you may be better off going on one of the expensive tours organized by travel agents (see **Tours,** p. 270). Unless your karma is so bad that you end up on a crowded weekend outing, you'll probably find that you're one of the only people on the trip anyway. (Minimum 2 people.)

The tour to **Krakatau,** through the Hotel Beringin in **Kalianda** (see p. 272), visits **Pulau Sebesi, Sebuku,** and **Harimau,** a few of the islands dotting Lampung Bay. Alternatively, you can take a boat from **Canti,** a small town 10km from the Bakauheni port, for travel to Sebesi. Accommodations are available in Canti. **Pasir Putih,** a delightful beach with pricey hotels looking out onto **Pulau Condong,** sits southeast of Bandar Lampung—get there via the Rajabasa-Bakauheni bus.

Wild elephants are tamed at the **Way Kambas National Park and Elephant Training Center,** a 2hr. drive northeast of the city. The center also harbors a small population of Sumatran tigers and rhinos (see **Myanmar: Wildlife,** p. 453). To the dismay of the tigers, camping is prohibited. Instead, travelers can stay in **bungalows** ❷ (doubles Rp30,000-40,000) and play Hannibal with an elephant-powered jaunt through the jungle. The nearby **Way Kanan River** shelters 258 documented species of birds. To the west, the **Bukit Barisan** mountain range stretches along the coast, accessible by bus from Bandar Lampung, via Way Jepara. **Bukit Barisan National Park** begins at the southernmost tip at Tampang and climbs up the west coast. Travelers can explore the **Danau Menjukut** area by boat from Kota Agung to Tampang, or use the camping area near **Wonsobo.** The beaches at **Krui,** near the border with Bengkulu Province, offer decent waves for surfing. **Pugang Raharjo Archaeological Site,** which can be reached from Talang Padian, houses Buddhist-period megaliths.

KALIANDA ☎0727

Small, charming, and unspoiled, Kalianda overlooks a South Sumatran inlet, 30min. from the ferry port of Bakauheni and 1½hr. from Bandar Lampung. In addition to offering the cheapest trips to Krakatau, Kalianda is a good base for strenuous climbs through the surrounding hillside and also lies within easy reach of a number of relaxing beaches and seldom touristed hot springs.

The Sukarno-Hatta Highway passes Kalianda between Bandar Lampung and Bakauheni. Ask to be let off there (1½hr. from Bandar Lampung, Rp6000). From the main road, a Rp5000 motorcycle ride will bring you to town. Minibuses to Bakauheni run frequently (7am-3pm, Rp7000). There's **no currency exchange** or English-language **ATM** in town; bring all the rupiah you'll need. The main **police** office is at Jl. Kol. Makman Rasyid 142 (☎322 110), on the way to Pantai Laguna. The **hospital** is close by, at Jl. Lettu Rohani 14B. The attached **pharmacy** is open 24hr. There are several **wartel** in town, and the Telkom office on Jl. Kesuma Bangsa (on the left as you head uphill from the Beringin Hotel) is open daily 7am-11pm.

There are a couple of decent places to stay. The **Hotel Beringin** ❷, Jl. Kesuma Bangsa 55, on the town's major thoroughfare, has a pleasant family atmosphere and huge rooms. (☎322 008. Doubles, some with squat *mandi*, Rp15,000-25,000.) At the top of the hill on the same street, the **Hotel Kalianda** ❸, Jl. Kesuma Bangsa 163 (☎322 392), has shiny clean doubles with (seat) *mandi* for Rp32,000-55,000. For a bite to eat, hit up the host of foodstalls and seafood restaurants all along **Jl. Kasuma Bangsa.** The scene is even more lively down at the bottom of **Jl. Veteran.**

Up the road 1.5km, **Pantai Way Urang** is a decent beach with a gorgeous view, overlooked by scenic **Gunung Rajabasa. Way Belerang Hot Springs,** 2km in the other direction, offer a pleasant soak. Both can be reached by motorbike (Rp2000). Farther afield is **Pantai Laguna Beach,** 3km up from Way Urang. Motorbikes can be rented from the Hotel Beringin for around Rp50,000 per day.

The islands of **Krakatau** mark the edge of a huge underwater crater. In ancient times, Krakatau was over 2000m high. The biggest island left after the colossal explosion of 1883 was **Rakata,** which is what tourists come to look at today. Meanwhile, the next geological generation continues to edge its way toward rock-spitting maturity, in the shape of **Anak Krakatau** (Child of Krakatau), which has been the site of increasingly violent seismic activity over the past 100 years (see **The Wrath of Krakatau,** above). Constantly growing and erupting since it appeared in 1930, this island of ash and rock entices adventurous souls to stroll around its base and peak. This can be dangerous, however, despite guides' assurances to the contrary. In 1993, Krakatau performed unexpectedly and killed two climbers.

Boats for Gunung Krakatau leave from nearby fishing villages. An overnight trip leaving at 8am from the Hotel Beringin costs Rp200,000 per person, including meals. The three- to five-hour boat ride stops at the jungle-covered "coral garden" islands of Sebuku and Sebesi for snorkeling. You then spend a night on the beach at Sertung, less than 1km away from Krakatau.

LAOS

HIGHLIGHTS OF LAOS

CULTURAL HERITAGE. Serene **Luang Prabang** (p. 297) is Laos's spiritual center. The **Plain of Jars** (p. 305) is anything but ordinary. For vibrant hill-tribe culture, **Muang Sing** (p. 308) and the far north are unparalleled. Pakse's **Wat Phu** (p. 320) is the largest Angkorian temple complex outside of Cambodia.

NATURAL WONDERS. Surreal **Nam Ngum Lake** (p. 293) and **Vang Vieng's jagged cliffs** (p. 294) are within striking distance from Vientiane. The **Bolovens Plateau** (p. 321) and the **Nam Tha National Biodiversity Conservation Area** (p. 308) outside Luang Nam Tha are tops for natural beauty.

HANGING OUT. Don Det Island (p. 323), in the **4000 Islands** region (p. 322), is a great spot to put down your rucksack, string up a hammock, and relax over the Mekong.

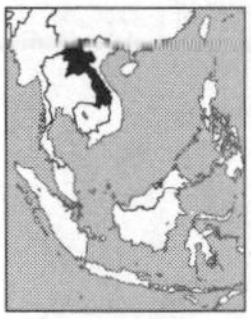

Many visit Laos and expect to find a land untouched by tourists, with opium dens hanging off limestone cliffs ripping through jungle. Though, as one of the poorest countries in the world, Laos is far from developed, it is not the mythic Shangri-la sought by all backpackers. Since the early 90s, this small jewel of Southeast Asia has followed neighboring Thailand's model by promoting itself as a new tourist destination. Guesthouses, restaurants, and sites are springing up like weeds in a garden, threatening Laos's natural and cultural resources. Yet Laos remains one of the most captivating and enchanting countries you'll ever visit. Whether traveling the mountainous regions near the Chinese and Burmese borders, exploring the jeweled temples of Luang Prabang, venturing into the thick jungles of the Bolovens Plateau, or kicking back in the 4000 Islands region, visitors are often content to sit back and let the journey take its course.

FACTS AND FIGURES

Official Name: Lao People's Democratic Republic.

Government: Communist state.

Capital: Vientiane.

Land Area: 236,800km^2.

Geography: Borders Thailand, China, Myanmar, Vietnam, and Cambodia. 85% of the country is mountainous. River systems: Mekong River.

Climate: Dry (high season) Dec.-Apr., rainy (low season) May-Nov.

Phone Codes: Country code: 856. International dialing prefix: 14.

Population: 6,068,117.

Major Cities: Vientiane, Luang Prabang, Pakse, Savannakhet.

Language: Lao (official), French, English, hill-tribe languages.

Religion: Theravada Buddhism (60%), Animist and other (40%).

Literacy Rate: 52.8% overall; 67.5% of men, 38.1% of women.

Major Exports: Timber, coffee, tin, textiles, electricity, opium.

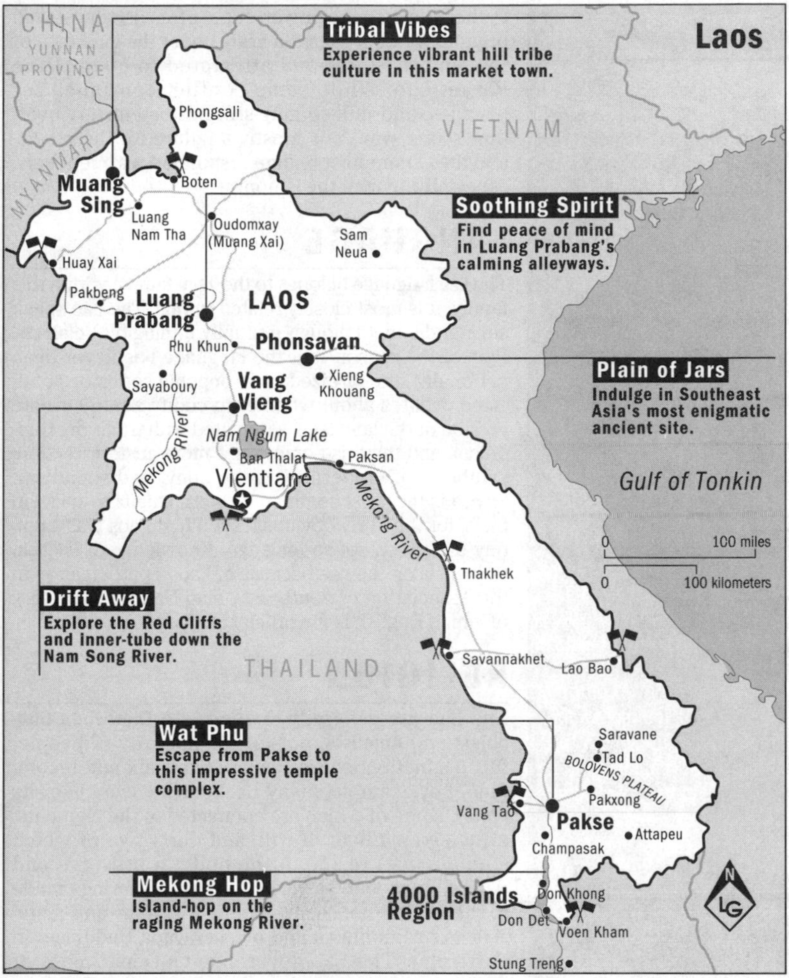

LIFE AND TIMES

DEMOGRAPHICS

Traditionally, the Lao people divide into three ethnicities: the **Lao Loum,** who form more than two-thirds of the current population; the **Lao Theung,** who account for about a fifth; and the highland **Lao Soung,** who include the **Hmong** and **Yao.** The Lao Loum, the ethnic Lao, live in the lowlands of the Mekong River. The semi-nomadic Lao Theung live in the mountains along the Lao-Vietnamese border and on the Bolovens Plateau. The Lao Soung are relatively recent newcomers to Laos (they arrived from China in the 19th century) and tend to be marginalized politically and economically. Some Lao Soung groups underwent diaspora as the Communist

Pathet Lao came to power; some of those who stayed organized into a guerrilla army under the guidance of the United States and attempted to combat the Pathet Lao. While some conflict continued for decades, and indeed may still not be entirely over, the "secret war" was mostly a failure for the rebels, and the Communist regime responded with reprisals, especially against the Hmong.

LANGUAGE

The **Lao** language belongs to the Thai family; within this family, it is most closely related to **Thai.** The Lao speak several distinct (though mutually intelligible) **dialects.** Part of the reason that the language has never been nationally standardized is an ongoing series of politicized debates about whether to codify a more ornate version of the language, associated with tradition, Buddhism, and the aristocracy, or a more austere version, symbolic of modernity, technology, and socialism. **French** is the most common Western language in use in Laos, for the fairly obvious reason that Laos was a colony of France not so long ago. Knowledge of **English,** though, is on the rise because of Laos's participation in the Association of Southeast Asian Nations (ASEAN), of which English is the official language.

RELIGION

The Lao are generally divided into **Theravada Buddhists** and **Animists,** but for the majority of people, this distinction is hazy, as practices mix and recombine. For example, many Laotians believe in spirits *(phi)*, some of which are connected to the elements, others which bear ill will, and thirty-two of which (the *khwan*) reside in the body to preserve and defend it, as well as various others. Offerings made to the *phi* are not seen to conflict with the anti-materialism of Buddhism and of Theravada Buddhism in particular. The Lao government's Department of Religious Affairs oversees the teachings of Buddhist monks in Laos. Unlike Cambodian Buddhist monks under the Khmer Rouge, Buddhists in Laos seem not to have been targeted as enemies by the Communist government. If anything, the oppression goes the other way—monks are required to teach the compatibility of Communism with Buddhism and the non-compatibility of either with the traditional Animistic practices. Similarly, they are required to use herbal or Western medicine in cases of sickness instead of the magical blessings of the old days. While this system is clearly not based on the conception of freedom of religion that is known in the West, many in Laos consider it a step forward for their people.

HAIR DYE CRIMES

Lao authorities have added yet another item to their laundry list of dangerous cultural influences. In an interesting move, they have set hair products by the likes of L'Oréal and Garnier, among others, in the same danger bracket as the drugs, sex, and rock-and-roll feared to be corrupting Lao youth.

According to a March 2004 article in *Le Renovateur*, Vientiane's French-language newspaper, hair dye has been working as a miasmic influence on Lao women and adolescents, subverting the natural order, and destroying the fabric of everyday life. People of all ages have contributed to the growing trend of swapping black and white locks for more varied hues, causing a stir in the Lao government. Police in Vientiane stop Lao people with colored hair, examine their government-issued identification cards, and then confiscate the ID cards until the colorations have been removed.

Resistance persists, however. And although it may seem like a trivial issue, the ban does make a statement about Laos, its government and its people. In the face of corrupt officials that they see overstepping bounds, everyday citizens are engaging in this unique form of civil disobedience. One head of hair at a time, they are making a push for justice.

LAND

Bordered by Thailand, Cambodia, Vietnam, Myanmar and China, Laos is the only landlocked country in Southeast Asia. The land is mostly forested and mountainous, with the tallest mountains located in Xieng Khouang province. Two-thirds of Laos is forested and a mere 10% is fertile. The largest river, the Mekong (Nam Khong), more than half of which originates in Laos, comprises a large part of Laos's border with Thailand and part of the border with Cambodia.

WILDLIFE

Mosquitoes will be your main source of agony in Laos. Mosquitoes can bite through thin fabric, so cover up as much as possible with thicker materials. **100% DEET** is useful, but the mosquitoes are so ravenous that nothing short of a **mosquito hood** and netting really stops every jab. **Geckos** have no boundaries, so plan on seeing them everywhere you go. If you plan to venture into remote forests, be wary of wildcats, and even leopards.

HISTORY

LANE XANG (1353-1694) AND BEFORE

IMPORTANT DATES			
8th Century Tai Kadai emigrate from China.	**14th Century** Prince Fa Ngum founds Lane Xang.	**16th Century** The great King Setthathirat moves the capital from Luang Prabang to Vientiane.	**1637-1694** Lane Xang's Golden Age, which ends abruptly upon the death of King Souligna Vongsa.

According to legend, the Lao sprang from three gourds—nobility from one, peasants from another, and indigenous hill-tribes from the third. The proto-Laotians of the Tai Kadai emigrated from China in the 8th century to escape the Mongols in the mountains. The first recorded date in Lao history is 1316, when Angkor's Prince Fa Ngum was born. With Khmer aid, he united a collection of small principalities to found Lane Xang, the "Kingdom of a Million Elephants." His capital, Luang Prabang, was named after **Pha Bang,** a golden Buddha given to him by his Khmer father-in-law. The statue symbolized Lane Xang's rulers' spiritual and temporal power and the importance of Theravada Buddhism. For the next 300 years, Lane Xang prospered; at its zenith, it spanned all of north Indochina. Threatened by Burmese and Siamese invasions, **King Setthathirat** moved the capital to the more defensible Vientiane and brought the **Emerald Buddha,** the most revered Buddha in Thailand, from Lanna. Under the enlightened **King Souligna Vongsa,** Lane Xang experienced its Golden Age—its borders expanded to Yunnan to the north, Shan Myanmar to the west, Cambodia to the south, and Vietnam to the east.

INTERNAL DIVISION AND SIAMESE CONTROL (1694-1885)

IMPORTANT DATES			
18th century Prolonged harassment by Vietnamese, Burmese, and Thai forces.	**1791** Bangkok gains control of most of old Lane Xang.	**1805** Prince Chou Anou attempts to restore Lane Xang to Lao rule.	**1827** The Thai sack Vientiane.

Many crises after King Vongsa's death in 1694 caused Lane Xang to fragment into three weak principalities: Vientiane, Luang Prabang, and Champasak. Vietnamese warlords threatened all borders, and chaos resulted. In the 1700s, the Burmese

LAOS

and Thai attacked the divided kingdoms, beginning Bangkok's control over much of Laos. In 1805, **Chou Anou,** a Vientiane prince, tried to end Thai rule. In turn, Bangkok sacked Vientiane in 1827 and depopulated the area—an event that still haunts Thai-Lao relations today. By the mid-19th century, only Luang Prabang maintained a modicum of independence.

COLONIAL RULE (1885-1954)

IMPORTANT DATES			
1880s The French enter Laos and arbitrarily cede the Khorat Plateau to Thailand.	**1941** Japan invades Indochina.	**1941-1945** Anti-French movements, including the Communist Pathet Lao, arise.	**1945** King Sisavangvong declares independence for Laos.

As the French consolidated their rule over Vietnam, they also assumed traditional Vietnamese interests in Laos. After establishing a protectorate over Luang Prabang, the French expanded their territory in Laos and, blithely ignoring traditional boundaries, divided it at the Mekong, ceding all of the Khorat Plateau to Bangkok. French rule in Laos was *laissez-faire;* they used the area primarily as a buffer between British interests to the west and their colonial claims in Vietnam. Health care and education were, for the most part, ignored. Nationalism came slowly, but the 1941 invasion of Indochina by Japan catalyzed independence movements. Several anti-French movements, including the **Lao Issara** (Free Lao) and the Communist **Pathet Lao** (Lao Nation), arose to counter French imperialism. **King Sisavangvong,** initially reluctant to break with France, declared independence for his country in 1945, backed by Japanese support.

THE WAR YEARS (1954-80)

IMPORTANT DATES			
1954, 1962 International attempts to form an independent, neutral Laos.	**1965-1975** During the Second Indochina War, the US bombs Laos and supports rivals of the Communist insurgents.	**1975** The Pathet Lao take Vientiane and establish the Lao PDR.	**1980s** Laos becomes a puppet of Vietnam.

The first attempt to establish a neutral Lao, conceived at the Geneva Conference in 1954, lasted only eight months. Another attempt in 1962 failed after the small kingdom was dragged into the Vietnam War. The North Vietnamese would accept a neutral Laos only if they could transport supplies along Laos's portion of the Hồ Chí Minh Trail, while the US remained intent on shutting the trail and preventing the Pathet Lao from seizing power. The US waged a secret war in Laos, pouring aid to the right-wing government, recruiting highland minorities, and waging a destructive air campaign. From 1964 to 1972, US bombers dropped more than two billion kilograms of bombs on Laos, making it the most heavily bombed country in history. In 1975 after 30 years of division and war, the Pathet Lao marched into Vientiane and established the **Lao People's Democratic Republic (LPDR),** with the **Lao People's Revolutionary Party (LPRP)** as the sole political party. Abolishing Laos's 600-year-old monarchy, they gave leadership to **Kaysone Phomvihane.** Fear of Communism sparked a mass exodus of educated lowland Lao in the 70s and left the LPDR with very few educated bureaucrats and technicians. Hmong rebels continued to wage guerrilla wars against the LPDR. In the 1980s, Laos was a puppet state of Vietnam, with upward of 60,000 Vietnamese troops still on Lao soil.

LAOS TODAY

Corruption and economic mismanagement contribute to Laos's status as one of the world's poorest countries. The LPRP followed Hà nội's lead in 1986 by approving an economic liberalization program dubbed "New Thinking." In November 1992 after Kaysone's death, **Nouhak Phoumsavan** came to power. At the Sixth Party Congress, held in 1996, the LPRP upheld "New Thinking" but reaffirmed the state's role in the economy and its monopoly of power. Laos joined the **Association of Southeast Asian Nations (ASEAN)** in July 1997. In February 1998, the pro-reform **General Khamtay Siphandone** replaced Nouhak. Today, the Lao government remains committed to shielding the country from foreign influence. Since 1986, however, the government has made strides in decentralizing economic control and encouraging private enterprise; consequently, the average economic growth rate grew 7% from 1988 to 1996. The Asian economic crisis dealt the Lao economy a strong blow due to its close ties to Thailand. By September 1999, Lao currency had lost most of its value, and, although it has stabilized at the level it reached then—about 9000kip to US$1—the Lao government hasn't taken strong actions to try to reverse the foreign-exchange problems. Thus, Laos continues to reel from a years-past economic blow. Vientiane has earned US praise for its cooperation in the "war on drugs" (though Laos remains the world's third-largest producer of opium) and the search for American MIAs. Laos receives aid as one of the world's 20 least developed nations, but the government has trouble distributing and implementing programs to help its people. Up to 80% of employed Laotians are subsistence farmers who benefit little from the country's fledgling capitalist economy.

CUSTOMS AND ETIQUETTE

TABOOS. The head is considered the highest part of the body and the feet the lowest, literally and figuratively. Pointing to people with your feet and placing your feet on a table are unacceptable. Women must not touch Buddhist monks or give them offerings as they cannot accept anything from a woman's hand. It is considered disrespectful to visit religious monuments in shorts, miniskirts, or hot pants.

PUBLIC BEHAVIOR. Displays of affection, wild gesticulation, shouting, or anger in public are frowned upon.

HOSPITALITY. Traditionally, Lao people greet each other with a prayer-like gesture called a *nop*. A smile and a slight bow of the head is always considered polite—though shaking hands has become more common in recent years. Remove shoes before entering homes or temples. On a traditional low cushion, sit with the legs folded to one side. (Men may also sit cross-legged.) A guest is expected to accept offers of tea or fruit when visiting a home.

LAO UNCOOKED. Traditional Lao food is very simple: sticky-rice, meat or fish, and vegetables. Many dishes are cooked in order to suit the Western palate, but if you want to eat in the authentic Lao way, go raw.

Laap: finely chopped meat—usually raw—mixed with spices, broth, and crushed, uncooked dry fried rice grains. Served with raw vegetables and sticky-rice.

Foe: noodle soup usually served with a dish of raw vegetable leaves.

Tam Makk Houng: spicy salad of raw papaya, chilli, garlic, sugar, peanuts, lime juice, and *pa daek*, a highly pungent, fermented fish sauce.

Som moo: fermented pork sausage usually eaten raw. Barbecued *som moo*, known as **Naem Nuang,** is served in spring rolls, Vietnamese-style.

ARTS AND RECREATION

Influenced by Thai, Burmese, and Khmer styles, Lao art is unique and expressive, frequently inspired by Buddhist themes. Sadly, however, much of the country's artistic heritage has been lost or destroyed. While attempts at a resurgence of Lao art go on, notably in the area of cinema, the poverty and instability that linger from a war that it theoretically never entered and that theoretically ended over 25 years ago make progress barely perceptible.

ARCHITECTURE. Lao architecture is religious in nature. Buddhist temples, Laos's architectural forte, come in three chief styles. High, pointed, and layered roofs distinguish the **Vientiane style** of architecture found in the capital city. The **Luang Prabang style,** with multi-layered roofs and graceful, sweeping eaves that nearly touch the ground, is similar to that of Northern Thailand. A third temple style, **Xieng Khouang,** was irrevocably lost when American bombers razed Laos during the war.

LITERATURE. Lao literature, recorded in the Lao and Tham scripts, is based on the *Jataka* tales from India and oral traditions. The 17th century was the golden era of Lao literature. The razing of Vientiane by the Thai in the early 19th century and the subsequent imposition of French as the official language under colonialism, coupled with recent declines in the membership of monasteries and the advent of radio and television, have served to sharply curtail Lao literary tradition.

DANCE AND DRAMA. Classical dance and drama came to Laos from India via Cambodia in the 14th century, but not until the 16th and 17th centuries was **classical theater** fully developed. The Royal Court organized dance and drama, which were accompanied by a grand orchestra of xylophones, gongs, trumpets, tambourines, violins, mandolins, and, later, chanting. **Mimic dancers** wore rich and vibrant costumes with masks and diadems. Today, classical dance is pretty well extinct. The Royal Lao Ballet, which also performs a number of Lao folk dances, is the only remaining court troupe in Southeast Asia.

MUSIC. Songs and music are indispensable accompaniments to all celebrations and are prominent features of everyday life. Live **mor lam** performances, involving singing jousts of Lao epic poems, occasionally take place at markets and temple fairs. The haunting, hollow sound of the **khaen,** a complex bamboo reed organ that Lao musicians play at celebrations and funerals, is the center of Lao traditional music. The Hmong are renowned for the *khaen* players who often perform at New Year festivals. A Lao orchestra consists of the *khaen*, the **so** (a two-stringed cello), the **khouy** (a bamboo flute), and the **nang-hat** (a wooden xylophone). Traditional music is becoming less popular as Thai pop and Lao imitations gain favor.

FILM. Laos had a bustling film culture during the mid-20th century. In the 1960s and 70s, before Laos was equipped to process its own films, it sent them to Vietnam instead, which meant that the negatives of these films joined the comprehensive National Archiving Film Collection of Vietnam. In 1998, after the construction of a suitable film vault in Laos, the Lao portion of this collection—1192 films—was repatriated. However, since the end of the Vietnam war, despite efforts to revive the industry, Laos has produced only two feature-length films.

WEAVING AND HILL-TRIBE ART. Young girls learn the traditional art of weaving cotton and silk with shimmering gold and silver threads (called **tdinjok**); a woman's ability to weave is considered an asset during courtship. The **pha sin** (Lao sarong), **pha baeng** (Lao shawl), and **sin** (bridal skirt with an elaborately embroidered hem), are made from these cloths. The Yao and Hmong are renowned for their excellent **silversmiths.** Both groups traditionally assessed their wealth in terms of family silver. The Hmong are the only people in Laos who make **batik,** created by dyeing fabric with resistant wax designs. **Appliqué** is a craft form in which cloth is layered and stitched to create a rich collage of contrasting colors, textures, and geometric shapes. Most hill-tribes, such as the Akha, make beautiful appliqué.

OUTDOORS. In Laos, you can visit hill-tribes in the Nam Tha Biodiversity Area, outside Luang Nam Tha, or in Muang Sing. For those who want to explore a less beaten track, the remote Attapeu region in Southern Laos sees few tourists and is home to many endangered animals. **Swim** in Nam Ngum Lake and **raft** down the Nam Ngum River. The cliffs near Vang Vieng offer **spelunking, underground swimming, waterfalls,** and **inner-tubing** down the Nam Song River. For a laid-back experience, go **boating** in the 4000 Islands Region and spot rare Irrawaddy dolphins.

HOLIDAYS AND FESTIVALS (2005)

Government offices and banks are closed on Lao public holidays as well as on festival days. These often coincide. Public holidays are listed below. Festivals in Laos are largely linked to historical Buddhist holidays. The word for festival in Laos is *boun* (merit), which means doing good deeds in order to acquire merit for a life after death. Banks based in Thailand may also close on Thai holidays.

DATE	NAME	DESCRIPTION
Jan. 1	International New Year's Day	Celebration often includes paying visits to loved ones.
Jan. 6	Pathet Lao Day	Honors the victory of the Communist Pathet Lao in 1975.
Jan. 20	Army Day	Commemorates Laos's army, its veterans, and its casualties.
Feb. 5	Boun Maka Boucha	The celebration of Buddha's speech. Go to the Khmer ruins of Vat Phou near Champasak.
Feb. 9-10	Chinese New Year	Vietnamese and Chinese populations celebrate with feastings and rice wine.
Feb.	Boun Khao Chee	A morning temple ceremony at which a special sticky-rice bread is offered.
Mar. 8	Women's Day	An international holiday. Women do not have to work.
Mar. 22	People's Party Day	Celebrates the ruling party of Laos.
Apr. 13-15	Boun Pimailao	Lao New Year.
May 1	International Labour Day	Known as "May Day" in many parts of the world.
May 4	Boun Visaka Boucha	One of the most important festivals in celebration of the birth, the enlightenment, and the death of Buddha.
Mid-May	Boun Bangfai	Festival celebrating rain and fertility.
June 1	Children's Day	Pays honor to children.
July 2	Boun Khao Phansa	The first day of the Buddhist Lent. Go to a large temple, like *That Luang*.
Aug. 13	Lao Issara Day	Commemorates the "Free Lao," an early movement that, with the Pathet Lao, struggled for independence from France.
Aug. 23	Liberation Day	A Lao independence celebration.
Sept. 29	Boun Ok Phansa	The final and most important day of the Buddhist Lent.
Oct. 2-3	Boat Racing Festival in Vientiane	A two-day water festival culminating in a boat race on the Mekong.
Oct. 12	Freedom from France Day	Celebrates the 1953 naming of Laos as a "fully independent and sovereign" state within the French Union.
Oct. 26-28	That Luang Festival	A colorful procession between Wat Si Muang and Pha That Luang.
Dec. 2	National Day	Yet another Lao independence celebration—maybe the most important.

ADDITIONAL RESOURCES

GENERAL HISTORY

The Politics of Heroin in Southeast Asia, by Alfred McCoy (1972). A fascinating account of the opium trade in Southeast Asia, focusing on America's role in opium smuggling during the Vietnam War. Since republished as *The Politics of Heroin*.

Indochina's Refugees: Oral Histories from Laos, Cambodia, and Vietnam, by Joanna C. Scott (1989). Tells a story of the Vietnam War from the point of view of citizens of the Indochinese countries—mostly civilians and almost half of them Lao who chose to flee and then had to find ways of doing so.

The Ravens—Pilots of the Secret War of Laos, by Christopher Robbins (1989). Exposes many aspects of America's secret war.

A History of Laos, by Martin Stuart Fox (1997). One of the few general histories of Laos. The author covers all of Lao history, emphasizing the colonial and modern periods.

Tragedy in Paradise: A Country Doctor at War in Laos, by Charles Weldon (1999). Describes the efforts of the author and others to administer aid in Laos from 1963 to 1974, during the time of the American CIA's "secret war" there.

FICTION AND NON-FICTION

The Spirit Catches You and You Fall Down, by Anne Fadiman (1998). A carefully researched account of the tension between the traditional beliefs of a real-life Hmong family—refugees to the United States from Laos—and their Western doctors over the case of the treatment of their epileptic daughter.

The Yao: The Mien and Mun Yao in China, Vietnam, Laos, and Thailand, by Jess G. Pouret (2002). Fifteen years went into preparing this work on the many facets of the society of the various branches of this subset of the Lao Soung people.

Atlas des ethnies et des sous-ethnies du Laos, by Laurent Chazee (1995). A study of Laos's ethnic groups written in French. Sold in Bangkok and Vientiane.

TRAVEL BOOKS

Stalking the Elephant Kings: In Search of Laos, by Christopher Kremmer (1998). The author describes his travels through contemporary Laos and his interviews with a wide range of Laotians as he searched for the truth about the fate of the Lao royal family, who were abducted by the Communist Pathet Lao in 1977.

Lao-English/English-Lao Dictionary and Phrasebook, by James Higbie (2001). The options for Lao phrasebooks are slim, but, for travelers, this is one of the most useful out there.

A Dragon Apparent, by Norman Lewis (2003). A travel writer's account of a journey through Cambodia, Laos, and Vietnam in 1950. Lewis paints a portrait of the region before it changed out of all recognition.

ON THE WEB

Laos News.net (www.laosnews.net). Links to Lao history and updates on daily news and current events.

Visit Laos (www.visit-laos.com). Practical tips and hotel, tour, and travel info.

ESSENTIALS

LAOS PRICE ICONS					
SYMBOL:	❶	❷	❸	❹	❺
ACCOMM.	Under US$2 Under 1300kyat	US$2-5 1300-3250kyat	US$5-10 3250-6500kyat	US$10-20 6500-13,000kyat	Over US$20 Over 13,000kyat
FOOD	Under US$0.25 Under 150kyat	US$0.25-0.50 150-300kyat	US$0.50-1 300-650kyat	US$1-3 650-1950kyat	Over US$3 Over 1950kyat
Please note that currency is converted at free-market rates for the purposes of this chart.					

EMBASSIES AND CONSULATES

LAO CONSULAR SERVICES ABROAD

Laos has only a limited number of diplomatic missions worldwide. If your country has no mission from Laos, try contacting the embassy geographically closest to you. All Lao embassies will provide visa services for any foreign national.

Australia: Embassy, 1 Dalman Cres., O'Malley, Canberra, ACT 2606 (☎262 864 595; fax 262 901 910). Also accredited to **New Zealand.**

France: Embassy, 74 Avenue Raymond-Poincaré, Paris 75116 (☎33 1 4553 0298; www.laoparis.com). Also accredited to **Ireland** and the **United Kingdom.**

Thailand: Embassy, 520/502/1-3 Soi Sahakarnpramoon, Pracha Uthit Rd., Wangthonglang, Bangkok 10310, Thailand (☎662 539 6667/8; www.bkklaoembassy.com). Recommended for citizens of **South Africa** (to which no Lao embassy is formally accredited).

United States: Embassy, 2222 S St. NW, Washington, DC 20008 (☎202-332-6416; www.laoembassy.com). Also accredited to **Canada.**

CONSULAR SERVICES IN LAOS

Australia: Embassy, Rue Jawaharlal Nehru, Quartier Phone Xay, P.O. Box 292, Vientiane (☎856 21 413 600; www.laos.embassy.gov.au).

Canada: For limited emergency consular services, contact the Australian Embassy in Vientiane (see above). Otherwise, use the Canadian Embassy in Bangkok, Thailand (see p. 664), which is also accredited to Laos.

Ireland: Use the Irish Embassy in Kuala Lumpur, Malaysia (see p. 339), which is also accredited to Laos.

New Zealand: For limited emergency consular services, contact the Australian Embassy in Vientiane (see above). Otherwise, use the New Zealand Embassy in Bangkok, Thailand (see p. 664), which is also accredited to Laos.

United Kingdom: For limited emergency consular services, contact the Australian Embassy in Vientiane (see above). Otherwise, use the British Embassy in Bangkok, Thailand (see p. 664), which is also accredited to Laos.

United States: Embassy, 19 Rue Bartholonie, Vientiane (☎856 21 213 966; http://usembassy.state.gov/laos/).

TOURIST SERVICES

Lao National Tourism Authority (LNTA; ☎856 21 212 248; mekongcenter.com) is the official tourism promotion agency of the Lao government. Perhaps marginally more useful are the private-sector websites **visit-laos.com** (www.visit-laos.com) and **visit-mekong.com** (www.visit-mekong.com), both run by **ETC Asia.**

DOCUMENTS AND FORMALITIES

PASSPORTS AND VISAS. A valid passport is required to enter and leave the country, and all foreign travelers must obtain visas. Tourist visas, generally good for 15 days, are issued at **Wattay Airport** and **Friendship Bridge** in Vientiane; and at **Luang Prabang Airport** for a fee of US$30. Bring two passport-size photos. The Department of Immigration in Vientiane will only extend tourist visas for one day. Thirty-day visas are only issued at Lao embassies. It is sometimes possible to acquire a 15-day extension through a tourist agency. Visas are not available at the Chong Mek border crossing. Travelers who overstay their visit without a valid visa risk arrest and must pay a fine of US$5 per day. Double-check entrance requirements at the nearest embassy or consulate of Laos (listed under **Embassies and Consulates** on p. 283) for up-to-date info before departure. US citizens can also consult www.pueblo.gsa.gov/cic_text/travel/foreign/foreignentryreqs.

MONEY

CURRENCY AND EXCHANGE

The currency chart below is based on August 2004 exchange rates between local currency and Australian dollars (AUS$), Canadian dollars (CDN$), European Union euros (EUR€), New Zealand dollars (NZ$), British pounds (UK£), and US dollars (US$). Check the currency converter on websites like www.xe.com or www.bloomberg.com, or a large newspaper for the latest exchange rates.

CURRENCY (KIP)

AUS$1 = 7,435.68KIP	10,000KIP = AUS$1.43028
CDN$1 = 8,038.93KIP	10,000KIP = CDN$1.34252
EUR€1 = 12,853.09KIP	10,000KIP = EUR€.821328
NZ$1 = 6,922.27KIP	10,000KIP = NZ$1.58049
UK£1 = 19,019.40KIP	10,000KIP = UK£.549203
US$1 = 10,000KIP	10,000KIP = US$1

The Lao kip comes in denominations of 100, 500, 1000, and 5000 and is divided into 100 cents. Thai baht and US dollars are the most widely exchanged currencies, especially since the government devalued the kip in 1998. Vendors in markets are eager to change US dollars and Thai baht into kip, often at better rates than in the banks. Traveler's checks are only accepted at major banks and businesses. Credit, debit, and ATM cards are not accepted. There are also no money wiring services. In serious emergencies, US citizens can have the US State Department forward money to the nearest consular office, which will then disburse it according to instructions for a US$15 fee. For this service, you must contact the Overseas Citizens Service division of the US State Department (☎317-472-2328; nights, Su, and holidays 202-647-4000). It's customary to **tip** guides, but tipping in restaurants and hotels is uncommon. Feel free to **bargain** whenever a price isn't indicated.

GETTING TO LAOS

BY PLANE. Laos has two **international airports:** Wattay International Airport in Vientiane (p. 288) and Luang Prabang Airport in Luang Prabang (p. 297). Entry to Vientiane is possible via Cambodia, China, Thailand, and Vietnam; to Luang Prabang via Cambodia, Thailand, and Vietnam; to Pakse via Cambodia. Lao Airlines, Thai Airways, Vietnam Airlines, and China Yunnan Airways offer flights to Laos. **Lao Aviation** (www.laoaviation.com) runs the most international flights between major Southeast Asia gateways, but the US State Department has issued a warning (http://travel.state.gov/laos.html) regarding Lao Aviation's safety record, advising visitors to limit their use of the carrier to essential travel only. Consult your embassy for the latest safety reports. Alternatively, use **Thai Airways** or **Vietnam Airlines** for flights to Bangkok, Hà nội, and Hồ Chí Minh City.

BY LAND. Refer to the following table for overland border crossings in Laos.

BORDER CROSSINGS. Always be sure to get up-to-date information before trying to cross any border.

CAMBODIA. The only border passage is at Koh Chheuteal Thom to Voen Kham in Laos. The border crossing between **Don Khong** in southern Laos and **Stung Treng** (p. 101) in northern Cambodia was officially closed in March 2004.

CHINA. The only legal crossing is from the small town of **Boten** in northern Laos to **Mohan/Mengla** in southwest China.

MYANMAR. It isn't currently possible to travel overland to Myanmar from Laos.

THAILAND. There are 5 border crossings from Laos to Thailand: **Huay Xai** (p. 311) to **Chiang Khong** (p. 791); **Vientiane** (p. 288) to **Nong Khai** (p. 747); **Thakhek** to **Nakhon Phanom** (p. 742); **Savannakhet** (p. 313) to **Mukhadan** (p. 740); and **Pakse** (p. 316) to **Chong Mek.**

VIETNAM. Travelers pass between **Savannakhet** (p. 313) in Laos and **Đà Nẵng/Huế** (p. 920) in Vietnam via **Lao Bao** (7hr. from Savannakhet, 8hr. from Huế). The crossing at **Điện Biên Phủ** is open to locals but not foreigners. Check with an embassy for up-to-date information. You may be denied passage, especially if your visa doesn't specify the correct points of entry and exit.

GETTING AROUND LAOS

BY PLANE. During the rainy season, air travel may be the only way to reach remote areas like Luang Nam Tha. **Lao Aviation** has domestic flights that link the capital with every region of the country, but be aware that the US State Department (http://travel.state.gov/laos) has issued a warning regarding the carrier's safety record, especially over mountainous areas. Buy your ticket several days in advance and confirm your flight one day in advance, as some routes only run occasionally, and other forms of transportation aren't always available. Foreigners must pay in US dollars. Check out the following airlines in Laos:

Lao Airlines, Th Pang Kham, Vientiane (☎021 21 2051; www.laoarlines.com).

Bangkok Airways, 57/6 Th Sisavangvong, Ban Xiengmuan, Luang Prabang (☎071 25 3334).

THAI, Th Pang Kham, Vientiane (☎021 21 6143).

Vietnam Airlines, 1st fl., Lao Plaza Hotel, Th Samsenthai, Vientiane (☎021 21 7562).

BY BUS AND TUK TUK. Buses are generally available for travel between cities. However, they are unreliable. The only thing to do is hope that one is departing when you need it. *Tuk tuks*, three-wheeled, open-sided taxis are most common for travel around town. Both buses and *tuk tuks* tend to be in poor condition.

AIRCRAFT SAFETY. The airlines of developing world nations do not always meet safety standards. The *Official Airline Guide* (www.oag.com) and many travel agencies can tell you the type and age of aircraft on a particular route. This can be especially useful in Laos, where less reliable equipment is often used for internal flights. The International Airline Passengers Association (US ☎800-821-4272, UK ☎020 8681 6555) provides region-specific safety information. The Federal Aviation Administration (www.faa.gov) reviews the airline authorities for countries whose airlines enter the US. US State Department travel advisories (☎202-647-5225; travel.state.gov/travel_warnings.html) sometimes involve foreign carriers, especially when terrorist bombings or hijackings may be a threat.

BY CAR, MOPED, AND BICYCLE. Driving or riding any kind of bike in Laos is not recommended. Roads are tenuous, rough, and generally in poor condition. Few roads have lane markings, few drivers are licensed and insured, construction sites are poorly marked, and most traffic regulations are ignored. It is extremely dangerous traveling on roads at night. Many vehicles do not have working lights and few bikes have reflectors. Law requires that any driver coming upon a road accident transport all injured persons to a hospital.

BY BOAT. Travel by boat is common in Laos. However, travel by specialist (locally known as "fast boat") should be avoided, especially during dry season. Lao militia have shot at boats on the Mekong River after dark, so do not cross it at night.

TIP **SLOW BOAT 101.** Travel by slow boat is the most authentic way to get around Laos. Some are frustrated by the slow pace of river travel, but the alternatives include ear-splitting speedboats or spine-shattering bus rides, so the slow boat is worth a try. The Mekong is the heart and soul of this country, and it's worth seeing river life first-hand. Here are some tips for your first lazy ride:

Pick the less-traveled direction. The boats upstream from Luang Prabang have plenty of room to stretch out and nap; travelers going south from Huay Xai generally aren't as lucky.

Bring a camera. There's nothing like the sun setting over a group of water buffalo in a remote bend on the Mekong.

Bring food and water. Boats stop irregularly and often not for hours at a time. Restaurants in river towns know what's up and can prepare a lunch and give it to you to go.

Bring layers and a blanket. It can be quite cool on the river in the early morning and after the sun sets, whereas at midday it can be sweltering.

Be first off the boat. In small river towns, guesthouses fill up quickly; the early bird gets the worm.

HEALTH AND SAFETY

EMERGENCY NUMBERS: Police: ☎191. Fire: ☎190. Ambulance: ☎195.

MEDICAL EMERGENCIES. Laos does not have extensive medical facilities, and most travelers seek medical attention in neighboring Thailand. Foreigners seeking help can cross The Friendship Bridge connecting Vientiane with Nong Khai, Thailand between 6am-10pm or after hours in the event of an emergency.

HEALTH RISKS. The usual immunization requirements apply. In particular, malaria and Dengue fever are a problem in Laos. Avoid them by sleeping with a mosquito net at all times, wearing long sleeves and pants around dusk, and going crazy with insect repellent.

EXPLORING AND TRAVELING. Be careful, especially if alone. Laos has a low rate of violent crime. However, for many years, there have been attacks by armed gangs on vehicles traveling on Rte. 13 between Vang Vieng and Luang Prabang. A bus attack in February 2003 left 13 people, including two Western cyclists, dead. Two months later, there was another bus attack in which 12 people were killed and 31 injured. Ambushes along Rte. 13 continued through 2003, in Hua Phan province and southern Laos, and there was a bomb attack at Vientiane's bus station.

WOMEN TRAVELERS. In general, women are safe traveling in Laos. It's highly recommended, however, that women wear wedding rings, travel in lit areas, and keep a low profile.

MINORITY TRAVELERS. In general, there are few minority travelers in Laos. More than anything else, locals are intrigued by minorities. Don't be alarmed if people treat you like an alien from Mars, gawk at you, or ask to touch your skin or hair. In general, once you show respect, you'll gain respect.

GLBT TRAVELERS. Homosexuals should be discreet. There have been reports that homosexuals have been picked up in police raids and detained.

DRUGS AND ALCOHOL. Penalties for possession, trafficking, or use of illegal drugs are strict. Before April 2001, offenders could expect jail sentences and fines. Today, the penalty for certain drug crimes is death. Those who are caught violating the law, even unknowingly, will be punished. Sometimes a caller is informed that the police are not authorized to respond or not equipped with transportation.

KEEPING IN TOUCH

BY MAIL. Mail from Laos is unreliable and slow. Postage is cheap, but many prefer to send overseas packages from Thailand. Receiving mail in Laos is possible through *Poste Restante* in Vientiane. Postal officers will inspect anything that's not a letter.

BY TELEPHONE. Making phone calls over the Internet from a cafe is usually cheaper than using a telephone. The next cheapest option is using a phone card. Post offices in medium-sized towns sell US$3, US$6, and US$9 phone cards, stock English-language white pages, and invariably have a card phone outside. The new **Lao Telecom** phone service has made international calls from Laos possible for the first time for a steep price. Cities like Luang Prabang and Vientiane have telecommunication bureaus that place calls but charge more for fewer services (no collect, credit card, or incoming calls allowed). For **Home Country Direct (HCD)** numbers from Laos, refer to the table on the inside back cover of this book.

Calling within Laos is like calling anywhere else. If you're planning to stay in the country for a long time, you might want to consider purchasing a **cell phone.**

Cell phones are available in Laos. However, they are not cost-efficient; a call to the US will cost US$2-3 per minute. If you purchase a cell phone, you have the option of adding as much value as you need. To make and receive calls in Laos you will need a **GSM-compatible phone** and a **SIM (subscriber identity module) card.**

BY EMAIL AND INTERNET. Internet access is the best way to stay in touch. Internet cafes are found surprisingly often, but are by no means everywhere.

NORTHERN LAOS

VIENTIANE ☎21

Laos's sleepy capital feels more like an extensive village than an Asian metropolis. To adventurers from a bygone era, Vientiane was an exotic colonial backwater where days melted into years, and life was as sluggish as the Mekong in the dry season. Today, wine shops and French restaurants still dot the streets near the Nap Phou Fountain, but the "City of Sandalwood" has begun to shed its colonial legacy. For most travelers, this capital's chief appeal is its provincial feel; most linger a day or two before heading into rural Laos.

TRANSPORTATION

Flights: Wattay International Airport (international ☎512 028, domestic ☎512 000), on Luang Prabang Rd. Taxi to downtown US$5 (expect to tip; *tuk tuk* 30,000kip plus tip. Departure tax: 5,000kip domestic, US$10 international. **Lao Air Booking Co.,** 43/1 Setthathirat Rd. (☎216 761). Open M-F 8am-noon and 1-4:30pm, Sa 8am-noon. AmEx/V. **Lao Aviation,** 2 Pang Kham Rd. (tickets ☎212 051). Open M-F 8am-noon and 1-4pm, Sa 8am-noon. MC/V. To: **Bangkok** (2 per day, US$95); **Chiang Mai** (3 per week, US$85); **Hà Nội** (1 per day, US$108); **Hồ Chí Minh City**(1 per week, US$168); **Huay Xai** (4 per week, US$80); **Luang Nam Tha** (daily, US$74); **Luang Prabang** (2 per day, US$57); **Oudomxay** (3 per week, US$66); **Pakse** (1 per day, US$87); **Phonsavan** (1 per day, US$46); **Phnom Penh** (1 per day, US$140); **Savannakhet** (3 per week, US$57). **Thai Airways,** 27/1 Pang Kham Rd. (☎222 527). Open daily 8:30am-noon and 1-5pm. V (3% fee). To **Bangkok** (1 per day, US$100). **Vietnam Airlines,** 63 Samsenthai Rd. (☎252 618; fax 222 379), Lao Plaza Hotel. Open M-F 8am-noon and 1:30-4:30pm, Sa 8am-noon. To **Hà Nội** (US$110) and **Hồ Chí Minh City** (US$165).

Buses: Northern Bus Terminal (☎216 507), on the corner of Mahosot and Khou Vieng Rd. To: **Ban Thalat** (2hr., every hr. 6:30am-3:30pm, 5000kip); **Friendship Bridge** (#45, 30min., every 20min. 7am-5pm, 1500kip); **Paksan** (#18; 3hr.; 7, 11am, 1:30pm; 6000kip); **Pakse** (#35, 13hr., 7 per day 10am-4pm, 47,000kip); **Savannakhet** (#36, 8hr., 7 per day 5:30-9:30am, 30,000kip); **Tha Deua** (#14, 1hr., every 20min. 7am-5pm, 2000kip); **Vang Vieng** (#1; 4hr.; 7, 10:30am, 1:30pm; 6000kip). Other buses leave from **Thalat Laeng** (☎413 297), accessible by *tuk tuk* (about 3000kip). To: **Luang Prabang** (10hr.; 6, 10:30am, 12:30, 3:30, 7pm; 50,000kip); **Oudomxay** (15hr., 6am, 60,000kip); **Phonsavan** (10hr.; 6:30, 7:30, 9am, 3pm; 60,000kip); **Xamnena** (30hr.; 7, 9:30am; 120,000kip).

Boats: Erratic schedules—particularly during dry season—make buses a preferred means of transport. **Speedboats** go from **Kao Liao Pier,** to **Luang Prabang** and **Pak Lay.**

Local Transportation: Taxis congregate at the morning market on Lane Xang Ave. and in front of the Novotel on Luang Prabang Rd. (10,000-15,000kip per hr. or 200,000kip per day). To **Tha Deua** (Buddha Park) 50,000kip. **Tuk tuk** to Buddha Park US$2-8, depending on your bargaining ability. **Saysouly Guest House** (☎218 383), on Manthatulath Rd. 1 block west of Pang Kham Rd., rents **motorbikes** (US$8 per day).

ORIENTATION AND PRACTICAL INFORMATION

The **Nam Phou Fountain,** on **Setthathirat Road,** serves as a convenient landmark. Vientiane's three main thoroughfares are: **Samsenthai Road,** one block north of the fountain; Setthathirat Rd., one block south of the fountain; and **Lane Xang Avenue,** which runs perpendicular to the **Mekong River** until the **Anousavari Monument.** Lane

Xang Ave. is home to **Talat Sao** (the morning market) and the **GPO.** Many restaurants are on **Quay Fa Ngum Road,** which runs parallel to Mekong River. The **Northern Bus Terminal** is on **Mahosot Road,** parallel to and one block east of Lane Xang Ave.

TOURIST AND FINANCIAL SERVICES

Tourist Offices: National Tourism Authority (☎212 251), on Lane Xang Ave. 300m before Anousavari Monument. Flight and bus schedules and travel info. Open M-F 8am-noon and 1-4pm. **Inter-Lao Tourism** (☎214 832), on Luang Prabang Rd. near the Novotel. Open M-F 8am-4pm. **A Rasa Tour** (☎213 360), on Setthathirat Rd. 1 block past PlaNet on the right, has information on public buses, flights, and tourist buses. English, French, and Japanese spoken. Open M-F 8:30am-5:30pm, Sa 8:30am-4pm.

Tours: Diethelm Travel (☎213 833), on Setthathirat Rd. beside the Nam Phou Fountain. Open M-F 8am-noon and 1-5pm. **Sadetour,** 114 Quay Fa Ngum Rd. (☎213 478). Laos's oldest tour company. Open M-F 8am-6pm, Sa 8am-noon.

Embassies: Australia, Nehru Rd. (☎413 600), at the intersection with Phon Xay Rd. Open M-Th 9am-noon and 1:30-5pm, F 9am-noon. Serves **Canada, NZ,** and **UK** citizens in emergencies. **Cambodia** (☎314 952), on Tha Deua Rd., 2km outside the city center. 3-day visas US$20. Open M-F 7:30-11:30am and 2-4pm. **China** (☎315 100), on Wat Nak Rd. past Myanmar Embassy. 30-day visas US$50; allow 3 working days. Open M-F 9-11:30am. **Myanmar** (☎314 910), on Sok Paluang Rd. 500m past Wat Sokpaluang on the left. Tourist visas US$20; 3-day processing. Bring 4 photos. Open M-F 8:30am-noon and 1-4:30pm. **Thailand** (☎214 582), on Thanon Phone Kheng Rd.; consular office (☎217 154), Lane Xang Rd. 60-day tourist visas 1000฿, transit visas 800฿. Bring 2 photos and photocopies of passport; 2-day processing. Open M-F 8:30am-noon and 1-4:30pm. **US** (☎213 966), 19 Bartholomie Rd. Open M-F 8-11:30am and 1-4:30pm. **Vietnam,** 60 Thanon That Luang Rd. (☎413 400). Tourist visas US$55; 3-day processing. Bring 2 photos. Open M-F 8-11:30am and 2:30-4:15pm.

Currency Exchange: Banque Pour le Commerce Extérieur Lao, 1 Pang Kham Rd. (☎213 200). Traveler's checks cashed. V cash advances. Open M-F 8:30am-3:30pm. **Lao Development Bank** (☎213 300), 39 Pang Kham Rd., provides similar services. Open M-F 8:30am-3:30pm. There's another branch on Setthathirat Rd., next to Wat Mixayram, with an exchange booth open daily 8:30am-6pm.

American Express: Diethelm Travel (see **Tours,** above) is the Lao representative. They will issue **traveler's checks** (1% commission) for AmEx cardholders.

LOCAL SERVICES

Bookstores: Bookshop, on Chantha Kuman Rd., next to That Dam, has a luck-of-the-draw selection of used guidebooks and novels in English and French. Buys used books. Open daily 9am-4pm. **Vientiane Book Center** 54/1 Pang Kham Rd. (☎212 031), across from the Lao Airlines office. They also sell up-to-date maps of Laos and neighboring countries. Open M-F 9am-5:30pm, Sa 9am-4pm.

Photo Store: Master Color Lab 110/4-5 Samsenthai Rd. (☎217 425), takes passport photos (25,000kip per 6 prints) and will burn images from a digital camera to a CD (20,000kip). Open M-Sa 8am-7pm.

EMERGENCY AND COMMUNICATIONS

Emergency: Police: ☎191. **Fire:** ☎190. **Ambulance:** ☎195.

Pharmacy: Seng Thong Osoth Pharmacy (☎213 732), on the road between the morning market and the Northern Bus Terminal, is one of many. Heading away from the river, it's on the right. Friendly staff; some English spoken. Open daily 8am-8pm.

Medical Services: Australian Embassy Clinic (☎413 603), on Nehru Rd. near the Australian Embassy. Serves Australian, British, Canadian, and NZ citizens. Initial consultation US$50. By appointment only. Open M-Th 9am-noon and 2-4pm, F 8:30am-12:30pm. **International Clinic, Mahosot Hospital,** emergency room (☎214 023), on Mahosot Rd. past Wat Pha Kaew. Little English spoken. Open 24hr. In emergencies, contact **Aek Udon International Hospital** (☎66 42 342 555) in nearby Thailand; their ambulances can cross into Laos, and they have evacuation services. English spoken.

Telephones: Central Telephone Office (☎214 977), on Setthathirat Rd. Facing Nam Phou Fountain, head 1 block right on Setthathirat Rd.; it's a yellow building on the left. Cash calls only. **Fax** 14,000kip per min. to US and UK. Open M-F 8am-5pm, Sa 8:30am-5pm. International phones also at **GPO** (card calls only). Several of the Internet cafes along Setthathirat Rd., opposite Sabaidee Restaurant, offer international calls over the Internet; 2000kip per min. to the US.

Internet Access: PlaNet Online, 205 Setthathirat Rd. (☎218 972). Facing Nam Phou Fountain, walk to the left down Setthathirat Rd. for a little more than a block; it's on the right. PlaNet has many terminals and fast connections. 200kip per min. Open daily 8:30am-11pm. Other Internet cafes line Setthathirat Rd.

Post Office: GPO (☎/fax 217 327), on Lane Xang Ave.; from the river, it's just before the morning market on the right. *Poste Restante*. Open M-F 9am-1:30pm and 2:30-4pm.

ACCOMMODATIONS

Thawee Guest House, 64 Ban Ann. (☎217 903), a comfortable guesthouse with energizing orange walls; A/C rooms are a nice splurge. Singles with outside hot-water bath US$6-8; doubles US$12-14. ❸

Lane-Xang Hotel (☎214 102), on Quay Fa Ngum Rd., near the Royal Palace along the river. An upscale hotel with a swimming pool, large rooms, and quality service. Doubles with satellite TV, breakfast, hot water, and A/C US$25. Surcharge for paying in kip. ❺

Praseuth Guest House, 312 Samsenthai Rd. (☎217 932), next to the Cultural Hall. Amicable, family-run business with small but spotless rooms in the heart of the city. Laundry. Rooms US$6-7, with A/C US$7, with bath US$8. ❸

Vannasinh Guest House, 051 Phnom Penh Rd. (☎222 020). Near the intersection of Samsenthai Rd. and Hanoi Rd. Surprisingly quiet, considering its central location. Backpacker-friendly. French- and English-speaking staff manage clean, pleasant rooms; they will also help you arrange bus tickets. Singles US$7; doubles US$8. ❹

Phonepaseuth Guest House, 97 Pang Kham Rd. (☎212 263; http://phonepaseuthgh.tripod.com). A little pricey but well located. Rooms are cool and clean, with hot showers. Rooms US$10; with A/C and satellite TV US$15. ❹

Mixok Guest House, (☎251 600), on Setthathirat Rd., 2 blocks west of the Nam Phou Fountain. Small rooms with dorm bunk beds. Some rooms have a balcony that looks out onto the street and a temple. All rooms have shared bath. Internet access. Dorms 16,000kip; singles 30,000kip; doubles 40,000kip; triples 54,000kip. ❶

FOOD

For cheap and delicious Lao food, head to one of the many eateries along the river. Most are open from dawn until late evening and serve a mix of Lao, Thai, and Western-style dishes (10,000-20,000kip). French bakeries and restaurants cluster near the Nam Phou Fountain.

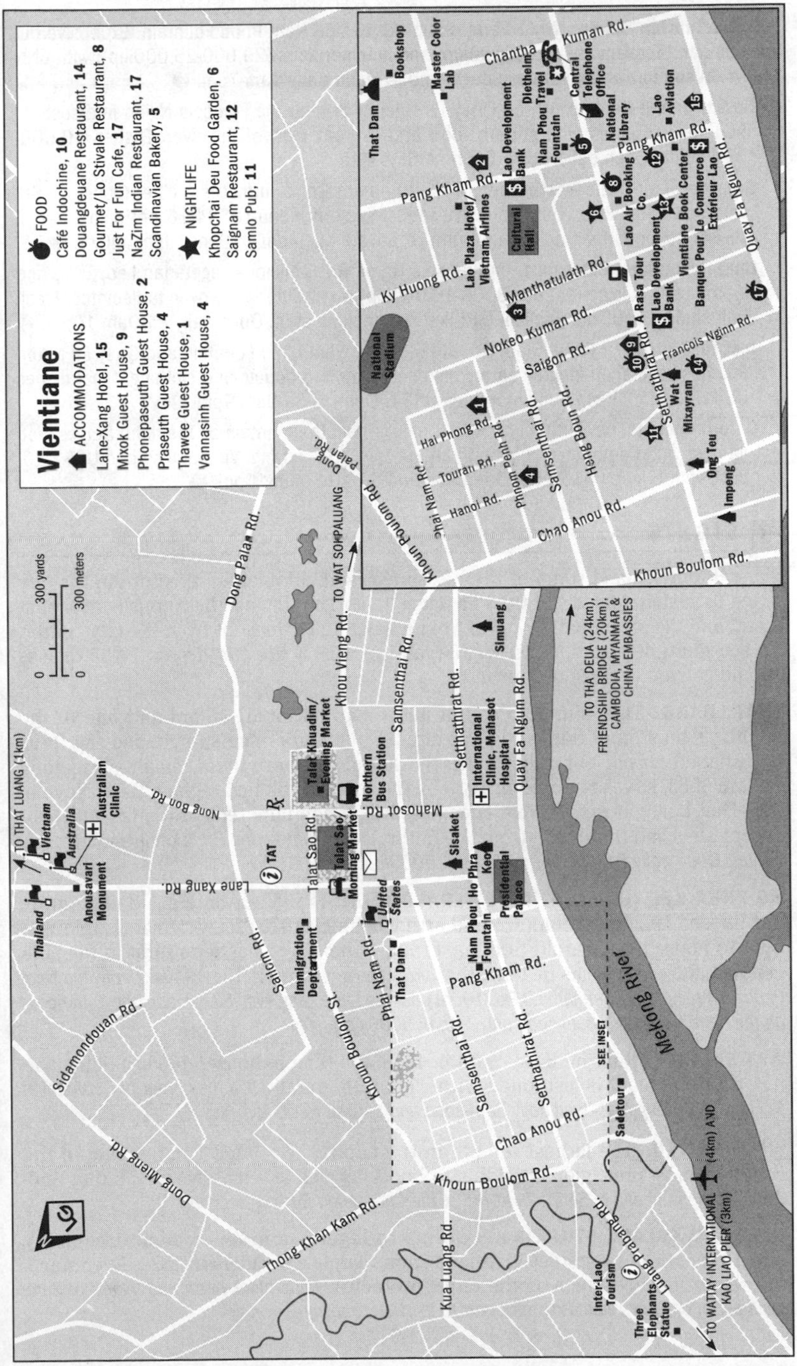
Vientiane
ACCOMMODATIONS
Lane-Xang Hotel, 15
Mixok Guest House, 9
Phonepaseuth Guest House, 2
Praseuth Guest House, 4
Thawee Guest House, 1
Vannasinh Guest House, 4
FOOD
Café Indochine, 10
Douangdeuane Restaurant, 14
Gourmet/Lo Stivale Restaurant, 8
Just For Fun Cafe, 17
NaZim Indian Restaurant, 17
Scandinavian Bakery, 5
NIGHTLIFE
Khopchai Deu Food Garden, 6
Saignam Restaurant, 12
Samlo Pub, 11
0 300 yards
0 300 meters
TO THAT LUANG (1km)
Thailand
Vietnam
Australia
Australian Clinic
Anousavari Monument
Lane Xang Rd.
Nong Bon Rd.
TAT
Talat Sao Rd.
Talat Sao/ Morning Market
Talat Khuadim/ Evening Market
Northern Bus Station
Mahosot Rd.
Khou Vieng Rd.
TO WAT SOKPALUANG
Dong Palan Rd.
Dong Palan Rd.
Samsenthai Rd.
Setthathirat Rd.
Simuang
International Clinic, Mahasot Hospital
Quay Fa Ngum Rd.
TO THA DEUA (24km), FRIENDSHIP BRIDGE (20km), CAMBODIA, MYANMAR & CHINA EMBASSIES
Sisaket
Ho Phra Keo
Presidential Palace
United States
Immigration Department
Sailom Rd.
Phai Nam Rd.
That Dam
Nam Phou Fountain
Pang Kham Rd.
Khoun Boulom St.
Samsenthai Rd.
Setthathirat Rd.
SEE INSET
Sidamondouan Rd.
Dong Mieng Rd.
Chao Anou Rd.
Khoun Boulom Rd.
Sadetour
Mekong River
Thong Khan Kam Rd.
Kua Luang Rd.
Luang Prabang Rd.
Inter-Lao Tourism
Three Elephants Statue
TO WATTAY INTERNATIONAL (4km) AND KAO LIAO PIER (3km)
That Dam
Bookshop
Master Color Lab
Chantha
Kuman Rd.
Diethelm Travel
Central Telephone Office
Nam Phou Fountain
National Library
Lao Aviation
Lao Development Bank
Pang Kham Rd.
Pang Kham Rd.
Lao Plaza Hotel/ Vietnam Airlines
Cultural Hall
Lao Air Booking Co.
Vientiane Book Center
Banque Pour Le Commerce Extérieur Lao
Quay Fa Ngum Rd.
Ky Huong Rd.
National Stadium
Manthatulath Rd.
A Rasa Tour
Lao Development Bank
Nokeo Kuman Rd.
Saigon Rd.
Setthathirat Rd.
Francois Nginn Rd.
Wat Mixayram
Hai Phong Rd.
Touran Rd.
Hanoi Rd.
Phai Nam Rd.
Phnom Penh Rd.
Samsenthai Rd.
Heng Boun Rd.
Ong Teu
Impeng
Chao Anou Rd.
Khoun Boulom Rd.
Khoun Boulom Rd.

LAOS

Scandinavian Bakery, 74/1 Pang Kham Rd. beside Nam Phou Fountain. Expensive but popular. Excellent pastries (5000kip) and lunch options (20,000-25,000kip), with CNN on TV and foreign magazines strewn about. Open daily 7am-7pm. ❷

NaZim Indian Restaurant, on Quay Fa Ngum Rd. near the François Nginn intersection. Popular Lao chain with superb food and a great view of the river. Dishes 10,000-20,000kip. Open daily 11am-11pm. MC/V. ❷

Gourmet/Lo Stivale Restaurant, 44 Setthathirat Rd. Gourmet is a cafe; Classy Lo Stivale serves delicious but expensive food. Western menu (US$4-16 per dish). *Panini* US$4. Gourmet open daily 7am-8pm; Lo Stivale open daily 10am-10pm. MC/V. ❺

Douangdeuane Restaurant, on François Nginn Rd. Delicious vegetarian Lao, Thai, and Vietnamese cuisine (entrees 8000-16,000kip) on traditionally woven tablecloths. Fresh fruit shakes 3000kip. English- and French-speaking staff. Open daily 8:30am-10pm. ❶

Just for Fun, 15/2 Pang Kham Rd. between the Nam Phou Fountain and Quay Fa Ngum Rd. This vegetarian-friendly eatery also sells ethnic products and clothing. Most dishes US$1.50-2.50; fresh fruit smoothies US$1. Open M-Sa 9am-9pm. ❶

Café Indochine, on Setthathirat Rd., 2 blocks past the fountain on the right. Serves Vietnamese and Cambodian cuisine in an upscale, A/C setting. Vietnamese phô US$1.20; duck with 5 herbs US$2.50. Open M-F and Su 10:30am-10pm. ❶

SIGHTS

Several temples and some of the best-preserved colonial architecture in the city grace **Setthathirat Road** and **Quay Fa Ngum Road.** That Luang, the Anousavari Monument, and the steam baths of Wat Sokpaluang lie farther out from the city center. To see multiple sights, consider bargaining with a *tuk tuk* driver; US$5 or less should get you to three or four *wats*.

THAT LUANG. This 45m gold *stupa* is the Lao national symbol and one of the country's most important religious sites. Four *wats* once surrounded the lotus bud-shaped *stupa*, but only the northern and southern *wats* remain. Originally built in 1566, it was restored in 1935 by the French colonial regime. Each November, That Luang hosts the **That Luang Festival,** when hundreds of monks gather to accept alms and floral gifts from the faithful. *(On That Luang Rd. 1km inland from city center. Open daily 8am-noon and 1-4pm. 5000kip.)*

HO PHRA KEO (HALL OF THE EMERALD BUDDHA). Vientiane's oldest temple has housed Buddhist sculpture and artifacts since 1970. The original temple was built to house the Emerald Buddha, brought there by King Settathirat in the 16th century. Razed by Thais in 1827, the *wat* was restored in the 1940s. *(From the Nam Phou Fountain, follow Setthathirat Rd. 100m past the Lane Xang Ave. intersection; the entrance is on the right. Open daily 8am-noon and 1-4pm. 5000kip.)*

WAT SISAKET. Built by King Anou in 1818, the temple houses 7000 Buddha statues. The sanctuary is festooned with elaborate murals. *(On the corner of Setthathirat Rd. and Lane Xang Ave. Open daily 8am-noon and 1-4pm. 5000kip.)*

WAT ONG TEU. The largest temple in the capital, Wat Ong Teu has one of the country's most prestigious Buddhist schools, as well as a massive meditating Buddha. *(At the west end of Setthathirat Rd. at the Chao Anou Rd. intersection.)*

THAT DAM (BLACK STUPA). According to legend, a seven-headed dragon lay under this *stupa* to protect Vientiane from Siamese invaders in 1828. Ever since, the *stupa* has been seen as the city's protector. *(One block north and inland of Samsenthai Rd. on Pang Kham Rd., right next to the US embassy.)*

WAT SOKPALUANG. This *wat* offers wonderfully refreshing herbal saunas and rigorous 40min. massages for 30,000kip (1-7pm). They also conduct *vipassana* (insight) meditation sessions that are open to newcomers and experienced practitioners alike (Su 4-5:30pm). For more information ask at the temple for English-speaking monk KooBa Khun. *(1.5km southeast of the city center. Take a* tuk tuk *(5000kip) or walk away from Lane Xang Ave. on Khou Vieng Rd. The turn-off for the wat is unmarked; it is visible through the trees from the main road. Open daily late morning-8pm.)*

WAT SIMUANG. Built by King Setthathirat in 1566, this *wat* houses the foundation pillar of Vientiane. According to legend, it crushed a pregnant woman—named Nang Si—as it was lowered. As a result, Nang Si is revered as the guardian spirit of the city. *(On Quay Fa Ngum Rd. at the east end of town. Open Tu-Sa 8am-8pm.)*

ANOUSAVARI MONUMENT (VICTORY GATE). This bizarre-looking monument, at the inland end of Lane Xang Ave., is a concrete mix between Paris's *Arc de Triomphe* and a wedding cake. It was built in 1969 by the government in memory of those who died during the Lao struggle for independence. When builders ran out of concrete, they completed the memorial with US cement earmarked for use in construction of Wattay International Airport. Known to some as the "vertical runway," it has an unparalleled panoramic view of town. *(At the north end of town on Lane Xang Ave. Open daily 8am-5pm. 1000kip.)*

MARKETS. Talat Sao (morning market) and **Talat Khuadim** (evening market) are two of Vientiane's main attractions. Talat Sao is in two green-roofed buildings off Lane Xang Ave., the first selling electrical and silver goods, and the second selling clothes and wall-hangings. (Open daily 6am-6pm.) Talat Khuadim is the large open-air market behind the Northern Bus Terminal. **Magninom Market,** on Khoun Boulom Rd., is geared more toward tourists. (Open daily 8am-9:30pm.)

ENTERTAINMENT

Nightlife is tame in Vientiane, since bars and clubs must close by midnight. **Khopchai Deu Food Garden,** next to the Nam Phou Fountain on Setthathirat Rd., has a beautiful courtyard surrounding an aging French colonial building. Its nighttime barbecues are one of the town's most popular afternoon and nighttime hangouts. Travelers sit around drinking Lao beer, listening to a looped mix tape of Radiohead, Buena Vista Social Club, and REM. Sit at the outside bar, enjoy a Lao wine cocktail (8000kip), and snack on some Pad Thai (13,000kip). If you're there on Friday or Saurday, kick back and listen to the live band. (Barbecue open M-Sa 9am-11:30pm, Su 5:30-11:30pm.) **Saignam Restaurant,** across the street from Khopchai Deu and down a small road to the right, shows recent movies in English around 7:30pm every day (food 15,000-20,000kip). British **Samlo Pub,** 101 Setthathirat Rd., caters to a crowd of tourists and expats. Hang out, shoot pool, watch European football, or play foosball. (☎222 308. Open daily 11:30am-2pm and 5pm-midnight.)

DAYTRIPS FROM VIENTIANE

NAM NGUM LAKE. Nam Ngum Lake, 70km northeast of Vientiane, is a vast reservoir that was formed by the damming of Nam Ngum River in the late 1970s. Today the hydroelectric power plant supplies electricity to much of Laos and parts of Thailand. Nam Ngum's natural setting is spectacular and serene; emerald islets, many of which were prisons during the 1980s, dot the lake. In the hurry to complete the dam, no one thought to harvest the surrounding forest, which was soon submerged. Ingenious Lao loggers have now developed underwater chain saws, and lumberjacks have traded their boots for flippers. Travelers seeking peace and quiet head to **Santipap Island,** the site of a dilapidated but charming **guesthouse ❷.** Great swimming and gorgeous sunsets compensate for the simple lodgings and sporadic electricity (rooms 10,000kip). If it's full you can sleep in hammocks outside for free. The only **restaurant ❷** on the island serves fresh fish (10,000-18,000kip). Hire a boatman with a small wooden boat to get to the island (15min.; 40,000kip per boat; ask people in the village: "Santipap?"). Alternatively, pay more for a slower boat at the pier (30-40min.; 70,000kip). Private boatmen also make one- or two-day tours on the lake; tours could include tribal villages, rock islands, Santipap Island, swimming, and diving. Mr. Ley organizes such trips for US$25-40; you can ask for him in the village. To reach the lake, take a bus from Vientiane's Northern Bus Terminal (see **Transportation,** p. 288) to Ban Thalat. From there, *songthaew* and *tuk tuks* run to the lake (10min., 5000kip), passing the dam complex. To continue farther north of Nam Ngum Lake, head back to Ban Thalat and take a *tuk tuk* (30min.; 10,000-20,000kip) to **Phon Hong,** or wait for a full *songthaew* (3000kip). From Phon Hong, a bus goes to **Vang Vieng,** or you can take a full *songthaew*. The last bus from Ban Thalat to Vientiane leaves at 5pm; *songthaew* leave until 6pm.

THA DEUA. Buddha sculptures are everywhere in this sculpture park, built by the same "half-man, half-animal" Lao mystic who designed Sala Kaew Ku. Both temples feature a blend of Hindu and Buddhist themes brought to life in cement sculptures. Fat Buddhas, thin Buddhas, big Buddhas, little Buddhas, Buddha family scenes, and reclining Buddhas all make an appearance. *(Tha Deua, 24km from Vientiane, can be reached by bus from the Northern Bus Terminal (#14, 50min., every 30min., 2000kip) or* tuk tuk *(45min., bargaining starts around US$10, 1000kip for parking.) Open daily 8:30am-5:30pm. 3000kip; 2000kip photo-ticket.)*

BAN PAKO. A small ecotourist lodge 50km from Vientiane, **Ban Pako ❶** is popular with Vientiane's expatriates. Austrian owner Mr. Pfabigan organizes treks, river-rafting expeditions, and village visits. The restaurant/bar is popular but expensive; bring your own food and drink if you're staying for a few days. *(☎451 970, office in Vientiane 451-841. Ban Pako, 50km northeast of Vientiane, can be reached by bus from the Northern Bus Terminal (#19 to Paxxap; get off at Som Sa Mai; 1½hr.; 6:30, 11am, 2pm). Once there, take a motorboat (25min.; 25,000kip per boat.) to Ban Pako resort. Dorms US$3.80; doubles US$11-17.50; bungalows US$20.)*

VANG VIENG ☎23

The Song River winds through a countryside full of dramatic limestone cliffs and caves before coming to the small town of Vang Vieng, the destination for backpackers en route to Luang Prabang or Vientiane. Spend your days tubing or caving and while away the evenings watching pirated DVDs or practicing your Swedish, Hebrew, or French. A short walk from the tourist strip to the bus station wanders across a deserted airstrip—during the Vietnam War this area was a stronghold for Vang Pao's Hmong guerrillas, recruited by the US Central Intelligence Agency to fight the Pathet Lao and Vietnamese communists. The area is now home to Hmong and Yao minority communities. Due to bandit attacks in recent years, the US State Department has advised its citizens not to travel on the road between Vang Vieng and Luang Prabang, nor along Rte. 7 from the Rte. 13 junction to Phonsavan.

TRANSPORTATION

All **buses** leave from the **bus station** next to the old airstrip on Rte. 13. Arrive at least 30min. in advance to ensure a seat on the crowded Luang Prabang buses. VIP buses run to **Luang Prabang** (9hr.; 10am; 55,000kip) and **Vientiane** (4-5hr.; 10am,

1pm; 35,000kip). Buses also go to **Phonsavan** (9-9:30am; 55,000kip). Minibuses, used almost exclusively by tourists, go to **Luang Prabang** (9am; 70,000kip) and **Vientiane** (9am, 1:30pm; 45,000kip). To visit **Nam Ngum Lake,** take a *songthaew* to **Phon Hong** (3hr., 8-9am, 6000kip), a *tuk tuk* to **Ban Thalat** (20min.; 20,000kip), and then another *tuk tuk* to the reservoir (5000kip).

ORIENTATION AND PRACTICAL INFORMATION

Vang Vieng lies along **Route 13,** which runs between Vientiane and Luang Prabang. The town spans two unnamed roads west of the airstrip. One road runs along the **Nam Song River;** the second is one block east, between the river road and the deserted airstrip. At the north end of the river road is the **market.** The **Vang Vieng Resort** and **Tham Chang Cave** are 2km south of the river road. Hand-colored maps are available from shops all over town (2000kip). The **post office,** on the river road next to the market, sells international phone cards. (☎511 009. Open M-F 8-11:30am and 2-4:30pm.) A **card phone** is outside. Heading away from the market is the **district hospital,** 1km down on the left. (☎551 019. Open M-F 8-11am and 2-4pm.) Facing the market, **Souk Pharmacie** is on the right. (☎511 444. Open M-Sa 7am-9pm.) Currency and AmEx Traveler's Cheques can be exchanged at **Banque Pour Le Commerce Extérieur Lao** (☎511 434; change window open daily 8:30am-3:30pm; AmEx/MC/V accepted only M-F), on the cross-street with Wildside Bar on the corner, and also at the **Lao Development Bank** (☎511 158; open M-F 8:30am-4pm), at the north end of town on the road between the river road and the airstrip. International calls can be made from **Lao Telecom,** next to the post office and market. (☎511 000. Open M-F 8am-noon and 1:30-3:30pm.) Facing the market on the right side, **Book Shop** (☎511 303) has an eclectic collection of secondhand books in English and other languages. You can rent **bicycles** (US$1 per day) and **motorbikes** (US$5-6 per day) from most guesthouses and restaurants in town. **Internet** access is available pretty much everywhere for roughly the same price. One place to check email is **PlaNet Online,** on the same road as Banque Pour Le Commerce Extérieur Lao. (300kip per min. Remove shoes before entering.)

ACCOMMODATIONS AND FOOD

Across from the Sunset Restaurant is **Hotel Namsong ❺,** a guesthouse with attractive rooms, a beautiful garden, and a river view. (☎511 016. Singles US$20; doubles with bath, hot water, and breakfast US$30.) Follow the river road about 750m from the market, and then follow the sign leading you down a to the river's edge. **Phaserdsay Guest House ❶,** 100m east of the market and across the street from the bank, has clean, new rooms. (☎511 052. With hot-water bath US$3.) Next door, **Doukkhoun 1 Guest House ❸,** also has clean rooms. (Doubles with hot-water bath US$4.) At the south end of town, on the road that runs parallel to and east of the airstrip, the **Nana Guest House ❶** has clean, quiet rooms. (Rooms with bath and hot shower 40,000kip.) For a chance to see traditional silkworm breeding and the production of green tea and starfruit wine, head 3km north of Vang Vieng to **Mr. T's Phondindaeng Organic Farm ❷.** Spending a night in Mr. T's WWOOF-affiliated guesthouse is the ideal way to experience farm life firsthand. (☎511 220; suanmone@hotmail.com. Rooms US$6 for the first 5 days, including all meals.)

The **Organic Farm Cafe ❶,** just north of Lao Telecom, serves delicious food made from the produce grown on the Phonindaeng Organic Farm. (Tasty vegetable curry stew 10,000kip; mulberry shake 5000kip; starfruit wine 5000kip; fill up your water bottle for 500kip. Open daily 8:30am-10:30pm.) The **Sunset Restaurant,** an old favorite, is 300m south of the hospital down a lane to the left off the river road. It offers gorgeous views of the Nam Song River. Near the market, **Fathima Restaurant ❷** cooks up fresh *roti* in front of your eyes and dishes out quality Indian food. (Dishes 10,000-20,000kip. Open daily 11am-9pm.)

SIGHTS

By far the most popular activity around Vang Vieng is **inner-tubing** down Nam Song River. Ask about excursions at shops along the river road or at shops along the road west of the airstrip (30,000kip should include *tuk tuk* and tube rental). The **limestone caves** in the cliffs surrounding Vang Vieng are a spelunker's dream. Apart from **Tham Chang,** the caves are unspoiled, beautiful, and easy to get lost in. Mr. Keo, based in the Nang Bot Restaurant across from Wildside Bar, is a reputable guide. His tours include spelunking, hikes to waterfalls, swimming, and inner-tubing (☎511 018. 1-day US$10; 2-day, 1-night US$30). The **Wildside Bar** also offers excursions, including **rock climbing** (US$20-28). Sturdy footwear and a flashlight (sold in the market) are a must for spelunking. Many shops near the market sell maps of Vang Vieng and its environs (2000kip) for those wishing to venture alone.

> **!** Many travelers explore the caves on their own and return home safely. Still, unaccompanied foreign explorers make tempting targets for rogues and bandits in more remote areas around Vang Vieng. Consider hiring a guide from one of the restaurants or guesthouses on the main road; doing so reduces your chances of getting lost, hurt, or robbed.

Tham Xang (the Elephant Caves) are the largest and most spectacular. They are 15km north of town and are accessible by motorbike (US$5-6 per day), bicycle (US$1 per day), or *tuk tuk*. Take Rte. 13 north to the village of Nadao. Proceed through the village; 50m after a small bridge, look for a dirt road on the left with a sign for Phoub A Num Caves. At the end of the road, park your ride (bicycles 1000kip; motorbikes 2000kip) and cross the bridge (toll 2000kip; cave entrance 2000kip.) During the rainy season, villagers may run an informal ferry service across the river in lieu of the bridge. The first Elephant Cave rises out of the rice fields like a shark fin. Images of Buddha, a single footprint, and a stalactite bearing an uncanny resemblance to an elephant's head all await inside. Vang Vieng's largest cave, **Tham Nang Phomhorm** (Cave of the Fragrant-Haired Woman), is 4km past Ban Tham Xang. Take the turn-off right at the village of **Ban Patthang.** The cave is 15km down this road, which passes **Ban Nam Yen,** a Yao hill-tribe village 3km before the cave entrance, accessible by *tuk tuk*. It's a good idea to pay extra to get the *tuk tuk* driver to wait while you explore. The most popular way to visit the caves is by tours (1-day tour of caves and local villages US$9-11) offered by guides around Vang Vieng. Some companies also offer whitewater rafting and rock-climbing trips (about US$20 per day). South of town and across the Nam Song River lies **Tham Phou Kham** (Cave of the Golden Crabs). To reach the caves, head south of town toward the river and turn right down the path next to the Sunset Restaurant. In the dry season it's possible to cross the bridge to get to the caves (2000kip toll), but in rainy season you'll need to cross by boat (2000kip, bicycles 1000kip). **Tham Chang** is 2km south of town, in the Vang Vieng Resort. Follow the river road away from the market, and 1.5km past the hospital, then follow the signs to Vang Vieng Resort. (Resort entrance 2000kip per motorbike or 1000kip per person; cave entrance 9000kip. Cave open daily 8:30-11:30am and 1-4:30pm.)

Ethnic villages, best visited by bicycle, are another highlight of the countryside. Across the river, west of town, are the Hmong villages of **Naxom** and **Namouang.** South of town, off Rte. 13 toward Vientiane, are the Yao villages of **Namone** and

Vangheua, which offer splendid views of the surrounding mountains and paddy fields. A Hmong village of some 300 households, composed mainly of repatriated Thai refugees, is 13km north of Vang Vieng. The village is south of Tham Xang village, west of Nam Song River. The United Nations High Commissioner for Refugees (UNHCR) oversees their reassimilation. Ask before taking photos.

NIGHTLIFE

Nightlife is less than riotous in Vang Vieng. Start your evening by watching the sunset along the river, and then move to one of the restaurants along the main road; most have nightly showings of bootlegged American DVDs. The bar scene centers around two establishments across the street from each other at the north end of the main road, **Wildside Bar** and **Xayoh Downtown Bar and Restaurant,** which has a pool table. (Cocktails 17,500kip. Both open daily 10am-midnight.) The movies end and the restaurants close at about midnight; those who are still feeling festive head to **Mantra Bar** or **Happy Bar** by the river.

LUANG PRABANG ☎71

Luang Prabang's name is synonymous with Lane Xang—the magnificent "Kingdom of a Million Elephants" that stretched across Indochina from the 14th to the 17th centuries. Substitute palanquins and pachyderms for bicycles and *tuk tuks*, and it seems like the city hasn't changed much since. From Mt. Phousi in the center of town, the gold peaks of Luang Prabang's many *wats* shine through a palm-tree canopy. King Setthathirat shifted the capital to Vientiane in 1556, leaving Luang Prabang in peaceful isolation, which has helped it resist the urbanization that has swept other Lao cities. Today, Luang Prabang is an UNESCO World Heritage site and an ideal springboard for both trips north and lazy rides down the Mekong.

TRANSPORTATION

Flights: Luang Prabang Airport (☎212 173), on Airport Rd., 5km from the town center. *Tuk tuks* to Central Station on Chao Xomphou Rd. 55,000kip. Flights to **Chiang Mai** (Th and Su, US$75) and **Vientiane** (2-3 per day, US$56). Departure times vary, so ask at **Lao Aviation** (☎212 172) on Wisunalat Rd., near the Kitsalat Setthathirat Rd. intersection. Open M-Sa 8-11:30am and 2-4:30pm.

Buses: Northern Bus Terminal (☎252 729), 5km north of the city in Ban Don. *Tuk tuks* 5000kip. Buses leave when full after 7:30am for: **M. Vieng Kham** (9am; 25,000kip); **Nong Khiaw** (9am; 12,000kip); **Oudomxay** (5hr.; 3 per day 8-11:30am; 30,000kip); **Pakmong** (2½hr.; 12,000kip). **Southern Bus Terminal** (☎252 066), south of the city off Phothisane Rd. next to the city stadium. *Tuk tuks* from town center 10,000kip. Buses to: **Phonsavan** (8:30am; 60,000kip); **Vang Vieng** (6-7 hr.; daily 10am; 45,000kip); **Vientiane** (10-11hr.; daily 6:30, 7, 7:30, 8:30, 10:30am, 12:30, 3:30pm; 50,000kip). Arrive before 8am to ensure a seat.

Boats: Book tickets for **slow boats** at the Navigation Office (☎212 237) on Souvanabalang Rd. Service to: **Huay Xai** (next to **Chiang Khong**, Thailand; 2 days with a night in Pakbeng; 150,000kip); **Pakbeng** (1 day; 75,000kip); **Tha Souang** (1 day, 60,000kip); **Nong Khiaw** (7hr., 65,000kip); **Vientiane** (3 days; 234,000kip). **Charter boats** for up to 20 people go to **Paklay** (2 days, 68,000kip) and **Tha Deua** (1 day, 40,000kip). **Speedboats** leave when full from **Ban Don** (*tuk tuk* 5000kip), 5km north of Luang Prabang; tell the driver "speedboat." Boats go to: **Huay Xai** (7hr.; 280,000kip); **Pakbeng** (3hr., 156,000kip); **Pak Ou Caves** (20min.; 40,000kip). Speedboats can also be chartered if the water is high enough. Prices listed are per boat for at most 8 passengers;

boats for fewer passengers may cost nearly the same. To: **Muang Ngoi** (2hr., US$50); **Paklay** (4hr., US$80); **Tha Deua** (1½hr; US$30); **Vientiane** (9hr., 8300₿). For long journeys (to Huay Xai or Vientiane), arrive before 10am or you'll have to stop overnight.

Local Transportation: Fishing **boats** run across the river to and from **Ban Chiang Man** (5min.; 25,000kip round-trip), the gateway to **Wat Long Khoune** and **Wat Tham,** to **Ban Chan Pottery Village** (40min.; 30,000kip round-trip), and to **Pak Ou Caves** (160,000kip per boat). **Songthaew** run to: **Ban Phanom Pottery Village** (15min.; 10,000kip); **Khouang Si Waterfalls** (2hr.; 100,000-120,000kip); **Pak Ou Caves** (100,000-120,000kip); **Xae Waterfall** (100,000kip).

Rentals: Many guesthouses and rental shops across the city rent **motorbikes** (US$6 per day) and **bicycles** (US$1 per day).

ORIENTATION AND PRACTICAL INFORMATION

Luang Prabang is small enough to navigate easily. The main road, running southwest to northeast from the **Nam Phou Fountain** to the **Nam Khan River,** is **Sisavangvong Road.** Between the fountain and the post office, Sisavangvong Rd. is briefly called **Chao Fa Ngum Road;** after the tourist strip, between PlaNet Online and the river, Sisavangvong Rd. is also called **Sakkarine Road.** The **post office, tourist office, national museum, Wat Xieng Thong,** and the entrance to Mt. Phousi all lie along this road. **Souvanabalang Road** runs parallel to Phothisarath Rd. and the Mekong River. The main cross-street, **Setthatilath Road,** runs away from the waterfront, eventually intersecting **Naviengkham Road.** Lao Aviation, the **police,** the Rama Hotel, and numerous restaurants sit on **Wisunalat Road,** parallel to Naviengkham Rd.

Tourist Office: Luang Prabang Tourism Office (☎212 487), on Wisunalat Rd. near the intersection with Chao Xan Phon Rd. Friendly staff arranges tours (but guesthouses will do the same for less). Open M-F 8-11:30am, 2-4pm.

Tours: Wildside, 44 Sisavangvong Rd. (☎212 043; www.lao-wildside.com) has daytrips to local attractions (US$5 and up), a 7-day kayak trip to Vientiane, and minivan service to Vang Vieng and Vientiane. Open daily 8am-10pm. **Diethelm Travel** (☎212 277), on the right walking toward Wat Xieng Thong on Sisavangvong Rd., helps arrange airline tickets. MC/V. Open M-F 8am-noon and 1-5:30pm, Sa 8am-noon. **Tiger Trail** (☎252 655) on Sisavangvong Rd. across from Luang Prabang Bakery, has local excursions, including trips with elephant rides (US$27). Open daily 8:30am-9:30pm.

Currency Exchange: Bank for Exterior Commerce (☎252 983), next to the Scandinavian Bakery. MC/V cash advance (3% commission). Open M-F 8:30am-7pm and Sa-Su 8:30am-3:30pm. **Lao Development Bank** (☎212 185), on Sisavangvong Rd. across the street from Moung Market. Open M-F 8:30am-4:30pm.

Red Cross (☎212 259), on Wisunalat Rd. Herbal saunas (10,000kip) and aromatic massages (30,000kip). Massages 9am-9pm, steam bath 4-8pm.

Pharmacies: Many on Kitsalat Setthathirat Rd. next to the hospital, on the Mekong side of Phothisarath Rd., although not much English spoken. Open daily 8am-7pm.

Medical Services: Clinique Internationale (☎252 049) on Samsenthai Rd.; from the intersection with Setthatilath Rd., walk 100m. Open daily 8-11:30am and 1:30-4pm.

Internet Access: All over town. About 350kip per min. **PlaNet Online,** on Phothisarath Rd. offers free coffee and tea and shows CNN. Open daily 8am-11pm. **Luang Prabang Internet,** across from an elementary school 50m before Wat Xieng Thong on Sakkarine Rd. 300kip per min. Open daily 8:30am-10:30pm.

Post Office: (☎212 255). Corner of Sisavangvong Rd. and Setthatilath Rd. *Poste Restante.* International calls US$3 per min. Open M-Sa 8am-noon and 1-5pm.

LAOS

ACCOMMODATIONS

Paphai Guest House (☎212 752), on Savang Vathana Rd. off Sisavangvong Rd. Charming wooden guesthouse. Centrally located, on a quiet sidestreet. Friendly English- and French-speaking staff. All rooms have shared bath. Singles US$5; doubles US$8. ❷

Pathoumphone Guest House (☎212 946), on Sakkarine Rd. From the base of Mt. Phousi, head up the riverbank 75m; it's on the left. Small, quiet guesthouse overlooking the Nam Khan River. Reception next door. Doubles US$5, with bath US$10. ❸

Kounsavan Guest House (☎212 297), on Chaotonkham Rd., the 1st right off Setthatilath Rd. when heading away from the Mekong River. Like a Swiss chalet. Clean rooms with shared bath and hot water. Singles US$3; doubles US$4, with bath US$10.❸

Phounsab Guest House, 6/7 Sisavangvong Rd. (☎212 975), 1 block right of the Royal Palace. Airy, clean, friendly. English spoken. Rooms US$3, with bath US$6. ❷

Tanoy Guest House (☎252 101), on Watthat Rd., near the Nam Phou Fountain. Clean and family-run. Rooms US$4-6. ❷

Jaliya Guest House (☎252 154), on Wisunalat Rd., across from Lao Airlines. Spacious, spotless bungalow-style rooms behind main building. Convenience store in reception area. Rooms US$3, with bath US$6. ❸

FOOD

Luang Prabang offers hungry travelers a wide range of satisfying options. Those on a budget need only stray off the tourist streets to find the same inexpensive staples common throughout Laos (*fôe* noodle soup in a market, 5000kip). Sakkarine Rd., though touristy, is a good place to start. There you will find wood-oven pizzerias, upscale Lao food, and bakeries alongside more common guesthouse restaurants. A little farther away from Mt. Phousi, on the leafy sidestreets off of Sakkarine Rd., are several upscale French cafes and restaurants; though it's expensive for Laos, you can treat yourself to a heavenly French-Lao meal for a fraction of what it would cost you at home. At Lao restaurants, look for traditional dishes like chicken steamed in banana leaf, *laap kai* (spicy chicken salad), watercress salad, and brown sticky rice. In the evenings, the night market on Sisavangvong Rd. has inexpensive street vendor food (daily dusk-9:30pm). Noodle vendors and *khao jii pâté* sellers gather at **Talat Dara.**

Indochina Spirit Restaurant (☎252 372), on Chao Fa Ngum Rd. next to Nam Phou Fountain. In a traditional wooden stilt house. Cushioned floor seating as well as tables. Wide selection of Lao, Thai, Western dishes. Delicious selection of *tom yam* (Lao soup), curries, and grilled dishes 25,000-39,000kip. *Lau lao* (rice wine) 3000kip per glass. Traditional Lao music in the evenings (after around 7pm). Open daily 10am-11pm. ❸

Somchan Restaurant, on Souvanabalang Rd. by the Mekong River. Wooden house with gorgeous sunsets. Tasty hot papaya salad. Traditional Lao dishes 8000-15,000kip; fresh fruit shake 3000kip. Open daily 7am-10pm. ❷

Nazim Restaurant, on Sisavangvong Rd., next to the Bank for Exterior Commerce. Great Indian food and friendly service. Vegetarian options. Entrees 10,000-20,000kip; pineapple *lassi* 6000kip. Open daily 11am-11pm. ❸

Café Ban Vat Sen, on Sakkarine Rd. across from Wat Sen. Parisian cafe with a breakfast combo including a melt-in-your-mouth croissant, baguette, and jam 27,000kip. Happy hour 5-8pm; *apéritifs* 13,000-15,000kip; wine 10,000kip. Open daily 7am-10pm. ❸

Luang Prabang Bakery, on Sisavangvong Rd. 50m east of the Royal Palace. Superb home-baked goodies. Lao and Western menu. Big baguette sandwiches 12,000-15,000kip; pastries 5000kip and up; pizza 38,000kip. Open daily 7am-10pm. ❷

Indochina Restaurant, on Sisavangvong Rd. across from Luang Prabang Bakery, is a backpacker haven with simple decor but tasty food; delicious yellow mushrooms with chicken in coconut milk (25,000kip). ❸

ENTERTAINMENT

Luang Prabang's many cafes and the restaurants along Sisavangvong Rd. are popular and pleasant places to have a beer or a cup of coffee in the evening. **Café Ban Vat Sen** (see **Food,** above) has happy hour daily 5-8pm (*kir* 15,000kip; red wine 10,000kip). The cool kids go to uber-hip **Hive Bar,** on Chao Sisouphan Rd. on the east side of Mt. Phousi. Hive has happy hour with two-for-one drinks daily 5-9pm.

Next door to Hive is **L'Etranger Books and Tea,** a laid-back, tasteful place to trade in your novels and have a cup of tea; their book selection is way above average, but the best books are only for rent. They show classy films nightly at about 7pm ("We favor art to action!" appears on their business card), and they'll fill up your water bottle for free. (Open M-Sa 8am-10pm, Su 10am-10pm.)

SIGHTS

The former capital of a great Buddhist kingdom, Luang Prabang still bears the vestiges of its glorious past. Most notable are its many *wats*, which show off the Luang Prabang-style five-tier roofs that dot the city. Many of the most interesting sights line **Sisavangvong Road,** which culminates with the magnificent Wat Xieng Thong. If you have time for only a few sights, start there and work your way up to the Royal Palace and Museum, Wat Mai, and Mt. Phousi. *Wats* are locked to prevent theft, but a polite request can open them.

WAT XIENG THONG (TEMPLE OF THE GOLDEN CITY). Built by King Setthathirat in 1559, the temple is widely regarded as the *magnum opus* of Lao religious architecture, boasting elaborate golden reliefs and a mosaic of the Buddhist Tree of Life. The pagoda on the right when entering from Sisavangvong Rd. houses King Sisavangvong's funeral chariot, used to transport the funerary urn after his death in 1959. *(On Souvanna Khampong Rd. near the Mekong River. Open daily 6am-5pm. 5000kip.)*

ROYAL PALACE AND NATIONAL MUSEUM. Built by King Sisavangvong in 1904, the Royal Palace was the home of the royal family until the monarchy was abolished in 1975. It houses a copy of the **Pha Bang,** a golden Buddha that is Lao Buddhism's most revered image. A gift to Lane Xang's first king from the Khmer court in the 1300s, the original figure is made of 50kg of pure gold and is sealed in a Vientiane bank vault. The elephant motif seen in much of the palace symbolizes the kingdoms of Luang Prabang, Champasak, and Vientiane, which were unified under Lane Xang in the 15th century. Inside the Royal Palace is the National Museum, a fine collection of Lao art. *(Next to Wat Mai. Museum open M and W-Su 8-11am and 1:30-4pm; last entry 3:30pm. No bare thighs, upper arms, or midriffs. No photos. 10,000kip.)*

MOUNT PHOUSI (MARVELOUS MOUNTAIN). Despite its name, "Mt." Phousi is not very high. A leisurely climb up 329 steps takes visitors to the small **Wat Chom Phousi,** whose glittering *stupa* is visible from miles away. There is no better spot to take in Luang Prabang's sunsets, as every tourist in town well knows. Past the *wat* and up a staircase on the left, a rotund Buddha sits at the entrance of a cave. Bring a flashlight. Beyond the pavilion is a deep footprint of the Buddha. Continuing along the path down the mountain leads to an exit onto Sisavangvong Rd. *(Open daily 6am-6pm. 8000kip.)*

WAT MAI. It took 70 years to construct this impressive *wat*. It was completed in 1797 and housed the Pha Bang Buddha from 1894 to 1947. The north side of the *wat* is adorned with gold bas-reliefs depicting the story of *Veisantara*, Buddha's ultimate mortal reincarnation. *(Opposite Mt. Phousi. Open daily 6am-late.)*

WAT WISOUNNARATH. Built in 1523, this *wat* was razed by Chinese mercenaries and then rebuilt at the turn of the 19th century. The towering *sim* houses Buddhist art, overseen by the largest Buddha in the city. Stacked haphazardly along the walls are hundreds of Buddha images. Also on the temple grounds, **That Mak Mo Stupa** (aptly named the **"Melon Stupa"**) was constructed in 1504 and held many Buddha statues that are now on display in the National Museum. *(Opposite the tourist office and the Red Cross. Open daily 5am-5:30pm.)*

OTHER SIGHTS. **Wat That Luang,** the final resting place of many royals, including King Sisavangvong, is another sunset-viewing spot. *(Start at Nam Phou Fountain and walk out of town on Phothisarath Rd.; That Luang is 3 blocks down on the left, behind a soccer field.)* **Wat Prabouthabat** was built in the 1950s with money from local Chinese and Vietnamese communities. Be sure to see the beautiful river view at the back of the temple. *(Starting from Nam Phou Fountain, walk out of town on Phothisarath Rd. At a large intersection after 500m, pass a Shell station on your left and the Kaysone Monument on your right; take your next right after 25m down a dirt road. The wat is at the end of the road.)*

SHOPPING

Luang Prabang's **markets,** though not large by Southeast Asian standards, are some of the city's most engrossing sights. **Talat Dara,** at the intersection of Kitsalat Setthathirat and Samsenthai Rd., sells everything imaginable. (Open daily 6am-6pm.) **Talat Tha Heua** is on Kitsalat Setthathirat Rd. near the waterfront. It's hard to miss the easygoing **night market,** geared almost exclusively toward tourists, on Sisavangvong Rd. (between Mt. Phousi and the Royal Palace). It's a great place to buy souvenirs: silk tapestries, paper lanterns, and, yes, Beerlao t-shirts. (Open daily dusk-9pm or later.) **Handicraft** and **textile shops** along **Phothisarath Road** display a wide range of products crafted from traditional woven fabrics including silks and cottons. This industry accounts for much of Luang Prabang's trade.

DAYTRIPS FROM LUANG PRABANG

KHOUANG SY WATERFALL. Numerous pools of cool, crystal water dot the slope of the hill making the waterfall a popular swimming spot for travelers despite "Do Not Swim" signs next to the pools at the base of the falls. Climb the steps cut into the clay slope to the pool at the first tier. From here you can cross the river and climb natural, water-eroded steps to the top. The view of the jungle from the top pool is amazing, but be careful—the steps are steep and slippery. Look for the tiger in a cage on the right of the path up to the falls. *(30km south of the city. Take a* tuk tuk *(50min., US$10) or a minibus (US$15-20). 15,000kip.)*

PAK OU CAVES. **Tham Ting** (lower) and **Tham Phum** (upper), are home to hundreds of Buddha statues. The boat journey has fantastic scenery and is worth the trip in itself. Every April during **Phimai** (Lao New Year), thousands flock to the caves to pray, a tradition dating back to King Setthathirat's discovery of the caves in the 1500s. Bring a flashlight. Close to the caves is **Xang Hai Village,** famed for its *lao khao* (rice whiskey) distillation industry. Locals brew the liquor from sticky-rice in oil drums along the riverbank. Traditionally, women drink the less abrasive colored whiskey, but locals are happy to provide the stronger variety to anyone who dares. *(At the confluence of the Mekong and Nam Ou Rivers, 25km upriver from Luang Prabang. Charter a boat on Souvanna Khamg Rd., at the bank of the Mekong River (1hr., US$10 per boat, up to 4 people; larger boats may cost more) or* tuk tuk *(1hr., US$10-12, up to 6 people) to Pak Ou Village and hire a boat to the caves (5000kip per person). 8000kip.)*

LAOS

ACROSS THE RIVER. Few temples match the excellent location of **Wat Long Khoune,** in a tranquil tropical garden above the Mekong. **Wat Tham** (Temple Cave) is 20m up the path from Wat Long Khoune. A passageway twists 50m underground, ending at a thick quartz stalactite\. Monks guide spelunkers and point out Buddha statues and rock formations along the way. Bring a flashlight. *(To get to the other bank, hire boats (bargaining starts at 15,000kip each way) all along the Mekong River.)*

CRAFT VILLAGES. Each of the craft villages near Luang Prabang specializes in a specific item. **Ban Phanom,** a weaving village 4km east of the city on the banks of the Nam Khan River, is a 300-year-old Lu village where many villagers have served as royal weavers and tailors. Come early before tour groups arrive. In **Ban Chan,** 45km south of Luang Prabang, on the opposite of the Mekong River, the entire village participates in making large *thong* (water jugs) and clay roofing tiles. Visitors can watch the entire process, from grinding clumps of clay into fine sand to baking the pots and tiles in large underground kilns. **Ban Xang Chang,** 7km east of Luang Prabang, is home to a traditional paper-producing workshop. A small shop sells paper products, like notebooks for 8000-20,000kip. *(To get to Ban Phanom by bicycle, head away from Mt. Phousi on Chao Xomphou Rd. Just after passing Mittaphab Market on the right, take a left at a large intersection. Follow the road for 1km; after Vannaphone Guest House, at a green sign reading "B. Phanom," take a right onto a dirt road. Follow the road into the village. To get to Ban Chan, hire a boat (40,000kip) from Luang Prabang or Ban Chiang Man.)*

> **!** The US Department of State issued a Public Announcement (one step below a travel advisory) in February 2000 advising its citizens to avoid travel to Xieng Khouang Province (except for Phonsavan and the districts of Muang Kham and Muang Nong Haet) due to ongoing insurgent and bandit activity. Ask your embassy for up-to-date conditions before traveling there. Also note that Rte. 7, the main road to Phonsavan from Vientiane, is periodically closed due to bad conditions. It is always closed during rainy season.

PHONSAVAN (XIENG KHOUANG)

The terrain of Xieng Khouang Province, northeast of Vientiane along the Vietnamese border, is composed of rugged mountains and beautiful rolling hills, more reminiscent of Ireland than Indochina. During November and December, the mountains near the border blaze with poppy blossoms; opium, grown by the hilltribes, is the province's chief cash crop. Xieng Khouang is best known for its history, both ancient and modern. On the ancient side is Thong Hay Hin (Plain of Jars), an area scattered with mysterious 3000-year-old stone vessels that continue to puzzle archaeologists today. In the 20th century, Xieng Khouang was one of two Lao provinces heavily bombed during the Vietnam War. US B-52s damaged Xieng Khouang City so severely that after the war the provincial capital was moved from there to Phonsavan, 36km north. The landscape is pocked with craters, and cluster bombs that litter the countryside still exact a gruesome toll on limbs and lives.

> **!** All listings in Phonsavan, including Plain of Jars, Xieng Khouang Province, and Muang Kham District were updated as of January 2004.

TRANSPORTATION

Flights: Xieng Khouang Airport, 5km from town down Rte. 4 (5000kip by *tuk tuk*). To **Luang Prabang** (3 per week, US$35; may be cancelled if demand is low) and **Vientiane** (1 per day, US$46). **Lao Airlines** (☎312 027) is about 1km out of town, next door to the bank. Book a day before departure. Open M-F 8am-12:30pm and 1:30-4pm, Sa-Su 8am-12:30pm.

Buses: Ramshackle buses and trucks leave from an empty lot on Rte. 7 adjacent to the market. Buses go to: **Ban Thatcho** (1hr.; noon, 3pm; 500kip); **Luang Prabang** (10hr.; 8am; 60,000kip or more); **Vientiane** (8-10hr.; 7:15, 8:45am, 8pm; 60,000kip); **Oudomxay** (8:30am; 70,000kip); **Vang Vieng** (7:30am; 55,000kip); **Vang Vieng VIP bus** (7:45am; 80,000kip).

SWALLOW IT DOWN

Phonsavan's rolling hills are pockmarked by craters—a reminder of the bombing it suffered during the Indochina War. If you look closely, though, you can see depressions that are not circular (as bomb craters are), but rectangular. These are man-made and used by locals to catch swallows (a migratory bird), which are an unusual and important part of Xieng Khouang Province's traditional cuisine.

Locals catch the swallows in large nets, often scores of them at once. In order to lure the birds into the snares, they light fires, driving swarms of insects from the grass. The swallows show up for an easy meal, but end up becoming one themselves.

Once caught, the swallows are pickled (hence their Lao name, *nok ann tong,* or "sour swallow"), and then fried or stewed. The birds are a seasonal favorite, particularly among the older people in the province. The best time of year to enjoy these delicacies is usually in late August or early September.

Nok ann tong is not only an important local specialty in Xieng Khouang, it also serves as a source of cultural common ground among natives. While traveling, for example, if someone from Xieng Khouang sees someone else he suspects is also from Xieng Khouang, he will walk up and softly say, "swallow." If he is understood, the two know that they came from the same place.

Local Transportation: Tuk tuks go anywhere except the Plain of Jars. 10,000kip or less.

Rentals: Tour companies rent **cars** and 4WD vehicles with driver. Prices vary from US$25-50 or more, depending on destination. Minibus with room for 8, US$120. Available at guesthouses, tour agencies, or the tourist office.

ORIENTATION AND PRACTICAL INFORMATION

Phonsavan is organized around the T-shaped intersection of **Route 7,** which runs east-west, and **Route 1** (also called **Phonsavan Road**), which runs north-south. The **bus station** is a dirt lot at the top of the T; just east on Rte. 7 is the **dry market,** and across the street is the **post office.** Continuing east on Rte. 7 there are several guesthouses and restaurants and **Internet** cafes. Heading east on Rte. 7, away from the bus station, turn left down a dirt road opposite Doukkhoune Guest House to get to the **tourict information office.** To get to **Lao Airline** and the **bank,** walk about 1km south on Rte. 1 from the main intersection; on the right will be the airline office, and then the bank. Follow Rte. 7 west a few kilometers out of the center of town to get to **Route 4;** to the south on Rte. 4 are the orphan school, government buildings, a **hospital,** and, eventually, the **airport.**

Tours: The **Xieng Khouang Tourism Office** (☎312 217), 50m down the road across the street from Doukkhoune Guest House, is the best place to start (6-8hr. tours, US$6-34 per person). Open daily 8am-4pm. Vong, who works for **Lanexang Travel and Tour** (☎312 171; at Doukkhoune Guest House) is reliable but expensive (full day US$40). **Indochina Travel** (☎312 121; www.indochhinatracel.com), across from the bus station, has tours and rents vans, cars, and 4WD vehicles (car to old capital US$25).

Currency Exchange: Lane Xang Bank (☎312 041), on Phonsavan Rd, 1km away from the main intersection. Exchanges traveler's checks. Open M-F 8:30am-4pm. Closer to town, in the market across the street from the post office, is a **Lao Development Bank,** but they won't change traveler's checks. Open M-F 8am-4pm.

Markets: Central market, on Rte. 7 next to the bus station, has clothes, electronics, and everything in between. Open daily around 7:30am-5pm. The nearby **wet market,** on Rte. 1 next to the post office, has fruits, vegetables, and other edibles. Look for the local specialty, *nok an toong* (pickled swallow). Open approximately 6am-sunset.

Police: Xieng Khouang Provincial Police (☎3152 001 and 312 152), on Phonsavan Rd., in a 2-story concrete building in the field opposite the hospital. No English spoken.

Medical Services: Xieng Khouang Military Hospital (☎312 014), on Phonsavan Rd., southwest of town past the provincial hall on the right. Some English spoken. In emergencies, call **Lao Mongolia Hospital** (☎312 166).

Telecom Office: (☎312 001), on Phonsavan Rd., between the post office and wet market. International phonecards and card phone. Open M-F 8am-5pm. AmEx/MC/V.

Internet Access: Available from a couple of shops across Rte. 7 from the dry market. The going rate is 500kip per min.

Post Office: (☎212 208), on the corner of Rte. 7 and Phonsavan Rd. opposite the market. Currency exchange. Open M-F 8:30-11:30am and 1-4:30pm.

ACCOMMODATIONS AND FOOD

Fifty meters past the tourist office, by a cement field, lies the lovely **Kong Keo Guest House ❶**, which has a garden replete with bombshells, bandoliers, and a bamboo thatched-roof bar. (☎211 354; www.kongkeojar.com. Bungalows include breakfast. US$2-3 for rooms; US$5-10 for cute bungalows.) At **Doukkhoune Guest House ❸**, on Rte. 7 near the market, the lobby is decorated with (fake) defused bombs, and they use expended cartridges for keychains. Some rooms are near a disco, and can be noisy at night. (☎312 189. Rooms with bathroom US$2-10 per night.) Despite its unencouraging exterior, **Venearoun Guest House ❸**, on Rte. 750m east of the market, has fine rooms with bath and hot water for US$5 (☎312 1890).

The **wet market** behind the post office sells produce, French bread, and prepared snack foods. (Open daily 6am-sunset.) There are **noodle stands ❶** here and across the street in the **dry market. Sanga Restaurant ❷**, on Rte. 7, is the most popular stand in town. The extensive menu has huge portions. (Steak with fries 12,000kip; most entrees 10,000-20,000kip. Open daily 6:30-9pm.) **Phone Keo Restaurant ❶**, across the street by Photo Express, serves good sweet-and-sour pork (13,000kip) and fruit shakes. (Most entrees 10,000-15,000kip. Open daily 11am-11pm.)

DAYTRIPS FROM PHONSAVAN

THONG HAY HIN (PLAIN OF JARS)

The best way to see the plains is a day-tour of the 3 main jar sights. Tours cost US$6-34 per person depending on group size. Seen individually, sights cost 7000kip each.

The Plain of Jars, an archaeological puzzle, consists of 3000 jars scattered in clusters on hilltops. The largest jars are up to 3.5m high and weigh as much as three cars. They are believed to be between 2500 and 3000 years old. One theory, strengthened by the discovery of human remains in one of the jars in 1963, holds that the jars are funerary urns hewn from solid stone by ancestors of the Khamu people. Others guess that an ancient civilization used the jars to store rice or wine; some locals claim that the jars were Stone Age kegs, used to brew vats of *lao khao* for the troops of a Chinese king after their victory on the Bolovens Plateau. The most impressive sight is **Hay Hin 1,** 12km from town down Rte. 4: over 200 urns cover three hilltops marked by bomb craters, including the heaviest urn (3.7 tons) and a cave where locals took shelter during the American War. **Hay Hin 2** (24km) and **Hay Hin 3** (32km) are accessible by car, and, during the rainy season, by Russian jeeps. The jars are smaller than those of Hay Hin 1, but Hay Hin 2 boasts the longest jar (3.5m) and a sweeping view of the landscape. Hay Hin 3, reachable by foot through paddy fields and villages, is known for the Buddha statues in its jars.

SHAKY GROUND. Laos is still fighting a war that ended nearly three decades ago for its primary combatants. Officially neutral, Laos allowed North Vietnamese troops on its land to start the Hồ Chí Minh Trail, a conduit for supplies that eventually spelled ruin for both the South Vietnamese and US troops. Neutrality came with a price: nearly three million tons of explosives dropped in a never-ending series of raids, one every eight minutes every day for nine years. Around 30% of that ordnance—only 4% of it actual mines—never exploded and is still there, experts reckon. International NGOs have tried to help, but the Lao government thinks it can do the job with locally trained staff. Time will tell, but it's not on the Lao side. The largest building in Phonsavanh, one of the target areas during "The War," is an orphanage with 500 residents, their parents the victims of ordnance in supposedly clear paddies. The school plans to accept another 300 students soon. Areas immediately surrounding the jars are clear of mines and cluster bombs, but the rest of the countryside is not safe. Permission from the local Department of Commerce and Tourism (on Rte. 4 near the governor's office) is required to get to the official sights. Though *tuk tuk* drivers will offer to take you to the Plain for cheaper prices than most package tours, it is recommended to stick to well-trodden paths and to go with an authorized guide.

XIENG KHOUANG PROVINCE

Most travelers choose from the many tour options found at the Tourist Information office, or at private agencies like Lane Xang Travel or Indochina Travel. It's cheapest to get a group of people interested in seeing the sights together and then organize a tour. If hiring a guide is too expensive, look into hiring a car and driver (US$25 and up). You may also be able to persuade a tuk tuk *to take you to some of the closer attractions.*

MUANG KHA/XIENG KHOUANG CITY (ANCIENT CAPITAL)

Thirty-six kilometers from Phonsavanh, but access is difficult in the rainy season; take a tour, tuk tuk, *or see if the local bus is running.*

Despite major bombing during the American War, the city boasts two temples and a few Buddhas; beyond are Hmong villages, hot springs, and waterfalls, best reached by foot (with a guide to avoid bombs).

BAN DONG AND BAN THATCHO

Ban Dong is near Hay Hin 2, and Ban Thatcho is 24km outside of Phonsavan.

Ban Dong and Ban Thatcho are commonly visited Hmong villages; travelers go to see village life and shop for souvenirs. If you're lucky, you may see the Hmong in their beautiful costumes.

MUANG KHAM AND ENVIRONS

The people of Muang Kham District have put war scraps to clever use and have molded scrap metal and discarded shells into farmyard troughs, fences, and souvenirs. **Tham Phyu,** a cave 56km from Phonsavan, was a civilian bomb shelter until an aircraft fired a rocket into the cave in 1968, killing all 400 people. The nearby Hmong villages are also worth exploring. Despite the Lao government's war on drugs, these villages are interspersed with poppy fields. It is best to go with a guide.

LUANG NAM THA ☎86

Relaxed and friendly Luang Nam Tha is the principal city of Laos's most ethnically diverse region. Surrounded by luscious landscapes and home to the Nam Tha National Biodiversity Conservation area, it's a picturesque gateway to surrounding villages and also to the Chinese border crossing at Boten.

eTravel
exploration
education
excitement
experience
STA TRAVEL
www.statravel.com
CST #1017560-40
(800) 351.3214
WE'VE BEEN PLANNING ONE TRIP FOR 25 YEARS. YOURS.
STUDENT TRAVEL & BEYOND

TRANSPORTATION. The **airport** is 7km south of town. The offices of **Lao Aviation** are located there (☎312 180. Open daily 8-11:30am and 1:30-4pm). Flights go to Luang Prabang (F, US$39) and Vientiane (daily, US$74). Low-season flights may be cancelled due to demand; check for current schedules. The tourist information boards at the **bus station** (☎211 977) and guesthouses list up-to-date travel info. Most **buses** depart by 8:30am or when full, and they fill up quickly; show up around 7 or 7:30am. Buses and **songthaew** depart daily from the bus station for: Bokeo (8hr.; 8:30, 10:30am; 65,000kip); Boten (2hr.; every 2hr. 9am-3pm; 12,000kip); Muang Long (4hr.; noon, 7pm; 32,000kip); Muang Sing (2-2½hr.; 6 per day 8am-4pm; 10,000kip); Nalae (3hr.; 9:30am; 30,000kip); Oudomxay (4-5½hr.; 8:30, 11:30am; 23,000kip). During the rainy season, the road to Huay Xai is impassable, but *songthaew* may ply the route during the dry season (8-11 hours). **Boat** information is posted at the bus station. Call the Boatmen's Association (☎211 305) to arrange transport to Nalae, Pak Tha, and Huay Xai. The suggested price is US$100 per boat, which carry 4-10 people. The landing is 7km south of Luang Nam Tha; to get there, take a *tuk tuk* (10,000kip). It may be quicker to hire a boat to Pak Tha on the Mekong (US$65-95) and then a faster boat to Huay Xai or Luang Prabang. Ask what supplies to bring; trips are lengthy and the boats stop infrequently.

ORIENTATION AND PRACTICAL INFORMATION. Luang Nam Tha lies along the main north-south road **(Route 3)** 217km northeast of Huay Xai and 117km northwest of Oudomxay via Rte. 2. Boats and *songthaew* will drop you off at the **bus lot,** at the south edge of town. To get to the town center from the ticket office, walk left out of the bus lot, then take your next left, and then the next right. This will bring you to Rte. 3, the main drag. The **airport** and **boat landing** on the Nam Tha River both lie off this road 7km south of town; heading north on the same road leads to **Muang Sing. Lao Development Bank** is a few blocks down this road, and changes US dollars, Thai baht, Chinese yuan, and traveler's checks into kip. (☎312 292. Open M-F 8:30am-3:30pm.) **Bank for Exterior Commerce,** across from Manychan Guest House on the same road, offers Visa cash advances. (☎211 141. Open daily 8:30am-3pm.) Stores next to Manychan Guest House **rent bicycles** (10,000-18,000kip per day; US$50 deposit). The **Telecom Office,** 100m past Lane Xang Bank, provides international phone and fax service. (☎312 004. Open M-F 8am-noon and 1-5pm.) Phone cards are available at the Telecom Office and various shops; look for the green "INT" sign. The yellow **post office** (☎312 007) is opposite the Telecom Office. The bus lot and **hospital** are at the southern edge of town. The covered **market,** easy to miss, is across from Manychan Guest House and set back back from the street about 20m. **Phonxay Pharmacie** (☎312 238) and **Sivilang Pharmacy** (☎312 438) are next to Manychan Guest House and Wildside. The **Nam Tha Ecotourism Office** (☎312 047) is off the main road, behind the post office. They organize excursions to hill-tribe villages and sell maps of Luang Nam Tha and its surroundings. For **Internet** access head to **Just For Fun,** across the street a block down from Manychan Guest House. (Open daily 7:30am-10pm; 600kip per min.) They also have tasty banana cake (5000kip) and can burn digital photos onto a CD.

ACCOMMODATIONS AND FOOD. Luang Nam Tha has many budget accommodations near the bus lot and on the main road (Rte. 3) north of the lot. The best value is **Buonthaxong Guest House ❶** (☎312 356), where clean rooms with mosquito nets are 25,000kip; shared bathrooms have squat toilets and a hot shower. From the bus station ticket office, turn left and walk until you come to Buonthaxong. **Manychan Guest House ❶** is on the main road across from the post office. The friendly staff speaks English and offers comfortable rooms with clean, shared baths. (☎312 209. Curfew 10pm. Doubles with hot water and squat toilets

30,000kip.) Facing the post office, turn right and walk about 500m to find **Darasavath Guest House ❸** on your left. Darasavath features bungalow-style rooms and a garden restaurant/bar. (Rooms 40,000kip.) At the north end of the main road, past Kaysone Monument, is **Sing Savananh Guest House ❶**, set apart by its clean rooms and family feel. (☎211 141. Rooms with squat toilets and mosquito nets US$3.)

Many guesthouses have restaurants serving Lao and Western dishes. **Chit ta Phorne ❶**, three doors to the right of Palanh Guest House and across the street from Manychan, serves delicious Lao food. Fried noodles with egg and pineapple come with soup and tea (7000kip). **Panda Restaurant ❶**, on the road parallel to Rte. 3, has excellent Chinese and Lao food. (Entrees 6000-15,000kip.)

SIGHTS. The town itself offers little, but superb excursions and scenery are a few minutes away by bicycle. Keep to roads and well-trodden paths. The **Nam Tha National Biodiversity Conservation Area** is one of the best places to hike pristine forests and see hill-tribes and many endangered animals. Since Nam Tha has only recently been opened to foreigners, you must go with a guide. **Wildside Eco Groups,** on Rte. 3, organizes excursions into the Nam Tha area for groups of four people. (☎211 594; www.lao-wildside.com. 2-day trip US$26 per person.) These trips involve hiking, rafting down the Nam Tha River, and visiting Hmong tribe villages. One popular excursion is to **Hmong Had Yao Village,** 3km down the road to Muang Sing. Head north out of town and continue past the turn-off with the bridge. The **waterfall** at Ban Nam Dee (bargaining starts at 30,000kip for *tuk tuk*), 6km north of Luang Nam Tha off Rte. 3, is worth a detour. From December to March, the waterfall is the site of local paper-making. A visit to **Ban Thong Tai,** past the bridge north of town, affords views of **weaving** and **silk** production. Behind the Kaysone Monument, the local **museum** displays local textiles, clothing, and religious artifacts.

BORDER CROSSING: BOTEN/MOHAN. Boten Village, 60km northeast of Luang Nam Tha and northwest of Oudomxay, is the only legal border crossing between Laos and China, open daily from 8am to 6pm. Boten has two roads: a paved road leading to the border checkpoint and a parallel dirt road with most of the town's buildings. Before the checkpoint, on the left, sits a **Lao Development Bank** that trades Chinese yuan, US dollars, Thai baht, and kip, but no traveler's checks. (Open daily 8am-noon and 1-4pm.) Noodle shops on the dirt road have dorm-style **rooms** (5000kip per person), but you don't want to spend the night here if you can avoid it. For those coming from China, **songthaew** leave, when full, into the early afternoon, to **Luang Nam Tha** (2hr.; 12,000kip) and **Oudomxay** (4hr.; 20,000kip). Walk past the bank on your right; buses leave from a dirt lot 100m down the road on the right side. Remember that, while Chinese yuan are generally negotiable in Boten, they are not commonly used elsewhere in Laos. Bring dollars or baht, or buy some kip. Those crossing into China must have a Chinese visa, available from the Chinese embassy in Vientiane, on hand. After the border checkpoint, you can board a *tuk tuk* to Mohan, China (1-2km, 5 yuan), and proceed to Mengla, the closest sizable town in China's Xishuangbanna region.

MUANG SING

Muang Sing attracts two types of visitors. Travelers make the bumpy journey north from Luang Nam Tha to find a sleepy, one-road town nestled among small villages and rice paddies, just a short walk from rural northern Laos's world of age-old traditions. Villagers, on the other hand, come to Muang Sing as a commercial center—

climbing steep trails to get to the town's lively market, where they conduct their business. The opportunity to witness village life adds to the town's appeal for travelers, who greatly benefit village commerce.

TRANSPORTATION. Muang Sing is 58km northwest of Luang Nam Tha on a bad road (prone to mudslides in the rainy season) that continues 10km to the Chinese border. Arriving from Luang Nam Tha, the **bus** drops off passengers at Muang Sing's large **market,** on the main road. From here, **songthaew** return to Luang Nam Tha when full (2½-3½hr.; 6 per day; 12,000kip). *Songthaew* departure times vary; inquire at the ticket office, and be prepared to wait. **Bicycle** rentals are available from guesthouses (5000-10,000kip per day).

PRACTICAL INFORMATION. Opposite the market, **Lao Development Bank** exchanges currency. (Open M-F 8am-3:30pm.) Left of the bank sits a tiny **post office;** look for the "La Poste" sign. (Open M-F 8am-4pm.) With the market on your right, head up the main road through the center of town. After 200m the road crosses a small bridge; 200m farther down on the left is the **hospital,** a cluster of wooden buildings with blue shutters. (Open 8:30am-4pm). Make **international phone calls** from a small wooden building across the street from the tourist office.

ACCOMMODATIONS AND FOOD. Many cheap accommodations line Muang Sing's main road. **Muang Sing Guest House ❶** offers small but charming double rooms with mosquito nets for US$2 (US$3 with bath). From the market (which is also the bus station) take a right onto the main road; it's 100m past the tourist office on the left. Take a right onto the main road from the market and 20m down on the right you'll find the **Viengxay Guest House ❶.** It has friendly management and a restaurant. (Some rooms with hot water. Rooms 25,000kip.) Out of the way, 7km north of town (*tuk tuk* 5000kip), the **Adima Guest House ❸** is a great base for hikes and visits to hill-tribes. Overlooking rice paddies and mountains 2km from the Chinese border, this guesthouse couldn't be more idyllic. (Restaurant. Rooms US$4-6.) A few **foodstalls ❶**, especially around the market, offer cheap meals.

SIGHTS. Most travelers come to Muang Sing for its remoteness and proximity to ethnic villages. Take a right onto the main road and 50m down on the left-hand side is the **tourist office** (open daily 8-11:30am and 1:30-5pm), which organizes treks to hill-tribe villages (1-day trek US$10 per person; 3-

THE LOCAL STORY

*BETEL*JUICE, *BETEL*JUICE, *BETEL*JUICE!

Few things are as prevalent in Southeast Asia as the chewing of *betel* (pronounced "beetle").

Betel chewers wrap *betel* leaves around slices of areca nut and limestone to form a quid, which produces a mouthful of brick-red juice and a mind full of mellow vibes. When one woman was asked why she chewed *betel,* she laughed and said, "If I don't chew, I won't want to go out to the field and work."

In the past, rulers had *betel*-bearing slaves, and the *betel* trade did great things for Penang. *Betel* is used in all manner of social functions, from offerings in the Thai Water Festival to Vietnamese courtships to Burmese divorces. In many languages, *betel* and marriage are linked, and in many cultures, the exchange of *betel* is the starting point for a romantic relationship and a necessity for mind-melting sex. (The *betel* chewer's red lips and stained teeth were once considered sexy throughout Southeast Asia.)

Nobody knows whether *betel* is addictive or carcinogenic, though many believe that it is outmoded. Thailand tried to outlaw it in 1945, and in the 1950s the Vietnamese Communists launched a campaign against this supposed *hu tuc* (backward custom). As Southeast Asia continues to Westernize, *betel*-chewing has declined, and few now sport the telltale ring around the mouth.

days, 2-nights US$34). If you're interested in trekking, make friends on the bus up to Muang Sing or in the tourist office, as you generally need a group of 3-6 people. A bike ride through the surrounding countryside is also a nice way to spend a day. The **morning market** offers another chance to experience local culture. Market activity dies down by 7:30-8am, so come early. During the rainy season, market activity may drop, as travel gets difficult. Muang Sing also has a small museum with a few photographs and artifacts (5000kip). Turn right out of the market and walk 300m; it's on the left.

OUDOMXAY (MOUNG XAI) ☎81

Oudomxay, located halfway between Luang Prabang and Luang Nam Tha, is convenient as a transportation hub. Although it's a pleasant little town, it has few tourist attractions. Most travelers, eager to make the most of the limited time their visas allow, spend the night only if the bus schedule necessitates it.

TRANSPORTATION. The **airport** is 1km outside town off the road to Pakbeng. **Lao Aviation** (☎312 146) flies to Vientiane (Tu, Th, Sa; US$66). Buy tickets at least a day in advance from the Lao Aviation desk at the airport. Scheduled flights may be cancelled if demand is low. **Buses, trucks,** and **songthaew** leave—but only when full—from a lot near the bridge. Departures start between 8 and 9am, and continue into the afternoon, going to: Boten (5hr.; up to 3 per day; 19,000kip); **Luang Nam Tha** (4-5hr.; 8, 11am, 2pm; 23,000kip); Luang Prabang (5-6hr.; 3-4 per day; 30,000kip); Pakbeng (7hr.; 8-9am or later; 26,500kip). To get to Nong Khiew take a Luang Prabang-bound bus to Nambak and continue from there. You can also reach Luang Prabang from via Pak Mong (3hr.; 3-4 per day; 12,000kip).

ORIENTATION AND PRACTICAL INFORMATION. Oudomxay lies at the intersection of **Route 1,** which leads east to Nambak and Nong Khiew, and **Route 2,** which heads north to Boten and Luang Nam Tha, and south to Pakbeng. **Lao Development Bank,** about 400m up Rte. 1 from the intersection (☎312 059. Open M-F 8:30am-4pm), and the **Bank for Exterior Commerce,** on Rte. 1 600m out of the intersection (☎211 263; open M-F 8:30am-3:30pm), **exchange currency** and traveler's checks. The **hospital** is 3km south on Rte. 1., 400m down the first road on the right after Rte. 1 becomes a dirt road (☎312 043; open M-F 8am-noon and 1-4pm); the **Telecom Office,** on Rte. 2, 100m from the main intersection away from the pagoda hill on the right, with international phone/fax (☎312 001; open M-F 8-11:30am and 1:30-4:30pm); a box for **international calls,** opposite the Bank for Exterior Commerce; a few **Internet** shops across the bridge, all of which charge 700kip per min.; and the **post office,** next to the Telecom Office (☎312 007; open M-F 8-11:30am and 1:30-4:30pm). **Postal Code:** 0400. Just before the bridge is the **Tourist Office,** which rents bicycles and motorbikes and organizes excursions (☎211 797; not much English spoken). Also, **Oudomxay has electricity from 6pm-6am.**

LAOS

ACCOMMODATIONS AND FOOD. A family feel and friendly owners sets **Sivankham Guest House ❶,** across the bridge after the main intersection, apart from others. Follow signs to "Chilas Children Feed School," which is next door. (☎312 253. Shared baths, squat toilet. Rooms US$3.) **Pholay Guest House ❷,** on Rte. 2 100m past the bridge on the right before the gas station, has clean rooms with private baths and a restaurant downstairs. (☎312 324. Doubles 30,000kip.) Pricey but very comfortable and close to the bus station is **Litthavixay Guest House ❷** (☎212 175; rooms with bathroom US$6); Litthavixay has Internet access when the power is on (700kip per minute). From the intersection, cross the bridge and 200m down on the left to the simple **Linda 2 Guest House ❷** (☎211 242. Doubles US$4).

The **market** in Oudomxay offers fresh fruit and vegetables, and every morning **vendors on bicycles** ❶ serve baguettes with condensed milk filling (2000kip). From the main intersection, walk across the bridge and after 100m look down a side-street on the left for **Kanya's Restaurant** ❷ (☎312 077. Entrees 6000-18,000kip). Pleasant **Phonsay Guest House Restaurant** ❶ serves good, simple food (fried rice 8000kip). **Sainamkor Restaurant** ❷, at the bridge on Rte. 2, takes its name from the river it overlooks. It serves substantial meals ranging from eel to duck.

SIGHTS AND ENTERTAINMENT. To ease the pain inflicted by bumpy roads, the **Red Cross** operates an **herbal sauna and massage** center behind Phon Xay Hotel down the road from Sivankham Guest House. (☎312 391. Sauna 10,000kip. 1hr. massage 20,000kip. Open daily 3-7pm.) A **snooker hall** next to Sainamkor Restaurant has four tables. The large **market** (open daily 7am-7pm), a block off Rte. 2, sells colorful wall-hangings and clothes and, because it attracts fewer tourists, presents a different dynamic from the markets in Luang Nam Tha or Vientiane. The eye-catching **pagoda,** with a panoramic view of the town and countryside, is the only other site worthy of a detour. As with all the northern towns, beautiful landscapes await those who walk along the roads leading away from town.

PAKBENG

On the threshold of dense primary forest at the confluence of the Nam Beng and Mekong Rivers, tiny Pakbeng is a colorful respite from a long, lazy day on the Mekong. Most travelers stay one night on their way heading northwest to the Thai border or east to Luang Prabang, and find it enough to soak in Pakbeng's ambience; others find its remoteness enticing enough to extend their visit.

One-road Pakbeng winds along Rte. 2 for 2km. **Buses, trucks,** and **songthaew** depart when full from a lot out of town (*tuk tuks* leave from the pier; 5000kip to get there) for Oudomxay (7hr.; 8am until passengers stop showing up; 27,000kip). **Slow boats** leave for Luang Prabang (7-10hr.; 75,000kip) and Huay Xai (9-11hr.; 75,000kip). **Speedboats** depart to Luang Prabang (3hr.; leave 8am-4pm when full; 156,000kip) and Huay Xai (3hr.; leave 8am-4pm when full; 156,000kip). There is no official currency exchange in Pakbeng, although you can try the market 1km from the pier to the left. A **pharmacy** is on the main road 500m from the pier on the right-hand side opposite an improvised cinema. (Open daily 8am-10pm.) The local **hospital,** 1km from the pier on the right, sits opposite the **post office.** Pakbeng has no telephone office, and has **electricity from 6pm to 6am.**

Sarika Guest House ❶, the large white building next to the ticket office, is pricier but larger than most other accommodations. (Doubles with private bath US$5.) Its **restaurant** (entrees 8,000-15,000kip) overlooks the Mekong. Of the dozens of guesthouses near the pier, a few stand out for cleanliness and service. **Mon Savan Guest House** ❶, 300m left from the pier, has clean, small doubles in bamboo houses (20,000kip with mosquito net and fan). A dozen restaurants cluster around the guesthouses in and around town. All offer standard, though greasy, Lao rice and noodle dishes. Most open daily 6:30am-10pm. **Pine Kham Restaurant** ❷, 200m left from the pier, and **Bounmy Restaurant** ❷, 100m farther, serve large fried rice dishes and soup (10,000-15,000kip). The **main market,** 300m left from the pier, is excellent for fruits and other munchies; don't forget to buy food and water for the boat.

HUAY XAI ☎084

Huay Xai is a Thai border town and Laos's little link to the infamous Golden Triangle. Most travelers stay just long enough to arrange the rest of their stay in Laos, but those who linger get a glimpse of a country where children play in the streets, the power goes out during storms, and a short walk brings you to hill-tribe villages.

TRANSPORTATION. Ferries to and from Chiang Khong (20฿) dock right by the town center, down behind the Maniratn Hotel. They leave when full from 8am-6pm, which are the official hours of the **border passport control** by the landing. **Speedboats** to Luang Prabang (6-7hr.; 8-9am; 280,000kip) via Pakbeng (3-4hr.; 115,000kip) depart from a small pier 5km south of town (2000kip per person by *tuk tuk*). **Slow boats** heading north and south share a landing 1.5km north of the town center (past Aramid Guest House, down a short road to the left). Boats go to Luang Prabang (2 days, overnight in Pakbeng; 130,000kip) and Pakbeng (5½hr.; 65,000kip). Speedboats heading upriver dock north of the slow boats. During the dry season, **passenger trucks** and **buses** leave from a station by the market for Luang Nam Tha (up to 7hr.; leaves early; 65,000kip). **Lao Aviation** has flights (subject to weather conditions and frequently postponed during rainy season) to: Luang Prabang (1hr.; W, Sa; US$43); Vientiane (4-5 per week, US$81). The airstrip is 7km south of town; pay 4000kip per person for a *tuk tuk*. With your back to the Maniratn Hotel, head right, then take the first left; the Lao Aviation office is 30m down. (☎211 026. Open daily 8am-4pm.) Many travel agents line the main street and can arrange excursions and further travel within Laos. **Udomkai Travel** (☎211 277), across the street from the post office, is open daily 8am-3:30pm.

ORIENTATION AND PRACTICAL INFORMATION. North of Luang Prabang and a few hundred meters east of Chiang Khong, Thailand, tiny Huay Xai hugs the Mekong. The main road runs north-south parallel to the river, and a small road passes shops and the customs to the pier on the Mekong. Perpendicular to the main road and opposite the pier, steps lead up the hill to a **Buddhist temple.** Heading south, the main road also passes a **market** to the left and forks west (away from the river) toward the old French **Fort Carno,** now occupied by Lao officials. A dirt track on the way (to the left) leads uptown to the **post office.**

The **Bokeo Tourism Authority Office** has free maps. (Open M-F 9am-4pm.) The **police** are in a stucco house on the hill above the slow boat landing. **Lane Xang Bank** (☎312 020), opposite Aramid Guest House's back entrance, cashes traveler's checks and exchanges US dollars and Thai baht. A counter by the customs office on the Mekong provides similar services. (Open M-Sa 8:30am-5pm.) A smaller market sits at the center of town opposite the post office. **Pharmacies** dot the main road and **Bokeo Hospital** is on a back road, 1km south of the bank. The **post office** is to the left on a dirt track when you are heading south on the main road. (☎312 026. Open M-F 8am-noon and 1-4pm.) An **international card phone** is outside.

ACCOMMODATIONS AND FOOD. Most places in town are similar, the nicest being **Aramid Guest House ❸**, on the main road, 1km north of the border ferry, and close to the slow boat dock. From the slow boats, take a right at the top of the road from the pier and go straight for 200m. Aramid rents bicycles and has a decent restaurant. (☎211 040. Doubles US$5.) **Maniratn Hotel ❸** (☎312 040), on the main road, has wood-floored doubles with private baths for US$3-4. **Keochampa Hotel ❸**, left from the border pier, is a comfortable, modern option with decent rooms. (☎312 035. Doubles US$5.) Restaurants cluster along the main road; **Nutpop Restaurant ❶**, toward the slow boat pier and just before the bridge, serves delicious meals for 6000-15,000kip in an attractive outdoor garden. Next to the pier for the ferry to Thailand, **KhemKhong Restaurant ❶** offers good food for 8000-15,000kip, accompanied by beautiful sunset views of the Mekong. The **Lao-Chinese Restaurant ❶** north of the pier also serves entrees for 8000-15,000kip. There are two good **foodstalls ❶** at the pier (soup 5000kip); the market has lunchtime **foodstalls ❶**.

SOUTHERN LAOS

SAVANNAKHET ☎41

Nearly 500km south of Vientiane and on the west bank of the Mekong, Savannakhet—"Savan" to locals—is the center of Laos's most populated province. The town's charm lies in its odd mix of both colonial French and modern architecture and its idyllic riverside walk. Many say that the "PDR" in "Lao PDR" stands for "Please Don't Rush"; those who live in Savannakhet can tell you why. Most travelers don't stop for long en route to the Vietnamese cities of Huế and Đà Nẵng or to Wat Phu and the 4000 Islands region farther south.

TRANSPORTATION

Flights: Purchase tickets at the airport. Flights to **Pakse** (3 per week, US$42) and **Vientiane** (2 per week, US$57). Schedule is erratic; buy tickets at least 1 day ahead and confirm your seat the day of the flight.

Buses: The **bus station** (☎213 920) is at the intersection of Sisavangvong and Visouthat Rd., 1.5km north of the town center. Buses to **Pakse** (4-6hr.; 7, 9am, noon, 1:30, 4:30, 11:30pm; 25,000kip) and **Vientiane** (9hr.; several per day 6am-12:30pm; 30,000kip). Buses along the unpaved road will eventually lead you to **Vietnam: Đà Nẵng** (18-21hr.; Tu-W, F-Sa 4pm; 110,000kip); **Hà nội** (27hr., Sa 7pm, US$20); **Huế** (14hr.; M-Tu 4pm; 90,000kip). Buses also leave daily for border town **Lao Bảo** (6-7hr.; 6:30, 11:30am; 45,000kip), where further transportation to Vietnam is available.

Ferries: Pier is at the immigration office, across from Simuang-Tha Heua Rd. intersection. Buy tickets at the desk downstairs to **Mukdahan, Thailand** (15min.; M-F 9:10, 10, 11:10am, 1:30, 2:30, 4:30pm; 12,000kip or 50฿). Get your exit stamp for Laos at the window, buy a ferry ticket, cross the river, and get your entrance stamp for Thailand. Once in Mukdahan, you can catch a bus to destinations like **Bangkok** (p. 664), or you can stay the night. (See **Mukdahan,** p. 740.) You can get a Thai visa in Savannakhet.

Local Transportation: Tuk tuks roam streets in large numbers 4am-10pm. Around town, don't pay more than 8000kip during daylight hours. To **That Inheng** (40min.; round-trip bargaining starts at 50,000kip) and **That Phon** (2hr.; bargaining starts at 100,000kip).

Rentals: Most guesthouses rent **bicycles** for US$1 per day.

ORIENTATION AND PRACTICAL INFORMATION

The town's main road is **Photisalath Road,** north-south parallel to the river and several blocks away. **Tha Heua Road,** along the bank, **Khanthabouli Road,** a block east, and **Sisavangvong Road,** farther east, are also important. They are linked by east-west streets, the main one being **Oudomsinh Road** at the north end of town, which passes the deserted **old market** (a good landmark). **Simuang Road,** five blocks south, is home to the immigration pier and cheap restaurants. The **bus station** and **new market** are at Sisavangvong Rd.'s north end, and the **airport** is at the south.

Tourist Office: (☎212 755). From the post office, head 2 blocks north and 2 blocks east. Info about Savannakhet and nearby attractions. Open M-F 8-11:30am and 2-4pm.

Tours: Savan Banhao Tour, 644 Senna Rd. (☎/fax 212 944), in Savan Banhao Hotel. Tours are the best way to visit the Hồ Chí Minh Trail near Xepon, 160km east of Savan. Car with driver US$100 and up outside the city; 1200฿ around town. Open M-Sa 8am-noon and 1-4pm.

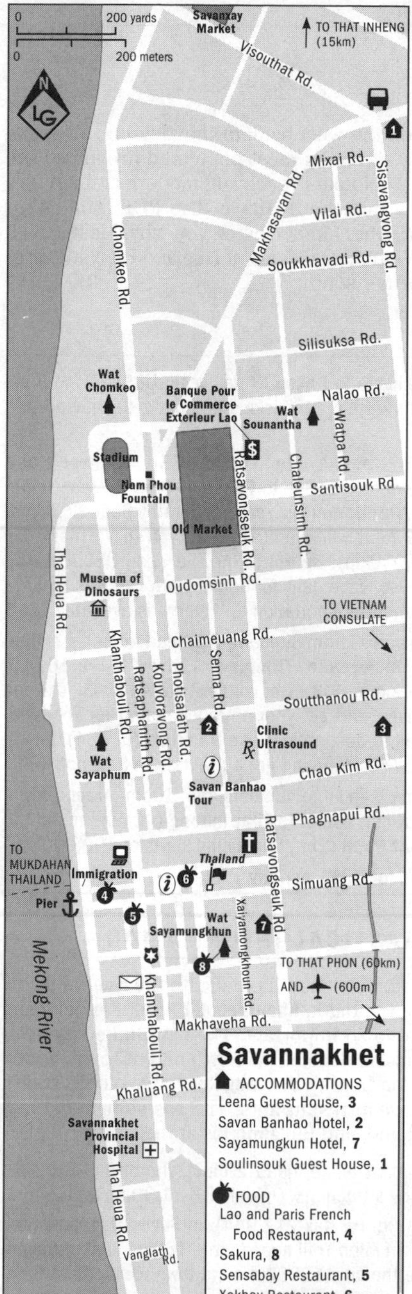

Consulates: Vietnam (☎212 418), on Sisavangvong Rd. From the south end of the old market, head away from the river on Oudomsinh Rd. and take the 1st right onto Sisavangvong Rd.; it's ½ block down. **30-day visas** for crossing at Lao Bảo (US$50; bring 1 passport photo. 3-day processing. Open M-F 7:30-11am and 1:30-4:30pm). **Thailand** (☎212 373), ½ block east and 1 block south of Xokhay Restaurant. **60-day visa** (1000฿. 25hr. processing: drop your passport off M-F 8am-noon, and pick it up the next day, M-F 1-3:30pm. Bring 2 passport photos, 1 copy of your passport, and make sure your passport doesn't expire within the next 6 months).

Currency Exchange: Banque Pour le Commerce Extérieur Lao (☎212 261), opposite the old market. AmEx and V traveler's checks, V cash advances (3% commission). Open M-F 8:30am-3:30pm.

Markets: Savanxay market, 200m toward the river from the bus station, near the north end of Sisavangvong Rd. A sight to behold. Open about 6am-6pm.

Police: (☎212 212), on Khanthabouli Rd., opposite the post office.

Pharmacies: Many near the old market. **Clinique Ultrasound** (☎212 711), on Ratsavongseuk Rd., near the market. Open daily 7:30am-6pm.

Medical Services: Savannakhet Provincial Hospital (☎212 131), on Khanthabouli Rd. 5 blocks south of Simuang Rd. on the right. English spoken.

Internet Access: On Photisalath Rd., facing the Catholic Church. Look for signs. 10,000kip for 30min. Open daily 9am-10pm.

Post Office and Telecom: (☎212 295), on Khanthabouli Rd. From the intersection with Simuang Rd., the post office is 1 block south, beside the radio tower. Cash, **overseas telephone,** and fax service. *Poste Restante.* Open M-F 8am-5pm, some Sa.

Postal Code: 1300.

BORDER CROSSING: LAO BẢO. The border town of Lao Bảo lies 200 buttock-bruising kilometers east of Savannakhet on Rte. 9, which winds around the slopes of the Annamite Mountains, on the Lao-Vietnamese border. If you opt to stay the night (or are stuck), there are simple lodgings (20,000-30,000kip). For those heading into Vietnam, Lao customs at Lao Bảo is a formality, though travelers must show passports and pay a US$5 fine for each day they have overstayed their visa. Vietnamese immigration requires a visa stamped with the right entry point (get the stamp in Vientiane, Savannakhet, or Pakse). Passing through Vietnamese customs can take up to 4hr., as officials may search bags and comb the bus for contraband. You can also bus from Savannakhet to Lao Bảo, pass through customs on foot, and then catch a motorcycle-taxi to the next town. The border opens at 8am. However, buses leave Savannakhet for Huế and Danang at 10pm, and also leave Huế and Đà Nẵng for Savannakhet at 10pm. You may be stuck in your bus at the border for the night. If you just go to the border, you can catch buses into Laos, or into Vietnam at 8am.

ACCOMMODATIONS AND FOOD

Sayamungkun Guest House ❷, 85 Ratsavongseuk Rd., one block south of the Simuang Rd. intersection, has tiled floors, towering ceilings, a large terrace, and a lovely second-floor patio. (☎212 426. Doubles with bath and fan 40,000kip, with A/C 60,000kip.) **Leena Guest House ❷** has great management and charming rooms. (☎212 404. Rooms with fan 40,000kip, with A/C 50,000kip, with A/C and hot water 60,000kip.) The comfortable **Soulinsouk Guest House ❷** is ideally located for catching an early bus—opposite the Makhasavan Rd. station. (☎213 436. Doubles with bath 40,000kip.) Sometimes called the Silan Hotel, **Savan Banhao Hotel ❷** has four "classes" of rooms, from tiny with shared bath and hot water (45,000kip) to decent with bath (75,000-95,000kip). From the side of the old market nearest the Mekong, walk 1½ blocks south. (☎212 202.)

There aren't many decent restaurants in Savannakhet; most are between the river and the Catholic church. The **market ❶** boasts a large food section with *phở*, spring rolls, and other Lao and Vietnamese snacks. On Simuang Rd., around the corner from Sayamungkun Guest House, is **Sakura ❸**, which serves up tasty Korean-style barbecue (called "fondue" on the menu; 25,000-35,000kip) on a breezy, outdoor patio. The owner is half-Vietnamese and half-Lao, and has traveled widely as a lounge singer. If you're lucky, you'll get to hear his to-die-for Elvis Presley imitation. Near the immigration office, in a Chinese-style house at the corner of Simuang Rd. and Tha Heua Rd., **Lao and Paris French Food Restaurant ❶** serves popular Asian and European dishes. (Entrees 8000-15,000kip. Open daily 8am-11pm.) On Simuang Rd., past the Internet cafe, **Xokhay Restaurant ❶** serves decent Vietnamese and good Chinese fare. (Dishes 8000-15,000kip. Open daily 10am-9pm.) **Sensabay Restaurant ❶** has rice and noodle dishes as well as steaks and french fries. (Most entrees 10,000kip. Open daily 8am-11pm.)

SIGHTS

Wat Sayaphum, on Tha Heua Rd. north of the pier, is Savannakhet's only historically significant *wat*. The complex dates to 1896 and contains two main *sim;* the largest is a secondary school for monks decorated with murals depicting scenes from the *Ramakien*. **That Inheng,** the city's most revered shrine, is 15km north of

Savannakhet. The 25m *stupa*—built to hold the Buddha's spine—is all that remains of the ancient city of Sikhottabong. The road is poor; biking isn't advisable. (*Tuk tuk* to That Inheng 50,000kip.) **That Phon** stands 60km south of Savannakhet on Rte. 13. with a tall, white *stupa*. It isn't awe-inspiring, but it is sacred. One of the most unusual Buddhist legends, dating from the Angkor period, explains that Buddha was in mid-sermon when nature's call came on strong. Exercising the prerogative of the "World-Honored One," he had a *naga* build him a toilet on the spot. That Phon's white spire now commemorates the momentous site. **The Museum of Dinosaurs,** on Khanthabouli Rd. near some tennis courts (head north from Hotel Santyphab on Simuang Rd.), is a surprising sight. The local archaeologist gives an interesting tour of the remains found northwest of Savannakhet in the early 1990s. *(☎212 597. Open daily 8am-noon and 2-4pm. 2000kip.)*

PAKSE ☎031

Quiet and unassuming, Pakse ("pak-SAY") is a worthwhile prelude to the Emerald Triangle region, where the natural beauty of Laos builds to a crescendo of mountains, gorges, and islands. Its lively market has just been built a shiny new home—the old one burned down in 1998—complete with escalators. Pakse also boasts the largest Vietnamese population in Laos and an assortment of eateries serving Vietnamese fare. Many travelers use Pakse as a springboard to the far-flung Saravane and Attapeu provinces, and to the laid-back 4000 Islands region farther south.

TRANSPORTATION

Flights: Pakse Airport, on Rte. 13, 1km west of Xedone River Bridge. To **Savannakhet** (2-3 per week, US$42) and **Vientiane** (1 per day, US$87). Departure tax 5000kip domestic, US$15 international. **Lao Airlines office** (☎212 751, airport 251 460), before the airfield on the left, and in town, on Rd. 11 near Banque Pour le Commerce Extérieur Lao and the pier. Open M-F 8-11:30am and 1:30-4:30pm, Sa 8-11:30am.

Ferries: Ferries cross the Mekong to **Ban Muang Kao** (7am-6pm; 10,000kip). **Boats** to **Don Khong** (8hr.; 50,000kip) via **Champasak** (1½hr.; 30,000kip) leave when full from the waterfront right of the ferry pier (daily 8:30am and on).

Buses: The southbound bus station is 8km east off Rte. 13; northbound buses depart from a station 10km west of town on Rte. 13. *Tuk tuks* run to either for 4000-5000kip per person.

Southbound Station: Buses leave daily for: **Attapeu** (4-7hr.; 6:30, 8, 10:30am; 25,000kip); **Champasak** (1-2hr.; 9am, noon; 10,000kip); **Muang Khong** on the island of Don Khong (2-3hr.; 8, 9, 10, 11am, noon; 20,000kip); **Pakxong** (1-2hr., every hr. 6am-noon, 8000kip); **Saravane** via **Thad Lo** (3hr.; 10am, noon, 1:30pm; 13,000kip).

Northbound Station: Buses leave daily for **Vientiane** (15-17hr.; up to 6 per day roughly 6am-12:30pm; 47,000kip) via **Savannakhet** (8hr.; 35,000kip). To get to **Vang Tao border crossing** with Thailand, charter a *tuk tuk* from the central market (45min.; 10,000kip).

Local Transportation: The **tuk tuk** hang-out is the parking area on Xedone Quay from the pier to Lao Aviation Office. *Tuk tuks* will take you anywhere in town for 3000-5000kip.

LAOS

ORIENTATION AND PRACTICAL INFORMATION

Pakse is confusing to navigate and many streets aren't labeled; maps are available. The **Xedone River** borders the town to the north and west. The **Mekong River** borders it to the south. **Route 13,** the main road, goes past the **airport** and over the Xedone at the western end of town, passes by Lankham and Phonsavan hotels, Lao Devel-

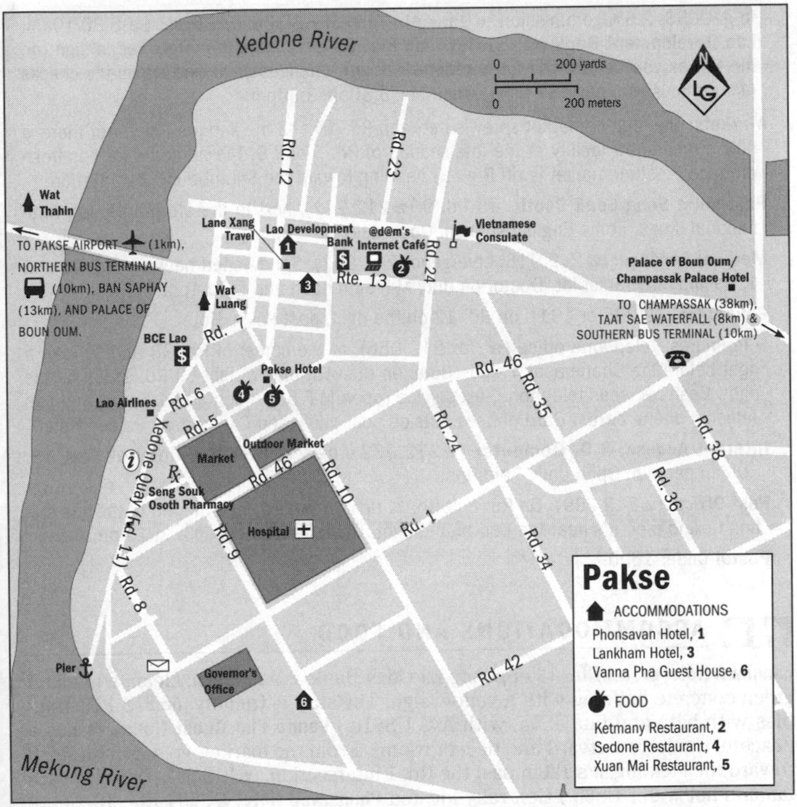

opment Bank and the impressive Champasak Palace Hotel before leaving town at the eastern end. Most budget hotels, restaurants, and shops are along Rte. 13, around the central market, and on the Xedone. All streets are numbered along Rte. 13. **Xedone Quay** (also known as **Road 11**) runs along the Xedone from Rte. 13 to the **ferry pier**. **Unhila market** is between Rd. 9 and 10.

Tourist Office: Lao National Tourism Authority (☎/fax 212 021), on Rd. 11 near the ferry pier. Map of Pakse 5000kip. Open M-F 8–11:30am and 2-4pm.

Tours: Inter-Lao Tourism, #121 Rte. 13 (☎/fax 212 226). 4WD pickup tours of coffee plantations and waterfalls US$80-90 per day. Open M-F 8am-noon and 1-4pm, Sa 8am-noon. **Lane Xang Travel** (☎212 002), on Rte. 13 near Phonsava Hotel. Bus and ferry schedules and organizes tours. Open M-F 8am-noon and 2-5pm, Sa 8am-noon.

Consulates: Vietnam (☎212 058), on Rd. 24 past Ketmany Restaurant on the right as you head toward Xedone River from Champasak Palace Hotel. Visas US$50. Passport and 2 photos required. 3-day processing. Open M-F 8-11am and 2-4:30pm.

Currency Exchange: Banque Pour Le Commerce Extérieur Lao (☎213 697), in the concrete and glass building on Xedone Quay (Rd. 11), 150m from Xedone Bridge. Exchanges currency. AmEx/V traveler's checks, and V cash advances (3% commission to get US$; 2.5% commission to get kip). Open M-F 8:30am-3:30pm, Sa 8:30-10am. **Lao Development Bank** (☎251 326), on Rte. 13 just before the large Honda sign (on the left as you head away from Xedone Bridge), changes cash and traveler's checks (1% commission into US$ only.) Open M-F 8:30am-3:30pm.

Markets: The regular market sprawls between Rd. 10 and the Xedone River, but there is now a brand-new facility at the intersection of Rd. 5 and 9. The adjacent lot has fresh produce. Another market is off Rte. 13 heading toward the Southbound Bus Station.

Pharmacy: Seng Souk Osoth, #5 Rd. 9 (☎212 272), next to the old market lot. Anti-malarial drugs. Some English spoken. Open daily 7am-6pm.

Medical Services: (☎212 018, emergency 212 041). Sandwiched between Rd. 46 and 1, behind old market lot. Doctor on duty M-F 8am-noon and 1:30-4pm.

Police: (☎212 235 or 191), on Rd. 12 on the right, past Pakse Hotel.

Telephones: Telephone office (☎/fax 212 056), at the corner of Rd. 38 and 1. Take a right before the Champasak Palace Hotel on Rte. 13, then a right on Rd. 1; it's on the right. Cash overseas telephone, fax service (open M-F 8am-noon and 1-5pm), and Lao Telecom **phone cards.** Card phones outside post office and Champasak Palace Hotel.

Internet Access: S.D. Computer (☎212 232), next to Lankham Hotel on Rte. 13. 300kip per min. Open daily 7am-8pm.

Post Office: (☎212 299). On Rd. 8 at Rd. 1. Head down Rd. 8 to the left of the gas station next to pier; it's near the end on the right. Open M-F 8am-noon and 1-5pm.

Postal Code: 1600.

ACCOMMODATIONS AND FOOD

Lankham Hotel ❷, on Rte. 13 opposite Lao May Bank, is a modern, clean, white and green concrete building with a yellow sign. The staff is friendly. (☎212 125. Doubles with bath and fan US$5, with A/C US$10.) **Vanna Pha Guest House ❷** has a peaceful shaded courtyard and decent rooms. From the market, go south on Rd. 9 toward the Mekong; it's 120m past the Rd. 1 intersection. (☎212 502. Doubles with fan and hot water US$5.) Centrally located **Phonsavan Hotel ❶,** 294 Rte. 13, opposite the Lankham Hotel, is the town's cheapest option. (☎212 842. Basic rooms US$2, with hot water US$4, with A/C US$6.)

Pakse has the largest Vietnamese population in Laos; *phở* shops are abundant. The evening market features a pavilion that sells very cheap *kai ping*, *khao niaw*, and noodle soups. **Sedone Restaurant ❶,** #110 Rd. 5, two shops to the left of Pakse Hotel and opposite the empty market lot, has great Vietnamese food and decent Lao and Thai fare. (Most dishes 7000-10,000kip. Open daily 6am-10pm.) **Xuan Mai Restaurant ❶,** at the intersection of Rd. 5 and 10, opposite Pakse Hotel, serves satisfying Vietnamese food. (Spring rolls 5000kip. Entrees 8000-20,000kip; most under 16,000kip.) On Rte. 13 past the Honda sign, **Ketmany Restaurant ❶** serves good Lao, Vietnamese, and Western food for 8000-15,000kip. (☎212 615.)

SIGHTS

The **Palace of Boun Oum,** between the Xedone River and the bus station on Rte. 13, is one Laos's more bizarre landmarks. Construction of the former residence of the Prince of Champasak began in 1969 and had not been completed when the Communists deposed the prince in 1975. The huge white structure now houses the **Champasak Palace Hotel.** Visitors can take the elevator to the top floor for a view of the Bolovens Plateau. **Taat Sae Waterfall,** 8km east of town on Rte. 13, makes for a pleasant half-day trip. Large artificial pools lead to three waterfalls, two of which fall a steep 40m. (Easiest to take a *tuk tuk*. Bargaining starts at around US$5.) **Ban Saphay,** a weaving village 13km west of town off Rte. 13, is renowned for *ikat* silk and *mutmee* cotton. Two shops along the main road sell fabric by the meter and a few ready-made garments. The **Lao Women's Union** operates one, but the privately owned **Lao Homemade Silk Skirt Shop** carries a better selection. *Mutmee* cotton costs 10,000kip per meter, *ikat* silk 8000kip per meter. Materials are cheaper and often better from the producers in nearby homes. Take a *songthaew* from the ferry pier (30min., leaves when full, 5000kip) or a *tuk tuk* (about US$4 round-trip).

BORDER CROSSING: VANG TAO/CHONG MEK. The **Thai** border lies 45km west of Pakse, and crossing between the two countries is quite easy. The border is open 8am-4:30pm, but note that it takes at least 45min. to get from Pakse to the border. To get to the border from Pakse go to the market near the Xedone River and charter a *tuk tuk* to **Vang Tao** (45min.; bargaining starts at US$10). You will then go through Lao customs and pay US$5 for every day you outstayed your visa. Once you get your exit stamp, cross the bridge and go through Thai immigration. From Chong Mek, *songthaew* (overgrown *tuk tuks*) run to Phibun (see **Khong Chiam,** p. 739); from here, buses head to Warin Chamrap station at **Ubon Ratchathani** (p. 734). Buses depart from another station in Ubon, the Ubon Ratchathani Bus Station, to **Mukdahan** (p. 740), from where further bus connections to **Bangkok** (p. 664) can be made.

CHAMPASAK

The quiet little town of Champasak offers a nice stopover for travelers on their way south. It lies 38km downriver from Pakse, sandwiched between the Mekong and steep, craggy limestone hills. Its main attraction is Wat Phu, a magnificent and relatively untouristed—albeit crumbling—Khmer temple, 11km south of Champasak proper.

TRANSPORTATION AND PRACTICAL INFORMATION. Buses leave the Southern Bus Station in Pakse 8km east of town on Rte. 13 (1hr.; 8, 9, 10, 11am, noon; 20,000kip). *Songthaew* leave from Rte. 13 (7000kip). Champasak lies across the river from Pakse—your bus will be ferried across. Buses leave Champasak for Pakse (1-2hr., 7:30am, 8000kip). If you miss that bus, cross the river (7000kip) and take a *tuk tuk* to Junction 30 on Rte. 13 (5km, 10,000kip). From there buses come by around every hour going to Pakse. If you want to head south to **Don Khong** or **Don Det,** go to the same junction and catch a bus in the opposite direction (20,000kip). Boats heading upriver to Pakse stop at the landing near the center of town (3hr.; last boat at about 3pm; 10,000kip), as do boats continuing downriver to **Don Khong** (6-8hr.; leave around 8:30am; 20,000kip). A **bank** on the left before the roundabout changes US dollars and Thai baht. (Open M-F 8:30am-3:30pm.)

ACCOMMODATIONS AND FOOD. Once in Champasak, the buses will continue 2km to the town center, a small roundabout. Driving into town from the dock, **Anouxa Guest House ❶** (☎213 751) is on the left just before the roundabout. It has generic bungalows (US$3) and beautiful, tiled-floor rooms with bathrooms, hot water, and porches overlooking the Mekong (US$10-15). Nearby **Dok Champa Guest House ❶** offers basic rooms with fans in little bamboo houses (20,000kip). Across the road and down 500m past the roundabout is **Mr. Seng's Guest House ❶,**

an agreeable spot overlooking the Mekong; grab a hammock and nap by the river. (Singles 15,000kip; large doubles with bath 25,000kip.) A few kilometers out of the roundabout, toward Wat Phu, is **Khem Khong Guest House ❶**, which has relaxing bungalows with sit-down toilets (☎213 248. 15,000kip; 30,000kip overlooking the river). Champasak's tiny size, limited options, and lazy, riverside atmosphere make it the sort of place where you're likely to just eat at your guesthouse. The **Say Thong Restaurant ❶** at Mr. Seng's Guest House serves a mix of Lao and Vietnamese food. (Entrees 7000-12,000kip.) The attached **Dok Champa Restaurant ❶** serves Lao, Vietnamese, and French food, and offers great curries, fruit salad, and many breakfast options. (Entrees 8000-10,000kip.)

SIGHTS. Wat Phu (Hill Temple), or rather its ruins, lie 11km south of Champasak. An ancient Khmer temple known as **Muang Kao** (Old City) constitutes one of the finest examples of Khmer art outside of Cambodia. Archaeologists believe the site dates to the 500s, although construction was completed in the 12th century by Angkor's King Suryavarman II (1113-50). The temple bears stylistic similarities to Angkor Wat, and may have served as its prototype. Some of the walls are unstable; exercise caution while exploring. The temple's access road skirts a large **baray,** which symbolized the waters of the earth and irrigated surrounding rice fields. The causeway is now fenced off; two large rectangular galleries flank the entrance. Crowning a series of moss-covered laterite tiers is a small central **sanctuary.** A rather incongruous Buddha sits where the *linga* once did, reflecting the empire's overlapping Hindu-Buddhist influences. The temple's main gate is 8km south. *(Tuk tuks to Wat Phu run 15,000kip per person round-trip. It is also a nice bike ride to Wat Phu. Guesthouses rent bicycles for 10,000kip. Entrance fee US$3, including admission to the small but informative museum; open daily 8am-4:30pm.)*

BORDER CROSSING: VOEN KHAM/STUNG TRENG. As of March 2004, the border between Laos and Cambodia at Voen Kham was officially closed. Check in the guesthouses of Don Det and Don Khong for the most up-to-date information. The border is open M-F 8am-5pm, and all travelers must have a valid Cambodian visa (get one at the embassies in Vientiane, Bangkok, Hà Nội, or Hồ Chí Minh City). Those willing to try crossing need first to get to Veunkhsam. The cheapest way is to take a boat from Don Khong to **Hat Xai Khun** (5000-15,000kip), or from Don Det to **Ban Nakasang** (5000-15,000kip), walk or take a *tuk tuk* to the main road (500m from Hat Xai Khun, about 2km from Ban Nakasang), and then catch a Voen Kham-bound bus. In Don Khong or Don Det, motorbike drivers will journey to Voen Kham (about US$8), or, if you're lucky, you might be able to tag along with a tour group going to see the dolphins (about US$5 from Don Khong). For US$1-2, Lao immigration will give you an exit stamp. Walk down to the river and charter a boat to **Stung Treng,** the nearest town on the Cambodian side of the river (2hr., US$40 for a 4-5 person boat). Your driver will take you across the river to Cambodian immigration and wait for you. Cambodian immigration will charge you US$5 for an entry stamp. Some travelers report that they have successfully refused to pay this bribe. You **cannot** obtain a visa at the border. Once you have your stamp, go back to your boat and on to Stung Treng. **There is no bank in Stung Treng,** and you will almost certainly be stuck there for a night. Bring US dollars or baht.

THAD LO

Idyllic Thad Lo sits on a bend in the Xedone River against the backdrop of the Bolovens Plateau, 80km northeast of Pakse and 30km from Saravane. Travelers soak their weary bodies in natural pools, visit out-of-the-way villages, or kick back in bungalows, lulled to sleep by the sound of waterfalls. Attractions in Thad Lo include great hiking, which starts at the waterfall (guides 30,000kip from Tim Restaurant or Sisapaseuth Guest House), and some of the cheapest elephant rides in Southeast Asia (50,000kip for 90min. at Tim Restaurant or Tad Lo Resort.) There are tribal villages and more waterfalls within an hour's walk of the bridge. The owner of the restaurant next to Sapyasath Guest House will provide a map of a good 3hr. walk. The river above the first waterfall is a nice place to swim.

Buses run from Pakse to Thad Lo (2hr.; 10am, noon, 1:30pm; 13,000kip) and continue on to Saravane. Buses leave Saravane for Pakse (3hr.; 6:30, 7:30, 10am, 12:15, 1:30pm; 13,000kip), and stop at the main road at Thad Lo (around 8:30, 11, 1:15, 2:30pm). Make sure to arrive early to catch them. Buses drop passengers off on the road; Thad Lo village is 2km down a dirt road to the right (follow the signs). **Saise Guest House ❸**, across the bridge, offers comfortable rooms with bath for US$6-15. They also have much nicer lodging in their **Green House ❹**. Clean rooms with a gorgeous view of the falls run 60,000-120,000kip. **Sapyasath Guest House ❸**, right before the bridge across from Thad Lo Resort, has clean bungalows and an attached restaurant overlooking the river (bungalows 25,000kip). Next to Sapyasath, there are several sets of bungalows without a river view (15,000-20,000kip). From the bridge, head past Tad Lo Resort in the woods to **Tim's Restaurant, Guesthouse, and Tourist Information Center ❸**. Bungalows run 25,000kip, email costs 800kip per min. and a 4hr. guided trek is 30,000kip; there's also a book exchange, and they'll drive you to the bus stop on the main road for 3000kip. The best restaurant in Thad Lo is the **Sapyasath Guest House Restaurant ❷**, which serves good Lao and Western fare at steep prices (entrees 15,000-20,000kip). The restaurant at **Saisie Guest House ❷** also offers delicious eats. Try the vegetable curry (20,000kip).

SARAVANE AND BOLOVENS PLATEAU

Northeast of Pakse looms the Bolovens Plateau, one of Southeast Asia's last frontiers. The plateau is inhabited by ethnic minorities, many of whom were forced to flee their homelands in Vietnam's Central

NO WORK, ALL PLAY

CHILD'S PLAY

If you spend much time in Laos you'll soon notice the ubiquity of children's games. All over the country, little children gather together in hallways and dusty alleys to take turns expertly throwing their sandals at stacks of cards. Their focus is intense, the stakes clearly high. This is the game of *makjaat.*

You, too, can play *makjaat;* you can play with any number of people, from two to 10 or even more. All you need is an open space, sandals, and a stack of little cards. Like many good things, these cards come from Thailand, and they feature cartoons; a pack of 20 or so will usually run 500kip.

The players all contribute the same number of cards to form one stack, which is placed at the end of the passage/alleyway. To determine who gets to go first, a line is drawn on the ground and the participants throw one sandal apiece at the line. The player whose sandal lands closest to the line, without going over, goes first; the next closest goes second, and so on. If you throw your sandal over the line, you go last.

Once the throwing order has been determine, the players take turns throwing their sandals at the pile of cards. Every time you hit the stack, you get all the cards that are knocked off; the goal, of course, is to get as many cards as possible.

Highlands during the war. Among the larger groups are the Ngai, Suk, Katou, and Alak. Tea, coffee, fruit, and cardamom are still grown here, as they have been since the days of the French. Although there is nothing to see or do in Saravane proper, it is a good base for exploring the **Attapeu region.** This remote border area is home to many ethnic tribes, as well to as tigers, gaur, Asian elephants, crocodiles, and other Lao endangered species. Travel to Attapeu is difficult, especially during the rainy season, and the region is rife with **malaria.** Inquire at the Saise Guest House about hiring transport and a guide. An easier trip is to the waterfalls at **Pakxong** (1hr.; 7, 9, 11am, 1pm; 8000kip).

On the vast plateau, 113km northeast of Pakse, lies the provincial capital **Saravane** (or "Salavan") on the bank of the **Xedone River.** The road from Pakse passes the **bus station** and **airport** on the southwestern edge of town, then rings the town center. Daily **buses** and **trucks** go to: Kongsedone (1hr.; 10am, noon, 2pm; 75,000kip); Pakse (3hr.; 6:30, 7:30, 10am, 12:15, 1:30pm; 13,000kip); and Sekong (2-3hr.; 7am, 1:30pm; 35,000kip). The main attraction, the **market,** is the center of town, with the **post office** and **bank** to the west and the **hospital** and football field to the north. The post office sells phone cards, and has a card phone out front. (Open M-F 8am-4:30pm.) The bank exchanges US dollars, Thai baht, and traveler's checks. (Open M-F 8am-3:30pm.) The road along the market has several guesthouses, including **Thippaphone Guest House ❶,** where the rooms have mosquito nets (☎211 063; 30,000-80,000kip), and **Silsamay Guest House ❶,** which has a balcony overlooking the market and simple rooms (☎211 056; rooms 30,000-70,000kip). **Saise Guest House ❶,** at the northeastern corner of town, has a helpful hand-drawn map of the town (☎213 171. Dorms 20,000kip; rooms with A/C 40,000-50,000kip). *Tuk tuks* from the bus station cost 3000kip to the market or to Saise Guest House. Next to the market, **Vilaivoue Restaurant ❶** serves up savory food in three sizes: small, medium, and bigmax (☎211 014. Small entrees 10,000kip; bigmax entrees 30,000kip). There are *phở* shops around the market, fruit vendors abound.

4000 ISLANDS REGION ☎31

The area from Ban Munla Pamok to the Cambodian border is a tropical paradise. Here the lazy waters of the Mekong become a raging torrent; this is the sleepiest part of a very sleepy country. Thousands of islets dot the branches and tributaries, earning the region its nickname. The larger, inhabited islands remained untouched by caustic mainland affairs, and life's pace is dictated only by the cycles of the river. Muang Khong, on the island of Don Khong, is the biggest of the little towns in the region, but Don Det is by far the most popular destination: travelers there pay a dollar for a bungalow on an almost unsettled island and sleep their worries away on a hammock by the Mekong.

> **WARNING.** There is a serious risk of both **Dengue fever** and **malaria** in this area. Take anti-malarial drugs before coming, and bring bug spray.

TRANSPORTATION AND PRACTICAL INFORMATION. The largest island, and a good starting point for explorations, is **Don Khong.** There are several guesthouses in the main village, **Muang Khong.** To get to Don Khong from Pakse, take a **boat** (8hr.; several 7am-noon; 50,000kip) or **bus** (3½hr.; several 8am-noon; 20,000kip). The boat stops at Muang Sen, on the west side of the island. The 20min. *tuk tuk* ride to Muang Khong costs up to 6000kip per person. Buses stop in Hat Xai Khun; take a skiff to Muang Khong (5000-15,000kip per person, depending on group size). Buses return to Pakse from Hat Xai Khun daily (3hr.; ask at the pier for times). Boats also go back to Pakse, but schedules are erratic. Ask at the pier in Muang Sen in advance. A **post office** and **telephone office** is a few meters upriver from Don Khong's pier and can make cash-only **international calls.** (☎212 073. Open M-F 8am-noon and 1-5pm.) A **morning market** is upriver from Muang Khong pier.

ACCOMMODATIONS AND FOOD. On **Don Khong,** Muang Khong has pleasant budget guesthouses and there are currently many more under construction. The first, in front of the pier, is **Don Khong Guest House** ❶ (☎214 010). The French-speaking proprietor offers basic, tidy doubles with shared bath (30,000kip), and doubles with private bath (40,000kip). Her English-speaking son runs **Don Khong Guest House No. 2** ❶, 200m up the road past the post office, which has a beautiful veranda overlooking rice fields. (Rooms 20,000kip and up.) Down the road, past Pou's Restaurant, is the **Souksan Hotel** ❷ (☎212 071), which has bungalows with bath and hot water for US$3. **Kang Khong Villa** ❷, a large wood and concrete building with balcony and front garden, is 30m past the original Don Khong. (☎213 529. Rooms 30,000kip and up.) Every guesthouse rents **bicycles** for 8000kip per day.

Mr. Pon, formerly a chef in Vientiane, now operates **Pon's Restaurant** ❷, 50m upstream from Muang Khong pier. Delicious steamed fish (15,000kip) must be ordered 2hr. in advance. (Open daily 6am-10pm.) Mr. Pon organizes boat tours of the islands (20,000kip per person) and trips to see the dolphins (25,000kip). Don Khong Guest House has a good **restaurant** ❶ that serves quality Vietnamese and Lao food (8000-15,000kip). The cheapest option in town is the nondescript **Phou Khong Restaurant** ❷, right across the small bridge from Don Khong Guest House. (☎213 673. Mouth-watering fried spring rolls 7000kip; most entrees 8000kip.)

Don Det Island, 20km downriver from Don Khong, lacks Don Khong's modern facilities, but the tropical haven has become the region's most popular destination. Take a bus from Pakse to Ban Nakasang (3½hr.; 7, 9am; 20,000kip), and then a boat to Don Det Island (5000-15,000kip, depending on group size). From Don Khong or Muang Khong, charter a **boat** (1½hr.; US$10) to the main beach, or take the boat back to Ban Nakasang (5000-15,000kip) and hire a *tuk tuk* to Hat Xai Khun (bargain hard to get it for about US$3), and then a ferry across to Muang Khong (5000-15,000kip). **Khampong Bungalows** ❶, next to the boat landing, has bungalows overlooking the river (15,000kip) and friendly owners. For slightly cheaper digs, continue walking left from the boat landing. 200m down the town's only road, and then down a side path to the right (follow the signs) is popular waterside **Sunset Bungalows** ❶ (bungalows 10,000kip). For food, try the **Khampong Guest House Restaurant** ❶, across from its bungalows, which serves delicious Lao and Western food (most entrees 10,000kip). The restaurant's owner, Kampai, helps arrange transport and crossing into Cambodia and gives tours to see the dolphins and waterfalls at **Don Khone Island** (20,000kip). Near the boat landing there are a few information boards offering tours (Don Khone 20,000kip), visa services (US$75 Vietnam; US$45 Cambodia; some travelers report lengthy processing time), and info on crossing into Cambodia. If you continue to the left from the boat landing, you will reach the bridge to Don Khone Island (45min. walk from main boat landing). There is a small fee to cross the bridge.

SIGHTS. One of the main attractions of the 4000 Islands are the **Li Phi Falls,** on the southwestern tip of Don Kone Island. All of the waterfalls are accessible by boat. Don Khone shelters a 5km **railroad line** (now inoperative). Both sights are part of a government-owned resort. (Organized excursions to see both about US$5.) **Khone Pha Pheng** (Voice of the Mekong), the largest cascade in Southeast

Asia, is farther south on the left bank, off Rte. 13. This so-called "Niagara of the Mekong" is (once again) little more than large rapids. Both waterfalls can be visited in a day with an early start. Guesthouses and Pon's Restaurant (see **Accommodations and Food,** p. 323) organize trips (group of 4-10 people and boat with skipper 10,000kip per person). Since the final stretch of river is not navigable, travelers stop on the mainland 12km away and take a *tuk tuk* to Khone Pha Pheng (whole *tuk tuk* 60,000kip). This region is home to endangered freshwater **Irrawaddy dolphins,** who come upriver to spawn between January and March. Guesthouses in Don Khong or Don Det will arrange day tours to see the dolphins for US$5-7 (see **Accommodations and Food,** p. 323).

MALAYSIA

HIGHLIGHTS OF MALAYSIA

BEACHES. **Pulau Langkawi** (p. 375) harbors budget haunts, but **Pulau Tioman** (p. 406) and the **Perhentian Islands** (p. 385) take the prize. **Similajau National Park** (p. 426) proves there's more to Borneo than jungle.

NATURAL WONDERS. **Taman Negara National Park** (p. 382) provides cool respite. Spelunk in **Niah National Park** (p. 427) or scale **Gunung Kinabalu** (p. 441), Southeast Asia's highest peak.

URBAN BEAT. Slick and never dull, **Kuala Lumpur** (p. 339) boasts capital sights, services, and after-hours elan. **Melaka** (p. 350) blends east and west both in the kitchen and on the street. **Georgetown** (p. 368) exudes the feel of a Chinese city. **Kota Bharu** (p. 389) is the heart of Malay culture. **Kuching's** (p. 411) vibrant waterfront scene and sights on the edge of the jungle are the cat's meow.

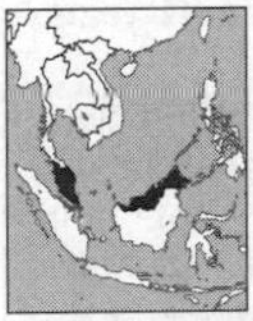

Malaysians have much to be proud of: the most sophisticated transportation infrastructure in Southeast Asia; clean, diverse cities; and a reasonably well-protected natural environment. For the traveler, Malaysia offers the comforts of rapid modernization as well as the grandeur of carefully preserved traditional cultures. Although the interaction between the country's Malay majority and sizable Chinese population isn't without tension, it's a credit to the Malaysians that in the wake of regional depression their society has remained unified. Malaysia's ethnic mix prevails in the cities of the cosmopolitan west coast, but the sparsely populated east coast remains a bastion of seafaring Malay culture. While fantastic island beaches beckon eager travelers to both coasts, the eastern states of Sabah and Sarawak offer a chance to explore the wilds of Borneo, Malaysian-style, with accessible national parks, efficient tourist services, and buses that never run late.

LIFE AND TIMES

DEMOGRAPHICS

Malaysia's true natives are the **Orang Asli** (original people), who probably migrated to the peninsula from China some 10,000 years ago. Today most of Malaysia's 23 million residents live on the peninsula, and the rest inhabit Sabah and Sarawak to the east. The terms "Malaysian," "Malayan," and "Malay" are distinct. "Malaysian" is a reference to a citizen of the country, "Malayan" denotes anyone from the peninsula, while "Malay" is a term for the ethnic Malay who constitute roughly 60% of the population. Almost all Malays are Muslim. Sarawak is home to the **Dayak,** Malaysia's small Christian population. The ethnic **Chinese** and **Indian** populations comprise one-third and one-tenth of the total population, respectively.

LANGUAGE

Bahasa Malaysia is the official language of Malaysia. Malay is taught in all schools and used in all governmental institutions including Parliament and the courts. Malay is tied very closely to the Malaysian national identity, and its cultural importance has been emphasized by the government since the founding of the Federation of Malaysia in 1957. Several different dialects of **Chinese** are spoken in Malaysia, including Cantonese, Foochow, Hokkien, Hakka, Hainan, and Mandarin. Although **English** is recognized as Malaysia's second language, more people speak Chinese. English is much more common in the larger cities on the western coast of Peninsular Malaysia. **Tamil** is spoken almost exclusively in Peninsular Malaysia due to the Indian population there. **Iban** is the largest language group in Sarawa, spoken on some radio programs and schools. Four different dialects of **Dusun** are spoken in Sabah. Dialects of both Iban and Dusun are spoken in the Polynesian islands. **Bajau,** spoken on the western coast of Sabah, is related to but distinct from other languages of Borneo like **Sama** (also known as East Coast Bajau).

FACTS AND FIGURES

Official Name: Malaysia.

Government: Constitutional Monarchy with an elected federal parliamentary government.

Capital: Kuala Lumpur.

Land Area: 328,550km².

Geography: Separated from the mainland by the South China Sea; borders Thailand to the north and Singapore to the south. Sabah and Sarawak occupy the northern one-third of the island of Borneo, which borders Brunei, Indonesia, and the South China Sea.

Climate: Tropical and humid year-round. Monsoon season in east coast Peninsular Malaysia and Sabah/Sarawak Nov.-Mar.

Phone Codes: Country code: 60. International dialing prefix: 00.

Major Cities: Kuala Lumpur, Penang, Ipoh, Malacca, Johor Baru, Georgetown, Kota Kinabalu, Kuching.

Population: 23,500,000.

Life Expectancy: Women: 74.81 years. Men: 69.29 years.

Language: Bahasa Malaysia (official), Chinese dialects, English, Tamil, Telagu, Malayalam, Panjabi, Thai. Dominant indigenous languages are Iban, Kadazan.

Religion: Islam 52%, Buddhism 17%, Taoism 12%, Christianity 8%, Hinduism 8%, tribal 2%.

Literacy Rate: 88.9% overall; 92.4% of men, 85.4% of women.

Major Exports: Petroleum, natural gas, electronic equipment, wood and wood products, palm oil, rubber, chemicals, textiles.

RELIGION

ISLAM. Islam is the official state religion of Malaysia and is practiced by 52% of the population. Religious freedom for all faiths is guaranteed by the constitution for all but ethnic Malays, who are born Muslim by law. Malaysia is a miracle of cultural fusion, and Muslim Malay culture has borrowed many customs from other cultural and religious traditions. Islam still exerts a conservative influence on Malay culture, and the government strongly supports Muslim values and favors ethnic Malays in housing, education, and business. Those who convert from Islam to another religion are usually fined or imprisoned for rehabilitation.

BUDDHISM. The Buddhist influence in Malaysia was stronger before the rise of Islam, but due to the significant Chinese population, Buddhism still retains importance in Malaysian culture. **Confucianism, Taoism,** and ancestor worship also belong to the school of Buddhism and are associated with the Chinese community.

OTHER RELIGIONS. Christianity is practiced by approximately 8% of Malaysia. Many Christians in Malaysia are converted Chinese. Malaysia's large Indian population (roughly 8% of the total population) practices **Hinduism.** Trade brought the religion to Malaysia's shores nearly one millennium before Islam, and continued trade with India reinforced Hinduism's importance to Malaysian culture.

PLANTS

Malaysia's plantlife alone is more than enough reason to visit the country. Malaysia has more endangered plant species than any other country in the world. While all of Europe contains approximately 5000 species of plants, Malaysia alone, at a fraction of the size, boasts an estimated 12,000-15,000. The national flower is the **hibiscus** and there are over 800 species of **orchids.** Native to Sarawak, the **bitahgor tree** is one of three plant species that pharmaceutical companies believe may generate a cure for AIDS. Nearly 20% of Peninsular Malaysia's tree species and slightly over 20% of the tree species in Sabah and Sarawak are endangered. Thirteen species of plants have become extinct since the 1920s due to logging. Of particular note, the plant life on **Mt. Kinabalu** (see p. 441) makes up 10% of all vascular plants in Malaysia. The **coconut palm** can grow to be 25-30m tall and is heavily harvested throughout Malaysia for its oil, as is the **oil palm.** Two other important crops in Malaysian agriculture are **rubber** and **cocoa.**

WILDLIFE

While the number of animal species in Malaysia is not as impressive as the bulk of plant species, many of the animals are just as precious. **Orangutans** and **hawksbill turtles** are two endangered animals in Malaysia. There are no more than 4000 orangutans in East Malaysia, and of endangered marine turtles, the hawksbill population is the smallest. Also native to Malaysia is the **Asian elephant.** The first Asian elephant equipped with satellite tracking equipment was Mek Penawar, who in 1995 was relocated after she raided a starfruit plantation in southern Malaysia. A few other highly endangered species are the **Malaysian sun bear,** with a population of only 600-1000 in all of Malaysia, Myanmar, Thailand, and Sumatra (Indonesia); the **Javan rhino,** with only an estimated 150 left in Malaysia; and the **storm stork,** which may have a population of less than 200.

HISTORY

EARLY KINGDOMS (100-1400)

As early as the first century AD, the Straits of Melaka facilitated gold-seeking Chinese and Indian traders who spread Indic influences throughout Malaya. The Javanese Empire seized Malaya around AD 1080 and ruled until the Chinese, fleeing from the threatening Siamese, founded Melaka in the early 15th century. Melaka then grew quickly as a naval port and trading center for merchants from Arabia, China, Java, India, and Myanmar.

RISE OF ISLAM AND WESTERN EXPLORATION (1400-1795)

IMPORTANT DATES		
15th Century Melaka converts to Islam.	**1511** Muslim loyalists flee as Portuguese invade.	**16th Century** Dutch overthrow Portuguese rule.

The 15th century witnessed the spread of Islam under Muslim **Muzaffar Shah,** who helped Melaka eliminate Thai vassals. By the late 15th-century reign of **Mahmud Shah,** Melaka included modern-day peninsular Malaysia, Singapore, parts of Thailand, and northern Sumatra. The **Portuguese invasion** in 1511 marked the beginning of Malaysia's "age of exploration." Unruffled by the Portuguese presence, locals remained loyal to the Shah Dynasty and fled south to establish the state of **Johor.** The chaos following the assassination of Melaka's **Sultan Mahmud** attracted the **Bugis** and other groups from southern Sulawesi. They competed with the Sultan of Johor and the **Dutch,** who replaced the Portuguese in the 16th century.

COLONIAL RULE (1795-1945)

IMPORTANT DATES			
1795 British rule begins.	**1819** British claim uninhabited Singapore.	**1824** Anglo-Dutch Treaty gives Malaysia to Britain.	**1879** Treaty of Pangkor brings British residents to Malaysia.

The Dutch gave up the island of Penang to British occupation in 1786, and the English acted as a stabilizing—though oppressive—force in the region. The Dutch, in turn, took control of the islands south of Singapore. The **Treaty of Pangkor of 1879** saw the import of ill-prepared English "residents" to Malaysia. By World War I, all of Peninsular Malaysia had submitted to some sort of British control, though not without resistance. Throughout the 150 years of British rule, anti-colonial sentiment grew, evinced by the frequent popular uprisings and subsequent periods of repression that characterized the colonial period.

FORGING A NATION (1942-1957)

IMPORTANT DATES		
1942-45 Japanese occupation, British desertion, and Malay nationalism.	**1946** United Malay National Organization established.	**1957** Independence: Federation of Malaya formed.

During WWII, the Japanese moved into Malaya and returned the northern states to Thailand, hoping to exploit Malaya's resources and strategic location. The British, who had fled and left the country defenseless, returned to Malaya after the war but were unable to return the country to its former calm. In 1946, Britain's plan for refederation—which proposed that all Malayan territories except for Singapore be included in a single union—was opposed by the newly formed **United Malay National Organization (UMNO)** and the **Malay Communist Party.** But Communist hopes were soon dashed, in part due to the deportation of 500,000 Chinese. The government plan then shifted to unifying Malaya and guaranteeing Malay rights. In 1957, the independent **Federation of Malaya** was established under Prime Minister **Tunku Abdul Rahman.**

THE TUMULTUOUS 1960S (1960-1970)

IMPORTANT DATES			
1960s Government tries to enforce Islam and Malay language.	**1963** Indonesian President Sukarno declares *Konfrontasi*.	**1965** Singapore secedes.	**1969** Ethnic riots in Kuala Lumpur.

Supporting insurgency in Malaysia's eastern states and border skirmishes between Sabah/Sarawak and Kalimantan, Indonesian President **Sukarno** declared **Konfrontasi** ("confrontation") against Malaya in January 1963. With

England's support, the Federation of Malaya combined with Sabah, Sarawak, and Singapore to become the Federation of Malaysia on September 16, 1963. This union infuriated the Philippines, which held an ancient claim to Sabah. Indonesia, meanwhile, regarded Malaya's action as covert British neo-colonialism. Within the newly formed Malaysia, ethnic tensions rose. The official attitude toward Singapore's predominantly Chinese population created more problems for the Malay-oriented government, which had established Islam and Bahasa Malaysia as its official religion and language, respectively. In 1965, Malaysia passed an amendment allowing Singapore to secede. In May 1969, **ethnic riots** erupted in Kuala Lumpur after the Malay majority party, **Alliance** (which consisted of the UMNO and the conservative Malayan Chinese Association), lost a number of seats to non-Malay-supported parties. Feeling their own culture should be adopted, at least in part, by other nationalities, the Malay forced the use of the Malay language in official contexts. Malay political leaders called mass meetings but quickly lost control of the armed mobs that gathered. Ensuing riots lasted four days, leaving over 200 Chinese dead and more than 5000 homeless. Some Malays blamed the prime minister, but most blamed the concessions made to non-Malay groups rather than their own racial attitudes.

MALAY DOMINATION (1970-2004)

IMPORTANT DATES			
1971 Islamic National Culture Policy established.	**1981** Mahathir elected Prime Minister, consolidates power.	**1996** First satellites launched.	**1999-2000** Ibrahim convicted of sodomy; receives six-year prison sentence.

Under Prime Minister **Tun Abdul Razak's** rule (1970-1976), UMNO's power increased, and the country continued to promote Malay interests. Additional political alliances increased the status and political clout of Malay citizens, and economic policies were implemented to support Malay business ownership. The **Islamic National Culture Policy,** established in 1971, defined "national culture" as encompassing the indigenous traditions of the Malay people, which disregarded not only pre-Islamic Chinese and Indian influences but also those of the Orang Asli, who had populated the region thousands of years before the proto-Malay. Policy makers insisted on education in Bahasa Malaysia alone and provided federal support only for ethnic-Malay art and literature. Though he faced allegations of human rights violations and a court declaration that the UMNO was unconstitutional, **Mahathir Mohamad** (who became prime minister in 1981) prevailed and organized the **UMNO Baru (New UMNO).** Mahathir intertwined Western economic models with a **"Look East"** policy when seeking foreign investment and trade to pull Malaysia out of financial crisis. Under Mahathir's administration, the country became less dependent on tin and rubber resources and moved toward industrialization. As part of the **Vision 2020** plan, which aims to attain developed-nation status by 2020 by improving technology, Malaysia launched its first two space satellites in August 1996. In April 1999, Deputy Prime Minister **Anwar Ibrahim** was condemned to a six-year prison sentence for corruption, and then in 2000 was sentenced to nine years in prison after being convicted of sodomy. Many viewed the ordeal as a direct result of Ibrahim's differing opinions about Malaysia's economic policies. In June 2002, Mahathir announced his impending resignation, and in October 2003 he was succeeded as Prime Minister by his deputy, **Abdullah Ahmad Badawi.** Badawi won the general election in March 2004 in a landslide victory for the ruling Barisan National.

MALAYSIA TODAY

BUMIPUTRA. In 1970, in response to the race riots of May 1969, the government introduced the **New Economic Policy (NEP)** a state-run program dedicated to redistributing wealth to the native Malay, known as the *bumiputra* (literally "sons of the soil"). The goals of the NEP were to eradicate poverty regardless of race and to end identification of ethnicity with economic function. The NEP extended the *bumiputra* certain privileges to help them compete with the wealthy ethnic Chinese majority. The program was replaced in 1991 by the still pro-*bumiputra* **National Development Policy (NDP).** In 2000, then deputy Abdullah Ahmad Badawi expressed concern that the government's continuing Malay favoritism would ultimately harm smaller Malay business interests by patronizing more prominent *bumiputra* businessmen. Badawi accused this practice of ultimately weakening the Malay economy. Both foreign and domestic Malaysian companies are required to have at least 30% Malay shareholders and are encouraged to hire Malays over Chinese for top positions. Malays also get discounts on housing and loans. Consequently, Malays have risen economically, though critics denounce the NDP for its limited Malay favoritism and discrimination against the Chinese.

ECONOMIC DEVELOPMENT. By 1998, the Asian Financial Crisis of 1997 had slowed Malaysia's economy by 7.5%. To help ameliorate IMF regulations, Deputy Prime Minister Anwar Ibrahim called off Mahathir's high-growth policies in December 1997 to help stabilize the ringgit and the plummeting stock market. A significant increase in exports, especially in electronics and electrical products going to the United States, resulted in a surge of economic growth between 1999 and 2000, followed by the threat of yet another recession in 2001 due to global trends. Malaysia's economic recovery has since paralleled that of the U.S. Continued expansion of the ICT sector led to a 5.3% growth rate in 2003, with a 6% growth rate projected for 2004.

DOWNSIDES OF DEVELOPMENT. The downside of development has been severe **environmental degradation.** Once-beautiful bus rides are now marked by hills scarred from mining, single-crop plantations, factories, and construction sites. Environmental awareness has gained popularity, but much of it is little more than rhetoric. Another drawback to development is the ever-widening gap between rich and poor. In the 2004 election, Abdullah Ahmad Badawi faced serious opposition from the **Parti Islam SeMalaysia (PAS),** which won the northern state of Terengganu for the opposition in 1999 and has since also spread its influence through the state of Kedah. The leader of PAS in Selangor, **Hassan Ali,** believes Islam promotes a socially responsible government that could help close Malaysia's large economic gap. Badawi had to turn his attention to small and medium-size businesses as well as the agricultural sector (both Terengganu and Kedah are agricultural) in order to beat out the opposition in the election. The government also relies on widespread fear of Islamic fundamentalism to downplay its opponent. Hassan Ali claims, however, that the strict Islamic *hudud* penal code—which mandates chopping off thieves' hands, stoning adulterers, and flogging women with unproven rape claims—would not be enforced in Selangor, where there is a considerable non-Muslim majority, and would instead be limited to Malay Muslim-dominated areas. Hassan Ali may have been responding to the controversy surrounding the *hudud* laws that in the summer of 2002 were successfully passed in eastern Terengganu State, where 95% of the population is Muslim. Malaysian police were instructed not to enforce the laws on the basis on unconstitutionality.

HUMAN RIGHTS. In its quest for unity, the Malaysian government has used a heavy hand regarding freedom of expression. **Amnesty International** has criticized Malaysia for its heavy censorship of the media, use of capital punishment, and restrictions on religion. Though the constitution provides for religious freedom, the practice of Islamic sects other than Sunni Islam is severely restricted, and religious minorities like Buddhists, Hindus, and Christians frequently face restrictions. In addition, criminals under arrest face a very high death rate.

THE WAR ON TERROR. Fourteen suspected members of **al Qaeda,** the group responsible for the September 11, 2001 attacks on New York City, were arrested in Malaysia in 2002. In addition, the **Abu Sayyaf Group (ASG),** the terrorist group responsible for kidnapping several Americans in 2002, is believed to have at one time had a training ground in eastern Sabah (see **The Philippines Today,** p. 533). In summer 2002, Malaysia joined nine other ASEAN countries in a pledge to "prevent, disrupt, and combat" global terrorism through increased sharing of information and intelligence. In April 2004, Islamic nations met at an emergency summit in Putrajaya, Malaysia to examine the situation in Iraq. Malaysia was among 20 Muslim countries that pledged peacekeeping aid to Iraq if the UN were to take over Iraq's transition to sovereignty. The Human Rights Watch has recently criticized Malaysia for the abuse of some 100 terror suspects linked with the regional radical group Jemaah Islamiah, who are allegedly being held without charge under the auspices of the Malaysia Internal Security Act.

CUSTOMS AND ETIQUETTE

As in most Muslim countries in Southeast Asia, the standard conservative codes of conduct apply. Remove shoes before entering a home or place of worship, dress modestly, and use your right hand when handling food or greeting someone. As part of the traditional Muslim handshake, or *salam*, the younger person usually grasps the hands of the older person. Malays extend this gesture by retracting the hand and placing it over the heart to indicate sincerity. Handshakes are suitable between men and between women, but be forewarned that Muslims discourage physical contact with the opposite sex. **Longhouses** observe a specific code of politeness with foreigners. Visitors should never enter a longhouse without an invitation. Upon entering, one proceeds directly to the elder's room to announce one's presence. It is not polite to enter a family's sleeping quarters without permission, nor is it acceptable to walk over a person. Before departing, it is expected that one stay and converse with the inhabitants of a longhouse while sampling the local wine, which is usually made from fermented rice.

IN RECENT NEWS

BAG-SNATCHERS

Travelers beware: Petty crime is on the rise in Malaysia. In the past year, the nation has had an average of 43 snatch-thief cases per day. Most thefts have occurred in major cities but there have been several in less metropolitan areas as well. Usually, shoulderbags are grabbed by hoodlums on motorcycles, who then speed off before their victims are fully aware of the crime. Popular targets include foreign travelers and female pedestrians.

In the first half of 2004, 434 snatch-thief cases involved foreign tourists, and some of these offenses went beyond petty theft. In two separate incidents, women who tried to hold on to their bags were dragged along the road by motorcycles, and died from head injuries. In general, Malaysia's citizens are outraged by the increase in such crimes, and many have staged protests. In one incident in Klang, a suspected snatch-thief bore the brunt of the crowd's frustration and was beaten to death. While the Malaysian police have increased efforts to curb snatch-theft, travelers in Malaysia should be on constant alert when walking.

Some tips for safer travel:

- Walk facing the flow of traffic to avoid exposing your bag to a passing cyclist.
- Carry your bags under your arms, not slung over your shoulder.
- Walk a safe distance from road traffic.
- Walk in groups, and stay alert.

MALAYSIAN COOKING. Malaysia's exotic cuisine offers the novice an endless gastronomic adventure. It is composed of three main groups–Malay, Chinese and Indian–in addition to the fusion cuisines of the Nyonya and Indian Muslim communities. Hit up roadside foodstalls or food bazaars for some of Malaysia's most popular dishes. Ice-blended fruit slushes are especially cheap and refreshing, and milky bubble teas are also common. Everything is *halal* unless otherwise specified.

Laksa: spicy curry broth over noodles, bean sprouts, chicken, and seafood.

Satay: bite-sized pieces of skewered meat marinated in spices and barbecued. Usually served with rice cake, salad, and a sweet and spicy peanut gravy.

Nasi Lemak: rice cooked in coconut milk. Served with *sambal* boiled egg, anchovies, fried peanuts, and cucumbers.

Roti Canai: an all-time breakfast favorite made from wheat-flour dough, occasionally with beaten egg and diced onions.

Roti Puri: Fried bread with savory filling (looks like a big pancake).

Murtabak: *roti canai* stuffed with minced beef, egg, and onion.

Rojak: salad of pineapple, cucumber, bean curd, prawn fritters, and boiled egg served with peanut sauce.

ARTS AND RECREATION

DRAMA AND DANCE. Malaysian dance and drama are closely related, as exemplified by the **Ma'Yong** (also **Mak Yong**), a Malay dance-drama that gained prominence as a court tradition over 400 years ago. Roles are traditionally reserved for young women, except for that of the buffoon or clown. **Malay shadow play** is an ancient and elaborate form of puppetry. The central story is the **Ramayana,** Valmiki's epic Hindu poem, in which Rama leads an army of monkeys from India to Ceylon to rescue his wife. **Malay dance** comes in many forms. Two of the most popular are the **candle dance,** in which dancers hold candles on small plates, and **silat,** which started as a deadly martial art. The most popular Malay dance is the **Joget,** derived from Portuguese folk dance. Also popular in the state of Johor is the **Kuda Kepang,** a form of drama-dance brought by Indonesian immigrants in the 20th century. The Kuda Kepang depicts Islam holy wars and is thought to be connected to the world of spirits. Another dance specifically for women, the **Datan Julud** is found in Sarawak and is used most often to greet visitors to the longhouses.

MUSIC. Traditional Malaysian music exhibits Middle Eastern, Indonesian, Portuguese, Filipino, and Chinese influences and usually contains some combination of the drum and gong. Thought to be of Arab origin, the **kompang** is an instrument similar to a tambourine and consists of goat hide stretched across a circular frame made from the wood of the balau tree. It is usually played at social events in ensembles of two or more *kompang.* Another traditional instrument to listen for is the **sape** (pronounced "sa-peh"), a carved, wooden guitar-like lute of the Orang Ulu people in central Borneo. Musical compositions for the *sape* are designed to accompany specific ceremonies of the **rumah panjang** (longhouses) in concert with the **jatung ulang** (wooden xylophone) and **keluai** (mouth organ). Among the most well-known instruments is the **rebab,** a spike fiddle. The large Arabic **gendang** drums provide the tempo for Malay drama and dance events. The popular music scene in Malaysia is dominated almost entirely by Indonesian artists.

HOLIDAYS AND FESTIVALS (2005)

DATE	NAME	LOCATION AND DESCRIPTION
Jan. 1	New Year's Day	National.
Jan. 21	Hari Raya Haji	Muslim-National; marks the end of the *haj* pilgrimage period.
Feb. 9-10	Chinese New Year	Chinese-National. Book accommodations and transportation well in advance if visiting at this time.
Feb. 10	Maal Hijrah	Muslim New Year–National.
May 1	Labor Day	National.
May 12	Prophet Mohammed's birthday	Muslim-National.
June 4	The King's Birthday	National (Birthday of Yang di-Pertuan Agong).
Aug. 31	National Day	Celebrates the anniversary of Malaysia's independence from colonial rule on August 31, 1957–National.
Oct. 4	Start of Ramadan	Muslim–National.
Nov. 3	Hari Raya Puasa	Festival celebrating the culmination of Ramadan.
Dec. 25	Christmas Day	Christian community observes Advent, the 4-week period prior to Christmas, with prayers, Bible-reading, and fasting.

ADDITIONAL RESOURCES

GENERAL HISTORY

A History of Malaysia, by Barbara Watson Andaya and Leonard Y. Andaya (2001). An in-depth look at the historical phenomena that have contributed to the formation of modern Malaysia.

FICTION AND NON-FICTION

Joss and Gold, by Shirley Geok-lin Lim (2001). Portrays the uncertainty of newly independent Malaysia and the country's search for a definite identity.

The Malay Dilemma, by Mahathir bin Mohamad (1970). A controversial treatise on Malaysia's racial issues. Banned in Malaysia until Mahathir's election.

The Ordeal: My Ten Years in a Malaysian Prison, by Beatrice Saubin, translated from the French by Barbara Brister (1994). A personal account of time spent in a Malaysian prison for a crime she never committed.

ON THE WEB

Malaysia Tourism Promotion Board (www.interknowledge.com/malaysia). Where to go, what to see, and how to do it.

ESSENTIALS

MALAYSIA PRICE ICONS					
SYMBOL:	❶	❷	❸	❹	❺
ACCOMM.	Under US$3 Under RM12	US$3-6 RM12-24	US$6-10 RM24-40	US$10-17 RM40-68	Over US$17 Over RM68
FOOD	Under US$1 Under RM4	US$1-2 RM4-8	US$2-4 RM8-16	US$4-8 RM16-32	Over US$8 Over RM32

EMBASSIES AND CONSULATES

MALAYSIAN CONSULAR SERVICES ABROAD

Australia: High Commission, 7 Perth Ave., Yarralumla, ACT 2600, Canberra (☎02 6273 1543/44/45; fax 6273 2496; malcanberra@netspeed.com.au). **Consulate,** Hyatt Regency Perth, Room 203, 204, 206, 99 Adelaide Terrace, Perth, WA 6000 (☎08 9225 1234; fax 9225 1701; mwperth1@bigpond.com).

Canada: High Commission, 60 Boteler St., Ottawa, ON K1H 8Y7 (☎613-241-5182/5206/5210; fax 241-5214; malottawa@kln.gov.my). **Consulate,** 1805-1111 W. Georgia St., Vancouver, BC V6E 4M3 (☎604-685-9550; fax 685-9520; mwvcouvr@axionet.net).

Ireland: Embassy, Level 3A-5A, Shellbourne House, Shellbourne Rd., Ballsbridge Dublin 4. (☎353 1667 7280; fax 1667 7283; mwdublin@mwdublin.ie).

New Zealand: High Commission, 10 Washington Ave., Brooklyn, P.O. Box 9422, Wellington (☎04 385 2439; fax 385 6973; mwwelton@xtra.co.nz).

UK: High Commission, 45-46 Belgrave Sq., London SW1X 8QT (☎020 7235 8033; fax 7235 5161; mwlondon@btinternet.com).

US: Embassy, 3516 International Court, N.W., Washington, D.C. 20038 (☎202-572-9700; fax 572-9882). **Consulate,** 313 E. 43rd St., New York, NY 10017 (☎212-490-2722/3; fax 490-2049; malnycg@kln.gov.my); 550 S. Hope St., Ste. 400, Los Angeles, CA 90071 (☎213-892-1238; fax 892-9031; mwla@pacbell.net).

CONSULAR SERVICES IN MALAYSIA

Australia: Embassy, 6 Jl. Yap Kwan Seng, 50450 Kuala Lumpur (☎03 2146 5555, emergency 2146 5575 or 800 80 88 49; www.australia.org.my).

Canada: Embassy, 17th fl., Menara Tan and Tan, 207 Jl. Tun Razak, 50400 Kuala Lumpur (☎03 2718 3333; www.dfait-maeci.gc.ca/kualalumpur). **Consulate,** 3007 Tingkat Perusahaan 5, Prai Industrial Park, 13600 Prai, Penang (☎04 389 3300; fax 3892300; tyt@lbsb.com).

Ireland: Embassy, Ireland House, Amp Walk, 218 Jl. Ampang, 50450 Kuala Lumpur (☎03 2161 2963; www.irlgov.ie/iveagh).

New Zealand: Embassy, Level 21, Menara IMC, 8 Jl. Sultan Ismail, 50250 Kuala Lumpur (☎03 2078 2533; www.nzembassy.com). **Consulate,** Lot 8679, Section 64, Pending Commercial Centre, 93762 Kuching, Sarawak. P.O. Box 3201 Kuching, Sarawak (☎082 482 177; fax 482 279; shazwi69@tm.net.my).

UK: Embassy, 185 Jl. Ampang, 50450 Kuala Lumpur (☎03 2170 2200; www.britain.org.my).

US: Embassy, 376 Jl. Tun Razak, 50400 Kuala Lumpur (☎03 2168 5000; http://usembassymalaysia.org.my).

TOURIST SERVICES

Tourism Malaysia: 17th fl., Menara Dato'Onn, Putra World Trade Centre, 45 Jl. Tun Ismail 50480 Kuala Lumpur (☎03 2693 5188; http://tourism.gov.my).

The Malaysia Tourism Centre (MTC): 109 Jl. Ampang, 50450 Kuala Lumpur (☎03 2163 3664 or 2164 3929; www.mtc.gov.my).

Australia: 56 William St., Perth WA 6000 (☎08 9481 0400; fax 9321 1421; tourmal@omen.com.au); 65 York St., Sydney NSW 2000 (☎02 9299 4441; fax 9262 2026; Amir@iaccess.com.au). **Canada:** 830 Burrard St., Vancouver, B.C. V6Z 1X9 (☎604-689-8899; fax 689-8804; mtpb-yvr@email.msn.com). **UK:** 57 Trafalgar Sq.,

London WC2N 5DU (☎020 7930 7932; fax 7930 9015; razally@tourism.gov.my). **US:** 120 E. 56th St., Ste. 804, New York, NY 10022 (☎212-754-1113; fax 754-1116; mtpb@aol.com); 818 W. 7th St., Ste. 802, Los Angeles, CA 90017 (☎213-689-9702; fax 689-1530; mtpb.LA@tourism.gov.my).

DOCUMENTS AND FORMALITIES

Citizens of Australia, Canada, Ireland, New Zealand, the UK, and the US do not require a visa for stays of up to three months and can obtain two-month visit extensions without a visa. Most European citizens do not need a visa for stays of up to three months. Greek and Portuguese citizens can stay for one month. Enquire about visa requirements at the nearest Malaysia embassy or consulate. **Visa extensions** are available in Johor, Kuala Lumpur, and Penang, as well as at any international airport. As of the beginning of 2003, Malaysian immigration authorities have been detaining foreigners who over-stay visas. Travelers who leave Malaysia and come back must apply for a US$10 **re-entry permit.**

MONEY

CURRENCY AND EXCHANGE

The currency chart below is based on August 2004 exchange rates between local currency and Australian dollars (AUS$), Canadian dollars (CDN$), European Union euros (EUR€), New Zealand dollars (NZ$), British pounds (UK£), and US dollars (US$). Check the currency converter on websites like www.xe.com or www.bloomberg.com or a large newspaper for the latest exchange rates.

CURRENCY (RM)		
	AUS$1 = RM2.61	RM1 = AUS$0.38
	CDN$1 = RM2.80	RM1 = CDN$0.36
	EUR€1 = RM4.60	RM1 = EUR€0.22
	NZ$1 = RM2.38	RM1 = NZ$0.42
	UK£1 = RM6.92	RM1 = UK£0.14
	US$1 = RM3.80	RM1 = US$0.26

Malaysia's **ringgit (RM)** is issued in denominations of RM1, 2, 5, 10, 20, 50, 100, 500, and 1000. Each ringgit is equivalent to 100 **sen,** which is divided into coins of 1, 5, 10, 20, and 50 (there are also RM1 coins). UK£ and US$ are the most widely accepted foreign currencies. Traveler's checks are accepted at all banks, hotels, and major department stores. A 5% government tax and 10% service charge is added to most bills, making **tipping** unnecessary but appropriate for good service.

GETTING THERE

BY PLANE. Malaysia's four largest **international airports** are: Bayan Lepas International Airport in Georgetown (see p. 367), Kuala Lumpur International Airport (KLIA) in Kuala Lumpur (p. 339), Kuching International Airport in Kuching (p. 411), and Malaysia Airport Berhad in Kota Kinabalu (p. 434). Airports in Kota Bharu, Langkawi, Kuala Terengganu, and Kuantan also have international flights. **Malaysia Airlines** (**MAS;** www.malaysiaairlines.com.my) flies from KLIA to over 100 domestic and international locations. Kuala Lumpur, Penang, and Singapore are the major international gateways.

BORDER CROSSINGS: Always acquaint yourself with current events before crossing the border. Below are widely used border crossings.

BRUNEI. From Kuala Baram in **Sarawak** (near Miri, p. 428) take the bus that stops at the border in Kuala Belait and have your passport stamped before going on into Seria and **Bandar Seri Begawan** (p. 66). Alternatively, from Lawas or Limbang (also in Sarawak), cross over to Temburong or Bangar, stopping by the immigration post near Bangar. From **Sabah,** take a ferry to **Pulau Labuan.**

INDONESIA. Buses connect Tebedu in **Sarawak** (near Kuching, p. 411) with **Entikong** (near Pontianak) in West Kalimantan. The border crossing is open daily 6am-5pm; Indonesian visas are available in Kuching. Ferries run from Tarakan/Nunukan in East Kalimantan to **Tawau** in Sabah. To reach Sumatra from Peninsular Malaysia, take a ferry from **Penang** (p. 366) to **Medan** (p. 234).

SINGAPORE. Most travelers take the 1km causeway that connects Singapore (p. 625) to **Johor Bahru** in Malaysia. Buses and trains from Malaysia run over this causeway into Woodlands town.

THAILAND. Most Western tourists can travel to Thailand from Malaysia without buying a visa before crossing borders. Obtain transit visas at the border stops instead. By ferry, you can travel from **Kuala Perlis** and **Pulau Langkawi** (p. 375) to **Satun;** stop by the immigration office at Thammalang pier to have your passport stamped. Other common crossings are (listed from Malaysia to Thailand): **Rantau Panjang/Kota Bharu** (p. 389) to **Sungai Kolok** in the east and **Kangar** to **Padang Besar, Alor Setar** to **Sadao,** and **Keroh** to **Betong** in the west.

BY LAND. Refer to the above table for overland border crossings in Malaysia.

GETTING AROUND

BY PLANE. Malaysia's abundance of domestic airports makes plane travel between cities easy and safe. **Malaysia Airlines** monopolizes the domestic market.

BY BUS OR TRAIN. Buses are the most popular mode of domestic transportation. Both A/C and non-A/C **buses** run between major towns at reasonable prices. **Malayan Railways (Keretapi Tanah Melayu Berhad, KTM)** runs up and down the west coast from Alor Setar to Singapore. KTM railpasses allow unlimited travel on passenger trains in Malaysia and Singapore for 10 days (US$55, children US$28) or 30 days (US$120, children US$60). The slow but scenic **Jungle Train** connects Wakat Baru (near Kota Bharu, see p. 389) to Singapore via Jerantut. Bus travel is quick and efficient along **Hwy. 3,** a well-maintained road connecting Johor Bahru in the south to Kota Bharu in the north.

BY CAR. Fixed-rate inter-city **taxis** connect many towns and cities. Split the ride with up to three others. Local taxis are often unmetered, so agree on a price beforehand. Surcharges apply to taxis booked by phone, trips between midnight and 7am, and rides for more than two passengers. Malaysia's roads are some of the best in Southeast Asia. Travel the North-South Highway along the west coast from Singapore to Thailand in 10-12 hours. To **rent a car,** you need an **International Driver's Permit (IDP)** or a government-issued license (see p. 37). Some hotels rent cars for RM160-350. Malaysians drive on the left side of the road.

HEALTH AND SAFETY

EMERGENCY NUMBERS: Police/Ambulance: ☎999 **Fire:** ☎994.

MEDICAL EMERGENCIES. Pharmacies are open daily 9:30am-7pm. **Private Clinics** are available throughout Malaysia with visits costing around RM30, not including medications. Each town's **general hospital** will see foreigners in the emergency department for RM1, but the cost will rise if there is extended treatment or overnight stays. Most staff speak English and modern technology is available most everywhere.

HEALTH RISKS. Standards for hygiene and medical care in Malaysia are better than in most other Southeast Asian countries. Travelers from **yellow fever** endemic areas require vaccination documentation. Urban and coastal areas are free of **malaria**, but it is still found in more inland regions. **Dengue fever** occurs in both urban and rural areas, so be careful to avoid mosquito bites. The tap water is safe to drink in Malaysia, but bottled water is recommended.

SPECIFIC CONCERNS. Most Malaysians are Muslim, so women should dress conservatively. The east and west coasts of peninsula Malaysia are dangerous for women traveling alone, while travel to Borneo is comparatively safer. Exercise caution in rural areas.

There is a general threat of terrorism for Westerners traveling to all countries in Southeast Asia. Be especially vigilant at tourist sites and in public places. In the coastal area of Sabah there is an ongoing risk of kidnapping. Possession of any kind of **drugs** can lead to **imprisonment** or the **death penalty.**

Homosexuality is illegal in Malaysia and punishable by imprisonment, fines, or whipping. Travelers should exercise discretion. In spite of widespread Islamic fundamentalism, Malaysia does have a gay community. For more information, try **Pink Triangle,** an NGO that handles sexuality issues and HIV/AIDS. The staff has information on GLBT venues in Kuala Lumpur and holds socials: 7C-2 Jl. Ipoh Kechil, Kuala Lumpur (☎603-444-4611; hotline ☎603-444-5455 and 444-5466; fax 444-4622; isham@pop7.jaring.my. Open M-F 10am-7pm, hotline open M-F 7:30-9:30pm.)

KEEPING IN TOUCH

Malaysia's **postal system** does quality work. Airmail across the globe should take one to two weeks. **Long-distance calls** are easiest from cell phones. Card phones that offer International Direct Dialing (IDD), are also convenient, but you'll have to pay local charges in addition to long-distance fees. Telephone offices and convenience stores sell **phone cards.** The most convenient is the Telekom Malaysia card, except in Kuala Lumpur, where the Uniphone card is most useful. For **Home Country Direct (HCD)** numbers from Malaysia, refer to the table on the inside back cover of this book.

PENINSULAR MALAYSIA

WEST COAST

Rich with colonial history and natural beauty yet polished and with a cosmopolitan veneer, Peninsular Malaysia's west coast offers plenty of sights and modern amenities. With user-friendly transportation, tourist facilities, and many English

Peninsular Malaysia
Monk Mystique
Climb the Pagoda of 10,000 Buddhas at Kek Lok Si, Malaysia's largest temple.
Coral Corral
Snorkel among the coral deposits and exotic sea life in Long Beach.
Pulau Perhentian Kecil
On the DL in KL
Indulge in the wild dancing that characterizes Kuala Lumpur's popular nightlife.
Truly Trekking
Hike the breathtaking nine-day route to and from Gunung Tahan, Malaysia's highest peak.
Cultural Heritage
Soak up Malaysian culture in Melaka's Chinese, Dutch, & Portuguese villages.
Pulau Langkawi
Kangar
Alor Setar
Keroh
THAILAND
South China Sea
Kota Bharu
Rantau Panjang
Kuala Besut
Pulau Perhentian Besar
Pulau Redang
Pulau Penang
Penang
Lake Temenggor
Kuala Terengganu
Marang
Taiping
Kuala Kangsar
Ipoh
Kenyir Dam
Rantau Abang
TAMAN NEGARA NATIONAL PARK
Cameron Highlands
Pulau Pangkor
Tapah
Fraser's Hill
Jerantut
Cherating
Kuantan
Temerluh
Kuala Lumpur
Shah Alam
Andaman Sea
Lake Bera
Seremban
Pulau Tioman
Melaka
Mersing
Muar
Batu Pahat
Straits of Melaka
INDONESIA
Johor Bahru
SINGAPORE
0 40 miles
0 40 kilometers
N
LG

speakers, the west coast may well be the best introduction to Southeast Asia. The west coast also represents Malaysia's ethnic mix well: sizable Chinese and Indian communities coexist with ethnic Malay. Many tourists complain that industrialization has hindered local culture, but it has also created many jobs and comforts.

KUALA LUMPUR ☎03

The skyline of Kuala Lumpur is awesome seen from a distance. In the teeming urban streets, however, this quiet grandeur dissolves into the kinetic activity of an efficient capital city. Kuala Lumpur displays its patriotism through "Proud to be Malaysian" songs, ubiquitous Malay flags, and the highest flagpole in Asia. A country that has been in the hands of every country from India to Portugal, from The Netherlands to Britain, Malaysia's multi-ethnic history is still visible: up to 7% of the population is of mixed European and Asian blood, and there is a national obsession with inter-racial marriage. And as Malaysians chant *"Malaysia Boleh!"* ("Malaysia Can!") at sports events, the rumblings of numerous construction projects throughout the city reiterate the same sentiment.

INTERCITY TRANSPORTATION

BY PLANE. Ultra-modern **Kuala Lumpur International Airport** (**KLIA;** ☎8776 4311) lies 70km southwest of the city. The most efficient way to reach KLIA is the new **KLIA Ekspres** (☎2267 8000), which checks-in baggage at **KL CAT** (Kuala Lumpur City Air Terminal) inside **KL Sentral** and then drives you directly to the KLIA departure hall (28min. non-stop; every 15min. 5am-1am; RM35, child RM15; wheelchair accessible). KL CAT is an official destination recognized by the International Air Transportation Association, so luggage that's checked-in at KL CAT (at least 2hr. in advance) will be loaded onto its routed flight. The alternative route from **KL Sentral** is **KLIA Transit,** a high-speed train that leaves from the station for KLIA (37min., every 30min. 5:33am-12:03am, RM35). You can also catch the KLIA Transit at any of its three stops along the way: **Bandar Tasik Selatan** (Star LRT and Komuter Station, RM26.50), **Putrajaya-Cyberjaya** (RM6.20), or **Salak Tinggi** (RM3.20). If you are not leaving from **KL Sentral,** you can take Intrakota bus #47 from Platform 4 in Klang Bus Station (every 30min., RM2). Other KLIA-bound buses leave from certain LRT and commuter rail stations (from **Nilai Komuter Station:** 40min., every 30min. 6:30am-10:15pm, RM2; from **Chan Sow Lin Star LRT Station:** 45min.; every hr. 6:30am-9:30pm; RM14, child RM10). Airport taxis between Kuala Lumpur and KLIA charge exorbitant rates (☎9223 8915. 1-1½hr.; RM60-70 to KLIA, RM70-90 from KLIA). Don't ride in a taxi without a meter.

DESTINATION	FREQUENCY	PRICE	DESTINATION	FREQUENCY	PRICE
Bangkok	2 per day	RM643	**Jakarta**	2 per day	RM533
Hà nội	4 per week	RM860	**Manila**	2 per day	RM1230
Hong Kong	2 per day	RM1080	**Singapore**	10 per day	RM304

Airlines that serve Kuala Lumpur include: **Air Asia,** B-812 Kelana Sq., 17 Jl. SS7/26 Kelana Jaya (☎7809 6888); **Garuda Indonesia,** 19th fl., Citibank Bldg., 165 Jl. Ampang (☎2162 2811); **Malaysian Airlines (MAS),** MAS Bldg., Jl. Sultan Ismail (☎7846 3000); **Royal Brunei Airlines,** 2nd fl., UBN Tower, 10 Jl. P. Ramlee (☎2070 7166); **Singapore Airlines (SIA),** Wisma Singapore Airlines, 2/4 Jl. Dang Wangi (☎2692 3122); **Thai Airways,** Ste. 3001, 30th fl., Wisma Gold Hill, 67 Jl. Rajah Chulan (☎2031 2900); **Vietnam Airlines,** Wisma MPL 1st fl., Jl. Raja Chulan (☎2141 2416).

BY TRAIN. The **railway station,** known as **KL Sentral,** is in front of the National Museum, off Jl. Travers. (☎2267 1200; http://ktmb.com.my. Open daily 7pm-midnight.) Take the LRT Putra line or Komuter train to KL Sentral. Express trains run to **Singapore** (7hr.; 8:30am, 3, 10:30pm; RM34) and **Jerantut** (6½hr.; 2, 7:55am; economy seat RM18, 2nd-class sleeper RM35). Regular trains leave for **Hat Yai** (12hr.; daily 8pm; 2nd-class seat RM36, 2nd-class sleeper RM46) via **Butterworth** (10hr.; 2nd-class seat RM30, 2nd-class sleeper RM40) and **Singapore** (9hr.; 10:30pm; economy seat RM19, 2nd-class seat RM30, 2nd-class sleeper RM37.50-40).

BY BUS. Puduraya Station on Jl. Pudu is KL's long-distance bus station. Take the **LRT Star** line to **Plaza Rakyat.** Dozens of express bus companies sell tickets for destinations all over Malaysia. The counters inside the station and across the street near 7-Eleven are better for last-minute purchases. **Transnasional Express** is one of the largest bus companies. (☎2070 3300. Open daily 6am-midnight.) Buses go to: **Butterworth** (5hr.; midnight, 9, 10, 11am, 3, 4:30, 6, 11pm; RM20.40); **Ipoh** (3hr., every hr. 7.30am-11:30pm, RM11.30); **Kota Bharu** (7hr., 9:10am, RM26); **Kuala Kangsar** (4hr.; 1:30, 2:30, 9, 10, 11:30am, 4, 6:30, 9:30pm; RM14); **Kuala Terengganu** (8hr.; midnight, 9, 10:30, 11am, noon, 9:30, 10:30, 11pm; RM25.10); **Kuantan** (4½hr., 17 per day 9am-midnight, RM14.30); **Melaka** (2½hr., 23 per day 7am-10pm, RM8); **Mersing** (4hr.; 9, 11am, 12:30, 6, 11, 11:30pm; RM9.50); **Pulau Penang** (5hr.; midnight, 9, 10:30, 11:30am, 4, 5:30, 11pm; RM22.80); **Singapore** (6hr.; 9:45, 10:30, 11:15am, 1:30, 3:45, 5:30pm; RM31.10). Express coaches cost more. Other bus companies including Eltabina, Indah Ekspres, Plusliner, Triton, and Warisan specialize in buses to the same cities mentioned above. **Hantian Putra Station,** which serves Malaysia's east coast, has the same prices as Puduraya Station.

BY TAXI. Above Puduraya Bus Station, five taxi companies serve various regions. These companies have different rates for each destination—ask all of them to find the best price for your destination. The following rates are the lowest rates for four-person cabs with A/C, excluding toll, from the taxi station: **Butterworth** (RM250); **Cameron Highlands** (RM180); **Genting Highlands** (RM45); **Ipoh** (RM140); **Jerantut** (RM180); **Johor Bahru** (RM250); **Kota Bharu** (RM400); **Kuala Kangsar** (RM160); **Kuala Terengganu** (RM380); **Kuantan** (RM200); **Melaka** (RM120); and **Muar** (RM160). Expect higher rates on nights and weekends.

ORIENTATION

Most sites within the city are accessible by the LRT trains (see **Local Transportation,** below), and the central city is more walkable that one might think judging from the map. Budget accommodations are clustered near the **Puduraya Bus Station** and in **Chinatown.** To the east of **Puduraya Bus Station, Jln Bukit Bintang** runs from Jl. Pudu through the **"Golden Triangle,"** a posh area of luxury hotels, expensive restaurants, and large shopping malls. The Golden Triangle is roughly bordered by **Jl. Imbi** to the southeast, **Jln Raja Chulan** to the north, and Jln Bukit Bintang and **Jl. Sultan Ismail** to the west. Heading west from **Puduraya Bus Station, Jln Pudu** splits into **Jln Cheng Lock,** which runs along the northern edge of Chinatown, and **Jln Tun Perak,** which leads to **Masjid Jamek,** where the LRT station of the same name connects both Star and Putra LRT lines. South of Masjid Jamek, **Jln Sultan Hishamuddin** runs through **Merdeka Square** and past the **GPO** before reaching the **old railway station. KL Sentral,** to the south, is a major transportation hub for trains to other cities and for KLIA Ekspress to KL's international airport. While restaurants and shops are open late along Jl. Bukit Bintang and in the Golden Triangle, **Bangsar Baru,** south of KL Sentral, is *the* center of nightlife. North of Masjid Jamek, **Jln Tuanku**

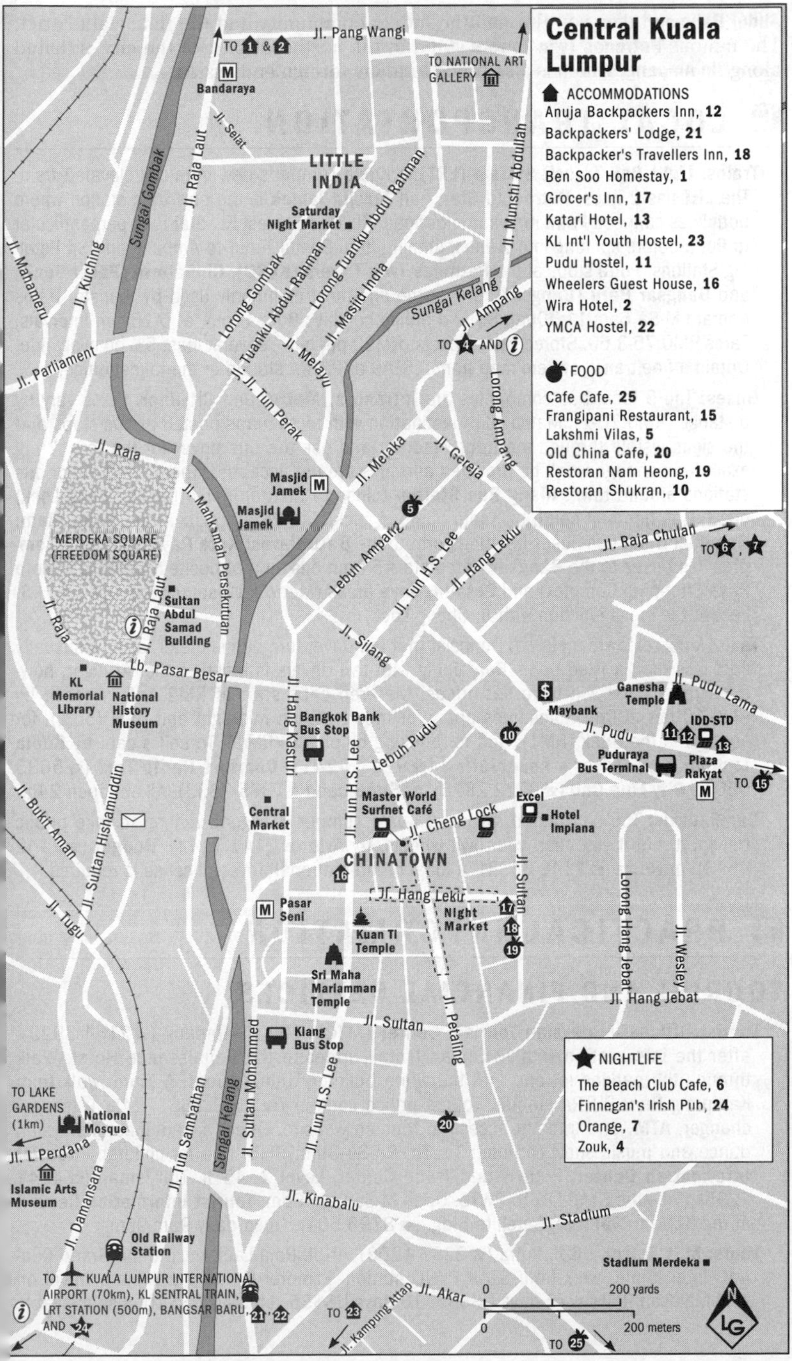
Central Kuala Lumpur
ACCOMMODATIONS
Anuja Backpackers Inn, 12
Backpackers' Lodge, 21
Backpacker's Travellers Inn, 18
Ben Soo Homestay, 1
Grocer's Inn, 17
Katari Hotel, 13
KL Int'l Youth Hostel, 23
Pudu Hostel, 11
Wheelers Guest House, 16
Wira Hotel, 2
YMCA Hostel, 22
FOOD
Cafe Cafe, 25
Frangipani Restaurant, 15
Lakshmi Vilas, 5
Old China Cafe, 20
Restoran Nam Heong, 19
Restoran Shukran, 10
NIGHTLIFE
The Beach Club Cafe, 6
Finnegan's Irish Pub, 24
Orange, 7
Zouk, 4
Jl. Pang Wangi
TO 1 & 2
TO NATIONAL ART GALLERY
Bandaraya
Jl. Selat
Jl. Raja Laut
Sungai Gombak
LITTLE INDIA
Saturday Night Market
Jl. Tuanku Abdul Rahman
Lorong Tuanku Abdul Rahman
Jl. Munshi Abdullah
Jl. Mahameru
Jl. Kuching
Lorong Gombak
Jl. Masjid India
Sungai Kelang
Jl. Ampang
TO 4 AND
Jl. Parliament
Jl. Melayu
Jl. Tun Perak
Lorong Ampang
Jl. Raja
Jl. Melaka
Jl. Gereja
Masjid Jamek
Jl. Mahkamah Persekutuan
MERDEKA SQUARE (FREEDOM SQUARE)
Lebuh Ampang
Jl. Tun H.S. Lee
Jl. Hang Lekiu
Jl. Raja Chulan
TO 6, 7
Sultan Abdul Samad Building
Jl. Silang
KL Memorial Library
National History Museum
Lb. Pasar Besar
Jl. Hang Kasturi
Bangkok Bank Bus Stop
Maybank
Ganesha Temple
Jl. Pudu Lama
IDD-STD
Jl. Pudu
Lebuh Pudu
Puduraya Bus Terminal
Plaza Rakyat
TO 15
Jl. Bukit Aman
Jl. Sultan Hishamuddin
Central Market
Master World Surfnet Café
Jl. Cheng Lock
Excel
Hotel Impiana
CHINATOWN
Jl. Hang Lekir
Night Market
Jl. Sultan
Lorong Hang Jebat
Jl. Wesley
Jl. Tugu
Pasar Seni
Kuan Ti Temple
Sri Maha Mariamman Temple
Jl. Hang Jebat
Jl. Sultan
Jl. Petaling
Klang Bus Stop
Jl. Sultan Mohammed
TO LAKE GARDENS (1km)
National Mosque
Jl. L Perdana
Jl. Tun Sambathan
Sungai Kelang
Islamic Arts Museum
Jl. Damansara
Jl. Kinabalu
Jl. Stadium
Old Railway Station
Stadium Merdeka
TO KUALA LUMPUR INTERNATIONAL AIRPORT (70km), KL SENTRAL TRAIN, LRT STATION (500m), BANGSAR BARU, AND 24
TO 23
Jl. Kampung Attap
Jl. Akar
0
200 yards
0
200 meters
TO 25

Abdul Rahman takes you through the Indian community and the financial district. The famous **Petronas Twin Towers** stand in the northeast part of the city, situated along **Jln Ampang,** which is also home to many foreign embassies.

LOCAL TRANSPORTATION

Trains: Light Rail Transit System (LRT) is Kuala Lumpur's new intra-city elevated train. The **LRT** has 2 lines, **Putra** and **Star,** and **Masjid Jamek** is the only train station where both lines connect. Putra runs from northeast KL to southwest KL. Star runs perpendicular to Putra before splitting into 2 lines, running from Sentul Timur to Ampang and Sri Petaling Stations. Putra stops at the **Petronas Twin Towers (KLCC), Chinatown (Pasar Seni),** and **Bangsar Baru (Bangsar),** and is the line most commonly used by tourists. Trains operate M-Sa 6am-11:30pm, Su and public holidays 8am-11pm, at 5-15min. intervals. Fares RM0.75-3.60. Stored value tickets (RM20 per min.) save at least 5% on every ride. Obtain a free transit system map from a STAR or PUTRA station or the tourist office.

Buses: The 3 local bus companies are **Intrakota, Metro,** and **Cityliner.** Fares vary by distance (RM0.70-2). Match your destination with route maps posted at bus stops and the signs visible through the front windows and ask the bus driver for the fare. Bring exact fare; change won't be provided and bills are not accepted. There are 3 major bus stations around town: **Klang Bus Station** (close to Central Market on Jl. Cheng Lock) has buses heading south of Kuala Lumpur, including **Petaling Jaya** and **Shah Alam; Bangkok Bank** has buses heading north to the **Batu Caves; Kota Raya Shopping Complex** has buses to the **Bangsar** (Interkota #5 from bus stop opposite Starbucks in Kota Raya Shopping Complex) and **Petaling Jaya** areas (Metro #12 southward along Jl. H.S. Lee, at the cross junction with Jl. Cheng Lock).

Taxis: Most taxis are metered. Do insist that the driver turn on his meter, as it will usually cost less than a fixed price. Bargaining with taxi drivers is mostly futile. At night, however, most cabs will have set prices. Metered cabs start at RM2 and increase by RM0.10 per 200m. Surcharges apply for trips between midnight and 6am (50%), for luggage in the trunk (RM1), and for booking by phone (RM1). To call a cab, try **Kuala Lumpur Taxi Driver's Association** (☎9221 4241), **Comfort Radio Taxi** (☎5633 0507), **City Line Cab** (☎9222 2828), or **Supercab** (☎7875 7333). All are open 24hr.

Car Rentals: The convoluted layout of Kuala Lumpur is a good reason to take public transport, but if you need your own wheels, try **Avis** (☎2141 7144), **Budget** (☎2142 4693), or **Hertz** (☎2148 6433). A local or international driver's license is required.

PRACTICAL INFORMATION

TOURIST AND FINANCIAL SERVICES

Tourist Offices: Malaysian Tourism Center (MTC), 109 Jl. Ampang (☎2164 3929), after the intersection with Jl. Sultan Ismail opposite the Renaissance Hotel. Walk through the parking lot and into the white building with red roof. A 5min. walk from Kampung Baru PUTRA station. Tourist police counter (☎2163 3657; 24hr.), moneychanger, **ATM,** and Internet access to tourism website. Offers a traditional Malaysian dance and music show (45min.; Tu, Th, Sa-Su 3pm; RM5, free for children). **Tourist Information Center,** Putra World Trade Center, Level 2, 45 Jl. Tun Ismail (☎4041 1295). Take the STAR LRT to PWTC. Open M-Sa 9am-6pm. **Tourist Information Center,** at the **KLIA arrival hall,** Satellite Bldg. (☎8796 564). Open daily 9am-9pm.

Tours: MSL Travel, 66 Jl. Putra (☎2267 1200), off Jl. Raja Laut, next to the Grand Central Hotel. 5min. walk from STAR PWTC station. Explorer Pass for unlimited travel on KTM-Malayan Railway (5 days US$35, 10 days US$55, 15 days US$70; also available at KL Sentral ☎2274 3125). Offers airfare discounts for students. Issues International Student Identity Cards (ISIC), Teacher's Identity Cards (RM20 including photo), and Youth Travel Cards (RM15 with photo). Open M-F 9am-5pm, Sa 9am-1pm.

Embassies: Australia, 6 Jl. Yap Kwan Seng (☎2146 5555). Open M-F 8:30am-12:30pm and 1:30-4:30pm. **Brunei,** MBF Plaza, 172 Jl. Ampang (☎2161 2800). **Canada,** 17th fl., Menara Tan and Tan, 207 Jl. Tun Razak (☎2718 3333). Open M-Th 8am-4:30pm, F 8am-1:30pm. **Indonesia,** 233 Jl. Tun Razak (☎2145 2011). Open M-Th 8:30am-1pm and 2-4:30pm, F 8:30am-1:30pm and 2:30-4:30pm. **Ireland,** The Amp Walk, 218 Jl. Ampang, 50450 Kuala Lumpur (☎2161 2963). **Laos,** 12A Persiaran Madge, off Ampang Hilir (☎4251 1118). Open M-F 8:30am-noon and 2-5pm. **Myanmar,** 10 Jl. Meng Kong off Jl. Ru (☎4256 0280). Visas RM70; 3-day processing. Open M-F 9am-1pm. **New Zealand,** 21st fl. Menara IMC, 8 Jl. Sultan Ismail (☎2078 2533). Open M-F 8am-12:30pm and 1:30-4:30pm. **Singapore,** 209 Jl. Tun Razak (☎2161 6277). Open M-F 8:30am-5pm. **Thailand,** 206 Jl. Ampang (☎2148 8222). Open M-F 9:30am-5pm; consul open M-F 9am-12:30pm. **UK,** 185 Jl. Ampang (☎2170 2200). Open M-F 8am-12:30pm and 1:30-4:30pm. **US,** 376 Jl. Tun Razak (☎2168 5000). Open M-F 7:45am–4:30pm. **Vietnam,** 4 Persiaran Stonor (☎2148 4036). Open M-F 9am-noon and 2-4:30pm, Sa 9am-noon.

Currency Exchange: Moneychangers are on Jl. Pudu, directly across from Puduraya Bus Station, as well as in Chinatown along Jl. Tun H.S. Lee. Banks are ubiquitous–especially along Jl. Hang Kasturi, near Central Market. **MayBank,** 100 Jl. Tun Perak (☎2070 8833), close to Puduraya Station, opposite Metrojaya. Traveler's check fee RM5 plus RM0.20 per check. Open M-F 9:30am-4pm, Sa 9:30-11:30am. 24hr. **ATMs.** Most ATMs accept Cirrus/MC/PLUS/V.

American Express: 18th fl. of Weld Bldg. on corner of Raja Chulan and Jl. P. Ramlee (☎2050 0888). Mail-holding services offered. Open M-F 9am-5pm.

LOCAL SERVICES

Luggage Storage: Yakin Enterprise (☎2070 0052), on the 1st fl. toward the back of Puduraya Bus Station. RM2 per bag per day. Open daily 8am-11pm. **Matang Lockers** (☎013 343 7939), on the 2nd fl. of KL Sentral. Small bag RM3 per day, large bag RM5 per day. Open daily 7am-10:30pm.

English-Language Bookstores: MPH Bookstores has branches at 2 Jl. Telawi, Bangsar Baru (☎2282 7300), and the ground fl. of Mid Valley Megamall (☎2938 3812). Open daily 10am-10pm. **Kinokuniya,** 4th fl., Suria KLCC (☎2164 8133). Open daily 10am-9:30pm. Both bookstores have a wide selection of books and magazines.

EMERGENCY AND COMMUNICATIONS

Emergency: ☎999. **Fire:** ☎994.

Tourist Police: (☎2146 0522). Main office at corner of Jl. Pudu and Jl. Hang Tuah. Branch office at Puduraya Bus Terminal (☎2078 9496). 24hr.

Police: (☎2146 0522). Kuala Lumpur Police HQ, 13th fl., Jl. Hang Tuah.

Pharmacies: All around Jl. Sultan and Cheng Lock. **Guardian Pharmacy,** 123 Jl. Sultan (☎2031 4013), on the corner with Jl. Cheng Lock. Open daily 10am-10pm.

Medical Services: Kuala Lumpur General Hospital (☎2692 1044), in city's north end, on Jl. Pahang near Grand Seasons Hotel. **City Medical Center,** 415-427 Jl. Pudu (☎9221 1255), is privately run. Most doctors speak English.

Telephones: Pusat Telekom (☎2079 6025), Jl. Raja Chulan. **Perkhidmantan Biro,** at the corner of Jl. Rajah Chulan and Jl. Bukit Mahkamah. Open daily 8:30am-9pm. HCD phones, fax. Across from Puduraya Bus Terminal, **Internet Express IT Center,** 10 Jl.

Pudu, 2nd fl. (☎2070 7377), has **IDD.** RM2.30-6 per min. Open 24hr. **Assisted International Calls:** ☎108. **Directory Assistance:** ☎103.

Internet Access: Internet Express IT Center, 10 Jl. Pudu, 1st fl. (☎2070 7377), across from the Puduraya Bus Terminal. RM3 per 30min., RM4 per hr., RM1 per additional 15min. Guests of Pudu Hostel (see **Accommodations,** p. 344) receive discounts (RM3 per hour). Overnight special RM15 10pm-6am. **IDD-STD Internet Cafe,** 18 Jl. Pudu, ground fl., across from the Puduraya Bus Terminal. RM4 per hr. Open 24hr.

Post Offices: GPO, 9 Jl. Sultan Hishamuddin, Dayabumi Complex (☎2274 1122). *Poste Restante.* Open M-Sa 8:30am-6pm. Closed 1st Sa of each month and public holidays. **Pos 2020** on the ground fl. is usually sufficient.

Postal Code: 50670.

ACCOMMODATIONS

CHINATOWN AREA

Pudu Hostel, 10 Jl. Pudu, 3rd fl. (☎2078 9600; www.puduhostel.com), opposite Puduraya Bus Terminal; look for the tall pink building. Large A/C lounge with Western food, cable TV, pool table, beer, and movies. Clean, comfortable rooms with A/C, lockers, and hot common showers. 24hr. reception. Towels and blankets for rent RM10. 4-bed dorms RM12; 2-bed dorms RM20; singles RM30; doubles RM40; triples RM40. ❶

Anuja Backpackers Inn, 28 Jl. Pudu (☎2026 6479; anujainn@sgsmc.com), across the street from Puduraya Bus Terminal. Rooms are inexpensive and spacious, but have weak A/C and poor ventilation. Hang out in the rooftop beer garden. Cafe next door. Internet (RM2 per hr. 9am-noon and 8-11pm, RM2.50 per hr. noon-8pm). Safe at reception. Hot common showers. Laundry. Dorms with A/C RM10; singles and doubles RM10-30, with A/C RM30-40; triples RM38/RM50. ❶

Backpacker's Travellers Inn, 60 Jl. Sultan, 2nd fl. (☎2078 2473 or 2032 1855; backpacker_inn@hotmail.com), 1½ blocks from Jl. Cheng Lock on the right; look for a red sign. Rooftop bar encourages partying. Books bus tickets. Owner runs great half-day tours. Bakery downstairs. Lockers RM1. Laundry RM9. Dorms with A/C RM10; singles and doubles RM25-36, with A/C RM28-60. 10% discount for *Let's Go* users. ❶

Grocer's Inn Lodge, 78 Jl. Sultan, 1st fl. (☎016 308 2307). Clean rooms have high ceilings and good ventilation. Common bathrooms with cold showers. Cafe downstairs. Newly renovated. 2-bed dorm with fan RM15-20; 4-bed dorm with A/C RM25. ❶

THE BIG SPLURGE

FRANGIPANI

Housed in a sleek, snow-white building, **Frangipani** ❺ is a feast for the senses. Every aspect of the interior is awesome, particularly the central staircase. Elegantly reaching up to the glass ceiling, it serves as the perfect vantage point for watching the torrential rains of the region's frequent, dramatic thunderstorms.

Begin an evening with drinks at the upstairs lounge, where velvet-covered chaises yield the perfect combination of casual and luxurious. Housepours are priced 10-15% less from 6-9pm. Late in the evenings, the lounge converts into a crowded dance floor, where local DJs spin downtempo and house tracks.

Downstairs, with Billie Holiday singing quietly over the stereo, diners find fusion cuisine at its finest. Standout dishes include the pan-seared *foie gras* wrapped in egg noodles with porcini dust in lettuce soup (RM48) and a sumptuous grilled heart of sirloin with fresh corn humita (RM68). If you have a sweet tooth, or any room left, don't miss Frangipani's dessert menu, which boasts fabulously rich chocolates and delicious cheeses and fruits. With excellent cuisine, a richly appointed interior, and attentive service, Frangipani is a choice destination for a special night out.

(25 Changkat, Bukit Bintang, Malaysia (☎2144 3001). Open Tu-Su 5pm-1am.)

Wheelers Guest House, 131-133 Jl. Tun H.S. Lee (☎2070 1386), off Jl. Cheng Lock on the right. Clean rooms; A/C is slightly weak. Manager provides excellent travel advice. Laundry RM9. 6-bed dorms with A/C RM10; singles and doubles RM25, with A/C RM40, with A/C and private bath RM60; triples RM30; quads with A/C RM45. ❶

Katari Hotel, 38 Jl. Pudu (☎2031 7777; www.katari.com.my), opposite the Puduraya Bus Terminal. New, clean facilities. Rooms with TV and Astro Channel. Laundry and dry cleaning. Safety deposit boxes. Breakfast included. 24hr. reception. Doubles RM88. ❺

KL SENTRAL

Backpackers' Lodge, 84 Jl. Tun Sambanthan (☎2272 3736), opposite KL Sentral. Convenient place to stay for a night, with 20-person. Common showers only. Dorms RM15; singles and doubles RM40; triples RM45. ❷

YMCA Hostel, 95 Jl. Padang Belia (☎2274 1439), a 5min. walk from KL Sentral/LRT. Great facilities, comfortable rooms. Unmarried couples may not share a room. Tennis court. Hot showers. Laundry next door. Doubles with A/C and private bath RM66-72; triples RM90. MC/V. ❸

Kuala Lumpur International Youth Hostel (HI), 21 Jl. Kampung Attap (☎2273 6870; myha@pd.jaring.my). Turn off Jl. Attaponto Jin Manau. Clean, single-sex baths and dorms. Midnight curfew. Reservations advisable May-Aug. and Nov.-Dec. HI cards for foreigners RM30 (1-year membership). Dorms RM25, members RM20. MC/V. ❸

FARTHER AFIELD

Ben Soo Homestay and Travelers Service, 61B Jl. Tiong Nam, 2nd fl. (☎2691 8096; bensoohome@yahoo.com), is highly recommended. Travel tips by Ben Soo, ex-travel agent and taxi driver extraordinaire. Call ahead to arrange pick-up. Breakfast included. Singles with fan RM30, with A/C RM38; doubles with fan RM36, with A/C RM44. ❸

Wira Hotel, 123 Jl. Thamboosamy (☎4042 3333; www.wirahotel.com.my), off Jl. Putra near the PWTC LRT Station. Spacious rooms with A/C, TV, and private hot showers. Breakfast included. Laundry. Safe deposit. Singles RM85-95; doubles RM95-105; family rooms RM115. Discounts for ISIC holders: singles and doubles RM80-90. ❺

FOOD

Head to **Chinatown** for delectable meal options around the clock. **Jln Sultan** and **Jln Hang Lekir** host an open-air carnival of steamboat restaurants, *satay* sellers, and exotic fruit-juice vendors, while the **Chinatown night market** bustles on along Jl. Petaling. **Little India,** north of Chinatown around **Jln Masjid India,** tantalizes travelers with a blend of South Indian and Malay flavors.

THE KING OF FRUITS. Among Malaysia's variety of tropical fruits is the famous (or infamous) durian. Recognizable by its spiky exterior and pungent aroma, the flesh comes in fist-sized, pulpy, yellow sacks. The texture is one-of-a-kind and the taste is indescribable, although it has been likened to the sting of fresh garlic. You'll either love it or hate it, but do give it a try. Higher-end hotels usually post signs forbidding the possession or consumption of durian on their premises (again, the smell!). Public consumption of durian is banned in Thailand. The finest grade is D24. Durian are sold as a whole fruit or by the kg at street vendors. They are sometimes pre-cut and pre-wrapped in plastic; insist on having a freshly cut one. A note of warning: simultaneous consumption of durian and alcohol may be fatal because of the chemical combination.

Restoran Nam Heong, 56 Jl. Sultan (☎2078 5879), off Jl. Cheng Lock, next to the Backpackers Traveller's Inn, has a reputation for having the most authentic chicken rice in town (it sells out by mid-afternoon!). Hainanese chicken rice with cucumbers RM3.60. Kampung chicken rice RM6.70. Open daily 10am-3:30pm. ❷

Restoran Shukran, at the roundabout off Jl. Pudu, next to Metrojaya Shopping Complex. Buzzing with activity around the clock. *Roti canai* RM0.80. Buffet of white rice and curried meats RM3-5. Great spot for city-watching at any time of the day. Open 24hr. ❷

Old China Cafe, 11 Jl. Balai Polis (☎2072 5915), off Jl. Petaling, preserves the feel of early 20th-century Chinese social life and serves delicious Melakan-style *nyonya* and Portuguese fare. The interior is quite dim, but the special *pie-tee* top-hat appetizers (RM3.90) and *Nyona laksa* (RM7.90) are sure to please. Expect to spend RM15-40 for a full meal. Wines available RM48-90 per bottle. Prices subject to tax and service charge. Open daily 11am-11pm. MC/V. ❹

Lakshmi Vilas, 57 Lebuh Ampang (☎2078 3523), near Masjid Jamek LRT Station. Best vegetarian and South Indian cuisine in town. *Dosai* RM1; *lassi* RM2.50; set vegetarian meals RM5.50-6. *Biryani* RM6. Open daily 7:30am-8:30pm. ❷

Cafe Cafe, 175 Jl. Maharajalela, at the intersection with Jl. Lapangan Terbang (☎2141 8141 or 012 212 5701). This Francophile's haven boasts an attentive waitstaff and thousands of crystals suspended from the ceiling. The French cuisine includes delights like pan-seared *foie gras* with apple and grape sauce (RM38) and pan-fried duck breast (RM48). Divine desserts abound—try the tiramisu (RM15). Open daily 6pm-midnight. ❹

SIGHTS

MERDEKA SQUARE (FREEDOM SQUARE)

Kuala Lumpur's most architecturally rich area, this expansive square was once a colonial cricket field, the site of Malaysia's independence ceremonies in 1957, and is now home to the tallest flagpole in Asia.

SULTAN ABDUL SAMAD BUILDING. Adorned with shiny copper domes and a 40m high clocktower, this stately Moorish-inspired building stretches along the eastern side of Merdeka Square. Built in 1897, it now serves as the High Court. While visitors are free to admire the exquisite exterior, they are not allowed inside.

NATIONAL HISTORY MUSEUM. Originally Kuala Lumpur's first bank (and later used as a telecommunications base during the Japanese occupation), the museum now exhibits artifacts dating from the pre-historic period to the present. The displays, while very informative, are rather unexciting. *(29 Jl. Raja. ☎2694 4590. Near the southeastern edge of Merdeka Square. Open daily 9am-6pm. Free.)*

MASJID JAMEK. This mosque, built in 1909 by the same architect who designed the railway station, stands where the first settlers landed in KL. Its full splendor is best viewed from the banks of the Kelang and Gombak Rivers. *(Follow Jl. Hang Kasturi north. Proper attire is required: long pants for everyone, long sleeves and head shawl for women. Open M-Th and Sa-Su 8:30am-12:30pm and 2:30-4pm, F 8:30-11am and 2:30-4pm. Free.)*

SOUTH OF MERDEKA

NATIONAL MOSQUE (MASJID NEGARA). This white marble mosque contrasts starkly with the Masjid Jamek across the river. Its most notable features are a 73m high minaret from which the faithful are called to prayer and a multi-fold, umbrella-like roof. The upper deck houses the main prayer hall and a reflecting pool. Visitors may borrow a robe *(jubah)* or a head scarf (*tudong*, for women) and explore. *(Enter at the intersection of Jl. Sultan Hishamuddin and Jl. Perdana. Open Sa-Th 9am-noon, 3-4pm, and 5:30-6:30pm, F 3-4 pm and 5:30-6:30pm. Free.)*

ISLAMIC ARTS MUSEUM. The building itself is testament to the elegant beauty of Islamic architecture. Inside are exhibits on the evolution of mosque architecture, complete with models of mosques from throughout Asia. Arab pottery, coins, textiles, and a collection of Qur'ans are also on display. *(On Jl. Lembah Perdana, across from the National Mosque carpark. ☎2274 2020. Open Tu-Su 10am-6pm. RM8, students RM4.)*

KUALA LUMPUR OLD RAILWAY STATION. Built by a British architect in 1900, this station is a collection of domes, minarets, and archways that house everything from a tourist office to a hostel. It is well worth a visit to admire Moorish architectural influences. KTM Komuter trains stop here. *(On Jl. Sultan Hishamuddin. Open 24hr.)*

NATIONAL MUSEUM. This museum houses the usual weapons, royal paraphernalia, and Orang Asli crafts and artifacts. Most interesting are the shadow puppet display and the natural history section, which features stuffed wildlife, including the largest crocodile ever caught. *(On Jl. Sultan Hishamuddin, 500m past the Kuala Lumpur Visitors Center. ☎2282 6255. Open daily 9am-6pm. RM2, children and senior citizens RM1.)*

LAKE GARDENS. Next to the National Museum, a pedestrian overpass leads to the Lake Gardens—91.6 hectares of greenery. The complex draws visitors with a **planetarium, orchid and hibiscus garden,** and **sculpture garden.** The popular outdoor aviary **Taman Burung,** houses tropical birds (RM5). In the northern section of the garden, the **National Monument** is dedicated to Malaysians who died during the two World Wars and the Emergency of 1948-1960. Many people come here to jog or run, as the park provides a haven from KL's mad traffic. Rowboats, paddleboats, and surf bikes can be rented to cruise the lake. *(☎2698 3253. Gardens open daily 9am-5pm. Rowboats RM3 per hr., paddleboats RM6 per hr., surf bikes RM3 per 30min. Boathouse open M-Th 9am-12:30pm and 2-5:30pm, F 9-11:30am and 2:45-5:30pm, Sa-Su 8am-noon and 2-5:30pm.) Musicians usually perform at the band shell on Sundays around 5:30pm.)*

NEAR CHINATOWN

SRI MAHA MARIAMMAN TEMPLE. In the heart of Chinatown, this temple is the center of Kuala Lumpur's Hindu community and is known as "The Mother Temple." According to Hindu belief, Mariamman, the Mother Goddess, is wife of Lord Shiva and mother to

A DRINKING CLUB WITH A RUNNING PROBLEM

In 1938, a small group of British expats founded the Hash House Harriers in Kuala Lumpur. These first inspired "Hashers," named for the grub at the Selangor Club, joined the traditional Paper Chase with ample alcohol.

The group leader, or "hare," would blaze a tangled trail across challenging terrain, leaving behind scraps of paper and the occasional case of beer for his friends, the "hounds," to pick up.

During the Emergency of 1948, some hashers followed a path straight past a group of dangerous bandits, informed the police, and received enough bounty to buy two new cars. In the 60s, Hash House chapters spread throughout Malaysia and then to the rest of Southeast Asia.

There are over 1300 confirmed Hashes worldwide. They all send their constituents over 6-8km courses with a tipsy cry of "On-on!" Though a safer English-style sport than, say, ferret-legging, at least one death has occurred in the history of Hashing. In Myanmar, one hapless hound toppled from a waterfall. A mega-Hash in KL in 1998 celebrated the 60th anniversary of the first Hash. For chapter contacts throughout the globe, see www.gthhh.com. Tally-ho and bottoms up!

Murga, the deity to whom the annual **Thaipusam Festival** is dedicated. The prize of the 124-year-old temple is a silver chariot. *(163 Jl. Tun H.S. Lee. From the Central Market, turn left on Jl. Cheng Lock and then right on Jl. Tun H.S. Lee. Daily* pooja *at 7:30am, 12:30, 5:30pm. Open daily until 9pm.)*

KUAN TI TEMPLE. This 114-year-old Chinese temple was restored in 1994 by the Kwong Siew Association. The temple's rooftop architecture is particularly striking. *(168 Jl. Tun H.S. Lee, across the street from Sri Maha Mariamman Temple. Incense RM1.)*

SIN SZE YA TEMPLE. Tucked in a back alley, this Chinese temple was founded in 1864—before the existence of a "Chinatown." Its patron deities are Sin Sze Ya and Si Sze Ya, who helped Yap Ah Loy defeat their enemies and defend Kuala Lumpur during the Civil War (1870-1873). Their two sedan chairs flank the entrance. *(113A Jl. Tun H.S. Lee. Walk through the inconspicuous gateway to the temple.)*

GANESHA TEMPLE. Thirty-two figures of the elephant-head god decorate the upper walls inside this Hindu temple. Devotees crack coconuts before entering—symbolic of purging one's sins. *(Cross Jl. Pudu from the Puduraya Bus Terminal and walk left. Turn right at 7-Eleven; the temple is near the top of the hill. Open daily 7am-9pm.)*

OTHER SIGHTS

Along with Asia's tallest flagpole, Kuala Lumpur boasts two of the tallest buildings in the world. The 88-story **Petronas Twin Towers,** in the northeast part of the city, rank as the loftiest twin towers and the fourth-tallest buildings in the world (452m). The lowest floors hold the largest mall in the country and show off Malay arts and crafts next to fancy boutiques like Escada and DKNY. Tourists are permitted to go as far as the Sky Bridge. *(Take the PUTRA LRT to KLCC. ☎ 2058 8181. Mall open daily 10am-10pm. Sky Bridge open Tu-Su 9:30am-5:15pm. 1300 free tickets are issued daily; the line begins forming at 8:30am and it is recommended to get in line by 10am.)* The **Menara Kuala Lumpur,** or **KL Tower** as it is commonly called, offers a spectacular view of the city. There is a revolving restaurant at the top. *(Walk or take a taxi. ☎ 2020 5448. Open daily 9am-10pm. RM15, children RM9.)* The **National Art Gallery (Balai Seni Lukis Negara)** houses a diverse collection of Malaysian artwork, a sculpture garden, and a photography studio. Call ahead for updates on special contemporary art exhibitions. *(On Jl. Temerloh, off Jl. Tun Razak. ☎ 4025 4980. Open daily 10am-6pm. Free.)*

MARKETS

Chinatown, south of Jl. Cheng Lock and east of the Kelang River, is the liveliest place in KL. At dusk, central Jl. Petaling becomes a **pasar malam (night market).** Foodstalls and open-air restaurants roll their tables onto Jl. Hang Lekir and Jl. Sultan, as do traders selling pirated movies and CDs, designer watches, handbags, and clothing. Audio CDs are RM10, DVDs RM12. For other items, bargaining is the name of the game. **Central Market,** on Jl. Hang Kasturi, off Jl. Cheng Lock, is an arts and crafts haven with over 150 shops selling *batik* dresses, Muslim pajamas, intricate silver jewelry, and Malay kites and masks. Free cultural performances are held here some evenings. (☎ 2274 6542 for performance dates and times. Sarongs RM17; *kaftans* RM30; kites RM39; portraits RM50, color RM120. Open daily 10am-10pm.) **Night Markets** set up in different locations each night of the week. (**M:** section 1 in Wangsa Maju, northeast of town toward the zoo; **Tu:** Seri Petaling, south toward Serembau; **Th:** Jl. Kaskas in Taman Cheras; **F:** Taman Melati Gombak; **Sa:** 5-10pm on Jl. Tuanku Abdul Rahman between Jl. Tun Perak and Jl. Dang Wangi.) Markets are difficult to reach—ask at your guesthouse for directions.

NIGHTLIFE

The mix of yuppies, expatriates, and rich teens means that Kuala Lumpur has many nightlife options. The life span of clubs here is typically six to 12 months. There is also a growing interest in theater and dance, and major hotels host performances. For information, call **MTC** (☎2164 3929) or **Istana Budaya** (☎4025 2525).

The Beach Club Cafe, 97 Jl. P. Ramlee (☎2166 9919), off Jl. Sultan Ismail. All-ages crowd loosens their collars under a large "hut"—enjoying brick-oven pizza outside or bopping around the bar's shark tank. Try the beach party margaritas on Th, when ladies get in for free. Beers RM14.50. "Cover" is a 1st drink charge: Su-Th RM18, F-Sa RM25. Happy hour noon-9pm, beers RM8. Open daily noon-3am.

Orange, 1 Jl. Kia Peng (☎2141 4929). Best reached by taxi. A young, local crowd dances to the latest hip-hop tunes. Beer RM8. No cover for ladies W-Th and Sa. Cover W-Th RM20, F-Sa RM25 with drink coupons. Open W-Sa 7pm-3 or 4am.

Zouk, 113 Jl. Ampang (☎2171 1997; www.zoukclub.com.my). The sister club in KL to the original Zouk in Singapore. Made up of three sections: Zouk, Velvet Underground, and Terrace Bar. Housed in a cave-like warehouse, the decor is a cross between a Moorish palace and *A Space Odyssey: 2001*. W New Wave, 70s and 80s music on W, cover RM25 (includes 1 drink); Tu hip-hop and R&B; ladies free; cover RM28-30. Ladies and aircrew get into Velvet Underground free Tu and Th; cover Tu RM20 (includes 1 drink) and Th RM28 (includes 1 drink). All are 1-for-1 Th-Sa, 11pm-midnight at Zouk and Velvet Underground and daily 6-10pm at the Terrace Bar.

Alexis Bistro & Wine Bar and SINO: Bar Upstairs, 29 Jl. Telawi 3 (☎2284 2880). The sophisticated, clean-cut bistro attracts the well-heeled crowd, while bar on the 2nd fl. delights the senses with ambient lighting, kitschy wallpaper, comfy armchairs, and dark parquet flooring. Happy hour daily 6-9pm with housepours and half-price draft beer. Open weekdays noon-midnight and weekends noon-1:30am.

Finnegan's Irish Pub, 6 Jl. Telawi 5 (☎2284 9024), in Bangsar Baru. This Official English Premier League Bar pumps the best retro tunes and serves select beers like Kilkenny and Cream Ale. Ladies' night Th and Sa 9pm-2am, with selected drinks on the house. Beer RM18 per pint. Happy hour 5-8pm. Open Su-M 5pm-2am, Tu-Th 5pm-3am.

DAYTRIPS FROM KUALA LUMPUR

BATU CAVES. The most famous attractions near KL are the Batu Caves. In January and February, hundreds of Hindu devotees from around the world descend here for the annual **Thaipusam Festival,** armed with hooks and needles with which to pierce their skin in a ritual of penance. After checking out the Hindu temple at the base, visitors can climb 272 steps to the main cave temple, where Thaipusam participants remove the *kavadis* (shrines) that are attached to the hooks and needles. A pile of last year's *kavadis* lies to the left of the final staircase inside the cave; they are removed every January or February in preparation for a new set. *(Take Intrakota bus #11D 45min. from Bangkok Bank or Central Market. ☎6189 6284. Open daily 7:30am-midnight. Donations of RM4 or more appreciated.)*

KUALA SELANGOR. Fireflies are attracted to the berembang trees that flank both sides of the river in Kampung Kuantan. Watch thousands of them flash in unison on a nocturnal boat tour along the Selangor River. The **Nature Park,** covering over 200 hectares and including a bird sanctuary, is another popular destination within Kuala Selangor. *(From Puduraya Bus Station, take Selangor Omni Bus #141 from Platform 23* *(leaves every hour). Returning to Kuala Lumpur requires chartering a taxi for RM60. Boat tours (☎3289 1439) leave from the Kampung Kuantan jetty daily 7:30-11pm, RM10. Ferries from Bukit Belimbing RM2. Seafood restaurant on the premises.)*

NATIONAL ZOO AND AQUARIUM. This complex is home to 500 species of animals and fish. *(Intrakota bus #170 or 17 from Lh. Ampang (45min., RM1.60). ☎4108 3422. Open daily 9am-5pm. Weekdays RM7, children RM3; weekends RM9/RM5.)*

SUNWAY LAGOON. This water theme park promises wet (and wild) fun, with giant waterslides, speed slides, twister slides, a waterfall garden, and a wave pool. Park recently updated with the addition of larger and more thrilling rides in the Waters of Africa, Wild Wild West and World of Adventure. *(Take bus #10 (RM1.40) from in front of Hotel Impiana at corner of Jl. Sultan and Jl. Cheng Lock. ☎5635 6000. Open M and W-Th noon-9pm, F noon-10:30pm. RM38, children RM25.)*

MELAKA ☎06

Founded around 1400 by an exiled Sumatran prince, Melaka succumbed to the Portuguese in 1511. The Dutch and British would later hold Melaka for almost four centuries, until Malaysia's first Prime Minister, Tunku Abdul Rahman, proclaimed independence at Padang Pahlawan in the heart of Melaka. The many layers of Merlaka's past are displayed in Chinatown, where visitors can walk past the crimson hues of the Dutch Square, and around the waterfront abodes of the Portuguese Settlement. Soak in Melaka's easygoing charm and let your tastebuds sample *nyonya* food, an often spicy blend of Chinese and Malay cooking—full flavors that capture Melaka's rich heritage.

TRANSPORTATION

Trains: The nearest station is at **Tampin** (☎441 1034), 38km to the north. Take bus #26 from the local bus station (50min., every 15min. 6:30am-9pm, RM2.50) or take a taxi (45min.; shared RM10, charter RM40). Trains to: **KL** (2¼hr.; M-F 5am, 12:38, 7:54pm, Sa-Su 2:18am and 3:26pm; economy seat RM9, 2nd-class seat RM13-17, 2nd-class bunk RM20.50-23), where connecting trains go up the west coast to **Hat Yai** and **Singapore** (express 5hr., regular 6½hr.; M-F 12:58, 9:34am, 4:04pm, Sa-Su 1:37pm; economy seat RM15, 2nd-class seat RM23-27, 2nd-class bunk RM30.50-33).

Buses: Melaka Sentral Bus Station, on Jl. Tun Abdul Ruzak (☎288 1321). Long-distance buses run by private companies. Purchase tickets at any of the counters surrounding the station. Compare prices first, as they vary between companies. Different companies also depart for similar destinations at different times. **Express Delima** (☎284 8908) goes to **KL** (2hr., every 30min. 6am-7pm, RM7.90) and **Singapore** via **Johor Bharu** (3hr.; 8, 9, 11am, 1, 3, 5, 7, 8pm; RM14.70, to J.B. RM12.50). Several bus companies go to: **Alor Setar** (8hr.; 9:30am, 9:30pm; RM33.35); **Butterworth** (10hr., 6 per day, RM26-28); **Ipoh** (5hr.; 9:30am, 9:30pm; RM20); **Kangar** (9hr.; 9:30am, 9:30pm; RM36); **Kota Bharu** (10hr.; noon, 8pm; RM32); **Mersing** (4½hr.; 8am, 12:45, 6:30pm; RM14.80); **Penang** (7hr.; 9am, 9:30pm; RM30); **Perlis** (8hr., 9pm, RM36); **Seremban** (2hr., every 30min. 7am-7pm, RM5); **Sungei Petani** (7hr.; 9am, 9pm; RM30-33); **Taiping** (6hr., 3 per day, RM20-28).

Taxis: Jl. Tun Ali, down the street from the bus station. All cabs are shared by 4 passengers unless they are chartered. Shared cabs to: **Batu Pahet** (RM15, charter RM80-90); **Johor Bharu** (RM40-45, charter RM180); **KL** (RM40, charter RM120); **Muar** (RM10, charter RM40); **Port Dickson** (RM20, charter RM80). These are standard rates; successful bargaining is unlikely. Weekend and night rates may be up to 30% higher.

Local Transportation: The town is compact enough to cover by foot, but take a break and hire a **trishaw** from Jl. Kota (RM25-30 per hour). All local **buses** that leave from Melaka Sentral meet at the roundabout in front of Hotel Equatorial and they converge at the bus stop behind **Mahkota Parade Mall** before heading back to **Melaka Sentral.** Bus #17 goes to the **Portuguese Settlement** (every 10min., RM0.50). Bus #19 heads for the zoo at **Ayer Keroh** (every 30min., RM1.70).

Bicycle Rentals: Muhibbah Enterprise (☎283 0631), on Jl. Munshi Abdullah in Intan Plaza Shopping Arcade. RM10 per day. Open daily 10am-6pm.

ORIENTATION AND PRACTICAL INFORMATION

The city sprawls on both sides of the **Melaka River,** which winds southwest as it empties into the **Straits of Melaka.** The streets extending from **Lorong Hang Jebat** lead to the heart of **Chinatown.** Buddhist temples, art galleries, antique shops, and the Baba-Nyonya homes of **Old Melaka** run along **Jln Tun Tan Cheng Lock, Jln Hang Jebat (Jonkers Walk),** and **Jln Tokong,** all of which parallel the southern coast. The bridge that extends from Jl. Hang Jebat leads to a cluster of many historical museums and sights, easily recognizable by the bright red **Christ Church** and the **Stadthuys,** former home of the governor of Melaka. South of the numerous sights and east of the **Mahkota Parade Mall** lies the gateway to backpacker heaven: **Jln Merdeka. Taman Melaka Raya 1-3,** a series of side streets off Jln Merdeka, offer some of the best values for budget accommodations in Malaysia. Farther east is the **Portuguese Settlement.**

Tourist Office: Melaka Tourist Information Center (☎281 4803), on Jl. Kota near bridge connecting Jl. Laksamana and Lorong Hang Jebat. Free maps. Open daily 9am-5pm. Closed some public holidays. Sometimes closes for lunch.

Tours and Travel: The **Tourist Center** runs 45min. boat tours on the Melaka River (RM8). Frequency depends on tide and demand. **NH Travel and Tours,** 209 Jl. Melaka Raya (☎281 4242), offers city tours (RM35, children RM25), plantation tours (RM40, children RM30), heritage tours (RM35, children RM25), Ayer Keroh/nature tours (RM35, children RM25), and night tours (RM55, children RM50). Open daily 9am-5pm.

Currency Exchange: MayBank, 6 Jl. Hang Tuah (☎282 2477), near the bus and taxi stations. Open M-F 9:30am-4pm, Sa 9:30-11am. Closed 1st and 3rd Sa of the month. **Branch** on Jl. Melaka Raya 1, off the roundabout. Open M-F 9am-4:30pm, Sa 9am-12:30pm. Currency exchange service stops 1hr. before closing. Both have **ATMs** (Cirrus/MC/V). **Bank Simpanan Nasional** in the Mahkota Parade Mall is open M-F 10am-5pm, Sa 10am-1pm.

English-Language Bookstore: MPH (☎283 3050), ground fl. of Mahkota Parade Mall. Open daily 10am-10pm.

Emergency: ☎999. **Fire:** ☎994.

Tourist Police: (☎285 4115). On the pedestrian mall section of Jl. Kota, opposite the Tourist Center. Open daily 8am-11pm.

Pharmacies: Guardian Pharmacy (☎282 9499), on the ground fl. of Mahkota Parade Mall. Open daily 10am-10pm.

Medical Services: Mahkota Medical Center, 3 Mahkota Melaka (☎281 4071), next to Mahkota Parade Mall. Private hospital with 24hr. **emergency care.** Open M-F 9am-5pm, Sa 9am-2pm.

Telephones: Purchase **Telekom cards** at any communications store, to use on the public card phones.

Internet Access: Budget Communication Centre, 259A-B Jl. Melaka Raya 3 (☎286 7718), offers Internet access at RM3 per hr. Between Jl. Melaka Raya 1 and 3, **Kiosk Internet,** 155 Taman Melaka Raya, off Jl. Banda Hilir (☎286 9397); provides access in an A/C room behind **Kiosk design+print.** RM3 per hr. Printing, scanning, and faxing.

Post Offices: GPO (☎283 3860), on Jl. Bukit Baru, 6km north of town center. Take bus #17 20min. from the local bus station. *Poste Restante.* Open M-Sa 9am-5pm, closed 1st Sa of month. **Pos 2020** (☎284 8440; **Postal Code:** 75670), in the Youth Museum on Jl. Laksamana next to Christ Church and off south Jl. Merdaka. *Poste Restante.* Open M-Sa 8am-5pm.

Postal Codes: Old Melaka 75200; business district 75100.

ACCOMMODATIONS

Budget options cluster in the area known as **Taman Melaka Raya,** to the east of Mahkota Parade Mall off Jl Merdeka. Closer to the Melaka Sentral, several inexpensive hotels are located near **Jln Munshi Abdullah.** Taxis go to Taman Melaka Raya (20min., RM12-15) from the Melaka Sentral Bus Terminal.

TAMAN MELAKA RAYA

Traveller's Lodge, 214B Taman Melaka Raya 1 (☎226 5709). At night, travelers relax in the Japanese-style living room or in the new rooftop common area. Small kitchen, laundry, lockers, and a cafe downstairs. Hot showers. Clean 3-bed dorms RM11; singles with fan RM18, with A/C RM35, with A/C and private bath RM45; doubles RM20-25, with A/C RM34-35, with A/C and private bath RM45-50. ❸

Travelling Inn, 238 and 239B Taman Melaka Raya (☎286 6697). Although not particularly well lit, inexpensive rooms and the favorable location make this hostel a great value. 3-bed dorms with fan RM10; singles with fan RM15; doubles with fan RM18-22; triples RM27-30. ❸

Samudra Inn, 348B Taman Melaka Raya 3 (☎282 7441; www.geocities.com/samudrainn). Clean, slightly cramped rooms with a bright stairwell connecting 2 converted shophouses. Easy-going owner, kitchen facilities, common area with TV. 3-bed dorms RM10; singles with fan RM16-18, with A/C RM28; doubles with fan RM20-24, with A/C 30. RM7-10 more for private bath. ❶

Sunny's Inn Guest House, 270 and 271A/B Taman Melaka Raya 3 (☎226 5446; www.geocities.com/sunny_inn2002). Friendly staff, lounge, laundry, travel info board, book exchange library, and 2 movies every night. Bicycle rental RM5 per day. Laundry RM3 for 5 pieces. Dorms RM9; singles RM16, with A/C RM25; doubles RM18-25, with A/C RM30-35; triples RM30, with A/C RM40, attached shower RM10-20 extra. ❶

OLD MELAKA

Hotel Puri, 118 Jl. Tun Tan Cheng Lock (☎282 5588; www.hotelpuri.com). Beautiful yellow Peranakan-style manor house. All rooms with TV, A/C, phone, and hot shower. Breakfast included. Doubles RM110-200; triples RM230; quads RM305; Puri Suite and Suite Royal RM450-500. Includes tax and service charge. AmEx/MC/V. ❺

Sama-Sama Guest House, 26 Jl. Tukang Besi (☎012 305 1980). Spacious entrance has tons of reggae records strewn all over. Towels, sarongs, and sheets provided. All have shared bathrooms. Central courtyard has lovely fish pond. Laundry service RM2. 3-bed dorms RM10; 4-bed dorms RM8; singles RM18; doubles RM15-35. ❶

MALAYSIA

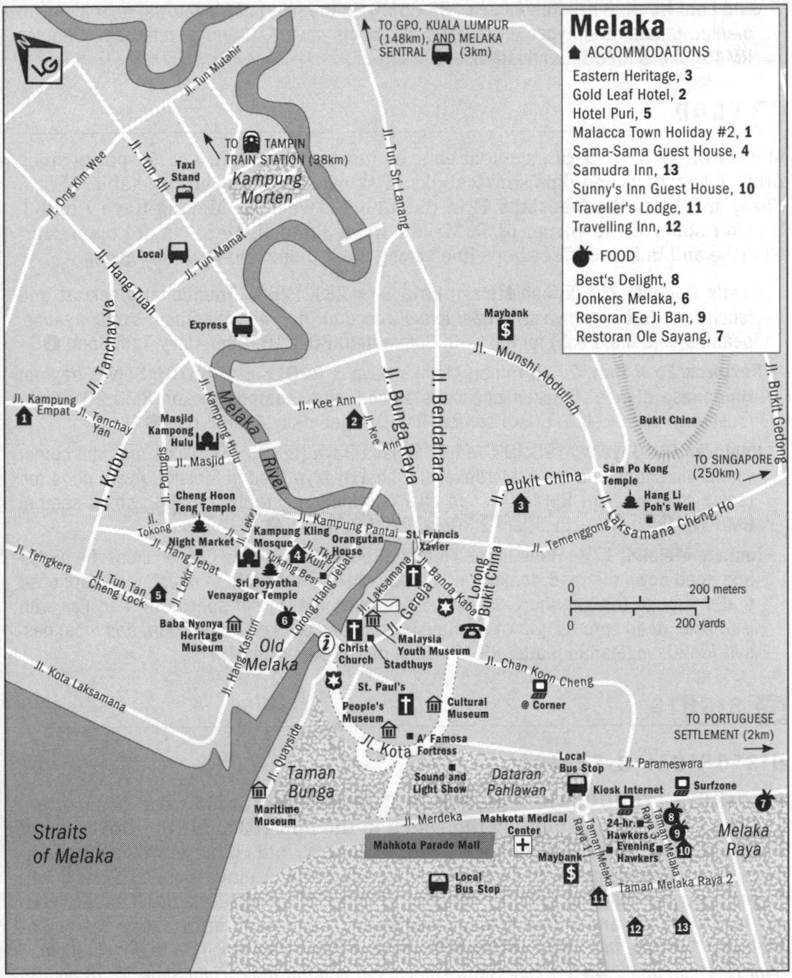

NEAR BUKIT CHINA

Eastern Heritage, 8 Jl. Bukit China (☎283 3026; eastern_heritage@hotmail.com). Chinese architecture and paintings in the rooms give a distinct Eastern flavor. Guests can try out the *batik* studio (RM30). Small dipping pool downstairs. Midnight lockout. 10-bed dorms RM8; singles with fan RM18-22; doubles RM20-26; triples RM27-30. ❸

NEAR THE EXPRESS BUS TERMINAL

Malacca Town Holiday Lodge #2, 52 A, B, C Jl. Kampung Empat (☎284 6905; jasmine_M12@hotmail.com), in the Wine and Spirits building. Walk down Jl. Kubu from the bus terminal, turn right on Jl. Tanchay Yan, and stay left on Jl. Kampung Empat as the road forks. They'll buzz you in. Western breakfast, kitchen, laundry (RM5). Singles and doubles with fan RM18-20, with private bath RM25-30, with A/C RM35-40. ❸

Gold Leaf Hotel, 31 Jl. Kee Ann (☎283 6555), in the heart of Chinatown, near the night market. Caters to all types of travelers. All rooms have A/C and private bath. Doubles RM45; triples RM55; quads RM65. ❹

FOOD

Melaka offers a range of excellent eats, including *satay celup*, a hot-pot of spicy broth into which one dips *satay* sticks of skewered meat and vegetables. For a cheap meal, try the **foodstalls** ❶ in the alley between Jl. Melaka Raya 1 and 3. Hawker stalls at the corner of Jl. Melaka Raya 3 and Jl. Merdeka are open 24hr. Chinese and Indian coffee shops line **Lorong Bukit China** and **Jln Temenggong.**

Best's Delight, 268 Taman Melaka Raya 3 (☎281 1268). Traditional breakfast and lunch fare. *Baba nyonya*-style *nasi lemak* (coconut rice with fried egg, *sambal* sauce, peanuts, and dried fish) for RM1.80. Coffee RM0.80-1.10. Open daily 7am-3pm. ❶

Restoran Ee Ji Ban, 270A Taman Melaka Raya 3 (☎012 625 6670). Serves fragrant Hainanese dishes. Chicken rice balls served with roasted chicken RM3.20; whole roasted chicken RM20; prawn *sambal* RM10. Open daily 10am-9pm. ❶

Restoran Ole Sayang, 198-199 Taman Melaka Raya (☎283 1966), on the right corner where the shops end on Jl. Merdeka. The best *nyonya* food in Melaka. *Ayam pong teh* (spicy chicken dish) RM7.50, *chap chai* (stir-fried vegetables) RM5-9, squid sambal RM5-10. Open Th-Tu 11:30am-2:30pm and 6-9:30pm. ❸

Jonkers Melaka, 17 Jl. Hang Jebat. From the Tourist Information Center, cross the bridge and head down the road. Jonkers is 10 doors down on the left, in a restored shophouse that's through the gift shop. Soup and sandwich RM15; set special of fried rice with *ikan bilis,* bean sprouts, prawn *sambal,* lemongrass chicken, lamb soup, and local dessert RM20; vegetarian platter RM17. Open daily 10am-5pm. ❹

SIGHTS

HISTORICAL DISTRICT

STADTHUYS ETHNOGRAPHICAL AND HISTORICAL MUSEUMS. The *Stadthuys*, a dark pink residence built by the Dutch in the mid-1600s for the Governor of Melaka, now displays Melakan porcelain, weaponry, and coins, as well as the boxing gloves of **Muhammad Ali.** Downstairs, an exhibit on Melaka's code of law documents corporal punishments for various offenses. If the exhibits don't satisfy you, the nightly **"Light and Sound Spectacular"** show features an informative history of Melaka. *(Opposite the Tourist Information Center. ☎284 1934. Open Sa-Th 9am-5:30pm, F 9am-12:15pm and 2:45-5:30pm. RM5, students in uniform RM2. Light show M, Th and Su 8:30pm, Tu-W and F-Sa 9pm. Tickets sold at Cultural Museum booth; RM10, children RM2.)*

CHRIST CHURCH. One of the most famous landmarks in Melaka, this church was built by the Dutch in 1741 to commemorate a century of colonial rule in Melaka. Check out the Dutch, Armenian, and Portuguese inscriptions, dating back to 1776, in the stone floor near the entrance. *(Between Jl. Gereja and Jl. Laksamana. ☎284 8804. Su service in English 9am.)*

THE MALAYSIAN YOUTH MUSEUM. Housed in the old Melaka General Post Office, this museum celebrates and documents the activities of youth organizations in Malaysia and abroad. Inside there is also an **art gallery** showcasing captivating watercolors and prints by famous Malaysian artists. *(430 Jl. Laksamana, next to Christ Church. ☎282 7533. Open Su-Th 9:30am-5:30pm, F 9:30am-12:15pm and 2:45-5:30pm. Closed M. RM1, children RM0.50.)*

RUINS OF ST. PAUL'S CHURCH AND A' FAMOSA FORTRESS. Built by a Portuguese captain grateful for his safe arrival, this church was originally dedicated to Mary and dubbed Our Lady of the Hill. The name changed to St. Paul's under Dutch rule in 1641. Before falling into ruin due to British neglect, the building served as a fortress, lighthouse, Dutch burial ground, Catholic chapel, and Protestant church. Near the altar is an open crypt that housed the body of **St. Francis Xavier,** missionary extraordinaire, for nine months before he was sent to Goa, India. *(Climb steps from Jl. Kota.)* Down the steps from St. Paul's Church and through an English cemetery, the last remnants of the **Porta de Santiago** act as a gateway to what remains of the Portuguese fortress of **A' Famosa.** The Dutch used the fort, but the British demolished it in the early 1800s to ensure that Melaka could not compete with Penang for controlling trade in the Strait of Melaka.

MUZIUM RAKYAT (PEOPLE'S MUSEUM). The "Enduring Beauty" exhibit displays the lengths to which humans will go for beauty, from male corsets and lip plates to cranium manipulations and Padong neck coils. *(Down Jl. Kota away from the clocktower. ☎282 6526. Open daily 9am-5:30pm, closed F 12:15-2:45pm. RM2.)*

OTHER SIGHTS. Inside a Portuguese ship, the **Maritime Museum** has three floors of ship models and exhibits on Melakan sea trade and piracy. The museum is on Jl. Quayside toward the river's mouth. *(Open Sa-M and W-Th 9am-5:30pm, F 9am-12:15pm and 2:45-5:30pm. RM2, children RM0.50.)* The **Cultural Museum,** in a replica of the old sultan's palace, displays costumes and headwear of Malay high society. *(On Jl. Parameswara, near Jl. Kota at the foot of St. Paul's Hill. ☎282 7464. Open Su-Th and Sa 9am-6pm, F 9am-12:15pm and 2:45-6pm. RM2, children RM0.50.)* Across the river is **Old Melaka,** a district of winding streets and architecturally interesting Chinese homes.

CHINATOWN

BABA NYONYA HERITAGE MUSEUM. Constructed in the 1890s as a private residence and converted into a museum in 1985, this home tells the tale of Chinese Malays. *(48-50 Jl. Tun Tan Cheng Lock. From the Tourist Information Center, cross the river and turn left on Jl. Kasturi; take the next right and it's on the right. ☎283 1273. Open daily 10am-12:30pm and 2-4:30pm. Admission and tour RM8, children RM4.)*

CHENG HOON TENG TEMPLE. The oldest functioning temple in the country (founded in 1673), the Cheng Hoon Teng Temple also served as a city hall and courthouse for Melakan Chinese during the Portuguese and Dutch control of the city. Carefully maintained by a board of trustees, the temple is still an active place of worship for Confucians, Taoists, and Buddhists. The main hall contains the altars of the Goddess of Mercy (Kwan Yin) in the center, the Guardian of Fishermen (the goddess Ma Cho Po) to the left, and the God of Justice (Kwan Ti) to the right. *(On Jl. Tokong, near the intersection with Jl. Lekiu. ☎282 9343. Open daily 7am-7pm. Obtain an English brochure from the office in the back, to the right.)*

MASJID KAMPUNG HULU. Built in 1748, Kampung Hulu is Malaysia's oldest mosque. Like Kampung Kling, Hulu has a pagoda-like minaret and a three-tiered roof, a combination of Sumatran and Chinese architectural styles. *(On the corner of Jl. Kampung Hulu and Jl. Masjid. Open Su-Th 7am-8pm.)*

KAMPUNG KLING MOSQUE. Built in 1784, Kampung Kling's construction was influenced by Sumatran, English, Greek, Portuguese, Chinese, Indian, and Moorish architectural styles. Intricately sculpted cast-iron lamps surround the outdoor pools for cleansing before prayer. *(1 block down from Cheng Hoon Teng on the opposite side of Jl. Lekiu. Open Su-Th 7am-8pm.)*

SRI POYYATHA VENAYAGER MOORTHI TEMPLE. The third holy building on the "Street of Harmony," this Hindu temple contains the shrine of Venayager, the remover of obstacles and the god of filial piety. *(Next door to Kampung Kling. Daily prayers 7, 11:30am, 6, 8:30pm.)*

BUKIT CHINA. This site housed Princess Hang Li Poh's hundreds of attendants when she came from China to marry the sultan. Now it's the largest Chinese cemetery outside of China. Many of its 12,000 tombs date back to the 12th century. At the foot of the hill are **Sam Po Kong Temple** and **Hang Li Poh's well.** Legend has long held that anyone who drinks from the well will someday return to Melaka; Dutchmen and the forces of the Johor Sultanate cruelly disproved this by poisoning the well during the wars of the 1500s and 1600s. *(At the end of Jl. Temenggong, northeast of the city center. Open 24hr. Due to the isolation of the cemetery, it is advisable to visit during daylight hours and preferably with some company, particularly for female travelers.)*

FARTHER AFIELD

PORTUGUESE SETTLEMENT. Three kilometers east of historic Melaka, the Portuguese Settlement's main attractions are the seafood restaurants around the **Portuguese Square** and a look at the Portuguese houses adorned with images of both Jesus and Buddha. The **Festa San Pedro,** an extravagant festival with Portuguese dancers, singers, and beauty pageants, takes place during the weekend closest to June 29. *(Take bus #17 (RM0.50) from the roundabout near Hotel Equatorial.)*

IPOH ☎05

Historically, Ipoh was used as a transit point for the region's natural resources. attracting traders, laborers, and devious marauders. Today, Ipoh's prostitution problem and turbulent thoroughfares strike anxiety into the hearts of trekkers, many of whom give the town short shrift in favor of Malaysia's island paradises. Those prepared to delve a little will find several points of interest. As the capital of the state of Perak, Ipoh offers excursions to Buddhist cave temples and has 25 heritage buildings in the old town. Always on the cutting edge, it hosts a hodge-podge of industries, several modern mega-malls, and a mother-lode of fast-food chains.

TRANSPORTATION

Flights: Sultan Azlan Shah Airport, on Jl. Lapangan Terbang, 7km outside of town. Taxi to town RM10. Airport tax RM5. **MAS,** Lot 108, Bangunan Seri Kinta, Jl. Sultan Idris Shah (airport ☎2414 4155, reservations 312 2459). Open M-Sa 8:30am-5:30pm. Flights to **KL** (35min., 3 per day 6:45am-7pm, RM66).

Trains: KTMB Ipoh (☎254 0481), in Majestic Ipoh Station Hotel on Jl. Panglima Bukit Gantang Wahab. To: **Hat Yai** via **Butterworth** (express 9hr. (5hr. to **Butterworth**) 1:13am; 2nd-class seats RM23, 2nd-class bunks RM33); **KL** (express 5hr.; 1:50am; 3rd-class seats RM10, 2nd-class seats RM18, 2nd-class bunks RM26-28).

Buses: Medan Kidd Bus Terminal, on Jl. Kidd in the southwest corner of town. **Jelita Transportation** (☎241 4413) runs buses to: **Alor Setar** (4hr., 11 per day, RM15); **Melaka** (5hr., 5 per day, RM20); **Penang** (3hr., 9per day, RM12). **Kurnia Bistari** (☎012 566 1145) runs buses to: **Butterworth** (11:15am, 12:15, 6:15pm; RM9.50); **Cameron Highlands** (11am; 5:30, 6:45pm; RM15). **Rhino Ekspres** (☎243 6119) runs buses to: **KL** (3hr., 25 per day, RM11.30); **Singapore** (7hr.; 9am, 8:30pm; RM38). **Azra Ekspres** (☎241 8013) runs buses to **Kuala Kangsar** (50min., 11 per day, RM2.90); **Penang** via **Butterworth** (3hr.; 8:30, 9:45, 10:45am, 1:30, 3:30, 5:30, 7:15, 8:30, 10:15pm; RM11.30). **Indah Ekspres** (☎255 3306) runs buses to: **Hat Yai**

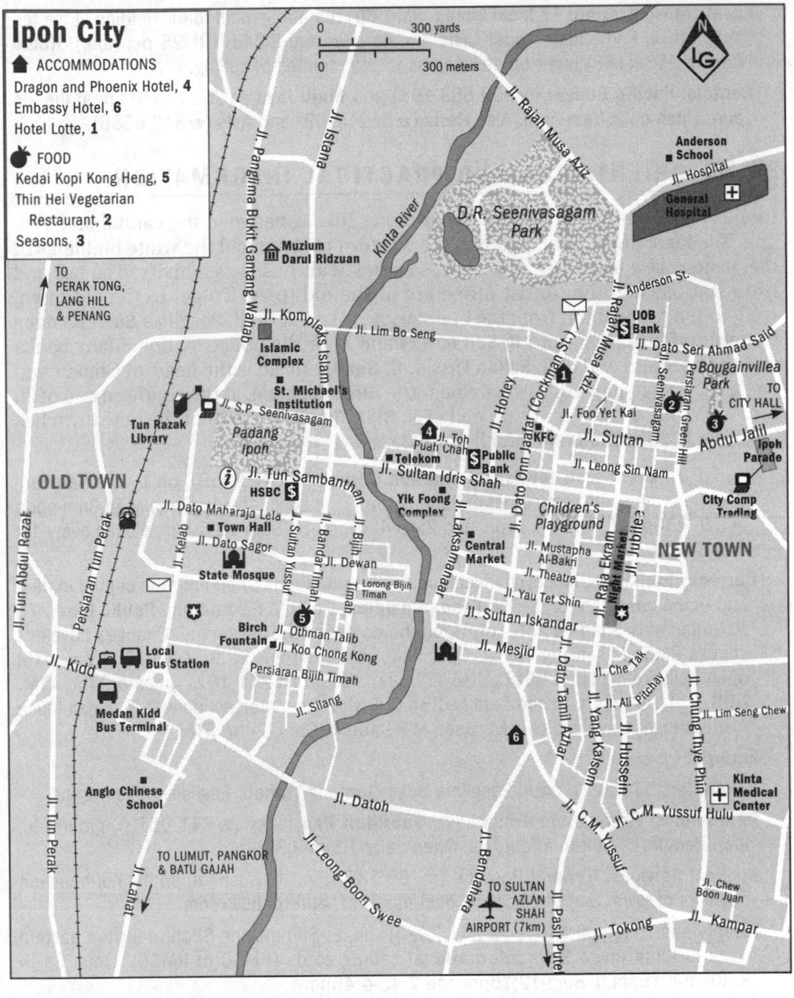

(7hr.; midnight, 1am; RM33); **Johor Bahru** (6hr.; 12:15, 9:30am, 1, 8:15pm; RM35); **Kota Baru** (6hr., 9:30pm, RM21.50); **KL** (3hr.; 7:30, 8:30, 9am, every 30-45min. 12:15-4, 4:15, 5:15, 5:30, 6:30, 8:15, 8:45, 10pm; RM11.30); **Kuala Terengannu** (12hr., 9:30pm, RM34); **Kuantan** (6hr.; 8, 8:45pm; RM25.50); **Lumut** (1¾hr.; 1:30am, 1:30, 4, 6:30, 11:30pm; RM4.70). **Restu Interstate Ekspres** runs buses to: **KL** via **Port Dickson** (3hr.; 1, 7, 10:45am, 12:30, 1:30, 3:30, 6:30pm; RM11.30); **Lumut** (1½hr.; 1:30am, 1:30, 4, 6:30, 10, 11pm; RM4.65). **Konsortium Ekspres** runs buses to **Batu Pahat** via **Melaka** (6hr.; 9:30am, 11:30pm; RM35); **KL** (3hr.; 2, 3am, every 30min. past the hr. 4:30am-8:30pm); **Singapore** via **Johor Bahru** (7hr.; 9, 9:30, 10am, 8:30, 9:30, 11:30pm; RM38).

Taxis: Long-distance taxi stand, opposite the Medan Kidd Terminal. To **KL** (RM110 per car) and **Penang** (RM100 per car). Fares have set minimum, but drivers may ask more.

Local Transportation: 12 **local buses** (RM0.80) run along main roads, ending at the terminal on Jl. Perhentian. **Local taxis** around town are RM4-6 (RM25 per hour). **Radio Cab** (☎253 4188) picks up passengers within minutes of calling.

Rentals: Pacific Budget (☎800 883 191) and **Maju Jaya** (☎255 5510) are at the airport. Open daily 8am-5pm. Also **Hertz** (☎312 7109) and **Avis** (☎312 6586).

ORIENTATION AND PRACTICAL INFORMATION

Ipoh is 205km north of Kuala Lumpur along Rte. 1, between the capital and Penang. The **Kinta River** splits Ipoh into the western **old town** and the white buildings of the eastern **new town.** The new town scurries with business activity. The **bus** and train stations and the tourist office are in the old town. To get to the old town, walk to the roundabout from the bus station, turn left on **Jl. Panglima Bukit Gantang Wahab,** and turn right onto **Jl. Sultan Iskandar** after the police station. Many banks line the northern end of **Jl. Sultan Yussuf. Jl. Bandar Timah** is the heart of Chinatown, while the Indian parts of town are near the **Birch Fountain,** at the southern end of Jl. Sultan Yussuf and the northern end of **Jl. Bijih Timah.** The hub of the new town lies between **Jl. Dato Onn Jaafar** and **Jl. Raja Ekram.**

Tourist Offices: Perak Tourist Information Center (☎241 2959), on Jl. Tun Sambanthan near the southwest corner of Padang Ipoh (the soccer field). Open M-Th 8am-noon and 2-4:30pm, F 8am 12:15pm and 2:45-4:30pm, Sa 8am-12.50pm; closed every 1st and 3rd Sa.

Currency Exchange: Moneychangers are on Jl. Sultan Idris Shah near the central market and in the basement of the **Yik Foong Complex.** Open M-F 9am-5pm. **Public Bank,** 76 Jl. Sultan Idris Shah (☎255 1068), on the corner of Jl. Laksamana. Changes traveler's checks RM5; 15sen per check. Open M-F 9:30am-4pm, Sa 9:30am-12:30pm. **ATM** open daily 7am-11pm. **HSBC,** 138 Jl. Sultan Yussuf (☎241 1022), has a 24hr. **ATM. UOB**, 2 Jl. Dato Seri Ahmad Said (☎254 0008), at the intersection with Jl. Rajah Musa Aziz. Changes traveler's checks. Open M-F 9am-4:30pm. 24hr. **ATM.**

Emergency: ☎999.

Police: (☎253 5522), on Jl. Panglima Bukit Gantang Wahab. English spoken. 24hr.

Pharmacies: *Farmasi* are everywhere. **Guardian Pharmacy** (☎241 0673), ground fl., Ipoh Parade, Jl. Sultan Abdul Jalil. Open daily 10am-9:30pm.

Medical Services: General Hospital (☎253 3333), on Jl. Hospital, on the northeastern outskirts of town. English-speaking doctors. 24hr. **emergency room.**

Telephones: Telekom Office (☎241 2825), on Jl. Sultan Idris Shah, near the eastern bank of Kinta River. Sells **international** calling cards (RM30 or RM60). Open Sa-Th 8:30am-4:15pm, F 8am-12:15pm and 2:45-4:45pm.

Internet Access: City Comp Trading (☎241 7612), in Ipoh Parade, 1st fl., on Jl. Sultan Abdul Jalil. Email RM2 per 30min., RM3 per hr. Open daily 10am-10pm. **Tun Razak Library** has an Internet cafe, RM2 per hr. Open daily 9am-9pm.

Post Office: Ipoh GPO (☎254 6555), opposite the police, next to the train station. *Poste Restante.* Open M-Sa 8:30am-6pm.

Postal Code: 30670.

ACCOMMODATIONS

Inexpensive accommodations congregate in the new town. **Jl. Raja Musa Aziz** (Anderson Rd.) has the best options. Cheaper places line **Jl. Yang Kalsom** in the south, but numerous massage parlors lend it a seedy air.

Hotel Lotte, 97 Jl. Dato Onn Jaafar (☎254 2215/2216/2217), on the corner of Jl. Foo Yet Kai. Clean and spacious rooms fully equipped with mini-fridge, dresser, and bathtub. Towels provided. Doubles RM63; quads RM125. MC/V. ❹

Dragon and Phoenix Hotel, 23-25 Jl. Toh Puah Chah (☎253 4661). Equally close to new and old towns, near the Kinta River. All rooms have A/C, TV, phone, and private bath. Free parking. Doubles RM59.80; twins RM62.10; quads RM96.50. ❸

Embassy Hotel, 33-37 Jl. C. M. Yusuff (☎254 9496 or 254 9497), housed in a converted Chinese shophouse. Rooms are old and provide basic amenities at a good value. For the true budget die-hards. Singles with fan RM25.30, with A/C and TV RM38.60; doubles with fan RM30.50, with A/C 44. ❶

FOOD

Find the best and widest variety of options at **The Food Center (Pusat Makaran Majestic)** ❶, on Jl. Dato Tahwil Azar, which serves Ipoh's signature *koey teow* (RM2.50; open daily 9am-11pm), and at **Pusat Penjaja Podeng Kanak (The Children's Playground)** ❷, on Jl. Raja Musa Aziz, south of Jl. Sultan Idris Shah, which serves various Malay dishes (RM3-5). For Malay cuisine, look for shop names preceded by *kedai kopi*, meaning "coffee shop." Although coffee is served, the name literally refers to a space where hawkers set up stalls. The best place for Ipoh's famous white coffee *(pak kopi)* is at the southern end of Jl. Bandar Timah, where numerous Chinese-run coffee shops serve packed houses all afternoon. *Pak kopi* is not exactly white (although it is whiter than regular *kopi*); the locals roast the coffee beans in a more gentle manner to produce a less fragrant, more bitter brew. For fast-food fiends, **Kentucky Fried Chicken** has a 24hr. outlet at the corner of Jl. Dato Onn Jaafar and Jl. Sultan.

Restaurant Lou Wong Tauge Ayam Kuetiau, 49 Jl. Yau Tet Shin (☎012 501 8384), along Jl. Dato Tahwil Azhar. A somewhat preppy atmosphere, but with downright delicious food. Serves local favorite *koey teow* in chicken broth (RM1), with soy sauce chicken (RM3). Try iced local fruit drinks like *longan* (sour plum) and *luohanguo* (barley) for RM1. Open daily 5pm-3am. ❶

Thean Chua, 73 Jl. Bandar Timah. Popular with locals, the marble tables heave under their weight during lunch hour. Order the *gai see hor fun* (literally, "chicken shreds–flat noodles;" RM3), which usually sells out by 3-4pm. *Satay* is served in abundance, and you pay for however much you eat–signal the owner when you have had enough (RM0.50 per stick). Open daily 10am till whenever the food runs out. ❶

Thin Hei Vegetarian Restaurant, 25 Persiaran Greenhill (☎253 7388), in the northern part of the new town. Laid-back, family atmosphere. Tofu and vegetable dishes RM5, noodle dishes RM3-6. Open daily 10:30am-2:30pm and 5:30-9:30pm. ❷

Seasons, 88 Jl. Sultan, at the Syuen Hotel, features an international menu in an elegant setting. Spaghetti carbonara RM17, burger with fries RM14, mixed fruit RM8, Guinness RM13.50. Open 24hr. ❸

SIGHTS

Ipoh's significant sights are mostly architectural, but the cave temples on the outskirts of the city are worth a visit. There is a night market that sells all kinds of goods and offers foot reflexology. (Along Jl. Dato Tahwil Azhar, between Jl. Sultan Idris Shah and Jl. Theatre. Open daily 8:30pm-1am.)

COLONIAL BUILDINGS AND PARKS. Jl. Panglima Bukit Gantang Wahab has many impressive colonial buildings, including the train station and town hall. The **Ipoh Railway Station,** also designed by A. B. Hubback, rivals the one in Kuala Lumpur in grandeur. The imposing **St. Michael's Institution** was initially designed by LaSallean Brother Vernier Auguste, also the architect for the St. John's Institution in KL. **D.R. Seenivasagam Park** spans the strip between the YMCA and the roundabout on Jl. Rajah Musa Aziz and has soccer fields, gazebos, and a Japanese garden. Smaller but more stylish, **Bougainvillea Park** flanks Ipoh City Hall southeast of D.R. Seenivasagam Park. For detailed information on the history of Ipoh, the Perak Tourist Information Center provides heritage maps.

LIMESTONE CAVES. Limestone caves, used as Buddhist temples by Chinese immigrants, surround the city. Six kilometers north of Ipoh on the road to Kuala Kangsar is **Perak Tong,** a temple known for its paintings and endless stairwell. *(Accessible by bus #141; 15min., every 30min.; RM0.55. Open daily 8am-6pm.)* Other cave temples are **Sam Poh Tong,** 6km south of Ipoh on Jl. Gopeng, and **Kek Lok Tong,** near Gunung Rapat *(Sam Poh Tong open daily 8am-4.30pm. Kek Lok Tong open daily 8am-7:30pm.)* Both cave temples are accessible by buses #66 and #73 (15min., RM0.55). Sam Poh Tong is the oldest in the region and shelters ponds brimming with fish and turtles. To get to Kek Lok Tong from Sam Poh Tong, back-track to the roundabout and make a right. Walk for 15min. and turn right before the first traffic light, where signs will direct the way to the temple. Farther south, about 25km from Ipoh, are the impressive limestone formations of **Gua Tempurung.** Visitors walk through the cave along paved pathways. *(☎545 8834. Accessible by taxi RM25. Open daily 9am-5pm.)*

OTHER SIGHTS. The road to **Lumut,** southwest of Ipoh, passes by Chinese cemeteries, open-cast mines, and small mining towns gone bust. One such town is **Papan.** Built in the 1890s, it has become a near-ghost town since the demise of the tin industry. **Kellie's Castle,** 30min. outside town, is the beautiful mansion of William Kellie Smith, a wealthy Scottish planter who died before its completion in 1926. Take a peek at the castle's empty rooms and rubble walls, fashioned in a mix of Moorish and Greco-Roman styles. *(Accessible by taxi or by a short ride on the Batu Gajah bus from Gopeng (RM2). Admission RM3, children RM1.)* In the **Clearwater Century Golf Resort,** you can tour the set of *Anna and the King*. The RM15 fee includes high tea at 4pm (accessible by City Bus or taxi). Northeast of Ipoh is the **Tanjung Rambutan Waterfall** (accessible by the Tanjung Rambutan bus, 50min.).

LUMUT ☎05

Lumut is the gateway to **Pulau Pangkor. Buses** drop off visitors opposite the ferry terminal. From the bus terminal, buses run to KL (4hr.; every 30min. past the hr. 8:30am-8:30pm, 12:30am; RM15.90), Butterworth (4hr.; 9:30am, 2, 6:30pm; RM12.70), and Ipoh (1hr.; every 45min. 9:30am-7:45pm; RM4.70). **Ferries** run from Lumut to Pangkor (20min.; 7, 7:45am, every half hr. 8:30am-4:30pm, 5:30, 6:30, 7:30, 9pm; RM5). Return trips from Pangkor (20min.; 6:40, 7:45am, every half hr. 8:30am-4:30pm, 5:30, 6:30, 7:30, 9pm). The **Pangkor Tourist Information Center,** in Lumut across the street from the jetty, can answer any questions and has an assortment of brochures about other destinations in Malaysia. (Open M-F 9am-5pm, Sa 9am-1:45pm.) As you walk from the bus station or the Tourist Information Center toward the sea, the road ahead running along the shore is **Jl. Titi Panjang,** which meets **Jl. Iskandah Shah** at the jetty. If you miss a ferry, don't despair—there are a few decent hotels near the Lumut-Pangkor jetty. **Indah Hotel ❹,** 208 Jl. Iskandar

Shah, a couple blocks from the bus station right near the beach, offers clean, spacious rooms with TV and private bath. (☎683 5064. RM40, with sea view RM50.) Next door, **Hotel Putra ❹**, 211-213 Jl. Islandah Shah, has well-kept rooms with TV, A/C, and mini-fridge. (☎683 8000. Doubles RM60-134; quads RM162.) **Harbor View Hotel ❹**, 13 and 14 Jl. Titi Panjang, a short walk from the bus station and next to a primary school, has a wider range of rooms. (☎683 7888. Doubles RM40; triples RM55; quads RM70. Extra bed RM10.) Malay foodstalls between the two hotels serve *nasi goreng* (fried rice) well into the night. **Capri ❸**, 4174 Jl. Sultan Idris Shah, behind Bank Simpanan Nasional, serves homemade Italian cuisine for travelers and homesick American marines. (☎683 3112. Pizzas RM19-29; pasta RM10-20; steaks RM30-36. Open M-Tu, Th, and Sa-Su 11:30am-3pm and 6-11pm.)

PULAU PANGKOR ☎05

Despite the island's commercial success, much of Pulau Pangkor's coastline and jungle interior remain untouched. The island's 25,000 inhabitants reside mostly on the east coast, while travelers flock to west coast beaches to view the vibrant sunsets and watch black hornbills flit from tree to tree. Rustling breezes, deserted sands, and shops brimming with sacks of dried fish create a laid-back atmosphere. Pulau Pangkor's waters reveal the diversity of its travelers; Muslim women swim fully-clothed next to bikini-clad Westerners, but all unite to relax and enjoy.

TRANSPORTATION. The **Pangkor jetty** is on the island's southeast side (the local ferry will stop first at the **Sungai Pinang Jetty,** where locals usually disembark). Ferries arrive frequently from Lumut. Pangkor's main road, **Pekan Pangkor,** generally follows the coastline; coming from the jetty it's to the left. Heading west, Pekan Pangkor goes past the fishing village of **Teluk Gedung** and **Kota Beland (Dutch Fort).** Turning right at the **Teluk Gudung** sign leads to **Jl. Pasir Bogak,** which goes to the **post office, police station,** and the beaches of **Pasir Bogak** (3km), **Teluk Nipah** (6km), and **Coral Beach** (7km). Pink **taxivans** at the Pangkor jetty and by the south end of Pantai Pasir Bogak go anywhere for RM10. Taxivans line up on the main roads in Teluk Nipah and Pasir Bogak starting at 6am to shuttle passengers to the ferry. Several shops and hotels on the main road rent **motorcycles** (RM30 for 24hr., RM40 for 48hr.) and **bicycles** (RM15 for 12hr.). Wear a helmet and make sure rented bikes have good brakes. **Ah Thim** hires motorcycles at the jetty and is usually waiting as travelers disembark (☎012 388 7076).

PRACTICAL INFORMATION. Opposite the jetty, **Maybank** changes currency and has an **ATM.** (☎685 1494. Open M-F 9:30am-4pm, Sa 9:30-11:30am.) On **Jl. Pasir Bogak** 150m past the post office is **Hospital Desa P. Pangkor,** which has a prescription counter and an English-speaking assistant. There is also a 24hr. sick bay. (☎685 4048. Consultation RM2, overnight stays RM5. Clinic open 8am-4:30pm.) **JH Pharmacy,** Lot 14A Taman Desa Pangkor, is just across from the police station. (☎685 5322. Open daily 9:30am-9:30pm.) The **police** can be reached 24hr. (☎685 1222.) **Internet** access is at **Purnama Beach Resort** in **Teluk Nipah,** across from **TJ Chalet and Restoran** (RM8 per hr.; open daily 8am-11pm) and at **Pangkor Laser Internet,** located in a row of shophouses diagonally opposite the police station. (☎685 5744. RM2 per hr. Open daily 10am-1am.) The staff at the **post office** is very helpful. (☎685 1281. Open M-F 8:30am-4:30pm, Sa 8:30am-3:30pm.)

ACCOMMODATIONS. Pulau Pangkor's budget accommodations cluster on two side streets at Teluk Nipah. Travelers gather here for the beautiful sunsets and proximity to **Coral Beach** and secluded **Monkey Bay,** and for the kayaking, fishing, and island-hopping. Prepare to bargain, as many mediocre hotels charge ridiculous prices. **Horizon Inn ❺**, on the main road in Teluk Nipah, is a well run mini-resort with rooms overlooking the beach and a fabulous restaurant downstairs. Each room has its own porch. (☎685 3399. A/C doubles with hill view RM80, with sea view RM90. Discounts apply for stays over 2 days. Expect a 20% price increase on weekends and public holidays.) **Nazri Nipah ❶**, at the end of the lane from Restoran Horizon in Teluk Nipah, provides true backpacker camaraderie. Travelers come here for Western breakfasts and the cheapest beds in town. (☎685 2014. A-frames RM25; chalets with bath RM35.) Nazri Nipah also offers trekking trips to Pangkor Hill (RM30). On the same road, before reaching Nazri Nipah, **Ombak Inn ❸** provides clean, spacious rooms with TV and attached bath. (☎685 5223 or 019 573 4977. Doubles RM30-40.) **O La La Chalets ❷**, at the end of the first lane in Teluk Nipah (turn at the Seagull Beach Resort sign), has neat baths and quiet chalets, although some of the rooms have a dank ocean smell. (☎685 5112. Bike rental RM3 per hr., RM15 per 24hr. Motorbikes RM10 per hr., RM30 per 24hr. Doubles RM25-30.) On the same road, **Takana Juo (TJ Chalet and Restoran) ❸**, 4458 Teluk Nipah, has delicious food and comfortable rooms 50m from the beach. (☎685 4733. Singles and doubles with toilet and shower RM30; for stays over 2 nights RM20 per person, RM25 per couple.)

FOOD. A few stalls sell burgers and snacks at Teluk Nipah. The south end of Pasir Bogak, 5min. from Pangkor Paradise Village Holiday Resort, has night hawkers. Most accommodations have attached restaurants. **TJ's Restoran ❶**, at Teluk Nipah (connected to Takana Juo), is known for its Malay and Indonesian dishes. (Chicken or beef *rendang* in spicy coconut milk RM4; Western breakfast RM3-5. Open daily 8:30am-11pm.) One of Pangkor's culinary specialties is fish, purchased fresh from the piers each morning. **Restoran Horizon ❸**, 4438 Teluk Nipah, the best restaurant in town, has excellent *tom yam* (spicy Thai soup; RM17), Chinese-style cooked vegetables (RM5-8), and seafood dishes starting from RM8. (☎685 3388. Open M-F and Su noon-10pm, Sa 11am-10pm.) Across the street from Chuan Full Hotel, **Sin Nam Huan Restaurant ❸** serves tantalizing garlic butter prawns (RM16).

SIGHTS. Pulau Pangkor's best sights are its beaches and green hills. A leisurely island tour takes 45min. by motorcycle or 2hr. by bicycle. Taxivans charge RM40 to circle the island, so share the ride to offset costs. **Trekking** through the island's jungle interior makes for a good daytrip, but pay for a guide, as many of the trails are unmarked and overgrown. **Nazri Nipah** (see **Accommodations,** p. 361) offers trekking trips to Pangkor Hill. **Pangkor Hill,** 371m above sea level, can be reached by a 2km trail marked with a sign reading "Hulan Simpan Sg. Pinang" on the hill's north side near the airport. On the western side of the island, between Teluk Nipah and Pasar Bogak, is the trailhead to **Tortoise Hill** and to the **Jungle Information Center,** which provides tips on trekking through the island's interior.

For swimming and sunbathing, there are some nice beaches on the west coast, including the beautiful **Coral Beach,** north of Teluk Nipah and with a small Chinese temple at its northern end, and **Turtle Bay,** a deserted stretch of golden sand just south of Teluk Nipah, separated from the main road by waves of wild grass. There are quite a few monkeys lounging around both Turtle Bay and **Monkey Bay.** Although it's rarely on maps, the bay is just off the main road after the bridge from Nipah. Off Teluk Nipah's coast lies **Giam Island,** which has another small beach. Boats from Teluk Nipah motor here for RM30. You can also hire a boat to island-hop and **snorkel** for several hours (RM50). Arrange boats with **Lambaian Pulau Water Sports,** which also rents kayaks for RM10 per hour and snorkel gear for RM10 per day. (On the main road at Teluk Nipah. Open daily 8am-7pm.)

As for Pulau Pangkor's "sights," the **Fu Lin Kung Chinese Temple,** north of Pangkor town, should not be missed. From Pangkor town go toward the town of **S. Pinang Besar,** and pass **Chawangan Sekola,** a primary school. Turn left after passing **Restoran Hong Tong** on your right and go to the end of the road. Nestled at the base of a hill and surrounded by dense jungle, the temple contains pools of turtles and orange *koi* fish, a garden, and statues of the 12 animals in the Chinese zodiac. About 100m north of Fu Lin Kung on the right side of the road is **Sri Pathira Kaliamman,** a Hindu temple that has fallen into disrepair. About 1.5km south of Pangkor town is **Kota Beland,** a Dutch fort built in 1680. Today the fort stands in ruins due to a number of attacks from locals and pirates. It has been marked as a national monument, and souvenir stands have dutifully accompanied its restoration.

KUALA KANGSAR ☎05

Perak state's royal riverside town is home to the Istana Iskandariah, also known as the royal palace, and to the magnificent Masjid Ubudiah. Aside from a handful of architectural and royal monuments, Kuala Kangsar has little to offer. Kuala Kangsar makes a good daytrip from nearby Taiping, but extended visits are discouraged by the limited backpacker accommodations.

TRANSPORTATION. The **Express Bus Terminal** is along Jl. Kuala Kangsar. Buses go to: Butterworth (2hr.; 11:45am, 4:15pm; RM6.30); Ipoh (1½hr., every 10-15min. 6:15am-9:30pm, RM4); KL (4hr; 9, 10, 11:30am, 1:30, 2, 2:30, 4, 5:30, 6:30, 9pm; RM14.10-16); Kota Bahru (5hr.; 10:30am, 10:30pm; RM18.80); Lumut (1¾hr.; 11am, 3:30, 8pm; RM6.70); Taiping (1hr., every 20min. 6:40am-7:40pm, RM2.50).

ORIENTATION AND PRACTICAL INFORMATION. Kuala Kangsar has a main roundabout, from which **Jl. Istana** branches out toward the Masjid Ubudiah and the Istana Kenangan. **Jl. Datok Sago** meets Jl. Istana at the main roundabout and meets **Jl. Kuala Kangsar** at the smaller one. Jl. Kuala Kangsar leads to the bus station from the smaller roundabout. Coming out of the bus station, make a left to reach the smaller roundabout. Make another left on Jl. Datok Sago and walk along this road to reach the larger roundabout; Jl. Istana is to the right, while **Jl. Daeng Selili** is to the left and contains the post office, police station and several banks.

Currency exchange is available at **Public Bank,** 12 Jl. Daeng Selili, also known as Jl. Taiping. Exchange traveler's checks and currency. (☎776 9895/9896. Open M-F 9:30am-4pm, Sa 9:30am-12:30pm.) The **police** are on Jl. Raja Chulan, off Jl. Daeng Selil. (☎776 2222. 24hr.) For **emergencies,** dial ☎999. **Cardphones** are scattered across town. The **post office** is at the roundabout corner of Jl. Datok Sago and Jl. Daeng Selili. (*Poste Restante.* Open M-Sa 8:30am-5pm. Closed 1st Sa of each month.) **Postal Code:** 34000.

ACCOMMODATIONS AND FOOD. Double Lion Hotel ❷, 74 Jl. Kangsar. At the small roundabout behind a small bakery —go around back to find reception. Offers comfortable and clean rooms. (☎776 1010. Doubles with fan RM25-40, with A/C RM50, with A/C and private bath RM70-80; triples with fan RM30-50/RM60/RM100.) **Hotel Da Resto ❷,** along Jl. Daeng Selili next to the post office. Adequate rooms with good amenities. (Doubles with A/C, TV, cable, and private bath RM59; triples RM99.) *Kedai kopi* (coffee shops) selling local dishes can be found along Jl. Datok Sago between both roundabouts. The **bakery ❶** in front of the Double Lion hotel serves delicious coconut, sausage, and tuna buns (RM0.40-0.80).

SIGHTS. Masjid Ubudiah is a must-see, dazzling viewers with its size and attention to detail. Walk about 1250m from the large roundabout down Jl. Istana. The mosque's dome should be easily visible on the left side of the road. The absolutely resplendent building is both elaborate and extensive. (Open daily 9am-noon, 3-4pm, and 5:30-6pm.) **Istana Kenangan** (also known as Istana Lembah or Istana Tepas) is located at the end of Jl. Istana. From Masjid Ubudiah, walk 400m away from the roundabout, take the right fork when you reach the Istana Iskandariah, and walk another 400m. Built in 1926 without the use of a single iron nail, the Istana Kenangan served as the residence of the Sultan of Perak while the larger Istana Iskandariah was being constructed. Architecturally more interesting than the larger palace, Kenangan features lattice decorations, elaborate weaved patterns, and resembles a *kris* (a short dagger) in its scabbard when viewed from above. Currently, it functions as the Perak Royal Museum. (Open M-Th 9:30am-5pm, F 9:30am-12:15pm and 2:45-5pm.) **Malay College,** opened in 1905 as a school for aristocratic boys, and where Anthony Burgess once taught, is located on Jl. Tun Razak. Take the second left off Jl. Daeng Lelili when walking from the larger roundabout; the college is located just past the first junction, on the right side of Jl. Tun Razak. Today the college still boasts an immaculate rugby field and well-maintained buildings—it stands as a symbol of pride for higher education in Malaysia.

TAIPING ☎05

Once the capital of Perak, proud Taiping is a city of firsts: the country's first museum, railway line, newspaper, post and telegraph office, zoo, hill station, and public garden. Downtown Taiping displays the hallmarks of Chinese influence, as the city was originally settled by Chinese workers who came from Penang to mine the rich tin-fields. It was named Taiping ("Eternal Peace") in 1874 as part of a treaty between rival Chinese secret societies that were fighting for control of a water-course. For those who like long strolls among lake gardens and cool hills, Taiping provides an ideal break from the rigors of traveling.

TRANSPORTATION

Trains: Stesyen Keretapi Taiping (☎807 5584), on Jl. Stesyen 700m west of the downtown area near the hospital. Office open 24hr. Trains to **Hat Yai** via **Butterworth** (7hr.; 3:20am; economy seats RM7, 2nd-class seats RM17, bunks RM24.50-27) and **KL** (8hr.; 12:36am; economy seats RM14, 2nd-class seats RM24, bunks RM31.50-34).

Buses: Stesyen Bus, at the west end of Jl. Panggong Wayang. To **Kuala Kangsar** (every 15min. 6am-9:30pm, RM2.50). **Express Bus Terminal** is in **Kamunting,** a 20min. bus/taxi ride from Taiping (take the red Omnibus from **Steysen Bus**). To: **Butterworth** (every 30min. 6:30am-8:30pm, RM5) via **Alor Setar; Ipoh** (1hr., every 30min. 6:30am-6:30pm, RM5.45); **Johor Bahru** (8hr.; 9:30am, 9, 10:30pm; RM35); **KL** (4½hr., 26 per day 7:30am-11pm, RM13.30); **Penang** (1½hr.; 9, 11:30am, 1:30, 4, 6:30, 7:30, 8:30pm; RM7.35); **Singapore** via **Johor Bahru** (9hr.; 9:30am, 9pm; RM40).

Taxis: (☎808 1691). In Kamunting at Express Bus Terminal and in Taiping on Jl. Iskandar between West Jl. Kota and Jl. Panggong Wayang. From Taiping to: **Bukit Larut** (RM5); **Ipoh** (RM48, with A/C RM52); **Kamunting** (RM5); **Kuala Kangsar** (RM28).

ORIENTATION AND PRACTICAL INFORMATION

Taiping's center is set up in a grid. From south to north, the main streets running from east to west are **Jl. Panggong Wayang (Theatre Street), Jl. Kota, Jl. Pasar (Market Street), Jl. Taming Sari (Main Street), Jl. Barrack,** and **Jl. Stesyen.** From west to east, the cross-streets are **Jl. Masjid, Jl. Idris, Jl. Iskandar/Jl. Yusof, Jl. Chung Thye Phin, Jl. Pang Lin Ah Chong, Jl. Lim Teong Chye/ Jl. Kelab Cina, Jl. Lim Tee Hooi, Jl. Ong Saik/ Jl. Sultan Abdullah,** and **Jl. Maneckha.** A warning about street names: many have two—the older, British name, and the more recent, Malay name. Most maps will print the Malay names, but locals often refer to what they've known the longest. The local bus station, **Steysen Bus,** is located at the western end of the southernmost main street, **Jl. Panggong Wayang.** This street intersects two consecutive cross-streets, **Jl. Iskandar** and **Jl. Chung Thye Phin.** The taxi station is located on **Jl. Kota** between these two adjacent streets. The tourist information center is on **Jl. Kota,** three blocks eastward from the taxi station.

Tourist Office: Taiping Visitor and Information Center (☎805 3245), on Jl. Kota, under the cream-colored clocktower at the intersection with Jl. Lim Tee Hooi. Very helpful. Provides transportation info and maps. English-speaking staff; ask for Annuar. Open M-F 8:30am-5:30pm, Sa 8:30am-3pm.

Currency Exchange: Bank Bumiputra Commerce (☎807 2422), on Jl. Kota, next to the cream-colored clocktower. Open M-F 9:30am-4pm, Sa 9:30am-noon. **Maybank,** on Jl. Panggong Wayang, has **ATMs.** Open M-F 9:30am-4pm, Sa 9:30-11:30am, ATMs 6am-midnight. **HSBC** (☎807 5400), on the western end of Jl. Kota, has 24hr. **ATMs.**

Emergency: ☎999.

Police: (☎808 2222.) On Jl. Taming Sari, in front of the white and stately district office. Attentive and helpful. 24hr.

Medical Service: Hospital Taiping (☎808 3333), at the west end of Jl. Taming Sari. English spoken. 24hr. **emergency care.**

Telephones: Telekom (☎809 9841), uptown on the far east side of Jl. Barrack. IDD/fax. Open M-F 8:45am-5pm, Sa 8:45am-1pm.

Internet Access: Helmi Computer Technology Centre (☎808 2454), 200 Jl. Kota, at the western end of Jl. Kota, between Jl. Mosque and Jl. Idris. Internet RM3 per hr. Open daily 9am-midnight. **Pusat Computer,** Jl. Panggong Wayang, at the east end near the intersection with Jl. Kelab Cina. Internet RM2 per hr. M-F 10am-11pm, Sa 9am-11pm.

Post Office: (☎807 7555). Next to the Telekom office. *Poste Restante.* Open M-Sa 8:30am-5pm.

Postal Code: 34000.

ACCOMMODATIONS AND FOOD

Persatuan Hin Aun ❷, 218, 220, and 222 Jl. Chung Thye Phin, at the first intersection as you walk south along Jl. Chung Thye Phin from Jl. Panggang Wayang. Offers guest rooms on the second floor with A/C and bath. (☎808 3582. Doubles and triples RM22-25; quads RM29.) In the heart of Taiping at 52 Market Sq., **Hotel Malaya ❸** has clean rooms with A/C, phones, and bathrooms. From the bus station, walk east along Jl. Panggong Wayang, make a left on Jl. Chung Thye Phin before the film-developing shop, and take the first right onto Jl. Boo Bee. (☎807 3733. Laundry. Doubles RM30, with TV RM35; quads RM40, with TV RM45.) **Hotel Fuliyean ❺,** 14 Jl. Barrack, at the intersection with Jl. Ong Saik. On the corner next to the post office, the hotel has new rooms with hot showers, A/C, TV, towels, and soap. (☎806 8648. Doubles RM50; triples RM60; quads RM75.) **Panaroma Hotel,** 61-79 Jl. Kota, between Jl. Lim Tee Hooi and Jl. Kelab Cina. All rooms with A/C, TV, and private bathrooms. (☎808 4111. Doubles RM75; triples RM85-105; quads RM140.)

The central **day market** is along Jl. Chung Thye Phin, between Jl. Taming Sari and Jl. Panggong Wayang. The **night market** is southeast of Jl. Panggong Wayang, near Jl. Maharaja Lela. Walking east along Jl. Panggong Wayang, make a right onto Jl. Tupai. (Open daily 6am-midnight.) Taiping's best food is at the huge center in **Market Square ❶** near the local bus station. Look for the large *Fajar* sign. (Open daily 6am-midnight.) *The* choice for dim sum is **Kum Loong ❷**, 45-47 Jl. Kota, east of the cream-colored clocktower. (☎807 2649. Rice and vegetables RM6. Open daily 5am-11pm.) **Bismillah Restaurant ❶**, 138 Jl. Taming Sari at the intersection with Jl. Chung Thye Phin, is an authentic Malay/Indian restaurant. (*Roti canai* RM0.60. Open daily 6am-9pm.) At the Legend Inn near the local bus station at 2 Jl. Long Jaafar, **Legend Cafe ❸** is perhaps the fanciest restaurant in town. (☎806 0000. Sirloin steak RM26.50, broiled salmon RM19.)

SIGHTS

The **Taiping Lake Gardens and Zoo,** Jl. Tmn. Tasik Taiping (☎808 6577; www.zoottaiping.gov.my). This was Malaysia's first recreational garden, and it is also one of the country's most delightful. Near the entrance is the world's smallest monkey, *pygmy marmoset*, situated next to its fellow primate *tamarins*. (Paddle boat RM10 per 30min. Zoo open daily 8am-10pm. Feeding time 10am-noon. RM4, children RM2. Tram ride around the zoo 9:30am-5:30pm; RM2, children RM1.) On the new **Night Safari,** faux moonlight allows visitors to view nocturnal animals in their evening routines. (Open Su-F 8-10pm; Sa and eve of public holidays 8-11pm. Adults RM10, children RM6, camera RM5.) Malaysia's oldest hill station, **Bukit Larut,** formerly known as Maxwell's Hill, is popular for its cool temperatures, mountain greenery, and seclusion. Government-operated Land Rovers ply the route to the hill station from the base in Taiping on Jl. Air Terjun, past the northeast end of the Lake Gardens (35min., every hr. 8am-5pm, round-trip RM5). Taxi drivers will tell you that the station base is within walking distance, but it's a 45min. walk. For an extended stay on the hill, **Larut Hill Resort ❷** (☎807 7241) runs 10-person bungalows for RM150-200, while guest rooms cost RM15. Reserve in advance. **Muzium Perak,** built in 1883, is Malaysia's first museum. One kilometer east of the town center, follow Jl. Taming Sari east past the Telekom building and the prison. The museum is on the left after the intersection with Jl. Muzium. It maintains an eclectic exhibit that includes a Vietnam War-era CAC Avon Saber, royal garb, a collection of Orang Asli tools, and an array of animal taxidermy. There is also a *kris* (a traditional Malay dagger) collection celebrating Malaysian and Indonesian knife-dueling. (☎807 2057. Open Sa-Th 9am-5pm, F 9am-12:15pm and 2:45-5pm. Free.)

PENANG (PULAU PINANG)

Those with illusions of a sweet little island are in for a shock. The second-largest economic center in Malaysia, Penang is more powerhouse than paradise. The island is home to a number of multinational corporations, five colleges, and Malaysia's largest Buddhist temple, as well as numerous Malaysian *kampongs* (villages) and *kongsi* (clans) in the rural areas. The dense jungles contain *durian*, jackfruit, and nutmeg plantations, and tourists can visit the prestigious Butterfly Farm, new aquarium, botanical garden, and Forestry Museum and Arboretum. Other delights include relaxing by Batu Ferringhi's beaches, temple-hopping in Georgetown, and devouring one of Penang's culinary contributions to the world—the minty yet spicy *assam laksa*.

THE VIEW FROM ABOVE

Major Cities: Georgetown, Batu Ferringhi, Teluk Bahang.

The Lowdown: A bustling island off the west coast with a life of its own and the most Chinese in Malaya.

Highlights: Penang cuisine, lush jungles, colorful seasonal festivals, Malaysia's largest Buddhist temple.

TRANSPORTATION

Flights: Bayan Lepas International Airport (☎643 0811), 20km south of Georgetown. Yellow bus #83 (every hr. 6am-10pm) and minibus #32 run between the airport and Pengkalan Weld in Georgetown. **MAS** (☎262 0011) flies to **KL** (45min., every hr.,

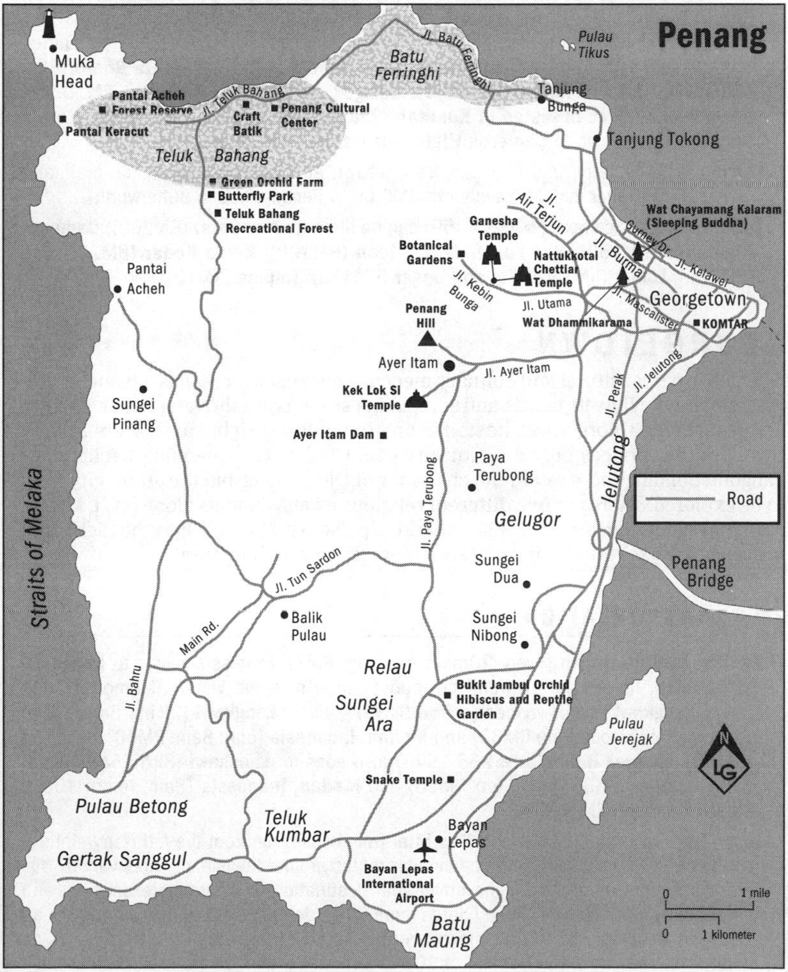

RM109) and **Medan, Indonesia** (45min., 12:55pm, RM253). **Singapore Airlines** (☎226 3201) flies to **Singapore** (1hr., 3 per day, RM295). **Thai Airlines** flies to **Bangkok** (2hr., 8am, RM499).

Trains: The **train station** (☎261 0290; www.ktmb.com.my) is below the ferry landing in Butterworth. Train schedules change biannually. To: **Bangkok** (21½hr., 2:20pm, 2nd-class bunks RM88-94.20) via **Hat Yai** (4½hr.; 3rd-class seats RM4, 2nd-class seats RM13); **KL** (10½hr.; 9:55pm; 3rd-class seats RM17, 2nd-class seats/bunks RM30/RM37). Transfer to **KL** for trains to **Johor Bahru** and **Singapore.**

Buses: There are two **bus stations:** one at KOMTAR in Penang, and the other below the Butterworth ferry landing. From KOMTAR, **Supercoach** buses run to: **KL** (5hr., 11 per day, RM22); **Kuantan** (8½hr., 10pm, RM35); **Singapore** via **Johor Bahru** (10hr.; 8:15, 9am, 12:30, 7:30, 8:30, 9:30, 10pm; RM42); **Taiping** (1hr.; 11am, 1:30, 4, 6pm; RM7.50). **Sri Maju** buses go to **Ipoh** (3hr.; 7:30, 9:30am, 2, 4:30, 7, 9pm; RM12.50). **Kurnia Bistari** buses go to **Cameron Highlands** via **Ipoh** (6hr.; 8am, 3pm; RM22), while their minivans go to **Hat Yai** (4hr.; 5, 8:30am, noon, 4pm; RM20). From Butterworth, **Transnasional** buses go to **KL** (5hr., 13 per day, RM20) and **Kota Bharu** (8hr.; 10am, 10, 10:30pm; RM20). **Sri Maju** buses go to **Lumut** (3hr., 7 per day, RM10.50). **Sri Jengka Ekspres** buses go to **Kuantan** (7½hr.; 8:30, 9, 10pm; RM30-35). **Kurnia Bistari** buses also go to **Cameron Highlands** via **Ipoh** and **Tapah.**

Ferries: A 24hr. ferry runs between **Georgetown** and **Butterworth** on the mainland (every 20min., after midnight every hr.; RM0.60 to Penang, free to Butterworth).

Taxis: Long-distance taxis (☎333 4459) can be hired to: **Alor Setar** (RM200); **Cameron Highlands** (RM250); **Hat Yai** (RM220); **Ipoh** (RM120); **Kuala Kedar** (RM200); **KL** (RM250); **Lumut** (RM180); **Padang Besar** (RM150); **Taiping** (RM70).

GEORGETOWN ☎04

Georgetown is a cultural and culinary mecca, where each street has a blend of ethnic influences. While its debris and screeching street noise threaten Penang's tropical-resort feel, Georgetown hosts fascinating cultural sights and offers budget travelers the services only a major city can. Chulia St. is the main backpacker hangout; buildings here retain the character of Old Penang, but the entire city begs to be explored. There are five different religious establishments alone on Jl. Masjid Kapitan Keling. Narrow streets and markets pulse with life late into the night, and wandering walks reveal some of Asia's most diverse architecture.

TRANSPORTATION

Ferries: To **Butterworth** (every 20min.; free cars RM7). Express services to **Langkawi** and **Medan, Indonesia** run from the tourist center near the Victoria Memorial Clock Tower. **Langkawi Ferry Services** (☎966 9439) goes to: **Langkawi** (2½hr.; 8am, return 5:30pm; RM35, round-trip RM60) and **Medan, Indonesia** (5hr.; 8am; RM90, round-trip RM160). **Ekspres Bahagia** (☎263 1943) also goes to: **Langkawi** (8, 8:45am, return 2:30, 5:30pm; RM35, round-trip RM60) and **Medan, Indonesia** (8am, return 10am; RM90, round-trip RM160).

Local Transportation: Buses and **Bas Mini** (minibuses) run from the *jeti* (ferry station) and KOMTAR (6am-11pm), making circular routes around the island. Fares vary by distance and bus company; tell the driver your destination to determine exact fare, and always carry loose change. *Beca* charge more for guided tours of Georgetown but are an ideal way to take in the city's atmosphere. **Yellow** buses go south while **blue** buses go north. Take **red and white** bus #1 or 101 to Central Penang, blue bus #93 and transit line #202 to the north shore. Both taxi and *beca* are RM20 per hr. and taxis charge 20% more at night. Lh. Chulia to the *jeti* RM5. **Taxis** from the airport are hired through a coupon system. Purchase a coupon at the Teksi counter (Georgetown RM25-30).

Rentals: A valid driver's license with photo is required for all car rentals. **New Bob Car Rental,** at 11 Gottlieb Rd. and at the airport (☎642 1111), also has cars from RM170.50. Rental services also provide car delivery.

ORIENTATION AND PRACTICAL INFORMATION

Penang's **ferry terminal** and one local **bus station** are on **Pengkalan Weld Quay,** along Georgetown's southeast coast. Parallel to Pengkalan Weld Quay is **Lh. Pantai (Beach Street),** the financial district, administrative buildings, **police station,** and the main **post office.** Lh. Pantai runs north to the **Victoria Memorial Clock Tower,** at the intersection with Lebuh Light. Here **Fort Cornwallis** guards the city while boats leave from the jetty near the **Penang Tourism Centre.** Running northwest from the Penang-Butterworth ferry terminal is **Lh. Chulia.** At the west end of Lh. Chulia, **Jl. Penang** runs north to hotels and south to **KOMTAR,** the cylindrical building that dominates Penang's skyline. At KOMTAR are shopping malls, the **long-distance bus station,** and the **local** bus station. Buses run northwest from KOMTAR to Batu Ferringhi and Teluk Bahang, as well as south toward the **airport.**

Tourist Offices: Penang Tourist Center (☎261 6663), on Pesara King Edward by the clocktower. Maps and info. Open M-Th 8:30am-1pm and 2-4:30pm, Sa 8:30am-1pm. **Penang Tourist Guides Association** (☎261 4461), 3rd fl. of KOMTAR, has extremely helpful staff. Follow the signs near McDonald's in the KOMTAR building. Open M-Sa 10am-6pm; closed for irregular lunch breaks. **Tourism Malaysia** (Northern Region), 10 Jl. Tun Syed Sheh Barakbah (☎262 0066), near the Penang Tourist Center. Open M-F 8am-4:30pm, Sa 8am-1pm. Closed 1st and 3rd Sa of each month.

Tours and Travel: MSL Travel, Agora Hotel, Jl. MacAlister (☎227 2655). Malay and Thai rail-passes available with ISIC. Smaller companies along Lh. Pantai and Lh. Chulia offer tours. **Newasia Tours and Travel,** 35-36 Pangkalan Weld (☎261 7933), offers plane tickets, a variety of tours, and minibuses to Thailand. Branch offices at KOMTAR ground fl., off Jl. Ria (☎261 5558), and at 27 Lh. Chulia (☎264 3930).

Consulates: Indonesia, 467 Jl. Burma (☎227 4686). Open M-F 8:30am-1pm and 2-4:30pm. **Thailand,** 1 Jl. Tuanku Abdul Rahman (☎226 8029). Open M-F 9am-noon and 2-4pm. Visa applications accepted until noon. 2-month tourist visa RM33. Accommodations also help issue visas, but it is advisable to go through a consulate.

Currency Exchange: Several moneychangers on Lh. Chulia and major banks along Lh. Pantai have good rates. **OCBC Bank,** on Lh. Pantai near Lh. Chulia, has 24hr. **ATMs** (PLUS/V). Bank open M-F 9:30am-3:30pm, Sa 9:30-11:30am. **HSBC,** down the road, also has a 24hr. **ATM.** There are also banks with **ATMs** at KOMTAR and on Lh. Pantai.

Emergency: Police: ☎999. **Fire:** ☎994.

Tourist Police: ☎261 5522, ext. 409.

Directory Assistance: ☎103.

Pharmacies: A few large pharmacies are on Lh. Pantai. **Ego Pharmacy,** 448 Penang Rd. (☎226 4529), has a wide selection. Open M-Sa 9:30am-7:30pm. The **Guardian Pharmacy** at KOMTAR is open daily until 10pm.

Medical Services: General Hospital (☎229 3333), on Jl. Hospital. English spoken. 24hr. **emergency room.** Consultation fee RM2. Performs minor surgery.

Telephones: Telekom office (☎220 9321), on Jl. Downing next to the post office. Open M-F 8:30am-4:30pm. **HCD**/fax. **IDD** from any card phone.

Internet Access: Many on Lh. Chulia. RM3 per hr. **Eighteen Internet Cafe,** 18 Lh. Cintra, off Lh. Chulia, has speedy connections. Open M-Sa 10:30am-10pm.

Post Office: GPO Penang (☎261 9222), on the corner of Lh. Downing and Pengkalan Weld. Open M-F 8:30am-6pm, Sa 8am-4pm. *Poste Restante.*

Postal Code: 10670 (for post office only).

ACCOMMODATIONS

Budget hotels abound on and near Lh. Chulia. Love Lane, named for the Chinese matchmakers who once lived there, intersects the center of Lh. Chulia.

Olive Spring Hotel, 302 Lh. Chulia (☎261 4641), above Rainforest Restaurant. Lovely walls awash with Caribbean purples and blues. No skimping on cleanliness here. Lockers available. Laundry. Dorms RM8; singles with fan RM15; doubles RM22-25. ❶

37 Inn, 37 Love Ln. (☎264 4337), located directly on the left of Wan Hai Hotel. Brand new and well maintained. Dorms RM8; doubles with fan RM16, with A/C RM28. ❶

Cathay Hotel, 15 Leith St. (☎262 6271). Traveling buddies and couples enjoy this famous antique colonial with lofty ceilings and white sheets. Doubles with fan RM57.50; standards with A/C RM69; deluxe with A/C RM92. ❹

Hotel Noble, 36 Lh. Pasar (☎261 2372), off Jl. Masjid Kapitan Keling behind Lh. Chulia. Featured in a scene of Michelle Yeoh's film, *The Touch.* Close to the Indian part of town. Rooms have private showers and common toilets (RM18). ❷

FOOD

Street-side *nyonya* cuisine reigns supreme in Penang. The **foodstall** on the corner of Lh. Cintra and Lh. Kimberley dishes out samples of Penang specials. (Open daily 6pm-1am.) Another favorite is the oxtail soup at a **foodstall** across from Hotel Continental on Penang Rd. The best spring rolls can be found at the **Popia Lazat Enak** ❶ stall with the Tweetie Bird decoration (on Gurney Dr., RM1.10 each). Malaysian **foodstalls** line Lh. Tamil. Join locals for dinner at the **night market.** (Call ☎263 8818 for current location.) Lh. Carnavan, between Lh. Chulia and Lh. Campbell, hosts a bustling **morning market.**

Hameediyah, 164A Lh. Campbell. Terrific Indian Muslim restaurant with a selection of *murtabak* curries. Signature "Curry Kapitan" dish RM3.50. Open M-Th and Sa-Su 10am-10pm. ❶

The Tandoori House, 34-36 Jl. Hutton, 2 blocks north of the intersection with Penang Rd. Georgetown's finest Mughal restaurant. 19 types of *naan* and 11 types of rice. *Tandoori thali* with choice of meat RM14, vegetarian *naurattan qurma* RM11, homemade ice-cream *kulfi payalla* RM6. Tax 15%. Open daily 11:30am-3pm and 6:30-10:30pm. ❸

Hard Life Cafe, 363 Lh. Chulia, 400m from Lh. Penang. Pool table and reggae. Beer RM6. Mostly vegetarian dishes (RM5-10). Rooms RM10, for 2 RM12. Open late. ❷

PIPIN' HOT IN PENANG. These are a few dishes you might find:
Char Kuey Teow: Flat rice noodles stir-fried with bean sprouts, seafood, and spicy sauce.
Popia: A fresh spring roll.
Top Hats: Crispy bite-size pastries filled with cooked turnips.
Ais Kacang: Shaved ice, sweet corn, sweet red beans, saso, and syrup.
Chendol: Shaved ice with green pea noodles in coconut milk and pandan syrup.
Bubur Cha Cha: Sweet coconut milk over ice with chunks of fruit and colorful rice gummies.

SIGHTS

All sights listed except for Wat Chayamang Kalaram, Fort Cornwallis, and the State Art Gallery are near Jl. Masjid Kapitan Keling (formerly Lh. Pitt).

WAT CHAYAMANG KALARAM. The 33m reclining Buddha at this Thai temple is Malaysia's largest and reputedly the third largest in the world. *(Accessible by blue bus #93, 94, 102, 202, and minibus #26, 31, and 88. Off the main road to Batu Ferringhi on Lg. Burma. Open daily 8:30am-5:30pm.)* Opposite the temple is **Dhammikarama Burmese Temple,** the only Burmese temple in Malaysia, with intricately carved decorations. *(Meditation class and dharma lecture W 8-9:30pm. Open daily 8am-6pm.)*

PENANG MUSEUM AND ART GALLERY. Fantastic displays give a flavor of Penang's history and culture without the dusty aftertaste of many museum exhibits. Soundbyte displays lend insight into the city's heritage. *(On Lh. Farquar, between St. George's Church and the Cathedral of the Assumption. Open Sa-Th 9am-5pm. RM1.)*

KHOO KONGSI TEMPLE. Signs for various *kongsi*, meaning "clan house," are visible throughout the island. This one stands out for its lavish decorations and innumerable ancestral pillars, whose beauty won it the honor as a location set for

Anna and the King in 1999. *(On Jl. Masjid Kapitan Keling, near Lh. Acheh. Go through the temple entrance; the meeting hall is on the right, and the temple is down the drive.)* Nearby, on the corner of Lh. Cannon and Lh. American, **Yap Temple** proudly displays intricately hand-carved stone pillars at its entrance. *(Open daily 8am-5pm.)*

FRANCIS LIGHT CEMETERY. Formed in 1789, it contains the remains of most of the founding fathers of Penang, including Francis Light, and most of the early expatriate British families. The fun is in hunting for the Francis Light tomb. (Hint: It's in the Catholic section. The cemetery is divided into Protestant and Catholic halves.) It also contains the grave of Thomas Leonowens, husband to the Anna Leonowens portrayed in *Anna and the King.*

CHEONG FATT TZE MANSION. The preserved home of wealthy Chinese merchant Cheong Fatt Tze. Striking in its use of different architectural details—Art Nouveau steel, stained-glass windows, venetian shutters, Victorian cast-iron work, and gold-leaf timber—this is an extremely *"feng shui"* house according to geomancers from all over Asia. It won the UNESCO Conservation Award and has been the location for several films, including *Indochine.* Painted an iridescent electric blue, the mansion contains two museums, 38 rooms, five courtyards, seven staircases, and 220 windows. *(14 Leith St. ☎ 262 5289. Open daily 9am-5pm. RM10)*

KUAN YIN TENG. Built in 1800, the temple is devoted to the Buddhist Goddess of Mercy. Devotees at Penang's oldest Chinese temple burn *joss* paper money for prosperity in the afterlife, offering up prayers for health, wealth, and longevity in a fog of sandalwood incense. Catch the temple at its liveliest during the feast days for Kuan Yin, on the 19th day of the second and sixth lunar months. *(1 block from St. George's. Open daily 9am-6pm.)*

SRI MARIAMMAN TEMPLE. Lord Shiva and his consort Parvati preside over this active Hindu temple, which also shelters the Shrine of the Nine Planets. During the Thaipusam Festival in January or February, the lavish Lord Subramanian statue is paraded from the temple. *(The back of the temple is down Jl. Masjid Kapitan Keling near the intersection with Lh. Chulia. The entrance is one block over on Lh. Queen. Open daily 8am–9pm.)*

DAYTRIPS FROM GEORGETOWN

Kek Lok Si Temple and Penang Hill are accessible from the town of Ayer Itam, while the Botanical Gardens are a 2hr. hike from the top of Penang Hill. The Snake Jungle and the Bukit Jambul Orchid, Hibiscus and Reptile Garden are near the Penang airport.

KEK LOK SI TEMPLE. Blending Chinese, Thai, and Burmese architecture, Kek Lok Si is a must-see. Buddhist laity from all over Malaysia and Thailand flood the temple on Buddhist holidays. Remove your shoes in all sanctuaries; photographing nuns and monks is forbidden. The seven-tiered **Pagoda of 10,000 Buddhas** has six flights of stairs leading to a narrow balcony, which offers a bird's-eye view of Ayer Itam and the countryside as well as a closer look at the giant bronze statue of Kuan Yin at the top of the hill. *(Take bus #1, 85, 91, 101, 351, or minibus #84, 21. (25min.). Open daily 9am-6pm. Pagoda RM2.)*

PENANG HILL. Offering cool temperatures and wonderful views of Georgetown, this hill has a Hindu temple and an unspectacular mosque. You can stop halfway up the cable train to view the rubber plantations of old. Before going home, stop by the Ayer Itam market to try one of the best *laksa* (RM2.50) in front of the red sign. *(Take bus #1, 91, 101, 85, 351, or minibus #21 from Georgetown to Ayer Itam's Roundabout Junction, then take bus #8 (RM0.70) to the foothill. There, a train creeps up*

830m Penang Hill (45min.; every 30min., every 15min. in late afternoon, M-F 6:30am-9:30pm, Sa-Su 6:30am-11:45pm; RM3, round-trip RM4). From the top, you can walk 3hr. down a jungle path. Ask for directions and watch the weather.)

BOTANICAL GARDENS. Northwest of Georgetown, the 30-hectare Botanical Gardens are great for a stroll, jog, or picnic, but on the weekend you will likely have the rest of Georgetown to keep you company. Admire the rhesus monkeys roaming amid the greenery, but don't feed them. During Hindu festivals, the **Ganesha Temple** on Jl. Waterfall becomes the site of many activities. Stray from the main paths to avoid crowds. *(Take bus #7 from the jeti, Lh. Chulia, or KOMTAR. Alternatively, the hike from atop Penang Hill takes approximately 2hr. Open daily 5am-8pm.)*

BUKIT JAMBUL ORCHID, HIBISCUS, AND REPTILE GARDEN. As the name suggests, this outdoor site houses orchid and hibiscus plants, but the highlight is a set of giant tortoises—the elder of which is 150 years old—from the Seychelles Islands. The reptile house is a good spot for observing snakes, though the tanks could be better maintained. *(Take yellow bus #69 or 83 to Jl. Dr. Awang at Bukit Jambul, then walk 10min. to the garden. ☎644 8863. Open daily 9:30am-6:30pm; last entry 5:30pm. Free snake show Sa-Su 11:30am, 3:30pm. RM5, children RM2. Camera fee RM1.)*

BATU FERRINGHI

Graced with the natural beauty that has earned Penang the nickname "Pearl of the Orient," Batu Ferringhi ("Portuguese Rock") is a seafood dining mecca and local hangout. From the main road toward Teluk Bahang, look for the Coca-Cola sign with "Bayu Senja Kompleks 50m." Keep in mind that taxi drivers may bad-mouth certain guesthouses and send you elsewhere for a commission. To avoid the hassle, ask to be dropped off at the Coca-Cola sign. Better yet, bus #93 or 202 (50m from KOMTAR) will drop you at the police station.

You can roll out of bed and onto the sand from any of the following guesthouses. For **Baba Guest House ❷**, 52 Batu Ferringhi, turn right down this road and left at the end. Baba is the first guesthouse on this lane. Laundry, tickets to Langkawi and Thailand, and motorbike rental (RM53 per day) are available. (☎881 1686. Singles RM20; doubles RM25-30, with bath and A/C RM40-60.) **Shalini's ❷**, 56 Batu Ferringhi, has clean rooms and a restaurant serving inexpensive Malay, Indian, and Chinese food. (☎881 1859. Doubles with fan RM20-30, with A/C and bath RM60. Discounts available.) **Ah Beng Guest House ❸** offers great deals for A/C rooms. The fan rooms are simpler and more faded. (☎881 1036. Doubles RM50, with A/C, fridge, and bath RM70; triples with A/C, fridge, and bath RM80.)

Hawker stalls ❶ and waterfront **cafes ❶** are scattered amid high-class restaurants; nearly everywhere, a plate of *mee* or a bowl of *laksa* goes for RM3. For the cheapest food in town, try **Bayu Senja Corner Cafe ❶**, on the corner of Jl. Teluk Bahang and Bayu Senja, which serves Malaysian, Chinese, and Thai food. (Fried noodles RM3. Open daily 4pm-5am.) **Poker III Bayu Senja Food Court ❸**, to the right of the guesthouses, is a popular beachfront dining spot offering everything from pizza (RM12-25) to Hainanese chicken rice for RM4. (Open daily noon-11pm.)

TELUK BAHANG

Known as "The End of the World" to local Malays because the road out of Georgetown once ended here, Teluk Bahang counterbalances the pressure-cooker atmosphere of Georgetown. Along the tree-lined streets, free-range roosters dodge school children, and laid-back vendors arrange piles of durian and rambutan. At the far end of town lies a *kampung nelayan* (fishing village). Rickety piers, a few weather-beaten boats, and a handful of equally weather-worn folks panning for *goleng* (tiny clams) are all that keep the *nelayan* in this *kampung*. Many travelers stay to enjoy the seafood and explore the nearby monkey beach, **Pantai Acheh Forest Reserve,** and the **Butterfly Farm.** To reach Teluk Bahang from Georgetown, take blue bus #93 or 202 from the jetty, Lh. Chulia, or KOMTAR.

The **Fisherman's Village Guest House ❷,** in a turquoise house in the fishing *kampung* off the main road to the right, has basic rooms in a longhouse. Ask for one of the better rooms upstairs. (☎885 29 36. Standards with fan RM18, with A/C RM30.) Near the roundabout on the main road toward Batu Ferringhi, **Hotbay Motel ❸,** 48 Jl. Teluk Bahang, has an attentive staff and brand-new rooms; the sheets are white and clean. All rooms have two twin beds. (☎012 558 6160. Doubles with fan RM55, with A/C RM65; family rooms RM110, on weekends RM130.) For the cheapest stay in town head to **Miss Loh's Guest House ❶.** Coming from Georgetown, turn left at the roundabout, continue 300m, and take the first right after the Telekom station; it's the first gate on the left after the bridge. (Singles RM25; doubles RM30.)

As you enter town, the main food center is before the roundabout on Teluk Bahang. Fare is simple but tasty (RM5). The **night market** by the roundabout vends *satay, nasi kandar*, chili burgers, and local desserts. (Open daily 7:30-10:30pm.) The **morning market** on the left, beyond the public park on Jl. Teluk Bahang, sells fruits and veggies. (Open daily 6:30am-noon.) **Sun Stall ❶,** on the right side of the main road before the roundabout, is a Malay and Indian Muslim restaurant open 24hr., serving *char koey teow* (fried flat rice noodles RM2) and banana *roti* with ice cream (RM3). **Fisherman's Village Restaurant ❹,** before Fisherman's Village Guest House, serves fresh seafood. Most restaurants open for dinner at 6pm.

Nature enthusiasts hike at the **Pantai Acheh Forest Reserve,** between Teluk Bahang and Balik Pulau. There the **Forestry Museum and Arboretum** displays the local species of rainforest trees and plants. (Open Tu-Su 9am-noon and 2:45-5pm.) The trail begins where Jl. Teluk Bahang ends, near the jetty at the fishing village. From the trailhead, walk 30min. to a sheltered campsite near a footbridge where the trail forks. The right branch leads to a **lighthouse,** while the left branch leads to **Keracut Beach,** where there are camping facilities. Those who take the adventurous 2hr. hike to the lighthouse should bring plenty of water. The dangerous parts of the trail are marked with white squares of paper pointing out the best path. The trail leads to an empty beach, beyond which stands an out-of-date "Do Not Enter" sign. (Forest Reserve open daily 7am-7pm.) Erected in memory of the Buddhist priest and healer Chor Soo Kong, the **Snake Temple** seethes with all kind of snakes, free to wind around the temple. Every traveler in Malaysia will ask whether you went, but the 45min. bus ride is not quite worth seeing a handful of slithery reptiles unless you're dying for a photo with them. (Take yellow bus #66 or minibus #32. Open daily 7am-7pm. Donations requested.) From the roundabout, the road leads south 500m to the **Penang Butterfly Farm,** 830 Jl. Teluk Bahang, which breeds 120 species of butterflies. The farm also has an insect museum, a mini-zoo, and an art gallery. (☎885 12 53. Open M-F 9am-5pm, Sa-Su 9am-5:30pm. RM12.50, children RM6.25. Cameras RM1.) Up the road 5min. is the **Teluk Bahang Recreational Forest,** which boasts **camping facilities ❶** (free), a swimming pool, a waterfall, and forest hiking trails. There is also a forestry **museum** near the entrance. (Open daily 7am-7pm.)

Craft Batik, 699 Mk. 2, across the main road from Mutiara Hotel, offers free tours of its factory and a gift shop showcasing traditional Malaysian crafts. (☎885 1302. Factory open daily 8am-5pm; gift shop 8:30am-5:30pm. The factory has been relocated here until renovations are complete at its permanent location, 651 Jl. Teluk Bahang.) The **Penang Cultural Center,** 288 Teluk Bahang Rd., on the way to Batu Ferringhi, is a bit touristy but has dinner shows with award-winning performances. (☎885 1175. Open M-Sa. Cultural show 9:30am-noon, RM48. Dinner and show 7:30-10:30pm, RM110. Cultural tour, dinner, and show 6-10pm; RM135.)

PULAU LANGKAWI

Expected to become the Phuket of Malaysia, sparsely populated Langkawi transformed from a fisherman's outpost into a touristed island resort in the early 1990s. The main attractions are eagle feeding and cave viewing, with hours and hours of relaxation to spare. Snorkelers and divers head south for daytrips to Pulau Payar to swim with black-tip sharks and schools of tropical fish.

THE VIEW FROM ABOVE

Major City: Kuah.

The Lowdown: A well-developed island with everything from parties to sandy beaches.

Island Mascot: The reddish-brown eagle, for which Langkawi is named.

Beaches: Pantai Cenang, Pantai Tengah, and—the best—Pantai Tanjung Rhu.

KUAH ☎04

Kuah lays claim to *chendol* (shaved ice) hawkers, duty-free and souvenir shops, and five out of Pulau Langkawi's six traffic lights. For the most part, it serves as a base from which to explore nearby beaches and the lush landscape.

TRANSPORTATION

Flights: Langkawi Airport (☎955 1311), at Padang Matsirat, 20km from Kuah. **MAS,** ground fl., Langkawi Fair Shopping Mall (☎966 6622), flies to: **KL** (1hr., 5-8 per day 6:35am-9:30pm, RM205); **Medan, Indonesia** via **Penang** (2hr., 11:35am, RM408); **Penang** (30min.; Su-M 11:35am, Th-F 7:45pm; RM77); **Singapore** (1½hr.; Tu-Th and Sa 4:45pm; Tu, F, Su 5:10pm; Su-M, F 8:40pm; RM448).

Boats: Ferry companies have counters at the **jetty** (☎966 5889). Ferries go to: **Kuala Kedah** (1¼hr., every hr. 7am-7pm, RM15); **Kuala Perlis** (45min., every hr. 7am-7pm, RM12); **Penang** (2½hr.; 2, 5:30pm; RM35, round-trip RM65); **Satun, Thailand** (1hr.; 9:30, 11am, 12:30, 3, 4pm; RM20).

Taxis: Fixed-fare taxis abound, offering rides from the jetty to **Kuah** (RM4) and **Pantai Cenang** (RM16), or chartered to circumnavigate the island (RM80-100).

Rentals: Major hotels and stores along Pantai Cenang rent **cars** (RM60-150 per day). **Motorcycle** (RM30-50 per day) and **bicycle** (RM3 per hr., RM10-15 per day) rentals are everywhere.

PRACTICAL INFORMATION

Tourist Office: Tourism Malaysia (☎966 7789), on Persiaran Putra. Coming from the jetty into Kuah, it's on the left across the road from the police station and library. Open M-W and Sa-Su 9am-5pm, Th 9am-1pm. English spoken.

Tours: Langkasia Travel and Tours (☎966 2429), at the jetty. Fishing, day and sunset cruises, snorkeling, and island-hopping tours. English spoken.

Currency Exchange: Moneychangers abound. **Bumiputra Commerce Berhat,** 1 and 3 Jl. Pandak Mayah 1 (☎966 6725), opposite the hawker stalls. Cirrus/MC 24hr. **ATM.** Open M-F 9:30am-4pm, Sa 9:30am-noon.

Markets: The nightly location of **Pasar Malam** rotates among Ulu Melaka (M), Kedawang (Tu), Kuah (W), Temoyong (Th), Air Hangat (F), Kuah (Sa), and Padang Matsirat (Su).

Emergency: ☎999.

Police: (☎966 6222), on Jl. Leboh Kisap opposite the old hospital. Open 24hr.

Pharmacy: MNY Multi-Pharmacy, 102 Persiaran Mutiara (☎966 0066). Open daily 8am-11pm.

Medical Service: The **hospital** (☎966 3333) is on Bukit Tekoh, 10km toward Pantai Cenang. English-speaking doctors. 24hr. emergency care.

Telephones: Telekom Office, Jl. Pandak Mayah 6 (☎966 7202), a few blocks off the main road. Sells international and domestic calling cards. Open M-W and Sa-Su 8:30am-4:30pm, Th 8:30am-1pm. **IDD** from public phones.

Internet Access: Atiera Computer, Lot 3, Bangunan Arked MARA, in Kuah across from the night hawkers. RM2.50 per hr. Open M-Th and Sa-Su 10am-midnight, 2hr. lunch break on F. On Pantai Cenang, **AB Motel** has Internet. RM5 per hr. Open daily 10am-midnight.

Post Office: (☎966 8690), from the jetty, it's 500m before the tourist office. *Poste Restante.* Open Sa-Th 9am-5pm.

Postal Code: 07000.

ACCOMMODATIONS AND FOOD

Most travelers stay in nearby Pantai Cenang. Consequently, **Hotel Langkawi ❸**, 6-8 Persiaran Putra, down from the tourist office, is Kuah's only budget accommodation. (☎966 6248. Singles RM30; doubles RM40-45). The new **Hotel Panggau Libau**

❺, 1592-1594 Persiaran Putra, offers a restaurant, lounge, and travel services. (☎967 2122 or 019 428 2356. Singles RM70, with A/C RM90; doubles RM80/RM100; triples RM90/RM110. Prices drop in low season.)

Despite the lure of nearby beaches, several of Kuah's restaurants remain packed with locals and tourists. For tastebud bliss, try **Prawn Village Restaurant ❷,** 7-10 Jl. Persiaran Putra, between Hotel Langkawi and the tourist office. (Noodle soup RM3. Fish fillet RM10. Open daily noon-2:30pm and 6-11pm.) **Rootian Seafood Restoran ❷,** at the corner of Jl. Pandak Mayah and Jl. Pandak Mayah 6, and its neighbor, **Water Garden Hawker Center ❷,** serve a variety of local fare. Crowds flock here on weekends. (Open M-Th and Sa-Su 5-11pm.) The **open-air hawker center ❶** lines up along Jl. Persiaran Putra with seafood. On the western end of Kuah is **Aquarium Seafood Garden ❹,** Lot 411, Kelibang, which hosts an evening Thai cultural show (F-W 8:45-9:30pm). Their own fresh seafood is cooked in an open kitchen. (☎966 8888. Open daily noon-11pm.)

SIGHTS AND BEACHES

WATERSPORTS. Pulau Langkawi is full of exquisite beaches, mountains, stone cliffs, and waterfalls. The clearest water and best snorkeling are at **Pulau Payar Marine Park** south of Langkawi, which has the best coral reefs off Malaysia's west coast. Full-day excursions can be arranged with several travel agencies at the Kuah jetty for RM130 (includes snorkel gear, nature guide, and ferry transport). Highly recommended by the tourist office, **Zarminda Holiday** (☎966 1550 or 966 1660; zttour@time.net.my) offers a beefy package that includes snorkeling gear, underwater chamber viewing, glass-bottom-boat rides, buffet lunch, and insurance. (RM220, children RM140.) Many hotels along Lh. Pantai Cenang arrange island-hopping tours around Pulau Beras Basah (4hr.; 9:30am, 2pm; RM45-60 not including snorkeling gear), tours of the wildlife park on Pulau Singa Besar, and a visit to the gorgeous Lake of the Pregnant Maiden on Pulau Dayang Bunting. Many hotels also offer waterskiing and jet skiing. Fishing boats travel between the Kuah jetty and **Pulau Tuba** (30min., every 30min., RM3). Tuba's beach, fishing village, and bungalows are popular among backpackers and are worth a daytrip.

Those seeking to get away from conventional tourism can turn to Jürgen Zimmerer, a German nature guide who leads jungle treks (RM70), village excursions to a local *kampung* (RM70), and river safaris around mangrove forests (RM160). Booking is available online. (☎955 4744 or 012 484 8744.)

BEACHES. On the road to Datai is **Pantai Pasir Tengkorak,** a small, clean beach that gets crowded on Fridays when families come to picnic by the water. Down the road is the **Temurum Waterfall.** A 10min. walk leads to the pool at its base. During the rainy season (June), the overflowing pool makes this a beautiful picnic spot; during the dry months, the waterfall is reduced to a trickle, but the beauty of the sheer cliff and surrounding trees still make the walk worthwhile. **Pantai Pasir Hitam,** a black-sand beach, is east on Rte. 113. Farther east, a road leads north from the roundabout to **Pantai Tanjung Rhu,** Langkawi's most secluded beach. At low tide, walk to the neighboring beach and watch fishermen cast their nets. Tours of nearby caves in the Killem River—**Gua Cerita** and **Gua Kelawar** (the bat cave)—are available. You can also see eagle feedings at a nearby mangrove swamp. (☎955 2745. Cave tours RM40. Feedings RM110 per person, RM250-350 per boat.)

OTHER SIGHTS. North of Pantai Cenang is **Laman Padi,** a rice paddy-turned-museum with guided tours. (Open daily 10am-6pm. No tours on F. Free.) Small roads off Rte. 115 between Pantai Cenang and Pantai Kok wind through fields, the

Kuala Teriang fishing village, and Padang Matsirat. By motorbike, you can follow the many small paths that lead off the main road between Padang Matsirat and Ulu Melaka to a quiet, traditional *kampung*. **Pantai Kok,** 15min. past the fishing village, was once one of the best beaches on the island, but is now merely another construction site. Its only redeeming quality is the Anna and the King palace set. (Open daily 10am-7pm. RM3.50, children RM2.) Northwest of Pantai Kok is **Telaga Tujuh,** the **Seven Wells Waterfall.** While the 20min. hike is steep, a splendid view of the surrounding mountains awaits at the top. For the more adventurous, in the wet season the full hike affords spectacular views, refreshing swims in the fall's six wells (the seventh, locals say, is found only by those who get lost in the village), and close contact with monkeys. Located west of Pantai Kok, near Burau Bay is the **Langkawi Cable Car,** the world's longest cable rope and the best way to see fantastic views of surrounding islands. In the center of the island, a road leads off Rte. 112 to the top of **Gunung Raya,** the tallest mountain on Langkawi. Off Rte. 113 east of the roundabout, a road leads to **Durian Perangin Waterfall,** where there is a large pool and thick foliage.

PANTAI CENANG

Pantai Cenang is an up-and-coming backpacker center. The easiest way to get here is by taxi from the airport (RM15) or from Kuah (See **Kuah: Transportation,** p. 375.) Family-run, backpacker-friendly **Amzar Motel Beachview Chalet ❸,** just steps from the beach, is an unbeatable deal. (☎955 1354. Chalet rooms for 2 with fan, TV, and bath RM35, with A/C RM45.) Beachfront **Charlie Motel ❹** has a wide variety of well-kept chalets. From Kuah, continue straight toward the beach—it's on the left near the lighthouse. (☎945 1200. All rooms with A/C and bath. Doubles RM65; triples RM75; quads RM65-85.) **AB Motel ❸,** 1km from the intersection of Lh. Pantai Cenang and the road from Kuah, has huts on the beach. (☎955 5278; abmotel@hotmail.com. All rooms with bath and A/C RM50-120.) **Gecko Hostel ❷,** offers very basic but clean rooms and a cup of coffee in the morning. (RM25, with private bath RM50, with A/C RM50. RM5-10 discount for a 3-day min. stay.)

TJays ❸, behind the moneychanger across from Underwater World, serves Italian recipes in a romantic setting. (☎012 451 2867. Delicious thin-crust pizzas RM12-24. Open daily 1pm-late.) For early risers, there's **Breakfast Bar ❷,** a favorite for its laid-back atmosphere and low prices. (☎955 6533. Breakfast from RM4; sandwiches RM5-7; fresh fruit juices RM1.50. Open M and W-Su 7am-2pm.) **Red Tomato Garden Cafe ❷,** near Charlie Motel, serves homemade bread, Western fare—pancakes, omelettes, pizza, and hashbrowns—and Lavazza coffee. (☎955 9118. Buttery bread rolls RM2. Open daily 9am-3pm and 6:30-10:30pm.)

The hottest spot is **Hideout,** 200m past Underwater World, hidden behind trees and bushes, where locals and tourists in-the-know gather for ice cold beer. For live music, check out **Reggae Bar,** down from Langkawi Tailors. (☎012 489 3275. Cocktails RM10. BBQ chicken and fish RM4-5. Open noon-2am.) **Coco Jam,** at the Langkawi Village Resort in Pantai Tengah blasts music until the early morning. (☎955 1511. Disco 11pm. RM15 cover includes 1 drink. Open daily 10pm-3am.) **Bananas Fun Pub,** in the Awana Hotel, has live music and a karaoke bar. (Beer RM10, pitcher RM34. Open daily 6pm-2am.) Ooh and ah at marine life at **Underwater World,** on the left as you come from Kuah. (☎955 6100. Open daily 10am-6pm. RM18, children RM10.) The **Taman Buaya Crocodile Park,** on the road to Datai, has croc shows and a 25 ft. python. (☎955 2559. Shows 11:45am, 2:15pm. Open Su-Tu and Th-Sa 9am-6pm. RM8.)

CAMERON HIGHLANDS

Cool breezes, lush giant ferns, and fuchsia orchids await travelers at this historic retreat. Since 1885, when government surveyor William Cameron hacked away wild jungles to a "fine plateau," the Cameron Highlands have provided a sweet escape for overheated, homesick Brits, and, more recently, ornithologists documenting bird species. Outside the cool jungle are vegetable and strawberry farms and vast tea plantations that supply lowlanders with their pekoe. There are three towns: Ringlet, the lowest, is primarily a farmers' hub; Brinchang, the highest, attracts locals for its weekend night market; and Tanah Rata, the main town and the most expensive of the three, offers jungle treks and the basic traveler needs.

TANAH RATA ☎05

In the clouds 14km north of Ringlet and 5km before Brinchang, Tanah Rata emerges with tall, mock-Tudor apartments and hotels interspersed around the main drag, which is lined with restaurants, entrances to jungle treks, and bus and taxi stands. Travelers come here for laid-back, late-night relaxation.

TRANSPORTATION

Buses: From the bus station (☎491 2978), on the main road, Regal Transport Co. operates local routes to **Brinchang** (10min.) and onward to **Kampung Raja** (35min., every hr. 6:30am-6:30pm, RM0.80) and **Tapah,** a stopover en route to the Cameron Highlands (2hr., 8 per day 8am-5:30pm, RM5). **Express buses** go to: **Butterworth** (6hr.; 8, 9am; RM19.50); **Kota Bharu** (9am, 10pm; RM38); **KL** (4½hr.; 8:30, 10:30am, 1:30, 3, 4:30pm; RM13); **Penang** (10hr.; 8, 9am, 3pm; RM19.50) via **Ipoh** (3hr.; 8, 9am, 3pm; RM15). A **minivan** at the bus station goes to **Gua Musang** (2½hr.; M, W, F 7:30am; RM68). From there, there's a train to Kota Bharu (4hr., RM7.40).

Taxis: ☎491 2355. Next to the bus station. RM18 per hr. is the lowest price. To **Brinchang** or anywhere between Tanah Rata and Brinchang RM4. **Outstation taxis** will go to all major cities, and even straight to KL's international airport.

ORIENTATION AND PRACTICAL INFORMATION

The town of Tanah Rata begins with a row of restaurants, hotels, and shops on both sides of the street. Two hundred meters down, the **bus station** and **Malay foodstalls** signal the end of central Tanah Rata. Past the heart of town, the road leads to Bala's Holiday Chalets 1km away, and a golf course before reaching Brinchang.

Tourist Offices: Souvenir shops sell maps (RM3). Guesthouses and booths at the bus station provide detailed tourist information. Guides and experienced trekkers at guesthouses are the best source of information on trails and trekking.

Currency Exchange: HSBC, 31-32 Main Rd. (☎491 1217). Open M-F 9:30am-3:30pm, Sa 9:30-11:30am. 24hr. **ATM** (Cirrus/MC/PLUS/V). **Maybank,** 69-70 Persiaran Camellia 4 (☎491 4897), by the cake house, exchanges currency. Open M-F 9:30am-4pm, Sa 9:30-11:30am. The **moneychanger** at Maybank exchanges traveler's checks (RM10 for the 1st check, RM0.15 per subsequent check). Open daily 9:30am-5:30pm.

Emergency: ☎999.

Police: (☎491 1222). Next to the hospital at the northern edge of town. 24hr. English-speaking officers available on call.

Medical Service: Hospital (☎491 1966), left of the main road at the end of town. During office hours (M-F 8am-4:30pm), check in at the registration room on the left. 24hr. emergency care. English spoken.

Telephones: No available Telekom office, but Telekom card phones are all over town.

Internet Access: Pusat Computer CL, 55B, 1st fl., Persiaran Camellia 3, near Maybank. RM2.80 per hr. Open daily 9am-11pm. Most guesthouses also offer Internet access for RM2-3 per hr.

Post Office: (☎491 1051), left of the main road near the Orient Hotel. Open M-Sa 8:30am-5pm.

Postal Code: 39000.

ACCOMMODATIONS

Nearly all guesthouses provide extra amenities, including free pick-up, bus reservations, international phone service, hot water (you'll need it), kitchen facilities, book exchange, movies, food, Internet access, and tourist information.

Father's Guest House, P.O. Box 15 (☎491 2484). Perks include: 5 acres of luscious greenery, 2 dalmatians, unique Nissen-hut dorms, and a volleyball court. Excellent Internet rates. Ask for pickup from the bus station. Reserve in advance. Dorms RM7; doubles RM25, with bath and shower RM50; triples RM40-55. Lower rates for longer stays. ❶

Twin Pine Chalets, Jl. Mentigi 2 (☎491 2169). Follow the signs from the main road or call for pickup. A variety of rooms, including simple attic rooms for longer stays. Clean facilities. Laundry. Restaurant. TV room. Internet RM3 per hr. Dorms RM7; attic rooms RM7.50-10; doubles RM16-30; family rooms RM40-60; rooms with bath from RM30. ❶

Daniel's Travelers Lodge, Lorong Perdah 9 (☎491 5823). The street is 1 block from the bus station. Bonfires every night. Trekking guide leads patrons into the jungle. Dorms with lockers RM7; singles and doubles RM16-35; triples RM25-45; quads RM35. ❶

Cameronian Inn, Jl. Mentigi 16 (☎491 1327), off the main road. Clean and comfortable. Trail maps, currency exchange, Internet access, and motorbike rentals. Dorms RM7; singles and doubles RM25-30, with shower RM45-60; triples and quads RM40-80. ❶

Bala's Holiday Chalets, Lot 55 (☎491 1660). Serene surroundings and elegant architecture make up for the distance from town. Free pick-up from the bus station. Reserve ahead. Doubles RM98, RM120 on weekends; family rooms from RM220. ❺

FOOD

Delicious, inexpensive food is everywhere. Don't miss the steamboat hot pot offered by most restaurants. As you enter town, head for the right side of the road before the bus station for foodstalls serving cheap, standard Malay and Chinese fare. The best of these are **Excellent FoodStall** ❶ (open daily 7am-5pm) and **Zainab San** ❶, which serves Malay food. Several good Indian and Chinese restaurants are on the left side of the road. Guesthouses serve food as well.

Mayflower Restaurant, 22 Main Rd. (☎491 1793). Locals agree it's the best in town. *Tom yam* RM10; steamboat hot pots RM10-13; fried rice or noodles RM5. ❸

Restoran Bunga Suria, 66A Persiaran Camellia 3, beyond the palm trees when facing Ringlet. The runner-up on the "local favorites" list. Buffet-style banana leaf meals RM5. Many vegetarian options. Open daily 7am-10pm. ❶

The Orient Restaurant, 38 Main Rd. (☎491 1633). Great atmosphere with a collection of red lanterns and Chinese opera paraphernalia. Steamboat RM12-13. ❸

Yong Teng Cafe, Stall G15, beside the taxi stand. Pancakes with fresh Highlands strawberries and ice cream RM2.50. Curry noodle soup RM2.50. Open daily 7am-5pm. ❶

SIGHTS AND OUTDOOR ACTIVITIES

The Highlands's best sights are agricultural. Picturesque tea plantations and terraced vegetable, strawberry, and dairy farms form a surreal "food pyramid." Check out the camouflaged leaf frogs and foot-long stick insects at the **Butterfly Park.** (Open daily 8:30am-5:30pm. RM3, children RM1.50.) Boh ("Best of Highlands") Tea Estates runs free factory tours at two locations. **Sungai Palas Boh Tea Estate,** north of Brinchang, is accessible by taxi, bus, or foot on Path #1. The cafe at the larger **Boh Tea Estate** also provides stunning views of the emerald carpet of tea plants. It is 5km from Paths #9 and 9A—a taxi is the best option. (Both open Su and Tu-Sa 9am-4:30pm.) Daily countryside tours, available at all accommodations, include a visit to the tea plantation and factory, and some combination of visits to a Buddhist temple, strawberry garden, vegetable farm, butterfly garden, honey-bee farm, rose center, and market center. (4hr.; 9am-2pm; RM15 not including admission to the rose center RM4 and butterfly farm RM3.)

Hiking is the preferred Highlands activity. Most guesthouses offer trail maps and answer questions about specific paths. Count on each hike being more difficult than its description, and be careful after it rains—trails are treacherous. The mountains of **Gunung Brinchang** (2000m) and **Gunung Perdah** (1550m) have excellent views from their peaks. The hikes' level of difficulty varies widely depending on the approach taken. Path #1 to Gunung Brinchang is very steep. A paved road from the viewpoint leads 7km to Sungai Palas Boh Tea Estate and it's another 6km to the main road. You can also climb up and arrange a car back. Path #10 goes to Gunung Jasar (1670m) before connecting with Path #12 to Gunung Perdah. Paths #3, 5, 7, and 8 lead to **Gunung Peremban,** with Path #8 being the steepest and most challenging. In contrast, the shortest and easiest is Path #4, a short-cut to the golf course that passes by **Parit Falls** before ending at **Taman Sedia,** which has a picnic area and trees with species-identifying labels. By far the most popular trek (highly recommended for people of average fitness level) are Paths #9 and 9A, which form a loop from **Robinson Waterfall** to vegetable farms and a mini dairy farm near the Boh Tea Estate. Path #9A is a pleasant downhill walk and the easier of the two. Budget 4-5hr. round-trip for all paths except #1, which may take a full day, and #4, which should take 1½-2hr. at most. Almost all the paths are within walking distance from Tanah Rata. Path #1 starts from Brinchang. For good maps, ask tourist information offices or guesthouses to show you the different trails.

INTERIOR PENINSULAR MALAYSIA

Malaysia's development has wrought enormous environmental harm throughout the peninsula. The protected parklands of Taman Negara, the interior's premier attraction, sometimes seem to be the lone pristine oasis. Eco-conscious travelers still sneer at the unabashed marketing and development of this "virgin jungle paradise," but this development is only in the main resort—the rest remains relatively untouched, and efforts to maintain Malaysia's natural heritage are ongoing.

JERANTUT ☎09

Jerantut is largely a gateway to Taman Negara and is the best place to stock up on supplies and information about treks and other adventures.

TRANSPORTATION AND PRACTICAL INFORMATION. Taman Negara can be reached by land (1½hr.) or by water (3hr.). Although the bus ride is faster, many travelers opt for the scenic boat ride. **Boats** leave for Taman Negara from

Kuala Tembeling, 25min. outside of Jerantut. To get there, take a **shuttle** from any of the hotels (from Hotel Sri Emas RM4, from Green Park Rest House RM5) or take a **taxi** (RM16). NKS Hotel & Travel at Hotel Sri Emas runs **minibuses** to Kuala Tahan headquarters in Taman Negara. The Agro Tour is highly recommended. (1½hr.; 2:30, 5:30pm, or anytime for a min. of 4 people; RM15, with Agro Tour RM23.) The **bus station** is on Jl. Diwangsa. Local buses go to Kuala Tembeling (30min.; 8:15, 11am, 1:45pm; RM1.50). Express buses run to Kuantan (3½hr.; 8:30, 11am, 2:30pm; RM10.50) and Temerloh (1½hr., 12 per day 6am-6:30pm, RM4.20). Express Perwira buses depart at 8:30, 10:30am, 2:30, and 4pm for: KL (3hr., RM10.85); Klang (4hr., RM12.65); Temerloh (1hr., RM3.50). The station in Temerloh serves some destinations that the Jerantut station does not. The **train station** (☎266 2219) is on Jl. Stesen Keretapi. Jungle trains crawl to: KL (6½hr.; daily 12:30am, Sa-Su 9:25pm; RM15-25); Singapore (8½hr., 9:05am, RM15-30; express 7¼hr., 2:20am, RM19-38); Wakaf Bharu near Kota Bharu (9hr., 12:20pm, RM12.60; express 6¼hr., 3:30am, RM18-32). Taxis go to: KL (RM120); Kota Bharu (RM240); Kuala Tahan (RM90); Kuantan (RM100). Share taxis to offset costs.

The two main roads are Jl. Besar and Jl. Diwangsa. **Bank Simpanan Nasional,** on Jl. Diwangsa, opposite the bus station, has a MC/PLUS/V 24hr. **ATM.** (☎266 5300. Open M-F 9am-4pm, Sa 9am-noon.) The **hospital** (☎266 3333) is outside town off of Jl. Besar. Turn left from the bus station onto Jl. Diwangsa and the **post office** is at the end of the street, near the intersection with Jl. Bomba. (☎266 2201. Open M-Sa 8:30am-5pm.) **Postal Code:** 27000.

ACCOMMODATIONS AND FOOD. In the center of town, **Sri Emas ❶,** 46 Jl. Besar, across from the police station, offers relatively clean rooms at great prices. Call ahead for 24hr. pick-up from bus and train stations. **NKS Travel** is based here and provides the usual run of park-related services. Ask for the fun and fearless Angie, the only female guide in the park. Sri Emas offers standard amenities including a restaurant, luggage storage, Internet access, and showers for guests on the go. (☎266 4499. All A/C rooms with bath. Dorms RM7; doubles RM15, with A/C RM38-48; triples RM21/56; quads RM64.) **Jerantut Rest House ❸,** on Jl. Besar past the mosque, has spacious rooms. (☎266 6200. Dorms RM8-10; doubles RM40.)

Dine at one of the outdoor restaurants across from the market on Jl. Pasar Besar. The **night market** offers the standard *kway teow*, fried rice, and *satay* standards for RM4-5. (Open Sa 4-10pm.) Look for *roti canai* stands with late-night snacks. **Restoran Al-Haj ❶,** next to Sri Emas, serves delectable Malay food like *nasi lemak* (RM0.80, with egg RM1.50) and white rice dishes—choose your own meat, fish, and vegetables for RM3-5. (☎266 2161. Open M-Sa 7:30am-10pm.)

TAMAN NEGARA NATIONAL PARK ☎09

However awesome this 130-million-year-old rainforest may be, due to heavy deforestation, it is all that is left of its kind on the peninsula. As Malaysia's first and largest national park, Taman Negara is one of the world's best-kept rainforests, yet it is teetering on the brink of ecological disaster.

TRANSPORTATION

Taman Negara and its gateways, **Jerantut** and **Kuala Tembeling,** are accessible by **bus** from KL or Kuantan, and by **train** from Wakaf Bharu or Singapore. The park can be reached by privately arranged bus or taxi, or by **boat** on the Tembeling River. Boats to the park (2-2½hr.; 9am, 2pm, return M-Th and Sa-Su 9am, 2pm, F 9am, 2:30pm; RM22 each way) leave from the village of Kuala Tembeling, accessible by bus (RM1.50), minibus from hotels (RM4-5), or share-taxi (RM4 per person, RM16

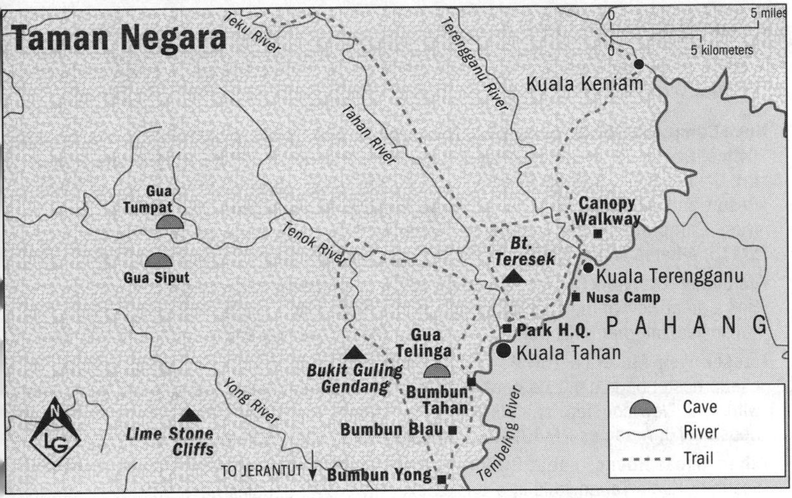

per car) from Jerantut. **Minibuses** from Jerantut (RM22) leave from Hotel Sri Emas (2:30, 5:30pm) and from Nusa Camp information center at the bus station (6:30am, 4pm). From Kuala Tembeling, fixed-price **share-taxis** (4-passenger max.) go to: Jerantut (RM16, with A/C RM18); KL (RM140); Kuantan (RM120). At Taman Negara, boats shuttle across the river for RM0.50 (7:30am-11pm). Nusa Camp runs **river-buses** (RM30-290 per day) within the park that are cheaper than private charters. Nusa Riverbus routes go from Kuala Tahan to: Nusa Camp (3, 6pm, F 12:30pm; RM3 for registered guests, RM7 for non-guests); Blau and Yong observation hides (8:30am, 5:30pm; RM7); Kuala Terengganu (10am, 3pm; RM15, round-trip RM20); the cave (9:30, 11:45am, 2:45pm; RM5, round-trip RM8).

ORIENTATION AND PRACTICAL INFORMATION

Book your boat ride and accommodations at least one night in advance, especially during weekends and holidays. **Permits** for cameras and entry to the park can be purchased at the Kuala Tahan bus station. Hold on to your permits (RM1, camera RM5), as you can be fined RM50-500 if caught without one during random checks; you will be asked to produce them when you leave. Bring extra cash; the only moneychanger is at the resort and has exorbitant rates. Make sure to stock up on insect repellent and a flashlight if planning to go for a jungle or night trek.

Park headquarters, next door to a minimart, is on the left of the Tembeling River, near the park's south entrance. Across the river is the village of **Kuala Tahan** with cheaper hostels and floating restaurants. The reception area at the resort offers **telephone** service at rip-off prices. **Internet** cafes in Kuala Tahan charge about RM6 per hr. Good maps (RM2) with trails and points of interest are available at the Wildlife Office at the park headquarters. The resort office next to reception rents hiking and camping gear (tent RM20; sleeping bag RM3; boots RM3). If you're undertaking a lengthy hike or are inexperienced, consider hiring one of the expensive but knowledgeable guides (around RM120 per day, RM600 per week). Guides specialize in different activities and areas of the park, so ask around. For the Taman Negara environs (including Kuala Tahan, Kuala Tembeling, and Jerantut), the **Postal Code** is 27000. Drop off mail at the resort reception desk.

ACCOMMODATIONS

For cheaper accommodations, cross the river to Kuala Tahan. It is advisable to make your own reservations rather than go through travel agencies in Jerantut.

Nusa Camp and SPKG Tours, 16 Jl. Diwangsa (☎266 2369), at Jerantut bus station. **KL Office:** Studio 2B, Arcadia Green, 1 Jl. Sultan Ismail (☎03 2070 5401). **Kuala Tembeling Office:** No. 5, Taman Negara Jetty (☎266 3043). Upriver from the Taman Negara Resort and more serene than jetty-area lodging. Rates include boat transfer between Nusa Camp and Kuala Tembeling. Camping RM2, with 2-person tent RM17; dorms RM15; A-frame chalet RM55; Malay cottages RM100; Malay house RM110. ❷

Tembeling Riverview Chalet (☎266 6766), first on the right up the stairs from the river. Has a great view of the scenic–though murky–river, and a homey campground feel. Few vacancies. Internet RM2 per 15min. Dorms RM10; doubles RM40; quads RM60. ❶

Teresek View Motel (☎266 9744). Although it is a bit of a hike to get up the hill, its cheap hostel beds can't be beat. A-frames for 2 people. Clean and cozy Malay houses with A/C. New concrete chalets with A/C. Internet and playstation RM4 per hr. Hostel beds RM10; A-frames RM40; Malay houses RM60; chalets RM60-70. ❶

Tahan Guest House, about 300m past the police station. Though far from the main scene at Kuala Tahan, this is a backpacker haven. All doubles have balconies. Dorms RM10; doubles RM50. ❶

Agoh's Chalets (☎266 9570), farther up the embankment past Teserek View. Neat rooms with bath and newly tiled floors surround a garden. Dorms RM20; doubles RM40; quads RM100. ❷

FOOD

Both **Nusa Camp** and **Taman Negara Resort** have pricey restaurants. The resort is the only place in town to get a beer, though at RM18 you have to question whether it's worth it. For snacks and soft drinks, mini-markets on the Kuala Tahan side are less expensive than the one at the resort. Several eateries line the river on the shore opposite the resort. For exotic cuisine, head to **Mawar's Cafe ❹,** the farthest upstream in the row of floating restaurants. Portuguese Malay chef José Monteiro creates Western and local fusions to die for. Try his caramelized banana (RM12) or baked pumpkin with coconut cream soup (RM15). The **Family Restaurant ❷** offers tasty Malay dishes and standard Western fare. (Burgers RM2.50; *tom yam* RM6; *satay* RM5 for 10 sticks. Open daily 8am-11pm.) The most romantic place to eat is at **Rumbia Restaurant ❸.** Their *soya* sauce fish (RM20) is excellent, as are their lychee shakes (RM3). Look for the thatched roof at the end of Kuala Tahan's riverfront. (Most dishes RM5. Open daily 8am-11pm.)

OUTDOOR ACTIVITIES

Taman Negara never experienced an ice age and, as a result, is the oldest rainforest in the world. Trails are clearly marked, so it's easy to slip away in the early morning and surround yourself in the virgin jungle. The larger mammals—elephants, tigers, rhinos, leopards, and cattle (oh my!)—are rarer sights these days, but amazing insects, birds, and lush forest make this a forest a must-see.

CAMPING AND HIKING. The nine-day trek to and from **Gunung Tahan,** Peninsular Malaysia's highest peak, and the nearby four-tiered waterfall is the best way to take in the ecological riches of the park. Purchase food and supplies in Kuala Tahan, or hire a porter (RM600 per week, including food and water). Travelers must consult with park authorities beforehand and hire a **guide** (RM600 for 1 week, RM70 for each subsequent day). The information desk at the resort has postings from people willing to split costs. Travel agencies in Kuala Tahan organize shorter hikes starting at two days and one night (RM200, including food, water, and shelter; min. 4 people). Another recommended trek is the 31km **Tenor Trail** through dense jungle; ask for Nizram, the guide who is most familiar with this path. When camping on your own, pitch tents away from the river to protect against unexpected floods. The primarily uphill climb to **Bukit Teresek** (1.7km, 1hr.) offers breathtaking panoramas. Bring plenty of water.

CANOPY WALKWAY. Suspended by a web of ropes, wires, cables, and wooden planks along the treetops, the canopy walkway is the longest crossing of its kind. This can be its selling point, although for those afraid of heights, it is 500m of sheer torture. The view 40m above the forest floor is tremendous; bring a camera. Authorities regularly test the safety of the walkway. It pays to go early to avoid crowds or long waits (only 4 people are allowed on the walkway at a time). The canopy walkway is 1.2km (25min.) from the headquarters. Set aside 30min.-2hr. total. (Open Sa-Th 11am-3pm, F 9am-noon. RM5.) The canopy walkway combined with a climb to Bukit Teresek is RM25. Book through NKS travel at Jerantut or at the main drop-off point.

GUA TELINGA. Also known as the "Ear Cave," this limestone cave is a tourist favorite. Look for bats and the non-poisonous snakes that feed them. The cave is slippery and dirty, so bring old clothes, sturdy shoes, and a flashlight. (2.6km, 1½hr. hike each way; 25min. by Nusa Riverbus). NUSA camp offers a package that includes the canopy walk, water, and food for RM100.

NIGHT ADVENTURES. The rainforest really comes to life at night. Explore it on a guided night hike (RM15), 4WD safari tour (RM25), or river cruise (RM35). Hikes focus more on insects and phosphorescent fungi, while safaris attempt to track the more elusive wildlife. Be forewarned that your chances of spotting wildlife around or during the full moon are slim, as animals are more cautious to avoid predators. Bring a flashlight. Check for times and book reservations through the Family Restaurant.

OBSERVATION HIDES. These *bumbun*, as they are called in Malay, are elevated viewing platforms in the midst of the jungle. The platforms are enclosed with a narrow opening for viewing wildlife. Travelers are encouraged to stay overnight for increased chances of seeing animals, although it is more likely that you will just enjoy the sounds of the forest. **Bumbun Tahan** is the closest to headquarters (200m) and the most frequently visited by night trekkers. It has a great view of a salt lick that attracts many animals. **Bumbun Blau** and **Bumbun Yong** are accessible by boat or by foot (3km and 3.9km from headquarters, respectively). Nusa Riverbus runs to Blau and Yong *bumbun* (15min. downstream and a 10min. walk; 8:30am, 5:30pm; RM7, round-trip RM10). Bring flashlights.

RIVER RAFTING AND TUBING. Ride the rapids in a "boat" or float down the river in a rubber tube for a new vantage point of the forest—on your back. Expect to get wet. Book trips at the Family Restaurant at least 1hr. in advance. (2hr.; 10am, 3pm; RM25 per person including life jacket with NKS; RM30 with NUSA).

PERHENTIAN ISLANDS ☎09

One of the world's most beautiful beaches, Long Beach has brought widespread fame to the Perhentian Islands. Tourists come in search of great snorkeling and scuba diving, and end up staying for the evening barbecues and starry nights.

Those hoping for a taste of indigenous culture will be disappointed, as vacationers flock to the islands during tourist season. In rainy months, however, visitors find cheap hostels, fewer tourists, and great surfing.

THE VIEW FROM ABOVE

The Lowdown: Eastern Malaysia's northernmost island group.
Islands: Pulau Perhentian Kecil ("Little Island") and Pulau Perhentian Besar ("Big Island").
Gateway City: Kuala Besut and Tok Bali.
Beaches: On Kecil: Coral Bay, Long Beach, Mira Beach, Petani Beach, Adam and Eve Beach. On Besar: Blue Lagoon, Flora Beach, Main Beach.

TRANSPORTATION

There are two embarkation points for the Perhentians—Kuala Besut and Tok Bali—which are easily accessed via Kota Bharu or Kuala Terengganu. From Kuala Besut or Tok Bali, take a boat to the islands. Tok Bali is about 20min. closer to Kota Bharu than Kuala Besut, but boats run more frequently from Kuala Besut.

TO KUALA BESUT: From **Kota Bharu,** take a taxi to Kuala Besut (1½hr., RM28 per 4 people). Booking a taxi from a guesthouse (they usually arrange for a carpool, even for non-guests) will certainly cost less than the whopping RM40 that you'll be charged at the bus station. If you can't find other passengers to split the cost, take bus #3 to **Pasir Putih** (1hr., every 30min. 6:30am-7:30pm, RM3) and catch bus #96 to Kuala Besut (30min., every 30min. 6:30am-6:30pm, RM1.20). From **Kuala Terengganu,** a direct bus now heads to Kuala Besut (2½hr.; 8, 10am, 2pm; RM5).

TO TOK BALI: From **Kota Bharu,** take a taxi to Tok Bali (70min., RM24 per 4 people). Or, call one of the boat services to be picked up from the bus station at **Pasir Puteh** (**KB Backpackers Holiday** can be reached at ☎743 2125).

TO THE PERHENTIANS: Boats leave for the islands from **Kuala Besut** (slow boats 1½-2hr.; 10am, 2pm; RM20 each way, children RM10; speed boats 30-45min.; 8, 9:30, 11am, 2, 4pm; RM30 each way, children RM15). From **Tok Bali,** speed boats depart at 7, 10:30am, and 2pm, while slow boats depart at 9:30am and 2pm (travel time and prices same as Kuala Besut). Boats bring passengers to their beach of choice on either **Besar** or **Kecil,** where motorboat taxis charge RM2 to drop passengers on shore. Returning from the Perhentians, slow boats leave at 8am and noon, and speed boats leave at 8am, noon, and 4pm (during the peak season). The Tourist Information Center and many guesthouses in Kota Bharu and Kuala Besut sell boat tickets.

ARRIVE EARLY. Accommodations can be difficult to find during the peak season (May-Sept. and public holidays). Arrive in Kuala Besut for the 8am boat departure, or in Tok Bali for the 7am departure, as island accommodations fill up quickly. Most accommodations close from Nov.-Jan. Reservations usually aren't accepted except at more upscale resorts, and scant telephone lines make local phone calls impractical. Also, accommodations' phone numbers are subject to change (literally every three months or so, since most use cellular phones). If you can't find a bed, check with reception for free rooms the next morning at 7:30 or 11:30am, when people usually check out. It is also common for backpackers to camp on the beach in peak season. Accommodations are cheaper during the low season.

PULAU PERHENTIAN KECIL ☎09

With the constant criss-crossing of motorboats, the monotone hum of generators, and hip, young backpackers kicking back on every available plot of land, Kecil is not a mecca of serenity. But crowds aside, Long Beach is arguably Malaysia's most beautiful locale.

TRANSPORTATION AND PRACTICAL INFORMATION. **Long Beach** is on the island's east coast. Accommodations span the entire length of the beach, while tourist services run up the center. On the west coast, a 15min. walk from **Mohsin Chalets,** is quieter than **Coral Bay.** A 25min. trek south through the jungle is **Mira Beach.** Another 20min. takes you to the southern coast and larger **Petani Beach. Perhentian Village,** on the island's southeast tip, 20min. from Petani, is home to fishermen, a **police station,** and **medical services. Motorboat taxis** line up along **Long Beach** and go to: Coral Bay (RM14); D'Lagoon (RM4); Mira Beach (RM12); Perhentian Village (RM8); Petani Beach (RM10); Pulau Perhentian Besar (RM7-15). Taxis are pricier in the evening due to rougher waves.

There is no official tourist office, although **Turtle Shop,** at the center of Long Beach, offers info on entertainment, transportation, and the turtle hatchery. Snorkeling trips run RM30 including equipment rental. (Open daily 8:30am-7pm.) Both Turtle Shop and **Mama's Place** in Coral Bay change traveler's checks. Major resorts on Pulau Besar change currency at poor rates. Don't count on plastic; credit card machines at hotels are unreliable. **Bring cash from the mainland.** The **police** can be found in the blue building along the village beach. (☎697 7722. Open daily 8am-4pm.) Basic medical services are available behind the police station and across a small bridge. English is spoken, but go to the mainland for emergency care. (☎697 7680. Open M-W and Sa 8am-4:50pm.) You can make international calls at high rates at some accommodations, usually around RM10 per min. A **Telekom Malaysia** booth is next to the police station. For mobile phone users, the best reception is at Coral Beach. Turtle Shop has stamps and better mail service than the village **post office. Postal Code:** 22200.

ACCOMMODATIONS. Most accommodations on Long Beach fill up during the tourist season (May to Sept.). Some travelers head to less-frenzied and more affordable Coral Bay or hire a boat to one of Besar's smaller beaches. Kecil offers secluded beaches. On Long Beach, **Mohsin ❸** has large bungalows on the hill above the beach. Linens and towels are provided, and a restaurant is attached. Rates in high season include dinner for two. (☎010 333 8897. 24hr. electricity. Dorms RM30. Doubles RM65, low-season RM40; twins RM74/RM55; family rooms RM85/RM65.) **Bubu Long Beach ❺,** a new addition to Long Beach, caters to tourists looking for luxury. There is an attached lounge and restaurant with a long list of cocktails, as well as a beach massage center. All rooms have balconies, A/C, fan, hot water, and towels. (☎032 078 0080. Rooms with 2 doubles RM240; rooms with 2 bunk beds and 1 double RM280.) **Rock Garden Chalet ❶** is up a hill next to Mohsin, and offers some of the cheapest rooms at RM20. The Lemongrass restaurant downstairs serves deeeelicious barbecue fish and chicken (RM12), milkshakes (RM6-10), and fried noodles (RM6). A 10min. stroll across the island from Long Beach is Coral Bay, Kecil's second most popular beach. **Maya Beach Resort ❷** has immaculate new chalets with Western toilets surrounding a hammock garden. (☎019 924 1644. Triples RM50. Extra bed RM10.) **Aur Bay Chalets ❸** sits where the trail to Long Beach starts. (☎019 908 8037 or 019 985 8584. Doubles with fan RM30; beautiful dark-red wooden chalets with fan and bath RM50-60.)

FOOD. Most accommodations have attached restaurants or cafes. By night, restaurants in the center of Long Beach set up barbecues with fresh seafood, chicken, and veggie options (meat, sauce, rice or fries, and fruit RM10-15). The restaurant at **Panorama ❷** makes pizzas with veggie or meat options (small RM10-20). **Shake Shack ❶** mixes up gigantic shakes for RM4 and serves mouthwatering banana and chocolate pancakes for RM3.50. On Coral Bay, try the homemade cakes (RM2-3) from the **Cake Lady ❶** in front of DJ Chalets. **Lily Restaurant** (☎019 222 4360), next to Spice Divers, serves yummy burgers for RM5 and hot plates of mean RM14-20. Next to the entrance path from Long Beach to Coral Bay is **Santai,** a great place for cocktails (RM18) and Japanese *oknomiyaki* (RM4-6).

OUTDOOR ACTIVITIES. Nearby coral reefs and clear waters make Kecil ideal for **snorkeling** and **diving.** Several dive shops near the beach offer PADI courses. **Turtle Bay Divers** (☎019 333 6647) is a popular shop offering two-day nitrox courses for RM500 on Long Beach, with branches at D'Lagoon and Mama's Chalets on Besar. **Sea Dragon Divers** (☎019 984 1181) offers new equipment and small groups. Almost all dive shops on the islands arrange open-water courses (standardized price RM800), advanced courses (RM650), discover scuba courses (RM250), fun dives for certified divers (2 dives RM140, 20% discount with own equipment), and daytrips to the marine park at Pulau Redang (includes 3 fun dives RM300, 15% discount with own equipment). MC and V are accepted. All certified divers receive a discount on breakfast and lunch at the **Safety Stop Cafe** at Chempaka Chalets on Long Beach. **Snorkeling** trips can be arranged at **Turtle Shop** (see **Practical Information,** p. 388) and most accommodations (4hr., RM30; gear rental RM5-10). From June to August, places around Long Beach will advertise evening trips to see **turtles laying eggs** (RM25).

Long Beach is perhaps one of the easiest places in Malaysia for a foreigner to find **employment.** Expatriates can extend their travels for several months to several years by waiting tables or teaching as a dive instructor. If you speak English and another European language, there are abundant opportunities on Kecil and Besar, as the dive shops (there are over 10 on the two islands combined) are always seeking multilingual staff. Restaurants along Long Beach post "help wanted" signs for wait staff in exchange for free room and board.

PULAU PERHENTIAN BESAR ☎09

Besar, "The Big Island," languidly awaits travelers looking for more space, calm, and waves. Dive shops along the west coast attract younger travelers, while peaceful beaches lull backpackers, newlyweds, and families alike. The local way of life remains less disturbed here than on Kecil, the budding Waikiki next door.

TRANSPORTATION AND PRACTICAL INFORMATION. Most services and accommodations cluster on two chief beaches, **Main Beach** and **Flora Bay.** There is no official **tourist office,** but most guesthouses and shops provide basic information. **Flora Bay** (see **Accommodations,** p. 388) and **Kamamoto Shoppe** (see **Activities,** p. 389) change money and make international phone calls. **Mama's Place** (see **Accommodations,** p. 388) exchanges **traveler's checks** at poor rates and runs **boats** to: Abdul's Chalets (RM4); Coral Bay (RM10); D'Lagoon (RM10); Flora Bay (RM10); Long Beach (RM7); and Perhentian Village (RM4).

ACCOMMODATIONS. Budget accommodations are concentrated along the south and west coasts on Main Beach and Flora Bay. Upscale resorts cluster farther north. On Main Beach, try **Coral View Island Resort ❺.** It has comprehensive facilities and attentive service. The restaurant has set barbecue meals for RM25-48, and there is a dive shop with snorkel rental. (☎019 948 0943, office in Kuala Besut 697 4943. Internet RM30 per hr. Reservations accepted. Doubles with fan RM100, with A/C RM150-210; triples RM230-280. MC/V.) **Abdul's Chalet ❸,** on the south end of the beach is popular with families. (☎697 7058. Doubles RM50, with sea view RM70; quads with sea view RM90.) In Flora Bay, **Wanderer's Inn ❶** is popular for its cheap rates, clean baths and delicious barbecue. (Camping RM5 (bring your own tent); A-frames RM20-28.) **Flora Bay ❺** offers a variety of well-kept rooms, a large cafe, and a friendly staff. Internet access and currency exchange are available. (☎697 7266. Reservations accepted. Doubles with fan RM50-60, with A/C RM120-150; triples with fan RM75; family rooms for 5 RM90. MC/V.) **Samudra Beach Chalet ❸** is at the eastern end of Flora Bay. All rooms come with fan and bath. (☎697 7608. Standard A-frames RM30; 2-person sea view bungalows RM50; 3-person bungalows RM45.)

FOOD AND NIGHTLIFE. Nearly all hotels have attached cafes. **Seaside Cafe ❷** at Abdul's dishes out delicious curry. (With veggies RM5.50; with beef, chicken, or seafood RM8. Open daily 7:30am-10pm.) On the Main Beach, **Kamamoto Shoppe** has a small bar where people gather until late. For the best Malay food in Flora Bay, try **Fauna Beach Cafi ❷.** (Deep fried squid, rice, soup, and fries RM7.50. Open daily 7:30am-10:30pm.) At night, hit **Wanderer's Cafe** for barbecue, and **Sea Horse Cafe** for beers.

OUTDOOR ACTIVITIES. Like Kecil, Besar boasts fabulous **snorkeling** and **scuba diving. Kamamoto Shoppe,** on Main Beach, rents snorkel gear (mask and snorkel RM5, flippers RM5) and kayaks (RM10 per hr., RM50 per day) and hosts snorkel trips (RM20). **D'Lagoon, Shark Point,** and the water in front of **Mama's Place** are the best snorkeling sites. The best place to see sharks is at **Shark Point. Bay Watch** arranges snorkeling trips (RM20) to **Rawa Island** (RM45) and **Redang** (RM60). **Blue Lagoon,** a deserted beach on the north shore (taxi RM12 from Main Beach), is a romantic snorkeling destination. **Turtle Bay,** where many turtles lay eggs, is on Besar's northern shore. **Terumba Tiga** ("Reef Three") offers a breathtaking swim. Purportedly one of the best dive sites is **Tokong Laut,** literally the "Temple of the Sea." There are two wreck dives: a 25m ship that sank while carrying Vietnam War refugees and a 75m cargo ship that carried Indonesian sugar. Dive shops have standard scuba prices (courses last from a half-day to 4 days; fun dives for certified divers RM140, with own equipment RM110; discover scuba course RM150-200; advanced course RM550; PADI open-water certification course RM750). **Sea Horse Dive Center** (☎019 923 8270), on Main Beach, and **Scuba Ayu** (☎019 395 1463), on Flora Bay, are small shops with easy-going staffs. **Flora Bay Divers** (☎697 7266) is the best choice on Flora Bay.

EAST COAST

The fishing villages of Peninsular Malaysia's east coast offer a remarkable contrast to west-coast city life. Visitors relax on endless stretches of white beaches and observe with awe the arrival of leatherback turtles on shore. The predominantly Malay communities adhere strongly to Muslim values; keep this in mind before stripping down to your skivvies on the beach.

KOTA BHARU ☎09

Among a handful of cities in Malaysia with a majority Malay population, Kota Bharu, the capital of Kelantan State, has recently seen a revival of traditional Muslim values—including separate check out-lines for the sexes in supermarkets, and gender-segregated seating at movies—most of which have not lasted. Some travelers complain that there's little to do, but if you're passing through to Thailand or the Perhentian Islands, consider staying a day or two to get a taste of true Malay.

TRANSPORTATION

Flights: Airport (☎773 7400), 9km northeast of town. Take bus #9 (RM1) into town. **MAS** (☎773 7600; 24hr. 1 300 88 3000), at roundabout on Jl. Gajah Mati, flies to **KL** (1 hr., 5-7 flights daily 6:45am-10:45pm, RM158).

Trains: Station (☎719 6986), 7km west of town in **Wakaf Bharu.** Take a taxi (RM10) or bus #19 or 27 from town. Jungle trains go to **Gemas** (13½hr., 5:25am, 3rd-class RM19.20) via **Jerantut** (10hr., 3rd-class RM12.60). Daily **express trains** go to: **Gemas** (9hr.; seats 24-30, bunks RM37.50-40); **KL** (13hr.; 6:39pm, also Sa-Su 3:50pm; seats RM28-38, bunks RM45.50-86); **Singapore** (13½hr.; 8:24pm; seats RM32-41, bunks RM48.50-51) via **Jerantut** (6hr.; seats RM18-22, bunks RM29.50-32).

Buses: Local and long-distance buses stop at the **Central Bus Station** (☎744 0114), on Jl. Doktor in the town center. The **Transnasional** office sells tickets for both stations. To: **Alor Setar-Sungai Petani** (7hr., 9:30pm, RM22.60); **Butterworth/Penang** (8½hr.; 9, 9:30pm; RM19.50); **Ipoh** (7½hr., 9:30pm, RM21.60); **Johor Bahru** (11hr., 9pm, RM34); **Kuala Terengganu** (3hr.; Su-W 6 per day, Th-Sa 7 per day; RM9); **Kuantan** (6½hr., 5 per day, RM20.50); **Temerloh** (8hr.; 10pm, RM26.50). The **Express Bus Terminal/Langgar Station** (☎748 3807), on Jl. Hamzah outside town, serves many of the same destinations for similar prices. To: **Ipoh** (8hr., 9am, 9pm; RM21.60); **KL** (9-10hr.; 9:30am, 8:30, 9pm; RM26); **Melaka** (7hr., 8pm, RM32); **Singapore** via **Johor Bahru** (12hr., 8pm, business class only RM46). Reserve at either bus station, regardless of destination, 1 day ahead. **Regional buses** also leave from or near the central station to the **Thai border** crossing at **Rantau Panjang** (opposite Sungai Kolok). To get to the central train station, catch local bus #29 (1hr., every 30min. 6:45am-6:30pm, RM3).

Taxis: Long-distance taxi stand, next to the bus station in town center. Drivers depart when full (4 people) for: **Butterworth** (RM40); **KL** (RM50); **Kuala Besut** (RM7); **Kuala Terengganu** (RM16); **Kuantan** and **Cherating** (RM35); **Marang Jeti** (RM23); **Rantau Panjang** (RM5); **Wakaf Bharu** (RM2.50). Chartered taxis cost 4 times the prices listed here. Always ride a registered, licensed taxi.

Local Transportation: Trishaw rides within town average RM5-8 (RM20 per hour).

Rentals: Avis Rent-A-Car (☎748 4457), operated out of Perdana Hotel on Jl. Mahmud. From RM150 per day. Credit cards only.

ORIENTATION AND PRACTICAL INFORMATION

Kota Bharu lies along the east bank of the north-south **Kelantan River.** Six major thoroughfares run roughly parallel to the river. **Jl. Post Office Lama** (called **Jl. Atas Banggol** on many maps) traces the river and runs into **Padang Merdeka** (Independence Square) in the northern part of the city. The next street east is **Jl. Sultanah Zainab,** with a roundabout at its southern end. **Jl. Temenggong** parallels Jl. Sultanah Zainab before hitting the clocktower roundabout and becoming **Jl. Sultan Ibrahim. Jl. Dato Pati** runs from the night market in the town center to Jl. Hospital near the clocktower. **Jl. Doktor** and **Jl. Kebun Sultan/Jl. Mahmud** are next, the latter converging with Jl. Sultan Ibrahim. The east-west avenues are **Jl. Tok Hakim/Jl. Padang Garong/Jl. Pengkalan Chepa,** which runs through the city center, and **Jl. Gajah Mati/ Jl. Hospital,** which wraps around the clocktower. Guesthouses and hotels are concentrated near Jl. Padang Garong, just 5min. from the Central Bus Station. On the northern edge of the city, **Jl. Wakaf Mek Zainab** runs toward **Pantai Cahaya Bulan.**

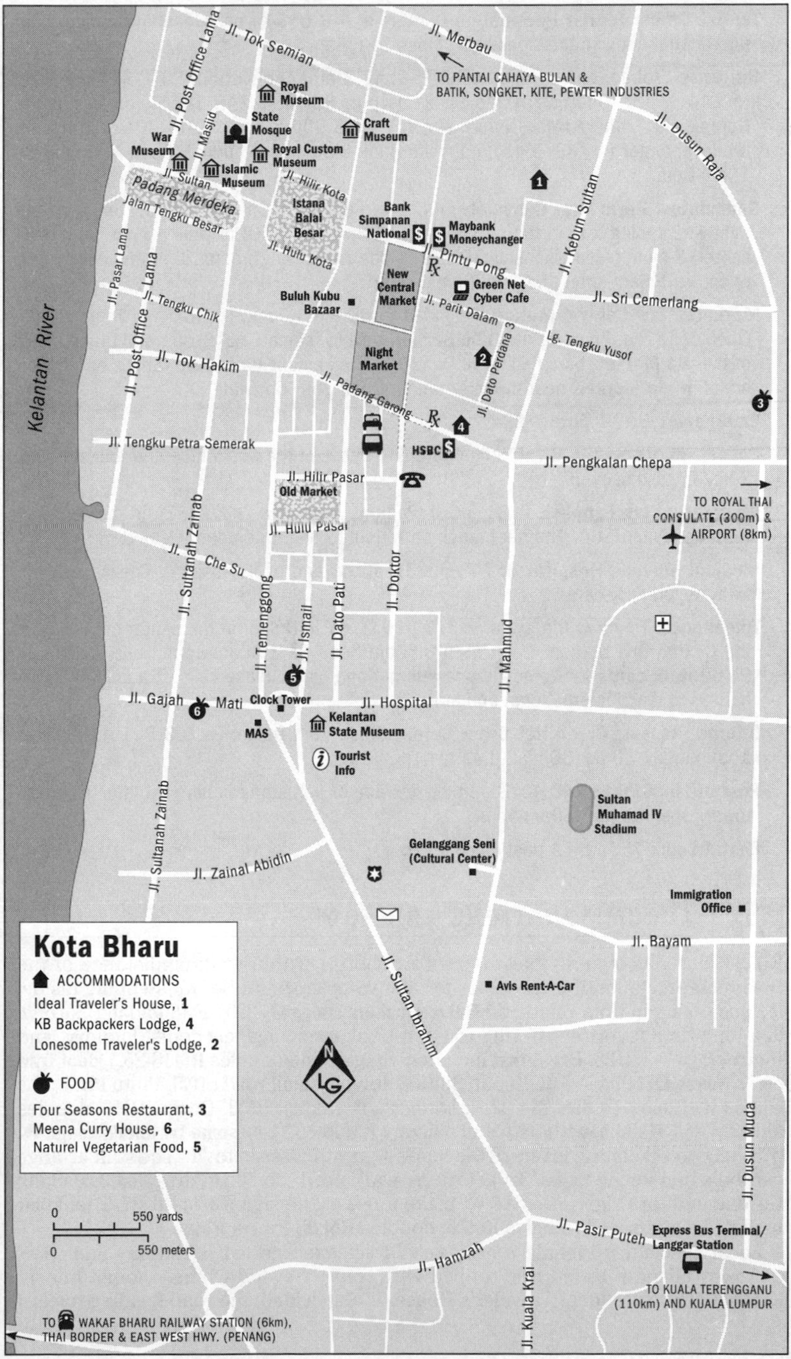
Kota Bharu
ACCOMMODATIONS
Ideal Traveler's House, 1
KB Backpackers Lodge, 4
Lonesome Traveler's Lodge, 2
FOOD
Four Seasons Restaurant, 3
Meena Curry House, 6
Naturel Vegetarian Food, 5
Jl. Tok Semian
Jl. Merbau
TO PANTAI CAHAYA BULAN &
BATIK, SONGKET, KITE, PEWTER INDUSTRIES
Jl. Post Office Lama
Royal Museum
State Mosque
Craft Museum
Jl. Masjid
War Museum
Royal Custom Museum
Islamic Museum
Jl. Sultan
Jl. Dusun Raja
Padang Merdeka
Jl. Hilir Kota
Jalan Tengku Besar
Istana Balai Besar
Bank Simpanan National
Maybank Moneychanger
Jl. Kebun Sultan
Jl. Hulu Kota
Jl. Pintu Pong
Jl. Pasar Lama
New Central Market
Green Net Cyber Cafe
Buluh Kubu Bazaar
Jl. Sri Cemerlang
Jl. Tengku Chik
Jl. Parit Dalam
Kelantan River
Lg. Tengku Yusof
Jl. Post Office Lama
Night Market
Jl. Dato Perdana 3
Jl. Tok Hakim
Jl. Padang Garong
Jl. Tengku Petra Semerak
HSBC
Jl. Pengkalan Chepa
Jl. Hilir Pasar
Old Market
TO ROYAL THAI CONSULATE (300m) & AIRPORT (8km)
Jl. Hulu Pasar
Jl. Che Su
Jl. Sultanah Zainab
Jl. Temenggong
Jl. Ismail
Jl. Dato Pati
Jl. Doktor
Jl. Mahmud
Jl. Gajah Mati
Clock Tower
Jl. Hospital
MAS
Kelantan State Museum
Tourist Info
Sultan Muhamad IV Stadium
Jl. Sultanah Zainab
Gelanggang Seni (Cultural Center)
Jl. Zainal Abidin
Immigration Office
Jl. Bayam
Jl. Sultan Ibrahim
Avis Rent-A-Car
N
LG
Jl. Dusun Muda
0
550 yards
0
550 meters
Jl. Pasir Puteh
Express Bus Terminal/ Langgar Station
Jl. Hamzah
TO KUALA TERENGGANU (110km) AND KUALA LUMPUR
TO WAKAF BHARU RAILWAY STATION (6km), THAI BORDER & EAST WEST HWY. (PENANG)
Jl. Kuala Krai

Tourist Office: Tourist Information Center (☎748 5534), on Jl. Sultan Ibrahim, near the roundabout with the clocktower. Open Su-F 8am-5pm.

Currency Exchange: No banks open F. **Bank Simpanan National,** 61 Jl. Pintu Pong (☎744 9433). Open M-Th and Sa 9am-4pm. **HSBC** (☎748 1451), on Jl. Padang Garong, has 24hr. **ATMs.** Open Sa-W 9:30am-3:30pm, Th 9:30-11:30am. **Maybank Moneychanger** (☎743 2615), opposite Bank Simpanan National. Open M-Th and Sa 10am-6pm.

Consulates: Royal Thai Consulate, 4426 Jl. Pengkalan Chepa (☎748 2545), on the right when going toward the airport. Take bus #4 (RM0.50) or walk 15min. from town center. 3-month visa extensions RM33 (1-day processing); bring 3 photos. Visa office open Su-Th 9am-noon and 2-3:30pm.

Markets: New Central Market, bounded by Jl. Pintu Pong, Doktor, and Tengku Chik. Open daily 7am-7pm. **Buluh Kubu Bazaar,** next to Istana Balai Besar, and the top floor of the **Old Market,** bounded by Jl. Dato Pati and Temenggong, have fabrics and handicrafts. **Night market,** near the bus station. Open daily 6pm-late.

Emergency: ☎999. **Fire:** ☎994.

Police: (☎748 5522). On Jl. Sultan Ibrahim, between the post office and tourist office. Some English spoken.

Pharmacy: Kian Farmasi, 2981 B-C Jl. Padang Garong (☎744 1267), in the center of town opposite HSBC. Another branch on Jl. Pintu Pong. Open daily 9am-10pm.

Medical Service: Hospital (☎748 5533), at the end of Jl. Hospital. English spoken. 24hr. emergency care.

Telephones: Telekom Malaysia (☎513 9191), on Jl. Doktor in the center of town near the Central Bus Station. Open M-Th 8:30am-5pm, Sa 8:30am-3pm. Sells RM30 and RM60 **italk cards** for domestic and international calls. Place calls at hotels or guesthouses to reach international operators.

Internet Access: Green Net Cyber Cafe, 166 Jl. Parit Dalam (☎753 2015). RM1 per 15min., RM1.50 per 30min., RM2 per 1hr.

Post Office: GPO (☎748 4073), on the left side of Jl. Sultan Ibrahim, south of the clocktower. Open Sa-Th 8:30am-5pm.

Postal Code: 15670 (for post office only).

ACCOMMODATIONS AND FOOD

Kotu Bharu has over 40 guesthouses and hotels within walking distance of the town center. Do kindly remember to take your shoes off before stepping inside; it's customary in Kota Bharu. **KB Backpackers Lodge ❷,** 2981-F Jl. Padang Garong, is a long-time favorite, offering tours, a book exchange, carpools, laundry, and Internet. (☎743 2125. Breakfast included. Singles and doubles RM18-25.) **Ideal Traveler's House ❶,** 3954 F-G Jl. Kebun Sultan, down a small road off Jl. Pintu Pong, has rooms with fans. (☎/fax 744 2246. Laundry. Breakfast RM3. Dorms RM6; doubles and triples RM20-25, with bath and balcony RM30-35.) **Lonesome Traveler's Lodge ❶,** 375 Jl. Dato Perdana 3, is one of the hippest guesthouses in town. The staff arrange carpools and jungle treks. To get there, walk north on Jl. Doktor past J. Padang Garong and turn right after A&W; make a left at the sign. (☎744 6637. Breakfast included. Dorms RM9; singles RM15; doubles RM20; triples RM25.)

Local specialties include *ayam percik* (chicken grilled on sticks) and *nasi dagang* (coconut-based rice topped with tuna). Several Chinese joints line Jl. **Kebun Sultan,** near Ideal Traveler's House. **Jl. Gajah Mati,** the road heading toward the river from the roundabout, has a handful of Indian eateries. The **night market ❶** has a dizzying assortment of food (try *murtabak*, a stuffed Indian pancake). For a sit-down culinary experience, head to **Meena Curry House ❷**, 3377-G Jl. Gajah Mati, east of Jl. Sultanah Zainab. (Vegetarian curry RM3.50, chicken curry RM5-6.50. Open daily 11am-9:30pm.) **Naturel Vegetarian Food ❶**, 2848 Jl. Ismail, near the roundabout, has buffet-style vegetarian delights for about RM3. (☎746 1902. Open daily 7:30am-5:30pm.) For delicious Chinese *halal* food, try **Four Seasons Restaurant ❹**, 5670 B/2 & B/3 Jl. Dusun Raja. Head down Jl. Pengkalan Chepa and left onto Jl. Dusun Raja. (☎743 6666. Steamboat for 2-4 people RM58. Open daily noon-2:30pm and 6-10pm. AmEx/MC/V.)

SIGHTS

Kota Bharu's sights are within walking distance of each other but require a good day or two to explore. The **Gelanggang Seni (Cultural Center)**, on Jl. Mahmud opposite the Perdana Hotel, sponsors free top-spinning, kite-flying, drum-beating, and *silat* demonstrations. From 9 to 11pm on Wednesdays and Saturdays, there are performances of *wayang kulit* (shadow-puppets), dance, and drama. (☎744 3124. M, W, Sa 3:30-5:30pm; all shows free.) **Padang Merdeka** (Independence Square) commemorates the Malay struggle against British rule. At the east end of the rectangle away from the river is the **Istana Balai Besar**, a large wooden hall built in 1844. Closer to the river to the right of the square are the **War Museum, Islamic Museum, Royal Custom Museum, Royal Museum,** and **Craft Museum. Kelantan State Museum,** next to the tourist office on Jl. Sultan Ibrahim, is worth a gawk for its cultural exhibits. (All open M-Th and Sa-Su 8:30am-4:45pm. RM2, children RM1.) The **Pantai Cahaya Bulan (PCB) Beach** is pleasant and has cheap accommodations (look for homes with signs that say *tempat penginapan* or *asrama*). **Buses** leaves from the Royal Museum for PCB (#10; every 20min., last returning bus 7pm, RM1).

OUTDOOR ACTIVITIES

If relaxing on the beach isn't enough, take a **river cruise** through the surrounding jungle. **Roselan Hanafiah,** award-winning guide, leads a half-day tour for three to 10 people through the canals and rivers of Kelantan. Check the tourist office to find Roselan. (☎748 5534. Runs 10am-1pm; RM75 per person with high tea.) Travelers on a smaller budget can cruise on a public boat and return by bus. Boats depart from **Kuala Krai,** accessible by bus #5 from the central terminal (RM3.40). Roselan can also help make reservations to stay with a family in the village, through a program called **The Kampung Experience.** Meals and transportation are included. (3-day packages: RM265 per person, 2-person min., or RM250, 4-person min. 1-day workshops RM125, including lunch.) Or, for a taste of Malaysia, try Roselan's Malay **cooking class** (RM55) taught in the comfort of his home. For more adventurous folk, KB Backpackers Lodge organizes **nature tours.** Choose among a trip to the **Jelawang Jungle,** site of the highest waterfall in Southeast Asia (RM230 for 3 days), and cave expeditions (RM99 for 1 day). Prices include meals, transportation, equipment, and in some cases insurance. There are also **city tours** or **country tours** that sample cultural sights (4-5hr., RM40, 2-person min.). Book trips at the KB Backpackers Lodge (see **Accommodations,** p. 392). Their website (www.kb-backpackers.com.my) provides information on transport within Peninsular Malaysia.

PULAU REDANG ☎09

Thanks to the concerted efforts of its marine park to preserve the ecosystem, Pulau Redang has the most vibrant coral and marine life in Malaysia. Compared to other destinations visiting Pulau Redang costs a few extra ringgit, but given the beauty of its crystal-clear waters, its many wonderful snorkeling and diving opportunities, and its higher-quality services, it's well worth it.

THE VIEW FROM ABOVE

The Lowdown: An archipelago of nine islands designated as a marine park off Malaysia's east coast.
Islands: Lima, Paku Besar, Paku Kecil, Kerengga Besar, Kerengga Kecil, Ekor Tebu, Ling, Pinang, and especially Redang.
Highlights: Snorkeling, diving, playing beach volleyball, sunbathing.

TRANSPORTATION. Everything at Pulau Redang runs on package deals, which include accommodation, food, activities, and transportation. These are available directly through resorts or through tourist agencies in Kuala Terengganu and other nearby locations (see **Pulau Perhentian Besar: Activities,** p. 388). Private resorts operate their own **boats** to Redang Island from the Merang jetty (45min.-1hr.; 9:30am, 1:30pm; RM40 one-way). Merang (not to be confused with Marang) is 30min. north of Kuala Terengganu by **taxi** (RM30) or **tourist bus** (RM10-20). **Ping Anchorage Travel and Tours,** 77A Jl. Dalo' Issacs, offers resort and camping packages and runs buses from Kuala Terengganu to the jetty. (☎626 2020. Open daily 8am-7:30pm.) Upon request, buses will pick up and drop off at the airport or bus station. For those who arrive at the jetty without reservations, many booths there also sell packages, but be warned that Redang is a popular destination for Malaysian and Singaporean tourists, so advance bookings are almost always necessary on weekends and school and public holidays.

ACCOMMODATIONS. Accommodations cluster on Pasir Panjang (Long Beach) on Redang Island. Rates below always include breakfast; the phrase "with amenities" below means that rates also include boat transport to and from the island, rooms with A/C, at least one guided snorkel trip for each night stayed, lunch, dinner (with barbecue options), snack, and beverages. Snorkel gear rental costs RM10-15. **Redang Lagoon Chalet ❺,** on the main beach, is the cheapest option and attracts a mixed crowd. (☎/fax 827 2116. Twins and doubles 2 days, 1 night with amenities RM460; additional nights RM100.) At the right end of the beach is **Redang Holiday Beach Villa ❺,** which respects guests' privacy and has a NAUI dive shop. Their new hillside villa rooms have the best views on the beach. (☎624 5500, office in Kuala Terengganu 622 6181. Twins 2 days, 1 night with amenities RM560, 3 days, 2 nights with amenities RM720; triples RM720/RM990; quads RM880/RM1200; additional nights RM100-120 per person. 50% discount for children.) As the classiest lodging on Long Beach, **Coral Redang Island Resort ❺** offers an outdoor swimming pool, a poolside bar, a dive shop, and a variety of chalets. (☎626 5011, office in Kuala Terengganu 623 6200. Closed Nov.-Feb. Singles RM225-415, 3 days, 2 nights with amenities RM680-1100, 3 days, 2 nights with amenities and 4 dives RM890-1310; doubles RM610-1160/RM1060-1720/RM1480-2140; triples 3 days, 2 nights with amenities RM1410-2250, 3 days, 2 nights with amenities and 4 dives RM2040.) Travel agencies generally offer better prices than these. For an off-the-beaten-path alternative, **Ping Anchorage** offers a **Redang Camping Adventure ❺** in a double tent with common bath on Long Beach or Kalong Beach. Packages include snorkeling trips, all meals, and round-trip boat tickets. (☎626 2020. 2 days, 1 night RM180; 3 days, 2 nights RM240; additional nights RM80.)

FOOD AND ENTERTAINMENT. Every resort has a restaurant, and package deals include all meals. Aside from the *mahjong*, chess, card, and dart games offered at most resorts, nightlife consists of loud music and expensive booze. A poolside **bar** at Coral Redang Island Resort sells beer (RM8) and is a quieter alternative to the karaoke bars. For information on diving and snorkeling, consult dive shops, which have maps of the best sites and experienced staff on hand. Snorkel gear rental is available everywhere (RM10-15). The **Marine Park Headquarters** at Pulau Pinang is definitely worth a visit for colorful snorkeling adventures, if not for informative exhibits on coral and marine life. (RM5, children RM2.50.) The NAUI dive shop at Redang Holiday Beach Villa (☎624 5500) has the best rates on Discover Scuba courses (RM150 for one dive), open water diver certification courses (RM750 for 5 dives), advanced diver courses (RM650 for 6 dives), and fun dives (1-4 dives RM50 each, 5-9 dives RM45 each, 10 or more dives RM40 each; regulator and BCD rental RM50 per day, wetsuit rental RM10 per day). Instructor Calin Sas (instructor #35042) emphasizes safety techniques.

KUALA TERENGGANU ☎09

Capital of the Muslim state of Terengganu, Kuala Terengganu lies beside the inlet of the Terengganu River. Until recently a large fishing village, KT, as it's commonly called, now thrives on oil, though it is often upstaged by the sunny beaches nearby. Though attractions and nightlife here are minimal, KT isn't just a gateway city to nearby Marang and Merang—its low-key seaside warrants exploration, as well.

TRANSPORTATION

Flights: Airport (☎666 4204), 18km from town. Taxi from the airport RM20. **MAS,** 13 Jl. Sultan Omar (☎622 9279; 24hr. hotline ☎1 300 88 3000), flies to **KL** (4-5 per day, RM158). Open M-W and Sa-Su 8:30am-4:30pm, Th 8:30am-12:30pm. AmEx/MC/V.

Buses: Local buses leave from the **large bus station** (☎623 6239) at the intersection of Jl. Masjid Abidin and Jl. Syed Hussain. To: **Dungun** (every 30min., 7:30am-6pm, RM4) via **Marang** (50min., RM1.50); **Duyong** (#16 or 20; every hr. 7:40am-5:40pm, RM0.60); **Kuala Besut** (2½hr.; 7, 8, 10, 11:30am, 2, 3, 4, 5:30pm; RM5); **Kamaman** (11am and 5pm; RM8.65); **Melaka** (8hr., 8:30pm, RM27.6); **Rantau Abang** (every 30min. 7:30am-6pm, RM3). **Express buses** stop at the large bus station and at the **express bus station** (☎622 5335) on Jl. Sultan Zainal Abidin near the Jl. Tok Lam intersection. To: **Ipoh** and **Lumut** (12hr., 9pm, RM37); **Kota Bharu** (3hr., 7 per day 8:30am-5:30pm and Th-Sa 7:30pm, RM9); **KL** (8hr.; 9, 9:30, 10am, 9:30, 10pm; RM25, with A/C RM35); **Kuantan** (3½hr., 7 per day 9am-10pm, RM11.60); **Mersing** (6½hr., 12:30 and 10pm, RM22); **Penang** (9hr., 9pm., RM29.80); **Singapore** (9-10hr.; 9am and 8:30pm; RM30.2, with A/C RM42).

Ferries: Pulau Duyong (Duyong Island), off the west coast, is accessible by boat from the jetty opposite the Tourist Information Center or from the jetty behind Hotel Seri Malaysia (15min., 7am-6pm, RM1).

Taxis: From the **taxi stand** (☎622 1581) on Jl. Masjid Abidin, near the large bus station, fixed-rate taxis go to: **Kota Bharu** (RM60); **Kuala Besut** (RM648); **KL** (RM280); **Kuantan** and **Cherating** (RM100); **Marang** (RM15); **Merang jetty** (RM25); **Mersing** (RM250); **Rantau Abang** (RM40); **Taman Negara** (RM280). Passengers can split fares 4 ways. No bargaining.

Local Transportation: Trishaw rides RM3-5. **Taxis** (☎626 5150) run RM5-10 in town.

ORIENTATION AND PRACTICAL INFORMATION

Jl. Sultan Zainal Abidin, on which sits the **post office, Tourist Information Center,** and **express bus terminal,** runs east-west along the city's shore. Major sights, including **Bukit Puteri** (Princess Hill), **Istana Maziah** (the Sultan's Palace) and the **Central Market,** also line the shore. Farther south along the shoreline, **Chinatown** lies near **Jl. Bandar.** The city's commercial spine and home to most moneychangers, **Jl. Sultan Ismail** runs parallel to Jl. Sultan Zainal Abidin. Its west edge begins with Hotel Seri Malaysia, while the **police station** and **immigration office** flank its eastern edge. These two streets sandwich **Jl. Dato' Isaacs.** From the city's center north to its shores, **Jl. Tok Lam** connects all three boulevards. Parallel and to the west is **Jl. Masjid Abidin;** walking from Jl. Sultan Ismail will lead to the **taxi stand** and **large bus station.** Accommodations flank the north and east sides of the mosque in the center of the city.

Tourist Office: Tourist Information Center (☎622 1553), on Jl. Sultan Zainal Abidin. Free maps and friendly staff. Open M-Th and Sa-Su 9am-5pm.

Tours: Ping Anchorage, 77A Jl. Dato' Isaacs (☎626 2020). Packages to Redang Island, Lang Tengah Island, Perhentian Islands, Taman Negara, and Kenyir Lake. Open daily 8am-7:30pm.

Currency Exchange: Bank Bumiputra (☎622 2611), on Jl. Sultan Ismail. AmEx/MC/V/ traveler's checks. Currency exchange upstairs next to **ATM.** Open M-W and Sa-Su 9:30am-4pm, Th 9:30am-noon. **Maybank Moneychanger,** 12 Jl. Sultan Ismail (☎624 7637). Open daily 9am-5:30pm.

Laundromat: Mr. Dhoby, 18A Jl. Masjid Abidin (☎622 1671), next to Seaview Hotel. RM3.50 per kg. Ironing RM1 per item. Open daily 9am-8:30pm.

Police: ☎622 2222. On the corner of Jl. Sultan Omar and Jl. Sultan Ismail. Some English spoken. 24hr.

Pharmacy: Formasi 2k, 10 Jl. Tok Lam (☎631 4677). Open M-Th and Sa-Su 8am-10pm.

Medical Service: General Hospital (☎623 3333), on Jl. Sultan Mahmud, south of the roundabout. English-speaking doctors. Consultation fee RM2. 24hr. emergency care.

Telephones: Telekom Malaysia (☎623 1191), on the corner of Jl. Sultan Ismail and Jl. Banggol. Sells international calling cards. Free access to international operators. Direct **international calls.** Open M-Th and Su 8:30am-4:30pm.

Internet Access: Golden Wood Internet Cafe, 59 Jl. Tok Lam (☎624 6171), near Jl. Dato' Isaacs. RM3 per hr. Open M-Th and Sa-Su 10am-12:30am.

Post Office: (☎622 7555). On Jl. Sultan Zainal Abidin. It's 100m left of Jl. Masjid Abidin if you face the river. *Poste Restante.* Open M-Th and Su 8:30am-5pm.

Postal Code: 20000.

ACCOMMODATIONS AND FOOD

Ping Anchorage Traveler's Homestay ❶, 77A Jl. Dato' Isaacs near the Jl. Tok Lam intersection, caters exclusively to backpackers and offers a rooftop lounge, cafe, and travel service. From the mosque, it's on the right; the reception is through the *batik* store. (☎622 0851. Dorms RM6; singles and doubles RM12-18, with A/C and bath RM30.) Across from the palace at 18A Jl. Masjid Abidin, **Seaview Hotel ❹** has clean, spacious rooms with bath, A/C, hot showers, and TV. (☎622 1911. Reserve in advance for weekends and holidays. Doubles RM65; triples RM75; quads RM85. MC/V.) **Hotel Seri Malaysia ❹**, 1640 Jl. Hiliran, a large pink building on the western

end of Jl. Sultan Ismail, has rooms facing the river and daily room service. (☎623 6454. Laundry. Breakfast included. Doubles RM120; family rooms RM140.) The only accommodation in the village of Pulau Duyong, **Awi's House ❶** is accessible by infrequent boats or by bus. Peaceful wooden rooms overlook the water. (☎624 5046. Cooking facilities. Dorms RM7; doubles RM17.)

Foodstalls ❶ crowd the first floor of the bus station on Jl. Syed Hussain, and **Chinese food spots ❷** line the shores of **Pantai Batu Buruk.** Try *keropok*, a Terengganu specialty of fried ground fish with chilli sauce. The **food court ❷** above the central market offers Malay dishes and a wide selection of fruits. **Golden Dragon ❹,** 198 Jl. Bandar in Chinatown near the Dragon Gate. (☎622 3034. Chilli *kang kong* vegetables RM10, fresh fish RM20-30. Open daily 11am-3pm and 6-9:30pm.) Next door to Golden Dragon, **Kedai Makan Soon Kee ❹** serves steamed buns (RM0.5-0.7) and a hearty five-spice pork soup called *bak kut teh* (RM10). **Ping Anchorage Travelers Café ❷,** 77A Jl. Dato' Isaacs on the ground floor. An oasis for weary travelers hungering for Western meals and thirsting for cold beer, it is mainly visited by tourists staying in the above hotel. (☎626 2020. 4-decker club sandwich RM5.50. Open daily 7am-midnight.) **Restoran Terapung Puteri ❶** overlooks the shoreline on Jl. Sultan Zainal Abidin opposite the Visitor Center. (☎631 8946. *Nasi lemak*—steamed coconut rice with spicy *sambal* sauce, peanuts, and anchovies RM2; *popiah*—spring rolls RM3.50. Open daily 6am-midnight.)

MALAYSIA

SIGHTS AND ENTERTAINMENT

Kuala Terengganu's main tourist attractions cluster near the **Tourist Information Center.** The **central market,** on Jl. Sultan Zainal Abidin, sells handicrafts and produce. Nearby, next to the GPO, are **Istana Maziah,** the sultan's stately palace, and **Bukit Puteri,** the "hill of the princess." Climb the stairs next to the Tourist Information Center for great views over the waterfront and the remains of a fort and a lighthouse. (Open M-Th and Sa-Su 9am-5pm. RM1.) Outside town, the **Muzium Negeri,** Malaysia's largest museum, features a set of Terengganu-style buildings on stilts. The main museum showcases the *batu bersurat,* an inscribed stone dated to AD 702 that states Islamic law regarding misdeeds. The complex also includes botanical gardens and an outdoor exhibit of traditional fishing boats. Bus #10 (20min., every 30min. 7:30am-6pm, RM0.70) runs between the large bus terminal and the museum. (☎622 1444. Open Sa-Th 9am-5pm. RM5.) Off the mainland, **Pulau Duyong's** locals still construct boats of all sizes with traditional techniques—without plans or diagrams. (For transportation, see **Ferries,** p. 395.) On the road south to Marang, 4.5km from KT (bus #13 or 13C; RM0.70), sits **Masjid Tengku Zaharah** (Floating Mosque), a striking white building that seems to float on the water. (Open 24hr. Best times to visit are 7am-noon and 3-4pm. Free.) Down the Ibai River from the Floating Mosque is the **Noor Arfa Craft Complex,** where visitors can witness the *batik-* and basket-making processes and browse through a large selection of souvenirs. (☎617 5700. Open M-Th and Sa-Su 9am-5pm.)

DAYTRIP FROM KUALA TERENGGANU

TASIK KENYIR. Located only 55km from Terranganu, Tasik Kenir offers respite from the more cosmopolitan Kuala Terengganu. Several waterfalls and caves make for excellent explorations, and the gorgeous lake itself is worth the trip. Although there are several overpriced resorts located on the lake, it may be easier on your wallet to simply base yourself in KT. *(Ping Anchorage offers package trips to Tasik Kenyir, which include a boat cruise, lunch and guide. Min. 2 people. RM105 per person. 10am-4pm. Or, take a taxi from Kuala Terengganu for RM45. There are no buses to the lake.)*

MARANG ☎09

Government bulldozers have ended Marang's peaceful days as a picturesque Malay fishing village. Construction projects have devastated half the town. Breakwaters line the beach, and good food and budget accommodations are scarce. The park near the main jetty is a pleasant place to have lunch and watch the boats pass, but for most, Marang is a transit town en route to Kapas Island.

Those who stay in Marang may enjoy the **Marang River Cruise,** which stops at **Jenang,** a traditional village where craftsmen make brown sugar and mangrove roofs. (4-person min. for the 4½hr. cruise, 8am, RM100 per boat.)

Marang is 20km south of Kuala Terengganu. From KT, get to Marang via Dungun **buses** (30min., every 30min. 7:30am-6pm, RM1.50) or **share-taxi** from the Terengganu-Kuantan Hwy. (RM15 to Marang jetty, RM20 to KT). The **bus stop** is on the highway. Most people get dropped off at the four-way intersection next to the squid-and-prawn statue. The main part of town is on **Kampung Paya,** the street parallel to and east of the highway, running close to the river and beaches. North of the jetty, Kampung Paya passes shop houses and two footbridges before reaching the budget accommodations. The **police station** is on the highway before the bridge. (☎618 2222. Some English spoken. Open 24hr.) Ask for English-speaking Dr. Mohamed Reze bin Rashid at the **Klinik Kesihatan Clinic** (☎618 2216; open M-Th and Sa-Su 8am-12:30pm and 2-4pm) on the highway opposite the **post office** (☎618 2215; open M-Th and Su 8:30am-4:30pm but closed the first Th of each month). **Postal Code:** 21600.

Marang Guest House and Restaurant ❷, Lot 1367 and 1368 Kampung Paya, up the hill next to Kamal Guest House near the second footbridge, has clean rooms, and offers laundry service (RM5), massages (RM30), Internet (RM3 per hr.), and travel information. (☎/fax 618 1976. Doubles with fan and squat toilet RM15, with fan and Western bath RM25, with TV, A/C, and Western bath RM50; 5-person family rooms with A/C, TV, and Western bath RM80.) **Kamal Guest House ❷,** B283 Kg. Paya, between the two footbridges north of the jetty and market area, has a variety of nice rooms. (☎618 2181. Doubles RM15, with bath RM25; triples with fan and bath RM35, with A/C RM60.) Devour the best meals at the **foodstalls ❶** opposite the market near the tourist boat agencies. **Hasnani Dinamik Bakery ❶** is on the highway near the squid-and-prawn statue intersection. (☎618 2976. Breads and pastries RM1-3. Rice and noodle dishes RM3-5. Open Sa-Th 9:30am-7pm.)

KAPAS ISLAND ☎09

Although fewer travelers have visited beautiful Kapas Island since Marang's storm of development destroyed much of the coral, many Malaysian families still vacation here and spend their time walking through the jungle or snorkeling.

Friendly Zakaria, who runs **Suria Link** at the **Marang Tourist Jetty,** can help arrange diving courses, sea sport rentals, and room reservations. **Aqua-Sport Diving Service** is a PADI dive shop to the right of the jetty on Long Beach. (Discover scuba courses RM80; 4-day open-water diver certification courses RM950; fun dives RM90 or less; kayak rental RM10 per hr.; guided jungle treks RM10; round-island boat trips RM10.)

Fast boats (☎983 9454 or 985 8869) can be requested in advance. **Tourist boats** to the island cost RM15-25 for a 15min. journey. Buy tickets from agents near the jetty or at guesthouses. Boats leave from 9am to 6pm when there are at least 4 passengers and return from 10am to 6pm. The **jetty** is between Gua Beach and Long Beach on Kapas Island, but boatmen sometimes drop off passengers at their chalets. **Batu Payong Beach** and **Pasir Cina Beach** on the west coast are the best on the island. (Pasir Cina is a steep climb over a small cliff from Batu Payong. Rope handrails aid the journey.) **Snorkel Bay** is a 30min. jungle trek to the north coast. You can rent snorkel gear almost anywhere for RM10-15. Kapas Island is closed from October 15 to February. July through August is turtle nesting season. Although the coral has been destroyed on Kapas Island, boats from each of the resorts will take you to see the coral at Pulau Gemjang for RM10.

The Lighthouse ❶ fosters a backpacker atmosphere at the eastern end of Long Beach, with cooking facilities, a reggae bar after 7pm (beer RM9), free snorkel gear, and a hammock garden. (☎019 983 9454. 12-person dorm RM15 per person; doubles with fan RM30.) The last chalet to the left of the jetty is **Kapas Garden Resort ❹,** which is run by a cheery couple who offer a 6hr. "sunset cruise" on their sailboat for RM150. (☎010 984 1686. Bar and restaurant. A-frames with fan and bath RM60; chalets with fan and bath RM75.) **Puta Puri Island Resort ❹** has beautiful Balinese-style chalets with baths. (☎624 6090. Breakfast included. Packages available. Backpacker's room RM60; doubles with fan RM100, with A/C RM140-200. AmEx/MC/V.) In addition, there are two **campsites ❶** on the island, located after the second bridge. (Sites RM10; tent rental RM5 per night.) The **restaurant ❸** at Puta Puri has banana pancakes (RM7.50) and fried vegetables with garlic (RM8). Their Western- and Malay-style meals average RM8-16. (Open daily 8am-9:30pm.) **Warong Pakya ❶** (019 968 3130) serves fresh juice (RM3) and Western breakfasts

(RM5), as well as local dishes (RM4-5). Food on the island is not cheap, so bring snacks from the mainland or try the **Payung Pelancungan Cafe Corner ❶** to the left of the jetty. *Nasi goreng* (fried rice) and *tom yam* noodle soup run RM3.50-4, and fruit salad is RM4. (Open daily 8am-1am.)

CHERATING ☎09

On Rte. 3 lies Cherating, the town Malaysia forgot. Cherating's more attractive aspects include a windsurfing beach, cultural diversions, a few bars, and an occasional leatherback turtle. Less than titillating are the omnipresent tourists.

TRANSPORTATION AND PRACTICAL INFORMATION. Cherating is 47km north of Kuantan, accessible by **local bus** (1hr., every hr. 8am-6pm, RM3). From Kuala Terengganu, take a bus from the main bus station (RM11.50) or a **taxi** (RM100). The beach road meets the highway at the two bus stops on the way. The west stop, closer to Kuantan, is near the Cherating River and marked by a "Culture Center" billboard. This stop is closer to Masnah and Mataheri Chalets. The east stop, 700m from the other bus stop, is marked by a "Residence Inn" billboard; get off here for the Moon Guest House. Buses leave to Kota Bahru (8:30, 10, 11:30am, 2, 4, 11pm; RM24) and Terranganu (10, 11:30am, 2pm; RM14.5). Boats to Perhentian leave at 8:30am (one-way RM50; round-trip RM50).

The town has two main roads: the **Kuantan-Terengganu Highway,** which bends east-west through town, and the U-shaped **beach road** that runs along the river and the sea. On the highway between the bus stops is the **police office** (☎581 9322). There are **no medical services** available in Cherating. Call hospitals in **Kemaman** (☎859 3333) or **Kuantan** (☎513 3333) for 24hr. emergency care. The closest **clinic** is in **Kampung Balok,** 10km south of Cherating. The beach road is lined with restaurants, accommodations, and bars. Toward the center of the road is **Travel Post,** which provides **Internet** (RM6 per hr.), **mail service, international phone** service (RM7 per min.), and **currency exchange. Capacity Dot Com,** near the eastern end of the beach road, has travel information, Internet (RM6 per hr.), **mountain-bike rental** (RM10 per hr.), and a library. Warm and friendly Firdaus speaks flawless English and provides travel info. (☎581 9330. Open M-Tu and Th-Su 10am-11pm.) Both Travel Post and Capacity Dot Com sell intercity bus tickets.

ACCOMMODATIONS AND FOOD. Guesthouses pack the beach road, offering standard A-frame or small chalet-style huts. **Matahari Chalet ❸,** 100m down the road from the west bus stop, maintains solid, well-kept huts. Friendly management and a range of amenities, including fans, a cozy TV room with books, and an attached do-it-yourself *batik* studio (RM25-35 per piece), make Matahari one of the best abodes in the village. (☎581 9835. Singles RM20; doubles RM25.) **Maznah Guest House ❶,** also near the west bus stop, has a cozy common area with TV and movies. (☎568 7180 or 513 9892. Internet RM5 per hr. Breakfast and kitchen facilities included. A-frame singles with fan RM15, with private bath RM30; chalet doubles RM20 for 1 person, 2 person RM2, doubles with bath RM35.) Roll out of bed and onto the beach at **Tanjung Inn ❸,** which has clean wooden chalets around an attractive lake toward the western end of the beach road. (☎581 9081. Breakfast included. 2-person rooms with fan RM45, with A/C RM90; 3-person rooms with fan RM60; 4-person rooms with A/C RM120.) **Payung Guest House ❷** is popular for its well-maintained gardens and porches. (☎019 917 1934. Chalet doubles with fan and bath RM30; 4-person family room RM50.)

Can't Forget Seafood ❷, on the beach road, serves superb Chinese fare. (Set meals for 2 RM16-22; sweet and sour chicken or squid RM6. Beer RM5. Open M-Tu and Sa-Su 11am-3pm and 6-11:30pm.) **Payung Cafe ❷,** down the beach road away from the center of Cherating, makes huge pizzas for RM9-13 and pasta for RM4.50-9.50. (Open daily 10:30am-2:30pm and 7-10:30pm.) **Ranting Resort ❷** has great breakfast options. (Homemade bread sandwiches RM4-6.)

ENTERTAINMENT AND OUTDOOR ACTIVITIES. **Watersports** rents watersports equipment. (☎019 917 1934. Double kayaks RM15 per hr., RM60 per day. Windsurfing RM25 per hr., RM30 with instructor. Surfboards RM15 per hr., RM60 per day. Fishing trips RM200. Snorkeling at Snake Island RM35. Firefly trip at 7:30pm RM15.) **Surfing** is best from January to March, but windsurfing is great anytime. Ibrahim and Raihman at **MAP Batik,** across the road from Maznah Guest House, offer *batik* lessons at their studio. (☎012 966 4565. Make-your-own *batik* RM35-40.) If you're in Cherating between June and September, don't miss the opportunity to see the **giant leatherback turtles** lay their eggs. The Fisheries Department has set up a hatchery near the Club Med Beach. (Open Tu-Su.) Upon request, most lodgings will wake you if there is a sighting and take you to the beach (RM15). Two kilometers east of Cherating is the breathtaking but members-only **Club Med Beach,** which can be reached from the main road. Alternatively, ask guesthouse managers about trails through the hills that will take you from the village beach to the promised shore. For those who want to venture to nearby villages, Firdaus at Capacity Dot Com (see **Practical Information,** p. 400) rents mountain bikes and recommends trails through rambutan and durian plantations. The best nightspots are **Pop Inn Pub** (live cover band F-Sa; open daily 6pm-late) and **Rhana Pippins** (2-for-1 drink specials 3-11pm). Both are on the same side of the beach road.

KUANTAN ☎09

Kuantan offers little in the way of cultural attractions or remarkable cuisine, and for those coming from elsewhere on the east coast, the capital of the state of Pahang will seem either rejuvenating or overwhelmingly cosmopolitan. Surrounded by waterfalls, caves, and beaches, the town itself is home to the beautiful State Mosque, and the beaches of Teluk Chempedak are only 4km away.

TRANSPORTATION

Flights: Airport (☎538 1291), 10km west of town. Take a local bus (every hr. 7am-5pm) or a taxi (RM20). **MAS** (☎515 6030, 24hr. ticketing ☎1 300 88 3000), on the ground floor of Wisma Persatuan Bola Sepak on Jl. Gambut, has flights to **KL** (40min., 4 per day 7:30am-10:10pm, RM112). Open M-F 8:30am-5:30pm. AmEx/DC/MC/V.

Buses: The **express bus terminal** is on Jl. Stadium. Buses to: **Butterworth** (10hr.; 8, 8:30, 9pm; RM32-35); **Jerantut** (4hr.; 10am, 1, 3pm; RM10.50); **Johor Bahru** (6hr.; noon, 1, 2:30, 4:30, 10:45pm, midnight, 1am; RM18); **Kota Bharu** (7hr., 7 per day 8am-11pm and F-Sa 1am, RM20.50); **KL** (5hr., every 30min. 12:30am-10pm, RM14); **Kuala Terengganu** (3½hr.; 9:30, 10, 11am, noon, 12:15, 1:30pm, every 30min. 2:30-5:30, 11:15pm; RM11.60); **Melaka** (6hr.; 1, 9am; RM17.60); **Mersing** (4hr.; 9, 10:30am, 5pm; RM10.90); **Singapore** via **Johor Bahru** (8hr.; 9, 10:30am, 10:30, 11pm; RM19.40). **Luggage storage** on 2nd fl. (RM1 per day; open daily 8am-12:30am). The **local bus terminal** on Jl. Besar, 1 block toward the river from Jl. Mahkota next to the tourist information office, runs buses to **Cherating** and **Kemaman** (1hr. and 1¼hr., every 30min., RM3 and RM3.70). Buses to the **airport** leave from both terminals (every hr. 7am-5pm) but it is quite a hike to the terminals. **City buses** ply the streets at RM0.70-0.90.

Taxis: Taxis leave from the express bus terminal or **city taxi stand** on Jl. Mahkota, near the tourist office. Taxis go anywhere in town for RM5-10, RM20 hourly. **Share-taxis** also leave from the stand. Fare per car (4-person max.) to: **Jerantut** (RM100); **Johor Bahru** (RM300); **Kota Bharu** (RM180); **KL** (RM160); **Mersing** (RM160).

ORIENTATION AND PRACTICAL INFORMATION

Kuantan lies at the crossroads of **Routes 2** and **3.** The city sprawls in a flurry of high-rises, but the main points of interest are in the southwestern parts of town along the **Kuantan River.** The two main streets, **Jl. Besar** and **Jl. Mahkota,** run parallel along the river. The town's central landmark is the large blue and white mosque, **Masjid Negeri,** beside the town *padang* (square) on Jl. Mahkota. Jl. Bukit Ubi runs perpendicular to Jl. Mahkota and takes you to the **central market,** near the express bus terminal. Budget hotels lie along or near Jl. Bukit Ubi and Jl. Mahkota.

Tourist Office: (☎516 1007), on Jl. Mahkota, near the taxi station. Free maps and tour info from a friendly, English-speaking staff. Open M-Th 9am-1pm and 2-5pm, F 9am-12:15pm and 2:45-5pm, Sa 9am-5pm.

Currency Exchange: Many banks are near the intersection of Jl. Mahkota and Bank St. **HSBC,** Jl. Mahkota (☎552 4666), has Cirrus/MC/Plus/V 24hr. **ATMs.** Open M-F 9:30am-3:30pm, Sa 9:30-11:30am.

Markets: Outside the **central market,** near the express bus terminal, is a bustling **day market** mostly selling Chinese hawker food. Open daily 2-9:30pm. On Su, there is a market on Jl. Mahkota, opposite the town square.

Laundry: Pusat Dobi Unik, 119 Jl. Mahkota (☎516 2403), opposite the town square. Laundry priced per item; roughly RM6 for a small load. Extra fee for same-day service.

Emergency: ☎999.

Police: (☎513 2222), on Jl. Mahkota. Open 24hr.

Medical Service: Hospital Tengku Ampuan Afzan (☎513 3333), on Jl. Tanah Putih, opposite Kompleks Terantun. Head southwest on Jl. Besar, away from Teluk Chempedak; the road becomes Jl. Tanah Putih. English-speaking doctors. RM2. Open 24hr.

Telephones: Telekom Office (☎513 9292), next to the post office. Sells phone cards. Open M-F 8:45am-4:15pm, Sa 8:30am-12:30pm. **Cyberpoint** on Jl. Besar, 3rd fl. RM2.50 per hr. Open 9am-9pm.

Internet Access: Terminal (☎516 4500), on the 2nd fl. of Kompleks Makmur, next to the express bus terminal. RM2 per hr. Open 8am-1am.

Post Office: Pejabat Pos Besar (☎552 1032), on Jl. Mahkota at Jl. Merdeka intersection. Turn left coming from Jl. Bukit Ubi. *Poste Restante,* at the side of the building, open Su-Th and Sa 8:30am-5pm. Post office open M-Sa 8am-4:30pm.

Postal Code: 25670.

ACCOMMODATIONS AND FOOD

New Campital Hotel ❷, 55-59 Jl. Bukit Ubi, 350m from Jl. Makhota, is worth the extra ringgit. (☎513 5222. Rooms RM16, with bath RM17.90, with bath and A/C RM26.) **Hotel Kristal ❸,** 2nd fl. 59-61A Jl. Mahkota, is down the street from the Standard Chartered Bank across from the mosque. (☎516 2577. Doubles RM30, with TV and bath RM38; triples with shower and TV but no toilet RM45.) Near the local bus station, **Hotel Sungei Wang ❸,** 86 Jl. Besar, has tidy and spacious rooms with bath. (☎514 8912. Doubles RM30, with A/C RM35-37; triples with A/C RM45; quads RM50.) For really cheap rooms, head to **New Evergreen Hotel ❶,** 63 Jl. Bukit Ubi. (Singles with bath RM13; doubles with bath and fan RM20.)

Foodstalls on Jl. Mahkota near the State Mosque on Jl. Tun Ismail are great for cheap, convenient meals. For scenic late-night eats, head to the river behind the local bus terminal. Try the steamed shredded coconut with *gula melaka* inside a short bamboo cylinder (RM0.50). **Restoran Chan Poh ❷,** 52 Bukit Ubi, opposite the Snooker Bistro and a few stores down, is a great place for late-night dim sum. (Shrimp dumplings RM1.80; fried noodles RM3. Beer RM6. Open daily 6pm-midnight.) **Restoren Parvathy ❶,** 75 Jl. Bukit Ubi, has the old standbys: *dosai, roti, chapati,* and a host of curry selections for RM0.40-4. Heading away from Jl. Mahkota, it's seven stores past the Snooker Bistro. (Open daily 7am-10pm.) One of the finer Chinese restaurants in town, **Kum Leng Restaurant ❶,** E-897-901 Jl. Bukit Ubi, north of the roundabout, has delicious dinners for RM10-20. (☎513 4446. Sweet and sour pork RM8. Been curd RM6. Fried rice RM4.)

SIGHTS

The only noteworthy attraction is the **Masjid Negeri** (State Mosque) on Jl. Mahkota; its blue domes are the most colorful on the peninsula. Visitors are allowed inside if they are dressed appropriately (long pants or skirt, no bare shoulders) and do not walk on the elevated areas. Admission is free, but you must ask to enter at the front desk. The best times to visit are before 11:30am or between 3-5pm. The most popular attraction is **Teluk Chempedak,** 4km from town on the east-coast shore. Teluk Chempedak's sandy 2km beach is bound by rocky headlands. Walk over the bridge for the **Denai Tebling Pelindung** (cliff walk), which leads to a secluded beach inhabited by monkeys and tiny crabs. From here, you can scramble over a cluster of rocks to venture to beaches farther north. Although the only budget accommodation recently closed, the **Kuantan Hotel ❹** (☎568 0026), opposite the Hyatt, is comfortable. (Upper-level rooms have sea views and bathtub. Doubles with fan RM46, with A/C RM58-68; quads RM77-88.) Get to Teluk Chempedak on the Rahmat Alam Bus (30min., 7am-10pm, RM1).

DAYTRIPS FROM KUANTAN

For even more scenic, relaxing activities, check out several worthwhile daytrips from Kuantan. **Sungai Pandan Waterfall** is a 50m cascade with eight tiers and a large pool at the bottom. Take a bus (45min., every hr., RM3) from the local bus station to **Felda Panching** (30km); from there it's a 3km hike to the falls along a paved road. Nearby is **Panchang Cave,** a four-million-year-old limestone cavern enclosing a statue of the "Natural Buddha" carved by water drops (RM2). Take bus #48 (toward Sungai Lembing) from the local bus station to Panching (RM3). From town, it's a 4km hike through palm-oil plantations. A taxi takes you closer to the mouth of the cave for about RM50 round-trip. Travelers are discouraged from making the trip alone due to thugs in the area. **Tasik Chini,** Malaysia's second-largest lake, is well worth a side trip for one or two days. The lake and its environs are a natural playground; you can fish, jog, trek, take a boat ride through twelve interconnected lakes, or absorb the serene landscape. To get there, take a taxi (round-trip RM120) or a bus to Chini Town (8, 10, 11am, 1:30, 3:45, 5:30pm; RM5.20), which will bring you 12km from the lake. From here you can walk, take an unlicensed taxi at exorbitant rates (RM30), or try to catch a ride—*Let's Go* does not recommend hitchhiking. "Uncle" Rajan Jones runs a homestay in an Orang Asli village (RM18). There is no phone, but locals should be able to direct you.

MERSING ☎07

The bustling town of Mersing is cluttered with signs of travelers in transit. The main departure point for those going to Tioman, Mersing hosts backpackers roaming the sidewalks in search of foodstalls, moneychangers, cheap housing, and short-term distractions. Most hostels and hotels offer river cruises and day trips to the nearby islands or national parks. ATMs are rare on Tioman Island, so it is recommended that you get some cash in advance.

> **TIP** Bus drivers sometimes drop off passengers at the entrance to Mersing city, and not at the jetty that is on the other end of town along Jl. Abu Bakar (the main street and departure point for ferries). At the city entrance, tourist agency employees will jump up on the bus and aggressively hawk ferry/speedboat tickets, while insisting that they can offer you the best deals on rooms on Tioman Island. They don't charge extra for ferry tickets, and if you buy one you will save a 750m walk to the jetty since they drive you there. However, avoid buying a return ticket (you can get them from most hostels or hotels on each beach on Tioman), and definitely avoid reserving rooms through these hawkers. You can find much nicer and less expensive accommodation once you reach the islands.

TRANSPORTATION

Buses: Express Bus Terminal in **Plaza R&R,** on the left side as you exit the jetty. **Transnasional Express** (☎799 3155) goes to: **Kota Bharu** (8hr., 10pm, RM29.10); **KL** (5½hr.; 11, 11:30am, 12:30, 6, 10, 10:30pm; RM19.50); **Kuala Terengganu** via **Cherating** (6-7hr.; noon, 10pm; RM22.10); **Kuantan** (3hr.; noon, 10pm; RM10.60); **Singapore** via **Johor Baru** (3hr.,1:30pm, RM12.50).

Ferries: Buy boat tickets to **Pulau Tioman** in Plaza R&R. **Ferries** are the cheapest but also the slowest (2-2½hr., 5 per day 7:30am-4:30pm, RM30). **Speedboats** are most efficient (1½-2hr., multiple rides per day 9:30am-5.30pm, RM35). Don't buy round-trip tickets—they may not be honored on the return journey.

Taxis: (☎799 1393), on Jl. Sulaiman next to the local bus station. From the jetty or Plaza R&R, walk down Jl. Abu Bakar, turn right at 1st intersection and then left at the end of the road. Fares are measured from one taxi station to another city's taxi station. Open daily 7:30am-6pm.

ORIENTATION AND PRACTICAL INFORMATION

Walking out from the **jetty,** the blue and white tiled **Plaza R&R** is to the left, and houses a **tourist center** and the **Express Bus Terminal.** Also within the plaza are travel agencies, a hawker center, and an Internet cafe. **Jl. Abu Bakar** runs across as you walk out from the jetty; make a right onto this main road to reach the main part of town. The **post office** is on the left, about 200m down from the jetty, and the **tourist information center** is across the road from the post office. Farther down, after you reach the first of two roundabouts, are guesthouses, casual restaurants, and Internet cafes. The other major road, **Jl. Ismail,** runs parallel to Jl. Abu Bakar farther away from the jetty and holds **banks,** a **supermarket,** and pricey **hotels.**

Tourist Offices: Mersing Tourist Information Center (☎799 5212), on Jl. Abu Bakar. Open M-Th 2-4:30pm, F 2:45-4:30pm. English-speaking staff at **Island Connection Travel and Tours,** 2 Jl. Jemaluang (☎799 2535), at the corner opposite where Jl. Abu Bakar and Jl. Ismail intersect at the 2nd roundabout. Open M-F 9am-6pm. **Sun and Sand Holiday** (☎799 4995), at the Embassy Hotel, also has English-speaking staff.

Tours: Omar's Backpacker's Hostel (☎019 774 4268; see **Accommodations and Food,** p. 405) offers 1-day tours to nearby islands (RM60; includes guide, transport, lunch, and snorkeling gear; 4-12 people). **East Coast Hotel** (☎012 762 4983; see **Accommodations and Food,** p. 405) offers an Endau Rowpin National Park tour (2 days, 3 nights RM400 per person; 3 days, 2 nights RM550; 4 days, 3 nights RM650; group discounts available), an Endau River Cruise (RM110 per person, 4-8 people) and tours of Gunning Berlumut jungles, fruit farms, and rubber and tea plantations (about RM250; at least 2 people).

Currency Exchange: Bank Bumiputra Malaysia Berhad, 4-5 Jl. Ismail (☎799 1600), next to Embassy Hotel. Cashes traveler's checks for RM2.15. MC/V cash advances RM4. Open M-F 9am-4:30pm, Sa 9:30am-noon. **Maybank,** on Jl. Ismail next to Parkson Supermarket. **ATM** (Cirrus/MC). Open M-F 9:30am-4pm, Sa 9:30-11:30am. **Money-changers** line Jl. Abu Bakar. Generally open daily 9am-6pm. **Giamso Safari,** 23 Jl. Abu Bakar (☎799 2253). Licensed moneychanger inside. Open daily 8am-6pm.

Emergency: ☎999.

Police: (☎799 2222). From jetty, walk down Jl. Abu Bakar and turn left on Jl. Sultanah.

Medical Services: Hospital Daerah (☎799 3333), at end of Jl. Ismail. English spoken. 24hr. emergency care. Open daily 8am-4:15pm.

Telephones: Card phones everywhere, especially around jetty and inside Plaza R&R. Many shops along Jl. Abu Bakar sell phone cards.

Internet Access: Easy Internet Cafe, 9 Jl. Dato Mohammed Ali (☎799 7319) and **Eddy Internet Cafe,** 13 Jl. Dato Mohammad Ali (☎799 7140). From the jetty, turn left onto Jl. Abu Bakarand then left at the 1st roundabout. Both open daily 9:30am-11:30pm. Rates are the same: RM1.50 per 30min., RM2.50 per hr. Eddy offers extra services like printing, scanning and faxing, and Easy Internet Cafe tends to be more crowded.

Post Office: 670 Jl. Abu Bakar (☎799 1031). Open M-Sa 8:30am-5pm.

Postal Code: 86800.

ACCOMMODATIONS AND FOOD

Embassy Hotel ❷, 2 Jl. Ismail, near the roundabout by Bank Bumiputra, has good, clean rooms. All rooms—except the doubles with fan—have hot showers and cable. (☎799 3545. Doubles RM16, with bath RM30, with A/C RM48; triples with bath RM35, with A/C RM55; quads with A/C RM65.) **East Coast Hotel ❶,** 43A Jl. Abu Bakar, has a rooftop common area, laundry service, and Internet (RM3 per hour). The staff also provides travel info, travel packages (see **Tours,** p. 405), and can book onward travel. Rooms are old but clean and well maintained; all rooms have private sinks and share a common bathroom. Hotel provides free mineral water, sheets, towels and soap. (☎799 3546; www.geocities.com/anwarkinin. 6-bed dorms RM10; doubles RM20; triples RM30.) Opposite the post office and 5min. from the jetty, **Omar's Backpacker's Hostel ❶,** 1D-1 Jl. Abu Bakar, has basic, musty rooms with fan and shared bath, as well as a simple cooking area. (☎799 5096. Dorms RM8; doubles RM20.)

Foodstalls ❶ at Plaza R&R sell cheap Malay food. White rice with vegetables, chicken, or fish costs RM20-5, while *mee goreng* is RM2. (Open daily 5:30am-8pm.) For freshly cooked food, try the Chinese seafood or Indian restaurants. **Restoran Ee Lo ❷,** at the first roundabout where Jl. Abu Bakar and Jl. Mohammad Ali meet, cooks up special dishes, including fried wild boar meat with ginger and onion, and lemon chicken, both for RM6. (☎799 3050. Open daily 10am-11pm.) **Restoran Al-Arif ❶,** 44 Jl. Ismail, has excellent *roti canai* for RM0.60 and *roti telur* for RM1.20 (savory crispy pancakes eaten with a curry dip, with or without an egg). Fried noodles or rice are RM3-5. (☎799 4518. Open daily 7am-11pm.) **Restoran Halina ❶**, 53 Jl. Abu Bakar, between the two roundabouts, offers a wide variety of Malaysian favorites, including *murtabak ayam* (savory pancake with chicken filling; RM4), *mee goreng* (fried noodles; RM2.50), and *nasi briyani* (rice cooked in saffron with various curry dishes; RM4.50), among others. (☎799 7350. Open daily 6am-10pm.)

PULAU TIOMAN

According to legend, a magical dragon princess inhabits the island, presiding over its peaceful beauty. The princess is certainly doing her job, given the island's tranquil beaches and clear waters, transparent to depths of over 20m. Indeed, Tioman has been rated as one of the world's top ten island destinations. There is something here for everyone, from snorkeling and diving spots to resorts or secluded bays. The locals are infinitely generous and friendly. Whether it's action or relaxation you are seeking, you might end up staying longer than expected.

TRANSPORTATION

The **airport** is in Kampung Tekek. **Berjaya Air** (☎419 1309) has daily flights to **KL** (1hr.; 11:30am, 1:50pm; RM141, children RM71) and **Singapore** (40min., 11am, RM280). Make reservations one day in advance (AmEx/MC/V).

Most travelers catch a **boat** from **Mersing** (see p. 404) to get to Pulau Tioman. Buy tickets at a travel agency for a **ferry** (2-2½hr., 5 per day 7:30am-4:30pm, RM30) or **speedboat** (1½-2hr., 2 per day 9:30am-5.30pm, RM35). Ferries to Mersing leave from **Kampung Salang** (6:30am) and pick up passengers at **Kampung Air Batang** (7am) and **Kampung Tekek** (7:30-8am). Speedboats to Mersing also leave from all three piers (9:30am-noon). Buy tickets from most hostels and hotels. Ferries leave for **Singapore** from the **Berjaya Resort** (4-4½hr.; 2:30pm; RM150-170, child RM100-110, not including seaport tax or weekend surcharges). Schedules vary with the tides. Check with ticket sellers and locals. Don't buy round-trip tickets, as they may not be honored upon return. An expensive local **sea taxi,** booked at any hostel, travels between beaches (RM10-45 depending on travel distance). A daily ferry leaves from **Juara** at 3pm to: **Berjaya Resorts** (RM30); **Kampung Salang** (1hr., RM20); **Kampung Tekek** (2hr., RM25). Chartering a boat runs upward of RM200.

KAMPUNG TEKEK ☎09

Despite being Pulau Tioman's largest village, Kampung Tekek remains less touristed than other destinations on the island; it feels more like a residential village than a tourist destination. A few diving centers attract enthusiasts, but accommodations are expensive and the beaches are nothing to write home about. Still, Tekek is popular for its duty-free shops and cheap foodstalls.

ORIENTATION AND PRACTICAL INFORMATION. The walk between Tekek and Kampung Air Batang takes 30min.—turn left as you come out from the jetty. To the right lies the main village center, where there are hotels, hostels, duty-free shops, and small restaurants. The **police station** is in the center of town, 500m down from the jetty. (☎419 1167. Open 24hr.) A **clinic** is several doors down in a pale yellow building (☎419 1880; open M-Th 8am-1pm and 2-4:30pm, F 8am-12:15pm and 2:45-4:30pm, Sa 8am-1pm) and charges foreigners RM1 for medical consultation. English-speaking staff is available. For emergencies, an on-site doctor is available 24hr. On the second floor of the **Airport Terminal Complex,** across from the jetty, there is a **currency exchange** bureau that cashes traveler's checks at poor rates—**bring cash from the mainland.** Next door is the **post office** (☎419 1145; open daily 8.30am-6pm), which sends to and receives mail from Mersing twice a week. Its *Poste Restante* address is: Kampung Tekek, Pulau Tioman, 86800 K. Rompin, Pahang Darul Mamur, Malaysia. An **Internet** cafe is on the second floor, inside **Featherlight.** (☎419 1609. RM3 for the first 5min. and RM0.11 for each min. after, RM9 per hr. Open daily 9am-midnight.) **Telekom card phones** are clustered at the jetty and near the Airport Terminal Complex; purchase phone cards at the moneychanger. To the left of the Airport Terminal Complex is the **tourist information** center. (Open daily 9am-4pm.)

ACCOMMODATIONS AND FOOD. Persona Island Resort ❺ has the cleanest rooms in town, but no beachfront property. All rooms have fan and A/C. Van service and discounts are available. (☎419 1213. Doubles RM90; triples RM110; sea view RM130.) A 700m walk, heading right coming out of the the jetty, **Coral Reef Holidays ❹** has rooms facing the sea or a garden. Discounts are available for groups; try to bargain since prices are flexible. (☎419 1628. High-season doubles RM70, low-season RM40; triples RM60-80/50; larger rooms RM120-180/80.) **Monte Chalets ❹,** 100m closer to the jetty, offers complete luxury with bathrobes, A/C, carpeting, and hot water in all the rooms. (☎419 1648. Doubles RM80, with sea view RM100; triples RM150; family rooms RM200; VIP rooms RM250.) **Barbura Seaview Resorts ❸** has considerably more spartan rooms that look quite unappealing. It is located about 1km from the jetty. (☎419 1139. Doubles with fan RM55, with A/C RM80; triples with A/C RM132-160.) The hotel also has an excellent seafood restaurant, **Seafood Restaurant Babura ❷,** that specializes in steamed *karupa,* a local fish, and sweet and sour styles (RM6-10). **Foodstalls ❶** at the Airport Terminal Complex serve excellent *roti canai* (RM1.20), *nasi lemak* (RM2.50), and fried eggs with toast (RM3.50), as well as fried rice (RM3.50) and fried noodles (RM3.50) of your choice. Numerous small **supermarkets** line the road to the right of the jetty, before you reach Sri Tioman.

ENTERTAINMENT AND OUTDOOR ACTIVITIES. Eco-Divers (☎419 1250; www.divemalaysia.i8.com), next to Tekek Inn and Sri Tioman Resorts, is run by a friendly couple, Michelle and Jeffree. The diving center is PADI-registered; they offer three- to four-day open-water courses for RM600, advanced open-water courses for RM650, as well as night dives and dive master courses. Eco-Divers also offers underwater video-taping of your dives. They will pick you up from other beaches at ABC and Berjaya. Next door to Sri Tioman Resort and past the police station is **Tioman Dive Centre,** which offers PADI courses (☎419 1228; www.tioman-dive-centre.com). All levels of instruction available: 2hr. intro dive course RM140; 2-day scuba dive course RM550; 4-day basic open-water course RM800; advanced diver 650; rescue diver RM850; dive master RM850 and up. Gear rental available as well as discounts for large groups. **Cheers Souvenirs,** next to Coral Reef Holidays, rents **bicycles, motorbikes,** and **snorkel gear.** (☎419 1425. Bikes RM5 per hr., RM25 per day; motorbikes RM15 per hr., RM75 per day; mask and snorkel RM10 per day. Open daily 9am-7pm.)

KAMPUNG SALANG ☎09

Kampung Salang sits at the north tip of Tioman Island. The small, dreamy beach is delightful, and most travelers spend their days sunbathing, snorkeling, or diving at nearby Coral Island.

ORIENTATION AND PRACTICAL INFORMATION. The beaches and chalets stretch out on both sides of the pier. Most restaurants, shops, and budget accommodations are to the left of the jetty as you get off the boat and walk toward the beach. Exchange **currency** at most budget hotels or to the left of the jetty at **Salang Indah minimart,** which cashes traveler's checks, sells phone cards, and will let you make **international calls** (prices vary according to call destination). For **medical assistance,** take a sea taxi to the clinic in Kampung Tekek, or seek simple first aid from one of the dive centers. The 24hr. **police** office is next to B&J Diving Centre, to the left of the jetty (☎013 983 9244). **A-D Internet Service** lies next to **Salang Indah Resorts** away from the jetty. (RM1.50 per 15min. Open daily 9am-11:50pm.)

ACCOMMODATIONS AND FOOD. Half a dozen inexpensive hotels line Salang's beach, and many have restaurants with Malay, Chinese, and Western cuisine. Coming out of the jetty, most of the budget accommodations are to the left, while the pricier resorts with chalets are to the right. The first resort to the right, **Salang Pusaka Resort (Khalid's Place) ❹,** offers quiet accommodations that seem to be less crowded than the other resorts. (☎419 5317, 419 5034; www.salangpusakaresort.tripod.com. Doubles with fan and attached bathroom RM45, with A/C and attached bathroom RM70-130; rooms for 3-5 people RM150-200.) Farther down in the same direction, **Salang Sayang (Zaid's Place) ❹,** at the southern end of the village by the beach, has clean rooms with great views. Restaurant, library, moneychanger, Internet, and snorkel gear rental are all available here. Reserve in advance for August. (☎419 5020; info@salangsayangtioman.com. Singles RM80; doubles RM60-80; Banana Hill doubles RM75, with A/C RM100; triples with A/C and hot shower RM150; 4-person family rooms with A/C and hot shower RM180.) Just to the left of the jetty is **Salang Indah Resorts ❸,** which operates a restaurant, sea taxis, ferries, a sports center, minimart, bar, and dive shop. (☎419 5015; www.salangindah.com. Internet access RM2 per 15min. Doubles with fan RM30; triples with A/C RM60; quads with A/C RM60-150. Extra mattresses RM10.) Close to Dive Asia Dive Center and White House, **Salang Beach Resort ❺** offers well-appointed rooms in a quieter part of the beach, and serves well as a family vacation destination. Clean rooms and lovely gardens. (☎07 799 2337; www.tioman-salang.com. Doubles with fan RM80, with A/C RM110; quads with fan RM100, with A/C RM145.)

Right off the jetty, **Salang Dreams Restaurant ❸** serves *nasi lemak* (RM2), chocolate pancakes (RM4), seafood fettucine (RM10), and beer (RM2.50-5). Try the "special milkshake." (☎419 5040. Open daily 7.30am-11pm.) Next door, **Salang Indah Restaurant ❷** dishes up Chinese, Malay, Thai, and Western food. The Thai chef recommends Thai fried rice (RM4) or *laksa penang* for RM3. (Open daily 8am-10:30pm.) A short walk from Salang Indah away from the jetty, nightlife stumbles on at **Four-S Cafe** with RM5-8 beers. (Open daily 6pm-1am. MC/V.) On the north end of Kampong Salang, the **Chinese Restaurant ❹** at Salang Beach Resort has an extensive menu of seafood. Try the chilli crab (RM15-28) or claypot Indonesian prawns (RM18-38). Vegetarian options available. (Open daily 8am-3pm and 6-10pm.) After 7pm, **White House Cafe ❸,** near Dive Asia, fills with the smell of barbecue seafood and meat. Main dishes run between RM7 and RM30. (☎013 729 0658.)

OUTDOOR ACTIVITIES. Near Salang Indah Resorts, the **Fishermen Dive Center** is well equipped and offers PADI courses as well as daytrips. (☎419 5014; www.fishermenscuba.com. Shore dive RM60, night dive RM90, scuba dive RM140; 2 dives RM160, 3 dives RM220, 4 dives RM270; underwater photography course RM400; prices include equipment, food, and drink. Open daily 9am-6pm. MC/V.)

Farther down, **Dive Asia** offers similar day trips and PADI courses. (☎419 1654; www.diveasia.com.my. 2 dives RM130-160; shore dives RM70; 3- to 4-day open-water course RM750; rescue course RM750; prices vary, depending on whether you have your own equipment, and bring your own lunch. Open daily 8:30am-6:30pm. AmEx/MC/V.) Salang Indah Resorts also has badminton courts and fishing gear at its sports center.

KAMPUNG AIR BATANG (ABC) ☎09

Kampung Air Batang is a backpacker haven, buzzing with affordable accommodations, food, and souvenir shops. Life is slower paced here; most travelers come here to relax. The beach is wider and sandier south of the jetty, while resorts to the north face a pile of uninviting rocks.

The **tourist information hut** is opposite the ferry landing spot but is rarely open. Luckily, the boatman at **Zinza's Place,** to the right just off the jetty, can provide all the information you need on transportation. Diving and snorkeling expeditions are led by **B&J Diving.** (☎419 1218. Kayak rental RM15 per hr. Open daily 8:30am-6pm.)

Bamboo Hill Chalets ❺, at the northernmost end of the beach about 750m left of the jetty, offers picturesque accommodations with sea views, Internet access (RM2.5 per 15min.), and international calls. All proceeds from library book rentals (RM1 per book) are donated to the local school. Reserve several days in advance over the Internet. (☎419 1339; www.geocities.com/bamboosu. 2-person bungalows with hot showers RM70; triples RM100; quads RM120.) Next door, **ABC Chalets ❸** is owned by the same family and has the same type of chalets (but without the elevated views of the sea). Rooms are clean and have clear views of the beachfront. (☎013 922 0263; www.geocities.com/abcbeachtioman. Doubles with fan RM35; triples with A/C RM120.) Following ABC Chalets, backpackers flock to **Johan's House ❷,** which offers cheap and well-maintained accommodations (☎419 1359; 4-6 person dorm RM10; doubles with fan RM35; 3-5 person rooms RM80-120) and **South Pacific Chalets ❷,** which has less impressive but still inexpensive accommodations (doubles with fan RM15, triples with fan RM30). To the right of the jetty, the hostels enjoy nicer beaches, and are quite affordable. **Mawar Beach Chalets ❸** has a cozy restaurant in addition to standard chalets with showers. For RM35 per person, Mawar offers a daytrip to Coral Island for groups of four or more; reservations must be made one day in advance. (☎419 1153. Laundry RM5 per kg. Doubles RM25.) About 500m to the right of the jetty are the best value accommodations in Air Batang. **Yang Puang (YP) Chalet ❷** has chalets with brightly patterned sheets and curtains. (☎419 1018, 013 609 4628; hussinkhan@hotmail.com. Doubles RM15-20; triples RM30-35.) Also quite inexpensive is **My Friend's Place ❷,** which has eight chalets that are clean and spacious. (☎419 1150. Doubles RM18-25, with A/C RM35.) The southernmost hostel, **Nazri's Place ❸,** has more luxurious rooms and a restaurant with a lively atmosphere in the evenings. (☎419 1329; bungur@tm.net.my. Laundry priced per item. Internet RM1 per 5min. Camping RM3; doubles with A/C and hot shower RM80-120.)

People flock to **Nazri's Cafe ❷,** at the south end of ABC, for excellent Malay and Western meals. For breakfast, try *roti canai* (RM1), pineapple pancakes (RM3), or the continental breakfast (RM6). Entrees cost around RM6. At night, Nazri's Cafe does a huge barbecue cookout that attracts almost all the backpackers on Batang. (Open daily 8am-10:30pm.) Nearby, the restaurant at **Mawar Beach Chalets ❷** serves similar fare, but with more creative flair. Try a Malaysian omelette with chilli and onion (RM2.50) or grilled fish with garlic butter, salad, and chips for RM12. (Open daily 9am-4pm and 7-10pm.) The cheapest food on this side of the jetty is at **My Friend's Place ❶.** Many travelers stop here for a breakfast of toast and scrambled eggs (RM2.50) with coffee or tea (RM1). For a more romantic setting, **Restoran Hijau ❸,** to the left of the jetty, provides serene seaview dining atop a small hill. Hijau has steeper prices for a sophisticated dining experience. (☎419 1375. Barbecue RM13-18, burgers RM8. Open 8am-4pm and 7-10:30pm.)

KAMPUNG JUARA ☎09

Kampung Juara, on the east coast of Tioman, is the hardest place to reach on the island. Those who make the trek will be rewarded with some of Pulau Tioman's best beaches.

Bushman Dive Centre offers PADI courses (open-water RM750; advanced-diver RM600, dive master RM1200) in addition to regular dives for RM70-150. (☎419 3109; www.members.tripod.com/bushman42.)

The most scenic route to Juara is a cross-island trek through the jungle from **Kampung Tekek** (2½hr., 7km). From the jetty, turn left on the cement path and walk 500m, turning right at the sign on the paved path before the minimart. Past the mosque, the trail narrows to a thin dirt path. Get a motorbike ride (RM15-20) up to the top and trek back down; or from Juara, take a **sea bus** (3pm, RM25) back to Kampung Tekek. Sea buses do not run regularly; it is wise to check with your hotel owner and ensure you have transportation back. The road set back from the beach meets the **jungle trail** to Tekek south of the jetty. **Happy Market,** next to the jetty, exchanges traveler's checks and major currencies, but rates are unpredictable. **Internet** costs RM12 per hr. (☎419 3137. Open daily 7:30am-9pm.) **Ferry** and **sea bus tickets** are sold at the counter on the jetty. Rent **snorkeling equipment** at the hut next to Mini Cafe, left of the jungle trail as you come out. (RM10. Open daily 8:30am-5pm.) The Juara **clinic** is off the path to the left of the jetty (open daily 2-4:30pm).

Paradise Point ❷, to the right of the jetty, has basic two-person chalets with private bath (RM20). The **restaurant ❶** serves an extensive menu (fried noodles with peanut sauce RM4) and has outdoor seating. (☎419 3145. Laundry RM4 per kg. Restaurant open daily 7am-10:30pm.) Next door is **River View Chalets ❷,** also with basic two-person rooms (RM20) and a pleasant open-air seafood **restaurant ❷** offering fried fish in *sambal* sauce for RM13.50 and *Tom Yam* noodle soup for RM5.50. (☎419 3168. Doubles with bath, fan, and mosquito net RM20.) **Juara Mutiara Resort ❸** is left of the jetty, with newly built chalets, a cafe, boat service, and a minimart. (☎419 3161. Doubles RM25; quads RM40. Group packages and daytrips available.)

NEAR KAMPUNG SALANG

Coral Island, even more beautiful than Pulau Tioman, has reefs with abundant marine life that are perfect for snorkeling. **Salang Beach Mini Market** organizes snorkeling trips to Coral Island. (☎419 5016. 10:30am-3:30pm or 1:30-5:30pm; RM25, 2-person min., includes snorkel gear; RM40, 4-person min., includes gear and lunch. Reserve 24hr. in advance.) Many resorts and dive centers in Salang offer daytrips to Coral Island as well. **Penuba** and **Monkey Beach** are dreamy secluded bays halfway between Kampung Salang and ABC. Follow the well-marked jungle trails going in each direction (40min. to Monkey Bay from Kampung Salang, 1½hr. to Monkey Beach from ABC). Where the trail is not distinct, follow the power cables overhead to find your way back to the path. Alternatively, you can take a sea taxi to Monkey Bay from Kampung Salang (RM10). The hike is steep; bring water and look out for monkeys. If you're exhausted from the effort of lying around on the beach all day, try the **Mukut Waterfalls** at the southern tip of Tioman island. **Salang Indah Resorts** organizes a waterfall trip. (☎419 5015. RM50.) **Nazri's Place 2** in ABC also has a trip there. (☎419 1375. RM50.)

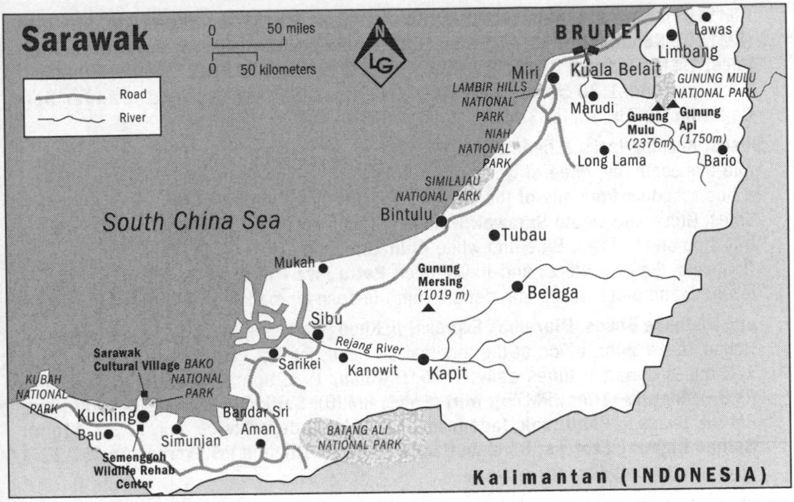

SARAWAK

Sarawak earned its name when the Sultan of Brunei handed it over to James Brooke, the first White Rajah, with the words "*Serah kapada awak*" ("I give this to you"). Though he really doesn't need the money, the sultan is probably kicking himself now—Sarawak is Malaysia's richest state and boasts nine national parks, lush jungles, secluded beaches, and a series of giant limestone caves recognized by UNESCO as a World Heritage Site. The state is also home to 26 ethnic groups, including the famed Iban who live in longhouses along the Rajang River. See it soon, as environmental degradation is threatening Sarawak's natural beauty and its indigenous cultures, though major conservation efforts are now underway.

KUCHING ☎082

Kuching means "cat" in Malay, and residents celebrate that appellation with gleaming feline statues. Easily the most modern city in Borneo, Kuching successfully preserves the relics of its past: Chinese temples and Muslim mosques stand in the shadow of hip cafes, towering skyscrapers, and luxury hotels. A meticulously landscaped waterfront esplanade invites people to unwind after touring world-renowned museums or sorting through piles of handicrafts. An ideal base from which to explore Bako National Park, the Sarawak Cultural Village, and Iban and Bidayuh longhouses, this cat bites hard and leaves visitors craving more.

TRANSPORTATION

Flights: Kuching International Airport (☎457 373), 10km south of the city. Take Sarawak Transport Company bus #12A (30min., every hr. 6am-7:20pm, RM1) or Chin Lian Long bus #8A (30min., every hr. 6am-8pm, RM0.90). Coupons for taxis (RM17.50) are available at the stand outside customs. Storage lockers RM3 per day. **Air Asia** (www.airasia.com), the region's biggest budget airline, flies daily to Kuala Lumpur (RM70), with flights connecting to **Singapore, Bangkok,** and **Jakarta** (from RM119). **MAS** (☎246 622), on Jl. Song Thian Cheok. To: **Bintulu** (RM150); **Hong Kong**

(RM1167); **Kota Kinabalu** (RM228); **KL** (am flights RM197, pm flights RM262); **Miri** (RM180); **Sandakan** (RM284); **Sibu** (RM72); **Singapore** (RM286). **Royal Brunei Airlines,** 1st fl., Rugayah Building, Jl. Song Thian Cheok (☎243 344). Open M-F 8:30am-12:30pm and 1:30-5pm, Sa 8:30am-12:30pm, Su 9am-1pm. To: **Bandar Seri Begawan** (Tu, Th, Su; RM334).

Buses: Kuching lacks a central bus terminal. Departure points depend on destination and bus company, three of which serve both Kuching and southwest Sarawak. Pick up a bus schedule from any of the city's tourist offices for the latest fares and departure times. Green and cream **Sarawak Transport Company** (☎242 967) buses run from the bus stop on Lh. Jawa. Blue and white **Chin Lian Long** (☎422 767) buses depart from Jl. Masjid, the post office, and Jl. Gambier. **Petra Jaya Transport** (☎429 418) has yellow, red, and black buses that depart from the open-air market on Jl. Khoo Hun Yeang.

Long-Distance Buses: Biaramas Express, Jl. Khoo Hun Yeang (☎429 418), near Electra House, has a 24hr. office at the terminal on Penrissen Rd. (☎452 139). Comfortable A/C buses depart 5 times daily (7:45, 9:45am, 1, 5, 9pm). To: **Batu Niah** (12hr., RM85); **Bintulu** (10hr., RM75); **Miri** (15hr., RM90); **Sarikei** (6hr., RM39); **Sibu** (7hr., RM46). Buses to **Pontianak, Indonesia** (7hr., RM45) depart twice daily (7:30, 11am). **Borneo Highway Express,** 63 Main Bazaar (☎413 595), and **PB Express** (☎461 277) also provide long-distance service.

> **TIP** Buses can get extremely cold with the A/C blasting, so be sure to bring blankets (or sub-zero rated sleeping bags).

Ferries: Express ferries depart from **Bintawa Express Wharf** in Pending, accessible by CLL buses #17 and 19 (30min., RM1), or taxi (RM10). **Express Bahagia,** 50 Padungan Rd. (☎421 948), runs boats to **Sibu** (4hr.; 8:30am; RM40, 1st-class RM50). Purchase tickets at the wharf. It is advisable to arrive at the wharf 30min. prior to departure. Seats regularly sell out.

ORIENTATION AND PRACTICAL INFORMATION

Kuching's city center unfolds along the southern banks of the **Sarawak River.** Its western border is **Jl. Gambier,** which becomes **Jl. Main Bazaar** and runs along the waterfront. **Fort Margherita** stands across the river. The **central district** begins past the souvenir shops on Jl. Main Bazaar near **Tua Pek Kong Temple.** Turning right leads to **Lh. Temple** and most budget accommodations. Tourists should not walk along the waterfront alone after midnight as this is a favorite spot for pickpockets.

Tourist Offices: The airy, hardwood-floored **Visitors Information Center,** Sarawak Tourism Complex in the Old Court House (☎410 944; stb@sarawaktourism.com) offers assistance with bookings, maps, and information for the entire province. Entrance at the corner of Jl. Main Bazaar and Jl. Tun Haji Openg, opposite the main post office. Book accommodations for Bako and Gunung Mulu National Parks here (see p. 418). **Sarawak Tourism Association,** Kuching Waterfront, Jl. Main Bazaar (☎240 620). Walking away from the Tua Pek Kong Temple, this octagon-shaped building is on the right. Maps, advice, and brochures available from a friendly staff.

Consulates: Chinese Consulate (PRC), Lot 3719 Dogan Garden, Jl. Dogan (☎453 344), off Jl. Batu Kawa. **Indonesia,** 111 Jl. Tun Abang Hj. (☎241 734; fax 424 370), opposite the hospital.

Currency Exchange: Passport required for all currency exchange. **Public Bank,** 28-30 Jl. Tun Haji Openg (☎417 922), opposite the post office. RM3 for cashing first traveler's check; RM0.15 per additional check. **Standard Chartered Bank** on Jl. Padungan near

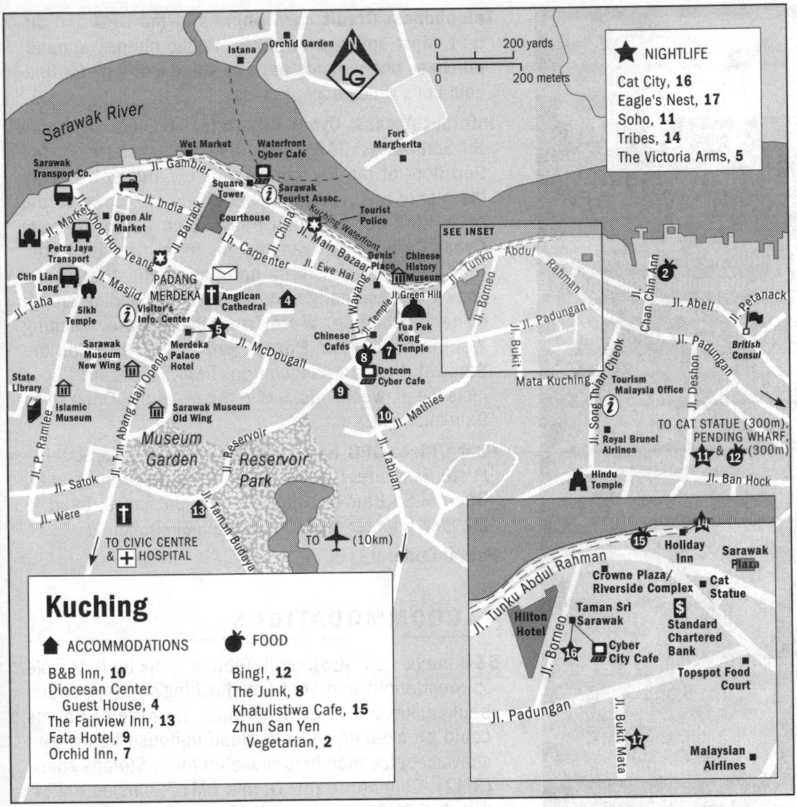

Holiday Inn. 24hr. **ATM. Bumiputra Bank** (☎236 809), next door, offers Western Union services. All banks open M-F 9:30am-4pm, Sa 9:30-12:30am. After hours, head to the licensed moneychangers in the Riverside Complex or to the major shopping centers.

American Express: At **CPH Travel Agency,** 70 Jl. Padungan (☎243 708), off the intersection with Jl. Chan Chin Ann. Open M-F 8:30am-5pm, Sa 8:30am-noon.

English-Language Bookstore: Times Bookshop, 1st fl., 103 Crown Plaza Complex, Jl. Tunku Abdul Rahman (☎412 231). Proceed up escalator; the store is on your right. Open daily 10am-9:30pm. AmEx/MC/V.

Emergency: ☎999.

Police: ☎241 222. At the corner of Jl. Khoo Hun Yeang and Jl. Barrack. **Tourist Police Unit,** Kuching Waterfront, Jl. Main Bazaar (☎250 522). English spoken. The staff can help with any problem. Open daily, including public holidays, 8am-midnight.

Hospital: Sarawak General Hospital (☎257 555), on Jl. Ong Keattwi. English spoken. Taxi RM10.

Pharmacies: Apex Pharmacy, No. 125, first fl., Sarawak Plaza (☎413 605). Open daily 10am-9pm. AmEx/MC/V. **Guardian Pharmacy,** Lower Ground Floor, Riverside Plaza. Open daily 10am-9:30pm. AmEx/MC/V.

ONE FLUSH, TWO FLUSH, NO FLUSH, YOU FLUSH

Visitors flock to Sarawak for its exoti[redacted]nd fauna. While most of th[redacted]e is harmless, travelers [redacted]ed! A strange and mysterious creature native to Southeast Asia lurks quietly in public parks, shopping malls, and less modern hotels. You will inevitably encounter it and are advised to be prepared.

What is it? The Sarawak species of toilet.

My first encounter with this beast occurred during a moment of urgency along a waterfront esplanade. How convenient that a public *tandas* (restroom) was set up in a small hut only a few meters away.

A male stick figure directed me to the left when I entered, and I was greeted by a smiling woman holding a glaring sign: "20 sen." Ugh. When you're a traveler, everything seems to have a price. I mi[redacted] America, Land of the Free (Toilets).

I grudgingly bought my way into the bathroom and rushed to a stall. I opened the door and stared at the oddity before me.

Rather than a gleaming bowl of porcelain, I saw a bizarre metallic depression in the tiled floor. I checked the next stall just in case this was a practical joke. Alas, the toilet was identical.

Why was the floor covered in water? And *what* was that orange hose protruding from the wall?

After surveying the locals and

Telephones: Credit card phones at the GPO and airport. Most hotels send faxes. Public phones abound; purchase phone cards at news stands, or look for Telekom units which accept coins.

Internet Access: Cyber City Cafe, 46 Block D, Taman Sri Sarawak (☎243 549). Take the escalators to the 2nd floor of the Riverside Complex, and exit through the rear of the building. Cyber City is 1/2 down on the right. RM4 per hr. Open daily 10am-11pm. **Dotcom Cyber Cafe,** Jl. Tabuan, across from the Fata Hotel. RM4 per hr. Open daily noon-midnight, though it's known to close early and open late depending on the owner's schedule. **Waterfront Cyber Cafe,** Kuching Waterfront, Jl. Main Bazaar (☎271 176), beside the Sarawak Tourism Association. RM4.50 per hr. Prices increase on weekends and in the evenings. Open Th-Tu 9am-midnight.

Post Office: GPO (☎241 311), on Jl. Tun Haji Openg. *Poste Restante*. Closed 1st and 3rd Sa of the month. Open M-Sa 8am-4:30pm. To ship packages, head to the EMS counter adjacent to the main building.

Postal Code: 93100.

ACCOMMODATIONS

B&B Inn (☎237 366), on Jl. Tabuan. Walk up Jl. Temple to roundabout and veer left. Kuching's most popular backpacker inn is also its most affordable. Rooms could be cleaner, but the small in-house library and convenient location help make up for it. Storage space (RM2). Common bath. Dorms RM17; singles RM24, with A/C RM30; doubles RM32, with A/C RM38; 3-person family room RM42. ❷

Diocesan Center Guest House (☎240 188), on Jl. McDougall. Enter driveway right of the Anglican cathedral parking lot and veer right at the end. Basic rooms with fan and hardwood floors. Clean and quiet. Open Jan.-late Aug. and early Sept.-Dec. Singles RM18-20; doubles RM23-25; apartments with A/C RM30, double occupancy RM45. ❷

The Fairview (☎429 2251), 6 Jl. Taman Budaya, behind the old Sarawak Museum near Reservoir Park. Situated in a renovated colonial building, the Fairview offers comfort and style. Reading room, TV room, Internet access and laundry service available. Dorms RM20; doubles with A/C and private bath RM80, with fan and shared bath RM55. ❹

Orchid Inn (☎411 417), 2 Jl. Green Hill, past Furama Lodging House. Rooms have A/C, hot water, and private bath. Laundry. Singles RM28; doubles RM35; triples RM45. ❸

FOOD

Latte lovers and *satay* addicts alike will enjoy Kuching's culinary offerings, which range from posh cafes to delicious, cheap waterfront stalls. Sarawak's signature dish and breakfast staple, *laksa mee*, consists of noodles cooked in a spicy curry broth laced with shredded chicken, prawns, bean curd, and bean sprouts; try it at any of the restaurants along **Lh. Temple** opposite the Medan Pelita Complex. **Vendors** cluster in the western end of town, south of the **Jl. Gambier** terminals and opposite the Chinese temple on **Jl. Carpenter.** After breakfast, try *apam*, a sizzling pancake that vendors stuff with coconut, peanut butter, and sugar. In the evening, vendors along the Kuching Waterfront grill up *satay* (marinated meat served on a skewer; RM0.40 per stick) and fast food. Visit the **Top Spot Food Court** on Jl. Bukit Mata Kuching, a favorite local eating place, for more varied choices.

The Junk, 80, Ground and 1st Fl., Wayang St. (☎259 450). Follow L. Temple away from the waterfront to Wayang, and keep left. The only "junk" you'll find in this restaurant is the owner's collection of vintage memorabilia. Candlelit surroundings and artfully prepared dishes are worth every *sen*. Favorites include homemade spaghettini with prawns and vodka cream sauce (RM22) and lamb shank (RM26). Extensive cocktail list (from RM18). Open nightly 6:30pm-12:30am, closed Tu. ❸

Bing!, 84 Pandungan Rd. (☎410 188). Follow Pandungan from the city center and bear right after the cat statue. Kuching's newest cafe is also its most stylish—the spectacular interior boasts mod leather sofas and minimalist Asian-inspired decor. Impressive line-up of specialty coffees, freshly baked cakes (from RM12) and wraps (RM15). Caramel machiatto RM9. Bring your laptop for wireless internet access. AmEx/MC/V. ❷

Hornbill's Corner Cafe, 85 Jl. Ban Hok (☎252 670). Communal cooking at its best; patrons crowd around tables to pile prawns, noodles, and an array of vegetables into "steamboats"—boiling pots of water. Attached barbecue plates allow you to grill marinated lamb, beef, or chicken. Leave room for the fresh fruit and ice-cream bar. Unlimited portions, RM16 per person. Beer RM20 per jug. Open daily 5pm-12:30am. ❸

Zhun San Yen Vegetarian, Lot 165, Jl. Chan Chin Ann (☎230 068). Follow Jl. Tunku Abdul Rahman past Sarawak Plaza and turn left at Pizza Hut. Vegetarian heaven with over 30 dishes (RM1.40 per 100g). Savory white fungus and straw mushroom soup RM1.10. Fresh fruit juices RM2.50. Open M-Sa 7:30am-2:30pm and 5-8:30pm. ❶

some good ol' fashioned practice, I finally understood. As it turns out, these seemingly strange creations are quite practical. The absent bowl reduces clean-up; you won't see automated machines that cover the seats in plastic here.

While squatting will be difficult at first, rest assured that it does eventually get easier. Practice makes perfect—or just more comfortable. Plant your heels firmly on the ground for balance. If you have a backpack or large purse, place it in front of you and grasp it with your hands. The illusion of stability works wonders. And practice eliminates potentially painful leg cramps.

Back home, the next logical step involves toilet paper. In some cities in Malaysia, you'll be able to purchase it at public toilets, but at others, you are on your own. The strange hose snaking out of the wall is used for cleaning with the left hand, which is considered dirty by Muslims.

The hose explains why most Sarawak bathroom floors are completely drenched in water. Don't worry, your 20 sen usually includes soap with which to wash your hands, so the experience is as hygienic as possible. Finally, you're ready to flush. While most toilets come equipped with a flushing device, many have fallen into disuse and thus into disrepair. If this is true, a bucket will be located adjacent to the hose. Simply fill with water, and pour.

-William Lee Adams

Khatulistiwa Cafe (☎248 896), on Jl. Tunku Abdul Rahman, across from the Crowne Plaza complex on the waterfront. House specialty is *Sarawak laksa* served with *bee hoon* (RM8.50). Pineapple rice RM7.90. Creamy ice-blended milkshakes RM6.50. Breakfast served 24hr. Upstairs bar houses DJs and dancing on weekends from 9pm onwards. AmEx/DC/MC/V. ❷

SIGHTS

Kuching's colonial architecture was spared from the bombing that leveled other cities on Malaysia's east coast during WWII. All the sights lie along the **Kuching Heritage Trail.** Admission to all sights is free. Along the esplanade and Jl. Main Bazaar, the **courthouse** faces the **Square Tower,** built in 1879 as a fortress and prison. Across the river are the pavilions of the **Istana,** built by Charles Brooke as a gift to his wife, which are now used as the residence of Sarawak's head of state. On Jl. Tun Haji Openg is the **Round Tower,** constructed in the 1880s as a hospital and fortress. Sarawak's oldest Taoist temple, **Tua Pek Kong,** stands on Jl. Temple opposite the esplanade. The region's best **museums** are within the city center. Follow Jl. Tun Haji Openg away from the river and past the town green to get to the **Sarawak Museum.** The pedestrian overpass to the new wing, which houses temporary exhibits and the museum gift shop, is visible from the road; for the permanent collections, turn left and walk to the main entrance in the old wing. The exhibits upstairs focus on Sarawak's 27 ethnic groups. Downstairs, stuffed relics of colonial-era taxidermy provide a fascinating insight into the island's fauna. The splendid grounds of the museum house an impressive **Aquarium,** the **Botanical Gardens,** and the **Heroes' Memorial,** built in honor of Malay soldiers. (Open daily 9am-6pm.) The **Sarawak Islamic Museum** showcases seven galleries of Muslim art centered around an attractive garden courtyard. (Open M-Th and Sa-Su 9am-6pm.) The real treat, however, is Kuching's **Cat Museum,** in the North City Hall in the Petra Jaya district. Take Petra Jaya Transport bus #2B or 2C (RM1). The museum houses a tribute to "Hello Kitty" products and a mummified cat (circa 3500 BC) from ancient Egypt. The cat-crazy converge each November for **Pesta Meoww,** seven days of cat bazaars, cartoons, and competitions (see **Mastijah Masleh, Organizer of "Pesta Meoww,"** p. 422). The corpse of the 1995 recipient of the "Best Dressed Cat" award is even on display at the museum. (☎446 688. Open daily 9am-5pm. Free. Camera fee RM1.) To get to the nearby **Timber Museum,** take Kuching Matang Transport Company bus #8 (RM1). The museum was established by timber companies as a response to foreign environmentalists and exhibits traditional wood items and forest products. (Open M-Th 8:30am-4pm, F 8:30-11:30am and 2:30-4:30pm, Sa 8:30am-12:30pm.)

The long **street market** on **Jl. Main Bazaar** offers great deals if you can bargain hard. Small shops deal in ethnic crafts including the popular *pua kumbu* (rugs handwoven by the Iban, RM20-180, depending on size), hanging tapestries, woven handbags, and elaborate beadwork and wood carvings by the Orang Ulu.

For upscale art, head to **Atelier Gallery** (☎243 492), designer Lucas Goh's über-stylish showroom at the east end of Jl. Bazaar. The **Sunday Market,** which actually starts on Saturday afternoon, is held on Jl. Satok on the outskirts of town. The best times to go are Saturday night and Sunday morning. (Open all night.) Across the river, **Fort Margherita,** named after Charles Brooke's wife, houses a **Police Museum.** (Open Tu-Su 10am-6pm.) Take local *sampans* (RM0.30) from the esplanade across the river and walk past the park to the road beyond. Turn right and head up the hill. At the gate, surrender your passport and pick up a pass. The **Chinese Museum,** along the esplanade opposite Tua Pek Kong Temple, traces the history of Sarawak's diverse Chinese community, which is comprised of over 8 dialect groups. (Open daily 9am-6pm.)

ENTERTAINMENT AND NIGHTLIFE

Kuching's bar culture is Borneo's best and rivals that of cities triple its size. With over 30 bars in the city center, visitors have no excuse to go to bed early. Many residents head to the **esplanade** along the Sarawak River in the evening to people-watch; bars and clubs don't get busy until 11pm. *Sampan* boats (RM20-25 per hr. day or night) provide a relaxing welcome to the city as they meander past *kampungs* (Malay villages), the gold-domed **Sikh Mosque,** and picturesque mountains.

Soho, 64 Jl. Padungan (☎247 069), 2 blocks west of Bing Cafe near the cat statue. Kuching's cosmopolitan set converges at this self-proclaimed "hip gastrobar," where live DJs pump downbeat jazz and chill-out music through the trendy red interior. Cocktails from RM15. Steamed mussels RM18; Spanish omelette RM12. On weeknights, turntables are swapped for staff members' iPods; bring yours along to join the party. Open Su-Th 4pm-1am, F-Sa 4pm-2am. Kitchen closes at midnight. AmEx/MC/V.

The Victoria Arms, Jl. Tun Abang Haji Openg (☎258 000), in the Merdeka Palace Hotel. Posh English pub featuring live bands each night and Kuching's most original cocktails (RM23), including the "Monkey Gland" and the "Hair of the Dog." Over 50 imported whiskeys. The adjacent wine cellar and lounge boasts Borneo's most extensive selection, including a 1967 bottle of California red at RM10,000. Free drinks for ladies W and F-Sa 7-8:30pm. Cover RM25 F-Sa. 2-for-1 happy hour daily 5-9pm. Open Su-Th 11am-2am, F-Sa 11am-3am. AmEx/MC/V.

Eagle's Nest, No. 19 and 20, ground fl., Jl. Bukit Mata (☎234 745), behind the Top Spot Food Court. Famed for its lively bar staff, scrumptious "bamboo chicken" and a variety of bottled wines (RM59-126). Excellent live bands play nightly from 9:30pm. 2-for-1 happy hour daily 4-9pm on house beers (RM6-8). Open M-Th 4pm-1am, F-Sa 4pm-2am. AmEx/MC/V.

Tribes, Jl. Tunku Abdul Rahman (☎423 111), outside the Holiday Inn. Lavish tribal decor and performances by some of Southeast Asia's hottest groups. Hearty "elephant ribs" (300g of grilled marinated beef) RM30. "Kremlin vodka" RM18.50. Drinks are 2-for-1 daily 7-10pm; if you arrive before 9, you'll have the place to yourself. Open M-Th 7pm-1am, F-Sa 7pm-2am. AmEx/MC/V.

Cat City, Block H, Taman Sri Sarawak (☎243 699), opposite the Hilton. Nocturnal pleasure-seekers fill the pub to capacity well past 3am; the surrounding area is packed with cheap late-night eateries and bars. Live bands complement the daily happy hour (beer RM6). Gay-friendly. Open Tu-Su 5pm-4am. AmEx/DC/MC/V.

DAYTRIPS FROM KUCHING

SARAWAK CULTURAL VILLAGE. This award-winning "living museum" claims you can "experience Sarawak in half a day." Spread over a spectacular 17-acre site in nearby Damai, the village highlights seven reconstructions of Bidayuh, Iban, Penan, Orang Ulu, Melanau, Malay, and Chinese dwellings. English-speaking actors and storytellers inhabit each reconstruction, interpreting traditional lifestyles while engaging in typical domestic activities. Each day ends with tribal dancing and singing in the village theater. A 5min. walk opposite the village and through the Holiday Inn leads to a pristine public beach. If you arrive in July, don't miss the spectacular **Rainforest World Music Festival,** Kuching's answer to Glastonbury and Ozzfest. Over 15,000 visitors converge at the Sarawak Cultural Village for three days of afternoon workshops and nightly outdoor performances from the *crème de la crème* in world music. At the Sunday evening finale, performers combine instruments as diverse as the Iraqi *oud* and Malian *kamele n'goni* in an all-out jam session, treating listeners to rare improvised fusion music. The RM50 day-pass includes access to all workshops and a 4hr. evening concert; 3-day passes for RM120 are also available. Biaramas runs a special shuttle for the event (tickets at the tourist office, RM10). For concert schedules and performers, check out the Festival's website (www.rainforestmusic-borneo.com).

PJ bus #2B departs from Jl. Khoo Hun Yeang for Damai and the Sarawak Cultural Village (45min., 6 per day 7:20am-7pm, RM2.70). For the return trip, PJ buses depart from the roundabout in front of the village entrance (6 per day 8:20am-7pm). When the buses stop running, catch a shuttle from the Holiday Inn at Damai to Kuching (5 per day 10am-9:30pm, RM10). It is advisable to purchase an all-inclusive day package from the Holiday Inn (RM60, children RM45). Buses depart from the hotel at 9am and return in the late afternoon. *(Village open daily 9am-5pm, dances 11:30am and 4:30pm. RM45, under 12 years RM22.50. For more information, check out www.sarawakculturalvillage.com.)*

SEMENGGOH WILDLIFE REHABILITATION CENTER. Sarawak's orphaned and injured animals find sanctuary at the Semenggoh Wildlife Rehabilitation Center. Here, specialists take care of orangutans, proboscis monkeys, and honey bears until they can survive on their own in the surrounding forest. Semi-wild orangutans halfway through rehabilitation are the main attraction. They return for daily meals at 9am and 3pm; park guests take visitors from the center on a short walk through the forest to reach the jungle feeding platform. Do not bring water bottles, and hold tight to your bags—mother orangs take delight in claiming "gifts" from unwitting guests. Arrive at least 30min. early. The morning feeding is best, as afternoon buses sometimes stop running at 3:30pm

STC bus #6 departs from the bus stop at the west end of the esplanade on Jl. Gambier (45min.; 7, 8:10, 10, 11, 11:30am, noon, 1:15, 2pm; RM1.50) and drops passengers off at the Forest Department nursery. From here it's a 30min. stroll to the feeding stations. Buses return from Semenggoh nursery at 7:55, 8:50, 11am, noon, 12:30, 2, and 4pm. RM3 park permit, available at the main entrance. *(Center open daily 8am-4:15pm.)*

MATANG WILDLIFE CENTER AND KUBAH NATIONAL PARK. Most orangutan rehabilitation actually takes place at Matang, Semenggoh's less touristed equivalent. Also housed on the grounds are hornbills, deer, crocodiles, sun bears and civet cats. Animal feedings offer prime observation. Most are fed daily at 8:30am and 3pm; the crocs eat Sundays at 2:30pm. Kubah, one of the state's smaller parks, contains excellent jungle trails suitable for daytrips. The best of these is the **Pitcher Trail,** named for the several species of carnivorous pitcher plants visible along the path (2hr., start near Park HQ). Accommodation is also available in a 10-bed Forest Lodge (RM150) or dorms (RM15). Camping RM5. Transport to Kubah from Kuching is via Matang Transport Co. bus #11, on Manlee Rd. opposite the Sikh Temple. There is no set bus schedule; check with the tourist office for departure and return times. To get to Matang, walk from the Park Office along the Ulu Rayu trail (3-4hr each way), or take a taxi for RM30-35—minivans sporadically ply the route, but you may be in for a wait (RM3). Alternatively, arrange a daytrip with a local tour company.

BAKO NATIONAL PARK. Within Bako's 2700 hectares, trails meander to cliff-lined beaches through almost every type of vegetation in Borneo—swamp forest, mangroves, and more. The park is home to 150 rare proboscis monkeys, active during early mornings and late evenings. Arrange accommodations well in advance for forest lodges with 2 rooms and 6 beds (RM150), double rooms (RM50), or dorms (RM18) from Kuching's Visitor's Information Center. Camping is also possible;

bring your own tent (RM5). All rooms and dorms have cooking facilities. The **park office,** where all visitors must purchase entrance permits (RM10, RM5 for students and seniors), is over the wooden pedestrian bridge, a 5min. walk from the boat drop-off. Obtain free maps of the park here. A **canteen** ❶ serves up basic meals (RM3-5) and sells snack food and drinks. (Open daily 8am-10pm.) There's a limited selection, so **bring your own rations.** Macaques will raid dustbins in rest houses and steal food and unguarded bags at the canteen. Famed for sightings of proboscis monkeys, the **Lintang Trail** (5.25km., 3½hr.) is great for a dayhike. **Telok Pandan Kecil** (2.5km. one way, 1½hr.) takes you to a breathtaking beach with views of Bako's renowned sea stacks.

PJ bus #6 departs from Jl. Khoo Hun Yeang (45min., every hr. 7am-6pm, RM2.50). Return buses follow the same schedule (8am-5pm), or charter a minivan for RM40 (seats 8). Take buses and taxis to Kampung Bako, and charter a boat (30min., RM40, 7 person max.) to park headquarters. Low tides may interfere with transport, so check before heading out.

LONGHOUSES. Several tour companies in downtown Kuching can arrange day and overnight trips to **local longhouses.** Freelance guides are often villagers themselves; travelers recommend **Abba** (ask for him at B&B Inn. RM350 for 3 day/2 night trip including transport, accommodations, and food). **Borneo Inbound Tours and Travel** (☎082 237 287), No. 98, 1st fl., Main Bazaar, offers a variety of trips including daytrips on the Lemanak River with a visit to an Iban longhouse (RM300), half-day trips to Land Dayak longhouses (RM130), and overnight trips (RM400-600). Homestays in Malay fishing villages can also be arranged.

SIBU ☎084

In the early 20th century, immigrants from southern China flooded into Sibu to escape persecution. Gradually they transformed this river town into Sarawak's second-largest city and an economic dynamo. Sibu's Chinese influence remains strong in two of the city's stunning attractions: the colorful seven-story pagoda and historic Tua Pek Kong Temple. Recent public works projects entice visitors en route to Kuching, Similajau, or Niah to spend a night—for a taste of the conveniences they thought they could do without. From chic designer boutiques to indigenous handicrafts sold along the palm tree-lined streets, Sibu has it all.

TRANSPORTATION. The **airport** (☎307 770) is 23km outside town. Take Bus #3A from Lanang Rd. (every 1½hr., 6:30am-6pm; RM2.50) or a taxi (RM25). MAS, 61 Jl. Tuanku Osman, has daily flights to: Bintulu (RM72); Kota Kinabalu (RM193); KL (RM335); Kuching (RM65); Miri (RM100); Sandakan (RM198). (☎326 166. Open M-F 8:30am-4:30pm, Sa 8:30am-12:30pm.) Buy tickets at the terminal. **Air Asia** flies to KL from Sibu (from RM79.99). Book online at www.airasia.com. The **Sungei Antu Express Bus Terminal** is on the outskirts of town. Take bus #2, 7, or 9 (all RM0.70) from the local bus station on Lanang Rd or a taxi for RM8. Buses run to Bintulu (3½hr., every hr. 6am-11:30pm, RM20); Kuching (6hr., 12 per day 6:30am-10pm, RM40); Miri (6½hr., every 2hr. 6am-11:30pm, RM40). **Express Bahagia boats** to Kuching depart from the wharf near the Chinese temple (4½hr., 11:30am, RM35-40). Boats to **Kapit** depart upriver, near the Sungei Antu Express Bus Terminal (3hr., 6am-2:30pm, RM20). Buy tickets on the boat.

PRACTICAL INFORMATION. The **Sarawak Visitor's Information Center,** 32 Jl. Tukang Besi, ground fl., is helpful and offers free maps and info on Belaga, Kapit, and Sibu. (☎340 980; vic-sibu@sarawaktourism.com. Open M-F 8am-4pm, Sa 8am-12:45pm.) **Sazhong Travel,** 4 Jl. Central, arranges air tickets and longhouse tours. A two-day tour for two to four people is RM275; a three-day tour runs from RM450. (☎336 017. Open M-F 8am-noon and 1:30-4:45pm, Sa 8am-noon and 1:30-4:15pm, Su 8:30am-noon. AmEx/MC/V.) The **Public Bank,** on Jl. Pulau in a tall white building close to the Chinese temple, cashes traveler's checks. (RM3.15 for the 1st, RM0.15 per additional check. Open M-F 9:30am-4pm, Sa 9:30am-12:30pm.) **Standard Chartered Bank** near the Visitor's Information Center has a 24hr. **ATM.** The **police,** (☎322 222), are on Jl. Kampung Nyabor near the post office. **Zhunian Pharmacy,** on the first floor of Wisma Sanyon, has English-speaking staff. (☎328 392. Open daily 9:30am-9pm.) **Lao King Howe Hospital,** (☎343 333), is at the west end of Jl. Pulau. To get there, take a taxi (RM10) or Sungei Merah bus #9 (6:30am-7:30pm, RM1.20). The **Telekom Office** is on Persiaran Brooke near the communications tower 200m from Jl. Kampung Nyabor. (☎329 292. Open M-F 8:30am-12:45pm and 2-4:45pm, Sa 8:30am-1pm.) **IDD phones** are along Jl. Tuanku Osman. There are several **Internet** cafes on the fourth floor of Wisma Sanyon, a tall white building at the west end of town. All cost 3RM per hr. and close at 10pm. The **post office** is on Jl. Kampung Nyabor. (☎337 700. *Poste Restante.* Closed first and third Saturday each month. Open M-Sa 8am-5pm.) **Postal Code:** 96000.

ACCOMMODATIONS. Most accommodations are scattered between Jl. Kampung Nyabor and Raman Way, near the post office and cineplex. **Hoover House ❷** is a faded white structure with blue trim on Jl. Pulau to the left of the Methodist church, near the Chinese temple. All rooms have A/C, hot water, and a private bath. (☎332 491. Dorms RM18; singles RM30; doubles RM35.) More comfortable rooms with A/C, TV, and private shower and bathtub are available at **Hotel Zuhra ❹** (☎310 711. Laundry service. Check-out 1pm. Singles and doubles RM64.) The **Sarawak Hotel ❸,** on Ramin Way near Jl. Wong Nai Siong just before the Sugarbun Restaurant, is all smiles. Rooms have A/C, TV, phones, and private baths. The taxi stand behind the hotel is an added bonus. (☎333 455. Singles RM40; doubles RM50.) For pure convenience, nothing beats the **River View Hotel ❸,** near the Lanang Rd. bus station and the wharf. Rooms all have A/C, private bath, and hot water. (☎325 241. Laundry service. Singles RM35; doubles RM40.)

FOOD. Chinese **kedai kopi ❶** (coffee shops) line Ramin Way, Jl. Wong Nai Siang, and Jl. Morshidi Sidek. Don't leave Sibu without sampling *foochow* noodles, served in a broth of soy and oyster sauce, with onions and shrimp. All *kedai kopi* serve them—ask for *kampua mee.* **Sin Yung Kiaw Cafe 98 ❶,** No. 5 Ramin Way, opposite Kee Supermarket, serves *kampua mee* for RM1.60. (Open daily 6am-10pm.) *Kong bian,* Sibu's version of a sesame bagel, is another *foochow* specialty. Pick up a freshly baked dozen at **Seng Kee Agencies** on Jl. Tinggi. **Hawker stalls ❶** line the first floor of the **SMC Market** on Jl. Channel. At the end of Jl. Market is the circular **SEDC Food Center ❶,** commonly known as "Bulatan Tanahmas," which serves *mee soto* (noodle soup with shredded chicken, RM2) and other *halal* Malay food. The **Pasar Malam** (night market) serves a smorgasbord of *satay,* cakes (about RM4), roast corn and steamed dumplings. **All The Best Vegetarian Restaurant ❶,** No. 39 Jl. Tuanku Osman, is on the left if you're coming from Jl. Kampong Nyabor walking toward the MAS Office. Their sweet and sour tofu (RM2.50) and fresh scallion pancakes (RM0.40 each) are not to be missed. (Open daily 6am-4pm and 6-10pm. Closed Th nights.)

SIGHTS. **Tua Pek Kong Temple and Seven-Story Pagoda** (Great Uncle's Temple), built in 1870, withstood the fire that swallowed Sibu in 1928, only to be destroyed during WWII bombing. The altar, however, somehow survived. Ask caretaker Tan Teck Chiang for the keys to climb the seven-story tower. The **Civic Center Museum** displays informative exhibits on historic Sibu (dubbed "New Foochow" during the influx of Chinese immigrants) and showcases Orang Ulu and Iban handicrafts. (Located off Jl. Suarah in the northeast part of town, past the federal government complex. Open daily 9am-4:30pm. Free.)

DAYTRIPS FROM SIBU: REJANG RIVER LONGHOUSES. Sibu is the starting point for all longhouse tours along the mighty Rejang River, which stretches to a mile wide at some points. This area is also home to Sarawak's largest Iban population. Most people arrange tours either in Sibu or Kapit, choosing from simple daytrips to strenuous week-long expeditions. Sazhong Travel (see **Practical Information,** p. 419) offers a large variety of trips and will custom-design itineraries; contact Frankie Ting two weeks in advance. For those attempting a visit on their own, Kapit is a good starting point. Hang out in the coffee shops and chat with locals for advice. Permits, available for free at the Resident's Office in Kapit, are required for travel beyond Kapit. The same is true for Belaga.

KAPIT ☎084

A frontier town along the mighty Rejang River, Kapit serves as a jumping-off point for the surrounding jungles and for Orang Ulu and Iban longhouses. Unfortunately, most of these longhouses have become modernized, and traditional dances are seen only on special holidays. Although the city itself offers little in terms of cultural enrichment, travelers with plenty of time, money, and a tolerance for leeches can venture upriver to the most remote reaches of Borneo.

TRANSPORTATION. From the jetty to the right (Wharf A), **Express Bahagia** sends **boats** downriver to Sibu (3hr., frequently 6am-3pm, RM20 and up). Sit on the roof of the boat to see longhouses along the way. Boats upriver depart from the jetty to the left (Wharf B). During the rainy season, **Balui Express** boats leave from Kapit and Sibu to Pelagus Rapids and Belaga (5-6hr., RM30); when the river is low, take a **speedboat** (2 daily before 11am, RM50-80). **Longboat** rentals run about RM200 per day and can be arranged from the farthest jetty, near Fort Sylvia.

ORIENTATION AND PRACTICAL INFORMATION. Kapit stretches south of the **Rejang River. Jl. Wharf** leads from the main jetty into the town center. The New Rejang Inn is a block down on the right. Another block up at the **Public Bank,** Jl. Wharf intersects the main road, **Jl. Teo Chow Beng.** The **town square** is on the right, bounded to the east by **Jl. Tan Sit Leong** and to the west by **Jl. Kapitan Chua Leong Kee. Jl. Tiong Ung Hong** runs past the square to the west. Farther along where Jl. Teo Chow Beng intersects **Jl. Temenggong Jugah** is the **post office** and the Meligai Hotel. **Jl. Airport** is past the roundabout beyond the hotel.

The **Resident's Office** is on the first floor of the State Government building. From Jl. Wharf, go past Hock Hua Bank, continue straight through a small playground and onto a road beside the Telekom. You can obtain free, mandatory permits for upriver travel to Balleh and Belaga; bring your passport. (☎796 963. Open M-Th 8am-12:45pm and 2-4:15pm, F 8-11:30am and 2:30-4:45pm, Sa 8am-12:45pm.) There is a **Public Bank,** at 63-64 Jl. Wharf , at the east end of Jl. Teo Chow Beng. They cash traveler's checks (RM2.15 for the 1st check, RM0.15 per additional; up to 5) and have a Cirrus/MC/PLUS/V **ATM.** (☎797 677. Open M-F (9:30am-4pm, Sa 9:30am-12:30pm.) The **day market** is on Jl. Teo Chow Beng, past the town square on the right. Stalls set up between Rejang Hotel and the river on Jl. Temenggong Jugah. The **night market** is on Jl. Penghulu Nyanggau, behind the post office. The **hospital** is at the east end of town on Jl. Hospital. (☎796 333. English spoken.) The **police** are past the lake and the turn-off for Jl. Hospital. (☎796 222, for **emergencies** dial 999.) Pick up basic necessities at **James Pharmacy,** 17 Jl. Tan Sit Leon. (☎798 382.

MASTIJAH MASLEH, ORGANIZER OF "PESTA MEOWW"

LG: What goes on during Pesta Meoww?
A: We have our live cats competition, and then we have our cat show... But then we also have human[s] dressed [as] cat[s]... and we have the [cat] imitation[s]. Everything.

LG: What kind of competition is for the live cat?
A: We have Siamese, local crossbreeds, all types... We have the best, fancy-dressed cat.

LG: They wear dresses?
A: It's up to the owner.

LG: Is there any costume that you remember very well?
A: Yes, a few. Some putting on gowns like Lady Diana. Or Queen Margaret. And then cowboy. There are all sorts of styles they have.

LG: Could you talk about the judging of the best-dressed cat?
A: It's up to the judge... Some of the cats, they are shy. And they don't like [clothes] put on them... But some cats are very good...

LG: So the cat has to be confident?
A: Yes. I think the owner has [to] train the cat.

LG: It's about more than looks?
A: Looks and personality itself.

LG: Is there a swimsuit competition?
A: Oh, I would like that, but so far we don't have that. I will suggest it later on.

English spoken. Open M-Sa 7:30am-6:30pm, Su 7:30am-noon.) You can make calls at **Telekom Kapit,** on a hill opposite resident's office. (☎796 991. Open M-F 8:30am-4:45pm, Sa 8:30am-1pm.) Access the **Internet** at **Lee Cyber Center,** Lot 65, 1st fl., No. 14 Jl. Tang Sit Leong, above the Wan Chew Market. (☎013 820 0891. RM3 per hr. Open daily 9am-11pm.) The **post office** is on Jl. Teo Chow Beng, west of the square. (☎796 332. Open M-F 8am-noon and 2-5pm, Sa 8am-noon. Closed the 1st and 3rd Sa of each month.) **Postal Code:** 96800.

ACCOMMODATIONS AND FOOD. Many budget hotels have degenerated into brothels, but you can still find some less seedy options. **Rejang Hotel ❷,** No. 28 Jl. Temenggong Jugah, near the morning market and opposite Hiap Chiong Hotel, has clean rooms with A/C and private bath. (☎796 709. Singles RM25; doubles RM30.) Facing Jl. Wharf at No. 104 Jl. Teo Chow Beng, **New Rejang Inn ❹** has spotless rooms with A/C, phone, and mini-fridge. (☎796 600. Laundry. Singles and doubles RM45.) **Hotel Meligai ❹,** at the western end of Jl. Teo Chow Beng near Malayan Bank, past the post office, oozes refinement. Look for the "Meligai Kapit" sign. All rooms have A/C, TV, phones, and carpeting. (☎796 611. Laundry. Singles RM70; doubles RM80.) **Greenland Inn ❹,** Lot 463-464 Jl. Teo Chow Bang, above the Sugarbun Restaurant facing the Town Square, has rooms with hot water, A/C, TV, fridge, and complimentary coffee. (☎796 3888. Singles RM65; doubles RM75.) For the cheapest eats in town, try the **food court** at the end of Jl. Tiong Ung Hong, one block uphill from the **hawker stalls** by the day market on Jl. Teo Chow Beng; look for the "Gelanggang Kenyalang" sign. (Open until 6pm.) A **night market** serving *halal* Malay staples sets up by the post office. Local cuisine includes *babi hutan* (wild boar) and *rusa.* (Open 7pm-midnight.) **Foodstalls** line the Town Square side of Jl. Koh; in the evenings, stop here for chicken wings (RM1) or *satay* skewers. (Open until 9pm.) **Siong Seng Coffee Shop ❷,** No. 23 Jl. Teo Chow Beng, opposite the town square, has excellent Chinese coffee (RM1) and *kampua mee* for RM2. *Pau ayam* (chicken steam bun) RM1.20. (☎796 687. Open daily 8:30am-5pm.) **99 Seafood Cafe ❶,** uphill behind Hotel Meligai and the post office, is one of the few restaurants open all afternoon and evening. (☎797 321. *Nasi udong,* shrimp rice; RM2.50. Selection of teas. Open daily 1pm-midnight.)

SIGHTS AND ENTERTAINMENT. **Fort Sylvia** was built in 1880 as a demonstration of the government's intent to end intertribal hostilities and head-hunting. The **museum,** within the Civic Center on the east edge of town, displays local handicrafts, ethnic arts, and watercolors depicting life along the Rejang. (Open M-F 9am-12:45pm and 2-4:15pm, Sa 9am-12:45pm.) Evening entertainment varies from karaoke clubs and snooker halls to the more insidious brothels staffed by Indonesian immigrants. The **Fullmoon Music Cafe** is a lively pub where locals gather for beer (RM6) and live music. (☎797 818. Jl. Penghulu Nyangau, behind the post office. Open daily 5pm-2am.) If you hear loud drumming near Rejang Inn, children may be practicing Lion Dancing at the Chinese Temple.

DAYTRIPS FROM KAPIT: LONGHOUSES. Home to an entire Malay community, longhouses are built from ironwood and bamboo and are raised off the ground for safety and to take advantage of cooling drafts. Each family occupies a separate apartment, called a *bilik;* the outside verandah, or *ruai,* is used for communal gatherings and to house male visitors (females are permitted to stay inside with the family). A *tuai rumah* (headman) presides over the longhouse community and enforces strict rules to maintain harmony. In the past, a visit to east Malaysia was not complete without a trip to a longhouse. Guests who brought news to the isolated longhouses were welcomed with raucous parties. As these communities became more affluent, they built sturdier tin-roofed cement structures—much to the dismay of tourists. Longhouse dwellers started to resent the well-to-do foreign travelers who showed up on their doorstep expecting to be feted like a Rajah in exchange for cigarettes. Needless to say, remoter areas have more traditional longhouses and less cynical residents.

TIP **PASS THE POTATOES, PLEASE.** Don't throw your manners out the window at a longhouse. The Orang Ulu will warm up to visitors once they are comfortable. *Let's Go* offers some basic dos and don'ts for your visit:

1. Wait for an invitation to enter a longhouse.
2. Take off your shoes before entering.
3. Dress modestly. When bathing, men should wear their underwear and women should wear a sarong.
4. At meals, be sure to sample any food that is offered. Evenings sometimes culminate in a small celebration with *tuak,* a traditional rice wine (take at least a small sip), and plenty of dancing and music. Visitors are expected to join in the fun, and your hosts will love it if you participate wholeheartedly, even if it means making a fool of yourself.
5. Gifts are appreciated. Bring pencils and crayons for children, and practical clothing, like shirts or hats, and luxuries, like foreign cigarettes, for adults. Avoid giving sweets and alcohol. It's also nice to bring some pictures of your family, postcards, coins, stamps, or a book about your home country. For instant and enduring fame, bring a Polaroid camera and lots of spare film.
6. Overall, basic courtesy is the rule: don't enter any rooms, touch anything, or take pictures of anyone without first quietly asking permission.

Those looking for a traditional longhouse stay should try **Bareo** in eastern Sarawak (accessible from Miri) or **Belaga** farther upriver from Kapit. For those short on time, less remote longhouse stays can be arranged through tour guides in Kuching and Kapit. Before you go, confirm the price, mode of transportation, and name and location of the longhouse to assure safety. Most trips include full board, lodging, and transport. **Mr. Tan Teck Chuan** at Kapit Adventure Tours, 11 Jl. Tan Sit Leong, on the western edge of the town square, is one of the area's most reputable guides. (☎796 352. P.O. Box 16, 96807 Kapit, Sarawak, Malaysia. 1-day trip to Iban longhouse RM400 per person, 2-day RM650 per person. 2-person min.) For extensive treks into the extreme hinterlands, Chuan requests one to two months' advance notice. **Mr. Joshua M. G.,** at Regang Travel and Tours, is another experienced guide who offers daytrips (RM320) and longer treks. (☎796 600. New Regang Inn, 104 Teo Chow Beng Road, 96807 Kapit, Sarawak, Malaysia.) The best time to visit longhouses is in early June during the **Dayak Gawai** (harvest festival) celebrations that begin on June 1, but the best weather is from July to September. Bring a plastic bag for cameras, raingear, toilet paper, flashlight, sunscreen, mosquito repellent, aspirin, and basic toiletries. **Permits** from the Resident's Office are required for journeys upriver from Kapit. Most guides can help you obtain one.

BINTULU ☎086

Bintulu was once listed by the *Guinness Book of World Records* as the closest city in the world to an airport—the runway cut through the middle of town. Alas, Bintulu's one claim to fame was demolished in May 2003, when a RM350,000,000 airport was opened 20km outside of the city. Beyond its convenient location halfway between Kuching and Kota Kinabalu, Bintulu offers little of interest. Still, for those awaiting connections to the sands of Similajau National Park or other alluring destinations, attractions do exist to help pass the time.

TRANSPORTATION

Flights: Airport (☎331 958), 20km southwest of the city. **MAS** (☎332 898), 129 Taman Sri Dagang. Open M-F 8:30am-4:30pm, Sa 8:30am-1pm. AmEx/MC/V. Flies daily to: **Kota Kinabalu** (RM152); **Kuching** (RM137); **Miri** (RM74); **Sibu** (RM82).

Buses: Medan Jaya Bus Terminal, on the outskirts of town. Accessible by local bus (RM0.80) or taxi (RM8) from downtown. **Syarikat Bus Suria** operates to: **Batu Niah** (2½hr., 7 per day 7am-3pm, RM10) and **Miri** (3½hr.; 7:30, 10:30am, noon, 1:30, 3, 6pm; RM18). **Biaramas Express** traverses the Pan-Borneo expressway to **Kuching** (6, 10:30am, 3, 5:30pm; RM52) via **Sarikei** (RM24). For **Sibu,** take Syarikat Bas Express (3½hr; noon, 1:30, 6pm; RM18). Obtain a detailed schedule of local and long distance bus routes from the tourist office.

Boats: Express boats leave from the waterfront daily at 8am and 1pm to **Binyo** (RM18), and at 7, 9, 10:30am, noon, and 1pm to: **Labang** (RM12); **Pandan** (RM9); **Sebauh** (RM8); **Tubau** (RM18).

Local Transportation: The local **bus terminal** is next to the markets on Jl. Main Bazaar/ Masjid. Buses shuttle to **Medan Jaya Bus Terminal** (20min., every 15min. 6:15am-10:15pm, RM0.80). **Taxis** congregate opposite the station and charge high fares. To **Medan Jaya** (RM8) and **Similajau National Park** (RM40).

ORIENTATION AND PRACTICAL INFORMATION

Bintulu has two parallel main streets: **Jl. Abang Galau,** which becomes **Jl. Keppel,** and **Jl. Masjid,** which becomes **Jl. Main Bazaar.** The markets, taxi station, and bus terminal are clustered around the center of **Jl. Masjid.** Beaches and parks line **Jl. Tanjung Batu,** accessible by taxi (RM10), in the city's west end.

Tourist Offices: Visitor's Information Center, 1 Jl. Tanjung Kidurong (☎332 011), on the ground fl. of the **Bintulu Development Authority,** a white, cone-shaped building. Open M-F 8am-12:30pm and 2-5pm, Sa 8am-12:45pm. Assists with bookings for Similajau and Niah National Parks.

Currency Exchange: Public Bank, 29-32 Jl. Sommerville (☎337 751). Cashes traveler's checks (RM1.15 for the 1st, RM0.15 per additional check). Open M-F 9am-3:30pm, Sa 9:30-11:30am. **Standard Chartered Bank,** on Jl. Keppel, down the street from the Capital Hotel, has a 24hr. **ATM** (Cirrus).

Markets: The twin cones of the **day market** (Pasar Utama and Pasar Taru) reach skyward along Jl. Main Bazaar. The **night market** (Pasar Malam) lights up at the end of Jl. Pedada.

Emergency: ☎994.

Police: (☎311 121), on Jl. Tun Razak.

Pharmacies: L.T. Ling Pharmacy, 61 Medang Sebadoh (☎335 773), near the Plaza Hotel. Open M-Sa 8:30am-9pm, Su 8:30am-1pm.

Medical Services: Bintulu Regional Hospital (☎225 899), on the outskirts of town at the northern end of Jl. Bukit Nyabau. English-speaking staff. 24hr. emergency care.

Telephones: Telekom office (☎319 292), on Jl. Law Gek Soon, north of the intersection with Jl. Keppel. International phone/fax. Open M-Th 8:30am-12:30pm and 2-4:15pm, F 8:30-11:30am and 2:15-4:15pm, Sa 8:30am-noon.

Post Offices: GPO (☎332 375), on Jl. Tun Razak, opposite the airport. *Poste Restante.* Open M-F 8am-4pm, Sa 8am-3pm. A reliable **courier service** (☎339 164), on Jl. Sommerville opposite Hock Hua Bank, offers good rates. Open M-F 8am-5pm, Sa 8am-1pm. Also, a **branch** is in the Medan Jaya Bus Terminal.

Postal Code: 97000.

ACCOMMODATIONS AND FOOD

Summer Inn ❸, 1st fl., 19 New Commercial Centre, behind the Plaza Hotel, has snug and spotless rooms with A/C, TV, private shower, and free bottled water. (☎331 223. All rooms RM42.) Facing the Chinese temple, at 78 Jl. Keppel, **Kemena Inn ❹** is worth the extra ringgit. The large rooms have fancy showers, carpeting, and A/C. (☎331 533. Singles RM60; doubles RM65.) **City Inn ❸,** 150 Jl. Aban Galau near the Plaza Hotel, has clean A/C rooms with TV in a central location. (☎337 711. All rooms RM43.) **Night markets** at the local bus terminal and at the former long-distance bus terminal east of Jl. Sommerville, beside the old airport runway, offer an excellent selection of *satay,* grilled fish, and fruit. (Open daily 7-10pm.) An alley near the Plaza Hotel and the mini post office at the eastern end of town hosts a variety of open-air restaurants. Most popular is **Famous Mama Cafe ❶,** serving up a delicious array of meat and veggie selections, *bacadile* (veggie potato puff; RM2), freshly made *roti canai* (RM0.80), and *nasi campur* (RM2.50). **Sea View Restaurant ❶,** next to the Riverfront Inn on the east edge of the waterfront, serves fried rice and various *nasi* (noodle) dishes for RM2.50. (Open daily 6am-10pm.) **Honey Bakery ❶,** 63 Medan Sepadu, on Jl. Abang Galau, has rows of appetizing savory and sweet pastries, including the chicken curry puff (RM0.90) and deep caramel-colored honey cake for RM1. (Open daily 7:30am-10pm.)

SIGHTS

The only zoological and botanical park in Sarawak, **Taman Tubina Bintulu** describes itself as an "animal garden." Lions, macaques, and hornbills (Malaysia's state bird) reside among the 57 hectares of unique flora and fauna, including the Borneo Giant Orchid, peacocks, crocodiles, and pythons. Borneo's only tigers are also found here. (1 Jl. Tanjung Kidurong. ☎337 709. Open daily 8am-6pm. RM2, children RM0.50.) Down the road, the modest but scenic **Tanjung Batu Beach** is lined with impressive children's playgrounds, gazebos, and foodstalls. Described as a "retrospective walk down memory lane," the **clocktower** on Jl. Abang Galau was the site of Sarawak's first state legislature, convened by Charles Brooke, the second white Rajah of Sarawak.

SIMILAJAU NATIONAL PARK

Some of Sarawak's finest beaches are 30 min. northeast of sleepy Bintulu, nestled in Similajau National Park. Only 1.5km wide, the park encompasses 30km of sand and coastal cliffs, inlaid with exotic fauna like the pitcher plant, a carnivorous flower known as "The Assassin of the Plant World." The 9km of trails that snake through coastal forest lead to the fine sands of Turtle and Golden Beaches where turtles can be seen mating. Over 185 bird species nest in the park's lush jungles. Boats to the Kolam Sebubong pool drift through emerald water. Eager for some privacy? If you arrive during the week, you may have the entire park to yourself.

To reach park headquarters, contact **Mr. Syaidi,** who runs the park's canteen (☎010 884 18 88) and picks up guests in Bintulu for RM20. If you can't reach him, take a **taxi** from Bintulu (30min., RM40), and arrange a ride back with Mr. Syaidi (RM20). **Bus** #1322 leaves from the local bus station for Similajau (RM20); from here, it's a 1hr. (4km) walk to the park. Also negotiable is a chartered **minivan** from the park canteen to **Niah Caves** (around RM150, seats six). The **park office** (☎391 284) is down a path from the parking lot and to the right. Drop by to pick up brochures, maps, and **permits** for park entrance (RM10, students and seniors RM5, cameras RM5, video recorders RM10). The office assigns rooms and arranges transport to the mouth of **Sungai Sebubong** for trekking to **Koam Sebubong Pool.** Next door to the park office is a **Visitor Center** with a fine collection of photographs of the area's wildlife. A ranger is usually on duty, but try to arrive during office hours. (Open Sa-Th 8am-12:45pm and 2-4:15pm, F 8-11:30am and 2:30-4:45pm.)

Reserve accommodations at the Visitor's Information Center in Miri (☎085 434 184). The park has two identical **hostels ❶,** each with communal toilets, fans, and showers. Each room sleeps four in bunk beds with sheets, blankets, and storage cubbies (RM15.75; RM42 per room). Closer to park headquarters are three A/C **chalets ❹,** each with two 4-person rooms (RM105 per room; RM157.50 for the entire 8-bed chalet). Shaded **camping ❶** areas are nearby (RM5 per person). A simple open-air **canteen ❶** offers staples like snacks, bottled water (RM5), fried rice (RM3), and welcome extravagances like chocolate-dipped ice cream bars (RM1-4). Dinner consists of a set menu of fresh fish and vegetable stir-fries (RM10-15). For an extended stay, it's wise to bring your own supplies. (Opens daily at 8am; usually closes at 6pm.) For a late afternoon trek, notify the canteen of your destination to ensure an evening meal.

Many visitors are content to romp in the surf and loll on the sand near the park's accommodations. Farther afield are more secluded beaches accessible only by marked forest paths. Treks range in length and difficulty. A good full-day hike goes from the park office to **Setensur Rapids** (15km, 8hr. round-trip). The trail passes through beaches and dipterocarp forests. **Turtle Beach** is an 8km hike from headquarters (permit required). If you're lucky, you might spot a green turtle laying its eggs on the shore. **Kolam Sebubong** is an isolated pool on the upper reaches of the Sebubong River. Arrange with the park office to hire a boat for the day (RM175). Similajau has **saltwater crocodiles.** These ferocious beasts are hard to spot and attack with lightning speed. Do not wade across larger streams. Use boat transfers wherever possible. Safer **coastal cruises** can be arranged through the park office.

LAMBIR HILLS NATIONAL PARK

For weary city-dwellers and visitors to Miri, the pristine waterfalls of Lambir Hills are a welcome refreshment. The park boasts some of Borneo's finest scenery nestled in a mixed dipterocarp forest. All sights are scattered along one well-maintained (and relatively leech-free) trail originating at park headquarters; signposts mark the turn-offs. Kiss your masseur good-bye and ease tired limbs under the **Paku Waterfalls**—Lambir's most idyllic—in a moss-covered granite alcove 2km from the start of the trail. Bring swimwear if you plan to enjoy the clear pool below the falls; Malaysian officials have fined foreigners for public nudity. At only 30km from Miri proper, Lambir can easily be covered as a daytrip. Syarikat Bus Suria public **buses** depart from the main station on Jl. Padang opposite the Visitor's Information Center (40min.; 6:30, 9, 10am, noon, 3, 4pm; RM3). Exit at the sign-posted park entrance in Lambir. Alternatively, charter a **taxi** from town (30min.; RM40). Lodgings at the park are limited to fan-cooled double rooms (RM50-75) or chalets with three beds and A/C (RM100-150). Camping is also permitted on a small grassy patch near the headquarters (RM5 per person). A modest **canteen** sells baked goods, rice, and noodle dishes (RM3-10). Book accommodations in advance at the Visitor's Information Center in Miri (☎085 434 184).

NIAH NATIONAL PARK

It's a bird! It's a plane! No, it's a flying lizard. These and other air-borne creatures inhabit the extensive cave system of Niah National Park. Some visitors to these caves take away more than just photographs—licensed harvesters and illegal poachers shimmy up rickety, 30m long bamboo poles to gather highly prized swiftlet nests, which can fetch up to RM1200 per kilogram in Chinese soup markets. Archaeologists have garnered more morbid treasures: Iron Age coffins and 40,000 year-old intact skulls were discovered in the Great Cave in1958. Faint markings on the walls of the Painted Cave date back to AD 1 and depict the voyage of the dead into the afterlife. Niah is a spectacle not to be missed.

Batu Niah is the gateway to Niah Park. Buses from Miri and Bintulu deposit passengers near the town jetty on the Niah River. The park is a 10min. **longboat** ride downriver (RM10 for 1-5 people, RM2 per person for more than 5) or a 2km **taxi** ride (RM10). Returning to Batu Niah is possible by boat or taxi or via a shaded concrete path along the river. **Buses** depart from Batu Niah square for Bintulu (2hr., 6 per day 6am-4pm, RM10) and Miri (2hr., every hr. 6:30am-3:30pm, RM10). Buy tickets on board. Taxis make the trip 30min. shorter (RM60 from Miri or Bintulu). The **Park Reception Area** is a few hundred feet from the river's edge. If you don't have a reservation, pay the park entrance fee, and arrange accommodations here. (☎085 737 454. Entrance fee RM10, students and seniors RM5, cameras RM5, video RM10. Open Su-Th 8am-12:30pm and 2-4:30pm, F 8-11:30am and 2:30-4:45pm, Sa 8am-12:45pm.)

The park **hostel's** ❶ wood-paneled rooms and modern baths are a bonus for those who visit Niah. Each fan-cooled dorm has four beds and a bath with hot water. If visitors are scarce, ask for a room to yourself. (Dorms RM15.75, or RM42 for the entire room; 8-person chalets RM157.50.) A cheap **restaurant** ❶ on the park grounds has fried rice or noodles for RM4. (Open daily 8am-9pm.) The park has no minimart, so purchase snacks in Batu Niah.

A boat ride across the river ends at the start of the trail to **Niah Caves** (RM0.50, after 6pm RM1). Be sure to bring a flashlight, as the caves are unlit. Rent flashlights from the **museum** immediately on your right, which houses artifacts excavated from the caves. (Open daily 10am-5pm.) It's a pleasant 45min. walk from the museum through cool forest air to the caves. The sometimes slippery plank walk doesn't require a guide (RM35). The trail leads through the **Traders Cave** before arriving at the 60m by 250m mouth of the **Great Cave.** Here, in 1958, Tom Harrison and his staff from the Sarawak Museum unearthed a 40,000-year-old human skull. Excavations along the cave's left flank uncovered stone tools and other human relics. Next, the trail crosses the **Cave of Bones** and **Beunt Cave,** where bamboo poles are positioned by bird's nest collectors, and eventually leads to **Moon Cave.** It's impossible to proceed beyond this point without a flashlight, but fear not—a brief walk through the caverns leads visitors back to sunlight. The fern-covered plank walk continues to the **Painted Cave,** which originally contained coffins. The relics have since been removed for conservation, but faded paintings are faintly visible behind a locked gate. At dusk, nocturnal bats swoop out of their cave while sun-loving swiftlets return to the cave for sleep. Position yourself at the mouth of the cave to witness this dizzying aerial traffic jam. **Iban longhouses** are a 30min. walk from the main plank walk; turn left at the marked sign. Though the longhouses are not as traditional as some, the Iban, especially the English-speaking schoolchildren, still welcome visitors with traditional Dayak hospitality.

MIRI ☎085

Built by oil companies, Miri's bustling streets display new signs of wealth (the Mega Hotel prominent among them) but even they are soon to be eclipsed by bigger, glitzier projects. But Miri is more than the booming center of Sarawak's oil industry. As a gateway to Niah National Park, Lambir Hills Rainforest, and Gunung Mulu National Park, Miri offers the wilderness-bound a final chance to enjoy some creature comforts before descending into more remote, less comfortable terrain.

TRANSPORTATION

Flights: Airport (☎615 433), west of the city limits. Taxis (RM17; purchase a coupon at the desk near the arrivals area) and infrequent public buses run into town. **MAS office** (☎414 144), on the corner of Jl. Yu Seng. Open M-F 8:30am-4:30pm, Sa 8:30am-12:30pm. To: **Gunung Mulu National Park** (2 per day, RM80); **Kota Kinabalu** (5 per day 9:25am-9:10pm, RM115); **Kuching** (5 per day 8:40am-9:30pm, RM175); **Sandakan** (2 per day, RM163); **Sibu** (3-4 per day, RM123). **Royal Brunei Airlines,** ground fl., Lot 263, Jl. South Yu Seng (☎426 322). Open M-F 8:30am-noon and 1-5:30pm, Sa 8:30am-12:30pm. Budget-friendly **AirAsia** (www.airasia.com) fliers daily to Kuala Lumpur (from RM80); book in advance for the lowest fares.

Buses: Pujut Padang Kerbau Long Distance Bus Station, several kilometers outside of downtown Miri. The #33 Shuttle Bus (every 20min., RM1.20) takes you to the local **bus terminal** in town, opposite the Visitor's Information Center on Jl. Padang. Pick up a helpful bus schedule from the Center upon arrival. **SYKT Express** (☎439 325) and **Rejang Express** (☎435 336) are neighbors on Jl. Malay; **P.B. Express** and **Biaramas Express** are at the bus terminal. All go to **Bintulu** (3½hr., every hr. 6am-6pm, RM25). Frequent buses run to **Kuching** (RM86) and **Sibu** (RM43). **Miri-Belait Transport Co.** (☎419 129) sends buses to **Kuala Belait,** over the Brunei border (daily 7, 9, 10:30am, 1, 3:30pm; RM20). Bus changes at the border, so take all belongings off when getting your passport stamped, and hold onto your ticket. At Kuala Belait, board a purple bus outside the immigration building and continue onward to **Seria** (B$1.80). Switch to a bus bound for **Bandar Seri Begawan** there (B$1.80). Buses in Seria stop running at 3:20pm, so leave Miri before 10:30am to avoid getting stuck in Seria for the night. A more convenient option is to book a seat on a charter minivan through the Visitor's Information Center or Tropical Adventure (p. 429) The trip to Bandar takes 3hr. and includes door-to-door service (4 per day, RM50).

Local Transportation: local bus station, behind Wisma Pelita on Jl. Padang. Green and yellow Miri Transport Co. buses #30 and 28 go to the **airport** (every hr. 5:55am-7:10pm, RM1.50). **Taxis** (☎432 277) meet at the bus station and in front of the Fairland Inn. Syarikat Bus Suria departs for **Batu Niah and Lambir** (2hr.; 6:30, 9, 10am, noon, 3, 4pm; RM3 to Lambir; RM8.50 to Batu). Blue and red Miri City buses run to **Taman Selera** (#11 and 13: 5min. every 15min. 6:30am-9pm, RM10.80). All depart from bus stops across Jl. Padang, opposite the Visitor's Information Center.

ORIENTATION AND PRACTICAL INFORMATION

The heart of the old town lies adjacent to the towering **Wisma Pelita Tunku** complex. On the southern side of the complex lie the **bus station** and **Visitor's Information Center.** Most of Miri's streets are bounded by **Jl. Kingsway,** running northeast away from Wisma Pelita, and **Jl. Bendahara,** several blocks west along the edge of the **Miri River.** Jl. Bendahara leads to the bulky blue and white Mega Hotel. Opposite the hotel, which is now the center of the city, **Jl. Yu Seng** heads north past the **Imperial Mall Shopping Center** and the gold-domed **mosque,** where Jl. Yu Seng morphs into **Jl. Datuk Merpati. Jl. Miri Pujut** at the south end of Miri leads to the spectacular **Boulevard Shopping Center.**

Tourist Offices: Visitor's Information Center, Lot 452, Jl. Melayu (☎434 181; vicmiri@sarawaktourism.com). From Wisma Pelita, walk through the bus terminal; it's a white building in a park to the right. Staff provides maps, bus schedules and brochures. Reserve accommodations in Lambir, Niah, and Gunung Mulu Parks here. Open M-F 8am-5pm, Sa 8am-12:50pm. Closed holidays.

Tours and Travel: Transworld Travel Services, 2nd fl., Wisma Pelita Tunku Complex (☎422 277), offers similar packages. Open M-F 8:30am-5pm, Sa 8:30am-4:30pm. AmEx/MC/V. **Tropical Adventure** (☎419 337; www.tropicaladventuremart.com), in the shopping complex adjacent to the Mega Hotel, organizes treks and transport. Cash preferred. Open M-F 8:30am-5pm, Sa-Su 8:30am-1pm.

Currency Exchange: Bank Bumiputra (☎420 371), past Mega Hotel on Jl. Indica, off Jl. Bendahara. RM2.15 per check. 24hr. **ATM** (Cirrus/MC/V). Open M-F 9:30am-4pm, Sa 9:30am-noon. **Bank Utama** (☎411 882) is the futuristic building on Jl. Nahoda Gampar. Open M-F 9:30am-3:30pm, Sa 9:30-11:30am. Several licensed moneychangers operate around the Fairland Inn, behind J. Kingsway. Open M-Sa 9am-7pm.

Police: (☎433 222, ext. 204). On the corner of Jl. Kingsway and Jl. Chia Tze Chi.

Pharmacies: Guardian Farmasi, ground fl., Bintang Plaza, on the corner of Jl. Merbau and Jl. Min Pujut. Well-stocked prescription counter. Open daily 10am-10pm.

Medical Services: Hospital Umum Miri (☎420 033), on Jl. Cahaya-Lopeng, south of the city on the road to Bintulu. English spoken. 24hr.

Telephones: Telekom Office (☎421 010), next to the post office on Jl. Post, near the rear of the Imperial Mall. Open M-Th 8:30am-12:45pm and 2-4:15pm, F 8:30-11:45am and 2:30-4:15pm, Sa 8:30am-12:30pm. **IDD phones** opposite Wisma Pelita, on Jl. Padang.

Internet Access: Cyber Corner, 1st fl. Wisma Pelita. RM4 per hr. Open daily 9am-6pm. **Public library** (☎424 984) at Dewan Suarah also has access. Take Jl. Yu Seng-Datuk Merpati north and turn right on Jl. Persekutuan before the gold-domed mosque. Follow the street until it ends; the library is the glass and concrete creation. 10 terminals; free 30min. usage. Open Tu-F 9am-8pm, Sa 8am-8pm, Su 9am-3pm; closed holidays.

Post Office: ☎432 887. On Jl. Sylvia on the eastern edge of town. *Poste Restante.* Open M-F 8am-noon and 2-4pm, Sa 8am-noon. Closed 1st and 3rd Sa. A branch is also located on the 3rd fl. of the Boulevard Shopping Center.

Postal Code: 98000.

ACCOMMODATIONS

Brooke Inn, 14 Brooke Road (☎412 881; brookeinn@hotmail.com). Walking away from the Miri Central Market past Yulan Plaza along Jl. Kingsway, it's on the right. Impeccable service, newly carpeted rooms with hot water, A/C, TV, and free storage. Singles RM40; doubles RM45; family rooms RM50. ❹

Muhibba Inn, Lot 548, Jl. South Yu Seng (☎412 003), above Sin Mui Pin Restaurant. Gate locks at 1am, but someone is always on duty. Central location and clean, spartan rooms. Singles and doubles with private bath, A/C, and TV RM40. ❹

Tai Tong Lodging House, 26 Jl. Cina, 1st fl., (☎411 498), opposite the Chinese temple. Exhibitionists will love the lack of privacy; the main entrance is through the dorms. Pretty clean. Midnight lockout. Dorms (men-only) RM12; singles/doubles with shared bath RM28/32; doubles with A/C RM36, with private bath RM45. ❸

Fairland Inn, 21 Jl. Kingsway, 1st fl., (☎413 981). From Wisma Pelita, it's across Jl. Kingsway, down Jl. Anatto, above Sunmay Refreshment Center on left corner. Lockout 10pm. Singles/doubles with bath and hot water RM25, with A/C RM30. ❷

FOOD

North Indian eateries line the covered promenades of the aptly named **Beautiful Jade Center** on either side of **Jl. Nahkoda Gampar.** In the evenings, several excellent seafood restaurants along Jl. North Yu Seng beyond the Mega Hotel fry up the day's catch for RM5 and up. Nearby street vendors serve hot sandwiches and skewers of red chicken rump (fatty and best avoided). A few kilometers south of town, **Taman Selera** offers a wide range of outdoor restaurants and foodstalls to suit any taste.

Bilal Restaurant (☎420 105), near Mega Hotel on Persiaran Kabor. Savory Indian cuisine. English-language menu. Tandoori chicken (RM7). 4-piece kebab RM5. South Indian *dosai* (thin, savory rice-flour pancakes with various fillings) RM2-3. Tender *rogani naan* RM2. *Lassi* RM2.50. Open daily 6am-9pm. ❷

Michael Unlimited B.B.Q. Steamboat, Lot 2406, Boulevard Commercial Centre, Jl. Miri Pujut (☎436 608). Choose seafood, vegetables, or noodles from an all-you-can-eat buffet, and cook them in a steamboat (RM20 per person). Open daily 5:30-11pm. ❹

Hengyap Noodle Factory (☎412 977), on Jl. N. Yu Seng, near Standard Chartered Bank. Look for the yellow "vegetarian" sign. Vegetarian buffet with Chinese specialties. Vegetable *mee* RM2.50. Huge egg rolls RM1.50. Selection of Chinese teas RM2. Open daily 8am-10pm. ❶

Yi-Hah-Hai Seafood (☎413 883), on Miri Waterfront off Jl. Bendahara. Turn left after Bank Bumiputra; look for red tablecloths and orange chairs. Worth the extra ringgit. Exquisite *makan laut* (seafood) RM10-15. Open daily 9:15am-1:30am. ❸

ENTERTAINMENT AND NIGHTLIFE

When the heat becomes too much, locals rush to the **public swimming pool** on Jl. Kipas. (☎411 412. RM1 for adults, children under 12 RM0.50. Open M-F 9am-9pm, Sa-Su 9am-7:30pm.) The Righa and Holiday Inn hotels in Taman Selera open their fancier, less crowded pools to the public on Sundays. Take Bus#11 or 13 from the main bus station. In the evenings, stop here for a cheap dinner from the foodstalls and a stroll along the beach. Before partaking in Miri's vibrant nightlife, visitors can walk along Jl. Melayu to a roundabout, where a right turn leads to the free ferry across the Miri River. Follow the road 100m to **Long Jetty**—a perfect spot to catch Miri's pastel sunsets.

Karaoke-crazed locals head to the **bowling alley** (RM5 per game; open daily 9am-1am) on the fourth floor of Bintang Plaza, while others enjoy the **gaming arcade** or **movie theater** next door (RM8; shows every 2hr. 12:30-11pm). Miri's hip converge at **Cheerie Berries,** past the Bintang Plaza Shopping Center on Jl. Miri Pujit, for nightly live music. (Happy hour daily 9-11pm, buy one, get one free. Beer RM8.) The Rihga Royal Hotel's **Rigs Fun Pub,** before Taman Selera on the right, hosts more dancing fun. (☎412 128. No shorts or flip-flops. Beer RM15 M-Th. Cover RM20. Open M-Sa 9pm-1:30am.) Several bars also dot **Jl. Mebau.**

GUNUNG MULU NATIONAL PARK

As Sarawak's largest park, Mulu encompasses 544km² of peat swamp, heath, dipterocarp forest, moss thickets, and mountain vegetation. Over 3500 plant species—including 170 species of wild orchids and 10 varieties of carnivorous pitcher plants—and 20,000 animal species have been documented within the park. Treks include a three-day hike to the razor-sharp limestone pinnacles on the slopes of Gunung Api and a four-day ascent of Gunung Mulu. Perhaps most impressive, some 500km of mostly undiscovered caves lurk underground, including the world's largest cave passage, the Sarawak Chamber, which could house 18 Boeing 747s and then some. Recognized as a UNESCO World Heritage Site, Mulu is Borneo's biggest draw and one of the world's last unadulterated treasures.

TIP The recent privatization of the Park's management has led to a fee hike; to avoid blowing your budget, join other travelers in Miri or contact a travel operator–groups of 5 get the best rates. If you arrive solo, ask to post a notice at Park Headquarters. You may be forced to wait a day or two, but for some it's a step worth taking, to save a extra hundred ringgit.

TRANSPORTATION

Flights: The **airport** (☎011 205 285) is a 20min. walk from park headquarters along the main road. **MAS** runs flights from Miri to **Gunung Mulu** (2-3 daily, RM75; RM85 if booked in advance). Reserve early or try to fly stand-by. Vans drive visitors to park headquarters (3min., RM3) and to Royal Mulu Resort. **Vision Air** offers more scenic flights that travel just above and sometimes through the Pinnacles (3 per day, RM86). Arrange return transport at park headquarters the day before your departure.

Ferries: Returning to **Miri** by boat involves an entire day (and possibly night) of travel via longboat, starting with the trip to **Long Terawan.** Charter a boat (1-4 people, RM250 or RM45 per person, 5 or more people). To make the next connection, some travelers leave by 4pm the day before and arrange accommodation in longhouses in Long Terawan. Residents may let you sleep on their floor in return for a small gift or gratuity; ask at the park office. Or, leave from park headquarters by 4am and try to catch the boat to **Marudi** (express 3-4hr., 6am, RM20; speedboat 2½hr., 6am, RM22). From the Marudi jetty, take an express boat to **Kuala Baram** (3hr., 4-5 per day 7am-3pm, RM18). **Buses** from Kuala Baram go to **Miri** (45min., every 30min. 5:30am-9:30pm, RM2.50).

On Foot: After conquering the Pinnacles, you can hike from Camp 5, the Pinnacles' base camp, to the **Lubang Cina Cave** on the Terikan River. The next leg involves taking a boat, with an overnight stop at Bala Losong, to **Medamit** (RM450, 1-5 people). It's possible to catch a taxi from here into **Limbang,** with cheap sea and air connections to **Kota Kinabalu** and **Miri.** Trekking the Head-Hunters' trail requires prodigious logistical coordination; package tours are easiest. Alternatively, pre-arrange transportation before leaving park headquarters; solo travelers should consider joining groups to minimize costs. The boat ride to Camp 5 alone costs RM200, and you'll also have to hire a guide (RM160). Experienced trekkers have been known to ply the trail from the opposite direction (heading into park); this option is not for the navigationally challenged as many parts of the trail are not clearly marked.

PRACTICAL INFORMATION

Obtain all **permits** for Gunung Mulu at the park headquarters upon arrival. Gunung Mulu's airport, the Mulu Cafe at Park Headquarters, and the Royal Mulu Resort all harbor pricey minimarts for snacks and travel necessities; it's best to stock up in Miri before arrival, especially if you plan to hike to Camp 5. Head to the **park office,** left of the boat dock, to pay park fees and for accommodations, and to arrange (mandatory) guides and transportation for adventures within the park. There are no equipment rentals at the park, but lockers (RM5 deposit) are available for those staying in the dorms. (☎434 561. Open daily 8am-5pm.) The recreation center at **Royal Mulu Resort,** a 30min. walk farther down the main road away from the airport, rents kayaks and mountain bikes to non-guests from RM30 per hr. There are no ATM facilities anywhere in the park; bring enough ringgit for all permits, accommodation, food, and return flight. The **Royal Mulu Resort** accepts all major credit cards in its gift shop and restaurant.

ACCOMMODATIONS AND FOOD

Lodgings cluster near the park's office. An 18-bed **dormitory** ❷ with hot showers is the cheapest option in the park (RM18); the one-room setup makes it easy to meet other trekkers. A nicer **forest lodge** ❹ with fan and attached bath, has singles/doubles and triples (RM50 and RM70, respectively). Electricity is switched off between 1am and 6am. A mattress at Camp 5, the overnight stop for trekkers to the Pinnacles and Head Hunters' Trail, costs RM12.50. Cooking facilities and utensils are available; you'll have to carry all bedding and food into the camp. Along the summit trail, camps have no cooking areas and provide only thin sleeping mats (RM10). The sole **restaurant** ❷ on the park grounds offers tasty options like fried jungle fern (RM4) and *laksa* (RM5), as well as staples like fried rice and noodles (RM4), set breakfasts (RM7), bottled water (RM6), and beer (RM6). Across the park entrance bridge, **Melinau Restaurant** ❸ serves large set dinners (3 courses RM15) and beer (RM5) on an open deck with loud music. The award-winning **Royal Mulu Resort** ❹ (☎085 790 100; www.royalmuluresort.com) bathes guests in luxury and fantastic service. The complex includes a swimming pool, jacuzzi, in-house lounge and restaurant, and several limestone climbing walls. The recreation center, also available to non-guests, offer equipment rentals (from RM20 per hr.), traditional longboat rides (RM20, 5:30-7pm, 2-person min.), and supervised climbing (RM15, RM5 per additional wall). Superior rooms with A/C, TV, and private bath RM260; doubles are RM290. Substantial discounts available online. **The Wildflower Coffee House** ❺ at the Royal Mulu resort serves large gourmet burgers, steak, ice cream and local favorites (RM20-46). Try the Thai Beef Salad (RM14), laced with ginger and garlic. (MC/V.)

HIKING

Over five million years old, the **Pinnacles** point skyward from the upper reaches of Gunung Api. The trek begins with a scenic 2hr. longboat ride from park headquarters to **Kuala Berar.** In times of low water, you may spend more time pushing the boat than riding in it. From Kuala Berar, it's another 8km hike along muddy trails to **Camp 5,** the Pinnacles base camp, with basic lodging (claim your mat on the wood floor) and cooking facilities. Bring your own food, dishes, and water bottles. The next morning, trekkers tackle the steep, slick, stone-mired hillside of Gunung Api. Although the path is only 2.4km long, you need to be fit and focused to conquer the hike. With 400m to go, climbers are greeted with ropes and ladders, some nearly vertical and others horizontally bridging 20m chasms. Hikers find this part of the climb the easiest. The trail downhill is tricky and slippery after rain; it takes 3-5hr. to reach Camp 5. Most visitors spend another night here before returning to headquarters. Many of the trails are leech-infested; trekkers swear by Tiger Balm (spread on the legs as a repellent) and any spray containing DEET, which makes the parasites drop off on contact. Other recommended gear: climbing gloves (available for RM1.50 at the canteen), raingear, flashlight, and first aid supplies.

A boat to Kuala Berar, the first leg of the journey to the Pinnacles, costs RM350 for up to four people and RM85 per additional person; the permit fee is RM190 per group, which includes a guide for the three-day, two-night trek.

Rhinos were the first to enjoy the craggy summit of **Gunung Mulu,** and the trail used by most trekkers today follows their footsteps. The journey takes four days for moderately fit travelers. Visitors to Camp 1 deal with muddy trails. The second day is a tough uphill battle. It takes nine leech-infested hours to reach Camp 4 (1800m). The next day, the most zealous of climbers are up before sunrise. The journey up to the wind-scarred peak involves 2hr. of climbing, some of it using thick lengths of rope to steady wobbly legs. After capturing the sunrise and a spectacular panorama all the way to the Brunei Bay, most visitors return to camp for a night before trudging back to park headquarters on day four. Guides are mandatory (RM350 for groups of 1-5).

OUTDOOR ACTIVITIES

Gunung Mulu's numerous fees may seem high for the budget traveler, but permit fees are charged per group; cut costs significantly by joining other travelers. Permit fees for all attractions include a knowledgeable guide trained in first-aid.

SHOW CAVES. The Show Caves are Gunung Mulu's most accessible and least strenuous attraction. All have been equipped with boardwalks and dramatic lights highlighting the rock forms and passages. Bring a flashlight, a raincoat, and a plastic bag for cameras and video recorders. **Permits** are mandatory but nominal, even for solo travelers. Standard fees are RM4 per person at Deer Cave, Lang's Cave, Wind Cave, and Clearwater Cave. Moonmilk Cave, on the trail midway to Wind Cave, requires no permit.

Adventure caving requires special guides and at least 24hr. advance notice. Bring your own flashlight and shoes with traction. **Turtle cave** is the smallest and can be done in 45min. (RM20, groups of 1-10). The others are day-long affairs through tough unlit terrain, including narrow passes and chest-deep lagoons. Not for the claustrophobic. Slanted tree-like stalagmites give stunning **Drunken Forest Cave** its name; this is the hardest route along with Clearwater Connection (RM300, groups of 1-5). Other routes include easy-to-navigate **Langang's Cave** and the more challenging **Sarawak Chamber,** the world's largest (both RM200, groups of 1-5). The **Clear Water Cave** and **Wind Cave** systems (lit 9:30am-12:30pm) were first explored 16 years ago by a Sarawak Royal Geographic Society expedition that mapped 25km of passages. Over the past decade, exploration has brought the mapped terrain to over 107km, confirming Clear Water Cave as Asia's longest. To get there, walk 4km on wooden planks and up several hundred steps, through Moonmilk Cave (flashlight required). Alternatively, charter a boat (15min., 1-4 people, RM85) up the Melanau River. The first stop is Wind Cave, up a wooden plank walk to the right of the boat dock. Clear Water Cave is a 5min. walk along the river. The path first passes through **Young Lady's Cave** (named for the silhouette of the Virgin Mary visible near the entrance) and ends at a 50m chasm littered with the bones of boars who got lost in the caverns.

FERTILE GROUND. Those who examine the floor in the Niah Caves will find a bizarre feast of bat dung, attracting not only cockroaches and worms but humans as well. Guano collectors have gathered bat and swiftlet feces for local Iban farmers since 1929, who use the dung as fertilizer. Despite the availability of chemical fertilizer, guano remains the standard in Iban societies because of its low price and ability to prevent root-rotting disease in pepper vines. Today's harvests are nowhere near the 1950s recorded average of 476 tons per year, but professional collectors still work the cave floor. In case you were wondering, quality guano tastes salty.

The path into **Deer Cave** hugs the base of the mountain. Deer Cave has one of the world's largest caverns; at over 2km, even the shrill screeches of the two million wrinkle-lipped bats living in the cave are lost in the vast opening passage. The entrance to **Lang's Cave,** best known for its stunning limestone formations, is a few minutes walk from Deer Cave. A 3km boardwalk has been built from the park's office to these two caves; it makes for excellent hornbill spotting around dawn. The lush, scenic trip takes 30-45min. (Officially open daily 2:30-4:30pm, when the lights are on.) Just outside the two caves, the **bat observatory** is a good vantage point for watching the continuous stream of bats emerging from Deer Cave at 6pm (lasts about 20min.).

SABAH

Known as the "Land Below the Winds," Sabah was once rumored to be a storehouse of gems. Although none have been found, Sabah has proven to be rich in other natural treasures. Southeast Asia's highest peak, the world's most concentrated orangutan population, and the world's largest flower are all found in a jungle teeming with wildlife and vegetation. Shopaholics feast on handicrafts at the ubiquitous markets, while the adventurous partake in river treks and wilderness expeditions. In the south, the island of Sipadan sits atop a 700m coral-rimmed peak, ranked in 2001 as the top dive site in the world. Sabah's outdoor offerings trump those in neighboring countries, and should feature prominently on any adventurer's itinerary.

KOTA KINABALU ☎088

Kota Kinabalu (KK) is quickly becoming Borneo's biggest metropolis, bustling with nightclubs, tour operators, and travelers seeking city life. Chic coffeeshops and low-key Indian and Chinese restaurants pepper the city's main thoroughfare, which leads southward to several beachfront resorts. KK serves as a base of operations for those seeking the austere grandeur of Gunung Kinabalu and southern Sabah's spectacular dive sites. The charming beaches of nearby Tunku Abdul Rahman Park Islands are an off-beat surf-and-turf combo where divers and sunbathers alike come seeking sun, sand, and sea.

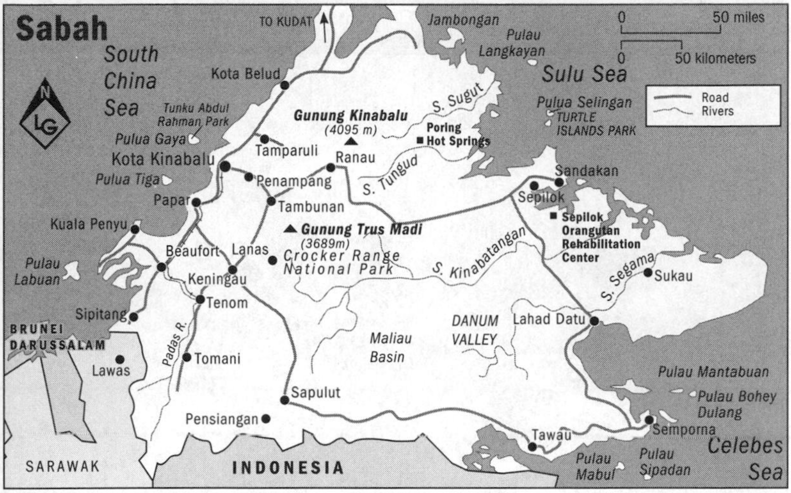

TRANSPORTATION

Flights: Malaysia Airport Berhad (☎238 555), 6km from the city. From the highway outside the terminal, minibuses, Putatan Buses (RM1), and taxis (RM13.50) go to the city center. **MAS offices** are in the departure hall (☎240 632; open daily 5:30am-7pm), and in the Kompleks Karamunsing (☎239 310). MAS flies daily to: **Bandar Seri Begawan, Brunei** (RM103); **Hong Kong** (RM750); **Jakarta** (RM785); **Johor Bahru** (RM320); **Kuching** (RM*250*); **Manila** (RM700); **Miri** (RM120); **Sandakan** (RM95); **Singapore** (RM584); **Tawau** *(*RM95). **Singapore Airlines,** Lot 12-13, ground fl., Block C, Kompleks Kuwasa (☎255 444), flies to **Singapore** (Tu and Th; RM315). **Dragon Air,** Lot CG01-CG04, ground fl., Block C Kompleks Kuwasa (☎254 733), flies to **Hong Kong** (RM825). **AirAsia** (www.airasia.com) flies direct to **Johol Baru** and **Kuala Lumpur** (from RM170)

Buses: Long-distance bus terminal, next to a field on Jl. Tunku Abdul Rahman opposite the library. Buses to **Kota Belud** (1hr., RM5) depart when full until 4pm. Buses to **Gunung Kinabalu Park** (2hr., RM15) and **Ranau** (2½hr., RM15) depart until noon. Buses to **Sandakan** (6hr., RM30) leave most frequently in the morning. Many hostel owners happily arrange bus and private transport for guests.

Ferries: Park boats leave from the **Harbour View Jetty** in the northern part of the city off Jl. Haji Saman to islands in **Tunku Abdul Rahman Park** (4 per day 8:30am-4:30pm, RM10 per person for groups of 4 or more). To get to **Bandar Seri Begawan, Brunei,** catch the Labuan Express ferry to **Pulau Labuan** (2½hr., 8am, RM28); from here take a ferry to BSB (1hr., 12:15pm, RM24). Purchase tickets at the jetty office (☎236 834). Open daily 7am-3pm. Outside the jetty, touts linger with promises of cheap accommodation; it's best to avoid them and reserve transport through your hostel. If you must take a taxi, insist that the driver use the meter.

Local Transportation: Local **minibus** terminals are opposite the post office on Jl. Tun Razak, **Putatan Buses** marked "Beach" go to **Tanjung Aru Beach** (RM1.20). **Taxis** congregate near hotels and charge RM5-10 for intra-city hops.

ORIENTATION AND PRACTICAL INFORMATION

Completely destroyed in World War II (save for the colonial building housing the tourist office), the center of KK was rebuilt in a grid system with three main north-south roads. **Jl. Tun Fuad Stephens** curves along the waterfront west of the city center and encompasses the waterfront area, Filipino Market, Pesar Besar, and Sabah Parks Office. The GPO and minibus terminal are on **Jl. Tun Razak,** the city's central road. At the north end of Jl. Razak, the **Wisma Sabah** complex houses several dive and tour operators. The police station, long-distance bus terminal, and immigration office all line **Jl. Tunku Abdul Rahman,** which leads to the airport, Lintas Plaza, and Tanjung Aru, along the city's southeast edge. Other major landmarks are the **Wisma Merdeka,** a six-story shopping complex opposite Wisma Sabah on Jl. Tun Razak, and **Centre Point,** on the same boulevard on the opposite side of town.

MALAYSIA

Tourist Offices: Sabah Tourism Board, 51 Jl. Gaya (☎212 121; www.sabahtourism.com), in the old post office adjacent to Stamford College. Multilingual pamphlets and reference brochures. Free comprehensive map. Open M-F 8am-5pm, Sa 8am-2pm. **Sabah Parks Office** (☎211 881), opposite the Filipino Market, has advice on Sabah's national parks. Open M-F 8am-1pm and 2-4:30pm, Sa 8am-12:50pm. Closed 1st and 3rd Sa of every month. **Tourism Malaysia,** ground fl., EON CMG Bldg. (☎211 732), opposite Sabah Tourism. Open M-F 8am-4:30pm, Sa 8am-12:50pm.

Tours: Sutera Sanctuary Lodges, G15, ground fl., Wisma Sabah (☎257 084; www.suterasanctuarylodges.com). Handles all accommodations in Gunung Kinabalu Park, Poring Hot Springs, and Tunku Abdul Rahman Park. Book at least 3 days in advance. Open M-F 9am-6:30pm, Sa 9am-4:30pm, Su 9am-noon. Pay in advance for accommodation. 20% cancellation fee if less than 24hr. before. ■ **Borneo Divers,** 9th fl. Stamford College (☎222 226), near Sabah Tourism. 5-star PADI dive center with excellent facilities and well-trained staff. 4-day open-water course RM900, min. 2 people. Day tours to Tunku Abdul Rahman Park RM180. Wreck dives off Pulau Labuan RM185-250 for 2 dives. Packages to Sipadan and Mabul Islands from RM400 per day.

Consulates: Indonesia (☎219 110), on Jl. Kemajuan, opposite Karamunsing Hotel, north of Jl. Tunku Abdul Rahman. Open M-F 8am-noon and 2-4pm.

Currency Exchange: Banks cluster by Wisma Merdeka on Jl. Tugu. **Standard Chartered Bank** and **Bank Bumiputra** have 24hr. **ATMs. Maybank** (☎254 295), at the corner of Jl. Pantai and Jl. 3. Open M-F 9:30-11:30am. Maybank airport branch (☎268 906) cashes traveler's checks. RM5 per transaction, RM0.15 per check. Open daily 8am-10:30pm. **Wisma Merdeka** has moneychangers on the 1st fl. Open daily 10am-6pm.

Emergency: ☎999.

Police: (☎242 111), on Jl. Balai, east of town .

Pharmacies: Doses Pharmacy, ground fl., KK Plaza, Lot G 39 (☎259 972). English spoken. Open daily 10am-9pm. AmEx/MC/V. **Pharmex,** ground fl., Lot 6, Block F, Kompleks Segama on Jl. Tun Razak (☎231 457). Open M-Sa 8:30am-7:30pm, Su 9:30am-1:30pm. **Syarikat Kaca Mata** (☎258 589), next door to Pharmex. Open daily 8:30am-7:30pm.

Medical Services: Perdana Polyklinik (☎235 100), on Jl. Pantai. **Queen Elizabeth Hospital** (☎218 166), near State Museum. English spoken. Both 24hr.

Telephones: Public phones place collect calls; some accept Foncards. **Telekom Office,** ground fl., Block I, Jl. Ikan Juara 1, Karamunsing (☎257 676). Open M-F 8:30am-4:45pm, Sa 8:30am-1pm. Telekom airport branch (☎261 261). Open daily 8am-5pm.

Internet Access: Vision De Net Cafe, 1st fl., Lot 91, Jl. Gaya (☎019 873 3475), near RHB Bank and Sabah Tourism. RM3 per hr., students RM2.50 per hr. Open daily 9am-2am. **PlayNet,** ground fl., Wisma Sabah. 9am-7pm RM3 per hr., 7pm-2am RM2 per hr. Open daily 9am-2am. **City Internet Cafe,** No. 1 Jl. Centre Point (☎255 255). RM3 per hr. Open daily 9am-1am.

Post Office: GPO (☎210 855), in large white building on Jl. Tun Razak, near Bank Negara and Kompleks Segama. *Poste Restante.* Open M-Sa 8am-5pm. Closed 1st and 3rd Sa of every month.

Postal Code: 88806.

▛ ACCOMMODATIONS

City Park Inn, Jl. Pasar Baru 2 (☎260 607 or 260 608; www.borneo-online.com.my/cityparkinn), near Kampung Air, across from Public Finance. Popular owner ■ **Jimmy Wong** arranges daytrips, offers helpful advice, and has been known to treat his guests to dinner. This hostel-hotel hybrid has clean rooms with lockers, A/C, and private bath. Internet (RM4 per hr.) and breakfast (RM3). Rooftop patio with free tea and coffee. Dorms RM15; singles RM45; doubles RM50. ❷

Lucy's Homestay, 1st fl., Lot 25, Lorong Dewan, Australia Place on Jl. Tun Razak (☎261 495). Common room with TV, stereo, and library. Breakfast included. Flexible curfew 11pm. Laundry. Single-sex, 12-bed dorms with shared bath RM18; doubles RM45. ❷

Kinabalu Daya Hotel, Lots 3/4, Block 9, Jl. Pantai (☎240 000; www.kkdayahotel.com), opposite Wisma Merdeka along Jl. Saman; entrance on Jl. Pantai. The latest addition to KK's slew of business hotels is also a fabulous bargain. In-house Hunter's Pub offers discounts to card-holding divers (RM17 for 5 beers, daily 4-9pm). 24hr. laundry, room service. Singles and doubles with breakfast RM88; 4-person family room RM180. AmEx/MC/V. ❸

The Jesselton Hotel, 69 Jl. Gaya (☎223 333; www.jesseltonhotel.com). In the style of "a refined English country house," this 4-star hotel dates from 1954 and bears KK's colonial name. Chinese antiques and an authentic London taxicab (exclusively for guests) lend a boutique atmosphere. A/C, private bath, satellite TV, IDD, and minibar in each room. Lavish junior suite has a rooftop garden. Singles and doubles with breakfast and fruit basket RM230; suite RM650. AmEx/MC/V. ❺

FOOD

Affordable Malay, Indian, and Chinese restaurants line every street. The **Kompleks Sedco ❷,** off Jl. Laiman Diki, is an open-air food court with the feel of a raucous family reunion. Choose fresh seafood from over 20 tanks (RM3-10 per 100g). Vegetarian dishes are available. (Open daily 6pm-1am.) The **waterfront esplanade ❷,** past the Filipino market, boasts 16 kiosks and has emerged as KK's trendiest eatery and one of the best places to find cheap seafood. (Open daily 4pm-1am.)

Ang's, on Jl. Haji Saman, opposite Wisma Merdeka and Trekker's Lodge, is packed with locals. Hefty portions of Chinese seafood and meat. Sizzling Japanese bean curd RM6; BBQ prawn RM15. Open daily 11am-11pm. ❸

Port View Seafood Restaurant, on Jl. Haji Sama opposite the old customs wharf. Follow Jl. Tun Razak east out of town, 200m past Wisma Sabah; look for the blazing blue and red neon sign on the right. Scrumptious Chinese seafood. Menu priced seasonally. Fried cuttlefish with chillies RM13; lobster RM90; grilled tiger prawn with butter sauce RM12-20. Open daily 10:30am-11:30pm. AmEx/MC/V. ❺

The Aru (☎269 915), on the Tanjung Aru waterfront adjacent to the white main complex. Mediterranean and fusion cuisine, and white-curtained cabanas for secluded outdoor dining. Budget travelers fill up at adjacent beachfront hawker stalls and slip in for a cocktail. Pan-seared bean curd with avocado salsa. RM9. Open daily 6pm-1am. ❶

SIGHTS

STATE MUSEUM AND ENVIRONS. KK's main cultural destination, the State Museum is a modern interpretation of traditional Rugus longhouses, housing exhibits on ethnography, natural history, ceramics, and archaeology. **Kampung Warisan** (Heritage Village) is at the compound's opposite end, past the waterfall. Visitors can pose with a Murut longhouse or a traditional Bajau or Chinese farmhouse before continuing to the nearby **Ethno-botanic Gardens,** where plants used for ornamentation, commerce, and medicine vie for space and sunlight. *(The State Museum is a 30min. walk southwest from the city center along Jl. Tunku Abdul Rahman. Walk 400m past the intersection with Jl. Kemajuan and turn left on Jl. Penampang. Through the small* *gate on the left, a path leads uphill to the museum. Alternatively, catch a minibus (RM1) from a bus stop along Jl. Tunku Abdul Rahman. Museum open M-Th and Sa-Su 9am-5pm, closed May 1. RM5, seniors free. Heritage Village and Ethno-botanic Gardens open M-Th and Sa-Su 10am-5pm.)*

TANJUNG ARU BEACH. While the warm water and soft sand make this beach ideal for relaxation, the newly renovated Tanjung Aru waterfront comes to life at sunset and on weekends. Hawkers sell steamed corn, peanuts, fried noodles, and chicken *satay*. Several open-air restaurants serve spicy grilled meats and vegetables; a branch of the Sugar Bun franchise caters to those with tamer palates. Kampung Nalayan Restaurant in Tun Fuad Stephens Park, several kilometers east of the town center, has daily Malay and Kandazan dance performances around 7:30pm. Take a minibus bound for Luyang. *(2.5km from the museum. Take one of the buses labeled "Tanjung Aru" or "Shangri-La Resort" opposite the post office. After 6pm, the trip costs RM12 in a taxi.)*

OTHER SIGHTS. The **City Bird Sanctuary** on Likas Bay has an impressive lookout tower and paths that meander through a mangrove forest. Bring your binoculars to see the Great Egret and the King Fisher. (☎246 955. Open Tu-Su 8am-6pm. Free; donations are appreciated.) **Tun Fuad Stephens Park,** off Jl. Tun Fuad Stephens, features impressive jogging trails where many locals train prior to hiking Mt. Kinabalu. A **waterpark** with a large slide is just inside the park's gates. Outside the park, a small **night market** serves up local favorites. (Open daily 12:30-9pm, RM5.)

ENTERTAINMENT

The **Poring** and **Kilan Cinemas,** at the intersection of Jl. Tunku Abdul Rahman and Jl. Laiman Diki, often show English-language movies. (RM6-8. Open daily noon-midnight.) Nightspots abound in central KK. **The Beach,** along the waterfront in the Coffee Bean complex, packs in sweating masses gyrating to house music starting at midnight. (RM15 cover on Sa includes 1 drink). An outdoor, tree-lined **courtyard** behind The Reef Project Bar is dotted with small bars and restaurants, including **BB Cafe,** a local hangout with pool tables. The courtyard is also a wireless Internet hot spot. (Monthly passes available at the Sugar Bun counter.) **Shenanigan's,** on the ground floor of the Hyatt Hotel, next to Wisma Sabah, is a popular backpacker hangout with live music. (No shorts or slippers. Beer from RM7.50. Cover RM15. Happy hour daily 5-9pm. Open M-Th 5pm-1am, F-Sa 5pm-2am, Su 5pm-midnight.)

MARKETS

KK's market area is along the waterfront and mainly specializes in food; souvenirs and artwork are best bought in Kuching, Sarawak. The **Pesar Besar** (big market) lays out fresh fruit, veggies, and cheap clothing. (Open daily 8am-6pm.) Upstairs, eager foodstall owners with KK's cheapest eats shout *"Macam!"* ("Eat!"). Follow the smell to the **fish market** behind Pesar Besar. If it swims, they have it. Next door, the **Filipino Market** sells souvenirs, t-shirts, and fruit. At night, hawkers barbecue fresh fish (RM8-15). Friendly conversation and sincere smiles invariably earn travelers a discount. On Sunday mornings, **street stalls** on Jl. Gaya sell everything from Chinese medicines to puppies. Beware of pickpockets.

DAYTRIPS FROM KOTA KINABALU

MONSOPIAD CULTURAL VILLAGE. Head to Monsopiad Cultural Village, where former resident and famed Kadazan warrior Monsopiad is still revered over 300 years after his death. His direct descendants run the village, vividly detailing the

THE BIG SPLURGE

THE JUMP-OFF: SIPADAN

Just 45min. by boat off the southern coast of Sabah, Sipadan's waters are a veritable underwater aquarium. No more than a stone's throw from shore, visitors have spotted hammerhead sharks, schools of silvery barracuda and jack fish, and an array of microlife that includes hundreds of nudibranch and coral species. Even giant Green and Hawksbill sea turtles become mundane sightings after a few dives. As if that wasn't enough, superb visibility—up to 50m in the dry season—lends a Technicolor effect to already vivid hues.

Most biologists suspect that Sipadan's beauty is due to its one-of-a-kind geography. The tiny island stands on a column of earth 700m above the ocean floor. Its thin rim of white sand stretches only about 10 meters from the shore, where it abruptly gives way to an immense coral-covered wall, known simply as the "drop-off." The wall provides a glimpse into both shallow- and deep-water environments, accommodating both inexperienced and advanced divers.

As of August 2004, plans were underway to close all accommodations in Sipadan due to problems with human waste management. However, diving will still be possible. To dive off Sipadan, contact Borneo Divers in Sabah. *(☎ 222 226; www.borneodivers.com. Packages start at RM400 per day for an unlimited number of dives .)*

warrior's adventures and showing off his 42 trophy heads that remain in the House of Skulls. A welcome drink of local rice wine, lessons on the blow pipe, and a taste of *hinava*—a local fresh pickle—await. *(The Cultural Village is several kilometers south of KK in Donggonggon. Take a taxi (RM20) or Penampang Bus from the local bus terminal in KK to the last stop in Donggonggon (RM1), connect to a minibus to Terawi (RM1), and ask to be let off at Monsopiad. ☎ 761 336; www.monsopiad.org. Open daily 9am-6pm. Cultural shows daily 11am, 2, 4pm. Guided tours 10am, noon, 3, 5pm. RM25.)*

KOTA BELUD. Coastal Kota Belud, 75km north of KK, is a welcome diversion from KK's urban rhythms. Surrounded by rubber plantations and shaggy dipterocarp forests, Kota Belud is famous for its lively *tamu* (market and trade fair), one of Sabah's largest. (Open Su 6am-noon.) Historically, *tamu* allowed the upland Rugus and Kadazan/Dusun people to meet and trade goods with the coastal Bajau community. The Bajau, Sabah's famed "cowboys of the east," wear brilliantly stitched garb on special occasions, like **Tamu Besar** in late November. The real attraction is the raucous atmosphere and bustling trade in the shaded fairgrounds.

Buses from the long-distance terminal in KK drop off passengers on the highway in the city center. Head for the pink spires and gilt dome of the city mosque and bear right down Jl. Hasbollah. The *tamu* grounds are a 5-10min. walk from town past the post office. **Minibuses** back to KK leave from the Esso gas station near the bookstore (1½hr.; depart when full, last bus 4pm; RM10). Most tour operators and hotels can arrange daytrips to Kota Balud, starting at RM50.

TUNKU ABDUL RAHMAN PARK. Idyllic Tunku Abdul Rahman Park is made up of five placid islands 3-8km from KK. Boats leave from the Harbour View Jetty for the park (9, 11am, noon, 1pm; RM14, children RM7). **Palau Gaya,** the largest island, is home to Filipino immigrants who have settled in the stilt village off the east coast. Over 20km of trails criss-cross the island through an intact dipterocarp forest; the trail from the park headquarters leads through a dense mangrove thicket. Though crowded and dirty, tiny **Pulau Sapi** (Cow Island), off Pulau Gaya's southwest coast, is also popular. **Police Beach,** once used as a police shooting range, is the most secluded, while **Manukan** and **Mamutik Islands**—the most scenic and the most popular—are crowded with large tour group barbecues. **Pulau Sulug** is the least developed and is popular with divers and snorkelers. (RM10 per island, children RM6.)

Camping ❶ is permitted on Pulau Sapi, Pulau Mamutik, and Pulau Sulug (RM5 per person, under 18 RM2). Campers must obtain written permission from park headquarters and bring their own food and equipment. Picnic tables and barbecue pits are available at the scenic campsites, many a stone's throw from the sand. Four-person **chalets** ❺ are available on Manukan (RM230). Make reservations with **Sutera Sanctuary Lodges** (p. 437). For more information on accommodation on Mamutik, consult **Sabah Parks Office** in Komplex Sinsuran. **Borneo Divers** arranges daytrips (RM170) to Mamutik Island for diving, snorkelling, and SCUBA courses. Contact the main office in KK (☎222 226; www.borneodivers.com) for schedules.

GUNUNG KINABALU

Gunung Kinabalu is the world's youngest non-volcanic mountain, Southeast Asia's highest peak, and Sabah's premier tourist draw. The surrounding park—which has an area larger than the nation of Singapore—encompasses four climate zones and showcases one of the world's richest flora collections, including giant rafflesia blossoms and several species of carnivorous pitcher plants. Whether watching the sunrise from atop Kinabalu's peak or discovering that a moving twig is actually a rare insect, visitors won't regret a trek to Sabah's most enticing attraction.

TRANSPORTATION

Regular **buses** run to Gunung Kinabalu Park from the long-distance terminal in Kota Kinabalu (1½hr., first bus departs at 7:30am, RM10) and from the smaller town of Ranau (RM5). **Minibuses** make the journey until noon. Flag down buses back to KK on the highway in front of the park entrance (2hr., last bus 4pm, RM10). Daily **shuttles** also make the trip (1hr., every 1½hr., RM10). Chartered **minivans** charge RM120-140 for up to six passengers. From Sandakan, buses to KK pass the park headquarters (4hr., RM30).

ACCOMMODATIONS AND FOOD

Sutera Sanctuary Lodges (see **Tours,** p. 437) has the monopoly on park accommodations, some of which are listed here. Make reservations at least one week in advance; in peak season (June-Sept.), mountain resthouses are booked for months. To the right of the park entrance, the **reception office** will give you a room assignment and a map of the park with directions to accommodations. (☎088 889 077. Open daily 7am-10pm.) Camping is not allowed. Many trekkers stay at **Medang Hostel** ❶ or **Menggilan Hostel** ❶. (Dorms RM18; doubles RM92; quads RM184; 5- and 6-person cabins RM230.) Halfway up the mountain is the popular **Laban Rata Rest House** ❶. (Dorms without heaters RM17, with heaters, hot water, and electricity RM34; doubles with bath RM115; quads RM230.) Rooms at **Gunting Lagadan Hut, Panar Laban Hut,** and **Waras Hut** ❶ are unheated but provide cooking facilities and sleeping bags. (Dorms RM12, under 18 RM6.) The most basic accommodations (cooking facilities only) are at **Sayat Sayat Hut** ❶, a 2hr. climb up the Panar Laban rock face. Many visitors rave about Sayat's camaraderie-fostering seclusion, where groups gather in sleeping bags under the stars and chat late into the cold night. Lock up food to avoid rats. (RM12, under 18 RM6.)

The **Kinabalu Balsam Canteen** ❷, below the park office, has excellent sunset views of the mountain from its veranda. (Dishes start at RM5. Open daily 6:30am-9:30pm.) Meals at **Mt. Kinabalu Restaurant** ❷, part of the Visitor Center complex, are comparable to those at canteens. (Entrees RM8. Open M-F 6:30am-10pm, Sa and holidays 6:30am-11pm.) Outside the park, **Restoran Tenompok** ❶ serves *laksa* (RM2.50) and *mee* dishes. (Open daily 9am-11pm.)

HIKING GUNUNG KINABALU

The **Visitor Center** is past the hostels before the access road loops back to the park reception, and has a small but intriguing exhibit on the park's history and wildlife. (Slide show daily 2pm, F-Su 7:30pm. RM2.) Learn about ecology at the **Sabah Parks Office** near the park entrance. Behind the Visitor Center is the **Mountain Garden,** home to flora endemic to the park and medicinal plants, as well as more common species. The garden has a beautiful selection of Kinabalu's 1200 orchid species, including the world's smallest flowering orchid, with a blossom the size of a pinhead. Tours are required. (Tours 9am, noon, 3pm. RM5.)

Be sure to arrive at the park headquarters by 9am at the latest, wallet in hand. You'll need to purchase a **permit** (RM100, under 18 RM40), **accident insurance** (RM3.50), and possibly a **porter** (RM50 for the first 10kg, RM5 per additional kg). The **conservation fee,** payable upon entrance at the main gate, is an additional RM15 (under 18 RM10). **Guides** are mandatory for climbing past Laban Rata. (Guides for 1-3 people RM80 round-trip, 4-6 people RM86 round-trip, 7-8 people RM92 round-trip.) Park officers place independent travelers in groups. Bring a change of warm clothes (temperatures can drop below freezing), gloves for the ropes at the summit, trekking poles or a walking stick, hat, rain gear, sunscreen, a small flashlight, comfortable shoes with traction, toilet paper, aspirin, bandages, a water bottle (taps line the trails), and hard candy or chocolate for quick energy. Some hikers swear by Tiger Balm as relief for sore muscles. The pricey Laban Rata Canteen also sells basic supplies. Store baggage at the park office; free lockers are provided for valuables.

DAY 1. The first day takes you halfway up the mountain in 3-6hr. The trail begins at the power station, a short bus ride (RM25) or 1hr. trek from the base. After a brief walk to the picturesque **Carson Falls,** it's all uphill along narrow but well-maintained trails. Six rest shelters are scattered along the trail. Over half of the plants above 912m, including the unusual **Kinabalu Balsam** with iridescent purple flowers, are unique to the park. **Pitcher plants,** with their large, liquid-filled leaves, attract insects that fall and drown in the plants' digestive juices. The largest of the species holds up to 2L of fluid. Gradually, the trail becomes more steep, rocky, and barren. The rare **Kinabalu Warbler** and **Mountain Blackbird** live in this terrain. In late August and early September, the **rafflesia,** the world's largest flower, blossoms to a striking 1m in diameter. Phone the park headquarters in advance to ensure that it is in bloom. The afternoon is spent recharging for the next day's push to the top. Most climbers spend the night at Laban Rata Guest House or at one of the nearby huts; a hardy few trek 1.5km farther to Sayat (see **Accommodations,** p. 441).

DAY 2. By 3am the next day, bundled-up climbers set out against the freezing cold to reach the summit by sunrise. Above Laban Rata is the **Panar Laban** rock face, where wooden staircases evolve into steep ladders that eventually give way to shelves of bare gray granite. Ropes aid climbers up the sheerest parts. The Kadazan guides of early explorers offered sacrifices to appease the spirits of the dead at Panar Laban (Place of Sacrifice). The treeline stops here, and thin air makes the rest of the climb much tougher. Take it slow and steady to avoid altitude sickness. **Low's Peak,** at 4101m, rises in a gentle curve from this austere landscape of windswept granite. Tourists vie for the ideal vantage point to capture the breathtaking sunrise over Borneo. The descent takes 4-8hr. Every climber is eligible to receive a certificate of achievement from the park office (RM10).

DAYTRIPS FROM GUNUNG KINABALU

PORING HOT SPRINGS. The sulphurous waters of Poring Hot Springs, 43km east of Kinabalu Park Headquarters, are advertised as a cure for Kinabalu-weary legs. The springs (glorified bathtubs) cost RM10 for a standard tub and RM15 for a larger "deluxe" tub. Poring's isolated setting makes for a soothing visit. Hot tubs, small swimming pools, and a seven-tiered swimming pool and waterslide are available for an additional fee. Walk past the baths to the **canopy walkway**—a series of boardwalks suspended 60m above the ground. Those intent on seeing wildlife eye-to-eye in the forest area can negotiate nocturnal visits for higher fees. (Canopy walkway open daily 9am-4pm. RM5, cameras RM5, video recorders RM30.) Many trails meander through bamboo thickets and caves formerly infested with bats. A 10min. stroll to the right of the baths leads to **Kepungit Falls.** Another taxing 2hr. trail rewards you with the 150m **Langanan Waterfall.** Take a break to watch the *Lepidoptera* flutter at the **Butterfly Farm.** (Open Tu-Su 9am-4pm. RM4.)

Reserve **accommodations** ❶ at Sutera Sanctuary Lodges in KK on the ground fl., Wisma Sabah. (☎243 629; www.suterasanctuarylodges.com. Dorms RM12, under 18 RM6; 4-person chalet with ceiling fan, bath, and cooking facilities RM92; 6-person chalet RM115; two 6-person chalets with A/C and a BBQ pit RM288.) Camping is possible, but facilities are limited to the hostel's common bathroom and a common BBQ pit. (RM6 per person.) The park **restaurant** ❷ serves excellent meals. (Banana milkshake RM3; clay pot bean curd RM9.) Several restaurants are outside the park and there are cooking facilities in the dorms.

SABAH TEA PLANTATION. Just a 1hr. bus ride from the base of Kinabalu, rocky mountain terrain gives way to lush green slopes harboring one of the region's proudest exports: tea leaves. The plantation, on the outskirts of Ranau, offers guests a relaxing break from the tourist-packed camps at Kinabalu's headquarters and Laban Rata. Daily tours led by local harvesters walk visitors through the various stages of the tea process. Tea is available for sale in the adjacent gift shop. Accommodations are also available in family bungalows (RM120) or longhouses (RM60). The plantation hosts an annual adventure bicycle race each August; tourists are welcome to participate. *(☎440 882; www.sabahtea.net. Contact the Sabah Tea main office in KK for reservations and to arrange transportation and tours.)*

SANDAKAN ☎089

Grim and artless, Sandakan's grid of numbered streets and concrete blocks of shops have the charm of army barracks. Indeed, the city served as a Japanese POW camp during WWII. The splendor the city lacks, however, is made up for in its surroundings, and Sandakan is slowly being recognized as a major ecotourism hub. Animal and nature lovers alike come seeking the orangutans of nearby Sepilok, the tortoises of the Turtle Islands National Park, and Kinabatangan River's virgin jungle, home to everything from proboscis monkeys to civet cats and rare leopards. Divers with thick wallets will find paradise on the nearby island of Langkayan, famed for its pristine coral reefs and peppered with pricey resorts.

TRANSPORTATION

Flights: The **airport,** Sabah Bldg., 1st fl. (☎669 969), is 11km outside town. **MAS** (☎273 966), on Jl. Pelabuhan at Jl. Lebuh Dua. Open M-F 8:30am-5pm, Sa 8:30am-1pm. Flights to: **Kota Kinabalu** (RM94); **Kuching** (RM300); **Miri** (RM168); **Tawau** (RM85).

Buses: Long-distance bus terminal, on Jl. Pryer on the west edge of town. Follow Jl. Tiga out of town and turn left before the pedestrian overpass. Buses to **Kota Kinabalu** (7½hr., 3 per day 6:30am-noon, RM20-25; A/C buses 4 per day, RM15-25; minibuses depart until 2pm, RM25) and **Ranau/Park Headquarters** (A/C buses 4hr., RM15-18; minibuses depart until 2pm, RM20).

Ferries: For up-to-date schedules, inquire at the main jetty. Slow-moving boats ply the strip of **Sulu Sea** that separates Borneo from the southern Philippines. Boats depart regularly from the **Sandakan boat terminal** at the main jetty, and deposit passengers in **Zamboanga, Mindanao** (16hr.; Tu, Th 5pm; RM119-200). It is possible to find boat transport from here to the westernmost islands; the terminal has weekly schedules.

Local Transportation: The local bus terminal sends green and red striped buses down Jl. Leila (RM0.50 to Bandar Ramai-Ramai). Blue *labuk* buses head north on Jl. Utara toward the **airport** (RM1.50); some buses cut the route short, so specify your destination before hopping on. Buses show how far they go from town in *batu* (miles). Any bus marked **Batu 14** and higher goes to the junction leading to **Sepilok Orangutan Rehabilitation Center** (RM1.80). **Taxis** traveling within a few kilometers of the city center cost RM3-5; taxis to **Sepilok** cost around RM30.

! Rebel separatist groups from Mindanao in the Philippines are the region's newest pirates; boatloads of armed men scout the seas surrounding the islands for boats with valuable cargo, including passengers. Rich foreign tourists, worth millions in ransom, are their most precious bounty. Though such events are very rare, exercise caution by traveling on regular ferries rather than small charters.

ORIENTATION AND PRACTICAL INFORMATION

Many of Sandakan's streets have similar names, but street signs are scarce. Pick up a tourist map at the Visitor Information Center, up the staircase opposite the Standard Chartered Bank. **Lh. Tiga,** or **Third Avenue** (not to be confused with **Jl. Tiga**, a cross-street at the east end of town) is the town's main thoroughfare; it becomes **Jl. Leila** near the post office. South of Lh. Tiga along the waterfront is Jl. Pryer. At the far east end of Lh. Tiga is the **Wisma Koo Siak Chew Building,** which houses the Sabah Park Office and Telekom Office. Jl. Leila leads west to the long-distance bus

FROM THE ROAD

ISLANDS IN THE STREET

After a long day of sweating along the black pavement, I was elated finally to come across a crosswalk. Small but busy roads usually lack crosswalks entirely, and major highways—regardless of how congested—are lucky to have more than one.

For a moment, it seemed that only four lanes of traffic separated me from the quickie marts and bottled water. But this crosswalk, like most, was a bit of a mirage. The quickie marts were across the street—and 4km to the east! This "convenient" crossing would take me only to a wheat field with abandoned houses. Still, thirst impelled me to cross the road, and so I waited.

And I waited. It seems that there is a mandatory 15min. waiting period before the red "don't walk" stick figure turns green. In the meantime, I watched businessmen on cellular phones, children dribbling basketballs, and elderly women balancing fruit on their heads nonchalantly step into traffic. They mounted the concrete islands that float in the middle of the mania. After a short wait, they simultaneously jumped into the first hole in traffic, no matter how small, and waded across the sea of cars.

If you're anything like I was for the first few days of my trip, you are probably still waiting for the red stick figure to turn green. Eventually, I sucked in my stomach and fearfully waddled across terminal, night market, post office, and **Bandar Ramai-Ramai,** home to many restaurants, banks, and budget accommodations.

Tourist Offices: Visitor Information Center (☎229 751), across the town square from the police station on Jl. Empat. Open daily 8am-4:30pm. **Crystal Quest Tours** (☎212 711), at the Sandakan jetty near the yacht club, arranges Turtle Island tours. Open daily 9am-5pm. Hostel owners are particularly helpful. The owners at **Sepilok Jungle Resort** and **Labuk B&B** are a great resource and can also book transport and tours.

Currency Exchange: Hong Kong Bank (☎213 122) cashes traveler's checks. First check RM2.15, each additional check RM0.15. 24hr. **ATM.** Open M-F 9:30am-3pm, Sa 9:30-11:30am. All major banks along Lh. Tiga exchange currency. Passport required.

Emergency: ☎999.

Police: (☎211 222). On Jl. Empat, north of town.

Pharmacies: Borneo Dispensary, 65 Lh. Tiga (☎213 981), 2 doors from KFC. English spoken. Open M-Sa 8am-5:30pm, Su 8am-12:30pm. AmEx/MC/V.

Hospital: (☎212 111). On Jl. Utara, 3km from the airport. English spoken.

Telephones: Near the long-distance bus terminal. No credit card phones. **Telekom Office,** 6th fl., Wisma Khoo Siak Chew (☎219 292), at the east end of Lh. Tiga. International phone/fax. Open M-F 8:30am-4:45pm, Sa 8:30am-1pm.

Internet Access: Internet Cybercafe, Lot 305, Wisma Sandakan (☎216 158), near Hotel Sandakan. Fast connections are coupled with the noise of Internet gamers. RM5 per hr. Open M-Sa 9am-10pm, Su 9am-8pm.

Post Office: (☎201 501). On Jl. Leila, next to the supermarket on the outskirts of town. *Poste Restante.* Open M-Sa 8am-5pm. Closed 1st and 3rd Sa of the month.

Postal Code: 90000.

ACCOMMODATIONS

May Fair Hotel, No. 24, Block 26, 1st fl., Jl. Pryer (☎219 892), in front of the market. Newly renovated rooms boast A/C and private baths. A central location compensates for pricey rooms. Laundry. Singles RM40; doubles RM50. 10% student discount. ❸

Paris Inn, Block 23, 1st fl., Lh. Tiga (☎218 488), opposite Hong Leong Finance Bldg. Spartan rooms have a central location close to the tourist office. Laundry. Singles RM30, with A/C RM35; doubles RM35/45. Discounts available. ❷

a road nowhere near a crosswalk.

Attaching yourself to a group makes getting to and from the concrete islands easie[illegible]t is an advantage to have other pedestrians as human shields against the threat of on-coming traffic.

That said, however, traveling in groups can make your stay on the island a bit unstable, as the laws of physics threaten even the most cohesive of groups.

The islands seem more like narrow isthmuses as SUVs, which act like urban death-machines, pass just a few centimeters from your face. Behind you, sporty sedans brush against your daypack.

To stop the circular spinning motion initiated by the traffic, clutch a wooden pole. Luckily, the children bouncing basketballs can often sense your [illegible]f they offer you a hand, don't be embarrassed to take it.

Attempting to cross four lanes of Malaysian traffic all at once is suicidal. Wait for a group; it's definitely your safest bet.

You won't get flattened, your feathers won't fly, and I promise, there will be no fried chicken.

—William Lee Adams

Travelers Rest Hostel, Apt. 2, Block E, 2nd fl. Bandar Ramai-Ramai (☎019 873 4289). 1 block from Jl. Leila, near MayBank. Turn left at the Esso gas station. Spacious, basic rooms with common bath. Breakfast included. Organizes trips to Turtle Island and the Kinabatangan River (RM130). Dorms RM12, with A/C RM18; rooms RM30. ❶

Rose B&B (☎232 582; rosebb@tm.net.my), opposite Travelers Rest Hostel. Clean rooms with common bath come highly recommended. Breakfast included. Communal TV. Dorms RM18; doubles RM25, with A/C RM38. ❷

FOOD

Sting ray-steak vendors compete with used-clothing stalls at Sandakan's **night market** on Jl. Tiga. (Open daily 7pm-late.) Several Indian restaurants and market stalls line Jl. Pryer (a.k.a. India Street); cafes and bakeries can be found at the intersection of Lh. Tiga and Jl. Tiga, near Wisma Sandakan.

The English Tea House, No. 2002 Jl. Istana (☎222 544; www.englishteahouse.org), opposite the Agnes Keith House. Take a taxi (RM5) from town. From the manicured croquet field (complete with wandering peacock) to the imported clotted cream, the Tea House is true English colonial style. Outdoor seating has spectacular views of Sandakan Bay. Morning or afternoon tea with 2 scones and fresh jam RM15. Free wireless Internet. 20% off during happy hour, 7-9pm daily. ❺

Supreme Garden Vegetarian Restaurant, Lots 2-3, Block 30, ground fl. Bandar Ramai-Ramai, off Jl. Leila (☎213 292). Look for a red and gold sign. Backpackers flock here for the faux-pork lunch specials (served M-Sa 11am-1:30pm; RM5.50). Stuffed bean curd RM9. Open daily 9:30am-1:45pm and 5:30-8:45pm; closed Tu evening. ❷

Kedai Minuman Shamrock, Lot 9, Block 20 (☎220 598), on the corner of Jl. Empat and Jl. Pryer. Excellent beer selection and an up-to-date jukebox. Beef chop with rice RM5. Chicken with mixed vegetable *mee* RM10. Local beers RM5. Open daily 8am-2am. ❷

Kedai Makanan King Cheong, Lot 5A, Block 19, 2 blocks from the MAS office. Cheap Chinese meals and an excellent veggie selection. Owner speaks English. Wonton soup RM1.50. Steam buns RM0.90-1.50. Dishes RM3-6. ❶

DAYTRIPS FROM SANDAKAN

SEPILOK ORANGUTAN REHABILITATION CENTER. As the world's largest orangutan sanctuary, the center reintroduces into nature infant orangutans taken from their mothers. Keep these rules in mind: don't leave trash anywhere; don't smoke or carry insect repellent; don't get closer than 2m to the animals; don't attempt to feed any of the animals on the trail. Orangutans are strong, and their idea of play could put you in traction—they aren't known as "the wild men of Borneo" for nothing. They'll jump on your head, steal your camera, strip you naked (as they did to a visitor in 1992), and drop your camera from the tree-tops. There are two daily feedings on platform A (10am and 3pm); arrive 30min. before feeding time.

The closest look you'll get at the animals may be on-screen; the park's informative video show is well worth an extra 20min. (8:40, 10:40, 11:15am, 2:10, 3:30pm). The park also offers several short trails (2hr. each way); register and pick up permits at the park office. The **reception office** (☎215 189) is to the right of the entrance. To reach the center from Sandakan, catch a blue-and-white Sepilok "Batu 14" **bus** (45min., 8 per day, RM1.50) from the long-distance bus station. Buses will drop you at the turn-off to the center; from there, it's a 3km walk. (☎081 531 180. Open daily 9-11am and 2-3:30pm. RM40, cameras RM10.)

Most visitors to the center stay at the **Sepilok Jungle Resort ❷** on Labuk Rd., 500m from the park entrance. It boasts an ideal location, a resort-style setting, and helpful management who offer trips and travel. Call for pick-up from the main road. Bus tickets to Kota Kinabalu can be reserved at the front desk. (☎533 031. Breakfast included. Dorms RM20; doubles RM50, with A/C RM60; family rooms RM100.) **Labuk B&B,** at *Batu* 15 just down the road from the Sepilok junction, is a cozy family home with guest bedrooms upstairs and a breezy patio. Owner Robert Chong is a one-man encyclopedia of tourism in Sandakan and the Kinabatangan River. (☎533 190. Airport transfer RM20. Dorms RM20 with breakfast.) **Uncle Tan's B&B ❷,** on Labuk Rd., Lot 8, Block B, SEDCO Complex/*Batu* 16, Gum Gum, is another great value. From Sandakan, take any bus going beyond *Batu* 16 and ask to be dropped off at Gum Gum. Uncle Tan was a local legend as a former newspaperman, environmental activist, and geography teacher; his children now run the family business. Uncle Tan's Wilderness Camp (see below) runs treks to the Kinabatangan River. (☎531 639; www.uncletan.com. Meals included. Reservations recommended. Rooms with mosquito nets and shared bath RM20.)

KINABATANGAN RIVER. Sabah's largest river, the Kinabatangan supports one of the densest concentrations of wildlife in the world. The proboscis monkey is the easiest animal to spot, wildly and loudly jumping through the jungle canopy every morning and evening. Other treetop denizens include gibbons, macaques, and the occasional orangutan. On the ground aardvarks, porcupines, and deer meander through the trees, and civet cats are frequent night visitors to the jungle camp kitchens. Feel an earthquake? It's probably just a herd of elephants passing by.

The most distinctive way to see the Kinabatangan River is on an excursion to a local jungle camp. **Uncle Tan's Wilderness Camp,** run by the eponymous B&B near Sepilok, draws rave reviews from guests. Most choose a 3-day, 2-night package including round-trip transport from Sandakan, a visit to Sepilok Rehabilitation Center, boat transport to the camp, three daily meals, and guided treks into the jungle. The river looks enticing, but would-be swimmers beware: crocs often swallow wild pigs whole. Accommodations are basic (no electricity or running water) but comfortable. Vans leave Uncle Tan's B&B at Gum Gum at 2:30pm daily, and return from the camp by 12:30pm, in time to catch the 2pm bus to Kota Kinabalu. (☎531 639; www.uncletan.com. 3-day, 2-night package RM200 per person. Reserve well in advance, especially from June-Aug.)

TURTLE ISLANDS PARK

Forty kilometers from Sandakan's coast, Turtle Islands Park is made up of three islands—**Selingaan, Gulisan,** and **Bakkungan Kecil**—jointly protected by the Malaysian and Philippine governments. It is a nesting home to **Green** and **Hawksbill Turtles,** whose eggs and flesh have been harvested for centuries by the local Cagayan people. Egg counts dropped from 700,000 in the late 1960s to less than 250,000 in 1987. The Green Turtles prefer to lay their eggs on Selingaan from July to September, while the more elusive Hawksbills nest at Gulisan from February to April. All eggs laid in Selingaan are collected each evening by park rangers and resettled at the park's turtle hatcheries. After 50-60 days, the turtles emerge and are released. It's estimated that a mere 3% survive into adulthood. Green turtles are seen year-round, and it's extremely rare for a night to pass without a sighting. The islands also offer opportunities to swim and **snorkel** in the Sulu Sea.

> **TIP** The success of turtle rehabilitation efforts hinges largely on visitor conduct. Campfires, the use of bright lights, and any singing or loud music on the beaches are prohibited at night—such action frightens the turtles. Guests are encouraged to stay in their chalets rather than wander the beaches at night; park rangers will inform visitors of the prime viewing times.

Many guesthouses offer package tours. Round-trip **transportation** from Sandakan to the park costs RM100 (2½-3hr; schedules vary). Contact the Tourist Information Centre (☎229 751) for information. Pricey accommodations are run by **Crystal Quest Sdn. Bhd ❺**. Make reservations one month in advance at their office at the Sabah Parks Jetty near the yacht club in Sandakan. (☎212 711; mailing address P.O. Box 848, 90709, Sandakan, Sabah, Malaysia. Doubles RM125 per person, with shared bath, A/C, 2 meals RM150.)

MYANMAR

HIGHLIGHTS OF MYANMAR

CULTURAL HERITAGE. **Bagan** (p. 46), the 11th-century capital of Myanmar, retains one of the most impressive collections of ancient archaeological sites in Southeast Asia. **Kyaiktiyo Pagoda,** (p. 28) also known as the Golden Rock Pagoda, perches precariously on a giant gold-sheathed boulder. Witness the entertaining Burmese **marionette theater,** *yok-thei pwe,* (p. 40) at Mandalay's Garden Villa Theater.

HANGING OUT. Take in the natural beauty and surrounding mountains of **Inle Lake** (p. 52). The fresh air and cooler temperatures make it an attractive retreat from the heat and chaos of the cities. Peruse the production processes of Myanmar's **artisan guilds,** from Pathein's parasol-makers to the Mandalay artists who produce the gold leaf that worshippers use to gild images of the Buddha.

BEACHES. While one does not usually travel to Myanmar to hang out at the beach, **Chaung Tha Beach** (p.33) is Myanmar's main white-sand attraction aside from the difficult to reach Ngapali Beach.

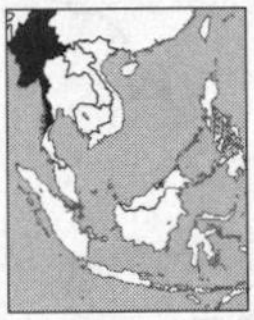

There are two views of Myanmar. One encompasses a country with glittering pagodas and a glorious past, where village life thrives undisturbed and the serenity of the country's Buddhist faith seeps into a culture of gentleness and respect. The other reveals one of the poorest countries in Southeast Asia, where real incomes are lower now than they were at independence in 1947, a government that represses and tortures its own people, the will of a people for democratic freedom is ruthlessly suppressed, and slave labor is the norm for public works. Both of these prospects illustrate in part the reality of Myanmar today. Known until recently as Burma, it has been a hermit state since the 1960s and was opened up to foreign investment and tourism only in 1989—a change that many hope will be the primary agent of some movement toward reform in the country. Travelers who step down at Yangon Airport will find golden *stupas*, picturesque lakes, and unspoiled mountain scenery. Myanmar's arid central plains gave rise to some of Southeast Asia's greatest civilizations, and the country's jewel, the ancient city of Bagan, is rivaled only by Angkor Wat as one of the most breathtaking sights in Southeast Asia. Perhaps the greatest treasure in Myanmar, however, is the grace of the Burmese people amidst the fierceness of their repression.

LIFE AND TIMES

DEMOGRAPHICS

Myanmar has one of the most intricate ethnic combinations in the world—the government officially recognizes over 135 different ethnicities—making any general breakdown by percentage largely superficial and politicized. That said, Myanmar's main ethnic groups are loosely defined to include the **Burman** majority (69%) and the seven minority populations of the **Shan** (8.5%), **Karen** (6.2%), **Rakhine** (4.5%), **Mon** (2.4%), **Chin** (2.2%), **Kachin** (1.4%), and **Karrenni** (0.4%). The term "Burman" refers to ethnicity, whereas "Burmese" refers to nationality. It is likely that the

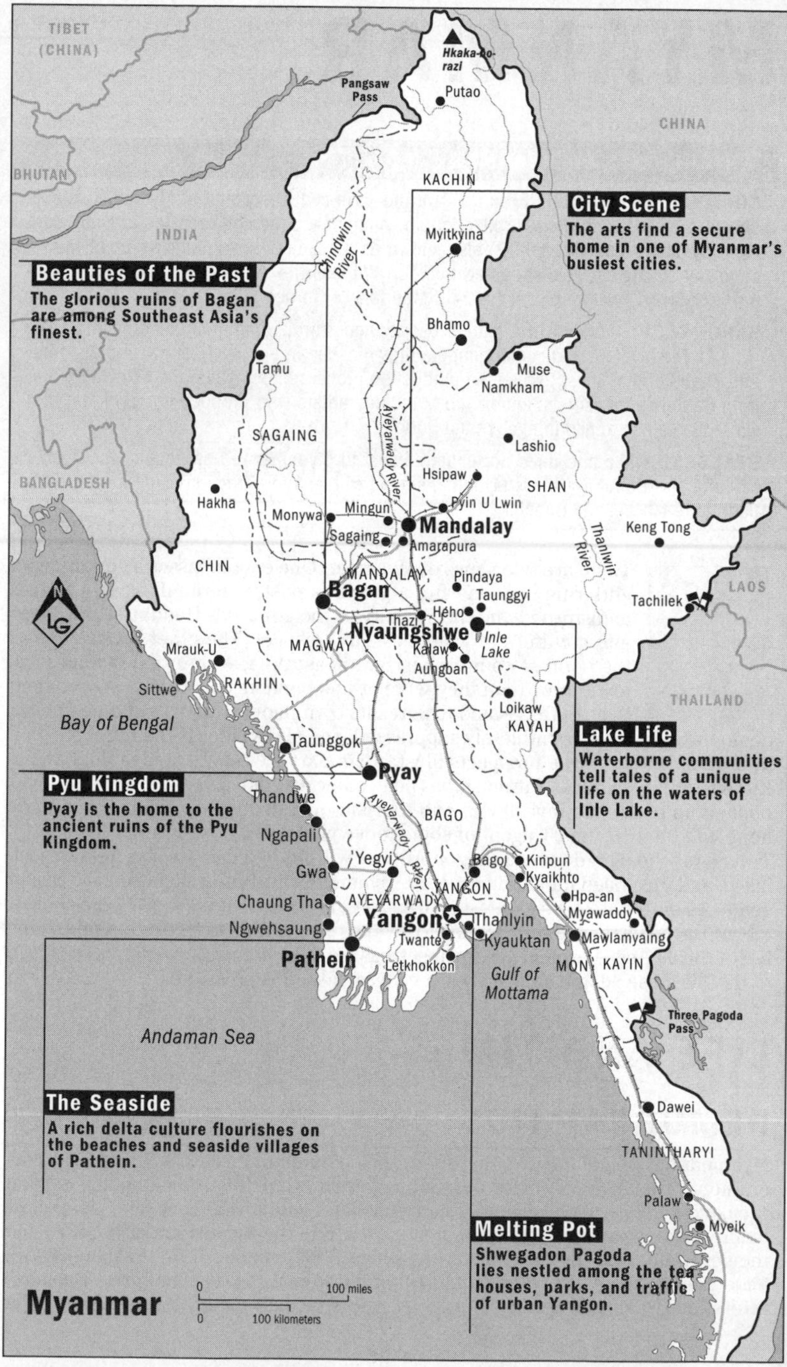

Myanmar
TIBET (CHINA)
CHINA
BHUTAN
INDIA
BANGLADESH
LAOS
THAILAND
Hkaka-Bo-razi
Pangsaw Pass
Putao
KACHIN
Myitkyina
Bhamo
Muse
Namkham
Lashio
Hsipaw
SHAN
Pyin U Lwin
Keng Tong
Tamu
SAGAING
Chindwin River
Ayeyarwady River
Thanlwin River
Hakha
Monywa
Mingun
Mandalay
Sagaing
Amarapura
CHIN
MANDALAY
Bagan
Pindaya
Taunggyi
Tachilek
Heho
Thazi
Nyaungshwe
Inle Lake
Kalaw
Aungban
MAGWAY
Mrauk-U
Sittwe
RAKHIN
Loikaw
KAYAH
Bay of Bengal
Taunggok
Pyay
Thandwe
Ngapali
BAGO
Ayeyarwady River
Yegyi
Gwa
Bago
Kinpun
Kyaikhto
YANGON
Chaung Tha
AYEYARWADY
Hpa-an
Myawaddy
Yangon
Thanlyin
Ngwehsaung
Twante
Kyauktan
Mawlamyaing
Pathein
Letkhokkon
MON
KAYIN
Gulf of Mottama
Three Pagoda Pass
Andaman Sea
Dawei
TANINTHARYI
Palaw
Myeik
0
100 miles
0
100 kilometers
City Scene
The arts find a secure home in one of Myanmar's busiest cities.
Beauties of the Past
The glorious ruins of Bagan are among Southeast Asia's finest.
Lake Life
Waterborne communities tell tales of a unique life on the waters of Inle Lake.
Pyu Kingdom
Pyay is the home to the ancient ruins of the Pyu Kingdom.
The Seaside
A rich delta culture flourishes on the beaches and seaside villages of Pathein.
Melting Pot
Shwegadon Pagoda lies nestled among the tea houses, parks, and traffic of urban Yangon.

FACTS AND FIGURES

Official Name: Union of Myanmar.

Government: Military Regime.

Capital: Yangon (Rangoon).

Land Area: 57,740 km^2.

Geography: Borders Bangladesh, India, China, Laos, and Thailand. River systems: Ayeyarwady, Chindwin, Mekong, Sittang, Salween. Mountain ranges: Himalayas in northern Myanmar.

Climate: Tropical, with average temperature 27°C (80°F). Rainy (low season) May-Oct., dry (high season) Nov.-Apr.

Major Cities: Yangon, Mandalay, Mawlamyaing, Bago, Pathein.

Population: 50 million.

Language: Burmese (official), over 100 different ethnic languages.

Religion: Buddhism (official), Islam, Christianity, Hinduism, animism.

Literacy Rate: 83.1% overall; 88.7% of men, 77.7% of women.

Major Exports: Rice, beans, pulses, teak, tobacco, rubber, gemstones, natural gas.

Phone Codes: Country Code: 95. International Dialing Prefix: 00.

actual percentage of the Burman population is closer to 50%, as the government counts as Burman anyone who is listed as Buddhist or anyone with a Burman name, which many Burmese citizens have adopted in order to avoid discrimination. The government continues to combat the lack of national unity in Myanmar. The Shan live in the mountain ranges near the border with Thailand and have been struggling for centuries to establish an autonomous state. The Karen also have a complex relationship with the Burman majority, but in early 2004 they agreed to end hostilities. The last **official census** to have any credibility was taken in 1931, which reveals more about the central Burmese authorities than it does about the country's population. A lack of reliable data makes Myanmar's population statistics ambiguous; most sources estimate a figure ranging from 48 to 51 million.

LANGUAGE

The official language is **Burmese,** although ethnic minority groups often have their own dialects and languages. The Burmese script has only recently been adapted to many of the tribal languages; these previously had no written form. The precise name of the country is a subject of much contention. In 1989, the ruling military junta outlawed the name **"Burma"** in an attempt to purge the nation of its past as a British colony. One of the earliest references to "Myanmar" appears on the stone inscription of a temple built in the 12th century A.D. The British corrupted the local word for the majority Burman ethnic group, *Bamar*, in order to create "Burma" in the first place, a gesture which overlooks the complexity of Myanmar's ethnic mix. In Burmese, the nation has always been referred to as **"Myanmar."** Still, the "r" at the end of Myanmar is merely a linguistic construct to lengthen the last syllable; most government-run organizations leave off the "r" in favor of a more accurate romanization of the Burmese word, **"Myanma."** Most of the international press, however, refuses to acknowledge these changes as a symbolic gesture of their non-recognition of the ruling military junta.

RELIGION

THERAVADA BUDDHISM. Brought by **Indian merchants** looking for commercial opportunities in the Ayeyarwady delta, Buddhism did not become the dominant religion until 1044, when **King Anawratha** ascended to the throne of the Burmese

Kingdom in Bagan. Today, about 89% of the Burmese population practices Theravada Buddhism, which is distinguished from Mahayana Buddhism in that it is the older of the two sects and its followers consider Theravada to be closer to the teachings of the Buddha. Over the centuries, the religion has become laced with aspects of **animism** and **spirit worship.** The Buddhist temple, which lies at the center of the community, has both educational and spiritual purposes. All men and women are required to enter a monastery or nunnery as a novice at least once for a period of nine days. Affiliation with Buddhism also often serves political ends, since the junta, infamous for its "whimsical" partiality, tends to favor Buddhists and Buddhism. As of June 2004, the World Buddhist Summit has been scheduled to take place in Yangon in December 2004. This has ignited controversy as to whether or not the Summit will benefit Buddhism in Myanmar or the repressive military regime.

CHRISTIANITY. A prominent 19th-century missionary to Myanmar, **Adoniram Judson**, translated the Bible from Hebrew into Burmese and worked successfully to convert a large portion of the **Karen** minority group to Christianity. Based on the mystique surrounding the Karen's history and creation myths, which many scholars believe echo Judeo-Christian stories, it has been suggested that the Karen may be a **lost tribe of Israel.** Their Christianity has fostered an uneasy relationship between them and the Burman majority and has resulted in waves of Karen refugees flooding across the Thai border to live in refugee camps.

MYANMAR: TO GO OR NOT TO GO? The question of whether to go to Myanmar echoes the debate that once plagued travelers to South Africa under apartheid. Tourism in Myanmar supports financially one of the world's worst military regimes, but in one of Southeast Asia's poorest countries, the fledgling tourist industry is, for many, the only alternative to state-sponsored slave labor. Increasingly relaxed tourist regulations mean that informed travelers can direct their money to Myanmar's people, not to its repressive government (see **Keep the Bucks Where They Belong,** p. 462). Many Burmese hope that more travelers will visit their impoverished nation and bring money with them; some also want travelers to witness the political situation and tell others about it. The Burmese government's abuses are not a new story, yet they have only recently come to the attention of the world after the country opened to foreign investment and tourism in 1989. Many argue that responsible and informed tourism is a far more effective means for change than isolating a military government that will then have no incentive to stop its abuse of power. However, it is important to note that Burmese citizens have disappeared or been beaten severely for discussing politics with foreigners, no doubt due to an insidious network of government informants. Military intelligence interrogated a family-restaurant owner for 24hr. after he spoke with travelers who tried to visit one of Myanmar's "no-go" areas. For the locals' sake, **avoid discussion of politics** and educate yourself about how to avoid empowering the military junta.

ISLAM. The government claims that Muslims enjoy freedom of worship. In the early 1990s, however, close to 250,000 Rohingya Muslims poured into Bangladesh to escape alleged government persecution in Myanmar; the **United Nations** intervened to send most of them home. In May 2003, with the aid of the Burmese government, Bangladeshi authorities began the process of speeding up the repatriation of thousands of refugees that remain living along the southeastern border. Between 1991 and 1992, about 2500 Muslims fled to Malaysia but were also largely repatriated with the help of the UN. Nevertheless, as of mid-2004 Malaysia retains a considerable population of Muslim refugees.

NAT WORSHIP. *Nat* worship is a pre-Buddhist practice that involves attributing a live soul to natural objects such as trees, lakes, or hills. Over time this concept evolved to include animistic spirits that exhibit power over a particular person, place, or type of experience. Despite King Anawrahta's 11th-century attempts to wipe out *nat* worship in favor of Theravada Buddhism, the practice still remains integral to the faith of among many Buddhists in Myanmar. The Burmese reconcile *nat* worship in conjunction with Buddhism with an easy maxim: *nat* worship tackles problems in this life, while Buddhism takes care of lives to come.

LAND

Like with much else in Myanmar, statistics on the country's plant and animal species are fuzzy. A few reports suggest that the flora and fauna of some regions have not been extensively studied since the 1800s. Myanmar exhibits a rich diversity of wildlife, from tropical reefs to the Himalayas. Unfortunately, deforestation and industrial pollution threaten these fragile ecosystems. In an effort to catch up with the other more economically developed countries of Southeast Asia, the government has contrived projects such as the **Yadana pipeline,** which involves the mining of gas fields in the Andaman Sea and the construction of a pipeline stretching from southeastern Myanmar to Thailand. This construction project combines damage to the environment with the mandatory slave labor of Burmese locals. Other such government plots to rapidly convert natural resources to hard currency have drastically depleted a great deal of rainforest and the plant and animal life within.

FLORA. Myanmar's **teak** forests, which account for over 80% of the world's teak, are being clear-cut at a rate that far outstrips that of the Amazonian rainforest. The forests were opened to Thai loggers so that the government could earn foreign credit, but this economically motivated plan has only temporarily bumped up the country's export statistics, and the countryside is now riddled with deforested areas. As fewer than 50,000 acres are replanted annually, deforestation has led to problems like erosion, flooding, and landslides. The government's agricultural policies have also forced Burmese farmers to increase rice production without crop rotation, leading to depletion of the soil and increased instances of pestilence.

WILDLIFE

The destruction of the teak forests has threatened many of Myanmar's endangered animal species, including the tiger, Asian elephant, silvered leaf monkey, and clouded leopard. The **Sumatran Rhino,** the only rhino with hair on its body and the only Asian rhino with two horns, is also on the brink of extinction; only a few remain, scattered throughout Myanmar, Malaysia, Thailand, and Sumatra. They live in the dense forests that are rapidly disappearing throughout the region. Also inhabiting these dense forests, the **binturong** fetches between US$1500-2000 in US exotic pet markets. Nocturnal and arboreal, the binturong is poached for its meat and for use in traditional aphrodisiacs. **Tigers** are another key ingredient in many traditional recipes, and hunting tigers is still legal in Myanmar, which contains 40% of Southeast Asia's priority tiger habitat. Myanmar is also home to one of the most diverse population of birds in Southeast Asia, including 47 endangered birds.

HISTORY

PREHISTORY

Five thousand years ago, the first humans settled in the **Ayeyarwady Valley.** The **Pyu** joined the upper valley around 200 BC and grew wealthy by controlling the lucrative trade route from China to India. Two centuries later, they were joined by the **Mon.** When their last major city fell to the Chinese in AD 832, the Burmese took over the Pyu River area and established the city of **Bagan** in 849.

BAGAN AND TOUNGOO DYNASTIES (1044-1776)

IMPORTANT DATES				
1044 Bagan Dynasty established under King Anawrahta.	**10-12th Centuries** 3000 temples constructed.	**1287** Mongol Invasion of lower Myanmar.	**1546** Tabinshweti reunifies nation.	**1752** The fall of the Toungoo Dynasty.

Myanmar's first unified kingdom arose during the **Bagan Dynasty,** founded in 1044 by **King Anawrahta,** who pronounced Theravada Buddhism the new state religion and expanded the kingdom. Under **King Alaungsithu,** Theravada Buddhism became increasingly dominant. Now seen as the **"classical age"** of Bagan, the dynasty spawned the building of an estimated 3000 temples, 100 of which still stand. The Mongol invasion of 1287, lead by **Kublai Khan**, marked the beginning of the empire's demise. Burmese forces rose again when, in 1546, **Tabinshwehti** declared himself king and reunified Myanmar under the **Toungoo Dynasty**, establishing the capital at Pegu. Frequent wars with Thai kings and Arakanese minorities led to the fall of the Toungoo rulers in 1752. **Alaungpaya** emerged as a powerful leader against the Toungoo and gained control of Myanmar, establishing the new city of Yangon. Following Alaungpaya's death in 1760, however, border conflicts escalated to war with Siam. **King Hsinbyushin** sacked Ayutthaya in 1776 and killed the king of Siam, creating an enmity that still festers today. After the Thais recaptured Ayutthaya, the tyrannical **King Bodawpaya** spent his reign embarking on several failed attempts to reinvade Siam. He channeled his frustrations by persecuting anyone who wasn't Buddhist and by strictly enforcing the death penalty for smoking opium.

COLONIALISM (1777-1945)

IMPORTANT DATES				
1824 First Anglo-Burmese war.	**1900-1930** British colonial rule.	**1930** Burmese Liberation movement.	**1937** New constitution adopted.	**1943** Aung San founds AFPFL.

The second Burmese invasion of the Arakan region, which bordered British colonial territory in India, instilled fear in the British that Myanmar would continue to expand and finally culminated in the Anglo-Burmese Wars of 1824 and 1852. Britain won both wars and subsequently annexed Pegu Province, renaming it Lower Burma. The third Anglo-Burmese War gave Britain control over Myanmar in 1886, at which time they renamed it "Burma" (see **Language,** p. 451) and made it a province of India with the capital at Yangon (Rangoon). During colonial occupation, Britain exploited Burma's rich oil and mineral deposits by building fledgling industries. However, the people of Burma didn't receive many benefits from these economic boosts. The British eliminated the monarchy and separated religion and government, thereby destabilizing Burmese society. An increase in the number of Indian immigrants (already over 7% of the population) displaced local labor and caused increasing economic duress. Resentment toward Indians culminated in the violent anti-Indian riots of the Burmese national liberation movement in 1930 as well as in the Burmese army's expulsion of over half-a-million

Indians during World War II. Dr. Ba Maw was elected Prime Minister in 1936 in the first and only election under British control. In 1937, Burma adopted a new constitution. The country's abundant natural resources and access road to China made it attractive to the Japanese during World War II; in March 1942, they seized Rangoon but were forced to withdraw in 1943. Meanwhile, Minister of Defense Aung San began a movement of organized resistance against the Japanese and planned to achieve complete independence for Burma with his Anti-Fascist People's Freedom League (AFPFL).

INDEPENDENCE (1945-1960)

IMPORTANT DATES		
1947 Burma gains independence.	**1948** Britain recognizes the Republic of the Union of Burma.	**1950** Civil war breaks out with minority rebel armies.

After World War II, the British took over, suspended the 1937 constitution, and implemented a governor system. As the new leader of the Council of Ministers, Aung San expelled the Communists from the AFPFL in 1946 and pressured the British to free Burma completely. Aung San was slain by right-wing politician U Saw in July 1947, just two months before the Burma Constituent Assembly, under Thakin Nu, achieved complete independence as the Republic of the Union of Burma. In opposition to the declaration, communists and other minority factions revolted, disrupting the government's control over most of the country. In 1948, minority Karen groups rebelled and cut off Rangoon's river, rail, and road communication systems. At the height of the civil war in 1950, many nations, including Britain and India, supplied the Burmese government with weaponry and money.

MILITARY RULE (1962-1995)

IMPORTANT DATES				
1962 First Military Government; BSPP established.	**1962** Military crushes protests.	**1988** SLORC takes over.	**1989** "Burma" becomes "Myanmar."	**1990** SLORC throws out election results.

In March 1962, **General Ne Win,** tired of the secession threats from ethnic groups, arrested prominent leaders, revoked the 1947 constitution, and established a military government. Citizens raged at restrictions on their freedoms, and students at Rangoon University demonstrated against the new regime. Acting on the indirect orders of General Ne Win, soldiers fired into the crowds and bombed the Students' Union, a Burmese nationalist symbol since 1930. Eyewitnesses reported hundreds of bodies strewn across the campus, but the official report cited only 15 dead and 27 wounded. To protect Burma from insurgent groups, the government established **Ka Kwe Ye (KKY),** or "Home Guard," a local militia group supported with the help of local druglords, who often bribed government drug enforcement officials to turn a blind eye to the area's thriving opium trade. After General Ne Win retired in 1972, the country sought foreign aid to combat serious economic stagnation caused by financial mismanagement and rampant corruption. By the late 1980s, resource-rich Burma had become one of the poorest nations in the world. Widespread anti-government riots erupted in Rangoon in October 1987, again accompanied by demonstrations and violent suppression by the military. By March 1988, **Aung San Suu Kyi,** daughter of the national hero Aung San, had become the driving force behind the democracy movement in Burma. One of General Ne Win's military groups, the **State Law and Order Restoration Council (SLORC),** took power and suspended the 1974 constitution, revoking the limited autonomy that had been granted to ethnic minority groups. The new dictatorship, under the rule of **General Saw Maung,** changed the name of the nation from "Union of Burma" to "Union of

Myanmar" in June 1989 in order to purge the country of colonial ghosts (see **Language,** p. 451). Aung San Suu Kyi was placed under house arrest in July 1989 for speaking openly against the government. Under the leadership of Aung San Suu Kyi, the **National League for Democracy (NLD)** won the national elections in 1990, but SLORC refused to honor the results and jailed most of the party leaders. Aung San Suu Kyi, though still under house arrest, won the **Nobel Peace Prize** in 1991.

MYANMAR TODAY

INTERNATIONAL FREE BURMA ACTIVISM. Latching onto the charismatic figure of Aung San Suu Kyi and her fight for democracy in Myanmar, international **human rights activists** have turned their attention to the plight of the Burmese. Numerous organizations have sprung up to agitate for **corporate divestment** from Myanmar, to sponsor educational activities, and to lobby the governments of Western nations to put political pressure on the military junta to improve the nation's human rights records. In the early 1990s, Levi-Strauss & Co. stated explicitly that business in Myanmar meant a tacit support of the repressive military junta. One company that has topped human rights activists' blacklists is **Unocal,** a California energy company that is invested in Myanmar. EarthRights International represented a group of Burmese peasants in a case that received high publicity from coverage on ABC's *20/20* show. These peasants claimed that Unocal was complicit in human rights violations allegedly committed by the Myanmar military on the construction site of the Yadana pipeline, which stretches from Southeastern Myanmar into Thailand. These accusations included forced labor and rape. In a corporate responsibility discussion paper, the company actively denied these allegations. The 1997 ruling, which stated that the case falls within American jurisdiction, set a precedent for holding American companies responsible for their actions overseas. More than 25 American cities and states have passed corporate divestment legislation with regards to Myanmar. As of June 2004, the United States renewed a one-year ban on Myanmar imports as a protest against the State Peace and Development Council's (the name changed from SLORC in November 1997) human rights violations. The ban was accompanied by a government increase in import taxes, which set of a frenzy of buying that resulted in a 4% decrease in value of the kyat against the dollar on the free-market.

DEMOCRACY UNDER HOUSE ARREST. A hero at home and abroad for her pro-democracy work and her leadership of the National League for Democracy (NLD), Aung San Suu Kyi has drifted in and out of house arrest since just before her party's electoral victory in 1990. Her release in 1995 was on the condition that she not travel outside of Yangon; violation of this restriction in 2000 landed her under house arrest for 19 months. Although her unconditional release in May 2002 was not publicized, a crowd of over 1000 gathered outside the NLD party headquarters to hear her speak. In late May 2003 Aung San Suu Kyi was the target of an orchestrated army attack while traveling with a convoy of her followers. Following the massacre, she was again placed under house arrest. The government claimed that it would release Aung San Suu Kyi in time for the beginning of the National Convention in May 2004, convened for the purpose of drafting a new, more democratic constitution. As of June 2004, the NLD has thus far boycotted this convention because Aung San Suu Kyi remains under house arrest. The government claims that the NLD leader is not essential to the progress of the National Convention. Many countries are skeptical of a pro-democracy constitution that suppresses the input of one who has pledged her life-long devotion to the cause of democracy in Myanmar. The government prohibits anyone from going anywhere near Aung San Suu Kyi's house, which is on University Ave. near Inya Lake in Yangon.

THAILAND-MYANMAR RELATIONS. The most recent controversy between the two neighbors erupted in May 2002 when officials in Yangon accused the Thai military of firing shells over the border during a routine Thai military exercise. Myanmar claimed that Thailand's actions supported ethnic Shan rebels and closed all **border checkpoints** with Thailand immediately, stepping up anti-Thai rhetoric and requiring citizens in Yangon to fly Myanmar's flag. A Myanmar writer, **Ma Ta Win,** published articles in the government mouthpiece *New Light of Myanmar* that Thailand interpreted as defamatory of their monarchy. Needless to say, this series of articles did little to improve the shaky relations. A subsequent Myanmar military offensive against the Shan accidentally crossed into Thai territory, which further angered the Thai. Myanmar aggression against minority groups in the border areas have precipitated waves of **refugees** into Thailand. By the end of 2001, Thailand was hosting 227,000 refugees, all but 700 of whom were from Myanmar.

DRUGS. For **United Nations International Narcotics Day** in 2002, Myanmar and Thailand incinerated a total of over US$1 billion worth of drugs—including 3000kg of **opium,** 240kg of pure **heroin** powder, and over 40 million **methamphetamines**–in a gesture to the international community that they are taking a no-nonsense attitude toward drug smuggling in the infamous **Golden Triangle** region. But after all, Myanmar and Afghanistan control 90% of the world's opium supply and are responsible for 60% of the heroin found on US streets. Most of these poppy products are grown and produced under the auspices of infamous drug lord **Wei Hsieo-kang,** leader of the Wa State Army. But even as Myanmar's opium and heroin production is on the decline due to increased governmental pressure, drug lords have shifted their focus to methamphetamines, which are more easily produced and smuggled. Today, Myanmar produces eight times as many pills as they did two years ago.

CUSTOMS AND ETIQUETTE

PUBLIC BEHAVIOR. Bamahasin chin describes the essential "Burmese-ness" that encapsulates Burmese ideals of good behavior. It prizes the subtle and quiet over the loud and direct, knowledge of Buddhist scriptures, respect for elders, discretion in dress and attitudes toward the opposite sex, and the ability to speak idiomatic Burmese. It is unseemly to show too much emotion, especially in public, and loss of temper is seen as a loss of face. The **head** is considered the most spiritual part of the body and is therefore protected at any cost in the rain; it is not unusual to see people walk down the street during a monsoon with nothing but a hand over their head. Images of the Buddha, however old, ruined, or broken, are sacred above all. When interacting with others, try to avoid using your left hand—it is considered polite to offer or accept things by extending the right arm while bending the left hand to touch the right elbow.

ARTS AND RECREATION

ARCHITECTURE. Much of Burmese art is associated with *nats*, deities ranging from ghosts of people to spirits of trees who wreak vengeance on those who frustrate them. The Buddha is the most important *nat*, and thus Buddhist **monasteries** and **temples** are lavishly adorned like divine palaces. **Stupas** and brick structures with bell-like apexes characterize architecture from the **Mon period.** Modern structures show an **Indian** influence, with thicker apexes that taper to the top.

DANCE AND DRAMA. All-female **dance shows** feature solo performers who sing a shrill-sounding song and dance using their feet, head, and arms to create thousands of movements. Dramatic **street-side performances** are often ceremonies portraying various *nat* stories. Men dressed as women (and vice-versa) are the main performers at these shows. **Marionette theater,** or *yok-thei pwe,* which flourished in the late 18th century, has almost ceased to exist with the exception of those puppeteers that appear regularly in Mandalay and more sporadically at temple fairs or local festivals.

BURMESE COOKING. There are not many restaurants in Myanmar that serve authentic Burmese food, since most locals prefer Indian or Chinese when dining out. However, don't miss the opportunity to sample some of Myanmar's unique offerings, available from street vendors or in the few Burmese restaurants. The base of Burmese cuisine is steamed rice or rice and wheat noodles, accompanied by a mild curry dish and two salad or vegetable dishes. Restaurants that serve Burmese curries only prepare them in the morning, which means that when served later in the day food is not reheated and usually has more oil added as a preservative. Common ingredients are: fried garlic, fermented tea leaves, coconut, shrimp paste, onions, fish sauce, lemongrass, ginger, chiles, turmeric, and coriander. On menus in Myanmar, "mutton" refers to goat-meat.

Ngapi: fish, shrimp, or prawns that have been left to rot and then dried and salted to form a paste used in flavoring many dishes.

Mohinga: a fish chowder that is typically eaten for breakfast but is available any time of day. Made from rice noodles, fish, egg, the soft core of the banana plant, and thickened with pea powder, cream of coconut, and, occasionally, ground peanuts. Seasoned with lemongrass, garlic, ginger, chiles, and turmeric.

Thok: fruit and vegetable salad.

Lephet Thote: a traditional green tea salad unique to Myanmar. Made with fermented green tea leaves, dried shrimp, toasted yellow peas or kidney beans, sesame seeds, fried garlic, green peppers, lime juice, and green chiles.

FILM. Those **cinemas** that haven't been privatized have fallen into ruins, complete with cockroaches, leaking toilets, jamming projectors, and no air-conditioning. Movies are often shown in teashops as a way to encourage customers to stay and eat and drink more. Despite recent government attempts to revitalize it, Myanmar's film industry has steadily declined. One problem is a lack of the money required to import foreign film supplies, but perhaps the greatest deterrent is the government's series of censorship guidelines. Previously producing approximately 80 movies per year, the Myanmar Motion Picture Enterprise released only 27 films for distribution in 2003.

MUSIC. The Burmese **orchestra** is dominated by its drummer, who sits within a railing enclosing 21 drums. Other instruments include a gong ensemble, bass and tenor drums, cymbals, and bamboo clappers. In larger orchestras, melodic instruments such as oboes or flutes are added.

TELEVISION AND RADIO. Myanmar has two main television stations: TV Myanmar, which is state-run by the Myanmar TV and Radio Department, and TV Myawady, which is army-run. A new entertainment station was released recently, the Myanmar Media Box, which will broadcast the 2004 Euro soccer championship, complete with celebrity and sports analyst commentary on the games. Myanmar's airwaves are also dominated by the government, with the exception of the Democratic Voice of Burma (an opposition, short-wave station run by Burmese exiles living in Norway), Voice of America (VOA), and the BBC.

SPORTS. The people of Myanmar love soccer, and images of David Beckham are everywhere. Rugby comes in a distant second.

HOLIDAYS AND FESTIVALS (2005)

DATE	NAME	DESCRIPTION AND LOCATION
Jan. 4	Independence Day	A 7-day fair is held at the Kandawgyi Lake in Yangon.
Jan. 10	Kachin Manao Festival	In Kachin State, the festival marks the day on which Kachin State joined the Union of Myanmar in 1948; there is also a traditional *nat* festival to ensure a good harvest.
Feb. 12	Union Day	Commemorates Aung Sang's attempts to unify Myanmar's many different ethnic groups. The government organizes early morning celebrations in People's Park in Yangon.
Mar. 2	Peasants' Day	Honors the country's workforce by commemorating the anniversary of the 1962 coup.
early-Mar.	Tabaung Full-moon Day	The lunar month of Tabaung is regarded as an auspicious time for building new pagodas. Pagodas all over the country hold local celebrations.
Mar. 27	Armed Forces Day	Also known as Resistance Day, commemorated with parades and fireworks.
mid-Apr.	Thingyan (Water Festival)	Commemorates the Burmese New Year and involves throwing water on passersby to "wash away" the sins and bad memories of the year.
Apr.-May	Watering the Sacred Bo Tree Festival	Held on the day of the full moon, this festival commemorates the Buddha's birthday.
July-Aug.	Buddhist Rains Retreat	The 3-month Buddhist Lent begins on the Waso full moon day, accompanied by donations to local monasteries and pagodas.
late Aug.	Taung Byone Nat Festival	Observe a traditional, 7-day *nat* festival in this village, around a 1hr. drive from Mandalay. Ceremonies are held mostly at night and include spirit dances and ceremonial reenactments.
Sept.-Oct.	Phaung Daw U Kyaung Festival	Images of the Buddha are loaded onto decorated barges and carried all along Lake Inle. The accompanying festival features music, dance, and boat races.
late Oct.	Kyaukse Elephant Dance Festival	In Kyaukse, 26 miles south of Mandalay, elaborately decorated, life-size elephant figures sing and dance to music on the day before the full moon of Thadingyut.
late Oct.	Thadingyut Full-moon Day; Thadingyut Light Festival	Marks the end of Buddhist Lent and is accompanied by the 3-day Festival of Lights, which celebrates the Buddha's return from preaching in the highest realm of heaven. All of Myanmar is illuminated with candles, fire balloons, and paper lanterns.
late Oct.-early Nov.	Shwezigon Pagoda Festival	In Bagan, candles and fireworks are offered to the pagoda. Entertainment consists of evening dances, songs, and plays.
late Nov.	Kahtein Robe-Weaving Festival	A weaving competition held from dusk to dawn before the Tazaungdaing full-moon day, in which teams of women weave robes, called "Ma Tho Thin Gan." The robes are subsequently offered to Buddha images in local pagodas.
late Nov.	Tazaungdaing Full-moon Day and Festival	Locals offer robes and other gifts to the monks of nearby monasteries in a ceremony known as "Kahtein." Sagaing, with its heavy concentration of monasteries, is an ideal place to observe the festival.

ADDITIONAL RESOURCES

GENERAL HISTORY

Living Silence: Burma Under the Military Rule, by Christina Fink (2001). A description of the impact of military rule on the Burmese people.

Burma in Revolt: Opium and Insurgency Since 1948, by Bertil Lintner (1994). Unravels the complex relationship between drug trade and the country's ethnic insurgencies.

FICTION AND NON-FICTION

Burmese Days, by George Orwell (1962). A classic. An insightful treatment of colonial Burma, drawing on Orwell's experience as a colonial official in the early 20th century.

Freedom From Fear and Other Writings, by Aung San Suu Kyi (1991). A must-read for anyone wishing to familiarize themselves with the struggle to bring democracy to Myanmar. This is the work for which Aung San Suu Kyi won the Nobel Peace Prize.

The Voice of Hope, by Aung San Suu Kyi (1997). Written by the Nobel Peace Prize winner and one of the world's spiritual and political leaders, this humorous personal narrative discusses the fight for democracy in Myanmar.

Singing to the Dead: A Missioner's Life Among Refugees from Burma, by Victoria Armour-Hileman (2002). The journal of a Catholic missionary working with displaced Mon refugees at an illegal camp in Thailand.

From the Land of Green Ghosts: a Burmese Odyssey, by Pascal Khoo Thwe (2002). The memoir of a Mandalay University student demonstrator, who successfully flees Myanmar's 1988 political upheaval to study English literature at Cambridge University.

Burma: Insurgency and the Politics of Ethnicity, by Martin Smith (1999). A highly regarded scholarly examination of the complexities of modern Myanmar's political and racial conflicts.

TRAVEL BOOKS

The Trouser People: A Story of Burma—In the Shadow of the Empire, by Andrew Marshall (2002). This travelogue describes the adventures of Sir George Scott, the British explorer and later administrator of Myanmar who introduced soccer to Burmese natives. Marshall retraces Scott's travels, establishing connections between British imperialism and Myanmar's current military regime.

FILM

Beyond Rangoon, dir. John Boorman (1995). A poignant portrayal of the fight for democracy in Myanmar. Based on actual events, this is the movie that is largely responsible for bringing the plight of the Burmese people to the attention of the world.

NO WORK, ALL PLAY

SEASON OF LIGHT

The end of monsoon season comes as a relief to Myanmar's people. After fending off the rain, being trapped indoors, and staving off rising flood waters for months, October brings new light. This is *Thadingyut*—Buddhism's second-largest festival.

In one key aspect of the holiday, participants pay respects to their elders. At dusk, with candles and lanterns lighting up homes, families pay visits to parents, teachers, and mentors. Students and children *kadaw* (crouch with clasped hands raised to the forehead) and give offerings.

Thadingyut is also the time of many weddings. It is considered bad luck to marry during the rains, so *Thadingyut* not only relieves the rainy season's pent-up emotions, but it is also believed that *Thadingyut* imbues new unions with the blessings of the Buddha, who descended to earth on a bejeweled ladder at this time of year.

Since Burma's people usher in the new season of warmth by lighting up their homes, *Thadingyut* is better known as the "Festival of Light." The lights welcome the Buddha into homes and show him reverence, while he in return spreads joy to the occupants. The best places to view the festival are smaller towns and villages, where homemade *see-see* lamps (sesame oil with cotton wicks) are used to light up houses and streets.

ON THE WEB

Irrawaddy Publishing Group (www.irrawaddy.org). Established in 1992 by Burmese citizens in exile, this website claims to promote freedom of the press and access to information free from political bias. Provides up-to-date news briefs pertaining to Burma and other countries of Southeast Asia.

The Golden Land of Myanmar (www.myanmar.com). This official government website has information steeped in propaganda, including a link to the Ministry of Defense that publishes an online nine-volume book called "The Truth."

Free Burma (www.freeburma.org). This website features links to pro-democracy and activists groups.

The Burma Project (www.burmaproject.org). A site dedicated to increasing international awareness about a range of issues in Myanmar, from education and the environment to promoting freedom and democracy.

ESSENTIALS

MYANMAR PRICE ICONS					
SYMBOL:	❶	❷	❸	❹	❺
ACCOMM.	Under US$2 Under 1300kyat	US$2-5 1300-3250kyat	US$5-10 3250-6500kyat	US$10-20 6500-13,000kyat	Over US$20 Over 13,000kyat
FOOD	Under US$0.25 Under 150kyat	US$0.25-0.50 150-300kyat	US$0.50-1 300-650kyat	US$1-3 650-1950kyat	Over US$3 Over 1950kyat
Please note that currency is converted at free-market rates for the purposes of this chart.					

EMBASSIES AND CONSULATES

MYANMAR CONSULAR SERVICES ABROAD

Australia: Embassy, 22 Arkana St., Yarralumla, ACT 2600, Canberra (☎02 6273 3811 or 6273 3751; fax 6273 4357; mecanberra@bigpond.com). Open M-F 9am-4pm.

Canada: Embassy, The Sandringham Building, 85 Range Rd., Ste. 902-903, Ottawa, Ontario K1N 8J6 (☎613-232-6434/46; fax 232-6435).

UK: Embassy, 19A Charles St., London W1J 5DX (☎020 7499 8841, 7629 9531, or 7629 4486; fax 7629 4169). Open M-F 9:30am-4:30pm.

US: Embassy, 2300 S St. N.W., Washington, D.C. 20008 (☎202-332-9044 or 332-9045/49; fax 332-9046; MEWashDC@aol.com). **Consulate,** 10 E 77th St., New York, NY 10021 (☎212-535-1310; fax 737-2421).

CONSULAR SERVICES IN MYANMAR

Australian: Embassy, 88 Strand Rd., Yangon (☎95-1 251-809/10; fax 246-159; dimarangoon@dfat.gov.au). Client counter hours M-F 9:30am-noon; staff office hours M-F 8am-4pm. Also serves **Canadian** citizens.

New Zealand: Embassy (in Thailand), M Thai Tower, 14th Floor, All Seasons Place, 87 Wireless Rd., Lumpini, Bangkok 10330 (☎66-2 254-2530; fax 253-9045 or 253-0249) Open M-F 7:30am-noon and 1-4pm.

UK: Embassy, 80 Strand Rd., P.O. Box 638, Yangon (☎95-1 380-322, 370-863-5, or 371-852-3; fax 370-866; chancery@Rangoon.mail.fco.gov.uk). Open M-F 8am-4:30pm, except W 8am-1pm. Also serves **New Zealand** citizens.

US: Embassy, 581 Merchant St., Yangon (☎95-1 379-880 or 370-963/65; rangoon-info@state.gov). Open M-F 8am-4:30pm. **Consular Services,** 114 University Avenue Rd., Kamayut Township, Yangon (☎95-1 538-037; fax 538-040; consular-rangoo@state.gov). Open M-Th 8am-4:30pm, F 8am-noon.

TOURIST SERVICES

Tourism greatly declined in Myanmar with the installation in 1988 of the SLORC (now SPDC). However, the government worked throughout the 1990s to regenerate the tourism industry, which led to an increase in the number of tourists, from 5000 in 1989 to roughly 206,000 in 2000. **Myanmar Travels and Tours (MTT)** does a good job but only provides information on government services. Guesthouse owners and travel agents are the next-best resources and can offer advice regarding non-government transportation and services.

! **KEEP THE BUCKS WHERE THEY BELONG.** Stupendous sights, vibrant cultures, and the friendliest people in the world aren't enough to draw more than a trickle of tourists to Myanmar each year. "Do not let your tourist dollars pay for SPDC's bullets," urge flyers in Bangkok guest houses, and socially conscious backpackers seem to listen. Many argue that visiting Myanmar may end up helping the vicious regime that controls it, but others counter that educated and responsible tourism may be an agent of change and, more importantly, may transfer valuable and scarce tourist dollars to Myanmar's impoverished citizens, who otherwise have no source of income (See **Myanmar: To go or not to go?,** p. 452). There are simple ways to minimize your contribution to SPDC and to maximize the portion that goes to citizens who make their livelihood from the tourist industry.

Government-owned agencies: Government-run agencies listed in *Let's Go* are marked with a **M**. Private alternatives are almost always listed.

Transportation: Use only privately run transport. Don't take trains, Myanmar Travels and Tours' boats, or Myanmar Airways, all of which are state-owned.

Accommodations: Stay in private guesthouses. Most accommodations listed in this guide are privately owned. Even private guesthouses must pay for an accommodations license, so some money is still going to the government.

Sights: Many of Myanmar's sights carry hefty entrance fees, and it's unclear where the cash ends up. If you have an ISIC card or student ID, wave it in front of every attendant you see; some will give discounts.

Myanmar Tourism Promotion Board, Marketing Committee c/o Traders Hotel, Level 3, Business Centre, 223 Sule Pagoda Rd., Yangon. (☎95-1 242-828; www.myanmar-tourism.com).

M **Myanmar Hotels and Tourism Services,** 77-91 Sule Pagoda Rd., Yangon 11141 (☎95-1 282-013; fax 254-417; mtt.mnt@mptmail.net.mm).

TOURIST SERVICES ABROAD

Myanmar Tourist Services, 36c Sisters Avenue, London SW11 5SQ (☎0171 223 8987).

DOCUMENTS AND FORMALITIES

Travelers seven years and older must obtain single-entry, 28-day tourist visas from Myanmar embassies abroad. Allow five to seven business days for processing. The most convenient embassies are in nearby Bangkok, Kuala Lumpur, and Hong Kong. Once in Myanmar, it is possible to obtain two **visa extensions** for 14 days each. Travelers may be asked to present their passports with valid visas at accommodations, airports, train stations, and at frequent security checkpoints. Journalists can rarely acquire visas, and tourists mistaken for journalists have been harassed or have had materials confiscated when leaving Myanmar. In order to stop international child abduction, government officials have been known to require documentation proving the relationship status of children to their adult traveling companions.

MONEY

CURRENCY AND EXCHANGE

The currency chart below is based on August 2004 exchange rates between local currency and Australian dollars (AUS$), Canadian dollars (CDN$), European Union euros (EUR€), New Zealand dollars (NZ$), British pounds (UK£), and US dollars (US$). Check currency converters on websites like www.xe.com or www.bloomberg.com or a large newspaper for the latest exchange rates. Dual exchange rates reflect disparity between the fixed government rate and the free-market rate. The official rate is listed first, followed by the free-market rate. Rates change as much as 20% daily. The Myanmar **kyat** (pronounced "chat") comes in

CURRENCY (KYAT)

AUS$1 = 3.97KYAT, 400KYAT	100KYAT = AUS$25.19, $0.243
CDN$1 = 4.24KYAT, 500KYAT	100KYAT = CDN$23.58, $0.2
EUR€1 = 7.01KYAT, 750KYAT	100KYAT = EUR€14.27, €0.133
NZ$1 = 3.61KYAT, 350KYAT	100KYAT = NZ$27.70, $0.286
UK£1 = 10.67KYAT, 1150KYAT	100KYAT = UK£9.37, £0.087
US$1 = 6.26KYAT, 920KYAT	100KYAT = US$15.97, $0.108

denominations of 1,5, 10, 15, 20, 45, 50, 90, 100, 200, 500, and 1000. Particularly in the tourism industry and international trade, US$ and their "one-to-one equivalent," **Foreign Exchange Certificates (FECs),** operate as legal tender. FECs are printed in denominations of 1, 5, 10, and 20 but as of late have become increasingly obsolete.

The government has fixed the exchange rate at 6.7kyat to US$1, but the free-market rate hovers around 900kyat, with each US$ reaping 50kyat more than an FEC. **Avoid exchanging currency at the airport;** the best places to change money at the free-market rate are officially licensed booths, guesthouses, and private travel agencies. Many people will solicit you to change money on the street; not only will you most likely be cheated, the police may attempt to interfere. Rates in larger cities like Yangon and Mandalay tend to be 10-20kyat better than in smaller towns like Kalaw or Nyaungshwe, so it pays to convert before heading into the countryside. Apart from government banks and a few luxury hotels and restaurants, credit cards and traveler's checks **are not** readily accepted in Myanmar, so it's necessary to carry US$ in cash. Budget travelers can expect to spend around US$15 per day. There is a US$10 departure tax for all international flights.

TIP **FECS NO MORE.** As of August 2004, individual travelers (called "Foreign Independent Travelers" in bureaucratic jargon") are no longer required to exchange US$200 into 200FECs upon arrival at Mandalay and Yangon International Airports. Foreign Exchange Certificates are the SPDC's means of keeping cash in government coffers. The former mandatory monetary exchange regulated how much visitors spent while traveling in the country, and only FECs bought in excess of the required amount could be changed back into US$ at departure. Since the government can no longer expect to bring in currency "tagged to the US dollar," they require purchases to be made in US dollars outright. As a result, most services run by the government (trains, Myanmar Airways, ferries), or those establishments that require permits from the SPDC to service foreigners (mostly guesthouses), only accept US$ in cash. Services used by both foreigners and locals (buses, most restaurants and food sellers) can be paid for in kyats.

GETTING THERE

BY PLANE. Mingaladon Airport (p. 466), near Yangon, is the international gateway to Myanmar for the majority of travelers. **Air Mandalay** (www.air-mandalay.com), **Myanmar Airways** (www.maiair.com), and **Yangon Airlines** (www.yangonair.com) are the major international and domestic carriers. **Bangkok Airways** (www.bangkokair.com) flies to Mandalay from Chiang Mai, Thailand.

BY LAND. Refer to the following table for overland border crossings in Myanmar.

BORDER CROSSINGS: FROM THAILAND Due to periodic fighting and fickle government regulations, the status of these border crossings changes with frustrating frequency. As the tourism mouthpiece of the SPDC, Myanmar Travels And Tours (MTT) will know the current status better than will locals or guesthouse staff. Foreigners can officially enter Myanmar by land from 3 points in Thailand: from **Mae Sai** (p. 788) to **Tachilek;** from **Mae Sot** (p. 777) to **Myawaddy;** and from **Sangkhlaburi** to **Phayathonzu** via the **Three Pagoda Pass.** In the past it has also been possible to take a ferry between **Ranong** in southern Thailand and **Kawthoung.** All 3 crossings include customs and immigration checkpoints. Depending on the level of insurgent activity, you may be confined to the immediate area near your point of entry.

GETTING AROUND

BY PLANE. Air travel is the fastest, safest, most comfortable, and most expensive means of getting around the country. Frequent connections and increasing competition for routes between major tourist destinations make flying very convenient. **Myanmar Airways** had two major accidents in 1998. Preferable are **Yangon Airways** and **Air Mandalay.** Travel agencies charge 10-15% less than airline offices.

TIP **DEPARTURE CARD.** This pink card is stapled into visitors' passports upon arrival. Without it fines are levied upon departure. If it gets lost, replacements can be purchased at Yangon and Mandalay post offices.

BY BUS. Bus travel is the cheapest mode of transportation. The recent proliferation of private bus lines has led to improvements in comfort and convenience, though no luxury can compensate for the condition of the roads, which are some of the worst in Southeast Asia. Tickets are always cheaper when purchased directly from the bus company or at the bus terminal. Book at least one day in advance to reserve a good seat; avoid rows in the back or over the wheels. During long journeys (up to 20hr.), the bus will (thankfully) stop several times for food and bathroom breaks.

BY TRAIN. Train travel in Myanmar is state-owned and operated. **Myanma Railways** has three classes: sleeper, upper, and ordinary; most find the last intolerable. Fares for beds in sleeper-class and reclining seats in upper-class are considerably more expensive but remain competitive internationally. Tickets must be reserved a day in advance (sleepers up to a week in advance) and must be paid in **US$ cash.** The most trafficked route is the **Yangon-Bago-Thazi-Mandalay** line. An extension from Thazi to **Shwenaung (Inle Lake)** is extremely slow but scenic. There is also service between Mandalay and **Bagan.**

BY BOAT. Powerful river currents render boat travel impractical for visitors on a limited tourist visa. The journey from Yangon to Pyay takes three days. The only exception is the **Inland Water Transport** boat service from Mandalay to Bagan, which takes 9-14hr. During the dry season, exposed sandbars have snagged boats—inquire about current conditions.

HEALTH AND SAFETY

EMERGENCY NUMBERS: Police/Fire/Ambulance: ☎999.

MEDICAL EMERGENCIES. Medical facilities in Myanmar are unreliable for even the most basic care. If in need of medical attention, go to a private clinic or hospital rather than to a larger, government-run facility. Many foreign medications have been smuggled into the country and are therefore not safe for consumption. Overseas medical insurance that covers medical evacuation in the event of an emergency is highly recommended.

HEALTH RISKS. The tap-water in Myanmar is not safe to drink. Drink plenty of bottled water, avoid unpasteurized dairy products, and make sure that all fruits and vegetables have been thoroughly cooked or peeled. Locals are accustomed to cooking with and drinking only bottled water, so the food served in restaurants is fairly safe. The fresh vegetable plates in Burmese meals are safe in reputable restaurants because they are changed often and are covered between customers. Utensils are often served in bowls of steaming water to ensure patrons of cleanliness. However, on the street one can never be certain. Malaria is widespread throughout Myanmar, so be sure to carry antimalarial medication. Protect against mosquito bites to prevent Dengue fever, Japanese B encephalitis, and plague. Avoid handling animals and swimming in fresh water.

WOMEN TRAVELERS. Women traveling alone in Myanmar are not as susceptible to harassment as in other Asian countries. Dress modestly to avoid undesirable attention.

MINORITY TRAVELERS. As long as you stay within government-regulated areas, travel in Myanmar is relatively safe. Avoid acts of political protest and be wary when discussing politics with Burmese locals.

GLBT TRAVELERS. There are no laws that prohibit homosexuality in Myanmar. However, discretion is advised.

KEEPING IN TOUCH

Myanmar's **postal system** is difficult and unreliable. Sending letters is straightforward and inexpensive, but mailing parcels is a convoluted, time-consuming process—set aside at least 1½hr. Customers are required to buy regulation boxes and tape at the post office and complete a host of customs and address forms. Fees amount to 900-1200kyat for a 10kg maximum limit to most parts of the world. DHL services are available in Yangon (at Traders Hotel) and Mandalay.

The **telephone system** further reveals the inadequacies of Myanmar's communications infrastructure. Overseas calls from Myanmar are among the most expensive in the world. Placing international calls can be accomplished using the expensive IDD services at government telephone offices and private telephone offices, hotels, and guesthouses. (Calls to North America about US$5-10 per min.) Savvy planners who manage to forward itineraries and guesthouse numbers to acquaintances can receive calls along the way.

There is **Internet** access in three cities: Mandalay, Taunggyi, and Yangon (500-1000kyat per hour). There is sporadic access to email in other locations, but you must send an email using the address provided. Yahoo! and Hotmail are both banned websites, so get another type of email account before you arrive.

SOUTHERN MYANMAR

YANGON ရန်ကုန် ☎1

Even amid the cacophony of a packed city bus, all heads turn, all conversations cease, and all hands move gracefully to bowed foreheads at the sight of Shwedagon Pagoda. The reverence shown Yangon's main landmark captures the extent to which the sacred and secular intertwine in the city's social fabric. With nearly 5 million residents, Yangon serves as the commercial, administrative, and transportation hub of Myanmar. But while other Southeast Asian capitals have developed into modernized metropolises, Myanmar's closed-door policies have diminished the city's colonial glory. Nevertheless, small delta villages persist despite the threat of being overshadowed by avenues surging with *longgyi*-clad locals. Visitors find themselves immersed in a capital whose rigors are both satisfying and exhausting. Just 33km from the ocean via the mighty Yangon River, Yangon is also one of the lesser-known port cities of Southeast Asia.

GOVERNMENT LISTINGS. Government listings are marked by a symbol. Money spent at such establishments goes directly into the government's hands. For information, see **"Keep the Bucks Where They Belong,"** p. 462.

INTERCITY TRANSPORTATION

BY PLANE. International and domestic flights arrive at **Mingaladon Airport,** 19km northwest of Yangon.

DESTINATION	FREQUENCY	PRICE	DESTINATION	FREQUENCY	PRICE
Bagan	3 per day	US$85	**Hong Kong**	2 per week	US$340
Bangkok	4-9 per day	US$80-128	**Kuala Lumpur**	2 per day	US$243-259
Dhaka	2 per week	US$131	**Mandalay**	6 per day	US$100
Heho	2-3 per day	US$85	**Singapore**	4 per day	US$260-280
Some prices fluctuate as demand changes for seasonal and other reasons.					

Prices are always cheaper through travel agents or **ticketing offices** (see **Practical Information**). Several flights and carriers serve each destination. Contact the airlines for exact schedules and official ticketing offices: **Biman Bangladesh,** 106 Pansodan Rd. (☎24 09 22; open M-F 9:30am-4pm); **Malaysian Airlines,** Central Hotel, Bogyoke Aung San Rd. (☎24 10 07; open M-F 8:30am-12:30pm and 1:30-5:30pm, Sa 8:30am-1:30pm); **Myanma Airways International,** 239 Bogyoke Aung San Rd., Sakura Tower, 8th fl., opposite Traders Hotel (☎25 52 60; open M-F 9am-5:30pm, Sa 9am-1pm); **Silk Air, Singapore Airlines,** Sakura Tower, 2nd fl. (☎25 52 87; open M-F 9am-5pm, Sa 9am-noon); **Thai Airways,** Sakura Tower, ground fl. (☎25 54 99; open M-F 9:30am-4:30pm, Sa-Su 9:30am-noon). Three major airlines serve domestic routes in Myanmar: **Air Mandalay,** 146 Dhammazedi Rd. (☎52 54 88; open M-F 8am-

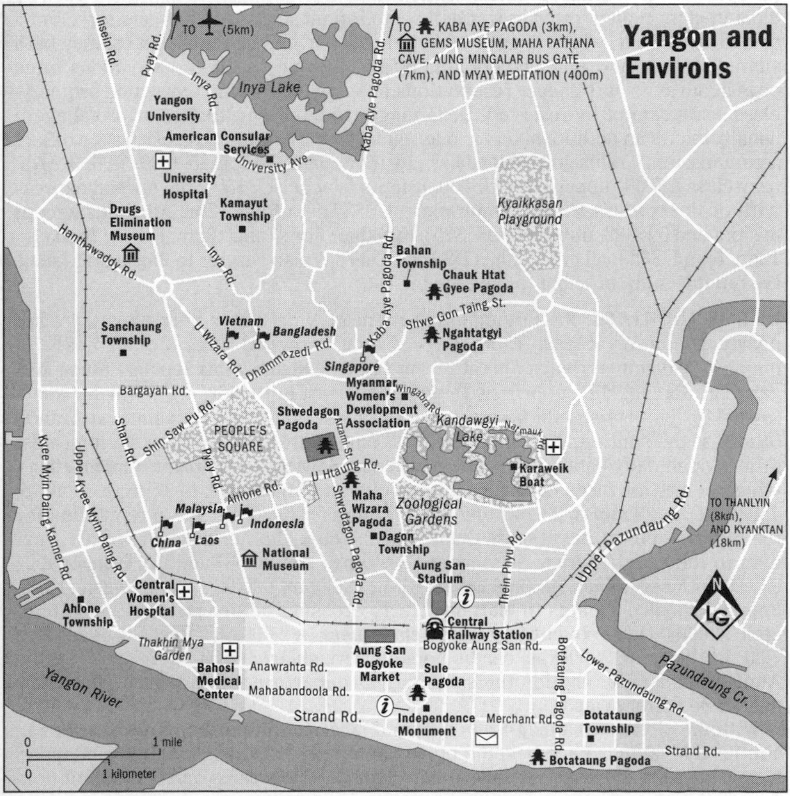

5pm); **Myanma Airways,** 104 Strand Rd. Tickets are sold M-F 8:30am-noon; **Yangon Airways,** MMB Tower, Level 5, Upper Pansodan Rd. (☎38 31 00; open daily M-F 9am-5pm, Sa 9am-noon).

Just past the customs counter, foreigners are greeted enthusiastically by several pre-paid taxi booths. Healthy competition keeps prices low (US$2-6) to most places in the city and provides options other than **Myanmar Travels and Tours (MTT)** (see **Practical Information**). All booths provide free maps. New arrivals can also take their chances outside, where it is necessary to compare prices and negotiate. Beware of anyone who mentions currency exchange. Since the removal of the requirement to purchase FECs, there is no need to change money in or outside the airport; all taxis will happily take US$. It is better to exchange money in the city once you find out the current free-market rate. Some guesthouses offer free transport for guests with advance notice.

BY TRAIN. Yangon Central Railway Station holds dominion over Kun Chan St., north of Bogyoke Aung San Rd., between Sule Pagoda and Pansodan Rd. Tickets are booked for the only train company, **Myanma Railways,** at the **Myanma Railways Booking Office** on Bogyoke Aung San Rd., across from Sakura Tower. (Open daily 6am-4pm.) Once inside the booking office's courtyard, counters for upper-class tickets are to the left, sleeper cars to the right, and ordinary-class tickets straight ahead. If the booking office is too much to tackle, the **Myanmar Travels and Tours (MTT)** office on the first platform, inside the train station, can help arrange tickets. **Ordinary-class** tickets provide wooden seats. An **upper-class** ticket gets a reclining seat in an A/C car, while a **sleeper** ticket means one bed in a four-bed cabin, a bath shared by four, and A/C. The booking office takes upper-class reservations three days in advance and sleeper reservations in advance or same day, while ordinary-class seats cannot be reserved. Reserving through a guesthouse or travel agent usually incurs an additional fee, and as usual, beware of touts whose prices reflect a commission. Trains go to: **Mandalay** (14-15hr., 6am, 3:15pm, 5, 6:30, 7:30, 9; ordinary-class US$11, upper-class US$30, 3:15pm, sleeper US$50; 5pm special express with ordinary-class US$15, upper-class US$35) via **Bago** (2hr. All times except 3:15pm and 5 US$2, upper-class US$5); **Kyaikhto** (6hr.; 7am, 10pm; US$8); **Thazi** (11-12hr., 5pm US$33, all other times US$27). There is also service to **Bagan** and **Taunggyi,** but it is more efficient to take the bus.

BY BUS AND LINECAR. Although they are more timely, Myanmar's buses are not nearly as comfortable as trains. Expect long, crowded rides. Companies with major long-distance routes operate from the **New Highway Bus Terminal (Aung Mingalar Bus Station),** 18km north of Yangon, northeast of the airport in North Okkala township. Tickets should be purchased at least one day in advance, at branch offices at the south end of Aung San Stadium, north of the railway station (most offices open daily 9am-5pm). **Rubyland Tourism Services** (see **Practical Information**), which books for three companies, has tickets to **Mandalay** (14-15hr.; 4:30pm, 5; 4300kyat). **Leo Express,** 23-25 Aung San Stadium (☎25 20 01), has a reputation for the roomiest buses, but at more than twice the cost of other tickets (US$10). Next door to Rubyland Tourism Services, **Ye Thu Aung** (☎24 30 53) and **TOE Express** (☎24 96 72) both serve **Taunggyi (Inle Lake)** (18hr., 12:30pm, 6000kyat) and **Bagan** (16hr., 3pm, 6000kyat). Tickets to **Mottama** (ferry crossing before **Mawlamyaing;** 10hr., 8pm, 2200kyat) are sold by **Zwe Marn Hein Express** (☎24 99 33). Buses to **Pyay** (6hr.; 7:30, 10, 10:30am; 2000kyat) can be booked through **Asia** (☎63 94 66, ext. 0) at the Aung Mingalar Bus Station the same day as departure, but advanced bookings guarantee better seats.

With the closure of a major bus terminal, buses and linecars to destinations in southern Myanmar have become quite disorganized. The information included here is a starting place; ask for current departure locations and times, and double-check with another travel agency. **Thein Than Zaw** (☎63 94 66, ext. 253) serves **Kyaiktiyo** (5-6hr.; 6:30am, 7:30, 9, 11; 2500kyat). Contact **Shwe Man Du** (☎57 96 55) for buses to **Pathein** (4hr., 8am, 1650kyat; 10am, noon, 12:30pm; 1250kyat). Buses to **Bago** (2hr., every hr. 6am-4pm, 1000kyat) don't have to be booked. All buses depart from Aung Mingalar Bus Terminal (take city bus **#43 white** from north of Mahabandoola Garden on Mahabandoola Rd., or north of Sule Pagoda on Sule Pagoda Rd. Buses to **Thanlyin** (45min-1hr., every 15min. 5:30am-6pm, 30kyat) leave from **Mahabandoola Road** between 37th and 38th St., in front of Nilar Win's Cold Drink and Yogurt Shop.

ORIENTATION

Flanked to the south and west by the Yangon River, the capital sprawls over 350 km^2. In the southern part of town near the Yangon River, the **downtown** area has the most accommodations, restaurants, and services. This area is made up of tightly packed blocks and follows an orderly grid layout—making navigation by foot feasible, if tiring. Downtown, the four east-west thoroughfares are, from north to south: **Bogyoke Aung San Road,** the site of the Bogyoke Aung San Market and the train station; **Anawrahta Road; Mahabandoola Road,** bisected by the **Sule Pagoda Rotary;** and **Merchant Road** (sometimes seen as Merchant St.), nearest the Yangon River to the south. The area circumscribed by Bogyoke Aung San Rd. and Anawrahta Rd. is the **Upper Block,** by Anawrahta and Mahabandoola Rd. is the **Middle Block,** and by Mahabandoola and Merchant Rd. is the **Lower Block. Sule Pagoda Road** divides the downtown area in half, creating areas east and west of the **Sule Pagoda.** The short north-south streets between the larger east-west thoroughfares are numbered from one to almost sixty. Every third or sixth street gets a proper name instead of a number.

The area between the Yangon River to the south and Inya Lake to the north is divided into **townships** the size of neighborhoods. **Shwedagon Pagoda** is 4km north of downtown; **Yangon International Airport** and **Aung Mingalar Bus Terminal** are about 19km north.

BURMESE NUMERALS

1	2	3	4	5	6	7	8	9	0
၁	၂	၃	၄	၅	၆	၇	၈	၉	၀

Cheat Sheet for major routes: #37=၃၇ #43=၄၃ #44=၄၄ #46=၄၆ #47=၄၇ #51=၅၁

LOCAL TRANSPORTATION

Trains: A circular train line—scenic but not particularly useful—follows a route from **Yangon Central Railway Station** to **Mingaladon** (near the airport) and back, via **Insein** to the west and **Okklapa** to the east (3 hr.; every 30 min. 4:30am-7:30pm, with trains leaving alternately east and west; US$1).

Buses: Dilapidated, archaic buses provide the cheapest—but sometimes most uncomfortable—transportation. **Since most bus numbers are labeled in Burmese, finding the right one can be challenging.** For your convenience, there's a Burmese numeral chart above. Open-air **linecars** with canvas-covered truck beds (front seat 30kyat, back seat 15kyat), and buses packed to the brim (20kyat anywhere in Yangon) follow mainly the same routes. Service begins between 5-5:30am and ends by 11pm, with higher linecar fares after 6pm. There are hundreds of bus routes, with buses that share the same number sometimes serving slightly different routes, but here are the most useful ones for tourists:

#3: Latha Rd. (Upper Block)-Shwedagon Pagoda

#43: Sule Pagoda Rd., north of Sule Pagoda–west end of Kandawgyi Lake–Kaba Aye Pagoda Rd.

#43 white: North of Mahabandoola Park, on Mahabandoola Rd.–north of Sule Pagoda, on Sule Pagoda Rd.–Aung Mingalar Bus Gate.

#47: Corner of Merchant Rd. and 30th St.–Shwedagon Pagoda (Southern Staircase)–Chauk Htat Gyee Pagoda.

#51: Corner of Merchant Rd. and 32nd St.–Pyay Rd.–Inya Lake (west side)–Airport.

#68: Sule Pagoda Rd., north of Sule Pagoda–Aung Mingalar Bus Gate.

#204: Corner of Merchant Rd. and 30th St.–Shwedagon Pagoda (Eastern Stairway).

Ferries: Cross the **Yangon River** to the small town of **Dalah,** known for its furniture, rice, fishing, and views of the Yangon skyline. From there take a pedestrian ferry to **Letkhokkon Beach** or **Twante.** Boats leave from the Pansodan St. jetty, at the intersection of Pansodan Rd. and Strand Rd., opposite the Port Authority building (every 20 min. 5:30am-8:30pm; one-way US$1).

Taxis: 4-door 1980s-style Japanese taxis provide the most convenient, albeit expensive, transport within Yangon. None have meters, so settle on a price before departing. 600-1200kyat within downtown. From Sule Pagoda to: **airport** (3000kyat); **Aung Mingalar Bus Terminal** (4000kyat); **Shwedagon Pagoda** (1000kyat). Longer excursions (US$25-35 per day).

Trishaws (or Sica): In Myanmar's version of the pedicab, the passenger sits next to the pedicab driver, sidecar-style. Though exiled from the downtown area, trishaws are easy to find west of Shwedagon Pagoda Rd. and east of Bo Aung Kyaw St. Good for a less crowded but slower ride to the city's pagodas. Short trips 500kyat.

PRACTICAL INFORMATION

TOURIST AND FINANCIAL SERVICES

Tourist Offices: Myanmar Travels and Tours (MTT), 77/91 Sule Pagoda Rd. (☎37 42 81). This organization arranges tours and transportation using government-operated services (planes, trains, and ferries). Cheap (free-40kyat) but quality maps of Yangon and Myanmar. **Tourist visa extensions** available (US$36 plus small service fee). Each visitor is eligible for two 2-week extensions, which are only available in Yangon; take 2 passport photos and allow 2-3 days for processing. 1-month extensions are sometimes available. (Alternatively, the airport charges US$3 per day for overstaying a visa. This is not recommended for stays longer than two weeks; be sure to arrive at the airport early to deal with the paperwork.) Open daily 8:30am-5:30pm.

Travel Agencies: Rubyland Tourism Services, 16 Aung San Stadium (☎24 50 51). One of Myanmar's most established travel companies. Adept at organizing tours outside Yangon (price depends on amenities and number of persons). Arranges buses for many private companies. A reliable source for currency exchange. Open M-Sa 9:30am-6pm. Many travel agencies deal with airline reservations, but **Seven Diamond Express Travel,** 65 Thein Phyu Rd. (☎20 33 98), is the most comprehensive since it reserves for both domestic and international airlines. Open daily 9am-5pm.

Embassies and Consulates: Australia, 88 Strand Rd. (☎25 18 10). Open M-F 8am-4pm. Visa services open M-F 9:30am-noon. **Bangladesh,** 11B Than Lwin Rd. (☎51 52 75). Consular services open M-F 9:30am-noon. **China,** 1 Pyidaungzu Yeiktha Rd., also called Halpin Rd. (☎22 12 80). Consular services open M-F 9-11am. **India,** 545-547

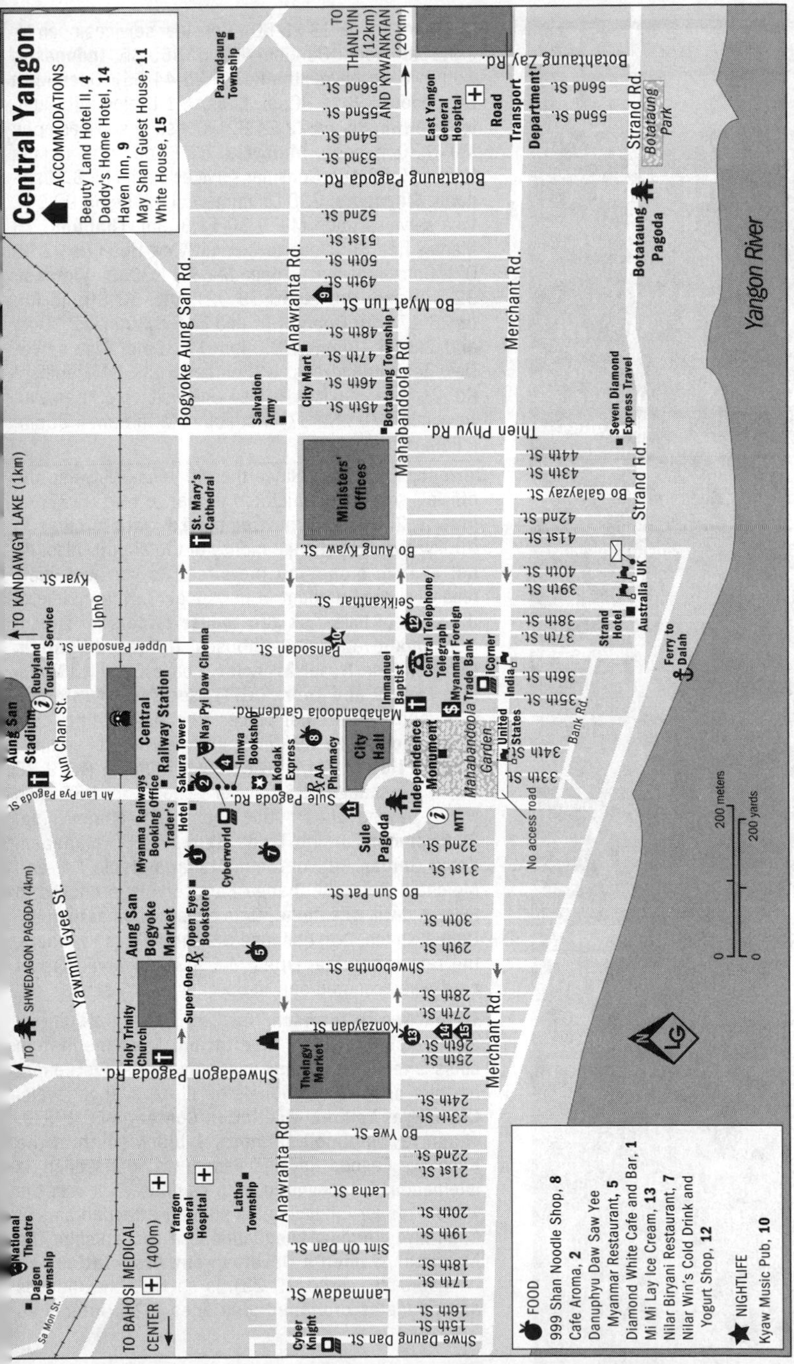
Central Yangon
ACCOMMODATIONS
Beauty Land Hotel II, 4
Daddy's Home Hotel, 14
Haven Inn, 9
May Shan Guest House, 11
White House, 15
FOOD
999 Shan Noodle Shop, 8
Cafe Aroma, 2
Danuphyu Daw Saw Yee Myanmar Restaurant, 5
Diamond White Cafe and Bar, 1
Mi Mi Lay Ice Cream, 13
Nilar Biryani Restaurant, 7
Nilar Win's Cold Drink and Yogurt Shop, 12
NIGHTLIFE
Kyaw Music Pub, 10
TO SHWEDAGON PAGODA (4km)
TO KANDAWGYI LAKE (1km)
TO BAHOSI MEDICAL CENTER (400m)
TO THANLYIN (12km) AND KYWANKTAN (20km)
Yangon River
Strand Rd.
Merchant Rd.
Mahabandoola Rd.
Anawrahta Rd.
Bogyoke Aung San Rd.
Shwedagon Pagoda Rd.
Sule Pagoda Rd.
Botataung Pagoda Rd.
Thien Phyu Rd.
Bo Myat Tun St.
Bo Aung Kyaw St.
Seikkanthar St.
Pansodan St.
Upper Pansodan St.
Mahabandoola Garden Rd.
Bo Sun Pat St.
Shwebontha St.
Konzaydan St.
Bo Ywe St.
Latha St.
Sint Oh Dan St.
Lanmadaw St.
Shwe Daung Dan St.
Bo Galayzay St.
Botataung Zay Rd.
Bank Rd.
Yawmin Gyee St.
Kun Chan St.
Ah Lan Pya Pagoda St.
Kyar St.
Sa Mon St.
Theingyi Market
City Hall
Ministers' Offices
Sule Pagoda
Independence Monument
Mahabandoola Garden
Central Railway Station
Aung San Stadium
Aung San Bogyoke Market
Holy Trinity Church
St. Mary's Cathedral
Immanuel Baptist
Botataung Pagoda
Botataung Park
Yangon General Hospital
East Yangon General Hospital
Road Transport Department
Central Telephone/Telegraph
Myanmar Foreign Trade Bank
Strand Hotel
Ferry to Dalah
Seven Diamond Express Travel
City Mart
Salvation Army
Rubyland Tourism Service
Myanma Railways Booking Office
Trader's Hotel
Sakura Tower
Nay Pyi Daw Cinema
Innwa Bookshop
Kodak Express
AA Pharmacy
Super One
Open Eyes Bookstore
Cyberworld
Cyber Knight
iCorner
MTT
Australia
UK
India
United States
No access road
National Theatre
Dagon Township
Latha Township
Botataung Township
Pazundaung Township
Upho
200 meters
200 yards

FROM THE ROAD

THE WORLD FROM A TRISHAW

Racing down Yangon's roads and dodging the potholes that attempted to derail us, my trishaw-driver glanced down at me. I was his side-kick. Seated directly next to his right knee, I could sense the palpable intensity and urgency coming from him. It was almost like we were on a mission to rescue a defenseless victim—except these "defenseless victims" looked an awful lot like pagodas, and our outfits were not nearly as snazzy as those of Batman and Robin.

Although I had never harbored childhood fantasies of being a superhero side-kick, I certainly felt like one as I was being whisked through the streets of Yangon. Unlike in India, where passengers sit behind the vehicle driver, or in Thailand, where they sit safely inside metal *tuk-tuk* grills, the trishaw brings its passenger face-to-face with the outside world. And for budget travelers like myself, riding a trishaw may be the closest thing to having a private car and tour guide.

Before landing in a trishaw, I did not fully realize what it must be like to live under Myanmar's oppressive government. Traveling on foot, there was a smile and someone to point me in the right direction on every corner. I often traveled using buses and trains, and when I did, it was easy for me to rely on this friendliness to help me locate the necessary station

Merchant Rd. (☎28 25 50). Consular services open M-F 9:30am-noon. 6-month visa US$65-85. **Indonesia,** 100 Pyidaungzu Yeiktha Rd. (☎25 44 65). Open M-Th 8am-noon, F 8-11:30am. **Laos,** A-1 Diplomatic Quarters, Tawwin Rd. (☎22 24 82). Consular services open M-F 8:30am-noon. **Malaysia,** 82 Pyidaungzu Yeiktha Rd. (☎22 02 48). Consular services open M-F 8:30am-noon. **Singapore,** 238 Dhammazedi Rd. (☎55 90 01). Visa services open M-F 9:30-11:30am. **Thailand,** 73 Manaw Hari St., close to Summit View Hotel (☎22 45 07). Consular services open M-F 9-11:30am. **Vietnam,** 32 U Wizara Rd. (☎50 19 92). **UK,** 80 Strand Rd. (☎28 17 00). Open M-Tu and Th-F 8:30am-12:30pm and 2:30-4:30pm, W 8:30am-12:30pm. Also serves **New Zealand** citizens. **US,** embassy at 581 Merchant Rd. Consular services at 114 University Ave., Kamayut Township (☎53 80 37). Both open M-Th 8am-4:30pm, F 8am-noon.

Currency Exchange: Since the difference between the official, government-dictated exchange rate (6.67kyat in June 2004) and the **free-market rate** is close to 900kyat, **do not** change money at the airport. Also, do not change money on the street as you will likely receive a good amount of newspaper in the middle of the stack of bills. **Ask guesthouse owners** for current free-market rates. Guesthouses, **Rubyland Tourism Services** (see **Travel Agencies,** above), and **Myanmar Travels and Tours (MTT)** (see **Tourist Information,** above) are safer places to change money, but they will only take US$ in cash; a few will take Euros. **Eastern Hotel,** 194/196 Bo Myat Htun St. (☎29 38 15) will exchange US$ traveler's checks for US$ cash with 1-day advance notice and a 10% commission. **Myanmar Foreign Trade Bank,** 80/86 Mahabandoola Garden Rd., between Mahabandoola Rd. and Merchant Rd., will change Euro traveler's checks to FECs and will wire money from countries other than the United States. Don't change US$ or FECs to kyat here; the rate is terrible. Open M-F 9:30am-3pm. **Credit cards** are accepted only in upscale jewelry stores.

Alternatives to Tourism: Travelers seeking a spiritual experience should try **meditation.** Most meditation courses require a 10-day min. stay for the first retreat and are open to individuals of all experience levels. **Chan Myay Yeiktha Meditation Center** (☎66 14 79; chanmyay@mptmail.net.mm), 1 block south of the Kaba Aye Pagoda Rd. and Parami Rd. intersection, is internationally recognized, with campuses all over the world. Free for foreigners. To plan an extended stay at Chan Myay, arrange meditation visa sponsorship. The **Myanmar Women's Development Association,** 17 Wingabra Rd. (☎54 29 25), is an NGO that houses and educates orphaned girls ages 5-25. Interested travelers (no Myanmar language skills necessary) should inquire about positions of any length—an English-speaking representative should be available M-F 9am-3pm.

LOCAL SERVICES

English-Language Bookstores: Innwa Book Shop, 232 Sule Pagoda Rd., Upper Block (☎24 32 16), next to Nay Pyi Daw cinema. Stocks new and old magazines (200-800kyat depending on publication date), including *Newsweek, Time,* and *Reader's Digest.* Weekly English newspaper, *Myanmar Times* (500kyat), and books on Myanmar available. Open daily 9am-5:30pm. **Open Eyes Bookstore,** 365 Bogyoke Aung San Rd., at the corner of Bo Sun Pat Rd., and the stalls that crowd it on either side also have a good selection of novels. Open daily 9am-6pm.

Libraries: British Council, 78 Strand Rd., in the same building as the embassy. Operates a small library with current newspapers, magazines, and BBC broadcasts. Open M-F 8:30am-5:30pm, Sa 8:30am-4:30pm. **American Center,** 14 Tawwin Rd., Dagon (☎22 31 40). Comparable facilities, but only open to those holding American passports. Open T-W and F-Sa 9am-4pm, Th 9am-7pm.

Grocery Store: City Mart, at the corner of Anawrahta Rd. and 47th St. With canned goods, refrigerated produce, and fixed prices, it is an alternative to street-side hawkers. Open daily 9am-9pm.

Developing Film: Kodak Express, corner of Sule Pagoda and Anawrahta Rd., isn't the cheapest, but offers digital processing and has English-speaking employees (film: 100kyat per picture plus 400kyat developing charges; digital: 250kyat per picture plus 400kyat developing charges). Open daily 9am-7pm.

EMERGENCY AND COMMUNICATIONS

Emergency: Fire: ☎191. **Ambulance:** ☎192. **Police:** ☎199.

Pharmacies: Super One Pharmacy, 394 Shwebontha St. (☎25 60 09), at the corner of Bogyoke Aung San Rd. So large it is almost a department store. Very little English spoken. Open daily 9am-7pm. **AA Pharmacy,** 146 Sule Pagoda Rd. (☎25 32 31), opposite Traders Hotel. Open 24hr.

Medical Services: Bahosi Medical Center, at the corner of Bogyoke Aung San Rd. and War Dan St., with entrance on War Dan St (☎21 29 33). Quality outpatient/inpatient services and emergency room. Fine English spoken. Open 24hr.

and car, settle into the reclining seat, and roll on—leaving the small, roadside towns (and the people who lived in them) in the exhaust.

Then one day I leapt into my first trishaw passenger seat and found myself not caring that it didn't recline or have A/C. We crossed the town I'd already been in for several days, but the driver took a route only a local would know. We moved from streets flanked with grandiose, multi story colonial homes to streets lined with ramshackle houses made from thatch, where the front yards served as barnyards, schools, toilets, and laundromats. In just one ride across town, I witnessed the full spectrum of Myanmar's economic classes to an extent that would not have been possible from the window of an air-conditioned vehicle. Together, my driver and I avoided pigs and cows, dodged games of soccer, and set our jaws against the heave of extremely unkempt roads, with nothing to shield us from the mud, rocks, or soccer balls.

As a result of my trishaw experience, I would never make the mistake of taking the warm Myanmar welcome for granted. Sometimes it takes seeing the depths of poverty to fully appreciate the towering heights of generosity and selflessness. The world whizzing past my trishaw's passenger seat will never seem the same.

—Kelzie E Beebe

Telephones: Calling from Myanmar isn't difficult, but it is extremely expensive. Street-side **private phone shops** and guesthouses with IDD telephones charge US$5-8 per min. to most parts of North America and Western Europe. Fax service is sometimes available; shop around for the best prices. **Central Telephone/Telegraph Office,** 393 Mahabandoola Rd., sends next-day delivery telegrams (3.6kyat per letter) and faxes (US$5 per minute). Open daily 9:30am-4pm. Local calls are cheapest (30kyat per minute) made from street-side phone stands that are not in private shops.

Internet Access: Internet in Myanmar is fairly cheap, but remains unreliable. Users can often check, but not send, email. Yahoo! and Hotmail are government-banned websites, so visitors should set up a freeware account before arriving. **iCorner Cyber Café,** in the dead-end street opposite the Indian embassy, is the cheapest at 500kyat per hr. Open daily 7am-8pm. **Cyber Knight,** Shwe Daung Dan St., Middle Block, costs 700kyat per hr. Open daily 8am-midnight. **CyberWorld,** Sule Pagoda Rd., next to Café Aroma, is most convenient but most expensive (1000kyat per hour). Open daily 8am-9pm. Smaller shops of variable quality dot the city.

Post Office: GPO, corner of Strand Rd. and Bo Aung Kyaw St. Open M-F 9:30am-4pm; closing time not set in stone. Utter chaos; arrive early for faster service and amiable employees. International airmail (letters 33kyat; registered 50kyat extra; paper up to 0.5kg 400kyat; 2 weeks) and Express Mail Service (Bangkok and Singapore only) available. *Poste Restante* on 2nd floor. Do not have valuables sent to you in Myanmar. DHL service is available on the 1st fl. of the Traders Hotel.

Postal Code: 11181.

ACCOMMODATIONS

Budget hotels are scattered on either side of Sule Pagoda Rd. downtown, and between Shwedagon Pagoda and Inya Lake. Establishments farther out from the city center are closer to some sights, and are priced comparably to downtown hotels. However, their guests miss the pulse of the city and spend more on transportation. Some prices drop by a dollar or two in the low season (June-September) and usually include breakfast. Most accommodation bills must be paid in US$ or FECs; very few places will accept Euros. A hotel is usually of higher quality if its lobby is air-conditioned (but not necessarily higher priced).

Beauty Land Hotel II, 188-192 33rd St., Upper Block (☎24 39 52; beautyland@goldenlandpages.com). In a city where windows are at a premium, Beauty Land II leads the budget pack. Clean and relatively airy rooms tucked away from noisy streets, yet in a great location. Smiling, English-speaking staff provides complimentary information, ticket reconfirmation, safety deposit box, and luggage storage. Burmese and Western breakfast included. IDD service (US$4-6) and currency exchange also available. Bills payable in Euros. Almost all rooms with A/C. Singles US$6-14; doubles US$12-25. ❸

White House, 69/71 Konzaydan St., Lower Block (☎24 07 80). Despite the lobby's oppressive feel, these rooms are brighter and cooler than most. Prolific, rooftop restaurant serves all-you-can-eat breakfast buffet (inclusive) and Burmese dinner buffet (US$2). Arranges transportation, including airport pick-up. Singles with fan and shared bath US$5, with A/C, window, and private bath US$10; doubles US$8/US$16. ❸

Haven Inn, 216 Bo Myat Tun St., Middle Block (☎29 55 00; phyuaung@mptmail.net.mm). With only 5 rooms, Haven Inn provides a cozy feel close to downtown but a decent distance from the hubbub. Large, immaculate wood-floored rooms have A/C, fridge, and hot-water bath, but no windows. Western and Burmese breakfast included. Free airport transport with advance notice. Singles US$10; doubles US$15. ❸

May Shan Guest House, 115/117 Sule Pagoda Rd. (☎25 29 86), just north of Sule Pagoda. A Chinese-run guesthouse with clean, comfortable rooms in a prime location. All rooms with bath, A/C, satellite TV, and refrigerator. May Shan has many different arrangements in terms of beds and having a window, so keep asking to see rooms until you find what you want at the right price. Expensive IDD and Internet access available. Singles US$10-15; doubles US$15-20; triples/family rooms US$25-30. ❹

Daddy's Home Hotel, 170 Konzaydan St., Lower Block (☎25 21 69). On the same block as White House. If you are desperately looking for an A/C room, those on the 6th floor tie for the cheapest in town. Its distance from downtown makes for a quiet atmosphere; the lack of windows makes it a troglodyte's dream. Singles US$4, with A/C US$6, with A/C and bath US$10; doubles US$8/$10/$20. ❸

FOOD

Yangon's Shan, Burmese, Chinese, and Indian cuisines deliciously reflect the city's ethnic diversity. The quintessential meal includes a curry of fish, meat, or vegetables, a soup dominated by gourd or bitter greens, and a plate of steamed rice and boiled vegetables. In the evenings, downtown Yangon overflows with vendors offering deep-fried snacks. Spilling out onto the streets, teahouses are also great places for cheap eats. Be sure to try a bowl of *mohinga*—Myanmar's favorite noodle snack—which consists of rice noodles in a fish broth, served with egg and seasoned according to individual specification (see **Burmese Cooking,** p. 458).

RESTAURANTS

999 Shan Noodle Shop, 130B 34th St., between City Hall and Anawrahta Rd. Comprehensive and tasty introduction to Shan noodle cuisine. *Shan Khauk Swai* (rice) and *Gyon Khauk Swai* (wheat), among many others, available in soup, with salad dressing or oil flavoring (400kyat). Vegetarians will find more than enough to eat. Open daily 6am-7pm. ❷

Danuphyu Daw Saw Yee Myanmar Restaurant, 175/177 29th St., Upper Block. Meals, which include sour soup, are a reputable introduction to Burmese cuisine. Make use of the available English menu to discover all the possible choices, as ingredients are varied and intriguing. Prices are unmarked, but generally under 800kyat. Chicken curry, Butter Fish Head sour soup, steamed butter beans, and more. Open daily 9am-9pm. ❸

Nilar Biryani Restaurant, 203 Anawrahta Rd., between 31st and 32nd St. Will serve anything as long as it is chicken, mutton, or vegetable *biryani* (650kyat). Dishes can be on the oily side; sit by the entrance and watch the colorful world of Anawratha Rd. pass you by. Cool beverages 450-550kyat. Open daily 4:30am-10pm. ❷

Cafe Aroma, on Sule Pagoda Rd., Upper Block, serves quality Western fare at decent prices in a ritzy coffeehouse setting. For those who don't take to tea, there's coffee and espresso (400-900kyat). Grilled chicken sandwich (1000kyat) and french fries (280kyat). Open daily 7am-10pm. ❺

TEAHOUSES AND CAFES

Diamond White Cafe and Bar, on Bogyoke Aung San Rd., between 31st and 32nd St., next to the Central Hotel. Hip teahouse by day, popular bar by night, and, simply, *the* place to hang out. Pastries and tea 150kyat. Open daily 7am-10pm. ❶

Mi Mi Lay Ice Cream, Konzaydan St., Lower Block, near Mahabandoola Rd. Relieve dry season heat or wait out a wet season's shower with a scoop or two of the usual (chocolate, vanilla) or unusual (grapefruit). 150kyat per scoop. Open daily 10am-10pm. ❶

Nilar Win's Cold Drink and Yogurt Shop, 377 Mahabandoola Rd., between 37th and 38th St. Good for breakfast (toast with egg 400kyat) or a healthy snack (yogurt with fruit 600-800kyat). One of the safer places to enjoy dairy. Open daily 8am-11pm. ❷

SIGHTS

A day in the life of a sightseer: Wake up early and take a trip to **Shwedagon Pagoda** for a glimpse of praying Buddhists before crossing the foot bridge to see the **Maha Wizara Pagoda,** commissioned by General Ne Win. After a morning stroll through the gardens around **Kandawgyi Lake,** stop to see the royal **Karaweik Boat.** After lunch, either visit some of the museums—**National Museum, Gems Museum,** or the **Drugs Elimination Museum**—or head downtown to the **Sule** and **Botataung Pagodas** and take in the sparkling **Strand Hotel.** Cap off the day strolling the markets or relaxing with a cup of tea at one of Yangon's many teahouses.

SHWEDAGON PAGODA AND ENVIRONS

SHWEDAGON PAGODA ရွှေတိဂုံဘုရား. Visible from many points in the city, Shwedagon Pagoda is Myanmar's most sacred structure and Yangon's marquee attraction. Legend has it that two traders from Okkala (as Yangon was known 2500 years ago) traveled to India, where they met the recently enlightened Siddhartha Gautama. When the travelers presented the Buddha with rice cakes and honey, he gave them a sermon and eight of his hairs. Upon the traders' return, King Okkalapa ordered that the hairs be enshrined in a pagoda on Singuttara Hill, where other Buddhist relics had been enshrined. The solid *stupa*—several different metallic facings and renovations later—still stands. Four stairways, one in each of the cardinal directions, lead to the top of the hill, but the Southern Staircase, flanked by a pair of *chinthe* (half lion, half dragon), is considered the main entrance and therefore hosts the most vendors of Buddhist paraphernalia. After stepping onto the curb, remember to remove all footwear, including socks, before mounting the first step. Bring a bag to put them in to avoid paying for their return to your ownership.

At the top of the stairs, circle clockwise (left) to show respect and see the 64 smaller pagodas, 4 main prayer pavilions, 8 zodiac prayer posts, and countless other shrines, pavilions, and buildings that surround the main *stupa*. Based on the day of the week and zodiac sign of their birth, pilgrims make offerings and pour cups of water on the heads of Buddha statues at the zodiac prayer posts, while others chant from the shade of a pavilion in front of their chosen shrine. In the southeast quadrant, near the walkway to Maha Wizara Pagoda across the street, there stands a *bodhi* tree, supposedly descended from the tree in India under which the Buddha gained enlightenment. The northwest corner, in a rare empty space, holds a "wish-fulfilling" spot around the inlaid marble star.

Early morning is the best time to come, when the tinkle of the *hti*'s gold-leafed leaves is only interrupted by low-octave chanting and the cawing of a few wayward crows. By 10am the distinct rumble of traffic starts to break through the calm. In the heat of the day it is best to stick to the mats placed in a track around the main *stupa*, as hot marble is unkind to bare soles.

As the heart and soul of religion in Myanmar, Shwedagon also serves as a sort of political icon. In 1988, the honorable **Aung San Suu Kyi** made her first public speech against the government here (see **Myanmar Today,** p. 456.) As a result, the military keeps a watchful eye on the pagoda, and government informers pay close attention to contact between locals and foreigners here. (*3km northwest of Sule Pagoda, at the northern end of Shwedagon Pagoda Rd. Accessible via buses #47 and #204. Private guides* *give tours for US$5; don't worry, they will find you. No sleeveless shirts or shorts. Remove shoes. Open daily 4:30am-9:30pm. US$5; counters on stairways open at 8am, but officials patrol starting at 6am to collect the admission fee.)*

DOWNTOWN YANGON

SULE PAGODA ဆူးလေဘုရား. In the center of downtown, 2000-year-old Sule Pagoda is a natural starting point for exploring the city's sights and is a good introduction to the city's social fabric. Its Mon name, *Kyaik Athok*, means "the pagoda enshrining the sacred hair." Sure enough, the pagoda enshrines one of the Buddha's hairs, brought by two missionaries from India. Like other pagodas, including Shwedagon, the octagonal shape reflects the eight planetary posts of the Burmese zodiac, but unlike its brother to the north, Sule carries these eight sides up into the construction of the *zedi*. Sule is best visited before 7am. *(On Sule Pagoda Rd. in the middle of a roundabout. Admission free.)*

MAHABANDOOLA PARK. Southeast from the Sule Pagoda roundabout, the gardens provide a visual refuge from the surrounding city. A hotbed of student activism during the late '80s, the park now hosts sedate morning tai chi and lively afternoon chats. The **Independence Monument** rests at its center. The colonial architecture of **City Hall,** the **Supreme Court,** and the **High Court** surrounds the park. *(5am-6pm; 15kyat.)*

BOTATAUNG PAGODA ဗိုလ်တထောင်ဘုရား. A contemporary of Shwedagon, the histories of these two pagodas are intertwined. The eight hairs of the Buddha first were enshrined here first for six months before being moved to Shwedagon. Legends then diverge, as one of those eight is said to remain at Botataung, while other reports say all eight are in Shwedagon. Its name, meaning "1000 officers," refers to the military escort these relics received upon their arrival in Botataung. Allied bombing in 1943 almost completely destroyed the temple, but it has been restored and now features a hollow, walk-in center. Mirror-enhanced views of some relics are available, but the most sacred ones are locked away from view. *(Along the Yangon River, at the intersection of Strand and Botataung Pagoda Rd. Open 6am-10pm. US$2.)*

NORTH TO INYA LAKE

CHAUK HTAT GYEE PAGODA ခြောက်ထပ်ကြီးဘုရား. The selling point of this "six-story" pagoda is its enormous, 70m long reclining Buddha, second only in size to the one in Bago. With a giant 8.5 carat diamond placed between its eyes, 551 smaller diamonds, and one ton of gold leaf stamped on its body, this Buddha image is worth US$18 million. Make sure to walk to the image's upturned feet; the soles are covered in traditional Buddha-footprint designs. Chauk Htat Gyee also lends its name to the **monastery** next door, connected by a covered walkway, where 600 monks study ancient Buddhist scriptures and Pali language and literature. On the opposite side of Shwe Gon Taing St. from Chauk Htat Gyee, the shorter **Ngahtatgyi Pagoda** sits on the grounds of **Ashay Tawya Monastery** and houses a several-story sitting Buddha backed by an ornately carved wooden screen. More open than Chauk Htat Gyee, Ngahtatgyi is cooler in the midday heat and is also less crowded. *(2km northeast of Shwedagon Pagoda on Shwe Gon Taing St. Accessible via bus #47. Chauk Htat Gyee Pagoda free; Ngahtatgyi US$2.)*

KANDAWGYI LAKE. This breezy lake and its sculpted parks are a godsend amidst Yangon's urban landscape. Yangon's **Zoological Park,** just off the southwest corner, is home to many animals only found in the restricted areas of Myanmar *(US$5; 6am-4pm).* At the eastern end is the picture-perfect **Karaweik Boat,** constructed in the 1970s as a replica of a royal barge. This 90m, nearly 2 million-kg structure doesn't actually float, but the main objective in its construction was the revival and preservation of traditional Burmese art. Today it has a restaurant featuring a titanic buffet and traditional dance performances. If animals and food don't interest you, pick a path and start strolling. *(The lake is accessible by bus #43, which lets passengers off at the west end. Restaurant entrance 100kyat. Dance performances 1000kyat. Open daily 8am-9pm, dinner buffet 6-9pm.)*

INYA LAKE. Despite their distance from downtown, Inya's surrounding parks and footpaths are worth an afternoon's exploration. Bordering **Yangon University,** the benches along the lake are often full of young couples. To escape the roar of traffic, head for Inya Rd., along the lake's southwest corner. *(Accessible by buses #51 (west) and #43 (east).)*

OUTLYING TOWNSHIPS

NATIONAL MUSEUM အမျိုးသားပြတိုက်. Although it lacks entertaining interactive displays or high-tech attractions, travelers interested in the history and culture of Myanmar will find the National Museum educational. Topics include royal regalia, neolithic stone artifacts, clay votive tablets, and other objects from the Bagan period, as well as diverse images of the Buddha, cave-paintings, and information on the cultures of national minorities. The big deal on the ground floor is the 180-year-old Great Lion Throne, originally used in the Mandalay Palace by the last Burmese king. *(66/74 Pyay Rd. in Dagon Township. Accessible by bus #51. ☎ 28 25 63. Open daily 10am-4pm; last ticket sold at 3:30pm. No cameras. US$5.)*

GEMS MUSEUM AND ENVIRONS. If you are gemstone-savvy, Myanmar is the place to shop. The mining of ruby, sapphire, jade, and other stones is a significant sector of the Myanmar economy. The first three floors of the Gems Museum building consist only of jewelry shops; those in need of gemstone education should head to the actual museum on the fourth floor, where there is a display for each stone mined in Myanmar. One can also view traditional jewelry settings and some of the biggest gemstones ever found. *(66 Kaba Aye Pagoda Rd. Accessible via bus #43. Open daily 9:30am-4:30pm. US$5 to enter the 4th fl.)* Just north of the Gems Museum is **Kaba Aye Pagoda.** Nicknamed the "world peace" pagoda, Kaba Aye was commissioned for the 1954-1956 Sixth Buddhist Synod. Shorter and squatter than Shwedagon or Sule, this pagoda's design is notably modern. Each of its five entrances correspond to a separate Buddha image, while an inner chamber shelters a 500kg silver Buddha image. *(11km north of downtown, past Inya Lake on Kaba Aye Pagoda Rd. Accessible via bus #43. Open daily 9am-5pm.)* Adjacent to Kaba Aye Pagoda, **Maha Pathana Cave** was built to hold 10,000 people for the Synod, which commemorated the 2500th anniversary of the Buddha's enlightenment.

DRUGS ELIMINATION MUSEUM. Housed in a beautiful colonial building all to itself, the museum boasts life-size, high-tech displays that document every step of Myanmar's drug history. The timeline starts with how drugs first entered and grew in Myanmar, focuses mainly on the government's drug destruction operations, and ends with rehabilitation programs to deal with those who became addicted. One indication of the museum's extravagant scale is the life-size opium den. *(Hanthawaddy Rd., in San Chaung Township. Open daily 10am-4pm. US$3, with camera US$5.)*

ENTERTAINMENT

Yangon's nightlife has since recovered from the 11pm curfew imposed in the mid-'90s and now boasts teahouses, karaoke venues, and a good amount of prostitution. To avoid the skin trade, head to **Nay Pyi Daw Cinema,** on the Upper Block of

Sule Pagoda Rd., which shows one recent Hollywood movie for a period of about three weeks. (Show times 10am, 12:30, 3:30, 6:30, 9:30pm. Tickets 400-800kyat.) **Kyaw Music Pub,** 190 Pansodan Rd., Middle Block, has live music and a fashion show every night from 7-11pm. Food and beer are priced for locals. (Pitcher of beer 1500kyat.) Most venues labeled KTV (Karaoke—TV) are candidates for a good time, but single travelers should check out the ambience during the day before arriving after dark. For a nice place to have some good, old-fashioned conversation, head to **Diamond White** (see **Food**).

MARKETS

Downtown Yangon has everything a traveler could need or want. Hawkers concentrate on the main east-west streets off **Sule Pagoda Road,** a few blocks in each direction. They set up at dawn, but business doesn't pick up until the evening rush hour (starting at 5pm), when sidewalks are crammed with clothing, produce, and fried snacks. **Street-side shops** provide an alternative to the ever-present vendors and can be found anywhere in the city. Those selling similar products tend to group together: books at the corner of Bogyoke Aung San Rd. and Bo Sun Pat St.; film where Sule Pagoda and Anawrahta Rd. meet; and prescription eyeglasses on Shwebontha St., between Bogyoke Aung San Rd. and Anawrahta Rd. Centralized **markets** are good both for rubbing elbows with locals and for doing some serious shopping. **Bogyoke Aung San Market** is on the street bearing its name west of the Central Railway Station. This massive, extremely organized space (indoors and out) hosts numerous clothing and textile stores, carvings and handicrafts sellers, and **government-registered** gem and jewelry shops. The market remains fairly empty midweek, but weekends are quite busy. Bargaining is recommended, as shopkeepers gear prices toward tourist crowds. Geared more toward locals, **Theingyi Market** takes up the few blocks between Konzaydan and 24th St., between Anawrahta Rd. to the north and Mahabandoola Rd. to the south. All markets are open daily 9:30am-5pm except on national holidays.

> **BUYERS BEWARE!** Buying jewelry in Myanmar essentially requires a purchase from a government shop, since exporting jewelry from the country requires an accompanying government-issued certificate. See **"Keep the Bucks Where They Belong,"** p. 462.

DAYTRIPS FROM YANGON

TWANTE တွံတေး: Pottery aficionados will enjoy the village of Twante and its craft industry. From the linecar stop, head away from Yangon for 10min. and take the left fork to reach the **Oh Bo pottery district.** This collection of loosely thatched huts houses a well-oiled pottery-making industry, turning out nearly 100,000 pots a year. Each pot starts half-coiled and half-thrown and then cycles through 15 days of glazing, air-drying, and kiln-drying. Warehouses of finished pieces on the way to the market can be seen on the banks of the canal. Most huts are open to exploring, and though it's not mandatory, workers all expect you to buy a small pot for their troubles.

At the main intersection by the market, head away from the canal for 1km. to reach **Shwesandaw Pagoda** (ရွှေဆံတော်ဘုရား). This 76m golden *stupa* rivals Shwedagon in antiquity and houses a small display of antique pottery and royal artifacts from the Mon and Burman kingdoms. A "wish-fulfilling" station in a corner of the pagoda commemorates the defeat of King Bayinnaung's uprising. Trishaws cluster around the marketplace and go to Oh Bo District or Shwesandaw Pagoda for 400-500kyat. A round trip to both Shwesandaw and Oh Bo runs 1000kyat. *(To get to Twante, cross the Yangon River to Dalah from the jetty on the intersection of Pansodan and Strand Rd. (every 20min. 5:20am-8:40pm, US$1) and take a linecar, bus, or jeep to Twante (1hr., every 30min. 6am-5pm, 200-300kyat). Taxis cost 1000-2000kyat.)*

THANLYIN ဿံလျှင AND KYAUKTAN တေံ. For those in need of a breath of country air, the tiny towns of Thanlyin and Kyauktan provide a daytrip's worth of sweet refuge. **Thanlyin** was the base for Portuguese explorer Philip De Brito, who tried to establish a kingdom here in the 1600s before meeting a violent death at the hands of the Burmese. Today Thanlyin has little more to offer than a bustling market and side-streets to wander. For the 3km journey south to **Kyaikkhauk Pagoda,** Thanlyin's primary attraction, stay on the bus or get on any transport heading away from Yangon; get off when you see the large pagoda staircase up the hill to the right of the road. Kyaikkhauk isn't as awe-inspiring as Shwedagon, but from the top you can see over the surrounding delta farms and peanut groves. The road in front of the pagoda continues 10km or so to **Kyauktan,** and the highlight of the greater Yangon area, **Yele Pagoda,** dominates the view from the village, which sits on an island in the middle of the river. To get to the pagoda, head to the waterfront from the bus stop and buy a round-trip boat ticket (1500kyat; 7am-5pm) at the pavilion on the shore opposite the pagoda. Remove shoes before stepping ashore. (US$1 if someone happens to be manning the admission booth, free otherwise.) Opposite Yele Pagoda on a small hill overlooking town, the pavilion of **Kyauktauk Pagoda** is a nirvana for the heat-sensitive, as it receives steady waves of cool, blustery wind. *(Thanlyin and Kyauktan, southeast of the capital, lie on the same bus route. Buses and linecars to Thanlyin (45 min., every 15min. 5:30am-6pm, 50kyat) leave from Mahabandoola Rd., between 37th and 38th St., in front of Nilar Win's Cold Drink and Yogurt Shop. Buses that return to Yangon (45-90min., every 20min. until early evening, 40-50kyat) leave from both the Thanlyin and Kyauktan marketplaces.* ***Do not*** *take bus #204 back to Yangon, as it does not return to downtown.)*

BAGO (PEGU) ပဲခူး ☎052

At first glance, Bago is just another blur on the highway between Yangon and Mandalay. Those who actually get off the bus here may have trouble seeing past the constant traffic. However, away from the Yangon-Mandalay highway, the city's pace slows to trishaw speed. The view from hotel rooftops or the upper levels of the Mahazedi Pagoda illustrates the pervasiveness of Buddhist culture: in every direction tree tops are overshadowed by *htis,* the wrought-iron spires that adorn pagodas. Amidst the shrines, teashops, monasteries, and cheroot factories, the people of Bago remind visitors that not everyone leads a hectic city life.

TRANSPORTATION

The **train station** is 4 blocks west of the river and 2 blocks north of the Main Rd., near where Main Rd. bridges the tracks. Connections to Bagan (18hr.; 11:50am; ordinary-class US$11, upper-class US$31); Mandalay (14hr., 4 per day 7:45am-10:45pm, US$11/US$30); Mottama (8hr.; 6, 8:50am, 11:50pm; US$4/US$11); Yangon (2hr., 6 per day 2:45am-7:55pm, ordinary-class US$2). The bustling Main Rd. has **linecar** and **bus service** to Kyaikhto (3hr.; pick-up truck, anytime after 6am, 800kyat; bus, every hr. 7:30am-6:30pm, 1000kyat); Kinpun (base camp for Kyaiktiyo Pagoda, only during the high season; 3½hr., every hr. 7:30am-6:30pm, 1500-2500kyat); Taunggyi (18hr., 1:30pm, 5000kyat); Yangon (2hr., frequent 6am-6pm, 400-500kyat). Many travelers stop in Bago to break up the long journey between Yangon and upcountry destinations. Those wishing to continue by bus to Mandalay (12hr., 6pm, 4500kyat) can arrange tickets at Myananda Guest House, Emperor Motel, or San Francisco Guest House. Book one day in advance during the high season.

ORIENTATION AND PRACTICAL INFORMATION

The **Yangon-Mandalay Highway** slices through the heart of Bago from southeast to northwest as **Main Road,** bridging over the train tracks and passing most of the accommodations before reaching the river. The turn-off to sights, on the east side of town, is on the southwest side of the train track bridge, heading away from the river. After the river, on the northwest side, Main Rd. first splits at a **clocktower.** The left fork splits 100m farther on at **Bogyoke Aung San Statue,** leading left to Mandalay and Mawlamyaing and right to **Shwemawdaw Pagoda.** The right fork at the clocktower leads to the **post office** (open M-F 9:30am-4:30pm), 5 blocks after the fork. On the ground floor of the Myananda Guest House (see **Accommodations**), **Myananda Pharmacy** is marked by a blue and white Burmese sign. (Open daily 7:30am-9:30pm.) The 24hr. **hospital** is to the left, 50m before the Bogyoke Aung San Statue. (Call ☎215 11 in an emergency.) **International phonecalls** are possible from the phone on the left side of Main Rd., 20m before the clocktower. (US$5 per min. to US. Open daily 6:30am-9pm.)

ACCOMMODATIONS

Three guesthouses and a motel line Main Rd., one block on either side of the bridge. **Emperor Motel ❷,** one block before the river as you come into town from Yangon, offers excellent views, friendly service, and well-furnished rooms. It's worth staying at the Emperor if for no other reason than to be under the wing of the manager, Mr. Yee, who knows virtually everyone in town. All rooms have A/C, TV, refrigerator, and hot showers, but breakfast is not included. (☎230 24. Singles in high season US$9-11, in low season US$5-7; doubles US$18-22/US$10-14.) If the Emperor is full, try across the street at **Myananda Guest House ❸,** where there are similar rooms but less tourist information and a staff that speaks very little English. (☎222 75. Singles with A/C US$3, with bath US$4; doubles US$7/US$8.)

FOOD AND NIGHTLIFE

A number of tourist-oriented restaurants line Main Rd. between the railroad tracks and the clocktower. For great Burmese food, try **Cho Pyone Family Restaurant ❸,** on Main Rd. before the clocktower; look for the orange "Crusher" sign. A full spread of curry, soup, and vegetable sides costs 600kyat. (Open daily 9am-8pm.) **Three Five Hotel ❸,** next to the Emperor Motel, serves up a massive array of chicken, beef, prawn, and noodle dishes (600-2000kyat). The adventurous can try goat testicles, prepared in the style of their choice. For breakfast, open-air **Ngwe Pon Gyi Cafe ❷,** on the right bank of the river after crossing the bridge toward the clocktower, serves mouth-watering pastries (60kyat), hard-boiled eggs, baked flat bread, and tea. (Open daily 6am-10pm.) Those who want to fend for themselves will find fresh fruit and sticky-rice dishes in the **market,** on the left bank of the river after crossing the bridge toward the clocktower. Early birds get the best selection.

SIGHTS

Though the town merits staying a few days, Bago's sights can be covered in a day or less. Energetic travelers can do a walking tour of the sights (about 8km total), but the best way to soak in the town's atmosphere is by bicycle or trishaw. Rent the former at the **Hadaya Cafe,** opposite Emperor Motel, for 800kyat per day. A round-trip trishaw ride to any one sight is 1000-1500kyat. **Tun Tun** at Emperor Motel offers a special deal of US$2 per day for *Let's Go* readers. He is quite knowledgeable about the town and speaks decent English and Japanese. Attractions are open daily 5am-9pm. Some cost US$2, but paying US$10 at any sight with an entrance fee buys a ticket to all of them. Ticket booths are open 7am-5pm at the latest. A morning journey to the **Shwethalyang Buddha** sheds light on Buddhist prayer rituals, while the nearby pagodas and **ordination hall** illustrate Buddhist history, daily culture, architecture, and **cheroot factories.** Stop for lunch after seeing **Kha Khat Wain Kyaung** and continue on to **Shwemawdaw Pagoda** and **Hinthagone Hill,** which are best visited in the late afternoon when locals come to pray.

SHWEMAWDAW PAGODA. Contrary to popular belief, Yangon's Shwedagon Pagoda is not Myanmar's tallest. Monopolizing Bago's skyline at 114m, impressive Shwemawdaw Pagoda wins the title by 5m. Over 1000 years old, it was constructed to enshrine two hairs of the Buddha bequeathed to two merchant brothers. After an earthquake leveled the structure in 1930, successive reconstruction propelled it to its present height in 1953. A piece of the former structure, on display in the northwest corner, gives a good idea of the damage inflicted by the quake. The pagoda is a fascinating combination of modernization and tradition, as the grounds also contain electrical contraptions with revolving boats and bobbing serpents designed to collect projectile coin and paper money donations. *(Take the right fork at the Aung San Statue; Shwemawdaw is visible at the end of the road. Subject to US$10 ticket 7am-5pm.)*

SHWETHALYANG AND MYATHALYANG BUDDHAS. Debate rages over which of Bago's sights is more awesome—the massive Shwemawdaw Pagoda, or the colossal 55m by 16m reclining Shwethalyang Buddha. Built in 994, the pagoda languished in decay until King Dhammaceti ordered its restoration in the 15th century. By 1900, it again stood in disrepair and underwent a sweeping facelift. Compared to the Chauk Htat Gyi Buddha in Yangon, Bago's is "relaxing" because its feet are askew rather than parallel. In 2006 Shwethalyang is scheduled to gain a partner in relaxation: the Myathalyang Buddha, 500m closer to downtown Bago. Until then Myathalyang is still an interesting stop, if only to see what goes into making such monstrous, yet artistic images. *(Heading away from the river, cross the train tracks and turn right at the turn-off; at the fork turn right. Subject to US$10 ticket 7am-4pm. Camera fee 50kyat; video fee 200kyat.)*

KHA KHAT WAIN KYAUNG. The second-largest monastery in Myanmar, Kha Khat Wain is a good stop any time for architecture buffs, but is especially noteworthy when it comes alive during lunch. Its 1300 monks and novices assemble, process, and eat in complete silence at the banging of a single gong. Visitors are allowed during this time, between 10:30-11am daily, but are asked to remain quiet and to dress respectfully (sleeves and long pants). Early risers can also watch the monks file out to collect their daily alms between 5-5:30am. *(After the bridge and heading toward the clocktower, take the second left, then the second left again, and then the first right. The entrance is 500m along, at the break in the yellow wall. Free.)*

HINTHAGONE HILL. The small pagoda perched atop Hinthagone Hill, east of Shwemawdaw Pagoda, is of particular importance to Bago's history. According to legend, two *hamsa* birds perched over the water here, fulfilling a prophecy of the Buddha. Eventually, the river and surrounding delta shifted course, and that fated spot emerged as the hill's summit and the center of the Mon kingdom. The guardian of this hill and therefore of the town of Bago is a former king who was raised, according to legend, by a buffalo. His statue, with buffalo horns on its head, can be found on the right as you walk up the steps. *(A walkway from the east side of Shwemawdaw leads to the steps up the hill. Free. Camera fee 100kyat.)*

CHEROOT FACTORY. Cheroots, cigarette lookalikes with a green leaf outer wrapping, pervade the daily life of Myanmar, and many of them are hand-wrapped in Bago. Each woman at **Kyaiksuu Cheroot Factory** makes 800-1000 per day and gets 1kyat per cheroot. Visitors are welcome as long as they don't disrupt production. *(Take the left turn onto the 2nd dirt lane before Maha Kalyani Sima and then the first right. The factory is a 2-story wooden building on the left, 20m down. Free. Open daily 9am-5pm.)*

MAHA KALYANI SIMA (SACRED ORDINATION HALL). A wooded respite from linecars and teashops awaits at these temple grounds on the way to Shwethalyang Buddha. While its present incarnation is only 48 years old, the hall stands on the site of one of the oldest structures of its kind in Myanmar. King Dhammaceti, an ardent supporter of Buddhism, sent monks to Ceylon in 1475 for re-ordination by the famed Mahavihara sect. Upon their return, he commissioned the building of Maha Kalyani Sima, and monks consecrated the site with sand from the sacred Kalyani River. To the left of and behind the ordination hall stand 10 huge stone pillars protected by a roof and fence and covered with inscriptions in Pali and Mon. For the monks who can read them, the pillars give insight into the early history of Buddhism in Myanmar and the role that the religion played in 15th-century Bago and Ceylon. *(On the road to Shwethalyang Buddha, before the fork and on the left.)*

MAHAZEDI PAGODA. In 1560 this pagoda enshrined a tooth of the Buddha obtained from Ceylon. Fifty years later, the relic was captured and taken north to Sagaing, near Mandalay. Male visitors are allowed to climb

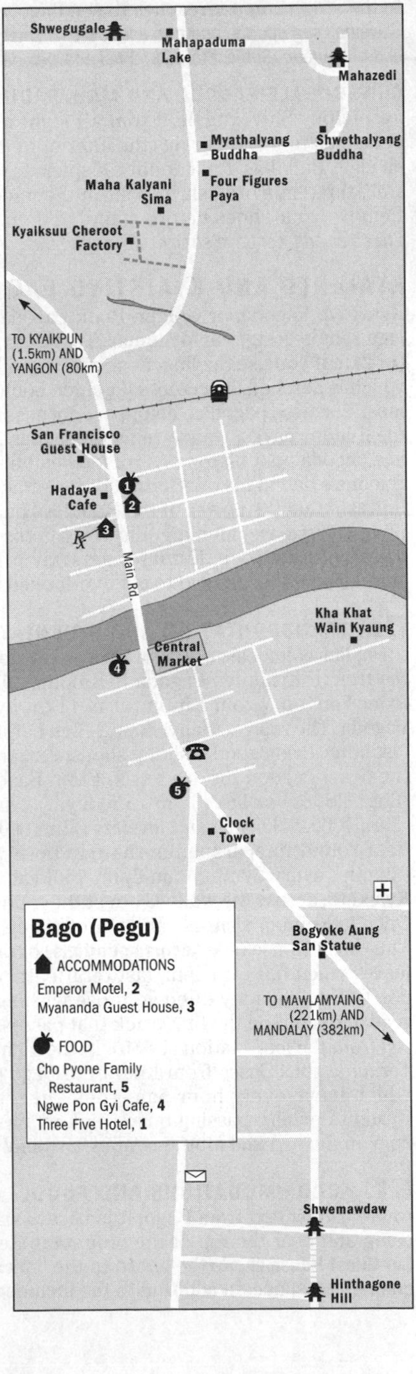

to the *stupa*'s upper reaches to see Bago's finest views. *(Continue past the front of the Shwethalyang Buddha and turn left at the "T" intersection; it's a few hundred meters down at the end of the road. Subject to US$10 ticket. Open daily 7am-4pm.)*

SHWEGUGALE PAGODA AND MAHAPADUMA LAKE. Near Mahazedi stands the auspicious Shwegugale. From all eight major directions, entrances lead to an octagonal tunnel that rings the interior of the pagoda. On each side of the octagon sit eight Buddhas, for a doubly auspicious total of 64. At the turn to reach Shwegugale, three mirrored shrines sit in the middle of lily-covered Mahapaduma Lake. Remove your shoes before stepping onto the walkway. *(At the right turn leading to Shwethalyang, continue straight. To reach Shwegugale, turn left at Mahapaduma. Free.)*

KYAIKHTO AND KYAIKTIYO PAGODA

Kyaiktiyo Pagoda, or Golden Rock Pagoda, is the most popular and most significant religious sight in Myanmar. Tourists and pilgrims alike make the steep 13km (or 2km if you use the linecar service from Kinpun) climb to marvel at the pagoda, which is perched on a colossal golden boulder balanced on the edge of a cliff. Like most Burmese pagodas, it supposedly enshrines a Buddha relic. As the story goes, the Buddha gave a wandering monk a lock of his hair and asked him to enshrine it in a pagoda built on top of a rock resembling his head. The monk tucked away the Buddha's hair in his own hair knot for safekeeping and set out to fulfill the request. It is said that the power of the Buddha's hair alone prevents the boulder from toppling off its base. Men are allowed to cross a small walkway and apply gold leaf directly to the rock. Kinpun's gateway town of **Kyaikhto,** and the other smaller shrines on the peak tend to get overlooked in the shadow of Kyaiktiyo Pagoda.

TRANSPORTATION AND ORIENTATION. Kyaikhto, the area's gateway town, lies 65km east of Bago, between Bago and Mawlamyaing. The base camp for the trek to Kyaiktiyo Pagoda is Kinpun, 20km north of Kyaikhto off the highway from Yangon. From Kinpun it is 11km by trail or 14km by road to Kyaiktiyo Pagoda. The road actually stops 2-3km before the top, so riders are left to walk the last hour. Bring good walking shoes. Entrance fee to the pagoda area is US$6, but the ticket is good for one week. From Bago it is possible to get to Kinpun by **taxi** (3hr., US$20) or **bus** (3-4hr., 1500kyat). During the **low season** (May-Oct.), **buses** (3hr., 1000-2000kyat) and **linecars** (3hr., 800kyat) from Bago only go to Kyaikhto. Year-round linecars make the trip both ways between Kyaikhto and Kinpun (30min., every 30min. 6am-6pm, 150kyat). These leave from the north side of Kyaikhto, across the walkway over the train tracks, and from the center of Kinpun. Once in Kinpun, visitors can either **walk** on the path that starts next to Pann Myo Thu Guest House (see **Accommodations**) or take a **jeep** to Kyaiktiyo Pagoda (45min.; leaves when full 6am-4pm, last return at 6pm; 400kyat). In the low season, jeeps don't fill to capacity often so those wishing to drive should start walking on the road and jump on the first truck that passes. It is also possible to be carried to the top from the jeep station (US$5). In the high season, **Win Express** in the Kinpun Bus Terminal runs buses from Kinpun to Bago (1500kyat) and to Yangon (2500kyat), which leave every hour 5am-1pm. Otherwise it is necessary to backtrack to Kyaikhto, where passing buses pick up passengers going to Bago/Yangon (7am-2pm on the hr.) and Mottama/Mawlamyaing (between 10am-noon daily).

ACCOMMODATIONS AND FOOD. Unless you visit the Golden Mount round-trip by taxi from Bago, it is best to stay in the accommodations at the base camp and near the top of the mountain. Recent additions have transformed **Sea Sar Guest House ❶,** up the hill from the linecar stop, into bungalows surrounding a quiet green space. In addition to the included breakfast, the guesthouse restaurant serves up great Bamar and Chinese dishes. (Singles US$3, with bath and fan US$5; doubles US$5-8/5-10.) Straight ahead from the linecar stop is **Pann Myo Thu Guest House** ❷, which offers cheaper rooms that are slightly more cramped. (Basic rooms $2; singles with fan and bath US$3; doubles with bath US$5, with fan and bath US$6.) For its luxurious rooms, proximity to the Golden Mount, and beautiful views at sunrise and sunset, try **Golden Rock Hotel** ❹. (Singles US$25, with A/C and TV US$36; doubles US$30/US$41.) In the base camp, English-speaking restaurants and tea shops fill out Kinpun.

MAWLAMYAING (MOULMEIN) ☎032

Squished by the Thanlwin River to the west and a pagoda-encrusted ridge to the east, Mawlamyaing is a cross-cultural city. As the capital of the Mon State, it thrives both as a major seaport and as the spiritual center for those who devote their lives to one of its numerous monasteries. Although travel to the south has been restricted in the past, this is changing and Mawlamyaing could soon lose its vestiges of culture and cleanliness. For now, however, it is far enough off the yellow-brick road of tourism to allow dedicated souls a few days of cool breezes and pagodas before launching a journey south.

TRANSPORTATION

Foreigners are not allowed to go south by land, but during the high season, **flights** go to: Dawei (US$50), Myeik (US$75), and Yangon (US$35) on Wednesdays. Ask any guesthouse to book tickets. The **train station** is in Mottama, but tickets can be purchased one day in advance from the **Northern Station Booking Office,** 3 blocks north of Breeze Guest House (see **Accommodations**), on Strand Rd. To: Yangon (10hr.; 7, 10am; ordinary-class US$8, upper-class US$17) via Bago (8 hours). **Buses** go to: Yangon (8-10hr.) from Mottama, across the river (express 8:30am, US$15; 9:30am, 7000kyat; 6:30pm, 4500kyat; 7:30pm, 5000kyat), and Mawlamyaing (8:30am, 5000kyat; 4:30pm, 2700-5000kyat). Heading south, buses run 18 mi. to the restricted-area checkpoint (every 30 minutes). **Pick-up trucks** leave from Mottama for Kyaikhto (every hr. 7am-noon, 700kyat). **Ferries** go to: Mottama (every hr. on the half hr. 6:30am-5:30pm; US$1, deck-chairs 50kyat) and Hpa-an (M, W-Sa noon; US$2). The Mottama ferry leaves from the jetty at the central market, while boats to Hpa-an leave from 3 blocks north of Breeze Guest House, next to the Northern Station Booking Office. Until the new bridge is finished in 2005, all tourists who arrive through Mottama have to take the ferry to reach town. From Hpa-an, either take the ferry back to Mawlamyaing at 7am the next day or take a pick-up truck to Thaton, on the Kyaikhto-Mottama road. Local transport is mainly by foot or trishaw. A trishaw from Strand Rd. to the base of the ridge should be 200kyat, and to the bus terminal, 6000kyat.

ORIENTATION AND PRACTICAL INFORMATION

Mawlamyaing is basically a grid, but a prison right in the middle of town and several large green spaces ensure that the roads do not run exactly parallel. In the west, hugging the river's shoreline, **Strand Road** runs south from the **central market.** One block east, just off the water, **Lower Main Road** runs the entire north-south length of town and has most of the shops. Farther east, **Middle (Baho) Road** splits off **Upper Main Road** (both run north-south) at the main east-west thoroughfare, **Kyaikthan Road.** Kyaikthan Rd. connects the waterfront to the ridge, intersecting with Strand Rd. at a set of traffic lights. **Sipin Thar Yar Street** and **Dawei Todar Street** run east from Strand Rd., intersecting with it at the central market and at the

Dawei Jetty respectively. No bank or guesthouse in town is licensed to do **currency exchange,** so it is best to leave Yangon prepared. The **central market,** given a boost by Mawlamyaing's water-way business, spans two blocks just north of Sipin Thar Yar St. (Open daily 7am-5pm.) The 24hr. **hospital** sits at the corner of Upper Main Rd. and Uzani Pagoda Rd., which heads west toward the river from Uzani Pagoda (see **Sights**). The **post office** offers expensive **IDD** but not much else. It is on Middle Rd., four blocks south of Kyaikthan Rd. (Open M-F 9:30am-3pm.)

ACCOMMODATIONS AND FOOD

Few foreign travelers come to Mawlamyaing, so budget options are limited, and overpriced hotels abound. **Breeze Guest House ❸,** on Strand Rd., seven blocks south of the central market, combines good prices with one of Mawlamyaing's most prized commodities: riverside rooms. The two managers are a visitor's godsend for local tourist information. (☎214 50. Singles and doubles with fan and clean shared bath US$4-6/8-10; singles/doubles with fan and bath US$6-12/10-18.) One block off the river and two blocks south of Breeze, **Aurora Guest House ❸,** 277 Lower Main Rd., offers comparable rooms, without river views, that range from very basic to amenity-packed. Though the staff is less capable at supplying tourist information, they will help arrange bus tickets. (☎244 54. Basic singles/doubles with fan US$4/8; singles and doubles with bath, A/C, TV, and refrigerator US$10/20.) Aimed at businessmen, **Ngwe Moe Hotel ❺,** on Strand Rd. three blocks south of the Myanmar Food Restaurant (see below), offers slightly overpriced comfort outside the budget spectrum. All room have carpet, bath, A/C, and TV. Front rooms have river views. (☎247 03. Singles and doubles US$27/36.)

Mawlamyaing suffers from a lack of quality eateries, with the most notable exception being the **Myanmar Food Restaurant ❸,** on Strand Rd. opposite Mya Thanlwin Restaurant, five blocks south of Breeze Guest House. Inside this building (with no English sign), Myanmar curries come with all the fixings for 600kyat. (Open daily 7am-9pm.) **Panzabé Bakery House ❶,** on Lower Main Rd., has some of the ingredients for a makeshift Western meal, in addition to homemade cakes for 100kyat per slice. (Open daily 7:30am-9pm.)

SIGHTS

The ridge that constricts Mawlamyaing to the east is the town's main attraction, which is best seen over the span of several days. The hefty number of monasteries and pagodas can be overkill for those who have already seen their fair share. On the northernmost point sits **Mahamuni Pagoda,** which houses an image in the likeness of its Mandalay-based namesake. The complex of covered walkways is quite extensive, including a southern path leading to **Kyaikthanlan Pagoda.** The most visible pagoda on the ridge, Kyaikthanlan sits at the eastern end of Kyaikthan Rd., which runs west to the river and Strand Rd. The long stairs to the tiled pavilions around the pagoda are worth it, if only for the spectacular eastward views of rice fields and delta farming. The stairs off the southern edge lead down to **Seindon Mibaya Kyaung,** a monastery where King Mindon's queen, Seindon, hid after King Thibaw Min took power. The resident monks are proud to show off their prized possession, a Buddha tooth entirely too large to be from the mouth of any normal man. Donations are welcome. One kilometer south along the road—past Thung Poak Kyaung, two pagodas called Law Ku Mhan Ku and Law Ka Oak Shaung, and Sarosa 2500 Monastery—stands **Aung Theikdi Pagoda.** Here are the best views of both sides of the ridge. Several hundred meters farther south is a signposted **viewpoint** of the Thanlwin River and its delta islands. **U Khanti Pagoda,** a large, white, squat building, and **U Zina Pagoda,** on the ridge's southernmost point, lie 500m past the viewpoint. The western stairs at U Zina lead to U Zina Pagoda Rd., which runs west all the way to the river. Some of the pagodas and monasteries are connected by stairs or pathways, but one road does run the length west of the ridge, just below the buildings. A trishaw from the river to this road is 200kyat.

Take a break from pagodas at the **Mon Cultural Museum.** Although most displays aren't in English, there is just enough to get an idea of what you're looking at. The pieces include everything from musical instruments to paintings of benefactor monks, to artifacts from ancient Mon villages. Just inside the door are mannequins dressed in the traditional Mon style. (Corner of Middle and Dawei Todar Rd. US$2. Open M-F 9:30am-4pm.)

There are several destinations for daytrips or overnight excursions. Most notable are **Shampoo** and **Ogre Islands,** which lie just offshore in the Thanlwin River Delta. Farther south between Mawlamyaing and Ye is a reclining Buddha and **Setse Beach,** which is nothing spectacular but a place to get away from things. Inquire at Breeze Guest House (see **Accommodations**) for transportation and guides.

PYAY ☎053

Pyay is much grander than its small downtown area might suggest, both in size and significance. The ruins at Thayekhittaya—much older than the temples in Bagan—were the seat of the Pyu Kingdom, from which both the town and its modern name derive. In central Pyay, overlooking the downtown, stands Shwesandaw Pagoda, one of the three major pilgrimage pagodas in Myanmar (the other two are Yangon's Shwedagon and Bago's Shwemawdaw). Pyay's bus stand brings further importance to the city, as it is the major transfer point between North and South Myanmar, and between the interior and Ngapali Beach. Whether coming or going, it's worth staying a few days in Pyay.

TRANSPORTATION

Trains: To **Hmawza (Thayekhittaya)** (30min.; 6:15am, return train at 5:30pm; ordinary-class US$2, upper-class US$5) and **Yangon** (7hr.; 10pm; ordinary-class US$6, 1st-class US$12, upper-class US$15).

Buses: To **Kyaukpadaung** (3pm, 2000kyat); **Mandalay** (12hr.; 3, 4, 5pm; 4000kyat); **Pathein** (10hr.; 8:30am; 7000kyat in front, 4000kyat in back); **Taunggok** (for **Ngapali Beach**) (10hr., 6pm, 4000kyat); **Yangon** (6hr.; 6:30, 7:30, 8:30, 9:30, 10:30am, 1, 9, 10pm; 1500kyat). For **Bagan,** take a bus to Kyaukpadaung and switch to one headed for Bagan. To get to **Inle Lake,** you can take a bus to Mandalay and get off at Meiktila, then switch to a bus to Taunggyi. However, *Let's Go* does not recommend this route as the Mandalay bus arrives in Meiktila in the middle of the night. A safer option is to backtrack through Yangon. All buses leave from the **Highway Bus Terminal.**

Linecars depart from the **Bogyoke Aung San** roundabout and run to different areas of town. Cars with **red** signs head to the Highway Bus Terminal, **green** signs denote cars that run to **Paya Gyi,** and **blue** signs denote cars that run to the **Northeast Quadrant,** a residential neighborhood. Fare is 50kyat for any distance on any line.

ORIENTATION AND PRACTICAL INFORMATION

The **Bogyoke Aung San Statue Rotary** marks the center of town. From here, roads radiate in four directions. A **market** fills the path going west for about 100m before it terminates at **Strand Road,** which runs along the massive **Ayeyarwady River.** The road to the east is **Bogyoke Street,** which eventually leads to the **Highway Bus Terminal** (2km, right fork), a 24hr. **hospital** (☎215 11; 2km; left fork), and

Thayekhittaya (9km; left fork). **Madaw Road** runs north from the roundabout toward restaurants and eventually residential neighborhoods. The **train station** lies on the wedge between Madaw and Bogyoke St., with the entrance on Bogyoke St. **Kan Road** runs parallel to the market, one block north on Madaw St. and west of the roundabout. The **post office** (open M-F 9:30am-4:30pm) only handles domestic mail. The **telephone office,** four blocks north of the market on Strand Rd. and left at the Pyay Traditional Hospital, makes international calls for US$4-6 per min. (Open daily 6:30am-9:30pm.) The road radiating south from the roundabout leads to **Shwedaung** (14km).

ACCOMMODATIONS

Pyay's relatively few guesthouses tend to be geared toward Burmese visitors. Spending a little extra can result in a large jump in quality. All those listed here include breakfast and are within a 5min. walk from the Bogyoke Aung San Statue.

Myat Lodging House (☎213 61). Take the 1st left going north from the Bogyoke Aung San Statue, then turn right at the post office. A bit pricier than other options, the money is well spent. The bungalow rooms are cleaner, and the shared bath has hot water. Breakfast and some tourist information included. Singles/doubles with fan US$4/5; with A/C and TV US$8/10; with A/C, TV, and bath US$10/16. ❸

Yoma Hotel (☎242 84). 3 blocks south of the statue. A step down from Myat, but the higher-end rooms are still a good choice. The cheapest rooms, although they include breakfast, are closet-sized. Singles/doubles with fan US$3/6; with A/C and bath US$12/16; larger room with fan US$8. ❸

Aung Gabar Guest House, at the southeastern corner of the Bogyoke Aung San Statue. These small but centrally located rooms are inexpensive and can be paid for with kyat. Private showers have hot water; no A/C. Singles 2000-3000kyat, with attached bath 4000kyat; doubles with or without attached bath 5000-6000kyat. ❷

FOOD

Numerous teashops cluster around the roundabout, and most restaurants are within a few blocks of the roundabout. The most popular restaurant is **Hline Ayar** ❸, on Strand Rd. just north of the intersection with the market path. Although main dishes (Burmese and Chinese) tend to be a bit expensive (1500-3000kyat), the chance to eat on an open veranda overlooking the Ayeyarwady is worth the extra few hundred kyat. On Kan Rd., across from the post office, **May Ywet War Restaurant** ❸ (the sign also designates it as **Aunty Moe's**) serves great sweet and sour chicken (1400kyat) and Bamar food—best had at lunchtime, since it is cooked throughout the morning. Some of the staff speaks excellent English. For a more down-to-earth dining experience, check out the **Indian Food Stall** ❸. Heading north from the roundabout, take the second right; it will be 50m ahead on your left. All-you-can-eat *thali* set-meals: vegetarian (450kyat) or meat (700kyat).

SIGHTS

SHWESANDAW PAGODA. Sitting on top of a hill near the center of town, Shwesandaw Pagoda is one of the most sacred and popular pagodas in Myanmar. Like Shwedagon Pagoda in Yangon, Shwesandaw is said to contain several Buddha hairs and is aptly named "Golden Hair Relic." The main (north) staircase leads up the hill from Bogyoke Rd., but there are also two elevators off to the right. Once at the top, look east toward **Sentatgyi Paya,** or "Big Ten-Story," a 10-story sitting Buddha that people pray to from its base and from a Shwesandaw pavilion. Leaving by a staircase other than the north will place you in the surrounding residential neighborhoods. With the surrounding skyline of pagodas, Shwesandaw and Pyay-from-above are best seen at sunrise or sunset, when the river and pagoda *zedis* glitter with gold. After dark, Shwesandaw itself is illuminated. *(Elevators 5am-9pm, staircase 6am-9pm. Free.)*

SHWEDAUNG. For travelers staying in Pyay for more than a day, Shwedaung, a village 14km south of Pyay, offers a relaxing tour of small-town life saturated with pagodas. The most fascinating of the three pagodas is perhaps **Muni Pagoda,** to the right as you enter the town limits and 1.5km before you reach Shwedaung proper. Hosting miniature replicas of Kyaiktiyo's Golden Rock and Thayekhittaya's Bawbawgyi Pagoda, as well as an image which closely resembles Mandalay's Mahamuni Golden Buddha (see p. 502), this pagoda seems to be a compilation of the major religious sights in Myanmar.

Known among the locals as the "glasses Buddha," **Shwemyetman Pagoda** and the image it holds comprise the most famous site in Shwedaung. To see this rare image, head back toward Pyay from the linecar stop about 50m and follow the sign pointing left. After a little over an eighth of a mile, the understated complex is on the right. The practice of putting a pair of glasses on a Buddha image originates in the fifth century AD. When King Duttabaung lost his eyesight after the construction of Shwemyetman, his sage prophets suggested that he donate a pair of spectacles to the image. Since then, it is believed that the bespectacled Buddha image has the special power of curing diseases or disorders of the eyes. As an extended prayer offering, local families also donate money to have the glasses cleaned and replaced when necessary.

The third pagoda and its neighbor lie 6km southwest of the village—a 4km walk or a 3000kyat round-trip horsecart ride. **Shwenattaung** and **Maeshin** stand on a hill surrounded by rice paddy fields. To the east, a Buddha image sits atop the coiled tail and under the head of a giant snake. This memorializes the story of a giant snake giving an enlightened Buddha protection from the rain. To the right of Shwenattaung, **Maeshin Pagoda** contains a small Buddha image with many colorful gems on its body. *(Pick-up trucks to Shwedaung (30min., every 15min., 100kyat) leave from 3 blocks south of Bogyoke Aung San Statue, opposite the Yoma Hotel in Pyay.)*

DAYTRIP FROM PYAY

THAYEKHITTAYA (SRI KSHETRA)

To get to Hmawza, take a taxi (round-trip 4500kyat), trishaw (round-trip 3000kyat), or train (30min., 6:15am, US$2). Linecars (50kyat) also run to Paya Gyi, but you will need to walk from there.

Dating back to as early as the fourth century AD, the Thayekhittaya ruins are perhaps the oldest archaeological discoveries in Myanmar. This ancient capital of the Pyu Kingdom encompassed about 7 mi.^{2} at the peak of its power—the boundary is still evident in the remaining brick walls. Today, life goes on in the form of little, sleepy Hmawza, a village more concerned with bull-carts than with kings and rulers. But only by walking the backroads and fields can one discover the ancient secrets of this modern nation. The first encounter with the ancient ruins of the Pyu Period is the conspicuous **Paya Gyi Pagoda,** on the right about 4km from Pyay and on the way to Thayekhittaya. Believed to enshrine the big toenail of Buddha's right foot, Paya Gyi was one of the nine pagodas constructed by King Duttabaung between the sixth and seventh centuries AD. Another cone-shaped pagoda that King Duttabaung built is **Payamar,** containing fingernail, toenail, and collarbone relics. It lies 500m off the highway, opposite the turn-off to Hmawza. Near the center of Hmawza lies the **museum,** the entrance point to the ruins. Though small, it holds all of the artifacts found at the ruins that date back to between the fourth and ninth centuries AD—gold leaves with Pyu writing, bronze figures of Pyu musicians, stone funeral urns, images of Vishnu and Buddha, and ancient coins. On an inside wall is a hand-painted map of the area; there are no paper copies to be had. Either ask the museum for a guide or use our Insider Feature, as getting lost is very easy. Places of interest include the **Old Palace Ground, Bebe Temple, Queen Beikthano's tomb,** and other **pagodas,** yet the most impressive is **Bawbawgyi Pagoda**—the prototype of Myanmar's ancient pagodas—audaciously rising 50m at the end of a long dirt path. *(You can either rent a bull-cart (1000kyat) or walk the 2-3hr. to visit the ruins. US$4 for the museum and beyond.)*

TAUNGGOK

Situated on the western edge of the Rakhaing Mountain Range, Taunggok is little more than a transfer point between Pyay and Thandwe. Thandwe is, in turn, the major transportation hub for the region and the gateway to Ngapali Beach. **Buses** run from the bus terminal to Pyay (10hr.; 5, 7pm; 2500kyat); Thandwe (3hr.; 6, 7:30, 10am, noon, 1, 2, 3, 4:30, 6pm; 800kyat); and Yangon (16hr.; 3:30, 4pm; 3000kyat). While it is possible to reach Taunggok in the rainy season, the bridges on the road to Thandwe are often impassable during this time. When buses aren't an option, take **motorcycle taxis** to Thandwe (3hr.,10,000kyat). For a bed (or the closest thing to it) head to **Royal Guest House** ❶ by turning right out of the bus terminal and continuing straight for two blocks. Small but adequate rooms with shared squat toilet and cold showers are 2500kyat per person. Though the guesthouse is not licensed to serve foreigners, it doesn't seem to make a difference. Teashops and foodstalls cluster at the intersection where Royal Guest House sits.

THANDWE (NGAPALI BEACH)

Ngapali Beach offers little besides several miles of pure white sand and a small village atmosphere. Yet this, along with the beach's beauty, is enough to make it one of Myanmar's foremost tourist destinations. Since most services are located in Thandwe (Sandoway)—the gateway to the coast—guests at the beachfront hotels are left to congregate in relative isolation, removed from most things Burmese. Low season offers a respite from flocks of foreigners and allows quiet exploration of the fishing villages of Lintha, Lontha, and Myabyin. Less developed than Chaung Tha Beach, Ngapali still has food and accommodations in every price bracket.

TRANSPORTATION. Air Mandalay flies to Yangon (US$75); tickets can be purchased from **Shwe Thantwe Express** (☎44 044 and 44 111), in Ngapali Junction, at the T-intersection between Ngapali Beach and the airport. Flight schedules change on a weekly basis; ask at any hotel. The same company sells **bus** tickets to Yangon (16-17hr., daily 3pm, 4500kyat) via Pyay (10hr., 4500kyat). **Dwarawady Express** runs daily buses to Yangon via Gwa; most hotels book these tickets. Local buses to Taunggok (3hr., frequently 6am-6pm, 800kyat) leave from Thandwe's bus terminal, on the right just after the bridge into town coming from Taunggok. All bus departures in the rainy season depend on the road conditions, so inquire a few days in advance; most express buses will pick passengers up at hotels. It is possible to reach Pathein by taking the bus via Gwa; ask to be dropped off at the Kyaunggon Bridge toll gate. Note that this bus reaches the bridge between midnight and 3am, and the connection to Pathein doesn't pass until 6am; *Let's Go* recommends backtracking through Yangon.

Linebuses run between Lontha and Thandwe throughout the day (200kyat), passing all the hotels on Ngapali Beach. They leave from the bus terminal in Thandwe and the main street in Lontha. **Bicycles** can be rented from most hotels (300-500kyat per hr.) during the high season. Between June and September, inquire at **Excellence** or **Best Friend Seafood Restaurants.** **Trishaws** hover in the area, and increase in number during the high season. Trips along the beach run 100-500kyat, into Thandwe 3000kyat. Locals use the beach as if it were just another street, so walking there is relatively safe, even at night (a flashlight is recommended).

ORIENTATION AND PRACTICAL INFORMATION. The road from Taunggok enters Thandwe from the east, passing the **bus terminal** on the left just after the bridge. After several jogs to avoid the **Central Market,** an old British prison, the road leaves town near the **hospital** and meanders through terraced fields as it heads for the coast. Five kilometers west of Thandwe and 3km north of Ngapali Beach, the road ends at **Ngapali Junction.** A **T-intersection** leads right (north) to the **airport** (2km) and left (south) to Lintha (1.5km), Ngapali Beach (3km), Myabyin (4km), and then Lontha (5km), the last town on the peninsula. **Email** (US$3 per address) and **international phone calls** (US$4-6 per min.) are available at the **Bayview Resort Hotel** (accepts MC/V, based on the Singapore exchange rate, when weather and the connection permit).

ACCOMMODATIONS. Guesthouses in Thandwe are not licensed to host foreigners, so, for better or worse, foreigners must search out a bed at the beach. Very few establishments stay open year-round, but the diamond in the rough during any season is **Linn Thar Oo Lodge** ❸ (☎22 99 28 in Yangon), on the right just south of Bayview Resort Hotel. Centrally located, the economy bungalows aren't much to look at, with shared squat toilets and cold showers, but even in the high season they are the cheapest accommodation in the area. Standard bungalows, with veranda, attached hot-water baths, and fans, put guests right on the beach. Breakfast at the attached restaurant, ticket booking, and book swap included. (High-season economy singles US$5, low-season US$10; standard singles US$10/$20; deluxe singles US$36; standard doubles US$15/$25; deluxe doubles US$40.) More than a kilometer south in Myabyin, **Royal Guest House** ❸ (☎42 411, in Yangon 24 38 80) is also a good value and is open year-round. Comfortable and well-kept rooms with breakfast, bath, and fan are US$10 in the low season and

THE BIG SPLURGE

A BAYVIEW OF THE SILVER BEACH

If you've been on the road for what feels like years, consider taking a "vacation from your vacation" along the Bay of Bengal. Tucked away from the cities and separated from the upcountry by the Rahkairy Mountains, Ngapali Beach provides a gorgeous haven for the weary traveler.

The staff of the **Bayview Resort Hotel** ❺ is waiting to soothe away the aches of traveling with a tender massage. Bayview's spotless rooms face either the ocean or a fresh-water pool, and offer a laundry list of amenities, including A/C and satellite TV. Guests dine on traditional Burmese or Western food in the house restaurant.

(Yangon reservation office: 289/A Pyay Rd., 50 44 71, hotel@bayview.com.mm. Singles high season US$120, low season US$50; doubles US$125/US$55.)

High-season visitors will find the **Silver Beach Hotel's** ❺ bungalow suites a better value. More like beach-front apartments, each suite has a bedroom, sitting room with flat-screen TV, full bath with hot water, and a refrigerator. Guests' privacy extends right up to the ocean view, as all nine bungalows have private verandas. *(Silver Beach: Yangon Reservation Office 838 18 98, 24 26 52. sbh01@goldenbrothers.com.mm; high season only, standard singles US$46, standard doubles US$55. Deluxe bungalows US$86/US$100.)*

US$20-45 in the high season, based on view and proximity to the beach. The **Bayview Resort Hotel** ❺ (☎50 44 71 in Yangon), which is open all year and accepts MC/V, and the **Silver Beach Hotel** ❺ (☎38 18 98 in Yangon), top out the price range with rooms and free-standing bungalow suites filled with all the amenities, including refrigerator and satellite TV, for US$50-125. Travelers who want to avoid government-owned establishments should not stay at **Ngapali Beach Hotel.**

FOOD. All of the hotels on Ngapali Beach have attached restaurants, but that hasn't stopped private ventures from serving the same menu: seafood, seafood, and Chinese. These establishments are spread fairly evenly along the beach, but the best cluster at the gates of the Bayview and Silver Beach hotels. **Best Friend Seafood Restaurant** ❸ and **Excellence Seafood Restaurant** ❹ stand out from the crowd for their selection of seafood (lobster available if ordered a day in advance) and mixed tropical drinks (500-1000kyat). Excellence serves pasta (1500kyat) and seafood salads (800-1500kyat), while Best Friend's coconut soup (500kyat) is not to be missed. Both are open daily 9am-10pm.

SIGHTS. Ngapali Beach, a strip of white sand bordered by swaying coconut trees, is home to the local fishing industry and a bull cart transportation lane. It also serves as the field for impromptu soccer games. When the high season starts and foreigners arrive, bull cart tracks fade into footprints and towels, but no matter the season, the beach remains a central part of village life. Ngapali's distance from Yangon keeps the area less commercialized and the sand more pristine, so for those who make the effort to visit it, relaxation is the prize.

The three villages of Lintha, Lontha, and Myabyin lie on the outskirts of Thandwe, with Lintha to the north and Myabyin and Lontha to the south. Fishing boats leave before dawn and can be seen continuously casting in the deeper waters off the beach. Around noon they return to the part of the beach adjacent to their village to sort fish and clean gear. From the sand, fishermen carry their day's catch into town via the lanes and paths that end at the sand's edge. In Lontha, visitors can head west through town to the other side of the peninsula, where the beach shows the signs of a people who make use of every available resource.

There are also several small and secluded islands in the area. **Linn Thar Oo Lodge** offers a half-day boat trip (10,000kyat), and other hotels will do so on request.

PATHEIN ☎42

The jewel of the Ayeyarwady Delta, Pathein was once a Mon stronghold but lost its prominence under the Burmese Empire. Today Myanmar's fourth-largest city is known for its rice production, parasol workshops, and Karen, Rahkine, and Burmese populations. There aren't many sights in the area, but with its fascinating home industry and as a gateway to Chaung Tha Beach, this relaxed urban center lures visitors year-round.

> **DON'T LEAVE HOME WITHOUT IT.** Unlike in other towns listed in this book, entering Pathein requires passing an immigration checkpoint. Buses stop upon entering town, and valid **visas** are required for entry. If you've overstayed your visa, you'll be sent back to Yangon.

TRANSPORTATION. Pathein's **airport** is currently for military use only but is under renovations for domestic use beginning in late 2005 or early 2006. The **Highway Bus Terminal** is several kilometers east of the town center. **Jeeps** run along Mahabandoola Rd., between the terminal and Shwezedi Rd. and between Merchant St. and Mingyi Rd. (200kyat). **Buses** leave daily for Pyay (15 hr., 4pm, 2500kyat). Companies sell tickets to Yangon (5hr.; 4, 6, 7, 8, 10am, noon, 2pm; 2500kyat) at the corner of Shwezedi Rd. and Merchant St., opposite the Myanmar Commercial Bank. These buses leave from the bus terminal, but the companies provide free transport from downtown. Buy tickets one day in advance. **Buses** to Chaung Tha Beach (3hr.; 7, 11am, 1pm; 2000kyat) leave from the Chaung Tha Bus Terminal. From the clocktower, go one block away from the river (intersection of Mahabandoola Rd. and Mingyi Rd.) and turn left. After one block, turn right; buses line up on the left. A **ferry** runs to Yangon (17hr., 5pm, US$7) from the intersection of Strand and Mahabandoola Rd. A ticket gives you access to a chair on the deck, under the stars. **Trishaws** charge 200-300kyat anywhere in the city.

ORIENTATION. **Pathein Highway** enters Pathein from the east and becomes **Mahabandoola Road** as it approaches the heart of the city. A **clocktower** stands at its intersection with **Merchant Street,** two blocks before Mahabandoola Rd. ends at the **Pathein River,** which runs north-south. **Strand Road** runs alongside the river, perpendicular to Mahabandoola Rd. **Shwemokhtaw Pagoda** sits in the block encompassed by Merchant St., Strand, Mahabandoola, and Shwezedi Rd. The **Central Market** (open M-Sa 7am-5pm) sits in the next two blocks south of the pagoda, spanning the small stream that winds through downtown.

PRACTICAL INFORMATION. Although it is best to change money before leaving Yangon, **Taan Taan Ta Guest House** (see **Accommodations**) will exchange US$ in a pinch. **Pharmacies** (open daily 7am-9pm) cluster on Mingyi Rd., just south of Mahabandoola Rd. opposite the 24hr. **hospital,** which sits on the corner of Mahabandoola and Mingyi Rd. In **emergencies,** call ☎215 11. The **telephone office** (open daily 7am-9pm) is on Mahabandoola Rd., one block toward the river from the clocktower. The **library** in City Hall, the white building south of the Strand-Mahabandoola Rd. intersection, will send **email.** One A4-sized page is 600kyat. (Open M-F 9:30am-4:30pm.) The **post office** (open M-F 9:30am-4:30pm) is next door but sends only postcards internationally (50kyat). **Postal Code:** 10011.

ACCOMMODATIONS. Several new accommodations have opened in Pathein, but the top few all have similar rooms. The front rooms at **Pamawady Inn ❷,** at the corner of Mingyi and Shwezedi Rd., are the best value in town. Very friendly service, but breakfast is not included. Tiled rooms with A/C and attached bath, some with TV. (☎211 65. Singles US$5; doubles US$10.) **Paradise Guest House ❷** offers more of the same for a few dollars more. Take a left immediately after crossing a small bridge as you walk south from the Shwemokhtaw Pagoda on Merchant St. (☎227 51. Singles US$8; doubles US$10.) The attentive and helpful staff at **Taan Taan Ta Guest House ❷,** on Merchant St. across from the Central Market, have older and much smaller rooms with A/C, bath, and breakfast included. (☎222 90. Singles US$5-10; doubles US$8-15.)

FOOD. **Kha Kha Gyi ❸,** 68 Mingalar St., opposite the east entrance to Shwemokhtaw Pagoda, serves excellent, full spreads of Burmese food for around 700kyat. (Open daily 9am-9pm.) The other notable restaurant in town is **Shwe Zin Yaw ❸,** on Shwezedi Rd. between Merchant St. and Mingyi Rd., which serves huge helpings of Myanmar food or *biryani* (800kyat) daily 7am-9pm. If Chinese food is more your style, try **Zee Bae Inn ❸,** 3 blocks south of the Central Market on Merchant St., or the slightly more expensive **Golden Land Restaurant ❸,** one block north of the clocktower. They share the exact same menu (basic rice dishes 800kyat). At Zee Bae, don't let them seat you on the airless upper floor.

SIGHTS AND ENTERTAINMENT. Shwemokhtaw Pagoda, with its southern entrance on Shwezedi Rd. opposite the north end of the Central Market, literally floated to Myanmar. The southern pavilion's image, **Thiho-Shin Phondaw-pyi,** was released on the ocean, along with several other images on separate rafts, to spread Buddhism from India. It worked, as Buddhists in the area pray here throughout the day. In the southwest corner of the compound, behind a painted yellow pagoda, is a very graphic display of the ailments Buddha envisioned before his renunciation. While the pagoda is not as big as its cousin in Yangon, the mirror inlay on the small pagoda in the southeast corner and the pillars in the eastern pavilion prove that size doesn't matter when it comes to beauty.

Pathein is well known throughout the country for its **parasols** (locally called umbrellas), made in the privacy of many private homes and backyards. One of the very few places the entire production process can be seen is **Pathein Shwe Sar,** 653 Twe Ya Kyang Rd. (Open daily 9am-5pm.) Although the final decoration and display is done in the open front yard, venture to the back to see the deft splitting of bamboo and weaving of strings that provide the internal support of the covering. Parasols for women and tourists come in brightly colored pinks and blues, with painted bouquets of flowers. The only waterproof parasols available are made for monks and nuns and come in simple, muted colors. Prices range from 500kyat for a small tourist souvenir to 50,000kyat for a parasol to cover an outdoor table. The building is on the road behind Settayaw Pagoda (see below). You can walk through the pagoda compound and turn left, where the workshop is another 100m ahead and on the left. Or you can take a trishaw (500kyat) from Mahabandoola Rd.

Settayaw Pagoda, to the left off Mahabandoola Rd. as you leave the city, but before the golf course (look for statues of two men), is a haphazard collection of shrines and statues that have accumulated throughout the ages. Spanning several small hills and valleys, the pagoda's big attraction is a Buddha footprint, found in an octagonal building just left of the peak of the farthest hill. The building is surrounded by statues of men enduring severe suffering and extremely graphic deaths. The top of the other, closer hill is filled with statues crowded so close together they almost touch. In the southern part of the city stands **Tagaung Pagoda,** a sprawling and well-maintained complex. About halfway up on the west side of the *zedi* is a small golden squirrel that symbolizes one of Buddha's previous lives. At this particular pagoda the planetary posts take the form of mirror-encrusted pillars in front of the usual, seated Buddha figure. Nearby is **Mahabodhi Mingala Pagoda,** built to look like the Mahabodhi *stupa* in Bodgaya, India. A horned animal sits where Tagaung's squirrel could be seen, and in true Indian fashion, statues of Ganesh grace surrounding shrines. (Tagaung, Mahabodhi, and the fork in the Merchant St. that leads to them form a triangle. Five blocks south of the Central Market, Tagaung Pagoda St. splits left off of Merchant St. and leads to Tagaung Pagoda. The right fork leads 1km to Mahabodhi Mingala. A 10min. walk left from Tagaung or right from Mahabodhi will reach the opposite pagoda).

CHAUNG THA BEACH ☎42

One of the prettiest beaches in Myanmar, and certainly the one most accessible to foreigners, Chaung Tha's prices and company change with the monsoons. In low season hotel representatives vie for clientele, offering rock-bottom prices, while in high season Myanmar's tourism is at its finest. However, the beach remains the same year-round—a wide mudflat at low-tide, and a soft, off-white strip otherwise. Behind the western beach-front facade of pearly, white sand is Chaung Tha the village—a quiet fishing community which comes into view as you walk east on Bogyoke St. Concrete turns to dirt and buildings elevate onto stilts as the world created for tourists fades into the eastern beach, home to the industry that supports most of the local inhabitants. Visitors come to Chaung Tha for surf, sand, and a relaxing break but are surprised when they find a dose of reality in the unadulterated lives of Myanmar locals.

TRANSPORTATION. Buses go to: **Pathein** (3hr.; 7, 11am, 1pm; 1500kyat) and **Yangon** (9hr., 6:30am, 5000kyat). Hotels can arrange tickets, which should be bought a day in advance, and all buses stop at hotels for passengers. A bridge scheduled to be completed by the end of 2006 will make the Shwe Myin Tin-Than Hylet Soon ferry obsolete, but until then foreigners must pay US$5 (round-trip) on the way to Chaung Tha. Distances within town are easily covered on foot, but a trishaw may be preferable at night (50-200kyat).

ORIENTATION AND PRACTICAL INFORMATION. The very bumpy road from Pathein passes through increasingly smaller bamboo-industry villages before coming from the east to the very northern end of the beach. At **Shwe Hin Tha Hotel** it takes a sharp left turn (south), becoming **Main Road** as it passes all the hotels and the **post office.** (Domestic mail only. Open M-F 9:30am-4:30pm.) After 1km Main Rd. intersects **Bogyoke Street,** which runs east-west between the peninsula's two beaches and is home to all the restaurants and the **Thien Than Aung Store,** a pharmacy that is open daily 7am-9pm. The **hospital** is on Bogyoke St., opposite the small pagoda, but it is highly recommended to seek medical care in Pathein. **Hotel Max,** at the intersection of Main Rd. and Bogyoke St., can place IDD calls (US$10/min.) when the line is working. After crossing Bogyoke St., Main Rd. continues south 700m to the **Whitesand Island Jetty** at the end of the peninsula.

ACCOMMODATIONS AND FOOD. With about twenty hotels lining the beach side of Main Rd., everyone, regardless of budget, has a shot at beachfront digs. **Shwe Hin Tha ❸,** which sits where the road from Pathein turns south, is the best value during low season. Its extensive services, including horse rides, bicycle rental, billiards, and hot water, make it worth the extra money year-round. The attentive staff tends huge bungalow rooms on the beach and smaller rooms away from the beach, all with a bath and veranda. (Yangon: ☎01 650 588; Chaung Tha: ☎042 24098; beachfront in high season US$20-25, in low season US$7; off the beach US$7/US$4.) **Chaung Tha Beach Hotel ❸** (☎248 80, ext. 324), just north of the Main Rd.-Bogyoke St. intersection, and **Golden Beach Hotel ❸** (☎241 26), a 5min. walk back toward Pathein from the intersection, both have more than 50 rooms ranging from economy rooms with sparse furniture and fan (singles US$8-10; doubles US$12-20) to superior suites with satellite TV, A/C, refrigerator, hot shower, and bathtub (singles US$24-30; doubles US$30-36). Golden Beach has nicer economy rooms, while Chaungtha Beach Hotel's upper-level rooms shine. A substantial discount off the superior room prices is common during the low season. The only hotel that could possibly overshadow these is the **Hotel Max ❺** (☎249 66; reservation@maxmyanmar.com.mm), right in the center of town. It meets international standards with a swimming pool, tennis court, mini-golf course, massage parlor, beauty parlor, karaoke room, business center, convenience store, and Asian/Continental dining room. Prices start at US$49 and rise steadily into the stratosphere.

The restaurants that line Bogyoke St. all dish up fresh seafood from the Bay of Bengal. **Pearl Restaurant ❹,** opposite Hotel Max at the intersection of Main Rd. and Bogyoke St., has attentive service and mainly local customers. **Thiriwai Restaurant ❹** serves decent Burmese food. For basic provisions, head to **Zaw Mart,** on the opposite side of Main Rd. from the Golden Beach Hotel (open daily 6am-9pm), or the **local market,** 1 block north of Bogyoke St. (closes at noon).

SIGHTS. Grab an inner tube (free at most hotels) and take to the surf, or choose a towel and stick to the sand—whichever way you want to relax, **Chaung Tha Beach** makes it possible. Local women patrol with snack foods for sale and fishermen break out soccer balls at dusk. Swimmers should beware of the monsoon season currents. Witness the local **fishing industry** along the eastern beach, where local inhabitants live and work. Fishing boats trawl all morning, pulling in to the south and east sides of the peninsula around noon for sorting and cleaning. Later in the day, bigger boats anchor off the beach while workers wade to shore for a game of *chinlon.* During the high season sunbathing is also possible on remote **Whitesand Island,** off the south end of Chaung Tha. Most hotels rent equipment for snorkeling, which is better at Whitesand. Boats leave from the jetty at the southern tip of the peninsula (every hr., US$5 round-trip).

NORTHERN MYANMAR

> **GOVERNMENT LISTINGS.** All government listings are marked with a **M** symbol. Money spent at such establishments goes directly into the government's hands. See **Keep the Bucks Where They Belong,** p. 462.

MANDALAY မန္တလေး ☎02

Sprawling, dusty Mandalay may not exactly be eye candy, but the joy of Myanmar's second-largest city lies not in its appearance but in its importance as a cultural center. The last capital of Myanmar before British rule, Mandalay retains the artistic traditions that were once the object of royal patronage, and quarters of the city still brim with performers and artisans. Daytime affords opportunities to observe local artisans, and the night brings out traditional theatrical performers. At the northeast and southwest corners of the city are Mandalay Hill and Mahumuni Pagoda, both of which deserve a visit, and four nearby towns provide escape from the bustle and invite travelers to linger for a few days before slipping off to a more sedate respite on Inle Lake or Bagan.

INTERCITY TRANSPORTATION

BY PLANE. Mandalay International Airport is a distant 35km south of the city center. (Blue taxi to and from southwest corner of Palace, 5000 kyat.) Maps indicating an airport between the Palace and highway bus terminal have not been updated recently. **Air Mandalay** (☎315 48; open M-F 8am-6pm, Sa-Su 9am-1pm), on 82nd St. between 26th and 27th St., flies to: Bagan (daily 4:25pm, US$38); Heho/Inle Lake (daily 9am, 4:40pm; US$38); Yangon (1½hr.; 4 times daily 9am-5pm; US$96). Tickets are several dollars cheaper at ticket sales agents. **M Myanma Airways** (☎362 21; open daily 9am-4pm), on 81st St. between 25th and 26th St., flies to: Bagan (20min.; Sa-M, W 6am; US$40); Bhamo (30min., F 8am, US$50); Kengtung (Th noon, US$60); Tachilek (1hr., M 9am, $70); Yangon (1hr., daily 6am, US$100). Tickets are bought one day in advance from the office and are only sold 9-10:30am. **Yangon Airways** (☎360 12 for reservations; open daily 9am-5pm), on 78th St. between 29th and 30th, opposite the train station, flies to Heho/Inle Lake (daily 8:35am, $US38) and Yangon (daily 8:35am, 4:55pm; US$96).

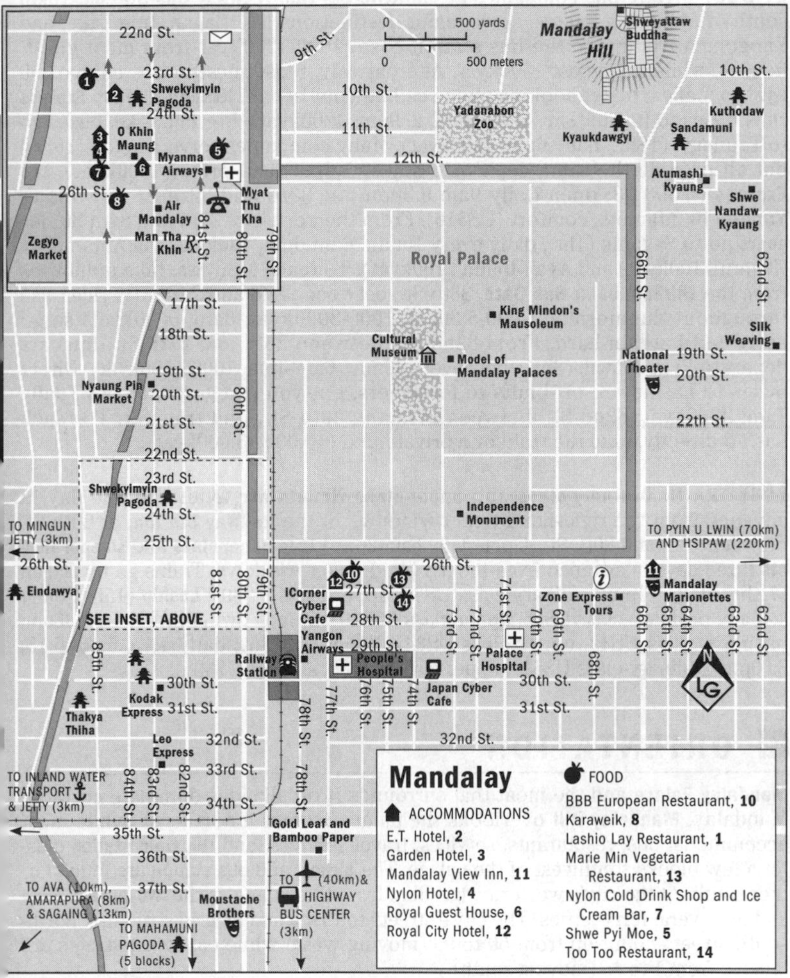

BY BOAT. Boats sail to Bagan (regular: 16hr.; W and Su 5:30am; deck US$11, cabin US$33; express: 9hr.; M-Tu, Th-Sa 6am; US$18). The **Inland Water Transport Jetty** (also known as **Gaw Wein Jetty**) on the west end of 35th St., a 500kyat trishaw ride from the palace area, and **Myanmar Travels and Tours (MTT)** (see **Practical Information,** p. 499), sell tickets to foreigners. Tickets purchased from the jetty cost US$1-2 less and can be bought on the day of departure. MTT will sell tickets at full price until 2pm the day before departure. The **Mayan Chan Jetty,** at the west end of 26th St., organizes a tourist boat to Mingun (1hr.; 9am, return 1pm; 1500kyat). Private charters to Mingun cost 8000-15000kyat.

BY BUS. Private bus companies at the **Kywe Ser Kan Highway Bus Station,** 10km south of Mandalay Palace, serve major destinations like Bagan, Inle Lake, and Yangon. A trishaw to the bus station costs 1000-1200kyat from most guesthouses, while taxis cost 1500kyat. Alternatively, most guesthouses charge 250 kyat to make a ticket-booking phone call on your behalf. **Nyaung U Mann Express** runs buses to Bagan (8hr.; daily 9am, 2, 9pm; 4200kyat). For **Inle Lake,** buses go to Taunggyi (18hr., daily 6pm, 4500kyat). Many companies serve Yangon (16hr.) but all provide the same departure times (5,6pm) and price (4500kyat). **Leo Express** (☎393 23; open daily 9am-6:30pm) at 83rd and 33rd St., travels to Yangon in infamous comfort (US$10). From the corner of 29th and 84th St., **linecars** go to Sagaing (1hr., daily every 15min. 6am-6pm, 100kyat) via Amarapura (30min., 100kyat) and Ava (45min., 100kyat). To reach Monywa, take minibuses from the **Thirimandalar Bus Gate,** 88th St., between 22nd and 23rd St. Prices rise throughout the morning (4:30-5:30am, 1000-3000kyat; 6am, 5000kyat) so go early and bargain hard. From 82nd St., between 26th and 27th St., linecars depart to Pyin U Lwin (3hr., daily every 30min. 6am-4pm, 1000-1500kyat). Direct buses to Lashio are off-limits to foreigners, but you can go to Hsipaw (daily 7am, 2300kyat; 82nd St., between 28th and 29th St.) and transfer. To reach Lashio directly, take the train or a private taxi (10,000-15,000kyat).

BY TRAIN. **Ordinary-class** and **upper-class tickets** are available one day in advance from the right-hand ticket windows in the **Railway Station,** at 30th St. between 78th and 80th St. (Open daily 6am-2pm.) Buy **upper-class** and **sleeper tickets** three days in advance from the left-hand ticket windows. Trains go to: Bagan (7½hr., daily 10pm; ordinary-class US$4, upper-class US$9); **Lashio** (15hr., daily 4:45am; ordinary-class US$5, upper-class US$10); Pyin U Lwin (4hr., daily 4:45am; ordinary-class US$2, upper-class US$4); Yangon (15hr.; daily 4:15, 5:15, 6:15, 8:00pm; ordinary-class US$11, upper-class US$30, sleeper US$35).

ORIENTATION

Mandalay Palace and the moat that surrounds it on all sides dominate northern Mandalay. **Mandalay Hill** overlooks the palace from the northeast, while most accommodations, restaurants, services, travel services, and the **train station** cluster a few blocks southwest of the palace. The **airport** and **bus station** are much farther south. At the city's western edge, 3km from the palace, is the **Ayeyarwady River** and its several ferry jetties. The city's streets follow a simple grid structure: north-south streets count up from 50 to 90 (moving west) while east-west streets are labeled from 1 to 45 (moving south).

LOCAL TRANSPORTATION

Unless you aren't comfortable negotiating through Mandalay's crazy traffic or it's too hot outside, go ahead and rent a bicycle. Otherwise, hire one of Mandalay's 17,000 trishaws. There is no such thing as a "short walk;" expect a 1½ hr. trip to Mandalay Hill from the Palace's southwest corner.

Taxis: Two types of taxis are available: small **blue** taxis that resemble mini linecars (1500kyat per hr., US$20 per day) and larger **white** taxis that are typically Japanese sedans (5000kyat per hr., US$30 per day). Rates can fluctuate with the cost of petrol. Settle on a price first.

hostelbookers.com
Great Hostels. Free Booking. No Worries.
Guaranteed lowest cost internet hostel booking
No booking fees
Genuine hostels featured
Fast and easy to use
Book Worldwide hostels online at
www.hostelbookers.com

Bicycles: Several guesthouses and hotels rent bicycles. **O Khin Maung,** opposite the Royal Guest House (see **Accommodations,** p. 500), charges 700kyat per day (8am-7pm) and 400kyat per half-day (8am-1pm).

Trishaws (or Sica): Hopping on a trishaw is a crucial part of the Mandalay experience. Use these pedicabs for short trips within the city, which will cost about 300kyat. Drivers charge 5000kyat for a day of sightseeing or 1000kyat to the bus terminal. Make your destination clear.

TIP **TOUR DE MANDALAY.** Without question, the most efficient way to get around Mandalay is by bicycle. Braving the bi-wheeled hordes can be test of self-determination, however. Here are some rules for the road:

1. Be assertive at intersections. Join a group of cyclists, and take cues from the cars next to you (or use them as a shield). If you wimp out you might just be stuck at 26th and 82nd street until next monsoon season.
2. Take note of the vehicle hierarchy. Motorized vehicles travel close to the center line, with bikes closer to the sidewalk. Trishaws and carts, the snails of the city streets, are basically in the gutter.
3. Due to their size and power, it's best to let motorized vehicles have the right of way if they want it. In you vs. the car, the car always wins.
4. At most stops there is a bike stand where attendants charge 50kyat to protect your ride. This is no substitute for the wheel lock.
5. Beware of linecars that pull over constantly to collect passengers.
6. Toot your horn like your life depends on it. Because it does, especially when you're about to pass a vehicle or enter traffic. Ain't nobody gonna do it for ya.
7. When deciding what route to take one seasoned local advises, "choose the best way—your own way." Sage advice for life, and a good rule of thumb for cycling in Myanmar.

PRACTICAL INFORMATION

Tourist Office: Myanmar Travels and Tours (☎603 56), on 68th St. between 26th and 27th St. Myanma Airways and boat bookings. Maps 100kyat. Will **exchange currency,** but at a less favorable rate than in Yangon. Open daily 8:30am-5:30pm.

Travel Agency: Zone Express Tours (☎/fax 611 36; ZONE.ETT@mptmail.net.mm), on 27th St. between 66th and 68th St. Friendly staff will happily assist with hiring cars (US$25 per day) and tour guides (US$15 per day) and setting up accommodations in other cities. Open daily 8am-6pm.

Currency Exchange: This is best done in Yangon, but in a pinch, ask at **MTT** or most guesthouses.

Emergency: Fire ☎191. **Ambulance** ☎192. **Police** ☎199.

Pharmacy: Man Tha Khin, on 81st St. between 26th and 27th St. Open daily 9:30am-9:30pm.

Medical Services: Most big hospitals in the city are government-run. For private care, go to **Palace Hospital** (☎361 28, ext. 810 for emergencies), at 79th and 29th St., or **Myat Thu Kha** (☎350 66), on 80th St. between 24th and 25th St. Both are open 24hr and have English-speaking staff.

Telephones: Telephone/Telegraph Office, on 26th St. between 80th and 81st St. Calls to the US cost US$5 per min. Callbacks cost US$1 per 3min. **IDD** at hotels costs a couple more dollars per min. **Telegraphs** (4kyat per word) arrive in one day. Open daily 7am-9pm.

Internet Access: iCorner Cyber Cafe, 77th St. between 27th and 28th St., has a fairly reliable server and charges 500kyat per hr. Open daily 7am-7pm. **Japan Cyber Cafe,** 30th St. between 73rd and 74th St., has A/C. 1000kyat per hr. Open daily 9am-11pm.

Film Developing: Kodak Express, at 83rd and 30th St., has film (800-1200kyat per roll) and developing services (70kyat per 4x6 print). No English. Open daily 7am-9pm.

Post Office: GPO, on 22nd St. between 80th and 81st St. *Poste Restante.* Open M-F 9:30am-4:30pm.

Postal Code: 05071.

ACCOMMODATIONS

Budget accommodations are west of Mandalay Palace, with the most popular ones concentrated near the intersection of 25th St. and 83rd St. Most accommodations include breakfast, laundry service, and transportation arrangements.

Royal Guest House, 41 25th St. (☎314 00), between 82nd and 83rd St. As the current epicenter of Mandalay backpackers, its reputation is well earned with spotless, tiled rooms and personable staff. Short-term luggage storage available. Cold drinks 100kyat. Singles US$3, with A/C and private bath US$5-10; doubles US$6/$8-14. ❷

Garden Hotel, 174 83rd St. (☎318 84), between 24th and 25th St., next to Nylon Hotel. Spacious rooms, all with A/C, hot shower, refrigerator, and TV. Will provide free pick-up from the train station, boat jetty, or bus terminal with prior notice. Singles US$5-10; doubles US$12-15; discounts during the low season. ❸

E.T. Hotel (☎665 47), on 83rd St. between 23rd and 24th St. Right in the backpackers' neighborhood, E.T. has mismatched rooms with bath, A/C or fans, and refrigerator, but no breakfast. Book exchange in the lobby. Singles US$6 in high season, US$5 in low season; doubles US$10/US$8. ❸

Royal City Hotel, 130 27th St. (☎318 05), between 76th and 77th St. Provides the same comfort and friendliness as the Royal Guest House, but with luxury. All rooms with TV, bathtub, and A/C. IDD telephone service (US$6 first min., US$4 every min. thereafter). Bicycle rental and laundry service. Singles US$15-20; doubles US$20-25. ❹

Nylon Hotel (☎334 60), at the corner of 25th and 83rd St. Pleasant staff manages cheap but older rooms with bath, A/C, and TV. Breakfast included and email available. Singles in high season US$4-6, in low season $US3-5; doubles US$8-12/US$6-10. ❷

Mandalay View Inn (☎611 19), on 66th St. between 26th and 27th St., across from Sedona Hotel. Convenient location at the southeast corner of Royal Palace. For those who want to escape the backpacker scene. Offers comfortable, quiet rooms with TV, refrigerator, phone, bath, and A/C. Breakfast included. Email and IDD telephone service. Standard rooms US$30; superior rooms US$35; discounts for longer stays. ❺

FOOD

Quality and culture find a rare but oh-so-tasty balance in Mandalay's restaurants. As Mandalay is situated at a regional crossroads, cuisines include Chinese, Shan, Burmese, Indian, and Thai. Most tourist places bunch off the southwest corner of the Palace, and several deviate from the sit-down-with-a-menu style.

Karaweik, on the sidewalk at the southeast corner of 26th and 83rd St. Once the corner shops close, out come the chairs, food, and locals. Point to order and rub elbows with the neighborhood. At local prices, the food is divine: coconut rice (400kyat), *kima* (meat in *parantha;* 350kyat), curry (500kyat). No beer. Vegetarians should look elsewhere. Open daily 5pm-1am. ❷

Nylon Cold Drink Shop and Ice Cream Bar (☎229 38), on the corner of 83rd St. and 25th St. Get your dairy fix here at low prices. Divine ice cream in both classic and unusual flavors 150kyat. Strawberry milkshake 200kyat. Open daily 8am-10pm. ❶

Marie Min Vegetarian Restaurant, on 27th St. between 74th and 75th St., opposite Too Too Restaurant. Refreshing drinks and guaranteed-safe vegetables make it an herbivore's favorite. Carnivores will enjoy the break from rice and curry. Breakfast served all day. Muesli, yogurt, and fruit 1500kyat. Lentil soup 800kyat. Open daily 8am-9pm. ❹

Shwe Pyi Moe, on 25th St. between 80th and 81st St., offers early service and easily the best milk-tea (80kyat) in town. *El Kyar Kway* (fried bread) is the house specialty, but the menu item "Myanmar Noodles" (300kyat) is a good choice at any time of day. Open daily 5am-5:30pm. ❷

Lashio Lay Restaurant (☎385 68), 65 23rd St. between 83rd and 84th St. One of the locals' favorite Shan restaurants. The menu changes daily, so get the rundown of what's available before picking your dishes from the front of the restaurant. A good choice for all diets with meat dishes (700-1000kyat) and several completely vegetarian options (300kyat). Heapings of rice come with your food for 250kyat per person. Large bottle of beer 1000kyat. Open daily 9am-9pm. ❸

BBB European Restaurant, 242 76th St. between 26th and 27th St. Don't let the name or ritzy appearance scare you away. BBB serves quality, reasonably priced Western food and wine in A/C surroundings. A good place for a nicer evening out. Burgers 800kyat. Chicken barbecue 3300kyat. Spaghetti 1300kyat. Open daily 9am-10:30pm. ❹

Too Too Restaurant, on 27th St. between 74th and 75th St., opposite Marie Min Vegetarian Restaurant. Locals say it's the best Burmese food in the area. Succulent meat and fish curries come with several side dishes of lentils and broadbeans. Meals 900kyat, veggie-only 700kyat. Open daily 10:30am-9pm. ❸

SIGHTS

Mandalay's historical sights are in the northeast, with the exception of Mahamuni Pagoda and the artisan quarters in the southern reaches. A ticket (US$10 per person, valid for five days) to the Archaeological Zone gains entry to: The Royal Palace, Kuthodaw Pagoda, Sandamuni Pagoda, Kyaukdawgyi Pagoda, Mandalay Hill, Shwe Nandaw Kyaung, Atumashi Kyaung, Mahamuni Pagoda, Amarapura, Innwa, Pinya, and Palaik. Ticket checks are conducted at The Royal Palace, Kuthodaw Pagoda, Shwe Nandaw Kyaung, and Atumashi Kyaung. Sites where tickets are checked are open daily 7:30am-5pm unless otherwise noted.

MANDALAY HILL မန္တလေးတောင်. Rising 236m above the northeastern corner of town, the 700-odd steps are well worth the 30min. climb. The less ambitious can use linecar (200kyat) and elevator (free) service to the top. The temples leading to the summit seem newfangled and lacking in distinction, but the Shweyattaw image, around halfway, is an exception. The towering 8m Buddha structure points toward the city. This is a representation of a famous legend in which the Buddha predicted that a great Buddhist city would arise at the base of the hill, under the rule of Sandamukhi Ogress, who, being poor, decided to cut off her own breasts and donate them as a gift to the Buddha. Also of note is the yellow, semi-circular prison visible from the northwest corner of the top platform: it has a pagoda in the middle. Especially at sunset or on the weekends, local teens come to practice their foreign languages with tourists. *(Main entrance between 2 white* chinthas. *Camera fee for the top 350kyat. Open daily 6am-9pm.)*

SHWE NANDAW KYAUNG (GOLDEN PALACE MONASTERY) AND ATUMASHI KYAUNG (INCOMPARABLE MONASTERY). The only teak building in Mandalay to survive WWII, the architecture and ornamentation of **Shwe Nandaw Kyaung** yields one of Mandalay's most impressive sights. Built by King Mindon and originally located in his Amarapura palace, it was moved to Mandalay and used as his private bedroom when he ascended to the throne. After he died in this room, it was disassembled, donated as a monastery, and reassembled in its current location. Its highlights include a royal medication couch and a replica of the great Lion Throne. It used to be covered in gold, hence the name "Golden Palace Monastery." **Atumashi Kyaung,** to the west of Shwe Nandaw Kyaung, is much less stunning. Before burning down in 1892, it was considered Mandalay's most beautiful monument, with elaborate stucco carvings, glass mosaics, fine masonry work, and a revered, diamond-encrusted Buddha image (which the British stole in 1885). The fruit of intense prison labor, the reconstructed building looks so modern and empty that it's difficult to imagine its prior splendor. Today both sites function only as tourist attractions. *(Corner of 60th and 12th St.)*

MAHAMUNI PAGODA. The "Pagoda of the Great Buddha Image" remains the holiest object in Northern Myanmar. According to legend, the Buddha brought this 3.8m bronze temple to life after embracing it seven times during a visit to the Rakhine (Arakan) State. Mahamuni was presented to Mandalay in 1784 by the Crown Prince of Amarapura, who had claimed it upon his victory over the Arakan King. Every morning around 4am, the head monk gives the image a ceremonial facial, right down to brushing its teeth. Women grind sandalwood for the ceremony in one of the side courtyards but are prohibited from entering the inner sanctuary. Male pilgrims flock to the podium to affix gold leaves to the Buddha. Over the years, the golden build-up has accumulated to a layer over 16cm thick. The face has reputedly expanded proportionally with this growth—stirring evidence, some say, that Mahamuni is a living entity. *Longgyi*-clad male visitors are welcome to place gold leaves on the image (*longgyi* rental 200kyat, 5 gold leaves 500kyat).

Behind the image and to the right stand **six bronze statues.** The interest here lies not so much in their artistic merit but in the statues' travels. Originating at Cambodia's Angkor Wat, the statues were moved to Ayutthaya in 1431, the Burmese Kingdom of Bago in 1564, the Arakan Kingdom in 1599, and finally to Mandalay along with the Mahamuni Pagoda in 1784. There is also a legend surrounding these bronze statues: after arriving in Mahamuni Pagoda, it was believed that they were alive as they cried at night longing for their Cambodian homeland. It is also thought that rubbing the figures in a particular place cures ailments in the corresponding part of the body. Artisans selling wood-carvings, miniature gongs, and other handicrafts crowd the walkways to the temple. Although beggars are prohibited in Myanmar by the government, you may encounter some here. *(In southern Mandalay. The main entrance is at the intersection of 82nd and 45th St. No sleeveless shirts, shorts, or photographs of the main image. Open daily 4am-4pm.)*

KUTHODAW PAGODA AND SANDAMUNI PAGODA. Crafted in 1857 on the model of Bagan's Shwezigon Pagoda, **Kuthodaw Pagoda,** a 5min. walk east of Mandalay Hill, holds the distinction of housing the world's biggest book, a tome with all Buddhist scriptures in Pali, an ancient language which today only the monks can read. The text is inscribed on 729 stone slabs, each sheltered in masonry shrines surrounding the pagoda. One hundred meters southwest of Kuthodaw, **Sandamuni Pagoda** marks where King Mindon's younger brother, hand-picked to succeed him, was murdered in 1866 by two of the King's miffed sons. Much more interesting than the pagoda's iron Buddha are the surrounding miniature *stupas*, which shelter 1774 marble slabs containing commentaries on the Tripitaka called *Sutta Vinaya Abidhamma*. *(Open daily 7am-6pm.)*

THE ROYAL PALACE မန္တလေးနန်းတော်. Surrounded by stately walls and a formidable moat, the Royal Palace, built in the 1860s, monopolizes northern Mandalay on a 3.2km² plot of land. The walls of King Mindon's teak palace and their associated guard towers are all that remain of the original structure after the destruction of WWII. A few concrete reconstructions—including the palace itself and a watch tower—make up the main tourist attractions, and visitors are restricted from other areas due to the fort's present incarnation as a military base. Although the views from the watch tower are good, the palace may not be worth the steep admission. Many travelers skip the palace or consciously boycott it to protest the forced labor involved in its reconstruction. The enormous moat, for example, is the result of the mass mobilization of Mandalay's citizens, who had to bring their own tools to the work site.

ARTISAN WORKSHOPS. Mandalay is known as Myanmar's center of culture and art thanks to the **artisan guilds. Marble and wood workshops** craft Buddha statues of every size in the south of the city. Come here if your personal pagoda needs a new image or you want to watch monks deck out their monastery. *(South of Mahamuni Pagoda on 84th St., between 45th and 46th St. Open daily 9am-5pm.)* At the **Gold Rose,** one family dedicates its energy to the production of **gold leaf,** which is used to gild *stupas* and sacred images, and **bamboo paper.** The labor-intensive hammering and delicate packaging processes are an eye-opening look into the effort required to make the 0.02cm thick leaves. Follow the noise and see the underground shelter where the bamboo paper is hammered. *(On 36th St. between 77th and 78th St. Gold leaf 100kyat, Bamboo paper 300kyat. Open daily 7am-11pm.)* The ancient art of **silk weaving** continues and can be observed in the eastern part of the city. The process is best viewed in Amarapura (see **Daytrips from Mandalay,** p. 504), but the Mandalay District's silk is reputed to be Myanmar's best. *(On 19th St. between 62nd and 61st St. Open daily 7am-6pm.)*

KYAUKDAWGYI PAGODA. Built by King Mindon from 1853 to 1878, this pagoda rests at Mandalay Hill's base, opposite the main southern walkway. The Buddha statue was cut from a 3.5 million kg block of green marble; moving it from the quarry required a Herculean effort of 10,000 laborers. Visitors should note that this image is unique in that unlike most other Buddha images which are coated in gold, this one bares its marble body.

MARKETS

Equidistant from India, Bangladesh, China, and Thailand, Mandalay serves as a major shopping hub. **Handicrafts**—teak, marble, and jade carvings, lacquer-ware, and metalworking—abound, particularly in the south of the city around Mahamuni Pagoda. **Zegyo Market,** a three-story shopping and socializing extravaganza, provides just about everything else, including hours of people-watching. Fruit and vegetable merchants set up around midnight, and locals crowd the side-streets around the building to buy produce each morning. Once the Zegyo opens at 7am, the inventory shifts gears: plastic and stainless steel kitchenware, *longgyi* (around 2000kyat), and bamboo weavings replace foodstuffs. (Open daily 7am-4:30pm.) The **night market** sets up before dark on 84th St., between 27th and 29th St., and continues the selling frenzy with less practical goods like military knives, brass knuckles, and fake designer watches. **Soe Moe,** on 84th St. about a 5min. bike ride south of Mahumuni Pagoda on the right side, specializes in antiques but also produces and sells new pieces. Workshops in back of the market provide a selection of embroidered tapestries, teak wood carvings, puppets, and bronze Buddhas. Prices vary greatly based on the age and condition of a piece. Open daily 6am-10pm.

IN RECENT NEWS

CAN'T TAKE A JOKE?

A-nyeint theater has a long history. Burmese people flock to its synthesis of cabaret, burlesque, and vaudeville. From the 1960s to 1996, Mandalay's Moustache Brothers were some of the art's most popular practitioners. A controversial incident in 1996, however, changed the lives of the Brothers forever. They have since become an international symbol for political opposition and for the human rights movement in Myanmar.

On January 4, 1996, two of the Moustache Brothers, Par Par Lay and his cousin U Lu Zaw, were invited to perform before government officials and dignitaries at Aung San Suu Kyi's compound in honor of the NLD's 48th anniversary celebration of Burmese independence. Par Par Lay prefaced his routine by declaring he would speak his mind despite the threat of reprisals. In one skit, he portrayed an imprisoned activist who refused to die after being shot multiple times by a general. The pun hinged on the homonym of "hit" and "right" in Burmese: in response to the general's insistence that he die after being hit, the prisoner responds, "Why should I die if I am right?" Three days after their return to Mandalay, security forces arrested dancers, musicians, comedians, and NLD attendees. After a short, undisclosed trial in Mandalay, the two comedians were handed a seven-year prison

ENTERTAINMENT

If you are in the mood for an artistic, cultural night, check out the **Mandalay Marionettes**, an entertaining traditional Burmese art form. Dating to 11th-century Bagan, Burmese puppetry adapts themes from stories of the Buddha and colorful events in Burmese mythology. Seasoned puppeteers deliver quality shows at the Garden Villa Theater, at 66th and 27th St. (1hr., daily 8:30pm, 3500kyat.) Mandalay also boasts its own **"Little Broadway."** Spanning 39th to 43rd St. between 80th and 81st St., this theater district has 50 *a-nyeint pwe* troupes, each advertised on colorful billboards. The government authorizes all but one of these troupes to perform all night long at weddings or other festivities for 200,000kyat per day. The one exception, which has attracted international attention, is the **Moustache Brothers,** on 39th St. between 80th and 81st St. Backed by 30 years' experience, this troupe performs a modified show that both exposes foreigners to this dying art form and gains exposure for Myanmar's plight. The performances interweave commentary, conjugal infidelity jokes, and traditional dances with elaborate costumes. The Moustache Brothers also welcome visitors after-hours to their home, which doubles as their theater due to government restrictions. (Shows daily 8:30pm. 2000kyat per person.)

DAYTRIPS FROM MANDALAY

Several daytrip destinations surround Mandalay, each catering to different interests: the three ancient cities **(Amarapura, Ava,** and **Sagaing)** embody the political, historical, and religious roots of the Burmese culture, at the same time providing beautiful scenery. A pile of bricks being the major sight, **Mingun** serves as a quick glimpse of an unsuccessful attempt at ancient glory. **Monywa** is a destination with a set of unique archaeological and religious attractions, including a staggering number of concentrated Buddha images.

Mingun is accessible only by boat, while the others can be reached by linecar or taxi. Amarapura, Ava, and Sagaing are also possible to see by a long but relatively flat bike ride. By hiring a blue taxi (US$6-10 per day) or starting early enough on your own, you can see the three downriver towns in one leisurely day. The natural progression of sights makes it best to work your way farther away from Mandalay over the course of the day from Amarapura to Ava to Sagaing, but it really depends on the season and where you want to view the sunset. In the winter, when the sun sets earlier, it is possible to catch sunset at Sagaing Hill, which is only open until 5pm. During the summer months, end the day at Amarapura and U Bein Bridge, as the locals return home in droves. Alternatively, it's possible to see Mingun by boat in the morning, return to Mandalay, catch a linecar or taxi to Sagaing in the afternoon, and visit Amarapura and Ava by linecar another day. Monywa requires a full day and sometimes even two. Pyin U Lwin has become a common day-trip destination because of its cooler air, but it is best to get an early start.

MINGUN မင်းကွန်း

Foreign tourists are limited to 3hr. visits and are required to use the daily MTT "tourist boat" that departs from the jetty at the west end of 26th St. in Mandalay (1½hr., 1hr. return; 9am, returns 1pm; 1500kyat). If you want to stay longer, charter a private boat (8000-15000kyat), but 3hr. is ample time to enjoy the town. Entrance fee US$3.

Once a quiet village along the great Ayeyarwady River, Mingun has been turned into a tourism production by the government. Thus, it is no surprise that Mingun's three main sights are often accompanied by hordes of children who greet tourists at the dock and hound visitors at every turn, scrapping their way through explanations of the sights in hopes of earning a few kyat. All it takes is one step off this well-beaten track, however, and the traveler is alone, free to wander Mingun's fields and hills and enjoy splendid views all the way to Mandalay and a worthwhile glimpse into Myanmar's rural life.

MINGUN PAGODA. Size mattered to King Bodawpaya. In 1790 he began construction of a 150m pagoda meant to dwarf the mountain range behind it. In truc autocratic fashion, he mobilized 20,000 Arakanese slaves for 39 years, but the pagoda only made it to 50m before suffering irreparable damage from the 1838 earthquake. Today the remains of the king's arrogance bear the dubious title of "largest stack of bricks in the world," and the temple carries an alternate tag, Patodawgyi Pagoda, or "Unfinished Pagoda." Brisk breezes and views extending to Mandalay make the steep, 174-step climb up the most crumbled portion worthwhile.

MINGUN BELL. A big bell meant for a big pagoda, it was completed in 1790 and continues to hang as King Bodawpaya's crowning achievement. The impressive 82,000kg bell, 4m high and 5m in diameter, is the largest un-cracked bell in the world. It is customary to hit

sentence, but first they were tortured in a labor camp. Meanwhile, the remaining Moustache Brother, Lu Maw, "kept the home fire burning," hosting the show in his home and continuing to make political jokes.

In 1997 10 Hollywood comedians wrote to the government to urge that Par Par Lay and Lu Zaw be released. In 1998 anti-government demonstrators created a 6m-by-4m portrait of the comedians in front of Myanmar's London embassy by applying 1.6 million thumbprints to a canvas. The portrait now hangs in London's National Gallery. Such domestic courage and international support resulted in the early termination of the comedians' sentence, and on July 13, 2001 they were released. More than 2000 people filled the streets around the theater and five government officials (whom Lu Maw refers to as KGB or military intelligence) came to view and tape their first show upon release. Having tolerated Lu Maw's political jokes for only 11 days, the government again deemed the performances subversive and on July 26th 2001 imposed strict curbs on *a-nyeint* artists that banned all-night performances, censored advertising, and required comedians to submit written copies of jokes for approval. Today, the three comedians, 10 dancers, and eight musicians continue to demonstrate their belief in freedom. Until they attain it, the Moustache Brothers will not back down.

the bell three times—one time each for your father, mother, and teacher—and finish with a final stroke for yourself. Thrill-seekers crawl underneath to hear its resonance from within

HSINBYUME PAGODA. North of Mingun Pagoda, Hsinbyume is humble in comparison. Built in 1816, it finds its architectural inspiration in the cosmological vision of Sulamani Pagoda atop the heights of Mount Meru. Its seven concentric terraces symbolize the mountain ranges surrounding Meru.

AMARAPURA အမရပူရ

Linecars to Amarapura leave from the intersection of 29th and 84th St. (45min., frequently 6am-6pm, 100kyat). From the market in Amarapura, it's easy to pick up linecar #8 onward to Ava and Sagaing or back to Mandalay (100kyat per ride).

From the late 18th century until the mid-1800s, Amarapura swapped roles with Ava several times as the Burmese capital before ultimately losing the title to Mandalay. In its heyday, one writer has contended, Amarapura stood as a "microcosm of Burmese civilization"—a center not only of wealth, fashion, and beauty but also of erudition and scholarship. Apart from a few structures and four pagodas marking the original corners of the city, Amarapura —"The City of Immortals"—has nothing to show for this regal legacy. Nonetheless, the lively market, provincial atmosphere, and opportunities for leisurely people-watching on the town's famous bridge will please those seeking respite from Mandalay's clamor.

U BEIN'S BRIDGE. At the west edge of town, U Bein's Bridge spans scenic **Lake Taungthaman.** Over 1km in length, it's the longest teak bridge in the world, all the more impressive given that it's nearly 250 years old. The materials to build it were salvaged from the Inwa Palace. Townspeople flock to the bridge during the rainy season to fish in the shallow lake, while the dry season sees farmers tilling and harvesting rice paddies where the lake once was. Regardless of the season, however, the relationship between the people and their land is worth a look, and foot traffic across the bridge is always high. *(From the linecar stop, weave through the market and follow the footpath to the lake's edge. Locals make sure tourists don't get lost. During the rainy season rowboats provide an alternate route across the lake for 1500kyat.)*

SILK WEAVING. With nearly every house in town weaving silk, Amarapura has emerged as one of Myanmar's premier weaving centers. Family-run silk businesses have functioned here for generations, and weaving households line the street from the market to the bridge. Generally, those with English signs accept visitors and will demonstrate the entire painstaking process. Beware of shops where the clacking is very rapid—a sign that machines, rather than humans, are doing the weaving. *(Cotton-and-silk* longgyi *US$3. Intricate silk skirts US$5.)*

OTHER SIGHTS. North of the bridge entrance lies **Mahagandhayon Monastery.** The 1000 monks uphold rigorous standards in the study of Pali and meditation techniques. A visit around 10:30am will allow you to witness the monks silently eating lunch, their last meal of the day. Rising at 4am, monks meditate and study the teachings of Buddha throughout the day, interrupted only by their two meals, one at 6am and the other at 10:30am, after which they ingest nothing but fluids.

AVA (INWA) အင်းဝ

Linecars from Amarapura drop off passengers at the end of a long road (trishaw 200kyat or 15min. walk). At its opposite end is a ferry landing where boats shuttle to Ava (5min., frequent 5am-5pm, 500kyat round-trip). Once in Ava, tourist booths at each of the three main sites sell and check one of two types of tickets: US$3 per person for Ava only, or US$10 per person for multiple sites (see Mandalay Sights, p. 501).

Ava (commonly referred to as Inwa) lies 20km southwest of Mandalay and 7km beyond Amarapura at the junction of the Ayeyarwady and the Myitnge Rivers. Thado Minbya established Ava as the capital of Burma in 1364, a position it retained until 1823—the longest streak in Burmese history. Today, disembarking on the triangular island—which has a handful of motorized vehicles, a legion of horsecarts, and one backwater village in the northeast—is like stepping back in time. Let the wondrous vibe of Ava take your imagination back to when this Burmese capital was the seat of a powerful, prosperous society in Southeast Asia. The old walls of the city remain intact, guarding cultivated land, tiny hamlets, abandoned monasteries, and crumbling pagodas. Pony carts provide the best means of navigation; flurries of them await arrivals at the dock landing. The circuit around the "hit parade" of sights—Bagaya Monastery, Okkyaung Monastery, and the "leaning" watch tower of King Bagyidaw's Palace—takes two hours and costs 3000kyat. It is also possible to walk the route in four hours, as locals are happy to give a point in the right direction. You can hire guides at Mandalay guesthouses (US$6-10), but both monasteries have plaques in English explaining their histories.

Bagaya Monastery, constructed in 1834, represents Myanmar's famous teakwood monasteries and maintains many of its original carvings despite its dilapidated present condition. It is supported by 274 teak posts, the largest of which is 60 ft. tall and 9 ft. in circumference. Bagaya is all the more notable because it is one of the few monasteries built entirely from teak to escape the triple threat: fire, earthquake, and renovation. A lone 30m watch tower marks the site of **King Bagyidaw's Palace,** inhabited from 1819 to 1837. Though an 1838 earthquake left the tower slanted, people are allowed to climb the reinforced stairways for a breezy panorama of the area. The nearby **Maha Aungmye Bonzan Monastery** (Okkyaung Monastery), was built in 1818 by Bagyidaw's notorious queen, Nanmadaw Me, to house her religious preceptor, Nyaunggan Sayadaw. The upper chambers are desolate and not particularly interesting, but navigating the dark, grotto-like series of walkways used for meditating provides a good idea of the building's construction. Most intriguing are the island's crumbling pagodas. They dot the landscape, popping up in fields and streams, with several supported by trees growing in the vicinity. Ruins enthusiasts may want to jump off the horsecart en route or may be better off just walking the island so as to be free to wander where they wish.

SAGAING စစ်ကိုင်း

Linecars depart for Mandalay (via Ava and Amarapura) from the train trestle area until 6pm (1.5hr., 100kyat).

Across the Ayeyarwady River from Ava, Sagaing is the religious center of the Mandalay District, teeming with *stupas* and monasteries, mostly scattered near Sagaing Hill. Sagaing is a good place to view sunset panoramas, but only in the winter, when the sun sets while Sagaing Hill is still open. Transportation back to town from Kaunghmudaw Pagoda is harder to find later in the day, so visit there first.

SAGAING HILL. With 300 temples and pagodas, Sagaing Hill rises majestically from the river's edge, with tremendous views of Mandalay, Ava, Amarapura, and Sagaing. The walk up the front of the hill is good exercise but offers far fewer lookouts along the way than the back staircase, which passes several pagodas. Due to the difficulty (for non-Burmese speakers) in finding the back stairs, the best route may be to head up the front and down the back before flagging down a horsecart back to the linecar terminal. Locals head directly up to the top to pray, but foreigners will get more out of wandering the paths that lace the area. *(The hill is 4km north of the town center; take a horsecart (500kyat one-way) or linecar (15min., every 20min. 8am-3pm, 100kyat) from downtown. Some go all the way to the top, while others stop at the main* *staircase. Covered walkways shelter the 30min. climb. From the top, linecars run to Mandalay (1½hr., every 1½hr. 8am-3pm, 200kyat). The back stairs are 50m down the road that leads away from the back entrance to the pagoda at the peak. Free.)*

KAUNGHMUDAW PAGODA. Sagaing's most renowned and biggest temple, Kaunghmudaw sits 10km outside town. In 1536, with Ceylon's Mahaceti Pagoda as his ambitious model, King Thalun of Ava built the Kaunghmudaw Pagoda, also known as **Rajamanicula,** which reputedly houses a Buddha tooth and hair relics transferred from Bagan's Mahazedi Pagoda. Some believe that its architectural signature, a 46m high white Indian-style dome, was made in the likeness of the voluptuous breast of King Thalun's queen. *(All linecars from Mandalay, Ava, or Amarapura that continue to Shwebo pass by Kaunghmudaw. Otherwise, flag down almost any transport heading through downtown. Free.)*

MONYWA

Minibuses to Monywa leave from the Thirimandalar Bus Gate, at 22nd and 88th St. (4½hr., 5:30am, 3000kyat; 6am, 5000kyat; bargaining is possible, especially on earlier buses). However, because the sights of interest require a bit of a drive out of Monywa, sharing a taxi with other tourists is the most convenient option (US$25 all day).

Monywa's heat is known to be the worst in Myanmar, reaching 40°C (104°F) in the months of April and May. Despite this, the town flourishes as a trade hub on the Chindwin River. **Shwe Zy Ghong Pagoda,** in the middle of town, is majestically illuminated when the lights get turned on after 7pm. On the road to Mandalay, **Thanbodday Pagoda** exhibits over 580,000 Buddhas that range in height from one inch to huge. (All transports going to Mandalay pass by Thanbodday.) Embedded in the hills a few kilometers from Thanbodday Pagoda, at 100m long **Shwe The Lakaung** is one of the largest reclining Buddhas in the world, if not *the* largest. Shwe The Lakaung is surrounded by other impressive Buddha images and pagodas, including **Bodi Tatoung** with 10,000 images. (To see both Thanbodday and Shwe The Lakaung, take a trishaw (7000kyat) or a taxi (5000kyat). Entrance fee US$3 for both, payable at Thanbodday.)

The area's most intriguing attraction is **Pho Win Taung.** The history of this site, which, it's claimed, hosts more than 400,000 Buddhas, dates back to the 13th-century Inwa Dynasty. Monks then spent the next four centuries carving images and small meditation chambers out of the bluffs. Step inside these small, serene caves (take your shoes off first!) and discover intricate wall-paintings from the 18th century. Monkeys inhabit the entire hillside, and locals sell monkey food for 200kyat. Be careful, however, how long the locals follow you, as they will ultimately demand a "guide fee." Also of interest near Pho Win Taung is **Shwebotha Hill,** with shrine caves fewer in number and much bigger. The rock faces of the entrances take the shape of colonial architecture, but inside are the usual gold-leafed images. Built on the slope of a hill, the main entrance gives a feeling of descending into an ancient underground city. First, take a boat (1500kyat one-way) to the opposite bank of the Chindwin. Due to restricted mines on either side of the road, foreigners are required to take taxis (5000-6500kyat per vehicle) from there. Entrance to Pho Win is US$2 per person and to Shwebotha US$2 or 1600kyat.

NORTHEASTERN MYANMAR

Shan State is one of the most diverse regions in Myanmar. Divided by locals into Northern Shan State and Southern Shan State (see **Inle Lake Region,** 519), it is geographically separated and isolated from the rest of the country by mountains. Penetrated only by one-lane switchbacks and a few train lines, its isolation allows the

Shan to keep their traditions intact, their agriculture flourishing, and their villages untouristed. However, it also protects military bases and opium fields from outside scrutiny, and much of the state is off-limits to foreigners. Tourists tend to concentrate in the plains below, including Mandalay and Bagan, but after one bus ride to the towns that aren't restricted, Myanmar will seem like a whole new country.

PYIN U LWIN (MAIMYO) ☎085

In the late 19th century, during their colonial rule, the British experienced the unbearable heat of summer in Myanmar and went looking for a resort-esque area that would relieve them from the scorching sun in Mandalay. What they found was a small village just 70km east of Mandalay at a cool elevation of 1000m. The subsequent development of Pyin U Lwin was only a matter of time and its British "origin" explains the colonial architecture, design, and feel of the town. Today the military has a large presence, bringing with it economic stratification, which is especially noticeable among the younger generations who sport leather jackets and toe-rings with traditional *longgyi*. But the Shan don't seem to take much notice, going about their daily market business the same way they did before the British came and the same way they will after the military leaves.

ORIENTATION AND TRANSPORTATION. Pyin U Lwin is a huge, sprawling complex, but visitors really never venture far off **Main Road.** Running west to Mandalay and east to Hsipaw, Main Rd. winds several kilometers past most shops and services. At the center of town stands a **clocktower,** where a small side-street splits off toward the Shan **market.** Three blocks west of the clocktower, on Main Rd., stands a **tree**—a major directional landmark. The **train station** is north of Main Rd., five blocks east of the tree, but taking the train is a very inefficient use of time. It is better to take **jeeps** from opposite the clocktower to Hsipaw (5:30am, 3000kyat) and Mandalay (2hr; leaves when full 6am-noon; 1000-1500kyat) via Anisagen Falls (20kyat). **Pick-ups** to Peik Chin Myaing (when full 8am-noon, 1000kyat) leave from the tree. **Bike rental** is 100kyat per hr. at the Golden Dream Hotel.

ACCOMMODATIONS AND FOOD. Most establishments cater to the military cadets and their families, but there are a few tourist-licensed options. In the center of town is **Grace Hotel II ❷,** opposite the clocktower on Main Rd. Rooms are clean and bright; those in back are much quieter. (☎220 81. Singles US$3, with bath US$4; doubles US$6/8.) Next door is the older yet still comfortable **Golden Dream Hotel ❷** (Singles US$3, with bath US$4). For visitors seeking a total getaway from urban life, **Grace Hotel ❸** is a 5min. bike ride out of town in a quiet, green neighborhood. (☎212 30. Singles US$5; doubles US$10.) When the stomach starts rumbling, head to **Family Restaurant ❸** by going toward the tree from the clocktower and turning left at the sign. All-you-can-eat Indian and Myanmar curry spreads with all the fixings and side dishes. (Vegetable 750kyat, meat 950 kyat. Served daily 10am-9pm.)

SIGHTS. The town itself does not offer many tourist sites other than the market and the botanical garden. The Shan market, one block behind the clocktower, is interspersed with military personnel in a weird mix of vibrant color and camouflage. Some of it is housed in a permanent structure, while other stalls are plopped down in any available space. The brand-new, 400-acre **botanical garden** can be reached by a nice, long stroll on foot or by bike. The route is a lesson in where all the money in Myanmar is located. (Botanical garden open 8am-6pm. 2000kyat.) Out of the many waterfalls surrounding Pyin U Lwin, **Anisagen Falls** is perhaps the most worthwhile to visit despite the hike to get there. Relax in front of the 45m waterfall after a 1hr. descent down a steep slope. (All linecars to Mandalay from Pyin U Lwin pass the drop-off point, 200kyat.) You can also be dropped off at the junction on the way from Mandalay to Pyin U Lwin to save time on a daytrip. For a more religious bent, visit the shrine cave of **Peik Chin Myaing.** In 1990, the government renovated and developed this 600m cave into a tourist attraction by adding many religious elements to it. Alternatively, the mountain scenery and plentiful rice paddies are great for a bike ride in almost any direction. Main Rd., lined with Indian and Pakistani confectioneries and teashops, is the perfect place to indulge in some after-biking relaxation; breathe in the cool mountain air and watch as the horsecart-filled world goes by.

HSIPAW ☎082

Many travelers haven't even heard of tiny Hsipaw until they reach Mandalay and are facing a fast-approaching visa expiration. However, those who plan ahead are greeted by a bustling town with a village atmosphere, where hill-tribes mix with townfolk and the tourist infrastructure is practically nonexistent. There isn't much to see in the conventional sense, leaving plenty of time to walk the edges of rice paddies and talk with locals. Situated in the mountains, Hsipaw is blessed with cool air and cultural and historical roots undisturbed by time or politics.

TRANSPORTATION. The **train station** acts as the western boundary of town, but the mountainous terrain renders the trains that stop in Hsipaw extremely inefficient for traveling anywhere besides the otherwise restricted Lashio (5hr.; 3pm; ordinary-class US$2, upper-class US$4). **Buses** leave from the southern edge of the market for Lashio (2hr., 6am) and Mandalay (6-7hr.; 5:30, 6am; 1800kyat) via Pyin U Lwin (4hr., 1800kyat). Purchase all tickets a day in advance. Local navigation is completely possible on foot.

ORIENTATION AND PRACTICAL INFORMATION. The **Dokhtawady River** forms the eastern border of town and fills the canals that line the streets. The road from Lashio enters Hsipaw in the southeast, forms the southern border of downtown, and heads to Pyin U Lwin and Mandalay from the southwest. Three blocks west of the river, on the road to Pyin U Lwin, sits a **clocktower.** The **central market** (open daily 6am-6pm) sits at the north end of the road that is one block east of the clocktower. The road that is one block west of the clocktower runs the entire north-south length of town and leads to the **Shan Palace** (see **Sights**) in the north. Inquire at Nam Khae Moe Guest House (see **Accommodations**) for town maps and to place IDD phone calls.

ACCOMMODATIONS AND FOOD. **Nam Khae Moe Guest House ❷,** opposite the clocktower, distinguishes itself from the cheaper Mr. Kid (Golden Doll) Guest House by offering off-the-beaten-path tourist amenities like free maps, bicycle rental (500kyat per day), and guide service. The clean, well-lighted rooms and several common spaces make for a comfortable stay. Breakfast is included. (☎800 77. Singles US$3, with bath US$6; doubles US$4/10.) **Mr. Kid ❶,** two blocks west of the clocktower, shares a central location with Nam Khae but does not include breakfast. (Singles 1500kyat, with bath 2500kyat; doubles 2500/3500kyat.)

As Hsipaw is smack in the middle of Shan State, you can't throw a stone anywhere without hitting a **Shan noodle stand ❶,** and it would be a shame not to sample their delicious and inexpensive fare (150-250kyat per bowl). Most are known only by the corner they have come to claim over time and specialize in making noodles a certain way—find a favorite and pull up a low, plastic chair. Lunch stalls fill the market and serve until early afternoon, while dinner stalls set up on corners and sidewalks at 4pm and serve until midnight in some cases. For breakfast noodles or *chapati*, head to **Duhtawadi Tea Shop ❷**, opposite the southern side of the central market, which opens at 4am. Try the Myanmar curries at **Akaung Kyaik Restaurant ❸**, one block west of the clocktower, where the huge vegetable spreads are to die for. (Curries 750kyat. Open daily 8am-9pm.)

SIGHTS. First and foremost is a visit to the **Shan Palace.** The home of the last Shan prince, it continues as a residence and stands as a relic of Myanmar's pre-SPDC history. Mr. Donald (Sao Oo Kya) and Fern (Sao Sarm Hpong) open their home to visitors daily at 4pm in order to tell the story of the Shan prince and his disappearance in 1962. (On the road that runs one block west of the clocktower, continue north to the police station and then turn right. At the three-way split, take the sharp left, which is paved, and follow it around to the Palace's gate. A 1000kyat donation is asked of each visitor.) **Mr. Book** is also an informative person to talk with. He uses any donations to his bookstand—located four blocks north of Akaung Kyaik Restaurant and next to the white picket fence—to buy books for the village schools. He often allows visitors to help him deliver the gifts.

Hsipaw is home to many cottage industries and factories. The **Yee Dar Port "Smile" Cheroot Factory,** two blocks west and one block north of the clocktower, houses the entire cheroot-making process, from leaf-cutting to rolling. **Shan bags** are made on the ground floor of a home two blocks east of Nam Khae Moe Guest House. In the town's southern neighborhood, several blocks from the clocktower, old tires are made into **sandals,** and the finished product can be seen in the central market. The **morning market** outshines the central market because of the absence of touristy merchandise. It provides a glimpse of the vast ethnic and agricultural diversity of the area, as people gather from far and wide.

BAGAN (PAGAN) ပုဂံ ☎062

If Myanmar were to have a World Heritage Site nominated, it would be Bagan—42km² dotted with over 3000 pagodas and temples. Bagan's early history is not completely clear, but scholars agree that its splendor prevailed for 250 years following King Anawrahta's ascension to the throne in 1044 (see **Bagan and Toungoo Dynasties,** p. 454). Dissatisfied with the religious practices of his people, Anawrahta launched a plan to rejuvenate Theravada Buddhism that was accompanied by a flurry of temple-building, and the number of pagodas is still increasing today.

> **GOVERNMENT LISTINGS** Government listings are marked by a **M** symbol. Money spent at such establishments goes directly into the government's hands. For more information, see **Keep the Bucks Where They Belong,** p. 462.

TRANSPORTATION

Flights: Nyaung U Airport, 4km southeast of Nyaung U, off the road to Mandalay. Taxis from the airport to most destinations in Bagan 2000kyat. **Air Mandalay** (☎671 16; open M-F 8am-5pm), off Bagan-Chauk Rd., 80m north of Main Rd. in New Bagan. Daily flights leave (8-10am) for **Thandwe** (only during high season, US$183) via **Heho/Inle Lake** (US$63); via **Mandalay** (US$38); via **Yangon** (US$85). **Yangon Airways** (☎061 602 01; open daily 9am-4pm), in Nyaung U on Anawrahta Rd. and on the right about 200m past the post office heading away from the market toward Old Bagan. Flights leave Bagan daily (8:05am) for **Thandwe** (only high season, US$189) via **Mandalay** (in the high season US$49, low season US$38); via **Heho/Inle Lake** (US$74/US$63); via

Yangon (US$109/US$85). ■ **Myanma Airways** (☎671 99; open Tu, Th, F 9am-4pm), 150m inside Tharaba Gate in Old Bagan, flies to **Mandalay** (daily 7:30am, US$40) and **Yangon** (daily 8:30am, US$90). Airline tickets are cheaper from agents that cluster on Bagan-Nyaung U Rd., 75m south of the market area. Most open daily 8am-6pm.

■ **Trains:** The **train station** is 6km south of Nyaung U and 10km east of New Bagan, off the road to Mandalay. Taxis 2000kyat. Buy tickets a day in advance at the station or at Shwe Taung Tarn Guest House, on Bagan-Nyaung U Rd., 200m west of the market in Nyaung U. (Shwe Taung charges US$1 commission; open daily 10am-5pm.) Trains to **Mandalay** (8hr.; 7am; ordinary-class US$4, upper-class US$9) and **Yangon** (24hr.; times vary; ordinary US$15, upper US$33).

Buses: Highway Bus Center, in front of Shwezigon Pagoda on Bagan-Nyaung U Rd., in Nyaung U. Book tickets at guesthouses or in person. **Nyaung U Mann Express** goes to **Mandalay** (8-9hr.; 7, 9am; 4000kyat) and **Taunggyi** (12hr., 5am, 6000kyat). Several companies serve **Yangon** (15-16hr.; 3, 3:30pm; 5000kyat, 6500kyat with A/C). **Bagan Minn Thar** runs to **Pyay** (3:30pm, 6500kyat), while **Popa Dagon Travel** goes directly to **Bago** (3pm, 5000kyat). Buy tickets 1-2 days in advance, especially in the high season.

■ **Boats:** Popular express boats to **Mandalay** depart from the Nyaung U jetty, where Bagan-Nyaung U Rd. meets the river north of the Nyaung U market (12hr.; W and F-Su 5:30am; US$16). Buy tickets at the jetty or through guesthouses one day in advance.

Local Transportation: Linecars depart from the market in Nyaung U to **New Bagan** (6am-6pm; less frequent in the afternoon; 100kyat) via **Old Bagan** (100kyat). **Pony-carts** are a comfortable way to skim the sights in one day (2-person max., 4000kyat per day). **Private taxis** can be hired through most guesthouses to **Inle Lake** (8hr., US$70), usually via **Mount Poppa** (1½hr., US$20-27). **Car rental** US$15 per day in the area. **Bicycles** available at guesthouses (500kyat). Nicer models are worth the extra kyat.

■ ▨ ORIENTATION AND PRACTICAL INFORMATION

The **Bagan Archaeological Zone** is along the banks of the **Ayeyarwady River.** At the bend in the river is **Old Bagan,** the historical and geographic focus of the town. Two parallel roads, **Bagan-Nyaung U Road** and **Anawrahta Road,** extending 5km northeast from Old Bagan, meet at **Nyaung U market. Shwezigon Pagoda** is 2km before the market on Bagan-Nyaung U Rd., set back by the usual covered walkway. Next to Shwezigon is the **Highway Bus Center,** which handles all long-distance buses. Opposite the bus center, **Yakhinthar Road** connects Anawrahta and Bagan-Nyaung U Rd. and is home to many of the Nyaung U's accommodations and restaurants. Heading south from Old Bagan, **Bagan-Chauk Road** runs 3km to **New Bagan.** Bagan-Chauk Rd. intersects with **Main Road,** which runs through the center of New Bagan and then continues east all the way to the **airport,** 4km south of Nyaung U. The historic village of **Myinkaba** lies between New Bagan and Old Bagan, 1km south of the latter.

Tourist Offices: ■ MTT, 400m north of Main Rd. on Bagan-Chauk Rd. Maps of Bagan 500kyat. Open daily 8:30am-4:30pm. Guides (US$15-20 per day) can help you understand Bagan's temples; it seems like every local is licensed to provide this service.

Currency Exchange: Money changers can be found in Taung Be and Wetkyi Inn, but rates are 50-100kyat less than in Yangon or Mandalay.

Pharmacies: The District Hospital has a basic pharmacy and can recommend places to buy what they don't carry.

Medical Services: District Hospital (☎02 672 19), 1.5km southeast of Nyaung U on the road to Mandalay. Western-trained, English-speaking doctors available 24hr.

Telephones: Telephone Office, at the post office in Nyaung U. **IDD** only (US$6-9 per min. to Western nations). Open daily 8am-8pm. Most guesthouses offer similar prices.

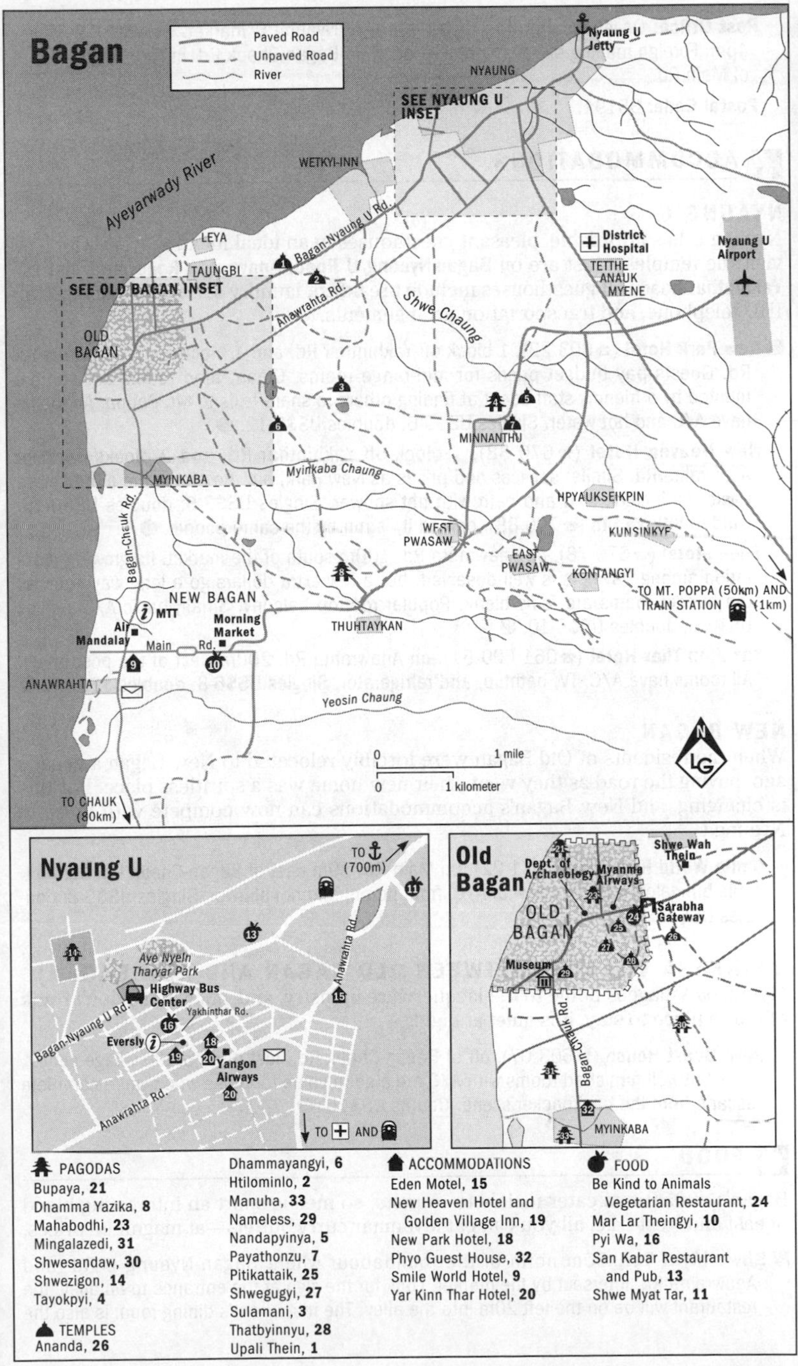

PAGODAS
Bupaya, **21**
Dhamma Yazika, **8**
Mahabodhi, **23**
Mingalazedi, **31**
Shwesandaw, **30**
Shwezigon, **14**
Tayokpyi, **4**

TEMPLES
Ananda, **26**
Dhammayangyi, **6**
Htilominlo, **2**
Manuha, **33**
Nameless, **29**
Nandapyinya, **5**
Payathonzu, **7**
Pitikattaik, **25**
Shwegugyi, **27**
Sulamani, **3**
Thatbyinnyu, **28**
Upali Thein, **1**

ACCOMMODATIONS
Eden Motel, **15**
New Heaven Hotel and Golden Village Inn, **19**
New Park Hotel, **18**
Phyo Guest House, **32**
Smile World Hotel, **9**
Yar Kinn Thar Hotel, **20**

FOOD
Be Kind to Animals Vegetarian Restaurant, **24**
Mar Lar Theingyi, **10**
Pyi Wa, **16**
San Kabar Restaurant and Pub, **13**
Shwe Myat Tar, **11**

Post Office: On Anawrahta Rd., 750m south of Nyaung U market. Open M-F 9:30am-4pm. Foreign mailing M-F 9am-noon. Branch on Bagan-Chauk Rd. in New Bagan, south of Main Rd.

Postal Code: 05191.

ACCOMMODATIONS

NYAUNG U

Nyaung U has affordable, pleasant guesthouses in an ideal location from which to visit the temples. Most are on **Bagan-Nyaung U Road, Anawrahta Road,** and just off **Yakhinthar Road.** All guesthouses include breakfast, laundry service, bicycle rental, IDD telephone, and transportation arrangements.

New Park Hotel (☎603 22), 1 block off Yakhinthar Rd. and 1 block north of Anawrahta Rd. Guests pay budget prices for mid-range rooms. Clean, tiled rooms are complimented by a friendly staff adept at finding others to share taxis to Mt. Poppa. All rooms have A/C and hot water. Singles US$3-6; doubles US$8-12. ❷

New Heaven Hotel (☎670 88), 1 block off Yakhinthar Rd. and 2 blocks north of Anawrahta Rd. Similar services and prices as New Park, but the rooms are a little more basic. All include A/C and bath with hot shower. Singles US$3-5; doubles US$6-10. **Golden Village Inn** (☎700 88), behind it, is run by the same people. ❷

Eden Motel (☎670 78), on Anawrahta Rd. 100m south of the market. Its growing reputation among travelers is well deserved, but a few extra dollars go a long way here, as the budget rooms are fairly bleak. Popular rooftop balcony. Small, basic A/C singles US$3-6; doubles US$6-10. ❷

Yar Kinn Thar Hotel (☎061 600 51), on Anawrahta Rd. 200m west of the post office. All rooms have A/C, TV, bathtub, and refrigerator. Singles US$6-8; doubles $10-12. ❸

NEW BAGAN

When the residents of Old Bagan were forcibly relocated to New Bagan a decade ago, paving the road as they went, their new home was a spiritless place. But this is changing, and New Bagan's accommodations can now compete with those in Nyaung U.

Smile World Hotel (☎02 671 22), on Main Rd. 50m east of Bagan-Chauk Rd. Comfortable bungalow-style rooms with A/C, front porch, and hot shower. Singles US$5-8; doubles US$10. ❷

MYINKABA VILLAGE (BETWEEN OLD BAGAN AND NEW BAGAN)

Myinkaba Village is home to the lacquerware industry, and since many don't think of it as a place to stay, it is quiet at night.

Phyo Guest House (☎603 07), off of Bagan-Chauk Rd., just north of the village center. Dark but well-furnished rooms with A/C are a good value for those who want a complete escape from the backpacker scene. Rooms US$15. ❸

FOOD

Bagan's restaurants cater mainly to tourists, so menus sport an interesting blend of east and west—i.e. all-you-can-eat Myanmar curry buffets—at magnified prices.

Shwe Myat Tar, 50m north of the roundabout where Bagan-Nyaung U Rd. and Anawrahta Rd. intersect by the market. Look for the sign at the entrance to an alley; the restaurant will be on the left 20m into the alley. The restaurant's dining room is also the kitchen of the family that owns and operates it. A good place to escape the tourist scene and to eat with locals. Vegetarian-friendly selection of Myanmar curries (1200kyat including dessert). Open daily 9am-9pm. ❹

San Kabar Restaurant and Pub, on Bagan-Nyaung U Rd. 800m east of Shwezigon Pagoda. Offers Italian food prepared by Italian-trained chefs. Outdoor seating is available. Pizza 2000-3000kyat, tortellini with fresh tomato sauce 1200kyat, and crêpe creations 800kyat. Open daily 9am-10pm. ❹

Be Kind to Animals Vegetarian Restaurant and Cold Drinks, 30m inside Tharaba Gate, on Bagan-Nyaung U Rd. An excellent alternative to the Myanmar rice diet. Serves freshly made yogurt. Mango *lassi* 300kyat. Yogurt with fruit 600kyat. Burmese meals 700kyat. Open daily 7am-9:30pm. ❸

Mar Lar Theingyi, opposite the morning market in New Bagan, serves all-you-can-eat Myanmar curry (1200kyat) but doesn't let quantity short-change quality. Its wall-less design gives customers sweet relief from the heat. Open daily 10am-7pm. ❹

Pyi Wa, on Yakhinthar Rd. Typical tourist fare served in an unbeatable atmosphere: candlelit, open-air tables in the shadow of a ruined temple. Free marionette show. Chinese, Burmese, and Italian food at a reasonable price with complimentary fruit salad 600-2000kyat. Open daily 7:30am-10pm. ❹

SIGHTS

For most visitors three days are enough to explore the 4000-plus ancient temples and pagodas adorning the **Bagan Plain.** A fourth day could be used to poke around the small villages and get a taste of the modern culture that thrives between the ancient pagodas. The US$10 admission to the archaeological zone is supposed to be per person, per day. However, after the fee is collected the first time at either a road checkpoint or the airport and the receipt is presented upon check-in at an accommodation, no one bothers to extract payment for subsequent days. This fee allows access to all of the temples from around sunrise to after sunset (roughly 6am-6pm, although the larger ones open earlier and close later).

To make the most of your time in Bagan, it's essential to talk to guesthouse owners, pony-cart drivers, and tour guides for insight into off-the-beaten-path destinations—valuable gems abound. It is most efficient to get around by **bicycle** (500kyat per day) or **horsecart** (all-day itinerary around 4000kyat for two people). Many travelers take a one-day horsecart ride first, then strike out on their own by bicycle. A guide is useful (most US$15 per day). Guesthouses may try to pressure you into using their in-house guide, but it is OK to go elsewhere. If you're pressed for time, be sure to see **Ananda Temple** and **Thatbyinnyu Temple** in Old Bagan, **Shwezigon Pagoda** near Nyaung U, and **Sulamani** and **Dhammayangyi Temples** between Old Bagan and New Bagan, before soaking in a red and purple sunset from atop **Shwesandaw.** If the western sky is clear, then there is nothing quite like being amid the ancient pagodas and golden landscape. **Mingalazedi Pagoda** offers a panoramic shot by the river and is well lit for good photography. **Tayokpyi Pagoda,** at the very eastern edge of the plain, gets almost no sunset visitors and puts all the giants in silhouette. Situated right in between the two, **Shwesandaw Pagoda** is rightfully the most popular (read: crowded) viewpoint.

OLD BAGAN

Old Bagan contains many of the archaeological zone's marquee temples. The area is navigable on foot and warrants a full day of exploration.

MYANMAR

ANANDA TEMPLE (အာန္ဒာ). The pride of Old Bagan, Ananda represents the pinnacle of Bagan's Early Period design, with its sweeping terraces and symmetrical square Greek cross design. The 12th-century temple is commanding and awe-inspiring, with 17 *stupas* rising from its walls and exterior structure. The interior features hundreds of Buddhas staring down from their alcoves, as well as four 10m standing Buddhas (one for each reincarnation of the Buddha), one in each entrance. *(Just east of the walls of Old Bagan, between Bagan-Nyaung U and Anawrahta Rd.)*

THATBYINNYU TEMPLE (သဗ္ဗညု). This 61m two-tier temple was built in 1144 by King Alaungsithu and is the tallest structure in Bagan. Its most interesting features are its exemplary brickwork and the intricate multi-level architectural design. As tourists are no longer allowed to go to the upper terraces, it is best seen from neighboring Shwegugyi Temple. *(Just inside the walls of Old Bagan, at the end of the dirt path that leads past Be Kind to Animals Restaurant (see Food, p. 514).)*

BAGAN MUSEUM. The Bagan Museum complex tells the story of the cataclysmic earthquake of 1975 and features Buddha images from the 10th and 11th centuries. It's worth it only for the dedicated museum hounds. *(Immediately inside the southern wall of Old Bagan. US$3. Open Tu-Su 9am-4:30pm.)*

NAMELESS TEMPLE. This tiny temple is worthy of mention. Attempting to find treasure in a plaster Buddha statue, a thief performed open-heart surgery on the image. He discovered a smaller plaster Buddha whose face emerged from the chest cavity. The smaller Buddha's owners had simply built a larger statue over it, craving the merit granted to grand figures. *(Opposite Bagan Museum.)*

PITAKATTAIK (LIBRARY). Legend has it that King Anawrahta built this structure in 1057 to house 30 sets of the Buddhist canon, carried by a caravan of 32 elephants from Thaton. Its design carries many similarities to a temple, with a central room surrounded by a processional hallway. The distinctive five-tier roof emerged as a later renovation at the hands of King Bodawpaya in 1783. If it is locked, ask at Shwegugyi for the key. *(Halfway to Thatbyinnyu on the dirt path that leads south from Be Kind to Animal Restaurant (see Food, p. 514).)*

MAHABODHI PAGODA. This pagoda maintains spiritual ties with Bodhgaya in India, where the Buddha attained Enlightenment under a *bodhi* tree. In 1215 King Zeya Theinkha modeled its design after the original Mahabodhi Pagoda in Bodhgaya, accounting for its pyramidal spire and many seated Buddhas occupying niches in horizontal shelves. *(North of Bagan-Nyaung U Rd. as it runs through Old Bagan.)*

BUPAYA PAGODA. Thought to have been built in the third century AD, Bupaya rests on a bank overlooking a bend of the Ayeyarwady River. It was destroyed in the 1975 earthquake but has since been restored. The real reason to visit isn't for the temple but for the views of the river and mountain scenery beyond. *(At the northern end of the dirt road that starts where Bagan-Nyaung U Rd. turns sharply south in Old Bagan.)*

BETWEEN OLD BAGAN AND NYAUNG U

HTILOMINLO TEMPLE. Built in AD 1218 by a three-named king and surrounded by much smaller structures, 150 ft. Htilominlo dominates the skyline halfway between Old Bagan and Nyaung U. Visitors can't go up to the higher levels, but the ground floor has numerous remaining stucco decorations and wall-paintings. *(Between Wetkyi-Inn village and Old Bagan, between Bagan-Nyaung U and Anawrahta Rd.)*

SHWEZIGON PAGODA (ရွှေစည်းခုံဘုရား). According to legend, Buddha's tooth, collar bone, and frontlet relics are enshrined in this pagoda. It's said that King Anawrahta placed the frontlet relic atop a white elephant and declared that wherever the elephant knelt would be the relic's resting place. Of all of Bagan's temples, Shwezigon is the most revered and the most frequently visited, but despite its glittering gold spire, it pales in comparison to the character of the crumbling giants. *(100m west of the intersection of Yakhinthar and Bagan-Nyaung U Rd.)*

UPALI THEIN (ဥပါလိသိမ်). Allegedly dating back to the 13th century, Upali Thein is the only ordination hall for monks *(sima)* in the Bagan area. *(Halfway between Nyaung U and Bagan on the north side of Bagan-Nyaung U Rd., near Htilominlo.)*

SOUTH OF THE OLD CITY: BETWEEN OLD AND NEW BAGAN

SHWESANDAW PAGODA (ရွှေဆံတော်ဘုရား). King Anawrahta built Shwesandaw in the late 11th century to shelter one of the Buddha's hairs. Archaeologists consider its design, featuring a white, bell-shaped dome atop five terraces, a forerunner to Shwezigon in the east, near Nyaung U. A steep climb to the top affords a spectacular sunset view (crowded—get there early to stake out a seat). Also interesting is the original top felled by the 1975 earthquake, left on the pagoda's south side. *(3km west of Nyaung U, south of Anawrahta Rd.)*

MANUHA TEMPLE. Manuha was named after the King of Thaton, who was exiled and imprisoned in Bagan after King Anawrahta sacked his kingdom in 1057. King Manuha sold his last possessions, even his crown jewels, to build the temple. Of interest is the claustrophobic nature of the Buddha images and temple—it's believed that the king chose to show his displeasure with imprisonment through the temple's design. *(In Myinkaba Village, south of Old Bagan on Bagan-Chauk Rd.)*

MINGALAZEDI PAGODA (မင်္ဂလာစေတီဘုရား). King Narathithapate inaugurated the construction of the "Auspicious Pagoda" in 1268 but held off completion for six years when he heard a prophecy foretelling that it would ultimately bring his kingdom's destruction. Lo and behold, the Mongols sacked Bagan 10 years later. Due to its smooth, precise design, archaeologists consider it the last great pagoda of Bagan. *(400m south of Old Bagan on Bagan-Chauk Rd.)*

SOUTHEAST OF OLD BAGAN

SULAMANI TEMPLE (ရူဠာမနိယ). King Narapatisithu built Sulamani, dubbed "Crowning Jewel" in Pali in AD 1183 . The name stems from the fact that he built it on the site where a small ruby was unearthed. This massive, two-story structure contains vaulted corridors of solid brickwork, each side sporting a Buddha image seated on a pedestal. Interesting wall-paintings adorn many walls and ceilings, but some believe they were added in the 18th century. *(South on the dirt path that starts on Anawrahta Rd., opposite Ananda Temple.)*

DHAMMAYANGYI TEMPLE (မ္မရံကြီး). This is one of Bagan's largest temples. Although its design, with porticos projecting from all sides of a square to form a Greek cross, follows Ananda's model, Dhammayangyi is loftier. Its unsurpassed brickwork, considered a crowning achievement of the Later Period, is airtight. As in the contemporary Sulamani, only the four porches and the outer corridors are accessible, while the upper levels are locked. *(South on the dirt path that starts on Anawrahta Rd., opposite Ananda Temple.)*

DHAMMA YAZIKA PAGODA. Set in a lush, botanical complex, Dhamma Yazika is far from crumbling like those around it. The golden *zedi* sparkles as the peaks in the roof support countless statues in red and gold. *(North of Main Rd., 1km east of Bagan-Chauk Rd.)*

TAYOKPYI PAGODA. It is one of the last buildings in Bagan that visitors are allowed to explore completely, including the two-tiered roof. Sunsets here throw the plain into dramatic silhouette. *(200m north of Minnanthu Village, just left off Main Rd.)*

NANDAPYINYA TEMPLE. Built by King Kyazawa in 1248, Nandapyinpya houses the best-preserved wall-paintings around, depicting scenes from the life of the most recent Buddha, Gautama. A racy picture on the west wall depicts women modeling see-through clothing in provocative postures; some postulate that this picture shows the temptation of Buddha by Mara. If the building is locked, ask at Payathonzu for the key. *(400m north of Minnanthu Village, on Main Rd. The farthest building to the right is the Nandamanyaw Complex.)*

PAYATHONZU TEMPLE (THREE TEMPLES). Payathonezu's structural design, involving a uniform trio of temples joined at the hip via narrow vaulted passages, evokes its share of curiosity. These temples also contain 11th-century wall-paintings depicting Gautama Buddha's life and mysterious deities from outside Theravada Buddhism. *(North of Minnathu Village on Main Rd., opposite Tayokpyi Pagoda.)*

HANDICRAFTS

When the government relocated residents of Old Bagan a decade ago, their livelihoods were altered drastically. Farmers, stripped of their land, went to work in the accommodations and restaurants of their new home, but most were given the choice of learning one of three handicrafts: lacquer-ware, wood carving, or wall-painting. At 16 years of age, artisans bought a license from the government and were assigned a temple or pagoda where they could sell their art. Therefore, at many of the major sites, visitors are met by government-created handicrafts. Reactions vary between buy and boycott, but it's important to remember that these trades present the only way for Bagan residents to support themselves, and often entire families are involved in a single handicraft industry.

Shwe Wah Thein, an antique souvenir store out of the price range of most backpackers and budget travelers, has a knowledgeable staff that can answer questions about bargaining at the temple-side stalls. (North of Bagan-Nyaung U Rd., just east of Tharaba Gate. Open daily 5am-10pm.) **Myinkabar Village,** between Old and New Bagan, is lacquer-ware central, hosting the majority of centralized shops and factories. Come here to buy quality pieces.

DAYTRIP FROM BAGAN: MOUNT POPPA ပုပ္ပားတောင်

Mount Poppa, 50km southeast of Bagan, is best reached by private car. Guesthouses and hotels in Nyaung U and New Bagan arrange transport (1½hr., US$15-25 depending on the number of people and type of vehicle) and can help find other travelers to split costs. Alternatively, a pick-up leaves daily from the Nyaung U Bus Terminal (3hr.; 8:30am, return 1pm; 2000kyat round-trip).

Volcanic Mount Poppa rose to 1518m above sea level after a colossal earthquake in 442 BC, its volcanic ash transforming the barren Myingan plains below into fertile soil. Today Mt. Poppa attracts religious attention and tourists thanks mostly to its natural wonder, **Taung Kalat**—a rock tower standing about halfway up the mountain. The mesa on top serves as the seat of all magical power and *nat* worship in Myanmar, adorned with *nat* shrines, monasteries, bells, and *stupas*. On a clear, sunny day stunning views and cool air await those who navigate the 20min. staircase to the top. Watch your step—the staircase houses mischievous monkeys. Visitors should do as the pilgrims do to avoid offending the *nat:* be careful not to wear red or black, speak ill of others, or carry meat on the climb. Those who visit using a private car should consider other possible stops along the way including **jaggery (palm sugar) factories** and the little, but touristy **Poppa Village.**

INLE LAKE REGION

NYAUNGSHWE ညောင်ရွှေ ☎081

Idyllic Nyaungshwe rests in a fertile plain between twin ranges of rolling hills that continue south to Inle Lake. Visitors frazzled by the bustle of the cities or enervated by the swelter of Bagan will find relief here despite the high concentration of touts trying to make a quick kyat. Intha, Pa-O, Shan, and Burmese traditions combine to create a congenial and multifaceted culture unlike any other in Myanmar. Nyaungshwe is not only the springboard to Inle Lake, Myanmar's most celebrated natural attraction, it's a destination in itself. With scenic treks to hill-tribe villages, motorboat forays on the lake, leisurely canoe paddles around the canals, and invigorating bike rides, plenty exists to occupy visitors, though for many the greatest appeal is the town's relaxed atmosphere.

GOVERNMENT LISTINGS Government listings are marked by a **M** symbol. Money spent at such establishments goes directly into the government's hands. For more information, see **Keep the Bucks Where They Belong,** p. 462.

TRANSPORTATION

Flights: Heho Airport lies 25km northwest (taxi 1hr., 8500-9000kyat). Airline offices are in **Taunggyi,** but guesthouses and travel agencies arrange tickets for the same price. **Air Mandalay** flies daily to: **Bagan** (US$59); **Mandalay** (12:10pm, US$37); **Yangon** (9:55am, US$80). **Yangon Airways** flies daily to **Mandalay** (9:55am, US$37) and **Yangon** (9:20am, US$80).

M Trains: The closest station is 11km away in **Shwenyaung,** from which a daily train winds its way to **Thazi** (8hr.; 8:30am; ordinary-class US$3, upper-class US$7) via **Kalaw** (3hr., 8:30am; ordinary-class US$1, upper-class US$3). From Thazi, connections run to **Mandalay** (3hr.; 8 per day; ordinary-class US$3, upper-class US$8) and **Yangon** (12hr.; 9 per day; ordinary-class US$10, upper-class US$25, sleeper US$33). Trains are often delayed in the rainy season. Buy tickets one day in advance.

Buses: Company offices are in **Taunggyi,** but guesthouses and travel agencies sell tickets with a 500kyat commission, which is included in the prices listed here. Passengers should arrive at least 30min. before scheduled departure. Buses leave from **Shwenyaung Junction,** 11km north. **Nyaung U Mann Express** runs minibuses to **Bagan** (10hr., daily 5:30am, 7000kyat). **Shwe La Min** and **Shan Maw Mye** run minibuses to **Mandalay** (9hr., daily 5:30am, 4500kyat). **Shwe Kabar** sells A/C bus tickets to **Mandalay** (9hr.; daily 7am, 7pm; 5000kyat). **Ye Thu Aung, Eastern State Express,** and **Taung Paw Thar** run parallel routes to **Yangon** via **Bago** on A/C, reclining-seat buses (17-20hr., daily 12:30pm, 7000kyat). Ye Thu Aung gets the nod for comfort and timeliness, but Eastern State Express does a drop-off closer to downtown Yangon than the Aung Mingalar Bus Gate.

Local Transportation: Linecars leave from the street 1 block west of the market for **Shwenyaung Junction** (30min., when full 7am-7pm, 200kyat) and **Taunggyi** (1hr., when full 7am-7pm, 250kyat). From Shwenyaung Junction, connections run to **Kalaw** (3hr., every hr. 6am-4pm, 1000kyat) via **Heho** (1hr., 500kyat) and **Aungban** (2hr., 700kyat); and to **Thazi** (7-8hr., every hr. 7am-noon, 1500kyat). Most services run daily 7am-7pm. **Taxis** can be hired at most guesthouses and travel agencies. To: **Bagan** (60,000kyat); **Heho Airport** (8500-9000kyat); **Kalaw** (20,000kyat); **Pindaya Cave** (25,000kyat);

THE LOCAL STORY

MARKET MERRY-GO-ROUND

The Shan people have established a system that rotates the location of the market, giving all villagers an equal opportunity to sell t[redacted]ir crops and to buy necessities[redacted]Every fifth day, villagers trek [redacted]ough the Shan hills bearing kilos of tea leaves, jack-fruits, strawberries, and *cheroot* (cigar) leaves mounted on their backs or heads. The bustling market travels according to the following schedule:

1. Kalaw, Shwenyaung, Kaungtaung, Indein
2. Pindaya, Nyaungshwe, Nampan
3. Heho, Kyone
4. Ywama (floating market), Aungban, Taunggyi homes
5. Pwayhla, Minethout, Phaung Daw Oo Pagoda

The floating market at Ywama is a stop [redacted] lake tour no matter what [redacted]u go. This has, essentially, [redacted] it into the local "souvenir market." Even on scheduled market days, floating souvenir stands far outnumber produce sellers. As of July 2004, Pwayhla and Pindaya's markets are still fairly untouristed, which allows the rare visitor an insightful look into the agricultural life of the area. Be sure to ask the managers at your guesthouse for recommendations and the current schedule.

Shwenyaung Junction (3000kyat); **Taunggyi** (10,000kyat); **Thazi** (US$40). Guesthouses and travel agencies rent **bicycles** (500kyat per day), **canoes** (500kyat per person per hr.), and **teak motorboats** (driver included, 5000-7000kyat per group per day).

ORIENTATION AND PRACTICAL INFORMATION

Nyaungshwe is set in a rectangular grid and is easily navigable on foot. Linecars from Shwenyaung Junction stop at the northwest corner of the **market,** which sits on the northern edge of town and is often used as a landmark for directions. **Main Road** forms the western edge of the market and heads south. Along the southern edge of the market is **Yonegyi Road,** home to countless **travel agencies, shops,** and **local cafes. Phaungdawseik Road,** which is one block south and recognizable by its numerous pagodas, runs parallel to Yonegyi and then west to the **canal. Phaungdawpyan Road** is one block south of Phaungdawseik Rd. and runs parallel to the west. Most **guesthouses** and **restaurants** are found east of the canal and southwest of the market. The canal (with **Canal Road**) forms the western edge of town and runs north-south along its length.

Tourist Office: **MTT,** 300m down Canal Rd. from Yonegyi Rd. They claim to be open daily 10am-3pm, but you may not find anyone there. It's better to ask at guesthouses or travel agencies.

Tours and Travel: Comet Travel Agency (inlay-comet@myanmar.com.mm), Yonegyi Rd., near the southwestern corner of the market. Run by friendly Nwe Ni Soe. Arranges bus, train, and airline tickets and rents boats, canoes, bikes, and taxis. **Treks** US$5-7 per day, including lunch. Open daily 8am-8pm. **Novelty Tour Services,** 1 block south of the market of Main Rd., finds groups to share transportation. Open daily 8:30am-8:30pm.

Currency Exchange: Guesthouses offer the most reliable rates, but at 50-80kyat less than in Yangon or Mandalay. Offers on the street are generally worse.

Markets: Mingala Market, at the corner of Main and Yonegyi Rd., is a ring of souvenir stalls surrounding the products locals buy. Relatively tame, except when the rotating market comes, but foreigners can expect a hard sell. Open daily 6am-6pm except on full moons and holidays.

Pharmacies: Win Htin (open daily 9am-8pm) and **Zizawa** (open daily 8am-7:30pm) are both on the southwest corner of the market.

Medical Services: Nyaungshwe Township Hospital, 3 blocks south of Phaungdawpyan Rd. and 1 block west of Main Rd. Although care here has improved, it is recommended that tourists go to Taunggyi to receive medical attention.

Telephones: Most guesthouses and travel agencies offer **IDD** phone service. US$6-8 per min. The **post office** (see below) allows free callbacks.

Internet Access: Internet and **email** are available at guesthouses and travel agencies, but prices fluctuate, sometimes daily. Internet is usually 1500-2000kyat per 30 min. and email 1500kyat per page.

Post Office: On Phaungdawpyan Rd., across from Aquarius Inn. Good for free IDD callbacks, but not much else. Open M-F 9:30am-4pm.

ACCOMMODATIONS

Splendid budget guesthouses and hotels offer clean, cozy rooms and reliable information on Inle Lake. Many options have opened recently so competition is fierce; managers will offer excellent deals if you switch mid-stay. However, to counteract this, some may ask for payment in advance. Establishments often provide free breakfast, laundry service, boat and canoe rentals, bus bookings, and taxi service.

Aquarius Inn (☎293 52), on Phaungdawpyan Rd., opposite the post office, only opened recently but already has a strong reputation for hospitality. Well-furnished rooms open onto a common sitting area where guests can chat and relax over free snacks. Breakfast and book-swap included. Singles US$7, with bath US$12; doubles US$4/US$6. ❷

Remember Inn, 80m east on the road that runs along the northern edge of the market. A 10min. walk from the canal, it's situated in a quiet area. A new addition more than doubled the size of rooms, so shop around until you find the right one. Friendly staff and fellow backpackers congregate in the TV-equipped common room. The bungalows are a good value. Singles US$5-15; doubles US$8-15/25. ❷

Bright Hotel, on Phaungdawseik Rd., 2 blocks east of the canal, is a good budget option for people who don't want to pay for frills. The triples are palatial, and there is a breezy common balcony overlooking the street. Singles US$5; doubles US$10; triples US$15; all with bath. ❷

Gypsy Inn, on the Canal Rd. about 200m south of the bridge. The sound of motorboats starts early, but it's in the middle of everything. The cheapest place in town. Singles US$3-5; doubles US$6-10. ❷

View Point Hotel, (☎290 62), on the right after crossing the bridge over the canal. For travelers who wanted to stay in one of the floating bungalows in Inle Lake but found them too expensive, View Point offers affordable, comfortable rooms built in the traditional Inle architectural style on the canal. Singles US$10; doubles US$15. ❸

Gold Star Hotel (☎292 00), on Phaungdawpyan Rd., opposite the Independence Monument. This large hotel has rooms that range from basic to family-size, bungalow-style rooms with TV and A/C. The high-rise rooms are newer and more expensive. Singles US$8-16; doubles US$12-20. ❹

FOOD

Golden Kite, 4 blocks east from the market on Yonegyi Rd., serves freshly made pasta with herbs grown in the family's backyard and Inle Lake tomatoes, the best in the country. Customers are welcome in the kitchen to watch as their meal is prepared. Pancakes 450-850kyat. Pasta dishes 1000-2000kyat. Open daily 8am-10:30pm. ❹

Big Drum Restaurant, across the bridge at the end of Yonegyi Rd. and left at the end of the path, shares a building with La Libellule. Shan specialties in A-frame bungalows on the canal. 7-course meals with curry, soup, and fried potato or salad 2000kyat. Open daily 9am-10pm. ❹

Pancake Kingdom, toward the canal on Yonegyi Rd.; follow the signposts. Good for a snack or a light meal. Homemade yogurt *lassis* 400kyat. Toasted sandwiches and crêpes 400-1000kyat. Open daily 7am-9:30pm. ❸

Four Sisters Restaurant, at the southern end of Canal Rd. Home-cooked Burmese meals. No menu: they serve what they make that day. Pay what you feel is appropriate (except for the set-priced drinks). Make a reservation before 4pm. Dinner served daily 6:30-9:30pm. They also have accommodations: singles US$7; doubles US$12. ❸

Aroma Restaurant, 100m down Canal Rd. from Yonegyi Rd. Slightly overpriced Indian food with a Burmese twist. Set dinners (1000-1500kyat) offer *chapaati* or rice, vegetable curry, and lentil soup. Finish the meal off with a spicy Masala Tea (500kyat). Open daily 10am-9:30pm. ❹

La Kabar, on Yonegyi Rd., 2 blocks from the canal, has good Indian food. English movies are often screened in the afternoon. *Puri* 200kyat, samosas and Indian sweets 50kyat each. Open daily 5am-7pm. ❷

ENTERTAINMENT

Check out **Kaung Kaung Restaurant,** on the west side of the market, for 350kyat taps of Myanmar draught beer. (Open daily until 10pm.) Those who missed the Mandalay Marionettes can take in a show at the **Aung Traditional Puppet Show,** on Yonegyi Rd. next to the Golden Kite Restaurant. The master puppeteer puts on excellent one-man, 30min. shows with historical explanations in English. (Shows daily 7, 8:30pm. 1000kyat per person.)

DAYTRIPS FROM NYAUNGSHWE

INLE LAKE အင်းလေးကန်

Inle Lake, 2km down the canal from Nyaungshwe, is the showpiece of the Shan Plateau. The Intha, as the lake area's residents are known, build homes on stilts over the water and succeed admirably in "living off the lake." There's little space on this lake that isn't harvested, fished, or lived on. Intha farmers tend to floating gardens that yield flowers, vegetables, and fruit (especially tomatoes) from their narrow teak canoes. Infamous leg rowers and fishermen patrol the open spaces, especially early and late in the day, when they appear silhouetted against the mountainous horizon. The Intha are also gifted weavers, carpenters, canoe-builders, and metalworkers; their workshops are very informative but a little touristy.

MOTORBOAT TRIP. If visitors do only one thing when they come to Inle Lake, it should be to take a motorboat trip on the lake (5000kyat per boat). There are numerous pagodas, monasteries, markets, and handicraft shops to visit, and itineraries can be worked out with motorboat drivers to suit individual interests. Destinations listed here are only a cross-section of the possibilities.

The village of **Ywama** was once an essential stop on any Inle Lake expedition. Its **floating market** appears in full vigor every fifth day. Recently, however, the market has been redubbed the "Souvenir Market." On official market days, it's an interesting lesson in nautical trade, but come early (7-8am) because by 9am souvenir boats vastly outnumber all others. On any other day, it is just you and the souvenir hawkers. The most sacred religious site in the northern Shan State, **Phaung Daw U Kyaung,** sits south of Ywama. Though the (reconstructed) exterior architecture is impressive, the structure's contents are not. Owing to generous gold-leaf donations over the years, the Buddha images have ballooned considerably in size, rendering their original dimensions a mystery and leaving five lumps of gold in their place. Every September and October, the 20-day **Phaung Daw U Kyaung Festival** features a procession of four out of the five images (one is left behind due to a sinking in a previous festival) in decorated barges, along with hundreds of accompanying vessels, around the lake's villages.

At the northern outskirts of Ywama stands the stilted **Nga Phe Kyaung,** the oldest monastery among the 268 that dot the lake's shores. The beautiful teak structure houses Bagan, Intha, Shan, and Tibetan Buddha images. For generations, the monks have trained cats to jump through hoops. Donations welcome.

The farther out you head on the lake, the better your chances are of escaping the souvenir scene. One good bet is **Indein,** known for its market, and **Shwe Inn Tain Pagoda.** At the lake's far southern end, the villages of **Taung Doe** and **Kyauk Taing,** known for *stupas* and pottery respectively, were recently opened to foreigners and therefore still retain some of their original atmosphere. Because of its distance from Nyaungshwe, adding Indein to an itinerary means paying 6000kyat per boat; adding the towns farther south raises the price to 7000kyat. *(Lake admission fee US$3, payable at the collection booth opposite Gypsy Inn.)*

CANOE TRIP. Another good way to avoid overly touristed areas is to take a human-powered canoe trip. Commonly lasting several hours around sunset, these boats (500-1000kyat per person, per hr.) only venture to canals around the northern edge of the lake. The number of passengers is limited, but trips are not subject to the US$3 lake admission fee.

WALKING/TREKKING. This is the best way to explore the edge of the lake and the villages that surround it. For a personal encounter with Inle Lake monastic life, wander to the village of **Nan The,** a 5min. walk south of Four Sisters Inn, where Canal Rd. becomes a dirt path. The village contains three monasteries—**Le Bien, Pien Tha,** and **Moke Thoke**—and one pagoda, **Pai An Gyi,** where a 10m Buddha image sits shoulders above the foundations of the crumbled walls that used to enclose it. For a more strenuous experience, day-trek guides are available for US$5-7 (lunch included). Most treks are similar and involve going through several villages on the way to the top of one of the mountain ranges for panoramic views of the lake. Half-day treks followed by half-day personalized boat trips start at 9000kyat (inquire at any travel agency). It is also possible to trek to Kalaw over 2½ days for US$10-15 per person, per day (inquire at Comet Travel Agency, see **Practical Information**).

BICYCLE. Alternatively, cyclists can pick a road out of Nyaungshwe and get lost in the villages on the lake's edge. It gets a bit muddy in the rainy season, but it is a good way to see the valley without trekking or paying the lake entrance fee. South of Nyaungshwe, on the western edge of the lake, **Inle Khaung Daing Spa** at Hu Pin Hotel provides solitude and comfort for weary travelers. *(Open daily 5am-6pm. Myanmar Swimming Pool US$7 per person. Hot Spring US$3 per person.)*

TAUNGGYI

*Take a pick-up truck or taxi from Nyaungshwe (**see* **Local Transportation,** *p. 519**). Pick-ups back to Nyaungshwe leave from just south of the market in Taunggyi (1hr., leave when full 7am-4:30pm, 100kyat).*

The capital of Shan State, Taunggyi used to be a culturally diverse frontier town nestled among the peaks of picturesque highlands at an altitude of 1430m, 28km northeast of Inle Lake. However, its status as a center of commerce has caused some of that diversity to fade, leaving only the services available in a big town and the cool air as reasons to visit. Regional instability makes Taunggyi the easternmost point accessible by land in Shan State. **Bogyoke Aung San Road,** the main street in Taunggyi, divides the city in half as it goes uphill from north to south. Pick-ups from Nyaungshwe may drop passengers in a lot on the northwest outskirts of town; from there, take another pick-up to the town center (10min., 50kyat). The town's main draw is the **central market,** on Bogyoke Aung San Rd., which sells everything from handicrafts to traditional Shan dress. Taunggyi's market is less touristed but busier than Nyaungshwe's, resulting in a larger selection of goods and better bartering opportunities. The other reason travelers might visit Taunggyi is for treatment at the private **Mandalar Hospital,** 222 Bogyoke Aung San Rd. (☎227 33), near the north end of town, which has an English-speaking staff and 24hr. emergency service. (Consultation with a physician US$20, M-F 8-9am and 6-9pm, Sa-Su 8-11am and 6-9pm.) At the opposite end of town, also on Bogyoke Aung San Rd., Taunggyi's **post office** offers the most services of any in the region (open M-F 9am-4pm), while the **telephone office** next door is fairly useless for foreigners. For those with time to spare, the **Shan State Museum,** south of the post office, manages to pack religious, cultural, and artistic artifacts into relatively few exhibits. (US$2. Open Tu-F 9:30am-3:30pm.) Clean, comfortable, and affordable accommodations are at **Khemarat Hotel ❷,** Bogyoke Aung San Rd., opposite Mandalar Hospital. (☎224 64. Singles US$6-10; doubles US$12-16.)

KALAW ကလော ☎081

The sedate alpine charm of Kalaw is nothing short of paradise for travelers coming from the dusty swelter of Bagan or the frenzied sprawl of Mandalay or Yangon. The British must have thought similarly when they founded a hill station here. Their colonial legacy lingers in the wide, uncluttered streets and missionary-built schools, even though most tourists do not. With trekking trails and traditional villages in the surrounding hills, Kalaw serves as a base camp for hikes or the perfect place to sit back, relish the air, and take in the scenery.

TRANSPORTATION. The **train station** at the southern end of Station Rd., which runs along the east side of the market, serves Thazi (4hr.; 11:30am, 1:30, 10:30pm; upper-class US$5) and Shwenyaung (for Nyaungshwe, 10:30am, upper-class US$3). Trains are often hours late in the rainy season. **Buses** originating in Taunggyi pass through Kalaw on their way to points west and south. Book tickets at numerous travel and trekking agencies near the market. Buses go to Bagan (8hr., 7:30am, 5000kyat); Mandalay (8-10hr.; 7:30am, 4500kyat; 8:30, 9am, 5000kyat); Yangon (16hr., 2pm, 7000kyat). Two buses depart from Parami Hotel, one block west of the market, for Taunggyi (3hr.; 6:30, 7, 7:30am; 1000kyat) via Shwenyaung Junction (for Nyaungshwe, 2hr., 1000kyat). Buy all tickets one day in advance. Tickets for Taunggyi are sold in the green shack half a block south of the banyan tree on Main Rd. If the buses to Taunggyi are full, **pick-ups** rattle eastbound on Union Rd. (6am-4 or 5pm, 1000kyat).

ORIENTATION AND PRACTICAL INFORMATION. Pye Htaung Su (Union) Road, which runs west to Thazi and east to Taunggyi, forms the northern boundary of Kalaw. Ten parallel streets extend southward. Just west of the **market, Main Road** intersects perpendicularly with Union Rd. and runs south. After one block

Main Rd. crosses **Merchant Street,** an intersection by a **banyan tree,** the town landmark. On Main Rd., about halfway between Union Rd. and the banyan tree on the market side, sits **December Store,** a well-stocked **pharmacy.** (Open daily 7am-7pm.) A doctor offers **private medical care** out of the **Eastern Paradise Hotel,** on the corner of Merchant St. and Natsin Rd. (☎503 15. Open W and F 5-8pm, Sa and Su 9am-5pm.) **IDD** calls can be made from the **Trunk Call Station** (7am-9pm) on the north side of the market next to Ye Baw Gyi (see **Accommodations and Food**) or from the **post office,** at the west end of Union Rd opposite Natsin Rd. (Open daily 9am-4pm.)

ACCOMMODATIONS AND FOOD. Hotel and guesthouse rooms outnumber visitors, so quality is high and prices are low. However, of the 22 guesthouses in town, only two are not owned in part by the government. **Golden Lily Guest House ❶,** at the town's west end on Natsin Rd., is a quiet, clean place run by a helpful family. (☎501 08. In the high season with bath US$5 per person, without bath US$3; in low season US$3/US$2.) It doesn't get any more basic than **Pine Land Inn ❶,** next to Winner Hotel. (☎500 20. Small rooms US$2 per person; nicer rooms with bath US$3.) **Winner Hotel ❷,** in the town center on Union Rd., has excellent rooms and a TV in the sitting area. (☎502 79. Basic singles US$3, with bath US$8; doubles US$16; rooms with bathtub, fridge, TV, and teak decor US$15-25.)

Ye Baw Gyi ❸, on Union Rd. at the north side of the market, is popular for its Myanmar curries and fried noodles. (Dishes 700kyat. Open daily 7am-9pm.) **Everest Nepali Food Center ❸,** on Aung Chan Tha St. (look for the sign near the banyan tree), offers quality Nepalese dishes, but make sure you look first at the menu listing the prices. (Dal Bhat set meal 900kyat. Cucumber salad 600kyat. Open daily 7am-9pm.) **Thirigayhar (Seven Sisters) Restaurant ❹,** Union Rd., 200m west of Winner Hotel, serves delicious but expensive Burmese, Chinese, Indian, and European food. (Dishes 1000-2500kyat. Open daily 7am-10pm.) Those who want something inexpensive and hearty after a day on the trail should head for the Indian teashops around the market.

DAYTRIPS FROM KALAW

The hillside outside Kalaw hosts several different one- to three-day treks. Routes focus on visits to the villages of four regional tribes. Guide fees (US$5-7 per person per day) cover food and accommodations in the villages, but ask at the **trekking agencies** that line Union Rd. in the vicinity of the market. It pays to shop around for a guide in Kalaw; ask locals for recommendations and try to find someone who speaks the languages of the peoples on the itinerary. Guides range from highly experienced and knowledgeable to utterly ignorant. **Sam Trekking** (☎502 37), on Union Rd. on the north side of the market, receives raves, as does **Eddie,** owner of the Golden Kalaw Hotel. Treks to the north visit tribes that live more traditionally than those in the south, but all routes have spectacular scenery. Hiking in the rainy season, however, means slippery conditions; hiking boots are highly recommended.

PINDAYA AND SHWE U MIN. Pindaya, 1180m above sea level and 39km north of the town of **Aungban,** has crisp air, excellent scenery, and fertile farmland. The town's reputation is built on **Shwe U Min Pagoda,** or "Golden Cave Pagoda" (US$3 for admission), which is just inside the cave's entrance. The rest of the limestone void is a maze of stalagmites, stalactites, and 8000 Buddha images crafted in every conceivable style. Over the years, pilgrims and adherents have donated these images to the caves, but the monument is now saturated, and trustees have put a cap on further offerings. Of the several interesting columns and images, make sure to find the "Perspiring Buddhas;" scraping the "sweat" off the Buddha images is supposed to be good luck. The **rotating market** comes through town every five days, making the trip even more worthwhile.

Pindaya is best reached from Kalaw, but public transportation is difficult, especially in the rainy season. When Pindaya hosts the market, a linecar makes the journey from Kalaw (1½hr.; leaves when full around 6am, returns around noon; 1000kyat). If it's not a market day, traveling to Pindaya by public transportation is nearly impossible; it involves an overnight stay and the possibility of having to return to Kalaw via an expensive taxi ride. This situation changes frequently, so ask in Kalaw. The more trustworthy option is to go by **taxi** (US$15-20 round-trip), which allows you to stop around Pindaya to view **handicraft centers** specializing in bamboo hats, tree-bark paper, and umbrellas. At the base of the bluff that holds the cave entrance, **Nan Cherry Umbrella Shop** is run by an extended family that gives a step-by-step demonstration of the umbrella-making process and sells fixed-price umbrellas (small paper 1000kyat, medium cloth 2000kyat, large cloth 5000kyat).

THE PHILIPPINES

HIGHLIGHTS OF THE PHILIPPINES

BEACHES. The sugar-fine sand of Boracay's **White Beach** (p. 608) lures jet setters and backpackers alike, while **Palawan** (p. 617) draws a decidedly adventurous crowd. **Bantayan** (p. 592) and **Malapascua** (p. 593) are restful island detours en route to Cebu.

DIVING. Visayan dive sites are Southeast Asia's best: **Moalboal** (p. 591), **Panglao Island** (p. 595), and **Apo Island** (p. 603) are all on the diver's pilgrimage trail.

CULTURAL HERITAGE. Manila's walled city of **Intramuros** (p. 552), **museums** (p. 551), and **Fort San Pedro** (p. 589) hark back to the drama between *conquistadores* and natives, while **Vigan's churches** (p. 568) attest to lasting Christian influence. Indigenous Cordilleran cultures around **Banaue** (p. 566) delight budding anthropologists.

NATURAL WONDERS. Mountain air cleanses Manila-marred lungs around **Bontoc's rice terraces** (p. 564). The **Mayon Volcano** (p. 574) in Legazpi and **Mt. Kanla-on** (p. 599) near Bacolod challenge with their height and fiery tempers. Palawan's **Cabayugan River** (p. 620) offers a surreal float through the bowels of the Earth. Hikers meander through Bohol's **Chocolate Hills** (p. 595) to peek at the precious primate, the *tarsier*.

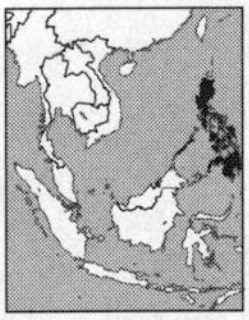

The Philippines has been permanently thrown out of sync with the rest of Southeast Asia. Described as a hodgepodge of "Malay, Madrid, and Madison Ave.," Filipino culture fosters a range of ethnicities, languages, and lifestyles among which natives have found unity and an unparalleled love for life. Their willingness to drop everything for a basketball game or a cockfighting match reflects the national philosophy of *bahala na*, roughly translated as "whatever will be, will be." At the heart of Filipino tradition is a strong sense of community that values family, friendliness, and personal loyalty. This cheerful attitude, along with convenient transportation, numerous English speakers, and inexpensive locales, makes the Philippines a budget traveler's paradise.

LIFE AND TIMES

DEMOGRAPHICS

Although they are spread out over more than 1000 different islands, Filipinos remain a relatively unified group. Christian Malays, known as **Filipinos,** account for 91.5% of the population of the Philippines. About 8.5% of the Philippine population is made up of ethnic and religious minorities, including tribal groups, Muslim Malays, ethnic Chinese, and **mestizo** populations (mostly Filipino-Spanish and Filipino-American). The dwindling **negrito** population, the Philippines's oldest surviving race, lives largely in the country's upland forests, subsisting by hunting and fishing. Similarly, the **Lumads—**a generic term for the indigenous people of various ethnic and linguistic backgrounds—inhabit Mindanao, living mainly by subsistence agriculture. Victims of the never-ending sprawl of development, the Lumads are gradually being pushed farther and farther into the Philippine hinterlands.

The Philippines
0 150 miles
0 150 kilometers
Batanes
Luzon Strait
Babuyan Islands
Babuyan Channel
Cape Bojeador
Laoag
Luzon Sea
Vigan
Tabuk
LUZON
Banaue
San Fernando (La Union)
South China Sea
Bolinao
100 Islands
Baguio
Dagupan
Mt. Pinatubo
Angeles
San Fernando
Polillo Island
Olongapo
Manila
Pasig
Cavite
Santa Cruz
Batangas
Lucena
Daet
Naga
Catanduanes Island
Puerto Galera
Mayon Volcano
Legazpi
Calapan
Marinduque
Mindoro
Sibuyan Sea
Romblon
Busuanga Island
Boracay Island
Masbate
Catarman
Calbayog
Calamian Group
Kalibo
Roxas
Biliran Island
Samar
Visayan Sea
Naval
El Nido
San Jose de Buenavista
Panay
VISAYAS
Ormoc
Tacloban
Iloilo
Bacolod
Cuyo Island
Guimaras Island
Toledo
Cebu City
Leyte
Maasin
Panay Gulf
La Carlota
Cebu
Siargao Island
Palawan Passage
Puerto Princesa
Bohol
Surigao
Negros
Tagbilaran
Quezon
Sulu Sea
Panglao
Mambajao
Camiguin Island
PALAWAN
Dumaguete
Siquijor
Bohol Sea
Bataraza
Dipolog
Cagayan de Oro
Tubbataha Reef
Ozamis
MINDANAO
Balabac Island
Pagadian
Cotabato
Davao
Cagayan de Tawi Tawi Island
Zamboanga
Mt. Apo
Isabela
Moro Gulf
Digos
Basilan Island
General Santos
Sandakan
Jolo
Jolo Island
Mindanao Sea
MALAYSIA (SABAH)
Tawi-Tawi Island
Sulu Archipelago
Celebes Sea
Philippine Sea
Cool Coral
Scuba dive at the world-famous Visayan dive sites.
Walled Wonder
Explore the walled city of Intramuros in Manila.
Soft Sands
Sunbathe on Boracay's gorgeous White Beach.
Hot Spot
Soak yourself in El Nido's Makinit Hot Springs.
Chocolate Paradise
Trek through the stunning Chocolate Hills in Bohol.

FACTS AND FIGURES

Official Name: Republic of the Philippines.

Government: Republic.

Capital: Manila.

Land Area: 298,170km^2.

Geography: A 7107-island archipelago stretching 1851km north-south and 1107km east-west. Divides into 4 zones: Luzon, the Visayas, Palawan, and Mindanao. Mountain ranges: Central Cordillera and Sierra Madre in Luzon. Mindanao's Mt. Apo (2954m) is the highest peak.

Climate: Tropical: Dry (high season) Nov.-Mar., and rainy (low season) Apr.-Oct.

Phone Codes: Country code: 63. International dialing prefix: 00.

Random Fact #1: The word "boondocks" comes from the Tagalog *bundok,* which means "mountain."

Major Cities: Manila, Bacolod, Cagayan de Oro, Cebu, Davao, Iloilo, Zamboanga.

Population: 84,619,974.

Life Expectancy: Women: 72.28 years. Men: 69.29 years.

Language: Filipino, English, and 8 major dialects.

Religion: Roman Catholic (83%), Protestant (9%), Muslim (5%), Buddhist and Other (3%).

Literacy: 95.9% overall; 96% of men, 95.8% of women.

Major Exports: Electronics, textiles, agricultural products.

Random Fact #2: The yo-yo was invented in the 16th century in the Philippines, for use as a weapon.

LANGUAGE

Although the official languages of the Philippines are **Filipino** and **English,** over 150 different dialects and languages are spoken throughout the archipelago. English is used mainly for legal, governmental, academic, and commercial purposes. The eight major spoken dialects are Tagalog, Cebuano, Ilocano, Hiligaynon or Ilonggo, Bicol, Waray, Pampango, and Pangasinense. Tagalog is thought to derive from *taga-ilog*, which means "people who live by the river;" it serves as the basis for the national language, Filipino, which boasts a vocabulary heavily influenced by Sanskrit, Arabic, Chinese, English, and Spanish.

RELIGION

CATHOLICISM. The Philippines boasts that it is the only Christian nation in Asia with over 80% of the population adhering to Roman Catholicism—a legacy of Spanish missionaries. The recent church scandals in America have led to a larger international discussion about sexuality and celibacy among Catholic priests. This discussion has uncovered some unpleasant aspects of Catholicism in the Philippines, which may challenge the Church's prominence in the future. However, the Philippines remains strongly rooted in its form of the Catholic faith, one which is colored by distinctive folk elements.

ISLAM. Islam was introduced to the Philippine archipelago by Arab traders in the 14th century, and has remained prevalent in the south, particularly on Mindanao. Because this area was not successfully colonized by the Spanish, the people of Mindanao have remained culturally distinct from the rest of the country, spurring demands for local autonomy and fueling separatist sentiment. More recently, Mindanao has been influenced by the **Wahabi** (more fundamentalist) branch of Islam, due to missions and projects funded by Saudi Arabia.

PROTESTANTISM. American influence in the 20th century oversaw the spread of Protestantism throughout the Philippines. Today, about 9% of Filipinos consider themselves Protestant. Under American colonialism, Protestant converts experienced a great deal of upward social mobility at the expense of the Catholics.

PHILIPPINE INDEPENDENT CHURCH. A nationalistic offshoot of Catholicism informally known as the **Aglipayan Church**, the Philippine Independent Church (PIC) was founded in 1902 by Gregorio Aglipay, a Roman Catholic priest who fought diligently for institutional reforms. Over the course of the 20th century, the church has become increasingly fractious, and dwindled in power from its originally impressive strength.

OTHER RELIGIONS. In recent years, many smaller sects have started challenging the supremacy of the Roman Catholic Church in the Philippines. There has been a proliferation of **Rizalist sects** that believe that Jose Rizal, the late 19th-century martyred nationalist leader, was the reincarnation of Christ. **Iglesia ni Kristo** is the Philippine version of Mormonism and was founded by Felix Manalo in 1914. The churches associated with Iglesia ni Kristo are architecturally distinctive, and serve as prominent landmarks in nearly all provincial capitals and metropolitan areas.

LAND

The 7107 Philippine islands (only 1000 of which are inhabited) are composed of volcanic rock and coral formations. Although the country lies on the Pacific Ring of Fire, only 10 of the 50 volcanoes in the Philippines are known to be active; most of these lie within the Luzon Volcanic Arc that runs along the south and west of Luzon. The most recent volcanic eruptions have been Mt. Pinatubo in 1991 and Mt. Mayon in 2001. The positive long-term effects of volcanic activity are evident in the form of fertile soil, enriched by volcanic ash and lava.

WILDLIFE

The Philippines is one of the ten most biologically diverse countries in the world, teeming with reefs, jungles, forests, and other lively ecosystems. Unfortunately, it is also one of the world's most environmentally endangered, thanks to the work of developers. The future of national parks and conservation efforts are sadly uncertain; ecologically minded travelers should go to as many national parks as possible and sign the guestbook to show their support for conservation projects.

ENDANGERED ANIMALS. The Philippines is home to several species of endangered animals, brought to the brink of extinction by the destruction of their natural habitats. The **Philippine Eagle,** the largest eagle in the world, has become a symbol of the mounting importance of habitat preservation. Five of the eight known species of **marine turtles** make their home in the Philippines. Hunted for their meat and leather, their eggs stolen as a purported aphrodisiac, and their nesting sites destroyed by development, these turtles are in imminent danger of extinction. The sanctuary at Turtle Island serves as one of the world's only breeding and resting grounds for the endangered marine turtle. The **Bleeding-Heart Dove,** a terrestrial pigeon, lives in the forests of Luzon. Found in public and private zoological collections the world over, the dove's population in the wild has currently dwindled to an indeterminate number. Widely considered the most beautiful of the peacock species, the **Palawan Peacock-Pheasant** is in danger of extinction as more of its natural habitat, the coastal lowland forest of Palawan, is destroyed. The species's wild population is estimated at less than 10,000.

DANGEROUS ANIMALS. Travelers who plan to dive should watch out for dangerous marine life and stick to reputable, often-frequented dive sites. The **Salt Crocodile** is one of the world's deadliest animals; it is usually found only in remote areas, favoring brackish water and large river mouths (although it has also been sighted in the open ocean). The venom of the common pale blue **Banded Sea Snake** is a deadly neurotoxin. In northern Palawan, Snake Island offers the opportunity to watch these sea snakes from a safe distance.

HISTORY

EARLY HISTORY

The original inhabitants of the Philippines archipelago were probably immigrants of Australo-Melanesian descent—ancestors of the pygmy people today known as the Aeta. One epic Philippine legend has it that the **Ten Datus** moved to the Philippine Visayas from Sabah Province in Malaysia (Borneo) during the early 13th century, fleeing the tyranny of the violent Sultan Makatunaw.

SPANISH YEARS (1521-1885)

IMPORTANT DATES		
1521 Magellan arrives; Spanish rule begins.	**1565** The Philippines becomes a Spanish colony with the capital at Manila.	**1762** The British seize Manila during Seven Year's War but promptly return it to Spain.

Ferdinand Magellan landed on the island of Samar in 1521, and the Philippines became a Spanish colony in 1565—laying the ground for great cultural and political transformations (as well as Magellan's spectacular death at the hands of unhappy natives). Although the takeover was turbulent, the rewards were magnificent: for merchants moving between Canton, China, and Acapulco, Manila served as a gateway to Asia; for the Spanish, Manila was an important commercial prize, attracting more and more international trade. In the process of claiming and colonizing this land, the Spanish made an indelible religious and social imprint on the Philippines, particularly through the spread of **Roman Catholicism** and the idea of a landed elite. Rural Catholic friars were left up to their own devices under Spanish rule, claiming control of religious life, government, and education. This "friarocracy" alienated wealthy Filipinos, causing tension and strife. These moneyed, educated Filipinos were known as the *ilustrados*, a group that would become the driving force in the revolution to come.

REFORM MOVEMENT AND EARLY NATIONALISM (1886-1896)

IMPORTANT DATES		
1886 Jose Rizal publishes "Noli Me Tangere."	**1892** Rizal returns to the Philippines to found The Philippine League.	**1896** Rizal's execution stimulates nationalism.

After several attempts to expel the friarocracy, the Filipino expatriate community in Spain organized the hot-blooded **Propaganda Movement,** circulating the revolutionary newspaper *La Solidaridad* (Solidarity) in both Spain and the Philippines. The most famous and perhaps most eloquent propagandist, **Jose Rizal,** led the fight for independence using literature as his weapon of choice; his most famous works are *Noli Me Tangere* (Touch Me Not) and *El Filibusterismo* (The Subversive). These were smuggled into the Philippines and read widely, galvanizing the *ilustrados* against the Spanish friarocracy. Returning to the Philippines in 1892, Rizal founded **The Philippine League,** an organization devoted to nonviolent reform. Rizal was arrested for revolutionary activity and executed in 1896 for these efforts. Still, his movement would live on, as budding Philippine nationalism—set in motion by Rizal's death—fueled the development of **Katipunan,** a radical organization dedicated to independence through revolution. Founded by **Andres Bonifacio,** Katipunan suffered a long spell of internal woes, as loyalties among the group's members divided between Bonifacio and **General Emilio Aguinaldo.** Aguinaldo was ultimately elected to replace Bonifacio as the group's leader, and after armed infighting, Bonifacio was arrested, tried, and executed on Aguinaldo's orders.

AMERICA IN THE PHILIPPINES (1896-1945)

IMPORTANT DATES		
1898 US defeats Spain and buys the Philippines in giant 3-for-1 bargain.	**1910** US crushes insurrection, changes tactics, and begins cultural invasion.	**1942-45** Japanese invade Luzon and defeat US General MacArthur.

Spanish-American relations went down with the *U.S.S. Maine* off the coast of Cuba in 1898, and shortly thereafter, the US Navy attacked the Spanish fleet in Manila Bay. This was the start of the **Spanish-American War,** known for both its brevity and intensity. Although the US had claimed no desire to commandeer Spain's crumbling colonial empire, fears of missing out on commercial trade in Southeast Asia changed its mind. In the peace treaty that ended the war, the US bought the Philippines, Guam, and Puerto Rico for a bargain: US$20 million. Despite the **Philippine Insurrection** initiated by Aguinaldo, the US adopted a policy of "benevolent assimilation" toward their "little brown brothers" (so dubbed by William Taft, the first American governor of the Philippines). Education became the main means of Americanization, emphasizing English literacy, a public health-care system, and the development of infrastructure. US involvement in the Philippines came at a heavy cultural price. Indigenous culture was devalued, and little was done to bridge the gap between the middle class and the rural *barrios*.

INDEPENDENCE (1946-1969)

IMPORTANT DATES		
1946 US grants the Philippines independence on July 4.	**1953** Suppressor of Huk Rebels, Magsaysay, elected president.	**1957** Magsaysay dies in freak plane crash.

The Japanese invaded the Philippines just 10hr. after their attack on Pearl Harbor. **General MacArthur,** sent packing by the Japanese, vowed, "I shall return," and did just that in 1945—defeating the Japanese occupying forces and liberating the Philippines. Then, on July 4, 1946, the US granted their pseudo-colony its independence, beginning the Philippines's long-standing position as a pseudo-independent puppet state. Elected to rehabilitate a country ravaged by strife and war, **Manuel Roxas** was inaugurated as the first president of the postwar commonwealth. Historians agree that life on the archipelago was not quite rosy during this time: WWII had given rise to bitter tensions between farmers and landlords, and landlords' attempts to collect rent often dissolved into armed conflict between members of the **Hukbalahap** peasant movement and the landlords' armed bands. The Huks, as the peasants were commonly known, fought against the Japanese as US-backed guerrilla forces, and hoped to be embraced by US leadership after the war. Communist tendencies among the Huks, however, caused the US to provide military aid to help quell their movement, under the heavy hand of Defense Secretary **Ramon Magsaysay.** Following Magsaysay's election to the presidency in 1953, he worked extensively for land reform. Unfortunately, he died in 1957 before accomplishing this, and the government passed from one inept regime to another.

THE MARCOS DYNASTY (1965-1986)

IMPORTANT DATES			
1965 Ferdinand Marcos elected president; wife's collection of shoes continues to grow.	**1968** NPA established; Marcos brands them Communist, calls coup, and declares martial law.	**1973, 1975, 1978** Referendums rigged by Marcos "okay" the extension of martial law.	**1979** The Philippine Peso plummets in a severe economic recession.

In 1965, **Ferdinand Marcos** came to power. His wife, former beauty queen **Imelda Marcos,** is known for her immense shoe collection (a mere 1000-2000 pairs now reside in the Marikina Shoe Museum). The tale of a president-turned-dictator began benignly with widespread admiration of his aggression in tackling the problems of education, poverty, transportation, and land reform; in 1969, he became the first Philippine president to win a second term. Claiming to root out the internal Communist threat of the **New People's Army (NPA),** he declared martial law and rigged plebiscites in 1973, 1975, and 1978 that "approved" its extension. As the unprecedented levels of corruption in Marcos's inner circle became clear, the public became increasingly disenchanted with the regime. In 1977, Marcos's rival, Senator **Benigno Aquino,** was accused on trumped-up charges of treason and murder. Upon arrival in Manila after years of exile, Aquino was assassinated.

PEOPLE POWER (1986-1998)

IMPORTANT DATES	
1968 EDSA Revolution overthrows Marcos; he escapes to Hawaii under US military escort.	**1992** *USS Belleau Wood* leaves Subic Naval Base, ending 94 years of US military presence.

Aquino's assassination marked the end of Marcos's rule. **Corazon Aquino,** Benigno's widow, ran against Marcos and received overwhelming support, although Marcos had the National Assembly declare him the victor. Growing steadily more disillusioned with the regime, Marcos's Secretary of Defense **Juan Ponce Enrile** and **Fidel Ramos,** Chief of Staff of the Armed Forces, led the **EDSA Revolution,** named for the street on which local masses faced Marines and tanks in support of "Cory" Aquino. The mass demonstrations forced Marcos to flee to Hawaii aboard a US Air Force plane, and international attention turned to focus on the Philippines as an example of one of the first successful pro-democracy revolutions in the developing world. President Aquino released all political prisoners of the Marcos regime and drafted a new constitution that reduced executive power. She also dealt with the continuing demands of Imelda Marcos, who was found guilty of stealing millions from the treasury. Succeeding Aquino in 1992, Fidel Ramos faced an economic crisis caused by volcanic eruptions and the termination of the US lease on the Subic Bay naval base—a move that cost the Philippines thousands of jobs. However, Ramos successfully courted foreign investment by lifting the foreign currency restrictions and liberalizing the Philippine economy. He also sought negotiations with the terrorist group **Moro National Liberation Front,** in an effort to bring peace to Mindanao.

THE PHILIPPINES TODAY

POLITICS. Though she still faced lawsuits for embezzlement and a 12-year prison sentence for corruption, **Imelda Marcos** entered the 1998 presidential race on a supremely ironic platform: strengthening the nation's economy. Unfortunately for Imelda, **Joseph Estrada,** a college drop-out and popular movie star, won the election and became president on May 11, 1998. After a series of massive resignations from his staff, however, the Philippines Supreme Court impeached Estrada on charges of corruption, removing him from office in January of 2001. In his place, the court installed Vice President **Gloria Macapagal Arroyo.** The biggest challenges facing Arroyo's administration are the swelling government budget deficit (estimated at US$2.87 billion), rampant corruption, poverty, and high crime rates. She must also deal with increasing domestic terrorism from left-wing groups and Muslim separatists, who have become more and more active as of late, claiming over 120,000 lives in the past three decades. Although critics maintain that Arroyo's reign has done little to stop poverty and terrorism, these opinions did not hinder her in her 2004 bid for reelection. She edged out competitor Fernando Poe—a 64-year-old political novice and former movie star—by a narrow margin. It is hoped that the resilient Arroyo, who has also survived an attempted ouster and military mutiny in 2003, will be able to shore up the nation's floundering economy. Presently, Filipino economic stability depends largely on money sent home by the huge number of Filipinos working abroad.

MILITANT SEPARATISTS AND TERRORIST GROUPS. Arroyo's administration sees a direct link between the country's terrorism problem and its extreme poverty, and hopes to redouble its efforts for sweeping social and economic change in its second term. The **Abu Sayyaf Group (ASG),** an Islamic separatist group, is viewed as one of her main targets. ASG leaders have been conclusively linked with several terrorist attacks in the southern Philippines. Presently, the US is training Filipino soldiers in terror-fighting tactics, in cooperation with requests from Arroyo. The **New People's Army (NPA)** is an armed wing of the Communist Party of the Philippines that seeks to overthrow the government through extended guerrilla warfare. Opposed to any US military presence, they have threatened violence to American troops participating in joint military exercises with the Philippines, as well as any other Americans who encroach on their sphere of influence in rural northern Luzon and parts of Mindanao.

The **Moro Islamic Liberation Front (MILF),** another Muslim insurgent group demanding the formation of an autonomous Islamic state on the southern Philippine island of Mindanao, has racked up impressive military forces. A deadly 2003 airport bombing in the populous southern city of Davao was initially attributed to MILF, although charges were recently dropped by the government. Despite the turmoil, it should be noted that these events are concentrated mainly in extremely rural areas of northern Luzon,

IN RECENT NEWS

RANSOM IN IRAQ

The Philippines, like other world nations, joined the US-led operation in Iraq. But when Iraqi dissidents kidnapped Angelo de la Cruz, a Filipino truck driver, in early July 2004, the Philippines military pulled out of Iraq early. Partly in the hope of saving de la Cruz's life, 51 Philippine troops left Iraq in July 2004 instead of August. This decision was the first of its kind.

While other nations have had their nationals kidnapped or killed during the fighting in Iraq (including Italy, South Korea, Bulgaria, and the US), none have so far agreed to accommodate the demands of the hostage-takers. Iraq's provisional government advises countries in the Philippines's situation not to negotiate with kidnappers, and the Philippine decision to do the exact opposite has caused some criticism. In this case, grabbing a foreigner off the streets of Baghdad and threatening to behead him was successful—the Philippines radically changed its Iraq policy.

In the Philippines itself, however, the debate over de la Cruz's fate did not focus on such broad issues or ideological doctrines. Instead, the discussion was extremely personal, with the local media focusing on the plight of his wife and eight children. News cameras documented their ordeal in agonizing detail, following the family's tense vigil in front of their television set, and watching the

Mindanao, and parts of Palawan; nearly 2,000,000 travelers journey to the Philippines each year and have safe, enjoyable trips.

THE SECOND FRONT OF THE US WAR ON TERROR. In the wake of the **September 11, 2001** attacks on the World Trade Center in New York City, the US has stepped up its offensive against international terrorist organizations. Despite postcolonial political sensitivities, the Philippines has been the site of the largest US troop deployment after Afghanistan in the Bush administration's **War on Terror.** These troops are meant to train Filipino soldiers to fight against ASG forces in Mindanao, and to prepare Filipino defense forces for UN peacekeeping missions. Officials in Manila, however, fear a broadening role of US troops in the Philippines. US Defense Secretary **Donald Rumsfeld** has expressed qualms about the participation of US troops in joint jungle patrols, hinting that putting Army Special Forces at such a risk demands a valid justification, and warning that such a commitment would probably bind the US to a protracted military role in Mindanao.

CUSTOMS AND ETIQUETTE

TABOOS. Pointing at or beckoning to someone by wiggling the index finger is considered rude; the accepted way to motion for someone to approach is to extend your arm with the palm facing down and make a scratching motion with your fingers. Because of the prevalence of Catholicism in the Philippines, it is considered impolite to swear with religious words. In general, avoid conversations on the touchy topics of politics, religion, corruption, and foreign aid. If ever truly at a loss for words, remember that Filipinos particularly enjoy discussing their families.

PUBLIC BEHAVIOR. Philippine values emphasize optimism, politeness, and respect. It is common to show even street beggars dignified respect with the phrase, *"Patawarin po,"* which means "Forgive me, sir." Filipinos are relatively conservative in social settings; while holding hands is acceptable, any other public displays of affection (including informal physical contact) are not. Social etiquette encourages a *laissez-faire* attitude, so show up about 20min. later than the appointed time, except for business transactions. Additionally, the concept of "losing face" is prevalent in the Philippines, so be sure to allow Filipinos a way out of an awkward situation.

clock as deadline after deadline passed and rumors of both his death and his release continued to mount. Protests in Manila and other cities took issue with the fighting in Iraq, but much of the attention remained focused on Cruz himself.

In many ways, the situation sheds light on the Philippines's unique position, and unique needs, when it comes to handling matters of foreign policy. de la Cruz is a temporary expatriate sending money back to his family. One in 10 Filipinos has worked or is working abroad, which means that almost everyone in the country knows someone like de la Cruz. Filipino crews man a good deal of the world's cargo ships, and their labor has helped build the modern face of the Middle East's oil states. Most Filipinos abroad work as nurses, construction workers, sales clerks, and in hundreds of other service positions; when they come back to the Philippines, they become the *Balikbayan,* or "those who return home." In large part, the Philippine troops left Iraq because the government can't afford to look weak when it comes to protecting its nationals—for them, writing off de la Cruz would be a short step away from writing off a tenth of the country, along with their families. Whether or not terrorists were appeased as a result, it seems that de la Cruz's freedom was a gesture of putting nationals first—a strong, affirmative message from the Philippine government.

TABLE MANNERS. Food is an important part of most social gatherings and engagements in the Philippines. Filipinos usually eat with a fork in the right hand and a spoon in the left. Slurping soup is a sign that you enjoy the taste, but leaving something on your plate after you have finished eating indicates that you did not enjoy the meal. To get a waiter's attention, raise your hand and draw a square in the air. Drawing a larger square indicates that you want to see a menu.

LEAN, MEAN PHILIPPINE CUISINE. Experimenting with Philippine cuisine is hit-or-miss. Taking the phrase "fusion cuisine" to a whole new level, food in the Philippines eschews the chilli peppers used in other Southeast Asian cuisines for more salty and sour flavors.

Adobo: A derivative of a Spanish dish made with chicken, pork, seafood, or vegetables stewed in vinegar, soy sauce, garlic, peppercorns, and bay leaf.

Lumpia: Local spring rolls filled with vegetables and meat are served with vinegar, soy sauce, and sweet sauce.

Sinigang: A sour soup made with tamarine leaves or unripe guavas.

Kinilaw: An unusually versatile dish that uses any meat or vegetable as a base ingredient, which is then "cooked" in a flavorful vinegar.

Lechon: A roast suckling pig served primarily on festive occasions in a sauce made of liver, vinegar, sugar, and seasonings.

Bistek: A Filipinized beef steak.

Halo-Halo: A fanciful creation with layers of preserved fruit, gelatin, custard, crushed ice, and ice cream.

Tuba: A local wine made with the sap of the coconut tree.

ARTS AND RECREATION

Philippine artistic traditions are particularly dynamic, and have been influenced by those of several other cultures. Visitors will find elements of Spanish, Moorish, Chinese, and American traditions incorporated into indigenous Filipino folk traditions. The result of this intermingling is today considered to be "the Philippine arts." Recently, there has been a push to bring the artistic traditions of isolated ethnic groups to light.

ARCHITECTURE. Like most of its other cultural traditions, Philippine architecture has absorbed international elements while managing to retain a distinctively Filipino feel. Under Spanish colonialism came European religious and military architecture; the *Intromuros* in Manila (p. 552) is a fantastic example of this unique blending. Today, **Bobby Manosa** and the late **Leandro V. Locsin** are the major figures in the world of Philippine architecture, with designs that stress the somewhat unlikely melding of the folk and postmodern aesthetics. Manosa in particular has championed the use of Filipino materials like bamboo, and has even helped foment the use of "plyboo"—bamboo plywood with a distinctive look and feel.

DANCE. The quintessential **barrio** dance is the mesmerizing **tinikling,** the national dance. Performers beat pairs of long bamboo sticks against the ground in steady rhythm, as couples skip and twirl in and out of the sticks. Another dance tradition comes from the Muslim areas of the Philippines, where dances are characterized by their theatricality. In the **Langka-batuang,** men act like angry monkeys, scuttling about and nimbly climbing poles propped up by other dancers. To this day, royal princesses in the Sulu archipelago are required to learn the noble **Singkil** dance, which dramatizes a legend of the Maranao people of Mindanao.

FILM. Introduced to the Philippines in the early 20th century, film has become an important medium for artists to respond to social, political, educational, and economic conditions. The world's third-largest film producer after India and China, the Philippines is one of the few nations whose domestic film industry can stand up to Hollywood in the box office; most local films, however, are of the sentimental or violent variety. **Yam Llaranas** and **Erik Matti** are touted as the country's most impressive filmmakers. Annual Filipino, French, and gay film festivals liven the scene in Malaysia.

LITERATURE. Though artistically hindered under Spanish rule, the Filipino *ilustrados* continued to write about their discontent with revolutionary results. After being exiled from Spain, many of them began writing in Tagalog to increase their mass appeal. The period of American cultural infiltration was a low point for Philippine literature. Written in English, it merely imitated the American greats; written in Spanish, it echoed trite nationalism; written in Tagalog, it found refuge in self-pity. The Marcos era brought little relief for the floundering literary tradition—reading or writing "subversive" literature meant indefinite imprisonment. In recent years, however, Philippine literature seems to have begun a second renaissance. Writers **Tess Uriza Holthe** and **F. Sionil Jose** have set about to revive the Filipino voice in writing, setting high standards for contemporary Filipino fiction.

MARTIAL ARTS. Refined over many centuries, Filipino martial arts stress efficiency and pragmatism. Different techniques have evolved in the country's disparate regions, including open and closed hand forms, stick fighting, and blade fighting. Although Spanish colonists banned the blade-fighting **Arnis** school (a.k.a. **Kali** or **Eskrima**), it has reappeared in the graceful steps of many folk dance routines. Today, Filipino martial arts schools dot the globe; many law enforcement officials the world over are trained in Filipino martial arts because of their flexibility and effectiveness.

DIVE FACTS. The Philippines boasts some of the world's best diving. Below are just some of the treasures to look out for under the sea.

1. Seven of the eight known species of giant clams are found in the Philippines.
2. 488 of the 500 known species of coral in the world are found in the Philippines.
3. Of the eight known species of marine turtles, five are found in the Philippines.
4. The world's largest pearl was found in the waters off Palawan in 1934.
5. There are roughly 12,000 types of seashells found in the Philippines, including the Conus Gloriam—the most expensive in the world.

HOLIDAYS AND FESTIVALS (2005)

DATE	NAME AND LOCATION	DESCRIPTION
Jan. 9	Feast of the Black Nazarene (Manila's Quiapo District)	Thousands of devotees escort a life-size blackwood statue of Jesus.
Jan. 16-22	Ati-Atihan (Kalibo) Sinulog (Cebu City)	The Philippine equivalent of Mardi Gras.
Feb. 22-25	People Power Days	Thanksgiving for the 1986 overthrow of the Marcos regime.
Mar. 24	Holy Thursday	The day of the Last Supper when Jesus washed the feet of his disciples.

DATE	NAME AND LOCATION	DESCRIPTION
Mar. 25	Good Friday	Day of mourning for the crucifixion of Jesus.
Mar. 27	Easter	Commemorates Jesus's rising from the dead.
Jun. 12	Independence Day	Military parades in major cities.
Oct. 19	Masskara Festival (Bacolod)	Masked parade, with dancing and carnivals.
Nov. 30	Bonifacio Day	Remembrance for the nationalist Andres Bonifacio, who launched the Philippine Revolution.
Dec. 22	Giant Lantern Festival (San Fernand)	Lantern parade, in honor of la Nuestra Señora de Guia.
Dec. 25	Christmas Day	Commemorates the birth of Jesus Christ.
Dec. 30	Rizal Day	Remembrance for the nationalist martyr, Jose Rizal.

ADDITIONAL RESOURCES

GENERAL HISTORY

The Loves of Rizal and Other Essays on Philippine History, Art, and Public Policy, by Pably S Trillana, III (2000). An eloquent collection of essays that examines many Filipino institutions.

America's Boy: A Century of Colonialism in the Philippines, by James Hamilton-Paterson (1999). Ponders the scandalous reign of Ferdinand and Imelda Marcos, approaching the regime's history from a Filipino perspective.

Muslim Rulers and Rebels: Everyday Politics and Armed Separatism in the Southern Philippines (Comparative Studies on Muslim Societies, No. 26), by Thomas M. McKenna (1998). A probing look at Muslim separatist movements, in the context of Muslim-Catholic relations in the Philippines.

FICTION AND NON-FICTION

Nelson's Run, by Peter Bacho (2002). Political and sexual satire exposing the intricacies of corruption and the effects of colonialism.

Babylon: An Anthology of Filipina and Filipina American Writers, Ed. Nick Carbo, Eileen Tabios (2000). Outstanding collection of Filipina and Filipina-American writers.

The Tesseract, by Alex Garland (1999). A thrilling tale of the streets of Manila. From the author of *The Beach.*

Noli Me Tangere, by Jose Rizal (1886), trans. by Ma Soledad Locson-Locsin (1997). The most famous and influential nationalist novel written under Spanish colonialism.

ESSENTIALS

PHILIPPINES PRICE ICONS					
SYMBOL:	❶	❷	❸	❹	❺
ACCOMM.	Under US$2 Under P100	US$2-4 P100-200	US$4-7.75 P200-400	US$7.75-11.50 P400-600	Over US$11.50 Over P600
FOOD	Under US$1 Under P50	US$1-2 P50-100	US$2-4 P100-200	US$4-5.75 P200-300	Over US$5.75 Over P300

EMBASSIES AND CONSULATES

PHILIPPINE CONSULAR SERVICES ABROAD

Australia: Embassy, 1 Moonah Pl., Yarralumla, Canberra, ACT 2600; mailing address: P.O. Box 3297, Manuka ACT 2603 (☎61-2 6273 2535; www.philembassy.au.com). **Consulates,** Sydney (☎61-2 9262 7377; www.sydneypcg.com/); Fortitude Valley (☎07 3252 8215; fax 07 3252 2840); Nightcliff (☎61-8 8922 4411; fax 61-8 8922 4440); Melbourne (☎/fax 03 9662 9702; phconsul@austarmetro.com.au); Canberra (☎ 61-2 6273 2535; fax 61-2 6273 3984).

Canada: Embassy, 130 Albert St. #606, Ottawa, ON K1P 5G4 (☎613-233-1121; http://members.rogers.com/embassyofphilippines/. Open 9am-noon and 1:30-5pm). **Consulates,** Toronto (☎416-922 7181; www.philcongen-toronto.com); Vancouver (☎604-685 7645, ext. 1619; www.vancouverpcg.net/).

New Zealand: Embassy, 50 Hobson St., Thorndon; P.O. Box 12-042, Wellington (☎04 472 9921; fax 00 644 472 5170).

UK: Embassy, 9A Palace Green, London W8 4QE (☎020 7937 1600).

US: Embassy, 1600 Massachusetts Ave. NW, Washington DC 20036 (☎202-467-9312; fax 202-466-6288; consular@philippinesembassy-usa.org). **Consulates,** New York (☎212-764-1330; www.pcgny.net); Chicago (☎312-332-6458); San Francisco (☎415-433-6666; phisf@aol.com); Los Angeles (☎213-639-0980; www.philcongenla.org).

CONSULAR SERVICES IN THE PHILIPPINES

Australia: Embassy, Level 23, Tower 2, RCBC Plaza, 6819 Ayala Ave., Makati City Manila (☎63-2 757 8100; www.australia.com.ph/).

Canada: Embassy, Levels 6-8, Tower 2, RCBC Plaza, 6819 Ayala Ave., Makati City, Manila (☎63-2 857-9001; fax 63-2 843-1082).

New Zealand: Embassy, 23rd fl., BPI Buendia Center, Sen Gil Puyat Ave.; near Makati Ave., Makati City, Manila (☎63-2 891 5358; fax 63-2 891 5357).

UK: Embassy, 15-17th fl., LV Locsin Bldg., 6752 Ayala Ave., Makati City, Manila (☎63-2 816-7116; fax 63-2 819 7206).

United States: Embassy, 1201 Roxas Blvd., Ermita 1000, Manila (☎ 63-2 52 6300; http://usembassy.state.gov/posts/rp1/wwwhmain.html).

TOURIST SERVICES

Philippines Department of Tourism: Philippines, Rm. 207 DIT Bldg. T.M. Kalaw St., Ermita, Manila (☎6-32 524 2345; www.tourism.gov.ph/). **Australia,** Tourism Information Officer, Level 1 Philippine Centre, 27-33 Wentworth Ave., Sydney NSW 2000 (☎02 9283 0711; pdotsydney@ozemail.com.au). **UK,** Embassy of the Philippines, Culture and Tourism Office, 146 Cromwell Rd., London SW7 4EF (☎ 44 20 7835 1100; tourism@pdot.co.uk). **US,** Philippine Center, 556 5th Ave., New York, NY 10036 (☎212-575-7915; fax 212-302-6759; pdotny@aol.com).

DOCUMENTS AND FORMALITIES

Citizens of Australia, Canada, the European Union, UK, and US may enter without visas and stay for 21 days, but must have proof of onward travel (plane or boat ticket) in order to board any plane to the Philippines. To avoid buying a ticket on the spot at the airport, travelers can purchase visas before they arrive. For longer

JOHN ABUL, MANILA BAKLA

Homosexuals are far more open and readily accepted in the Philippines than in other parts of Southeast Asia. The bakla, *as gay men are known, are considered arbiters of fashion, glamour, and humor.* Let's Go *sat down with clothing designer John Abul after a gay book opening in Manila to discuss the intersection of Philippine culture and sexuality:*

LG: Is homosexuality accepted in the Philippines?
A: In so many words, yes. [Filipinos] would rather not confront reality, but [homosexuality] has been around here for ages—even before the Spanish came.

LG: Would a *bakla* be accepted in a small town?
A: Oh, yes. If you go to the southernmost tip of this country, you'd see a parlor with a *bakla* in it... And at the northernmost part of the country... you'd see a parlor or a designer or a choreographer. Even [on] the highest mountain, you'd see a gay person here. You'd be surprised. I climb mountains, and I see them all over the place... within the minority groups—the indigenous groups...

LG: What about poor people and the *bakla*?
A: The poorer families... would rather have a *bakla* kid because he's a potential money-earner.

LG: How so?
A: [The *bakla* could] be an entertainer in Japan or even in this country in sing-along bars or

stays, obtain a 59-day visa beforehand (single-entry visas US$35; multiple-entry US$50) or get an **extension** from the immigration office (P510). Extensions for longer stays require approval from the government, which can take three weeks or more; express service is usually available for P500. Alternatively, travelers can pay a fee at the airport before departure, for each day they have outstayed their visa.

MONEY

CURRENCY CONVERTER

The currency chart below is based on August 2004 exchange rates between local currency and Australian dollars (AUS$), Canadian dollars (CDN$), European Union euros (EUR€), New Zealand dollars (NZ$), British pounds (UK£), and US dollars (US$). Check the currency converter on websites like www.xe.com or www.bloomberg.com or a large newspaper for the latest exchange rates.

CURRENCY (P)		
	AUS$1 = P28.36	P100 = AUS$3.53
	CDN$1 = P33.25	P100 = CDN$3.01
	EUR€1 = P50.92	P100 = EUR€1.96
	NZ$1 = P24.33	P100 = NZ$4.11
	UK£1 = P80.84	P100 = UK£1.24
	US$1 = P51.85	P100 = US$1.93

The Philippine **peso (P)** is divided into 100 **centavos.** In the text, the peso is denoted with "P," as in P45. Bills come in denominations of P5, 10, 20, 50, 100, 500, and 1000. Coins come in 1, 5, 10, and 25 centavos and P1, 2, and 5. Fares for taxis should be rounded up for a tip of P5-10. **ATMs** abound in most cities.

GETTING THERE

BY PLANE. The Philippines has two **international airports: Mactan Cebu International Airport** in Cebu (p. 585) and **Nino Aquino International Airport** in Manila (p. 543). **Philippine Airlines** (**PAL;** www.philippineair.com) operates international flights from dozens of countries.

GETTING AROUND

BY PLANE. Air travel is a godsend for island-hoppers in the Philippines. Multi-day land and sea journeys are shrunk down to 1-2hr. plane rides. PAL is the national airline, but competitors include **Air Philippines** (☎02-855 9000; www.philippineairlines.com/), which has some of the best student rates, **Asian Spirit** (☎02-851 8888; www.asianspirit.com), **Cebu Pacific** (☎02-632 7026; www.cebupacificair.com./), **Mindanao Express** (☎62-991 8739; www.jetlink.com.ph/~zambo/mindex.htm), **Seair** (☎02-851 5555; www.flyseair.com/), and **Philippine Airlines** (☎02-855 8888; www.philippineairlines.com/).

BY BUS AND JEEPNEY. A slew of competing bus companies, like **Autobus** and **BLTB,** service Luzon, with a few epic 45hr. journeys. "Ordinary" buses are hot and stuffy, while first-class and "premier" or "aircon" buses have A/C and more room; however, these upscale buses often don't depart until full. Jeepneys also offer cheap, convenient transportation.

BY BOAT. Ferry travel is a cheap (but sometimes dangerous) means of traversing the seas; many fatal ferry wrecks occur every year, and pirates have emerged as a recent threat to sea-travelers' safety. Regulation is improving steadily, and faster, safer catamarans now ply many popular routes; most are equipped with radar and night-vision equipment. Inter-island shipping schedules are published in daily newspapers. Journey times to the same destination vary significantly between different carriers. Check out WG&A Ferries (☎632 528 7979; www.wgasuperferry.com/) for information from one of the more reliable companies.

HEALTH AND SAFETY

EMERGENCY NUMBERS:
Police: ☎166. **Ambulance:** ☎117.

MEDICAL EMERGENCIES. Pharmacies and medical centers can be found in most major cities in the Philippines. When traveling in rural areas, be sure to have a supply of your medications, and know the location of the nearest hospital (sometimes on another island). If you need extensive medical care, check into a private hospital if possible (state-run hospitals often offer flawed and inferior service).

HEALTH RISKS. The rainy season the Philippines provides perfect conditions for a mosquito heaven. Recent outbreaks of mosquito-borne **Dengue fever** and the ever-looming threat of **malaria** make it more important than ever to avoid getting bitten. Wear a

beauty contests...

LG: Besides entertainment, what are some other common occupations for *bakla*?

A: Politicians. A lot of them.

LG: What about *baklas* and the beauty industry?

A: It's dominated by gay men. All of them are there.

LG: How does the gay life in the Philippines compare to gay life in other countries?

A: Here, I think there's more freedom [than in] other Asian countries. We're not a Muslim country. There's no one religion. Though we're predominantly Christian, Filipinos are, by nature, tolerant.

LG: Would you be comfortable being gay in, say, Malaysia?

A: You kidding? They'd kill me right there in the airport.

LG: You don't experience much discrimination here?

A: Luckily, no. I guess it's how you conduct yourself. At first, they might say, "Oh, he's a *bakla*...he's gay!" But if you project yourself properly like any other person, they would take you in.

LG: Are there different types of *baklas*?

A: Oh yes. From A to Z. The BPS—meaning "Beauty Parlor Swarthe"—they're the ones who look like they had a bad hair day.

LG: How do you classify yourself?

A: I'm regular on a daily basis, but at parties, I'm not. I did Rocky Horror Picture Show as Dr. Frankenfurter. I go in drag every now and then, just to shock people...

strong insect repellent and consider covering up arms and legs in areas where mosquitoes reign supreme. Travelers to Palawan should strongly consider getting malaria prophylaxis. **Rabies** is still fairly common in the north and south, so seek medical attention promptly if bitten or scratched by an animal. The usual rules concerning water apply: avoid drinking from lakes and streams, and when in doubt about the local water supply, drink purified or bottled water. Note that in the rural south, even swimming in some lakes and rivers means flirting with insidious **bacteria** and **parasites.** To avoid an extremely unpleasant gastronomical nightmare, exercise careful judgment. Be sure to have a note from your physician to explain any prescription drugs you may be carrying. Check the weather often, especially in the wet season; be sure to have a sweater in case a **typhoon** hits.

GBLT TRAVELERS. Homosexuality, far more accepted for men and women in the Philippines than in other parts of Southeast Asia, takes a unique form in Filipino communities. Gay men, known as *bakla*, consider themselves men with the souls of women and are attracted more to heterosexual men than other gay men. The *bakla* occupy a well-accepted niche within Philippine society, though many *bakla* fear being trivialized as superficial and appearance-obsessed. Travelers to the Philippines will have no trouble finding bars, clubs, and beaches that cater to a mixed crowd.

KEEPING IN TOUCH

The Philippine *Poste Restante* system is unreliable at best, even in the country's most sophisticated cities; use American Express mail holding service instead. Mail usually reaches Manila from the west in 5-10 days, but it takes a few more days to snake its way through the islands. For **telephone calls,** a number of public calling offices handle domestic and international communication. The **Philippines Long Distance Telephone Company (PLDT)** is most prevalent, but **RCPI/Bayantel, Islacom,** and a few smaller companies pick up the slack in more remote areas. When using PLDT, dial 105-11 before the number. Unfortunately, not all public calling offices allow phone card calls. PLDT has phone cards which can be used for international or domestic calls, but coin-operated payphones are still commonplace. A few resort areas still lack phone service, but cell phones keep the lines of communication open for reservations. For **Home Country Direct (HCD)** numbers from the Philippines, refer to the table on the inside back cover of this book. The Philippines is **8hr. ahead of GMT. Internet** access is found often, but is by no means everywhere.

LUZON

Home to half of the country's population, the island of Luzon extends north from Manila's sprawl, crisscossed by teeth-shattering rural roads. The Cordillera mountains peer out over Banaue's rice terraces—the world's eighth natural wonder. Gigantic stone staircases climb skyward, carpeted with emerald puffs of rice seedlings. Leisurely treks grant glimpses of indigenous traditions, and Pangasinan's Hundred Islands Park provides a taste of Filipino beaches. Nearby Baguio entertains a thriving student and artist community. While Legazpi's Mayon Volcano may be the hottest of Luzon's hot spots, the scene in Manila is no doubt the feistiest.

MANILA

☎2

In spite of a modern transit system and huge shopping malls, Manila's poverty is evident on the streets. Traffic—in a constant jam—includes honking jeepneys, neighing horses, and screaming men on tricycles. Street children line the sidewalks where vendors pitch cigarettes, fruits, and trinkets. Police guard the entry to nearly every restaurant and ATM to fend off the omnipresent threat of thieves, pickpockets, and hooligans. But despite the unmistakable poverty and pollution, Manila retains an energy that borders on exhausting. Visitors brave enough to battle the city's heat and noise will admire the well-preserved 16th-century Spanish colonial architecture of Intramuros and the beautifully landscaped parks. For all its vices, this city leaves its guests tired and frustrated, but eager to return.

! A combination of economic stagnation and rising unemployment has led many impoverished locals into a life of crime. Tourists are especially vulnerable and advised to take precaution, particularly in heavily visited areas. Aside from pickpockets, travelers should be wary of overly friendly locals who offer to buy them drinks or take them home to meet friends or discuss business deals. Several visitors have been robbed in recent years after ingesting drugs in their drinks or following a new acquaintance into an unfamiliar area. Taxi drivers and horse-drawn carriage operators have also been known to overcharge tourists; make sure to check rates with hotel staff or local police to avoid getting fleeced.

INTERCITY TRANSPORTATION

BY PLANE. Manila has separate international and domestic airports. International flights arrive at **Ninoy Aquino International Airport** (Dept. of Tourism ☎877 1109, international flight info 877 1200), off Ninoy Aquino Ave. in Parañaque, 9km south of Rizal Park. Banks in the arrivals hall change currency at poor rates, but ATMs near the car rental booths offer a fair alternative (Cirrus/MC/NYCE/V). Domestic flights arrive at **Manila Domestic Airport** (☎871 0000), off Domestic Rd. in Parañaque. The international departure tax is P550; domestic P100.

Taxis run between NAIA and Manila Domestic Airport (P85-90). Philippine Airline (PAL) passengers can take the **free shuttle** between terminals. Brave travelers can venture out to Ninoy Aquino Ave., where **jeepneys** and **buses** are available. Jeepneys head along Domestic Rd. to **Baclaran Market** and Manila Domestic Airport ("Baclaran-MIA" route, P4). To get to Manila from the market, take the **Light Rail Transit** (**LRT;** P12) or a "Sucat-Hwy." or "New MIA" jeepney. Jeepneys may charge extra for large baggage. Buses bound for **Fairview, Monumento,** or **Santa Cruz** pass by Ermita and Malate Districts along Taft Ave. (P17). Relatively inexpensive taxis are a better option for first-time visitors. To avoid being ripped off by pushy taxi drivers, head to the Philippine Tourism Authority booth in the arrivals hall for a **coupon taxi,** which will take you into **Metro Manila** (P150).

DESTINATION	FREQUENCY	PRICE	DESTINATION	FREQUENCY	PRICE
Bangkok	5 per week	US$638	**Jakarta**	4 per week	US$867
Bacolod	2 per day	P2343	**Kuala Lampur**	3 per week	US$801
Cebu	13-14 per day	P1736-2183	**Legazpi**	1 per day	P1611
Hồ Chí Minh City	3 per week	US$528	**Puerto Princesa**	2 per day	P2071
Hong Kong	4 per day	US$421	**Singapore**	1 per day	US$801
Iloilo	3 per day	P2342	**Tacloban**	3 per day	P2298

Most airlines have offices in the Makati Business District, though many have branches closer to Ermita and Malate. Major **international airlines** that serve Manila are: **Cathay Pacific,** 2nd fl., Tetra Global Bldg., 1616 Dr. Vasquez St., Pedro Gil, Ermita (☎848 2701); **Malaysia Airlines,** ground fl., Legazpi Towers, 300, Roxas Blvd. (☎525 9404); **Philippine Airlines,** 540 P. Faura St., Cov. Adriatico St., Ermita (☎855 8888); **Royal Brunei,** 7 Saville Bldg. (☎897 3309), at the corner of Gil Puyat Ave. and Paseo de Roxas St., Makati City; **Singapore Airlines,** 138 H.V. de la Costa St., Salcedo Village, Makati City (☎810 4951); **Thai Airways,** Escolta Twin Towers, 288 Escolta St., Paco (☎243 2645). Major **domestic airlines** that serve Manila are: **Air Philippines,** 15th fl., Multinational Bank Corporation Center, 6805 Ayala Ave., Makati (☎843 7770); **Asian Spirit,** ground fl., LPL Towers, 112 Legazpi St., Legazpi Village, Makati (☎840 3811); **Cebu Pacific,** Manila Midtown Hotel (☎636 4938), on the corner of Adriatico St. and Pedro Gil, Ermita; **PAL,** S&L Bldg. (☎521 8821, 24hr. info 816 6691), on Roxas Blvd., Ermita; **South East Asian Airlines (SEAIR)** 2nd fl., Doña Conception Bldg., 1020 Arnaiz Ave., Makati City (☎884 1521).

BY BUS. Buses are the main mode of transport in Luzon since the region is only comprised of one major island. In general, buses are safe (even at night), clean, and air conditioned (the non-A/C option is increasingly limited). Buses heading **north** leave from terminals clustered around **Epifanio de los Santos Ave. (EDSA)** in the Cubao District, accessible by a Cubao-bound jeepney or bus. Buses headed **south** leave from terminals along EDSA in Pasay City (LRT: EDSA), or from the station at Taft Ave. and Sen. Gil Puyat Ave., listed on placards as **"LRT: Taft/ Buendia" (LRT: Gil Puyat).** Call for schedules and specific prices. Major transit companies include: **Autobus** (☎ 735 8098), at the corner of Dimasalang and Laong-Laan St., Sampaloc; **Jam Transit** (☎831 4390), at the corner of Taft Ave. and Gil Puyat, Pasay City; **Dagupan Bus** (☎727 2287), at the corner of EDSA and New York St., Cubao, Quezon City; **Dangwa Tranco** (☎410 1991), at the corner of Aurora Blvd. and Driod St., Cubao, Quezon City; **Partas** (☎724 9820), at the corner of Aurora Blvd. and Arayat, Cubao, Quezon City; **Philippine Rabbit**, Santa Cruz Terminal (☎734 9836), at the corner of 819 Oroquieta St. and C.M. Recto; also at Quezon Terminal, 1240 EDSA (☎456 7659); **Philtranco** (☎832 2456), at the corner of EDSA and Apelo Cruz St., Pasay City; **Victory Liner,** Caloocan Terminal (☎361 1506), on Grays Park Ave.; also at Cubao Terminal (☎833 0293), 853 Immaculate Conception Rd. along EDSA, and Pasay City Terminal, 561 EDSA (☎727 4268). Bring a blanket on overnight A/C bus rides.

BY TRAIN. The **Philippine National Railway** (☎254 9772) runs between Manila and **Legazpi City** (from Tayuman Station: 8hr., daily 4pm, P179-234; from Blumentritt Station: daily 7:40pm, with A/C P234). Antiquated cars and slow speed make this government-backed operation a last resort for travelers.

DESTINATION	DURATION/ FREQUENCY	PRICE	DESTINATION	DURATION/ FREQUENCY	PRICE
Baguio	6½hr., 21 per day	P240	**Santa Cruz**	2hr., 25 per day	P78
Banaue	9hr., 2 per day	P257	**San Fernando**	8hr., 24 per day	P200
Batangas City	30min., 20 per day	P70	**Tagaytay**	1½hr., 15 per day	P78
Legazpi	12hr., 15 per day	P 433	**Vigan**	9hr., 20 per day	P321

BY BOAT

North Harbor District: In the North Port District on Marcos Rd., north of the Pasig River, accessible by taxi from Ermita (P65) or "North Harbor" jeepneys from Divisoria Market. **WG&A Lines,** Pier 4 and 14, North Harbor (☎528 7000) sends boats to: **Catbalogan,**

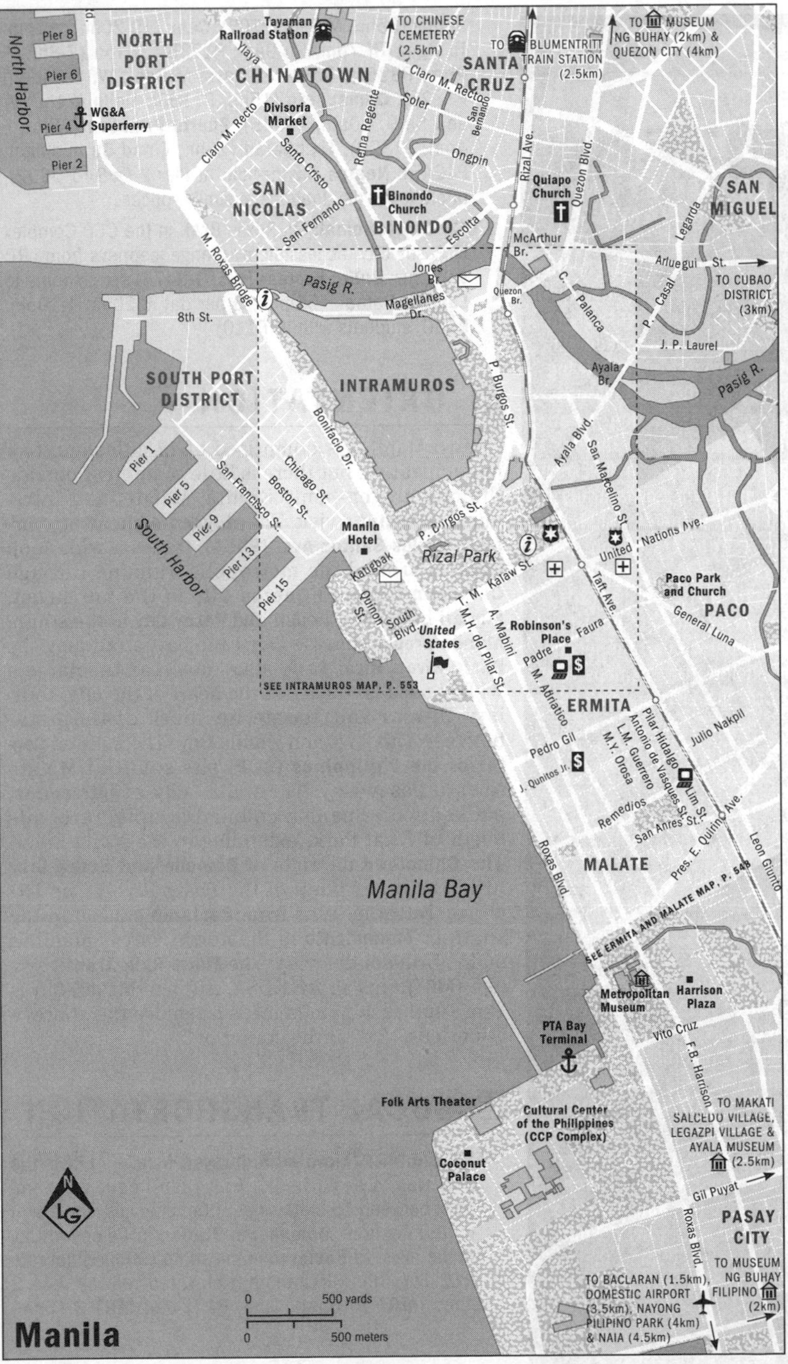
Manila
North Harbor
Pier 8
Pier 6
Pier 4
Pier 2
NORTH PORT DISTRICT
WG&A Superferry
Tayaman Railroad Station
TO CHINESE CEMETERY (2.5km)
TO BLUMENTRITT TRAIN STATION (2.5km)
TO MUSEUM NG BUHAY (2km) & QUEZON CITY (4km)
CHINATOWN
SANTA CRUZ
Ylaya
Claro M. Recto
Soler
Divisoria Market
Reina Regente
San Bernardo
Ongpin
Rizal Ave.
Quezon Blvd.
Santo Cristo
SAN NICOLAS
San Fernando
Binondo Church
BINONDO
Escolta
Quiapo Church
McArthur Br.
SAN MIGUEL
Legarda
Arluegui St.
TO CUBAO DISTRICT (3km)
M. Roxas Bridge
Jones Br.
Pasig R.
Magellanes Dr.
Quezon Br.
C. Palanca
P. Casal
J. P. Laurel
8th St.
SOUTH PORT DISTRICT
INTRAMUROS
P. Burgos St.
Ayala Br.
Ayala Blvd.
San Marcelino St.
Bonifacio Dr.
Pier 1
Pier 5
Pier 9
Pier 13
Pier 15
San Francisco St.
Chicago St.
Boston St.
South Harbor
Manila Hotel
P. Burgos St.
Rizal Park
United Nations Ave.
Katigbak
T. M. Kalaw St.
Taft Ave.
Paco Park and Church
PACO
General Luna
Quirino St.
South Blvd.
United States
M.H. del Pilar St.
A. Mabini
Robinson's Place
Padre Faura
M. Adriatico
SEE INTRAMUROS MAP, P. 553
ERMITA
Pedro Gil
J. Qunitos Jr.
Pilar Hidalgo Lim St.
Antonio de Vasques St.
L.M. Guerrero
M.Y. Orosa
Julio Nakpil
Remedios
San Anres St.
Pres. E. Quirino Ave.
Leon Giunto
Roxas Blvd.
MALATE
Manila Bay
SEE ERMITA AND MALATE MAP, P. 548
Metropolitan Museum
Harrison Plaza
Vito Cruz
F.B. Harrison
PTA Bay Terminal
Folk Arts Theater
Cultural Center of the Philippines (CCP Complex)
TO MAKATI SALCEDO VILLAGE, LEGAZPI VILLAGE & AYALA MUSEUM (2.5km)
Coconut Palace
Gil Puyat
PASAY CITY
Roxas Blvd.
TO MUSEUM NG BUHAY FILIPINO (2km)
TO BACLARAN (1.5km), DOMESTIC AIRPORT (3.5km), NAYONG PILIPINO PARK (4km) & NAIA (4.5km)
0 500 yards
0 500 meters
N
LG

Samar (25hr., M 9am, P705); **Cebu** (19-20hr.; M 7pm, Tu 3pm, Th 7pm, Su 9am; P1235); **Coron** (7-8hr., F 4pm, P825); **Davao** (2 days; M 9am, W, Sa noon; P1825); **Dumaguete** (15hr., P1185); **Iloilo** (21hr.; W and Sa 9, 10am; P1245); **Puerto Princesa** (28hr., F 4pm, P1320); **Tagbilaran** (28hr.; F and Su midnight; P1245). **Negros Navigation**, at Pier 2 (☎245 0602), offers fewer destinations at similar prices.

CCP Bay Terminal: On Roxas Blvd. in the CCP Complex in Pasay City, accessible by orange jeepneys from LRT: Vito Cruz. **Bullet Express** (☎551 0476) sends boats to **Lamao,** Bataan (55min.; 5 per day 6:20am-4:30pm; P130, students with ID P110).

ORIENTATION

"Metro Manila" is comprised of 12 cities and five municipalities, but there is little of interest outside the city center—only Ermita, Malate, and Intramuros warrant a visit. The clogged main artery, **Epifanio de los Santos Ave. (EDSA),** traces a wide loop (24km) around the metropolis, running through **Caloocan City** and **Quezon City** in the northeast, **Makati** in the southeast, and **Pasay City** in the south. **Manila proper** sprawls along the bay, straddling the **Pasig River. Rizal Park,** also known as **Luneta,** is a widely-used landmark in the heart of the city; touristy Ermita and Malate lie south of the park, between Taft Ave. and Manila Bay. The **Cultural Center of the Philippines (CCP)** sits south of Malate toward Pasay City. The walled city of **Intramuros,** packed with Spanish colonial architecture, sits north of Rizal Park, extending to the Pasig River. The **Chinatown** districts of **Binondo** and **Santa Cruz** form the other bank of the Pasig River. The **LRT** above Taft Ave. runs from **Baclaran** station in the south to **Monumento** in the north; Taft is Manila's main north-south artery. The **Metro Rails Transit** system **(MRT)** runs above EDSA. Affluent **Makati City** is 7km southeast. Manila maps often use the abbreviation "cor." for "at the corner of."

LOCAL TRANSPORTATION

LRT and MRT (Elevated Railways): Manila's LRT is the only way to avoid traffic. Trains run frequently 5am-9pm between 15 stations at 800m intervals. The 15km route runs from **Monumento Station** in Caloocan City in the north to **Baclaran** in the south (30min., flat rate P12-15). The MRT, another elevated railway, has 2 lines: **MRT 1** (6am-11pm, P12) and **MRT 3** (6am-

A JEEPNEY BY ANY OTHER NAME

I arrived in Manila with the confidence of a seasoned road warrior. I had traveled extensively in the developing world, encountering almost every form of moving vehicle that could possibly pass as public transportation. I had ridden in Senegal's *car rapides,* Ghana's *tros-tros,* and East Africa's *mutatus.* So naturally I thought I was prepared to handle the close quarters of Filipino jeepneys.

Map in hand, I casually inquired at my hostel about the nearest jeepney route. The receptionist faltered. "Uh...perhaps you should try the LRT, ma'am? It's only 12 pesos." I prickled at the mention of the metro; a bevy of sources pegged jeepney fares at P7 per ride, and the budget-seeker in me was not about to lose 5 pesos for want of decent advice. I headed to the nearest major intersection and waited.

A glimpse of gaudy silver zoomed around the corner, paused for about two seconds while a man leapt off the back, and sped away like a crazed beetle. Before I could ask him about my route, two more jeepney hurtled past, threatening to flatten me. There was no room for the faint of heart in this system. I managed to flag down a woman hurrying past me and inquired about how to get to my destination. She smiled. "Stand there," she said, pointing to a spot near

11:30pm, P9.50-16). MRT 1 has 18 stops along Rizal and Taft Ave. MRT 3, a.k.a. **Metrostar,** passes through Makati City, Pasig City, and Cubao via EDSA Ave. The first few cars of each train are reserved for women.

Taxis: An affordable and comfortable way to get around, and an ideal stepping stone for new travelers not yet ready to brave the the chaotic jeepney circuits. Beware of taxis that charge exorbitant rates as set down in a farebook with the deceptive title "meters." Some taxi drivers also take longer routes than necessary; carry a map and get a sense of the city's layout before going for a ride. Taxis charge a base fare of P25 plus P2 for every 200m or 1½min. wait in traffic. Insist that drivers use their meters—if they refuse, they can be fined and, in some cases, lose their licenses. A ride from Ermita to Malate should run about P40. From Malate to Intramuros, a taxi should cost P80.

Jeepneys: The cheapest transportation in town, jeepneys follow set routes all over the city (1st 4km P6, P0.50 per additional km). A signboard declares destinations, and the route and fares are listed on the front. A useful route connects Ermita and Malate to **Baclaran Market** in Pasay City. Others run from Baclaran or LRT: Buendia (Gil Puyat Ave.) along Taft Ave. to **Quiapo, Santa Cruz,** and **Monumento,** north of the Pasig River. Jeepneys marked **Project 2** and **3** head for the **Quirino District, Project 4** go to **Cubao,** and **Project 6** and **8** head to the center of **Quezon City.** The Cubao jeepney are useful for reaching several **EDSA bus terminals,** while Baclaran and Taft Ave. jeepneys intercept a cluster of **Pasay City bus terminals.** Jeepneys with the same destinations can take entirely different routes with different stops, depending on where you catch them from. Don't be afraid to ask the driver or other passengers for directions to your destination, and, as always, be aware of your surroundings and property inside a jeepney. Often overcrowded, they are prime pickpocketing locations and can be unsafe at night.

Other Moving Objects: Pedi-cabs, small BMX bikes with sidecars, roam Ermita and Malate's back streets (P20-30). In Binondo, Divisoria, Intramuros, and Rizal Park, **calesas** (horse-drawn carriages) cruise the city (P40 per km; signboards post fixed rate for families in Intramuros). Eight-seater Toyota Tamaraw FX **"mega-taxis"** run along similar routes as the jeepneys and have A/C—a life-saver during Manila's severe traffic jams. (rides from P15). **Local buses** travel major thoroughfares, particularly Taft Ave. and EDSA (about P10 per 4km); these are slow and best avoided. Destinations are posted in the front windows. "Ayala" buses run along Taft Ave. to Ayala Ave. in Makati City (P14). **Tricycles** run in Caloocan City (P7 per 2 minutes).

the curb, "raise your arm, and try to read the signboard. If you can't, just shout your destination at each one that passes. One will eventually stop." Five minutes and numerous jeepneys later, I was still standing at the curb feeling defeated. It turns out that jeepneys were quite different from their African cousins in terms of pace. To board a jeepney, I realized, I would literally have to step into oncoming traffic, holler out my destination at the top of my lungs, and take a running jump if I planned to get anywhere.

Frighteningly, this course of action worked. I soon found myself safely tucked between two schoolchildren and their mother. I breathed a sigh of relief and saw the driver shoot me an amused smile as he darted the vehicle through pedicabs, carriages, and colossal inter-city buses.

"Are you also headed to Pasay City?" I inquired of the woman next to me. She laughed.

"Pasay, you say? Ma'am, you are going in the opposite direction."

My eyes widened in disbelief. "But the driver told me to get on when I shouted Pasay! It took me half an hour to catch this jeepney!"

"Perhaps," she said gently, "you should consider taking the LRT."

—Leila Chirayath

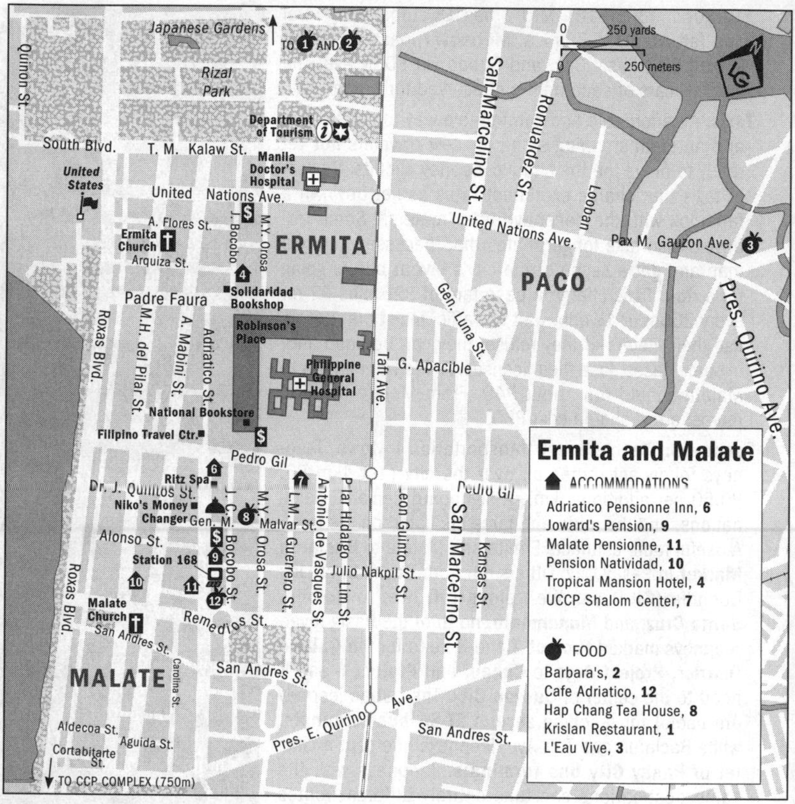

PRACTICAL INFORMATION

TOURIST AND FINANCIAL SERVICES

Tourist Offices: Head Office, #106, Dept. of Tourism Bldg., Teodoro Valencia Circle, T.M. Kalaw St., Ermita (☎525 2000), at the corner of Rizal Park near Taft Ave. and T.M. Kalaw St. LRT: UN Ave. Station. Free tourist map of the country plus street map of Manila. Open 7am-8pm. To reach **Airport Tourist Information,** head to the arrivals hall.

Intramuros Visitor's Center (IVC), (☎527 2961), inside Fort Santiago left of the main entrance, at the end of Gen. Luna St. Free Intramuros maps. Open daily 8am-5pm.

Travel and Tours: The Ermita and Malate areas have many travel agencies—make sure the agent you choose is accredited by the Dept. of Tourism. **Swagman Travel,** 411 A. Flores St., Ermita (☎524 5816), a well-established Aussie outfit with 15 outposts all over the Philippines, organizes local tours. Open M-F 8am-6pm. **Filipino Travel Center,** 1555 Adriatico St., Ermita (☎528 4504; www.filipinotravel.com.ph), at the corner of Pedro Gil, organizes city and day tours (P800-2400), as well as budget domestic and international packages. Open M-Sa 8am-6pm. AmEx/D/MC/V. **Aqua Travel and Tours,** Ste. #201, Manila Midtown Hotel, Pedro Gil St., Ermita (☎523 1989), specializes in scuba holidays. Open daily 9am-6pm.

Embassies: Australia, 23rd fl., RCBC Plaza, Tower 2, 6819 Ayala Ave., Makati (☎757 8100; www.australia.com.ph). Open M-F 8:30am-4:30pm. **Brunei,** 11th fl., Ayala Wing, BPI Bldg., at the corner of Ayala Ave. and Paseo de Roxas St. (☎816 2836). Open M-F 8am-4pm. **Canada,** 9-11th fl., Allied Bank Center, 6754 Ayala Ave., Makati (☎857 9000). Open M-Th 9-11:30am and 1-3pm, F 9am-1pm. **Indonesia,** 185 Salcedo St., Legaspi Village, Makati (☎892 5061). Open M-F 8:30am-5pm. **Ireland,** 3rd fl., Max's Restaurant, 70 Jupiter St., Bel-Air I, Makati (☎896 4668). Open M-F 9am-4pm. **Laos,** 34 Lapu-Lapu St., St. Magallanes Village, Makati (☎852 5759). Open M-F 8:30am-4:30pm. **Malaysia,** 107 Tordesillas St., Salcedo Village, Makati (☎817 4581). Open M-F 9am-noon. **Myanmar,** 8th fl., Xanland Center, 152 Amorsolo St., Legaspi Village, Makati (☎817 2373). Open M-F 9am-4:30pm. **New Zealand,** 23rd fl., Far East Bank Center, Sen. Gil Puyat Ave. near Makati Ave., Makati (☎891 5358). Open M-F 8:30am-12:30pm and 1:30-4:30pm. **Singapore,** 35th fl., Enterprise Tower 1, Ayala Ave. (☎751 2345). Open M-F 8:30am-5pm. **Thailand,** 107 Rada St., Legaspi Village, Makati (☎815 4219). Open M-F 9am-5pm. **UK,** 15-17th fl., L.V. Locsin Bldg., at the corner of Ayala and Makati Ave., Makati (☎816 7116). Open M-Th 8am-4:30pm, F 8am-2pm. **US,** 1201 Roxas Blvd. (☎523 1001). Open M-F 7:30am-4:30pm. **Vietnam,** 554 Vito Cruz St., Malate (☎524 0364). Open M-F 8:30am-5pm

Currency Exchange: Adriatico St. in Ermita and Malate is rife with late-night money-changers and 24hr. **ATMs. Niko's,** 1647 M. Adriatico St., Malate (☎522 5434) exchanges traveler's checks at lower rates than cash. Open daily 7am-11pm. **Equitable PCI Bank,** EBC Bldg., at the corner of J. Bocobo St. and UN Ave., Ermita (☎524 9661). Branches throughout the city. MC/V cash advances. 24hr. **ATM.** Open M-F 9am-4pm.

American Express: 1810 Mabini St. (☎524 8681), at the corner with Remedios St., Malate. Mail held for free. Open M-F 8:30am-4pm, Sa 9am-noon.

LOCAL SERVICES

Bookstores: National Book Store, Robinson's Mall, Pedro Gil St., Ermita (☎733 8265). English books, Filipinana section, maps, and travel guides. Metro Manila street map P80. Open daily 10am-9pm. **Solidaridad Bookshop,** 531 Padre Faura St., Ermita (☎523 0870). Owned by F. Sionil "Frankie" Jose, one of the Philippines's foremost contemporary novelists. *International Herald Tribune* and *Financial Times* delivered by 5:30pm. Open M-Sa 9am-6pm.

Women's Resources: Women in Travel Club, c/o Philippine Airlines, S&L Bldg., 1500 Roxas Blvd., Manila (☎525 5420). Info on safety and discounts.

Gay and Lesbian Resources: Library Foundation, 1066 Remedios St., coordinates gay activities in the capital. Ask at **The Library Bar,** 1779 Adriatico St. (see **Entertainment: Bars and Cafes,** p. 555). **Womyn Supporting Womyn Center (WSWC),** 43-44 University of the Philippines Shopping Center, U.P. Diliman, Quezon City (☎522 2484). Lesbian info service.

EMERGENCY AND COMMUNICATIONS

Emergency: ☎166.

Police: Western District Police (☎523 8391). Smaller police **branch** on the corner of UN Ave. and San Marcelino St., east of Taft Ave.

Tourist Police: Dept. of Tourism Bldg., #112, Teodoro Valencia Circle, T.M. Kalaw St., Ermita. **24hr. Tourist Assistance Hotlines:** ☎524 1728 or 524 1660.

THE PHILIPPINES

Pharmacies: Well-stocked **Mercury Drug** branches in every major shopping mall. Most branches open daily 7am-10pm. The branch in Plaza Miranda, Quiapo (☎733 2112) is open 24hr. **Manila Doctors Hospital Pharmacy** (☎524 3090, see below). Open 24hr.

Medical Services: Manila Doctors Hospital, 667 UN Ave., Ermita (☎524 3011), opposite the Philam Bldg., is close to most accommodations. Open 24hr.

Telephones: Payphones can be found on almost every street corner. Most shops and guesthouses also provide **local phone service** (P5 per 3 minutes). Prepaid PLDT **"Fonkards"** (P100-1000), available in stores throughout the city, make local or long-distance calls from PLDT card phones. Green Eastern **card phones** line the streets of Ermita and Malate as an alternative for international calls. SIM cards for tri-band cellular phones are available in all shopping malls; SMART (P90; recharge cards in units of P300 and P500) offers free national roaming.

Internet Access: Several Internet cafes line Pedro Gil St. in front of Robinson's Mall. P30 per hr. **Station 168,** opposite Malate Pensionne on Adriatico St. (☎522 2728), has high-speed connections for over 70 computers, laptop stations, and a snack bar. P60 per hr. Open 24hr. **Shuttle.com** on Pedro Gil St. and Adriatico St. has 20 stations for Internet and network gaming. The **Universe Cyber Cafe** (☎524 2575), on the 3rd fl. of Robinson's, charges P1.50 per min. Open daily 10am-9pm.

Post Offices: GPO, Liwasang Bonifacio, Intramuros (☎527 0085). LRT: Central Station. Walk 10min. past Manila City Library and through the Quezon Blvd. underpass. It's near MacArthur Bridge on Pasig River. *Poste Restante* at Counter 218. EMS expedited services. Open M-F 7am-5pm, Sa 8am-noon.

Postal Code: 1000.

ACCOMMODATIONS

Manila can be a carbon-monoxide sauna—**A/C rooms are worth the extra pesos.** Ermita and Malate, in the heart of Metro Manila, have the best locations amidst restaurants, sights, services, and entertainment. Bring cash; only the most modern hotels accept credit cards.

Malate Pensionne, 1771 Adriatico St., Malate (☎523 8304; fax 522 2389; info@mpensionne.com). Behind Starbucks. Beautiful lodgings in a superb location. Strong security precautions. Breakfast (P80-150), fax, Internet, airport transfer, tour packages, and laundry services available. Dorms with fan P250; economy singles P550; doubles with A/C, TV, and private bath P1050. ❹

Adriatico Pensionne Inn, 1612 Adriatico St., Malate (☎404 3430; r1612adriatico@skyinet.net). Luxury accommodation on a backpacker's budget. Rooms are small but elegantly furnished with double beds. Breakfast included in the adjacent restaurant. 24hr. massage and taxi service. Reservations recommended. Doubles with fan P584, with A/C and TV P700, with A/C, cable TV and bath P930. AmEx/D/MC/V. ❸

Pension Natividad, 1690 M.H. del Pilar St., near J. Quintos St., Malate (☎521 0524). The best-kept secret of backpackers, Natividad has clean, newly renovated rooms. Breakfast P80. Same-sex dorms P280; doubles P650, with common room P780, with A/C and bath P980. MC/V. ❸

Joward's Pension, 1730 Adriatico St., between J. Napkil and Alonso St., Malate (☎338-3191). Though you may leave smelling like the Chinese food served in the restaurant downstairs, Joward's offers the best value in Manila–A/C doubles are P440. Matchbox-sized singles with fan P210; doubles with fan P310, with A/C and private bath P550. ❷

UCCP Shalom Center, 1660 L.M. Guerrero St. (☎524 6242). All are welcome in this "Christian home in Manila," which offers clean rooms and heavenly service. A/C dorms P350; family room P1200; doubles with A/C and common room P1250. ❸

Tropical Mansion Hotel, 1242 J.C. Bocobo St., Ermita (☎523 1742). Neither tropical nor a mansion, but with murals of both. A/C in most rooms makes this urban hotel a temporary oasis from the city heat. 24hr. room service from the Tropical Mansion Cafe next door. Economy singles with fan P500, with A/C P750, with cable TV P950; family rooms with 2 twin beds, couch, and TV P1500. ❸

FOOD

Manila overflows with fast-food joints and expensive sit-down restaurants, offering little selection in between. Intramuros is the exception—the area behind Clamshell I is packed with outdoor stalls serving freshly grilled meat and fish, and Filipino specialties (P30-100). Most open at 7pm. The **Food Plaza,** on the corner of Padre Faura and Bocobo St., Ermita, lacks the charm of street vendors but offers a wide selection of Filipino dishes like chicken adobo (P35). Other stalls and canteens line **Santa Monica Street,** particularly between Adriatico and M.H. del Pilar St.

Krislan Restaurant, (☎536 7834) on Gen. Luna between Anda and Real opposite Clamshell II, Intramuros. Evening strolls around Intramuros would not be complete without a stop at this sumptuous outdoor buffet, set up in the middle of the street. Over 20 Filipino and international dishes are served beneath the stars. Try the Krislan fried chicken and fettucine. P160 buys you all you can eat. Open daily 6:30pm-midnight. ❸

Cafe Adriatico, 1790 Adriatico St. (☎525 2509), on the corner of Remedios Circle. Malate's swankiest joint, with none of the gimmicky kitsch of other cafes. Elitism oozes from this classy eatery. Indulge in beef fondue Bourguignonne (P385) or the fusion favorite, spare ribs adobo (P295). Sangria P119. Open daily 7am-6pm. MC/V. ❺

Hap Chang Tea House, 563 Gen. Malvar St. (☎525 1635), at the intersection with Adriatico St., Malate; you can't miss the neon signs. Hordes of hungry patrons flock at all hours to sample roasted soy sauce pork head (P90), fishcake squidball noodles (P80), and Hong Kong soy duck (P240). Open daily 10am-5am. ❸

L'Eau Vive, 1499 Paz. M. Gauzon Ave., Paco (☎563 8558). UN Ave. turns into Paz M. Gauzon Ave. 15min. east of Rizal Park. Run by nuns, "The Running Water" spreads the gospel through French cuisine. Among the sisters' favorites: ox tongue in a divine mushroom cream sauce (P340) and rabbit with vegetables (P380). Gluttony isn't a sin here. Open M-Sa 11am-3pm and 7-11pm. AmEx/MC/V. ❺

Barbara's Restaurant, (☎527 4090) on Gen. Luna opp. St. Augustin Church in the Casa Manila, Intramuros. The cavernous main dining hall is complete with gilt moldings and antique furniture. Succulent "Seafood Amelie" in lemon buttercream sauce, P350. Local *indios bravos* menu includes Filipino steak P225. Open Tu-Su 11am-3pm and 6pm-11pm. MC/V. ❺

SIGHTS

INTRAMUROS AND LUNETA

RIZAL PARK. Also known as "Luneta," or Little Moon, Rizal Park is where all of Manila meets. The park is verdant and provides a nice respite from the city's intolerable noise and bustle. Children run from 3D dinosaurs at the amusement park (open daily 10am-8pm; P10), and street performers sing, dance, and play among the beautiful Chinese and Japanese Gardens on the north side of the Park. The Spanish executed Filipino rebels here, including national hero Jose Rizal, whose remains are entombed in the Rizal Monument. The souls of other Filipino greats rest on canvas and in clay in the museum on P. Burgos St., in the northeast corner of the park. *(Museum ☎527 0278. Open Tu-Su 10am-4:30pm. Free.)*

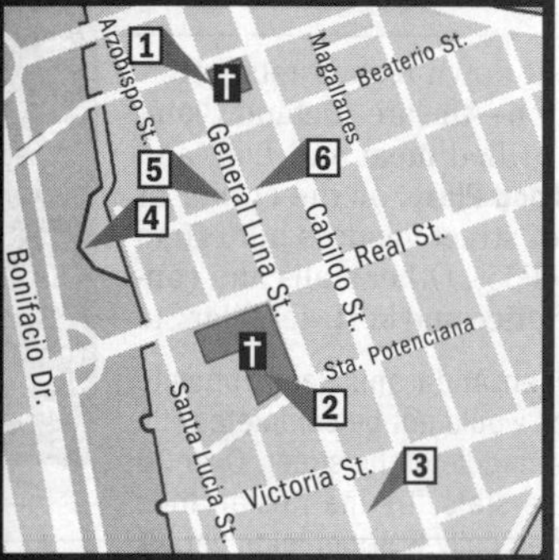

INTRAMUROS, INSIDE THE WALLS

Manila's sprawl may dwarf tiny Intramuros, but it can't hold a candle to the historical center. Below we bring you the best of everything within the walls.

1. Begin at **Fort Santiago,** where José Rizal took his final steps.
2. Check out the **Manila Cathedral.** Its 4500-pipe organ—the largest in Asia—is played at celebrity weddings.
3. Take in *trompe-l'oeil* paintings and Aztec frescoes at **San Augustin Church and Museum.**
4. Peruse handicrafts, books, and jewelry at **Silahis Center.**
5. Stop for a snack from the outdoor vendors under the **Baluarte Sta. Isabel.**
6. Bargain for mother-of-pearl bracelets and necklaces from Mindanao at the **Night Market.**
7. Finally, cross the street to the stand of horse-drawn *calesas* and ride home in style.

INTRAMUROS. Hundreds of years ago, the Spanish surrounded Manila with 4.5km of walls to protect the city from attack. All districts beyond this zone, including Malate, Ermita, and Binondo, were considered *extramuros*, Spanish for "outside the walls." During the occupation, American soldiers drained the moat that used to surround the city and made it into a golf course—ostensibly to prevent malaria. Soon after, WWII transformed the city into a barren ghost town until the Intramuros Administration began renovations in 1979. Today the area contains the best examples of 16th-century Spanish architecture in Asia; even the McDonald's resembles a hacienda. The crown jewel among these is the **San Augustin Church and Museum,** on the corner of Gen. Luna and Real St. UNESCO declared the church a World Heritage Site in 1993 for its exquisite baroque architecture and interior treasures, including Aztec frescoes and gilt altars. Spanish soldier and architect Juan Macias designed the building in 1587; it has since withstood five earthquakes and three national invasions. *(☎527 4061; samuseum.nsclub.net. Open daily 8am-noon and 1-6pm. Church and museum P50, college students P25, high school students P20, children P15; admission includes free drink or biscuits at museum cafe.)* **Fort Santiago,** wedged between Bonifacio Dr. and the Pasig River on the northwest promontory of Intramuros, houses the **Rizal Shrine,** which marks the beginning of Manila's "Freedom Trail." Follow the yellow footsteps showing Rizal's final walk on the day of his execution; the **Intramuros Visitor's Center (IVC)** on the first floor provides maps. *(IVC ☎527 2961. Fort open daily 8am-6pm. P40, students and children P15. Rizal Shrine open Tu-Su 8am-5pm.)* Strolling down Gen. Luna St. from Fort Santiago leads to several other points of interest. **Manila Cathedral,** in Plaza Roma on Postigo St., was rebuilt in 1958 by Fernando Ocampo after being razed in WWII. With imposing high arches and a 4500-pipe organ (Asia's largest), the cathedral now hosts the weddings of Manila's rich and famous. The **Casa Manila Museum,** on the corner of Real and Gen. Luna St., is a replica of an 1850 *ilustrado* home said to be haunted until several exorcisms were performed in the 1990s. *(Museum ☎527 4084. Open Tu-Su 9am-6pm. 2hr. guided tours depart every 2hr. starting at 9am. P40, children P15.)* A few blocks east of the Museum on Anda Street, a giant white tent dubbed **Clamshell I** houses food and craft stalls from each of the regions of the Philippines, plus nightly cultural shows. Call the **Dept. of Tourism** (see **Practical Information,** p. 548) for event schedules. Opposite the Clamshell, the **San Ignacio Church Ruins** are the site of nightly outdoor sermons, beginning just before sundown.

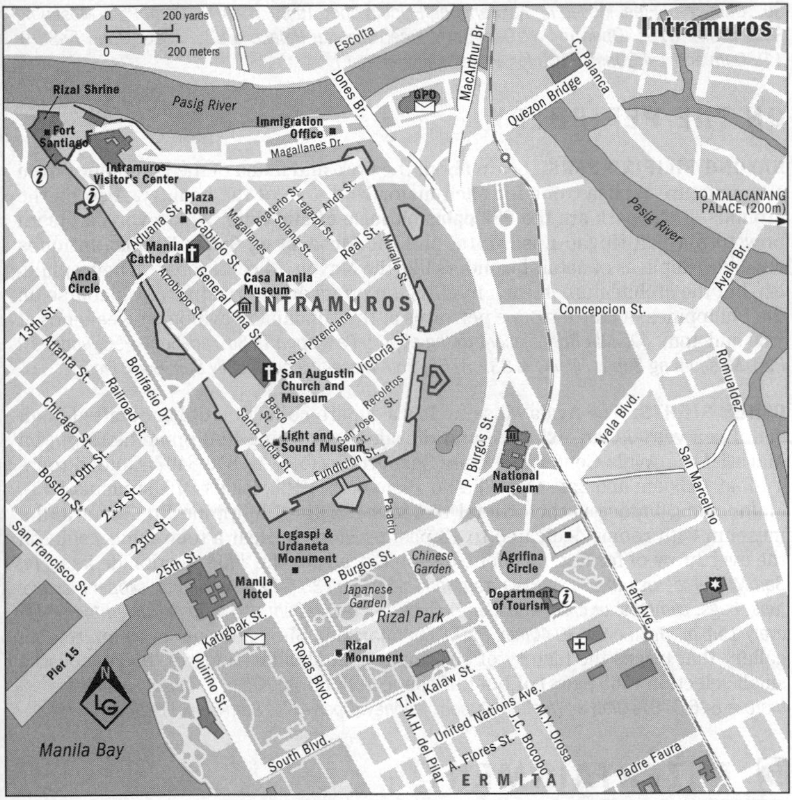

MANILA BAY. In May 1898, Spanish colonial rule ended suddenly when US Commodore Dewey wiped out the Spanish fleet in three hours in Manila Bay. Manila Bay cruises provide interesting lectures on the bay's history. The view of villagers living along the waters against the background of Makati's skyscrapers is a sobering reminder of the gap between Manila's rich and poor. *(Boats depart from CCP Bay Terminal at CCP Complex in Pasay City. ☎525 5698. Cruises 1 hr. Call for reservations, prices.)*

CCP AND ENVIRONS

CULTURAL CENTER OF THE PHILIPPINES (CCP) COMPLEX. The CCP is built on land reclaimed from Manila Bay. The main building has **three theaters,** an **ethnographic museum,** and a contemporary **Filipino art exhibit.** The ethnographic **Museo ng Kalinangang Pilipino** concentrates on local cultural traditions. **Museo ng Sinig,** in the GSIS Building, exhibits experimental art. The **Coconut Palace** was constructed at Imelda Marcos's request specifically for Pope John Paul II's visit to Manila. Approximately 70% of the structure is actually made of coconut products. The Pope was horrified by the extravagance of the palace and refused to stay there, counseling the Marcoses to put their money to better use. *(☎832 1125. On Roxas Blvd. in Malate. Take an orange jeepney with yellow stripes from LRT: Vito Cruz. Art exhibit open Tu-*

Su 10am-5pm. Free. Museo ng Kalinangang Pilipino open Tu-Su 10am-6:30pm. P50. Museo ng Sinig ☎891 6161. Open Tu-Sa 10am-5pm. Free. Coconut Palace ☎831 1756. Open Tu-Su 9-11:30am and 1-4:30pm. P100 for adults, children free.)

ON THE PERIPHERY

NAYONG PILIPINO PARK. Learn about the flora and fauna of the Philippines from six miniature replicas, one for each major land area of the country. Also on the grounds of the park are the **Philippine Museum of Ethnology,** where you can learn how to play an Ifugao nose flute, and the **Museum ng Buhay Filipino** antiques museum. Replicas of natural wonders like the Mayon Volcano verge on being childish, but the architecture in each mini-region offers an informative crash course on the Philippines. A dance troupe performs at the Mindanao Pavilion on weekends at 2:30 and 4pm. *(Off MIA Rd. adjacent to the airport. Park open Tu-Su 7am-6pm. P50, under 12 P25. Museum ng Buhay Filipino ☎832 3766. Both museums open daily 8am-6pm. Free.)*

OTHER SIGHTS. The Ayala Museum has a superb collection of handcrafted models of sea vessels, art exhibits, and dioramas depicting Philippine history. (On Makati Ave., Ayala Center, opposite Shangri-La Hotel. ☎ 810 8407. Guided tours Tu-F at 10:30am and 2pm Open Tu-Su 10am-6pm. P120, locals P75, students P45). Malacañang Palace is the official residence of the Philippine President and a museum with rooms dedicated to 13 past presidents. Hear a tour guide's spin on the overthrow of former president Joseph Estrada or the 2004 election debacle. *(In San Miguel, across the Pasig River from Intramuros. ☎733 3721. No shorts, slippers, singlet tops, bags, cameras, or children under 7. Open M-F 9-11:30am and 1-3pm. Guided tours M-W every 15min., Th-Su every 30-40min. P20.)* The Marikina Shoe Museum is an interesting gallery that traces the history of shoemaking in Manila—and yes, there is also a small selection (565 pairs) of Imelda's shoe collection. *(Off of P. Tauzon, near the shoemart. ☎646 3787. Grab a "Yale" or "Cubao" jeepney. Open W-Sa 8am-5pm. Free.)*

ENTERTAINMENT

Manila supports several venues for cultural performances—check the "Nocturnal Navigator" guide for monthly schedules and special events (☎896-6264; print version available at Dept. of Tourism offices). The **Cultural Center of the Philippines,** CCP Complex, Roxas Blvd., Malate, presents concerts, ballets, dramas, and films. (☎832 3704; box office 832 1125, ext. 240; www.culturalcenter.gov.ph. Open M-F 9am-5pm, Sa-Su 1-5pm. Tickets from P200.) Various plays grace the stages of the **William J. Shaw Theater,** Shangri-La Shopping Mall, 5th fl., EDSA, Mandaluyong. (☎633 4821. Box office open daily 10am-7pm.) **Intramuros Evenings** (formerly Puerto Real Evenings) feature music, dance, and madrigal singing. (☎527 3138. Shows about 6:30pm around Intramuros.)

The **Araneta Coliseum** (☎911 3101), on the corner of Gen. Roxas and Gen. Araneta Ave., stages **cockfights** in September (P100-450) and hosts **Philippine Basketball Association (PBA)** games the rest of the year. (Tickets from P100.) **Dragon Acupressure Center,** 2nd fl., 1811 LM Guerrero St., Malate, on the road that connects J.M. Nakpil St. and Remedios Cir., offers herbal steam baths with massage for P500. (☎526 7342. Open daily noon-1am.) **The Ritz Spa,** 1614 M. Adriatico St., Malate, offers a plethora of beauty treatments and types of massage; included in the price is use of the luxurious steamrooms, saunas, and jacuzzis. (☎523-3333. Swedish or Shiatsu massage, foot reflexology P650. Open daily noon-2am.) **Massages** from the blind are also available at Robinson's Mall at a booth on the first floor.

Film-lovers will enjoy **Manila's** diverse cinema scene, which ranges from tiny arthouse theaters to 11-screen multiplexes. The **Alliance Française** holds weekly screenings of international classics Wednesday 8pm and Saturday 2:30pm. (☎895 7585; www.alliance.ph. 209 Nicanor Garcia St., Bel-Air II, Makati City.) The films of Almodovar, Saura, and Bunuel grace the screens of the Salon des Actos at the **Instituto Cervantes.** (☎526 1482; http://manila.cervantes.es. 2515 Léon Guinto Ave. at Estrada St., Malate.) For a more alternative vibe, head to aptly named **Brash Young Cinema,** which screens student work and indie films. (In the basement of the Unisys Bldg. on Esteban and de la Rosa St. in Legaspi Village, Makati. www.brashyoungcinema.tripod.com.) The venue of choice for film festivals is the **U.P. Film Institute,** on Magsaysay Ave. in Quezon City (☎925 0286; www.upd.edu.ph/~film_ctr), bringing the best of Cannes to Manila. For the latest American blockbusters, head to the more mainstream movie theaters in any of the city's shopping malls. **Robinson's Place** in Ermita (☎536 7812) and **SM Megamall** in Makati City (☎633 1901) boast two particularly impressive theaters. (P65, balcony seats P95. Movies run 10am-10pm.)

SHOPPING

Malls are omnipresent. **SM Megamall** in Mandaluyong offers two behemoth six-floor buildings, enough to challenge even the most ardent shopper. If shopping wears you out, take a spin on its ice-skating rink or catch a flick at the theaters. Ooh-la-la your way through upscale boutiques at **Shangri-La Plaza** next door. **Robinson's Place,** conveniently located in the tourist district, has two levels of restaurants and a bowling alley. Use it as an A/C shortcut from Pedro Gil to Pedro Faura.

Beyond the malls and fixed-price shops, prices are negotiable. **Divisoria Market,** outside Binondo, is a bargain-hunter's mecca, as is **Baclaran Market** in Paranaque. The **Ilalim ng Tulay Market** in Quiapo hawks cheap tokens of Filipino culture, while Cubao's **Farmer's Plaza** is a collision of department stores and flea markets. In **Chinatown,** shops along Ongpin St. near Santa Cruz Church sell Chinese desserts, textiles, and herbal medicines. The heavyweight among antiques and handicraft stores is the **Silahis Center,** 744 Gen. Luna St., Intramuros (☎527 2111), near P. Burgos St. Vendors hawk handicrafts and inexpensive trinkets at the **Intramuros Night Market,** on Anda St. between Gen. Luna and Arzobispado St. (Open daily 7pm-midnight.) One block east on Anda St. lies the giant **Clamshell I,** which contains temporary craft stalls from various regions of the Philippines. Hours vary; obtain a schedule at the Dept. of Tourism or Intramuros Visitors Center.

NIGHTLIFE

> **!** In the Philippines, discos are often brothels in disguise. Prostitutes, and the men who love them, frequent the floors, looking for more than throbbing music. If you want to put on your dancing shoes, head to the dancefloor in a groovy bar.

A vibrant bar and cafe scene thrives in Manila, especially on **J. Nakpil Street** and **Remedios Circle** in Malate and on **P. Burgos Street** in Makati. Live music is standard at most places, and bands often invite members of the audience to join them. As one local bar owner puts it, "half of all Filipinos can sing, and the other half like to think they can." Famous names like Freddie Aguilar regularly perform in Manila nightspots; call ahead to check band schedules. Many bars have basic dress codes barring tank tops, shorts and rubber sandals—but patrons are often found wearing one or all of the above.

The Library, 1779 A.M. Adriatico St., Malate (☎522 2484), near Remedios Circle and adjacent to Starbucks. The country's funniest drag queens perform karaoke and nightly Tagalog standup comedy to sold-out audiences. Get there before 9:30pm to guarantee a good seat. The crowd is a mix of locals and tourists, though the latter are often prime targets for (relatively painless) jokes. Thirsty for a cocktail? Try the "Blowjob" (P150). Sizzling grilled "Chicken library" (P230) is another favorite. Cover P50, for special shows M-W P150 (call for schedule). Open daily 7pm-3am; standup starts at 9pm.

Café Havana, 1903 Adriatico St., Remedios Circle, Malate (☎521 8097). The Philippines' first Cuban restaurant/dance club serves all types of Latin fare. Swing with local salsa dancers to live Afro-Cuban music W-Sa from 11pm. "Mangojito" cocktail P145. Cuban cigars P400-1700. Che t-shirts P250. Open M-Th 11am-2pm and 5pm-2am, F 11am-2pm and 5pm-4am, Sa 5pm-4am, Su 3pm-midnight. MC/V.

Club Indios, 618 J. Napkil St., Malate (☎521 5406). Yuppies flock to this stylish new club, where talented bartenders concoct drinks with a native twist. The flaming *Indios Bravos* (P90) is a favorite. Tangy green mango shake P75. Beer P39. Nightly live music from 9:30pm in the upstairs patio. Tu open mic, W-F acoustic, Sa reggae. MC/V.

Hobbit House, 1801 Mabini St., Malate (☎521 7604). Live rock, blues, and country music from some of the biggest names in the nation. "The smallest waiters in the world"—all midgets and dwarves—serve excellent steaks (Australian Porterhouse P275) and cocktails (P100-120). *Lord of the Rings* gimmicks aside, this is one of the best bars in Manila. Local beers half off during happy hour (5-8pm). Imported beers P135. Weekday cover P100, weekends P150. Open Su-Th 5pm-1:30am, F-Sa 5pm-3am.

The Verve Bar, 607 J. Nakpil St. off Adriatico St., Malate. Musically one step above the rest. Bar and DJ compete for the most innovative mixes: trip-hop, progressive house, and acid jazz. The "Adios Motherfucker," an 8-alcohol blend, will knock your socks off (P165). Open Tu-Sa 8:30pm-5am.

Bedrock, 1782 Adriatico St., Malate (522 7279). One of Malate's most popular and unabashedly tacky bars, with a huge Korean following. Stone-age cocktails include the "Green Dino" (P260), and friendly waitresses dress as cavewomen. Live bands nightly. Open Su-Th 6pm-4am, F-Sa 6pm-5am. AmEx/D/MC/V.

DAYTRIPS FROM MANILA

PAGSANJAN FALLS

Pagsanjan is 5km from Santa Cruz, Laguna, accessible by JAM Transit buses leaving from Taft Ave. at Gil Puyat St., Pasay City (2hr., every 30min. 4am-10:30pm, with A/C P115). It's recommended to leave between 8 and 10am to get back before 8pm, as traffic is bad. Exit the bus at Santa Cruz Crossing, and board a jeepney for Pagsanjan (P7). From the jeepney stop, most hotels and boat operators are accessible by tricycle (P10-20).

The final scenes of Francis Ford Coppola's *Apocalypse Now* were filmed along this tropical gorge. Tourists pay high prices to have *banqueros* canoe them 7km up the Bumbungan River to **Magdapio Falls** and shoot the rapids back down. (2hr.; last trip 2hr. before sundown; one person P1080, 2-3 people P580 per person, plus P100-200 tip.) The rapids are most active in the rainy season. Float on a bamboo raft (P50 per person) underneath the waterfall to **Devil's Cavern,** named for the eerie shape of the cave's outline. Some boatmen have been known to pressure tourists into paying more, so it's advisable to arrange a boat through the PTA-operated **Pagsanjan Garden Resort,** Pagsanjan (☎049 808 4451; pjresortlag@yahoo.com), a short tricycle ride (P20) from town. The resort also offers free lockers, town maps (P100), and buffet lunches with Filipino cuisine (P200). Alternatively, obtain a list of recommended boat operators from the **Tourism and Cultural Development Office** (☎049 808 3544). Other accommodations line Rizal St., the town's main road, or Garcia St., which runs parallel to Rizal and the northern bank of the river.

BAGUIO ☎74

Baguio rests 1400m above sea level, sprawling in a rugged, pine-bedecked landscape. Its cooler temperatures make it the "summer capital" of the Philippines. Although popularity has put pressure on the mountain locale, highland tribes still subsist on the thriving produce market, which draws tourists looking for a taste of the Filipino way of life, as well as legions of artists and students attempting to study and protect the pre-colonial Cordilleran culture.

TRANSPORTATION

Flights: Take a taxi from Session Rd. to the **Loakan Airport** (P60). **Asian Spirit** (☎444 5413) flies M, W, F, Su to **Manila** (45min., 9:15am, P1583).

Buses: Several bus companies send out buses from different terminals in Baguio City. From the terminals on Gov. Pack Rd., near the corner of Session Rd., **Autobus** (☎444 9056) goes to Banaue (8-9hr., 7:30pm, P250); **Dagupan Bus Co.** (☎442 5391) runs buses to Manila (7hr., every hr., with A/C to Cubao District P230); **Partas** (☎444 8431) goes to Manila (5, 6, 10am, 2pm, midnight; with A/C to Cubao District P235) and Vigan (5hr.; 6:30, 10am, noon, 3:15, 6, 8:45pm; P154, with A/C P215); **Victory Liner** (☎442 6654) to Manila (6hr.; every hr.; with A/C to Cubao District P280, with A/C to Pasay City P285). From the terminal on Rajah Soliman St., behind Baguio Central Mall: **Dangwa Tranco** runs buses to Banaue (8-9hr., 7:30pm, P250) and Bontoc (7hr., every hr. 5-10am, P1450) and **Lizardo** goes to Banaue (8-9hr.; 2:30, 7:30pm; P230) and Sagada (6½hr.; every 30min. 7-9:30am 11am; P189, students P155). From the terminal on Otek St., **Eso-Nice Liner** (☎443 3076) runs buses to San Fernando (La Union; 1½hr., every 30min. 5:30am-6pm, P40). The **Philippine Rabbit** goes to Manila (every hr. 24hr., P225) and Vigan (5hr.; every hr. until 7pm; P150, with A/C P170).

Local Transportation: Taxis start at P20 for the 1st 250m, P1 for each 100m after. **Jeepneys** cost about P4 per trip but are slower than taxis.

ORIENTATION AND PRACTICAL INFORMATION

Rose-colored **Baguio Cathedral** overlooks the main commercial thoroughfare, **Session Road,** which climbs from its intersection with **Magsaysay Avenue** to the top of a hill. Session Rd. then splits into **Leonard Wood Road,** which leads to the Botanical Gardens, Wright Park, Mines View Park, and the **Session Road Extension.** Northbound highways leading into Baguio go to **Governor (Gov.) Pack Road,** which borders **Burnham Park.** Half a kilometer down the road is the **Department of Tourism Complex** in front of Baguio City High School. Another kilometer farther is the main **bus terminal** and a roundabout into Session Rd. Near City Hall, Rizal Park, and Malcom Sq., **Otek Street** forms an arc around the northwest end of Burnham Park. The *Baguio Road Guide*, which plots all major buildings in the city (P40) and the *Map of Baguio*, by Island Viewing Publishing are both useful. A free but quite useless map is available at the Department of Tourism (DOT).

Tourist Office: DOT Complex (☎442 6708). 10min. down Gov. Pack Rd. from bus terminals, opposite Baguio City High School. Open daily 7am-5pm.

Travel and Tours: Swagman Travel, Swagman Attic Inn, 90 Abanao St. (☎442 5139). 3hr. city tour P850. 4-day tour to Banaue, Sagada, and Bontoc depart from the inn at 6am daily. Visa extensions P2050. Open M-Sa 8am-5pm.

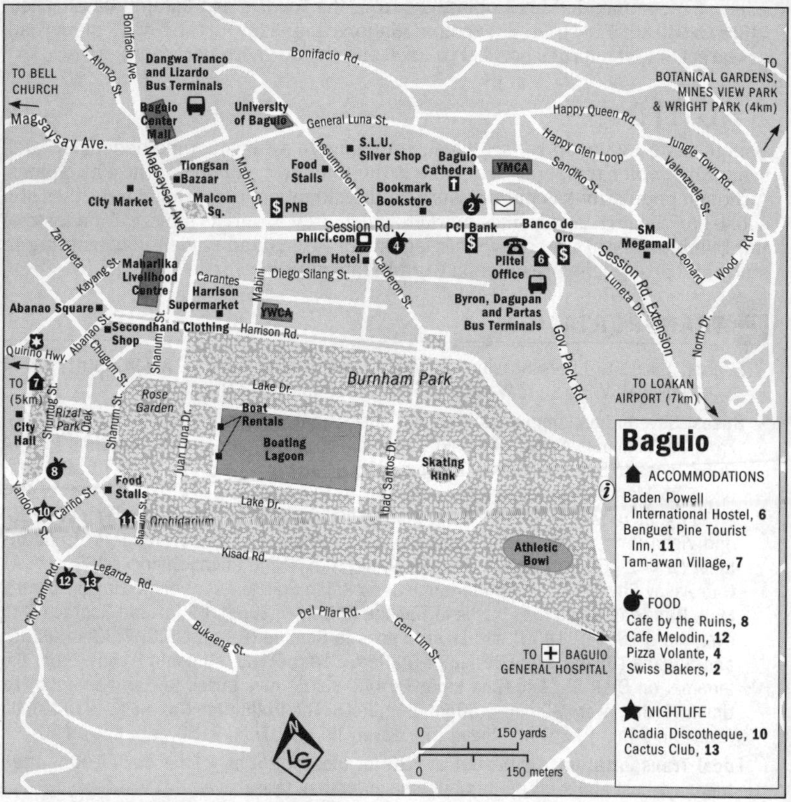

Banks: Philippine National Bank (PNB), on Session Rd. Open M-F 9am-3pm. (☎442 7795). Good exchange rates. AmEx/Cirrus/MC/V 24hr. **ATM. SM Department Store,** 3rd fl. SM Mall, Luneta Hill, Upper Session Rd. Open daily 9am-10pm.

Emergency: ☎117.

Police: ☎166. Station on Abanao St.

Pharmacy: Store Plus (☎442 8156), in YMCA building on Session Rd., at the top of the hill opposite Banco de Oro. Open 24hr.

Medical Services: Baguio Medical Center (☎442 7770), on Kennon Rd. English-speaking staff.

Telephones: Piltel Office (☎422 4567), on Session Rd., at the corner of Gov. Pack Rd. Accepts all Filipino and major international calling cards. Collect calls (deposit P50). Open daily 7am-8pm.

Internet Access: PhilCi.Com, Juniper Bldg., Bonifacio Ave., opposite Baguio City University. Quick access. P40 per hr. Telnet and webcam available. Open 24hr. Several Internet cafes vie for customers at SM Megamall, 3rd fl. P30 per hr. Laptop hookups available. Open daily 9am-10pm.

Post Office: At corner of Gov. Pack and Session Rd. Open M-F 8am-noon and 1-5pm, Sa 8am-noon. *Poste Restante* at counter in adjoining lockbox section (closed Sa). **FedEx** office at SM Megamall, 3rd fl. Open daily 9am-10pm.

Postal Code: 2600.

ACCOMMODATIONS

Walking down **Abanao Street** and onto Session Rd. will take you past many accommodations. Prices are higher than in other mountain locations, and are sensitive to seasonal demand. Ask for a discount in the low season. Prepare to pay 50% more than the prices listed below during high season and 30% more during Holy Week.

Benguet Pine Tourist Inn, 39 Shanum St. (☎442 7325). Clean rooms and great views of Burnham Park's *orchidarium* compensate for higher prices. Avoid a room facing Spirits Nightclub, or bad singers will keep you up all night. Breakfast included. Dorms P300; doubles P500, with bath P800, with TV P1000; quads P1350, with TV P1500. ❸

Baden Powell International Hostel, 26 Gov. Pack Rd. (☎442 5836), at the intersection with Session Rd. Proximity to bus stations guarantees early morning wake-up calls. Clean and comfortable. Breakfast included. Dorms P400; rooms for 1-2 with private bath and cable TV P1500; quads P1350. Suite for 7-8 with dining room and fireplace P5000. 50% discount in low season (June-October). MC/V. 10% surcharge. ❸

Tam-awan Village (see **Sights**, p. 560), Purok 1, Tam-awan, Pinsao Proper (☎446 2949), off Tacay Rd. on the way to La Trinidad (P35 taxi from Session Road). A more expensive form of camping. Traditional Ifugao huts rise 1.5m off the ground. Toilets are steps away. Singles P550; doubles P950. Extra person P200. ❹

FOOD

Fruits you won't find anywhere else in the Philippines thrive in Baguio's cool climate. Foodstalls on **Shanum Street** around Burnham Park sell spit-roasted chicken and sweet corn with condensed milk, a student favorite (P15), while those around **Otek Street** play the juiciest karaoke hits. For the cheapest eats around, head to the hidden **foodstalls** ❶ behind the vehicle-shaped Starbus Restaurant on Assumption Rd., opposite the University of Baguio. Meals with meat, rice, vegetables, and drink (P35).

Cafe by the Ruins, 25 Shuntug St. (☎442 4010; ruins@mozcom.com). Built from the ruins of a governor's mansion, Cafe by the Ruins is one of the best vegetarian selections in the region. Over 20 non-meat and meat offerings served in a garden patio. Freshly baked bread and rolls, delivered hot with homemade jam (P30-50). Set lunches P155-230. Try the eggplant caviar on toast (P45). Open daily 7am-9pm. MC/V. ❸

Pizza Volante, 82 Session Rd., Session Theater Bldg. (☎445 0777). Relax in this chic cafe known for its inventive pizzas. Pizza Marengo, with chicken, mushrooms and bell peppers (P80), was reportedly invented by Napoleon's Italian chef. With broccoli and basil, Veggie Dream (P60) is another favorite. Open 24hr. MC/V. ❷

Cafe Melodin (☎442 7734), on Legarda Rd., renews your appetite for Filipino cuisine. The all-day breakfast menu fills you up for the rest of the day. Seafood rice (P190) for 4. Crispy *pata* pork P275. Beef spare ribs P215. Open daily 7am-10pm. MC/V. ❸

Swiss Bakers (☎442 4010), on Session Rd., uphill from the steps to Baguio Cathedral. Dazzling cakes, buns, and bread. Tuna turnover P2523. Croissants P16. Cinnamon rolls P20. Bread from P10. Open daily 7am-8pm. ❶

SIGHTS

TAM-AWAN VILLAGE. Tam-awan, literally "vantage point" in the local dialect, is a gateway to the indigenous Cordilleran culture. The cluster of authentic Ifugao wood and *cogon* grass huts, dismantled from their original location and reconstructed less than an hour outside Baguio City, serves as a "living museum" and art gallery. Huts of this kind face extinction as mountain tribes switch to modern housing structures. Walk up the hill to "Batad" hut to get a glimpse of the South China Sea. Stay in the huts overnight (see **Accommodations,** p. 559) for a true taste of the culture. *(Purok 1, Tam-awan, Pinsao Proper, off Tacay Rd., on the way to La Trinidad. ☎446 2949. A P35 taxi ride from Session Rd. Open daily 9am-6pm. P20.)*

BELL TEMPLE. Bordering Trinidad Valley, the background of the Bell Temple combines Buddhist, Taoist, Confucian, and Christian beliefs. Ask a priest to tell your fortune (P4), or take a trip around the fountain of waterlilies as you ponder your existence. *(Off Magsaysay Ave. Take a jeepney (P5) from the corner of Bonifacio and Magsaysay Ave. Cameras prohibited. Open M-F 6am-5pm, Sa-Su 6am-10:30am and 1-5pm. Free.)*

ST. LOUIS UNIVERSITY MUSEUM OF ARTS AND CULTURE. Established in 1969, this museum, in the university's Msgr. Charles Vath building, conserves cultural artifacts of the Cordilleras. On display is a carabao-powered grinding machine called a *dadapilan*, normally used to squeeze juice from sugar cane but allegedly used during WWII to squeeze confessions out of prisoners. *(☎442 3043, ext. 260. Open M-Sa 7:30am-noon and 1:30-5pm. Free.)*

PARKS. Ride a horse through the **Botanical Gardens, Wright Park,** and **Mines View Park.** Set routes (up to 5hr.) take you to **Mt. Santo Tomas,** the limestone peak 8km away. Behind a blockade of tourist shops, a small promontory gives a wide-angled view of Amburayan Valley and Benguet's gold and copper mines. *(The Botanical Gardens and Wright Park are on the route to Mines View Park, 4km from the city. Open daily 6am-sunset. Horses P100 per 30min. P100 for guide.)*

MARKETS. For inexpensive clothing, secondhand shops can't be beat. A good selection is opposite Abanao Sq. Mall on Abanao St. Tiongsan Bazaar on Magaysay Ave. houses discount goods of all kinds, from cheap Chinese stereos to stationery. *(Open daily 8am-8pm.)* The **City Market,** also on Magsaysay Ave., showcases gruesome livestock parts as well as vegetables, fruit, *ube*-flavored jam, peanut and cashew brittle, and strawberry wine. For the skilled bargainer, all will be wondrously cheap. *(Open daily 5:30am-8pm.)* Across the street is the multi-story **Maharlika Livelihood Center.** Tourists' anti-modern predilections have made the traditional garb, personal adornments, and handicrafts of the mountain tribespeople highly marketable. The **Easter Weaving Room,** on Easter Rd. on the northwest outskirts of Guisad, is the commercial counterpart to the Easter Weaving School. Watch weavers stitch clothes and tablecloths. *(☎442 4972. Open M-F 8am-5pm. Tablecloths P800-1000. Stalls along the main mountain highway from Manila showcase stunning woodwork, including driftwood benches, coffee tables, and finely carved sculptures.*

OTHER SIGHTS. On top of a hill with a view of Session Rd., the rose **Baguio Cathedral** is a funky church with multicolored stained glass; enjoy an afternoon cappuccino in the cafe opposite the entrance. Less authentic than the Tam-awan Village, the **Ifugao Woodcarvers Village** churns out figurines and animals, including Buddhas, Ifugao warriors, and potency symbols for P35-150. **Asin Hot Springs** (16km northwest of Baguio) features a swimming pool surrounded by thermal springs, hanging bridges, and vegetation. *(Along Asin Rd. off Naguilian Rd. Take a San Luis jeepney or a taxi to Km 5 for P40, or ask to be let off at the hot springs.)*

ENTERTAINMENT AND NIGHTLIFE

City Center Burnham Park, named after American urban planner Daniel Burnham, boasts an **orchidarium** (open daily 6am-7pm), lake, playground, and roller-skating rink. (Roller-skating P50 per hr., inline skates P50 per hr.; available 8am-midnight. Boating P60 per boat, P25 per additional person, max. 5 per boat, available 8am-10pm.) The **Baguio Arts Festival,** held each November, features visual, performing, and folk arts, many of which are staged in the park. The **Modern Age Spa,** in the YMCA building on Session Rd. opposite Banco de Oro, offers shiatsu and Swedish massage (P350, with aromatherapy P450). **Reyes Salon,** near the intersection of Assumption and Session Rd., offers manicures, pedicures, and hot oil treatments starting at P75.

At night, beneath the Prince Plaza Hotel on Legarda Rd., the **Cactus Club** serves its 20-something patrons with a live band and a pulsating rock and blues mix from 7pm onward. (☎442 5082. Great whiskey sours P55. Live band 7-10pm. Open daily 5pm-2am.) Baguio's new disco **Acadia Discotheque,** on the corner of Cariño St. and Legarda Rd. is geared toward the hipper-than-thou college crowd. (☎300 1227. Cover P70; M-Th 7-10pm P25. Open daily 6pm-3am.)

BANAUE ☎74

Rice is king in Banaue. Generations of Ifugao farmers have constructed vast rice terraces on every mountainside in and around the city. The rugged terrain is now a spectacular gallery of geological sculptures, billed as the "Eighth Wonder of the World" in spite of swarming tourists and tricycles that slightly spoil the terrace panoramas. The indigenous artistic tradition, marked by an outpouring of jewelry, carvings, bronze works, and textiles, enjoys immense popularity—as do the elder tribeswomen with stooped backs posing for photos. A short but often steep trek to Batad affords even more spectacular terrace views and a chance to experience local culture in a more natural, less touristy setting.

TRANSPORTATION. **SEAAIR** (☎02 891 8708) flies to Bagabag Airport in Nueva Vizcaya from Manila; from there, it's a 90min. bus ride to Banaue (1hr.; M, W, F 11am; P2000). Most buses and jeepneys leave from the Sanafe Lodge. **Dangwa buses** run to Baguio (7am, 4pm; P240) and Manila (9hr.; 4, 4:30pm; P310). The dispatch office in Niclyn's Store at the marketplace makes reservations one day in advance 3-7pm. **Autobuses** leave from near the Banaue Hotel and go to Baguio (5:30pm, P230) and Cubao in Manila (5pm, P250). Make reservations at their office next to Tam-an village. A **KMS** bus that leaves from the top of the stairs near Cool Winds also goes to Baguio (9hr.; 3, 5pm; P180). Make reservations at the craft shop opposite Cool Winds. **Jeepneys** run to Bontoc (2½hr., 7am, P80).

ORIENTATION AND PRACTICAL INFORMATION. The main street starts at a parking area for **buses** and **jeepneys** surrounded by market stalls and shops. Nearby, the Town Hall houses a branch of the **post office** (☎386 4104; *Poste Restante;* open M-F 8am-noon and 1-5pm) and a desk where jeepneys and **tricycles** can be chartered. The **Tourist Information Center** is on the first floor of the Town Hall. (Open daily 8am-noon and 1-5pm.) Maps are available at **People's Inn** (P10). **RSR Merchandising** at the market exchanges US dollars and traveler's checks at poor rates. From the **market,** the main street runs beside the river before it crosses the river, and becomes a national road. This road heads back on the other side of the gully past the **Guihob Natural Pool** (4km) to the **Batad Junction** (12km). A left at the fork by the market leads uphill past the **Good News Clinic** to the Banaue Hotel overlooking **Tam-an Village** (15min. walk). At the top of the drive are the main **post office** and the **Digitel telephone office.** (☎386 9850. Open M-F 8am-6pm). **Postal Code:** 3601.

ACCOMMODATIONS AND FOOD. Hostels generally have hot water and a 10am check-out. **People's Inn and Restaurant** ❷ offers serene views of their terraces, a knowledgeable staff, and a restaurant and bakery. (☎386 401. Restaurant open daily 6am-9pm. Singles P100-150, with common room P300; doubles P200/500; quads with common room P500.) **Uyami's Green View Lodge** ❶ boasts spacious rooms with balconies but lacks the views available at People's. (☎386 4021. Rooms with shared common room P150 per person; twins with balcony, hot-water shower, and private common room P400-600; quads with common room P700; family room with common room P800.) **Cozy Nook Inn** ❷, opposite the Stairway Lodge, is a homey inn run by an affectionate woman and her family. (Doubles P350; triples P500; P100 less during the low season.) The most colorful rooms in Banaue can be found just outside the town center at the **Fairview Inn** ❸. The bright rooms have hot water, private baths, and a wrap-around terrace. (☎386 4002. Singles P300; doubles P600.) The **Banaue Hotel and Youth Hostel** ❸ is in Tam-an Village. Rooms other than dorms will cost you an arm and a leg. All rooms have a common room, hot water-shower, and pool access. (☎386 4087. Dorms P200, P175 for students; singles P2300/1200; doubles P2800/1200.)

Banaue has limited dining options, but a few places offer delicious, reasonably priced meals. The **Las Vegas Restaurant** ❶ delivers the finest in "Las Vegas" cuisine—whatever that means. (Israeli salad P40. Rum and coke P30. Open daily 6am-9:15pm.) Toward the Town Hall on the left side of the main street, **Jam Café** ❸ serves savory entrees like pork *adobo* (P110) and chicken curry (P110) with complimentary vegetables and rice. Start the morning with the "choc'lait n' toast"—creamed hot chocolate with buttered toast. (☎0917 394 5471. Open daily 6:30am-8pm.) **Cool Winds Restaurant** ❷ has a friendly staff that whips up fresh treats like fruit salad (P45). Meat eaters and sugar addicts are welcome too. (☎386 4023. Pork dishes P75. Chocolate and cheese pancakes P35. Open daily 6am-9pm.)

SIGHTS AND TREKKING. The established viewpoint of the famous **Banaue rice terraces** is 4km along the road to Bontoc (round-trip tricycle to Banaue Viewpoint P100, jeepney P350). These rice terraces produce much less than those in Batad, and subsidies from the United Nations are all that keep the land plowed and the villagers working (guide P300). If placed end-to-end, the terraced land would encircle half the globe. Before the viewpoint, turn left onto the Hapao-Hunguan Rd. to see the **mummified couple of Hiwang,** whose final wish was to be smoked and embalmed. Their son lives off of P20 donations from visitors. While the cloth-shrouded corpses are disappointing, the son's elevated hut is worth a visit. (No photos allowed.) The **Banaue Museum** at the Banaue View Inn (on the main street, 300m from Municipal Hall) holds the collection of anthropologist H. Ottley Beyer, one of the first outsiders to study Ifugao culture. (☎386 4078. Open M-Sa 8am-noon and 1-5pm. P25.) On sunny days, visitors cool off in the **Guihob Natural Pool** along the road to Batad. (Round-trip tricycle P120, jeepney P350.) **Bintakan Cave,** in Lagawe about 2km from the center of town, opens into three caverns with abundant stalagmite and stalactite formations. (Tricycle P100; from the main road, walk 20min. up to the cave along the marked trail.)

An established two day trek from Banaue includes the villages of Batad, Cambulo, and Pula. Cambulo, a village circumscribed by a river, has two guesthouses, the **Riverside Inn** ❶ and the **Friends Inn** ❶ (both P85 per person). The treks can be difficult during the rainy season. Arrange your trip at the Banaue Viewpoint or Banaue Hotel. (1-2 people P1200 per day, 3-4 people P500 per person per day.)

SAGADA

Chickens seem to outnumber people on Sagada's unpaved streets. Residents may chat on cell phones, but there is still no local phone service in the area. Sacred burial grounds, caves, limestone formations, and heavy waterfalls prove welcome alternatives to rice terraces. And while the road to Sagada is rocky, the bumpy ride is punishment worth enduring to reach this quiet town.

TRANSPORTATION AND PRACTICAL INFORMATION. **Lizardo buses** go to Baguio (7hr.; every hr. 5-10am, 6:30pm; P189). **Jeepneys** to Bontoc leave from the market (1hr.; every 20min. 6-7am, every hr. 7:45-8:45am and 10am-noon; P30). To reach Banaue from Sagada, you must go through Bontoc; catch a jeepney from beside Bontoc Municipal Hall (2-3hr., every 30min. 8am-1pm, P80). Alternatively, hire a jeepney to take you directly (P2500). The road that ascends into Sagada also serves as the town's main street. It passes **St. Theodore's Hospital,** then reaches the **town center** and **Municipal Hall** about 500m down the road. Also in the town center are: the **Tourist Information Center** (open daily 7am-5pm); **Sagada Rural Bank** (open Tu-Sa 8-11:45am and 1:15-4:30pm); the 24hr. **police station;** and the **post office** (*Poste Restante;* open M-F 8am-noon and 1-4:30pm). **Postal Code:** 2619.

ACCOMMODATIONS AND FOOD. **Masferré Inn and Restaurant ❶** (☎0918 341 0164) offers clean rooms in the center of town (P150 per person, shared bath). Laundry service is available, along with buckets of warm water (P15 per bucket; order 15min. before needed). The dining area serves decent sandwiches (ham or tuna P30) and lukewarm beer (P30). Other guesthouses can be found in the town center, including the **Sagada Guest House ❶** (☎0918 560 0849. Check-out 9:30am. Cafe open daily. P150 per person; private singles with common room P600, with hot-water P800.) **Greenhouse Inn ❷** is a cozy establishment run by an elderly woman. (Check-out 10am. P130 per person; private singles P200; doubles P220.) Next door, blind masseuses offer **scientific massages** for P140 per hr. To the right of the Town Hall is **Shamrock ❷,** which serves the hearty "Hangover's Anathema" (P65) breakfast of toast, eggs, and coffee, as well as "Shamrock meals" of soup, meat, vegetables, rice, and dessert for P110. (☎0918 341 1912. Open daily 6am-9pm.) Down the hill from Masferré is the **Yoghurt House ❷,** highly recommended for delicious veggie fried rice (P40) and (surprise) fresh yogurt with fruit (P50). Listen to great 80s music or rent a book while you wait. (Open daily 6:30am-9pm.)

SIGHTS. The **Masferré Gallery,** 1km down the road from St. Theodore's Hospital, displays the work of the late Eduardo Masferré, the son of a Spanish soldier who settled in the mountains at the turn of the century. His photographs of friends and neighbors have received international acclaim. (Open daily 6am-9pm. Free.)

TREKKING. The **Sagada Environmental Guides Association (SEGA)** has fixed rates, and only SEGA guides can be hired at the Tourist Information Center in the Municipal Hall. Typical tours include the **Sugong Hanging Coffins, Lumiang Burial Cave,** and **Sumaging Cave,** popularly known as "Big Cave." (4-5hr.; 1-4 people P300, group of 5 P350, group of 6-9 P600. Prices double after 5hr. Spelunking is possible at Big Cave; check with the tourist office about equipment and guides.) Another alternative is a one-day trek including the 1800m **Mt. Ampacao** (1½hr.), **Lake Danom,** and **Bokong Falls,** complete with a climb up the **Kiltepan Tower** to survey the rice terraces. (1-4 people P400, group of 5 P500, 6-9 people P600. Guides strongly recommended for novice hikers.)

If you'd prefer not to take a tour, try exploring some of the sights on your own. Fifteen minutes past the Igorot Lodge, the road forks. The left fork, leading to Suyo Rd., passes the **Sugong Hanging Coffins,** tethered to a cliff face. Thirty minutes farther along Suyo Rd., a path leads to the **Lumiang Burial Cave.** Friendly signs make all of this clear. Even if you don't take a tour, it is advisable to hire a guide for **Sumaging Cave,** 10min. past the Burial Cave. Inside the chamber, you must wade waist-deep in water, cling to ropes, and crawl through crevices; one wrong step and you become bat food. From Bontoc Rd., a path to the right leads past St. Mary's Episcopal Church to a **cemetery** and **Calvary Hill.** To the right, the path takes you to a boulder, while another path takes you to the floor of **Echo Valley.** The path is slippery; be prepared to come back drenched in mud. These trails are unmarked, and it's easy to get lost without a guide. Hanging coffins are visible in the limestone cliff faces, accompanied by a smattering of "death chairs." In certain rituals, the deceased body was placed in a chair while funeral-goers performed sacrifices and songs. Fifteen minutes along the road to Bontoc, the **Matangkib Burial Cave** is at the foot of a path opposite the Rocky Valley Inn. Passing to the left of the cave leads you to the **Latang Underground River.** With a strong flashlight, you can follow the river to the Bokong Falls. If you don't want to follow the underground river, you can take the concrete steps that lead up from Bontoc Rd. and wind down to the river. Cross the river, and head upstream to the falls. To visit the 40m high **Bomod-ok (Big) Waterfalls,** register with the Tourist Information Center and obtain a guide (P500). On school days, jeepneys go to the Banga-an Elementary School from the basketball court (30min.; 8am departure, 1pm return; P15), where a trail leads to the Bomod-ok Waterfalls. (1½hr. trek. Bring a bathing suit.) On weekends and holidays, hire a jeepney to Banga-an (P450 round-trip), or walk (2-3 hours). Follow the road to Banga-an for about an hour, turn down the steps beyond the Banga-an Elementary School, and take the path through Fidelsian village to the waterfalls.

BONTOC ☎74

Although primarily a commercial town, Bontoc retains the charm of a small village. The friendly people, inexpensive, quality accommodations, and proximity to the Maligcong rice terraces lure the adventurous traveler headed to nearby Banaue. The opportunity to observe local Igorot culture integrated with Western influence also makes it worth a visit—you'll be walking the streets alongside Levi-clad locals and tattooed members of the Kalinga tribes.

TRANSPORTATION. Several companies run **buses** to nearby towns. Dangwa buses, leaving from the **bus terminal** behind the Mountain Hotel, go to Baguio (7hr., every hr. 6-10am, P145) and Banaue (signs read "Tabuk," 2½hr., 8am, P80). **Rising Sun** buses leave from outside City Hall to Baguio (every hr. 7am-1pm, P130). **Von-Von** buses leave from opposite the culture station for Banaue (signs read "Tabuk" or "Paracelis," 8:30am, P70). **Jeepneys** depart from beside Municipal Hall to go to Banaue (8:30, 9:30, 11:30am, noon, sometimes 1pm; P80); those leaving from behind the Kodac building near Old Saints Mission Elementary School go to Sagada (1hr., every hr. or when full 8:30am-4:30pm, P40).

ORIENTATION AND PRACTICAL INFORMATION. Bontoc's streets are unmarked and, as far as the residents know, unnamed. **"Main Street"** runs parallel to the **Chico River** through the town center. Most transportation arrives at the town circle (marked by a large tree) on Main St. Adjacent to the circle and up the hill are **Rizal Plaza** and **Pines Kitchenette and Inn.** The latter gives helpful travel information, arranges guides, and sells the Bontoc-Kalinga trekking map (P10; also available at the Bontoc Museum). Five major roads intersect Main St. Between the circle and the first street lies **Xijen Computer School,** where you'll find **Internet** access on the second floor. (P2 per min. Open M-Sa 8am-7:30pm, occasionally Su 9am-2pm.) For cheaper rates, use computers at any of the numerous office supply stores (P50 per hour). Opposite the second street, a road curves back up the hill past the **post office.** (*Poste Restante.* Open M-F 8am-noon and 1-5pm. **Postal Code:** 2616.) The **Philippine National Bank** exchanges currency and AmEx Traveler's Cheques at no charge. (☎602 1078. Open M-F 8:30am-2:30pm.) **Bontoc General Hospital** has a 24hr. **pharmacy** and emergency care. (Open M-F 8am-noon and 1-4pm, Sa 8am-noon for consultation.) **International calls** can be placed from the **Bayantel** office on Main St. (Collect calls P50. Open M-Sa 8am-noon and 2-7pm.)

ACCOMMODATIONS AND FOOD. During the dry season, accommodations suffer from intermittent water supply. The road to Samoki, which runs across the river from the town circle, passes the newly furnished **Ridgebrooke Hotel, Cafe and Restaurant ❷** (☎0918 199 1901). Ridgebrooke offers Bontoc's brightest rooms and one of the few laundry services in town. (Laundry P25 per piece. Rooms P150 per person; private room P600.) **Pines Kitchenette and Inn ❶,** opposite Rizal Plaza (☎0919 429 9813), has large rooms and great service. (P100 per person; doubles P300, with common room P500.) Its restaurant features live bands each night starting around 6:30pm. **Eastern Star Hotel and Restaurant ❶,** near the Sagada Jeepney Station in Walter Clapp Centrum, has friendly management and sparkling private rooms. (☎0919 483 7684. Economy rooms P100; singles and doubles P300; family room with cable TV P600.)

Bluebirds Restaurant ❶, between the third and fourth streets intersecting Main St., provides large, flavorful portions. Forget your pets, and try the dog (P50). For P30, the "budget meal" includes meat, rice, and vegetables. (Open daily 7am-9pm.) Next door, **Crystal's Bakery ❶** fattens patrons up with pudding bread (P2), fruit pastries (P10), and cinnamon rolls (7 for P10) fresh from the oven. (Open daily 5am-8pm.) Across Main St., the **Cable Cafe and Bar ❸** claims it is "where great singers are born." Said singers perform country and pop with live bands each night starting at 6pm. (Cocktails P60-120. *pusit*—squid; P130. Open daily 6am-10pm.)

SIGHTS AND ENTERTAINMENT. Before heading into the villages, check out the **Bontoc Museum,** opposite the post office. (Open daily 8am-noon and 1-5pm. P40.) Artifacts reflect the distinct cultures of the four tribes in the area. A collection of photographs from 1908-09 record earnest Americans trying to introduce games of tug-of-war to the males of rival villages to divert them from head-hunting. At the end of the day, blind masseuses will rub your aches away at the **Massage Clinic,** next to the Provincial Capital Building. (Whole body P140, half-body P70, feet or back P35. Open daily 7am-7pm.) After the massage, visit **Cable Cafe and Bar,** Bontoc's PG-rated version of nightlife (see **Accommodations and Food,** above).

TREKKING. You're asking for trouble if you don't hire a guide to smooth out cultural and linguistic barriers. Ask Manuela Cofulan at Pines Kitchenette to contact private guide **Francis Pa-in,** a Kalinga who is highly recommended by several publications. (☎462 4225. Around P500 per day for groups of 1-5.) Treks last anywhere from one morning to three days. A typical dayhike could involve a 3hr. walk from Bontoc to the **Maligcong rice terraces,** a 2hr. trek from Maligcong to **Guina-ang,** and then a 45min. hike to the **Mainit Hot Springs,** where optimistic miners pan for gold. The return to Bontoc is a 3hr. downhill walk. **Jeepneys** leave for Maligcong from the town circle (8am, noon, 2:30, 4:30pm; P30). From the drop-off point, it's a 2km trek to the village. It is customary for trekkers to bring gifts—adults appreciate matches, while children are delighted by candy. A longer expedition might include a trip to the village of **Butbut.** From Bontoc, it's a long jeepney ride to **Basao** (P40), then a 2hr. hike up the mountain to reach Butbut. The views of Tinglayen village from along the ridge are unbeatable.

BATAD

Tiny and remote, Batad is a favorite destination of travelers. Visitors rave about the abundance of cheap rooms and some of the most phenomenal rice terraces in the Philippines. Only accessible by foot, Batad remains less touristed than Banaue and the surrounding towns. Snapshots of President Gloria Arroyo dot the walls of virtually every establishment, and with good reason: Arroyo recently promised US$10 million to revitalize Batad's prized landscape, which includes the spectacular 21m Tappia Waterfall.

TRANSPORTATION. The trek to Batad consists of a 50min. trip from Banaue to **Batad Junction,** a 1hr. hike up a winding, unpaved road to the **Batad Rest Area,** and a 1hr. walk down steep "stairs" and dirt paths to Batad. To reach the junction, catch the jeepney leaving from the market area outside Sanafe Lodge (10am-noon, P40). Unless you plan on spending a night in Batad, it is best to hire a round-trip tricycle (P400-500) to ensure transportation back to Banaue. Round-trip jeepneys can also be hired for P1000. Some tricycle drivers will brave the uphill road from the junction to the rest area for an extra fee (P200-300). From the rest area to Batad, there is no option but to walk. About 15min. into the hike from the junction, the "mountaineer's shortcut" veers left over the "saddle" to Batad, cutting the trek in half. The shortcut, however, is steep and dangerous, especially with a backpack.

ACCOMMODATIONS AND FOOD. Batad's hostels are quite similar to each other: dorm beds cost P50 everywhere, and there is no electricity—you'll need a flashlight for the outhouse. The only deviation in price occurs at **Hillside Inn ❶,** jutting out from the first hill you see entering Batad, where private singles (P100) and doubles (P200) are available in addition to dorm beds (P50). Hillside is run by the Orlando family, who entertain guests with board games, guitars, and village legends. They also arrange daytrips (P15-200). Laundry service is available (P50 per kg). Farther down the path, **Simon's Inn and Restaurant ❶** is the only hostel offering views of both sides of the valley. **Pension House ❶** is closest to the rice terraces, farther downhill from Simon's and Hillside. These hostels are preferable because of their spectacular views; additional guesthouses dot the village center deep in the valley, a 30min. walk away. Though they lack the vistas, village hostels afford a better chance to see Ifugao dwellings. The friendly **Foreigner's Inn ❶** on the hill is the most well established.

Even though the lack of electricity makes refrigeration impossible, Batad's cuisine is quite satisfactory. Most restaurants are found in the hostels themselves. **Terrace View Café and Souvenir Shop ❶** is the one exception. The shop is on your right when the valley first comes in sight. Ginger tea (P15), sautéed noodles with vegetables (P45), and garlic egg soup (P35) are all appetizing after the 2hr. trek. Handwoven bags (P25-30) and flip-flops (P35) are also available. (Open daily 6am-9:30pm.) Both **Simon's ❸** and **Hillside's ❶** restaurants serve sandwiches on *chapaati* (pita bread) and *malawach* (a flat Middle Eastern bread) for P30-60. Simon's makes a mean *pinikpikan* (chicken; P300) and delicious native coffee (P25), while Hillside's is known for its more sinful treats: chocolate banana pancakes (P50), cigarettes (P35 a pack), and 80-proof gin (P40). At both restaurants, order your dinner before 7:30pm.

THE WEST COAST

If Manila moves too fast and the mountain provinces too slow, the West Coast is just right. The beaches around San Fernando are popular with domestic tourists from Manila, but if beaches are your final goal, you would be better off heading south to Mindoro or the Visayas. Vigan's architecture, however, is second to none. Mess about on boats around the Hundred Islands National Park and unwind on the beaches around San Fernando on your way there.

SAN FERNANDO (LA UNION) ☎72

The capital of La Union Province, San Fernando emanates great civic pride. Tricycles buzz through the streets, festooned with slogans lauding the city, and residents are quick to extol the virtues of their hometown. The crowded streets and the air reek of pollution, however, and the hubub sometimes boils over into madness. Travelers who end up here can find peace at the spectacular Ma-cho Temple and at a stretch of beach between San Fernando and Bauang. Those familiar with other Visayan beaches, however, will not be too impressed with its paltry stretch of passable sand. Rougher waters to the north, at San Juan beach, support loyal surfers and wannabes between November and February.

TRANSPORTATION. **Partas** (☎242 0465), on Quezon Ave. 100m north of P. Burgos St. intersection, runs buses to Baguio (2hr., every hr. 5am-8pm, with A/C P70) and Manila (7-8hr., 6am-12:30am, P265). **Minibuses,** including Eso-Nice, depart from Gov. Luna St. to Baguio (2hr., every 15min. 5:30am-6pm, P50). For Dagupan, catch minibuses departing from Rizal Ave. (2hr., every 5min. 4:30am-6pm, P50). For Alaminos, change minibuses at Dagupan.

ORIENTATION AND PRACTICAL INFORMATION. San Fernando is 270km north of Manila, bracketed between the beaches of **Bauang** (6km) to the south and **San Juan** (10km) to the north. The town is arranged linearly, and the South China Sea makes north-south orientation easy. **Quezon Avenue** (which becomes **National Highway**) connects the beaches and the city's main road. Most accommodations lie north of the **town plaza** along Quezon Ave. The major streets running east-west include **Gen. Luna Street** (not to be confused with adjacent Gov. Luna St.), **Rizal Avenue,** and **P. Burgos Street.** The sights sit on polar ends of town, with the **Ma-cho Temple** at the northern extreme, and other sights (Freedom Park, Fil-Chinese Pagoda and the Museo de La Union) to the south. Taking Rizal Ave. west away from the hill leads to the coast.

The **tourist office** is connected to the left side of the Oasis Country Resort on National Highway (☎888 2411; open M-F 7am-6:30pm), and the **Office of the City Planner,** in the Marcos Building has maps. (Open M-F 7am-6pm.) The **Philippine National Bank,** on Quezon Ave., at Gov. Luna St. exchanges currency and has a Cirrus/MC/PLUS/V 24hr. **ATM.** (☎242 0908. Open M-F 9am-3pm.) The **bookstore, Triva** (☎888 2996), on Quezon Ave., is open M-Sa 7:30am-8pm. The police station (☎888 2577) is north of the town plaza on Quezon Ave. In an emergency, dial ☎166. For **medical services, Bethany Hospital,** on Widdoes St. past Union Christian College, off Gen. Luna St. toward the hill is open 24hr. English spoken. The **pharmacy, Mercury Drug,** on Quezon Ave., opposite Far East Bank is open daily 6:30am-9pm. **The NET Café,** on Quezon Ave., 30m from P. Burgos St. intersection offers **Internet** access for P30 per hr. (☎242 2222. Open M-Sa 8am-9pm, Su 1pm-7pm.) There are two **post office** branches; the first is in the Marcos Building, on Rizal Ave., at the corner of P. Tavera St., and the second branch is on Mabini St., Catbangen. (☎888 2965. *Poste Restante.* Open M-F 8am-5pm.) **Postal Code:** 2600.

ACCOMMODATIONS AND FOOD. **Hotel Mikka ❺** is on Quezon Ave., next to the Partas bus terminal, 150m north of P. Burgos St. intersection toward Ma-cho Temple. The staff is knowledgeable, and all rooms are fully equipped with phones, A/C, and cable TV. Room service available. (☎242 5737. Singles P625; doubles P750; family rooms P1250.) Also on Quezon Ave., 100m south of the town plaza, **Mandarin House Hotel ❷** is more budget-friendly. (☎888 5309. Doubles P165, with A/C and common room P435.) The lines are long, but the service is quick at the **Danish Baker ❶**, on Quezon Ave., past the plaza on the left. (Tuna turnovers P23. *Pandisuelo* bread, a local favorite, P3. Open daily 6am-8:30pm.) **Las Villas ❺**, 2514 San Juan, 400m toward the sea from the National Highway (Quezon Ave.) in San Juan, has fresh seafood that melts in your mouth as you cool in the shade. The "Fisherman's Basket"—well worth the trek from town—feeds two for P420.

SIGHTS. On the lush green hillside off Quezon Ave., 400m to the north of the town plaza, a joint group of Filipinos and Taiwanese fisherman built the **Ma-cho Temple** in gratitude for local hospitality. Ma-cho, the Taoist goddess of the sea, looks out upon the South China Sea from atop her hill; visitors can borrow her vista from the balcony, or step inside to ask her questions. A Chinese deity of the Sung dynasty, Ma-cho is known in the Philippines as the Virgin of Caysasay. In the second week of September, the original statue of the Virgin is brought to the temple from Taal for the **Feast of Our Lady of Caysasay.** (Open daily 6am-6pm.)

VIGAN ☎77

The Americans left behind McDonald's, the Japanese left behind bombed ruins, and the Spanish left behind Vigan—now a UNESCO World Heritage Site. Thankfully, the city was spared the devastation that gutted Manila's Intramuros, leaving one of the oldest and best-preserved of Spain's 16th-century colonial holdings in the Philippines. Glorious architecture, cobblestone pavements, unhurried pedestrians, and horse-drawn traffic give Vigan a time-capsule ambience.

TRANSPORTATION. **Dominion Bus Lines** (☎722 2053), near the south end of Quezon Ave., sends buses to Manila (8-10 per day 4:30am-10pm, A/C P400). The **Partas** terminal (☎722 2933) is south of the public market, with buses to Cubao in Manila (every 30-60min. 4:45am-10:30pm, P360). Catch a **tricycle** from here to the city center for P10.

ORIENTATION AND PRACTICAL INFORMATION. Vigan lies west of the Mestizo River. Its grid-patterned streets are easily covered by foot, tricycle, or horse-drawn *calesa*. **Quezon Avenue,** parallel to the river, intersects P. Burgos St. on the east side of the city's two main plazas. The main plaza area is beside Municipal Hall, which houses the **police station** (☎166). The newly restored **Mena Crisologo Street,** distinguished by cobblestones and antique shops, runs south of Plaza Burgos near the provincial **tourist office** (open daily 8am-4:30pm). One block south of Burgos St., Florentino St. runs east-west and passes a branch of **Philippine National Bank,** with a 24hr. **ATM.** (Cirrus/MC/PLUS/V. Open M-F 9am-3pm.) Gen. Luna St. is home to the **PT&T Telephone Office.** (☎722 2273. Open M-W 7am-8pm, Th-F 8am-8pm, Sa-Su 8am-5pm.)

The **Gabriela Silang General Hospital** is on Quirino Blvd., which runs north-south on the east side of town along the river. (☎169, office 722 2782. English spoken. Open 24hr.) Most tourists go to **Lahoz Clinic,** across from Mercury Drugstore on Jose Singson St. (☎722 2175. English spoken. Open 24hr.) **Farmacia Fernandina** is on Quezon Ave., between Bonifacio and Gen. Luna St. (☎722 2470. Open daily

7am-10pm.) **Internet** access is available at **Powernet,** 32 Gov. A. Reyes St., just west of Mena Crisologo St. (☎722 1830. 1st hr. P60, P0.83 each additional min. Open daily 8am-7:30pm.) The **post office** is one block past the bank on Bonifacio St., near the corner of Gov. A. Reyes St. **Postal Code**: 2700.

ACCOMMODATIONS AND FOOD. **Grandpa's Inn ❸,** 1 Bonifacio St., on the corner of Quirino Blvd. not far from the river, is an affordable way to experience old-world chic. Check out the giant suite with custom-built *calesa* beds. (☎722 2118. Laundry services. Doubles P400, with private bath P600, with A/C P1000. 20% discount for seniors.) The staff is warm and friendly and the adjacent **coffee shop** tempts guests with specialty coffees (ice-blended latteccino P60) and cakes. (Open daily 8am-10pm.) Farther along Quirino Blvd. away from the town center, **El Juliana Hotel ❹,** 5 Liberation, has far less friendly service; the A/C rooms border on sterile but come equipped with cable TV and private bathrooms. (☎722 2994. Singles and doubles P800.) The swimming pool, closed in the low season, is open to the public 7am-6pm (P35) and 6-11pm (P50). The comfortable **Gordion Inn ❸,** on V. Delos Reyes St., offers comfortable rooms with A/C, cable TV, private bath, and breakfast. (☎722 2526. A/C dorms P300; standard rooms P1200. MC/V.) The newly renovated **Vigan Heritage Mansion ❺,** on Crisologo St. at Liberation Blvd., offers stylish lodgings at prices that would make its colonial-era Spanish owners turn in their graves. (☎722 6479; viganheritagemansion@yahoo.com. Singles and doubles P1500; with TV and fridge P2000.) **Street vendors ❶** along Plaza Burgos serve Spanish *empañadas*, deep-fried rice tortillas filled with local vegetables (P10) or meat and eggs (P20), and *okoy*, crispy shrimp and onion pancakes (P20), from late afternoon until early morning. **Cafe Leona Restaurant and Videoke Bar ❸,** on Mena Crisologo St. next door to the tourist office, is Vigan's sole outlet for Thai and Japanese entrees. The "ice tea" (P25) is more like a popsicle in a cup. (☎722 2212. Sushi P90-190. Open daily 8am-10pm.) **Cafe Floresita ❸,** set within attractive arches by the Ancieto Mansion, has fabulous *longganiza* and a variety of Filipino dishes, including *pancit*. (Most dishes P40-180. Open daily 6am-9pm.) **Cool Spot Restaurant ❸** (☎722 2588), behind the Vigan Hotel on Quirino Blvd., is a local favorite known for its homemade *bagnet* (P200) and *longganiza* (P80). It's also a popular venue for armchair sports enthusiasts; check with the management for a schedule. The **8.88 Restaurant and Pool Hall ❶,** on Rizal Ave., draws a local crowd with pool tables and a variety of entrees for P55-70, from squid balls (P50) to *longsilog* (P46), a combination of egg, fried garlic rice, and *longganiza*. (☎722 2208. Open daily 8am-2am.)

SIGHTS. The legacy of the Spanish *conquistadores* is well preserved in the town's architecture, but Vigan has also been shaped by its participation in the lucrative galleon trade with Europe, Asia, and Mexico. **Rowilda's Hand Loom,** on Crisologo St. near Cordillera Inn, is reminiscent of the hand-weaving crafts that contributed to the international textile trade in colonial times. (Woven handbags P150-180. Open daily 8am-6pm.) **Pagburnayan Potteries,** on the corner of Liberation Blvd. and Rizal St., produces the stoneware *burnay* jar used by the Ilocanos to store everything from vinegar to wine. A water buffalo squashes the clay under its hoof, and wood-fired kilns bake the sculpted clay. **Padre Burgos House National Museum,** 6 Burgos St., adjacent to St. Paul's Cathedral, commemorates the death of Padre Burgos, one of the most famous Chinese *mestizo* residents of Vigan, whose 1872 martyrdom galvanized the revolutionary movement. On display, among other things, are ancient *itneg* (ovens) of the Tinggian tribe, which were recently discovered inside a bat cave in Ilocos Sur. (Open Tu-Su 8:30-11:30am and 1:30-4:30pm. P10.) **Crisologo Museum,** 23 Liberation Blvd., is another ancestral home that has evolved into a museum. This former residence of congressman, governor, and war hero Floro Crisologo contains dusty relics of the political family, including antique furniture and a few of Crisologo's war weapons. (Open daily 8:30-11:30am and 1:30-4:30pm.) **St. Paul's Metropolitan Cathedral,** the orange church on N. Segovia St., is an example of distinctive "Earthquake Baroque" architecture. Attached to it is the **Museo de San Pablo,** a religious museum with life-size figures of Jesus. West of the cathedral is **Plaza Salcedo,** an elevated elliptical plaza and former site of public executions that features a 17th-century statue—the oldest in Northern Luzon.

SOUTHERN LUZON

While Manila's appeal comes mostly from manmade venues, Southern Luzon is a natural wonder. A beautiful lake fills the formerly volatile crater of Taal Volcano while layers of recently released ash cover the still active Mayon Volcano. For those seeking adventure closer to sea level, the island of Mindoro offers beaches and world-class dive sites.

LAKE TAAL REGION ☎43

In prehistoric times, the Taal Volcano stood mighty at 18000m. A massive eruption blew off the volcano's top, however, and a crater lake formed in the new opening. Lava rising through this lake has created an island at its center (the tip of the volcano's cone) which, over thousands of years, has developed its own lake. Tagaytay Ridge, now an excellent spot from which to view the crater, was once part of the volcano's rocky base. The towns surrounding Lake Taal, however, are dreary and uncomfortable. No more than a daytrip is necessary to see the volcano and the neighboring Tagaytay Ridge.

TRANSPORTATION AND PRACTICAL INFORMATION. Lake Taal is located between the towns of Talisay and Leynes. **Buses** from Batangas and Manila pass through Tanauan, which has transportation connections to Taal. **Jeepneys** travel from the public market in Tanauan, adjacent to McDonald's, to Talisay (20min., 5am-7pm, P17). From there, **tricycles** (15min., P32) can be taken toward Leynes to reach the resorts. On an alternate route, buses heading to Nasugbu or Calatagan pass Tagaytay Ridge, which has the best views of the volcano. To get to the lakefront from the ridge, get off the bus at Olivares Plaza, catch a jeepney (P10) to the top of Ligaya Drive, and transfer to another jeepney down Ligaya Dr., which ends at the water (last trip 6pm, P20). Jeepneys turn left to Talisay, but you can catch a tricycle if you're heading toward Leynes. Jeepneys to Tanauan depart from the corner of Laurel and Wencislao St. (3am-5pm, P20). Buses to Batangas and Batangas Pier pass along J.P. Laurel St. in Tanauan (1½hr.; P4035, A/C P68). Buses also go the other way to Manila (1½hr.; P47, with A/C P78).

The **Tanauan Shoppers Market (TSM)** on A. Mabini St. exchanges **currency** and traveler's checks. (Open daily 7am-6pm.) For **Western Union** services, head to the **Luzon Development Bank,** opposite McDonald's on A. Mabini St. (Open M-F 9am-4:30pm.) One block away on the same side of the street, **Saudi@net** has six computers with reasonably fast **Internet** access. (☎778 5830. P30 per hr. Open daily 8am-11pm.) The **PLDT telephone office,** on the lakefront road near the Ligaya Dr. intersection, provides international phone service. In Talisay proper, the Municipal Hall on Wencislao St. houses the **police** (☎773 0241, **emergency** ☎166) and **post office** (open M-F 8am-5pm). **Postal Code:** 4220. Farther along the street (with the lake to your right), **St. Andrew's Hospital** (☎773 0196) has a 24hr. **pharmacy.**

ACCOMMODATIONS AND FOOD. Tourists flock here during summer months (Mar.-May); book well in advance. Resorts generally offer packages for guests, which include round-trip boat transfers and a guided walk around the crater. Outside peak season, the area resembles a ghost town and most hotels offer few services. It's wise to call ahead. Most resorts have in-house restaurants. Alternatively, head to any of the restaurants facing the lake around Talisay Junction for succulent Taal Lake tilapia (P50-150). **San Roque Beach Resort ❺,** 5min. from Ligaya Dr. off Tagaytay Rd., is a labor of love for owners Lita and Leo. (☎773 0271; sanroquebeacheresort@yahoo.com. *Nipa* huts with common room P850, with A/C and breakfast P1500; 3-bedroom guesthouse with living room and kitchen P4500.) Round-trip boat transport to Taal Crater P1000-1200. **Vista Hazel's Beach Resort ❸,** down the road from San Roque and situated on the beach, has a swimming pool. (☎773 0257. Cottages P500; doubles with A/C P1700.) **Buco Resort ❺,** next to the Taal Volcano Science House (see **Sights,** below), is a 5min. walk toward Leynes from San Roque. (☎773 0306. Doubles P800, with A/C P900; family room P2000.)

SIGHTS. Pick up some background knowledge on Taal and other Philippine volcanoes at the **Taal Volcano Science House,** next to the Buco Resort, halfway between Talisay and Leynes. (Open 24hr. Free.) **Taal Volcano** actually has two craters, the younger of which erupted in 1965. There are two popular ways to tackle the older crater. A boat can take you to the front of the island (30min., about P1000), where a trail (by foot or horseback) leads to the lip of the old crater, the smaller of the two. Don't shell out P300 for a guide; though rocky, the trail is easy to navigate. Veer right at the junction 500m from the base. Alternatively, you can pay extra for a boat to take you around the back of the island (45min., P750-1000), where islanders guide visitors into the crater to the water's edge (P300).

The Taal Lake Yacht Club (☎773 0192), on the lakeshore in Talisay, arranges boats for groups of up to six, plus a free guide and use of their *nipa* huts (and hot showers) for 2hr. upon your return (P1600). Kayak and sailboat rentals also available.

You're free to bathe in the sulfurous waters, which are said to have medicinal value, but don't swim to the rocky outcrop in the center of the lake, and avoid areas with rising steam—the water can scald. It takes 2-4hr. to visit Taal Volcano, so go early and bring water. Travel on the lake can be rough in the rainy season, and most boats only operate in the morning or early afternoon.

DAET ☎54

Daet (pronounced Dah-et), proclaims itself "A City of Character" on its welcome sign. However, the "character" this slogan references—outside a smoggy battalion of tricycles in the main square, perhaps—remains largely unknown. The nearby coastal village of Mercedes attracts more attention, drawing in a flotilla of fishing boats for its morning fish market. Four kilometers from Daet town center along J. Lukban St. (10min. tricycle ride P15), **Bagasbas Beach** stretches far and wide, with surfing on particularly rough days. The **San Jose Beach,** near the Talisay district (15min. tricycle ride north of Daet center) makes for a relaxing beach experience. An absence of shade, however, will keep any stay short.

Daet's main street, **Vinzons Avenue,** runs parallel to the north side of the river and is home to many hotels and restaurants. Several pay phones line Vinzons Ave. Further down, Vinzons Ave. becomes **Gov. Panotes Avenue,** which continues to **Mercedes.** The **Philtranco** bus terminal is on F. Martinez St., off Gov. Panotes Ave. (☎571 2718), a short jeepney ride from the town center (P4). Buses depart for Pasay and Cubao in Manila (8-9hr.; 9-12 per day 6:30am-9:40pm; P300, with A/C

P341). Buses also leave from **Superlines** bus terminal (☎721 2961), a short tricycle ride from Vinzons Ave. (P10), for Cubao in Manila (8-9hr.; every hr. 5:30am-9:30pm; P201, with A/C P245). J. Lukban St., across the river, leads past the **Rizal Monument** and **Freedom Park** to **Magana Street,** where the **Philippine National Bank** exchanges traveler's checks (☎571 2815; open M-F 9am-4pm). For the **police,** dial ☎166 or ☎571 2815. (☎440 0568. Open daily 7am-7:30pm.) The **post office** is in Camambugan, a P5 tricycle ride from the town center. (*Poste Restante*. Open M-F 8am-noon and 1-5pm.) **Postal Code:** 4600.

Karilagan Hotel ❷, on Moreno St. behind the elevated town plaza, is a well-established hotel with a 24hr. restaurant, piano, and beauty parlor. (☎721 2236. Singles with bath P200, with A/C P500; doubles P600; family room P900.) On Vinzons Ave. opposite the elevated town plaza, **Hotel Dolor ❸** has 24hr. room service and a nightclub upstairs. (☎721 2167. Economy singles P250, with TV, A/C, hot water, and fridge P450; doubles P450/P650, with A/C and cable P950.) Look for the distinctive red and yellow building on Zabala St., by Metroback off Vinzons Ave. where **Golden House ❸** (open daily 7am-10pm) serves Chinese delicacies like sea cucumber (P200). Set meals run P70-85. For Bicol treats like *pala tim* pork (P170) and *miki-bijon* noodles (P70), head to **Slennalo's ❷,** adjacent to the Palayok complex on Pimentel Avenue (open daily 9am-10pm). **Stroll Jazz Bar,** on the fourth floor of the Hotel Dolor Bldg. on Vinzons Ave., is better than other bars on Bagasbas Beach. (No sandals or shorts. Open daily 6pm-2am.) As much as it is a quaint, old-fashioned fishing village, **Mercedes,** 7km from Daet up Gov. Panotes Rd., is also a successful industrial outlet. Hundreds of fishing vessels congregate here for its seafood market; rumor has it local fisherman use an array of bizarre techniques, including whispering, to attract their catch.

LEGAZPI ☎52

> **!** Mt. Mayon is regarded as one of the world's most volatile volcanoes. Since 1616, it is known to have erupted at least 40 times; its most recent eruption was on June 25th, 2001. Check with the Department of Transportation in Legazpi, the local tourist office, or your embassy for updated news on safety.

Even the beautiful must belch from time to time. Mt. Mayon, whose name derives from the local word meaning "beautiful," has been violently spewing forth ash about every 10 years since 1968. Still, adventure-seekers flock to this friendly town to scale what is widely hailed as the world's most perfect cone. Legazpi also makes an ideal base for excursions into the eastern Visayas.

TRANSPORTATION

Flights: The airport is off Washington Dr., 3km northwest of the city center. **Philippine Airlines** (☎245 5024) serves Legazpi with daily flights to **Manila** (1hr.; 9:05am, 3:25pm; P2418). An agent is at **Hotel Victoria** (☎214 3476) on Rizal St. Open daily 8am-noon and 1:30-5pm.

Buses: There are two bus terminals. From the **Satellite Bus Terminal** on Imperial St., **Philtranco** (☎820 2794) buses depart for Taft. Ave. in **Manila** (6 times daily 6am-7pm; P546, with A/C P746). **Jam Transit** (☎480 4029) buses depart for **Manila** (2pm P330; 5:30pm A/C P530). Local buses and **jeepneys** leave from the **Old Market terminal** on Circumferential Rd. to **Donsol** (2½hr; 15 per day, last bus 4:30pm; P47).

ORIENTATION AND PRACTICAL INFORMATION

The main commercial district, also home to most of Legazpi's budget accommodations, lies between **Albay** to the south and **Rawis** to the north. **Rizal Street** links central Legazpi with Albay and is plied by hordes of **jeepneys** (most rides P4). The **Battle of Legazpi Monument** stands in the middle of central Legazpi. To the west, **Circumferential Road** leads to the local bus and jeepney terminal and **Satellite Bus Terminal.** One block east (toward the bay) is **Peñaranda Street,** Legazpi's principle commercial artery. The **airport,** accessible by tricycle (P50) or taxi (P100), is 2km northwest of town at the end of **Aquende Street,** which then becomes **Washington Drive.** The fishing quarter, known as **Victory Village,** lies along the black-sand beach south of central Legazpi, at the foot of **Kapuntaken Hill.**

The helpful **tourist office,** 3rd fl., RCBC Bldg., Rizal St., can arrange Mayon treks. (☎213 215; leg-cmo@globalink.net.ph. Open M-F 8am-5pm.) There are a number of **banks** on Rizal St. and Quezon Ave. in central Legazpi (most open M-F 9am-3pm). Many have 24hr. **ATMs. Tanchuling Hospital** serves central Legazpi and is in the Imperial Court Subdivision II off of Rizal St. (☎480 6372. Open 24hr.) **Ago General Hospital** is in Albay, past the provincial capitol on the left. (☎481 5807. Open 24hr.) Next door, **Mercury Drug** is on Rizal St. opposite the Bayantel office. (Open daily 6am-9pm.) The **Bayantel** office, on Rizal St. at the corner of Imperial St., provides **Internet** access. (☎180 6187. P33 for collect calls. Open daily 8am-5pm.) The **PLDT office** on Rizal St. in Albay has an **IDD phone.** (☎214 3896. Open daily 7am-9pm.) **Internet** access is also available at **Joycom** on Rizal St. (☎480 4777. P30 per hr. Open daily 9am-10pm.) The **post office** is on Lapu-Lapu St. near the corner of Quezon Ave. and Legazpi Tourist Inn. (Open M-F 8am-noon and 1-5pm.) **Postal Code:** 4500.

ACCOMMODATIONS

Most of Legazpi's accommodations cluster within a few blocks of the monument. The **Rex Hotel ❸** is at the corner of Peñaranda St. and Aguinaldo St., next to the church. (☎241 5290. Singles P240, with A/C P540; doubles P275/580.) The **Xandra Hotel ❷** on Peñaranda, one block north of the Rizal intersection on the left, is the cheapest bed in town. (☎820 4808. Singles with fan and common bath P150-270, with A/C, bath, and TV P500; doubles P180-600.) Among the city's more comfortable hotels, **Hotel Victoria ❺,** near the post office on Rizal St., is the most reasonably priced. (☎480 8041. Videoke bar and cafe inside. Singles and doubles with A/C, cable TV, and breakfast P1200.)

FOOD AND ENTERTAINMENT

Legazpi is a great place to sample the area's signature dish, "Bicol Express," a mildly vile concoction whose principal ingredient is chilli peppers. **Doña Alice ❸,** in Rawis 1km north of the bridge on the left, has a pleasant atmosphere and serves scrumptious Bikolano delicacies like *camolig*, an herbal leaf with coconut, and *pili*, an almond, honey, and sugar combination. (Open daily 10am-10pm.) Closer to town, on Peñaranda just beyond the BLTB bus terminal, the **Paayahayan Beer Garden ❸** serves delicious seafood in *nipa* huts. (Crabs in chilli sauce P180. Open daily 10am-1am.) There are also a number of fast-food joints and several nondescript Chinese restaurants in central Legazpi.

For after hours entertainment, locals hit the **Bicharra Entertainment Center** in central Legazpi, opposite the statue of Jose Rizal. Inside you'll find a movie theater (shows P30), cafes, and ice cream shops. **Bar 101** on the third floor features live bands. (Open daily 1pm-2am.) **Club Paparazzi,** on the fourth floor of Hotel Victoria, is a popular videoke bar. (☎214 3476. Cover P100. Open daily 6pm-2am.)

SIGHTS

During the 1814 eruption of Mt. Mayon, almost everything in the town of Cagsawa was destroyed. The eerie remains of the town church, including its forlorn belfry, can still be seen. Visitors seeking personal tours at cheaper prices should contact local tourist guru **Eddie Nolasco,** who hangs out in the lobby of the Xandra Hotel (☎820 4808) and has scaled Mt. Mayon numerous times.

CAGSAWA RUINS. Cagsawa National Museum features an exhibit about major volcanoes in the Philippines. *(Take a Guinobatan- or Camalig-bound jeepney and get off at the Cagsawa turn-off (20min., P5), marked by advertising for the Cagsawa 1814 Restaurant. It is 500m from the turn-off to the ruins. Open M-Sa 8-11am and 1-4pm. P6, students P5.)*

CAVES. The three-tiered **Hoyop-Hoyopan Caves** have crystal formations that guides insist resemble everything from the Banaue rice terraces to the Philippine eagle. Hoyop-Hoyopan literally means "blow-blow," supposedly the sound of the whispering wind at the caves' exit. Only guided tours are permitted. The **Calabidongan Caves** ("Cave of the Bats"), 3km from the Hoyop-Hoyopan Caves, are much more extensive. It takes 3hr. and a chest-deep dip in the underground river to get there. Bring a flashlight, and be prepared to get wet. *(For Hoyop-Hoyopan, take a Guinobatan-bound or Camalig-bound jeepney to Camalig town proper (30min., last trip 8pm, P10), and find a jeepney bound for Cotmon (6am-6pm, P8), 12km away. Tell the driver to stop at the junction for the Hoyop-Hoyopan Cave. It's an additional 100m to the entrance. Guided tours 45-60min.; P100. For Calabidongan, P500 for 1-2 people, each additional person P250.)*

BUSAY WATERFALLS. These seven-tiered falls in Malilipot are a godsend in the heat of the rainy season. Kids play in the larger pools at each tier, and dare you to stand under the pummeling waters of the highest waterfall. If you do, you'll earn their deepest respect and loudest laughter. *(Take a jeepney or bus to Malilipot (35min., P15) and get off when you see the large "Busay Falls" sign. It is a 35min. walk to the falls. P5.)*

MAYON VOLCANO. In northeast Albay, Mt. Mayon peaks at 2457m. A challenging but popular climb, it's normally scaled over two days. Base camps punctuate the climb at 750m and 1500m, serving as a place for climbers to pitch tents. The second day's trek begins at 6am and reaches the "knife edge," 2250m high, around 9:30am. Loose rocks make it risky for inexperienced mountaineers to cover the remaining 500m to the rim. Expeditions return to Legazpi by 6pm the second day. The climb is possible year-round, though March and April are ideal times. Temperatures can fall to 10-15°F on upper parts of the mountain. Guides charge P4500 for one or two climbers (each extra person P1500). The fee includes transportation, a five-person tent, rope, and food. The tourist office organizes guides (book before 5pm 1 day in advance). True penny-pinchers and the stamina-filled can consider attempting the peak in one day for P2500. In the third week of May, the DOT conducts the "Mayon Conquest"—a free, organized climb of the volcano. For travelers wishing to get close, but not *that* close, to the volcano, the ramshackle **Mayon Rest House** sits at 840m. To get there, take a jeepney to Tabaco, 26km north of Legazpi, and then transfer to a **Ligao**-bound jeepney; ask to be let off at the junction leading to the guesthouse—it's 8km from there.

DARAGA HILLTOP CHURCH. Established in 1773 by Franciscan missionaries, Daraga is a monumental reinterpretation of a traditional Basilican Church. Built of volcanic rock, it appears to be formed as much by geology as by the human hand. *(Jeepneys (20min., P5) head west into Daraga (Locsin). Get off at the Shell station on Gen. Luna St.; walk up St. Maria St.; or take the Daraga Water District stairs next to Sarko Cafe and Bookstore. Open daily 7am-midnight.)*

OTHER SIGHTS. Visitors can take a pre-dusk stroll through **Victory Village,** an old fishing enclave incongruously appended to the characterless city. From the end of Elizondo St., pass through the entrance to the covered fish market. On the other side, the village huddles on the black-sand beach. At the far end, steps take you up **Kapuntukan Hill** for a stunning view of the volcano, the sunset, and the city.

DONSOL

The sleepy fishing village of Donsol lies 30km southeast of Legazpi in neighboring Sorsogon province. With a single phone line shared by the entire village, Donsol remained an anonymous speck on the map until the discovery of mighty whale sharks (Rhicodon typus). Growing up to 20m in length, the sharks are the largest species of fish known to man. In the late 1990s, word of the *butanding* (as the sharks are locally known) spread, attracting divers and poachers alike. Local authorities promptly passed legislation banning the hunting of the sharks and, with the assistance of the United Nations Development Program, established what has become a model for ecotourism and sustainable development projects.

Prime *butanding*-watching season is December to May, though this varies from year to year. For more information, call the Bayantel phone in Donsol (☎56 411 1109), and ask for Nita Pedragoza at the Visitor Center. You will probably have to spend at least one night in Donsol. Check in at the **Visitor Center,** where officials will help you find a place to stay. There are several homestays in the village, including **Hernandez Lodging House** ❸ and **Santiago Homestay** ❸ (both P300 for a 3-person room). Pricier "beach resorts," **Amor Farm Beach Resort** ❹ and **Woodland Beach Resort** ❹ (both P500 per room), are accessible from Donsol by boat.

Donsol is accessible by local bus from Legazpi. Excursions leave at 8am and return at 5pm. It's wise to show up at the Visitors Center by about 7am to secure a spot (each boat holds 6 people). A "Butanding Interaction Officer" oversees each boat and advises you on safety. (P2500 per boat, plus a P300 fee per person. Snorkeling gear P220. Scuba-diving is banned.)

ORIENTAL MINDORO

Four hours by bus from Manila, the steamy smog gives way to the salty air of Mindoro, 26km off the coast of Luzon. Teeming marine life replaces the crowds, and sizzling sand, not hot asphalt, burns visitors' feet. Exquisite reefs, pristine water, and dazzling aquatic life make Mindoro's dive sites among the world's best in the peak season (Nov.-May); during the summer months frequent rainfall reduces visibility. While the island's wildlife and forests continue to thrive, so does an unfortunate sex industry. Stick to the diving, and steer clear of the discos.

THE VIEW FROM ABOVE

Main Towns: Batangas, Puerto Galera.

Beaches: Big Lalaguna, Sabang, Small Lalaguna, and White Beaches, all near Puerto Galera.

Something Fun: Hash House Harrier runs and treks to Mt. Calavite and Mt. Halcon.

PUERTO GALERA ☎43

The beaches surrounding Puerto Galera are the destinations of choice for island-hoppers from Luzon. Sabang Beach, the most popular in the area, lays the amenities and services on thick; other beaches are more tranquil. The cove of Big Lalaguna, offers the best swimming and snorkeling, while Sabang and Small Lalaguna boast the best venues for bar hopping. Windsurfers will enjoy the gentle waves of White Beach (highest during the summer months). The harbor at Puerto Galera proper is an option for those who don't want to be on the front line of tourism development or who don't plan to stay on the island for long. Dive sites lie near the coast, and the interior provides numerous trekking opportunities into wilderness that has successfully resisted development.

TRANSPORTATION

Buses: The **Si-Kat** office on Muelle Pier sells combined ferry and bus tickets to **Manila;** in Sabang, tickets are sold at a desk in front of Eddie's Place on the beach. Open daily 7:30am-4pm. **Si-Kat II** ferry departs from Muelle Pier and arrives at City State Tower Hotel in **Ermita** (5½hr.; 9:30am, 1pm; P550).

Ferries: Several operators go to **Batangas** from Muelle Pier, Balatero Pier, White Beach and Sabang Beach (1½-2 hours). From Muelle **Pier: Blue Eagle** (7am, 1:30pm; P125), **Blue Phoenix** (9am, 3:30pm; P140), and **Five J Ferry** (10:20am, 2:30pm; P140). Other boats depart hourly between 5:45am and 3:30pm. From **Balatero Pier: Car Karl** (6:30am, 1:30pm; P120), **Golden Hawk** (5:30, 6:30, 8:45, 11:30am, 3pm; P150). From **Sabang Beach: Princess Kay/Super Gigi Outriggers** (6, 7, 9, 11:30am; P120), **Blue Penguin** (1pm, P140). From **White Beach: MB Brian** (☎0917 426 8995; 8, 10:15am, 2, 2:30pm; P150). "Special Ride" to Batangas in a *banca* P1800. To get to **Boracay,** take a jeepney from the Puerto Galera market to **Calapan** (2hr., 5am-2:30pm, P70), then catch a bus from the wharf in Calapan to **Roxas** (3-4hr., 5am-5pm, P105). Spend the night in Roxas (a hotel is near the stone beach). In the morning, take the Flor B to **Boracay** (5hr., M-Tu and Th-F 10:30am, P300). Several **outrigger boats** also leave Roxas for **Romblon Island** and **Tablas Island** north of Boracay. From Romblon Island, ferries cross to Tablas Island. A jeepney to **Santa Fe** on Tablas Island and a ferry across to Boracay completes the journey. You can also reach Boracay via Batangas.

Local Transportation: Bancas to coastal destinations leave from Muelle Pier (P400-1000). **Tricycles** are common but pricey; hail one already in motion to avoid being charged the "special rate" (P5-20 within Población; P80-150 to Sabang or White Beach). From **Sabang: Jeepneys** to **Puerto Galera**'s town proper congregate around **Sabang Fast Food**—in the rainy season, muddy roads make the trip longer (15min., depart when full 6am-5pm, P20; return approx. every hr. 6am-5pm, P20). From **Puerto Galera:** take a tricycle to the Sabang jeepney stand from Muelle Pier (5min., P5). You can also hire a jeepney to make the trip for P100.

ORIENTATION AND PRACTICAL INFORMATION

Puerto Galera proper (or Población) is in **Muelle Bay** on the north coast of Mindoro, at the neck of a Y-shaped peninsula surrounded by coves and beaches. A lighthouse at **Escarcero Point** marks the easternmost tip of the peninsula. **Sabang Beach** stretches 1-2km west along the coast. A road connects Sabang Beach to Población, 5km away. A short walk west from Sabang Beach, with the sea to your right, leads around a rocky point to **Small** and **Big Lalaguna Beaches.** Small Lalaguna Beach is actually bigger than Big Lalaguna Beach—the names refer to inland lagoons, not to the beaches themselves. The west tip of the "Y" shelters ritzy and exclusive **Coco Beach.** From Población, a 7km ride west goes to **San Isidro. White Beach,** named for the color of its fine sand, lines the coast and boasts the island's swankiest resorts.

Tourist Office: (☎287 3059). On Muelle Pier in Población. Friendly staff provides bus and boat schedules, accommodations suggestions, and information on excursions. The Tourist Map, available from guesthouses, the tourist office, and travel agents, features resort listings and transport and diving information (P100). Open daily 8am-5pm.

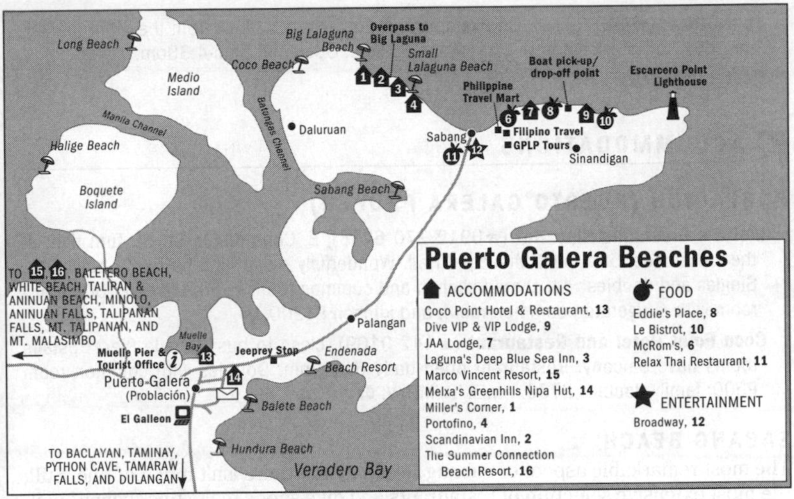

Travel and Tours: Tarzan Trek Tours (☎0919 410 1020), located at the Sunshine Coast Restaurant in Sabang Beach (p. 11), offers island-hopping (P800), waterfall-sighting (P1000), and mountain-trekking daytrips (P1500) around Mindoro and Lake Taal. Ask for Naty. **Going Places into the Land of Paradise (GPLP),** opposite Sabang Fast Food, has a variety of local tours, starting at P200. (☎0921 531 7878; adventures172001@yahoo.com.) Open daily 9am-6pm. **Filipino Travel Center,** in Sabang opposite Sabang Fast Food, arranges airfare as well as local packages. (☎287 3108; www.filipinotravel.com.ph.) Open daily 9am-6pm.

Currency Exchange: Filipino Travel Center offers cash advances on all major credit cards (7.5% commission) and exchanges traveler's checks and currency. Moneychangers abound on Muelle Pier in Población.

Markets: In Poblacion, **Parkway Mini Mart** (☎442 0144), opposite Muelle Pier, has the best selection of foods, toiletries, and other supplies. Open daily 6am-7pm. In Sabang, small markets line the major pedestrian street. **Philippine Travel Mart,** opposite McRom's Restaurant, is the most well stocked. Open daily 5:30am-3am.

Police: (☎487 3043). Municipal Hall, H. Axalan St., opposite Puerto Galera Academy. Open 24hr.

Medical Services: The privately run **Puerto Galera Lying-In Clinic** (☎0912 352 9531), next to the Municipal Hall, takes care of prescriptions. Open 24hr. **Dr. Carmelita Atienza** works in Sabang down the road that turns off near Tropicana Restaurant, leading to the town market. Open M-Sa 9am-5pm. **Ospital ng Mamamayan** (☎287 3049), the city's government hospital, also handles foreign patients. Open 24hr. **St. Patrick's Hospital Medical Center** (☎0917 536 2757, emergency 1111; www.divemed.com.ph) in Batangas City has a hyperbaric chamber for divers.

Telephone: Card pay phones are common in Sabang and Población. IDD available at outlet next to a minimart and Barangay Security office in Sabang (☎0912 318 2840). Open daily 6am-10pm. **Bayantel,** in Muelle, Población, has lowest fees for international collect calls. Open M-F 7am-8:30pm, Sa-Su 7am-6pm.

Internet Access: McRom's Restaurant, opposite Philippino Travel Mart in Sabang, has the cheapest access at P1 per min. (30min. free for patrons). In Población, **Cyber Galleon Computer Center** (☎287 3263), on the main road near the market opposite Ester Store, has 6 computers. P60 per hr. Open daily 8am-9pm. The only access in White Beach is at the Marco Vincent Resort (p. 579).

Post Office: (☎442 0215). On Axalan St. in Población, 1 block from the main market, next door to Hotel California. Pay phone outside. Open M-F 8am-4:30pm.

Postal Code: 5203.

ACCOMMODATIONS

POBLACIÓN (PUERTO GALERA PROPER)

Melxa's Greenhills Nipa Hut (☎0912 270 6248), E. Cobarrubias Sr. St. Turn right at the crossroads, 50m past Municipal Hall. Wonderfully rustic *nipa* huts with balconies. Singles and doubles with shared kitchen and common room P350; triples P400; family room with refrigerator, common room, and kitchen P1200. ❷

Coco Point Hotel and Restaurant (☎442 0109), close to busy Muelle Pier. Upstairs rooms have balcony. Restaurant open daily 6am-9pm. Doubles with common room P500; family doubles P700. AmEx/D/MC/V. ❹

SABANG BEACH

The most remarkable aspect of Sabang Beach is that there isn't much of one. Still, the most extensive selection of restaurants and dive shops make this "beach" popular among tourists.

VIP Lodge (☎0917 795 9062), behind Dive VIP and adjacent to Le Bistrot restaurant. No-nonsense rooms with the beach's lowest rates, not to mention a great owner. Flexible noon check-out. Laundry service. Budget doubles with cable TV, fan, and bath P300; standard doubles with kitchen P400-500. MC/V. ❸

JAA Lodge (☎0918 798 9778), west of Ed's Bar and Pool Hall, is a tropical mansion with well-equipped, comfortable rooms with balcony and couch. Doubles with TV, refrigerator, stove, and private common room P1000, P700 in low-season. ❹

SMALL LALAGUNA BEACH

Too often overlooked, Small Lalaguna is situated between Sabang and Big Lalguna. The lack of tourists translates to a more relaxed, more private getaway, provided you have the cash.

Portofino (☎287 3227; www.portofino.com.ph), toward the end of the beach adjacent to Action Divers, offers posh lodgings in a Mediterranean-style villa. Studios come with A/C, TV, and full kitchens; for a splurge, rent the 2-bedroom family suite, with stunning ocean views and a sitting room. Breakfast included. Laundry and international fax services available. Studios US$70/45; beachfront suite, max. 6 people US$145/120 35% discount for singles. AmEx/D/MC/V (10% surcharge). ❺

Laguna's Deep Blue Sea Inn (☎287 3209; dbsi@catsi.net.ph), toward the end of the beach. German-owned and Filipino-operated, this international inn can arrange direct transport to and from Batangas (P2000-2500). Doubles with refrigerator and bath US$14, with 2 beds US$16, with A/C, TV and hot water US$20. Prices higher for reservations made via email. MC/V (8% surcharge). ❺

BIG LALAGUNA BEACH

Big Lalaguna Beach is a 15min. walk from Sabang Beach. As you round the narrow stairs between Small and Big Lalaguna Beaches, you'll traverse "Penman's Mountain Pass." A stone notes the dizzying altitude—6.7m above sea level. The near-spotless beach has crystal-clear teal waters dotted with coral, ideal for swimming and snorkeling.

Scandinavian Inn (☎0919 452 4229; www.scandinaviandivers.com) is cozily tucked away toward the end of the beach. Relax in the small marble pool after a day of diving or sipping drinks on the oceanfront patio. Restaurant open daily 7am-midnight. Doubles with cable TV, fridge, and A/C P1500/1200, for divers P1000. MC/V. ❺

Miller's Corner (☎0919 789 2063) is as far away from Sabang as possible, with rooms on the rocks. Restaurant open daily 6am-7:30pm. *Nipa* huts with hammock P600/P500; doubles with common room P1200/P1000, with A/C P1300/P1150. MC/V. ❹

WHITE BEACH

This long and powdery stretch of beach is a 5min. walk from San Isidoro Rd. Jeepneys run from Puerto Galera to San Isidro and vice versa (depart when full 6am-5pm, P10). A *banca* trip from Sabang costs P500-1000. Nester Bhoymaranan (☎0912 316 5910) manages the beach, runs tours around Mindoro (rates negotiable), and can offer travel and accommodation advice.

The Summer Connection Beach Resort (☎0917 990 0181; www.thesummerconnection.com), at the farthest, most secluded end of the beach. Lattice-work cottages with hammocks. Reservations advised in peak season. Restaurant open daily 6am-10pm (closed in low season). Singles with private common room P2000/700; doubles with common room and porch P800/500; suites P3500. ❺

Marco Vincent Resort (☎0919 589 5854; www.marcovincent.com), at the entrance to White Beach from the jeepney drop-off on the main road. The only place to live up to the "resort" in its name, Marco Vincent resembles a brand-new Spanish hacienda. Luxurious rooms include A/C, cable TV, mini-bar and tiled bathrooms. Pool, jacuzzi, and rooftop bar. Satellite Internet access (P100 per 30min.; open daily 8am-10pm). Doubles P3395/P3895 (P4395 on weekends and major holidays). Discount packages available. AmEx/D/MC/V. ❺

FOOD

SABANG BEACH

Relax Thai Restaurant (☎0917 9985 917), west of the center. Bulwark against Sabang's tendency toward "anything-but-Asian" cuisine. *Aham talay* (stir-fried seafood and veggies) P295. Decent *pad thai* P160. Open daily 10:30am-10pm. ❹

Le Bistrot (☎0917 386 1425; lebistrot44@hotmail.com), on the beachfront next to Dive VIP. Varied menu is guaranteed to please Francophiles. Offerings include steak tartare (P330) and smoked salmon on toast (P250). Upstairs bar and pool table. Good selection of imported wine. MC/V. ❺

BALUUUT!

Balut, they say, gives you almost immediate sexual energy. An aphrodisiac, it oozes with protein and nutrients, and holds the promise of instant virility.

Interested? Just step into the street to find some of this wonderfood. In the humid evening hours, after dinner but before the shutters close, the *balut* kids toddle down the streets, swinging plastic buckets and wailing "Bah-luuuuut! Bah-luuuuuut!" Sometimes you will see whole stalls or pushcarts, filled with cartons of this marvel. *Balut* is everywhere.

What is *balut*, you ask? Forsooth, *balut* is a half-grown duck embryo, incubated for 18 days and then boiled, all for the express purpose of being gulped down. Season it with salt or *kalamansi* juice, then suck it straight from the egg. *Balut* embryos are intact; if you were to dump one out of the shell and onto a plate, you would see its beak, wings, and tiny eyeballs. Only healthy, developing embryos are sold on the streets.

Regardless of its potential gross-out factor, *balut* is in fact rather tasty, reminiscent of an undercooked sweet-and-sour omelette, full of gummy meat. There is little conclusive evidence as to whether Balut can deliver strength and "energy," but our researchers report that the strange tang of *balut* make it the true lodestar among Philippine snacks.

Eddie's Place, front and center on the waterfront. Spunky waitresses serve ice-blended mango shakes (P55) and sizzling meat and seafood platters (squid, P185). *Mai tai* P120. Sandwiches P70-110. Open 24hr. ❸

McRom's (☎0919 880 8899), on the southeast corner of the main street. Owner Romy now serves up more than burgers; the "stir-fried seafood with McRom's peanut sauce" (P175) will satisfy the pickiest palate. "Susi Q" sandwich P125. Spicy tuna nuggets P90. 30min. free Internet access for patrons. Open daily 8am-2am. AmEx/MC/V. ❸

ELSEWHERE

Pier Pub and Pizza Restaurant, on Muelle Pier, at end of the bay-side boardwalk. Sandwiches P50-110. Small pizza P145-205. Buttered shrimp P300. German *spaetale* noodles with meat sauce P160. Open daily 7am-10pm. ❸

ENTERTAINMENT AND NIGHTLIFE

If the sun's shining, most of Sabang is on the beach or in the reefs. When the moon comes out, however, so do the ladies of the night, and Sabang transforms into the Philippines's "Sin City." To avoid the prostitutes and their patrons, steer clear of discos and "go-go" bars. Stretch your lungs and join the **Hash House Harriers,** a beer-drinking and running club founded in 1938 in Kuala Lumpur that now has branches all over the world. Runs start from Cap'n Gregg's. (☎0912 305 0652. Su 4:30pm; P200 for first-time runners, including beer and t-shirt; P100 for repeat runners.

Broadway, on the main pedestrian walkway in Sabang, draws the largest crowds to its bar and pool hall. (Beer P50. Open 24hr.) **The Lounge** on Sabang Beach is a stylish and laid-back sports bar with soccer shirts on the walls and sports on the TV. (Happy hour 5-6pm. Open daily 9am-midnight.) There's no shortage of **pool halls** on the beaches (P10 per game).

Try **Eddie's Place** for excellent competition, but be wary of hustlers when betting on a game. If you need to supplement your budget, enter the high-season **pool tournament** at Le Bistrot restaurant, on Sabang Beach, where the winner takes all (Sa 5pm, P80). If you really want to be a shark (or at least look like one), you can purchase a beautiful handmade cue (P1700).

OUTDOOR ACTIVITIES

Thirty well-established dive sites—among the best in the Philippines—are within a 20min. boat ride from Sabang Beach. Abundant reef fish, including triggerfish, lionfish, frogfish, and scorpionfish populate the coral. A score of dive shops line the shore from Sabang to Big Lalaguna Beaches; prices are uniform. **South Sea Divers,** on Sabang Beach, stands out. Owners Sky and Paul define the word "laid-back," and divemasters Carlos and Rob will show you Sabang's nightlife. They offer dives with equipment, boat, and guide (US$25, night dives US$32) and PADI dive courses. (☎918 865 0264; www.southseadivers.com). Discover course US$50; open-water course US$300; advanced open-water course US$200. Beachside stands rent snorkels and masks (P50 per day). Also in Sabang, Dive VIP (☎0917 795 9062; www.divevip.com), in front of the VIP lodge, is slightly cheaper than other shops at US$20 per dive; inquire with John about long-term packages. Foreigners with an advanced certification may be able to find work at the center in exchange for room and free diving during the peak season. In White Beach, **Pacific Divers** (☎0920 606 2212; http://pacificdivers.free.fr) is the major adventure hub, offering snorkeling (P200 per day), windsurfing (P500 per hr.), and motorbike rentals (P600-800 per day; 18+, with valid foreign or international driver's license). Tamer travelers can take a trip on the banana boat (P250 per person, 6 person max.). PADI diving courses also available. Ask for Parra or Meldy.

WHOSE SIGN IS IT ANYWAY? Visitors to the Philippines may be taken aback by the blood-red flags emblazoned with "KKK" above government buildings. It's not in any way connected to the Ku Klux Klan in the United States, but rather a symbol of Philippine nationalism. Here, "KKK" stands for "Kataastaasan Kagalanggalangang Katipunan ng mga Anak ng Bayan" ("Highest and Respected Association of the Sons of the Country"). "Katipunan," for those challenged in the art of oral acrobatics, was founded in 1892. Like any respectable secret society, it boasted passwords, blood oaths of loyalty, and color-coded masks denoting rank. Unfortunately, founder Andres Bonifacio proved a better schemer than leader, and his troops were defeated repeatedly in the revolution against the Spanish. Co-founder General Emilio Aguinaldo proved himself more capable and became president of the Katipunan. Bonifacio indignantly crowned himself king, appointed a vice-king, and was later executed for treason by President Aguinaldo.

DAYTRIPS FROM PUERTO GALERA

The stunning **Tamaraw Falls** are only 30min. from Sabang Beach via jeepneys bound for Calapan; braver souls can swim beneath the falls in the small lagoon. (Jeepney P25; entrance P15.) Also within easy striking distance is the **Light House** on Escarcero Point, where cliffs fall away on three sides (jeepney to Sinandigan near Escarcero Point P15, "special" jeepney to the Light House P150). It's also a pleasant trek by foot. To escape the crowds, explore **Talipanan Beach** (35min. by jeepney from Muelle Pier, P20). Local tour companies (see **Practical Information,** p. 579) can assist with longer treks into Mindoro's more secluded beaches and interior wilderness. Past White Beach, where the road thins, large tracts of rainforest have yet to be penetrated by roads. With the exception of the village 1km behind White Beach, the Mangyan tribes in the interior are unaccustomed to tourists.

A trek from White Beach to **Mt. Malisimbo** (1230m) near Ponderosa, south of White Beach, takes 3hr. Guides should be arranged from the tourist office, at Muelle Pier, or via the **Summer Connection** on White Beach. **Island Trekking Tours** (☎ 0973 497 503; ask for Ralf) organizes treks into the interior. The **Bogdong Beach trek** leaves from Sabang Beach's Sunshine Coast Restaurant. A native outrigger takes trekkers to Bogdong Beach, followed by a 2hr. trek through Mangyan valleys that ends at a lagoon with waterfalls. (Sa and W; 7:30am, returns 6pm; US$40 per person including food, additional US$17 for overnight stay; 8-person min.) If there are enough people, Island Trekking Tours or Summer Connection can arrange more extensive treks. Longer treks might include **Mt. Calavite,** where communities live on bamboo rafts at the confluence of two rivers. One-week hikes head to **Mt. Halcon,** the highest mountain in Mindoro at 2587m. **Tarzan Trek Tours** (☎ 0919 410 1020) arranges daytrips to Lake Taal (P1000).

ROXAS ☎36

The waters off Panay's northeast coast swarm with fish, and Roxas gets first crack at the catch. Though it is the birthplace of Manuel Roxas, the country's first president and a national hero, Roxas prefers to sell itself as the "Seafood Capital of the Philippines." Its large riverfront park plaza, and quick access to Iloilo and Boracay make it a good spot to stop and do some eating.

TRANSPORTATION

Flights: The small airport is overshadowed by **Iloilo,** 2½hr. south. **PAL** (☎621 0618; www.philippineairlines.com) and **Cebu Pacific** (☎621 0671; www.cebupacificair.com) each fly to **Manila** (P3000) at 7:10am. The airport is 2km north of downtown on Arnaldo Boulevard. All other destinations require a Manila connection.

Buses: The main bus terminal is on Roxas Ave., less than 1km across the Panay River from downtown. **Ceres Bus Lines** has buses to **Iloilo** (3hr., every 30min. 7:15am-5:30pm, P110). **GM Liners** heads to **Kalibo** (2hr., every hr. 5:30am-3:30pm, P50). Some A/C **vans** headed to Kalibo (P80) may serve **Caticlan** (3hr.); the fare is typically P80 more for the Caticlan connection—check the signs and ask. Vans to **Iloilo** are P120. Van service to both destinations begins at 6am and ends at 5pm.

Ferries: Ferries leave from **Culasi Port,** 6km from downtown. Tricycles into town run P25, Culasi jeepneys P12. **Negros Navigation** (☎621 1473; www.negrosnavigation.ph) sails to **Manila** (19hr.; M and W 7pm, Sa 1pm; P1020). **WG&A** (☎621 5567; www.wgasuperferry.com) serves **Manila** (Tu, Th, and Su 12:30pm; P1350). The ticket office is on Rizal St. near the central plaza.

ORIENTATION AND PRACTICAL INFORMATION

Roxas is 5km from the Sibuyan Sea, on a loop extension of Panay Island's main highway. The city is located inland, at the beginning of a peninsula, and the port of **Culasi** is 6km away at the peninsula's end. The **Libas fishing port** is on another peninsula directly south. Roxas City is divided by the **Panay River.** The large **town square** sits at the center of Roxas, on the north riverbank. **Roxas Avenue** heads south from the square to the bus terminal, and **Arnaldo Boulevard** (also called **Hughes Street**) goes north to the airport and the huge Gaisano mall. **Burgos, Legazpi,** and **Rizal Street** are the major east-west roads.

Tourist Offices: The **Tourism Promotion Office** (☎621 5316), ground fl. City Hall Bldg. on Arzbispo St., by the town square. The regional **Provincial Tourism Office** (☎621 0042), located in the Provincial Capital Bldg. Both open M-F 9am-noon and 1-5pm.

Tours: Roxas City Tours (☎621 2344), on Roxas Ave., near the bridge. Handles local and regional travel arrangements. Open M-F 8am-noon and 1-5:30pm.

Banks: Banks and **ATMs** cluster on Arnaldo Blvd. (Hughes St.) and Roxas Ave. near the town square. **Metrobank** (☎621 0813) on Roxas Ave. near the bridge. Cashes AmEx Traveler's Cheques. **24hr. ATM.** Open M-F 9am-4:30pm.

English-Language Bookstore: Several in the **Gaisano Mall** (☎621 1227), located on Arnaldo Blvd. Mall open 8am-8pm.

Emergency: ☎117.

Police: (☎621 0222), on Arnaldo Blvd. near the town square.

Hospital: Roxas Memorial General Hospital (☎621 0431), on Arnaldo Blvd.

Telephones: PLDT and **RCPI-Bayantel** have phones at the Gaisano Mall on Arnaldo Blvd. **PLDT office** (☎621 2300) on McKinley St. near the town square. Open M-F 8:30am-5pm.

Internet Access: Gaisano Mall, lower level. P25 per hr. Open 9am-7pm.

Post Office: (☎621 0669), on Arnaldo Blvd. Open M-F 8am-noon and 1-5pm.

Postal Code: 5800.

ACCOMMODATIONS

Roxas has plenty of rooms, though they tend to be priced higher than elsewhere on mainland Panay. Make reservations for early December for the Sinadya sa Halaran festival.

President's Inn (☎621 0208; presinn@i-rox.net.ph), at the corner of Rizal and Lopez Jaena St., close to the town square. This combination of hotel, cafe, and antique gallery is one of Roxas's finest. Free breakfast and rooms with A/C and cable TV. Singles P950; doubles P1150; luxury suites P1650. MC/V. ❺

Villa Patria Cottages (☎621 0180), on Arnaldo Blvd., south of the Gaisano Mall. This quiet retreat offers easy access to Roxas. Singles with A/C and bath P600; doubles P750; large suite P1200. ❹

Capiz Bay Beach Resort (☎621 2165), in *barangay* Libas near the fishing port, 4km from downtown (tricycle P15). Clean resort upwind of the fish market. Small singles P550; larger singles with cable TV P750; doubles from P900. ❹

FOOD

If you want a taste of the fishing scene, stalls at the **Libas fishing port market,** 4km from town, sell every kind of fish—raw and cooked. Otherwise, the **Rockpoint Grill & Restaurant** ❸ (☎621 0713) on McKinley St., a few blocks from the square, will do the work for you. Try the tender *taniguie* steaks (P120) or crisp-fried boneless *bangus* (P90). The **Wayfarer Bar and Restaurant** ❹ (☎621 1479), on Hernandez Ave. in *barangay* Baybay 2km north of town, serves seafood specialties (whole buttered crabs P200) and adds alcohol (San Miguel P35) and late nights to the mix. **Maru Bar & Grill** ❷ on Hughes St. next to the square, is an affordable local hangout, with double portions of grilled chicken going for P90 and grilled *bangus* for P60.

SIGHTS AND FESTIVALS

The **Libas fishing port** is a sight to see in mid-morning, when the waves bear fishermen with loads of freshly caught fish. To get there from downtown, take a tricycle (4km, P15) or a jeepney marked "Libas" (P10). *Barangay* Baybay (Baybay Beach), is where the shore turns to soft beach peppered with seafood restaurants and grilling stands. Tricycles charge P13 for the 3km ride from downtown; jeepneys charge P8. The first weekend of December is the **Sinadya sa Halaran** festival. Its centerpiece is a "Seafood Festival" featuring a huge feast that follows a parade in which people compete to make the best sea-creature costumes.

THE VISAYAS

After endless bus rides in the mountains of north Luzon, island-hopping brings a welcome reminder that the Philippines is, in fact, an archipelago. The ancient coral beds and volcano tips of the Visayas include six major islands: Samar and Leyte in the Eastern Visayas, Negros and Panay in the Western Visayas, and Cebu and Bohol at the heart of the chain. All of these areas have their own dialects. Amid this confusing tropical Tower of Babel, the Visayas bore witness to two unifying events in Filipino history: the spread of Catholicism in the 16th century and the wresting of the islands from Japanese oppression in the 20th. Although travelers find it hard to leave the beaches, which are among the loveliest in Southeast Asia, Visayan cities try their best with a generous dash of frenzied charm. From Bohol's Chocolate Hills to Mt. Kanla on Negros, inland adventures also await. Whether bounding up a hill, frolicking on a beach, or jumping into a jeepney, friendly Visayans won't hesitate to greet you with a shriek of "Hey Joe!"

CEBU

Once upon a time, Ming vases and Spanish doubloons were the currencies of choice on Cebu. Nowadays, tourist cash runs the island, and resorts have mushroomed along its trendier beaches. The sandy northern islands of Bantayan and Malapascua run at a slower pace, jackhammered by dynamite fishing. Cebu City's nightlife lives on into the daylight, peddling excess and delirium all week long.

THE VIEW FROM ABOVE

Main Cities: Cebu City, Moalboal.

Island Fever: Diving off Mactan and Malapascua Islands, vegging out at deserted Bantayan Island.

Blast from the Past: Discover the lingering history from Cebu City's colonial era.

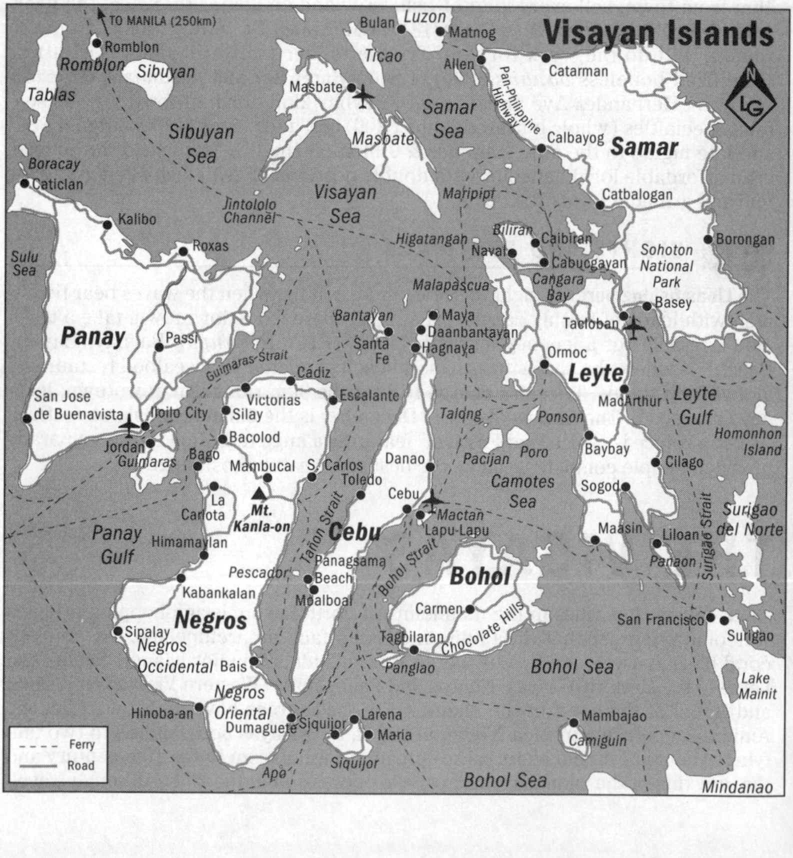

CEBU CITY ☎32

Spanish Conquistador Miguel Lopez de Legazpi anchored off the shores of Cebu in 1565, took one look at the droves of hostile natives, and aimed his galleons in the direction of friendlier shores. Two months later, he stormed back, set Cebu ablaze, and erected the first fortified settlement on the archipelago. Known as the "Queen City of the South," Cebu City sprawls from ocean to hills, speckled with churches from the age of conquest and the mudpits of future malls. Today's visitors can expect a warmer welcome than Legazpi received, pinballing between restaurants, nightspots, beaches, and easygoing locals.

TRANSPORTATION

BY AIR

Mactan Cebu International Airport (☎340 2468; www.mactan-cebuairport.com) serves all of Cebu Island. From Cebu City, **Metro Ferry** runs from Pier 3 to Mactan Island (45min., every 15min. 6am-7:30pm, P6). From the pier on Mactan, take a tricycle (25min., P30) or a taxi (15min., about P50 from downtown Cebu). Another option is to take the 23D jeepney from S.M. City Mall to Lapu-Lapu city (P5) and then a tricycle (P30) to the airport. Aircon "U-hires" minibuses leave from the terminal opposite the S.M. City Mall for Lapu-Lapu City (20 min, P14). The tourist info counter in the arrival area can help. (☎340 8229. Open M-F 8am-5pm.) Tickets are subject to a P10-40 airport departure fee.

INTERNATIONAL CARRIERS. Check the airport website for the latest carriers and schedules. **Cathay Pacific** (☎254 0740; www.cathaypacific.com) flies to **Hong Kong** (daily, US$205). **Malaysia Airlines** (☎231 3887; www.malaysiaairlines.com) has flights to **Kuala Lumpur** (Th, Su; US$311) via **Kota Kinabalu** (US$249). The ticket office is on 116 Gorordo Ave., on the second floor of the Export Bank Building. **Silkair** (☎254 0740; www.silkair.com) flies every other day to **Singapore** (US$499). The ticket office is in Suite 302, Cebu Holding Center in Cebu Business Park. However, travel agents can offer cheaper promotion fares.

DOMESTIC CARRIERS. Cebu is the principal transportation hub for the Visayas. Ticket booking agencies abound both downtown and uptown, around Fuente Osmeña. **PAL** locations include the airport (☎340 0191; open daily 8am-5pm), S.M. City Mall (☎232 8412; open daily 9am-5pm), and on Plaridel St. in downtown Cebu (☎254 4136; open M-F 8:30am-6pm, Sa 8:30am-noon). PAL has flights to **Manila** (7 per day, P3270). **Air Philippines** (☎341 0920; ticketing done through PAL) has daily flights to: **Bacolod** (P1674); **Davao** (P2735); **General Santos** (P2656); **Iloilo** (P1890); **Manila** (P2656). **Cebu Pacific** (☎255 4040; at the airport) flies to: **Bacolod** (daily, P1682); **Davao** (2 per day, P2383); **Iloilo** (daily, P1899); **Manila** (7 per day, P2657); **Zamboanga** (daily, P2614). **Asian Spirit** (☎341 2555) flies daily to: **Caticlan** (P2496); **Cagayan de Oro** (P2010); **Tagbilaran** (P529). **Seair** flies to: **Bantayan** (W, F, Su; P1100); **Camiguin** (M, F; P1434); **Caticlan** (daily, P2404); **Surigao** (Tu, F, Su; P 2178); **Tacloban** (M, W, F; P1623).

BY BOAT

For ferry schedules, go to the S.M. City Mall complex, which houses the **S.M. Traveler's Lounge** as well as independent ferry offices. (☎232 0291. Open daily 6am-8pm.) Take a jeepney from Colon St. headed toward "Colon, S.M., N. Terminal" (30min., P4). **Alboitiz Express** (www.alboitizone.com) operates a similar service on the third floor of the **Robinson Mall** at Fuente Osmeña. **SuperCat** catamarans (☎232 4511; www.supercat.com.ph) leave from Pier 4 to **Dumaguete** (3hr., 2 per day,

P570) via **Tagbilaran** (1½hr., 3 per day, P450); **Larena** on Siquijor (2½hr., daily, P720); **Ormoc** (2hr., 3 per day, P550). 15% student discounts on all fares. **WG&A Superferry** (☎232 0490; www.wgasuperferry.com) pulls out of Pier 6 for **Manila** (19hr.; daily except Tu, Sa; P1360-1950) and **Surigao** (5 hr., Tu, P480-870). **Trans-Asia** (☎254 6491), located on M. Cuenco Ave. by Osmeña Blvd (open M-Sa 8am-noon and 1:30-5pm, Su 8am-noon), goes to: **Cagayan de Oro** (8hr., M-Th and Sa-Su, P290-430); **Iloilo** (12hr., every other day, P540-810); **Maasin** (2 per week, P250-380); **Masbate** (14hr., 2 per week, P480-870); **Tagbilaran** (2hr., M, P155-270). **Cebu Ferries** (☎232 0291) goes to: **Cagayan de Oro** (10hr., daily, P290-800); **Ormoc** (5hr.; W, F, Su; P225-590); **Tacloban** (14hr.; M, F; P310-590).

BY BUS

Northbound buses leave from **Cebu North Bus Terminal,** outside the city center along the north coast, for: **Daan Bantayan** (3½hr., every 1½hr. 6:30am-10pm, P65); **Hagnaya** (3hr., every hr. 6am-10pm, P105); **Maya** (4hr., every 1½hr. 6am-10pm, P70). Schedules for other destinations are available at the station. For southbound and westbound buses, walk west 5min. down Del Rosario Ave. away from Osmeña Blvd. to **Cebu South Bus Terminal.** Buses to **Moalboal** (2½hr.; every 30min. 5am-6pm; P30, A/C P75) and other nearby destinations depart from here.

LOCAL TRANSPORTATION

Linking uptown and downtown, **jeepneys** (P4) are the most convenient way to get around town. To venture downtown, look for jeepneys headed toward "Colon," any of the piers, "Carbon Market," or "Sto. Niño." To head back uptown, look for "Capitol Bldg.," "Escario," or "Fuente Osmeña." These routes run along Osmeña Blvd. The "Colon-SM-H Terminal" covers S.M. City Mall complex, North Bus Terminal, and Colon. The "Colon-Ayala" jeepney will take you to the Ayala Mall and the Waterfront Hotel. **Taxi** meters start at P25 and click upward in P2 increments. Licensed taxis are white. (From the pier area into downtown P40, to Fuente Osmeña P70, across town to Beverly Hills P90.)

ORIENTATION AND PRACTICAL INFORMATION

Halfway down the east coast, Cebu City is about 600km south of Manila. **Mactan Island,** home of Mactan Cebu International Airport and **Lapu-Lapu City,** is accessible by ferry and bridge. Cebu City has two main sections: downtown and uptown. Downtown sprawls along the piers to **Del Rosario Avenue.** On the seafront, **Quezon Boulevard** passes all piers, **Fort San Pedro,** and **Carbon Market. D. Jakosalem** starts at City Hall and runs uptown to **Gen. Maxilom Avenue. Osmeña Boulevard** runs from **Plaza Independencia** (downtown, known as 'Juan Luna St.' south of Colon St.) though **Fuente Osmeña** (uptown) to **Escario Street.** Gen. Maxilom Ave. radiates east from Fuente Osmeña and intersects **F. Ramos, Jakosalem,** and **San José** on its way back to the sea and Quezon Blvd. The country's biggest mall outside Metro Manila, the **S.M. City Mall** is 1.5km east of downtown along the **J. Luna Extension.** The upscale **Ayala Mall** is 1km north of S.M. City and 1km east of uptown in the **Cebu Business Park.**

Tourist Office: The **main tourist office** (☎254 2811), is at the corner of Lapu-Lapu and Legazpi near Fort San Pedro. Head for glass doors midway down the block in the LDM Building. Free maps and brochures. Open M-F 8am-noon and 1-5pm. The **tourist info counter** at the airport (☎340 8229) offers the same services. Open M-F 6am-8pm.

Travel Agencies: Swagman Travel, 301 F. Ramos (☎254 1365; swgmn-ceb@mozcom.com). Very helpful Australian-owned agency. Open M-Sa 9am-5pm.

Consulates: US (☎231 1261), PCI Equitable Bldg., 3rd fl., on Gorordo Ave. Open M-F 8-11am.

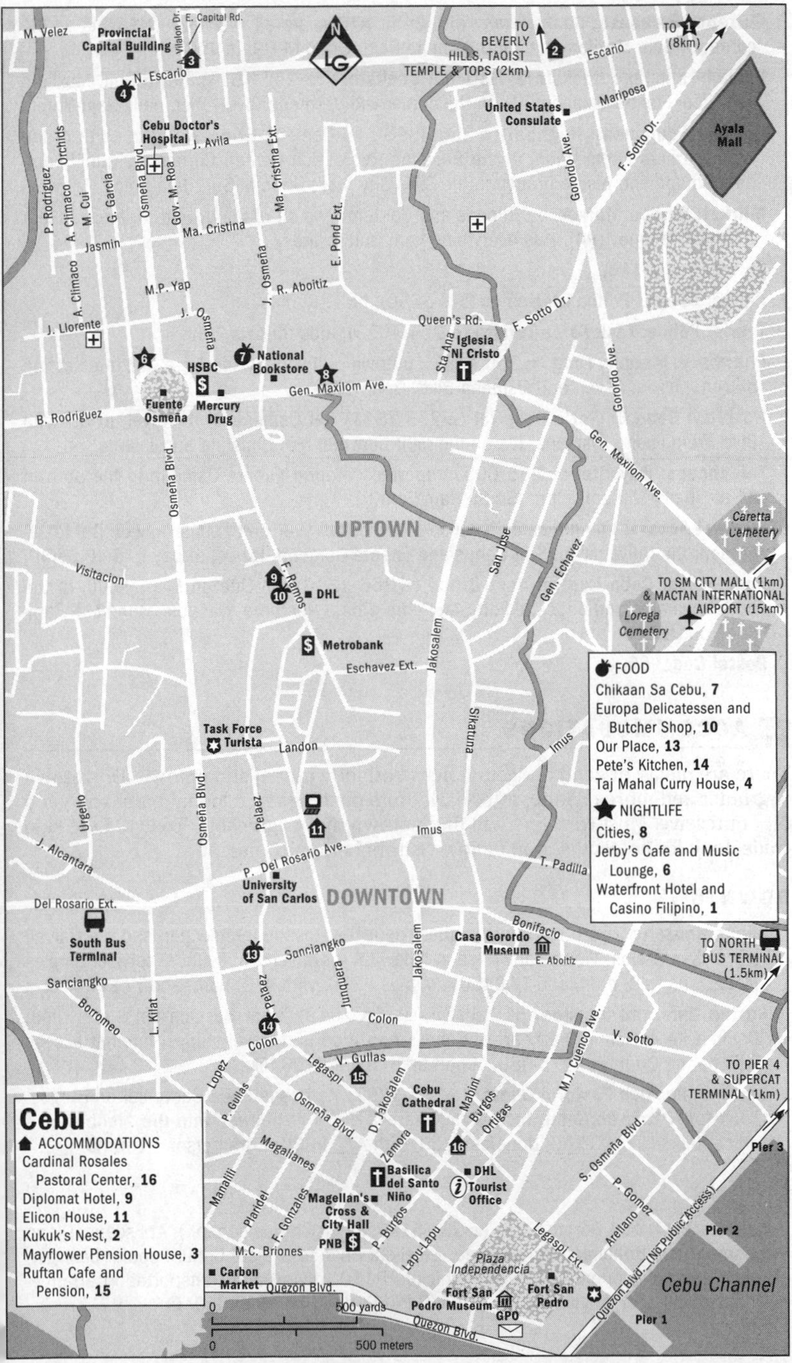

Cebu
ACCOMMODATIONS
Cardinal Rosales Pastoral Center, 16
Diplomat Hotel, 9
Elicon House, 11
Kukuk's Nest, 2
Mayflower Pension House, 3
Ruftan Cafe and Pension, 15
FOOD
Chikaan Sa Cebu, 7
Europa Delicatessen and Butcher Shop, 10
Our Place, 13
Pete's Kitchen, 14
Taj Mahal Curry House, 4
NIGHTLIFE
Cities, 8
Jerby's Cafe and Music Lounge, 6
Waterfront Hotel and Casino Filipino, 1
UPTOWN
DOWNTOWN
Provincial Capital Building
Cebu Doctor's Hospital
United States Consulate
Ayala Mall
TO BEVERLY HILLS, TAOIST TEMPLE & TOPS (2km)
TO 1 (8km)
National Bookstore
HSBC
Mercury Drug
Fuente Osmeña
Iglesia Ni Cristo
DHL
Metrobank
Task Force Turista
Caretta Cemetery
Lorega Cemetery
TO SM CITY MALL (1km) & MACTAN INTERNATIONAL AIRPORT (15km)
University of San Carlos
South Bus Terminal
Casa Gorordo Museum
TO NORTH BUS TERMINAL (1.5km)
TO PIER 4 & SUPERCAT TERMINAL (1km)
Cebu Cathedral
Basilica del Santo Niño
Magellan's Cross & City Hall
PNB
Tourist Office
Plaza Independencia
Fort San Pedro Museum
Fort San Pedro
GPO
Carbon Market
Cebu Channel
Pier 1
Pier 2
Pier 3
M. Velez
E. Capital Rd.
Vilalon Dr.
N. Escario
Escario
Mariposa
J. Avila
Orchids
P. Rodriguez
A. Climaco
M. Cui
G. Garcia
Osmeña Blvd.
Gov. M. Roa
Ma. Cristina Ext.
Ma. Cristina
Jasmin
E. Pond Ext.
Gorordo Ave.
F. Sotto Dr.
M.P. Yap
J. Osmeña
R. Aboitiz
J. Llorente
Queen's Rd.
Sta Ana
Gen. Maxilom Ave.
B. Rodriguez
Visitacion
F. Ramos
San Jose
Gen. Echavez
Jakosalem
Eschavez Ext.
Sikatuna
Landon
Imus
Urgello
Pelaez
J. Alcantara
P. Del Rosario Ave.
T. Padilla
Del Rosario Ext.
Bonifacio
E. Aboitiz
Sanciangko
Junquera
Borromeo
L. Kilat
Colon
V. Sotto
M.J. Cuenco Ave.
V. Gullas
Legaspi
Lopez
P. Gullas
D. Jakosalem
Mabini
Burgos
Ortigas
Magallanes
Zamora
S. Osmeña Blvd.
P. Gomez
Arellano
Manalili
Plaridel
F. Gonzales
P. Burgos
Lapu-Lapu
Legaspi Ext.
M.C. Briones
Quezon Blvd.
Quezon Blvd. (No Public Access)
0
500 yards
500 meters

Currency Exchange: Banks, many with **24hr. ATMs,** are all over town. **HSBC** is on the corner of Gen. Maxilom Ave. and Osmeña Blvd. Open M-F 9am-4pm.

English-Language Bookstore: National Bookstore (☎255 4644), down Gen. Maxilom Ave. from Fuente Osmeña; it's on the corner with Osmeña Blvd. Open daily 9am-8pm.

Outdoor Equipment: Hagabat (☎256 3896), on Osmeña Blvd., 3 blocks north of the Gen. Maxilom intersection, in the Baseline Recreation Center. Carries top-quality outdoor equipment. Also a branch in the S.M. City Mall. Open M-Sa 10am-8pm.

Market: Carbon Market, on Briones and Calderon, south of the downtown area. Take a "Carbon" jeepney (P4). Has everything from fruit to tires.

Emergency: ☎166.

Police: Central Police Station (☎253 5636), on F. Ramos.

Tourist Police: Task Force Turista (☎254 4023), aids tourists 24hr.

Pharmacy: Mercury Drug (☎255 4187), uptown on Fuente Osmeña, at the intersection of Gen. Maxilom Ave., and Osmeña Blvd. Open 24hr.

Hospital: Cebu Doctor's Hospital (☎253 7511), on Osmeña Blvd. Travel up Osmeña Blvd. from Fuente Osmeña; it's on the right between Ma. Christina and J. Avila.

Telephones: Bayantel (☎255 0057) operates around Fuente Osmeña in the uptown area. Open M-F 8am-10pm, Sa-Su 8am-5pm.

Internet Access: Internet cafes have sprouted up all over town, especially on Del Rosario near the University of San Carlos and Fuente Osmeña. Expect to pay P15-40 per hr.

Post Office: Cebu Central Post Office (☎256 1696), on Quezon Blvd., south of the downtown area and opposite Fort San Pedro. *Poste Restante* available. Open M-F 8am-noon and 1-5pm.

Postal Code: 6000.

ACCOMMODATIONS

There are plenty of good budget choices both downtown and uptown. Downtown is grimier and more chaotic; after-dark touts pushing their "bikini bars" can get a bit oppressive. Most travelers will find uptown more agreeable. To avoid the skin trade, look for hotels that don't allow visitors in their rooms.

DOWNTOWN

Ellcon House (☎255 0300), on Junquera near Del Rosario intersection and the University of San Carlos. Vibrant artwork and cafe with room service. Laundry service. Singles P212, with A/C, bath, and TV P450; doubles P309, with A/C, bath, and TV P500. ❷

Ruftan Cafe and Pension, 61 Legazpi (☎256 2613). Near Basílica del Santo Niño. Backpacker haven in the heart of Cebu. Good food and travel stories. Internet access P15 per hr. Doubles P175-380. "Short-time" room P100. ❷

Cardinal Rosales Pastoral Center (☎255 1269). Opposite Cebu Cathedral on Burgos. Look for "Patria de Cebu, Inc." sign. Share a dimly lit hallway with the Archbishop's office. Singles P170-220; doubles P250, with A/C P600. Extra person P100. ❷

UPTOWN

Kukuk's Nest, 157 Gorordo Ave. (☎231 5180; kukus@nexus.com.ph). At Escario. Clean rooms with a Bohemian atmosphere. Excellent base to explore Cebu. Popular beer garden/restaurant open 24hr. Roast chicken P110. Diving and transportation arrangements available. Singles P200, with A/C P460; doubles P520-580. ❷

Diplomat Hotel, 90 F. Ramos St. (☎254 6342; fax 254 6346; diplomat@cebu.pw.net.ph). Located in a quiet area in the center of Cebu. Next door is the Europa Delicatessen and Butcher Shop (see **Food,** below). Currency exchange. Laundry service. Room service. Caters mainly to business travelers and offers attractive, comfortable rooms with A/C, cable TV, and bath for a mere P750. ❺

Mayflower Pension House (☎255 2800; fax 255 2700; mayflower@cebu.weblinq.com), on Villalon Dr., off Escario east of the Capitol Bldg. TV in A/C rooms, cafe, tickets, and a library. Convenience store. Laundry service. Check-out 1pm. Small singles P240-490; doubles P300-610; triples P 390-750. MC/V. ❸

FOOD

You can get good food anywhere (though uptown restaurants are more consistently good than those downtown). Some of the tastiest and cheapest (P30-60) food can be found in the food courts of Cebu's many shopping malls, including the **Robinson** complex at Fuente Osmeña and the **Ayala Center.** The mother of all food courts can be found at the **S.M. City Mall.**

Pete's Kitchen (☎254 9910), **Downtown,** on Pelaez. With a vast array of great eats, Pete's is the place to be. From Colon, walk north; it's on the right. *Lumpia* P25. Grilled squid P65. Fried rice P15. Takeout counter open daily 6am-8:30pm; restaurant open daily 6:30am-10:30pm. ❶

Our Place (☎254 7196), **Downtown,** at the corner of Pelaez and Sanciangko. Locals and expats dine over savory Western dishes. Steak P110. Open M-Sa 10am-11pm. ❷

Europa Delicatessen, 91 F. Ramos St. (☎253 7012), **Uptown,** next to the Diplomat Hotel. One of the swankiest and priciest hot spots in town, with food worthy of its reputation. Imported Australian steak dinner is a whopping P850, but worth a night's splurge. Reservations not required, but swap sandals for shoes. Open daily 11:30am-2:30pm and 5pm-11pm. AmEx/MC/V. ❺

Taj Mahal Curry House (☎254 3788),**Uptown,** on Escario at the Osmeña Blvd. intersection. Facing the capitol, it's to the left. Tasty and cheap Indian food and lots of vegetarian entrees. Try the spinach *kofta* (P60) or the mushroom curry (P70). Also has a branch in the Ayala Center. Open M-Sa 5-11pm. ❷

Chikaan Sa Cebu (☎253 6221), **Uptown,** on Osmeña Blvd. From Fuente Osmeña, go down Gen. Maxilom Ave., turn left up Osmeña Blvd., then left into the shopping plaza. A worthwhile splurge. Seafood menus with *adobong kangkong* (sauteed vegetables) P145. Sizzling blue marlin P150. Open daily 11am-2pm and 6-10pm. AmEx/MC/V. ❷

SIGHTS

MAGELLAN'S CROSS. Planted on April 14, 1521 by Ferdinand Magellan, **Magellan's Cross** on Magallanes marks the location where missionaries baptized the first Filipinos as Christians. Two weeks later, after Chief Lapu-Lapu killed Magellan, the expedition fled and the Spanish influence waned until Legazpi returned to raze Cebu in April 1565. Located on Osmeña Blvd. *(Free.)*

FORT SAN PEDRO. Legazpi threw up this fortress in 1565 to thwart the attacks from shafted natives. There isn't much left to see within the eight-foot-thick walls besides a few old cannons, but there's a view of the city from the bastion towers. Archaeology buffs might want to take a look at the small exhibition of Ming dynasty artifacts in the **Fort San Pedro National Museum.** *(In the pier area in southern Cebu on Quezon Blvd. opposite the post office. ☎256 2284. Fort open daily 7am-11pm. Museum open Tu-Sa 8am-noon and 1-4pm. P15.)*

OTHER SIGHTS. A jaunt north to **Beverly Hills** (taxi P70-80) shows you the world of the wealthy Chinese Cebuanos. Lavish mansions surround the **Taoist Temple** high above the city. This is a great place to see the sunset. The **Casa Gorordo Museum** provides an unparalleled glimpse into Cebu's late colonial past. Built in the 1860s, this beautiful Spanish colonial house was constructed without a single nail. *(35 Lopez Jaena. ☎255 5630. Open M-Sa 9am-noon and 1-5pm. P25, students P10.)*

OUTDOORS. Outdoor enthusiasts usually strike out for other islands in search of adventure. Nevertheless, there are some activities in and around Cebu to catch the traveler's attention. **Swagman Travel** (see **Practical Information,** p. 586) organizes environmental and adventure daytrips, including **kayaking tours** and **trekking** through Cebu's mountainous interior. (Prices vary widely, but expect to spend at least P1500). The **Hagabat Outdoor Gear Shop** (see **Practical Information,** p. 588) is a meeting spot for the local hiking, climbing, and diving scene. There's also a climbing gym next door. The shop frequently organizes weekend daytrips—contact Warlito "Monski" Momongan (☎253 6292).

ENTERTAINMENT

Cities (☎255 4562), on the left side of Gen. Maxilom Ave. away from Fuente Osmeña. Cover bands and zany stage acts. Beer P55-90; pitchers P250. Ladies' night Tu and Th. Cover P100. Open M-Th 7pm-1am, F-Sa 7pm-2am. MC/V.

Jerby's Cafe and Music Lounge (☎253 5401), on the north corner of Fuente Osmeña, along Osmeña Blvd., next to Dunkin' Donuts. Live bands and karaoke. San Miguel P35. Cocktails P65-100. F-Sa cover P50. Happy hour 6-9pm. Open M-Sa 10pm-2am.

Waterfront Hotel (☎232 6888). Offers intriguing after-hours entertainment including the Casino Filipino with card tables, roulette, and slots (P100 cover). H_2O, a hip bar and nightclub, attracts a glamorous late 20s crowd. San Miguel P45. Cocktails P100. Cover P150. To get there, take a taxi (P70 from downtown) or a jeepney going to Lahug and tell the driver to drop you off at the Casino Filipino.

MACTAN ISLAND ☎32

Mactan is known for its diving, though the marine ecosystem has been hit hard by "dynamite fishing," a technique where fishermen detonate dynamite in the water to collect the fish as they float up to the surface. Other than its house reef, the island has no natural attractions. Travelers might enjoy being pampered in one of the luxurious resorts, but anyone on a smaller budget should skip the island; similar diving, better beaches and lower prices can be found elsewhere in the Visayas.

TRANSPORTATION AND PRACTICAL INFORMATION. Just off the east coast of Cebu Island, Mactan Island is linked to Cebu City by ferry and land. Two bridges connect Mactan to mainland Cebu in Mandaue, 8km north of Cebu City. Mactan's capital city, **Lapu-Lapu City,** is on the northwestern coast, facing Cebu. Beaches dot the east coast. The **airport** spreads through much of the island and serves Cebu City. **Jeepneys** leave from the S.M. City Mall in Cebu City and drop passengers at the jeepney terminal north of Lapu-Lapu City. (30-45 min., every 20 min. 4am-11pm, P5.) Airport services include a **tourist office** (☎340 8229; open M-F 8am-5pm) and a **post office** (open M-F 8am-5pm). **Postal Code:** 6015.

ACCOMMODATIONS AND FOOD. The **Buyong Hotel and Restaurant ❹,** on Maribago Beach, offers abodes that are small by Mactan standards. It has access to the sea but no beach. (☎492 0118. Doubles P500, with A/C P1200.) Alternatively, cheap and tasty seafood can be found at the **eateries ❷** around the Lapu-Lapu Monument in Punta Engano (squid P100 per kg).

SIGHTS AND DIVING. Mactan's diving isn't the hottest, but it is plentiful. **Marigondon Cave** is the Philippines's largest underwater cave, recommended for advanced divers only; **Kon Tiki Reef** is suitable for all levels. The waters off Mactan are home to jet-skiing Japanese businessmen as well as snapper, tuna, and occasionally, shark. **Snorkelers** can rent gear from most dive shops (US$10-20). The public beach at **Marigondon** offers everyone a taste of Mactan, on the rocks. A tricycle ride to Marigondon is P80 from Lapu-Lapu City and P50 from Maribago.

MOALBOAL ☎32

Sleepy Moalboal has attracted attention for its superb diving. Although ten years ago a typhoon devastated nearby reefs, marine parks lace nearby tropical islets. Affordable dives, friendly local families, and the outdoors draw tourists and Cebuanos. Non-divers should note that there is no sand to be found here; beach bums might find Bantayan and Malapascua islands more to their liking.

TRANSPORTATION AND PRACTICAL INFORMATION. The town of Moalboal shares a peninsula with Panagsama and White Beach, 89km southwest of Cebu City on the opposite shore. **Tricycle** drivers make the 1km hop to Panagsama Beach (10min., P30). **Buses** to Cebu (2½hr., every 30min. 3am-8pm, P40) cluster on the main drag. From Moalboal, ABC Liner buses continue south down the coast to **Bato** (2hr., P30), where rickety **ferries** make the short hop to Tampi, a port just a few kilometers north of Dumaguete. PADI-certified dive instructors should inquire via email for **job openings** at any of the Moalboal dive shops. Travelers willing to work as English or German **teachers** for young children should inquire via email with Jochen Hanika (planet@han-grp.de). **Eve's Kiosk** has **currency exchange.** (Open daily 6:30am-9pm.) A **market** lines the left side of the road where the bus stops. The **post office** is in the municipal building at the end of the road. (Open M-F 8am-noon and 1-5pm.) There's a **telephone office** in back of the post office. (Open M-F 8am-noon and 1-8pm, Sa-Su 8am-noon and 1-5pm.) **Postal Code:** 6032.

ACCOMMODATIONS AND FOOD. All accommodations are within walking distance of each other; accompanying **restaurants** ❸ serve fresh seafood for about P100-200. Ask about discounts if you dive with their shop. **Mollie's Place** ❷ is a simple but immaculate backpacker's haven. (☎917 254 7060. Singles P110-170; doubles P210. AmEx/MC/V.) **Pacitas Beach Resort** ❸ offers private *nipa* huts. (☎919 858 2502. Call ahead Oct.-Mar. Doubles P360, with A/C P720.) **Marcosas Cottages** ❹ has gorgeous bungalows for P550. (☎474 0064.) Restaurants along the shore await hungry divers from Pescador. Feast on the Asian table BBQ (P140) while sipping a refreshingly bitter *kalamansi* juice (P20) at the **Last Filling Station** ❸, which flanks the main path along the shore. With one of the largest menus in town including banana chocolate pancakes (P65) and *pancit canton* (P90), the **Little Corner Restaurant** ❷ (☎917 334 4096) is a little farther north.

SIGHTS AND DIVING. The skinny, pebbly beach makes Moalboal more of a diving than a sunning getaway. Several dive sites are accessible by a short *banca* trip. For the experienced diver, **Sunken Island** is the spot to see schools of tuna and large pelagics. The **Pescador Island Marine Park,** suitable for all divers, has vibrant coral life. **White Beach** has a coral wall that leads to a sunken airplane now piloted by turtles. Diving companies in Moalboal include: **Neptune Diving Adventure** (www.neptunediving.com); **Visaya Divers; Ocean Globe; Savedra Dive Center's** (www.savedra.com). Prices vary little among the well-established dive centers. One dive goes for around US$22 (nitrox US$30). Open-water courses and advanced courses cost US$210-265.

BANTAYAN ISLAND ☎32

Just northwest of Hagnaya, Cebu, Bantayan Island is indeed magical—it's not just the locals' mystic beliefs in *aswang* (witches). Although dynamite fishing has blasted the hopes of would-be divers, it has left the beaches relatively *banca* free, a god-send for sunbathing purists. Visitors get warm receptions in the two small towns, Santa Fe and Bantayan, and throughout the undertouristed countryside.

TRANSPORTATION. **Seair** (☎438 5612; www.flyseair.com) flies to Cebu (30min.; F 1:30pm, Su 3:30pm; P1085; 20% discount for students and senior citizens, 50% discount for children under 12). Bantayan is connected to Cebu by **Island Shipping Corp. ferries,** which depart from Hagnaya (1hr.; 4 per day 7:30am-6:30pm; P66, A/C P75-80) and land in Santa Fe. Buses run from Cebu City to Hagnaya (3hr., 6 per day, P65). When traveling from Santa Fe to Hagnaya, buy tickets on board (1hr., 4 per day 5:30am-2pm, P15). **Jeepneys** depart from the ferry pier to the market place in Bantayan Town (20min., every 20-30min. 6am-10pm, P10). The Island Shipping Corp. office in Bantayan Town is at the end of the road after City Hall. (☎352 5103. Open daily 8am-5pm.)

ORIENTATION AND PRACTICAL INFORMATION. Off Cebu's northwestern coast, Bantayan Island is a stepping stone to Negros and Panay. The main road connects southwestern **Bantayan Town** with southeastern **Santa Fe,** which is surrounded by beaches. For those who want to skip straight to coastal fishing communities, the road begins as **Pres. Osmeña Street** in central Bantayan Town. A trip by dirtbike to the northernmost community, **Madridejos,** takes 30-45min. **Nestor's Bike Rental,** on the main road in Santa Fe, rents out scooters (P150 per hr., P500 per half-day) and tricycles with a driver (P100 per hour).

Allied Bank, on the corner of Osmeña and Escario St., cashes AmEx Traveler's Cheques. (☎352 5144. Open M-F 9am-4pm.) There are no non-local ATMs on the island. The **police station** (☎352 5309) is in the town hall near the ferry pier. **Bantayan District Hospital** (☎352 5231) is 500m down the road to Santa Fe and offers basic care. The town hall hosts the **PLDT office** (☎198 5231; open M-Sa 8am-noon and 1-5pm) and the **post office** (open M-F 8-11:30am and 1-4pm). **Postal Codes:** Bantayan Town 6052. Santa Fe 6047. Small **Internet** cafes spring in and out of business, but if you can tolerate the slow connection, you can probably get online.

ACCOMMODATIONS AND FOOD. Santa Fe's resorts are far better than those in Bantayan. All resorts are a P5-10 tricycle ride from the Santa Fe pier. There are often discounts for longer stays. The most comfort can be found at the intimate **Ogtong Cave Resort ❺.** (☎438 0031; travelvision@skyinet.net. Cottages with fan and bath P1440; family villas P3200-4000.) Along the main road in Santa Fe, **Budyong Beach Resort ❹** has more affordable bungalows on the nicest beach in the area. (☎438 9040. Cottages for two with fan P500, with A/C P1000.) North of the pier, Danish-managed **St. Bernard's Resort ❸** features seven cottages and a small but pretty beach strip—a true bargain at P350-750.

Santa Fe has some very good food and, during the high season, a lively bar scene. **El Paso ❸,** on the second floor of a cosy *nipa* hut, serves excellent Thai food (coconut soup P70, chicken *piri-piri* P170). **Little Moby Dick's ❷** specializes in "volcano dishes," mountains of mashed potatoes with different meaty fillings (P120-140). The town **market** sprawls along the main drag, and specializes in fish. The main drag has a few **grilled chicken stalls** in the evening (P100 per chicken).

SIGHTS AND ENTERTAINMENT. Beyond the sand and surf in Santa Fe, Bantayan's sights are slim. The nearby community often holds afternoon **cockfights** behind Little Moby Dick's. Follow the men with the roosters. **"Jungle discos"** happen spontaneously in the forest, where all ages groove to 70s classics. Ask a tricycle driver or the guesthouse staff for directions.

MALAPASCUA ISLAND ☎32

Off the northeastern tip of Cebu, this tiny speck captures travelers' attention as they cross from Cebu City to Boracay. Malapascua's white beach freezes time; one might spend days reading in the shade of coconut trees, swimming in crystalline waters, or counting passing ships. Malapascua has become one of the Visayas' most popular dive destinations, its popularity fed by the regular appearance of thresher sharks in the channel between Cebu and Leyte.

The starting point from Cebu is Maya. **Bancas** head to Malapascua (10am and whenever full during the day, P50) and also ply the return journey (8am and whenever full during the day, P50). Chartered *bancas* can be hired anytime (around P500); from Santa Fe, hire one at a resort or at the pier (2hr., P1000-1500 per boat). Otherwise, the route is long—take the **ferry** to Hagnaya (1hr., P60), a **tricycle** to Bogo (30min., P10), and then hop on a **bus** to Maya (1hr., P15). From there you can catch the scheduled trips or charter a *banca*. Certified PADI instructors and dive masters should check www.malapascua.net for job postings.

During low season (late June-Sept.), activity slows down, prices drop, and some establishments close. Almost all accommodations are along **Bounty Beach**, which is also the *banca* drop-off point. **Cocobana Beach Resort** ❺ has spacious waterfront and garden cottages with fan, bath, and breakfast included. Check out their floating bar. (☎0918 775 2942 or 437 1040. Waterfront P1100 high-season, low-season P960; garden P780/600.) Next door, the **Malapascua Bluewater Resort** ❹ also has beachfront cottages, "garden rooms," and small rooms. (☎0919 481 8166 or 437 1053. Beachfront P1000, low-season P800; garden P800/600; small room P500.)

With specialties including crepes (P40-80), pasta (P130-190), and pizza (P140-200), **Sunsplash** ❸ (☎0919 633 3654 or 437 0982), next to the Cocobana, has great Euro-Filipino food and a floating bar to boot. Right behind it, **Ging Ging's Eatery** ❶ (☎1918 877 7765), run by a mother and her children, serves up excellent curries (P45-65) and fresh seafood; try the squid with *pancit canton* (P45).

Several dive shops have cropped up along the beach, capitalizing on thresher-mania. Dutch-owned **Exotic Divers,** at the far end of the beach, is a well-established operation that runs daily shark-watching excursions to Monod Point.

BOHOL

The island of Bohol is a nature lover's paradise. In the heart of the Boholano forest, goggle-eyed tarsiers swivel their heads and leap from tree to tree, clinging with elongated suction-cup fingers. To the north, the majestic Chocolate Hills pop out of the flat landscape and offer unparalleled sunrises and sunsets. Off southwest Panglao Island, porpoises and whales slip through world-class diving reefs in the Mindanao Sea. Although there is a fair amount of tourism here, Bohol remains undisturbed; the island's life and lifestyle endure in peace and quiet.

THE VIEW FROM ABOVE

Main towns: Carmen, Tagbilaran.

Highlights: Diving off the coast, swimming with dolphins, or just lounging on the Panglao Island beaches.

Something Sweet: North of Tagbilaran, the Chocolate Hills might be your true soul food.

TAGBILARAN ☎38

The rulers of the Bohol Kingdom once used Panglao Island, off the southeastern coast of Bohol, to hide from the *Bilaan*—Muslim raiders who swept north from Mindanao. Modern-day marauders find little in Tagbilaran but telephones, Internet terminals, and ATMs. Once these are plundered, you can explore the island's inspiring interior without further ado.

TRANSPORTATION

Flights: Tagbilaran airport, 1.5km north of the city. **Asian Spirit** (☎235 3541; www.asianspirit.com) flies to **Cebu** (daily 8:20am, M, F, Su 2:10pm; P555) and **Manila** (daily 9am, M, F, Su 2:30pm; P2880). Several ticketing offices on Carlos P. Garcia Ave. handle reservations. Tricycle from the airport into town P6.

Buses: Dao Integrated Bus Terminal serves all of Bohol's major sights. Take a jeepney from Grupo St. next to the Bohol Quality Mall downtown, or any marked "Dao" or "Int. Bus Terminal" (15-20min., P4). Buses to: **Baclayon** (15-20min., P5); **Bilar** (1½hr., P20); **Carmen** (2hr., every hr. 4am-5:30pm, P62), passing the **Chocolate Hills Complex** (6km before Carmen proper); **Loboc** (45min., P25); **Loon** (45min., P25). Buses marked "Talibon; Tubigon" follow the north-coast road to **Maribojoc** (25min., every 30min. 4am-6:30pm, P10).

Boats: The lengthy ferry pier extends from the northwest part of the city. Walking along the pier, turn right onto Gallares St. to head into town (1km). Take a tricycle to Tagbilaran center (5-10min., P4) or directly to **Alona Beach** on Panglao Island (1¼hr., P100). Ferries are operated by 4 companies with offices in the terminal (open 5am-9pm); all grant a 15% student discount. **SuperCat** (☎411 4906; www.supercat.com.ph) goes to: **Cebu** (1½hr., 3 per day, P450); **Dumaguete** (1½hr., 2 per day, P480); **Larena** (3hr., 5:15pm, P590). **WG&A** (☎411 3048; www.wgasuperferry.com) departs to: **Cagayan de Oro** (4hr., Sa midnight, P400); **Dipolog** (3hr., Su 9am, P380); **Dumaguete** (2hr., W 8am, P300); **Manila** (29hr.; M, W 10am; P1275). **Oceanjet** leaves for **Cebu** 4 times daily (2hr., P420). **Sulpicio Lines** departs for: **Iligan** (3hr., Th 8pm, P350) via **Dipolog** (2hr., P282), and **Manila** (27hr., M 6pm, P1052). Ferries to **Siquijor** (M, W, F 7pm; P160); purchase tickets on the pier.

Jeepneys: Leave from **Grupo Street** near Jacinto St. and from the **Cogon Public Market.** They go north to Punta Cruz in **Maribojoc** (40min., every 45min. 7am-5pm, P10) and south from **Dao Integrated Bus Terminal** to the Blood Compact site in **Bohol** (5-10min., 7am-5pm, P5) on their way to **Baclayon** (20min., P5). Flag down a jeepney leaving from Boholand near the cathedral in Tagbilaran. Those marked "Panglao" head to **Doljo Beach** (45min., every hr. 7am-5pm, P15). Those marked with the number 80 or "Panglao-Tawala" pass **Alona Beach** but stop running by 4pm (P15-25).

Tricycles: P4-5 per trip in town. To **Panglao** (P100-150).

Rentals: Most hotels and pension houses can organize a rental car with driver (P1500-2000per day).

ORIENTATION AND PRACTICAL INFORMATION

Tagbilaran, on the southwestern tip of Bohol, guards the narrow strait separating **Bohol** and **Panglao.** From the pier, **Gallares Street** follows the shore and terminates at **St. Joseph's Cathedral** and **City Hall.** In front of the cathedral, **Plaza Rizal** is bounded on the other side by **Carlos P. Garcia (CPG) Avenue,** Tagbilaran's main commercial street, on which you can find the **tourist office** (☎411 3666; open M-F 8am-8pm) opposite the **Bohol Quality Mall.** Come here to book whale-watching excursions or arrange for a tour of the Chocolate Hills. (Guided full-day tours P1500-

1800.) **Metrobank** (and its **ATM**) is just down the street. (☎411 2405. Open M-F 9am-4pm.) On the opposite side of the street is **Mercury Drug Pharmacy.** (Open daily 7am-9pm.) Private **Ramiro Hospital** (☎411 3515) is on Gallares St., on the way to the pier. There are **Internet** cafes (P20-30 per hr.) all over town, especially along Lesage St. near Divine World College. The hulking new **Island City Mall** is a P20 tricycle or a bumpy P4 jeepney ride away in the hills of *barangay* Dao. The **post office** is behind the cathedral. (Open M-F 8am-noon and 1-5pm.) **Postal Code:** 6300.

ACCOMMODATIONS AND FOOD

Tagbilaran has a number of cheap, forgettable budget accommodations. **Slim Pension House ❹**, on F.R. Ingles St. behind the Agora market, is the best value in town. (☎411 4858. Singles with A/C P500; doubles P640.) On CPG Ave., rooms in the friendly, tidy **Nisa's Traveler's Inn ❷** are a good value for the price, and are both-clean and cool. (Singles with fan P150; doubles P170, with A/C and bath P540.) The entrance is in a shopping arcade right across from the Bohol Quality Complex.

Seafood is the passion here, and fresh catch is abundant in the stalls and restaurants on the pier. With delicious *kinilaw* (P95) and marinated octopus (P55), **M-R Seafood ❷** occupies a prime location midway up the pier. (Open daily 6am-10pm.) **Fannie's Lechon ❹**, on Gallares St. near Y. Visarra St., swaps fish for hot and flavorful pork (*lechon* P140). The usual fast-food joints and eateries crowd the center of town. Check out the **night market** next to the Bohol Quality Complex for cheap, tasty barbecues (P15-30).

DAYTRIPS FROM TAGBILARAN

THE CHOCOLATE HILLS. The Chocolate Hills are Bohol's signature attraction. Dome-shaped limestone mounds preside over the hillside, resembling rows and rows of chocolate kisses when the grass dries up. Whether the hills live up to the tourist hype is questionable. Geologists believe that the 1268 coral and limestone mounds, which mysteriously materialized out of the relatively flat paddy land, have been sculpted into this bizarre topography by eons of erosion.

The hills are best viewed from **Carmen,** 59km northeast of Tagbilaran. To enjoy the spectacle at dawn, the best place to go is on top of one of the hills themselves. The **Chocolate Hills Complex ❸** perches atop the tallest hill 6km before Carmen; make sure the driver knows your destination. (Doubles P280-850; triples P380-900. Extra person P200.) The **observation patio,** 214 steps up from the complex, is the highest point in the hills. (☎0912 856 1559. Admission P10. Open daily 6am-9pm.) Motorcyclists congregate at the turn-off to the complex and take you on a meandering tour back to Tagbilaran, stopping to see the sights along the way. (Half-day P600 for two.) Visit **Nuts Huts** (walterken@hotmail.com), 3km after Loboc on the road to Carmen; a turnoff sign on your left marks the driveway. Backpackers hang out in *nipa* huts by the forested Loboc River. Savor fusion cooking with views at the **restaurant ❸** (Filipino "curry" P120), or clear your head in the herbal steam sauna. Ask Walter, Chris, or Rita about mountain biking, hiking, or river swimming. (Dorm beds P175; cottages P405; larger cottages P570.)

PANGLAO ISLAND. Some say the silky white sand and great diving make Panglao Island's beaches the best in the Visayas. Underwater fanatics dominate **Alona Beach,** the most developed of the island's beaches. For more seclusion, escape to **Doljo Beach.** Whales roam off the southern cost.

A well-paved central road connects Panglao with Bohol and the new bridge to Tagbilaran. Most amenities can be found only in Tagbilaran. Few roads are paved, so allow for extra travel time. International calls can be made from hotels or from the **PLDT** in Panglao town. (☎198 8109. Open daily 7am-10pm.) **Jeepneys** passing Alona Beach go to Panglao (15min., P4) but don't travel by jeepney on your way back; return by **tricycle** (15min., P40). **Dirt bikes** are for rent along Alona Beach (P100 per hr., P600 per day).

All of the following accommodations are near each other on Alona Beach, except for the Palm Island Beach Resort on Doljo Beach. Most lodgings have an attached restaurant, but local foodsellers offer cheaper meals. Prices rise during the high season. No shoes are allowed upstairs at **Peter's House ❸**, which boasts delicious pizzas (P100-150) and exotic rooms in a beautiful three-story *nipa* house. (☎502 9056. Singles with fan P420; doubles P580; discounts for divers.) Down the beach, the **Alona Kew White Beach Resort ❺** has private beach facilities and cottages in a well-tended garden. (☎502 9042; www.bohol-info.com/alonakew.html. Cottages with fan P850-1100, with A/C P2000-2300.) The cheapest option on the beach is the centrally located **Alonaville Beach Resort ❷.** (Doubles P210; cottages for 2 with fan P600/P500.)

For the best diving, head to **Balicasag Island,** southwest of Doljo Point. **Black Forest,** distinguished by its black coral, is an excellent site for drift-diving. **Pamalican Island** is known as the "nesting place of manta rays," and **Doljo Beach,** on the other side of Panglao, has rich coral walls. Dive shops along **Alona Beach** serve every hotspot and offer the entire range of PADI courses. (US$35 per dive; open-water courses US$300; advanced open-water US$195-220. Look for low-season discounts in July and Aug.) Friendly **Genesis Divers** (☎502 9056), owned by Peter's House, is a notch above the rest.

Whales save their best performances for early birds, but hyperactive dolphins perform at the drop of a hat. Ask your guesthouse about chartering a boat, or if you feel like haggling, local *bancas* clutter the shoreline. Organized tours leave **Bacloyan Pier** east of Tagbilaran City and cruise to **Pamalican Island.** (☎540 9279. 3-person boat P600 per person, 7-person boat P500 per person.)

BETWEEN TAGBILARAN AND CARMEN. Rajah Sikatuna National Park, south of the Chocolate Hills, covers 9000 hectares of *molave* forest and grasslands, and is honeycombed with caves (P20). Among the animals inhabiting the park is the petite **tarsier,** the world's smallest primate. To get there, take a Carmen-bound bus from the Integrated Bus Terminal; get out at the market in **Bilar** (1hr., P18). From there, hire a motorcycle (P15) or pedicab (P10) to cover the few kilometers to **Camp Magsaysay.** The park is best visited with plenty of time and your own transportation, so unless you've got an obsessive interest in tarsier habitats, it is best skipped altogether. Before going, groups should contact the National Park (☎032 411 2357). *Nipa* cottages are available for rent (P100), and camping is possible (P50).

The best and most humane place to view the tarsier is at the **Philippine Tarsier Breeding Center,** near Corella. It is 11km west of Loboc, and 16km northeast of Tagbilaran; from Tagbilaran or Loboc, take a jeepney bound for **Sikatuna** (P10-15) or **Corella** (P10-15). The Breeding Center is 2km west of Sikatuna. At **Supercarp's,** you can commandeer a small *banca* (local crew included) to head upriver to a waterfall that is ideal for swimming (15min., P500).

NEGROS

When Spanish missionaries deemed the mountains of Negros too formidable to traverse—even for the glory of God—they split the island into two halves. Vibrant Dumaguete, a lone Protestant outpost in a sea of Catholicism and the capital of Negros Oriental, is a great base for exploring the lush jungle around Mt. Kanla-on and the untouched volcanic Apo Island. The plains of Negros Occidental, with spotless Bacolod as their capital, are known for their sugar crops, but the worldwide sugar market crash has devastated that industry. The jarring economic conditions have contributed to the rise in popularity of the Communist New People's Army (NPA), an active force in the area.

THE VIEW FROM ABOVE

Major Cities: Bacolod and Dumaguete.

Nearby Islands: Apo Island, Siquijor Islands.

Beaches: Head south to Apo Island for, yup, you guessed it, another great dive.

Something Big: Mt. Kanla-on is the tallest peak in the Central Philippines.

BACOLOD ☎34

Bacolod is where Negros's denizens come to do business, and where tourists come to kick back. Apart from its convenient location, across the Guimaras Straight from Panay, Bacolod boasts great food and a lively bar and club scene. Historically the city was situated in the heartland of Negros's once thriving sugar industry. The Negros Museum resurrects the city's past glories even as the sugar barons' *haciendas* in Silay and Victorias slowly decay. South of the city, Mt. Kanla-on spikes out of the sugarlands, challenging hardcore trekkers.

TRANSPORTATION

Flights: The **airport** is south of the city, on Araneta St. Taxis to and from airport P50. To go downtown, flag down a jeepney marked "Pta. Taytay—Central Market" (P4). **PAL** (☎835 295; www.philippineairlines.com), in the main terminal, flies to **Manila** (1hr., 3 per day, P3391). **Air Philippines** ticketing is opposite the main terminal (☎433 9211; www.airphils.com; open M-Sa 8:30am-4:30pm). The downtown office is in Victorina Arcade on Rizal St. near the plaza (☎433 9570; open M-Sa 8:30am-6pm). To **Cebu** (30min., daily, P1430) and **Manila** (1hr., daily, P3019). **Cebu Pacific**'s terminal (☎434 2052; www.cebupacificair.com) is near Air Philippines's ticketing office. The downtown office (☎434 2020; open daily 9am-5:30pm) is on Rizal St. near the plaza. To **Cebu** (30min., daily, P2049) and **Manila** (1hr., 3 per day, P3079). All airlines offer a 20% discount to students and senior citizens. There are often additional promotions—inquire at travel agencies in town.

Buses: Ceres North Terminal, on Lopez Jaena St. near the corner of B.S. Aquino Dr. (15min. taxi from city center, P40). To: **Cadiz** (1½hr., P38); **Cebu City** (7-8hr.; 1:30, 5:45, 9:30, 9:45am; P125-150) via **Toledo; Dumaguete** (8hr., 8 per day 3am-midnight, P180) via **Silay** (20min., P10); **San Carlos** (2hr., every 30min. 4am-7:30pm, P83); **Victorias** (30-40min., P15). **Public North Bus Terminal,** a few meters down Lopez Jaena St., has buses and jeepneys to **Cadiz** (1½hr., every hr. 6am-7pm, P30) and **San Carlos** (2hr., every hr. 4am-4pm, P65) via **Victorias.** Down Lopez Jaena St., at the Luzuriaga and San Sebastian St. intersection, **Public South Bus Terminal** has buses to: **Canlaon** (3hr., every hr. 4am-4pm, P66); **Dumaguete** (5hr., 6 per day 5:30am-4pm, P205); **Hinoba-an** (6hr., 12 per day 3am-10pm, P118); **Kabankalan** (2½hr., 8 per day 6am-8:45pm, P64); **Sipalay** (3½hr., 8 per day 4am-3pm, P64). Jeepneys leave from across Robinson's Mall to: **Cadiz** (P38); **Silay** (P12); **Victorias** (P14).

Ferries: Passenger ferries leave from **Banago Port,** about 4 mi. west of downtown. **Bullet Express** (☎432 0118; open daily 6am-5pm) goes to **Iloilo** (1hr.; 4-5 per day, last trip 5pm; P190). **Negros Navigation** (☎434 4291; www.negrosnavigation.com.ph) runs to **Cagayan de Oro** (14hr., Tu 7pm, P1400) and **Manila** (18-24hr., 5 per week,

P1490). The branch office (☎432 3627; open M-Sa 8:30am-5pm), at the corner of Rizal and Gatuslao St., sells Negros Navigation and **SeaAngels** tickets. A complimentary **shuttle** to Banago leaves 2, 3, and 4hr. before scheduled departure times from the Ceres North Terminal and the Public South Bus Terminal. **SuperCat** (main office ☎434 2350, terminal 441 0659; www.supercat.com.ph) runs speedy ferries to **Iloilo** (1hr., 4 per day 6am-3:15pm, P270). There is another branch next to Negros Navigation at 6th St. off Lacson St. Open M-F 8am-5pm, Sa 8am-noon. **WG&A** (☎435 4965; www.wgasuperferry.com) sends ferries to **Cagayan de Oro** (13hr., F 9pm, P1390) and **Manila** (21hr.; W 3:30pm, Su 2pm; P1450). All shipping lines grant a 15% discount for students, a 20% discount for seniors, and half-price fare for ages 4-11.

Taxis: Fares start at P25. To the airport P50. To Banago ferry pier P50.

Local Transportation: Intra-city **jeepney** routes: "Pta. Taytay-Central Market" to airport; "Bata" and "Mandalagan" pass the Negros Museum to **Robinson's Mall** (15min., P4); "Shopping" to **Ceres bus terminals;** "Libertad" to **Libertad Market.** For **Mambukal,** take a jeepney from Libertad Market (2hr., every 15min. 7am-9pm, P30).

ORIENTATION AND PRACTICAL INFORMATION

Bacolod is on the northwestern tip of Negros Occidental. The **ferry pier** sits west of the **plaza. Lacson Street** runs straight across town. Three blocks closer to the coast, **Araneta Street** begins at the plaza and continues south to the airport. Between the two, **Gatuslao Street** passes the post office and Negros Museum. **Burgos Street** intersects Lacson and Araneta St. and ends at the ferry pier. In the east, Burgos St. cuts across **Lopez Jaena Street,** which hosts the **bus terminals,** 1km from downtown.

Tourist Offices: City Tourism Office (☎434 6571), from Bacolod Plaza on San Juan St. Open M-F 8am-noon and 1-5pm. **Provincial Tourism Office** (☎433 2515), in the provincial government complex, north of the lagoon near the Negros Museum. Open M-F 8am-5pm.

Budget Travel: Manna Travel Agency (☎433 9204; mannatrvl@yahoo.com), on San Juan St. near the plaza. Open M-Sa 9am-6pm.

Banks: BPI Bank (☎434 2751), on Araneta St. near the San Sebastian intersection. Cirrus/MC **24hr. ATM.** Open M-F 9am-4pm.

Markets: Fruit vendors line Ballesteros, **barbecue grills** clutter Gatuslao St. on the corner of Hernadez and Mabini St., and the **Libertad Market** has fresh fish and produce.

Emergency: Police ☎166. **Fire** ☎161. **Ambulance** ☎166.

Police: There is a **PNP** office (☎434 8776) next to the City Tourism Bldg. in the Plaza. The local police force is known as Bac Up. (Main office ☎434 1412, on Magsaysay Ave.)

Pharmacy: Mercury Drug (☎433 6604), on the corner of Araneta and Luzuriaga St. Open daily 7am-10pm.

Hospitals: Riverside Medical Center (☎433 7331), on B.S. Aquino Dr. in the northern part of the city.

Telephones: PLDT (☎433 6700), on Galo off Lacson St. Booths close at 4:30pm. Open M-F 8am-noon and 1-5pm.

Internet Access: Cyberworld, on Araneta St. near the Plaza. P25 per hr. Open daily 9am-midnight.

Post Office: (☎433 0436), on Gatuslao St. near intersection with Burgos St. *Poste Restante.* Open M-F 8am-noon and 1-5pm, Sa 8:30-11:30am.

Postal Code: 6100.

ACCOMMODATIONS

Pension Bacolod (☎433 7842), 11th St. on corner of Hilado St. This backpacker haven is situated in a quiet part of town. Cafe attached (shrimp *sinigang* P84). Singles P105-215, with A/C P350; doubles P170-262; triples P245-315. MC/V. 10% surcharge. ❶

Business Inn (☎433 8877; fax 434 2114; businn@bed.i-next.net), 28 S. Lacson St. Room service. Laundry service. Business center with Internet and fax. The cafe has a great all-you-can-eat breakfast buffet for P175. Doubles P840-2000❺

King's Hotel (☎433 0572), on Gatuslao St. at the corner of San Sebastian. Gleaming rooms. A/C, telephone, private common room. Singles P600; small doubles P670; bigger doubles P780. MC/V with 8% surcharge. ❺

FOOD

For quality and ambience, head to the **Goldenfield Commercial Complex,** which has bistros and cafes, or hit the area of **Lacson Street** between 20th and 24th St. **Cyberazia** ❷, on the corner of 22nd and Lacson St., is an Internet cafe and trendy bar. (Wings P75. Internet P25 per hr. Open M-Sa 9am-2am.) Nearby **Chicken House** ❶, on Lacson St. at the corner of 24th St., proves that not all chicken is created equal. Try the *pecho* (breast) or *paa* (thigh) for P50. (Open daily 10am-11pm.) Chicken is a Bacolod specialty—**Jo's Chicken Inato** ❸ on San Juan St. near the town square serves it up hot and tender (Open M-Sa 9am-9pm, Su noon-8pm.) The central **market** ❶ downtown offers sweet delicacies, including *piyaya* (hardened crêpe with melted sugar) and *bay ibayi* (sugar and coconut in a coconut half-shell).

SIGHTS AND ENTERTAINMENT

Nearly everything in the **Negros Museum** in the Old Capitol Building, relates to the colonial sugar industry. (☎434 9505. Open M-Sa 9am-6pm. P30, students P20.) The **Old Capitol Building,** built in 1921, sprawls from Gatuslao to Lacson St. Across the street from the Negros Museum is the Negros Forest and Ecological Foundation's **Biodiversity Center.** The center is devoted to preserving what small shreds remain of Negros's indigenous flora and fauna. (Open M-Sa 10am-5pm.) The **Masskara Festival,** a melange of Mardi Gras and Río party styles, is during the third week of October. In the Goldenfield Commercial Complex, **bars, karaoke joints,** and a new **casino** stay open daily 9pm-2am. **Quorum,** near the back of the complex at the Kundutel, is an enormous arena with space-tech flair. (Cover P100. Beer P35.)

DAYTRIPS FROM BACOLOD

MT. KANLA-ON NATURAL PARK

Take a jeepney from Bacolod to Mambukal (1½hr., every 30min. 7:20am-9pm, P30). The last jeepney back to Bacolod leaves Mambukal at 5pm. Guides cost around P530 per day. Package deals run about P4500 for 2 climbers including equipment, food, and transport. To secure a permit and find accredited guides, tourists should consult the tourist office in Bacolod. Or, check out the Mt. Kanla-on Natural Park Bacolod Liaison Office, in the Dept. of Environmental and Natural Resources in the Penro Compound on Gatuslao St., near the Hall of Justice (☎434 7769; open M-F 8am-5pm). Permits to explore the park and climb the volcano P300.

The tallest peak in the Central Philippines (2465m), Mt. Kanla-on offers challenge, natural beauty, and danger. Two expeditions got caught in a 1996 eruption, resulting in the deaths of one British trekker and two Filipino guides. Its unique structure consists of a small active opening on the southwestern edge of the larger collapsed caldera of the original volcano, also called the Margaja Valley. The rainy season creates a small lake inside this caldera. The surrounding rainforest is teeming with wildlife. The trails within 4km of the summit are treacherous during the rainy season (Jan.-Mar. and July-September). During these months, the mountain is closed for safety. The best entrance point into the park is from the **Mambukal Mountain Resort ❹**, near many hot springs and waterfalls. (☎433 8887. 2-person cottages P550; 4-person cottages P870.)

SILAY AND VICTORIAS

To either town, take a bus connecting Bacolod with Cadiz (Bacolod to Silay 20min., every 30min. 4am-7pm, P8; to Victorias 30-40min., P14) or a jeepney from opposite Robinson's Mall (P14).

Silay and Victorias are the centers of Negros's sugar industry. Silay, the "Paris of Negros," is also a longtime artist's haven. In Silay, hop on a jeepney at the corner of Rizal and Severino St. (10min., P4) to get to the **Hawaiian Philippines Sugar Corp.** (☎495 3200) and see the sugar trains. A letter of introduction from the Silay tourist office (located by the City Hall, near the highway; open M-F 9am-noon and 1pm-5pm) is recommended. The best time to visit the Sugar Corp. is between October and May. Sandals and shorts are not allowed. The **Tourism and Cultural Arts Office,** in the City Hall opposite the plaza, can point out ancestral homes and sights and give you the low-down on the **Kansilay Festival** held November 5-13. (☎495 0661. Open M-F 8am-noon and 1-5pm.) Don't miss the **El Ideal Bakery ❶** on the corner of National Rd. and Zulueta St. near the plaza. El Ideal satiates Silay's sweet tooth with local treats like *lumpia ubod* (fresh spring rolls, P25) and *piaya* (sesame cakes) for P15. (Open M-F 8am-5:30pm, Sa noon-5pm.)

The **Victorias Milling Company, Inc. (Vicmico)** is the largest sugar mill in Asia. It is accessible from the main road in Victorias by jeepney. Grab the one marked "VMC" at the corner of Osmeña and Jover St. (10min., every 30min. 5:30am-8:30pm, P4.) Ask to be let off at the **Vicmico Public Relations Office** on Ossorio Rd. below the Personnel Building. Tours can be arranged at the factory and the Church of St. Joseph the Worker, but call ahead. (☎399 3002. Open Tu-F 7am-noon and 1-4pm. Tours 30-40min.; M-F 9am and 2pm; P20, students P5.) Vicmico's real attraction is the **Church of St. Joseph the Worker** and its mural, known as the "Angry Christ," where Jesus sits in front of the hands of God, straddling a serpent-spewing skull. No miniskirts, shorts, or sleeveless shirts are allowed.

DUMAGUETE ☎35

Popularly known as the "City of Gentle People," Dumaguete keeps the peace at the southern tip of the Visayas. The capital of Negros Oriental, it sits across from turbulent Mindanao, and near the alleged witchcraft of Siquijor Island. Travelers will find it a convenient springboard for exploring Siquijor or lovely Apo Island, which shelters some of the finest diving in the country. Though Dumagete is a decidedly relaxed place, its student population brings vitality and energy to the waterfront, making it a city that promises something for almost everyone.

TRANSPORTATION

Flights: To get to the **airport,** take Dumaguete North Rd. (the National highway) off Silliman Ave. **Air Philippines** (☎225 4266; www.airphils.com) is at the airport, and the ticket outlet is in the Honeycomb Tourist Inn (☎225 9826). Open M-F 9am-noon and 1-

4:30pm. Daily flights to **Manila** (7:30am and 2:50pm, P2690). **Cebu Pacific** (☎225 8802; www.cebupacificair.com) also flies daily to **Manila** (3:30pm, P2260). Purchase tickets at the airport or from a travel agent in town.

Buses: Dumaguete Ceres Terminal is in the southern part of the city across the river on Calindagan South Rd. Follow Perdices St. (tricycle P2.50). To: **Bacolod** via **Cadiz** (6hr., P130); **Kaban Kalan** (5hr., every hr. 4am-10pm, P120); **San Carlos** (6hr., every hr. 3am-11pm, P145). Buses going north stop at **Ceres Sub Terminal Northbound,** near the ferry pier. Walking away from the pier, take a right up Flores St. Terminal; it's 5min. up on the right, in *barangay* Lo-oc. **Royal Express Bus Terminal** (☎225 2234) sends buses to **Bacolod** (6hr.; 6am, 2pm; P186) via **Mabinay** (2hr., P80).

Ferries: The **pier** is at the north end of Rizal Ave. Shipping companies send representatives to the pier area 1hr. before departure. There is a P15 terminal fee for most ferries. 15% student discount. **SuperCat** (www.supercat.com.ph) sends daily ferries to **Cebu** (2½hr., 11:45am, P570) via **Tagbilaran** (1½hr., P480). **Express** office (☎225 0735) on Ma. Christina St. behind the Metrobank Branch. Open M-Sa 8am-noon and 1-5pm. The branch office (☎225 5799) is near the pier opposite Ceres Sub Terminal in Lo-oc. **Delta Fast Ferries** (☎225 3128) whisks passengers to **Larena** on Siquijor (45min.; 9:15am, 1:30, 4:30pm; P120). The main ticket outlet is in the Gold Label Bakeshoppe on Perdices St. Open M-Sa 7:30am-noon and 1-7pm. **WG&A** (☎225 3538; www.wgasuperferry.com) sends ferries to **Cagayan de Oro** (6hr., F 6am, P540) and **Manila** (25hr.; W 5pm, Sa 9am; P1450). WG&A tickets can be purchased at SuperCat offices. **Negros Navigation** (www.negrosnavigation.ph) goes to **Manila** (24hr., Sa 5:30pm, P1400). Ferries leave from Tampi, several kilometers north of Dumaguete, for **Bato** on Cebu, a short ride from Moalboal (1hr., leaves when full, P55).

Local Transportation: Tricycles (P4) in town.

ORIENTATION AND PRACTICAL INFORMATION

Downtown is easily navigable by foot. **Rizal Avenue** borders the coast connecting the ferry pier in the north with roads heading inland. Silliman University sprawls north of nearby **Silliman Avenue,** which runs west from the shore. Originating at Silliman Ave., **Perdices Street** bisects the city, heads south, crosses the **Banica River,** and passes the main bus terminals. **Dr. V. Locsin Street** intersects Perdices midway through downtown; the market, park, and post office are a few blocks south.

Tourist Office: (☎225 0549), in the city hall and schools complex near the corner of Colon and Santa Catalina St. Open M-F 8am-noon and 1-5pm. Free map of town.

Budget Travel: Maganda Travel and Tours (☎225 8256), on the corner of Dr. V. Locsin and Santa Catalina St. Visa extension service, airline ticketing, and tour packages. P500 service charge over standard fares. Open M-F 8:30am-5pm, Sa 8:30am-4pm.

Currency Exchange: PCI Bank (☎225 4787), on the corner of Perdices and Legazpi St. Cashes traveler's checks. Cirrus/MC **24hr. ATM**. Open M-F 9am-3pm.

English-Language Bookstore: The Old San Francisco Bookstore (☎225 8230), on Real St., opposite the provincial capitol. Used books, paperbacks P50-80. Open M-Sa 9:30am-7:30pm.

Emergency: ☎116 or 166. **Fire:** ☎160.

Police: Philippine National Police (☎225 1766), corner of Cervantes and Locsin St.

Pharmacy: Mercury Drug (☎225 0425), on Colon St. opposite the fish market. The largest of several pharmacies. Open daily 6am-10pm. MC/V.

Hospitals: Holy Child Hospital (☎225 0247), on Legazpi St.

Telephones: RCPI (☎225 1733), at the corner of San Jose and Santa Catalina St. Open M-F 7am-9pm, Sa 8am-8pm.

Internet Access: Scooby's (☎422 8368), on the corner of Perdices and Silliman Ave., upstairs from the fast-food joint. P20 per hr. Open daily 8am-11pm.

Post Offices: GPO (☎255 5877), at the corner of Santa Catalina and Pedro Teves St. *Poste Restante.* Open M-F 8am-noon and 1-5pm.

Postal Code: 6200.

ACCOMMODATIONS

All accommodations are within walking distance of the market and town plaza. Tricycle drivers make the 5min. trip with baggage from the ferry pier (P10).

Silliman University Alumni Hall Dormitory (☎225 4323). Walk north along Perdices St., which becomes Campus Dr.; turn right at the 1st gate. A/C rooms with cable TV. Dine at the cafeteria next door. Doubles P540; quads P650. Open 6:30am-7pm. ❹

Home Quest Lodge (☎225 3327), on Silliman Ave. near the Perdices St. intersection, on the 2nd fl. Complimentary coffee 6-8am. Cable TV in lobby. Singles P191, with A/C P282; doubles with shared common room P302, with A/C P425-478. ❷

Vintage Inn (☎225 1076), on Legazpi St. opposite the public market, near the Real St. intersection. Clean rooms in a large, airy building. Restaurant open daily 7am-8pm. Singles P220, with A/C P330, with A/C and TV P440; doubles P330, with A/C P495, with A/C and TV P605. Family room P935. ❷

C and L Suites Inn (☎225 6219), on Colon St. near Perdices St., across from the cathedral. Big rooms overlooking a cathedral and a park make this an upmarket pleasure. All rooms with TV and A/C. Singles from P720; doubles P850. ❺

FOOD

Barbecue chicken reigns supreme in Dumaguete. There are several BBQ hot spots on Silliman Ave., and smaller operations set up along Rizal Blvd. in the evenings.

Silliman Avenue Cafe, opposite the university. Students come here to hang out and get some action. Try the *panini* and the sweet coffee concoctions (P30-110). ❷

Chin Loong, on Rizal Blvd. at the corner of San Jose St. A local favorite. Bird's nest soup (P115). Entrees P40-170. Huge portions make most dishes bargains. ❷

Don Atilano (☎225 4724), inside the Hotel La Residencia. Foreign meats attract Dumaguete's expats. Try the Serrano ham (P390 per 100g) or the Angus steaks (P315 per 100g) imported from Spain and America. AmEx/MC/V. ❺

Thrifty Chicken Alley, on Silliman Ave. between Rizal Blvd. and Perdices St. They grill, fry, filet, and boil this flightless bird into a moist and tender frenzy. Whole roasted chickens for P180, chopped BBQ chicken and rice for P80. ❸

ENTERTAINMENT

The seaside **Why Not Complex** (☎225 4488), on Rizal Ave., dominates local nightlife. Internet access (24hr.; 1hr. P60), a disco with live music (P50 cover, open Tu-Sa 9pm-2:30am), and a karaoke lounge with billiards (open daily 8pm-2am) fuel partiers. The **Rosante Bar** (☎225 3909) on Perdices St., downtown serves up plenty of beer (P30-70) to cheerful locals Monday to Saturday 2pm to midnight. The **Sandurot Festival,** in the third week of November, celebrates multiculturalism. After ceremonial gift-giving, various costumed Negrenses parade and celebrate their *sandurot* (friendship).

ISLANDS NEAR DUMAGUETE

APO ISLAND

Together with Moalboal (Cebu) and Panglao Island (Bohol), Apo Island is part of a trinity of world-class diving spots in the Visayas. Secluded, posh, and serene, this may be the finest dive destination in the country. Sheltered beaches dot the island coast, and cliffs poke through the green jungle. Fishermen inhabit a small village and tend to a lighthouse with over 300 steps leading down to the water. The reefs around **Coconut Point** are suitable for divers of all levels, while the crystal-clear waters of the sanctuary give snorkelers a view of this underwater community. Barracuda swim at Coconut Point, a site perfect for drift-diving. Humongous schools of jackfish are regularly spotted at **Mamsa Point.** To get to Apo, take a **jeepney** from the Zamboangita terminal, next to Judy's Bakeshoppe (ask a tricycle driver to bring you there for P4), and get off in Malatapay (40min., P15). The island's accommodations can arrange a pickup by *banca* (40min., P100); otherwise, bargain hard to have local fishermen make a "special trip" (P300-1000). From Apo, hire a *banca* to take you to **Siquijor** (P3000-3500).

Apo is becoming wealthier and more touristed, though deals still exist for those who look. At **Liberty's ❸**, the bamboo rooms usher in onshore breezes, and Paul, the English owner, guides divers to the Marine Sanctuary. (☎424 0888; www.apoisland.com. Dive with equipment US$30; PADI open-water certification US$315; advanced open-water US$255; Discover Scuba US$55. Restaurant open daily 6am-9pm. 5-bed dorms P200; doubles P500-900.) Several local families rent **cottages ❸** for P200-300 per night; make inquiries in the village. **Food** can be ordered on-site at the resorts (most dishes P100-200) or from a number of street-side establishments serving the usual dollops of *adobo* and fish soup (P30-60).

BAIS

About 40km north of Dumaguete, Bais is named for a species of eel—though most people slither to Bais to see whales and dolphins in the Tañon Strait between Cebu and Negros. Buses from the Ceres Northbound Terminal in Dumaguete headed for San Carlos or Cadiz go via Bais (1½hr., every hr. 4am-6pm, P24). The only way to get to the whales is through the tourist office (☎541 5161), which sends out daily tour boats. (20-seater P3000; 15-seater P2500 for a daytrip including whale-watching, lunch, scuba diving, snorkeling, and hiking.) To get to the wharf, take a pedicab (P10) or tricycle (P30) to Capiñahan. The best place to stay in Bais is the **Bahia Hotel ❺**, which has great views from its hilltop terrace. (☎402 8850. Doubles P900-1300.) **Elly's Place ❹**, directly on the wharf, is a breezy bamboo house on stakes. (☎402 8603. Doubles P530.) For rock bottom prices, go to **New Jacob's Eatery and Lodging House ❶**, on Mabini St. 100m from the BPI bank. (☎0919 492 9138. P110 per person. Grilled fish and rice P125.)

SIQUIJOR ISLAND

The smallest province in the Philippines, Siquijor sits 20km off the southeastern tip of Negros Oriental, patched with beaches, mountains, jungles, and rice fields. A fire road encircles the island, making it an excellent place to explore by motorbike, available at most accommodations (P500). Dubbed *"Isla del Fuego"* ("Island of Fire") by Spaniards who saw strange lights in the mountains, Siquijor's name is synonymous with the black-magic shenanigans of *aswang*, hideous witches who prey on children and pregnant women. Although mysticism is not immediately visible, healers dwell in the interior mountains, especially north of Siquijor Town in San Antonio. A handful of resorts are scattered around the island. **Casa de la Playa ❹**, 7km from Larena on **Sandugan Beach,** is a quiet retreat designed to calm

FROM THE ROAD

THE SPIRITS OF SIQUIJOR

Siquijor's alleged harboring of methods of witchcraft is its biggest draw. Tourists flow in from Negros and Bohol to dally with the island's purveyors of black magic. Some come out of mere curiosity, while others come seeking healing or guidance. There isn't much in Siquijor that points to its spirit healers—the workmanlike churches preach God's orthodox word, and crosses dangle in storefronts and streetstalls.

"There are no witches in our town," a local man explains to me. "But look over there—in the hills." The hills he indicates rise up from the coast and create forested coves and valleys throughout the interior of the island. This is where the sorcery supposedly takes place.

It's a tricky thing for a foreigner to go snooping for curiosities in someone else's backyard. The people of rural Siquijor know that many of the trekkers who come to their *barangays* are looking for new curios and more scalps to add to their travelogues. Some enterprising locals have taken to passing themselves off as traditional healers, offering to perform "secret" ceremonies for a fee. More will probably crop up as Siquijor's tourist industry develops.

For a price, these "healers" will sell the secrets of Siquijor's "witchcraft" to those travelers looking for a quick and novel

body and soul. Its owners offer personalized tours of the island as well as yoga and painting classes. The excellent restaurant specializes in exotic vegetarian fare. (☎397 2291; fax 484 1170; laplaya@gmx.net. Restaurant open 6am-9pm. Laundry service. Cottages for 2 P580-650, with kitchen and refrigerator P750, with A/C P850; 4-person family house P1200.) Still a little farther down the beach, **Kiwi Dive Resort** ❷ is the island's best-established dive shop. (1 dive US$26; PADI open-water course US$300; advanced open-water US$230. Dorm beds P180; cottages P400-730.) Rent motorbikes at any of these places for P500 per day.

PANAY

A Goliath of an island, Panay has never matched the quick-footed and savvy tourist tendencies of its David—little Boracay off its northwest tip. Tourism officials are developing Panay's potential attractions, including trekking in the mountains of Antique and diving off the southern coast. For now, though, the main attraction remains Kalibo's Ati-Atihan festival.

THE VIEW FROM ABOVE

Main Cities: Iloilo in the south and Kalibo in the north.

Nearby Islands: North of Panay, Boracay Island rivals some of the world's most beautiful tropical havens.

Tasty Mangos: Guimaras Island, only a daytrip from Iloilo, is famous for its luscious mangos and beaches.

ILOILO ☎33

Iloilo (pronounced 'Eelo-eelo') is the biggest, most stylish city in all of Panay. Its colleges keep things young, and its nightlife keeps the young sloshed and merry. Rivers, parks, and seabreezes also make Iloilo an expat favorite. Though the town shuttles travelers off to Boracay, it's got enough allure to keep them around for a while. More patient folks should consider making the short hop to Guimaras, which rewards visitors with idyllic beaches and the world's sweetest mangos.

TRANSPORTATION

Flights: Iloilo's **airport** is northwest of the city in Mandurriao. Take a "Mandurriao Iloilo" jeepney heading west on Gen. Luna (20-25min., P4); a pedicab goes the rest of the way (3min., P3). Taxis to the airport run P40-45. **PAL** (☎320 3030; www.philippineairlines.com) flies to: **Davao** (daily 8am, P3720) via **Cebu** (P1957) and **Manila** (4 per day, P4151). **Cebu Pacific** (☎320 6889; www.cebupacificair.com) goes to **Davao** (daily, P3620) and **Manila** (3 per day, P2745) via **Cebu** (P1965). All airlines have branch offices open daily 9:30am-6pm in the Atrium Mall at the Gen. Luna-Bonifacio intersection. Terminal fee P45.

Buses: Buses from 2 stations connect Iloilo with towns in the rest of Panay. **Ceres Bus Terminal** (☎337 0456), on Tanza St. near Ledesma St. intersection. To: **Caticlan,** the gateway to **Boracay** (6hr., 6 per day, P140); **Kalibo** (4hr., every 30min. 3am-4pm, P140); **Roxas** (3hr., every 30min. 4:15am-5:30pm, P77). 15% student discount. Buses to **Antique** leave from the **R. M. Panay Transport** office (☎336 8341) on Gen. Luna, opposite the John B. Lacson Colleges Foundation.

Ferries: Fast ferries dock on the river after the 1st bend, near City Hall. **Bullet Express** (☎338 0618; open daily 6am-5pm) goes to **Bacolod** (1hr.; 4-5 per day, last trip 5pm; P190). **SuperCat** (☎336 4259; www.supercat.com.ph) goes to **Bacolod** (1hr., 4 per day 7:30am-5pm, P270). 15% student discount. From Arrastre Pier by Fort San Pedro, **Negros Navigation** (☎336 2396; www.negrosnavigation.ph) serves: **Cagayan de Oro** (14hr., Sa 4pm, P1390) and **Manila** (19hr., 5 per week, P1470). **WG&A** (☎336 2776; www.wgasuperferry.com) has similar routes but also goes to **Davao** (20hr., Su 7am, P1410) via **General Santos** (17hr., P1410). Some schedules vary, so call ahead. **Cockaliong** (W, F, Su 7pm; P500) and **Transasia** (daily 6pm, P550) liners go to **Cebu.** All shipping companies' offices are on the 3rd fl., Atrium Mall. Outriggers to **Buenavista** and **Jordan** on Guimaras (15min., depart when full 6am-6pm, P15) leave from the pier to the right of the large ferries.

Local Transportation: Jeepneys cost P4 to most destinations. Southbound jeepneys gather at the corner of de Leon and Fuentes St. A/C **taxis** P25 plus P2 increments. **Tricycles** P5-10, though they are largely banished from downtown streets.

ORIENTATION AND PRACTICAL INFORMATION

The largest city on Panay, Iloilo sits on the southeastern coast, across the straits from Bacolod (on Negros Island). Iloilo covers five subdivisions, demarcated by the Iloilo and Batiano River system. The **Provincial Capitol** sits on the northern edge of downtown at the intersection of **Gen. Luna Street** and **Bonifacio Drive,** which leads north across the river into **La Paz** and **Jaro.** Separated by a tributary, **Mandurriao** lies west of Jaro and is home to the **airport. Molo** is west of down-

experience. Another approach is to visit Siquijor, get to know the people, and wait until a local requires some healing of his own. Many rites are performed in public in order to harness the energy of the whole community. Christianity is still an overwhelming force, and many of the rituals incorporate calls for prayer.

In my short time wandering Siquijor's hills, I saw only one public rite—a death rite for an older man who had been felled by illness. The people interred the man, offered prayers, and then performed a brief ceremony intended to help the man's spirit find rest. Spirit healers came to the community from nearby valleys to incant their own prayers. At the center were several chickens and a pig destined for roasting that the people of the neighborhood had slaughtered to express regard for the dead man and his family.

The whole affair ended with a few further prayers—concluded by "amens"—and a feast. Though there was nothing particularly shocking or dramatic about this ceremony, and though most spirit-healing is more low-key than many outsiders expect, the rite did manage to suture together the people of several small settlements, isolated from one another by mountains. That's not quite magic, though it says more about the nature of Siquijor's "voodoo" than the rite-peddlers would have tourists believe.

–Greg Schmeller

town and south of Mandurriao. Downtown revolves around the Gen. Luna St.-Bonifacio St. intersection, site of the **Atrium Mall.** From here, **jeepneys** head to the five subdivisions (P4-20). **Benigno Aquino Avenue** runs past the airport and the mastadonic **S.M. City Mall** complex.

Tourist Office: (☎337 5411), on Bonifacio Dr., a 2min. walk north of the capitol by the pedestrian bridge. Helpful staff. Free town maps. Open M-F 8am-5pm.

Budget Travel: Panay Island Holidays (☎336 8069), at the Casa Plaza Building on Gen. Luna St. downtown. Offers Boracay packages and city and Guimaras Island tours. Open M-F 8:30am-5pm, Sa 8:30-noon.

Bank: Dozens of banks and **ATMs** dot downtown. **Philippine National Bank** (☎337 0481), on the corner of Gen. Luna and Valeria St. MC/V 24hr. **ATM.** Open M-F 9am-4:30pm.

Emergency: ☎117.

Police: (☎337 3011). On Gen. Luna St. west of the Provincial Capitol building.

Pharmacy: Mercury Drug (☎335 0037), on Iznart St. near J.M. Basa St. Open 24hr.

Hospital: St. Paul's Hospital (☎337 2741), a 5min. walk from the Provincial Capitol building down Gen. Luna St. on the right.

Telephones: RCPI (☎336 2220), at the corner of Iznart and Yulo St. Open M-F 7am-7pm, Sa 8am-5pm, Su 9am-2pm. **PLDT** calling office on E. Lopez St. north of the Gaisano Mall.

Internet Access: IPX (☎508 8678), on the 2nd fl. of the Atrium Mall, has the speediest connection in town. P30 per hr. Open daily 9am-8pm.

Post Office: (☎336 2128), in the Old Customs House on Aduana St. *Poste Restante.* Open M-F 8am-noon and 1-5pm, Sa 9-11am.

Postal Code: 5000.

ACCOMMODATIONS

Family Pension House (☎335 0070), on Gen. Luna St. at the Mabini intersection. The best budget option in town. Treehouse restaurant and pool table (P10). Breakfast included. Singles P275; doubles P350, with A/C P575. ❸

Four Season Hotel (☎336 1070; fax 509 3888), at the Fuentes and Delgado St. intersection. Clean rooms and professional service make this hotel a great deal. Room service. Laundry service. Standard rooms P720; deluxe P1050/030. ❺

Castle Hotel (☎338 1022), on Bonifacio Dr. beyond the museum. Friendly place in a rambling 19th-century mansion. A/C and TV. Singles P545; doubles P640. ❹

FOOD

There is more to Iloilo cuisine than seafood—local specialties include bloody pig guts in "mud soup." **Foodstalls** ❶ along Valeria and Gen. Luna St. offer cheap, late-night eats. For finer dining, try the fresh-from-the-docks menu at local favorite **Nes and Tats Seafoods ❹,** on BS Aquino Ave., south of the SM City Mall. Whole buttered crabs with sauce (P200) or a whole stuffed eel (P170) are featured on a menu that changes with the catch. (Open daily 9am-11pm.) **Marina ❸, is** on Iloilo Diversion Rd. in Mandurriao, in an airy *nipa* pavilion on the river. (Delicious *kinilaw* P110; *adobo* P150; *lechon* P200. Open daily 9:30am-1am.) **Nena's Manokan ❷,** on Gen. Luna St. before the Diversion Rd. intersection, serves first-rate grilled chicken (P65) on balconies over the river. (Open daily 11am-11pm.)

SIGHTS AND ENTERTAINMENT

The **Dinagyang Festival,** held during the fourth weekend of January, pays tribute to the Santo Niño (Christ Child) and the heritage of tribes with colorful street dancing. The southwest coast of Panay offers Spanish churches, including **Molo** and **San Joaquin. Miag-ao,** a church built of coral, bedecked with palms and bananas, is a rare vernacular baroque. (Jeepneys to Miag-ao leave from the intersection of Gen. Luna St. and Bonifacio Drive; 30min., P18.)

Iloilo's student population ensures that there are plenty of nightlife options around town. Neighborhood **sing-along bars** abound downtown. For live music, a friendly, raucous crowd, and "San Miguels (P35), try the military-themed **Barracks,** on Iloilo Diversion Rd. past the S. M. City mall. (Open M-Sa 6pm-1am. Taxi P60.) Several bars and a disco are in the **Sarabia Manor** hotel complex on Gen. Luna St.

DAYTRIP FROM ILOILO

GUIMARAS ISLAND. The island of Guimaras is famous throughout the archipelago for its mangos, said to be the country's sweetest and juiciest. The island is home to a Trappist monastery whose monks produce candies and preserves from local produce. Other attractions include the **Macopo Falls** and, of course, the **Oro Verde Mango Plantation.** There are several beach resorts on **Alubihud Beach** in Nueva Valencia that offer picnic facilities as well as lodging (P350-900). Local boat owners can be hired to take you to the many outlying islands (P100-2000, depending on destination). On an idyllic islet off Lawi, the **Baras Beach Resort** ❺ offers its guests an array of aquatic activities, including sailing, snorkeling, and windsurfing. (☎0917 9387 159. Cottages P800-1000. Ask for Mike or Baby to arrange transportation to the island.) There is a very helpful **tourist information kiosk** on the pier in Jordan, the provincial capitol. (Open daily 9am-6pm.) All of Guimaras's sights can be seen in a daytrip from Iloilo (tricycles can be hired for P220-450) or by using one of Nueva Valencia's resorts as a base. Ask at the tourist kiosk about the **International Mountain Biking Tournament,** held every year in March. *(Guimaras is 15min. by banca from Iloilo harbor. Buses run every hr. 5am-5:30pm, P15).*

KALIBO ☎36

Once a year, Kalibo becomes a destination instead of a Boracay stopover. January's *Ati-Atihan* festival is Panay's Mardi Gras, with soot-faced revelers from all over the world jitterbugging down the avenues for a week. When this strange fusion of Catholic and tribal carnival rites ends, Kalibo sleeps again, and the party moves away. Travelers might spend some time here to re-stock and get big-city services, but beyond that, Kalibo is best at sending people on their merry way. The city of Kalibo has helpful festival information at www.ati-atihan.net.

TRANSPORTATION. Kalibo's **airport** is a major hub for the daily traffic from Manila to Boracay. **PAL** (☎262 3263; www.philippineairlines.com) and **Air Philippines** (☎262 4444; www.airphils.com) both fly to **Manila** (P2900). **Cebu Pacific** (☎262 5409; www.cebupacificair.com) also serves **Manila** (P2900). From the airport parking lot, **Southwest Tours** (☎268 5100) brings tourists to **Boracay** via **Caticlan** (1½hr., P350). The cheapest option from the airport to Boracay includes a tricycle to town (P20), a Ceres liner to Caticlan jetty (P40), and then a pumpboat to Boracay itself (P20). Buses congregate on Osmeña Ave. **Ceres Bus Terminal** has buses to **Iloilo** (4hr., every 30min.-1hr. 2:30am-3:30pm, P140). **Delmabel** offers three to four daily A/C vans to **Caticlan** (1hr., 7am-3:30pm, P100) and **Iloilo** (3hr., 7am-5pm, P120). **GM Liners** heads to **Roxas** (2hr., every hr. 4:30am-2:30pm, P50). Buses and **jeepneys** to Caticlan also depart from the corner of Roxas Ave. and Barrios St., and from the corner of Roxas and Pastrana Ave. when full (1½hr., P50). Ferries leave for Manila from Kalibo's Dumaguit port. To get there, take a jeepney from the Gonzalez St. market (45min., roughly every 30min., P15)—the last jeepney from Dumaguit leaves at 4:30pm. **Negros Navigation** leaves Saturdays at 3pm. (☎262 4943. Open M-F 8am-noon and 1-4pm, Sa 8am-noon. 18hr., P995). **WG&A** (☎268 4391; www.wgasuperferry.com) takes off on Tu, Th, and Su afternoons. The schedule changes frequently, so call their office to confirm.

ORIENTATION AND PRACTICAL INFORMATION. Kalibo lies along Panay's north highway, a few kilometers from the sea, at the confluence of the Sooc and Aklan Rivers. **Southwest Tours** (☎268 5100; open M-F 8am-noon and 1:30-5pm, Sa 8am-noon) offers connecting bus and boat transfers to and from **Caticlan,** and from Kalibo airport to **Boracay** (1½hr., P350). **BPI,** on Martelino St. at the corner of XIX Martyrs St. cashes American Express Traveler's Cheques, and has a 24hr. **ATM.** (☎262 3504. Open M-F 9am-3pm.) Other banks and ATMs cluster on Roxas Ave. In an **emergency** dial ☎166; the **police** station is in the city center on XIX Martyrs St. **Kalibo Provincial Hospital** (☎268 4565, emergency 141) is on Mabini St. **Web Center, Inc.,** next to Air Philippines on Roxas Ave. offers **Internet** access for P40 per hr. The nearest **post office** is **GPO,** in the capitol—a P5 tricycle ride. (☎262 3215. *Poste Restante.* Open M-F 8am-noon and 1-5pm.) **Postal Code:** 5600.

ACCOMMODATIONS AND FOOD. Rooms are usually easy to find except during the Ati-Atihan Festival in January, when you should make reservations weeks ahead and prepare for prices to launch into the stratosphere. **La Esperanza Hotel ❹,** on Osmeña Ave by the bus stop, is the picture of affordable luxury. All rooms have cable TV, A/C, and bath; most have waterbeds and bathtubs. (☎262 3989; fax 262 5858. Laundry service and cafe. Dorm beds P300; pension doubles P850; standard doubles in the main building P1100; deluxe triples P1500; suite P2500.) **Garcia Legaspi Mansion ❸,** on the fourth floor of 159 Roxas Ave., near the corner with Barrios St., has a convenient and central location. Rooms vary from comfortable to luxurious. (☎262 5588. Singles P400, with common room 475; doubles with A/C and bath P800.)

Cheap eats abound in Kalibo. Basic eateries and Filipino fast-food joints encircle the plaza. **Kusina sa Kalibo ❷** (☎262 3466), on D. Maagma St., is a peaceful beer garden escape serving favorites like shrimp tamarind soup (P140) and huge portions of crispy *pata* (P160). Some of the best food in town can be found at the **Perfect Combination Bar & Restaurant ❹** (☎268 4240) on L. Barrios St. Try the pineapple chicken (P150). The **sing-along bars** that crowd Roxas and Regala St. are lively local hangouts, even if you shun ballads for mere beer.

BORACAY ISLAND ☎36

Filipinos everywhere will tell you about Boracay's smooth, cool, salt-white sand, even if they've never felt it for themselves. Boracay boosts the entire country's tourism industry—shops and resorts clog the 4km White Beach, and in the high season everything fills up for months. The island's hard-charging nightlife feels more like Thailand's Ko Samui or Ko Phangan than like other places in the Philippines. Not quite as budget-friendly as it was in the 1970s, when dinner meant bartering with fishermen, you can still find affordable deals.

TRANSPORTATION

Flights: Many tourists fly to **Kalibo,** the capital of Aklan, and then take a van or bus to the small town of **Caticlan,** where outriggers run to Boracay. Vans to Kalibo's airport vary by season (1½hr., 10 per day in low season, P80). **Southwest** (☎288 3010), south of Boat Station 1 on Boracay, runs a boat- and bus-trip to the airport during the high season (1½hr., departs 4hr. before flight departure, P200). Several airlines link Manila with Caticlan's small airport, a 15min. walk from the ferry pier (P20-30 by tricycle). The tourist center books plane tickets. **Asian Spirit** (☎288 3465) and **Seair** (☎288 7272) both fly to **Manila** (1hr., P2500-2800).

Buses: Bus and van connections between Kalibo and Caticlan are frequent. **GM Liner** sends buses to **Iloilo** (6hr.; 7:30, 9:30am; P140). **Jeepneys** (P30) and buses (P36) run to **Kalibo,** but only some go to the **airport** (1½hr., 6am-4:30pm, P30).

Ferries: Outriggers link Caticlan with 3 boat stations on White Beach and stop at the south station first (30min., every 15min. 6am-5pm, P16.50). When the waves are choppy, the ferries dock on the southeast tip of the island; from there, it's a P20 tricycle to White Beach. Boats also run to: **Carabao,** north of Boracay (1hr., 3 per day, P20); **Roxas,** on Mindoro (6hr.; M, Th 10am; P150); **Santa Fe,** on Tablas Island of Romblon province (2hr., 9am, P150); **Tablas City** (2hr., P150). Check at the tourist office on the Caticlan pier for the latest schedules and prices—several **RORO** (roll-on, roll-off) ferry services to **Manila** and **Mindoro** (14hr., P760-900) are appearing as part of the "Strong Republic Nautical Highway" program, though low-season travel is trickier. **MBRS Lines** operates a ferry service to **Manila** (W, F, Su; P840).

Tricycles and Pedicabs: Tricycles sputter up and down the jeepney-free main road. Daytime rides P8 per person, at night P12. **Pedicabs** along White Beach P20-30.

Rentals: Mopeds can be rented everywhere. Bargain if the prices you hear seem too high (many run half-day P600, P500 low-season). **Mountain bike** rentals run about P50 per hr.

ORIENTATION AND PRACTICAL INFORMATION

Boracay is north of Panay between the Sulu and Sibuyan Seas. Its 4km **White Beach** stretches along the west coast. Boracay is shaped like a dumb-bell; the Main Road goes from end to end. **Barangay Yapak,** capped by **Puka Beach,** is on one end, and the forested **Barangay Manoc-Manoc** is on the other. **Bulabog Beach** is opposite White Beach, 1km away. White Beach, in **Barangay Balabag,** has three boat stations.

Tourist Office: DOT office (☎/fax 288-3289) in a *nipa* cottage in the Mall d'Boracay near Boat Station 2. Helpful staff. Immigration officer extends visas W 9am-3pm (P2000-3000). Open M-F 8am-noon and 1-5pm. The much bigger **Tourist Center** (☎288 3704) centralizes many helpful resources: telecommunication services (open daily 9am-10pm); currency exchange; Internet; safety deposit (P150 per month); activities desk (open daily 9:30am-7pm). Helpful staff. Open M-Sa 9am-6pm. **Tribal Adventures** (☎288 3207; www.tribaladventures.com), at Sand Castle Resort south of Boat Station 1. Mountain biking, kayaking, and windsurfing. Open daily 7:30am-10pm.

Currency Exchange: Allied Bank (☎288 3048), on the main road between Boat Station 2 and 3. Open M-F 9am-5pm. Branches lie beside Boat Stations 1 and 3. Moneychangers crowd Station 3 and offer decent rates.

Market: Talipapa Market, north of Boat Station 3.

Emergency: Police ☎166. **Medical** ☎141.

Police: Philippine National Police (☎288 3066), between Boat Stations 2 and 3.

THE PHILIPPINES

Medical Services: Boracay Island Emergency Hospital (☎141), on the main road; take the road next to Boracay Regency Hotel near Boat Station 2, then turn left at the main road. **Boracay Medical Clinic** (☎288 3147) is on the main road in Balabag. Open 24hr. Serious cases require treatment in Kalibo.

Telephones: Cruztelco phone booth near Lapu-Lapu Divers, north of Boat Station 2. **Pantelco,** north of Boat Station 2, opposite Mango Ray's. **RCPI-Bayantel** (☎/fax 288 3012), at Oro Beach Resort, Boat Station 3. Open M-Th 8am-6pm, F-Su 8am-noon and 1-5pm.

Internet Access: Tourist Center (see **Tourist Office**) has fast connections. P70 per hr.

Post Office: In Balabag, north of Boat Station 1 on the main road. Open M-F 8am-noon and 1-5pm. *Poste Restante.* **Tourist Center** (see above) has a postal center (letters only) with *Poste Restante* (address: P.O. Box 552, Manila 1099, Philippines), delivered from Manila every 2 days. P5 service charge per letter. Open daily in high season 9am-8pm; in low season 9am-6pm.

ACCOMMODATIONS

Heading north toward Boat Station 1, the sand gets finer and prices start rising. Always bargain, and ask for discounts for extended stays. Low season often brings discounts as high as 25%.

Michelle's Bungalows (☎288 3086). A short walk north of Boat Station 3. Between Beach Life Diving and La Isla Resort; take a right and head 35m from beach. Good service for low prices sets this lodge above the rest. Doubles P670/350. ❺

Trafalgar Garden Lodge (☎288 3711). From Boat Station 3, head north, turning right into the market at Beach Life. Trafalgar is 200m down on the left. Operated by a friendly British-Filipino couple, Trafalgar is one of the last truly budget accommodations on the island. Singles P250-550; doubles P350-800. ❸

Nigi Nigi Nu Noos 'e' Nu Nu Noos (☎288 3101). Between Tourist Center and Boat Station 2. Polynesian pagodas in a tropical garden. A great low-season deal. Free 30min. email session per day. Cashes traveler's checks. Huts with fan in high season P2000-3000, in low season P1000; huts with A/C P2500-3500/1500. MC/V. ❺

Paradise Lodge (☎288 5050), between Boat Station 3 and Beach Life. 7 spacious cottages near coconut and avocado trees—the attached cafe serves up the fruits (avocado shake P40). Porchside hammocks. Doubles with fan and private bath in high season P1800, in low season P700; doubles with A/C P2000/850. ❺

FOOD

Boracay serves up a dizzyingly diverse array of foods. Expats have globalized the dining scene and locals have started fusing styles together.

Shenna's Restaurant (☎288 6120), next to Lapu-Lapu Divers. Superb, inexpensive 3-course dinner combo P125; other seafood and grilled entrees P110-190. Smooth pineapple shake P50. Open daily 7am-10pm. ❸

Nigi Nigi Nu Noos 'e' Nu Nu Noos (see **Accommodations,** above). Pry the name's hidden meaning out of the owners. Big seafood variety basket P180. Happy hour 5-7pm. Jazz and blues Th-F. Open daily 6:30am-11pm. AmEx/MC/V with party of 5 or more. ❸

Mango Ray (☎288 3371), north of Boat Station 2. Savory BBQ and international grub. 4-course meal P230. Many grilled dishes from P150. "Mango Ray Baby" mixes *kalamansi,* mango, and rum (P75). Open daily 7am-1am. ❹

Paradise Restaurant and Coffee Shop (see **Accommodations,** above). Fresh fruits from the trees behind the restuarant add color to Filipino specialties like boneless bangus (milkfish; P90) or sizzling squid (P120). Shakes from P40. Open daily 8am-9pm. ❸

SIGHTS AND WATERSPORTS

The sunset on White Beach is Boracay's premier sight. Except for the outcrop of **Willy's Rock,** north of Boat Station 1, the sand is fine and uniform. The northern beaches are often forgotten and thus make great secluded escapes. **Puka Beach** is isolated on the northern shore (tricycle from White Beach 30min., P30). Snorkeling tubes crisscross the water off **Ilig-Iligan Beach** to the northeast. From the beach, the **Bat Cave** is easily reached (P50). The **windsurfing beach** sits a short walk across the narrowest point of the island from White Beach. Trails run through the **southern rainforest** in *barangay* Manok-Manok. **Watersports equipment** can be rented right off the White Beach path for negotiable rates, or at **Scuba World,** south of Boat Station 1. (☎288 3310. Windsurfing gear P300 per hr., with instruction P500. Kayaks P200-300 for the first hr., each additional hr. P75-150. Wakeboarding P650 per 30min. Open daily 8am-6pm.) The **Tourist Center** (see **Practical Information,** p. 429) rents waterskiing equipment (P800 per 15min.), wakeboarding equipment (P1300 per 30min.), and speedboating equipment (P2800 per hour). Local boat owners hawk snorkeling tours (P500).

Boracay is surrounded by wall dives, channel drift dives, plunges into bat- and snake-infested caves, and deep dives. One site ranks among the Philippines's best: **Yapak,** on the coast of Panay. At 35m, the strong currents attract pelagic fish, tuna, and whitetip sharks. On **Maniguin Island,** 18km southwest of Boracay, whitetip sharks sleep in caves. An overnight stay is recommended on Maniguin, although it can be reached in a day by boat (2hr., around US$90). To explore shallower reefs, divers head for **Crocodile Island** and the fish frenzy at **Friday's Rock** (30min., US$40).

Dive shops litter the sands of White Beach; be sure to shop around. Typically, dives cost US$20-25, PADI open-water courses are US$290-320, and advanced courses cost US$185-200. **The Beach Life Club,** near Boat Station 3, has a friendly multilingual staff and low-season discounts on courses. (☎288 5211; www.beachlifeclub.com. Open daily 8am-9pm.) **Victory Divers,** next to Nigi's and south of Boat Station 2, does regular live-aboard dive safaris to **Apo Reef** and **Busuanga** and claims that only they know the coordinates of some magnificent wrecks within daytrip distance. (☎288 3209; www.victorydivers.com. Open daily 7:30am-11pm.)

NIGHTLIFE

Boracay is a drinking island, and there are a lot of ways to get your drinking done. The neighborhood **sing-along bars** north of the Main Road are the best places to give other tourists the slip and meet locals. **Wave Disco,** near Boat Station 2, is the hot new White Beach nightspot. For a P100 cover you can drink tropical cocktails (P80-150) and dance in a cave with aquariums for walls. (Open daily 6pm-2am.) To the delight of some and the horror of others, several Boracay clubs have begun staging "full moon parties" like Thailand's Ko Phangan. Dare to drink two or more "coconut killers" (P130) and **Barracuda,** south of Boat Station 2, will enshrine you in their Hall of Fame. (Open daily 5pm-1am.) **Beachcomber,** north of Boat Station 1, is Boracay's premier open-air disco. (Beer P40. Open daily 5pm-3am.)

LEYTE

Sipping a blood cocktail with a local chieftain and planting the first of many crosses, Ferdinand Magellan staked his claim for the glory of Spain on the tiny Leyteno island of Limasawa in 1521. Four centuries later in 1944, American General Douglas MacArthur made his triumphant return to the archipelago here. Historical significance aside, there is little in Leyte to interest tourists. Travelers find most of the action outdoors—from siesta-friendly beaches to trails through the island's jungles. Leyte is also a useful departure point for visits to nearby islands.

THE VIEW FROM ABOVE

Major Towns: Tacloban at the edge of Samar, Ormoc on the western coast.

Something Different: Escape to the beach on Biliran Island, host to one of the Philippines' only hinterlands.

Natural Wonders: From Tacloban, head to Sohoton Natural Bridge National Park to see nature at its best.

TACLOBAN ☎53

Tacloban is the geographical and historical heart of the Eastern Visayas. Smog, *kamikaze* jeepneys, and a lack of sights don't give many reasons to linger. Travelers will want to follow MacArthur's lead, and island-hop from here.

TRANSPORTATION. Flights arrive and depart from the **Daniel Z. Romualdez Airport** (☎325 5893), 11km east of Tacloban in San Jose. Cross the parking lot for the cheapest jeepney to town (P5). Flights from Tacloban go to **Cebu** and **Manila. Cebu Pacific** (airport office ☎325 8486; www.cebupacificair.com; open 5:30am-4pm; downtown office on Sen. Enage St. 325 7747; open 8am-5pm) offers 3 flights per day (P3033). **Philippine Airlines** (☎321 2212; www.philippineairlines.com) has 2 flights per day (P2688; open daily 5:30am-4:30pm). **Seair** (☎323 8805 or 321 5578; www.flyseair.com) flies to **Cebu** (M, F; P1620).

To find the **bus** terminal, walk away from the city on Quezon Blvd. Buses go to: **Manila** (24hr.; 11 per day; P790, with A/C P892) via several destinations in **Samar,** including **Allen** (6hr., 6 per day, P164); **Catbalogan** (3hr., 15 per day, P60-70); **Calbayog** (5hr., 11 per day, P100); **San Isidro** (4hr.; 3 per day; P159, with A/C P173). San Isidro and Allen ferries run to **Matnog** on Luzon (1½hr., P74). Other destinations include: **Davao** (12hr., 2 per day, P375); **Naval** on Biliran (3-4hr., 4 per day, P100); **Ormoc** (2hr., every 20min. 6:30am-6:30pm, P65-72). **Jeepneys** strike out for **Basey** on Samar (45min.; depart when full, last return 3pm; P10). Jeepneys also head south to **Palo** (30min., every 20min. until 7pm, P5) and **Tolosa** (1hr., P10). Yet more buses depart from the **Philtranco Station.** To get there, take a jeepney to San José from Real St. and ask to be dropped off at the Philtranco Station. These buses leave for **Cebu** (11hr.; P220, with A/C P250); **Cubao** and **Pasay** via **Manila** (24hr.; P795, with A/C P896). **WG&A Lines** (☎321 2536; www.wgasuperferry.com) have **ferries** that go to **Cebu** (15hr.; Tu and Sa 4pm; P230). **Jeepneys** cruise Magsaysay Blvd., Real St., and Veteranos St. From the jeepney stop along Quezon Blvd., cross-town fare P4. For a **taxi,** call ☎321 4713.

ORIENTATION AND PRACTICAL INFORMATION. Tacloban is a portal to and from Samar, across the San Juanico Straits to the northeast. The city is sandwiched between **Panalaron Bay** to the north and **Cancabato Bay** to the south. The pier, market, and bus/jeepney terminal overlook Panalaron Bay. **Magsaysay Boulevard** wraps around the northern and eastern boundaries of the peninsula. It originates in the north by **Children's Park,** the **tourist office,** and Leyte's **Provincial Capitol Building,** and ends in the south at **Real Street.** Jeepneys blaze down southwest **Avenida Veteranos** and southeast Real St., converging to funnel passengers southward to **Palo** or the **airport** across Cancabato Bay.

The main **tourist office,** is across from the entrance to Leyte Park Resort compound on Magsaysay Blvd. (☎321 2048. Open M-F 8am-6pm.) **MacArthur Landing Tours and Travel,** at 122 Lopez Jaena St., off Saint Niño St. is very helpful in arranging tours. (☎321 5685. Open M-F 8:30am-noon and 1-5:30pm.) **ATMs** are available at most banks. The **Philippine National Bank,** at the corner of St. Niño St. and J. Romualdez St. cashes traveler's checks and has a Cirrus/MC/PLUS/V 24hr. **ATM.** A passport photocopy is required to cash traveler's checks. (☎321 2053. Open M-F 9am-3pm.) **PDCP Bank** is on Zamora St. (☎321 2881. Open M-F 9am-3pm.) The **markets** on Quezon Blvd., Torres St., and Tarcela St. sell fruit (P5-30), straw goods (P10-250), and clothes (P15 and up). **Police** (☎166), are on the Paterno Ext. In an emergency, dial one of the following numbers: **fire** ☎911; **ambulance** ☎325 6471; **medical** ☎321 2816. **Mercury Drug,** on Salazar St. near the intersection with P. Zamora is well stocked. (☎321 2852. Open daily 7am-10pm.) The **Eastern Visayas Regional Medical Center** (☎325 6471), near the gate of Children's Park on Sen. Enage St. is on-call 24hr. Telephones can be found at **Bayantel,** at 109 Romualdez St. (☎325 6608; open M-F 7am-6pm) and at the **PLDT** office on Zamora St. near Del Pilar St. (Open M-F 8am-7pm.) All **Internet** cafes, including **Continental Internet Cafe** on 170 Veteranos St. (☎321 3427) offer a rate of P25 per hr. Others are located on Real and Paterno St. The **post office** is on Trece Martirez St., along the harbor. (☎321 3509. Open M-F 7am-noon and 1-5:30pm, Sa 8am-noon.) **Postal Code:** 6500.

ACCOMMODATIONS AND FOOD. **LNU House ❹,** at the corner of Paterno and Santa Cruz St., is a working lab for tourism students at Leyte Normal University. All rooms have A/C and bath, a balcony, TV, tea rooms, and laundry service. (☎321 3175. TV P50. Refrigerator P50. Spacious singles P400; doubles P500; 4-bed family room P1150. Extra bed P120.) **Cecilia's Lodge ❷,** on 178 Paterno St. near Ave. Veteranos, has simple rooms and an amicable owner. (☎321 2815. Singles with fan P150, with fan and private bath P190, with A/C and private bath P450; doubles with fan and private bath P550.)

Visitors can slurp a San Miguel while watching Filipino soap operas at the **roadside barbecues ❶** along Real St. The **fish and vegetable market ❶** along the streets outside the bus terminal provide a great medium for the culinary artist. **Guiseppe's Restaurant ❸** on Ave. Veteranos at the corner of MH del Pilar St. is an unlikely blend of Italian and Filipino cuisine—the best in town. (☎321 4910. Steak P285. Mango shake P50. Open daily 10:30am-10:30pm. AmEx/MC/V.) Sample local cuisine like *giniling* (spicy chopped pork, P25) at **Join Us Cuisine ❶** on Ave. Veteranos, near the intersection with Real St. Or fall back on a classic burger (P17) or grilled-cheese sandwich. (☎321 6984. *Halo-halo* P35. Open M-Sa 7am-8pm.)

SIGHTS. South of Tacloban, the **General Douglas MacArthur Landing Memorial** commemorates the commander's return on October 20, 1944. Take a jeepney from Avenida Veteranos to Palo via Baras (20min., last return 4:30pm, P5). Ask the driver to drop you off in front of the memorial. Hide in foxholes on nearby **Hill 522.** The **Battle of Baluarte Marker,** 52km away in Barugo, commemorates a battle between guerrillas and Japanese troops. North of the city, the **San Juanico Bridge**—the longest spanning bridge of its kind in Southeast Asia—links Leyte to Samar.

DAYTRIP FROM TACLOBAN

SOHOTON NATURAL BRIDGE NATIONAL PARK. Sohoton is across the straits in Samar. A subterranean river snakes beneath two mountain ridges, creating the natural stone bridge for which the park is named. From Tacloban's bus terminal, take a jeepney to **Basey** (1hr., P10). Get off at Basey's Town Hall; the **Department of the Environment and Natural Resources (DENR)** is across the street. Francisco Corales Jr. arranges the necessary boat trip (1½hr., P700 per boat) and provides kerosene lamps (P50). The guide expects a tip (around P200). Boats do not go out in the rain. (☎276 1151. Open M-F 8am-5pm. Park US$2 or P110.)

IN RECENT NEWS

ORMOC'S REBIRTH

The streets of Ormoc look spiffy and new. While other towns' throughways are mottled with cracks, ditches, and potholes—made barely passable by years of uneven repairs—Ormoc's are smooth. Some even have fresh paint lines streaking down the middle. At the edge of each avenue, new-looking buildings congregate and spawn. The town has an airy feel, with park plazas and new municipal venues going up around the city.

Ormoc isn't simply a boomtown, though. The city looks relatively new because it was forced to regenerate 13 years ago, after one of the worst disasters to hit the Philippines in modern times. There isn't much evidence of it to view, but in November 1991, huge swaths of the city were swept right into the ocean, and Ormoc almost came to an end.

During this time, rain bulleted down on western Leyte, as Typhoon Uring (also known as Thelma) dumped out its Titan-sized waters over the Visayas. Ormoc's residents had prepared as best they could for strong winds, which are normally the biggest threat from passing typhoons. But the typhoon began to pass, the storm system began to break apart, and Uring slowed to a crawl. Over the course of a mere three hours, the storm bled off six inches of rain.

For accommodations, the best bet is **St. Michael's Lodging House** ❷ to the left of Elsie's Bakery, next to the jeepney stop in Basey. (☎276 1003. Dorm bed P150.) Another option is the **guesthouse** ❹ in the national park. (Call DENR for reservations. Singles P300; doubles with bath P400.)

While in Basey, wander the picturesque streets to **St. Michael's Church,** built in 1636. There are many attractions in **Western Samar:** the area around **Calbayog** is full of caves and waterfalls, while the **Samar Archaeological Museum and Research Center,** at Christ the King College in Calbayog, documents the island's history.

ORMOC ☎53

Ormoc was the stage for the decisive, if relatively unknown, WWII Battle of Ormoc Bay on November 11, 1944. This battle marked the beginning of the Japanese retreat. Floods again destroyed much of the town in 1991, but locals stuck it out and rebuilt. Today the WWII memorial, in an attractive waterfront park, is frequented by families during the day and is the center of festivities at night. Cleaner and friendlier than Tacloban, this transportation hub merits a day's stay.

TRANSPORTATION. At the **bus** terminal, Philtranco (☎255 2708) takes off for Manila at 5am (24hr., with A/C P930) and also at 9am and 5pm (26hr., P950). These buses stop at Allen (P349, with A/C P382); Calbayog (P213/280); Catbalogan (4hr., P211/230); San Isidro (P349/384); Tacloban (2hr., P110/122). **Ferries** connect San Isidro and Allen to Matnog on Luzon (1½hr., P81). **JD Bus Line** (☎255 2890) runs A/C vans to Tacloban (2hr., 4 per day 6am-8:30pm, P100), and Naval on Biliran (1½hr., 3 per day 6:30am-9pm, P100). **Eagle Star** (☎255 5166) and **Velmar** alternate service to Catbalogan (4hr.; 3, 5, 8, 9am; P132) and Tacloban (2½hr., every hr. 3:30am-5pm, P82). **Bachelor Express** runs to Davao (11:30am, 11pm; P490). **SuperCat ferries** (☎255 3511; www.supercat.com.ph; open 5am-7pm), at the end of the pier, chug to Cebu (2hr.; 8:30am, 1:30, 6:30pm; P550). 15% student discount with ID. **Sulpicio Lines** (☎255 2041) heads for Cebu (5hr., Su 11pm, P165) and Manila (52hr., Tu 7pm, P750). **Oceanjet** runs twice a day to Cebu (P450).

ORIENTATION AND PRACTICAL INFORMATION. Ormoc is in northwest Leyte, 109km across the central range from Tacloban. Tucked into the north coast of **Ormoc Bay,** the **city pier** juts southward. The bus terminal and jeepneys are to the left of the pier. The first road perpendicular to the pier is **Larrazabal Boulevard,** featuring street BBQs (P25-100) and fresh pineapple (P15). **Bonifacio Street** heads north, crossing Larrazabal Blvd. and **Aviles Street.** Farther east, **Navarro** and **San Pedro Street** run north-south from the memorial park along the water.

Services include: the **Philippine National Bank** (☎255 4538), on Bonifacio St. with an **ATM** (open M-F 9am-3pm); a **hospital** (☎255 2475); the **police** (☎166); **Internet** access at **CupNet** in the Ormoc Centrum mall on Aviles St. (open daily 9am-10pm; P25 per hr.); **telephones** in the PLDT office, on the corner of Bonifacio and Catag St. (☎/fax 255 4737; open daily 7am-10pm); and the Cogon district **post office** (☎255 3181; open M-F 7am-noon and 1-5:30pm, Sa 8am-noon). A **postal desk** accepts letters closer to downtown at the corner of Larrazabal Blvd. and San Pedro St. (Open M-F 9am-noon and 1pm-5pm). **Postal Code:** 6541.

ACCOMMODATIONS AND FOOD. Opposite the bus terminal is the **Hotel Don Felipe** ❹ with clean rooms, a comfortable lobby and friendly staff. (☎255 2460. Singles P360, with A/C P480; doubles P420/P630; deluxe rooms in a renovated building P800-2400; extra person P250.) Rooms at **Eddie's Inn Lodging House** ❷ on Rizal and Aviles St. have beds and nothing else. (Singles P125; doubles P250.)

The area near the bus stop is an all-night **roasted chicken and pork** event. Ginger-roasted whole chickens are P100 at the stalls. For more formal dining, head along Larrazabal Blvd. away from the bus terminal. **Chitos Chow** ❷ serves up Chinese and Filipino dishes for P45-200. (Open daily 9am-11:30pm.) The restaurant in the **Ormoc Villa Hotel** ❷ offers specialties like chicken pork *adobo* (P150) and *halo-halo* with ice cream (P80), as well as pan-Asian favorites. (Open daily 6am-11:30pm.)

SIGHTS AND ENTERTAINMENT. Magellan left behind the historic **bridge** by Larrazabal Blvd., which is worth a gander on your wanderings through town. For nature lovers, the **Leyte Mountain Trail** snakes east 40km to Mahagnao National Park, terminating in Burauen, 66km from Tacloban. A national park since 1992, **Lake Danao** is an oasis in the heart of a wild forest. From the Ormoc bus terminal, take a jeepney (1½hr., leaves when full, P30) to the Lake Danao stop. Walk (15min.) or take a *bangka* (5min., P5) to the Department of Environment and Natural Resources (DENR), where park ranger Quinciano Abiertas, Jr. arranges *banca* trips

With so much excess water, bare logging areas and shallow-rooted sugarcane plantations quickly turned to mud, and soon the waters rolled off the land in a gigantic sheet. The surge of mud and roots smashed right through the city, blitzing whole neighborhoods at the base of the hills. In just a few hours, much of the town was sinking into Ormoc Bay. Most of the victims were asleep when the torrents swept down on dozens of homes.

Though the true number of deaths will never be known, the government estimates that nearly 7000 people perished—around 5% of the population. Televisions showed pictures of relatives desperately trying to find loved ones, and rescuers digging up bodies of entire families. Indeed: the Ormoc floods were nine times deadlier than the eruption of Mt. Pinatubo that same year.

The months after November were brutally lean. People fled or fashioned themselves temporary shacks. Government aid was slow in coming, but reconstruction eventually got underway, giving the city its present modern face. And while flash floods still rip into Leyte Island from time to time, nothing nearly as disastrous has happened since the epic floods of 1991, for which the city's residents are extremely grateful.

around the lake (P40 per hr.) and treks in the forest (park entrance fee US$2 or P110; tip expected for forest treks). Camping is free. The station has showers, and huts cost P100 per person per day.

Ormoc's nightlife is low-key and local. **Fred's Bar,** on Jaena Lopez St. near the corner of J. Navarro St., provides the locals with a forum for karaoke. (☎255 2953. San Miguel P30. Open daily 8pm-1am.) Within the Don Felipe complex, the **Swing Disco** is mainly ballroom (Tu-F 8:30pm-2am) and disco (F 11:30pm-3am, Sa 9pm-3am, Su 11:30pm-2am). Cover is P100.

NAVAL

Naval is the main town on Biliran Island and connects to Leyte by a bridge. Most folks speak Waray in this relaxed town, which is more useful as a base than a destination. The hectic activity of the **pier/bus terminal,** with its eateries and large market, radiates east by way of two parallel roads—**Vicentillo Street** to the north, and **P. Inocentes Street** to the south. A 15min. hike down P. Inocentes or a 5min. pedicab ride will bring you to the **Naval Institute of Technology** on the right.

The **PLDT,** on P. Inocentes St., has phone booths for both domestic (P1-5 per min.) and international (P20-50 per min.) calls. (☎198 2029. Open daily 7am-10pm.) The **Philippine National Bank** is at the left end of Ballesteros St. looking toward the ocean. (Open M-F 9am-noon and 1-3pm.) At the other end of Ballesteros St., a right on Caneja St. leads to the **police station.** From another path leading down P. Inocentes, a right on Ballesteros St. will lead to a **hospital,** 2km outside Naval. **Chapeland Pharmacy** on Casfin St. is open 24hr. Naval's pier and bus/jeepney terminal has daily departures for coastal cities and nearby islands. From the pier, walk 10-15m along P. Inocentes St. and take a right through the market to reach the **post office.** (Open M-F 8am-noon and 1-5pm.) **Postal Code:** 6543.

Enroll in night school at the **Naval Institute of Technology ❷,** or stay at their spartan hostel for P200 (with A/C P300). **Marvin's Place Seaside Inn ❺** in Atipolo is a good place to spend extra cash. It has a pool and access to a little beach. (P600 per room with A/C and private bath.) Hire a pedicab (20min., P5) or a motorbike driver (10min., P20) to take you to Atipolo.

Serving up Filipino dishes like pork *adobo* (P25) and *halo-halo* (P25), as well as burgers and sandwiches (grilled cheese P20), the **Five Sisters ❶** cafe-restaurant on Inocentes St. across from the PLDT office is a great deal. Next to the CAP building at the market, **Benno's ❶** serves Filipino pork stews (P20-40) and cake (P20) in an equally relaxed setting. **Balondo Discopub** across from Brigida's Inn plays the Philippine dance charts up and down. (Open daily 7pm-2am.)

Naval's pier and bus terminal have daily departures for coastal cities and nearby islands. Outriggers run west to **Higatangan Island** (1hr., 11am, P30). Arrive early at the pier, as the boats fill up quickly. The only lodging option on Higatangan is the **Limpiado Tourist Inn ❹** (basic rooms with sea view P350). The snorkeling heaven of **Maripipi Island** can be reached by boat (3hr., 10am, P30). Inquire at the mayor's house near the beach by Maripipi town for a homestay on the island. **Caibiran** is convenient for launching an expedition to **Mt. Biliran.** Surrounding villages shelter sulfur hot springs: **Caibiran Falls,** and the spring-fed **San Bernardo** pool. Jeepneys cross the island every hour (P30). Daytrippers may hire a motorcycle with driver (P450 per day). Sunsets are wonderful at secluded **Agta Beach.** Take the jeepney bound for Kawayan and tell the driver to let you off at Agta (35min., P12.) Inhabited by a hospitable family, **Agta Beach Resort ❷** has thatched huts. (P150 per person, with A/C P500 per hut.) Agta Beach faces **Dalutan Island.** The resort rents boats to paddle to Dalutan (40min., P30). Alternatively, hire a pump boat to Dalutan (10min., P300) or **Tingkasan Bat Cave** on Tingkasan Island (10-15min., P350).

PALAWAN

Palawan Island is an outland, lush with the fauna that the rest of the Philippines lacks, and teeming with bizarre beasts, ranging from the scaly anteater and Palawan bearcat to the stink badger. Instead of volcanoes, the island has limestone cliffs similar to those of China and Vietnam. Outside Puerto Princesa, electricity and running water are rare. With over 80 tribes and rainforest bordered by velvety tropical beaches, Palawan offers a serene induction into one of the world's last remaining frontiers.

THE VIEW FROM ABOVE

Main city: Puerto Princesa.

Other towns: Coron, El Nido, Port Barton.

Highlights: Scuba diving at Tubbataha Reef or Coron's Japanese wrecks; visiting the Subterranean River National Park; island-hopping and snorkeling in Honda Bay or Bacuit Bay; visiting Maquinit Hot Springs.

PUERTO PRINCESA ☎48

The government of this lone urban outpost carefully tends its growing ecotourism industry—ferociously fending off loggers and establishing itself as the center from which to explore Palawan's outlands. The cleanest city in the Philippines, "Puerto" levies heavy fines on litterers. Travelers to Palawan may want to spend a night here to stock up on cash and supplies, which other towns lack. The city's tasty food, friendly locals, and liquored-up "sing-along" bars make many visitors stay and revel a bit before moving on.

TRANSPORTATION

Flights: The **airport** is 1km from where the National Hwy. intersects Rizal Ave. Tricycle rides to downtown around 5min. (P5). **PAL** (☎433 4565; www.philippineairlines.com; open daily 8-noon and 1-4pm), in the building to the right of the airport, flies to **Manila** (daily 10:30am, P3956). **Air Philippines,** 420 Rizal Ave. (☎433 7003; www.airphils.com; open daily 8am-5pm), flies to **Manila** (daily 11am, P3309). **Seair,** in the Moana Hotel at 430 Rizal Ave. (☎433 4753; www.flyseair.com; open daily 8am-noon and 12:30-5pm), goes to **Manila** (M, F 9:30am; P3290) and **Busuanga** (M, W, F 2:20pm; P2190) via **El Nido** (P1860).

Ferries: The **wharf** is on the western tip of the city. Walk uphill and to the right to find Rizal Ave. Tickets sold at the wharf, but reserve beforehand at the ferry offices downtown. **Negros Navigation** (☎/fax 433 7204 or 434 4735) has an office on Roxas St. near the corner with Rizal Ave. Open M-Sa 8am-noon and 1-5pm. Ferries sail to **Manila** (22hr., M 2pm, from P1325). **WG&A** (☎434 5734) is on the right side of Rizal Ave. in the ARL building, a 5-10min. walk from the airport. Open M-F 8am-5pm. WG&A's **Super ferries** sail to **Manila** (28hr., Su 9am; from P1310, with meals P1400) via **Coron** (14hr., P1015).

Local Transportation: Public transportation is spotty when demand is low; hiring a **private vehicle** is often necessary. A jeepney-derivative costs around P2500 per day. An A/C 4WD runs P5000 per day (P3000 in low season) to **Sabang** and the **Underground River.** A/C vehicles to **El Nido** cost up to P15,000. Rentals come with a driver unless you pay massive insurance premiums and deposits. Former motocross racer **Romel Gevela** (☎921 375 8796), owner of a garage at 134 Abad Santos St., arranges car, truck, and motorbike rentals at competitive rates (multi-day rentals to El Nido and beyond P12,000 and up). **Go Palawan** (see **Travel Agencies,** p. 618) rents **dirtbikes** for P850 per day.

ORIENTATION AND PRACTICAL INFORMATION

The Puerto Princesa region sprawls from **Sabang** in the north to **Long Point** in the south. The city is on a peninsula jutting into the Sulu Sea, south of Honda Bay on the east coast. Ferries dock on the western tip, where **Rizal Avenue,** the main east-west drag, ends. **Roxas, Burgos,** and **Valencia Streets** intersect Rizal Ave. The **airport** lies along Rizal Ave., 1km east of the city center. The **National Highway** intersects Rizal Ave. on the eastern tip of the commercial area near the **Provincial Capitol** and runs north, splitting into north- and south-bound highways outside the city's peninsula. The highway is paved spottily to both El Nido in the north and Quezon in the south, with large stretches of gravel and mud in between.

Tourist Offices: City Tourism (☎434 4211), at air and sea ports. Open daily 8am-noon and 1-5pm. Also helpful is the **Provincial Tourism Office** (☎433 2968; www.palawan.net/palawangovt), at the corner of Rizal Ave. and the National Hwy. Open M-F 8am-noon and 1-5pm. The unofficial tourist office at **Backpackers' Cafe** has a humorous and helpful "comments book" and a wall map of Palawan. Open daily 7am-11pm. **Pat Murray,** one of Palawan's original settlers, is a walking Palawan encyclopedia. He frequents Trattoria Inn and happily offers advice.

Travel Agencies: Go Palawan, 353 Rizal Ave. (☎433 4570; gopalawan@pal-onl.com). Phenomenal staff and brochures. Open M-Sa 9am-6pm. **Coron Tours and Travel,** 38-B R. San Juan St. at Unit 6 Bundal Business Center (☎/fax 434 2638), between airport and city in *barangay,* San Miguel. Info on north Palawan. Open M-F 8am-5pm, Sa 8am-noon. **Palawan Ecology Travel and Tours,** 11 Mabini St. (☎434 4179; leomonice@yahoo.com), near the corner of Roxas St., arranges trekking, mountaineering, cliff-climbing, and more from US$107. Open M-F 9am-5pm.

Banks: Many on Rizal Ave. near Valencia St. All banks open M-F 9am-3pm. **Bank of the Philippine Islands** has a Cirrus/Maestro/MC/Visa **ATM.**

Bookstore: Leonar's Merrimart Bookstore, in the Merrimart store on Rizal Ave. downtown, has English titles. Open M-Sa 8am-7pm.

Markets: The central market is on Malvar St. between Burgos and Valencia St.

Emergency: ☎166.

Police: Police Assistance Center (☎433 9826), on Rizal Ave. near Palawan Museum.

Pharmacies: Mercury Drug (☎433 2498), on Rizal Ave. Another branch on Valencia St. Open daily 7am-10pm.

Medical Services: Adventist Hospital (☎433 2156), on San Pedro National Hwy. near the Santa Monica Rd. intersection. Open 24hr.

Telephones: Bayantel, 293 Rizal Ave. (☎433 4892), near the Provincial Capital. International and domestic calls. Open M-F 8am-10pm, Sa 8am-5pm. **PLDT Calling Office,** on Rizal Ave. at Roxas St., has a bank of A/C indoor booths. Open M-Sa 8am-6pm.

Internet Access: Numerous cafes dot Rizal Ave. **Big Bad Wolf,** on Valencia St. next to the market. P40 per hr. Open M-Sa 10am-10pm, Su 2-10pm.

Post Office: (☎433 2556), on Burgos St. near the corner of Rizal Ave. *Poste Restante.* Open daily 8am-noon and 1-5pm.

Postal Code: 5300.

ACCOMMODATIONS

Trattoria Inn (☎433 2719), at the corner of Palay Rd. and P.E.O. Rd., 1km from the airport away from downtown. A laid-back expat hangout with superb service. Laundry service. Tourist information. Doubles with A/C, cable TV, and hot water P520; double occupancy P620. ❹

Puerto Pension (☎433 2969; ppension@pal-onl.com), 35 Malvar St., a 5min. walk to downtown. Gorgeous, bamboo rooms. Restaurant with panoramic view. Great Filipino breakfast P90. Singles-P300; doubles P430, with A/C and common room P750. ❸

Backpackers' Cafe, Bookshop, and Inn, 112 Valencia St., 5min. past the Palawan Museum. Equal parts cafe, bookstore, travel agency, guesthouse, and island-guru hangout. Fairly small rooms. Reception daily 7am-11pm. Singles P150; doubles P240. ❷

FOOD

Ka Lui Restaurant (☎433 2580), on Rizal Ave. toward the airport from the city center. Easily the best restaurant in Palawan, and possibly the Philippines's best seafood. Menu changes with daily catch, and includes soup and a dessert fruit plate served in a coconut. Meals start at P110. Open M-Sa 11am-2pm and 6-11pm. ❷

Baan Kanita (☎434-5768), on Jacana Rd. near DZRH Radio, 1km south from the airport. Big, hot servings of Thai food arrive at tables equipped with small grill-pits to keep things sizzling. Dine in the garden for a romantic escape. Pork *sateh* P75, combination platters from P95. Open M-Sa 10am-2pm and 5pm-11pm, Su 5pm-10pm. ❷

Vegetarian House, 79 Burgos St., at the corner of Manalo St. Wise sayings adorn the walls of this Buddhist eatery. "Beef steak" and other "meat" dishes keep critters alive for P50-120. Open M-Sa 9am-2pm and 4-10pm. ❶

SIGHTS

The **Palawan Museum,** at the corner of Rizal Ave. and Valencia St. behind Mendoza Park, has over 20,000-year-old artifacts from the Tabon Caves—the home of the first known Filipinos. Their library has English-language books on Palawan. (☎433 2963. Open M-Sa 8am-noon and 1:30-5pm, Su 9-11am. P10, students P5, children P2.) The **Kamarikutan Kape at Galeri,** on Rizal Ave. near the airport away from downtown, showcases abstract takes on tribal art. The complex, constructed in Palawan and Ifugao styles, exhibits area artists. (☎433 5182. Open daily 8am-11pm.) At the western end of Rizal Ave., by the cathedral, a **memorial** marks where 143 US POWs were herded into a tunnel, doused with gasoline, and set on fire by Japanese captors on December 15, 1944. Eleven men survived by jumping off the cliff and swimming across the bay.

YUMMY IN YA TUMMY AT KA LUI

Remove your shoes and slippers at the gate, then make your way to a bamboo table. Delicate chords play in the background, and the climate is perfect for a quiet conversation at **Ka Lui Restaurant** ❸. The menu is handwritten, and accounts for the chef's whims and the daily catch. Dozens of sample plates and main courses all appear by dinnertime, most featuring local seafood in novel arrangements.

Squid, milkfish, clams, and crabs are arrayed by hand and elegantly paired with sauces and vegetables. A notch above the rest, even the *buko* juice comes with the entire coconut (which, once drunk, is cut open and returned with a spoon and sugar), and every dinner entree includes a dessert bowl of fresh, sweetened fruit. The breezy, bamboo dining rooms lack air-conditioning, but a web of fans brushes away heat and flies.

The restaurant serves some of the best seafood in the entire country at unbeatable prices. A meal of grilled squid and vegetables, soup, *buko* juice, and dessert costs P180. Lunches and dinners start around P110, and even the biggest, most complicated dinner samplers don't rise much beyond P270. As a result, Ka Lui is one of Palawan's most popular restaurants for gatherings, celebrations, and dates.

(☎433 2580. Open M-Sa 11am-2pm and 6-11pm.)

NIGHTLIFE

Most Filipinos won't let foreigners sneak out of Puerto Princesa's innumerable **"sing-along" joints** without wailing a song. For a night free from the spotlight, the cozy **Tom-Tom Club** on Manalo Extension (tomtom@pal-onl.com) leaves the music to the professionals. **Nick's Venue,** in the Admiral Hotel on Rizal Junction, is the main hot spot for Palawan's 20-something jet setters. (Cover P100-150. Open daily 8pm-2am.) **Spice Bar and Disco,** on Rizal Ave., keeps the crowd hopping until early morning. (San Miguel P35. No cover, but P100 minimum tab. No shorts or slippers. Open M-Th 8pm-2am, F-Su 8pm-3am.)

OUTDOOR ACTIVITIES

Tubbataha Reef, 150km southeast of Puerto Princesa, is the archipelago's most sought-after dive site. Its remote location and limited accessibility (Mar.-June) make a trip to the reef difficult, but big, rare fish await. **Queen Anne Divers** (☎433 2719), on P.E.O. Rd. at the Trattoria Inn, operates two dive ships to Tubbataha Reef (5-7 days, US$700-900. Book 6 months in advance). Queen Anne also runs trips to **Busuanga** and the **Coron Islands** (famous for their Japanese wrecks), daytrips to reefs off the southern coast near Puerto Princesa (2-dive packages with lunch and boat US$60, with rentals US$65), and PADI courses (open-water US$300, advanced open-water US$250). **Island Divers,** 371 Rizal Ave., brings divers to southern Puerto Princesa Bay around Pete's Reef, Light House, and Table Head (2-dive daytrip US$55, with rentals US$60) and offers PADI courses for US$220-300. (☎433 5103. Open M-F 8am-5pm.)

In late June, Puerto Princesa enters its festival season. The **Baragatan festival,** on the third Friday of June, brings parades, food, dancing, and dozens of carnival stalls to the Provincial Capitol grounds. It is followed by the **Pista Y Ang Kagueban,** a big, strange combination of festival and reforestation efforts.

DAYTRIPS FROM PUERTO PRINCESA

HONDA BAY. North of the city the water is peppered with islands ideal for snorkeling, swimming, and sunbathing. Tourism has largely recovered since the Abu Sayyaf terrorist kidnappings from **Areceffi Island** in 2001; policeboats prowl the waters, and resorts (including Areceffi's upscale **Dos Palmas**) are open again. **Snake Island, Starfish Island,** and **Pandan Island** are reached by a short *banca* trip (P800). Visitors to **Señorita Island** can check out fish and seaweed farming. *(*Bancas *(P250-1200) leave for Honda Bay from Santa Lourdes Wharf, a 30min. tricycle ride from town (P180). A tourist shack organizes* bancas *and snorkeling gear rentals (P100 per day,* banca *prices vary).*

TABON CAVES. History reaches back 20,000 years in these jungly caves, the former home of Tabon Man, the "first Filipino"—although local stone artifacts say he wasn't quite the first. Only 14 of the 200 caves have been explored. They make for a great hike through creature-filled forests and cool batcaves. *(South of Puerto Princesa in Quezon. Charing Bus Lines runs trips to Quezon leaving from the market on Malvar St. (up to 4 buses daily, leave at 5am and when full, P142). From Quezon, hire a* banca *to go to the caves (P500 round-trip). Bring a flashlight and hiking shoes.)*

PUERTO PRINCESA SUBTERRANEAN RIVER NATIONAL PARK

Between Port Barton and Puerto Princesa, Puerto Princesa Subterranean River National Park gapes toward the South China Sea. The **Cabayugan River,** the world's longest underground river, weaves 8.2km through natural growth forest, home to macaques, monitor lizards, 40,000 bats, and thousands of birds. Its natural stone and stalagmite statues of Christ and the Virgin Mary are strange but captivating.

The park is best reached from Sabang. Four or five **jeepneys** to Sabang leave from Malvar St. near the Shell station in Puerto Princesa (3hr., 7am-2am, P75). From Sabang, the park now runs **motorboats** (round-trip P300) to the park entrance from the jeepney stop. Or hike along the 2hr. **Monkey Trail,** flush with surly macaques, that ends at the park entrance. Infrequent **boats** go to Port Barton (3hr., private P2500) and El Nido (7hr., private P5000), but prepare for a rough ride. **Jeepneys** to Puerto Princesa leave from the ferry pier (3hr., 3 per day 6:30am-2:30pm, P75) but aren't very reliable. Infrequent **A/C vans** offer a more comfortable ride (P400). If desperate hire a **jeep** (P2000) or A/C van (P2500) from the park office in Sabang, or hire one in Puerto Princesa for the whole day at a comparable price.

Stop by **St. Paul's Subterranean River National Park Office** on Manalo St., near the corner with Fernandez St. in Puerto Princesa, to get **permits.** (☎433 2409. Open M-F 8am-noon and 1-5pm. General entrance P50. Cave entrance P200, children P100.) Or grab a permit at the **Visitor's Assistance Center** in Sabang itself. (Open daily 8am-noon and 1-5pm.) Snorkelers should rent equipment in Puerto Princesa.

PORT BARTON

Perhaps it's the absence of phones, roads, and reliable electricity that draws travelers to the pristine islands off the coast of Port Barton. **Jeepneys** go to Puerto Princesa (5-6hr., up to 12hr. in low season; 8-9am; P150, private P4500). In high season, **boats** go from the town pier to El Nido (5hr.; M, W 9:30am, Th, Su 10:30am; P1000, private P5000) and Sabang (3hr.; Tu, Th noon, W, Sa 12:30pm; P650, private P2000). **Quezon, Mabini,** and **Ballesleros** cross Rizal Ave. toward the ocean. **The Adventist Health Care Clinic** on Bonafacio Ave., a block from **Rizal Avenue** between Quezon and Ballesleros Ave., provides very basic care M-F 9am-5pm and Sa 1-5pm. The nearest **post office** and public **phones** are in Roxas (2hr. by jeepney).

Port Barton rides the tide of tourism. During high season, the tourist swell necessitates tents, while in low season restaurants and cottages often shut down. **Swissippini Lodge and Resort ❺** (☎433 4757) has clean accommodations. One-room cottages for P500/300; cottages with a common room are P700/500. **El Dorado Sunset Cottages ❸** (☎433 2110) offers similar lodgings with cottages P350-500 and a delicious seafood buffet complete, with squid and fixings for P235. The **Bamboo House ❷** has entrees for P65-140. (Open daily 7am-10pm.)

Port Barton's **beach** is good, if a bit crowded by *bancas*, and the bay is great for swimming; more options hide in island coves. *Bancas* island-hop for P800-1000. **Cacnipa, Exolica,** and **Albaguin Islands** all have snorkeling sites, and scuba diving can be arranged through the **El Busero Inn** on Rizal Ave. (☎918 567 6669. US$55 for 2 dives. Front desk open daily 8am-4pm.) For a freshwater experience, walk 1½hr. inland to cascading waterfalls. Pick up a map from behind the bar at El Dorado Sunset Cottages (see above).

EL NIDO ☎48

El Nido is the frontier of travel on this "last frontier" island. Limestone cliffs ascend out of the jungle that laps at the edge of town. Every shoreward glance from downtown floods up with mist and the towering ivory islands of Bacuit Bay.

TRANSPORTATION. **Seair** flies to Manila (M, F 3:25pm, P4700) via Busuanga (P2300) and Puerto Princesa (M, W, F 9:45am, P1800). **Jeepneys** go to Puerto Princesa daily during high season and every 2-3 days during low season (8-10hr., 12-14hr. in rainy season, P400). Alternate routes to Puerto Princesa include taking a jeepney to Sibaltan (2-2½hr., daily 7am, P60) where a **boat** leaves for Taytay (3-4hr., 9:30am, P170); from Taytay, jeepneys head to Puerto Princesa (6-8hr.; 2, 4pm;

P190). During the high season, **boats** leave for Port Barton (4hr., F 6am, P650) and Sabang (7hr.; W, Sa 7am, P870). During the low season, private boats will take you anywhere if you pay enough (P1500 and up).

PRACTICAL INFORMATION. **Calle Hama,** which turns into **Palmera Street,** runs along the coast; **Calle Real** runs parallel to Calle Hama. **Rizal Street** cuts through the two and heads to the ocean. An increasing number of streets are being paved and marked with signs. Buy a **map** at El Nido Boutique. The **Municipal Tourism Office** (open M-F 8am-noon and 12:30pm-5pm) is across from the **post office** (open M-F 8am-5pm) on Calle Real. There are no banks, but **Palawan Pawnshop, El Nido Boutique and ArtCafe,** and **Lim's Store** exchange cash at competitive rates. The **police station** is in the Municipal Building. **Farmacia Comprendio** has most non-prescription drugs. (Open daily 7am-9pm.) There is also a **clinic** next to El Nido High School. (Open M-F 8am-noon and 1-5pm.) **Globe Telecom** offers **collect call** service for P70. (Open M-F 7:30am-10pm, Su 9am-10pm.) There is no public **Internet,** but dive shops, lodgings, and resorts may share theirs with patrons.

ACCOMMODATIONS AND FOOD. Like most of Palawan, El Nido is deserted in the low season but sees large crowds of backpackers and adventurers during peak months. During the low season, cottage prices are halved and many restaurants shut down. **Lally and Abet Cottages ❸,** at the far end of the beach, is popular and quiet. They offer island-hopping trips from P550. (Cottages P450/P350; beachfront P950/P750, with A/C P1300/P900). **Dolarog Beach Resort ❸** (www.dolarog.com), a short *banca* ride from town (P350), has upscale cottages in a well-tended palm garden. Edo, the Italian owner, cooks pastas and risottos for P150-300. Cottages run P1300-1600. Package deals include full board and a daily boat excursion for US$60. **Ric Son's ❸,** on the beachfront, has gorgeous views of Bacuit Bay and a large seafood menu. (Fish with black-bean sauce P130. Open daily 6am-10pm.) **Squido's Bar and Grill ❷,** toward the far end of the beach on Calle Real, serves seafood specialties like fried boneless bangus (P65) and grilled squid (P85), and the bar dishes up San Miguel for P30. (Open daily 6:30am-11pm.)

SIGHTS AND ENTERTAINMENT. The islands of **Bacuit Bay** are El Nido's prime attraction. These isles boast coral, three species of endangered giant turtles, and neon fish, all beneath rugged limestone cliffs. Among the best sights are the small lagoons of **Miniloc Island,** the secret beach of **Matinloc Island,** (hidden behind a stony cove) and **Pinsail Island,** where a skeleton of a WWII Japanese soldier lies within a marble cave. **Simisu Island** offers great snorkeling. Cottages have boats that will take you wherever you want for P1200 per day. Alternatively, Judith and Tani from the **El Nido Boutique and Artcafe** have set island-hopping trips for P375-450 per person (4-person minimum). Other tours include cliff-climbing (P150, scaled to experience level), island trekking on **Cadlao** (P300), and hiking to the **Maquinit Hot Springs** and **Nagkalit Kalit Waterfalls** (P400). All prices include lunch and are per person, with a 2-person minimum. Though not advised, intrepid hikers can pick up a rough but free map from the tourist center and set out on their own. Bring shoes and water. **Palawan Divers** on Calle Real offers dive trips around the archipelago, but Coron Island has better diving. On most Sundays, especially holidays, **cockfights** erupt at the cockpit on Rizal Ave. The **Shipwrecked Bar,** on Palmera St., is a popular tourist hangout. (San Miguel P30. Open daily 4pm-midnight.) Locals get down at **Bom Disco,** opposite Mac-Mac Restaurant. (Beers P30-50. Open daily 8pm-midnight.) The bar at **Bistro El Nido** has great mixed drinks (P60-110) and relaxed live guitar music. (Open daily 8am-1am.)

CORON ☎48

Northern Palawan is a wreck-diver's Shangri-La. The waters off Coron Island and the separate town of Coron hold the dubious distinction of housing the second-highest number of sunken Japanese WWII vessels after the Marianas Islands. Diving aside, the azure waters, countless islets, and gorgeous inland lakes are enough reasons to visit for one day or four.

TRANSPORTATION AND PRACTICAL INFORMATION. **Seair** flies to Manila (daily, P2450) and Puerto Princesa (P2400) via El Nido (M, F, P2300). **Asian Spirit** has daily flights to Manila (P1990). Both airlines fly out of the **YKR Airport** in **Busuanga,** about 14 mi. from Coron, and have offices in Coron Town. **Jeepneys** to the airport leave Coron Town 2hr. before departure (P150). **Pacific Airways** flies to Manila (P2030) from the more convenient **VAL Airstrip** behind the KokosNuss Resort, but only when there is an incoming plane from Manila. The airstrip office is sporadic; inquire at the **Coron Municiple Office.** (☎196 2508. Open M-F 8am-noon and 1-5pm.) **WG&A Superferry** (☎123 148) sails to Manila (14hr., Su, P1015) and Puerto Princesa (12hr., Sa, P700). **San Nicolas Lines** also goes to Manila (Su-M, F).

Side streets are unmarked, but this is slated to change. The **National Highway** connects Coron Town only to the western side of Busuanga Island, and the town's two main streets run parallel to the highway. **Real Street** is anchored by **Municipal Hall,** which also houses the **police station** and **post office** (open M-F 8am-noon and 1-5pm). At the opposite end of town is the **market** and small-boat **pier. Swagman Travel** (with a **Western Union** branch) lies at the intersection of **Don Pedro Street** and the National Highway. The **Coron District Hospital** is staffed 24hr. and lies 3km north along the highway, next to the KokosNuss Resort. **Netport,** next to Bayside Divers Lodge, has a relatively fast Internet connection. (P50 per hr. Open daily 8am-9pm.)

ACCOMMODATIONS AND FOOD. Most of Coron's accommodations are concentrated between its two ports. **Bayside Divers Lodge ❷** has cool rooms with breezes off the water and a very friendly staff. (☎02 817 3175. Doubles P255, with bath P330-500.) A 5min. *banca* ride across from Coron Town, on Uson Island, the **Dive Link Resort ❺** (☎02 371 9928) has package deals starting at US$70 per person (high season) and P1700 per person (low season), including board, daily boat trips, and airport transfer. The restaurant at the **Sea Dive Center ❸,** on the 2nd pier across from the Public Market, offers scrumptious seafood with menus that depend on the day's catch. (Dishes P80-250. Open M-Sa 8am-2pm, 4pm-10pm.) **Corong Galeri and Coffee Shop ❸,** on Real St. one block from City Hall, features local artists and plenty of sizzling seafood dishes like grilled squid for P80-180. (Open M-F 8am-9pm, Sa-Su 9am-8pm.)

SIGHTS. There are over 10 Japanese wrecks within **diving** depth in Coron Bay and beyond. Among the best are the **Irako,** the **Taiei Maru,** the **Olympia Maru,** and the **Kogyo.** Palawan's strangest dive has to be **Barracuda Lake.** Climb across sharp limestone rocks in full diving gear, then go from cold to hot water before swimming head-on into volcanic mud in an attempt to find mudfish and tube worms. Coron Town's many dive shops have fairly uniform prices (US$25 per dive with equipment and divemaster). PADI courses are also available (US$200-450). **SeaDive** offers the cheapest daytrip package for P1500, including lunch, equipment, divemaster, and two boat dives.

Island-hopping is the best way to enjoy the beauty of Coron Bay. Some of the wrecks can be explored by **snorkeling,** and secluded beaches abound. **Hike** around Coron Island's **lakes,** and you might stumble upon the elusive Tagbanua tribe.

(*Banca* with driver P800-1000.) Coron Town's **Maquinit Hot Springs** can be reached by a 3.5km walk or a 15min. tricycle ride (P150 round-trip). A boat trip up the **Busuanga River** is the most scenic way to get to the northern part of Busuanga Island. Inquire at the KokosNuss Resort (see **Accommodations,** above). **Caluit Island** lies 3-4hr. by boat from the northwest side of Busuanga Island. It is here that ex-President Marcos created his own private safari grounds. The animals flown in from Africa have multiplied since the 70s, and the park is now open to the public. Visitor's permit P300, children P100; purchase at the Municipal Hall in Coron. Private **boats** can be rented for P5000 and up; inquire at **Coron Tours** or **Swagman Travel.** For P5700, the KokosNuss Resort offers a 2-day trip on their live-aboard boat that includes meals and stops for snorkeling. (Open daily 5am-7pm.)

SINGAPORE

HIGHLIGHTS OF SINGAPORE

INHALE the spices and incense of Singapore's Little India district (p. 641), home to good eats, cheap souvenirs, and local mystics.

GO NOCTURNAL at the Singapore Zoological Gardens (p. 647), where a Night Safari leads the way through recreated rainforests and a trove of exotic animals.

SHOP like there's no tomorrow in the **Sim Lim Square Electronics Market** (p. 644), where six floors of inexpensive electronics await the gadget-geek in you. When finished, head outside to view the **Fountain of Wealth** (p. 645), the world's largest fountain.

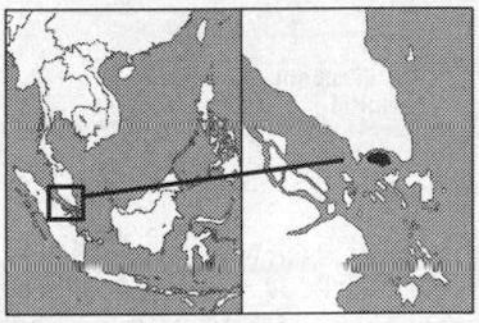

After trekking through Southeast Asia's more rugged regions, Singapore may come as a surprise to travelers. High-tech skyscrapers, clean streets, and potable tap water distinguish the "Lion City" from its neighbors. Though stringent laws and formidable wealth lend an imposing reputation, the city's streets sway to a decidedly convivial beat. Busy sidewalks serve as the dynamic meeting place of four ethnicities. Locals chatter on about the daily news, and debate the controversy surrounding the city-state's human rights violations. Known for its harsh gum-chewing penalties, Singapore has relaxed its laws slightly as of late—though many residents argue that there is little palpable change. Even so, the pleasures of Geylang Rd. and treks up Bukit Timah are worth toning down one's behavior.

LIFE AND TIMES

DEMOGRAPHICS

Singapore's ethnic makeup is 76.6% **Chinese,** 14% **Malay,** 7.9% **Indian** (the majority of whom are **Tamil,** originally imported by the British as laborers) and 1.4% other minorities. Singapore has welcomed immigrants since the 1300s, and with so many foreign-born residents, it's understandable why some express concern about the lack of Singaporean national unity. Recognizing this, the government strives to promote a vision of a unified, multicultural Singapore, free of Western influence.

LANGUAGE

Though **Malay** is the official language, virtually everyone in Singapore speaks at least one dialect of **Chinese**—Min Nan, Cantonese, Mandarin, and Hakka being the most common. Slightly over 10% of the population speaks Malay as a first language. The dialect spoken in Singapore is similar to that which is spoken in western peninsular Malaysia. Roughly 2% of Singaporeans speak **Tamil** as a first language. A legacy of British rule, **English** is also fairly common. Approximately 5% of the population speaks English as a first language, and English is the language of business and government. Its newer version in Singapore is **Singlish,** a mix of English and Chinese phrases or words. Often Singlish sounds much the same as English, but with an "a-lah" added to the end of each sentence.

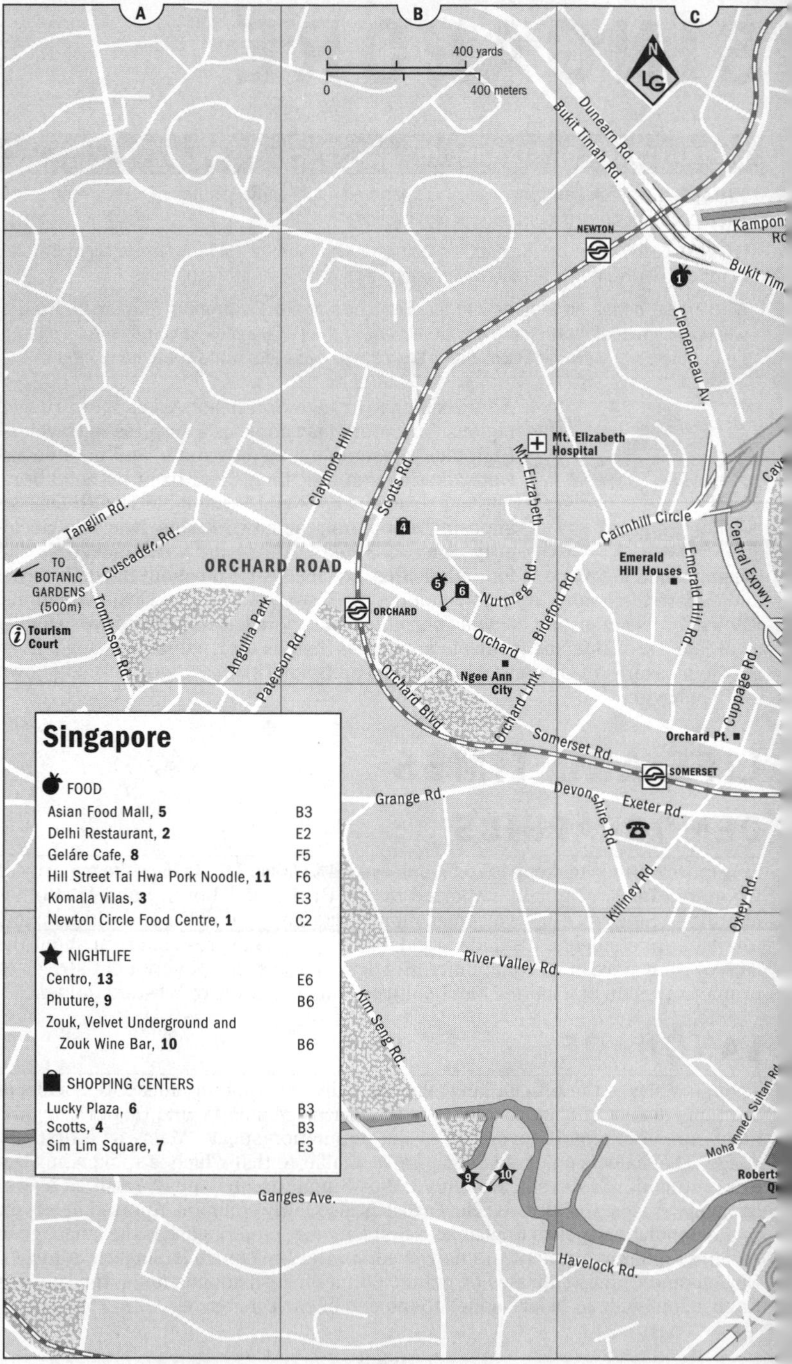
A
B
C
0
400 yards
0
400 meters
N
LG
Dunearn Rd.
Bukit Timah Rd.
NEWTON
Clemenceau Av.
Mt. Elizabeth Hospital
Mt. Elizabeth
Scotts Rd.
Claymore Hill
Tanglin Rd.
Cuscaden Rd.
ORCHARD ROAD
TO BOTANIC GARDENS (500m)
Tomlinson Rd.
Tourism Court
Angullia Park
Paterson Rd.
ORCHARD
Nutmeg Rd.
Orchard Rd.
Bideford Rd.
Cairnhill Circle
Emerald Hill Houses
Emerald Hill Rd.
Central Expwy.
Ngee Ann City
Orchard Link
Orchard Blvd.
Somerset Rd.
Orchard Pt.
Cuppage Rd.
SOMERSET
Grange Rd.
Devonshire Rd.
Exeter Rd.
Killiney Rd.
Oxley Rd.
River Valley Rd.
Kim Seng Rd.
Ganges Ave.
Havelock Rd.
Singapore
FOOD
Asian Food Mall, 5 B3
Delhi Restaurant, 2 E2
Geláre Cafe, 8 F5
Hill Street Tai Hwa Pork Noodle, 11 F6
Komala Vilas, 3 E3
Newton Circle Food Centre, 1 C2
NIGHTLIFE
Centro, 13 E6
Phuture, 9 B6
Zouk, Velvet Underground and Zouk Wine Bar, 10 B6
SHOPPING CENTERS
Lucky Plaza, 6 B3
Scotts, 4 B3
Sim Lim Square, 7 E3

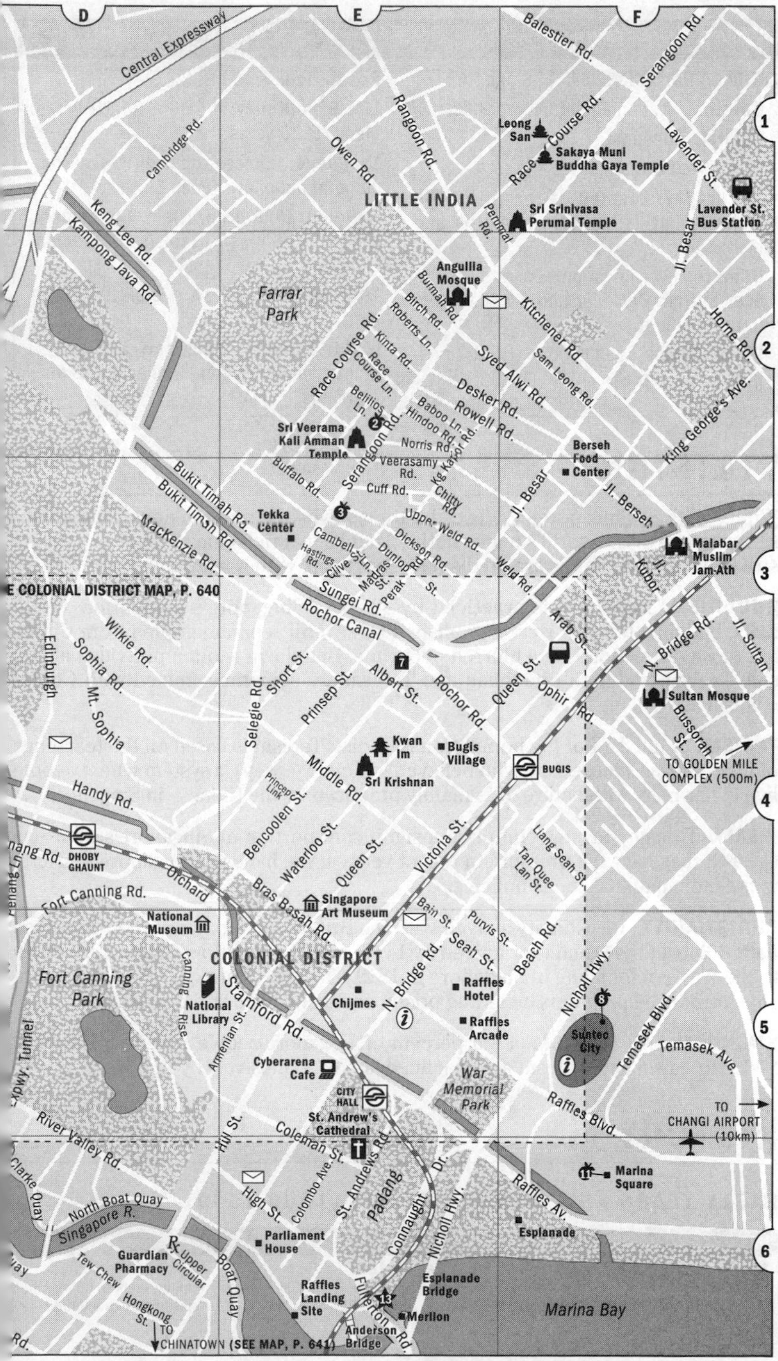
Central Expressway
Balestier Rd.
Serangoon Rd.
Cambridge Rd.
Owen Rd.
Rangoon Rd.
Leong San
Race Course Rd.
Sakaya Muni Buddha Gaya Temple
Lavender St.
LITTLE INDIA
Sri Srinivasa Perumal Temple
Perumal Rd.
Lavender St. Bus Station
Keng Lee Rd.
Kampong Java Rd.
Jl. Besar
Angullia Mosque
Farrar Park
Burmah Rd.
Birch Rd.
Roberts Ln.
Kitchener Rd.
Horne Rd.
Race Course Rd.
Kinta Rd.
Race Course Ln.
Syed Alwi Rd.
Sam Leong Rd.
Desker Rd.
Rowell Rd.
King George's Ave.
Belilios Ln.
Baboo Ln.
Hindoo Rd.
Kg Kapor Rd.
Sri Veerama Kali Amman Temple
Serangoon Rd.
Norris Rd.
Berseh Food Center
Veerasamy Rd.
Buffalo Rd.
Cuff Rd.
Chitty Rd.
Jl. Besar
Jl. Berseh
Bukit Timah Rd.
Bukit Timah Rd.
Tekka Center
Upper Weld Rd.
MacKenzie Rd.
Campbell Ln.
Dunlop St.
Dickson Rd.
Hastings Rd.
Clive St.
Madras St.
Perak Rd.
Weld Rd.
Malabar Muslim Jam-Ath
Jl. Kubor
COLONIAL DISTRICT MAP, P. 640
Sungei Rd.
Rochor Canal
Arab St.
Wilkie Rd.
Edinburgh
Sophia Rd.
N. Bridge Rd.
Jl. Sultan
Short St.
Albert St.
Rochor Rd.
Queen St.
Ophir Rd.
Selegie Rd.
Prinsep St.
Sultan Mosque
Mt. Sophia
Kwan Im
Bugis Village
Bussorah St.
TO GOLDEN MILE COMPLEX (500m)
Middle Rd.
BUGIS
Sri Krishnan
Princep Link
Handy Rd.
Bencoolen St.
Victoria St.
Waterloo St.
Liang Seah St.
Tan Quee Lan St.
DHOBY GHAUNT
Queen St.
Orchard
Bras Basah Rd.
Fort Canning Rd.
Singapore Art Museum
Bain St.
Purvis St.
National Museum
Seah St.
Beach Rd.
COLONIAL DISTRICT
Canning Rise
Nicholl Hwy.
Fort Canning Park
Stamford Rd.
N. Bridge Rd.
Raffles Hotel
National Library
Chijmes
Armenian St.
Raffles Arcade
Suntec City
Temasek Blvd.
Temasek Ave.
Cyberarena Cafe
War Memorial Park
CITY HALL
Raffles Blvd.
TO CHANGI AIRPORT (10km)
St. Andrew's Cathedral
Hill St.
Coleman St.
River Valley Rd.
Colombo Ave.
St. Andrews Rd.
Connaught Dr.
Raffles Av.
Marina Square
Clarke Quay
North Boat Quay
Singapore R.
High St.
Padang
Nicholl Hwy.
Esplanade
Parliament House
Guardian Pharmacy
Upper Circular
Tew Chew
Boat Quay
Raffles Landing Site
Esplanade Bridge
Fullerton Rd.
Merlion
Marina Bay
Hongkong St.
Anderson Bridge
TO CHINATOWN (SEE MAP, P. 641)
Expwy. Tunnel

FACTS AND FIGURES

Official Name: Republic of Singapore.

Government: Parliamentary Republic.

Capital: Singapore.

Land Area: 692.7km^2.

Geography: Located at the tip of the Malay Peninsula between Indonesia and Malaysia.

Climate: Two monsoon seasons: Northeastern from Dec.-Mar and Southwestern from June-Sept.

Phone Codes: Country code: 65. International dialing prefix: 001.

Population: 4,353,893.

Life Expectancy: Women: 84.29 years. Men: 78.96 years.

Language: Chinese (official), Malay (official and national), Tamil, English.

Religion: Buddhism, Islam, Christianity, Hinduism, Sikhism, Taoism, Confucianism.

Literacy Rate: 93.2% overall; 96.7% of men, 89.7% of women.

Major Exports: Machinery and equipment, consumer goods, chemicals, mineral fuels.

RELIGION

While 14.8% of Singaporeans describe themselves as "non-religious," most subscribe to one of the world's major faiths. Thanks to a rich immigrant legacy, many strikingly different faiths are on display, coexisting with remarkable ease.

BUDDHISM. Buddhism is practiced by 42.5% of Singapore's population. Originally, buddhist temples were established by several separate groups from China, but those distinctions have blurred over time. Buddhism is often practiced alongside Taoism, and both Buddhism and Taoism are sometimes mixed with Confucianism as well.

TAOISM. A full 8.5% of the population is Taoist. Taoism is based on the teachings of Lao Tsu—a Chinese sage who believed in *Tao* (the way), a system where people live in harmony with nature. It is mainly practiced by the Chinese in Singapore.

ISLAM. Though Muslims comprise a significant portion of Singapore's denizens (14.9%), they have felt pressure in recent years at the hands of Singapore's strictly non-denominational social policies.

CHRISTIANITY. Christianity arrived with the British and Sir Stamford Raffles (see **Raffles Hotel,** p. 644) and is practiced by 14.6% of the population. Catholicism dates to the Western founding of Singapore in 1819. The Protestant church in Singapore also introduced programs including prison counseling and anti-drug campaigns.

HINDUISM AND SIKHISM. Four percent of Singapore people are either Hindu or Sikh. Hinduism and Sikhism are practiced almost exclusively by Indians.

HISTORY

EARLY YEARS AND ISLAND COLONY (1300-1940)

IMPORTANT DATES

14th Century Tumasek established.	**1819** Sir Stamford Raffles docks in Singapore's harbor.	**1867** Singapore becomes British colony.	**1915** Singapore rules opium market, stifles Chinese secret societies.

The island state of Singapore, or **Tumasek** (sea town) as it was once known, was established in the 14th century. One legend says it was founded by a strapping Shrivijayan prince, who claimed relation to Alexander the Great. Another legend says that the island was named by an Indian prince, who saw a lion on the horizon and, in turn, named it **Singhapura** (Lion City). In the 15th and 16th centuries, Portugese raids and territory-hungry Southeast Asian empires took their toll: the small island-city sank into obscurity for two centuries. It remained little more than a pirate's pit stop, free of Europeans until **Sir Stamford Raffles** of the **British East India Company** docked in Singapore's harbor in January 1819. Raffles transformed Singapore into a thriving port city, and in 1867, it became a British colony. Piracy, trade, exploitation, and prosperity all swept through the area during the 19th century as waves of immigration created a cultural melting pot. British expatriates strolled about the *kampung*, Chinese traders grew rich off Malayan exports, and indentured Indian convicts built St. Andrew's Cathedral. By 1915, the government began to address opium abuse, fund public works, and improve social services.

JAPANESE INVASION AND INDEPENDENCE (1941-1965)

IMPORTANT DATES		
1941 Japanese invade on Chinese New Year.	**1959** New constitution written.	**1965** Independence for Singapore.

Despite its large British naval base, Singapore quickly surrendered to an unexpected **Japanese invasion** on the Chinese New Year in 1941. The ensuing years were ugly, as the Japanese proceeded to terrorize the colony—carting Europeans off to Changi Prison, and raping and slaughtering local Chinese. After the war, a battered Singapore fell into political disarray, welcoming back British governance (though its residents began yearning for independence). Strikes and demonstrations crescendoed in the 1950s, and for three years, **Lee Kuan Yew** negotiated for Singapore's independence; a new constitution was written in 1959. After Lee and the leftist **People's Action Party (PAP)** won the 1959 elections, Singapore became more stable and modernized. It dissolved British ties and pursued an alliance with the strongly nationalist **Federation of Malaysia.** This partnership, however, ended when Singapore assumed its present independent status in August 1965.

SINCE INDEPENDENCE (1965-2001)

IMPORTANT DATES			
1990 Lee Kuan Yew steps down, succeeded by Goh Chok Tong.	**1996** Singapore achieves developed nation status.	**1971** PAP opposition parties boycott elections in protest.	**2001** PAP wins its ninth consecutive term.

When Lee Kuan Yew became a de facto dictator, he masterminded Singapore's transformation into a city-state and economic powerhouse, complete with social-welfare trimmings. However, in doing so he was willing to sacrifice democracy and free speech. Yew maintained that while these freedoms were important, they meant little to individuals with nothing to eat and nowhere to live. Lee stepped down in 1990 to be succeeded by **Goh Chok Tong,** whose administration readmitted political exiles. Lee remains active in the Cabinet, however, and his popularity has waned little since his resignation. Many eye his son, Deputy Prime Minister **Lee Hsien Loong,** as the next heir to the dynasty. Since it boycotted elections in 1971, PAP has dominated politics, despite some growth in opposition parties. In one of the first major victories for Prime Minister Goh Chok Tong, PAP won the parliamentary elections of January 1997. In November of 2001, PAP swept its ninth term, winning 82 of 84 possible legislative seats. Scattered opposition was only able to muster candidates for 29 seats. Singapore is, in effect, a one-party state.

SEMI-AUTOCRATIC WEAPONS

While Singapore has recently relaxed its gum-chewing laws, the nation's yen for order is still striking. The government continues to sponsor "harmony-imposing" initiatives—Orwellian commands that aim to advance conservative ideals. These plans include:

Freedom from smut: The Undesirable Publications Act forbids hundreds of Western magazines, books, and websites with "controversial" sexual, political, and religious content.

Freedom from smog: High car prices, taxes, and a fantastic public transport system dissuade drivers. In 1998, Electronic Road Pricing (ERP) introduced a tax requiring debit cards on every windshield. Those driving without a card receive a fine by mail.

Freedom to schmooze: The state-sponsored Social Development Unit serves as a family planning service. Singapore has many matchmaking services, all of which offer singles' mixers. Recent events have included a High Tea, Swinging Love (i.e., golfing), and dance workshops.

Freedom from stench: There are no public toilets. Unfortunately, this leaves many bladder-heavy people stranded. Strangely enough, elevators have become the latrine of choice. Many elevators in Singapore now contain automated urine-sniffers that trap incontinent occupants until law enforcement agents arrive.

SINGAPORE TODAY

Unlike other Asian bureaucracies, efficiency is at the heart of Singaporean government. Its administration is able to quickly establish and fund programs to improve education, cultural pursuits, and economic growth—as well as fill potholes and keep the city clean. While 2000 saw a steep downturn in many Asian economies, Singapore has largely floated above fiscal crisis, with its robust economy, low inflation, and strong commercial banks. In addition, throughout 2001 and 2002 George Yeo, the minister of trade and industry, worked to establish a free-trade agreement with the US. Because of their meteoric success, Singaporeans are justifiably proud of their country and refute criticisms from Western governments. Still, not everything is perfect; today analysts are watching the city-state's increasing foreign debt with growing concern and advising financial leaders to curb foreign imports. The economy continues to grow at a healthy rate, but no longer outpaces the rest of Asia by such leaps and bounds.

Singapore has been less affected by the US-led **War on Terror** than its neighbors Malaysia and Indonesia. In January 2002, however, Singaporeans and Americans alike were surprised by the arrest of **al Qaeda** operatives, at least eight of whom were trained in Afghanistan. Earlier that month, 15 people intending to bomb military targets and other official buildings, including the US Embassy, were also arrested in Singapore. In August 2002, Singapore, along with eight other ASEAN countries, entered an agreement with the US to "prevent, disrupt, and combat" global terrorism by sharing information and intelligence. (For more information on regional terrorist activities see **The Philippines Today,** p. 533.). Tightly controlling the Singaporean image, Prime Minister Goh Chok Tong publicly declared his own war on terror in 2004—drawing a link between poverty in Singaporean Malay populations and terrorist support. Predictably, some Muslims bristled at his strongly worded remarks, which highlighted a claim of higher rates of drug abuse, divorce, and violent crime in the Muslim population.

Today, efforts to give Singapore a more relaxed image have met with mixed results. Gum chewing is no longer forbidden by law, and penalties for other minor offenses have been softened. Babies remain a pressing concern, as Singapore's birth rate inches further and further below population replacement levels, and the government steps up its campaign to encourage procreation.

CUSTOMS AND ETIQUETTE

HUMAN RIGHTS. Singapore's harsh stance on drugs and crime has been internationally publicized, coming under fire from human rights groups like Amnesty International. In May 1994, 18-year-old American **Michael Fay** was flogged for spray-painting cars and throwing eggs, putting Singapore in the international spotlight. Ever since, the Singaporean government has set about to loosen up Singapore's international image, relaxing some of the more absurd social codes—but residents claim that little has changed. The government indirectly controls the press by encouraging self-censorship among journalists. Though not technically censored, newspapers critical of the government are rarely allowed into the country. In 1997, the Singaporean government began censoring the Internet, denying access to "unsuitable" websites with references to sex, politics, or religion. Political freedom is limited by the virtual one-party system imposed by PAP. One obstacle facing potential opposition parties is the restriction on freedom of assembly and association. Jehovah's Witnesses and the Unification Church have both been banned. There are small but pervasive reminders of the government's tight clamp, including laws restricting those under 21 from watching movies with homosexual content, and government posters gently encouraging procreation. Yet, despite the restrictions, everyday life remains at least superficially liberal, with many residents simply choosing to ignore or skirt some of the government's limitations.

SINGAPORE COOKING. There is an vast array of flavors to satisfy any epicurean fancy. Below is a sampling of some of the most popular dishes.

Hainanese Chicken Rice: If Singapore had a national dish, this would be it! Chicken, roasted or boiled, served with steamed vegetables and fragrant rice. Usually, the dish is paired with a zesty chilli and lime sauce.

Kaya Toast: Toast served with a thick egg and coconut jam, accompanied with soft-boiled eggs in a teacup saucer and a fragrant cup of *kopi-o* (local coffee).

Rojak: A salad of fruit and vegetables mixed in dark prawn paste and nuts, includes dough fritters, bean curd, sprouts, turnip, pineapple, and mango.

Yong Tau Foo: Noodle soup with your choice of bean curd, eggplant, okra, spinach, fish paste, and mushrooms. Pick the ingredients you want and hand them to the hawker, who will prepare the noodles for you.

Sambal Stingray: Succulent stingray served with spicy *sambal* chillies and lime.

ARTS

Like Singapore's other art forms, traditional **pen and ink drawing** has been influenced by older Chinese styles. Local cultural shows present traditional art, such as **Malay shadow plays, kite-flying,** and **Chinese lion dances. Chinese opera** combines high (melo)drama with elaborate costumes. Singapore's **architecture** integrates Western, Indian, Arabic, and Chinese styles. The Emerald Hill area, off Orchard Rd., has beautiful shophouses. Colonial architecture is predominantly found in "black and white" style houses, like Adam Park, off Adams Rd. near the Bukit Timah crossing.

HOLIDAYS AND FESTIVALS (2005)

DATE	NAME	DESCRIPTION
Jan. 1	New Year's Day	National holiday.
Feb. 9	Chinese New Year	A 15-day festival with celebrations and feastings.
Jan. 21	Hari Raya Haji	Festival of sacrifice, usually four days long.
Feb. 22	Islamic New Year	Muslim.
2nd M in Mar.	Commonwealth Day	Annual celebration of the Commonwealth association and its members to promote global awareness.
May 1	Labor Day	National holiday.
May 15	Vesak Day	Commemorates the birth and enlightenment of Buddha.
Aug. 9	National Day	A line-up of celebratory events including fireworks, carnivals, and concerts to commemorate Singapore's birthday.
Dec. 25	Christmas Day	Christian–lights flood the city and many gifts are exchanged.

ADDITIONAL RESOURCES

LITERATURE

Fistful of Colours, by Su-Chen Christine Lim (1993). Celebrates the destinies of three women shaped by the uniqueness of Singapore's multi-ethnic society.

From Third World to First: The Singapore Story: 1965-2000, by Kuan Yew Lee (2000). Lee traces Singapore's ride from independence to the present day.

ON THE WEB

Singapore Tourism Board North America (www.tourismsingapore.com). Abounds with helpful links, and even has an advice center for planning trips.

ESSENTIALS

SINGAPORE PRICE ICONS					
SYMBOL:	❶	❷	❸	❹	❺
ACCOMM.	Under US$10 Under S$17	US$10-20 S$17-34	US$20-30 S$34-52	US$30-40 S$52-68	Over US$40 Over S$68
FOOD	Under US$3 Under S$5	US$3-7 S$5-11	US$7-13 S$11-22	US$13-20 S$22-34	Over US$20 Over S$34

EMBASSIES AND CONSULATES

SINGAPORE CONSULAR SERVICES ABROAD

Check out www.embassyworld.com for easy access to many embassy websites and to download forms. Embassies and consulates within Southeast Asia are listed in the **Practical Information** sections of individual cities.

Australia: High Commission, 17 Forster Cres., Yarralumla, ACT 2600 Canberra (☎02 6273 3944; sydney@iesingapore.gov.sg).

Canada: Consulate, 1305-999 W Hastings St., Vancouver, BC V6C 2W2 (☎604-669-5115; www.mfa.gov.sg/vancouver/).

New Zealand: High Commission, P.O. Box 13-140, 17 Kabul St., Khandallah, Johnsonsville, Wellington (☎64 4 470 0850; www.mfa.gov.sg/wellington/).

UK: High Commission, 9 Wilton Cres., Belgravia, London SW1X 8SP (☎020 7235 8315; www.mfa.gov.sg/london/).

US: Embassy, 3501 International Pl. NW, Washington, DC 20008 (☎202-537-3100; www.mfa.gov.sg/washington). **Consulates, New York:** 231 E 51st St., New York, NY 10022 (☎212-223-3331; ny_singcons@hotmail.com); **San Francisco:** 595 Market St., Ste. 2450, San Francisco, CA 94105 (☎415-543-0475; www.mfa.gov.sg/sanfrancisco/); **Miami:** 2061 South Bayshore Dr., Ste. 1775, Cicinut Grove, Florida 33133 (☎305-858-4225; fax 305-858-2334).

CONSULAR SERVICES IN SINGAPORE

For embassies and consulates of other countries in Singapore, please see **Practical Information: Embassies,** p. 638.

TOURIST SERVICES

Australia: 47 York St., Level 11, AWA Building, Sydney NSW 2000 (☎02 9290 2888; http://au.visitsingapore.com).

Canada: 2 Bloor St. W, Ste. 404, Toronto, ON M4W 3E2 (☎416-363-8898; AskMich@tourismsingapore.com). Also serves New Zealand.

UK: Carrington House, 1st fl., 126-130 Regent St., London W1B 5JX (toll-free ☎080 8065 6565 or 020 7437 0033; http://uk.visitsingapore.com).

US: New York: 590 5th Ave., 12th fl., New York, NY 10036 (☎212-302-4861; http://us.visitsingapore.com); **Los Angeles:** 4929 Wilshire Blvd., Ste. 510, Los Angeles, CA 90010 (☎323-677-0808; fax 323-677-4081; AskRoc@tourismsingapore.com).

DOCUMENTS AND FORMALITIES

All travelers to Singapore must obtain a **Social Visit Pass,** issued upon arrival and valid for six months (S$20). Citizens of Canada, Ireland, New Zealand, the UK, and the US must have a passport valid for at least six months after date of entry, and can stay for up to 30 days. The immigration office may provide **visa extensions** for up to 90 days. For stays over three months, travelers must apply for a **Long Term Social Visit Pass** and be backed by a Singaporean organization. **Work permits** are difficult to obtain unless you already have a job.

MONEY

CURRENCY AND EXCHANGE

The currency chart below is based on August 2004 exchange rates between local currency and Australian dollars (AUS$), Canadian dollars (CDN$), European Union euros (EUR€), New Zealand dollars (NZ$), British pounds (UK£), and US dollars (US$). Check the currency converter on websites like www.xe.com or www.bloomberg.com or a large newspaper for the latest exchange rates.

The **Singapore dollar (S$)** comes in denominations of S$2, 5, 10, 20, 50, 100, 500, 1000, and 10,000, and coins come in 1, 5, 10, 20, and 50 cents and S$1. **Credit cards** are widely accepted, and **ATMs** are abundant. Service charges are included, so **tipping** is uncommon. Clubs, bars, and classier restaurants and hotels label themselves either "plus," indicating a 10% service charge, or "plus plus," indicating a

CURRENCY (S$)		
	AUS$1 = S$0.96	S$1 = AUS$1.04
	CDN$1 = S$1.12	S$1 = CDN$0.89
	EURO€1 = S$1.72	S$1 = EURO€0.58
	NZ$1 = S$0.82	S$1 = NZ$1.22
	UK£1 = S$2.73	S$1 = UK£0.37
	US$1 = S$1.75	S$1 = US$0.57

14% tax. The 5% Goods and Services Tax (GST) can be partially refunded by shopping at stores with "Tax Refund" signs. Ask for a Global Refund Cheque and present it at airport customs before departure. Unless you see a "fixed price" sign, feel free to **bargain** (it is becoming less common) in outdoor markets, at most shops in Chinatown and Little India, and on trishaw rides. Little India is the best place to exchange money. For information on **currency exchange,** see p. 639.

HEALTH AND SAFETY

HEALTH RISKS. Malaria in not a risk in Singapore, but be careful of mosquito bites just the same—Dengue fever is a possibility. Emergency medical attention isn't difficult to find, and access to modern medical facilities is readily available.

GLBT. Homosexuality is illegal in Singapore and Singaporean media and government have been known to treat homosexuals harshly. Numerous clubs and hangouts, as well as a booming online community nonetheless make up a thriving gay scene (see **Adam and Steve, Darling!,** p. 650). For a complete listing of gay venues in Singapore and helpful tips, check out the **Utopia Asia Singapore** website (www.utopia-asia.com/tipssing.htm).

KEEPING IN TOUCH

Singapore's postal service is probably the most reliable in Southeast Asia. Many *Poste Restante* packages actually make it to the post office. It takes about 7-10 days to send for international mail. High-tech communications equipment make phone connections clear and consistent. The **international operator** number is ☎104; **directory assistance** is ☎100. For **Home Country Direct (HCD)** numbers from Singapore, refer to the table on the inside back cover. There are more cell phones in Singapore than there are people; getting a cell phone compatible with the Singapore wireless network (or getting a SIM card for your existing compatible phone) can be done at any of the electronics or phone stores that dot the streets.

THE CITY ☎65

INTERCITY TRANSPORTATION

BY PLANE. Changi Airport (☎800 542 4422, flight info 6542 4422), is 25min. east of the city center. A S$15 **airport tax** is usually included in your ticket price. To get downtown, take **bus** #36 (6am-midnight, S$1.50) to the **Raffles City** and **Orchard Road** areas, or take the **MRT** directly from the terminal (30min. one-way, last train departs airport 11:18pm, S$1.40). **Taxis** run S$15-20, plus a S$3

(S$5 on weekends) airport charge and a 50% surcharge from midnight to 6am. CityCab's **Maxicab**, an A/C, wheelchair-accessible, six-seat coach, takes you near any budget accommodation. (☎6542 8297; every 15min. in peak hours, every 30min. in off-peak hours; 6am-11pm from airport to city, S$7; 8:20am-10:30pm from city to airport S$8 in advance; consult shuttle desk at arrival halls of terminals 1 and 2.)

DESTINATION	FREQUENCY	PRICE	DESTINATION	FREQUENCY	PRICE
Bangkok	5-6 per day	S$664	**Jakarta**	7 per day	S$360
Brunei	1 per day	S$431	**Kuala Lumpur**	12-14 per day	S$182
Calcutta	3 per week	S$1249	**Manila**	3 per day	S$925
Cebu	1 per day	S$1044	**Mumbai (Bombay)**	1 per week	S$1516
Hà Ńỹĩ	1-2 per week	S$749	**Phuket**	2 per day	S$455
Hong Kong	6-7 per day	S$680	**Yangon**	1 per day	S$858

Singapore International Airlines (SIA) is in airport terminal 2, DBS tower, 290 Orchard Rd., and SIA building, 77 Robinson Rd. #01-01. (24hr. ticketing ☎6223 8888; www.singaporeair.com.) **Silk Air,** 8 Shenton Way #08-01 Temasek Tower, is a subsidiary of SIA. (Reservations ☎6223 8888; www.silkair.net. Ticketing open M-F 8:30am 5:30pm.) Air service also provided by: **Bangkok Airways,** airport terminal 1, #041-04F (☎6545 8481; www.bkkair.co.th); **Cathay Pacific Airways,** 10 Collyer Quay, #16-01 Ocean Building (☎6533 1333; www.cathaypacific.com); **Garuda Indonesia,** 101 Thomson Rd., #13-03 (☎6250 2888; www.indodirect.com/garunda); **Malaysia Airlines,** 190 Clemenceau Ave., #02-09/11 (reservations ☎6336 6777; www.malaysiaairlines.com.my; open M-F 9am-6pm); **Myanmar Airways,** Singapore Station, 50 HPL House, Cuscaden Rd., #07-00 (☎6235 5005); **Philippine Airlines (PAL),** 35 Selegie Rd., #10-02 Parklane Shopping Mall (☎6336 1611; www.pal.com.ph); **Royal Brunei Airlines,** 25 Scotts Rd., #04-08 Scottswalk (☎6235 4672); **Thai Airways,** 100 Cecil St. (Reservations ☎6224 9977, ticketing 6224 2024; www.thaiair.com); **Vietnam Airlines,** 260 Orchard Rd. #08-08 (☎6339 3552; www.vietnamair.com.vn).

BY TRAIN. The **railway station,** 30 Keppel Rd., near Cantonment Link, is on the southern tip of the main island, 20-30min. from downtown by bus. (24hr. automated schedules and fares ☎6222 5165. Open daily 6am-11pm.) Buses run every 5-15min. between the station and the **Raffles Hotel** (#97, 100, 131), **Little India** (#97, 131), **Orchard Road** (#167), and **Chinatown** (#80). Buy tickets 8:30am-7pm. The **KTM** (☎6222 5165) has two train routes: one runs along the west coast up to **Hat Yai** (Haadyai) in Thailand; the other cuts through the middle of Malaysia and **Taman Negara National Park,** and ends in **Tumpat,** the northeastern corner of Peninsular Malaysia. The Hat Yai (via Butterworth) line leaves from Kuala Lumpur—buy the ticket from there, (46R, if purchased in Singapore S$46). **Express trains** with A/C go to **Kuala Lumpur** (6½hr.; daily 8:30am, 3:25pm, Sa-Su also 10:30am; S$34) via **Tampin** (5hr., S$27). An overnight train runs daily to **Kuala Lumpur** (8½hr.; 10pm; seats S$19-30, bunks S$37.50-40). To go to **Taman Negara National Park,** take the Gua Musang train to **Jerantut** (8hr., 9:45am), or to **Tumpat** (13½hr.; 8:20pm; seats S$32-41, bunks S$48.50-51) via **Jerantut** (7½hr.; seats S$19-28, bunks S$35.50-38).

BY BUS. In addition to the stations below, buses also leave from the **Golden Mile Complex** on Beach Rd., near Lavender St. Bus Station.

SINGAPORE

Lavender St. Bus Station: On the corner of Lavender St. and Kallang Bahru north of Little India. Take the bus from **Bugis MRT** (#145) or **Raffle Hotel** (#82) and get off at Eminent Plaza. **Hasry Express** (☎6294 9306; open M-Sa 8am-7pm, Su 7:45am-2:30pm) goes to: **Ipoh** (8hr.; 9:30am, 10pm; S$33; board at Jl. Sultan); **Kuala Lumpur** (6hr., 12 per day, S$12; board at Jl. Sultan); **Melaka (Malacca)** (2½hr.; 8:30, 10:30am, 2:30, 4:30pm; S$11); **Batu Pahat** (3½hr.; 8am, 2pm; S$7.80); **Penang** (11hr.; 9:30, 10pm; S$38; board at Beach Road).

Transnasional Express (☎6294 7034; open daily 8am-8pm) to: **Mersing** (4hr.; 9, 10am, 10pm; S$11.10); **Kota Bahru** (12hr., 7:30pm, S$35.10); **Kuala Lumpur** (5-6hr.; 8, 9, 11am, 4:30, 6, 10pm; S$25-30); **Kuala Terengganu** (10hr.; 9am, 8, 9pm; S$26-33); **Kuantan** (7hr.; 9, 10am, 10pm; S$16.50). **Malacca Singapore Express** (☎6293 5915) runs coaches to **Melaka** (4½hr.; 8, 9, 10, 11am, 2, 3, 4, 5pm; S$11).

Johor Bahru Bus Depot: At Queen and Arab St., a 15-20min. walk from **Bugis MRT. Singapore-Johor Express** (☎6292 8151) to **Johor Bahru** (1hr.; every 10min. 6:30am-midnight; S$2.40, purchase an extra ticket for large luggage). **Kuala Lumpur-Singapore Express** (☎6292 8254) to **Kuala Lumpur** (6hr.; 9am, 1, 5, 10pm; S$23).

Copthorne Orchid Hotel: 214 Dunearn Rd. (☎6256 5755). To **Kuala Lumpur** (5½hr., every hr. 7:30am-9:30pm, S$37) and **Melaka** (3hr.; 9am, 3:30, 9:30pm; S$12).

BY BOAT

Changi Ferry Terminal: In the northeast, accessible by taxi. **Cruise Ferries** (☎6546 8518) sends boats to the gateway to the Peninsula's east coast, **Tanjong Belungkor** (30min.; M-Th 10am, 5, 8pm, F-Su 7:15, 10am, 5, 8pm; S$22 round-trip including seaport tax, children S$14). Check-in 1hr. in advance, closes 30min. before departure. Return from Tanjong Belungkor at 8:15am, 3:30, 6:45pm.

World Trade Center Ferry Terminal: At the southern tip of the island, accessible by bus from **Raffles Hotel** (#97, 131), **North Bridge Road** (#61, 145), **Orchard Road** (#143), or **HarborFront MRT** on the **NorthEast Line** in front of St. Andrew's Cathedral (#95). **Penguin Fast Ferry** (☎6271 4866) goes to **Tanjung Balai** (1hr.; 5 per day 7:50, 9:50am, 12:45, 3, 6:25pm; S$26, round-trip S$37); **Batam Center** (1hr., first boat at 7:25am and every 40min. thereafter, S$24). **Dino Shipping** (☎6270 2228) sends ferries to **Batam Center** (70min.; every hr. 7:35am-9:15pm; round-trip S$24) and **Sekupang** (1hr., every hr. 7:30am-8:45pm, round-trip S$27). **Widi Express** (☎6272 7540) has the most boats to **Batam Center** (45min., every 2hr. 8:40am-9:45pm, round-trip S$20).

ATTENTION ISLAND-HOPPERS. If you're off to Pulau Penyenget, take a ferry to Tanjung Pinang, the main city, and not to Bintan Resort. Transport from Bintan Resort to Tanjung Pinang involves a taxi and a 2hr. local bus ride.

Tanah Merah Ferry Terminal: On the southeast corner of the island. Take MRT to Tanah Merah station and bus #35 to the last stop. Gates close 10min. before departure. **IndoFalcon** (☎6270 6778) sends ferries to **Sebana** (45min.; 8:55, 11:55am, 6pm; round-trip S$25.20) and **Tanjung Pinang** (1½hr.; 10:20am, 2:20, 6:55pm; S$30).

ORIENTATION

The city center divides into four areas. **Orchard Road** stretches from west to east of the city center, where it forks into **Bras Basah Road** and a parallel street to the south, **Stamford Road.** These two streets are home to the **Raffles Hotel** and **Chijmes** in the heart of the **Colonial District.** When Selegie Rd., which protrudes from the eastern end of Orchard Rd., becomes Serangoon Rd. to the north, you've reached **Little India.** South of the Singapore River, below Upper Cross and Cross St., **Chinatown's** many shops and restaurants extend as far as Cantonment Rd. The **airport** is on the eastern fringe of the city. The **railway station** is south of Chinatown.

COLONIAL DISTRICT. The extensively renovated Raffles Hotel captures the grandiose splendor of colonial Singapore, as do all the neighborhood museums. Many visitors stop for a drink by the fountain at Chijmes, the convent-turned-shopping gallery. Backpackers flock to accommodations on North Bridge Rd., near Rochor Rd., in the Colonial District, which is gradually expanding northward. *(Take the MRT to City Hall to get to the center of the Colonial District.)*

BENCOOLEN STREET. Once a backpacker haven with a concentration of budget guesthouses, Bencoolen is rumored to be slated for development into a high-wattage strip of shops and hotels. Already most of the backpacker hostels have been vacated, and the few remaining tend to be operated without proper license. For now, it remains a land of discount stores, vacant lots, and unremarkable coffee houses. *(To reach Bencoolen St. from the airport, take the Maxicab, or take bus #36 to the YMCA on Orchard Rd.)*

ORCHARD ROAD. Shopaholics are free to roam about the street's numerous shopping centers and underground food courts. While designer boutiques are normally empty, shopping centers are usually packed with cosmopolitan consumers staying at the five-star hotels nearby. On weeknights and weekends, the energy on Orchard Rd. reaches its peak as people come here for late-night movies and seasonal outdoor events. Bars and pubs may be hard to find, since they are either underground or at the top of shopping centers. *(Take the MRT to Orchard.)*

CHINATOWN. Chinatown stands as a testament to Singapore's pride in its newfound national heritage—Chinese-colonial shophouses have been gutted, refurbished, and repainted in lively pastels. The MRT extension has skyrocketed property values; old coffee shops have yielded to new offices and boutiques. These streets are home to temples, Chinese medicine shops, and massage therapy centers. While refurbished Chinatown is touristy, the old market and side streets preserve much of old Chinatown's charm. *(From the airport, take public bus #36 to the Stamford and North Bridge Rd. intersection, then catch #81 to Sri Mariamman Temple.)*

LITTLE INDIA. Indian immigrants used to raise cattle on land north of the Rochor Canal, using the cattle's energy to power machines for wheat grinding, sesame oil production, and pineapple preservation. As more first generation Indian immigrants flocked to Singapore to be construction workers in the late 20th century, Little India grew into a thriving trade center and an Indian cultural haven. Scrubbed and purified in Singaporean fashion, Little India provides a fair compromise for budget travelers—accommodations are reasonable, worthwhile sights are within easy reach, and cheap food is everywhere. Desker St. and Petain St. to the north host two of the three red light districts in Singapore, the last being in Geylang. *(From the railway station, take public bus #97 or 131 to Little India.)*

LOCAL TRANSPORTATION

Buses: SBS Transit runs local bus routes (☎800 287 2727; www.sbstransit.com.sg). **Trans-Island Bus Services (TIBS)** runs longer distance buses and Night Rider buses (☎800 482 5433; www.tibs.com.sg). **Local buses** run 6am-midnight. Striped orange and white roofed stops have signs listing buses by street, frequency, and destination.

Night Rider buses usually run 11:30pm-4:30am; bus stops have yellow NR signs and the time of the last bus. NR buses charge a flat fare (S$3); regular bus fares are S$0.55-1.50 depending upon distance and payment type (cash or Farecard). Ask the driver for the fare to your destination and pay the exact fare, or insert your **Farecard** (see MRT, below). **TransitLink Guide** (S$1.50), with comprehensive information on the 100+ bus routes, is sold at any bookstore.

Mass Rapid Transit (MRT): (☎800 336 8900; www.smrtcorp.com.sg). 3 main A/C lines going east-west, north-south, and southwest-northeast (the Northeast Line, also known as NEL) run 6am-midnight. First train leaves around 5:30 or 6am; last train leaves at 11:30pm. Single-trip tickets start at S$0.80 and can cost up to S$1.80 depending on distance. Stored value **Farecards** save 5-10¢ per ride (S$10 plus S$2 deposit, returned when card is returned; unused portion is refunded) and are sold at MRT stations and 7-Eleven stores. Most MRT counters (open M-F 8am-9pm, Sa 8am-6pm) also sell TransitLink Guides (S$1.50) and provide free MRT maps.

Taxis and Trishaws: With an efficient bus and train system, there is little reason to use taxis. Taxis are semi-government-owned, so fares are standardized but surprisingly low. 7 major taxi companies: **CityCab** (☎6552 2222); **Comfort** (☎6552 1111); **TIBS** (☎6555 8888); **Premier Taxi** (☎6363 6888); **Smart Automobile** (☎6485 7777); **Sovereign** (☎6552 2828); **Trans-Cab** (☎6281 1047). Meter starts at S$2.10-2.40, depending on the cab company. Each additional 240m is S$0.10; most city fares cost S$3-7; 50% surcharge midnight-6am. Other surcharges for booking during peak hours, and within the city's restricted zones. Expensive **trishaws,** at Bras Basah Park on Orchard Rd. and outside of Bugis St. food market, are unnecessary for most travelers. Agree on the fare beforehand.

SINGAPORE

PRACTICAL INFORMATION

TOURIST AND FINANCIAL SERVICES

Tourist Offices: Singapore Visitors Center at Suntec City, 3 Temasek Blvd. #01-35/37/39/41 Suntec City Mall (☎800 332 5066). Open M-Sa 8am-6:30pm, Su 9am-6:30pm. **Singapore Visitors Center at Orchard,** Junction of Cairnhill and Orchard Rd. (☎800 736 2000). Open daily 8am-9:30pm. **Singapore Visitors Center at Plaza Singapura,** 1/F Plaza Singapura, 68 Orchard Rd. (☎6332 9298). Open daily 10am-10pm. **Singapore Visitors Center at Liang Court,** 177 River Valley Rd., Level 1, Liang Court Shopping Center (☎6336 2888). Open daily 10:30am-9:30pm.

Tour and Travel Agencies: Airpower Travel, 131A Bencoolen St. (☎6334 6571). Most competitive prices for regional flights. **STA Travel,** 33A Cuppage Rd. (☎6737 7188). Student and youth-rate tickets, ISIC cards, and train packages to Thailand and Malaysia. Open M-F 9am-6pm, Sa 9am-5pm. MC/V (3% surcharge). For international bus tickets, try **Five Star Tours,** 5001 Beach Rd. #01-27 Golden Mile Complex (☎6294 7011; www.fivestarsonline.com). Many other travel agencies are located at the **Golden Mile Complex.** Go in person to check routes and rates and to purchase tickets.

Embassies: Australia, 25 Napier Rd. (☎6836 4100). Open M-F 9am-12:30pm and 1:30-4:45pm. **Brunei Darussalam,** 325 Tanglin Rd. (☎6733 9055). Open M-Th 8:30am-4:30pm, F 8:30am-noon and 2:30-4:30pm. **Canada,** 80 Anson Rd., 14th-15th fl., IBM Towers (☎6325 3200). Open M-F 8am-noon and 2-4pm. **Indonesia,** 7 Chatsworth Rd. (☎6737 7422). Open M-F 9am-4pm. **Ireland,** 298 Tiong Bahru Rd., #08-06 Tiong Bahru Plaza (☎6276 8935). Open M-F 9:30am-12:30pm and 2:30-4pm. **Malaysia,** 301 Jervois Rd. (☎6235 0111). Open M-F 8am-5:15pm. **Myanmar,** 15 St. Martin's Dr. (☎6735 6576). Open M-F 9am-12:30pm and 2-5pm. **New Zealand,** 391A Orchard Rd., Ngee Ann City Tower A, 15th fl. (☎6235 9966). Open M-F 8:30am-5pm.

Philippines, 20 Nassim Rd. (☎6737 3977). Open M-F 9am-5pm. **Thailand,** 370 Orchard Rd. (☎6737 2158). Open M-F 9:30am-12:30pm and 2-5pm. Visas M-F 9:15am-noon. **UK,** 100 Tanglin Rd. (☎6424 4200). Open M-F 8:30am-5pm. Visas M-F 8:45am-noon. **US,** 27 Napier Rd. (☎6476 9100). Open M-F 8:30am-5:15pm. Visas M-F 9-11am. **Vietnam,** 10 Leedon Park (☎6462 5938). Open M-Sa 9am-noon.

Currency Exchange: Moneychangers are often the best deal; you can find this service at most shopping centers. The one at the airport is open 24hr. Most open daily 9am-9pm. Try **Saj Drug Store Money Change,** #01-09 Raffles City Shopping Center (☎6339 1723). Open M-Sa 8:30am-9pm, Su 10:30am-9pm. **Banks** mostly open M-F 9:30am-3pm, Sa 9:30am-12:30pm. **Citibank,** 268 Orchard Rd., #01-00 Yen Sen Bldg. (☎800 225 5221), opposite Mandarin Hotel.

American Express: Member Services, 300 Beach Rd., #18-01 Concourse Bldg. (24hr. ☎800 732 2244). Mail held 1 month for card or traveler's check holders. Replaces cards and cashes personal checks for members. Open M-F 9am-5pm, Sa 9am-12:30pm.

SINGAPORE

LOCAL SERVICES

Luggage Storage: Train Station (☎6222 5165). S$3 per piece per day. Open daily 7am-9pm. **Changi Airport** (☎6546 2738), in the basement and in both terminals; S$3.09-4.12 for 1st day, additional S$4.12-5.15 for subsequent days. Includes S$500 insurance. Follow the signs. Open 24hr.

Bookstores: MPH, 63 Robinson Rd. (☎6222 6423). Office supplies, English-language best-sellers, maps, magazines, and newspapers. Open M-F 10am-7pm, Sa 10am-3pm.

EMERGENCY AND COMMUNICATIONS

Emergency: Police ☎999. **Ambulance** ☎995. **Fire** ☎995. Toll-free from pay phones.

Pharmacies: Guardian Raffles City Pharmacy, 252 North Bridge Rd., Raffles City Shopping Center basement, #11 (☎6339 2137). MRT: City Hall. Knowledgeable staff. Call ahead for prescriptions. Open daily 10:30am-9:30pm. **Essentials Pharmacy** has branches throughout the city, usually in shopping malls.

Medical Services: Raffles Medical Group Clinic (☎6543 1118), in the basement of Changi Airport, passenger terminal 2. Doctors available 8am-midnight. S$30, after midnight S$180. Open 24hr. for consultations. **Singapore General Hospital** (☎6222 3322). MRT: Outram Park. Emergency clinic open 24hr. All major hospitals have 24hr. on-call doctors.

Directory Phone Info: ☎100.

Internet Access: Cybernet Cafe, in Changi Airport, passenger terminal 2. Open daily 8am-10pm. **Cyberarena Cafe,** 11 Stamford Rd. (☎6333 5739). Before 3pm, S$3 per hr.; after 3pm, S$5 per hr.

Post Office: GPO, 10 Eunos Rd. 8, Level 1 West Entrance, 408600 (☎6741 8857). MRT: Paya Lebar. *Poste Restante.* Open M-F 8am-9pm, Sa 8am-6pm, Su 10am-4pm. Dial ☎1605 for post office nearest you.

ACCOMMODATIONS

Tiny Singapore has enough hotel beds to house its 7 million annual visitors—no small feat, considering Singapore's resident population is under 3.5 million. Accommodations may not be as budget-friendly as those in the rest of Southeast Asia, but aside from those on ritzy Orchard Rd., most hotels are an excellent value. Many establishments add taxes, which are around 4%.

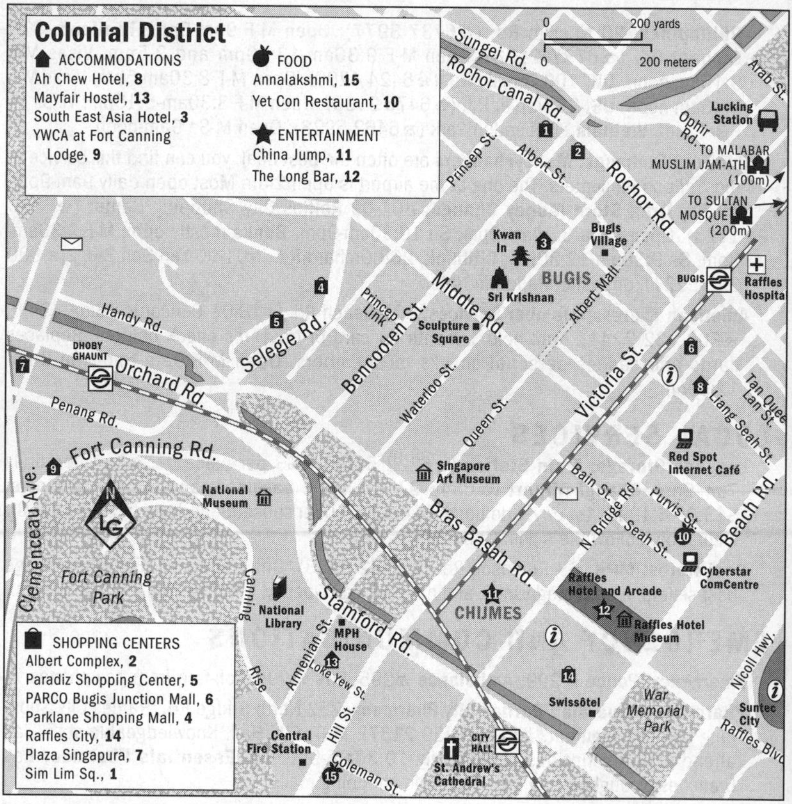

COLONIAL DISTRICT

New 7th Storey Hotel, 229 Rochor Rd. (☎6337 0251; www.nsshotel.com). MRT: Bugis (5min. walk). Views of the city from lawn-chaired patios. Rooms have A/C and TV. Very clean 4-bed dorms with lockers. Laundry. Reservations recommended. Dorms S$17; doubles S$52-79. Extra bed S$15. Reduced rates for extended stays. ❷

YWCA at the Fort Canning Lodge, 6 Fort Canning Rd. (☎6338 4222; reservations@ywcafclodge.org.sg). MRT: Dhoby Ghaut. Immaculate, new with great views. Pool, tennis, Internet, and karaoke bar. Rooms have A/C, TV, minifridge, phone, and bath. Breakfast included. Free lockers. Laundry. Reservations recommended. Women-only dorms S$45 (groups preferred); singles S$85+; doubles S$95+ ; family suites S$220. S$3.09 surcharge on 1st night for YMCA membership. ❸

South East Asia Hotel, 190 Waterloo St. (☎6338 2394; www.seahotel.com.sg). MRT: Bugis. Next to Sri Krishnan and Goddess of Mercy Temples. A family business for 48 years. Skip the overpriced coffee house attached to the hotel lobby; cheaper options abound nearby. Amenities include A/C, TV, hot-water boiler, and private bath. Reservations by email preferred. Doubles S$70-77; triples S$82-88; family rooms S$118. ❺

Ah Chew Hotel, 496 North Bridge Rd. (☎6837 0356), above Tong Seng coffeeshop among a sea of shopping centers. MRT: Bugis. For those who just want a place to sleep. Bare-bones cubby-sized dorms with bunk beds. Common pantry area for dining and relaxing. Laundry starts at S$5. Dorms S$10, with A/C S$20; singles and doubles S$26-30. ❶

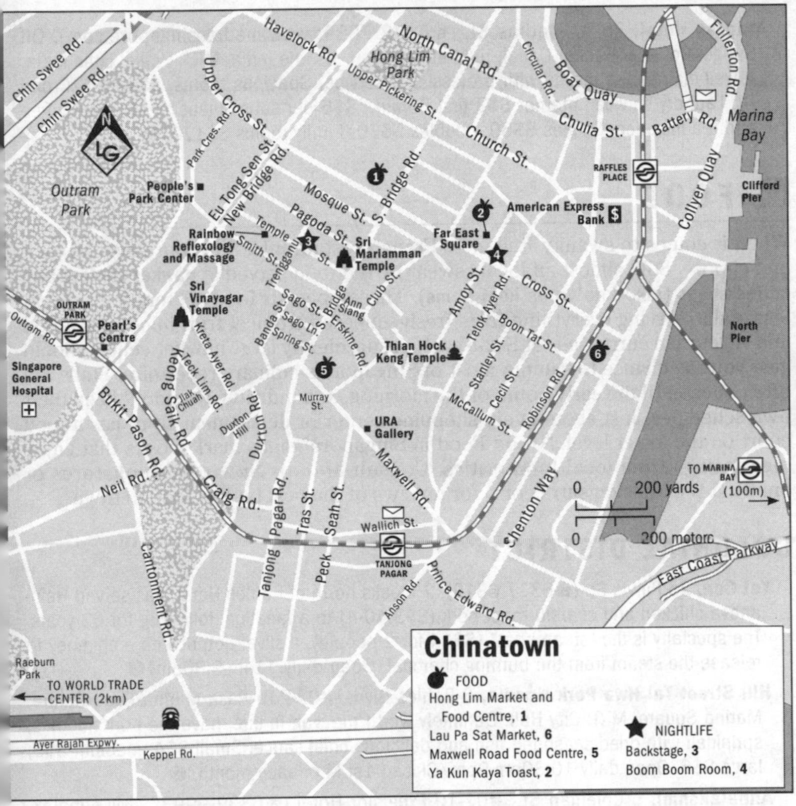

CHINATOWN

A Travellers Rest-Stop, 5 Teck Lim Rd. (☎6225 4812). On a triangular block about a 10min. walk from Outram Park MRT, this new hotel is popular among backpackers. Bright sun-lit rooms and a friendly atmosphere make this one of Singapore's more worthy hotels. All rooms (except dorms) include A/C, minifridge, TV, phone, and private shower and toilet. Laundry service (priced per item). Dorms S$18; doubles S$49-52. ❹

LITTLE INDIA

The InnCrowd Backpackers' Hostel, 73 Dunlop St. (☎6296 9169; reservations@theinncrowd.com). MRT: Bugis. The InnCrowd boasts a vibrant atmosphere and is full of young backpackers and travelers. Large rooms, with an open-air shower on the rooftop balcony and a patio overlooking the Singapore skyline. All rooms have A/C. 15min. free Internet per day. Breakfast included. Linen provided. Dorm S$18; doubles S$48. ❹

Little India Guest House, 3 Veerasamy Rd. (☎6294 2866), off Serangoon Rd. MRT: Little India. Rooms have TV and phones; slatted windows let in the bustling noise from the streets below. Spotless common baths. Locker service. 24hr. reception and check-in. Singles S$35, with A/C S$40; doubles S$40/50; family rooms that can sleep 5-6 people S$60/70. Bargain during the low season. ❹

Madras Hotel, 28-32 Madras St. (☎6392 7889; www.madrassingapore.com). Off Sungei Rd. near Rochor Canal, right in the heart of Little India. MRT: Bugis, Little India. A well-maintained facility with professional service. Spacious rooms, all with A/C and TV. Laundry service. Internet S$3 first 30min., S$5 per subsequent hr. Morning coffee and tea included. Singles S$60; doubles S$70; family rooms S$120. ❺

FOOD

When it comes to swanky Italian or French restaurants, Singaporeans can pick and choose. Still, almost all locals swear by the food served at **hawker centers** and **coffee shops** (also known as **kopi tiams**). These open-air food centers hold countless stalls, serving everything from fresh-squeezed tropical fruit juice to seafood and vegetarian curry—all for S$2-5 each. A sufficiently large hawker center should give you the chance to sample most of Singapore's culinary repertoire. Stalls are often open until the early hours of the morning, and individual vendors keep their own schedules. Just about every shopping center or department store has a food court on the lower level. "Good Food in Singapore" signs mark kiosks that enjoy high ratings from local food critics. Consult *Makan Sutra* (at bookstores or online at www.makansutra.com) for reviews of the best budget food in town.

SINGAPORE

COLONIAL DISTRICT

Yet Con, 25 Purvis St. (☎6337 6819), 2 blocks north of Raffles Hotel, has served Hainanese chicken and *charsiu* roast pork (S$3.40-4) to a fanatical following for 62 years. The specialty is the "steamboat" (S$14 for 2 people), a silver hotpot with a chimney to release the steam from the burning charcoal. Open daily 11am-9:30pm. ❷

Hill Street Tai Hwa Pork Noodle, 6 Raffles Blvd., #02-249 Rasa Marina Food Centre, Marina Square. MRT: City Hall. Definitely worth the wait in line; have the pork noodles, sprinkled with dried seasoned fish and delicious chilli sauce. Small S$4; medium S$5; large S$6. Open daily 10:30am-9pm. Closed 1st M of each month. ❷

Annalakshmi, 5 Coleman St., #02-10 Excelsior Hotel (☎6339 9993; www.annalakshmi.com.sg). No set prices; "Eat what you like, pay as you wish." Proceeds support the Temple of Fine Arts. Variety of *dosias* and *Sampoorna,* 7-course set meal. Reservations recommended. Open M-Sa 11:30am-3pm and 6-10pm. ❷

Geláre Cafe, 3 Temasek Blvd., Suntec City Mall #02-084 (☎6336 5615), has the best ice cream-topped waffles (though not much in the way of traditional Singaporean fare). One scoop S$6-8. Open daily 9:30am-10pm. ❷

ORCHARD ROAD

Newton Circle Food Centre, next to Newton MRT stop, Newton Food Circus exit. Post-clubbing open-air eats. Big helpings of fried rice or frog legs for S$3-5. *Satay,* barbecued meat on skewers, (S$5-10). Beer S$3.50; sodas S$2. Open 24hr. ❶

Asian Food Mall, 304 Orchard Rd., Lucky Plaza #B1-31-38/135-143/148. MRT: Orchard. A decent alternative to fancy joints and Western food chains on Orchard Rd. Local delicacies like beef noodles (S$4), claypot chicken rice (S$4), and *mee goreng* (S$4) grace the manifold menu. For dessert, don't miss the *burbur chacha*–a cold, sweet coconut soup with tapioca and yams. ❶

Scotts Picnic Food Court, 6 Scotts Rd., Scotts Shopping Center. MRT: Orchard. A more authentic food court. In addition the typical Singaporean noodle and rice dishes (S$3-4.50), Scott's has a terrific dim sum restaurant and sushi bar. ❶

CHINATOWN

Maxwell Road Food Centre, at the intersection of Maxwell and South Bridge Rd. MRT: Tanjong Pagar. Singapore's most recently refurbished hawker center. Try the River Valley *char kway teow* (S$2-3) at Stall 3, the *tian tian* Hainanese chicken rice (S$3-4) at Stall 10, and the *zhen zhen* porridge (S$2-3) at Stall 54. Try also the *orh-luak* (S$3-5) and local doughnut *hum jin pang* with red bean paste inside, powdered sugar outside (S$1 for 7 pieces). Open daily 6am-11pm; some stalls open 24hr. ❶

Lau Pa Sat Market, the oldest hawker center in the city, is a 24hr. carnival at Cross St. and Shenton Way. MRT: Raffles Place (5min. walk south). Crabmeat *popiah* S$2.50; cheapest bubble tea in town S$0.95. ❶

Hong Lim Market and Food Centre, on Upper Cross St. near South Bridge Rd., is right near the Speaker's Corner at Hong Lim complex. MRT: Raffles Place. A local lunch favorite. Rice dumplings (S$2-4). Open daily 9:30am-7pm. ❶

Ya Kun Kaya Toast, #01-01 Tanjong Pagar (☎6323 2528). MRT: Tanjong Pagar. Traditional Singaporean breakfast: heavily buttered *kaya* toast (S$1.40). Also order the soft-boiled eggs (S$1) and a cup of *kopi* (S$0.80) or *kopi-o* (black coffee). Open M-F 7:30am-6:45pm, Sa 7:30am-6pm, Su 8:30am-3pm. ❶

LITTLE INDIA

Komala Vilas, 76-78 Serangoon Rd., around the corner from Upper Dickson Rd. Head down the street at 12-14 Buffalo Rd. Vegetarian Indian food. Try the *Masala dosai*—a huge pancake with potato stuffing, served with curry and yogurt (S$1.80). Also try *teh terik*—local tea that is cooled by pouring it back and forth between 2 tin mugs (S$0.80). The bakery next door sells Indian sweets (S$0.80). ❶

Delhi Restaurant, 195 Serangoon Rd. (☎6297 1148), in Little India's center, has North Indian (Mugalai and Kashmiri) cuisine. Intimate setting. Favorites: chicken *tikka Masala* (S$9.90), *Gobi Manchurian,* a cauliflower dish (S$6.50). Open daily 7am-midnight. ❷

Banana Leaf Apolo, 54-58 Race Course Rd. (6293 8682). MRT: Little India. Famous for its fish head curry (S$18-25), which is served on a banana leaf with steamed rice, papadams, and vegetables. Wash the spicy meal down with a jug of local Tiger beer (S$18). Many vegetarian options. Open daily 10:30am-10:30pm. ❸

GEYLANG ROAD

GEYLANG ROAD: FISH AND FROLICKING. Famed not only as Singapore's *third* red light district, Geylang Rd. is also the best neighborhood for delicious seafood. Brothels are on even-numbered streets (e.g. Lorong 8, 12), and easy to identify—the building numbers are written inside hearts. Hawker stalls and seafood restaurants are on the main road and odd-numbered streets.

Sin Huat Seafood Restaurant, #659/661 Geylang Rd., off Lorong 35. Everyone visits Geylang for seafood, but celebrities like Michelle Yeoh come to Sin Huat for the best crab *bee hoon* and steamed scallops in black bean sauce—both cooked with plenty of garlic. Expect to spend between S$40-60 per person. Open daily 5pm-1am. ❺

SIGHTS

COLONIAL DISTRICT

SINGAPORE ART MUSEUM. Formerly St. Joseph's New School, the Singapore Art Museum houses an array of multimedia works by regional artists and hosts traveling exhibits by artists from Monet to Rodin. Don't miss *Oh, My Head,* a

SINGAPORE

piece by Singapore's foremost sculptor, Ng Eng Teng. *(71 Bras Basah Rd. ☎6332 3222. MRT: City Hall. Open M-Th and Sa-Su 10am-7pm, F 10am-9pm. Free guided tours Tu-F 11am and 2pm, Sa-Su 11am, 2, 3:30pm. S$3; students, children, and seniors S$1.50. Free admission F 6-9pm, as well as certain public holidays.)*

RAFFLES HOTEL. This pristine white behemoth, built in the late 19th century and designated a National Monument in the 20th century, is one of few remaining testaments to Singapore's colonial past. One of few hotels in the world to make it into its third century, legend has it a tiger once escaped from a circus and wandered into the hotel's billiard room, where a guest shot it dead. Lacking tigers, the shop prices in the **Raffles Arcade** are just as scary. Ambience and peanuts at the **Long Bar** are the only free things. **Raffles Hotel Museum,** on the 3rd fl., traces the hotel's history from its founding in 1887 to 1993. *(The block between North Bridge and Beach Rd. along Bras Basah Rd. ☎6337 1886. MRT: City Hall. Museum open daily 10am-7pm.)*

SINGAPORE

CHIJMES. This area was the home of the Convent of the Holy Infant Jesus, an orphanage run by French nuns. After five years of restoration, this four-acre city jewel is now an esplanade of outdoor shops and cafes, where you can purchase pashmina scarves starting at S$35, crafts from Myanmar starting at S$10, or a glass of sangria for S$10.50 at the Spanish tapas bar. Raffles City Shopping Center, across the park from Chijmes, has designer boutiques. *(30 Victoria St. between Stamford Rd. and Bras Basah Rd. MRT: City Hall.)*

SINGAPORE HISTORY MUSEUM. The museum's 117-year-old building at Stamford Rd. has closed for extensive redevelopment, and temporarily relocated to Riverside Point. The museum contains historical artifacts of Singapore's past, but has recently been used as a venue for urban walking tours, the Singapore International Film Festival, and an exhibition on the Singapore River's history. *(Riverside Point, next to Swissotel Merchant Court. ☎6837 9940. MRT: Clarke Quay, Exit B. Open M 1-7pm, Tu-Th and Sa 9am-7pm, F 9am-9pm. Free tours Tu-F 11am and 2pm, Sa-Su 11am, 2, 3pm. S$2, students S$1. Free admission F 7-9pm.)*

URA GALLERY. Wonder how Singapore grew into the modern city-state of today? Trace its urban development with 48 displays, interactive touch-screens, and a large-scale model of the country about half the size of a basketball court. The gallery emphasizes the "Concept Plan," a vision for the physical development of Singapore in the 21st century. *(45 Maxwell Rd., 2nd floor of the VRA Centre. MRT: Tanjong Pagar. Open M-F 9am-4:30pm, Sa 9am-12:30pm. Free.)*

BUGIS VILLAGE AND FOOD CENTRE. Always bustling with activity, the Bugis area, stretching over Waterloo and Queen St., used to serve as a stage where transvestites and transsexuals paraded openly. After a government crackdown, residents complained of decreased business and the demise of Bugis life, but government efforts to reintroduce Bugis culture failed. Today the atmosphere at the fruit market and adjoining market offers a glimpse of Singapore's street culture. Performances by Chinese singers or Thai dancers may be hidden on adjacent side streets, so go peek. *(Open daily 9am-10pm.)*

OTHER SIGHTS. Enter **Sultan Mosque,** on North Bridge Rd., off Arab St. from Bussorah or Muscat St. Inspired by Indian traditions, it was originally built with a S$3000 grant from Sir Stamford Raffles. The biggest mosque, it's home to Singapore's Muslim community. *(MRT: Bugis. Visiting hours M-Th and Sa-Su 9am-1pm and 2-4pm.)* **Malabar Muslim Jam-Ath,** a smaller mosque, sits to the north. *(471 Victoria St., on the corner of Victoria St. and Jl. Sultan. ☎6294 3862. Open 24hr. F prayer noon-2pm.)*

Near the Bugis area, the section of Waterloo St. between Middle and Rochor Rd. is closed to traffic. Wander among the flower vendors and fortune tellers on the street opposite the **Kwan In** and **Sri Krishnan Temples.** *Puja* (worship) ceremonies occur at 7am, noon, 5:30, and 9pm. Next door, **Kwan In Temple** shines in golden splendor. Take fortune sticks from the monks' desk, kneel in the middle of the floor, and shake the canister until a stick falls out. Tell the monks the number on your stick and they'll give you a sheet of paper with your fortune on it. *(Open daily 6am-6:15pm, 1st and 15th days of lunar month 5am-6:45pm, holidays 4am-6:45pm.)*

In **Sim Lim Square,** six floors of electronics are ready to be sold to the best bargainer. Digital cameras cost about S$300-1500, Playstation 2 S$400, portable CD players S$90-300, and Palm Pilots S$200+. *(1 Rochor Rd. Open daily 11:30am-8:30pm.)* Of all the shopping centers in Singapore, **Suntec City** has the most innovative design. The Suntec City complex is shaped like a human hand, with the International Convention and Exhibition Centre as its thumb, opposed by four office towers for fingers. What's more, it boasts the world's largest fountain, **The Fountain of Wealth,** designed according to the rules of *feng shui*. *(3 Temasek Blvd., off Raffles Blvd. MRT: City Hall. Free laser shows at the fountain daily 8-10pm.)* Take a ride with **Singapore River Cruises** in a traditional bumboat and learn about how the city went from merchant trading on the banks of the Singapore River to becoming the busiest port in the world. *(MRT: City Hall; walk to the Raffles Landing site along the northern bank, behind Parliament House. ☎6336 6111; www.rivercruise.com.sg. Open daily 9am-10:30pm. 30min. ride S$12, children S$5.)*

SINGAPORE

CHINATOWN

The **Chinatown Historic District,** on Telok Ayer St., parallel to Amoy St., used to be home to Chinese and Malay immigrants in the 19th century. It later became the Chinese commercial district and served as a slave-trade hub. The shophouses reflect architectural styles from the Transnational to Art Deco periods (1840-1960). For information on specific buildings, pick up a brochure at the Urban Redevelopment Authority, 45 Maxwell Rd.

THIAN HOCK KENG TEMPLE. Of the three monuments along Telok Ayer St., only the Escher-like "Temple of Heavenly Happiness" merits a true visit. The original **statue of Ma Cho Po,** goddess of the sea, was installed in 1840. A larger statue of her is behind, in the center. In the courtyard are statues (from left to right): Dr. Bao Sun Da Di, a countryside hero, Buddhisatra, Confucius, and Kwan Gong. Sailors donated tile and ironwork and a spate of stone dragons slinking on the roof, pillars, and walls. *(On Telok Ayer St. between Boon Tat and McCallum St. Open daily 6am-5:30pm. Free, donations accepted.)*

SRI MARIAMMAN TEMPLE. Locals say you know you're in Chinatown when you see the *gopuram* (entrance tower) of this colorful temple. It is dedicated to the generous goddess Mariamman who is believed to protect children. Nearby is a pit 4m wide for **Thimithi,** the **Firewalking Festival** during which Hindu stalwarts wrap their feet with faith alone for the October stroll over hot coals. *(242 South Bridge Rd. at the corner of Temple St. MRT: Chinatown. Take Eu Tong Sen St. past Pearl's Center and the People's Park complex; turn left onto Temple St.; walk to the end of the street. ☎6223 4064. Open daily 7am-noon and 6-9pm. Inner part closed noon-6pm. Camera S$3, video camera S$6.)*

OTHER SIGHTS. Evening visitors to the **Sri Vinayagar Hindu Temple,** at the intersection of Kreta Ayer and New Bridge Rd., may witness Hindus praying and cracking coconuts on the ground. This temple is dedicated to Ganesh, the elephant-headed god. Shops nearby, along Trengganu, Smith, and Temple St., sell clothes, fabric, medicine, and countless souvenirs. Bargain away! *(Open daily 5am-noon and 5-9:30pm. Donations of S$0.50 accepted for Afghan refugees.)* **Rainbow Reflexology and Massage,** performs reflexology, Thai, Chinese, Swedish, and injury massage. *(59 Temple St. Open daily 11am-10pm. Massage S$23 for 30min.; reflexology S$20 for 30min.)*

THE CHINESE OF SOUTHEAST ASIA

More Than an Ethnic Minority

Some say that visiting Chinatown in Singapore is redundant in a city-state where ethnic Chinese account for 75% of the population. In other Southeast Asian countries, ethnic Chinese constitute a substantial minority of the population and comprise a considerable majority of entrepreneurs. The largest Chinese populations are in Singapore and Malaysia, where British colonials recruited Chinese workers to their mines and plantations. Their descendants now dominate trade and commerce in much of Southeast Asia. Chinese-scripted shop signs and restaurant names highlight almost every business district, and Chinese employees range from itinerant street hawkers to the CEOs of multi-national conglomerates.

The status of the Chinese varies throughout Southeast Asia. In Malaysia, the government has tried to curb Chinese dominance in business by reserving particular sectors of the economy for the indigenous Malay population. In Indonesia, the government recently lifted the ban on Chinese writing and Chinese schools, initially imposed to sever perceived ties to Communists in China. In Thailand, the large ethnic Chinese population has integrated successfully with the indigenous population, taking Thai names and inter-marrying with Thais. In the Philippines, the Chinese-Filipino *mestizos* are prominent in politics, the economy, and other areas of society. Vietnam's Chinese have fared ill or well, depending on the current status of Vietnam's relationship with China—many of the "boat people" who fled Vietnam were in fact ethnic Chinese. The Chinese populations in Myanmar, Laos, Brunei, and Cambodia are much smaller. In Cambodia, the Khmer Rouge killed any ethnic Chinese unable to flee. The current development of Chinese business in Cambodia and Laos is a very recent phenomenon, supported by old networks and the arrival of new entrepreneurs from China, Taiwan, and elsewhere in Southeast Asia.

Not until the 20th century did the Chinese in China come to recognize their country as a single nation. Emigration from the southeast coastal provinces of Fujian and Guangdong long predated the political formation of a recognizable Chinese nation. As a result, Southeast Asia's ethnic Chinese have defined themselves according to linguistic group, place of origin, common surname, and occupation, rather than according to a common identity as "Chinese." Ask a Singaporean Chinese if she is Chinese, and she will likely reply, "I'm Singaporean However, you will be able to determine the Ch nese linguistic or regional group in which sh claims membership.

There are many languages and dialects th can be labeled as "Chinese." In general, th term refers to Mandarin, which is the form (Chinese taught in Chinese language schoo throughout Southeast Asia. Mandarin was fir introduced into schools in the 1920s as part of pan-Chinese movement. However, with th exception of Singapore, where it is one of fo national languages, Mandarin is rarely spoke by the oldest generation of Chinese in Southea Asia. A working knowledge of Mandarin ca still facilitate travel in the region, as young generations use it to converse across linguist boundaries and to travel in or do business wi China and Taiwan. The Chinese of Southea Asia often mix languages in their conversation using words in Chinese languages, Englis Indonesian, Vietnamese, and Thai, depending o where they live and on their level of education

Other major sources of coalescence amor ethnic Chinese are trades based on linguist groupings, which in turn are based on commc regional origins. The earliest immigrants fro Chaozhou engaged in trades and broug friends and relatives to join them in Southea Asia. Later immigrants preserved the languag and customs of Chaozhou by engaging in th same trades as earlier Chaozhou immigrant These networks resulted in the identification certain linguistic groups with particular trade

Early Chinese immigrants took on ar excelled at the manual work that others eith could not or would not do. And although ma are still laborers, immigration, hard work, and dedication to education have raised the Ch nese to the highest levels in art, literature, ed cation, commerce, and philanthropy countries where their success has not bee hampered by laws restricting their non-politic activities. Many Chinese customs, soci norms, and beliefs that were systematical obliterated in China during the Cultural Revol tion can still be witnessed in Southeast Asi particularly in locales with a high concentr tion of ethnic Chinese, like Singapor Bangkok, and Penang. However, they expre cultural rather than political ties to China; mo of them aligned their fate long ago with that their homeland—Southeast Asia.

Raymond Lum was a Peace Corps Volunteer in Malaysian Borneo. He holds an M.A. and a Ph.D from the Harvard Department of East Asian Languages and Civilizations. He regularly travels Southeast Asia to acquire new publications for the Harvard College Library.

LITTLE INDIA

Shops near Serangoon Rd. emit whiffs of incense, jasmine, and freshly ground spices. Proprietors fuss with displays of jewelry, gold, *saris*, and Hindu gods.

SRI SRINIVASA PERUMAL TEMPLE. An exact replica of a temple in India, Sri Srinivasa Perumal Temple is dedicated to Vishnu. Inside are statues of him and his consorts, Lakshmi and Andel. The temple is the launching pad for the **Thaipusam Festival.** On a decreed religious day in January or February, Hindus honor Lord Subramaniam with a pilgrimage from here to the Chettiar Hindu Temple. They carry a *kavadi* (metal cage) decorated with offerings and hooks, with which worshippers pierce their skin so the *kavadi* can hang from their flesh. Zealots never bleed, a phenomenon attributed to their trance-like state. *(397 Serangoon Rd., past Perumal Rd. ☎ 6298 5771. Open daily 6:30am-noon and 6-9pm.)*

SRI VEERAMA KALI AMMAN TEMPLE. The temple draws devotees of the fearsome goddess Kali, who purportedly grants material desires in exchange for the sacrificial blood of animals. Friday evenings see a steady stream of visitors. *(141 Serangoon Rd., on the corner of Belilios Rd. ☎ 6298 5053. Open daily 6am-noon and 4-9:30pm.)*

OTHER SIGHTS. **Sakaya Muni Buddha Gaya Temple** (Temple of 1000 Lights), boasts a 18m Buddha adorned in yellow and orange robes. In the back chamber is a reclining Buddha. The Thai temple was placed in Little India to recognize the Buddha's Indian background and to encourage Buddhist-Hindu dialogue. *(366 Race Course Rd. Open daily 8am-4:45pm.)* Across the street, the **Leong San Buddhist Temple** (Dragon Mountain Temple) has impressive fountains and a back room full of ancestral tablets of patrons. The main hall, built in 1917, replicates a Chinese palace. Reverend Zhuan Wu established the temple with a statue of Kwan Yin that he brought from Fujian Province. *(371 Race Course Rd. Open daily 6am-6pm.)* The neighborhood around **Desker Street** and **Petain Road** comprises two of Singapore's **red light districts.** On Desker St., turn onto the alleyway next to Sin Hup Kee Eating House at 120 Desker St. From Petain Rd., north of Desker, turn onto Flanders St. In house after house, red fluorescent lights shine on bored women reading or chatting. Transsexuals and transvestites pose and approach men in the streets. **Angullia Mosque,** on Serangoon Rd. near Birch Rd., is a unique specimen of religious architecture that mixes traditional and contemporary styles. Along Syed Alwi Rd. across from Angullia Mosque, **Mustafa Centre** hums with the activity of bargain shoppers, as electronics are particularly inexpensive at this shopping center.

NEAR SINGAPORE

SINGAPORE ZOOLOGICAL GARDENS AND NIGHT SAFARI. This award-winning zoo is renowned for its open-concept policy. Some animals wander at their leisure; others are separated from visitors by moats or trees. The zoo has a collection of four rare **Komodo dragons,** which are publicly fed at 2pm on the second and last Sundays of the month. Visitors come for breakfast or afternoon tea with the **orangutans.** Catch nocturnal creatures at their best on the **Night Safari,** next door to the zoo. Tour recreated rainforests and river valleys from the Himalayas to the Americas, communing with "pig bears," tigers, and rhinos. Well-lit footpaths offer the chance to get up close with the sights and smells. *(80 Mandai Lake Rd. ☎ 6269 3412. Go there in luxury on the Zoo Express (☎ 6481 0166). Buses run from Orchard Rd. (every 30min. 9:30am-11:30pm; S$5, children S$3). Or take the MRT to Ang Mo Kio and transfer to bus #138. Allow at least 1hr. of travel time on public transportation from the city center. Open daily 8:30am-6pm. S$12, ages 3-12 S$5. Breakfast 9am S$16, tea 4pm S$13; no tea on Su. Night Safari open daily 7:30pm-midnight; last entry 11pm. S$15.45, children S$10.30.)*

SENTOSA ISLAND. The Singaporean mother-of-all-tourist-traps includes Dolphin Lagoon, miniature golf, Fort Siloso, three beaches, Images of Singapore, Underwater World, a butterfly park, and an insect museum. Don't be tempted by a guided tour. Avoid Volcano Land like the plague—S$12 gets you an elementary school field trip experience. Most of the sights would thrill only either the very young, or the young at heart. To feel like you're escaping the city (at least for half the day), lounge around the white sand beaches or rent a bike for S$4 an hour. Saturday nights, **Siloso Beach** hops with expatriates and Singaporean yuppies at Bora Bora Beach Club. For island **camping,** reserve several days in advance. *(☎800 SENTOSA; www.sentosa.com.sg. Camping ☎6270 7888. 4-person tents S$14; 8-person tents S$19. To get to Siloso Beach, take Sentosa Bus E from Orchard Rd. or Raffles Hotel, Bus C from Tiong Bahru MRT (S$7, children S$5), or take the cable car (S$13.50, children S$7.90) or ferry (S$8.30, children S$6.30) from the World Trade Center. Prices include S$2 admission to the island.)*

SINGAPORE

JURONG BIRD PARK. This open-concept park contains over 600 bird species, including Antarctic penguins and the cassowary from Papua New Guinea, known for its ability to charge at humans and rip out their hearts with its bare claws. For a cheerful start to your day, have "breakfast with the birds" in the park, on Jl. Ahmad Ibrahim. *(Take the MRT to Boon Lay Station and transfer to bus #194 or 251. ☎6265 0022; www.birdpark.com.sg. Open daily 8am-6pm. S$12, children S$5.)*

SINGAPORE BOTANICAL GARDENS. This botanical haven shelters the world's largest orchid display, with over 700 species and 2100 hybrids. Perfect for an early morning stroll, the gardens have duck ponds, statues and gazebos at every turn. On weekends, the gardens are often used as a concert venue for jazz and symphonic performances. *(Take the MRT to Orchard, then bus #7, 105, or 106. ☎6471 7361. Open daily 5am-midnight. Free, except S$2 for Orchid Garden, which is open daily 8:30am-7pm.)*

JURONG REPTILE PARK. The park is next door to the Bird Park on Jl. Ahmad Ibrahim; you can gape at over 2500 crocodiles and see crocodile wrestling at 11:45am and 2pm. *(☎6261 8866. Open daily 9am-10pm. S$8, children S$7.50.)*

CHINESE AND JAPANESE GARDENS. Built in Jurong Lake on a pair of islands connected by a carved stone footbridge, the gardens are at Jurong Park on Yuan Ching Rd. *(Take the MRT to the Chinese Garden station and follow the signs. ☎6264 3455. Open daily 9am-6m. S$4.50, children S$2.)*

EAST COAST PARKWAY. Popular with local residents for biking, fishing and inline skating on weekends, this park tends to be quieter at other times. A 5 mi. stretch of uninterrupted walkway allows one to skate or bike from one end to the other. The parkway offers good seafood (pepper prawns and chilli crab are recommended) and ocean views. The best eateries are UDMC Seafood Centre (right) and East Coast Lagoon Food Center (left). **East Coast Park** is the most popular beach. *(Take bus #36 (S$1.20) from Bras Basah Rd. to Marine Crescent, Block 34, cross the street toward the main road; or take a taxi from Bedok MRT. Open daily 5-10pm.)*

OTHER SIGHTS. Changi Prison Chapel and Museum is a chilling reminder of World War II and the Allied POWs. The **Changi Murals,** recreated from originals painted by Bombardier Stanley Warren, are worth an extended visit. *(Take the MRT to Tanah Merah, then SBS bus #2 for 15-20min. and get off at the stop after Changi Women's Prison/Drug Rehabilitation Centre. ☎6214 2451. Open M-Sa 9:30am-4:30pm. Free.)* From the Changi Point Ferry Terminal, boats leave for **Pulau Ubin,** a quiet *kelong* fishing and *durian* plantation island that is ideal for hiking or biking. *(Take the MRT to Tanah Merah, then bus #2 to Changi Point, where you take a 10min. bumboat ride from Changi Jetty for S$2. Boats run daily 6am-11pm and leave when full.)* More island getaways lie south of Singapore. **Kusu Island** has a hill sacred to Muslims and Taoists that offers panoramic views. It also has a temple and quiet beaches. **St. John's Island** has serene beaches and walking paths. *(Ferries (M-Sa 10am and 1:30pm, Su 5 per day 9am-5pm) leave from the World Trade Centre to both islands. ☎6270 7888. S$9, children S$6; includes ferry ticket.)* Equip yourself with lots of water and sunscreen, and spend a day exploring Singapore's parks. The **Bukit Timah Nature Reserve** has the only real hike in Singapore. Bukit Timah "hill" rises 164m above sea level and is host to such wildlife as the long-tailed macaque monkey. The reserve is one of the only two rainforests in the world located within a city. The other is in Rio de Janeiro. *(177 Hindhede Dr. From Newton MRT take bus #171. ☎800 468 5736. Open 24hr.)*

NIGHTLIFE

There's no beirut or dancing on bar stools, but Singapore's classy club and bar scene still offers some great places to let your hair down. Check out www.danceandsoul.com for the most up-to-date listings.

COLONIAL DISTRICT

The Long Bar (☎6337 1886, ext. 1230), in the Raffles Arcade, is the birthplace of the Singapore Sling (S$16). Be fanned by palm leaves, engage in pleasant conversation, and drop peanut shells on the floor. Cover bands on the 3rd fl. Happy hour 5-9pm. Open Su-Th 11am-12:30am, F-Sa 11am-2:30am.

Harry's, 28 Boat Quay (☎6538 3029), near Tew Chew St. on Boat Quay. Live jazz and rhythm-and-blues Tu-Th and Sa-Su 9:30pm, F 10pm, with loads of expats and yuppies. Happy hour until 9pm. Beer S$6. The "Bank Breaker" is a popular drink. Bar/restaurant open Su-Th 11am-1am, F-Sa 11am-2am.

China Jump, #B1-07/08 Fountain Court (☎6338 9388), in Chijmes, has 1930s Shanghai-style furniture and bartenders who do fancy tricks. After 10pm, it's a hip night spot with contemporary music and dancing. W night, women get in free and enjoy drinks on the house. Men pay cover, but get free drinks from 11pm-midnight. Men: S$18 cover W and F-Sa. Women: S$15 cover F-Sa. Women 21+, men 25+. Open daily 5pm-3am.

MOHAMED SULTAN ROAD

Club-hopping is the local ritual on Mohamed Sultan Rd., particularly at the Robertson Quay end. Prepare yourself for a sensory experience.

IN RECENT NEWS

SINGAPORE SLINGERS

The Singapore Gun Club, a venerable institution of arms-bearing citizens, was founded in the early 1950s. In addition to offering introductory shooting courses and other full-day events, the club also has an esteemed civic duty: its members are responsible for culling crows, the city's largest urban pests.

Crows, a non-native species, inflict disease, contagion, and droppings on the otherwise sparkling clean city-state. Singapore's National Environment Agency began a crow elimination campaign in the early 1980s, and for the past several years has provided free ammunition to members of the gun club in return for their shooting services.

Members tote their shotguns to parks and shipyards, blowing away anything black and winged. As of August 2004 the club reported a death toll of approximately 2000 crows. This number is low compared to the roughly 15,000 crows killed in 2000 and 2001, but as the reported crow population is still around 100,000 birds, there is room for the numbers to go up.

Once the crow population decreases to about 10,000 (less than a tenth of the crows' heyday numbers) the city plans to stop the hunt, so as not to promote the increase of other refuse-eating pests, like rats and certain types of insects.

Zouk, 17 Jiak Kim St. (☎6738 2988), off Kim Seng Rd. Premier dance club in Singapore, set in an abandoned warehouse by the Singapore River. "We Love House" on F nights and "Mambo Jambo" on W nights always pull in the crowds. **Phuture,** connected to Zouk, is a hipper alternative to the crowded main dance floor, playing drum and bass and lots of hip hop. Cover S$15 before 9pm. Women S$23, men S$28. Open W-Sa 8pm-3am. **Zouk Wine Bar** (☎6738 2988) has an older crowd. Open daily 6pm-3am.

Velvet Underground, next door to Zouk, sports an older yuppie crowd. Stellar house beats and decor. Special events allow clubbers to play DJ for a day—bring your own records or pick from their library. Check out the "Healing Hand" Keith Haring painting, and Warhol-esque reprints of Botticelli's *Venus*. Cover women S$25, men S$35. W women get in free. Open W-Sa 8pm-3am.

Centro, 1 Fullerton Rd. (☎6238 0200). Competes with Zouk, drawing mostly 20-something yuppies and playing a wider variety of music, including house, garage, and Latin beats. Open W-Su 9pm-3am. Includes **Lola,** which plays deeper house music for a mature crowd. Open Su-W 5pm-2am, Th-Sa 5pm-3am.

GAY AND LESBIAN NIGHTLIFE

Backstage, 13A Trengganu St., 2nd fl. (☎6227 1712), on the corner of Trengganu and Temple St. Enter from Temple St. where you see the rainbow sticker. The theme is Broadway: snazzy show posters embrace the walls. An international crowd relaxes while chill music sets the mood. Beer S$9. Cocktails S$9.50. Open daily 7pm-2am.

Boom Boom Room, 130-132 Amoy St., Far East Square (☎6435 0030). Home to celebrated comedian and drag queen Kumar, this flamboyant club is best known for its risqué stand-up comedy routines and cabaret shows. Cover W-Th S$20, F-Sa S$25. Shows F-Sa 10pm and 1am. Open W-Th 8:30pm-1am, F-Sa 8:30pm-3am.

Taboo, 65/67 Neil Rd. MRT: Tanjong Pagar. Contains go-go bar poles and podiums for the trendy young. Drinks S$10-15. Open Su-Th 6pm-midnight, W and F-Sa 6pm-3am.

ADAM AND STEVE, DARLING! A gay rights forum was recently denied its permit, and Janet Jackson's previous album was not released here because of its racy lyrics, but the gay scene is blossoming despite Singapore's government. With limited access to gay and lesbian literature, many Singaporeans still view homosexuality as "unnatural," leaving individuals to find venues on the Internet (like www.sgboy.com, www.fridae.com, and www.maleculture.com). So while a gay pride parade is still a long way off, events and venues are slowly being publicized. Special one-off events like Nation, a large-scale foam party on Sentosa Island during Singapore's National Day, are organized without governmental intervention. Rainbow flags are also displayed prominently at these gay establishments. In addition to the gay- and lesbian-friendly bars listed here, a few clubs offer lesbian nights the first Wednesday of every month.

THAILAND

HIGHLIGHTS OF THAILAND

BEACHES. Idyllic **Ko Samet** (p. 698) and **Ko Chang** (p. 704) off the east coast are cheap and mellow. Down south, **Ko Samui** (p. 824), **Ko Phangan** (p. 829), and **Ko Tao** (p. 834) have a more raucous brand of sun and fun with a broader slate of aquatic activities. **Krabi**'s (p. 812) seaside cliffs offer world-class climbing.

HIKING AND TREKKING. Northern Thailand (p. 758) offers the greatest range of affordable treks. Less-touristed **Mae Hong Son** (p. 772) and **Sangkhlaburi** (p. 721) have activities ranging from elephant excursions to river rafting.

HANGING OUT. Towns along the Mekong, including **Nakhon Phanom** (p. 742), are unparalleled spots to unwind and take in stunning natural settings. Tiny **Pai** (p. 771), nestled in the northern highlands, has much to explore.

CULTURAL HERITAGE. The temples and palaces of **Bangkok** (p. 664), the ancient capitals of **Sukhothai** (p. 780) and **Ayutthaya** (p. 709), and the Khmer ruins of **Phimai** (p. 732) are engrossing and accessible.

NIGHTLIFE. Bangkok (p. 664), **Chiang Mai** (p. 759), **Ko Samui** (p. 824), and **Khon Kaen** (p. 754) keep rocking while the rest of the kingdom sleeps.

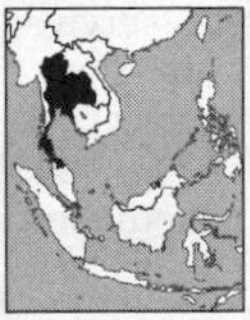

The only country in Southeast Asia never to have been colonized, Thailand has a proud and independent history. This historical influence infuses the spirit of Thai society even today, in spite of the hordes of tourists who tramp through the country's beaches, temples, and jungles. A period of economic depression has made living very cheap for foreigners, even as the Thai economy slowly begins the road to recovery. While 15 years ago, a million people descended on the "Land of Smiles" yearly, today that number has risen to an estimated 10 million, and catering to tourists has become the country's lifeblood. There are sights to suit every taste: beachgoers head to the picturesque islands off the eastern and southern coasts, while more adventurous travelers trek through hill-tribe homelands in the mountainous north. Others explore the ancient cities of central Thailand, where the ruins of once-great kingdoms now lie in silent majesty, a testament to a glorious past. For travelers new to Southeast Asia, there's no better place to start than "Amazing Thailand."

LIFE AND TIMES

DEMOGRAPHICS

Use of the word "Thai" began in the 20th century as a political and geographical designation referring to all citizens of Thailand. "Tai," however, refers to the ethnic Tai-Kadai people, who speak Tai-based languages, live mostly in China, Laos, and Myanmar (where they are known as the Shan), and who account for 75% of the population of Thailand. At about 12% of the population, the **Chinese** are Thailand's largest minority. Homeland starvation and poverty are the leading causes behind the high Chinese immigration rate over the past decades. Hill-tribe groups, including the **Karen, Hmong, Yao, Lahu, Akha,** and **Lisu,** are concentrated in the north, while the country's six million Muslims are concentrated mainly in the south.

FACTS AND FIGURES

Official Name: Kingdom of Thailand.

Government: Constitutional monarchy.

Capital: Bangkok.

Land Area: 513,000 km^2.

Geography: Borders Malaysia, Myanmar, Laos, and Cambodia. Chao Praya River flows through the fertile central plain. Northern Thailand and the Burmese border to the west are mountainous.

Climate: Dry (high season) Nov.-Mar., rainy (low season) Apr.-Oct.

Phone Codes: Country code: 66. International dialing prefix: 001.

Major Cities: Chiang Mai, Khon Kaen, Nakhon Ratchasima, Ubon Ratchathani.

Population: 64,850,000.

Language: Thai.

Religions: Theravada Buddhism (95%); Muslim, Christian, Hindu (5%).

Literacy Rate: 96% overall; 97.5% of men, 94.6% of women.

Major Exports: Textiles, rice, rubber, jewelry, electrical appliances, automobiles, footwear.

LANGUAGE

Like the people themselves, the Thai language has evolved with influences and adaptations from English, Chinese, and Sanskrit (to name only a few), while still retaining the characteristic five tones, monosyllabic words, and ancient alphabet. King Ramkhamhaeng of Sukhothai created the first **Thai alphabet** in 1283 as a combination of Sanskrit syntax and Khmer characters, and this alphabet has survived almost entirely intact to this day. This standardized language has lent the Thais a sense of cultural identity and national unity. **Grammar** is delightfully simple: there are no suffixes, genders, articles, declensions, or plurals in spoken Thai. Like English, it is written from left to right, but it lacks capital letters and punctuation.

RELIGION

THERAVADA BUDDHISM. The religion of more than 90% of the Thai people, Theravada Buddhism informs both their faith and their lifestyle. The Thai outlook is better understood in light of the **Four Noble Truths of Buddhism:** there is suffering; the source of suffering is desire; there is a cessation to suffering; and that cessation is achieved through an adherence to the **Eightfold Path,** which is a path of virtue, mental cultivation, and wisdom. Anti-materialism, forgiveness, and a vigorous spirit that has mastered tranquility are all characteristics of this highly scriptural religion and of the Thais themselves.

ISLAM. Thailand's largest religious minority, Muslims account for approximately 4% of the population. Thailand's Muslim inhabitants are overwhelmingly Sunni, with a Shi'a distribution of only 1 or 2%. They live mostly in southern Thailand, close to the Malaysian border, and many are originally of **Malay** descent. In fact, in the south there are more mosques than *wats*. Although Islamic law necessitates a lifestyle significantly different from that of Theravada Buddhists or nihilist backpackers, Muslims are well assimilated into Thai culture.

CHRISTIANITY. Christianity first appeared in Thailand in the 16th and 17th centuries, brought by missionaries of varying Christian sects. However, Thailand's Christian population remains proportionally the smallest of any Asian nation (at 0.5%), with almost half residing in Chiang Mai and the surrounding area. The reli-

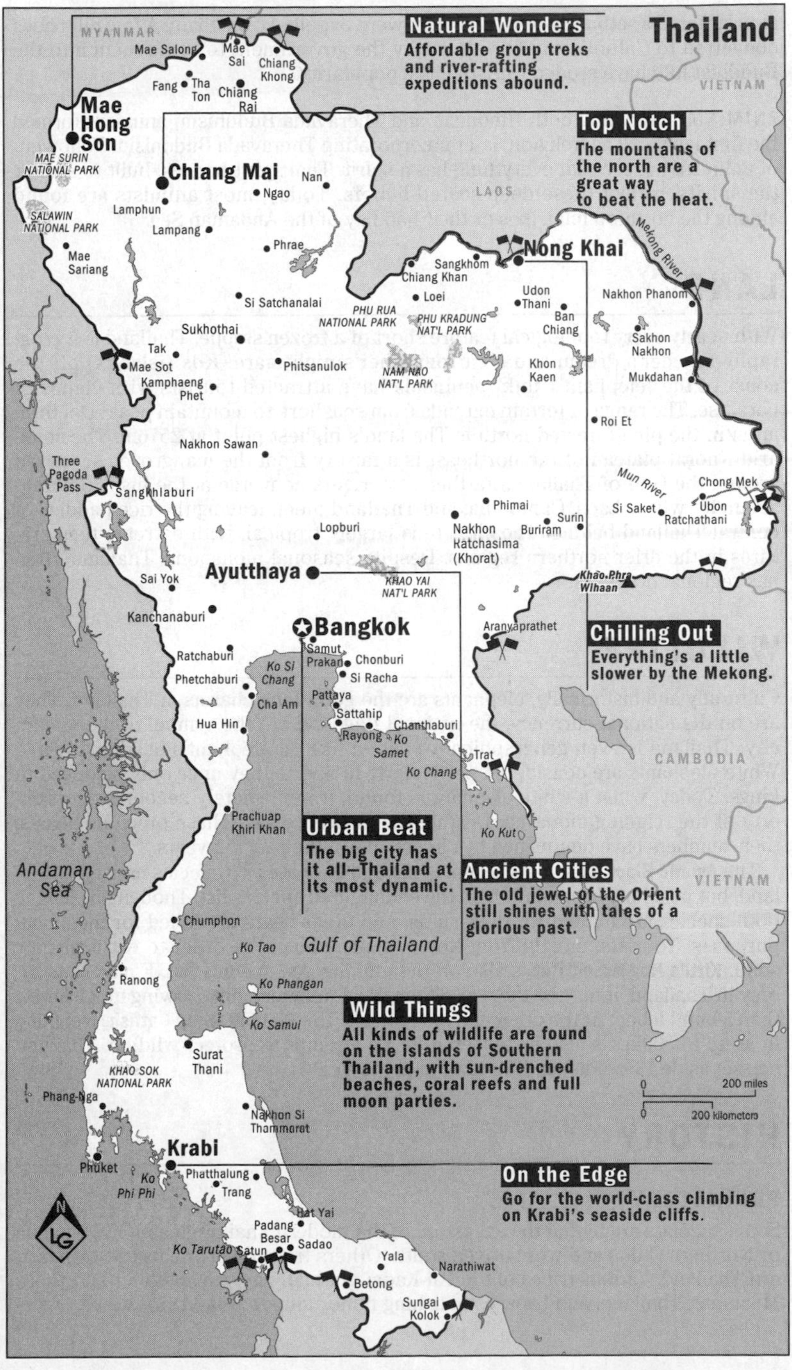
Thailand
Natural Wonders
Affordable group treks and river-rafting expeditions abound.
Top Notch
The mountains of the north are a great way to beat the heat.
Chilling Out
Everything's a little slower by the Mekong.
Urban Beat
The big city has it all—Thailand at its most dynamic.
Ancient Cities
The old jewel of the Orient still shines with tales of a glorious past.
Wild Things
All kinds of wildlife are found on the islands of Southern Thailand, with sun-drenched beaches, coral reefs and full moon parties.
On the Edge
Go for the world-class climbing on Krabi's seaside cliffs.
MYANMAR
LAOS
VIETNAM
CAMBODIA
Mae Salong
Mae Sai
Chiang Khong
Fang
Tha Ton
Chiang Rai
Mae Hong Son
MAE SURIN NATIONAL PARK
Chiang Mai
Nan
Ngao
Lamphun
SALAWIN NATIONAL PARK
Lampang
Phrae
Mae Sariang
Sangkhom
Chiang Khan
Nong Khai
Mekong River
Udon Thani
Nakhon Phanom
Loei
Si Satchanalai
PHU RUA NATIONAL PARK
PHU KRADUNG NAT'L PARK
Ban Chiang
Sukhothai
Sakhon Nakhon
Tak
Mae Sot
Phitsanulok
NAM NAO NAT'L PARK
Khon Kaen
Mukdahan
Kamphaeng Phet
Roi Et
Nakhon Sawan
Three Pagoda Pass
Sangkhlaburi
Mun River
Chong Mek
Phimai
Si Saket
Ubon Ratchathani
Surin
Lopburi
Nakhon Ratchasima (Khorat)
Buriram
Ayutthaya
KHAO YAI NAT'L PARK
Khao Phra Wihaan
Sai Yok
Kanchanaburi
Bangkok
Aranyaprathet
Ratchaburi
Samut Prakan
Chonburi
Ko Si Chang
Si Racha
Phetchaburi
Pattaya
Cha Am
Sattahip
Hua Hin
Rayong
Chanthaburi
Ko Samet
Trat
Ko Chang
Prachuap Khiri Khan
Ko Kut
Andaman Sea
Chumphon
Ko Tao
Gulf of Thailand
Ranong
Ko Phangan
Ko Samui
Surat Thani
KHAO SOK NATIONAL PARK
Phang-Nga
Nakhon Si Thammarat
Krabi
Phuket
Ko Phi Phi
Phatthalung
Trang
Hat Yai
Padang Besar
Ko Tarutao
Satun
Sadao
Yala
Narathiwat
Betong
Sungai Kolok
0
200 miles
200 kilometers
N
LG

gion suffered a setback when foreigners were expelled from Siam. A few hill-tribes converted to Catholicism, but efforts by the government to bring them into the Buddhist fold have eroded Christianity's popularity.

ANIMISM. Predating both Hinduism and Theravada Buddhism, animism formed the first layer of Thai religion, later incorporating Theravada Buddhism. Followers of animism believe that everything has a spirit. Thai spirit houses, built to shelter the spirits, reflect these deep-seated beliefs. Today, most animists are found among the northern hill-tribes or the Chao Lay of the Andaman Sea.

LAND

With nearly every topological feature short of a frozen steppe, Thailand is a geography teacher's dream and a cartographer's nightmare. *Kos* (islands) off the coast of the "elephant trunk" peninsula have attracted tourists with claims of paradise. The range of terrain extends from seashore to mountain peak: Doi Inthanon in the pine-forested north is Thailand's highest point at 2576m. The semi-arid Khorat plateau of the northeast is a far cry from the mangroves scattered around the Gulf of Thailand. Farther east, rivers converge at the lush "Emerald Triangle" where Laos, Cambodia, and Thailand meet, leaving the rice paddies of central Thailand behind. The climate is largely tropical, with extreme temperatures in the drier northern regions. Despite seasonal monsoons, Thailand often has regional droughts.

WILDLIFE

Culturally and historically, elephants are the good luck charms of Thailand. They are on the national currency, the national flag, and are the symbol of the monarchy. Thailand is even geographically shaped like an elephant's head and trunk. White elephants are considered particularly lucky, as they once only belonged to kings. Today, when a white elephant is found, it immediately becomes the property of the reigning monarch. Despite the efforts to save these precious beasts, their numbers have diminished by almost 40% in the past ten years.

The **Asiatic Black Bear** and the **Malaysian Sun Bear** are two species native to Thailand, but poaching has put both on the endangered species list. Though it is illegal, both species are hunted for their skins, and older bears are killed for medicinal purposes. Tourists, mostly from Korea, visit Thailand in order to eat bear-paw soup. **Kitti's Hog-Nosed Bat** is also on the endangered species list. Found thus far only in Thailand, it may be the world's smallest mammal, not growing much larger than a bumblebee. At the other end of the scale, the **Giant Mekong Catfish,** weighing in at up to 300kg, is also endangered. In an attempt to protect wildlife, Thailand has set aside 13% of its land for natural preserves.

HISTORY

PREHISTORY

Some scholars argue that the ancestors of the modern Thai originated in Mongolia or Northern China and were driven south. Others trace their origins to northeastern Thailand. Various tribes of the Tai-Kadai gradually moved south into northern Myanmar, Thailand, and Laos, establishing minor kingdoms and city-states.

THE SUKHOTHAI PERIOD (1238-1350)

IMPORTANT DATES		
1238 Kingdom of Sukhothai founded by King Si Inthrathit.	**1275** King Ramkhamhaeng ascends the throne.	**1283** Thai alphabet established by King Ramkhamhaeng.

In 1238, **King Inthrathit** founded the kingdom of **Sukhothai,** considered by most to be the first unified Thai polity. Sukhothai, meaning "Dawn of Happiness," reached its zenith in power and size in 1275, when **Ramkhamhaeng the Great** became king. Sukhothai is commonly celebrated as a utopian golden age in Thai history, which, to a certain degree, it was. It's no wonder everyone was smiling; after all, King Ramkhamhaeng levied no taxes. In 1283, he introduced the Thai **alphabet** as a symbol of the nation's cultural independence.

THE RISE AND FALL OF AYUTTHAYA (1350-1782)

IMPORTANT DATES			
1350 Kingdom of Ayutthaya founded.	**1688** Foreigners plot, lie, and steal; get expelled from the kingdom.	**1767** Burmese annex, sack, and burn Ayutthaya.	**1782** General Taksin claims to be the Buddha.

In 1350, **King Ramathibodi I** established the kingdom of **Ayutthaya.** The kingdom's rise coincided with a stampede of curious foreign visitors to Thailand—the **Portuguese, Spanish, Dutch, English, Danish,** and **French** all tramped through. But in 1688 the king's chief minister, a Greek named **Constantine Phaulkon,** was accused of conspiring with France, and that year, Thailand cut off all relations with France and had limited contact with other foreign counties. After a year-long siege, **Burmese forces** burned Ayutthaya to the ground. The Thai have never forgiven the Burmese or forgotten what they did to Ayutthaya. Within 15 years, the forces of **General Phraya Taksin** had successfully recaptured much of the lost territory, but soon afterward, Taksin began to suffer from the unfortunate misconception that he was a **reincarnation of the Buddha.** He also made the ill-advised decision to proclaim this publicly. Needless to say, his declaration was poorly received in court. He was executed in royal fashion: thrown into a velvet sack and beaten to death with a club. Commander-in-chief **Thong Duang** was recalled from his campaign in Cambodia and crowned **King Rama I** in 1782, founding the **Chakri dynasty.**

COLONIALISM AVERTED (1782-1932)

IMPORTANT DATES		
1785 Bangkok becomes the capital of Siam.	**1851** King Rama IV ascends the throne.	**1855** King signs treaty with British, imports Western technology.

For increased security, Rama I moved the capital to **Bangkok.** The major achievement of his reign was the codification of Thai law into the **Kotmai Tra Samdung (Three Seals Code).** The reign of King Mongkut, or **King Rama IV,** was one of the most significant transitional periods of modern Thailand. In 1885, he negotiated a foreign trade treaty with the British, reversing 150 years of virtual isolation. When malaria cut short his rule, the government fell into the hands of his teenage son, **Prince Chulalongkorn,** who was crowned **King Rama V.** His rule was marked by social reforms and a courageous foreign policy in an era of European expansion. A treaty with the French established Siam as a **buffer state** between English and French colonial holdings, guaranteeing its independence. By his death, Rama V had become the most admired Thai monarch in modern history. His successor **King**

Vajiravudh all but destroyed pride in the monarchy with dubious financial finesse that left the country riddled with debt long after his reign. Thailand joined **WWI** on the side of the Allies and was one of the original members of the **League of Nations.**

THE RISE OF THE MILITARY (1932-1976)

IMPORTANT DATES				
1932 Absolute monarchy abolished; People's Party comes to power in a bloodless coup.	**1935** King Rama VII goes into voluntary exile in England.	**1957** Military *coup d'état* during general elections.	**1973** Students and workers hold pro-democracy demonstrations.	**1976** Government quells demonstrations, resulting in the October Massacre.

Unheeded calls for a civil constitution led to a coup in 1932 organized by the **People's Party. King Rama VII,** unable to satisfy the demands of his people, abdicated in 1935 and went into a voluntary exile in England. Under **Ananda Mahidol** (later **King Rama VIII**), the country experimented with **constitutions** granting varying degrees of democracy. In 1946, after his brother was found shot dead in his bed, **King Rama IX** began his reign. Economic development spurred the country to become more actively involved in international affairs, joining the **United Nations** in 1946. In 1957, the military staged a *coup d'état* during the general elections. Field Marshal **Sarit Thanarat** took over, and the new government re-established full military control. However, the nation's patience with new constitutions, coups, and regime changes was wearing thin. In June 1973, students and workers held demonstrations in the streets, calling for a democratic government. In the largest protest in Thai history, 250,000 people converged on Bangkok's **Democracy Monument.** The military attacked the crowd the very next day, killing 75. In response, King Bhumibol called for the resignation of Field Marshal Thanom (who fled the country), and appointed **Professor Sanya Dharmasakti** as interim prime minister. A new constitution sparked a short-lived era of democratic rule, cut short by Thanom's return to Thailand. Responding to a sit-in at **Thammasat University** in October of 1976, military troops killed more than 300, in what was later called the **October Massacre.** The military seized power of the government that night. Even today, the events of 1971-76 are taboo and rarely taught in Thai schools.

TOWARD DEMOCRACY (1976-1992)

IMPORTANT DATES		
1988 First elected, non-military Prime Minister since 1977.	**1991** Army launches bloodless coup, dissolves legislature, abolishes Constitution.	**1992** Troops kill hundreds of protestors on Suchinda's orders.

An 11-year stretch of rotating prime ministers, failed constitutions, economic decline, and constant coups left the Thai people desirous of a new form of government. In 1988, after 16 coups in 40 years, public dissatisfaction and shrinking support for the military culminated in general elections and the end of military rule. Early in 1991, the army launched a successful bloodless coup under **General Suchinda Kraprayoon,** who abolished the constitution, dissolved the legislature, and curtailed general freedoms. Accusations that the army influenced the framing of the new constitution to institutionalize its rule spurred hundreds of thousands of pro-democracy protesters to hold a demonstration in May 1992. Under Prime Minister Suchinda's orders, the military killed or injured hundreds of people, many of whom were strategically located in front of the Democracy Monument and Western TV cameras. Horrified, King Bhumibol forced Suchinda out of office and appointed **Anand Panyarachun** as transitional prime minister.

END OF MILITARY RULE (1992-1997)

IMPORTANT DATES		
1992-96 Economic prosperity slows down.	**1996** Stock market crashes.	**1997** Asian Financial Crisis.

Panyarachun's administration tried to separate the government and the military. Subsequent regimes, however, faced charges of corruption and mismanagement, and the resulting political instability heavily damaged Thailand's economy. In 1996, Thailand had a 5.9% inflation rate, 0% export growth, and a drop of 30% in stock market prices. Tougher times were still to come. In July 1997, heavy external debts, financial deregulation, and an unsustainable fixed exchange rate culminated in the collapse of the Thai *baht* in what became known as the **Asian Financial Crisis.** Economists discovered the hard way that the national economic infrastructure was too weak to absorb the shock. The **International Monetary Fund (IMF)** initiated a US$17.2 billion emergency international rescue package for Thailand in August 1997. In spite of IMF intervention, the *baht's* value fell 40%, over 350 factories shut down, and Thailand's stock market hit a nine-year low.

THAILAND TODAY

A thriving sex and intravenous drug industry drove **Acquired Immune Deficiency Syndrome (AIDS)** to epidemic status in parts of Thailand during the late 1990s. By the end of 1999, 66,000 people had died of HIV/AIDS in Thailand, the first country in Southeast Asia to experience the epidemic. Many feared that the disease was spreading to new sectors of Thai society. Today, these trends are slowly reversing. The effects of **safe-sex practices** such as condom use, first advocated in the early 1990s by **Senator Mechai Viravaidya** (justly dubbed "Mr. Condom") and his "100 Percent Condom" plan, are now becoming apparent in HIV/AIDS statistics. The use of condoms in commercial sex is up from 14% to over 90%, and protective measures have resulted in a 90% decrease in the rate of sexually transmitted diseases (STDs). Traditionally, AIDS prevention efforts have focused on **prostitutes** and those intimately involved in the skin trade. Now, however, **drug users** are seen as the main obstacle in Thailand's victory over HIV. Recent budget cuts have also severely hampered the efforts of **AIDS awareness programs.** Thailand introduced an inexpensive **AIDS cocktail** during the summer of 2002 designed to consolidate patients' medications. As of now, however, only about 10% of Thailand's estimated 200,000 HIV-positive patients receive the drug cocktail from the government.

THAILAND-MYANMAR RELATIONS. Since Myanmar sacked the Thai capital of Ayutthaya in 1767 (p. 654), relations have been off-and-on at best. The issue of illicit drugs adds to tensions, as Myanmar drug lords have long been producing methamphetamine and smuggling it into Thailand, China, and India. The most recent controversy between the two neighbors erupted in May 2002 when officials in Yangon, Myanmar accused the Thai military of firing shells over the border in support of ethnic Shan rebels. Thailand denied the charges and Myanmar closed all border checkpoints with Thailand indefinitely. After a five-month closure of the border, however, the two countries managed to reestablish relations and have turned their attention to other issues, such as the flourishing drug trade. Currently, the two governments are discussing possible ways to curb drug trafficking.

SOUTHERN DISCOMFORT. In January 2004, armed men in the southern provinces of Narathiwat, Pattani, Songkhla, and Yala burned schools, looted weapons, and killed four Thai soldiers. In response, Thailand declared martial law, deploying troops to the region. Scattered bombings and shootings plagued the area until the conflict came to a head in April 2004, when militants raided police stations and government buildings. The police fought back, killing an estimated 112 fighters. The southernmost provinces, once the independent Sultanate of Pattani, only came under Thai rule in 1902 and have complained of religious, cultural and economic isolation. The population is largely Muslim, many of them ethnic Malays. In a recent statement, Prime Minister Thaksin Shinawatra declared his intentions to bring "peace and prosperity" back to the region through education reform and public works projects that would create jobs. By August 2004, more than 300 casualties had been reported.

CUSTOMS AND ETIQUETTE

THE THREE SPIRITS. The Thai attitude toward life rests on three major concepts. The first, *jai yen*, or "cool heart," explains an aversion to any sort of confrontation, especially in public. Most Thais avoid raising their voices or displaying any visible irritation, instead embracing the idea of *mai pen rai*, literally translated as "it can't be helped, so why bother?" This verbal equivalent of a shrug is complemented by the last of the three Thai spirits, *sanuk*, which literally means "fun."

HEADS UP. According to an ancient Hindu belief (now incorporated into Buddhism), the head is the most sacred part of the body, and by extension, the feet are the most unclean. A pat on the head in Thailand is neither playful nor cute—it's simply disrespectful. Similarly, don't point your feet toward an image of the Buddha in a temple or toward another person, especially if he or she is older. Shoes, even more unclean than feet, are unwelcome in temples and most private homes.

WAI NOT? To show respect, put palms together at chest level, pointing your fingers away from you, and gently bow your head. This is a traditional greeting, called a *wai*. The degree to which you should bend your waist while performing a *wai* is determined by your social status relative to the other person. Older people receive lower, more respectful *wais*. Younger people or those of inferior social standing *wai* first. Inanimate objects that should receive a *wai* include **spirit houses,** miniature temples blessed by Brahmin priests that house the spiritual guardians of the land on which the house resides.

TABOOS. Don't ever speak disparagingly of the monarchy, and avoid dropping, defacing, or stepping on currency or stamps, which carry the king's portrait. When near a portrait of King Bhumibol or any past Thai king, never raise your head above the head in the portrait. Always remove your **shoes** when entering a home or temple. Clothing should be modest: both men and women should wear long sleeves and long pants or skirts, especially when visiting a *wat*. Women should never touch a monk or give him anything directly, as this will violate an important part of his vows. Similarly, **public displays of affection** between lovers are frowned upon. Affectionate same-sex caresses or hugs are commonplace and rarely have sexual overtones. Despite its tolerance of different cultures, Thailand does imprison foreigners for actions considered sacrilegious.

STAND AND DELIVER. Whether they're in the bus station, on the street, or in the market, all Thai people stop what they're doing when they hear the national anthem (and they hear it often). In smaller cities, traffic comes to a screeching halt. Thailand's flag is raised each morning at 8am and lowered each evening at 6pm to the accompaniment of the anthem. Respect Thailand's national custom—be still and stand up when the anthem is played before movies and public events.

FETCH ME SOME FOOD. Thai cuisine is based primarily on a "throw-together" technique which produces delicious treats from fresh ingredients with incredible speed. Often vendors will make food right in front of you, as you dictate which ingredients should be used.

Some local delicacies are:

Pad thai: the national dish, pan-fried rice noodles, bean sprouts, peanuts, lime, bean curd, scallion, dried red chilli, egg, and the meat of your choice.

Pad ka-phrao: meat with chillies and basil, usually on rice.

Pad kee mow: stir-fried vegetables with chillies and meat (this is a spicy one).

Som tam: raw, unripe papaya salad; also available with unripe mangoes.

Sup nau mai: wet curry with bamboo shoots, squash, and mushrooms.

Tom kha kai: chicken coconut soup with galanga, lemon grass, black chilli paste, green chilli peppers, coriander, and sugar.

Khao niaw mamuang: sticky-rice and mango.

ARTS AND RECREATION

ARCHITECTURE. Classical Thai architecture focused primarily on **religious structures,** particularly the **wat.** The **bot,** or main chapel, is a tall, oblong building with a three-level, steeply sloped roof that houses the principal Buddha image. The **sala** is an open, gazebo-like structure for meditation and preaching. Above some monastic compounds looms a tapering, spire-like tower, called a **chedi,** the reliquary for the possessions and cremated remains of high priests, members of royalty, and the Buddha. By the 20th century, increased contact with Europeans led to the steady decline of traditional Thai architecture. Western styles and materials (often concrete) were adopted, making Thailand's modern architecture remarkably similar to that in cities elsewhere. However, some intrepid Thai architects still study historical styles, utilizing modern materials for the construction of traditional forms.

DANCE AND DRAMA. In their classical forms, Thai dance and drama are inseparable. The three main types of dramatic media in Thai culture are **khon, lakhon,** and **likay.** *Khon*, or masked dance drama, is based on Indian temple dances and rituals; its various stories come exclusively from the Indian epic, the *Ramayana*, known in Thai as the **Ramakien.** The *lakhon* form of drama is less structured and stylized. Like *khon*, *lakhon* is derived from the *Ramakien* but also adds stories from Thai folk tales and Buddhist *Jatakas*. The *likay* style is bawdy and humorous with loud, sharp music, lyrics sprinkled with sexual innuendos, improvisation, pantomime, and social satire.

FILM. Thai movies are traditionally low-budget productions packing a sensationalist punch. However, 2001 seems to have been a turning point for the industry, with Thai movies beginning to gain recognition on the international film circuit. *Tropical Malady*, by director Apichatpong Weerasethakul, won the 2004 Jury Prize at Cannes after being the first Thai film to be shown in competition there. Co-directed by the Pang brothers from Hong Kong, *Bangkok Dangerous* is a dramatic thriller to a frenetic techno beat—a change for Thai audiences, who usually favor upbeat comedies. Prince Chatreechalerm Yukol's much anticipated film, *Suriyothai*, details the life of a princess as a 16th-century battle for the throne of Thailand rages. The government actively promotes the shooting of foreign films in Thailand because it boosts state revenue, but all scripts have to be approved.

MUAY THAI (THAI BOXING). Muay Thai is a martial art that has been around since the early days of Thailand, but was especially encouraged to keep Thai soldiers battle-ready during the 15th and 16th centuries. The first boxer to win historic recognition was **Nai Khanom Tom.** Captured by the Burmese, he won his freedom after dispatching 10 Burmese soldiers one by one in a boxing challenge. Muay Thai reached the peak of its popularity in the first decade of the 18th century during the reign of Phra Chau Sua, when he promoted it as a national sport. Due to an alarming number of injuries and even deaths, Muay Thai was banned in the 1920s. It was reinstated in 1937, however, when it underwent a series of regulations that shaped the sport to its present form. Today these fights, full of ritual, music, and blood, are put on display throughout Thailand. Fighters exchange blows for five three-minute rounds; the winner either knocks out his victim or takes the bout by points (most bouts are decided in the latter manner).

WEAVING. For centuries, village women in the northeast bred silkworms and worked at hand looms to produce bolts and bolts of traditional Thai silk. However, cheaper fabrics imported from China and Japan devastated the industry in the second half of the 19th century. Jump-started by the famous American expatriate **Jim Thompson** after World War II, the silk industry soon became symbolic of Thailand on the international market. Each region has its own special style and technique; the most famous Thai silk, however, is still woven in the northeast.

HOLIDAYS AND FESTIVALS (2005)

DATE	NAME AND LOCATION	DESCRIPTION
Feb. 9-10	Chinese New Year	Celebrated by nearly all of Thailand.
Feb. 23	Makha Bucha	*Full moon of third lunar month.* Commemoration of the 1250 disciples of Buddha coming to hear him preach.
Apr. 6	Chakri Day	National holiday to commemorate the first king of the present dynasty to ascend to the throne.
Apr. 13-15	Songkran, Thai New Year	Best in Chiang Mai, this holiday is known for water; both for washing and throwing, consists of lots of water throwing.
May 1	Labor Day	Banks, factories, and offices closed.
May 5	Coronation Day	National holiday.
May	Royal Ploughing Ceremony, Bangkok	Official beginning of rice-planting outside the Royal Palace.
May 22-23	Wisakha Puja	*Full moon of sixth lunar month.* Birth, enlightenment, and death of Buddha. Holiest holiday, celebrated at every temple with candlelight processions.
July 21	Khao Pansa Day: Buddhist Lent begins. Candle Festival, Ubon Ratchathani	A time of giving up indulgences, the first day is commemorated with particular attention by students.
Aug. 12	The Queen's Birthday, Mother's Day	Thais celebrate their queen's birthday by honoring their own mothers.
Oct. 23	Chulalongkorn Day	Commemoration of King Rama V's death.
Dec. 5	His Majesty's birthday, Father's Day	Thais celebrate their king's birthday by honoring their own fathers.

ADDITIONAL RESOURCES

GENERAL HISTORY

Modern Thailand: A Volume in the Comparative Societies Series, by Robert Slagter and Harold Kerbo (1999). A review of contemporary Thai institutions and social change.

Thailand: A Short History, by David Wyatt (1982). Excellent history of Thailand.

CULTURE

Night Market: Sexual Cultures and the Thai Economic Miracle, by Ryan Bishop and Lillian Robinson (1998). Explores the trade-off between the lives of young Thai women who are lured into the prostitution industry and the country's economic recovery.

Peoples of the Golden Triangle: Six Tribes in Thailand, by Paul and Elaine Lewis (1998). A historiography of local hill-tribes in northern Thailand, with personal vignettes.

FICTION AND NON-FICTION

Jasmine Nights, by S.P. Somtow (1995). A brilliant and hilarious coming-of-age story that paints a colorful and rich picture of Thai culture, contrasting it with its Western counterpart. Thailand's most widely-published author.

Monsoon Country, by Pira Sudham (1988). Personal account of the period of tumult and revolution experienced by Thai culture and politics during 1954-1980. Sudham was nominated for the Nobel Prize for this work. His *People of Esarn* (1987) is highly informative background reading for those traveling to northeast Thailand.

FILM

The Bridge On the River Kwai, directed by David Lean, starring Sir Alec Guinness and William Holden (1957). A WWII epic based on a true story about Allied POWs forced to build a bridge connecting Thailand to Myanmar (Burma). The film won 7 Academy Awards, including Best Picture, and causes hundreds of tourists flock to Kanchanaburi each year.

Suriyothai, directed by Chatrichalerm Yukol (2001). Historical epic set in the Ayutthaya period that follows events in the life of Queen Suriyothai.

ESSENTIALS

THAILAND	❶	❷	❸	❹	❺
ACCOMM.	Under $2 Under 80฿	$2-7 80-280฿	$7-12 280-480฿	$12-18 480-720฿	Over $18 Over 720฿
FOOD	Under $0.75 Under 30฿	$0.75-2 30-80฿	$2-4 80-160฿	$4-6 160-240฿	Over $6 Over 240฿

EMBASSIES AND CONSULATES

THAILAND CONSULAR SERVICES ABROAD

Australia: Embassy: 111 Empire CTT, Yarralumla 2600, Canberra, ACT (☎06 273 1149; http://members.tripod.com/posit/index2.html). **Consulates:** 75-77 Pitt St., 2nd fl., Sydney, NSW 2000 (☎02 9241 2542); Silverton Place, 5th fl., 101 Wickham Terrace, Brisbane, QLD 4000 (☎07 3832 1999); 277 Flinders Ln., 6th fl., Melbourne, VIC 3000 (☎03 9650 1714); 72 Flinders St., 1st fl., Adelaide, SA 5000 (☎08 232 7474); 135 Victoria Ave., Dalkeith, WA 6009 (☎09 386 8092).

THAILAND

Canada: Embassy: 180 Island Park Dr., Ottawa, ON K1Y 0A2 (☎613-722-4444; www.magma.ca/~thaiott/mainpage.htm). **Consulate:** 1040 Burrard St., Vancouver BC V6Z 2R9 (☎604-687-1143; www.thaicongenvancouver.org).

New Zealand: Embassy: 2 Cook St., P.O. Box 17-226, Karori, Wellington 6005 (☎04 476 8617; www.thaiembassynz.org.nz).

UK: Embassy: 29-30 Queen's Gate, London SW7 5JB (☎020 7589 2944; www.thaiembassyuk.org.uk).

US: Embassy: 1024 Wisconsin Ave. NW, Ste. 401, Washington, D.C. 20007 (☎202-944-3600; www.thaiembdc.org). **Consulates:** 351 E. 52nd St., New York, NY 10022 (☎212-754-1770); 700 N. Rush St., Chicago, IL 60611 (☎312-664-3129); 611 N. Larchmont Blvd., 2nd fl., Los Angeles, CA 90004 (☎323-962-9574; www.thai-la.net).

CONSULAR SERVICES IN THAILAND

Australian Embassy: 37 S. Sathorn Rd., Bangkok 10120 (☎02 287 2680). Open M-Th 8:30am-12:30pm and 1:30-4:30pm.

Canadian Embassy: Abdulrahim Bldg., 15th fl., 990 Rama IV Rd., Bangkok 10500 (☎02 636 0540). Open M-Th 7:30am-4pm, F 7:30am-1pm. **Consulate:** 151 Moo 3 Superhighway, Tambon Tahsala, Chiang Mai 50000 (☎053 242 292).

New Zealand Embassy: M Thai Tower, 14th fl., All Seasons Place, 87 Wireless Rd., Lumphini, Bangkok 10330 (☎02 254 3856). Open M-F 7:30am-noon and 1-4pm.

UK Embassy: 103 Wireless Rd., Bangkok 10330 (☎02 305 8333). Open M-F 7:30am-noon and 1-3:30pm. **Consulate:** 198 Bumrung Rat Rd., Muang, Chiang Mai 50000 (☎053 263 015). Open M-F 9-11:30am.

US Embassy: 120-122 Wireless Rd., Bangkok 10300 (☎02 205 40 00). Consular services M-F 8-11am and 1-2pm. **Consulate:** 387 Witchayanond Rd., Chiang Mai 50300 (☎053 252 629). American citizen services open M and W 1-3:30pm.

TOURIST SERVICES

Tourism Authority of Thailand (TAT): www.tat.or.th or www.tourismthailand.org. 75 Pitt St., 2nd fl., Sydney 2000 (☎61 2 9247 7549); Brook House 98-99 Jermyn St., 3rd fl., London SW1Y 6EE (☎44 207 925 2511); 61 Broadway, Ste. 2810, New York, NY 10006 (☎212-432-0433); 611 N. Larchmont Blvd., 1st fl., Los Angeles, CA 90004 (☎323-461-9814). Web page regularly updated for dates of festivals and recent news.

Ministry of Foreign Affairs: www.mfa.go.th. Sri Ayudhaya Rd., Bangkok 10400 (☎66 2 643 5000). Provides info about traveling in Thailand as well as foreign policy updates.

DOCUMENTS AND FORMALITIES

American, Australian, British, Canadian, most European, New Zealand, and South African citizens can stay for 30 days without a visa. For longer stays, Thai consulates abroad issue 60-day tourist visas, or travelers can apply for **extensions** in Thailand. If you wish to sojourn to nearby countries, obtain a **re-entry permit** at an immigration office before departure.

MONEY

The currency chart below is based on August 2004 exchange rates between local currency and Australian dollars (AUS$), Canadian dollars (CDN$), European Union euros (EUR€), New Zealand dollars (NZ$), British pounds (UK£), and US dollars (US$). Check the currency converter on websites like www.xe.com or www.bloomberg.com or a large newspaper for the latest exchange rates.

CURRENCY (฿)

AUS$1 = 30.02฿	10฿ = AUS$0.33
CDN$1 = 31.98฿	10฿ = CDN$0.31
EUR€1 = 51.04฿	10฿ = EUR€0.20
NZ$1 = 27.91฿	10฿ = NZ$0.36
UK£1 = 75.45฿	10฿ = UK£0.13
US$1 = 41.46฿	10฿ = US$0.24

The Thai **baht (฿)** comes in paper money denominations of 20, 50, 100, 500, and 1000, and coins come in 1, 5, 10฿ and 25 and 50 satang. Thailand has a **10% VAT** (value-added tax) on most items, including hotel rooms and food; it's usually already included in stated prices. Menus, tariff sheets, etc., specify if VAT is not included in the listed price. **Tipping** is not customary but much appreciated; in restaurants that don't levy service charges, a 15% gratuity is appropriate. Foreigners should expect to pay higher entrance fees at some places.

GETTING THERE

BY PLANE. Thailand has four major **international airports:** Don Muang International Airport in Bangkok (p. 664), Chiang Mai International Airport in Chiang Mai (p. 759), Phuket International Airport in Phuket (p. 801), and Hat Yai International Airport in Hat Yai. Numerous international airlines, including **Thai Airways** (www.thaiair.com), fly to each of these destinations.

BY LAND. Refer to the following table for overland border crossings in Thailand.

BORDER CROSSINGS

CAMBODIA. Border crossings include: **Aranyaprathet** to **Poipet** (p. 709), from **Chong Jiam,** or via a **Trat-Sihanoukville** boat.

LAOS. Border crossings include: **Chiang Khong** to **Houay Xay** (p. 792), **Nong Khai** to **Vientiane** (p. 751), **Nakhon Phanom** to **Tha Kaek** (p. 743), **Mukdahan** to **Savannakhet** (p. 741), **Chong Mek** to **Vang Tao** (p. 739).

MALAYSIA. Border crossings include: **Satun** to **Kuala Perlis, Padang Besar** to **Kangar, Betong** to **Keroh, Sungai Kolok** to **Kota Bharu** (p. 389).

MYANMAR. Border crossings include: **Mae Sai** (p. 789), **Mae Sot** (p. 779), or the **Three Pagoda Pass** (p. 721). These border crossing points close the most frequently and unexpectedly, so check at the local embassy first.

GETTING AROUND

BY PLANE. Thai Airways (☎02 535 5173; www.thaiair.com) has a near-monopoly within Thailand with extensive domestic flights. An alternative is **Bangkok Airways** (☎2 229 3456), whose major routes go from Bangkok to Ko Samui and Phuket.

BY TRAIN. The **State Railway of Thailand** (☎2 225 0300) operates an efficient and cheap rail system with three main train routes that all start in Bangkok: north to Chiang Mai, south to Malaysia and Singapore, and northeast to Nong Khai and Ubon Ratchathani. Minor routes connect Bangkok to Kanchanaburi and cities north of the eastern seaboard. For long rides (over 3hr.), **third-class** travel can be uncomfortable. **Second-class** sleeping berths carry an additional charge of 100-

320฿ (depending on the type of train, fan or A/C, and upper or lower bunk) and often sell out. **Rapid** (40฿ extra), **Express** (60฿ extra), and **Special Express** (80฿) trains come next in price and are speedier than ordinary trains.

BY BUS. Public buses are the cheapest and easiest way to travel short distances but **A/C buses** are recommended for longer transits. These buses generally cost twice as much, make fewer stops, and are mostly used by tourists.

HEALTH AND SAFETY

DRUGS. First of all, it is important to remember that foreigners in Thailand are subject to Thai law. Drugs, no matter what anyone tells you, are illegal in Thailand and for severe infringements of this law, Thailand has imposed the death penalty.

HEALTH RISKS. Major health concerns in Thailand are malaria and Dengue fever. Both are transmitted by mosquitoes and precautions should be taken to avoid being bitten. Talk to your doctor about taking malaria medication if you are going to be traveling near Thailand's borders since this is the area where malaria is prevelant. The spread of HIV/AIDS is another health concern in Thailand, especially related to the skin trade. Travelers to Thailand should take extreme precautions to avoid exposing themselves to HIV/AIDS or other sexually transmitted diseases.

WOMEN TRAVELERS. Female travelers to Thailand should consider bringing feminine products with them as they may not be easy to procure in rural areas. Wearing loose clothing can help prevent yeast infections, which thrive in tropical climates.

MINORITY TRAVELERS. Thai society is generally very accepting and most travelers have had no reason for complaint. However, visitors of African descent have occasionally reported incidents of discrimination.

GLBT TRAVELERS. Gay, lesbian, bisexual, and transgendered individuals usually find Thailand largely accepting, if not actively supportive, of same-sex relationships.

KEEPING IN TOUCH

The Thai **postal system** is reliable and efficient. Airmail across the globe from Bangkok takes about 10 days. Overseas mail from rural areas takes two weeks but almost always gets to its destination. For 3-day overseas mail, **Express Mail Service (EMS)** is often available. Communications Authority of Thailand (CAT) and post offices usually offer international phone service.

BANGKOK ☎02

After a day or two, most travelers are amazed that Bangkok remains standing at each sunset. Bangkok wasn't fashioned by city planners; it was hewn from unsuspecting rice paddies by the double-edged sword of Thailand's growing economy. The consummate Western city, Nintendo has taken children permanently away from their mothers, 7-Elevens abound on every corner, and modern medicine, education, and technology are taken for granted. But this urban center of over 10 million people is the center of Thailand's government and culture, and has much to offer. Southeast Asia's best DJs blast the latest hits next to the pinnacles of royal Buddhism and ancient architecture in the Grand Palace. The Emerald Buddha poses contemplatively for praying worshippers as Muay Thai kickboxers battle it out in front of screaming fans. Chefs bargain for meat at the sunrise floating markets just hours after the "meat market" in the Patpong red light district closes down. It is a city of constant surprises—no two people know the same Bangkok.

INTERCITY TRANSPORTATION

BY PLANE. Most flights to Thailand arrive at **Don Muang International Airport,** 171 Vibhavadi-Ransot Rd. (the main northern highway), 25km north of the city center. The airport includes **International Terminal 1** (departure info ☎535 1149, arrival 535 1310), **International Terminal 2** (departure info ☎535 1386, arrival 535 1301), and **Domestic Passenger Travel** (departure info ☎535 1192, arrival 535 1253). The 24hr. **post office,** in the departure hall of International Terminal 1, has **international phones, EMS,** and **stamps.** Each terminal has **baggage storage** (70฿ per bag per day, over 3 months 140฿ per day). Departure tax is 500฿ for international flights, 60฿ for domestic. The prices below are based on a round-trip fare.

DESTINATION	PRICE	DESTINATION	PRICE
Chiang Mai	4500฿	Phuket	5500฿
Hà nội	12,500฿	Singapore	10,500฿
Kuala Lumpur	11,500฿	Udon Thani	4000฿
Phnom Penh	11,000฿	Vientiane	10,000฿

A new international hub, **Suvarnabhumi Airport,** is under construction east of the city. Upon its completion, it will handle all international traffic. Until then, Don Muang will continue to handle all air traffic in and out of Bangkok. The airport is scheduled to open in August 2005, but is currently behind schedule. Check www.suvarnabhumiairport.com for construction updates.

As you exit customs, take one of the waiting taxis (250-400฿) or one of the four A/C airport buses (100฿). A1, A2, and A3 run every 30min. 5am-midnight. A4 runs every hour, or when eight people get on. To get to Khaosan Rd., take A2.

ROUTE #	STOPS
A1: DON MUANG-SILOM	Don Muang Tollway, Dindaeng Rd., Pratunam, Ratchadamri Rd., Lumphini Park, Silom Rd., Charoen Krung Rd., Silom Rd.
A2: DON MUANG-SANAM LUANG	Don Muang Tollway, Dindaeng Rd., Rachavithi Rd., Victory Monument, Phyathai Rd., Phetchaburi Rd., Larn Luang Rd., Tanao Rd., Phrasumen Rd., Chakrapong Rd., Banglamphu (Khaosan Rd.), Democracy Monument, Ratchadamnoen Klong Rd., Sanam Luang.
A3: DON MUANG-THONGLOR	Don Muang Tollway, Dindaeng Expressway, Sukhumvit Rd., Asok, Eastern Bus Terminal (Ekamai), New Phetchaburi Rd., Thonglor Rd.
A4: DON MUANG-HUALAMPHONG	Don Muang Tollway, Dindaeng Expressway, Ploenchit Rd., Siam Sq., Phayathai Rd., Mahboonkrong, Rama IV Rd., Wongwien 2, Hualamphong.

A cheaper way to get from the airport to the city is to cross the bridge to the Don Muang Train Station and catch an inbound **train** to Hualamphong Railway Station (10-15฿), and then take a **city bus.** Night service is infrequent.

Suffocating **public buses** are available on the highway just outside the exit for 3.50-16฿ (regular #3, 24, 52; A/C #504, 510, 529), though other modes of transportation are more reliable. A list of fares and schedules can be found at the **Tourist Authority of Thailand (TAT)** in the arrivals area of Terminal 1. (Open 24hr.)

BY TRAIN. Second only to elephant transport in style and peanut-holding capacity, train travel is cheap, efficient, and safe. Four train lines, traveling north, northeast, east, and south, start and end at **Hualamphong Railway Station** (☎220 4334, 24hr. info 1690), on Rama IV Rd. in the center of the metropolis. *Klongs* (canal) and river ferries, coupled with public buses (p. 668), provide the easiest transportation to the station from the city. Metered taxis or *tuk-tuks* at the side entrance of the station are the best ways into town from the station. The new **subway** line also terminates at Hualamphong. Bus #29 runs from the airport through Siam Sq. to the station. Otherwise, walk down Rama IV Rd. to a bus stop from which A/C bus #501 and regular buses #29 and 34 go to Siam Sq. Walk down Sukhumvit Rd. for regular bus #53 to Banglamphu (Khaosan Rd. area), which continues to Thewet.

Daily ticket booking is left of the main entrance; advance booking is to the right. The lower information counter has train schedules. Upper-class seats have bathrooms and A/C; lower-class seats put you right in the middle of many friendly Thai people. Sleeper berths are popular, so buy tickets eight to ten days before departure. In order of increasing speed, price, and service, the trains are: ordinary *(rot thamada)*, rapid *(rot reaw)*, express *(rot duun)*, and special *(rot phooset)*.

THAILAND

THE PRICE IS RIGHT! Prices listed are ranges of fares. Add 40฿ for rapid trains, 60฿ for express trains, and 80฿ for specials. Sleeper cars cost 100-500฿ extra, depending on class. Duration listed is for rapid trains; add 2-3hr. per 10 hr. for normal trains.

Platform 12 has a **luggage storage center.** (☎215 1920. 10-30฿ per day depending on bag size. 4-month max. Open 4am-11pm.) Other services include: an **information booth;** a 24hr. **ATM** near the main entrance; a **police booth** (☎225 0300), left of the main entrance; and a **post office** outside. (Open M-F 7am-7pm, Sa 8am-4pm.)

DESTINATION	DURATION	FREQUENCY/TIME	PRICE
CHIANG MAI LINE (NORTHERN)			
Ayutthaya	2hr.	20 per day 6am-11:40pm	15-20฿
Chiang Mai	10-14hr.	7 per day 6am-10pm	181-1253฿
Don Muang Intl. Airport	1hr.	20 per day 6am-11:40pm	5-10฿
Lampang	13hr.	7 per day 6am-10pm	166-1172฿
UBON RATCHATHANI LINE (NORTHEASTERN)			
Nong Khai	13hr.	daily 8:45am, 10pm	183-1117฿
Surin	8hr.	8 per day 5:45am-11:40pm	173-946฿
Ubon Ratchathani	12hr.	5 per day 5:45am-11:25pm	175-1080฿
BUTTERWORTH LINE (SOUTHERN)			
Hua Hin	4hr.	12 per day 7:45am-10:50pm	164-842฿
Surat Thani	12hr.	11 per day 12:25-10:50pm	227-1179฿
EASTERN LINE			
Aranyaprathet	5½hr.	daily 5:55am, 1:05pm	48฿
Pattaya	3½hr.	daily 6:55am	31฿

BY BUS. Government buses depart from four terminals. The **Eastern Bus Terminal** (**E;** ☎391 2504) is on Sukhumvit Rd., and accessible via the Skytrain's Ekamai Station, local A/C bus #1, 8, 11, or 13, and regular bus #2, 23, 25, 38, 71, 72, or 98. The **Northern** (**N;** ☎936 2852), **Central** (**C;** ☎936 1972), and **Northeastern** (**NE;** ☎936 3660) **Bus Terminals** are in a new building west of Chatuchak Park. Take the Skytrain's Sukhumvit Line to Mo Chit and a motorcycle taxi (5min., 30฿) from there to the terminals. The **Southern Bus Terminal** (**S;** ☎435 1199) is on Boromat Chonnani (Pinklao-Nakhonchaisi) Rd. across the river in Thonburi. Tickets for government and **private buses** can be bought at the Southern Bus Terminal. To get there, take A/C bus #503 or 511 from the Democracy Monument, regular bus #19 from Phra Athit Rd., or regular bus #30 from Sanam Luang. Although private companies can be cheaper and more convenient, and sometimes offer more modern accommodations, they have higher scam and accident rates.

DESTINATION	DURATION	TERMINAL, FREQUENCY	PRICE
Ayutthaya	1½hr.	C, every 20min. 5:40am-7:20pm	41-52฿
Ban Phe (to Ko Samet)	3½hr.	E, every hr. 5am-8:30pm	124฿
Chanthaburi	4hr.	E, every 30min. 4am-midnight	115-148฿
Chiang Mai	9hr.	N, 74 per day 5:30am-10pm	314-625฿
Chiang Rai	11-13hr.	N, 32 per day 7am-9:30pm	264-700฿
Khon Kaen	7½hr.	NE, 27 per day	202-400฿
Krabi	12hr.	S, 1 per day	459-710฿
Mae Hong Son	14hr.	N, 1 per day 6pm	569฿
Nong Khai	7½-10hr.	NE, 19 per day 4:10am-9:45pm	195-545฿
Pattaya	2½hr.	E, every 20-30min. 4:40am-11pm	73-90฿
Phang-Nga	12hr.	S, 7 per day	441-685฿
Phrae	8hr.	N, 30 per day 6am-9:30pm	177-319฿,
Phuket	11½hr.	S, 8 per day	486-755฿
Si Racha	2hr.	E, every 20-30min. 5am-9pm	55-70฿
Sukothai	7hr.	N, 32 per day 7am-10:50pm	142-256฿
Surat Thani	9hr.	S, 7 per day	380-590฿
Surin	6-8hr.	NE, 30 per day 7am-11pm	146-385฿
Trat	5hr.	E, every hr. 4am-midnight	147-221฿
Ubon Ratchathani	5hr.	NE, 18 per day 7am-10:40pm	297-570฿

THAILAND

ORIENTATION

Beyond the backpacker-infested shelters of **Khaosan Road** lies a bastion of unclaimed sights. The north-south **Chao Phraya River** is a good landmark. To the river's east rests **Banglamphu,** the heart of the city. Home to Khaosan Rd., it's immediately north of **Ratchadamnoen/Ko Rattanakosin,** the location of Bangkok's major sights, including Wat Pho, Wat Phra Kaew, and the Royal Palace. Farther north is **Thewet/Dusit,** a backpacker area and the location of the Dusit Zoo and the former royal mansions. Heading southeast along the river leads to **Pahurat** the Indian district, **Chinatown,** and the **Hualamphong Railway Station.** Farther south is the wealthy **Silom** financial district and its less-upstanding bedfellow, the **Patpong** red light district. East of the Hualamphong Railway Station is **Siam Square,** the hub of the BTS Skytrain and home to huge shopping malls and cinemas. **Rama I Road** slices through the city, connecting Wat Phra Kaew in the west with Bangkok's eastern edge and the **Sukhumvit Road** area, where everyone parties until the wee hours. The *Bangkok Tourist Map* (40฿) or Nancy Chandler's *Map of Bangkok* (200฿) will make all of this clearer than we ever could.

LOCAL TRANSPORTATION

Maneuvering through Bangkok traffic is enough to drive anyone crazy. Traffic has decreased recently, but getting from north to south is still frustrating. Taking canal boats and river taxis means less time sweating on buses and breathing exhaust. Travelers hoping to utilize public transportation will love the **Bangkok Tourist Map** (40฿), which has bus, water taxi, and Skytrain routes, as well as sight info.

BY BUS. The shiny, happy bus system, run by the **Bangkok Metropolitan Transit Authority (BMTA),** is extensive and cheap. Red-and-cream and white buses have no A/C (4-5฿); orange, blue-and-white, and yellow-and-white buses all have A/C (10-20฿). Pea-green **minibuses** (3.50฿) supposedly run the same routes as the buses but tend to stray easily. **Microbuses** cover long distances and stop only at designated places (5am-10pm, 30฿); the higher price guarantees a seat and fewer stops. A/C buses run 5am-midnight; regular buses run 24hr. Make sure you get on the right type of bus, not just the right route number. Below is a sample listing; there are many, many buses, so for more options, pick up a free **bus map** at any **TAT office** (see **Practical Information,** p. 676).

THAILAND

TIP **BACKPACKER'S BUS.** Regular bus #15 is especially important for those staying in Khaosan. It connects that area with Siam Sq., where passengers can hop onto the Skytrain to access the eastern parts of the city, like Sukhumvit, Silom, and Chatuchak. Alternatively, a taxi from Khaosan to Siam costs 60-90฿.

REGULAR BUSES WITH NO A/C (RED-AND-CREAM OR WHITE)

#1: Wat Pho–Yaowarat Rd. (Chinatown)–General Post Office (GPO)–Oriental Hotel

15: Banglamphu (Phra Athit Rd., Phrasumen Rd.)–Sanam Luang–Democracy Monument–Wat Saket–Siam Sq.–Ratchadamri Rd.–Lumphini Park–Silom Rd.

18 and **28:** Vimanmek Teak Museum–Dusit Zoo–Chitralada Palace–Victory Monument

25: Wat Phra Kaew–Wat Pho–Charoen Krung Rd.–Rama IV Rd. (near Hualamphong Railway Station)–Phayathai Rd.–Mahboonkrong Center–Siam Sq.–World Trade Center–Ploenchit Rd.–Sukhumvit Rd. to outer Bangkok

48: Sanam Chai Rd.–Bamrung Muang Rd.–Siam Sq.–along Sukhumvit Rd.

59: Don Muang International Airport–Victory Monument–Phahonyothin Rd.–Phetchaburi Rd.–Larnluang Rd.–Democracy Monument–Sanam Luang

70: Democracy Monument–TAT–Boxing Stadium–Dusit Zoo

72: Ratchaprarop Rd.–Si Ayutthaya Rd.–Marble Temple–Samsen Rd.–Thewet

74: Rama IV Rd. (outside Soi Ngam Duphli)–Lumphini Park–Ratchadamri Rd.–World Trade Center–Pratunam-Ratchaprarop Rd.–Victory Monument

115: Silom Rd.–Rama IV Rd.–along Rama IV Rd. until Sukhumvit Rd.

116: Sathorn Nua Rd.–along Rama IV Rd. (passes Soi Ngam Duphli)–Sathorn Tai Rd.

204: Victory Monument–Ratchaprarop Rd.–World Trade Center–Siam Sq.–Bamrung Muang Rd.

A/C BUSES (BLUE-AND-WHITE, YELLOW-AND-WHITE, OR ORANGE)

#501: Wat Pho–Charoen Krung Rd.–Rama IV Rd. (near Hualamphong Railway Station)–Phayathai Rd. (Mahboonkrong Center)–Siam Sq.–along Sukhumvit Rd.

508: Sanam Luang–Bamrung Muang Rd.–Rama I Rd.–Ploenchit Rd.–outer Bangkok

510: National Assembly (Ratchavithi Rd.)–Dusit Zoo–Chitralada Palace–Victory Monument–Phahonyothin Rd.–Don Muang International Airport

511: Khaosan Rd.–Phra Sumen Rd.–Democracy Monument (Ratchadamnoen Klong Rd.)–Phetchaburi Rd.–World Trade Center–Sukhumvit Rd.

BY BOAT. **Chao Phraya River Express ferries** (6am-6:40pm, 4-25฿) are the best way to travel along the river and provide easy access to the Skytrain. Buy tickets at the booth on the pier or from the ticket collector on board. Specify your stop, as boats will otherwise stop only if there are passengers waiting. Disembark quickly and carefully.

The main stops, from north to south, are **Thewet** (for the National Library and Dusit guesthouses), **Phra Athit** (for Khaosan Rd./Banglamphu), **Thonburi Railway Pier** (for Thonburi Railway Station and Royal Barges), **Chang** (for Wat Phra Kaew and the Royal Palace), **Tien** (for Wat Pho), **Ratchawong** (for Chinatown and Hualumphong Railway Station), **Si Phraya** (for GPO), **Oriental** (for the Oriental Hotel and Silom), and **Sathorn** (for the Skytrain to Silom). During peak transit times special rush-hour express ferries with orange (10฿) or yellow (15-25฿) flags stop at only some of the major piers (6:30am-9pm and 4-7pm). Small, brown, box-like ferries with bench seats, easily confused with river taxis, shuttle across the river to every major stop (2฿). A small sign identifies each *tha* (pier).

Klongs are small canals that zig-zag through the city's interior. Thonburi, west of Chao Praya, has an extensive network, and Bangkok proper has two useful lines. **Klong Saen Saep** links Democracy Monument near Banglamphu with the area around Siam Sq. and the World Trade Center (10min.). Another route links **Klong Banglamphu** and **Klong Phadung Krung Kasem.** From Tha Banglamphu, at the Chakraphong and Phrasumen Rd. intersection, you can reach Hualumphong Railway Station (15min.). Boats run every 30min. during peak hours and every 45min. 6am-6:40pm during off-peak hours and weekends. A single trip costs 7-20฿.

Longtail boat rentals are available at almost every pier for tourist destinations on the river and *klongs*. Agree on a price before setting off. Usual rates are 600฿ for the first hour, 400฿ each additional hour.

BY SKYTRAIN. The **Skytrain** (Bangkok Mass Transit System, **BTS**), a monorail train launched on December 5, 1999 to celebrate the King's 72nd birthday, is an A/C delight. Incredibly useful for navigating Siam Sq., Silom, and Sukhumvit, the train has two lines that meet at Siam Sq. The **Sukhumvit Line** runs from Mo Chit, next to Chatuchak Market, goes past the Victory Monument to Siam Sq., continues through Sukhumvit Rd., and terminates at On Nut, beyond the Eastern Bus Terminal. The **Silom Line** runs from the National Stadium past Siam Sq. and Lumphini Park, and along part of Silom Rd., before terminating at Taksin Bridge. All stations have useful **maps. Fares** are based on distance (10-40฿), and ticket purchase is automated. Trip passes (10-15-, and 30-ride) are the most cost-effective for students; show your ISIC card (200-540฿, with ISIC 160-360฿; passes must be used within 30 days of purchase). Unlimited one-day (100฿) and three-day (280฿) passes are also available. Insert the card at the turnstile to enter the station; **hold onto it and insert it at the turnstile at your destination to leave the station.** The Skytrain operates daily 6am-midnight. There is a BTS information office in the Siam Center stop. (☎617 7340. Open daily 8am-8pm.)

THAILAND

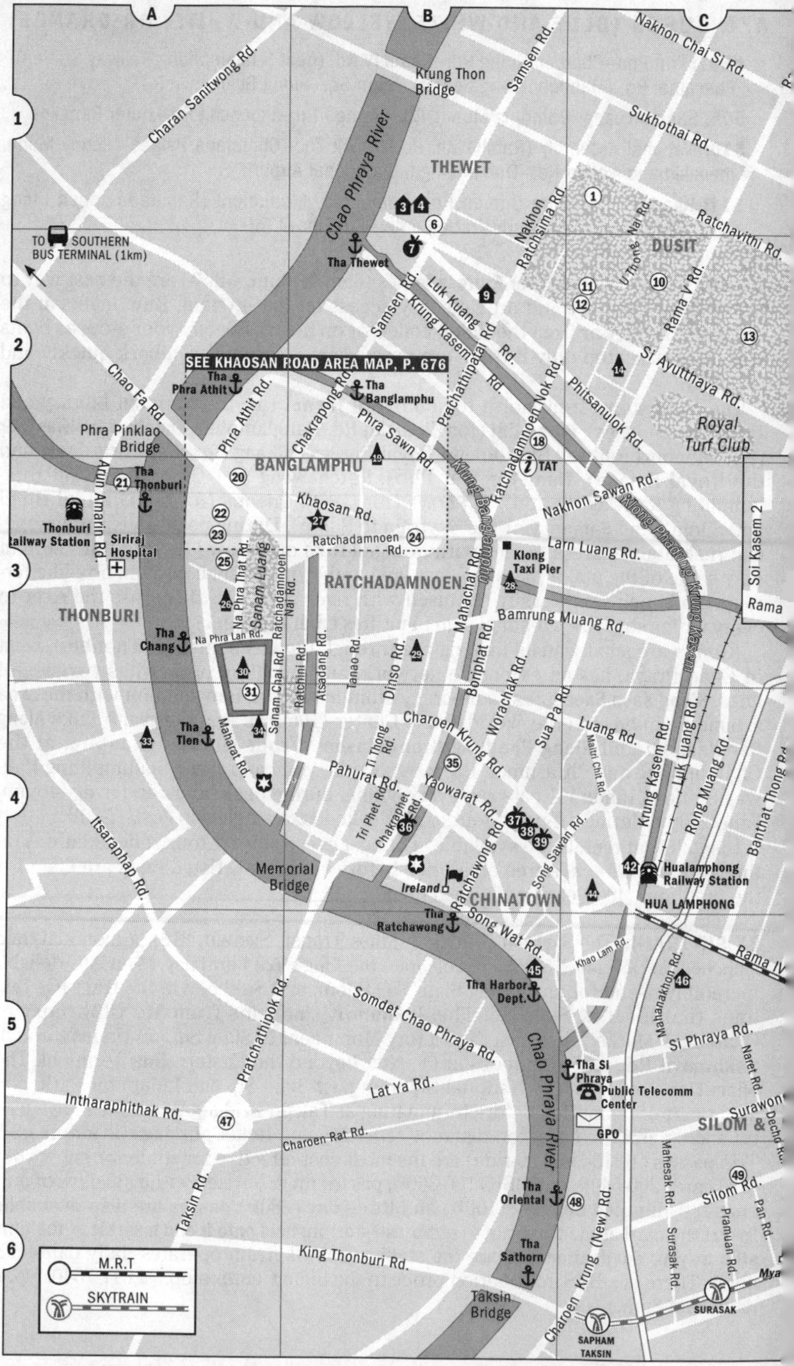

A
B
C
1
2
3
4
5
6
Charan Sanitwong Rd.
Krung Thon Bridge
Samsen Rd.
Nakhon Chai Si Rd.
Sukhothai Rd.
Chao Phraya River
THEWET
Nakhon Ratchsima Rd.
U Thong Nai Rd.
Ratchavithi Rd.
DUSIT
TO SOUTHERN BUS TERMINAL (1km)
Tha Thewet
Samsen Rd.
Krung Kasem Rd.
Luk Kuang Rd.
Prachathipatai Rd.
Rama V Rd.
Si Ayutthaya Rd.
Phitsanulok Rd.
SEE KHAOSAN ROAD AREA MAP, P. 676
Tha Phra Athit
Tha Banglamphu
Chao Fa Rd.
Phra Athit Rd.
Chakrapong Rd.
Phra Sawn Rd.
Ratchadamnoen Nok Rd.
Royal Turf Club
Phra Pinklao Bridge
TAT
BANGLAMPHU
Tha Thonburi
Arun Amarin Rd.
Khaosan Rd.
Klong Banglamphu
Nakhon Sawan Rd.
Klong Phadung Krung Kasem
Thonburi Railway Station
Siriraj Hospital
Ratchadamnoen Rd.
Larn Luang Rd.
Soi Kasem 2
Klong Taxi Pier
Na Phra That Rd.
Sanam Luang
Ratchadamnoen Nai Rd.
RATCHADAMNOEN
Mahachai Rd.
Rama
THONBURI
Bamrung Muang Rd.
Tha Chang
Na Phra Lan Rd.
Sanam Chai Rd.
Ratchini Rd.
Atsadang Rd.
Tanao Rd.
Dinso Rd.
Boriphat Rd.
Worachak Rd.
Sua Pa Rd.
Charoen Krung Rd.
Luang Rd.
Maitri Chit Rd.
Krung Kasem Rd.
Luk Luang Rd.
Rong Muang Rd.
Banthat Thong Rd.
Tha Tien
Maharat Rd.
Ti Thong Rd.
Pahurat Rd.
Yaowarat Rd.
Itsaraphap Rd.
Tri Phet Rd.
Chakraphet Rd.
Ratchawong Rd.
Song Sawan Rd.
Hualamphong Railway Station
Memorial Bridge
Ireland
CHINATOWN
HUA LAMPHONG
Tha Ratchawong
Song Wat Rd.
Khao Lam Rd.
Rama IV
Mahanakhon Rd.
Tha Harbor Dept.
Pratchathipok Rd.
Somdet Chao Phraya Rd.
Chao Phraya River
Si Phraya Rd.
Naret Rd.
Tha Si Phraya
Public Telecomm Center
Lat Ya Rd.
Intharaphithak Rd.
Surawong
GPO
SILOM &
Decho Rd.
Charoen Rat Rd.
Mahesak Rd.
Silom Rd.
Taksin Rd.
Tha Oriental
Charoen Krung (New) Rd.
Pan Rd.
Pramuan Rd.
Surasak Rd.
King Thonburi Rd.
Tha Sathorn
Mya
M.R.T
SKYTRAIN
Taksin Bridge
SURASAK
SAPHAM TAKSIN
1
3
4
6
7
9
10
11
12
13
14
18
19
20
21
22
23
24
25
26
27
28
29
30
31
33
34
35
36
37
38
39
42
44
45
46
47
48
49

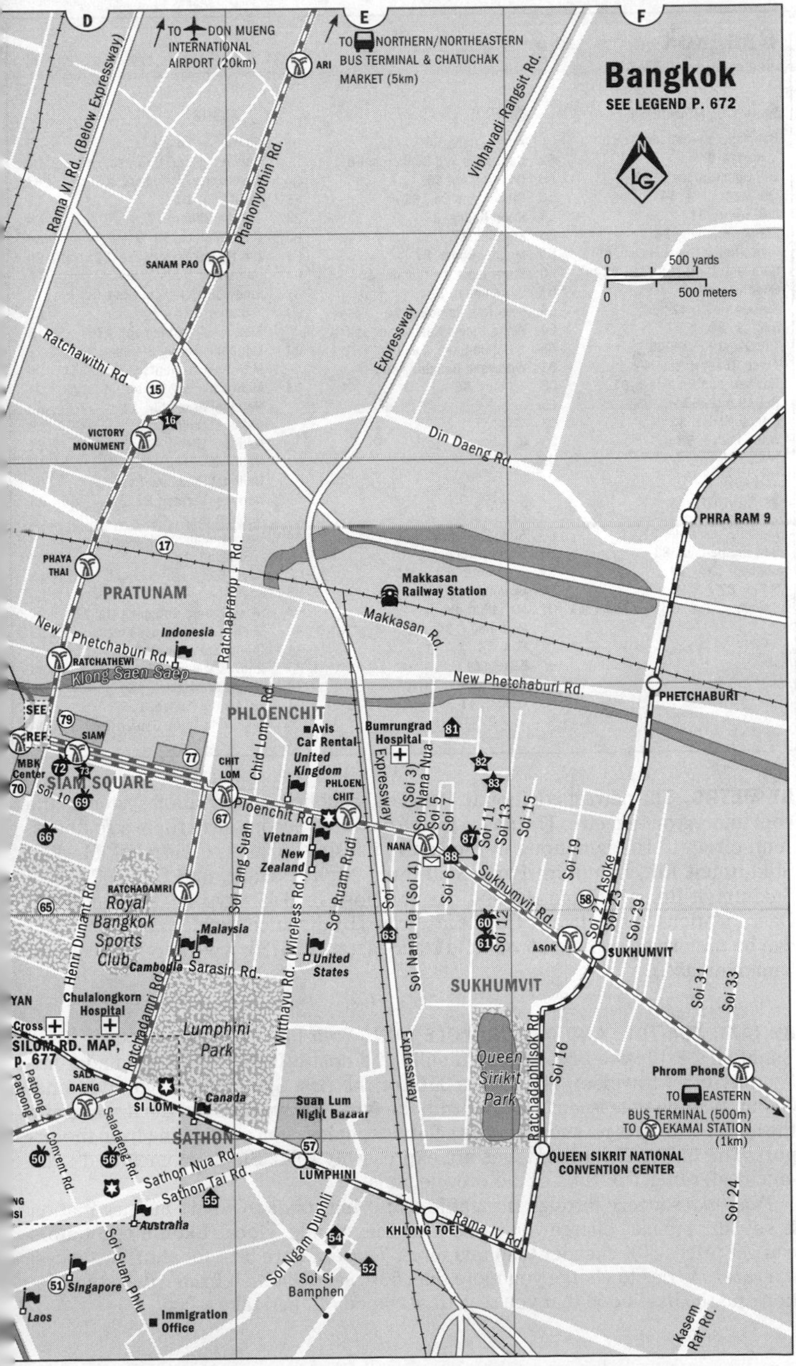
Bangkok
SEE LEGEND P. 672
D
E
F
TO DON MUENG INTERNATIONAL AIRPORT (20km)
TO NORTHERN/NORTHEASTERN BUS TERMINAL & CHATUCHAK MARKET (5km)
ARI
Rama VI Rd. (Below Expressway)
Phahonyothin Rd.
Vibhavadi Rangsit Rd.
SANAM PAO
0
500 yards
500 meters
Ratchawithi Rd.
Expressway
VICTORY MONUMENT
Din Daeng Rd.
PHRA RAM 9
PHAYA THAI
Makkasan Railway Station
PRATUNAM
Ratchaprarop Rd.
Makkasan Rd.
New Phetchaburi Rd.
Indonesia
RATCHATHEWI
Klong Saen Saep
PHETCHABURI
SEE REF
PHLOENCHIT
Chid Lom Rd.
Avis Car Rental
Bumrungrad Hospital
SIAM
MBK Center
SIAM SQUARE
CHIT LOM
United Kingdom
PHLOENCHIT
Soi 10
Ploenchit Rd.
Soi Nana Nua (Soi 3)
Soi 5
Soi 7
Soi 11
Soi 13
Soi 15
Vietnam
New Zealand
NANA
Soi Lang Suan
Soi Ruam Rudi
Sukhumvit Rd.
Soi 19
Soi 6
Soi 21 Asoke
Soi 23
Soi 29
RATCHADAMRI
Royal Bangkok Sports Club
Henri Dunant Rd.
Witthayu Rd. (Wireless Rd.)
Soi 2
Soi Nana Tai (Soi 4)
Soi 12
ASOK
SUKHUMVIT
Malaysia
Cambodia
Sarasin Rd.
United States
SUKHUMVIT
Soi 31
Soi 33
Chulalongkorn Hospital
Ratchadamri Rd.
Lumphini Park
Queen Sirikit Park
Ratchadaphisok Rd.
Soi 16
SILOM RD. MAP, p. 677
SALA DAENG
SI LOM
Canada
Suan Lum Night Bazaar
Phrom Phong
TO EASTERN BUS TERMINAL (500m)
TO EKAMAI STATION (1km)
Patpong
Saladaeng Rd.
SATHON
LUMPHINI
QUEEN SIKRIT NATIONAL CONVENTION CENTER
Convent Rd.
Sathon Nua Rd.
Sathon Tai Rd.
Australia
KHLONG TOEI
Rama IV Rd.
Soi 24
Soi Ngam Duphli
Soi Si Bamphen
Singapore
Soi Suan Phlu
Laos
Immigration Office
Kasem Rat Rd.

THAILAND

Bangkok

see map pp. 670–671

ACCOMMODATIONS

Bangkok International Youth Hostel, **9**	B2
Lee Guest House 3, **53**	E6
Lee Mansion 4, **54**	E6
P.B. Hotel, **81**	E4
Pranee Building, **96**	C3
River House Guest House, **45**	B5
Sala Thai Daily Mansion, **52**	E6
Shanti Lodge, **3**	B1
Station Hotel, **42**	C4
Suk 11, **88**	E4
T.T. Guest House, **46**	C5
Tavee Guest House, **4**	B1
The Bed and Breakfast, **91**	C3
The Atlanta, **63**	E5
Wendy House, **92**	C3
White Lodge, **94**	C3
YWCA, **55**	D6

NIGHTLIFE

Banana Leaf Cafe, **27**	B2
Bed Supperclub, **83**	E4
Concept CM^2, **73**	D4
Q Bar, **82**	E4
Saxophone Pub and Restaurant, **16**	D2

FOOD

Anna's Cafe, **56**	D6
Cabbages and Condoms, **60**	E5
Cha Cha An, **69**	D4
Crepes and Co., **61**	E5
Hoon Kuang, **38**	B4
KP Suki, **37**	B4
Moghul Room, **87**	E4
Royal India Restaurant, **36**	B4
Si Amnouai, **7**	B2
Sam Tam Paradise, **72**	D4
White Orchid Restaurant and Coffee Shop, **39**	B4
Witthyakit Building Food Court, **66**	D4

WATS

Arun (Temple of Dawn), **33**	A4
Benchamabophit (Marble Temple), **14**	C2
Bowonniwet, **19**	B3
Mahathat, **26**	A3
Phra Kaew, **30**	A3
Pho, **34**	A4
Saket, **28**	B3
Suthat, **29**	B3
Traimit, **44**	C4

SIGHTS

Chitralada Palace, **13**	C2
Chulalongkorn University, **65**	D4
Democracy Monument, **24**	B3
Dusit Zoo, **10**	C2
Erawan Shrine, **77**	D4
Grand Palace, **31**	A4
Jim Thompson's House, **80**	D4
Kamthieng House, **58**	F4
King Chulalongkorn (Rama V) Statue, **12**	C2
King Taksin Monument, **47**	A5
Lumphini Boxing Stadium, **57**	E6
M.R. Kukrit's Heritage Home, **51**	D6
Mahboonkrong Center, **70**	D4
National Assembly, **11**	C2
National Gallery, **20**	A3
National Library, **6**	B1
National Museum, **23**	A3
National Stadium, **71**	D4
National Theater, **22**	A3
Oriental Hotel, **48**	C6
Ratchadamnoen Boxing Stadium, **18**	B2
Royal Barge Museum, **21**	A3
Ruen Thep, **49**	C6
Siam Square Shopping Mall, **79**	D4
Suan Pakkad Palace Museum, **17**	D3
Thammasat University, **25**	A3
Thieves Market, **35**	B4
Victory Monument, **15**	D2
Vimanmek Palace, **1**	C1
Zen World Trade Center, **77**	D4

BY METRO. The newest addition to Bangkok's public transportation system is the cool underground metro. The metro runs from Bang Sue in the north in a southeast semi-circle to Hualamphong in the south, passing through Chatuchak Market, Sukhumvit Rd., Lumphini Park, Suan Lum Night Bazaar, and Silom Rd. The Sukhumvit Rd. and Silom Rd. stations are close to BTS Skytrain Asok and Sala Daeng stations, respectively. Tickets are priced by distance (single ride 14-36฿) and can be purchased in the underground stations. (☎246 6733; www.mrta.co.th. Open 6am-midnight.)

BY TAXI, TUK-TUK, AND MOTORCYCLE TAXI. Your lungs will thank you for using Bangkok's extensive taxi system. Simple and cost-efficient, taxis are under-utilized by most travelers. The fare is 35฿ for the first 2km and 2฿ per additional 0.4km. Waiting time is also factored into the fare. Always insist on the driver using the meter—there is no such thing as a flat rate, unless you are coming from the airport. The only official extra fees are expressway tolls. Single women find taxis much safer than *tuk-tuks* or motorcycle taxis.

Tuk-tuks squeeze through the traffic that brings taxis to a halt, but negotiation is key: drivers may charge you twice what they would a local. Skillful negotiators can get prices 30% cheaper than taxi fares. *Tuk-tuks* are best for short distances; if a *tuk-tuk* tries to charge you more than 50฿, save yourself from exhaust inhalation and the likelihood that you're getting ripped off, and take a taxi.

Motorcycle-taxi drivers loiter on street corners in brightly colored vests. Though faster in traffic and 10-25% cheaper than *tuk-tuks*, motorcycle taxis carry only a single passenger, are dangerous, and require calm nerves. Travelers should insist on a helmet, as police will fine non-wearers.

TOURIST SCAMMING. *Tuk-tuk* drivers are often con artists and have been known to harass women travelers. Drivers have also been known to drive off with passenger luggage, push the skin industry, deliver passengers to expensive restaurants, or tell travelers that sights are closed and take them to jewelry and tailor shops instead. To entice ***farang,*** they offer tours of the city for low rates (10-20฿ per hr.), but all you'll get is a sales pitch and inflated prices. Beware of these words: *free, sexy, massage, jewelry, tailor shop*, and *go-go* (unless, of course, you really want to go to a masseur, jeweler, tailor, or prostitute). *Tuk-tuks* aren't all bad—just be firm and make it clear that you want to go to your intended destination and nowhere else.

BY CAR. Travelers should avoid cars, as driving in Bangkok can be dangerous. An **International Driver's Permit** and major credit card are required. Rental agencies include **Avis,** 2/12 Witthayu Rd. (☎255 5300). Renting a small sedan costs 1400-2000฿ per day, including collision insurance. Personal accident insurance costs an extra 160฿ per day. A passport, driver's license, and major credit card are needed to rent. (☎535 4052. Branch at airport. Open M-F 7am-7pm, Sa-Su 7am-6pm.)

THAILAND

PRACTICAL INFORMATION

TOURIST AND FINANCIAL SERVICES

Tourist Office: TAT, 4 Ratchadamnoen Nok Rd. (☎282 1672; www.tourismthailand.org). Ratchadamnoen Nok is the broad boulevard that begins at the 8-way intersection east of the Democracy Monument; the office is on the right, just past the tourist police station. Open daily 8:30am-4:30pm.

Tourist Information: (☎1672). Receives calls 8am-8pm. Tourist information booths are scattered throughout the city: Chakrapong Rd., opposite Khaosan Rd. (☎281 5538; open M-Sa 8:30am-5pm); and Chakraphet Rd., near the Grand Palace (☎225 7612; open daily 9:30am-5pm).

Embassies and Consulates: Cambodia, 185 Ratchadamri Rd. (☎254 6630). Consular services around the corner off Sarasin Rd. on the first *soi* on the left. 30-day visa; 2-day processing (1000฿). Open M-F 9-11am and 1:30-4pm. **China,** 57 Ratchadaphisek Rd. (☎245 7043). Open M-F 9-11:30am. **Indonesia,** 600 Phetchaburi Rd. (☎252 3135). Take regular bus #2 or 11; or A/C bus #505, 511, or 512. Open M-F 8am-noon and 1-4pm. **Laos,** 502/1-3 Soi Ramkhamhaeng 39 (☎539 6667). Visa 300฿; 2-day processing. Open M-F 8am-noon and 1-4pm. **Malaysia,** 33-35 Sathorn Tai Rd. (☎679 2190). Open M-F 8:30am-noon and 1-4pm. **Myanmar,** 132 Sathorn Nua Rd. (☎233 2237). Consular services on Pan Rd., off Sathorn Nua Rd., 1½ blocks from the Skytrain Surasak Station. 30-day visa 800฿ (inquire at embassy for up-to-date status of land crossings); 24hr. processing. Open M-F 8:30am-noon and 2-4:30pm. **Singapore,** 129 Sathorn Tai Rd. (☎286 2253). Open M-F 8:30am-noon and 1-4:30pm. **Vietnam,** 82/1 Witthayu Rd. (☎251 5836). Visa 2050฿; 2- to 3-day processing. Open M-F 8:30-11:30am and 1:30-4:30pm. (For other embassies see **Essentials,** p. 661.)

Currency Exchange: 24hr. **ATMs** abound. Those with "ATM" spelled in blue dots or with a purple hand holding an ATM card accept AmEx/Cirrus/MC/V. You can't throw a stone in Bangkok without hitting a bank, particularly in **Silom.**

American Express: Offices in Terminal 1 (☎504 3181) and Terminal 2 (☎504 3176) at Don Muang Airport. Open 24hr. Also branches at **G.M. Tour and Travel,** 273 Khaosan Rd. (☎282 3979; fax 281 0642; open M-F 9am-7pm, Sa 9am-4pm) and Sukhumvit Soi 7 (☎655 7719; open daily 10am-9pm).

LOCAL SERVICES

Luggage Storage: The **airport** is the most reliable but a bit pricey (70฿ per day). Open 24hr. Also available at **Hualamphong Railway Station** for 10-30฿ per day. Open daily 4am-11pm. Guesthouses may also offer this service, but it may not be as secure.

Bookstores: Aporia Books, 131 Tanao Rd. (☎629 2552), opposite the end of Khaosan Rd. One of the best bookshops in Bangkok, with new and used books for sale, trade, or rent. Open daily 9am-8pm. **Used bookstores** are very common in the Khaosan area; Mango Lagoon Hotel runs a great one (open daily 9am-7pm).

GLBT Resources: *Metro* (above) has extensive gay nightlife listings. *Thai Guys* is a gay newsletter and guide to gay life in Bangkok, published 10 times yearly and distributed free at most gay venues.

THAILAND

EMERGENCY AND COMMUNICATIONS

Tourist Police: Tourist-specific complaints handled. Most useful office located next to TAT, 4 Ratchadamnoen Nok Rd. (☎282 1144). All others will refer you here. **Branches** at 2911 Unico House Bldg., Soi Lang Suan (☎652 1721), off Ploenchit Rd. in Siam Sq., and at the corner of Khaosan and Chakraphonh Rd. English spoken. 24hr. booths opposite Dusit Thani Hotel in Lumphini Park and at Don Muang International Airport.

Pharmacy: Fortune Pharmacy (Banglamphu), in front of Khaosan Palace Hotel on Khaosan Rd. Open daily 9am-2am. **Siam Drug** (Silom/Financial), at the cul-de-sac of Patpong 2 Rd. Open daily 11am-3:30pm. Many pharmacies cluster on **Sukhumvit Road** between Soi Nana and Soi II. Most open daily 8am-late.

Medical Services: Bumrungrad Hospital, 33/3 Sukhumvit Soi 3 (Soi Nana; operator ☎667 1000, emergency 667 2999). BTS: Nana. Thailand's only internationally accredited hospital. Open 24hr. **Chulalongkorn Hospital,** 1873 Rama IV Rd. (☎252 8181). Ambulance service. The best public hospital is **Siriraj Hospital** (Thonburi), 2 Pran Nok Rd. (☎411 0241). Take regular bus #19 from Sanam Luang. 24hr. ambulance. Cheapest vaccinations at **Red Cross Society's Queen Saovabha Institute** on Rama IV Rd.

Telephones: Make domestic calls at "cardphone" booths (5฿ per 3min.) and international calls at yellow "international cardphone" booths. Upper right metal button connects directly to an AT&T operator. Offices offering 10-15฿ international calls abound on Khaosan Rd. The **Public Telecommunication Service Center** (☎614 2261), next to GPO, offers fax and telex. Open 24hr.

Internet Access: Try **Khaosan Road** and all other guesthouse areas listed. Khaosan rates 40฿ per hr. Elsewhere in Bangkok 60฿ per hr.

Post Offices: GPO (☎233 0700), in CAT building on Charoen Krung Rd. near Soi 32. *Poste Restante*. Mail held for 2 months. Pick-up fee 1฿ per letter, 2฿ for parcels. Open M-F 8am-8pm, Sa-Su 8am-1pm. **Banglamphu Office,** off Khaosan Rd.; turn left onto Tanao Rd. and walk to the corner of Kraisi Rd. *Poste Restante.* Open M-F 8:30am-5:30pm, Sa 9am-noon. **Patpong Office,** 113/6-7 Thanon Surawong Center. Head up Patpong 1 Rd. and turn left on Surawong Rd.; the post office is at the end of the next dead-end *soi* on the left. Open M-F 8:30am-4:30pm, Sa 9am-noon. **Sukhumvit Rd.**

Office, 118-122 Sukhumvit Rd. (☎251 7972), between Soi 4 (Nana Tai) and Landmark Plaza. International calls 8am-10pm. Open M-F 8:30am-5:30pm, Sa 9am-noon. To track packages, go to www.thailandpost.com.

Postal Code: GPO 10210; Banglamphu 10203; Patpong 10500; Sukhumvit 10110; *Poste Restante* 10112.

ACCOMMODATIONS

Accommodations in Bangkok are as varied as the exotic fruits lining its streets. Options range from dirt-cheap flophouses to five-star hotels and every level of guesthouse in between. Always ask to see rooms to discern differences in quality.

BANGLAMPHU AND KO RATTANAKOSIN

Within walking distance of Wat Phra Kaew, Wat Pho, the Grand Palace, and the National Museum, this hub functions as a kind of decompression chamber for international travelers and budget backpackers as they enter Thailand. **Khaosan Road,** a dubious backpacker mecca, has cheap digs, free-flowing *Chang* beer, and fake designer clothing. Rooms are often cramped, noisy, and full—reserve ahead by phone. The area just west between Chakrapong Rd. and Phra Athit Rd. is less noisy, just as popular with the *farang*, and can have more rooms available. To get to Banglamphu, take the Chao Phraya River Express to Banglamphu Pier. You can also take Airport Bus AB2, regular bus #15, or A/C bus #511.

New Siam Guest House, 21 Soi Chana Songkram (☎282 4554). On the small *soi* that connects the *wat* to the river. This recently renovated guesthouse is worth the extra *baht*. Very popular, and the sheets have maps of Thailand on them. 24hr. Internet 1฿ per min. Singles 200฿; doubles 245฿, with bath 395฿, with bath and A/C 500฿. ❷

Wild Orchid Villa, 8 Soi Chana Songkram (☎629 4378), across from New Siam. The brightly colored rooms are a welcome change from many Khaosan guesthouses. Extremely popular 24hr. restaurant and bar. Singles with fan 200฿; doubles with fan 290฿, with bath and A/C 550฿. ❷

D & D Inn, 68-70 Khaosan Rd. (☎629 0526). Rooftop pool here is party central. New section offers Khaosan address and impersonal room with A/C and bath. Very popular: book ahead by phone. Singles 450฿; doubles 600฿. Low-season discounts. ❸

DUSIT AND THEWET

Just a quiet bus ride, boat trip, or walk from the sights of Ko Rattanakosin and Banglamphu, the guesthouses behind the National Library in Thewet are some of Bangkok's best-kept secrets. Some taxi and *tuk-tuk* drivers don't even know where this area is; be sure to tell them to go to Thewet, behind the National Library. Conversely, Dusit is dominated by heavily trafficked, wide avenues and large government buildings, and does not have many accommodation options. To get to Dusit, take the Chao Phraya River Express to Thewet. You can also take regular buses #16, 23, 30, 32, 33, 72, or A/C bus #505. One bus from each *soi* stops near Thewet; check local listings for more complete schedules.

Shanti Lodge, 37 Si Ayutthaya Soi 16 (☎281 2497). Billed as "The Oasis of Bangkok," Shanti is one of the best choices in the city. With smoking and shoes prohibited inside, the place feels like paradise. In high season reserve 1-2 weeks ahead. Dorms 100฿; doubles 300฿, with shower 400-500฿, with A/C and shower 600฿. ❷

Tavee Guest House, 83 Si Ayutthaya Soi 14 (☎280 1447). Cozy common spaces with natural wood furniture and a popular restaurant open 24hr. Rooms are clean and tidily decorated. Dorms 90฿; singles 200฿; doubles 250฿, with bath 300฿, with A/C 350฿. ❷

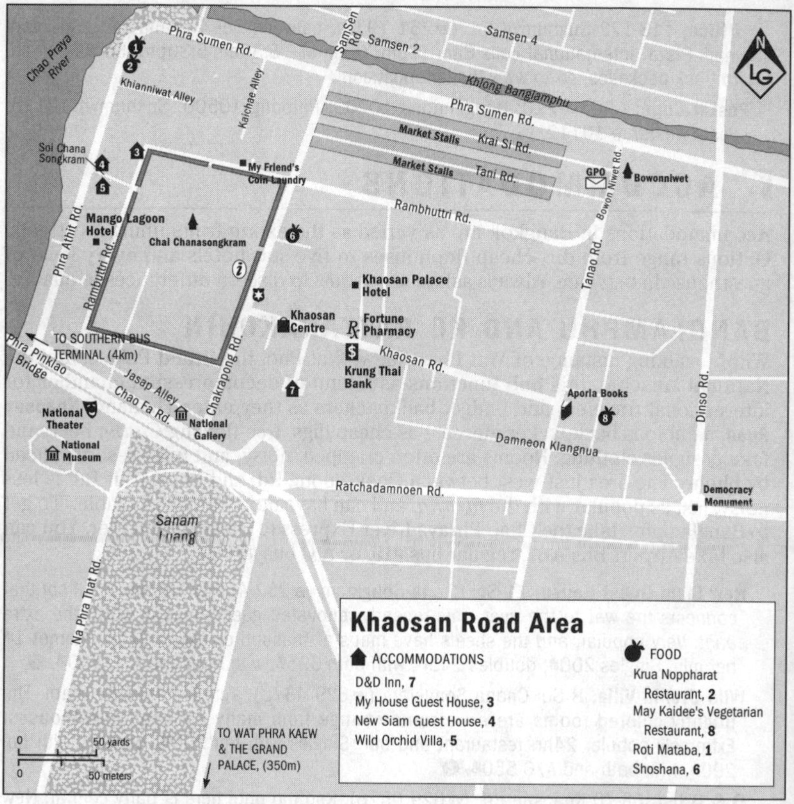

Bangkok International Youth Hostel (HI), 25/2 Phitsanulok Rd. (☎281 0361). Head south on Nakhon Ratchasima Rd. and turn right on Phitsanulok Rd.; it's 20m on the right. Spacious dorm rooms. Sex-segregated. No alcohol, and smoking in permitted areas only. HI members only; non-members can buy a year-long membership on the spot for 300฿ or 50฿ per night. Dorms 70฿, with A/C 120฿; singles with A/C and bath 280฿; doubles with fan 250฿, A/C, and bath 350฿. ❶

CHINATOWN, PAHURAT, AND HUALAMPHONG

A notch below those in other neighborhoods, Chinatown accommodations line **Yaowarat Road, Pahurat Road, Chakraphet Road,** and **Rong Muang Road.** Travelers staying here are either evading *farang* hordes or jumping on and off early-morning trains. Chinatown offers few budget rooms that are clean and safe. Some are rip-offs, others welcome only Asians, and many are brothels. To get to Chinatown, Pahurat, and Hualamphong, take the Chao Phraya River Express to Ratchawong. You can also take regular buses #1, 4, 25, 73, or A/C bus #501. The boat taxi is easy and enjoyable.

T.T. Guest House, 516-518 Soi Sawang, Si Phraya Rd. (☎236 2946; ttguesthouse@hotmail.com). Exit Hualamphong, take a left on Rama IV Rd., turn right on Mahanakhon Rd., and take the 1st left; it's a 15min. walk or 30฿ *tuk-tuk* ride total. Midnight lockout. Reserve ahead. Dorms 100฿; singles 160฿, with window 200฿; doubles 250฿. ❷

River House Guest House, 768 Soi Panurangsri (☎234 5429). From Tha Harbor Department, exit the pier, turn left on Soi Duang Tawan, and follow the noise. The neighborhood is every bit as colorful as Chinatown. Women walking alone in the area at night may feel uncomfortable. Spacious rooms with A/C and TV. Doubles 690฿. ❹

Station Hotel (☎214 2794), opposite the Hualamphong Railway Station. Entrance is down the small *soi.* Good for those with a train to catch, but there's no other reason to stay here. All rooms have private bath. Singles 250฿; doubles 250฿, with A/C 400฿. ❷

SILOM ROAD

Although towering skyscrapers dominate **Silom Road,** the surrounding area is home to diverse neighborhoods. On **Pan Road,** a Burmese community lives between the Myanmar Embassy and the Hindu temple. The world-famous **Patpong** red light district explores the raunchier side of Bangkok, while the wealthy saunter in and out of the Oriental Hotel. To get to Silom Rd., take the Chao Phraya River Express to Oriental or Sathom/Central Pier to access the Skytrain. Take the Skytrain to Saladaeng. You can also take regular buses #15, 76, 77, 115, or A/C buses #502, 504, 505, 515.

Sala Thai Daily Mansion, 15 Soi Sapankoo (☎287 1436). From Rama IV Rd., walk up Soi Ngam Duphli and turn left onto Soi Si Bamphen; take the 1st *soi* to the left and then turn right. Sizable rooms and rooftop garden. Singles 200-300฿; doubles 300-400฿. ❷

Lee Mansion 4, 9 Soi Sapankoo (☎286 7874). All rooms are clean and bright with small balconies and private baths. Small rooms 160฿; large 200฿. ❷

Lee Guest House 3, 13 Soi Sapankoo (☎679 7045), next to Sala Thai, offers clean rooms with fan. Singles 120฿; doubles 150฿, with private bath 200฿. ❷

YWCA, 13 Sathorn Tai Rd. (☎679 1280), accessible through BMW dealership on Sathorn Rd. Women only. Bookstore, badminton courts, and restaurant. Singles 750฿; doubles 1000฿. Monthly rate: singles 8000฿; doubles 9500฿, plus service and utilities. 5% discount for members. 3% credit card charge. ❺

SIAM SQUARE

In the shadow of Bangkok's ritziest malls, **Soi Kasem San 1** lies off Rama I Rd., opposite the National Stadium. Quieter than Khaosan, Siam Sq. claims a loyal following of travelers. Prices run high, but accommodations are a good deal for those willing to splurge a little. Proximity to the Skytrain makes much of Bangkok's nightlife and the Eastern Bus Terminal easily accessible. Guesthouses can be reached by taking Exit 3 at the National Stadium Skytrain stop, one stop away from Siam Sq. To get to Siam Square, take the Skytrain to Siam Sq. You can also take regular buses #15, 25, 204, or A/C bus #501.

Wendy House, 36/2 Soi Kasem 1 (☎214 1149). This popular guesthouse is clean and simple. Convenience sets it apart from its neighbors. All rooms have A/C and private hot water bath. Internet 65฿ per hr. Laundry 50฿ per kg. Reserve ahead. Doubles 550฿, weekly 3465฿, with TV and fridge 650฿/4095฿; triples 750฿/4725฿. ❹

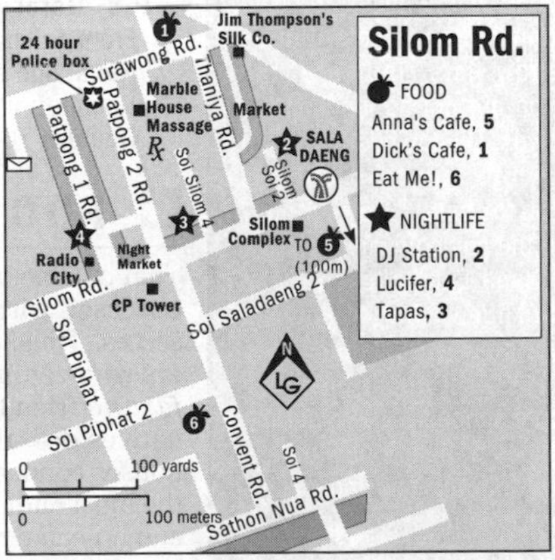

RED LIGHT, GREEN LIGHT

Love it or loathe it, Bangkok's red light district cannot be denied. Three Bangkok locales—Patpong, Nana, and Soi Cowboy—host a concentration of "entertainment centers."

Most innocent are regular bars staffed by Thai women, who sit with male customers as they drink. Next are hostess bars, almost exclusively for Japanese tourists. Well-dressed Japanese women wait to accompany their clients into karaoke bars for food, drinks, and singing. Third are go-go bars, which feature topless and/or bottomless dancing, in addition to topless and bottomless girls for "company." Many of these have back rooms for live sex shows. Needless to say, additional "services" can be purchased at any of these locations.

At first sight, Patpong appears to be another of Bangkok's tourist attractions, with families and couples roaming the streets. But as the "show lists" indicate, the goings-on are not as innocent as the crowds. Go-gos host plenty of older white men and curious younger tourists. "Boy go-gos" provide the gay equivalent.

The Nana Entertainment Complex (Sukhumvit Soi 4) and Soi Cowboy (between Sukhumvit Soi 21 and 23) set about their mission more seriously. There are the same types of bars, but with less wide-eyed *farang* and more business proceedings.

The Bed and Breakfast, 36/42-43 Soi Kasem 1 (☎215 3004). Fairly clean rooms and steel frame beds. A/C, phone, and hot shower. For the price, it's a respectable enough place to hang your hat. Breakfast included. Reserve ahead Nov.-Feb. Singles 380฿; doubles 480-550฿; triples 650฿. ❸

White Lodge, 36/8 Soi Kasem 1 (☎216 8867). Bright white halls and the odd nice piece of furniture give this place a cheery feel. All rooms with A/C, private bath, and telephone. Singles and doubles 400฿. ❸

Pranee Building, 931/12 Soi Kasem 1 (☎216 3181). You pay more for location, not luxury. Doubles 400฿, with hot-water bath 450฿; triples 500฿. ❸

SUKHUMVIT ROAD

Beneath the Skytrain, Sukhumvit Rd.'s accommodations boast proximity to some of Bangkok's trendiest nightlife and great restaurants. The area also hosts a red light scene second only to Patpong. The area is popular with expats and is one of the best places to find long-term accommodation. To get to Sukhumvit Rd., take the Skytrain to Nana or Asok. You can also take regular buses #2, 25, 38, 40, 48, 90, or A/C buses #501, 508, 511, 513.

Suk 11, 1/13 Sukhumvit Rd. Soi 11 (☎253 5927; www.suk11.com), 10m down the *soi* on the left. All rooms have A/C, and are worth every *baht;* baths have hot water. Internet access. Dorms 250฿; singles 450฿, with bath 500฿; doubles 550฿/600฿. ❷

The Atlanta, 78 Sukhumvit Rd. Soi 2 (☎252 6069), at the very end of the road. 60s character, style, and sass. Singles with fan, balcony, and bath 330฿, with A/C and hot water 450฿; doubles 450฿/570฿; triples 570฿/690฿. Funky, spacious suites also available–singles 500฿; doubles 620฿; triples 740฿. ❸

P.B. Hotel, 40 Sukhumvit Rd. Soi 3 (☎651 1525). From Sukhumvit Rd., head up Soi 3, also called Soi Nana, and turn down the alley across from Bumrungrad Hospital; it's on the left. Very nice hotel-style rooms. Doubles 700฿. ❹

FOOD

Thai cuisine is world-renowned, but no one is more obsessed with and proud of it than the Thais themselves. Thus, they become visibly excited by travelers who venture away from the Thai-Western fare of *farang*-friendly restaurants to eat food the way the natives do—right from the street. While most guesthouses connect to overpriced Thai and Western cafes, the most authentic Thai victuals are served from carts and no-name restaurants lining back alleys.

BANGLAMPHU AND KO RATTANAKOSIN

For good foodstalls, stroll down **Soi Rambuttri, Krai Si Road** (in the evening), or **Phra Chan Road** (during the day) opposite **Thammasat University.** The university's **cafeteria** has good cheap grub. During the weekday lunch hour, vendors catering to Thai professionals serve a diverse selection of food. On weekends, hawkers hang out in the area around **Sanam Luang. Khaosan Road** bursts with overpriced Thai and Western cuisine. One or two blocks north on **Tani Road** and at **Wat Chai Chanasongkram,** foodstalls fry noodles and rice dishes all day and into the night.

Roti Mataba, at the bend in Phra Athit Rd. where it becomes Phra Sumen Rd. This roadside corner is home to some of the best Muslim Thai food in the area. Abundant breakfast *roti* options (8-20฿). Open Tu-Su 7am-10pm. ❶

May Kaidee's Vegetarian Restaurant (☎282 5702). Walk to Tanao Rd., at the end of Khaosan Rd. Turn right, a quick left, and left again down the first *soi;* it's 50m down. Sit on a street-side stool and suck on a sweet Thai specialty like black sticky-rice with coconut milk and fruit (35฿). May Kaidee has a book of recipes (350฿) and offers cooking classes (1000฿) that focus on healthy vegetarian cooking. Open daily 9am-11pm. ❷

Shoshana, on Chakrapong Rd. Facing the temple at the end of Khaosan Rd., turn right and right again at the first alley. Specializes in Israeli and Middle Eastern cuisine. *Falafel* (50฿). *Shawarma* (60฿). Vegetarian options. Open daily 11am-11pm. ❷

Krua Noppharat Restaurant, 130-132 Phra Athit Rd. (☎281 7578). Thai professionals pack in at lunch to enjoy the authentic Thai food at this award-winning restaurant. Fried rice with pork 30฿. Chicken with cashew nuts 60฿. Open M-Sa 10:30am-9pm. ❷

DUSIT AND THEWET

The pavement opposite the guesthouses on **Si Ayutthaya Road** bustles with foodstalls, as does the market at the end of the road by Thewet pier. Shanti Lodge, Tavee Guesthouse, and Sri Ayuttaya (p. 675) all serve quality Thai food at reasonable prices. With no English sign, **Si Amnouai** ❶, on Si Ayutthaya Rd. at the intersection with Samsen Rd. opposite the National Library, serves the same dishes as the stalls outside at the same prices (20฿)—only indoors. (Open daily 5am-late.) **Bangkok Youth Hostel Cafe** ❷, 25/2 Phitsanulok Rd., has a mostly Thai clientele despite international flags. The menu features noodles, curries, and Western treats (60-130฿). Open daily 11am-10:30pm.

CHINATOWN, PAHURAT, AND HUALAMPHONG

The center of **Yaowarat Road** is a treasure of outdoor dining, and the *sois* that branch off it overflow with culinary delights prepared right on the street. This area requires more adventurous tastes: shark-fin soups and abalone dishes are specialties. Sampling these delicacies on the street is much cheaper than trying them in a restaurant (sharkfin soup in a restaurant runs 2000฿ and up; on the street it's 300-600฿). As you move down Yaowarat it shifts from Chinese to Indian; excellent Indian restaurants are plentiful near where **Chakraphet Road** meets **Pahurat Road.**

Royal India Restaurant, 392/1 Chakraphet Rd. (☎221 6565), near the river; look for the sign on the left as you come from Yaowarat Rd. Menu features delicious Indian dishes (some vegetarian) at 50-100฿. The *thali*–curry, *masala,* and *naan* set menu (150-190฿)–saves you from making a difficult choice. Open daily 10am-10pm. ❸

Hoon Kuang (☎623 0640), on Yaowarat Rd. a block west of the White Orchid Hotel. Delicious Chinese classics in the heart of Chinatown. Extensive vegetarian and seafood options. Sweet-and-sour tofu 100฿. Prawn with asparagus 200฿. Open 11am-10pm. ❸

White Orchid Restaurant and Coffee Shop, 415 Yaowarat Rd., in the White Orchid Hotel. Famed *dim sum* (30฿ per dish, buy 5 get 1 free) and Friday night all-you-can-eat dinner buffet (6-10pm, 160฿) are reliably delicious. The upstairs restaurant specializes in expensive delicacies like sharkfin soup (2200฿) and bird's nest soup with seafood (135฿). Open 24hr. for late-night snacking. ❷

KP Suki, 233 Yaowarat Rd. (☎222 6573), at the intersection with Ratchawong Rd. Serves a sanitized version of the noodle and soup dishes found on the street. Their specialty is a chicken broth soup you cook at your table to which you add meat, dumplings, and veggies. Most noodle and rice dishes 35-70฿. Open 10:30am-10pm. ❷

SILOM ROAD

Silom Road brims with delicious, expensive restaurants, particularly near Silom Center. Small tourist cafes set up at night on **Surawong Road** opposite Patpong. Look for local fare along **Convent Road** and inside **Soi Ngam Duphli.** If you feel daring, try the food cart opposite Dick's Cafe—it serves fried scorpions, grasshoppers, and milky white grubs. For some power protein, try the worm salad.

Eat Me!, 1/6 Soi Piphat 2 (☎238 0931), off Convent Rd. to the left. Creativity and food collide in this stylish restaurant. Photography and sculpture downstairs, delicious entrees upstairs (300-500฿). Live jazz F-Su 8-11pm complements shots of chocolate vodka. As luxurious as a Thai massage. Open daily 3pm-1am. AmEx/MC/V. ❺

Anna's Cafe (☎632 0619; reservations at www.annascafes.com), toward the end of Saladaeng Rd. heading away from Silom Rd. Named after Anna Leonowens, the English governess to the children of King Rama IV (made famous first in the book *Anna and the King,* and then in *The King and I*), this restaurant has some of the best dining in Silom for some of the lowest prices. Entrees 75-200฿. Open 11:30am-10pm. ❹

Dick's Cafe, 894/7-8 Soi Pratoochai (☎637 0078; www.dickscafe.com). From Patpong, cross Surawong Rd. and walk two *sois* to the right. This classy gay cafe and bar draws a *farang* male clientele of all ages. Well-lit with wicker chairs, sofas, and modern-art decor, it's perfect for lunch or late-night socializing. Thai and Western food 60-130฿. Beer from 70฿. Cocktails 140฿. Open 11am-2am. ❸

THAILAND

SIAM SQUARE

Siam Sq. is bursting with great restaurants—if you like American fast food. If not, in the afternoon and evening, vendors grill up juicy meats in front of the **National Stadium** on Rama I Rd., at the mouth of **Soi Kasem 1,** and along the *soi* weaving through Siam Sq. Cafes punctuate the *soi* around the square while fast-food chains and Ramen shops pop up in the shopping centers. The **MBK** has an inexpensive Asian food court on the sixth floor. Sidewalk restaurants dot **Ratchaprarop Road** and **Soi Wattanasin** opposite the Indra Regent Hotel.

Sam Tam Paradise, 392/14 Siam Sq. Soi 5 (☎251 4880). Young university students come here in droves to enjoy exotic salads in this hip new restaurant. No English menu, but waiters will help you pick out a good selection of dishes. Usually includes a mango or papaya salad (55฿), a meat dish (70฿), and soup (50฿). Open 11:15am-9pm. ❸

Cha Cha An, 484 Siam Sq. (☎252 5038), across from the Novotel Hotel in the parking lot at the end of Soi 6. As lively as a karaoke bar, but without the discordant singing, Cha Cha An serves up steaming hot *yakitori* (50-200฿), finger foods, and well-portioned pieces of sushi (set dinners 200-350฿). Open daily 11am-10:30pm. AmEx/MC/V. ❹

Witthyakit Building Food Court. Walk down Siam Sq. Soi 4, cross Soi 10, and at the next intersection, enter the basement of the tall building resembling a parking structure. Students and faculty from nearby Chulalongkorn University pack this food court for dozens of Thai dishes at 15฿ per plate. Open daily 11:15am-12:45pm. ❶

SUKHUMVIT ROAD

Sukhumvit Rd. brims with expensive quality restaurants and tourist cafes for wealthier travelers. If you want to burn *baht* for a fancy meal and get your money's worth, this is where to do it. The usual foodstalls set up on many *soi* at lunchtime to sell Thai dishes for 20-40฿. **Soi 3/1** specializes in Middle Eastern cuisine.

Cabbages & Condoms, 10 Sukhumvit Rd. Soi 12 (☎229 4632). Whether you eat the exceptional Thai food in the beautiful garden or in the A/C restaurant, it is guaranteed not to cause pregnancy. Free condom with the bill. Most dishes 80-250฿. Open daily 11am-10pm. Reserve on weekends. AmEx/V. ❷

Crepes and Co., 18/1 Sukhumvit Rd., Soi 12 (☎653 3990), past Cabbages & Condoms. Every type of crepe: sweet, rich, Western, Thai–or design your own (80-250฿, most around 150฿). Spanish-style *tapas* 90-130฿. Incredibly friendly and service-oriented staff. Open daily 9am-midnight. AmEx/MC/V. ❷

Moghul Room, 1/16 Sukhumvit Rd. Soi 11 (☎253 4465), down the *soi* opposite "Sea Food Center." One of Bangkok's best Indian restaurants. Muslim and Indian curries. Vegetarian dishes 80-90฿. Vegetarian set menu 180฿, with meat 220฿. Open daily 11am-11pm. AmEx/MC/V. ❷

SIGHTS

BANGLAMPHU AND KO RATTANAKOSIN

With its many points of interest, Ko Rattanakosin requires at least an entire day to explore fully. Although extremely touristed, **Wat Phra Kaew** and the **Grand Palace** remain two of the most impressive sights in Bangkok. Chao Phraya River Express (Tha Chang) and buses (#1, 25, 47, 82; A/C #543, 544) stop near the compound. History and art lovers will be glued to the treasures in the nearby **National Museum.** A circuit of **monasteries** is also nearby.

WAT PHRA KAEW (TEMPLE OF THE EMERALD BUDDHA) AND THE GRAND PALACE. The Temple of the Emerald Buddha was initially the Royal Chapel of the Chakri Dynasty. Inside the *bot* is the actual **Emerald Buddha,** Thailand's most sacred Buddha figure. The Emerald Buddha was discovered in 1434, when lightning shattered a *chedi* in Chiang Rai and an abbot found a stucco Buddha inside. He removed all the stucco and found the glorious Emerald Buddha, made of precious jade, hidden underneath. The figure stayed in Lampang until 1468 before being carted off to Vientiane, Laos. Two hundred and fourteen years later, General Chao Phraya Chakri captured Vientiane and reclaimed the statue. In 1782, King Rama I ascended the throne, moved the capital to Bangkok, and built the Royal Chapel—Wat Phra Kaew—for the Buddha. Take a look at the frescoes that encircle the compound; the scenes are taken from the ancient Indian epic *Ramayana.*

Next door to the Temple of the Emerald Buddha is the **Grand Palace,** accessible through a gate connecting the two compounds. Heading right, the first is **Amarinda Vinichai Hall,** which once held court ceremonies. Next, **Chakri Mahaprasad Hall,** the residence of King Chulalongkorn, is a hybrid of European and Thai design. Today, the reception areas and central throne hall are used for royal ceremonies and are off-limits to mere mortal backpackers. Farther on, **Dusit Hall** is a symmetrical Thai building with a mother-of-pearl throne. Take a right after the gift shop to find the **Wat Phra Kaew Museum,** inside the Grand Palace. (*☎ 623 5500. No pictures allowed inside Wat Phra Kaew, although they are allowed elsewhere in the complex. Polite dress required: full shoes, pants, and shirts with sleeves. Shirts, long pants, and shoes are available at the entrance. Complex open daily 8:30am-3:30pm. Museum open daily 8:30am-4pm.*

200฿. Admission to Wat Phra Kaew and the Grand Palace includes admission to the Royal Thai Decorations and Coins Pavilion and the Vimanmek Palace in Dusit within 7 days of purchase. Audio guide 100฿ for 2hr.)

WAT PHO (THE TEMPLE OF THE RECLINING BUDDHA). Wat Pho is the oldest (technically, although it was completely renovated by Rama I), largest, and most architecturally spectacular temple in Bangkok. Its grounds are divided by Soi Chetuphon: one side is home to the monastery, while the other contains temple buildings. Wat Pho is also home to Thailand's first university, a monastery that taught medicine a century before Bangkok was founded. A world-famous **Thai massage school** (p. 686) is its latest achievement. *(From Wat Phra Kaew, walk around the block and take 3 left turns from the entrance. ☎ 225 9595. Open daily 9am-5pm. 20฿.)*

WAT MAHATHAT. Also known as the Temple of the Great Relic, this *wat* houses a large sitting Buddha and was home to King Rama I, who was an abbot before he took up military campaigning. Today, the temple is a famous center of Buddhist teaching and home to one of Thailand's two Buddhist colleges. The southern part of the complex offers daily English instruction in Buddhist meditation 7-10am, 1-4, and 6-8pm. *(Between Silpakorn University and Thammasat University on Na Phra That Rd., opposite Sanam Luang. For more info on meditation call ☎ 222 6011. Open daily 9am-5pm.)*

SANAM LUANG. Sanam Luang is the "national common" of Thailand and kite-fighting contests—in which the large "male" kites *(chula)* pursue fleeing smaller "female" kites *(pukpao)*—are a common sight here. *(On Na Phra That Rd.)*

NATIONAL MUSEUM. As Southeast Asia's largest museum, it is the crown jewel of Thailand's national system. King Chulalongkorn (Rama V) founded it in 1874 with the opening of a public showroom inside the Grand Palace to exhibit collections from the reign of his father. The museum has three permanent exhibition galleries: the Thai History Gallery, the Archaeology and Art History Collection, and the Decorative Arts and Ethnological Collection. *(On Na Phra That Rd. past Thammasat University. ☎ 224 1333. Open W-Su 9am-4pm, tickets sold until 3:30pm. Free tours in English W-Th 9:30am. 40฿.)*

NATIONAL GALLERY. The National Gallery contains a very small collection of classical and contemporary Thai artwork. Rooms upstairs display paintings of scenes from epics and classical plays. Downstairs, works by the novice artist King Rama VI and the considerably more talented King Rama IX are on display. *(On Chao Fa Rd. opposite the National Theater. ☎ 282 2639. Open W-Su 9am-4pm. 30฿.)*

DEMOCRACY MONUMENT. Commemorating Thailand's transition from absolute to constitutional monarchy after the Revolution of 1932, the monument is built on the site of the bloody demonstrations of May 1992, when students and citizens protested the dictatorial rule of General Suchinda Kraprayoon. *(At the intersection of Ratchadamnoen and Dinso Rd.)*

WAT SAKET. Notable for its Golden Mount (an artificial hill topped with a gilded pagoda) soaring 80m high, this popular mount was once the highest point in the city. Today, Wat Saket's 360° panoramic view and golden *chedi* reward those fit enough to make the trek to the top. *(On Worachak Rd. Open daily 7:30am-5:30pm. 10฿.)*

WAT SUTHAT. This *wat* is famous for its association with the Sao Ching Cha (Giant Swing) directly in front of the temple, and for housing Thailand's largest cast-bronze Buddha. In the past, Sao Ching Cha was the scene of several of the more curious Brahmin rituals, including one in which a priest would swing on a rope and use his teeth to try to catch money suspended 25m high. Many priests lost their lives performing this feat until a law was passed to prohibit the ritual. *(On Tithong Rd. near the Giant Swing. Open daily 8:30am-9pm. 20฿.)*

WAT BOWONNIWET. King Rama IV spent 27 years as chief abbot here, and the current king, King Bhumibol Adulyadej, spent several months as a monk here in 1956 shortly after his marriage and coronation. The *wat* is home to Thailand's second Buddhist college, Mahamakut University. Be polite and discreet. *(On the corner of Phra Sawn and Bowon Nivet Rd. in Banglamphu, near Khaosan Rd. Open daily 9am-5pm.)*

DUSIT AND THEWET

The sights of Dusit and Thewet are quieter than those in the heart of the city and make for a relaxing morning or afternoon of sightseeing.

VIMANMEK PALACE. Built of golden teak during the reign of King Chulalongkorn (Rama V), the palace is the largest teak mansion in the world. Held together with wooden pegs, the 72-room structure was the king's favorite palace from 1902 to 1906. The museum in Aphisek Dusit Hall houses an impressive collection of silver jewelry, silk, and soapstone carvings. *(Entrance is on the left on U Thong Nai Rd. Bus #70 stops nearby. Shorts and sleeveless shirts not allowed. Open daily 9:30am-4pm, last admission 3pm. 45min. tours in English every 30min. 9:30am-3:15pm. Thai dancing daily 10:30am and 2pm. 100฿, students 20฿, under age 5 free, with a Wat Phra Kaew and Grand Palace admission ticket free. Admission to the palace includes a visit to the museum, open daily 10am-4pm.)*

DUSIT ZOO. Once part of the gardens of the Chitralada Palace, Thailand's largest zoo hosts a collection of regional animals, as well as rare species, including white-handed gibbons and white bengal tigers. *(On the right on U Thong Nai Rd. Entrances also on Rama V and Ratchavithi Rd. ☎ 282 9245. Open daily 9am-6pm. 30฿, under age 10 5฿.)*

WAT BENCHAMABOPHIT (MARBLE TEMPLE). This *wat*'s symmetrical architecture and white Carrara marble walls were built in 1899 by King Chulalongkorn. The courtyard is lined with 52 bronze Buddhas that represent styles from different periods, while the garden contains sacred turtles given to the temple by worshipers. Early in the morning (6-7:30am), the monks line the streets to accept donations of food and incense. In February and May, the *wat* hosts Buddhist festivals and candlelight processions around the *bot*. *(On the right of Si Ayutthaya after the Ratchadamnoen Nok Rd. intersection. Take bus #72. Open daily 8:30am-5:30pm. 20฿.)*

OTHER SIGHTS. Past the Si Ayutthaya Rd. traffic light, Ratchadamnoen Nok Rd. opens into Suan Amphon, site of the revered **statue of King Chulalongkorn (Rama V).** This beloved king, who ruled from 1868 to 1910, is remembered for abolishing slavery, modernizing Thai society (he introduced the first indoor bathroom, among other things), and fending off power-hungry British and French colonialists. On October 23, the anniversary of his death, patriotic citizens pay homage here.

Behind the statue, guarded by an iron fence and a well-kept garden, stands the former **National Assembly** (Parliament Building). This domed building was commissioned as a Royal Palace by King Chulalongkorn in 1908 to replace his old residence. Originally called Anantasamakhom, it was patterned after St. Peter's Basilica in Rome. Following the 1932 coup, the palace became the National Assembly building, but the Assembly has since been moved to Dusit.

CHINATOWN, PAHURAT, AND HUALAMPHONG

Chinese immigrants settled southeast of the royal center along the Chao Phraya River in the 18th century, after construction of the Grand Palace evicted them from Bangkok's first Chinatown. Today, this area is called **Yaowarat,** after the road that runs through Chinatown, or **Sampaeng,** after the smaller road that runs parallel to Yaowarat one block south. On the western edge of Chinatown is the Pahurat District, where the population abruptly turns from Chinese to Indian and textiles take over as the main ware.

WAT TRAIMIT. The only major temple in this area is home to the Giant Golden Buddha—a 3m, five-ton, 700-year-old Sukhothai-style gold statue. It is the largest pure-gold Buddha image in the world. When the Burmese sacked Ayutthaya, residents saved the statue by covering it with stucco. Its identity remained secret until 1955, when the statue slipped from a crane while being transported to Wat Traimit. Cracks developed in the plaster, the stucco was removed, and the Golden Buddha was rediscovered. *(Main entrance on Yaowarat Rd. near Charoen Krung Rd.; a smaller entrance on Traimit Rd., accessible by bus #73. ☎225 9775. Open daily 8am-5pm. 20฿.)*

SILOM ROAD

M.R. KUKRIT'S HERITAGE HOME. M.R. Kukrit is one of the most colorful characters of 20th-century Thailand. Born in 1911 to a princely family descended from Rama I and II, Kukrit was of the last generation to be raised in the Grand Palace during the time of the absolute monarchy. Kukrit was an influential political leader, founder of Thailand's first political party, prime minister, and amateur actor, dancer, and author. He died in 1995. The home consists of five traditional Thai houses set on two beautiful acres and preserved largely as they were during Kukrit's lifetime. *(19 Soi Phra Pinit. From BTS: Chong Nonsi, walk south down Norathiwat Rajanakarin, cross busy Sathon Rd., and take the 2nd left. ☎286 6185. Open Sa-Su and holidays 10am-5pm. 50฿. Free 30min. guided tour in English.)*

THAILAND

LUMPHINI PARK. Lumphini Park, the largest park in Bangkok and an oasis in its glass and steel, makes for some of the best people-watching in the city. In the mornings, the Chinese practice tai chi while others rent paddle boats and cruise the park's lakes. During the day, locals and expats relax at cafes along Ratchadamri Rd. The early evening sees a virtual carnival of runners, jazzercisers, and sports enthusiasts crowding the paths. *(The park is bordered by Ratchadamri, Rama IV, Sarasin, and Witthayu Rd. and is accessible from Silom by regular bus #15, 77, or 115, or from Siam Sq. and Banglamphu by regular bus #15. Skytrain: Sala Daeng. Open daily 5:30am-7pm.)*

ORIENTAL HOTEL. Founded by two Danish sea captains, the Oriental is one of the world's most famous hotels. H.N. Andersen built the grand Italianate building in 1887, which still stands as the "Authors' Residence" wing and shelters some of the hotel's finest, most expensive rooms. Some suites are available "on application" only. *(48 Oriental Ave. along the Chao Phraya River. Chao Phraya River Express: Tha Oriental.)*

SIAM SQUARE

Famed for its shopping malls, Siam Sq. has some sights and easy Skytrain access.

JIM THOMPSON'S HOUSE. This elegant house was home to American Jim Thompson, who revitalized the Thai silk industry after World War II and later disappeared in 1967 during a trip to Malaysia. Actually a combination of six teak buildings, the house is home to one of Thailand's best collections of Ayutthaya- and Rattanakosin-period art. Admission includes a tour in English. Jim Thompson's flagship store, 9 Surawong Rd., is open daily 9am-9pm. *(Soi Kasem San 2, opposite the National Stadium. Take any Rama I Rd. bus. Skytrain: National Stadium. ☎612 3744. Tours required; every 10min. Open daily 9am-4:30pm. 100฿, students 50฿.)*

SUAN PAKKAD PALACE MUSEUM. Suan Pakkad's eight traditional Thai houses hold the private collections of their Royal Highnesses Prince and Princess Chumbhot of Wagara Svarga. A very comprehensive and informative guided tour takes visitors through rooms filled with artifacts from the Ban Chiang civilization and the Sukhothai, Ayutthayan, and Bangkok Periods. *(352 Si Ayutthaya Rd. Take regular bus #54, 73, or 204 from Siam Sq. past the Indra Regent on Ratchaprarop Rd. Get off near the corner of Ratchaprarop and Si Ayutthaya Rd. and turn down Si Ayutthaya Rd.; it's on the left. Skytrain: Phayathai. ☎245 4934; www.suanpakkad.com. 40min. guided tours in English leave frequently. Open M-Sa 9am-4pm. 100฿, students 50฿.)*

CHULALONGKORN UNIVERSITY. Thailand's most prestigious academic institution is worth a visit. The buildings are an architectural representation of Thai classicism, and the bookstore contains a fine selection of English books. *(On the eastern side of Phayathai Rd., south of Siam Sq. From MBK, cross Phayathai Rd. on the footbridge or take any bus heading south on Phayathai Rd. until you see the campus on the left.)*

OTHER SIGHTS. Opposite Jim Thompson's House is the **National Stadium,** the most noticeable landmark on Rama I Rd. aside from the Mahboonkrong Shopping Complex and the Siam Sq. Shopping Center. Used mostly for sporting events, the stadium holds 65,000. The famous **Erawan Shrine** is farther along Rama I Rd., where it becomes Ploenchit Rd. After accidents causing the deaths of several workers, the Erawan Hotel built this memorial. The shrine was intended to correct the hotel's karma, as it was determined that the original foundation stone had been laid at an inauspicious hour. Dancers often perform around the shrine.

SUKHUMVIT ROAD AREA

When Rama I/Ploenchit Blvd. crosses Witthaya Rd., it becomes Sukhumvit Rd., stretching southeast out of the city. This area hosts trendy nightlife, upper-crust travelers, red light districts, and nice restaurants, but few traditional tourist sights.

KAMTHIENG HOUSE. This ethnological museum is home to the Siam Society, a cultural society supported by the royals. The museum reconstructs daily life in 19th-century Thailand for people of the matriarchal Lanna culture. Videos and exhibits in English help to explain rituals, cooking, courtship, rice farming, and water sharing in Lanna villages. The exhibit area is small and takes only 1hr. to visit. *(131 Soi 21 Asoke, on the left as you walk from Sukhumvit Rd. Near Asok Skytrain station. ☎661 6470. 100฿, students 50฿, ages 18 and under 20฿. Open daily 9am-5pm.)*

THONBURI: WEST OF THE RIVER

WAT ARUN (TEMPLE OF DAWN). Named for Aruna, the Hindu god of dawn, this *wat* was built in the Ayutthaya period and embellished during the reigns of Kings Rama II and III into its present Khmer-style form. The distinctive 79m *prang* is inlaid with ceramic tiles and porcelain. The best view of the *wat* is from the Bangkok side of the Chao Phraya River in the early morning or in the evening; the top of the *prang* affords beautiful views as well. *(In Thonburi, from Wat Pho, take a right from Chetupon Rd. onto Maharat Rd. and a left at Tani Wang Rd. This path goes to Tha Tien pier. From an adjacent pier, ferries cross to the wat for 2฿. ☎465 5640. Open daily 7am-6pm. 20฿.)*

ROYAL BARGE MUSEUM. The museum displays seven long, glittering royal barges and their ceremonial accoutrements. The most impressive barge in the museum is the Suphannahongsa, a 46m vessel requiring 50 oarsmen, reserved for the king when he makes his annual offering of robes to the monks during the Kathin Ceremony. *(On Arun Amarin Rd., under the bridge over Klong Bangkok Noi. Take a river ferry to Tha Pra Pinklao and walk down river, then follow the signs through the narrow sois to the museum. ☎424 0004. Open daily 9am-5pm. 30฿. Camera 100฿.)*

ENTERTAINMENT

NATIONAL THEATER

Dedicated in 1965, the National Theater, on Na Phra That Rd. past the national museum, has regular drama and dance shows. The performance program changes monthly but usually includes at least one *lakhon* dance-drama performance and a concert by the Thai National Orchestra every Friday. Contact the theater for the month's schedule. (☎224 1342. Open M-F 9am-3:30pm and 1hr. prior to performances. Tickets 40-100฿ for government-sponsored shows.)

THAI CLASSICAL DANCE DINNERS

Missed the National Theater show? Don't worry, many restaurants offer Thai classical dance dinners with half a dozen traditional dances in an hour-long show. Shows usually include *khon* dances from the *Ramakien*. No shorts, sandals, or tank tops are allowed. Reserve at least a day in advance. At **Ruen Thep,** Silom Village, 286 Silom Rd., enjoy a dance dinner in a garden of turtle pools. Performances begin at 8:30pm and include seven dance styles that change monthly. (☎234 4581; www.silomvillage.co.th. Opens at 7pm; set Thai dinner at 7:30pm. Tickets 450฿. AmEx/MC/V.)

THAILAND

TRADITIONAL THAI MASSAGE

Quality among massage parlors varies tremendously, and many are fronts for prostitution. Pictures of women in the window are giveaways for the latter. Ask other backpackers about their favorites, in addition to using the following listings. At Wat Pho, **The Traditional Massage School** (p. 682) offers massages for 300฿ per hr., as well as a 10-day, 30hr. course for 7400฿. (☎221 2974. Open daily 8am-6pm.) **Bann Phuan,** 25 Sukhumvit Soi 11, offers the traditional triumvirate of Thai, foot, and oil massage (☎253 5963. 1hr. 200฿, 300฿, and 400฿, respectively. Open noon-2am.) **Marble House,** 37/18-19 Soi Surawong Plaza, one *soi* up Surawong Rd. from Patpong 2, is one of the few massage parlors in Patpong that doesn't have a VIP room. It even has some blind masseurs, who are reputed to be the best in the business. (2hr. Thai massage 330฿. 1hr. head and shoulder massage 280฿.) A popular standby in the Banglamphu area is **Pian Massage Center and Beauty Salon,** 108/15 Soi Rambuttri, Khaosan Rd., down the tiny *soi* next to Nat Guest House on Khaosan Rd. (☎629 0924. Massage 80฿ per 30min., 140฿ per hr. 30hr. certification course 4000฿. Open daily 7am-3am.)

MUAY THAI (THAI BOXING)

One of the world's more brutal sports, Thai kickboxing is generally fought with opponents close together, constantly defending against a kick to the head, which would entail not only a concussion but also a sure knockout. For those who don't care for the actual fighting, the rituals and fervor that surround these matches are fascinating aspects of Thai culture (p. 660).

On Mondays, Wednesdays, Thursdays, and Sundays, the action is at **Ratchadamnoen Boxing Stadium,** on Ratchadamnoen Nok Rd. near the TAT office. Take regular bus #70 from Sanam Luang. (☎01 317 9917 or 629 9856. Fights begin at 6:30pm. Open 9am-11pm. Foreigner tickets 500-800฿, ringside 1500฿.)

On Tuesdays or Saturdays, head for **Lumphini Boxing Stadium** on Rama IV Rd. near Lumphini Park and the night market, which stages better fights. (☎247 5385. M: Lumphini. Take regular bus #115 from Silom Rd. Fights Tu 6:30pm; Sa 5, 6:30, 8:30pm. Same prices as above.)

SHOPPING

After a while in the Bangkok sun, the **Siam Square** and **Silom Road** areas begin to look like one big air-conditioned shopping mall. Siam Sq. houses five immense shopping centers, four movie complexes, 200 restaurants, and a few discos. (Most open daily 10am-10pm.) The area is a hangout for Bangkok teenagers and college students trickling in from Thailand's prestigious Chulalongkorn University. The undisputed heavyweight of Bangkok's shopping centers is **Mahboonkrong Center (MBK),** on the corner of Rama I and Phayathai Rd. in the Siam Sq. area. With seven floors of department stores, arcades, electronics, music stores, fast-food joints, and a cinema, MBK puts most Western shopping malls to shame. MBK is also by far the cheapest of the Siam malls. Outside MBK, the malls are name-brand and pricey. Connected by a skyway across Phayathai Rd. is the crowded and more upscale **Siam Discovery Center and Siam Square.** Spread over several *soi* are outdoor clothing and music stores, restaurants, two movie theaters, and a hotel. **Amarin Plaza,** at the intersection of Rama I and Ratchadamri Rd., and MBK's main competitor for the largest mall, the **Zen World Trade Center,** up Ratchadamri Rd. toward Phetchaburi Rd., have the same shops as the Siam Center but are a little less busy.

THAILAND

MARKETS

Chatuchak Market, Bangkok's infamous weekend market, is a bargain-hunter's dream and a great example of market culture in Southeast Asia. Come armed with plenty of free time and patience, bargain ruthlessly, and watch your wallet. *(Skytrain: Mo Chit. Open Sa-Su 7am-6pm.)* The frenzied, late-afternoon **Banglamphu Market** branches onto Chakrapong, Krai Si, and Tani Rd., but the tourist-oriented section is along Khaosan Rd. Between Lumphini Park and Lumphini Boxing Stadium, the **Suan Lum Night Bazaar** is one of the best markets in Bangkok. The best time to go is 6-10pm. *(Entrances on Wireless Rd. and Rama IV Rd. M: Lumphini.)* At the market, the Hun Lakhon Lek Joe Louis Troupe performs daily puppetry shows in the Joe Louis Theater. *(600฿, children 300฿.)* **Thewet Market** is on Krung Kasem Rd. along the Chao Phraya River. The selection is not as diverse, but it's the one-stop shopping center for food or garden landscaping. *(Chao Phraya River Express: Thewet.)* A sweet and brilliant sight is **Pakklong Market,** a wholesale flower market, southwest of Pahurat District over Triphet Ave. The best time to go is early in the morning or late at night. In Chinatown the **Sampaeng Lane Market** runs through the heart of Chinatown one block south of Yaowarat Rd. Extending northwest from the corner of Yaowarat and Chakrawat Rd. is the **Nakhon Kasea,** or **Thieves Market,** best known for its machinery and ninja weaponry. The **Pratunam Market** operates during the day along Ratchaprarop Rd., opposite the Indra Hotel. In the **Silom** area, vendors set up along **Patpong 1 Road** after nightfall.

NIGHTLIFE

Bangkok's entertainment and nightlife need little introduction. The city's reputation as the epicenter of Southeast Asia's internationalism is rooted in its effortless mix of traditional art and culture with the hip, connected youth who want to party until dawn. Like other global metropolises, Bangkok offers a wealth of activities, from sophisticated bars and shady massage parlors to dance shows and kickboxing—something to entertain and enlighten every type of traveler. Check out the free *BK Magazine* (available at many bars and restaurants) or the *Metro* (100฿ at newsstands) for the latest in "cool." Places listed here are not associated with the skin trade.

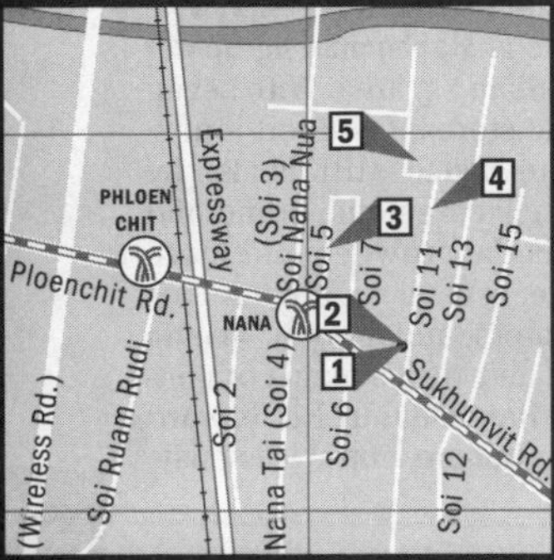

ONE NIGHT IN BANGKOK

Savvy tourists often head to Silom and Patpong at night in search of something more sophisticated than the 60฿ street cocktails and hair-braiding stalls of Khaosan Rd. Those truly in the know (and willing to spend some *baht*), however, visit oft overlooked Sukhumvit for the best of Bangkok after dark. Cover prices can be steep, so bar-hopping may not be feasible for those on a budget, but the area is well worth visiting for a taste of the hottest nightlife Thailand has to offer.

1. Suk II Guest House is the perfect base for your Sukhumvit adventure. Prices are low—save up now so you can party later.
2. Fuel up with a delicious Indian dish from Moghul Room.
3. Warm up at Gulliver's—no cover and happy hour until 9pm.
4. Dine in bed or rock to the music of the hottest DJs at ultra-trendy Bed Supperclub.
5. Sip martinis with the beautiful and privileged at Bangkok's standard of nightlife excellence, Q Bar.

Q Bar, 34 Sukhumvit Soi 11 (☎252 3274; www.qbarbangkok.com). At the end of Soi 11, take a left. Well-to-do expats and even wealthier Thais mix and mingle in this classic institution of the Bangkok social scene. An upscale place, but the darkness and blacklights give it a relaxed feel. Food 150-200฿. Cocktails 200-260฿. Singha 150฿. Strict ID policy—20+. Cover F-Su 600฿, M-Th 400฿ includes 2 drinks. Open daily 8pm-2am.

Bed Supperclub (☎651 3537), at the end of Sukhumvit Soi 11. This all-white, futuristic club is perhaps the hottest new thing in Bangkok. One side has the beds and supper (supper served in bed F-Sa 9pm, 1190฿; Su-Th 7:30-10:30pm, 990฿; reserve ahead); the other, the bar and DJs. No shorts or flip-flops. Strict ID policy—20+. Cover Tu and F-Sa 500฿, Su-M and W-Th 400฿ includes 2 drinks. Open daily 7:30pm-1:45am.

Tapas, 114/7 Silom Soi 4 (☎632 7982). Resident DJs spin house in this "room club" bar. Sink into a couch or get up and groove wherever there's space. Outdoor seating for fresh air. Beer 120฿. No cover downstairs, 300฿ cover upstairs. Open daily 8pm-2am.

DJ Station (☎235 1227), on Silom Soi 2, is awarded "Best Gay Disco" every year by *Metro*. With the metal decor, great house/techno, and a full range of openness, it's no wonder. Also features a nightly cabaret (11:30pm). No shorts or sandals. 20+. Cover F-Sa 200฿, includes 2 drinks; Su-Th 100฿, includes 1 drink. Open daily 11pm-2:30am.

Lucifer, on Patpong 1 Rd., next to Radio City, is delightfully and elaborately designed to look like hell; the club surely takes in its share of devils from the street and bars below. Regardless, this venue still gets kicking around midnight with dance remixes and happy house. Drinks 120฿. Cover F-Sa 130฿, includes 1 drink. Open daily 10pm-2am.

Banana Leaf Cafe, 34/1 Khaosan Rd. (☎629 3343). One of the best bars on Khaosan Rd., and the tourists haven't quite discovered it yet. Comprehensive Thai/Western menu 60-120฿. Drinks 60-140฿. Open daily 10am-2am.

Concept CM² (☎255 6888), as in "Siam Squared," in the basement of the Novotel Hotel on Soi 6, is as classy as it gets. The city's most recognizable "club" features postmodern decor and talented bartenders. Dance to Thai and Western techno or dine in the restaurant area 6:30-10pm. Beer 170฿. Food 150-600฿. Live music M-W and F-Su. No shorts or sandals. 20+. Cover F-Sa 550฿, includes 2 drinks; Su-Th 220฿, includes 1 drink. Officially open daily 7pm-2am, but the doors sometimes don't open until after 10pm.

LIVE MUSIC

Bangkok's most rewarding nightlife centers on jazz establishments with live music and classy Thai and foreign clientele. Off Ratchadamri Rd., Soi Sarasin, just north of Lumphini Rd., has restaurant/bars that play live music nightly. Bands generally start around 8pm, but things get cooking after 11pm. Brown Sugar Jazz Pub and Restaurant, 231/20 Sarasin Rd. (☎250 1826), opposite Lumphini Park, is regarded as one of the best jazz clubs in the city, with bands every night. (Food 90-360฿. Cocktails 150฿. Live music 9:45-1am. Open daily 5pm-1am.) Another one of the city's best, **Saxophone Pub and Restaurant,** 3/8 Phayathai Rd. (5246 5472; www.saxophonepub.com), away from Siam Sq. at the southeast corner of the Victory Monument, has a mostly funk/jazz/blues band rotation. The Thai and Western food is delicious. (Food 100฿. Beer 120฿. Open daily 6pm-2am.)

DAYTRIPS FROM BANGKOK

Travel agencies offer pricey daytrips to attractions outside Bangkok, but these sights can be seen more cheaply independently.

NONTHABURI. Nonthaburi Province straddles the Chao Phraya River 20km north of Bangkok. The town of Nonthaburi, on the east bank, is known for its fruit and earthenware. On the west bank, in Amphoe Bangkluai, stands **Wat Chalerm Phra Kliad Wora Wihaan,** known to locals simply as Wat Chalerm. Chinese styles influence the statues around the grounds as well as the ceramics and flowering decorations. Both the eastern and western piers are bordered by **fruit markets,** where a greater variety and better quality of fruits is available than anywhere in Bangkok. *(The best way to get to Wat Chalerm is by the Chao Phraya River Express ferry, which ends at the Nonthaburi Pier. From here, take another ferry to the west bank (2฿) and hire a motorcycle to Wat Chalerm (10฿). Open daily 9am-5pm.)*

SAMUT PRAKAN. The center of Thailand's leather industry, Samut Prakan is also home to **Muang Boran** and the **Crocodile Farm.** Muang Boran, the "Ancient City," is an open-air museum in the shape of Thailand that contains replicas of monuments and sights from around the kingdom. Highlights include the Ayutthaya-style **Saphet Prasat Palace,** the **Dusit Maha Prasat Palace,** and **Khao Phra Wihan,** which sit atop a hill affording a spectacular view. The Crocodile Farm houses the largest crocodile in captivity. At the "Crocodile Wrestling" show, trainers taunt the toothy behemoths. Other attractions include an aviary, snake pits, a dinosaur museum, and go-carts. *(A/C bus #511 runs to Samut Prakan. Take a songthaew from the center of Samut Prakan to Muang Boran or the Crocodile Farm (shared 5฿, one person 20฿). Tuk-tuks and taxis run between the 2 parks (50-60฿). Muang Boran: ☎323 9253. Open daily 8am-6pm, last entry 5pm. 100฿, children 50฿. Crocodile Farm: ☎703 4891. Crocodile shows every hr. 9-11am and 1-4pm; additional shows on weekends and holidays at noon and 5pm. Elephant shows 9:30, 10:30, 11:30am, 1:30, 2:30, 4:30pm. Open daily 7am-6pm. 300฿.)*

DAMNOEN SADUAK. Damnoen Saduak's **floating market,** though touristy, captures a quick snapshot of a transient canal economy. A boat tour (300฿ per hr.) is a must, but service and quality vary greatly. A ride through the actual market is included in any tour. Browse through the woodcarvings and cowboy hats, then head to the sugar farm and sample some palm flower juice or honey. Depicted on postcards and picture books, the bustling scene has become the poster child for traditional Thai life. Some visitors may find the not-so-picture-perfect reality—murky waters, swarming flies, and spitting vendors—disappointing, but it's a great place to practice bargaining. *(Buses leave from Bangkok's Southern Bus Terminal for Damnoen Saduak and drop off passengers in the thick of the action (2hr., every 20min. 6am-9pm,*

52฿). Upon arrival, locals approach, offering 1hr. boat tours for 300฿. The best time to visit is 8-10am. The market is open daily 6am-2pm. To return to Bangkok, take a yellow songthaew *(5฿) into the center of Damnoen Saduak and wave down one of the buses as it turns around.)*

NAKHON PATHOM. Historians speculate that Nakhon Pathom was first inhabited in the third century BC by Buddhist missionaries from India, which would make it one of the oldest cities in Thailand; the city's name comes from the Pali word *Nagara Pathama,* which means "first city." This claim to antiquity is disputed, but undisputed is the fact that Nakhon Pathom is home to one of the world's tallest Buddhist monuments, **Phra Pathom Chedi,** which rises to 127m. Also note the stone reliefs of angels and demons on lions below the Chinese temple, the intriguing Lab Lae Caves on the southeastern part of the grounds, and the temple's small museum, which is bursting with old amulets, statues, pottery, and other artifacts. Nakhon Pathom's other local attraction is the **Sabaan Chan Palace,** a 335-acre complex with several residences restored to their original Rama VI condition, open to tour. *(Chedi open 9am-5pm. 20฿. Palace ☎03 424 4237. Open daily 9am-4pm, last entry 3:30pm. 50฿. Buses leave the Southern Bus Terminal for Nakhon Pathom (A/C buses 1hr., every 10min. 4:10am-9:30pm, 34฿; buy a ticket for the return bus 2 blocks north of the chedi on Thanon Phayaphan, the road bordering the northern side of the canal. If you want to visit both the floating market and Phra Pathom Chedi in the same day, take a bus from Bangkok to Damnoen Saduak early and stop in Nakhon Pathom on the trip (1hr., every 20min.) back to Bangkok.)*

LOPBURI. Remarkably well-maintained ancient *wats* and traces of civilization that date back 4500 years are found around virtually every corner of Lopburi, relics of its past as a major cultural and political center during the Ayutthaya period. Continuing in this tradition, the new city is an important site for military training and higher education. Check out **Wat Phra Sru Rattanamahathat** and **King Narai's palace,** both used by King Narai when Lopburi was the second capital of Thailand. **Wat Prang Khaek** is Lopburi's oldest historical sight, dating back to the 9th century AD. *(The best way to get to Lopburi is by train (3hr.) via Ayutthaya (1½ hours).)*

PHETCHABURI. Phetchaburi remains largely undiscovered. Visitors enjoy a small-town atmosphere along with several outstanding cultural sights. In 1858, King Rama IV built a royal retreat on the hilltops overlooking Phetchaburi. A unique mixture of Chinese and Western architecture, **Phra Nakhon Khiri** (or Khao Wang) spreads across the hill's three peaks. Other sights include several *wats* and Wat Khao Banda-It and Khao Luang Cave, both impressive due to the sheer number of Buddhas ensconced in them. Nearby Kaeng Krachan National Park is Thailand's largest, enveloping 3000km^2 of rain forest. Since the park's opening in 1981, four white elephants, long considered symbols of royal prestige, have been captured here. *(Catch a bus to Phetchaburi (3hr., every 20min. 5am-5pm, 70฿). Most arrive at the intersection of Damnerkasem Rd. and Rot Fai Rd. Khao Wang ☎401 006. Museum open daily 9am-4pm. 40฿. Park open M-F 8:15am-5pm, Su-Sa 8:15am-5:15pm. To get to Kaeng Krachan, take a dark blue* songthaew *to Tha Yong, 20฿. There, switch to a Koeng Krachan* songthaew *to park headquarters, 20฿.)*

CENTRAL THAILAND

From Bangkok to Trat, the coastal highway follows the progression of economic development. Shiny new refineries, power stations, and petrochemical plants dominate the coast from Si Racha to Rayong. East of Rayong, construction sites and highway traffic give way to groves of durians and mangosteens. The fertile Chao Phraya River Basin stretches from Hua Hin in the south to Nakhon Sawan in

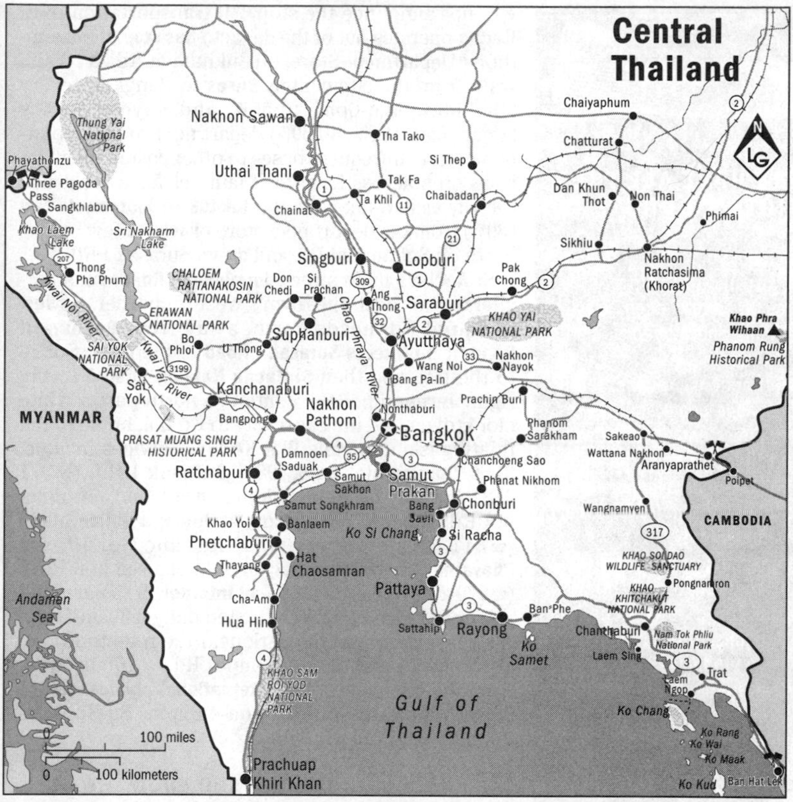

the north. The region's attractions include the awe-inspiring ruins of Ayutthaya and the lush landscapes fanning west of Bangkok around Kanchanaburi, as well as the River Kwai and the province's national parks. Southbound buses and trains wind through the beginnings of peninsular Thailand, a teaser for the sandy playgrounds farther south.

SI RACHA ☎038

Thailand may be a culinary heaven, but few towns celebrate the taste buds like Si Racha does. The maritime heritage of this fishing-village-turned-bustling-town lives on in the restaurants and foodstalls, whose blinking lights tempt visitors to sample Thailand's finest and most traditional seafood. Besides its culinary appeal, the town is also home to one of Thailand's best zoos. If neither fish nor caged animals strike your fancy, make sure to arrive early enough to catch the ferry to Ko Si Chang; there are few other reasons to dawdle in Si Racha (and few tourists do).

TRANSPORTATION AND PRACTICAL INFORMATION. Buses heading from Bangkok to Si Racha leave from the Eastern Bus Terminal accessible from the Skytrain's Ekamai Station (2hr., every 20-40min. 5:40am-9pm, 50-70฿). Be on the lookout for a large, glossy-white department store on the right, as the driver

IN RECENT NEWS

WHERE HAVE ALL THE TIGERS GONE?

They are some of the most majestic, powerful, and impressive creatures on earth. Feared as full-grown adults and adored as cuddly cubs, tigers make for great tourist attractions. Yet the same brilliant orange coats and powerful physiques that draw crowds also lure Thai poachers and dealers of animal materials, causing a great deal of concern from animal rights watch groups.

The poaching of tiger products is sadly indicative of a larger, woldwide trend toward using exotic animals for health, food, and novelty products. Speculative reports have ignited concern that tigers are being shipped to the lucrative Chinese market for tiger bone (to treat rheumatism), kidney fat (to prolong erections), and even tiger penis, which is soaked in liquor and served at high-end brothels.

Alarmingly, the use of tiger parts has become unabashedly mainstream in Thailand. Though Thailand has all the proper laws in place to protect tigers, failure to enforce these laws only increases Thailand's notoriety as an offender in wildlife trafficking.

will not announce the stop. All transportation in Si Racha operates out of the de facto **bus stop,** the Laemthong Department Store, on Sukhumvit Rd., a 20min. walk from the city center. **Buses** to Bangkok (every 20-40min. 5am-6pm, 40-55฿) and Rayong (every 20min. 5am-10pm, 40-60฿) depart next to the department store. Infrequent buses to other eastern destinations stop across from the main entrance. To reach the **city center,** take either a **tuk-tuk** or **motorcycle taxi** (30฿) from the department store or walk a few blocks north on Sukhumvit Rd. and down Surasak I Rd.

Si Racha's main street, **Jermjompol Road,** runs parallel to the coast, the town's western border. As Jermjompol Rd. heads north, away from **Sukhumvit Road,** it intersects **Surasak I Road** to the right, Soi 10 to the left, and then **Si Racha Nakhon Road 3** to the right. Jermjompol Rd. continues north past a white clocktower and the causeway to Ko Loi, home of the floating island temple Wat Ko Loi. Services include: **Siam Commercial Bank,** 98/9 Surasak I Rd. (☎311 313), halfway between Sukhumvit Rd. and Jermjompol Rd. (open daily 8:30am-3:30pm); a **police booth** (☎311 800) at Jermjompol Rd. and Soi 10; the **Phayathai General Hospital,** 90 Si Racha Nakhon Rd. 3 (☎770 200; open 24hr.); **Naoni Internet,** 1/15 Surasak I Rd. (☎511 064; 25฿ per hr., open daily 8:30am-7pm); the **post office,** past the park near the road to Ko Loi at the north end of Jermjompol Rd., a 10min. walk from the city center, has **international phones.** (☎311 202. Open daily M-F 8:30am-4:30pm, Sa-Su 9am-noon.) **Postal Code:** 20110.

ACCOMMODATIONS AND FOOD. Hotels near the bus stop at the Laemthong Department Store tend to be on the expensive side. Budget rooms line the salty sea near the Ko Si Chang ferry, a 20min. walk or 30฿ *tuk-tuk* ride from the bus stop. **Siri Watana ❷** (☎311 037), off Jermjompol Rd. one block north of Soi 10, opposite Si Racha Nakhon Rd. 3, has plain, immaculate rooms with towels, a ceiling fan, and a squat toilet. (Singles 160-200฿; doubles 300฿.) Busier **Samchai Hotel ❷** (☎311 131), at the end of Soi 10 off Jermjompol Rd., across from Surasak I Rd., has similar amenities. (No English spoken. Singles 200฿; doubles 400฿.)

Si Racha is famous for its **seafood,** often prepared with Si Racha sauce, a spicy red dressing which appears as ซอสศรีราชา on Thai menus. The prime location for gorging oneself on local cuisine is **Si Racha Nakhon Road 3** after it branches off Jermjompol Rd., one block north of Soi 10. This road overflows with foodstalls, small restaurants, and larger open-air eateries. The best place to go to sample a variety of fresh seafood is the **market ❶,** where you can peruse the exotic dishes of literally hundreds of vendors. To get to the market, turn right on Si Racha Nakhon Rd. 3 from Jermjompol Rd. Take the first left; the market is across from the end of the road. **Hanamoto ❷,** 7 Si Racha Nakhon Rd. 3 Soi 8 (☎322 274), is a clean, cool oasis in a strip of Japanese restaurants and karaoke clubs. From Jermjompol Rd., turn right on Si Racha Nakhon Rd. 3 and make the first left—Hanamoto is on the left. (Most dishes 50-180฿. Large Singha beer 110฿. Open daily 6-11:30pm.)

SIGHTS. Si Racha's main attraction is the **Si Racha Tiger Zoo,** a rather gimmicky, amusement-park-style affair 9km east of town. A *tuk-tuk* from anywhere in the city should take 25min. and cost 100฿. The zoo's shows (in Thai only) are quite entertaining; take your pick from elephant, crocodile, and tiger shows or the pig-racing extravaganza. There are several opportunities to get a close look at the animals, including taking a picture with a baby tiger (150฿). It's an unusual zoo and an interesting way to kill time while waiting for the ferry. (☎296 556; www.tiger-zoo.com. Open daily 8am-6pm. Several shows per hr. 300฿, children 150฿.)

Those with less time can head to the temples nearer to town. From Jermjompol Rd., **Wat Radniyomtum** is several blocks down Surasak I Rd. on the right. Near the market, Surasak Suguan leads to **Wat Mahasiracha,** on the corner of Tesabarn Rd. The town's most touristed temple is **Wat Ko Loi** (Floating Island Temple), reached via a pleasant walk to the causeway at the northern end of Jermjompol Rd. Release a pair of finches at the top (20฿), watch enormous **sea turtles** in the nearby moat, or just wander around the base of the *wat,* where foodstalls and trinket shops draw the picnicking Thais who flock here on weekends. A shady, well-landscaped park stretches along the waterfront on Jermjompol Rd.

KO SI CHANG ☎038

A tourist boom years back encouraged the residents of this 5000-person fishing village to spruce up their island with new bungalows and English signs and maps. But as the rest of Southeast Asia opened up, more and more visitors cut Ko Si Chang from their itineraries. Accordingly, Ko Si Chang remains a pretty island with good tourist services, friendly locals, and hardly a trace of commercialism.

Ferries to Ko Si Chang depart from Si Racha's main pier at the end of Jermjompol Rd. Soi 14 (40min., every 2hr. 8am-6pm, 30฿). Boats returning to Si Racha (6, 8, 11am, 2, 4, 6pm; 30฿) leave from **Ta Lang Pier** or **Ta Bon Pier,** based on the tide.

Assadang Road runs north along the water past the two piers, curves past the Chinese temple on the hill, and finally doubles back onto itself 4km later next to the Tiew Pai Guest House. The road then runs south to **Hat Ta Wang** and **Hat Sai Kaew** and branches off to **Hat Tampang,** the island's best beach. To get there, take a right onto **Chakra Pong Road** up the hill, then follow the signs. Motorized *samlor* (a motorcycle-drawn variation unique to Ko Si Chang) go anywhere on the island for 20-50฿, but the best way to see the island is to hire a *tuk-tuk,* regular *samlor,* or motorcycle taxi to take you on an all-inclusive tour of the island sights. The **Tiew Pai Guest House** rents **motorbikes** (200฿ for 12hr., 250฿ for 24hr.), a pickup truck that seats up to 15 people (500฿), and a limo bike (an extended version of the local *samlor,* 250฿), and conducts **boat tours** (3-4hr., 1500฿ for a group of 10). Just 25m up Assadang Rd. from Tiew Pai Guest House to the right, a family (☎01 949 1819) rents **mountain bikes,** though be forewarned—Ko Si Chang is extremely hilly!

The **Thai Farmers Bank,** 9-9½ Assadang Rd., between the piers, exchanges traveler's checks and has a 24hr. **ATM** (☎216 132. Open M-F 8:30am-3:30pm.) The local **police** can be reached at ☎216 218. Ko Si Chang also has a general **hospital** (☎261 000), to the right up Assadang Rd. from the pier. Very slow **Internet** access is available from a nameless shop. From the pier, make a left on Assadang Rd.; when the road curves sharply up to the right, the shop is on the left. (30฿ per hr. Open variable hours, usually 11am-5pm.) Across from the hospital, the **post office** has an **international phone.** (☎216 227. Open M-F 8:30am-4:30pm.) **Postal Code:** 20120.

Ko Si Chang's only budget-minded guesthouse is **Tiew Pai Guest House ❷,** to the left of the pier on Assadang Rd. Fortunately, it's cheap and well-kept. (☎216 084. Singles 150฿; doubles 350฿, with A/C and fridge 450฿; triples and family rooms 750-1000฿.) For those who want to spend a day at the beach, **Tampang Beach Resort ❷** is just above Hat Tampang. Rooms are drab but the location is unbeatable. (☎216 179. Dorm-style rooms for 10 or more 150฿; doubles 450-700฿; triples 1200฿.) To **camp** for free, bring your own tent.

Food vendors ❶ sell noodle and rice dishes along **Assadang Road.** Try the breakfast (70฿) or the entrees, which range from typical rice dishes (25-30฿) to "fish 'n' fixin's" (180-200฿), at Tiew Pai Guest House's **restaurant ❶.** (Open daily 7:30am-1am.) The rice dishes (40-50฿), fresh fish (54-220฿), and steamed fresh grouper in black bean sauce (60฿ per 100g) at the **Sichang View Resort ❸** are simple and satisfying. (Open daily 8am-9pm.)

Touring Ko Si Chang takes a few hours by motorbike or *samlor* (200-250฿). From the pier, Assadang Rd. winds up and to the right to the Chinese Temple, a 163-step climb from the road. Four hundred steps farther up is an enshrined **Buddha footprint,** whose size matches the **Yellow Buddha**'s on the island's west side. Beneath this 10m-high statue are several caves accessible from the lower platform in front of the Buddha. On the road between the Chinese Temple and Yellow Buddha are the striking **Khao Khat Cliffs,** where Rama V built a pavilion to enjoy the horizon and write poetry. A path by the Sichang View Resort leads down to the cliffs, which are best visited at sunset.

Toward the southern end of Assadang Rd. are the ruins of King Rama V's **summer palace.** Here you can still see pagodas, reservoirs, and European-influenced buildings. To get there, continue south on Assadang Rd. through the gate of the Marine Research Institute. Continue to **Hat Tampang,** Ko Si Chang's most swimmable beach, by taking the right branch of the road next to the gate, climbing over a steep hill, and then making a right on Chalerm Prakariat Rd.

PATTAYA ☎038

From the early days when American servicemen first came here for "rest and recuperation" during the Vietnam War, Pattaya has been "hospitable" to *farang*. Beer bars and go-gos filled with Thai women and single—or single enough—foreign men pervade the city. In recent years, efforts to clean up the city have made some headway. Diving, snorkeling, jet skis, and speedboats are welcome diversions for willing tourists, and Pattaya is even advertised as a family vacation spot. Remarkably, Pattaya does have its charms, but they must coexist with its seedier aspects.

TRANSPORTATION

Trains: Arrive and depart from the **train station** off Soi 45 on Sukhumvit Rd., north of the intersection between Sukhumvit Rd. and Central Pattaya Rd. From Hualamphong Station in Bangkok (3¾hr., 7:10am, 40฿).

Buses: Buses from Bangkok depart from **Ekamai Station** (2½hr., every 30min. 6am-10:30pm, 90฿) and **Mo Chit Station** (2½hr., every 30min. 6am-9pm, 90฿). Public buses run from **Rayong** (1hr., every 30min. 3am-6:20pm, 50฿) and **Si Racha** (1hr., every 10-12min., 40฿). In Pattaya, buses to Bangkok's **Ekamai Station** (2½hr., every 30min. 5:40am-9pm, 90฿) and **Mo Chit Station** (2½hr., every 30min. 5:40am-7pm,

90฿) depart from the station on North Pattaya Rd., 2 blocks from Sukhumvit Hwy. A/C buses to **Rayong** and **Si Racha** (1hr., 40฿) leave from the bus stop on Sukhumvit Rd., close to the intersection with Central Pattaya Rd.

Local Transportation: Songthaew (10-200฿) travel up Pattaya 2nd Rd. and down Beach Rd. **Motorcycle taxis** (20-50฿) also abound.

Rentals: Thanyamat Rent (☎415 892), in front of Kangaroo Bar on Central Pattaya Rd., close to Beach Rd. Automatic motorbikes 200฿ per day, jeeps 500฿ per day.

ORIENTATION AND PRACTICAL INFORMATION

Pattaya's main strip, **Pattaya Beach Road** (Beach Road), runs north-south, parallel to the coast. Toward the southern end of the city, Beach Rd. turns into **Walking Street,** an area closed to traffic after 9pm and the center of the city's nightlife. **Pattaya 2nd Road** (2nd Rd.) runs parallel to Beach Rd.; between these two streets is the heart of Pattaya. They are intersected to the north by **North Pattaya Road** and in the south by **South Pattaya Road.** Small numbered *sois* also run between Beach and 2nd Rd., increasing in number as they go south. North Pattaya is the quiet neighborhood of Naklua; south is Jomtien Beach, a center for water sports.

Tourist Office: TAT, 609 Moo 10, Soi Pratamnak (☎428 750; fax 429 113), on the mountain near Big Buddha at the southern end of Pattaya. Open daily 8:30am-4:30pm.

Laundromat: On the small *soi* connecting Soi 7 and 8, across from the Della Vista. Shirt 15฿, pants 15฿, shorts 10฿, underwear 5฿. Open 8am-8pm.

Tourist Police: Two 24hr. stations: one in North Pattaya on Pattaya 2nd Rd. just north of Soi Tropicena (☎425 957), and one in the south off South Pattaya Rd. (☎425 937).

Medical Services: Pattaya Memorial Hospital, 328/1 Central Pattaya Rd. (☎422 741) is centrally located. **Pattaya International Hospital** (☎428 374), on Soi 8 in North Pattaya, has a fantastic reputation and a 24hr. **pharmacy** (☎428 374). Both hospitals have English-speaking staff and are open 24hr. for emergencies.

Telephones: Many small shops advertise overseas calls. Most in central Pattaya charge 20฿ per min. to call America, Australia, or Europe, but a few blocks outside this area you will find 10฿ shops, like the one at the back of Mike's Shopping Center, facing Pattaya 2nd Rd., which is small but air-conditioned with comfy chairs (minimum 3min.).

Internet Access: Virtually identical Internet cafes can be found in the entrance courtyards at the Easting and Sunshine Hotels on Soi 8. 1฿ per min., 20฿ minimum. Printing 10฿ per page. Fax to USA, Europe, or Canada 50฿ per min. Open 8am-3am.

Post Office: ☎429 341. On Soi Post Office. **Western Union.** *Poste Restante.* Open M-F 8:30am-4:30pm, Sa-Su 9am-noon.

Postal Code: 20260.

ACCOMMODATIONS

Accommodations are easy to find in Pattaya, but, unfortunately, budget accommodations are another story altogether. Many hotels lower their prices significantly during the low season. Often, if you ask for a discount, slow summer hotels will be very accommodating. Usually, Pattaya's upscale hotels have websites where you can book online, and, if you plan ahead, you can get great deals.

Sawasdee Sea View, 327/1 Moo 10 Soi 10 (☎710 566). One of the cheapest options in Pattaya. The rooms are small and the shower is basically right over the toilet, but the hotel is still well-run. Rooms with fan 280฿, with A/C 500฿; low-season 250฿/350฿. ❷

The Green Hotel, 217/10 Beach Rd. Soi 9 (☎423 555). Located on a quiet stretch of Soi 9, the hotel is peaceful and has a plant theme. Doubles 650฿, low-season 500฿. ❹

THAILAND

Apex Hotel, 216/2 Soi 11 2nd Rd. (☎428 281; www.apexhotelpattaya.com). An incredibly popular budget hotel. Famous for its extensive breakfast (95฿) and dinner (160฿) buffets. The hotel has a pool and parking lot. In high season book 1-2 months in advance. Rooms 500-555฿; low-season 450-500฿. ❹

FOOD

Unless you're looking for beer or meat on a stick, good food (especially good Thai food) can be hard to find in Pattaya. Many restaurants are in quieter northern Pattaya. Central Pattaya has notoriously few places to eat, though as you head south there is a cluster of restaurants, largely American chains, around the Royal Garden Plaza. Street vendors traverse Pattaya at all times, serving Westernized dishes as well as typical Thai offerings. If Western-style food isn't what you're in the mood for, stick to the carts and nameless restaurants peppering the streets.

PIC Kitchen (☎428 374), on Soi 5. An excellent Thai restaurant. Choose from open gardens, air-conditioned rooms, or low tables with pillows on the floor. Home to the **Jazz Pit,** a piano bar, open 7pm-1am. 20% off 8am-4pm. Restaurant open 8am-midnight. ❹

Alibaba Tandoori and Curry Restaurant, 1/13-14 Central Pattaya Rd. (☎429 881), 2 blocks from Beach St. The most popular Indian restaurant. A tandoori platter of assorted meats, seafood, and vegetables for 2 is 450฿. Open daily noon-midnight. ❹

English Pig and Whistle, 217/34 Moo 9 Soi 7 (☎361 315). Very popular restaurant and pub with A/C in the midst of a sea of beer bars. Full English breakfast 135฿. Other English dishes 150-200฿. Also rents rooms for 600฿. Open 8:30am-2am. ❸

SIGHTS

All sights in Pattaya are outside the city on the far side of Sukhumvit Rd. Pattaya's most popular attraction, the **Million Year Stone Park and Crocodile Farm,** has a collection of rock gardens and rare plants and animals on its 10 acres, as well as thousands of crocodiles. The park puts on several performances per day, including crocodile, monkey, magic, and fire-swallowing shows. For a couple extra *baht* you can ride an elephant or have your picture taken with tame tigers, bears, and lions. (22/2 Moo 1, Tamban Nong Pla Lai. Turn left at Km 140 on Sukhumvit Rd. ☎549 347. Open 8:30am-6:30pm. 300฿, children 150฿.) The principal event at the **Pattaya Elephant Village** is the elephant show, which takes place daily at 2:30pm (450฿). The village also offers two half-day elephant treks through the brush. Prices vary depending on where your hotel is, as they pick you up and drop you off at the end of the trek. (☎249 818. Off Siam Country Club Rd., 20min. from central Pattaya). If your trip to Thailand doesn't have enough sights for you, check out **Mini Siam** for recreations of famous landmarks from around the world. Alongside the River Kwai Bridge and the Emerald Buddha are icons like the Eiffel Tower, Statue of Liberty, and Leaning Tower of Pisa. Mini Siam is especially popular at night when the miniatures are lit up. (☎421 628. At Km 143 on Sukhumvit Hwy. 250฿.)

BEACHES AND WATERSPORTS

The beach in central Pattaya tends to be disappointing to visitors. While it is not as polluted as it was a few years back, very little swimming goes on. For a more pleasant beach experience, most people head north to Naklua. For watersports, Jomtien is the best spot to hit; while the water is still not clear, there are more swimmers bobbing around and families on the beach. A variety of jet skis (600฿ per 30min.), boats (600-1000฿ per 30min.), and sailboats (700฿ per hr.) are available for rent. Parasailing trips are also popular (500฿). Jomtien is also the only

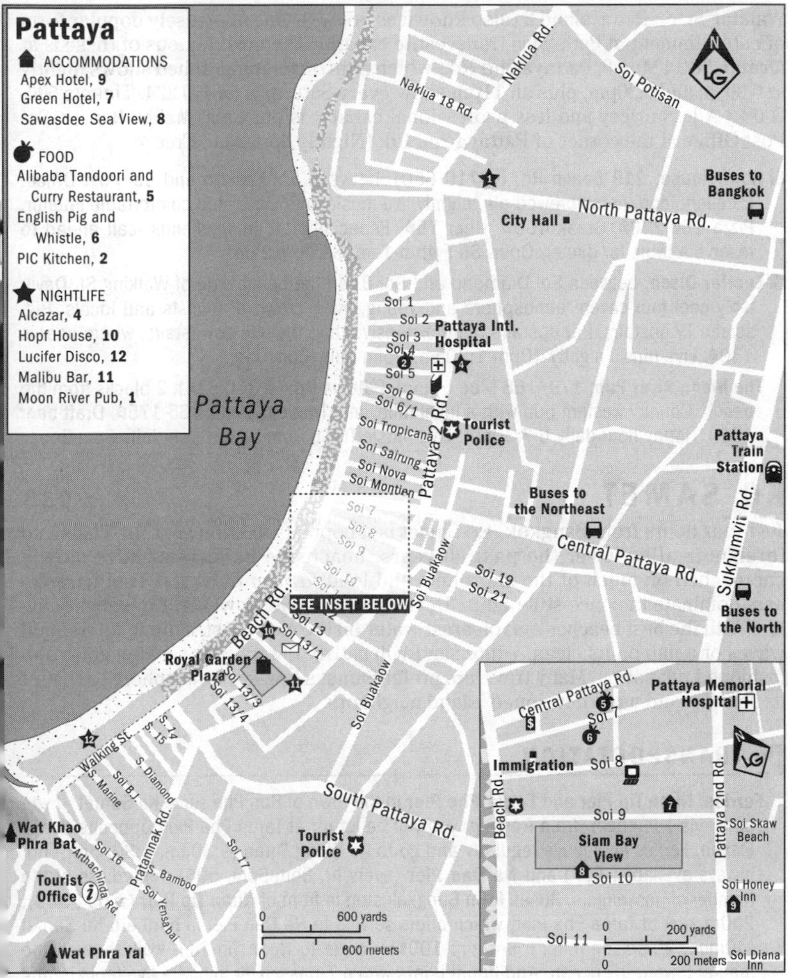

beach in Pattaya where windsurfing is available; renting a board costs 500฿ per hr. Another 100฿ will get you a 1hr. lesson. **Scuba diving** and **snorkeling** are both popular activities in Pattaya. There are many dive shops in the area that offer both PADI certification courses in scuba diving and daily dive trips to one of Pattaya's islands or to one of the two shipwrecks offshore (Ko Larn and the *HMS Khran* are among the best dive destinations). Visibility is best during the high season, generally around 15m. During the low season visibility shrinks to 5-9m due to rain.

ENTERTAINMENT AND NIGHTLIFE

Pattaya's nightlife is dominated by beer bars (open-air pickup joints) and go-go bars. Fortunately, not all of Pattaya's nightlife is focused (overtly) on commercial sex; classier bars and clubs dot the city. Gay nightlife is centered slightly north of

Walking St. on Pattayaland 2 (also known as Soi 3/4). One immensely popular form of entertainment in Pattaya is transvestite cabaret. The most famous of these is at **Alcazar,** 78/14 Moo 9, Pattaya 2nd Rd., which puts on choreographed shows nightly at 6:30, 8, and 9:30pm, plus an 11pm show every Saturday. (☎410 224. Tickets 500-600฿.) A less pricey and less professional cabaret is put on at **Malibu Bar,** on Soi Post Office at the corner of Pattaya 2nd Rd. (Nightly 8pm-2am. Free.)

Hopf House, 219 Beach Rd. (☎710 650), between Soi Yamato and Soi Post Office. Excellent food, home-brewed ale, nightly live music, and classy but comfortable interior. Pizza 160-220฿. Steak 400฿. Beer 75฿. Especially full on weekends—call ahead to reserve a table for dinner. Open Su-F 4pm-1am, Sa 4pm-2am.

Lucifer Disco, between Soi Diamond and Soi BJ on the beach side of Walking St. Devilishly cool faux-cavern atmosphere and young, lively crowd of tourists and locals. Big-screen TV upstairs. Bar upstairs more expensive than the one downstairs, where beer is 130฿. Live music nightly 10pm-1:30am. Open daily 6pm-3am.

The Moon River Pub, 179/168 Moo 5 North Pattaya Rd. (☎370 614), 2 blocks from the beach. Country-western pub with a loyal following. Tropical drinks 165-175฿. Draft beer 120฿. Happy hour daily 6-7:30pm. Live music Th-Su 9pm-2am. Open daily 6pm-2am.

KO SAMET ☎038

Just four hours from Bangkok, Ko Samet is a popular vacation spot for Thais and foreigners alike. Over the past 20 years, beachside bungalows have slowly encroached on much of the shoreline, and loud *farang* pubs and Thai karaoke bars dominate the once-still nights. Development aside, however, Ko Samet delivers. With the best beaches and clearest water on the east coast, a dip in its tranquil waves or a nap on its clean, white sand will satisfy the traveler seeking good old-fashioned relaxation. Many travelers prefer Samet's low-key atmosphere to that of its rowdier and more developed island neighbors.

TRANSPORTATION

Ferries: Nuan Tip Pier and **Tarua Phe Pier** in the town of Ban Phe serve Ko Samet. If you arrive via *songthaew* from Rayong, you will be let off at Tarua Phe Pier, opposite the 7-Eleven. Ferries here leave regularly and go to **Ao Wong Duan** (9:30am, 1:30, 5pm—not always available; 60฿) and **Na Dan Pier** (every hr. 8am-5pm, 50฿), regardless of the number of passengers. Buses from Bangkok stop in front of **Nuan Tip Pier** (☎651 508), 200m east of Tarua Phe Pier, which offers service to Na Dan Pier in northern Ko Samet (40min., 20-person min., round-trip 100฿). To get to Nuan Tip Pier, walk through the market toward the ocean. Additional boats with a 7-passenger min. are available during peak months to: **Ao Kiu/Ao Pakarang** (200฿); **Ao Phrao** (45min., 120฿); **Ao Wai** (50min., 200฿); **Ao Wong Duan** (45min., 120฿).

Buses: Ban Phe Bus Station (☎651 528), opposite Nuan Tip Pier on the mainland. Buses go to **Bangkok** (3½hr., every hr. 4am-7pm, 124฿). If you're heading elsewhere, grab a *songthaew* to **Rayong** (30min., every 15min. 6:15am-6pm, 20฿) and transfer.

Local Transportation: Songthaew generally wait for 8-10 people before leaving. More remote destinations may require chartering the entire car—prices listed are per person and to charter. From Na Dan Pier to: **Ao Kiu** (50฿, 700฿); **Ao Phai** (20฿, 150฿); **Ao Phrao** (30฿, 300฿); **Ao Thian** (40฿, 300฿); **Ao Tup Tim** (20฿, 150฿); **Ao Wai** (40฿, 500฿); **Ao Wong Duan** (30฿, 300฿); **Hat Sai Kaew** (10฿, 100฿). *Songthaew* returning to the pier or offering taxi service wait at Ao Phai in front of Silver Sands Resort. The island is generally walkable—it's only a 500m stroll from Na Dan Pier to Hat Sai Kaew, and the walk from Ao Wong Duan to Ao Phai takes just 30min.

Rentals: Shops renting **motorbikes** cluster near Na Dan Pier and along the road to Hat Sai Kaew. 100-150฿ per hr., 300-400฿ per day with passport or 500฿ deposit. Open daily 8am-8pm. The only part of the island with paved roads is where the rental shops are; as soon as you leave the pier area the roads are extremely rutted and rocky.

ORIENTATION AND PRACTICAL INFORMATION

With only two roads stretching through its 16km, Ko Samet does not require much orientation. Boats disembark at **Na Dan Pier** on the island's northeast corner. A paved road runs south to the Park Service entrance booth, where you must pay a hefty **admission fee** to enter the island, technically a Thai national park (200฿, ages 10 and under 100฿). Here, the path forks. Directly ahead is **Hat Sai Kaew,** while the right-hand fork continues south, behind the bungalows of the eastern beaches: **Ao Cho, Ao Hin Klong, Ao Kiu, Ao Nuan, Ao Phai, Ao Thian, Ao Tup Tim, Ao Wai, Ao Wong Duan,** and **Hat Lung Dum.** To get to these beaches, bear left at the fork after Ao Phai. Head straight to go to Ko Samet's only west-coast beach, **Ao Phrao.** Beachside paths and jungle trails link all the beaches except Ao Phrao and Ao Kiu.

Tourist Office: Visitors Center, next to the park entrance by Hat Sai Kaew, provides info on local wildlife. English-speaking Mr. Nan can be reached 24hr. in case of emergency (☎01 663 5055). Open daily 8am-4pm, often much later in high season.

Tours: Many of Ko Samet's larger guesthouses offer air ticketing, domestic minibus service, and snorkeling tours.

Currency Exchange: Exchange as much money as you think you'll need at the banks in **Ban Phe,** west of the pier. Otherwise, the **post office** at Naga Bungalows offers the most competitive rates for currency, traveler's checks, and cash advances.

Local Tourist Police: (☎651 669). On the mainland, a block east of the market at Nuan Tip Pier. English spoken. Open 24hr.

Medical Services: Health Center (☎644 123), halfway between Na Dan Pier and the park entry. Some English spoken. Open M-Sa 8:30am-4:30pm. In emergencies, phone the **hospital** in Rayong (☎611 104); Ko Samet's emergency services are inadequate.

Telephones: Pay phones are near the Visitors Center and the pier. **Miss You Coffee Corner** offers international calls starting at 60฿ per min.

Internet Access: The large bungalows at Ao Phai, Ao Phrao, Ao Wong Duan, and Hat Sai Kaew all offer Internet access for 2฿ per min. Fast connections are available at **Miss You Coffee Corner,** just before the park entrance. (☎644 060. Internet 2฿ per min. Open 7:30am-midnight.)

Post Office: Naga Bungalows (☎353 257) operates a licensed **post office** next door to the hotel. Address *Poste Restante* to: "POSTE RESTANTE, Ko Samet, Ban Phe, Rayong 21160." Open daily 8:30am-9:30pm.

Postal Code: 21160.

ACCOMMODATIONS AND FOOD

All of Ko Samet's beaches offer some bungalow-type accommodation. In general, **Ao Cho** and **Ao Phai** offer the cheapest accommodations, while **Hat Sai Kaew** and **Ao Phrao** cater to older travelers with fatter wallets. Hat Sai Kaew, Ao Phai, and **Ao Wong Duan** are the most heavily touristed beaches; **Ao Kiu** and **Ao Nuan** the most secluded. Be prepared for major crowds on weekends and holidays, and expect prices to jump accordingly. **Camping** is available on all beaches, although your best bets are on secluded Ao Kiu, the rocks between Ao Phai and Ao Tup Tim, and the knoll behind the Visitors Center near Hat Sai Kaew. Prices fluctuate between high and low season, so call ahead for the most up-to-date figure.

AO PHAI. A 5min. walk from Hat Sai Kaew, Ao Phai is a backpacker haven. Free of the litter and bobbing boats that sometimes plague Hat Sai Kaew and Ao Wong Duan, Ao Phai's white beaches are wide and its waters are good for swimming, despite the crowds. Accommodations, while plentiful, fill up quickly, so arrive before 3 or 4pm. At the northern end is the cheapest of the accommodations, **Naga Bungalows ❸**, a Ko Samet institution that remains the most popular spot on the island. The plain bamboo bungalows sit on stilts. (☎644 035. Internet 2฿ per min. Reception 8:30am-9:30pm. Bungalows with fan 300฿, with private bath 400฿; low-season 200฿/400฿.) The **restaurant ❸** serves fresh bread, sundaes, tofu-veggie options, and more. (Entrees 30-250฿. Open 8am-10pm.) The **bar** is one of the most popular hot spots on the beach. **Tok's Little Hut ❸**, south of Naga and just as popular, but slightly more upscale, has wood-paneled bungalows with fans and baths. (☎644 072. Bungalows 300฿, with A/C 800฿; low-season 250฿/700฿.) Tok's **bar** rivals Naga for most popular—crowds usually depend on who has the better promotion that night. (Open until 2am).

AO KIU. With glistening white sand, good swimming, and a coral reef nearby, secluded Ao Kiu is Ko Samet's best beach. The beauty and seclusion come at a price, though; Ao Kiu is relatively hard to reach. A taxi from the pier will cost you a hefty 500฿, and from neighboring Ao Wai it's a 20-30min. walk along the back road. In 2004, Ao Prao Resorts bought and renovated the old bungalows on Ao Kiu. The new, luxurious complex is set to open in early 2005. While the gentrification of Ao Kiu largely prevents budget travelers from staying there, a trip down to the beach is still rewarding for those who want the best snorkeling on the island. For up-to-date information on the new resort, visit www.aopraoresort.com.

AO PHRAO. Ko Samet's only western-facing beach is a smooth crescent of sand with the island's most luxurious accommodations and delectable fine dining. Bungalows line this long stretch of beach, punctuated by massage mats and ocean kayaks. Make a right when the road forks just after the last resort; 25min. later, you will arrive at the pearly gates of **Le Vimarn Cottages ❺**, the island's ultra-expensive, nothing-but-luxury, 7000฿ bungalows. (40% low-season discount. Price includes transfer from Seree Ban Phe Pier.) The international **restaurant ❺** has the finest dining on the island. (Open 7am-11pm.) Next up is **Lima Coco Resort ❺**, a newer establishment not as nice as its neighbors, but also slightly less expensive. (☎02 938 1811; www.limacoco.com. Rooms 2500฿ and up. Low-season discounts. Price includes transfer from Ban Phe.)

AO NUAN. The best way to get to this beautiful, secluded spot is to ascend from the main road (take the next left after the turn-off for Ao Tup Tim) to a small hill overlooking the rocky beach below and then to descend upon the rustic **Nuan Bungalows ❸**. Waves crash onto the rocks that make up the tiny beach. Behind it are immaculate wooden huts with mattresses on the floor and mosquito nets hanging from the ceiling—this place is like no other on the island. Usually full from November to April, so come early in case you have to go elsewhere. (No telephone or reservations. Small huts 250฿; doubles 500-700฿.)

HAT SAI KAEW. A 10min. walk from Na Dan Pier, Hat Sai Kaew caters mostly to package tours from Europe and Asia and is usually packed with sarong vendors, ferries, and seniors bobbing in the water. Consequently, the beach, though good for swimming, is usually crowded. Budget accommodations are scarce. Your best bet is the rather glum **Ploy Thalay Resort ❹**, halfway up the beach. (☎01 451 1387. Doubles with fan 600฿, with A/C 1000฿; low-season 500฿/800฿.) Farther south on the beach is the large **White Sands Resort ❹.** The sprawling complex has several convenience stores, a restaurant, and tours to the other islands. Electricity runs 5pm-9am only. (Rooms with fan 600฿, with A/C 1200฿; low-season 400฿/1000฿.) **Jirawan Restaurant ❸**, at Saikew Villa III, has vegetarian options and pricey seafood on the beach. (Seafood entrees 120-250฿. Open 7am-11pm.)

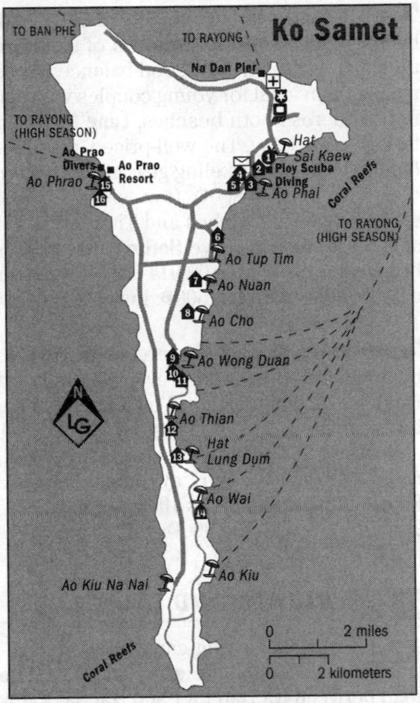

Ko Samet

BUNGALOWS AND RESORTS
Ao Phai Hut, **7**
Ao Prao Resort, **20**
Ploy Thalay, **2**
Horizons Resort, **12**
Jep's, **6**
Le Vimarn Cottages, **16**
Lima Coco Resort, **15**
Lung Dum Bungalows, **13**
Naga Bungalows, **4**
Nice and Easy, **10**
Nuan Bungalows, **7**
Samet Cabana, **9**
Samet Ville Resort, **14**
Sea-Breeze Bungalows, **8**
Sea Horse Bungalows, **11**
Tok's Little Hut, **5**
Tubtim Resort, **6**
White Sands Resort, **3**
Wonderland Resort, **8**

FOOD
Jirawan, **1**

AO TUP TIM. This pretty beach is an easy 5min. walk along the coast from Ao Phai. Although it's usually less crowded than Ao Phai, it's fairly congested compared to the beaches farther south. **Tubtim Resort ❹**, on the southern end of the beach, offers the best deal on accommodations. The comfortable thatched bungalows all have private baths. (☎644 025. Doubles with fan and shower 500฿, with A/C 1200฿.) The **restaurant ❸** has an extensive menu of European and Thai options (40-300฿) in a green area with lots of large trees.

AO CHO. Small, secluded Ao Cho is the most whimsical of Ko Samet's beaches. The quaint pier on the shore is complemented by tree swings and flowered bushes on the grounds of the beach's only accommodation, **Wonderland Resort ❷.** (☎01 996 8477. Snorkel rental 50฿ per day. Motorbike rental 400฿ per day. Doubles with fan 150฿, with A/C 900-1200฿.) The **restaurant ❷** is open daily 7am-10pm.

AO WONG DUAN. "Half Moon Bay" is a spacious beach filled with restaurants, bars, tour operators, traffic, and congestion. The huge mother/daughter-owned **Nice and Easy** and **Sea Horse Bungalows ❺** complex offers not just a place to stay, but motorbike rental (100฿ per hr., 400฿ per day), jet ski rental (900฿ per 30min.), boat tours, and some of the best beachside dining on the island. (☎653 740. Doubles with fan 600฿, with A/C 800-1200฿; low-season 300฿/600฿. Extra person 100-150฿.) The lowest-priced option on the beach is **Samet Cabana ❸**, at the north end of the beach, which has rooms in red bungalows, equipped with two small beds. (☎01 838 4853. Rooms 400฿, with bath 700฿; low-season 300฿/600฿.)

AO THIAN (CANDLELIGHT BEACH) AND HAT LUNG DUM. Though these beaches have shorter stretches of sand broken up by longer intervals of rocks, they manage to strike a good balance between seclusion and accessibility, which makes them ideal for young couples who want to frolic in relative privacy. Stretching out across both beaches, **Lung Dum Bungalow ❸** is both remote and mellow, though quite busy. The well-priced, plain bungalows have private baths and patios facing the sea. Snorkeling gear can be rented for 50฿ per day. (☎01 652 8056. Doubles with fan 300-800฿; low-season 250-600฿.) Lung Dum's **restaurant ❸** offers inexpensive sandwiches and Thai food. (Entrees 60-200฿. Open 7am-10pm.) The slightly more expensive **Horizons Resort ❹,** on the Candlelight Beach side, offers hot water and TVs. (☎09 914 5585. Kayak rental 150฿ per hr. Snorkel gear 50฿ per day. Doubles with fan 600฿; low-season 400฿.)

AO WAI. Though remote, Ao Wai's clear water and clean, white sand backed by green vegetation make every second of the 25min. coastal hike from Ao Wong Duan to Ao Wai worth it. You'll have to charter a taxi from the pier (500฿), since few people venture so far south. The ride itself is a real off-road journey and is almost worth the high fare. Targeting package tourists, **Samet Ville Resort ❺** dominates the beach with pricey rooms. The **restaurant ❹** serves Thai dishes (40-300฿). Snorkeling gear rental is 100฿ per day. (☎651 681. Restaurant open daily 7:30am-9pm. Rooms with fan 900฿, with A/C 1300฿. 10% low-season discount.)

SIGHTS AND NIGHTLIFE

A thirst for sightseeing can be satisfied at the 14m high **Sitting Buddha** and the smaller Buddha images at his knees. A gate next to the **Golden Buddha** abuts the road between Na Dan Pier and Hat Sai Kaew; follow the path to the statue.

Ko Samet boasts a lively **nightlife** scene on Ao Phai. The bar at **Naga Bungalows,** which occasionally features a free dancing show, battles **Tok's** next door to attract crowds with nightly promotions. Nearby **Silver Sands Resort,** at the southern end of the beach, offers a beachside bar that becomes an impromptu disco when crowds are large enough. The other beaches tend to quiet down when their restaurants close. The bars on Ao Phai are famous for serving **drinks** by the bucket.

WATERSPORTS

With an abundance of coral reefs and clear water, it's no wonder that Ko Samet is popular for **snorkeling.** At Ao Phrao, Ao Kiu, and Ao Wai, reef communities are a 5min. swim from shore. Less-disturbed coral live in more remote reaches of the archipelago. Many establishments offer snorkeling tours of Ko Samet and the surrounding islets. There are now several **scuba diving** operations on the island, so it pays to shop around. **Ao Prao Divers,** based in the lobby of the Ao Prao Resort on Ao Phrao, runs a PADI-certified scuba diving school year-round. The school makes daytrips around Ko Samet and to Ko Thalu from November to May. (☎644 100. 2 dives 2500฿. 4- to 5-day certification courses 12,000฿. Specialty and more extensive dives 10,000-13,000฿. 3-4hr. introductory courses 2500฿. Open daily 8am-4pm.)

Ploy Scuba Diving (☎06 143 9318) on Hat Sai Kaew by Ploy Thalay, also offers certification courses (2-4 per day, 7000-10,500฿), dive trips for those already certified (2 dives 2500฿) and snorkel trips for 300฿ for a half day and 600฿ for a full day. (Open high-season 8am-8pm; low-season 8am-5pm.)

CHANTHABURI ☎039

Chanthaburi, the "City of the Moon," is famous for its waterfalls, fruit, and gemstones. Between May and July, the city's fruit market bulges with mouth-watering produce. Year-round, rubies and sapphires from all over the world are cut and sold right before your eyes in the city's gem district, before being distributed across the globe. These attractions, in addition to the neighboring national parks, make Chanthaburi a worthwhile visit.

TRANSPORTATION AND PRACTICAL INFORMATION. The **bus station** (☎311 299), on Saritidet Rd., sends buses to: Aranyaprathet (8hr., 15 per day 3am-10pm, 80-180฿); Bangkok (4hr., 12 per day 7:30am-11pm, 115฿); Khorat (6hr., every 2hr. 6am-10pm, 116-209฿); Pattaya/Si Racha (2½hr., 10 per day 5am-5pm, 90฿); Trat (1½hr., every hr. 9:30am-9:30pm, 30-42฿). **Taxis** in town are 30฿.

To get downtown from the bus station, head left onto **Saritidet Road.** Saritidet Rd. ends at **Benchamarachuthis Road,** at the Kasemsarn 1 Hotel. The alley to the left of the hotel leads to **Sukhaphibal Road,** which runs parallel to Benchamarachuthis Rd. along the river. Heading right at the Kasemsarn 1 Hotel brings you to the commercial heart of town. Branching off Kasemsarn 1 to the right on **Si Rong Muan Road** leads to the **market.** The **gem district** is one block past Si Rong Muan Rd. on Kasemsarn 1; it is to the right down **Kwang Road** and left on **Si Chan Road.**

Services include: **Krung Thai Bank,** next to the post office on Benchamarachuthis Rd. (☎311 111; Cirrus/MC/V 24hr. **ATM;** open daily M-F 8:30am-4:30pm); 24hr. **police booth** at the bus station; a **clinic,** 20m to the left of the bus station on Saritidet Rd. (☎321 378; open 8am-8pm; for emergencies, call Taksin Hospital, ☎351 467); **Telecomm Center,** next to GPO on Thung Dondang Rd., a 3km walk or a 30฿ taxi ride from town (☎325 916; open daily 7am-11pm); **Perfect Net and Print,** on Saritidet Rd. 40m past the bus station toward town, has Internet (☎351 403; 20฿ per hr.; open daily 8:30am-midnight); and **GPO,** on Thung Dondang Rd. near the Eastern Hotel. (☎311 013. *Poste Restante.* Open M-F 8:30am-4:30pm, Sa-Su 9am-noon.) **Postal Code:** 22000. The more conveniently located **Chantani Post Office** is on Benchamarachuthis Rd. across from the Kasemsarn 1 Hotel. (☎350 247. Open M-F 8:30am-4:30pm, Sa-Su 9am-noon.) **Postal Code:** 22001.

ACCOMMODATIONS AND FOOD. Accommodations of any sort are scarce in tourist-free Chanthaburi. To reach two budget spots, continue down the alley at the end of Saritidet Rd. on Benchamarachuthis Rd., and turn left onto Sukhaphibal Rd. On the left is the **Arun Sawat Hotel ❷,** which features drab rooms with fans and A/C. (☎311 082. Doubles with fan 120-150฿, with A/C 250฿.) The **Chantra Hotel ❷,** 248 Sukhaphibal Rd., across the street, offers slightly more spartan accommodations. The clean rooms are a sterile white. Ask for the room by the river. (☎312 310. Doubles 120-150฿.) The **Eastern Hotel ❹,** 899 Thachalab Rd., is far from the bus station and market but offers mid-range hotel rooms with flush toilets and A/C. (☎312 218. Rooms 550฿.)

Take your grumbling stomach to Chanthaburi's immense **market ❶,** centered on the low-lying fountain one block west of Benchamarachuthis Rd., down Si Rong Muang Rd. The **coffee shop and bakery ❶,** 33/4 Saritidet Rd., has some of the best pastries and cake anywhere. (Coffee 15฿. Sweets 10-20฿. Open M-F 6:30am-6pm, Sa-Su 7am-5pm.) **Dream Restaurant ❷,** 22/1 Saritidet Rd., by the bus station, is one of the few places in town that has both A/C and English translations. Try their specialty, milky crab spring rolls (75฿).

SIGHTS. Chanthaburi's more spectacular sights are outside the city limits, but a few treasures within town keep travelers entertained for a day or two. On weekends, shoppers head to **Si Chan Road,** the heart of Chanthaburi's **gem district.**

Some 50-60% of the world's rubies and sapphires pass through Chanthaburi on their way from Cambodia, Laos, Myanmar, and even Africa. Though Chanthaburi's mines no longer produce as many gems as they used to, the city is still the center for cutting and buying. Be wary of buying, however, as it is easy to be swindled. The 19th-century **Cathedral of the Immaculate Conception,** across the footbridge near the southern end of Sukhaphibal Rd., was built by French soldiers who occupied Chanthaburi from 1893 to 1905. It is the largest Catholic edifice in Thailand. On the southwest side of town, **Taksin Park** occupies many well-pruned acres. (Open daily 5am-9pm.) In order to celebrate the area's renowned produce, Chanthaburi holds a 10-day **fruit festival** at the peak of the spring fruit season.

NIGHTLIFE. Chanthaburi boasts a surprisingly happening nightlife scene. Its epicenter is at the enormous **Diamond Pub,** on the southwestern side of town. Live bands belt out Thai pop while a beautiful young crowd looks on. It rocks all week, but is packed Fridays and Saturdays. Bottles of soda go for 30฿, and Singhas are 120฿. Grab a taxi from the city center for 20฿. (Open daily 9pm-2am.)

BORDER CROSSING: BAN HAT LEK/SIHANOUKVILLE. To enter Cambodia, you must have a Cambodian visa, available at the border at **Hat Lek** for 1200฿. To be on the safe side, it is best to obtain your visa at the Cambodian embassy in **Bangkok** (p. 664). Crossing the border takes 9-13hr. Depending on the departure time of the boat to **Sihanoukville,** an overnight stay may be necessary. Either way, it pays to get an early start. To get from Trat to **Ban Hat Lek,** take a blue *songthaew* from behind the market (1½hr., every hr. 6am-6pm, 35฿) or a minivan from 2 blocks north of the market (1½hr., every hr. 6am-6pm, 80-100฿). When you exit Thailand at the border, remember to obtain an exit stamp. After crossing the border, you can hire a taxi to cross the newly finished bridge to **Ko Kong,** where overnight accommodations can be found. Daily minibuses leave from outside the Cambodian immigration office at 9am for Phnom Penh (650฿) or Sihanoukville (550฿). Leave Trat by minibus by 7am to catch these minibuses. A boat departs daily at 8am (sometimes earlier) for Sihanoukville (3½-4hr., 600฿). To catch the boat, leave Trat at 6am. Stay the night in Sihanoukville or catch a bus to Phnom Penh (3½hr.; 10,000 *riels*).

THAILAND

KO CHANG ☎039

Ko Chang (Elephant Island) is rapidly going the way of its southern cousins. A steady stream of development promises lots of tourists, high prices, piles of garbage, and resort commercialism. But for the moment, the island is still bursting with leafy rain forests, towering waterfalls, isolated beaches, and unexplored territory on its eastern coast. A new road skirting the border of the island makes it much easier to access even the most remote patches of sand. Unfortunately, the amount of trash washing up on beaches and coral increasingly renders the water less swimmable.

TRANSPORTATION

To reach Ko Chang, take a bus to **Trat,** then a *songthaew* (every 30min. or when full 6am-6pm, 30฿) from the front of the municipal market on Sukhumvit Rd. to whichever pier has a ferry leaving next, usually either **Laem Ngop Pier** or **Center Point Pier.** (Basic one-way tickets 30฿.) The ferry will arrive at one of the piers on

Ko Chang's northern end (30-50min.). From Ko Chang, pickup-truck **taxis** run frequently to the west-coast beaches: **Hat Kai Bae** (50min., 40฿); **Hat Khlong Phrao** (30min., 40฿); **Hat Sai Khao** (15min., 30฿); **Lonely Beach** (1¼hr., 70฿).

Ferries: Ferries run frequently from Pier 2 on Ko Chang to **Center Point Pier** (30min., every hr. 6am-7pm, 30฿) and **Laem Ngop Pier** (50min.; every hr. 6am-7pm, low season every 2hr. 7am-5pm; 30฿). Center Point is 5min. from Laem Ngop by *songthaew;* your driver will take you to whichever pier has the next ferry leaving. Ferries also go between **Ao Thammachat** (20min. from Laem Ngop) and Piers 1 and 3 on **Ko Chang** (25min., every hr. 7am-6:30pm, 30฿; high season only). Ao Thammachat and Center Point can accommodate vehicle crossings.

Local Transportation: Songthaew rule. A ride between beaches is 30-70฿. In theory, *songthaew* leave from Hat Kai Bae 1hr. before ferry departure, hit the other 2 beaches on the way up, and reach the pier just in time for departure.

Rentals: Motorbike rentals are available on any of the 4 beaches. A good rate is 150฿ per day for manual and 200฿ per day for automatic. The roads between Hat Sai Khao and the pier and Kai Bae and Lonely Beach are extremely steep and curvy, and very dangerous to ride on. Usually a day rental will require a deposit of 500฿.

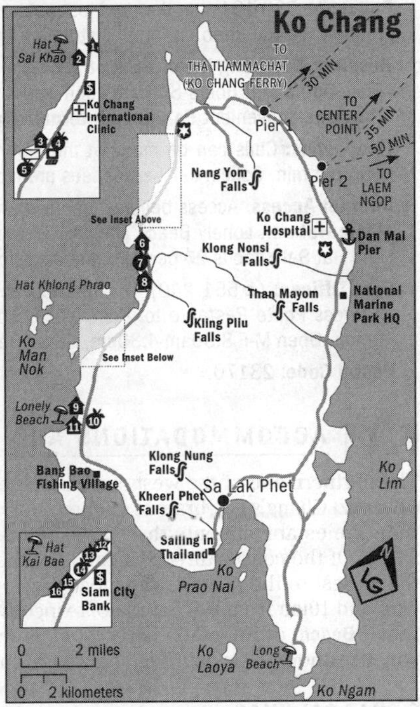

Ko Chang

ACCOMMODATIONS
Cookie Bungalows, **2**
K.B. Bungalow, **16**
K.P. Bungalows, **6**
Kai Bae Hut, **15**
Magic Bungalows, **8**
Nature Beach Resort, **9**
Paloma Cliff Resort, **3**
Treehouse Bungalows, **11**

FOOD
Guitar House, **10**
Hungry Elephant, **5**
Invito, **4**
Morgan Restaurant, **14**
O_2 Bar, **13**
Tropicana Restaurant, **7**

NIGHTLIFE
Lek Bar and Diner, **12**
Oodie's, **1**

ORIENTATION AND PRACTICAL INFORMATION

Ko Chang's interior is a trackless rain forest. There is a well-paved road around the perimeter of the island, except for the very southern part. From the pier area at the island's northeast end, the road goes south to the east coast, passes waterfall trails, and branches into a western road that almost reaches Bang Bao and an eastern road that ends in the fishing village of Sa Lak Pet. A right turn at the pier leads past the west coast's four beaches: **Hat Sai Khao, Hat Khlong Phrao, Hat Kai Bae,** and **Lonely Beach.** The road ends in the picturesque fishing village of Bang Bao.

Tourist Office: Ko Chang National Park Headquarters (☎09 251 9244), in Than Mayom, 20km from Hat Sai Khao. Open daily 8:30am-4:30pm. Also in Laem Ngop.

Police: (☎586 191), on the road just before Dan Mai. A police box is also on the main road in Hat Sai Khao, far north just before the road begins to climb the mountain.

Hospital: Ko Chang Hospital (☎586 131), on the eastern side of the island by Dan Mai Pier. Outpatient hours 8:30am-noon and 1:30-4:30pm. Open 24hr. for emergencies. The more convenient **Ko Chang International Clinic** (☎551 151) is open 9am-8pm.

Telephones: Calls can be made at most bungalows and Internet cafes. A good rate is 60฿ per min. Collect call service fees are typically 10฿ per min. with a 15min. limit.

Internet Access: Access becomes more sparse and expensive the farther south you go. **Siam Huts** on Lonely Beach charges 3฿ per min. Access at Kai Bae, Hat Khlong Prao and Hat Sai Khao is 2฿ per min.; the occasional gem in Hat Sai Khao offers 1฿ per min.

Post Offices: (☎551 240). On the main road at the southern end of Hat Sai Khao. Address *Poste Restante* to: Post Office, Ko Chang Island, Thailand 23170, Western Union. Open M-F 8:30am-4:30pm, Sa-Su 9am-noon.

Postal Code: 23170.

ACCOMMODATIONS AND FOOD

The northern end of the west coast is spiked with soaring cliffs, which soon level off to Ko Chang's celebrated beaches. Much of the new development is far pricier than the establishments that came before, squeezing budget travelers farther south. Of the coast's three principal beaches, **Hat Sai Khao** (White Sand Beach) is the closest to the pier and the most developed. **Hat Khlong Phrao** and **Hat Kai Bae,** 6km and 10km from Hat Sai Khao, respectively, offer more privacy. Farther south, **Lonely Beach,** of full-moon party fame, is the most laid-back. During the low season, guesthouses slash prices and are willing to negotiate.

THAILAND

HAT SAI KHAO. Prices have skyrocketed in recent years at Hat Sai Khao. While budget accommodations are virtually non-existent, Hat Sai Khao offers the most services. Dive shops, motorbike rentals, bars, restaurants, and Internet cafes are plentiful here. At the southernmost point, **Plamola Cliff Resort ❺** has a pool and bamboo huts overlooking the rocky point south of Hat Sai Khao. (☎551 119. Rooms with fan 800฿, A/C 1500-2500฿. Up to 50% low-season discount.) **Cookie Bungalows ❺,** 300m south, has renovated bungalows. (☎01 861 4227. Bungalows with fan 700฿, with A/C 1500฿; hotel rooms 1800฿. Low-season 300฿/500฿/1000฿.)

The **Hungry Elephant ❸** has a reputation for great steaks and French food. Walk 10min. south from Hat Sai Khao; it's on the right. (☎09 985 8433. Steaks 175฿. Open daily 11:30am-11:30pm.) **Invito ❹** serves oven-baked pizza and pasta in a intimate setting, just across from Plamola Cliff Resort. (☎551 326. Pizza 200-290฿. Pasta 160-280฿. Open daily 11am-11pm.) **Oodie's** has live music nightly, beginning at 10pm. (Cocktails 80-150฿. Small beer 40-60฿. Open daily 4pm-1am.)

HAT KHLONG PHRAO. Although not the most remote, Hat Khlong Phrao is the most serene and sparsely settled of Ko Chang's three main beaches. Bungalows are widely spaced on broad expanses of sand punctuated by rock outcroppings and creeks from the interior. Each establishment has its own entrance, but all are connected by a walk along the beach. **K.P. Bungalows ❷,** toward the center of the beach, has cute, rustic, thatched bamboo huts. (☎01 863 7262. Doubles with fan 400฿, with private bath 600฿; low-season 200฿/400฿.) **Magic Bungalows ❸** offers clean, recently renovated rooms, and 3hr. snorkeling trips to Ko Yauk for 250฿ per person. (☎01 861 4829. Motorbike rentals 250฿ per day. Doubles 300฿, with private bath 500฿, with A/C 1300฿; low-season 150฿/300฿/700฿.)

For a nice meal, head to one of the brand-new resorts on the beach. The **Tropicana** has a **beachside restaurant ❸** with slightly pricey but well-prepared Thai food. (Seafood 150-250฿. European and Thai food 70-270฿. Open 6am-11pm.)

HAT KAI BAE. Hat Kai Bae has a nice selection of restaurants, bars, Internet cafes, and bungalows without the overcrowding and conspicuous consumption characteristic of Hat Sai Khao. **K.B. Bungalow ❹** is a step above the typical mid-range accommodation, with spacious baths. (☎01 862 8103. Doubles with fan 600฿, with A/C 1500฿; low-season 400฿/1200฿.) **Kai Bae Hut ❹** is conveniently located right next to the *songthaew* stop. (☎01 062 8426. 2-person fan rooms 500฿; beachside 4-person bungalows 1500฿; low-season 300฿/800฿.) The **restaurant ❷** serves Thai food. (Entrees 60-100฿. Breakfast 40฿. Open daily 7am-10pm.)

The **O_2 Bar ❷** is a popular place to enjoy delicious Thai food. (Breakfast 40-70฿. Entrees 40-70฿. Beer 45฿. Cocktails 90-140฿. Open daily 8am-midnight.) **Morgan Restaurant ❷** is especially popular for breakfast. (Breakfast 35-60฿. Veggie options. Open daily 7:30am-11pm.) **Lek Bar and Diner ❹** is a bit more expensive, but its loud pop music and festive lighting draw an energetic crowd. (☎07 131 0308. Thai food and grill 160-300฿. Heineken 65฿. Cocktails 70-140฿. Open 5pm-2am.)

> **TIP** If you want to escape the crowds but can't afford the boat transportation to the outlying islands, try walking to one. Off the southern part of Kai Bae, there is a small island where, at low tide, the waters recede enough so that it's possible to walk there and spend a couple hours on your own private island paradise. Mind the rising waters, though, or you'll be stranded out there until the next low tide.

LONELY BEACH. A new road connects this once-secluded beach to the rest of the world, but it remains one of the most chilled-out, tailor-made backpacker hideouts in Thailand. The best place to go to see fellow backpackers is the **Treehouse Bungalow ❶**, at the far southern end of the beach. (☎01 847 8215. Motorbikes 250฿ per day. Rooms 100-200฿. Low-season discount.) For a slightly more comfortable experience, the beachside bungalows at the **Nature Beach Resort ❸** are of the well-kept bamboo variety and have their own baths. (☎01 803 8933. Huts 300฿; bigger rooms 400-500฿. Low-season 150-300฿.) The **Guitar House ❶**, on the main road behind Treehouse, serves simple and cheap Thai food (open 11am-10pm). The most consistent nightlife can be found at Treehouse's bar (open until 2am). During the high season, **Nature Bar** and **Monkey Bar**, on the beach by Nature Beach Resort, are popular nightspots.

THE WEST COAST. Popular **Mama's Very Famous Snorkel Trips** (☎09 831 1059) is just north of the road's end on Hat Kai Bae. A trip to Ko Yuak costs 150฿; special three-island trips cost 450฿ and leave at 9am. Fishing boats can be rented for 500฿ per hr. Diving and snorkeling tend to be poor during the rainy season; many operations shut down entirely.

The west coast of Ko Chang also provides some opportunities to see the island's interior. **Khlong Pliu Falls,** just 500m from the park entrance, is popular, accessible, and swimmable. (Open daily 8am-5pm. 200฿, students 100฿.) **Chutiman Chuayrum** offers tourists the chance to enjoy jungle treks while seated comfortably on top of an elephant. (☎09 939 6676. Open 8am-5pm. 1hr. 500฿, 2hr. 900฿.)

THE EAST COAST. The picturesque east coast is short on beaches but long on scenic beauty. The town of **Dan Mai** hides a path to **Khlong Nonsi Falls,** a 30min. walk inland. **Than Mayom,** 4km to the south, is home to the **National Park Headquar-**

THAILAND

ters (☎03 952 1122), with little to offer save a visitors center. Across the street, **Than Mayom Falls,** a favorite of King Rama V, still bears his initials. Clear mountain water gushes over a 7m high rock into a jungle pool. (Only in rainy season, June-Dec. Accessible 8am-5pm. 200฿, 14 and under 100฿.) On the west coast of the island's southeast peninsula, **Long Beach** is secluded. There are 16 bungalows available, beginning at 100฿ per night. Call Tom, the owner (☎01 848 5052), ahead of time. A right at the fork and another quick right will lead to **Khlong Nung Waterfall;** a right at the fork and straight leads to **Kheeri Phet Waterfall.** The right fork ends at the homestay village and the pier where **Sailing in Thailand** can be found. From here, you can charter a sailboat from Frank, the captain, for a day-trip visiting islands (☎01 833 7673; www.sailing-in-thailand.com; 1800฿ per person), or charter a speedboat (800฿) or hire a local (around 300฿) to take you to one of the nearby islands to spend the day. One of the most beautiful islands is **Ko Wai,** home to the exceedingly popular Thai restaurant **Paradise.** Getting to the east coast can be tricky. There are no motorbike rentals north or east of Hat Sai Khao, which means if you plan to take a motorbike you'll be traversing a very steep and curvy stretch of road. Alternatively, you can try to find a taxi or someone to drive you (400฿).

ARANYAPRATHET ☎037

Aranyaprathet is the border town for the Cambodia-bound. The savvy traveler will arrive early enough to push straight on through without staying the night. The first train from Bangkok arrives with plenty of time for those heading to Siem Reap to reach it on the same day. In the center of town, **Mahadthai-Suwannasorn Road** and **Chaoprayabodin Road** intersect at a clocktower. The **railway station** (☎231 698) sits nearby at the north end of **Suwannasorn Road. Trains** leave Bangkok for Aranyaprathet at 5:55am and 1:05pm and depart Aranyaprathet for Bangkok at 6:40am and 1:40pm (5½hr., 48฿). The bus station is on the west side of town: walk three blocks straight out and one block to the right to reach the clocktower. **Buses** run to Bangkok (4hr.; 6:30, 10:30am, 1:30, 3pm; 164฿). **Tuk-tuks** and **samlor** putter to hotels from the bus and train stations (20฿). The border **market,** on Weruwan Rd., mainly sells a dull mix of jeans and other faux-Western items. (Open daily 6am-7pm.) Motorcycle rides to the market should cost 25-30฿; *tuk-tuks* run 40-50฿. Other services include: the **pharmacy,** one block north of the Aran Garden I Hotel (open M-Sa 6:30am-8pm); the **Telecom Office,** near the corner of Mahadthai and Raduthid Rd., 500m south of the clocktower (open M-F 8:30am-4:30pm); and **Internet** access at **I-net,** 2 Raduthid Rd., one block before Aran Gardens (20฿ per hr.; open 10am-11pm). At the clocktower, the **GPO** has a **Lenso** phone card machine. (*Poste Restante.* Phone cards 300฿ and 500฿. Open M-F 8:30am-4:30pm, Sa 9am-noon.) **Postal Code:** 27120.

Aranyaprathet has no guesthouses and few accommodations of any sort. Many travelers stay at the **Aran Garden I Hotel ❷,** 59/1-7 Raduthid Rd. Walk 500m south from the clocktower to Raduthid Rd. and then 600m east to Chitsuwarn Rd.; it's on the corner. Rooms are clean and plain. (☎231 105. Doubles 150฿, with TV 200฿.) Down Raduthid Rd. one block, **Aran Garden II ❸,** 110 Raduthid Rd., has much nicer, quieter rooms with Western toilets. (☎231 070. Singles 230฿, with A/C 370฿; doubles 300฿/450฿.) In the low season, many travelers crash for free on the office floor of their Siem Reap-bound tour company. Restaurants are dismal; it's best to enjoy noodles or rice at a street stall. (Open daily 5am-8pm.) For those skipping straight to the border there is the **Star Grill ❷,** a fast-food joint with fried chicken. (Combo meal 55฿. Open daily 8:30am-5:30pm.)

BORDER CROSSING: ARANYAPRATHET/POIPET. To enter Cambodia, you must have a Cambodian visa. Travelers can obtain visas either at the Cambodian embassy in **Bangkok** (p. 664) or quickly and conveniently at the border (1200฿). In Aranyaprathet, touts materialize at the train and bus stations offering trips to Siem Reap and Angkor Wat. They are helpful in navigating the chaotic bridge and boarding a public pick-up for the painful 5hr. ride ahead (in the cab 350฿, in the back 200฿). Trucks leave 500m beyond the Cambodian border on the left. Be sure to obtain an exit stamp from Thai immigration (open daily 7:30am-5:30pm) at the bridge. Border open daily 7am-8pm. A *tuk-tuk* from anywhere in town to the bridge costs 60฿.

AYUTTHAYA ☎035

For four centuries Ayutthaya was the capital of Siam, raising 33 kings, withstanding 23 Burmese invasions, and extending its rule west to Myanmar and east to Cambodia. In 1767, however, good times turned bad when Ayutthaya was sacked by the Burmese, and the capital was moved to Bangkok, leaving the city a mere shadow of its former regal self. In 1991 UNESCO named Ayutthaya a World Heritage Site, but today *farang* and Thai alike walk by ancient royal palaces without so much as batting an eye.

TRANSPORTATION

Trains: Ayutthaya Railway Station (☎241 521), on the mainland east of the island. Take the ferry from U Thong Rd. (2฿) and walk up the street. Otherwise, it's a long walk across **Pridi Damrong Bridge** and up your 1st left (*tuk-tuk* 30฿). Trains to: **Bangkok** (1½-2hr., 20 per day, 15-20฿); **Chiang Mai** via **Phitsanulok** (12-13hr., 4 per day, 161-1253฿); **Lopburi** (1½hr., 7 per day, 13฿); **Saraburi** (1hr., 15 per day, 9฿); **Udon Thani** (9hr., 5 per day, 145-306฿).

Buses: Ayutthaya has 3 bus stations.

Naresuan Rd. has a small station 1 block east of Chikum Rd., with buses that go to **Bangkok** (#901; 1½hr., every 20min. 4:30am-7:10pm, 41฿).

Chao Phrom Market, also on Naresuan Rd., has a chaotic mess of buses leaving from the west end of the market to **Saraburi** (#358; 2¼hr., every 30min. 6am-5pm, 30฿), connecting to destinations in the northeast, and **Suphanburi** (#703; 1¾hr., every 25min. 6am-5pm, 40฿), connecting with #411 to **Kanchanaburi.**

Mainland bus terminal, 5km east of the island (*tuk-tuk* 50฿). Buses go to: **Chiang Mai** (9½hr., 9 per day 6:30am-9pm, 283-625฿); **Phitsanulok** (5hr., 7 per day 7am-7pm, 140฿); **Sukhothai** (6½hr.; standard 11 per day 7am-8:30pm, VIP 11:30am, 10pm; 169฿/256฿.)

Ferries: Continuous **ferries** to the mainland (and the train station) leave from an alley off U Thong Rd. near the intersection with Horattanachai Rd. (2฿). **Longtail boats** and **cruisers** can be hired at the Chantharkasem Palace pier at the island's northeast tip for a 1hr. trip around the island (500฿, with 2 temple stops 600฿).

Local Transportation: Tuk-tuk/songthaew hybrids wheel around the island for 30-100฿. Rent by the hr. (100฿) or for a full day (500-700฿). Most guesthouses rent **bicycles** (50-60฿ per day).

ORIENTATION AND PRACTICAL INFORMATION

The Ayutthaya **city center** is an island at the intersection of the **Chao Phraya, Pa Sak,** and **Lopburi Rivers. U Thong Road** encircles the entire island. **Buses** from nearby cities stop next to the **Chao Phrom Market** at the corner of **Naresuan** and **U Thong Roads,** near **Khlong Makham Rieng Road** in the island's northeastern corner. Buses from northern Thailand arrive east of the island, 5km beyond the **Pridi Damrong Bridge.** Although *wats* are found all over the island, most tourist attractions cluster north of the Tourist Information Center on **Si Sanphet Road.** Guesthouses are concentrated in the eastern part of the island, north of the Chao Phrom Market.

Tourist Offices: Tourist Information Center (☎322 730), Si Sanphet Rd., a 5min. walk south of Wat Phra Si Sanphet. 2nd fl. has Ayutthaya Historical Exhibition Hall. Office open M-Tu and Th-Su 8:30am-5pm.

Tours: KanKitti Travel (☎321 583), across from Tony's Place, right before Ayutthaya Guest House, has **Internet** (20฿ per hr.) and arranges bike tours (50฿) and nighttime *tuk-tuk* tours (100฿ per person) of the *wats.* Open daily 8am-10pm.

Markets: Chao Phrom Market, at the corner of Naresuan and U Thong Rd. Open daily 7am-7pm. **Hua Ro Night Market,** farther north along U Thong Rd. from Chao Phrom. Open daily 4-10pm. **Bang Lan Night Market** is off Chikun Rd. Open daily 5-9pm.

Local Tourist Police: (☎241 446), on Si Sanphet Rd. Some English. Open 24hr.

Medical Services: Ayutthaya Hospital, 46 U Thong Rd. (☎241 686), at the intersection of Si Sanphet and U Thong Rd. English spoken. Open 24hr. No credit cards.

Telephones: International telephone booths outside GPO and at U.P. Inn

Internet Access: Internet Game, on Pamapro Rd., 30m from U Thong Rd., has fast connections and lots of games. 20฿ per hr. Open daily 9am-1am.

Post Offices: GPO, 123/11 U Thong Rd. (☎252 246), on the island's northeast corner. *Poste Restante.* Open M-F 8:30am-4:30pm, Sa 9am-noon.

Postal Code: 13000.

ACCOMMODATIONS AND FOOD

Budget accommodations cluster north of **Naresuan Road,** near the Chao Phrom Market bus stop. Rates increase during festival season (Nov.-Dec.), and lodgings are harder to find. Most places have laundry and bike rental. The best option in Ayutthaya is **U.P. Inn ❷,** 20/1 Soi Thor Korsor. From Naresuan Rd., head up the *soi* opposite the bus station next to Chao Phrom Market, and make a left following the signs. The large rooms all have private bath. (☎251 213. Motorbike rental 250฿ per day. Internet 30฿ per hr., min. 15฿. Nighttime tours of ruins. Singles 200฿; doubles 250฿, with A/C 400-500฿.) **Tony's Place ❶,** 12/18 Naresuan Soi 1 Rd. (☎252 578), sits across from Ayutthaya Guest House, with clean rooms above a common garden area. (Motorbike rental 250฿ per day. Reserve ahead. Dorms 80-100฿; doubles 160฿, with bath 250฿, with A/C 400฿.) **Chantana Guest House,** 12/22 Naresuan Rd. (☎323 200), next to Tony's Place, is a quiet spot. All rooms have bath. Reserve ahead. Singles and doubles 300฿, with A/C and hot shower 450฿. ❸

Foodstalls ❶ serving 20฿ chicken and rice are interspersed with tables of plastic toys, dried fish, and piles of fruit at **Chao Phrom Market,** one block east of the local bus stop. More stalls line U Thong Rd., particularly on the eastern side of the island, after the post office. For dinner, try the foodstalls at the **night markets** such as the **Hua Ro Night Market** and the **Bang Lan Night Market.** For a cool breeze and views of a nearby *wat,* try **Saihong River Restaurant ❷,** 45 Moo 1 U Thong Rd. (☎241 449), close to the intersection of U Thong Rd. and Chikun Rd. (*Tom yam,* a hot-and-sour soup with prawns, 120฿. Entrees 50-120฿. Open daily 10am-9:30pm.) **Thai House Restaurant (Ruenthai Maisuay Restaurant) ❷,** 8/2 Moo 3 Klongsuanplu District, down the road from Wat Yai Chai Mongkhon and around the bend on the left, has tasty curry (80-120฿) set in traditional Thai houses and mossy gardens. (Entrees 80-250฿. Open daily 10am-10pm.)

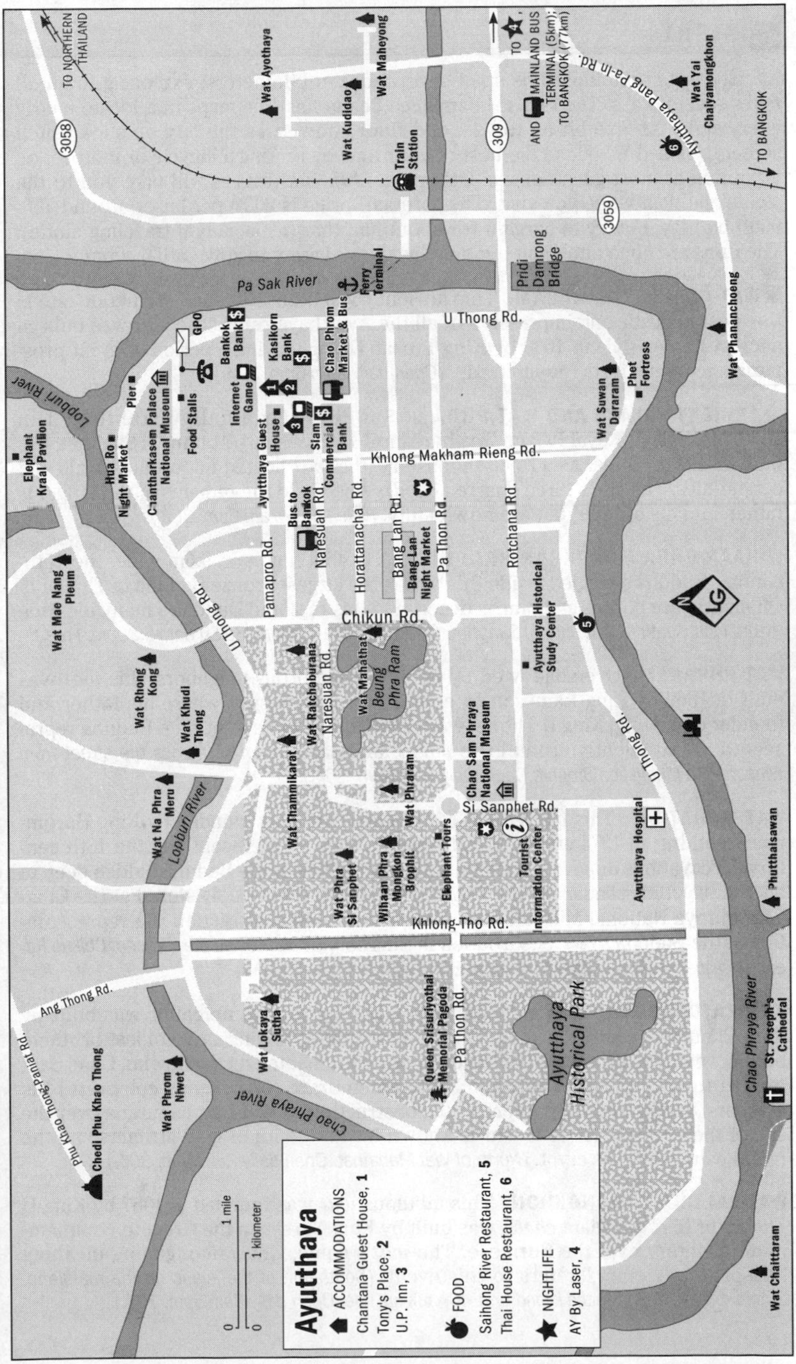
Ayutthaya
ACCOMMODATIONS
Chantana Guest House, 1
Tony's Place, 2
U.P. Inn, 3
FOOD
Saihong River Restaurant, 5
Thai House Restaurant, 6
NIGHTLIFE
AY By Laser, 4
0
1 mile
0
1 kilometer
TO NORTHERN THAILAND
3058
309
3059
TO 4
TO BANGKOK
MAINLAND BUS TERMINAL (5km); TO BANGKOK (77km)
AND
Ayutthaya Pang Pa-in Rd.
Wat Yai Chaiyamongkhon
Wat Ayothaya
Wat Maheyong
Wat Kudidao
Train Station
Pa Sak River
Ferry Terminal
Pridi Damrong Bridge
U Thong Rd.
GPO
Bankok Bank
Kasikorn Bank
Chao Phrom Market & Bus
Internet Game
Siam Commercial Bank
Ayutthaya Guest House
Pier
Food Stalls
Chantharakasem Palace National Museum
Lopburi River
Elephant Kraal Pavilion
Hua Ro Night Market
Wat Phananchoeng
Phet Fortress
Wat Suwan Dararam
Khlong Makham Rieng Rd.
Bus to Bankok
Naresuan Rd.
Pamapro Rd.
Horattanacha Rd.
Bang Lan Rd.
Bang Lan Night Market
Pa Thon Rd.
Rotchana Rd.
Wat Mae Nang Pleum
U Thong Rd.
Chikun Rd.
Wat Rhong Kong
Wat Khudi Thong
Wat Ratchaburana
Wat Mahathat
Beung Phra Ram
Ayutthaya Historical Study Center
Wat Na Phra Meru
Wat Thammikarat
Wat Phraram
Chao Sam Phraya National Museum
Si Sanphet Rd.
Ayutthaya Hospital
Wat Phra Si Sarphet
Wihaan Phra Mongkon Bophit
Elephant Tours
Tourist Information Center
Phutthaisawan
Khlong-Tho Rd.
Ang Thong Rd.
Phu Khao Thong-Paniat Rd.
Chedi Phu Khao Thong
Wat Lokaya Sutha
Queen Srisuriyothai Memorial Pagoda
Pa Thon Rd.
Ayutthaya Historical Park
Wat Phrom Niwet
Chao Phraya River
St. Joseph's Cathedral
Wat Chaittaram

THAILAND

SIGHTS

Ayutthaya's crumbling ruins span several dozen kilometers; exploring them all takes several days. The **Tourist Information Center** has free maps that locate nearly every sight. An exhibit on the second floor showcases the city on slick touch screens (closed W). Make the best of your time by renting a bicycle or motorbike, an option at most guesthouses. Otherwise, *tuk-tuk* drivers will take you to the sights and wait while you visit. The "official" price is 200฿ per hr. or around 700-900฿ per day, but try to bargain for about half that (especially if traveling alone). The ruins are open until 6pm but usually allow visitors to stay until 6:30pm.

WAT CHAIWATTHANARAM. This ancient royal monastery and cremation site is the most majestic and impressive of all the Ayutthaya ruins. The *wat* was built in ancient Khmer-style in 1630 by King Prasat Thong, during a period of great prosperity stemming from foreign trade. *(Open daily 8am-6pm. 30฿.)*

ANCIENT PALACE AND WAT PHRA SI SANPHET. Originally established in 1350, the ancient Royal Palace was here until 1448, when Wat Phra Si Sanphet was built on the grounds. As a royal monastery, the *wat* hosted important rituals and ceremonies. The site's three charred *chedis* once held the remains of the king, his father, and his brother, but are now empty. *(Open daily 7am-6pm. 30฿.)*

WIHAAN PHRA MONGKHON BROPHIT. At 12.45m high and 9.5m wide, the 15th-century Buddha snuggled inside this *wat* is the largest bronze Buddha in Thailand. On display are photos and blurbs describing this restored Buddha's many incarnations. *(Just south of Wat Phra Si Sanphet. Open M-F 8am-4:30pm, Sa-Su 8am-5:30pm. Free.)*

WAT PHRARAM. Overshadowed by its more glamorous neighbors, this *wat* was built in 1369 by King Ramesan to commemorate the spot where his father and founder of the city, King U Thong, was cremated. Dozens of broken Buddha representations sit silently around the *wat*'s landmark *prang*. *(Across the street from Wihaan Phra Mongkhon Brophit. Open daily 8am-6pm. 30฿.)*

WAT MAHATHAT. This impressive royal monastery was founded by King Borommarachathirat in 1374 and restored several times, most recently in the 18th century. Excavations done in the 1950s uncovered relics of the Buddha hidden deep in a seven-layered reliquary in the *stupa*. With those finds safely stored at the Chao Sam Phraya National Museum, the *wat*'s most famous attraction is a representation of the Buddha's face enshrouded in the roots of a tree. *(At the corner of Chikun Rd. and Naresuan Rd. Open daily 8am-6pm. 30฿.)*

WAT RATCHABURANA. Wat Mahathat's most impressive neighbor was built by King Chao Sam Phraya in 1424. Legend has it that the king's two oldest brothers both coveted the throne and killed each other in a heated duel, allowing Chao Sam Phraya to ascend to the throne. To commemorate (or perhaps celebrate) his brothers' deaths, the king ordered the construction of Wat Ratchaburana over the site of their cremation. This *wat* is known for its wealth of gold artifacts and the mural paintings in its crypt. *(North of Wat Mahathat. Open daily 8am-6pm. 30฿.)*

WAT YAI CHAIYAMONGKHON. This fabulous *wat* was founded in 1357 by King U Thong. In 1592, the giant *chedi* was built by King Naresuan the Great to commemorate a victory over the Burmese. The *wat*'s name, Chaiyamongkhon, meaning "Auspicious Victory," refers to this event. *(Southeast of the island on the mainland. 20min. bicycle ride from the island or a 40฿ tuk-tuk ride. Open daily 8am-5pm. 20฿.)*

WAT PHANANCHOENG. This massive gold Buddha is the largest in Thailand and dates back to 1324, 26 years before Ayutthaya was founded. Legend has it that tears formed in its eyes when the city was sacked by the Burmese in 1767. *(West of Yai Chaiyamongkhon, about 2km farther down the road. Open daily 8am-5pm. 20฿.)*

AYUTTHAYA HISTORICAL STUDY CENTER. This US$8 million research institute funded by the Japanese government features displays on the ancient city's political, economic, and social practices. Scale models of villages during the Ayutthaya period give insight into daily life. Touring the surprisingly small upstairs exhibition hall shouldn't take more than 45min. *(On Rotchana Rd., 2 blocks east of the Chao Sam Phraya National Museum. Open M-F 9am-4:30pm, Sa-Su 9am-5pm. 100฿, with student ID 50฿.)*

CHAO SAM PHRAYA NATIONAL MUSEUM. An old-school presentation complete with wood-and-glass display cases, dusty artifacts, and missing labels, the Chao Sam Phraya Museum has little to recommend itself besides the splendid jewels taken from Wat Ratchaburana. *(On Rotchana Rd., near the intersection with Si Sanphet Rd. A 5min. walk from the Tourist Information Center. Open W-Su 9am-4pm. 30฿.)*

OTHER SIGHTS. A short bike ride north of the train station are the impressive **Wat Maheyong, Wat Kudidao,** and the smaller **Wat Ayothaya.** All three are devoid of tourists. *(Free.)* North of the island, the king used to watch his elephant army train at the **Elephant Kraal Pavilion.** The Kraal now serves as a home for abused elephants; it supports itself in part by making paper out of elephant dung and offering elephant tours of the city center. Visitors are welcome to the Kraal but they should not go up to the elephants without talking to the staff. *(☎321 982. On Pathon Rd., south of Wihaan Phra Mongkhom Brophit. 400฿ for 20min. elephant tour. Open daily 9am-4pm. Donations appreciated.)* Ayutthaya also has one of the country's largest **Loi Krathong** festivals (p. 709), which usually takes place in November during the full moon.

THAILAND

ENTERTAINMENT AND NIGHTLIFE

After a hard day of *wat*-hopping, treat yourself to a **massage** at the Chao Phrom Market bus station. (From Naresuan Rd., it's the second building on the right. ☎244 582. 2hr. Thai massage 300฿. Foot massage 200฿ per hr. Open daily 10am-midnight.) From 7:30 to 9:30pm nightly, **Wat Phra Si Sanphet, Wat Mahathat, Wat Ratchaburana, Wat Phraram,** and **Wat Chiawatthanaram** are illuminated by floodlights. Note that entering the grounds of the *wats* after dark is illegal and dangerous. There is a limited amount of nightlife around the guesthouses—**Tony's Place** is always hopping—but to get to the real hot spots, head to the mainland east of the island to the area around the Grand Hotel (*tuk-tuk* 60฿). **AY By Laser** (☎06 525 2742) is a massive disco with Thai pop singers and dancers. (Open daily 9am-1am.)

KANCHANABURI ☎034

The Japanese invasion during WWII immortalized the otherwise undistinguished town of Kanchanaburi and the humble River Kwai. Backpackers now use the city—once of strategic importance in the overland route between Singapore and Yangon, Myanmar—as a base for exploring the surrounding waterfalls, caves, and jungles. They return in the evenings to their lively guesthouses beside the peaceful river to swap travel stories with Thai tourists hoping to escape hectic Bangkok life.

TRANSPORTATION

Trains: Kanchanaburi Train Station, (☎511 285), on Saeng Chuto Rd. To **Namtok** via the **River Kwai Bridge** (2½hr.; 6:10, 10:50am, 4:30pm; 17฿) and Thonburi Station in **Bangkok** (3hr.; 7:25am, 2:50pm; 25฿). Call (☎561 052) for info on weekend trains to **Bangkok** and other destinations (2hr., Sa-Su 5pm, 28฿). For short trips, such as the River Kwai Bridge, it is more convenient to take a bus, as they depart more frequently.

Buses: The **Kanchanaburi Bus Station** (☎511 182) is in Ban Noue Village at the southern end of Kanchanaburi. To: **Bangkok** (#81; 2nd-class with A/C 2hr., every 20min. 3:50am-6:50pm, 62฿; 1st-class with A/C 2hr., every 15min. 4am-7pm, 79฿) via **Nakhon Pathom** (1½hr., 40฿); **Erawan National Park** (#8170, 1½hr., every 50min. 8am-5:20pm, 26฿); **Sangkhlaburi** (#8203: 5hr.; 6, 8:40, 10:20am, noon; 84฿. VIP bus #8203: 4hr.; 9:30am, 1:30, 3:30pm; 151฿. A/C Van #8203: 3hr., every hr. 7:30am-4:30pm, 118฿, departs across from main bus terminal).

Local Transportation: Orange **songthaew** run up and down Saeng Chuto Rd. including in their route the River Kwai Bridge (10฿). **Samlor** cost 10-20฿ from the railway station to TAT. **Motorcycle taxis** to guesthouses from bus station cost 30฿. A **ferry** crosses the river (5฿) at the end of Chai Chumphol Rd.

Rentals: Bicycles available from almost all guesthouses and on Mae Nam Kwai Rd. with deposit of some form of ID. 20-50฿ per day. **Motorbikes** are permitted on Mae Nam Kwai Rd. with passport deposit. 200฿ for 24hr., 150฿ for 9am-5pm. Cruising motorbikes 500฿ per day. Motocross bikes are difficult to find.

ORIENTATION AND PRACTICAL INFORMATION

Kanchanaburi is 129km from Bangkok and stretches roughly 4km along the banks of the **Kwai River,** which flows parallel to **Saeng Chuto Road,** the city's main drag. North of town is the famous **River Kwai Bridge;** 2km south of the bridge is the **train station** and the riverside **guesthouse area,** where *farang* congregate. **Mae Nam Kwai Road** connects the guesthouses to the River Kwai Bridge and is lined with Internet cafes, bike rentals, tour companies, and bars. Two kilometers farther south of the guesthouse area is **Ban Noue Village,** the city's main commercial area and home to the **bus station.** West of the bus station are the **city gate, day markets,** and **river wharf area.** Because Kanchanaburi is quite spread out, consider renting a bicycle to avoid the long, dusty walks between one part of town and the other.

Tourist Office: TAT, (☎/fax 511 200), on Saeng Chuto Rd., a 5min. walk south of the bus station. Friendly, English-speaking staff deals out leaflets. Excellent regional map (20฿ donation). Bus and train schedules. Lenso phone. Open daily 8:30am-4:30pm.

Work Opportunity: Teach English at the local private Catholic school. 1-month, 3-month, and 1-year commitments. Teachers receive room and board plus stipend. Contact the school directly (☎09 889 0050, ask for Orawan).

Markets: The **Dalat Kao Market,** bounded by Chao Khunnen and Burakamkosol Rd., offers fresh produce and meat. **Phasuk Market,** across from the bus station near Lak Muang Rd. in Ban Noue Village, sells clothing and accessories. Both open daily dawn-dusk. The closest **night market** to guesthouses is the haphazard roadside affair just north of the train station on Saeng Chuto Rd. Open M, Th, Sa-Su 5-10pm. There is also a night market by the bus station on Tu, W, F nights. 10min. walk.

Tourist Police: (☎512 795). 1.5km north of the train station on Saeng Chuto Rd., on the right. Free **luggage storage.** English spoken. Open 24hr. 3 helpful **booths** at the foot of the River Kwai Bridge, on Song Kwai Rd. at Burakamkosol Rd., and on Mae Nam Kwai Rd. 50m past Apple's Guest House toward cemetery. Open daily 8:30am-6pm.

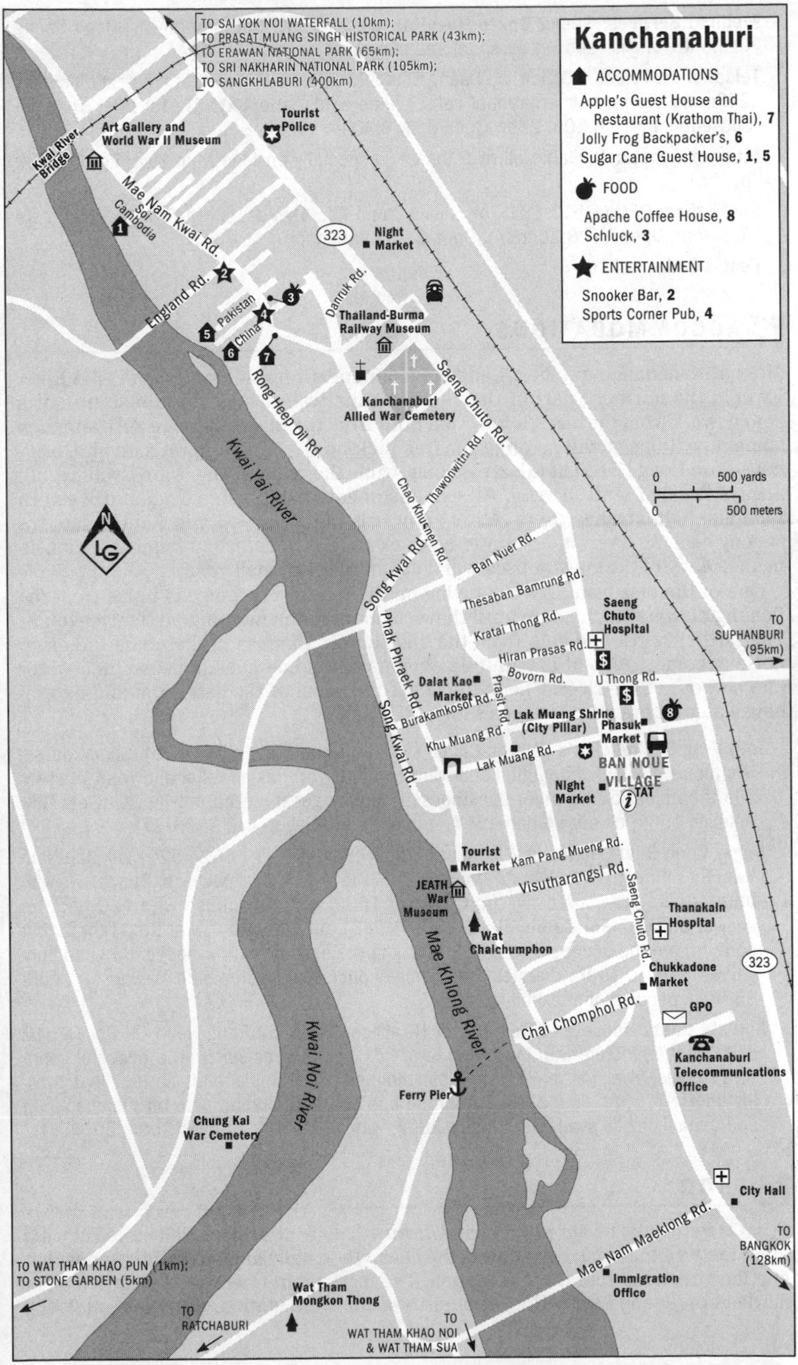
Kanchanaburi
ACCOMMODATIONS
Apple's Guest House and Restaurant (Krathom Thai), 7
Jolly Frog Backpacker's, 6
Sugar Cane Guest House, 1, 5
FOOD
Apache Coffee House, 8
Schluck, 3
ENTERTAINMENT
Snooker Bar, 2
Sports Corner Pub, 4
TO SAI YOK NOI WATERFALL (10km);
TO PRASAT MUANG SINGH HISTORICAL PARK (43km);
TO ERAWAN NATIONAL PARK (65km);
TO SRI NAKHARIN NATIONAL PARK (105km);
TO SANGKHLABURI (400km)
Kwai River Bridge
Art Gallery and World War II Museum
Tourist Police
Mae Nam Kwai Rd.
Soi Cambodia
323
Night Market
England Rd.
Pakistan
China
Danruk Rd.
Thailand-Burma Railway Museum
Kanchanaburi Allied War Cemetery
Rong Heep Oil Rd
Saeng Chuto Rd.
Thawonwitri Rd.
Chao Khunnen Rd.
Kwai Yai River
0 500 yards
0 500 meters
Song Kwai Rd.
Ban Nuer Rd.
Thesaban Bamrung Rd.
Kratai Thong Rd.
Saeng Chuto Hospital
Hiran Prasas Rd.
TO SUPHANBURI (95km)
Bovorn Rd.
U Thong Rd.
Phak Phraek Rd.
Dalat Kao Market
Burakamkosol Rd.
Prasit Rd.
Lak Muang Shrine (City Pillar)
Phasuk Market
Song Kwai Rd.
Khu Muang Rd.
Lak Muang Rd.
BAN NOUE VILLAGE
Night Market
TAT
Tourist Market
Kam Pang Mueng Rd.
Visutharangsi Rd.
JEATH War Museum
Saeng Chuto Rd.
Thanakain Hospital
Wat Chaichumphon
323
Chukkadone Market
Mae Khlong River
GPO
Chai Chomphol Rd.
Kanchanaburi Telecommunications Office
Ferry Pier
Kwai Noi River
Chung Kai War Cemetery
City Hall
Mae Nam Maeklong Rd.
TO BANGKOK (128km)
TO WAT THAM KHAO PUN (1km);
TO STONE GARDEN (5km)
Wat Tham Mongkon Thong
Immigration Office
TO RATCHABURI
TO WAT THAM KHAO NOI & WAT THAM SUA

THAILAND

Medical Services: Saeng Chuto Hospital (☎621 129), 500m north of TAT on Saeng Chuto Rd. English spoken. Hospital and **pharmacy** open 24hr. MC/V.

Telephones: Telecom Office, on Saeng Chuto Rd., Soi 38. Turn left at the post office; it's 200m on the right. International calls, phone cards, and **CATNET.** 1st min. 3฿, each subsequent min. 0.50฿. 24hr. Open daily 8:30am-10pm.

Internet Access: Available all over the city, especially on Mae Nam Kwai Rd. (25-40฿ per hr.)

Post Office: GPO (☎511 131), on Saeng Chuto Rd., 1km south of TAT on the left. *Poste Restante.* Open M-F 8:30am-4:30pm, Sa-Su 9am-noon.

Postal Code: 71000.

ACCOMMODATIONS

Most of Kanchanaburi's best budget accommodations sit along (or in) the River Kwai in the northern part of the city, a 10min. walk from the train station or a 25min. walk from the bus station. Taxi rides from the bus station are 30฿, although some guesthouses will arrange for free pick-up if you call upon arrival. Guesthouses on Rong Heep Oil Rd. are quieter, while the ones on Mae Nam Kwai Rd. are always flooded with *farang*. All establishments listed serve Thai and Western food and help arrange tours. A hot shower is not a necessity in Kanchanaburi's steamy heat. As a result, hot water costs extra or is nonexistent in most establishments. Many of the guesthouses will do laundry for a small charge.

One of the disadvantages to staying on the river is the raucous noise from the floating discos, which boom until the wee hours of the morning on the weekends. The farther north one gets from the bus station, the less bothersome the disco noise becomes. Also, it is painfully obvious that some guesthouses pump water into and out of the river. Check the color and smell of the bathroom and its running water before agreeing on a room.

Jolly Frog Backpacker's, 28 Soi China, Mae Nam Kwai Rd. (☎514 579). Clean, attractive rooms overlook a beautiful courtyard and the river. Has a livelier and younger clientele than most of the other guesthouses. Nightly guest-picked movies. Singles 70฿; doubles 150฿, on-raft portion 150฿, with bath 200฿, with A/C 290฿. ❶

Sugar Cane Guest House in 2 locations. **22 Soi Pakistan** ❷ (☎624 520), off Mae Nam Kwai Rd., turn-off 1 block north from turn-off to Jolly Frog Backpacker's. Bungalows with bath around manicured riverfront garden 150-250฿; raft house with A/C and hot shower 550฿. **7 Soi Cambodia** ❸ (☎514 988), off Mae Nam Kwai Rd., 1km farther north toward the bridge, is quieter, if not as upscale. Laundry 20฿ per kg. Bamboo bungalows, singles 150฿; doubles 200฿; huge concrete bungalow with TV and A/C 400-550฿, depending on proximity to river.

Apple's Guest House and Restaurant (Krathom Thai), 52 Rong Heep Oil Rd. (☎512 017), at the juncture with Mae Nam Kwai Rd. Clean rooms surround a peaceful courtyard but lack riverside real estate. Hospitable co-owner Apple leads an excellent cooking course (750฿). Free pick-up from the bus and train station. Info on Kanchanaburi and tourist sites is available. Singles 200฿, with A/C 500฿; doubles 250฿/500฿. ❷

FOOD

From May to July, be sure to try the *khanun* (jackfruit), a Thai delicacy. This and other tasty victuals can be found in the cheap foodstalls and open-air eateries that line the streets around the bus station. The markets in town, including two night markets on Saeng Chuto Rd. (one north of the train station, one north of TAT), make for cheap and authentic Thai eats. If market eating is not your style, head for **Song Kwai Road,** where dozens of indistinguishable restaurants cater almost exclusively to locals. Most tourists get meals at the guesthouse they are staying at, where convenience and location make up for average quality and value.

One of the best guesthouse restaurants is **Apple's Thai Restaurant** ❷ (p. 716), which offers fabulous food (entrees 30-60฿). For a Thai-style Indian dish, try chicken massaman curry (65฿). Tofu can be substituted in all meat dishes. **Schluck** ❷, on Mae Nam Kwai Rd., stands out from the rest, offering A/C dining comfort. The delicious chicken schnitzel baguette (45฿) is drenched in mayonnaise dressing. (Open daily 4pm-1am.) By the bus station, **Apache Coffee House** ❸ provides a quiet meal in air-conditioned comfort. Though a bit expensive, the food is some of the best in town. Entrees cost 80-120฿, coffee and desserts 40-60฿.

SIGHTS

Today, World War II's Allies and their old opponents join forces, packing into A/C buses to see the Death Railway Bridge and the graves of thousands of Allied soldiers. Several interesting museums quickly dispel (or confirm) myths associated with the war, and all stand as testament to the strength of the POWs.

Kanchanaburi's attractions are spread over 6km. To take it all in over a couple of days, rent a bicycle or motorbike—it's infinitely faster and easier than walking, cheaper than taking a taxi, and more convenient than trying to catch a bus.

RIVER KWAI BRIDGE (DEATH RAILWAY BRIDGE). Constructed between 1941 and 1942, the original River Kwai Bridge was the Japanese army's final attempt at completing the 415km Thai-Myanmar railway line (the "Death Railway") for transporting war materials to military camps in Myanmar. Roughly 16,000 POWs and 96,000 Asians died building the bridge, which was subsequently destroyed by British air raids in 1945. Engineers predicted that it would take five years to construct the bridge, but the Japanese forced POWs and local laborers to complete this vital section of the railway in 16 months. The bridge you see, although impressive, is a reconstruction built as a memorial to those who lost their lives. Kanchanaburi celebrates the **River Kwai Bridge Week** during the first week of December. Activities include archaeological and historical exhibitions, performances, musical events, and a spectacular light and sound show. *(3km northwest of train station. Orange minibus #2 runs from Focus Optic shop, 2 traffic lights from TAT (10min., 6am-7pm, 6฿). Approx. 2.5km walk north of guesthouses on Mae Nam Kwai Rd. Songthaew to bridge 10-20฿. Many local tour companies arrange rides on a train that crosses the River Kwai Bridge.)*

THAILAND-BURMA RAILWAY CENTER. This fairly new museum (opened in 2003) tells the bitter story of the 415km Death Railway, which was crucial to Japanese expansion into Asia during WWII. The museum has a 3-D model of the railway, video displays, historical artifacts, and details on the POWs. *(73 Chao Kunnen Rd., across from the Allied War Cemetery. www.tbrconline.com. Open daily 9am-5pm. 60฿.)*

ART GALLERY AND WORLD WAR II MUSEUM. Luring bridge visitors with claims of World War II exhibitions, the museum is actually a bizarre collection of odd, dusty exhibits. Everything from Thai stamps to dresses of former Miss Thailands can be found here. Follow the "toilet" signs to the basement, where cobwebs hide life-sized portrayals of the bridge construction, as well as automobiles and motorbikes used in the war. It's mildly interesting and very unusual, but skip it if you're pressed for time. *(50m toward town from the bridge. ☎ 512 596. Signs imply this is the JEATH museum; do not be confused, the JEATH museum is in town. Open daily 8am-6pm. 30฿.)*

JEATH WAR MUSEUM. Established in 1977 by the abbot of Wat Chaichumphon to honor victims of the Death Railway Bridge, JEATH (Japan, England, America/Australia, Thailand, and Holland) sits in a bamboo hut like those used to house POWs. The collection of pictures, artifacts, and drawings is modest but nevertheless intriguing. Newspaper articles posted on the walls highlight the accomplishments of famous POWs and their efforts to raise awareness of wartime events. *(500m south of the town gate on Phak Phraek Rd. ☎515 203. Open daily 8:30am-4:30pm. 30฿.)*

KANCHANABURI ALLIED WAR CEMETERY. This is the final resting place of 7000 Allied POWs, mostly British and Dutch, who died working on the Death Railway Bridge. Western tour groups often seem to outnumber the headstones. *(2km north of the bus station on Saeng Chuto Rd., a 5min. walk from the train station. Free.)*

CHUNG KAI WAR CEMETERY. Farther afield, Chung Kai holds the remains of 1700 Death Railway POWs in a setting more peaceful and pleasant than its larger counterpart in town, although the tranquility is often broken by the ruckus from the party boats. The trip makes a nice escape from the congestion of Kanchanaburi City. *(4km across the bridge at Song Kwai Rd.'s northern end. Free.)*

STONE GARDEN. Grassy oases sit among barren rocks in the Stone Garden, where the rock formations supposedly look like animals. This takes a bit of imagination, but the Stone Garden is nonetheless ideal for a picnic. *(On the same road as Chung Kai War Cemetery and Wat Tham Kao Pun, 5km farther than the cemetery and 4km farther than the wat.)*

WATS. Wat Chaichumphon (also called **Wat Dai**), next to JEATH, is most often frequented by townspeople. **Wat Tham Khao Pun,** 1km beyond Chung Kai War Cemetery, has a cave full of Buddhist shrines (5-20฿ donation suggested). Four kilometers across the river, Chinese-influenced **Wat Tham Mongkon Thong,** (Cave Temple of the Golden Dragon) is renowned for its "floating nun," a woman who can lie on water without sinking. Early weekend mornings are the best time to catch her in action. Private shows are 200฿, or 10฿ per person with a minimum of 20 people, to see her 10-15min. performance (which might be worth 10฿ but is probably not worth 200฿). The temple also features a small **museum** of Kanchanaburi's history. Behind the museum, dragon-shaped steps lead up the mountain and into a **limestone cave** that affords views of the surrounding mountains and valleys. Motorcycle taxis make the trip for 30฿; by motorbike, follow the road out over the bridge past immigration.

NIGHTLIFE

At night, most *farang* stick to bars, discos, and restaurants in the well-trodden area around the guesthouses along Mae Nam Kwai Rd. The small but popular **Sports Corner Pub,** at the corner of China Rd. and Mae Nam Kwai Rd., entertains Commonwealth folk with nightly showings of football, rugby, and cricket. (Open daily 9am-late.) Farther north on Mae Nam Kwai Rd. toward the bridge, **Snooker Bar** has three recent movie releases per night starting at 6pm. The staff is more than happy to let you sit and watch with just the purchase of a drink. (Large Singha 55฿. Open daily 9am-2am.) Though some report the atmosphere is inhospitable to *farang*, head to the **karaoke** and **live music bars** that line the east side of Song Kwai Rd. to experience a more authentic Thai night out. For dives that float, check out the tacky and charmingly mobile floating discos that launch from the west side of Song Kwai Rd. and cruise merrily down the river toward the bridge. You'll probably have to talk (or motion) your way onto these, as they're mainly for Thai tour groups, but it might be worth the effort.

DAYTRIPS FROM KANCHANABURI

Kanchanaburi is an ideal base for exploring the waterfalls, caves, and parks that stretch all the way to Sangkhlaburi and the Thai-Myanmar border. **Routes 3199** and **323** bisect the province at the northern end of Kanchanaburi and make good points of reference. 3199 is a well-paved passage to the Erawan waterfalls. 323 heads west to Sangkhlaburi and the Thai-Myanmar border (Three Pagoda Pass), passing Sai Yok National Park and Hellfire Pass.

ALONG ROUTE 3199

ERAWAN NATIONAL PARK. The foremost tourist destination near Kanchanaburi is **Erawan** ("Three-Headed Elephant") **Waterfall.** The seven-tiered waterfalls may not be the biggest cascades, but they're certainly the most accessible. It's best to arrive early to beat the crowd of locals and *farang*. The first three levels are a 5-10min. walk from the trailhead. The challenging 2.2km trail to the top (1hr.) leads past enticing, clear-water swimming holes, rewarding the intrepid with greater seclusion. But watch out—the trail at the seventh tier is slippery. Sturdy shoes are recommended. The **visitors center,** next to where the Kanchanaburi bus stops, has maps, photos, and a slide show. **Accommodations ❶** range from camping (30฿ per person; 100฿ per tent) to dorms (mattresses 10฿; dorms 30฿) and bungalows (4 beds and bath 250฿ per person; 800฿ per bungalow). **National Park Headquarters,** opposite the visitors center, handles accommodations and emergencies. *(65km from Kanchanaburi. Take public bus #8170 (1½hr.; every 50min. 8am-5:20pm, last bus back at 4pm; 26฿). Open daily 8am-4:30pm. 200฿; motorbikes 20฿; cars 30฿.)*

SRI NAKHARIN NATIONAL PARK. Sri Nakharin has more animals and fewer tourists than Erawan, but getting there demands considerable time, money, and effort. About 105km from Kanchanaburi, **Huay Mae Khamin Waterfall**'s nine tiers are best reached from **Erawan.** Only motocross bikes and 4WD vehicles can traverse the 42km dirt road, parallel to the reservoir, that leads from Erawan (about 2 hours). If you insist on taking your Honda Dream into this area, be advised that it may turn into your Nightmare: the first few kilometers of dirt track are a good indication of the roughness of the road. Service facilities are available along the way, so you won't run out of gas. A romantic alternative is to charter a boat (1-2hr., up to 10 people, 1000-1500฿) from **Tha (Pier) Kraden,** 13km northeast of the Sri Nakharin Dam, 5km past Mongatet Village. The pier is accessible over dirt road from Ban Kradan, but boat options may be limited. Continue the rough journey to Sisawat if this is the case. The National Park at Huay Mae Khamin has **accommodation ❶** options ranging from camping (30฿ per person) to bungalows with restaurant. *(Park open daily 8am-4:30pm. 200฿, children 100฿. Motorbikes 20฿, cars 30฿.)*

ALONG ROUTE 323: BAN KAO AREA

PRASAT MUANG SINGH HISTORICAL PARK. Muang Singh (City of the Lion) is an ancient city dating back to the 13th century. Once part of the Angkor Empire, the city features Khmer design and artwork. The ruins sprawl across almost 74 hectares, surrounded by moats, city walls, and the Kwae Nai River. The most notable structure in the park is Monument No. 1 (Prasat Muang Singh), which sits at the center of the city and towers above the rest of the park. An interesting exhibition hall near the park office has Buddhist sculptures found at the site. There is also an ancient burial site dating back 2000 years. The park is a worthwhile stop, especially for those interested in the Angkor Empire but not able to go to Cambodia. *(Located 43km northwest of Kanchanaburi. If driving, take Rte. 323, then turn onto Rte.*

THAILAND

3455; turn is about 40km from Kanchanaburi. The park is a 7km drive southwest on 3455 and well posted. Trains (1¼hr.; leave Kanchanaburi 6:10, 10:50am, 4:35pm; return 6:20am, 1:50, 4:30pm; 10฿) come closer to the park than buses. Get off at Thakilen; from the train station, walk 1km to the main road, then 1km to the right. Bus #8203 stops 7km from the park; transportation for the final leg may be hard to find. Return buses are best caught before 4pm. ☎ 591 122. Open daily 8:30am-4:30pm. 40฿, cars 30฿, motorbikes 20฿.)

BAN KAO NEOLITHIC MUSEUM. This small museum houses artifacts and findings from the Thai-Danish excavations in the Ban Kao area in the 1960s. They discovered a Neolithic-era settlement, including a burial site with 44 human skeletons and evidence of rituals and social stratification. While the museum is an interesting example of the Southeast Asian Neolithic culture of 3000-4000 years ago, its small exhibits can be easily seen in an hour. *(Ban Kao is 6km south of Muang Singh, on 3455. See Muang Singh for directions.)*

WAT LUANGTA-MAHABUA FOUNDATION. This foundation runs a tiger conservation project and wild animal rescue park. The grounds of the *wat* contain Indo-Chinese tigers, a leopard, water buffalo, deer, gibbon monkeys, and all types of farm animals. The best time to visit is in the late afternoon, when the tigers are brought out of their cages for feeding. If you arrive in the morning, the monks will gladly bring the tigers out for photo ops (suggested donation 20-40฿). The tigers are very tame, having been raised by the monks since birth; however, a few large scars on the shoulders of the monks suggest that they sometimes misbehave. *(Take 323, and turn off for the Muang Singh Historical Park. After 5km, a large billboard marks the next turn-off onto a 1.5km dirt road leading to the wat's impressive green gated entrance.)*

ALONG ROUTE 323: HELLFIRE PASS

In their quest to complete the Thai-Myanmar railway, the Japanese Imperial Army would not let a mere mountain stand in their way. Thousands of oppressed laborers worked for months, chipping away rock to create the **Hellfire Pass,** so named for the ghostly campfire shadows that would dance on the mountain walls at night. Today the pass is a trail leading down the former railway on a 3km circuit around the area. The adjoining **Hellfire Pass Memorial Museum** is a showcase of the POWs who died in the construction of the pass. *(Between Sai Yok Noi and Sai Yok Yai. Take bus #8203 from Kanchanaburi and tell the attendant where you want to get off (1½hr.; every 30min. 6am-6:30pm, last return bus at about 4:45pm; 38฿). Open daily 9am-4pm. Suggested donation 30-100฿.)*

ALONG ROUTE 323: SAI YOK NATIONAL PARK

Sai Yok National Park is a 500km^2 park that stretches almost 70km alongside Route 323 and the Mae Nam Kwai River. The first attraction is the Sai Yok Noi Waterfall, 60km from Kanchanaburi, and the last attraction is the Hin Dat Hot Springs, 130km from Kanchanaburi. All of the sights, with the exception of Lawa, are easily accessible from 323. *(Public bus #8203 to Sangkhlaburi leaves Kanchanaburi every 30min. 6am-6:30pm and returns at similar intervals for 25-40฿. The National Park is open daily 6am-6pm. 200฿, children 100฿. Motorbikes 20฿, cars 30฿.)*

LAWA CAVE. The electrically lit 200m cavern is the region's largest. Unfortunately, it's not easily accessible. Hire a longtail boat (45min. one-way, up to 10 people 800฿; landing is 350m from caves) from Pak Saeng Pier, 2km southwest of Sai Yok Noi. Boats can continue up to Sai Yok Yai Waterfall and National Park. Alternatively, complete the 30min. trip on motorbike. After crossing the bridge next to Pak Saeng Pier, turn right just past the 3km marker and follow the partially sealed road to the caves. *(Open daily 6am-6pm. National Park entrance fee 200฿, children 100฿.)*

SAI YOK YAI WATERFALL AND NATIONAL PARK ENTRANCE. Celebrated in poetry and song, the Sai Yok Yai Waterfall dribbles unimpressively, except between July and September, when it gushes unimpressively. One of the world's smallest mammal species, Kitti's Hog-Nosed Bat (p. 654), lives in the park's Bat Cave, 2km from the visitors center and accessible by trails. Pick up maps and leave gear at the visitors center (3km off 323). Accommodations include **camping** ❶ (30฿) and **rooms** ❹ (500-1000฿) for two to 12 over the river . *(Open daily 6am-6pm. 200฿, children 100฿. Motorbikes 20฿, cars 30฿.)*

HIN DAT HOT SPRINGS. The two springs are rather small but are popular with Thai tourists. One stays a constant 40°C, while the other fluctuates between 35 and 38°C. *(1km off 323. Pools have no English road signs, but the turn-off is 127km from Kanchanaburi and 15km before Thong Pha Phum. Bus #8203 goes from Kanchanaburi (2¾hr; every 30min. 6am-6:30pm, last return bus 4pm; 54฿). Hot springs 5฿, private room 20฿.)*

ALONG ROUTE 323: SANGKHLABURI

Unlike its neighbor Kanchanaburi, Sangkhlaburi's natural beauty attracts tourists. In 1989 the border was closed due to fighting between Shan and Wa separatist troops. Travelers are now beginning to trickle back into the region. Most attractions in Sangkhlaburi are far away from the town center. Arrange **trekking trips** through **P. Guest House** ❸, 81/2 Tumbon Nong Loo, 300m beyond the turn-off to the **Burmese Inn** ❶, 52/3 Tambon Nong Loo, 1km to the right of the bus station if facing the Siam Bank. The **longest wooden bridge** in Thailand, the 400m bridge of the Reverend Auttamo, crosses the massive Lake Khao Laem and connects the city of Sangkhlaburi to **Mon Village.** The border crossing to **Phayathonzu** in Myanmar is marked by three stunted pagodas—hence the name **Three Pagoda Pass.** Due to poaching, the wildlife that inhabits **Thung Yai Sanctuary Park,** Thailand's largest conservation area, have retreated deep into the forest. *(To get to Sangkhlaburi, catch a bus from Kanchanburi's main terminal (5hr.; 6, 8:40, 10:20am, noon; 84฿). Songthaew travel the 22km from Sangkhlaburi to Three Pagoda Pass 6am-6pm (30min., 30-35฿). The clearly marked turn-off to Thung Yai Sanctuary Park is 18km from Sangkhlaburi along the road to Three Pagoda Pass. In general, it is possible to get to the pass without personal transportation, but the same is not true of Thung Yai Sanctuary Park. The turn-off to Three Pagoda Pass from the highway is 3km from Sangkhlaburi toward Kanchanaburi.)*

BORDER CROSSING: THREE PAGODA PASS. About 24km from Sangkhlaburi, the Three Pagoda Pass is an anticlimax for those with visions of border intrigue. The border crossing from Three Pagoda Pass to Phayathonzu, Myanmar is sporadically open to foreigners, with several caveats. Prior authorization and a permit from the immigration office in Sangkhlaburi are required. Two passport-sized photos, photocopies of the front page of your passport and Thai visa, and US$10 are required for a permit. Return to immigration by 5pm to collect your passport. The US$10 is paid at the Myanmar border, and allows you to enter 2km into the country. Since this is not an official border crossing, your passport is not stamped and visa extensions are not available. Myanmar time is 30min. behind Thailand's. Immigration office open daily 8:30am-6pm. Recent tensions between Thailand and Myanmar have resulted in frequent closings of the border. Be sure to check with the Thai embassy for updates. The area is also occasionally considered dangerous (see **Thailand-Myanmar Relations,** p. 657)–yet another reason to get the latest update from the Thai embassy or your home nation's embassy; both keep close tabs on the border situation.

CHA AM ☎032

During the week, Cha Am looks like someone built an elaborate beach town but forgot to tell anybody. However, upper-middle-class Thais pour in come late Friday. The **Cha Am Railway Station** at the end of Narathip Rd. has **trains** to Bangkok (3½hr., 6 per day, 49฿) and Chumphon (4½hr., 6 per day, 53฿). Catch a **bus** out of on Phetkasem Hwy. at Narathip Rd. to go to Bangkok (3½hr., every 20min., 95-113฿) and Hua Hin (30min., every 20min., 20-30฿). Buses for Hua Hin and Bangkok also leave from the station at the intersection of Chaolai and Ratchaplhi Rd., one block south of Narathip Rd. Note that only buses whose origin or terminus is Cha Am stop here, so the frequency of service is low. For Phetchaburi, take a Bangkok-bound bus (40min., 20-30฿). **Motorcycle taxis** travel in town for 20฿. Cook Travel and Tours arranges **bicycle rentals** for 30฿ per hr. or 150฿ per day.

Ruamjit Road is home to most of the hotels and restaurants in town. The road runs north-south adjacent to the beach; heading north the beach is on the right. **Chaolai Road** runs parallel to Ruamjit Rd. **Narathip Road** meets Ruamjit Rd. on the southern end of Cha Am Beach and leads to the railway station, town center, and **Phetkasem Highway.** More information on the city, accommodations, and nearby sights is available at www.chaam-beach.com. Cha Am services include: **TAT** (☎471 005), on Phetkasem Hwy. 500m south of Narathip Rd. (open daily 8:30am-4:30pm); the 24hr. **tourist information booth,** inside the **tourist police station** on the beach side of Ruamjit Rd. at Narathip Rd.; **Siam Commercial Bank,** on Ruamjit Rd. just north of Narathip Rd. (open M-F 8:30am-3:30pm); **Cha Am Hospital** (☎471 007), on Klongtien Rd. northwest of the beach, with very little English but 24hr. **emergency** service; **Internet** at **Cook Travel and Tours,** just south of Jolly & Jumper (1฿ per min., 30฿ minimum.). The **post office,** on Ruamjit Rd., has international phones. (Open M-F 8:30am-4:30pm, Sa 9am-noon.) **Postal Code:** 76120.

Jolly & Jumper ❸, 274/3 Ruamjit Rd., in the middle of town, just north of the post office and just south of Gems Hotel, is *the* backpacker dive in Cha Am. There is free bicycle use for guests. (☎433 887. Basic rooms with fan and shared bathrooms 150฿, with amenities up to 450฿.) The **Cha Am Villa Hotel ❷,** 241/1 Ruamjit Rd., about four blocks north of Narathip Rd. and a block south of the post office, offers large, clean, cable TV-equipped rooms and a swimming pool free for guests. (☎471 241; www.chaamvilla.com. Rooms 250฿, with A/C 300-500฿.)

Poom ❸, 274/1 Ruamjit Rd., in front of Gems and just north of Jolly & Jumper, has a fantastic seafood menu. (Entrees 40-200฿. Open daily 9am-10pm.) **Da Vinci's ❸,** 274/5 Ruamjit Rd., just north of Jolly & Jumper, serves authentic Western cuisine in a wood-paneled setting. (Entrees 80-400฿. Open daily 10am-midnight.)

Hat Cha Am (Cha Am Beach) is clean, white, and wide. During the week, you need only compete with dogs for control of the beach. Mondays through Thursdays are the best days for those seeking a peaceful vacation. Beach chairs (5฿ per hr.) line the strand—just find one and sit, and its owner will come around to you. The same is true for motorboats, which are generally 100฿ per 30min., although the price varies with demand. Multi-person flotation devices and one-, two-, and three-person bicycles are available on the beach.

HUA HIN ☎032

Long before Phuket and Pattaya were catapulted into jet-set stardom, Hua Hin (Head Rock) catered to the Thai upper crest. Following the example of King Rama VI, wealthy Thai families vacationed here, mingling with local fishermen and squid vendors. Today, affluent Europeans have joined the Thais, and towering resorts share the waterfront with the fishermen.

TRANSPORTATION

Flights: Hua Hin Airport (☎522 305), on the north side of the city, is served by **Bangkok Airways.** 4 flights per week to **Bangkok** (40min.; Su-M, W, F 7:20pm; 950฿) and **Ko Samui** (1hr., 9am, 2080฿).

Trains: Railway Station (☎511 073), at the end of Damnernkasem Rd. A 10min. walk from town center. To: **Bangkok** (4hr., 16 per day, 54฿); **Chumphon** (4hr., 16 per day, 48฿); **Phetchaburi** (1hr., 12 per day, 34฿); **Surat Thani** (7hr., 12 per day, 73฿).

Buses: VIP bus station (☎511 654), 1st fl. of the Siripetchkasem Hotel on Srasong Rd. near Decharnuchit Rd. A/C buses to **Bangkok** (3½hr., every 40min. 3am-9pm, 120฿) via **Cha Am** (20min., 30฿). Southbound A/C buses and everything else depart from the **regular bus station** (☎511 230), a dusty roundabout at the end of Liab Tang Rodfai Rd., about 500m north of the railway station. To: **Bangkok** (4hr., every 20min., 100฿) via **Cha Am** (20min., 15฿); **Chumphon** (4hr., 12 per day, 120฿); **Phuket** (12hr., 6 per day 10am-11pm, 305-486฿); **Prachuap Khiri Khan** (1½hr., every hr. 6:30am-4pm, 50฿); **Surat Thani** (8hr.; 10am, 210฿; 11pm, 340฿).

Local Transportation: Samlor go round-trip to **Khao Krailas** and **Khao Takieb** (every 15min. 6am-7pm, 7฿). Green **songthaew** leave from the motorcycle shop at Decharnuchit and Srasong Rd. (every 15min. 6am-7pm, 7฿). **Tuk-tuks** and **motorcycle taxis** can be found on most street corners. No trip within town should cost more than 30฿ by *tuk-tuk* or 20฿ by motorcycle.

ORIENTATION AND PRACTICAL INFORMATION

Despite its immense popularity as a tourist destination, Hua Hin is surprisingly small and generally walkable. **Phetkasem Highway** and the train tracks run north-south through town. **Damnernkasem Road** leads from the train station to the beach and forms the southern boundary of the town proper, although the beach and resort area extends far beyond. To the north and running parallel to each other are **Decharnuchit Road** and **Chomsinthu Road,** both of which lead from the beach to Phetkasem Hwy. Most hotels, restaurants, and bars cluster around **Naresdamri Road,** which branches off Damnernkasem Rd. close to the beach and passes by the Hilton. Free maps are available at the tourist office, restaurants, or bars.

Tourist Office: Tourist Information Service Center, 114 Phetkasem Hwy. (☎532 433), on the ground fl. of the municipal building at the Damnernkasem Rd. intersection. Open daily 8:30am-4:30pm.

Markets: The **night market,** on Donamuchit Rd. between Srasong Rd. and Phetkasem Hwy., is a bit touristy but has excellent Thai food. **Chatchai Market,** between Srasong Rd. and Phetkasem Hwy., is a great place to sample local street culture during the day.

Local Tourist Police: (☎515 995.) In the little white building on the left side of Damnernkasem Rd. just before the beach. English spoken. Open 24hr.

Medical Services: All services listed provide 24hr. care. **San Pau Lo Hospital** (☎532 576), on Phetkasem Hwy. 400m south of the Tourist Center. Credit cards accepted. **Hua Hin Hospital** (☎520 371), 4km north of town on Phetkasem Hwy. A **Red Cross station,** next door to the municipal building, provides basic services.

Telephones: Next to the GPO. **International phone**/fax. Open daily 8am-midnight.

Internet Access: Sunshine Internet Cafe, beneath Hotel Thanawit in a *soi* off Amnuaysin Rd. near Phetkasem Hwy. Very fast access for 20฿ per hr. Open daily 9am-midnight.

Post Office: GPO (☎511 063), opposite the police station on Damnernkasem Rd., as soon as you turn off Phetkasem Hwy. toward the beach. *Poste Restante.* Open M-F 8:30am-4:30pm, Sa-Su and holidays 9am-noon.

Postal Code: 77110.

ACCOMMODATIONS

Most budget hotels cluster around Naresdamri Rd. and on the alleys that branch off it. While prices are similar, style varies, so shop around. Reservations are recommended during the high season, which is late November to mid-March.

All Nations Guest House, 10-10/1 Decharnuchit Rd. (☎512 747; cybercafehua-hin@hotmail.com), on the left about 100m from the beach. Clean rooms. Rooms 150-250฿, with A/C 350-450฿; triples with A/C and cable TV 600฿. ❷ Just around the corner on Leung Lom Soi is **All Nations 2** (☎531 240), offering quieter surroundings. Smaller rooms have no hot water. Singles and doubles 150฿. ❷

HI-Hua-Hin/Euro Hua-Hin City Hotel, 5/15 Srasong Rd. (☎513 130), a half-block from the train station toward Phetkasem Hwy. All rooms have private bath and A/C. 8-bed dorms 130฿; 6-bed dorms 160฿; 4-bed rooms 200฿ per person; 3-bed rooms 250฿ per person; singles and doubles 700-800฿. ❷

Pattana Guest House, 52 Naresdamri Rd. (☎513 393). Look for the sign pointing down an alley off Naresdamri Rd. 10m to the left of the pier. Traditional 200-year-old Thai home with teak furnishings. Rooms 240฿, with private bath 375฿. ❸

FOOD

Every morning, Hua Hin's fishing fleet returns to the pier with a fresh catch. The lively **night market** is the best place to sample authentic Thai seafood, cooked right in front of you. (Entrees 10-50฿. Open daily 5pm-midnight.) **Chatchai Market** sets up during the day. For something sit-down, head to Naresdamri Rd., where quality restaurants line the entire length of the street. **Amadeus ❸,** 23 Naresdamri Rd., across from Memory Guest House, serves delicious *pad thai* (85-95฿). (Most dishes 95-140฿. Open daily 9am-midnight.) **Maharaja ❸,** 25 Naresdamri Rd., between Amadeus and Fulay Guest House, has great Indian food. (Extensive vegetarian menu. Most dishes 90-160฿. Open daily 11am-11pm.) **Siam Restaurant ❷,** on Poolsuk Rd., serves cheap Western and Thai dishes in a relaxed setting. (Great drink specials. Entrees 40-100฿. Drinks 25-110฿.)

NIGHTLIFE

Notorious "girlie bars" dot the Hua Hin nightlife landscape, and it isn't hard to tell when you've seen one. There are, however, a number of regular bars on Damnernkasem Rd. and adjacent Selekam Rd. Several, including **Coconuts** (also called the Hard Kok Cafe), 85 Selekam Rd., are expat-run and have pool tables and televisions tuned to soccer games at any time of day. (Open daily until 1am.) For non-sporting entertainment, **Hua Hin Brewery,** inside the Hilton, offers overpriced drinks and nightly performances of Thai bands playing Western hits. (Beers 125-215฿. Starts getting crowded around 9:30-10pm.) The **Star Planet Pub** inside the City Beach Hotel is similar but more reasonably priced and offers more Thai-themed live music acts. (Open daily until 2am.)

SIGHTS

Hua Hin's major attraction is **Hua Hin Beach,** which rolls along for kilometers in either direction. The fishing pier, at the base of Chomsinthu Rd., dominates one area; the prettier part of the beach begins just past the entrance to the Sofitel Hotel. Farther south, vendors wander the sand offering massages, food, and pony rides (100-400฿ for 30min.). The **Sofitel Central Hotel** is 1.5km south of the pier. Built by Prince Purachatra, the former Director General of State Railways, it was cast as Phnom Penh's leading hotel in the film *The Killing Fields.* One of Southeast Asia's grandest five-star hotels (rooms start at 6000฿), Sofitel has beautiful grounds worthy of a stroll. Tourists on a budget can come for high tea (130฿) and meander through the green elephant herds in the topiary gardens. Head north past the Hilton Hotel and the pier to see **Klai Kang Won (Far From Worries) Palace.** A royal summer residence in the 1920s, the palace now houses the ailing king, and the grounds are closed to visitors. The twin hills of **Khao Takieb** (Chopstick Hill) and **Khao Krailas,** 6km south of Hua Hin on Phetkasem Hwy., are accessible by motorbike or *songthaew* (7฿). Khao Takieb features a temple, hundreds of monkeys (monkey grub sold on the spot for 120฿), and an excellent view. Khao Krailas has a small lighthouse and a decent view of Hua Hin. Tree-lined **Suan San Beach** is farther south and has unbeatable swimming. Charter a *songthaew* or *tuk-tuk* (150฿). Still farther south is **Khao Tao** (Turtle Hill).

DAYTRIP FROM HUA HIN: PRACHUAP KHIRI KHAN

Catch a southbound bus from Hua Hin (1½hr.) to Phrachuap Khiri Khan.

Flanked by verdant rock formations jutting sharply out from its bay, Prachuap Khiri Khan is an unassuming fishing town with two remarkable sights: caves, which hide a pair of magnificent reclining Buddhas, and a hilltop *wat*, which overlooks the bay. What makes them even more exhilarating is their complete seclusion. It's 421 steps to the golden *chedi* of **Khao Chong Krajok** (Mirror Tunnel Mountain), which offers a glorious 360° panorama of the surrounding bay and province. Overlooking Ao Khan Kradai are two impressive complexes of **caves,** the larger of which holds the two **reclining Buddhas.** Though the cave is lit, you should bring a flashlight. If you're looking for a beach, **Ao Manao** is a scenic 2km stretch of sand enclosed by cliffs and very popular among Thais.

NORTHEAST THAILAND

Encompassing nearly one-third of Thailand's landmass and supporting an equal proportion of the nation's population, this plateau is called *Isaan,* meaning "vastness and prosperity." Ironically, largely agrarian Isaan is one of the country's poorest regions. Historically, the region has had stronger ties to Laos and the Khmer across the Mekong River than to the central plains. So close is this relationship culturally that the Isaan dialect carries striking similarities to Lao, and in some areas Thai is spoken as a second language. Travelers are drawn to the region for its lack of large tour groups, fiery foods, captivating hospitality, and intoxicatingly slow pace of life. For skeptics who hold that any statement containing both "Thailand" and "off the beaten path" is oxymoronic, Isaan emerges as a buried treasure.

KHAO YAI NATIONAL PARK

Only 160km from Bangkok, Khao Yai, Thailand's first (and perhaps best) national park, opened in 1962. The humbling 2168km² park ranges from stark prairie to thick evergreens and boasts one of the world's largest monsoon rain forests. Wild elephants, tigers, and bears and more than 300 species of birds, including the great hornbill, also make their home in Khao Yai. Khao Yai is most conveniently reached via Pak Chong, an urban strip featuring little more than basic lodging and supplies.

PAK CHONG ☎044

Primarily a market town, Pak Chong is of little interest to travelers except as a base for Khao Yai National Park. Since the construction of the rail line and the Mittaphap Hwy., Pak Chong has developed into the center of the region.

Songthaew leave for Khao Yai National Park around the corner from the 7-Eleven on Tesabarn 19 (every 20min. 6am-3pm, every 30min. 3-5pm; 20฿). The **train station** (☎311 534) lies at the end of Tesabarn 15. **Trains** go to Bangkok via Ayutthaya (3½-4hr., 9 per day 10am-2:30am, 36-262฿) and Khorat (1-1½hr., 11 per day 9am-4am, from 18฿). At the first **bus station,** beside the Thai Farmers Bank just after Tesabarn 19, you can catch **A/C buses** en route from Bangkok to Khorat (1½hr., every 20min. 5am-9pm, 46฿) and make connections to northern and northeastern destinations. An **A/C bus station** is between Tesabarn 18 and the overpass, with service to Bangkok (3hr.; newer orange and red bus 74฿, blue bus 110฿). A second **A/C bus terminal** between Tesabarn 21 and 23 has service to Nakhon Sawan via Lopburi (6hr., 4 per hr. 7:20am-12:20pm, 150-180฿). Ordinary buses for Khorat also leave from this terminal (2hr., every hr., 34฿). A third **A/C bus station** next to the Shell station serves Chayaphurn (2½hr., 10 per hr. 9:30am-7:30pm, 83฿).

Pak Chong extends approximately 2km along the main strip, **Mittaphap (Friendship) Highway,** parallel to the railway. Sidestreets are designated "Tesabarn Rd.," followed by a number. Odd-numbered Tesabarns parallel even-numbered ones on either side of the strip. Landmarks include the stoplight at Tesabarn 16/17, the 7-Eleven store, the pedestrian overpass, and the gas station at Tesabarn 25.

The **Bank of Ayudhya,** centrally located between Tesabarn 18 and the overpass, gives cash advances, cashes traveler's checks, and has a MC/Plus/V 24hr. **ATM.** (☎311 411. Open M-F 8:30am-3:30pm.) Other services include: the **day market,** which starts near Tesabarn 21 and extends one block uphill from the main road (open daily 6am-4:30pm); the **supermarket,** at the corner of Tesabarn 16, which sells flashlights, batteries, and toiletries for Khao Yai treks (open daily 8:30am-9:30pm); the **night market,** between Tesabarn 17 and 19, with rows of food carts and young Thais on motorbikes; **CAT,** on the corner of Tesabarn 24, which handles faxes, has sporadic **Internet,** receives collect calls, and places domestic and international phone calls (☎312 209; Internet 15฿ 1st hr., 12฿ every hr. after; collect calls 50฿; open M-F 8:30am-4:30pm); **Internet access,** between Tesabarn 15 and 17 (20฿ per hr.; open daily 9am-11pm); the **post office,** directly across from CAT. (☎311 736. Open M-F 8:30am-4:30pm.) **Postal Code:** 30130.

Khao Yai Garden Lodge ❶, Thanon Thanarat Km 7, is on the left side of the road from Pak Chong to Khao Yai (Rte. 2090). A pleasant garden with an eclectic collection of small pools and Lamyai trees weaves through a series of charming houses. An artificial waterfall cascades into the swimming pool. The quality of rooms ranges from decent to spectacular. (☎365 167; www.khaoyai-garden-lodge.com. Also runs park tours (see p. 728). Singles 100฿; doubles with bath 500฿; suites with marble bath and A/C 1800฿. Discounts for suites are negotiable.) Along the 30km stretch of road between Pak Chong and the park are luxury resorts, like **Juldi's Khao Yai Resort and Spa ❺,** Thanarat Rd., Km 17. A swimming pool and tennis courts sit amid beautifully landscaped grounds. The spa offers Thai herbal steam saunas for 300-450฿, rice and tumeric scrubs for 600-900฿, and traditional 90min. Thai massages for 500-750฿. (☎297 297; www.khaoyai.com. Great choice for a group. Breakfast included. 4-person bungalows, Nov.-Apr. Su-Th 3630฿; low-season 3267฿. AmEx/MC/V.) **Jungle Guest House ❶** is at 63 Kong Vaccine Soi 3, 1 Rd. Head on to Tesabarn 16 at the stoplight; the road forks, veer left onto Thanon Kong Vaccine Soi 1; the guesthouse is 50m on the right. Jungle is run by an amiable family that organizes expeditions to the park; reservations recommended. (☎09

917 6044; malivan65@yahoo.com. Coffee included. Breakfast 25฿. 200฿ for 2-day excursion. Basic dorms with mattresses on wooden floors and no fan 100฿; private singles and doubles with limited hot water shower and fan 150฿.)

The **night market** has many foodstalls, and some of the guesthouses have restaurants. Khao Yai Garden Lodge's restaurant serves both Thai and Western dishes.

THE PARK

Home to one of the last wild elephant herds and some of the world's few remaining wild tigers, the park has over 40km of **hiking** and **biking** trails through rainforest and grasslands. The **visitors center** rents bikes for 40฿ per hr. To avoid leeches, don't trek in sandals and steer clear of salty water. Leech-guards (70฿ to buy, 20฿ to rent) are available at the souvenir shop near Park Headquarters. **Haew Narok** ("awful cliff"), a three-tiered cascade, is the tallest waterfall in the park. Its impressive 150m height can be deadly; elephants have been known to slip and fall from the surrounding cliffs. **Haew Suwat Falls** and **Pha Kluai Mai Falls** (named for the surrounding red orchids) are also noteworthy. **Nong Pak Chi Watch Tower** (11km from the north entrance) is the place to observe deer, and **Elephant Crossing** is the spot to view elephants. For a tour of the park, try **Jungle Adventure**—a 1½-day tour operated by Jungle Guest House in Pak Chong. The tour, which includes Buddhist meditation caves, waterfall swims, elephant-trail treks, and a night safari, moves at a blistering pace and costs 950฿. Trips leave at 3pm and end the next evening. Leisurely 2hr. family **rafting** trips on Lam Tak Hong are offered May to September. Contact the Khao Yai Elephant Camp, Thanarat Rd. Km 19.5 (☎297 183). *Songthaew* leave the north park entrance for Pak Chong every hr. 7am-4pm. After stepping off the *songthaew* at the northern park entrance (☎04 429 7406), it's another 14km to Park Headquarters and the visitors center. You can arrange a pick-up at the entrance to headquarters (☎04 429 7406). Although *Let's Go* does not recommend it, most travelers find they have to hitchhike to headquarters. (Park Headquarters and visitors center open daily 8am-6pm. For longer treks, a guide is recommended; usually around 300-800฿. Park open daily 6am-9pm. 200฿, students 100฿, vehicles 50฿.) To stay overnight in the park call the Royal Forest Department in Bangkok (☎02 506 2076) for permission—bookings must be made by 6pm. Two campgrounds, **Lamtakong ❶**, 6km from the visitors center, and **Orchid ❶** *(Pha Kluai Mai)*, 9km from the visitors center, offer campsites for 30฿ as well as tent rentals (1-person tent 80฿, 3-person 150฿). Alternatively, **Suratsawadee Lodge ❷**, 1km from the visitors center, offers dorm beds for 100฿ a night.

THAILAND

NAKHON RATCHASIMA (KHORAT) ☎044

Known locally as Khorat, Nakhon Ratchasima straddles the main corridor to all other destinations in Isaan. Although it's one of Thailand's largest cities, the texture of urban life found here is worlds away from the manic snarls of Bangkok. Designed by French engineers for Ayutthayan King Narai, the city was once fortified by a wall and surrounded by a moat (the remains of which are still visible). Khorat enjoys close proximity to the silk-weaving of Pak Thong Chai, the pottery manufacturers of Dan Kwian, and the ruins of Phimai and Phanom Rung.

TRANSPORTATION

Flights: Airport (☎259 534), 28km east of town. Catch a **Buriram**-bound bus (10฿) at **Bus Terminal 2,** or a **shuttle bus** (70฿) with pick-up at your hotel. A van to the airport is also available on Asadang Rd. in front of Klang Plaza I (30min., 2-3pm, 50฿). **Thai Airways** (☎257 211), at the corner of Suranaree and Buarong Rd., has at least 1 flight to Bangkok per day. Open M-F 8:30am-4:30pm. **Air Asia** flies to Bangkok daily (4:50pm, 590฿ including taxes and fees).

Trains: Nakhon Ratchasima Train Station (☎242 044), on Mukkhamontri Rd. From the center of town, the station is 500m west on Mukkhamontri Rd., with an old locomotive out front. For a complete list of fares and departures, ask for an English timetable at the ticket booth. To: **Bangkok** (5-6hr., 11 per day 6:50am-11:25pm, 50-315฿).

Buses: The easiest way to find your bus is to inquire which platform it departs from. Purchase tickets on the platform or on the bus.

Terminal 1 (☎245 443), on Burin Lane. To: **Bangkok** (3hr., every 30min., 157฿); **Nakhon Sawan** (#572; 6hr., every hr. 5am-11pm, 95-113฿); **Pak Thong Chai** (#1303; 1½hr., every 30min. 5:30am-8:30pm, 12฿); and numerous stops within the province.

Terminal 2 (☎268 899), is on Rte. 2 north of town beyond Takhong River. Take a motorcycle, *tuk-tuk* (40-50฿), or *songthaew* from in front of the Mae Kim Heng Market on Suranaree Rd. To: **Bangkok** (#21; 4hr., every 30min., 157฿); **Buriram** (#273; 3hr., every 30min., 57-80฿); **Chiang Mai** (#635; 12hr., 11 per day 3:30-9:45am and 2-8:30pm, 437-510฿); **Chiang Rai** (#651; 13hr., 6 per day 5am-6pm, 472-550฿); **Nong Khai** (#22; 3½hr., every 2hr. 9am-3pm and 10pm-3am, 215฿) via **Khon Kaen** (2hr., every hr., 104฿) and **Udon Thani** (3hr., every hr., 184฿); **Phimai** (#1305; 1½hr., every 30min. 5am-10pm, 36-40฿); **Surin** (#274; 4hr., every 30min., 70-97฿); **Ubon Ratchathani** (#25; 4½hr., 6 per day 8am-4pm, 250฿).

Local Transportation: Samlor and **tuk-tuks** are omnipresent. From TAT to the Thao Suranaree Memorial should cost no more than 50฿. City buses are just as convenient (6am-8pm, 5-7฿). Buses #1, 2, and 3 start on Mukkhamontri Rd. near TAT and all go into the center of town. They split where Mukkhamontri forks into Phoklang Rd. (#1), Suranaree Rd. (#2), and Jomsurangyard Rd. (#3). **Songthaew** run routes more frequently and coincide with bus-route numbering.

ORIENTATION AND PRACTICAL INFORMATION

Khorat is enclosed on the west and north by **Mittraphap Road,** on the east by **Pol Lan Road,** and on the south by the railroad. **Ratachadamnoen Road** and **Chumphon Road,** separated by a narrow park, divide the city into two halves, a quieter western half and a more commercial eastern half. In the middle of this divider and marking the center of the city stands the dramatic **Thao Suranaree Memorial.** A rectangular moat, a remnant of the city's old fortifications, circumscribes the city's east half. **Chomphon Road,** not to be confused with Chumphon Rd., begins behind Thao Suranaree Memorial and cuts east-west through the center of the old city.

Tourist Offices: TAT, 2102-2104 Mittraphap Rd. (☎213 666; tatsima@tat.or.th), near the intersection with Mukkhamontri Rd. next to the Sima Thani Hotel. English spoken. Free brochures and a useful map. Info on cultural events and the Cambodian border. Open daily 8:30am-4:30pm.

Tours: Supatha Tour, 138 Chainarong Rd. (☎242 758).

Currency Exchange: Bank of Ayudhya, 168 Chomphon Rd. (☎242 388). MC/V cash advances and traveler's check exchange M-F 8:30am-3:30pm. 24hr. **ATM.** Cirrus/MC/Plus/V. Other ATMs line Chomphon Rd.

Markets: Mae Kim Heng Market, between Suranaree and Phoklang Rd. about 1 block beyond the city gate. **Supermarket** on the ground fl. of Klang Plaza II department store, Jomsurangyard Rd. Open daily 10am-9pm. The 2nd and 3rd floors have the English-language section of a bookstore, with limited magazines. **The Mall,** on Mittraphap Rd., is one of northeast Thailand's largest shopping plazas. The **night bazaar** fills 2 blocks of Marat Rd., between Chomphon and Mahatthai Rd. Open daily 6-10pm.

Local Tourist Police: (☎341 777). To the right of the Thao Suranaree Memorial. Additional location across Mittraphap Rd., across from Bus Terminal 2.

Pharmacy: Amarin, 122 Chumphon Rd. (☎242 741), behind the memorial to the left. "Rx" on the glass doors. Adequate English. Open daily 8:30am-8:30pm. Also on the lower level of Klang Plaza II, on Jomsurangyard Rd., just off Ratchadamnoen Rd.

Medical Services: St. Mary's Hospital, 307 Mittraphap Rd./Rte. 2 (☎261 261), 50m south of Bus Terminal 2. Private hospital with English-speaking staff. **Khorat Memorial Hospital,** 348 Suranaree Rd. (☎265 777). From the Thao Suranaree Memorial, it's past the Sri Pattana Hotel on the right. Look for the new white building proclaiming "KMH." English spoken. Open daily 24hr. Accepts Visa.

Telephones: CAT (☎259 707), next to the post office on Jomsurangyard Rd. Overseas calls, fax, and telex. Open daily 8:30am-4:30pm.

Internet Access: Internet Services, 768 Ratchadamnoen Rd., near the clocktower. Open daily 10am-midnight. 20฿ per hr. **Soft and Ware,** 438/2 Phoklang Rd. (☎267 766), near Yotha Rd. 1st hr. 20฿, each additional hr. 15฿. Open daily 10am-9pm.

Post Office: 48 Jomsurangyard Rd. (☎256 670). Facing the memorial, go right on Ratchadamnoen Rd. until Jomsurangyard Rd. Turn right and pass Klang Plaza II; it's on the right. Open M-F 8:30am-4:30pm, Sa 9am-noon.

Postal Code: 30000.

ACCOMMODATIONS

Budget digs in Khorat are generally dingy and run-down. Cheap and pleasant do not necessarily go together here, so if you are sick of grimy squat toilets and have a few extra *baht* saved up, this is one place to splurge on nicer accommodations.

Doctor's Guest House, 75 Sueb Siri Rd. Soi 4 (☎255 846). On the western edge of the city, past the train station and near TAT. The oldest and only real guesthouse in town. Distant location, but quiet. The best place in its price range. Laundry service 5-15฿ per item. Strict 10pm lockout. Small, clean rooms with fan 180฿. ❷

Sripatana Hotel, 346 Suranaree Rd. (☎251 652-4; www.sripatana.com). Clean rooms in an impersonal hotel. The curved hallways makes you feel like you're in a 70s futuristic movie. All rooms have A/C and TV. Internet and coffee shop. 460-615฿. MC/V. ❸

Sima Thani Hotel (☎213 100; sales@simathani,co.th), on Mittraphap Rd. Khorat's most luxurious hotel, miles above the rest. Traditional Thai dancing, pool, gym, spa, cafe. Enjoy it while it lasts. Deluxe rooms 2500-3000฿. MC/V. ❺

FOOD

The **markets** are fine places to sample regional specialties, such as *sai klog* (grilled pork sausages stuffed with rice; 5฿) and *kanom bueng* (small, taco-shaped, coconut-stuffed crepes; 1฿). An alternative is the **food courts** in the basement and fifth floor of the Klang Plaza II shopping center on Jomsurangyard Rd., which offer western fast-food, cheap Chinese-Thai dishes (20-35฿) and hybrid pizza crepes (20฿). Purchase food coupons before ordering. (Open daily 10am-9pm.)

Ran Ahaan Jay Con Im, 191/2 Suranaree Rd., serves vegetarian entrees (10-20฿). Open daily 8am-midnight. ❶

Suan Sin, 163 Washarsarit Rd. Heading south on Chumphon Rd. behind Thao Suranaree shrine, take a left onto Mahatthai Rd. and then a right onto Washarsarit Rd. Open-air storefront serves Isaan specialties. Entrees around 60฿. Open daily 10am-8pm. Next door is **Samram Lap,** which serves similar food outdoors (open 10am-11pm). ❷

Suan Pak (SPK), 154-158 Chumphon Rd., behind the shrine and to the left, past Dok Som. Sweet cafe serving cakes and an extensive menu (13 pages) of Thai, Chinese, and Western food. Entrees 45-120฿. Open daily 4pm-12:30am. ❷

Cabbages & Condoms (C&C Restaurant), 86/1 Sueb Siri Rd., just past Soi 4 and before the train tracks near Doctor's Guest House. Same food as its Bangkok sibling (p. 681). Open daily 10am-10pm. ❷

SIGHTS

Khorat's handful of sights can be visited in a single afternoon. A good starting point is the **Thao Suranaree Memorial.** Constructed in 1934, the memorial is a source of identity and inspiration for generations of Khorat citizens. Shaped like a Chinese ship, **Wat Sala Loi's** unique symbolism adds to its appeal. Look for its sign on Mittraphap Rd., at the old moat's northeast corner. Every Thai city has a sacred pillar from which distances are measured. Khorat's is enshrined at **Wat Phra Narai Maharat** on Prajak Rd., between Assadang and Chompon Rd. inside the city moat. This *wat* contains a sandstone image of the Hindu god Narayana as well as a *shiva linga* (phallus-shaped pillar). The **Mahawirawong Museum,** Khorat's branch of the National Museum, is on Ratchadamnoen Rd., one block past the clocktower from the shrine. Its small collection contains artifacts from the Angkor and Ayutthaya periods. (☎242 958. Open W-Su 9am-4:30pm. 10฿.)

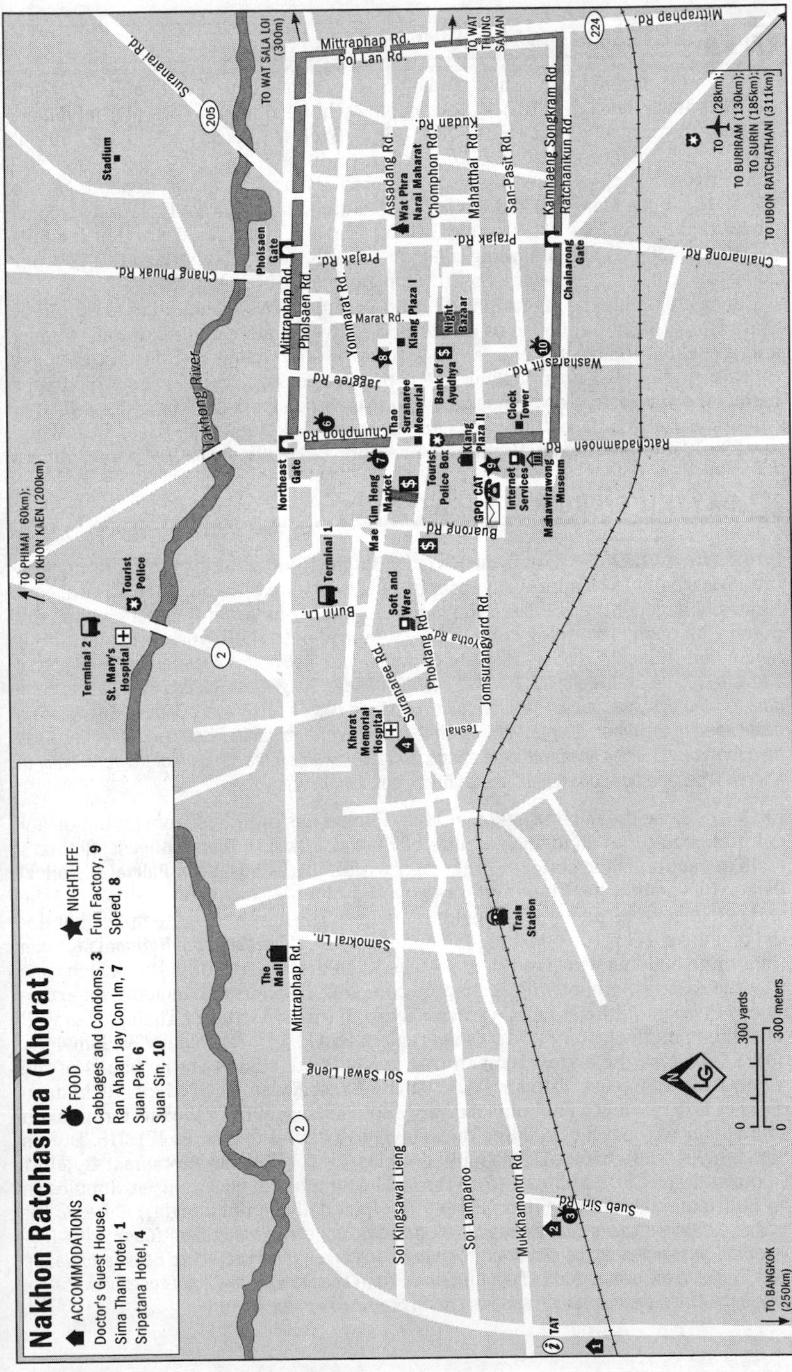
Nakhon Ratchasima (Khorat)
ACCOMMODATIONS
Doctor's Guest House, 2
Sima Thani Hotel, 1
Sripatana Hotel, 4
FOOD
Cabbages and Condoms, 3
Ran Ahaan Jay Con Im, 7
Suan Pak, 6
Suan Sin, 10
NIGHTLIFE
Fun Factory, 9
Speed, 8
TO PHIMAI 60km);
TO KHON KAEN (200km)
TO WAT SALA LOI (300m)
TO WAT THUNG SAWAN
TO BURIRAM (130km);
TO SURIN (185km);
TO UBON RATCHATHANI (311km)
TO (28km)
TO BANGKOK (250km)
Suranarai Rd.
Stadium
Pholsaen Gate
Chang Phuak Rd.
Takhong River
Northeast Gate
Chainarong Gate
Tourist Police
Terminal 2
St. Mary's Hospital
Terminal 1
Mittraphap Rd.
Pol Lan Rd.
Pholsaen Rd.
Prajak Rd.
Yommarat Rd.
Marat Rd.
Jaggree Rd
Chumphon Rd.
Assadang Rd.
Wat Phra Narai Maharat
Chomphon Rd.
Kudan Rd.
Mahatthai Rd.
San-Pasit Rd.
Kamhaeng Songkram Rd.
Ratchanikun Rd.
Chainarong Rd.
Klang Plaza I
Night Bazaar
Bank of Ayudhya
Washarasit Rd.
Thao Suranaree Memorial
Clock Tower
Klang Plaza II
Ratchadamnoen Rd.
Mae Kim Heng Market
Tourist Police Box
GPO CAT
Internet Services
Mahawirawong Museum
Buarong Rd.
Burin Ln.
Soft and Ware
Phoklang Rd.
Yotha Rd.
Jomsurangyard Rd.
Suranaree Rd.
Khorat Memorial Hospital
Teshal
Train Station
Samokral Ln.
The Mall
Soi Sawai Lieng
Soi Kingsawai Lieng
Soi Lamparoo
Mukkhamontri Rd.
Sueb Siri Rd.
TAT
205
224
2
300 yards
300 meters
0

THAILAND

ENTERTAINMENT AND NIGHTLIFE

The karaoke plague has reached epidemic proportions here. For temporary relief, the **Sima Thani Hotel,** next to TAT, occasionally holds dinner shows of Thai dance. Call ahead for availability. (☎213 100. 7-8pm. Free with *à la carte* dinner, about 250฿.) Performances of *phleng khoraat*, a traditional folk song, occur sporadically next to the clocktower. Lyrics are improvised and the drama depends on the wit of the singer. **Muay Thai** kicks off at the stadium; inquire at TAT. Khorat also has **movie theaters** on the 6th floor of Klang Plaza II, with Thai movies for 60฿ (10:30am-6:30pm) and a **bowling alley** on the 8th floor of the plaza (40-70฿ per game; open M-F 11:30am-1am, Sa-Su 10am-1am) on Mittraphap Rd.

Dance clubs rule the nightlife in Khorat. **Speed,** 191 Assadang Rd., next to the K Stars Hotel, has a full house of dance floors, live music, private karaoke rooms, and a cocktail lounge. Set the mood with some slow dancing (8-11pm), then get down to glittering disco until 2am. (☎248 944. No cover. Karaoke rooms 1000฿ per night.) **The Fun Factory,** on Jomsurangyard Rd. across from the Klang Plaza II, also celebrates the great age of disco. There is a one-drink minimum. (Beer 80฿. Whiskey 290-1350฿. Live music. Hip-hop dance floor F-Sa. 20+. Open daily 9pm-2am.)

DAYTRIPS FROM KHORAT

DAN KWIAN VILLAGE. Tiny Dan Kwian Village, 15km southeast of Khorat, was the crossroads for traders traveling in bull-cart caravans between Khorat and Khmer. Villagers have collected the clay from the Moon River for years, giving the pottery its distinctive rusty color. The geometric-patterned work is beautiful but heavy and fragile. *(From Khorat, follow Chomphon Rd. behind the Thao Suranaree Memorial and turn right on Chainarong Rd. Turn left onto Kamhaeng Songkhram Rd. and walk past the vendors. On the right, you should see a small blue-striped bus (#1307; every 30min., 5฿). Indicate destination to the driver. Alternatively, catch the bus from Terminal 2. Disembark when the small road forks into 3 lanes lined with little shops. To return, wait on the left side of the road back to Khorat. When the bus comes (last one at 6pm), gesticulate wildly.)*

PHIMAI. Since the fall of Angkor in 1432, Phimai has morphed from an important cultural center into an idyllic satellite of Khorat, 60km to the southeast. Phimai's main attraction is the stately Khmer ruin within the **Prasat Hin Phimai Historical Park.** At its zenith, the Khmer empire covered much of mainland Southeast Asia, and evidence of its power and wealth remains in the hundreds of temples that dot the region. (☎471 568. Open daily 7:30am-6pm. 40฿.) The **Phimai National Museum** (in a white building with a red-tiled roof) is 500m down Songkhran Rd., which runs past the eastern perimeter of the temple complex. The museum includes an extensive collection of Khmer and Dvaravati art from lower northeast Thailand, as well as exhibits on the history of the Isaan region. (☎471 167. Open daily 8:30am-4pm. 40฿.) **Sai Ngam,** the largest banyan tree in Thailand, stands on the banks of the Moon River 2km east of town. **Old Phimai Guest House ❶,** 214 Moo 1 Chomsudasaget Rd., two and a half blocks down Chomsudasaget from the bus terminal on a small *soi* to the right (look for the sign), has palatial rooms. (☎471 918. Dorms 80฿; singles 130฿, with A/C 300-350฿; doubles 160฿.) **Baitiey Restaurant ❷,** 246/1 Chomsudasaget Rd., a block before the *soi* leading to the guesthouses, doubles as an informal tourist info center. (☎471 725. Open daily 7am-midnight.) *(Buses to Phimai depart from Khorat's Bus Terminal 2 (#1305; 1½-2hr., every 30min. 5am-10pm, 34฿). They first drop passengers at the center of town, once you cross the Moon River. Be sure to get off here. To get to the center of town from the Phimai Town bus station, take a red songthaew (5฿) or take a right from the bus station and walk down Sra Kaew Rd. for 1km.)*

TIP **WHERE'S THE BE IN BC?** You may wonder why many Thai historical markers date the fall of Angkor to the same year as the end of the Vietnam War. Many Thai brochures and historical markers use the traditional Buddhist Era (BE) calendar, marking year 1 as the year of Buddha's death. To convert from Buddhist (BE) to Gregorian calendars (BC), subtract 544 from the BE year.

SURIN

☎044

For one week each November, hordes of Thai and *farang* flood Surin to watch dancing, bejeweled, soccer-playing pachyderms on parade in the Surin Elephant roundup. The other 51 weeks of the year, Surin remains a rare stop on itineraries, as most travelers press on to the Mekong River. Their loss is your gain; this peaceful town, boasting one of the niftiest night markets around, is a springboard for the many small Khmer ruins and traditional villages by the countryside. Only 50km from the Cambodian border, Surin reflects the province's unique mixture of Lao, Khmer, Thai, and indigenous Suay cultures.

TRANSPORTATION

Trains: Surin Railway Station (☎511 295), beside the elephant statue on Tanasan Rd. Trains to: **Bangkok** (4½-9hr., 9 per day, 299฿) via **Khorat** (2-3hr., 32-204฿); **Ubon Ratchathani** (3hr., 11 per day, 31-150฿).

Buses: Surin Bus Terminal (☎511 756), on Chit Bam Rung Rd. From the roundabout, go 1 block east past Mr. Donut, and then 2 blocks to the left; it's on the right. Buses to: **Bangkok** (7-8hr., 10 per day 7:30am-10pm, 280-380฿); **Chiang Mai** (15hr., 6 per day 2:45-10:45pm, 275-685฿); **Khorat** (4hr., about every 30min. 4am-6pm, 64-97฿); **Pattaya** (9hr., 9 per day 9am-10:30pm, 170-300฿); and **Ubon Ratchathani** (4hr., 9 per day 7:30am-9:30pm, 60-110฿) via **Si Saket** (40฿).

Local Transportation: Samlor around town 20-25฿; **tuk-tuk** 30-40฿.

ORIENTATION AND PRACTICAL INFORMATION

The main street, **Tanasan Road,** runs north-south. At its north end is the **train station,** which faces an elephant statue. Several blocks down Tanasan Rd. from the train station is a **roundabout.** To reach the roundabout from the bus station, go left, pass the *soi* with the sign for the Petchkason Hotel, and take the next right. Tanasan Rd. is the first intersection. One block past the roundabout on Tanasan is the intersection with **Krung Sri Nai Road.**

Tourist Offices: Brochure and Surin map available at **TAT** in Khorat. **Surin City Hall** (☎516 075), on Lakmuang Rd., can also offer tourist info. Open M-F 8:30am-3:30pm. Mr. Pirom at **Pirom's House** (p. 734) is an invaluable English-speaking resource.

Currency Exchange: Bangkok Bank, 252 Tanasan Rd. (☎512 013), just past the roundabout on the right. 24hr. **ATM** AmEx/MC/Plus/V. Open M-F 8:30am-3:30pm. Several other banks and ATMs also lie along Tanasan Rd.

Markets: Day and **night markets** are in the same location along Krung Sri Nai Rd. From the train station, walk 1 block past the roundabout. The permanent market is on the right; the left side of the street comes to life at dusk. 24hr.

Police: Surin Police Station (☎511 007), on Lakmuang Rd. Walking from the train station down Tanasan Rd., take a left. It's on the 2nd block on your left.

Pharmacy: Kayang Chelan Pesat, 294 Tanasan Rd. (☎513 055). Near Krung Sri Nai Rd. Open daily 8:30am-9pm.

Medical Services: Ruam Paet, Tesabarn 1 Rd. (☎513 192), a tall building with a blue-and-white sign. Facing the train station at the roundabout, turn right; it's after the 2nd stoplight on the right. English-speaking doctor. **Surin Hospital** (☎511 757), on Lakmuang Rd. From the roundabout, head from the train and take a left; it's on the left.

Internet Access: Internet is available on Krung Sri Nai Rd., between Tesabarn 3 and Tanasan Rd., across from the day market. 15฿ per hr.

Post Office/Telephones: Surin Post Office (☎511 009), on the corner of Tanasan and Tesabarn 1 Rd. at the roundabout. **Phone** and **fax** available 7am-10pm. Open M-F 8:30am-4:30pm, Sa-Su 9am-noon.

Postal Code: 32000.

ACCOMMODATIONS AND FOOD

During the elephant roundup, rates can soar 50% and finding a room is nearly impossible. One of the best options in town is **Pirom's House ❶,** 242 Krung Sri Nai Rd. From the roundabout, head away from the train station on Tanasan Rd. Make a right onto Krung Sri Nai Rd.; it's two blocks down when the road bends a sharp left. Mr. Pirom offers several tours in his SUV (from 750฿ per day). At the time of this write-up, Mr. Pirom was in the process of moving to a new location. Take another right over the train tracks and the first left onto Muangleng Rd. Look for **Pirom's Guesthouse No. 2** on the left at the end of the dirt driveway. (☎515 140. Laundry 5-20฿. Strict 11pm lockout. Dorms 70฿; singles 100฿; doubles 150฿.)

Surin has some of the best Isaan food around, especially at the **day** and **night markets**. Try the Hoi Hut, fried river oysters in a crispy batter over bean sprouts, flavored with sweet-and-sour sauce (20-30฿). From the train station, take the second left onto Sanitnikhomrat Rd. and **Wai Wan Restaurant ❷,** 44-46 Sanitnikhomrat Rd., is on the right. (☎511 614. Open daily 8am-10pm.) Inside Surin Plaza, across from the suspension bridge, **Hot Pot: Suki Shabu Restaurant ❹** is a Pan-Asian chain serving *dim sum* and hot pot combinations of pork, seafood, and beef for 199-219฿. From the roundabout, walk west toward the KFC sign; take a right and enter Surin Plaza on the left. (Open daily 11am-9:30pm. AmEx/MC/V.)

SIGHTS AND ENTERTAINMENT

Surin is a pleasant place to relax and enjoy Isaan life, but there aren't many "official" sights unless you're there for the annual **Elephant Roundup** in mid-November (check with TAT for exact dates). The stars of this two-day festival honoring the national animal are the 200 pachyderms who awe audiences with feats of strength and skill. For those who want to dance, **Sparks** is the place. From the roundabout, head down Tesabarn Rd. toward the Mr. Donut sign. Take a left at Sirirat Rd. and proceed 300m; look up high for the red sign, next to Thong Tarin Hotel. (☎514 088. Cover 70฿. Open daily 9pm-2am.)

UBON RATCHATHANI ☎045

The trading and communications hub for the northeast corner of Thailand, Ubon Ratchathani (or simply "Ubon") attracts few travelers except during the Candle Festival in July. This festival features processions of beeswax serpents, saints, and Buddhas—some larger than the monks that carry them. This "royal city of lotuses"

THAILAND

has a fine museum and is famed for its silk and cotton cloth. Those interested in monastic Buddhism can visit many of the region's secluded forest monasteries. Not far downstream, the Moon River flows into the "emerald triangle," where Laos, Cambodia, and Thailand converge in the lush jungle.

TRANSPORTATION

Readily accessible by air, bus, or train, Ubon is the last stop on the northeastern branch of the national rail network. To go farther east or north, take the bus.

Flights: Ubon Ratchathani International Airport (☎245 612), on Thepyothi Rd. **Thai Airways,** 364 Chayangkun Rd. (☎313 340), 2km north of the river on the right. Open M-F 8am-4pm. Flights to **Bangkok** per day (2 per day 8:30am, 7:45pm; 1405-2205฿). **Air Asia** also flies to Bangkok (6:45am, 6:25pm; 600฿).

Trains: Railway Station (☎321 276, advance ticketing 321 004), on Sathani Rd., Warin Chamrap District. Buses #2 and 6 run to the station from Upparat Rd. (5฿). Trains go to: **Bangkok** (9-12hr., 6 departures 7:05am-7:15pm, 301-641฿) via **Si Saket** (13-50฿), **Surin** (31-152฿), and **Khorat** (58-313฿). Additional trains head to **Khorat** (6:25am, 4:45pm) via **Si Saket** and **Surin.**

Buses: Ubon has 2 main bus stations.

Ubon Bus Station (☎316 089), at the far north end of town; take city bus #2, 3, or 11. To: **Bangkok** (10-12hr., every 20-30min. 4am-9:30pm, 267-431฿); **Chiang Mai** (17hr., 6 per day 12:15-6:20pm, 325-685฿) via **Surin** (3hr., 60-160฿); **Nakhon Phanom** (4½-6hr., 5 per day 6am-2pm, 91-164฿) via **Mukdahan** (2½hr., 9 per day 5:45am-5pm, 60-108฿) and **That Phanom** (3½hr.); **Pattaya** (12hr., 9 per day 6:30am-7:30pm, 215-455฿) via **Khorat** (6hr., 115-340฿); **Udon Thani** (6hr., 6 per day 5:45am-1pm, 140-232฿) via **Khon Kaen** (4hr., 169฿) and **Yasothon** (1hr., 68฿). Purchase tickets at the kiosks in the terminal. For destinations within the province, buy tickets on the bus. To: **Det Udon** (platform #23, 25, and 27; 6:30am-5pm; 20฿); **Kantaralak** (platform #19; 5:30am-6pm, 30฿); **Khong Chiam** (platform #26, 28; 8, 9am, 12:30, 4:30pm; 30฿); **Na Cha Luai** (platform #25; 9:30, 10:30, 11:30am; 30฿); **Phibun** (platform #22, 24; 6:30am-4:30pm, 25฿). Local tour companies have booths at the bus terminal, making it easy to shop around and compare prices.

Warin Chamrap Station, south of the Moon River. Take *songthaew* #1, 3, 6, or 7 (5฿) to the station. Buses to: **Na Cha Luai** (every hr. 10am-1pm, 30฿); **Phibun** (every 20min. 5am-7:40pm, 20฿); **Surin** (every 30min. 7am-5pm, 43฿). From Phibun, *songthaew* run to **Chong Mek** (every hr. 6:30am-5:30pm, 25฿) and **Khong Chiam** (every 30min. 8am-4:30pm, 20฿).

Local Transportation: City buses (numbered *songthaew*) run 5am-6pm (5฿). From Upparat Rd., buses #2 and 6 run to the train station and buses #2, 3, and 11 go to the Ubon bus station. Buses #1, 3, and 9 go near the Warin Bus Station. **Tuk-tuks** and **samlor** roam the streets (up to 60฿ from the Moon River to Sahamit Bus Station).

Rentals: Thai Yont, 300-316 Khuanthani Rd. (☎243 547), across from the Ratchathani Hotel. Reliable and well-maintained. **Motorbikes** 300฿ per day. Open M-Sa 8am-5pm, Su 8am-noon. **Ubon Rental Cycle,** 115 Sinarong Rd. (☎242 813), across from the Krungtong Hotel. **Bicycles** 20฿ per hr. 100฿ for 5-24hr. Open M-Sa 8am-3pm.

ORIENTATION AND PRACTICAL INFORMATION

Ubon's main thoroughfare, **Upparat Road,** stretches north-south for 12km; at its north end it is called **Chayangkun Road.** To the south, it crosses the **Moon River** into the **Warin Chamrap District,** where the train station is located. Buses #1, 2, 3, and 6 go there from Ubon proper. North of the river, Upparat Rd. passes the riverside **market** and intersects **Khuanthani Road,** two blocks up.

Tourist Office: TAT, 264/1 Khuanthani Rd. (☎243 770). Turn right onto Khuanthani Rd. at the National Museum; TAT is on the left, 2 blocks down. Free, useful maps. Fluent English spoken. Open daily 8:30am-4:30pm.

Currency Exchange: Bangkok Bank, 13 Ratchabut Rd. (☎262 453). **ATM.** AmEx/MC/Plus/V. Open M-F 8:30am-3:30pm. Banks line Upparat Rd.

Markets: The **riverside market** is open 24hr. As you cross the bridge into Ubon, the market is immediately to the right of Upparat Rd.

Local Tourist Police: (☎244 941), at the corner of Suriyat and Thepyothi Rd., near the airport. English spoken.

Pharmacy: Chai Wit, 87 Promathep Rd. (☎254 077). From TAT, walk 2 blocks toward the river. Chai Wit is 1 block to the left; look for the yellow-and-green sign across the street. Open M-F 7am-7:30pm, Sa 7am-noon.

Medical Services: Rom Klao, 123 Upparat Rd. (☎244 658), 2 blocks north on Upparat Rd. From the bridge, it's on the left before Khuanthani Rd. English spoken. Open 24hr.

Internet Access: One of the fastest and cheapest places to surf the web is **PR Net.Com,** 100/1 Chung Konnithan Rd. From Upparat Rd. with your back to the river, take a left onto Sapasit Rd. Walk 2 blocks and take a right. 10฿ per hr. Open daily 8am-9pm.

Post Offices/Telephones: GPO, 145 Sinarong Rd. (☎254 001). From the museum, walk past TAT and turn left on Luang Rd. *Poste Restante* behind the office. Open M-F 8:30am-4:30pm, Sa-Su 9am-noon. AmEx/MC/V. **Telephone** service available M-F 8:30am-4:30pm at a 2nd post office at 159-163 Phadaeng Rd., between Suriyat and Sapasit Rd. The **Warim Chamrap** postal branch (☎324 333) is at 88 Tahar Rd.

Postal Code: 34000.

THAILAND

ACCOMMODATIONS AND FOOD

The town's best accommodations are at the **Sri Isaan Hotel ❹,** 62 Ratchabut Rd., across from the riverside market. Clean but small rooms are strung along a mosaic-tiled staircase and bright sky-lit atrium. This option is not for the miser. (☎261 011. Laundry service 5-20฿. Singles 550฿; doubles 600฿.) The **Ratchathani Hotel ❸** is on Khuanthani Rd., one block over from the National Museum, with bright, clean rooms. (☎244 388. Singles 330฿, with A/C 500฿; doubles 450฿/650฿. AmEx/MC/V.) Farther away is **River Moon House ❷,** 21 Si Saket 2 Rd., Warin Chamrap. Walk out the train station past the golden horse statue and take the 2nd left. It's on your right, across from the fire station. River Moon organizes one-day tours to Khao Pravihaan for 350฿ plus the admission fee. All rooms have shared baths. (☎286 096. Breakfast 50฿. Singles 120฿; doubles with twin beds 150฿.)

The **market,** off Promathep Rd. east of Upparat Rd., serves duck salad, *kuay chap*, and other Isaan and Vietnamese dishes around the clock. At night, **vendors** also gather on Ratchabut Rd., off Khuanthani Rd. near the Ratchathani Hotel. Diagonally across from the National Museum is **Chiokee Restaurant ❷,** 307 Khuanthani Rd. Wooden screens open onto the street for a breezy meal. (☎254 017. Breakfast porridge with fish 40฿. Most dishes 30-120฿. Open daily 6am-6pm.) **Muang Buffet (Vegetarian Buffet) ❶** is at the corner of Prathumthepphakdi and Thetsuban 81 Rd. *Songthaew* often park in front. Meat is replaced with a soybean derivative, and all dishes come with brown rice. (☎323 360. Sweet herbal teas. Open M-Sa 6am-2pm.) On the upscale side is **The Gold Fish Restaurant ❸,** 142/1-2 Khuanthani Rd., 50m east of Ratchawong Rd. (☎242 394. Thai menu only. Owner speaks English. Steamed catfish with vegetables in *isaan* sauce 120฿. Red ant eggs (in season) 80฿. Most dishes about 60-180฿. Open daily 10:30am-10pm.)

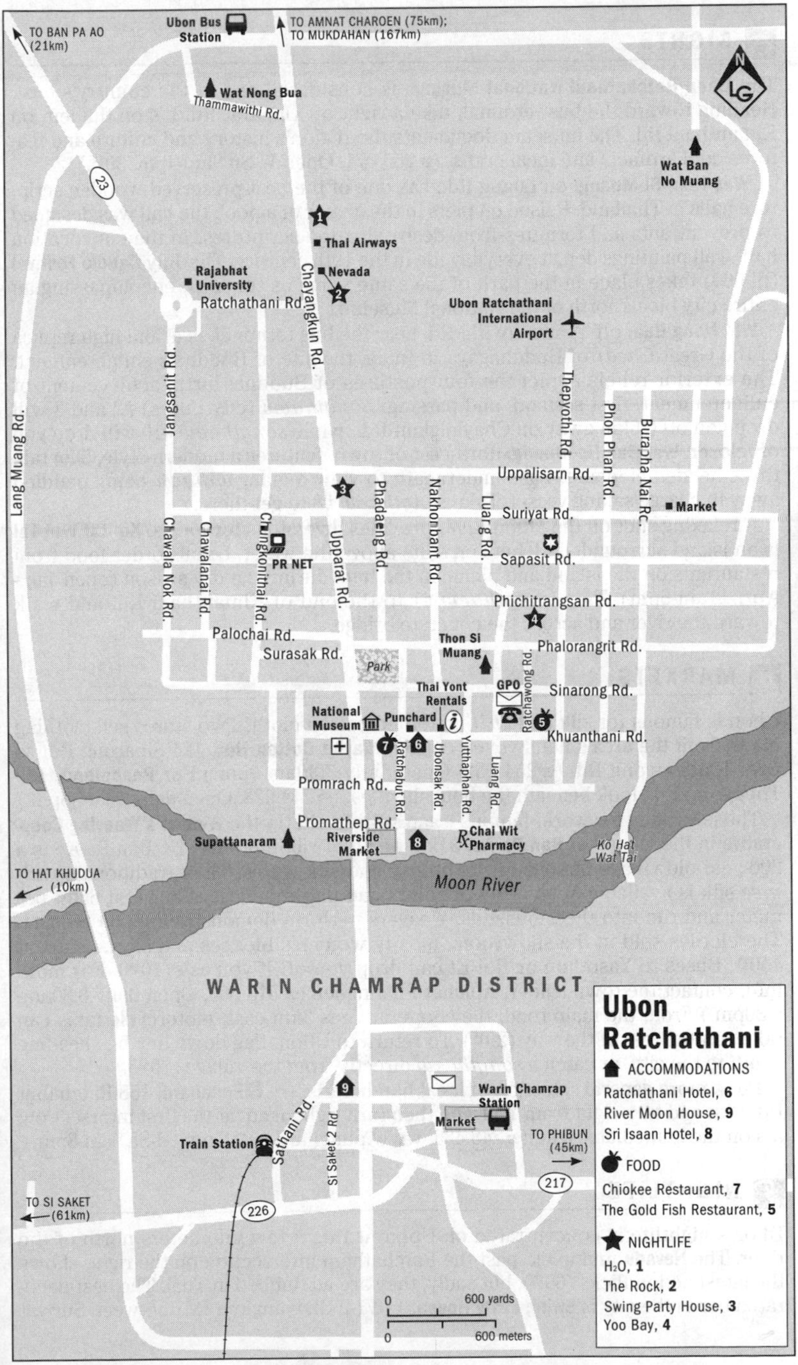

TO BAN PA AO (21km)
Ubon Bus Station
TO AMNAT CHAROEN (75km); TO MUKDAHAN (167km)
Wat Nong Bua
Thammawithi Rd.
23
Wat Ban No Muang
Thai Airways
Nevada
Rajabhat University
Ratchathani Rd.
Chayangkun Rd.
Ubon Ratchathani International Airport
Jangsanit Rd.
Lang Muang Rd.
Thepyothi Rd.
Phon Phan Rd.
Buraha Nai Rd.
Uppalisarn Rd.
Suriyat Rd.
Market
Phadaeng Rd.
Nakhonbant Rd.
Luang Rd.
Sapasit Rd.
Chawala Nok Rd.
Chawalanai Rd.
Chingkonithai Rd.
PR NET
Upparat Rd.
Phichitrangsan Rd.
Palochai Rd.
Surasak Rd.
Park
Thon Si Muang
Phalorangrit Rd.
Thai Yont Rentals
GPO
Sinarong Rd.
Ratchawong Rd.
National Museum
Punchard
Khuanthani Rd.
Ratchabut Rd.
Ubonsak Rd.
Yutthaphan Rd.
Luang Rd.
Promrach Rd.
Promathep Rd.
Supattanaram
Riverside Market
Chai Wit Pharmacy
Ko Hat Wat Tai
Moon River
TO HAT KHUDUA (10km)
WARIN CHAMRAP DISTRICT
Warin Chamrap Station
Market
Sathani Rd.
Si Saket 2 Rd.
Train Station
TO PHIBUN (45km)
217
TO SI SAKET (61km)
226
0 600 yards
0 600 meters
Ubon Ratchathani
ACCOMMODATIONS
Ratchathani Hotel, 6
River Moon House, 9
Sri Isaan Hotel, 8
FOOD
Chiokee Restaurant, 7
The Gold Fish Restaurant, 5
NIGHTLIFE
H2O, 1
The Rock, 2
Swing Party House, 3
Yoo Bay, 4

SIGHTS

The **Ubon Ratchathani National Museum** is considered one of the country's best. Heading toward the bus terminal, take a right off Upparat Rd. It's on the left, on Khuanthani Rd. The museum documents the region's history and culture and features cool artifacts and local crafts. (☎255 071. Open W-Su 9am-4pm. 30฿.)

Wat Thon Si Muang, on Luang Rd., has one of the best-preserved wooden scripture halls in Thailand. Raised on piers in the center of a pool, the hall was designed to prevent ants and termites from destroying the scriptures. In the convocation hall, wall paintings depict everyday life in the 19th century. The July **Candle Festival** (p. 660) takes place in the park of the same name as the *wat*, encompassing an entire city block north of the National Museum.

Wat Nong Bua, off Thammawithi Rd. near the bus terminal, is a 56m high replica of the Great *Chedi* of Buddhagaya in India, the site of Buddha's enlightenment. The exterior reliefs depict the four postures of Buddha: birth, achievement of enlightenment, first sermon, and passing. *Songthaew* (city buses) #2 and 3 will drop you off 0.6km away on Chayangkun Rd., while *songthaew* #10 will drop you off closer. **Wat Ban No Muang,** northeast of town, features a modern-style, 50m tall, three-headed elephant. Pass underneath to view a giant *wihaan* being paddled away in a large sailing vessel. Take *songthaew* #8 to get there.

A relaxing spot on the Moon River provides diversions for locals. **Ko Hat Wat Tai** is an island surrounded by huts on stilts above the water. Locals order food from restaurants on the island and picnic in the huts during the dry season (open Jan.-Apr. 11am-6pm). Take *songthaew* #1 to the end of Khuanthani Rd. and walk toward the river and across the concrete bridge.

MARKETS

Ubon is famous for silk and *khit*-patterned cotton cloth. Two stores sell clothing made from the area's handwoven cotton. **Maybe Cotton Hut,** 124 Sinarong Rd., is near Ratchawong Rd. (☎254 932. Open daily 7:30am-9pm.) For **Peaceland,** 189 Thepyothi Rd., look beneath the bougainvillea. (☎244 028. Open daily 10am-8pm.)

Those looking for world-famous Isaan silk should try the **Women's Weaving Cooperative** in the village of **Ban Pa Ao,** 21km north of Ubon on Rte. 23. Ban Pa Ao is a 200-year-old village famous for its bronze and silk wares. Their traditional *mudmee* silk is available in an array of colors and patterns. Prices begin at 650฿ per meter and run into the thousands. Weavers perform demonstrations on request. The clothes sold in the showroom, mostly women's blouses and skirts, start at 450฿. Buses to Yasothon or Roi Et can drop you off if you ask (10฿). For more info, contact the town leader, Apichat Phanngoen (☎313 505. Open daily 8:30am-6:30pm.) From the main road, the cooperative is 3km east; motorcycle taxis can take you the rest of the way (20฿). To return to Ubon, flag down any bus heading south to the city, or catch a *songthaew* directly from the village (20฿).

For a more general selection of local handicrafts, try **Punchard,** 158 Ratchabut Rd. Exit and turn right from TAT and then turn right again at the first intersection; it's on the immediate right. (☎243 433; www.punchard.net. Open M-Sa 9am-8pm.)

NIGHTLIFE

Ubon's nightlife is concentrated on Upparat Rd., a few kilometers north of the river. The **Nevada** multiplex, past the Ratchathani intersection on the right, shows the latest action flicks (60฿), but sadly, they are all dubbed in Thai. The best-decorated bar in the city is **Swing Party House,** 140/1-2 Chayangkun Rd., between Suriyat and Uppalisarn Rd. Facing the bus station, it's on the right. (☎265 145. Singha 100฿. Live music nightly at 9:30pm. Open daily 7pm-1am.) **The Rock** is a pumping disco in the basement of the Nevada Hotel on the northern end of Chayangkun Rd. (☎280 999. Large Singha 99฿. Open daily 9pm-2am.) Housed in a glass and metal box, chic **H_2O,** 488/1 Chayangkun Rd., 100m north of the Nevada Hotel, is Ubon's trendy epicenter, with leopard-skinned bar stools and chrome chairs. (☎280 315. Jug of Singha 140฿. Open daily 7pm-2am.) Ubon's most popular discotheque for 20-somethings is **Yoo Bay,** on Phichitrangsan Rd. between Thepyothi and Luang Rd.

BORDER CROSSING: CHONG MEK/VANG TAO. Travelers can enter Laos at the village of Chong Mek, 44km from Phibun. From the village of Vang Tao on the Lao side, it is one hour to Pakse, an excellent springboard for exploration of southern Laos. From Ubon, take a bus from the Warin Chamrap station to **Phibun** (1hr., 5am-6pm, 20฿). At the Phibun market, locals can direct you to *songthaew* heading to **Chong Mek** (1¼hr., 7am-5pm, 20฿). Purchase a 15-day visa on arrival for US$30, or a heftier 1500฿ (1 passport photo required). 30-day visas are available from the Lao embassy in Bangkok or the consulate in Khon Kaen (3-day processing 1100฿, expedited processing up to 1400฿). Before crossing the border, you must register your departure from Thailand at the **immigration office,** 30m before the fence on the right. Once in Laos, present visas to immigration, just beyond the border on the right. From Vang Tao, take a *songthaew* to **Pakse** (10฿). Border open daily 8:30am-4pm. The Lao entry tax varies but currently stands at 50฿.

THAILAND

DAYTRIPS FROM UBON RATCHATHANI

FOREST MONASTERIES. **Wat Pa Nanachat** has the unique mission of training non-Thai monks. Those studying meditation and Buddhism are welcome to visit 10am-noon. Serious students may be able to arrange a stay lasting overnight or several weeks, but must write in advance. The *wat* is a branch of nearby **Wat Nong Pa Pong,** known primarily for meditation teacher **Ajahn Chah.** A major branch of the controversial **Santi Asok** sect resides 6km to the east of town; ask in town for details. *(Wat Pa Nanachat is behind a rice field off the highway to Si Saket, near Bung Wai village. Catch a Si Saket-bound bus or* songthaew *from Warin Chamrap Station, and ask to get off at Wat Pa Nanachat (13km, 7-8฿). It's located about 500m from the road, inside a walled, forested compound. Wat Nong Pa Pong temple is 10km south of Ubon and off the road to Katharalak.)*

PHU CHONG NAYOI NATIONAL PARK. Covering 686km² in the Emerald Triangle, this national park stretches through the forested region bordering Thailand, Cambodia, and Laos. Highlights of the park include the **Huay Luang Waterfall** (Bak Taey), which plunges 30m into a basin of emerald-green water (3.5km south of headquarters), and **Phu Hin Dang,** a cliff offering views of the two neighboring countries, accessible only by car or motorbike. *(From Warin, take a bus to Na Cha Luai (every hr. 10am-1pm, 30฿). From Ubon, buses run less frequently (Platform #25; 9:30, 10:30, 11:30am; 130฿). The park is another 15km from Na Cha Luai. You can hire a motorcycle taxi for 120฿ or a* songthaew *(200฿ round-trip). Campsites 20฿ per person; bungalows 100฿ per person. Park admission 200฿. Open 6am-6pm. Although TAT states that the area has been de-mined, stay safe and do not venture off well-trodden paths.)*

KHONG CHIAM. This tranquil hamlet is known for the *mae nam song si*, or convergence of the "Two-Color" river, an effect created by the different levels of silt suspension from the blue Moon and brown Mekong Rivers. At the end of Klaewpradit Rd., walking through the temple grounds leads to a pavilion with an excellent view of the two rivers. About 20km north of Khong Chiam is **Pha Taem National Park,** housing a 200m stretch of prehistoric rock-paintings. (☎249 780. Open 6am-6pm. Admission 200฿.) Two kilometers before the cliffs at Sao Chaliang, erosion has created chantral-shaped rock formations. During the high season, two or three *songthaew* may depart to Nawng Pu Poi (15฿). It's a 2km walk from the road. Ask about departures and private transportation rentals at Apple Guest House. A motorbike can be hired for 100฿ one-way. Once at Pha Taem, it's a 500m walk to the paintings. **Tana Rapids National Park,** 3km south of Khong Chiam, is named after a cataract on the Moon River. Accommodations in the park include **bungalows** (100฿ per person) and **campsites** (20฿ per person). Tent rental (20฿) is also available. A *tuk-tuk* can be hired one-way from Khong Chiam for 50฿. (☎243 120. Open 6am-6pm. Admission 200฿.) Take a boat via the Mekong from Khong Chiam to **Pha Taem** (800฿), **Kaeng Tana** (400฿), or **"Two-Color" river** (200฿). *(Take a bus from the Warin or Ubon Ratchathani bus station to Phibun Mangsahan (platform #22 or 24; 1hr., every 30min. 5am-6pm, 20-25฿). From the Phibun market, take a samlor to the songthaew station on the Moon River (10฿ at most). You can also walk. From the bus stop, head toward the market. Turn right onto Thiboon Rd. and walk 3 long blocks. At the traffic signal, take a left and walk until you reach the river. Songthaew are in a parking lot on your right and go to Khong Chiam (45min., every hr., 25฿). A direct bus runs infrequently from Ubon (platform #26 or 28; 2hr.; 8, 9am, 12:30, 4:30pm; 50฿). It takes a similar route but doesn't require a bus change.)*

MUKDAHAN ☎042

The 1893 demarcation of the Mekong River as an international boundary politically separated Mukdahan from Savannakhet, Laos. However, the region remains unified by its culture, food, and lifestyle, as evidenced by the golden baguettes sold in shops and the annual boat races in October enjoyed from both sides of the river. A bridge (expected to open in 2006) spanning the Mekong will further strengthen the economic links between the two sides.

TRANSPORTATION. The main **bus station,** 33 Chayangkong Rd. (☎671 478), is 3km away on the side of the highway opposite town. To walk into town, take a left out of the terminal and a right at Wiwitsurakan Rd., the first major intersection, 500m ahead. Follow this street as it merges to the right. Make a left at Phitak Phanomket Rd. and walk 0.5km into the heart of town. *Tuk-tuks* to the river are 20-40฿. **Buses** run to: Bangkok (platform #1; 10-12hr.; 8, 8:30, 8:50am, 2:40pm, every 30min. 3:30-8:30pm; 202-590฿) via Khorat (6hr., 175-243฿); Khon Kaen (platform #3; 4½hr., every 30min. 3:30am-4:30pm, 115฿); Nakhon Phanom (platform #8; 2½hr., 6 per day 5am-5pm, 40-56฿); That Phanom (1hr., 22฿); Ubon Ratchathani (platform #2; 2½hr., 10 per day 6:15am-5:20pm, 60-108฿); and Udon Thani (5½hr., 7 per day 8:30am-3:30pm, 93-167฿). With a 30-day Lao visa, obtainable at the Lao embassy in Bangkok or the consulate in Khon Kaen, you can take a **ferry** to Savannakhet. You can also obtain a 14-day visa on arrival for US$30 (p. 673).

ORIENTATION AND PRACTICAL INFORMATION. The town is laid out on a grid, with streets running roughly parallel (north-south) and perpendicular (east-west) to the Mekong, the town's east border. Along the river bank is **Samron Chaikhong Road,** site of the **Indochine Market,** the *wat*, and the pier. Parallel to Samron Chaikhong, heading from the river, are **Samut Sakdarak (Mukdahan-Domton) Road** and **Phitak Santirad Road.** Perpendicular to these are **Song Nang Sathit Road,** which runs from the pier past the Huanum Hotel to the night market, and, one road south, **Phitak Phanomket Road,** where the **post office** is located. The **roundabout** is located at the intersection of Phitak Phanomket and Phitak Santirad Rd. The **bus terminal** is on the main highway **Chayangkong Road (Route 212),** 3km northwest.

Thai Farmers Bank, 191 Song Nang Sathit Rd., two blocks up the road from the pier and one block past Huanum Hotel, has a 24hr. **ATM** and exchanges currency. (☎611 056. Open M-F 8:30am-3:30pm, except holidays. AmEx/MC/V.) Other services include: the **Indochine market,** which sets up every day at the waterfront and sells trinkets like mini disco balls, Buddha images, and dinnerware; the **day market,** off Phitak Phanomket Rd. heading away from the river; the **night market,** four blocks from the river on Song Nang Sathit Rd.; the **police station** (☎611 333), on Phitak Santirad Rd. between the roundabout and Song Nang Sathit Rd.; **Mukdahan International Hospital** (☎611 983), 1km south of downtown on Samut Sakdarak Rd. past Mukdahan Hotel; **Internet** access at 44 Phitak Phanomket Rd., 400m from the roundabout heading away from the river, past the Ploy Palace Hotel (15฿ per hr.; open daily 9am-11pm); the **post office,** 18 Phitak Phanomket Rd. (☎611 065. Open M-F 8:30am-4:30pm, Sa-Su 9am-noon.) **Postal Code:** 49000.

ACCOMMODATIONS AND FOOD. **Saensuk Bungalows ❸,** 136 Phitak Santirad Rd. Heading toward the river on Phitak Phanomket, take a right on Phitak Santirad Rd.; it's two blocks down on the right with a Thai sign. It offers A/C rooms with TV, all set around a stone parking lot. (☎611 214. Rooms 300-350฿.) **Huanum Hotel ❷,** 36 Samut Sakdarak Rd., is on the corner of Samut Sakdarak and Song Nang Sathit Rd., one block from the pier. It is a labyrinth of staircases and fairly clean rooms. (☎611 137. Singles 120฿, with bath 220฿, with A/C 280฿; doubles 300฿, with A/C 320฿.) Next to Pith Bakery, **Hong Kong Hotel ❷,** 108 Phithaksantirat Rd., provides clean, worn rooms with firm beds and Western toilets. From the roundabout facing the river, make a left; it's on the left. (☎611 143. Rooms 160฿.)

The **night market** along Song Nong Sathit Rd. is especially good. French-Lao bakeries sell tasty goods. **Foremost Restaurant ❸** on 74/1 Samut Sakdarak Rd., serves noodle soup as well as more substantial Thai and Western meals. From Huanum Hotel, walk one block past the pharmacy; it's at the next intersection. (☎612 251. Entrees 40-150฿. Open daily 7am-10pm.) The small **Mumsabai Restaurant ❷** has good food. Walk to one block before the river on Song Nong Sathit Rd.; it's on the right. (☎633 616. Vegetable coconut soup 60฿. Open daily 10am-10pm.) **Pith Bakery ❷,** 703 Phithaksantirat Rd., serves Western breakfasts (35-45฿) and the only brownies this side of the Mekong. (☎611 990. Open daily 8:30am-9pm.) Next to the bakery, a food stand serves Vietnamese rice-flour dumplings.

SIGHTS. A larger-than-life golden Buddha contemplates the Mekong from **Wat Si Mongkan Tai,** on Samron Chaikhong Rd. **Chao Fa Mung Shrine,** far up Song Nang Sathit Rd., houses the city pillar. If you happen to arrive at the end of Buddhist Lent (in late fall), you'll catch boat races on the Mekong.

BORDER CROSSING: MUKDAHAN/SAVANNAKHET. Purchase a 15-day visa on arrival for US$30, or a heftier 1500฿ (1 passport photo required). 30-day visas are available from the Lao embassy in Bangkok or the consulate in Khon Kaen (3-day processing 1100฿, expedited processing up to 1400฿). From Mukdahan, take a **ferry** to Savannakhet. (M-F 7 per day 9am-4:30pm, Sa 6 per day 9am-2:30pm. 50฿ ferry fare, 50฿ surcharge for Sa arrivals, and 50฿ if only staying one night.) The Lao entry tax varies (currently 50฿).

DAYTRIPS FROM MUKDAHAN. Aside from being a border town, Mukdahan is conveniently located near several worthwhile sights.

MUKDAHAN NATIONAL PARK. Known for its rock formations and caves, **Mukdahan National Park** also boasts prehistoric rock art, wildlife, and cliff-top views of the Mekong. The collection of huge, oddly shaped rocks at the main entrance is the chief crowd-pleaser. Trail maps are available from the park office at the entrance. Trails are marked in Thai; arrows pointing straight ahead direct hikers along the main 2km hike to the **Buddha Cave Waterfall.** During the dry season, the falls shrink to a trickle. Rickety wooden stairs lead to the **Buddha Cave,** lined with thousands of Buddha images. *(The park can be reached from Mukdahan by bus and songthaew leaving town on Samut Sakdarak Rd. toward Dontan (Rte. 2034), past Mukdahan Hotel on the right (2 per hr. 6am-6pm, leaves when full; 10-15฿). The entrance is a 15min. walk down a small paved road on the right. 200฿. Camping fee 20฿. Open daily 8am-6pm.)*

THAT PHANOM. Many travelers would overlook this tranquil town if it were not home to **Wat That Phanom,** the most sacred religious structure in northeast Thailand. Legend says it was built to house one of the Buddha's clavicle bones transported from India. Topped by a 110kg gold spire, the shrine has been restored seven times since its initial construction. At the beginning of February, thousands come to pay their respects during the annual **Phra That Phanom Homage Fair.** About 15km northwest is the silk-weaving village of **Renu Nakhon.** Isaan music and dance at **Wat Renu Nakhon** are performed sporadically during the winter and holidays; contact TAT in Nakhon Phanom for more information. Take any Nakhon Phanom-bound *songthaew* to the Renu Nakhon junction 8km north of town; from there, hire a *tuk-tuk*. *(That Phanom, midway between Nakhon Phanom and Mukdahan, is easily reached from either town by bus or songthaew (20฿), which stop along Chayangkun Road (Highway 212) and at a small bus station (☎547 247) south of town.)*

THAILAND

NAKHON PHANOM ☎042

Nakhon Phanom, the city of mountains, is named for its view of the jagged green limestone outcroppings across the river in Laos. Indeed, the picturesque vista dominates the city and creates a dramatic backdrop for ordinary life here; around sundown, the riverside promenade comes alive with women sweating to an aerobics workout and young teens gossiping, while the occasional elephant, a light reflector attached to its tail, traces a flashing red line in its wake.

TRANSPORTATION AND PRACTICAL INFORMATION. Nakhon Phanom Airport (☎587 444), 15km out of town, has flights to Bangkok (M and Sa 7:30am, Tu-F 10:20am, Su 11am; 2455฿). **PBAir** (☎511 265) is on Aphibanbuncha Rd. From Fuang Nakhon Rd. with your back to the river, take a left; it's one long block on the right. The **bus terminal** (☎513 444), on Piya Rd., is in the southwest corner of town. **Buses** go to Bangkok (11-12hr., 8 per day 7:20am-6pm, 319-635฿); Khon Kaen (4hr., 6 per day 6:10am-4pm, 97-175฿); Mukdahan (2½hr., 13 per day 5:45am-5am, 40-56฿) via That Phanom (1hr., 26-30฿); Sakhon Nakhon (1½hr., every hr. 7am-5pm, 36-50฿); Udon Thani (4½hr., 13 per day 5:15am-3pm, 87-120฿). **Tuk-tuks** hang out near the night market on Aphibanbuncha Rd. Getting around town costs about 20฿.

Two main roads run parallel to the river; smaller roads perpendicular to the river connect the two. **Sunthon Wichit Road** is adjacent to the river and lined with a promenade. Farther south, past the intersection with **Fuang Nakhon Road,** is the **clocktower** and the immigration office. **Aphibanbuncha Road** runs parallel to Sunthon Wichit. At the end of Fuang Nakhon Rd. is **Piya Road,** where the **bus terminal** is located. Services include: **TAT,** one block north of the post office (☎513 490; open daily 8:30am-4:30pm); **Bangkok Bank,** on Srithep Rd. behind the Indochine market (☎511 209; open M-F 8:30am-3:30pm); a **day market** off Aphibanbuncha Rd.; a **night**

market on Fuang Nakhon Rd. (opens around 6pm); the **police** (☎511 266), on Sunthon Wichit Rd., one long block north of the clocktower; **Nakhon Phanom Hospital** (☎511 424), on Aphibanbuncha Rd., a few blocks north of the intersection with Fuang Nakhon; **CAT,** on Salaklang Rd., two blocks north of the post office (open M-F 8:30am-4:30pm); **Internet** access at **Cybernet,** 37 Sunthon Wichit Rd., 50m off Fuang Nakhon Rd. (☎513 633; 15฿ per hr.; open daily 8:30am-10pm); the **post office,** 341 Sunthon Wichit Rd., next to the police station. (☎512 945. *Poste Restante.* Open M-F 8:30am-4:30pm, Sa-Su 9am-noon.) **Postal Code:** 48000.

ACCOMMODATIONS AND FOOD. Generally, accommodations are mid-sized hotels showing signs of age. Some rooms at the **Windsor Hotel ❸,** 272 Bamrungmuang Rd., have a view of the Lao mountains. From Aphibanbuncha Rd., walk toward the river on Fuang Nakhon Rd. and take a right; the hotel is on your right. (☎511 946. Singles with TV 250฿, with A/C 350฿; doubles with A/C 400฿.) **Grand Hotel ❸,** 2210 Si Thep Rd., is a few blocks south of the clocktower. The A/C rooms are better-kept than the fan rooms. (☎511 526. Singles 180฿, with A/C 320฿; doubles 280฿/380฿.) Riverfront restaurants dominate Nakhon Phanom's culinary scene. A few open-air restaurants line Sunthon Wichit Rd. south of the immigration office, and there's always a 20฿ bowl of noodles at the **night market** on Fuang Nakhon Rd. The **Golden Giant Catfish Restaurant ❷,** 257-261 Sunthon Wichit Rd., is on the riverside beside the clocktower, toward the immigration office. (☎09 421 8491. Entrees 60-120฿. Open daily 7am-10pm.) **Sweet Home ❸,** 281 Buangrungmuang Rd., is famous for its *nam neung,* or Vietnamese spring rolls (60฿). From Fuang Nakhon Rd. with your back to the river, take a left onto Buangrungmuang Rd. It'll be on your left before Nittayo Rd. (☎511 654. No English sign. Open daily 9am-4pm.)

SIGHTS AND NIGHTLIFE. Wat Okatsribuaban, adjacent to the promenade south of the clocktower, houses two highly revered images of the Buddha. Tourists come to Nakhon Phanom for the view and to take relaxing evening strolls along the **riverfront promenade.** And if all this *wat*-hunting and pleasure-strolling has worn you down, recharge with pumping MP3s and an ice-cold Heineken (small 50฿) at the **Duck Pub,** Piya Rd., one block toward the city center from the bus terminal. (Open daily 8pm-1:30am.)

BORDER CROSSING: NAKHON PHANOM/THA KHAEK. You can purchase a 15-day visa on arrival for US$30, or for 1500฿ (1 passport photo required). 30-day visas are available at the Lao embassy in Bangkok or the consulate in Khon Kaen (3-day processing 1100฿, expedited processing up to 1400฿). Before crossing the border, ' an exit stamp from the **immigration office** just opposite the Indochine market on Sunthon Wichit Rd. (☎511 235. Open M-F 8:30am-4:30pm.) A **boat** behind the office shuttles passengers to Tha Khaek (14 per day 8am-4pm, 60฿). The Lao entry tax varies but is currently 50฿.

UDON THANI ☎042

Home to a six-digit population, Udon Thani is one of the most prosperous cities in the northeast and Isaan's chief agricultural, commercial, and transportation center. Once the site of a US Air Force base during the Vietnam War, the American presence can still be felt in its Western restaurants and expatriate community.

TRANSPORTATION

Flights: Udon Thani Airport (☎246 567), on the Udon Thani-Loei Hwy., 5km southwest of town. **Air Asia** (☎02 515 9999) flies to **Bangkok** (3:45, 8:20pm; 459-850฿). Open daily 8am-9pm. **Thai Airways,** 60 Makkhaeng Rd. (☎243 222), also has flights to **Bangkok** (8:20am, 2:45, 8:25pm; 1890฿). Open M-F 8-11:30am and 1-4:30pm.

Trains: Train station (☎222 061), at the east end of Prajak Rd. Booking office open daily 6am-8pm. To: **Bangkok** (10-11hr.; 8:16am, 6:40, 8:03pm; 175-1077฿) via **Khon Kaen** (3hr., 25-50฿); **Nong Khai** (1hr., 7 per day 5am-8:50pm, 11฿).

Buses: Buses to **Ban Phu** (1½hr., 20 per day 6:30am-5:30pm, 25฿) leave from Rangsima Market, as do buses to **Nong Khai** (every 20min. 5:20am-8pm).

Bus Terminal #1 (☎222 916), near Charoensri Shopping Complex off of Sai Uthit Rd. To: **Ban Chiang/Sakhon Nakhon** (#230; 3hr., every 30min. 4am-7pm, 58-80฿); **Bangkok** (#407; 9-10hr., every hr. 6am-11pm, 179-500฿) via **Khorat** (4½hr., 102-184฿); **Khon Kaen** (2hr., every 30min. 7am-5pm, 44-79฿); **Ubon Ratchathani** (#268; 6hr., 8 per day 5:15am-1:15pm, 141-230฿) via **Mukdahan** (4hr., 91-167฿).

Bus Terminal #2 (☎247 788), 2km west of town on the ring road, has northbound buses to: **Chiang Mai** (11hr.; 8:15, 10:15am, 7, 8:30pm; 300-540฿); **Loei** (#220; 3½hr., every hr. 4am-5pm, 55฿); **Nong Khai** (#221; 1hr., every hr. 5:45am 3:45pm, 21฿).

Local Transportation: Songthaew #7 runs between bus terminals #1 and 2 as well as TAT (5฿); #6 along Udondutsadee Rd. from the fountain, north of Rangsima Market and Bus Terminal # 2; #14 from the train station to TAT. Free *songthaew* route maps available from TAT. Plenty of **samlor** (20-30฿) and **tuk-tuk** (20-50฿) run around town.

ORIENTATION AND PRACTICAL INFORMATION

Udon Thani, 562km northeast of Bangkok, lies between Khon Kaen and Nong Khai along the railroad line and **Friendship Highway.** Navigating the city requires a decent map, flexibility in interpreting street signs, and an eternal awareness of the **Nong Prajak Reservoir,** a large park on the town's west side and a good landmark. **Prajaksinlapacom Road** (commonly known as Prajak Rd.), **Posri Road,** and **Srisuk Road** run east-west. Each road sports a roundabout where it diagonally intersects **Udondutsadee Road.** Away from the reservoir, Prajak Rd. ends at the **train station** near **Bus Terminal #1.** The **airport** and **Bus Terminal #2** are on the far side of the reservoir, west of the town center.

Tourist Office: TAT, 16/5 Mukkhamontri Rd (☎325 406, ext. 27), at the edge of the reservoir. Look for the back door on Tesa Rd. Open daily 8:30am-4:30pm.

Currency Exchange: Bangkok Bank, 154 Prajak Rd. (☎221 505). Open M-F 8:30am-3:30pm; currency exchange open daily 8:30am-5pm. 24hr. **ATM.**

Markets: The **Ban Huay Market** at the north end of Udondutsadee Rd. The largest **night market** is located just outside the train station entrance at the east end of Prajak Rd.

Local Tourist Police: (☎240 616), in front of TAT.

Police: (☎328 515), at Srisuk and Naresuan Rd.

Pharmacy: Somsak, 194 Posri Rd. (☎222 478). Well-stocked pharmacy carries gauzes and sports braces. Open daily 7am-8pm.

Medical Services: Aek Udon International Hospital, 555/5 Posri Rd. (☎342 555). One of the best hospitals in the northeast. English-speaking doctors. 24hr. **pharmacy.** AmEx/MC/V.

Telephones: CAT, 108/2 Udondutsadee Rd. (☎222 805). North of the clocktower before Wattananuvong Rd. **Lenso international** phone. Open M-F 8:30am-4:30pm.

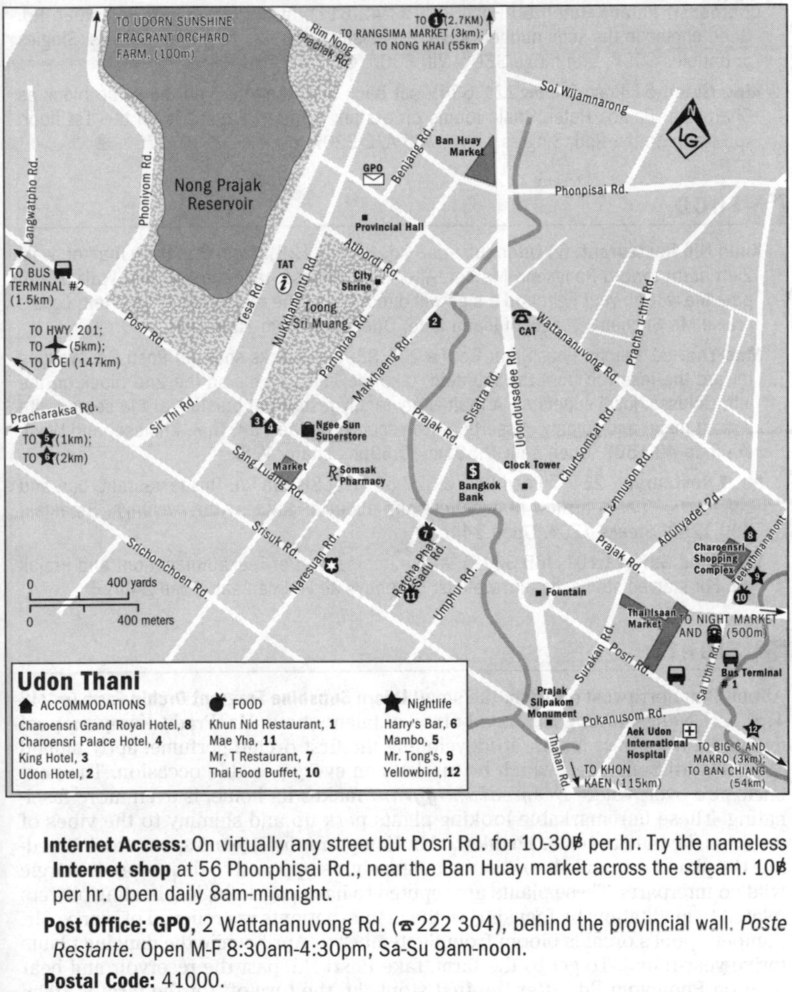

Internet Access: On virtually any street but Posri Rd. for 10-30฿ per hr. Try the nameless **Internet shop** at 56 Phonphisai Rd., near the Ban Huay market across the stream. 10฿ per hr. Open daily 8am-midnight.

Post Office: GPO, 2 Wattananuvong Rd. (☎222 304), behind the provincial wall. *Poste Restante.* Open M-F 8:30am-4:30pm, Sa-Su 9am-noon.

Postal Code: 41000.

ACCOMMODATIONS

If you're looking for a nice room at a good price, you've come to the wrong town. However, a number of hotels do exist and if you have the *baht*, luxury is just around the corner.

Charoensri Grand Royal Hotel, 277/1 Prajak Rd. (☎343 555), behind the Charoensri Shopping Complex. Nothing gritty or budget here; this is Udon's most luxurious hotel. Bar, garden, pool, gym. Breakfast included. Singles and doubles 1100฿. ❺

Udon Hotel, 81-89 Makkhaeng Rd. (☎248 160). A good value with those little luxuries—A/C, hot water, tub, TV. Breakfast included. Singles in old wing 460฿, new wing 500฿; doubles 500฿/550฿. ❸

Charoensri Palace Hotel, 60 Posri Rd. (☎242 611), at the corner with Parnphrao Rd. Good choice in the semi-budget range, especially if you like bright red carpets. Singles or doubles 300฿, with fridge 360฿; VIP 600฿. ❸

King Hotel, 57 Posri Rd. (☎221 634), set back from the street on the same block as Charoensri Palace Hotel. Basic rooms on a stark corridor. Parking is on the 1st floor; you sleep on the 2nd. Singles 190฿, with A/C 220฿; doubles 230฿/270฿. ❷

FOOD

Khun Nid Restaurant, 64 Udondutsadee Rd. (☎246 128). From Ban Huay market, walk 2km north toward Rangsima Market. After the overpass, take the 2nd left. Walk 700m past the *wat* on your right and a sign will direct you to the restaurant on your left. Locals praise Mr. Srichan's variety of Isaan food. Open daily 9am-10pm. ❷

Mae Yha, 81 Ratcha Phat Sadu Rd. (☎223 889), 4 blocks south of Posri Rd. Walking toward the reservoir from the fountain, take the 2nd left; it's on the 2nd block on the left. Colossal local superstar. A multi-story family restaurant bursting at the seams with a giant menu and yummy desserts. Seven-scoop sundae 75฿. Thai, Chinese, and Western food 40-150฿. Open daily 9:59am-10:59pm, sharp. V. ❷

Mr. T Restaurant, 254/7 Posri Rd. (☎327 506), at Sisatra Rd. This restaurant, bar, and coffee shop has a mellow atmosphere and acoustic guitar in the evenings. Breakfast 100-120฿. Steaks 120฿. Open 24hr. ❸

Thai Food Buffet (☎01 965 3819), at the intersection of Teekathmananont and Prajak Rd. For starved stomachs and wallets: 50฿ buys all you can eat. Open 24hr. ❷

THAILAND

SIGHTS

About 2km northwest of town, the small **Udorn Sunshine Fragrant Orchid Farm** (☎242 475), 127 Nongsamrong Rd., is a botanical talent show. Mr. Pradit Kampermpool devoted a decade of his life to developing the first orchid perfume, aptly named "Miss Udorn Sunshine," which he markets on every possible occasion. The next enclosure over, where *Desmodium gyrant* makes its home, is even more fascinating. These unremarkable-looking plants perk up and shimmy to the vibes of music or the human voice. Thanks to Mr. Kampermpool's years spent cross-breeding, the plants respond almost instantaneously, as opposed to their more lethargic wild counterparts. These plants are reputed to have psychological healing powers related to meditation: by focusing on the plants, patients are relieved of worry. Mr. Kampermpool's orchids bloom from September to April, while the dancing plants thrive year-round. To get to the farm, take Posri Rd. past the reservoir and bear right on Phoniyom Rd. After the first stoplight, the turn-off for the farm is 100m ahead on the left and the farm is another 100m to your right. *Songthaew* #5 and 16 pass by the turn-off. (Open daily 7am-6:30pm. The suggested 30฿ donation goes toward food and clothing for the poor and for AIDS patients.) **Nong Prajak Reservoir,** in the northwest section of town, is full of benches, pavilions, and footbridges.

ENTERTAINMENT AND NIGHTLIFE

The theater at the top of the Charoensri Shopping Complex screens Thai films (90฿ and up). Udon's nightlife revolves around two clubs: **Mambo** and **Yellowbird.** To get to Mambo in the Napalai Hotel, 572 Pracharaksa Rd. (☎347 444), head west toward the reservoir on Srisuk Rd. and walk left where Pracharaksa Rd. branches off Srisuk for 1km. Bathe yourself in fluorescent blue light to the pounding beats of Thai pop. (Open daily 9pm-2am.) Closer to town, but less popular, Yellowbird disco at the Charoen Hotel also plays Thai pop. (Open daily 10pm-1:30am.) About 200m past the discos, **Mr. Tong's** outdoor bar, on Teekathmananont Rd. across from the Charoensri Complex, is a great place to finish the evening if you don't mind incandescent color schemes. The town's expats and the locals who love them swear by **Harry's Bar,** 19/4 Banliam Bypass. Heading past the reservoir on Srisuk Rd., take a left on Pracharaksa Rd. and a right on Suk Rd. *Tuk-tuks* from the town center cost 80฿. (Both bars: beer 60-80฿, mixed drinks 100-110฿; no cover; open nightly until 1-2am.)

DAYTRIPS FROM UDON THANI

BAN CHIANG. Ban Chiang, 54km east of Udon Thani, is one of Southeast Asia's most significant archaeological discoveries and a UNESCO World Heritage Site in 1992. The story of its discovery begins in 1966, when Stephen Young, a Harvard University archaeology student, tripped over a large root and found the rim of a partially unearthed pot staring him in the face. Upon closer scrutiny, he found that the area was littered with half-buried pottery. By the time excavation began in the mid-1970s, many valuable artifacts had been sold to collectors in trading centers worldwide. The skeletons and numerous bronze artifacts found here have shed light on the lives of the inhabitants of the area between 3000 and 1000 BC. They also indicate that the civilization possessed knowledge of metallurgy much earlier than originally estimated, casting doubt on the theory that metallurgy came to Thailand from China. The **national museum** documents the unearthing of Ban Chiang. The second-floor exhibits have comprehensive captions in English. (☎208 340. Open daily 8:30am-5pm. 30฿.) At the other end of the village, **Wa Phosi Nai** displays a well-preserved burial site with intact artifacts. *(Exit left from the museum; the excavation site is 600m down on the right. Orange and blue songthaew leave from Posri Rd. for Ban Chiang (1½hr., every 30min., 25฿). On Sai Uthit Rd., walk past the bus station on your left and make a right onto Posri Rd. You will see the songthaew on the right side of the road opposite a small supermarket. Usually the bus driver will drop you off at the turn-off for Ban Chiang. If so, take a tuk-tuk for the remaining 6km (30-40฿). Buses and songthaew return to Udon from the museum entrance every 1½hr. until 2pm. If you miss these, hire a tuk-tuk to the main road; there are frequent buses from Sakhon Nakhon to Udon.)*

ERAWAN CAVE. Visible from several kilometers away, this towering limestone outcrop is pierced by a gaping crevice sheltering a large Buddha. While the few stalagmites in the cave aren't that impressive, the interior lunar landscape makes a trip worthwhile. At the base of the outcrop is a *wat* from which a series of stairs ascends to the cave entrance. Eventually the steps branch; take the flight to the left. A path with a view of the nearby peaks runs through the mountain to the other side. *(Erawan Cave is just off the Udon Thani-Loei Hwy. (Hwy. 210). Any Loei-bound bus will drop you at the turn-off between Km 30 and 31 (93km, 30-35฿). From there, another* tuk-tuk *will transport you the additional 2km from the entrance to the cave.)*

NONG KHAI ☎042

If Khaosan Rd. is a noisy, spunky kid, then Nong Khai's riverfront is its calm, cool older brother. Travelers end up staying on to see one of Thailand's most unique Buddhist temples—Sala Kaew Ku. The large influx of foreigners, along with the greatest number of temples per capita, makes for one of Thailand's most authentic tourist towns, bringing Thais and *farang* alike.

TRANSPORTATION

Trains: Nong Khai Railway Station (☎411 592), on Hwy. 212, 1.5km west of town. *Tuk-tuk* ride from Rimkhong Rd. 30-50฿. Trains to **Bangkok** via **Khon Kaen** and **Udon Thani** (10-12hr.; 7:30am, 7:05pm; 183-1177฿) and **Khorat** (6hr., 1pm, 64฿). Booking office open daily 7am-7pm.

Buses: Nong Khai Bus Terminal, off of Prajak Rd. at the east end of town. To: **Bangkok** via **Khon Kaen, Khorat,** and **Udon Thani** (#23; 12hr., 12 per day 5:30am-5:30pm, 273-545฿); **Nakhon Phanom** (#224; 5-7hr., 6 per day 6:40-9:50am, 106-148฿) via **Beung Khan** (2hr., 50-70฿); **Udon Thani** (#221; 1hr., 16 per day 5:30am-4pm, 21฿). Green buses go to **Loei** (#507; 6-8hr., 5 per day 6-11:35am, 84฿) via **Si Chiangmai** (1hr., 22฿), **Pak Chom** (5hr., 57฿) and **Sangkhom** (2-3hr., 37฿). To get to **Chiang Khan,** switch buses at **Pak Chom.**

Local Transportation: For those who just want to walk, **tuk-tuks** are abundant to the point of distraction, as drivers assume all *farang* are desperately in need of their services (20-50฿).

Rentals: Bicycle rental at Mut Mee Guest House (43฿ per day) or at the front of the *soi* leading to Mut Mee (30฿ per day). **Motorbike rental** 200฿ per day at **Nana Motor,** 1160 Meechai Rd. (☎411 998), opposite Chayaporn Market. Open daily 7:30am-6pm.

THAILAND

ORIENTATION AND PRACTICAL INFORMATION

Nong Khai is a major border crossing to **Vientiane, Laos**—the **Friendship Bridge** joins the two countries. In the north, Nong Khai is bordered by the **Mekong River,** while **Highway 212** marks the town's southern boundary. Parallel to Hwy. 212, from south to north, are **Prajak Road, Meechai Road,** and **Rimkhong Road.** The **train station,** on Hwy. 212, 2.5km west of the town center, is a bit of a hike. The **bus station** is off Prajak Rd., southeast of the main tourist area. Guesthouses are scattered to the northeast, and most have maps.

Currency Exchange: Bangkok Bank, 372 Soi Srisaket (☎412 675), in the ground fl. office next to the ATM. Open M-F 8:30am-3:30pm. Currency exchange open Sa-Su 8:30am-4pm.

Markets: The **Indochine market,** along Rimkhong Rd. near the Mekong River, features a cornucopia of scented soaps, electronics, binoculars, and, of course, massive grilled fish. Open daily 9am-5:30pm. **Prochai Market,** adjacent to the bus terminal, and **Chayaporn Market,** to the west, sell the usual produce and meats.

Police: (☎411 020). On Meechai Rd., facing the hospital.

Pharmacy: Tong Tong Pharmacy, 382/2 Meechai Rd. (☎411 690). Exit left from the post office; it's on the corner. Open daily 7:30am-9pm.

Medical Services: Nong Khai Hospital, 1158 Meechai Rd. (☎411 504), near City Hall and opposite the police station.

Internet Access: Sitai Cha Computers, 269/1 Soi Wat Nak, next to the Kiwi Cafe. If the owner, Malinee, challenges you to a game of Scrabble, let her win. 20฿ per hr. Open daily 9am-9pm. **Oxynet,** 569/2 Mecchai Rd. 25฿ per hr. Open daily 9am-midnight.

Telephones: Lenso phones in the **GPO** and along Meechai Rd.

Post Office: GPO, 390 Meechai Rd. (☎411 521). **International phone.** *Poste Restante.* Open M-F 8:30am-4:30pm, Sa-Su 9am-noon.

Postal Code: 43000.

ACCOMMODATIONS

Mut Mee Guest House, 1111/4 Kaeworawat Rd. (☎460 717; www.mutmee.net). From the bus station, take a left onto Prajak Rd. for 1km. Take a right onto Haisok Rd. and a left before the *wat*. The guesthouse is around the corner, down a well-posted *soi*. Dorms 90฿; singles with shared hot shower 130฿; doubles 150-450฿. ❷

Sawasdee Guest House, 402 Meechai Rd. (☎412 502). From the post office, 5 blocks toward the bus station behind Wat Srikunmuang. This rickety-looking wooden guesthouse has clean rooms with flavor. Singles 100฿; doubles 140฿, with A/C and hot water 300฿. ❷

Ruan Thai Guest House, 1126/2 Rimkhong Rd. (☎412 519; www.ruanthaihouse.com). From the Indochine market, walk 3 blocks toward Wat Haisok. Clean rooms in the white building; cleaner (and pricier) rooms in the wooden buildings. Singles 120฿ and doubles 200฿ both with shared cold shower; rooms with private hot shower 300-400฿. ❷

FOOD

For the homesick traveler, many co-*farang*-owned establishments provide some Western comfort. Good, inexpensive Thai food can also be found. **Chayaporn Market** ❶, on the west side of town, has loads of prepared eats available. More **foodstalls** ❶, some offering fresh seafood, crowd the intersection of **Rimkhong** and **Haisok Road.** Two blocks south, where **Prajak Road** meets Haisok Rd., the smell of *pad thai* and skewered meats wafts down the street. **Dang Nam Neung** ❷, 1062/1-2 Banterngit Rd., half a block toward the river from Mecchai Rd., serves *nam neung*—Vietnamese spring rolls—that you make yourself. (50฿ per person or 155฿ for 4 buys a platter. Open daily 6am-7pm.) **Savoy Restaurant** ❷, 242/2 Moo 3 Sri Lang Tuan, has an assorted meat platter *(jambon, rillettes, pâté)* for 100฿. From Prajak Rd., take a right onto Haisok Rd., then take the first left before the Pantawee Hotel. (Entrees 80-140฿. Open daily 10am-10pm.)

THAILAND

SIGHTS

SALA KAEW KU (WAT KHAEK). The city with the most *wats* per capita, Nong Khai can boast another superlative, as it's home to one of Thailand's most unique temples. Towering concrete statues of Hindu and Buddhist figures represent various levels of Buddhist cosmology: the good and the evil, the mundane and the fantastic, the innocent and the freaky—all the brainchild of a Lao mystic, **Luang Poo Boun Leya Sourirat.** After building a park in Vientiane, Sourirat fled to Thailand when the Communists came to power in 1975. Most of the temple's gravity-defying figures are gods, goddesses, demons, and Buddhas found in the Indian pantheon of mythical deities. Enter the giant mouth in back to learn about *samsara*, the Buddhist belief in the endless life cycle of rebirth and suffering. A series of sculptures arrayed in a circle represents the events of one life cycle. Near the entrance of the circle is a statue of Buddha stepping over the enclosure walls, conveying the message that the way to step outside of this cycle is to follow the teachings of Buddha. *(Head east on Rte. 212, past "St. Paul Nong Khai School" on the right; Sala Kaew Ku is 2 turn-offs later. 4km outside of town. 15-20min. bike ride. Tuk-tuks can be hired for 100-120฿ round-trip. Open daily 8am-5pm. 10฿.)*

WAT PO CHAI. Another more sedate but equally famous statue is housed in Wat Po Chai. Murals in the *wat* illustrate the story of how this gold and bronze Buddha image, known as Luang Pho Phra Sai, sank into the Mekong after the raft that was transporting it from Laos capsized. Twenty-five years later, it resurfaced—many believed it to be a miracle. *(Off Prajak Rd., down Prochai Rd. Open daily 7am-5pm.)*

VILLAGE WEAVER HANDICRAFTS. Seekers of handwoven *mudmee* fabrics can visit Village Weaver Handicrafts, off Prajak Rd. near the Honda dealership. This 22-year-old project promotes local industry and offers lucrative work to Isaan women who are at risk of turning to brothels for their livelihood. Seamstresses tailor outfits at warp speed and ship them everywhere in the world. *(1151 Soi Jittapunya. ☎411 236; village@udon.ksc.co.th. Open daily 8am-5pm. Weaving demos M-F.)*

DAYTRIPS FROM NONG KHAI

PHU PHRA BAT HISTORICAL PARK. Some 85km southwest of Nong Khai, not far from the dusty village of Ban Phu, the eerie wizardry of prehistoric hunter-gatherers lingers at Phu Phra Bat Historical Park. On 5.5km² of forested mountains in the Phu Pan Range, the park boasts a fine collection of prehistoric cave paintings and rock shelters that date back to 1500 BC. Over a dozen excavations lie scattered along a shady, well-marked path. Buddhas abound in **Tham Phra** (Cave of Buddha Images). At the top of the mountain, the 800m path yields an astounding vista of **Pha Sadet Cliff,** which has a perfect picnic area overlooking the Lao mountains. *(☎910 107. Open daily 8:30am-sunset. Admission 30฿. Camping fee 20฿, tent rental 50฿. 1-2 person bungalows 300฿; each additional person 100฿. To have enough time to see the park and get back, catch a bus to Ban Phu (#294; 1½hr., 7:15am, 30฿) from the Nong Khai Bus Terminal. Take a left from the Ban Phu station and walk 100m over the bridge to where songthaew (15min., every 15min., 5฿) take you to Ban Tiu. From there, hike 4km to park headquarters or grab a motorcycle taxi (50฿). Leave the park by 2pm; the last bus to Nong Khai leaves Ban Phu at 3pm. Take Hwy. 2266 from Si Chiangmai to Ban Tiu via Ban Klang Yai (32km) if you have a motorbike.)*

THAILAND

WAT PHU TOK AND BUENG KHAN. Although it's one of northeast Thailand's most spectacular sights, **Wat Phu Tok** (meaning "single mountain") remains untouristed because of its remote location. The shrine stands on a red sandstone outcropping, rising to seven levels, each representing a stage of enlightenment. Level five has a sanctuary built into the cliff. Reaching the top involves climbing stairs into a maze of paths that cut into the rock and wooden platforms. When traversing the platforms, be careful of the gaps between the lower planks. The view of the Isaan plains makes the sweaty ascent more than worth it, though climbing the stairs isn't recommended in windy weather. The sheer isolation of Wat Phu Tok makes tackling it in one day difficult. If you're coming from Nakhon Phanom, heading to Nong Khai, you'll probably want to spend the night in Beung Khan, the largest town between Nakhon Phanom and Nong Khai on Hwy. 212, and the only place between Nong Khai and Phu Tok for overnight stays. Hwy. 212 becomes **Thaisamok Road,** home to a small bus stop, a roundabout, and a clocktower. To reach the guesthouses from the bus stop, head toward the roundabout, turn right onto **Maesongnang Road,** and left onto **Prasatchai Road.** Two hotels are 100m down at the first intersection. **Santisuk Hotel ❷,** 21/2 Prasatchai Rd., is on the right. (☎491 114. Singles with TV and Thai-style bath 150฿, with A/C 280฿.) **Samanmit Hotel ❷,** 34/3 Prasatchai Rd., is directly across from Santisuk. (☎491 078. Singles 100-140฿, with A/C 200฿.) *(From the Nong Khai Bus Terminal, take bus #224 to Bueng Khan (2hr., every hr. 6am-3pm, 45฿). From the Bueng Khan bus stop (across from the Kasikorn Bank), catch a bus to Ban Similai (40min., 12฿). Hire a motorcycle taxi (30min., 40-50฿) or a tuk-tuk (100฿) for the remaining 20km to Phu Tok.)*

PHU WUA WILDLIFE SANCTUARY. Jungle and evergreen forest protect the elephants, bears, palm civets, monkeys, and gibbons that call the park's 187km² home. Visit **Tham Fun Waterfall,** or check out the more impressive waterfalls, like the 50m **Tham Phra (Chanaen) Waterfall,** with its first tier cascading over one large boulder, and the **Chet Si Waterfall** ("Seven Colors Waterfall"), so named because it often reflects the colors of the rainbow. The latter two are accessible by car or motorbike (at 30km, the distance is too far to walk) and difficult to reach during the late rainy season. All the waterfalls are best seen from August to September, when they are at their full strength. *(From Beung Khan, take a bus to Nakhon Phanom. At Ban Chaiyaporn (24km from Bueng Khan), get off the bus. Take a right at the turn-off for Ban Phu Sawat (5km from the turn-off); turn right and continue on for 2.5km to the park office. The waterfalls are 3km from this point.)*

BORDER CROSSING: NONG KHAI/VIENTIANE. 15-day Lao tourist visas are issued on the **Friendship Bridge** for US$30 or a heftier 1500฿ (1 passport photo required). 30-day visas are available from the Lao embassy in Bangkok or the consulate in Khon Kaen (3-day processing 1100฿, expedited processing up to 1400฿). Ask at Mut Mee Guest House for the latest info. A *tuk-tuk* from Nong Khai to the bridge should cost 30-50฿. A bus shuttles people across the bridge for 10฿. On the other side, public buses run the 25km to Vientiane (50฿), or you can take a taxi (100-150฿). The Lao entry tax varies, but currently stands at 50฿.

LOEI ☎042

A big billboard on Hwy. 201 greets visitors to Loei with, "Welcome to Loei, Land of the Sea of Mountains and Coldest in All Siam." Grammar aside, the sign captures the essence of this seldom-visited but appealing province. It is the only base from which to venture into the cloud-frosted mountains in search of hermit caves and Thailand's version of the vineyards of southern France—the Chateau de Loei Vineyards. At the end of June, the three-day, rain-making **Phi Ta Khon Festival** in Dan Sai transforms the western district into a shamanistic orgy of brightly colored costumes and masks, parading spirits, and dancing fueled by drinking shots of *lao khao* ("white spirit"), culminating in a final day of Buddhist sermons at the *wat*. Those who make the trip to Loei find a perfect place to unwind after a day exploring the countryside and national parks.

TRANSPORTATION

Buses: All buses leave from the **main bus terminal** (☎833 586), off Maliwan Rd., south of the city center. Green buses go to **Nong Khai** via **Pak Chom, Sangkhom,** and **Si Chiangmai** (#507; 7hr., every hr. 5:40-10:40am, 84฿). If you're going to Nong Khai, take a bus to **Udon Thani** (platform #2; 3hr., every 20min. 4am-8pm, 55฿) and then catch a bus to Nong Khai; it's at least 2hr. faster. Buses also run to: **Bangkok** (9-10hr., every hr. 6am-8pm, 200-495฿); **Chiang Mai** (10hr., 5 per day 10:15am-10:30pm, 184-410฿); **Chiang Rai** (11hr., 5 per day 6:30-10:30pm, 286-367฿). Chiang Mai and Chiang Rai buses travel via **Phitsanulok** (5hr.) and **Lom Sak** (4hr., 6 per day 5am-5pm, 58฿). **Long-distance buses** may be full upon arrival; guarantee a seat by buying a ticket at the bus terminal counter. *Songthaew* go to **Chiang Khan** (1hr., every 30min. 5:30am-5:30pm, 20฿).

Local Transportation: Samlor and **tuk-tuk** 20-40฿. **Motorbike** rental (200฿ per day) at the **bike shop,** between Chum Saai and Ruam Jai Rd., 20m north of the roundabout.

ORIENTATION AND PRACTICAL INFORMATION

Loei town is a tangled mess of streets on the Loei River's western bank. **Charoen Rat Road** runs the length of the river, beginning near the bus terminal at the **market.** Moving north into town on Charoen Rat Rd., you'll see the **post office** and a white suspension footbridge, followed by **Chum Saai Road,** which becomes **Nok Kaew Road** three blocks down at a busy roundabout. Continuing up Charoen Rat Rd., you reach **Ruam Jai Road,** a major east-west thoroughfare. **Maliwan Road (Highway 201),** forms the town's western border.

Tourist Office: Loei Tourism Co-ordination Center (☎812 812), on Charoen Rat Rd., opposite the GPO. Maps and brochures of Loei province. Open M-F 8:30am-4:30pm.

Currency Exchange: Bangkok Bank, at the intersection of Oua Aree and Charoen Rat Rd. Open M-F 8:30am-3:30pm. 24hr. **ATM.** AmEx/MC/Plus/V.

Markets: Loei has 2 **day/night markets.** One, at the northern end of Charoen Rat Rd., opposite the 7-Eleven, has grilled meat and plastic items. The night market gets going around 6pm and closes between 9 and 10pm. The 2nd market sets up at the southern end of Charoen Rat Rd. and offers the usual meat and produce. Open daily 10am-9pm.

Police: (☎811 254). On Pipat Mongkon Rd., the city's northern border.

Pharmacy: Bun Jung Pesat Pharmacy, 83 Charoen Rat Rd. (☎830 634), on the corner of Ruam Jai Rd. Open daily 3am-8pm.

Medical Services: Loei Provincial Hospital (☎811 541), at the intersection of Maliwan Rd. and Nok Kaew Rd., opposite provincial offices. Some English spoken. Cash only.

Internet Access: PA Computers (☎814 761), on Charoen Rat Rd. between Chum Saai and Oua Aree Rd. 20฿ per hr. Open daily 9am-8pm. Internet available between Chum Saai and Ruan Jai Rd. 15฿ per hr. Open daily 10am-10pm.

Telephones: International calls from **CAT,** next door to the GPO on Charoen Rat Rd.

Post Office: GPO (☎812 0222), on Charoen Rat Rd., between the footbridge and night market. Open M-F 8:30am-4:30pm, Sa-Su 9am-noon.

Postal Code: 42000.

ACCOMMODATIONS AND FOOD

The **Sugar Guest House ❷**, 4/1 Wisuttiep Rd., down Soi 4 on the right, has clean rooms with white-tiled floors in a new house. (☎09 711 1975. Bike rental 30฿ per day, motorbikes 200฿ per day. English spoken. Singles 150฿; doubles 200฿.) The **King Hotel ❹**, 11/9-12 Chum Saai Rd., has the cleanest rooms in town, which are decked out in tile with phone, TV, A/C, and hot shower. (☎811 701. Singles 380฿; doubles 399฿; VIP rooms with fridge 1200฿.) **Thai Udom Hotel ❸**, 122/1 Charoen Rat Rd. on Oua Aree Rd., has decent, clean rooms that are slightly worn down and furnished with a desk, phone, and TV. (☎811 763. Singles 240฿, with A/C 350฿; doubles 320฿/500฿; VIP rooms 600฿.)

Some of the best places to eat are the **open-air restaurants ❷** in front of the movie theater just off Oua Aree Rd., opposite Thai Farmers Bank, and at the main bus terminal. Pyromaniacs can order *pak boong fai daeng* (flaming morning glory vine), leafy water spinach that the chef sets on fire before hurling toward your plate. A couple of **foodstalls ❶** line Chum Saai Rd. where it turns into Nok Kaew Rd., just after the roundabout. All of them serve fine noodle and rice dishes for about 30฿. **Charcoal ❷**, at the roundabout at the intersection of Sathon Chiang Khan Rd. and Chum Saai Rd., has a patio and serves heaps of Thai classics. (Chicken with cashews 80฿. Most entrees 40-90฿. Open daily 5pm-midnight.) **Moon Aroi ❷**, 22/1 Sert Si Rd. (☎833 660), is a great late-night option. (Vegetarian dishes upon request. Fried river oysters with bean sprouts 60฿. Open daily 4pm-5am.)

ENTERTAINMENT

There is a **cinema** on Sathon Chiang Khan Rd. between Ruam Jai Rd. and the roundabout. Western-style pubs line **Rhuamphattana Road.** As you walk west on Nok Kaew Rd. toward the highway, Rhuamphattana Rd. is the first right after the roundabout. Halfway down on the left is **Ban Muang Loei Pub,** and across the street is its twin, **Oasis.** Both bars offer live music after 8:30pm (small Singha 50฿); Ban Muang has Thai country music. Continuing down the street, you'll see two robot statues on your right; a large, glowing spaceship marks the entrance to **Robot 2029.** Rock bands play nightly at 10:15pm in a neon-lit hall (large Singha 90฿).

DAYTRIPS FROM LOEI

CHATEAU DE LOEI VINEYARDS. One of Thailand's first wine-producing vineyards (there are now multiple wine producers), Chateau de Loei is large by any standard. After a long process of securing permits to import foreign grapevines into Thailand, a thriving vineyard now stands in the middle of Loei's mountains. The wine itself is not for the connoisseur, but a walk through the vineyards is pleasurable. The rolling landscape offers views of marching rows of grapes, a small reservoir, and a private runway. *(Take a bus bound for Lom Sak (1½hr., 60km, 30฿) and get off when you see the blue metal sign in English on your left and the Km 60 marker on your right. The cream-colored vineyard shop sells fresh grapes, organic produce, local crafts, and, of course, bottles of wine (300-1100฿). The actual vineyard is another 1km down the road beneath the sign. ☎809 521. Open daily 8am-5pm.)*

PHU KRADUNG NATIONAL PARK. A ringing bell inspired the name of this popular sanctuary ("Bell Mountain"). Trails criss-cross the 60km² plateau's pine forests and grassy meadows. Bamboo stairways facilitate the 5km hike (2-6hr.) from the mountain base to park headquarters on the plateau rim. Porters can tote your gear for 10฿ per kg. Views of the sunset reward visitors who reach **Pha Lom Sak** or **Pha Daeng.** Explorers bid the Khon Kaen bus adieu at Nong Hin, the turn-off for **Suan Hin Pha Ngam,** a stone forest where limestone outcroppings form a natural labyrinth. Guides promise not to lose you for 100฿ per group. The 18km to Ban Pha Ngarm are traversed only by chartered *songthaew* for 500฿. *(☎801 900. Suan Hin Pha Ngam open M-F 9am-4:30pm, Sa-Su 8am-5pm. Buses (70km, 25฿) to Khon Kaen drop you off at the Amphoe Phu Kradung Administrative Office. From here, catch a minibus (15฿) to the National Park Office. The park is packed on weekends and holidays, but closes June-Sept. You'll probably want to spend a night at the park. The camping fee runs 30฿ per person. Tents are available for 100-200฿. Mountaintop lodging ❺ starts at 2000฿ per bungalow. Reservations should be made weeks in advance with the National Park Division of the Forestry Department in Bangkok. (☎02 561 4292, ext. 724.) Park admission 200฿.)*

PHU RUA NATIONAL PARK. Small nurseries cultivate a rainbow of flowers along the road, culminating in a January flower show near the turn-off to **Phu Rua National Park,** 50km from the city center. The majestic centerpiece of this park is a 1375m **mountain.** Personal vehicles can travel to the top, where a large Buddha surveys the scene below. Routes include a 2km trek to a **waterfall,** from which it's 5.5km to the peak. It is possible to complete the circuit in a day, but an overnight stay at the park is recommended. (Camping fee 30฿ per person. Tents 100-200฿. Lodging for 3-6 people 250-500฿.) Large groups should contact the **National Parks Division** in Bangkok (☎02 561 4836). Alternative accommodations are available at the **Song Pee Nong Bungalow** ❹ (☎899 399), about 2km away from the park entrance on the right heading toward Loei. Bungalows are simple and clean, with shared

THAILAND

Western toilets. (Wooden bungalows 500฿; larger concrete bungalows 700฿.) *(To get to the park, catch bus #14 to Lom Sak (1hr., every hr. 5am-5pm, 25฿) via Phu Rua; watch for the large English sign on the right. Although* Let's Go *doesn't recommend hitchhiking, the easiest way to get to the park headquarters, 3.5km away, is to hike up the road and try to snag a lift. Otherwise,* songthaew *charge an outrageous 300฿. Park open year-round. Park admission 200฿.)*

NAM NAO NATIONAL PARK. Nam Nao, meaning "cold water," stretches for 1000km² at the junction of Loei and Phetchabun provinces. Its sandstone hills and sandy plains make it ideal for hiking. During the 6-7hr. ascent to the park's highest peak, **Phu Pha Chit** (1271m), a landscape of low shrubs and small yellow flowers rolls down the mountain. The park also has verdant bamboo forests and a waterfall and cave. (Camping fee 30฿ per person. Tent rental for one to three people 250฿.) **Resorts** line Hwy. 12 near the park, but these are more expensive choices. *(A daytrip to the park is possible but inadequate, especially if you are using public transportation. From Loei, catch a bus to Lom Sak (runs regularly 6am-5pm, 63฿). At the Lom Sak bus terminal, take a Khon Kaen-bound bus and get off at park headquarters on the left. Hwy. 12 (connecting Lom Sak and Khon Kaen) cuts through the park. As most trailheads start from this road, buses to Lom Sak or Khon Kaen can help traverse the long distances between trailheads. Park headquarters is 55km from Lom Sak and 103km from Khon Kaen. (☎05 672 9002.) Park admission 20฿.)*

KHON KAEN ☎043

Like other Isaan cities, Khon Kaen lacks a "big" tourist attraction. Nevertheless, its festive nightlife, open-air markets, and efficient transportation system give visitors the means to enjoy themselves. The 7200 students of Khon Kaen University, northeastern Thailand's largest, are a vibrant young crowd and make for a hip evening scene. The city also serves as a base for daytrips to the rest of the province.

TRANSPORTATION

Flights: Khon Kaen Airport (☎246 305), 8km west of town off Maliwan Rd. **Air Asia** (☎02 515 9999) has flights to **Bangkok** (daily 2:30pm, 399-850฿). Open daily 8am-9pm. **Thai Airways,** 9/9 Prachasamran Rd. (☎227 701), inside the Hotel Sofitel, flies to **Bangkok** (3 per day, 1605฿).

Trains: Khon Kaen Railway Station (☎221 112), where Ruen Rom Rd. ends at Darunsamran Rd. To: **Bangkok** (8hr.; 9:43am, 8:13, 9:56pm; 259-978฿); **Khorat** (3-4hr., 1:40 and 8:13pm, 38฿); **Nong Khai** (3hr.; 3:36, 4:14, 5:50, 9:50am, 2:33pm; 35฿) via **Udon Thani** (25฿); **Udon Thani** (2hr., 7 per day 3:36am-6:44pm, 25฿).

Buses:

Bus terminal (☎237 472), on Pracha Samoson Rd., by the pedestrian overpass. Buses to: **Bangkok** (7hr., every 25min. 6:30am-9:30pm, 129฿); **Khorat** (3hr., every 30min. 5:20am-7pm, 95฿); **Mukdahan** (5hr., every 30min. 4am-6:30pm, 115฿); **Nakhon Phanom** (6hr., 6 per day 7:30am-4:30pm, 175฿) via **Kalasin** (1½hr., 80฿) and **Sakhon Nakhon** (4hr., 124฿); **Nakhon Sawan** (7hr., 6 per day 5:30am-1:30pm, 72฿); **Phitsanulok** (6hr., 3 per day 9am-3pm, 150฿); **Ubon Ratchathani** (4½hr., every hr. 5:40am-2pm, 115฿); **Udon Thani** (2hr., every 20min. 5:20am-7pm, 65฿).

A/C bus terminal (☎239 910), on Glang Muang Rd. Buses to: **Bangkok** (7hr., every hr., 259-400฿) via **Khorat** (3hr., 121฿); **Chiang Mai** (12hr., 8 and 9pm, 394฿) via **Phitsanulok** (5hr., 203฿); **Loei** (5hr., 11:30am and 3:30pm, 139฿); **Nakhon Phanom** (5hr.; 7:30, 10am, 4pm; 175฿) via **Sakhon Nakhon** (4hr., 124฿); **Nong Khai** (3hr.; 5:30am, 1, 3, 5pm; 110฿); **Ubon Ratchathani** (5hr., every 2hr. 9am-5pm, 169฿).

Local Transportation: Look for **samlor** (20-30฿), **tuk-tuks** (20-50฿), and **songthaew** (5฿). TAT lists all 20 *songthaew* routes. *Songthaew* #4 runs along Nah Muang Rd.; #11 from Khon Kaen Railway Station to TAT; #17 from TAT to the National Museum.

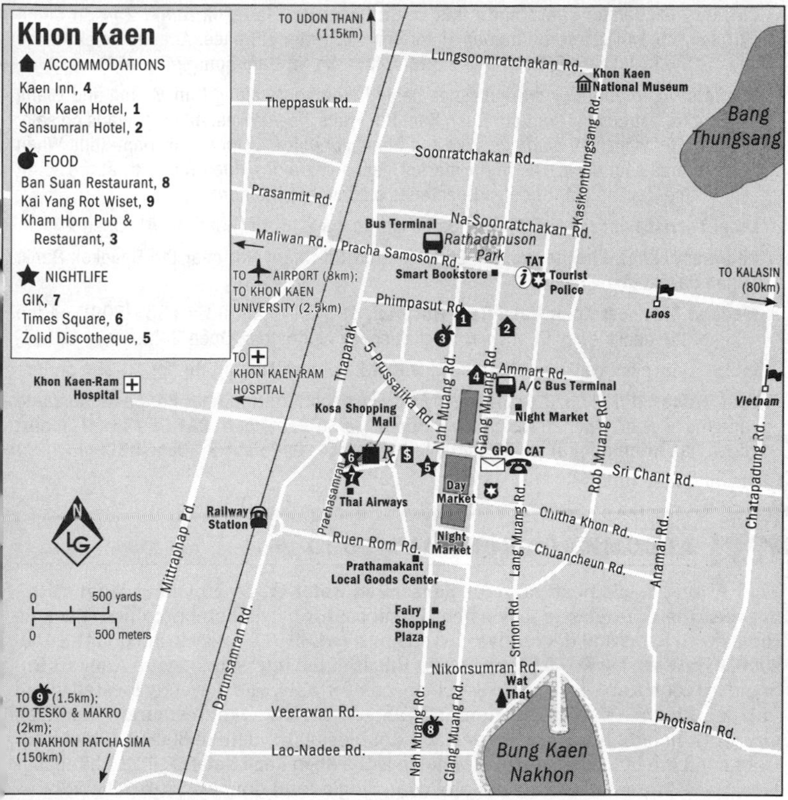

ORIENTATION AND PRACTICAL INFORMATION

Khon Kaen, 450km from Bangkok, is easily accessible by plane, bus, or train. The main north-south thoroughfares, **Nah Muang Road** and **Glang Muang Road,** are lined with hotels, restaurants, and the A/C bus terminal. Farther south, the parallel Muangs cross **Sri Chant Road,** home to the best nightspots. Past Sri Chant Rd. on Glang Muang Rd. are the post office, police station, and day market, leading to **Ruen Rom Road.** A right turn onto Ruen Rom Rd. from Nah Muang Rd. leads to the train station. The **regular bus terminal** and **TAT office** are on **Pracha Samoson Road.**

Tourist Office: TAT, 15/5 Pracha Samoson Rd. (☎244 498). A brown-and-white building several blocks from the regular bus terminal. Maps and guides of Khon Kaen and surrounding provinces. Open daily 8:30am-4:30pm.

Consulates: Laos, 171 Pracha Samoson Rd. (☎242 856). 30-day visas US$40 (1600฿) are available same-day if you come early. Open M-F 8:30am-noon and 1-4pm. **Vietnam,** 65/6 Chatapadung Rd. (☎235 264). 15-day visas about US$40 (1600฿); 2-3 working days to process. Open M-F 8-11:30am and 1:30-4:30pm. Light-blue *songthaew* #10 runs to both consulates.

Currency Exchange: Banks and ATMs on Sri Chant Rd. **Bangkok Bank,** 254 Sri Chant Rd. (☎225 144), next to Charoen Thani Princess Hotel entrance. After-hours exchange during the high season. Open M-F 8:30am-7pm, Sa-Su 9am-5pm. 24hr. **ATM.**

Markets: A sizeable **day market** hides behind storefronts along Nah Muang and Glang Muang Rd., stretching south to Ruen Rom Rd. Fruits, vegetables, and pig heads on sale. Popular items include *mudmee* silks and triangular pillows. Open daily 5am-6pm. When other shops shut down, the **night market** gets going along Ruen Rom Rd. at the south end of the day market. Street-side eateries stretch into the horizon.

Local Tourist Police: 15/5 Pracha Samoson Rd. (☎236 937), left of TAT. Open 24hr.

Pharmacy: Phon Phesad (☎228 260), just off Sri Chant Rd. near the Bangkok Bank. Open daily 8am-midnight.

Medical Services: Khon Kaen-Ram Hospital, 193 Sri Chant Rd. (☎333 800), on the side of the tracks away from town. English-speaking doctors. Open 24hr.

Internet Access: Available on Glang Muang Rd. north of Ammart Rd. for 10-15฿ per hr.

Post Office: GPO, 153/8 Glang Muang Rd., just south of Sri Chant Rd. *Poste Restante* on ground floor. Open M-F 8:30am-4:30pm, Sa-Su 9am-noon. **CAT** (☎236 097), next door, has **international** calling and Internet service. Open M-F 8:30am-4:30pm.

Postal Code: 40000.

THAILAND

ACCOMMODATIONS AND FOOD

Find Khon Kaen's best value at **Sansumran Hotel ❷,** 55-59 Glang Muang Rd., between the giant plastic tusks, near Phimpasut Rd. The hotel provides spacious rooms with baths and decorative carved lions. (☎239 611. Singles and doubles 150-250฿.) The **Kaen Inn ❹,** 56 Glang Muang Rd., is at the intersection with Ammart Rd. Standard rooms are the best deal—clean, comfortable, and perfectly located in the middle of town. (☎245 420; kaeninn@yahoo.com. Karaoke, restaurant, and free airport transfers. Standard singles and doubles 500฿; deluxe 800฿.) A block up from Kaen Inn but a step down in upkeep is the **Khon Kaen Hotel ❹,** 43/2 Phimpasut Rd. (☎333 222; www.khonkaen-hotel.com. Singles and doubles 550฿. MC/V.)

Sidewalk **eateries ❶** cluster on Phimpasut and Ammart Rd. Cheap Isaan meals tempt hungry passersby at **night markets** on Lang Muang and Ruen Rom Rd. Korean barbecue restaurants, like **Ban Suan ❷,** 539/3 Nah Muang Rd., surround Bung Kaen Nakhon. Exiting Fairy Plaza, take a left and walk for 1km. Look for the tall Kawasaki sign on your left; the restaurant, serving Chinese, Thai, Isaan, and outdoor Korean barbecue, is immediately before it. (☎227 811. Stir-fried asparagus with shrimp 80฿. Barbecue platter 150฿. 5% *Let's Go* discount. Open daily 4pm-2am.) Buffet is easy for the linguistically challenged at **Kai Yang Rot Wiset ❶,** 177 Mittraphap Rd. Take blue *songthaew* #10 toward Tesco Lotus (5฿); it's just beyond the PTT gas station on the left. (Entrees 20฿. Open daily 7am-10pm.) The **Kham Horm Pub & Restaurant ❷,** 38 Nah Muang Rd. between Phimpasut and Ammart Rd., is an outdoor barbecue with nightly live music. (☎243 252. Stir-fried chicken with baby corn 60฿. Most entrees 40-120฿. Open daily 10am-2am.)

SIGHTS

The only noteworthy sight here is the well-presented **Khon Kaen National Museum,** at the Lungsoomratchakan and Kasikonthungsang Rd. intersection. Lime-green *songthaew* #14 stops here. The museum documents the history of central northeast Thailand. The second floor has articles from the olden days (Lopburi period) while the first floor is devoted to the really olden days (Ban Chiang period and earlier). Particularly impressive are the *semas*, or carved boundary stones. (☎246 170. Open W-Su 9am-4pm. 30฿.)

In the southeast corner of Khon Kaen is **Bung Kaen Nakhon,** a lakeside recreational area enclosed by four *wats* and numerous foodstalls. Every April it hosts the **Dok Khoon Song Kran Festival,** featuring Isaan music, floral processions, and dances. On the southeast shores of the lake is **Wat Nong Waeng,** where you can climb to the top of the nine-story *chedi* for panoramic views of the city.

Prathamakant Local Goods Center, 79/2-3 Ruen Rom Rd., is 30m from the Nah Muang Rd. intersection. Those unable to visit **Chonabot** (p. 757) can enjoy silk handicrafts here. You can find lots of *mudmee* silks, classy and funky shirts and skirts, wooden carvings, and instruments for sale. (☎224 080. Open daily 9am-8:30pm.)

ENTERTAINMENT AND NIGHTLIFE

The arcade near The First Choice Restaurant is packed with karaoke bars, beer gardens, and pubs. All the major hotels behind Sri Chant Rd. have some sort of nightlife, like the **GIK** discotheque at the Hotel Sofitel. Across the street is the Kosa Shopping Center, a generic mall showing Hollywood **movies** (dubbed in Thai, 80฿). There's also a **cinema** at the more popular Fairy Plaza Shopping Center, on Nah Muang Rd. Adjacent to the Sofitel Hotel on Prachasamran Rd. is the **Times Square** complex with six small bars. (Small Singha 50฿. Open 9pm-1am.) The **Zolid Discotheque,** on the bottom floor of the Charoen Thani Princess Hotel, off Nah Muang Rd., has three levels of dancing and huge screens showing music videos. (☎240 400. Small Singha 80฿. Open daily 9pm-2am.)

DAYTRIPS FROM KHON KAEN

PHUWIANG NATIONAL PARK. Those interested in ancient reptiles should swing by Phuwiang, home to the largest dinosaur fossils in the country. Fossils dug from the nine quarries located in the area have added weight to the theory that *Tyrannosaurus rex* existed first in Asia Minor before crossing the Bering Strait to North America. (Camping fee 30฿; 2-person tent 120฿; bungalows 300฿ per person.) *(Buses to Phuwiang (25฿) leave daily before 1:30pm from the regular bus terminal. From Phuwiang Station, hire a* tuk-tuk *for the remaining 20km (100฿). Open daily 8:30am-4:40pm. Park admission 200฿.)*

CHONABOT. Chonabot's livelihood comes from hand-woven silk. Besides the small factories peppering the town, the Sala Mai Thai, located 3km from town toward Nakhon Sawan on the left, sells local wares and presents exhibits on the silk-making process. *(☎286 160. Prices vary depending on the thickness and weight of the material.* Mudmee *silk costs 1300฿ for 4 yards. Open daily 9am-5pm. Catch a bus to Nakhon Sawan (1hr., every hr. until 1:30pm, 22฿) from Khon Kaen's regular bus terminal and ask to be let off at Chonabot police station. Facing the station, walk right to the 1st intersection and turn left. The 1st silk factory is on the right after the post office. The last bus back to Khon Kaen leaves at 5pm. Most factories open M-Sa 8am-5pm.)*

BAN KOK SA-NGA. Villagers in "King Cobra Village" have been taming deadly cobras since 1951, using them as attention-getters for herbal medicine businesses. Villagers stage "boxing" exhibitions: after tempting the snakes to strike, the masters deftly sidestep death. Performances must be scheduled in advance. Contact Mr. Prayoon Yongla. *(☎06 219 0428. 45km from Khon Kaen. From the regular bus station, take a bus to Kra Nuan (1½hr.; every 30min., last return 6pm; 15฿) on Rte. 2039. Get off at Km 14 and ride a* tuk-tuk *to the village (30฿) or walk the 2km. Snake-breeding center 20฿.)*

NORTHERN THAILAND

Northern Thailand's mountains constitute the lowest crags of the Himalayan foothills. Its Salawin River flirts with Myanmar before flooding into the Bay of Bengal, and its northeastern border is formed by none other than the mighty Mekong. Central **Chiang Mai,** formerly the capital of the prosperous Lanna Kingdom, serves as the first stop for many visitors. The magnificent historical ruins of **Sukhothai** break up the journey from Bangkok. The hill-tribe haven of **Mae Hong Son** is to the west. Many choose to savor a peaceful piece of **Pai,** accessible by the renowned Mae Hong Son Loop. **Chiang Rai,** in the north, har-

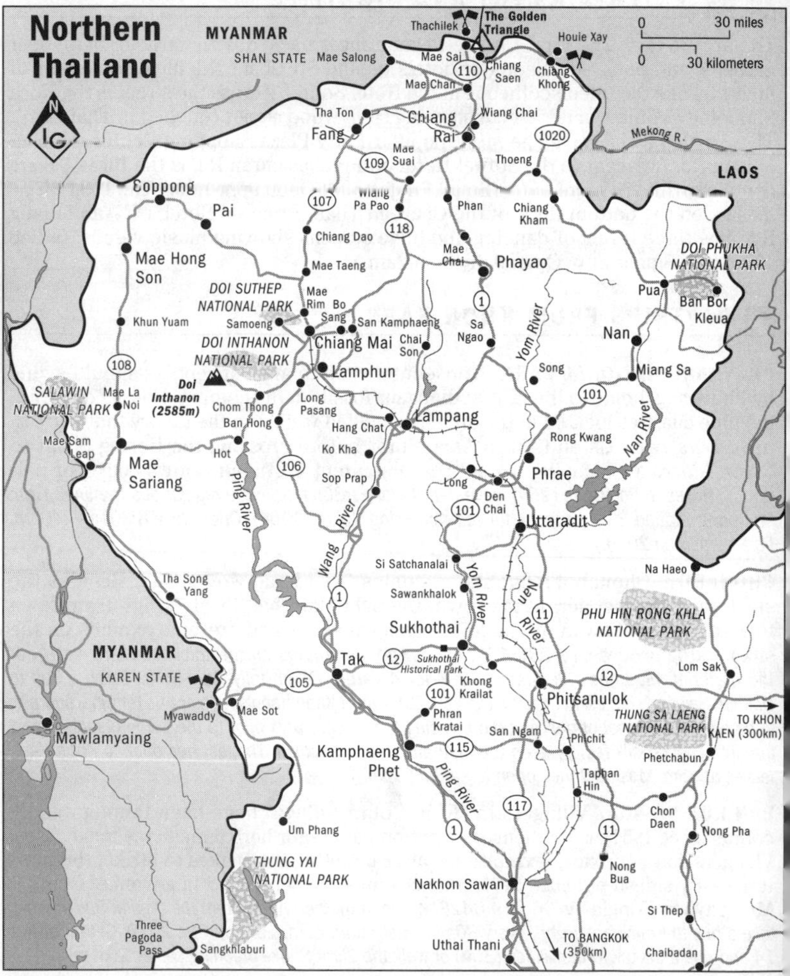

bors poppy fields and the Golden Triangle. To the east, **Nan,** which borders Laos, is a good place for *wat*-lovers and those seeking locales off the beaten path. Throughout the region, Chinese immigrants display pictures of the Thai Royal Family, tribal minorities inhabit remote mountainsides, and camps swell with refugees from Myanmar. The dialect, cuisine, dance, and *wat* architecture of Northern Thailand owe much to this fusion of cultures, reflecting the myriad influences of the region.

CHIANG MAI ☎053

The sighting of several good omens convinced King Mengrai to establish the seat of his great Lanna Kingdom in Chiang Mai in 1296—an auspicious beginning for a city that has become Thailand's second-largest, both in population and in tourist crowds. Thousands of *farang,* drawn by the promise of adventure and a cooler climate, clog the narrow streets of this ancient city. The distinctive dialect, Burmese-influenced art and architecture, and an abundance of sticky-rice (a northern specialty) prove that the city is not about to surrender its heritage.

INTERCITY TRANSPORTATION

BY PLANE. Chiang Mai International Airport (☎270 222), on Sanambin (Airport) Rd., 3km southwest of the city center, is accessible by **taxi** (100฿), **tuk-tuk** (50฿), or **songthaew** (20฿). **Thai Airways,** 240 Phra Pokklao Rd., has branches around the city. (☎211 044. Open daily 8am-5pm.) It flies to: Bangkok (11 per day 7am-9:15pm, 2170฿); Kunming, China (Tu and Su 2:30pm); Mae Hong Son (5 per day 10am-4:10pm, 765฿); Phuket (daily 11:15am, 4640฿). **Bangkok Airways,** at the airport (☎281 519), flies to: Bangkok (1-2 per day, 2170฿) via Sukhothai (940฿); Jinghong (Tu and Th 4:10pm, 4540฿); **Xian** (W and Su 7:50pm, 10,910฿). **Lao Airlines** (☎223 401) flies to Vientiane (Tu, F, Su 1:30pm; 3360฿) via Luang Prabang. **Air Mandalay,** 148 Charoen Prathet Rd. (☎818 049), flies to Mandalay (Th 2:55pm, 3200฿) and Yangon (Tu, Su 2:55pm; 2895฿). **Mandarin Airlines** (☎201 268), 2nd floor at the airport, flies to Taipei (Tu and Sa 10:45am). **Silk Air,** 153 Sri Donchai Rd. (☎276 459), at the Imperial Maeping Hotel, flies to Singapore. (Tu and Th-F 10:55am, Su 5:30pm; 7000฿. Open M-F 8:30am-5pm, Sa-Su 8:30am-1pm.) A branch of STA Travel is **Trans World Travel Service Co., Ltd.,** 259/61 Tha Pae Rd. (☎272 416), which may offer cheaper student tickets than carriers do. You'll need a student card (200฿ with passport and proof of student status). All international flights are subject to a 500฿ (cash) departure tax.

BY TRAIN. The **Chiang Mai Railway Station,** 27 Charoen Muang Rd. (☎244 795), on the eastern outskirts of the city, is accessible by *songthaew* (10-20฿) and *tuk-tuk* (40-50฿). Trains run daily to Bangkok (11-14hr., 7 per day 6:55am-9:50pm, 161-1193฿). Most Bangkok-bound trains also stop in Lampang (2hr., 23-53฿) and Phitsanulok (6-7hr., 105-190฿). Reserve sleeper tickets well in advance (this must be done in person); lower berths are pricier. (Ticket window open daily 6am-8pm.)

BY BUS. *Tuk-tuks* (30-50฿) and *songthaew* (20฿) shuttle between the old city and **Arcade Bus Station** (☎242 664), 3km to the northeast. **Chang Phuak Bus Station** (☎211 586), on Chang Phuak Rd. 1km north of the old city, runs provincial buses.

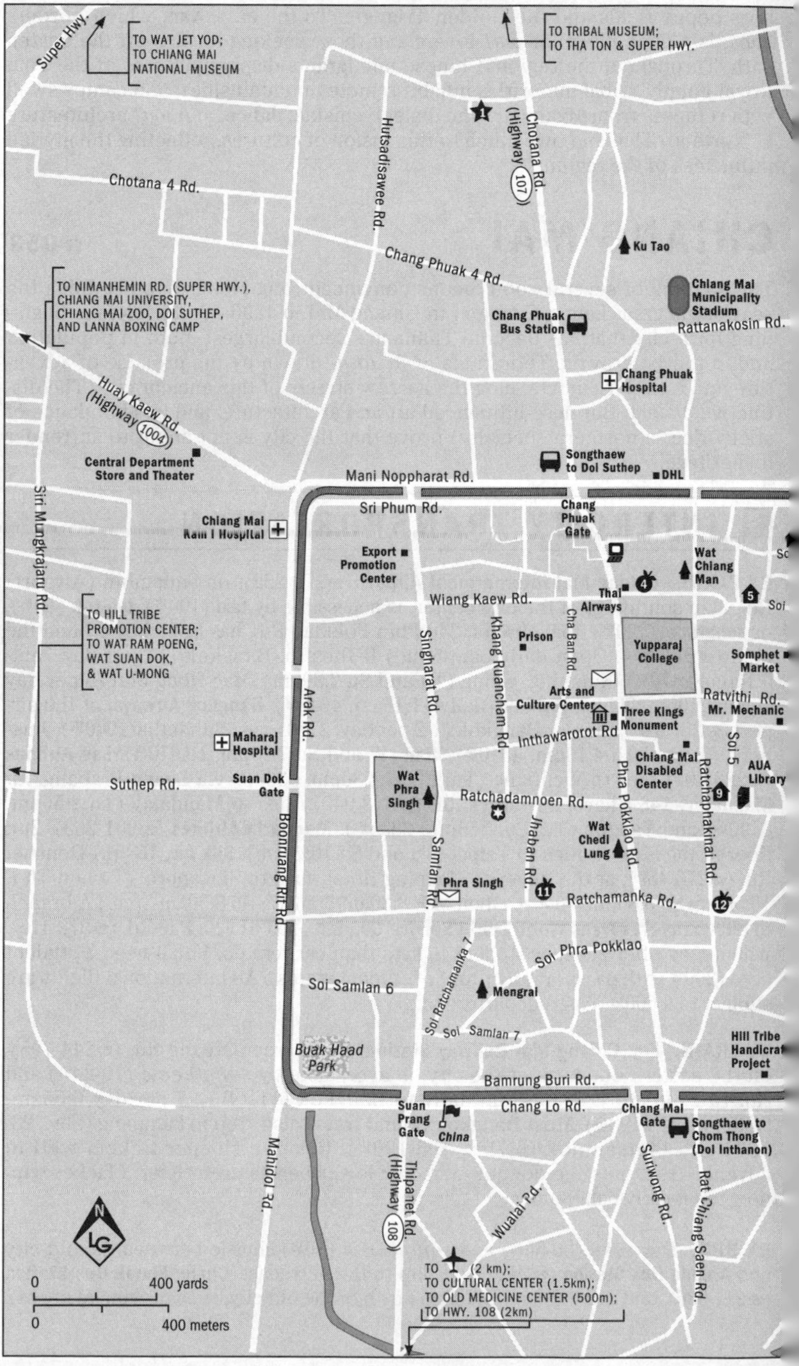

Super Hwy.
TO WAT JET YOD; TO CHIANG MAI NATIONAL MUSEUM
TO TRIBAL MUSEUM; TO THA TON & SUPER HWY.
Hutsadisawee Rd.
Chotana Rd. (Highway 107)
Chotana 4 Rd.
Ku Tao
Chang Phuak 4 Rd.
Chiang Mai Municipality Stadium
Rattanakosin Rd.
TO NIMANHEMIN RD. (SUPER HWY.), CHIANG MAI UNIVERSITY, CHIANG MAI ZOO, DOI SUTHEP, AND LANNA BOXING CAMP
Chang Phuak Bus Station
Chang Phuak Hospital
Huay Kaew Rd. (Highway 1004)
Central Department Store and Theater
Songthaew to Doi Suthep
DHL
Mani Noppharat Rd.
Sri Phum Rd.
Siri Mungkrajaru Rd.
Chiang Mai Ram I Hospital
Chang Phuak Gate
Export Promotion Center
Wat Chiang Man
Thai Airways
Wiang Kaew Rd.
Soi
TO HILL TRIBE PROMOTION CENTER; TO WAT RAM POENG, WAT SUAN DOK, & WAT U-MONG
Khang Ruancham Rd.
Cha Ban Rd.
Prison
Singharat Rd.
Yupparaj College
Somphet Market
Arts and Culture Center
Three Kings Monument
Ratvithi Rd.
Mr. Mechanic
Arak Rd.
Inthawarorot Rd
Maharaj Hospital
Chiang Mai Disabled Center
Soi 5
AUA Library
Suthep Rd.
Suan Dok Gate
Wat Phra Singh
Ratchadamnoen Rd.
Ratchaphakinai Rd.
Phra Pokklao Rd.
Boonruang Rit Rd.
Wat Chedi Lung
Jhaban Rd.
Samlan Rd.
Phra Singh
Ratchamanka Rd.
Soi Ratchamanka 7
Soi Phra Pokklao
Soi Samlan 6
Mengrai
Soi Samlan 7
Buak Haad Park
Hill Tribe Handicraft Project
Bamrung Buri Rd.
Chang Lo Rd.
Suan Prang Gate
China
Chiang Mai Gate
Songthaew to Chom Thong (Doi Inthanon)
Mahidol Rd.
Thipanet Rd. (Highway 108)
Wualai Rd.
Suriwong Rd.
Rat Chiang Saen Rd.
N
LG
0 400 yards
0 400 meters
TO (2 km); TO CULTURAL CENTER (1.5km); TO OLD MEDICINE CENTER (500m); TO HWY. 108 (2km)

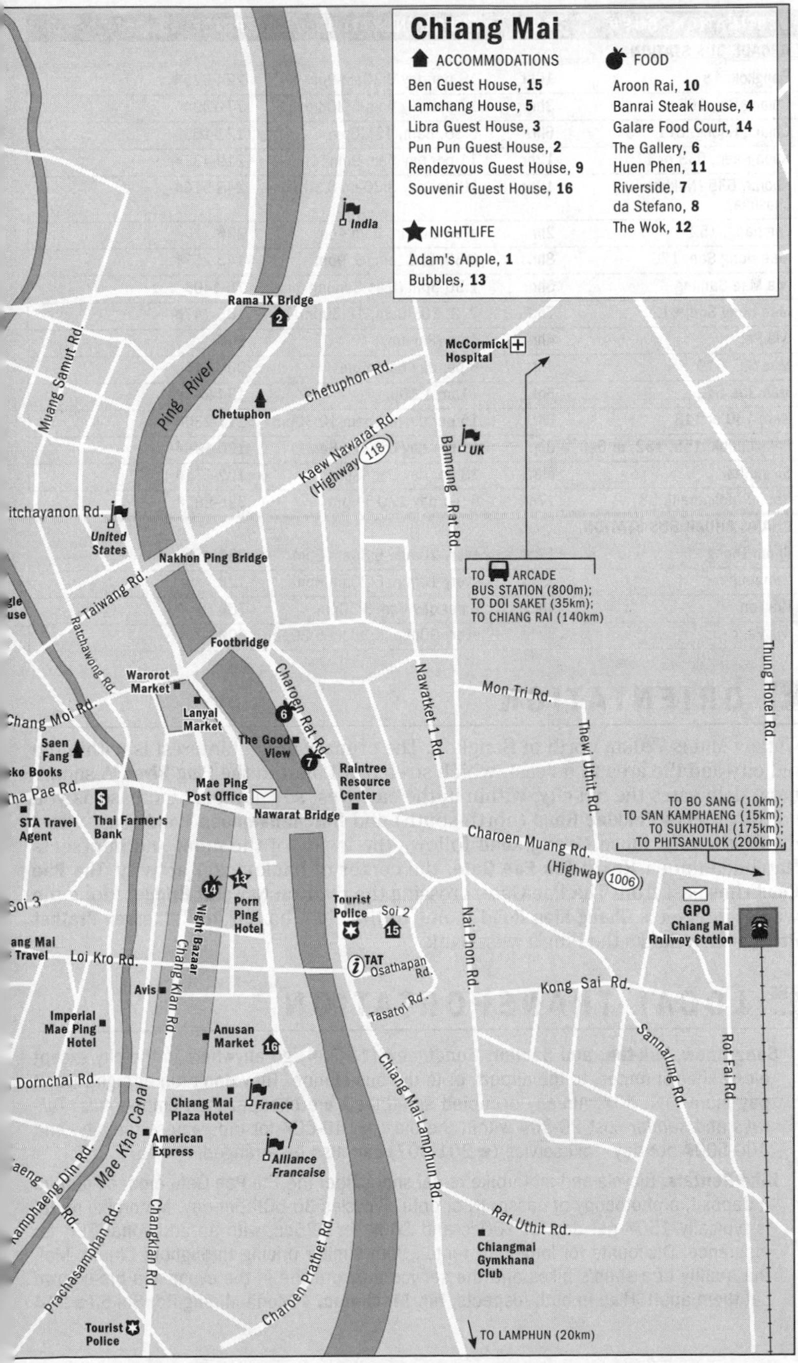
Chiang Mai
ACCOMMODATIONS
Ben Guest House, 15
Lamchang House, 5
Libra Guest House, 3
Pun Pun Guest House, 2
Rendezvous Guest House, 9
Souvenir Guest House, 16
FOOD
Aroon Rai, 10
Banrai Steak House, 4
Galare Food Court, 14
The Gallery, 6
Huen Phen, 11
Riverside, 7
da Stefano, 8
The Wok, 12
NIGHTLIFE
Adam's Apple, 1
Bubbles, 13
India
Rama IX Bridge
Muang Samut Rd.
Ping River
Chetuphon Rd.
Chetuphon
McCormick Hospital
Kaew Nawarat Rd. (Highway 118)
Bamrung Rat Rd.
UK
itchayanon Rd.
United States
Nakhon Ping Bridge
Taiwang Rd.
TO ARCADE BUS STATION (800m);
TO DOI SAKET (35km);
TO CHIANG RAI (140km)
Ratchawong Rd.
Footbridge
Warorot Market
Lanyai Market
Charoen Rat Rd.
Chang Moi Rd.
Nawatket 1 Rd.
Mon Tri Rd.
Thewi Uthit Rd.
Thung Hotel Rd.
Saen Fang
The Good View
Raintree Resource Center
Tha Pae Rd.
Mae Ping Post Office
Thai Farmer's Bank
STA Travel Agent
Nawarat Bridge
Charoen Muang Rd. (Highway 1006)
TO BO SANG (10km);
TO SAN KAMPHAENG (15km);
TO SUKHOTHAI (175km);
TO PHITSANULOK (200km)
Soi 3
Porn Ping Hotel
Night Bazaar
Tourist Police
Soi 2
GPO
Chiang Mai Railway Station
Nai Phon Rd.
Loi Kro Rd.
Chang Klan Rd.
TAT
Osathapan Rd.
Kong Sai Rd.
Avis
Tasatoi Rd.
Imperial Mae Ping Hotel
Anusan Market
Sannalung Rd.
Rot Fai Rd.
Dornchai Rd.
Chiang Mai Plaza Hotel
France
Mae Kha Canal
American Express
Alliance Francaise
Chiang Mai-Lamphun Rd.
Kamphaeng Din Rd.
Prachasamphan Rd.
Changklan Rd.
Charoen Prathet Rd.
Rat Uthit Rd.
Chiangmai Gymkhana Club
Tourist Police
TO LAMPHUN (20km)

DESTINATION, BUS#	DUR.	FREQUENCY/TIME	PRICE
ARCADE BUS STATION			
Bangkok, 18	10hr.	19 per day 6:30am-9pm	224-625฿
Chiang Rai, 166	3hr.	17 per day 6am-5:30pm	77-139฿
Chiang Khong, 671	6hr.	6:30, 8am, 12:30pm	121-169฿
Khon Kaen, 633 or 175	12hr.	11 per day 5am-9pm	219-437฿
Khorat, 635 (Nakhon Ratchasima)	12hr.	10 per day 3:30am-8:30pm	243-510฿
Lampang, 152	2hr.	every 30min. 6am-4pm	29฿
Mae Hong Son, 170	8hr.	6:30, 8, 11am, 8, 9pm	143-257฿
via Mae Sariang	5hr.	1:30 3pm (Mae Sariang only)	78-140฿
Mae Hong Son, 612	7hr.	7, 9, 10:30am, 12:30pm	105-147฿
via Pai	4hr.	4pm (Pai only)	60฿
Mae Sai, 619	4hr.	8 per day 6am-5pm	95-171฿
Mae Sot, 672	6hr.	11am 1:10pm	134-241฿
Nan, 169 or 113	6hr.	15 per day 6:15am-10:30pm	117-230฿
Phitsanulok, 155, 132, or 623	6hr.	11 per day 6:30am-8pm	120-196฿
Sukhothai	5hr.	13 per day 5am-8pm	122-171฿
Ubon Ratchathani, 587	17hr.	6 per day 12:15-6pm	325-685฿
CHANG PHUAK BUS STATION			
Chom Thong	1¼hr.	every 20min. 6:30am-6pm	23฿
Lamphun	1hr.	every 10min. 6:20am-6pm	12฿
Tha Ton	4hr.	6 per day 6am-3:30pm	70฿
via Fang	3½hr.	every 30min. 5:30am-5:30pm	60฿

THAILAND

ORIENTATION

Chiang Mai is 720km north of Bangkok. The primary area of interest is within the old city and the area to its east, which stretches 1.5km to the **Ping River.** A square moat delineates the old city; within it, the east-west *soi* numbers increase as you go north. **Phra Pokklao Road** (north-south) and **Ratchadamnoen Road** (east-west) divide the city. **Moon Muang Road** follows the inside of the moat and intersects Ratchadamnoen Rd. at **Tha Pae Gate,** the center of backpacker activity. **Tha Pae Road** runs east from Tha Pae Gate, crossing the river on **Nawarat Bridge.** Along the way, it intersects **Chang Klan Road,** home to the night bazaar, and **Charoen Prathet Road,** which flanks the Ping's west bank.

LOCAL TRANSPORTATION

Songthaew, Tuk-tuk, and Samlor: *Songthaew* (10-20฿) go anywhere in the city except along special routes, to the airport, or to the bus station. They don't run at night. Don't pay more than 40฿. Already occupied *songthaew* are cheaper than empty ones. *Tuk-tuks* and *samlor* cost 20-30฿ within the old city, 40-60฿ for trips across the city, and 400-500฿ per day. **Taxi** service (☎201 307) can also be arranged.

Bike Rentals: Bicycle and motorbike rental shops litter the Tha Pae Gate area; all require a deposit, a photocopy of passport, or both. Bicycles 30-60฿ per day. Motorbike rental is typically 150฿ per day for 100cc and 200฿ for 125cc, with an additional 50฿ for insurance. Discounts for long-term rental. With similar pricing throughout Chiang Mai, the quality of a shop's bikes and the service they provide in the event of a breakdown set them apart. High in both respects, **Mr. Mechanic,** 4 Moon Muang Rd. Soi 5 (☎214

708), also has comprehensive insurance. Motorbike 120฿, with insurance 170฿, and a full range of options 300-700฿ per day. **The Chiang Mai Disabled Center,** 133/1 Ratchaphakhinai Rd., rents mountain bikes (40฿ per day).

Car Rentals: Avis, Royal Princess Hotel, 112 Chang Klan Rd. (☎281 033), and the airport (☎201 574) both rent Toyota Corollas (1790฿ per day) and Suzuki 4WDs (1290฿ per day). Open daily 8am-5pm. In the Old City is **North Wheels,** 127/2 Moon Muang Rd. (☎216 189).

PRACTICAL INFORMATION

Tourist Office: TAT, 105/1 Chiang Mai-Lamphun Rd. (☎248 604), across from the 1st bridge 500m south of Nawarat Bridge. On the 2nd fl. Chock-full of maps, current transportation schedules, and brochures. English spoken. Open daily 8:30am-4:30pm.

Consulates: Australia, Canada, China, France, India, UK, and the **US** offer visas and consular services. See **Embassies and Consulates,** p. 661, for contact info.

Visa Services: Travel agents around town can organize visas. **Laos** (same price as in Bangkok): 4-day processing 750฿ for 15-day visa, 2-day wait 1050฿. **Vietnam** (slightly more expensive than in Bangkok): 4-day processing 2400฿ for a 1-month visa.

American Express: Sea Tours Company, 2/3 Prachasamphan Rd. (☎271 441). The only AmEx affiliate in Northern Thailand. Will replace American Express Traveler's Cheques. Open M-F 8:30am-4:30pm, Sa 8:30-11:30am.

Luggage Storage: At the **train station** (☎245 363) it's 10฿ per piece per day for the first 5 days, 15฿ per additional day, 20-day max. Open daily 4:50am-8:45pm. At the **airport** it's 30฿ per day, 14-day max. Open daily 6am-10pm. Most guesthouses store luggage for free, although security is questionable; never leave valuables in luggage.

Markets: The **night bazaar,** a must-see of Chiang Mai, dominates Chang Klan Rd. 6pm-midnight and is stocked with hill-tribe handicrafts, expensive furniture, and designer rip-offs. The southern end leads to sit-down food joints at Anusan Market where the English dishes may be double the price. Head north to the **nightly foodstalls** at Warorot Market for a cheap, quick bite.

Ambulance: ☎1669.

Tourist Police: (☎248 130). On Chiang Mai-Lamphun Rd. Open 24hr.

Pharmacy: Pharma Choice 2 (☎280 136), in Suriwong Plaza at Tha Pae Gate. Open daily 9am-7pm.

Medical Services: McCormick Hospital, 133 Kaew Nawarat Rd. (☎241 010), has ambulance service and a 24hr. **pharmacy.** English-speaking doctors. MC/V. On the other side of town, the plush **Chiang Mai Ram I Hospital,** 9 Boonruang Rit Rd. (☎224 861), has the same services.

Telephones: Overseas calls at post offices. Internet cafes around town offer collect (30฿) and overseas calls. The cheapest rates are for calls placed via the Internet.

Internet Access: Internet cafes line the northern half of Ratchaphakhinai Rd. 20฿ per hr. Around Tha Pae Gate 30฿ per hr. **The Chiang Mai Disabled Center,** 133/1 Ratchaphakhinai Rd., 20฿ per hr. Open daily 8am-8pm.

Post Offices: GPO (☎245 376), on Charoen Muang Rd. 150m toward the old city from the train station. *Poste Restante.* Open M-F 8:30am-4:30pm, Sa-Su 9am-noon. **Mae Ping Post Office** (☎252 037), on Charoen Prathet Rd. just north of Nawarat Bridge. Open M-F 8:30am-4:30pm, Sa 9am-noon. **Phra Singh Post Office** (☎814 062), on Samlan Rd. south of Wat Phra Singh. Open M-F 8:30am-4:30pm, Sa 9am-noon. All 3 provide **CATNET** with PIN or card. GPO and Phra Singh have **international phone**/fax. **DHL Worldwide Express,** 160/1 Mani Noppharat Rd. (☎418 501), east of the Chang Phuak Gate. Open M-F 8:30am-6pm, Sa 8:30am-5pm.

Postal Code: 50000.

ACCOMMODATIONS

Guesthouse signs sprout from almost every *soi* entrance within a 1km radius of **Tha Pae Gate.** Guesthouses inflate prices and reservations are recommended during festival periods (p. 661), the largest of which are the three-day **Flower Festival** in early February and the four-day **Songkran Water Festival** (Thai New Year) in mid-April. The easiest way to choose from among accommodations is to pick a neighborhood. Many guesthouses make their money from treks. In the high season, if you don't sign up for your guesthouse's trek, you may be asked to sign out.

THA PAE GATE AREA

Libra Guest House, 28 Moon Muang Rd. Soi 9 (☎/fax 210 687). Tidy, small rooms, a nice garden, and attentive service. Some backpackers may be annoyed by the rules and pressure to use Libra's services. Consistently praised treks (3-day, 1600฿, 12 people max.). Cooking school 700฿ per day. Laundry service 25฿ per kg. Check-out 10am. Reservations recommended. Doubles with bath 100฿, with hot water 150฿. ❶

Rendezvous Guest House, 3/1 Ratchadamnoen Rd. Soi 5 (☎213 763), 50m left off Ratchadamnoen Rd. Superb value with bath, TV, cable, and fridge in every room. Safety deposit box. Laundry service 30฿ per kg. Rooms 280฿, with A/C 380฿. ❹

Lamchang House, 24 Moon Muang Rd. Soi 7 (☎210 586). Charming house in a concrete jungle. The handful of comfy, 1st-fl bamboo rooms are always full. All rooms with shared bath. Singles 90฿; doubles 160฿; 3-person private outdoor house 300฿. ❶

NEAR THE PING RIVER

Ben Guest House, 4/11 Chiang Mai-Lamphun Rd. Soi 2 (☎244 103, soiphet99@hotmail.com), down a *soi* adjacent to the tourist police, signposted for Ben's. Large beds, hot showers, and fans. Nice garden. Internet 30฿ per hr. Laundry service 40฿ per kg. Check-out 10am. Motorcycle rental 150฿, with insurance 200฿. All rooms 150฿. ❷

Pun Pun Guest House, 321 Charoen Rat Rd. (☎243 362; www.armms.com), at Rama IX Bridge. The only budget accommodation by the river, though a bit far from city center (about a 30min. walk). Small restaurant/bar with cable TV and pool table. Carlsberg 30฿. Bungalows by the river 175฿; rooms with hot water and Western toilet 225฿. ❷

Souvenir Guest House, on Charoen Prathet Rd. (☎818 786; www.souvenir-guesthouse.com) at the Sri Donchai Rd. intersection. Nice rooms on a busy street. Table tennis and weight room (30฿ for 2 hours). Best-values are A3 and A4 with shared bath and patio. Singles 170฿, with bath 220฿, with A/C 370฿; doubles 200฿/260฿/410฿. ❷

FOOD

Chiang Mai has the widest variety of restaurants in Thailand. Diners can alternate between quick markets and elaborate dining rooms. All options have one thing in common: great value. Thanks to the large expat community, you can find Western dishes around Tha Pae Gate. The culinary highlight of Chiang Mai, however, is northern Thai food. Dishes are served with sticky-rice, and regional curries, characterized by a lack of coconut milk, are generally spicier. The food connoisseur will love the *Chiang Mai Restaurant Guide Book* (40฿), available at the **Chiang Mai Restaurant Club,** 128/1 Rattanakosin Rd. (☎233 297; open M-F 10am-5pm), or at any of the member restaurants around town.

Somphet Market, on Moon Muang Rd. between Soi 6 and 7, serves banana pancakes (10-15฿), fried noodles (20-40฿), and *kuay tiaw lu chin plaa* (fishball noodle soup, 20฿). It's open all day, but foodstalls don't get going until after 7pm. **Anusan Market,** between Chang Klan and Charoen Prathet Rd. north of Sri Dornchai Rd., is an overpriced nocturnal snack zone. Dining is cheaper at the **Galare**

Food Court in the middle of the night bazaar, where a casual dinner is served with nightly entertainment. In the evening, the road that runs between **Warorot Market** and **Lanyai Market** on the west bank of the Ping River is crammed with foodstalls offering Chiang Mai's best Thai take-out. For a serious culinary experience, try a *khantoke* dinner. At this formal meal, diners sit on the floor and use their hands to eat rice, two meat dishes, and two vegetable dishes from bowls placed on a *khantoke*, a low tray table. The **Old Chiang Mai Cultural Center,** 185/3 Wualai Rd. (☎275 097), 1.5km south of the old city, offers vegetarian and Muslim versions. Call ahead for reservations and to state your preference. Beginning at 7pm and accompanied by traditional dancing, dinner lasts 3 hr. (270฿, transportation included).

Huen Phen, 112 Ratchamanka Rd., west of Phra Pokklao Rd. Northern Thai dining at its finest. Locals come here for the spicy *num phrik* (chilli paste with meat, 35฿). *Farang* with soft palates may prefer the curries (50-60฿). Portions are small but have exquisite flavor and allow you to sample more. Open daily 8am-3pm and 5-10pm. ❷

Riverside, 9-11 Charoen Rat Rd. From Nawarat Bridge, take a left on Charoen Rat Rd.; it's the 1st building on the left. Attentive staff serves beef salad with mint leaves (60฿). Entrees 80-120฿. Romantic evening dinner on boat ride down the Ping River. Board 7:15pm and depart at 8pm; 70฿ minimum fee. Open daily 10am-1:30am. ❷

The Wok, 44 Ratchamanka Rd., east of Ratchaphakhinai Rd. Owners run the Chiang Mai Thai Cookery School. Impeccable "special Northern style food." Spicy Chiang Mai sausage 60฿, Thai-style fishcakes 60฿, Chiang Mai curry 60฿, black sticky-rice pudding 30฿, iced *panadanus* leaves drink 20฿. Open daily 11am-10pm. ❷

Banrai Steak House, Phra Pokklao Rd. Soi 13, around the corner from Thai Airways. This Chiang Mai institution lives up to its boast of having "the best steak in town." Barbecued steak and chicken 99฿. Fried rice 50฿. Open daily noon-midnight. ❸

Aroon Rai, 45 Kotchasarn Rd., south of Tha Pae Rd. and before Loi Kroa Rd. The food here is tasty and cheap—a dangerous combination. Open daily 8:30am-10pm. ❷

da Stefano, 2/1-2 Chang Moi Kao Rd., off Tha Pae Rd. High-quality Italian restaurant. Gnocchi with asparagus pesto and ricotta cheese 120฿. Open daily 11am-11pm. ❸

The Gallery, 25 Charoen Rat Rd. (☎241 866), next to The Good View. Excellent Thai food in a classy, intimate setting—a 100-year-old teak house overlooking the Ping River. The restaurant also exhibits local artwork. Excellent chicken wrapped in banana leaves. Entrees 80-120฿. Open daily noon-midnight. ❸

THAILAND

SIGHTS

WITHIN THE MOAT

WAT CHIANG MAN. The oldest *wat* in the city, Chiang Man was built by King Mengrai in 1296. With its low-sloping roofs and intricate facade, the temple is a classic example of Northern Thai design. The *wihaan* on the right contains two Buddha images: **Phra Setangamani** (Crystal Buddha), thought to have come from Lopburi 1800 years ago, and **Phra Sila** (Stone Buddha), imported from India some 2500 years ago. *(At the north end of Ratchaphakhinai Rd. Open daily 9am-5pm.)*

WAT CHEDI LUANG. Built by King Saen Suang Ma in 1401, the temple walls hold the spectacular remains of Chiang Mai's largest *chedi*, once spiraling 86m toward the sky before being destroyed by an earthquake in 1545. Legend holds that Wat Chedi Luang was home to the Emerald Buddha during the statue's stay in Chiang Mai. On the east side of the *wat* (right side from entrance) is **Monk Chat,** a unique opportunity for tourists to talk to monks about Buddhism, the monk lifestyle, and more. *(From Tha Pae Gate, head west on Ratchadamnoen Rd. and turn left onto Phra Pokklao Rd.; it's opposite the Yamaha music store. Monk Chat open M-Sa noon-6:30pm. Free.)*

WAT PHRA SINGH. This *wat*'s chief attraction is the bronze **Phra Singh Buddha** in **Phra Wihaan Lai Kam,** left of and behind the main *wihaan.* Experts aren't sure if this is the genuine Phra Singh Buddha, as there are identical statues in Bangkok and Nakhon Si Thammarat. The image is the focus of Songkran festivities when incense is lit and offerings are made to the Phra Singh Buddha, which is cleansed with holy water. *(On the western side of the old city, at the end of Ratchadamnoen Rd.)*

OUTSIDE THE MOAT

WAT JED YOT. Inspired by the Mahabodhi Temple in Bodhgaya, India, King Tilokaraja built this shrine in 1455. In 1477, the Eighth World Buddhist Council met here to revise the *Tripitaka* scriptures of Theravada Buddhism. The two *bodhi* trees are said to be descendants of the one Gautama sat under during his enlightenment. *(On the super-highway, 1km from the Huay Kaew Rd. intersection.)*

WAT U-MONG. Another remnant of King Mengrai's building spree, this peaceful forest temple has serene footpaths that lead through the trees. Tunnels leading into the hill at the site of the original *wat* are lined with niches housing Buddha figures. Other points of interest on the grounds are the **Herbal Medicine Garden,** a handicapped **vocational training center,** and the *wat*'s **library** (open daily until 4pm). On Sundays from 3 to 6pm, enjoy a *dhamma*'s lecture in English. *(Off Suthep Rd., on the outskirts of town. Following Suthep out of town, the turn-off is marked by a faded green sign and is the 3rd left after the super-highway. It's 2km farther down the road.)*

THAILAND

WAT SUAN DOK. King Ku Na constructed the "Temple of Flower Gardens" (also known as Wat Buppharam) in 1383. The enormous Chiang Saen-style bronze Buddha inside the *bot* dates from 1504. Originally, the grounds served as a pleasure garden for the first kings of Chiang Mai; they later became a cemetery for their remains. Today tai chi is practiced in the gardens daily at 6:30am. Suan Dok hosts **Monk Chats** (www.monkchat.net); follow the signs to the building in the back. *(On Suthep Rd., after the Hill-Tribe Products Promotion Center. Monk chats M, W, F 5-7pm.)*

CHIANG MAI NATIONAL MUSEUM. This museum features art and artifacts collected from Northern Thai royalty, commoners, and hill-tribes. Chronological dioramas depict the rise and fall of the Lanna Kingdom (*Lanna*, referring to the region of Northern Thailand, literally means "a million rice fields"). At its peak in the 13th and 14th centuries, the kingdom, a contemporary of the Sukhotai Kingdom, encompassed modern-day Northern Thailand, eastern Myanmar, and western Laos. Lanna encompasses Phrae, Nan, Phayao, Mae Hong Son, Lamphun, Chiang Rai, and Chiang Mai. *(☎221 308. On the super-highway, 500m past Wat Jet Yod on the left side of the road if coming from Huay Kaew Rd. Open daily 9am-4pm. 30฿.)*

TRIBAL MUSEUM. The polished exhibits, collected by the Tribal Research Institute, explore daily life, language derivation, gender roles, and costumes of various hill-tribes in Northern Thailand. The museum also helps visitors interested in arranging a homestay in a hill-tribe village. *(☎210 872. On Chotana Rd. in Ratchamangkhla Park, 4km north of Chang Phuak Gate, the same entrance as the Chiang Mai Shooting Club. Tuk-tuk from Chang Phuak Gate 30-50฿. Open M-F 9am-4pm. 20฿ suggested donation.)*

CHIANG MAI UNIVERSITY. Though architecturally uninspiring, the university's 725 park-like acres offer a pleasant break from the city's urban sprawl. The library is in the center of the grounds, just south of the central roundabout. The university's Art Museum often hosts major exhibits. *(Museum ☎944 833. 6km northeast of the old city off Huay Kaew Rd.)*

CHIANG MAI ZOO AND ARBORETUM. You can find everything from black bears to zebras housed somewhere along the network of roads that crisscross the zoo. The paths are both confusing and exhausting to walk; pick up a map before heading into this civilized safari. The star attraction in the zoo is the Giant Panda exhibit, which was introduced in late 2003. The two pandas are a gift from China and are advertised as a symbol of Thai-Chinese friendship. *(☎358 166. On Huay Kaew Rd. at the base of Doi Suthep, after Chiang Mai University. Open daily 8am-6pm. Last ticket sold at 5pm. 30฿, .8 5฿, an additional 100฿ to see the pandas. Bicycles 1฿, motorbikes 10฿, cars 30฿.)* Next door, the **Huay Kaew Arboretum** provides a shady respite or an invigorating workout (if you opt to use the fitness track).

CHIANG MAI ARTS AND CULTURE CENTER. Located in the old Provincial Hall, the museum has 13 rooms of permanent exhibits documenting the history and culture of Chiang Mai and Northern Thailand. The museum is geared more toward local youth, and while the building itself is remarkable, those interested in the art and history of the area would be better served by the Chiang Mai National Museum (see above). *(☎217 793. Located just behind the Three Kings Monument on Phra Pokklao Rd. Open Tu-Su 8:30am-5pm. 90฿, 40฿ students.)*

TREKKING AND SPORTS

Chiang Mai has over 200 companies itching to fulfill the trekking desires of eager *farang*. 3-day/2-night treks (4-person min.) run 1500-1800฿ per person to the **Maeteang, Phrao, Sameong, Doi Inthanon,** or **Chiang Dao** areas. Extra days can be negotiated. These five are the only legal trekking areas around Chiang Mai and with 200 companies tromping through them, there is no such thing as a non-touristed area. Maeteang, with its bamboo rafting, hosts the most trekkers; Chiang Dao gets the fewest because it runs along the questionable Myanmar border. Chiang Mai's areas encompass Akha, Lisu, Karen, Meo, Yao, and Padong villages. Some Chiang Mai-based companies also run treks to **Mae Hong Son** and **Pai.** If either of these locales tickles your fancy, it's better to hop on a bus and book from there, where a three-day trek will cost 1500-1800฿. During the low season, it's easier for solo travelers to join a trek in Chiang Mai. In Pai or Mae Hong Son, you might need to assemble your own group or end up paying more. All guesthouses either run their own treks or have an affiliated partner (usually TAT-certified) that they recommend to guests. It is important to understand exactly what the trek price includes—like sleeping bags and food. Travel-

THE LOCAL STORY

LADY KILLER

The words Muay Thai conjure up images of a bloodbath; certainly no place for a drop-dead-gorgeous woman. Nong Toom tenaciously disproved these assumptions, forcing her opponents to drop at her pedicured feet. But when she burst onto the kickboxing scene at the age of 16, Nong Toom wasn't quite so feminine. A *katoey* (transvestite), she fought as a man, but dressed as a woman. Known to wear red lipstick and a bra in the ring, Nong Toom was anything but lady-like in her disposal of opponents, amassing a 50-3 record. At the beginning of one match, her opponent mockingly kissed her on the cheek. After Prinaya crushed him, she returned the kiss. As her celebrity grew, she assumed the name Prinaya Kiatbusaba, to honor her trainers at the Lanna Boxing Camp in Doi Suthep, Chiang Mai.

In 1999, Prinaya underwent a sex-change operation to become physically attuned to her inner gender. The operation officially ended her professional kickboxing career, however, as Muay Thai regulations do not allow men to fight women. Having retired from one stage, Prinaya ascended another. In 2002, she was singing at the Icon Club in Bangkok. Unsurprisingly, her incredible story of beating adversity and discrimination has been immortalized in film in 2003's *A Beautiful Boxer.*

ers looking for extreme adventure can go **rock climbing,** regardless of experience. Most trips go to Crazy Horse Buttress. Two companies that run these trips are **The Peak Adventure** (☎516 529; www.thepeakadventure.com) and **Chiang Mai Rock Climbing Adventures** (☎111 470; www.thailandclimbing.com).

WELCOME TO THE JUNGLE. As of early 2004, less than half the trekking companies met TAT and **Northern Thailand Jungle Club** regulations, which include stipulations that guides have at least 10 years experience and speak both English and some hill-tribe dialects; that all costs (e.g. food, transportation, insurance, and elephants or bamboo rafts, if offered) be included in the stated price; that treks have no more than 12 participants; and that the company employ men from the villages they visit as porters and charge the prices set by the Northern Thailand Jungle Club. Not every company with a Jungle Club Plaque is actually a member; many have been expelled for having three or more lawsuits brought against them. For updated info on legitimate outfits, contact the tourist police or Sangduen Chailert, the president of the Northern Thailand Jungle Club and manager of **Gem Travel,** 29 Charoen Prathet Rd. Soi 6 (☎272 855). The Jungle Club's website (www.thaifocus.com/jungle) has information on trekking and hill-tribes.

Chiang Mai has abundant opportunities to watch or participate in sports such as Muay Thai (Thai Boxing), bowling, ice skating, jogging, cycling, and tennis. **Lanna Muay Thai Boxing Camp** (☎892 102; www.lannamuaythai.com), off Huay Kaew Rd., is Chiang Mai's premier boxing training center for both foreigners and Thais. The **Bar Beer Center,** on Moon Muang Rd. at the Tha Pae Gate, lets you watch the So Anucha Thai Boxing School train from 4 to 7pm. Muay Thai matches are held every night in the same arena at 10:30pm. Galare II of the **Galare Food Center** (☎272 067) in the night bazaar has live Thai boxing from 9 to 11:30pm.

COURSES AND FORUMS

Chiang Mai offers several popular courses to tourists, including Thai cooking, massage, meditation, and language.

COOKING CLASSES. Most popular are the one- to five-day **cooking courses,** which usually cost around 700฿ per day and include a trip to the market, materials, and a recipe book. **The Chiang Mai Cooking School,** 1-3 Moon Muang Rd., Chiang Mai 50200 (☎05 320 6388; www.thaicookeryschool.com), is the most widely known in all of Thailand. Another school was established in 1993 and is housed at The Wok. (☎05 320 8287. 44 Ratamanka Rd., Chiang Mai 50200. 1-day 900฿, 2-day 1800฿, 3-day 2600฿, 4-day 3400฿, 5-day 4200฿.) **Baan Thai Cooking School,** 11 Ratchadamnoen Rd. Soi 5 (☎357 339; www.cookinthai.com), is located in the heart of Chiang Mai. Run by Eagle House, **Chili Club Cooking Academy,** 26 Rathwithi Rd. Soi 2 (☎874 126; www.eaglehouse.com) has one-day courses.

MASSAGE CLASSES. Try the **Old Medicine Hospital,** 238/8 Wuolai Rd., opposite the old Chiang Mai Cultural Center. (☎275 085. 10-day certified course 4000฿.) Several others include **Mama Nit,** 1 Chaiyaphum Rd., Soi 2 is at Baan Nit (☎668 289; 2-day course 1000฿, 10-day course 3000฿), **International Training Massage,** 17/7 Maraket Rd. (☎218 632; www.infothai.com/itm), and **Thai Massage School,** 238/8 Wualai Rd. (☎275 085; www.thaimassageschool.ac.th.)

MEDITATION COURSES. Whether you'd like to stay for one day or for one month, there's a meditation program that fits your needs. **Northern Insight Meditation Center** (☎278 620), at Wat Ram Poeng near Wat U Mang, offers 10-day retreats and 26-day meditation courses. At Wat Pratat Sri Chom Thong, 60km southwest of Chiang Mai, **Voravihara Insight Meditation Center** (☎826 869) has a 26-day course followed by a suggested 10-day retreat. For *preksha* meditation and other spirituality courses try **Hatha Yoga,** 129/79 Chiang Mai Villa 1, Pa Daed (☎271 555).

LANGUAGE COURSES. American University Alumni Language Center (AUA), 73 Ratchadamnoen Rd. (☎278 407; www.auathailand.org), offers a small variety of courses, including a 30hr. course in survival Thai and a more intense 60hr. course. **Payap University** (☎243 164; www.payap.ac.th) has similar offerings. Or check out **Chiang Mai Thai Language Center,** 131 Ratchadamnoen Rd. (☎277 810; cmat@loxinfo.co.th).

SHOPPING

Chiang Mai has a wide selection of local handicrafts. **Tha Pae Road** is one of the best daytime hunting grounds, but rampant consumerism takes off only after dark. The famed **night bazaar** on **Chang Klan Road** showcases a variety of antiques, silver jewelry, hill-tribe embroidery, Thai textiles, pottery, designer clothing knock-offs, and pirated DVDs. It is a spectacle to see even if you are not intending to buy anything. **Warorot Market** is a multi-story complex containing food, textiles, and clothing. Next door in **Lanyai Market,** on the river side, flower stalls abound, spilling out onto the road. Buy a *poung ma lai* (festive flower necklace) for 5฿. The **Hill Tribe Handicraft Project,** 1 Moon Muang Rd., in a brick building at the southeastern corner of the old city, sells Karen, Lisu, Akha, Lahu, Yao, and Hmong quilts, bags, pullovers, and sculptures. (☎274 877. Open M-F 9am-4:30pm.) The better-known **Hill Tribe Promotion Center,** 21/17 Suthep Rd., next to Wat Suan Dok, has a greater selection of traditional and innovative crafts. (☎277 743. Embroidered bag 280฿, Karen dress 650฿. Open daily 9am-5pm. MC/V.) Both government-run stores seek to shift tribal economies away from opium cultivation by providing alternative means of income. The **Export Promotion Center,** 29/19 Singharat Rd., opposite Cathay Pacific Airways, showcases high-quality Thai products for export. (☎216 350. Open M-F 8:30am-noon and 1-4:30pm.)

THAILAND

NIGHTLIFE

Several wildly popular **bars** and **clubs** line Ping's east bank, just north of Nawarat Bridge. The 30฿ *tuk-tuk* from Tha Pae Gate is well worth it. *Farang* pubs line **Moon Muang Road.** Those immediately at Tha Pae Gate attract backpackers, while those to the south on Loi Kro Rd. are a bit sketchier. There are very few outright go-go bars in Chiang Mai; "karaoke" bars fill the void. The **night bazaar** hosts the most relaxed gay bars and attracts a mixed crowd. Other gay nightlife clusters in the *sois* west of Chang Phuak Bus Station, north of the old city. **Riverside,** 9-11 Charoen Rat Rd. (☎243 239), has long been the most popular club. Live music acts play nightly at 8pm. (Screwdriver 110฿, large Singha 95฿, Corona 140฿, pitcher of beer 300฿. Open daily 10am-1:30am.) **Bubbles,** 46-48 Charoen Prathet Rd. (☎270 099), in the Porn Ping Tower Hotel, is Chiang Mai's premier disco with a mixed gay and straight crowd. (Cover Su-Th 100฿, includes 1 free drink. 200฿ F-Sa and holidays includes 2 drinks. Drinks 100฿. Open daily 9pm-2am.) **Inter Bar,** on Tha Pae Rd. near Art Cafe, always has a solid crowd, a chill atmosphere and pool table. (Small Singha 60฿, screwdriver 110฿. Music nightly 7:30pm-1am. Open daily 2pm-2am.) **Adam's Apple,** on Wiang Bua Rd., is indisputably the most popular gay venue in Chiang Mai. The turn-off from Chofana Rd. is 300m past the Novotel. (Restaurant, bar, and karaoke downstairs; go-go boys upstairs. Singha 130฿. Raunchy cabaret F-Sa 11pm).)

DAYTRIPS FROM CHIANG MAI

DOI INTHANON NATIONAL PARK. Doi Inthanon National Park is $482km^2$ and is located about 60km southwest of Chiang Mai. It is one of Thailand's best national parks and is home to the country's highest peak (2585m), the most bird species (400), several beautiful waterfalls, scenic vistas, and well-paved roads to the summit. It also has some of the best tourist information; pay the national park entrance fee and pick up a map from either the vehicle checkpoint (500m after the turn-off to Mae Klang Waterfall), the visitors center (1km from the vehicle entrance on Hwy. 1009), or park headquarters (at Km 31 of Hwy. 1009). The cool season (Oct.-Feb.) is the best time to visit. The average park temperature then is 12°C (50°F). Bring raingear and warm clothing, especially if you intend to hike. The park has **guesthouses** ❹ (500-2000฿), **camping** ❶ (30฿), **tents** ❶ (70฿), and a **restaurant** at park headquarters, just past Siriphum Falls. *(To get from Chiang Mai to the summit of Doi Inthanon using public transportation, go to Chom Thong, then to Mae Klang Waterfall, and then to the summit. To get to Chom Thong, take either a bus from Chang Phuak Station (1¼hr., every 20min. 6:30am-6pm, 23฿) or yellow* songthaew *from Chiang Mai Gate (leave when full, 20฿). From Chom Thong,* songthaew *head to the national park and Mae Klang Waterfall, an 8km ride up Hwy. 1009 to the turn-off.* Songthaew *cost 10-20฿ and leave when full—which may take a while—6am-5pm. Catch another* songthaew *from Mae Klang to the summit (30฿). If relying on public transportation, you will need to make plans to stay overnight in the park. All inquiries: ☎355 728. Office open M-F 8:30am-4:30pm. Park and facilities open daily 6am-6pm. Park admission 200฿, students 100฿. Motorbikes 20฿, cars 50฿.)*

THAILAND

WAT DOI SUTHEP AND DOI SUTHEP NATIONAL PARK. If you only have time to visit one of Chiang Mai's 300 *wats*, it should be Wat Phra That Doi Suthep, one of Thailand's most sacred pilgrimage sights, built in 1383. The glint of the brilliant gold *chedi* is visible from the city's limits, and the sweeping survey of the city from the temple's observation deck (1676m high) is sublime. Upon reaching the *wat*, voyeurs have the option of ascending either via cable-car (round-trip 20฿) or the 297 steps. Encompassing a $261km^2$ area surrounding Wat Suthep, Doi Suthep National Park contains an amazing range of wildlife. *(Wat Doi Suthep 30฿ admission for foreigners; does not require national park admission. The national park is 16km northwest of Chiang Mai.* Songthaew *leave when full from Chang Phuak Gate (6am-5pm, 30฿) and the Chiang Mai Zoo (6am-5pm, 30฿), located on Huay Kaew Rd. The park headquarters (☎295 117), 1km past Wat Phra That Doi Suthep, provides trail maps and accommodations. Camping ❶ in the national park costs 10฿ per night. Available for rent are 2-person (200฿) and 5-person (500฿) tents, and 2-person (200฿) and 10-person (2000฿) cabins ❸. Reserve at least a week in advance. National park admission 200฿.)*

LAMPHUN. Tiny Lamphun, 26km southeast of Chiang Mai, has a handful of worthwhile sights. The most exciting event of the year is the **Lum-Yai Festival** in August, celebrating the *lum-yai* (longan) season. **Wat Phra That Haribhunchai** is one of the most sacred temples in Thailand. *(Loosely enforced admission 20฿.)* The **Haribhunchai National Museum** houses a small collection of Buddhas, bells, and other bric-a-brac. With your back to the *wat* on Inthayongyot Rd., it's to the left. *(Buses to Lamphun leave from the Chang Phuak Station in Chiang Mai and from just south of the footbridge near Warorot Market (1hr., every 10min. 6:20am-6pm, 12฿). Get off as the bus passes through the walled city; the Lamphun bus station is 2km south of town, where buses depart for Chiang Mai* *(every 30min. 6am-6pm). Electric blue* songthaew *leave from Chiang Mai-Lamphun Rd., south of TAT (every 20min. 5am-6pm, 15฿).* Songthaew *back to Chiang Mai depart just south of the museum, on Inthayongyot Rd. (15฿). Museum ☎511 186; open W-Su 9am-4pm; 30฿.)*

MAE SA VALLEY. The Mae Sa Valley stretches 30km from Mae Rim to Samoeng along the Mae Sa River on Hwy. 1096. The first 15km from the Mae Rim are littered with tourist attractions: poisonous snake farms, bungee jumping, ATV trails, and lavish spas. The final 15km is picturesque and peaceful, as the well-paved road weaves through rural villages and up stunning mountainsides. Much of the Mae Sa Valley is also part of **Doi Suthep National Park.** The cascades in the park tumble down the 10-tier **Mae Sa Falls.** *(National park open daily 6am-6pm. Entrance 200฿, students 100฿.)* Another popular attraction is the **Mae Sa Elephant Training Center,** 3km past the national park entrance. *(☎206 247. Admission 80฿.)* There are also daily **elephant-back jungle tours** from 7am to 2:30pm (600฿ per hour). Just two kilometers past the training center is the 2600-acre **Queen Sikrit Botanic Garden,** established in 1993 as a research and conservation center. *(Songthaew to Mae Rim, 17km north of Chiang Mai, leave from Chotana Rd. north of Chang Phuak Gate. Alternatively, take a bus headed toward Fang. Once in the Mae Rim district, transportation can be arranged to all the sights. Songthaew to Samoeng also leave from Chang Phuak Gate, (2½hr., 30฿). By car, head north out of Chiang Mai along Chotana Rd. (Hwy. 107) and pass through the tiny town of Mae Rim. After the town, take the turn-off to the left onto Mae Rim-Somoeng Rd. (Hwy. 1096). To get back from Chiang Mai, either return the way you came (52km from Samoeng) or take Hwy. 1269 through the Chang Valley (43km from Samoeng). Botanical Garden ☎298 171. 20฿.)*

BO SANG AND SAN KAMPHAENG. Bo Sang, 9km east of Chiang Mai, is world-famous for its umbrella production; mulberry paper is stretched over bamboo frames. Silk and cotton parasols, sporting bright floral, feral, and bucolic designs, are manufactured in Chiang Mai. Seeing the artisans at work is worth a trip, but prices are no better than those in established stores near the night bazaar in Chiang Mai. In the third week of January, Bo Sang hosts the colorful **Umbrella Festival,** which has a parade and a beauty pageant. **San Kamphaeng,** 4km down the road from Bo Sang and 13km from Chiang Mai, is famous for cotton and silk weaving. Duck into a side-street to catch a glimpse of production. Choose from a wide variety of fabrics and patterns. Other handicrafts are available as well. *(Located east of Chiang Mai on Route 1006, both Bo Sang and San Kamphaeng are extremely easy to reach. White songthaew at the market on the west bank of the Ping River make the 15-20min. trip regularly during the day (10฿), as do those at the Chang Phuak bus station (10฿).)*

PAI ☎053

An oasis halfway between Chiang Mai and Mae Hong Son, tiny Pai (pop. 3000) attracts both artists and trendy pilgrims. Behind the scenes, however, a clandestine drug culture has come to the attention of local authorities, who are starting to crack down on nefarious activities. The **bus station** is on Chaisongkhram Rd. and has buses to Chiang Mai (4hr.; 8:30, 10:30am, noon, 2, 4pm; 60฿) and Mae Hong Son (4hr.; 8:30, 10:30am, noon, 2, 4pm; 48฿, with A/C 67฿) via Soppong (2hr., 35฿). **Motorcycle taxis** are at the corner of Chaisongkhram and Rungsiyanon Rd. at Ban Pai and travel to hot springs (50฿), a waterfall (60฿), and Tham Lot (2hr., 300฿). Look along Chaisongkhram Rd. for **motorbike** rental. **Aya Service,** 21 Chaisongkhram Rd., offers 100cc for 100฿ and 110cc for 120฿. Turn left out of the bus station; it's 50m down on the left. (☎699 940. Open daily 7:30am-10:30pm.)

Pai is 136km northwest of Chiang Mai and 111km northeast of Mae Hong Son. **Highway 1095** cuts through town, turning into **Ketkelang Road,** which forms the town's western border. Parallel to the border (one block east) is **Rungsiyanon Road,** with the market and many restaurants. The two main east-west roads are **Chai-**

songkhram Road, and (two blocks south) **Ratchadamrong Road,** which crosses the **Pai River** to the town's east side, a popular guesthouse area. Services include: **Krung Thai Bank,** 90 Rungsiyanon Rd. (☎699 028; open M-F 8:30am-3:30pm); the **night market,** on Rungsiyanon Rd. between Chaisongkhram and Ratchadamrong Rd.; the **day market** on Ketkelang Rd., south of Ratchadamrong Rd.; the **tourist police** after Ketkelang and Rungsiyanon Rd. merge; the **Pai Hospital** 500m west of the bus station. (☎699 031; open 24hr.); a **pharmacy** on Rungsiyanon Rd. near Chez Swan (open daily 6am-9pm); **Internet** on Chaisongkhram Rd.,(1฿ per min.; open daily until 11pm); and a **post office,** 76 Ketkelang Rd., south of the day market. (☎699 208. *Poste Restante.* Open M-F 8:30am-4:30pm, Sa 9am-noon.) **Postal Code:** 58130.

Follow the road to the hot springs to find **Sun Hut ❷,** in the small town of Mae Yen. Once you cross the second bridge, it's on your right. All the huts are clean and have towels, mosquito nets, and a fan. (☎699 730; thesunhut1999@yahoo.com. Singles 150฿; doubles 200฿. Deluxe huts with bath and porch 350-400฿.) **Pai Radise ❸,** 98 Moo 1 Ban Mae Yen (☎09 38 7521; www.pairadise.com), has some of Pai's best accommodations. The pristine rooms all have baths. Turn left after the bridge over Pai River; it's located 200m on the right. (450฿ for 1 or 2 people; 400฿ if staying 2 days or more.) In the evenings, head to the **night market** on Rungsiyanon Rd. Just south of the tourist police next to BeBop, **Baan Benjarong ❷** serves the best Thai food in Pai. (Entrees 40-80฿. Open daily 11am-10pm.) **Nong Beer ❷,** 39/1 Chaisongkhram Rd. at the intersection with Ketkelang Rd., serves panaeng curry pork and rice for 30฿. (Open daily 7am-10pm.)

Wat Phra That Mae Yen has sublime views. To get there, head east on Ratchadamrong Rd. and cross the Pai River; the 360 steps to the *wat* are 1km up, or you can take the easier, paved route. Continuing past the Mae Yen River leads to the **hot springs,** 7km from town. For a more luxurious experience, the local resorts (2km before the hot springs) pump the spring water to their grounds. **Natural Hot Spring Bungalows** has individual baths (40฿), while nearby **Thapai Spa Camping** has larger pools for lazing (50฿). It's possible to pitch a tent for free at the hot springs, or for 100฿ at either of the resorts. About 2km before the hot springs (5km from town), there are three **elephant schools.**

Trekking outfitters in Pai offer everything from hiking and rafting to elephant rides (300฿ per hr.), so shop around. **Back Trax,** 27 Chaisongkhram Rd., leads groups around the Pai and Soppong areas, giving 15-20% of their proceeds to the villages. The owner Chao, a member of the Lahu tribe, speaks excellent English. (☎09 759 4840; trek@yahoo.com. 3 days 1500฿. Open daily 8am-8pm.) **Duang Trekking,** at Duang Guest House, offers treks that visit Karen, Lisu, and Shan villages, along with several waterfalls. (2-day treks 1000฿, with rafting and elephants 1450฿; 3-day treks 1500฿, with rafting 1750฿.) Bamboo rafting is usually only possible from November to May. Whitewater rafting fills the void in the wet season, although by February the water level is too low for rafting. **Thai Adventure Rafting** (☎699 111), next to Chez Swan, and **Northern Green** (☎699 385), on Chaisongkhram Rd. next to Aya Service, have similar adventures down the Khong and Pai Rivers. By the time you've finished paddling, you're in Mae Hong Son. (2-day trips stay in established campsites, 1800฿. 4-person min.)

MAE HONG SON ☎053

Lush valleys, rocky streams, and forested mountains dotted with hill-tribe villages and temples have visitors flocking to Mae Hong Son. *Farang* come for some of Thailand's best trekking, and Thai tourists come to soak up the rural lifestyle. The best time to visit is during the Bua Tong Blossom Festival in the beginning of November, when the local wild sunflower turns hillsides golden.

TRANSPORTATION

Flights: Mae Hong Son Airport (☎611 367), on Nivit Pisan Rd. Turn left at the hospital at the east end of Singhanat Bumrung Rd. **Thai Airways,** 71 Singhanat Bumrung Rd. (☎612 220). Open M-F 8am-5pm. Flies to **Chiang Mai** (35min.; 12:45, 3:10, 5:30pm; 870฿). **Air Andaman** (☎620 451), with offices at the airport, flies to **Bangkok** (1¾hr., 4 per week, 2055฿).

Buses: 33/3 Khunlum Praphat Rd. (☎611 318). To: **Chiang Mai** (7½-8½hr., 11 per day 6am-9pm, 105-261฿) via **Mae Sariang** (4hr., 4 per day 6am-9pm, 78฿; with A/C, 6, 10:30am, 9pm; 140฿) and **Khun Yuam** (2hr., 35฿); or via **Pai** (3½hr., 4 per day 7am-12:30pm, 53฿; with A/C, 8am, 105฿) and **Soppong** (2hr., 33฿).

Local Transportation: Songthaew leave for points north of Mae Hong Son from the day market on Punit Watana Rd. **Motorcycle taxis** and **tuk-tuks** wait at the bus station and airport (10-40฿).

Rentals: Numerous places around the traffic light on Khunlum Praphat Rd. rent **motorcycles. Highway,** 67/2 Khunlum Praphat Rd. (☎611 620), opposite Thai Farmers Bank south of the lights, has "as new" motorcycles with good service facilities. 150฿ per day; passport or 500฿ and passport photocopy required for deposit. Open daily 8am-7pm. **TN Tour,** 107/17 Khunlum Praphat Rd. (☎620 059), rents Suzuki 4WD.

ORIENTATION AND PRACTICAL INFORMATION

Mae Hong Son is 348km from Chiang Mai via Mae Sariang (Hwy. 108, the southern route), and a meandering 274km via Pai (Hwy. 107 and 1095, the northern route). Buses stop on **Khunlum Praphat Road,** which is home to restaurants, trekking outfitters, and banks, and runs north-south through the center of town. As you turn left out of the bus station and head south, the second intersection is **Singhanat Bumrung Road.** Another block south, guesthouses dot **Udom Chao Nithet Road,** which borders the **Jong Kham Lake.**

Tourist Office: TAT (☎612 982), on Khunlum Praphat Rd. 200m south of traffic light, opposite post office. Eager staff hands out tourist brochures and excellent maps. Open M-F 8:30am-noon and 1-4:30pm.

Currency Exchange: Bangkok Bank, 68 Khunlum Praphat Rd. (☎611 275). Open M-F 8:30am-3:30pm. 24hr. **ATM.** AmEx/MC/PLUS/V.

Bookstore: Saksarin Tour, 88/5-6 Khunlum Praphat Rd. (☎612 124), next to La Tasca. Small selection of English fiction and travel books. Comprehensive map selection.

Markets: The **day market** is on Panit Watana Rd. next to Wat Hua Viang. Street-side stalls sell fruits and vegetables; the covered market sells mainly meat. Cookies mix with hill-tribe bags and cartoon-character umbrellas in the nearby *sois.*

Ambulance: ☎1669.

Local Tourist Police: (☎611 812). At the corner of Rachadamphitak and Singhanat Bumrung Rd. Helpful. Same excellent maps as TAT, and good English is spoken. Open daily 9am-9pm. 24hr. emergency.

Pharmacy: 37 Singhanat Bumrung Rd. (☎611 380). Open daily 7am-8pm.

Medical Services: Srisangwal Hospital (☎611 378), at the end of Singhanat Bamrung Rd. English-speaking doctors. 24hr. emergency care.

Telephones: Telecom Office, 26 Udom Chao Nithet Rd. (☎611 711), just west of Khunlum Praphat Rd. **International phones** and fax. **Lenso** phone at post office. **CATNET.** Open M-F 8:30am-4:30pm.

THAILAND

Internet Access: Cheapest (and slowest) is the **CATNET** at the Telecom Office. 11฿ per hr.; buy 100฿ card. Several places around the traffic light. **Kai Comp,** just north of the post office. 1฿ per min., 40฿ per hr. Open daily 8am-11pm.

Post Offices: Mae Hong Son Post Office, 79 Khunlum Praphat Rd. (☎611 223). Open M-F 8:30am-4:30pm, Sa-Su 9am-noon.

Postal Code: 58000.

ACCOMMODATIONS AND FOOD

All of the town's guesthouses are in two areas: the central area around the lake, and the less convenient but quieter northwest outskirts of the city. Standard hotels cluster along Khunlum Praphat Rd. Turn left out of the bus station, take the first left after the traffic light, and then the first right; **Friend House ❶,** 20 Paditchongkam Rd., is just off the intersection with Udom Chao Nithet Rd. The cleanest of the lakeside joints, Friend House has upstairs rooms with lake-view balconies. (☎620 119. Laundry 30฿ per kg. Rooms 100฿, with shower 250฿.) To get to the **Mae Hong Son Guest House ❷,** 295 Mucksanti Rd., turn right out of the bus station and left on the first street. The guesthouse has a garden and a relaxed atmosphere. (☎612 510. Singles 150฿; doubles 200฿, with bath 250-300฿. Private bungalow with bath 450-500฿.) The **Yok Guest House ❸,** 14 Sirimongkol Rd., is set back from the main road. Turn right out of the bus station, then take the second left; it's 300m on the right after the *wat.* (☎611 532. Free transportation from airport and bus station. Clean rooms with fan, towels, and bath 200฿, with carpet 300฿, with A/C 400฿.)

Most restaurants in Mae Hong Son offer Western specialties, but the best options are still the Northern Thai dishes. **Fern Restaurant ❷,** on Khunlum Praphat Rd. just south of the post office, serves what locals call the best Thai food in town. (Entrees 40-80฿. Local chicken with herbs 70฿. Live Thai music nightly until 9pm. Open daily 10am-11pm.) **Baimon Kitchen ❶,** on Khunlum Praphat Rd. south of the bus station, has good, cheap Thai entrees. Try their specialty *khao soy,* a Northern Thai coconut curry noodle dish, for 20฿. (Pineapple chicken 25฿. Lots of tofu dishes 10-40฿. Open daily 7am-11pm.) Stop by the **Sunflower Cafe ❶,** Soi 3 Khunlum Praphat Rd., at 8am for oven fresh bread and a delicious breakfast. To get there, face the post office and follow the road's left fork 100m; it's on the left. The comfy, cushioned seating is a great place to put together a trekking group. (☎620 549. Cheesecake 25฿. Papaya shake 15฿. Open daily 7:30am-11:30pm.)

THE LOCAL STORY

THE PLIGHT OF THE PADONG

Perhaps the most ubiquitous of all Thailand's attractions are the Padong long-necked women. It is impossible to leave Bangkok without seeing them on postcards or hearing stories about them. In reality, the total number of Padong is only about 7,000, out of which a mere 300 live in Thailand, in Mae Hong Son Province.

The women are famous for the brass coils they wear around their necks. The coils—weighing 5kg or more—push down the woman's collarbone, which creates the illusion of a very long neck. Research shows that Padong women's necks are actually normally sized; if the brass coils were removed, the neck would revert from its elongated state.

Padong legend holds that in their golden age, a pack of tigers attacked a village and bit several tribal members on the neck, killing them. This so worried the village leader that he forced girls and unmarried women to wear neck coils. Originally, the coils were made of gold, but as that became too expensive, brass was substituted. Girls receive their first set of coils at age five , and three more are added every three years until the girl is 25 or is married. The tradition began dying out in Myanmar, but once groups fled to Thailand, entrepreneurs seized on the women as a tourist gold mine.

The Padong tourist villages are quite controversial, as critics see

SIGHTS AND TREKKING

Wat Phra That Doi Kongmu, 474m above town, has a panoramic view of the city. Nearby **Wat Phra Non** houses a 12m Burmese-style reclining Buddha and the ashes of Mae Hong Son's kings. To get to either *wat*, head west on Udom Chao Nithet Rd. and turn left at the end. On the right is Wat Phra Non; take the right before the stadium for the road to Wat Phra That Doi Kongmu.

Visit the **Jong Kham Lake**'s south side to see two famed *wats*. **Wat Chong Klang** is on the right, with Buddhist glass-paintings and wooden dolls. (Open daily 8am-6pm.) **Wat Chong Kham,** built in 1827, shines with gold-leaf.

The **Pa Bong Hot Springs** offer a different type of soul-cleansing. The relaxation center, 10km south of town toward Mae Sariang, pipes spring water into private baths. (Small bath 40฿, large 200฿. Thai massage available. Open daily 9am-7pm.)

Mae Hong Son has some of the best trekking in Thailand—several Chiang Mai-based treks descend here. The surrounding hills support villages of Lisu, Lahu, Hmong, and Karen tribes, as well as Shan and Kuo Min Tang (KMT) zones. During the low season, putting together your own crew can lower prices, since Mae Hong Son draws fewer travelers than Chiang Mai and there aren't always organized groups. TAT can provide you with a list of the 28 licensed travel agents in Mae Hong Son. Once you decide on a company, it doesn't hurt to check their status with the tourist police. For those heading out by themselves, TAT still has the best free regional map. Detailed trekking routes are found on the regional map produced by the **Pai Association for Travelers** (available at some restaurants and trekking agencies; 10฿). **Sunflower Tours,** run out of Sunflower Cafe, offers consistently good butterfly- and bird-watching tours, as well as treks featuring elephants, bamboo rafts, and visits to hill-tribes. (1- to 5-day trips 600฿ per person per day, 4-person minimum). Treks with **Mae Hong Son Guest House** (see **Accommodations,** p. 774) also receive favorable reports. (☎620 105. 3-day trek 1800฿; 4-person min.)

DAYTRIPS FROM MAE HONG SON

NAI SOI (LONG-NECKED KAREN VILLAGE). Travelers to Mae Hong Son Province can't miss hearing about the Myanmar refugees who make this village their home. At the age of five, the girls in this subset of the Karen tribe are fitted for their first brass neck rings. By adulthood, the rings have compressed the

them as exploitative. Proponents of the coils counter that th[redacted]vil-lage has increased income[redacted]he biggest and most touristed [redacted] the Padong villages is Nai So[redacted]near Mae Hong Son. It is clear [redacted] any-one who has been there that the women do not lead an authentic village life. Instead, they pose for pictures, superficially play together in the river, and weave baskets for tourist souven[redacted]Con-tradicting their detract[redacted], the Padong women themselves say that they don't mind the photographs and that life in Thailand is much better than in Myanmar.

Indeed, the Padong don't have much more appealing alternatives. The Padong could live in intense poverty in Myanmar, under an oppressive government that persecutes them. They could flee to Thailand, perform taxing farm labor, and lead a life of bare subsistence. Or they could establish tourist villages in Thailand, where they strive to pleas[redacted]pho-tographers all day, all th[redacted]while making more money than by traditional methods. While the tourist village is not a perfect way of life for the Padong, it surpasses their next-best option.

If you are interested in seeing the Padong, go to Hoy Sen[redacted]ao, Huay Ma Khen Som, or No[redacted]oi—all in Mae Hong Son Province. All of the villages can be reached by private transportation. The entrance fee is 250฿, some of which goes directly to villagers. Tour companies charge much more.

woman's collarbone and rib cage so that her neck appears stretched. Many visitors find the zoo-like atmosphere disturbing. *(Take a songthaew from Mae Hong Son's day market to the Shan town (leaves when full, 30฿); then walk or hail another for the 3km to Nai Soi. Returning can be tricky; a motorcycle taxi is your best bet (250฿). For those with their own transportation, the turn-off is Km 199 on the highway to Pai. Turn left at this point, and take the 1st left 500m down. There is a sign at this 2nd turn-off, but it is obscured. Entrance 250฿. Open daily 6am-6pm.)*

SOPPONG (PANG MA PHA). Soppong stretches over 4km of Hwy. 1095; at the end closest to Pai is the turn-off to **Tham Lod** (Lod Cave). Follow the 9km road to its end to reach the cave. Visitors must hire a guide to take them through the three gigantic underground caverns (100฿ for 1-4 people). Rafts can be chartered either at the beginning of the cave (round-trip 400฿ for 1-4 people) or before the subterranean river crossing (round-trip 200฿ for 1-4 people). The best time to visit the cave is about 1½hr. before sunset, so that the tour will conclude with the aerial display put on by swifts as they return to the cave. (☎617 218. Open daily 8am-5pm.) To get to the cave from Soppong, catch a motorbike taxi (60฿) or rent your own transportation. The repair shop opposite Little Eden and Soppong River Inn has motorcycles (200฿ per day). *(Buses stop in Soppong on their way between Mae Hong Son (2hr., 4 per day 10am-5:30pm, 30฿) and Pai (1½hr., 4 per day 9am-6pm, 30฿). The last bus to Chiang Mai (5½hr.) is at 2:30pm. Soppong is 43km from Pai and 66km from Mae Hong Son.)*

THAILAND

MAE SARIANG ☎053

Mae Sariang, a small, peaceful town (pop. 8000), is a good base for exploring nearby hill-tribe villages. Teak, rice, and heroin trade with Myanmar has fueled a small building boom, and the town is prepared for tourism: information markers clutter every street corner. But neither the construction nor the as-yet-to-materialize tourist flood has managed to disrupt Mae Sariang's drowsiness. Charming countryside and quiet nights await those willing to leave the beaten path. Visiting Mae Sariang is a worthwhile way to complete the loop instead of backtracking.

TRANSPORTATION AND PRACTICAL INFORMATION. The **bus terminal** (☎681 347) is on Mae Sariang Rd., 100m north of the traffic light, opposite the PTT gas station. **Buses** run to Chiang Mai and Mae Hong Son (4hr., 5 per day 7am-1:30am, 80฿-140฿). **Yan Yont Tours** (☎681 532), offers **VIP buses** to Bangkok (12hr.; 4, 7pm; 420฿). **Songthaew** head to Mae Sot (6hr., every hr. 7:30am-12:30pm, 150฿). **Motorcross-bike rental** is just south of the PTT gas station (250-400฿ per day).

Mae Sariang is bordered by the **Yuam River** to the west and **Highway 108** to the east. The two main roads run north-south. The bus station and numerous shops are on **Mae Sariang Road.** One block west, **Langpanit Road** runs parallel to the river and hosts the best guesthouses. **Wiangmai Road** stretches from the river to Hwy. 108 and intersects Mae Sariang Rd. at the traffic light in the town center. **Saritpol Road,** site of the morning **market,** connects Mae Sariang and Langpanit Rd. one block south of the light. Also south of the traffic light, **Wai Suksa Road** heads west out of town across the town's only bridge to Mae Sam Laep. Services include: an **immigration office,** 200m north of the hospital on Hwy. 108, for visa extensions (☎681 339; open M-F 8:30am-4:30pm); **Thai Farmers Bank,** on Wiangmai Rd. west of Mae Sariang Rd., with **ATM** and **currency exchange** (Cirrus/MC/PLUS/V; open M-F 8:30am-3:30pm); **police** (☎681 308), on Mae Sariang Rd. 150m south of the traffic light; a **pharmacy,** on the corner of Siritpol and Langpanit Rd. (open daily 8am-9pm); the **hospital** (☎681 027), on Hwy. 108, 200m toward Mae Hong Son from the intersection with Wiangmai Rd.; **Internet** access on Wiangmai Rd., east of the traffic light (30฿ per hr.; open daily 9am-10pm); and the **post office,** 31 Wiangmai Rd., which has **international phone**/fax. (☎681 356. Open M-F 8:30am-4:30pm, Sa-Su 9am-noon.) **Postal Code:** 58110.

ACCOMMODATIONS AND FOOD. For a view of the river, try the **Riverside Guest House ❷,** 85 Langpanit Rd., 300m north of Wiangmai Rd. From the bus station, turn left onto Mae Sariang Rd., right at the first intersection, and right again on Langpanit Rd.; it's 100m down on the left. The cheapest rooms are in the dark basement. (☎681 188. Bicycles 50฿. Check-out 11:30am. Basic singles 100฿; doubles 180฿. Tiled-floor singles with private bath 280฿, with A/C 450฿; doubles 350฿/550฿.) Budget-friendly **Northwest Guesthouse ❶** is across the street. Trade the river view for exceptionally clean rooms. (Bicycle rental 50฿; motorbike rental 250฿. Singles with fan 100฿; doubles 150฿.)

Of all the open-air eateries along Wiangmai Rd., the popular **Renu Restaurant ❷,** 174/2 Wiangmai Rd. 50m toward the highway from the traffic light, has the best eats in town. (Cashew nuts with some chicken thrown in for good measure 60฿. Most entrees 40-50฿. Open daily 6am-midnight.) Across the street, **Intira Restaurant ❷** offers good Thai and Chinese entrees for 25-60฿. (Chicken in oyster sauce 50฿. Open daily 8am-10pm.) The **stands** that set up in the evening on Mae Sariang Rd. around the bus station sell cheap, tasty food.

DAYTRIPS FROM MAE SARIANG. The country around town is perfect for excursions. The 6km to **Pha Maw Yaw** is particularly scenic. To get there, take Langpanit Rd. north and follow the left bend around the *wat.* This Karen village is set among green fields, and its temple, **Phra That Chom Mawn,** has a panoramic view of Mae Sariang. On the other side of town, on the road south to Mae Sot, the **Big Buddha** is an intriguing sight. Those daring enough to make the trip up the hill are rewarded with another panorama of Mae Sariang. Follow Wiangmai Rd. out of town. Just before the highway, turn right on the road to Mae Sot. It's impossible to miss the 10m Buddha. The Riverside and See View Guesthouses and the Riverside Hotel have decent regional maps and can organize day or overnight trekking, rafting, and elephant-riding trips (800-1200฿ per day, 4-person min.).

To reach **Mae Sam Laep,** 46km west of Mae Sariang on the border, take the *songthaew* which leave Mae Sariang from just east of the bridge near the morning market. The first *songthaew* (1½hr., 50฿) leaves around 7am; others depart when full. The last comes back in the afternoon—ask your driver for a return time. You'll need a motorcross bike in the wet season; roads can be muddy and there are several creek crossings. (River boats from Mae Sam Laep depart by 9am, return 3pm; 100฿. Chartered boats 750-850฿.) All guesthouses can arrange trips to Mae Sam Laep and Salawin National Park.

On the route to Mae Hong Son are the **Mae Surin National Park** and **Mae Surin Waterfall**—Thailand's tallest, located about 120km north of Mae Sariang and 45km northeast of Khun Yuam. Hop off the Mae Sariang/Mae Hong Son bus when it stops in Khun Yuam. Catch a *songthaew* for the remaining distance in front of Ban Farang, 100m toward Mae Sariang from the bus stop, at the curve in the main road.

MAE SOT ☎055

Mae Sot is a small city 7km east of Myanmar. The border leads to a volatile influx of Myanmar refugees and black-market goods. All routes to Mae Sot pass through police border checkpoints. Mae Sot's day market is a sight to behold, where "Union of Myanmar" currency notes, hill-tribe headdresses, and precious gems mingle with pig heads and mangoes.

THAILAND

TRANSPORTATION

Flights: Mae Sot Airport (☎563 620), 3km west of town. Take a *songthaew* toward the Moei River Market (10฿). Daily minibus service from the airport (80฿). **Thai Airways,** 110 Prasatwithi Rd. (☎531 440), books flights with **Air Andaman** and **Phuket Air.** To **Bangkok** (Tu, Th, Sa 9:55am, F, Su 2:20pm; one-way 1915฿) and **Chiang Mai** (Su-M, W, F 3pm; one-way 1185฿).

Buses: There are 5 bus stations within 200m of town center. The station (☎532 949) for trips to and from **Bangkok** (10hr.; 8per day 8-8:30am, 7-9:45pm; 211-420฿) is 2 blocks north of the police station. Ticket office open daily 9am-5pm. Orange *songthaew* to **Mae Sariang** (6hr., every hr. 6am-noon, 160฿) leave from behind the covered market area south of the bus station for Bangkok. Orange-and-white **minivans** to **Tak** (1½hr., every 30min. 6am-5:30pm, 44฿) gather on the east side of the same market. The station (☎532 331) for green buses to **Chiang Mai** (6½hr.; 8am, 9am; 115-207฿) is 1 block east of the police station on Intharakhiri Rd. Head south from the police station and take the 1st left after the mosque and you'll see a cluster of blue *songthaew* to **Um Phang** (5hr., every hr. 7:30am-3:30pm, 100฿). White **vans** to **Phitsanulok** (4hr., 7 per day 7am-3pm, 125฿) via **Sukhothai** (2½hr., 100฿) leave from the station at the southern end of the main market.

Local Transportation: To go to the **Moei River Market** and the **border,** catch a blue **songthaew** (10฿) opposite Bank of Ayudhya near the west end of Prasatwithi Rd. Last one returns at 6pm.

Rentals: Guesthouses rent **bikes** (50฿). **Motorbike** rental (☎532 099) is next to Bangkok Bank on Prasatwithi Rd. 160฿ per day. Open daily 8am-5:30pm. To keep your passport for Myanmar, you must put down a 5000฿ deposit and take an old motorbike.

THAILAND

ORIENTATION AND PRACTICAL INFORMATION

Mae Sot is 165km west of Sukhothai and 7km east of Myanmar. The two main roads run east-west: **Intharakhiri Road,** heads east and runs parallel to **Prasatwithi Road,** where traffic heads west toward the Myanmar border. **Asia Highway** bypasses town a few blocks north of the two major roads. The **police station** is on Intharakhiri Rd. in the center of town; guesthouses primarily lie on the same road to the west. The **market** sprawls south of Prasatwithi Rd. Free maps with varying degrees of accuracy are available at guesthouses.

Tours: Go to Um Phang to book a trek. To book in Mae Sot, try TAT-approved **Mae Sot Conservation Tours,** 415/17 Tang Kim Chiang Rd. (☎532 818; maestco@cscoms.com). 3 days, 2 nights 5500฿ per person; min. 3 people.

Currency Exchange: Banks line Prasatwithi Rd., most with 24hr. **ATMs.**

Markets: The **day market** stretches south from Prasatwithi Rd. on either side of the Siam Hotel. You can find frogs, vegetables and every kind of shirt, from collared to tie-dye. The bustling **gem and jade market** on Prasatwithi Rd., stretching east from the Siam Hotel, heats up by noon and closes at 4pm. The **night market** at the east end of Prasatwithi Rd. is mostly foodstalls. The **Moei River market,** at the border 7km west of town, sells everything from Myanmar fabrics to Sony Playstations.

Laundry: On both ends of Intharakhiri Rd.: next to the DK Hotel, and at the other end, next to Bai Fern Guest House (30฿ per kg).

Local Tourist Police: (☎533 523), near Asia Hwy. in the vicinity of the Bangkok bus station. With your back to the police station, head left, take the 1st left, and follow it to the end; it's on the left. City map and good bus schedules. Minimal English. Open 24hr.

Medical Services: Pawo Hospital (☎544 397), south of town past the market, near the vans to Sukhothai. Some English spoken. Hospital and **pharmacy** open 24hr. MC/V.

Telephones: Telecom Office, 784 Intharakhiri Rd. (☎533 364), 10min. walk west of guesthouses. Standard 33฿ for assisted collect call. Lenso phone and **CATNET.** Open M-F 8:30am-4:30pm.

Internet Access: 112/9 Prasatwithi Rd. (☎531 909), 2 doors west of Thai Airways. 25฿ per hr. Open daily 9am-8pm, Internet access often until midnight.

Post Office: GPO (☎531 277), on Intharakhiri Rd. With your back to the police station, head left; it's 150m down the road on the right. *Poste Restante.* Lenso phone. Open M-F 8:30am-4:30pm, Sa-Su 9am-noon.

Postal Code: 63110.

BORDER CROSSING: MOEI-MYAWADDY. A 7km *songthaew* ride away from Mae Sot, this Thai/Myanmar border crossing is a relatively hassle-free way to extend your Thai visa. Blue *songthaew* leave from Prasatwithi Rd., opposite the Bank of Ayudhya (10min., every 15min. 7am-5pm, 10฿). Show up at the Thai-Myanmar Friendship Bridge, present your passport to the Thai authorities to get an exit stamp, walk over the bridge, present US$10 or 500฿ and your passport to Myanmar officials to be stamped, then walk back over the bridge, and receive your new visa. If you intend to pay in US dollars, bring them with you, as authorities are frequently out of change. If you want to see Myawaddy, just leave your passport with Myanmar officials and be sure to return by 5pm. Myawaddy's main attractions are **Shwe Muay Wan Temple** and a fairly typical market. Myanmar touts are even more relentless than Thai ones—be prepared to have unwanted "guides" on your trip. Get updated on the political situation in Myanmar before crossing the border.

ACCOMMODATIONS

The number of guesthouses in Mae Sot is growing by the day. Most are located at the west end of Intharakhiri Rd., about 0.5-1km from the police station.

KK Guesthouse, 668 Intharakhiri Rd.; just east of Bai Fern (☎737 101; glamax007@hotmail.com). This new guesthouse has clean, tiled rooms, all with bath and nice beds—specify your preference, hard or soft. Its innovative and artsy Bar Kong has a pool table and serves food and drinks. Singles 150฿; doubles 200฿. ❷

Bai Fern Guest House, 660/2 Intharakhiri Rd. (☎533 343). With your back to the police station, it's 400m to the right. Wonderfully friendly staff. All rooms with fans and shared hot-water bath. Small singles 100฿; large but noisy upstairs doubles 150฿. ❶

Ban Thai Guest House, 740 Intharakhiri Rd. (☎531 590; banthai_mth@hotmail.com), 25m farther west from No. 4 Guest House. Well off the main road, it's Mae Sot's nicest guesthouse. Beautifully decorated rooms with comfy mattress, table, and cushioned seating. All rooms have shared bath. Bike rental 50฿. Singles 250฿; doubles 350฿. ❷

FOOD AND NIGHTLIFE

The day and night markets have a huge selection of cheap eats. Various other restaurants are scattered throughout the town.

Bai Fern Restaurant serves incredible *farang* fare. The "Bai Fern delight" pizza (ham, veggies, and pineapple, with bacon- and cheese-stuffed crust; 120฿) is delicious. Plenty of baked goods and espresso. Thai entrees 30-40฿. Open daily 7am-10pm. ❷

THAILAND

Tea Shop, opposite the mosque, has an English menu and serves up cheap and tasty samosas (2฿ each), *roti,* and curries. Open daily 8am-8pm. ❶

Khrua Canadian, on Tong Kim Chiang Rd., serves good *farang* and Thai food under the watchful eyes of the Toronto-born owner. Has satellite TV and fair-trade hill-tribe coffee. Chicken cheeseburger 50฿, fries 40฿. Open daily 7am-10pm. ❷

SUKHOTHAI ☎055

In 1238 the Thais established the new capital of the Lanna Kingdom near the Yom River and drove the Khmer to the east. Named "Sukhothai," or "Dawn of Happiness," the city marked the birth of the first Thai nation. Sukhothai's period of glory is preserved in its spectacular ruins. Old Sukhothai and Ayutthaya are Thailand's two premier ancient sites. Nearby Si Satchanalai, Old Sukhothai's twin city (with its own impressive ruins) remains untrafficked.

TRANSPORTATION

Flights: The **airport** (☎612 448) is 26km out of town. **Bangkok Airways** (☎613 075), at the Pailyn Hotel nestled on the road to the old city, flies to: **Bangkok** (daily 12:50pm; Su-M, W, F 4:40pm; 1500฿); **Chiang Mai** (daily 10:40am, 1040฿); **Luang Prabang** (Su, M, W, F 1:10pm; 4300฿). 100฿ departure tax. Shuttle bus to the airport from Sukhothai Travel Service 90฿.

Buses: There is a brand new **bus station** (☎614 529) 1.5km north of town on Bypass Rd. It is possible to walk into town using the shortcut path behind the bus station (see map). White, pink, and blue *songthaew* run along Bypass Rd. into town (5฿ before 4pm). *Tuk-tuks* to town are 30฿. Buses go to: **Bangkok** (7hr., every hr. 7:50am-11pm, 199-256฿) via **Ayutthaya** (5hr., 169฿); **Chiang Mai** (6hr.; 1:30, 2:30am, 14 per day 7:15am-5:30pm; 171฿) via **Tak** (1hr., every hr. 7:30am-6:15pm, 31-43฿); **Chiang Rai** (6-7hr.; 6:40, 9, 11:30am; 190฿); **Phrae** (4hr.; 8:40, 11:40am, 1:40, 4:10pm; 92฿); **Phitsanulok** (1hr., every 30min. 6:20am-8pm, 23-32฿). **Minibuses** to **Mae Sot** (2½hr., 7 per day 8am-4pm, 100฿) leave from a traffic triangle off Charot Withi Thong Rd., 2 blocks north of the main traffic light.

Local Transportation: Tuk-tuks 20-30฿. **Samlor** 10-20฿. At the terminal on Charot Withi Thong Rd., 200m west of the bridge, red-, white-, and blue-striped **songthaew** run to Old Sukhothai (every 20min. 6am-6pm, 10฿). A **bus** to **Si Satchanalai** runs from the bus station (every 30min. 7am-4:30pm, 30฿).

Rentals: Lotus Village and **Ban Thai Guest House** rent **bicycles** for 30-50฿ per day. Bicycles cost 20-30฿ per day at the Historical Park and 20฿ per day at Si Satchanalai. **Thanin Motorbikes,** 112 Charot Withi Thong Rd. (☎613 402), 20m past Thai Farmers Bank with 24hr. bell service, rents **motorbikes.** (150฿ per day. open daily 7am-8pm.) Guesthouses rent them for 200฿.

ORIENTATION AND PRACTICAL INFORMATION

New Sukhothai city, 12km east of the old city (*muang gao*) and 427km north of Bangkok, appears at an L-shaped bend in the Yom River. **Charot Withi Thong Road** and **Singhawat Road** each run parallel to the river (about three blocks east of it) and converge at Sukhothai's largest intersection, near the bend in the "L." From there, Charot Withi Thong Rd. crosses **Praruang Bridge** and continues into the old city, intersecting **Nikorn Kasaem** and **Pravet Nakhon Road** along the way. **Highway 101** bypasses the town at its northern end.

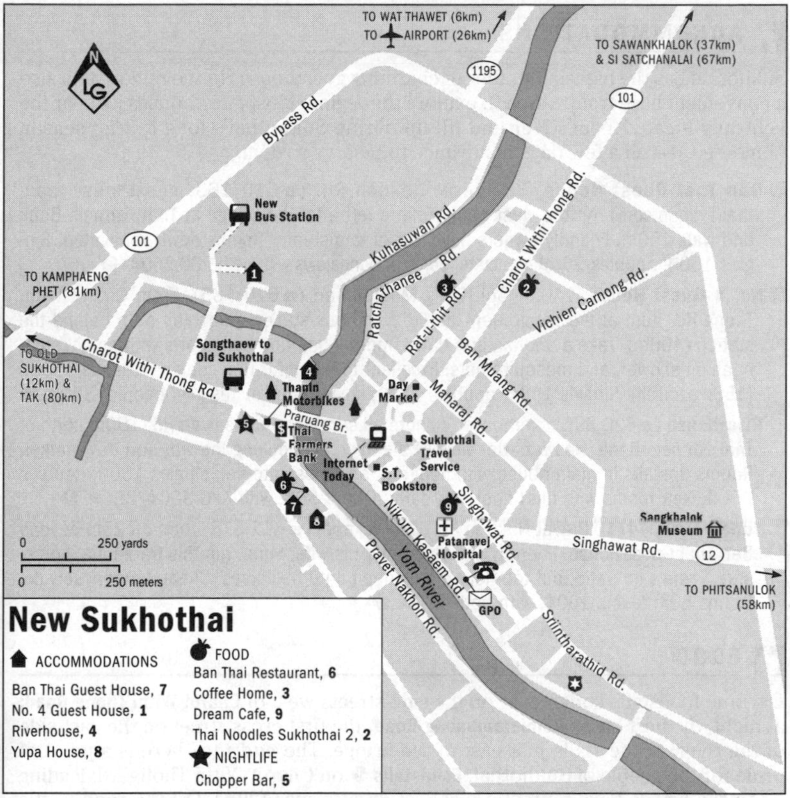

Tourist Offices: The small tourist office on the east side of Praruang Bridge gives out timetables and brochures. Open M-F 8am-4:30pm. The bus counter has the same info. The guesthouses–especially Ban Thai and No. 4–have the best tourist advice.

Tours: Sukhothai Travel Service, 327/6-7 Charot Withi Thong Rd. (☎613 075), books domestic and international flights. Open daily 8am-5pm.

Currency Exchange: Most banks exchange currency and traveler's checks. **Thai Farmers Bank,** 134 Charot Withi Thong Rd. (☎611 932) at the base of the bridge, has a 24hr. **ATM.** Cirrus/MC/Plus/V. Open M-F 8:30am-3:30pm. Other banks on Singhawat Road.

Police: 263 Nikorn Kasaem Rd. (☎613 110), 250m beyond the post office.

Medical Services: Patanavej Hospital, 89/9 Singhawat Rd. (☎621 502), 200m from the intersection of Singhawat and Charot Withi Thong Rd., on the right. Some English spoken. Hospital and **pharmacy** open 24hr. V.

Telephones: At the GPO. **International telephone,** fax, and **CATNET** upstairs. Open M-F 8:30am-4:30pm, Sa 9am-noon. Lenso telephone at 7-Eleven.

Internet Access: Cafes on Nikorn Kasaem Rd. near the bridge. **Internet Today,** on Charot Withi Thong Rd. 100m into town from the bridge. 1฿ per min., 40฿ per hr. Open until 11pm.

Post Office: GPO, 241 Nikorn Kasaem Rd. (☎611 645), 1km south of the bridge. *Poste Restante.* Open M-F 8:30am-4:30pm, Sa-Su 9am-noon.

Postal Code: 64000.

ACCOMMODATIONS

Sukhothai has the highest number of charming guesthouses in the region. It is also a convenient base from which to explore the region. Most guesthouses lie near the centrally located Yom River and fill up during Sukhothai's long tourist season (June-Feb.)—call a few days in advance to reserve a room.

Ban Thai Guest House, 38 Pravet Nakhon Rd. (☎610 163; guesthouse_banthai@yahoo.com), on the west bank. Take a left after the bridge at Thai Farmers Bank and walk 150m. Friendly owners have lots of tourist info. Rooms newly renovated. Singles 150฿; doubles 200฿; concrete rooms or bungalows with bath 200-250฿. ❷

No. 4 Guest House, 140/4 Soi Klong Maelampan (☎610 165). From Charot Withi Thong Rd., turn at the *songthaew* lot. From the bus station follow the path behind the station (400m). Take a *tuk-tuk* after dark. Tranquil bamboo bungalows with porch, sofa, open-air shower, and mosquito nets. Excellent tourist info. Thai cooking lessons 1500฿ (150฿ per dish). Singles 150฿; doubles 180฿; nice 3-room suites (1-4 people) 350฿. ❷

Riverhouse (☎620 396; riverhouse_7@hotmail.com), on Kuhasuwan Rd. 150m north of Thai Farmers Bank. Has a better view of the river, overlooking the *wat* and day market. Rooms upstairs in main house with floor mat and mosquito net: singles 150฿; doubles 200฿. New rooms with tiled floor and bath 200฿/250฿, with A/C 300฿/350฿. ❷

Yupa House, 44/10 Pravet Nakhon Rd., Soi Mekapat (☎612 578). Turn-off 25m beyond Ban Thai Guest House. Friendly Mr. Chuer and his wife, Yupa, run this traditional home-stay. There's no patio, but top-floor rooms open onto balconies. Cheap laundry service. Dorms 60฿; rooms 100฿, with bath 150฿. ❶

FOOD

Daytime foodstalls congregate on the side-streets west of **Charot Withi Thong Road;** at night, the best bet is **Ramkhamhaeng Road,** the first cross-street on the east side of the river, or the stalls just east of the bridge. The *pad thai* here is a point of pride for the people of Sukhothai. **Foodstalls** ❶ on Charot Withi Thong Rd. leading up to the bridge have fantastic meals at great prices (20฿). Off the road to the north in front of the *wat* are a variety of **fruitstalls** ❶ (watermelon 10฿).

Dream Cafe, 96/1 Singhawat Rd., next to Patanavej Hospital. The best restaurant in town–the price tag is worth it. The owner, Chaba, will gladly walk you through the extensive menu and explain the subtleties of Thai herbs. Ask her to brew a fruit tea (not on the menu) or take a stamina shot, which improves everything from strength to sexual desire. Roasted eggplant and basil with shrimp 120฿. Entrees 100-150฿. Open daily 10am-midnight. MC/V. ❸

Coffee Home, on Rat-u-thit Rd., next to Lotus Village. Pleasant outdoor candlelit dining with elegantly presented food. *Kiao krop* (pork wonton in plum sauce) 65฿. Chicken sauté in oyster sauce 80฿. Coffee 20-50฿. Open daily 11am-11pm. ❷

Thai Noodles Sukhothai 2, 139 Charot Withi Thong Rd. It's 300m past the school on the right, at the turn-off to Ruean Thai. Look for a restaurant with small ivy-covered fountains and a "2" on the sign in all-Thai script. The specialty is *kuay tiaw sukhothai* (noodle soup with pork, green beans, coriander, and chilli; 15฿). Phenomenal *pad thai* (20฿). Top half of Thai menu is noodles, bottom half rice dishes. Open daily 10am-3pm. ❶

Ban Thai Restaurant, 38 Pravet Nakhon Rd., at Ban Thai Guest House. Serves great food on a nice patio. A great place to get tourist info and meet other travelers. Tofu can be substituted for meat. Sweet and sour pork with pineapple, papaya, and mango 60฿. Milk and fruit shakes 15฿. Open daily 7am-9pm. ❷

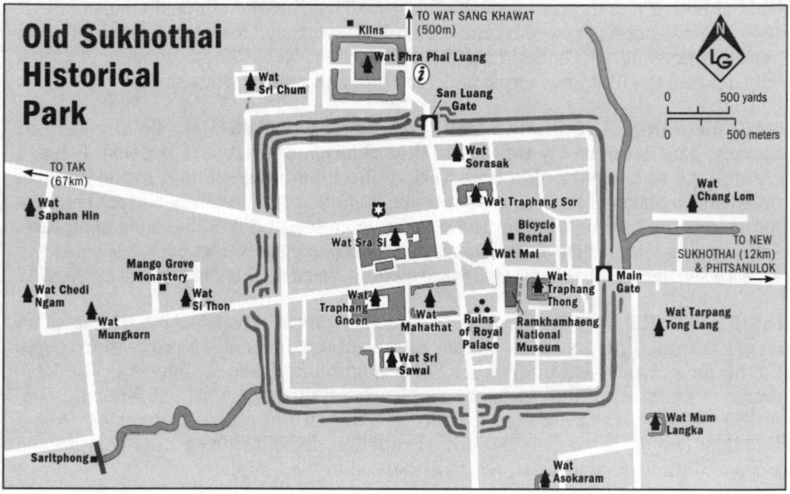

SIGHTS AND ENTERTAINMENT

Wat Thawet is surrounded by a three-dimensional maze of statues that morbidly illustrate the punishments awaiting disobedient Buddhists. Inspired entirely by the dream of the *wat*'s now-deceased monk, highlights include a woman with a rooster head and a man being forced to eat his own intestines. To get there, go on Charot Withi Thong Rd. Turn left on Bypass Rd., go over the bridge, and take the first paved right. The turn-off is 6km down the highway on your right, 700m after the major intersection with another highway. Great fried bananas are sold along the highway.

The **Sangkhalok Museum** displays hundreds of artifacts detailing the daily lives of people who inhabited the nearby ruins. Ceramic masterpieces from the Lanna Kingdom, around 700 years old, are also on display. It's 1.5km outside of town. Follow Singhawat Rd. out of the city as it turns into Hwy. 12 (toward Phitsanulok). Turn left at the first major intersection (Hwy. 101); it's 100m on the left. (☎614 333. Open daily 8am-5pm. 100฿, children under age 17, 50฿.)

A nightspot for *farang* and Thais alike is the **Chopper Bar,** 101 Charot Withi Thong Rd., on your left walking from the river to the old city bus stop. Transsexuality is not the theme—it's incidental—but adds flavor nonetheless. (Large Singha 65฿. Folk music 8-10pm. Open daily 1pm-midnight.)

DAYTRIPS FROM SUKHOTHAI

OLD SUKHOTHAI HISTORICAL PARK

To reach the park, located 12km west of New Sukhothai, take the red-, white-, and blue-striped songthaew *that leave from the lot 200m west of Praruang Bridge (20min., every 20min. 6am-6pm, 10฿). Park ☎697 310, museum 612 167. Park open daily 6am-7pm; museum open daily 9am-4pm. Old City Entrance 40฿, Museum 30฿, North/West/South Entrances an additional 30฿ each. Bike 10฿, motorbike 20฿, car 50฿ extra fee. Combined pass, which includes all of Old Sukhothai's attractions, plus those of Si Satchanalai, is a great value at 150฿ and is good for visits within 30 days.*

Old Sukhothai was the center of the first true Thai Kingdom. It peaked around AD 1300 and was soon annexed by the expanding Ayutthaya Kingdom. The Sukhothai period is considered Thailand's golden age, when King Ramkhamhaeng supposedly devised the first Thai script and Thai arts and culture flourished.

MAIN ENTRANCE AND RAMKHAMHAENG NATIONAL MUSEUM. To the left of the east gate is the newly renovated **Ramkhamhaeng National Museum.** It has a chronology of ancient Sukhothai, various Buddha images found in the excavations, and replicas of ancient inscriptions, including the first Thai script. The centerpiece is the bronze Walking Buddha, an example of Sukhothai-style sculpture. (*The east gate serves as the main entrance and is where* songthaew *from Sukhothai arrive. This entrance sells excellent brochures for 3฿. Bikes can be rented close to the entrance for 20-30฿.*)

INSIDE THE OLD CITY WALL. The town centerpiece is **Wat Mahathat.** The main *chedi* is famed for its lotus shape, an architectural feature particular to the Sukhothai period. Also unique are several standing Buddha images in the Ceylonese style. Many of the ornate carvings around the *wat* remain in fantastic condition. Nearby **Wat Sri Sawai,** a south-facing Hindu shrine converted into a Buddhist temple, is the only Sukhothai ruin that doesn't face east. Its centerpiece is a set of three huge *prangs*, which shoot out of the temple.

NORTH OF THE OLD CITY WALL. North of **San Luang Gato** is **Wat Phra Phai Luang,** where there is more room to explore and fewer tourists. Situated on an island, the *wat* has a magnificent Khmer-style *stupa* and plaster reliefs of Buddha. The *wat* is treasured by archaeologists for its traces of pre-Sukhothai period art. **Wat Sri Chum** sits just to the west. Its *mondop*, a cone-shaped structure, houses the must-see 15m "talking" Buddha. The great King Ramkhamhaeng, assembling his troops for war, brought them in front of the massive Buddha image at the *wat*. In a terrifying supernatural display, he compelled the image to speak and urge the soldiers to fight bravely. (Since those days of yore, a hidden staircase has been discovered that leads to an opening behind the Buddha's mouth.) The tunnels on your right and left as you enter the temple were escape passages for the king.

WEST OF THE OLD CITY WALL. At **Wat Mungkorn,** with its distinctively circular *chedi*, the road splits. To the left lies **Saritphong (Phra Ruang Dam),** an earthen dam 487m long and 4m wide, which today can hold up to 400,000m³ of water. The water was necessary in Sukhothai's glory days to keep the moats full and the gardens green. The road to the right leads back to the main road between Sukhothai and Tak, but not before passing the entrance to **Wat Saphan Hin,** 200m up the hill. The *wat* contains a towering Buddha in standing position, known as **Phra Attharot.**

SI SATCHANALAI AND CHALIANG

Old Si Satchanalai is 56km north of Sukhothai, and the park entrance is 1km west off Hwy. 101. Take a public bus from Sukhothai bus station (1hr., every 30min. 7am-4:30pm, 30฿). Make sure the driver knows you are getting off at the old city, as new Si Satchanalai is 8km farther north. Last bus returns before 5pm from Hwy. 101. ☎679 211. Park open daily 8am-5pm. 40฿. Admission to Chaliang is included in Si Satchanalai admission, and park hours are the same. Kilns open daily 8am-4:30pm. 30฿.

During the 13th century, Thailand's golden age, Si Satchanalai rivaled Sukhothai in wealth and sophistication. When Ayutthaya rose to preeminence in the late 14th century, however, Si Satchanalai sank into anonymity. A UNESCO World Heritage Site, Si Satchanalai has excellent tourist facilities, including a **Visitors Information Center** marked by signs from the roads entering the park. Near the entrance, you

THAILAND

can rent bikes for 20฿, tents for 80฿, and sleeping bags for 20฿. Despite its historical significance and impressive ruins, Si Satchanalai does not receive many visitors; at times, it will feel like you have the park all to yourself. The unearthing of 200 **kilns** at **Ban Ko Noi,** 5km beyond the park, challenged conceptions of ancient Siam as isolated and technologically simple. The city's kilns produced advanced celadons (ceramics known today as *sawankhalok* or *sangkhalok*) for export to countries as far away as the Philippines. The Siam Cement Company has spent 2-3 million *baht* making a few of these kilns accessible to tourists. Kiln #61 is located in Chaliang and has an adjacent museum. Kilns #42 and 123 (together) are northwest of Si Satchanalai, along the river, and are covered for protection from the elements. Only one ticket is necessary to see both kiln sites.

KAMPHAENG PHET

Songthaew run from Sukhothai (35฿) to the bus station in Kamphaeng Phet. Ask to be dropped off on the east side of the river, opposite the bus station, for convenience. Sights open daily 8am-4pm. 40฿ entrance fee gets you into both the Old City and Arunyik Temples.

Kamphaeng Phet ("diamond wall"), 77km south of Sukhothai, attracts daytrippers wishing to see the three UNESCO World Heritage Sites in northern Thailand (the other two being Sukhothai and Si Satchanalai National Parks). The history of this northern town begins with the Sukhothai period of the 14th century and the Ayutthaya period of the 15th century, when it was a principal city, strategically located to defend itself against the kingdoms of Lanna (Chiang Mai) and Myanmar (Burma). A northern section of Kamphaeng Phet was once surrounded by a fort and a moat, some of which are still visible. The main attractions of the Old City are **Wat Phra Kaew** and **Wat Phra That,** both situated in a beautifully maintained park. Hundreds of years ago, Wat Phra Kaew was the biggest and most important temple in Thailand, supposedly housing the Emerald Buddha (now in Bangkok). The **Arunyik (Forest) Temples** are another sight of interest, a couple hundred meters behind Wat Phra Kaew. These temples, built by Sukhothai-era monks, were originally constructed in the woods to foster a meditative calm for the monks. Today the area is a park suitable for a leisurely walk or bike ride.

THAILAND

PHITSANULOK

Buses from Sukhothai to Phitsanulok run every 30min. 6:20am-8pm.

Phitsanulok is a gateway to northern Thailand. **Wat Phra Si Ratana Mahathat (Wat Yai),** at the northern end of Puttaboocha Rd., shelters Phitsanulok's jewel. Cast in 1357, the spectacular **Phra Buddha Chinnarat** ("Victorious King") is one of the world's most commonly reproduced Buddha images. The left wing of the *wat* (if you're facing Phra Buddha Chinnarat) has been turned into a mediocre museum. (Museum open W-Su 9am-4pm. *Wat* open daily 7am-6pm. Suggested 20฿ entrance donation includes brochure. Sarongs provided free of charge to the bare-legged.) Other sights include: the **Sgt. Maj. Thawee Folk Museum,** 26/43 Wisutkasat Rd., which preserves local traditions (☎212 749; open Tu-Su 8:30am-4:30pm; free, but donations accepted); the **Buranathai Buddha Image Foundry,** where you can see handcrafted bronze Buddhas (☎258 715; open daily 8am-5pm); and **Wat Chulamanee,** built in 1464, 6km outside the city, best reached by motorcycle taxi (100฿).

LAMPANG ☎054

This sprawling city isn't impressive—its concrete-banked Wang River, congested streets, and mediocre sights don't attract many visitors. The few tourists who do wander through will agree that Lampang's friendly citizens are its redemption.

TRANSPORTATION

The **airport** is on Sanambin Rd. 2km south of town center. **Thai Airways,** 236 Sanambin Rd. (☎217 078; open daily 8:30am-5:30pm), flies to Bangkok (M, Sa 11:15am; 2055฿). **PB Air,** at the airport (☎226 238; open daily 8am-6pm), also flies to Bangkok (M-F and Su 9:55am, 5:10pm; 2055฿, departure and insurance tax 105฿). The **Lampang Railroad Station** (☎318 648) is on Prasanmaitri Rd. 2km southwest of the clocktower. To reach the station, flag down a westbound *songthaew* (10-20฿). Trains go to Bangkok (10-12hr., 6 per day, 146-284฿) via Phitsanulok (5hr., 88-151฿) and Ayutthaya (9hr., 135-261฿); Chiang Mai (2hr., 9 per day, 23-53฿). The **bus station** (☎227 410) is off Asia 1 Hwy., 2km southwest of the clocktower, with buses to: Bangkok (8hr., 7:30am-9pm, 193-540฿); Chiang Mai (2hr., every 30min. 2am-9pm, 39-70฿); Chiang Rai (5hr., every 45min. 5am-5pm, 81-113฿); Nan (4hr., 11 per day 8am-midnight, 86-154฿); and Sukhothai (4-5hr., every hr. 6:30am-4:30pm, 91-164฿) via Phitsanulok (4hr., 91-196฿). Blue **songthaew** go anywhere in town (10฿). Trips to and from the bus and train stations cost 10฿ more. **Samlor** usually cost around 50฿. The guesthouses on the river rent **motorbikes** (200฿ per day with passport deposit) and **bicycles** (30-40฿ per day).

THAILAND

ORIENTATION AND PRACTICAL INFORMATION

Most roads radiate from the **clocktower roundabout** near the town center. **Boonyawat Road,** the town's main commercial road, heads east past hotels, banks, and shops. In the opposite direction, **Tah Krao Road** runs past the **Aswin Market. Suren Road,** off the west end of Tah Krao Rd., runs to the **train station. Thipchang Road** lies one block north of the clocktower. **Talad Gao Road,** one block north of Thipchang Rd., runs alongside the **Wang River** and is the location of the town's most popular guesthouses and restaurants. The bus station, on **Jantsurin Road,** and the train station, on **Prasanmaitri Road,** are both about 2km southwest of the clocktower.

Services include: a **tourist office** on Boonyawat Rd. just past Praisanee Rd. (☎218 823; open daily 8:30am-4:30pm); tours leave from the horsecart stand opposite the police station on Boonyawat Rd. (30min. 200฿; 1hr. 200-300฿); **Bangkok Bank,** 36-44 Thipchang Rd., with a 24hr. **ATM** (☎228 135; AmEx/Cirrus/MC/PLUS/V; open M-F 8:30am-3:30pm); **Tesaban Market 1,** at the intersection of Boonyawat and Rajawang Rd.; **Aswin Market** next to the clocktower; **night foodstalls** open until 11pm; **police** (☎217 017), on Boonyawat Rd. opposite City Hall; a **pharmacy** on the corner of Boonyawat and Praisanee Rd. (☎223 869; open daily 8am-10pm); **Khelang Nakorn-Ram Hospital,** 79/12 Phaholyothin Rd. (☎225 100; open 24hr.; AmEx/MC/V); **Lampang Telecommunication Center,** 99 Phaholyothin Rd., 500m before the hospital (☎221 700; **international phone** and fax; open daily 7am-8pm); **CATNET** at the GPO or Telecom Center (11฿ per hr.) and the **GPO** on Thipchang Rd.; follow Boonyawat Rd. to City Hall and then turn left on Praisanee Rd. (☎224 069. *Poste Restante.* **Lenso** telephone. Open M-F 8:30am-4:30pm, Sa-Su 9am-noon.) **Postal Code:** 52000.

ACCOMMODATIONS AND FOOD

Hotels are clustered along Boonyawat Rd., and the few guesthouses are near the Wang River. **Boon Ma Guesthouse ❷,** 256 Talad Gao Rd., is 100m east of Riverside Guest House (away from the clocktower). Its enormous, clean rooms are Lampang's best value. (☎322 653. Motorbike rental 200฿. Singles 100฿, larger rooms with hot bath 150฿; doubles 150฿/200฿.) The nearby **Riverside Guest House ❷,** 286 Talad Gao Rd., has a veranda over the river. From the clocktower, walk along

Boonyawat Rd. with the river on your left, then turn left on the *soi* with the sign to the guesthouse. (☎227 005. Laundry. Motorbike rental 200฿ per day. Tours of surrounding sights 350฿ each, 800฿ min. Doubles 250฿, riverside 350฿; suites 600฿.)

For strongly flavored Thai dishes try **Riverside Restaurant ❷,** on Thipchang Rd. From the clocktower, walk to the river; it's 250m to the right. (Dishes 40-80฿. Pizza on W and Sa-Su. Band starts at 7:30pm. Open daily 10am-midnight.) Next door is **Relax By Anytime Pub and Restaurant ❷,** the current hotspot for young and trendy locals. Fried rice with meat is 45฿, seafood soups 60-80฿. (Band starts at 9pm. Open daily 6am-1pm.)

SIGHTS

Wat Phra Kaew Don Tao, in the northeastern corner of town, housed the Emerald Buddha during the reign of King Anantayot (r. 1436-68). A large reclining gold Buddha is in a building to its left. The *wihaan* is open to visitors on Buddhist holidays only. (*Wat* open daily 6am-6:30pm. 20฿.) The **Lampang Herb Conservation Center** (☎350 787; www.herblpg.com), a spa and research center, is one of the most fascinating places in Lampang. Though it's only a few kilometers outside town, its off-the-beaten-path location makes private transportation the best option. Go approximately 2km west on Jamatawee Rd. (Hwy. 1039). When you see signs for the center, veer right on the street across from the 7-Eleven, go 400m, and turn left on the dirt road just before the bridge; the center is 200m down on your left. Organic shampoo is available in the vapor rooms and should be enjoyed after the free barefoot health walk in the gardens. (Open daily 8am-8pm.)

DAYTRIPS FROM LAMPANG

WAT PHRA THAT LAMPANG LUANG. Eighteen kilometers southwest of Lampang in the town of Ko Kha is **Wat Phra That Lampang Luang,** one of northern Thailand's finest displays of religious architecture. The *wat* also hold Lampang's most sacred Buddha. Constructed in 1486, the chapel houses two important images: **Phra Jao Lan Tang,** cast in 1563, is enclosed in a golden *mondop* near the rear of the temple, and **Phra Jao Tan Jai** sits behind the *mondop*. A Buddha footprint lies behind Haw Phra Phutthabat, constructed in 1149. Beyond the back wall, a shrine showcases the temple's most valuable Buddha image, a **jade Buddha** from the Chiang Saen period (1057-1757). To the south of the complex are several small but interesting museums. *(Songthaew to Ko Kha leave from Robwiang Rd., 1 block west of Praisanee Rd. (20฿). The wat is about 3km north of Ko Kha—negotiate with a driver in Ko Kha (20-30฿) or catch a songthaew bound for Hang Chat and tell the driver to stop at the wat (10฿). If driving from Lampang, take Asia Hwy. 1 south and take the exit for Ko Kha, then look for signs to the wat.)*

THAI ELEPHANT CONSERVATION CENTER. The Thai Elephant Conservation Center, 37km west of Lampang, is on the highway between Chiang Mai and Lampang, outside the Thung Kwian Forest. The center was established to employ elephants and their *mahouts* (handlers), given their decreasing importance in traditional labors such as logging and construction. Bundles of sugar cane or bananas sell for (10฿), and an extra 50฿ buys a 10min. elephant ride. A 30min. ride through the forest costs 400฿. (Rides daily 8am-3:30pm.) The center has a homestay program that lets you stay and work with *mahouts*. *(Take a Chiang Mai-bound bus; ask to be let off at the Center (35min., 20฿). The show ground is 2km farther on foot. The center is located on Hwy. 11, 37km west from Lampang. (☎229 042). Shows daily 9:30, 11am; weekends 1pm. 80฿.)*

CHAE SON (JAE SORN) NATIONAL PARK AND KEW LOM DAM. This national park boasts modern facilities and **hot springs.** The springs' main draw is not the **bubbling sulfurous pools,** but rather the luxurious **private baths** (20฿; 5฿ for shower). **Chae Son Waterfall,** plummeting 150m, is 1km farther up the road. The concrete staircase leading to the fall's origin is more imposing than the waterfall itself. An easy 3km nature trail along the river links the two sites (fish food 10฿). The **Kew Lom Dam** is a relaxation spot favored by Thai and *farang* alike. Packed during the holidays, the island can be reached by boat (50฿). Make **bungalow** reservations with the Royal Irrigation Department (☎02 241 4806) or Kew Lom Resort (☎223 772). *(To get a songthaew to Chae Son Falls, 70km from Lampang, look for the dirt parking lot 100m down the soi running between Thipchang and Talad Gao Rd., 1 block toward the GPO from Bangkok Bank (1½hr., 50฿). Returning will be difficult;* Let's Go *does not recommend hitchhiking, but families visiting on the weekend may offer rides. If driving, take Pratum Rd. (Hwy. 1035) north from Lampang. Park open daily 6am-6pm. Park admission 200฿, students 100฿. Waterfall 200฿. Camping permitted (30฿). Tent rental 180฿ for 2 people, 250฿ for 3. 3- to 15-person bungalows 600-3000฿ (☎229 000). Songthaew to Kew Lom Dam do not run regularly; you will have to charter one or use private transportation. Take Asia Hwy. 1 north, then follow the signs for the turn-off. Kew Lom Dam is 38km north of Lampang. Boat from Lampang 50฿. Open daily 6am-6pm.)*

MAE SAI ☎053

With an established opium trade and a burgeoning gem trade due to a new sapphire mine in the Shan State, Mae Sai's future looked bright—until a full-scale battle broke out in February 2001 among the Shan, Thai, and Myanmar troops. Three Thai civilians died, and the resulting tensions closed the border for four months. A similar situation occurred in early 2002. While the precious stone- and antique-trade is no longer what it was, it's hard to tell this from the bustling streets.

TRANSPORTATION

The **Mae Sai Bus Terminal** is 4km south of the bridge along Phahonyothin Rd. Red *songthaew* head there every 10min. (5฿). **Buses** go to: Bangkok (14hr.; 7am, 5:30, 5:45pm; 481฿); Chiang Mai (5hr.; 8, 9, 11am, 2, 3:10pm; 95-171฿); Chiang Rai (1½hr., every 15min. 6am-6pm, 25฿) via Ban Pasang (45min., 15฿). South of Thai Farmers Bank, blue *songthaew* go to Chiang Saen (1hr., every hr. 7am-2pm, 30฿) via Sop Ruak (40min., 20฿). **Motorcycle taxis** and **samlor** pepper Mae Sai. Rides within the city cost 10-30฿. A trip from the guesthouses to the bus terminal should cost 30฿. Green *songthaew* go up and down Phahonyothin Rd. (5฿). **The Honda Shop** (☎731 113), on Phahonyothin Rd. nearly opposite the Bangkok Bank, rents 110cc motorbikes for 150฿ with passport deposit.

ORIENTATION AND PRACTICAL INFORMATION

Mae Sai is 61km north of Chiang Rai, 68km northeast of Mae Salong, and 35km northwest of the Golden Triangle. Hwy. 110 becomes **Phahonyothin Road** and runs north to the **border,** marked by a gate and **Friendship Bridge.** Phahonyothin Rd. hosts banks and shops. **Silamjoi Road** follows the river west toward guesthouses.

Services include: the **Immigration Office,** on Phahonyothin Rd., 2km south of bridge (☎731 008; 10-day visa extension 1900฿, 1-month visa extension for 60-day tourist visas; bring 2 photos and 2 photocopies of passport; open daily 8:30am-4:30pm); the Immigration Office at the **border** (☎733 261); **Thai Farmers Bank,** 122/1 Phahonyothin Rd. (☎640 786; open M-F 8:30am-3:30pm; 24hr. Cirrus/MC/V **ATM**); **ambulance** (☎731 300); **tourist police** in a booth next to the bridge (☎733 850; open daily 8am-5pm); **Drugstore,** next to and south of the police station (owner speaks excellent English; open daily 8am-8pm); the **Mae Sai Hospital,** 101 Moo 10 Pomaharat Rd. (☎751 300), off Phahonyothin Rd. 2km south; the **Telecom Center,** next to the post office (Fax; **CATNET;** open M-F 8:30am-4:30pm); **Internet** (take the last right before the bridge, look for the sign leading to the 2nd fl.; 20฿ per 30min., 30฿ per hr.; open daily 9am-9pm); and the **post office,** 230/40-41 Phahonyothin Rd., 4km south of the bridge and, despite the address, not on the main road. (☎731 402. *Poste Restante.* Open M-F 8:30am-4:30pm, Sa-Su 9am-noon.) **Postal Code:** 57130.

BORDER CROSSING: MAE SAI/TACHILEK. Thirty-day and 60-day visas can be renewed by crossing into Tachilek and returning to Mae Sai on the same day. Go to passport control at the border gate and get a departure stamp. Proceed across the bridge and hand over 250฿ or US$5 and your passport. The Myanmar border control will stamp your passport and keep it until you exit the country. When you re-enter Thailand, you'll be able to stay another 30 or 60 days, depending on your visa. When you surrender your passport in Myanmar, you will get a thin **piece of paper.** That piece of paper is your passport, so hold onto it. The border is open daily 6:30am-6:30pm. Myanmar time is 30min. behind Thailand, so its border is open daily 6am-6pm. Thai immigration officials ask that you cross back by 5pm. (See **Myanmar, To Go or Not To Go?,** p. 452.)

ACCOMMODATIONS AND FOOD

Mae Sai Guest House ❷, 688 Wiengpangkam Rd. (☎732 021), 500m west of the border, has thatched bungalows and a restaurant overlooking Myanmar. (Singles and doubles 100฿-150฿; doubles with bath 300฿; bungalows on the water 400-500฿.) West of the border, the **King Kobra Guest House ❷,** 135/5 Silamjoi Rd. (☎733 055), has a restaurant, laundry, and nightly movies. (Singles 120฿, with bath 200฿; doubles 150฿/250฿; "VIP" room 350฿.)

The **night market** along Phahonyothin Rd. has dishes on display, so point to what you want. (Open daily 7-10pm.) Pamper your palate at **Jo Jo Coffee House ❷,** 233/1 Phahonyothin Rd., opposite the Thai Farmers Bank. (Open daily 6am-5pm.) **Rabieng Kaew Restaurant ❸,** 150m south of the bridge on Phahonyothin Rd., is one of the few restaurants open at night. (Open daily 9am-10pm.)

DAYTRIPS FROM MAE SAI

THAM LUANG (GREAT CAVE) NATIONAL PARK. The national park lies 8km south of Mae Sai, 2.5km off Hwy. 110. Its 200m deep caverns include the very manageable **Buddha Cave** and the 7km deep **Royal Luang Cave.** (Open daily 7am-5pm.) Maps of the area are available at the entrance, but you should bring a flashlight. Two more caves are inside **Wat Tham Plaa,** 12km south and 3km west of Mae Sai along Hwy. 110. *Samlor* along the highway will take you for 20฿. Fresh water runs through **Tham Plaa (Fish Cave),** also called "Monkey Cave." The adventurous can explore **Tham Gu Gaeo,** rumored to lead to Myanmar. The path to the right of the temple leads to attendants who will take visitors to a Buddha village 2km away (50-70฿ per person). Bring a flashlight. *(There are two marked entrances to Tham Luang on Hwy. 110; take the well-paved one. After the 3-headed dragon, continue straight for Khun Nam Nang Non (Sleeping Lady Lagoon), or take the 1st right and then the next left (about 1km) to Tham Luang. It may be possible to find a motorcycle taxi or samlor at the entrance from the highway. There are no guides, sometimes you can convince locals to join you for a nominal fee.)*

THAILAND

DOI TUNG. The **Royal Villa,** located in Doi Tung, is 32km from Mae Sai and was the home of the Princess Mother (mother of King Rama VIII and King Rama IX) from 1988 until she died 1994. The palace has an exquisite carving of the zodiac in the reception hall. Please dress conservatively. The **Mah Fah Luang Gardens,** a beautiful blend of Thai and European garden styles, flow down the hill from the villa. The brand-new **Princess Mother Commemorative Hall** is located at the entrance. (All open 6:30am-5:30pm. Royal Villa 70฿, garden 80฿, Commemorative Hall 30฿, all three 150฿.) About 8km past the villa is the peak of Doi Tung (1500m), with **Wat Phra That Doi Tung** and its twin *chedi*. The staircase provides beautiful views over the valley. There is a stunning back route to Doi Tung from Mae Sai but it is extremely dangerous if you stray into Myanmar. Ask at your guesthouse for current info about the border situation. The route leading from Hwy. 110 to Doi Tung is heavily touristed and safe to travel. *(To reach Doi Tung, take a green* songthaew *to Mae Chan (15฿). At the turn-off from Hwy. 110, purple* songthaew *take visitors the other half of the trip.)*

SOP RUAK. Sop Ruak may be its official name, but most refer to where Myanmar, Laos, and Thailand meet as **Sam Liam Tongkham** (Golden Triangle). In the middle of town, the **House of Opium** features exhibits on the history and cultivation of opium. After showing how to grow and smoke opium, it closes with a message about the dangers of drug addiction. Dioramas on the **Padong** (longneck villagers) and *plaa buek* (giant catfish) are thrown in for good measure. The museum does not have the same quantity of info on opium nor quality of organization as the Hill Tribe Museums in Chiang Mai and Chiang Rai. (☎784 062. Open daily 7am-6pm. 20฿.) For a view of the three countries, head up the five-dragon-headed staircase next to the bank, then follow the road behind **Wat Phra That Doi Pu** up the hill to the viewpoint. Just 2km north of Siam Bank, toward Mae Sai, is the world's largest opium research center. The state-of-the-art complex opened in 2004, and its **Hall of Opium** (☎784 444; www.goldentrianglepark.com; open Tu-Su 10am-3:30pm) not only presents the history of opium, but also attempts to recreate the emotional experience that opium addicts face through multimedia exhibits and sensory stimulation. *(To get to Sop Ruak catch a* songthaew *(45min., 25฿).)*

THAILAND

MAE SALONG ☎053

Fifty years after the Chinese Nationalists fled to this mountaintop village in the wake of Communist victory, Mae Salong maintains its Chinese identity. Chinese characters adorn door frames, lanterns decorate teahouses, and the dialect of China's southern province, Yunnan, is more common than Thai. The slopes surrounding the town, once covered by jungle, now lie barren to accommodate the year-round tea harvest. Pockets of natural beauty still exist, making Mae Salong a nice daytrip. Try to visit in January, when the cherry trees are blossoming.

TRANSPORTATION AND PRACTICAL INFORMATION. *Songthaew* run frequently early in the morning and leave when full; if the wait is unbearable, you can pay the full fare (300฿). To get to Chiang Rai, take a light blue *songthaew* to Ban Pasang (1hr., 7am-2pm, 50฿), and then flag down a passing bus (1hr., every 30min. 6am-6pm, 20฿). To get to Mae Sai, take the light blue *songthaew* to Ban Pasang, then catch a bus heading north (45min., every 20min. 7am-7pm, 20฿). Yellow *songthaew* to Tha Ton (1½hr., 7am-2pm, 50฿) leave from the small **day market,** 1km toward Tha Ton from the town center. The market features Akha wares and Chinese herbs. The **main road** through Mae Salong stretches 2.5km and is a continuation of roads from Tha Ton (Rte. 1234) and Ban Pasang (Rte. 1130).

The town center is near the guesthouses and has **food vendors** and a **mosque.** The **morning market** is off the road to Mae Salong Resort. Other services include: **Thai Military Bank,** opposite Khumnaipol Resort (☎765 159; open M-F 8:30am-3:30pm; AmEx/Cirrus/MC/PLUS/V **ATM** open daily 6am-10pm); a **police booth** (☎767 7109) near the Mae Salong Villa; and **Internet** at the Golden Dragon. (60฿ per hr.) The nearest **hospital** is in Mae Chan and there are **no international phones.**

ACCOMMODATIONS AND FOOD. Since few travelers choose to stay the night in Mae Salong, the accommodation options are somewhat disappointing. **Golden Dragon ❷,** on the main road between the Mae Salong Resort and Akha Guest House, has clean rooms with hot showers and balconies. (☎765 009. Singles 200฿; doubles 300฿.) The family-style **Akha Mae Salong Guest House ❷,** just off the main road near the mosque, has four huge rooms with a common bath. The owner sells Akha wares, distributes useful maps (10฿), arranges trips to hill-tribe villages (400฿), and speaks English. (☎765 103. Singles and doubles 130฿; triples 150฿.)

Yunnanese **noodle shops** and **vendors** abound (5฿ per serving). **Teashops** provide a relaxing ambience; a kettle of Mae Salong tea soothes for 50฿. **Mini ❷,** 300m toward Tha Ton from the Golden Dragon, serves *kanom jiin naam ngiaw* (Yunnanese noodle soup, 25฿), the town specialty. Ask for vegetarian options. The store also rents motorbikes for 200฿ per day. (Lao beer 50฿. Open daily 7am-10:30pm.) **Sakura Restaurant ❸** is a popular Thai/Chinese restaurant in Mae Salong Resort. (Chicken with cashew nuts: small 80฿, large 120฿. Open daily 7am-10pm.)

SIGHTS. For an awesome view, follow the road to the Mae Salong Resort and walk up the steps to the **pagoda** at the top of Doi Mae Salong. Take the side road, not the steps leading up the front of the *wat.* From here, a road continues 4km through the mountains, finally curving back into town via the day market. Area hill-tribes include **Akha, Lahu, Lisu,** and, in smaller numbers, **Hmong** and **Yao.** There aren't many organized trekking groups. The intrepid can set off alone, but don't wander too far; in addition to hill-tribe villages, pockets of Shan and KMT groups line the Myanmar border. Drug trade and clashes have erupted between Khun Sa's Shan United Army and the Wa National Army. Pick up a map at Akha Mae Salong or Shin Sane Guest House (10฿) and ask in town about the current situation. The foot-weary can inquire about 4hr. **horseback rides** at Akha Mae Salong or Shin Sane Guest House (400฿ per person). For those who don't have the time or resources to stay overnight in a hill-tribe village, **Ban Lorcha** is more illuminating than a visit to a museum. The Akha village, with the help of the PDA, has established a **"Living Museum"** in order for the villagers to benefit from tourism without drastically changing their lifestyles. An entrance fee of 40฿ includes a guide who will walk you through the village. There are also two other villages between Ban Lorcha and Tha Ton that travelers can visit. Ban Lorcha is on Rte. 1089 between Tha Ton and Mae Chan, 1km toward Tha Ton from the turn-off to Mae Salong. From Mae Salong, take yellow *songthaew* headed to Tha Ton (20min., 15฿).

CHIANG KHONG ☎053

Chiang Khong (pop. 10,000) is the archetypal border town. **Buses** go to Chiang Mai (6hr., 6am, 121฿; with A/C 8am, 218฿ and 11am, 169฿) and Bangkok (12-13hr.; 7am, 3:30, 4pm; 390-491฿). The **booking offices** (☎655 732) are next to each other, between the bridge and service station. Buses to Chiang Rai leave from the market across from the Esso Station (3hr., every hr. 5am-5pm, 50฿). The main **Saiklang Road** runs northwest to southeast, parallel to the Mekong River. **Soi 13** is at the southeast end near the bridge and day market. **Soi 1,** home to several guesthouses, is a 25min. walk northwest from the market at the northwestern end of town. Services include: the **Immigration Office** next to the ferry pier to Laos (daily 7am-5pm); the **main immigration office** located next to Soi 13 (☎791 322; visa extensions 1900฿; open M-F 8:30am-noon and 1-4:30pm); **Thai Farmers Bank,** 20m south of Soi 7 (open M-F 8:30am-3:30pm); the **police** (☎791 426), next door to the immigration office; the **Chiang Khong Hospital,** 354 Moo 10, 3km outside of town (☎791 206; no credit cards; open 24hr.); **@Net.com,** across from Bamboo Riverside Guest House (40฿ per hr.); and the **post office** near Soi 3 with **international phones.** (☎791 555. Open M-F 8:30am-4:30pm, Sa-Su 9am-noon.) **Postal Code:** 57140.

BORDER CROSSING: CHIANG KHONG/HOUIE XAY. The ferry (20฿) across the Mekong leaves from the old pier and takes less than 15min. Frequent daily departures 8am-5pm. As of February 2004, 15-day visas are obtainable on arrival in Houie Xay for 1200฿. Check in with the immigration office by the pier to get your departure stamp, then board the ferry. The cheapest option is to get a visa in Bangkok or Chiang Mai (15-day visa with 2- to 3-day delay 700-800฿). If in Chiang Khong, try **Traveler Corner** (☎655 374; open daily 8am-9pm) or **Ann Tour** (☎655 198; open daily 7am-8pm), which both have offices on Saiklang Rd. near Soi 2. 15-day visas are 1500฿ for same-day service and 900฿ with a 3-day wait. 30-day visas are 1900฿ with a 3-day wait and 1500฿ with a 4-day wait. Going through a guesthouse instead of a travel agency may raise the price. Once in Houie Xay, catch a speedboat (6-9hr., 8am-1pm, 1100฿) or a slow boat (2 days, 10:30am, 650฿) to Luang Prabang. If you do the latter, pack food, water, and a book; the boats stop intermittently before docking overnight in Pakbeng. Special boats that stop along the Mekong may be organized in Chiang Khong for those who want to see more—ask at Traveler Corner for info. It is usually cheaper to cross the river to buy your tickets, though the boats may fill up. The Lao entry tax varies but currently stands at 50฿.

THAILAND

Bamboo Riverside Guest House ❶, 71 Huaviang Rd., 75m northwest of Soi 1, is very popular with backpackers. (☎791 621; saweepatts@hotmail.com. Dorms 70฿; singles 100฿; bungalows 150฿; doubles with bath 200-250฿.) **Ban Tammila ❸,** by Soi 2, has bungalows with private showers and sells a compact tent that can also function as a hammock. (☎/fax 791 234. Tents 1350฿; bungalow singles 200-400฿; doubles 300-400฿.) Noodle-and rice-shops line Saiklang Rd. A morning treat from the **day market,** south of the bridge, is *kanon ton kanon niaw* (rice-flour balls with coconut filling; 5฿). By the river between Soi 7 and 9, **Rimkhong ❷** offers freedom from *farang*, but at a price—the menu is only partially translated. (Green curry 50฿. Open daily 7am-11pm.)

Ask at guesthouses about bike rides to **Hmong villages,** though they may prove inaccessible in the rainy season (3hr., 3:30pm, 100฿ includes bike and guide). In April and May, **Ban Haadkhrai** hosts the annual giant catfish competition. Lao and Thai boats take turns trawling the river in search of the 2.5m, 200kg beasts.

CHIANG RAI ☎053

Chiang Rai has always played second fiddle to its southern neighbor, Chiang Mai. King Mengrai built Chiang Rai in 1262, using it as his central command post for three decades. The rivalry between the two cities began when the king abandoned his original capital city for Chiang Mai. Those staying overnight in Chiang Rai leave feeling they've glimpsed authentic Thai city life without having to deal with the characteristic tourist traps of popular destinations.

TRANSPORTATION

The **Chiang Rai International Airport** (☎798 202) is 9km out of town on Hwy. 110 with flights to Bangkok (1hr., 6 per day, 2645฿) and Chiang Mai (25min.; 8:40am, 8pm; 880฿). **Thai Airways,** 870 Phahonyothin Rd., is one block south of Teepee Bar. (☎711 179. Open M-F 8am-noon and 1-5pm.) **Chiang Rai Bus Station** (☎711 224) is on Prasopsuk Rd., one block east of the intersection with Phahonyothin Rd., next to the night market. Buses go to: Bangkok (12hr., 4pm, 264฿; A/C 10 per day 8am and 4:30-8pm, 351฿-370฿; VIP 8am, 6:30, 7pm, 700฿; private companies 8am-7:15pm, 452฿); Chiang Khong (2½-3hr., every 30min. 6am-5:45pm, 42-54฿); Chiang Mai (3½hr., 6 per day 6:15am-5:30pm, 77฿; A/C 13 per day 7:30am-5pm, 139฿); Mae Sai (1½hr., every 15min. 6am-6pm, 25฿); and Mae Sot (10hr., 7:20am, 200฿; A/C 9:20am, 360฿) via Tak (8hr., 165-297฿). **Songthaew, tuk-tuk,** and **samlor** cluster on Uttarakit Rd. around the market and in the evening on Phahonyothin Rd. near the night bazaar. Fares in city 10-20฿. Within 10-15km radius, *songthaew* and *tuk-tuk* should cost under 50฿. Practically every guesthouse rents motorbikes through **Soon Motorcycle,** 197/2 Trairat Rd. (☎714 068. New motorbikes 200฿, secondhand 150฿, 4WD Suzuki Jeep 1000฿, with insurance 1500฿. Reduced rates for longer rentals. Open daily 8am-7pm.) **Avis** car rental is at the airport (☎793 827).

ORIENTATION AND PRACTICAL INFORMATION

The **Mae Kok River** flows west to east, forming Chiang Rai's northern border. **Singhaklai Road,** site of TAT and guesthouses, skirts the river. The northern part of town lies between the river and **Banphraprakan Road,** 500m south and parallel to Singhaklai Rd. The most helpful landmark, the **Haw Nariga** (clocktower), stands in the middle of Banphraprakan Rd., forming a chaotic roundabout. **Jet Yod Road,** full of bars, leads south from there. One block east, a portion of **Phahonyothin Road** runs parallel to Jet Yod Rd., while the upper half curves around above the bus station. More info is available online at www.chiangraiprovince.com.

The **TAT** office, 448/16 Singhaklai Rd., is receptive and organized, and offers free maps with bus schedules, brochures, a list of trekking outfits, and regional info. English is spoken, and there is a **Lenso** phone outside. (☎744 674. Open daily 8:30am-4:30pm.) Other services include: a **Thai Military Bank,** 897/7-8 Phahonyothin Rd. (☎715 657; 24hr. AmEx/Cirrus/MC/PLUS/V **ATM;** open daily 8:30am-9pm); a massive **day market** that borders the post office on Uttarakit Rd. and a **night market** whose streets are closed to all but pedestrian traffic; an **ambulance** (☎711 366); the **local tourist police,** downstairs from TAT, will gladly give a background check on tour agencies (☎717 779; 24hr.); the **Overbrooke Hospital,** 444/3 Singhaklai Rd., 250m west of TAT has a 24hr. **pharmacy** (☎711 366; AmEx/MC/V); a **Telecom office,** on Ngam Muang Rd. has **CATNET,** fax, and international call services (☎776 738; open M-F 8am-8pm, Sa-Su 8:30am-4:30pm; AmEx/MC/V); **Internet** access at **Mae Salong Coffee & Internet,** on Phahonyothin Rd. opposite Thai Airways (30฿ per hr.; open daily 9am-10:30pm); and a **post office** at 486/1 Moo 15 Uttarakit Rd., 200m south of TAT and 300m north of the clocktower. (☎711 421. *Poste Restante.* Open M-F 8:30am-4:30pm, Sa-Su and holidays 9am-noon.) **Postal Code:** 57000.

ACCOMMODATIONS AND FOOD

Over 30 guesthouses and hotels have opened recently. Down the *soi* directly across from the Overbrooke Hospital on Trairat Rd., **Chat House ❶,** 3/2 Sangkaew Rd., is cheap and quiet. (☎711 481. Laundry and trekking service. Bicycle rental 80฿ per day. Bargain during the low season. 3-bed dorms 70฿; singles 80฿; doubles 120฿, with bath 160-180฿, with A/C 250฿.) Despite its proximity to bars, **Baan Bua Guest**

House ❷, 879/2 Jet Yod Rd., has immaculate rooms. South of the clocktower, the guesthouse is 3 blocks down on the left. All the rooms have a fan, Western toilet, and hot water. (☎718 880; baanbua@yahoo.com. Tiled rooms with bath 200฿, with A/C 300฿; larger rooms 220฿/350฿.) At **Mae Hong Son Guest House ❶,** all rooms have fans and mosquito nets. From TAT, head east on Singhaklai Rd.; take the second left on Santirat Rd. (☎715 367. Singles 80฿; doubles 100฿; triples 150฿. Rooms with bath and Western toilet single 150฿, double 200฿.)

Chiang Rai's culinary scene is between Jet Yod, Banphraprakan, and Phahonyothin Rd. The **day** and **night markets** both serve a variety of cheap food. At the night market, try the Thai-style sweet and sour grilled fish from the back stall (60-80฿). Most guesthouses have restaurants. The elegant buffet feast at **Wiang Inn ❸,** 893 Phahonyothin Rd., seems too good to be true. (☎711 533. 100฿. Open M-F noon-2pm.) **Nakon Pathon ❶,** 869/25-26 Phahonyothin Rd., just south of Teepee Bar, caters almost exclusively to the Thai working crowd. (No English sign. Small English menu. Unbeatable *khao moo dang* (barbecue pork with rice) 30฿, iced Milo 10฿, noodle soups 30฿. Open daily 6am-3pm.) On the ground floor of the Hill Tribe Museum is **Cabbages and Condoms ❸,** 620/25 Thanalai Rd. (See **Bangkok,** p. 681. Open daily 11am-midnight. AmEx/MC/V.)

SIGHTS

According to local lore, the *stupa* of **Wat Phra Kaew** was struck by lightning in 1434 to reveal an Emerald Buddha; the temple's name became "Wat of the Emerald Buddha" as a result. Today, the original is Thailand's most important Buddha image and sits in Bangkok's Wat Phra Kaew (p. 681). A new image, commissioned in China in 1991 and carved from Canadian jade, sits in its place. (At the west end of town on Trairat Rd., opposite Overbrooke Hospital. Open daily dawn-dusk.) At the west end of town, walking from Trairat Rd. past Chat House on Sang Kaew Rd., is **Wat Ngam Muang.** Its *stupa* contains King Mengrai's ashes and relics. **Wat Phra Singh,** on Singhaklai Rd. near TAT, dates from the 14th century. The **PDA Hill-Tribe Museum,** 620/25 Thanalai Rd. 300m east of Pintamorn Guest House, isn't nearly as informative as the one in Chiang Mai. The museum focuses on opium issues, sells local handicrafts, and arranges treks. (☎740 088. Open M-F 9am-6pm, Sa-Su 10am-6pm. 50฿ admission includes coffee. Slide show 50฿.)

Teepee Hippie Happy Bar, 542/4 Phahonyothin Rd. south of Banphaprakan Rd., offers a vegetarian menu and occasional acoustic blues after 10pm in high season. (Open daily 11am-5pm and 6:30pm-1am.) Head to **Cat Bar,** 1013/1 Jet Yod Rd., for jamming sessions or a game of pool. (☎714 637. Small beer 50฿. Open daily noon-1am.) The most popular disco in town is the **Par Club** in the Inn Come Hotel, 172/6 Rajbamrung Rd., accessible by *tuk-tuk*. (☎717 850. Cover 100-150฿, includes free drink. Open daily 9pm-1am.)

TREKKING

Chiang Rai's bucolic province has trekking routes less traveled than those around Chiang Mai. Trek prices should include food, transportation, and an informed guide. Typical treks run 3-days, 2-nights (2-4 people around 2500฿ per person, 5-7 people around 2000฿ per person), but they can be as short as a day or as long as a week. Many companies have access to horses, elephants, rafts, and mountain bikes; decide where you want to go and mix and match your itinerary. Ben's Guest House, Chat House, Chian House, and Mae Hong Son Guest House all run flexible treks with guides who are registered with TAT. **Population and Community Development Association (PDA),** 620/26 Thanalai Rd., which funds rural development, family planning, and AIDS education programs among hill-tribes, offers treks and one-day

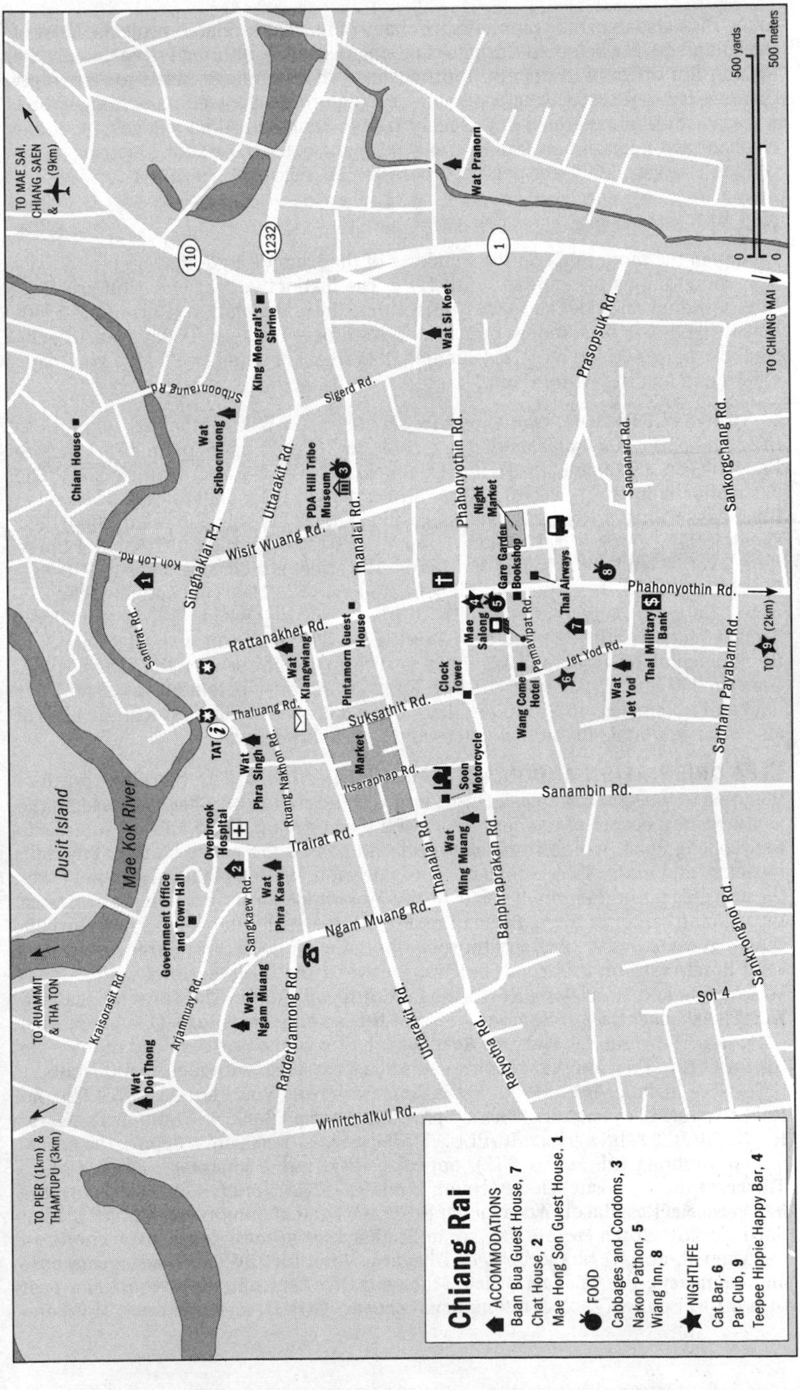
Chiang Rai
ACCOMMODATIONS
Baan Bua Guest House, 7
Chat House, 2
Mae Hong Son Guest House, 1
FOOD
Cabbages and Condoms, 3
Nakon Pathon, 5
Wiang Inn, 8
NIGHTLIFE
Cat Bar, 6
Par Club, 9
Teepee Hippie Happy Bar, 4
TO MAE SAI, CHIANG SAEN & (9km)
TO RUAMMIT & THA TON
TO PIER (1km) & THAMTUPU (3km)
TO CHIANG MAI
TO 9 (2km)
500 yards
500 meters
0
110
1232
1
Dusit Island
Mae Kok River
Wat Pranorn
Wat Si Koet
King Mengrai's Shrine
Chian House
Wat Sriboonruang
Sriboonruang Rd.
Sigerd Rd.
PDA Hill Tribe Museum
Uttarakit Rd.
Singhaklai Rd.
Koh Loh Rd.
Wisit Wuang Rd.
Thanalai Rd.
Phahonyothin Rd.
Night Market
Gare Garden Bookshop
Prasopsuk Rd.
Sanpanard Rd.
Sankorgchang Rd.
Santirat Rd.
Rattanakhet Rd.
Wat Klangwiang
Pintamorn Guest House
Mae Salong
Pamavipat Rd.
Thai Airways
Thai Military Bank
Clock Tower
Wang Come Hotel
Jet Yod Rd.
Wat Jet Yod
Satham Payabarn Rd.
Thaluang Rd.
TAT
Wat Phra Singh
Ruang Nakhon Rd.
Suksathit Rd.
Market
Itsaraphap Rd.
Soon Motorcycle
Sanambin Rd.
Overbrook Hospital
Trairat Rd.
Wat Ming Muang
Thanalai Rd.
Banphraprakan Rd.
Government Office and Town Hall
Sangkaew Rd.
Wat Phra Kaew
Ngam Muang Rd.
Wat Ngam Muang
Arjamnuay Rd.
Kraisorasit Rd.
Ratdetdamrong Rd.
Uttarakit Rd.
Ratyotha Rd.
Sankhongnoi Rd.
Soi 4
Wat Doi Thong
Winitchaikul Rd.

THAILAND

tours. PDA also accepts volunteers for many of its health-related projects. Most of the volunteers are selected through the Bangkok office, although occasionally the Chiang Rai office will accept applications. Thai language skills are strongly favored. If interested, bring a resume and plan to wait a week. (☎/fax 740 088; www.pda.or.th/chiangrai. 3-day, 2-night trek to Lahu and Akha villages, including elephant and longtail boat rides, 3700฿ per person, 2-person min. Daytrips to the Golden Triangle 1500฿ per person, 2-person min. Max. group size is 12.)

NAN ☎054

Hidden in the mountains on the outskirts of the Lanna Kingdom, Nan remained a semi-autonomous principality until 1931. The distinctive and beautiful architecture of the mural-bedecked *wats* reflect this cultural isolation. During the 1960s and 1970s, Nan's remoteness made it a haven for smugglers. Today, Nan's seclusion provokes nothing more threatening than frequent shouts of "I love you" from children unfamiliar with *farang*.

TRANSPORTATION. **Nan Airport** (☎771 308) is on Worawichai Rd., 4km north of town center. **Air Andaman** at the airport (☎711 222; open 10am-2pm) flies to Bangkok (daily 1:30pm, 2240฿) and Chiang Mai (M, W, F, Su 12:30pm; 1025฿). The **bus station** is located just off Chao Fah Rd. (Hwy. 101), 200m north of the Nan River as you enter town, with buses to: Chiang Rai (blue bus; 5hr., 9am, 90฿); Phitsanulok (5hr.; 7:45, 9:45, 11:45am, 1:45pm; 140฿) via Uttaradit (101฿), and Phrae (2hr., every 45min. 5am-5pm, 47฿). Across the street is a **booking office** (☎710 737) for Chiang Mai (6-7hr., 9 per day 7:30am-10:30pm, 117-211฿) via Lampang (4hr., 86-154฿). Buses to Bangkok (☎710 027; 10-13hr.; 8 per day 8-9am, 6-7pm; 236-600฿). **Sombat Tours** (☎710 122) and **Prae Tour** (☎710 348) also run buses to Bangkok. Book Bangkok buses in the morning to ensure an evening seat on the fastest route. **Oversea,** 490 Sumon Thewarat Rd. (☎710 258), rents **mountain bikes** (30-50฿ per day) and **motorbikes** (150-180฿ per day). Open daily 8am-5:30pm. Guesthouses will also arrange rentals for similar prices and a passport deposit.

ORIENTATION AND PRACTICAL INFORMATION. The **Nan River** borders the town to the south and east. Buses arrive at the station off **Chao Fah Road,** in the southwestern corner of the city. North of the bus station, Chao Fah Rd. intersects **Suriyaphong Road,** which runs east-west and passes the **police station, City Hall,** museum, and *wats.* Two blocks north of Suriyaphong Rd., **Mahawong Road** passes the **post office.** Another block north, **Anonta Worarittidit Road** runs roughly east-west through the center of town. **Sumon Thewarat Road,** which runs north-south through the town center, is the primary thoroughfare. A useful point of reference, the **Dhevaraj Hotel** rests on this road, halfway between the intersections with Anonta Worarittidit and Mahawong Rd. At the far north end, Sumon Thewarat Rd. leads to **Worawichai Road.** East of Sumon Thewarat Rd. is **Khao Luang Road.** One block west of Sumon Thewarat lies **Mahayod Road,** which runs to the northern end of town via the turn-off to Pua; another block west is **Pha Kong Road,** with nightly foodstalls.

Services include: **TAT,** on Pha Kong Rd. across from Wat Phumin (☎751 029; no English spoken; open daily 8:30am-5pm); **Thai Farmers Bank,** 434 Sumon Thewarat Rd. (☎710 162; 24hr. Cirrus/MC/PLUS/V **ATM;** open M-F 8:30am-3:30pm); the **police,** 52 Suriyaphong Rd. (☎751 681), opposite City Hall; a **pharmacy,** 347/5 Sumon Thewarat Rd., opposite Thai Farmers Bank (☎710 452; open daily 8am-7pm); the **Nan Provincial Hospital** on Worawichai Rd. at the bend in Sumon Thewarat Rd., 3km north of downtown (☎710 138; some English; *songthaew* leave from the Nara department store, 1 block north of Dhevaraj Hotel for 10฿; 24hr. **emergency** care and **pharmacy**); the **Telecom Office,** Mahayod Rd., 2km outside town, 200m past turn-off to Pua (☎773 214; **international phones, CATNET,** and fax; open M-F 8am-

6pm, Sa-Su 9am-4:30pm); **Easy Internet,** 345/8 Sumon Thewarat Rd., opposite and north of Thai Farmers Bank. (20฿ per hr.; generally open daily 9am-10pm); and the **GPO,** 70 Mahawong Rd., west of Sumon Thewarat Rd. (☎710 176. *Poste Restante.* Open M-F 8:30am-4:30pm, Sa-Su 9am-noon.) **Postal Code:** 55000

ACCOMMODATIONS AND FOOD. Most of Nan's guesthouses are located northeast of the bus station and town center, making bicycle or motorbike rental very convenient. **PK Guest House ❷,** 33/12 Premphachraj Rd., has nice rooms and a pond. Walk north 1.5km on Sumon Thewarat Rd. and turn left after the school; it's down the second *soi* on the right. (☎751 416. Bicycle and motorbike rental 30฿/150฿. Laundry. Shared bath and Western toilet. Wacky singles in oxcarts 100฿; larger singles 150฿; doubles 200฿; VIP suites 300-350฿.) **Nan Guest House ❷,** 57/16 Mahaphrom Rd., is a 15min. walk from the bus station. Follow Chao Fah Rd. for four blocks (500m), then take a right on Mahaprhom Rd.; it's 500m on your left. (☎771 849. Laundry 5-10฿ per piece. Singles 150฿; doubles 230฿. Smaller rooms in back house: singles 80฿; doubles 150฿.) 150m past the PK Guest House on the left is **Amazing Guest House ❷,** 25/7 Soi Snow White, with spacious rooms. (☎710 893. Singles 100-120฿; doubles 160-200฿; triples 210฿; new private bungalows with bath 200-250฿. 1-week 10% discount, 1-month 25% discount.)

Dining in Nan is an adventure. The region is known for its dog farms as well as **Nan River dining:** in an effort to keep cool (temperatures exceed 40°C), locals sit up to their waists in the Nan River eating from **foodstands** at firmly fixed tables. To get to the river dining, turn onto Nokham Rd., one block north of the **produce market** directly opposite the Dhevaraj Hotel. Several counters serve over 20 dishes, which you can point at and buy by the bag (10-15฿). The tiny **night market,** on Anonta Worarittidit Rd. outside the 7-Eleven, starts around 6pm and serves cheap noodle and rice standards for 20฿. Don't miss the fabulous **fruit stand** at the end of the foodstalls on Pha Kong Rd. The regional specialty is crispy fried dog—if you really want to try it, ask for *mah* or *soonahk.* One block beyond Pha Kong Rd. from the bus station on the right is **Tanaya Kitchen ❷,** 75/23-24 Anonta Worarittidit Rd. The friendly owner has an English menu with separate vegetarian options. (Open daily 7am-8:30pm.) Next to Amazing Guest House is a little piece of Italy, **Ristorante Da Dario ❸.** (☎710 636. Spaghetti Pesto Genovese 100฿. Tasty small pizza 70-90฿, large 110-130฿. Open Tu-Sa noon-2pm and 3-10pm.)

SIGHTS. The **Nan National Museum,** in the palace at the intersection of Suriyaphong and Pha Kong Rd., features informative exhibits on Nan's history and Thailand's hill-tribes. (☎710 561. Open daily 9am-4pm. 30฿.) Nan's ornate, detailed *wats* are among the most beautiful in northern Thailand. Across the street is **Wat Phra That Chang Kham,** which houses a walking gold Buddha. The 400-year-old **Wat Phumin,** on Pha Kong Rd. south of the museum, contains murals depicting Lanna culture. The distinctive golden *chedi* of **Wat Phra That Chae Haeng** shines 2km beyond the Nan River bridge. Constructed nearly 700 years ago, the *wat* is the oldest in the region. Southwest of town, **Wat Phra That Khao Noi** has a standing Buddha surveying the valley below. The attraction at **Wat Phaya Wat** is the slightly lopsided old pagoda that leans parallel to a bending coconut palm. Go west on Suriyaphong Rd. to Hwy. 101 and turn right after the bridge onto Hwy. 1095. Wat Phaya Wat is on the plain, while Wat Phra That Khao Noi is 2km up the road on top of a hill.

Back in town, the **Thai Payap Project** sells hill-tribe **handicrafts** from 15 villages. Follow the road opposite the Dhevaraj Hotel past the market; it's 400m down on the right. The project arranges **homestays,** during which travelers may live and work with a family. All proceeds go to community development projects. (☎772 520. Open daily 8:30am-5pm.) The project may move a few blocks north to Nokham Rd. in the near future. The best place to purchase **silver** is directly from the hill-tribes, but if you can't make the trip, **Chompu Phuka** has a showroom with hill-tribe silverware and fabrics. Follow Suriyaphong Rd. west toward Phayao; the showroom is opposite PT Gas Station. (Open daily 9am-5:30pm.)

DAYTRIPS FROM NAN. Nan is now almost entirely safe—some mines remain buried in remote areas, but risks are negligible, especially on roads. Getting lost is actually a greater danger, as English signs are sparse. Try to bring the name of your destination written in Thai. **Fhu Travel Service,** 453/4 Sumon Thewarat Rd., south of the intersection with Mahawong Rd., leads expeditions around the province. A **trek** with Mr. Fhu is the best way to visit the **Mrabi** (*Phi Tong Lueng*, "Spirit of the Yellow Leaves"), a tribe found only in Nan and Phrae provinces.

DOI PHUKHA NATIONAL PARK AND ENVIRONS. Dozens of waterfalls and caves dot **Doi Phukha National Park,** home to Hmong and Mien tribes. (Open daily 6am-6pm. 200฿.) The most easily accessed point from which to see the prized **Chomphu Phukha tree** *(Bretschneidera sinensis)* is 5km past the park office. Turn left off the highway and north from Ban Bor Kleua; a road leads to **Ban Sapan,** 10km away. Crossing the bridge just before the village and turn right on a dirt road to reach the **Sapan Waterfall,** off the road to the right, marked by a red Thai sign and a smaller English one. The dry-season flow will probably leave you unimpressed, but it's worthwhile in the wet season. The **park office** (☎701 000), 25km up the road from Pua, can sometimes provide **accommodations ❶;** call the National Park Division of the Forestry Service in Bangkok first to check. (☎02 579 0529. Tent rental 250฿. Camping 30฿; bungalows for 2 200฿.) A better choice is **Bamboo Huts ❶,** nestled on the ridge of the mountain looking over Laos. It features basic huts with shared facilities. (3 meals per day 130฿. Great-value treks 1-day 500฿, 2-day 1000฿, 3-day 1500฿. Huts 100฿.) *(Orange buses speed to Pua from the bus station in Nan (1½hr., every hr. 5am-6pm, 25฿).* Songthaew, *which leave from near Pua's market for Ban Bor Kleua, can drop you at the park office (1st* songthaew *departs between 8 and 10am, and others leave infrequently throughout the day; 30฿). Once you're at the park, there's not much to do without private transportation. It's possible to loop your way back from Ban Bor Kleua to Nan taking back routes; pick up the regional map from TAT. If you're driving, take Hwy. 1080 from Nan for 60km to Pua. Here, turn right just before the market (you'll have to loop back), then left 100m up the road at the English sign for the park (Hwy. 1256). The road stretches 47km over a mountain peak and through the park to Ban Bor Kleua. The road to Doi Phukha is steep and windy.)*

PHRAE. Phrae is a quiet, peaceful town. One of its main attractions, **Phae Muang Phi,** is billed as a mini-Grand Canyon. The mystery of its origin and location has superstitious locals convinced that phantoms haunt the area. (Open 7am-5pm.) Its 33m-high gilded pagoda and Phra Jao Than Jai Buddha image have established **Wat Phra Chaw Hae** as one of the most important pilgrimage sites in northern Thailand. (Open 7am-5pm.) Both of these attractions lie on the outskirts of town and it's easiest to rent a *songthaew* (200฿ round-trip for either) for the trip. *(To get to Phrae catch a bus. The trip takes 2hr. and buses leave every 45min. between 5am and 5pm for 47฿.)*

SOUTHERN THAILAND

Southern Thailand is a full-blown vacation mecca. With some of the world's best dive sites, thousands of kilometers of white-sand beach, rock climbing, a steady nightlife, and a well-developed tourist infrastructure, the number of tourists isn't surprising. The steady stream of dollars means that nearly every island welcomes visitors and English is an unofficial second language, but the development has also begun to overwhelm both the environment and Thai culture. Farther south, the ethnic mix goes from Thai to Malay, and the number of tourists dwindles.

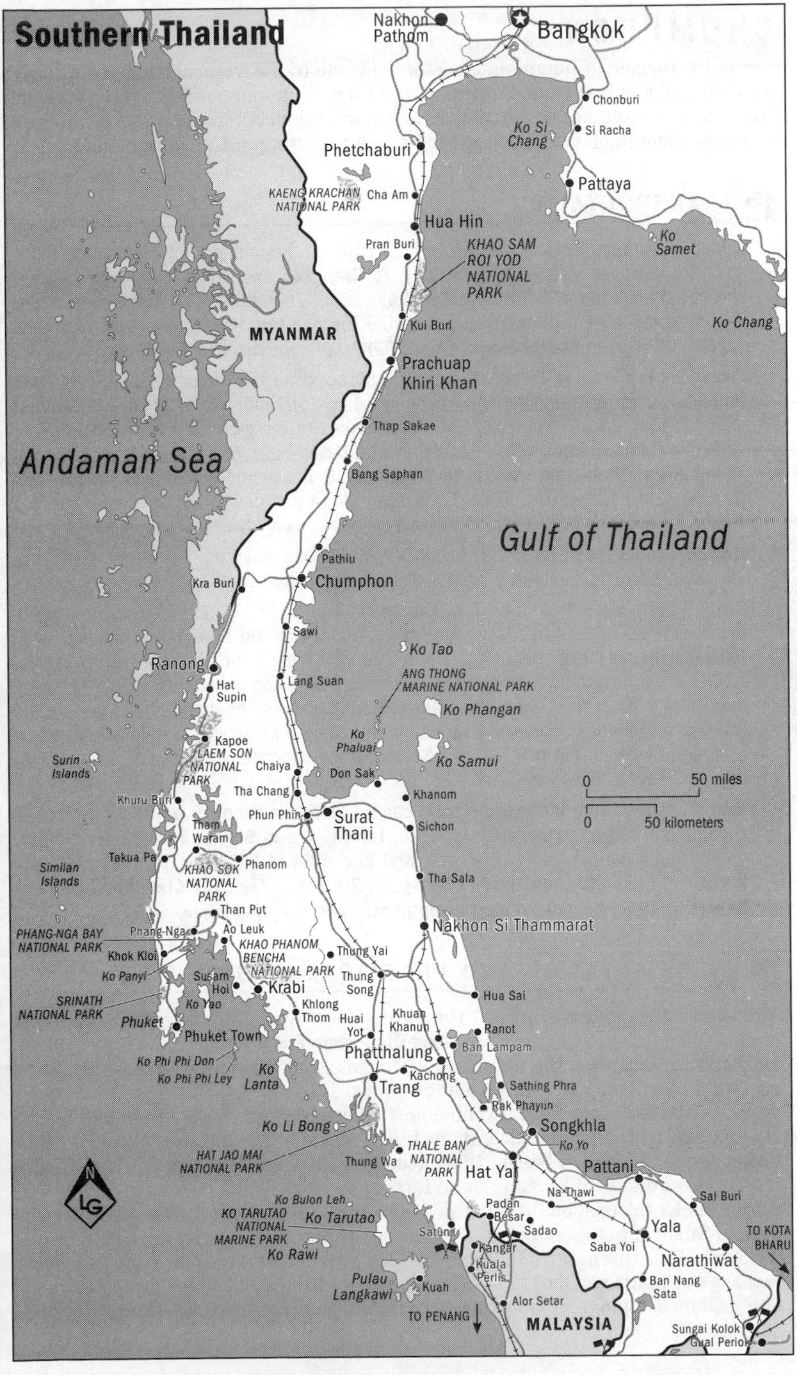
Southern Thailand
Nakhon Pathom
Bangkok
Chonburi
Ko Si Chang
Si Racha
Phetchaburi
Pattaya
KAENG KRACHAN NATIONAL PARK
Cha Am
Hua Hin
Ko Samet
Pran Buri
KHAO SAM ROI YOD NATIONAL PARK
Ko Chang
Kui Buri
MYANMAR
Prachuap Khiri Khan
Thap Sakae
Andaman Sea
Bang Saphan
Gulf of Thailand
Pathiu
Kra Buri
Chumphon
Sawi
Ko Tao
Ranong
ANG THONG MARINE NATIONAL PARK
Lang Suan
Hat Supin
Ko Phangan
Kapoe
Ko Phaluai
LAEM SON NATIONAL PARK
Ko Samui
Surin Islands
Chaiya
Don Sak
50 miles
0
Tha Chang
Khanom
Khuru Buri
Phun Phin
Surat Thani
0
50 kilometers
Sichon
Tham Waram
Takua Pa
Phanom
Similan Islands
KHAO SOK NATIONAL PARK
Tha Sala
Than Put
Nakhon Si Thammarat
PHANG-NGA BAY NATIONAL PARK
Phang-Nga
Ao Leuk
KHAO PHANOM BENCHA NATIONAL PARK
Thung Yai
Khok Kloi
Ko Panyi
Susarn Hoi
Krabi
Thung Song
Hua Sai
SRINATH NATIONAL PARK
Ko Yao
Khlong Thom
Phuket
Huai Yot
Khuan Khanun
Ranot
Phuket Town
Ban Lampam
Ko Phi Phi Don
Phatthalung
Ko Phi Phi Ley
Ko Lanta
Trang
Kachong
Sathing Phra
Rak Phayun
Ko Li Bong
Songkhla
Ko Yo
HAT JAO MAI NATIONAL PARK
Thung Wa
THALE BAN NATIONAL PARK
Hat Yai
Pattani
Na Thawi
Sai Buri
Ko Bulon Leh
Padan Besar
KO TARUTAO NATIONAL MARINE PARK
Ko Tarutao
Sadao
Yala
Satun
TO KOTA BHARU
Kangar
Saba Yoi
Ko Rawi
Narathiwat
Kuala Perlis
Pulau Langkawi
Kuah
Ban Nang Sata
Alor Setar
TO PENANG
MALAYSIA
Sungai Kolok
Gual Periok

CHUMPHON ☎077

For most travelers, Chumphon is a stop en route to the tropical trinity of Ko Tao, Ko Phangan, and Ko Samui. For those with time, Chumphon offers numerous local travel and ecotourism opportunities. With quality accommodations and tourist services, Chumphon is a fine stop for refueling, regrouping, or simply relaxing.

TRANSPORTATION

Trains: Chumphon Railway Station (☎511 103), at the west end of Krumluang Chumphon Rd. Luggage storage 10฿ per day. To: **Bangkok** and **Surat Thani** (3hr., 10 per day, rapid and express 243฿). To: **Bangkok** (10hr., 7am, 80฿; rapid and express trains 7-10hr., every hr. 11:30am-10:30pm, 330-370฿) via **Hua Hin** (3-4hr.; 49฿, rapid and express 293฿) and **Phetchaburi** (4-5hr.; 62฿, rapid and express 308฿).

Buses: Tha Tapoa Road Terminal (☎502 725), opposite Tha Tapoa Hotel, runs A/C and non-A/C buses to: **Bangkok** (8hr., every hr. 6am-2pm and 10pm, 211฿) and **Phuket** (6hr.; 4:30am, 4:30, 10pm; 196฿). Most buses to Bangkok stop in **Hua Hin** (5hr., 126฿) and **Phetchaburi** (6hr., 160฿). Orange buses leave from across the street for **Hat Yai** via **Surat Thani** (3hr.; every 30-60min. 5:30-11am and 4:30pm; 65-102฿) and **Ranong** (3hr., 12 per day, 70฿). For **Krabi,** take a bus to Chumphon Mueng Mai bus station and change for a Krabi-bound bus.

Minivans: To **Ranong** (2hr., every hr., 90฿). **Minibuses** make the trip in 2hr. instead of the usual 3 by bus. Minibuses leave across from Infinity Travel.

Boats: 3 boats leave daily to **Ko Tao. Express boats** (2¼hr., 7:30am, 400฿) and **speedboats** (1¾hr., 7:30am, 400฿) leave from piers at **Hat Sai Ree,** 10km outside town. **Midnight boats** ("slow boats") leave at midnight from a different pier (6hr., 200฿). Tickets are available in Chumphon at tourist agencies and guesthouses. The best deal in town is through **New Chumphon Guest House.** Express boat and speedboat tickets 350฿ with full refund. Free wake-up call and pick-up from anywhere in town and transportation by car to the pier. To visit **Ko Maphraw** (Coconut Island), contact a tourist office 15 days in advance.

Local Transportation: Motorcycle taxis can be found on almost every street in town. It should cost 10฿ to go anywhere in town. **Infinity Travel Service** (see **Tourist Office,** below) rents **motorbikes** (150฿ per day) and **cars** (1000฿ per day). **Suda Guest House** (p. 801) also rents motorbikes (150-200฿ per day). The **Chumphon Cabana Resort** (☎504 442) rents **diving equipment.** Open daily 9am-8pm.

ORIENTATION AND PRACTICAL INFORMATION

Chumphon lies 498km south of Bangkok. The town is compact, and its main streets roughly follow a grid. **Krumluang Chumphon Road,** home of the town's night market, runs east from the train station, forming the northern edge of town. **Poraminthra Manka Road** marks the southern limit. The bus station and several travel agencies line **Tha Tapoa Road,** running north-south through the western part of the city. Parallel to Tha Tapoa Rd. and one block east is hotel- and eatery-studded **Sala Daeng Road.** "V"-shaped **Pracha Uthit Road** straddles the city center with the day market, *songthaew* to Ko Tao-bound ferries, and Hat Thung Wua Laen.

The **Tourist Information** office is near the post office. The staff is friendly and speaks English, but most questions can be answered at tourist agencies. (☎511 024, ext. 120. Open daily 8:30am-4:30pm.) Other services include: **currency exchange** at Bangkok Bank, 111/1-2 Sala Daeng Rd. (☎511 446; 24hr. **ATM.;** open M-F 8:30am-3:30pm; pick up extra cash if you are heading to Ko Tao); a **day mar-**

ket, between Pracha Uthit and Poraminthra Manka Rd. (open daily 5am-5pm), and a **night market** on Krumlaung Chumphon Rd. (open daily 6-11pm); the **police,** on Sala Daeng Rd., 50m north of the intersection with Krumluang Rd; little English is spoken (☎511 505; open 24hr.); **Virajsilp Hospital,** at the south end of Tha Tapoa Rd., a 5min. walk from the bus station, with great service and a **pharmacy** (☎503 238); **Chumphon Hospital,** on Phisit Phayaban Rd. where it curves to Krumlaung Rd., offers emergency care (☎503 238; 24hr.); several guesthouses and tourist offices have **international phone** service. Access the **Internet** at **Suwan Internet,** on Pracha Uthit Rd. at Phinit Khadi Rd. near the market (20฿ per hr.; open daily 9am-10pm) or at **Infinity Travel** (1฿ per min.; 20฿ min.). The **GPO** is at 192 Poraminthra Manka Rd., southeast of town, past the tourist office, on the left. *Poste Restante* is available. (☎511 041. Open M-F 8:30am-4:30pm, Sa 9am-noon.) **Postal Code:** 86000.

ACCOMMODATIONS AND FOOD

Most hotels and guesthouses are near the bus station, either on Tha Tapoa Rd., Sala Daeng Rd., or in the alleys between the two. **Suda Guest House ❷,** 8 Bangkok Bank Thatapao Rd., is just around the corner from Infinity Travel near the bus station. Immaculate facilities and a homey atmosphere add to the charm. Spotless bathrooms have hot showers. (☎504 366. Singles 180-250฿; doubles 300-350฿. Add 80฿ for A/C.) **Sri Chumphon Hotel ❷,** 127/22-24 Sala Daeng Rd., has impersonal but spacious rooms with luxuries like TVs, private baths, and hot water. (☎570 536. Tea and coffee downstairs. Singles and doubles with fan 250฿, with A/C 350฿.)

For Chumphon's finest victuals, head to the markets. The **day market** offers a variety of fruits, while the **night market** on Krumluang Chumphon Rd. has Thai staples. (Open daily 5-11pm.) The **bakery ❶** on the corner of Sala Daeng and Pracha Uthit Rd. sells great pastries. (Open daily 6am-5pm.) Restaurants line Krumluang Chumphon Rd. Several offer live entertainment. **Papa 2000 ❸,** 188 Krumluang Chumphon Rd., is two blocks from the Sala Daeng Rd. intersection. Outdoor seating and live music make this a relaxed dining experience. (Delicious Thai dishes 80-100฿. Open daily 10am-11pm.) **Rin Garden Restaurant ❷,** on Krumluang Chumphon Rd. at Suksamoe Rd., has affordable dishes in a pleasant outdoor setting. (Curried crab with vegetables 70฿. Most dishes 50-70฿. Open daily 10am-10pm.)

PHUKET ☎076

A tropical playground of international renown, Phuket draws tourists looking for anything but a cultural or solitary experience. Most visitors arrive by plane and are swiftly shepherded to five-star resorts. Here they frolic, safely avoiding almost everything having to do with Thailand. Phuket can be less than friendly for the budget traveler, but there are still some good deals to be found, especially if you travel in the low season. Backpackers relax on beaches like Hat Kamala and Hat Karon by day and cruise the discos of Hat Patong by night. Give up your dreams of idyllic seclusion for a few nights, soak up a raucous good time with fellow *farang*, and make the most of the "Jewel of the South."

TRANSPORTATION

Phuket lacks public transportation, so getting around is expensive. The cheapest and most convenient way to explore the island is by motorbike. However, it is also the most dangerous and results in many casualties every month.

THAILAND

Flights: Phuket International Airport, 28km outside of Phuket Town on Rte. 4026. **Bangkok Airways,** 158/2-3 Yao Warat Rd. (☎225 033; open daily 8am-5pm), and **Thai Airways,** 78/1 Ranong Rd. (☎211 195; open daily 8am-5pm), across from the local bus station, run most domestic and international flights. To: **Bangkok** (1½hr., every hr. 8am-8pm, 2730฿); **Hat Yai** (45min., 12:50am, 1180฿); **Ko Samui** (40min.; daily 11:15am, 4:20pm; 1480฿; M, W, F, Su 11:10am; 1480฿); **Kuala Lumpur, Malaysia** (1½hr., daily, 3730฿); **Penang, Malaysia** (Tu, F, Su 12:30pm; 2230฿); and **Singapore** (4 per day, 6085฿).

Buses: Intercity bus station (☎211 480), off Phang-Nga Rd. in eastern Phuket Town, behind a shopping plaza. TAT office has a good, free bus schedule. A/C and non-A/C buses to: **Bangkok** (14hr., 21 per day 6am-7pm, 278-755฿); **Hat Yai** (7hr., 14 per day, 150-270฿); **Khao Sok National Park** via **Takua Pa** (7:30, 9am; 70-100฿); **Krabi** (4hr., 22 per day, 65-117฿); **Phang-Nga** (1½hr., 26 per day, 36฿); **Surat Thani** (5hr., 14 per day, 104-180฿); **Trang** (6hr., 20 per day 6am-6:30pm, 105-189฿).

Boats: Boats to **Ko Phi Phi** depart from Tonsai Bay (9am, 2:30pm; 250-450฿), the deep-sea port on the southeast coast. The cheapest way to buy tickets is through **Mark Travel Service** inside the On On Hotel. Transportation from in-town hotels to the pier is included. Tickets are cheaper in Phuket Town than elsewhere on the island. They are also less expensive in Ko Phi Phi, so unless you're getting a round-trip discount, it is best to buy your return ticket there.

Local Transportation: Local bus station on Ranong Rd. in Phuket Town, near the market. Labeled **songthaew** (every 30min. 7am-5pm) to: **Hat Kamala** (25฿); **Hat Karon** (20฿); **Hat Kata** (20฿); **Hat Patong** (15฿); **Hat Rawai** (20฿); **Hat Nai Yang** (30฿); **Hat Surin** (20฿). **Tuk-tuks** to: **Hat Kamala** (250฿); **Hat Kata** (150฿); **Hat Nai Yang** (300฿); **Hat Patong** (150฿); **Hat Rawai** (100฿); and **Hat Surin** (250฿). **Taxis** (from airport to Phuket Town 300฿) and **tuk-tuks** cruise between the beaches and airport. Blue-and-yellow **metered taxis** are hard to find, but they are comfortable and not a bad deal (30฿ for the first 2km and 4฿ for each additional km). Within Phuket Town, *tuk-tuks* charge 10-20฿; rates are negotiable to other points on the island and go up after 5pm.

Rentals: Motorbikes (150-300฿ per day) and **jeeps** (600-1000฿ per day) are available all over the island. Vehicle rentals are cheapest in Phuket Town and more expensive near the beaches. All vehicles are uninsured, and accident rates are alarmingly high. Helmets are required for all drivers, and the rule is strictly enforced. Cops sometimes run stings to ensure that all *farang* drivers possess an International Driver's Permit.

THAILAND

ORIENTATION

Given the island's size (570km²), traveling can take some time. Phuket is connected to the mainland by **Route 402,** the island's main north-south artery, and the **Sarasin Bridge.** Bordered by the Andaman Sea, the west coast is lined with beaches. The northern beaches, especially **Hat Kamala, Hat Surin,** and **Laem Sing** are quieter and prettier, while south of Kamala, party central **Hat Patong** has bars, cabaret shows, and tourist stalls. Farther south are the gentle duo **Hat Karon** and **Hat Kata.** On the island's southeast corner, **Phuket Town,** the island's lifeline, offers financial, postal, and telecom services in addition to a bevy of budget restaurants.

PRACTICAL INFORMATION

Tourist Office: TAT, 73-75 Phuket Rd. (☎212 213), in Phuket Town northwest of the clocktower and hidden among furniture stores. Open daily 8:30am-4:30pm.

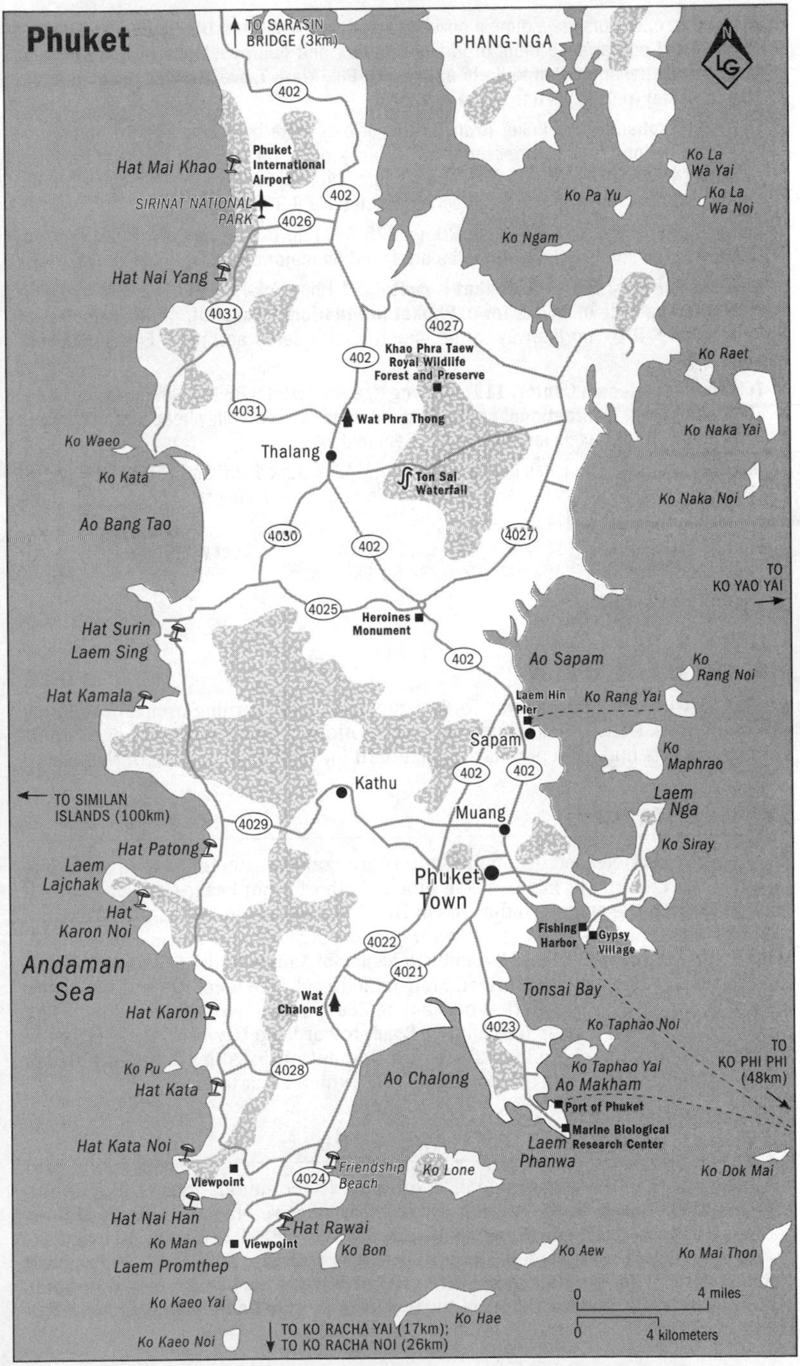
Phuket
TO SARASIN BRIDGE (3km)
PHANG-NGA
LG
402
Hat Mai Khao
Phuket International Airport
SIRINAT NATIONAL PARK
4026
Ko La Wa Yai
Ko La Wa Noi
Ko Pa Yu
Ko Ngam
Hat Nai Yang
4031
4027
Khao Phra Taew Royal Wildlife Forest and Preserve
Ko Raet
Wat Phra Thong
Ko Waeo
Thalang
Ko Naka Yai
Ko Kata
Ton Sai Waterfall
Ko Naka Noi
Ao Bang Tao
4030
TO KO YAO YAI
4025
Heroines Monument
Hat Surin
Laem Sing
Ao Sapam
Ko Rang Noi
Hat Kamala
Laem Hin Pier
Ko Rang Yai
Sapam
Ko Maphrao
TO SIMILAN ISLANDS (100km)
Kathu
Laem Nga
Muang
4029
Hat Patong
Ko Siray
Laem Lajchak
Phuket Town
Hat Karon Noi
Fishing Harbor
Gypsy Village
Andaman Sea
4022
4021
Tonsai Bay
Wat Chalong
Hat Karon
4023
Ko Taphao Noi
TO KO PHI PHI (48km)
Ko Pu
4028
Ko Taphao Yai
Hat Kata
Ao Chalong
Ao Makham
Port of Phuket
Marine Biological Research Center
Hat Kata Noi
Laem Phanwa
Friendship Beach
Ko Lone
Ko Dok Mai
Viewpoint
4024
Hat Nai Han
Hat Rawai
Ko Man
Viewpoint
Ko Bon
Ko Aew
Ko Mai Thon
Laem Promthep
0
4 miles
Ko Kaeo Yai
Ko Hae
0
4 kilometers
TO KO RACHA YAI (17km); TO KO RACHA NOI (26km)
Ko Kaeo Noi

THAILAND

Tours: Tour operators are a dime a dozen in Hat Karon, Hat Kata, Hat Patong, and Phuket Town. Most can arrange tours to Phang-Nga Bay and nearby islands (450-650฿) and bus or ferry transportation to Krabi and Ko Phi Phi. **Mark Travel Service,** located in the **On On Hotel** (p. 804) is one of the cheapest.

Currency Exchange: In Phuket Town, a slew of banks are on Phang-Nga Rd. in front of the On On Hotel, and several more are 1 block down on Ratsada Rd. **Thai Farmers Bank,** 14 Phang-Nga Rd. (☎216 928), has a 24hr. **ATM.** Currency exchange booths and ATMs abound on the larger beaches. Open daily 8:30am-5pm.

Local Tourist Police: 81-83 Satun Rd. (☎225 361), in the far northwest part of town. 24hr. English spoken. Smaller booths are found on major beaches.

Medical Services: Bangkok Phuket Hospital, 21 Hong Yok-H-Thit Rd. (☎254 421), on the northwest side of Phuket Town. **Phuket International Hospital,** 44 Chalerm Prakiat Rd. (☎249 400), on the way to the airport. Credit cards accepted. English spoken. Both 24hr.

Telephones: Telecom Center, 112/2 Phang-Nga Rd. (☎216 861), in the building under the radio tower. **International phone**/fax and Internet. Generally cheaper than services provided by travel agencies. Open daily 8am-midnight.

Internet Access: Cybercafes line Montri Rd. and Tilok Uthit 1 Rd. and charge 25฿ per hr. **Hi-Tel,** on Ong Sim Phai Rd. at Tilok Uthit 1 Rd., has particularly fast connections. Open daily 8am-midnight. Also available in the On On Hotel (p. 804).

Post Offices: GPO, 12/16 Montri Rd. (☎211 020), on the corner with Thalang Rd. *Poste Restante.* Open M-F 8:30am-4:30pm, Sa-Su 9am-noon.

Postal Code: 83000.

THAILAND

PHUKET TOWN ☎076

Phuket Town is the place to stay for late-night or early-morning transit or to stock up on supplies. Despite scant entertainment options, Phuket Town's budget hotels and restaurants make it a popular springboard for exploring the rest of the island.

ORIENTATION

Most tourist services and accommodations are concentrated in a small area. The island's intercity bus terminal is one block north of main **Phang-Nga Road,** which runs west from the station to the On On Hotel and many banks. Past the Telecom Center (distinguished by its clocktower), Phang-Nga Rd. intersects **Phuket Road,** which runs south past **TAT** and **Navamindra Memorial Square** to the **Seiko Clock Tower,** next to the towering and overpriced Metropole Hotel. The local **bus** and **songthaew station** is adjacent to the market on **Ranong Road,** on the west side of town. The newer part of town is near **Tilok Uthit 1 Road,** toward the bay from the Metropole Hotel. It has dining, shopping, and entertainment options, including the **Ocean Shopping Mall** and **Robinson's Department Store,** which cater to *farang.*

ACCOMMODATIONS AND FOOD

Phuket Town has the widest selection of budget accommodations on the island. **Talang Guest House ❷,** 37 Thalang Rd., is clean and well-maintained. Third-floor rooms cost more, but fresh air and views are worth it. (☎211 154; www.talangguesthouse.com. Breakfast included. Rooms 260-300฿, with A/C 360-400฿.) At **Pengmen Hotel ❷,** 69 Phang-Nga Rd., rooms are old but fairly clean. (Singles and doubles 120฿.) Past the Pengmen away from the bus station, is **On On Hotel ❷,** 19 Phang-Nga

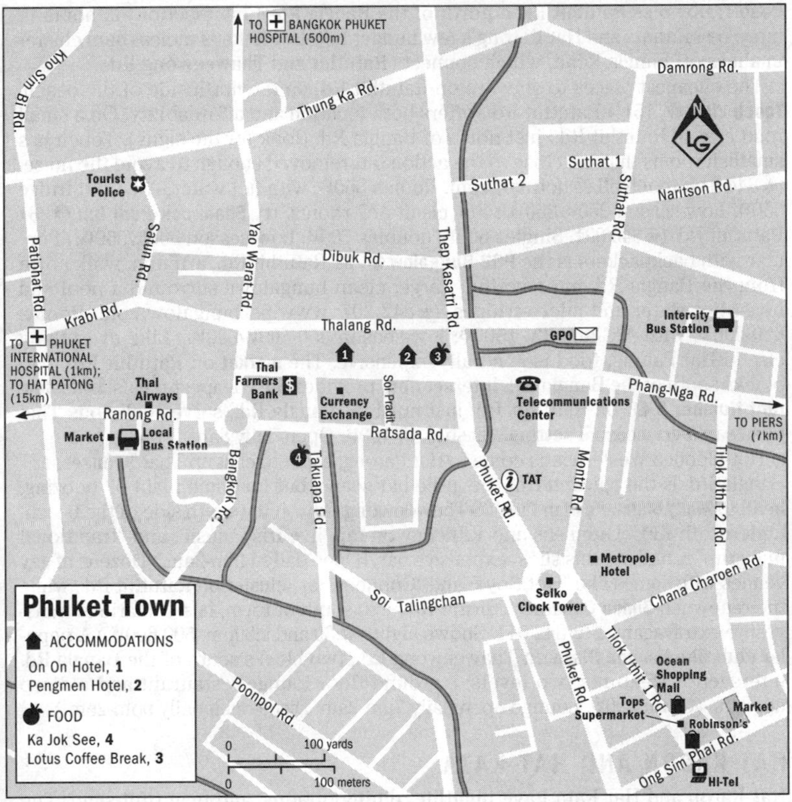

Rd. (☎211 154. Internet 25฿ per hr. Rooms 150฿, with bath 250฿, with A/C 360.) Phuket is famous for its cuisine, including *tao sor* (Chinese crepes) and *kanom jin Phuket* (breakfast noodles in spicy curry). The day and night **markets** are at the junction of Tilok Uthit 2 and Ong Sim Phai Rd. **Baan Thalang ❷**, on Talang Rd. a few doors down from Talang Guest House toward Phang-Nga Rd., is a quiet Muslim restaurant that serves great Thai dishes (40-120฿), curries (85฿), and fantastic *roti* (20฿). Grab a Western breakfast or a sandwich is **Lotus Coffee Break ❶**, at the corner of Phang-Nga and Phuket Rd. (Tea 10฿. Thai dishes 35-65฿. Shakes 20-25฿. Open daily 7:30am-9:30pm.) The excellent **Ka Jok See ❹**, 26 Takuapa Rd., is several shops south of the Ratsada Rd. intersection. (Try the *tom yam* or *goong-sarong*, both 150฿. Chinese and Thai dishes 80-380฿. Open Tu-Su 6-11pm.)

HAT PATONG

If you're looking for peace and relaxation, don't come to Hat Patong. But, if you're in the market for seedy drunken revelry and a crowded beach full of *farang*, then you've come to the right place. On Phuket's west coast, Hat Patong is the island's nightlife and entertainment center. Hat Patong has two roads that run parallel to the beach. Closest to the water is **Thaweewong Road,** crowded with expensive seafood restaurants, outdoor bars, and souvenir stalls. One block east, **Song Roi Pee**

Road (known as **Ratuthit Road** north of the **Bangla Road** intersection) is home to more restaurants and Hat Patong's few budget hotels. Phuket's raciest bars cluster in alleys off Bangla Road, which connects Ratuthit and Thaweewong Rd.

The cheapest places to stay are on Ratuthit Rd. on the north side of the beach. **Touch Villa ❸**, 151/4 Ratuthit Rd., offers both location and affordability. On a small road east of Ratuthit Rd., just north of Bangla Rd. (look for the signs), Touch has smallish rooms that are close to the action but removed enough to avoid the noise. (☎344 011; touchvilla@hotmail.com. Rooms 350฿, with hot water, A/C, and fridge 550฿. Low-season 250฿/350฿.) For clean A/C rooms, try **Shamrock Park Inn ❹**, 31 Ratuthit Rd. (☎340 991. Singles 600฿; doubles 700฿. Low-season 500฿/550฿.) Popular with backpackers is the **PS2 Bungalow ❹**, 21 Ratuthit Rd., a 15min. walk north from the Bangla Rd. intersection. Large, clean bungalows surround a pool and boast hot water and micro-fridges. (☎342 207; www.ps2bungalow.com. Rooms 600-900฿, with A/C and TV 1500฿; low-season 350-500฿/600฿.) Like everything else in Hat Patong, food is generally expensive. The **market** on Ratuthit Rd., two blocks south of the Bangla Rd. intersection, provides the cheapest meals. **Restaurant Number 6 ❷**, on Ratuthit Rd. just north of Bangla Rd., serves delicious Thai dishes in a very casual setting. (Dishes 40-100฿. Open daily 8am-11pm.)

THAILAND

Hot-blooded Western lads come to Hat Patong, eager to chat up Thai "waitresses." Bangla Rd. is the epicenter of the girlie bar scene, but for some plain ol' boozing, head to **Molly Malone's Irish Pub**, 68 Thaweewong Rd., on the south side of the beach, underneath KFC. Guinness and Kilkenny on tap, live Irish music, and "traditional pub grub" round out this slick, expensive bar. (Open daily 11am-2am.) Dozens of gay venues with names like "Hot Boys" and "Connect Bar" cluster on Ratuthit Rd., while the renowned **Simon Cabaret**, 8 Sirirat Rd., just south of town, has a hilarious transvestite extravaganza. (☎342 011. Shows nightly 7:30 and 9:30pm. 500-600฿.) A popular club, **The Banana Disco** on Thaweewong Rd., two blocks south of the Bangla Rd. intersection, features two levels: a ground-floor lounge/restaurant and a disco upstairs. (Cover 200฿. Lounge open daily 7pm-2am. Disco open daily 9pm-2am.)

HAT KARON AND HAT KATA

Hat Karon and Hat Kata have nightlife, dining options, and beautiful sand. The adjacent destinations are actually three separate beaches. To the north, luxury resorts dot Hat Karon. To the south, a rocky cape separates Hat Karon from Hat Kata. Here, budget restaurants and hotels cluster around **Taina Road**, which winds inland from the beachside **Patak Road**. Hat Kata itself is split into the beaches of **Hat Kata** and **Hat Kata Noi**. While Hat Kata is monopolized by **Club Med**, Hat Kata Noi is the most solitary beach of the three. The tiny tree-covered island of **Ko Pu** lies a few hundred meters offshore between Hat Kata and Hat Karon; the distance is manageable for experienced swimmers when the green flags are flying.

Budget accommodations are on the beach along Taina Rd. between Hat Karon and Hat Kata. One of the best is Scandinavian-themed **Little Mermaid Guest House ❹**, on Taina Rd. at the far end of the block of establishments. Rooms have hot water, phones, and optional fridges and TVs, each for 50฿ extra. (☎330 730; www.littlemermaidphuket.net. Rooms with fan 365฿, with A/C 500฿; bungalows with A/C 590฿; low-season 265฿/365฿/850฿. Discounts for long-term stays.) A great escape is **Kata On Sea ❸**. On Taina Rd., turn up the driveway next to 7-Eleven, and walk to the top of the hill. Stay in large, basic bungalows with fans, or in recently renovated rooms with A/C, cable TV, and hot water. (☎330 594. Motorbikes 300฿ per day. Reservations recommended in high season. Basic bungalows 400฿; deluxe rooms with A/C 600฿. Low-season 300฿/450฿.) Karon lacks the superb budget options of Kata, but there are a number of mid-level selections.

Both Hat Karon and Hat Kata have a good selection of inexpensive restaurants. In Karon, they are on Patak Rd., just inland from the roundabout. The best of the bunch is **Papaya Restaurant ❷,** which serves Thai dishes out-of-doors. Papaya has an extensive vegetarian menu and selection of cocktails (100-140฿). From the beach, turn left on the side-street at the Crystal Beach Hotel and walk 2min. (Dishes 60-210฿. Open daily 9am-midnight.) In Kata, restaurants line Taina Rd. close to the beach. **The Kwong Seafood Shop ❷,** on Taina Rd., is a no-frills place. (Chicken and beef dishes 50-80฿. Seafood dishes 80-200฿. Open daily 9am-midnight.) **La Banana ❷,** also on Taina Rd., offers great Italian dishes in a setting best described as "Venetian jungle." (Dishes 80-380฿. Open daily 9am-midnight.)

For those with the cash, Hat Karon and Hat Kata have some of the world's best **snorkeling** and **diving** around the Similan and Racha Islands. Head to PADI-certified **Siam Dive n' Sail,** 68/14 Patak Rd. Moo 2, behind Club Med near the Jiva Resort. They specialize in live-aboard diving trips. Four-day trips to Similan and Surin start at 14,500฿ per person, seven-day trips to Myanmar start at 57,000฿, and day-trips start at 2000-3100฿. Gear rental costs 700฿ per day. All trips include transport from your hotel, tanks, weights, and most meals and drinks. (☎330 967; www.siamdivers.com. Open M-Sa 11am-8pm. MC/V.) Hat Kata center's **nightlife** consists of nondescript bars blasting loud music. **Dino Park Mini-Golf** provides more innocent fun. (Open daily 10am-midnight. 240฿, children 180฿.)

HAT SURIN, AO BANG TAO, AND HAT NAI YANG

The island's northwestern shore has exploded with luxury resorts, and **Hat Surin** is no exception, though there are some cheaper guesthouses closer to the highway. Swimming is not recommended due to the winds and surf. **Surin Sweet Hotel ❺,** 107/8 Moo 3, on the beach road, has rooms with sea views and top-notch amenities. The higher the floor, the less the noise and better the view. (☎270 863; surinhotel@hotmail.com. Rooms 1700฿; low-season 400฿.) Outdoor restaurants crowd the beach area (Western and Thai dishes 80-180฿). On the southern end of Surin Beach, **Diver's Place ❷** is a beachfront pub with a friendly expat crowd (beers 60฿).

Attractive **Ao Bang Tao** makes a decent daytrip, especially between May and July. Two resorts monopolize access to the water. Squeezed between the two beaches on the road from Surin to Ao Bang Tao, **Bangtao Lagoon Bungalows ❺,** 72/3 Moo 3 T. Cherngtalay, has comfortable huts with marble floors. Ask the bus driver from Phuket Town to drop you off here. (☎324 260; http://phuket-bangtaolagoon.com. Bungalows 680-1780฿; low-season 400-1000฿. Extra bed 200฿.)

Sirinat National Park, farther north at **Hat Nai Yang,** spans hundreds of kilometers of coconut trees and coral reefs. In the rainy season, Hat Nai Yang has Phuket's most dangerous riptides. The **Visitor Office** is near the entrance. (☎327 407. Open daily 8:30am-4:30pm.) It's possible to rent **tents ❷** (2-to 3-person tent 200฿; camping 20฿). Beachside **park bungalows ❹** are popular among vacationers (600-1200฿).

HAT KAMALA

Escape to quiet **Hat Kamala** on the way to Hat Surin from Phuket Town (*songthaew* 20฿). There are no luxury hotels and the beaches are decent. Rooms at **Benjaim Resort ❺,** 83 Moo 3, have ocean views, A/C, TV, and hot water. Low-season discounts make this place a steal. (☎385 145; www.phuketdir.com/benjaminresort. Rooms 1200-1500฿; low-season 350-500฿.) To get to the spotless **Malinee House ❺,** 74/7 Moo 3, follow the beach road from the south end of the beach until it curves inland; the restaurant and guesthouse are on the right. An Internet cafe is below. (☎324 094. A/C singles and doubles 1000฿; low-season 500฿.) The excellent **Gourmet Restaurant ❸,** at the corner where Moo 3 turns inland, serves Thai and Western food and has great beach views. (Dishes 80-210฿. Open daily 8am-11pm.)

HAT RAWAI AND AO CHALONG

On the southeastern tip of Phuket, **Hat Rawai** caters mostly to locals. The narrow strip of sand and muddy water render it unappealing; try its more attractive neighbor **Hat Nai Han.** Hat Nai Han slows down considerably during rainy season, and Rawai shuts down altogether. At Hat Rawai, **Pornmae Bungalows ❸,** 58/1 Wiset Rd., inside the hair salon opposite the central part of the beach, has simple rooms with fridges. (☎/fax 381 300. Singles and doubles 300-400฿.)

Pleasant **Ao Chalong,** north of Hat Rawai on the island's southeastern side, is the largest bay on Phuket. The swimming is only mediocre, but it's a good place to stay if you want to learn about Andaman Sea yachting culture. Meet other sailors at **Friendship Beach ❺,** 27/1 Soi Mittrapap, 2km north of Hat Rawai toward Phuket Town on the southern side of the bay, across from the Phuket Shell Museum. Friendly and relaxed, it has bungalows, a **restaurant ❸,** a pool table, cable TV, and **Internet** for 1฿ per min. (☎381 281. Bungalows 800฿; low-season 400฿.)

SIMILAN ISLANDS ☎076

Ko Similan, a national park consisting of nine small islands, remains the beauty of the Andaman Sea. Relative inaccessibility and high prices have helped preserve Ko Similan both below and above water. Its 30m underwater visibility and magnificent coral gardens make the Similan Archipelago one of the best deep-water dive sites in the world. Known for diving and snorkelling, Ko Similan has spectacular beaches and rock formations, and fascinating wildlife (only open Nov.-Apr.).

There are three ways to access the Similan Islands by boat: from **Ban Thap Lamu** pier (3hr., 8am, 2100฿) closest to Phang-Nga Town, from **Amphoe Khuru Buri** pier (3hr.) farther north, or from Phuket (1½hr., 8am, 700฿). **Met Sine Tours** (☎443 276), at Ban Thap Lamu, is the most reliable booking agent. In Phuket, contact **Songserm Travel Center** (☎076 222 570). Rough seas might result in cancellation or nausea.

The nine islands 60km off the west coast of Phang-Nga are numbered north to south. The second-largest island, **Ko Miang,** is where boats dock and is the only island that allows overnight guests. It's also the site of the **Visitor Center, Park Headquarters,** and the only drinking water. Irregular boat trips between the islands cost 250฿ per person. Contact the **Similan National Park Office** (☎411 913) at Thap Lamu pier for questions regarding transportation and practicalities. There's a 40฿ admission fee to the park, collected at upon arrival.

Ko Miang has the only accommodations, a **campground** offering both **tents ❷** (150฿) and **bungalows ❺** (4 beds 600฿). There's a small fee if you bring your own tent. Elsewhere in the islands camping and campfires are prohibited. If you're not camping, book in advance through the Park Headquarters. Ko Miang also has the only restaurant, so bring your own food.

From November through February, sea turtles lay eggs on the beach at **Ko Hu Yong. Khao Lak,** on the mainland, is the launching point for tours of the underwater landscape. A typical dive leaves from Phuket, lasts four days and three nights, and includes 10 dives (10,000-20,000฿). If you're not interested in diving, there's superb snorkeling and hiking (with fantastic views).

PHANG-NGA TOWN ☎076

From Phang-Nga Bay to Buddhist temple caves at Suwan Kuha and the nearby rainforest, Phang-Nga remains largely undiscovered. Buses come from Bangkok, Hat Yai, Ko Samui, Krabi, Phuket, and Trang, arriving at the bus station on **Phetkasem Highway** near the center of town. **Phang-Nga Guest House ❷,** on Phetkasem Hwy. near Krug Thai Bank, two blocks to your right as you exit the bus station, has the best budget digs in town. (☎411 358. Singles with fan 200฿, with TV and A/C

300฿; doubles 250฿/400฿.) **Phang-Nga Inn ❸**, owned by the same family, is at the other end of the price spectrum. Just off Phetkasem Hwy. on the opposite side of the bus station, most of the rooms have hot water and cable TV. (☎411 963. Rooms 450-1200฿.) **Duang Restaurant ❷**, at 122 Phetkasem Hwy. next to Thai Farmers Bank and opposite the night market, serves hot and sour seafood soup. (Dishes 50-100฿. Open daily 9am-10:30pm.) **Bismilla ❸**, 247 Phetkasem Hwy. on the same side of the street as the bus station, is a Muslim restaurant with good *roti*, curry, and soup. (Breakfast *roti* 30฿. Entrees 80-120฿. Open daily 7am-11pm.)

PHANG-NGA BAY NATIONAL PARK. The park stretches over 400km², 80% of which is water, and encompasses more than 120 limestone islands. Most tourists make a beeline for the park's twin jewels: beautiful Ko Khao Ping Gan and its satellite, Ko Tapu, better known as "James Bond Island" (scenes from *The Man With The Golden Gun* were filmed here). While the image of Ko Tapu (literally, "Nail Island") slicing into the bay is quite striking, be prepared to throw elbows at shell-vendors and tourists to stake out a prime photo-taking spot. If it gets too crowded, head to Ko Khao Ping Gan for more spectacular panoramas. If you have time, be sure to paddle through the Tam Lod Grotto, a sea-level, open-ended cave dripping with stalactites. Ko Khien displays 300-year-old drawings of boats and animals on the mountain's edge. (*Songthaew* 20฿) run from Phang-Nga bus station to the pier, where longtail boats are chartered (300-400฿ for a few hours; be prepared to bargain). While larger boats come from Krabi and Phuket, the most common tours from Phang-Nga are on **longtail boats**, which are able to maneuver through the narrower caves and waterways. Most tours include a swim and lunch on the beach. **Sayan Tour** offers half-day (200฿), full-day (500฿), and overnight trips (extra 250฿), which include a stay at Ko Panyi. The latter option, tacked on after a half-day or full-day tour, is highly recommended. You can also tour the bay by **kayak.** This pricey alternative (roughly 2000-3000฿ for a full day) allows you to fully explore the hidden lagoons without the deafening buzz of the longtail motor. *(Park admission 200฿.)*

KO PANYI AND THE MUSLIM FISHING VILLAGE. Technically part of the Phang-Nga Bay National Park, Ko Panyi is certainly worth a visit by itself. About 250 years ago, Muslim fishermen from Indonesia settled on the island, constructing homes and businesses on stilts. Other than the prominent town **mosque**, there's not much to see (besides a gorgeous sunset and sunrise); the real fascination is ambling down the rickety, suspended streets to watch the inhabitants go about their chores in the unusual setting. You can arrange a room with the locals or book an overnight stay through a travel agency for 250-350฿. The best accommodations in town are at the brand-new **bungalows** operated by Sayan Tour. The rooms are tidy and run by a friendly staff; dinner and breakfast are included with your stay. (Rooms with private bath 250฿, with full-day park tour 350฿.) For a more authentic, if somewhat less comfortable experience, **M.T. Tour** can arrange **homestays.** (150-250฿ per night.) The company's owner, Mr. Hassim, is a native of Ko Panyi and knows almost everyone—walking the streets with him is a particular pleasure.

KO PHI PHI DON ☎075

Beautiful Ko Phi Phi Don (generally known as Ko Phi Phi)—once an untouristed island surrounded by shimmering turquoise waters—is now second only to Phuket as a destination for *farang* in southern Thailand. Nearby, the island preserve of Ko Phi Phi Ley, accessible by boat from Ko Phi Phi Don, provides a somewhat more serene atmosphere, although it too has suffered, especially since its role in the 2000 Leonardo DiCaprio film, *The Beach*. Ko Phi Phi may no longer be a secluded island paradise, but it still promises a relaxing visit.

TRANSPORTATION AND PRACTICAL INFORMATION

Ferries depart regularly to and from Ko Phi Phi and Ko Lanta, Krabi, or Phuket. Some ferries may not operate May to September. From Ko Phi Phi's Thon Sai Pier, boats head to: Ko Lanta (2hr.; 11:30am, 2pm; 200฿); Krabi (1½hr.; 9am, 1:30, 2:30pm; low season no 2:30pm boat; 200฿); and Phuket (1½hr.; 9am, 1:30, 2:30pm; low season no 1:30pm boat; 250฿). Purchase tickets at any of the travel agencies in Thon Sai Village. Boats to Ko Phi Phi Ley depart from the pier. It is best to hire longtail boats for more remote beaches (prices vary, generally 150฿ per hour).

Ko Phi Phi is small and devoid of roads. It's easy to walk the entire island, save for the high cliffs. The main port of call is pretty but polluted **Ao Thon Sai,** where travelers come to eat, check email, and party. A narrow isthmus connects the two main chunks of island, Ko Nok to the west (left as you exit the pier) and larger Ko Nai to the east. On the other side of the village, beautiful **Ao Lo Dalam** has several pricey bungalows. Less-developed beaches ring the island's outer peninsulas, the most popular of which is **Hat Yao** (Long Beach), east of Ao Thon Sai on Ko Nai.

There is no tourist office on the island; **TAT** in Krabi serves Ko Phi Phi. Ao Thon Sai agencies arrange trips to Ko Phi Phi Ley and boat/train/bus combos to Bangkok and Malaysia. **Maya Tour & Travel** (☎612 403), in Tonsai Bay, offers tours, including a good snorkeling excursion. From the pier, take a right; it's 20m on the right. The **Siam Commercial Bank** in Ao Thon Sai exchanges currency and gives credit card advances. (Open daily 9:30am-7:30pm.) There are scattered **ATMs** in the village. Other services include: the **local tourist police,** off the pier in Ao Thon Sai (☎622 369; English spoken; open daily 8:30am-7:30pm); a 24hr. **police booth** past the Chao Khao Lodge in Ao Thon Sai; **Phi Phi Islands Hospital,** in Ao Thon Sai to the left of the pier, with basic medical services and relief from swimming injuries (☎622 151; English spoken; open 24hr.); and expensive **telephone** connections from private travel agencies in Ao Thon Sai. **Internet** access is abundant in Ao Thon Sai. Unfortunately, it's not cheap—the going rate is 2฿ per min.

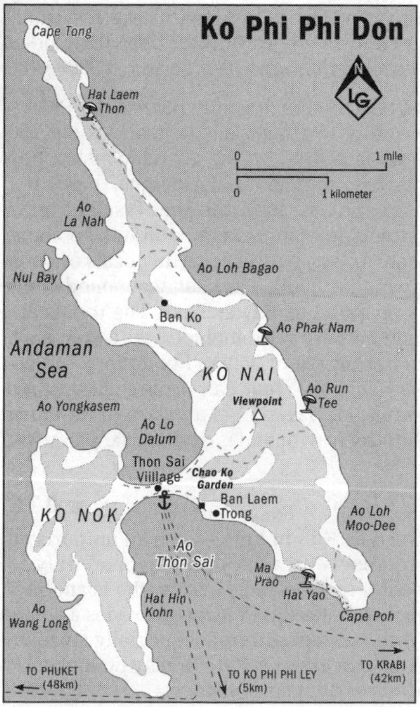

ACCOMMODATIONS

Ko Phi Phi's accommodations are plentiful but vary widely in price and quality. Rooms are cheaper on the edges of the village and on the more isolated beaches. Don't trust the touts who meet your boat at the pier and tell you there are no accommodations below 300-400฿ on the island.

AO LO DALAM AND AO THON SAI. There is a row of cheap accommodations on the east side of the village. From the pier, turn right, walk about 100m, and then turn left at the bronze statue of the big fish. Go past the V Shop, a 24hr. minimart. On your left there are a number of restaurants and tattoo parlors that double as **guest-houses** offering spartan rooms with private baths for 250-400฿ per night. On your right is **The Rock Backpacker ❷**, with the cheapest beds in town. Rooms are bare and hardly large enough to hold the rock-hard bed. All baths are shared and have cold water. (☎612 402. Singles 150฿; doubles 300฿.) If you keep walking and turn left at the sign for Rim Na Villas, you'll cross a small bridge and, 20m later, find the unmarked, unlabeled **Ammarin House ❸**. The fan rooms are spotless, reasonably priced, and come with private bath. (Rooms 400-600฿; low-season 200-250฿.) Popular on the island, the upscale **Charlie Beach Resort ❺** is located on the quieter and cleaner Ao Lo Dalam, across the isthmus from the pier. The bungalows have great views and a lively **restaurant ❷**. Bungalows in the back are a bit noisier. (☎620 615; www.ppcharlie.com. Bungalows with fan 750฿, with A/C 1200-1400฿.)

HAT HIN KOHN AND LAEM HIM. Just southeast of Ao Thon Sai, a path leads to flat Hat Hin Kohn, a long stretch of sand sprinkled with bungalows. The beach is decent, but far from the island's best. **Andaman Guest House ❹** has new rooms that are plain but fairly clean. (Singles and doubles 500-600฿.) The similarly named **Andaman Resort ❹**, at the end of the beach, has clean bungalows in a quiet spot by the island's primary school. (Bungalows 500-800฿, with A/C 1000-2900฿.) Heading right from the pier next to the coast takes you around a small promontory known as Laem Him. Past Laem Him is a stretch of quieter beach, which is completely overrun with longtail boats. **Gypsy 1 ❸**, inland from the path after the mosque and about 100m from the shore, has clean and basic bungalows with baths at rock-bottom prices by Phi Phi standards, as does **Gypsy 2 ❸**, 50m farther on. (☎01 229 1674. Bungalows 350-600฿.)

MA PRAO AND HAT YAO (LONG BEACH). The best option in the area is just before Long Beach on a lush promontory called Ma Prao. **Ma Prao Resort ❸** has wood and bamboo huts only a stone's throw from the water. The **restaurant ❷** has excellent food, drink, and music. (☎622 485. Basic bungalows 300-800฿.) Just over the hill, past Ma Prao, is Hat Yao, commonly known as Long Beach. It has Ko Phi Phi's best sand and swimming, and the lack of nightlife keeps partiers away. Hat Yao's good mix of accommodations complements its pleasant beach. The cheapest is the cheerful, expat-run **Long Beach Resort ❷**, offering little more than four walls and a bed, but with a smile. (☎612 217. Singles and doubles 150-350฿.) Farther up the beach, away from Ma Prao, is the pricey but pleasant **Phi-Phi Natural Resort ❺**. Spacious, well-equipped bungalows offer water views. (☎07 622 3636; www.phiphinatural.com. Bungalows with A/C 1400-3800฿.)

FOOD AND ENTERTAINMENT

Ko Phi Phi offers an outstanding range of international cuisine. The cream of the crop is **Cosmo Resto ❸**, an Italian restaurant with exceptional pasta. Run by an Italian expat, the restaurant is only open for dinner and closes on random days of the week. When open, the unassuming place is one of Thailand's best restaurants. (Dishes 120-380฿. Open roughly 5 days per week.) The **Lemongrass Restaurant ❷**, off the main road in Ao Thon Sai, is one of the only places to get good Thai food. (Rice dishes 60-80฿. Curries 70-120฿. Open daily 9am-11pm.) **Pee Pee Bakery ❷** offers delicious baked goods and cheap Western and Thai dishes. The film showings are a huge favorite. (One location on the pier road and another on the path to The Rock Backpacker at the east end of the village. Pastries 5-20฿. Dishes 40-120฿. Open daily 7am-10pm.) **Garlic 1992 Restaurant ❷**, proud of its relative old age (as compared to other Phi Phi restaurants), sure loves its garlic. Everything is spicy and delicious. (Located just past V Shop in the village. Dishes 40-90฿.)

THAILAND

By night, Ao Thon Sai a hotbed of activity. **Jordan's Irish Bar** relinquishes anything Irish in favor of music that will make *farang* wave their hands in the air. The **Rolling Stoned Bar** blasts chill music, much of it live, until sunrise. The **Reggae Bar** has a large dance floor and a boxing ring featuring nightly matches (around 10pm). **Carlito's Bar,** on the walkway toward Long Beach, has live entertainment. Look for drink specials at all of the above bars.

OUTDOOR ACTIVITIES

Bamboo Island and **Mosquito Island** are famous dive sites, and there are many dive shops and tour agents eager to serve you. PADI certification courses generally cost 10,000฿ (far more than Ko Tao). **Visa Diving Center** is one of the best. **Hippo Divers,** an expat-run outfit left from the pier, offers a range of area dives for 800-3200฿. (☎618 200; www.hippodivers.com. Open daily 10am-9:30pm.) Snorkeling is also popular and far cheaper (usually 500฿ for a daytrip including lunch and gear). **Maya Tour & Travel** (p. 810) runs quality half-day and full-day tours.

KRABI ☎075

Tourists come to this area for the beaches of Ao Nang, Rai Ley, and Ko Lanta; Krabi itself is little more than a necessary transit point. However, its mellow vibe and excellent budget accommodations more than justify an overnight stay.

TRANSPORTATION

Buses: The **bus station** (☎611 804) is 5km north of town along Utarakit Rd. Buses to: **Bangkok** (12hr., 8 per day 8am-5:30pm, 378-710฿); **Hat Yai** (5hr., every hr. 9am-3:20pm, 173฿); **Phuket** (5hr., every hr. 9am-5pm, 117฿); **Satun** (5hr.; 11am, 1pm; 175฿); **Surat Thani** (4½hr., every hr. 9:30am-1:30pm, 80฿; A/C 3½hr., 5 per day 7am-1pm, 120฿); **Trang** (2½hr., every 2hr. 9am-5pm, 90฿).

Minivans: Private travel agencies operate A/C minibuses to various towns in Thailand and Malaysia. They are the primary mode of transit to **Ko Lanta** when ferries aren't running. Usually every hr. 7am-7pm, but in low season only 4 times per day (2hr., 100฿).

Ferries: Longtail boats leave from **Chao Fah Pier** on Kongka Rd. to: **Hat Rai Lay** (30min., 8am-5pm, 70฿) and **Ko Lanta** (2½hr.; 10:30am, 1:30pm; 200฿). From the shiny new **Passenger Marine Port** 5km south of town, **express boats** go to **Ko Phi Phi** (1½hr.; 10:30am, 2:30pm; 200฿). In the low season, service decreases and the Ko Lanta ferry service shuts down altogether.

Local Transportation: Songthaew run up and down Utarakit Rd. and go to: the **bus station** (20฿ from the center of town); **Ao Nang** (after 6pm 50฿); the **Shell Cemetery** (16-20฿); **Wat Tham Sua** (20฿); other places near Krabi. **Tuk-tuks** go to the center of town from: the new passenger pier (30฿); the bus terminal (50฿); the airport (100฿).

Rentals: Travel agencies and guesthouses on Utarakit Rd. rent **motorbikes** for 150-200฿ per day. Some also rent **jeeps** (1200-1500฿ per day).

ORIENTATION AND PRACTICAL INFORMATION

Central Krabi is compact and easily walkable. **Utarakit Road,** the city's main street, runs parallel to the **Krabi River** and is home to most services. Parallel to Utarakit Rd. and one block over, **Maharat Road** has shops and eateries. Boats to Hat Rai Lay and Ko Lanta leave from **Chao Fah Pier** on **Kongka Road,** which branches off Utarakit Rd. and runs along the river. **Chaofa Road,** running from the pier past Utarakit Rd. is home to several *farang*-oriented hotels and restaurants.

The local **TAT** office is on Utarakit Rd. near Chaofa Rd. The staff speaks English and has good maps. (☎612 740. Open daily 8:30am-4:30pm.) A **market** sets up on Sukhon Rd. across from City Hotel. (Open daily 8am-11pm.) Other services include: the **police,** 500m past the post office (☎637 208; little English spoken); **Krabi Hospital,** on Utarakit Rd., 2km north of town (☎611 227; some English spoken; 24hr.); **Internet** access on Utarakit Rd. in cafes and guesthouses (1฿ per min. or 40฿ per hr., with a 10฿ min.); the **post office,** on top of the hill on the left. (☎611 497. *Poste Restante.* Open M-F 8:30am-4:30pm, Sa 9am-noon.) **Postal Code:** 81000.

ACCOMMODATIONS AND FOOD

Most of Krabi's budget choices lie near the pier along **Utarakit Road.** Room prices are generally 100-200฿ cheaper in the low season. **K Guest House ❷,** on Chaofa Rd. one block from the intersection with Utarakit Rd., is very comfortable. (Singles and doubles 200-250฿, with private bath 300฿.) Just past K Guest House and across the street is **Ban Chaofa ❹,** 20/1 Chaofa Rd. This elegant hotel is worth visiting just for the bathrooms. (☎630 359; banchaofa@hotmail.com. TV downstairs. Rooms with A/C 500-800฿; low-season with fan 300฿, with A/C 400-500฿.) **Chan-Cha-Lay Guest House ❸,** 55 Utarakit Rd. up the hill, is one of the hippest digs in town. (☎620 952. Popular restaurant. Laundry. **Internet.** Reservations recommended. Prices may rise after renovations. Singles and doubles 200฿; doubles with twin beds 250฿.) There are two **night markets,** one opposite the City Hotel (open until 9pm) and one by the pier. Several *farang*-friendly restaurants and cheap foodstalls are on **Kongka Road,** just north of the pier. For an interesting dining experience, try **Ruenmai Thai ❷** on Maharat Rd., 2km from town past the hospital (motorcycle taxi 30฿). This huge outdoor restaurant has tables surrounded by jungle-like vegetation. For 60฿, try the blissful coconut-cream prawn soup with *pak mieng* or edible ferns with fish. (Open daily 10am-10pm.) The **restaurant ❷** in Ban Chaofa specializes in pizza and pasta dishes and also serves a delicious vegetarian *pad thai.* (Thai dishes 40-70฿. Italian dishes 130-170฿. Open 7am-10pm.)

THAILAND

SIGHTS

Krabi's most impressive sight is **Wat Tham Sua,** 8km north of town along Utarakit Rd. An operating monastery comprised of monks, nuns, and tourists, the *wat* is best known for its **Tiger Cave.** Legend has it that a large tiger once lived here, and its footsteps adorn the *wat*'s entrance (donation requested). Outside, stairs by the rear of the monastery lead up the mountain (30-45min.) to a pair of **Buddha's footprints.** One benefit of the hike is a fantastic view of Krabi and the surrounding area from the top. Utarakit Rd. *songthaew* (15min., 10฿) drop you off at an access road 2km from the *wat.* Or, walk or take a motorcycle taxi (5min., 10฿) to the entrance.

DAYTRIP FROM KRABI

KHLONG THOM

To get to the trail, take a motorbike from Krabi or a songthaew to Khlong Thom. Mr. Koyou at the Krabi Bird Club, 24 Phetkasem Rd., will haul tourists around in his pick-up truck (300฿). Contact him by calling the park's tourist office (☎622 124); TAT can also track him down. If hiring a motorcycle taxi from Khlong Thom (100฿), be sure to arrange return transportation.

The **Khao Nawe Choochee Lowland Forest** is one of the last remaining forests of its kind in Thailand. Among the 290-plus bird species that nest in the forest is *Pitta gurneyi*, a brightly colored, ground-dwelling bird of which only 150 remain. The **Thung Tieo Nature Trail** (2.7km) traverses some of Thailand's most lush and undisturbed slices of nature. Hop into the natural pool or hot spring for relaxation.

HAT RAI LAY AND HAT PHRA NANG ☎075

With spectacular limestone cliffs dropping onto sand beaches and luminous, turquoise waters, Hat Rai Lay has become a haven for both climbers and beach lovers. Hat Rai Lay also offers hiking trails, a mellow nightlife, and peaceful beaches, while Hat Phra Nang's caves provide hours of exploring potential. Hat Rai Lay is actually two beaches, **Hat Rai Lay East** and **Hat Rai Lay West,** which occupy opposite sides of a peninsula. Rai Lay East is little more than a littered mangrove forest, but Rai Lay West's beach is a good deal nicer. The best way to get to Hat Rai Lay is by **longtail boats** docking at Hat Rai Lay East from Ao Nang (20min.; shared 50฿, chartered 200฿) or Krabi (30min., 70฿/300฿). In the low season, Ao Nang becomes inaccessible by longtail boat; they instead go to Ao Nam Mao (15min., 40฿/200฿), a short *songthaew* ride from Ao Nang (15min., 10฿). The east side of the peninsula has a few budget accommodations, climbing schools, mangrove trees, and the gorgeous and largely undisturbed **Hat Phra Nang.** To get to Hat Phra Nang from Hat Rai Lay East, with your back to the boats turn left and walk to the end of the beach; a dirt path to your right leads to Hat Phra Nang. Hat Rai Lay West can be reached easily by cutting through Sand Sea Bungalows or Rai Lay Bay Bungalows.

Finding good deals on Hat Rai Lay between October and May can be difficult, but during the low season prices plummet by 50 percent or more. **Ya-Ya Bungalow ❸** has the best off-beach location and a lively **restaurant.** (☎622 593. Closed in low season.) On the northern end of Hat Rai Lay East, **Viewpoint Bungalow ❸** has clean, modern bungalows with enormous windows that put the "view" in Viewpoint. (☎622 588. The only **Internet** access on the beach. Bungalows with fan 400฿, with A/C 1200-2000฿; low-season 200฿/400-700฿.) Hat Rai Lay West has more upscale accommodations. **Rai Lay Village Resort ❺** charges twice as much as Hat Rai Lay East digs for posh bungalows with nicer baths and landscaping. (☎622 578. Bungalows 1500-3000฿; low-season 500-1200฿.) The expensive **Dusit Rayavadee Resort ❺** dominates Hat Phra Nang, though there never seems to be anyone staying there. It's much more practical to find cheaper accommodations on Hat Rai Lay East and daytrip to Hat Phra Nang.

The hotels have their own restaurants, and most of them serve similar, reasonably priced Thai and Western dishes. After a day of climbing, many travelers flock to **CoCo Restaurant ❷** on the northern part of Hat Rai Lay East for tasty Thai dishes. (Chicken wrapped in steamed leaves 60฿. Open daily 8am-10:30pm.) **Cholay Pancakes ❶,** in a booth outside Ya-Ya Bungalow, serves delicious *roti* for 15-30฿. (Open daily 9am-midnight.) Nightlife options include **Yaya's Bar, Last Bar,** or the **beachfront,** where fire dancers light up the beach to pulsing music.

The Rai Lay beaches and environs have become the **rock climbing** capital of Southeast Asia, especially for beginners, and several schools have cropped up to meet the increasing demand. **Krabi Rock Climbing,** on Hat Rai Lay East, is known for its friendly staff. (☎01 676 0642. Half-day course 800฿, 1-day 1800฿, 3-day 5000฿. Equipment rental available.) **Hot Rock Climbing** (☎01 677 3727), next to CoCo Restaurant on Hat Rai Lay East, is also popular. Adventures closer to sea level await you on Hat Phra Nang. Extending past the water, dagger-like stalagmites protect **Princess Cave,** which can be explored by land or sea with a flashlight. About halfway down the dirt path to Hat Phra Nang from Hat Rai Lay East, another dirt path leads to a few mountain viewpoints and a lagoon best visited at high tide. Bring sturdy footwear, expendable clothing, and company for the challenging climb to the top. Closer to Hat Rai Lay East beach, a hidden path leads to the popular **Diamond Cave,** whose walls sparkle with the precious stone.

AO NANG ☎075

Ao Nang's accessibility by car gives it a completely different atmosphere from either secluded Rai Lay or Phang-Nga. With brightly colored shops, beachfront hotels, and a boardwalk perfect for a stroll, Ao Nang has a pleasant holiday feel.

Sea Canoe Krabi (☎612 740), near Gift's Bungalows, offers half-day (500-800฿) and full-day (800-1200฿) self-paddled trips along the coast as well as equipment rental. A guided trip includes meals, fruit, and water (1200-1600฿). Rent **mountain bikes** (30฿ per hr.) at **Ao Nang Adventure Travel and Tour** on the corner before the main shops, coming from Krabi. Ask for a map. Full-day snorkeling tours of the nearby islands by speedboat cost 1000-1200฿, but only 300฿ by the slower and noisier longtail boat. Low-season speedboat discounts (500-600฿) are available from **J. Mansion** (see below). **Nosy Parker's Elephant Trekking and River Camp** (☎637 464) offers elephant treks (700฿) and half-day tours (1600฿). On the road that runs past the beach there are **moneychangers, ATMs,** a **minimarket,** restaurants, and **tour offices.** There is a **police** substation on the town's main road across from PK Mansion. (☎695 163. Open daily 8am-midnight.) Find white Krabi-bound **songthaew** on the beach road during the day (30฿ before 6pm, 50฿ thereafter).

Many lodgings in Ao Nang offer services besides room rental. **Blue Bayou ❸,** in the quiet outskirts of town, has kayak rentals (200฿ per 2 hours). The **restaurant ❸** serves Thai and Western cuisine. (☎637 148. Single and double bungalows with fan 350-500฿, with A/C 750฿; low-season 200-400฿/500฿.) The twin steals of **J. Mansion** and **J. Hotel ❺,** 302 Moo 2, are located about a 2min. walk from the beach. Rooms are big, clean, and come with hot shower, minifridge, and TV. Try to get a fourth-floor room at J. Hotel for sea views. (☎695 128; www.krabidir.com/j_mansion. Fan rooms 600฿, with A/C 800฿; low-season 300฿/400฿.) The best Thai food from the beachfront restaurants is available at **Ao Nang Cuisine ❷,** in the middle of the strip. (Thai entrees 45-75฿. Western dishes 80-200฿. Open daily 9am-11pm.) The ideally situated **Poda Restaurant ❷,** in Felix Phra Nang Inn in the circular building, is an alternative to bungalow basics. The green curry soup with shrimp is exceptional. (Most dishes 70-90฿. Open daily 7am-10pm.)

KO LANTA YAI ☎075

While the northern part of Ko Lanta Yai is fairly developed, more serene parts can be found to the south, especially in the area surrounding the national marine park. During the high season, **boats** arrive regularly from Krabi at Ban Sala Dan Pier (2½hr.; 10:30am, 1:30pm, return 8am; 200฿), at the northern tip of the island. Boats also leave from Ko Phi Phi for Ko Lanta (1½hr.; 10am, 1pm; 200฿). Otherwise, minivans depart year-round from Krabi and connect via ferry with Ko Lanta (2hr.; 11am, 1, 4pm; 200฿). **Ban Sala Dan** is the island's largest town, with a police booth, a post office, **Internet** cafes, banks, a health center, and other conveniences. Much of the town closes down during the low season, however.

Most resorts offer free pick-up from minivan and ferry drop-off points, as well as a free return, as long as you purchase your ticket through them. Reservations are recommended during the high season. The roads on the island are extremely poor and can be dangerous even for experienced drivers, but for those who insist on going it alone, most tour agencies rent motorbikes for 200-250฿ per day. Around the corner from Ban Sala Dan is Ko Lanta Yai's **Hat Klong Dao,** a 2km beach sprinkled with quality resorts. Klong Dao has decent coral at its north end and the beach faces directly west, making for stellar sunsets. **Golden Bay Cottages** ❺ offers spacious accommodations with huge price swings based on the season. (Bungalows with fan 800฿, with A/C 1500฿; low-season 100฿/300-600฿.) Toward the more rugged south, overlooking the scenic Kanthiang Bay, the **Marine Park View Resort** ❷ offers an excellent range of accommodations, from television-equipped A/C bungalows to more rustic rooms, all with private baths. The three-tiered **restaurant** ❷ overlooks the peaceful bay. Most entrees are between 60-180฿. (☎01 397 0793; www.krabidir.com/lantampv. Rooms 150฿; bungalows with fan 400-900฿, with A/C 1500฿. Low-season 150฿/200฿/400฿.) Off the same drive as Marine Park View, the **restaurant** ❷ at Top View Koh Lanta, precariously perched atop a west-facing cliff, has small portions but absolutely jaw-dropping sunset views. Most dishes are between 50 and 120฿. There are eight other beaches on the island, including the beautiful **Nin** and **Kanthiang** beaches, and **Hin** beach, renowned for its snorkeling. There is also excellent diving and snorkeling at the offshore islands. A few outstanding daytrips to the interior head to the **Tham Mai Ka** caves or to **waterfalls,** and visitors can take **elephant treks.**

TRANG ☎075

Trang offers no special attractions but its relatively *farang*-free atmosphere provides relief from the southern Thailand tourist circuit. What's more, the province contains 119km of beaches and a formidable collection of small islands, mostly undisturbed by large-scale development.

TRANSPORTATION

Flights: Trang Airport (☎210 804), on Trang-Palian Rd., 7km south of the city. Take Trang Travel's airport vans (30฿) or a *tuk-tuk* (50฿) into town. **Thai Airways,** 199/2 Visetkul Rd. (☎218 066). Turn right at the clocktower onto Visetkul Rd.; it's several blocks down on the left, just past Soi 5. Open daily 8am-noon and 1-4:30pm. Daily flights to **Bangkok** (9:15pm, 2855฿).

Trains: Railway station (☎218 012), at the west end of Phraram 6 Rd. Train service is quite limited; buses and minivans are a better bet. Fares listed are 2nd-class express. Trains to: **Bangkok** (16hr. sleeper; 2:30, 5:20pm; 970฿) via **Chumphon** (7hr., 571฿) and **Surat Thani** (5hr., 201฿).

Buses: Bus station (☎215 718), on Huay Yod Rd., north of downtown. Check with TAT for buses that leave from other parts of city. Buses to: **Bangkok** (10hr., 4:30pm, 565฿); **Hat Yai** (4hr., every hr. 7am-7pm, 60-100฿); **Krabi** (2hr., every hr. 6am-8pm, 50-80฿); **Phuket** (5hr., every hr. 6am-6pm, 100-189฿).

Minivans: Leave from various parts of town. **Beach** minivans leave from Taklang Rd. near the railroad tracks (1½hr., every hr. 8am-5pm, 50฿). Service is less frequent during the low season. **Kantang Pier** minivans leave from Kantang Rd. in the opposite direction from Phraram 6 Rd. Minivans to **Surat Thani** (3hr., every hr. 9:30am-5pm, 125฿) leave from the train station. Check with hotels or travel agencies in town for departure location of minivans to: **Hat Yai** (every 30min. 6am-6pm, 70-99฿); **Krabi** (2hr., every hr. 7am-6pm, 90฿); **Nakhon Si Thammarat** (2½hr., every 2hr. 9am-5pm, 80฿); **Phang-Nga** (4hr., every hr. 7am-6pm, 139฿); **Phuket** (5hr., every hr. 7am-6pm, 189฿); **Satun** (3hr.; 1:30, 3:30pm; 101฿).

Local Transportation: Pastel green **tuk-tuks** within the city run at a fixed 15฿ per person. They're a little difficult to find, but definitely the way to go since they cost the same as **motorcycle taxis,** which line every street corner. **Taxis** (15฿) and **minivans** (10฿) leave when full from different parts of town (every 20min. 5am-7pm).

ORIENTATION AND PRACTICAL INFORMATION

Buses arrive at the **bus station** near the intersection of **Ploenpitak Road** and **Huay Yod Road,** a 20min. walk north of town or 5min. by motorcycle taxi or *tuk-tuk* (both 20฿). The **railway station** sits at the west end of **Phraram 6 Road,** a large hotel-lined avenue with a landmark **clocktower** and most other tourist services. North of Phraram 6 Rd., **Ratchadamnoen Road** (which becomes **Pattalung Road**) winds roughly parallel to the main day market and connects to Phraram 6 Rd. by **Kantang Road** to the west and **Visetkul Road** to the east by the clocktower.

Tourist Office: The **TAT** office in Nakhon Si Thammarat handles Trang queries. In town, try the **Trang Tourist Association** (☎/fax 215 580), next to the Trang Hotel on Phraram 6 Rd. Very helpful staff and free maps. Open daily 8am-5:30pm.

Tours: Travel agencies offering organized tours and transportation line Phraram 6 Rd.

Currency Exchange: Bangkok Bank, 2 Phraram 6 Rd. (☎218 203), 1 block from the train station on the right. 24hr. **ATM.** Open M-F 8:30am-3:30pm.

Markets: The **day market** sells mostly produce and is near the train station. One **night market** is outside the Diamond Department Store near the train station; another, bigger one between Pattalung and Phraram 6 Rd., near the police station.

Police: 6 Pattalung Rd. (☎211 311). Some English spoken. Open 24hr.

Medical Services: Wattanapat Hospital, 247 Pattalung Rd. (☎218 585), at the intersection with Ploenpitak Rd., northeast of the clocktower. English spoken. Open 24hr.

Internet Access: Gigabyte, 126 Phraram 6 Rd. 30฿ per hr. Open daily 9am-10pm.

Post Offices: GPO (☎218 521), at the bend on Jermpanya Rd., which branches north from Phraram 6 Rd., a 20min. walk from train station. *Poste Restante.* **International phones.** Open M-F 8:30am-3:30pm. **Branch office** on Phraram 6 Rd., 1 block from train station. Open M-F 8:30am-4:30pm, Sa-Su 9am-noon.

Postal Code: 92000.

ACCOMMODATIONS AND FOOD

Koh Teng Hotel ❷, 77-79 Phraram 6 Rd., five blocks from the train station on the left and one block before the clocktower, pitches itself as the best place in town for backpackers. The large rooms are clean and comfortable. (☎218 148. Singles and doubles 180฿, with TV 220฿, with A/C 280฿.) Another excellent guesthouse is **Yamawa Bed and Breakfast ❸,** 94 Visetkul Rd., offering TVs, a terrace, **Internet,** and a massage parlor. (☎07 521 6617; www.trang-yamawa.com. Breakfast 50฿. Closes periodically in low season. 200฿ per person.) Trang has two **night markets,** both open daily 6-10pm. There's also a **day market** by the train station. **Kanok Restaurant ❷,** 31/1 Visetkul Rd., just down the street from the Queen Hotel, has standard Thai fare in a low-key atmosphere. (Dishes 40-80฿. Open daily 9am-9pm.) **Koh Teng Restaurant ❶,** below the hotel of the same name, serves tasty Chinese and Thai dishes for lunch or an early-bird special. (Dishes 30-90฿. Open daily 7am-5pm.)

ENTERTAINMENT

Trang offers a different kind of entertainment. Traders sell colorful **fighting fish** on Phraram 6 Rd. Makeshift **cock fighting** arenas are below stilt houses, and **bullfights** are staged a few times a year. (Direct *tuk-tuk* drivers to Sanam Wuah Chon (10฿) near the bullfight field. Tickets from 100฿.) The Trang Chamber of Commerce organizes events like the **Cake Festival** (August) and **Barbecue Festival** (September).

DAYTRIPS FROM TRANG

The area surrounding Trang offers a bevy of attractions, from caves to oceanside Edens. Expect few tourists even in places like **Ko Mook** and **Pakmeng,** and only a smattering of locals on isolated **Hat Yong Ling.** Most towns are accessible from Trang by **minivan. Boats** to islands near Pakmeng, such as **Ko Hai** and Ko Mook, leave from **Pakmeng Pier** (100-600฿). Boats to **Ko Sukorn** leave from the pier at Tasae Cape in southern Trang Province.

HAT YONG LING NATIONAL PARK. The park has two coves sheltered by mountain-covered orchids. Trek through the forest to reach one of the best sand-and-sea combos around. Hat Yong Ling's **National Park Headquarters,** actually located on the southern end of **Hat Chang Lang,** also serves its distant neighbor **Hat Chao Mai.** (☎213 260. Open M-F 9am-5pm.) There is a **ranger station** in the center of Ban Yong Ling. *(Minibuses to Hat Yong Ling for 50฿ leave every hr. or when full from near the beach. During low season, it may be necessary to hire a taxi or minivan from Trang or Pakmeng for 400฿.)*

HAT PAKMENG. Busy Hat Pakmeng's beach is long but shallow. Although not good for swimming, there are several picturesque limestone formations dotting the horizon. Numerous seafood stalls and restaurants serve customers reclining in their beach chairs. The popular **Pakmeng Resort ❹,** farther south, offers tidy bungalows and private baths. *(☎210 321. Singles and doubles 400฿, with A/C 750-800฿. Minivans (45min.; every hr., low-season every 2hr.; 50฿) from Trang will take you to the center of the beach or to Pakmeng Resort. To return, flag down a van on the main road.)*

THAILAND

KO MOOK. Easily accessible from Pakmeng Pier, Ko Mook is the most developed of the Trang Province islands. **Emerald Cave,** so named for its tinted waters, is a spectacular sight. Visitors must swim to the lagoon at the center. The nicer and cheaper western side of the island boasts a great white-sand beach. Of the island's four resorts, **Had Farung Bungalows ❷** is the least expensive (bungalows 200฿, with bath 300฿), and **Sawatdee Resort ❷** has a highly recommended restaurant. On the west side, similarly-priced **Muk Resort ❷** (☎214 441) and **Muk Garden Resort ❷** (☎211 372) can arrange transport to the island from their offices in Trang. *(Take a minivan to Pakmeng Pier (1hr., 50฿) and hop on a boat to the island (1hr.; 11am; 400฿, alone 600฿). Bungalows at Sawatdee, Muk Resort, and Muk Garden 300฿.)*

KO HAI (KO NGAI). With white-sand beaches and three pricey resorts, teardrop-shaped Ko Hai (sometimes spelled "Ko Ngai") is an excellent dive and snorkeling spot. **Koh Ngai Villa ❹** has the cheapest rooms and arranges trips to and from the island. (☎210 496. Bungalows with fan 500-800฿; low-season 300-500฿.) More upscale **Koh Ngai Resort ❺** has a diving center. *(☎210 317. Bungalows 600-780฿. The ferry to Ko Hai leaves from Pakmeng Pier at 11:30am and returns at 8am the following day (150฿). Otherwise, charter a longtail boat (600฿ each way) for the 1hr. ride.)*

KO KRADAN. Pristine Ko Kradan, under the protection of the **Hat Jao Mai National Park,** contains only one high-end resort. Since **Ko Kradan Paradise Beach ❺** knows you're a hostage, the food is as expensive as the rooms; bring your own from the mainland. (☎211 391. Bungalows 600-2500฿, low-season 400-1000฿.)

NAKHON SI THAMMARAT ☎075

Located off the backpacker circuit, Nakhon Si Thammarat is a bustling city whose long cultural history is evident in the town's markets and *wats,* including the largest temple in all of southern Thailand. Buddhists come here from all over the world to visit the massive Wat Phramahathat. Known for its fine jewelry and basketry, Nakhon Si Thammarat is a perfect choice for those looking for the chance to stock up on souvenirs.

TRANSPORTATION

Flights: Airport (☎346 976), 20km north of town. **Thai Airways,** 1612 Ratchadamnoen Rd. (☎312 500), flies daily to Bangkok (1hr., 8:15am, 2525฿). Open daily 8am-7:30pm. Thai's "competitor," **PB Air,** is located in the same office, reached via the same phone number, and does the Bangkok flight daily at 1:35pm for the same price.

Trains: Railway station, on Yommarat Rd. at Pagnagon Rd., 1 block from downtown. Nakhon Si Thammarat is on a spur off the Southern line, so service is somewhat limited. Fares given are 2nd class. Trains to: **Bangkok** (15-16hr.; 1, 2pm; 488-728฿); **Sungai Kolok** (9hr., 6:10am, 372฿); **Phatthalung** (2½hr.; 6:10, 10:20am, 3pm; 213฿).

Buses: The **bus terminal** (☎341 125) is off Phaniant Rd. past the mosque and across the railroad tracks. Buses go to: **Bangkok** (12hr.; 7am, 4-7pm; 350-454฿); **Hat Yai** (3hr., every hr. 4:30am-4:30pm, 73-102฿); **Ko Samui** (5hr.; 11:30am; 135฿, includes ferry fare); **Phatthalung** (3hr., 7 per day 6am-3:30pm, 43฿); **Phuket** (8hr., 7 per day 5:20-11am, 125-175฿); **Ranong** (6hr., 7:30am, 252฿); **Surat Thani** (2½hr., frequent 5am-5pm, 55-60฿); **Trang** (2hr.; 6, 9:10am, 2:50pm; 65฿).

Minivans: Leave from stands and travel agencies all over town, most within 1 block of Ratchadamnoen Rd. near downtown. Inquire at TAT or your hotel.

Local Transportation: An impressive and efficient **songthaew** fleet has rendered *tuk-tuks* obsolete in Nakhon Si. Blue *songthaew* ply linear routes on virtually every major street in town (every 2min. 6am-8pm, 6฿). **Motorcycle taxis** do the same for more *baht* and more adventure (20-40฿).

THAILAND

ORIENTATION AND PRACTICAL INFORMATION

Most of the city's sights and services are on or within a block of **Ratchadamnoen Road,** the main street. The town's commercial center is in the northern part of town. Here **Yommarat Road** runs parallel to the west of Ratchadamnoen Rd. and **Si Prat Road** runs to the east. The **train station** is on Yommarat Rd. Si Prat Rd. is the site of more **banks, hotels, restaurants,** and **shops.** Between Ratchadamnoen Rd. and Yommarat Rd. is **Jamroenwithi Road,** home to the **night market. Pagnagon Road** is the city's largest east-west street. It runs from the train station past Ratchadamnoen Rd. downtown to some good eateries, **hotels,** and a **day market.** A new part of town is east of the center near **Phatthanakarn-Khukhwang Road** and contains a number of Western-style shopping centers.

Tourist Office: Two official tourist offices in town. The more useful is **TAT** (☎346 515; tatnksri@tat.or.th), near Sanam Na Meuang Park, a few blocks south of downtown past the police station along Ratchadamnoen Rd. English-speaking staff dispenses a full range of city information. Ask for Bom, the office manager. Open daily 8:30am-4:30pm.

Currency Exchange: Banks line Ratchadamnoen Rd. in the downtown area. Off the main road, try **Krung Thai Bank** on Pagnagon Rd., 1 block from Ratchadamnoen Rd. heading away from the train station. Open M-F 8:30am-4:30pm.

Markets: Two produce-oriented **day markets,** one on Yommarat Rd. south of the train station, the other on Pagnagon Rd. past the Nakorn Garden Hotel, a few blocks east of Ratchadamnoen Rd. heading away from the train station. **Night market** on Jamroenwithi Rd., near intersection with Pagnagon Rd., between Ratchadamnoen Rd. and Phatthanakarn-Khukhwang Rd. to the east. **Souvenir markets** selling local jewelry, basketry, and pottery at good prices across the street from Robinson's department store east of downtown, and near TAT on Si Thammarat Rd. south of downtown.

Police: (☎356 500). On Ratchadamnoen Rd. a few blocks south of downtown. Very little English spoken. Open 24hr.

Hospital: Christian Hospital (☎356 214), at Si Prat and Phaniant Rd., is the best bet in terms of location and English skills. Open 24hr.

Internet Access: Several places offer 20฿ per hr. Try **Java,** near Robinson's department store off Phatthanakarn-Khukhwang Rd. east of downtown. Open daily 8am-10pm.

Post Offices: GPO, on Ratchadamnoen Rd. across the street from the police. *Poste Restante.* Open M-F 8:30am-4:30pm, Sa-Su 9am-noon. Branch office on Pagnagon Rd. 3 blocks from Ratchadamnoen Rd., past the Nakorn Garden Hotel on the right.

Postal Code: 80000.

ACCOMMODATIONS AND FOOD

There are two types of places in Nakhon Si Thammarat: middle-class A/C hotels and dirt-cheap digs. **Thailee Hotel ❷,** 1128-30 Ratchadamnoen Rd., is at the corner with Boh-Ang Rd., one block before City Hall from the train station. Clean rooms and professional service make this a good deal. There are squat toilets, but the rooms are comfortable. (☎356 948. Singles and doubles 120฿.) Just past Krung Thai Bank, one block from Ratchadamnoen Rd. away from the train station, is **Nakorn Garden Hotel ❸,** 1/4 Pagnagon Rd. The greenery lets you forget you're in the city. All rooms come with A/C, hot shower, minifridge, and TV. (☎313 333. Attached restaurant. Singles and doubles 445฿.) **Kanokinn Hotel ❷,** 30/307-8 Ratchapruk Rd., east of Robinson's department store past Phatthanakarn-Khukhwang Rd. is convenient to the newer part of town, Kanokinn offers clean, comfortable rooms with A/C, TV, and hot showers. (☎318 555. Singles and doubles 280฿.)

The **night market** offers curries, rice, and fried whole chickens. The **foodstall** on Jamroenwithi Rd. at the corner with Pagnagon Rd. has particularly good *roti* and green tea for 15฿. (Open daily 6pm-midnight.) The **foodstall** nearest to Phatthanakarn-Khukhwang Rd. on Pagnagon Rd. is the best place for curried rice dishes. (Most everything 15฿. Open daily 10am-midnight.) **Khrua Nakhon ❷,** inside Bavorn Bazaar just off Ratchadamnoen Rd., is in the heart of downtown; turn into the small alley at the 7-Eleven. Come here at lunchtime for a real taste of Nakhon Si. (Fish curries served with coconut rice 40฿. Open daily 6am-3pm.) **A&A Restaurant ❷** is on Pagnagon Rd. just past Si Prat Rd., heading away from the town center. A large, pleasant Western-style cafe. (Delicious ice cream 7฿. Thai dishes 40-90฿. Fresh-brewed coffee 20฿. Open daily 7am-midnight.)

SIGHTS

WAT PHRAMAHATHAT WORAMAHA WIHAAN. The largest temple in the south, Wat Phramahathat is said to be over 1000 years old. The *wat*'s compound houses the Phra Borom That Chedi, built around AD 757, during the Si Wichai period. The base diameter is 23m and it is 53m high, making it the second tallest pagoda in Thailand. *(Located 2km south of downtown on Ratchadamnoen Rd. Take any songthaew heading south on Ratchadamnoen Rd. from the center of town (10min., 6฿). Open daily 7am-4pm.)*

NATIONAL MUSEUM. The museum contains a number of interesting and historically significant artifacts, the most impressive being the throne of King Rama V, with intricate carvings exemplifying the craftwork of Nakhon Si Thammarat artisans. The museum also contains Hindu and Sri Lankan Buddhist images and artifacts. *(3km south of town on Ratchadamnoen Rd. Southbound Ratchadamnoen Rd.* songthaew *(6฿) go past the museum entrance. Open W-Su 8:30am-4pm. 30฿.)*

SHADOW PLAYHOUSE. One of Nakhon Si Thammarat's most famous residents is the puppet maker, Suchart Sabsin. From his small shop on the southern end of town, Sabsin and his apprentices work on enormous buffalo-hide puppets. When enough people gather, he will even give a free demonstration. Also on the premises is the International Puppet Museum, featuring puppets from around the world. *(On Thammasok Soi 3, 2km south of the city center. Take a blue* songthaew *(6฿) south from the city, or walk over 2 blocks from Wat Phramahathat. Open daily 8:30am-4:30pm. Free.)*

SURAT THANI ☎077

Surat Thani's tourist industry caters to those waiting for the next boat to Ko Samui or the next bus heading west or south. Few travelers stay here long enough for more than a stroll down the river promenade or a snack at the day market. While overnight visitors are able to indulge in the vibrant night market, there is not much more to do in Surat Thani than check your watch and re-examine your ticket out.

THAILAND

TRANSPORTATION

Flights: Airport (☎253 500), 30km outside of town. **Thai Airways,** 3/27-8 Karoonrat Rd. (☎441 137), flies daily to **Bangkok** (1hr.; 12:40, 7:15pm; 242฿). The office, 2km inland from the pier, is remote; **Phantip Tour** (p. 822) handles bookings from the city center. More destinations are accessible from Ko Samui's airport, but with an added 800฿ departure tax. Vans leave from the Thai office and Phantip Travel for the airport 2-2½hr. prior to departure and head to town 30-60min. after flight arrivals 70฿.

Trains: Railway station (☎311 213), in Phun Phin, 13km from Surat Thani. Orange buses run between Talaat Kaset 1 in town and the station; catch them on Talaat Mai Rd. (25min., every 5min., 10฿). Fares given are 2nd class. To: **Bangkok** (12hr., 11 per day 11:25am-11pm, 47-508฿) via **Chumphon** (3hr., 138฿); **Butterworth, Malaysia** (11hr., 1:34am, 880฿); **Hat Yai** (6hr., 7 per day 9:20am-1:20am, 186-306฿); **Sungai Kolok** (10hr.; 1:20, 3, 4am; 231฿); **Trang** (5hr.; 6, 8am; 115฿).

Buses: There are 3 bus stations, and tour agencies will try to lure you to **private buses,** which often cost 50-100฿ more than public buses but take significantly less time.

Talaat Kaset 1: On Talaat Mai Rd. behind Phantip Travel at Nokkon Rd. To: **Chumphon** (3hr., every 30min. 7am-6pm, 80฿) and **Surat Thani Province,** with frequent buses to the railway station.

Talaat Kaset 2: (☎272 341), behind Thai Tani Hotel next to the market, has regular and A/C buses departing for: **Hat Yai** (4-5hr., 120-380฿); **Krabi** (4hr., 80฿); **Phang-Nga** (3½hr., 60-130฿); **Phuket** (5hr., 100-160฿), and other southern destinations (roughly every 30min. 6am-5pm).

New station: Just outside of town toward the train station, with **Bangkok** buses (9-11hr., every 30min. 7am-11pm, 211-380฿).

Minivans: Run from Talaat Kaset 2 to **Nakhon Si Thammarat** (2hr., every hr. 7am-5pm, 95฿) and **Penang, Malaysia** (6hr., every hr. 6am-5pm, 450฿), among others.

Boats: Ferries depart from several points around town. **Songserm Travel Center** operates a **daily express boat** from the **Tha Thong Pier** 8km outside of town to **Ko Phangan** (4hr., 7:30am, 250฿) and **Ko Samui** (3hr.; 7:30, 8am, 2pm; 150฿); ticket includes transport to the pier. Also operates a **night ferry** from the Surat Thani pier (Ban Don) at 11pm for **Ko Phangan** (6hr., 200฿) and **Ko Samui** (6hr., 100฿). **Samui Tours** offers buses (1hr., 7 per day 6:15am-4:30pm, 45-65฿) to the **Donsak Car Port,** 60km from Surat Thani, where **Raja Car Ferry** goes to **Ko Phangan** (2½hr., 120฿) and **Ko Samui**

(1½hr., every 2hr. 6am-6pm, 45฿). **Seatran** operates car and passenger ferries that leave from Donsak for **Ko Samui** (ferry 2hr.; 7am, 12:30pm; 250฿), with bus service included. The 7am boat goes to **Ko Phangan**. An agent will add a 50-100฿ surcharge.

Local Transportation: Few tourists stray from the bus-train-ferry station triangle, which is well served by the orange railway station bus. However, **tuk-tuks** (10-40฿), **motorcycle taxis** (10-20฿), and **songthaew** (10฿) roam the streets.

ORIENTATION AND PRACTICAL INFORMATION

Trains arrive at **Phun Phin Railway Station.** Phun Phin and Surat Thani are connected by **Talaat Mai Road,** which enters town from the southwest and passes the **tourist, police,** and **post offices.** Local buses leave from two separate **markets,** each a block off Talaat Mai Rd., near the town center. Ferries depart from the pier on **Ban Don Road,** which runs along the **Ta Pi River,** and from piers outside town.

Tourist Office: TAT, 5 Talaat Mai Rd. (☎288 817). A 20min. walk on Talaat Mai Rd. from the town center; jump on an orange local bus heading to the train station. Friendly staff, good info, and maps. English spoken. Open daily 8:30am-4:30pm.

Tours: Many agencies near the pier and on Talaat Mai Rd. between the 2 markets. Ask questions and choose wisely. A well-respected, full-service travel agency is **Phantip Tour** (☎272 230), located between the 2 bus terminals on Talaat Mai Rd.

Currency Exchange: Banks with 24hr. **ATMs** line Na Muang Rd. Most open M-F 8:30am-3:30pm, although a few open longer. **Bangkok Bank,** 195-7 Na Muang Rd. (☎281 298), has a booth in front. Open daily 8:30am-5pm.

Markets: A **day market** is on Na Muang Rd., near the Ban Don Hotel. The popular **night market** sprawls on a single street (Ton Pho Rd.) between Na Muang Rd. and Ban Don Rd. From the bus stations, head toward the river.

Police: 188 Na Muang Rd. (☎272 095). Little English spoken. Open 24hr.

Hospitals: Surat Thani Provincial Hospital (☎284 700), 1km past TAT on Talaat Mai Rd., on the way to privately-run **Phun Phin Taksin Hospital** (☎273 239). Staff at Taksin speak somewhat better English. Credit cards accepted. Open 24hr.

Telephones: Telecom Center (☎283 050), on Donnok Rd., 2km from hotels. Walk down Talaat Mai Rd. toward TAT from the intersection with Chonkasem Rd. and turn left on Donnok Rd.; it's 20min. down on the left under the radio tower. Open daily 8am-10pm.

Internet Access: Next to the Muang Tai Hotel, **Welcome Internet** charges 20฿ per hr. Open daily 9am-midnight. Other places are on Chonkasem Rd. and Talaat Mai Rd. Expensive Internet access (2฿ per min.) is available at travel agencies around the pier.

Post Offices: GPO (☎272 013), near the corner of Talaat Mai Rd. and Chonkasem Rd. *Poste Restante*. Open M-F 8:30am-4:30pm, Sa-Su 9am-noon.

Postal Code: 84000.

ACCOMMODATIONS AND FOOD

The **Ban Don Hotel ❷,** 268/2 Na Muang Rd., is hidden between 7-Eleven and the day market, a block from where the river meets the road. Clean, well-maintained rooms make this your best bet. The cheap Thai-Chinese **restaurant ❶** downstairs is open daily until 5pm. (☎272 167. Singles and doubles officially 250฿, with A/C and TV 450฿, but 50-100฿ can be bargained off the nightly rates.) The **Muang Tai Hotel ❷,** 390-2 Talaat Mai Rd., at the intersection with Chonkasem Rd., is a good option, but some rooms are noisy. Large rooms come with TVs, tables, cushy chairs, and private baths. (☎273 586. Singles with fan 220฿, with

A/C 360฿; doubles 260฿, with A/C 390฿, with A/C and hot water 440฿.) The **Thai Tani Hotel ❷,** 442/306-308 Talaat Kaset 2 off Talaat Mai Rd. between the markets, is in the middle of things. The facade hides a fairly clean and popular establishment. (☎272 977. Rooms include private bath. Singles 240฿, with A/C 320฿; doubles with twin beds 260-380฿.)

The **night market** is reason enough to spend the night in Surat Thani. From crunchy bugs and duck eggs to enormous oysters and oil-drenched crepes, this is the place to sample Thai cuisine. **Talaat Kaset 1** and **Talaat Kaset 2** both have stalls displaying curries, meats, and vegetables over rice. For Thai dishes and seafood in an English tea garden, try the **Ploy Pilim Restaurant ❷,** 100 Chonkasem Rd. in front of the Tapee Hotel, which has an impressive 25 vegetarian options. (Standard dishes 40-70฿. Specialties 60฿ and way up. Open daily 7:30am-11pm.) **Future@Internet ❶,** across from the Thai Tani Hotel, has mostly 30฿ items, good for a quick bite between buses. The *tom yam* (35฿) is particularly good. (Open daily 8am-9:30pm.) Next door to Ploy Pilim is **Valaisak Bakery ❶,** which has fresh, mouth-watering donuts for 9฿. (Open daily 8am-8pm.)

DAYTRIPS FROM SURAT THANI

CHAIYA. Chaiya, once an important city-state on the southern coast, boasts several *wats*, museums, and ruins, including a revered Buddhist sight, **Wat Phra Borommathat.** This 1200-year-old pagoda is surrounded by 174 Buddha images. The elaborate stone *chedi* is an example of Srivijaya art, and the *wat* is the best-preserved in this style in Thailand. Its three tiers are decorated with small *stupas*.

Next door, the **National Museum** houses artifacts dating from Chaiya's heyday. (☎431 090. Open W-Su 9am-4pm. 30฿.) In a forest along Hwy. 41, **Wat Suan Mokkha Phalaram** (Suan Mok) is more working monastery than tourist attraction. A daytrip offers a glimpse of beautiful paths and a bizarre collection of modern Buddhist art. Anyone can attend the **meditation retreats** that start on the last day of each month and run to the 11th day of the following month. Reservations are unneccessary; you need only show up a few days before the end of the month. *(☎431 552. 1200฿ covers food, accommodations, and expenses for the 12-day retreat. Take a Chumphon-bound bus from Surat Thani's Talaat Kaset 1 bus station, get off at Suan Mokkha, and catch a northbound* songthaew *to Wat Phra That. (1½hr.) Alternatively, you can catch a* songthaew *from Surat Thani to Chaiya town (1½hr., 25-30฿) and walk the 15min. to the wats from there.)*

KHAO SOK NATIONAL PARK. Splendid Khao Sok National Park is one of the more worthwhile interior destinations in southern Thailand. The 160-million-year-old rain forest (some date it as far back as 380 million years) covers roughly 650km² and is mostly comprised of jungle-covered foothills and limestone formations. It is also home to diverse wildlife, including gibbons, bears, elephants, and guars, and native flora, exemplified by dozens of species of orchids and ferns.

The **park headquarters** are near the entrance, and two major trails depart from behind the **Visitor Center.** A fairly easy 7km trek to **Ton Gloy Waterfall** leads through picturesque falls and gorges. A somewhat trickier 4km hike to **Sip-et-Chan,** a majestic, 11-tiered waterfall, takes you through dense rainforest and has six river crossings. The headquarters offer a **camping area ❶** (pitch your own tent) and **bungalows ❺** (sleeps 4; 1000฿). Just inside the park at the Visitor Center is **Tree Tops River Huts ❷,** a set of treehouses and bungalows on the river just a stone's throw from the trailheads. (☎395 129. Free bus station pick-up available. Reservations recommended. Tree houses and bungalows 200-1800฿.) For a more remote experience, come to **Lost Horizons Jungle House ❸,** off a dirt road 1km before the park entrance. (Make reservations through **Lost Horizons Asia**; ☎02 860 3936; www.losthorizonsasia.com. Bungalows 400฿; treehouses 500-600฿.) Park admission is 200฿ for three days. *(For more information on the park call ☎299 150. To get to Khao Sok, find a bus on the Phuket-Surat Thani route (2hr., every hr. 6am-5pm, 50-70฿) and make sure it goes to Khao Sok—some buses bypass the park. The buses drop you off at the Khao Sok road, which goes to the park entrance (3km). The road is full of bungalows: you're sure to find a room by walking along it.)*

KO SAMUI ☎077

Thailand's third-largest island has come a long way since its "discovery" by backpackers in the 1970s. Ko Samui is a major exporter of coconuts, the main source of income for its 40,000 occupants. Thousands of travelers rush to the beaches, which range between loud, shop-crammed Hat Chaweng and Hat Lamai to the tropical enclaves of Hat Bo Phut and Hat Choeng Mon. Those looking for entertainment and sunbathing options will not be disappointed.

TRANSPORTATION

Flights: Samui Airport, between Hat Chaweng and Hat Bangrak (Big Buddha Beach). **Bangkok Airways,** in Chaweng (☎422 234, at the airport 245 601), flies daily to: **Bangkok** (1-1½hr., every hr. 6am-9:20pm, 4200฿); **Krabi** (50min., 4 per week 1:30pm, 3200฿); **Phuket** (50min.; 9:20am, 3:20, 7:20pm; 2600฿); **Singapore** (1½hr., 3:50pm, 5500฿). Book tickets at Bangkok Airways or any travel agency on the island. There is an 800฿ departure tax at the Bangkok Airways-owned airport. **Thai Airways** offers cheaper flights to Bangkok through Surat Thani.

Trains and buses: Most travel agents can book joint boat/train or boat/bus tickets to the mainland. Packages to **Bangkok** (16hr.; ferry and A/C bus 480฿, ferry and sleeper train 800฿) and **Kuala Lumpur, Malaysia** (22hr., ferry and A/C bus 1000฿).

Boats: Three piers in Ko Samui. Main pier in **Na Thon** dominated by **Songserm Travel Center,** runs boats to: **Chumphon** (6½hr., 11am, 745฿); **Ko Tao** (2½hr.; 9, 11am; 345฿); **Krabi** (7hr., 2pm, 250฿); **Surat Thani** (3hr.; 12:30, 3:30pm; 150฿; night boat 7hr., 9pm, 150฿); Ko Phangan's **Thong Sala** (45min.; 9, 11am, 5pm; 115฿). **Seatran** sends express boats from Na Thon to **Donsak Pier,** 60km away from **Surat Thani** (1hr., plus 1hr. by bus; 8am, 3pm; 250฿ including bus to Surat Thani). Slower but cheaper **car ferry** runs between Na Thon and **Donsak Pier** (5hr., 120฿). The **Raja Car Ferry** runs between a pier 10km south of Na Thon and Surat Thani (3hr., every hr. 5am-6pm, 200฿). The pier at **Hat Bangrak** has direct service to **Hat Rin** on **Ko Phangan** (1hr.; 10:30am, 1, 4pm; 100฿).

Local Transportation: Yellow A/C cabs will charge 200-800฿. The most convenient way to explore is by **motorbike.** Clearly labeled **songthaew** congregate near the piers and circle the island 5am-6pm. From Na Thon to: **Hat Bangrak** (30฿); **Hat Bo Phut** (20฿); **Hat Chaweng** (40฿); **Hat Lamai** (40฿); **Hat Mae Nam** (20฿). These are official rates, but actual rates tend to be higher. **Motorcycle taxis** also circle the island. From Na Thon to: **Hat Bo Phut** (150฿); **Hat Chaweng** (200฿); **Hat Mae Nam** (100฿).

Rentals: Motorbikes 150฿ per day (200฿ for 150cc automatic bikes); **jeeps** 800฿ per day, with insurance 1000-2000฿. Rental places everywhere, but choose a reputable vendor. Your hotel is usually a good choice.

ORIENTATION AND PRACTICAL INFORMATION

Ko Samui is encircled by one road **(Route 4169),** making getting around fairly easy but still time-consuming. The transportation hub and service center, **Na Thon,** is on the west coast. From here, Rte. 4169 runs to **Ao Bang Po** and **Hat Mae Nam** on the northern coast and cuts down the east coast to **Hat Chaweng,** the island's most cel-

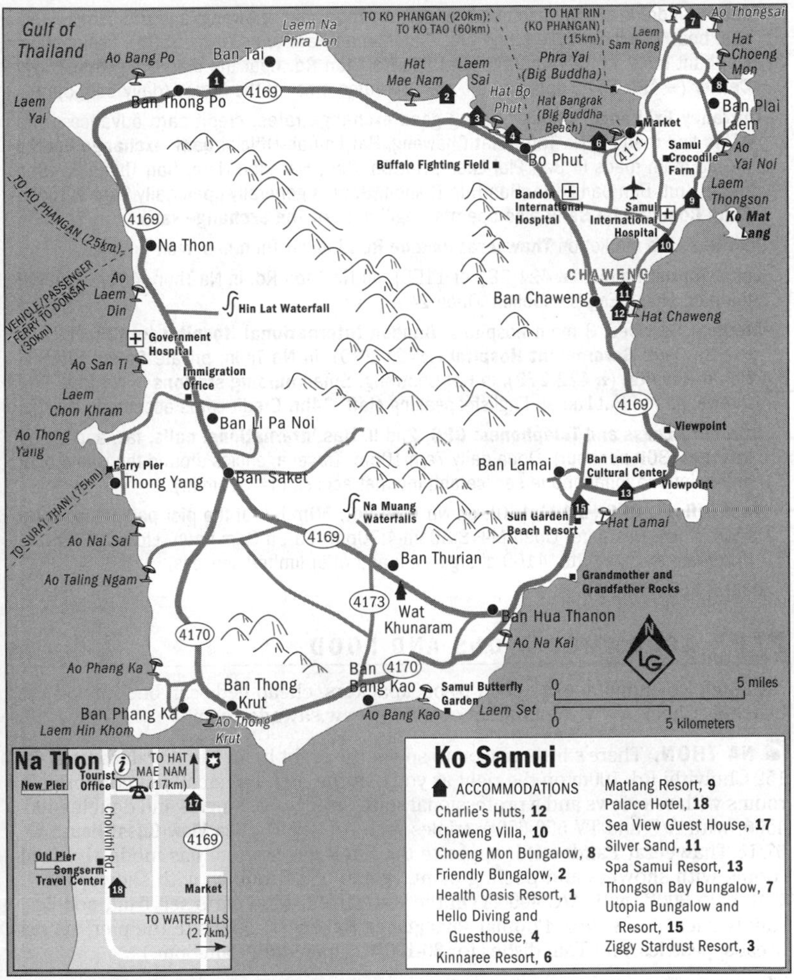

ebrated beach, and **Hat Lamai,** Hat Chaweng's budget-oriented sibling. **Route 4171,** enveloping the island's northeastern peninsula, branches off Rte. 4169 past Hat Mae Nam and reconnects in Chaweng. It passes through **Hat Bo Phut (Fisherman's Village), Hat Bangrak (Big Buddha Beach),** and the beaches of **Ao Thongsai, Ao Yai Noi,** and **Hat Choeng Mon.** *Songthaew* circle Rte. 4169 and 4171, Hat Chaweng, and Hat Lamai; elsewhere find a taxi or ride a motorbike. In general, Na Thon, Hat Chaweng, and Hat Lamai are the liveliest and offer the most services, while Hat Mae Nam, Hat Bo Phut, and Hat Choeng Mon are quieter.

Tourist Office: TAT (☎/fax 420 504; tatsamui@samart.co.th), on Na Thon Rd. in Na Thon. Turn left from the pier and follow signs to the new buildings behind the post office. English-speaking staff provides maps and brochures on the island and environs. Open daily 8:30am-4:30pm.

Tours: Hundreds of establishments all over Na Thon, Hat Chaweng, and Hat Lamai. Identical boat/bus/train tickets and Ang Thon Marine Park tours (from 550฿), fishing trips, elephant treks. In Na Thon, agencies line Na Thon Rd. near the pier. **Songserm Travel Center** (☎420 157), opposite the pier, operates most of the ferries (daily 5am-5pm).

Currency Exchange: Banks offering good exchange rates, credit card advances, and **ATMs** line roads in Na Thon, Hat Chaweng, Hat Lamai. Official **bank exchange booths** on the main roads in Ban Plai Laem, Hat Bo Phut, Hat Mae Nam, Ban Thong Po, Ban Thong Krut, Ban Bang Kao, Ban Hua Thanon. Booths generally open daily 9am-9:30pm. **Siam Commercial Bank** also operates legitimate **roving exchange vans.**

Markets: The market on **Thaweerat Pakdee Road** in Na Thon has fresh produce.

Local Tourist Police: (☎421 281 or 1155), on Na Thon Rd. in Na Thon, 400m south of the pier. Fluent English spoken. Open 24hr.

Medical Services: 3 main hospitals: **Bandon International Hospital** (☎425 382), in Hat Bo Phut; **Government Hospital** (☎421 230), in Na Thon; private **Samui International Hospital** (☎422 272), in Hat Chaweng. Small **nursing stations** in Na Thon, Hat Chaweng, and Hat Lamai. English-speaking staff. 24hr. Credit cards accepted.

Internet Access and Telephones: GPO, 2nd fl. Has **international calls,** fax, and cheap **Internet** (30฿ per hour). Open daily 7am-10pm. Travel agencies around the island offer pricier international phone service and Internet access (1฿ per min.).

Post Offices: GPO (☎421 130), on Na Thon Rd., 50m left of the pier parking lot in Na Thon. *Poste Restante.* Open M-F 8:30am-4:30pm, Sa-Su 9am-noon. Licensed, private **branches** all along Rte. 4169 charge extra and offer limited services.

Postal Code: 84140.

THAILAND

ACCOMMODATIONS AND FOOD

Although Ko Samui doesn't cater to backpackers, cheap beds can be found at the beaches. Check www.samuidirect.com and www.sawadee.com.

NA THON. There's little reason to spend the night in Na Thon. **Palace Hotel ❸,** 152 Cholvithi Rd. 100m on the right as you exit the pier, has small but comfortable rooms with sea views and a professional staff. (☎421 079. Singles and doubles 400-450฿, with A/C and TV 550-650฿; triples with A/C 800฿.) **Sea View Guest House ❷,** 67/15 Thaweerat Pakdee Rd. opposite the Shell gas station, has modestly sized rooms with showers and peeling paint. (☎420 052. Doubles with shower 200฿, with bath 300฿, with A/C 400฿.) On the waterfront, food carts sell fruit, noodles, sandwiches, and *satay.* Popular **Ruangthong Bakery ❶,** opposite the pier, serves breads, pastries, and Thai dishes for 20-100฿. (Open daily 6am-8pm.)

HAT MAE NAM AND AO BANG PO. With its narrow strip of wet sand, Hat Mae Nam is the island's least spectacular beach. Thanks to its seclusion (there is no road running along the beach and the way to access it is via dirt paths off Rte. 4169), Mae Nam draws long-term visitors and those looking for tranquility and respite from the bustle of the island's more popular beaches. On the way to Hat Bo Phut, popular **Friendly Bungalow ❸** has beachside huts with baths and mosquito nets. (☎425 484. Small huts 300฿, large huts 400฿. 3-night min. during busy months.) On the other side of Hat Mae Nam at Ao Bang Po, the **Health Oasis Resort ❹** has clean, modern bungalows, although the high-end ones aren't a great value. (☎420 124; www.healingchild.com. Rooms with fan 600฿, with A/C 1000-3000฿.)

HAT BO PHUT. The charming Bo Phut, or Fisherman's Village, offers white sand and a quiet atmosphere, as well as seafood restaurants and trendy shops. Bo Phut is on one road that branches off Rte. 4169 (Samui's main road) and runs along the coast before reconnecting with the main road farther west. **Hello Diving and Guesthouse ❷**, a few meters from the pier, boasts cheap dorm beds in a restored wooden house. It doubles as a dive shop. Those enrolled in diving classes stay free. (☎09 872 7056; www.hello-diving.com. Dorms with fan 100฿, with A/C 150฿.) The old-time favorite, **Ziggy Stardust Resort ❹**, farther down the road, has spacious rooms with carved wooden furniture and clean full baths. The beachfront bar and restaurant features fabulous homemade yogurt. (☎425 173. Bar and restaurant open daily 7:30am-10pm. Small doubles with fan 400฿; larger rooms with A/C 1000฿.) Of all the restaurants serving up excellent seafood, try the **Summer Night Restaurant ❸**, in the heart of Bo Phut village on the beach. (Breakfast 80-110฿. Seafood 50฿ per 100g. Thai dishes 60-140฿. Open daily 7:30am-11:30pm.)

HAT BANGRAK (BIG BUDDHA BEACH). Big Buddha Beach lies north of Samui's northeastern peninsula, along Rte. 4171. The rocky, boat-filled beach is not conducive to swimming. **Kinnaree Resort ❸**, close to the Big Buddha pier and across from the school, is a villa with gardens and beach views. (☎245 111. Motorbike rental. Singles and doubles 400฿, with hot shower and A/C 800฿.) Try **Picnic Basket ❸**, 150m to the left as you exit the pier. Quiet and friendly Scottish owner Jimmy offers tasty breakfasts and build-your-own *à la carte* picnic offerings. (2 eggs cooked to order 30฿. Fresh fruit, vegetables, meats, cheese, and fresh baked bread each 30-120฿. Open daily 6am-7pm.) 100m farther down the road toward the airport turn-off, the open-air **One Dollar Cafe ❷** delivers three-course breakfasts and Thai and Western entrees. (All cost 40฿. Open daily 7am-10pm.)

NORTHEASTERN PENINSULA: LAEM THONGSON, AO THONGSAI, HAT CHOENG MON, AO YAI NOI. The northeastern cape has some of the island's best views and most secluded coves. Beaches are down dirt roads highway connecting northern Hat Chaweng to Rte. 4171 and best accessed by motorbike. Solitude seekers should follow the signs 2km down to **Thongson Bay Bungalow ❸**, on the tip of the promontory. The beach is rocky and scenic, but not suitable for swimming. (☎01 891 4640. Rustic bungalows with bath 250-500฿, on the beach 1000฿.)

North of Ao Yai Noi, bordering Ao Thongsai and 4km north of Hat Chaweng, Hat Choeng Mon's serene beaches make it worth visiting, especially to escape crowds. **Choeng Mon Bungalow ❸** has modern, concrete bungalows with baths. (☎425 372. Singles 300฿, with A/C and hot water 600฿; doubles 450฿/1200฿.)

HAT CHAWENG. The biggest of Ko Samui's beaches, Hat Chaweng is 5km on the eastern coast. The sunbathing and party capital of the island, it is loud and happy, with superb sand, clean water, cheap booze, and loud music. Hat Chaweng's main **Chaweng Road,** where most services are located, parallels the beach and connects to Rte. 4169 via three access roads.

Affordable accommodations in Hat Chaweng are scarce and fill up quickly. The best option for those on a budget is **Charlie's Huts ❸**, in the middle of the beach near the turn-off for the lagoon. Movies play every evening at 6pm. Spartan bungalows have thatched roofs, bamboo walls, and mosquito nets. (☎422 383. Doubles 300฿, closer to the beach and with bath 500฿, with A/C 700฿.) Next door, **Silver Sand ❷** has a few budget bungalows close to the water. **Matlang Resort ❸**, 1541 Chaweng Rd. in North Chaweng by the end of the cape, is away from the main drag. The beach here is too shallow for swimming at low tide but is more picturesque than anywhere else on Chaweng. (☎/fax 422 172. Singles and doubles with bath and fan 300-370฿, with A/C 1200฿.) A good higher-end options is **Chaweng Villa ❺**, on the beach toward the northern end of Hat Chaweng. Well-maintained, modern bungalows are near the water and have a pool and nice bars and restaurants. (☎231 123; www.chawengvilla.com. Bungalows with A/C 1700-2600฿.)

Inexpensive foodstalls cram the road by the Green Mango, serving pizza, sandwiches, and Thai favorites to night revelers. **Los Gringos Cantina ❹**, on an alley across from Pizza Hut toward the northern end of Hat Chaweng, does Tex-Mex very well. (Strawberry frozen margaritas 120฿. Tostadas, enchiladas, and burritos 160-200฿. Open daily 2-11pm.) **The Deck Restaurant ❸**, before the Green Mango as you approach from Na Thon, has great food (including vegan and vegetarian options), music, and three levels from which to enjoy it all. (☎230 898. 3-course breakfast 99฿. 5-course dinner 175฿. Thai dishes 60-80฿. Open daily 8am-2am.)

HAT LAMAI. Hat Lamai has a family-friendly environment, good body surfing, and fewer crowds than Hat Chaweng. **Spa Samui Resort ❷**, on Rte. 4169 before the Hat Lamai turn-off, has simple bungalows with fan and fancier ones with A/C. Many come here for the cheap rooms and for the excellent health spa, which features tai chi and yoga programs starting at 3000฿. (☎230 855. Bungalows with fan 250-600฿, with A/C 600-1800฿.) Most establishments in south Lamai, the busier part of the beach, are mid-range or above. The centrally located **Utopia Bungalow & Resort ❹** has nice bungalows, an upscale clientele, and beautifully groomed gardens. (☎233 113. Bungalows 500฿, with A/C and hot water 1000฿.)

Most bungalows serve meals until 10pm and let more expensive restaurants and pubs pick up the slack late at night. **Il Tempio ❸**, in central Lamai just down the road from the Sun Garden Beach Resort, has good Italian food in a casual setting. (Pizzas and pastas 130-230฿. Open daily 9am-2am.) **Will Wait Bakery ❷**, in the center of Lamai Beach Rd., serves Thai and Western favorites. (Most dishes 50-150฿. Open daily 7:30am-10:30pm.) The **day market** at Ban Hua Thanon sells snacks.

THAILAND

SIGHTS

Most non-beach sights are located off Rte. 4169 and are easily accessible by *songthaew*, foot, or motorbike. Travel agencies also offer one-day tours of the island for around 1000฿.

WAT KHUNARAM. Rather sensational as far as *wats* go, this temple, off Rte. 4169 in the island's southeast corner, is known for a mummified monk who died in 1973 and supposedly evaded decomposition via complex pre-death meditation.

THE BIG BUDDHA IMAGE (PHRA YAI). Ko Samui's most prominent landmark, the golden "Big Buddha" is located on a small island connected by causeway to Rte. 4171 on the island's northeast corner. Overlooking Samui Island from its location near Hat Bangrak (Big Buddha Beach), the 15m-tall statue was built in 1972.

SAMUI CROCODILE FARM. The most fear-inspiring of the novelty animal sideshows on Samui, the Crocodile Farm, located near the airport, features 84 crocs in several holding pens, dozens of poisonous snakes, and several friendly monkeys who will perform acrobatic stunts in exchange for a rambutan and a back rub. The daily shows at 2:30 and 5pm are a must-see. *(Off the airport road between Hat Bangrak and Hat Chaweng. ☎01 894 4228. Open daily 9am-6pm. 270฿ admission includes shows.)*

SAMUI BUTTERFLY GARDEN. One of Samui's most popular non-beach attractions, the Butterfly Garden maintains over 24 species of southern Thai butterflies in addition to less spectacular (and less popular) species of insects. *(Off Rte. 4170, opposite central Samui Village. ☎424 020. Open daily 8:30am-5:30pm. 120฿, children 60฿.)*

NIGHTLIFE

With dozens of pubs and go-go bars, Hat Chaweng is Samui's nightlife capital. Most places are open until at least 2am. The mega-pub **Green Mango** is a massive bar complex that draws a raging young drink-and-dance crowd. The mood picks up at around 11pm and doesn't fade until 4am. (Beer 80-100฿. Cocktails 120-150฿. Red Bull and vodka 130฿. Champagnes 800-2000฿. Open daily from 8pm.) **Reggae Pub** is a popular bar, attracting an older, mellow crowd. To get there, follow the signs to the boxing stadium across the lagoon.

Hat Lamai has fewer nighttime options than Hat Chaweng, but bars and strip-joints are cropping up by the dozen. **Bauhaus Pub, Bistro and Disco,** south of the go-go area, is *the* hot spot for Lamai's young and restless. The foam party takes over on Friday nights, while the Saturday night Gin and Vodka party offers half-price cocktails. (Drinks 30-100฿. M-Tu and Th buy-1-get-1-free. Open daily 6pm-2am.)

DAYTRIP FROM KO SAMUI

ANG THONG MARINE PARK

The only way to visit is on a tour through one of Ko Samui's travel agencies. Songserm sends boats daily at 8:30am from Na Thon's pier (return around 5pm, 550฿ includes lunch). If you have the money, kayaking (1800฿) allows you to explore the island inlets.

The infamous setting for Alex Garland's *The Beach*, Ang Thong Marine National Park is a collection of over 40 limestone islands 60km north of Ko Samui. Among the islands are **Ko Mae Ko** (Mother Island), popular for lake **Thalay Nai** (Lake Crater); **Ko Sam Sao** (Tripod Island), famous for its huge rock arch and fantastic snorkeling; and **Ko Wua Talap** (Sleeping Cow Island), home to the **park office. Ko Lak** and similar limestone formations tower 400m above the water. If you end up staying, the park office (☎286 025) rents modest **bungalows** ❸ for 1000฿; **camping** is free.

THAILAND

KO PHANGAN ☎077

Ko Phangan is a backpacker's heaven and hell. The island's beaches range from unspoiled beauties like Hat Khuat (Bottle Beach) to the insanely overdeveloped backpacker universes like Hat Rin Nok. Don't come to Ko Phangan to get away—come here to be in the middle of it all.

TRANSPORTATION

Boats: Ferries run between Ko Phangan and **Ko Tao, Ko Samui,** and **Surat Thani.** From Ko Tao, ferries leave from Mae Hat's southern pier (5 per day 9:30am-2:30pm, 180-350฿). From Ko Samui, boats leave from Big Buddha Pier for **Hat Rin** (1hr., 4 per day 9:30am-5pm, 100฿) and from Na Thon Pier for **Thong Sala** (9, 11am, 5:30pm; 95฿). Boats from Surat Thani leave from the Tha Thong Pier for Thong Sala. You can also head to Ko Phangan directly from Surat Thani via the **Donsak Car Port** (2½hr.; leaves Donsak 7, 10am, 2, 5:30pm; returns 6, 10am, 1, 7pm; 300฿) or the **town pier** (7:30am, 205฿; 11pm, 400฿). Ferries from Ko Phangan depart Hat Rin Nai and Thong Sala. From Hat Rin Nai, boats to: Ko Samui's **Hat Bangrak** (Big Buddha Beach; 1hr., 4 per day 10am-4pm, 100฿); **Hat Tian** (12:40pm, 50฿); **Than Sadet** (12:40pm, 80฿); **Thong Nai Paan** (12:40pm, 100฿). From Thong Sala, boats to: **Chumphon** (12:30pm, 650฿); **Hat Bangrak** (1hr., noon, 115฿); **Ko Samui's Na Thon** (30-60min., 7 per day 7:30am-4:30pm, 115-250฿); **Ko Tao** (2hr.; 10, 11:30am, 12:30pm; 180-350฿); **Surat Thani** (night boat 7hr., 10pm, 400฿; express boat via Ko Samui 4hr.; 7, 11am, 12:30, 1pm; 205฿).

Local Transportation: Getting around can be a bit. **Songthaew** meet ferries at the pier in Thong Sala and run to the island's major beaches. To: **Ban Kai** (20-30฿); **Ban Tai** (20฿); **Chalok Lam** (50฿); **Hat Rin** (50฿); **Hat Yao** (50฿); **Thong Nai Paan** (100฿). In Hat Rin Nai, *songthaew* wait across from the police booth and go to **Thong Sala** (min. 3 passengers, 50฿). In addition, **longtail boats** make trips between the major beaches.

Rentals: Motorbikes are available for rent around the pier and on Thong Sala's main street as well as from guesthouses in Hat Rin Nai (150฿ per day with passport deposit).

ORIENTATION AND PRACTICAL INFORMATION

A few boats dock at the Hat Rin pier, but most arrive at the island's unsightly main city and port of call, **Thong Sala,** where tourist services abound. From the Thong Sala pier, three paved roads cover most of the island; one runs 10km southeast along the coast to the beach at **Hat Rin,** split into **Hat Rin Nai** to the west and **Hat Rin Nok** to the east. Midway, a bumpy dirt road heads to the northeastern beaches of **Thong Nai Paan Yai** and **Thong Nai Paan Noi,** and other dirt trails stretch to more remote coves. A second paved road from Thong Sala cuts 10km north to **Ao Chalok Lam,** a departure point for boats going to **Hat Khuat (Bottle Beach).** The third road runs a scenic course west along the coast to the less-developed bays of **Ao Mae Hat.**

THAILAND

Tours: The helpful **Mr. Kim** (☎377 274), usually found a few meters from the Thong Sala pier on the right, is knowledgeable and can help book tickets. **Songserm Travel Center** (☎377 096), on the left side of the main road in Thong Sala. Boat and A/C bus packages to: **Bangkok** (450฿); **Krabi** (350฿); **Phuket** (350฿). Open daily 8:30am-5pm.

Currency Exchange: Several exchange booths on the street from the main pier in Thong Sala. **Siam Commercial Bank,** 30m from the Thong Sala pier on the left, has a 24hr. **ATM.** Open M-F 8:30am-3:30pm. In Hat Rin, there are several bank exchange booths and ATMs on the road that leads from Hat Rin Nok to Hat Rin Nai.

Police: Main office (☎377 114), 2km north of Thong Sala on the road to Ao Chalak Lam. English spoken. A small **police booth** operates at Hat Rin off Haadrin Rd., opposite the school. Some English spoken. Both open 24hr.

Medical Services: Koh Pha-Ngan Hospital (☎377 034), 3km north of Thong Sala. English spoken. 24hr. In Hat Rin, private **nursing stations** provide basic medical services. For serious medical attention, take a boat to Ko Samui.

Internet Access: The cheapest Internet providers (1฿ per min.) are on the road stemming from Thong Sala's main pier. More expensive places in Hat Rin charge 2฿ per min.

Post Office: GPO (☎377 118), in Thong Sala. From the pier, walk down the main road, take 1st right, and continue to the end and turn left; the office is on the right. *Poste Restante.* In Hat Rin, a **branch** (☎375 204), on the southern road connecting Hat Rin Nok and Hat Rin Nai, offers limited postal and courier services. Open daily 9am-midnight.

Postal Code: 84280.

ACCOMMODATIONS AND FOOD

Most travelers to Ko Phangan head immediately to the southern coast and the beaches of Hat Rin. Those looking for more secluded beaches should head north to Hat Khuat (Bottle Beach) or mellow Thong Nai Paan Noi. Accommodation prices and availability fluctuate. The island fills to capacity in the days surrounding the full moon and its notorious party. If you come for the party, arrive a few days early or be prepared to sleep on the beach.

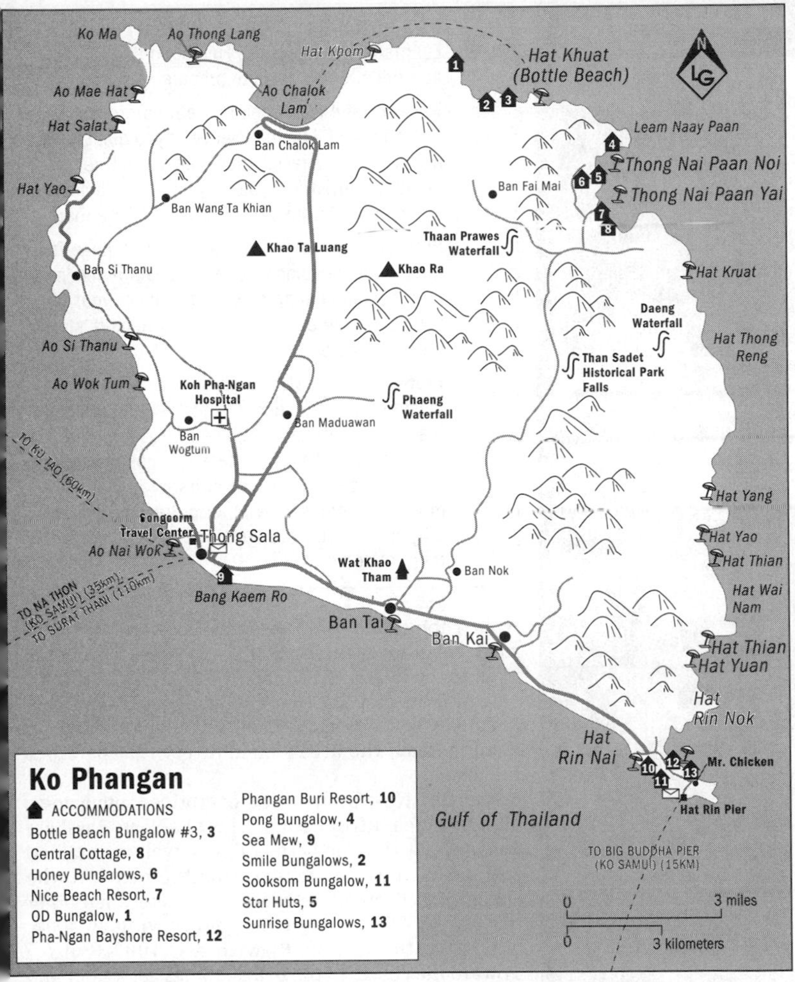

THONG SALA. Thong Sala is a lifeline for the island, boasting the cheapest Internet, most tourist services, and aggressive *songthaew* drivers waiting at the pier. Near the waterfront, **Sea Mew ❷,** to the right heading from the pier, has a great staff. Enjoy the quirky restaurant and the cable TV. Mattresses may be hard, but rooms are clean. (Singles with fan 200฿.) The **Corner Kitchen ❷,** diagonally across from the post office, serves extensive Thai, European, and Chinese cuisine (35-60฿). (Dishes 30-200฿. Open M-Sa 6pm-5am.)

HAT RIN NOK. Introducing "Backpacker Land," where the average age is 21 and the average personal savings are approaching zero. With all that's going on in the village, the boat-covered beach seems like almost an afterthought—until the night of the Full Moon Party, when the waterfront takes center stage. *Songthaew*

IN RECENT NEWS

CRAZY MEDICINE

Recently, Thailand has discovered that curbing the demand for one drug does not mean curbing drug demand.

In the mid-90s, opium use declined dramatically in Thailand because social and economic programs reduced both supply and demand. The big push worked—but only for opium. Just at the moment heroin became the world's hip drug, it was abundant, too—produced right in the Golden Triangle.

But heroin was only a passing fancy compared to the meteoric rise in the use of methamphetamines. Locally known as *"ya ba"* (crazy medicine), speed is Thailand's latest drug scourge. *Ya ba* became the intoxicant of choice among laborers during the boom years, but its use skyrocketed among disillusioned youth after the Asian Financial Crisis.

Ya ba is the perfect narcotic to attract new young drug users. Heroin prices are generally out of reach for new customers (price fluctuations influence the buying behavior of new users much more than addicts). *Ya ba* also fits the pop cultural trend: it's a club drug and cheap substitute for ecstasy, producing temporary hyperactivity, euphoria, confidence, alertness, and tremors. Users' heart rate, temperature, breathing, and blood pressure increase.

Violent behavior is common among drug users, as are anxiety, panic, paranoia, drowsiness, and

TIP

SEX, DRUGS, AND LUNAR CYCLES. For many, the fun of the Full Moon Party comes at a price. Some ways to prepare:

Reserve ahead. Accommodations on Hat Rin Nok and Nai fill up in advance. If you don't have a week to burn, reservations are strongly recommended. Otherwise, you may be stuck commuting from Ko Samui or paying 4000฿ for a room.

Protect your stuff. Full moon night is huge for theft. Avoid keeping valuables in your bungalow or in obvious hiding places, like under your pillow. Leave the expensive footwear behind: shoe theft is a major problem.

Protect your health. Drug use is rampant; the most popular offenders are ecstasy, opium, and the local methamphetamine, *ya ba*. Hundreds of people are forced to check into hospitals due to overdoses of impure substances. What's more, an increasing number of travelers reportedly have been drugged or tranquilized and then robbed.

from Thong Sala drop passengers off on the main road, just above Hat Rin Nai. From here, it's a 5min. walk to the beach or a 10min. walk to Hat Rin Nok's quieter twin, Hat Rin Nai. The two beaches are connected by several dusty roads, all of which intersect **Haadrin Road,** the area's main artery that parallels the beach.

Hat Rin Nok brims with overpriced bungalows along its beachfront road. The **Pha-Ngan Bayshore Resort ❸,** at the northern end, is a well-maintained set of bungalows reaching from the beach to the *songthaew* drop-off. At night, it's quieter than other resorts. (☎375 227. Basic bungalows with fan 400฿, with private bath 600฿, with A/C 1000-1800฿.) Toward the center of the beach, things get louder and more crowded, especially at night. **Sunrise Bungalows ❸,** in the middle of the beach, has breezy bamboo cottages with large beds. (☎375 145. Bungalows 250฿, with bath 350฿, with A/C 1000-1200฿.) **Mr. Chicken ❷** is something of a landmark and local meeting place. It has chicken sandwiches (40฿) that will make you forget about *pad thai* for a while. Around the corner is **Niras Beach Kitchen and Bakery ❷,** which caters both to health-spa types and those with a sweet tooth. (Excellent chocolate croissant 40฿. Hummus sandwich on homemade bread 50฿. Kitchen open daily 8am-10pm. Bakery open 24hr.) Across the street is **Sao's Kitchen ❷,** which dishes out decent tofu-based vegetarian food. (☎375 166. Vegetable curries 40฿. Pumpkin soup with coconut milk 40฿. Open daily 8:30am-10:30pm.)

Hat Rin Nok's nightlife takes place in open-air bars right on the beach itself. The most popular spot is the **Cactus Club,** which creates an outdoor ambience with oil lamps and bottle-spinning bartenders. The **Outback Bar,** on the road between Hat Rin Nok and Nai, offers a laid-back yet sophisticated atmosphere and large crowds on most nights. The **Full Moon Party** is the stuff of legend. Each month under the full moon, thousands gather on this strip of sand, bodies gyrate to the latest mixes, and minds dance to the beat of illicit substances. Even when the moon isn't full, don't come here for a quiet beach. Hat Rin Nok is loud, brash, and proud of it.

HAT RIN NAI. The strip of muddy sand at Hat Nai is hardly attractive, but the location does have its perks, including a good selection of bungalows, pretty sunsets, and a location that's close enough to take advantage of Hat Rin Nok's nightlife but far enough to retreat from it. Basic accommodations, restaurants, and ticket agencies line the main road. Budget beachside bungalows lie at the northern end of the beach, a 15min. walk from the pier and past a rocky outcropping. **Sooksom Bungalow ❷,** just past the outcropping, has simple, wooden huts and a vegetarian-friendly restaurant. (☎375 230. Bungalows 150-250฿, with bath 300-350฿.) Next door, **Phangan Buri Resort ❸** has more expensive, cleaner concrete bungalows with tiled patios. (☎375 330. Bungalows 300-800฿.)

HAT KHUAT (BOTTLE BEACH). This gorgeous and quiet **beach lures** visitors into spending weeks or months here. Take a *songthaew* from Thong Sala to **Ao Chalok Lam** (10km, 20min., 100฿). The bay is the departure point for boats to **Hat Khuat** (9:30am, 3, 6pm; return 8am, 1, 5pm; 50฿.) It's also possible to walk the 4km from Ao Chalok Lam to Bottle Beach. **Bottle Beach 1 ❶,** in the middle of the beach, has the cheapest accommodations in the area, with bathless bungalows starting at 100฿. **Bottle Beach 3 ❸** and **Smile Bungalows ❸,** at the far end of the beach, have bungalows with private baths and hammocks between 250฿ and 400฿. **OD Bungalow ❶,** removed from the beach on a cliff, has great views. (Rooms 100฿.)

THONG NAI PAAN NOI AND THONG NAI PAAN YAI. With sparkling water and a relaxed atmosphere, these twin beaches offer ample reward for those who endure the hour-long *songthaew* ride

depression. Effects on the mind may include moodiness and lack of interest in friends, sex, and food. Continued use can cause personality changes, chronic paranoia, increased blood pressure, and brain damage.

The Thai Health Ministry estimates that 2.4 million of Thailand's 62 million people use the drug. Most users are ages 15-24, but addicts as young as 5 and as old as 68 have been documented. A *ya ba* tab, which can be smoked, injected, or swallowed, can cost as little as a dollar. Tabs have even become a form of currency—Bangkok taxi drivers short on *baht* have been known to return *ya ba* instead.

Ya ba is a supplier's dream. With no fickle crop to deal with, labs can be quickly and easily dismantled. Runners can carry as many as 200,000 tabs in a backpack across the border from Myanmar. An estimated 700 million tablets—more than 10 per person in Thailand—entered Thailand in 2001, mostly crossing the 1300-mile border with Myanmar.

Officials believe *ya ba* use is plateauing. The Thai government is in the midst of a Southeast Asia-wide crackdown on the drug.

—Derek Glanz is a freelance journalist and has written and edited extensively for Let's Go.

from Thong Sala or the boat ride from Hat Rin. *Songthaew* stop first at Thong Nai Paan Noi, the more populated of the two and the one favored by backpackers. Near the drop-off, the popular **Star Huts ❷** is the largest operator on the beach and teems with long-term guests. (☎299 005. Bungalows 200฿, with bath 300-400฿.) Younger backpackers frequent **Honey Bungalows ❸,** behind Star Huts and away from the beach. At the northern end of the beach, a 15min. walk from the *songthaew* drop-off, **Pong Bungalow ❷** is well known for its popular bar. (Bungalows 150-180฿, with bath 250-300฿.) Most travelers take their meals at bungalow restaurants, though many recommend **Banglangon Vegetarian Restaurant ❷,** halfway up the beach and famous for its 150฿ pizzas.

To the south, Thong Nai Paan Yai is longer, less populated, and more suitable for swimming and snorkeling than Thong Nai Paan Noi. Ask the *songthaew* driver to let you off here, or make the 20min. walk across the small promontory from Thong Nai Paan Noi. At the end of the road to Thong Nai Paan's easternmost point, **Nice Beach Resort ❹** has bright, whitewashed rooms with mosquito nets, high ceilings, and private baths. (☎238 542. Bungalows 200-600฿, with A/C 1000-1600฿.) Toward the middle of the beach, **Central Cottage ❸** provides simple but comfortable thatched bungalows and a **restaurant** (☎299 059; bungalows 350-400฿).

THAILAND

SIGHTS

After full moons and beaches, **waterfalls** are Ko Phangan's major attraction. The most famous stretches of river run through **Than Sadet Historical Park,** a good daytrip from the beach. Longtail boats from Hat Rin (50฿) drop passengers off at the mouth of the river. From here, travel north on the road parallel to the river for 2.5km. **The Sanctuary** is a spa that comes highly recommended, noted for its seclusion, clean facilities, attentive staff, and free evening meditations. Many are happy to pay 60฿ for a dorm bed and splurge on yoga classes (150฿), oil massages (400฿), and 10-day fasts. Only accessible by **longtail boat,** 50฿ from Hat Rin. (☎01 271 3614; www.thesanctuary-kpg.com. Singles and doubles with bath 300-1000฿.)

KO TAO ☎077

One of Southeast Asia's most renowned dive sites, tiny Ko Tao lures an international crowd of underwater enthusiasts, ranging from scuba neophytes drawn to cheap certification courses to veterans who relish clear gulf waters and outstanding reefs. For non-divers, the island offers superb sun-baked coves, many of which are so secluded they can only be reached by boat or a long hike. Despite its popularity, it remains a laid-back destination for scuba fans and backpackers alike.

TRANSPORTATION

Boats: Ferries leave Ko Tao's **Mae Hat** for **Chumphon** (slow boat: 5hr., 10am, 200฿; faster boat: 2-3hr.; 10:30, 11am, 3pm; 300-400฿); **Ko Phangan** (3hr., 9:30am, 180฿; 1-2hr.; 9:30, 10:30am, 2, 3:30pm; 250-350฿); **Ko Samui** (4hr., 9:30am, 280฿; 2-3hr.; 9:30, 10:30am, 2, 3pm; 350-550฿); **Surat Thani** (6½hr., 10:30am, 500฿; 8hr., 9pm, 400฿). For **Bangkok,** there are ferry/bus combos (9½hr., 11am, 550฿; 15hr., 3pm, 800฿). Boat service thins out somewhat in the low season.

Local Transportation: The best way to explore is to rent a **motorbike,** available everywhere (150฿ for 24hr., passport deposit required). Otherwise, **pickup-truck taxis** go from Mae Hat to anywhere that's accessible by the island's few paved roads (30-60฿). **Taxis** between Mae Hat and Hat Sai Ree cost 30฿ per person. **Longtail boats** go to **Nang Yuan** (100฿) and **Chalok Ban Kao** (150฿).

ORIENTATION AND PRACTICAL INFORMATION

Boats arrive at **Mae Hat** (Mother Beach), where most services are located. Facing the island from the pier, a paved road heads left over a hill to **Hat Sai Ree,** the heart of the backpacking and scuba scene (3min. by taxi or 20min. on foot). The same paved road eventually bends right, leading to **Ao Chalok Ban Kao,** the main southern beach, and, 500m farther, to **Ao Thian.** Dirt roads branch off the paved road to more beaches, including **Ao Leuk, Ao Tanote** (a fantastic snorkeling destination), **Ao Hin Wong** (on the east coast), and **Hat Sai Daeng** (in the island's southeastern corner).

Tours: Private agencies line the pier in Mae Hat and the main road in Hat Sai Ree. **Mr. J** (☎456 066) claims to provide any type of service, from obtaining visa extensions to arranging emergency loans. Find him at any of his 3 offices and shops on the hill just north of the pier, a 5min. walk down the dirt path right off the pier in Mae Hat, and before the Buddha View Dive Center in Hat Sai Ree. All open daily 8am-10pm.

Police: (☎456 260), a 10min. walk north of the pier on the hill heading toward Hat Sai Ree opposite the school. Some English spoken. Open 24hr.

Medical Services: Nursing stations offering basic services are abundant around Ao Chalok, Hat Sai Ree, and Mae Hat. Dive shops recommend the **Chintana Nursing Unit** at the top of the hill to the left, on the road to Hat Sai Ree. Open daily 8am-8pm.

Telephones: Nearly all travel agencies and bungalows offer **international phone** service. About 80฿ per min.

Internet Access: Facilities in Mae Hat or Hat Sai Ree charge 1 or 2฿ per min. A couple places in Sai Ree Village offer 1฿ per 2min. access, but that's because of very slow dial-up connections.

Post Office: There is 1 privately licensed post office (☎456 122) on Ko Tao, on the main road in Mae Hat. *Poste Restante* (quite reliable). Open daily 8:30am-midnight.

Postal Code: 84280.

THAILAND

ACCOMMODATIONS AND FOOD

Dive agencies rent bungalows almost exclusively to clients, but there are still plenty of budget places to stay if you're not here to scuba dive. The cheapest rooms, usually with fan, overnight electricity, and attached bath, run 200-300฿. Prices reflect high-season rates; in the low season, it's usually 100-150฿ cheaper.

MAE HAT. Mae Hat is the food, fuel, and ferry center of Ko Tao. The beach here is covered with boats, so it is unsuitable for swimming. If an early-morning ferry departure keeps you on Mae Hat, accommodations cluster south of the pier. Just before the Sensi Resort, **Kanlapangha Resort ❷** has friendly management and cheerful bungalows complete with hammocks. (☎456 058. Bungalows 250฿, with private bath 300-1000฿.) More bungalows are north of the pier on the hill between Mae Hat and Hat Sai Ree, a 15min. walk from the pier. Jack-of-all-trades Mr. J owns several clean **bungalows ❸** across from the school. (Rooms with private bath and new fixtures 300-400฿.) Mae Hat may not be the best place to stay, but it's one of the better places to eat. The best place to get bread is the **Swiss Bakery ❷,** just a few steps up from the pier on the right. Try the delicious tuna sandwich for 60฿. (Open daily 6am-6:30pm.) **Yang's ❶,** next to the Swiss Bakery, has fried noodles with chicken (40฿) and breakfast omelettes (30฿), among other cheap Thai eats. (Open daily 6am-10pm.) At night, **Whitening ❸,** on the southern end of Mae Hat along the beach road, is the new place to be seen. (Thai-Indian fusion dishes 80-220฿. Open daily 5pm-1am.)

HAT SAI REE. Ko Tao's busiest bit of sand, Hat Sai Ree still manages to be laid-back. For better-quality swimming and snorkeling, however, head elsewhere. To get to the relatively inexpensive **Pranee's Bungalows ❸,** head to the northern end of Hat Sai Ree, a 20min. walk on sand from the start of the beach. (☎456 080. Bungalows 300-700฿.) The deservedly popular **Sai Ree Cottage ❷** is just past Scuba Junction. Their charming wooden bungalows get points for cleanliness, as does their beachside restaurant. (☎456 374. Bungalows 250-600฿.)

For culinary offerings, Hat Sai Ree is second-best to Mae Hat. The **Lotus Restaurant ❷,** past Sai Ree Cottage at the northern end of the beach, specializes in Thai cuisine. (Dishes 60-100฿.) The restaurant is romantic, quiet and serves up affordable grilled food. (Open daily 6:30am-midnight.) **El Toro/The Little Mermaid ❸,** despite its apparent identity crisis, has inauthentic but tasty Mexican and Swedish dishes. (Dishes 60-200฿. Open daily 5-11pm.) **AC Bar,** at the south end of the beach, draws partiers from all over the island with its theme nights.

LAEM NAM TOK. The walk to Laem Nam Tok is deceptively long; it's best to take a taxi from Mae Hat (40฿) or inquire about boat transport. The most scenic of the bungalows along the paved road is **CFT Bungalow ❷,** which is at the very end. Its simplistic huts offer spectacular views of Ko Nang Yuan and the sunset. The attached **Here and Now** offers massage and classes. (Massage 550฿ for 2hr. Yoga 12-day courses. Electricity only available 6-10:30pm. Bungalows with outdoor showers 100-600฿.) On the way to CFT is one of the only luxury resorts on the island, **Thipwimarn Resort ❺,** a collection of bungalows overlooking the water. The attached **restaurant** is quite reasonably priced. (☎456 409; www.thipwimarnresort.com. Bungalows 1650-4250฿. 30% low-season discount.)

AO LEUK AND AO TANOTE. The two major bays on the eastern side of Ko Tao are ideal for solitude seekers and offer fantastic **snorkeling.** They are accessed by a paved road branching off Ko Tao's main road just south of Mae Hat. **Taxis** to both bays cost 50฿ from Mae Hat. Tiny Ao Leuk has a rocky beach but is much more peaceful than the ever-packed Hat Sai Ree. The best choice for lodgings is **Leuk Bungalows ❷,** which has airy, wooden bungalows with porches scattered about sprawling grounds. (Restaurant open daily 7am-10pm. Rooms 200-400฿.)

About 2km farther north from Ao Leuk along a dirt road is **Ao Tanote,** which has a better beach than its neighbor. On the north end of the beach is upscale **Tanote Bay Resort ❹,** with bungalows dotting the hill overlooking the bay. (☎01 970 4703. Basic bungalows 400฿, with shower and fan 500฿, on the beach 600-1000฿, with A/C 2500฿.) Nearby **Diamond Beach Resort ❸** has reasonably priced rooms. (☎01 958 3983. Bungalows 400-600฿.) For food, vacationers recommend **Mountain Reef ❷,** a popular spot in the middle of the bay. (Thai and Western entrees 50-160฿.)

AO CHALOK BAN KAO. The bay is a distance away from Mae Hat (45min. by foot, 50฿ taxi ride). A dense concentration of bungalows, dive shops, Internet cafes, and restaurants overwhelm the beach, making the bay more convenient than scenic. Solution: head to gorgeous Ao Thian, a 10min. walk away. Most bungalows are affiliated with dive shops, but non-divers seek happy refuge in the new **JP Resort ❸,** in the center of the beach. Its cliffside bungalows are squeaky clean, with private baths. Second-floor rooms have nice sea views, and a relaxed **restaurant** rounds out this relative newcomer. (☎456 099. Internet 2฿ per min. Rooms with fan 300-400฿, with A/C 1000฿.) **Sunshine Bungalows ❸** is conveniently located but features less glamorous bungalows with private baths (250฿). The mellow, beachside **Reggae Bar,** at the left end of the beach when facing the water, serves drinks for 120-150฿. (Open daily 6:30pm-2am.)

AO THIAN. An uphill walk south from Ao Chalok leads to a fork in the dirt road. The left path leads downhill to the small but stunning Ao Thian, also known as Rocky Bay or Shark Bay. The outstanding white-sand beach (perhaps the island's best), is ideal for both swimming and snorkeling (equipment rental including fins 100฿, available on the beach). The only accommodation is **Rocky Resort ❸**, on the bay's east end, with simple bungalows. Rocky also doubles as the beach's only **restaurant,** with decent, relatively inexpensive fare. (Bungalows 300-500฿.)

LAEM TAA TOH. This cape juts into the gulf, separating Ao Chalok from Ao Thian. Follow the dirt road from Ao Chalok, and take the right path leading uphill at the fork. The **Taa Toh Lagoon Dive Resort ❸,** on Taa Toh Beach halfway around the cape, has simple bungalows and a **scuba school.** (☎377 792; www.taatohdivers.com. Bungalows 300-100฿.) Stop at **New Heaven Restaurant ❸,** which has a delicious menu and near-celestial views of Ao Thian. (Excellent Thai dishes 60-120฿. Seafood 200฿. Drinks 100-120฿. Open daily 11am-11pm.)

OUTDOOR ACTIVITIES

Scuba diving is popular year-round in Ko Tao, although late September through December often brings heavy rains and choppy waters. September to May is high-tide season and better for snorkeling, while May to September is low-tide season and better for basking on the beach. Ko Tao has over 20 dive sites. **Chumphon Pinnacle,** where a granite tower rises 14m above the surface, is a favorite for deep dives. **Southwest Pinnacle** and **Shark Island** are known for gorgeous coral and leopard sharks. **Green Rock** and **Sail Rock** on the way to Ko Phangan are famous for rock "swim-throughs." Closer to Ko Tao, **Hin Wong Pinnacle** and **Ko Nang Yuan** (see below) have coral in waters suitable for snorkeling.

Scuba prices are standardized, so friendliness and professionalism are the key elements of a good dive shop. Beginners can choose from the four-day open-water certification course (8500฿) or the supervised one-day "discover scuba" dives (2000฿, additional dives 800฿ each). Certified divers can hone their skills with the two-day advanced open-water course (6600฿) or tag along with any dive class on a one-day "fun dive" (1 dive 1000฿, 2-5 dives 900฿ each, 6-9 dives 800฿ each, 10 or more dives 700฿ each). Bring your own equipment for a 15% discount. Prices include accommodations for the duration of the course. If you choose to stay in a non-affiliated lodging, however, prices only drop by 150฿. Snorkelers can tag along on shallower dives for around 50฿. There are plenty of dive shops from which to choose, all with PADI certification. The following is an abbreviated list of dive shop operations: **Ban's Diving Resort & Sunshine Divers** (☎456 061; www.amazingkohtao.com); **Big Blue Diving Center** (☎377 750; www.bigbluediving.com); **Buddha View Dive Resort** (☎456 074; www.buddhaview-diving.com); **Scuba Junction** (☎456 164; www.scuba-junction.com); **Taa Toh Lagoon Dive Resort** (☎456 192; www.taatohdivers.com). The larger shops have representative offices on Mae Hat.

VIETNAM

HIGHLIGHTS OF VIETNAM

CULTURAL HERITAGE. Hà Nôi (p. 850) is a 1000-year-old city steeped in history and tradition. Hill-tribe cultures are the chief attractions of **Mai Châu** (p. 879) and **Sapa** (p. 868) in the northwest. The **Perfume Pagoda** (p. 865) ranks as one of the region's most unique shrines. Gentle **Huế** (p. 920) stewards an array of palaces and tombs. **Hội An**'s (p. 936) ornate Chinese architecture is some of the best-preserved in Southeast Asia.

URBAN BEAT. Hồ Chí Minh City (p. 965) flaunts a vibrant market culture, colonial architecture, and extravagant nightlife.

BEACHES. Nha Trang (p. 946), "the Vietnamese Riviera," features infamous pleasure cruises and fine food. **Phú Quốc Island** (p. 987) remains tourist-free...for now.

HANGING OUT. Đà Lạt (p. 953) boasts cool vibes, an eclectic avant-garde scene, and friendly locals. The livin' is easy on the Mekong in **Cần Thơ** (p. 981) and **Châu Đốc** (p. 983). Remote **Hà Tiên** (p. 986) is likely the most mellow town on earth.

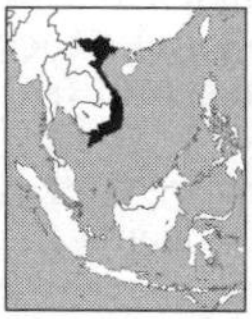

Whether drifting along the slow-moving Mekong or battling the rush of motorbikes in Hà Nội, travelers are surrounded by Vietnam's hardworking and friendly people. Vietnam prides itself on its unique heritage and strong survival instinct; after centuries of invasion and forcible influence by the Chinese, French, and Japanese, Vietnamese culture is anything but simple. Vietnamese soil has hosted over a dozen wars. The country's history of struggle against imperialism and desire for independence has created a culture distinct from that of its Southeast Asian neighbors—the nuances can be hard for visitors to grasp. Tourist cafes whisk travelers around on sputtering minibuses, usually providing only spoon-fed doses of local color. A truer taste of contemporary Vietnam hides in alleyway eateries, in *bia hơi* stalls, and amid the plastic furniture of streetside cafes.

FACTS AND FIGURES

Official Name: Socialist Republic of Vietnam.

Government: Communist State.

Capital: Hanoi.

Land Area: 325,360km^2.

Geography: Borders Cambodia, China, Laos, Gulf of Thailand, Gulf of Tonkin, and the South China Sea.

Climate: Rainy (low season) May-Oct., dry (high season) Oct.-March.

Average Height of a Vietnamese Man in His Twenties: 5 ft. 4 in.

Liters of Fish Sauce Consumed Annually by the Average Vietnamese Person: 11.

Population: 83 million.

Language: Vietnamese (official), English, French, Chinese, Khmer.

Religion: Buddhism, Christianity (mostly Roman Catholic), Islam.

Literacy Rate: 94% overall; 95.8% of men, 92.3% of women.

Major Exports: Crude oil, rice, coffee, rubber, tea.

Phone Codes: Country Code: 84. International Dialing Prefix: 00.

LIFE AND TIMES

DEMOGRAPHICS

Ethnic Vietnamese, or **Kinh,** make up roughly 90% of the country's population of 82.8 million; the remaining 10% is split among 53 ethnic minority groups. Most ethnic minority groups live in rural areas, particularly the Central and Northwest Highlands. The Vietnam War's death toll dramatically shifted the country's demographics: Today, over 60% of the population is under 25 years old.

LANGUAGE

Vietnamese is the only official language of Vietnam and is spoken by the great majority of the population (around 90%); those who don't speak it are largely ethnic minorities in the rural highlands. Vietnamese itself was originally written in Chinese characters called **Nôm.** Seventeenth-century French Jesuit missionary **Alexandre de Rhodes** adapted Vietnamese to the Latin alphabet, using diacriticals to transcribe the tonal qualities of words. The result was called *quốc ngữ* ("national language"), and today it is the exclusive written form of Vietnamese. The language has six separate tones, and Western speakers require substantial practice before they can approximate tones in a way that sounds natural to native speakers. For a tantalizingly cursory Vietnamese primer, flip to our Appendix (p. 990) and peruse the **Pronunciation Key** and the **Phrasebook.**

RELIGION

Buddhism, Taoism, and Confucianism are the big players in Vietnamese religious practice, alongside the smaller forces of animism, astrology, and other local superstition. No church or organization wields any profound nation-wide influence, largely due to governmental suppression. Today, religious persecution is uncommon, except in the Central Highlands, where ethnic minority **Protestants** are still subject to harassment by local police. Vietnam's home-grown **triple religion** derives from Mahayana Buddhism, Taoism, and Confucianism. Most of its adherents classify themselves as Buddhists. Established in 1939 by So Phu Huynh, **Hòa Hảo** ("harmony") is a quietist form of Buddhism. **Cao Đài** ("High Palace") was founded in 1926, seven years after Ngo Van Chieu was visited by an enormous floating eye (see **Someone To Watch Over You,** p. 977). The **Roman Catholic Church** enjoys official recognition by the Vietnamese government, and roughly 6 million followers.

LAND

For a country with so much waterfront real estate, Vietnam is surprisingly hilly—roughly 75% of the country is composed of hills and mountains. Much of the inland north is dotted with towering limestone cliffs and monoliths (called karsts). Central Vietnam north of Huế is blanketed in forest. Inland, the central highlands reach lower extremes than those of the northwest but are just as striking in some places. Approaching Ho Chi Minh City from the northeast, the landscape flattens out; southwest of HCMC, the land sinks into the swamps and mangrove jungle of the Mekong Delta, an area kept arable by the delta's industrious denizens.

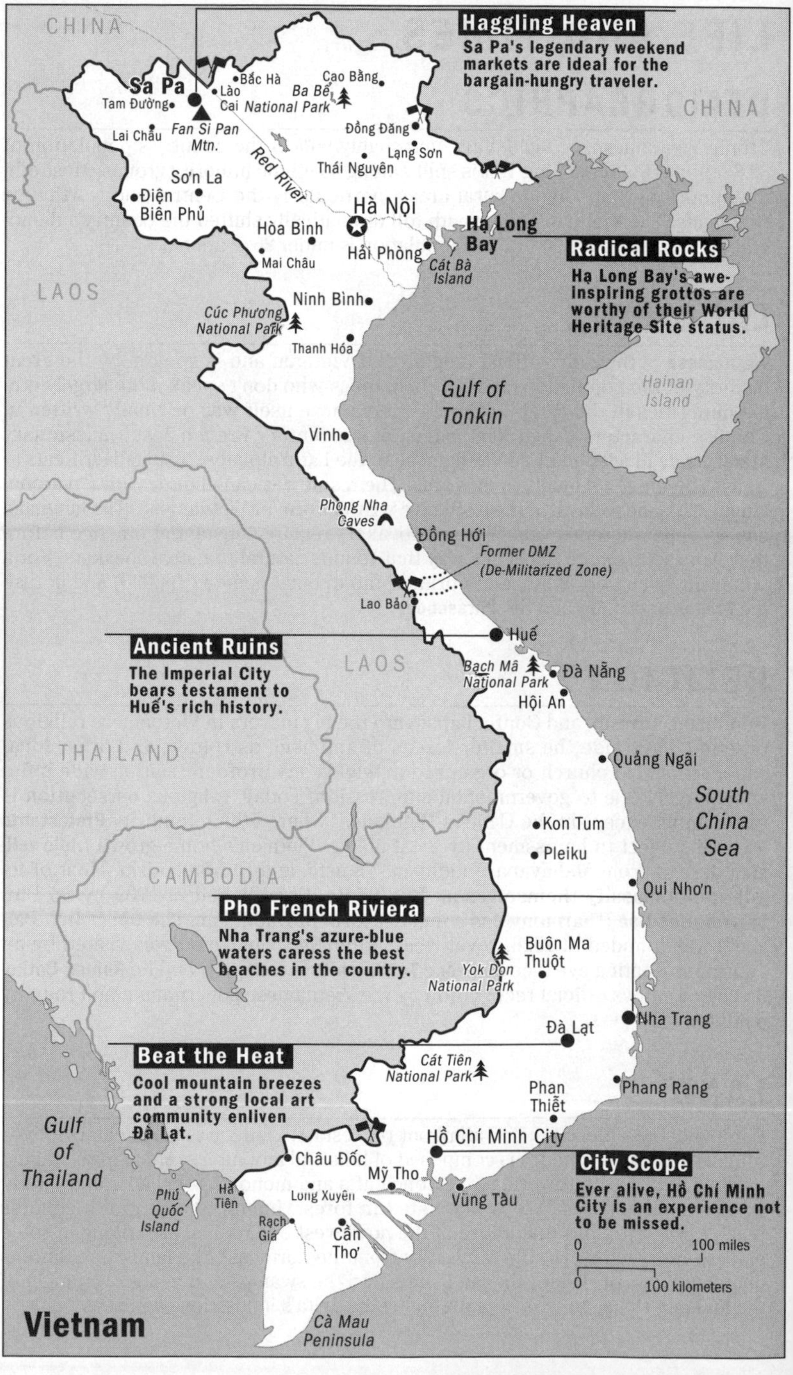
CHINA
Haggling Heaven
Sa Pa's legendary weekend markets are ideal for the bargain-hungry traveler.
CHINA
Sa Pa
Bắc Hà
Lào Cai
Cao Bằng
Ba Bể National Park
Tam Đường
Fan Si Pan Mtn.
Lai Châu
Đồng Đăng
Lạng Sơn
Red River
Thái Nguyên
Sơn La
Điện Biên Phủ
Hà Nội
Hạ Long Bay
Hòa Bình
Hải Phòng
Radical Rocks
Hạ Long Bay's awe-inspiring grottos are worthy of their World Heritage Site status.
Mai Châu
Cát Bà Island
LAOS
Ninh Bình
Cúc Phương National Park
Thanh Hóa
Gulf of Tonkin
Hainan Island
Vinh
Phong Nha Caves
Đồng Hới
Former DMZ (De-Militarized Zone)
Lao Bảo
Huế
Ancient Ruins
The Imperial City bears testament to Huế's rich history.
LAOS
Bạch Mã National Park
Đà Nẵng
Hội An
THAILAND
Quảng Ngãi
South China Sea
Kon Tum
Pleiku
CAMBODIA
Qui Nhơn
Pho French Riviera
Nha Trang's azure-blue waters caress the best beaches in the country.
Buôn Ma Thuột
Yok Đon National Park
Nha Trang
Đà Lạt
Beat the Heat
Cool mountain breezes and a strong local art community enliven Đà Lạt.
Cát Tiên National Park
Phan Thiết
Phang Rang
Gulf of Thailand
Hồ Chí Minh City
Châu Đốc
City Scope
Ever alive, Hồ Chí Minh City is an experience not to be missed.
Mỹ Tho
Hà Tiên
Phú Quốc Island
Long Xuyên
Vũng Tàu
Rạch Giá
Cần Thơ
0
100 miles
0
100 kilometers
Vietnam
Cà Mau Peninsula
VIETNAM

WILDLIFE

The country does not lack for biodiversity and natural wealth. Vietnam is considered one of the top 25 biodiversity locales in the world. Over 800 species of bird decorate the skies, land, and waters of the country. And that's not even touching on the thriving marine life—there are more than 1000 species of fish and shellfish—that feed the country and its economy. The water buffalo is a popular domesticated mammal; among more common wild animal species are deer, bears, leopards, foxes, mongeese, wildcats, crocodiles, lizards, iguanas, cobras, and pythons. According to a 1996 World Wildlife Fund report, 10% of Vietnam's wildlife is in danger of extinction; a dozen endangered species call Vietnam home, including four types of monkeys. Deforestation, overfishing, unchecked tourism, and habitat infringement brought on by population growth are taking their toll. On the other hand, the extensive and ever-expanding national park system, as well as several centers for endangered animals and research, are steps in the right direction.

HISTORY

CHINESE OCCUPATION AND THE LÝ-TRẦN PERIOD (111 BC-AD 1400)

IMPORTANT DATES			
111 BC Chinese armies capture Nam Việt.	**AD 939** Đại Việt established.	**1009** Lý Thái Tổ establishes the Lý Dynasty.	**13th-14th Centuries** Chinese Ming Dynasty gains further control, attacks Vietnamese culture.

Much of Vietnam's early history revolves around the struggle with Chinese forces over territorial control. The Chinese began their quest to acquire Vietnamese land in the 2nd century BC, when Hán armies captured Nam Việt from the Hùng kings. Power shifted back and forth until AD 939, when Ngô Quyền defeated the Chinese army and his successor founded the independent state of **Đại Việt.** Đại Việt was ruled by the **Lý Dynasty,** founded in 1009 by Lý Thái Tổ; the Trần Dynasty also held power (1225-1400), managing to defeat the Mongols under Kublai Khan. During the 12th century, however, Chinese forces once again gained a foothold in Vietnamese territory. As Chinese leaders gained power, they enslaved the Vietnamese and attempted to eradicate their culture through the process of "Sinicization."

THE LATER LÊ DYNASTY (1428-1776) AND THE TÂY SƠN REBELLION (1772-1802)

IMPORTANT DATES			
1418 Lê Dynasty defeats Ming, establishes Confucian state.	**16th Century** Nguyễn Dynasty gains control of Champa Kingdom.	**1772-1802** Tây Sơn Rebellion.	**1790** Nguyễn Anh comes to power and brings back Chinese influences.

In 1418, **Lê Lợi,** an aristocrat, and **Nguyễn Trãi,** a brilliant military strategist, drove out the Chinese and founded the Later Lê Dynasty, which instituted a highly centralized state founded upon Confucian principles. The country expanded south to include the Champa Kingdom during the early 16th century. In 1545 the country was partitioned into three, with the Nguyễn Dynasty controlling the southern third. Modern-day Vietnam was briefly unified as Đại Việt when **Nguyễn Huệ** (not a member of the similarly-named ruling dynasty) and his brothers capitalized on widespread peasant discontent to spark the **Tây Sơn Rebellion.** After crushing a Chinese army dispatched to prop up the Nguyễn Dynasty rulers, Nguyễn Huệ declared himself emperor, but died soon afterward. With the aid of the Chinese and Europeans, **Nguyễn Anh** of the Nguyễn Dynasty reclaimed the throne and renamed the country Nam Việt, which the Chinese later reversed to Việt Nam.

CONTACT WITH THE WEST AND COLONIALISM (1857-1925)

IMPORTANT DATES

1857 French ships sail into Vietnam.	**1867-83** French gain control of Mekong Delta and then entire country.	**19th Century** French landlords exploit Vietnamese.

The first Westerners to visit Vietnam were the **Portuguese,** who established a trading center at Faifo (Hội An). Missionaries and Jesuits, never far behind, began proselytizing in Northern and Central Vietnam. Among them was Alexander de Rhodes, a Portuguese priest who devised a system of transliterating the Vietnamese language into Latin characters, an early version of today's *quốc ngữ* (national language) script (see **Language,** p. 839). **France**'s interest in *Indochine*—the area of Cambodia, Laos, and Vietnam—lay in trade, natural resources, and a chance to compete with Britain's rapidly expanding Asian empire. In 1857, Napoleon III decided to colonize Vietnam; by 1867 the French had seized the entire Mekong Delta region. With the signing of the Treaty of Protectorate in 1883, the French gained control of the whole country and established the capital in Saigon.

The French *mission civilisatrice,* as they euphemistically dubbed their colonial endeavor, was anything but civil. Landless tenancy skyrocketed in the south as ownership became concentrated in the hands of wealthy landlords. In Northern and Central Vietnam, the French forced peasants to work on rubber plantations. Apologists for the colonial regime claimed that the French had made great strides in the areas of medicine and education. Some experts, however, say that reforms were largely cosmetic. Only one doctor was available for every 50,000 Vietnamese, and literacy rates actually declined during the colonial period—only an estimated 10% of all school-age children received an education.

NATIONALISM AND REVOLUTIONARY MOVEMENT (1920-45)

IMPORTANT DATES

1920s Resistance movements grow.	**1930** Hồ Chí Minh establishes Indochinese Communist Party.	**1941** Vietnam Independence League formed.	**1941** Japanese annex Indochina, place Vietnamese government in charge.

By the 1920s, a new generation of young Vietnamese assumed control of a rising nationalist movement. In 1930, **Hồ Chí Minh** founded the **Indochinese Communist Party (ICP),** which helped instigate a series of violent uprisings in the central provinces of Nghệ An and Hà Tĩnh; both were brutally suppressed by the French. In the early 40s, the Communists shifted from a platform of class struggle to a more moderate approach that emphasized independence; the **Vietnam Independence League (Việt Minh)** was established in 1941. That same year, the Japanese gained permission to occupy Indochina militarily, hastily deposing the French and placing an ill-prepared Vietnamese government in charge.

THE FIRST INDOCHINA WAR AND ITS AFTERMATH (1946-65)

IMPORTANT DATES

1944 Việt Minh leads August Revolution.	**1945-46** Vietnam gains independence. First Indochina War begins.	**1954** French defeated at Điện Biên Phủ. Geneva Accords, division of Vietnam.	**Late 1950s** Ngô Đình Diệm rules South Vietnam.	**Early 1960s** US involvement increases as North Vietnam allies with USSR. Diệm assassinated in 1963.

Power struggles began with the largely peaceful August Revolution, in which the Việt Minh forces occupied most of the country. The culmination of the Việt Minh anti-colonial movement occurred on September 2, 1945, when Hồ Chí Minh read Vietnam's **Declaration of Independence** in Hà Nội's Ba Đình Square. The French were not content to watch their empire slip away, however, and in October they drove the Việt Minh out of South Vietnam. After a year of failed negotiations, the First Indochina War officially began. In the spring of 1954, after a bloody eight-year struggle, Việt Minh forces defeated the French at **Điện Biên Phủ,** an isolated valley in the northwest. Humiliated, the French agreed to begin a peace process.

At the Geneva Convention in July of 1954, both sides agreed to an interim compromise and partitioned Vietnam along the 17th Parallel. Plans were drawn up calling for national elections to reunify the country two years after the treaty. In the meantime, the Communists gained control of the north while a coalition of non-Communists came to power in the south. The **Republic of Vietnam (RVN)** in the south became an American client-state ruled by the dictatorial Catholic Ngô Đình Diệm, who refused to hold the elections agreed upon at the Geneva Convention. In fall 1963, Diệm's own generals assassinated him; General Nguyễn Văn Thiệu seized power. The **Democratic Republic of Vietnam (DRV)** in the north sought to build a socialist state, carrying out a disastrous land reform campaign in the late 1950s. Hà Nôi maintained good relations with both the USSR and China, receiving military and economic aid from both.

In the early 1960s, things began to heat up as the north gave support to the popular **National Liberation Front of South Vietnam (NLF)**—guerrilla forces in the south. The NLF was modeled on the Việt Minh, with front organizations accommodating women, students, and peasants. The fighting arm of the NLF, known as the Việt Cộng (pejorative slang meaning Vietnamese Communist), with military aid from the north's DRV, marched down the Hồ Chí Minh Trail through Laos and Cambodia into Southern Vietnam. The anti-Communist US, alarmed at the accelerated wave of Việt Cộng violence, began to increase its presence in the south.

THE SECOND INDOCHINA WAR (1965-75)

IMPORTANT DATES

1965 US officially enters Second Indochina War, bombs the north.	**1968** NLF forces launch Tet Offensive.	**1972** Christmas bombings.	**1973** Paris Peace Accords finally end war.	**1975** North Vietnamese enter Saigon, form Socialist Republic of Vietnam.

Known in Vietnam as the "American War," the Second Indochina War marked the pinnacle of destruction and violence on Vietnamese soil. The US officially entered the war in 1965, when President Lyndon Johnson approved regular bombings of North Vietnam and deployed American troops to the south. By 1968, half a million US troops were fighting in South Vietnam. During the first part of 1968, NLF forces launched the **Tet Offensive,** attacking more than 100 cities and military bases over the course of the Vietnamese New Year (early February). Although a military defeat, the bloody offensive was a propaganda victory for Hà Nôi and fueled American dissatisfaction with the war. The US stepped up bombing campaigns against the north, culminating in the 1972 **Christmas bombings,** an attempt to force the Vietnamese to come to the negotiating table. Without popular support to sustain the conflict, the US terminated active participation in the war with the **1973 Paris Peace Accords.** On April 30, 1975, North Vietnamese tanks rolled into Saigon, reunited the country under Communist rule, and renamed the capital Hồ Chí Minh City. At the Hà Nội Citadel, travelers can see the tank that crashed through the gates of the presidential palace (see p. 861).

THE SOCIALIST REPUBLIC OF VIETNAM (1975-98)

IMPORTANT DATES				
1976 War continues: conflict with the Khmer Rouge.	**1979** Foreign relations weaken after a brief war with China.	**1986** *đổi mới* reforms sweep the country.	**1990** Vietnamese forces leave Cambodia.	**1995** Relations with US normalized; Vietnam joins ASEAN.

The decade following the end of the war was one of the darkest in modern Vietnamese history. More than a seventh of the population had been wounded or killed in the war; millions were left homeless. Thousands of "boat people" fled the country, a flight that lasted until the mid-80s. Immediately after the **Socialist Republic of Vietnam (SRV)** was established, the country began a protracted war with the Khmer Rouge in Cambodia. Worsening relations with Beijing climaxed in a brief but destructive border war with China in 1979. South Vietnam's agricultural production declined precipitously. In the north, conditions approached famine.

In 1986, at the historic **6th Party Congress,** the Communist Party approved sweeping economic reforms, dubbed **đổi mới (Renewal).** Frightened by events in the former Soviet Union and by the Tiananmen Square pro-democracy uprising in China, the Vietnamese Politburo sought to grant the Vietnamese economic freedom while maintaining a tight grip on political power. Since *đổi mới*, Hà Nội has pursued a foreign policy aimed at reintegrating the country into regional and global affairs. Vietnam's withdrawal from Cambodia in 1990 cleared the way for better relations with its Southeast Asian neighbors. On July 11, 1995, Vietnam normalized relations with the US and joined the Association of Southeast Asian Nations (ASEAN) 17 days later.

VIETNAM

VIETNAM TODAY

Vietnam stands at a crossroads. While the first 10 years of *đổi mới* have brought impressive results, talk of "the next Asian Tiger" now appears to have been premature. The government has been reluctant to push economic reforms too far, especially in the wake of the region's recent economic crisis. While the January 1998 Politburo reshuffle brought two pro-reform officials to power—President **Trần Đức Lương** and Prime Minister **Phan Văn Khải**—conservative elements within the Politburo (led by the military) have succeeded in keeping reforms in check. A series of demonstrations in Thái Bình and Đồng Nai provinces over local government corruption prompted President Lương to call for the elimination of "immoral and incapable officials." The response is part of a nationwide effort to reduce corruption, rife within the government and businesses.

In November 2000, US President Bill Clinton visited Hà Nội, the first trip a US president has made to a reunified Vietnam. The US had begun crafting new relations with its former adversary when President Clinton lifted the trade embargo from Vietnam in 1994. Two years later, the US embassy in Hà Nội reopened, and diplomatic relations slowly resumed. Even with other foreign investors taking interest in Vietnam, however, the average Vietnamese income remains only about US$1 a day. The government hopes to further strengthen the economy by capitalizing on the resource-rich Spratly Islands. The archipelago is claimed by China, Taiwan, Vietnam, the Philippines, Brunei, and Malaysia and remains a heated source of debate.

Large-scale prisoner absolution in 1998 was a step toward human rights protection in Vietnam. However, the same laws under which peaceful political protestors were arrested still exist. Open letters to the Politburo calling for political reform have been tacitly tolerated. However, groups remain intent on keeping out foreign powers, mimicking a long history of similar struggle with foreign counterparts. Many human rights activists are pushing for democracy. Persecution of the Montagnards in the central highlands peaked in 2003 and remains a problem.

In January 2004, an avian influenza (birdflu) outbreak swept through the country, killing six people, but was brought under control. In the summer of 2004, after reports of the increase in the AIDS epidemic, the government increased its education program and even christened the country's first condom machine in Hà Nội.

CUSTOMS AND ETIQUETTE

In Vietnam, a smile goes a mile. Be polite, courteous, and patient—if you expect promptness, you will be disappointed. If you must criticize, try to find a way to express your complaint as a joke. Outbursts, known as "losing face," are frowned upon and are something to be avoided at all costs, particularly when bargaining.

A LITTLE RESPECT. As a gesture of respect, take off your hat and bow your head slightly when addressing elders or monks. Remove your shoes before entering a temple; when invited into someone's home, note whether your host takes off his shoes, then do the same. The Vietnamese value family tremendously; in conversation with locals, be attentive to family details. When you give or receive gifts, use both hands and wrap them in lucky green or red paper; black and white are considered inauspicious.

TABOOS. The feet are regarded as the least holy part of the body; don't point the bottoms of your feet at any person or Buddhist image, as this is considered rude. Conversely, Vietnamese regard the head as the most sacred part of the body; never touch a person's head, even a small child's.

TABLE MANNERS. Chopsticks sticking out of a rice bowl are thought to resemble the incense burned for the dead. Never leave your chopsticks in this position, as it is considered a negative omen. Dog lovers should avoid *thịt cho* (dog meat). Vietnamese puppies are man's best lunch, not man's best friend.

GLBT. Homosexuality is not openly discussed in Vietnam, though major cities like Hồ Chí Minh City and Hà Nôi have a small but growing gay scene. The importance of procreation in Vietnamese society, however, means that most gay men remain closeted, so the gay community stays underground. Public displays of romantic affection are frowned upon for both heterosexuals and homosexuals. *The Men of Vietnam*, by Douglas Thompson, is the first comprehensive account of Vietnamese gay subculture. Utopia-Asia (www.utopia-asia.com) also offers tips for gay travelers in Vietnam.

ARTS AND RECREATION

DANCE AND DRAMA. Vietnam has many traditional musical genres, especially **folk music** and **theater/opera,** that remain popular today. Folk songs *(dân ca)* originated in the countryside and were sung at festivals and in the fields. One common style, the *quan họ* tradition of Bắc Ninh Province north of Hà Nôi, was sung in a call and response fashion between young men and women as an important element in courtship. **Musical theater** is also characterized by regional variation. Most famous in the north is *hát chèo*, which combines singing, acting, and dancing. Central and southern Vietnam see more *hát tuồng* and *cải lương* (reformed opera). *Tuồng* was influenced by Chinese opera in plot, costumes, and instrumentation, while *cải lương* combines elements of *tuồng* with Western traditions. A third popular genre, *múa rối nước* (water puppetry), originated in the north. Wooden puppets cavort across the surface of a shallow pool, acting out fairy tales. Puppeteers, standing knee-deep in water behind a screen, manipulate the puppets with rods. Witness this exquisite art form in Hà Nôi (see **Entertainment,** p. 863).

LITERATURE. Literature is Vietnam's most treasured legacy of the pre-modern period. Early literature was written in classical Chinese and the *nôm* demotic script. During the 17th and 18th centuries, one of Vietnam's greatest *nôm* writers, poet **Hồ Xuân Hư'o'ng,** was famous for her innuendo-laden poems about the lives of court women. **Nguyễn Du** is recognized as Vietnam's greatest writer. His *Truyện Kiều (Tale of Kieu)* is an epic in verse about the tragic life of an aristocratic woman. Vietnamese of all ages and social classes can recite passages from the epic. When the French occupied Vietnam, they sought to curtail Chinese influence by banning Chinese and instituting the *quốc ngữ* script. Literature written in the vernacular flourished by the 1920s and 30s and played a significant role in the nationalist struggle by highlighting the injustices of the colonial regime.

HOLIDAYS AND FESTIVALS (2005)

Government offices and businesses are closed on public holidays.

DATE	NAME AND LOCATION	DESCRIPTION
Jan. 1	Western New Year's Day	Happy New Year!
Feb. 9-12	Tet	Vietnamese and Chinese New Year, taking place during the first week of the new lunar calendar. The most important Vietnamese celebration of the year.
Feb. 3	Anniversary of the Founding Day of the Communist Party of Vietnam	Anniversary of the Founding Day of the Communist Party of Vietnam.
Apr. 13	Thanh Minh	Vietnamese All Soul's day; the 5th day of the 3rd lunar month. Families gather to worship the dead.
Apr. 30	Liberation of South Vietnam and Saigon	Celebrate the reunification of Vietnam!
May 1	International Labour Day	Celebrate Labour!
May 19	Ho Chi Minh's Birthday	It's Ho Chi Minh's birthday!
May 28	Celebration of the Buddha	Celebrate the Buddha!
Sept. 2	National Day	Vietnam... yes!
Sept. 3	President Ho's Anniversary	It's Ho Chi Minh's anniversary!
Oct. 17	Mid-Autumn Festival	The 15th day of the 9th lunar month. This celebration is dedicated to children, who parade through the streets carrying paper lanterns.
Dec. 25	Christmas Day	Not a government holiday; only celebrated by Christians.

ADDITIONAL RESOURCES

GENERAL HISTORY

Postcolonial Vietnam: New Histories of a National Past, by Patricia Pelley (2002). A postmodern critical perspective on a well-known past.

Vietnam: A History, by Stanley Karnow (1983). A straightforward modern Vietnamese history, focusing on the Second Indochina War. Winner of the Pulitzer Prize.

Vietnam, Now, by David Lamb (2003). A comprehensive look at modern Vietnam through the eyes of a reporter returning for the first time since the war.

FICTION AND NON-FICTION

A Bright, Shining Lie: John Paul Vann and America in Vietnam, by Neil Sheehan (1988). Winner of the National Book Award. A scathing indictment of America's involvement in Vietnam by a war correspondent.

Catfish and Mandala, by Andrew X. Pham (2000). A Vietnamese-American returns to his homeland many years after leaving for California and takes on the country by bike. A poignant, insightful account of contemporary Vietnam.

Dispatches, by Michael Herr (1991). Vivid stories from the front as recorded by *Esquire* correspondent Herr render this one of the must-reads on the subject of the Vietnam War. It served as the inspiration for a number of movies, including *Apocalypse Now.*

FILM

Apocalypse Now, dir. Francis Ford Coppola (1979). One of the greatest war films ever made, depicting hopelessness and insanity on the American side during the war.

VIETNAM PRICE ICONS					
SYMBOL:	❶	❷	❸	❹	❺
ACCOMM.	Under US$4 Under 64,000Đ	US$4-8 64,000-128,000Đ	US$8-15 128,000-240,000Đ	US$15-25 240,000-400,000Đ	Over US$25 Over 400,000Đ
FOOD	Under US$0.75 Under 10,000Đ	US$0.75-2 10,000-30,000Đ	US$2-4 30,000-60,000Đ	US$4-7 60,000-105,000Đ	Over US$7 Over 105,000Đ

ESSENTIALS

EMBASSIES AND CONSULATES

VIETNAMESE CONSULAR SERVICES ABROAD

Australia: 6 Timbarra Cres., O'Malley, ACT 2606 (☎02 6286 6059 or 6290 1556; http://members.iinet.net.au/~vembassy/); **Consulate General:** 489 New South Head Rd., Double Bay Sydney 2028 (☎02 9327 1912 or 9327 2539; fax 9328 1653).

Canada: 470 Wilbrod St., Ottawa, ON K1N 6M8 (☎613-236-1398; vietem@istar.ca).

New Zealand: Level 21 Grand Plimmer Tower, 2-6 Gilmer Terr., P.O. Box 8042, Wellington (☎473 5912; embassyvn@paradise.net.nz).

UK: Victoria Rd. 12-14, London W8 5RD (☎020 7937 1912; www.vietnamembassy.org.uk/).

US: 1233 20th St. NW, Ste. 400, Washington, DC 20036 (☎202-861-0917; www.vietnamembassy-usa.org); **Consulate General:** 1700 California St., Ste. 430, San Francisco, CA 94109 (☎415-922-1707; www.vietnamconsulate-sf.org/).

CONSULAR SERVICES IN VIETNAM

Australia: 8 Đạo Tan, Ba Đinh District, Hà Nội (☎4 831 7755; www.ausinvn.com). Open M-F 8:30am-noon and 1-4pm. **Consulate:** 5th fl. Landmark Bldg., 5B Tôn Đức Thắng, Hồ Chí Minh City (☎8 829 6035; fax 829 6035). Open M-F 8:30am-noon and 1-5pm.

Canada: 31 Hùng Vương, Hà Nội (☎4 734 5000; www.dfait-maeci.gc.ca/vietnam/menu-en.asp). **Consulate:** 61 Nguyễn Du, Ste. 1002, Hồ Chí Minh City (☎8 824 5025; hochi@dfait-maeci.gc.ca).

New Zealand: 32 Hàng Bài, Hà Nội (☎4 824 1481; nzembhan@fpt.vn). **Consulate:** 5th fl. YOCO Bldg., 41 Nguyễn Thị Minh Khai, Hồ Chí Minh City (☎8 822 6907; fax 822 6905).

UK: Central Bldg., 31 Hai Bà Trưng, Hà Nội (☎4 936 0500). **Consulate:** 25 Lê Duẩn, Hồ Chí Minh City (☎8 829 8433; bcghcmc@hcm.vnn.vn).

US: 7 Láng Hạ, Ba Đình District, Hà Nội (☎4 772 1500). **Consulate:** 4 Lê Duẩn, District 1, Hồ Chí Minh City (24hr. ☎8 822 9433; http://hochiminh.usconsulate.gov/).

VISAS

All travelers must obtain a one-month single-entry tourist visa at any Vietnamese consulate or embassy. A one-month single-entry visa is US$65 or an equivalent, multiple-entry visa is US$110; a three-month single-entry visa is US$130, multiple-entry is US$150. **Extensions** can be arranged by tour agencies or hotels. Travelers can enter and depart from any international airport or port; see the box on overland border crossings (xref). Entering Vietnam to work requires a letter from a sponsor organization—they can obtain a visa for you in Vietnam. If you find a job while in Vietnam, the organization can transfer your visa status.

MONEY

The Vietnamese **đồng (Đ)** comes in denominations of 100; 200; 500; 1000; 2000; 5000; 10,000; 20,000; 50,000; and 100,000Đ. US$ are widely accepted in accommodations and restaurants in larger towns, where prices are frequently quoted in dollars. However, for other expenses, paying in đồng allows more room to bargain. *Let's Go* lists prices according to the currency cited by the establishments. Many establishments list prices in US$ but accept đồng as well. Credit cards are generally accepted in major cities, especially at expensive restaurants, hotels, and travel agencies. Banks give credit card advances in dollars. **Tipping** is not necessary but is appreciated and occasionally expected at touristy establishments. At expensive restaurants and hotels, a 10% service charge is added.

CURRENCY (Đ)		
	AUS$1 = 11,431Đ (ĐỒNG)	100,000Đ = AUS$8.75
	CDN$1 = 12,146Đ	100,000Đ = CDN$8.24
	EUR€1 = 19,487Đ	100,000Đ = EUR€5.13
	NZ$1 = 10,592Đ	100,000Đ = NZ$9.44
	UK£1 = 28,868Đ	100,000Đ = UK£3.46
	US$1 = 15,753Đ	100,000Đ = US$6.35

GETTING THERE

BY PLANE. The two primary international airports are **Nội Bài International Airport** in Hà Nội and **Tân Sơn International Airport** in HCMC, although there is a smaller airport in Đà Nẵng **(Đà Nẵng International Airport). Don't lose your baggage claim tickets**—you won't be allowed to take your luggage without them. **Vietnam Airlines** (www.vietnamair.com.vn) runs the most flights to these airports.

BY LAND. Refer to the table below for overland border crossings to Vietnam.

BORDER CROSSINGS. On your visa application, be sure to specify the correct point of entry and exit.

LAOS. There is a crossing open from **Đà Nẵng/Huế** (p. 920) through **Lao Bảo** to **Savannakhet.** The **Keo Nưa** (Cầu Treo) **Pass** is 80km southwest of Vinh on Highway 8, near Tây Sơn.

CHINA. Borders are open from **Đồng Đăng,** near Lạng Sơn (p. 903), to **Pingxiang** (Guangxi Province) and from **Lào Cai** to **Hekou** (Yunnan province). A third border crossing is at **Móng Cái** in northeastern Vietnam. You can get there by hydrofoil direct from Hải Phòng or Hạ Long City, 178km south.

CAMBODIA. The border at **Mộc Bài** provides a cheap way to get between Vietnam and Cambodia. The ferry that departs from **Châu Đốc** crosses the border at Vĩnh Xương and is well worth it for a trip through the Mekong Delta.

GETTING AROUND

BY PLANE. If you can afford it, travel by plane is the fastest and most comfortable way to get from one end of the country to the other. **Vietnam Airlines** has extensive domestic connections from hubs in Hồ Chí Minh City and Hà Nội.

BY TRAIN. Trains exist in Vietnam, but solely for the joy of existing. They move slowly and require patience. Passengers should retain their tickets, lest they be charged a fee upon disembarking. A journey on the "**Unification Express**" from Hà Nội to HCMC or vice versa is a scenic way to visit most of Vietnam's major cities and offers much more contact with local culture than travel by tourist minibus.

BY BUS. Vietnam's public bus system is the cheapest way to travel off the beaten path. Buses go everywhere, and foreign faces are rare. To avoid getting stuck with ridiculous "tourist prices," try to learn numbers and phrases for "how much is it to..." and "no, it is..." (See **Appendix,** p. 990.) Buses are not for the impatient, faint of heart, or claustrophobic. Expect to be packed in with bikes, fruits, vegetables, and sweating commuters. The rides tend to be exciting, loud, dusty, and tiring. **Open-tour buses** cost more than public buses, but run more regularly, boast A/C and more comfortable seating, and don't require haggling. Regrettably, you will see 80% of Vietnam through a window and your fellow riders will all be backpackers; your choice of destinations is also limited to those along the open-tour bus path from HCMC to Hà Nội, passing over many out-of-the-way destinations.

BY MINIBUS. Many backpackers use minibuses operated by budget travel cafes based in Hồ Chí Minh City and Hà Nôi. Minibuses, which cost a bit more than public buses, reduce the headaches of public transportation. The downside is that they limit your contact with locals as well as the places you can visit, since many of the destinations *Let's Go* lists lie off the well-trodden minibus path.

WE BE SCAMMIN'. In any major city, you'll likely be surrounded by *cyclo* and motorbike drivers. They'll attempt to bring you to a hotel that is paying them a commission instead of wherever it is that you want to go. Be adamant about your intended accommodation and quoted price. It's a good idea to write down your destination (with accent marks) and the fare before you negotiate.

VIETNAM

BY BICYCLE OR MOTORBIKE. Despite safety risks, traveling by motorbike is a good alternative for getting from city to city without the hassle of public transportation. Travelers can flag down motos (called "*xe ôm*," literally "hugging bike," because the passenger hugs the driver to stay on) for intercity travel. Bicycles are readily available for rent, but helmets aren't; bring your own. Vietnamese drivers tend to be much more attuned to cyclists than drivers in the West; nonetheless, be sure to ride defensively, signal clearly, and avoid highways.

BY CYCLO. Ubiquitous three-wheeled bicycle rickshaws ply the streets. Passengers sit in front while the driver pedals behind. As most drivers can't speak English, a map or written address will prove helpful to communicate your destination. Agree on a fare in advance.

KEEPING IN TOUCH

The Vietnamese **postal service** is reliable when letters are sent to or from major cities, although letters to most Western countries can take anywhere from 10 days to three weeks to arrive. All overseas packages must be processed through customs before they can be received. **Poste Restante** is available in Đà Lạt, Đà Nẵng, Hà Nội, Hồ Chí Minh City, and Nha Trang, but isn't always reliable.

Long-distance calls placed from Vietnam can cost an arm and a leg. Make international calls at the local post office. **International phone cards,** such as those issued by AT&T and MCI, can be used for no fee, but rarely work. **Credit card calls** are available in Hà Nôi and Hồ Chí Minh City.

Internet access is available in most tourist destinations. Average prices hover around 100 đồng per minute, though Internet service may cost twice that in Nha Trang and Hội An. Log on in Hà Nội for the best rates in the country.

HÀ NỘI ☎4

The idea of Hà Nội evokes images of a stern, austere bastion of Vietnamese Communism, ravaged by war and closed to the world. Visitors to the capital, however, will be surprised to find themselves in one of Southeast Asia's most charming cities. With its Chinese architecture, majestic French colonial buildings, and tree-lined lanes, this ancient city of lakes extends a reserved but genuine welcome—the essence of the North Vietnamese. Less cosmopolitan than Hồ Chí Minh City, Hà Nội is kinder and gentler than its southern rival. Fewer skyscrapers tower overhead and less traffic clogs the streets. The Old Quarter has stepped up as the city's tourist enclave, with tourist hotels, travel cafes, and Western restaurants popping up left and right. The hard-core Communist era appears to be on the wane; the almost overnight transformation of the infamous "Hanoi Hilton" prison into the Hà Nội Tower Commercial Center has been an omen of things to come. Hammers and sickles still adorn the cityscape, but the *đổi mới* "renovation" policies are slowly reshaping the face of the city.

INTERCITY TRANSPORTATION

BY PLANE. Flights into Hà Nội land at **Nội Bài International Airport,** 35km north of the city. There's a 25,000Đ domestic departure tax and a US$14 tax for international flights. The white Nội Bài Transport Co-op booth right outside the airport runs **taxis** to town (US$10) and from town (US$7.50). Most travelers split the fare with one or two others, so ask around. **Minibuses** run US$1.50 (20,000Đ if you purchase tickets on board), though they're mostly reserved for locals. Where you get dropped off depends on the whim of your latest friend, the hotel commission hound. The more disinterested you seem in your choice of lodging, the more likely it is that you will get a better value. **Vietnam Airlines minibuses** (☎886 5054) also run between the airport and city every 30min. (45min.-1hr., US$2), stopping at the Vietnam Airlines office on Quang Trưng. To head back to the airport, call Nội Bài Airport Taxis (☎886 5615) or Vietnam Airlines Airport Taxis (☎883 3333) to arrange for pickup.

DESTINATION	FREQUENCY	PRICE	DESTINATION	FREQUENCY	PRICE
Đà Nẵng	3 per day	825,000Đ	**Hong Kong**	1-2 per day	US$272
Hồ Chí Minh City	6-8 per day	1,525,000Đ	**Kuala Lumpur**	2-3 per day	US$250
Huế	3 per day	825,000Đ	**Manila**	1 per day	US$280
Nha Trang	1 per day	1,325,000Đ	**Singapore**	1-2 per day	US$310
Bangkok	3 per day	US$155	**Vientiane**	2 per day	US$100

Several airlines operate domestic and international flights from Hà Nội: **Cathay Pacific Airways,** 49 Hai Bà Trưng (☎826 7298); **China Airlines,** 18 Trần Hưng Đạo (☎824 2688); **Lao Aviation,** 269 Kim Ma (☎846 4873); **Malaysia Airlines,** 15 Ngô Quyền (☎826 8820); **Pacific Airlines,** 100 Lê Duẩn (☎733 2162); **Singapore Airlines,** 17 Ngô Quyền (☎826 8888); **Thai Airways,** 44B Lý Thường Kiệt (☎826 6893); **Vietnam Airlines,** 1 Quang Trưng, at the intersection with Trang Thi (☎825 0888; open M-F 7am-6:30pm, Sa-Su 8-11:30am and 1:30-5pm). Sometimes two airlines will share one plane leaving from Hà Nội. In that case, purchase your ticket from Vietnam Airlines, as it is usually around US$20 cheaper. Be aware that the prices listed in the chart below vary with the season.

! Keep your baggage tags or you won't be allowed to claim your bags. **Keep your stamped immigration card with your passport at all times;** you'll need it to leave the country.

BY TRAIN. Trains are the safest, most comfortable mode of domestic transport in Vietnam. Reserving a sleeper is well worth the extra cost, since the seating compartments sometimes get quite crowded.

Hà Nội Railway Station (Ga Hà Nội), 120 Lê Duẩn (☎825 3949), at the west end of Trần Hưng Đạo, a 10min. cyclo ride from the city center (5000-10,000Đ). Travelers arriving in Hà Nội from Lạng Sơn, Lào Cai, and southern Vietnam disembark here. Purchase tickets for points south at Counter 1, the special booking window for foreigners in the main building (open daily 7am-12:30pm and 1-8:45pm). Counter 2, beside the tourist window, exchanges foreign currency. Always buy tickets at least one day in advance to get the seat or sleeper you want, especially for special events like the Saturday market in Sa Pa. **Save your ticket** or you will be forced to pay again upon arrival. Fares vary by speed. Prices listed reflect the full range of comfort, from hard seats to soft sleepers, with or without A/C. To: **Hải Phòng** (2hr.; 6am; 22,000Đ); **Hồ Chí Minh City** (32-41hr.; 11pm; 380,000-900,000Đ); **Huế** (12-16hr.; 11pm; 170,000-400,000Đ); **Nha Trang** (24-32hr.; 11pm; 340,000-800,000Đ); **Ninh Bình** (2½-3hr.; 11pm; 26,000-31,000Đ); **Sa Pa** via **Lào Cai** (9hr.; 10am, 9:30pm; 65,000-200,000Đ).

Other Departure Points: Buy tickets for **Hải Phòng, Lạng So'n,** and **Lào Cai** at Hà Nôi Railway Station, at the booth near Gate 5 (open daily 7am-12:30pm and 1-7pm), up to 2hr. before departure; otherwise buy them at the station itself. On the opposite side of the tracks from the main station (accessible via Trần Quý Cáp), daily trains run to **Lạng So'n** (5:40am, 10pm; 78,000Đ). Trains to **Hải Phòng** (2hr.; 22,000Đ) leave from **Long Biên Station (Ga Long Biên)** near Đồng Xuân Market, accessible from **Trần Nhat Duat** (2hr.; 9:35am, 3:10, 5:45pm; 20,000Đ). Trains also leave from **Gia Lâm Station (Ga Gia Lâm)** across the Red River (2 blocks north of the **Gia Lâm** bus station) and head to: **Hải Phòng** (12:40pm, 3:35pm; 11,000Đ); **Lạng So'n** (6½hr.; 6:10, 7:10am, 1:47pm; 28,000Đ); **Lào Cai** (6:35am, 10:28pm; 54,000-61,000Đ).

BY BUS. Using public buses requires patience for overcrowded, jostling rides that leave only when full, regardless of quoted departure time. In true Vietnamese style, the prices below are approximations, but be sure not to be overcharged: current prices are usually clearly listed in the bigger stations. Always try to buy your ticket at the station; onboard, the collector may demand an inflated fare.

Gia Lâm Bus Station: 3km across the Red River on the left. To: **Hải Phòng** (2½hr.; about every hr. 6am-4:30pm; 20,000Đ); **Hạ Long City** (3hr.; every hr. 6am-3pm; 35,000Đ); **Lạng So'n** (5hr.; every hr. from 7am; 30,000Đ). Moto to the station 10,000Đ.

Southern Bus Station (Bến Xe Nam Hà Nội): On Đường Giải Phóng, the extension of Lê Duẩn, 5km south of the train station. For all destinations south of Hà Nội. To: **Điện Biên Phủ** (16-20hr.; 4, 9am, 1pm; 100,000Đ); **Ninh Bình** (2½hr.; every 2hr.; 20,000Đ).

Há Đõng Bus Station: Down Tôn Đức Thắng, a 20min. cyclo ride from the city center (10,000-15,000Đ), in the suburb of Há Đõng. To **Lào Cai** (20hr.; 5am; 70,000Đ) and **So'n La** (8hr.; 5:30am; 55,000Đ). To get to **Mai Châu,** head toward So'n La and ask to get off at **Tòng Đâu.**

Tourist buses: More comfortable and reliable, albeit more expensive. An established bus line departs daily at 7pm from **Sinh Cafe,** 18 Lương Văn Can (☎828 7552 or 928 6631; www.tosercohanoi.com) to: **Đông Hà** (12½hr.; US$8); **Huế** (14½hr.; US$9) via **Ninh Bình** (2hr.; US$3); **Quang Bình** (10hr.; US$7); **Vinh** (6hr.; US$7). A popular **open-tour ticket** to **HCMC** (US$23) via **Đà Nẵng, Hội An,** and **Nha Trang** lets you get off at any of these towns and then jump back on the bus to the next destination southward at your leisure. For those who also want to get off at **Đà Lạt,** buy the special US$25 open ticket. There are almost 70 other tourist cafes in Hà Nội, many by the name of "Sinh Cafe," so beware of frauds.

ORIENTATION

Hà Nội divides into seven districts *(quận)*: **Hoàn Kiếm** (the **Old Quarter** to the north, and the **French Quarter** to the south), **Hai Bà Trưng** to the south, **Ba Đình** and **Đống Đa** to the west, **Cầu Giấy** and **Thanh Xuân** to the far southwest, and **Tây Hồ** to the north. Most streets in Vietnam are called "đường," though Hà Nội still sometimes uses the word "phố" and, in the Old Quarter, "hàng." Downtown Hà Nội is small but disorganized, with streets changing names almost every block; a good map is helpful. Large color maps (5000-20,000Đ) are available from guesthouses, bookstores, the international post office, and hawkers around **Hoàn Kiếm Lake,** the heart of central Hà Nội. The Old Quarter, enclosed between the **Hà Nôi Citadel Military Complex, Sông Hồng** (the **Red River**), and Hoàn Kiếm Lake, is divided in two by twin one-way streets going north from Hoàn Kiếm Lake (starting as **Lương Văn Can** and **Hàng**

Đào) which form good points of reference in the district's confusing labyrinth. A backpacker's heaven of small shops, restaurants, bars, tourist cafes, and hotels—the area north of and around Hoàn Kiếm Lake—is also the oldest and most interesting district, although nightlife, cuisine, and accommodations in the area south of Hoàn Kiếm Lake and even west of the Citadel also increasingly attract visitors. From the Citadel, **Đường Lê Duẩn** leads south to **Bẩy Mẫu Lake** in the more residential Hai Bà Trưng district, and west (down Khâm Tiên) to Đống Đa's pagodas and small lakes. Farther north, up Đường Hùng Vương, the Ba Đình district overlooking **Hồ Tây** (the **West Lake**) hosts the **Hồ Chí Minh Mausoleum,** the **Temple of Literature,** most embassies, and the majority of Hà Nội's expats.

LOCAL TRANSPORTATION

Bicycles (Xe Đạp) and Motorbikes (Xe Máy): In spite of Hà Nội's hectic and challenging traffic, driving a motorcycle is a convenience that many think is worth the woe. Most hotels, guesthouses, and rental shops in the Old Quarter, north of Hoàn Kiếm Lake, rent **motorbikes** (US$5-9 per day). Check out the rental shops on **Hàng Bạc** and **Ta Hiềm** (US$3-5). **Bicycles** are less glamorous but sufficient for getting around town. Rent them from most lodging or rental shops for around 20,000Đ per day. If you plan to ride a bike or motorbike for a long time, wear something over your face and eyes to protect them from insects and exhaust. Be prepared to fork over 1000-2000Đ when you park your bike or motorbike in busy areas: a parking guard will write a number on your seat with chalk and give you the corresponding ticket when you pay.

Cyclos and Motorcycle Taxis (Xe Ôm): Abundant and cheap 3-wheeled **cyclos** (a.k.a. pedicabs) are the bastard children of rickshaws, tricycles, and bicycles. Banned from most major thoroughfares, they are nonetheless a must for any traveler, with chatty drivers and winding routes. Perfect for 1 person, a little cramped for 2. Agree on a price beforehand (10,000-15,000Đ per hr.; usually 5000Đ is a fair rate within town). Hire **motorcycle taxis** for longer rides (2000-3000Đ per km; 10,000Đ around town). Within town few people wear helmets, but you should anyway. If you're persistent enough, someone will get you a helmet. Also keep in mind that to many of your fellow road users, traffic rules are more of a suggestion than anything else—if they even know them in the first place. Never let the scenery distract you from traffic. **Hũng Motorcycles,** 5 Đinh Liệt (☎926 0938; open daily 7am-7pm). The guys here rent both modern Honda motorbikes and Minsks for 50,000-60,000Đ per 24hr. or US$50 per month. They also rent bicycles for 15,000Đ per 24hr., provide raincoats, and do motorcycle repair.

Taxis: Everywhere in Hà Nội. Lines form outside the Vietnam Airlines office, the train station, and major hotels. **Hà Nôi Taxi** (☎853 5252) or **Huong Lua Taxi** (☎825 2525) will pick you up curbside (7000Đ per km). Insist that the driver use the meter. **Airport Taxi** (☎873 3333) runs to and from the airport (40,000Đ).

PRACTICAL INFORMATION

TOURIST AND FINANCIAL SERVICES

TOURIST SERVICES

Tourist cafes and most hotels and guesthouses organize cheap package tours, which provide a hassle-free opportunity to see Northern Vietnam. For the less adventurous and those with less time to spare, such short tours are the best way to explore Vietnam's less-touristed regions. Services and prices vary only slightly but

TIP **ZEN AND THE ART OF MOTORCYCLE HAGGLING.** Haggling with *xe ôm* drivers is indeed an art. Though it may seem cheap to haggle over a petty 1000Đ difference, you'll soon discover the fun of it.

1. Never look for a motorbike close to a museum, station, or other touristy area. Walk one or two blocks and prices will fall drastically.
2. Never seem in dire need of transport. The best approach is to respond to their "Motobai?" beckoning with some feigned doubt and then walk on a little and wait for a motorbike rider to come after you. That way, he will also be away from his buddies and less afraid to lose face while haggling.
3. Never let your driver know that you don't know exactly where your destination is. Show him a business card of your destination and point in its direction if you know it. However, always be sure he does understand exactly where you want to go.
4. Never get on the bike without first agreeing on a price. The best way is to use a notepad–"thirteen" may sound like a lot like "thirty" in the driver's ears.
5. Unless you're in the Old Quarter, never be the first to name a price. Wait for his offer, divide it by three and name that as your price. Be firm in your haggling and never concede to more than half their original price. Within the Old Quarter, immediately propose 5000Đ and don't concede a single đồng.
6. Never be afraid to walk out of negotiations, even if there are no other motorbikes around. Chances are he will come after you and give in with a smile.
7. Never accept rides from female bikers. If you're male, they may want to offer you a whole different service.

Also keep in mind that you're not at the mercy of the motorbike. Cyclos are often cheaper and great for sightseeing on the road. Once you're familiar with greater Hà Nội's bus routes, the bus is a more reliable and cheaper way of getting around. And at night, sharing a metered taxi is probably a lot cheaper (and safer) than taking a motorbike.

VIETNAM

quality can vary considerably. The best and only way of verifying the quality of a tour provider is to approach tourists returning from a tour. Flags on the shop window don't imply that the corresponding language is spoken, and logos on the window don't guarantee the tourist cafe is an official representative or dealer—consider both mere decoration. Be aware of exactly what is included and what isn't, since some tourist cafes cut corners left and right to lower costs. Going on a tour with a small group is more expensive, but enables a more personalized and flexible experience; those few extra đồng could prevent a lot of frustration and annoyance. Check whether your guides or drivers speak at least a little English, even if just for emergencies. Lastly, it is expected that you tip your guide a small amount if satisfied. Most tourist cafes also arrange **visas** to China (1 month US$25-35) and Laos (1 month US$60) and 30-day Vietnam **visa extensions** (US$25-40). Allow about 3-4 days for processing, even if they tell you it's 2 days.

Standard packages: Hạ Long Bay (1 night US$18-35; 2 nights including **Cát Bà Island** US$28-53); **Hoa Lư-Tam Cốc** (daytrip US$15-20); **Mai Châu** (1 night US$20-25); **Perfume Pagoda** (daytrip US$9-16); **Sa Pa** (3 nights including **Bắc Hà** US$30-70).

Established tourist cafes: Ocean Tours, 51 Hàng Bè (☎926 0463); **Kangaroo Cafe,** 18 Bảo Khánh (☎828 1996); **Queen Cafe,** 50 Hàng Bè, 13 and 65 Hàng Bạc (☎826 0860); **TF Handspan Cafe,** 116 Hàng Bạc (☎828 19 96), smaller branch at 18 Bảo Khánh (☎828 9931); **Hà Nôi Tour,** 23 Yên Thái (☎928 7978); **Green Bamboo Cafe,** 24 Đương Thành (☎828 6504).

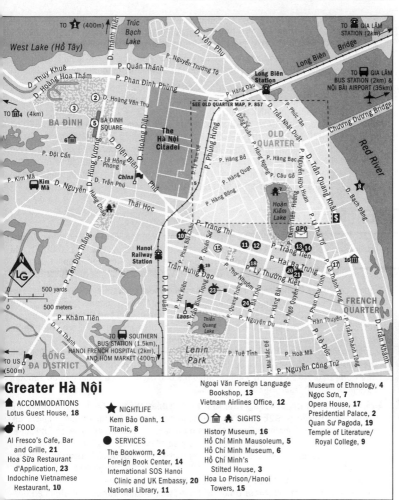

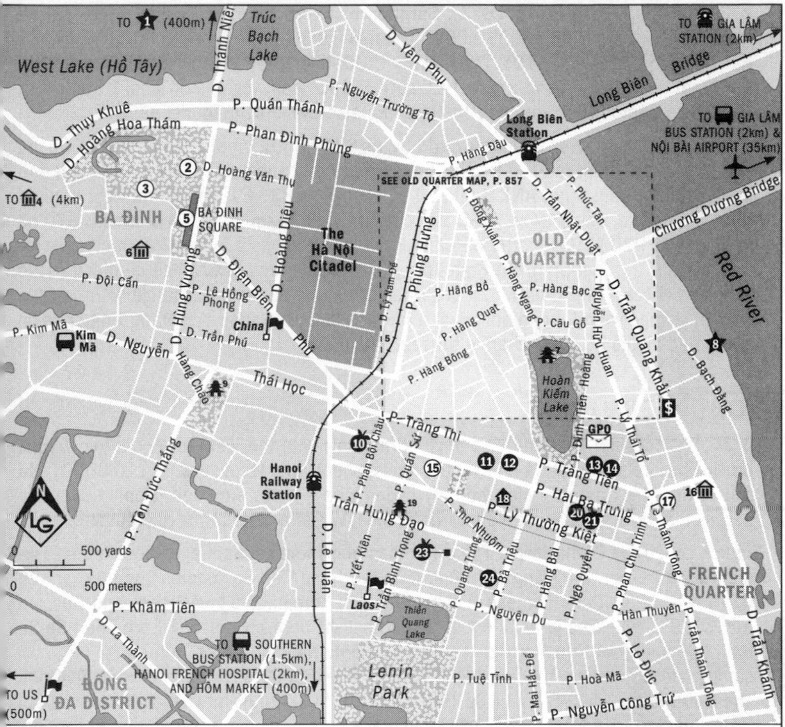

Greater Hà Nội

ACCOMMODATIONS
Lotus Guest House, **18**

FOOD
Al Fresco's Cafe, Bar and Grille, **21**
Hoa Sữa Restaurant d'Application, **23**
Indochine Vietnamese Restaurant, **10**

NIGHTLIFE
Kem Bảo Oanh, **1**
Titanic, **8**

SERVICES
The Bookworm, **24**
Foreign Book Center, **14**
International SOS Hanoi Clinic and UK Embassy, **20**
National Library, **11**
Ngoại Văn Foreign Language Bookshop, **13**
Vietnam Airlines Office, **12**

SIGHTS
History Museum, **16**
Hồ Chí Minh Mausoleum, **5**
Hồ Chí Minh Museum, **6**
Hồ Chí Minh's Stilted House, **3**
Hoa Lo Prison/Hanoi Towers, **15**
Museum of Ethnology, **4**
Ngọc Sơn, **7**
Opera House, **17**
Presidential Palace, **2**
Quan Sư Pagoda, **19**
Temple of Literature/Royal College, **9**

EMBASSIES AND FINANCIAL SERVICES

Embassies: Australia, 8 Đạo Tan (☎831 7755), behind Hà Nôi-Daewoo Hotel. Open M-F 8:30am-5pm. **Cambodia,** 71 Trần Hưng Đạo (☎942 4788). Visa US$20, 1-day processing. Bring a photo. Open M-F 8-11:30am and 2-4:30pm. **Canada,** 31 Hùng Vương (☎823 5000). Open M-F 8am-noon and 1-4:30pm. **China,** 46 Hoàng Diệu (☎845 3736). For visas, go to the consulate (☎823 5569) on Trần Phú. Visa US$30, 4-day processing; US$47, 2-day processing. Bring 2 photos. Open M-F 8:30-11am. **Indonesia,** 50 Ngô Quyền (☎825 3353). **Laos,** 22 Trần Bình Trọng (☎942 4576). Visa US$60, 1-day processing. Bring a photo. Open M-F 8-11:30am and 1-4pm. **Malaysia,** Fortuna Hotel, GB Lang Ha (☎831 3400). Open M-F 8am-4:30pm. **Myanmar,** Block A3 Vạn Phúc, on Kim Ma (☎845 3369). Open M-F 8:30am-noon and 1:30-5pm. **New Zealand,** 32 Hàng Bài (☎824 1481). Open M-F 8:30am-noon and 1-5pm. **Philippines,**

27B Trần Hưng Đạo (☎943 7873). **Singapore,** 41-43 Trần Phú (☎823 3965). **Thailand,** 63-65 Hoàng Diệu (☎823 5092). Open M-F 8:30am-noon and 1:30-5pm. **UK,** 31 Hai Bà Trưng (☎825 2510). Open daily 8:30am-4:30pm. Visa applications 8:30-11:30am only. **US,** 7 Láng Hạ (☎772 1500). Open daily 8am-noon and 1-5pm. Visa services to Cambodia, Laos, and Thailand are also available in tourist cafes.

Currency Exchange: Vietcombank Building (☎824 0880), on the corner of Trần Quang Khải and Lê Lai. Best rates in Hà Nội. For currency exchange, open M-F 8-11:30am and 1-3:30pm, Sa 9am-3pm. **ANZ Bank,** 14 Lê Thái Tổ (☎825 8190), on the west bank of Hoàn Kiếm Lake, has a 24hr. **ATM.** Bank open M-F 8:30am-4pm. **Sacombank,** 87 Phố Hàng Bạc (☎926 1392), north of Hoàn Kiếm Lake, also has a 24hr. ATM. Bank open M-F 8am-8pm, Sa 8am-5pm, Su 8am-4pm. All of these banks exchange currency, issue traveler's checks, and offer MC/V cash advances. For currency exchange with half the hassle, change your đồng to dollars at a **jewelry shop.** The shop at 5 Hàng Trong has an authorized Vietcombank exchange bureau.

LOCAL SERVICES

Local Publications: The Guide, published monthly with the *Vietnam Economic Times,* provides useful information on events, hotels, shops, and local services (10,000Đ). **Hà Nôi Pathfinder** has a similar monthly listing with a map, although it only lists businesses that advertise. Available for free at most Western restaurants and guesthouses.

English-Language Bookstores: Tráng Tiền has many foreign languages bookstores. **Foreign Book Center,** 44 Tráng Tiền, 2nd fl. in the Tráng Tiền Bookstores complex (☎826 0313, ext. 228). Sells Chinese, English, French, Korean, Japanese, Lao, and Russian books, but specializes in a variety of "learn English" books. Open M-F 8am-9pm, Sa-Su 8am-10pm. **Ngoại Văn Foreign Language Bookshop,** 64 Tráng Tiền (☎825 7376), carries books and paperbacks. Open daily summer 8am-9:30pm; winter 8am-7:30pm. **The Bookworm,** 15A Ngo Van So (☎943 7226; bookworm@fpt.vn), 1 block south of Trần Hưng Đạo. Hà Nội's only English-language bookstore with a second-hand section. Buys paperbacks. Open Tu-Su 10am-7pm.

VIETNAM

Alternatives to Tourism: Trung Tâm Anh Ngữ Sydney (Sydney Center of English), 26 Lương Ngọc Quyến (☎926 0762; sydneycentre@fpt.vn), and many other English language schools hire mostly native speakers on a case-by-case basis to teach English to Vietnamese locals. Wages and hours will vary significantly for each teacher and each week, but hours usually include weekends and evenings. **VUFO-NGO Resource Center,** Building L at the back of the La Thánh Hotel on 218 Đội Cấn (☎832 85 70; www.ngocentre.netnam.vn). The first and best place to find volunteering opportunities in Vietnam, this office of the **Vietnam Union of Friendship Organizations** and affiliated non-governmental organizations functions as a platform and liaison between volunteers and numerous aid and development organizations, complete with a large library of past and present NGO projects. The friendly office is under the guidance of the governmental People's Aid Coordinating Committee (PACCOM). Open daily 8am-noon and 1:30-5pm.

EMERGENCY AND COMMUNICATIONS

Emergency: ☎115.

Police: ☎113. Hoàn Kiếm District Headquarters, 2 Lê Thái Tổ (☎824 4141), in the booth on the northwest corner of Hoàn Kiếm Lake.

Pharmacy: There are many small pharmacies all over Hà Nội. A strip of pharmacies lines Quán Sứ near the intersection with Tràng Thi southwest of Hoàn Kiếm Lake. The **24hr. pharmacy** at 14 Phu Doan (☎825 5934) is small but well stocked.

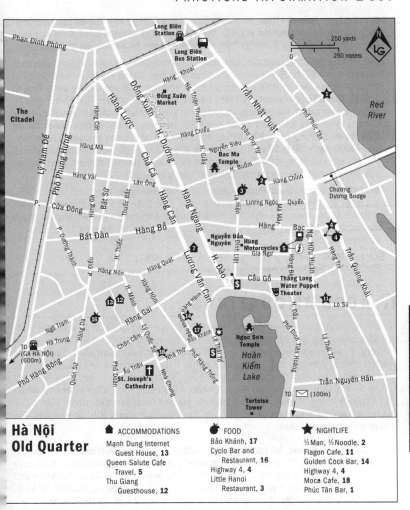

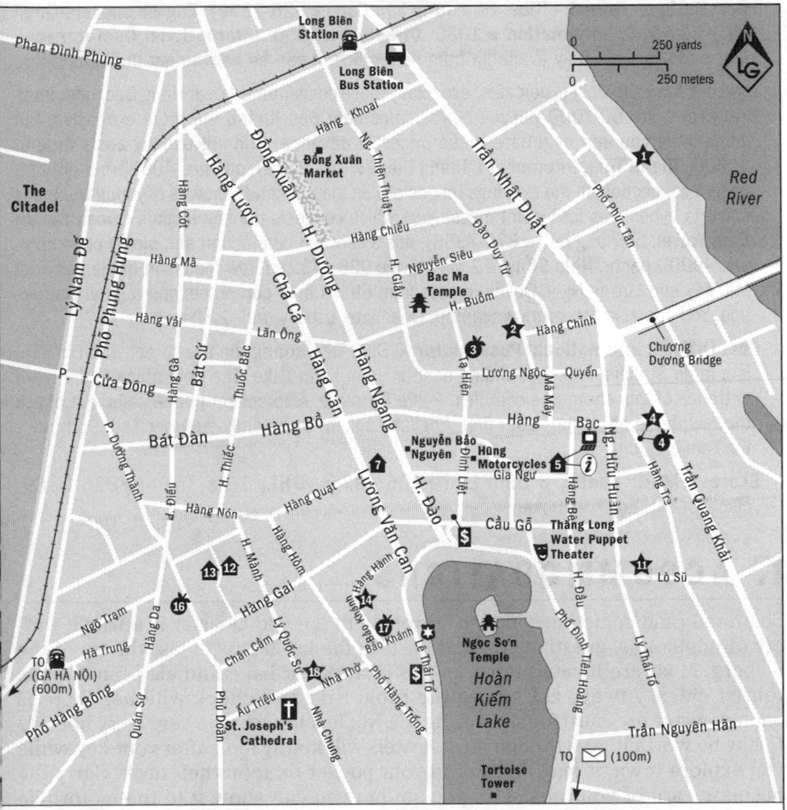

Hà Nội Old Quarter

ACCOMMODATIONS
Mạnh Dung Internet Guest House, **13**
Queen Salute Cafe Travel, **5**
Thu Giang Guesthouse, **12**

FOOD
Bảo Khánh, **17**
Cyclo Bar and Restaurant, **16**
Highway 4, **4**
Little Hanoi Restaurant, **3**

NIGHTLIFE
½Man, ½Noodle, **2**
Flagon Cafe, **11**
Golden Cock Bar, **14**
Highway 4, **4**
Moca Cafe, **18**
Phúc Tân Bar, **1**

Medical Services: International SOS Clinic, 31 Hai Bà Trưng (☎934 0555; www.internationalsos.com/). From south of Hoàn Kiếm Lake, walk 1 block down Bà Triệu. Large office signpost. A reliable medical service for expats, with doctors who speak English, French, Japanese, Dutch, Mandarin and, of course, Vietnamese. **24hr. emergency care.** US$69 per consultation (US$59 for a Vietnamese physician), US$55 for dental, US$29 for vaccine (US$49 for families). Medivac service (from anywhere in Vietnam to Bangkok or Singapore) available for members, but exceptions can be made for serious cases and an extra fee. **Hà Nôi French Hospital,** 1 Phuong Mai (☎570 0740). Expat doctors provide **24hr. emergency care.** US$25-30 per consultation.

Telephones: Telephone office, 75B Đinh Tiên Hoàng (☎826 0977), next to the international post office. International calls 13,000Đ per min. Fax and AT&T/MCI card calls are free but don't always work. English spoken. Open daily summer 6am-10pm; winter

6am-9:30pm. **Branch office,** 66 Lương Văn Can (☎826 2999). English spoken. Open daily 6am-9pm. **Information** ☎1080. **Directory** ☎1080. **International Operator (collect calls)** ☎110. Only available from post office. It can be hard to get through.

Internet Access: Most cybercafes, especially those concentrated near Hàng Bạc, offer Internet access for 50-100Đ per min. Cybercafes near Bảo Khánh are more expensive, but sometimes you can negotiate these prices in advance. Printing usually costs around 1000Đ. **Thanh Tùng Internet,** 71 Thàng Điếu (☎828 9172), charges 4000Đ per hr. for a decent connection. In the evenings (especially on the weekend), crowds of young Hanoians come to cybercafes for instant messaging, which congests the connection. **Queen Salute Cafe Travel,** 50 Hàng Bè (☎826 7356), has a very fast connection and plenty of computers. 4000Đ per hr. **Nhip Sống,** 72 Mã Mây (☎926 1432). A few meters from the corner of Mã Mây and Lương Ngọc Quyến, across from 69. Modern computers and a good connection. You can also use your own laptop. Open late, usually until 1:30am.

Post Offices: International Post Center, 6 Đinh Tiên Hoàng, on the corner with Đinh Le, is a large Stalinist-looking building east of Hoàn Kiếm Lake. The post office is the main entrance of this enormous complex. *Poste Restante.* Also collect phone calls, but check the telephone office next door first. English spoken. Open daily summer 7am-9pm; winter 7am-8:30pm.

Express Mail: FedEx, 6 Đinh Le (☎826 4925). **DHL,** 1 Bà Triệu (☎826 5389; ctsc@fpt.vn). English spoken.

ACCOMMODATIONS

VIETNAM

Scattered (and sometimes hidden) throughout the Old Quarter is a whole variety of minihotels, guesthouses, and hostels; the list below is just the tip of the iceberg. Most are located north of the Hoàn Kiếm Lake and also function as tourist cafes. Always ask to see the room first and check whether there is enough water pressure for showering. Hà Nội in summer gets very, very hot—A/C may be worth it. And though most hostels will kindly look after your key while you explore town, it may be safer in your pocket than on their desk. Carry the business card of your hostel on you so that you can show it to the motorbike driver on your way home.

Thu Giang Guesthouse, 5A Tạm Thương (☎828 5734; thugiangn@hotmail.com), down a small alley off Hàng Bông near Hàng Đào Market. The family-run guesthouses in this cozy and quiet alley are all popular with backpackers. The owners of Thu Giang are friendly and helpful. Small and quiet rooms with balconies and in-suite showers. Doubles US$4-7, with A/C US$5-8. Bigger doubles on 35A Hang Dieu (☎923 2078) US$6-8. ❷

Cát Tương Hotel, 10C Đinh Liệt (☎934 3797). Conveniently located hotel with very accommodating staff. Rooms are large and include TVs, fridges, spacious private bathrooms (some with bathtub), closets, and couches. Doubles without window US$6, with balcony US$8. With A/C US$2 extra. ❷

Lotus Guest House, 42V Lý Thường Kiệt (☎/fax 826 8642). Walking south from the lake on Bà Triệu, turn right at the intersection with Lý Thường Kiệt and walk 2 blocks down. Enter the Safari Bar and go through the camouflaged door in the back wall. Idiosyncratic, cozy, popular, and inexpensive. Food served until midnight (27,000-45,000Đ). 4-bed dorms US$4; singles US$6-7; doubles with fan US$8, with A/C US$10-15. ❷

Queen Salute Cafe Travel, 50 Hàng Bè (☎826 7356). From Đinh Tiên Hoàng on the eastern shore of Hoàn Kiếm Lake, walk up Hàng Dầu, which becomes Hàng Bè; it's on the left. Queen Salute is Hà Nội's prime backpacker haunt. Offering tours, visas, Western food (pizza 35,000-39,000Đ; breakfast 8000Đ), pool table, dart board, cybercafe (4000Đ per hr.), laundry service (US$1 per kg) and, of course, rooms. Dorms 40,000Đ; singles US$4; doubles US$5, with A/C US$7. ❶

Mạnh Dung Internet Guest House, 2 Tam Thường (☎826 7201). Like the other guesthouses in the alley, this small and quiet one is run by a friendly English-speaking household. Cozy rooms with private bath. Doubles US$5, with A/C US$7-8. ❷

Youth Hotel, 33 Lương Văn Can (☎828 5822; trekking-travel@hn.vnn.vn). Centrally located. Popular with younger crowds. Internet 12,000Đ per hr. in a buzzing backpacker cafe. Connected to Sinh Cafe for tour booking. Doubles US$7-15. ❷

FOOD

Backpackers can easily find the usual spaghetti and pancake fare in the Old Quarter, but the most rewarding dining experiences are found on the street. Street stalls around the markets dish up delectable staples like phở (noodles) or cơm (rice) and plenty of vegetarian options. Vendors set up all day long in the **Dong Xuan Market** north of the Old Quarter. If the heat's bothering you, try the second floors; most restaurants have an air-conditioned space upstairs.

THE OLD QUARTER

Bảo Khánh, 10 Bảo Khánh (☎828 8333), on the corner and just 1 block from the lake. A small restaurant where locals and visitors line up for a wide variety of authentic Vietnamese food for killer prices. Try anything from pigeon or frog to tortoise or cock testicles, all from 20,000-50,000Đ. Open daily 9:30am-9pm. ❷

Little Hà Nôi Restaurant, 25 Ta Hiền (☎926 0168). A hospitable Vietnamese restaurant. Quite popular with tourists, and for good reason: service is friendly, the food is great and prices are fair. Roll your own spring roll for 30,000Đ. Other dishes mostly 28,000-30,000Đ. Open daily 10:30am-10:30pm. ❷

Cyclo Bar and Restaurant, 38 Dường Thành (☎828 8333). Dường Thành intersects Hàng Gai as it becomes Hàng Bông; the restaurant is 100m down on the left from this crossing. Serving both Vietnamese and French cuisine in an elegant setting, Cyclo Bar revives Hà Nội's French epoque. Cyclo chairs and a pleasant garden add to the ambience. Set lunch menu 50,000Đ. A la carte 45,000-75,000Đ; French dishes around 100,000Đ. Open daily 9am-11pm. ❸

THE FRENCH QUARTER

Hoa Sữa Restaurant d'Application, 28A Phố Ha Hoi (☎942 4448). The Hoa Sữa training school is a stylish French restaurant founded by *La Maison de la Jonque,* where youth from underprivileged backgrounds obtain practical training for the real world. The students try their very best to provide top-quality service and cuisine. Set menu 75,000Đ for 2 courses, 85,000Đ for 3. Open daily 11am-10pm. ❹

Indochine Vietnamese Restaurant, 16 Nam Ngư (☎942 4097). High-quality local specialties with impeccable service. The house spring rolls have achieved crispy-fried yet un-oily perfection. Entrees start at US$3. Open daily 11:30am-2pm and 5-10pm. Reservations recommended. ❸

Al Fresco's Cafe, Bar and Grille, 23L Hai Bà Trưng (☎826 7782), 2 blocks south of the main GPO. A local expat hangout run by a fun-loving Australian, specializing in huge ribs. Big portions of pizza and buffalo wings go for US$4.50-11. Root beer US$2.50, fish and chips US$7. Free delivery. Open daily 9am-11pm. MC/V. ❺

SIGHTS

HOÀN KIẾM

HOÀN KIẾM LAKE (HỒ HOÀN KIẾM). The lake takes its name from a 15th-century legend of a magic turtle who loaned a sacred sword to Lê Lợi, the nobleman who led the Vietnamese against the invading Ming army. Paddling in the lake following the victory, the newly crowned emperor encountered the turtle, who demanded the sword back. The Tortoise Tower on a tiny island in the lake's center commemorates the event. Several mammoth turtles still live in the lake and occasionally surface, an event that locals believe is a sign of the impending death of one of the country's leaders. Persistent children sell postcards and t-shirts on the north side of the lake.

NGỌC SƠN TEMPLE (ĐỀN NGỌC SƠN). Generations have added more and more frills to this shrine since its construction during the Trần Dynasty (1225-1400). Last renovated in 1865, this Chinese-style temple is located on a wooded island in Hoàn Kiếm Lake and is dedicated primarily to Văn Xương, the god of literature. Thirteenth-century hero Trần Hưng Đạo and physician La To are also honored. The entrance to the temple is through Tam Quan (Three Passage) gate on the northeast shore on Đinh Tiên Hoàng. Behind the Hall of the Cult, the sanctuary to Văn Xương offers a beautiful view of the lake. *(Open daily 8am-6pm. 12,000Đ.)*

HISTORY MUSEUM. The History Museum (Bảo Tàng Lịch Sử), housed in a stately French-designed building, elaborately presents Vietnam's past from prehistory to Communism. The almost incessant foreign aggression that the Vietnamese have withstood over the centuries makes for an impressive read. Don't miss the Đông Sơn bronze drums and ceramics or the Khmer and Chàm artifacts. *(One block behind the Opera, across from the Revolutionary Museum on Phố Tráng Tiên. Enter through the gates on Phố Tráng Tiên. Open Tu-Su 8-11:45am and 1:30-4:30pm. 15,000Đ, students 8000Đ, children 2000Đ. Cameras an additional 15,000Đ, camcorders 30,000Đ.)*

VIETNAM

QUAN SƯ PAGODA. During the old days, foreign delegates—mostly monks—would stay at the Ambassador's Pagoda, or Quan Sư. Even today, dignitaries visit the pagoda on official occasions. Quan Sư is the center of Buddhism in Vietnam; many monks live and study here in Hà Nội's most bustling religious center. Enter through the gate on Quan Sư. *(73 Quan Sư. Open daily 7:30-11:30am and 1:30-5:30pm.)*

HOA LO PRISON. Hoa Lo Prison has a long history of stern punishment. Built by the French in 1896, it was quickly filled with political prisoners. After they achieved their goal, though, the Vietnamese imprisoned American POWs here—among them US Air Force Captain Pete Peterson and US Senator John McCain—until their release in 1973. These days, however, little remains of the notorious prison, nicknamed the "Hanoi Hilton." Today, the Hà Nôi Towers are the most prominent reminder of the former French colonial period, but a small part remains as a museum. Most information is in Vietnamese. *(1 Phố Hoa Lo, on the corner with Phố Hai Bà Trưng. Open Tu-Su 8-11:30am and 1:30-4:30pm. 10,000Đ.)*

BA ĐÌNH

Ba Đình district, the area west of the Old Quarter and south of West Lake, contains Hà Nội's principal sights, including the Hồ Chí Minh Mausoleum, the Presidential Palace, and the Hà Nội Citadel, making it a quarter few visitors miss.

HÀ NỘI CITADEL. Vietnam's Ministry of Defense occupies this restricted area, once the Thăng Long Citadel, home to the imperial city. Inside its gates is the **Army Museum (Bảo Tàng Quân Đội),** which details the exploits of the People's Army of Vietnam. Highlights include a light-and-sound diorama of Điện Biên Phủ Valley and the tank that crashed through the gates of the Presidential Palace in Saigon in April 1975. Next door is the 31m high **Hà Nŏi Flag Pillar,** a former guard tower, built in 1812 under the Nguyễn Dynasty. *(Museum: 28A Điện Biên Phủ. Open Tu-Th and Sa-Su 8-11:30am and 1-4:30pm. 10,000Đ, cameras 2000Đ.)*

HỒ CHÍ MINH MAUSOLEUM (LĂNG HỒ CHÍ MINH). Despite his wish to be cremated, poor Hồ Chí Minh couldn't escape his well-preserved fate. Completed in 1975, the sober granite structure serves as a receiving stand for officials and party leaders, upholding the slightly macabre Communist tradition of constructing glass sarcophagi for their idols. Almost every morning, a procession of pilgrims and curious visitors solemnly passes under the Communist and Vietnamese symbology that adorns the mausoleum. You, too, can join them, braving the cold sanitized air of the building and the white-uniformed soldiers guarding his earthly remains to venerate the late president's corpse. *(Up Điện Biên Phủ, away from the Army Museum; approach from Dương Hùng Vương. Open Apr.-Oct. Tu-Th 7:30-10:30am, Sa-Su 7:30-11am; Nov.-Mar. Tu-Th 8-11am, Sa-Su 8-11:30am. Get there early to avoid lines, especially on May 19, Uncle Ho's birthday, and Sept. 2, the date in 1945 he declared Vietnam's independence on that very spot. Closed briefly every Nov. for the make-up artist/embalmer to touch him up a bit. Wear respectable attire—no shorts, short skirts, or tank tops. No bags or cameras allowed; stash them at the visitors' entrance at the south end of the square. Free; brochures 5000Đ.)*

PRESIDENTIAL PALACE AND HỒ CHÍ MINH'S STILTED HOUSE. The former residence of the Governor-General of French Indochina, the **presidential palace** has served as a state guesthouse since 1954, when the Việt Minh defeated the French. You can't actually get a look inside, unless, of course, you're a guest of the Vietnamese government. Hồ Chí Minh believed the building should belong to the people and chose to live in an **electrician's hut** on the grounds. His personal area in the hut is as he left it. In 1958, he moved into a simple **stilted house** near a carp pond, which remained his residence until his death in 1969. The home was built for Uncle Ho near the Presidential Palace so he would feel more "with the people." Note the picture of Lenin on his desk and the military helmet next to the phone—a silent reminder that

THE BIG SPLURGE

SOUL ART

Truyền Thần is an ancient art form deeply rooted in Vietnamese ancestor worship. Many houses have little shrines with depictions of late ancestors in quiet, prominent corners. On the first and middle days of the lunar month and during anniversaries and celebrations, valuable offerings are put under them and incense is burned to invoke the souls of the departed and respectfully ask for their protection.

The delicate art of *Truyền Thần,* or "delivering the spirits," refers to the drawing of these portraits. They are meant to transfer the spirit of a person using only pencil and paper. A *Truyền Thần* portraitist invests immense feeling and concentration in his work, which takes a lot of talent and many years of practice to master.

Mr. Nguyễn Bảo Nguyên is perhaps the greatest of the remaining masters. He has practiced his art for over 45 years, for which the UN gave him a special award. Those who want their own soul or that of a loved one eternalized in a real *Truyền Thần* portrait can leave a photograph with Mr. Nguyên for him to draw. His fee depends on the size and image of the picture. The minimum is US$25, while a very large drawing may cost several hundred dollars. Be warned: Mr. Nguyên will not be rushed in his trade. Portraits may take anywhere from a couple of days to a couple of weeks.

47 Hàng Ngang. ☎ 926 03 64. Open daily 8:30am-5pm.

American bombers were still active when Vietnam's leader died. The house overlooks the carp pond where Uncle Ho used to summon the fish for feeding by clapping his hands. Living proof of Pavlovian conditioning, the fish still respond to clapping tourists. *(North of the mausoleum, across from the mausoleum's exit. Open daily 8-11:30am, also Tu-Th and Sa-Su 2-4pm. 5000Đ buys a guided tour of the palace, electrician's hut, and stilted house. Wait for a tour guide at the entrance.)*

ELSEWHERE IN HÀ NỘI

MUSEUM OF ETHNOLOGY. If you visit one museum in Hà Nội, this should be it, even if it's out of the way. Inaugurated in 1997, the museum is designed to enhance visitors' understanding of Vietnam's 54 ethnic groups and diverse cultures. The exhibits include clear and interesting presentations of objects and dress from everyday life. The signs in Vietnamese, French, and English give ample information about the daily lives and traditions of these peoples. The best part, though, is the enormous backyard, where eight traditional houses from different ethnic groups have been reconstructed. You can climb into them and explore them on your own. There are also replicas of a traditional gravesite (check out the interesting wood carving), a puppet theater, a pottery workshop, and hydraulic rice pestles. Students live here year-round, serving as guards at night. *(To get to the museum, go west from Quán Thánh Pagoda down Đường Hoàng Hoa Thám. At its end, take a left and 50m later a right onto Đường Hoàng Quốc Việt. Then take the fourth left onto Đường Nguyễn Văn Nguyên. The museum will appear right in front of you. It takes about 15min. to get there by motorbike. Plan ahead: there are very few motorbike taxis in the area around the museum. Alternatively, take bus #14 from the fountain north of Hoàn Kiếm Lake in the direction of Cầu Giấy, get off at Nghĩa Tân, and walk east down Đường Hoàng Quốc Việt, taking a right onto Đường Nguyễn Văn Nguyên. ☎756 2193. Open Tu-Su 8:30am-5:30pm. 10,000Đ. After passing through the gate, take a left to park your motorbike for 2000Đ or bicycle for 1000Đ.)*

LENIN PARK. Beautiful and peaceful Lenin Park (Công Viên Lenin) is the largest park in Hà Nội, 1km south of the train station on Lê Duẩn. This well-manicured getaway from urban noise, featuring Bảy Mẫu Lake, attracts many joggers, exercisers, and couples all hours of the day and into the late evening. *(Enter off Trần Nhân, under the enormous pillars. Open daily 7am-11pm. 2000Đ, children 1000Đ.)*

TEMPLE OF LITERATURE AND ROYAL COLLEGE. The Temple of Literature (Văn Miếu) was allegedly built in 1070 during the reign of Emperor Lý Thánh Tông to honor scholars and literary men. The Emperor dedicated this peaceful sanctuary to Khổng Tử (Confucius). Six years later, the Royal College (Quốc Tử Giám), Vietnam's first university, was founded here in order to educate the children of court mandarins. The university remained in use until 1802, when the national university was moved to the new capital, Huế. The buildings remain in pristine condition. To enter, pass through the Four Pillars on Quôc Tử Giám. Please remember to dismount your horses, in compliance with an ancient inscription on this gate. The following succession of open courts was established by a series of open gates. The first set is the Gates of Talent and Virtue. The next set heading north leads to one of the 82 Tortoise Stelae, all erected between 1442 and 1778, on which the names, places of birth, and achievements of 1306 successful triennial examination candidates are inscribed. Lastly come the Gates of Synthesis and the sanctuary, housing statues of Confucius and his four greatest disciples. *(At the intersection of Tôn Đức Thắng and Nguyễn Thái Học, 2km west of Hoàn Kiếm Lake. Enter off Quôc Tử Giám on the southern side. Open daily summer 7:30am-5:30pm; winter 8am-5:30pm. 5000Đ, students 2000Đ.)*

ENTERTAINMENT

You can't come to Hà Nội without visiting the **Thăng Long Water Puppet Theater,** 57 Đinh Tiên Hoàng (☎824 9494). This ancient art form unique to northern Vietnam, which traces its origins to rice-farmer folk culture, became court entertainment during the Lý and Trần dynasties. The puppets move and dance in a shallow pool of murky water (to hide the mechanisms operating them) and are accompanied by the voices and instruments of a group of traditional Vietnamese musicians. Since the puppets wear out after a few months of working their magic, you can buy the used ones in souvenir shops all over the Old Quarter. The theater offers both first-class seats (40,000Đ) and second-class seats (20,000Đ), the only difference being that first-class seats are in the front of the theater. Shows are daily at 5:15, 6:30, and 8pm, and last roughly 1hr.

SHOPPING

In the olden days, each of the Old Quarter's 36 streets had its own specialty trade. Today, the legacy continues on some streets, although many stores carry a larger variety of goods. **Hàng Dầu** specializes in cheap shoes (though many of them are exported to Europe, so larger sizes are hard to find) while its continuation, **Hàng Bè,** makes funeral stones. Best known are the silk shops on **Hàng Gai** and **Lương Văn Can,** which sell ready-made and tailored clothing of varying quality. **Phùng Khắc Khoan,** a few blocks south from Hoàn Kiếm Lake, sells much cheaper fabric and has several tailors, but don't expect Hội An prices or one-day service. **Hà Trung** sells leather products; **Hàng Quạt** peddles colorful funeral flags and religious objects; **Hàng Mã** specializes in paper products, including votive candles burned for ancestors; **Lãn Ông** exudes the sweet scent of medicinal herbs; and **Hàng Đào** features clothing. **Chợ Đồng Xuân** (Đồng Xuân Market) is a night marketplace in the northern part of the Old Quarter, off the extension of Hàng Đào, selling a variety of wholesale goods in the daytime and fruits, vegetables, and flowers from midnight onwards, when the market moves east onto Trần Nhât Duât. North of the market on Hàng Khoai are many little eating stands—the perfect place for a snack after 10pm. On the west side, Đồng Xuân Market (on Hàng Đào) stands open up after 10pm for **glitter drawing,** a favorite for Vietnamese couples. Shower bright-colored glitter over sticky paper to fill in cute (if somewhat cheesy) drawings. Sticky paper drawings go for 5000-10,000Đ—unless you want your souvenir to lose its glitter, be sure to ask for a plastic cover afterwards. After you've shopped till you've dropped, recover with a coffee in one of Hà Nội's coffee shops on **Hàng Hanh** or **Nhà Thờ** (also known as Church Street, east of St. Joseph Cathedral), or have ice cream either on **Phố Tráng Tiên** or at the evening street vendors on the northern shore of Hoàn Kiếm Lake.

NIGHTLIFE

BARS AND CAFES

Hà Nội's bar and cafe scene is huge. Some establishments cater exclusively to foreigners, some would be surprised to see a non-Vietnamese guest, and most are somewhere in between. Travelers will have no problem finding a bar to quench their thirst: every other street corner has a *bia hơi* streetbar, selling cheap, watered-down beer for as little as 1500Đ. Alternatively, the Old Quarter has many bars and cafes luring in tourists and their dollars. To tap into Hà Nội's authentic bar culture, though, an outsider must walk the extra mile, alley, and staircase.

VIETNAM

Kem Bảo Oanh, 7 Đường Thánh Niên (☎823 9688). On the northern shore of Trúc Bạch Lake in Tây Hồ, next to the Sofitel Plaza Hotel. A very popular ice cream joint. 4 floors provide a majestic view of West Lake, Trúc Bạch Lake, and Hà Nội behind them. Their delicious specialty—coconuts filled with fruit and home-made coconut ice-cream (11,000Đ)—is what every table around you will be ordering. All kinds of fruit juices 5000-10,000Đ. Open daily 8am-midnight.

Highway 4, 5 Hàng Tre (☎926 0639; www.highway4.com). Named after the highway along the Chinese border, this laid-back restaurant/bar serves traditional medicinal Son Tinh liquor from the northwest hill-tribes. The bartender will help match a Yin-Yang liquor to your ailment or taste. Doses run 5000Đ-25,000Đ. Open daily 9am-2am.

Flagon Cafe, 36 Lò Sũ (☎824 8205). From the corner of Lò Sũ and Lý Thái Tố, go 20m toward the highway; it's on the left side. Go down the hallway and (quietly!) up 2 flights of stairs. Students gather up and play on the acoustic guitars lying around. Sit outside on the roof terrace or inside on woven mats. Cages with tropical birds adorn the walls. Friendly service. All drinks 5000Đ or less. Open daily 8am-11pm.

Moca Cafe, 14-16 Nhà Thờ (☎825 6334), 50m east of St. Joseph Cathedral. The kind of coffeehouse you'd expect to find in America or Europe. Two spacious floors with white and brick walls, filled with chatter and the smell of fresh coffee. A small selection of novels in English are available for US$5 each. Breakfast 10,000-38,000Đ; entrees around 59,000Đ. International coffees 8000-20,000Đ. Open daily 8am-10:30pm.

½ Man, ½ Noodle, 52 Đào Duy Từ (☎926 1943), on Ta Hiền. Walk into the alley next to Labyrinth Bar; it's on your right. The poster on the door says it all: "Drink here or we shoot the puppy!" A small but popular pub for backpackers. Beer 15,000Đ; cocktails 35,000-50,000Đ; big bowl 60,000Đ. Open daily 6pm until the puppy gets it.

Golden Cock Bar, 5A Bảo Khánh (☎825 0499). Commonly referred to as the GC, Hà Nội's only gay bar is also one of the most comfortable drinking holes for all persuasions, which explains its large straight male (local and foreign) following. Happy hour until 9pm: most beers 12,000Đ. Otherwise 18,000Đ. Open daily 5:30pm-whenever.

VIETNAM

CLUBS

Phúc Tân Bar, Số 49-Tổ 4A (☎932 3244), in Phúc Tân. This club on the bank of the Red River is certainly worth the quest. Get on the dike road (parallel to the highway) in between the Long Biên and Chương Dương bridges, and pass through the dike entrance. Then go straight and turn left at the end of the alley; it's on your right after 100m. A European-flavored club where locals and foreigners mix on a great dance floor, at a bar area with pool table, and best of all, on an enormous terrace overlooking the Red River. Beer 18,000-20,000Đ; cocktails 35,000-50,000Đ. Open daily 7pm-very late.

Titanic, 42 Chương Dương Độ, is one of Hà Nội's newest clubs. On the Red River, Titanic keeps rocking the boat until the early morning. The DJ spins mostly dance music and R&B, while clubbers blow off steam on the outside terrace. Occasional live music. Happy hour 5-9pm: every beer 12,000Đ. Otherwise 20,000Đ. French wine 25,000Đ per glass. Open daily 5pm-5am.

KARAOKE

Karaoke is one of Hà Nội's favorite pastimes and a "great" way to begin a night on the town. Karaoke bars offer living-room-like spaces with several TV screens and microphones, allowing small groups to practice their singing talents while enjoying a drink. Neon signs for karaoke bars dominate the Old and French Quarters, especially on and around Nguyễn Hữu Huân (northwest of Hoàn Kiếm Lake) and in the alleys on Lý Quốc Sư (north of St. Joseph's Cathedral). They are almost as identical as *bia hơ'is*, and all have a similar selection of songs in English, French, and Vietnamese. Expect to pay 50,000-80,000Đ. Most karaoke bars open in the late afternoon and close at midnight. Sometimes men take "loose girls" to karaoke bars, but the bars themselves have no affiliation with prostitution.

DAYTRIPS FROM HÀ NỘI

PERFUME PAGODA

The wisest way to see the Perfume Pagoda is by tour. A typical tour to the Perfume Pagoda from Hà Nội includes transport over the 60km from Hà Nội to Yên Vô village, a boat ride and rower across the waterway, and the 4km hike to the main temple. (US$9-16 includes transport, lunch, and admission.) Alternatively, travelers can take a public bus south to Hà Dōng (30min., 5000-7000Đ) and catch another bus to Yên Vô village, or rent a motorbike for the day in Hà Nội (US$4-6)–go south down Hwy. 1 and take a left after 14km. Renting a boat and rower costs an additional 30,000-50,000Đ per person (depending on how many people are in the group, including admission, excluding tip). Lunch at one of the many stands along the path up the mountain can be quite pricey too. We recommend that you save yourself the hassle and take a tour.

Set in lush rice paddies studded with jagged limestone karsts like the ones found in Hạ Long Bay, Chùa Hương—the Perfume Pagoda—is one of the main Buddhist destinations in Vietnam. As with most pilgrimages, the journey is as important as the destination, and the Perfume Pagoda lives up to this principle. The journey begins at Yên Vô village, where lotus sculptures adorn the shores of a long channel. First is a beautiful 1hr. ride to the foot of the mountain in a narrow, red boat along a meandering waterway surrounded by cliffs, shrines, and jungle. The second part is a steep hike on a twisty, stony trail. Don't let physical exhaustion or the many souvenir and snack stands distract you from the surrounding natural beauty. Bring good hiking boots. After at least 1hr., a staircase down to the Perfume Pagoda will suddenly appear. It derives its name from the huge grotto in the Hương Tích Mountains (Mountains of the Fragrant Traces) in which it resides. At the bottom of the cave is a tiny sanctuary with statues, a small waterfall, and a cloud of incense. A flashlight can help you see the shrine more clearly. Aside from the Perfume Pagoda itself, the complex of temples at the bottom of the mountain, known as the **Thiên Trù Pagodas,** is also serene and beautiful. **Thiên Chù** and **Giải Oau Chù** are especially worth the small detour. The pagoda area, where over 100 temples once stood, was destroyed during the First Indochina War. Although it was partly rebuilt in 1968, only seven temples remain today.

For a month after the Lunar New Year, thousands of Buddhist pilgrims flock to the temple during the **Perfume Pagoda Festival** (Lễ Hội Chùa Hương). To avoid shuffling shoulder-to-shoulder for 2hr. up the mountain, check out the pagoda Monday to Wednesday during this month. Also, there will be less of a crowd on odd dates of the lunar calendar. And don't forget to dress a little conservatively—you're walking on holy ground. You can save your sexier outfits for Hà Nội's nightlife.

THẦY AND TÂY PHƯƠNG PAGODAS

Only about 10km apart, a joint visit to these two pagodas makes for a pleasant trip from Hà Nội. The easiest way to get there is either on an organized tour or by hiring a motorbike driver (about 70,000Đ), but riding over there yourself is also possible if you're familiar with Hanoian traffic.

TÂY PHƯƠNG PAGODA. The Pagoda of the West is, unsurprisingly, the westernmost of the two, situated on a steep limestone cliff, adorned by sanctuaries for centuries. The pagoda complex consists of a main pagoda on the top of the cliff

VIETNAM

and two shrines on its side. Walk up the steep stairs for about 10min. to arrive at the main pagoda. Inside its walls, you'll find a small monastery and several shrines (and the usual flock of hawkers). Enter through the small wooden doors on the left of the main building to discover the pagoda's treasure: a group of huge, antique, wood-carved figures representing all the emotional states of man—some in an almost caricature-like fashion. Then pass through the small gate in the right pagoda wall and follow the big white arrows down a winding path on the cliff's side, passing by the two smaller and simpler pagodas. When you reach the bottom of the cliff, take a right onto the concrete path that crosses the settlement. You'll find yourself back at the entrance, surrounded by its numerous snack stands. All in all, the walk down takes about 45min. *(About 30km from Hà Nội. Watch out for the big sign on your right on Hwy. 6. Open daily 7am-6pm. 3000Đ. Dress conservatively.)*

THẦY PAGODA. The Master's Pagoda lies practically on the next cliff over, in the direction of Hà Nội. Like its neighbor, Thầy Pagoda is actually a complex of pagodas and shrines, but its main pagoda is at the foot of the cliff. From the ticket booth, walk past a few stands and small shrines until you reach the chief pagoda in front of a big pond filled with lotus flowers. This pond is used for water-puppet theater performances during religious festivals. Take off your shoes and enter the pagoda to behold the many statues and shrines inside. Be sure not to miss the impressive central altar. The pagoda is also used as a classroom for the young monks who reside behind it. Past the main structure, a steep path ascends the cliff, leading to the other pagodas and shrines in the complex. In addition to the beauty of these man-made places of worship, the forest, caves, and natural rock formations along the meandering path are also quite a sight. The top of the cliff can be reached in about 15min., but plan some extra time to walk around and see the entire complex. Guides will flock eagerly to all visitors; it may be a good idea to hire an English-speaking one for 5000-20,000Đ, depending on the duration of the tour. *(About 25km from Hà Nội. Take a right after the toll booth on Hwy. 6 and follow the signs down 1km of unpaved road. Open daily 7am-6pm. 3000Đ. Dress conservatively.)*

HANDICRAFT VILLAGES

The more immediate area around Hà Nội contains many artisan villages, each specializing in a particular craft. Comprehensive tours are available for all of these villages, but with a good map you can also visit them by yourself.

VAN PHÚC (SILK VILLAGE). This village is probably the most accessible without a tour guide. Pretty much all the silk in tourist shops in the Old Quarter is woven here; Walk into any of the alleys and see the looms in operation. A row of little shops offers silk products at prices that would wipe all of Hàng Gai out of business. If you ask nicely, they might even custom-make silk products for you. *(Just southwest of Hà Nội in Hà Đông, 1km from Hwy. 1. Take a right after the bridge.)*

BÁT TRÀNG (POTTERY VILLAGE). Here you can see the whole pottery and ceramic production process; make your own pottery if you're feeling creative. There are also many stores selling a wide selection of Vietnamese- and Western-style products. *(13km down the Red River from Hà Nội.)*

LỆ MẬT (SNAKE VILLAGE). Every restaurant in this neighborhood specializes in serpent cuisine. You only get to see the serpent's "preparation" if you purchase a meal. Due to cutthroat (ha ha!) competition, any foreigner coming into the village will be approached by a flock of hawkers on motorbikes trying to lure you into their restaurants. *(7km across the Red River from Hà Nội, just off highway 1A. Take a motorbike there for 30,000Đ round-trip, including wait.)*

THE NORTHWEST HIGHLANDS

Travelers often discuss the development of the tourism industry in northwestern Vietnam. Adventure-seekers now shuttle up to trek through gorgeous valleys and visit dazzling Montagnard markets. Travelers with limited time can get a taste of the region with a trip to highly touristed Sa Pa or Mai Châu. More time allows detours off of the standard track, leading to worlds that are remote in a way no map can define. Beyond the city of Sa Pa, the Hoàng Liên Sơn Mountains present some of the most desolate territory and challenging travel opportunities in Vietnam. The roads wind through a magnificent array of highland populations and colors, free from the chemically dyed kitsch and the tourist-chasers that are now part of the package in more frequently-visited destinations.

The northwest affords a look at the Vietnam that has yet to reap the benefits of modernization. The region's people struggle and perservere on less than a dollar a day. It is a landscape of tattered homes, limp *phở* and *cơm* signs, and pyramids of luscious fruit set along the roadside, all of it simmering with a flavor distinctly different from anywhere else in the country. Local Montagnards coax water buffalo through soft, lush hills and over unforgiving mountain tops. Thick clothes designed to weather long winters sparkle in the harsh sun. Grandmothers sit hunched over intricate embroidery in meditative concentration while grandfathers puff away on bamboo water pipes. The crumbling road behind you will only push you onward into a mercilessly difficult and startlingly beautiful world.

LÀO CAI ☎20

Lào Cai is one of two border crossings into Yunnan Province, China, and the chief point of access to Sa Pa and Bắc Hà. Despite a boom in trade between China and Vietnam, there isn't a great deal to do here; most travelers hardly pause before speeding north across the border, south to Hà Nội, or directly into the mountains.

Most travelers arrive in Lào Cai by train from Hà Nội or China. Train ticket stubs are collected at the gate on arrival; don't lose them. Trains run to Hà Nội (10hr.; 10:20am, 7, 8:50, 9:15pm; 65,000Đ hard seat, 170,000Đ soft sleeper). Plenty of transfer options await at the Lào Cai train station to take you to guesthouses in Sa Pa. Some guesthouses have **minibuses** (35,000Đ per person); you are not obliged to stay at the assigned address, only to look. An official from Hà Nôi Tourism also has a makeshift desk selling 30,000Đ Sa Pa bus tickets redeemable at most private vans outside the station. Purchase directly from drivers outside, however, and you'll likely pay only 25,000Đ. **Tickets cheaper than 25,000Đ are likely to be fraudulent.** Other Sa Pa-bound transport includes **motorcycle taxis** (1hr.; 50,000Đ), **taxis** (150,000Đ or less), or **minibuses** from the bus station in town (2hr.; frequently 6am-4pm; 25,000Đ), though buying a ticket from the counter may prove difficult. **Buses** also depart to: Bắc Hà (2-3hr.; 5:30am; 35,000Đ); Hà Nội (10-12hr.; 3:30am; 70,000Đ); and Lai Châu (8hr.; 7am; 45,000Đ). There is another bus station located 150m down the street in front of the train station. Here, the prices are usually fixed and there are fewer hawkers than in town. Buses leave for: Hà Nội (4 and 5am; 53,000Đ); Bắc Hà (6:30am and 12:30pm; 20,000Đ); Điện Biên Phủ (7am; 75,000Đ). The train service into China has been temporarily discontinued, but there are buses available just over the border to Kunming (9-11hr.; 7, 9am, 12:30, 7pm Vietnam time—you gain an hour in China; soft seat 200,000Đ, soft sleeper 250,000Đ).

Lào Cai suffers from poor urban planning; the three locations tourists frequent are inconveniently far apart. The **train station** lies 2km south of the **border** (open daily 7:30am-4pm). Other services include: the train station and the **bank** (☎830 013; open 7-11:30am and 1:30-5pm), on Nguyễn Huệ across from the border, and

currency exchange offices (US$, Œ·ng, Chinese yuan accepted; open daily 7am-4pm). The **bus station** sits between the train and customs, immediately over the Côc Lên Bridge on the other side of the river. Motorcycle taxis will go anywhere in Lào Cai for 5000Đ. The **Sông Hông Guest House** ❷ is 10m down Phan Bội Châu, which jogs east when Nguyễn Huệ terminates by the Chinese border. It has all the amenities (which may or may not work) in big rooms. Some have terraces on the Nam Thi River, overlooking China. (☎830 004. Rooms 80,000-120,000Đ.)

SA PA (SAPA) ☎20

The common sentiment among visitors seems to be: "this place is beautiful—hopefully it doesn't lose its charm." Once a remote hill station, Sa Pa is now the premier spot for weekend package tours. In the center of town is the spectacle of Sa Pa's famed market, which has become a fixture on standard Southeast Asian tourist itineraries. Local Hmong girls approach travelers with high fives and questions in English; suspicious travelers assume this to be the lead-in to a sales pitch, which it often is. However, their kindness and spirited enthusiasm is genuine.

To escape the capitalistic frenzy of it all, more and more visitors choose to come mid-week to see Sa Pa's true idyllic beauty. Treks through the surrounding mountainside are an opportunity to visit picturesque villages, most notably those of the Hmong and Red Dao people. With the recent inundation of tourism, many of these villages have transformed into glorified shops where locals sell traditional garments to sweaty trekkers. A little respect on the part of travelers goes a long way. Leaving Sa Pa, though, might just be the best part, but be sure to leave the right way; the Sa Pa valley's magnificent mountains beckon dramatically westward to the untamed splendor of the provinces beyond.

TRANSPORTATION

Buses: Tourist minibuses to **Lào Cai** leave from the large square in front of the church (1½hr.; every hr. from 6am; 25,000Đ). Buy tickets at the post office or in any of the tourist cafes a day in advance. **Public buses** (2hr.; 7:30am and 3:30pm; 30,000Đ), as well as **jeeps, sedans,** and **minibuses** (2hr.; depart when full; no more than 30,000Đ) leave for Lào Cai from the church. Other transportation to Lào Cai can be secured through your hotel. The public bus to **Lai Châu** (8hr.; 45,000Đ for Vietnamese, more for foreigners) must be flagged down at the petrol station on the road toward Lào Cai. Facing the main post office, walk left down the road out of town 1km and wait at the traffic triangle. Start waiting at 7:30am; the bus usually comes between 8 and 9am and may come as late as 11am. **Demand a ticket with Lai Châu written on it.** Buses also run to **Tam Đường** (2-4hr.; every hr. 6am-2pm; 15,000Đ), where buses can be caught to Lai Châu and then Hà Nội. Since the bus to Lai Châu has no official price, travelers must pay what they ask. Bring a trusted Vietnamese friend (someone from your guesthouse is good) to purchase a ticket before boarding.

Local Transportation: Motos can take you anywhere in town, but it's best to walk.

Rentals: Many hotels rent **minsks** (old Russian motorcycles) and smaller **motorscooters** (US$1 per hr., US$5-8 per day). Check that the price of the bike includes petrol and a helmet. **Jeeps** with drivers are also available (from US$30 per day).

ORIENTATION AND PRACTICAL INFORMATION

The Sa Pa Church faces a grass field at the town's center. From the church, it takes 10min. to reach anywhere in town. Facing the church, the **GPO** is one block to your left and the lake is up a block from the post office. A stairway 100m to the right of

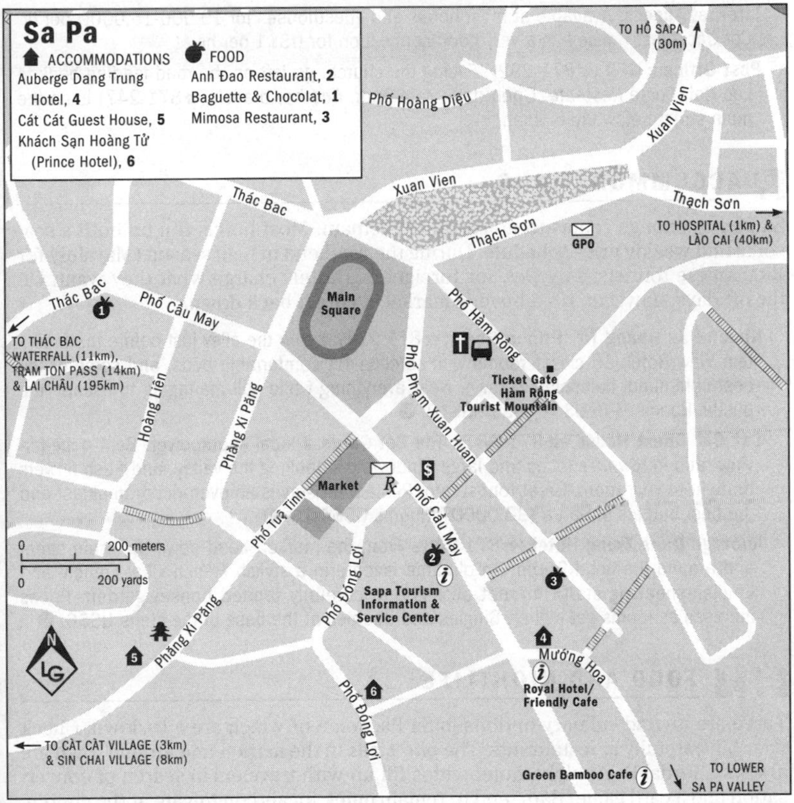

the church leads down to the **market** and **Cầu May,** the main street. Tourist services cluster on the main street before the road heads out of town. The other road that winds down the valley (toward Càt Càt Village) runs perpendicular to the main street and originates at the fruit and vegetable end of the market.

Tours: The best way to ensure a good daytrip is to ask other travelers to recommend a guide. Most companies offer competitively priced treks to minority villages or up Fan Si Pan Mountain (US$40-100). Most daytrips US$8-15, depending on the group size. Overnight trips generally US$10 per day. The **Mountain View Hotel** (☎871 914) serves travelers well on treks, especially trips to Fan Si Pan. Another reputable company is a branch of Hà Nội's **Green Bamboo Cafe** (☎871 556). Two offices in Sa Pa; better service inside the Green Bamboo Hotel. They do plane tickets. Next door to the Mountain View Hotel, inside the Royal Hotel, **Friendly Cafe** (☎871 313) offers similar treks.

Currency Exchange: The bank, 01 Cầu May (☎871 107), will exchange US$ for đồng, but the rate is poor. Most guesthouses will also change US$ and traveler's checks at high rates (5-7% commission).

Hospital: ☎871 237. 1km down the road from the main GPO toward Lào Cai.

Telephones: Call from the post offices. US$2.35 per min. Pay in cash; no phone cards.

VIETNAM

Internet Access: Available at most hotels and guesthouses for 10,000-15,000Đ per hr. Cát Cát Guest House has a very good connection for US$1 per hr.

Post Offices: GPO (☎871 292). Facing the church, go left on the road leading back to Lào Cai. *Poste Restante.* Open daily 7am-9pm. Another branch (☎871 247) is on the main street below the market.

ACCOMMODATIONS

Sa Pa has enough rooms to house all of Vietnam. Most hotels run on both a seasonal and weekly price schedule. During the weekend in high season (May-July for Vietnamese tourists, July-Oct. for foreigners), hotels charge what they want. On the off days, however, it's a buyer's market, so don't back down.

Khách Sạn Hoàng Tử (**Prince Hotel;** ☎871 274). Down the alley just before the Mountain View Hotel. 15 classy rooms with satellite TV, comfortable beds, and some of the best communal balconies in town. Near everything while still managing to escape the bustle. Rooms M-Th US$7, F-Su US$10. ❷

Cát Cát Guest House (☎871 387). The Cát Cát is a local superpower. Best price-for-view ratio in town. Terraces and large windows overlooking the valley, and fresh flowers brought to your room. Great tourist info. Restaurant serves an overpriced breakfast and the best burgers in Sa Pa (30,000Đ). Rooms US$4-15. ❷

Auberge Dang Trung Hotel (☎871 243). From the market, head down the main street and around the bend 200m. An old-time favorite in a stylish French villa. French- and English-speaking staff. Internet access and carefully tended bonsai garden. Prices increase as rooms get higher. Singles and doubles at the base of the stairs US$6. ❷

VIETNAM

FOOD AND NIGHTLIFE

There are myriad culinary options in Sa Pa, some of which are a letdown. Check your bill carefully at restaurants. The *phở* **stalls** in the market and around town are always affordable. At night, hotel patios fill up with travelers in search of conversation and a card game. Bars tend to remain quiet; locals congregate at the church. Mellow much of the time, this meeting place can become raucous on Saturday nights, when rice wine, musical instruments, and crowds tend to converge.

Baguette & Chocolat, up the stairs past the turn-off for the Cầu Mây Hotel. Take off your shoes, step up onto the wooden platform, and sit at one of the cushioned benches. The menu is very French with a dash of Vietnam. Wonderful pastries and a nice spread of sandwiches (21,000-38,000Đ), quiche (18,000Đ), pastas (25,000-35,000Đ, carbonara recommended), and more. Open daily 7am-10pm. ❷

Anh Đao Restaurant, across from the Mimosa Restaurant, by Cha Pa Restaurant. Service can be dodgy, but the price is right. The fried potato with vegetables (10,000Đ) is excellent. Steer clear of the fish dishes. Open daily 7am-10pm. ❶

Mimosa Restaurant, on the left side of the main street down from the market; a sign points up a stairway to the restaurant. Relaxed and away from the noise. Have the beef kebab in BBQ sauce or the frog's legs with bamboo shoots. Open daily 7am-10pm. ❸

MARKETS

Sa Pa's main attraction is its market. On Saturday afternoons and Sunday mornings, minority villagers (primarily Hmong) come to sell their goods, including colorful shirts, musical instruments, and jewelry. The Dao instituted the market as a

"Love Market," where friends from villages near and far came to meet, sing, impress, and entertain each other. Unfortunately, with tourists filming the villagers' every move, the event ceased. Now the market is geared toward tourists, who come by the busload and leave wearing silver bracelets and packing Hmong embroidery. For weekday visitors, there are still plenty of trinket sellers—so many that it is now difficult to distinguish which day is the official "market day." The second floor of **Chợ' Sa Pa** (town market) is the gathering spot all week.

DAYTRIPS FROM SA PA

Hikes to ethnic villages, past waterfalls, and through green rice fields offer magnificent views and an escape from Sa Pa's commercialism. Many visitors opt for a Hmong guide and later report that they are the best insight into the customs and life of local minority groups. Some routes can be navigated solo; if you're going alone, don't be afraid to ask the way, as most villagers will be pleased to point you in the right direction. If you want to take an overnight trip, you must obtain a permit, which should be organized through a hotel; most have a relationship with the police. Some of the remote areas around Sa Pa are not open to visitors.

HIKES TO MÁ CHA AND TẢ PHÌN VILLAGES

Finding the way between the trailhead and Má Cha village is difficult; we recommend hiring a guide. If you wish to visit the area on your own, pay the 5000Đ entry fee to start from Tả Phìn. Walk past the school into the Hmong part of town. The large trail leading toward Má Cha Village is easy to pick out. There is also a series of routes up the surrounding hills, all of which provide awesome views of the valley. A motorcycle taxi to Tả Phìn costs 50,000Đ round-trip.

This little village tour showcases the verdant fields and cultural splendor found throughout the Sa Pa area. From Sa Pa, travel 5km north of town to the major trail leading into the valley. One hundred fifty meters down from the road, cut right onto a narrow path, passing small Hmong homes and large vats of water stuffed with indigo, which are used to dye cloth. A 20min. walk down into the valley will bring you to a small bridge under a rice wheel. The path continues: climb through rice paddy fields, hop over bamboo pipes, and pass waterlilies. In the valley, the trail becomes a complex web, and hikers have to shuffle along terrace walls deeper into the hollow. Just past a hemp patch, there is a looming rock from which **Má Cha** village is visible. Má Cha is a small collection of tin-roofed Hmong homes with a modern school and a few water buffalo roaming the streets. A wide trail continues through town down into the valley.

An hour beyond Má Cha is the Hmong side of **Tả Phìn** village. Bales of hemp lie in the front yards of well-maintained homes. On the other side of the rice paddies, there are larger, taller buildings. This is where Tả Phìn's Red Dao people live. The Red Dao are easily identifiable by the large red headdresses worn by many of the women. Babies wear small red and blue beanies with metal beads. Their pants are resplendent with intricate geometrical embroidery atop dyed cloth. From Tả Phìn, most visitors choose to drive the 30min. back to Sa Pa.

THE LOWER SA PA VALLEY

The most popular trips in Sa Pa are accessed on the road out of town, past the Auberge Hotel. This road (admission 5000Đ) is presently undergoing construction. It's so treacherous that tourists on motorbikes often turn around, and xe ôms *should but don't. Ask at your hotel about the condition of the road. If it's being widened, head down on foot or by jeep. It's possible to hire a Hmong girl en route to be your guide; many speak English, and she may bring you to meet her family for an enjoyable visit. If you choose to visit independently, motorcycle taxis are available from the turn-off to Lảo Chai for 15,000Đ.*

FROM THE ROAD

POPULAR MECHANICS

In Vietnam, motorbikes have given all-terrain a new name. Drivers navigate the roads with alarming speed, rounding turns better-suited to sports cars and traversing floods that would look impassable even in a Jeep commercial.

Secretly I had wondered how these machines would respond to damage in a remote locale. Afraid that vocalizing my concern might render it a reality, I let it linger. But when a rock caught our bike's tire a day's hike from the closest repair shop or phone, my silent question was answered.

The driver and I rolled the bike to a small collection of Thài stilt homes. Everyone quickly emerged to see what was happening. A teenage boy magically produced a bicycle patch and glue. The village watched as we looked for a leak in the tube. Finally, we found the break and fixed it. The town laughed and smiled.

But we weren't home free. We filled the tire with air and... it popped. No patch could fix it. While the driver went to hitch a ride to a repair shop, I settled in for lunch. The local children showed me how to mount a water buffalo, and I sipped tea with the crafty boy's family, engaging in a dialogue of different tongues. While I may not have processed a word, I finally knew what can happen when you get a flat. By never making it to where I needed to go, I ended up where I wanted to be.

—J Zac Stein

About 7km down into the valley, a bridge appears far below and a trail leads downhill toward the river and across a footbridge to **Lảo Chai.** There is also a scenic and less-traveled route to Lảo Chai. From the entrance gate, head downhill for 40min. to the first convenience store. Nearby, there is a trail into the valley that slowly makes its way toward Lảo Chai. This "route" is actually a series of small local trails that slowly weave down toward and then along the river. Five minutes past the convenience store, just 30m beyond the first small hut, there is another clay path that meets the bridge to Lảo Chai. It's a beautiful walk through rice paddies and farmers' fields down into the valley.

The Hmong village of Lảo Chai experiences more traffic than Times Square, and visitors are constantly bombarded with goods. By the bridge, there are some wonderful spots to swim. From Lảo Chai, the river leads 4km to the village of **Tã Van.** The Dao and Hmong here have tile and tin-roofed homes, often with small drink stands out front. For a light day, backtrack across the bridge from Tã Van and return to the main road. It's about 2hr. back to town.

CÀT CÀT AND SIN CHAI VILLAGES. The most accessible village circuit from Sa Pa is approached on the road that runs downhill past Càt Càt Guest House. Follow the path northwest along the valley (5000Đ entrance fee), and you'll see a French villa built in the 1930s, which is now a center for wildlife protection. About 15min. later, a set of steps splits off to the left. This path leads down to the small Hmong village of **Càt Càt,** which has adapted a little too eagerly to the tourist trade. Continuing deeper into the valley, the stairs lead to an old hydroelectric power station and **Càt Càt Waterfall,** which is attractive but unspectacular. After snapping a photo, most tourists opt to retrace their steps back to the road. From there you can hike back to Sa Pa or take one of the *xe ôms*, which are strategically placed to prey on exhausted tourists. From the bottom of the gorge, however, the path continues over the river and up onto the other side of the valley, providing even more impressive views of both the waterfall and the surrounding countryside. This short addition to the trek circles back to the main road over a suspension bridge, which revisits the original turn-off to Càt Càt village after 1km. Walk 100m up the paved road to a smaller paved road. This leftward turn-off travels 4km to the Hmong village of **Sin Chai.** After 45min., Sa Pa is out of sight, the pavement ends, and you enter town. Sin Chai sees its share of tourists, mostly those visiting on their descent from Fan Si Pan; nonetheless, it remains beautiful and remote. *(Guided tours of Càt Càt and Sin Chai last a half-day. Most tourists choose to make the trip on their own; the road is paved and easily navigable. Walking round-trip to both villages takes 4-5hr.)*

FAN SI PAN MOUNTAIN. Fan Si Pan Mountain (3143m), across the valley from Sa Pa, is Vietnam's highest peak and a popular expedition for those willing to brave its deceptively steep slopes. The trail starts at the pink building just 1km before Tram Ton Pass. From that permit checkpoint, it's a 3-4hr. hike up to the base camp (2200m). Everyone sleeps in the small hut at base camp, and you will be provided with a sleeping bag, but you should bring your own or a liner for the one you're given. Trekkers reach the summit and return to base camp on the second day. The round-trip from base camp to the summit takes roughly 8hr. and there are great vantage points along the way. On top, you can take a picture holding the Vietnamese flag or a photograph of Hồ Chí Minh. *(Provisions and a competent guide are necessary for the 2-4 day trip to the summit and back. Weather is impossible to predict, but rain often renders the route impassable. A headlamp, bug spray, and snacks are all worth bringing. All guesthouses can arrange tours complete with sleeping bags, tents, rain gear, guide, porter, and 3 meals per day. Most guides, however, do not bring medical kits.)*

BẮC HÀ ☎20

One hundred kilometers northeast of Sa Pa, Bắc Hà recently came into the crosshairs of Hà Nội's tourist cafes, which tout it as an "alternative to Sa Pa." Once a mountain hamlet of hill-tribe traders and old wooden homes, the village is now adapting to its post as a tourist destination. But since few travelers attempt to visit on their own, from Monday to Saturday Bắc Hà really does become an alternative for those who wish to encounter north Vietnam's ethnic minorities and mountain scenery, without having to fend off busloads of tourists in the process.

TRANSPORTATION. Bắc Hà has one main road that splits into three near the north side of town. The right fork leads to the **bus station** (☎880 510). Buses run to Lào Cai (2-4hr.; 6am, noon, 2:30, 4pm; 20,000-30,000Đ) and Phô Lu (1½hr.; 7am, 9, 11, 11:30am; 12,000-20,000Đ), where buses or trains can be caught to Hà Nội (the 9:15pm train from Lào Cai does not stop in Phô Lu). Be suspicious of buses with signs saying "Bắc Hà-Phô Lu-Lào Cai"; they've been known to charge full price and then terminate in Phô Lu. The easiest way to leave Bắc Hà is by **xe ôm** to: Phô Lu (1hr.; 55,000Đ); Lào Cai (2hr.; 70,000Đ); Sa Pa (3hr.; 130,000Đ). Sundays, a **tourist bus** leaves for Sa Pa from the Sao Mai Hotel (3-4hr.; 2:30pm; 120,000Đ.)

PRACTICAL INFORMATION. The **post office** is on the right side of the main road, 150m before the three-way fork. (☎880 262. Open daily 7:30am-9pm.) You can make **international calls** from inside, but phone cards don't work. A road cuts right just past the post office and heads to the front of the market. Also on the main drag are several **Internet** parlors. Expect to pay 12,000-20,000Đ per hr. for a mediocre connection. The right fork leads past the **bus station** to the rear entrance of the **market.** The middle fork heads out of town toward minority villages and then on to Can Cau. A 5min. walk down this road brings you to the **police** (☎880 204) and soon after the **bank,** which exchanges currency. (☎880 226. Open 7:30-11:30am and 1:30-5pm.) The left fork runs past the Sao Mai Hotel to the **hospital** (☎880 263).

ACCOMMODATIONS AND FOOD. Prices are high during the weekends and very negotiable during the week. The **Sao Mai Hotel** ❸ is 150m down the left branch of the road described above. The Sao Mai empire is on the rise, with two buildings and a stately third under construction. Rooms are spacious and some have great views of the surrounding peaks. The **restaurant ❷** and bar (entrees 10,000-20,000Đ; open only when the hotel is busy) are connected to Hà Nội's Sinh Cafe and run tours and arrange transportation to Sa Pa or Hà Nội. (☎880 288. Doubles with TV and consistently hot water US$10-30; the new building will offer even more plush options for US$40-50.) The **Dang Khoa Hotel ❷,** on the main road on the left 75m up from the post office, has rooms with TV, fan, and terraces. Some of the front rooms look out over the Bắc Hà Valley. Ask to be on one of the top floors. (☎880 290. Singles US$5-8; doubles and triples US$10-15; prices highly negotiable.)

Restaurants include **C®ng Phú ❷,** just off of the main intersection on the street veering right toward the bus station. They'll hand you a pen and an oversized menu. The food is greasy but fresh. (☎880 254. Fried rice 10,000Đ; spring rolls 10,000Đ; beef with Sa Pa mushrooms 15,000Đ. Open daily 6am-10pm.) **Thanh S£n Restaurant ❷** is across the street from the bus station, 30m from the main intersection. A friendly family will hand over the English menu, which includes tofu stuffed with ground pork and tomato, omelettes with veggies and mushrooms, and pork with onions and bean sprouts. (☎880 407. Open daily 6am-10pm.)

MARKETS. In Sa Pa, you will see locals arriving at the market by motorbike. In Bắc Hà, the journey is made by hoof or foot—for now, at least. The hills surrounding Bắc Hà are home to the Flower Hmong, Red Dao, Black Dao, Tay, Nũng, La Chi, and Phu La people. Each market has its own distinct flavor, but most visitors opt to visit **Bắc Hà** for its own **Sunday** market (open 6am-3pm). While the town is adapting to an influx of tour buses, the market remains genuine: Flower Hmong come from all around to buy animals, clothes, and accessories. The market is also known for its food stalls, which serve cheap dishes. At 9:30am, things begin to get crowded, and the tour buses from Sa Pa arrive; coming early allows you to watch as locals stream in from the surrounding hillside with dogs, pigs, and other goods to sell. If you visit the Bắc Hà market and you're eager for more, head 12km north to **Lũng Phìn.** This small market is predominantly attended by the Phu La minority. The Phu La are of the Tibetan-Burman language group; they dress colorfully and often wear coins, metals, beads, and bits of animal fur. There are several other markets scattered throughout the area. These countryside markets tend to see fewer tourists and Kinh.

TREKS. Many visitors choose colorful markets over lacing up and heading off for a trek. Visiting villages, however, provides a fuller understanding of daily life in a Montagnard community. If you have the time, it is possible to stay overnight with any of the ethnic groups around Bắc Hà. There are endless options for multi-day treks. There are also routes in the area that can be done unguided—be sure to obtain a permit (US$10) beforehand and prepare for an adventure. English-speaking guides, fluent in some of the hill-tribe languages, can be hired at the Hoàng Vũ Hotel or the Sao Mai Hotel. They lead one- and multi-day treks through nearby minority villages, markets, and mountains. (All-inclusive, US$6 for day treks and US$18-20 per day for longer treks with overnights in villages.) Daytrips tend to be hassle-free, but overnight stays require a **permit** (US$10) purchased from the police office (no English spoken) or through one of the tourist offices.

LAI CHÂU ☎23

Lai Châu has fallen on rough times. A decade from now, the entire region is to be abandoned in order to make a colossal hydroelectric dam. Already, the town seems to have given in to its poignant, pre-determined fate. Business has slowed and visitors rarely stop for more than a meal and a night's sleep. Despite the utter lack of excitement in town, the Lai Châu Valley is home to some of the best trips in the northwest. The surrounding villages and treks remain breathtakingly unspoiled and worth a stay in the town.

Buses leave from a lot marked by a sign labeled "Bến Xe Thị Xã Lai Châu," 3km toward Điện Biên Phủ from Lai Châu proper (☎852 182). They head to: Hà Nội (18-30hr.; 6am; 90,000Đ) via Điện Biên Phủ (3hr.; 5, 6, 7, 8, 9:15, 10:30am; 30,000Đ); Lào Cai (10-14hr.; 6am; 45,000Đ) via Sa Pa (7hr.; 45,000Đ); Tam Đường (3-4hr.; 5, 10:30, 11am; 35,000Đ). You can also flag down buses to Điện Biên Phủ and Tam Đường along the road throughout the day. The **GPO,** at the far end of town toward Sa Pa, has *Poste Restante* and **international phones.** (☎852 301. Open daily 7am-9pm.)

The most popular accommodation is town is the **Lan Anh Hotel ❸.** The hotel is just off of the main street, immediately before the bridge over the Nam Na River. Free bananas, rooms with all-wood interiors, TV, fan, and private bath are all part of the package deal. Shop the hotel rooms to avoid getting thrown in claustrophobic quarters. (☎852 370. Motorbike rental US$6 per day. Internet 20,000Đ per hr. Currency exchange at fair rates. Singles and doubles US$7-15.) The hotel also boasts the only **restaurant ❸** in town. It serves a superb set menu (40,000-80,000Đ). The portions are enormous and include spring rolls, pork, fried noodles, vegetables, rice, and fruit. Main dishes are also available—most cost 30,000-40,000Đ. Simple breakfasts cost 10,000Đ.

DỚ AND NẬM CẢN VILLAGES

The closest and easiest trip from Lai Châu starts directly over the first suspension bridge on the main street. Turning right leads to the hospital, police, and boat landing. Turning left quickly leads to **Dớ**, home to White Thài villagers. While there are plenty of locals wearing Western clothes and driving motorbikes, the stilt houses with firewood stacked below the floors are lovely. Many homes have looms and some women continue to dress in traditional garb.

Past Dớ, the path goes by one suspension bridge (30min.) and then another (30min.) before turning inward to hug the mountainside. Trekking between the second and third bridges takes about an hour, and the road is generally flat. Roughly 300m before the third bridge, a small path leads up to the high reaches of **Nậm Cản,** which is inhabited by the White Hmong. Visiting the Hmong takes almost 4hr. round-trip; unlike the riverside path, this route is uphill and difficult to follow. Going solo? Prepare to say "Hmong" to many, many Thài people, in hope that they'll point the way. If getting lost isn't your thing, cross the third bridge to Hwy. 12; from here, it's an easy 4km back to Lai Châu. It is also possible, though not always easy, to take a *xe ôm* back to town or catch a bus arriving from Điện Biên Phủ. Another option is to continue along the far riverbank to (surprise, surprise) the next suspension bridge. This extension takes about 1½hr.

VIETNAM

ROUTE 6 FROM LAI CHÂU TO TUẦN GIÁO

Directly across the street from the Lai Châu post office, a Montagnard path pretending to be a road called **Route 6** eases up into the mountains. Rte. 6 is an empty, scenic alternative to the highway, and its beauty rivals any found in Vietnam. It connects Lai Châu with Tuần Giáo, an uninteresting town 80km from Điện Biên Phủ on the road to Sơn La. Buses run daily from Tuần Giáo to Điện Biên Phủ (3-4hr.; 7am and noon; 25,000Đ) and Sơn La (3hr.; 5:30 and 6:30am; 25,000Đ). The pavement is in a state of slow decay and disrepair, much like Lai Châu. The road quickly climbs out of the Lai Châu Valley, revealing fantastic views as rice paddies shrink into nothingness. Even if you only have a few hours, a quick trek or motorbike ride 5km up Rte. 6 is worthwhile for the panoramas alone.

The farther Rte. 6 continues, the more magnificent it becomes. Corn and rice fields converge with tangled jungles, high mountains, and a sliver of road. Jutting peaks conjure images of an arid, waterless Hạ Long Bay. Montagnards, machetes strapped loosely about their hips, walk their livestock along the road. Baskets or babies are latched to locals with intricately embroidered baby-carriers. The drive from Lai Châu to Tuần Giáo takes 4hr. in good weather. It is possible to take a *xe ôm* round-trip (roughly 3hr.) from Lai Châu to Pa Ham for 70,000-80,000Đ.

ĐIỆN BIÊN PHỦ ☎23

Điện Biên Phủ (ĐBP) is a destination for history buffs and a stopover for everyone else. Set in a beautiful valley, this unattractive but historically significant town is easy for foreign tourists to miss. As the site of the French defeat in 1954 at the hands of Hồ Chí Minh's Việt Minh, Điện Biên Phủ remains one of the best-known symbols of the collapse of European colonialism in Southeast Asia.

TRANSPORTATION. The **airstrip** runs parallel to Hwy. 12 and the **terminal** is on the left, 1km north of the bus station on the road to Lai Châu. Flights to **Hà Nội** leave daily at 10:30am and 4:30pm (465,000Đ). Flights to all other destinations require connections through Hà Nội. You can buy tickets at the **Vietnam Airlines** office in the Airport Hotel on Phuong Thành Bính, left off the main street between the bus station and the Mường Thanh intersection on Hwy. 12. (☎824 692. Open daily 7-11am and 1:30-4:30pm.) **Buses** leave from the station beside Hwy. 12 and run to: Hà Nội (20-30hr.; 4:30, 8:30, 10:30am; 115,000Đ); Lai Châu (3hr.; 8, 9, 10, 11am, 1:30pm; 30,000Đ); Lào Cai (8-10hr.; 6am; 75,000Đ) via Sa Pa (70,000Đ); Sơn La (6-7hr.; 4:30am and noon; 50,000Đ); Tam Đường (5-6hr.; 5, 7am, 12:30pm; 62,000Đ); Tuần Giáo (2hr.; 6:30 and 11am; 25,000Đ). Buy tickets from the booth before boarding. (☎825 776. Open daily 3:30am-7pm.)

PRACTICAL INFORMATION. Over 450km northwest of Hà Nội and 34km from the Lao border, Điện Biên Phủ is in the **Mường Thành Valley.** The **bus station** is west of town on **Highway 12,** which continues northwest to Lai Châu. As Hwy. 12 heads east from the bus station, it bridges the **Nam Yum River** and passes the **police** station (☎827 240). After 300m, it intersects **Dường Mường Thành,** the town's main drag. From this main intersection, a right leads toward the rest of town and on to Laos (34km), the hospital, the post office, the Điện Biên Phủ Museum, and the majority of the military sights. The **Bank for Investment and Development of Vietnam,** 3 Dường Mường Thành, halfway to the post office, exchanges foreign cash. (☎825 774. Open M-F 7-11am and 1:30-5pm.) A **hospital** (☎825 463) is on Hoàng Văn Thái, left off of the main street between A1 Hill and the Vietnamese cemetery. The **GPO** is just past the bank on the right. It has *Poste Restante* and an **international telephone office.** (☎825 833. Open daily 7am-9:15pm.) Back at the main intersection, a left leads into the **market.** Several hundred meters farther is a cluster of **Internet** cafes, of which **Trung Tâm Tin Học Trẻ** has the best connection. (5000Đ per hr. Open daily 7am-8pm.) **Công Ty TNHH Dược Phâm Hoa Ban,** located a few hundred meters farther, is the best pharmacy in town. (☎824 445. Open daily 7am-10pm.)

ACCOMMODATIONS. Hotels in Điện Biên Phủ are similar to the sights gracing its valley: numerous and unexciting. Some pleasant establishments have sprung up far from the city center, sacrificing convenience for solitude. More generic hotels survive closer to the action. While it's a trek, **Mường Thành Hotel ❸,** 25 Phương Him Lam, on the main drag by the 78km road marker to Tuần Giáo, boasts a swimming pool, massage parlor, and restaurant. Most rooms have A/C, TV, water cooler, and terrace. (☎810 043. Doubles US$10-20.) **Mây Hồng Hotel** ❷ is opposite the bus station but set off the loud street in an alleyway. A gloomy lobby leads up to pleasant rooms with TV, fan, and niftily enclosed balconies. (☎826 300. Doubles 100,000Đ.) **Lottery Hotel** ❸ has pleasant rooms that are close to the action but manage to remain quiet. Walking from the market toward A1 Hill and the Lao border, bear right on the street before the post office. Rooms feature bathtub, TV, and fan. (☎825 789. Doubles 150,000Đ; triples 200,000Đ.)

FOOD. *Phở* and *cơm* are best in the market, but can also be bought along Mường Thành. Stalls past the GPO offer a wider selection of eats, and Bế Văn Đàn, the second street on the right after the bridge, has little restaurants serving dog *(cho)* meat. **Hạnh Khôi Restaurant** ❷ is on the main street toward Sơn La between the Internet parlors and the Mường Thành Hotel. This friendly eatery is anything but glamorous and unique, but an enormous meal costs only 20,000Đ. The *Bó săo* is recommended. (Open daily 5am-11pm.) In the Mường Thành Hotel, **Mường Thành Restaurant** ❸ offers set breakfasts (15,000-20,000Đ), pastas (30,000-40,000Đ), fried tofu with veggies (20,000Đ), and a range of meats including frog and chicken. The delicious grilled duck in honey (35,000Đ) is a highlight. (☎810 043. Open daily 6am-9pm.) **Nhà Hàng Van Tuế** ❷ is just off the main drag on Đương Trường Chinh, on the way toward the Mường Thành Hotel and Sơn La. The restaurant has the ambience of a parking garage, but the beer (4000Đ) is fresh and the food is good but spicy. (☎829 652. Soup 6000Đ; meat dishes 30,000Đ. Check on the prices of non-listed foods like rice to ensure there are no surprises. Open 24hr.)

SIGHTS. For travelers who come to Điện Biên Phủ by bus, it is not difficult to imagine why the French reckoned the valley too remote to be threatened by the Việt Minh. In 1953, the French air-dropped 9000 troops into the region, thereby securing 8 hills surrounding Điện Biên Phủ, and constructed an airbase. Less than one year later, General Giap, commander of the Việt Minh, dragged artillery to the ridges ringing the Điện Biên Phủ Valley. On March 13, 1954, the Việt Minh unloaded roughly 9000 shells on the French troops. For 56 days a battle ensued; the French desperately tried to fly in supplies and reinforcements, but the Việt Minh successfully hindered their efforts. Rough estimates suggest that 2500 French and 8000 Vietnamese died during the battle. On May 6, 1954, the French lowered the *tricouleur* and hoisted another flag—the white one. A day later, negotiations began in Geneva.

In the yellow building across from the cemetery, on the main street heading toward the Lao border, lies the city's **museum**, chronicling the battle of ĐBP. Serving as a battle primer, this collection of pictures, models, and artifacts has descriptive plaques in English, French, and Vietnamese. Vietnamese and French weapons and equipment are on display outside. (Open daily 7-11am and 1:30-5pm. 5000Đ.)

Opposite the museum, 60m toward Hwy. 12, is **A1 Hill,** "Elaine 2" to the French. Some of the fiercest fighting of the campaign took place here, and today it stands as a scarred reminder of the war. A1 is a large network of paths, bunkers, and tangled barbed wire. Plaques dish out information along the way, but unless you read Vietnamese, they are of little service. At the top of the hill (accessible via the second small path branching left) are a tank, memorial, and bunker you can enter. A1 also provides good views of the valley. (Open daily 7-11am and 1:30-5pm. 5000Đ.)

Directly opposite the museum, the **Điện Biên Phủ Cemetery** was constructed in honor of fallen soldiers on both sides of the conflict. Inside the entrance is a long wall of names; the grounds are filled with nameless gravestones, many of which are lit with incense to honor the dead. The landing, accessible by a flight of steps near the entrance, has a good view over the grounds. The entire complex is beautifully designed, and along the outside wall is a gold-tinted Vietnamese pictorial representation of the war. (Open daily 7-11am and 1:30-5pm. Free.)

SƠN LA ☎22

Sơn La is a vaguely interesting town used by travelers as an intermediary point between Hà Nội and Điện Biên Phủ. Political prisoners were incarcerated here by the French, and even now the town has a self-contained, claustrophobic air. The surrounding natural beauty—where Black Thài and Hmong were wise enough to settle—offers an escape from the construction and rattling motorbikes that remain caged up in town.

TRANSPORTATION AND PRACTICAL INFORMATION. Sơn La is 320km west of Hà Nội and two-thirds of the way from the capital to ĐBP on **Route 6.** The **bus station** is 7km outside of town on Rte. 6 toward Mai Châu. From the bus station, buses and minibuses leave for Điện Biên Phủ (6-7hr.; 4 and 11am; 39,000Đ) and Hà Nội (8-10hr.; every hr. 4am-noon; 70,000Đ). Occasional buses plying the Hà Nội-Điện Biên Phủ route can be hailed as they cross the bridge. To get to Lai Châu, you must take the bus bound for Điện Biên Phủ and transfer in Tuần Giáo (25,000Đ).

On the right side of the street, 100m down Chu Văn Thinh from the main intersection, is the **Bank for Agriculture and Rural Development,** where you can change currency. (☎852 409. Open M-Sa 7:30-11:30am and 1:30-4:30pm.) **Internet** magically occurs 100m farther down Chu Văn Thinh. (☎853 012. 4000Đ per hr. Open daily 7:30-11:30am and 1:30-6:30pm.) A large **market** (Chợ Trung Tam) sits 1km down Chu Văn Thinh from the main intersection, and sells fresh fruit, meat, and vegetables as well as clothes and all kinds of goods. The **GPO,** 200m down Tô Hiệu, has an **international telephone** office. (☎852 421. Open daily 6:30am-9pm.)

ACCOMMODATIONS AND FOOD. There are dozens of hotels in Sơn La, ranging from dingy dens of prostitution to snazzier digs. Competition to fill rooms makes good deals even better. **Sơn La Trade Union Hotel (Nhà Khách Công Đoàn) ❹** is 200m off Tô Hiệu on Dương 26/4. The turn-off for the hotel is 300m past the GPO. It's popular—the competent staff speaks English and the rooms are spacious. If the price isn't right, ask to see a room and bargain it down. (☎852 804. Doubles with fan US$10, with A/C, TV, and phone US$12-20.) **Nhà Nghỉ Phương Bắc ❷,** 260 Tô Hiệu, is between the post office and the park. The lobby is cramped, but the hotel has pleasant rooms with new amenities and access to a rooftop terrace. (☎857 589. Doubles with fan 100,000Đ; triples with A/C 120,000Đ.) Walk past the post office on Tô Hiệu and bear right at the first street.

For a local gastronomic specialty, head 500m up Điện Biên from the bridge; as the road curves past the Tô Hiệu Monument, look for the sign on the left indicating **Hải Phi Thịt Dê ❷.** The name means "goat meat," which the cook will whip up in a kebab for 25,000Đ. (Open daily 11am-9pm.) **Nhân Đặt Cơm ❶,** a good local joint where you can eat a large Vietnamese meal for 10,000-15,000Đ, is on Tô Hiệu across from the park. They're happy to fry up your favorite meat and veggie combo or, better yet, their delicious stew of *thịt heo với dưa* (pork with bamboo shoots) for a measly 8000Đ. (☎854 444. Open daily 6am-noon and 5-8pm.)

SIGHTS AND DAYTRIPS. The French constructed a small local **prison** here in 1908. Later, it was used to hold thousands of Vietnamese patriots and now stands as a reminder of the French oppression of the Việt Minh during the 1930s and 1940s. To get to the prison, head toward Điện Biên Phủ on Điện Biên for 500m. Along the way, **Tô Hiệu Monument,** on the left, is dedicated to the favorite son of Sơn La.

Roughly 75m beyond the monument, take the first right on Khâu Cả and follow it to the top. The museum is the yellow building on the right before the radio tower. The entrance to the prison is down a path to the right. The complex was bombed in 1952 and most of the grounds have been left to stand in ruin. The left wing, however, has been reconstructed and now hosts an exhibit containing blueprints, artifacts, and photography explaining the prison's history. You can venture downstairs into the small, claustrophobic cells where leg irons and darkness remain. The main yellow building, which once housed the prison guards, now hosts a small cultural museum. (Prison and museum open daily 7-11am and 1:30-5pm. Joint entrance fee 5000Đ.)

Bản Bó is the closest Black Thài village to Sơn La, and makes for a pleasant walk. Head down Tô Hiệu straight past the post office and out of Sơn La toward the town limits, where it becomes Lò Văn Giá. Roughly 3km down you will see a sign on the left side of the road with an arrow pointing to "Di Tích Hang Thẩm Tat Toòng," 450m farther. Follow the path, passing a swimming pool on your right. On the left side of the road you will see a small shack in the rice paddies and a path beside it. This trail leads to **Tat Toòng Caves,** which, at the time of publication, had been placed off-limits. Ask at your hotel if they are again open for exploration. Back on the small paved road, turn left and continue toward Bản Bó. Stilt houses begin springing up soon after the path to the caves, and the road terminates by a football pitch after 3km. The area is beautiful and the village of Bản Bó is a charming and quiet place to visit.

MAI CHÂU ☎18

Surrounded by steep mountains and stunning rice paddies, tiny Mai Châu is a refreshing holiday from a region packed with challenging travel opportunities. Just outside town, the White Thài villages of Bản Làc and Pom Coọng allow visitors to step into Thài life by spending nights in stilt houses, eating home-cooked meals, and observing rural Thài and Vietnamese culture. Whether sipping tea with your host family or venturing out to nearby hills and villages, Mai Châu is an accessible gateway into the slow and peaceful White Thài lifestyle.

TRANSPORTATION AND PRACTICAL INFORMATION

Mai Châu is 140km west of Hà Nội and 6km from Tòng Đậu, which lies on Rte. 6 roughly halfway to Sơn La. The entire town stretches along 1.5km of **Route 15,** from the post office at the end of town nearer to Tòng Đậu to the Mai Châu Guest House at the opposite end of town. About halfway between the two, at the zero kilometer marker, is the **market** and, on the other side of the street, the **bus station.** At the time of publication there was no bus service in Mai Châu. Bus service is planned to recommence at the beginning of 2005, at which time there will be daily buses to Hòa Bình (2-3hr.; 6am and noon; 20,000Đ). From there, you can catch buses to Hà Nội. When service on Rte. 6 resumes, you can also take a **motorcycle taxi** to Tòng Đậu (6000-10,000Đ) and catch buses traveling to Sơn La (via Mộc Châu) or Hà Nội. Locals can tell you when to expect buses (as early as 6am).

In the meantime, Hà Nội-bound travelers will have to take a **boat** to **Hòa Bình** from **Bai Sang pier,** roughly 12km from Mai Châu. To reach the boat landing, take Rte. 15 to Tòng Đậu and continue straight. Soon after the town, there is a sign to Bai Sang along the right side of Rte. 6. The turn-off is 4km from the pier and at the time of publication this brief stretch was undergoing heavy construction—allow 45min. at the least. A **xe ôm** from Mai Châu costs 15,000-20,000Đ. There are three daily departures from Bai Sang to Hòa Bình: 6 (2hr.), 9am (1hr.), and noon (2 hours). Expect to pay 50,000Đ for all three boats. The ride is gorgeous—one of the best boat rides in the northwest.

There is no formal currency exchange in Mai Châu, but some residents will change dollars into đồng. The town's largest **pharmacy** is on the main road 100m past the market toward Mai Châu Guest House. (☎867 129. Open daily 6am-7pm.) There are three **Internet** cafes in town: one charges foreigners US$1 per hr., another 7000Đ per hr., and the last 4000Đ per hr. This last option is near the hospital on the way to the market. (Open daily 8-11:30am and 1:30-11pm.) The **post office** is 500m from the market toward Tòng Đậu, with international telephone and fax but no calling card access. (☎867 000. Open daily 7am-9pm.)

ACCOMMODATIONS AND FOOD

Mai Châu's accommodations are its primary attraction. **Pom Coọng** and **Bản Lác** are the most popular White Thài villages that provide lodging to tourists. The villages are next to each another off Rte. 15 on a semicircular detour. Pom Coọng is the closer and quieter of the two, located a few hundred meters into the rice paddies on the road branching right beside the Mai Châu Guest House. A majority of the traditional stilt houses now serve as **guesthouses ❶,** and for 50,000Đ visitors can sleep on a mat on the floor in the main room; mosquito nets are provided. The fee includes breakfast, which can range from eggs to banana pancakes. The meals are generally quite good. In Bản Lác, the nicest views are available from the **guesthouse ❶** at the entrance (☎867 019). For an extra 20,000Đ, Bản Lác families also serve up a filling Vietnamese dinner with a dash of local Thài flavor.

Culinary choices in Mai Châu itself are slim. The market sells fruit, vegetables, and deep-fried pastries. Full meals can be purchased at any of a handful of *phở* shops. **Hoàng Anh Cóm Phở ❷,** just after the bridge on the right heading toward the post office, offers generous portions of standard Vietnamese fare. The *bo sáo* comes with soup and rice for 20,000Đ. (☎867 752. Open daily 7am-11pm.) If you've been in rural Vietnam and are used to local prices, prepare to be frustrated in Mai Châu—even after intense bargaining, the cost of goods will remain inflated.

VIETNAM

DAYTRIPS FROM MAI CHÂU

The town is an excellent hub from which to explore the surrounding hills and valleys, which are densely populated with White Thài homes. Some roads are paved, while others are no more than narrow muddy lanes and rough mountain trails. There are also two caves close to town. All villages can be reached by foot and many are accessible by bicycle. You can rent a bike from the **guesthouse** at the entrance to Bản Lác, or at **Nhà Nghỉ Soẫ 19,** just down the lane. Bikes cost 20,000-25,000Đ per day. The villages listed below are only a few of the myriad options. Mai Châu is one of Vietnam's few locales where getting lost isn't the end of the world—everyone will happily point the way. Guides are necessary on more remote routes and multi-day treks in the Mai Châu area (100,000Đ per day). Once construction is complete on Rte. 6, tour companies in Hà Nội will again run trips to Mai Châu (US$30 for a 2-day, 1-night trip). Another option is to plan your trip with the Hòa Bình Hotel I (☎858 796 or 858 910).

HIKES THROUGH CHIỀNG SAI, XÒM CHA, BẢ CHA LONG, XĂM PÀ, NÀ CỤT, AND BẢ NA TÀNG VILLAGES

All of the villages on these trails have seen their fair share of visitors. Nonetheless, you're more likely to hear a "hello" in English than the all-too-familiar call of "money, money" that echoes along the more frequented circuits.

Take the street across Rte. 15 from the road to Bản Văn, which runs directly into **Chiềng Sại** village. Continue straight over the bridge to where the road forks. The road to the left terminates along the mountainside; the right path is an access route to rice paddies used by local farmers. Stretching for nearly 2km, this muddy route offers the chance to work in the paddies too. You'll receive brief instructions and a wide smile before being put to work in the knee-deep slosh.

The path eventually reaches **Xòm Cha,** where you'll be confronted by three roads. The paved road to the right leads to Rte. 15, exactly 2km from the Mai Châu Market. The dirt path to the left, which cuts deeper into the mountains, soon reaches **Bả Cha Long.** Here, the path narrows as it skirts corn fields before arriving at a small drainage in the brush, with a rusty blue sign secured overhead. This drainage is used by locals as a bridge; crossing it and heading farther up leads to **Xăm Pà.** On the side of the river on which you arrive, there is another small herd path cutting through brush. The trail curves left and climbs to **Nà Cụt.** If you've managed to make it this far on a bike, you'll be forced to ditch it here and go by foot. Unless you hike to Nà Cụt and circle back down to Mai Châu on the other side of the mountains to a paved road, you'll have to retrace your steps to Bả Cha Long—the village where three roads converge with the one that brought you here. The last, undiscovered road at this intersection acts almost as an extension of the trail from Mai Châu to Bả Cha Long, running perpendicular to Rte. 15 through rice paddies. Crossing a decrepit, wood-planked bridge onto the knife-edge path, you'll soon come to **Bả Na Tàng,** which leads out to Rte. 15.

HANG CHIỀU CAVE. The stairmaster never burned as bad as this climb does, but it also never rewarded you with such spectacular views. Hang Chiều itself is an impressive cave hidden by thick brush and a twisting bonsai tree. Large stalagmites drop from the ceiling. After catching your breath, it's possible to head into the cave. The path drops steeply to the chamber floor, from which point you can explore freely. Be careful—it's a very long walk down to Mai Châu and getting injured would make your life particularly unpleasant. While the first compartment receives plenty of light, venturing farther into the cave requires a flashlight. *(Across Rte. 15 from the hospital, a paved side-street is marked with a sign pointing to "Hang Chiều." This street soon meets a massive stairway ascending a mountain slope. Over 1000 steps later, you will arrive at a tiny landing that marks the entrance to the cave.)*

VIETNAM

NORTHEASTERN VIETNAM

With a rich history influenced by the occupation of imperial China and centuries of international trade, Vietnam's northern seaboard is a picture of serenity, laced with ancient temples and pagodas overlooking popular beaches. Foreign and Vietnamese visitors alike are charmed by the poetic grandeur of limestone treasures that protrude from the bay's frothing waters, foam-capped and washing picturesquely against the shore. Hạ Long Bay and Cát Bà Island play host to one of the country's biggest tourism scenes. Farther inland, the tables are turned. The provinces east of the famous Northwest Highlands are the least-touristed in Vietnam—a curse to those seeking an effortless travel experience, but a blessing to those with the time and energy to explore uncharted territory and meet its inhabitants.

HẢI PHÒNG (HAIPHONG) ☎31

A quiet city of wide, shady avenues and crumbling colonial buildings, Hải Phòng offers little to travelers en route to Cát Bà Island and Hạ Long Bay. Built by the French in the early 1900s, it was meant to imitate the cityscape of quiet towns in the south of France, and some areas do retain that tranquil touch. However, the city also has a darker history. Because of its key role as a conduit for Soviet aid to Northern Vietnam during the Vietnam War, Hải Phòng suffered severe US bombing; in some places it seems as though it has yet to recover. Fledgling industries have also changed the face of the Hải Phòng that the French designed, making it a commercial center that drives most travelers toward the beaches and parks of nearby Cát Bà Island. Remnants of the city's old pace still remain, though, in its food-laden alleys, away from the inevitable forces of change.

TRANSPORTATION

Flights: Cát Bà Airport (☎728 209), 7km southwest of the town center. Take a taxi (50,000Đ), motorcycle taxi (US$4), or cyclo (15,000-20,000Đ) from the town center. **Vietnam Airlines,** 30 Trần Phú (☎921 242; open M-Sa 8-11:30am and 1:30-6pm) offers flights to **HCMC** (1hr.; W-F 2pm; 1,800,000Đ).

Trains: Haiphong Railway Station, 75 Lương Khánh Thiện (☎846 433), at the end of Phạm Ngũ Lão. Trains to **Hà Nôi Central Station** (2-2½hr.; 8:50am and 6:40pm; hard seat 20,000Đ, soft seat 22,000Đ, soft seat with A/C 24,000Đ); **Hà Nôi Long Biên Station** (2-3hr.; 6, 8:50am, 2:35, 5:05pm; same prices as to Hà Nôi Central Station); **Hà Nôi Gia Lâm Station** (2-2½hr.; 8pm; hard seat 19,000Đ, soft seat 21,000Đ).

Buses: Tam Bạc Bus Station, opposite the steel market. Buses to Hà Nội's **Kim Ma Station** (2-3hr.; every 15min. 5:30am-7pm, every 30min. after 7pm; 25,000Đ). Buses also go to **Hạ Long City** (2¾hr.; 6am-4pm; 50,000Đ).

Ferries: Pier on Bến Bính on the Cấm River. From the west end of Điện Biên Phủ, head north toward the port. Companies typically run a morning slow boat and hydrofoil and early afternoon slow boats to Cát Bà. Exact times vary, prices don't. To **Cát Bà** (slow boat: 2-3hr., 70,000Đ; hydrofoil: 45min.-1hr., 90,000Đ). To **Hạ Long City,** Hòn Gai port (3hr.; 6:30am-2:30pm; 60,000Đ). In summer, purchase tickets a day in advance.

Local Transportation: Cyclos should get you anywhere in the city for 5000-10,000Đ. **Motorbikes** cost only a little more. **Haiphong Taxi** (☎641 641) charges around 6000Đ per km (depending on the car); ask the driver to use the meter. There's a cab stand at the flower stalls on Hoàng Văn Thụ, and cabs can be flagged down on Điện Biên Phủ.

VIETNAM

ORIENTATION AND PRACTICAL INFORMATION

On the Red River Delta 103km east of Hà Nội on **Highway 5,** Hải Phòng has a compact, densely populated center flanked by industrial zones. After crossing the **Lạc Long Bridge,** Hwy. 5 becomes **Điện Biên Phủ,** Hải Phòng's main drag, and runs past a number of hotels. One block east of the Lạc Long Bridge, Điện Biên Phủ intersects **Hoàng Văn Thụ. Trần Hưng Đạo, Trần Phú,** and **Lương Khánh Thiện** run diagonally between Điện Biên Phủ and Hoàng Văn Thụ. This area, called "Center," is home to the train station, a park, and **Tam Bạc Lake.** From the Municipal Theater, at the intersection of Trần Hưng Đạo and Hoàng Văn Thụ, **Quang Trưng** runs along Tam Bạc Lake before ending at the Tam Bạc Bus Station and steel market.

Tourist Office: Haiphong Tourist Company, 57 Điện Biên Phủ (☎747 216), in the Tháng Năm Hotel. Open M-Sa 7-11:30am and 2-5pm. Don't expect English speakers.

Currency Exchange: Vietcombank, 11 Hoàng Diệu (☎842 658). Heading east on Điện Biên Phủ, turn left onto Minh Khai; it's at the end on the left. Open M-F 7:30-11:30am and 1:30-4pm. The only **ATM** in town is within its gates, on the left. Open 24hr.

Emergency: Police: ☎113. **Ambulance:** ☎115.

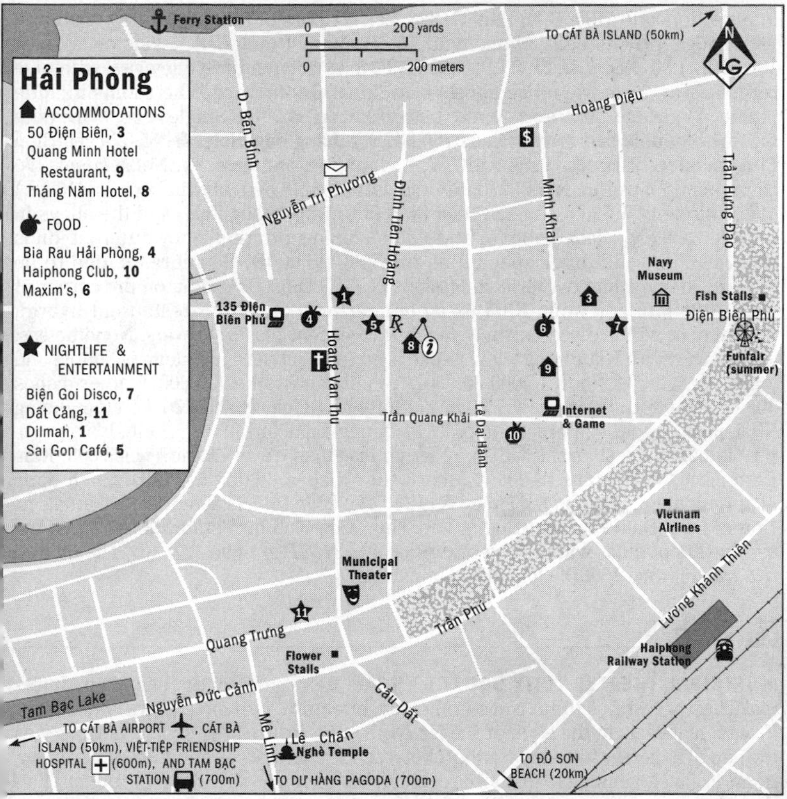

Pharmacy: Hoàng Lê Pharmacy, 63 Điện Biên Phủ (☎841 605). Reasonably stocked. Open M-Sa 8am-7pm, Su 8am-2pm. There are a few small pharmacies that are open until 9pm on Trần Quang Khải, east from the intersection with Hoàng Văn Thụ.

Medical Services: The best option may be to contact the **International SOS Clinic** (see p. 857) in Hà Nội, which can transport you to Hà Nội or Bangkok to be treated.

Telephones: Inside the GPO. International phone and fax. Open daily 6:30am-9pm.

Internet: Choices are few. **135 Điện Biên Phủ** (☎746 168) charges 3000Đ per hr. for Internet use and 2000Đ per hr. for computer games. In the back are 2 phone booths for Internet phone calls (3000Đ per min.). Open daily 8am-11pm. **Internet & Game,** 36 Minh Khai (☎745 598), charges the same rates. Open daily 8am 11pm.

Post Office: GPO, 5 Nguyễn Tri Phương (☎842 563). A big colonial building at the intersection with Hoàng Văn Thụ. *Poste Restante.* Open daily 6:30am-9pm. **DHL** inside GPO.

ACCOMMODATIONS AND FOOD

Almost all the city's hotels are around Điện Biên Phủ and cater mostly to businessmen. Still, most hotels are reasonably priced, and haggling helps. **Quang Minh Hotel ❸,** 20 Minh Khai, is the tall building halfway down the block from the intersection with Điện Biên Phủ. (☎823 404. 6 floors of rooms with big windows, A/C, fridge, private bath, phone, and TV. Breakfast included. Twins or doubles 180,000Đ.) **50 Điện Biên ❸**, 50 Điện Biên Phủ, is down a little alleyway, with nice rooms away from the noise and overlooking a courtyard. The rooms include phone, TV, fridge, A/C, and private bathroom. (☎842 409. Singles 150,000Đ; doubles with double bed or twin beds 160,000Đ.) **Tháng Năm Hotel ❹**, 55-57 Điện Biên Phủ, has decent-sized rooms with TV, A/C, phone, and balcony. Noise comes c/o Điện Biên Phủ traffic. (☎747 216. Rooms with double bed or twin beds US$15-18.)

The street is the place to eat. **Điện Biên Phủ, Trần Quang Khải,** and the alleys in between are especially good for streetside cuisine, offering many different kinds of *phở*, *cơm*, and other specialties for 5000-20,000Đ. Restaurants tend to be generic, kitschy, and overpriced. **Maxim's ❷**, 51B Điện Biên Phủ, on the corner of Điện Biên Phủ and Minh Khai, is an endearingly tacky bar-restaurant hybrid, resplendent with a disco ball and garish fluorescent plastic flowers. Nonetheless, it's popular with Hải Phòng's few expats and local jet-set. The menu is simple and bland. (☎822 934. Soup 15,000-30,000Đ; small sandwiches 30,000Đ; other dishes 30,000-100,000Đ. Open daily 7:30am-midnight.) **Haiphong Club ❸**, 17 Trần Quang Khải, is close to the intersection of Trần Quang Khải and Lê Dại Hành. It's a popular Vietnamese restaurant with live Vietnamese music every night. (☎822 603. Kangaroo 100,000Đ; soup 18,000Đ. Most other dishes 30,000-60,000Đ. Open daily 10am-midnight.) **Bia Rau Hải Phòng ❶**, 123 Điện Biên Phủ, is 50m from the intersection of Điện Biên Phủ and Hoàng Văn Thụ. This well-lit restaurant and its street terrace are popular with ferry workers. (☎402 243. *Phở* 8000-12,000Đ. The coldest *bia hơi* in town 1500Đ. Open daily 7am-11pm.)

VIETNAM

SIGHTS

MUNICIPAL THEATER (CITY SQUARE THEATER). The recently renovated Municipal Theater testifies to Hà Nội's French architectural influence. It was built using French materials in the style of the Hà Nôi Opera House. The square in front was the site of a bloody four-day standoff between French forces and Việt Minh revolutionaries in November 1946; more recently, it's been the site of street football battles. *(At the intersection of Quang Trưng/Trần Hưng Đạo and Hoàng Văn Thụ. Ticket prices vary.)*

NGHÈ TEMPLE. The many little compartments and the large courtyard of this red-gold temple commemorate Lê Chân, a leader of the Trưng sisters' insurrection against the Chinese. The Vietnamese celebrate the heroine's birth and death at the temple on the eighth day of the second lunar month and the twenty-fifth day of the twelfth lunar month, respectively. Special offerings are made at the shrine, and there seems to be an incense-burning contest in front of the statues of elephants and horses outside. Check out the ornate bronze sedan chair to the right of the entrance. *(55 Lê Chân. Best reached by cyclo. Open daily 6am-9pm.)*

ĐỒ SƠN BEACH. The beach attracts tourists from all over Vietnam and is cleaned regularly in a government-led effort to boost the local economy. In summer, get there early to find a good spot. Đồ Sơn also boasts Vietnam's sole casino, which serves foreigners only. *(22km southeast of Hải Phòng. Motorcycle taxi (30,000Đ) is the best way to get there. Buses depart to Đồ Sơn daily from Hải Phòng's bus stations when full. To reach the beach and casino, make a right at the ocean and continue 4km.)*

OTHER SIGHTS. Pagoda-like **Flower Stalls,** built in 1944, imbue the squares near Tam Bạc Lake with vibrant colors. Farther west, hawker shops flank Quang Trưng and its side-streets. At the end of Quang Trưng by the bus station, on the site of old rice markets, is the modern behemoth known as **Chợ' Sắt** (Steel Market). On Điện Biên Phủ, a block from the Navy Museum and across from the funfair, are some fish stalls with many aquaria of lively fish. Also check out the **Navy Museum,** 38 Điện Biên Phủ, which contains some poignant remnants of the city's battles with foreigners. *(Open Tu-Su 8am-5pm. 10,000Đ.)*

NIGHTLIFE

Despite being a port city, Hải Phòng has a pretty quiet nightlife. Cafes are very popular, especially those on Minh Khai and Đinh Tiên Hoàng, which become huge street terraces on weekend nights. Relaxing cafes at night include **Dilmah,** 84 Điện Biên Phủ (juices 500-10,000Đ, beer 12,000Đ), and **Dất Cảng,** 28 Quang Trưng, across from the flower stalls (cocktails around 35,000Đ). Good bars include **Maxim's,** 51B Điện Biên Phủ, which has live music until late every night plus cocktails (30,000-40,000Đ; see **Food,** above). Other happening places are the plush **Sai Gon Café,** 107 Điện Biên Phủ (☎823 314), which has live Vietnamese music every night, and nearby **Biện Goi Disco,** 31 Điện Biên Phủ, the only place to dance in town. (Cover 20,000-40,000Đ. Open daily 8am-2am.)

CÁT BÀ ISLAND ☎31

Home of **Cát Bà Island National Park** (see p. 888), 50km east of Hải Phòng and 60km west of Ha Long City, the island is the site of a recent tourism boom, as backpackers and Vietnamese vacationers alike have descended in increasing numbers on its 350km² of natural splendor. Guides and locals are quick to point out that Cát Bà is not just a larger version of Hạ Long Bay. The island is an impressive array of limestone mountains, overgrown with jungle and ringed by fine sand beaches. Despite the hordes of Vietnamese and foreign tourists wandering through the streets, especially in July and August, Cát Bà is the ideal place to go on rigorous hikes or boat excursions into Hạ Long Bay, or simply to relax on the beach.

TRANSPORTATION

This little island paradise is most easily and cheaply reached via a cafe tour from Hà Nội. Independent travelers can take a ferry from Hải Phòng or piggyback on the bus and boat of a tour heading to the island.

Ferries: Public ferries from Cát Bà run only to Hải Phòng.

Hạ Long City: Hitch a ride with an organized tour heading for Hà Nội (US$3-4). The tour boats arrive at and leave from the dock in the old harbor, past **Cát Cò Beaches I** and **II.** To find the dock, head up the road past the GPO and veer left at the top of the hill. The road runs about 1km to the old harbor and tour dock.

Hải Phòng: Purchase tickets at the **Sông Biền Hotel** to the left of Sunflower One, on the last street turning left before the road heads to the beach. (☎888 671; fax 888 671. Open daily 6am-8pm.) Alternatively, head to the office on the main stretch just past the corner of the last northward branch of the road. All offices have stable prices. Slow boat 2½hr.; daily 5:45am and 1pm; 70,000Đ. Hydrofoil 1hr.; daily 3:15pm; 90,000Đ.

When on the island, motorbikes and organized tours are the easiest and often only option for getting around.

Buses: To reach the national park, hitch onto a tour bus (US$6-10). Otherwise, public buses run from Cát Bà town to the park. Bus drivers assume all foreigners to be part of an organized tour and usually don't charge anything. The official fare starts at 500Đ.

Motorcycle: Many hotels and some restaurants rent motorbikes for US$4-5 per day. Some rent motorbikes with a driver for 70,000-80,000Đ per day. When hiring motorbike drivers, start with 2000-3000Đ and use 1000Đ-2000Đ per km as a rule of thumb.

VIETNAM

PRACTICAL INFORMATION

Tourist Office: Tourist services are offered at most hotels and restaurants. The excellent English-speaking owner at **Hoang Anh restaurant** and Mr. Lơ at the **Mý Ngọc Restaurant and Hotel** are both locals who organize and lead tours around the bay, and can provide information about the surrounding area. The Australian owner of the **Noble House** sells alternative tours of the bay (led by an English-speaking captain) that are adaptable to customer's wishes. Tour lengths can range from a few hours to overnights. The daughter of the owners at the **Quang Đuc Family Hotel** speaks excellent English and books bay tours, as well as transportation and guest rooms on Cát Ông Island.

Currency Exchange: Most hotels will exchange dollars for đồng, but at damaging rates. Though currently there is no **ATM** on the island, a Vietcombank ATM is rumored to be arriving at the **Prince Hotel** in September 2004.

Police: ☎888 239.

Ambulance: ☎888 239.

Pharmacy: Hiệu Thốc (☎888 896) is in the center of town, next to the Flightless Bird bar. Open daily 6am-11pm.

Telephones: Inside the GPO and inside smaller offices scattered around the town. Open M-F 7am-1pm, Sa-Su 9:30am-9pm.

Internet Access: Along both the main beachfront road and its main artery, which shoots off from across the dock next to the GPO. Most shops charge 200-300Đ per min. for the slow dial-up connection. For slightly lower prices, head to the town market.

Post Office: ☎888 566. Across the street from the ferry dock and on the corner of the main road that flows from the beach and into the island. Calls to the Canada, UK, and US US$0.70 per min. for the first 6min., then US$0.07 per second; Su and holidays US$0.55/US$0.05. Open daily 7am-10pm.

ACCOMMODATIONS

Since the introduction of electricity in 1998, hotels have sprung up all over. Though options are numerous, Vietnamese tourists take over the island on weekends. Independent travelers should book ahead on those nights and be prepared to pay a hefty price. Though some hotels and guesthouses standardize costs throughout the week and sometimes even throughout the year, others triple or quadruple their prices for the summer weekends. Nonetheless, plenty of affordable and quality options remain open from Sunday to Wednesday or Thursday. But beware—while some hotels and guesthouses are happy to accommodate budget travelers during summer weeks, some expect such visitors to vacate their rooms for high-paying or pre-booked customers. Ask ahead to avoid unpleasant surprises.

Quang Đuc Family Hotel (☎888 231), directly across from the dock. The owner's daughter speaks excellent English, provides tourist info about the island, and books tours. Rooms with balcony summer US$10-15, winter US$8-12. ❸

Giang So'n Hotel (☎888 214; giangsonhotelcb@hp.vnn.vn) sits opposite the fishing dock. There are 2 kinds of rooms, both with snow-white twin beds, dark wood frames, satellite TV, and clean bathrooms with shower: the front rooms have balconies, but their neighbors lack windows. All rooms with fan US$7, with A/C US$10. ❷

The Noble House (☎888 363; fax 888 570), next door to the GPO. Run by a friendly Australian and Vietnamese couple, this self-styled hotel, restaurant, and bar has pleasant doubles with twin beds that can turn into a double. Rooms with refrigerator, satellite TV, A/C, and homemade furniture. Sparkling new private baths. Back rooms with fan US$8, with A/C US$10; front rooms with balcony and bay view US$10/US$12. ❸

FOOD

Most visitors eat inferior hotel food as part of their deal. Still, seafood restaurants populate the island, all offering the freshest fare. Head down the pier along the railing. Two restaurants sit in the water and allow customers to grace their swishing floor by making the short sea-excursion on a floating walkway. **Cát Tiên ❸,** the second restaurant on the walk from the town toward the beach, has fair prices and flavorful seafood dishes. (☎887 855. Soup 10,000-15,000Đ, crab 150,000-200,000Đ per kg; fish 140,000-150,000Đ per kg, individual servings 30,000-40,000Đ; Tiger Beer 12,000Đ. Open daily 6am-midnight.) More options with floating sidewalks are available at the old harbor, where tour boats dock.

Hoang Y Restaurant, on the waterfront strip past the Quang Đuc Family Hotel, serves tasty seafood dishes (30,000-60,000Đ) and huge portions of soup (8000-15,000Đ). The pineapple and banana pancakes (8000Đ) topped with chocolate (10,000Đ) will seduce the most obstinate sweet tooth. Don't let its popularity with guidebooks turn you away. Open daily 6am-midnight. ❸

The Noble House Restaurant (☎888 363; fax 888 570), right next to the GPO. Popular with longer-term independent travelers and praised by visitors in search of a splash of variety. The fresh fish is highly recommended. The bar and terrace upstairs can make for a quiet evening or a rowdy night if a tour group stumbles in. Free pool table is an added bonus. Entrees 15,000-35,000Đ, all-day breakfast 15,000Đ, fruit shakes and Tiger Beer 15,000Đ. Open daily 6am-11pm or last customer (even if that means dawn). ❷

Đức Tuân (☎888 783), on the main stretch, 10-15m down from the Family Hotel. Popular with Vietnamese weekend tourists. Friendly service and fair portions of tasty soups. As everywhere, the seafood is fresh and good. Sit upstairs on the terrace. Spring rolls 15,000Đ; crab 45,000-55,000Đ. Open daily 6am-midnight. ❸

SIGHTS

In order to visit the island at your own pace, rent a motorbike (US$4-5) or hire a driver (US$5-6) from a hotel or restaurant. For a picturesque view of the ocean and waves crashing against the steep limestone shores, ask to make one leg of the journey along the coast. Otherwise, join up with a tour and ride in their minibus (US$5-6). Apart from the bay, Cát Bà's main attraction is its lush **national park** see (xref).

CÁT CÒ BEACHES. Deserted on most weekdays, Cát Bà's beaches become crowded in the evenings and on weekends. However, the beaches remain quiet in the earlier and hotter hours of the day. Heading east along the main road leads to a fork. Turn left and go up a hill to get to Cát Cò I and II.

A favorite spot of most Vietnamese, **Cát Cò I** lies closest to the town and is most crowded. For solitude, sneak up the stairs at the back or follow the red and white walkway, which winds about 700m around the limestone precipice and leads to **Cát Cò II,** accessible only by foot. It remains the quieter beach, even when crowds rush for a swim on weekends. A walk through the thin tunnel in the mountainside or through the ocean and along its edge leads to the other half of the beach, where a partly hidden entrance leaves it the best-protected of the town shores. Though there are no guesthouses on the beaches, you can ask the beach staff for permission to set up camp. *(Prices are standardized on Cát Cò I and II. A day on the beach's lounge chairs will cost 20,000Đ, use of the toilet an additional 1000Đ, the changing rooms 2000Đ, and showers 5000Đ. Stow your stuff in a small locker for 5000Đ. Camping on Cát Cò II 100,000Đ per 24hr. Open daily during the summer 6am-7pm.)*

VIETNAM

FROM THE ROAD

LONELY LADY

Women traveling alone in Vietnam are unlikely to encounter any special danger. Violent crimes against foreigners, women included, are relatively rare here. The biggest hassles most single foreign women face from the local men are stares and catcalls. Occasionally, men will also suck at their teeth, which seems to be the Vietnamese version of whistling, although it feels slightly more offensive—if only because it's different.

What may be more challenging for some single women is everyone's sheer pity concerning their solo status. Vietnamese cultural norms emphasize couplehood and marriage, so a woman traveling alone appears rather pathetic, like someone who has a birthday party but no guests. The question about one's relationship status comes up early on in conversations, and women who say they're alone are usually met with sorrowful looks and statements like, "It's very sad for you," or "But where is your friend?" Even the most independent woman may feel a bit lonely after this treatment. Try not to let it get you down; instead, let people know that you're happy to be alone, and explain that you chose to travel that way. If that doesn't work, you can always create a wonderful (albeit imaginary) boyfriend/husband who is waiting for you in your home country.

—Marianne Cook

NIGHTLIFE

After dinner, head to the main drag that runs along the water. Beer and refreshment stalls on the dock offer outdoor seating and an almost Riviera-like ambience.

Flightless Bird Cafe (☎888 517), toward the park, past Hoang Y Restaurant. Backpackers and foreign tourists gravitate to this tiny, laid-back Vietnamese/Kiwi-owned bar. Inside, darts, games, and a book exchange provide welcome low-key entertainment. Bicycles for rent US$1 per hr., US$4 per day. Book exchange US$1. Orange juice 15,000Đ; Tiger Beer 16,000Đ; cocktails 48,000Đ. Open daily 6:30-11:30pm.

Sóng Xanh Disco (☎888 637), 10m down the road from the Blue Note Bar. Try this one if you ever wondered how Public Enemy can blend with Canto-pop in a remix that features Celine Dion. In the evening, the more daring sing karaoke in front of a neon-lit stage, while after dark, Vietnamese teens shake it to disco beats alongside the occasional middle-aged foreigner. Tiger Beer a refreshing 10,000Đ.

CÁT BÀ NATIONAL PARK

Established in March 1986, the park is 17km from the pier and encompasses an area of 15,200 hectares—over 50% of Cát Bà Island. Its terrain is composed of limestone mountains which average 150m in height, with its highest peak, Cao Vong, measuring in 322m. The park is also home to a botanical garden, fields of lychee trees, and over 120 animal species; visitors are advised, however, to watch for small snakes slithering along the trails. While it is a little warmer from May to October, it is also the rainy season on Cát Bà.

ACCOMMODATIONS AND FOOD. Spending the night at the park is highly feasible and facilitates hiking during the day. Musty but clean **guesthouses** ❷ at the park headquarters have large rooms with twin beds and private baths with hot water and shower. (☎888 741; fax 821 249. US$8.) To camp in the park, bring your own equipment (25,000Đ per person per day). Those staying at the park can order **meals** ❷ through the park service. (Breakfast 10,000Đ; lunch and dinner 20,000-50,000Đ.) Those going on long hikes or planning to spend the day in the park are advised to bring along food and water. Though there are vendors along the path into the forest, they sell little but drinks, ice cream, and assorted snacks.

HIKES. Though the park provides numerous hikes, both relaxed and rigorous, the two trails (Ngủ Lâm and Việt Hải Village) which have been adopted by tourist companies enjoy the most popularity, especially with foreign visitors. Other, less-touristed routes allow visitors to walk through the forest en route to caves or simply to wander through the park. Though guides are not required, they are available and recommended for longer and more arduous hikes. (Guides 20,000-100,000Đ depending on the trail.)

Probably the least intense hike open to visitors is a walk to the timber forest of **Kim Giao** (1km; 30min.). From the park headquarters, head straight along the cement path until you reach the steps that mark the beginning of the mountain hike. Climb up into the forest. At the intersection, a sign points you left to Ngủ Lâm Peak (1.5km; 2 hours). Turning right leads to Trung Trang Cave (1½-2 hours).

HẠ LONG CITY ☎33

Hạ Long City, the popular launchpad for excursions into Hạ Long Bay (see p. 891), happily testifies to the recent boom in Vietnam's tourism industry. Once trade and fishing kept this outpost alive; now the tourist sector runs and rules town. To many visitors, though, its unbridled commercialism creates quite a distraction from Hạ Long Bay's quiet beauty.

TRANSPORTATION. Buses depart from **Bãi Cháy Bus Station,** 600m south of the Hòn Gai Ferry on Hạ Long Rd. Destinations include: Đà Nẵng (daily 7am; 138,000Đ); Hà Nội (3-4hr.; every 15min. 5:30am-6pm; 35,000Đ); Hải Phòng (2¾hr.; every 30min. 6am-5pm; 22,000Đ); Vinh (7-8hr.; 6:30am; 66,000Đ). Minibuses leave from across the street and can be flagged down along Hạ Long Rd., especially in front of the GPO. Catch one to Hải Phòng (2½hr.; 6am-5pm; 18,000Đ) or Hà Nội (4hr.; 6am-5pm; 35,000Đ). Ferries leave from Bãi Cháy to Hòn Gai (every 10min. until 10pm, then every 30min.; 500Đ). The Hòn Gai pier (Bến Tàu Hòn Gai), 1.5km down Lê Thánh Tông from the bridge, at the end of the road to the right at the first small roundabout, has ferries to Hải Phòng (2½hr.; daily 6am and 1pm; 60,000Đ); and occasional ferries to Cát Bà Island. Since many companies offer ferry services at Hòn Gai pier, it may be confusing to find the right boat and the right time. Always check in advance. The **Tourist Hydrofoil** is a better option. It runs to Cát Bà (40min.; daily 7:30am, return 4:15pm; US$7) and Móng Cái (3hr.; 8am and 1pm; US$12). Obtain your tickets at the counter 100m down Hạ Long Road from the bus station (away from the center of Bãi Cháy) and catch the boat at the dock 400m back toward town. Due to its small size and simple layout, Hạ Long City is a reasonably walkable city. **Motorbike** drivers are everywhere (especially at the ferry) and will take you anywhere you need to go for 3000-4000Đ.

ORIENTATION. Hạ Long City lies 165km east of Hà Nội and 55km northeast of Hải Phòng. The city is divided up by the **Cửa Lục Strait** into two districts: the more tourist-oriented **Bãi Cháy** on its western shore, and the more industrial **Hòn Gai** on its eastern shore. Most buses, signs, and maps refer to these two districts.

Bãi Cháy stretches out along the coast of Hạ Long Bay and is basically composed of two roads. Its main road is **Hạ Long Road (Đường Hạ Long),** which runs along the entire bay front from the **tourist boat pier** in the west, to the center of Bãi Cháy, 2km east, and the ferry, 2km farther east. All chartered boats to the grottos leave from the tourist boat piers, all the way in the west. Extending 1km between here and the town center is the **Royal Amusement Park,** on a strip of land between Hạ Long Rd. and the bay. In the center of Bãi Cháy, "Restaurant Row" and the general post office crowd the intersection of **Vườn Đào** (Bãi Cháy's second-most important road, a.k.a. "Hotel Alley") with Hạ Long Rd., which continues 2km farther northeast to the bus station and local ferry.

Being the main port district, Hòn Gai has very little to offer for visitors. Its reliance on coal exports has made the area dirty and unappealing. The only reason to go through Hòn Gai is to catch the ferry to Hải Phòng and Cát Hai Island.

PRACTICAL INFORMATION. **Hạ Long Tourist Company,** at the tourist pier, organizes 4hr. boat trips (US$20-27) and gives useful information. (☎846 272. Open M-Sa 7:30-11:30am and 1-5pm.) **Vietcombank** (Commercial Bank of Quảng Ninh; ☎825 297), on Hạ Long Rd. down the road from the tourist pier, changes major currencies and traveler's checks. The **ATM** is accessible during opening hours. The main branch is in Hòn Gai, 1.5km east down Lệ Thánh Tông at the first major roundabout. (☎628 692. Open M-F 8-11am and 1-5pm.) In case of **emergency,** call ☎825 486 for immediate local assistance. The usual numbers (emergency ☎115, police ☎113) may take a little longer. **Quảng Ninh Provincial Hospital,** 651 Lê Thánh Tông, is 1km beyond the Hòn Gai GPO on the road that forks to the right. The director speaks English. (☎825 494. US$50 per visit.) Surf the **Internet** at **Emotion Cyber Cafe,** 500m from the GPO (☎847 354; 300Đ per min.), the small Internet section of the Hạ Long City Post Office (3000Đ per hr., fills up quickly), and various cybercafes on Anh Đào (up Vườn Đào; take a right just before Restaurant Asia) for 3000-4000Đ per hr. Internet phone is also available on this street. The **Hạ Long City Post Office** or **GPO** (☎846 201), at Vườn Đào intersection, has **telephones;** you must purchase a phone card (100,000Đ) first. Open daily 6:30am-9:30pm.

ACCOMMODATIONS. To catch a sight like no other, veer off to the left from the GPO and walk 400m up the hill on Vườn Đào, the notorious "Hotel Alley." **Mini-hotels** line the street with a vengeance—there are over 75 on the small hill alone. All ask US$8-15 depending on amenities; all rooms include two beds, hot showers, and A/C. Enjoy making your choice. **Vân Anh ❷** is across from the ferry dock. Walk underneath the sign saying Vân Anh and up a steep path to this amazing location with a commanding view of the bay. Rooms include TV, fridge, and phone. (☎847 618. Doubles 120,000Đ, with balcony 140,000Đ.) **Hương Trầm Hotel ❷** is a comfortable mini-hotel overlooking the bay; the local military police supposedly have a hand in running it. From the GPO, walk down Hạ Long Rd. and take third left, where a dirt path leads up the bluff. (☎846 365. Doubles 120,000-150,000Đ.) **Hồng Minh Hotel ❸** has clean rooms in a great location. Facing the GPO, walk 100m on Hạ Long Rd. toward the ferry. Rooms include A/C, TV, fridge, and phone. (☎847 643. Doubles 150,000Đ, with balcony 180,000Đ.)

FOOD. **Seafood** is the specialty in Hạ Long Bay, but it doesn't come cheaply. **Restaurant Row** around the GPO is the culinary epicenter for tourists. If seafood is your thing, this is where you'll eat. Live lobster, crabs, fish, and clams await customers in water tanks outside each eatery. (Seafood entrees 25,000-200,000Đ.) Basic Western fare is also available. Keep in mind that the farther you walk away from the row, the cheaper the food becomes. In this lot, **Phướng Oanh** (☎846 145) is recommended for its cheap prices. A small **market** hides in the shadows of the hotels. From the GPO head up Vườn Đào; the first road branching right peters out at the market. As with urban markets all over the country, this one has various street eateries. A third alternative is the small **Restaurant Asia ❸,** 24 Vườn Đào, featuring a mean *phở* (15,000-25,000Đ) and many simple seafood dishes (30,000-35,000Đ). The operation is run by Quang Vinh, a friendly former Berliner. (Up Hotel Alley, on your right. ☎846 927. Open daily 7am-11pm.)

ENTERTAINMENT AND NIGHTLIFE. The beachfront is the place to go for entertainment. At the artificial "beach," there are wooden chairs under palm trees and stands every few meters that offer beer (15,000-20,000Đ), sodas (10,000Đ), and snacks from 8am to 11pm. Though the beach itself may be small and a little dirty in places (due to the nearby port), Hạ Long City tries to compensate: on the beachfront, travelers can rent jet skis (US$17-20 per 15min.), parasailing gear (US$100 per hr.), speedboats (US$100 per hr.), and other aquatic paraphernalia.

All nightlife in Hạ Long City centers around the beachfront and along Hạ Long Road. Don't expect too happening of a scene, as most visitors and locals hit the sack early, since tours of Hạ Long Bay leave early in the morning. **Number One (Thủy Long)** is about 1km west from the GPO. Go up the road to the Hạ Long Hotels; it's on your right after 30m. You'll find relaxed cocktail bar away from the crowds and Hạ Long traffic. (☎844 771. Beer 18,000-20,000Đ; cocktails 30,000-35,000Đ. Open 7am-11pm.) **Dilmah Cong Đoán** is right next to the Congdoan Hotel, and about 500m west of the GPO. Go up the greenly lit staircase. This small cafe-bar sports a relaxed terrace overlooking the bay, as well as an Internet corner. (☎848 309. Juices 6000-7000Đ; beer 12,000Đ; soda 6000Đ. Open daily 7am-11pm.) **Oh La La Bar,** a huge can't-miss bar on the beachfront, blasts Tchaïkovsky and the Titanic theme song in bamboo-decorated bliss. (Beer 15,000-18,000Đ. Open daily 3-11pm.)

HẠ LONG BAY (VỊNH HẠ LONG) ☎33

With its 1969 limestone islands and 23 grottoes, this natural marvel has twice been proclaimed a national heritage site, thus remaining under the watchful eye of UNESCO. In 1994, the committee first considered the bay a natural wonder, confirming its appointment because of its overwhelming beauty. In 1998, a British geologist ventured to explore the Bay, finding what the Vietnamese government had proclaimed since 1962—that the bay had rare and precious geological features. Following his report, UNESCO once more placed Hạ Long under consideration and in July 1999 recognized the site for its geological and geomorphic value.

The legends of the origins of the bay's name are as numerous as the guides and locals who tell them. Literally, Hạ Long means "Dragon Descending." As one story goes, the inhabitants of Hạ Long once lived in peace with a family of dragons. The mother and her children would descend over the bay to play over the waters. When a drought came, the dragons would spit rainwater to fill the bay. One day, according to the legend, a group of pirates pillaged the village and attacked its inhabitants. Hearing the cries of the villagers, the dragons rushed to their rescue, spitting fire into the bay to ward off the invaders. When the fire hit the water, it turned into the gray limestone rocks that now fill the bay.

The bay is most effectively and inexpensively reached by tour from Hà Nội. It's also possible to skip Hạ Long City altogether and explore the bay from Cát Bà Island via Hải Phòng. However, as Hạ Long City lies north of the bay and Cát Bà is couched on its southern tip, the destinations accessible from both towns vary and are mainly decided by the proximity of each to specific bay attractions.

VIETNAM

TRANSPORTATION

There are three ways to explore the bay. The cheapest way is to explore via a tour from Hà Nội. However, travelers can undertake a more thorough adventure independently and at their own pace from either Hạ Long City or Cát Bà. No matter what option is taken, though, renting a boat is necessary. Tourists can arrange their own plans (though such ventures are often costly) or buy a packaged, preplanned option. Below are the tour options:

FROM HÀ NỘI

Agencies sell packages with pre-arranged hotels, meals, and set schedules. Options available run from one to three days in the bay. One-day tours include transportation, food, and a boat tour of Hạ Long that stops at two caves. Two-day trips allow visitors an overnight stay on Cát Bà Island or a night on the boat. Those who stay for three days can enjoy a trek into the national park. Prices of tours vary widely. The most expensive agencies are **TF Hanspan,** 116 Pho Hang Bạc (☎828 1996), its sister organization **Kangaroo Cafe,** 18 Pho Bảo Khánh (☎828 9931), and **Ocean Travel,** 51 Hang Be (☎926 0463; www.oceantour.com). Three-day trips, including Cát Bà, cost around US$40-50. (All-inclusive. Max. group size 16.) Cheaper tours, often in larger groups and via lower-quality transportation, are run by **Queen** and **Sinh Cafes,** and run US$20-30 for three-day, two-night trips, with higher costs including a night or two on the boat, single rather than shared hotel rooms, and a long trek through the national park in Cát Bà. The large volume of travel agencies and frequent trips make it easy to book as little as a day in advance. However, as bookings are often made through hotels and secondary agents, mix-ups are frequent, sometimes depriving travelers of their coveted night on the boat if the available quarters are overbooked. Similarly, a long trek might be canceled or modified due to a dearth of travelers or if bad weather occurs.

FROM CÁT BÀ

Though making the trip solo is generally more expensive, some travelers prefer paying extra in order to visit the bay at their own pace. Tours are available on site, and allow a choice between the slightly varied programs that pitch Hạ Long to visitors. Most slow-boat tours begin at 8am and end around 5pm and visit two to three caves, deserted beaches, and Monkey Island. Unlike the tours organized from Hà Nội, the smaller boat sizes allow for a closer look at fishing villages and floating fish farms. Some avoid the more touristy grottoses, illuminated by colorful lights, and present visitors with smaller but natural caves, still unsullied by electricity and swarms of tourists. A trip will cost at least US$37-40. Ask around the restaurants and hotels along the stretch of the beach and the main perpendicular branch that houses the GPO. Tours change with time of the year and whim of the guides. Sometimes flashy sales pitches fail to offer the quality that comes with an English-speaking captain accompanying the boat.

FROM HẠ LONG CITY (BÃI CHÁY TOURIST WHARF)

Those who choose not to see the bay with a tour can rent boats at the **Bãi Cháy Tourist Wharf.** (☎846 592. Boats priced by length of tour, desired destination, and the number of passengers onboard. 4hr. with 10-15 passengers 280,000Đ per boat or 30,000Đ per person; 6hr. tour 380,000Đ/42,000Đ; 8hr. tour 490,000Đ/54,000Đ. Entrance tickets not included. Open daily 6am-6:30pm.) Local boats can be rented at the pier, but often for higher prices (70,000-100,000Đ per hour). Overnight excursions can be arranged at the center. The price, which includes all meals and entrance tickets, runs around US$100.

PRACTICAL INFORMATION

Located in a tropical monsoon zone, Hạ Long is at its most beautiful in the early summer and autumn, when temperatures hover around the mid-twenties and blue skies are the norm. Though summers bring heat waves, late July and August also bring heavy rain and winds. During the stormy season, boats and tours can be canceled. Visitors are advised to check with the **tourist center** at Bãi Cháy Wharf before heading out. The tourist center also provides free maps of the bay, as well as information about the bay and the various tours that are available. (Bãi Cháy Wharf. ☎847 481. Open daily 7am-4pm.)

BÁI TỬ LONG BAY ☎33

Bái Tử Long Bay shares the overwhelming majesty of its neighbor. As in Hạ Long Bay, the waters near the main land are spotted with limestone rocks projecting from the calm bay waters. A passage farther into the heart of the bay slithers out of the rocks and travels between more distinct, flatter islands. Gentler landscapes reveal smooth hills covered with rich forests, gently rolling over the water. The floating fishing villages of Hạ Long are traded for colorful houses perched on the shores of the green islands. Though life can be spotted along the edges of many of the larger islands, only a handful have erected any sort of tourist infrastructure; the others are suitable for one-day excursions.

TRANSPORTATION

One way of exploring Bái Tử Long Bay is to arrange a two- or three-day tour through a hotel or restaurant on Cát Bà. Most can arrange an excursion into Hạ Long's sibling on a sailboat, including one overnight on the boat and one on Quán Lạn Island, in a bungalow on the gorgeous white sand beach. However, chartering your own boat can be pretty expensive. The hotels and restaurants along the main drag usually ask for US$30-40 per person for a group of three or four. The **Noble House** (see p. 886) books tours (three days and two nights; two people US$120, four people US$180). While **Mý Ngọc Hotel** presents its price as US$30 per person, students and budget travelers can inquire about a US$5 discount. All tours include transport, room, and board. Travelers wishing to explore the area on their own can island-hop with the help of public ferries, which make infrequent but inexpensive and reliable trips between Bái Tử Long's populated islands.

ORIENTATION

Situated 10km from **Cua Ong** (on the mainland), **Cái Rồng** on **Vân Đồn Island** is the closest port in Bái Tử Long Bay to the rest of Vietnam. It's also the most developed and populated one. Connected on the west by the Ta Xai ferry to the mainland shore, and to the southern and eastern parts of the bay with ferries, Vân Đồn serves as the transportation hub of the bay. While limestone islands are scattered throughout the bay, the closest populated island east of Cái Rồng is **Bến Sen,** which takes about 1½hr. to reach by boat. Twenty kilometers from Cái Rồng, and slightly northeast of Ben Sen, is **Ba Mun National Park.** Heading straight east into the sea takes boats out of the cluster of islands and into the open ocean. A ferry ride of about 3hr. zigzags around the islands and then shoots straight out to **Cô Tô,** the farthest outlying inhabited island. Closer to the mainland and farther south is the peaceful island of **Quán Lạn.** Daily ferries traverse the southern part of the bay on their way to and from Hạ Long City and Quán Lạn.

VÂN ĐỒN (CÁI RỒNG) ☎33

Though it is the major city on Vân Đồn Island and the most developed one in the Bái Tử Long archipelago, Cái Rồng is far from the tourist spectacle of Hạ Long's Cát Bà town and from the ambitions of Vietnamese tourist officials. The town is a true communications and transportation hub, with boat service connecting Bái Tử Long's outlying islands. The nearby Ta Xai ferry runs to the mainland, though a lack of attractions fail to entice tourists to stay for more than a day or two.

TRANSPORTATION. To get to Cái Rồng, take the **hydrofoil** that runs daily to and from Hạ Long City (2hr., 3:50pm, US$6). In Cái Rồng, purchase tickets at the Tourist Information and Hydrofoil Desk 30m from the pier. Alternatively, from Hạ Long, catch a bus to Cua Ong, where public ferries run to Phà Tài Xã Pier on Vân Đồn, about 8km from Cái Rồng Town. (15min. Ferries daily 4:30am-9pm; the car and motorbike ferry runs every hr.; passenger and motorbike ferry every 30min. 1000Đ.) Public ferries connect Cái Rồng to the outlying islands. With service to: Quán Lạn (2½-3hr., daily 7am and 4pm; for Vietnamese 20,000Đ, for foreigners 30,000-50,000Đ), and Cô Tô (2½hr.; daily 7am and 2pm; 25,000Đ). Bến Xe Khách, the **bus station** (☎874 074), is adjacent to the left side of the market, about 8m in from the main road. Buses run to: Hạ Long (45min.; 5 and 7am; 12,000Đ); Hà Nội via Hà Đông (4 and 4:45am; 40,000Đ); Hải Phòng (45min.; 4:45am; 25,000Đ). You can charter **boats** near the town pier. Along the road heading into town and about 15m from the pier is the hydrofoil ticket booth. The owners charter a small tourist boat to go along the bay or to visit specific destinations (70,000-80,000Đ per hour).

PRACTICAL INFORMATION. Tourist information in English is scarce. One agency operates in the Duy Khánh Guesthouse, but is focused mainly on providing boat tours of the bay. Bring your own itinerary or risk floating around in circles. An English-speaking guide works with the agency. Though there is no bank and no ATM, you can exchange currency at the **Tiêm Vàng Thằng Rồng** jewelry store, directly to the right of the town market. (☎874 236. Open daily 6:30am-8pm.) Cái Rồng's proximity to the mainland has allowed it to plug into the Internet, while its outlying neighbors lag behind. Internet parlors with DSL access clutter the intersection that leads from the dock to the center of town. Heading from the dock, steer left when the road ends at the GPO. Continue for about 100m. The first Internet cafe on the left has new equipment and friendly staff. (☎874 419. Open daily 7:30am-11pm. 3000Đ per hr.) Follow the road from the dock to the town center for about 1.5-2km; the road comes to a stop at the steps of the **GPO,** which provides international mail and parcel services. (☎874 290. Open daily 7am-9pm.)

ACCOMMODATIONS. While there are some guesthouses in the center of Cái Rồng, most accommodations are clustered near the dock, suggesting that the majority of visitors just spend the night and move on in the morning. An eerie similarity in quality and price characterizes the town's accommodations. **Việt Linh Hotel ❸** is about 400m from the dock, and offers the nicest and freshest rooms in Cái Rồng, with pleasant wooden decor and large windows. Back rooms have bay views. All rooms have A/C, refrigerator, satellite TV, and private bath. (☎793 898. Rooms with double bed 180,000Đ; with 2 twins 200,000Đ.) **Duy Khánh Guesthouse ❷** features large and clean doubles with fresh furniture and new TVs, as well as sparkling bathrooms. (☎874 316. Rooms in winter without A/C 80,000Đ, with A/C 100,000Đ; in summer 100,000Đ/120,000Đ.) **Hùng Cường Guesthouse ❶** is on the left side of the road when heading from the dock to the post office and the second guesthouse from the intersection. It's probably the best option in the center of town. (☎874 001. Small, basic rooms with tiny private baths, fan, and TV 60,000Đ.)

FOOD. *Cơm* shops cluster around the pier and near the town center. All are run by locals and serve delicious seafood. The few restaurants that dare to go by the title cater to Vietnamese passersby; hence, they don't provide English menus. **Sỹ Long Cơm ❶** is run out of the hotel with the same name right next to the pier.

VIETNAM

The shrimp is praised as the best in Vietnam. If you come after the pre-cooked meal is over, design your own dish and decide on a price. *Phở* 7000Đ, bowl of *cơm* 3000Đ. Open daily 6am-11pm. **Kim Liên Restaurant** ❷ is 20m from the pier, on the right side. Clean, light-colored wooden tables and white tablecloths draw those in search of a break from streetside or home-run *phở* and *cơm* shops. (☎874 199. Bread with eggs 7000Đ; fried rice with chicken 15,000Đ; shrimp 15,000Đ; Coke 8000Đ. Open daily 8am-midnight.)

SIGHTS. There is little to see in the town of Cái Rồng and its surroundings. Locals and tourists can head to Long Beach or find respite in an old and rarely frequented temple hidden in the busy town. The best thing to do in Cái Rông is leave; the port is the best place to launch an excursion into the rest of Bái Tử Long's 15,000 hectares of sea and islands.

QUÁN LẠN

Found near the eastern side of Bái Tử Long's network of inhabited islands, the beautiful island of Quán Lạn remains largely unexplored. Though there are no more than 7000 inhabitants spread throughout a few small villages, the undeveloped island has been tagged for major investments aimed at expanding its tourist infrastructure. For now, visitors can stay in bungalows on the beach and enjoy a blessed reprieve from noisy motorbike traffic. The possibility of touring the island, however, signals that crowds will soon discover the gorgeous shores, and its unsullied, beautiful beaches won't be isolated for much longer.

TRANSPORTATION. You can only reach the island by boat. Though you can bring along a motorbike, the relatively small size of the island makes intra-island transportation relatively easy, if sometimes overpriced.

If traveling from Hạ Long City is Quán Lạn, take the public boat that runs from the Bến Tâiu dock in Hòn Gai. It is about 2km down the road from the public ferry, at the end of a thin and cluttered street that shoots off to the right. Bypass the station itself and just head to the dock. Look for a boat with a sign that reads "Quán Lạn." The boat will stop at Thắng Lợi (1½-2hr., 30,000Đ) and Cống Yên (2-2½hr., 40,000Đ) islands (4hr.; daily 7am and 1pm; 50,000Đ). Though the boat has a scheduled time to depart, it usually lounges around until it is full. The boats arrive at the dock about 1.5-2km from Quán Lạn town center and the village's accommodations. Motorbike drivers are happy to take travelers to the center for 3000-4000Đ.

Boats headed north and south depart from the dock 1.5km down the main road from Quán Lạn town. They run to Hạ Long City (4hr.; daily 6am and 1pm; 50,000Đ) and Cái Rồng (2½-3hr.; daily departures scheduled for 7am and 2pm, but in reality, they leave when the boat fills up; official fare for Vietnamese 20,000Đ, foreign travelers get charged, 50,000Đ; negotiation is difficult).

You can get around the island on foot or by hiring a motorbike driver. However, the secluded location means a hike in regular prices. To rent your own transport, head to **Nhà Nghỉ Huyền Trang** (bicycle 20,000Đ per day, motorbike 80,000Đ per day) or ask at your hotel. Located near its northwestern tip, Quán Lạn is the major town. The pier lies about 1.5-2km from the center of Quán Lạn.

PRACTICAL INFORMATION. As there is **no bank** or place to exchange currency, make sure to bring enough cash. The **post office** is on the left side of the main street in the heart of the village. **Telephones** await combat inside. (☎877 309. Calls to Australia, Canada, New Zealand, the UK, and the US US$1.50 per min. for the first 5min., US$1.20 on Su and holidays; US$0.15/US$0.12 for each 6 seconds after. Open daily 7-11:30am and 1-4:30pm.)

ACCOMMODATIONS AND FOOD. There are two options: guesthouses in the town of Quán Lạn or bungalows on the beach. If you choose the former, the village is blissfully unaware of the luxuries of hot water and A/C. The village generator runs from nightfall (6pm in the summer, 5pm in the winter) until 11pm, when the town (including the fan in your room) falls completely asleep. **Nhà Nghỉ Huyền Trang** ❷ is on the main street, a few meters from the post office and across from the village doctor. Immaculate well-lit rooms have pristine shared baths and sometimes views of the bay. (☎877 351 or 877 505. Motorbike for rent 80,000Đ per day; bicycle 20,000Đ. Singles 75,000-80,000Đ; doubles 100,000Đ.) Homemade **meals** ❶ are taken by order with the aid of a English-Vietnamese phrasebook. (Tasty fried noodles with vegetables 10,000Đ; *cơm* with rice, veggies, soup, and eggs or meat 30,000Đ for two.) Just past the post office when heading to the village center from the dock is **Hotel Phưởng Hoàng** ❷, one of the best offers in the small town. This new hotel has fresh rooms and sparkling private baths. (☎877 345. Rooms with 2 twins or double bed 100,000Đ.)

SIGHTS AND BEACHES. A **pagoda** in town and sundry **beaches** are the highlights of Quán Lạn. Located about 1km from Quán Lạn village, **Việt Mỹ** is the most frequented of the island's beaches. (To reach Việt Mỹ from Quán Lạn village, head along the main road and toward the dock. About 600m from the post office is the town generator, a yellow bunker-like house surrounded by water rice fields. Turn left onto the sand covered path. A short walk will take you to the beach.) Most call **Sơn Hào** the most beautiful of the island's beaches. White-sand dunes with meandering streams and tiny lakes border the narrow tropical green stretch that marks the edge of the stunning shore. (Follow the road that runs from the corner of the Ngân Hà hotel and passes the Robinson Guesthouse. When you pass a construction with a pink cement fence about 5km from Quán Lạn, hook a left into the white-sand dunes. Follow the sandy path toward the shore. A motorbike ride will cost around 7000-10,000Đ one-way.)

VIETNAM

BA MUN ISLAND

While Hạ Long Bay has the natural park located on Cát Bà Island, Ba Mun Island is Bái Tử Long Bay's version of protected wildlife. The whole of the thin island, which is 18km in length but only 1km in width, is classified as a nature reserve. Deep crimson and bright yellow flowers blanket the island. Along the slippery, rocky shores, patient visitors can see tiny crabs, while those who dare to walk into the forest can spot huge spiderwebs and their owners, whose rich red bodies and legs can span a ten-year-old's palm. Unlike the preserve on Cát Bà, however, this island is as yet untouched by tourism and there are no plans for development. As such, the landscape is wild and has no paths to guide visitors in and out. Slippery shores and steep hills make it difficult to venture onto the island while it rains. Those willing to step into the vine-covered vegetation should arrive dressed in long sleeves and pants and armed with a compass and water. There are no public ferries to the island, making it necessary to rent a boat in Cái Rồng. The island lies 20km from Cái Rồng town, the trip takes around 1½-2hr. each way.

NGỌC VỪNG ISLAND (PEARL HALO)

Characterized by small villages and soft sand beaches, Ngọc Vừng is also the location of the Cống Yên commercial harbor that boomed with trade in the 11th century, as well as the remnants of ancient citadels erected during the Mạc Dynasty in the 16th century and the Nguyễn Dynasty that ruled Vietnam in the 1800s. The orange and blue houses of Cống Yên rest peacefully on the island's shore. The island derives its name from the ancient occupation of its inhabitants, who harvested pearls along the island's shores.

The island can be reached by the **public ferry** that runs daily from Hòn Gai to Quán Lạn and back (about 2hr. each way; 30,000Đ). It departs both Hạ Long and Quán Lạn at 7am and 1pm, allowing visitors to explore the island between the arrival of the morning boat and the departure of the afternoon one, or as a half-day trip from either direction.

MÓNG CÁI ☎33

Made popular mostly because of the border crossing at the northwestern corner of the city, Móng Cái's bustling atmosphere seems to revolve around the juncture between China and Vietnam. Both languages grace signs and restaurant menus. Móng Cái is popular for its market with imported Chinese goods, as well as for its gorgeous beach 10km from town. Prices in Móng Cái cater to wealthy Chinese visitors and are surprisingly higher than in most of Vietnam.

TRANSPORTATION. Fast-paced **hydrofoils** connect Móng Cái to Vân Đồn Island and Hạ Long City. Ferries run: to Hạ Long (3hr., daily 9am and 2pm, US$12); from Hạ Long (3hr., daily 8am and 1pm, US$12); to Hải Phòng (9½hr., daily 6:30pm); from Hải Phòng (9½hr., daily 6:30pm); to Vân Đồn (2½hr., daily 2pm, US$6); from Vân Đồn (2½hr., daily 8:30am, US$6). Buy tickets at the **hydrofoil office,** 1 Trần Phú, at the intersection past the bridge, on the corner to the left of the post office. (☎883 988. Open daily 6am-5pm.) The **bus station** (☎881 226) lies on the southwestern edge of town, over the bridge and about 1km from the post office and town center (open daily 4am-5pm). Frequent buses run to: Hạ Long (5-6hr.; every 30min. 4:30am-5pm; 35,000Đ); Hà Nội (8-10hr.; every 30min. 4:30am-7:30pm; 42,000-62,000Đ); Hải Phòng (7-9hr.; 18 per day; 32,000-50,000Đ).

PRACTICAL INFORMATION. The **post office** sits across from the bridge in the town center. (☎881 101. Open daily 7am-9pm. Telephones and international mail/telegrams inside.) There is a large **pharmacy** on 7 Trần Phú, to the left of the hydrofoil office. (☎770 536. Open daily 7am-11pm.) To cash traveler's checks, get MC/V cash advances or change American, Australian, British, or Canadian currency, go to the **Vietcombank,** on 2 Vân Đồn. (☎881 211; fax 881 676. Open M-F 7-11:30am and 1-4:30pm. MC/V cash advances for a 22,000Đ fee.) There is a **24hr. ATM** outside. To reach the bank from the post office, hook a left onto Trần Phú and then take the next left onto Vân Đồn. The bank is at the end of the street on your right. There are plenty of Internet parlors around the city, all charging 4000Đ per hr. **Coffe Internet,** 1 Nguyễn Dứ Hoà Lạc, is about 1m down from the Internet room and has new equipment, A/C, and a selection of refreshments. (☎886 060. Refreshments 3000-5000Đ. Internet 4000Đ per hr. Open daily 8am-11:30pm.)

ACCOMMODATIONS AND FOOD. Accommodations in Móng Cái are scattered throughout the city; every corner reveals a *nha nghi* or hotel sign. Some of the better options are found near the bus station. On the street parallel to the left side of the bus station, the middle **guesthouse ❷** has good and pleasant rooms with immaculate bathrooms and a pleasant staff. Rooms run 100,000Đ, but singles can be bargained down (70,000-80,000Đ). **Hoàng Tiến Hotel ❷,** 105 Trần Phú, is near the town market. Though the friendly staff speaks no English, when in need, they can hunt down someone who can. Rooms are pleasant and clean, with A/C and neat private baths. (☎887 916. Small, cheap windowless options with double bed and TV 100,000Đ; larger rooms 150,000Đ.)

Phở and *cơm* shops can be found all over town. There is a cluster of them next to the town market and around the bus station. Good and carefully made dishes can be found at the last shop (right before the second guesthouse) on the street to the left of the bus station when walking up from the main road. Steaming *phở* 5000Đ. Open daily 4am-7pm. Another good *phở* and *cơm* **restaurant** can be found near the town market, at 99 Trần Dương. When heading up Trần Phú, go right just before arriving at the main square market. The restaurant is about 15m down the street, on the right. (☎770 912. *Phở* 5000Đ; popular and tasty *cơm* 5000-10,000Đ. Open daily 10:30am-8:30pm.)

MARKETS. After the border crossing, the town market just might be the town's biggest attraction. Stalls upon stalls of vendors sell fruits and foods, as well as imported Chinese goods. On the southern edge of the main market square, booths of tailors make for a warped imitation of Hội An. Electronic and appliance stores fill the streets near the market and line the way to the border crossing. To reach the market from the bus station, head down toward the post office and hook a left onto Trần Phú. Continue straight for a few minutes, passing streetside stores until you see the roof-covered market on the left. Some stalls spread into nearby streets and alleys, so hunt around. (Market open daily 6:30am-6pm.)

TRÁ CỔ BEACH

Stretching for 17km along the Vietnamese coast and overwhelmingly popular with the Chinese, Trá Cổ is correctly considered one of Vietnam's most beautiful beaches. The few extra hours of commute are well-justified by the gorgeous sight of the powdered shore littered with jewel-like seashells and the turbulent waves that dance in the ocean.

Trá Cổ lies about 10km from the Móng Cái bus station, from which it is easily reachable by motorbike. Drivers are willing to whisk you away for 10,000-15,000Đ. To reach the beach on your own, follow Hùng Vương over the bridge and into town. Continue straight until the road flows out of town and heads straight for the beach. Alternatively, a taxi ride one-way costs around 50,000Đ. The village that controls Trá Cổ's shore is a rural version of a beach resort, with practically every sign along the town road advertising lodging or edibles. The main road that leads to the beach from Móng Cái traverses the town parallel to the shore. Smaller roads branch off into the sand and sea.

Hotel Toàn Truyền ❸, across from the beach resort entrance, offers some of the highest quality rooms at fair prices. (☎780 187. Clean doubles with TV and large private bath; some with balconies. Set prices throughout the year. With fan 140,000Đ, with A/C 200,000Đ.) While *phở* and *cơm* shops populate the

THE TRUTH ABOUT CATS AND DOGS

Ever been bothered by your pets scrounging under the table for scraps of food? Rest assured that in Northern Vietnam, pets wouldn't want to—they would be eating their childhood playmates. In Vietnam, dogs are multi-purpose animals, serving as both man's best friend and his best meat—making for some surprisingly tasty entrees. The smell and taste of dog meat is fairly powerful, and well complemented by alcohol. Fido is generally fried up and served with a raw green called *lámơ*. You can order *thịt chó,* which is a stir-fried dog meat, but the most supple part of a dog is *loñg chó,* the stomach.

Think again if you imagine that cute little kitties get off the hook. Given the recent rat problem, eating cats has actually been outlawed in Hà Nội. Farther north, however, you can feast on *con mèo* in local establishments. The meat from these introspective animals is fatty and can be difficult to chew, but stir-fried with some veggies it's actually a real treat.

Even travelers who consider themselves oblivious to animal rights may be a bit unnerved to witness dogs experiencing the same treatment as chickens or cattle. If the house pets up north seem a bit timid, understand the psychological stress they're suffering. Friend and food have never been so close.

village road that runs parallel to the beach, the boardwalk that flows along the sand is lined with seafood restaurants. **Sâm Lợi** ❷ is a fancy eatery right on the beach in front of Hotel Trà Long. There are no menus, but the staff has a listing of prices by kilogram, and some of the younger workers speak some English. (☎883 081. Soup 10,000Đ; individual serving of steamed fish 15,000Đ; rice 5000Đ. Glass of Halida 9000Đ. Open daily 7am-11pm.)

BA BỂ NATIONAL PARK ☎281

Located in the Bàc Can province, Ba Bể National Park was established in 1992 to preserve some of Vietnam's most diverse wildlife and thrilling natural beauty. Covering over 20,000 hectares of land and water, the park is home to 40 species of reptiles and amphibians, 45 types of mammals (27 of which are bats), 87 varieties of fish, 350 genus of butterfly, and 200 types of bird. Communities comprised of 2800 Tay, Dao, Hmong, Nũng, and Kinh people share the natural wealth of the area. All three of the park's habitats—lake, limestone forest, and lowland evergreen forest—are accessible either by foot or boat. The park's major attraction is Ba Bể Lake, which is composed of three smaller, interconnected bodies of water.

Ba Bể's personal highlights will be determined by your approach. It is possible to take a nice room and do a professionally operated tour that scans the natural and cultural wonders within the park. Others might choose to have a *xe ôm* drop them at the boat landing or someplace remote and rely on intuition and the kindness of strangers to get them through.

TRANSPORTATION AND PRACTICAL INFORMATION

Heading into Ba Bể is relatively simple—just arrive with cash (the hotel inside the park is moderately willing to change small sums of money). There is a 10,000Đ entrance fee into the park and a mandatory 1000Đ insurance fee, both payable at the park entrance just past Chợ Rã, a small town 15km from park headquarters.

Getting anywhere from Ba Bể using public transport takes faith, effort, and time. Buses to **Hà Nội** leave from the three-way intersection in Chợ Rã. By *xe ôm* from Ba Bể, the ride to Chợ Rã (30min.) should cost 20,000Đ; hard bargaining is necessary. Have the hotel call up to an hour ahead of time for the motorcycle, since nobody seems to be in a rush. From Chợ Rã, the direct bus to Hà Nội leaves once daily (5am; 7hr.; 50,000Đ). It is also possible to get to Hà Nội during the morning and early afternoon via Bàc Can (2hr.; minibuses leave frequently; 15,000Đ). No buses leave from Chợ Rã to Cao Bằng, so it's best to take a *xe ôm* to Nà Phăc (1½hr.; 60,000Đ) and then hop one of the buses heading north on Rte. 3 toward Cao Bằng. If you're on a tight budget, you can take a minibus from Chợ Rã bound for one of the southern destinations and have it drop you on the highway.

ACCOMMODATIONS AND FOOD

If you're tackling Ba Bể by public transportation, it's best to stay at the **Ba Bể National Park Guesthouse** ❸ (☎894 026), located just past park headquarters, 2km from the lake. Ask for the Type 3 rooms (150,000Đ); they're by far the cheapest. On weekdays the place is a ghost town, but call ahead and reserve for weekends since the park fills up with Vietnamese tourists. For those who have private transportation, it is possible to stay in Chơ Rã and commute into the park, but the accommodations in Chơ Rã are no better than those in the park. Instead, stay at one of the **stilt houses** ❶ along the lake, where prices are about 40,000-70,000Đ and the experience is more fun. They can arrange overnight stays at park headquarters; if you prefer, it's possible to drive in and discover a guesthouse on your own.

VIETNAM

There is a **restaurant** ❶ on the park premises, which is also run by the government and is conveniently located beside one of the hotel buildings. The food compensates for the slim pickings—the fish (20,000Đ) is fried up fresh. For breakfast, there are noodles with beef or a fried egg (7000Đ) and at lunchtime, *phở* (10,000Đ) and dinner-type edibles are available. It is also possible to purchase drinks and snacks at the hotel or the boat landing, but the laws of supply and demand inflate the price; it's a good idea to stock up on fruit and water before entering the park.

SIGHTS AND HIKING

Whether or not you intend to take a guided tour, the park headquarters can be instrumental in planning your stay. Make sure you wear good footwear and bring lots of water wherever you go. There are three guides in Ba Bể National Park, and the rate is 75,000Đ for a half-day, 150,000Đ for full-day boat tour, and up to 300,000Đ per day for strenuous treks (although, in contrast to the boat tours, this price is negotiable). It's best to get a group together, since trips are the same price regardless of the group size. It is also possible to go without a guide, but communication and trails can prove tricky, particularly on less-established routes.

If you're averse to guided tours, take a boat across the lake (open daily 6am-6:30pm; 10,000Đ each way) and strike out from there. If you hope to visit certain minority groups, check the map by tourist headquarters with information on each village. As a general rule of thumb, **Tay, Nūng,** and **Kinh** live by rivers and do not dress in traditional garb. The **Dao** live in middle mountain regions, and the **Hmong** villages are the most remote, located in the upper mountains.

CAO BẰNG ☎26

Financially poor but culturally rich, Cao Bằng remains the archetypal undiscovered gem for travelers. Cao Bằng town, the capital of the province, acts as an ideal hub from which to venture out into the picturesque countryside. Rough roads cross corn fields and wind up high mountain passes to modest villages. Along the Băng Giang River, boys fish with bamboo poles and talkative women sell lychee fruit. Though the nine different ethnic minorities who live in the province differ in many ways, from dress to customs, they all share an unusual enthusiastic energy that makes the region feel oddly homey and familiar. In heavy rain you might be handed an umbrella, and at an impassable road (which isn't rare), you'll undoubtedly be offered a cigarette.

TRANSPORTATION

Motorcycle taxis will take you anywhere in Cao Bằng for 2000-4000Đ. The **bus station** (☎852 248) is across the river, 50m north of the bridge. Buses go to: Hà Nội (direct 60,000Đ; via Thài Nguyên 6:30am and 7pm; 45,000Đ) and Lạng Sơn (5:30am; 40,000Đ). It is also possible to get to Ba Bể National Park by taking the Hà Nội bus to Nà Phăc (2½hr.; 30,000-40,000Đ) and then taking a motorcycle taxi the rest of the way (1½hr.; 60,000Đ). Minibuses and provincial buses leave from Cao Bằng's bus station sporadically throughout the day, including afternoon trips to Hà Nội. The schedule changes frequently, so it's best to call and confirm times.

PRACTICAL INFORMATION

Tourist Office: In one of the offices through the yellow gate on Sô Nhà, accessible either from Nguyễn Du or the southern side of the goods market. Very little English spoken.

Currency Exchange: 1 block north of the bridge, turn left for the **Bank for Foreign Investment and Development,** 49 Xuân Trương (☎852 163), which is open daily 7am-4:30pm.

Police: Behind the goods market. Walk west on Đàm Quang Trưng 1 block and turn left onto Hoàng Như. The station will be on the right side of the street. **Emergency:** ☎113.

Pharmacies: Scattered all throughout the city; 2 are located on Nguyễn Du, south of the market off Kim Đông (☎855 069 and 852 338). Open daily 5am-7pm.

Hospital: 3km south of town on highway 4A. **Emergency:** ☎115.

International Telephone: Available at the post office or at the small calling center, 39 Chợ Xanh (☎841 147), just north of the bridge by the entrance to the food market.

Internet Access: Cao Bằng Network Club, 378 Hoàng Văn Thụ (☎858 044). Walking north of the bridge, take your first left onto Xuân Trường and then take your first right. Well lit, with a fast connection for 3000Đ per hr.; keep track of your time, since the employees will happily throw in some extra minutes. Open daily 7am-10:30pm.

Post Office: On Hoàng Đìng Ging, which intersects Kim Đông just south of the bridge. The post office is 2 blocks down the street, diagonally across from the Hồ Chí Minh statue. Open daily 7am-5pm.

ACCOMMODATIONS AND FOOD

Generally, hotels in Cao Bằng are both attractive and expensive. Bargaining takes some effort, but is nonetheless a worthwhile endeavor, given the asking prices. **Hoàng Anh Hotel ❷,** 131 Kim Đông, is the best deal in town. The hotel has a sleepy lobby, nice owners, and pleasant rooms; some overlook the water. (☎858 969. Doubles 100,000Đ.) **Thàn Loan Hotel ❸,** 159 Vườn Cam, is 100m north of the bridge, starring an enthusiastic staff and spacious rooms with high ceilings and wide wooden beds. (Simple breakfast included. Rooms US$15; less for extended stays.)

Restaurants in Cao Bằng offer some of the north's tastiest culinary treats. Those on a tight budget might choose to capitalize on the endless *phở* options throughout the city, or frequent the food stands that set up every evening in front of the food market. Most of Cao Bằng heads home around 8pm—be sure to eat early. **Việt Béo ❹,** 28 Lý Tư Trọng, is a 10min. walk north of the bridge, past the Thàn Loan Hotel. Turn left at the soon-to-be stadium; the restaurant is halfway down the block. Most fish are around 90,000Đ per kg; the *cá qúa* is excellent. (☎850 087. Open daily 6am-11pm.) **Phô Núi ❷,** 3-10 Nà Cạn, is across the river, a 10min. walk south of the bridge on the first street. The lengthy menu includes crab (85,000Đ per kg) and the best beef in town (25,000Đ). The tiki-torch atmosphere, with fruit hanging from the ceiling, somehow manages to make this place even more charming. (☎850 878. Open daily 9am-8pm.) **Hợp Trường Restaurant ❸,** 8 Băng Giang, is a 5min. walk north of the bridge along the riverbank. This place specializes in those meats you've been dying to try, including cat (40,000Đ for a healthy, delicious portion) and snake. (☎854 788. Open daily 9am-10pm.)

SIGHTS AND DAYTRIPS

Pulsing waterfalls, breathtaking caves, soothing lakes, and lively villages provide much more than a day's worth of sight-seeing. The below are just a sampling; Montagnard markets, particularly, are too numerous to list. Sights are most easily accessible by *xe ôm*, which generally runs 180,000-200,000Đ for a full day. Water, sunscreen, snacks, and a camera are essential.

THANG SEN LAKE. Crossing the Băng Giang Bridge and climbing alongside a creek, the road to Thang Sen Lake goes over Mã Phục Pass. The views alone are worth the trip. Above the pass a small road with a bamboo gate overhead branches off of the main highway. Thang Sen is a 15min. drive down this road.

The lake is still—no artificial sound, no ugly telephone poles, and no pushy vendors. No other tourist spot so fluently captures the sacred quiet of Cao Bằng's countryside. The best views are available from one of the bamboo rafts dotting the lake. Finding someone who is willing to take you out is tricky but well worth the effort. Ask around at the tiny settlement by the head of the road and expect to pay 10,000Đ. Once you find a boatman, staying on the raft (four bamboo logs tied loosely together) is even trickier. The highlight of Thang Sen Lake—a beautiful domed **cave** with an entrance and a small skylight—is accessible only by boat. *(Thang Sen Lake is a 1hr. drive from Cao Bằng. Most of the road is paved. The trip costs 60,000Đ by motorbike and an exorbitant 400,000Đ by SUV. It is also possible to make the trip using minibuses headed for Trá Lính. The return trip costs roughly 30,000Đ but involves a hike of several hours from the turn-off (marked by a bamboo gate). There are no facilities at the lake.)*

BÁN GIỐC WATERFALL AND NGƯỜM NGAO CAVE

Bán Giốc requires a permit that is available in Cao Bằng at the immigration office, 54 Kim Đông, in a large building south of the goods market. Open daily 7-11:30am and 1:30-5pm. Strangely, a permit is the same price (US$10) regardless of whether you're traveling solo or in a pair. The cave requires no paperwork, but there is an 18,000Đ entrance fee that includes both a guide and a flashlight. A motorcycle costs roughly 200,000Đ for the full-day trip. During the rainy season, the road is sometimes impassable, so check at your hotel before leaving.

Bán Giốc Waterfall and **Ngườm Ngao Cave** are a 3hr. drive northwest of Cao Bằng. The road, most of which is paved, climbs past Montagnard towns and villages—most notably those of the Nũng—before opening into even more vast and beautiful territory. Twenty-five kilometers past Trùng Khánh, the road splits; a sign directs you right toward the cave, failing to mention that the waterfall is to the left.

Bán Giốc, which is fed by the river Quay Xuan, is the largest waterfall in Vietnam and acts as an indistinct boundary with China. The approach from the parking lot is gorgeous—the road weaves through rice paddy fields and crossing bridges (which charge a frustrating 1000Đ) before arriving at the base of the trembling falls. The riverbank is a great place to swim, picnic (food and snacks are available on the road from Cao Bằng), watch the fisherman, or survey the intense Chinese tourist infrastructure across the waters.

The nearby **Ngườm Ngao Cave** is also a worthy and impressive sight. A 10min. walk through corn fields leads to a subtle opening in a rock face. Inside, the cave is an elaborate and dizzying system of tunnels—to get through, one must pass under arches, climb slopes, and dodge columns. A guide, required for good reason, will point out various stalagmite formations resembling cacti and waterfalls. As the cave deepens, the rooms increase in size and the rocks begin to sparkle under the glow of the torch. The final cavity, which is by far the largest and is illuminated by beams of natural light, leads back outside. Don't be fooled by the guide's sandals—the path is treacherous and proper shoes are a must.

LẠNG SƠN ☎25

Over the last 2000 years, the pass at Lạng Sơn has seen many uninvited, heavily armed Chinese guests. Most recently, Chinese troops razed Lạng Sơn in 1979 as part of Deng Xiaoping's effort to "teach the Vietnamese a lesson"—the lesson, however, was ultimately taught to the Chinese instead. Today, most travelers pass through only briefly while en route to China.

Buses drop people at the **Ngộ Quyền bus station**—left off Trần Đăng Ninh, 1km north of the Lê Lợi intersection—unless they have to transfer buses en route from Hà Nội, in which case they terminate at the **Lạng Sơn bus station** off Lê Lợi on Ngộ Quyền, 2km east of the intersection with Trần Đăng Ninh. Buses run from Ngộ

Quyền bus station to Đồng Đăng on the border (20-30min.; 20,000Đ) and Cao Bằng (5am; 6hr.; 40,000Đ). Buses from Lạng Sơn bus station leave for Hà Nội (3½-4½hr.; buses leave when full 6am-1pm; 35,000Đ). **Minibuses** to Hà Nội (4hr.; 50,000-80,000Đ for foreigners) and the border (20min.; up to 50,000Đ) ply the streets. **Trains** from Lạng Sơn Station (☎873 452), at the end of Lê Lợi, leave for Hà Nội (5-6hr.; 2 and 6am; 25,000Đ hard seat, 32,000Đ soft seat). For merchandise and comestibles featuring delicious fruit (pears, plums, and persimmons are all grown locally), try the **market** on Bâc Sơn, which runs north from Lê Lợi near the major intersection. Turn left off of Bâc Sơn when the stalls thin out; straight ahead will be Trần Đăng Ninh with another marketplace selling wares imported from China.

Most hotels are scattered along Trần Đăng Ninh near the center of town. A 10min. walk north of the major intersection, **Khách Sạn Hoàng Vũ ❸**, 240 Trần Đăng Ninh, has airy rooms and amicable service. (☎873 738. Doubles 130,000Đ; triples 160,000Đ.) **Hoàng Sơn Hải Hotel ❹**, 57 Tam Thanh, might just be worth the steeper price. Turn onto Tam Thanh just north of Lê Lợi's intersection with Trần Đăng Ninh and walk 100m. The entrance is up a set of marble stairs, past the goldfish tanks and colorful mural. Rooms are very well kept, with spectacular views overlooking all of Lạng Sơn. (☎870 199. Doubles US$20; triples US$25.) Trần Đăng Ninh and Lê Lợi host the usual *phở* shops (full meals 10,000-20,000Đ). Walking south on Trần Đăng Ninh, turning left by the bridge onto Nguyễn Tri Phương leads to a **market.** Toward the back of the first aisle a woman sells particularly tender chicken feet sandwiches (3000Đ)—which is to say, as tender as chicken feet get. Another good street kitchen can be found on Bắc Són, which intersects with the northern side of Lê Lợi near the main intersection. Under a blue tent across from the neon Bào Việt sign, boys and girls cook up hefty portions of fried rice; just point at what you want included (10,000Đ). **Minh Quang Restaurant ❷**, 44 Ngộ Quyền, offers a peaceful refuge from Lạng Sơn's noisy streets. Walk east on Lê Lợi and bear right when the road splits. Walk through the alley and turn into the dining room. The grilled beef is topped with sesame seeds and then fried with chunks of pineapple and garlic. Also available are snake head and sparrow. Bon appetit! Most entrees are 15,000-20,000Đ; be sure to check prices before you order. (☎870 417. Open daily 8am-8pm.)

BORDER CROSSING: ĐỒNG ĐĂNG/PINGXIANG. Just north of Lạng Sơn at the northern terminus of Rte. 1 lies the tiny border town of Đồng Đăng. The border is past two checkpoints, 3km beyond Đồng Đăng at the Hữu Nghị (Friendship) Crossing. To enter China here, your **visa** must have a Đồng Đăng **exit stamp.** Tourist cafes in Hà Nôi can procure Chinese visas (US$34, plus US$20 extra for American, Canadian, German, and Japanese citizens) and can change the exit stamp on Vietnamese visas (US$30). **Trains** to **Beijing, China** leave from Đồng Đăng train station, just south of town. Book tickets in Hà Nội. Travelers have found Chinese customs here low-key, quick, and easy.

NORTHERN CENTRAL VIETNAM

Rushing from Hà Nội or Hội An, most visitors opt to skip over the treasures of northern central Vietnam. They should at least look out the window. The landscape is unbelievable, comprised of limestone cliffs and lonely mountain passes tumbling east into the sea. Removed from the traditional backpackers' beat, and deprived of the safe comforts of catered travel packages, a zigzag through the region also offers foreign visitors a truer taste of Vietnamese life.

NINH BÌNH ☎30

One day, travelers will wise up and notice that Ninh Bình is more than just a place to stop for breakfast on the way to Hà Nội from Huế or vice versa. Until then, one of the most beautiful parts of Vietnam is yours for the taking. Dramatic scenery, historical intrigues, religious pilgrimage sites, and an endangered animal sanctuary, all within 50km of town, constitute a region that deserves to be explored. A slowly blossoming city, Ninh Bình itself is not overflowing with alluring sights, but instead serves as an ideal jumping-off point. Accommodations here are among the best in Vietnam; an intense (and hilarious) rivalry among lodging choices has kept prices reasonable and quality high.

TRANSPORTATION. The bus station is on Lê Đại Hành opposite the bridge that leads into Trần Hùng Đạo. **Buses** leave for: Hà Nội (1½-2hr.; every 15min. 5am-4pm; 20,000Đ); HCMC (42hr.; 6am 3-5 times per week; 211,000Đ); Hải Phòng (6hr.; 5:45am; 20,000Đ); and Kim Sơn/Phát Diệm (50min., every hr. 7am-5:30pm, 5000Đ; return from Kim Sơn 4pm). Additional buses to Hà Nội can be flagged down anywhere along the radio-tower side of Trần Hùng Đạo. An easier option is to get **tourist buses** which run daily to **Hà Nội** (1½-2hr., 7pm, US$3-4) and Huế (11hr., 9pm, US$5-7). Seats can be booked at any hotel, but the best seats are usually already taken. The **train station** lies at the end of Hoàng Hoa Thám. Walk up the street from the bus station on Lê Đại Hành, turn right, and walk 200m or so until the road ends at the foot of the station's stairs. Trains go north to Hà Nội (2-3½hr.; 3 per day; 26,000-282,000Đ) and south to Vinh (3½-4½hr.; 28,000-130,000Đ), followed by Huế (12½-15hr.; 134,000-282,000Đ) and HCMC (40hr.; 366,000-768,000Đ). If traveling to Huế and HCMC, buy your ticket at least a day in advance. To get to Vinh, arrive no later than 15min. before the train's scheduled departure. Train times and prices are posted on a bulletin outside the main entrance. The local **taxi** service can also get you where you want to go. (☎876 876; www.universe.fpt.vn. 14,000Đ per km for first 2km, 7000Đ per km for next 3-20km, 5000Đ per km for the following 21-50km, and 2000Đ per km or negotiable for longer journeys.)

ORIENTATION AND PRACTICAL INFORMATION. Ninh Bình lies 96km south of Hà Nội on Hwy. 1A. Most of the town lies along the highway **(Trần Hưng Đạo).** The slightly less hectic part of the town stems alongside **Lê Đại Hành,** the second main street. The streets appear to run parallel to each other until they merge past the bus station at a bridge at the south end of town that leads travelers on the highway to Hồ Chí Minh City and Huế. **Hải Thượng Lãn Ông** intersects Trần Hưng Đạo next to the radio tower at the south edge of town. Just south of the radio tower, **Lý Tự Trọng** heads west from Trần Hưng Đạo and terminates in front of the **hospital** (☎871 030). The **post and telephone office** (with fax) is inside the **GPO,** which is two buildings to the right of the radio tower and near the bridge, on Trần Hưng Đạo; look for the red "Bưu Điện" sign. (☎871 104. Open summer M-F 6am-10pm, Sa-Su 7-9pm; winter daily 6:30am-9:30pm.) Hotels will exchange *đồng* for dollars, but to exchange traveler's checks or obtain a cash advance, head up Trần Hưng Đạo, past the Star Hotel. On the right is the brand new **Industrial and Commercial Bank of Vietnam,** 1 Lương Văn Tuý, in a large yellow building. (☎872 675. Open M-Sa 7-11am and 1-4:30pm.) All the hotels provide easy **Internet** access, though it's slow and expensive compared with the cybercafes in town. Those staying on the main Trần Hưng Đạo can visit the new and spacious cybercafe **Sáu Mủoi,** 60 Trần Hưng Đạo (500Đ per 10 min., 3000Đ per hour).

ACCOMMODATIONS. In response to the town's increasing popularity, new hotels pop up daily, adding themselves to the already existing slew of accommodations, all of which include restaurants, Western bike rentals for US$1 per day, motorbikes for US$4-5 per day, and tourist information and tours.

Popular with budget travelers and returning guests, **Queen Mini Hotel ❶**, 21 Hoàng Hoa Thám, 150m directly outside the station, has the best deals in town, a helpful and smiling staff, and, like most other low-end Vietnamese hotels, the occasional insect friend. (Tiny but sunny single with fan and no tub US$3, comfortable rooms with bathtubs and A/C US$5-15.) Though removed both from the town and the train and bus stations, **Thanh Thuy's Guest House ❶**, 128 Lê Hồng Phong, assures guests quiet and replenishing rest. The German- and (sort of) English-speaking owners have just added a new wing with sparkling bathrooms to join their older rooms. (☎871 811; fax 880 441. Sturdy Japanese mountain bikes 15,000Đ per day, Chinese models 8000Đ. Internet 3000Đ per hr. Laundry 10,000-15,000Đ per kg. Tiny attic single with fan US$2; old doubles with fan and bathtub US$5-6; new, spacious doubles with private bath and fan US$8, with A/C US$15.)

Right next door to the train station is the small family-run **New Guest House ❶,** where the friendly service reflects its overall homey atmosphere. Like in most hotels, the older rooms are cheaper, while the freshly renovated ones start at a slightly higher price. Most rooms are doubles and sport tubs in the bathrooms. All rooms have a TV. (☎872 137; fax 874 252. Older singles with fan US$3-6, with A/C US$5-15; Newer rooms US$6/US$7-9.) Mr. De at **Thuy Anh Hotel ❸,** 55 Trương Han Sieu, off Trần Hưng Đạo in the center of town, leads the quality hotel pack with luxurious rooms and hefty prices. Full tourist service includes full-day tour (US$14), motorbike rental (US$5), and Internet (500Đ per min.). More expensive rooms come with 30min. of free Internet, and the priciest provide 2 free bikes per day and complimentary laundry service. (☎871 602; fax 876 934. Free transport to and from train and bus stations. Tourist information and expensive tours of the surroundings. Doubles with A/C and bath from US$10-25. MC/V.)

FOOD. For the famed local specialty *miện lúón* (eel in vermicelli noodle soup; 10,000Đ), or *canh cua* (crab soup; 10,000Đ) with *cà ghém muố* (a local pickled vegetable delight), stop by **Co'm Bính Dân ❷,** at the intersection of Trần Hưng Đạo and Van Giang, diagonally across from the Thuy Anh and directly across from the Star Hotel. Extra seating awaits upstairs. Grab the purple paper on the table to wipe off your chopsticks and bowl like the local guests do. The tree-shaded street in front of Queen Hotel has numerous local *phở* and *cơm* shops. The one at 22 Đường 7 Trần Phú, with its kitchen-turned-cafeteria look, caters to friendly young twenty-somethings on break or returning from work. (Open daily 11am-8pm. Serving of tofu, veggies, or various meats 1000-4000Đ.) Numerous **cafes** line the streets off of Trần Hưng Đạo. For a cool mid-afternoon or late evening snack, stop by the clean and friendly **Sinh Tổ ❶,** 49 Phúc Lôc Phúe Thánh. Try the Sinh Tổ Bo (guava ice cream, 7000Đ) or just ask for some mango or orange juice to cool you off (3000Đ). You might be served a slew of friendly questions along with your drink. (☎880 709. Open daily 7am-11pm.)

SHOPPING. Turning onto Van Giang at the Star Hotel will lead you to the largest market in Ninh Bình. Fresh fruits and vegetables are sold alongside slabs of meat, snails, and even eel. Amid the numerous stalls are locals selling hats and clothes. If you left any article of clothing at home, the market is the place to purchase a stylish hat like the ones worn by local women (6000-8000Đ) or dress shirts that range as much in price as they do in material quality (30,000-70,000Đ). Don't forget to ask around and don't fear to state a lower price, as a foreign face will rarely evoke a reasonable quote. (Open daily 5am-7pm.)

TAM CỐC ☎30

Ninh Bình's rice fields become otherworldly in the Tam Cốc (Three Caves) area. The mountains have earned the area the nickname "Hạ Long Bay without water," a moniker borne out by the limestone karsts which dominate the landscape. Bamboo skiffs float to and through the caves and past spectacular cliffs, Lilliputian villages, and lonely farming communities. Much of the town itself thrives on the work of local artisans who embroider cloth and line the stalls of Nhân Cơm Dật on the way to and from the three-cave tour.

The best way to visit Tam Cốc is by motorbike, bicycle, or car. To reach Tam Cốc from Ninh Bình, head 4km south on Hwy. 1, veering right at the Tam Cốc turn-off. Cross a short bridge and follow the road 4km to where it ends in the center of the town—the boat drop-off and pickup point.

Though most travelers choose to explore Tam Cốc in one day, some—especially those traveling from Hà Nội—stay overnight. The **Chu Vân Báu ❸**, on Văn Lâm, is the only hotel in town, providing guests with clean doubles with refrigerators, A/C, and private bath (US$10). The **restaurant** has good prices. (☎618 058. French- and English-speaking staff.) Numerous *phở* shops line the street alongside the boat-docking end of the river. For a set menu, join the groups heading into **Thế Long Restaurant ❸**, on Nhân Cơm Dật. Though the set menu is targeted at groups of four, just ask to mix a few options into a serving for one. (☎618 077. 15,000-100,000Đ. Open M-Sa 6:30am-11pm.)

NEAR NINH BÌNH AND TAM CỐC

VIETNAM

KENH GA

The most picturesque and breathtaking way to reach any of the local sights is to hop on a moped with a local tour guide. If you book a guide, ask to take the longer but worthwhile back-road way that passes villages and majestic golden limestone mountains. If you decide to venture to Kenh Ga by yourself, you can ask one of the hotel tour guides to sketch you a map of the back road, though sticking to major roads might be a safer bet. From the Ninh Bình bus station, head north up Đường Trần Hưng Đạo 11km out of town. Head left 400m after passing a bridge, following the sign to Cúc Phương National Park. Continue straight for another 10km. In the center of Me town look for the yellow "Bưu Điện" sign pointing visitors toward Kenh Ga. Turn left onto the road. 2km will bring you to the end of the village and a cafe with a green sunroof. You can buy tickets for the boat tour inside. The boats that take travelers to Kenh Ga can only be reached by motorbike. ☎868 560. 2½-3hr. trips available daily 7am-4pm. 40,000Đ per person; 80,000Đ if you take the tour solo.

The magnificent natural beauty of the town's surroundings knows no equal. Still largely undiscovered, though gaining popularity with backpackers looking for hidden treasures, Kenh Ga remains an amazing sight to explore without getting lost in flocks of tourists.

Though its name means "chicken canal," no chickens graze the canals of this river city. Rather, its inhabitants subsist off surrounding rice fields and the snails, crabs, and fish that get tangled in their nets. The best time to catch Kenh Ga at its utmost natural beauty is in July, the first of three months when the river floods, simultaneously swallowing many village homes and leaving locals to roam the river on houseboats until the water level falls. Though the **boat tour** (see below) is named after the floating village, the excursion captures more than that: it encompasses a trip past the spectacular **limestone mountains** that jut out from the rice fields and the river that gently meanders through them.

After passing the village, Vietnamese guides land the boat to embark on a 2km walk along rice fields and a short hike along the mountainside to reach the entrance to a water-carved **cave** that lies inside. Bring your own lunch or wait to return to the mainland, where you can snack at slightly inflated prices or try your bargaining skills at the local food stands sprinkled throughout the town.

FLOATING TOUR OF THE THREE CAVES OF TAM CỐC

To take a floating tour of the three caves and Tam Cốc's rice fields, buy a ticket at one of the green metal booths that stand at the junction of the paved road that leads into the town and the dirt bank where local merchants sell hats and drinks. 55,000Đ per person, including the nearby temple and pagoda. Open daily 7am-6pm. Arrive early to beat the crowds, sun, and boat vendors.

While floating in and out of passages carved in limestone by the now-peaceful river, visitors with a keen eye can spot locals working atop the jutting mountains, and a glance at the river bank provides a look into the lives of locals who work the golden rice fields under the blazing sun. Midway through the trip, the boat stops at a small shrine before returning along the same path. Floating alongside tourists, boat vendors approach boats and try to cajole visitors into buying drinks or food, if not for themselves then for their rower; tourists should know that many times the rowers simply sell the drinks back to vendors at a lower price. Tipping the driver might be a more direct option for those wanting to thank him or her. Remember to bring an umbrella, sunscreen, and camera. Lest you forget, local merchants who crowd the launching point for the boats have umbrellas ready for rent (5000Đ), while locals with camera in hand paddle boats alongside tourists.

HOA LƯ

A guide can bring you through fields of rice and local villages on the way back from Kenh Ga. From Ninh Bình, head north on Hwy. 1 for 6km, then take a left at the "Welcome to Hoa Lư ancient capital" sign and continue 6km farther, until the ticket booth and parking lot filled with souvenir and food stands pops up on your left. From the parking lot, continue straight and hook a right over the bridge. The entrance to the first temple is about 30m further. Bring a lunch to enjoy in the quiet gardens or grab something at the stand in the parking lot or in the local village. Open daily 7am-6pm. 10,000Đ for access to both temples and the mountain stairway, children 12 and under 3000Đ. To catch a ferry, wave the villagers on the opposite side to the foot of the bridge and ask for a ride. 30,000Đ per person.

Hoa Lư, the capital of Đại Cồ Việt, the first independent Việt state following the millennium of Chinese rule, lies 12km north of town in a valley ringed by volcanic peaks. It was chosen for its geographic location, which made it virtually impregnable, and served as the capital from AD 968 until Lý Công Uẩn, founder of the Lý Dynasty, moved the capital to Thăng Long (modern-day Hà Nội) in 1011. Nothing remains of the citadel. Two **temples** date back to the 17th century. The first, on the way from the ticket booth, commemorates Đinh Bộ Lĩnh (Đinh Tiên Hoàng), the first Vietnamese king to declare himself emperor. On each side of the temple stand two smaller structures. The one on the right is an imperial exhibit where those who don't speak Vietnamese can admire shots of the surrounding countryside, while the second is a simple display of nearby fauna that includes 577 various species of plants. While modest on the outside, the interior of the temple is carved from dark wood and decorated with golden signs and numerous dragons.

PHÁT DIỆM

You can reach the town and its main attraction—the cathedral—with an organized tour from any of the Ninh Bình hotels, or simply by renting a motorbike and a guide for the day (US$4-5, with guide US$6-9). The town is 28km southeast of Ninh Bình. From Trần Hưng Đạo, head east over the river, pass the bus station, and cross over the railroad tracks. Head straight into Phát Diệm (Kim Sơn), then continue 1km and veer left at a blue sign with an arrow heading straight into the Phát Diệm Cathedral. Mass is held daily at 5am and 5:30pm, though curious onlookers should come during visiting hours only. ☎862 058; tgmpdiem@hn.vnn.vn. Open daily 7:30-11:30am and 2:30-5pm. Free tour, although it's customary to give a 10,000Đ offering.

The center of Vietnamese Catholicism is the **Phát Diệm Cathedral,** one of the 30 or so churches in this area built by French Jesuits. Built between 1875 and 1899 by Vietnamese **Father Sáu,** it was nearly destroyed in 1972 by American bombs but was quickly repaired afterward. The edifice blends Chinese styles (pagodas on the rooftops and belltower, Buddhist lotuses carved on the walls of the Stone Chapel) and Western ones (neo-Romanesque columns and layout). Thousands of Vietnamese Catholics from the Ninh Bình diocese and elsewhere come to visit the cathedral, its peaceful grounds (which encompass a lake that rests ahead of the belltower), and the beautiful gardens found near the back of the monastery. Wander into the monastery grounds and ask for an English- or French-speaking guide to give you a tour of the small museum of Vietnamese Catholic culture that rests behind the cathedral, as well as a glimpse of the cathedral's interior, where you'll find a 2-ton bell that resounds across a 10km radius. Even if you forego the detailed tour of the one-room museum and the cathedral and its surroundings, you can still sneak a peek at the wooden interior and the ornate golden altar through the windows next door to the cathedral's main entrance.

BÍCH ĐỘNG PAGODAS

To reach the pagodas, take the road on your left when you face the loading point; this road winds past the boats and through the town, curving once more as it passes the only official-looking building in town—a memorial to veterans of the French and Vietnam Wars. Continue past Tam Cốc for 2km until the road terminates in a small square in front of the pagodas, where once more you can purchase souvenirs and eat or drink at one of the small cafes. For the backdoor entrance, backtrack 50m and take a right on the narrow path. Follow this for another 100m around the mountain, until you see the boats and the cave entrance. Open daily 7am-5pm. Price included in the floating tour, above.

These pagodas date back to AD 1428, when two Buddhists, Chí Klên and Chí Hể, became brothers in search of a place where they could continue their religious studies. When they found the breathtaking sights of Ngũ Nhạc Sơn, or "fire mountain," they built the first and highest of the three Bích Động Pagodas, which perch at varying heights on the mountainside. A stairway leads past these beautiful temples and through a grotto, yielding fantastic views of the cliffs and surrounding farmlands. They are especially beautiful during harvest season in June, when the fields resemble a yellow sea. Inside, take notice of the tablets carved in Chinese—once the only language studied in Vietnam. It's possible to enter the pagodas from the rear, via a torchlight boat trip through the low-hanging cave followed by a short climb over the front side of the mountain.

CÚC PHƯƠNG NATIONAL PARK

Nature-lovers may escape to the Cúc Phương National Park, 45km north of Ninh Bình. The park is an excellent daytrip, offering hikes and wildlife. The **Endangered Primate Rescue Center** provides a much-appreciated antidote to over-exposure to sad caged bears in local zoos.

TRANSPORTATION AND ORIENTATION. Since it's beyond the limits of local transportation, the best way to reach the park is on motorbike. To get there, follow the directions to Kenh Ga, but pass over the left turn at Bưu Điện and continue straight for another 20km. If you can't drive yourself, the price for a local to take you there and back is hefty (around 80,000Đ); it may be wiser to hop on an organized tour from Ninh Bình. (Motorbike US$10 at Queen Mini Hotel, US$14 at Thanh Thuy's; two-day trip by car US$42-65 at the Thuy Anh Hotel.)

Once inside, it is easy to maneuver around the park. The main road splits the park in two, with trails branching off in either direction. The park "center" and the starting point of six of its trails lies 20km from the entrance gate, while the first trail open to visitors without a park guide begins after a 10min. ride into the heart of the forest. A road open to cars and cyclists lies on the park's southern periphery. The **Visitor Information Center** resides in the first building on the left. The ticket **booth** and **gate** are perched 50m down the road.

PRACTICAL INFORMATION. Local hotels offer one- or two-day **tours** of the park, the latter including a night at the Mường Village. However, only tours led by a guide and arranged through the park authorities have full access to both marked and unmarked trails. These can last from one day to six days, for those wishing to fully exhaust the park's possibilities. (One-day hikes US$10-15. Groups and full-day guide US$20 per day.) The **entrance fee** for adults is 40,000D, for children 20,000Đ. Bring a meal; food in the park is scarce and overpriced.

ENDANGERED PRIMATE RESCUE CENTER. Hidden behind a metal fence, the Center lies just beyond the Park Gate, and before the Visitor Center. Inside reside 15 of Vietnam's 25 species of primates, which are brought to the center for rehabilitation before being set free into the wild. Some of the residents have been confiscated from hunters, who sell the monkeys to restaurants where they are consumed illegally as a delicacy, or to China, where the primates are killed and used to make medicine. Opened in 1993, the Center, once strictly a research facility, now allows animal lovers to visit its current residence. (Open daily 9-11am and 1:30-4pm. 15-30min. tours every 30 min. Buy tickets at entrance gate (40m past Visitor Center. English guided tour 10,000Đ.) On the way back to the entrance gate stop by the Visitor Center to sneak a peek at small ecological exhibits and illegal poaching exhibits as well. (Open daily 8am-4:30pm. Free.)

HIKING. You can pick up a free brochure with a map of the park's routes at the ticket booth. The trails open to visitors who opt out of a park guide are limited to the Cave of Prehistoric Man, the Ancient Tree, the Thousand-Year-Old Tree, and the Palace Cave. After a 30min. climb up the mountain from the trail head, you can enter the **Cave of Prehistoric Man** (Don Nguoi Xua). Once inside, crawl through small passages to reach the innermost enclosure, where tapping on stalactite-like formations on the wall fills the cave with sounds of drums.

INIQUITOUS DELICACIES

Vietnam is renowned for rare culinary delicacies, including monkeys' brains. Most accounts of the dish fail to mention, however, that the practice is neither legal nor common. Poachers capture the animals and sell them to Chinese tradesmen and Vietnamese restaurants. The former use the brains and blood for medication, while the latter prepare them as gourmet meals for the wealthy.

The process is far from pleasant: the scalp and brain are removed from the stunned animal. This practice has caused several species to dwindle in numbers; some are even endangered. Their survival lies in the hands of educators, rescue centers, and those willing to sacrifice an adventurous appetite.

Other "exotic" delicacies are also problematic. *Rượu den*, snake-blood vodka, is a famed Vietnamese alcoholic rite of passage. The two available types are white and yellow snakes: yellow ones taste like chicken and need no special preparation. Their poisonous white counterparts must be neutralized before being dropped in vodka. More than just a delicacy, vodka mixed with snake blood is believed to have healing properties against health problems like rheumatism. Unfortunately, locals and travelers fail to realize that endangered species get mixed up in the lot. The message, as always, is: think before you drink.

Another local favorite is a walk in the forest that leads from the Park Center (to the right of the pillar house) to the monumental **Thousand-Year-Old Tree.** After 3km along the path you can take the 10-15min. climb up the mountain to the smaller **Palace Cave,** then backtrack to the original trail. When you reach the tree, continue along the trail on the other side. Three kilometers farther, those with a park or hotel guide can hook a right in the fork in the road and embark upon the 5-6hr. walk to the **Mường Village.** (US$10 for park tour. Return 16km by foot to center or take a US$20 bus back to Ninh Bình.) If you veer left, you'll pass by the luxurious government-owned bungalows and then back to the small parking lot.

VINH ☎38

Historically a poor region, the Nghệ An province—and its capital Vinh—hosted the first Communist rebellion, the Xô Viết Nghệ Tĩnh uprisings. A convenient hub from which to explore the nearby home of Uncle Ho in Làng Kim Liên or the newly emerging resort town of Cửa Lò, Vinh caters both to history buffs and beachgoers.

TRANSPORTATION. A **travel agency** across from the booking office offers tours (open M-F 7:30-11am and 2-5pm). You can pick up a map of Vinh here or at the hotel's reception desk (20,000Đ). The interprovince **bus station** (☎844 127; open daily 4am-5pm), on Lê Lợi, sends early risers to: Hải Phòng (8hr.; 5am; 61,000Đ); Hà Nội (5-6hr.; every 30min.-1hr. 5-10am; 46,000Đ); Huế (5-6hr.; 5am; 57,000Đ). The **train station** (☎824 924) is northwest of the bus station. To get there, turn left from the bus station on Lê Lợi and make another left onto Phan Bội Châu. The station is 1km from the intersection. Trains head daily to: Hà Nội (4½-7hr.; 71,000-171,000Đ); Huế (6-8hr.; 130,000-215,000Đ); Ninh Bình (4-6hr.; 48,000-100,000Đ); Thanh Hóa (3-4hr.; 34,000-81,000Đ).

PRACTICAL INFORMATION. Most of Vinh's restaurants, hotels, and shops are concentrated along Lê Lợi and Quang Trưng, with clusters of cheaper hotels on the north and south fringes of the highway. Cash-starved foreigners should hit the **Vietcombank,** 9 Nguyễn Sỹ Sách, north of the bus station and just east off of Lê Lợi. (☎842 304; www.vietcomebank.com.vn. Cash traveler's checks and get a MC/V advance. Open M-Sa 7:30-11:30am and 1:30-4:30pm.) A DC/MC/V ATM stands outside, ready for battle. The **post office,** 2 Nguyễn Thị Minh Khai, has been newly renovated. To reach it, turn right out of the bus station onto Lê Lợi, veering left onto Nguyễn Thị Minh Khai, then turn right before the small park. The post office is 2km down the road. **Telephones** await inside. **Internet** access and Internet phones are to the left of the main entrance. (☎833 711. Open summer 6:30am-10pm; winter 7am-9pm. Internet 4000Đ per hr.) For fresh fruit and veggies, stop by the town **market,** at the intersection of Quang Trưng and Trần Phú.

ACCOMMODATIONS AND FOOD. If you don't mind a 20min. walk from the heart of city life, settle down at the **Đông Đô Hotel ❷**, 9 Nguyễn Trãi, which boasts cheap, clean, brightly lit, and well-kept doubles with balconies and private baths. (Breakfast included. Doubles with A/C and TV 100,000-160,000Đ.) The hotel's *phở* and *cơm* shop serves hearty meals. (Open daily 7am-9pm.) Those who want to sleep smack in the center of town can easily find a bed at one of the hotels sprinkled around the bus station on Lê Lợi. A left out of the bus station and a short walk down the street leads to the family-run **Hotel Huệ Lộc 1 ❷,** 147 Lê Lợi. Large rooms with private baths and tubs, TV, fridge, and A/C are of better quality than

Huệ Lộc's centrally-located counterparts. (☎585 183. Doubles 150,000Đ.) Across the highway from the bus station and a few doors down is **Hồng Ngoc 2 ❸,** a cabin-like arrangement hidden behind a restaurant. The rooms are dark and worn, but have A/C, TV, and fridges. The accompanying **restaurant ❷** serves up exotic dishes along with old standards. A filling plate of *cơm ga* costs 15,000Đ. Vegetarians may delight in tofu cooked in tomato sauce. (☎841 314; cell 913 548 661. Doubles 120,000Đ; quads 180,000Đ.)

DAYTRIP FROM VINH: LÀNG KIM LIÊN. Communist party members flock from across the country to pay homage to Hồ Chí Minh at his birthplace in the village of **Hoăng Thi,** as well as the thatched house to which his family returned for his formative years (ages 5-10) in **Làng Sen** or **Làng Kim Liên (Lotus Village).** The villages seem to have barely changed from the time when the socialist hero spent his childhood there. Save for a **post office** set on the way to Hồ Chí Minh's birth house, there is little else apart from the historical allure; also, don't expect much in the way of tourist information for English speakers, except for a few signs. The attraction itself is composed of two sights. The first, 2km along the road past the post office and local fish farms, are three hatched huts that form Hồ's proper birth house in **Hoăng Thi.** While two are furnished exactly as the socialist leader knew them during the first years of his life—showing his truly modest roots—the third contains a shrine where visitors are requested to place the first of three bouquets of flowers. The second sight contains the structure of three thatched houses in **Làng Kim Liên;** Hồ Chí Minh's family settled here in 1901 after returning from Huế, where Hồ's father had traveled to study. Here you'll find another shrine awaiting your second bouquet. Ahead on the same path is a museum which pays homage both to the leader and to the socialist movement itself. The most interesting and telling exhibit is located in the center building of the museum. Flowers, food, and burning incense lie at the feet of modern Vietnam's founding father, just as in the temples of the ancient kings. (Open M-Sa 6:30-11am and 2-5pm. Free.)

Snack and souvenir shops crowd both sights. To purchase flowers, head to the museum office located across from the entrance to the leader's birth house in Hoăng Thi. (5000-15,000Đ per bouquet. ☎825 962. Open daily summer 7-11:30am and 1:30-5pm, winter 7:30am-noon and 1:30-5pm.) To reach Làng Kim Liên, which lies 14km from Vinh, you can hop on a bus to Nam Đàm, although it might be easier and quicker to flag one down on Dình Phùng, off of Quang Trưng about 3km south of the bus station (20min., every 30min., 3000Đ). Alternatively, ask a local to give you a lift on his motorbike (20,000-25,000Đ). Hop off when you see a huge blue billboard welcoming you to Làng Kim Liên. The first sight is about 1km down the road that winds past the post office and fishing fields. Make the journey to each sight on foot, or hire a local to drop you off and pick you up at each place. Negotiate a price in advance (5000-15,000Đ).

CỬA LÒ ☎38

A short distance northwest of Vinh, Cửa Lò is one of the most beautiful and newly developed resort towns of the north. Most of the restaurants and hotels lie on one main road, which runs alongside the cafe-packed shore, making Cửa Lò accessible and easy to maneuver. Though the water lacks the crystal-clear quality that Vietnam's northern resorts invariably promise but fail to deliver, it still makes for a pleasant getaway, especially during the week. Weekends tend to see the beach get much more crowded. Since prices are high and the beach spans 7km, though, it's never difficult to find a quiet spot to relax. Three islands surround the beach, two lying on its northern tip and the third protruding from the middle of the ocean.

VIETNAM

Only 17km from Vinh, the new beach resort is easily accessible by motorbike. From the bus station, take a left onto Lê Lợi, hooking the next right onto Nguyễn Sỹ Sách. Continue until the road meets its end and head right on Lê Viết Thuật. About 11km down the road, a sign will indicate a left turn onto Đăc Sản Biển at the light. The road comes to a stop at Cửa Lò's main drag, Bình Minh, about 9km farther down. A one-way trip to or from Vinh on a stranger's seat costs about 20,000Đ. To take the hourly bus to Cửa Lò, just stand along Nguyễn Trãi and flag one down as it heads north, and then west, to Cửa Lò. Be advised that the bus returns less frequently, with the last bus passing through Bình Minh at 5pm. There's **no ATM;** make sure to bring enough cash to last throughout your stay. For **Internet** access, go to 26 Bình Minh, just across the street from the post and telephone office. (☎951 224. Open daily 7am-10pm. 4000Đ per hr.) If you're on the south side, you'll find a packed **Phóng Net** cybercafe in the small park situated in the middle of the beach. (☎949 793. Open daily 7am-11pm. 4000Đ per hr.) The **post office,** 1 Bình Minh, lies on the beach side of Bình Minh. (☎824 105. Open daily 7am-9pm.)

Peace, beauty, and inflated prices are a package deal in Cửa Lò. Cheap lodging is difficult to find; you might be better off daytripping to the resort. Those who would rather avoid the commute can find plain, clean, and well-lit rooms at **Hotel Hồng Tấn ❷,** Bình Minh. (☎824 387. Doubles with TV, A/C, and baths 200,000-250,000Đ.) For a luxurious splurge, look up the **Nghệ An II Hotel ❷,** 100 Bình Minh. Four-person grand suites with bedrooms, roomy private baths, dark paneled sitting rooms, and a private balcony come at a hefty price but can be bargained down (50,000-75,000Đ). Similarly, fully-equipped luxurious triples with pristine private baths run from 350,000-400,000Đ. (☎951 881; fax 824 779. Rooms include satellite TV, refrigerator, A/C, and phone.) A clean and friendly **phở and cơm shop** lies on the way from Vinh on Đăc Sản Biển, on the road's right corner where it intersects Bình Minh when coming in, and to the left when leaving the beach. (☎951 861. Open daily 7am-8pm.) If you're looking for Vietnamese cuisine with a tropical atmosphere, then settle down at the *phở* and *cơm* shop of **Hồng Thắng Hotel ❷,** near the beach park. (☎951 171. Open daily 5am-11pm. Entrees 7000-20,000Đ.)

VIETNAM

HÀ TĨNH ☎39

Visiting Hà Tĩnh, one might be hard-pressed to find examples of the alleged vast strides made by the province to improve tourist services. But a stable tourism infrastructure, by all accounts, is coming soon—in the meantime, visitors shouldn't be dissuaded from seeking out the treasures scattered around the province. The natural beauty of the province is a reward for those who wish to traverse a path as yet untouched by foreign feet.

TRANSPORTATION. As there is no train that passes through the city, Hà Tĩnh is only accessible by bus. The **bus station** stands across from the post office on the main road, Trần Phú. Buses leave daily for: Đồng Hới (3hr.; 5, 6am; 50,000Đ); Đồng Hà (4-5hr.; 5, 6am; 80,000Đ); Hà Nội (5-6hr.; every hr. 4am-10pm; 40,000Đ); Huế (6hr.; 5am; 70,000Đ). For interprovincial travel, flag down buses yourself; otherwise, they may speed past the station without making a stop.

ORIENTATION AND PRACTICAL INFORMATION. While most of Hà Tĩnh's centers of communication are concentrated along the main road **Trần Phú,** alias the infamous Hwy. 1, the town branches east toward the ocean. Both the bus station and the **post office,** 4 Trần Phú (☎855 312; open daily summer 6am-10pm, winter 6:30am-9:30pm), lie along the highway, facing each other. The Hà Tĩnh **tour-**

ist office, 9 Trần Phú, lies to the left of Bình Minh Hotel. The friendly, English-speaking staff provides brochures and information on all sights of natural or historical interest in the province, as well as available modes of transportation. (☎853 610; vkchi2003@yahoo.com. Open M-F 7-11am and 2-9pm.) To change currency and get AmEx/MC/V advances, turn left out of the post office and hook the first left onto Phan Đình Phùng. **Vietcombank,** 11 Phan Đình Phùng, is about 50m down the street. (☎821 202 or 857 002. Open daily summer 7-11:30am and 2-5:30pm; winter 7-11:30am and 1:30-5pm.) A 24hr. **ATM** hides behind the bank. To check email, turn right out of the post office and make a right onto Nguyễn Huy Tự. About 1km down the road you'll find an **Internet** cafe. (Open daily 7am-10pm. 4000Đ per hr.) For pharmaceutical needs, head to the town **market,** where vendors are ready to heal your aches and pains.

ACCOMMODATIONS AND FOOD. As the tourism industry is only beginning to take hold, so far there are only three hotels in all of Hà Tĩnh. The helpful, English-speaking owner at **Hotel Bình Minh ❸,** 9 Trần Phú, rents out motorbikes (10,000Đ per hr.) and provides affordable, comfortable, and fully equipped rooms with private bath. (☎857 890; fax 857 857. A/C, TV, refrigerator, and breakfast included. Three 3rd-class twin-bed singles 80,000Đ; reserve well in advance. Twin-bed doubles 155,000Đ. Double-bed double 300,000Đ.) Budget travelers can try to negotiate a discount at the **Thành Sen ❸,** 1 Nguyễn Côn Trứ. The doubles are spacious and the singles comfortable and clean. (☎855 706; fax 855 484. Singles 120,000Đ; doubles 140,000Đ.) Decent cuisine can be ordered at the restaurant on the ground floor of **Hotel Bình Minh ❷.** (Open daily 6am-9pm. Entrees 7000-20,000Đ.) Popular shops that remain busy into the night line the left of Phan Đình Phùng, near its intersection with the main Trần Phú.

DAYTRIPS. Ethereal white-sand beaches and surreal mountaintop pagodas are all within a day's traveling distance. Allegedly the most beautiful beach in Hà Tĩnh province, **Thiên Cầm** is a popular beach resort in the initial stages of development. Cut off from the eastern coast by mountains on the north and the south, Thiên Cầm's golden shores entertain weekend vacationers looking to escape the hassle of city life, with amenities for unprepared travelers. (Though accessible by paved roads, the beach lies 9km away from the closest bus stop on Hwy. 1, and as such must be reached by motorbike. One-way ride to or from Hà Tĩnh Town costs 25,000-30,000Đ. To reach the beach on your own, turn right out of the bus station and head south along Hwy. 1. Continue for about 20km until you reach the center of a town and a southward facing sign that signals a left turn to Thiên Cầm (east). A 9km drive leads to the resort.) At the top of the mountain which marks the northern tip of the beach is the **Cầm Sơn Pagoda,** built in 600 AD on the Thiên Cầm, or "sky guitar," mountain. Paved steps lead visitors on a 20-30min. ascent to the top of the mountain, while the less patient can reach the peak in half the time via a hike through the woods that breaks off at the stairs and heads left. Though the pagoda itself is a simple structure, the view of the beach below is worth the climb.

Though not as popularly acclaimed as Thiên Cầm beach, **Thạch Hải,** with its crystal-clear waters, is just as beautiful. Sans resort, the white shore stretches along a green forest, with merely a few refreshment stands (coconut milk 4000Đ) and seafood restaurants with fresh clams and crabs. (Easily accessible by motorbike, the trip lasts about 20min. and costs 10,000-15,000Đ one way. To reach the beach on your own, turn into Phan Đình Phùng and continue down the road until a blue billboard on your right invites you to head right and visit the shore.)

Situated in Thien Loc village, 15km northwest of Hà Tĩnh, **Hương Tích Pagoda** lies atop Ngàn Hống mountain. The pagoda remains a site of pilgrimage for local Buddhists, whose signs of worship—freshly burned incense and gifts of food—remain visible for visitors. (Boats run daily 7am-5pm. To reach the launch point of the boat, head north out of Hà Tĩnh (turning left out of the bus station) and continue straight on Hwy. 1 for about 10km until you spot a yellow sign on the right urging you to follow the dirt road for 5km to reach Hương Tích. A motorbike with a driver will cost around 15,000-20,000Đ. Arrange pickup in advance.)

Once you have reached the launch point, the journey begins with a short boat trip on the lake (20,000Đ per person) that brings you to the base of the steps that lead to the pagoda. You can forego the boat trip by searching out the steps that lie to the right of the launch point, and instead traverse the side of the mountain on foot (1km, 30-50min.). Once you begin to mount the steps, the 2km climb passes picturesque rivers and forest to the first attraction and a favorite spot of picnickers—the statue of a Buddhist monk atop a dragon, emerging from a small pool of water. Here the path crosses the river, allowing visitors to cool off by splashing their hands in the mountain stream. As the climb continues, the steps become progressively steeper, leading to spectacular views. Just the ascent to the top can take anywhere from 1½-3hr. Visitors are advised to bring sunscreen and covering and to avoid a midday climb when the blazing sun burns the rocky steps.

ĐỒNG HỚI ☎52

While the province mostly boasts historical importance as a focal point of the Vietnam War, its major city, Đồng Hới, provides peace for those looking to escape the noise and tumult of most of Vietnam's major cities and towns. It's an ideal rest stop before the requisite trip to Vietnam's famed Phong Nha Caves or to the head of the Hồ Chí Minh Trail.

VIETNAM

TRANSPORTATION. The easiest way to head north or south is to flag down one of the buses heading to Huế (25,000Đ) or Hà Nội (55,000-70,000Đ), most of which don't bother to stop at the city's out-of-the-way bus station, rumbling instead through town on Hwy. 1. The **train station** lies 3km west of town. (☎836 789. Open daily 7:30-11am and 1:30-5pm.) Continue past the bus station (1km west of town, on the corner of Trần Hưng Đạo and Nguyễn Hưu Canh) on Trần Hưng Đạo and take the first right after the bridge, turning right again into the path that leads to the station's steps. Trains depart for Hà Nội (9-13hr.; 4-9 per day; 122,000-304,000Đ); Huế (3-4hr.; 2 per day; 39,000-98,000Đ); Vinh (4hr.; 2 per day; 48,000-115,000Đ). To hail a **taxi,** dial ☎82 82 82.

PRACTICAL INFORMATION. Exchange US dollars at **Vietinde Bank,** 3 Nguyễn Trãi St. (Open M-F summer 7-11:30am and 1:30-4:30pm; winter 7-11:30am and 1-4pm.) To reach the bank, turn right onto Nguyễn Trãi St., a small road off Quang Trưng right after a bridge when heading south from the post office, which is marked by a sign for the Nhà Khách Hotel. To reach the **tourist office,** 20 Quách Xuân Kỳ, continue straight from Vietinde Bank until Nguyễn Trãi ends at Quách Xuân Kỳ, which runs parallel to the small harbor. Here you can find information about the town and the province, purchase tourist guide books, hire some English-speaking tour guides with motorbikes (150,000Đ, in addition to transportation costs), or ask about joining a different group heading for a cave excursion. (☎828 228; www.quangbin.gov.vn/qbtourist.com.) There's a Vietcombank **ATM** inside the post office. Check out the new equipment at the **Internet** cafe at 3 Lê Trực, on a small road off Quang Trưng, facing the shops between the historical gate and the Đồng Hới Hotel. (☎837 653. Open daily 9am-11pm. 3000Đ per hr.)

ACCOMMODATIONS AND FOOD. Hiding behind the Quảng Bình Gate is the **Kim Liên Hotel ❸**, 2 Lê Văn Hưu. Spacious and pristine rooms with older and pleasantly well-kept private baths, as well as a friendly staff, make for an enjoyable stay. (☎822 154. A/C, TV, refrigerator. Singles 120,000Đ; doubles 150,000Đ; triples 180,000Đ.) Cheap, old, but clean doubles with fan and a friendly and helpful staff reside at the hotel's neighboring **Nhà Khách ❶**, 30 Quang Trưng. (☎828 453. Doubles with TV 60,000-80,000Đ.) The **Nhà Nghi Điện Ảnh ❷**, 1 Lê Trực, next to the Internet cafe, has old triples with toiletless baths. However, their old and dark but clean A/C rooms are the cheapest cool chambers in town. (☎821 839. Triples with fans 60,000Đ, with A/C 100,000Đ.) For a decent bite, explore the popular shops and cafes that crowd the market area on Mẹ Suốt near the river, 300m east of the Quảng Bình Gate on Quang Trưng. The constantly crowded **cơm shop**, at 14 Mẹ Suốt, is run right out of the family kitchen and has a friendly staff. (☎822 234. Open daily 5am-9pm.) For delicious fruit-and-ice cream smoothies, settle down at one of the street cafes across from the province's prized gate. The restaurant at the **Đồng Hới Hotel ❷** serves guests a variety of traditional and international meals at slightly inflated prices. (Fried egg with bread 10,000Đ; fried cuttlefish 50,000Đ.)

SHOPPING. The major town market lies on the western outskirts of town, near the train station. Inside the **Chợ Ga market** you'll find stalls filled with clothing, shoes, books, bags, pharmaceuticals, and food. Outside, more vendors crowd the market to sell fruits, vegetables, seafood, and slabs of meat. To reach the market, turn onto Trần Hưng Đạo at the post office and head west for about 2.5km. The second and smaller market, the **Chợ Cá**, lies near the river bank, at the end of Mẹ Suốt, which faces the Quảng Bình Gate.

DAYTRIP FROM ĐỒNG HỚI: PHONG NHA CAVES. The Phong Nha Caves are some of Central Vietnam's most interesting natural land formations, or at least the tourism authorities think so. The attraction consists of several caves, of which only two larger enclosures are open to tourists. The first stop on the tour, the kilometer-long **Đồng Tiên Sơn Cave**, was discovered by a local villager in 1935 but wasn't opened to visitors until 1999. Inside, colorful red, green, and yellow lights illuminate various formations.

Natural beauty aside, the caves are an important historical site for Vietnamese visitors. The abandoned houses on the river leading to the cave and the small, difficult-to-spot bomb marks remind visitors and inhabitants alike of the conflict waged a generation and a half ago. Most of the caves of the region are difficult to reach and are therefore closed to visitors. They served as Vietnamese havens during the country's wars, filling the roles of military bases, hospitals, and even banks.

There is no public transport to the caves. Possible means of transportation include joining an organized tour (400,000Đ car rental for up to 4 people, see the tourist office), taking a taxi (300,000Đ one-way), or getting a lift on a motorbike (100,000-150,000Đ round-trip). To reach the caves by motorbike, head onto the Hồ Chí Minh Trail and continue north until it ends at Kẻ Bàng National Park. Follow the signs that lead you through the small town and toward the parking lot, ticket booth, and surrounding vendors and restaurants. (☎675 021; phongnhanp@dng.vnn.vn. The tour, including the boat trip to the entrance and visit to the caves, lasts 3½-5½hr. 25,000Đ. Boat into caves for 10 people or fewer 75,000Đ; 11-15 people 85,000Đ; 16-20 people 100,000Đ. If you are traveling solo, wait for a group to assemble or ask if you can join one.)

CENTRAL VIETNAM

ĐÔNG HÀ ☎53

Largely unimpressive, Đông Hà's claim to fame is its military history; a major US base dominated the area three decades ago. The town is also a prime jumping-off point for tours of the DMZ, and is conveniently near the Vietnamese-Lao border.

Located next door to Đông Hà Hotel, the bus station, 68 Lê Duẩn, runs **buses** to: Hà Nội (14-15hr.; 5am; 74,000Đ); Huế (2hr.; every 30min. 7am-6pm; 15,000Đ); Lao Bảo (2hr.; every 30min.-1hr.; 12,000Đ). The train station is 1.5km farther south, with its tracks on Lê Duẩn. **Trains** run daily to: Đồng Hới (1½-3hr.; 6 per day; 29,000-100,000Đ); Hà Nội (9½-10hr.; 7 per day; 176,000-622,000Đ); HCMC (23-28hr.; 5 per day; 312,000-1,104,000Đ); Huế (1-1½hr.; 6 per day; 19,000-66,000Đ); Vinh (6-8hr.; 5 per day; 86,000-303,000Đ). Various offices of the Sinh Cafe and the Quảng Trị Tourist Company sell open-tour tickets to Hà Nội (US$7-8), HCMC (US$17), Huế (US$3), Laos (US$11), and Ninh Bình (US$5). Pulsing from north to south, **Highway 1** (known in Đông Hà as **Lê Duẩn**) is the city's main artery.

The bus station is right next door to the **Quảng Trị Tourist Company,** which operates from the Đông Hà Hotel. (☎852 927; dmzqtri@dng.vnn.vn. Excellent English speakers. Organized one-day DMZ tours US$10. Solo or small group two-day tours of all sights with guide and car US$45-50. Guide with motorbike US$20 per day. DMZ and Minority Village Homestay tours for 1 person 1 day 150,000Đ, 2 days 275,000Đ; 2 people 190,000Đ/359,000Đ; 3 people 240,000Đ/435,000Đ. Internet 700Đ per min. Open M-Sa 7-11am and 1:30-5pm.) Sixty-five meters past the bus stop, facing the bridge, is **Internet Café,** 201 Lê Duẩn. Though you won't find any computers there, you can book **Sinh Cafe** DMZ tours and open-tour buses. (☎852 972. DMZ tours in English daily 8am-4pm. US$10. Breakfast included. Open-tour to Savannakhet, Laos US$12. Open daily 5-11am and 1:30-5pm.) The main office of the **Sinh Cafe** is hidden inside the city center at 1 Phan Bội Châu. From the town market, head west and down the curving road. About 80m down, Phan Bội Châu swings right. From the bank, continue straight for 1km until you reach a large intersection with train tracks on the left. The huge glass tower in the center of the colliding streets is the main **post office,** 20 Trần Hưng Đạo (☎852 206; open daily 6am-9pm).

Backpackers might feel most comfortable at the original **Phụng Hoàng ❷,** 295 Lê Duẩn, halfway between the bus and train stations. The rooms may be old and the furniture worn and broken, but A/C, private showers, and a clean public toilet make its singles (70,000-80,000Đ) the most quality affordable option. Higher-priced doubles (100,000-120,000Đ) have TV and private bath with shower and toilet. (☎854 567; victoryqt@dng.vnn.vn.) **Hotel Hữu Nghị ❸,** 16 Trần Hưng Đạo, stands opposite the Buddhist temple, down the street to the right of the town market. It contains colorful, spacious, fresh rooms with TV, A/C, refrigerator, and private bath. (☎551 670; fax 855 746. Doubles US$12; triples US$15.) To live in luxury, stay a night at the **Phụng Hoàng II ❹,** 146 Lê Duẩn, where a spacious king-sized room with bed to match, refrigerator, living room, and whirlpool costs 400,000Đ per night. Less upscale are rooms with twin beds, refrigerator, and a sparkling private bath, or smaller doubles with clean baths. (☎854 567. All rooms with A/C and TV. Internet 20,000Đ per hr. Twin bed rooms 300,000Đ; smaller doubles 200,000Đ.)

A stretch of Lê Duẩn heading south right after the bus station hosts a few inviting restaurants. On the corner right across from the bus stop is the **Tân Ngọc Sang ❶,** 72 Lê Duẩn, where the friendly owner is equipped with an English phrasebook so as to prevent any mix-ups. (☎853 366. Soup 5000Đ, with noodles 7000Đ. Bean curd soup 5000Đ. Milk 3000Đ. Open daily 5am-9pm.) Many DMZ tour and open-tour buses make a rest stop at the Đông Hà Hotel **restaurant ❷**, where decent meals come at acceptable prices. (☎852 292. Breakfast 7000-10,000Đ. Vegetarian noodle soup 7000Đ. Rice and meat dishes 12,000-16,000Đ. Open daily 6am-11pm.)

BORDER CROSSING TO LAOS: LAO BẢO. To reach Lao Bảo, head west on Hwy. 9, which runs perpendicular to Hwy. 1, traversing Vietnam from Đông Hà into Laos. **Buses** for the border leave the Đông Hà bus station every hour (12,000Đ). Tourist companies in Huế and Đông Hà run buses between the two countries for US$11-15. Most of the town itself lies on Hwy. 9. The bus station (☎877 503; open daily 5am-6pm) lies in the center of town, off the main road about 400m before the border crossing. Daily buses run to Đông Hà (2hr.; every hr. 6am-5pm; 12,000Đ). The border crossing lies at the end of Hwy. 1, about 1.5km from the center of town and the town market and a short 15-20min. walk from the bus station (or a 5000Đ motorbike ride). You can cross into Laos daily from 7am-7:30pm. If you don't have a **visa,** it will cost you an hour's wait and US$22 to get one.

THE DEMILITARIZED ZONE (DMZ)

US troops came to central Vietnam in 1965 to aid the South Vietnamese Army and government. The Americans built a string of bases in the area known as the DMZ to prevent the Northern Vietnamese Army from entering the country from Laos and descending into the South. With sights scattered along and around Hwy. 9 as it traverses the countryside from Đông Hà to the border with Laos, the DMZ covers a radius of about 25km south and north of the town. A complete visit to the sites approved for tourism takes time, energy, and a fair amount of money if you're planning to go with a guide. *Let's Go* recommends that independent explorers take at least two days in the area. A good motorcycle, excellent map, and patience are also useful—it can be tricky to spot sights whose importance and distinction from their surroundings now remain merely in national memory.

STAY ON THE BEATEN TRACK. As per the guidelines of the Geneva Accords of 1954, Vietnam was divided at the 17th parallel, which runs through the DMZ. After the war, locals attempted to clear the area by looking for mines by hand or with sticks. Since then, 5000 Vietnamese lives have been claimed by mines once planted by US troops to stop the Northern Vietnamese Army from progressing southward. Live mines and undetonated shells still litter the area. Be careful and stick to well-established paths.

TRANSPORTATION

You can book tours or find guides with excellent English skills at the tourist agencies in **Đông Hà** (see p. 916), thereby avoiding the 2hr. commute from Huế. Nonetheless, most tourists opt to visit the DMZ as an easy, pre-arranged daytrip from **Huế.** Tourist offices and many hotels offer half-day tours (US$6-10) and full-day trips with transport, A/C, and breakfast (US$7-13). Smaller agencies often offer tours of equivalent quality for lower prices, but sketchy, disreputable outfits abound. The **Phu Xuan Tourist Office,** 21 Trần Cao Vân, offers full-day tours with breakfast, guide, and A/C transport for US$7, while Mr. Do at the **Stop and Go Café,** 4 Bến Nghé, arranges motorbike trips for US$15 per person. Tours leave at 6am and return around 7pm, with drop-off at your hotel.

VIETNAM

ORIENTATION AND PRACTICAL INFORMATION

Former military bases and other sights that now comprise the area known to tourists as the DMZ lie west of Đông Hà on Hwy. 9, itself a historical landmark. Paved by the US military, it was designed to facilitate the transport of ammunition and supplies from the east to the bases that stretched toward the mountains of Laos. **Cam Lộ** lies 13km from Đông Hà, while another 7km reveals a dirt road which leads to the spot where **Camp Carroll** once stood. Head 15km west from Cam Lộ town to get a glimpse of the **Rockpile.** From here, it's another 30km to the former **Khe Sanh** combat base and the memorial museum that stands in its place. About 20km farther, the remains of the **Làng Vây Special Force Camp** rest on a ridge 9km before the Lao border. To visit the sights that rest north of Đông Hà, head back on Hwy. 9 past Camp Carroll, and about 15km west of Đông Hà town (after the **Đa Krông Bridge**), turn left onto Hwy. 15, built by the French before the war and now known throughout Vietnam as the **Hồ Chí Minh Trail.** Fourteen kilometers north is a dirt path 2km long which leads to the bunker at **Cồn Tiên.** Continuing 7km north on Hwy. 15 leads to the **Trường Sơn National Cemetery.** From here head right back to Hwy. 1. Heading north will take you to **Gio Linh,** a former military base and now a town. The DMZ tour continues with a stop at the **Bến Hải River** and the **Hiến Lương Bridge.** Two kilometers after the bridge, turn right onto **Cai Lai.** A 15km drive east will take you to the **Vĩnh Mốc Tunnels.** To get to **Quảng Trị Citadel** and **church,** head back south to Hwy. 1 and, after passing Đông Hà, continue for 13km. Or, flag down a bus heading south and make sure to exit when you hit town (5000-10,000Đ).

SIGHTS

Though the actual De-Militarized Zone spans 5km north and 5km south of the Bến Hải River, the sights in the area known as the DMZ reach as far as 60km west, 15km south, and over 25km north of Đông Hà.

CAMP CARROLL. Five kilometers west of Cam Lộ, an unpaved road turns left off Hwy. 9 to the old US base at Camp Carroll. Four kilometers farther from the paved road lies a pile of rocks that marks the spot of the former military base, whose function was to supply the Rockpile and Khe Sanh with artillery 175. When the DMZ was attacked in 1972 by the northern Vietnamese troops arriving from Laos, Camp Carroll was where Colonel Phạm Văn Đính of the southern army surrendered to the North.

THE ROCKPILE. Thirty kilometers from Đông Hà and 7km from Camp Carroll, a green mountain, alias "the Rockpile," looms in the distance. The valley in between it and its neighboring mountain, Razor Back, harbored a military base. From 1965-1972, 200 US Marines were stationed at the foot of the mountain. Some troops remained at the top, which was used both as an observatory and a radio tower. The US Marines thought the base to be an unassailable helicopter landing pad until 1967, when it was stormed one night by Việt Minh commandos, who managed to reach the base and engage the troops in hand-to-hand combat. Now nothing remains of the old base except for the mountains that harbored it.

BRU MINORITY VILLAGE. Though it wasn't a site of battle itself, the village of the Bru minority, who call themselves the Vân Kiều ("mountain people"), has become a popular stop on tours of the DMZ. The minority village is woven into the region's military history. During the Vietnam War, the Bru people took up arms to fight alongside the South Vietnamese government and the US troops. As the members of the minority group only went by their given first names, after the war they were all ironically surnamed Hồ to commemorate the northern hero, Hồ Chí Minh.

KHE SANH COMBAT BASE. The base is 10km from the bridge toward Khe Sanh. Established in 1966, the base housed 5000 US marines whose main mission was to prevent the Northern Vietnamese Army from descending into southern Vietnam on the Hồ Chí Minh Trail, which ran from the northern Phong Nha Caves (see p. 915) through the mountainous regions of Laos. The base was intended as a defensive stronghold in the South; its poor location betrayed it. Two years after American troops settled the area came the Tet Offensive of 1968. Getting word of large numbers of northern Vietnamese troops coming toward Khe Sanh, the US Army pulled its troops from the South to assemble at the Marine base. However, the North's true target was not Khe Sanh but rather HCMC itself. With much of the American Army concentrated in the DMZ, the Northern Vietnamese Army came through Laos and attacked HCMC. As the US troops pulled back to return south and aid their compatriots in an attempt to fend off the invaders, 40,000 northern Vietnamese soldiers descended upon Khe Sanh. The fighting continued until American airborne reinforcements came from Thailand. About 500 US soldiers and over 10,000 northern Vietnamese soldiers died during the Tet Offensive.

LÀNG VÂY SPECIAL FORCES CAMP. This Special Forces Camp housed only 24 US soldiers, who fought along with the Bru and Southern Vietnamese Army. This camp is known for the infamous 1968 northern Vietnamese attack that was launched with the help of Russian tanks. The northern army brought tanks along the river from Laos via bamboo ferries without being detected by the US or southern Vietnamese forces. During the battle, the Northern Vietnamese Army captured the Lao border, located a mere 7km away from the Special Forces Camp, and 11 US soldiers and 25-30 from the Southern Vietnamese Army fell.

TRƯỜNG SƠN NATIONAL CEMETERY. Farther north on Hwy. 15 there are signs that point visitors to the gate of Trường Sơn, one of the three national cemeteries in Vietnam. Named after the landscape, the name of the cemetery means "long mountain range." Composed of 11 separate cemeteries, the sight commemorates fallen northern Vietnamese soldiers, as well as their Việt Cộng comrades. During the war, when a soldier or fighter fell, he was buried on the spot of his death. However, since neither the Northern Vietnamese Army nor the southern rebels wore identification tags, friends of the fallen would write down the deceased soldier's name and the name of his village. In 1975, when the war was over, the government began to exhume corpses of those northern army soldiers and supporters of the northern army and government. The cemetery was constructed in 1976 and remains of northern supporters were brought to one of the 11 burial sites. Thanks to the efforts of their comrades, many remains were retrieved, along with the names of those who fell, allowing families to identify their loved ones and engage in proper ancestor worship. Most graves are marked by tombstones with the words "Liệt Sĩ," meaning "martyr," followed by the name of the deceased, his home village, the year that he entered the army, and the year in which he fell.

VĨNH MỐC TUNNELS. Located on the northern side of the Hiền Lương Bridge and thus in Northern Vietnam, the tunnels were built by locals in an effort to shield themselves from the US forces. While the American Army never crossed the northern border, the area was under constant aerial attack. The network of tunnels you can visit today is only one of the 11 that was built in the area, but it's the only one that survived. While the underground village took 18 months to construct, its inhabitants remained in the dark corridors for four years during the war. Over the four years, 300 people occupied the 2km long tunnels of Vĩnh Mốc. Before entering the tunnels, visitors can peruse pictures of inhabitants and other images of the war that fill the walls of the small museum. *(Museum ☎053 823 238. Open daily 7am-5pm. Entrance for foreigners 25,000Đ. The bookstore sells information booklets in Vietnamese and English for 10,000Đ, and collections of war pictures for 30,000Đ.)*

QUẢNG TRỊ CITADEL. Thirteen kilometers south of Đông Hà, the Citadel lies in the city of Quảng Trị. Constructed in 1820 by King Minh Mạng, it was occupied by the Southern Vietnamese Army during the Vietnam War. In May of 1972, the Citadel was attacked and taken by northern forces. The next month, the southern army attempted to reclaim the citadel. Intense warfare lasted 81 days, at the end of which American bombs and the severe back-and-forth had claimed the lives of the northern attackers along with the Citadel walls. Though the structure was totally devastated by the war, a war memorial commemorating those who fought and perished has been built in its place. *(Open daily 7am-5pm. Entrance for foreigners 25,000Đ.)* Just outside of the town on Hwy. 1 stands an old church. Its bullet- and mortar-marred walls testify to the overwhelming attack that was launched on the region.

HUẾ ☎54

Huế is delightful. As Vietnam's spiritual, artistic, and cultural center, the city has an incredible concentration of sights and ruins. In the 19th century, under the rule of the Nguyễn Dynasty, Huế reached prominence as the seat of Vietnam's first united court. Home rule was short-lived, however, as French ships blockaded the city and prepared to attack in 1833. Recognizing the might of the French, the emperor relented, and Vietnam became a French protectorate. Despite efforts to protect the city's treasures and to preserve its historical integrity, over 100 years later, Huế became a combat zone again; during the 1968 Tet Offensive, the Citadel was under the possession of both sides as fighting raged in the Imperial City.

Outside of Huế, history resounds through monumental tombstones of intricate design. The occasional grandiosity of the countryside's gorgeous, ostentatious architecture is softened by picturesque lotus ponds and majestic mountains.

TRANSPORTATION

Flights: Phú Bài Airport, 15km south of the city off Hwy. 1. **Taxis** (75,000-100,000Đ) and Vietnam Airlines airport **buses** (25,000Đ) run between the airport and city center. There are several booking offices on the Perfume River's southern shore. **Vietnam Airlines,** 7 Nguyễn Tri Phương St. (☎824 709), in Thuận Hóa Hotel. Open M-Sa 7-11am and 1:30-4:30pm, Su 7:30-11am and 2-4:30pm.

Trains: Huế Railway Station, 2 Bùi Thi Xuân (☎822 175 or 822 686), at the southwest end of Lê Lợi and over the small bridge that spans the canal. Trains to: **Đà Nẵng** (2½-3hr.; 3 per day; 25,000-60,000Đ); **Đông Hà** (1-1½hr.; 2-5 per day; 18,000Đ); **Đồng Hới** (3hr.; 2-6 per day; 39,000-98,000Đ); **Hà Nội** (12½-18hr.; 6 per day; 161,000-401,000Đ); **HCMC** (19½-26hr.; 3-5 per day; 243,000-604,000Đ) via **Nha Trang** (12-17hr.; 3-6 per day; 147,000-365,000Đ). Purchase tickets early.

Buses: Travel agencies, most hotels, and some cafes in the tourist center on Hùng Vương and Bến Nghé book minibuses to: **Đà Nẵng** (3hr.; 8am and 1pm; US$1.50-3); **Hà Nội** (16hr.; 5:30 and 6pm; US$6-7); **HCMC** (20hr.; 2:30pm; US$15-20); **Hội An** (4hr.; 8am and 1pm; US$1.50-3); **Nha Trang** (16hr.; 2:30pm; US$7-8); **Lao Bảo** (4hr.; 6am; US$11); **Savannakhet, Laos** (6hr.; 9pm; US$12-15). Huế has three bus stations:

An Hòa Bus Station (☎822 716), outside the Citadel at the northwest corner off Hwy. 1, 2km from town center. Buses go north to: **Đồng Hới** (5hr.; 5 and 6am; 25,000Đ); **Hà Nội** (24hr.; 6am; 80,000Đ); **Khe Sanh** (5½hr.; 5am; 40,000Đ); **Vinh** (11hr.; 6am; 70,000Đ). To get to **Lao Bảo,** catch a bus to **Đông Hà** (5-10am) and transfer to a bus bound for the Lao border.

Phía Nam Bus Station, 97 Hùng Vương (☎810 954 or 825 070), 2.5km southeast of the Perfume River and on Hwy. 1 as it heads south to Đà Nẵng. Primarily serves southern destinations. Buses to: **Buôn Ma Thuột** (18hr.; 6am; 78,000Đ); **Đà Lạt** (20hr.; 5am; 100,000Đ); **Đà Nẵng** (3hr.; every 30-40min. 5:40am-4:30pm; 20,000Đ); **HCMC** (30hr.; 6am; 120,000Đ). Open daily 4:30am-5pm.

Đông Ba Bus Station, on Trần Hưng Đạo (☎823 055), on the Citadel side of the Perfume River. Buses to **Đống Hà** (2hr.; 8:30, 10:30am, 8pm; 20,000Đ); **Thuận An Beach** (20min.; roughly every 45min. 7am-4pm; 4000-10,000Đ).

Cyclos swarm around the city. 10,000Đ per ride. Bargain like it's going out of style. **Motos** are often cheaper. 3000-7000Đ per ride; around the city 10,000-15,000Đ per hr. For longer distances, approximate 1000-1500Đ per km.

Taxis: ATC Taxi (☎833 333). Unmetered rides to almost anywhere. Agree on a price before you get there. **Gili Taxi** (☎828 282).

Boats: Agent offices where you can book boat trips are scattered along the northern shore of the southern city. **Tourist Boat Pier,** 7 Lê Lợi. 1-day tour up Perfume River to **Thiên Mụ Pagoda** and the **Royal Tombs** or to **Thuận An Beach** (8am-5pm; 10- to 15-person boat 200,000Đ). Individual tickets (25,000Đ per person) are available from tourist agencies, hotels, or at the Mandarin and Stop and Go Cafés. The acclaimed **Folk Songs of Huế** boat tour and performance leaves every night (1½hr.; 7 and 8:30pm; 350,000Đ for 10-15 people). Booking booth open daily 6am-10pm.

Rentals: Most guesthouses, hotels, and outfits on Hùng Vương rent motorbikes for US$4 per day. Some also rent them with hired drivers, US$5-6 per day. **Minh & Coco Mini Restaurant,** 1 Hùng Vương (☎821 822) provides **motorbikes with drivers** for US$4 or 60,000Đ per day. However, probably the easiest and most enjoyable way to get around Huế is to pedal around on a **bicycle.** Hotels and cafes, like the **Mandarin Café,** 3 Hùng Vương (☎821 281; mandarin@dng.vnn.vn), **Stop and Go Café,** 4 Bến Nghé (☎889 106), and **Minh & Coco's** provide Vietnamese model bikes with locks for 10,000Đ per day. **Phu Xuan Tourist** (see p. 921) rents **cars** with drivers for US$25 per day.

ORIENTATION

Over 16km inland from the South China Sea, Huế is bisected by the **Perfume River (Sông Hương).** The northern bank is home to the Old City, hidden within Citadel walls. The **Flagpole of Huế,** which marks the front gate of the Royal Palace and the Imperial City, is inside the Citadel. Across the river on the southeast side is the commercial capital known as **New Huế,** overrun with hotels, restaurants, and Westernized services. On the Citadel side, **Lê Duẩn/Trần Hưng Đạo** runs between the river and the Citadel wall. On the southeast bank of the Perfume River, **Lê Lợi,** the main tourist strip, runs parallel to the water. **Bến Nghé** is known for pricey shops and other services geared toward foreigners; it runs from the intersection of **Trần Cao Vân** and **Đội Cung,** one block south near the eastern tip of Lê Lợi, and continues until it merges with **Hùng Vương,** the other major tourist drag. Heading north toward **Thuận An Beach,** Lê Lợi becomes **Nguyễn Sinh Cung,** which runs through the city's northeast.

PRACTICAL INFORMATION

Tourist Offices: Nearly all tourist agencies offer identical services (1-day tours US$7-8; half-day Perfume River tour 25,000Đ). The smaller agencies frequently offer cheaper prices. Most guesthouses also book tours and open-tour bus tickets, often at lower costs. **Phu Xuan Tourist,** 21 Trần Hưng Đạo, is a small office that offers English-language guided city tours (US$10), DMZ tours (11hr.; departs 6am; breakfast and tickets included; US$7), boat trips on the river 25,000Đ. Open-tour to **Hà Nội** (US$6) and **HCMC** (US$13). **Mandarin Cafe,** 3 Hùng Vương (☎845 022 or 848 626). Sells **Sinh Cafe** open-tour tickets to **Hà Nội** (US$7) and **HCMC** (US$16) and arranges full-day DMZ tours (US$7) and Dragon Boat excursions (25,000Đ). **DNTN Tours,** 3 Phạm Ngũ Lão (☎824 010, cell 0914 007 316; huongsweets@yahoo.com), offers low prices, with Dragon Boat trip (20,000Đ), full day DMZ tours (US$8, US$40 for private car), and city tour (US$6). Open daily 8am-9pm.

Banks: Foreign Exchange Desk, 18 Lê Lợi (☎848 707), charges a 1% commission on exchanges of US$ into đồng, and a 2% commission to change đồng into US$. 3% commission on MC/V cash advances and cashing traveler's checks. Open M-F 7-11am and 1:30-4pm. **Vietcombank,** 78 Hùng Vương (☎824 209; fax 846 320). 3% commission on MC/V cash advances. Cashes traveler's checks (US$2.50 per check). Open M-Sa 7-11am and 1:30-4:30pm, Su 7:30-11am and 2-4pm. 24hr. **ATM** outside.

ATMs: Bank for Foreign Trade of Vietnam, across the street from 98 Lê Lợi. 24hr booth. **Duy Tân Hotel,** 12 Hùng Vương. In front of the hotel.

Police Station: 42 Hùng Vương (☎822 160). **Immigration Police:** 77 Bến Nghé (☎889 192). Visa extensions US$10. Open M, W, F summer 7-11:30am and 1:30-5pm; winter 7-11:30am and 1-4:30pm.

Pharmacies: Khánh Duy, 37 Bến Nghé (☎832 079), at the intersection with Nguyễn Tri Phương. On the southern bank of the Perfume River. Open daily noon-11pm. **Ngọc Diệp,** 75 Phan Đăng Lưu (☎527 609), just outside the eastern old city wall. On the northern bank. Open daily 7am-9pm.

Medical Services: Huế City Hospital, 16 Lê Lợi (☎822 325, ext. 2247). General check-ups and services open M-F 7-11am and 1:30-4:30pm. Emergency entrance on Nguyèn Huy Tá open 24hr.

Internet Access: With the arrival of DSL, cheap and numerous Internet cafes have sprung up in Huế, though prices near hotels and popular tourist areas are often inflated. For cheap and easy access, join local teens at **4 Võ Thị Sáu** (☎828 070). When heading up from Bến Nghé, hook left just before the tourist office. The computers in the first cafe have AOL Instant Messenger. 2000Đ per hr. Open daily 8am-8pm. To check email in the comfort of A/C, head to the main **post office** (GPO; see below). 3000Đ per hr. Open daily 6:30am-9:30pm. The Internet cafe right in the middle of the booming business at **51 Bến Nghé** charges 50Đ per min., with a 1000Đ min., and allows Internet calls for 70,000Đ per hr. Open daily 7am-8pm.

Post Office: Mini-post offices abound. **GPO,** 8 Hoàng Hoa Thám (☎821 220; bdt-thue@dng.vnn.vn), 1 block southwest of Hùng Vương, on the southern bank.

ACCOMMODATIONS

Popular with backpackers, the alley at 46 Lê Lợi has a dense cluster of inexpensive and quality accommodations—some of the best for the budget traveler. Venture elsewhere for more luxurious quarters and to forgo the foreign traffic that passes through the area. In guesthouses and less-established hotels, bargain until the quality matches the price. Most establishments arrange tours.

Mimosa Guest House, 46/6 Lê Lợi (☎828 068), down a small alley just off of the eastern tip of Lê Lợi. Friendly owner and lovely, quiet rooms. Breakfast on the terrace US$1. Tiny but precious singles US$3. Doubles US$4-6, with A/C US$7-10. Prices fluctuate depending on the season. ❷

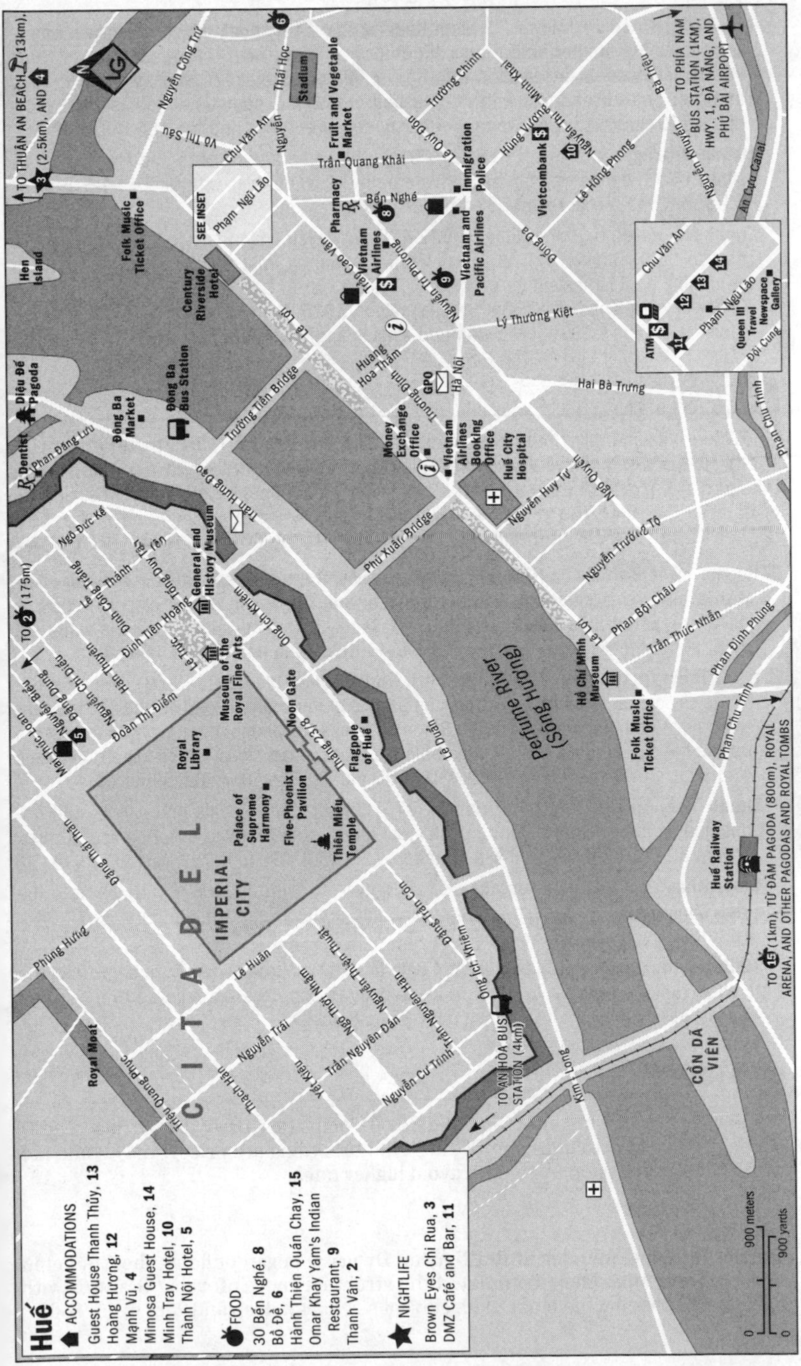
Huế
ACCOMMODATIONS
Guest House Thanh Thủy, 13
Hoàng Hương, 12
Mạnh Vũ, 4
Mimosa Guest House, 14
Minh Tray Hotel, 10
Thành Nội Hotel, 5
FOOD
30 Bến Nghé, 8
Bồ Đề, 6
Hành Thiện Quán Chay, 15
Omar Khay Yam's Indian Restaurant, 9
Thanh Vân, 2
NIGHTLIFE
Brown Eyes Chi Rua, 3
DMZ Café and Bar, 11
900 meters
900 yards
0
CITADEL
IMPERIAL CITY
Palace of Supreme Harmony
Five-Phoenix Pavilion
Thiên Miếu Temple
Royal Library
Museum of the Royal Fine Arts
Noon Gate
Flagpole of Huế
General and History Museum
Royal Moat
Perfume River (Sông Hương)
Cồn Dã Viên
Hen Island
Diệu Đế Pagoda
Đông Ba Market
Đông Ba Bus Station
Dentist
Century Riverside Hotel
Folk Music Ticket Office
SEE INSET
Phạm Ngũ Lão
Trường Tiền Bridge
Phú Xuân Bridge
Money Exchange Office
Vietnam Airlines Booking Office
Huế City Hospital
GPO
Vietnam Airlines
Pharmacy
Fruit and Vegetable Market
Stadium
Immigration Police
Vietnam and Pacific Airlines
Vietcombank
Hồ Chí Minh Museum
Huế Railway Station
ATM
Queen III Travel
Newspace Gallery
TO THUẬN AN BEACH (13km), 3 (2.5km), AND 4
TO 2 (175m)
TO AN HÒA BUS STATION (4km)
TO PHÍA NAM BUS STATION (1KM), HWY. 1, ĐÀ NẴNG, AND PHÚ BÀI AIRPORT
TO 15 (1km), TỪ ĐÀM PAGODA (800m), ROYAL ARENA, AND OTHER PAGODAS AND ROYAL TOMBS
Mai Thúc Loan
Nguyễn Biểu
Đặng Dung
Nguyễn Chí Diểu
Hàn Thuyên
Đinh Tiên Hoàng
Lê Thánh
Đinh Công Tráng
Ngô Đức Kế
Tống Duy Tân
Lê Trực
Đoàn Thị Điểm
Ông Ích Khiêm
Tháng 23/8
Lê Duẩn
Lê Huân
Phùng Hưng
Đặng Thái Thân
Triệu Quang Phục
Thạch Hãn
Nguyễn Trãi
Ngô Thời Nhậm
Nguyễn Thiện Thuật
Đặng Trần Côn
Nguyễn Hàn
Trần Nguyên Hãn
Trần Nguyên Đán
Nguyễn Cư Trinh
Yết Kiêu
Kim Long
Phan Đăng Lưu
Trần Hưng Đạo
Lê Lợi
Huang Hoa Thám
Trương Định
Hà Nội
Nguyễn Huy Tự
Ngô Quyền
Nguyễn Trường Tộ
Phan Bội Châu
Trần Thúc Nhẫn
Phan Đình Phùng
Phan Chu Trinh
Hai Bà Trưng
Lý Thường Kiệt
Đống Đa
Nguyễn Tri Phương
Trần Cao Vân
Bến Nghé
Trần Quang Khải
Lê Quý Đôn
Hùng Vương
Lê Hồng Phong
Nguyễn Thị Minh Khai
Trường Chinh
Bà Triệu
Nguyễn Khuyến
An Cựu Canal
Chu Văn An
Võ Thị Sáu
Nguyễn Công Trứ
Nguyễn Thái Học
Đội Cung

VIETNAM

Minh Tray Hotel, 27 Nguyễn Thị Minh Khai (☎828 148; khoithanh@dng.vnn.vn). Somewhat dark but comfortable rooms hidden on a street near the western tip of Hùng Vương, just past its intersection with Hà Nội. All rooms with A/C, most with refrigerator and tub. Smaller quarters with double bed or 2 twins, sometimes tubless and older baths 120,000Đ; spacious rooms with 2 queen sized beds and tub 150,000Đ. ❷

Hoàng Hương, 46/2 Lê Lợi (☎828 509), in the same alley. Cheap and friendly. Small single US$3; dorms with fan and private bath US$3; doubles with fan US$4-6, with A/C US$6-8. Motorbike rental US$4 per day. ❶

Thành Nội Hotel, 57 Đặng Dung (☎522 478; www.vietnamtourism.com/thanhnoihotel), next to the Forbidden City in the old town. A worthy upscale choice. Small outdoor swimming pool is heaven on a hot day. Rooms with A/C, satellite TV, and refrigerator. Check-in 2pm. Check-out noon. Small singles US$15. Somewhat cramped doubles and triples with bath US$20. Less cramped singles and doubles with tub US$25-30. ❸

FOOD

Huế's food is arguably the best in Vietnam. Try *bánh nam* (shrimp and pork with sticky rice in a banana leaf), *nem lụi* (grilled pork and greens in rice paper with peanut sauce), or *bánh khoái*, usually called the "Huế pancake" on menus. Scores of eateries on **Hùng Vương** and **Lê Lợi** entice patrons with greasy dishes. Venture farther afield for more authenticity.

Bồ Đề, 35/1 Bà Triệu (☎832 594). Easy to miss, the restaurant hides in a small alley, with a black sign showing the way. Don't be put off by the plastic decor. Delicious dishes prepared by a hospitable Buddhist family. A priced menu is on the wall—just point at what looks best. Selections 3000-4000Đ. Open daily 7am-10pm. ❶

Hành Thiện Quán Chay (Vegetarian Inn), 98 Điện Biên Phủ (☎884 569), lies far south of the city center, but the trip is quick on bicycle or motorbike. Head down Lê Lợi toward the train station, turn left onto Điện Biên Phủ, cross the bridge, then the train tracks. It's up the hill on your left. Try the vegetable soup or the delicious potato-filled dumplings (*bánh lọc;* 3000Đ). Dishes 20,000-30,000Đ per kg. Open daily 6am-9pm. ❷

Thanh Vân, 137 Lê Thánh Tôn (☎511 776). Popular with locals and expats and frequented by foreign chefs. During peak meal times, arrive early to ensure a seat. Grilled shrimp 30,000Đ; fresh squid with pineapple 30,000Đ. Open daily 11am-10pm. ❸

Omar Khay Yam's Indian Restaurant, 10 Nguyễn Tri Phương (☎821 616), next to the Binh Minh hotel. Huế's best Indian cuisine and a classy atmosphere. Entrees 12,000-43,000Đ. Open daily 10am-10:30pm. ❷

30 Bến Nghé (☎848 532), across from Binh Minh II Hotel. Head here for a break from the grease. Delicious and filling freshly squeezed juices and desserts, enjoyed by locals and tourists alike (2000-4000Đ). Open daily 11am-8pm. ❶

SIGHTS

The ancient Citadel, Imperial City, and Royal Tombs (see **Daytrips from Huế,** p. 929) dominate the tourist landscape of Huế. All attractions are pricey; only some are worth it. Pay admission in đồng to avoid higher rates.

THE CITADEL

Emperor Gia Long, founder of the Nguyễn Dynasty, began building the Citadel in 1805. **Emperor Minh Mạng** completed the structure by reinforcing the wall with brick and expanding the moat to its current size of 4m deep and 23m wide. Today,

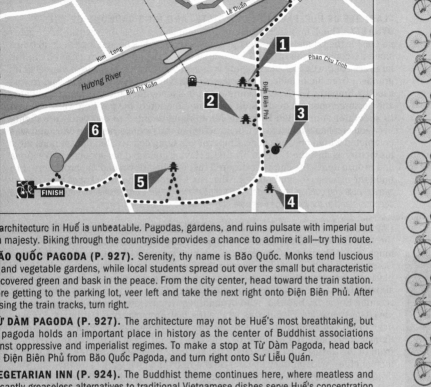

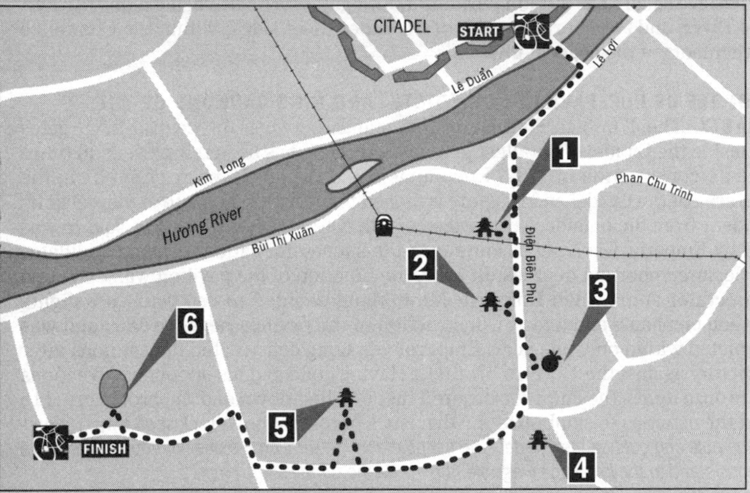

architecture in Huế is unbeatable. Pagodas, gardens, and ruins pulsate with imperial but n majesty. Biking through the countryside provides a chance to admire it all—try this route.

ĂO QUỐC PAGODA (P. 927). Serenity, thy name is Bão Quốc. Monks tend luscious and vegetable gardens, while local students spread out over the small but characteristic covered green and bask in the peace. From the city center, head toward the train station. re getting to the parking lot, veer left and take the next right onto Điện Biên Phủ. After sing the train tracks, turn right.

Ừ DÀM PAGODA (P. 927). The architecture may not be Huế's most breathtaking, but pagoda holds an important place in history as the center of Buddhist associations nst oppressive and imperialist regimes. To make a stop at Từ Dàm Pagoda, head back Điện Biên Phủ from Bão Quốc Pagoda, and turn right onto Sư Liễu Quán.

EGETARIAN INN (P. 924). The Buddhist theme continues here, where meatless and santly greaseless alternatives to traditional Vietnamese dishes serve Huế's concentration racticing Buddhists and other vegetarian visitors. From the pagoda, head back to Điện Phủ and backtrack a few meters down the hill to reach the Vegetarian Inn.

LTAR OF NAM GIAO (P. 927). After lunch, get back onto Điện Biên Phủ and follow it it ends at the park and the Altar of Nam Giao. Take a stroll in the heart of the park, an ern representation of the cosmos in which the three levels represent humanity, earth, and respectively. The trees around the altar were planted by Minh Mạng and his subjects. se that were tended by the king bear a plaque commemorating their royal treatment.

U HIEU PAGODA (P. 927). From the altar, veer right and continue straight for about until an imposing gate leading to a forest appears on the right. Follow the road to the nds of the Tu Hieu Pagoda. Monks and visitors mingle in the forest and lotus ponds, a ure of serenity. The grounds harbor a temple as well as school for young monks-to-be.

OYAL ARENA. Pedal through the streets along Huế's periphery and soak in the bucolic s. The Royal Arena, itself hidden amid homes and shops and secluded from Huế's other ctions, is a mini-coliseum where elephants and tigers were once forced to fight for the eror's viewing pleasure. To reach the arena, continue straight past the Tu Hieu Pagoda, ng right at the road's end. About 1km down the road before it flows into Bùi Thị Xuân, a ll path leads through the bustle of local houses that surround the arena

BIKE TOUR

the massive square has a 10km perimeter, four gates on its front side along the Perfume River, and two more on each of the other three sides. Within the Citadel lie the remnants of the **Imperial City.**

FLAGPOLE OF HUẾ, PAVILION OF EDICTS, AND NINE CANNONS OF THE DYNASTY. The 47m high **Flagpole of Huế** stands between the central front gates just inside the Citadel. The tallest pole in Vietnam, it has been rebuilt several times since its construction in 1807. Encompassing three levels, each 17.5m high, the large area of the citadel and flagpole is closed to visitors, who instead marvel at its grandeur from the outside. The **Pavilion of Edicts** was built in 1810. The square was used by Emperor Gia Long to announce the successful national exam candidates and declare important decrees. In 1929, the function of the pavilion was extended to spectator sport when Emperor Minh Mạng decided to use it to view fights between elephants and tigers. Construction of the pavilion began in 1809 and was completed within only one year. Emperor Gia Long constructed the cannons after his victory against the Tây Sơn brothers. Having collected his opponents' weapons and bronze items, the emperor ordered them melted down and the bronze used to build the cannons to symbolize the dynasty's perpetual power. *(Just off Hwy. 1, opposite the pole and outside the Citadel. The flagpole and the pavilion are open-air monuments. Five cannons stand to the left of the Flagpole and inside the Citadel Wall. Free.)*

IMPERIAL CITY. The red and saffron **Noon Gate** (Ngọ Môn), the grand entrance to the Imperial City, is opposite the flagpole. The city was modeled after China's much larger Forbidden City in Beijing, which was built during the Qing Dynasty. Constructed in 1833, the **Five-Phoenix Pavilion,** which sits at the gate, served as a platform from which the emperor could observe ceremonies. Only men were allowed to enter the pavilion during official ceremonies, and it was only the last reigning Emperor, Bảo Đại, who brought his wife to join his side during ceremonies. On August 30, 1945 it was where the last Emperor Bảo Đại handed power over to Hồ Chí Minh and the new government. Behind it, the **Palace of Supreme Harmony** once housed the emperor's throne. The different heights of the courts in front of the throne corresponded to the status of the mandarins (the court's intellectual elite), with military leaders on the right and civil leaders on the left. Nine dragons decorate the roof, symbolizing the perfect power of the emperor. The **Forbidden Purple City,** the formerly walled-in residence of the royal family, is in line with the Imperial City and Citadel. Elaborate inscriptions explain what once stood in place of the piles of rubble that are the unpleasant reminder of bombings during the Vietnam War. The **Royal Library,** on the right side as you face west, is one of the few structures still intact, and stands surrounded by a lush garden. South of the city are the residences of the Queen Mother and Great Queen Mother. In the south corner of the Imperial City is **Thiên Miếu Temple,** dedicated to Gia Long and his successors. These structures are undergoing extensive renovations with funds from UNESCO, which has declared Huế a World Heritage Site. *(Imperial City open daily 6:30am-5:30pm. English-language tour 40min.-1hr. 55,000Đ. Tours 50,000Đ.)*

VIETNAM

MUSEUM OF THE ROYAL FINE ARTS. Justly known as one of the most beautiful examples of Vietnamese architecture, the Long An Palace was built in 1845 under Triệu Tri, Emperor of the Nguyễn Dynasty. In 1923, the Palace became the showroom of the museum, where visitors can peruse 300 ancient artifacts. The museum courtyard displays cannons, statues, bronze cauldrons, and bells. *(Nearly directly north of the Imperial Museum. 3 Lê Trực. ☎ 524 429. English-speaking guide inside the museum available for questions 7-11am and 2-5:30pm. Museum open Tu-Su 7am-6pm. 22,000Đ.)*

OTHER SIGHTS

THIÊN MỤ PAGODA. On a high hill overlooking the Perfume River, this pagoda is dedicated to a legendary 16th-century woman who declared that a time of great prosperity would come if a Buddhist pagoda were to be built on the site. Lord Nguyễn Hoàng heard her decree and constructed the pagoda in 1601. Past the seven-story pagoda is an active monastery. The first monk to immolate himself publicly in Saigon during Ngô Đình Diệm's presidency, due to the discrimination against Buddhists and the violation of religious freedoms, came from this temple. Leaving the pagoda by car, he arrived in Saigon on June 11, 1963, stopped at an intersection in the city center, sat down in the lotus position, and set himself on fire. The car is on display. Monks chant periodically in the well manicured wooden temple behind the golden Buddha statue; tourists stream through constantly at a decidedly less spiritual pace. *(3km southwest of the Citadel. An easy and enjoyable riverside bike ride. Head west on Lê Duẩn and continue across the train tracks on Kim Long.)*

TU HIEU PAGODA. Located 5km southwest of the city and on the way to the Tự Đức Tomb, Tu Hieu should not be missed. Hidden amid woods and lotus ponds, its grounds are often visited by local friends out for a stroll or students trying to escape the city and delve into the serene beauty of Tu Hieu's gardens. Constructed in 1843, at first the pagoda was relatively modest. In 1848, however, it was expanded to include a cemetery reserved for the eunuchs of the Nguyễn Dynasty. *(To reach the pagoda, travel west toward the Altar of Nam Giao. When Điện Biên Phủ comes to its end, veer right. About 1km down the road a gate waits on the right. Pass through into the woods and take the second, marked path, to the pagoda grounds.)*

BĂO QUỐC PAGODA. Built in 1670, this pagoda sits atop stairs in a quiet sanctuary. Its altar is flanked by classrooms where monks have taught for 50 years. Behind the pagoda, monks tend their own fruit and vegetable gardens, while the peaceful garden on the side lends itself to students looking for a quiet spot to study or for a short respite. *(Walking toward the city center, head north on Phan Bội Châu, take a left on Điện Biên Phủ, and then take another left just before the train tracks.)*

ALTAR OF NAM GIAO. Sitting in the corner of a quiet park on the southwestern fringes of Huế's southern bank is the Altar of Nam Giao, a giant open-air monument. Its name means "Plane of Worshipping Heaven"; this now abandoned and desolate-looking structure was once the sight where the emperors of the Nguyễn Dynasty would make an annual journey to worship their fathers and perform Confucian rituals. The three layers represent heaven, earth, and man. The surrounding trees were planted by Emperor Minh Mạng and his subjects. Those planted by the Emperor himself proudly bear a bronze mark. The park and altar remain open to visitors looking for a quiet spot to read, promenade, or soak up the mid-morning sun. *(To reach the park, head west on Lê Lợi, then left on Điện Biên Phủ. Following it all the way down leads you straight to the park gates. Open daily 7am-5pm. Free.)*

TỪ ĐÀM PAGODA. Less impressive architecturally than its neighbors, the pagoda holds an important position in Vietnamese and Buddhist history. First founded in 1695 under the name An Tôn, in 1842 Emperor Thieu Tri renamed it Từ Đàm. In 1945, Từ Đàm became the center of Buddhist anti-colonial activism, while from 1960 to 1963 it harbored the Buddhist movement against the regime of Ngô Đinh Diệm. Now it is a place of learning, where monks study and impart their knowledge—especially of languages—to others. The pagoda remains an active place of worship, as yet unmarred by flocks of visitors; those wishing to view the simple interior can ask one of the monks for a peek. *(1 Sư Liễu Quán. Head west on Lê Lợi, turning left onto Điện Biên Phủ directly before hitting the train station. Continue straight. About 1km down the road, veer right onto Sư Liễu Quán.)*

THE TOMB OF PHAN BỘI CHÂU. Two small tombs are accompanied by a giant bust of the famous Vietnamese philosopher's head. A small museum with photos stands beside the relics. *(119 Phan Bội Châu. The museum is just across the street from the Từ Đàm Pagoda. Open Tu, Th, and Sa-Su 7:30-11am and 1:30-4:30pm. Free.)*

MARKETS

The sole source of fruits and veggies, as well as cheaper shoes and clothes, the city's larger markets make shopping easy. To avoid higher prices, venture farther from the center and away from tourist-flocked markets like Đông Ba.

NORTHERN BANK

Đông Ba Market, Huế's largest, sprawls on the Citadel side of the Perfume River at the far northeast end of Trần Hưng Đạo. (Open daily 6am-7:30pm.) The **Tây Lác Market** is across from 47 Nguyễn Trãi, about 1.7km from the Citadel's westernmost gate along the Perfume River. Food, clothes, toys, and shoes abound in the clutter of shops. (Open daily 7am-7pm.)

SOUTHERN BANK

Slightly smaller then the other two, but nonetheless equipped to meet almost any need is the **An Cựu Market,** near the southern end of Hùng Vương, 2.5km from Lê Lợi and before the small bridge. (Open daily 7am-8pm.) Shoppers are enticed by fresh fruit, meat, and veggies, as well as electronics, gadgets, and all sorts of apparel and accessories. The **Bến Ngự Market** is near the southwest edge of the Southern Bank. Heading down on Lê Lợi, veer left at the HCM museum onto Trần Thúc Nhẫn. The market sits at the road's end. A small **fruit and veggie market** sits near the intersection of Bến Nghé and Nguyễn Tri Phương.

NIGHTLIFE

Night owls take warning: Huế is known for its lack of a late-night scene. While locals and Vietnamese tourists crowd street cafes near the Citadel, restaurants, and street-corner *phở* and *cơm* shops, the city's streets quiet down by 10 or 11pm, leaving late-night, thrill-seeking tourists thirsting for entertainment. Most people simply wander the streets and congregate at the few late-night bars on the southern bank of the Perfume River.

DMZ Café and Bar, 44 Lê Lợi. Popular with backpackers, tourists, and locals refusing to give in to Huế's sleepy streets. An unpretentious hangout with free pool, cheap beer, and a lively crowd by 11pm. Beer 8000-15,000Đ. Open 2:30pm-2am.

Cafe Hóang Phưo'ng, 292B Chi Lang (☎524 879), on the thin strip east of the Citadel. Good coffee and a great location overlooking the Perfume River. Get here before dark to grab a water-side seat, as the cafe fills up with friends and couples early, even on weeknights. From Đông Ba market, head up across the bridge, veering left into the last road. White coffee 4000Đ. Open daily 7am-11pm.

Brown Eyes Chi Rua, 55 Nguyễn Sinh Cung (☎827 494). Open late and until it clears out, Brown Eyes livens up when the city goes to sleep at night. Locals and wandering tourists unwilling to call it a night mingle, dance, drink, and cheer for the cup all night. Corona 50,000Đ; Huda 15,000Đ; flaming B52 45,000Đ.

DAYTRIPS FROM HUẾ

A trip to Huế isn't complete without a short excursion to the historical, ruin-strewn countryside. You can choose from a full-day adventure into the heart of Vietnam's imperial history, or a relaxing day of fun in the sun on a nearby beach.

THUẬN AN. Heading east from Huế leads to the turbulent Pacific shore of Thuận An. Only 13km from the city center, the pristine sand beach is abandoned during weekday mornings and early afternoons, but visitors flock in the evening and on weekends. The golden, burning sand stretches south along the rough waters. Covered lawnchairs provide protection from the beating sun and a comfortable respite from the sea. Venturing farther east along the beach usually decreases the number of visitors, vendors, and seaside eateries with whom you share the beach. *(You can reach the beach by bus, taxi, or motorbike. Buses leave from the Đông Ba Market every hr. from 5:30am-3pm, 5500Đ. Only one bus makes a journey back into the city. To catch it, walk back from the beach onto the main road that run to Huế. Flag down the bus as it rumbles back at 3 or 4pm. Alternatively, hop on a motorbike (15,000Đ one-way) or call a taxi to drop you off and pick you up (90,000Đ one-way). To reach the water by yourself, follow Lê Lợi as it makes its way east and turns into Nguyễn Sinh Cung. Continue on the winding road for 12km until you spot signs for the beach directing you to hook a left into a sandy path.)*

ROYAL TOMBS

Huế is home to the tombs of seven emperors of the Nguyễn Dynasty. Designed by the rulers themselves, each tomb represents the expressive spirit of the emperor as well as the architecture of the time; most are a mix of Vietnamese and French styles. A few kilometers southwest of the city center, the tombs are accessible by motorcycle or bike. Most visitors, however, opt for a US$2 dragon-boat trip, which, though charming, throws all sorts of sales pitches at tourists. For some tombs, the additional motorbike ride from the river may cost upwards of 50,000Đ. Poorly marked roads connect most of the sights. The locals are usually helpful in pointing confused tourists in the right direction. *(All tombs open daily summer 6:30am-5:30pm; winter 7am-5pm. English-speaking guides inside can answer questions, provide some information, or take tourists on a guided tour. Requested tour donation 50,000Đ.)*

TOMB OF TỰ ĐỨC. The tomb of Tự Đức, whose indecisive rule was one of the factors in the Nguyễn's quick capitulation to the French, is one of the most striking. Its attractions include a temple dedicated to his wives and predecessors, ruins of the houses that held the Emperor's concubines, and the Minh Kiêm Theatre, where the concubines once performed and where visitors can now dress up to take their own royal photos. *(Train station 300m farther on a dirt road heading to the right. Follow this for 2km, then take 2nd left. 55,000Đ.)*

TOMBS OF ĐỒNG KHÁNH AND THIỆU TRI. At the age of 25, after only three years of royal control, Emperor Đồng Khánh died. Without a tomb, his remains were placed in the temple dedicated to his father. When Thành Thái, his son, ascended to the throne, he chose a palace constructed in 1845 for the worship of his father, and the hill 30 meters to the west as his resting place. The less-visited tomb of Đồng Khánh, dedicated to the late emperor, contains portraits of many of his nine wives as well as one of himself. *(200m from the tomb of Tự Đức. 22,000Đ.)* One and a half kilometers down the gravel track is the tomb of Thiệu Trị, the oldest son of Emperor Minh Mạng. As he died seven years after claiming power, he did not build his own tomb. Instead, his son, Tự Đức, found land at the foot of a mountain 8km from the city, suitable for his father's burial place. Rather than placing his

VIETNAM

father's remains among mountain peaks, as his ancestors had done, Tự Đức located them in a valley of calm, meandering streams. Though the tomb stands in ruins and the temple suffers from lack of renovation and interest, the grounds of Thiệu Trị's resting place remain peaceful and picturesque. *(From the tomb of Đồng Khánh, follow the road you arrived on as it flows into the fields and small forest, and passes unmarked ruins on the right. At its end, take a left onto the main road. Close ahead, a sign points to the tomb of Thiệu Trị. 22,000Đ.)*

TOMB OF MINH MẠNG AND TEMPLE OF MINH LẦU. Built between 1841 and 1843, Minh Mạng's tomb has the greatest architectural balance and poise of all Huế's tombs. Three sets of stairs lead to a steel pavilion that bears Minh Mạng's eulogy. The Minh Lầu Temple, opposite the courtyards at the tomb, houses an altar to the king's prosperity and longevity. Over a stone bridge is the tomb proper; look for a dirt mound. *(From Thiệu Trị, take a left on the paved road and continue for 2km. Go over the bridge and go back down toward the river bank. Take a right onto the dirt path and cross under the bridge. Minh Mạng is 1km farther on your left. Minh Lầu Temple 55,000Đ.)*

TOMB OF GIA LONG. Gia Long's tomb was built between 1814 and 1820. Eighteen kilometers from the city, this rarely visited mausoleum has a courtyard surrounded by a lotus pond and a chain of 42 hills. To peek inside the tomb, ask the keeper to open the gate. Inside, the Emperor and his wife are buried in what now seems like a desolate maze. Below the steps to the tomb stand figures of soldiers, elephants, and horses, mimicking the style of the king's court. *(Several kilometers from the tomb of Minh Mạng. Follow the access road southeast through Minh Mạng Village to a tributary of the Perfume River. Construction is underway on a bridge connecting the banks; until its completion, cross the river on a ferry for 10,000Đ per person round-trip. After reaching the other bank, turn left and follow the path, turning right into the fields (and directly after a small temple) and left again to reach a small road parallel to the first. Continuing straight toward a mountain streaked with red leads to the temple and tomb. Open daily 7am-5pm.)*

TOMB OF KHẢI ĐỊNH. With grounds a bit lacking in the luscious green appeal of those of his predecessors' tombs, Khải Định's tomb is smaller but also grander in its design. Only four years after he came to power, the French colonized the country, leaving the Emperor as no more than a ceremonial figurehead. With little power, but anxious to ensure a luxurious afterlife, Khải Định raised the country's taxes by 30% so as to collect the funds necessary to complete his final resting place. The last of the tombs to be built, it shows a distinctly European architectural influence, as well materials gathered from all over the world, including French tiles and Chinese and Japanese glass. At the top, the inside of the tomb is ornately decorated with gorgeous mosaics, and houses an altar with a gilded statue of Khải Định, making it the only tomb with a visual representation of the emperor. *(From the tombs of Gia Long, head toward the ferry dock and backtrack across the Perfume River. Turn right at the top of the bluff and left after 200m. Khải Định looms atop a hill, 1km down the road on the right. 55,000Đ.)*

BẠCH MÃ NATIONAL PARK

Travelers speeding along Hwy. 1 in the Huế-Hội An corridor rarely notice the turn-off leading to Bạch Mã National Park. It's their loss—Bạch Mã offers sights exceeding anything that can be found in Vietnam's cities and towns. Its ecotourism infrastructure is relatively well-developed and visitor numbers remain low. Bạch Mã has long been valued: the French built a resort here in the 1930s and the Americans built a helicopter base in the 1960s. They left ruins of each—ripe for exploring—as well as an outstanding road connecting the summit to Hwy. 1. Along this road, the park service has established several well-maintained trails and villas, a post office, and a water purification plant at the summit. Much has been done at the park to allow for responsible ecotourism opportunities. The magnificent sight of languorous clouds drifting among the valleys of Vietnam's coastal mountains is a welcome break from highway traffic; take an hour and get off the road.

TRANSPORTATION. The entrance to the park is just 3km from Hwy. 1. If you have your own transportation, simply turn off Hwy. 1 at the sign reading "Bạch Mâ" in the center of Cầu Hai Village (40km south of Huế, 60km north of Đà Nẵng). Follow the road through the village to the gate 3km away. Another option is to take a bus from Huế or Đà Nẵng and tell the driver to let you off in Cầu Hai, or simply say "Bạch Mâ." (A tourist bus should cost US$2-3; a local one, US$1-2.) Once you've been dropped off along the highway, a motorbike can take you the rest of the way for 5000Đ or less. No motorbikes are allowed to drive up the steep mountain road, but there are no restrictions on other private vehicles; if you don't want to walk, bring your own four wheels or rent some at the park headquarters.

ORIENTATION AND PRACTICAL INFORMATION. Comprised of Bạch Mâ's mountain (1450m) and its environs, the park climbs from Cầu Hai Lagoon to the summit, taking the visitor through tropical monsoon evergreen forest to the subtropical rainforest of the higher altitudes (the peak is one of Vietnam's wettest spots, with 800mm of rain per year). The park boasts well-maintained trails, and most of the trailheads are along the road to the summit. Bring plenty of water a, use lots of insect repellent, and be sure to check ankles and waistlines for leeches after you hike. The entrance fee is 10,500Đ and 5500Đ for students. Maps and trail information can be picked up at the **headquarters** (☎54 871 330; www.bachma.vnn.vn). Guides are also available for hire here, though they're not necessary. The best time of year to visit Bǎch Mâ is during the north's dry season: February to August. Hike in the afternoon, after the morning fog has burned off.

HIKING. Five Lakes Trail (2km+) is by far the most interesting trail in the park. It takes you along five small lakes and several cascades, and eventually links up with the Rhododendron Trail. The shores of the lakes are crowded by ferns, bamboo, and Lá Nón plants. Bring a guide on this trail; there are so many natural wonders on this trail that you could otherwise miss a lot of them.

Rhododendron Trail (3km+) is another excellent trail, and it connects up with Five Lakes Trail. Being above 100m, you have the chance to see flora and fauna not found in the lowlands, including the special orchids and the Samba Deer. Reaching the 300m high Rhododendron Falls is the climax of the trail: you have a clear view of Mt. Mang, the highest peak in the area (1713m). You can climb down to the bottom of the falls, but be aware that it's difficult and slippery. The best time to do this trail is the spring, when the top of the falls is framed by blooming flowers. The trail begins 14km up the summit road (2km short of the guesthouse).

ĐÀ NẴNG ☎511

For years a keystone of foreign designs on Vietnam, as both the primary French port in central Vietnam and a nerve center of the Vietnam War machine, Đà Nẵng today has shifted into a low-key role. Between Huế to the northwest and Hội An to the southeast, Vietnam's fourth-largest city is skipped over completely by most tourists. Though it's a booming seaport and commercial center, Đà Nẵng itself offers little to captivate; not so the surrounding countryside. The environs of Đà Nẵng include mountaintop resorts with spectacular vistas, secluded beaches with fresh seafood restaurants, and rice paddies melting into jungle.

TRANSPORTATION

Flights: Đà Nẵng International Airport (☎827 286), 4km west of town. **Vietnam Airlines,** 35 Trần Phú (☎811 111). Open daily 7:30-11am and 1:30-5pm. Flights to: **Bangkok** (Tu, Th, Sa 11:10am; US$170); **Buôn Ma Thuột** (M, W, Sa 2:10pm, F 10:10am; 550,000Đ); **Hà Nội** (3 per day; 975,000Đ); **HCMC** (4 per day; 975,000Đ); **Nha Trang** (daily 10:15am; 575,000Đ); **Pleiku** (M, W, Sa-Su 10:15am; 545,000Đ); **Vinh** (M, W, Sa 10:20am; 700,000Đ). **Pacific Airlines,** 135 Lê Lợi (☎825 136; fax 810 144).

Trains: Đà Nẵng Railway Station, 4 Hải Phòng (☎823 810). To **Hà Nội** (15-22hr.; 6:30am-9pm; 246,000-639,000Đ) and **HCMC** (17-23hr.; 5:30am-8pm; 284,000-740,000Đ). Ticket office open daily 6am-5pm.

Buses: Full-sized **public buses** make the frequent trip to **Hội An** from well-marked stops all over town; there's one outside Đà Nẵng Cathedral (20,000Đ). **A/C tourist minibuses** can be booked at most hotels to: **Hà Nội** (24hr., 2pm, US$10); **HCMC** (24hr., 5:30am, US$17); **Hội An** (1hr.; 7, 9am, 2pm; US$3); **Huế** (3hr.; 7, 9am, 2pm; US$3); **Nha Trang** (10-12hr., 5:30am, US$7); **Savannakhet, Laos** (19hr.; 6 and 9pm; US$18). There are two formal bus stations in Đà Nẵng:

Interprovince bus station, 33 Điện Biên Phủ (☎821 265), 2km west of town. Buses to: **Đà Lạt** (19hr.; 4am; 107,000Đ); **Hà Nội** (24hr.; 5-9am; 87,000Đ); **HCMC** (24hr.; 5:30-9:30am; 104,000Đ); **Huế** (3hr.; every 30min. 6am-4pm; 22,000Đ); **Nha Trang** (13hr.; 5am; 57,000Đ); **Qui Nhơn** (9hr.; 4:30-9:30am; 32,000Đ); **Savannakhet, Laos** (19hr.; 8pm; 300,000Đ).

Intraprovince bus station, 29 Điện Biên Phủ (☎823 715), next to the interprovince station. Sends tiny buses to **Hội An** (10,000Đ).

Local Transportation: Motorbike and **cyclo** drivers will gladly take you to the airport (8000Đ), the **bus stations** (7000Đ), China Beach (30,000Đ), Marble Mountains (30,000Đ), and elsewhere. **Taxi** service is most easily arranged through your hotel; try **Hương Lua Taxi** (☎828 282) or **Sông Hàn Taxi** (☎655 655). Metered taxi to the airport runs 30,000Đ.

ORIENTATION AND PRACTICAL INFORMATION

Almost at the center of Vietnam, 750km south of Hà Nội and 990km north of HCMC, Đà Nẵng is bounded in the east by the **Hàn River** and in the north by **Đà Nẵng Bay. Bạch Đằng,** the beautiful main boulevard, runs along the river's west bank. One block inland, **Trần Phú** runs parallel to Bạch Đằng, but traffic is one-way going south. Three blocks inland, **Lê Lợi/Phan Chu Trinh** is the major north-south artery. These three streets are intersected by **Điện Biên Phủ/Lộ Thái Tổ/Hùng Vương,** the busy east-west road that branches off Hwy. 1 and bisects the city. The city's southern boundary, **Nguyễn Văn Trỗi,** runs east over the Hàn River and toward the Marble Mountains, China Beach, and Hội An.

Tourist Offices: Most hotels offer basic tour services. State-run **Danatours** (danamarle@dng.vnn.vn) has offices all over town. Branch at 100 Bạch Đằng (☎834 515; fax 828 262). Private companies also abound. **An Phu Tourist** has offices in the center, 147 Lê Lợi (☎818 366), and the north end of town, 9 Đông Đa (☎818 366).

Consulates: Laos, 16 Trần Quộ Cáp (☎821 208). Issues tourist visas to cross into Laos at Lao Bảo; 1-day processing. Open M-F 8-11:30am and 2-4:30pm.

Banks: Vietcombank, 140 Lê Lợi (☎823 503) cashes traveler's checks and does credit card advances. Open M-Sa 7:30-11am and 1-4pm. 24hr. **ATM** outside. The **Investment and Development Bank,** 40-42 Hùng Vương (☎829 683; fax 827 693), is on the main drag in the center of town. Open M-Sa 7-11am and 1-4pm.

Markets: Chợ Hàn is on the river by the intersection of Hùng Vương and Trần Phú. Open daily 6am-8pm. **Chợ Côn** hulks near the intersection of Hùng Vương and Ông Ích Khiêm. Open daily 6:30am-6:30pm. Hùng Vương itself is lined with Western-style goods at Vietnamese prices.

Pharmacies: One on every other block.

Police: 1 Nguyễn Thị Minh Khai (☎828 371).

Medical Services: Central Đà Nẵng Hospital, 124 Hải Phòng (☎821 118), 1 block north of Lê Duẩn. Has a Foreign Relations Affairs Office affiliated with AEA International.

Internet Access: Every block has an **Internet** parlor: the going rate is 3000Đ per hr. Three options are: 131 Nguyễn Chí Thanh, 26 Quang Trưng, and 61 Trần Quốc Toản. Almost all places have Internet phones for cheap international calling.

Post Offices: General Post Office, 60 Bạch Đằng, north of the intersection with Hùng Vương. **Foreign Services Post Office,** 64 Bạch Đằng (☎821 327), across the street. International phones, fax, and *Poste Restante.* Open daily 6am-10pm.

ACCOMMODATIONS

Budget travelers usually bypass Đà Nẵng, so most hotels tend to cater to the resort crowd; cheap beds are few and far between. You may need to splurge.

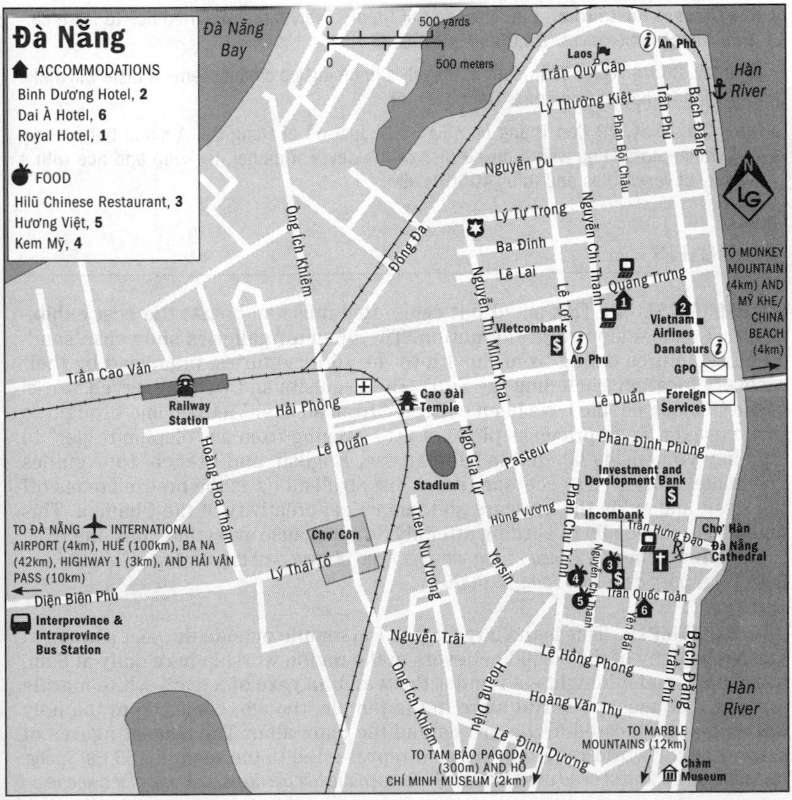

Dai À Hotel, 51 (27) Yên Bái (☎827 532; daiahotel@dng.vnn.vn). Great central location and clean rooms for some of the lowest prices in the city. You'll have to put up with the cathedral bell tolling at 4:30am, though. Rooms US$10-20. ❸

Binh Dư'o'ng Hotel, 32-34 Trần Phú (☎821 930; ngtbinh@dng.vnn.vn). The exceedingly friendly owner has arranged for a "no honking" sign to be put right outside. All rooms have A/C and satellite TV. Singles US$12; doubles US$15; apartment-style suites with breakfast US$22-30. Brand new restaurant downstairs. ❸

Royal Hotel, 17 Quang Trư'ng (☎823 295; royalhotel@dng.vnn.vn). A prototype of the legions of 3-star hotels in the city, yet in a quieter location than all the others. Caters to the foreign business crowd with mini-bars and meeting rooms. US$25-35. ❺

FOOD

Food options in Đà Nẵng are slim: you can choose from the ever-present food stalls selling rice, soup, and grilled meat, or from a bunch of Chinese restaurants. In the mix are a few Western offerings.

Hư'o'ng Việt, 89 Trần Quốc Toản. Relatively cheap English-language Chinese menu with some treats at the end. The fried chicken (15,000Đ) is excellent, but may not be satisfying enough for some. ❷

Hilu Chinese Restaurant, 225 Nguyễn Chí Thanh. Everything from fried rice to fresh catfish. Reasonable prices: 30,000-70,000Đ. ❸

Kem Mỹ, 86 Trần Quốc Toản. Part of the city's booming ice cream scene. A taste will make you pine for home. Open daily 8am-9pm. ❷

Cafe Giải Khát, 29 Cao Thắng (☎530 353). Just off of Đống Đa. A small but friendly vegetarian *co'm* shop with a mixed dish of the day. For dinner, try soup and rice with a variety of vegetables and tofu (4000Đ). ❶

VIETNAM

SIGHTS

CHÀM MUSEUM. This small but celebrated museum boasts the best exhibition of Chàm sculpture in the nation. The open-air galleries showcase sandstone sculptures dating from the 4th to the 16th centuries, organized by their recovery location (including Mỹ Sơn). The exquisite and well-preserved works of the Champa people have been collected from all over Vietnam and brought to this museum. Each priceless piece of art—ranging from an "elephant-tiger" to dancing women—is labeled in Vietnamese, English, and French; tour guides and guidebooks aren't necessary here. Just stroll along as the breeze comes off the river, and enjoy the intricate and fantastical creativity of the Champa. This museum is especially rewarding after Mỹ Sơn, because everything missing from there is found here. *(2 Trieu La, on the south end of town past the merging of Trần Phú and Bạch Đằng. Open daily 7am-5pm. 20,000Đ.)*

CAO ĐÀI TEMPLE. This is the largest Cao Đài temple outside the sect's home in Tây Ninh. Many of the 50,000 believers in the region worship here daily at 6am, noon, 6pm, and midnight—all under the watchful gaze of a giant white marble Buddha. The most powerful stare in the temple, though, comes from the holy all-seeing eye, located in the orb behind the main altar. The central figures of several major world religions are also represented in the temple. *(63 Hải Phòng, parallel to Lê Duẩn; just head one block north. To open the temple doors, ask one of the keepers.)*

HỒ CHÍ MINH MUSEUM. A slightly more upscale version of the generic HCM museum, dedicated to commemorating the life and achievements of Vietnam's famous political leader. A small garden encompasses the exhibition gallery of Uncle Ho's life and a military museum filled with wartime photographs. The museum also has a replica of the man's childhood home in Làng Kim Liên. *(☎069 775 0921. Duy Tân. Open daily 8-10:30am and 2-4:30pm. 20,000Đ.)*

DAYTRIPS FROM ĐÀ NẴNG

The real draw of Đà Nẵng is its surroundings: within an hour's ride are a variety of noteworthy locales, from mountain-top resorts to secluded beaches to ancient cave shrines.

MARBLE MOUNTAINS (NGŨ HÀNH SƠN). The Marble Mountains are named after the five fundamental elements: the popular Water Mountain, the thin Metal Mountain, the subtle Wood mountain, the double-peaked Fire Mountain, and the Earth Mountain. Limestone and marble quarries cluster around the foot of **Water Mountain (Ngon Thủy So'n),** with grand temples, eerie grottos, and idols hewn from the rock. In the 1960s, the mountain served as a base for the NLF. From the entrance closest to the beach, stairs lead past a white Buddha to the towering **Linh Ủng Pagoda.** The Tàng Chôn Cave, in the back, contains a shrine flanked by a Chàm sculpture and a square stone platform, on which, according to legend, fairies and gods played checkers. For a grand panorama of China Beach from the mountain's highest accessible point, ascend **Động Vân Thông,** the "Way to Heaven." Back on the path, the **Tam Thái Pagoda** sports some beautiful bas-relief carvings. To the pagoda's right, a stone representation of Quan Âm—a buddha who is Vietnam's patron saint—is carved from **Oa Nghiêm Cave,** but the best sight lies behind it: the light that penetrates the **Huyền Không Cave** through large holes above. Four warrior statues at the cavern's entrance, dating from Minh Mạng's time, protect it from evil spirits. Near the left stairwell, a path leads past two small pagodas to **Vọng Giang Đài,** the perfect place to take in the "Five-Mountain View." The Marble Mountains can provide a uniquely spiritual atmosphere if you visit when the place isn't overrun with tourists; consider visiting by motorbike in the early morning or at sunset. *(17km north of Hội An and 12km south of Đà Nẵng. Motos and cyclos make the trip for 30,000Đ. Most tourist buses stop here for an hour. Open daily 7am-6pm. 10,000Đ.)*

CHINA BEACH. Along the low-lying stretch of land to the east of Đà Nẵng and north of the Marble Mountains are kilometers of deserted beach. The southernmost beach is China Beach, famous for being the location of a US Marine landing in 1965—however, it's unlikely that it actually was. Mỹ Khê Beach, to the north, slightly more developed but still relatively deserted, is more likely the real landing place. Development has been blessedly minimal, and the white-sand beaches remain wide and clean. *(20,000Đ motorbike ride from Đà Nẵng or the Marble Mountains.)* Guesthouses line the thin forest near the water, while the beach's proximity to the Marble Mountains ensures a variety of tourist-oriented **restaurants** ❷ that provide decent meals (soup 7000-10,000Đ, main courses 10,000-35,000Đ). **Hoa's Place** ❷, 215/14 Huyền Trân Công Chúa (☎969 978), is a 10m walk from China Beach. A friendly English-speaking owner helps guests arrange bookings and prepares terrific spring rolls. The rooms are small but clean and feature private baths. (Spring rolls 20,000Đ. Singles with fan US$4; doubles with fan US$6, with A/C US$8-10.)

HẢI VÂN PASS. To move north from Đà Nẵng and on to Huế, you must first negotiate the Hải Vân Pass. A finger of the Trường Sơn Mountain range sticks into the South China Sea, forming a dramatic natural barrier. In the winter, the difference in climate is quite striking: north of the pass it will be cold and wet and pouring rain, while the south side will be clean and warm. The mountain pass, at the height of 500m, produces spectacular cloud formations and views of sprawling Đà Nẵng to the south and picture-perfect beaches to the north. There are two options to get through the "Pass of the Clouds." Buses take Hwy. 1, which goes over the summit, and many tour buses stop here in the shadow of an old French fort. Alternatively, the train winds around the edge of the mountain and brings you close enough to the breaking surf to feel its refreshing spray.

THE SOUTHERN CENTRAL COAST

The Southern Central Coast is where foreigners and nationals alike come to play. Gorgeous, secluded beaches begin around Quảng Ngãi, but many tourists head farther south for the well-groomed sands of Mũi Né or the bustling scene of Nha Trang. People have been enjoying the coastal sun for centuries: the Chàm were the first to flourish here, as evidenced by their many imposing towers. Sadly, this lovely region did not escape the ravages of war. Quảng Ngãi province saw intense fighting during the Vietnam War, including the infamous Mỹ Lai Massacre. Today, though, it seems that the tempestuous past has been forgotten, at least in part. Fishing communities have become resort towns, and battlefields have been reclaimed by rice paddies. Tourists flood the coast, gorging themselves on spectacular seafood, clean azure waters, and fine white sand.

HỘI AN ☎510

VIETNAM

Although it traces its trading roots to the Chàm era, Hội An (known to Europeans as "Faifo") gained its reputation as a central port frequented by Chinese, Japanese, and European merchants from the 16th to the 19th centuries. As the river began to silt up in the 1800s, the French chose nearby Đà Nẵng as the next commercial center of Central Vietnam. Today, Hội An does a brisk business in the tourist trade. Merchants' mansions, ornate Chinese assembly halls, and laid-back charm—plus over 100 quality tailoring shops—win over travelers' hearts. Hội An is also a UNESCO World Heritage Site, as is nearby Mỹ Son with its Champa ruins. Tourists overrun the town and tend to stay twice as long as they'd planned.

TRANSPORTATION

The **public bus station,** 81 Huỳnh Thúc Kháng (☎861 284), is 400m west of town. Tiny open-air trucks (2hr.; every hr. 5am-4pm; 10,000Đ) and full-size red and white buses run to Đà Nẵng via Marble Mountain or China Beach (1hr.; every hr. 5:30am-5:30pm; 20,000Đ) from less than 1km northwest of town at the intersection of Nhị Trưng and Lê Hồng Phong. For Nha Trang and Quảng Ngãi, head to Hwy. 1, about 10km away, and flag down a bus. **Tourist minibuses** are available at any hotel and head to: Đà Nẵng (1hr.; 8am; US$3); Hà Nội (14hr.; 6am and 8pm; US$15); Huế (3hr.; 8am; US$3); Nha Trang (10hr.; 6am and 8pm; US$7-12). Most hotels rent **cars** with drivers (from US$20 per day), **motorbikes** (US$5 per day including petrol), and **bicycles** (4000-7000Đ per day). **Taxis** and **freelance minibuses** hang out at the intersection of Phan Chu Trinh and Hoàng Diệu.

ORIENTATION AND PRACTICAL INFORMATION

Hội An is 25km south of Đà Nẵng and 102km north of Quảng Ngãi. Most public buses drop passengers at the side of **Highway 1;** from here, it's a 10km, 10,000Đ motorbike ride east to Hội An along **Huỳnh Thúc Kháng.** Just before town, the street

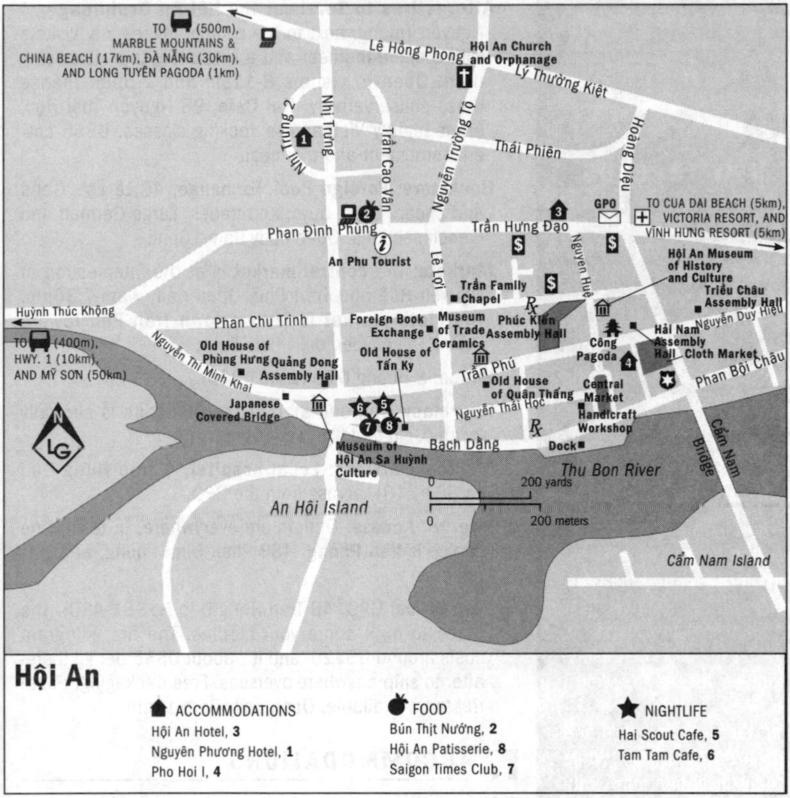

breaks into three branches. **Phan Đình Phùng** marks the north edge of town, eventually becoming **Trần Hưng Đạo,** home to the **post office** and Hội An Hotel, and ultimately leading to the beach (4km). The middle branch is **Phan Chu Trinh.** The last branch, **Nguyễn Thị Minh Khai,** heads southeast toward the **Japanese Covered Bridge.** After the bridge it becomes **Trần Phú,** the town's most sight-packed road. **Lê Hồng Phong** forms the northernmost boundary for visitors. The major north-south streets, from west to east, are **Nhị Trưng, Lê Lợi, Nguyễn Huệ,** and **Hoàng Diệu,** which leads over the Cẩm Nam Bridge to Cẩm Nam Island.

Tourist Offices: Every hotel can arrange local and national tours and tourist bureaus are everywhere. **An Phu Tourist Company,** 29 Phan Đình Phùng (☎862 643; www.anphutourist.com). Open tickets, guides, local tours (Mỹ Son US$150), currency exchange, and bus and plane tickets. Open daily 6am-10pm. **Hội An Tourist,** 37 Trần Phú (☎861 327; ttuhutt@dng.vnn.vn). Specializes in local sights (UNESCO sights 50,000Đ; Cham Island 800,000Đ; pottery village 75,000Đ; traditional music show 9pm, 40,000Đ).

Banking: Vietincom Bank, 4 Hoàng Diệu (☎862 675). Currency exchange, traveler's checks services, MC/V cash advances. Open daily M-Sa 7:30am-7pm. The fastest way to get a fistful of đồng is the **ATM** at 37 Trần Hưng Đạo (open daily 8am-8pm).

FROM THE ROAD

HOT NEW THREADS

I first heard about Hội An a month before I arrived in Vietnam. I was talking to a previous *Let's Go* Vietnam researcher and he remarked that he had really enjoyed Hội An, in part because he had had a couple of suits made there—he wished he had ordered more. I didn't pay much attention; clothing, as a regional attraction, didn't strike me as all that compelling. This sentiment didn't change much through my first weeks in the country, even as I closed in on Hội An and met travelers decked out in their new suits. I pulled into town with tailoring low on my list. Then everything changed for me—as well it should have.

Having tailored clothes made for you in a day is a rush. While the constant invitation into clothing shops may try one's patience, all is forgotten as the imagination runs wild with the prospect of creating a new outfit.

The process begins with the selection of the desired article of clothing. Almost all shops have a collection of Western catalogues to help with selection. You can either choose something exactly as shown or mix and match, creating completely unique gear. After you select the item and the fabric (from a remarkable variety), it's time to settle on the price.

I chose to have two suits and a pair of pinstripe trousers made, and I got the price down from US$145 to US$115. After negoti-

Alternatives to Tourism: The **Hội An Orphanage,** 4 Nguyễn Truong, next to the church, invites any visitors with a spare moment and a kind smile to visit its children. Open to visitors 8-11am and 2-5pm. Please dress conservatively. **Hai Cafe,** 98 Nguyễn Thái Học, offers nightly Vietnamese cooking classes. US$5 covers enrollment and the meal.

Bookstore: Foreign Book Exchange, 48 Lê Lợi. Good and cheap; sells, buys, and trades. Large German and French sections. Open daily 9am-10pm.

Markets: The **central market** is at the intersection of Nguyễn Huệ and Trần Phú. Open daily 6am-7:30pm. The **cloth market** is farther down Trần Phú toward Hoàng Diệu. Open daily 6am-5pm.

Police: 8 Hoàng Diệu (☎861 204).

Pharmacy: The one at 19 Phan Chu Trinh is centrally located. Open daily 7am-10pm.

Medical Services: Local hospital, 4 Trần Hưng Đạo (☎861 218), across from the GPO.

Internet Access: Outlets are everywhere. In town, one choice is **Vân Phòng,** 48B Phan Đình Phùng, at 100Đ per min.

Post Office: GPO, 4B Trần Hưng Đạo (☎861 480). The place to mail home your clothes. The first kilogram costs around US$20, and it's about US$5 per kg thereafter to ship anywhere overseas. Free packaging. *Poste Restante* available. Open daily 6am-10pm.

ACCOMMODATIONS

Hội An will never have a room shortage. The center of town offers older, more convenient, and more expensive establishments. The northwest corner of town, marked by Lê Hồng Phong and Nhị Trưng, has seen large-scale development of hotels. These tend to be newer, cheaper, and only a short 5min. walk from the center of town. You'll find most backpackers here.

Nguyên Phương Hotel, 6 Nhị Trưng (☎916 588). One of the best deals in Hội An. Small guesthouse in the hotel district provides comfortable rooms at the right price. Singles with hot water and satellite TV US$5; doubles US$8. ❷

Pho Hoi 1, 7/2 Trần Phú (☎861 633; www.phohoiriversidehoian.com). The best deal in the city center. Rooms are cheap and adequate. Staff is backpacker-friendly and speaks English. The proximity to the market brings early morning wake-ups and a cockroach or two. Singles with hot water and satellite TV US$8; doubles US$10. ❸

Hội An Hotel, 6 Trần Hưng Đạo (☎861 373; hoianhotel@dng.vnn.vn). The most plush sleep in downtown Hội An. The sprawling compound—almost a village in itself—offers tennis courts, tourist offices, a restaurant, and a swimming pool. Rooms US$40-100. ❺

FOOD

Hội An has both quantity and quality when it comes to food. The city's local culinary specialties are famous throughout the country. Every nook and cranny yields a new restaurant or cafe. The cheapest eats radiate out from the market in the center of town. A waterfront stroll reveals a string of seafood restaurants.

For seafood lovers, the delicate taste of **white rose,** tasty shrimp steamed in a light flour wrapping, is a find. **Fried wonton noodles** also draw connoisseurs from around the country. The real treat, however, is *cao lẫu,* served at almost every Hội An restaurant. It's a thick and flat rice noodle served with sprouts, greens, and crispy fried rice paper in a light soup, enhanced with mint, anise, and small chilies.

If you need a break from shopping or want to watch life go by, Hội An offers two outstanding windows on the world. **Cafe King ❶**, 10 Phan Chu Trinh, is located literally in the center of town (coffee 6000Đ). **Quán Dần Lang ❶** is tourist-free and stares down Hội An from the opposite side of the river. To reach it, cross Cam Nam Bridge, take the first right 20m down the road, and walk 150m to the end of the residential street. You'll find a beer here for 5000Đ.

Hội An Patisserie, 107-109 Nguyễn Thái Học. With a real French pastry chef and a wide selection of delectable treats, this is what you've been craving. Take the coffee and crème brulée (12,000Đ) to the terrace and be transported back to French Indochina. Located at the western edge of town by the river. Gourmet sandwiches 30,000Đ. ❷

Bún Thịt Nướng, Phan Đình Phùng, across from the Italian restaurant. Pull up a plastic stool and join the locals. This street stall is a true hidden gem of the city. Your choice is between a small bowl (8000Đ) or large bowl (10,000Đ) of noodles with meat cooked in an excellent peanut chili sauce. ❶

Saigon Times Club, 119-121 Nguyễn Thái Học. Hội An's finest eatery seems like a relic from the French colonial era, but it's actually brand new. Overlooks the river and a quiet plaza. Gourmet seafood and steak 150,000Đ and up. ❺

ations were over, I was measured and sent happily on my way, thinking only of my next opportunity to make clothing, as my creative tendencies had been awakened. I gave the seamstresses two days and they were very thankful; most requests are for 24hr. I returned the following day and tried on the suits. They looked great but were a little tight. I didn't think much of it, but realizing that this was the place to have any altering done, I mentioned the problem and they were more than happy to make the corrections. The following day, everything was finished—I almost wished that I was returning home to a professional job, or at least a job interview.

I headed up the street to the post office to mail everything home—I wasn't planning to carry around a couple suits for another month—and the mail clerks were helpful, being quite accustomed to visitors' needs. While they packaged my clothes (for free), I filled out several customs forms and paid an exorbitant amount to ship them home. Still, even after the US$75 charge, I was getting a great deal. The entire experience began stressfully, with eager vendors and tough decisions, but after the leap was made, I had to exercise serious discipline. Any trip to Hội An should include a trip to the tailors, if for nothing but the experience of the long-forgotten art of custom-making wardrobes.

—Danny Koski-Karell

SIGHTS

UNESCO SIGHTS

Hội An's official sights hold less interest for most travelers than the town's narrow streets do. The most beautiful sights demand an **entry ticket** (50,000Đ), available 7am-6pm at **Hội An Tourist Offices:** 12 Phan Chu Trinh (☎862 715); 5 Hoàng Diệu (☎861 114); 37 Trần Phú (☎862 118); 78 Lê Lợi (☎861 982); and 19 Nhị Trưng (☎861 984). Each ticket provides access to the Japanese Covered Bridge or the Công Pagoda, your choice of one old house, one assembly hall, one museum, and one additional sight. Government tour guides (free for groups over 8; 50,000Đ per 2hr. tour for smaller groups) have a sweeping knowledge of local history.

OLD HOUSES

TRẦN FAMILY CHAPEL. Devoted to ancestor worship, the 200-year-old Trần Family Chapel incorporates Chinese, Japanese, and Vietnamese design. The 10th generation of the Trần family, who live next door, explain their heritage and serve refreshments. *(At the corner of Lê Lợi and Phan Chu Trinh. Open daily 7am-6pm.)*

OLD HOUSE OF PHÙNG HƯNG. This 200-year-old home shelters eight people from the family's 8th generation. The spacious house stands in serene contrast to the busy street scene outside the Japanese Bridge. *(4 Nguyễn Thị Minh Khai, just west of the bridge. Open daily 7am-6pm.)*

OLD HOUSE OF TẤN KY. Visitors can only enter the stunning front chamber, as the 7th-generation family lives there today. Nonetheless, there is plenty to see—the 200-year-old house displays an impressive fusion of Chinese, Japanese, and Vietnamese architecture. A worthy selection for your ticket, since the owner speaks English and invites visitors to tea. *(101 Nguyễn Thái Học. Open daily 8am-5pm.)*

OLD HOUSE OF QUÂN THẮNG. Built by a Chinese captain in the 18th century, this well-preserved house is said to be the oldest in Hội An. Take the owner's advice and come after 6pm, when entrance is free. *(77 Trần Phú. Open daily 7am-9pm.)*

ASSEMBLY HOUSES

When Chinese merchants came to Hÿi An centuries ago, they formed congregations *(bang)* according to native region. The halls follow similar patterns and purposes: four open chambers surround a courtyard, providing an ornate environment for meeting peers, worshipping gods, and honoring ancestors.

PHÚC KIẾN ASSEMBLY HALL. This one is the best choice for your ticket. Hội An's oldest, largest and most complex structure, this hall was built in 1697 by Fukienese immigrants. Past the Red Phoenix Gate, look down to see the symbol for longevity surrounded by five bats of happiness. *(46 Trần Phú. Open daily 7am-6pm.)*

QUẢNG DONG ASSEMBLY HALL. This hall serves the families of Cantonese merchants who arrived during the 17th century. To the right of the main building, an alley takes you to a serene sculpture garden. *(176 Trần Phú. Open daily 6am-6pm.)*

TRIỀU CHÂU ASSEMBLY HALL. Intricate wood carvings lure visitors to this 150-year-old hall. Inside the sanctuary, a first-century Han emperor sits surrounded by tiny figures carved and painted on wooden panels. *(157 Nguyễn Duy Hiệu, the eastern extension of Trần Phú. Open daily 6am-6pm. Free, despite what the official entry ticket says.)*

MUSEUMS

MUSEUM OF TRADE CERAMICS. The front room introduces Western visitors to the global maritime network through rather boring displays. More engaging exhibits on modern-day architectural preservation efforts, along with a section of Hội An's signature *yin* and *yang* roof tiles, await visitors in the back room. *(80 Trần Phú. Open daily 7am-5:30pm.)*

HỘI AN MUSEUM OF HISTORY AND CULTURE. This 300-year-old museum (which used to be a Quan Âm Pagoda) provides a decent, albeit somewhat meager, overview of the city's history. Sadly, a poster and an old cannon are the main attractions. *(7 Nguyễn Huệ, connected to the Công Pagoda. Open daily 7am-6pm.)*

MUSEUM OF HỘI AN SA HUỌNH CULTURE. This museum displays remnants of the Sa Huỳnh civilization which were first unearthed around Hội An in 1993. Much of the history of this prehistoric, pre-Champa culture remains elusive. *(159 Trần Phú, opposite the Quảng Dong Assembly Hall. Open daily 6am-6pm.)*

OTHER UNESCO SIGHTS

JAPANESE COVERED BRIDGE. The pink Japanese Covered Bridge, Hội An's most famous symbol, is known locally as Chùa Cầu ("Pagoda Bridge"). Japanese traders built it in the early 17th century. Walking across the bridge today is free; entering its inner room requires your ticket but offers little to see.

CÔNG PAGODA. This pagoda honors Quan Công, a general of the Han Dynasty during the second and third centuries. The 350-year-old temple has the distinction of housing the largest deity statue in Hội An. *(24 Trần Phú. Opens into the Museum of History and Culture. Open daily 7am-5:30pm.)*

OTHER HỘI AN SIGHTS

The sights listed below are independently run; as such, they do not require the official entry ticket.

HỘI AN CHURCH AND ORPHANAGE. A church services the area's Catholic population and supports the orphanage next door. While the church is unimpressive, a visit to the orphanage is rewarding. Visitors taking a break from shopping are more than welcome to stop by and play with the children. *(See **Alternatives to Tourism**, p. 938. Corner of Nguyễn Trưng To and Lê Hồng Phong. Mass services: Su 5:30am and 4pm; M, W, F 6:45am; Tu, Th, Sa 4:45pm. Orphanage visiting hours: daily 8-11am and 2-5pm.)*

LONG TUYỀN PAGODA. This pagoda, whose name means "dragon's stream," is the largest and youngest of Hội An's pagodas. At the back of the compound is the entrance to the cemetery and a statue of a bearded white man who looks suspiciously like Jesus. *(Head 1km down Lê Hồng Phong from its intersection with Nhị Trưng, away from town. The pagoda is down a dirt path on the left—follow the towers.)*

SHOPPING

In a region renowned for its tailors and dressmakers, Hội An's couture scene shines. While those oblivious to quality can find US$20 suits, a good suit should cost about US$40, and a pair of silk pajamas US$10—all made within a day and according to the shopper's specifications. Shops are concentrated on Lê Lợi. Most have old pattern books and fashion magazines to aid the designing process. The **cloth market,** on Trần Phú near Hoàng Diệu, is also worth exploring. Inside the market, **Mai,** stall number 7, produces superb work, and its vendors speak excellent English. Most tailoring places offer great value and quality, but make sure you talk to the dressmakers, look at their previous work, and ask other customers' opinions. While linings might cost extra, double-stitching (which prevents fraying) shouldn't. Remember you can take off the extra inch; you can't add one. "Chinese silk," "Japanese silk," and "Vietnamese silk" mean different things, but when all is said and done, real silk burns in a flame, while synthetics melt away. Ask for a fabric sample to test.

Yet while Hội An makes its name with tailors, its **artists and craftspeople** should not be overlooked. This remarkable community produces brightly colored images reflecting the sparse beauty of Hội An and Vietnam. Most artists' shops line Nguyễn Thái Học. Also be sure to stop by the handicraft shop called **Reaching Out** (☎862 460; www.tbonet.f2s.com), which sells work made by the town's disabled population. (Open daily 8am-5pm.)

NIGHTLIFE

Hội An is full of tourists, but at heart it remains a quiet riverside town. Nightlife centers around bars, billiards, and cafes. For those bent on liver destruction, rice whiskey flows on the corner of Lê Lợi and Trần Phú until 4am most nights; most other bars are hopping until 2am, with happy hour lasting from 4-9pm.

Tam Tam Cafe, 110 Nguyễn Thái Học, one block toward the river from Trần Phú. The early evening is quiet as diners enjoy pricey but superb Western cuisine (Australian steak US$9). By 10pm every Westerner in town has elbowed his way in; by 1am the French owners begin coaxing out the raucous crowd. A bottle of LaRue drops from 18,000Đ to 10,000Đ during happy hour.

Hai Scout Cafe, 98 Nguyễn Thái Học. The quieter neighbor of Tam Tam. Equally popular with tourists, this place nonetheless promotes a more relaxed, elegant atmosphere. Pools, darts, and excruciatingly slow Internet. Inquire about Vietnamese cooking classes.

VIETNAM

DAYTRIPS FROM HỘI AN

CUA DAI BEACH. A picturesque 5km down the road from Hội An, Cua Dai warrants at least one lazy afternoon. **Boat tours** depart from near the market on Bạch Đằng between 7am and 10pm. Independent operators charge 30,000Đ per hour; Hội An Tourist's Tours are more expensive but better planned. Stops are made at three handicraft villages: **Ceramics Village** (Làng Gốm), **Carpenter's Village** (Làng Mộc), and **Carpet Village** (Làng Chieu). Staying on the beach is not cheap. **Victoria Hội An ❺** is the most lavish option, and also one of the priciest (US$100 and up), but it offers a variety of watersports, free shuttle service to and from downtown Hội An, and a buffet dinner every night. **Vĩnh Hưng Resort ❺** offers more affordable rooms but sits on the Hoai River instead of the beach. (☎910 577; www.vinhhung-hotels.com. Rooms US$45-110.) *(Cua Dai is located 5km east of town on Trần Hưng Đạo.)*

MỸ SƠN. Declared a UNESCO World Heritage Site in 1999, the ruins of Mỹ Sơn were once the major religious center of the ancient Champa Kingdom. The walls and pillars rising out of the jungle are a meeting point of Hindu and indigenous culture. The earliest artifacts date from the fourth century, though more permanent temples were not built until the seventh century. From the seventh to the 13th centuries, over 70 towers were built. Today, the ruins are organized into groups A-H. Regrettably, there is little written description of the sights. The path from the entrance leads first to the E (7-8th century) and F groups, then to the G group. These groups do not offer much to see. The C1 *kalan* (main tower) is the most prominent; the broad, rectangular D1 and D2 were once *mandrapart* (meditation chambers) for the B and C temples, respectively. Now they house a motley assortment of sculptures—unfortunately, the best have been moved to Đà Nẵng's Chàm Museum. US bombs reduced the A1 tower to a sad perimeter of stone. Today A1's best offering is a small rise which offers a picturesque view of the B-C-D group. It is recommended to pay a visit to the Chàm Museum in Đà Nẵng first—this helps you to imagine the site in its full majesty. It is advisable to arrive early to beat the swarms of visitors. *(Mỹ Sơn is located 50km west of Hội An. Minibus tours allow 2hr. at the ruins (leave 8am, return by 2pm). Smaller tourist offices put you on the same tours for less (US$1-5). To beat the crowds, hire a motorbike driver to take you there early (US$5-6 round-trip). The ruins are open daily 6:30am-4:30pm. To reach them, visitors must take a bus ride from the entrance and proceed 300m on foot. 50,000Đ entry fee. English-speaking guides cost an extra 30,000Đ (up to 4 people) or 50,000Đ (5 or more); they're rarely available on the spot, Try to book them in Hội An.)*

QUẢNG NGÃI ☎55

Straddling National Highway 1, this unremarkable provincial capital has little to boast except for its tradition of nationalistic resistance. The area first saw an uprising against French and Japanese troops in 1945 and became a Việt Minh stronghold in the 1950s. Heavy fighting took place in Quảng Ngãi province during the Vietnam War, including the tragic Mỹ Lai Massacre of 1968. Today, most tours of Mỹ Lai originate in Hội An instead of here.

TRANSPORTATION. The **bus station,** 26 Nguyễn Nghiêm (☎822 895) is located in front of the market. Buses head to: Buôn Ma Thuột (13hr.; 5:30am; 62,000Đ); Đà Lạt (16hr.; 3am; 74,000Đ); HCMC (24hr.; 8am; 100,000Đ); Hội An/Đà Nẵng (3-4hr.; approx. every hr. 5-8am; 18,000Đ); Kon Tum (11hr.; 5am; 43,000Đ); **Nha Trang** (9hr.; 5am; 49,000Đ); Pleiku (10hr.; 5am; 37,000Đ); Qui Nhơn (4hr.; 5am-noon; 19,000Đ). Another option is to flag down buses in front of the **Petro-Song Tra Hotel** on the north side of town as they travel the new Hwy. 1 bypass. The **train station** (☎820 272) is 2km west of Hwy. 1, at the end of Hùng Vương. Trains go to all major stops in either direction on the **Reunification Express,** including Hà Nội (24-35hr.; hard seat 230,000Đ, soft sleeper 460,000Đ) and HCMC (20-30hr.; hard seat 145,000Đ, soft sleeper 295,000Đ).

ORIENTATION AND PRACTICAL INFORMATION. Quảng Ngãi is 180km north of Qui Nhơn, 102km south of Hội An, and 117km south of Đà Nẵng. National Hwy. 1 runs north-south through town, where it's called **Quảng Trung.** The town, which stretches north-south, is bordered on the north end by the **Tra Khuc River.** Running east-west along this river is **Nguyễn Huệ.** The main east-west road running through the center of town has two names: west of Quảng Trung it's called **Hùng Vương** and east of Quảng Trung it's called **Lê Trung Đình.** The center of town is about 1km south of the river.

Quảng Ngãi Tourist Company, 310 Quảng Trung, is the only tourist outfit in town. They speak little English but have helpful pamphlets. (☎825 293; fax 922 836. Open M-Sa 7-11am and 1:30-5pm.) **Foreign Currency Exchange,** 89 Hùng Vương, cashes traveler's checks and changes money. (☎822 626. Open M-Sa 7-11:30am and 1:30-4:30pm.) The slow **P and T Internet,** 415 Quảng Trung, is the only Internet kiosk in the center of town. (4000Đ per hr. Open daily 7am-10pm.) The **General Post Office,** 70 Phan Đình Phùng, at the intersection with Hùng Vương, has international phone service. (☎815 598. Open daily 6:30am-9pm.)

ACCOMMODATIONS AND FOOD. There are two locales for hotels in Quảng Ngãi, which are plentiful due to the stream of Vietnamese traveling along Highway 1. On the north end of town, hotels line the river and are pricier. In the center of town, hotels cluster around the intersection of Quảng Trung (Hwy. 1) and Hùng Vương. **Thăng Long ❸**, 259 Lê Trung Đình, is a new place with clean rooms and a central location. It's near the highway and noisy. (☎818 877; fax 0913 447 377. Rooms US$8-15.) **Petro-Song Tra ❺**, 2 Quảng Trung, is the cheaper of two three-star hotels on the river. As this complex is rarely full, you're bound to get a deal. (☎822 665; PVSTC@dng.vnn.vn. Rooms US$30-55.)

Food stalls line Quảng Trung and Nguyễn Nghiêm and are the cheapest and tastiest options in town. Along the latter, **Hué** (at 314) and **Quàm Ràm** (at 324) are popular with the locals. Soup and rice dishes with your choice of meat are all under 10,000Đ. Actual restaurants are scarce. **Cơm Vietnam ❷**, 21 Hùng Vương, is located in the city center and has an English menu. They serve basic meals as well as Western breakfasts. (Dishes 15,000-25,000Đ. Open daily 7am-11pm.)

DAYTRIPS FROM QUẢNG NGÃI. Site of the 1968 Mỹ Lai Massacre, the **Sơn Mỹ Memorial** is one of Vietnam's most moving experiences, especially for Americans. At the back of the grounds lies an untouched artillery shelter used by one of the village families. This space, along with bullet-ridden trees and an irrigation ditch where more than 100 villagers were executed, convey the horror of the massacre as well as anything could. Head to the small museum (the second building from the parking lot) to view personal items and chilling photographs. While the captions are obvious government propaganda, the photographs do not hide the gruesomeness of death—avoid them if you have a weak stomach. The museum also provides a one-sided view of the US attempt to cover up the massacre, and the investigation that followed it. (Open daily 7am-5pm. Admission 10,000Đ. To get to Sơn Mỹ from Quảng Ngãi, go 1km north of Hùng Vương along Quảng Trung, cross the highway bridge and take the first right (My Tra Hotel sits at the intersection). Sơn Mỹ sits 15km down the road. From the center of town, a motorbike trip should cost 40,000-50,000Đ round-trip. No buses service this route.)

VIETNAM

QUI NHƠN ☎56

This charmless seaport town is the capital of Bình Định Province, but its current decrepit state masks its former glory. In the 18th century, the Tây Sơn brothers led the great Tây Sơn Rebellion. Contemporary Qui Nhơn is a hectic seaport attempting to be a resort destination. Still, Qui Nhơn has its highlights. Someday it may rival Nha Trang, but today it remains a gray industrial city, free of busloads of tourists bathing in the coastal sun.

TRANSPORTATION AND ORIENTATION. Any tourist **bus** originating in Hội An or Nha Trang will drop passengers off on Hwy. 1, 10km west of Qui Nhơn. Motorized vehicles headed to the city center hover at the junction (3000-15,000Đ). For **trains,** ignore the cargo transport station and head to Ga Diêu Trì (☎833 255), 10km outside the city (15,000Đ by motorbike). Tickets and schedules are available at **Ga Qui Nhơn** on Lộ Thường Kiệt, across from Quảng Trung Park. (☎822 036. Open daily 7am-4:30pm.) Trains go to: Đà Nẵng (6hr.; 8:20am; 87,000-129,000Đ); HCMC (12½hr.; 5:45pm; 138,000-282,000Đ); Nha Trang (4½hr.; 5:45pm; 69,000-101,000Đ). The **bus station,** 2km west of Quảng Trung Park on Lam Son, runs buses to: Buôn Ma Thuột (9hr.; 43,000Đ); HCMC (15hr.; 78,000Đ); Huế (11hr.; 6am; 48,000Đ) via Đà Nẵng; Nha Trang (6hr.; 28,000Đ); Pleiku (4hr.; 20,000Đ). Minibuses arriving in Qui Nhơn may drop passengers off along Trần Hưng Đạo on the north side of the city, rather than at the bus station.

PRACTICAL INFORMATION. The staff at the state-run **Bình Định Tourist Office,** 385-387 Trần Hưng Đạo, speak little English (☎822 189; tmdlbd@dng.vnn.vn). The two **Barbara Hostels** (see **Accommodations and Food**) provide great tourist services. **Vietcombank,** at the corner of Lê Lợi and Trần Hưng Đạo, has an **ATM** and does currency exchange. (☎822 408. Open M-F 7-11am and 1-4pm, Sa 8am-noon.) The city **market** is found at 1 Tháng 4 between Phan Bội Châu and Tăng Bạt Hổ. The **pharmacy** is at 345 Lê Hồng Phong. The central **hospital** (☎822 900) is located at 108 Nguyễn Huệ; there is a branch at 255 Trần Hưng Đạo. **Internet** access is abundant. The **General Post Office,** 197 Phan Bội Châu, has international phone service. (☎821 441. Open daily 6:30am-10pm.)

ACCOMMODATIONS AND FOOD. There are large, old, and noisy hotels frequented by Vietnamese tourists in the city center; and there are newer beachside accommodations that house foreign tourists. Of the latter, it is best to stay at the quieter southern end of the beach. **Barbara's on the Beach ❶,** 492 An Duong Vương, is the best deal in town. The older **Barbara's Backpackers** is down the road. A transplanted New Zealander's second offering has sprouted right on the beach and features clean, airy rooms. (☎846 992; nzbarb@yahoo.com. Dorm beds 50,000Đ; private rooms 100,000Đ and up.) **Thanh Binh ❸,** 6 Lộ Thường Kiệt is the best option in the city center. If it isn't full, prices drop. (☎822 041; thanhbinhhotel@dng.vnn.vn. Breakfast included. Rooms US$10-40.) **Hai Au (Seagull Hotel) ❹,** 489 An Duong Vương, is one of Qui Nhơn's two resort hotels. This aging juggernaut's cell-like rooms could use a face-lift. Nonetheless, it's on the city's attractive southwest beach. (☎846 473; kshaiau@dng.vnn.vn. Rooms US$20-50.)

Fresh seafood can be found along the beach. The cheapest eats are at the foodstalls in the beachside fishing village and at the brand-new **Qui Nho'n Trade Center,** one of Vietnam's first western-style supermarkets. It's on Nguyễn Tat Thanh; you can't miss it. **Hồng Phat Thai Food ❷,** 261 Lê Hồng Phong, is right in the main square and serves above-average Thai food in filling portions for a decent price. (Pad Thai 30,000Đ.) **Ngọc Nga ❶,** 324 Phan Bội Châu, on Quảng Trung Park, is one of Qui Nhơn's few gems. Hipsters love the ice cream. (Bowls 4000-8000Đ. Coffee and shakes 2500Đ.) Near the city's main pagoda, **Thanh Minh ❶,** 151 Phan Bội Châu, serves up tasty vegetarian food. (Most dishes 10,000Đ and under.)

BEACH. Qui Nhơn's big draw is its long, curved beach. With heavy fishing just offshore, the water isn't the cleanest along the coast, but the sands remain clean and well-loved by locals and visitors alike. The central portion of the shore is marred by a fishing village which needs to improve its sanitary infrastructure. At the southwest end is Genh Rang Beach, the least-visited portion of sand. Stretching from Qui Nhơn to Nha Trang, are fleets of electric blue fishing boats form the core of Vietnam's fishing industry: Qui Nhơn is the center for their production.

DAYTRIPS FROM QUI NHƠN. The countryside around Qui Nhơn is dotted with huge **Chàm towers** that dwarf the most visited Chàm site, Mỹ Sơn; they are impressive but differ little from one another. Located down a maze of dirt roads, they are reachable through tours organized at the Bình Định Tourist Office, or via motorbike hire. Inquire at Barbara's Hostels (see **Accommodations,** p. 945) or call the excellent Mr. Chu Nguyễn Vản. (☎091 413 0992. Day tour around US$10.)

Bánh Ít is the best Chàm site around Qui Nhơn. Built at the end of the 11th century, the site is a collection of four towers at the summit of a solitary hill. Each tower has been built in a completely different style. (20km north of Qui Nhơn, just east of Hwy. 1. Towers are visible from the road. Open daily 7:30-11am and 1-5pm.)

NHA TRANG ☎58

Nha Trang is party central. The city has recently exploded into a full-fledged resort spot, feeding rapaciously on tourist dollars. Unchecked growth threatens to choke the city with over-development—on bad days, smog completely blocks the nearby islands from view—but good times still abound. Budget hotels and luxury resorts are packed with visitors enjoying cheap, high-quality snorkeling and scuba diving, daily jaunts to offshore islands, and nightly parties care of the city's lively club scene. Vietnam's best municipal beach and a laid-back, tourist-friendly population round out the closest thing the country has to a Pacific-flavored island resort atmosphere; the sparkling turquoise water is the stuff of dreams. The best time to visit is from March to September—rain and high winds prevail the rest of the year.

TRANSPORTATION

Flights: Nha Trang Airport (☎827 286), just south of the city center, off of Trần Phú. **Vietnam Airlines,** 91 Nguyễn Thiện Thuật (☎826 768) or 1 Trần Hưng Đạo (☎822 753). Open daily 7-11:30am and 1:30-5pm. Flights to: **Đà Nẵng** (Sa-Tu and Th 2pm; 555,000Đ); **Hà Nội** (daily 10am; 1,450,000Đ); **HCMC** (3 per day; 650,000Đ).

Trains: Nha Trang Station, 17 Thái Nguyễn. Open 24hr. except 12:30-1:30pm. To **HCMC** (7-10hr.; frequent; 86,000-166,000Đ). Northbound trains leave 5 times per day for: **Đà Nẵng** (9-12hr.; 113,000-222,000Đ); **Hà Nội** (25-34hr., 320,000-632,000Đ); **Huế** (12-16hr.; 136,000-263,000Đ).

Buses: Northbound buses depart from the end of **2 Tháng 4,** 10km north of the city center. Southbound buses leave from **Liên Tỉnh Station,** 58 23 Tháng 10 (☎822 347). Buses run to: **Buôn Ma Thuột** (4-6hr.; 4 per day; 36,000Đ); **Đà Lạt** (5hr.; frequent; 40,000Đ); **Đà Nẵng** (14hr.; 1 per day; 36,000Đ); **HCMC** (10hr.; 7 per day 5:30am-8pm; 65,000Đ) via **Phan Thiết** (5hr.; 45,000Đ); **Huế** (15hr.; 5am; 68,000Đ); **Pleiku** (7hr.; Tu and Sa; 54,000Đ); **Quảng Ngãi** (8hr.; 1 per day; 43,000Đ); **Qui Nhơn** (6hr.; 1 per day; 33,000Đ). A "no tickets to foreigners" policy means you'll have to negotiate with the driver. Faster private **minibuses** leave from many hotels for **Đà Lạt** (US$5); **Hội An** (US$8); **HCMC** (US$8).

Rentals: Hotels rent **motorbikes** (US$3-6 per day) and **bicycles** (8000-10,000Đ).

ORIENTATION

Nha Trang lies 450km northeast of HCMC and 175km northeast of Đà Lạt. Two-lane **Trần Phú** runs north-south along the length of the 6km beach; its north end offers spectacular views from the **Trần Phú Bridge. Hùng Vương,** a block inland, becomes **Trần Hưng Đạo** and then **Pasteur** on its way northward. **Lê Thánh Tôn** shoots northwest from Trần Phú's **memorial tower,** hits a six-way intersection, and becomes **Thái Nguyễn,** which continues west as **23 Tháng 10** past the train and bus stations. Near the northern end of Trần Phú, **Yersin** heads inland toward another six-way hub; from here, **Quang Trưng** runs north and continues out of town as **2 Tháng 4. Lê Lợi** runs west from Trần Phú's north end to the town market.

PRACTICAL INFORMATION

Tourist Offices: Nha Trang is bursting with agents. Most line Biệt Thự and Trần Hưng Đạo; typically, they open between 6 and 7am and close at 10pm. **Sinh Cafe,** 10 Biệt Thự (☎811 981; sinhcafent@dng.vnn.vn), handles everything under the sun. **An Phu Tour,** 4 Trần Quang Khải (☎524 471; anphutour@yahoo.com). **TM Brothers,** 26 Trần

Hưng Đạo (☎814 556), and **Hanh Cafe,** 22 Trần Hưng Đạo (☎829 015), provide typical services. **Holiday Office,** 92 Trần Phú (☎828 803; cuong-thinh@yahoo.com), is a friendly local outfit frequented by Vietnamese tourists.

Banks: Vietcombank, 17 Quang Trưng (☎824 093). Currency exchange and MC/V cash advances. Open daily 7:30-11am and 1:30-4pm. **Branch** at 5 Hùng Vương has an **ATM.** Open daily 7am-9pm. **Sacombank,** 54 Yersin, has a 24hr. **ATM;** Yasaka Saigon Nha Trang Hotel and Nha Trang Lodge Hotel have ATMs in the lobby as well (see **Accommodations,** p. 948). Most hotels and tourist offices exchange cash and traveler's checks at punishing rates.

Markets: Chợ Đàm, west of the post office (take Lê Lợi from Trần Phú) at the end of Hoang Hòa Tham. Known for its dried squid. Western-style markets provide necessities: **Maximark,** at the intersection of Quang Trưng and Lê Thánh Tôn, and **Đại Thuận,** 17A Biệt Thự. The latter specializes in seafood. Both open daily 7am-6pm.

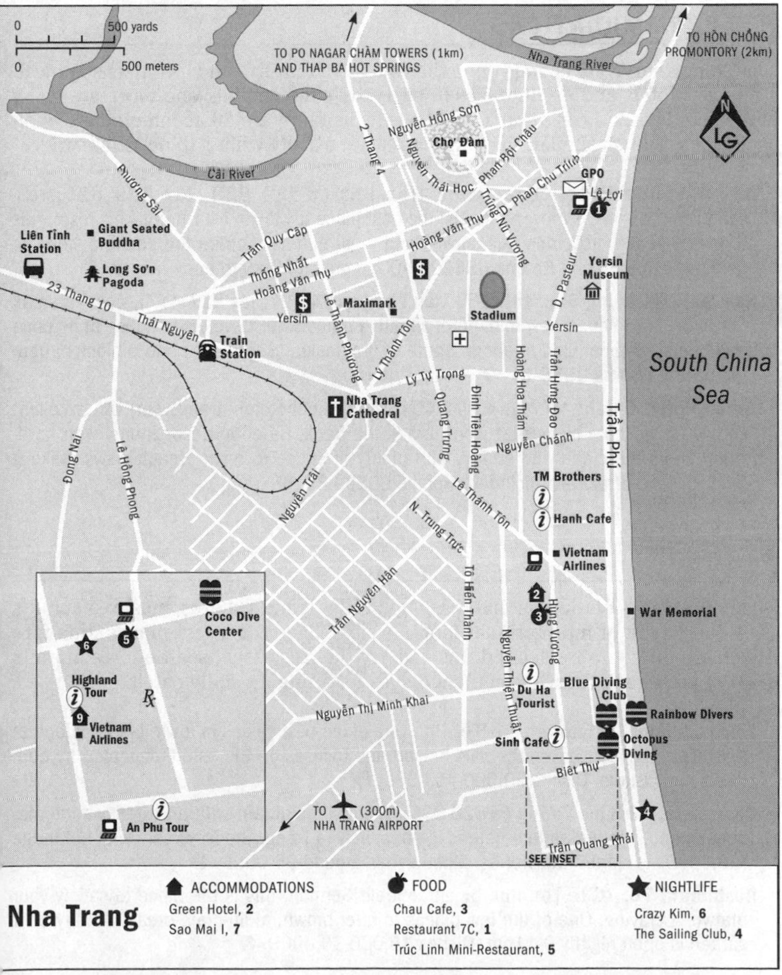

Emergency: ☎115.

Pharmacy: 7 Hùng Vương (☎812 857). Open daily 8am-6pm.

Medical Services: Khánh Hòa General Hospital, 94 Yersin (☎822 168), at the intersection with Quang Trưng. Some English and French spoken. 24hr. emergency service.

Internet Access: Most tourist offices charge 100Đ per min. **8C Biệt Thự,** 10 Pasteur, and **2 Hùng Vương** provide the best access at this rate. For the best price (3000Đ per hr.) and fastest speed, follow the locals to **3/10 Trần Quang Khải,** down the side-street. Cheap Internet phones and decent music, too. Open until 11pm.

Post Offices: General Post Office, 4 Lê Lợi (☎829 657). *Poste Restante,* Internet access, and international calling, as well as a DHL Express office. Open daily 6:30am-10pm. Smaller branch at 46 Nguyễn Thiện Thuật.

ACCOMMODATIONS

Nha Trang's survival depends upon the volume of tourists, and its citizens know it. There are hotels and guesthouses in every style imaginable, and more are being built each day. You can shop around easily, as there are 20 accommodations on each block, though similar; the empty ones are usually willing to negotiate prices.

Ana Miranda Hotel, beachside Trần Phú (☎829 829; fax 829 629; resvana@dng.vnn.vn). Simply gorgeous; the best place to stay in Nha Trang. This resort has a private beach, luxurious bungalows, and regal buffets. Admire the emerald views or take a dip in the pool. Rooms US$200-400; more late Dec. to early Jan. ❺

Sao Mai ("Morning Star") II, 96B Trần Phú (☎524 227; fax 827 412), down a small road from Trần Phú. A new mini-hotel already popular with travelers because of its price and quality. Typical tiled interiors. South of the backpacker quarter and a block in from the beach. Rooms US$6-12. ❷

Green Hotel, 6 Hùng Vương (☎821 404; www.greenhotelnhatrang.com). An excellent choice for upscale living that won't break the bank. Bamboo-decor rooms with hardwood floors are clean and sunny, with plenty of space to relax. Beach views make it hard to leave. Breakfast included. Rooms US$39-89. ❺

VIETNAM

FOOD

Due to the waves of tourists that crash upon Nha Trang's shores, most restaurants offer every type of international food possible. Save for a few places, this fare leaves something to be desired. Instead, try the fresh local seafood; restaurants in every price range serve succulent dishes featuring the daily catch.

Trúc Linh Mini-Restaurant, 11 Biệt Thự. One of the best values in town: tasty seafood at reasonable prices. Leaves the frills behind and focuses on the fish. Frequented by both locals and visitors. Dishes 20,000-40,000Đ. ❷

Chau Cafe, 42 Hùng Vương (☎826 336). A small restaurant with an extensive international menu. The Indian fare here is the best in Nha Trang. The ice cream with hot fudge (20,000Đ) is worth the calories. Most dishes around 25,000Đ. ❷

Restaurant 7C, 7C Lê Lợi. Run by an amiable German, this is the place to satisfy your bratwurst craving. One of the few places to offer brown, multi-grain bread. An airy beer garden is open nightly 9-11pm. Dishes 15,000-30,000Đ. ❷

SIGHTS AND SAND

The city's most splendid attraction is its **public beach.** Ample sand and azure water run the length of town, with plenty of beach chairs and roving vendors offering everything from fresh mangoes and English books to oil massages. Cushions and beach umbrellas start at 10,000Đ per day. For a more remote seaside experience, head north on 2 Tháng 4 to the beaches of **Hòn Ch·ng Promontory.** After crossing the two harbor bridges, turn right onto Nguy[n Đình Chi€u and left before the fishery university. Besides its beach, Hòn Ch·ng's most striking sight is the yellow boulders that form part of the shore. (Open daily 6am-6pm. Admission 3000Đ.)

BOAT TOURS

Boat tours (approx. US$6) are big business in Nha Trang. Back when the city was a tourist frontier, the tours were raucous, lawless affairs specializing in sun-soaked hedonism. Today they have become much tamer package deals, but they still provide an opportunity to cruise the South China Sea, snorkel among tropical fish, eat excellent seafood, and meet other travelers. After you buy a ticket, a minibus picks you up at your accommodation between 8 and 9am. You're then shuttled to the hectic dock and packed onto a wooden boat. The cruise takes you and 30-40 others to **Mun Island** (Black Island) for an hour of snorkeling and then anchors at **Mot Island,** where a fantastic lunch is served. Next comes Nha Trang's signature "floating bar," essentially free-flowing complimentary Vietnamese wine. Then it's off to **Tam Island** (admission 5000Đ) with its zoo-like beach, overpriced drinks, and jetskiing and parasailing opportunities. A refreshing fruit buffet helps you absorb the alcohol on the way to the fishing village on **Meiu Island,** where a ride in a bamboo basket boat costs 10,000Đ. Some boat tours also stop at Trí Nguyễn Aquarium. You should be back no later than 5pm. (Tickets can be booked at nearly every hotel and tourist office, or you can go directly to the operators: **Mama Hanh,** 44 Lê Thánh Tôn; Mỹ A, 10 Hùng Vương; or **Mama Linh,** 2A Hùng Vương.)

More sophisticated travelers—as well as many families—opt for a calm, educational **glass-bottom boat tour.** The journey begins with a hotel pickup around 8am, followed by a visit to the **Oceanographic Institute.** Then you're whisked away to **Mun Island** in a glass-bottom boat. Lunch is taken at a secluded "floating village" which also offers a variety of activities, including kayaking, swimming, and jetskiing. Next up is a trip to the Trí Nguyễn Aquarium. You'll be back in the city by 3pm. (Inquire at **VN Seaworld Offices,** 110A/14 Trần Phú. ☎828 242; www.vnseaworld.com. Adults 145,000Đ; children 85,000Đ.)

OTHER SIGHTS

The **Long So'n Pagoda,** Nha Trang's postcard picture of choice, stands at the west end of Yersin. The pagoda is dedicated to the Buddhists who gave their lives protesting the US-supported Diệm regime. Its renowned 9m high hilltop white **Buddha statue** has a commanding view of the city. The **Po Nagar Chàm Towers,** or **Tháp Bà,** are just north of the Xóm Bóng Bridge and south of Hòn Chồng. The temple is a fascinating example of the appropriation of one faith's deity (the Hindu goddess Po-negar) by Mahayana Buddhists. From the entrance, a brief ascent leads from the former *mandapa* (meditation hall) to the towers. A sculpture of Shiva marks the entrance to the north tower. Buddhists place offerings before Po-negar's image and the *linga* in the smaller towers. (Open daily 6am-6pm. 4000Đ; free during Tet.) At the west end of Lê Thánh Tôn, 1km from Trần Phú, is the **Nha Trang Cathedral,** a brilliant French Gothic relic of the colonial era. South of Lê Lợi on Trần Phú, the yellow Pasteur Institute houses the **Yersin Museum.** Alexandre Yersin, a French doctor remains one of the most revered Europeans in Vietnam. Artifacts include the microscope he used to discover the black plague bacillus. (Open M-Sa 8-11am and 2-4:30pm. 25,000Đ.)

NIGHTLIFE

People come to Nha Trang to party, and there is no shortage of options. Local expats know what the tourists want, and the result is a bustling nightlife scene dominated by Western-style bars and clubs. Most are found at the southern end of town, along Trần Quang Khải and Biệt Thự.

The Sailing Club, beachside Trần Phú, across from Trần Quang Khải. Unassuming Italian restaurant and bar by day; the ultimate place to be by night. Everyone's evening somehow ends here. Spacious dance floor, pumping beats, and a big seating area. Young crowd of sweaty bodies and endless shots. Open daily until very late.

Crazy Kim, 19 Biệt Thự. A large, hip bar in the center of the action. The crowd tends to be more laid-back but no less inebriated. Huge MTV-style lounge complete with a dance floor and pool table. Also has outdoor seating. Happy hour 6-10pm. Open daily until 1am.

DAYTRIP FROM NHA TRANG

JUNGLE BEACH. Jungle Beach is three acres of undeveloped land sandwiched between an isolated white-sand beach and the jungle-covered Hòn Hèo (813m). It is not a resort in the typical sense, but is the home of a socially and environmentally conscious French-Canadian. Guests stay in basic rooms and eat around a communal table, enjoying the exquisite food prepared by the *madame* of the home. A relaxed atmosphere permeates everything—a result of the hammocks down by the beach, the outdoor four-post beds (covered with mosquito netting) and the treks through virgin forest to nearby waterfalls. There is no other place like this in Vietnam, and it's only going to get better. Teepees are in the works, as well as running water, and—most impressively—an organic garden to provide nutritious meals. Although it's a bit hard to reach, Jungle Beach has a stellar reputation, so reservations are recommended. *(☎622 384; syl@dng.vnn.vn. Take a motorbike from north up Hwy. 1 about 36km and turn off at the huge Hyundai-Vinashin sign. You can also have tour buses. Follow the road about 20km down to its terminus. Food and bed US$15.)*

MŨI NÉ BEACH ☎62

Mũi Né is technically a small fishing village on a peninsula 19km east of Phan Thiết. In between the two villages is a long broad stretch of beach with fine white sands. Mũi Né Beach is the subject of myriad postcards—the waves are sparkling, and coconut palms sway along the beach's edge. It's the tropical paradise that many are seek in Southeast Asia, though numerous developers realized this and saturated the area with resorts. The disadvantage is that Mũi Né lacks a social fabric; the resorts are spread out and closed off from one another.

TRANSPORTATION. Tour buses shuttle visitors in from HCMC, Đà Lạt, and Nha Trang. There is a local bus station currently under construction in Mũi Né village. A motorbike ride to Phan Thiết or the sand dunes should cost around 20,000Đ each way. Most hotels rent out **motorbikes** (US$5 per day) and **bicycles**

(US$2 per day). One lone street, **Highway 707** (also called **Nguyễn Đình Chiểu** and **Huỳnh Thúc Kháng,** west and east respectively of the **Fairy Stream Bridge**), runs parallel to the beach and connects Phan Thiết and Hwy. 1 to Mũi Né village.

PRACTICAL INFORMATION. Mũi Né is serviced by the major nationwide **tour** agencies. Most places can book you tickets from Mũi Né to the surrounding tourist destinations (HCMC, Đà Lạt, and Nha Trang). They also rent out jeeps, motorbikes, and bicycles. **Sinh Café,** 144 Nguyễn Đình Chiểu (☎847 542; www.sinhcafevn.com), is located inside the Sinh Café Mũi Né Resort. **An Phu Tourist,** 45B Huỳnh Thúc Kháng (☎847 543; www.anphutouristhoian.com) is also popular. There are no **ATMs** as yet in Mũi Né. For currency exchange and MC/V cash advances, try **Incombank,** which has branches at Swiss Village Resort, 44B Nguyễn Đình Chiểu, and Tropico Resort, 73 Nguyễn Đình Chiểu. Both open daily 7am-5pm. **Internet** access is slow and expensive, the fastest and cheapest (200Đ per min.) is Hồng Di Resort, open daily 7am-10pm. Full Moon Resort charges the same rate. There is also a branch of Phan Thiết's **postal service** at Swiss Village Resort.

ACCOMMODATIONS. Mũi Né is all accommodations. The entire beach is lined with resorts of every shape, size, and smell. There are plenty of upper-end places, and budget accommodations are fewer but not impossible to find. No resort ever wants their guests to leave the grounds, so they're outfitted with restaurants, and entertainment venues. Constant construction means the number of rooms is growing rapidly.

The beach on the western (Phan Thiết) side is the nicest one. **Blue Ocean Resort ❺,** 54 Nguyễn Đình Chiểu, is as good as it gets, with gorgeous, expansive grounds and a wide, flat beach—a manufactured tropical paradise. (☎847 322; www.blueoceanresort.com. Rooms US$65-110.) The beach in the center of the strip tends to be the most battered by winds and surf; it's also quite narrow and steep on account of erosion. **The Sanctuary Resort ❹,** Km 4, lives up to its name, set far back from the road and boasts exquisite rooms in a large coconut grove facing the sea. (☎847 232; www.asiatravel.com/vietnam. Rooms US$20.) **Sinh Café Mũi Né Resort ❺,** 144 Nguyễn Đình Chiểu, is a new resort built with Sinh's tourism expertise. Everything is nice—beach, pool, rooms, decor—but lacks in character. (☎847 542; www.sinhcafenvn.com. Tourism service in the lobby. Bungalows M-F US$25-30; Sa-Su US$30-35; villas US$30-40/US$35-45.) The beach on the eastern (Mũi Né) side is also pleasant; budget accommodations are concentrated on this end. **Hải Gia ❷,** 72A Huỳnh Thúc Kháng, is new and kept immaculately clean by its friendly owner. Spacious rooms, all with bath, are set into long concrete units with thatched roofs. (☎847 555; haiga_muinc@yahoo.com. Rooms US$6-10.) **Thai Hòa ❸,** 56 Huỳnh Thúc Kháng, is popular with backpackers. The individual bungalows face into a large open space, creating a communal atmosphere—a rarity in Mũi Né. The owner speaks superb English. (☎847 320; vngold.com/mn/thaihoa. Bungalows with outdoor shower US$5, with private indoor shower US$12.)

FOOD. All the resorts provide their own private restaurants; outside food options in Mũi Né are scarce, and not necessarily better than the resort menus. Along the road near the village, there are many small seafood shacks frequented by locals. **Luna D'Autonno ❹,** Km 12, has some of the best Italian food in Vietnam. (Quality jazz played in the background Su-F; Sa night is festive salsa night. Dishes 70,000Đ and up.) The roadside restaurant at **Song Hai ❷,** 72 Nguyễn Đình Chiểu, serves up tasty Vietnamese dishes for unusually reasonable prices. (Dishes 15,000Đ and up.) **Trung Duong ❷** is on the village end of Coco Beach Resort, invites guests off the street to try special Vietnamese-style barbecue, fresh meats and veggies, lemon and salt, and a table-top grill. (Barbecue 25,000-50,000Đ.)

SIGHTS. The area east of Phan Thiết has a fascinating climate. Besides strong heat and winds, it receives only a fraction of the rainfall of surrounding provinces and of the city itself. This has created a unique landscape famous throughout Vietnam. A few kilometers northeast of Mũi Né village are large yellow **sand dunes,** just off the main road. Visitors can climb over the dunes and slide down them on sheets of plastic. There are bigger "white" dunes another 35km down the road. (To reach the first dunes, head down the highway toward the village. After entering the outskirts of town, take a left at the market immediately after the blue-and-yellow "Chợ" sign. The dunes will be on the left about 5km down the road.)

Fairy Spring is a colorful sight which truly deserves its name. The warm, clear stream has created a narrow gorge among some dunes, exposing a fantastical geological display of reds, pinks, oranges, and whites. Hollywood could not have created a better alien world. Local tour agencies arrange "expeditions" to the spring and the surrounding waterfalls. You can get there on your own by following the stream from where it flows underneath the bridge on the highway; go along the right bank, past some fences and shrubs, and then drop down to the stream and walk another 1km to the source. Guides can usually hire on the spot.

ENTERTAINMENT. **Jibe's Beach Club,** 90 Nguyễn Đình Chiểu, was the first in Mũi Né and is still the most reputable place to get your adrenaline rush. It offers equipment rental, lessons with experienced instructors, and of course, a bar. (Windsurf equipment US$12 per hr., US$45 per day; kitesurf equipment US$20/US$75; surfboard/boogie board US$2.50/US$10. Kitesurfing lessons plus equipment cost US$85.)

NIGHTLIFE. Since most vacationers choose to stay in their resorts, nightlife here is nowhere near as happening as in Nha Trang, Vietnam's other premier beach destination. But that doesn't stop the few local bars from pumping music and flashing lights all night long. If you go out, be aware that in the wee hours you'll be at the mercy of the very few motorbike drivers who stay up—gross overcharging is not unusual. Night owls play pool and enjoy music at Aussie-themed **Hot Rock,** across from Small Garden. The funky interior is a welcome change from the resorts. (Open late.) A youthful crowd mellows out at **Jibe's Beach Club,** 90 Nguyễn Đình Chiểu, with a comfy atmosphere, quality music, and seaside views. (Drinks 30,000-50,000Đ. Open late.)

VIETNAM

THE CENTRAL HIGHLANDS

Most foreigners, if they're familiar with the Central Highlands at all, heard about them 35 years ago, when the region saw some of the bloodiest combat in the Vietnam War. Today, some veterans return here on remembrance tours, but the region's beauty and native cultures—are its real attractions. Natural wonders thrive in Vietnam's largest national park, Yok Don, and along Hwy. 14, the original Hồ Chí Minh Trail. However, the region has struggled to combat the effects of toxins dumped during the war and the current slash-and-burn campaigns of coffee planters. Of Vietnam's 54 ethnic minorities, many make their homes in the Central Highlands: the Banar, Jarai, and Sodang live around Pleiku and Kon Tum, and the K'Long dwell outside Đà Lạt. Unfortunately, most (if not all) minority villages live under a destructive policy of "Vietnamization," which is erasing their unique cultures and keeping them in miserable poverty. Violent uprisings in the region have moved officials to close some villages to tourists. Enlightened and relaxed Đà

Lạt, is the region's crown jewel and the main tourist spot. Most other cities in the Central Highlands are all but devoid of visitors, so they offer images of the reality of Vietnam: an industrious nation struggling to recover from the past and determined to create a better future at all costs.

ĐÀ LẠT ☎63

Forget everything you know about Vietnam—Đà Lạt is different. The mountainous city's flourishing artistic community, easygoing atmosphere, and frankly bizarre "Đà Lạt Eiffel" have led to the affectionate nickname "Le Petit Paris." Doctor/adventurer Alexandre Yersin was smitten by the alpine climate and pine forests during a 1892 expedition. Following his suggestion that they build a city, the French displaced ethnic Vietnamese and K'ho people and established the resort city in 1910. Today, the hills are alive with the sounds of tourism. Known as "The City of Flowers" for its abundant flower market, Đà Lạt has perfected the art of the vacation destination. Romantic lakes and a booming flower industry make this the honeymoon capital of Vietnam; the clean air and abundant cafes still captivate the French. Simpler pleasures come from meandering the streets (closed to traffic on weekends) and enjoying mountain views. Recently, Đà Lạt has become the epicenter of adventure tourism and ecotourism in southern Vietnam, flinging eager backpackers into ravines and onto mountaintops.

TRANSPORTATION

Flights: Fly into **Đức Trong Airport,** 30km south of the city. The Vietnam Airlines booking office is in Hotel Hàng Khôi, 40 Hồ Tung Mâu (☎822 895). Daily flights via **HCMC** (40min.; 3:10pm; 430,000Đ) to: **Đa Nẵng** (950,000Đ); **Hà Nội** (2,230,000Đ); **Huế** (1,380,000Đ).

Buses: The public **bus station** (☎822 077) is at 3 Tháng 4, southwest of the city center. Haggle directly with departing drivers; they don't usually sell tickets to foreigners, but you can wait outside, hop aboard, and bargain. Local buses to: **Buôn Ma Thuột** (10hr.; 1 per day; 63,000Đ); **Đà Nẵng** (15hr.; 1 per day; 105,000Đ); **HCMC** (6hr.; frequent; 50,000Đ); **Huế** (26hr.; 1 per day; 120,000Đ); **Nha Trang** (7hr.; 3 per day; 32,000Đ); **Quảng Ngãi** (8½hr.; 3 per day; 86,000Đ). **Minibuses**, leaving when full, depart to **Buôn Ma Thuột** (10hr.; 50,000Đ); **Đà Nẵng** (15hr.; 105,000Đ); **HCMC** (6hr.; 50,000Đ); **Nha Trang** via **Phang Rang** (6hr., 7:30am, US$5). Arrive before 8am for longer trips.

Rentals: Motorbikes (US$4 per day) and **mountain bicycles** (70,000Đ per day) are easy to rent at any tourist office or hotel.

ORIENTATION

The capital of Lâm Dồng Province, Đà Lạt is 300km north of HCMC on Hwy. 20. Built on several adjoining mountaintops, the streets twist, turn, rise, and fall, making initial ventures a bit disorienting. The slope rising north out of the west end of Xuân Nương Lake supports the city's center and the central market. To the left of the market, steps lead up to **Hoà Bính Square,** dominated by the 3/4 Cinema. **Trương Công Định** heads roughly north from the cinema to **Phan Đình Phùng,** which also runs roughly north-south. Most of Đà Lạt's backpackers stay in this area. The slope facing it, marked by the "Đà Lạt Eiffel" and the cathedral, is the location of the post office and high-end accommodations. In this neighborhood, **Trần Phú** runs east-west, from which **3 Thàng 4** runs southwest out of the city.

PRACTICAL INFORMATION

Tourist Offices: Sinh Cafe, 49 Bùi Thi Xuân (☎822 663; sinhcafe2dl@hcm.vnn.vn) has it all. Confirm your open-tour ticket. **Đà Lạt/Kim Travel,** 09 Lê Đai Hành (☎822 479; dltoseco@hcm.vnn.vn), is the government agency, with slightly cheaper prices. It is on the south side of town. **TM Brothers,** 02 Nguyễn Chi Thanh (☎828 383; dalat.tmbrother@yahoo.com), is another HCMC-based outfit.

Currency Exchange: Incombank, 46-48 Khu Hoà Bính, is right on Hoà Bính Square (☎824 495; fax 822 827). Traveler's checks cashed. MC/V advances. Open M-Sa 7-11:30am and 1-4:30pm.

Markets: Chợ Đà Lạt, in the town center down the steps from Hoà Bính Square, converts into a cheap food stall and bargaining heaven after dark. Open daily 4am-1am.

Emergency: ☎115. **Police:** 19 Trần Phú (☎113). **Fire:** ☎114.

Hospital: The hospital is located at 04 Phạm Ngọc Thạch (☎827 550).

Pharmacy: On the square at 34 Khu Hoà Bính (☎822 570). Open daily 7am-10pm.

Internet Access: The cheapest option is in the second story of the **bookstore** at 18-20 Khu Hoà Bính (3,000Đ per hour). Open daily 7:30am-10:30pm. After the bookstore closes, enter through the propped-open side door. **Viêt Hưng,** 07 Nguyễn Thanh, is a true Internet cafe–30min. free if you order food.

Post Office: 14-16 Trần Phú, under the Đà Lạt Hotel (☎822 580). Fax, telex, Internet, international phone calls, and *Poste Restante*. Open daily 7am-9pm.

ACCOMMODATIONS

Like Vietnam's other tourist meccas, rooms are plentiful and there is a wide price range. Trương Công Định and Phan Đình Phúng, north of Hoà Bính Square, form Đà Lạt's backpacker quarter. The area south of the city center—under the "Eiffel"—has more upscale offerings.

Peace II Hotel (Hoà Bính II), 67 Trương Công Định (☎822 982; peace12@hcm.vnn.vn) is a smaller, more homey offshoot of its larger, older sibling. Rooms are large and bright. Popular with backpackers. Rooms US$5-10. ❷

Á Châu, 13 Trăng Bat Hố (☎823 974; fax 188 884). Perched on a hillside, this alpine villa wannabe offers large, open rooms, with lots of light and breeze. Its upscale appearance must scare off backpackers–it's rarely full, which leads to great discounts. Rooms US$4-10; off-season as low as US$2. ❷

Dreams Hotel, 151 Phan Đình Phùng (☎833 798; dreams@hcm.vnn.vn), is a hybrid budget/mid-range hotel. Clean, modern rooms for a low-end price. Its great reputation keeps the place full. Exceedingly friendly staff and (slow) Internet. Breakfast included. Rooms US$8-15. ❸

Empress Hotel, 05 Nguyễn Thái Học (☎833 888; www.empresshotel.vn.com). Sitting across from the lake, the villa-style Empress belongs in the French Alps. The courtyard, lobby, and rooms feature dark wood of the alpine world. Rooms US$50-200. ❺

FOOD

As befits a holiday destination, Đà Lạt's restaurants tend to be either relatively pricey Western-style restaurants for tourists or *phở* eateries for locals. Đà Lạt is the place to make your mom proud and eat your greens. The surrounding hills produce a variety of vegetables among the highest quality in the country. The most

VIETNAM

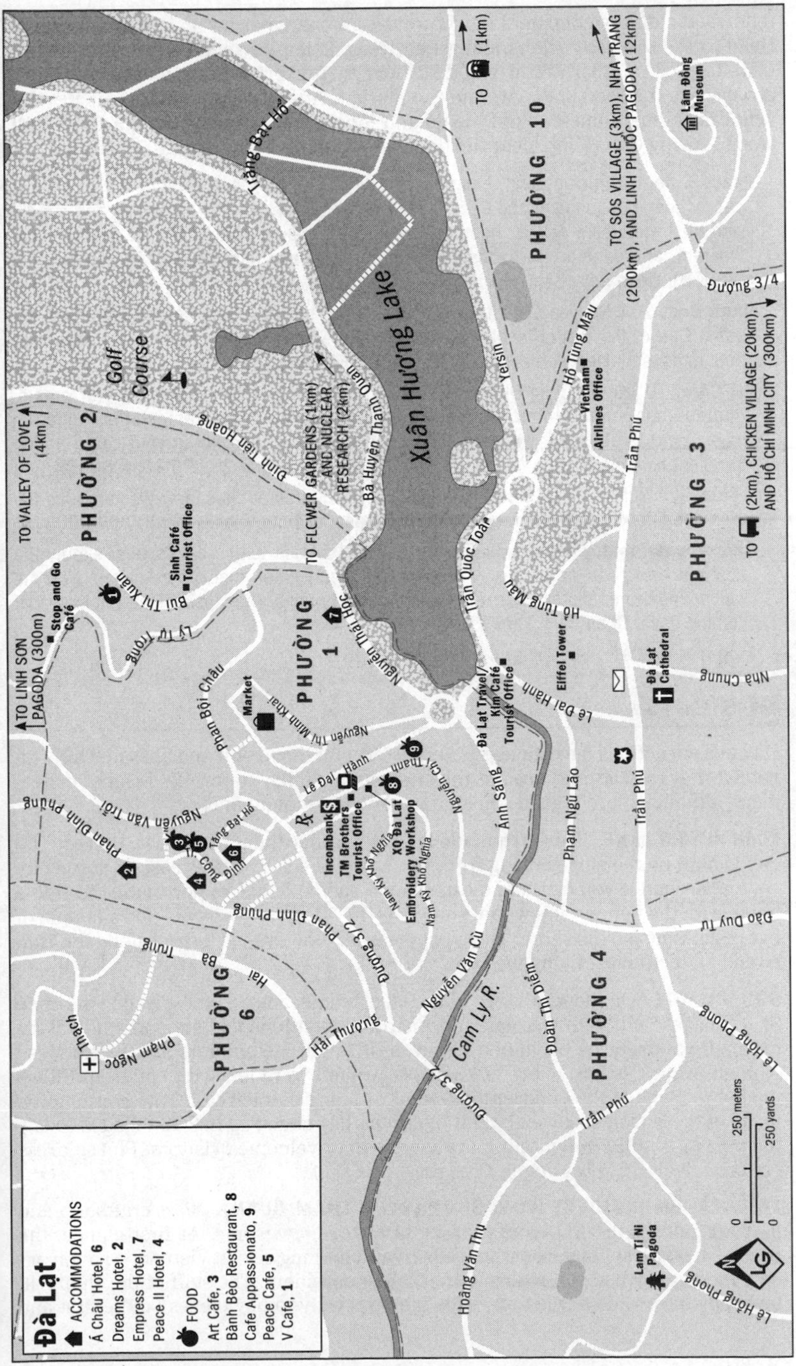
Đà Lạt
ACCOMMODATIONS
Á Châu Hotel, 6
Dreams Hotel, 2
Empress Hotel, 7
Peace II Hotel, 4
FOOD
Art Cafe, 3
Bánh Bèo Restaurant, 8
Cafe Appassionato, 9
Peace Cafe, 5
V Cafe, 1
Xuân Hương Lake
Golf Course
Cam Ly R.
PHƯỜNG 1
PHƯỜNG 2
PHƯỜNG 3
PHƯỜNG 4
PHƯỜNG 6
PHƯỜNG 10
TO LINH SƠN PAGODA (300m)
TO VALLEY OF LOVE (4km)
TO FLOWER GARDENS (1km) AND NUCLEAR RESEARCH (2km)
TO (1km)
TO SOS VILLAGE (3km), NHA TRANG (200km), AND LINH PHƯỚC PAGODA (12km)
TO (2km), CHICKEN VILLAGE (20km), AND HỒ CHÍ MINH CITY (300km)
Stop and Go Café
Sinh Café Tourist Office
Market
Incombank
TM Brothers Tourist Office
XQ Đà Lạt Embroidery Workshop
Đà Lạt Travel/ Kim Café Tourist Office
Eiffel Tower
Đà Lạt Cathedral
Vietnam Airlines Office
Lâm Đồng Museum
Lam Tí Ni Pagoda
Trần Quốc Toản
Nguyễn Thái Học
Bà Huyện Thanh Quan
Đinh Tiên Hoàng
Bùi Thị Xuân
Lý Tự Trọng
Phan Bội Châu
Nguyễn Thị Minh Khai
Lê Đại Hành
Nguyễn Chí Thanh
Nam Kỳ Khởi Nghĩa
Nguyễn Văn Trỗi
Phan Đình Phùng
Tăng Bạt Hổ
Trường Công Định
Đường 3/2
Hải Thượng
Nguyễn Văn Cừ
Ánh Sáng
Phạm Ngũ Lão
Hồ Tùng Mậu
Trần Phú
Nhà Chung
Đào Duy Từ
Đoàn Thị Điểm
Lê Hồng Phong
Hoàng Văn Thụ
Yersin
Trần Hưng Đạo
Đường 3/4
Trương Bạt Hổ
Hai Bà Trưng
Thạch
Phạm Ngọc
250 meters
250 yards

VIETNAM

renowned culinary contributions, however, are strawberries and strawberry jam. Head to the specialty shops along Phù Đổng Thiên Vương, north from the golf club, to pick up a jar of unrivaled strawberry preserves. The cheapest eats, as always, are the food stalls around the market. After dark, the market is lit with vendors selling home-cooked meals and local specialties. Nearby, a food stall along Trương Công Định, near the bookstore, sells superb pastries for 1000Đ.

Peace Cafe, 66 Trương Công Định (☎822 787), is literally the center of Đà Lạt's backpacker scene doubling as the Easy Rider clubhouse. Travelers swap stories and mingle with their motorbike drivers, hosted by exuberant manager/cook Tú Anh. Vietnamese, Western, and vegetarian dishes. The banana pancake hits the spot in the morning (8000Đ). Open daily 6am-10pm. ❶

Bành Bèo, 20A Nguyễn Chí Thành. Heading from the Hoà Bính cinema, it's past the bank. One of the tastier local eateries, it's named after its specialty: rice cakes with pork rinds, sprinkled with shrimp powder (3000Đ). Open daily 6am-6pm. ❶

Art Cafe, 70 Trương Công Định (☎510 089). A restaurant exclusively for Westerners, this one has tapped into the French vibe. Immaculate white tablecloths, romantic music, and the hushed whispers almost make you feel bad about your cargo pants. Excellent fish and coconut sauce (30,000Đ). French cuisine 25,000-40,000Đ. ❷

V Cafe, 1/1 Bùi Thị Xuân (☎837 576). This casual restaurant has tasty Western food figured out. Friendly staff and English menu. Outdoor seating. Dishes 25,000-50,000Đ. ❷

Cafe Appassionato, Nguyễn Chí Thanh. Part of Đà Lạt's terrific cafe scene; simply the best place to pass the time over excellent coffee. A great atmosphere begins with the welcoming owner and extends to the pastries and drinks. The music alone will have you coming back. Open daily 7am-11pm.

Stop and Go Cafe. See **Artist Community,** p. 957.

SIGHTS

Đà Lạt's attractions have gained notoriety around the nation and abroad. Unfortunately, they're scattered around the surrounding hills; motorbike is most convenient, although more rugged souls often choose a mountain bike.

XUÂN HƯƠNG LAKE. This man-made lake is the first thing you see in Đà Lạt. The city is built on the slopes rising from its shores; the lake curves east from the city center. Around it you can find swan-shaped paddle boats, opportunities to ride a horse with the famous and wonderfully kitschy "Đà Lạt Cowboys," and a couple of bar-restaurants on the shore. The most pleasant, however, is a stroll along the 7km sealed path circumscribing the lake.

SOS VILLAGE. On the south side of the lake, hidden among pines, is the villa-style SOS Village. Built with German and Austrian donations and support, the village originally housed the orphaned children of American soldiers and Vietnamese women. After GIs left, many Vietnamese women were left with children. Either unable to support the children or fearful of being ostracized by the community, many of these women gave up their children; they ended up in SOS Village. Today, the village is still a functioning orphanage that welcomes visitors. Please dress conservatively. *(67 Hùng Vương. Open daily 7am-5pm.)*

XQ ĐÀ LẠT EMBROIDERY WORKSHOP (DIỂM THAM QUAN). Part craftshop and part art gallery, the XQ Workshop is, in a word, awesome. At first glance, the framed artwork spilling from the walls rivals anything else in Vietnam—its impact only increases when you realize that it's all embroidery. The staff of the shop will be happy to provide a free tour, showing you ready-to-buy pieces on the first and third floors. The second floor houses the actual workshop. XQ employs 250 women but only 20 work at a time. The chosen few must go through a selection process and then a six-year training course before they put needle to silk. The second floor also has a small exhibit showing how the intricate patterns are made. *(56-58 Hoà Bịnh. ☎ 830 042; www.xqhandembroidery.com. Open daily 7am-5pm.)*

CHICKEN VILLAGE. This K'ho village located outside of Đà Lạt is widely known by its nickname because of the two-story concrete chicken in the center of the village. The people of the village chose to memorialize the animal because of a local legend. The story—or at least a variation of it—tells of a young couple in love who wanted to marry. The girl struggled to find a dowry, since the boy's family did not approve of her. In an effort to derail the marriage, the parents of the boy demanded that the girl present a chicken with nine spurs on the back of its legs. The girl searched throughout the village unsuccessfully and, just about as she was going to lose all hope, she heard a rumor that such a chicken lived on the nearby mountain. She left for the mountain and never returned. Stricken with grief, the villagers built the monument in memory of her. Today, the K'ho village is an excellent indigenous community to visit. Unlike the ethnic minority villages of the Central Highlands, the K'ho do not live in crushing poverty; they maintain a clean village and are comfortable with visitors. *(Located 18km south of Đà Lạt off Hwy. 20, in the shadow of Elephant Mountain.)*

ARTIST COMMUNITY. The Đà Lạt Artist Community is as famous as it is expansive, awash in relaxed, enlightened attitude and crisp invigorating mountain air. The scene here is dominated by three very different—and very eccentric—titans. All welcome tourists, but the result is that they have been swamped by visitors; meeting them has become less personal. **Hang Nga Guesthouse,** called the "The Crazy House," is comprised of a squat building and two towers. There are currently ten rooms that are designed in a unique way; the buildings themselves are unlike anything else. Imagine Gaudí gone wild or Disneyworld on acid. The artist who gave birth to this craziness is Mrs. Dang Viêt Nga, an architect trained in Moscow and still happily living in the 60s. She also happens to be the daughter of Vietnam's second president, Trương Chinh—there is an elaborate memorial room in his honor. *(3 Huỳnh Trúc Kháng. Open daily 7am-5pm. 5000Đ.)* **Lam Ti Ni Pagoda,** is an old, uncompleted pagoda where the famous "crazy monk" Viên Thức is holed up. Exceedingly friendly, the prolific painter, poet, and musician has turned this pagoda into his studio, gallery, and home, which is situated among shanties and dirt roads. Show yourself through the gate and unkept garden to the sealed doors. A knock will bring Viên Thức to the door, unless he is busy. He will happily show (and sell) his work, as well as talk about himself in fluent English, French, or Thai. Unfortunately, waves of visitors have turned this more into an attraction than an authentic experience, but it is still unlike anything else in the country. *(2 Thiện My.)* **Stop and Go Cafe,** hidden down a windy street, is a must on the artist circuit. Local poet, painter, and ex-mayor Duy Viêt has opened a cafe in the living room of his home. Squirreled away among flowers, greenhouses, and pine trees, this is one of the rare quiet urban hideaways in the country. Speaking English or French, and sporting his signature beret, Duy Viêt will show you his work while serving up excellent home-made cakes; you are also free to explore his greenhouse. Duy Viêt has hosted a multitude of visitors, including John F. Kennedy, Jr.; once you get settled in, it's hard to leave. *(2 Lý Tư Trong. Follow the unmarked Lý Tư Trong from the Buì Thi Xuân/Phan Bội Châu intersection to the end; the cafe is on the right.)*

PAGODAS. The hills around Đà Lạt are sown with pagodas, and after awhile they begin to blend together, even though each one is beautiful and peaceful. There are a few truly remarkable ones, including **Trưc Lam Pagoda,** one of Đà Lạt's newest pagodas. It was built in the last decade using donations from around the world, and the donors' names appear on the benches all around the grounds. Trưc Lam lacks character; it is noteworthy because it is actually a renowned zen meditation center, though how the monks can meditate with the noisy influx of tourists remains a mystery. Down the hill sits **Tuyễn Lam Lake** and small hamlets selling crafts, drinks, and boat rides. The hilltop Trưc Lam is accessible by cable car, connecting it to the bus station nearly 2km away (one-way 30,000Đ, round-trip 50,000Đ). Trưc Lam is 2km from Hwy. 20, 5km south of town. Follow the signs. **Thiên Vương Pagoda** (Chinese Pagoda), built by Đà Lạt's Chinese community in 1958, sits on a lonely pine-covered hilltop. The entrance building, at the end of a short, steep walk, beckons visitors with the arias of songbirds. The main pagoda holds three large, gold-painted wooden statues brought from China and thought to date from the 16th century. They are each 4m high and weigh 1500kg; from left to right, they represent power, infinite light, and mercy. Behind the pagoda is a large statue of Buddha. *(5km southeast of town on Khe Sanh.)* **Linh Sơn Pagoda** is Đà Lạt's oldest and most centrally located pagoda. Inside the central sanctum is a uniquely human Tích Ca (Gautama Buddha). Vien Nhu, an elder monk at the pagoda, speaks good English and is happy to explain Mahayana Buddhism's basic tenets. *(On Nguyễn Văn Trỗi, 1km north of the city center.)* **Linh Phước Pagoda** is a bustling, colorful pagoda in the nearby village of Trai Mát. Newly renovated, the ancient pagoda is the site of nationwide pilgrimages, and the intricate beauty of the building only begins to explain why. Inside the main building sits a giant gold Buddha under a massive molded bodhi tree. Visitors can climb the tower of the main building for a stunning view and climb the tower of the smaller building to see the 8400kg bell, featuring images of Vietnam's most revered pagodas. Between the two buildings lies a sculpture garden exhibiting a phantasmagorical dragon made of over 20,000 bottles of beer. The pagoda can be reached by train from Đà Lạt's historical station. *(1 Nguyễn Trãi, east of the lake; trains 7:30, 9am, 2, 3:30pm; 30min.; 70,000Đ. Or drive the 8km east to 120 Tư Phước Pagoda. Open daily 6am-7pm.)*

OUTDOOR ACTIVITIES

Đà Lạt's rugged environs make it the adventure and ecotourism capital of Vietnam. Fueled by backpacker dollars—and an increasing number of young Vietnamese—the industry has overrun the city. There are a number of companies to choose from, but they offer the same basic services and tours for nearly the same price. Going with a guide keeps things interesting, as there is much flora and local lore to discover; just make sure you aren't talked into being driven to the summit.

Đà Lạt Holidays/Phat Tire Ventures, 73 Trương Công Định (☎829 422; www.phattireventures.com). These two teams joined forces in 1996 to establish the most reputable operation in the area. Canyoning trips offered. Open daily 7:30am-8:30pm.

Hardy Dalat, 66 Phan Đình Phúng (☎836 840; www.hardyadventuretours.com). Another experienced institution.in Đà Lạt. Long excursions into the Central Highlands by jeep and down to Mũi Né by bike. Most daytrips are under US$15. Open daily 7:30am-8pm.

CÁT TIÊN NATIONAL PARK ☎61

Easily reached from HCMC or Đà Lạt, Cát Tiên National Park offers a much-needed haven from the noisy, overtouristed coast. It also provides a meaningful glance into Vietnam's young national park system and its growing efforts at environmental conservation. Though you probably won't see the Javan rhinoceros, biologists—lured by the endangered animal—abound.

VIETNAM

TRANSPORTATION. Cát Tiên is 125km north of HCMC and 175km south of Đà Lạt, and lies 24km off National Hwy. 20. From HCMC, take the Đà Lạt public bus from Miền Đông Station (4hr.; frequent departures; 40,000-60,000Đ) or a tourist bus (4hr.; 7:30 and 8:30am; 77,000Đ); tell the driver that you are going to Cát Tiên and ask to be let off at Ma Đu Guí Junction. If you're coming from Đà Lạt, use the same procedure as above; take an HCMC-bound bus and ask to be let off at the junction. Once there, hire a motorbike (15,000-30,000Đ) to take you the remaining 24km. The driver will take you to the ferry to the park headquarters.

PRACTICAL INFORMATION. At the entrance office to Cát Tiên, visitors must pay 20,000Đ. Across the river is the park headquarters. (☎/fax 791 288 or 791 227; cattien_nationalpark@fptnet.com. Daily 7am-evening.) You can rent Jeeps and trucks inside the park, but trips must be accompanied by a guide. (Jeeps 70,000Đ; trucks 100,000Đ.) Guided boat rentals are also available (100,000-150,000Đ). Hiking in the park must be done with a ranger. (Daytime 60,000-100,000Đ; nighttime 250,000Đ.) Rates vary depending on time of day and trip length.

ACCOMMODATIONS AND FOOD. Staying in Cát Tiên overnight for an extended period is easy. The park has double and triple **rooms** for rent ❷, as well as private wooden huts for two. The rooms are large and impersonal, but they get the job done with private bath, mosquito nets, and fans or A/C. All rooms are located at Park Headquarters and can be rented at the reception building, but not at the entrance office. (Doubles with fan 100,000Đ; triples 120,000Đ; slightly more for rooms with A/C.) There are two canteens located at the park headquarters compound, attracting giant geckos in addition to most visitors. The food and drink are decent but overpriced—a result of its being almost 30km from a major road. (Food 10,000-20,000Đ; beers 12,000Đ.)

HIKING. The park offers a range of ways to explore, but they differ in accessibility. Near Park Headquarters are **trails** that lead you among an impressive variety of flora, ranging from trees bearing mangoes to trees with eight-foot-high roots. Also easily reachable are the **Heaven Rapids,** a relaxing place to sunbathe, though not very striking in the dry season. These places should officially be explored with a ranger; they lie just off the main road. To have any chance of seeing animals, one must either push deeper into the forest or head to the **Crocodile Swamp.** A **nightspotting** trip (around 90,000Đ) through the park also allows you the opportunity to find local creatures, but odds are that you will only see deer, if anything. However, the drive through the jungle under the stars is well worth the price.

BUÔN MA THUỘT ☎50

Buôn Ma Thuột (BMT) was developed in 1899 by the French colonial *Compagnie d'Agriculture d'Asie* for the production of coffee and rubber, which grow well in the fertile red soil. On March 10, 1975, the North Vietnamese Army swept through the region, signaling the inception of their Hồ Chí Minh Campaign and the beginning of the end for the South Vietnamese forces. Today in BMT, rubber is still stripped, coffee is still grown, and the first tank to arrive on "Liberation Day" sits at the town center. Around this imposing monument, Buôn Ma Thuột has grown into a bustling provincial capital. Tourists find little of interest except fresh wholesale coffee at bargain prices. BMT is also a convenient staging area for trips to nearby waterfalls, tribal villages, and Yok Don National Park.

TRANSPORTATION. **Buôn Ma Thuột Airport** (☎862 248) is 13km northeast of town via Hwy. 14. The **Vietnam Airlines Booking Office** is at 67 Nguyễn Tất Thàn (☎855 055), just before the bus station. **Flights** go to: Hà Nội (4 times per week; 975,000Đ) via Đà Nẵng (545,000Đ) and HCMC (5 times per week; 635,000Đ). Reserve early. **Buses** leave the station at 71 Nguyễn Tất Thàn (☎852 603) for: Đà Lạt (6hr.; 6am; 56,000Đ); Đà Nẵng (19hr.; 11am, noon, 8pm; 80,000Đ); HCMC (9hr.; frequent; 91,000Đ); Huế (25hr.; 6am; 70,000Đ); Kon Tum (7hr.; 6am; 35,000Đ); Nha Trang (5hr.; 6am; 28,000Đ); Pleiku (4hr.; 6am; 28,000Đ); Quảng Ngãi (16hr.; 6am; 48,000Đ); and Qui Nhơn (11hr.; 6am; 34,000Đ). Travel time varies seasonally. **Minibuses** head to all of the above destinations for 10,000-20,000Đ less than the regular buses; negotiate prices with the driver and expect a cramped ride.

ORIENTATION. Buôn Ma Thuột is 190km south of Pleiku, 180km northwest of Nha Trang, and 350km northeast of HCMC. National Hwy. 27 connects BMT to Đà Lạt, but this route can only be traveled by private means. The big tank in the center of BMT is a navigational godsend. The turret, in its current position, points north down **Nguyễn Tất Thàn (Highway 14)** toward the bus station, 3km away. The back left corner of thc tank points down **No' Trang Long,** which runs west past the market and through the central district of cheap rooms and eats. Heading down this street, the first three rights are **Hai Bà Trưng, Lý Thường Kiệt,** and **Y Jut.** The right side of the tank faces **Lê Duẩn,** going south toward Dray Sap Falls and Tua Village.

PRACTICAL INFORMATION. **Daklak Tourist,** 3 Phan Chu Trinh, is located in the center of town next to the Thang Loi Hotel. They offer maps (10,000Đ) and book group tours of the area. (☎852 108; daklaktour@dng.vnn.vn. Open M-Sa 7:30-11am and 1:30-11pm, Su 7:30-11am and 1:30-5pm.) **Dam San Tourist,** 212-214 Nguyễn Công Trú (☎851 234; damsantour@dng.vnn.vn) is located in the Dam San Hotel, about 1km from the town center. The English-speaking staff gives out free city and regional maps and arranges group tours. Buôn Ma Thuột also has many English-speaking motorbike drivers who will be happy to guide for the right price. A trip from BMT to the Dray Sap Falls should run 60,000-100,000Đ round-trip.

Vietcombank, 2 Nguyễn Tất Thàn, faces the tank in the center of town and has a 24hr. **ATM.** The Đắk Lắk **General Hospital** is at 2 Mai Hắc Đé (☎852 662) off of Lê Duẩn going south out of town. The **Central Post Office,** 4 Lê Duẩn (open daily 6:30am-9pm), provides regular post service and international calling. Internet cafes have slow access but are open late. **Internet 045,** 119 Quang Trưng (☎858 643), and **Internet,** 45 Bà Triệu, both charge 3000Đ per hr.

ACCOMMODATIONS. Rooms are typically bare and soulless. All prices, even at the upscale hotels, are negotiable. The multiple lower-end hotels are all located in the city center and tend to be multi-story buildings with concrete cells, but they're all clean and outfitted with fan or A/C. **Thành Phát ❷,** 41 Lý Thường Kiệt, seems to be where the few backpackers congregate. Little English is spoken. (☎854 857; thanhphat@pmail.vnn.vn. Basic rooms US$6; with toilet US$8; with A/C and hot bath US$12.) **Hong Kong Hotel ❷,** 35 Hai Bà Trưng, is an older and sparser version of its neighbors, but the staff speaks English. (☎852 630. Same prices as Thànf Phát.) The upper-end hotels tend to be on the periphery of the city center. They all boast English-speaking staff, satellite TV, and hot water. **Thành Công Hotel ❹,** 51 Lý Thường Kiệt, is in the city center next and the market. (☎858 243 or 858 375; daklaktour@dng.vnn.vn. Rooms US$20-30.)

FOOD. Buôn Ma Thuột offers plenty of dining options, but not a lot of variety: there are cafes and street-side eats. The best value in a sit-down restaurant is traditional *phấn*. These can be found along Lý Thường Kiệt, of which **Thành Hùng ❶,** 14 Lý Thường Kiệt is the most popular with the locals, probably because it gives noodles to go with the rice-paper rolls. (☎83 910.) For a filling meal, try **Bò Né Bốn Triệu ❶,** 33 Hai Bà Trưng. Ask for *bò né* (10,000Đ), the breakfast specialty: eggs, beef, scallions, and a porkball on a sizzling cow-shaped plate. (Open daily 6am-10pm.) The **market** is also located along Quang Trưng, as well as **wholesale coffee shops** (20,000Đ per kg).

No visit would be complete without a trip to one of the myriad local cafes. Most cafes serve the generic brand-name Trung Nguyễn; a few, however, serve from a private stock. A string of cafes sit along Nguyễn Công Trú, between Lê Duẩn and the Dam San Hotel. **Cafe Daly ❷,** 188 Nguyễn Công Trú (☎812 243), and **Cafe Dồng Xanh ❷,** 157 Nguyễn Công Trú (☎853 104), are the most comfortable but also commercial. At the other end of the street (literally and figuratively), is **Cafe Xúa & Nay ❷,** 1 Lê Duẩn (☎850 143), a large, vine-covered patio haven for the locals. **Cafe 54,** 9 Nơ Trang Long, has sidewalk seating in the bustling center.

SIGHTS AND DAYTRIPS. Any sight-seeing tour of Buôn Ma Thuột proper begins and ends at the **Victory Monument.** Examine the tank. You're done!

South of Buôn Ma Thuột, along Hwy. 14, are daytrips that make BMT well worth the trek from the coast. About 30km down Hwy. 14 are the **Dray Sap Falls** (entrance 8000Đ entrance fee). Descend into a small rainforest, complete with strangler figs and hanging vines, then follow the path along the Krông Knâ river to the lower falls. The best view of the falls is from the suspension footbridge, several developing trails bring you within misting distance. The trails are unmarked but easy to follow. The upper falls can only be reached by foot, as a 3km road is under construction. Follow the machinery at the branch right after the entrance gate.

A bit closer to BMT, yet equally relaxing, is **Tua village** (also called Buôn Tuôr; pop. 415). Its Êđê inhabitants are Protestant; they live in longhouses made of wood and farm the surrounding land for potatoes, coffee, and corn. The village is quiet and immaculately clean, and the people are welcoming. A visit to the village is free, but small gifts like cigarettes are always appreciated. Try to go on a Sunday—the village is much more festive than during the work week. **Lak Lake,** 56km south of BMT, is accessible by a straight shot along Hwy. 27. A M'nong community lives by the water, growing rice and raising livestock beneath elevated longhouses. Visitors enjoy touring by elephant (1hr., 2 people US$30). The most memorable aspects of Lak Lake, though, are free: children playing soccer, boats on the water, and description-defying dawns and dusks.

The best way to get to Dray Sap Falls, Tua village, and Lak Lake is by motorbike from BMT. Either rent one yourself or hire one with a driver. A one-hour trip should cost 30,000-50,000Đ because of poor road conditions. The Dray Sap Falls are 27km south of BMT along Hwy. 14. Head south to Ea Tling Village and take a left at the intersection. Another 6km down this semi-paved road, you will come to the entrance gate. Tua Village is 14km south of BMT off of Hwy. 14. You must turn off at an unmarked road, so your best bet is to hire a local driver. Lak Lake is 56km south on Hwy. 27—you can't miss it, as the highway runs right along the lake.

YOK DON NATIONAL PARK

Yok Don is Vietnam's largest national park. This expansive wildlife preserve now encompasses over 100,000 hectares, stretching from 37km northwest of Buôn Ma Thuột to the Cambodian border. The park is primarily a nature reserve and—like many of Vietnam's national parks—hosts an abundance of animals, including elephants, monkeys, buffalo, and deer. There are dozens of endangered species, some of which have only just been discovered, like the *carnisauvus* (a type of wild dog). Except for a thin strip of rainforest along the regal Serepok RIver and the inaccessible mountains along the Cambodian border, grasslands and a sparse hardwood forest comprise most of Yok Don's landscape.

Several ethnic minority communities eke out a living in the area. The Ēdē and the M'nong are the most common; the M'nong have made a name for themselves in Đắk Lắk Province as skilled elephant catchers and tamers. Khonsonuk (1850-1924) is famed for having caught 244 elephants in his lifetime. His tomb, lying just outside of Ban Don Village, is worth a visit. There are a few master elephant catchers still living in the area. In contrast to the villagers who hang out in kitschy Bar Don, most M'nong families work the land as their ancestors have for centuries. You'll stumble on a few fields and families if you follow the river upstream from Ban Don 500m-1km.

TRANSPORTATION. Visitors must arrange their own transport to Yok Don National Park. The park is best reached from Buôn Ma Thuột, where groups can arrange transportation at **Daklak Tourist** or **Dam San Tourist** (p. 960). The cheapest and most convenient way (if you do not have your own transportation) is to rent a motorbike at a hotel or hire a motorbike and driver (US$5-7 for the 40km ride). The entrance to the park cannot be missed from the road that continues west from Buôn Ma Thuột's Phan Bội Châu. The turn-off for Ban Don Village is 2km up the road on the left and is also well-marked.

PRACTICAL INFORMATION. Arranged tours are, unfortunately, the only way you're guaranteed to see anything. The heavily traveled trails in the park are devoid of any wildlife except for a few lizards and insects, or perhaps a herd of buffalo. **Park Headquarters** (☎783 049; yokdon@dng.vnn.vn) offers informational treks and overnight stays, but visits do not penetrate the park very deeply and are overpriced. For longer and more in-depth excursions (upwards of US$60), permits are necessary; contact headquarters for information. Another option for prearranged touring is to inquire at **Daklak Tourist** in BMT, but they only deal with groups. The best bet for short, budget stays is to show up at **Ban Don village,** 2km past the park entrance. At Ban Don motorbike, boat, or trekking can be arranged. There are also elephant rides and demonstrations, as well as traditional elephant competitions in late winter. Tours from Ban Don range from 3hr. to three days; a half-day tour runs about US$5.

ACCOMMODATIONS AND FOOD. **Yok Don Guesthouse ❷** (☎853 110) is located at Park Headquarters and is serviced by a small canteen. The concrete guesthouse offers limited amenities but easy access to the park's tourist services. (Rooms 120,000Đ; tents 50,000Đ.) **Ban Don Village ❷** offers an ethnic alternative. Guests can stay in traditional-style M'nong longhouses, but they'll have to fend off other tourists. If there is a large enough group, locals will put on a traditional ceremony at night. The canteen there serves typical Vietnamese food. (Rooms US$5. Dishes 10,000-20,000Đ.)

KON TUM ☎60

Kon Tum, the capital of Kon Tum Province, is the last city before the Central Highlands swell into jungle mountains. Lying at the foot of these mountains along the Dakbla River, Kon Tum offers the most stunning scenery of the Central Highlands. Like its southern neighbors, however, the city of Kon Tum is an overcrowded provincial capital. Still, it's the best tourist option in the Central Highlands: it attracts some returning veterans of the Vietnam War due to its proximity to Đắk Tô and Charlie Hill, offers access to nearby Banar Villages, and is the start of an unrivaled drive up Hwy. 14 to the coast. Since it lies off the beaten path, you'll be the rare tourist and have many chances to practice your Vietnamese language skills. Don't speak Vietnamese? Yeah, we know.

TRANSPORTATION. The **interprovince bus station** is 2km north of the town center on Phan Đình Phùng. All buses head south through Pleiku. You must arrange for your transportation in town to move north along Hwy. 14. The ticket office won't serve foreigners; the bus driver is the man for non-Vietnamese to talk to. The following are local prices—use them to begin bargaining. **Buses** go to: Buôn Ma Thuột (6hr.; 7am; 26,000Đ); Đà Nẵng (14hr.; 6:30am; 56,000Đ); HCMC (14hr.; 7am; 40,000Đ); Huế (17hr.; 7am; 73,000Đ); Quảng Ngãi (11hr.; 7am; 40,000Đ); and Qui Nhơn (6hr.; 7am; 25,000Đ). Buses leave all day for Pleiku (1hr.; 8000Đ).

PRACTICAL INFORMATION. Kon Tum Tourist, located in the Dakbla Hotel (see below), is a government-owned agency that handles tours, permits, and transportation. A guide and driver to Đắk Tô costs US$15. Guide, driver, and permit to restricted hill villages runs about US$30. (☎861 826; www.kontumtourist.com.vn. Open daily 7-11am and 1-5pm.) **Investment and Development Bank,** 2 Trần Phú on the river, boasts an English-speaking staff. The bank can only offer credit card advances when the director is in. (Open daily 7am-6pm.) There is no ATM in town. **Police** stations are eerily omnipresent. There's one at 90 Phan Chu Trinh. The **hospital** is at 71 Phan Đình Phùng. (☎824 125.) Access the **Internet** for 3000Đ per hr. at **Vĩnh Lộc,** 99 Trần Hưng Đạo. The **General Post Office** is at 206 Lê Hồng Phong, at its intersection with Bà Triệu; look for the giant radio tower. (☎862 361. Open daily 7am-9pm.)

ACCOMMODATIONS. Family Hotel ❷, 55 Trần Hưng Đạo, is brand-spanking new. Privately owned, with bright and modern rooms, this is the best value in town. (☎862 448. Rooms US$7-15, negotiable.) **Dakbla Hotel ❹,** 2 Phan Đình Phùng, is Kon Tum's upper-end hotel. Situated across the bridge into town, it's a great place for tourists, but not necessarily backpackers. (☎863 333; ktourist@dng.vnn.vn. Rooms US$25-35.) **Quang Trung Hotel ❷,** 168 Bà Triệu, is the state-owned budget offering in Kon Tum: Everything you need, but in slight disrepair.

THE HIDDEN DEAL

APOCALYPSE REDUX

For a fraction of the cost paid by the characters in Francis Ford Coppola's movie, you can take your own boat trip through the Vietnamese jungle toward the Cambodian border. Outside of Kon Tum, the young Banar boys of Konkoitu (see p. 964) pass the day floating up and down the muddy, lazy Dakbla in their long dugout canoes, bringing goods up from town or sometimes just idling the day away. For 5000-10,000Đ, they will be more than happy to take you along for the ride.

The best place to catch the canoes is on the beach of Konkoitu village (walk past the village center and then bear left). From here you can either head upstream or downstream. Choosing the latter will conveniently bring you back to Kon Tum. However, heading upstream is the more interesting option; in this direction, the mountains close in and the road and cultivated lands fade from the shore. With the smallest bit of imagination, you begin to feel like a modern-day Dr. Livingston. The river becomes narrower and eventually branches into two, one branch heading north and the other heading south; both lead into the jungled peaks of the Annam highlands. This is a rare chance in Vietnam to explore virgin territory, free of any noise and other people. There are few better daytrips in Vietnam for less than US$1.

(☎862 249 or 863 961; fax 862 763. Rooms US$6-12.) **Dakbla Hotel 2 ❷**, 163 Nguyễn Huệ, by the river, is the more spartan sibling of Dakbla Hotel. (☎863 335; ktourist@dng.vnn.vn.)

FOOD. Dakbla's ❸, 168 Nguyễn Huệ, is Kon Tum's best tourist option, with reasonable prices and an extensive Vietnamese and Western menu. It's one of the few places in the Central Highlands that serves dessert. Decorating the walls are cultural artifacts from Banar villages, all for sale. (☎862 584.) **Hiệp Thành ❹**, 29 Nguyễn Huệ, is a nicer restaurant along the river, with an immaculate eating area and typical menu. (☎862 470.) **Hoàn Vũ ❹**, 81 Nguyễn Huệ, is a shiny upscale restaurant catering to Western tourists and prosperous government officials. The second-story seating area has a commanding view of the river and surrounding countryside. The cheapest eats in Kon Tom are in the **market** or at nearby hole-in-the-wall restaurants, such as **Phơ' Bò Cuoí ❷**, 70A Trần Phú, and **Restaurant 88 ❷**, 145 Trần Hưng Đạo.

SIGHTS. Kon Tum does not offer many in-town sights. **Wooden Church and Orphanage,** at the intersection of Nguyễn Huệ and Lý Tự Trọng, is Kon Tum's most-used church, and the orphanage is a living relic from the French colonial era, rare in today's Vietnam. The church, constructed in 1913, is made completely of wood and beautifully combines French and Vietnamese styles. The congregation worships in an airy, sublime space within pastel blue walls, framed in dark wood. The orphanage is behind the church and is full of friendly and curious children, mostly from local Banar villages. The nuns who run the orphanage still speak French, make their own baguettes, and are more than happy to show you around. (Free, but donations greatly appreciated.) **Rong House,** on Trần Hưng Đạo as you head east out of town, is an example of a traditional Banar "community center." Perched on stilts, *rong* houses stretch skyward for several stories. They're built using only wood, bamboo, lashing, and a thatching for the roof. This *rong* house, like all others, is an impressive sight, but empty unless there is a community festival.

DAYTRIPS FROM KON TUM. The best way to see and identify sights is to hire a motorbike and a knowledgeable guide. You can also arrange a tour at Kon Tum Tourist (see p. 963). **Konkoitu village,** a mere 5km to the east of Kon Tum, is the only hill-tribe village in the area that you are allowed to visit without a permit. Unfortunately, there isn't much there except a few huts, a *rong* house, and poor Banar families. But the friendliness of the inhabitants, their willingness to show you their skills in weaving and fishing, and the stunning scenery make the short trip worthwhile. To get there you can take private transport or rent a motorbike or bike. To reach Konkoitu, leave town heading east on Trần Hưng Đạo, cross over the bridge, take a left at the fork, and then follow the road to its terminus.

Đắk Tô, 40km north of Kon Tum on Hwy. 14, was a strategic area during the Vietnam War—valued for its proximity to the Laos and Cambodian borders. Today Đắk Tô is a booming village that nevertheless recognizes its unfortunate past. A Victory Monument dominates the center of the town. This Stalinist marble tower and the two tanks parked beside it are the most commanding sight in town. Next door is a pleasant *rong* house.

Five kilometers north of Đắk Tô are the remains of a **US Airbase** (Phượng Hoàng). The airstrip, now used to dry various tubers, is down the road on the left. In the distance you can see **Rocket Ridge,** the location of a heavily used and heavily bombed US/RVN helicopter base. **Skull Hill,** the site of a clash between Northern DVN and Southern RVN forces in the spring of 1972, stands on the road to Đắk Tô, 17km from Kon Tum. By overtaking the hill, the Communists severed the land route to Kon Tum. The location of the bloody attack is marked by a concrete shrine and three piles of stones where the locals burn incense. **Charlie Hill,** 5km south of Đắk Tô, was the location of a Southern RVN fortification. Although the base was rather small, the fight for control of Charlie Hill became infamous. The South Vietnamese officer commanding the base refused to surrender or retreat in the face of the superior Việt Cộng force. The officer, Colonel Ngoc Minh, and his 150 soldiers endured a siege that lasted two months before the VC were finally able to overrun the hill and kill them all. The hill is considered unsafe to climb, as it was heavily mined during the war, but it can be viewed from Hwy. 14.

HỒ CHÍ MINH CITY (HCMC) ☎8

Hồ Chí Minh City (formerly Saigon) has long been a hotbed of activity, but it only recently became the overcrowded powerhouse that it is today. The French made it the capital of colonial *Indochine*, endowing it with wide boulevards and grand architecture. During the Vietnam War, the city served as headquarters for US forces and international journalists, many of whom were captivated by its exotic nature. Today Hồ Chí Minh City is the country's largest and most populous city, and it continues to remain on the cusp of all things new and en vogue. Although the city was renamed after the national Communist hero, HCMC has since come down with capitalist fever. Merchants crowd every inch of sidewalk space, businesspeople broker international deals over their cell phones, and sparkling shopping centers cater to a growing number of upwardly mobile Vietnamese. People work around the clock, without weekend breaks. Yet despite all the commercial mania, Hồ Chí Minh City is also home to magnificent pagodas, lush gardens, and charming cafes. For visitors, these may be a welcome respite from the city's frenetic pulse, which races at the same speed as the thousands of motorbikes zipping down its streets. Given the way his namesake has turned out, Hồ Chí Minh is probably rolling over in his tomb. But the locals here aren't fazed—after all, everyone still calls it Saigon anyway.

INTERCITY TRANSPORTATION

FLIGHTS

Whatever else you do when you land, don't forget to keep your entry/exit form in a safe place, as you will need it upon your departure. When flying out, be sure to have the US$14 departure tax. There are several means of transportation to and from Tân Sơn Nhất International Airport, including the buses and the more expensive taxis.

Tân Sơn Nhất International Airport (☎844 6662; www.saigonairport.com), 5km northwest of the city center. ATM and currency exchange available. Flights to: **Bangkok,** Thailand (1½hr.); **Hà Nội,** Vietnam (2hr.); **Hong Kong,** China (2½hr.); **Kuala Lumpur,** Malaysia (2hr.); **Phnom Penh,** Cambodia (50min.); **Siem Reap,** Cambodia (1¼hr.); **Singapore** (2hr.); **Seoul,** Korea (5hr.); **Taipei,** Taiwan (3¼hr.); **Tokyo,** Japan (4½ hour).

TRAINS

Ga Sài Gòn, in District 3 at 1 Nguyễn Thông (☎843 6528). Tickets can be purchased at the station, or at the visitor-friendly **Saigon Railway Tourist Service,** 275C Phạm Ngũ Lão (☎836 7640). Express train leaves nightly at 11pm for **Đà Nẵng** (15hr.; 307,000-509,000Đ); **Hà Nội** (30hr.; 534,000-886,000Đ) via: **Nha Trang** (6½hr.; 135,000-224,000Đ); **Huế** (18hr.; 341,000-565,000Đ); **Vinh** (24½hr.; 487,000-809,000Đ).

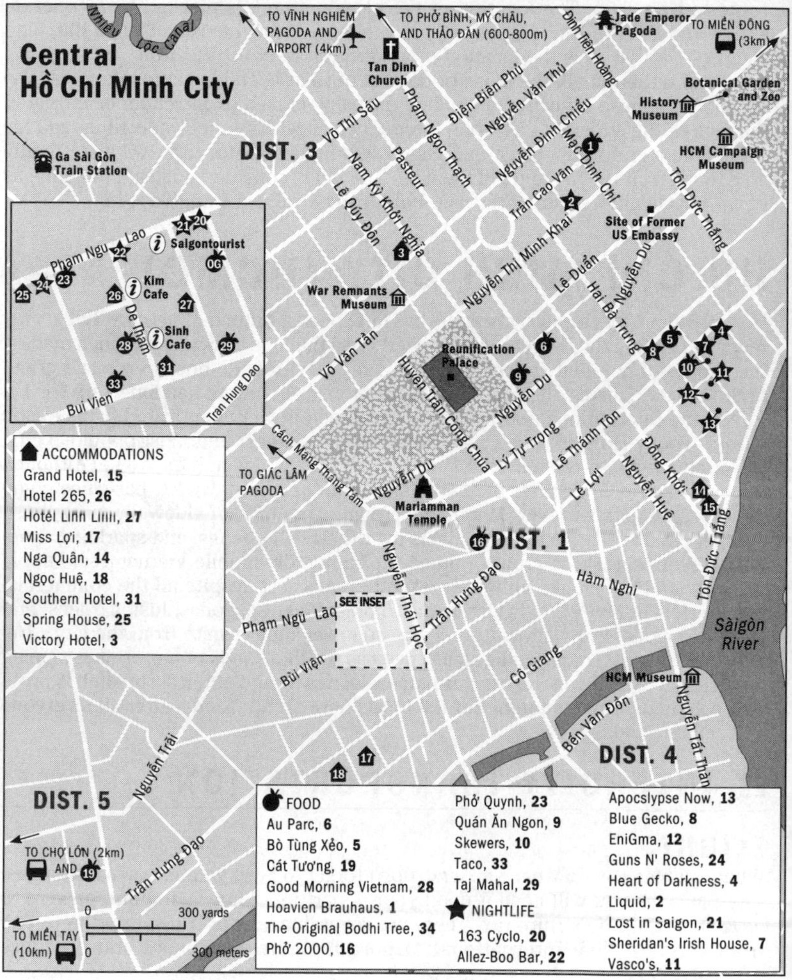

BUSES

There are two major bus stations in Hồ Chí Minh City. **Miền Đông** serves destinations to the north, while buses going south (except to Vũng Tàu) depart from **Miền Tây.** Both stations are quite far from District 1; take a motorbike or taxi.

Miền Đông Station, in Bình Thạnh District on Xô Việt Nghệ Tinh (Quốc Lộ 13). In most cases, the earliest bus departs at 6am and the latest bus departs at 6pm. Buses go to **Vũng Tàu** (2hr.; 22,000Đ) and to destinations in the north: **Đà Lạt** (6hr.; 43,000Đ); **Đà Nẵng** (24hr.; 102,000Đ); **Hải Phòng** (52hr.; 200,000Đ); **Hà Nội** (48hr.; 182,000Đ); **Huế** (27hr.; 120,000Đ); **Kon Tum** (14hr.; 100,000Đ); **Mũi Né** (4hr.; 35,000Đ); **Nha Trang** (9hr; 63,000Đ); **Phan Thiết** (3½hr.; 28,000Đ); **Pleiku** (12hr.; 85,000Đ).

Miền Tây Station, in Bình Chánh District on Kinh Dương Vương. In most cases, the earliest bus departs at 6am and the latest bus departs at 6pm; some buses depart as late as 9:30pm. Buses go south to the Mekong Delta: **Bạc Liêu** (8hr.; 47,000Đ); **Bến Tre** (2hr.; 22,000Đ); **Cà Mau** (10hr.; 47,000Đ); **Cần Thơ** (4hr.; 30,000Đ); **Châu Đốc** (6hr.; 43,000Đ); **Rạch Giá** (6hr.; 42,000Đ); **Sóc Trăng** (6hr.; 39,000Đ); **Trà Vinh** (4hr.; 34,000Đ); **Vĩnh Long** (3hr.; 24,000Đ).

Other Stations: Chợ Lớn Station, in District 5 (Chợ Lớn) on Hải Thượng Lãn Ông. Earliest buses depart at 4am and latest buses depart at 6pm. Buses go to **Mỹ Tho** (2hr.; 15,000Đ) and **Củ Chi** (1½hr.; 12,000Đ). **An Súong Station,** in Tân Bình District on Trường Chinh. Buses go to **Tây Ninh** (1½hr.; 18,500Đ).

OPEN-TOUR BUSES

The easiest and most popular way to tour Vietnam over land is on open-tour buses. Operated by most of the tour companies in HCMC (see p. 968), these air-conditioned buses traverse the country from HCMC to Hà Nội with stops in major cities and resorts en route. Passengers can buy a ticket to Hà Nội (US$20-30) and hop on and off whenever; alternatively, they can buy tickets for individual legs of the trip.

FERRIES

Hydrofoils leave from the pier on Tôn Đức Thắng, near the end of Hàm Nghi. Contact Petro Express (☎821 0650) or Vina Express (☎825 3888). To: **Vũng Tàu** (1¼hr., 11 per day 6:15am-5pm, US$10); and **Cần Giờ** (6hr., 6:30am, US$20).

ORIENTATION

Hồ Chí Minh City is divided into 12 numbered urban districts (**quận,** sometimes abbreviated **Q**), 5 named urban districts, and 5 named suburban districts. Most of the action takes place in **District 1;** not only is it home to the majority of tourist attractions and services, but it also contains the city's burgeoning commercial scene. On its western side, the area between **Phạm Ngũ Lão** and **Bùi Viện** is popular with budget travelers for its cheap accommodations and food. Expatriates and luxury travelers tend to congregate further east, between **Đồng Khởi** and **Tôn Đức Thắng.** North of District 1, a number of other sights and the train station are located in **District 3.** West of District 1, the ethnic Chinese population of the city is concentrated in **District 5,** also called **Chợ Lớn.**

Streets are sometimes labeled Đ for *đường* or ĐL for *đại lộ*. Alleys are often labeled *hẻm*. Street numbering can be quite confusing in HCMC. Street numbers on either side of a road are not necessarily close together; it is possible that 34 might be across from 67, for instance. Furthermore, some numbers have a slash in them. This usually means one of two things: either the place occupies several properties (e.g., 17/13 Lê Thánh Tôn, occupying lots 17 and 13) or it is located on an alley (e.g., 40/5 Bùi Viện, located at number 5 on an alley off 40 Bùi Viện).

LOCAL TRANSPORTATION

Buses: The city bus system can be confusing to foreigners. Many stops are unmarked and route maps are not available. However, most buses are labeled with their main stops. The two major depots in District 1 are Bến Thành (across from Bến Thành Market) and Mê Linh Square (on the riverfront, where Hai Bà Trưng and Tôn Đức Thắng meet). Most bus routes run between the large city bus stations (Miền Đông, Miền Tay, Chợ Lớn, and An Súong; see **Intercity Transportation,** p. 965) and make stops at these depots. Tickets are 1000-4000Đ.

TIP **TRAFFIC TRAUMAS.** Crossing the street in Hồ Chí Minh City is a daring and dicey proposition. Cars, motorbikes, and other vehicles typically do not stop if they see a pedestrian waiting to cross. Not all busy intersections have traffic signals, and even if they do, the drivers turning left and right do not tend to observe them. The trick is to walk at a slow, steady pace and trust in the inscrutable god of traffic. Most drivers are accustomed to dodging pedestrians (and one another), so if they spot you in their path, they will veer out of your way. If you try to dart around them, they will only get confused, making a horrible accident more likely. On the other hand, don't stop dead in your tracks, or you will face a wave of oncoming drivers, all honking at you angrily. Of course use crosswalks and follow traffic signals when available. Also, try to cross when as few drivers as possible are coming your way; take care to avoid large numbers of cars and trucks, which are more likely than motorbikes to simply plow ahead regardless of what's in front of them.

Taxis: There are a number of taxi companies in HCMC, but not all are trustworthy. Check that your taxi has a meter, and make sure the driver turns it on. Most meters start at 12,000Đ. A trip within District 1 shouldn't cost more than 20,000Đ. **Yellow Vina** taxis (☎811 1111) and green-and-white **ML** taxis (☎823 2323) are considered reputable.

Motorbikes: Tourists in HCMC will constantly be offered the services of motorbike drivers, who transport people on the back of their vehicles. Motorbikes are not metered, so the fee involves some bargaining. A typical rate is around 2000-3000Đ per km, and within District 1 should cost no more than 10,000Đ; agree on the price before you get onto the bike. Almost nobody in HCMC wears a **helmet,** but you should.

Cyclos: Popular with tourists, cyclos are bicycles with a seat attached to the front. Although slower than motorbikes, drivers may charge more because they work harder to transport passengers. Consider paying around 3000-4000Đ per km. Many cyclo drivers speak English and give city tours (15,000Đ per hour). Unfortunately, cyclos are banned on some major streets.

Motorbike and Bicycle Rental: Many hotels and guesthouses rent motorbikes and bicycles to those brave enough to face the traffic alone.

VIETNAM

PRACTICAL INFORMATION

Tours: There are countless tour companies in Hồ Chí Minh City, and many offer similar packages and rates. Most companies arrange city and regional tours. You can also buy **open-tour** bus tickets (see p. 967). Two well-known players in the Phạm Ngũ Lão area are **Sinh** (246-248 Đề Thám; ☎837 6833; www.sinhcafevn.com; open daily 6:30am-11pm) and **Kim** (270 Đề Thám; ☎836 9859; www.kimtravel.com; open daily 7:30am-9:30pm). **SaigonTourist** (49 Lê Thánh Tôn; ☎824 4554; www.saigontourist.net; open daily 7:30am-6:30pm) is the government-operated tourist agency, as well as also the owner of many city businesses.

Consulates: Australia, 5B Tôn Đức Thắng (☎829 6035). Open M-F 8:30am-noon and 1-5pm. **Cambodia,** 45 Phùng Khắc Khoan (☎829 2751). Open M-F 7:30-11:30am and 2-5pm. **Canada,** 235 Đồng Khởi (☎824 5025). Open M-Th 8am-noon and 1-5pm, F 8am-noon. **China,** 39 Nguyễn Thị Minh Khai (☎829 2457). Open M-F 8-11am and 2-5pm. **Laos,** 93 Pasteur (☎829 7667). Open M-F 8:30-11:30am and 1:30-4:30pm. **New Zealand,** 41 Nguyễn Thị Minh Khai (☎822 6907). Open M-F 8:30am-5pm. **Thai-**

land, 77 Trần Quốc Thảo (☎932 7637). Open M-F 8:30-11:30am and 1-4:30pm. **UK,** 25 Lê Duẩn (☎823 2604). Open M-F 8:30-11:30am and 1-3pm. **US,** 4 Lê Duẩn (☎822 9433). Open M-Th 8:30-11:30am and 1:30-3:30pm.

Visas: Most tour companies can arrange tourist visas to neighboring countries; this is usually quicker and easier than going to the consulate, and the price is comparable.

Banks: Sacombank, 211 Nguyễn Thái Học (☎836 4133). Open M-F 7:30-11:30am and 1-4:30pm, Sa 7:30-11:30am. **HSBC,** 235 Đồng Khởi (☎829 2288). Open M-Th 8:30am-4:30pm, F 8:30am-5pm, Sa-Su cash advance 8:30am-noon and 1-4:30pm. **ANZ,** 11 Mê Linh (☎825 8190). Open M-F 8:30am-4pm. All have 24hr. **ATMs.**

American Express: Exotissimo, Saigon Trade Center, 37 Tôn Đức Thắng (☎825 1723), is a registered AmEx Travel Service office. Open M-F 8:30am-5:30pm, Sa 8:30am-noon.

Alternatives to Tourism: Thảo Đàn, 451/1 Hai Bà Trưng (☎846 5410), on the alley that runs off 451 Hai Bà Trưng. An organization for street children, Thảo Đàn runs several safehouses, a drop-in center, education and counseling programs, and other services. Volunteers welcome. Call before visiting.

Bookstores: Fahasa, 185 Đồng Khởi (☎822 4670). Huge, with a large selection of English and French literature. Open daily 8am-10pm. **Thu Vân,** 179 Phạm Ngũ Lão (☎837 3288). Used books, including travel guides, language guides, and popular novels in abundance. Buys and exchanges books. Open daily 8am-10pm.

Library: 69 Lý Tự Trọng. Open Tu-Su 7:30am-7pm. Free **Internet** access in the room to the right of the central staircase.

Publications: *Vietnam Pathfinder* is a free monthly expatriate magazine which lists essential info and popular shops, restaurants, and clubs. Available in many hotels.

Laundromat: Almost all hotels and guesthouses have laundry service around 6000-10,000Đ per kg.

Emergency: Fire ☎114. **Ambulance** ☎115. Not all operators speak English. If you have a medical emergency, it is better to call the emergency number at one of the medical services below, or have a taxi take you directly.

Police: ☎113. If you run afoul of the law, contact your national consulate immediately.

Pharmacies: In most cases, you do not need a prescription; just ask for the medicine you need by its generic name. For its large selection, hospitals recommend **Mỹ Châu,** located at 389 Hai Bà Trưng (☎822 2266; open daily 6:30am-10:30pm).

Medical Services: The following all have 24hr. emergency service. **International SOS,** 65 Nguyễn Du (☎829 8424; emergency 829 8529). Open M-F 8am-8pm, Su 8am-6pm. **Family Medical Practice,** Diamond Plaza, 34 Lê Duẩn (☎822 7848). Open M-F 8:30am-5:30pm, Sa 8:30am-12:30pm.

Telephones: General Assistance: ☎**1080.** International direct calls are pricey (18,000-20,000Đ per min.); fortunately, **Internet phone** calls are cheaper and usually work just as well. Many hotels and guesthouses offer this service for 5000-10,000Đ per min. You can also purchase an Internet phone card (1000-5000Đ per min.) at many convenience stores; you'll need to find a computer that has an Internet phone attached to it.

Internet: Access is everywhere, especially around Phạm Ngũ Lão and other tourist areas. Typical rate 1000Đ per min.

Post Office: Central Post Office, 2 Công Xã Paris (☎829 9601), opposite Notre Dame Cathedral in a huge colonial-style building—a tourist attraction in its own right. Open daily 7am-10pm. **Branch:** 14 Bùi Viện (☎837 7715). Open daily 7am-10pm.

Postal Code: 70000.

VILLAGE OF THE DAMNED

One of the most delightful sounds in Vietnam is the laughter of children. Whether strolling home from school, darting around the sidewalks, or sharing in private jokes, they exude a contagious glee.

Several days a year, the whole country gets swept up in this mood as it celebrates *Tết Trung Thu,* the Mid-Autumn Festival. The festival is held at the time of year when the moon appears largest. This moon symbolizes the fullness of life, including the blessings that children bring to the world. During the festival, which lasts several days, children parade through the streets wearing masks, banging drums, and toting lanterns. They also perform traditional dances and participate in contests. The festival is filled with Vietnamese folklore, most of which relates to the moon. One prominent character is Ra Hu, a demon who eats pieces of the moon, thus creating its monthly phases. Children wear masks and growl like beasts in order to keep Ra Hu from gobbling up the moon altogether.

Tết Trung Thu provides a chance for parents to express their love and appreciation for their children; they honor them with cakes called *bánh trung thu* which are filled with lotus seeds, orange peels, and ground beans. *Tết Trung Thu* begins on the 15th day of the 8th lunar month; in 2005, it will start on Sept. 18.

ACCOMMODATIONS

Most budget accommodations in HCMC have a variety of room options: with or without A/C, bathtub, etc. A few dollars more will get you a larger room with better facilities. Also, many places do not make a distinction between singles and doubles; there is often one double bed, and the number of people you share it with is up to you. Unless otherwise indicated, the price ranges below reflect the cost of one or two people staying in a room. Check out rooms before you book them.

PHẠM NGŨ LÃO

This area is a budget travel mecca. Every street is packed with cheap hotels; the ones listed here are just a fraction of the total number. As a result, it's buyers' market, so negotiate before you settle in. If you'd like to stay in the area but want some peace and quiet, try one of the alleyways off the main streets; many have decent guesthouses.

Spring House, 221 Phạm Ngũ Lão (☎836 8859), between Đề Thám and Đỗ Quang Đẩu. Bright, lemon-yellow rooms with rattan furniture and a cheery atmosphere. Some rooms have excellent views of the park. Rooms US$12-15; triples US$25; quads US$40. ❸

Hotel Linh Linh, 175/14 Phạm Ngũ Lão (☎373 0004), on the alley that runs off 175 Phạm Ngũ Lão and connects to Bùi Viện. Spacious rooms with decorative touches. Larger rooms have lovely balconies. Rooms US$11-12. ❸

Hotel 265, 265 Đề Thám (☎836 7512; hotelduy@hotmail.com), between Phạm Ngũ Lão and Bùi Viện. The four-person dorms, spacious and well-maintained, are a great value. Large shared bath. US$3 per person. ❶

Southern Hotel, 216 Đề Thám (☎837 0922; www.vngold.com/hcm/southern), between Phạm Ngũ Lão and Bùi Viện. Sleek, sparkling accommodations. Some rooms have beautiful cityscape views. Breakfast included. Rooms US$15-20; special suite (with living room or personal garden) US$30. ❹

NEAR PHẠM NGŨ LÃO

Between Cô Bắc and Cô Giang is a network of alleyways filled with guesthouses. Less than a 10min. walk from the backpacker zone, this area has a considerably calmer feel. As a result, it's quite popular for longer stays; ask about discounts.

Miss Lợi, 178/20 Cô Giang (☎837 9589; missloi@hcm.fpt.vn), on the alley that runs off 178 Cô Giang and connects to Cô Bắc. One of the first and best in the guesthouse business. Warm staff and a great common area with inviting couches. TVs have HBO. Breakfast included. Rooms US$8-10. ❸

Ngọc Huệ, 171/22 Cô Bắc (☎836 0089; ngochuehotel@yahoo.com), on the alley that runs off 171 Co Bắc and connects to Cô Giang. Gorgeous rooftop garden terraces with excellent views. Long-term rooms are especially elegant; breakfast and Su dinner (with free beer) included. Rooms US$6-10. ❷

Thanh, 171/1E Cô Bắc (☎836 8469; huutri2001@hcm.vnn.vn), on the alley that runs off 171 Cô Bắc and connects to Cô Giang. Refreshingly clean rooms and a social atmosphere. Breakfast included. Rooms US$6-8. ❷

ĐỒNG KHỞI

If you want to be close to the museums and other attractions, and you don't mind paying a bit more than the average budget traveler, then Đồng Khởi may be the place for you. Rooms are typically a step up from the backpacker zone.

Nga Quân, 10/1 Ho Huan Nghiệp (☎824 2471), on the alley that runs off 10 Ho Huan Nghiệp. Rooms are spacious and tiled baths are impressive. An excellent value. Rooms US$15-20. ❹

Grand Hotel, 8 Đồng Khởi (☎823 0163; www.grandsaigon.com), near the riverfront. Constructed in 1930, this luxury hotel (both one of the best and one of the most affordable) lives up to its name. Highlights are the restored colonial elevator and the lovely tiled atrium with swimming pool. Breakfast included. Rooms US$55 and up. ❺

ELSEWHERE IN HCMC

Victory Hotel, 14 Võ Văn Tần (☎930 4989; victoryhotel@hcm.vnn.vn), at its intersection with Nam Kỳ Khởi Nghĩa. A stone's throw away from the War Remnants Museum and Reunification Palace. Rooms are comfortable and feature balconies; hotel has a swimming pool. Breakfast included. Basic rooms US$15-30. ❹

Tien An, 22 Trương Định (☎822 4834; ctytmkstienan@hcm.vnn.vn), near its intersection with Lê Thánh Tôn. Clean rooms with warm wood accents. Popular with Vietnamese-Americans. Rooms US$20-25. ❹

FOOD

Pull up a plastic chair—the true taste of HCMC is in the streets. Sidewalk stands and market stalls may lack ambience, but the taste and price (most dishes under 10,000Đ) are unbeatable. For those looking to stock up on food, there are several Western-style supermarkets, including **Maximark** (Saigon Center, 65 Lê Lợi; ☎821 0320; open daily 9am-9pm) and **Coopmart** (168 Nguyễn Dình Chiểu; ☎930 7384; open daily 8am-10pm).

PHẠM NGŨ LÃO

This backpacker haven offers dishes to make every world-weary traveler feel at home. Pizzas, curries, pancakes, and tacos are just a few of the comfort foods available. Don't dismiss the quality Vietnamese restaurants in the area either. An open-air produce market, **Thai Bình,** is at the intersection of Phạm Ngũ Lão and Cống Quỳnh.

The Original Bodhi Tree, 175/4 Phạm Ngũ Lão (☎837 1910), on the alley that runs off 175 Phạm Ngũ Lão (marked by a Chinese arch) and connects to Bùi Viện; there are two Bodhi restaurants next to each other, so take note of the exact address. A quality vegetarian eatery with a social conscience. Most meals under 15,000Đ; try the banana pancakes or Buddha's delight. Sells artwork made by and benefiting disadvantaged children; inquire with the staff. Open daily 7:30am-10pm. ❷

Taj Mahal, 26 Bùi Viện (☎836 9363), near its intersection with Trần Hưng Đạo. Bollywood music videos and authentic, mutton-intensive South Asian Halal fare. Sample a variety of tasty dishes with the *thali* platter (40,000-60,000Đ for 2 people). Meals 25,000-35,000Đ. Open daily 8am-midnight. ❷

Taco, 180 Bùi Viện (☎836 1947), between Đề Thám and Dổ Quang Đẩu. Don't be misled by the name—this cute little place serves Japanese cuisine in a cartoon-like red and blue setting. Rice dishes with soup, salad, and pickles 28,000-30,000Đ; sushi and sashimi 20,000-40,000Đ; Japanese cocktails (yum!) 6000-10,000Đ. Open daily 11am-2pm and 5pm-midnight. ❷

Vân, 103B Phạm Ngũ Lão (☎914 2208), near its intersection with Yersin. Wrap up the crispy seafood fritters and accoutrements (herbs and pickled vegetables) in big lettuce leaves, then dip your creations in sweet *nước mắm* sauce. Single serving 12,000Đ. Open daily 8:30am-10pm. ❷

Good Morning Vietnam, 197 Đề Thám (☎837 1894; www.goodmorningviet.com), between Bùi Viện and Phạm Ngũ Lão. This Italian eatery serves up decent pizzas (70,000-90,000Đ for 2 people). Impressive selection of Italian liquor (35,000-55,000Đ). Open daily 9am-12:30am. ❸

Phở Quynh, 323 Phạm Ngũ Lão (☎836 8515), at its intersection with Dổ Quang Đẩu. This local favorite serves flavorful phở with an almost comically large garnish plate of fresh herbs and chilies. Phở 12,000Đ. Open daily 6am-midnight. ❷

Gia Gia Lạc, 147 Trần Hưng Đạo (☎836 8708), at its intersection with Đề Thám. A great snack stop with standing room only; good for breakfast on the run. Sweet and savory pastries, most 3000Đ. Open daily 6am-10pm. ❶

VIETNAM

ĐỒNG KHỞI AREA

Many of the restaurants in this area cater to expatriates, middle-class Vietnamese, and luxury tourists. Prices may be a bit higher here than in the budget zone, but the quality of food and atmosphere is often superior.

Quán Ăn Ngon, 138 Nam Kỳ Khởi Nghĩa (☎825 7179; www.quananngon.com), between Hàn Thuyên and Nguyễn Du, right near the entrance to Reunification Palace. Actually run by a collective of cooks, this laid-back Vietnamese restaurant serves up exquisite dishes at remarkably affordable prices. Dishes 15,000-25,000Đ. Open daily 7am-11pm; kitchen closes at 10pm. ❷

Au Parc, 23 Hàn Thuyên (☎829 2772), near its intersection with Pasteur. This upscale deli makes fantastic sandwiches with ingredients like baked brie and smoked salmon. Treat yourself to a meal here amid the colorful North African decor lit up by the skylights. Sandwiches 35,000-60,000Đ; salads 45,000-70,000Đ. Take-out and delivery available. Open daily 7am-9pm. ❸

Bò Tùng Xẻo, 31 Lý Tự Trọng (☎825 1330), between Thái Văn Lung and Hai Bà Trưng. The place to experience Vietnamese barbecue. Patrons grill delectable beef slices over hot coals at their tables. The rest of the menu covers the whole animal kingdom, from crickets to clams. Dishes 30,000-60,000Đ. Open daily 10am-10pm. ❸

Skewers, 8A/1D2 Thái Văn Lung (☎829 2216; www.skewers-restaurant.com), between Cao Bá Quát and Lê Thánh Tôn. The place to go to be treated like royalty for an evening. Impeccable service and exquisite Mediterranean cuisine make your experience here fabulous and well worth the price (entrees 60,000-80,000Đ). Open M-F 11:30am-2pm and 6-10:30pm, Sa-Su 6-10:30pm. ❹

ELSEWHERE IN HCMC

Cát Tưởng, 105 Trần Hưng Đạo (☎853 7869), near the intersection with Trần Xuân Hòa in District 5 (Chợ Lớn). Outdoor Chinese eatery serves excellent dim sum with musical accompaniment by a traditional Chinese ensemble. Dim sum 10,000-15,000Đ; noodles 15,000-20,000Đ. Dinner 40,000-90,000Đ. Open daily 6am-11pm; dim sum served until 2pm. ❷

Phở 2000, 1-3 Phan Chu Trinh (☎822 2788), at the end of Lê Lai, next to Bến Thành Market. A modern take on an old classic. Phở dishes 15,000-20,000Đ. Former US President Bill Clinton stopped here during his 2000 visit to Vietnam. Open daily 6:30am-1:30am. ❷

Hoavien Brauhaus, 28 Mạc Đinh Chi (☎829 0585; www.hoaviener.com), near its intersection with Trần Cao Vân. Vietnam's first microbrewery serves up quality Pilsner (draught 14,000-24,000Đ; bottle 20,000-24,000Đ) at this classic Czech beerhall. Enjoy Bohemian and Bavarian cuisine (most dishes 40,000Đ and up) or a tour of the brewery facilities. Open daily 7am-midnight. ❸

SIGHTS

Most of the city's major sights lie within a short walking distance of one another in District 1. However, there are a few outside this area that are worth visiting; it is easiest to hire a motorbike or taxi to reach them. If you have only have a couple days in HCMC and would like to hit the city's main attractions with utmost efficiency, most tour companies (see p. 968) arrange one-day sightseeing tours.

MUSEUMS

WAR REMNANTS MUSEUM. This museum takes a brutal and disturbing look at the atrocities committed during the Vietnam War. Among its collection are bottled fetuses deformed by Agent Orange and gruesome photographs of the Mỹ Lai massacre. An intriguing exhibit on international opposition to the war (including the American resistance movement) provides other perspectives on the conflict. *(District 3. 28 Võ Văn Tần, between Trần Quốc Thảo and Lê Qúy Đôn. ☎930 6235. Open daily 7:30-11:45am and 1:30-5:15pm. 10,000Đ.)*

HISTORY MUSEUM. This museum boasts a comprehensive collection of national artifacts dating as early as the primitive period (circa 500,000 years ago). Don't miss the mummified Vietnamese woman. There are also some splendid relics from other Southeast Asian countries. A brief but charming water puppet show is performed daily. *(District 1. Nguyễn Bỉnh Kiêm at its intersection with Nguyễn Thị Minh Khai. ☎825 8784. Second entrance through the Botanical Garden. Open M-Sa 8-11am and 1-4pm, Su 8:30am-4pm. 10,000Đ. Water puppet show 9, 10, 11am, 2, 3, 4pm; also 1pm Su; 15,000Đ.)*

HỒ CHÍ MINH MUSEUM. Everyone's favorite Vietnamese national hero and icon, Hồ Chí Minh, is the subject of this collection, which is housed in a pink French colonial building (called Nhà Rồng) on the Saigon River. Besides a lot of photographs, a number of Hồ Chí Minh's personal items and letters are on display. Not surprisingly, the museum takes an non-controversial view of the president; however, the international journal articles may give insight into how the rest of the world saw him. *(District 4. 1 Nguyễn Tất Thàn, just across the river from District 1. ☎940 2060. Open Su and Tu-Sa 7:30-11:30am and 1:30-4:30pm. 10,000Đ.)*

HOUSES OF WORSHIP

GIÁC LÂM PAGODA. Over 260 years old, Giác Lâm is worth the hike from the city center. The path to the pagoda leads visitors past a modern religious tower, a gigantic Buddha, and monks' tombs. The pagoda itself, supported by dark teak pillars, is a dizzying maze of altars. The funeral hall contains photos of the deceased, while the main sanctuary houses an enormous and complicated altar to a host of Buddhist and Taoist deities. Here monks perform their rituals and worshippers offer prayers. Around the pagoda are several courtyards, one of which holds a sacred Bodhi tree. *(District 11. 118 Lạc Long Quân, near its intersection with Âu Cơ. Open daily 7am-noon and 2-10pm. Free.)*

JADE EMPEROR PAGODA. Considered by many to be the best pagoda in District 1, Jade Emperor Pagoda was built by the city's Cantonese population in 1909. Elaborately decorated in the Chinese style, the complex includes a courtyard with several shrines and a turtle pond, as well as sanctuaries where worshippers pray to Buddhist and Taoist deities. The Taoist Jade Emperor (Ngọc Hoàng), guardian of heaven, is located on the central altar just inside the main sanctuary doors. *(District 1. 73 Mai Thị Lựu, between Điện Biên Phủ and Nguyễn Văn Gia. Open daily 5am-7pm. Free.)*

NOTRE DAME CATHEDRAL. The main seat of Catholicism in Southern Vietnam, this cathedral features red bricks and stained glass imported from France during the colonial era. Inside, figures of national saints and plaques donated by parishioners provide insight into Vietnamese Catholic practices. *(District 1. On a paved square opposite the Post Office, near the intersection of Lê Duẩn and Đồng Khởi. Open daily 5-11am and 3-5:30pm. Mass in English Su 9:30am. Mass in Vietnamese M-Sa 5:30am and 5pm; Su throughout the day. Free.)*

MARIAMMAN HINDU TEMPLE. Although unassuming from the outside, this temple boasts an elaborate and gaudy interior that shocks the senses. Hindu gods and goddesses painted in neon colors adorn the walls and altars, and Mariamman sits in the center shrine amid numerous decorations and offerings. Not only Hindus worship here; the temple is also considered sacred by many Vietnamese and Chinese. Remove your shoes upon entering. *(District 1. 45 Trương Định, between Lê Thánh Tôn and Lý Tự Trọng. Open daily 7am-8pm. Free.)*

OTHER SIGHTS

CHỢ LỚN. District 5 (often called Chợ Lớn, meaning Big Market) is home to HCMC's large ethnic Chinese population. It has a rather different feel than the rest of the city. As the name suggests, mercantilism is the way of life here; two major indoor markets (**An Đông** and **Bình Tây**) are located in the area. **Chinese medicine shops** lie along Hải Thượng Lãn Ông. Some other shops around the neighborhood sell brilliantly colored **ceremonial decorations,** most notably dragon heads. There is a slew of pagodas in Chợ Lớn, each one constructed and operated by a different Chinese group. **Thiên Hậu** is the most active; pagoda enthusiasts may also want to check out **Tam Sòn.** *(118 Triệu Quang Phục; open daily 6am-6pm.)*

REUNIFICATION PALACE. First built by the French in 1868, then reconstructed by South Vietnamese President Ngô Đình Diệm after a 1962 bombing, this palace was home to several South Vietnamese heads of state before Việt Cộng tanks crashed through its gates on April 30, 1975. When a South Vietnamese general told the VC officers that he was prepared to transfer power to them, one officer famously replied, "You cannot give up what you do not have." Visitors to the palace today will find it frozen in its 1975 state, complete with residential rooms, subterranean war chambers, and an entertainment complex. *(District 1. Entrance on Nam Kỳ Khởi Nghĩa, between Nguyễn Thị Minh Khai and Nguyễn Du. ☎822 1716. Tours available. Open daily 7:30-11am and 1-4pm. 15,000Đ.)*

PHỞ BINH. In the late 1960s, while American soldiers and officers slurped soup on the ground floor of this diner, the Việt Cộng leadership met one floor above and devised its secret plans for the Tet Offensive, including an attack on the US Embassy. Today the place is still operated by the same man, a former Communist revolutionary who now greets visitors from all countries warmly and enthusiastically shares his stories. Be sure to look through the scrapbook and sign the guestbook. *(District 3. 7 Lộ Chính Thắng, near its intersection with Hai Bà Trưng. Open daily 7am-11pm. Phở 15,000Đ.)*

LÂM SỎN SQUARE. In French colonial times, **Lâm Sỏn Square** was the center of high society. The **Hotel Continental** is featured in Graham Greene's novel, *The Quiet American;* here the characters Fowler and Pyle became friends. Across from the hotel on a wide plaza is the **Municipal Theater** (sometimes called the Opera House). Constructed by the French at the turn of the 20th century, this pink Neoclassical theater was designed as an opera house, though it later housed the National Assembly, after the division of the country. It was restored in 1998 and now hosts Vietnamese theater performances, in addition to a variety music, dance, and opera productions. Inquire at the lobby (☎829 9976) for current performances. *(District 1. At the intersection of Đồng Khởi and Lê Lợi.)*

SHOPPING

Hồ Chí Minh City is a shopaholic's dream come true. Shops crowd every block, particularly in District 1. The most fun places to shop are the city's indoor markets, which sell everything imaginable under one roof. Bargaining, as per usual, is the norm here; estimate how much an item is worth and then offer a lower price. Most markets open between 6 and 7am and close between 6 and 7pm. If you know what you're looking for, it shouldn't be hard to find an entire section of a market devoted to the specific item you have in mind—just ask around or inquire at your lodging. The possibilities may, in fact, render your choice more difficult than you imagine.

Bến Thành, a city landmark and popular tourist stop, is located at the big roundabout where Lê Lợi, Trần Hưng Đạo, and Hàm Nghi meet. In the evenings, there are lively foodstalls outside. **An Đông,** in District 5 (Chợ Lớn, or "Big Market"), is absolutely massive and offers everything from plastic fruit to gold jewelry. It's located on An Đương Vương, between Sư Vạn Hạnh and Nguyễn Duy Đương. **Bình Tây,** right outside District 5 on Hậu Giang, is an impressive Chinese structure.

NIGHTLIFE

The nightlife around Phạm Ngũ Lão tends to consist mostly of budget travelers, while the Đồng Khởi area is where expatriates and young Vietnamese party. To find out which bars and clubs are hottest at the moment, pick up *Vietnam Pathfinder* or check out www.elephantguide.com. Many of the bars below double as restaurants during the day.

AROUND PHẠM NGŨ LÃO

Allez Boo, 187 Phạm Ngũ Lão (☎837 2505), on the corner of Phạm Ngũ Lão and Đề Thám. Extremely popular with the backpacker crowd. Friendly staff and good music. Beers 15,000-25,000Đ; mixed drinks 40,000-50,000Đ. Open daily 6:30am-3am.

Lost in Saigon, 169 Phạm Ngũ Lão (☎090 381 7182), near its intersection with Nguyễn Thái Học. Bowls and jugs filled with mixed liquor (110,000-130,000Đ) and designed for up to 6 people—a fast way to make new friends. Open daily 8am-4am.

163 Cyclo, 163 Phạm Ngũ Lão (☎920 1567), near its intersection with Nguyễn Thái Học. The highlight is the house band. Drinks are a bit pricey for the area (beers 17,000Đ; cocktails 45,000Đ), but the atmosphere is classy. Open daily 9am-1:30am.

Guns N' Roses, 207 Phạm Ngũ Lão (☎836 0845), between Đề Thám and Dổ Quang Đẩu. This biker bar plays nothing but G'n'R all night long. Free pool. Beers 14,000-17,000Đ; mixed drinks 25,000-30,000Đ. Open daily 8pm-6am.

ĐỒNG KHỞI

EniGma, 20 Thi Sách (☎842 4922), near its intersection with Lê Lợi. HCMC's first wine bar. World music, contemporary art, suede couches, and an extensive wine selection. Wine 45,000-70,000Đ; mixed drinks 62,000Đ and up. Open daily 5pm-midnight.

Apocalypse Now, 2B-2C Thi Sách (☎825 6124), near its intersection with Đông Du. An old standard in Saigonese nightlife. Draws a mixed crowd and features great music and attractive open-air seating. Mixed drinks 30,000-40,000Đ. Open daily 7am-1am.

Vasco's (Club Camargue), 16 Cao Bá Quát (☎823 2828), near its intersection with Thi Sách. House band keeps feet tapping and fingers snapping on weekends (Th-Sa). Free pool. Ladies' night (free vodka, gin, rum, and whiskey) Th 9-10pm. Beer 35,000-50,000Đ; mixed drinks 55,000-70,000Đ. Open daily 11am-midnight.

Heart of Darkness, 17B Lê Thánh Tôn (☎823 1080), between Thái Văn Lung and Chu Mạnh Trinh. The sign says 007 but it's the same club. Officially shuts down at midnight, but that's just when the wild party gets started. Ladies' time (free vodka and gin) nightly 7-9pm. Beers 20,000Đ; mixed drinks 40,000Đ. Open daily 7pm-4am.

Sheridan's Irish House, 17/13 Lê Thánh Tôn (☎823 0793), near its intersection with Thái Văn Lung. Authentic Irish pub features live music Th-Tu after 8pm; Irish tunes Sa. Quiz night W 7:30pm. Two 320ml cans of Guinness 80,000Đ. Open daily 11am-midnight.

Blue Gecko, 31 Lý Tự Trọng (☎824 3483), between Hai Bà Trưng and Thái Văn Lung. Play pool, throw darts, or watch rugby at this laid-back Aussie hangout. Beer 20,000Đ. Happy hour (20% off) nightly 5-7:30pm. Open daily 5pm-1am.

Liquid, 104 Hai Bà Trưng (☎822 5478), near its intersection with Nguyễn Thị Minh Khai. The DJ pumps out the rhythms amid colored lasers and psychedelic video images. Packs a huge crowd (mainly Vietnamese) on the weekends. Beers 52,000Đ; mixed drinks 80,000-90,000Đ. Open daily 8pm-midnight.

DAYTRIPS FROM HỒ CHÍ MINH CITY

CỦ CHI TUNNELS

Many tour companies in the Phạm Ngũ Lão area organize guided trips to the tunnels (US$4.) This is the easiest way to access them. You can also take a public bus from Chợ Lớn station to Củ Chi town (1½hr.; 12,000Đ); once there, you'll need to hire a motorbike or taxi to the tunnels. ☎794 6442. Open daily 7:30am-5pm. 65,000Đ.

Few sights capture the tenacity and ingenuity of the Vietnamese guerrillas better than the Củ Chi tunnels. The Việt Cộng developed this elaborate network of narrow passageways, which allowed them to infiltrate enemy camps while remaining almost completely hidden. At one point the multi-level subterranean system stretched all the way from Củ Chi to the Cambodian border, and included field hospitals, weapons facilities, and even kitchens. Today visitors can climb through the reconstructed 100m portion of the tunnels, although if claustrophobia sets in, there are closer escape routes. Above ground, there are gruesome exhibits of the booby traps used against enemy forces, some recreations of life in the tunnels, and also a shooting range, where visitors can fire authentic military rifles at a target (US$1 per bullet).

CAO ĐÀI HOLY SEE

Many tour companies in the Phạm Ngũ Lão area organize guided trips to the temple (US$4.) You can also take a public bus from An Súong station to Tây Ninh (1½hr.; 18,500Đ); once there, you'll need to hire a motorbike or taxi to the temple. Open 24hr.; ceremonies are held daily at 6am, noon, 6pm, and midnight. Free; donations accepted.

This enormous temple, constructed between 1933 and 1955, is the main seat of the Cao Đài religion in Vietnam. While the ornate exterior is rather impressive, it is the interior that truly dazzles. No color of the rainbow has been spared. The expansive main hall boasts pink columns decorated with mythical creatures, celestial ceilings sparkling with silver stars, and an immense globe from which the divine eye observes worshippers. During the daily ceremonies, visitors look down from the balcony as the many worshippers (clad in white, red, blue, or yellow based on their level of experience with the religion) process into the hall and perform their synchronized practices, accompanied by instruments and choral singing.

VŨNG TÀU ☎64

With its sun-drenched beaches, scenic vistas, and handsome promenades, Vũng Tàu is a popular weekend getaway for Saigonese. French colonists began vacationing here around the turn of the last century, and aside from the many pagodas dotting the landscape, the peninsula still resembles the French Riviera.

On the northwest corner of the peninsula is **Mulberry Beach** (Bãi Dâu), a quiet area with rocky cliffs. Along the western coast lies **Front Beach** (Bãi Trước); here fishing boats dock and ferries arrive and depart. Most of the city's main activity takes place in the streets behind Front Beach. Sunbathers and swimmers flock to **Back Beach** (Bãi Sau) on the opposite coast. While less comely than Front Beach, Back Beach has more sand and is more developed than its counterpart. Besides miles of beaches, Vũng Tàu also has an unusually large number of enormous religious statues. The **Madonna** and **Buddha** stand watch over Mulberry Beach, while **Jesus** faces the ocean with

THE LOCAL STORY

SOMEONE TO WATCH OVER YOU

In 1919 on Phú Quốc Island, a huge disembodied eye floated before Ngo Van Chieu, a colonial bureaucrat and occult enthusiast. This sign sparked a series of heart-to-hearts between Ngo and God, who allegedly expressed frustration that all the messages he had sent to humankind had been misunderstood or ignored. HIs agents of the gospel had included Buddha, Lao Tse, Confucius, Mohammed, and Jesus. He was disappointed by the discord among religious groups. Inspired by this message, Chieu founded a religion incorporating elements from multiple religions, most notably Buddhism, Taoism, Confucianism, Islam, Christianity, and Hinduism. The ever-watchful eye became the symbol.

Today, the religion (called Cao Đài, meaning "High Palace") has several million followers in Vietnam, mostly in the south. The clerical structure is similar to the Catholic church; worshippers wear different robes depending upon their rank. Adherents seek to escape the cycle of reincarnation by acting lovingly toward others and avoiding sinful behavior. They believe that divine messages can be communicated during seances; Victor Hugo, William Shakespeare, and Joan of Arc have all been in touch with Caodaists in the past. Worship ceremonies take place four times daily; the best place to see Caodaism in action is the Holy See complex in Tây Ninh.

open arms at the tip of the peninsula. At **Thích Ca Phật Đài Pagoda** on Trần Phú, the main attraction is a large Buddha meditating on a lotus leaf. **Niết Bàn Tịnh Xá Pagoda** features a massive stone Buddha reclining peacefully among jungle animals, an ancient bronze bell upon which visitors can leave written prayers (donation requested), and a mosaic-covered dragon boat containing an elaborate miniature landscape made of stone.

Buses arrive at **Vũng Tàu Station,** 192A Nam Kỳ Khởi Nghĩa, and go to **HCMC** (2½hr.; every 15min. 5am-5pm; 25,000Đ) and **Mỹ Tho** (4hr.; 11am; 25,000Đ). **Ferries** arrive at the pier on Hạ Long (opposite Hải Âu Hotel) and go to **HCMC** (1¼hr.; 11 per day 6:15am-5pm; US$10). Many hotels and guesthouses rent **bicycles** (10,000-20,000Đ per day) and **motorbikes** (US$5-7 per day).

Since Vũng Tàu is primarily a resort city, accommodations tend to be expensive, and many are booked solid on weekends. Mulberry Beach is the cheapest place to stay, as it is removed from most of the action. **Sao Mai ❷,** 80 Hoàng Hoa Thám, has well-maintained rooms and is located about halfway between Front Beach and Back Beach. (☎852 215. Rooms US$10.) Those on a tighter budget will appreciate **Mỹ Tho ❶,** 47 Trần Phù. Although not exactly luxurious, there is a large common terrace built right over the water, and the proprietor is friendly and speaks English well. (☎835 004. Laundry service included. Rooms US$6.)

Vũng Tàu is known for its seafood; restaurants serve crab, fish, squid, and other marine cuisine. If seafood isn't your thing, **Good Morning Vietnam ❸,** 6 Hoàng Hoa Thám, makes decent pasta and pizzas (40,000-60,000Đ) and offers Swensen's premium American ice cream at 16,000Đ per scoop. (☎856 959. Open daily 10am-11pm.) **Lăng Ký ❷,** 173 Lý Tự Trọng, is popular with locals for its flavorful hot-pot dishes. (20,000-30,000Đ per person. ☎856 807. Open daily 6am-10pm.)

VIETNAM

THE MEKONG DELTA

The Vietnamese call this region *Cửu Long* (Nine Dragons), in reference to the Mekong River's nine principal tributaries. As the river fans out across the land in its final push to the sea, it forms countless canals, the backdrop of life for delta residents. Boat tours around the region reveal bustling river markets, colorful fishing vessels, and a variety of floating homes. The flat, moist land is ideal for harvesting rice, making the region one of the world's largest rice producers. Fruit orchards, coconut groves, and sugar cane plantations also dot the landscape. The Vietnamese are relative newcomers to the delta—the region was dominated by the Cambodian Khmer people until the 18th century. Tensions between Cambodia and Vietnam over the area have persisted since then, reaching a boiling point in the late 1970s when Khmer Rouge forces invaded Vietnamese territory. However, the two countries seem to be at peace nowadays, and the delta population is a fascinating mix of Vietnamese and Khmer, along with some Chinese and Chàm influences. Tour companies in Hồ Chí Minh City offer trips to see the highlights of the region; an extensive bus and boat network allow you to explore on your own.

MỸ THO ☎73

Just a short bus ride away from Hồ Chí Minh City, Mỹ Tho serves as the traveler's gateway to the Mekong Delta. Don't be fooled by the fact that it's a provincial capital—the streets are quiet and you can cover the entire town by foot in about an hour. Its attractions are mostly in and along the Tiền River, but travelers may also enjoy the laid-back feel of the streets, where kite-flying is the most popular pastime for children and adults alike.

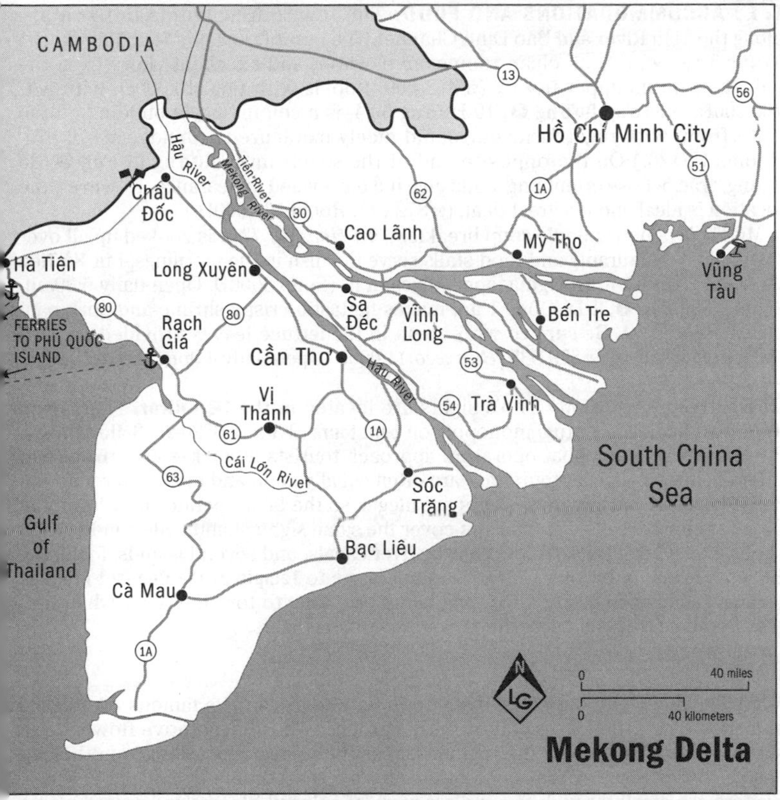

TRANSPORTATION AND PRACTICAL INFORMATION. **Buses** arrive at **Tiền Giang Station,** 42 Ấp Bắc (☎855 404), about 3km northwest of the city center. Buses go to HCMC (1½hr.; every 30min. 5am-5pm; 15,000Đ), Mỹ Thuận (2hr.; every hr. 5-8am; 15,000Đ), and Cần Thơ (3hr.; every hr. 5-8am; 14,500Đ). The small **city center** is laid out in a simple grid. **Nam Kỳ Khởi Nghĩa,** a north-south thoroughfare, intersects with Ấp Bắc and runs to the **Tiền River** (part of the Mekong). Along the main waterfront is **Đường 30/4,** which runs east-west and ends at the mouth of **Bảo Định Channel** (marked by a statue). **Trưng Trắc** runs along the channel, parallel to Nam Kỳ Khởi Nghĩa. Between the two bridges is a colorful **outdoor market.** The large **indoor market** is located at the corner of Lê Đai Hành and Lê Lợi.

Tiền Giang Tourist Office, 8 Đường 30/4, provides free, handy **maps.** (☎873 184; www.tiengiangtourist.com. Open daily 7am-5pm.) There is a **bank** at 2C Thủ Khoa Huân. (Currency exchange, MC/V cash advances, and Western Union. Open daily 7:15-11:15am and 1:30-4:30pm.) The **hospital** (along with a **pharmacy**) is located at 4 Thủ Koa Huân. (☎883 888. 24hr. emergency service.) **Internet** access is available at 80 Nam Kỳ Khởi Nghĩa. (☎883 993. Open daily 7am-9:30pm.) The main **post office,** 59 Đường 30/4, offers fax and phone services. (☎873 214. Open daily 6am-9pm.) **Postal Code:** 82100.

ACCOMMODATIONS AND FOOD. The few tourist hotels in town are along the Tiên River and Bảo Định Channel. The best of the lot is **Sông Tiền ❷**, 101 Trưng Trắc, with neat, clean rooms, an elevator, and excellent views from the balconies on its upper floors. (☎872 009. Rooms with fan 110,000Đ; with A/C 160,000Đ.) **Chương Dương ❹**, 10 Đường 30/4, is a colonial-style building on the waterfront, with regal furnishings and nicely manicured grounds. (☎870 875. Rooms US$20.) On the opposite end of the spectrum is **Hương Dương ❶**, 33 Trưng Trắc, whose crumbling walls give it a disheveled appearance. However, the location is ideal and it a great deal. (☎872 011. Rooms 60,000Đ.)

Mỹ Tho's famous noodle soup breakfast, *hủ tiếu Mỹ Tho*, is cooked up all over town. Most restaurants and food stalls serve the dish in the mornings, but **Hủ Tiếu 24 ❶**, 24 Nam Kỳ Khởi Nghĩa, specializes in it. (Soup 3000Đ. Open daily 6:30am-11am.) **Sáu Bảo ❶**, 1 Lý Công Uẩn, makes fantastic crispy shrimp-and-pork pancakes *(bán xeò)*. Be sure to wrap them in the lettuce leaves provided and dip them in fish sauce. (☎879 835. *Bán xeò* 11,000Đ. Open daily 4-9pm.)

SIGHTS. Most of Mỹ Tho's sights are located in the **Tiên River.** Tiên Giang Tourist Office has a virtual monopoly on **boat tours** (2-3hr. US$20-25; 3-4hr. US$30-35). However, many boat operators approach tourists along the waterfront and offer cheaper unofficial tours that are often equally good and more catered to the individual. Technically these tours are illegal, so the boat operator may have you board somewhere else. Most tours cover the same sights: handmade candy workshops, honeybee farms, fruit orchards, river canals, and several islands, including Phoenix Island, a bit of a tourist trap but home to **Temple of the Coconut Monk** is located (admission 5000Đ). Evening is the best time to tour the river, when fireflies flood the trees and give the effect of twinkling lights.

SA ĐÉC ☎67

Many Mekong Delta tours make a stop in Sa Đéc to view its famous **botanical nurseries.** The little city is full of these gardens, whose decorative flowers and shrubs are sold all across the region. Across the bridge about 2km from the city center, **Vương Hồng Tư Tôn** is one of the area's lushest and most popular gardens. Visitors can stroll through the endless rows of colorful blooms and potted plants and relax by the fishpond under the shade of palm fronds. The nursery is free and open from sunrise to sunset. The best time to go is Nov.-Dec., when the nurseries are in full bloom. If you're walking there, cross the metal bridge at Trần Phú, turn left onto Lê Lợi, and continue along for about 2km; the nursery will be easy to spot on your right. Sa Đéc is also notable for being the childhood home of French author **Marguerite Duras**—she set one of her novels *(The Lover)* here. You can admire her slightly dilapidated house from a distance, though you can't go in, as it is now a police station.

Buses arrive at the station in the city center on Quốc Lộ 80 and go to: HCMC (3hr.; every 30min. 6-9am; 25,000Đ); Cao Lãnh (2hr., 6am, 7000Đ); Trà Vinh (2hr.; 6:30am; 15,000Đ); Rạch Giá (4hr.; 6am; 18,000Đ); Cà Mau (6hr.; 5am; 36,000Đ).

If you're going to stay the night, **Sa Đéc Hotel ❸**, 108/5A Hùng Vương, is a good choice; although the outside is a bit tarnished, the rooms are well-maintained. Its location close to the peaceful botanical nurseries makes it even more appealing. (☎861 430. Rooms US$8-15.) The newly built **Bông Hồng ❷**, 251A Nguyễn Sinh Sắc, is flashier. The rooms on the upper floors have excellent city views. (☎868 287. Rooms US$6-16.) For grub, **Chánh Kộ ❶**, 193 Quốc Lộ 80, is a friendly place that serves Chinese noodle and rice dishes. (8000-12,000Đ. Open daily 6am-6pm.) **Thủy ❷**, 439 Hùng Vương, does some quality fish dishes and has a Western breakfast menu. (Most dishes 15,000-30,000Đ. Open daily 8am-9pm.)

VIETNAM

VĨNH LONG ☎70

Somewhat grittier than its delta neighbors, Vĩnh Long attracts tourists because of its prime location on the Cổ Chiên River. A trip down this attractive waterway will take visitors through lush island canals and past floating markets, bonsai gardens, and village homes. Cửu Long Tourist Office runs **boat tours** (4hr.; US$15-25) of the Cổ Chiên River. You may also be able to find private boat operators offering cheaper rates. The main attraction along the river is the **Cái Bè floating market.** In the mornings, boats laden with fruit and grain gather in the channel to await customers. The best time to visit is in the early morning, when the market is busiest. Most boat tours include visits to bonsai gardens, handmade candy workshops, and traditional homes. You'll be hard-pressed to find a more enchanting spot along the Mekong.

Many buses go to Mỹ Thuận, not Vĩnh Long; from there, it's a 10km motorbike ride. There are two **bus** stations in Vĩnh Long. From the one in the city center, on the corner of Doàn Thị Điểm and Dại Lộ 3/2, buses go to HCMC (3hr.; every hr. 3am-5pm; 30,000Đ) and Cần Thơ (1hr.; every 15min. 5am-5pm; 10,000Đ). Vĩnh Long's **city center** is surrounded on by water on all four sides. Most of the action takes place on **Đường 1/5,** which runs along **Long Hồ Canal,** and **Phan Bội Châu,** which runs along **Cổ Chiên River.** There is a rambling **market** behind Đường 30/4, concentrated between Nguyễn Công Trứ and Dại Lộ 3/2. **Cửu Long Tourist Office,** 1 Đường 1/5, books boat tours and rents bicycles and motorbikes. (☎823 616; cuulongtourist1@hcm.vnn.vn. Open daily 7am-5pm.)

Most tourist hotels are located on or near Cổ Chiên River. **Vân Trâm ❸,** 4 Đường 1/5, boasts large sparkling rooms with all the amenities. (☎823 820. Rooms US$10.) Set back from the river, **Phượng Hoàng ❷,** 2H-2R Hùng Vương, has cheerful sunny rooms on its upper floors. (☎825 185. Rooms 120,000-140,000Đ.) Another popular option is a **homestay.** Cửu Long Tourist Office can arrange for visitors to stay on one of the islands in the home of a Vietnamese family, an old colonial building, or a farmhouse. Most homestays include meals, transportation, and mosquito nets for US$15-65 per night. The restaurants along the river cater mainly to tour buses. Fill up at the **market** a block away instead. There are sit-down **food stalls** along Nguyễn Công Trứ and Nguyễn Văn Nhã (open during daylight hours) and on Dại Lộ 3/2 (open at night). Elsewhere, **Tài Có ❸,** 40A Đường 2/9, draws crowds of locals to its awesome hotpot and barbecue. (☎824 845. Dishes 40,000-60,000Đ. Open daily 10am-9pm.)

VIETNAM

CẦN THƠ ☎71

Cosmopolitan without the grit and grime, Cần Thơ is the unofficial capital of the Mekong Delta, as well as its most popular tourist destination. The wide boulevards and elegant waterfront are well-suited for strolling and have some of the better restaurants in the region. Boat tours of the surrounding canals bring travelers past floating markets, fruit orchards, and peaceful villages.

TRANSPORTATION AND ORIENTATION. Buses arrive at the station about 1km northwest of the city center on Nguyễn Trãi, and go to: HCMC (3½hr.; every 30min. 5am-2pm; 45,000Đ); Mỹ Tho (2hr.; 10am; 22,000Đ); Long Xuyên (1½hr.; every hr. 6am-3pm; 17,000Đ); Châu Đốc (3hr.; every 15min. 3am-5pm; 29,000Đ); Rạch Giá (4hr.; every 45min. 5am-5pm; 28,000Đ). Mai Linh (☎822 266) is a reputable **taxi** service in town. From the bus station, **Nguyễn Trãi** leads into the city center and curves to become **Hòa Bình,** the city's main thoroughfare. The city center lies at the confluence of **Cần Thơ River** and **Hậu River.** From this meeting point, **Hai Bà Trưng** runs along the main waterfront, past a statue of Hồ Chí Minh, and into the **market** area. **Hai Bà Trưng** and **Hòa Bình** are connected by another major road, **Châu Văn Liêm.**

PRACTICAL INFORMATION. Cần Thơ Tourist Office, 20 Hai Bà Trưng, offers handy maps (5000Đ), currency exchange, MC/V cash advance, Vietnam Airlines booking, and lots of advice on the city and region. They also arrange river tours and trekking and cycling trips. (☎821 852; www.canthotourist.com.vn. Open daily 7am-8pm.) There are a several **banks** in the city center. **Vietcombank,** which cashes traveler's checks, is located at 7 Hòa Bình. (☎820 445. 24hr. **ATM.** Currency exchange, MC/V cash advance. Open M-F 7-11am and 1:30-4pm.) **Pharmacies** are everywhere. The **hospital** is at 4 Châu Văn Liêm. (☎821 288. 24hr. emergency service.) **Internet** awaits you right by the market at 9 Châu Văn Liêm. (3000Đ per hr. Open daily 7:30am-10:30pm.) Phone and fax services are available at the **post office,** 2 Hòa Bình. (Open daily 6am-8pm.)

ACCOMMODATIONS AND FOOD. The most expensive hotels are along the waterfront. There are several popular backpacker spots on Ngô Đuc Kê. **Hotel 31 ❷,** 31 Ngô Đuc Kê, features spacious and airy rooms, enthusiastic staff, and a quality restaurant. (☎825 287. Rooms US$5-10.) **Hien Guesthouse ❷,** 118/10 Phan Đình Phùng, is a quirky little place on a narrow alley (Hẻm 118). The English-speaking staff can arrange boat tours and motorbike rentals. (☎812 718. Rooms US$4-8.) A step up from budget digs, **Hòa Bình Hotel ❹,** 5 Hòa Bình, boasts suites with bathtubs, minibars, and other special treats. (☎810 217; www.hoabinhct.com. Rooms US$18-45.) **Golf Hotel ❺,** 2 Hai Bà Trưng, overlooks the river and is one of the most luxurious hotels in the city. Bathrooms are equipped with full-body massage showers! (☎812 210; www.vietnamgolfhotel.com. Rooms US$50 and up.)

Cần Thơ is blessed with a number of good restaurants. If you need to stock up on snacks or booze, try the **minimart** at 19 Đồng Khởi. (Open daily 6am-9pm.) **Nam Bộ ❸,** 50 Hai Bà Trưng, is set in a restored French villa and provides decadent Western and Vietnamese dishes at reasonable prices. The upper terrace is particularly elegant. (☎823 908. Most dishes under 50,000Đ. Open daily 9am-2pm and 5-10:30pm.) **Mé Kong ❷,** 38 Hai Bà Trưng, is a long-standing tourist favorite. Inexpensive Western breakfasts (including pancakes and omelettes) are a big draw. (☎821 645. Breakfast 10,000-20,000Đ; other meals 20,000-30,000Đ. Open daily 7am-2am.) **Nam Đô ❷,** 186-188 Nguyễn An Ninh, packs a crowd eager for its local dishes and friendly atmosphere. (☎820 772. Most dishes 15,000-35,000Đ. Open daily 8am-10pm.) **Du Thuyền ❸** is a restaurant-boat that cruises the river and docks across from the Golf Hotel on Hai Bà Trưng. Departs 8pm and returns 9pm. Most dishes 30,000-50,000Đ.

SIGHTS. For many people, exploring the network of canals around Cần Thơ by boat is the highlight of their visit to the area. **Motorboat operators** congregate around the pier on Hai Bà Trưng, near its intersection with Ngô Quyền. Most charge 30,000Đ per hour, and travelers can decide how much time they want to spend on the water. There are four main **floating markets** in the region: **Cái Răng** (7km, 3-4hr. round-trip); **Phong Điền** (18km, 4-5hr. round-trip); **Trà Ôn** (20km, 5-6hr. round-trip); and **Phụng Hiệp** (33km, 8hr. round-trip). Cái Răng is the most popular tourist destination, while Phụng Hiệp is known for its trade in snakes and snake products. The best time to visit the markets is 6-8am, when they are most active. If you head out early enough, you can catch the sunrise over the river. Boat tours also typically include stops at **fruit orchards,** where you can sample the bounty for a small fee (10,000-20,000Đ). As far as presentation goes, **Cần Thơ Museum,** 6 Phan Đình Phùng, is one of the best museums in southern Vietnam. Although there are no signs in English, the diverse and detailed exhibits provide clear insight into the history and culture of the province. (Open Tu-Th 8-11am and 2-5pm, Sa-Su 8-11am and 6:30-9pm. Free.)

LONG XUYÊN ☎76

For those travelers looking to explore An Giang Province (whose attractions include Châu Đốc, Tức Dụp Hill, Ba Chúc, and the Óc Eco ancient ruins), capital city Long Xuyên can serve as a useful jumping-off point, with the provincial tourist office located in the city. Unfortunately, the city itself doesn't have much to offer tourists, although a river tour is an enjoyable way to spend a few hours. **Motorboats** are available for hire (30,000Đ per hr.) at the end of Nguyễn Huệ. Not far from this docking area is the lively **floating market.**

Buses arrive at the Long Xuyên station about 1km outside the city center on Trần Hưng Đạo, and head several times each morning to: HCMC (4½hr.; 34,000Đ); Châu Đốc (1½hr.; 10,000Đ); Cần Thơ (1½hr.; 12,000Đ); Rạch Giá (3hr.; 13,500Đ). From the bus station, **Trần Hưng Đạo** runs along the edge of the city center and meets the **Catholic church,** whose massive spire serves as a helpful navigational landmark. Perpendicular to Trần Hưng Đạo, major thoroughfare **Nguyễn Huệ** runs from the church, past a Tôn Đức Thắng statue, and up to the **Hậu River,** whose waterfront is crowed with market stalls. There is a **post office** on Ngô Gia Tự, near its intersection with Nguyễn Văn Cưng. (Phone and fax services. Open daily 6am-10pm.) The main **bank,** one of few in the Mekong Delta to cash **traveler's checks,** is located at 1 Hùng Vương. (Also has an **ATM,** currency exchange, and MC/V cash advance service. Open daily 7-11am and 1-5pm.) **Internet** can be found at 312/4 Trần Hưng Đạo. (3000Đ per hr. Open daily 7:30am-10pm.) Right across the street, **An Giang Tourimex Travel Service Center,** 80E Trần Hưng Đạo, is the best place to get information on the province. The office also books tours around the region and homestays on Mỹ Hòa Hưng Island. (☎841 036; www.angiang-tourimex.com. Open daily 7-11am and 1-5pm.)

Long Xuyên Hotel ❸, 19 Nguyễn Văn Cưng, has clean and comfortable rooms at reasonable prices. (☎841 927; longxuyenhotel@hcm.vnn.vn. Breakfast included. Rooms US$9-16.) A more basic budget option with friendly staff is **Xuân Phượng ❷,** 68 Nguyễn Trãi. (☎841 041. Rooms 77,000-187,000Đ.) Cheerful **Hồng Phát ❷,** 242/4 Lương Văn Cù, serves a variety of delicious meals. (Most dishes 20,000-40,000Đ. Open daily 10am-9pm.) The restaurant atop **Đông Xuyên Hotel ❸** offers elegant ambience, excellent city views, and a surprisingly affordable menu. (Most meals under 40,000Đ. Open daily 6am-10pm.)

VIETNAM

CHÂU ĐỐC ☎76

Most travelers in Châu Đốc are just passing through on their way to or from Cambodia. However, those who choose to linger here will find pilgrimage sites, floating homes, and one of the most attractive waterfronts in the Mekong Delta. It's ideal if you've been navigating the quiet towns in the Mekong and crave a slightly more cosmopolitan feel, or if you simply wish to laze by the river in the well-manicured park.

TRANSPORTATION AND PRACTICAL INFORMATION. Buses arrive at the station about 2km southeast of the city center on Lê Lợi, and go to: HCMC (6hr.; every hr. 4-9am; 43,000Đ); Long Xuyên (1hr.; 6am and 7am; 11,000Đ); Cần Thơ (3hr.; every hr. 5-7am; 20,000Đ); Vĩnh Long (4hr.; 6am; 28,000Đ). **Lê Lợi** (also called **Trần Hưng Đạo**) runs along the **Hậu River.** The waterfront is dominated by the **Victoria Hotel,** a huge, yellow, colonial-style building. Beside the hotel is a lovely **park** with flower arrangements, vine-covered archways, and an impressive **fish statue.** At night, the walkways and fountains here are lit up. From the waterfront, **Nguyễn Văn Thoại** (also called **Núi Sam**) runs through the city center toward **Sam Mountain. Market stalls** crowd the streets near the riverfront between Nguyễn Văn Thoại and Bạch Đằng, and the **indoor market** is located between Bạch Đằng and Chi Lăng. There is **no tourist office** in Châu Đốc, since the one in Long Xuyên serves the whole province. However, the first three guesthouses listed below all offer tour services, including **boats to Cambodia.** Most boats bound for Phnom Penh depart around 7am. (Fast boat 2½hr., US$15; slow boat 4hr., US$7.) See **Border Crossing,** p. 984, for more information. The **hospital** is at 5 Lê Lợi, just across from Victoria Hotel. (☎867 184. 24hr. emergency service.) The main **post office** is located at 73 Lê Lợi. (Phone and fax services. Open daily 6am-10pm.) Connected to the post office is an **Internet** center. (3000Đ per hr. Open daily 7am-9pm.)

ACCOMMODATIONS AND FOOD. **Trung Nguyễn ❷**, 86 Bạch Đằng, is a great new minihotel boasting bright, clean rooms, each with a private balcony. (☎866 158; trunghotel@yahoo.com. Rooms US$7-15.) **Hàng Châu II ❷**, 10 Nguyễn Văn Thoại, has spacious, rooms and a friendly staff. (☎868 891; hangchau2agg@hcm.vnn.vn. Rooms 110,000-280,000Đ.) The English-speaking proprietor of **Vĩnh Phước ❷**, 12-14 Quang Trưng, can provide information on Châu Đốc and the area. (☎866 242. Rooms US$4-6.) **Mỹ Lộc ❶**, 51B Nguyễn Văn Thoại, is another decent budget option. (☎866 455. Rooms 60,000-120,000Đ.)

The popular local joint **Trương Vân ❷**, 15 Quang Trưng, specializes in hotpot and claypot dishes. (Most dishes 20,000-30,000Đ. Open daily 6am-9pm.) **Bày Bông ❷**, 22 Thượng Đăng Lễ, draws crowds of tourists for its good service and flavorful fare. (Most dishes 15,000-35,000Đ. Open daily 9am-10pm.) **Mékong ❷**, 41 Lê Lợi, is in the lovely courtyard of an old French colonial villa; through the gates across from the Victoria Hotel. (Most dishes 20,000-40,000Đ. Open daily 6am-10pm.)

SIGHTS AND NIGHTLIFE. The most fascinating sights in Châu Đốc can be found on the **Hậu River.** Motorboat tours can be arranged at many guesthouses, but a much better way to cruise the river is by canoe, as it gives you more access to the sights. Canoe operators congregate around the pier at the end of Nguyễn Văn Thoại, and most charge 30,000Đ per hour. The chance to admire the somewhat precarious-looking technique of the rowers themselves is worth the trip. A typical tour begins with the **floating villages.** Here people reside in **boathouses** of all shapes and sizes—some are complex, multi-room structures afloat on steel drums, while others are little more than corrugated metal shacks atop canoes. Many residents catch fish in cages right underneath their floors. Amazingly, most of these river homes have electricity, and some even have computers! The other main stop on the tour is the nearby **Chàm community.** The Chàm minority people practice Islam and are widely known for their textiles. Visitors to their community can view the **textile weaving** process and visit the **mosques,** where locals worship and children learn to read the Qur'an in Arabic.

About 5km from Châu Đốc's city center stands **Sam Mountain** (Núi Sam). The most popular way to handle the mountain is to take a motorbike up to the summit (260m) and then walk down. From the summit, you can view the Cambodian border amid wide stretches of rice fields. You might wonder about the loud noises echoing from atop the summit, but no fear, they're only monkeys—the noises are not emanating from the bizarrely placed model T-Rex partway down the mountain. There is also a military post here; you should avoid photographing the building and the soldiers. Around the base of the mountain are a number of pagodas, including massive **Bà Chúa Xứ.**

BORDER CROSSING. Travelers can pass from Vietnam to Cambodia by boat at the **Vĩnh Xương** border crossing, about 40km from Châu Đốc. Travelers who do not yet have a Cambodian visa can obtain one here for US$26. One passport photo is also required. The trip can be arranged at many guesthouses in Châu Đốc or at tour offices in Hồ Chí Minh City.

DAYTRIPS FROM CHÂU ĐỐC. Tức Dụp and Ba Chúc are both located near the town of Tri Tôn, about 45km south of Châu Đốc. They are most easily reached by motorbike. A complicated cluster of huge boulders and deep caves, **Tức Dụp** served as a Việt Cộng base during the Vietnam War. Here the VC forces managed to hold off the US military against 3-to-20 odds between 1968 and 1976. Tức Dụp earned its nickname of Two Million Dollar Hill after the US spent that much money on weapons and yet still failed to capture the area. Visitors can climb over the boulders and wander through the caves, which served as meeting rooms, living quarters, and hospitals. The top of the hill provides great views of the surrounding countryside. Toward the bottom, there is a room with photographs of the soldiers and their camps. (Open daily 7am-5pm. 4000Đ.) Between 1975 and 1978, the area along the Cambodian border from Châu Đốc to Hà Tiên was routinely invaded by Khmer Rouge forces. Seeking to claim the territory as their own, the Khmer Rouge marched into Vietnamese towns and slaughtered civilians. In April 1978, they massacred 3157 people at **Ba Chúc.** Today a glass case containing hundreds of victims' skulls (from infant to elderly) memorializes of the tragedy. Nearby, a collection of horrifying photographs documents the event in an all-too-visceral manner. There are also Khmer Rouge weapons on display, including the clubs that they used to clobber children. (Open daily 7am-5pm. Free.)

RẠCH GIÁ ☎77

Fishing and marine commerce have brought prosperity to Rạch Giá, and this shows in the seaport city's handsome, paved waterfronts, well-lit streets that are ideal for evening strolls, and stately public buildings. There aren't many tourist attractions here, however, and most travelers just pass on their way to Phú Quốc Island. Still, Rạch Giá makes for an enjoyable stopover point and you shouldn't pass up the chance to savor a meal on the enchanting waterfront.

TRANSPORTATION. Most long-distance **buses** depart from the station in nearby **Rạch Sỏi,** 7km outside the city center on Nguyễn Trung Trực. Buses go from here to: HCMC (6hr.; every hr. 4am-5pm; 53,000Đ); Cần Thơ (3hr.; every 30min. 5am-5pm; 21,000Đ); Long Xuyên (3hr.; every 30min. 5:30am-4:30pm; 14,000Đ); Châu Đốc (5hr.; 4 per day 5am-3pm; 23,500Đ). Buses to Hà Tiên (3½hr.; every hr. 6am-4pm; 20,000Đ) leave from the station on Nguyễn Bỉnh Kiêm. There are also **minibuses** that leave for HCMC and Cần Thơ from various points around the city center. The bus and minibus system is a bit confusing, so ask your hotel receptionist about it if you can't seem to figure it out. **Boats** depart for Phú Quốc Island from the pier at the end of Nguyễn Công Trứ. The tourist office runs excellent **high-speed ferries** (2½hr.; 8:30am; top deck 160,000Đ, bottom deck 130,000Đ); their booking office is at 6 Tự Do. Get tickets at least a day in advance. Be prepared for high-tech TVs airing DVDs of the latest pop hit en route. (☎879 455. Open daily 6-11am and 1-6pm.) There are also **slow boats** (7hr.; early morning departure; 70,000Đ) that make the journey. Ask the tourist office staff for more info. **Flights** depart once daily for Phú Quốc (45min.; US$17 one-way) from the airport near Rạch Sỏi bus station.

ORIENTATION AND PRACTICAL INFORMATION. The city center contains two branches of the **Rạch Giá River** that flow southwest into the **Gulf of Thailand. Nguyễn Trung Trực** is one main avenue in the city center; coming in from the bus station, it crosses a canal and turns into **Lê Lợi,** which passes a public park, crosses over a second canal, and ends when it intersects with **Trần Phú.** Trần Phú is another important street that crosses both canals.

VIETNAM

KienGiang Tourist Office, 5 Lê Lợi, is one of the better tourist offices in the Mekong Delta. The capable staff can provide handy **maps** (includes Rạch Giá, Hà Tiên, and Phú Quốc Island) and explain transportation to Phú Quốc Island. (☎862 018; www.kiengiangtouristmap.com. Open daily 7-11am and 1:30-5pm.) Across the street is **Vietcombank,** 2 Mạc Cưu, which has an **ATM** and changes traveler's checks. (Also does currency exchange and MC/V cash advances. Open daily 7-11am and 1-4pm.) There is a **hospital** with emergency service at 46 Lê Lợi, and a **pharmacy** (open daily 7am-9pm) at 46 Hoàng Hoa Thám. A memorable place to access the **Internet** is inside **Children's Palace** on Nguyễn Công Trứ, where you'll probably catch a few karate lessons or even a quiz show in action. Once you enter the park, follow the path until you get to the opposite end; signs point to the Internet room. (100Đ per min. Open daily 7-11am and 1:30-9pm.) The **post office** is located at the intersection of Lê Lợi and Trần Phú. (Phone and fax. Open daily 6:30am-10pm.)

ACCOMMODATIONS AND FOOD. Due to the tourist traffic en route to Phú Quốc Island, Rạch Giá has a large number of lodging options. In the city center, **Kim Có ❸,** 141 Nguyễn Hùng Son, boasts large, brightly painted, modern rooms that have an art-deco feel to them. All rooms have bathtubs. (☎879 610. Rooms 160,000-200,000Đ.) **Trung Quyên ❸,** 20 Hoàng Hoa Thám, also has attractive rooms, plus perks like makeup tables and glass-walled showers. (☎876 757. Rooms 200,000Đ and up.) If you want to be near the ferries, head to Tự Do, where *nhà trọ* and *nhà nghỉ* signs indicate rooms for rent. **Phượng Hồng ❷,** 5 Tự Do, has friendly staff and decent rooms. (☎866 138. Rooms 90,000-140,000Đ.)

The lovely waterfront terrace at **Hải Âu ❷,** 2 Nguyễn Trung Trực, makes it the nicest place to eat in Rạch Giá, especially at sunset. (Most dishes 30,000-60,000Đ. Coffee and tea 3000-7000Đ. Open daily 6am-10pm.) **Tây Hồ ❶,** 6 Nguyễn Du, looks a bit shabby, but it dishes out ample portions of quality Vietnamese fare. (Most dishes 10,000-20,000Đ. Open daily 10am-10pm.) **Áo Dài Mới ❷,** 26 Lý Tự Trọng, is popular for its hearty soups. (Most dishes under 15,000Đ. Open daily 5am-2pm.)

SIGHTS AND ENTERTAINMENT. The city's one major sight is the **Nguyễn Trung Trực Temple,** 18 Nguyễn Công Trứ. Its namesake is a local hero who led fierce resistance efforts against French invaders in the 1860s—his most famous victory is the sinking of the French warship *Espérance.* Only when French forces took his mother hostage in 1868 did he agree to surrender himself, after which he was publicly executed in Rạch Giá. Right next door, machete-wielding women chop up plants for use in **traditional medicine.** A stunning array of dried stems and leaves covers every sun-exposed surface in sight.

VIETNAM

HÀ TIÊN ☎77

Picturesque Hà Tiên, set on the Gulf of Thailand amid a landscape of rolling hills dotted with temples, is a favorite Mekong Delta stop for many travelers. Colorful houses, cheerful residents, a small-town atmosphere, and a well-kept appearance add to its appeal and render it a sweet relief. The most famous attraction in Hà Tiên is **Thạch Động** (Stone Cave), 4km northwest of town off Quốc Lộ 80. This large outcrop of granite contains several Buddhist shrines within its caverns, and is also home to a colony of teeny bats. Openings in the rock provide lovely views of the town, the surrounding rice fields, and the Cambodian border.

Buses arrive at the station across the floating bridge from the town center, and head to Rạch Giá (3hr.; every 30min. 6:30am-6:30pm; 15,000Đ); Châu Đốc (4hr.; 4 times daily 6:15am-2pm; 25,000Đ); Long Xuyên (3hr.; 11pm; 30,000Đ); Cần Thơ (4hr.; 5:30am and 10pm; 25,000Đ); HCMC (8hr.; 8pm and 9pm; 50,000Đ). To find out about **boats** to Phú Quốc Island, ask at your hotel for more information; availability depends on the season. Hà Tiên is a small town, and many tourists enjoy exploring it by bicycle (rentals available for 20,000Đ per day at Đông Hồ Hotel).

Đông Hồ Hotel (☎951 031) is run by KienGiang Tourist Office; the staff gives out free town maps and answers general questions. **Vietcombank,** which has an **ATM** and changes traveler's checks, is at 40 Mạc Công Du. (Also currency exchange and MC/V cash advance. Open M-F 7-11am and 1-5pm.) The **post office** is located on Tô Châu. (Phone and fax services. Open daily 6:30am-9pm.) There is a hospital on Mạc Cửu and a **pharmacy** (open daily 7am-9pm) at 32 Trần Hầu. The almighty **Internet** awaits you at 33 Tham Tướng Sanh. (4000Đ per hr. Open daily 9am-11pm.)

Hà Tiên offers a range of accommodation choices, from scrubby to snazzy. **Hoàng Dũ ❷**, 30 Lam Sơn, is a spiffy minihotel with clean and fragrant rooms. (☎851 463. Rooms 90,000-180,000Đ.) **Ngọc Quan ❷**, 24 Mạc Công Du, is another minihotel with high standards, and its triples are a bargain deal. (☎852 652. Rooms 120,000-150,000Đ.) **Hải Vân ❷**, 55 Lam Sơn, is one of the most attractive hotels in town, and guests can enjoy lobby Internet access. (☎852 872. Rooms 70,000-220,000Đ.) For food, head to **Xuân Thạnh ❷**, located on Trần Hầu, which offers a great view of the market and is always bustling with locals. (Most dishes 15,000-25,000Đ. Open daily 6am-10pm.) **Hư'ơng Bien ❷**, 974 Tô Châu, is a popular place to sample local seafood dishes. (Open daily 6am-8pm.)

PHÚ QUỐC ISLAND ☎77

As one local put it, Phú Quốc has got the whole package. From fantastic beaches to wild forests to enchanting marine life, the island offers treasures for every visitor. It's no wonder that Thailand, Cambodia, and Vietnam have all laid claim to it in the past. Not too long ago, the island was largely undeveloped, except for a few villages and some military bases. However, the tourist industry has since caught on to Phú Quốc's enormous potential, and new resorts and services are now cropping up every minute.

VIETNAM

TRANSPORTATION. Phú Quốc has three main entry/exit points. **Flights** to HCMC (1hr., 2 per day, US$38 one-way) and Rạch Giá (45min., 1 per day, US$17 one way) take off at the airport right outside Dương Đông. **Boats** depart for Rạch Giá from An Thới. High-speed ferries operated by KienGiang Tourist (2½hr.; first class 160,000Đ, second class 130,000Đ) depart daily at 1:30pm. Their booking office is at 16 Trần Hưng Đạo. There is also a slow boat (7hr.; early morning departure; 70,000Đ); inquire with the staff at Hương Biển (see below). **Boats** head to Hà Tiên from Hàm Ninh. High-speed ferries (1½hr.; 120,000Đ) only operate for part of the year, when the water level is high enough. Otherwise, there are usually slow boats (4hr.; 60,000Đ) that make the journey to nearby Bà Hòn. Ask your hotel receptionist for more information.

ORIENTATION AND PRACTICAL INFORMATION. The island measures 48km from northern to southern tip. **Dư'ơng Đông,** on the western coast of the island, is the main town, and most travelers stay there. The fishing hamlet of **An Thớ'i** is about 28km south of Dương Đông, on the southern tip of the island. **Hàm Ninh,** another fishing town, is on the eastern side of the island, almost opposite Dương Đông. Dirt and some paved roads connect smaller villages around the island. **Dư'ơng Đông** itself is hardly more than a few streets. Many travelers rent a **motorbike** (80,000-100,000Đ per day) and explore the island themselves. The other option is to hire a **motorbike driver** (ask your hotel receptionist); some speak excellent English and are useful guides. The typical rate is US$10 per day.

Hương Biển (☎846 113), on Trần Hưng Đạo, is a hotel run by KienGiang Tourist Office, and the staff there can provide you with free maps and general information. **Tours** and **rentals** (motorbikes, boats, etc.) are most easily arranged through the resorts. **Vietcombank** is the place to go to cash traveler's checks and exchange currency. They also handle MC/V advances, and expect to get an ATM before 2005. (Open daily 7-11am and 1-5pm.) Around the corner on Trần Hưng Đạo, the **hospital** (☎846 074), 1km outside of town on Đường 30/4, has emergency service. There is a **pharmacy** at 55 Ngô Quyền. (Open daily 7am-7pm.) Satisfy your never-ending desire to surf the **Internet** in an adjoining room. (6000Đ per hr. Open daily 7am-8pm.) The **post office**, on Đường 30/4, has phone and fax services. (Open daily 6:30am-10pm.)

ACCOMMODATIONS. Currently, the most popular places to stay are the **resorts along Long Beach**, just south of Dương Đông. Many of them have their own restaurants and bars, as well as Internet access. In most cases, guests have the option of staying in bungalows (large furnished huts, often made of bamboo) or hotel rooms. The resorts don't have numbered addresses, but they're clearly marked by signs. The hotels in town tend to be more expensive and less convenient than those on the beach. **Kim Hoa ❸** features clean and comfortable digs, plus a nice shady piece of beach. The proprietor also owns a local fish sauce factory; you can pick up a bottle of the stuff here. (☎848 969. Rooms US$10-15. Bungalows US$15-20.) Nearby **Tropicana ❹** is a bit pricier, but guests can enjoy extra perks like the swimming pool, the beach huts, and the international reading rack. (☎847 127. Rooms US$20. Bungalows US$28-56.) **Beach Club ❸** claims a more distant stretch of sand. The proprietors are a very helpful source of information about the island. (☎980 998; beachclubasia@yahoo.com. Rooms US$10. Bungalows US$12-15.) **Nam Phương ❷** is another popular budget option, with warm-hearted staff and decent rooms. (☎846 319. Rooms US$7-8. Bungalows US$15.)

For those looking to get away from it all, the resorts along **Ông Lang Beach**, 10km north of Dương Đông, offer a more remote setting; most have restaurants and bars. **Thang Loi ❸** has cozy bungalows, and guests can celebrate the sunset with cheap drinks (most under 20,000Đ) at happy hour. (Cell ☎0908 297 413; thangloiresort@hotmail.com. Bungalows US$10-15. Happy hour nightly 5-7pm.)

FOOD. The restaurants at the **resorts** typically offer both Vietnamese and Western cuisine. Aside from this option, there are several good eateries in Dương Đông. **Lê Giang ❷**, 289 Trần Hưng Đạo, is very popular with both locals and tourists for its delicious Vietnamese fare. (Most dishes under 50,000Đ. Open daily 10am-10pm.) You can sample local seafood right on the harbor at **Góp Gió ❷**, 145 Bạch Đằng. (Most dishes 20,000-40,000Đ. Open daily 7am-10pm.) If you're planning a beach picnic, head to the **outdoor market** on Ngô Quyền for fresh fruits and veggies.

BEACHES AND OUTDOOR ACTIVITIES. Phú Quốc's beaches are considered to be some of the very best in Vietnam. The military has unfortunately claimed a number of them, but ample stretches of sand still remain open to travelers. **Long Beach** (Bãi Trưởng) stretches from Dương Đông to An Thới. Soft sand and a smooth shoreline make it the most popular tourist beach. Ten kilometers farther up the coast, **Ông Lang Beach** (Bãi Ông Lang) is somewhat rockier than Long Beach, which makes it great for marine life. **Sao Beach** (Bãi Sao), on the eastern side of the island, is worth the ride down a bumpy dirt road. This tranquil cove features crystal blue waters and powdery white sand. In the center of Phú Quốc are several **natural springs**. One of the local favorites is **Suối Đá Bán**, a series of waterfalls and bathing pools. The hilly northern part of the island is dominated by **lush forests**—they're environmentally protected but open to exploration.

Beyond the southern tip of Phú Quốc are the **An Thới Islands,** an archipelago of smaller islands which offer excellent snorkeling and scuba diving. Some of the resorts rent boats (US$20-30 per day), and most can arrange transportation.

A wealth of colorful and exotic creatures dwell in the waters around Phú Quốc. **Rainbow Divers** (☎0913 400 964; www.divevietnam.com) recently opened up a PADI-authorized **scuba diving** center in Phú Quốc. They offer a wide range of diving trips, from newbie outings to advanced courses. Contact them to arrange an info meeting, or else drop by their booth in Rainbow Bar (see below) during the evening. **Snorkeling** equipment can be rented or borrowed from many of the resorts, and Rainbow Divers also runs snorkeling trips.

SIGHTS AND ENTERTAINMENT. Phú Quốc is widely renowned for its superb fish sauce *(nước mắm)*. There are a number of **fish sauce factories** around Dương Đông, and many owners are willing to let visitors wander around the gigantic wooden vats. **Pepper groves** are another common sight (and smell) on the island. They're easily distinguished by their neat rows of wooden posts. Again, the owners generally don't mind visitors.

The spot to mix and mingle with other travelers is **Rainbow Bar,** located next to the entrance to Kim Hoa. Besides plenty of booze, the bar features TVs and a pool table. Charismatic Welsh bartender Brett has lived in Vietnam for several years and is a great person to chat with. (Open nightly 6pm-midnight, sometimes later.)

APPENDIX

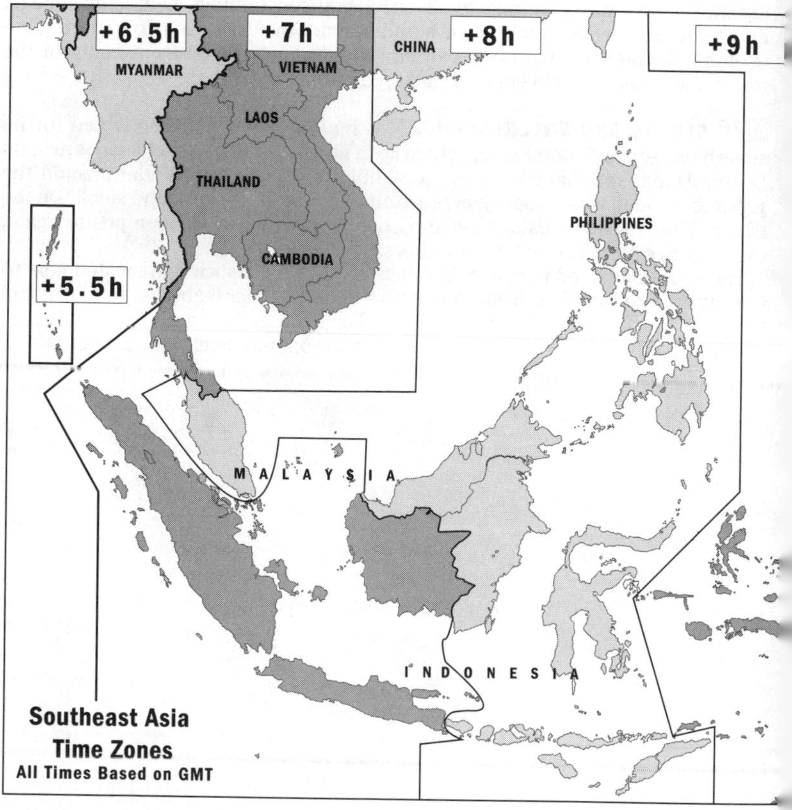

APPENDIX

COUNTRY CODES

Australia	61
Brunei	673
Cambodia	855
Canada	1
Indonesia	62
Ireland	353
Laos	856
Malaysia	60

Myanmar	95
New Zealand	64
Philippines	63
Singapore	65
South Africa	27
Thailand	66
United Kingdom	44
United States	1

MEASUREMENTS

1 meter (m) = 1.09 yards (yd.)	1 yard = 0.92m
1 meter (m) = 3.28 feet (ft.)	1 foot = 0.305m
1 kilometer (km) = 0.625 miles (mi.)	1 mile = 1.6km
1 kilogram (kg) = 2.2 pounds (lb.)	1 pound = 0.45kg

LANGUAGES

Languages in Southeast Asia are extremely different from English. Even gifted learners won't be able to pick up more than the barest rudiments of Thai during a short trip, although the rewards of making an effort to learn local languages are great.

PRONUNCIATION KEY

TONES: Thai, Lao, Burmese and Vietnamese are tonal languages; word meanings are partially determined by intonation and pitch. The five tones in Thai and Lao are neutral, low, high, falling, rising (the phrasebook doesn't distinguish between high- and low-falling tones in Lao); these tones are distinguished in the phrasebook by diacritical markings over the vowels to which they apply. Neutral tones (unmarked) are spoken in a level voice in the middle of the speaker's vocal range. Low (marked thus over the letter "a": à) and high (á) tones are spoken in level pitch from the bottom and top of the speaker's range, respectively. Falling tones (â) begin high and end low, as in the English pronunciation of "Hey!" Rising tones (ä) begin low and end high, as in the English interrogative "What?" The six Vietnamese tones are neutral, high (á), low (à), stopped (ă), rising-falling (ã), broken (ạ).

VOWELS: Vowels are very roughly pronounced as in English, except the "eu" sound in Thai and Lao, which represents the vowel sound in the French "bleu."

CONSONANTS: Consonants are pronounced (very roughly) as in English. Exceptions: in Bahasa Indonesia and Bahasa Malayu, "c" is pronounced "ch" as in "cherry." In Vietnamese, "d" is pronounced "z" as in "Zulu" in North, or "y" as in "yankee" in South, while "đ" and "Đ" are pronounced "d" as in "delta." "X" and "x" are pronounced "s" as in "sierra"; "s" and "S" pronounced "sh" as in "shovel"; "ph" pronounced "f" as in "foxtrot." "Th" is usually pronounced as in "tango."

ENGLISH	THAI//LAO	BURMESE
one	nèung // neung	ti
two	säwng // säwng	hni
three	sähm // sähm	thoun
four	sèe // see	le
five	hâh // hâh	nga
six	hòk // hók	chau
seven	jèt // jét	khun ni
eight	pàet // pâet	shi
nine	gâo // kâo	ko
ten	sìp // síp	tahse
eleven	sìp-èt // síp-ét	she
twelve	sìp-säwng // síp-säwng	seh-hni

APPENDIX

ENGLISH	THAI//LAO	BURMESE
twenty	yêe-sìp // sáo	hna se
thirty	sähm-sìp // sähm-síp	thoun ze
forty	sèe-sìp // see-síp	lei ze
fifty	hâh-sìp // häh-síp	nga ze
one hundred	róy // hâwy	taya
one thousand	pun // pán	taya fahse
hello	sàwatdee // sábài-dèe	mingala ba
good-bye	sawàtdee // pai jao	thwabi
yes / no	chai / mai chai // ya / baw	hou ke / hin in
thank you	khàwp khun // khâwp jài	kye zui tin ba de
excuse me	khäw tôht // khäw thôt	(m) khin mya, (f) shin
How are you?	ben yahng ngai // sábài-dèe baw	nei kaun ye la
fine/well	sabai-dee // sábài-dee	nei kaun ba de
Help!	chûay dûay // suay dae	lai kya ba oun
doctor	mäw // mäw	hsaya wun
police	tham ruat // tham ploh	ye sa khan
hocpital	rohng paiahhan // hóhng mäw	hsei youn
toilet	sûam // sûam	ein tha
Where is . . . ?	. . . yòo têe näi // . . . yôo säi	. . . bema shi th a le
to the right	khwä meu // lîaw khwaa	nya be cho
to the left	saí meu // lîaw sâai	be be cho
straight ahead	throng bai // pai seu seu	te da thwai
How much?	tâo rài // tao dài	da be lan le
bus	rót meh // lót meh	ba saka
train	rót fai // lot duan	mi ya tha
plane	krêuang bin // héua bìn	lei yin byan
car	rót yon // lot	twei
restaurant	ráhn ah-hän // lán ah-han	sa than hsain
guesthouse	bâhn pák // häw hap kháek	e yei tha
market	thah làt // thah làt	zei
bank	tanahkhan // thanáhkháhn	ban
post office	praisanee // pài-sá-née	sa dai
yesterday	mêua wahn née // mêu wáhn nêe	manei ga
today	wan née // mêu nêe	dinei
tomorrow	prûng née // mêu eun	ne hpan

KHMER	VIETNAMESE	MALAY/INDONESIAN
mouy	một	satu
pee	hai	dua
bei	ba	tiga
boun	bốn	empat
bram	nâm	lima
bram-mouy	sáu	eman

APPENDIX

KHMER	VIETNAMESE	MALAY/INDONESIAN
bram-pee	bảy	tujuh
bram-bei	tám	delapan
bram-boun	chín	sembilan
duop	mười	sepuluh
duop-mouy	mười một	sebelas
duop-pee	mười hai	duabelas
maphei	hai mươi	duapuluh
samseb	ba mươi	tigapuluh
sairseb	bốn mươi	empatpuluh
hahseb	năm mươi	limapuluh
mouy-rouy	một trăm	seratus
mouy-paun	một ngàn	seribu
suas dei	Chào ông (to males) Chào bà (to females)	selamat siang (good afternoon)
lia soon hao-i	Chào ông/Chào bà	selamat tinggal (to one staying)/ selamat jalan (to one going)
baht (males), chaat (females) / te	Dạ / Không	ya / tidak
aw kohn	Cám ơn	terima kasih
sohm toh	Xin lỗi	ma'af
niak sohk sabah-ay tay	ần/aẩ	Apa kabar?
khnyohm sohk sabah-ay	ần/aẩ	baik
juay khnyohm pawng	Cứu với	Tolong!
kroo paet	bác sĩ	dokter
po'leez	cảnh sát	polisi
mun'ti peyt	bệnh viện	rumah sakit
bawng-kohn	buồng tắm	kamar kecil
. . . neuv ai nah	ở đâu	Di mana . . . ?
bawt chweng	rẽ trái	ke kanan
bawt sdam	rẽ phải	ke kiri
teuv trawng	đi thẳng	terus menerus
nee tlay pohnmahn	Giá bao nhiêu	Berapa?
lahn chnual	xe buýt	bas (Mal.)/bis (Ind.)
roht plirng	xe lửa	kereta api
yohn haw	máy bay	kapal terbang
laht	xe ô tô	mobil
restoorahn	tiệm ăn	rumah makan
oh-tail	nhà khách	wisma
psah	chợ	pasar
thniakia	ngân hàng	bank
praisuhnee	bưu điện	pejebat pos (Mal.) kantor pos (Ind.)
m'sool mein	hôm qua	kemarin
thngay nee	hôm nay	hari ini
thngay saik	ngày mai	besok

APPENDIX

CLIMATE

High and low tourist seasons roughly correspond with rainy and dry seasons in Southeast Asia. There is no uniform seasonal pattern for the region; see the **Facts and Figures** section in each chapter for country-specific variations. Keep in mind that the monsoon is rarely an impediment for travel in the region, except for in rural Laos and Cambodia. Generally, rainfall peaks from May to September north of Singapore (including the Philippines), and between December to March south and east of Singapore (including Indonesia). To roughly convert Celsius to Fahrenheit, double the Celsius and add 30.

	January			April			July			October		
City	**High (F/C)**	**Low (F/C)**	**Rain (in)**	**High (F/C)**	**Low (F/C)**	**Rain (in)**	**High (F/C)**	**Low (F/C)**	**Rain (in)**	**High (F/C)**	**Low (F/C)**	**Rain (in)**
Bali	90/32	76/25	13.9	91/33	76/24	3.5	87/31	74/23	2.1	90/32	76/24	3.6
Bangkok	91/33	71/22	0.4	96/36	80/27	2.4	92/33	78/26	5.7	91/33	78/25	7.2
Bandar S.B.	87/30	74/23	11.7	88/31	77/25	6.9	90/32	77/25	8.8	88/31	76/24	11.9
Hà Nội	70/21	54/13	0.9	79/26	68/20	4.0	90/32	82/28	10.2	85/29	74/23	5.9
Hong Kong	68/20	59/15	1.2	79/26	71/22	5.6	90/32	82/28	14.4	85/29	76/25	4.8
Jakarta	90/32	75/24	13.1	93/34	75/24	8.3	93/34	72/22	3.4	95/35	74/23	6.3
Kuala Lumpur	91/33	74/23	6.5	93/34	76/24	10.6	92/33	74/24	5.2	91/33	75/24	10.3
Manila	88/31	71/22	0.7	96/35	76/24	1.0	91/33	77/25	17.7	90/32	76/24	7.2
Phnom Penh	74/23	62/17	0.2	84/29	75/24	3.3	82/28	77/25	10.5	80/27	74/23	3.4
Phuket	90/32	73/23	1.8	93/34	77/25	6.1	88/31	78/25	10.2	88/31	76/24	14.3
Singapore	87/30	77/25	6.5	91/33	79/26	10.6	89/32	80/27	5.2	89/32	79/26	10.3
Vientiane	82/28	58/15	0.4	91/33	74/23	3.6	88/31	78/25	9.9	88/31	70/21	3.4
Yangon	91/33	67/19	3.5	101/38	78/25	3.6	87/30	78/25	3.5	90/32	79/26	2.9

INDEX

C

INDEX

INDEX

U

V

W

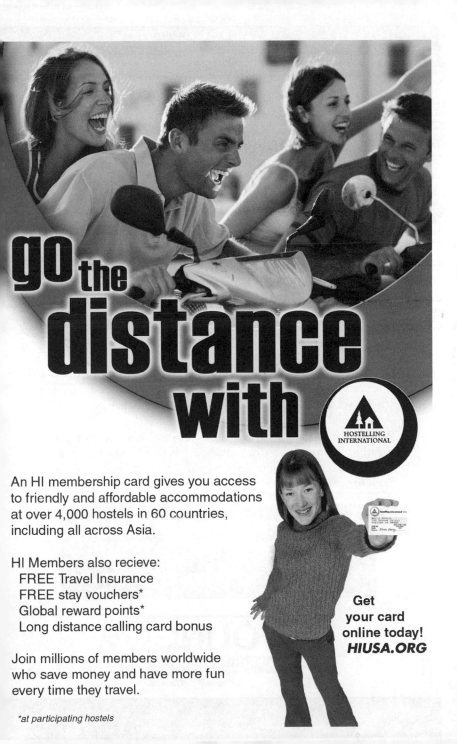

ABOUT LET'S GO

GUIDES FOR THE INDEPENDENT TRAVELER

At Let's Go, we see every trip as the chance of a lifetime. If your dream is to grab a machete and forge through the jungles of Brazil, we can take you there. If you'd rather bask in the Riviera sun at a beachside cafe, we'll set you a table. We write for readers who know that there's more to travel than sharing double deckers with tourists and who believe that travel can change both themselves and the world—whether they plan to spend six days in London or six months in Latin America. We'll show you just how far your money can go, and prove that the greatest limitation on your adventures is not your wallet, but your imagination. After all, traveling close to the ground lets you interact more directly with the places and people you've gone to see, making for the most authentic experience.

BEYOND THE TOURIST EXPERIENCE

To help you gain a deeper connection with the places you travel, our researchers give you the heads-up on both world-renowned and off-the-beaten-track attractions, sights, and destinations. They engage with the local culture, writing features on regional cuisine, local festivals, and hot political issues. We've also opened our pages to respected writers and scholars to hear their takes on the countries and regions we cover, and asked travelers who have worked, studied, or volunteered abroad to contribute first-person accounts of their experiences. We've also increased our coverage of responsible travel and expanded each guide's Alternatives to Tourism chapter to share more ideas about how to give back to local communities and learn about the places you travel.

FORTY-FIVE YEARS OF WISDOM

Let's Go got its start in 1960, when a group of creative and well-traveled students compiled their experience and advice into a 20-page mimeographed pamphlet, which they gave to travelers on charter flights to Europe. Four and a half decades later, we've expanded to cover six continents and all kinds of travel—while retaining our founders' adventurous attitude toward the world. Our guides are still researched and written entirely by students on shoestring budgets, experienced travelers who know that train strikes, stolen luggage, food poisoning, and marriage proposals are all part of a day's work. This year, we're expanding our coverage of South America and Southeast Asia, with brand-new *Let's Go: Ecuador*, *Let's Go: Peru*, and *Let's Go: Vietnam*. Our adventure guide series is growing, too, with the addition of *Let's Go: Pacific Northwest Adventure* and *Let's Go: New Zealand Adventure*. And we're immensely excited about our new *Let's Go: Roadtripping USA*—two years, eight routes, and sixteen researchers and editors have put together a travel guide like none other.

THE LET'S GO COMMUNITY

More than just a travel guide company, Let's Go is a community. Our small staff comes together because of our shared passion for travel and our desire to help other travelers see the world. We love it when our readers become part of the Let's Go community as well—when you travel, drop us a postcard (67 Mt. Auburn St., Cambridge, MA 02138, USA) or send us an e-mail (feedback@letsgo.com) to tell us about your adventures and discoveries.

For more information, visit us online: www.letsgo.com.

MAP INDEX

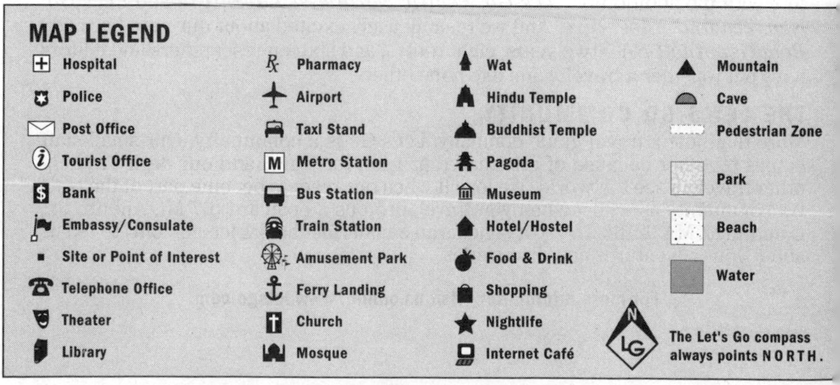

MAP LEGEND
Hospital
Police
Post Office
Tourist Office
Bank
Embassy/Consulate
Site or Point of Interest
Telephone Office
Theater
Library
Pharmacy
Airport
Taxi Stand
Metro Station
Bus Station
Train Station
Amusement Park
Ferry Landing
Church
Mosque
Wat
Hindu Temple
Buddhist Temple
Pagoda
Museum
Hotel/Hostel
Food & Drink
Shopping
Nightlife
Internet Café
Mountain
Cave
Pedestrian Zone
Park
Beach
Water
The Let's Go compass always points NORTH.